CAMBRIDGE LIBRARY COLLECTION

Books of enduring scholarly value

British and Irish History, Nineteenth Century

This series comprises contemporary or near-contemporary accounts of the political, economic and social history of the British Isles during the nineteenth century. It includes material on international diplomacy and trade, labour relations and the women's movement, developments in education and social welfare, religious emancipation, the justice system, and special events including the Great Exhibition of 1851.

A Dictionary, Practical, Theoretical and Historical, of Commerce and Commercial Navigation

A friend, correspondent and intellectual successor to David Ricardo, John Ramsay McCulloch (1789–1864) forged his reputation in the emerging field of political economy by publishing deeply researched articles in Scottish periodicals and the *Encyclopaedia Britannica*. From 1828 he spent nearly a decade as professor of political economy in the newly founded University of London, thereafter becoming comptroller of the Stationery Office. Perhaps the first professional economist, McCulloch had become internationally renowned by the middle of the century, recognised for sharing his ideas through lucid lecturing and writing. The present reference work, first published in 1832 and later revised, expanded and updated multiple times, made McCulloch considerable sums of money. His critical and analytical treatment of the data he had largely compiled himself made this much more than a mere book of facts. Several other works written or edited by McCulloch are also reissued in the Cambridge Library Collection.

Cambridge University Press has long been a pioneer in the reissuing of out-of-print titles from its own backlist, producing digital reprints of books that are still sought after by scholars and students but could not be reprinted economically using traditional technology. The Cambridge Library Collection extends this activity to a wider range of books which are still of importance to researchers and professionals, either for the source material they contain, or as landmarks in the history of their academic discipline.

Drawing from the world-renowned collections in the Cambridge University Library and other partner libraries, and guided by the advice of experts in each subject area, Cambridge University Press is using state-of-the-art scanning machines in its own Printing House to capture the content of each book selected for inclusion. The files are processed to give a consistently clear, crisp image, and the books finished to the high quality standard for which the Press is recognised around the world. The latest print-on-demand technology ensures that the books will remain available indefinitely, and that orders for single or multiple copies can quickly be supplied.

The Cambridge Library Collection brings back to life books of enduring scholarly value (including out-of-copyright works originally issued by other publishers) across a wide range of disciplines in the humanities and social sciences and in science and technology.

A Dictionary,

Practical, Theoretical and Historical,
of Commerce and
Commercial Navigation

J.R. McCulloch

CAMBRIDGE
UNIVERSITY PRESS

CAMBRIDGE
UNIVERSITY PRESS

University Printing House, Cambridge, CB2 8BS, United Kingdom

Cambridge University Press is part of the University of Cambridge.

It furthers the University's mission by disseminating knowledge in the pursuit of
education, learning and research at the highest international levels of excellence.

www.cambridge.org
Information on this title: www.cambridge.org/9781108078719

© in this compilation Cambridge University Press 2015

This edition first published 1832
This digitally printed version 2015

ISBN 978-1-108-07871-9 Paperback

This book reproduces the text of the original edition. The content and language reflect
the beliefs, practices and terminology of their time, and have not been updated.

Cambridge University Press wishes to make clear that the book, unless originally published
by Cambridge, is not being republished by, in association or collaboration with,
or with the endorsement or approval of, the original publisher or its successors in title.

The original edition of this book contains a number of colour plates,
which have been reproduced in black and white. Colour versions of these
images can be found online at www.cambridge.org/9781108078719

DICTIONARY

OF

COMMERCE

AND

COMMERCIAL NAVIGATION.

LONDON :
Printed by A. & R. Spottiswoode,
New-Street-Square.

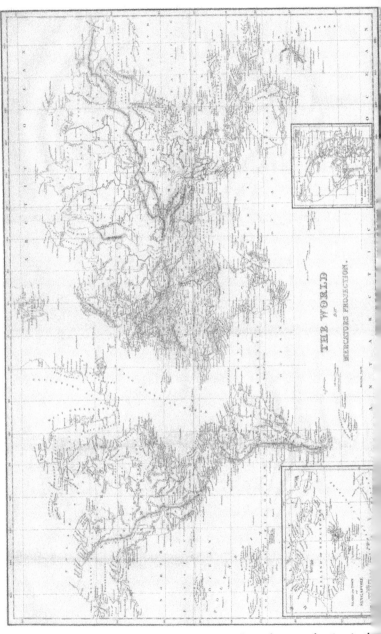

THE WORLD
ON
MERCATORS PROJECTION.

The material originally positioned here is too large for reproduction in this reissue. A PDF can be downloaded from the web address given on page iv of this book, by clicking on 'Resources Available'.

A

DICTIONARY,

PRACTICAL, THEORETICAL, AND HISTORICAL,

OF

COMMERCE

AND

COMMERCIAL NAVIGATION:

ILLUSTRATED WITH MAPS.

By J. R. McCULLOCH, Esq.

Tutte le invenzioni le più benemerite del genere umano, e che hanno sviluppato l'ingegno e la facoltà dell' animo nostro, sono quelle che accostano l' uomo all' uomo, e facilitano la communicazione delle idee, dei bisogni, dei sentimenti, e riducano il genere umano a massa.

VERRI.

LONDON:

PRINTED FOR

LONGMAN, REES, ORME, BROWN, GREEN, & LONGMAN.

MDCCCXXXII.

Though immediately and primarily written for the merchants, this Commercial Dictionary will be of use to every man of business or of curiosity. There is no man who is not in some degree a merchant; who has not something to buy and something to sell, and who does not therefore want such instructions as may teach him the true value of possessions or commodities. The descriptions of the productions of the earth and water which this volume contains, may be equally pleasing and useful to the speculatist with any other Natural History. The descriptions of ports and cities may instruct the geographer as well as if they were found in books appropriated only to his own science; and the doctrines of funds, insurances, currency, monopolies, exchanges, and duties, is so necessary to the politician, that without it he can be of no use either in the council or the senate, nor can speak or think justly either on war or trade.

JOHNSON, *Preface to Rolt's Dict.*

PREFACE.

It has been the wish of the Author and Publishers of this Work, that it should be as extensively useful as possible. If they be not deceived in their expectations, it may be advantageously employed, as a sort of *vade mecum*, by merchants, traders, ship-owners, and ship-masters, in conducting the details of their respective businesses. It is hoped, however, that this object has been attained without omitting the consideration of any topic, incident to the subject, that seemed calculated to make the book generally serviceable, and to recommend it to the attention of all classes.

Had our object been merely to consider commerce as a science, or to investigate its principles, we should not have adopted the form of a Dictionary. But commerce is not a science only, but also an *art* of the utmost practical importance, and in the prosecution of which a very large proportion of the population of every civilised country is actively engaged. Hence, to be generally useful, a work on commerce should combine practice, theory, and history. Different readers may resort to it for different purposes; and every one should be able to find in it clear and accurate information, whether his object be to make himself familiar with details, to acquire a knowledge of principles, or to learn the revolutions that have taken place in the various departments of trade.

The following short outline of what the Work contains may enable the reader to estimate the probability of its fulfilling the objects for which it has been intended: —

I. It contains accounts of the various articles which form the subject matter of commercial transactions. To their English names are, for the most part, subjoined their synonymous appellations in French, German, Italian, Russian, Spanish, &c.; and sometimes, also, in Arabic, Hindoo, Chinese, and other Eastern languages. We have endeavoured, by consulting the best authorities, to make the descriptions of commodities as accurate as possible; and have pointed out the tests or marks by which their goodness may be ascertained. The places where they are produced are also specified; the quantities exported from such places; and the different regulations, duties, &c. affecting their importation and exportation, have been carefully stated, and their influence examined. The prices of most articles have been given, sometimes for a lengthened period. Historical notices are inserted illustrative of the rise and progress of the trade in the most important articles; and it is hoped, that the information embodied in these notices will be found to be as authentic as it is interesting.

II. The Work contains a general article on COMMERCE, explanatory of its nature, principles, and objects, in which there is an inquiry into the policy of restrictions intended to promote industry at home, or to advance the public interests by excluding or restraining foreign competition. Exclusive, however, of this general article, we have separately examined the operation of

the existing restrictions on the trade in particular articles, and with particular countries, in the accounts of those articles, and of the great sea-port towns belonging to the countries referred to. There must, of course, be more or less of sameness in the discussion of such points, the principle which runs through them being identical. But in a Dictionary this is of no consequence. The reader seldom consults more than one or two articles at a time; and it is of infinitely more importance to bring the whole subject at once before him, than to seek to avoid the appearance of repetition by referring from one article to another. In this Work such references are made as seldom as possible.

III. The articles which more particularly refer to commercial navigation are AVERAGE, BILLS OF LADING, BOTTOMRY, CHARTERPARTY, FREIGHT, MASTER, NAVIGATION LAWS, OWNERS, REGISTRY, SALVAGE, SEAMEN, SHIPS, WRECK, &c. These articles embrace a pretty full exposition of the law as to shipping: we have particularly endeavoured to exhibit the privileges enjoyed by British ships; the conditions and formalities, the observance of which is necessary to the acquisition and preservation of such privileges, and to the transference of property in ships; the responsibilities incurred by the masters and owners in their capacity of public carriers; and the reciprocal duties and obligations of owners, masters, and seamen. In this department we have made considerable use of the treatise of Lord Tenterden on the Law of Shipping, — a work that reflects very great credit on the learning and talents of its noble author. The registry act and the navigation act are given entire. To this head may also be referred the articles on the COD, HERRING, and WHALE fisheries.

IV. The principles and practice of commercial arithmetic and accounts are unfolded in the articles BOOK-KEEPING, DISCOUNT, EXCHANGE, INTEREST AND ANNUITIES, &c. The article BOOK-KEEPING has been furnished by one of the official assignees under the new bankrupt act. It exhibits a view of this important art as actually practised in the most extensive mercantile houses in town. The tables for calculating interest and annuities are believed to be more complete than any hitherto given in any work not treating professedly of such subjects.

V. A considerable class of articles may be regarded as descriptive of the various means and devices that have been fallen upon for extending and facilitating commerce and navigation. Of these, taking them in their order, the articles BANKS, BROKERS, CANALS, CARRIERS, COINS, COLONIES, COMPANIES, CONSULS, CONVOY, DOCKS, FACTORS, LIGHT-HOUSES, MONEY, PARTNERSHIP, PILOTAGE, POST OFFICE, RAIL-ROADS, ROADS, TREATIES (COMMERCIAL), WEIGHTS AND MEASURES, &c. are among the most important. In the article BANKS the reader will find besides an exposition of the principles of banking, a pretty full account (derived principally from official sources) of the Bank of England, the private banks of London and the English provincial banks; the Scotch and Irish banks; and the most celebrated foreign banks: to complete this department an account of Savings' Banks is subjoined, with a set of rules which may be taken as a model for such institutions. There is added to the article COINS a table of the assay, weight, and sterling value of the principal foreign gold and silver coins, deduced from assays made at the London and Paris Mints, taken, by permission, from the last edition of Dr. Kelly's *Cambist*. The article COLONIES is one of the most extensive in the work: it contains a sketch of the ancient and modern systems of colonisation; an examination of the principles of colonial policy; and a view of the extent, trade, population, and resources of the colonies of this and other countries. In this article, and in the articles QUEBEC, SYDNEY, and VAN DIEMEN'S LAND, recent and authentic information is given, which those intending to emigrate will find worthy of their attention. The map of the British possessions in North America

is on a pretty large scale, and is, if not the very best, second to none, of those countries, that has hitherto been published in an accessible form. It will be a valuable acquisition for emigrants to Canada, Nova Scotia, &c. The article COLONIES is also illustrated by a map of Central America and the West Indies. An engraved plan is given, along with the article DOCKS, of the river Thames and the docks from Blackwall to the Tower; and the latest regulations issued by the different dock companies here and in other towns, as to the docking of ships, and the charges on that account, and on account of the loading, unloading, warehousing, &c. of goods, are given verbatim. The statements in the articles LIGHT-HOUSES and PILOTAGE have been mostly furnished by the Trinity House, and may be implicitly relied upon. In the article WEIGHTS AND MEASURES the reader will find tables of the equivalents of wine, ale, and Winchester measures, in Imperial measure.

VI. Besides a general article on the constitution, advantages, and disadvantages of Companies, accounts are given of the principal associations existing in Great Britain for the purpose of conducting commercial undertakings, or undertakings subordinate to and connected with commerce. Among others (exclusive of the Banking and Dock Companies already referred to) may be mentioned the EAST INDIA COMPANY, the GAS COMPANIES, the INSURANCE COMPANIES, the MINING COMPANIES, the WATER COMPANIES, &c. The article on the East India Company is of considerable length; it contains a pretty complete sketch of the rise, progress, and present state of the British trade with India; a view of the revenue, population, &c. of our Indian dominions; and an estimate of the influence of the Company's monopoly. We have endeavoured, in treating of insurance, to supply what we think a desideratum, by giving a distinct and plain statement of its principles, and a brief notice of its history; with an account of the rules and practices followed by individuals and companies in transacting the more important departments of the business; and of the terms on which houses, lives, &c. are commonly insured. The part of the article which peculiarly respects marine insurance was contributed by a practical gentleman of much knowledge and experience in that branch.

VII. In addition to the notices of the excise and customs regulations affecting particular commodities given under their names, the reader will find articles under the heads of CUSTOMS, EXCISE, IMPORTATION AND EXPORTATION, LICENCES, SMUGGLING, WAREHOUSING, &c. which comprise most of the practical details as to the business of the Excise and Customs, particularly the latter. The most important customs acts are given with very little abridgment, and being printed in small letter, they occupy comparatively little space. The article TARIFF contains a account of the various duties, drawbacks, and bounties, on the importation and exportation of all sorts of commodities into and from this country, as they stood on the 1st of January, 1832. We once intended to have also given the tariffs of some of the principal continental states; but from the frequency of the changes made in them, they would very soon have become obsolete, and would have tended rather to mislead than to instruct. We have, however, given the existing tariff of the United States.

VIII. Among the articles of a miscellaneous description, may be specified APPRENTICE, AUCTIONEER, BALANCE OF TRADE, BANKRUPTCY, CONTRABAND, CREDIT, HANSEATIC LEAGUE, IMPORTS AND EXPORTS, IMPRESSMENT, MARITIME LAW, PATENTS, PAWNBROKING, PIRACY, PRECIOUS METALS, PRICES, PRIVATEERS, PUBLICANS, QUARANTINE, &c.

IX. Notices are given, under their proper heads, of the principal emporiums with which this country has any immediate intercourse; of the commodities

usually exported from and imported into them; of their monies, weights, and measures; and of such of their institutions, customs, and regulations, with respect to commerce and navigation, as seemed to deserve notice. There are occasionally subjoined to these notices of the great sea-ports, pretty full accounts of the trade of the countries in which they are situated; as in the instances of AMSTERDAM, BORDEAUX, CALCUTTA, CANTON, HAVANNAH, HAVRE, NEW-YORK, PETERSBURGH, RIO DE JANEIRO, VERA CRUZ, &c. To have attempted to do this systematically would have increased the size of the Work beyond all reasonable limits, and embarrassed it with details nowise interesting to the English reader. The plan we have adopted has enabled us to treat of such matters as might be supposed of importance in England, and to reject the rest. We believe, however, that, notwithstanding this selection, those who compare this work with others, will find that it contains a larger mass of authentic information respecting the trade and navigation of foreign countries than is to be found in any English publication.

The reader may be inclined, perhaps, to think that it must be impossible to embrace the discussion of so many subjects in a single octavo volume, without treating a large proportion in a very brief and unsatisfactory manner. But, in point of fact, this single octavo contains about as much letter-press as is contained in two ordinary folio volumes, and more than is contained in Macpherson's Annals of Commerce, in four large volumes quarto, published at 8l. 8s.! This extraordinary condensation has been effected without any sacrifice either of beauty or distinctness. Could we suppose that the substance of the book is at all equal to its form, there would be little room for doubt as to its success.

Aware that, in a work of this nature, accuracy in matters of fact is of primary importance, the authority on which any statement is made is invariably quoted. Except, too, in the case of books in every one's hands, or Dictionaries, the page or chapter of all works referred to is generally specified; experience having taught us that the convenient practice of stringing together a list of authorities at the end of an article is much oftener a cloak for ignorance than an evidence of research.

Our object being to describe articles in the state in which they are offered for sale, we have not entered, except when it was necessary to give precision or clearness to their description, into any details as to the processes followed in their manufacture.

Besides the maps already noticed, the work contains a map of the world, on Mercator's projection, and a map of Central and Southern Europe and the Mediterranean Sea. These maps are on a larger scale than those usually given with works of this sort; and have been carefully corrected, and compared with the best authorities.

Such is a rough outline of what the reader may expect to meet with in this Dictionary. We do not, however, flatter ourselves with the notion that he will consider that all that has been attempted has been properly executed. In a work embracing such an extreme range and diversity of subjects, as to many of which it is exceedingly difficult, if not quite impossible, to obtain accurate information, no one will be offended should he detect a few errors. At the same time we can honestly say that neither labour nor expense has been spared to render the Work worthy of the public confidence and patronage. The author has been almost incessantly engaged upon it for upwards of three years; and the previous part of his life may be said to have been spent in preparing himself for the undertaking. He has derived valuable assistance from some distinguished official gentlemen, and from many eminent merchants; and has endeavoured, wherever it was practicable

to build his conclusions upon official documents. But in very many instances he has been obliged to adopt less authentic data; and he does not suppose that he had sagacity enough always to resort to the best authorities, or that, amidst conflicting and contradictory statements, he has uniformly selected those most worthy of being relied upon, or that the inferences he has drawn are always such as the real circumstances of the case would warrant. But he has done his best not to be wanting in these respects. We have had no motive to induce us, in any instance, to conceal or pervert the truth. What we have considered wrong, we have censured freely and openly; but we have not done this without assigning the grounds of our opinion; so that the reader may always judge for himself as to its correctness. Our sole object has been to produce a work that should be generally useful, particularly to merchants and traders, and which should be creditable to ourselves. Whether we have succeeded, the award of the public will show; and to it we submit our labours, not with " frigid indifference," but with an anxious hope that it may be found we have not misemployed our time, and engaged in an undertaking too vast for our limited means.

The following notices of some of the most celebrated Commercial Dictionaries may not, perhaps, be unacceptable. At all events, they will show that there is at least room for the present attempt.

The *Grand Dictionnaire de Commerce*, begun and principally executed by M. Savary, Inspector of Customs at Paris, and completed by his brother, the Abbé Savary, Canon of St. Maur, was published at Paris in 1723, in two volumes folio; a supplemental volume being added in 1730. This was the first work of the kind that appeared in modern Europe; and has furnished the principal part of the materials for most of those by which it has been followed. The undertaking was liberally patronised by the French government, who justly considered that a Commercial Dictionary, if well executed, would be of national importance. Since a considerable, and, indeed, the most valuable, portion of M. Savary's work is compiled from Memoirs sent him, by order of government, by the inspectors of manufactures in France, and by the French consuls in foreign countries. An enlarged and improved edition of the *Dictionnaire* was published at Geneva in 1750, in six folio volumes. But the best edition is that of Copenhagen, in five volumes folio; the first of which appeared in 1759, and the last in 1765. More than the half of this work consists of matter altogether foreign to its proper object. It is, in fact, a sort of Dictionary of Manufactures as well as of commerce; descriptions being given, which are, necessarily perhaps, in most instances exceedingly incomplete, and which the want of plates often renders unintelligible, of the methods followed in the manufacture of the commodities described. It is also filled with lengthened articles on subjects of natural history, on the bye laws and privileges of different corporations, and a variety of subjects nowise connected with commercial pursuits. No one, however, need look into it for any developement of sound principles, or for enlarged views. As valuable as a repertory of facts relating to commerce and manufactures at the commencement of last century, collected with laudable care and industry; but the spirit which pervades it is that of a customs officer, and not that of a merchant or a philosopher. " *Souvent dans ses réflexions, il tend plutôt à égarer ses lecteurs qu'à les conduire, et des maximes nuisibles au progrès du commerce et de l'industrie obtiennent presque toujours ses éloges et son approbation.*"

The preceding extract is from the Prospectus, in one volume octavo, published by the Abbé Morellet, in 1769, of a new Commercial Dictionary, which was to extend to five or probably six volumes folio. This Prospectus is a work of ster-

ling merit; and from the acknowledged learning, talents, and capacity of its
author for laborious exertion, there can be no doubt that, had the projected
Dictionary been completed, it would have been infinitely superior to that of
Savary. It appears (Prospectus, pp. 353—373.) that Morellet had been engaged
for a number of years in preparations for this great work; and that he had
amassed a large collection of books and manuscripts relative to the commerce,
navigation, colonies, arts, &c. of France and other countries. The enterprise
was begun under the auspices of M. Trudaine, Intendant of Finance, and was
patronised by Messrs. L'Averdy and Bertin, Comptrollers General. But whether
it were owing to the gigantic nature of the undertaking, to the author having
become too much engrossed with other pursuits, the want of sufficient encouragement, or some other cause, no part of the proposed Dictionary ever appeared.
We are ignorant of the fate of the valuable collection of manuscripts made by the
Abbé Morellet. His books were sold at Paris within these few years.

A Commercial Dictionary, in three volumes 4to, forming part of the *Encyclopédie Méthodique*, was published at Paris in 1783. It is very unequally executed,
and contains numerous articles that might have been advantageously left out.
The editors acknowledge in their Preface that they have, in most instances, been
obliged to borrow from Savary. The best parts of the work are copied from the
edition of the *Traité Général du Commerce* of Ricard, published at Amsterdam
in 1781, in two volumes 4to.*

The earliest Commercial Dictionary published in England, was compiled by
Malachy Postlethwayt, Esq., a diligent and indefatigable writer. The first part
of the first edition appeared in 1751. The last edition, in two enormous folio
volumes, was published in 1774. It is chargeable with the same defects as that
of M. Savary, of which, indeed, it is for the most part a literal translation. The
author has made no effort to condense or combine the statements under different
articles, which are frequently not a little contradictory; at the same time that
many of them are totally unconnected with commerce.

In 1761, Richard Rolt, Esq. published a Commercial Dictionary in one volume
folio. The best part of this work is its Preface, which was contributed by Dr
Johnson. It is for the most part abridged from Postlethwayt; but it contains
some useful original articles, mixed, however, with many alien to the subject.

In 1766, a Commercial Dictionary was published, in two rather thin folio
volumes, by Thomas Mortimer, Esq., at that time Vice-Consul for the Netherlands. This is a more commodious and better arranged, but not a more valuable
work than that of Postlethwayt. The plan of the author embraces, like that
of his predecessors, too great a variety of objects; more than half the work being
filled with geographical articles, and articles describing the processes carried on in
different departments of manufacturing industry: there are also articles on very
many subjects, such as architecture, the natural history of the ocean, the land
tax, the qualifications of surgeons, &c., the relation of which to commerce,
navigation, or manufactures, it seems difficult to discover.

In 1810, a Commercial Dictionary was published, in one thick octavo volume,
purporting to be by Mr. Mortimer. We understand, however, that he had but
little, if any thing, to do with its compilation. It is quite unworthy of the subject, and of the epoch when it appeared. It has all the faults of those by which
it was preceded, with but few peculiar merits. Being not only a Dictionary of
Commerce and Navigation, but of Manufactures, it contains accounts of the different arts: but to describe these in a satisfactory and really useful manner,

* This, when published, must have been a very valuable work. It is now, however, in a great measure
obsolete.

would require several volumes, and the co-operation of many individuals: so that while the accounts referred to are worth very little, they occupy so large a space that room has not been left for the proper discussion of those subjects from which alone the work derives whatever value it possesses. Thus, there is an article of twenty-two pages technically describing the various processes of the art of painting, while the general article on commerce is comprised in less than *two* pages. The articles on coin and money do not together occupy four pages, being considerably less than the space allotted to the articles on engraving and etching. There is not a word said as to the circumstances which determine the course of exchange; and the important subject of credit is disposed of in less than *two lines!* Perhaps, however, the greatest defect in the work is its total want of any thing like science. No attempt is ever made to explain the principles on which any operation depends. Every thing is treated as if it were empirical and arbitrary. Except in the legal articles, no authorities are quoted; so that very little dependence can be placed on the statements advanced.

In another Commercial Dictionary, republished within these few years, the general article on commerce consists of a discussion with respect to simple and compound demand, and simple and double competition: luckily the article does not fill quite a page; being considerably shorter than the description of the kaleidoscope.

Under these circumstances, we do think that there is room for a new Dictionary of Commerce and Commercial Navigation: and whatever may be thought of our Work, it cannot be said that in bringing it into the field we are encroaching on ground already fully occupied.

We do not presume to cast the horoscope of this Work. But we are exceedingly anxious, in the event of its arriving at another edition, to be possessed of the means of rectifying such errors as may have insinuated themselves into our statements, and of completing those parts that are defective. We, therefore, hope that merchants in this and other countries, and that all those into whose hands this Dictionary may happen to come, who take an interest in the diffusion of accurate information on subjects of great practical importance, will be kind enough to transmit to Messrs. Longman and Co. such remarks, observations, and documents, as may seem to them of any material importance in regard to the above mentioned objects. They will be gratefully received, and will not be thrown away.

ERRATUM.

Page 149. line 35. (BOOK-KEEPING AND ACCOUNTS). *For the words* " is left out of the balance. Exclusive of Stock" *read* " is put in the balance sheet exactly as it was in the beginning of the year. Including Stock," &c.

The material originally positioned here is too large for reproduction in the reissue. A PDF can be downloaded from the web address given on page i of this book, by clicking on 'Resources Available'.

A

DICTIONARY

OF

COMMERCE,

AND

COMMERCIAL NAVIGATION.

AAM, Aum, or Ahm, a measure for liquids, used at Amsterdam, Antwerp, Hamburgh, Frankfort, &c. At Amsterdam it is nearly equal to 41 English wine gallons, at Antwerp to 36¼ ditto, at Hamburgh to 38¼ ditto, and at Frankfort to 39 ditto.

ABANDONMENT, in commerce and navigation, is used to express the abandoning or surrendering of the ship or goods insured to the insurer.

It is held, by the law of England, that the insured has the right to abandon, and to compel the insurers to pay the whole value of the thing insured, in every case "where, by the happening of any of the misfortunes or perils insured against, the voyage is lost, or not worth pursuing, and the projected adventure is frustrated; or where the thing insured is so damaged and spoiled as to be of little or no value to the owner; or where the salvage is very high; or where what is saved is of less value than the freight; or where further expense is necessary, and the insurer will not undertake to pay that expense," &c. — (*Marshall*, Book I. cap. 13. § 1.)

Abandonment very frequently takes place in cases of capture: the loss is then total, and no question can arise in respect to it. In cases, however, in which a ship and cargo are recaptured *within such a time that the object of the voyage is not lost*, the insured is not entitled to abandon. The mere *stranding* of a ship is not deemed of itself such a loss as will justify an abandonment. If by some fortunate accident, by the exertions of the crew, or by any borrowed assistance, the ship be got off and rendered capable of continuing her voyage, it is not a total loss, and the insurers are only liable for the expenses occasioned by the stranding. It is only where the stranding is followed by *shipwreck*, or in any other way renders the ship incapable of prosecuting her voyage, that the insurer can abandon.

It has been decided, that damage sustained in a voyage to the extent of forty-eight per cent. of the value of the ship, did not entitle the insured to abandon. If a cargo be damaged in the course of a voyage, and it appears that what has been saved is less than the amount of freight, it is held to be a total loss. —(*Park Insurance*, cap. 9.)

When by the occurrence of any of the perils insured against the insured has acquired a right to abandon, he is at liberty either to abandon or not, as he thinks proper. He is in no case bound to abandon; but if he make an election, and resolve to abandon, he must abide by his resolution, and has no longer the power to claim for a partial loss. In some foreign countries specific periods are fixed by law within which the insured, after being informed of the loss, must elect either to abandon or not. In this country, however, no particular period is fixed for this purpose; but the rule is, that if the insured determine to abandon, he must intimate such determination to the insurers within a *reasonable period* after he has

B

got intelligence of the loss, any unnecessary delay in making this intimation being interpreted to mean that he has decided not to abandon.

No particular form or solemnity is required in giving notice of an abandonment. It may be given either to the underwriter himself, or the agent who subscribed for him.

The effect of an abandonment is to vest all the rights of the insured in the insurers. . The latter become the legal owners of the ship, and as such are liable for all her future outgoings, and entitled to her future earnings. An abandonment, when once made, is irrevocable.

In case of shipwreck or other misfortune, the captain and crew are bound to exert themselves to the utmost to save as much property as possible ; and to enable them to do this without prejudice to the right of abandonment, our policies provide that, " in case of any loss or misfortune, the insured, their factors, servants, and assigns, shall be at liberty to sue and labour about the defence, safeguard, and recovery of the goods, and merchandises, and ship, &c. without prejudice to the insurance; to the charges whereof the insurers agree to contribute, each according to the rate and quantity of his subscription."

" From the nature of his situation," says Mr. Serjeant Marshall, " the captain has an implied authority, not only from the insured, but also from the insurers and all others interested in the ship or cargo, in case of misfortune, to do whatever he thinks most conducive to the general interest of all concerned; and they are all bound by his acts. Therefore, if the ship be disabled by stress of weather, or any other peril of the sea, the captain may hire another vessel for the transport of the goods to their port of destination, if he think it for the interest of all concerned that he should do so ; or he may, upon a capture, appeal against a sentence of condemnation, or carry on any other proceedings for the recovery of the ship and cargo, provided he has a probable ground for doing so ; or he may, upon the loss of the ship, invest the produce of the goods saved in other goods, which he may ship for his original port of destination ; for whatever is recovered of the effects insured, the captain is accountable to the insurers. If the insured neglect to abandon when he has it in his power to do so, he adopts the acts of the captain, and he is bound by them. If, on the other hand, the insurers, after notice of abandonment, suffer the captain to continue in the management, he becomes their agent, and they are bound by his acts."

As to the sailors, when a misfortune happens, they are bound to save and preserve the merchandise to the best of their power ; and while they are so employed, they are entitled to wages, so far, at least, as what is saved will allow ; but if they refuse to assist in this, they shall have neither wages nor reward. In this the Rhodian law, and the laws of Oleron, Wisby, and the Hanse Towns, agree.

The policy of the practice of abandonment seems very questionable. The object of an insurance is to render the insurer liable for whatever loss or damage may be incurred. But this object does not seem to be promoted by compelling him to pay as for a total loss when, in fact, the loss is only partial. The captain and crew of a ship are selected by the owners, are their servants, and are responsible to them for their proceedings. But in the event of a ship being stranded, and so damaged that the owners are entitled to abandon, the captain and crew become the servants of the underwriters, who had nothing to do with their appointment, and to whom they are most probably altogether unknown. It is admitted that a regulation of this sort can hardly fail of leading, and has indeed frequently led, to very great abuses. We, therefore, are inclined to think that abandonment ought not to be allowed where any property is known to exist; but that such property should continue at the disposal of the owners and their agents, and that the underwriters should be liable only for the damage really incurred. The first case that came before the British courts with respect to abandonment was decided by Lord Hardwicke, in 1744. Mr. Justice Buller appears to have concurred in the opinion now stated, that abandonment should not have been allowed in cases where the loss is not total.

For further information as to this subject, see the excellent works of Mr. Serjeant Marshall (book i. cap. 13.); and of Mr. Justice Park (cap. 9.) on the Law of Insurance.

ABATEMENT, or REBATE, is the name sometimes given to a discount allowed for prompt payment ; it is also used to express the deduction that is some

mes made at the custom-house from the duties chargeable upon such goods as re damaged. This allowance is regulated by the 6 Geo. 4. c. 107. § 28. No batement is made from the duties charged on coffee, currants, figs, lemons, ranges, raisins, tobacco, and wine.

ACACIA, or GUM ARABIC, (Fr. *Gomme Arabique*; Ger. *Arabischen Gummi*; . *Gomma Arabica*; Arab. *Tolh*,) a gum which exudes from the trunk and ranches of the *Acacia vera*, a tree growing in Arabia, Barbary, and other places. It is hard, brittle, transparent, of a pale yellowish hue; insipid and inodorous. is imported from Barbary and Morocco in large casks. Its specific gravity ries from 1·31 to 1·43. It is often mixed with gum Senegal, which is nearly pure, but in larger masses, of a darker colour, and more clammy and te-acious.

ACAPULCO, a celebrated sea-port on the western coast of Mexico, in t. 16° 50½′ N., long. 99° 46′ W. Population uncertain, but said to be from 000 to 5,000. The harbour of Acapulco is one of the finest in the world, d is capable of containing any number of ships in the most perfect safety. Pre-ously to the emancipation of Spanish America, a galleon or large ship, richly den, was annually sent from Acapulco to Manilla, in the Philippine Islands; d at her return a fair was held, which was much resorted to by strangers. But is sort of intercourse is no longer carried on, the trade to Manilla and all other ices being now conducted by private individuals. The exports consist of llion, cochineal, cocoa, wool, indigo, &c. The imports principally consist of tton goods, hardware, articles of jewellery, raw and wrought silks, spices, and matics. Acapulco is extremely unhealthy; and though it be the principal port the west coast of Mexico, its commerce is not very considerable. The navi-ion from Acapulco to Guyaquil and Callao is exceedingly tedious and difficult, that there is but little intercourse between Mexico and Peru. The monies, ghts, and measures are the same as those of Spain; for which see CADIZ.

ACIDS, are a class of compounds which are distinguished from all others by following properties. They are generally possessed of a very sharp and sour te: redden the infusions of blue vegetable colours; are often highly corrosive, l enter into combination with the alkalies, earths, and metallic oxides; forming npounds in which the characters of the constituents are entirely destroyed, l new ones produced differing in every respect from those previously existing. e quality or strength of an acid is generally ascertained, either by its specific vity, which is found by means of the hydrometer, if the acid be liquid, or by quantity of pure and dry subcarbonate of potass or soda, or of carbonate of e (marble), which a given weight of the acid requires for its exact neutralisa-. This latter process is termed Acidimetry, or the ascertaining the quantity eal acid existing in any of the liquid or crystallised acids.

he principal acids at present known are, the Acetic, Benzoic, Boracic, Bromic, bonic, Citric, Chloric, Cyanic, Fluoric, Ferroprussic, Gallic, Hydrobromic, driodic, Iodic, Lactic, Malic, Margaric, Meconic, Muriatic or Hydrochloric, ous, Nitric, Oleic, Oxalic, Phosphoric, Prussic or Hydrocyanic, Purpuric, cholactic, Suberic, Sulphurous, Sulphuric, Tartaric, Uric, and many others ch it would be superfluous to detail. It is the most important only of these, ever, that will be here treated of, and more particularly those employed e arts and manufactures.

etic or pyroligneous acid. — This acid, in its pure and concentrated form, is obtained the fluid matter which passes over in distillation, when wood is exposed to heat in iron cylinders. This fluid is a mixture of acetic acid, tar, and a very volatile ether; these the acid may be separated, after a second distillation, by saturating with chalk, vaporating to dryness; an acetate of lime is thus procured, which, by mixture with ate of soda (glauber salt), is decomposed, the resulting compounds being an insolu-ulphate of lime, and a very soluble acetate of soda; these are easily separated from other by solution in water and filtration; the acetate of soda being obtained in the alline form by evaporation. From this, or the acetate of lime, some manufacturers oying the former, others the latter, the acetic acid is obtained by distillation with uric acid (oil of vitriol); as thus procured, it is a colourless, volatile fluid, having y pungent and refreshing odour, and a strong acid taste. Its strength should be ained by the quantity of marble required for its neutralisation, on account of its ic gravity not giving a correct indication of its strength. It is employed in the

preparation of the acetate of lead (sugar of lead), in many of the pharmaceutical compounds, and also as an antiseptic.

Vinegar is an impure and very dilute acetic acid, obtained by exposing either weak wines or infusions of malt to the air and a slow fermentation; it contains besides the pure acid, a large quantity of colouring matter, some mucilage, and a little spirit; from these it is readily separated by distillation. The impurities with which this distilled vinegar is sometimes adulterated, or with which it is accidentally contaminated, are oil of vitriol, added to increase the acidity, and oxides of tin or copper, arising from the vinegar having been distilled through tin or copper worms. These may be easily detected; the oil of vitriol by the addition of a little solution of muriate of barytes to the distilled vinegar, which, should the acid be present, will cause a dense white precipitate; and the oxides of tin or copper, by the addition of water impregnated with sulphuretted hydrogen. Vinegar is employed in many culinary and domestic operations, and also very largely in the manufacture of the carbonate of lead (white lead).

Benzoic acid—exists naturally, formed in the gum benzoin, and may be procured either by submitting the benzoin in fine powder to repeated sublimations, or by digesting it with lime and water, straining off the clear solution, and adding muriatic acid, which enters into combination with the lime, and the benzoic acid, being nearly insoluble in water, falls as a white powder; this may be further purified by a sublimation. Benzoic acid is of a beautiful pearly white colour when pure, has a very peculiar aromatic odour, and an acrid, acid, and bitter taste; it is used in making pastiles and perfumed incense. This acid also occurs in the balsams of Tolu and Peru and in the urine of the horse and cow.

Boracic acid—is found in an uncombined state in many of the hot springs of Tuscany as also at Sasso in the Florentine territory, from whence it has received the name of Sassolin. In Thibet, Persia, and South America, it occurs in combination with soda, and is imported from the former place into this country in a crystalline form, under the name of Tincal. These crystals are coated with a rancid, fatty substance, and require to be purified by repeated solutions and crystallisations; after which it is sold under the appellation of borax (bi-borate of soda); from a hot solution of this salt the boracic is readily obtained, by the addition of sulphuric acid in slight excess; sulphate of soda is formed, and the boracic acid crystallises as the solution cools. When pure, these crystals are white, and have an unctuous greasy feel; they are soluble in alcohol, communicating a green tinge to its flame; when fused it forms a transparent glass, and has been found by Mr. Faraday to unite with the oxide of lead, producing a very uniform glass, free from all defects, and well adapted for the purpose of telescopes and other astronomical instruments. Borax is much employed in the arts, particularly in metallurgic operations as a flux, also in enamelling, and in pharmacy.

Carbonic acid. — This acid occurs very abundantly in nature, combined with lime, magnesia, barytes, aerial acid, fixed air, mephitic acid; from any of these it is easily separated by the addition of nearly any of the other acids. In its uncombined form, it is a transparent, gaseous fluid, having a density of 1·53, atmospheric air being unity; it is absorbed to a considerable extent by water, and when the water is rendered slightly alkaline by the addition of carbonate of soda, and a large quantity of gas forced into it by pressure, it forms the well known refreshing beverage, soda water. This gas is also formed in very large quantities during combustion, respiration and fermentation. Carbonic acid gas is destructive of animal life and combustion, and from its great weight accumulates in the bottoms of deep wells, cellars, caves, &c., which have been closed for a long period, and numerous fatal accidents arise frequently to persons entering such places incautiously; the precaution should always be taken of introducing a lighted candle prior to the descent or entrance of any one; for should the candle be extinguished, it would be dangerous to enter until properly ventilated. The combination of carbonic acid with the alkalies, earths, and metallic oxides are termed carbonates.

Citric acid — exists in a free state, in the juice of the lemon, lime, and other fruit combined however with mucilage, and sometimes a little sugar, which renders it, required to be preserved for a long period, very liable to ferment; on this account, the crystallised citric acid is to be preferred. It is prepared by saturating the lemon juice with chalk: the citric acid combines with the lime, forming an insoluble compound while the carbonic acid is liberated; the insoluble citrate, after being well washed, is be acted upon by dilute sulphuric acid, which forms sulphate of lime, and the citric acid enters into solution in the water; by filtration and evaporation the citric acid is obtained in colourless transparent crystals. The chief uses to which it is applied are a preventive of sea scurvy, and in making refreshing acidulous or effervescing drinks for which latter purpose it is peculiarly fitted from its very pleasant flavour.

Fluoric acid is found in the well known mineral fluor spar in combination with lime, from which it is procured in the liquid form, by distillation with dilute sulphuric acid, a leaden or silver retort; the receiver should be of the same material as the retort, and kept cool by ice or snow.

This acid is gaseous in its pure form, highly corrosive, and intensely acid ; it is rapidly absorbed by water, communicating its properties to that fluid. Its chief use is for etching on glass, which it corrodes with great rapidity. For this purpose a thin coating of wax is to be melted on the surface of the glass, and the sketch drawn by a fine hard-pointed instrument through the wax, the liquid acid is then poured on it, and after a short time, on the removal of the acid and the coating, an etching will be found in the substance of the glass. A very excellent application of this property, possessed by fluoric acid, is in the roughing the shades for table lamps. All the metals, except silver, lead, and platina, are acted upon by this acid.

Gallic acid. — The source from which this acid is generally obtained is the nut gall, a hard protuberance produced on the oak by the puncture of insects. The most simple method of procuring the acid in its pure form, is to submit the galls in fine powder to sublimation in a retort, taking care that the heat be applied slowly and with caution ; the other processes require a very long period for their completion. When pure, gallic acid has a white and silky appearance, and a highly astringent and slightly acid taste. The nut galls, which owe their properties to the gallic acid they contain, are employed very extensively in the arts, for dyeing and staining silks, cloths, and woods of a black colour ; this is owing to its forming with the action of iron an intense black precipitate. Writing ink is made on the same principle : a very excellent receipt of the late Dr. Black's is, to take 3 oz. of the best Aleppo galls in fine powder, 1oz. sulphate of iron (green vitriol), 1oz. logwood finely rasped, 1oz. gum arabic, one pint of the best vinegar, one pint of soft water, and 8 or 10 cloves; in this case the black precipitate is kept suspended by the gum.

Hydriodic acid, — a compound of iodine and hydrogen, in its separate form is of very little importance in the arts ; its combinations with potass, soda, and other of the metallic oxides, will be treated of hereafter.

Malic acid — exists in the juices of many fruits, particularly the apple, as also in the berries of the service and mountain ash.

Meconic acid — is found in opium, in combination with morphia, forming the meconate of morphia, on which the action of opium principally depends.

Muriatic acid, or spirits of salts. — This acid (the hydrochloric of the French chemists) is manufactured from the chloride of sodium (dry sea salt), by the action of sulphuric acid (oil of vitriol). The most economical proportions are 20 pounds of fused salt, and 10 pounds of oil of vitriol previously mixed with an equal weight of water ; these are placed in an iron or earthen pot, to which an earthen head and receiver are adapted, and submitted to distillation ; the muriatic acid passes over in the vaporous form, and may be easily condensed. The liquid acid thus obtained should have a specific gravity of 1.17, water being equal to 100 ; it has a strong acid taste, and a slight yellow colour ; this is owing to a small quantity of oxide of iron. By re-distillation in a glass retort at low temperature, it may be obtained perfectly pure and colourless. It sometimes contains a little sulphuric acid ; this is detected by a little solution of muriate of barytes. Muriatic acid, in its uncombined state, is an invisible elastic gas, having a very strong affinity for water, that fluid absorbing, at a temperature of 40° Fahrenheit, 480 times its volume, and the resulting liquid acid has a density of 121. So great is this attraction for water, that when the gas is liberated into the air, it combines with the moisture always present in that medium, forming dense white vapours. Its combinations with the alkalies, &c. are termed muriates ; those of the greatest importance are, the muriates of tin, ammonia, barytes, and sea salt. The test for the presence of muriatic acid in any fluid is the nitrate of silver (lunar caustic), which causes a curdy white precipitate.

Nitric acid, or aquafortis. — This, which is one of the most useful acids with which the chemist is acquainted, is prepared by acting upon saltpetre (nitre or nitrate of potass), with oil of vitriol : the proportions best suited for this purpose are, three parts by weight of nitre and two of oil of vitriol ; or 100 nitre, and 60 oil of vitriol, previously diluted with 20 of water ; either of these proportions will produce a very excellent acid. When submitted to distillation, which should be conducted in earthen or glass vessels, the nitric acid passes over in the form of vapour, and a bi-sulphate potass (sal mixum), remains in the retort.

Nitric acid of commerce has usually a dark orange red colour, giving off copious fumes, and having a specific gravity of 150, compared with water as 100. Strongly acid and highly corrosive, it may be obtained perfectly colourless by a second distillation, rejecting the first portion that passes over. It is much employed in the arts, for etching on copper-plates for engraving ; also, for the separation of silver from gold, in the process of quartation. In pharmacy and surgery it is extensively used, and is employed for destroying contagious effluvia. Combined with muriatic acid, it forms aqua regia (nitro-muriatic acid), used as a solvent for gold, platina, &c. This acid is frequently contaminated with the muriatic and sulphuric acids ; these may be detected by the following methods. A portion of the suspected acid should be diluted with three or four times

its volume of distilled water, and divided into two glasses; to one of which nitrate of silver (lunar caustic in solution) is to be added, and to the other, nitrate of barytes: if muriatic be present, a white curdy precipitate will be thrown down by the former; and if sulphuric, a white granular precipitate by the latter.

Oxalic acid — occurs in combination with potass as binoxalate of potass in the different varieties of sorrel, from whence the binoxalate of potass has been termed salt of sorrel. This acid is usually prepared by the action of nitric acid upon sugar, evaporating the solution, after the action has ceased, to the consistence of a syrup, and re-dissolving and re-crystallising the crystals which are thus procured.

It is sold in small white acicular crystals, of a strongly acid taste and highly poisonous, and sometimes in its external appearance bears a strong similarity to Epsom salts (sulphate of magnesia), which it has been unfortunately frequently mistaken for. It is instantly distinguished from Epsom salts by placing a small crystal upon the tongue; when its strong acid taste, compared with the nauseous bitter of the sulphate of magnesia, will be quite a sufficient criterion. In cases of poisoning however by this acid, lime, or chalk, mixed with water to form a cream, should be immediately administered, the combinations of oxalic acid with these substances being perfectly inert. It is employed in removing ink stains, iron moulds, &c., from linen and leather: the best proportions for these purposes are: 1oz. of the acid to a pint of water. The most delicate test of the presence of oxalic lead is, a salt of lime or lime water, with either of which it forms a white precipitate, insoluble in water, but soluble in acids. Its combinations are termed oxalates.

Phosphoric acid — is of very little importance in a commercial point of view, except as forming with lime the earth of bones (phosphate of lime.) It is prepared by heating bones to whiteness in a furnace; from this phosphoric acid is obtained by the action of sulphuric acid, still combined, however, with a small quantity of lime. The action of nitric acid upon phosphorus, the latter being added gradually and in small pieces, yields this acid in a state of purity; its combinations are termed phosphates.

Prussic acid, or hydrocyanic acid. — This acid, which is the most virulent and poisonous acid known, is contained in peach blossoms, bay leaves, and many other vegetable productions, which owe their peculiar odour to the presence of prussic acid. For the purposes of medicine and chemistry, this acid is prepared either by distilling one part of the cyanuret of mercury, one part of muriatic acid of specific gravity 1·15, and six parts of water, six parts of prussic acid being collected; or, by dissolving a certain weight of cyanuret of mercury, and passing a current of sulphuretted hydrogen through the solution, until the whole of the mercury shall be precipitated; if an excess of sulphuretted hydrogen should be present, a little carbonate of lead (white lead), will remove it; on filtering, a colourless prussic acid will be obtained. By the first process, which is the one followed at Apothecaries' Hall, the acid has a density of 995, water being equal to 1000; by the latter, it may be procured of any required strength, depending on the quantity of cyanuret mercury dissolved. The best test for the presence of this acid is, first to add a small quantity of the protosulphate of iron (solution of green vitriol), then a little solution of potassa, and lastly diluted sulphuric acid; if prussic acid be present, prussian blue will be formed. Its combinations are called prussiates or hydrocyanates; when in its concentrated form, it is so rapid in its effects that large animals have been killed in the short space of 80 seconds, or from a minute to a minute and a half.

Sulphurous acid — is formed whenever sulphur is burnt in atmospheric air: it is a suffocating and pungent gas, strongly acid, bleaches vegetable colours with great rapidity, and arrests the process of vinous fermentation. For these purposes it is therefore very much employed, especially in bleaching woollen goods and straw. Fermentation may be immediately arrested by burning a small quantity of sulphur in casks, and then racking off the wine while still fermenting into them; this frequently gives the wine a very unpleasant taste of sulphur, which is avoided by the use of sulphite of potass, made by impregnating a solution of potass with sulphurous acid gas.

Sulphuric acid, or oil of vitriol — called oil of vitriol from its having been formerly manufactured from green vitriol (sulphate of iron). In some parts of the Continent this process is still followed. The method generally adopted in this country, is to introduce nine parts sulphur, intimately mixed with one part of nitre, in a state of active combustion, into large leaden chambers, the bottoms of which are covered with a stratum of water. Sulphurous and nitrous acid gases are generated, which entering into combination form a white crystalline solid, which falls to the bottom of the chamber; the instant that the water comes in contact with it, this solid is decomposed with a hissing noise and effervescence, sulphuric acid combines with the water, and nitrous gas is liberated, which combining with oxygen from the air of the chamber, is converted into nitrous acid gas, again combines with sulphurous acid gas, and again falls to the bottom of the chamber; this process continues as long as the combustion of the sulphur is kept up, or as long as atmospheric air remains in the chamber; the nitrous

cid merely serving as a means for the transference of oxygen from the atmosphere to ¬e sulphurous acid, to convert it into sulphuric acid. The water is removed from the ¬amber when of a certain strength, and replaced by fresh. These acid waters are then ¬vaporated in leaden boilers, and finally concentrated in glass or platina vessels. As ¬us manufactured, sulphuric acid is a dense oily fluid, colourless, intensely acid, and ¬ghly corrosive, and has a specific gravity of 1846, water being equal to 1000. This acid the most important with which we are acquainted ; it is employed in the manufacture the nitric, muriatic, acetic, phosphoric, citric, tartaric, and many other acids ; also in ¬e preparation of chlorine, for the manufacture of the bleaching powder (oxymuriate of ¬ne or chloride of lime), for the preparation of sulphate of mercury, in the manufacture calomel and corrosive sublimate, and in innumerable other chemical manufactures. ¬ the practice of physic it is also very much employed. It usually contains a little ¬ide of lead, which is readily detected by diluting the acid with about four times its ¬lume of water, and allowing the sulphate of lead to subside. Its combinations are ¬nominated sulphates. The fuming sulphuric acid, as manufactured at Nordhausén, ¬ntains only one half the quantity of water in its composition.

Tartaric acid. — This acid is procured from the cream of tartar (bi-tartrate of potass), ¬tained by purifying the crust which separates during the fermentation of wines by ¬lution and crystallisation. When this purified bi-tartrate is dissolved, and lime or ¬rbonate of lime added, an insoluble tartrate of lime falls, which after washing should be ¬ted upon by sulphuric acid ; sulphate of lime is thus formed, and the tartaric acid enters ¬to solution, and may be obtained by evaporation and crystallisation. It is employed ¬ry much in the arts, in calico-printing, as also in making effervescing draughts and ¬wders in pharmacy.

Uric acid — is an animal acid of very little importance, except in a scientific point of ¬w : it exists in the excrement of serpents, to the amount of 95 per cent, and forms ¬ basis of many of the urinary calculi and gravel.

¬N.B. *This article, and that on alkalies, has been furnished by an able practical chemist.*

ACORNS (Ger. *Eicheln, Eckern* ; Du. *Akers* ; Fr. *Glands* ; It. *Ghiande* ; ¬. *Bellotas* ; Rus. *Schedudü* ; Lat. *Glandes*), the seed or fruit of the oak. ¬orns formed a part of the food of man in early ages, and frequent allusion is ¬de in the classics to this circumstance (*Virgil, Georg.* lib. i. line 8. ; *Ovid, ¬t.* lib. i. line 106., &c.). In some countries they are still used, in periods of ¬rcity, as a substitute for bread. With us they are now rarely used, except for ¬ening hogs and poultry. They are said to make, when toasted, with the ad- ¬on of a little fresh butter, one of the best substitutes for coffee. Their taste is ¬ingent and bitter.

ACORUS (*calamus aromaticus*), sweet flag, or sweet rush, a red or knotty root, ¬ut the thickness of the little finger, and several inches long. " The root of ¬ sweet flag has a pleasant aromatic odour, similar to that of a mixture of ¬namon and allspice. The taste is warm, pungent, bitterish, and aromatic." ¬omson's Dispensatory.) The root, which is used in medicine, was formerly ¬orted from the Levant, but it is now obtained of an equally good quality from ¬folk.

¬ACORUS, blue coral. The true acorus of this kind is very rare. Some ¬it is, however, found on the coasts of Africa, particularly from Rio del ¬ to the river of the Camarones. It grows in the form of a tree, in a rocky ¬om.

¬CRE, a measure of land. The Imperial or standard English acre contains ¬ods, each rood 40 poles or perches, each pole 272¼ square feet; and conse- ¬tly each acre 43,560 square feet. Previously to the introduction of the new ¬em of weights and measures by the act 5 Geo. IV. cap. 74. the acres in ¬in different parts of England varied considerably from each other and from ¬ standard acre; but these customary measures are now abolished. The ¬ch acre contains four roods, each rood 40 falls, and each fall 36 ells ; the ¬eing equal to 37·06 Imperial inches. Hence the Imperial is to the Scotch ¬ nearly as 1 to 1¼, one Scotch acre being equal to 1·261 Imperial acres. ¬ Irish acre is equal to 1 acre 2 roods and 19$\frac{21}{121}$ poles, 30¼ Irish being equal ¬ Imperial acres.

¬ADAMANTINE SPAR, (*spath adamantine, corundum, corivindum,*) a stone ¬d in India and China; crystallised, or in a mass. The Indian is the best. ¬olour is grey, with shades of green and light brown; its fracture is foliated ¬parry, sometimes vitreous. It is brittle, and of such hardness as to cut rock ¬al and most of the gems. Specific gravity from 3·71 to 4·18. The Chi-

nese variety differs from the Indian in containing grains of magnetic iron ore disseminated through it; in being generally of a darker colour, and having externally a *chatoyant* lustre: its specific gravity is greater, and its hardness somewhat inferior. There are two varieties known of corundum in mass. That from Bengal is of a purplish hue: specific gravity 3·876. It is called by the natives *corone*. That from the coast of Coromandel is a foliated texture, and seems to be confusedly crystallised: its specific gravity is 2·785. This stone is employed for polishing gems.

ADJUSTMENT, in commerce and navigation, the settlement of a loss incurred by the insured.

In the case of a total loss, if the policy be an *open* one, the insurer is obliged to pay the goods according to their *prime cost*, that is, the invoice price, and all duties and expenses incurred till they are put on board, including the premium of insurance. Whether they might have arrived at a good or a bad market, is held by the law of England to be immaterial. The insurer is supposed to have insured a constant and not a variable sum; and in the event of a loss occurring, the insured is merely to be put into the same situation in which he stood before the transaction began. If the policy be a *valued* one, the practice is to adopt the valuation fixed in it in case of a total loss, unless the insurers can show that the insured had a colourable interest only, or that the goods were greatly over-valued. In the case of all partial losses, the value of the goods must be proved.

" The nature of the contract between the insured and insurer is," says Mr. Justice Park, " that the goods shall come safe to the port of delivery; or, if they do not, that the insurer will indemnify the owner to the amount of the value of the goods stated in the policy. Wherever then the property insured is lessened in value by damage received at sea, justice is done by putting the merchant in the same condition (relation being had to the prime cost or value in the policy) in which he would have been had the goods arrived free from damage; that is, by paying him such proportion of the prime cost or value in the policy as corresponds with the proportion of the diminution in value occasioned by the damage. The question then is, how is the proportion of the damage to be ascertained? It certainly cannot be by any measure taken from the prime cost; but it may be done in this way. Where any thing, as a hogshead of sugar, happens to be spoiled, you can fix whether it be a third, a fourth, or a fifth worse, then the damage is ascertained to a mathematical certainty. How is this to be found out? Not by any price at the port of shipment, but it must be at the port of *delivery*, when the voyage is completed and the whole damage known. Whether the price at the latter be high or low, it is the same thing; for in either case it equally shows whether the damaged goods are a third, a fourth, or a fifth worse than if they had come sound; consequently, whether the injury sustained be a third, fourth, or fifth of the value of the thing. And as the insurer pays the whole prime cost if the thing be wholly lost, so if it be only a third, fourth, or fifth worse, he pays a third, fourth, or fifth, not of the value for which it is sold, *but of the value stated in the policy*. And when no valuation is stated in the policy, the invoice of the cost with the addition of all charges, and the premium of insurance, shall be the foundation upon which the loss shall be computed."

Thus, suppose a policy to be effected on goods, the prime cost of which, expenses included, amounts to 1000*l.*; and suppose further, that these goods would, had they safely reached the port of delivery, have brought 1,200*l.*, but that, owing to damage they have met with in the voyage, they only fetch 800*l.*; in this case it is plain, inasmuch as goods that would otherwise have been worth 1,200*l.* are only worth 800*l.*, that they have been deteriorated *one third;* and hence it follows conformably to what has been stated above, that the insurer must pay one third of their *prime cost*, (1,000*l.*) or 333*l.* 6*s.* 8*d.* to the insured.

In estimating the value of goods at the port of delivery, the *gross* and not the *nett* proceeds of the sales are to be taken as the standard.

A ship is valued at the sum she is worth at the time she sails on the voyage insured, including the expenses of repairs, the value of her furniture, provisions and stores, the money advanced to the sailors, and, in general, every expense of the outfit, to which is added the premium of insurance.

When an adjustment is made, it is usual for the insurer to indorse upon the policy " adjusted this loss at (so much) per cent." payable in a given time, generally a month, and to sign it with the initials of his name. This is considered

a note of hand, and as such is *primá facie* evidence of the debt not to be shaken, but by proving that fraud was used in obtaining it, or that there was some misconception of the law or the fact upon which it was made. See, for a further discussion of this subject, the article MARINE INSURANCE, *Park on the Law of Insurance,* (cap. 6.) and *Marshall* (book i. cap. 14).

ADMEASUREMENT. See TONNAGE.

ADVANCE implies money paid before goods are delivered, or upon consignment. It is usual with merchants to advance from one half to two thirds of the value of goods on being required to do so, on receiving invoice, bill of lading, and orders to insure them from sea risk, &c. &c.

ADVERTISEMENT, in its general sense, is any information as to any fact or circumstance that has either occurred, or is expected to occur; but, in a commercial sense, it is understood to relate only to specific intimations with respect to the sales of articles, the formation and dissolution of partnerships, bankruptcies, meetings of creditors, &c. Until this year, a duty of 3s. 6d. was charged upon every advertisement, long or short, inserted in the Gazette, or in any other newspaper; and of 5s. 6d. on every advertisement inserted in any literary work published in parts or numbers. This duty has been so very oppressive as to add full 100 per cent. to the cost of advertising, for the charge (exclusive of the duty) for inserting an advertisement of the ordinary length in the newspapers rarely exceeds 3s. or 4s. According, however, to the new scale, the duty is to be only 1s. on advertisements of ten lines or under, and 2s. 6d. on those of greater length. The duty produced in 1829, 153,636l. 12s. 11d. in Great Britain, and 14,985l. 6s. in Ireland. We have little doubt that the reduced duty will yield a larger sum. For an account of the operation of the duty on literature, see BOOKS.

ADVICE, is usually given by one merchant or banker to another *by letter,* informing him of the bills or drafts drawn on him, with all particulars of date, or sight, the sum, to whom made payable, &c. Where bills appear for acceptance or payment, they are frequently refused to be honoured for *want of advice.* It is also necessary to give advice as it prevents forgeries: if a merchant accept or pay a bill for the honour of any other person, he is bound to advise him thereof, and this should always be done under *an act of honour* by a notary public.

AGARIC, a fungus growing on the trunks of trees. That produced in the Levant from the larch is accounted the best. It is brought into the shops in irregular pieces of different magnitudes, of a chalky whiteness, and very light. The best is easily cut with a knife, is friable between the fingers, and has no hard, or gritty, or coloured veins. It is used in medicine and dyeing. (*Lewis. Mat. Med.*)

AGATE. (Ger. *Achat;* Du. *Achaat;* Fr. *Agate;* It. *Agata;* Rus. *Agat;* Lat. *Achates.*) A genus of semi-pellucid gems, so called from the Greek αχατες, from its being found on the banks of the river of that name in Italy. It is never wholly opaque like jasper, nor transparent as quartz-crystal; it takes a very high polish, and its opaque parts usually present the appearance of dots, eyes, veins, lines, or bands. Its colours are yellowish, reddish, blueish, milk-white, honey-orange, or ochre-yellow, flesh-blood, or brick red, reddish brown, violet blue, and brownish green. It is found in irregular rounded nodules, from the size of a man's head to more than a foot in diameter. The lapidaries distinguish agates according to the colour of their ground; the finer semi-transparent kinds are called oriental. The most beautiful agates found in Great Britain are commonly known by the name of *Scotch pebbles,* and are met with in different parts of Scotland, but principally on the mountain of Cairngorm; whence they are sometimes termed cairngorms. The German agates are the largest. Some exquisitely fine ones have been brought from Siberia and Ceylon. They are found in great plenty the eastern extremity of the settlement of the Cape of Good Hope; and they are still met with in Italy.

AGENT. See FACTOR.

AGIO, a term used to express the difference between metallic and paper money; the difference between one sort of metallic money and another.

ALABASTER. (Ger. *Alabaster;* It. *Alabastro;* Fr. *Albâtre;* Rus. *Alabastr;* Lat. *Alabastrites.*) A kind of stone resembling marble, but softer. Under this name are confounded two minerals, the *gypseous* and *calcareous* alabasters; they are wholly distinct from each other when pure, but in some of the varieties are occasionally mixed together. The former, when of a white or yellowish, or greenish colour,

semi-transparent, and capable of receiving a polish, is employed by statuaries. It is very easily worked, but is not susceptible of a polish equal to marble. Calcareous alabaster is heavier than the former; it is not so hard as marble, but is notwithstanding susceptible of a good polish, and is more used in statuary. The statuaries distinguish alabaster into two sorts, the common and oriental. Spain and Italy yield the best alabaster. That produced at Montania, in the papal states, is in the highest esteem for its beautiful whiteness. Inferior sorts are found in France and Germany. Alabaster is wrought into tables, vases, statues, chimney pieces, &c.

ALCOHOL, ARDENT SPIRIT. (Fr. *Esprit de Vin;* Ger. *Weingeist;* Ital. *Spirito ardente, Spirito di Vino, Acquarzente.*) Alcohol is the name given to the *pure spirit* obtainable by distillation, and subsequent rectification, from all liquors that have undergone the vinous fermentation, and from none but such as are susceptible of it. It is a light, transparent, colourless liquor, of a sharp, penetrating, agreeable smell, and a warm stimulating taste. It is quite the same, whether obtained from brandy, wine, whiskey, or any other fluid which has been fermented. The specific gravity of alcohol when perfectly pure is from ·792 to ·800, that of water being 1,000; but the strongest spirit afforded by pure distillation is about ·820; alcohol of the shops is about ·835 or ·840. Alcohol cannot be frozen by any known degree of cold. It boils at 174°. It is the only dissolvent of many resinous substances; and is extensively used in medicine and the arts. (*Drs. A. T. Thomson, Ure,* &c.)

ALE and BEER, well known and extensively used fermented liquors, the principle of which is extracted from several sorts of grain, but most commonly from barley, after it has undergone the process termed malting.

1. *Historical Notice of Ale and Beer.* — The manufacture of ale or beer is of very high antiquity. Herodotus tells us, that owing to the want of wine, the Egyptians drank a liquor fermented from barley (lib. ii. cap. 77.). The use of it was also very anciently introduced into Greece and Italy, though it does not appear to have ever been very extensively used in these countries. Mead, or metheglin, was probably the earliest intoxicating liquor known in the North of Europe. Ale or beer was, however, in common use in Germany in the time of Tacitus (*Morib. Germ.* cap. 23.). " All the nations," says Pliny, " who inhabit the West of Europe have a liquor with which they intoxicate themselves, made of corn and water (*fruge madida*). The manner of making this liquor is somewhat different in Gaul, Spain, and other countries, and it is called by many various names; but its nature and properties are every where the same. The people of Spain, in particular, brew this liquor so well that it will keep good for a long time. So exquisite is the ingenuity of mankind in gratifying their vicious appetites, that they have thus invented a method to make water itself intoxicate." (*Hist. Nat.* lib. xiv. cap. 22.) — The Saxons and Danes were passionately fond of beer; and the drinking of it was supposed to form one of the principal enjoyments of the heroes admitted to the hall of Odin. (*Mallet's Northern Antiquities,* cap. 6, &c.) — The manufacture of ale was early introduced into England. It is mentioned in the laws of Ina, King of Wessex; and is particularly specified among the liquors provided for a royal banquet in the reign of Edward the Confessor. It was customary in the reigns of the Norman princes to regulate the price of ale; and it was enacted, by a statute passed in 1272, that a brewer should be allowed to sell two gallons of ale for a penny in cities, and three or four gallons for the same price in the country.

The use of hops in the manufacture of ale and beer seems to have been a German invention. They were used in the breweries of the Netherlands in the beginning of the fourteenth century; but they do not seem to have been introduced into England till two hundred years afterwards, or in the beginning of the sixteenth century. In 1530 Henry VIII. enjoined brewers not to put hops into their ale. It would, however, appear that but little attention was paid to this order; for in 1552 hop plantations had begun to be formed. (*Beckmann's Hist. Invent.* vol. iv. pp. 336—341. Eng. ed.) — The addition of hops renders ale more palatable, by giving it an agreeable bitter taste, while, at the same time, it fits it for being kept much longer without injury. Generally speaking, the English brewers employ a much larger quantity of hops than the Scotch. The latter are in the habit of using, in brewing the fine Edinburgh ale, from a pound to a pound and a half of hops for every bushel of malt.

2. *Distinction between Ale and Beer, or Porter.* — This distinction has been
ly elucidated by Dr. Thomas Thomson, in his very valuable article on Brewing, in
e Supplement to the Encyclopædia Britannica : — " Both ale and beer are in Great
ritain obtained by fermentation from the malt of barley ; but they differ from each
her in several particulars. Ale is light-coloured, brisk, and sweetish, or at least free
om bitter ; while beer is dark-coloured, bitter, and much less brisk. What is called
rter in England is a species of beer ; and the term "porter" at present signifies what
as formerly called *strong beer.* The original difference between ale and beer was owing
the malt from which they were prepared. Ale malt was dried at a very low heat, and
nsequently was of a pale colour ; while beer or porter malt was dried at a higher tem-
rature, and had of consequence acquired a brown colour. This incipient charring had
veloped a peculiar and agreeable bitter taste, which was communicated to the beer
ong with the dark colour. This bitter taste rendered beer more agreeable to the
late, and less injurious to the constitution than ale. It was consequently manufac-
red in greater quantities, and soon became the common drink of the lower ranks in
igland. When malt became high priced, in consequence of the heavy taxes laid upon
and the great increase in the price of barley which took place during the war of the
ench revolution, the brewers found out that a greater quantity of wort of a given
ength could be prepared from pale malt than from brown malt. The consequence
is that pale malt was substituted for brown malt in the brewing of porter and beer.
e do not mean that the whole malt employed was pale, but a considerable proportion
it. The wort, of course, was much paler than before ; and it wanted that agreeable
ter flavour which characterised porter, and made it so much relished by most palates.
e porter brewers endeavoured to remedy these defects by several artificial additions.
the same time various substitutes were tried to supply the place of the agreeable bitter
mmunicated to porter by the use of brown malt. Quassia, cocculus indicus, and we
ieve even opium, were employed in succession ; but none of them was found to answer
purpose sufficiently. Whether the use of these substances be still persevered in we do
know ; but we rather believe that they are not, at least by the London porter brewers."

. *Adulteration of Ale and Beer* — *substitution of Raw Grain for Malt.* — The
of the articles other than malt, referred to by Dr. Thomson, has been expressly
idden, under heavy penalties, by repeated Acts of Parliament. The Act 56 Geo. 3.
8. has the following clauses : —

No brewer or dealer in or retailer of beer shall receive or have in his possession, or make, or use, or
with, or put into any worts or beer, any liquor, extract, calx, or other material or preparation for the
ose of darkening the colour of worts or beer ; or any liquor, extract, calx, or other material or pre-
tion other than brown malt, ground or unground, as commonly used in brewing ; or shall receive, or
 in his possession, or use, or mix with, or put into any worts or beer, any molasses, honey, liquorice,
ol, quassia, cocculus indicus, grains of paradise, Guinea pepper, or opium, or any extract or prepara-
of molasses, honey, liquorice, vitriol, quassia, cocculus indicus, grains of paradise, Guinea pepper, or
m, *or any article or preparation whatsoever for or as a substitute for malt or hops,* upon pain that all
liquor, extract, calx, molasses, honey, vitriol, quassia, cocculus indicus, grains of paradise, Guinea
er, opium, extract, article, and preparation as aforesaid, and also the said worts and beer, shall be
ited, together with the casks, vessels, or other packages, and may be seized by any officer of excise ;
such brewer of, dealer in, or retailer of beer so offending, shall for each offence forfeit 200*l.*
No druggist, or vender of or dealer in drugs, or chemist, or other person whatever, shall sell, send, or
er to any licensed brewer of, or dealer in, or retailer of beer, knowing him to be so licensed, or
ted to be so licensed, or to any other person for, or on account of, or in trust for, or for the use of
brewer, dealer, or retailer, any colouring, from whatever materials made, or any other material or
aration other than *unground brown malt,* for the purpose of darkening the colour of worts or beer ;
y liquor or preparation heretofore or hereafter made use of for darkening the colour of worts or beer,
y molasses or other articles, as mentioned in the first section, for or as a substitute for malt or hops
ctively ; and if any druggist, or vender of or dealer in drugs, or any chemist, or other person what-
shall so do, all such liquor called colouring, and material or preparation for the purpose aforesaid,
quor and preparation used for darkening the colour of worts or beer, molasses, and article or prepar-
to be used as a substitute for malt or hops, shall be forfeited, and may be seized by any officer of
e ; and the druggist, vender, dealer, chemist, or other person so offending, shall forfeit 500*l.*"
the act 1 Will. 4. c. 51. for the repeal of the ale and beer duties, it is enacted (§ 17.), that no brewer
have in his brewery, or in any part of his entered premises, or in any mill connected with such
ery, any raw or unmalted corn or grain ; and all unmalted corn or grain which shall be found in such
ng premises or mill, and all malted corn or grain with which such unmalted corn or grain may
been mixed, shall be forfeited, and may be seized by any officer, together with all vessels or
ges in which such raw or unmalted corn or grain shall be contained, or in which such unmalted
or grain, and the malted corn or grain with which the same may have been mixed, shall be con-
 ; and every brewer shall for every such offence forfeit 200*l.*"

Descriptions of Ale and Beer. — Previously to 1823 there were only two sorts of
allowed to be brewed in England, viz. *strong beer,* that is, beer of the value of
and upwards the barrel, exclusive of the duty ; and *small beer,* or beer of the
 of less than 16*s.* a barrel, exclusive of the duty. In 1823, however, an act was
d (4 Geo. 4. c. 51.) authorising the brewing, under certain conditions, of an *inter-
ate* beer. But this sort of beer was either not suited to the public taste, or, which
re probable, the restrictions laid on the brewers deterred them from engaging
sively in its manufacture.

is limitation and classification of the different sorts of ale and beer, according to
strengh, originated in the duties laid upon them ; and now that these duties have

been repealed, ale and beer may be brewed of any degree of strength. This is an immense advantage.

5. *Regulations as to the Manufacture of Ale and Beer.* — Since the abolition of the beer duties, these regulations are very few and simple; and consist only in taking out a licence, entering the premises, and abstaining from the use of any article, other than malt, in the preparation of the beer. A brewer using any place, or mash tun, for the purpose of brewing, without having made an entry thereof at the nearest excise office, forfeits for every such offence 200*l.*; and all the worts, beer, and materials for making the same, together with the mash-tun, are forfeited, and may be seized by any officer. — Brewers obstructing officers shall, for every such offence, forfeit 100*l.* — (1 Will. IV. c. 51. §§ 15, 16.)

6. *Licence duties.* — *Number of Brewers.* — The licence duties payable by brewers of ale and beer, under the act 6 G. IV. c. 81., and the number of such licences granted during the year 1829, are as follow: —

	Sums charged for Licences.	Number of Licences granted.	
		For a Year.	For Periods of a Year.
	£ s. d.		
Common brewers of strong beer, not exceeding 20 barrels	0 10 0	2,854	42
Exceeding 20, and not exceeding 50 barrels	1 0 0	4,871	0
— 50 — 100 —	1 10 0	6,997	0
— 100 — 1000 —	2 0 0	11,526	123
— 1,000 — 2000 —	3 0 0	297	1
— 2,000 — 5000 —	7 10 0	249	0
— 5,000 — 7500 —	11 5 0	63	0
— 7,500 — 10,000 —	15 0 0	24	0
— 10,000 — 20,000 —	30 0 0	32	0
— 20,000 — 30,000 —	45 0 0	5	0
— 30,000 — 40,000 —	60 0 0	2	0
Exceeding — 40,000 —	75 0 0	12	0
Beginners	0 10 0	29	15
and a surcharge according to the quantity brewed.			
Brewers of table beer only, not exceeding 20 barrels	0 10 0	22	4
Exceeding 20 and not exceeding 50 barrels	1 0 0	8	0
— 50 — 100 —	1 10 0	13	0
Exceeding — 100 —	2 0 0	111	0
Retail brewers of strong beer	5 5 0	1,279	353

N. B. The barrel contains 36 gallons, or 4 firkins of 9 gallons each, Imperial measure. It is enacted 1 Will. 4. c. 51. § 7., that from the 10th October 1830, brewers are to pay their licence duty according to the malt used by them in brewing, and that every brewer shall be deemed to have brewed *one* barrel beer for every *two* bushels of malt used by such brewer.

In the year ending 5th January, 1830, there were of *public brewers* in the country collections 1442; in Scotland, 84; in Scotland, 168; being in all 1694. — Of *retail brewers* there were in the country 1184; in London, 85; in Scotland, 26; total 1295 — Of *intermediate brewers*, there were in the country 14; in London, 8; in Scotland none; total 22. — Of *victuallers*, there were in the country 45,981, of whom 23,2?? brewed their own beer; in London, 4461, of whom 17 brewed their own beer; in Scotland, 17,713, of whom 268 brewed their own beer: total of victuallers, 68,155, of whom 23,172 brewed their own beer.

It is enacted, 1 Will. IV. c. 51., that every person who shall sell any beer or ale in less quantities than four and a half gallons, or two dozen reputed quart bottles, to be drunk elsewhere than on the premises where sold, shall be deemed a dealer in beer.

7. *Progressive Consumption of Ale and Beer.* — Malt liquor early became to the labouring classes of England what the inferior sorts of wine are to the people of France, at once a necessary of life and a luxury: the taste for it was universally diffused. There are, however, no means by which an estimate can be formed of the quantity actually consumed, previously to the reign of Charles II. But duties, amounting to 2*s.* 6*d.* a barrel on strong, and to 6*d.* a barrel on small ale or beer, were imposed, for the first time, in 1660. These duties being farmed until 1684, the amount of the revenue only is known; and as there are no means of ascertaining the proportion which the strong bore to the small beer, the quantities that paid duty cannot be specified. But, since the collection of the duty was intrusted to officers employed by government, accurate accounts have been kept of the quantities of each sort of beer on which duty was paid, as well as of the rate of duty and its amount. Now, it appears, that at an average of the ten years, from 1684 to 1693 inclusive, the amount of ale annually charged with duty was as follows: — Strong ale - - 4,567,293 barrels

Small do. - - 2,376,278 do.

Soon after the Revolution several temporary duties were imposed on ale and beer

but in 1694 they were consolidated, the established duties being then fixed at 4s. 9d. a barrel on the strong, and at 1s. 3d. on the small beer, instead of 2s. 6d. and 6d., which had been the rates previously to 1690. This increase of duty had an immediate effect on the consumption, the quantity brewed during the ten years from 1694 to 1703 being as follows:—

Strong ale	- - -	3,374,604 barrels
Small do.	- - -	2,180,764 do.

The whole of this decrease must not, however, be ascribed to the increase of the beer duties only; the duties on malt and hops having been, at the same time, considerably increased, operated partly, no doubt, to produce the effect.

During the five years ending with 1750, the ale brewed amounted, at an average, to 3,803,580 barrels of strong, and 2,162,540 barrels of small. (*Hamilton's Principles of Taxation,* p. 255.)

The ale brewed in private families for their own use has always been exempted from any duty; and it may, perhaps, be supposed that the falling off in the consumption, as evinced by the statements now given, was apparent only, and that the decline in the public brewery would be balanced by a proportional extension of the private brewery. But, though there can be no doubt that the quantity of beer brewed in private families was increased in consequence of the peculiar taxes laid on the beer brewed for sale, it is abundantly certain that it was not increased in any thing like the ratio in which the other was diminished. This is established beyond all dispute, by the fact of the consumption of malt having continued *very nearly stationary*, notwithstanding the vast increase of population and wealth, from the beginning of last century down to 1750, and, indeed, to the present day! (*See art. Malt.*) Had the fact, as to malt, been different, or had the demand for it increased proportionally to the increase of population, it would have shown that the effect of the malt and beer duties had not been to lessen the consumption of beer, but merely to cause it to be brewed in private houses instead of public breweries : but the long continued stationary demand for malt completely negatives this supposition, and shows that the falling off in the beer manufactured by the public brewers has not been made up by any equivalent increase in the supply manufactured at home. The following is

I. AN ACCOUNT of the Quantity of the different Sorts of Beer made in England and Wales, in each Year from 1787 to 1825, both inclusive, the Rate of Duty and the total Produce of the Duties (English Ale Gallons).

Years ended 5th July.	Strong Beer.		Table Beer.		Small Beer.		Total Amount of Duty.
	Barrels.	Rate of Duty.	Barrels.	Rate of Duty.	Barrels.	Rate of Duty.	
1787	4,426,482	8s. 0d.	485,620	3s. 0d.	1,342,301	1s. 4d.	£1,952,922 10s. 8d
1788	4,304,895	—	524,176	—	1,334,947	—	1,389,580 17 4
1789	4,437,831	—	514,900	—	1,244,046	—	1,935,303 16 0
1790	4,525,950	—	546,260	—	1,282,157	—	1,977,796 2 8
1791	4,754,588	—	579,742	—	1,347,086	—	2,078,602 4 8
1792	5,082,293	—	625,260	—	1,401,870	—	2,220,164 4 0
1793	5,167,850	—	620,207	—	1,414,255	—	2,254,454 14 4
1794	5,011,320	—	586,554	—	1,446,939	—	2,188,973 14 0
1795	5,037,804	—	576,464	—	1,453,036	—	2,198,460 5 4
1796	5,504,453	—	565,630	—	1,479,130	—	2,385,234 7 4
1797	5,839,627	—	584,422	—	1,518,512	—	2,524,748 4 8
1798	5,784,467	—	622,064	—	1,547,570	—	2,510,267 14 8
1799	5,774,311	—	611,151	—	1,597,139	—	2,507,872 19 8
1800	4,824,306	—	574,995	—	1,360,502	—	2,106,671 15 8
1801	4,735,574	—	500,025	—	1,191,930	—	2,048,695 7 0
1802	5,345,884	9 5	392,022	—	976,787	—	2,321,198 0 4
1803	5,582,516	—	1,660,828	—			2,782,263 13 4
1804	5,265,623	10 0	1,779,570	—			2,810,768 10 0
1805	5,412,131	—	1,776,807	—			2,883,746 4 0
1806	5,443,502	—	1,771,754	—			2,898,926 8 0
1807	5,577,176	—	1,732,710	—			2,961,859 0 0
1808	5,571,360	—	1,710,243	—			2,956,704 6 0
1809	5,513,111	—	1,682,899	—			2,924,845 8 0
1810	5,753,319	—	1,635,588	—			3,040,218 6 0
1811	5,902,903	—	1,649,564	—			3,116,407 18 0
1812	5,860,869	—	1,593,395	—			3,089,774 0 0
1813	5,382,946	—	1,455,759	—			2,837,048 18 0
1814	5,624,015	—	1,432,729	—			2,955,280 8 0
1815	6,150,544	—	1,518,302	—			3,227,102 4 0
1816	5,982,379	—	1,514,867	—			3,142,676 4 0
1817	5,236,048	—	1,453,960	—			2,763,420 0 0
1818	5,364,009	—	1,434,642	—			2,825,468 14 0
1819	5,629,240	—	1,460,244	—			2,960,644 8 0
1820	5,296,701	—	1,444,290	—			2,792,779 10 0
1821	5,575,830	—	1,439,970	—			2,931,912 0 0
1822	5,712,937	—	1,492,281	—			3,005,696 12 0
1823	6,177,271	—	1,419,589	—			3,230,594 8 0
1824	6,188,271	—	1,401,021	—	Intermediate Beer.		3,234,237 12 0
1825	6,500,664	—	1,485,750	—	9,559	5 0	3,401,296 15 0

II. An Account of the Quantity of all the different Sorts of Beer stated in Barrels, made in each Year, from 5th January 1825 to 5th January 1830 ; the Rates of Duty per Barrel in each Year, and Total Amount thereof in each Year in England and Scotland. (Par. Paper, No. 190. Sess. 1830.)

Years ended 5th January	ENGLAND.						
	Number of Barrels, Imperial Measure. *						Total Amount of Duty.
	Strong.	Rate per Barrel	Table.	Rate per Barrel.	Intermediate.	Rate per Barrel.	
		s. d.		s. d.		s. d.	£. s. d.
1826	7,008,143	9 10	1,606,899	1 11½	6,160	4 11	3,492,779 10 4
1827 {	4,177,225	9 0	1,040,726	1 9½	7,707	—	3,265,441 14 6
	2,512,767	9 10	562,927	1 11½			
1828 {	3,895,226	9 0	989,827	1 9½	17,158	—	3,128,047 9 0
	2,500,043	9 10	542,481	1 11½			
1829 {	3,941,519	9 0	977,962	1 9½	62,617	—	3,217,812 2 11
	2,617,691	9 10	552,457	1 11½			
1830 {	3,569,364	9 0	879,879	1 9½	55,498	—	2,917,828 8 4
	2,379,930	9 10	500,590	1 11½			
	SCOTLAND.						
		s. d.		s. d.			
1826	133,903	9 10	264,035	1 11½	- .	—	91,731 2 2
1827 {	116,594	9 0	219,722	1 9½	-	—	79,931 4 7
	5,545	9 10	51,613	1 11½			
1828 {	102,769	9 0	187,873	1 9½	-	—	72,855 4 4
	9,250	9 10	53,420	1 11½			
1829 {	101,475	9 0	178,530	1 9½	-	—	76,885 9 11
	17,248	9 10	68,913	1 11½			
1830 {	94,387	9 0	161,488	1 9½	- .	—	71,733 17 5
	16,566	9 10	67,896	1 11½			

III. An Account of the Number of Barrels of Strong Beer exported in each Year, from 5th January 1825 to 5th January 1830.

		Number of Barrels (Imperial Measure) Exported from		
		England.	Scotland.	Ireland.
Years Ended 5th January {	1826 -	53,013	1,827	9,855
	1827 -	42,602	1,679	10,800
	1828 -	59,471	2,509	11,261
	1829 -	71,842	3,304	14,499
	1830 -	74,902	3,131	15,207

It appears from these tables, that the quantity of strong beer manufactured by the public brewers had increased about a third since 1787 ; but the quantity of malt consumed in 1787 was quite as great as in 1828 ; a fact, which shows conclusively, either that the *quality* of the beer brewed in the public breweries has been deteriorated since 1787, or that less, comparatively, is now brewed in private families ; or, which is most probable, that both effects have been produced.

It has been contended by some, that the condition of the bulk of the people has declined since the commencement of the late French war ; and that this decline, and not the duties and restrictions on the manufacture and sale of malt and beer, has been the real cause that the consumption of malt liquors has continued stationary during the last thirty years. But nearly *four* millions of persons were added to the population of England and Wales during the eighteenth century, and it is admitted, on all hands, that the condition of the middle and lower classes was, at the same time, vastly improved. Instead, however, of increasing, as no doubt it would have done but for some very powerful counteracting cause, we have seen that the consumption of ma

---

* The ale gallon contains 282 cubic inches, and the Imperial gallon 277¼ ; the latter being $\frac{1}{60}$ part less than the former.

juor continued stationary during the whole of *last century ;* so that the fair presump-
n is, that it has continued stationary during that period of the *present century* already
apsed, not because the people have become less able to purchase beer, but because
e same causes which formerly prevented the increase of consumption have continued
operate. If we except a portion of the peasantry in some of the southern counties,
here the pernicious practice of paying wages out of the poor's rates has been intro-
iced, it will be found that the condition of the labouring classes has been, speaking
nerally, changed very much for the better during the last thirty years. Their health
s been remarkably improved ; a result which could hardly have taken place without
improvement in their habits as to cleanliness, and in their ordinary accommodations ;
d, independent of this circumstance, the fact that the lower classes have lodged up-
rds of *fifteen* millions sterling in Savings' Banks, and that upwards of a million of
em are members of Friendly Societies, shows pretty clearly that, though they may
t be anywhere so comfortable as could be wished, and though, in Kent, Hampshire,
d some other southern counties, they are exposed to very great privations, their con-
ion is, on the whole, superior to what it has ever previously been. It has further
en contended, that if the decline in the consumption of beer cannot be ascribed to any
ling off in the condition of the people, or in their power to purchase malt liquors,
fair inference is, that it has originated in a change of taste ; and the increased con-
mption of spirituous liquors that has taken place of late years has been appealed to
proof that such is the fact. But this increase has been very greatly exaggerated :
mitting, however, that the circumstances are really such as have been represented,
question instantly recurs, to what is this change of taste owing? How comes it
t the people of England should be less partial than heretofore to that palatable
nutritious beverage to which they have been long accustomed, and that they
uld be resorting to ardent spirits and other deleterious compounds, destructive
e of their health and morals? If we mistake not, it will be found to be wholly
ng to the duties and restrictions that have been laid on the manufacture and sale
eer.

. *Duties on Ale and Beer : old licensing System.* — The duty on malt is 20s. 8d. a
rter; on hops 2d. a pound; and on strong beer, which forms five tenths of the
le quantity brewed, the duty was 9s. 10d. a barrel. It is commonly estimated,
from three to three and a half barrels of beer are manufactured from a quarter of
t; and that each quarter of malt requires twelve pounds of hops. Now, supposing
three and a quarter barrels of beer are produced from a quarter of malt, the duties
cting it, down to the 10th of October, 1830, were

	s.	d.
Duty laid directly on malt - - -	20	8
Beer duty on three and a quarter barrels -	31	11
Hop duty - - - - - -	2	
	54s.	7d.

dividing this sum of 54s. 7d. by 3¼, the duties affecting each barrel of beer will be 17s.
uch duties are obviously oppressive. The price of barley does not at an average
ed 35s. per quarter. But the duties on malt or beer produced from a quarter of
y (exclusive of the hop duty) amounted to 52s. 7d., being equal to 150 per cent.
the cost of the barley employed ! Need we seek elsewhere for the cause of the
nary demand for malt liquors? The taxes on wine, British spirits, tea, and coffee,
ot, in any case, exceed 100 per cent. Nor can there be a doubt that the dispro-
onately heavy burden that has thus been imposed on the natural and healthy beverage
e lower classes has principally contributed to lessen its consumption, and to cause
to resort to less salubrious substitutes.
another point of view, the beer duties were still more indefensible. They affected
that description of beer which was *brewed for sale ;* and as all the higher classes
ed their own beer, the duty fell only on the lower and middle ranks of the com-
ty, and particularly the former. It is singular, that a tax so grossly unequal and
essive should have been so long submitted to. Should the public necessities require,
y future period, that an effort should be made to increase the revenue from beer,
ir and proper method would be to increase the malt duties. They affect alike those
brew the beer which they consume, and those who buy it from a public brewer.
increase would not require the employment of any additional officers ; for it is
us, that the same officers and regulations that serve to collect a duty of 20s. 8d.
d equally serve to collect a duty of 30s. ; and, what is most important, an increase
s sort would not require any interference with the process of brewing.
t besides the obstacles to the consumption of beer arising from the oppressive duties
which it was burdened, the system recently in force of granting licences for its
pposed obstacles that were hardly less formidable. Previously to the present year

(1830), no one could open a house for the sale of beer without first obtaining a licence renewable annually from the magistrates; and as these functionaries were accustomed only to grant licences to the occupiers of *particular houses*, the brewers naturally endeavoured, in order to ensure the sale of their beer, either to buy up those houses or to lend money upon them: and in many extensive districts a few large capitalists succceded in engrossing most of the public houses; so that even the appearance of competition was destroyed, and a ready market and good prices secured for the very worst beer!

We, therefore, look upon the late abolition of the beer duties, and the granting permission to all individuals to retail beer upon taking out an excise licence costing 2*l.* 2*s.* as highly advantageous measures. The repeal of the duty has put an end to the unjust distinction that previously obtained; the poor man is no longer burdened with a heavy tax, from which the noble and affluent of the land were exempted; but all classes are placed, in so far at least as the duties on beer are concerned, in the same situation. The fall of price caused by the abolition of the duty, by rendering beer more easily obtainable, will do much to check the consumption of spirits; and will, at the same time, powerfully contribute to the health and comfort of the poor. The change in the mode of licensing houses for the retail of beer has introduced into the trade that system of free competition that is so advantageous. It is no longer in the power of any combination of brewers to maintain the price of beer at an unnatural elevation and the public may now depend on being supplied with malt liquors at the lowest price that will serve to indemnify the brewers.

9. *Existing Regulations with respect to the Sale of Beer.* The sale of ale, beer, &c. by retail in England, is now regulated by the act 1 Will. 4. c. 64. of which we subjoin a pretty full abstract. Licences to be granted by commissioners of excise, or by persons authorised by them; to cost 2*l.* 2*s.* a year; not to authorise the sale of wine or spirits; not to be granted to sheriffs' officers, nor to any person executing the legal process of any court of justice, nor to any person not being a householder assessed in the parish. § 2.

The party requiring such licence to enter into a bond to the commissioners, with one sufficient surety in the penalty of 20*l.*, or with two sufficient sureties in the penalty of 10*l.* each, for the payment of any penalty or sum of money, not exceeding the amount of such 20*l.* or 10*l.* respectively, which shall be incurred for any offence against this act by the party to whom such licence shall be granted; and a person licensed to sell beer by retail, or not being a householder paying the poor rates, shall be surety in any such bond. — § § 4, 5.

Every person who shall be licensed under this act, shall cause to be painted, in letters three inches least in length, in white upon a black ground, or in black upon a white ground, publicly visible and legible, upon a board, to be placed over the door of the house in which such person shall be licensed, the Christian and surname of the persons mentioned in such licence, at full length, together with the words " Licensed to sell Beer by Retail;" and every such person shall keep up such name and words during all the time that such person shall continue so licensed, upon pain of forfeiting for every omission 10*l.* — §

No person to sell any beer by retail, under this act, after the expiration of any licence granted, nor any house not specified in such licence; and any person selling beer by retail, not being duly licensed, the keeper of a common inn, ale-house, or victualling-house; or if any such person, so licensed, shall deal in or retail any wine or spirits, he shall, for every such offence, forfeit 20*l.*, half to go to the informer and half to the king; such penalty to be recovered as other excise penalties; and the powers of the excise as 7 & 8 G. 4. c. 53, &c. extended to this act. — § § 7, 8, 9.

Persons trading in partnership, and in one house, shall not be obliged to take out more than one licence in any one year: provided also, that no one licence shall authorise any person to sell any beer, in any other than the house mentioned in such licence. — § 10.

In cases of riot or expected riot or tumult, every person licensed under this act, and keeping any house situate within their jurisdictions, shall close his house at any time which the justice or justices shall direct; and every such person who shall keep open his house at or after any hour at which such justice shall have so ordered or directed such house to be closed, shall be deemed to have not maintained good order and rule therein, and to be guilty of an offence against the tenor of his licence. — § 11.

Every person licensed to sell beer by retail, shall sell (except in quantities less than a half pint) by the gallon, quart, pint, or half pint measure, sized according to the standard; and in default thereof, he shall for every such offence forfeit the illegal measure, and pay not exceeding 40*s.*, together with the costs of the conviction, to be recovered within thirty days next after that on which such offence was committed before two justices; such penalty to be over and above all penalties to which the offender may be liable under any other act. — § 12.

Every seller of beer by retail, having a licence under this act, who shall permit any person to be guilty of drunkenness, or disorderly conduct, in the house mentioned in such licence, shall forfeit the sum following: for the first offence, not less than 40*s.* nor more than 5*l.* as the justices, before whom such retailer shall be convicted, shall adjudge; and for the second offence, any sum not less than 5*l.* nor more than 10*l.*; and for the third offence, any sum not less than 20*l.* nor more than 50*l.*; and it shall be lawful for the justices, before whom any such conviction for such third offence shall take place, to adjudge, if they shall think so fit, that such offender shall be disqualified from selling beer by retail for the space of two years next ensuing such conviction, and also that no beer shall be sold by retail, by any person in the house mentioned in the licence of such offender; and if any person so licensed shall, knowingly, sell beer, ale, or porter, made otherwise than from malt and hops, or shall mix, or cause to be mixed, drugs or other pernicious ingredients, with any beer sold in his house, or shall fraudulently dilute, or any way adulterate, any such beer, such offender shall, for the first offence, forfeit not less than 10*l.* nor more than 20*l.*, and for the second such offence such offender shall be adjudged to be disqualified from selling beer, ale, or porter, by retail, for the term of two years, or to forfeit not less than 20*l.* nor more than 50*l.*, and shall be subject to a like penalty at every house where he shall commit such offence; and if any person shall, during any term in which it shall not be lawful for beer to be sold by retail on the premises of any offender, sell any beer by retail on such premises, knowing that it was not lawful to be sold, offender shall forfeit not less than 10*l.* nor more than 20*l.*; every person suffering the conditions of licence to be infringed to be deemed guilty of disorderly conduct. — § 13.

Retailers' houses not to be open before four in the morning, nor after ten in the evening; nor between the hours of ten in the forenoon and one in the afternoon, nor at any time between the hours of three and five in the afternoon, on any Sunday, Good Friday, Christmas day, or any day appointed for a public fast or thanksgiving; and any person offending herein shall forfeit 40s. for every offence; every separate sale to be deemed a separate offence. — § 14.

All penalties under this act, except for selling beer by any person not duly licensed, shall be recovered, upon the information of any person before two justices, in petty sessions; and every such penalty shall be prosecuted for within three calendar months next after the offence; and every person licensed under this act, who shall be convicted before two justices, shall, unless proof be adduced to the satisfaction of such justices, that such person had been theretofore convicted before two justices, within the space of twelve calendar months next preceding, be adjudged by such justices to be guilty of a first offence against this act, and to forfeit and pay any penalty by this act imposed for such offence, or if no specific penalty be imposed, then any sum not exceeding 5l., together with the costs of the conviction; and if proof be adduced to the satisfaction of such justices, that such person had been previously convicted, within the space of twelve calendar months next preceding, of one such offence only, such person to be adjudged guilty of a second offence against this act, and to forfeit and pay any penalty by this act imposed for such offence, or if no specific penalty be so imposed, then any sum not exceeding 10l., together with the costs of conviction; and if proof shall be adduced that such person had been previously convicted within the space of eighteen calendar months next preceding, of two such separate offences, and if proof be adduced that such person, so charged, is guilty of the offence charged against him, such person shall be adjudged to be guilty of a third offence against this act, and to forfeit and pay any penalty imposed by this act, in respect of such offence, or if no such specific penalty shall be imposed, then to forfeit and pay the sum of 20l., together with the costs of conviction. — § 15.

The party, convicted of any such third offence, may appeal to the general sessions, or quarter sessions, then next ensuing, unless held within twelve days after conviction, and in that case, to the then next subsequent sessions; and, in such case, the party convicted shall enter into a recognizance, with two sureties, personally to appear at the said general or quarter sessions, to abide the judgment of the court; and to pay such costs as shall be by the court awarded; or, in failure of the party convicted entering into such recognizance, such conviction shall remain good and valid; and the said justices, who shall take such recognizance, are also required to bind the person who shall make such charges to appear at such general or quarter sessions, then and there to give evidence against the person charged, and, in like manner, to bind any other person who shall have any knowledge of such offence; and it shall be lawful for the said general or quarter sessions to adjudge such person to be guilty of such third offence against this act, and such adjudication shall be final; and it shall be lawful for such general or quarter sessions to punish such offender by fine, not exceeding 100l., together with the costs of such appeal, or to adjudge the licence to be forfeited, or that no beer be sold by retail in the house for the term of two years, and if such licence shall be adjudged to be forfeited, it shall henceforth be void; and whenever, in such case the licence of such offender shall be adjudged to be void, such offender shall be deemed incapable of selling beer, ale, or porter, by retail, in any house kept by him, for the space of two years, to be computed from the time of such adjudication; and any licence granted to such person during such term shall be void. — § 16.

In default of payment of penalties, proceedings may be had against the sureties. — § 19.

Any person summoned as a witness, who shall neglect or refuse to appear, and not make such reasonable excuse for such neglect, &c. as shall be admitted by such justices of sessions, or who, appearing, shall refuse to be examined, shall, on conviction, forfeit not exceeding 10l. — § 20.

Offenders refusing or neglecting, within seven days after conviction, to pay the penalty imposed, and any costs assessed, such justices may issue their warrant, to levy the amount by distress and sale, together with the costs of distress and sale; and in every such case, such offenders, if in custody, shall be forthwith discharged; but if the goods and chattels are not sufficient, such justices may commit the offender to the common gaol or house of correction for not exceeding one calendar month, if the penalty shall not be above 5l.; for not exceeding three calendar months, if the penalty shall be above 5l., and not more than 10l.; and for not exceeding six calendar months, if the penalty shall be above 10l.; provided, that whenever such offender shall pay to the gaoler or keeper, or to whomsoever such justices shall have appointed, the penalty and costs, together with all the costs of apprehension and conveyance to gaol, at any time previous the expiration of the time for which such offender shall have been committed, such offender shall be forthwith discharged. — § 21.

No conviction under this act, nor any adjudication made upon appeal therefrom, shall be quashed for want of form, nor removed by *certiorari*. — § 27.

Every action against any justice, constable, or other person, for any thing done in execution of his duty under this act, to be commenced within three calendar months, and not afterwards: and if any person be sued, he may plead the general issue, and give the special matter in evidence. — § 28.

This act not to affect the two universities, nor the vintners' company in London; nor to prohibit the sale of beer at fairs, as heretofore.

10. *Scotch ale and beer duties.* — The duties on ale and beer in Scotland have been for a lengthened period the same as in England.

At the union in 1707, the English duties on ale and beer were introduced into Scotland. But, besides strong and small beer, the Scotch had an intermediate species, which they called *two-penny*, and which was their favourite beverage. The duty on this description of beer was fixed, at the union, at 2s. 1¼d. a barrel. For *thirty* years after its imposition the quantity of two-penny that paid duty was always above 400,000, and sometimes exceeded 500,000 barrels a year. But in 1760 the duty on two-penny was increased to 3s. 4¼d. and the consumption immediately fell off to between 100,000 and 200,000 barrels! The quantity that paid duty in 1800 amounted to 149,803 barrels. The manufacture of this species of beer ceased entirely in 1802.

No account has been kept of the quantity of beer brewed in Ireland since 1809, when it amounted to 960,300 barrels. (*Morewood on Intoxicating Liquors*, p. 353.) Perhaps it may now amount to from a 1,000,000 to 1,200,000 barrels.

11. *Regulations as to the exportation of beer.* — Ale or beer exported to foreign parts as merchandise is allowed a drawback of 5s. the barrel of 36 gallons, Imp. meas. But before any debenture for the above drawback shall be paid, the exporter or his principal clerk or manager shall make oath thereon, before the proper officer of excise, that such ale or beer was put on board the exporting ship as merchandise to be sent beyond sea, and no part thereof for the ship's use; and that, according to the best of his knowledge and belief, the same has been brewed wholly from malt which has been charged and paid the duty of 2s. 7d. a bushel, and shall also specify in such oath the

C

timo when and the place where; and the brewer, being an entered and licensed brewer for sale, by whom such beer or ale was brewed, and that the quantity of malt used in brewing was not less than two bushels (Imp. meas.) for every 36 gallons of such beer or ale. Persons making false statements forfeit the sum of 200*l.* and the debenture is void. (1 Wil. 4. cap. 51. § 11.)

ALEXANDRIA — so called from its founder, Alexander the Great; the principal sea-port town of Egypt, in lat. 31° 16′ N., and long. 30° 5′ E. Under the Ptolemies and the Romans, Alexandria was the first commercial city of the world, being the *entrepôt* through which the commerce between the East and West was principally carried on. It suffered greatly from its reduction by the Saracens in 640; but it continued to be a place of great commercial importance till the discovery of the route to India by the Cape of Good Hope, and the despotism of the Turks and Mamelukes completed its ruin. Latterly, however, the vigorous government of Mohammed Ali, by introducing comparative good order into Egypt, has revived the commerce of Alexandria. But the pacha has not even an idea of the principles by the adoption of which industry can alone be rendered really flourishing. He interferes with every thing; and has monopolised the whole trade of the country, fixing the price to be paid for every article to the cultivator, and the price at which it is to be sold to the foreigner. The population of Alexandria varies with the seasons of the year, but may at present amount to from 14,000 to 25,000. Under the Ptolemies it was supposed to amount to 300,000. The imports principally consist of hardware, iron and tin, tobacco, timber, machinery, silk, woollens, slaves, cotton stuffs, &c. The exports consist of cotton, rice, wheat and other grain, flax, linseed, sugar, coffee, drugs, &c. In 1823 no fewer than 140 vessels, loaded with grain, were despatched from Alexandria for Constantinople and the islands of the Archipelago.

Money. — Accounts are kept at Alexandria, as at Cairo, in *current piastres,* each piastre being equal to 40 paras, or medini, and each medino to 30 aspers. The medino is also divided into 8 borbi, or 6 forli. A purse contains 25,000 medini. The piastres struck in 1826 contain a great deal of alloy; 15½ or 16 piastres = 1 Spanish dollar; hence 1 piastre = 3½*d.* sterling, very nearly. Payments in transactions of any importance are generally made in Spanish dollars.

Weights and Measures. — The yard, or *pik,* = 26·8 English inches; hence 100 piks = 74·438 English yards. The measures for corn are the *rhebebe,* and the *quillot* or *kisloz;* the former = 4·364 English bushels, the latter = 4·729 ditto. The *cantaro* or *quintal* = 100 *rottoli,* but the rottolo has different names and weights: 1 *rottolo forforo* = ·9347 lib. avoirdupois; 1 *rottolo zaidino* = 1·335 lib. ditto; 1 *rottolo zauro* or *zaro* = 2·07 lib. ditto; 1 *rottolo mina* = 1·67 lib. ditto. — (*Manuel. Universel de Nelkenbrecher.*)

The following is an account of the foreign vessels that arrived at Alexandria in 1822, 1823, and 1824 : —

	1822.	1823.	1824.
Venetian and Tuscan	292	351	600
Danish	15	25	13
French	57	52	111
English, American, and Ionian	223	230	251
Romish	—	—	2
Russian	10	59	100
Sardinian	143	98	77
Hollanders	3	1	5
Spaniards	54	24	70
Swedes	76	81	47
Sicilians	28	12	14
	901	933	1,290

(*Bulletin des Sciences Géographiques,* v. p. 78.)

ALICANT, a sea-port town of Spain, in Valencia, in lat. 38° 35′ N., long 9° 24′ W. Population about 17,000. Alicant has a considerable foreig trade. Its principal exports are barilla, which is here of the finest quality, win brandy, oil, olives, raisins, soap, wool, silk, almonds, figs, saffron, anise, & The *vino tinto,* or tent wine, is much esteemed in France. Benicarlo wine, larg quantities of which are shipped at Alicant, is somewhat similar to claret, but full bodied. It is for the most part sent to Cette, whence it is conveyed by the can

Languedoc and the Garonne to Bordeaux, for the purpose of being mixed with
e poorer wines of the Bordelais. The imports principally consist of salted
h, grain, iron, hemp and flax, timber, coffee, sugar, cochineal, indigo, cotton,
nd cotton stuffs, &c.

Money. — Accounts are kept at Alicant in libras of 20 sueldos; each sueldo contain-
g 12 dineros; the libra, also called the peso, = 10 reals; and a real of Alicant =
½ maravedis of plate, or 51½ maravedis vellon. The libra may be valued at 3s. 6d.
rling, and the real at 4¼d. ditto.

Weights and Measures. — The carga = 2½ quintals = 10 arrobas. The arroba con-
ts either of 24 large pounds, or of 36 small ditto; the latter having 12 Castilian
nces to the pound, the former 18. The arroba = 27 lb. 6 oz. avoirdupois; but at
e custom-house the arroba = 25 lbs. of 16 oz. each.

The principal corn measure is the cahiz or caffise, containing 12 barchillas, 96
dios, or 192 quartillos. The cahiz = 7 Winch. bushels, nearly.

The principal liquid measure is the cantaro of 8 medios, or 16 quartillos. The can-
o = 3 1/10 English wine gallons. The tonnelada or ton contains 2 pipes, 80 arrobas, or
) cantaros.

The yard or vara, divided into 4 palmos, is = 29 33/100, or very nearly 30 English inches.
(*Dr. Kelly's Cambist,* art. " Alicant.")

ALKALIES. The distinguishing characters of these bodies are, a strong acrid,
d powerfully caustic taste, a corrosive action upon all animal matter, destroying
texture with considerable rapidity; exposed to the atmosphere, when in their
ustic state, they absorb carbonic acid with great rapidity, and become car-
nated (or mild). Their action upon vegetable colours also affords us means
which the presence of an uncombined or carbonated alkali may be detected;
e yellow colour of turmeric is changed to a red brown tint when im-
rsed into solutions containing them; the blue colour of the litmus, after being
dened by an acid, is again restored; the infusions of the red cabbage, the violet,
d many other purple vegetable colours, are converted to green. Litmus paper
dened by carbonic acid is, however, the most delicate test of the presence of
alkali. With the various acids they also combine, forming the very important
d extensive class of compounds generally called salts; a salt being any com-
nd formed by the union of an acid with an alkali, or a metallic oxide.

Alkalimetry. — The method by which the value of the alkalies, or carbonated alkalies,
etermined being of considerable importance in a commercial point of view, we shall
treat it somewhat in detail. It is an established fact, that 49 parts by weight of
of vitriol of the specific gravity 1·8485, are exactly equivalent to the neutralisation
0 parts by weight of pure carbonate of potash, or 48 pure potass, or 54 carbonate
oda, or 32 of soda; and that 70 parts of oil of vitriol will therefore be necessary
eutralise 100 parts of carbonate of potass: Hence, by employing a glass tube of
ut two ounces' capacity, and accurately divided into 100 equal parts, taking
grains of oil of vitriol, and diluting it with water, to make the 100 measures
plete, every measure of this dilute acid must be equal to a grain of pure carte of potass. The per centage of real carbonate of potass existing in any
ple of pearlash may be at once ascertained by taking 100 grains of the sam-
dissolving it in hot water, straining, and adding by degrees 100 measures of
test acid above mentioned; the point of neutralisation (when it ceases to affect
us paper or reddened litmus) being accurately ascertained, the residual acid will
the per centage of impurities: for instance, say that 75 measures of the dilute acid
been employed to render 100 grains of a sample of pearlash perfectly neutral,
we have ascertained that it contains 25 per cent. impurities. The same process
urse must be followed in examining samples of barilla or kelp, except that the
i contained in them, being carbonate of soda, 90·75 of oil of vitriol must be em-
d instead of 70. The process recommended by Mr. Faraday, and in which he
only one test acid, is as follows. Into a tube about three-quarters of an inch in
eter, and nine and a half long, and as cylindrical as possible throughout its whole
h, 1000 grains of water are to be weighed, and the space occupied marked on the
by a fine file, this space is then divided from above downwards into 100 equal
At 23·44, or 76·56 parts from the bottom, an extra line should be made, and
marked opposite to it; at 48·96 potass should be marked in the same way; at
carbonate of soda; and at 65 carbonate of potass. A diluted acid is now to
pared, which shall have a specific gravity 1·127; and this is made by mixing
ately together 19 parts by weight of oil of vitriol, and 81 of water. The method
followed in the employment of this acid is as follows: the dilute acid is to be
ured in the tube up to the line opposite to which the alkali sought for is marked;
illa, which contains carbonate of soda, 54.63 measures are to be taken. The 100

C 2

measures are then made up by the addition of water, and is then ready for use, following the method before stated.

The alkalies are four in number, namely, ammonia (or volatile alkali), potass (or vegetable alkali), soda (or mineral alkali), and lithia, which last is of so little importance that we shall not treat of it here.

The combinations of these alkalies with the various acids, whenever they form compounds of any importance, will be noticed.

Ammonia, or spirits of hartshorn, or volatile alkali, — in its uncombined form, is an elastic gaseous body, having a very pungent and suffocating odour, destroys animal life, converts the yellow of turmeric paper to a brown, which, from the volatility of the alkali, is again restored by a gentle heat to its original colour. This gas is rapidly absorbed by water, which takes into solution about 780 times its volume, forming the liquid ammonia, or what is commonly called hartshorn. Ammonia is liberated whenever any of the compounds of this alkali are acted upon by potass, soda, lime, and many other alkaline earths. Lime, from its being the most economical, is generally employed: the best proportions for its preparations are equal weights of sal ammoniac (muriate of ammonia), and fresh slaked lime. When these are introduced into a retort and heat applied, ammonia is liberated in the gaseous form, and is conducted by a Wetter's safety-tube into a vessel of water, by which the gas is instantly absorbed. Muriate of lime remains in the retort: sometimes water is added to the mixture, and then distilled. As thus obtained, it has a specific gravity of ·930 or ·940 water being equal to 1·000. The most concentrated solution of ammonia has the specific gravity ·875.

Carbonate of ammonia, or volatile salt, or subcarbonate of ammonia. — This salt, which is very much employed in various processes of the arts, was formerly obtained by the action of chalk (carbonate of lime) upon muriate of ammonia ; a double decomposition takes place. Carbonic acid and ammonia are sublimed in vapour, and muriate of lime remains in the vessel. A much less expensive process is, however, now followed namely, from the waste gas liquors obtained in the purification of coal gas ; these are evaporated, and the black impure sulphuric acid added. By this means a sulphate of ammonia is formed, and the carbonate procured from it by the action of powdered chalk as in the former process.

Its uses are principally in forming other compounds of ammonia, as smelling salts and is likewise employed rather extensively by pastry-cooks for making light pastry which is caused by the volatile carbonate of ammonia escaping and raising up the pastry by the heat of the oven. It is entirely dissipated during the baking, so that no ill effect can arise from its use.

Both this compound and the preceding act as violent stimulants on the animal system.

Muriate of ammonia, or sal ammoniac, — was formerly brought to this country from Egypt, where it was procured by submitting the soot of camels dung (there employed for fuel) to sublimation in closed vessels ; it is, however, at present manufactured in very large quantities in this country in a variety of ways. The most economical processes are either submitting sulphate of ammonia mixed intimately with muriate of soda ('sea-salt) to sublimation, or by subsituting the bittern of sea-water, which consists chiefly of muriate of magnesia, for the sea-salt. In the first process a sulphate of soda is formed, and the muriate of ammonia, which, being volatile, rises in the vaporous form, and is condensed in the cool parts of the apparatus : in the latter process, a sulphate of magnesia (Epsom salts) results. It is generally from this salt (muriate of ammonia) that the liquid ammonia is manufactured : it is also employed in tinning and soldering, to preserve the metals from oxidation. It is a semi-transparent, tough salt, having an acrid and cool taste, and is usually met with in the form of hemispherical masses.

Sulphate of ammonia. — The preparation of the sulphate has been already given under the head of ammonia, it is employed in the manufacture both of the carbonate and muriate.

Acetate of ammonia. — The spirit of mindererus is obtained by acting upon the carbonate of ammonia by acetic acid ; the carbonic acid escapes with effervescence, and an acetate of ammonia is formed : it is employed in medicine as a febrifuge.

All these salts of ammonia have the following properties : — they are volatile at low red heat, the fixed alkalies decompose them, combining with their acid, and the ammonia is liberated.

When combined with a fixed acid, such as the boracic or phosphoric, they are decomposed, the ammonia alone being volatilised, and the acid remaining pure. *The process was described for obtaining pure phosphoric acid.*

Potass, or vegetable alkali. — The original source of this alkali is in the vegetable kingdom, from whence is derived its name of vegetable alkali. When wood is burnt and the ashes lixiviated with water, boiled, strained, and evaporated to dryness,

intensely alkaline mass is obtained, which is known by the name of potash, from this process being conducted in iron pots. It is then removed to a reverberatory furnace, and submitted to heat, and a current of air. This burns out extractive matter and other impurities, and the salt assumes a pearly white colour, and is hence called pearlashes. Care should be taken, during this process, that the potashes do not enter into fusion, as this would destroy the full effect of the operation.

Pearlashes. — Pearlashes generally contain about from 60 to 83 or 84 *per cent.* of pure carbonate of potas. Its uses in manufactures are numerous and important. It is employed in making flint-glass, of which it constitutes about one sixth of the materials employed; in soap-making, especially for the softer kinds of soap: for this purpose, however, it is first rendered caustic by means of lime. In the rectification of spirits, large quantities are employed to combine with the water previously in union with the spirit.

Subcarbonate of potass, or salt of tartar. — In preparing the subcarbonate of potass of the pharmacopæia, (carbonate potass of the chemical nomenclature,) and likewise in rendering hard spring waters soft, and in cleansing substances from grease, it is sometimes called salt of wormwood ; and when made by the deflagration of two parts of tartar or argol and one of nitre, it is called black flux, and is used extensively in metallurgic operations.

From the subcarbonate of potash the pure and uncombined potass is obtained, by adding an equal weight of fresh burnt lime, previously slaked, and boiling them with half their weight of water. By this process the lime combines with the carbonic acid, and the potass remains in solution in its caustic state ; by boiling the clear solution rapidly in iron vessels, and submitting it to fusion, we obtain the fused potass.

If it be required perfectly pure for chemical purposes, it is necessary to evaporate in silver vessels, and dissolve in strong alcohol. This takes up the pure potass, and leaves any portion of the subcarbonate that may not have been acted upon by the lime ; then the alcohol is to be distilled off, and the potass fused at a red heat, and poured out in its liquid state on a cold slab. As thus procured, it is a white, brittle mass, highly deliquescent, absorbing moisture and carbonic acid rapidly from the atmosphere. When evaporated in iron vessels it has a dirty colour, and lets falls a quantity of oxide of iron, when dissolved in water, from its having acted upon the iron boilers.

Potass acts with great rapidity upon animal substances, destroying their texture, and on this account employed as a caustic, and was formerly called *lapis infernalis.*

Carbonate (or bicarbonate of potass in the chemical nomenclature), — is prepared by passing carbonic acid gas through a solution of the subcarbonate : and evaporating a temperature below 212, and crystallising. It is used in making effervescing draughts. It loses one proportion of its carbonic acid when heated, and is converted into the subcarbonate.

Sulphate of potass, or sal polychrest, or vitriolated tartar, — is obtained by submitting the salt, which remains after the manufacture of nitric acid from nitre and sulphuric acid, to a red heat, or by neutralising the excess of acid contained in that salt by bcarbonate of potass.

Bisulphate of potass, or sal enixum. — This is the salt mentioned above, as the residue from the process for obtaining nitric acid. It is employed, in very large quantities, the manufacture of alum; also in tinning iron, for pickling, as it is termed ; it is sometimes also used as a flux.

Nitrate of potash, nitre, or saltpetre. — This salt, which is of so much importance in every branch of the arts, is found native in many parts of the world, especially in the East Indies. It is obtained from soils composed of decomposing granite, the felspar which gives rise, as is supposed, to the potass. The nitric acid is not so easily accounted for, except it is by a union of the nitrogen and oxygen gases of the atmosphere taking place in those hot climates; for, from authenticated accounts, no decaying animal or vegetable matter exists in the nitre districts of India. By lixiviation with water the nitre is dissolved from the soil, which is again thrown out into the air, again to be washed the following year; so that it is formed continually. These liviations are then evaporated, and when of a certain strength, a quantity of common salt separates, which is removed as it falls; and the nitre is then crystallised and imported to this country, always containing a certain quantity of impurities, which are deducted in the purchase of large quantities of the article, being termed its refraction. It is generally used for the manufacture of gunpowder and pure nitric acid, refined or crystallised.

Nitre may be also made artificially, in beds of decaying vegetable or animal substances, mixed with old mortar, or other refuse calcareous earth ; these are watered occasionally, too much moisture being hurtful ; after a certain period, depending on the rapidity with which the process has gone on, the whole is submitted to lixiviation together with wood-ashes, which contain subcarbonate of potass, and which decomposes any

nitrate of lime formed, of which there is generally a considerable quantity. After the lixiviation is complete, which takes some time, the solution is separated and boiled down ; the salt separates as in the other process, and the nitre is then crystallised. It was from this source that the whole of the nitre, nearly, employed by the French during the long protracted war with the continental powers was obtained.

Nitre has a cold, penetrating, and nauseous taste ; enters into igneous fusion at a gentle heat, and is then moulded into round cakes called sal prunella. It is employed in the manufacture of nitric acid ; of gunpowder, which is composed of 75 parts by weight of nitre, 16 of charcoal, and 9 of sulphur (the nitre for this purpose should be of great purity) ; and in the manufacture of oil of vitriol : as a flux it is one of the most powerful we possess ; it is also used for the preservation of animal food, and in making frigorific mixtures : 1 oz. of nitre dissolved in 5 ozs. of water lowers its temperature 15 degrees of Fahrenheit's thermometer. See SALTPETRE.

Oxalate and binoxalate of potass. — The binoxalate of potass, or salt of lemon, or sorrel, by both which last names it is very commonly known, is procured from the juice of the common sorrel (rumex acetosa), or the wood sorrel (oxales acetosella), by crystallisation, after the feculent matter has been separated by standing a few days. Its chief uses are, in removing ink spots or iron moulds ; and also as a refreshing beverage when mixed with sugar and water.

The neutral oxalate is obtained from this salt by combining the excess of acid which it contains with a solution of subcarbonate of potass. Is very much used in chemistry, as the best test of the presence of lime.

Tartrate and bitartrate of potass. — Bitartrate of potass or cream of tartar is, when in its crude and impure state, called argol, and is deposited in the interior of wine casks during fermentation, and from this source the whole of the cream of tartar is obtained. It is generally of a very dark brown colour, but may be purified and rendered perfectly white by solution and crystallisation. It is employed very extensively in dyeing, hat-making, and in the preparation of tartaric acid, and many of the compounds of tartaric acid, as tartar emetic, soluble tartar (tartrate potass) : when heated to redness it is converted into carbonate potass, and charcoal ; mixed with half its weight of nitre and thrown into a red hot crucible it forms the black flux, and with its own weight of nitre the white flux, both of which are very much employed in metallurgic operations. The tartrate is made by the addition of subcarbonate of potass to a solution of the bitartrate until perfectly neutral : it is used in medicine as a mild purgative.

Ferrocyarate or prussiate of potass. — This salt is obtained by the action of subcarbonate potass, at a low red heat, upon refuse animal matter, such as hoofs, horns, skin, &c. in the proportion of two of subcarbonate, to four or five of the animal matter. But the process recommended by M. Gautier is preferable ; he finds, that when animal matter is heated with nitre, it yields a much larger quantity of the ferroprussiate than when either potass or subcarbonate of potass are employed ; the proportions he finds most economical, are 1 part by weight of nitre, 3 parts of dry blood, and iron scales or filings, equal to a fiftieth of the blood employed.

The coagulum of blood is mixed intimately with the nitre and iron filings, and dried by exposure to the air ; they are then submitted to a very low red heat, in deep iron cylinders, as long as vapours continue to be liberated ; when cold, the contents are dissolved in 12 or 15 times their weight of water and strained. On evaporation, till of the specific gravity 1·284, and allowing it to cool, a large quantity of bicarbonate of potass crystallises, and by further evaporation till of the specific gravity 1·306, the ferroprussiate of potass crystallises on cooling. This is to be recrystallised. It is a beautiful yellow salt, very tough, having a tenacity similar to spermaceti, and is decomposed at a red heat. It is employed very extensively in dyeing blues, and in calico printing, also in the manufacture of Prussian blue, which is a compound of the ferroprussic acid and oxide of iron, prepared by adding 1 part of the ferroprussiate of potass dissolved in water, to 1 part of copperas, and 4 parts alum in solution.

Chromate of potass. — This salt is obtained from the native chromate of iron by the action of nitre at a full red heat in equal proportions. By solution, filtration, and evaporation, a beautiful lemon-yellow coloured salt results. It is very much employed in dying, calico printing, and calico making, from its producing bright yellow precipitate with solutions of lead.

Bichromate of potass — is prepared from the above-mentioned salt, by the addition of nitric acid to the yellow solution obtained from the heated mass by the action of water on evaporating this, a dark red coloured salt crystallises, which is the bichromate. This is also very largely employed by the calico printers, and when mixed in solution with nitric acid, posseses the property of destroying vegetable colours ; on this account it is of great importance, as it at the same time removes a vegetable colour, and forms a base for a yellow dye.

Chlorate or hyperoxymuriate of potass. — The preparation of this salt is attended with

me little difficulty, and requires a great deal of nicety. It is obtained by passing a
rrent of chlorine gas through a solution of caustic potass ; then boiling and evaporat-
g ; the first salt that separates is the chlorate of potass, and by further evaporation,
uriate of potass is obtained. It is used in making matches for instantaneous light
xes, which are prepared, by first dipping the wood in melted sulphur, and then into a
in paste, formed of 3 parts chlorate potass, 2 parts starch, and a little vermilion ; with
phur it forms a very explosive compound, generally employed for filling the percus-
n caps of fowling pieces.

Soda or mineral alkali. — The sources of this alkali in nature are various. It is ob-
ned in combination with carbonic acid, when plants which grow by the sea-side are
rnt. The ashes thus obtained are called barilla and kelp ; and also in some countries
s found as an efflorescence upon the surface of the earth, and is called nitrum or na-
n ; this occurs particularly in Egypt and South America. Trona is also another native
bonate of soda, and is exported from Tripoli. In combination with muriatic acid it
also found in immense abundance, forming the rock salt, and sea salt, or muriate of
la. It is obtained from the carbonate exactly in the same way as potass is obtained
m its carbonate, namely, by boiling it with fresh burnt lime previously slaked, de-
ting the clear solution, and evaporating and fusing. It is a white brittle substance,
l by exposure to the air becomes converted into a dry carbonate. Its uses in the arts
l manufactures are of considerable importance. In soap making it is employed in
y large quantities, and for this purpose is generally procured from barilla or kelp, by
xing them with lime, and by the infusion of water procuring a caustic soda ley ; this
nixed with oil and fatty matters in various proportions, and boiled ; the saponification
the fatty matter takes place, and the soap formed rises to the surface ; the ley is then
wn from beneath, and fresh leys added, until the soap is completely free from oil ; it
hen allowed to dry. Soda is also employed in the manufacture of plate, crown, and
tle glass, though for this purpose it is generally in the form of carbonate or sulphate.

Subcarbonate of soda. (In the chemical nomenclature it is called carbonate.) — This
enerally prepared from barilla, which contains about from 16 to 24 per cent. Ba-
a is procured by incinerating the *salsola soda*, and other sea-side plants ; it is made in
ze quantities on the coast of Spain. Kelp is another impure carbonate of soda, but
s not contain more than 4 or 5 per cent. ; it is the ashes obtained from sea-weeds by
neration, and is made on the northern shores of Scotland. From these, the crystal-
l carbonate (or subcarbonate, as it is more frequently called) is made by the addition
small quantity of water, boiling, straining, evaporating, and skimming off the com-
salt as it forms on the surface ; on cooling, the subcarbonate of soda crystallises.
ther method is by heating the sulphate of soda with carbonate of lime and charcoal,
then dissolving out the soluble carbonate ; also, by the action of carbonate potass
rlash) upon solutions of sea salt. See BARILLA and KELP.

icarbonate of soda — is procured by driving a current of carbonic acid gas through
tions of the carbonate, and then evaporating at a temperature below 212° Fahren-
; employed chiefly in making soda-water powders. This is the carbonate soda of
Pharmacopœia. By the application of a red heat it loses carbonic acid, and is con-
ed into the subcarbonate.

ulphate of soda, or Glauber salts. — This salt, which has received the name of
uber, from its discoverer, is the residue of a great many chemical processes ; for ince, when muriate of soda is acted upon by oil of vitriol, muriatic acid and sulphate
da result ; in making chlorine gas for the manufacture of the chloride of lime, or
ching powder, sulphate of soda and sulphate of manganese result ; the materials
loyed being sea salt, sulphuric acid (oil of vitriol), and black oxide of manganese.
, in the preparation of acetic acid from the acetate of soda, and in the preparation
uriate of ammonia from sea salt and sulphate of ammonia. Sulphate of soda is a
arless, transparent salt, effloresces readily when exposed to the air, and becomes con-
d into a dry powder ; it has a cold, bitter taste. It is used for the preparation of
onate soda, and as a medicine. It is found native in some countries, particularly in
ia and South America — frequently as an efflorescence upon new walls.

itrate of soda. — This salt is found native in some parts of the East Indies, and is
l from its square form, cubic nitre ; it is, however, very little used.

uriate of soda, or sea salt. — This compound is found in immense quantities in the
, and is called from this circumstance rock salt, or sal gem. The mines of Cheshire
Droitwich, in this country, and those in Poland, Hungary, and Spain, and many
s, afford immense quantities of this compound. It is also obtained by the evapora-
f sea water, both spontaneously in pits formed for the purpose, and in large iron
s ; the uncrystallisable fluid is called the bittern ; basket salt is made by placing
lt after evaporation in conical baskets, and passing through it a saturated solution
t, which dissolves and carries off the muriate of magnesia or lime. Pure salt should
come moist by exposure to the air ; it decrepitates when heated ; it is employed for

the preparation of muriatic acid, carbonate soda, muriate of ammonia, and many othe operations; also in glazing stone-ware, pottery, &c., and from its great antiseptic proper ties, is used largely for the preservation of animal food; as a flux also in metallurgy.

Borate of soda, or borax. — This salt is found in Thibet and Persia, deposited from saline lakes; it is called tincal, and is imported into this country, where it is purified by solution; the fatty matter with which the tincal is always coated being removed, and the solution evaporated and crystallised; its principal uses are as a flux, from its acting very powerfully upon earthy substances.

ALKANET, Anchusa, or Bugloss (Ger. *Orkanet;* Du. *Ossetong;* Fr *L'Orcanette;* It. *Ancusa;* Sp. *Arcaneta*), a species of bugloss. The greates quantities are raised in Germany and France, particularly about Montpellier whence we are chiefly supplied with the roots. The alkanet of this country is very inferior. The root imparts an elegant deep red colour to pure alcohol, to oils to wax, and to all unctuous substances; also improves the colour of mahogany — (*Ure.*) The duty on alkanet root is very heavy.

ALLOWANCES, Tares, &c. In selling goods, or in paying duties upon them, certain deductions are made from their weights, depending on the nature o the packages in which they are enclosed, and which are regulated in most instance by the custom of merchants, and the rules laid down by public offices. These allowances, as they are termed, are distinguished by the epithets *Draft, Tare Trett,* and *Cloff.*

Draft is a deduction from the original or gross weight of goods, and is subtracte before the tare is taken off.

Tare is an allowance for the weight of the bag, box, cask, or other package, in which goods are weighed.

Real or *open tare* is the actual weight of the package.

Customary tare is, as its name implies, an established allowance for the weight of the package.

Computed tare is an estimated allowance agreed upon at the time.

Average tare is when a few packages only among several are weighed, their mean c average taken, and the rest tared accordingly.

Super-tare is an additiona allowance, or tare, when the commodity or package exceed a certain weight.

When tare is allowed, the remainder is called the nett weight; but if trett be allowed it is called the *suttle weight.*

Trett is a deduction of 4 lb. from every 104 lb. of suttle weight.

This allowance, which is said to be for dust or sand, or for the waste or wear of th commodity, was formerly made on most foreign articles sold by the pound avoirdupois but it is now nearly discontinued by merchants, or else allowed in the price. It wholly abolished at the East India warehouses in London; and neither trett nor dra is allowed at the Custom-house.

Cloff, or *Clough,* is another allowance that is nearly obsolete. It is stated in arithme tical books to be a deduction of 2 lb. from every 3 cwt. of the *second suttle;* that is, t remainder after trett is subtracted; but merchants, at present, know cloff only as a sma deduction, like draft, from the original weight, and this only from two or three article — (See *Kelly's Cambist,* art. "London.")

For an account of the tares and allowances at London, see Tare; for the tares a allowances at the great foreign trading towns, see their names.

ALMONDS (Ger. *Mandeln;* Du. *Amandelen;* Fr. *Amandes;* It. *Mandor.* Sp. *Almendra;* Port. *Amendo;* Rus. *Mindal;* Lat. *Amygdalus communis*), a kind medicinal fruit, contained in a hard shell, which is enclosed in a tough sort cotton skin. The tree which produces this fruit nearly resembles the peach bo in leaves and blossoms; it grows spontaneously only in warm countries, Spain, and particularly Barbary. It flowers early in the spring, and produces fr in August. Almonds are of two sorts, sweet and bitter. They are not d tinguishable from each other but by the taste of the kernel or fruit. " T Valentia almond is sweet, large, and flat-pointed at one extremity, and co pressed in the middle. The Italian almonds are not so sweet, smaller, and l depressed in the middle. The Jordan almonds come from Malaga, and are best sweet almonds brought to England. They are longer, flatter, less pointed one end and less round at the other, and have a paler cuticle than those we have scribed. The sweet almonds are imported in mats, casks, and boxes; the bitte which come chiefly from Mogadore, arrive in boxes."— (*Thomson's Dispensator*

Almonds are among the most grossly over-taxed articles that enter into British tariff. The duty on Jordan almonds amounts to 95s. a cwt.; on sw

lmonds it is 47s. 6d.; and even on bitter almonds, the price of which in bond ~~m~~ay be set down at 30s., the duty is 31s. 8d. Notwithstanding these enormous ~~d~~uties, which seem to have been intended to prevent the use of almonds alto~~g~~ether, there are about 1,900 cwts. of Jordan almonds imported, and about 11,000 ~~c~~wts. of other sorts. The nett duty on almonds in 1830 produced 18,610l., which ~~is~~ little more than its amount in 1807, when the duties were a good deal lower. ~~W~~ere the duty on Jordan almonds reduced to 20s. a cwt., and on other sorts in ~~p~~roportion, there are the best reasons for thinking that, instead of being dimi~~n~~ished, the revenue would, in a very short time, be increased to 100,000l. a year.

We subjoin an account of the quantities of the different descriptions of almonds im~~p~~orted in the year 1830, the rates of duty thereon, the produce of the duties, the coun~~tr~~ies from which the almonds were brought; and specifying the quantities brought from ~~ea~~ch country.

Almonds imported into the United Kingdom in 1830.

	Bitter Almonds.	Jordan Almonds.	Almonds of other Sorts.	Total of all Sorts.
	Cwts. qrs. lbs.	Cwts. qrs. lbs.	Cwts. qrs. lbs.	Cwts. qrs. lbs.
The Netherlands - - -	35 1 4	- -	- -	35 1 4
France - - -	86 0 7	0 0 10	760 0 21¼	846 1 10¼
Portugal - - -	- -	0 0 7	95 2 24	95 3 3
Spain - - -	3 0 8	1880 0 16	1149 1 17	3032 2 13
———— The Canary Islands -	- -	- -	3 1 11	3 1 11
Gibraltar - - -	- -	58 2 17	15 3 15	74 2 4
Italy, viz. Sardinian Territories -	8 0 18	0 0 17	- -	8 1 7
———— Naples and Sicily	12 2 18	5 1 2	118 2 15	136 2 7
Malta - - -	- -	0 1 2½	0 0 10	0 1 12½
Turkey - - -	- -	- -	0 0 7	0 0 7
Africa, viz. Morocco - -	3407 3 20	- -	5249 1 23	8657 1 15
———— Cape of Good Hope -	- -	- -	0 1 3	0 1 3
East India Company's Territories -	- -	0 1 1	- -	0 1 1
Guernsey, Jersey, and Alderney -	0 3 19	- -	27 3 24	28 3 15
Total of Importations -	3554 0 10	1944 3 16½	7421 0 2½	12,920 0 1
	£ s. d.	£ s. d.	£ s. d.	
Rates of Duty ⎰ Of British Possessions - ⎱ Of other Places -	0 15 10 per cwt. 1 11 8 per cwt.	2 7 6 per cwt. 4 15 0 per cwt.	2 7 6 per cwt. 2 7 6 per cwt.	
	£ s. d.	£ s. d.	£ s. d.	£ s. d.
Amount of Duty received -	2246 8 9	9470 5 0	6893 14 7	18,610 8 4

Quantities imported.

ALOES (Du. *Aloe*; Fr. *Aloés*; Ger. and Lat. *Aloe*; Rus. *Sabir*; Sp. *Aloè*; ~~Ar~~ab. *Mucibar*), a bitter, gummy, resinous, inspissated juice, obtained from the ~~lea~~ves of the plant of the same name. There are four sorts of aloes met with in ~~co~~mmerce; viz. *Socotrine, Hepatic, Caballine,* and *Cape.*

1. *Socotrine* — so called from being brought from Zocotora, or Socotra, an island ~~in~~ the Indian Ocean, opposite the south coast of Arabia. The real socotrine ~~alo~~es is now rarely met with in the market; the greater part of the aloes sold ~~un~~der that name is, however, brought from Arabia through Bombay. Genuine ~~soc~~otrine aloes is of a reddish brown colour; glossy, as if varnished; and in ~~so~~me degree pellucid. When reduced to powder, it is of a bright golden colour. ~~Its~~ taste is intensely bitter; and it has a peculiar aromatic odour, not unlike that ~~of~~ the russet apple decaying. It softens in the hand, and is adhesive; yet is ~~suf~~ficiently pulverulent. It is brought to this country by way of Smyrna and ~~Ma~~lta, in chests and casks.

Hepatic.—The real hepatic aloes, so called from its liver colour, is imported from ~~Ara~~bia by Bombay, and has nearly the same characters (except that it is duller ~~an~~d browner) as the Socotrine, for which it is usually substituted. The Barbadoes ~~alo~~es, which is often passed off as the hepatic, is brought home in calabashes, or ~~th~~e gourd shells, containing from sixty to seventy pounds' weight. It is duskier ~~in i~~ts hue than the Bombay or real hepatic aloes, and is intensely bitter and nau~~seo~~us. It is for the most part harder and drier; but the worst sort, imported in ~~cas~~ks, is frequently soft and clammy.

Caballine, or horse aloes, is the coarsest species. Its smell is decidedly ~~stro~~nger and ranker than the Barbadoes hepatic, for which, however, it is some~~tim~~es substituted.—(*Thomson's Dispensatory; Lewis's Mat. Med.*)

~~Ca~~pe aloes — so called from being produced in the vicinity of the Cape of Good

Hope. When reduced to powder, this species is yellow; when in a mass, it has nothing of the dark, cloudy, or opaque appearance of the others, but looks as if it were a piece of yellowish brown glass. It should be chosen bright, pure, and free from any impurity. The less rank the smell the better.—(*Milburn's Oriental Commerce.*)

The duty on Cape aloes (3*d*. per pound) being only *one fifth* of that on Barbadoes aloes, and *one tenth* of that on aloes from Socotra, it is imported to the nearly total exclusion of the others. The revenue derived from aloes in 1828 amounted to 5,971*l*. 11*s*. 11*d*.

ALOES-WOOD (Ger. *Aloeholz*; Du. *Alo̊chout, Paradyshout*; Fr. *Bois d'aloés*; It. *Legno di Aloe*; Sp. *Aloe chino*; Lat. *Lignum Aloes*; Sans. *Aguru*; Malay, *Agila*; Siam. *Kisna*), the produce of a large forest tree, to be found in most of the countries between China and India, from the twenty-fourth degree of north latitude to the equator. It seems to be the result of a diseased action confined to a small part of a few trees, of which the rest of the wood is wholly valueless. It appears to be more or less frequent according to soil and climate, and from the same causes to differ materially in quality. It is produced both in the greatest quantity and perfection in the countries and islands on the east coast of the Gulf of Siam. This article is in high repute for fumigations, and as incense, in all Hindu, Mohammedan, and Catholic countries. It formerly brought a very high price, being at one time reckoned nearly as valuable as gold. It is now comparatively cheap, though the finest specimens are still very dear. The accounts of this article in most books, even of good authority, are singularly contradictory and inaccurate. This is the more surprising, as La. Loubere, (Royaume de Siam, i. p. 45., 12mo ed.) has distinctly stated, that it consisted only of " *certains endroits corrumpus dans des arbres d'une certaine espèce. Toute arbre de cette espèce n'en a pas; et ceux qui en ont, ne les ont pas tous en même endroit.*" The difficulty of finding those trees which happened to be diseased, and of getting the diseased portion, has given rise to the fables that have been current as to its origin. The late Dr. Roxburgh introduced the tree which yields this production into the Botanical Garden at Calcutta, from the hills to the eastward of Sylhet, and described it under the name of *Aquillaria Agalocha.*

ALUM (Ger. *Alaun*; Du. *Aluin*; Fr. *Alun*; It. *Allume*; Sp. *Allumbre*; Rus. *Kwasszä*; Lat. *Alumen*; Arab. *Sheb*), a salt of great importance in the arts, consisting of a ternary compound of *aluminum*, or pure argillaceous earth, potass, and sulphuric acid. Alum is sometimes found native; but by far the greater part of that which is met with in commerce is artificially prepared. The best alum is the Roman, or that which is manufactured near Civita Vecchia, in the Papal territory. It is in irregular, octahedral, crystalline masses, about the size of a walnut, and is opaque, being covered on the surface with a farinaceous efflorescence. The Levant, or roch-alum, is in fragments, about the size of the former, but in which the crystalline form is more obscure; it is externally of a dirty rose-colour, and internally exhibits the same tinge, but clearer. Smyrna is the place whence it is usually shipped for Europe, but it was anciently made at Roccha, or Edessa, in Syria; and hence its name, Roch-alum. English alum is in large, irregular, semi-transparent, colourless masses, having a glassy fracture; not efflorescent, and considerably harder than the others. It is very inferior to either the Roman or roch-alum.

The principal use of alum is in the art of dyeing, as a mordant for fixing and giving permanency to colours which otherwise would not adhere at all, or but for a very short time; but it is also used for a great variety of other purposes.

Beckmann has shown (*History of Inventions*, vol. i. art. "Alum") that the ancients were unacquainted with alum, and that the substance which they designated as such was merely vitriolic earth. It was first discovered by the orientals who established alum works in Syria in the thirteenth or fourteenth century. The oldest alum works in Europe were erected about the middle of the fifteenth century. Towards the conclusion of the reign of Queen Elizabeth, Sir Thomas Chaloner established the first alum work in England, near Whitby, in Yorkshire, where the principal works of the sort in this country are still carried on. There is a large alum work at Hurlett, near Paisley. Alum is largely exported from China, but is very apt to be adulterated.

AMBER (Ger. *Bernstein*; Du. *Barnsteen*; Da. *Bernsteen, Rav.*; Fr. *Ambre jaune*; It. *Ambra gialla*; Sp. *Ambar*; Rus. *Jantar*; Pol. *Bursztyn*; Lat. *Su-*

um, *Electrum*), a brittle, light, hard substance, usually nearly transparent, sometimes nearly colourless, but commonly yellow, or even deep brown. It has considerable lustre. Its specific gravity is 1·065. It is tasteless, without smell, except when pounded or heated, when it emits a fragrant odour. It is highly electric. Most authors assert that amber is bituminous; but Dr. Thomson states, that " it is undoubtedly of a vegetable origin; and though it differs from resins in some of its properties, yet it agrees with them in so many others that it may without impropriety be referred to them."—(*Chemistry*, vol. iv. p. 147. 5th ed.) Pieces of amber occasionally enclose parts of toads and insects in their substance, which are beautifully preserved. It is principally found on the shores of Pomerania and Polish Prussia; but it is sometimes dug out of the earth in Ducal Prussia. It is also met with on the banks of the river Giaretta, in Sicily. Sometimes it is found on the east coast of Britain, and in gravel pits round London. The largest mass of amber ever found was got near the surface of the ground in Lithuania. It weighs 18 lbs., and is preserved in the royal cabinet at Berlin. Most of the amber imported into this country comes from the Baltic, but a small quantity comes from Sicily. Amber was in very high estimation among the ancients, but is now comparatively neglected.

AMBER-GRIS, or AMBER-GREASE (Ger. *Amber*; Du. *Amber*; Fr. *Ambre-gris*; It. *Ambra-grigia*; Sp. *Ambar-gris*; Lat. *Ambra, Ambra grisea*) — is a solid, opaque, generally ash-coloured, fatty, inflammable substance, variegated like marble, remarkably light, rugged and uneven in its surface, and has a fragrant odour when heated; it does not effervesce with acids, melts freely over the fire into a kind of yellow rosin, and is hardly soluble in spirit of wine. It is found on the sea-coast, or floating on the sea, near the coasts of India, Africa, and Brazil, usually in small pieces, but sometimes in masses of 50 or 100 lbs. weight. Various opinions have been entertained respecting its origin. Some affirmed that it was the concrete juice of a tree, others thought it a bitumen; but it is now considered as pretty well established that it is a concretion formed in the stomach or intestines of the *physeter macrocephalus*, or spermaceti whale."— (*Thomson's Chemistry*, 5th ed. vol. iv. p. 441.)

Ambergris ought to be chosen in large pieces of an agreeable odour, entirely grey on the outside, and grey with little black spots within. The purchaser should be very cautious, as this article is easily counterfeited with gums and other drugs.

AMETHYST (Ger. *Amethyst*; Du. *Amathiststeen*; Fr. *Amethyste*; It. *Ama-tisto*; Sp. *Ametisto*; Lat. *Amethystus*), a gem of a violet colour and great brilliancy, said to be as hard as the ruby or sapphire, from which it only differs in colour. This is called the oriental amethyst, and is very rare. When it inclines to the purple or rosy colour it is more esteemed than when it is nearer to the blue. These amethysts have the same figure, hardness, specific gravity, and other properties, as the best sapphires or rubies, and come from the same places, particularly from Persia, Arabia, Armenia, and the West Indies. The occidental amethysts are merely coloured crystal or quartz. — (*Ure*.)

AMIANTHUS, ASBESTOS, or MOUNTAIN FLAX, a mineral, of which there have varieties, all more or less fibrous, flexile, and elastic. This mineral was highly esteemed by the ancients. They manufactured it into cloth, which, from its being inconsumable by a high degree of heat, they employed to wrap the bodies of the dead when exposed on the funeral pile. Some moderns have succeeded in making this cloth; but the art, if it be not entirely lost, is but rarely practised.

AMMONIACUM (Fr. *Gomme Ammoniaque*; It. *Gomma Ammoniaco*; Sp. *Goma Ammoniaco*; Lat. *Ammoniacum*; Arab. *Teshook*), a concrete, resinous juice. It has a faint but not ungrateful smell; and a bitter, nauseous, sweet taste. The fragments are yellow on the outside and white within, brittle, and break with a glassy fracture; their specific gravity is 1·207. The best ammoniacum is brought from Persia by Bombay and Calcutta, packed in cases and chests. It is in large masses, composed of small round fragments or tears; or in separate tears, which is generally considered a sign of its goodness.—(*Thomson's Dispensatory*.)

AMMUNITION, a term expressive of the various implements used in war.

Ammunition can be imported into the United Kingdom by way of merchandise, but by licence from his majesty, and such licence is to be granted for furnishing his majesty's stores only, under penalty of forfeiture. 6 Geo. 4. c. 107. His majesty may

forbid, by order in council, the exportation of any saltpetre, gunpowder, or any so
of ammunition.   Any master of a vessel exporting ammunition when so forbidden, sha
for every such offence forfeit 100*l.* (29 Geo. 2. c. 16.)

AMPHORA, a measure used at Venice for liquids.   It is equal to about for
English wine gallons.

AMSTERDAM, the principal city of Holland, is situated on an arm of th
Zuyder Zee, in lat. 52° 25′ N. and long. 4° 40′ E. From 1580 to 1750 Amsterda
was, perhaps, the first commercial city of Europe ; and though her trade has expe
rienced a great falling off since the last-mentioned epoch, it is still very conside
able. The population is at present about 200,000. In 1785 it amounted to 230,00
The harbour is spacious, and the water deep ; but on acccount of a bank (th
Pampus) at its entrance, large vessels are obliged to load and unload a part of the
cargoes in the roads.   The imports principally consist of sugar, coffee, spice
tobacco, cotton, tea, indigo, cochineal, wine and brandy, wool, grain of all sort
timber, pitch and tar, hemp and flax, iron, hides, linen, cotton and woollen stuff
hardware, rock salt, tin plates, coal, dried fish, &c. The exports consi
partly of the produce of Holland, partly of the produce of her possessions in th
East and West Indies and other tropical countries, and partly of commoditie
brought to Amsterdam, as to a convenient *entrepôt*, from different parts of E
rope. Of the first class are cheese and butter (very important articles), madde
clover, rape, hemp, and linseeds, rape and linseed oils, Dutch linen, &c.   Genev
is principally exported from Schiedam and Rotterdam ; oak-bark principally fro
the latter.   Of the second class are spices, Mocha and Java coffee, sugar of Jav
Brazil, and Cuba, cochineal, indigo, cotton, tea, tobacco, and all sorts of Easter
and colonial products.   And of the third class, all kinds of grain, linens from Ge
many, timber and all sorts of Baltic produce, Spanish, German, and English wool
French, Rhenish, and Hungarian wines, brandy, &c.   The trade of Amsterda
may, indeed, be said to comprise every article that enters into the commerce
Europe.   Her merchants were formerly the most extensive dealers in bills
exchange.   And though London be now, in this respect, far superior to Amste
dam, the latter still enjoys a respectable share of this business.

The Bank of the Netherlands was established at Amsterdam in 1814.   It
not, like the old Bank of Amsterdam, which ceased in 1796, merely a bank of d
posit, but a bank of deposit and circulation formed on the model of the Bank
England. (*See* BANKS, FOREIGN.)

For an account of the Dutch fisheries, see the articles HERRING FISHER
WHALE FISHERY.

Of the imports into Amsterdam during the year 1825, were the following : —

Coffee	2,569	barrels.	Wine	790	barrels.
	99,579	bags.	Spirits	275	pieces
Sugar	16,845	casks.	Brandy	156	ditto.
	8,262	boxes.	Rum	28	puncheons
	1,509	canisters.	Wool	2,502	bags.
	9,118 }	sacks and	Flax	2,299	bundles.
		mats.	Stockfish	42,002	wags.
Tobacco	6,064	hhds.	Whale oil	6,760	barrels.
	2,883	bags.	Tar	3,045	gunnies.
	175,872	rolls.	Pitch	1,769	tons.
Rice	7,552	barrels.	Tallow	71	casks.
	945	bags.	Potash	5,514	tons.
Cotton	7,871	serons.	Ashes	3,142	ditto.
Cacao	823	bags.	Wheat	5,101	lasts.
Indigo	73	chests.	Linseed, flaxseed, &c.	6,361	ditto.
	28	serons.	Barley	2,519	ditto.
Hides	11,703		Oats	526	ditto.
Tea	26,024	chests.	Maize	485	ditto.
Pepper	1,113	bags.	Beans	554	ditto.
Wine	14,835	oxhofts	Rye	4,169	ditto.
	4,653	casks.			

(*Bulletin des Sciences Géograph.* vi. p. 18

The ships entering the port of Amsterdam, during each of the five years, end
with 1828, have been as follows : —

1824	1,729	1827	1,982
1825	1,606	1828	2,132
1826	1,887		

Captains of ships are bound to make, within twenty-four hours of their arrival at Amsterdam, or any Dutch port, a declaration in writing, of the goods of which their cargo consists. If the captains be not acquainted with the goods of which the cargo consists, they must make their declaration under the general term of *merchandise*, and exhibit the bills of lading along with the declaration. The custom-house officers are instructed to inform the captains of all formalities required by law.

All goods, whether for transit or newly imported, may be bonded or placed in *en-epôt*.

The business of insurance is extensively practised at Amsterdam; the premiums are moderate, and the security unexceptionable. The high duty imposed in this country on policies of insurance has contributed to the increase of this business in Holland.

Credit, Discount, &c.— Holland is, and has always been, a country of short credit. A discount is usually given for prompt payment, at the rate of one per cent. for six weeks, and of two per cent. for two months; but the terms of credit on most articles, and the discount allowed for ready money, have been fixed by usage, and are regarded as essential conditions in every bargain. Some of the more important of these terms and discounts are specified in the following table. In consequence of the preference given in Holland to ready money transactions, it is not a country in which adventurers without capital have much chance of speedily making a fortune. " Rien, en effet, de plus facile que de s'établir à Amsterdam; mais *rien de plus difficile que de s'y soutenir sans les grandes résources*. Dans cette ville, où l'argent abonde, où on le prête contre des suretés à si bon marché, *il est pourtant impossible de s'en procurer à crédit ;* et sans argent il n'y a pas plus de possibilité d'y travailler, que de trouver quelqu'un qui veuille de se charger d'un papier nouveau qui ne seroit pas appuyé d'un credit que l'opinion, la protection, ou des effets réels feroient valoir à la bourse. Les Hollandois suivent là-dessus les maximes très austères, même à l'égard des maisons d'une certaine considération." *Encyclopédie Méthodique, Commerce,* ii. p. 650.) But this *austerity* is not a disadvantage, but the reverse. It prevents commerce from degenerating, as it has too often done in other places, into gambling adventures, and places it on a comparatively solid foundation. And it should be mentioned to the honour of the Dutch, and as a proof of the excellence of this system, that notwithstanding the distress and loss of trade occasioned by the invasion and occupation of their country by the French, the bankruptcies in 1795 and subsequent years were not, comparatively, so numerous as in England in ordinary seasons!

It has long been the practice in Holland to make, on selling articles, considerable deductions from their weight, particularly from those of large bulk, as compared with their value. These tares and drafts, as they are termed, are now fixed by ancient usage; and the most important amongst them are here specified.

Tares and Allowances on the principal Articles sold at Amsterdam.

	Tares.	Allowances. (Draft and Discount.)
...shes	42 lbs. per cask	18 months' discount, and per cent.
...arilla	4 per cent.	2 per cent. and 2 per cent.
...coa, Caraccas	2 lbs.	1 per cent.
Maranham	ditto	
Cayenne	ditto	
Martinique	ditto	
Surinam	6 per cent.	
...ffee, East and West India in general	bags 3 per cent., casks real tare	2 per cent. and 2 per cent.
Bourbon	10 lbs. per original mat	
Java	14 lbs. per gunny	
Mocha	24 lbs. per bale	
...tton, Surat and Bengal	8 per cent.	2 per cent. and 1 per cent.
All other kinds	6 per cent.	
...tton yarn twist	—	1 per cent.
...digo, Bengal	real tare	1 per cent. 2 per cent. and 1 per cent.
...chineal	3 à 4 lbs.	4 per cent. augment. 1 per cent. deduct.
...lls	6 lbs. or 20 lbs.	2 per cent. and 2 per cent.
...ms, Senegal	6 lbs. 14 lbs. or 21 lbs.	2 per cent. and 2 per cent.
...rbary		
Arabic	14 lbs. or 30 lbs.	
...gwood	2 and 3 per cent.	2 per cent.
...stic	2 per cent.	

	Tares.	Allowances.
Hides, Buenos Ayres, &c.	} 2 lbs. per hide	2 per cent. and 1 per cent.
Linens, Flemish	———	2 per cent. and 1 per cent.
All other kinds	———	1 per cent.
Oils	———	1 per cent.
Rice, Carolina	real tare	} 2 per cent. and 2 per cent.
East India	6 lbs.	
Saltpetre	8 à 14 lbs.	1 per cent. and 1½ per cent.
Liquorice	real tare and 4 lbs.	2 per cent. and 1 per cent.
Spices, pepper	} 25 lbs. or 13 lbs.	
cinnamon		
cloves and mace		1 per cent.
pimento	12 lbs. and above 100	} 1 per cent.
nutmegs	12 per cent.	
ginger	8 lbs. à 16 lbs.	2 per cent.
Sugars, Martinique		
St. Domingo	} 18 per cent.	
St. Croix		
Surinam	} 20 per cent.	
English colonies		2 per cent. and 2 per cent.
Demerara		
Berbice	} 18 per cent.	
Essequibo		
Brazil, white		
Ditto Muscovado	———	18 months' discount, 2 per cent. and 2 per cent.
Havannah	80 lbs.	} 2 per cent. and 2 per cent.
Java	48 lbs.	
Salt,	———	1 per cent.
Tea, bohea		
congo	} 21 lbs. à 24 lbs.	
souchong		
campoi		1 per cent.
hyson	18 lbs.	
pekoe	} 18 lbs. à 42 lbs.	
tonquin		
Tobacco, Maryland	casks tared	2 per cent. and 4 per cent. damaged, and 1 per cent.
Virginia	2 and 8 per cent.	
Tin plates	2 per cent.	1 per cent.
Wool, Spanish	bags tared and 24 lbs. per 175 lbs.	21 months' discount, and 1 per cent.
Wines	———	1 per cent.
Madder	casks tared	10 lbs. per cask, and 2 per cent.
Herrings	3 or 5 per cent.	1 per cent., 2 per cent. and 2 per cent.
Smalts	36 lbs.	2 per cent.
Flax, hams, seeds, geneva, grain	———	} 1 per cent.
Butter	———	none.
Hides	———	2 and 1 per cent.
Cheese, Edam	———	2 per cent.
Gouda	———	1 per cent.

The above are the customary tares and other allowances made by the merchants in their transactions with each other. But in paying the import duties at the custom-house, the tare upon goods paying duty by weight is, with the exceptions undermentioned, fixed at 15 per cent. for such as are in casks or barrels, and at 8 per cent. for such as are in packages, canisters, mats, baskets, &c. Merchants dissatisfied with these allowances may pay the duty according to the *real* weight, ascertained by the customs officers at their expense.

Exceptions. — The tare upon grain imported in sacks is fixed at 2 per cent.
Porcelain, 15 per cent.

Indigo { in chests, 25 per cent.
{ in serons, 15 per cent.

Sugar { chests from Havannah, 18 per cent., other places 20 per cent.
{ canisters, 10 per cent.
{ casks and packages, 15 and 8 per cent. The tare upon sugar refined in the
{ interior and exported, is 12 per cent. per barrel, 8 per cent. per package.

n allowance for leakage is made upon all liquids, including treacle and honey, as
ows, viz.

oming from England, the northern ports of Europe, and France, by inland navi-
on, 6 per cent.

rom France by sea, and from other countries by the rivers Rhine and Waal, 12
cent.

rom any other port or place, 14 per cent.

inally, from whatever place the same may come, upon train oil, 12 per cent.;
bber, 6 per cent.

n case liquids shall have experienced, upon the voyage, such leakage as shall cause
importer to be dissatisfied with the allowance before specified, he is permitted to pay
duty upon the actual quantity, to be ascertained by the officers at the importer's
ense.

Tonnage duty. — Foreign vessels pay, each time that they enter a port of the king-
n, two florins twelve sous per last of two tons.

National vessels, sailing under the flag of the Netherlands, pay per last, on entering,
ty sous, and on their departure, fifteen sous : but for these last the duty is due but
e a year, reckoning from the 1st of January to the 31st of December.

Foreign vessels, belonging to any nation where the vessels of the Netherlands are
ted on the same footing as the ships of that nation, shall enjoy the same favour, with
ect to the tonnage duty, as the vessels of the Netherlands. Ministers *to* and *from*
ign courts exempt from duty.

Money. — Accounts used to be kept at Amsterdam by the pound Flemish = 6 florins
0 schillings = 120 stivers = 240 groats = 1920 pennings. But in 1820, the deci-
system was introduced. In order, however, to cause as little inconvenience as
sible, the florin = 1s. 8¾d. sterling, was made the unit of the new system. The florin
upposed to be divided into 100 equal parts or cents ; and the other silver coins are
al multiples or sub-multiples of it. The new gold coin is called the florin piece
is worth 16s. 6½d. very nearly. But accounts are still sometimes kept in the old
, or by the pound Flemish. Par of exchange between Amsterdam and London is 11
58 cent. per pound sterling.

Weights and Measures. — In 1820, the French system of weights and measures was
oduced into the Netherlands, the names only being changed.

he *pond* is the unit of weight, and answers to the French *kilogramme*. Its divisions
he ons, lood, wigtje, and korrel.

he *elle*, which is the unit or element of long measure, equals the French *metre*. Its
mal divisions are the palm, duim, and streep ; and its decimal multiples, the roede
mijle.

he *vierkante elle*, or square ell, is the unit of superficial measures ; and answers to
centiare or *metre carré* of France. Its divisions are the vierkante palm, vierkante
n, and the vierkante streep ; and its multiples, the vierkante roede and vierkante
der.

he *kubicke elle* is the unit of measures of capacity ; and equals the French *stere*. Its
ions are the kubicke palm, kubicke duim, and kubicke streep.

he term *wisse* is given to a kubicke elle of fire-wood.

he *kop* is the unit of measures for dry wares, and is the cube of the palm ; answering
e French *litre*. Its division is the maatje, and its multiples the schepel and mudde ;
atter is also called the *zak*, and equals the French hectolitre. 30 mudden make
.

he *kan* is the unit for liquid measure, and is the cube of the palm ; it corresponds
e French *litre*. Its divisions are the maatje and vingerhoed, and 100 kans make a
r cask, which equals the French hectolitre.

he apothecary's new pound is 12 ounces, 96 drachms, 288 scruples, or 5760 grains ;
answers to 375 grammes, or 5787 English grains.

y the old method of calculating, which is not yet entirely superseded, the pound of
terdam was = to 1·09 lib. avoirdupois, or 100 lib. Amsterdam = 108·923 lib. avoir-
is.

he *last* or measure for corn = 27 mudden = 10 qurs, 5¼ bushels Winchester measure.

aam liquid measure = 4 ankers = 8 steckans = 21 viertels = 64 stoops or stoppen =
ningles = 256 pints = 41 English wine gallons.

e stoop contains 5⅛ pints English wine measure.

0 mingles are equal to 32 English wine gallons, or 26⅓ English beer gallons, or 26⅞
rial gallons.

ench wine is sold per hogshead of.................................. 180 mingles.

anish and Portuguese wine, per pipe, of .... 349 ditto.

ench brandy, per hogshead, of .... 30 viertels.

Beer, per barrel, (equal to the aam) of .... 128 mingles.
Vegetable oils, per aam, of .... 120 ditto.
Whale oil,   per ditto .... 16 ditto.
Rum is sold per *anker*, of 2 steckan = 10¼ English wine gallons.
The foot of Amsterdam = 11¼ English inches.
The Rhineland foot ...... = 12   ditto.
The ell, cloth measure... = 27¹⁄₁₃ ditto.
Rock salt is sold per hondert of 404 maaten, making 20 tons, or 4000 lb. Dutch.
Pit coal is sold per hoed of 38 maaten; nine hoeds are five chaldrons of Newcastle, six hoeds are five chaldrons of London.
Butter is sold per barrel; the barrel of Leyden is 320 lbs. net. — that of Frieslan 28 lb. net — and the common Dutch barrel 336 lbs. gross.
A *last of herrings* is reckoned at 12, 13, or 14 barrels.
A *last of pitch* is 12 barrels.
A *last of tar*, 13 barrels.
A bag of seed = 2½ Winchester quarters.
A last for freight is reckóned 4000 lb. equal to two English tons.

Eight hogsheads (or oxhofts) of wine
Twelve barrels of pitch
Thirteen barrels of tar
Twenty chests of lemons, &c.   } are reckoned as one last in settlin
4000 lbs. of iron, copper, and colonial produce   the freight of ships.
4000 lbs. of almonds
2000 lbs. wool or feathers

A last of wheat is considered ten per cent. higher than one of rye, and the latter twen and a half per cent. higher than oats, and ten per cent. higher than seed.   A last of ba last is only 2000 lbs. — (*Steel's Shipmaster's Assistant.*)

Magnitude of the commerce of Holland in the seventeenth century. — Causes of prosperity and decline. — We believe we need make no apology for embracing th opportunity to lay before our readers the following details with respect to the commer and commercial policy of Holland. It forms one of the most instructive topics investigation; and it is to be regretted that so little attention should have been paid to in this country.

Previously to the commencement of the long-continued and glorious struggle ma by the Dutch to emancipate themselves from the blind and brutal despotism of o Spain, they had a considerable marine, and had attained to distinction by their fisheries a commerce; and the war, instead of being injurious to the trade of the republic, co tributed powerfully to its extension. After the capture of Antwerp by the Spaniard in 1585, the extensive commerce of which it had been the centre was removed to t ports of Holland, and principally to Amsterdam, which then attained to the distinctio she long enjoyed, of the first commercial city of Europe.

In 1602, the Dutch East India Company was formed; and notwithstanding t pernicious influence of that association, the Indian trade increased rapidly in magn tude and importance. Ships fitted either for commercial or warlike purposes, a having a considerable number of soldiers on board, were sent out within a few years the establishment of the company. Amboyna and the Moluccas were first wrest from the Portuguese, and with them the Dutch obtained the monopoly of the spi trade. Factories and fortifications were in no long time established, from Balsora, the mouth of the Tigris, in the Persian gulf, along the coasts and islands of India far as Japan. Alliances were formed with several of the Indian princes; and in ma parts, particularly on the coasts of Ceylon, and in various districts of Malabar a Coromandel, they were themselves the sovereigns. Batavia, in the large and fert island of Java, the greater part of which had been conquered by the Dutch, formed centre of their Indian commerce; and though unhealthy, its port was excellent, and was admirably situated for commanding the trade of the Eastern Archipelago. 1651, they planted a colony at the Cape of Good Hope, which had been strang neglected by the Portuguese.

Every branch of commerce was vigorously prosecuted by the Dutch. Their tr with the Baltic was, however, by far the most extensive and lucrative of which th were in possession. Guicciardini mentions that the trade with Poland, Denma Prussia, &c. even before their revolt, was so very great, that fleets of 300 ships arriv twice a year at Amsterdam from Dantzic and Livonia only; but it increased pro giously during the latter part of the sixteenth and the beginning of the seventeer centuries. The great population of Holland, and the limited extent and unfruit nature of the soil, render the inhabitants dependent on foreigners for the greater part their supplies of corn. The countries round the Baltic have always furnished th

ith the principal part of those supplies; and it is from them that they have been in
e habit of bringing timber, iron, hemp and flax, pitch and tar, tallow, ashes, and other
ilky articles required in the building of their houses and ships, and in various ma-
ifactures. Nothing, however, redounds so much to the credit of the Dutch, as the
olicy they have invariably followed with respect to the trade in corn. They have, at
I times, had a large capital embarked in this business. The variations which are
erpetually occurring in the harvests, early led them to engage very extensively in a
rt of speculative corn trade. When the crops happened to be unusually productive,
d prices low, they bought and stored up large quantities of grain, in the expectation
profiting by the advance that was sure to take place on the occurrence of an un-
vourable year. Repeated efforts were made in periods when prices were rising, to pre-
il on the government to prohibit exportation; but they steadily refused to interfere.
consequence of this enlightened policy, Holland has long been the most important
uropean *entrepôt* for corn; and her markets have on all occasions been furnished with
e most abundant supplies. Those scarcities which are so very disastrous in countries
ithout commerce, or where the trade in corn is subjected to fetters and restraints, have
t only been totally unknown in Holland, but became a copious source of wealth to
r merchants, who then obtained a ready and advantageous vent for the supplies ac-
mulated in their warehouses. "Amsterdam," says Sir Walter Raleigh, "is never
ithout 700,000 quarters of corn, none of it of the growth of Holland; and a dearth
only one year in any other part of Europe, enriches Holland for seven years. In
e course of a year and a half, during a scarcity in England, there were carried
vay from the ports of Southampton, Bristol, and Exeter alone, nearly 200,000*l*.;
d if London and the rest of England be included, there must have been 2,000,000*l*.
ore." (*Observations touching Trade and Commerce with the Hollander*, Miscel. Works,
l. ii.)
The very well informed author of the *Richesse de la Hollande*, published in 1778,
serves, in allusion to these circumstances, "Que la disette de grains regne dans les
atre parties du monde; vous trouverez du froment, du seigle, et d'autres grains à
nsterdam; *ils n'y manquent jamais*."—(Tome i. p. 376.)
The Bank of Amsterdam was founded in 1609. The principal object of this
ablishment was to obviate the inconvenience and uncertainty arising from the
culation of the coins imported into Amsterdam from all parts of the world. The
rchants who carried coin or bullion to the Bank obtained credit for an equal value in
books: this was called bank-money; and all considerable payments were effected
writing it off from the account of one individual to that of another. This establish-
nt continued to flourish till the invasion of the French in 1795.
Between the years 1651 and 1672, when the territories of the republic were invaded
the French, the commerce of Holland seems to have reached its greatest height.
Witt estimates its increase from the treaty with Spain, concluded at Munster in
13, to 1669, at fully a half. He adds, that during the war with Holland, Spain lost
greater part of her naval power; that since the peace, the Dutch had obtained most
the trade to that country, which had been previously carried on by the Hanseatic
rchants and the English; that almost all the coasting trade of Spain was carried on
Dutch shipping; that Spain had even been forced to hire Dutch ships to sail to her
nerican possessions; and that so great was the exportation of goods from Holland to
iin, that all the merchandise brought from the Spanish West Indies was not suffi-
it to make returns for them.
At this period, indeed, the Dutch engrossed, not by means of any artificial monopoly,
by the greater number of their ships, and their superior skill and economy in all
: regarded navigation, almost the whole carrying trade of Europe. The value of the
ds exported from France in Dutch bottoms, towards the middle of the fourteenth
tury, exceeded forty millions of livres; and the commerce of England with the
v Countries was, for a very long period, almost entirely carried on in the same way.
he business of marine insurance was largely and successfully prosecuted at Amster-
i; and the ordinances published in 1551, 1563, and 1570, contain the most judicious
ilations for the settlement of such disputes as might arise in conducting this difficult
highly useful business. It is singular, however, notwithstanding the sagacity of
Dutch, and their desire to strengthen industrious habits, that they should have pro-
ted insurance upon lives. It was reserved for England to show the advantages
might be derived from this beautiful application of the science of probabilities.
n 1690, Sir William Petty estimated the shipping of Europe at about 2,000,000
ons, which he supposed to be distributed as follows: — viz. England, 500,000;
nce, 100,000; Hamburgh, Denmark, Sweden, and Dantzic, 250,000; Spain, Por-
il, and Italy, 250,000; that of the Seven United Provinces amounting, according
im, to 900,000 tons, or to nearly one half of the whole tonnage of Europe! No

great dependence can, of course, be placed upon these estimates; but the probability is, that had they been more accurate, the preponderance in favour of Holland would have been greater than it appears to be; for the official returns to the circulars addressed in 1701 by the commissioners of customs to the officers at the different ports, show that the whole mercantile navy of England amounted at that period to only 261,222 tons, carrying 27,196 men. *

It may, therefore, be fairly concluded, that, during the seventeenth century, the foreign commerce and navigation of Holland was greater than that of all Europe besides; and yet the country which was the seat of this vast commerce had no native produce to export, nor even a piece of timber fit for ship-building. All had been the fruit of industry, economy, and a fortunate combination of circumstances.

Holland owed this vast commerce to a variety of causes: partly to her peculiar situation, the industry and economy of her inhabitants, the comparatively liberal and enlightened system of civil as well as of commercial policy adopted by the republic; and partly also to the wars and disturbances that prevailed in most European countries in the sixteenth and seventeenth centuries, and prevented them from emulating the successful career of the Dutch.

The ascendancy of Holland as a commercial state began to decline from about the commencement of last century. After the war terminated by the treaty of Aix-la-Chapelle, the attention of the government of Holland was forcibly attracted to the state of the shipping and foreign commerce of the republic. The discovery of means by which their decline might be arrested, and the trade of the republic, if possible, restored to its ancient flourishing condition, became a prominent object in the speculations of every one who felt interested in the public welfare. In order to procure the most correct information on the subject, the Stadtholder, William IV., addressed the following queries to all the most extensive and intelligent merchants, desiring them to favour him with their answers: —

" 1. What is the actual state of trade? and if the same should be found to be diminished and fallen to decay, then, 2. To enquire by what methods the same may be supported and advanced, or, if possible, restored to its former lustre, repute, and dignity ?'

In discussing these questions, the merchants were obliged to enter into an examination, as well of the causes which had raised the commerce of Holland to the high pitch of prosperity to which it had once attained, as of those which had occasioned its subsequent decline. It is stated, that, though not of the same opinion upon all points, they, speaking generally, concurred as to those that were most important. When their answers had been obtained, and compared with each other, the Stadtholder had a dissertation prepared from them, and other authentic sources, on the commerce of the republic, to which proposals were subjoined for its amendment. Some of the principles advanced in this dissertation apply to the case of Holland only; but most of them are of universal application, and are not more comprehensive than sound. We doubt, indeed, whether the benefits resulting from religious toleration, political liberty, the security of property, and the freedom of industry, have ever been more clearly set forth than in this dissertation. It begins by an enumeration of the causes which contributed to advance the commerce of the republic to its former unexampled prosperity; these the authors divide into three classes, embracing under the first those that were natural and physical; under the second, those they denominate moral; and under the third, those which they considered adventitious and external; remarking on them in succession as follows: —

" I. The natural and physical causes are the advantages of the situation of the country, on the sea, and at the mouth of considerable rivers; its situation between the northern and southern parts, which, by being in a manner the centre of all Europe, made the republic become the general market, where the merchants on both sides used to bring their superfluous commodities, in order to barter and exchange the same for other goods they wanted.

" Nor have the barrenness of the country, and the necessities of the natives arising from that cause, less contributed to set them upon exerting all their application, industry and utmost stretch of genius, to fetch from foreign countries what they stand in need of in their own, and to support themselves by trade.

" The abundance of fish in the neighbouring seas put them in a condition not only to supply their own occasions, but with the overplus to carry on a trade with foreigners and out of the produce of the fishery to find an equivalent for what they wanted, through the sterility and narrow boundaries and extent of their own country.

" II. Among the moral and political causes are to be placed, The unalterable maxim and fundamental law relating to the free exercise of different religions; and always to consider this toleration and connivance as the most effectual means to draw foreigners

* Macpherson's Annals of Commerce, anno 1701.

n adjacent countries to settle and reside here, and so become instrumental to the
pling of these provinces.

The constant policy of the republic to make this country a perpetual, safe, and
are asylum for all persecuted and oppressed strangers. No alliance, no treaty, no
rd for or solicitation of any potentate whatever, has at any time been able to
ken or destroy this law, or make the state recede from protecting those who have
to it for their own security and self-preservation.

Throughout the whole course of all the persecutions and oppressions that have
rred in other countries, the steady adherence of the republic to this fundamental
has been the cause that many people have not only fled hither for refuge, with their
le stock in ready cash, and their most valuable effects, but have also settled, and
blished many trades, fabrics, manufactories, arts, and sciences, in this country, not-
standing the first materials for the said fabrics and manufactories were almost
lly wanting in it, and not to be procured but at a great expense from foreign parts.

The constitution of our form of government, and the liberty thus accruing to the
en, are further reasons to which the growth of trade, and its establishment in the
blic, may fairly be ascribed; and all her policy and laws are put upon such an
table footing, that neither life, estates, nor dignities, depend on the caprice or
rary power of any single individual; nor is there any room for any person, who, by
, frugality, and diligence, has once acquired an affluent fortune or estate, to fear a
ivation of them by any act of violence, oppression, or injustice.

The administration of justice in the country has, in like manner, always been clear
impartial, and without distinction of superior or inferior rank,—whether the parties
been rich or poor, or were this a foreigner and that a native; and it were greatly
e wished we could at this day boast of such impartial quickness and despatch in all
legal processes, considering how great an influence it has on trade.

To sum up all, amongst the moral and political causes of the former flourishing
of trade, may be likewise placed the wisdom and prudence of the administration;
ntrepid firmness of the councils; the faithfulness with which treaties and engage-
ts were wont to be fulfilled and ratified; and particularly the care and caution
ised to preserve tranquillity and peace, and to decline, instead of entering on a
e of war, merely to gratify the ambitious views of gaining fruitless or imaginary
uests.

By these moral and political maxims was the glory and reputation of the republic
r spread, and foreigners animated to place so great a confidence in the steady deter-
tions of a state so wisely and prudently conducted, that a concourse of them
ed this country with an augmentation of inhabitants and useful hands, whereby its
and opulence were from time to time increased.

III. Amongst the adventitious and external causes of the rise and flourishing state
r trade may be reckoned—

That at the time when the best and wisest maxims were adopted in the republic as
eans of making trade flourish, they were neglected in almost all other countries;
ny one, reading the history of those times, may easily discover, that the persecutions
count of religion throughout Spain, Brabant, Flanders, and many other states and
loms, have powerfully promoted the establishment of commerce in the republic.

To this happy result, and the settling of manufacturers in our country, the long
nuance of the civil wars in France, which were afterwards carried on in Germany,
and, and divers other parts, have also very much contributed.

t must be added, in the last place, that during our most burdensome and heavy
with Spain and Portugal (however ruinous that period was for commerce other-
, these powers had both neglected their navy; whilst the navy of the republic, by a
ct directly the reverse, was at the same time formidable, and in a capacity not only
tect the trade of its own subjects, but to annoy and crush that of their enemies in
arters."*

e believe our readers will agree with us in thinking, that these statements reflect
reatest credit on the merchants and government of Holland. Nothing, as it
rs to us, could be conceived more judicious than the account they give of the
s which principally contributed to render Holland a great commercial common-
h. The central situation of the country, its command of some of the principal
to the continent, and the necessity under which the inhabitants have been placed, in
quence of the barrenness of the soil and its liability to be overflowed, to exert all
ndustry and enterprise, are circumstances that seem to be in a great degree peculiar
olland. But though there can be no doubt that their influence has been very
lerable, no one will pretend to say that it is to be compared for a moment with the

e Dissertation was translated into English, and published at London in 1751. We have quoted
e translation.

influence of those free institutions which, fortunately, are not the exclusive attributes [of] any particular country, but have flourished in Phœnicia, Greece, England, and Ameri[ca] as well as in Holland.

Many dissertations have been written to account for the decline of the commerce [of] Holland. But, if we mistake not, its leading causes may be classed under two pr[o]minent heads, viz. first, the natural growth of commerce and navigation in oth[er] countries; and second, the weight of taxation at home. During the period when t[he] republic rose to great eminence as a commercial state, England, France, and Spai[n] distracted by civil and religious dissensions, or engrossed wholly by schemes of forei[gn] conquest, were unable to apply their energies to the cultivation of commerce, or [to] withstand the competition of so industrious a people as the Dutch. They, therefo[re] were under the necessity of allowing the greater part of their foreign, and even of the[ir] coasting trade, to be carried on in Dutch bottoms, and under the superintendence [of] Dutch factors. But after the accession of Louis XIV. and the ascendancy of Cro[m]well had put an end to internal commotions in France and England, the energies [of] these two great nations began to be directed to pursuits of which the Dutch had hither[to] enjoyed almost a monopoly. It was not to be supposed, that when tranquillity wa[s] regular system of government had been established in France and England, their acti[ve] and enterprising inhabitants would submit to see one of their most valuable branches [of] industry in the hands of foreigners. The Dutch ceased to be the carriers of Euro[pe] without any fault of their own. Their performance of that function necessarily termi[n]ated as soon as other nations became possessed of a mercantile marine, and were able [to] do for themselves what had previously been done for them by their neighbours.

Whatever, therefore, might have been the condition of Holland in other respects, t[he] natural advance of rival nations must inevitably have stripped her of a large portion [of] the commerce she once possessed. But the progress of decline seems to have been co[n]siderably accelerated, or rather, perhaps, the efforts to arrest it were rendered ineffectu[al] by the extremely heavy taxation to which she was subjected, occasioned by the unavoidal[le] expenses incurred in the revolutionary struggle with Spain, and the subsequent wa[rs] with France and England. The necessities of the state led to the imposition of ta[xes] on corn, on flour when it was ground at the mill, and on bread when it came from t[he] oven; on butter, and fish, and fruit; on income and legacies; the sale of houses; an[d] in short, almost every article either of necessity or convenience. Sir William Tem[ple] mentions that in his time — and taxes were greatly increased afterwards — one fish sau[ce] was in common use, which directly paid no fewer than *thirty* different duties of excis[e,] and it was a common saying at Amsterdam, that every dish of fish brought to table w[as] paid for *once* to the fisherman, and *six* times to the state.

The pernicious influence of this heavy taxation has been ably set forth by the auth[or] of the *Richesse de la Hollande*, and other well-informed writers; and it has also be[en] very forcibly pointed out in the Dissertation already referred to, drawn up from t[he] communications of the Dutch merchants. "Oppressive taxes," it is there stat[ed] "must be placed at the head of all the causes that have co-operated to the prejudice a[nd] "discouragement of trade; and it may be justly said, that it can only be attributed [to] them that the trade of this country has been diverted out of its channel, and transferr[ed] to our neighbours, and must daily be still more and more alienated and shut out fr[om] us, unless the progress thereof be stopt by some quick and effectual remedy: nor is [it] difficult to see from these contemplations on the state of our trade, that the same will [be] effected by no other means than *a diminution of all duties.*

" In former times this was reckoned the only trading state in Europe; and foreign[ers] were content to pay the taxes, as well on the goods they brought hither, as on th[ose] they came here to buy; without examining whether they could evade or save them, [by] fetching the goods from the places where they were produced, and carrying others [to] the places where they were consumed: in short, they paid us our taxes with pleas[ure] without any farther enquiry.

" But, since the last century, the system of trade is altered all over Europe: fore[ign] nations, seeing the wonderful effect of our trade, and to what an eminence we had ri[sen] only by means thereof, they did likewise apply themselves to it; and, to save our du[ties] sent their superfluous products beside our country, to the places where they are m[ost] consumed; and in return for the same, furnished themselves from the first hands w[ith] what they wanted."

But, notwithstanding this authoritative exposition of the pernicious effects result[ing] from the excess of taxation, the necessary expenses of the state were so great as to ren[der] it impossible to make any sufficient reductions. And, with the exception of the tra[nsit] trade carried on through the Rhine and the Meuse, which is in a great meas[ure] independent of foreign competition, and the American trade, most of the other branc[hes] of the foreign trade of Holland, though still very considerable, continue in a c[om]paratively depressed state.

In consequence principally of the oppressiveness of taxation, but partly, too, of the cessive accumulation of capital that had taken place, while the Dutch engrossed the rrying trade of Europe, profits in Holland were reduced towards the middle of the venteenth century, and have ever since continued extremely low. This circumstance ould of itself have sapped the foundations of her commercial greatness. Her capitalists, ho could hardly expect to clear more than two or three per cent. of nett profit by any rt of undertaking carried on at home, were tempted to vest their capital in other untries, and to speculate in loans to foreign governments. There are the best reasons r thinking that the Dutch were, until very lately, the largest creditors of any nation in urope. It is impossible, indeed, to form any accurate estimate of what the sums ving them by foreigners previously to the late French war, or at present, may amount ; but there can be no doubt that at the former period the amount was immense, and at it is still very considerable. M. Demeunier (*Dictionnaire de l'Economie Politique*, n. iii. p. 720.) states the amount of capital lent by the Dutch to foreign governments, clusive of the large sums lent to France during the American war, at *seventy-three* llions sterling. According to the author of the *Richesse de la Hollande* (ii. p. 292.), e sums lent to France and England only, previously to 1778, amounted to 1,500,000 res tournois, or sixty millions sterling. And besides these, vast sums were lent to ivate individuals in foreign countries, both regularly as loans at interest, and in the ape of goods advanced at long credits. So great was the difficulty of finding an vantageous investment for money in Holland, that Sir William Temple mentions, at the payment of any part of the national debt was looked upon by the creditors as evil of the first magnitude. "They receive it," says he, "with tears, not knowing w to dispose of it to interest with such safety and ease."

Among the subordinate causes which contributed to the decline of Dutch commerce, which have, at all events, prevented its growth, we may reckon the circumstance of e commerce with India having been subjected to the trammels of monopoly. De Witt presses his firm conviction, that the abolition of the East India Company would have led very greatly to the trade with the East; and no doubt can now remain in the nd of any one, that such would have been the case.* The interference of the ministration in regulating the mode in which some of the most important branches of lustry should be carried on, seems also to have been exceedingly injurious. Every ceeding with respect to the herring fishery, for example, was regulated by the orders government, carried into effect under the inspection of officers appointed for that rpose. Some of these regulations were exceedingly vexatious. The period when fishery might begin was fixed at five minutes past twelve o'clock of the night of the th of June! and the master and pilot of every vessel leaving Holland for the fishery, re obliged to make oath that they would respect the regulation. The species of salt be made use of in curing different sorts of herrings was also fixed by law; and there re endless regulations with respect to the size of the barrels, the number and thick-s of the staves of which they were to be made; the gutting and packing of the rings; the branding of the barrels, &c. &c. (*Histoire des Peches*, &c. *dans les rs du Nord*, tom. i. cap. 24.) These regulations were intended to secure to the llanders that superiority which they had early attained in the fishery, and to prevent reputation of their herrings from being injured by the bad faith of individuals. But ir real effect was precisely the reverse of this. By tying up the fishers to a system of tine, they prevented them from making any improvements; while the facility of interfeiting the public marks opened a much wider door to fraud, than would have n opened had government wisely declined interfering in the matter.

n despite, however, of the East India monopoly, and the regulations now described, commercial policy of Holland has been more liberal than that of any other nation. d in consequence, a country not more extensive than Wales, and naturally not more ile, conquered, indeed, in a great measure from the sea, has accumulated a population upwards of two millions; has maintained wars of unexampled duration with the most erful monarchies; and, besides laying out immense sums in works of utility and ament at home, has been enabled to lend hundreds of millions to foreigners.

During the occupation of Holland by the French, first as a dependent state, and sequently as an integral part of the French empire, her foreign trade was almost rely destroyed. Her colonies were successively conquered by England; and, in ition to the loss of her trade, she was burdened with fresh taxes. But such was the accumulated wealth of the Dutch, their prudence, and energy, that the influence of e adverse circumstances was far less injurious than could have been imagined; and, withstanding all the losses she had sustained, and the long interruption of her commer-pursuits, Holland continued, at her emancipation from the yoke of the French in 1814,

---

* For proofs of this, see the article on the Commerce of Holland in the Edinburgh Review, No. 102., which most part of these statements have been taken.

to be the richest country in Europe! Java, the Moluccas, and most of her other colonies were then restored, and she is now in the enjoyment of a large foreign trade.   Her connection with Belgium was an unfortunate one for both countries.   The union was not agreeable to either party, and has been injurious to Holland.   Belgium was an agricultural and manufacturing country; and was inclined, in imitation of the French, to lay restrictions on the importation of most sorts of raw and manufactured produce.   A policy of this sort was directly opposed to the interests and the ancient practice of the Dutch.   But though their deputies prevented the restrictive system from being carried to the extent proposed by the Belgians, they were unable to prevent it from being carried to an extent that materially affected the trade of Holland.   Whatever, therefore, may be the consequences as to Belgium, there can be little doubt that the late separation between the two divisions of the kingdom of the Netherlands will redound to the advantage of Holland.   It must ever be for the interest of England, America, and all trading nations, to maintain the independence of a state by whose means their productions find a ready access to the great continental markets.   It is to be hoped that the Dutch, profiting by past experience, will adopt such a liberal and conciliatory system towards the natives of Java, as will enable them to avail themselves to the full of the various resources of that noble island: And if they do this, and freely open their ports, with as few restrictions as possible, to the ships and commodities of all countries, Holland may still be the centre of a very extensive commerce, and may continue to preserve a respectable place among mercantile nations.   Even   this moment, after all the vicissitudes they have undergone, the Dutch are, beyond all question, the most opulent and industrious of European nations.   And their present, no less than their former state, shows that a free system of government, security, and the absence of restrictions on industry, can overcome almost every obstacle; " can convert the standing pool and lake into fat meadows, cover the barren rock with verdure, and make the desert smile with flowers."

ANCHOR, a well-known maritime instrument used in the fastening or mooring of ships.   The iron of which anchors are made ought to be of the best quality, and the very toughest that can be procured.   Their price varies according to their size.

By the 1 & 2 Geo. 4. c. 75. pilots and other persons taking possession of anchors, cables, and other ship materials, parted with, cut from, or left by any vessel, whether in distress or otherwise, shall give notice of the same to a deputy vice-admiral, or his agent, within forty-eight hours, on pain of being considered as receivers of stolen goods; and if any person shall knowingly and wilfully purchase any such anchor, &c. that shall have been so obtained, without its being so reported, he shall be held to be a receiver of stolen goods, and suffer the like punishment as for a misdemeanor at common law, or be liable to be transported for seven years, at the discretion of the court.   Any master of a ship or vessel outward bound finding or taking on board any anchor, &c. shall make a true entry of the circumstance in the log book of such ship or vessel, reporting the same by the first possible opportunity to the Trinity House, and on his return shall deliver the article to the deputy vice-admiral, or his agent, nearest to the port where he shall arrive, under a penalty of not more than 100l. nor less than 30l., on conviction before a magistrate on the oath of one witness; one half to go to the informer, the other half to the Merchant Seamen's Society established by 20 Geo. 3. c. 38.: he shall also forfeit double the value of the article to the owner.   An every pilot, hoveller, boatman, &c. who shall convey any anchor, &c. to any foreign harbour, port, creek, or bay, and sell and dispose of the same, shall be guilty of felony, and be transported for any term not exceeding seven years. — (See SALVAGE.)

ANCHORAGE, or anchoring-ground, a place where a ship may cast anchor.   The best anchoring-ground is stiff clay or hard sand; and the best place for riding at anchor, is where a ship is land-locked, and out of the tide.

The anchorage of ships, especially ships of war, being a subject of great importance to the naval and commercial interests of the kingdom, several statutes have been enacted with respect to it.   The first which it is necessary to notice here is 19 Geo. 2. c. 22.   It prohibits masters of ships from casting out ballast, or rubbish of any kind, into any harbour or channel, except on the land where the tide never comes, on pain of forfeiting not more than 50s., nor less than 50s., on conviction before a justice on view, or on the oath of one witness, or of being committed to prison for two months; which penalty is increased to 10l. over and above the expense of removing the same, by 54 Geo. 3. c. 159.   In pursuance of the same object 54 Geo. 3. c. 159. enables the Lords of the Admiralty to establish regulations for the preservation of the king's moorings or anchorage, as well as for those of merchant ships, in all the ports, harbours, channels, &c. &c. of the United Kingdom, as far as the tide flows, where or near to which his majesty has, or may hereafter have, any docks, dock-yards, arsenals, wharfs, or moorings.   It prohibits all descriptions of private ships from being moored, or anchored, or placed in any of his majesty's moorings, &c. without special licence obtained from the Admiralty, or other persons appointed to grant such licences, on pain of forfeiting not exceeding 10l., one moiety to his majesty, the other to the informer, on conviction before any justice of the peace or commissioner of the navy.

It further prohibits the breaming of private vessels in such places, otherwise than appointed by the same authority of the Admiralty; and the receiving or having gunpowder, beyond a certain limited quantity, under a penalty of 5l. for every five pounds' weight of such powder beyond the quantity allowed.   It prohibits, likewise, all such private vessels, in any such places, having any guns on board shotted or loaded with ball, as well as firing and discharging any such before sun-rising and after sun-setting, under penalty of 5l. for every gun so shotted, and 10l. for every gun so fired.   It further gives to every officer of vessels of war, to harbour-masters, and others in their aid, a right of search in all private vessels so moored in such places, and inflicts a penalty of 10l. on resistance.

Anchorage also means a duty laid on ships for the use of the port or harbour.

ANCHOVIES (Fr. *Anchois*; It. *Acciughe*; Lat. *Encrasicoli*), small fish common in the Mediterranean, resembling the sprat.   Those brought from Go

a in the Tuscan Sea are esteemed the best. They should be chosen small,
h pickled, white outside and red within. Their backs should be round. The
line, a fish which is flatter and larger than anchovies, is frequently substituted
them.

NGEL, the name of an ancient gold coin in England, derived from the figure
n angel represented on it. It was originally 23¾ carats fine, and weighed four
nyweights. Its value differed in different reigns.

NISE, or ANISUM (Fr. *Anis ;* It. *Anice ;* Lat. *Anisum*), a small seed of an
ng shape. It is cultivated in Germany, but the best comes from Spain. It
so a produce of China, and is exported from that country. It should be
sen fresh, large, plump, newly dried, of a good smell, and a biting aromatic
e, without any bitterness. There is extracted from anise-seed a kind of white
called essence of *anise.*

NKER, a liquid measure at Amsterdam. It contains about 10¼ gallons
lish wine measure.

NNOTTO, or ANNATTO (Fr. *Rocou ;* Ger. *Orlean ;* It. *Oriana*), a red dye
ared in the West Indies from the seed capsules of the *Bixa Orellana*, a tree
South America. The seeds are contained in a pod similar to a chestnut,
osed in a pulp of a disagreeable smell and a bright colour. It is used in the
ies of England and Holland to colour cheese and butter. It is also exten-
ly used in dyeing and painting. The Spanish Indians used it medicinally.

NNUITIES. See INTEREST AND ANNUITIES.

NTIMONY (Ger. and Du. *Spiesglas ;* Fr. *Antimoine ;* It. *Antimonio ;* Rus.
monia ; Lat. *Antimonium*). Antimony, when pure, is of a greyish-white co-
, and has a good deal of brilliancy, showing a radiated fracture when broken ;
converted by exposure to heat and air into a white oxide, which sublimes
pours. It is found in Saxony, and the Hartz, also in Cornwall, Spain, France,
ico, Siberia, and the Eastern Islands. We are at present wholly supplied
this metal from Singapore, which receives it from Borneo. It is about as
as gold ; its specific gravity is about 6·7 ; it is easily reduced to a very fine
der ; its tenacity is such that a rod of $\frac{1}{10}$th of an inch diameter is capable of
orting 10 lbs. weight. Antimony is used in medicine, and in the composition
etal for types for printing. The ores of antimony are soft ; and vary in colour
light lead to dark lead grey ; their specific gravity varies from 4·4 to 6 8 ;
possess a metallic lustre, are brittle, and occur in the crystallised massive
s. — (*Thomson's Chemistry. Joyce's Mineralogy.*)

NTWERP, in the Netherlands, long. 4° 22′ E., lat. 51° 14′ N. A large, well-
, and strongly-fortified city, situated on the Scheldt. It has about 63,000
itants. Previously to its capture by the Spaniards, under Farnese, in 1585,
verp was one of the greatest commercial cities of Europe ; but it suffered
ly by that event. In 1648, at the treaty of Westphalia, it was stipulated by
n and Holland, that the navigation of the Scheldt should be shut up ; a sti-
ion which was observed till the occupation of Belgium by the French, when it
abolished. In 1803, the improvement of the harbour was begun, and extensive
docks and warehouses have since been constructed. Ships of the largest
en come up to the town, and goods destined for the interior are forwarded
the greatest facility by means of canals. Almost all the foreign trade of
ium is at present centred at Antwerp, which has again become a place of
commercial importance. By a decree issued in 1814, all goods are allowed to
arehoused in Antwerp *en entrepôt*, and may be exported on paying a charge
per cent. *ad valorem.* The exports from Antwerp chiefly consist of corn,
, linen, lace, carpets, flax, tallow, hops, &c. The imports principally consist
tton, wine, hardware, sugar, tobacco, coffee, and all sorts of colonial produce.

ney. —Accounts are now commonly kept in *florins* of 1816, worth 1s. 8¾d. sterling.
orin is divided into 20 sous, and the sou into 5 cents. Formerly accounts were kept
pound Flemish = 2¼ rix dollars = 6 florins = 20 schillings = 120 stivers = 240
= 1920 pennings. (See TABLE of COINS.) The par of exchange between Ant-
and London, is 11 florins 58 cents per pound sterling.

ights and measures. — By a law of 1816, the French system of weights and mea-
was adopted in the Netherlands on the 1st of January, 1820 ; but the old deno-
ions are retained. The *pond* is the unit of weight, and answers to the French
amme, &c. See AMSTERDAM.

D 4

Of the old weights, which are still occasionally referred to, the *quintal* of 100 lb
is equal to 103₃ lbs. avoirdupois, 100 lbs. avoirdupois being consequently equal to 96·81
of Antwerp.   A schippound is equal to 3 quintals, or 300 lbs. ; a stone is equal to 8 lb

Of the old measures, a viertel of corn = 4 macken ; 37½ viertels = 1 last ; and
viertels = 10½ Imperial quarters very nearly.   The aam of wine contains 50 stoop
or 36½ English wine gallons.

Of the weights and measures now current, 50¾ lbs. = 112 lbs. English ; 100 lbs.
100 kilogrammes of France, or 212¾ Antwerp old weight.   One barrel = 26½ gallo
English = 100 litres French.

Custom House Regulations. — Captains of ships arriving at Antwerp, or any of t
Netherlands ports, must make, within twenty-four hours, a declaration in writing, of t
goods of which their cargo consists ; specifying the marks and numbers of the bal
parcels, &c. ; their value, according to the current price at the time when the declarati
is made ; the name of the ship or vessel, as well as that of the captain, and of the cou
try to which she belongs, &c.

Shipping. — The ships entering the port of Antwerp, during the five years endi
with 1828, have been as follows : —

Years.	Ships.	Years.	Ships.
1824	681	1827	822
1825	800	1828	955
1826	928		

Of the 800 ships entering Antwerp in 1825, 114 were from Liverpool, 119 fro
London, 44 from Hull, 48 from Havre, 41 from Bordeaux, 24 from Petersburgh,
from New York, 25 from Cuba, 26 from Rio Janeiro, 11 from Batavia, &c. (*Bulle
des Sciences Géographiques*, for January, 1829, and February, 1826.

The following is an account of some of the principal articles imported into Antwe
since 1821 : (*See opposite side.*)

APPLES, a well-known and extensively cultivated fruit.   An immense varie
of apples are raised in Great Britain.   Those imported from New York are t
best ; and considerable quantities are imported from France.   The nett duty
apples imported into Great Britain, in 1828, amounted to 8,918*l*. 12*s*. 6*d*.

APPRENTICE, a young person of either sex, bound by indenture to ser
some particular individual, or company of individuals, for a specified time, in ord
to be instructed in some art, science, or trade.

According to the common law of England, every one has a right to empl
himself at pleasure in every lawful trade.   But this sound principle was alm
entirely subverted by a statute passed in the fifth year of the reign of Queen E
zabeth, commonly called the statute of apprenticeship.   It enacted that no pers
should, for the future, exercise any trade, craft, or mystery, at that time exercis
in England and Wales, unless he had previously served to it an apprenticeship
seven years at least ; so that what had before been a bye-law of a few corporatio
became the general and statute law of the kingdom.   Luckily, however, the cou
of law were always singularly disinclined to give effect to the provisions of t
statute ; and the rules which they established for its interpretation served m
terially to mitigate its injurious operation.   But though its impolicy had been lo
apparent, it was continued till 1814, when it was repealed by the 54 Geo
c. 96.   This act did not interfere with any of the existing rights, privileg
or bye-laws of the different corporations ; but wherever these do not interpo
the formation of apprenticeships, and their duration, is left to be adjusted by
parties themselves.

The regulations with respect to the taking of apprentices on board ship,
only part of this subject that properly comes within the scope of this work,
embodied in the 4 Geo. 4. c. 25.   They are as follow : —

From the 1st January, 1824, every master of a merchant ship exceeding the burthen of 80 tons
have on board his ship, at the time of such ship clearing out from any port of the United Kingdom,
apprentice or apprentices, in the following proportion to the number of tons of her admeasurem
according to the certificate of registry ; viz.

For every vessel exceeding 80 tons, and under 200 tons, 1 apprentice at least,

	200		400	—	2	
	400		500	—	3	
	500		700	—	4	
	700 and upwards	-	-		5	

who shall, at the period of being indentured, respectively be under the age of 17 years ; provided
every apprentice so to be employed on board any vessel, as above described, shall be duly indented f
least four years ; and the indentures of every such apprentice shall be enrolled with the collector
comptroller at the custom-house of the port whence such vessel shall first clear out after the executi
such indentures. — § 2.

Comparative Statement of Imports at Antwerp since 1821.

	Coffee.			Sugar.						Cotton.	Hides.		Pepper.	Pimento.	Ashes.		Rice.		Oil, Whale.	Indigo.		Rum.	Tobacco.		Dyewoods, Tons.	
	Casks.	Barrels.	Bags.	Casks.	Brazil. Chests.	Cuba. Boxes.	Barrels.	Canisters.	Bags.	Bales.	Ox and Cow.	Buff and other.	Bags.	Bags.	United States.	Baltic.	Tierces.	Bags.	Barrels.	Chests.	Serons.	Punch.	Hhds.	Pks. Bls.	Camp.	Fustic.
1821	2552	- -	88837	421	- -	10630	1347	6842	11439	13228	214310	- -	1277	732	4542	952	6369	17315	- -	435	20	231	664			
1822	372	- -	68929	784	- -	20812	385	2369	21774	9431	100131	- -	3012	1114	4982	1723	5988	- -	42	590	119	355	267			
1823	1505	- -	134250	1258	- -	33716	264	3115	22633	14284	188996	58747	4662	407	5335	2074	6658	3008	20	708	362	153	833			
1824	370	- -	81331	478	- -	24067	97	2913	29535	3247	80822	17891	1900	644	3421	233	5900	2240	343	645	181	46	341			
1825	1260	- -	145570	78	1056	19090	337	320	12121	5300	135863	1834	580	590	6752	2130	8388	384	704	647	233	15	43			
1826	1716	1432	211495	578	1188	26156	42	774	16879	15764	215155	1582	12664	398	3790	1072	9166	1044	333	522	351	- -	109			
1827	1526	804	187703	1732	1797	31367	540	1706	89551	20450	137838	11244	11121	682	5329	1301	12240	4267	- -	925	407	190	622	- -	595	375
1828	2319	925	235463	1148	3033	29976	1785	2699	48464	9110	65063	11215	1353	821	4634	771	13553	7518	- -	857	220	33	883	348	1491	533
1829 (to July 31st)	517	1598	248917	1921	5770	42624	257	3488	65416	22665	279326	9067	11420	551	6734	327	16452	57220	1237	1102	398	40	1323	508	656	963

Conditions under which goods are sold. — On goods generally 2 per cent. is allowed for payment in 20 days, and 1½ per cent. on credit of 6 weeks or 2 months. On Cottons, at 20 days' credit, 2 per cent. are allowed, and 1½ per cent. on a credit of 2 or 3 months. On Ashes, Hides, and Sugar, 3 per cent. for 20 days, and 1½ per cent. for three months' credit.

Tares. — West India, Brazil, and Java Coffee, in single bags, 2 per cent., and Havanna in joncs, ½ lb. per bag extra. Bourbon, in whole bags, 4½ lbs., and in ½ do. 2½ lbs. Pimento Pepper and Ginger, in bags, 2 per cent.; on these articles, as also Coffee, in casks and barrels, real tare. Cassia Lignea, and Cinnamon, in bales, 10 per cent.; and in chests, 6 to 6½ lbs. per chest. Ashes, 12 per cent. Quercitron Bark, 10 per cent. Cotton, in bales, 4 per cent., exclusive of ropes; and in serons, 6 lbs. per seron. Horse Hair, real tare. Indigo, in chests or barrels, real tare; and in serons, 6½ to 7 lbs. per seron. Rice, in casks, 12 per cent.; and in bags, 2 per cent. Muscovado sugars, in casks and barrels, and Havanna clayed, in boxes, 14 per cent.; Brazil, in chests, 16 per cent.; Java, in canisters and baskets, 9 per cent.: Siam and Manilla, in bags, 3 per cent.: Bengal, in triple bags, 5 lbs. each: Bourbon, in mats, 6 per cent. Bohea Tea, exclusive of wrappers, 46 lbs. per chest, 24 lbs. per ½ ditto, and 13 lbs. per ¼ ditto, 14½ lbs. per ½ ditto; fine black and green Tea, 12 to 13 lbs. per ¼ chest, 9 lbs. per ⅙ ditto, 7 lbs. per ⅛ ditto, 5 lbs. per $\frac{1}{12}$ ditto, 3 lbs. per $\frac{1}{16}$ ditto, and 2 per cent. in boxes. Tobacco, real tare: no draft or other deduction allowed. (*From the Circular of Dalmahoy and Co. of Antwerp, 31st July, 1829.*)

Every apprentice so enrolled is hereby exempted from serving in his Majesty's navy until he shall have attained the age of 21 years; provided he is regularly serving his time either with the first master or ship-owner, or some other master or ship-owner to whom his indentures shall have been regularly transferred ; and every owner or master neglecting to enrol such indentures, or who shall suffer any such apprentice to leave his service, except in case of death or desertion, sickness, or other unavoidable cause, to be certified in the log-book, after the vessel shall have cleared outwards on the voyage upon which such vessel may be bound, shall for every such offence forfeit 10*l.*, to be paid in manner following; that is to say, one moiety by the owners of such vessel, and the other moiety by the master thereof, to be levied, recovered, and applied, in manner hereinafter mentioned. — § 4.

Every person to whom such apprentice shall have been bound may employ him, at any time, in any vessel of which such person may be the master or owner ; and may also, with the consent of such apprentice, if above 17, and if under that age, with the consent of his parents or guardians, transfer the indentures of such apprentice, by endorsement thereon, to any other person who may be the master or owner of any registered vessel. — § 5.

No stamp duty shall be charged on any such transfer by endorsement. — § 6.

And by 6 Geo. 4. cap. 107. § 138. it is enacted, that no person shall be deemed to be an apprentice for the purposes of the preceding act (4 Geo. 4. cap. 25.), unless the indenture of such apprentice shall have been enrolled with the collector and comptroller of the port from which any such apprentice shall first go to sea after the date of such indenture ; or in default of such enrolment, until the same shall have been enrolled at some port from which the ship in which such apprentice shall afterwards go to sea shall be cleared.

By stat. 7 & 8 Geo. 4. cap 56. § 7. it is enacted that no higher duty than 2*s.* shall be charged upon the indenture of any apprentice bound to serve at sea in the merchant service.

AQUA FORTIS (Ger. *Scheidewasser ;* Du. *Sterkwater*; Fr. *Eau-forte ;* It. *Acqua-forte ;* Sp. *Agua-fuerte ;* Rus. *Wodka Krepkaja ;* Lat. *Aqua fortis*). See ACID, *Nitric.*

AQUA VITÆ, (Ger. *Aquavit ;* Fr. *Eau-de-vie;* It. *Acqua vite ;* Sp. *Agua de vida ;* Rus. *Wodka ;* Lat. *Aqua vitæ,*) answers to the *eau de vie,* or brandy, of the French, the *whisky* of the Scotch and Irish, the *geneva* of the Dutch ; and is a name familiarly applied to all native distilled spirits. In this way it is used in the excise laws relating to the regulation of the distilleries.

ARANGOES, a species of beads made of rough cornelian.

ARCHANGEL, the principal commercial city of the north of Russia, in lat. 64° 34′ N., long. 38° 59′ E. Its situation at the mouth of the Dwina renders Archangel the *entrepôt* of a large extent of country. Previously to the foundation of Petersburgh, it was the only Russian port accessible to Europeans, and it still enjoys a pretty extensive commerce. The principal articles of export are hemp, grain, pitch and tar, deals, tallow, linseed, iron, bristles, &c. Deals from Archangel, and Onega in the vicinity of Archangel, are considered superior to those from the Baltic. Hemp is not so good as at Riga, but it is proportionally cheaper. Tallow is also of an inferior quality. Iron is the same as at Petersburgh, sometimes cheaper and sometimes dearer. The quality of the wheat exported from Archangel is about equal to that from Petersburgh. The imports are not very extensive. They consist principally of sugar, spices, salt, woollens, hardware, &c. The merchants of Archangel are said by Mr. Coxe to be distinguished for honesty and intelligence. — (*Travels in the North of Europe,* iii p. 150.)

Monies, weights, and measures, are the same as at Petersburgh ; which see.

ARGOL, or ARGAL (Ger. *Weinstein ;* Du. *Wynsteen ;* Fr. *Tartre ;* It. Sp and Port. *Tartaro ;* Rus. *Winnui kamen ;* Pol. *Waystin ;* Lat. *Tartarus*), or Tartar is a hard crust formed on the sides of vessels in which wine has been kept ; it is red or white according to the colour of the wine, and is otherwise impure. On being purified, it is termed *cream* or *crystals of tartar.* It consists of a peculiar acid combined with potash. White argol is preferable to red, as containing less drossy or earthy matter. The marks of good argol of either kind are, its being thick, brittle, hard, brilliant, and little earthy. That brought from Germany is the best, on account of its being taken out of those great tuns wherein the salt has time to come to its proper consistence. Argol is of considerable use among dyers, as serving to dispose the stuffs to take their colours the better.

Argol, when pure, or cream of tartar, is extensively used in medicine. The net duty on argol imported into Great Britain, in 1828, amounted to 1,410*l.* 15*s.* 7*d*

ARISTOLOCHIA (Fr. *Serpentaire ;* Ger. *Schlangenwurzel ;* It. *Serpentaria* Lat. *Aristolochia serpentaria*), the dried root of Virginia snake-root, or birthwort it is small, light, and bushy, consisting of a number of fibres matted together sprung from one common head, of a brownish colour on the outside, and pale o yellow within. It has an aromatic smell something like that of valerian, but mor agreeable ; and a warm, bitterish, pungent taste, very much resembling camphor — (*Ency. Metrop.*)

RMS. See FIRE-ARMS.

RQUIFOUX (Ger. *Bleyglanz*; Fr. *Arquifou*; It. *Archifoglio*; Lat. *Galena*),
ed also Alquifou or Arquifou, a sort of lead ore, very heavy, easily reduced
owder, and hard to melt; when it is broken, it parts into shining scales of
nitish colour. The potters use it to give their works a green varnish; and
England it is commonly called *potters' ore*. The *arquifoux* is exported
n England in large lumps; it should be chosen heavy, the scales bright and
mbling tin-glass.

RRACK, or RACK (Fr. *Arac*; Ger. *Arrach, Rack*; Du. *Arak, Rak*; It.
cco; Sp, *Arak*; Port. *Araca*; Rus. *Arak*), a spirituous liquor manufactured
ifferent places in the East Indies.

he term arrack is applied in most part of India to designate every sort of
ituous liquor; a circumstance which accounts for the discrepancy in the state-
ts as to the materials used in making it, and the mode of its manufacture.
ack of Goa and Batavia is most esteemed; that of Columbo is very inferior.
re is said to be as great differences in the flavours of the several species of
ck, as in those of rum, brandy, and whisky.
oa arrack is invariably made from a vegetable juice called toddy, which flows
ncision from the cocoa-nut tree; after the juice is fermented, it is distilled
rectified. It usually has but a sixth or an eighth of pure spirit. Batavia
ck is obtained by distillation from molasses and rice; it is stronger than that
ioa. The legger of arrack contains 160 gallons. Very little is imported as
rticle of trade. — (*Milburn's Orient. Commerce.*)

RROW-ROOT, the pith or starch of the root *Maranta arundinacea*. It
received its common name from its being supposed to be an antidote to the
oned arrows of the Indians. The powder is prepared from roots of a year
It is reckoned a very nutritious food; but is often adulterated, when in the
s, with the starch or flour of potatoes. It is a native of South America, and
ltivated in the West Indies. The nett duty on arrow-root imported into
t Britain, in 1828, was 1,717*l*. 12*s*. 4*d*.

RSENIC (Ger. *Arsenik*; Fr. *Arsenic*; It. and Sp. *Arsenico*; Rus. *Müsch-*
Lat. *Arsenicum*). This metal has a bluish white colour not unlike that of
, and a good deal of brilliancy. It has no sensible smell while cold, but
heated it emits a strong odour of garlic, which is very characteristic. It is
oftest of all the metallic bodies, and is so brittle that it may easily be reduced
very fine powder by trituration in a mortar. Its specific gravity is 5·76. —
mson's Chemistry.)

etallic arsenic is not used in the arts, and is not, therefore, extracted from the
except for the purposes of experiment or curiosity. The arsenic of com-
e is the white oxide, or *arsenious acid* of chemists. It is a white, brittle,
act substance, of a glassy appearance; is inodorous; has an acrid taste, leav-
n the tongue a sweetish impression; and is highly corrosive. In its metallic
arsenic exerts no action on the animal system; but when oxidised, it is a
virulent poison. The arsenic of the shops is sometimes adulterated with
sand, chalk, or gypsum: the fraud may be detected by heating a small
on of the suspected powder; when the arsenic is dissipated, leaving the im-
ies, if there be any, behind. Though the most violent of all the mineral
ns, the white oxide of arsenic, or the arsenic of the shops, is yet, when judi-
ly administered, a medicine of great efficacy. It is also used for various pur-
in the arts. It is principally imported from Saxony and Bohemia. — (*Dr.*
son's Chemistry, Dr. A. T. Thomson's Dispensatory.)

AFŒTIDA (Ger. *Teufelsdreck*; Du. *Duivelsdreck*; Fr. *Assa-fetida*; Sp. *Asa-*
; Lat. *Asa-fœtida*; Per. *Ungoozeh*), " is obtained from a large umbelliferous
growing in Persia. The root resembles a large parsnep, externally of a black
ir: on cutting it transversely, the asafœtida exudes in form of a white thick
like cream; which, from exposure to the air, becomes yellower and yel-
, and at last of a dark brown colour. It is very apt to run to putrefaction;
ence those who collect it carefully defend it from the sun. The fresh juice
n excessively strong smell, which grows weaker and weaker upon keeping;
le dram of the fresh fluid juice smells more than a hundred pounds of the
safœtida brought to us. The Persians are commonly obliged to hire ships

on purpose for its carriage, as scarcely any one will receive it along with oth
commodities, its stench infecting every thing that comes near it.

" The common asafœtida of the shops is of a brownish colour, unctuous a
tough, of an acrid or biting taste, and a strong disagreeable smell, resembling th
of garlic." — (*Dr. Ure.*)

ASARUM (Fr. *Asaret;* Ger. *Hazelwurzel;* Sp. *Asaro de Europa*), the ro
or dried leaves of the asarabacca. The leaves are nearly inodorous; their tas
slightly aromatic, bitter, acrid, and nauseous. The powder of the leaves is th
basis of most cephalic snuffs. A good deal of their acrimony is lost in keepin
they should, consequently, be used in as recent a state as possible, and dried wit
out the application of much heat. Asarabacca grows in several parts of Englan
particularly Lancashire and Westmoreland.

ASHES (Fr. *Vedasse;* Ger. *Waidasche;* Du. *Weedas;* Da. *Veedaske;*
Feccia bruciata; Sp. *Alumbre de hez;* Rus. *Weidasch;* Lat. *Cineres infectori*
the residuum, or earthy part of any substance after it has been burnt. In cor
merce, the term is applied to the ashes of vegetable substances; from whi
are extracted the alkaline salts called potash, pearlash, barilla, kelp, &c
which see.

ASPHALTUM, BITUMEN JUDAICUM, or JEW's PITCH (DA. *Jödeberg;* D
Jodenlym; Fr. *Asphalte, Bitume de Judée;* Ger. *Judenpech;* It. *Asfalto, Bitur*
Giudaico; Lat. *Asphaltum;* Sp. *Asfalto*), a smooth, hard, brittle, black or brov
substance, which breaks with a polish, melts easily when heated, and when pu
burns without leaving any ashes. It is found in a soft or liquid state on th
surface of the Dead Sea, but by age grows dry and hard. The same kind
bitumen is likewise found in the earth in other parts of the world; in Chin
America, particularly in the island of Trinidad; and some parts of Europe,
the Carpathian hills, France, Neufchâtel, &c. The asphaltum of the shops is
very different compound from native bitumen; and varies in its properties a
cording to the substances made use of in forming it. It is used as a cement, a
by watch and clock-makers. — (*Ure,* &c.)

ASS (Fr. *Ane;* Ger. *Esel;* It. *Asino;* Lat. *Asinus*), the well-known quadrup
of that name.

ASSETS, goods or property in the hands of a person, with which he is e
abled to discharge an obligation imposed upon him as executor, &c. Lands,
general, are *real* assets; personal estate, or goods which come to the execut
are *personal* assets.

ASSIENTO, a Spanish word signifying a contract. In commerce, it mea
the contract or agreement by which the Spanish government ceded first tc
company of French, and afterwards (by the treaty of Utrecht) to a compa
of English merchants, the right to import slaves into the Spanish colonies.
(*Brougham's Colonial Policy,* vol. i. p. 439.)

ASSIGNEE, a person appointed by another to do, act, or transact so
business, or exercise some particular privilege or power.

Assignees may be created by deed, or by law : by deed, where the lessee o
farm assigns the same to another; by law, where the law makes an assign
without any appointment of the person entitled, as an executor is assignee in l
to the testator, and an administrator to an intestate. The term is most commo
applied to the creditors of a bankrupt appointed to manage for the rest, a
who consequently have the bankrupt's estate assigned over to them. £
BANKRUPT.

ASSIZE. See BREAD.

ASSURANCE. See INSURANCE.

AUCTION, a public sale of goods to the highest bidder. Auctions are
nerally notified by advertisement, and are held in some open place. The biddi
may be made either by parties present, or by the auctioneer under authority gi
to him; the sale is usually terminated by the fall of a hammer.

AUCTIONEER, a person who conducts sales by auction. It is his dut
state the conditions of sale, to declare the respective biddings, and to termir
the sale by *knocking down* the thing sold to the highest bidder. An auctionee
held to be lawfully authorised by the purchaser to sign a contract for him, whe
it be for lands or goods. And his writing down the name of the highest bidde

s book, is sufficient to bind any other person for whom the highest bidder pur-
~ased, even though such person be present, provided he do not object *before*
~try.

Every auctioneer must take out a licence, renewable annually on the 5th of July, for which he is
~arged 5*l.*; and if he sell goods for the sale of which an excise licence is specially required, he must also
~ce out such licence, unless the goods be the property of a licensed person, and sold for his behalf and
his *entered* premises, in which case such additional licence is not required. (6 Geo. 4. c. 81.)
Auctioneers within the limits of the chief excise office in London are bound, when they receive their
~ence, to give security to the excise by bond, themselves in 1000*l.* and two sureties in 200*l.* each, to
~liver in within twenty-eight days of any sale a true and particular account of such sale, and to pay the
~ties on the same. Auctioneers refusing or delaying to pay the duties within the specified time forfeit
~ir bond and the bonds of their sureties, and double the amount of the duties. (19 Geo. 3. c. 56.)
Auctioneers carrying on their trade without the limits of the head office give bond, themselves in 500*l.*
~d two sureties in 50*l.* each, to render an account of the duties accruing on sales, and to pay them within
~ weeks, under the penalties already mentioned. (19 Geo. 3. c. 56. and 38 Geo. 3. c. 54.)
A licensed auctioneer going from town to town by a public stage coach, and sending goods by a public
~nveyance, and selling them on commission by retail or auction, is a *trading person* within the 50 Geo. 3.
~. 1. § 6., and must take out a hawker's and pedlar's licence.
~he following duties are payable on goods sold by auction : —
For every 20*s.* of the purchase money arising or payable by virtue of any sale at auction for the benefit
~f the growers or first purchasers respectively of any sheep's wool, the growth or produce of any part of
~e United Kingdom, 2*d.*
For every 20*s.* of the purchase money arising or payable by virtue of any sale at auction of any interest
~f possession or reversion in any freehold, customary, copyhold, or leasehold lands, tenements, houses, or
~reditaments, and any share or shares in the capital or joint stock of any corporation or chartered com-
~ny, and of any annuities or sums of money charged thereon, and of any ships and vessels, and of any
~ersionary interest in the public funds, and of any plate or jewels, and so in proportion for any greater
~less sum, 7*d.*
For every 20*s.* of the purchase money arising or payable by virtue of any sale at auction of furniture,
~tures, pictures, books, horses, and carriages, and all other goods and chattels whatsoever, and so in pro-
~tion for any greater or less sum, 1*s.*
~he duties to be paid by the auctioneer, agent, factor, or seller by commission.
~y stat. 29 Geo. 3. c. 63. §§ 1, 2. no duty shall be paid for piece goods sold by auction, wove or fabricated in
~s kingdom, which shall be sold entire in the piece or quantity as taken from the loom, and in lots of
~ price of 20*l.* or upwards, and so as the same be sold in no other than entered places, and openly shown
~ exposed at such sale.
~ect. 3. And the auctioneer shall, besides the bond given on receiving his licence, give a further bond
~5000*l.* with two sureties, that he will, within fourteen days after every such sale, deliver an account
~reof at the next excise office, and will not sell by auction any goods woven out of this kingdom, or
~ven in this kingdom, which shall not be sold in the entire piece, without payment of the proper duty.
~y stat. 41 Geo. 3. c. 91. § 8. all corn and grain of every sort, flour, and meal, and all beef, pork, hams,
~on, cheese, and butter imported into Great Britain, shall be free of the duty on the first sale thereof by
~ction on account of the importer, so as the same be entered at some custom house at the port of import-
~n, and the sale thereof be within twelve months and by a licensed auctioneer.
~y stat. 30 Geo. 3. c. 26. all goods imported by way of merchandise from *Yucatan*, and by 32 Geo. 3. c. 41.
~ whale-oil (and by 41 Geo. 3. c. 42. all elephant-oil, produced from sea-cows or sea-elephants, and commonly
~ed "elephant's oil,") whalebone, ambergris, and head-matter, and all skins of seals and other animals
~ng in the sea, and also elephants' teeth, palm-oil, dyeing-wood, drugs, and other articles for dyers' use,
~ all mahogany and other manufactured wood for the use of cabinet-makers and other manufacturers,'
~orted in *British* ships from *Africa* and (by 42 Geo. 3. c. 93. § 3.) *America*, or any *British* settlement
~oad, shall be free of the excise duty on the first sale thereof at auction by or for the account of the
~inal importer to whom the same were consigned, and by whom they were entered at the custom-
~se, so as such sale be made within twelve months after such goods are imported, and the same be sold
~ licensed auctioneer.
~y stat. 19 Geo. 3. c. 56. § 13. no duties shall be laid (1.) on any sale by auction of estates or chattels made
~rder of the Court of Chancery or Exchequer, or courts of great sessions in Wales : nor (2.) on any sale
~e by the *East India* or *Hudson's Bay* companies : nor (3.) by order of the commissioners of customs
~xcise : nor (4.) by order of the board of ordnance : nor (5.) by order of the commissioners of the navy
~ictualling offices : nor (6.) on any such sales made by the sheriff, for the benefit of creditors, in
~cution of judgment : nor (7.) on sales of goods distrained for rent : nor (8.) on sales for non-payment
~thes : nor (9.) on sales of effects of bankrupts sold by assignees : nor (10.) on goods imported by way of
~chandise from any *British* colony in *America*, the same being of the growth, produce, or manufacture
~ch colony, on the first sale thereof on account of the original importer to whom they were consigned,
~by whom they were entered at the custom-house, so as such sale be made within twelve months after
~ortation (see 59 Geo. 3. c. 54. s. 3.) : nor (11.) on any ships or their cargoes condemned as prize, and sold
~he benefit of the captor : nor (12.) on any ships or goods wrecked or stranded, sold for the benefit of
~nsurers or proprietors : nor (13.) on the sale of any goods damaged by fire, and sold for the benefit of
~insurers : nor (14.) on any auction to be held on the account of the lord or lady of the manor for
~ting any copyhold or customary messuages, lands, or tenements for the term of a life or lives, or any
~ber of years : nor (15.) on any auction to be held for the letting or demising any messuages, lands, or
~ments for the term of a life or lives, or any number of years, to be created by the person on whose
~unt such auction shall be held : nor (16.) on the sale of any wood, coppice, produce of mines or quar-
~ or materials for working the same ; or on the sale of any cattle, and live or dead stock, or unmanu-
~red produces of land, so as such sale of woods, coppices, produce of mines or quarries, cattle, corn,
~, or produce of land, may be made whilst they continue on the lands producing the same, and
~e owner of such lands, or proprietor of or adventurer in such mines or quarries, or by their steward
~ent.
~stat. 52 Geo. 3. c. 53. §. 1. all coffee imported in any *British* ship from any *British* colony in *America*
~be sold by auction, free of the auction-duty, whilst the same shall remain in warehouses, under the
~3 Geo. 3. c. 132. or any other act.
~rtain articles from the United States, as regulated by the act 59 Geo. 3. c. 54. §. 3., and goods from
~ugal imported under stat. 51 Geo. 3. c. 47. may also be sold by auction free of duty, if on account
~e original importer, and within twelve months of their importation.
~stat. 19 Geo. 3. c. 56. §. 9. the auctioneer, if the sale be within the limits of the chief office of excise in
~ton, shall give two days' notice at the said office, elsewhere three days' notice to the collector or at the
~ excise office, in writing, signed by him, specifying the particular day when such sale shall begin ;
~shall at the same time, or within twenty-four hours after, deliver a written or printed catalogue,
~ted and signed by such auctioneer or his known clerk, in which catalogue shall be particularly

enumerated every article, lot, parcel, and thing intended to be sold at such auction. And if he shall presume to make such sale without delivering such notice and catalogue, or sell any estate or goods not enumerated therein, he shall forfeit 20*l.*

By stat. 32 Geo. 3. c. 11. every auctioneer who shall have delivered such notice or catalogue shall, within twenty-eight days (if within the limits of the chief office of excise, elsewhere within six weeks,) after the day specified in such notice for such sale, deliver at such chief office, or to the collector of excise in whose collection such sale has been or was intended to be, a declaration in writing, setting forth whether or not any such sale had been or was opened or begun under such notice, or any article, lot, parcel, or thing contained in such catalogue was bid for or sold at such auction; and such auctioneer, or person acting as his clerk as aforesaid, shall make oath to the truth of such declaration before the said commissioners or collector, on pain of forfeiting 50*l.* for every neglect or refusal of delivering such declaration, verified as aforesaid.

The real owner of any estate, goods, or effects put up to sale by way of auction, and bought in either by himself or by his steward or known agent employed in the management of the sale, or by any other person appointed *in writing* by the owner to bid for him, shall be allowed the duties, provided notice in writing be given to the auctioneer before such selling, both by the owner and person intended to be the bidder, of such person being appointed by the owner; and provided such notice be verified by the oath of the auctioneer, as also the fairness of the transaction to the best of his knowledge and belief. (19 Geo. 3. c. 56. 28 Geo. 3. c. 37.) An auctioneer employed in a case of this sort, and neglecting to take the proper steps to prevent the duties from attaching, may be obliged to pay them himself. (19 Geo. 3. c. 56.)

If the sale of an estate be void through defect of title, the commissioners of excise, or justices of the peace in the county, may, on oath being made, grant relief for the duties paid. Claim must be made within twelve months after the sale, if rendered void within that time; or if not rendered void within that time, within three months after the discovery.

The auctioneer is by law liable to pay the auction duties, but he may recover the same from the vendor. The conditions of sale usually oblige the buyer to pay the whole, or a part of the duties; and upon his refusing or neglecting to pay them, the bidding is void.

An auctioneer who declines to disclose the name of his principal at the time of sale, makes himself responsible. But if he disclose the name of his principal he ceases to be responsible, either for the soundness of or title to the thing sold, unless he *have* expressly warranted it on his *own* responsibility.

If an auctioneer pay over the produce of a sale to his employer, after receiving notice that the goods were not the property of such employer, the real owner of the goods may recover the amount from the auctioneer.

It has long been a common practice at certain auctions (called for that reason *mock* auctions) to employ *puffers*, or mock bidders, to raise the value of the articles sold by their apparent competition, and many questions have grown out of it. It was long ago decided, that if the owner of an *estate* put up to sale by auction employ puffers to bid for him, it is a fraud on the real bidder, and the highest bidder cannot be compelled to complete his contract. (6 *T. Rep.* 642.) But it would seem as if the mere employment of puffers under any circumstances were now held to be illegal. " The inclination of the courts at the present time is, that a sale by auction should be conducted in the most open and public manner possible; that there should be no reserve on the part of the seller, and no collusion on the part of the buyers. Puffing is illegal, according to a late case, even though there be only one puffer; and it was then decided that the recognised practice at auctions of employing such persons to bid upon the sale of horses could not be sustained." — (*Woolrych on Commercial Law*, p. 262.)

A party bidding at an auction may retract his offer at any time before the hammer is down. Another clearly established principle is, that verbal declarations by an auctioneer are not to be suffered to control the printed conditions of sale; and these, when pasted up under the box of the auctioneer, are held to be sufficiently notified to purchasers.

Auctioneers, like all other agents, should carefully observe their instructions. Should those who employ them sustain any damage through their carelessness or inattention they will be responsible. They must also answer for the consequences, if they sell the property entrusted to their care for less than the price set upon it by the owners, or in way contrary to order.

An auctioneer who has duly paid the licence duty is not liable, in the city of London, to the penalties for acting as a *broker* without being admitted agreeably to the 6 Ann. c. 16.

The establishment of mock auctions is said to be a common practice among swindlers in London. Persons are frequently placed at the doors of such auctions, denominated *barkers*, to invite strangers to come in; and puffers are in wait to bid up the article much beyond its value. A stranger making an offer at such an auction is almost sure to have the article knocked down to him. Plated goods are often disposed of at these auctions, but it is almost needless to add, that they are of very inferior quality. Attempts have sometimes been made to suppress mock auctions, but hitherto without much success.

We subjoin an account of the number of auction licences granted from 5th January 1819, with the amount of duty received on sales by auction; distinguishing each year

specifying those who have taken out such licences for town, country, and town country, to the latest period. (Parl. Paper, No. 138. Sess. 1831.)

Years ended 5th January.	Number of Auction Licences.	Amount of Duty received on Sales by Auction.	Number of Licences taken out		
			For Town.	For Country.	For Town and Country.
		£ s. d.			
1820	2,557	256,534 16 9	327	2,124	106
1821	2,770	225,630 5 9	338	2,323	109
1822	2,939	202,317 18 2½	309	2,523	107
1823	2,897	206,322 8 1	343	2,433	121
1824	2,939	223,835 4 9	334	2,493	112
1825	2,941	279,264 1 9¾	338	2,496	107
1826	2,910	308,591 12 7¼	357	2,437	116
1827	2,981	225,061 9 11	607	2,325	49
1828	3,119	250,239 10 3	—	2,577	542
1829	2,972	235,447 18 10½	—	2,422	550
1830	3,043	225,258 11 4½	—	2,519	524
1831	2,467	203,090 17 0	—	2,478	489

VERAGE, a term used in commerce and navigation to signify a contribu- made by the individuals, when they happen to be more than one, to whom ip, or the goods on board it, belong, or by whom it or they are insured ; in r that no particular individual or individuals amongst them, who may have forced to make a sacrifice for the preservation of the ship or cargo, or both, ld lose more than others. " Thus," says Mr. Serjeant Marshall, " where the s of a particular merchant are thrown overboard in a storm to save the ship sinking ; or where the masts, cables, anchors, or other furniture of the ship, ut away or destroyed for the preservation of the whole ; or money or goods given as a composition to pirates to save the rest ; or an expense is incurred claiming the ship, or defending a suit in a foreign court of admiralty, and ining her discharge from an unjust capture or detention; in these and the cases, where any sacrifice is deliberately and voluntarily made, or any ex- e fairly and *bonâ fide* incurred, to prevent a total loss, such sacrifice or expense e proper subject of a general contribution, and ought to be rateably borne ie owners of the ship, freight, and cargo, so that the loss may fall equally on ccording to the equitable maxim of the civil law — no one ought to be hed by another's loss : *Nemo debet locupletari alienâ jacturâ.*"

pon this fair principle is founded the doctrine of average contributions ; ations with respect to which having been embodied in the Rhodian law, were e adopted into the Roman law; and form a prominent part of all modern ms of maritime jurisprudence. The rule of the Rhodian law is, that, " if, ie sake of lightening a ship in danger at sea, goods be thrown overboard, the ncurred for the sake of all, shall be made good by a general contribution." *Dig.* lib. 14. tit. 2. § 1. *Schomberg on the Maritime Laws of Rhodes,* p. 60.) rmerly it was a common practice to ransom British ships when captured by emy, the ransom being made good by general average. But this practice g been deemed disadvantageous, it was abolished by statute 22 Geo. 3. 25. which declares, " That all contracts and agreements which shall be ed into, and all bills, notes, and other securities which shall be given by any n or persons, for ransom of any ship or vessel, merchandise, or goods cap- by the subjects of any state at war with his Majesty, or by any person com- g hostilities against his Majesty's subjects, shall be absolutely void in law, f no effect whatever ;" and a penalty of 500*l.* is given to the informer, for offence against this act.

erage is either *general* or *particular;* that is, it either effects all who have any st in the ship and cargo, or only some of them. The contributions levied cases mentioned above, come under the first class. But when losses occur ordinary wear and tear, or from the perils naturally incident to a voyage, ut being *voluntarily* encountered, such as the accidental springing of masts, ss of anchors, &c., or when any peculiar sacrifice is made for the sake of ip *only,* or of the *cargo only,* these losses, or this sacrifice, must be borne

by the parties immediately interested, and are consequently defrayed by a *particular* average.

There are also some small charges called *petty* or *accustomed* averages; it usual to charge one third of them to the ship and two thirds to the cargo.

No general average ever takes place, except it can be shown that the danger was imminent, and that the sacrifice made *was indispensable, or supposed to be indispensable, by the captain and officers, for the safety of the ship and cargo.* The captain, on coming on shore, should immediately make his protests; and he, with some of the crew, should make oath that the goods were thrown overboard, masts or anchors cut away, money paid, or other loss sustained, for the preservation the ship and goods, and of the lives of those on board, and for no other purpose. The average, if not settled before, should then be adjusted, and it should be paid before the cargo is landed; for the owners of the ship have a *lien* on the goods on board, not only for the freight, but also *to answer all averages and contributions that may be due.* But though the captain should neglect his duty in this respect the sufferer would not be without a remedy, but might bring an action either against him or the owners.

The laws of different states, and the opinions of the ablest jurists, vary as to whether the loss incurred in defending a ship against an enemy or pirate, and the treatment of the wounded officers and men, should be made good by general or particular average. The Ordinance of the Hanse Towns (art. 35.), the Ordinance of 1681 (liv. iii. tit. 7. § 6.), and the *Code de Commerce* (art. 400. § 6.) explicitly declare that the charges on account of medicine, and for attendance upon the officers and seamen wounded in defending the ship, shall be general average. A regulation of this sort seems to be founded on reason. But other codes are silent on the subject; and though the contrary opinion had been advanced by Mr. Serjeant Marshall, and by Mr. Justice Park in the earlier editions of his work, the Court of Common Pleas has unanimously decided, that in England neither the damage done to a ship, nor the ammunition expended, nor the expense of healing sailors wounded in an action with an enemy or pirate, is a subject of general average. — (*Abbott on the Law of Shipping*, part iii. cap. 8.)

Much doubt has been entertained, whether expenses incurred by a ship in an intermediate port in which she has taken refuge, should be general average, or fall only on the ship. But on principle, at least, it is clear, that if the retreat the ship to port be made in order to obviate the danger of foundering, or some other great and imminent calamity, the expenses incurred in entering and during the time she is forced by stress of weather, or adverse winds, to continue in it, ought to belong to general average. But if the retreat of the ship port be made in order to repair an injury occasioned by the unskilfulness the master, or in consequence of any defect in her outfit, such, for example, deficiencies of water, provisions, sails, &c. with which she ought to have been sufficiently supplied before setting out, the expenses should fall wholly on the owners.

When a ship (supposed to be *seaworthy*) is forced to take refuge in an intermediate port, because of a loss occasioned by a peril of the sea, as the springing of a mast, &c.; then, as the accident is not ascribable to any fault of the master or owners, and the retreat to port is indispensable for the safety of the ship and cargo, it would seem that any *extraordinary expense* incurred in entering should be made good by general average.

Supposing, however, that it could be shown, that the ship was not, at her outset, seaworthy, or in a condition to withstand the perils of the sea; that the mast, for example, which has sprung, had been previously damaged; or supposing that the mischief had been occasioned by the incapacity of the master, the whole blame would, in such a case, be ascribable to the owners, who, besides defraying every expense, should be liable in damages to the freighters for the delay that would necessarily take place in completing the voyage, and for whatever damage might be done to the cargo.

These, however, are merely the conclusions to which, as it appears to us, they must come who look only to principles. The law with respect to the point referred to, differs in different countries, and has differed in this country at different periods. "A doubt," says Lord Tenterden, "was formerly entertained as to the expenses of a ship in a port in which she had taken refuge, to repair

...mage occasioned by a tempest; but this has been removed by late decisions. ...nd it has been held, that the wages and provisions of the crew during such a ...riod must fall upon the ship alone. But if a ship should necessarily go into ...a intermediate port for the purpose only of repairing such a damage as is in ...self a proper object of general contribution, possibly the wages, &c. during the ...riod of such detention, may also be held to be general average, on the ground ...at the accessory should follow the nature of its principal." — (*Law of Shipping*, ...rt iii. cap. 8.)

Perhaps the reader who reflects on the vagueness of this passage will be dis- ...sed to concur with Lord Tenterden's remark in another part of the same ...apter, " That the determinations of the English courts of justice furnish less ...authority on this subject (average) than on any other branch of maritime ...w."

The question, whether the *repairs* which a ship undergoes that is forced to put ...to an intermediate port ought to be general or particular average, has occasioned ...great diversity of opinion; but the principles that ought to regulate our deci- ...on with respect to it are abundantly obvious. Injuries voluntarily done to the ...ip, as cutting away masts, yards, &c. to avert some impending danger, are uni- ...rsally admitted to be general average. It seems, however, hardly less clear, ...d is, indeed, expressly laid down by all the great authorities, that injuries done ...the ship by the violence of the winds or the waves should be particular ...erage, or should fall wholly on the owners. The ship, to use the admirable ...ustration of this principle given in the civil law, is like the tool or instrument of ...workman in his trade. If in doing his work he break his hammer, his anvil, or ...y other instrument, he can claim no satisfaction for this from his employer. ...*ig.* lib. xiv. tit. 2. § 2.)—The owners are bound, both by the usual conditions ...all charter-parties and at common law, to carry the cargo to its destination; and ...ey must consequently be bound, in the event of the ship sustaining any acci- ...ntal or natural damage during the voyage, either to repair that damage at their ...n expense, or to provide another vessel to forward the goods. In point of ...t, too, such subsidiary ships have often been provided; but it has never been ...etended that their hire was a subject of general average, though it is plain it ...s quite as good a right to be so considered as the cost of repairing the damage ...ne to the ship by a peril of the sea. Hence, when a ship puts into an interme- ...te port for the common safety, the charges incurred in entering the port, and ...*vn to the earliest time that the wind and weather become favourable for leaving it*, ...ght to be general average; but the repair of any damage she may have sus- ...ned by wear and tear, or by the mere violence of the storm, or an accidental ...il, and the wages of the crew, and other expenses incurred after the weather ...moderated, should fall wholly on the owners.

It has been, however, within these few years decided, in the case of a British ...p that had been obliged to put into port in consequence of an injury resulting ...m her accidentally coming into collision with another, that so much of the repair ...then underwent as was *absolutely necessary to enable her to perform her voyage*, ...uld be general average. The Judges, however, spoke rather doubtfully on the ...ject; and it is exceedingly difficult to discover any good grounds for the ...gment. (Plummer and Another *v.* Wildman, 3 *M. & S.* 482.) — It seems ...ectly opposed to all principle, as well as to the authority of the laws of ...odes (*Dig.* 14. tit. 2.), of Oleron (art. 9.), of Wisby (art. 12.), and to the ...mmon law with respect to freight. Lord Tenterden has expressed himself as ...e were hostile to the judgment. It is, indeed, at variance with all the doc- ...es he lays down; and the terms in which he alludes to it, " *yet in one case*," ...ear to hold it forth as an exception (which it certainly is) to the course of ...isions on the subject.

...t is now usual in this country, when a vessel puts into port on account of a ...nage belonging to particular average, which requires to be repaired before she ...safely proceed on her voyage, to allow in general average the expense of ...ering the port and unloading, to charge the owners of the goods or their ...erwriters with the warehouse rent and expenses attending the cargo, and to ...w the expense of reloading and departure on the freight.

...ccording to the law of England, when a ship is injured by coming into colli- ...with or *running foul* of another, if the misfortune has been accidental, and no

E

blame can be ascribed to either party, the owners of the damaged ship have to bear the loss; but where blame can be fairly imputed to one of the parties, it, of course falls upon him to make good the damage done to the other. The regulations in the *Code de Commerce* (art. 407.) harmonise, in this respect, with our own. According, however, to the laws of Oleron and Wisby, and the famous French ordinance of 1681, the damage occasioned by an accidental collision is to be defrayed equally by both parties.

The ship and freight, and every thing on board, even jewels, plate, and money, except wearing apparel, contribute to general average. But the wages of seamen do not contribute; because, had they been laid under this obligation, they might have been tempted to oppose a sacrifice necessary for the general safety.

Different states have adopted different modes of valuing the articles which are to contribute to an average. In this respect the law of England has varied considerably at different periods. At present, however, the ship is valued at the price she is worth on her arrival at the port of delivery. The value of the freight is held to be the clear sum which the ship has earned after seamen's wages, pilotage, and all such other charges as come under the name of petty averages, are deducted. It is now the settled practice to value the goods lost as well as those saved, at the price they would have fetched in ready money, *at the port of delivery*, on the ship's arrival there, freight, duties, and other charges being deducted. Each person's share of the loss will bear the same proportion to the value of his property, that the whole loss bears to the aggregate value of the ship, freight, and cargo. The necessity of taking the goods lost into this account is obvious; for otherwise their owner would be the only person who would not be a loser.

When the loss of masts, cables, and other furniture of the ship, is compensated by general average, it is usual, as the new articles will, in all ordinary cases, be of greater value than those that have been lost, to deduct *one third* from the value of the former, leaving two thirds only to be contributed.

But the mode of adjusting an average will be better understood by the following example, extracted from Chief Justice Tenterden's valuable work on the Law of Shipping (part iii. cap. 8.)

" The reader will suppose that it became necessary, in the Downs, to cut the cable of a ship destined for Hull; that the ship afterwards struck upon the Goodwin, which compelled the master to cut away his mast, and cast overboard part of the cargo, in which operation another part was injured; and that the ship being cleared from the sands, was forced to take refuge in Ramsgate harbour, to avoid the further effects of the storm.

AMOUNT OF LOSSES.	£	VALUE OF ARTICLES TO CONTRIBUTE.	£
Goods of A. cast overboard -	500	Goods of A. cast overboard -	500
Damage of the goods of B. by the jettison - - -	200	Sound value of the goods of B., deducting freight and charges	1000
Freight of the goods cast over board - - -	100	Goods of C. - - -	500
		—— of D. - - -	2000
Price of a new cable, anchor, and mast - - £300 Deduct one third - 100	200	—— of E. - - -	5000
		Value of the ship - -	2000
Expense of bringing the ship off the sands - - -	50	Clear freight, deducting wages, victuals, &c. - -	800
Pilotage and port duties going into the harbour and out, and commission to the agent who made the disbursements -	100		
Expenses there - -	25		
Adjusting this average -	4		
Postage - - -	1		
Total of losses - - £	1180	Total of contributory values - £	11,800

Then, 11,800*l*. : 1,180*l*. : : 100*l*. : 10*l*.

That is, each person will lose 10 per cent. upon the value of his interest in cargo, ship, or freight. Therefore, A. loses 50*l*., B. 100*l*., C. 50*l*., D. 200*l*., ₅00*l*., the owners 280*l*.; in all, 1,180*l*. Upon this calculation the owners to lose 280*l*; but they are to receive from the contribution 380*l*., to make d their disbursements, and 100*l*. more for the freight of the goods thrown ℸboard; or 480*l*., minus 280*l*.

hey, therefore, are actually to receive - - £200
ᵣ. is to contribute 50*l*., but has lost 500*l*.; therefore A. is to receive 450
ᵣ. is to contribute 100*l*., but has lost 200*l*.; therefore B. is to receive 100

Total to be actually received - - - £750

ᵢn the other hand, C., D., and E., have lost nothing, and are ⎰ C. £50
    to pay as before; viz. - - - - - ⎱ D.   200
                                         E.   500

Total to be actually paid - - - £750

ᵗh is exactly equal to the total to be actually received, and must be paid by to each person in rateable proportion.

In the above estimate of losses I have included the freight of the goods ᵥwn overboard, which appears to be proper, as the freight of the goods is to ᵢaid, and their supposed value is taken clear of freight, as well as other ₉es. In this country, where the practice of insurance is very general, it is ᵈ for the broker, who has procured the policy of insurance, to draw up an ₛtment of the average, which is commonly paid in the first instance by the ᵣers without dispute. In case of dispute, the contribution may be recovered ᵣr *by a suit in equity*, or by an action at law, instituted by each individual ᵈed to receive, against each party that ought to pay for the amount of his ₑ. And in the case of a general ship, where there are many consignees, it is ᵈ for the master, before he delivers the goods, to take a bond from the ᵣent merchants for payment of their portions of the average when the same be adjusted."

ₕe subject of average does not necessarily make a part of the law of insur- ; though as insurers, from the terms of most policies, are liable to indemnify ₙsured against those contributions which are properly denominated *general* ₐge, its consideration very frequently occurs in questions as to partial losses. ᵢn order to confine assurances to that which should be their only object, ₗy, an indemnity against real and important losses arising from a peril of the ₐs well as to obviate disputes respecting losses arising from the perishable ᵗy of the goods insured, and all trivial subjects of difference and litigation, it ₛ to be the general law of all maritime states, and is expressly indeed pro- ᵈ by the famous ordinance of 1681 (see liv. iii. tit. 6. § 47. and the ela- ₑe commentary of M. Valin), that the insurer shall not be liable to any ₙd on account of average, unless it exceed *one* per cent. An article 408.) to the same effect is inserted in the *Code de Commerce*; and, by stipu- ₐ, this limitation is frequently extended in French policies to *three* or *four* ₑnt. A similar practice was adopted in this country in 1749. It is now ₐntly stipulated in all policies, that upon certain enumerated articles of a ᵗy peculiarly perishable, the insurer shall not be liable for any partial loss ₑver; that upon certain others liable to partial injuries, but less difficult to ₑserved at sea, he shall only be liable for partial losses above *five* per cent.; ᵗhat as to all other goods, and also the ship and freight, he shall only be liable ᵤrtial losses above *three* per cent. This stipulation is made by a memoran- inserted at the bottom of all policies done at Lloyd's, of the following ᵣ: — " N.B. Corn, fish, salt, fruit, flour, and seeds, are warranted free from ₉e, unless general, or the ship be stranded; sugar, tobacco, hemp, flax, ₎, and skins, are warranted free from average under 5*l*. per cent.; and all goods free from average under 3*l*. per cent., unless general, or the ship be ᵈed."

The form of this memorandum was universally used, as well by the Royal E change and London Assurance Companies as by private underwriters, till 175 when it was decided that a ship having run aground, was a stranded ship with the meaning of the memorandum; and that although she got off again, the und writers were liable to the average or partial loss upon damaged corn. This de sion induced the two Companies to strike the words, "*or the ship be stranded* out of the memorandum; so that now they consider themselves liable to losses which can happen to such commodities, except general averages and to losses. The old form is still retained by the private underwriters. (S STRANDING.)

The reader is referred, for the further discussion of this important subject, the article MARINE INSURANCE; and to *Mr. Stevens's Essay on Average, Abb on the Law of Shipping* (part iii. cap. 8.), *Marshall on Insurance* (book cap. 12. s. 7.), *Park on Insurance* (cap. 7.), and Mr. Benecke's elaborate and a work on the *Principles of Indemnity in Marine Insurance.*

AVOIRDUPOIS, a weight used in determining the gravity of bulky co modities. See WEIGHTS AND MEASURES.

B.

BACON (Ger. *Speck*; Du. *Spek*; Fr. *Lard*; It. Sp. and Port. *Lardo*; R Solo ; Lat. *Lardum*) is made from the sides and belly of the pig, which are fi thoroughly impregnated with salt, then suffered to remain for a certain period brine, and, lastly, dried and smoked. The counties of England most celebrat for bacon are Yorkshire, Hampshire, Berkshire, and Wiltshire. Ireland p duces great quantities of bacon; but it is neither so clean fed, nor so well cur as the English, and is much lower priced. Dumfries and those counties Scotland on the borders of England, have recently cured large quantities of po and bacon, which principally come to the Liverpool and London markets. It excellent in quality.

The imports of bacon and hams from Ireland have increased rapidly of late yea The average quantity imported during the three years ending the 25th of Mar 1800, only amounted to 41,948 cwts ; whereas during the three years end with 1820, the average imports amounted to 204,380 cwts.; and during the th years ending with 1825, they had increased to 338,218 cwts. In 1825, the tr between Ireland and Great Britain was placed on the footing of a coasting trad and bacon and hams are imported and exported without any specific entry at custom-house. We believe, however, that the imports of these articles i Great Britain from Ireland amount, at present, to little less than 500,000 cwts year. The quantity of bacon and hams exported from Ireland to foreign co tries is inconsiderable; not exceeding 1,500 or 2,000 cwts. a year.

The duty on bacon, being 28*s.* the cwt. is in effect prohibitory. The duty hams is the same as on bacon. By the 7 Geo. 4. c. 48. bacon is not to be ente to be warehoused except for exportation only; and if it be so warehoused cannot be taken out for home use.

BAGGAGE, in commercial navigation, the wearing apparel and other artic destined for the sole use or accommodation of the crews and passengers of sh The following are the Custom-house regulations with respect to baggage : —

Baggage and apparel accompanied by the proprietor, worn and in use (not made up for the purpo being introduced into this country) exempted from all duty on importation.

Articles in baggage subject to duty or prohibited may be left in custody of the officers of customs a period of six months, to give the party an opportunity of paying the duty or taking them b Customs Order, August 6. 1822.

If unaccompanied by proprietor, proof must be made by the party that it is as aforesaid, and not ported as merchandise, otherwise it is subject to a duty of 20 per cent.

If not cleared at the expiration of six months from the date of landing it is liable to be sold for and charges, the residue (if any) to be paid to the right owner on proof being adduced to the satisfa of the honourable board.

One fowling-piece and one pair of pistols accompanying the party, *bonâ fide* in use, free per Cus Order, July 5. 1825.

Spirits, being the remains of passengers' stores may be admitted to entry, 6 Geo. 4. c. 107. § 107.

One pint drinkable spirits of whatever strength, or half pint of cordial or Cologne water, in bag for private use — free. Treasury Order, October 20. 1820.

Carriages of British manufacture, in use — free. Treasury Order, September 26, 1817.

Glass, in dressing or medicine cases, of British manufacture, free upon proof that no drawback been received. Treasury Order, December 5. 1821. — (*Nyren's Tables.*)

BAHIA, or St. Salvador, a large city of Brazil, at the entrance of Todos os antos bay, lat. 12° 58′ S., long. 38° 32¼′ W. Population (*Edin. Gazet.*) about ¼0,000. Bahia enjoys an extensive commerce. The imports and exports are milar to those of Rio de Janeiro; to which the reader is referred for some ac-»unt of the commerce of Brazil. The exports of sugar from Brazil, in 1830, mounted to about 76,000 tons, of which Bahia exported 44,000, and Rio »,000 tons. The monies, weights, and measures of Brazil are the same as those `Portugal; for which, see Lisbon. The *alquiere*, or measure for corn, rice, &c. ffers in different provinces, being in some 1¼ bushel Winch. meas., and in others ¼e only. At Bahia it is estimated at one. Wine and olive oil pay duty on being ported by the pipe, hogshead, or barrel: they are retailed by the frasco or case-»ttle = 4½ pints English wine measure. In 1828, 122 British ships, carrying »,166 tons, entered Bahia.

BAIZE (Du. *Bay, Baay;* Fr. *Bayette;* Ger. *Boy;* It. *Bajetta;* Port. *Baeta, ʒetilha;* Rus. *Baïka;* Sp. *Bayeta*), a sort of coarse open woollen stuff having a ʒng nap, sometimes frized, and sometimes not. This stuff is chiefly manufactured Colchester and Bocking, in Essex; Rochdale, in Lancashire, &c. The breadth of *baize* is commonly from a yard and a half to two yards, by forty-ʒo to forty-eight in length.

BAKER, a person whose business it is to manufacture or prepare all sorts of ʒead. For an account of the regulations to which bakers are subject, see Bread.

BALANCE, a well known instrument used to determine the comparative ʒights of different bodies.

BALANCE, in accounts, is the term used to express the difference between ʒe debtor and creditor sides of an account.

BALANCE, in commerce, is the term commonly used to express the difference ʒtween the value of the exports from and imports into a country. The balance said to be favourable when the value of the exports exceeds that of the im-ʒrts, and unfavourable when the value of the imports exceeds that of the ʒports. According to the custom-house returns, the official value of the exports ʒm Great Britain, exclusive of foreign and colonial merchandise, during the ʒr ending 5th January, 1830, amounted to 55,465,723*l.*; and the official value the imports during the same year amounted to 42,311,648*l.*; leaving a ʒurable balance of 13,154,075*l.*

ʒhe attainment of a favourable balance was formerly regarded as an object of the ʒatest importance. The precious metals early acquired, in consequence of their being ʒd as money, an artificial importance, and were long considered as the only real wealth ʒer individuals or nations could possess. And as countries without mines could not ʒain supplies of these metals except in exchange for exported products, it was con-ʒded, that if the value of the commodities exported exceeded that of those imported, ʒ balance would have to be paid by the importation of an equivalent amount of the ʒcious metals; and conversely. A very large proportion of the restraints imposed on freedom of commerce, during the last two centuries, grew out of this notion. The ʒortance of having a favourable balance being universally admitted, every effort was ʒde to attain it; and nothing seemed so effectual for this purpose as the devising of ʒemes to facilitate exportation and to hinder the importation of almost all products, ʒept gold and silver, that were not intended for future exportation. But the gradual ʒugh slow growth of sounder opinions with respect to the nature and functions of ʒney, showed the futility of a system of policy having such objects in view. It is now ʒceded on all hands that gold and silver are nothing but commodities; and that it is ʒo respect necessary to interfere either to encourage their importation, or to prevent ʒr exportation. In Great Britain they may be freely exported and imported, whether ʒhe shape of coin or bullion. See articles Bullion and Coin.

ʒhe truth is, however, that the theory of the balance of trade is not erroneous merely ʒn the false notions which its advocates entertained with respect to money; it proceeds ʒradically mistaken views as to the nature of commerce. The mode in which the ʒnce is usually estimated is, indeed, completely fallacious. Supposing, however, ʒ it could be correctly ascertained, it would be found, in opposition to the common ʒion, that the imports into every commercial country generally exceed the exports; ʒ that when a balance is formed, it is only in certain cases, and those of rare ʒurrence, that it is cancelled by a bullion payment.

ʒ The proper business of the wholesale merchant consists in carrying the various ʒlucts of the different countries of the world, from the places where their value is ʒ to those where it is greatest; or, which is the same thing, in distributing them

according to the effective demand. It is clear, however, that there could be no motive to export any species of produce, unless that which it was intended to import in its stead were of greater value. When an English merchant commissions a quantity of Polish wheat, he calculates on its selling for so much more than its price in Poland, as will be sufficient to pay the expense of freight, insurance, &c., and to yield besides the common and ordinary rate of profit on the capital employed. If the wheat did not sell for this much, its importation would obviously be a loss to the importer. It is plain, then, that no merchant ever did or ever will export, but in the view of importing something more valuable in return. And so far from an excess of exports over imports being any criterion of an advantageous commerce, it is directly the reverse; and the truth is, notwithstanding all that has been said and written to the contrary, that unless the value of the imports exceeded that of the exports, foreign trade could not be carried on. Were this not the case — that is, were the value of the exports always greater than the value of the imports—merchants would lose on every transaction with foreigners, and the trade with them would be speedily abandoned.

In England, the rates at which exports and imports are officially valued were fixed so far back as 1696. But the very great alteration that has since taken place, not only in the value of money, but also in the cost of most part of the commodities produced in this and other countries, has rendered this official valuation of no use whatever as a criterion of the true value of the exports and imports. In order to remedy this defect, an account of their *real* or *declared* value is annually prepared, from the declarations of the merchants, and laid before parliament; but even this is very far from accurate: most imported commodities being loaded with heavy duties, it is, speaking generally, the interest of the merchant to conceal and under-rate their real value; while, on the other hand, it is sometimes for his interest to exaggerate the value of those which are entitled to a drawback on being exported; and as few commodities are subject to a direct duty on exportation, it may be fairly presumed that their value is, if not over-rated, at least stated at its full amount.

But if perfectly accurate accounts could be obtained of the value of the exports and imports of a commercial country, there can be no manner of doubt that, in ordinary years, the latter would always exceed the former. The value of an exported commodity is estimated at the moment of its being sent abroad, and *before* its value is increased by the expense incurred in transporting it to the place of its destination; whereas the value of the commodity imported in its stead is estimated *after* it has arrived at its destination, and, consequently, after its value has been enhanced by the cost of freight, insurance, importer's profits, &c.

In the United States the value of the imports, as ascertained by the custom-house returns, always exceeds the value of the exports. And although our practical politicians have been in the habit of considering the excess of the former as a certain proof of a disadvantageous commerce, "it is nevertheless true," says Mr. Pitkin, "that the real gain of the United States has *been nearly in proportion as their imports have exceeded their exports.*" (*Commerce of the United States*, 2d ed. p. 280.) The great excess of American imports has in part been occasioned by the Americans generally exporting their own surplus produce, and, consequently, receiving from foreigners not only an equivalent for their exports, but also for the cost of conveying them to the foreign market. "In 1811," says the author just quoted, "flour sold in America for *nine dollars* and *a half* per barrel, and in Spain for *fifteen dollars.* The value of the cargo of a vessel carrying 5,000 barrels of flour would, therefore, be estimated at the period of its exportation at 47,500 dollars; but as this flour would sell, when carried to Spain, for 75,000 dollars, the American merchant would be entitled to draw on his agent in Spain for 27,500 dollars more than the flour cost in America, or than the sum for which he could have drawn, had the flour been exported in a vessel belonging to a Spanish merchant. But the transaction would not end here. The 75,000 dollars would be vested in some species of Spanish or other European goods fit for the American market; and the freight, insurance, &c., on account of the return cargo, would probably increase its value to 100,000 dollars; so that, in all, the American merchant might have imported goods worth 52,500 dollars more than the flour originally sent to Spain." It is as impossible to deny that such a transaction as this is advantageous, as it is to deny that its advantage consists entirely in the excess of the value of the goods imported over the value of those exported. And it is equally clear that America might have had the real balance of payments in her favour, though such transactions as the above had been multiplied to any conceivable extent.

II. In the second place, when a balance is due by one country to an other, it is but seldom that it is paid by remitting bullion from the debtor to the creditor country. the sum due by the British merchants to those of Holland be greater than the sum due by the latter to them, the balance of payments will be against Britain; but this balance will not, and indeed cannot, be discharged by an exportation of bullion, *unless bullion be, at the*

, *the cheapest exportable commodity;* or, which is the same thing, *unless it may be more* ~~ntageously exported than any thing else.~~ To illustrate this principle, let us suppose that balance of debt, or the excess of the value of the bills drawn by the merchants of Am-dam on London over those drawn by the merchants of London on Amsterdam, amounts ~~0,000l.~~ : it is the business of the London merchants to find out the means of dis-ging this debt with the least expense ; and it is plain, that if they find that any less , as 96,000l., 97,000l., or 99,900l. will purchase and send to Holland as much cloth, ~~n, hardware, colonial produce, or any other commodity, as would sell in Amster-~~ for 100,000l., no gold or silver would be exported. The laws which regulate the e in bullion are not in any degree different from those which regulate the trade in r commodities. It is exported only when its exportation is advantageous, or when more valuable abroad than at home. It would, in fact, be quite as reasonable to ~~ct that water should flow from from a low to a high level, as it is to expect that~~ ~~on should leave a country where its value is great, to go to one where it is low !~~ never sent abroad to destroy but always to find its level. The balance of pay-~~ts might be ten or a hundred millions against a particular country, without causing~~ exportation of a single ounce of bullion. Common sense tells us that no merchant remit 100l. worth of bullion to discharge a debt in a foreign country, if it be pos-to invest any smaller sum in any species of merchandise which would sell abroad .00l. exclusive of expenses. The merchant who deals in the precious metals is as h under the influence of *self-interest*, as he who deals in coffee or indigo; but what hant would attempt to extinguish a debt, by exporting coffee which cost 100l., if ~~ould effect his object by sending abroad indigo which cost only 99l. ?~~ ~~he argument about the balance of payments is one of those that contradict and con-~~ themselves. Had the apparent excess of exports over imports, as indicated by the sh custom-house books for the last hundred years, been always paid in bullion, as supporters of the old theory contend is the case, there ought at this moment to be t 450,000 000 or 500,000,000 of bullion in the country, instead of 50,000,000 or ~~00,000, which it is supposed to amount to ! Nor is this all. If the theory of the~~ ~~nce be good for any thing — if it be not a mere idle delusion,—it follows, as every~~ try in the world, with the single exception of the United States, has its favourable ~~ce, that they must be paid by an annual importation of bullion from the mines~~ sponding to their *aggregate amount.* But it is certain, that the entire produce of ~~ines, though it were increased in a *tenfold* proportion, would be insufficient for this~~ ose ! This *reductio ad absurdum* is decisive of the degree of credit that ought to tached to the conclusions respecting the flourishing state of the commerce of any try drawn from the excess of the exports over the imports !

t only, therefore, is the common theory with respect to the balance of trade erro-, but the very reverse of that theory is true. In the *first* place, the value of the nodities imported by every country which carries on an advantageous commerce no other will be prosecuted for any considerable period), invariably exceeds the value ~~se which she exports.~~ Unless such were the case, there would plainly be no fund ~~ce the merchants and others engaged in foreign trade could derive either a profit~~ ~~eir capital, or a return for their outlay and trouble; and in the *second* place, whether~~ ~~alance of debt be for or against a country, that balance will neither be paid nor re-~~ ~~l in bullion, unless it be at the time the commodity by the exportation or import-~~ of which the account may be most profitably settled. Whatever the partisans of octrine as to the balance may say about money being a preferable product, a *mar-tise par excellence*, it is certain that it will never appear in the list of exports and im-while there is any thing else with which to carry on trade, or cancel debts, that ield a larger profit, or occasion a less expense to the debtors.

s difficult to estimate the mischief which the absurd notions relative to the balance ~~de have occasioned in almost every commercial country ; — here they have been~~ ularly injurious. It is principally to the prevalence of prejudices to which they ~~iven rise, that the restrictions on the trade between this country and France are to~~ ribed. The great, or rather the only, argument insisted upon by those who pre-on the legislature, in the reign of William and Mary, to declare the trade with e a *nuisance*, was founded on the statement that the value of the imports from that om considerably exceeded the value of the commodities we exported to it. The e was regarded as a *tribute* paid by England to France ; and it was sagaciously , what had we done, that we should be obliged to pay so much money to our natural ? It never occurred to those who so loudly abused the French trade, that no ant would import any commodity from France, unless it brought a higher price in ~~untry than the commodity which had been exported to pay it ; and that the profit~~ merchant, or the national gain, would be in exact proportion to this excess of price. ery reason assigned by these persons for prohibiting the trade affords the best at-~~le proof of its having been a lucrative one ; nor can there be any doubt that an~~

unrestricted freedom of intercourse between the two countries would still be of greatest service to both.

BALE, a pack, or certain quantity of goods or merchandise; as a *bale* of silk, cloth, &c.

Bales are always marked and numbered, that the merchants to whom they belong may know them; and the marks and numbers correspond to those in the bills of lading, &c. Selling under the *bale*, or under the *cords*, is a term used in France and other countries for selling goods wholesale, without sample or pattern, and unopened.

BALKS, large pieces of timber.

BALLAST (Du. *Ballast*; Fr. *Lest*; Ger. *Ballast*; It. *Savorra*; Sp. *Lastre*; Sw. *Ballast*), a quantity of iron, stones, sand, gravel, or any other heavy material laid in a ship's hold, in order to sink her deeper in the water, and to render her capable of carrying sail without being overset. All ships clearing outwards, having no goods on board other than the personal baggage of the passengers, are said to be in ballast.

Ships that have cargoes of light goods on board require a quantity of ballast; increasing, of course according to the greater lightness of the goods. Flat vessels require most ballast. The following table shows the quantity of ballast allowed to ships of war: —

Ballast allowed to the following Ships.

Guns.	Tonnage.	Iron, Tons.	Shingle, Tons.
110	2,290	180	370
100	2,090	180	370
98	2,110	160	350
90	1,870	160	350
80	1,620	140	300
74	1,700	80	270
64	1,370	70	260
50	1,100	65	170
44	900	65	160
38	930	70	170
36	870	65	160
32	700	65	140
28	600	60	100
24	500	50	80
22	450	50	70
20	400	50	60
Sloop - -	300	50	40
Brig -	160	30	15
Cutter - -	—	20	} seldom any.
Sloop - -	—	15	

The iron ballast is first stored fore and aft, from bulk-head to bulk-head; then the shingle ballast spread and levelled over the iron.

The soil of the river Thames from London Bridge to the sea is vested in the Trinity House corporation, and a sum of 10*l.* is to be paid for every ton of ballast taken from the channel of the river with due authority from the said corporation. Ships may receive on board land ballast from the quarries, &c. east of Woolwich, provided the quantity taken in a year do not exceed the number of tons notified the Trinity corporation. Land ballast must be entered, and 1*d.* paid per ton on entering. No ballast to be put on board before entry at the ballast office, under a penalty of 5*l.* a ton. The Trinity corporation are authorised by the 3 Geo. 4. c. 111. to charge the following rates for all ballast demanded entered at the ballast office, viz. : —

For every ton (20 cwt.) of ballast, not being washed ballast, carried to any ship or vessel employed in the coal trade, the sum of 1*s.*

For every such ton carried to any other British ship or vessel, the sum of 1*s.* 3*d.*

For every such ton carried to any foreign ship or vessel, the sum of 1*s.* 7*d.*

For every ton of washed ballast carried to any ship or vessel employed in the coal trade, the sum of For every ton of washed ditto carried to any other British ship or vessel, the sum of 2*s.* 6*d.*

For every ton of washed ditto carried to any foreign ship or vessel, the sum of 3*s.* 2*d.*

And for every ton of ballast delivered in or unladen from the Inward West India Dock, the further sum of 10*d.* ; and for every ton of ballast delivered in or unladen from the Outward West India Dock the further sum of 4*d.* ; and for every ton of ballast delivered in or unladen from the London Docks, the further sum of 4*d.* ; and for every ton of ballast delivered in or unladen from the Inward East India Dock the further sum of 10*d.* ; and for every ton of ballast delivered in or unladen from the Outward East India Dock, the further sum of 4*d.* ; and for every ton of ballast delivered in or unladen from the Commercial Dock, the further sum of 4*d.* ; and for every ton of ballast delivered in or unladen from the Country Dock, the further sum of 4*d.* ; and for every ton of ballast delivered in or unladen from the City Canal, the further sum of 4*d.* ; and for every ton of ballast delivered in or unladen from the Surrey Canal, the further sum of 4*d.* ; and for every ton of ballast delivered in or unladen from the Regent's Canal, the further sum of 4*d.*

Which further rates or prices shall be payable and paid over and above the respective rates mentioned.

The ballast of all ships or vessels coming into the Thames is to be unladen into a lighter, at the charge of 6*d.* a ton. If any ballast be thrown or unladen from any ship or vessel into the Thames, the captain, master, &c. shall for every such offence forfeit 20*l.* No ballast is to be received on board otherwise than from a lighter. By the stat. 54 Geo. 3. c. 149. it is enacted, that no person shall, under a penalty of over and above all expenses, discharge any ballast, rubbish, &c. in any of the ports, harbours, roadsteads navigable rivers, &c. of the United Kingdom; nor take ballast from any place prohibited by the Lords of the Admiralty.

The masters of all ships clearing out in ballast, are required to answer upon oath any questions that ay be put to them by the collectors or comptrollers, touching the departure and destination of such ships. (6 Geo. 4. c. 107. § 75.)

If a *foreign* ship clear out in ballast, the master may take with him British manufactured goods of the lue of 20*l.*, the mate of the value of 10*l.*, and 5*l.* worth for each of the crew.

BALSAM (Ger. *Balsam;* Du. *Balsem;* Fr. *Baume;* It. and Sp. *Balsamo;* at. *Balsamum*). Balsams are vegetable juices, either liquid, or which sponta- ously become concrete, consisting of a substance of a resinous nature, combined ith benzoic acid, or which are capable of affording benzoic acid, by being heated one, or with water. The liquid balsams are copaiva, opobalsam, balsam of Peru, orax, and tolu; the concrete are benzoin, dragon's blood, and red or concrete orax. — (*Dr. Ure.*)

1. *Copaiva* (Fr. *Baume de Copahu;* Ger. *Kopaiva Balsam;* Sp. *Copayva*), obtained om a tree (*Copaifera*) growing in South America and the West India Islands. The rgest quantity is furnished by the province of Para in Brazil. It is imported in small sks, containing from 1 to 1½ cwt. Genuine good copaiva or copaiba balsam has a culiar but agreeable odour, and a bitterish, hot, nauseous taste. It is clear and trans- rent; its consistence is that of oil; but when exposed to the action of the air it becomes lid, dry, and brittle, like resin. — (*Thomson's Dispensatory.*)

2. *Opobalsam* (Fr. *Balsamier de la Mecque;* It. *Opobalsamo;* Lat. *Balsamum verum* um, *Ægptiacum,* Egypt. *Balessan*), the most precious of all the balsams, com- only called Balm of Gilead. It is the produce of a tree (*Amyris Gileadensis*), indige- us to Arabia and Abyssinia, and transplanted at an early period to Judea. It is tained by cutting the bark with an axe at the time that the juice is in the strongest culation. The true balsam is of a pale yellowish colour, clear and transparent, about e consistence of Venice turpentine, of a strong, penetrating, agreeable, aromatic smell, d a slightly bitterish pungent taste. By age it becomes yellower, browner, and cker, losing by degrees, like volatile oils, some of its finer and more subtile parts. It rarely if ever brought genuine into this country; dried Canada balsam being generally ostituted for it. It was in high repute among the ancients; but it is now principally ed as a cosmetic by the Turkish ladies. — (*Drs. Ure and Thomson.*) The Canada balsam, now referred to, is merely *fine turpentine*. It is the produce of e *Pinus Balsamea,* and is imported in casks, each containing about 1 cwt. It has a ong, but not a disagreeable odour, and a bitterish taste; is transparent, whitish, and the consistence of copaiva balsam. — See TURPENTINE.

3. *Balsam of Peru* (Fr. *Baume de Peru;* Ger. *Peruvianischer Balsam;* Sp. *Balsamo* *Quinquina;* Lat. *Balsamum Peruvianum*), the produce of a tree (*Myroxylon Perui- um*) growing in the warmest parts of South America. The balsam procured by isions made in the tree is called *white liquid balsam;* that which is found in the shops obtained by boiling the twigs in water: it is imported in jars, each containing from to 40lbs. weight. It has a fragrant aromatic odour, much resembling that of izoin, with a warm bitterish taste. It is viscid, of a deep reddish brown colour, and the consistence of honey. — (*Thomson's Dispensatory.*)

4. *Storax* (Fr. *Storax;* Ger. *Stryaxbroom;* It. *Storace;* Sp. *Azumbar;* Lat. *Styrax;* ab. *Usteruk*), the produce of a tree (*Styrax officinale*) growing in the south of Europe the Levant. Only two kinds are found in the shops: storax in tears, which is pure; storax in the lump, or red storax, which is mixed with sawdust and other impurities. th kinds are brought from the Levant in chests and boxes. Storax has a fragrant ur, and a pleasant, sub-acidulous, slightly pungent, and aromatic taste; it is of ddish brown colour, and brittle. — (*Thomson's Dispensatory.*)

5. *Tolu, Balsam of* (Fr. *Baume de Tolu;* Ger. *Tolutunischer Balsam;* Sp. *Balsamo* *Tolu*). The tree which yields this balsam is the same as that which yields the balsam Peru; it being merely the white balsam of Peru, hardened by exposure to the air.

6. *Benzoin,* or *Benjamin* (Fr. *Benzoin;* Ger. *Benzoe;* Sp. *Bengui;* It. *Belzuino;* Lat. zoinum; Arab. *Liban;* Hind *Luban;* Jav. *Menian;* Malay, *Caminyan*), is an article much greater commercial importance than any of those balsams previously mentioned. s obtained from a tree (*Styrax Benzoin*) growing in Sumatra and Borneo. It has a very eeable fragrant odour, but hardly any taste. It is imported in large masses packed hests and casks. It should be chosen full of clear, light-coloured, and white spots, ing the appearance of white marble when broken: it is rarely, however, to be met h in so pure a state, but the nearer the approach to it the better. The worst sort is kish, and full of impurities. — (*Milburn's Orient. Com.*)

Mr. Crawfurd has given the following interesting and authentic details with respect his article: — " Benzoin, or frankincense, called in commercial language Benjamin, more general article of commerce than camphor, though its production be confined he same islands. Benzoin is divided in commerce, like camphor, into three *sorts,* id, belly, foot), according to quality, the comparative value of which may be ex-

pressed by the figures 105, 45, 18. Benzoin is valued in proportion to its whiteness, semi-transparency, and freedom from adventitious matters. According to its purity, the first sort may be bought at the *emporia* to which it is brought, at from 50 to 100 dollars per picul (133¼ lbs.); the second from 25 to 45 dollars; and the worst from 8 to 20 dollars. According to Linschoten, benzoin, in his time, cost, in the market of Sunda Calapa or Jacatra, from 19$\frac{48}{100}$ to 25$\frac{40}{100}$ Spanish dollars the picul. By Niebuhr's account, the worst benzoin of the Indian islands is more esteemed by the Arabs than their own best *olibanum*, or frankincense. In the London market, the best benzoin is fourteen times more valuable than *olibanum*, and even the worst 2¼ times more valuable. Benzoin usually sells in England at 10s. per pound. The quantity generally imported into England, in the time of the monopoly, was 312 cwts. The principal use of this commodity is as incense, and is equally in request in the religious ceremonies of Catholics, Mohammedans, Hindus, and Chinese. It is also used as a luxury by the great in fumigations in their houses; and the Japanese chiefs are fond of smoking it with tobacco. Its general use among nations in such various states of civilisation, and the steady demand for it in all ages, declare that it is one of those commodities, the taste for which is inherent in our nature, and not the result of a particular caprice with any individual people, as in the case of Malay camphor with the Chinese." — (*Indian Archipelago*, III. p. 418.)

7. *Dragon's Blood* (Fr. *Sang-Dragon*; Lat. *Sanguis Draconis*; Arab. *Damulākhwain*, Hind. *Heraduky*), the produce of a large species of rattan (*Calamus Draco*) growing on the north and north-east coast of Sumatra, and in some parts of Borneo. It is largely exported to China, and also to India and Europe. It is either in oval drops, wrapped up in flag-leaves, or in large and generally more impure masses, composed of smaller tears. It is externally and internally of a deep dusky red colour, and when powdered it should become of a bright crimson; if it be black, it is worth little. When broken and held up against a strong light, it is somewhat transparent: it has little or no smell or taste; what it has of the latter is resinous and astringent. Dragon's blood in drops is much preferable to that in cakes; the latter being more friable, and less compact, resinous, and pure than the former. Being a very costly article, it is very apt to be adulterated. Most of its alloys dissolve like gums in water, or crackle in the fire without proving inflammable; whereas the genuine dragon's blood readily melts and catches flame, and is scarcely acted on by watery liquors. Its price at Bajarmassin in Borneo where large quantities are manufactured, is, according to quality, from 50 to 70 Spanish dollars per picul, or at an average 11*l*. 6*s*. 9½*d*. per cwt. Its price in the London market is usually about 30*l*. per cwt. — (*Milburn's Orient. Com. Crawfurd's East. Archip.*)

The net duty on balsams imported into Great Britain in 1828 amounted to 5,543*l*. 7*s*. 8*d*.

BALTIMORE, a large and opulent city of the United States, in Maryland, situated on the north side of the Patapsco river, about fourteen miles above its entrance into Chesapeake bay, in lat. 39° 17′ N. long. 76° 30′ W. Population 81,000. The harbour is spacious and convenient. The exports principally consist of tobacco, wheat, and wheat-flour (exported in large quantities), hemp and flax, flax-seed, Indian corn, and other agricultural products, timber, iron, &c. The imports principally consist of cottons and woollens, sugar, coffee, tea, wine, brandy, silk goods, spices, rum, &c. There are eight banks at Baltimore. The capital of the Union Bank is said to amount to 3,000,000 of dollars. The registered, enrolled, and licensed tonnage belonging to Baltimore, in 1828, amounted to 106,303 tons, of which 37,898 tons were employed in the coasting trade. The total value of the articles imported into Maryland, in the year ending the 30th of September, 1829, was 4,804,135 dollars; the total value of the exports during the same year being 4,804,465 do. (*Papers laid before Congress the 5th of February, 1830.*) In Maryland the dollar is worth 7s. 6d. currency, 1*l*. sterling being = 1*l*. 13*s*. 4*d*. currency. For an account of the currency of the different states of the Union, with a table of the value of the dollar in each, see NEW YORK. See EXPORTS and IMPORTS for an account of the foreign trade of the United States. Weights and measures same as those of England.

BAMBOO, (Fr. *Bambou, Bambochés*; Ger. *Indianischer Rohr*; It. *Bambu*, the *arundo bambos*, one of the most useful trees in the world, at least in the tropical regions. There are above fifty varieties, all of which are of the most rapid growth, rising from fifty to eighty feet in the first year, and in the second perfecting their timber in hardness and elasticity. It grows in stools, which are cut over every two years. Its uses are almost without end. It is employed in the construction of houses, furniture, bridges, boats, masts, rigging, all sorts

lements, &c. &c. Macerated in water it forms paper. The juice when issated is a favorite medicine of the natives. The canes imported into rope are principally small ones used for walking sticks.

BANDANAS, silk handkerchiefs, generally red spotted with white. They e formerly manufactured only in the East Indies; but they are now manufac-ed of a very good quality at Glasgow and other places.

BANK. — BANKING. Banks are establishments intended to serve for the custody of money, to facilitate its payment by one individual to another; and etimes, for the accommodation of the public with loans.

I. BANKING (GENERAL PRINCIPLES OF).
II. BANK OF ENGLAND (ACCOUNT OF).
III. BANKS (ENGLISH PROVINCIAL).
IV. BANKS (SCOTCH).
V. BANKS (IRISH).
VI. BANKS (FOREIGN).
VII. BANKS (SAVINGS).

I. BANKING (GENERAL PRINCIPLES OF).

GENERAL PRINCIPLES OF BANKING. — Banks are commonly divided into two great es; banks of deposit, and banks of circulation. This division is not, however, a distinct one; for there is no bank of deposit that is not, at the same time, a bank of lation, and few or no banks of circulation that are not also banks of deposit. But erm banks of deposit is meant to designate those who keep the money of individuals circulate it only; while the term banks of circulation is applied to those who do thus confine their circulation, but issue notes of their own payable on demand. The k of England is the principal bank of circulation in the empire; but it, as well as orivate banks in England and Scotland that issue notes, is also a bank of deposit. private banking establishments in London do not issue notes, and there are many ar establishments in Lancashire, and other parts of the country.

.) *Utility of Banks. Private banking companies of London.* The establishment of s has contributed, in no ordinary degree, to security and facility to all sorts of mercial transactions. They afford safe and convenient places of deposit for the ey that would otherwise have to be kept, at a considerable risk, in private houses. y also prevent, in a great measure, the necessity of carrying money from place to on purpose of making payments, and enable them to be made in the most con-nt and least expensive manner. A merchant or tradesman in London, for example, employs a banker, keeps but very little money in his own hands, making all his con-able payments by drafts or checks on his banker; and he also sends the various s, bills, or drafts payable to himself in London, to his bankers before they become

By this means he saves the trouble and inconvenience of counting sums of money, avoids the losses he would otherwise be liable to, and would no doubt occa-lly incur, from receiving coins or notes not genuine. Perhaps, however, the great tage derived by the merchant or tradesman from the employment of a banker, sts in its relieving him from all trouble with respect to the presentation for ent of due bills and drafts. The moment these are transferred to the banker, are at his risk. And if he either neglect to present them when due, or to have properly noted in the event of their not being paid, he has to answer for the con-nces.

This circumstance alone must cause an immense saving of expense to a mercantile in the course of a year. Let us suppose that a merchant has only two bills due day. These bills may be payable in distant parts of the town, so that it may take a half a day to present them; and in large mercantile establishments it would take up hole time of one or two clerks to present the due bills and the drafts. The salary of clerks is, therefore, saved by keeping an account at a banker's: besides the saving pense, it is also reasonable to suppose that losses upon bills would sometimes occur mistakes, or oversights, from miscalculation as to the time the bill would become - from errors in marking it up — from forgetfulness to present it — or from pre-g it at the wrong place. In these cases the indorsers and drawees are exonerated; the acceptor do not pay the bill, the amount is lost. In a banking house such kes occur sometimes, though more rarely; but when they do occur, the loss falls the banker, and not upon his customer."—(*Gilbart's Practical Observations on ng.*)

s on other grounds particularly desirable for a merchant or tradesman to have an nt with a banking house. He can refer to his bankers as vouchers for his re-

spectability.   And in the event of his wishing to acquire any information with resp
to the circumstances, or credit, of any one with whom he is not acquainted, his bank
will render him all the assistance in their power.   In this respect they have gr
facilities, it being the common practice amongst bankers in London, and most oth
trading towns, to communicate information to each other as to the credit and solver
of their customers.

To provide for the public security, the statute 7 & 8 Geo. 4. c. 29. § 49. "for the punishment of e
bezzlement committed by agents intrusted with property," enacts, "That if any money, or security
the payment of money, shall be intrusted to any banker, merchant, broker, attorney, or other agent, w
any direction *in writing* to apply such money, or any part thereof, or the proceeds, or any part of the p
ceeds of such security, for any purpose specified in such direction, and he shall, in violation of good fai
and contrary to the purpose so specified, in any wise convert to his own use or benefit such money, see
rity, or proceeds, or any part thereof respectively, every such offender shall be guilty of a misdemean
and being convicted thereof, shall be liable, at the discretion of the court, to be transported beyond se
for any term not exceeding fourteen years, nor less than seven years, or to suffer such punishment by f
or imprisonment, or by both, as the court shall award ; and if any chattel or valuable security, or a
power of attorney for the sale or transfer of any share or interest in any public stock or fund, whether
this kingdom, or of Great Britain, or of Ireland, or of any foreign state, or in any fund of any body cor
rate, company or society, shall be intrusted to any banker merchant, broker, attorney, or other agent,
safe custody, or for any special purpose, *without any authority* to sell, negotiate, transfer, or pledge, a
he shall, in violation of good faith, and contrary to the object or purpose which such chattel or security,
power of attorney, shall have been intrusted to him, sell, negotiate, transfer, pledge, or in any manner c
vert to his own use or benefit such chattel or security, or the proceeds of the same, or any part thereof,
the share or interest in stock or fund to which such power of attorney shall relate, or any part there
every such offender shall be guilty of a misdemeanor, and being convicted thereof, shall be liable,
the discretion of the court, to any of the punishments which the court may award as hereinbefore
mentioned."
This act is not to affect trustees and mortgagees, nor bankers receiving money due upon securities, w
securities upon which they have a lien, claim, or demand, entitling them by law to sell, transfer, or oth
wise dispose of them, unless such sale, transfer, or other disposal, shall extend to a greater number
part of such securities or effects than shall be requisite for satisfying such lien, claim, &c.—§ 50.
Nothing in this act is to prevent, impeach, or lessen any remedy at law or in equity, which any pa
aggrieved by any such offence might or would have had, had it not been passed.   No banker, mercha
&c. shall be convicted as an offender against this act, in respect of any act done by him, if he shall at a
time previously to his being indicted for such offence have disclosed such act on oath, in consequence of a
compulsory process of any court of law or equity, in any action *bond fide* instituted by any party aggriev
or if he shall have disclosed the same in any examination or deposition before any commissioner of ba
rupt.—§ 52.

The Bank of England, and the private banking companies of London, as well
some of the English provincial banks, charge no commission on the payments ma
and received on account of those who deal with them.   But they allow no interest
the sums deposited in their hands ; and it is either stipulated or distinctly understo
that a person employing a banker should, besides furnishing him with sufficient fur
to pay his drafts, keep an average *balance* in the banker's hands, varying, of course,
cording to the amount of business done on his account ; that is, according to the numb
of his checks or drafts to be paid, and the number of drafts and bills to be received
him.   The bankers then calculate, as well as they can, the probable amount of ca
that it will be necessary for them to keep in their coffers to meet the ordinary demar
of their customers, and employ the balance either in discounting mercantile bills, in
purchase of government securities, or in some other sort of profitable adventure ; so t
their profits result, in the case of their not issuing notes, from the difference between
various expenses attendant on the management of their establishments, and the pro
derived from such part of the sums lodged in their hands as they can venture to emp
in an advantageous way.

The Directors of the Bank of England do not allow any individual to overdraw
account.   They answer drafts to the full extent of the funds deposited in their han
but they will not pay a draft if it exceed their amount.   Private bankers, at least in
country, are not generally so scrupulous ; most of them allow respectable individuals
whom they have confidence, to overdraw their accounts.   Those who are entitled to
this have what is called an *overdrawing account*, paying interest at the rate of 5 per ce
on whatever sums they overdraw.   The possession of this power of overdrawing is of
a great convenience to merchants, while it is rarely productive of loss to the banker.
money which is overdrawn is usually replaced within a short period ; sometimes, inde
in the course of a day or two.   It is not very easy to see why the directors of the Ba
of England should so strictly enforce the rule against overdrawing.   There can
little doubt that it prevents them from getting a considerable accession of valua
business.

The facility which banks afford to the public in the negotiation of bills of exchan
or in the making of payments at distant places, is very great.   Many of the bank
companies established in different districts have a direct intercourse with each oth
and they have all correspondents in London.   Hence an individual residing in
part of the country, who may wish to make a payment in any other part, however dist
may effect his object by applying to the bank nearest to him.   Thus, suppose A
Penzance has a payment to make to B of Inverness : to send the money by post wo

hazardous; and if there were fractional parts of a pound in the sum, it would hardly practicable to make use of the post: how then will A manage? He will pay the m to a banker in Penzance, and his debtor in Inverness will receive it from a banker ere. The transaction is extremely simple: the Penzance banker orders his corre-ondent in London to pay to the correspondent of the Inverness banker the sum in estion on account of B; and the Inverness banker, being advised in course of post of at has been done, pays B. A small commission charged by the Penzance banker, and e postages, constitute the whole expense. There is no risk whatever, and the whole air is transacted in the most commodious and cheapest manner.

By far the largest proportion both of the inland bills in circulation in the country, d also of the foreign bills drawn upon Great Britain, are made payable in London, e grand focus to which all the pecuniary transactions of the empire are ultimately ought to be adjusted. And in order still further to economise the use of money, the incipal bankers of the metropolis are in the habit of sending a clerk each day to the *aring house* in Lombard-street, who carries with him the various bills in the possession his house that are drawn upon other bankers; and having exchanged them for the ls in the possession of those others that are drawn upon his constituents, the balance the one side or the other is then paid in cash or Bank of England notes. By this ntrivance, the bankers of London are enabled to settle transactions to the extent several millions a day, by the employment of not more, at an average, than from 0,000*l.* to 300,000*l.* of cash or bank notes.

In consequence of these and other facilities afforded by the intervention of bankers r the settlement of pecuniary transactions, the money required to conduct the business an extensive country is reduced to a trifle only, compared with what it would other-se be. It is not, indeed, possible to form any very accurate estimate of the total ving that is thus effected; but, supposing that 50 or 60 millions of gold and silver d bank notes are at present required, notwithstanding all the devices that have been orted to for economising money, for the circulation of Great Britain, it may, one uld think, be fairly concluded, that 200 millions would, at the very least, have been uired to transact an equal extent of business but for those devices. If this statement nearly accurate, and there are good grounds for thinking that it is rather under than r rated, it strikingly exhibits the vast importance of banking in a public point of w. By its means 50 or 60 millions are rendered capable of performing the same ctions, and in an infinitely more commodious manner, that would otherwise have uired four times that sum; and supposing that 20 or 30 millions are employed by bankers as a capital in their establishments, no less than 120 or 130 millions will altogether disengaged, or cease to be employed as an instrument of circulation, and de available for employment in agriculture, manufactures, and commerce.

2.) *Substitution of Bank Notes for Coins. Means by which the value of Bank Notes y be sustained.* Not only, however, does the formation of banking establishments ble the business of a country to be conducted with a far less amount of money, but lso enables a large portion of that less amount to be fabricated of *the least valuable erials,* or of paper instead of gold. It would, however, alike exceed the limits and inconsistent with the objects of this article, to enter into lengthened details with respect he mode in which this substitution originally took place. It is sufficient to observe, : it naturally grew out of the progress of society. When governments became iciently powerful and intelligent to enforce the observance of contracts, individuals sessed of written promises from others that they would pay certain sums at specified ods, began to assign them to those to whom they were indebted; and when those by m such obligations are subscribed are persons of whose solvency no doubt can be rtained, they are readily accepted in payment of the debts due by one individual to her. But when the circulation of obligations or bills in this way has continued for hile, individuals begin to perceive that they may derive a profit by issuing them in a a form as to fit them for being readily used as a substitute for money in the nary transactions of life. Hence the origin of bank notes. An individual in whose lth and discretion the public have confidence being applied to for a loan, say of 5000*l.*, ts the applicant his bill or note payable on demand for that sum. Now, as this note es, in consequence of the confidence placed in the issuer, currently from hand to hand ash, it is quite as useful to the borrower as if he had obtained an equivalent amount of ; and supposing that the rate of interest is 5 per cent., it will yield, so long as it inues to circulate, a revenue of 250*l.* a year to the issuer. A banker who issues s, coins as it were his credit. He derives the same revenue from the loan of his ten promise to pay a certain sum, that he would derive from the loan of the sum ; and while he thus increases his own income, he at the same time contributes to ase the wealth of the society. Besides being incomparably cheaper, bank notes are incomparably more commodious than a metallic currency. A bank note for 1,000*l.* 00,000*l.* may be carried about with as much facility as a single sovereign. It is of

importance, too, to observe, that its loss or destruction, whether by fire, shipwreck, or otherwise, would be of no greater importance in a public point of view, than the loss or destruction of as much paper.   No doubt it might be a serious calamity to the holder; but to whatever extent it injured him, it would proportionally benefit the issuer, whereas the loss of coin is an injury to the holder without being of service to any one else ; it is in fact, so much abstracted from the wealth of the community.

Promissory notes issued by private individuals or associations circulate only because those who accept them have full confidence in the credit and solvency of the issuers, or because they feel assured that they will be paid when they become due.   If any circumstances transpired to excite suspicions as to their credit, it would be impossible for them to circulate any additional notes, and those that they had issued would be immediately returned for payment.   Such, however, is not the case with paper money properly so called, or with notes that are declared *legal tender*.   It is not necessary, in order to sustain the value of such notes, that they should be payable at all ; the only thing that is required for that purpose is, that they should be issued in *limited quantities*. Every country has a certain number of exchanges to make ; and whether these are effected by the employment of a given number of coins of a particular denomination, or by the employment of the same number of notes of the same denomination, is, in this respect, of no importance whatever.   Notes which have been made legal tender, and are not payable on demand, do not circulate because of any confidence placed in the capacity of the issuers to retire them ; neither do they circulate because they are of the same real value as the commodities for which they are exchanged ; but they circulate because, having been selected to perform the functions of *money*, they are, as such, readily received by all individuals in payment of their debts.   Notes of this description may be regarded as a sort of tickets or counters to be used in computing the value of property, and in transferring it from one individual to another.   And as they are no wise affected by fluctuations of credit, their value, it is obvious, must depend entirely on the quantity of them in circulation as compared with the payments to be made through their instrumentality, or the business they have to perform.   By reducing the supply of notes below the supply of coins that would circulate in their place were they withdrawn, their value is raised above the value of gold ; while, by increasing them to a greater extent, it is proportionally lowered.

Hence it appears, that were it possible to obtain any security other than immediate convertibility into the precious metals, that notes declared to be legal tender would not be issued in excess, but that their number afloat would be so adjusted as to preserve their value as compared with gold nearly uniform, the obligation to pay them on demand might be done away.   But it is needless to say that no such security can be obtained.   Wherever the power to issue paper, not immediately convertible, has been conceded to any set of persons, it has been abused, or, which is the same thing, such paper has uniformly been over-issued, or its value depreciated from excess.   It is now admitted on all hands to be indispensable, in order to prevent injurious fluctuations in the value of money, that all notes be made payable, at the pleasure of the holder, in an unvarying quantity of gold or silver.   This renders it impossible for the issuers of paper to depreciate it value below that of the precious metals.   They may, indeed, by over-issuing paper depress the value of the whole currency, gold as well as paper, in the country in which the over-issue is made ; but the moment that they do this, gold begins to be sent abroad and paper being returned upon the issuers for payment, they are, in order to prevent the exhaustion of their coffers, compelled to lessen their issues ; and thus, by raising the value of the currency, stop the drain for bullion.

It does, however, appear to us, that it is not only necessary, in order to prevent the over-issue of paper, to enact that all notes should be payable on demand, but that it is farther necessary, in order to insure compliance with this enactment, to prohibit any one from issuing notes until he has satisfied the government of his ability to pay them. The circumstances that excite public confidence in the issuers of paper are often of the most deceitful description ; and innumerable instances have occurred, of the population of extensive districts having suffered severely from the insolvency of bankers in whom they placed the utmost confidence.   In 1793, in 1814, 1815, and 1816, and again in 1825, a very large proportion of the country banks were destroyed, and produced by their fall an extent of ruin that has hardly been equalled in any other country.   And when such disasters have already happened, it is surely the bounden duty of government to hinder, by every means in its power, their recurrence.   It is no exaggeration to affirm, that we have sustained ten times more injury from the circulation of worthless paper, or paper issued by persons without the means of retiring it, than from the issue of spurious coin.   It is said, indeed, by those who are hostile to interference, that coin are legal tenders, whereas, notes being destitute of that privilege, those who suspect them are at liberty to refuse them : but, whatever notes may be in law, they are, in very many districts, *practically*, and *in fact*, legal tenders ; and could not be rejected without

sing the parties to much inconvenience. It should also be observed, that labourers, en, minors, and every sort of persons, however incapable of judging of the stability anking establishments, are dealers in money, and consequently liable to be imposed . This then, is clearly a case in which it is absolutely imperative upon govern- t to interfere, to protect the interests of those who cannot protect themselves, either ompelling all individuals applying for stamps for notes, to give security for their ent, or by making sure, in some other way, that they have the means of paying , and that the circulation of the notes will be a benefit and not an injury to the ic.

security of this sort has been exacted in the case of the Bank of England; and whole 14,686,000*l.* lent by the Bank to government, must be sacrificed before the ers of her notes can sustain the smallest loss. Her stability has, therefore, been said, by Dr. Smith, to be equal to that of the British government. The system aking securities having been found to answer so well in the case of the Bank of land, is a powerful argument in favour of its extension. Were securities taken the country banks, their ultimate failure, in the capacity of banks of issue, would ndered impossible; and a degree of solidity would be given to our money system, h it is idle to expect it can ever attain, so long as it continues on its present ng.

is exceedingly difficult to prevent the issue of forged notes. Various schemes been suggested for this purpose; and though it is hardly possible to suppose that *imitable* note will ever be produced, it is contended, that by judiciously combining ent sorts of engraving, forgery may be rendered so difficult, as to be but rarely pted. But however this may be, during the period from 1797 to 1819, when the of England issued one-pound notes, their forgery was carried on to a great t. And the desire to check this practice, and to lessen the frequency of capital shments, appears to have been amongst the most prominent circumstances which the return to specie payments in 1821, and the suppression of one-pound notes. Table No. I.)

cording to the existing law, all descriptions of notes are payable at the pleasure of older, in coin; but the policy of such a regulation is exceedingly questionable. ay, we think, be easily shown, that it would be a very great improvement were it ed, that country bank notes should be payable only in those of the Bank of England. ng as the latter are convertible at the pleasure of the holder into coin, such an gement would, it is obvious, effectually prevent any over-issue of country paper, same time that it would be free from many very serious disadvantages that attach present plan. The unjust liabilities imposed upon the Bank of England by the ng system, place her in a situation of great difficulty and hazard. They oblige provide a supply of coin and bullion, not for her own exigencies only, but for of *all* the country banks; and, what is harder still, they expose her to be deeply ed by any misconduct on the part of the latter, as well as by the distress in which nay accidentally be involved. In consequence, her free action is at all times in some e impeded; and her power to render assistance to the banking and mercantile sts in periods of discredit is materially diminished. The country banks keep but ll supply of coin in their coffers. They are all, however, holders, to a greater or xtent, of government securities; and whenever any circumstance occurs, to oc- a demand upon them for coin, they immediately sell or pledge the whole or a n of their stock, carry the notes to the Bank to be exchanged, and then carry the to the country. Hence, when any suspicions are entertained of the credit of the ry banks, or when a panic originates amongst the holders of their notes, as was se in 1793 and 1825, the whole of them retreat upon the Bank of England, and 800 conduits are opened, to draw off the specie of that establishment, which hus, it is evident, incur the risk of stoppage without having done any thing wrong. not the drain for gold from abroad, but the drain for gold from the country, that exhausted the Bank's coffers in 1825, and forced her to issue about a million of d two pound notes. The currency cannot possibly be in a sound healthy state, the Bank of England, and, through her, public credit, are placed in so perilous ation. And as nothing whatever is gained by the present system, as it is pro- e of great insecurity and expense to all parties, without having a single counter- g advantage to recommend it, it should certainly be put an end to, by making of England paper legal tender for the paper of the country banks.

anker who issues notes must keep beside him such a stock of cash and bullion, be sufficient to answer the demands of the public for their payment. If the of the cash and bullion in his coffers were equal to the value of his notes in cir- n, he would not, it is plain, make any profit; but if he be in good credit, a a fourth, or even a fifth part of this sum will probably be sufficient; and his consists of the excess of the interest derived from his notes in circulation, over

the interest of the sum he is obliged to keep dormant in his strong box, and the
penses of managing his establishment.

(3.) *Legal Description of Bank Notes.* Bank notes are merely a species of promiss
notes. They are subscribed either by the parties on whose account they are issued
by some one in their employment, whose signature is binding upon them. A Bank
England note for *5l.* is as follows: —

Bank of England.

N°   *I Promise to pay to Mr. Thomas Rippon, or Bearer,*   N°

on Demand, the Sum of Five *Pounds.*

1831. *March* 22, *London,* 22 *March,* 1831.

*For the Gov' and Comp*ʸ *of the*

£ Five.   BANK of ENGLAND.

A. B.

_____

No particular form of words is necessary in a bank note. The essential requisites a
that it should be for a definite sum (in England and Wales not less than *5l.* and
Scotland and Ireland not less than *1l.*), that it should be payable to bearer on dema
and that it should be properly stamped. Promissory notes, though issued by bankers
not payable to bearer on demand, do not come under the denomination of bank not
they are not, like the latter, taken as cash in all ordinary transactions; nor are they, l
them, assignable by mere delivery.

The circulation of notes for less than *5l.* was restrained by law (stat. 15 Geo. 3.
51.) from 1766 to 1797. In 1808 it was enacted by stat. 48 Geo. 3. c. 88., that
bank notes, promissory notes, or other negotiable instruments for less than 20s. sho
be absolutely void: a penalty of from 20s. to *5l.* at the discretion of the justices, bei
imposed on their issuers. It was enacted by the 7 Geo. 4. c. 6., that the issue of
bank notes or promissory notes for less than *5l.* by the Bank of England, or by a
licensed English bankers, and stamped on the 5th of February, 1826, or previou
(after which period such notes were not stamped), should terminate on the 5th of Ap
1829.

The stamp duties on bank notes or promissory notes payable on demand, are,

	£. s. d.		£. s. d.	£.	s.	d.
Not exceeding	1 1 0	....		0	0	5
Exceeding	1 1 0	and not exceeding	2 2 0	0	0	10
Exceeding	2 2 0	and not exceeding	5 5 0	0	1	3
Exceeding	5 5 0	and not exceeding	10 0 0	0	1	9
Exceeding	10 0 0	and not exceeding	20 0 0	0	2	0
Exceeding	20 0 0	and not exceeding	30 0 0	0	3	0
Exceeding	30 0 0	and not exceeding	50 0 0	0	5	0
Exceeding	50 0 0	and not exceeding 100 0 0		0	8	6

Which notes may be re-issued after payment, as often as shall be thought fit, provi
they be issued by a banker or person who has taken out a licence, renewable annua
and costing 30*l.*, to issue notes payable to bearer on demand. Any banker or o
person issuing such re-issuable notes, without being duly licensed, shall forfeit 100*l.*
every offence. (55 Geo. 3. c. 184. § 27.)

These conditions do not apply to the Bank of England, the stamp duties on the n
of that establishment being compounded for at the rate of 3,500*l.*, per million of its n
in circulation.

Notes or bills *not* payable to bearer on demand, are not re-issuable, under a pen
of 50*l.* For the stamp duties affecting them, see EXCHANGE.

By the 9 Geo. 4. c. 23., English bankers not in the city of London, or within th
miles thereof, are authorised to issue promissory notes, and to draw and issue bills
exchange, on unstamped paper, for any sum of *5l.* or upwards, expressed to be pay
to the bearer on demand, or to order at any period not exceeding seven days after si
(*bills* may also be drawn at any period not exceeding twenty-one days after date,) u
obtaining licences, costing 30*l.*, to that effect, provided such bills of exchange be dr
upon bankers in London, Westminster, or Southwark; or provided such bills be dr
by any banker or bankers at the place which he or they shall be licensed to is
unstamped notes and bills, upon himself or themselves, or his or their copartner
copartners, payable at any other place where such banker or bankers shall be licer

issue such notes and bills. Bankers having such licences, are to give security by
nd, that they will keep a true account of all promissory notes and bills so issued, and
count for the duties on them at the rate of 3s. 6d. for every 100l., and also for the
actional parts of 100l. of the average value of such notes and bills in circulation. Per-
ns post-dating unstamped notes or bills shall, for every such offence, forfeit 100l.

(4.) *Legal Effect of the Payment of Bank Notes.*—Notes of the Bank of England are
t, like bills of exchange, mere securities, or documents of debt, but are treated as
oney or cash in the ordinary course or transactions of business. The receipts given upon
eir payment are always given as for money. They are not, however, legal tender, and
ay be objected to when offered in payment; but when once accepted, they are held to
equivalent to a money payment, and the transaction is closed. All notes payable to
arer are assignable by delivery. The holder of a bank note is *primâ facie* entitled to
ompt payment of it, and cannot be affected by the previous fraud of any former holder
obtaining it, unless evidence be given to show that he was privy to such fraud. Such
vity may, however, be inferred from the circumstances of the case. To use the words
Lord Tenterden, " If a person take a bill, note, or any other kind of security, under
cumstances which *ought to excite suspicion* in the mind of any reasonable man
quainted with the ordinary affairs of life, and which ought to put him on his guard to
ke the necessary enquiries, and he do not, then he loses the right of maintaining pos-
sion of the instrument against the lawful owner." (*Guildhall*, 25th October, 1826.)
Country bank notes, like those of the Bank of England, are usually received as cash.
ut though taken as such, if they be presented *in due time* and not paid, they do not
ount to a payment, and the deliverer of the notes is still liable to the holder. It is
c easy to determine what is a due or reasonable time, inasmuch as it must depend in
reat measure on the circumstances of each particular case. On the whole, the safest
e seems to be to present all notes or drafts payable on demand, if received in the place
ere they are payable, on the day on which they are received, or as soon after as possible.
aen they have to be transmitted by post for payment, no unnecessary delay should be
owed to intervene.—(*Chitty's Commercial Law*, vol. iii. p. 590., and the art. " Check.")

II. BANK OF ENGLAND (ACCOUNT OF).

1.) *Historical Sketch of the Bank.*—This great establishment, which has long been the
ncipal bank of deposit and circulation, not in this country only, but in Europe, was
nded in 1694. Its principal projector was Mr. William Paterson, an enterprising
l intelligent Scotch gentleman, who was afterwards engaged in the ill-fated colony at
rien. Government being at the time much distressed for want of money, partly from
defects and abuses in the system of taxation, and partly from the difficulty of bor-
ving, because of the supposed instability of the revolutionary establishment, the Bank
w out of a loan of 1,200,000l. for the public service. The subscribers, besides
eiving *eight* per cent. on the sum advanced as interest, and 4,000l. a year as the
oense of management, in all 100,000l. a year, were incorporated into a society deno-
aated the *Governor and Company of the Bank of England.* The charter is dated the
h of July, 1694. It declares, amongst other things, that they shall " be capable in
» to purchase, enjoy, and retain to them and their successors, any manors, lands, rents,
ements, and possessions whatsoever; and to purchase and acquire all sorts of goods
. chattels whatsoever, wherein they are not restrained by act of parliament; and also
rant, demise, and dispose of the same.

That the management and government of the corporation be committed to the
ernor, deputy governor, and twenty-four directors, who shall be elected between the
h day of March and 25th day of April, each year, from among the members of the
apany duly qualified.

That no dividend shall at any time be made by the said governor and company,
e only out of the interest, profit, or produce arising by or out of the said capital
k or fund, or by such dealing as is allowed by act of parliament.

They must be natural born subjects of England, or naturalised subjects; they
l have in their own name and for their own use, severally, viz. — the governor, at
t 4,000l., the deputy governor 3,000l., and each director 2,000l. of the capital stock
he said corporation.

That thirteen or more of the said governors and directors (of which the governor
leputy governor must be always one) shall constitute a court of directors, for the
aagement of the affairs of the company, and for the appointment of all agents and
ants which may be necessary, paying them such salaries as they may consider
onable.

Every elector must have, in his own name and for his own use, 500l. or more,
tal stock, and can only give one vote. He must, if required by any member present,
the oath of stock, or the declaration of stock, in case he be one of the people called
kers.

F

" Four general courts to be held in every year; in the months of September, December, April, and July. A general court may be summoned at any time, upon the requisition of nine proprietors, duly qualified as electors.

" The majority of electors in general courts have the power to make and constitute by-laws and ordinances for the government of the corporation, provided that such by laws and ordinances be not repugnant to the laws of the kingdom, and be confirmed and approved, according to the statutes in such case made and provided."

The corporation is prohibited from engaging in any sort of commercial undertaking other than dealing in bills of exchange, and in gold and silver. It is authorised to advance money upon the security of goods or merchandise pledged to it; and to sell, by public auction, such goods as are not redeemed within a specified time.

It was also enacted, in the same year in which the Bank was established, by statute 6 William and Mary, cap. 20, that the Bank " shall not deal in any goods, wares or merchandize (except bullion), or purchase any lands or revenues belonging to the crown, or advance or lend to their majesties, their heirs or successors, any sum or sum of money by way of loan or anticipation, or any part or parts, branch or branches, fund or funds of the revenue, now granted or belonging, or hereafter to be granted to their majesties, their heirs and successors, other than such fund or funds, part or parts, branch or branches of the said revenue only, on which a credit of loan is, or shall be, granted by parliament." And in 1697 it was enacted, that the " common capital and principal stock, and also the real fund of the governor and company, or any profit or produce to be made thereof, or arising thereby, shall be exempted from any rates, taxes, assessments, or impositions whatsoever, during the continuance of the Bank; and that all the profit, benefit, and advantage, from time to time arising out of the management of the said corporation, shall be applied to the uses of all the members of the said corporation of the Governor and Company of the Bank of England, rateably and in proportion to each member's part, share, and interest in the common capital and principal stock of the said governor and company hereby established."

It was further enacted, in 1697, that the forgery of the company's seal, or of any sealed bill or bank note, should be felony without benefit of clergy, and that the making of any alteration or erasure in any bill or note, should also be felony.

In 1696, during the great recoinage, the Bank was involved in considerable difficulties, and was even compelled to suspend payment of her notes, which were at a heavy discount. Owing, however, to the judicious conduct of the directors, and the assistance of government, the Bank got over the crisis. But it was at the same time judged expedient, in order to place her in a situation the better to withstand any adverse circumstances that might afterwards occur, to increase her capital from 1,200,000l. to 2,201,171l. In 1708, the directors undertook to pay off and cancel one million and a half of exchequer bills they had circulated two years before, at 4½ per cent., with the interest on them amounting in all to 1,775,028l.; which increased the permanent debt due by the public to the Bank, including 400,000l. then advanced in consideration of the renewal of the charter, to 3,375,028l, for which they were allowed 6 per cent. The Bank capital was then also doubled, or increased to 4,402,343l. But the year 1708 is chiefly memorable in the history of the Bank, for the act that was then passed, which declared, that during the continuance of the corporation of the Bank of England, " it should not be lawful for any body politic, erected or to be erected, other than the said Governor and Company of the Bank of England, or for other persons whatsoever, united or to be united in covenant or partnerships, exceeding the number of six persons, in that part of Great Britain called England, to borrow, owe, or take up any sum or sums of money on their bills or notes payable on demand, or in any less time than six months from the borrowing thereof." — This proviso, which has had so powerful an operation on banking in England, is said to have been elicited by the Mine-adventure-Company having commenced banking business and begun to issue notes.

The charter of the Bank of England, when first granted, was to continue for eleven years certain, or till a year's notice after the 1st of August, 1705. The charter was further prolonged in 1697. In 1708, the Bank having advanced 400,000l. for the public service, without interest, the exclusive privileges of the corporation were prolonged till 1733. And in consequence of various advances made at different times, the exclusive privileges of the Bank have been continued by successive renewals, to year's notice, after the 1st of August, 1833. The last renewal was made in 1800, by the act 40 Geo. 3. cap. 28., in consideration of an advance by the Bank to the public of *three* millions for six years without interest. The following is an account of the various *permanent* advances made by the Bank to government, of the occasions on which they were made, and of the increase in the capital of the Bank.

neral Statement of the Affairs of the Bank of England, from its Establishment in 1694, to the present Time.

		Advanced to the Public.			Bank Capital on which the Stockholders divide.		
		£.	s.	d.	£.	s.	d.
4. 5 & 6 & M. c. 20.	Amount of original subscription lent to the government at 8 per cent. interest, and 4,000l. for management. Charter to continue to 1st August, 1705.	1,200,000	0	0	1,200,000	0	0
7. 8 & 9 3. c. 20.	Exchequer tallies and orders for payment, having, in 1696, been at a discount of 40, 50, and 60 per cent. and Bank notes at a discount of 20 per cent., the Bank was empowered to receive subscriptions for the enlargement of their stock, ⅘ in tallies and orders, the remaining ⅕ in bank notes. The increase of stock was, in consequence	....			1,001,171	10	0
	* Interest at the rate of 8 per cent. was received on amount of tallies and orders, brought in from 24th June, 1697. Charter extended to 1st August 1710.				2,201,171	10	0
708. ne, c. 7.	Advanced, by the Bank, part of the grants for this year without interest, after the 1st August, 1711; thus reducing the interest on the whole sum lent to government, per cent.	400,000	0	0			
	* Charter extended to 1st August, 1732.	1,600,000	0	0			
	The Bank had, by 5 Anne, cap. 13., undertaken to circulate exchequer bills for 0,000l.; and they now agreed to cancel same, making, with interest due upon	1,775,027	17	10½			
	* They received 6 per cent. interest on from Michaelmas, 1710.	3,375,027	17	10½			
	y authority conveyed to them by the same they took in subscriptions for doubling capital	....			2,201,171	10	0
Feb.	A call of 15 per cent. made stock	....			4,402,343 656,204	0 1	0 9
Dec.	A call of 10 per cent. made stock				5,058,547 501,448	1 12	9 11
3. 12 , c. 11.	* Had charter renewed to 1st August, 1742, then, as before, having 12 months' notice, and re-payment of sums lent.				5,559,995	14	8
717.	Cancelled exchequer bills, and received interest at 5 per cent. on the amount	2,000,000	0	0			
	* Reduced interest on 1,775,027l. 17s. from 6 to 5 per cent., after Midsummer,	5,375,027	17	10½			
722. . c. 21.	Purchased of South Sea Company of their stock	4,000,000	0	0			
	* Interest on this till Midsummer, 1727, cent.; after that, 4 per cent.	9,375,027	17	10½	5,559,995	14	8

	Advanced to the Public.			Bank Capital on which the Stockholders divide	
	£.	s.	d.	£.	s.
Brought forward - -	9,375,027	17	10½	5,559,995	14
June 24. Increased their capital to enable them to make said purchase	....			3,400,000	0
1727. 1 G. 2. c. 8. Had repaid to them out of the sinking fund, part of the 1,775,027l. 17s. 10½d.	1,000,000	0	0	8,959,995	14
⁎ Reduced the interest on the 2,000,000l. from 5 to 4 per cent.	8,375,027	17	10½		
1728. Midsummer. Advanced on duties on coal and culm, at 4 per cent. in pursuance of above act	1,750,000	0	0		
2 G. 2. c. 2. Received remainder of above sum of 1,775,027l. 17s. 10½d. from sinking fund	10,125,027 17 10½ 775,027	17	10½		
Received out of the sinking fund part of the 2,000,000l. lent to government in 1717	9,350,000 0 0 500,000	0	0		
Advanced on lottery, at 4 per cent. interest, from Midsummer, 1729, per same act	8,850,000 0 0 1,250,000	0	0		
1738. 11 G.2. c.27. Received out of the sinking fund, a farther part of the 2,000,000l.	10,100,000 0 0 1,000,000	0	0		
1742. 15 G.2.c.13. Advanced without farther interest, thus making the interest which was before 6 per cent. on 1,600,000l., 3 per cent. on 3,200,000l.	9,100,000 0 0 1,600,000	0	0		
⁎ Charter renewed to 1st August, 1764.	10,700,000	0	0		
In consequence of above advance, they increased their capital stock by subscriptions ...	....			840,004	5
1746. 19 G.2. c. 6. Agreed to cancel exchequer bills issued on licences for retailing spirituous liquors, on being allowed 4 per cent. interest	986,800	0	0	9,800,000	0
A call of 10 per cent. made stock	....			980,000	0
1749. 23 G.2. c. 6. Agreed to a proposition made by parliament, to receive 4 per cent. on 8,486,800l. to Christmas, 1750; then 3½ per cent. to Christmas, 1757; and after that 3 per cent. on the whole.	11,686,800	0	0	10,780,000	0
⁎ Charter renewed to 1st Aug. 1786, for which they advanced 1,000,000l. 1764. 4 G.3. c.25. on exchequer bills, till 1766, and paid into the exchequer 110,000l.					
1781. 21 G.3. c.60. Added to capital stock 8 per cent.	....			862,400	0
⁎ Charter renewed to 1st August, 1812, for which they advanced 2,000,000l. for 3 years, at 3 per cent.	11,686,800	0	0	11,642,400	0

	Advanced to the Public.			Bank Capital on which the Stockholders divide		
	£.	s.	d.	£.	s.	d.
Brought forward - -	11,686,800	0	0	11,642,400	0	0
Charter renewed to 1st August, 1800.						
1833, for which they advanced 0 G.3. c.28. 3,000,000l. without interest for 6 years, which was continued, ursuant to the recommendation of the com- mittee of 1807, till 6 months after a definitive eaty of peace.						
1816. Advanced to government, at 6 G.3. c.96. 3 per cent.	3,000,000	0	0			
Were allowed to add 25 per cent. from their accumulated profits, to their capital stock	....			2,910,600	0	0
	14,686,800	0	0	14,553,000	0	0

The Bank of England has been frequently affected by panics amongst the holders of notes. In 1745, the alarm occasioned by the advance of the Highlanders under the etender as far as Derby, led to a run upon the Bank ; and in order to gain time to ncert measures for averting the run, the directors adopted the device of paying in llings and sixpences ! But they derived a more effectual relief from the retreat of Highlanders ; and from a resolution agreed to at a meeting of the principal mer- ants and traders of the city, and very numerously signed, declaring the willingness of subscribers to receive bank notes in payment óf any sum that might be due to them, l pledging themselves to use their utmost endeavours to make all their payments in same medium.

During the tremendous riots in June, 1780, the Bank incurred considerable danger. ad the mob attacked the establishment at the commencement of the riots, the con- quences might have proved fatal, Luckily, however, they delayed their attack till e had been afforded for providing a force sufficient to ensure its safety. Since that iod a considerable military force is nightly placed in the interior of the Bank, as a tection in any emergency that may occur.

In the latter part of 1792 and beginning of 1793, there was, in consequence of a pre- us over-issue on their part, a general run on most of the private banks ; and about *one* *d* of these establishments were forced to stop payment. This led to a considerable mand for coin from the Bank.

The year 1797 is, however, the most important epoch in the recent history of the Bank. ing partly to events connected with the war in which we were then engaged — to loans the emperor of Germany — to bills drawn on the treasury at home by the British nts abroad — and partly, and chiefly, perhaps, to the advances most unwillingly made the Bank to government, which prevented the directors from having a sufficient con- over their issues, — the exchanges became unfavourable in 1795, and in that and the owing year large sums in specie were drawn from the Bank.* In the latter end of 6 and beginning of 1797, considerable apprehensions were entertained of invasion, rumours were propagated of descents having been actually made on the coast. In sequence of the fears that were thus excited, runs were made on the provincial

So early as December, 1794, the court of directors represented to government their uneasiness on unt of the magnitude of the debt due by the government to the Bank, and anxiously requested a re- nent of at least a considerable part of what had been advanced. In January, 1795, they resolved to t their advances upon treasury bills to 500,000l. ; and at the same time they informed Mr. Pitt that it their wish that he would adjust his measures for the year *in such a manner as not to depend on any* her assistance from them. On the 11th of February, 1796, they resolved, " That it is the opinion of court, founded upon the experience of the late Imperial loan, that if any further loan or advance of ey to the emperor, or to any of the foreign states, should in the present state of affairs take place, it in all probability, prove fatal to the Bank of England. The court of directors do, therefore, most stly deprecate the adoption of any such measure, and they solemnly protest against any responsibility he calamitous consequences that may follow thereupon." But notwithstanding these, and many other ar remonstrances, fresh advances of money we remade to our foreign allies, and fresh demands uponthe ; the directors reluctantly abandoning their own better judgment to what they truly termed the essing solicitations " of the chancellor of the exchequer, and their desire to avert " the probable dis- which a refusal (on their part) might occasion, in the then alarming situation of public affairs." notwithstanding the difficulties of the Bank were greatly aggravated by that conduct on the part of nment against which the directors had so strongly protested, she could hardly, in any state of her s, have got safely over the crisis of 1797. The run upon the Bank that then took place, was occa- d by alarms of invasion ; and it is clear, as remarked in the text, that while they continued, no paper ediately convertible into gold could remain in circulation.

banks in different parts of the country; and some of them having failed, the panic became general, and extended itself to London. Demands for cash poured in upon the Bank from all quarters; and on Saturday the 25th February, 1797, she had only 1,272,000l. of cash and bullion in her coffers, with every prospect of a violent run taking place on the following Monday. In this emergency an order in council was issued on Sunday the 26th, prohibiting the directors from paying their notes in cash until the sense of parliament had been taken on the subject. And after parliament met, and the measure had been much discussed, it was agreed to continue the restriction till six months after the signature of a definitive treaty of peace.

As soon as the order in council prohibiting payments in cash appeared, a meeting of the principal bankers, merchants, traders, &c. of the metropolis, was held at the Mansion-house, when a resolution was agreed to, and very numerously signed, pledging, as had been done in 1745, those present to accept, and to use every means in their power to cause bank notes to be accepted as cash in all transactions. This resolution tended to allay the apprehensions that the restriction had excited.

Parliament being sitting at the time, a committee was immediately appointed to examine the affairs of the Bank; and their report put to rest whatever doubts might have been entertained with respect to the solvency of the establishment, by showing that at the moment when the order in council appeared, the Bank was possessed of property to the amount of 15,513,690l., after all claims upon it had been deducted.

Much difference of opinion has existed with respect to the policy of the restriction in 1797; but, considering the peculiar circumstances under which it took place, its expediency seems abundantly obvious. The run did not originate in any over-issue of bank paper; but grew entirely out of political causes. So long as the alarms of invasion continued, it was clear that no bank paper immediately convertible into gold would remain in circulation. And as the Bank, though possessed of ample funds, was without the means of instantly retiring her notes, she might, but for the interference of government, have been obliged to stop payment; an event which, had it occurred, must have produced consequences in the last degree fatal to the public interests.

It had been generally supposed, previously to the passing of the Restriction Act, that bank notes would not circulate unless they were immediately convertible into cash; but the event showed, conformably to principles that have since been fully explained, that this was not really the case. Though the notes of the Bank of England were not at the passing of the Restriction Act, publicly declared to be legal tender, they were rendered so in practice, being received as cash in all transactions on account of government, and of the vast majority of individuals. For the first three years of the restriction, their issues were so moderate, that they not only kept on a par with gold, but actually bore a small premium. In the latter part of 1800, however, their quantity was so much increased that they fell to a discount of about 8 per cent. as compared with gold, but they soon after rose nearly to par; and it was not until 1808 that the decline of their value excited any considerable attention. Early in 1810, they were at a discount of about 13½ per cent.; and this extraordinary fall having attracted the attention of the legislature, the House of Commons appointed a committee to enquire into the circumstances by which it had been occasioned. The committee examined several witnesses and in their report, which was drawn up with considerable ability, they justly ascribe the fall to the over-issue of bank paper, and recommended that the Bank should be obliged to resume cash payments within two years. This recommendation was not however, acted upon; and the value of bank paper continued to decline, as compared with gold, till 1814.

At the period when the restriction on cash payments took place in 1797, it is supposed that there were about 280 country banks in existence; but so rapidly were these establishments multiplied, that they amounted to above 700 in 1813. The price of corn, influenced partly by the depreciation of the currency, and the facility with which discounts were obtained, but far more by deficient harvests, and the unprecedented difficulties which the war threw in the way of importation, had risen to an extraordinary height during the five years ending with 1813. But the harvest of that year being unusually productive, and the intercourse with the Continent being then also renewed, prices, influenced by both circumstances, sustained a very heavy fall in the latter part of 1813, and the beginning of 1814. And this fall having proved ruinous to a considerable number of farmers, and produced a general want of confidence, such a destruction of provincial paper took place as has rarely been paralleled. In 1814, 1815, and 1816 no fewer than 240 country banks stopped payment; and *ninety-two* commissions of bankruptcy were issued against these establishments, being at the rate of *one* commission against every *seven and a half* of the total number of banks existing in 1813.

The great reduction that had been thus suddenly and violently brought about in the quantity of country bank paper, by extending the field for the circulation of Bank of England paper, raised its value in 1817 nearly to a par with gold. The return to cash

ments being thus facilitated, it was fixed, in 1819, by the act 59 Geo. 3. c. 78., monly called Mr. Peel's Act, that they should take place in 1823. But to prevent future over-issue, and at the same time to render the measure as little burdensome ossible, it was enacted, in pursuance of a plan suggested by the late Mr. Ricardo, the Bank should be obliged, during the interval from the passing of the act till the rn to specie payments, to pay her notes, if required, in bars of standard bullion of less than sixty ounces' weight. This plan was not, however, acted upon during the od allowed by law ; for, a large amount of gold having been accumulated at the k, the directors preferred recommencing specie payments on the 1st of May, 1821. See Table II. for an account of the price of bullion, the depreciation of paper, &c. ■ 1800 to 1821.)

great diversity of opinion has been entertained with respect to the policy of the rn to the old standard, in 1819. By one party it has been represented as a wise and ic measure: they contend that Mr. Peel's Act not only put an end to those fluctu-us in the value of money, which had previously been productive of great mischief, gave effect to the solemn engagements into which the public had entered with the nal creditor, but that it did this without adding anything material to the national ens. But another, and, perhaps, a more numerous party, take a totally different of this measure: they contend that the public was not really bound to return to payments at the old standard at the termination of the war ; that the return has greatly enhanced the value of the currency ; and that this enhancement, by adding ortionally to the fixed burdens, laid on the industrious classes, has been most inju-s to their interests. It will, however, be found in this, as in most cases of the sort, the statements of both parties are exaggerated ; and that if, on the one hand, the ure has not been so advantageous as its apologists represent, neither, on the other, ■t been nearly so injurious as its enemies would have us to believe.

discussing this question, it is material to observe that the value of paper, which been in 1815 and 1816 about 16¾ per cent. below that of gold, rose in 1817 and , from the causes already mentioned, without any interference whatever on the part vernment, to within little more than 2⅓ per cent. of the value of gold ; and that in 1819 epreciation only amounted to 4½ per cent. (See Table II.) It is, therefore, quite rous to ascribe to the act of 1819, as is often done, the whole rise that has taken in the value of the currency since the peace, seeing that the currency had been for years previously to its enactment from 12½ to 14½ per cent. above its value in 1815, rom 21 to 23 per cent. above its value in 1814! The main object which the pro-rs of the act of 1819 had in view, was to sustain the value of the currency at the to which it had recovered itself without legislative interference. This, however, ■ not be done without recurring to specie payments ; and the difference of 4½ per that obtained in 1819 between the value of gold and paper, was not deemed suffi-y considerable to warrant a departure from the old standard, and from the acts ∶ing to restore it.

■t it is alleged, that those who suppose that the act of 1819 added only 4½ per cent. ∶ value of the currency, mistake altogether the effect of the measure. It is ad-d, indeed that paper was then only 4½ per cent. less valuable than gold ; but by ∶ing to specie payments, we made an unexpected purchase of thirty millions of gold ; ■ is affirmed, that this novel and large demand, concurring simultaneously with the ∶ction of paper in several of the continental states, and with a falling off in the ∶y of bullion from the mines, had the effect of adding very greatly to the value of ∶tself, and consequently to that of the currency. It is very difficult, or rather, per-∶ impossible, to determine the precise degree of credit that ought to be attached to ∶atement ; but while we incline to think that it is well founded to a certain extent, ∶ no grounds for believing that it is so to anything like the extent that has been ∶. The gold imported into Great Britain, to enable the Bank to resume specie ∶nts, was not taken from any particular country or district, but was drawn from ∶arket of the world ; and considering the vast extent of the supply whence it was d, it is against all reason to suppose that its value could be materially influenced ∶r purchases. We doubt, too, whether the contraction of the paper currency of ∶of the continental states, and the substitution of specie in its stead, was not more ∶balanced by the cessation of the demand for specie for the military chests of the ∶nt armies, by the stoppage of the practice of hoarding, and the greater security ∶uent to the return of peace. And with respect to the falling off in the supplies ∶he mines, it is not a circumstance, supposing it to have had a considerable influ-∶that parliament could take into account. It could neither determine the extent to bullion had been raised, nor at what point the rise would stop, nor how soon it ∶ again begin to decline. The diminution in the supply of bullion had then conti-∶or too short a period, and its influence on the value of gold was much too uncertain, ∶e it a ground for interfering in any degree with the standard.

The decline in the price of most articles that has taken place since the peace, has be
often referred to, as a conclusive proof of the great enhancement in the value of bulli
But the inference is by no means so certain as has been represented.   The prices
commodities are as much affected by changes in the cost of their production, as
changes in the quantity of money afloat.   Now, there is hardly one of the great artic
of commerce, the cost of which has not been considerably reduced, or wh
has not been supplied from new sources, within the last few years.   The growth
corn, for example, has been vastly extended in France, Prussia, and genera
throughout the Continent, by the splitting of large estates, and the complete sv
version of the feudal system; and the reduction of its price in this country is,
least, as much owing to the extraordinary increase of imports from Ireland, as
any other cause.   The fall in the price of wool is most satisfactorily accounted for
the introduction and rapid multiplication of Merino sheep in Germany, where they se
to succeed even better than in Spain; and by the growing imports from N
Holland and elsewhere.   And a very large portion, if not the whole, of t
fall in the price of colonial products, is admitted, on all hands, to be owing to the c
struction of the monopoly system, and the vast extension of cultivation in Cuba, Bra
Louisiana, Demerara, &c.   Although, therefore, we do not deny that the falling off
the supply of bullion from the mines must have had some influence on prices,
hold it to be the greatest imaginable error to ascribe to it the entire fall that has tak
place since the peace.   Were its effect rated at 10 per cent. we believe it would be co
siderably overstated.

On the whole, therefore, we are disposed to approve of the conduct of those w
framed the act of 1819.   That it added to the burdens of the industrious classes, a
has been in so far hostile to the public interests, it seems impossible to doubt; but it b
not done this in any thing like the degree which its enemies represent.   The peri
too, when it was passed, is now so distant, that the existing engagements amongst in
viduals have almost all been formed with reference to the altered value of the currenc
so that whatever injury it may have occasioned in the first instance, must be nearly gc
by.   To modify or change the standard at this late period, would not be to repair inj
tice, but to commit it afresh.   At the end of the war, the circumstances were consid
ably different.   The standard had been really abandoned for the previous eighteen yea
and, perhaps, we may now say, that it would have been better, all things considered, l
the mint price of bullion been raised, in 1815, to the market price.   But having s
mounted all the difficulties attendant upon the restoration of the old standard, a
maintained it for a dozen years, it would be in the last degree impolitic to subject it
new alterations.   Should the country become, at any future period, unable to make gc
its engagements, it will better consult its honour and its interest, by fairly compoun
ing with its creditors, than by endeavouring to slip from its engagements by resorting
the dishonest expedient of enfeebling the standard.

The price of corn, which had been very much depressed in 1821 and 1822, rall
in 1823; and this circumstance contributed, along with others peculiar to that peri
to promote an extraordinary rage for speculation.   The issues of the country banks be
in consequence far too much extended, the currency became redundant in 1824; and
exchanges having been depressed, a drain for gold began to operate upon the Bank
England.   The Bank does not appear to have taken any steps for upwards of a twel
month, by contracting her issues, to check the drain; but being at length compelled
order to prevent the exhaustion of her coffers, to lessen her paper, a violent revulsion tc
place.   Such of the country banks — and they were a numerous class — as had b
originally established without sufficient capital, and such as had conducted their b
ness upon erroneous principles, began to give way the moment they experienced an
creased difficulty of obtaining pecuniary accommodations in London.   The alarm o
excited, soon became general; and confidence and credit were, for a while, almc
wholly suspended.   In the short space of six weeks, above seventy banking establi
ments were destroyed, notwithstanding the very large advances made to them by
Bank of England; and the run upon the Bank, for cash to supply the exigencies of
country banks, was so heavy, that she was well nigh drained of all the coin in her c
fers, and obliged, as already remarked, to issue about a million of 1l. and 2l. notes

In order to guard against a recurrence of the wide-spread mischief and ruin, produ
by this and the previous bankruptcies of the country banks, it was resolved, in 1826, v
consent of the Bank of England, to make a change in the law of 1708, limiting
number of partners in banking establishments to six only.   And it was accordingly
acted, that henceforth any number of partners might form themselves into associati
to carry on the business of banking, any where not within *sixty-five miles* of Lonc
The directors of the Bank of England came, at the same time, to the resolution of
tablishing branches in some of the principal towns; and, at this moment, branch ba

e established in Gloucester, Manchester, Birmingham, Leeds, Liverpool, Bristol,
xeter, Newcastle-upon-Tyne, Hull, Norwich, &c.*
The branch-banks cannot fail of being highly useful: but we believe that the benefit
pected to result from the formation of joint stock banks will not be nearly so great
has been anticipated. Even were they organised in all large towns, which there is
tt little reason to expect, seeing that every individual taking a share in one of them is
und, to the whole extent of his fortune, for their engagements, the lesser towns and
untry districts would be left to deal with inferior banks. But, supposing them to be
iversally established, so long as every one is allowed to issue notes without any sort
check or control, a thousand devices may be fallen upon to ensure a certain cir-
lation to those that are most worthless. At best, this measure is but a feeble palliative
inveterate disorders. It is quite illusory to expect to make any real improvement
on the system of country banking in England, by the mere introduction of a plan for
'owing banking establishments with large capitals to be set on foot. There have always
en, and are at this moment, a great number of such establishments in England.
hat is really wanted, is the adoption of a system, that will exclude the possibility of
tes being discredited, by *preventing* all individuals or associations from issuing such as
ve not been previously guaranteed.
Besides attempting to lessen the frequency of bankruptcy among the country banks,
repealing the law limiting the number of partners, it was further resolved, in 1826,
prohibit the future issue of 1*l.* notes. The policy and effects of this measure have
ven rise to much dispute. It seems clear, that it will go far to shut up one of
e most convenient channels by which the inferior class of country bankers contrived
get their notes into circulation, and will, in so far, do good. But there are many
er channels that are still open to them; and to imagine that this measure will place
 provincial currency on that solid basis on which it ought to be placed, is quite
ionary. There were no notes under 5*l.* in circulation in 1792; and yet fully *one*
rd of the country banks then in existence became bankrupt! The truth is, as already
ted, that it is not possible to guard against loss and fraud, from the proceedings of
 country bankers, otherwise than by compelling them to give security for their
ues; and, as security may as easily be given for 1*l.* notes as for those of 5*l.*, the sup-
ssion of the former does not appear to have been at all essential. No doubt can,
vever, be entertained, that the representations as to the extreme injury occasioned by
 withdrawal of the 1*l.* notes have been very greatly exaggerated; — though it is at
same time obvious, that the means of the bankers to make advances, as well as the
fit derived from making them, must both have been diminished by the suppression of
small notes; and it would be foolish to deny that this circumstance must have
asioned some loss and inconvenience to many individuals.
These remarks are meant to apply only to the case of the country banks. The ex-
ordinary extent to which the forgery of the 1*l.* notes of the Bank of England was
ried, affords, perhaps, a sufficient vindication of the policy of their suppression. But
comparatively limited circulation of the country banks, and, perhaps we may add,
greater attention paid to the manner in which their notes were engraved, hindered
r forgery from becoming injuriously prevalent.
2.) *Bank of England in its Connexion with Government and the Public.* — The Bank
England conducts the whole banking business of the British government. " It acts
only," says Dr. Smith, " as an ordinary bank, but as a great engine of state. It
eives and pays the greater part of the annuities, which are due to the creditors of the
lic; it circulates exchequer bills; and it advances to government the annual
unt of the land and malt taxes, which are frequently not paid till some years there-
r."
The greater part of the paper of the Bank has generally, indeed, been issued in the
 of advances or loans to government, upon security of certain branches of the
nue, and in the purchase of exchequer bills and bullion; but her issues through the
ium of discounts to individuals have, notwithstanding, been considerable. Among
papers laid by the Bank before parliament in 1797, was a scale of the cash and
ion in her coffers during every quarter of a year, for several years previously to the
riction. In this scale the real numbers were not given; and it was some time before
as ascertained what was the actual value of the numbers of which the proportional
es only were expressed. At length, however, it was discovered that in the scale of
 and bullion, the number 660 represented four millions; and that in the scale of
 discounted, the unit was two millions. The key being thus found, the real amounts
ash and bullion in the possession of the Bank, and of bills discounted, were easily
puted, and were, during the undermentioned periods, as follows: —

ee Table III., for an account of the total amount of the outstanding claims on the Bank of England,
of her funds for discharging the same, on the 30th of January, 1819, as given in the report of the
mittee of the House of Commons, on the resumption of cash payments.

Account of Cash and Bullion in the Bank, Bills discounted, and Advances to Government from March, 1793, to Feb. 26th, 1797.

Dates.	Cash and Bullion in hand. £	Bills Discounted. . £	Average Advance to Government. £
1793 March - -	3,508,000	4.817,000	8,735,200
June - -	4,412,000	5,128,000	9,434,000
September -	6,836,000	2,065,000	9,455,700
December - -	7,720,000	1,976,000	8,887,500
1794 March - -	8,608,000	2,908,000	8,494,100
June - -	8,208,000	3,263,000	7,735,800
September -	8,096,000	2,000,000	6,779,800
December -	7,768,000	1,887,000	7,545,100
1795 March - -	7,940,000	2,287,000	9,773,700
June - -	7,356,000	3,485,000	10,879,700
September -	5,792,000	1,887,000	10,197,600
December -	4,000,000	3,109,000	10,863,100
1796 March - -	2,972,000	2,820,000	11,351,000
June - -	2,582,000	3,730,000	11,269,700
September -	2,532,000	3,352,000	9,901,100
December -	2,508,000	3,796,000	9,511,400
1797 February 26th	1,272,000	2,905,000	10,672,490

Subsequently to 1797, the advances to government were still larger. During the five years ending with 1818, they were as follows : —

	£			£
1814 - - -	30,149,000	1817 - - -		27,347,000
1815 - - -	26,494,000	1818 -	-	28,061,000*
1816 - - -	23,544,000			

In 1819. provision was made for reducing the amount of these advances; and they are not at present, excluding the permanent advance on account of the dead weight, much above a third of their amount in 1818. On the 26th of February, 1828, they amounted, inclusive of 10,416,859*l.* then paid to the above account, to 20,963,395*l.* I should also be observed, that during the greater part of the war the advances were no nearly so great ; and did not, indeed, reach eighteen millions until the latter part of 1811.

In point of fact, however, a very large part of these advances has been nominal only or, which is the same thing, has been virtually cancelled by the balances of public money in the hands of the Bank. Thus, from 1806 to 1810, both inclusive, the average advances to goverment amounted to 14,492,970*l.* But the average balance of public money in possession of the Bank during the same period amounted to about 11,000,000*l.* so that the real advance was equal only to the difference between these two sums, or to about 3,500,000*l.* This statement completely negatives, as Mr. Tooke has justly stated, the supposition so commonly entertained and reasoned upon as a point beyond doubt, that the Bank was rendered, by the restriction, a mere engine in the hands of government for facilitating its financial operations. — (*First Letter to Lord Grenville* p. 64.)

The Bank being enabled to employ the greater part of the balances of public money in her hands as capital, they have formed one of the main sources of the profit she has derived from her transactions with the public. This subject was brought very prominently forward in the Second Report of the Committee of the House of Commons on Public Expenditure in 1807. And it was agreed in the same year, that the Bank should, in consideration of the advantages derived from the public balances, continue the loan of three millions made to government in 1800 for six years, without interest on the same terms, till six months after the signature of a definitive treaty of peace. In 1816, this sum was finally incorporated with the debt due by government to the Bank at an interest of 3 per cent. In 1818, the public balances had fallen to about seven millions ; and they have been still further reduced, in consequence of measures that were then adopted. . In 1825, they amounted at an average to 5,247,314*l.* ; and in 1826 to 3,862,656*l.*

A part of the public balances is formed of the dividends payable at the Bank, but un

* These are the averages of the total advances on the 26th of February, and the 26th of August, each year.

ned. The balance arising from this source has sometimes amounted to above a
ion; but in 1808 and 1811, arrangements were made by which the balances grow-
out of this fund have been much reduced.

reviously to 1786, the Bank received an allowance on account of the management
e public debt; that is, for trouble in paying the dividends, superintending the trans-
f stock, &c. of 562*l.* 10*s.* a million. In 1786, this allowance was reduced to 450*l.*
llion, the Bank being, at the same time, entitled to a considerable allowance for her
ble in receiving contributions on loans, lotteries, &c. This, however, had been long
rded as a very improvident arrangement on the part of the public; but it was acqui-
d in till 1808, when the allowance on account of management was reduced to 340*l.*
illion on 600 millions of the public debt; and to 300*l.* a million on all that it ex-
ed that sum, exclusive of some separate allowances for annuities, &c. The impres-
, however, seems still to be entertained, that the allowances for management should
rther reduced.*

: is necessary, however, to observe, that the responsibility and expense incurred by
Bank in managing the public debt are very great. The temptation to the com-
ion of fraud in transferring stock from one individual to another, and in the
nent of the dividends, is well known; and notwithstanding the skilfully devised
m of checks adopted by the Bank for its prevention, she has frequently sustained
great losses by forgery and otherwise. In 1803, the Bank lost, through a fraud
mitted by one of her principal cashiers, Mr. Astlett, no less than 300,000*l.* And
readers are all aware of the large sums she recently lost by the forgeries of
ntleroy the banker.†

he total sum paid by the public to the Bank on account of the loans raised, exche-
bills funded, transfer of three and a half per cent. stock, &c. from 1793 to 1820,
included, amounted to 426,795*l.* 1*s.* 11*d.* — (*Parl. Paper*, No. 81. sess. 1822.)

esides the transactions alluded to, the Bank entered, on the 20th March, 1823, into
agagement with government with respect to the public pensions and annuities, or,
ey have been more commonly termed, the *dead weight.* At the end of the war,
naval and military pensions, superannuated allowances, &c. amounted to above
),000*l.* a year. They would, of course, have been gradually lessened and ulti-
ly extinguished by the death of the parties. But it was resolved, in 1822, to
apt to spread the burden equally over the whole period of *forty-five* years, during
h it was calculated the annuities would continue to decrease. To effect this
ose, it was supposed that upon government offering to pay 2,800,000*l.* a year for
-five years, capitalists would be found who would undertake to pay the entire
ities, according to a graduated scale previously determined upon, making the
year a payment of 4,900,000*l.*, and gradually decreasing the payments until the
-fifth and last year, when they were to amount to only 300,000*l.* This suppo-
was not, however, realised. No capitalists were found willing to enter into
distant engagements. But in 1823 the Bank agreed, on condition of receiving an
ity of 585,740*l.* for *forty-four* years, commencing on the 5th April, 1823, to pay,
count of the pensions, &c. at different specified periods, between the years 1823
828, both inclusive, the sum of 13,089,419*l.* (4 *Geo.* 4. c. 22.)

e Bank discounted private bills at 5 per cent. during nearly the whole period from

---

e Table IV. for an account, printed by order of the House of Commons (12th March, 1830), of the
aid by the public to the Bank, for the management of the public debt during the year 1829.
e subjoin an abstract of the principal provisions in the late statute with respect to the forgery of
otes, powers of attorney, &c.

enacted, 1 Will. 4. c. 66., that if any person shall forge or alter, or shall offer, utter, dispose of, or
, knowing the same to be forged or altered, any exchequer bill or exchequer debenture, or any in-
ment on or assignation of any such bill or debenture, or any East India bond, or indorsement upon
gnation of the same, or any note or bill of the Bank of England, or a bank post bill, or any inent on or assignment of any bank note, bank bill of exchange, or bank post bill, with intent to
d any person whatsoever, he shall be guilty of felony, and shall upon conviction suffer death as a
— § 3.

ns making false entries in the books of the Bank of England, or other books in which accounts of
stocks or funds are kept, with intent to defraud, shall suffer death as felons. — § 5.
he same act, the forging of any transfer of any share of, or interest in, or dividend upon, any public
or of a power of attorney to transfer the same, or to receive dividends thereon, is made capital. If
son, falsely personating the owner of any share, interest, or dividend of any of the public funds,
r transfer such share, &c., and receive the money due to the lawful owner, he shall upon conviction
eath as a felon. — § 6.
any person *endeavouring* by such false personation to procure the transfer of any share, interest,
the public funds, may, upon conviction, be transported beyond seas for life, or for any term not
an seven years, or be imprisoned for any term not more than four, nor less than two years. —

forgery of the attestation to any power of attorney for the transfer of stock is to be punished by
rtation for seven years, or by imprisonment for not more than two and not less than one year.

s or servants of the Bank of England knowingly making out or delivering any dividend warrant
eater or less amount than the party in whose behalf such warrant is made out is entitled to, may,
nviction, be transported beyond seas for the term of seven years, or imprisoned for not more than
less than one year. — § 9.

her establishment till 1824, when the rate was reduced to 4 per cent.   In 1826 it
raised to 5 per cent. ; but was again reduced to 4 per cent. in 1828, at which it co
tinues.   It may well be doubted, however, whether the rate of discount ought not
be more frequently varied, as occasion may require.   When the currency happens, fr
any cause, to become redundant, its contraction, always a matter of some difficulty
to be effected only by the sale of bullion or public securities by the Bank, or b
diminution of the usual discounts, or all.   But were the Bank to throw any consid
able amount of public securities upon the market, the circumstance would be ap
excite alarm; and, even though it did not, it would be difficult to dispose of th
without a heavy loss.   Hence, when a reduction is determined upon, it is most co
monly effected partly by a contraction of discounts ; and it is plain, that such c
traction cannot be made except by rejecting altogether some of the bills sent in
discount, or, which is in effect the same thing, by shortening their dates, or by rais
the rate of interest, so that fewer may be sent in.   Of these methods, the last seems
be in every respect the most expedient.   When bills are rejected for no other rea
than that the currency may be contracted, the greatest injury is done to individua
who, entertaining no doubt of getting their usual accommodations from the Bank, m
have entered into transactions which they are thus deprived of the means of co
pleting.   Were the reduction made by raising the rate of interest, it would principa
affect those who are *best able to bear it ;* at the same time that its operation, instead
being, like the rejection of bills, arbitrary and capricious, would be uniform and
partial.   It does, therefore, seem that the Bank should never throw out good bills th
she may contract her issues ; but that when she has resolved upon such a measure,
should, provided the contraction cannot be made by the sale of bullion and public se
rities, raise the rate of discount.   The Bank cannot, however, act in the way now su
gested, so long as the usury laws are in existence ; and this circumstance forms
powerful argument in favour of their repeal.   But if it should be deemed hazard
(though we cannot see in what the hazard would consist), totally to annihilate th
laws, there can, it is plain, be nothing to fear from exempting the Bank from th
operation.   She does not advance money to the landlords.   They, therefore, could
nowise affected by her raising the rate of discount ; and it must be admitted by ev
one, that it would be infinitely more for the advantage of the mercantile class, that
should be allowed to do this, than that she should be driven, as is every now and th
the case under the present system, to the necessity of arbitrarily rejecting good bills.
The dividends on Bank stock, from the establishment of the company to the prese
time, have been as follows : —

Dividends on Bank Stock, from the Establishment of the Company to the present time.

Years.	Dividend.		Years.	Dividend.
1694	8 per cent.	Lady-day	1747	5 per cent.
1697	9 —	Ditto	1753	4½ —
1708 ⎱ Varied from 9		Michaelmas	1753	5 —
1729 ⎰ to 5½ per cent.		Lady-day	1754	4½ —
Lady-day	1730	6 —	Michaelmas	1764	5 —
Michaelmas	1730	5½ —	Ditto	1767	5½ —
Lady-day	1731	6 —	Ditto	1781	6 —
Michaelmas	1731	5½ —	Lady-day	1788	7 —
Lady-day	1732	6 —	Ditto	1807	10 —
Michaelmas	1732	5½ —	Ditto	1823	8 —

Previously to 1759, the Bank of England issued no notes for less than 20*l.*
began to issue ten pound notes in 1759; five pound notes in 1793 ; and one and
pound notes in March, 1797.   The issue of the latter ceased in 1821.
The Bank of England does not allow, either at the head office in London, or at
branches, any interest on deposits ; but it would be exceedingly desirable were sh
make some alteration in this respect.   The want of the power readily to invest sm
sums productively, and, at the same time, with perfect security, tends to weaken
motives to save and accumulate.   Nothing has contributed more to diffuse a spiri
economy, and a desire to save, amongst all classes of the population of Scotland, t
the readiness with which deposits of small sums are received by banks of undoub
solidity in that part of the country, and the allowance of interest upon them. (See *Ba*
Scotch.)   This advantage is in some degree, indeed, secured in England, by the in
tution of savings banks.   These, however, are but a very inadequate substitute.   T
are not open to all classes of depositors ; and of those to whom they are open, no one
deposit more than 30*l.* a year, and 150*l.* in all. (See *Banks, Savings.*)   But it is
sirable that every facility should be given to safe and profitable investments.   "Were
English banks, like the Scotch banks, to receive deposits of 10*l.* and upwards, and al
interest upon them at about one per cent. less than the market rate, they would co

immense advantage upon the community, and open a source of profit to themselves.
his is, in fact, a part of the proper business of a bank. A banker is a dealer in
pital, an intermediate party between the borrower and the lender. He borrows of
e party, and lends to another; and the difference between the terms at which he borrows
d those at which he lends is the source of his profit. By this means, he draws into active
eration those small sums of money which were previously unproductive in the hands
private individuals, and at the same time furnishes accommodation to another class,
o have occasion for additional capital to carry on their commercial transactions." *

In further corroboration of what has now been stated, it may be mentioned that it
s estimated by a very well-informed witness (Mr. J. G. Craig), before the Lords'
mmittee, on Scotch and Irish banking, in 1826, that the deposits in the Scotch banks,
that period, amounted to about 24,000,000l, of which more than a half consisted of sums
m 10l. to 200l.! This is a most satisfactory proof of the vast importance of the
stem. Perhaps it is not going too far to affirm, that but for the receiving of deposits
the banks, and the allowing of interest upon them, not one third of the sums under
0l., and not one half of those above it, would ever have been accumulated. (*See Scotch
nks.*)

[See Tables VI. and VII. for an account of the Bank of England notes, post bills,
. in circulation at certain periods from 1718 to 1830.]

The composition paid by the Bank at the rate of 3,500l. per million, as an equivalent
r the stamp duty on her notes, amounts, at an average, to about 75,000l. a year.

All accounts kept at the Bank with individuals are termed *drawing accounts*; those
th whom they are opened being entitled to draw checks upon them, and to send the
lls and drafts in their favour to be presented by the Bank, exactly as if they dealt with
ivate bankers. There is no fixed sum with which an individual must open a drawing
count; nor is there any fixed sum which the Bank requires him to keep at his credit
indemnify them for their trouble in answering his drafts, &c.

A person having a drawing account may not have a *discount account*; but no person
have the latter without, at the same time, having the former. When a discount ac-
int is opened, the signatures of the parties are entered in a book kept for the purpose,
d powers of attorney are granted, empowering the persons named in them to act for
ir principals. No bill of exchange is discounted by the Bank *in London* under 20l.,
London *note* under 100l., nor for a longer date, under existing regulations, than
ee months.

The number of holidays formerly kept at the Bank has recently been reduced about
alf, in the view, as stated by the directors, of preventing the interruption of business.
ere are no holidays in the months of March, June, September, and December, ex-
ting Christmas; Easter Monday and Tuesday are no longer kept.

We subjoin an account of the days for transferring stock, and when the dividends are
e at the Bank, the South Sea House, and the East India House:—

Transfer Days at the Bank, &c.

	Dividends due.		Dividends due.
nk Stock. — Tues. Thurs., nd Frid. .... er Cent. Reduc. — Tues. Wed. Thurs. and Frid. ... per Cent. — Tues. Thurs. nd Frid.	April 5. Oct. 10.	New 3½ per Cent. Annuit. — Tues. Wed. Thurs. and Frid.	Jan. 5. July 5.
er Cent., 1726. — Tues. nd Thurs. .... per Cent. Cons. — Tues. Wed. Thurs. and Frid.	Jan. 5. July 5.	New 5 per Cent. Annuit. — Tues. Wed. and Frid.	
per Cent. Cons. — Tues. Wed. Thurs. and Frid. ... g Annuit. to Jan. 1860. — Mon. Wed. and Sat.	April 5. Oct. 10.	Annuit. for Terms of Years, ending 10th Oct., 1859, pursuant to 10 Geo. IV. — Tues. Thurs. and Sat.	April 5. Oct. 10.
er Cent. New. — Tues. Wed. Thurs. and Frid. ...	Jan. 5. July 5.	Annuit. for Terms of Years, ending 5th Jan. 1860, pur- suant to 10 Geo. IV. — Tues., Thurs., and Sat.	Jan. 5. July 5.
er Cent. 1826. — Mon. Wed. and Frid.	April 5. Oct. 10.	Life Annuit., if transferred between Jan. 5. and April 4, or between July 5. and Oct. 9.	Jan. 5. July 5.

* See Gilbart's Practical Observations on Banking, p. 52.

	Dividends due.		Dividends due.
Life Annuit. if transferred between April 5. and July 4., or between Oct. 10. and Jan. 4.	April 5. Oct. 10.	3 per Cent. New Annuit.— Tues. Thurs. and Sat. .... 3 per Cent. 1751.— Tues. and Thurs.	Jan. 5. July 5.

At the South Sea House.

At the East India House.

| 3½ per Cents.— Mon. Wed. and Frid. .... | Jan. 5. July 5. | India Stock.— Tues. Thurs. and Sat. .... | Jan. July |
| 3 per Cent. Old Annuit.— Mon. Wed. and Frid. .... | April 5. Oct. 10. | Interest on India Bonds, due | Mar. 31. Sept. 30. |

Tickets for preparing transfer of stock must be given in at each office before one o'clock: at the East India House, before two o'clock. Private transfers may be made at other times than as above, the books not being shut, by paying at the Bank and India House 2s. 6d. extra for each transfer; at the South Sea House, 3s. 6d.

Transfer at the Bank must be made by half-past two o'clock: at the India House, by three: at the South Sea House by two; on Saturday, by one.

Expense of transfer in Bank Stock, for 25l. and under, 9s.; above that sum, 12s.

            India Stock, for 10l. .... £1 14s.

            South Sea Stock, if under 100l....9s. 6d. .... 12s.

Powers of attorney for the sale or transfer of stock to be left at the Bank, &c. for examination, one day before they can be acted upon; if for receiving dividends, present them at the time the first dividend is payable.

The expense of a power of attorney is 1l. 1s. 6d. for each stock; but for Bank, India and South Sea stocks, 1l. 11s. 6d. If wanted for the same day, half-past twelve o'clock is the latest time for receiving orders. The boxes for receiving powers of attorney for sale close at two.

Probates of wills, letters of administration, and other proofs of decease, must be left at the Bank, &c. for registration from two to three clear days, exclusive of holidays.

Stock cannot be added to any account (whether single or joint) in which the decease of the individual, or one or more of a joint party, has taken place; and the decease to be proved as soon as practicable. Powers of attorney, in case of the death of a party or parties granting it, become void.

The unaltered possession of 500l. or upwards Bank stock, for six months clear, gives the proprietor a vote.

The clear unaltered possession for a year of 1000l. India stock, entitles the proprietor to one vote; of 3000l., to two votes; of 6000l. to three; of 10,000, to four votes.

(3.) *Branch Banks of the Bank of England.*—The Bank of England, as already observed, has within these few years established branch banks at several of the most considerable towns throughout the country. The mode and terms of conducting business at these establishments have been described as follows: —

" The branch bank (of Swansea, and the same is true of those established in other places) is to be a secure place of deposit for persons having occasion to make use of a bank for that purpose; such accounts are termed *drawing accounts.* The facility to the mercantile and trading classes of obtaining discounts of good and unexceptionable bills founded upon real transactions, two approved names being required upon every bill or note discounted; these are called *discount accounts.* The application of parties who desire to open discount accounts at the branch are forwarded every Saturday to the parent establishment for approval, and an answer is generally received in about ten days. When approved, good bills may be discounted at the branch without reference to London. Bills payable at Swansea, London, or any other place where a branch is established, are discounted under this regulation. The dividends on any of the public funds, which are payable at the Bank of England, may be received at the branch, by persons who have opened ' drawing accounts,' after signing powers of attorney for that purpose, which the branch will procure from London. No charge is made in this case except the expense of the power of attorney and its postage. Purchases and sales of every description of government securities are effected by the branch at a charge of one quarter per cent., which includes brokerage in London, and all expenses of postage, &c. A charge of one quarter per cent. is also made on paying at the Bank of England, bills accepted by persons having drawing accounts at Swansea, such bills to be advised by the branch; also for collecting payment of bills at the other branches, and granting letters of credit on London, or on the other branches. The branch grants bills on London, payable at twenty-one days' date, without acceptance, for sums of 10l. and upwards,

sons having drawing accounts at Swansea may order money to be paid at the Bank
London to their credit at this place, and *vice versâ*, without expense. The branch
be called upon to change any notes issued and *dated* at Swansea; but they do
change the notes of the Bank in London, nor receive them in payment, unless as a
ter of courtesy where the parties are known. Bank post bills, which are accepted
due, are received at the branch from parties having drawing accounts, and taken to
unt without any charge for postage; but unaccepted bank post bills, which must be
to London, are subject to the charge of postage, and taken to account when due.
interest is allowed on deposits. No advance is made by the branch upon any
cription of landed or other property, nor is any account allowed to be overdrawn.
notes are the same as those issued by the parent establishment, except being dated
nsea, and made payable there and in London. No note issued exceeds the sum of
., and none are for a less amount than 5l."

he existing charter of the Bank of England expires on the 1st of August, 1833.
question as to its renewal is one of very great importance, and is not without diffi-
y. This, however, is not the proper place for entering upon its discussion; but the
or of this work has, in a pamphlet (from which part of this article is taken), enti-
" Historical Sketch of the Bank of England, with an Examination of the Ques-
as to the Prolongation of the Exclusive Privileges of that Establishment," fully
d his opinions on the subject. He has endeavoured to show that the privileges at
ent enjoyed by the Bank ought, with certain modifications, to be continued; and
it would be highly inexpedient to concede the power of issuing notes in the metro-
to all individuals, or to vest it in a body acting under authority of government.
his pamphlet he, therefore, begs to refer such of his readers as take an interest in the
ssion of this question.

E I. A return of the Number of Persons convicted of Forgery, or passing
forged Notes and Post Bills of the Bank of England, in each Year, from 1791 to
1829, inclusive.

Years.	Capital Convictions.	Convictions for having Forged Bank Notes in Possession.	Total Number of Convictions each Year.	Years.	Capital Convictions.	Convictions for having Forged Bank Notes in Possession.	Total Number of Convictions each Year.
1791—1796	nil.	nil.	nil.	1813	9	49	58
1797	1	- -	1	1814	5	39	44
1798	11	- -	11	1815	8	51	59
1799	12	- -	12	1816	20	84	104
1800	29	- -	29	1817	33	95	128
1801	32	1	33	1818	62	165	227
1802	32	12	44	1819	33	160	193
1803	7	1	8	1820	77	275	352
1804	13	8	21	1821	41	93	134
1805	10	14	24	1822	16	- -	16
1806	nil.	9	9	1823	6	- -	6
1807	16	24	40	1824	5	- -	5
1808	9	23	32	1825	2	- -	2
1809	23	29	52	1826	18	4	22
1810	10	16	26	1827	24	- -	24
1811	5	19	24	1828	10	- -	10
1812	26	26	52	1829	13	1	14

e Bank of England does not possess the means of stating or distinguishing the
uments inflicted for the said crimes.

TABLE I. *continued.* — A Return of the Number of Persons convicted of Forgery
the Bank of England connected with the Public Funds, Bills of Exchange,
otherwise, except Bank Notes, &c. in each Year, from 1791 to 1829, inclusive.

Convictions.			Convictions.			Convictions.		
1790	-	- 1	1804	-	- 1	1817	-	- 3
1791	-	- nil.	1805		- 1	1818 ⎫		
1792	-	- 2	1806	-	- nil.	1819 ⎪		
1793 ⎫			1807		- 1	1820 ⎬		- nil.
1794 ⎬		- nil.	1808	-	- nil.	1821 ⎭		
1795 ⎭			1809		- 1	1822	-	- 1
1796	-	- 2	1810	-	- nil.	1823		- nil.
1797	-	- nil.	1811		- 2	1824	-	- 1
1798	-	- 3	1812	-	- nil.	1825 ⎫		
1799		- nil.	1813		- 2	1826 ⎪		
1800	-	- 1	1814	-	- 1	1827 ⎬		- nil.
1801		- nil.	1815		- nil.	1828 ⎭		
1802	-	- 1	1816	-	- 2	1829	-	- 2
1803		- 1						

The Bank of England does not possess the means of stating or distinguishing
Punishments inflicted for the said Crimes.

FRESHFIELD AND SON,
Solicitors to the Governor and Compan
of the Bank of England.

20th May, 1830.

TABLE II. — An Account of the Average Market Price of Bullion in each Year, fr
1800 to 1821, (taken from official Documents) of the average Value per Cent. of
Currency, estimated by the Market Price of Gold for the same Period, and of
average Depreciation per Cent.

Years.	Average Price of Gold per oz.			Average per Cent. of the Value of the Currency.			Average Depreciation per Cent.		
	£	s.	d.	£	s.	d.	£	s.	d.
1800	3	17	10½	100	0	0		Nil.	
1801	4	5	0	91	12	4	8	7	8
1802	4	4	0	92	14	2	7	5	10
1803	4	0	0	97	6	10	2	13	2
1804	4	0	0	97	6	10	2	13	2
1805	4	0	0	97	6	10	2	13	2
1806	4	0	0	97	6	10	2	13	2
1807	4	0	0	97	6	10	2	13	2
1808	4	0	0	97	6	10	2	13	2
1809	4	0	0	97	6	10	2	13	2
1810	4	10	0	86	10	6	13	9	6
1811	4	4	6	92	3	2	7	16	10
1812	4	15	6	79	5	3	20	14	9
1813	5	1	0	77	2	0	22	18	0
1814	5	4	0	74	17	6	25	2	6
1815	4	13	6	83	5	9	16	14	3
1816	4	13	6	83	5	9	16	14	3
1817	4	0	0	97	6	10	2	13	2
1818	4	0	0	97	6	10	2	13	2
1819	4	1	6	95	11	0	4	9	0
1820	3	19	11	97	8	0	2	12	0
1821	3	17	10½	100	0	0		Nil.	

TABLE III.—An Account of the total Amount of Outstanding Demands on the Bank of England, and likewise the Funds for discharging the same; 30th Jan. 1819.

Dr. - - The Bank, - - 30th January, 1819. - - Cr.			
	£		£
To Bank Notes out	26,094,430	By Advances on Government Securities; viz.	
To other Debts; viz.		On Exchequer Bills, on Malt, &c. 1818	
Drawing Accounts		Bank Loan, 1808	
Audit Roll		Supply, 1816, at 4l. per cent.	
Exchequer Bills deposited	7,800,150	Growing Produce of the Consd. Fund to 5th April, 1819, and Interest due, and Loans to Government on Unclaimed Dividends.	8,438,660
And various other Debts			
	33,894,580		
Balance of Surplus in favour of the Bank of England, exclusive of the Debt from Government, at 3l. per cent. £11,686,800		By all other Credits; viz. Cash and Bullion .... Exchequer Bills purchased, and Interest .... Bills and Notes discounted Treasury Bills for the Service of Ireland. .... Money lent, and various other Articles	30,658,240
And the Advance to Government, per 56 Geo. 3. cap. 96. at 3l. per cent. £3,000,000	5,202,320		
£	39,096,900	£	39,096,900
		By the permanent Debt due from Government, for the Capital of the Bank, at 3l. per cent. per annum	11,686,800
		By the Advance to Government, per Act 56 Geo. 3. cap. 96. at 3l. per cent. per annum	3,000,000

Bank of England, 2d February, 1819.

WILLIAM DAWES, Accountant General.

TABLE IV.—An Account of Money paid or payable at the Bank of England, for the Management of the Public Debt, in the Year 1829, together with an Account of all the Allowances made by the Public to the Bank, or charged by the Bank against the Public, for transacting any Public Service in the Year 1829; describing the Nature of the Service, and the Amount charged thereon in the said Year, and including any sum under the Denomination of House-money, or House Expenses; and also, any sum under the Denomination of Charges of Management on South Sea Stock, and stating the aggregate Amount of the whole.

	£	s.	d.
Charge for Management of the Unredeemed Public Debt for one year, ending the 5th April, 1830, being the annual Period at which the Accounts are made up, as directed by the Act 8 Geo. 3. c. 4. - - - - - - -	248,417	17	2¾
Do. ditto, for one year ending ditto, on sundry Annuities transferred to the Commissioners for the Reduction of the National Debt, for the Purchase of Life Annuities per Act 48 Geo. 3. and subsequent Acts - - - - - -	2,922	11	9
Carried forward - - £251,340		8	11¾

G

	£	s.	d.
Brought forward - -	251,340	8	11.

Charges of Management, being part of an entire yearly Fund of 100,000*l.* enjoyed by the Governor and Company of the Bank of England, originally by the Act of the 5th and 6th of William and Mary, c. 20. confirmed to the said Governor and Company by several subsequent Acts, and lastly, by the Act of the 39th and 40th Geo. 3. c. 28. as per Return made to the Honourable House of Commons, on the 21st June, 1816 - -   **4,000 0 0**

Ditto, ditto, on 4,000,000*l* South Sea Stock, purchased by the Governor and Company of the Bank of England of the South Sea Company, and transferred by them to the said Governor and Company, in pursuance of the Act of the 8th Geo. 1. c. 21., and which charges of management were assigned by the said South Sea Company, to the said Governor and Company, out of a Sum of 8,397*l.* 9*s.* 6*d.* per annum, then paid by the Public to the said South Sea Company, for charges of management on their funds, as per Return made to the Honourable House of Commons, on the 21st June, 1816 - - - - -   **1,898 3 5**

£257,238 12 4

Bank of England,
11th of March, 1830.

T. RIPPON,
Chief Cashier.

———

TABLE V.—The following is an Account of all Distributions made by the Bank of Eng land amongst the Proprietors of Bank Stock, whether by Money Payments, Transfer o 5 per Cent. Annuities, or otherwise, under the Heads of Bonus, Increase of Dividend and Increase of Capital, betwixt 25th February, 1797, and 31st March, 1830, i addition to the ordinary Annual Dividend of 7 per Cent. on the Capital Stock o that Corporation, existing in 1797, including therein the whole Dividend paid sinc June, 1816, on their increased Capital; stating the Period when such Distribution were made, and the aggregate Amount of the whole.

	£
In June, 1799:	
10*l.* per cent. Bonus in 5 per cents. 1797, on 11,642,400*l.*, is · -	1,164,24
May, 1801:	
5*l.* per cent. ditto, in Navy 5 per cents. ditto - - -	582,12
November, 1802:	
2*l.* 10*s.* per cent. ditto, ditto, ditto - - - -	291,06
October, 1804:	
5*l.* per cent. ditto, Cash, ditto - - - - -	582,12
October, 1805:	
5*l.* per cent. ditto, ditto, ditto - - - - -	582,12
October, 1806:	
5*l.* per cent. ditto, ditto, ditto - - - - -	582,12
From April, 1807, to Oct., 1822, both inclusive { Increase of Dividend at the rate of 3*l.* per cent. per annum on 11,642,400*l.*, is, 16 years - - -	5,588,3
From April, 1823, to Oct. 1829, both inclusive { Increase of Dividend at the rate of 1*l.* per cent. per annum on 11,642,400*l.*, is, 7 years - - - - -	814,9
In June, 1816 - - Increase of Capital at 25 per cent., is -	2,910,6
From Oct. 1816, to Oct. 1822, both inclusive { Dividend at the rate of 10*l.* per cent. per annum on 2,910,600*l.*, increased Capital, is, 6½ years -	1,891,8
From April, 1823, to Oct. 1829, both inclusive { Dividend at the rate of 8*l.* per cent. per annum on 2,910,600*l.* increased Capital, is, 7 years - - - - -	1,629,9
Aggregate Amount of the whole - -	£16,619,5

ual Dividend payable on Bank Stock in 1797, on a Capital of
,642,400*l.* at the rate of 7*l.* per cent. per annum - - - £ 814,968

ual Dividend payable since June, 1816, on a Capital of 14,553,000*l.*,
October, 1822, inclusive, at the rate of 10*l.* per cent. per annum - £ 1,455,300

ual Dividend payable from April, 1823, to 31st March, 1830, both
clusive, on a Capital of 14,553,000*l.*, at the rate of 8*l.* per cent. per
num - - - - - - - - £ 1,164,240

WILLIAM SMEE, Dep. Acct.

k of England, 26th April, 1830.

ABLE VI.—An Account of the Amount of Bank of England Notes, &c. in Circulation at the following Periods :—

In the Year	Notes of 5*l.* and upwards.	Notes under 5*l.*	Bank Post Bills.	Total.
	£		£	£
1718	1,829,930	—	—	1,829,930
1721	2,054,780	—	—	2,054,780
1730	4,224,990	—	—	4,224,990
1754	3,836,870	—	186,920	3,975,870
1761	5,863,290	—	138,520	6,001,810
1762	6,012,150	—	119,620	6,131,770
1763	6,716,660	—	173,020	6,889,680
1772	5,881,960	—	319,070	6,201,030
1778	7,030,680	—	509,390	7,540,070
1783	6,354,070	—	353,470	6,707,540
1784	6,074,930	—	317,800	6,392,730
1791	10,027,600	—	661,910	10,689,510
1792	10,277,990	—	724,865	11,102,855

E VII.—An Account of the Amount of Bank Notes in Circulation on the under-
ntioned Days ; distinguishing the Bank Post Bills, and the Amount of Notes
der Five Pounds, with the Aggregate of the whole.

	Notes of 5*l.* and upwards.	Bank Post Bills.	Bank Notes under 5*l.*	Total.
	£	£	£	£
792 February 25	10,394,106	755,703	- - -	11,149,809
August 25	10,281,071	725,898	- - -	11,006,969
793 February 26	10,780,643	647,738	- - -	11,428,381
August 26	10,163,839	674,375	- - -	10,838,214
794 February 26	10,079,165	618,759	- - -	10,697,924
August 26	10,060,248	567,972	- - -	10,628,220
795 February 26	12,968,707	570,456	- - -	13,539,163
August 26	10,939,880	518,502	- - -	11,458,382
796 February 26	10,266,561	643,133	- - -	10,909,694
August 26	8,981,645	549,690	- - -	9,531,335
97 February 25	8,167,949	474,615	- - -	8,601,964
August 26	9,109,614	524,587	934,015	10,568,216
98 February 26	10,856,188	551,549	1,442,348	12,850,085
August 25	9,997,958	553,236	1,639,831	12,191,025
99 February 26	10,576,510	607,907	1,451,728	12,636,145
August 26	11,260,675	653,766	1,345,432	13,259,873
800 February 25	13,106,368	723,600	1,406,708	15,236,676
August 26	12,221,451	823,366	1,690,561	14,735,378

Table VII. — *continued.*

		Notes of 5*l.* and upwards.	Bank Post Bills.	Bank Notes under 5*l.*	Total.
1801	February 26	12,975,206	954,982	2,647,526	16,577,514
	August 26	11,715,665	759,270	2,495,386	14,970,321
1802	February 26	12,038,970	803,499	2,616,407	15,458,876
	August 26	12,801,746	772,577	3,312,790	16,887,113
1803	February 26	11,796,424	820,039	2,960,469	15,576,932
	August 26	12,413,924	776,030	3,846,005	17,035,959
1804	February 25	12,054,943	848,894	4,673,515	17,577,352
	August 25	11,766,628	743,841	4,813,525	17,323,994
1805	February 26	11,403,290	1,029,580	4,801,596	17,234,466
	August 26	11,182,188	718,510	4,395,480	16,296,178
1806	February 25	11,994,350	725,736	4,428,360	17,148,446
	August 26	14,141,510	702,425	4,228,958	19,072,893
1807	February 26	12,274,629	724,485	4,206,230	17,205,344
	August 26	15,077,013	725,262	4,231,837	20,034,112
1808	February 26	13,746,598	742,671	4,103,785	18,593,054
	August 26	12,440,930	795,102	4,129,234	17,365,266
1809	February 25	12,730,999	944,727	4,338,951	18,014,677
	August 26	13,255,599	880,104	5,221,538	19,357,241
1810	February 26	13,650,592	907,620	5,871,069	20,429,281
	August 25	16,078,390	1,145,832	7,221,953	24,446,175
1811	February 26	15,110,688	1,133,419	7,140,726	23,384,833
	August 26	15,203,611	1,016,303	7,573,201	23,723,115
1812	February 26	14,523,049	1,059,854	7,415,294	22,998,197
	August 26	14,873,705	987,880	7,621,325	23,482,910
1813	February 26	14,567,267	1,034,882	7,705,322	23,307,471
	August 26	14,975,479	1,015,616	8,033,774	24,024,869
1814	February 26	15,632,250	1,091,242	8,371,923	25,095,415
	August 26	18,066,180	1,246,479	9,667,217	28,979,876
1815	February 25	16,394,359	1,184,459	9,094,552	26,673,370
	August 26	16,332,275	1,115,079	9,576,695	27,024,049
1816	February 26	15,307,228	1,336,467	9,036,374	25,680,069
	August 26	16,686,087	1,286,429	9,103,338	27,075,854
1817	February 26	17,538,656	1,376,416	8,143,506	27,058,578
	August 26	20,388,502	1,712,807	7,998,599	30,099,908
1818	February 26	19,077,951	1,838,600	7,362,492	28,279,043
	August 26	17,465,628	1,627,427	7,509,782	26,602,837
1819	February 26	16,307,000	1,622,330	7,317,360	25,246,690
	August 26	16,972,140	1,468,920	7,216,530	25,657,590
1820	February 26	15,402,830	1,421,160	6,745,160	23,569,150
	August 26	16,047,390	1,633,730	6,772,260	24,453,380
1821	February 26	14,372,840	1,615,600	6,483,010	22,471,450
	August 26	16,095,020	1,634,260	2,598,460	20,327,740
1822	February 26	15,178,490	1,609,620	1,384,360	18,172,470
	August 26	15,295,090	1,610,600	862,650	17,768,340
1823	February 26	15,751,120	1,742,190	683,160	18,176,470
	August 26	17,392,260	1,763,650	550,010	19,705,920
1824	February 26	17,244,940	2,198,260	486,660	19,929,800
	August 26	18,409,230	2,122,760	443,970	20,975,960
1825	February 26	18,308,990	2,334,260	416,880	21,060,130
	August 26	17,091,120	2,061,010	396,670	19,548,800
1826	February 26	21,100,400	2,487,080	1,367,560	24,955,040
	August 26	18,172,160	2,040,400	1,175,450	21,388,010
1827	February 26	18,787,330	2,052,310	668,910	21,508,550
	August 26	19,253,890	2,270,110	483,060	22,007,060
1828	February 26	19,428,010	2,329,880	416,890	22,174,780
	August 26	19,016,980	2,417,440	382,860	21,817,280
1829	February 26	17,402,470	2,444,660	357,170	20,204,300
	August 26	17,164,940	2,030,280	334,190	19,529,410
1830	February 26	17,862,990	2,284,520	320,550	20,468,060
	August 26	19,403,610	2,217,870	313,460	21,934,940

III. Banks (English Provincial).

Besides charging the usual rate of interest on bills discounted, the provincial bankers ~~e~~ mostly in the habit of charging 5s. or 6s. per cent. as commission. They also ~~c~~arge a commission on all payments; and derive a profit from charges for the trans~~m~~ission of money, &c. They usually allow from 2 to 3 per cent. on money deposited; ~~bu~~t the numerous failures that have taken place amongst them have, by generating a ~~fe~~eling of insecurity in the minds of the depositors, confined this branch of their busi~~ne~~ss within comparatively narrow limits. When one of their customers overdraws his ~~ac~~count, he is charged with interest at the rate of 5 per cent.

When country banks are established by individuals possessed of adequate funds, and ~~ar~~e managed with due discretion, they are productive of the greatest service They ~~for~~m commodious reservoirs, where the floating and unemployed capital of the surround~~in~~g districts is collected, and from which it is again distributed, by way of loan, to those ~~wh~~o will employ it to the best advantage. It is, therefore, of the utmost importance, in ~~a~~ public point of view, that these establishments should be based upon solid foundations. ~~B~~ut in England, unfortunately, this has been but little attended to; and the destruction ~~of~~ country banks has, upon three different occasions, in 1792, in 1814, 1815, and 1816, ~~an~~d in 1825 and 1826, produced an extent of bankruptcy and misery that has never, ~~per~~haps, been equalled, except by the breaking up of the Mississippi scheme in France. ~~G~~overnment is bound to interfere to hinder the recurrence of such disastrous results. ~~Th~~e repeal of the act of 1708, preventing the association of more than six persons for ~~ca~~rrying on the trade of banking, has already led to the formation of joint stock banking ~~com~~panies in a few of the large towns, and will, in so far, improve the existing system. ~~Bu~~t it is quite visionary to suppose that the power to establish such banks is *all* that is ~~req~~uired to establish the provincial currency on a secure foundation. What is really ~~wa~~nted, is not a regulation to *allow* banks with large capitals to be set on foot, (for there ~~ha~~ve, at all times, been many such banks in England,) but a regulation to *prevent* any ~~ban~~k, be its partners few or many, from issuing notes without previously giving secu~~rit~~y for their payment. This would render the bankruptcy of such banks impossible, and ~~wou~~ld give a degree of security to the money system of the country that it can never ~~oth~~erwise attain. (The reader is referred, for a full discussion of this important question, ~~to~~ the Note on Money, in my edition of the *Wealth of Nations*, vol. iv. pp. 280—292.)

The following is an account of the number of commissions of bankruptcy issued ~~aga~~inst country bankers in England, from 1809 to 1826, both inclusive, and the num~~ber~~ of partners in the bankrupt firms since 1816: —

Years.	Commissions.		Years.	Commissions.	Partners.
1809	7		1816	37	75
1810	26		1817	3	9
1811	4		1818	5	8
1812	17		1819	12	25
1813	8		1820	4	8
1814	29		1821	11	20
1815	26		1822	9	15
			1823	9	11
			1824	9	15
			1825	37	96
			1826	22	48
			Totals -	158	330

~~E~~xclusive of the above, many banks stopped payment, to the great injury of their ~~cred~~itors and the public, that afterwards resumed them; at the same time that the affairs ~~of s~~ome bankrupt concerns were arranged without a commission. During the whole of ~~this~~ period not a single Scotch bank gave way.

~~T~~he stamp duties on country bank notes have been already specified. (p. 64.) ~~B~~esides the stamp duties payable on notes, each individual or company issuing them ~~mus~~t take out a licence, renewable annually, which costs 30*l*. This licence specifies the ~~nam~~es and places of abode of the body corporate, person or persons, in the firm to whom ~~it is~~ granted, the name of such firm, the place where the business is carried on, &c.; and ~~a se~~parate licence is to be taken out for every town or place where any notes shall be ~~issu~~ed by or on account of any banker, &c. Unless the licence granted to persons in ~~part~~nership set forth the names and places of abode of all the persons concerned in the ~~part~~nership, whether their names appear on the notes issued by them or not, such licence ~~shal~~l be absolutely void. (55 Geo. 3. c. 184. s. 24.) For the regulations as to the ~~issu~~e of unstamped notes, see *ante*, p. 64.

~~T~~he issue of notes for less than 5*l*. was prohibited in England, as previously ~~show~~n, from 1777 to 1797; but they continued to be issued from the latter period down

to the 5th of April, 1829, when their further issue ceased in consequence of an act passed in 1826. This act did not extend to Scotland or Ireland, and was intended to give greater stability to the system of country banking in England, by shutting up one of the principal channels through which the inferior class of bankers have been in the habit of getting their notes into circulation. But notwithstanding it will certainly have this effect, the policy of the measure seems very doubtful. It is idle indeed, to imagine that it can give that stability to the banking system which is so desirable; and in proof of this, it is sufficient to state, that though none of the country banks existing in 1793 had any notes for less than 5*l.* in circulation, upwards of *one third* of their entire number stopped payment during the revulsion that then took place. The truth is, that nothing but the exaction of security for payment of notes can ever place the country banking system on that solid foundation on which it ought to stand; and as security may be taken for 1*l.* notes as easily as for those of 5*l.*, there would, were such a system adopted, be no ground for suppressing the former.

It is not possible to obtain any accurate account of the number of country notes in circulation at different periods. But the following Table, drawn up by the late Mr. Mushet, of the Mint, founded partly on official returns, and partly on the estimates of Mr. Sedgwick, late chairman of the Board of Stamps, is the most complete and comprehensive hitherto published.

TABLE I. — An Account of the Number of Country Bank Notes, of all Denominations stamped in each Year, ending Oct. 10, from 1804 to 1825, inclusive, with the per centage of Increase and Decrease, comparing each Year with the Year preceding; together with an Estimate of the Total Amount in Circulation, according to Mr. Sedgwick's Tables, in each year, from 1804 to 1825, inclusive, with the per centage of Increase and Decrease, comparing each Year with the Year preceding.

	The Amount of Country Bank Notes of all Denominations stamped in each year, ending Oct. 10, from 1804, to 1825.	The per centage of Increase, comparing each year with the year preceding.	The per centage of Decrease, comparing each year with the year preceding.	The Amount of Country Bank Notes in Circulation, according to Mr. Sedgwick's Tables, in each year, ending Oct. 10, from 1804 to 1825, inclusive.	The per centage of Increase, comparing each year with the year preceding.	The per centage of Decrease, comparing each year with the year preceding.
1805	11,342,413					
1806	11,480,547	$1\frac{2}{10}$				
1807	6,587,398		$42\frac{6}{10}$	18,021,900		
1808	8,653,077	$23\frac{8}{10}$		16,871,524		$6\frac{3}{10}$
1809	15,737,986*	$81\frac{8}{10}$		23,702,493	$40\frac{5}{10}$	
1810	10,517,519		$33\frac{1}{10}$	23,893,868	$\frac{8}{10}$	
1811	8,792,433		$16\frac{4}{10}$	21,453,000		$1\frac{6}{10}$
1812	10,577,134	$20\frac{3}{10}$		19,944,000		7
1813	12,615,509	$19\frac{2}{10}$		22,597,000	$13\frac{3}{10}$	
1814	10,773,375		$14\frac{6}{10}$	22,709,000	$\frac{5}{10}$	
1815	7,624,949		$29\frac{2}{10}$	19,011,000		$16\frac{3}{10}$
1816	6,423,466		$15\frac{7}{10}$	15,096,000		$20\frac{6}{10}$
1817	9,075,958	$41\frac{1}{10}$		15,898,000	$5\frac{3}{10}$	
1818	12,316,868	$35\frac{7}{10}$		20,507,000	29	
1819	6,180,313		$50\frac{2}{10}$	17,366,875		$15\frac{3}{10}$
1820	3,574,894		$41\frac{1}{10}$	11,767,391		$32\frac{2}{10}$
1821	3,987,582	$11\frac{5}{10}$		8,414,281		$28\frac{6}{10}$
1822	4,217,241	$5\frac{7}{10}$		8,067,260		$4\frac{1}{10}$
1823	4,657,589	$10\frac{4}{10}$		8,798,277	9	
1824	6,093,367	$30\frac{8}{10}$		10,604,172	$20\frac{5}{10}$	
1825	8,532,438	40		14,147,211	$23\frac{4}{10}$	

* In 1809 the duty on 1*l.* notes was increased from 3*d.* to 4*d.*, and may account for the great increase this year, the notes bearing a 3*d.* stamp being no longer issuable.

TABLE II.—Number of Country Bankers' Notes Stamped in each Year, from 1819, and up to the 5th April, 1828.

	ENGLAND AND SCOTLAND.								IRELAND.				
	Not exceeding 1l. 1s.	Exceeding 1l. 1s. and not exceeding 2l. 2s.	Exceeding 2l. 2s. and not exceeding 5l. 5s.	Exceeding 5l. 5s. and not exceeding 10l.	Exceeding 10l. and not exceeding 20l.	Exceeding 20l. and not exceeding 30l.	Exceeding 30l. and not exceeding 50l.	Exceeding 50l. and not exceeding 100l.	Amounting to 1l. and under 5l.	Amounting to 5l. and under 10l.	Amounting to 10l. and under 50l.	Amounting to and not exceeding 50l.	Amounting to 50l. and under 100l.
	5d.	10d.	1s. 3d.	1s. 9d.	2s.	3s.	5s.	8s. 6d.	3d.	6d.	8d.	2s.	3s.
England	1,684,741	41,855	260,149	79,667	19,102	500	140	555	.....	.....	.....	.....	.....
Scotland	99,596	.....	4,000	.....	1,000				.....	.....	.....	.....	.....
Ireland	.....	.....							704,114	48,800	33,667	1,325	.....
	1,784,337	41,855	264,149	79,667	20,102	500	140	555	704,114	48,800	33,667	1,325	.....
England	1,660,824	22,181	202,173	49,280	7,150	.....	71	1,060	.....	.....	.....	.....	.....
Scotland	23,000	.....	1,500		100				.....	.....	.....	.....	.....
Ireland	.....	.....	.....						435,369	26,800	19,523	240	110
	1,683,824	22,181	203,673	49,280	7,250		71	1,060	435,369	26,800	19,523	240	110
England	2,167,624	20,180	243,739	49,226	8,838	50	417	1,000	.....	.....	.....	.....	.....
Scotland	46,999	.....	11,100	2,000	1,900			600	.....	.....	.....	.....	.....
Ireland	.....	.....	.....						354,041	5,700	6,146	75	24
	2,214,623	20,180	254,839	51,226	10,738	50	417	1,600	354,041	5,700	6,146	75	24
England	1,853,559	11,700	259,213	63,032	10,156	100	206	660	From 15th Aug. 1822, 1½d. By Act 3. Geo. 4. 334,570	.....	.....	.....	.....
Scotland	35,400	.....	8,000	2,000	3,600			400		.....	.....	.....	.....
Ireland	.....	.....	.....							10,000	8,849	120	100
	1,888,959	11,700	267,213	65,032	13,756	100	206	1,060	334,570	10,000	8,849	120	100
England	1,905,359	25,110	263,184	73,232	9,323	199	292	992	.....	.....	.....	.....	.....
Scotland	64,400	.....	10,000	1,000	250			400	.....	.....	.....	.....	.....
Ireland	.....	.....	.....						270,301	5,800	5,925	30	20
	1,969,758	25,110	273,184	74,232	9,573	199	292	1,392	270,301	5,800	5,925	30	20
England	2,449,353	21,500	434,512	130,196	18,789	14	528	1,861	.....	.....	.....	.....	.....
Scotland	52,496	.....	7,600	1,000	3,400				.....	.....	.....	.....	.....
Ireland	.....	.....	.....						669,602	16,000	12,200	200	.....
	2,501,849	21,500	442,112	131,196	22,189	14	528	1,861	669,602	16,000	12,200	200	.....
England	3,038,875	39,511	510,946	155,833	35,092	12	381	1,845	.....	.....	.....	.....	.....
Scotland	133,602	.....	47,000	2,400	11,300				.....	.....	.....	.....	.....
Ireland	.....	.....	.....						1,213,486	28,814	26,000	500	300
	3,172,477	39,511	557,946	158,233	46,392	12	381	1,845	1,213,486	28,814	26,000	500	300
England	119,604	.....	139,603	45,399	1,971	341	12	375	.....	.....	.....	.....	.....
Scotland	128,513	.....	2,000	.....	.....				.....	.....	.....	.....	.....
Ireland	.....	.....	.....						558,231	30,405	14,450	.....	.....
	248,117	.....	141,603	45,399	1,971	341	12	375	558,231	30,405	14,450	.....	.....
England	.....	.....	245,911	57,683	6,933	.....	95	208	.....	.....	.....	.....	.....
Scotland	291,377	.....	.....	.....	.....				.....	.....	.....	.....	.....
Ireland	.....	.....	.....						406,435	3,300	5,259	.....	.....
	291,377	.....	245,911	57,683	6,933		95	208	406,435	3,300	5,269	.....	.....
England	.....	.....	60,451	13,867	4,250	.....	140	1,020	.....	.....	.....	.....	.....
Scotland	16,090	.....	1,100	.....	.....				.....	.....	.....	.....	.....
Ireland	.....	.....	.....						9,200	100	100	.....	.....
	16,090	.....	61,551	13,867	4,250		140	1,020	9,200	100	100	.....	.....

Scotch banks obtain their note stamps chiefly through their London agents, and which are not dis-able from those obtained through the same medium for the country bankers in England. The which is made for Scotland is necessarily confined to the notes sent up from Scotland, through the tor, to be stamped, except the notes of a lesser value than 5l. stamped since the 3d February, 1826; plicable only to Scotland. The chartered banks obtain the stamps for their notes chiefly through ndon agents, in like manner as the other Scotch banks: no return can, therefore, be made of the of notes stamped for them.

TABLE III.—An Account of the Number of Licences taken out by Country Bankers
England and Wales, for the Years ending 10th October, 1824, 1825, 1826, and 182
specifying such as have been given to Firms carrying on Business in more Pla
than one.

	Total Number of Licences taken out in each Year.	Number given to Firms carrying on Business in more Places than one in each Year.
Year ending 10th October, 1824	788	162
Year ending 10th October, 1825	797	164
Year ending 10th October, 1826	809	166
Year ending 10th October, 1827	668	131

Stamp Office, Somerset Place,   TEASDALE COCKELL,
8th February, 1828.   Distributor.

IV. BANKS (SCOTCH).

The act of 1708, preventing more than six individuals from entering into a partn
ship for carrying on the business of banking, did not extend to Scotland. In con
quence of this exemption, several banking companies, with numerous bodies of pa
ners, have always existed in that part of the empire. The Bank of Scotland w
established by act of parliament in 1695. It enjoyed, by the terms of its charter,
twenty-one years, the exclusive privilege of issuing notes in Scotland. Its origi
capital was only 100,000*l.* It was increased to 200,000*l.* in 1744; and now amou
to 1,500,000*l.* The partners are liable only to the amount of the shares they respe
ively hold.

The Royal Bank of Scotland was established in 1727. Its original capital v
151,000*l.* At present it amounts to 1,500,000*l.*

The British Linen Company was incorporated in 1746, for the purpose, as its nar
implies, of undertaking the manufacture of linen. But the views in which it origina
were speedily abandoned; and it became a banking company only. Its capital amou
to 500,000*l.*

None of the other banking companies established in Scotland are chartered as
ciations; and the partners are jointly and individually liable, to the whole extent of th
fortunes, for the debts of the firms. Some of them, such as the National Bank,
Commercial Banking Company, the Dundee Commercial Bank, the Perth Banki
Company, &c. have very numerous bodies of partners. Their affairs are uniform
conducted by a board of directors, annually chosen by the shareholders.

The Bank of Scotland began to issue one pound notes so early as 1704; and th
issue has since been continued without interruption. " In Scotland," to use the sta
ment given in the Report of the Committee of the House of Commons of 1826, on
Promissory Notes of Scotland and Ireland, " the issue of promissory notes payable
the bearer on demand, for a sum of not less than twenty shillings, has been at all tin
permitted by law; nor has any act been passed, limiting the period for which such iss
shall continue legal in that country. In *England*, the issue of promissory notes fo
less sum than five pounds was prohibited by law from the year 1777 to the period
the Bank Restriction in 1797. It has been permitted since 1797; and the permiss
will cease, as the law at present stands, in April, 1829."

There have been comparatively few bankruptcies among the Scotch banks. In 1
and 1825, when so many of the English provincial banks were swept off, there was
a single establishment in Scotland that gave way. This superior stability seems to
ascribable partly to the formation of so many banks with numerous bodies of partn
which tends to prevent any company with only a few partners, unless they are know
possess considerable fortunes, from getting paper into circulation; partly to the
risk attending the business of banking in Scotland; and partly to the facility afforded
the law of Scotland of attaching a debtor's property, whether it consist of land
moveables, and making it available to the payment of his debts.

In the Report already quoted, the last-mentioned topic is touched upon as follo
— " The general provisions of the law of Scotland bearing upon this subject are
culated to promote the solidity of banking establishments, by affording to the cred
great facilities of ascertaining the pecuniary circumstances of individual partners,
by making the private fortunes of those partners available for the discharge of
obligations of the bank with which they are connected. There is no limitation u

e number of partners of which a banking company in Scotland may consist, and,
cepting in the case of the Bank of Scotland and the two chartered banks, which
ve very considerable capitals, the partners of all banking companies are bound
ntly and severally, so that each partner is liable, to the whole extent of his fortune,
r the whole debts of the company. A creditor in Scotland is empowered to attach
e real and heritable, as well as the personal estate of his debtor, for payment of per-
nal debts, among which may be classed debts due by bills and promissory notes; and
course may be had, for the purpose of procuring payment, to each description of pro-
rty at the same time. Execution is not confined to the real property of a debtor merely
ring his life, but proceeds with equal effect upon that property after his decease.

" The law relating to the establishment of records gives ready means of procuring
'ormation with respect to the real and heritable estate of which any person in Scotland
ay be possessed. No purchase of an estate in that country is secure until the seisine
aat is, the instrument of actual delivery has been given) is put on record,
r is any mortgage effectual until the deed is in like manner recorded.

" In the case of conflicting pecuniary claims upon real property, the preference is not
gulated by the date of the transaction, but by the date of its record. These records are
cessible to all persons, and thus the public can with ease ascertain the effective means
ich a banking company possesses of discharging its obligations; and the partners in
at company are enabled to determine, with tolerable accuracy, the degree of risk and
ponsibility to which the private property of each is exposed."

As was previously observed, all the Scotch banks receive deposits of so low a value as
., and sometimes lower, and allow interest upon them.

" The interest," say the committee, " allowed by the bank upon deposits varies from
e to time according to the current rate of interest which money generally bears. At
sent, 1826, the interest allowed upon deposits is four per cent." (At this moment,
31, the interest allowed on deposits is only two or two and a half per cent.) " It
been calculated that the aggregate amount of the sums deposited with the Scotch
ks amounts to about twenty or twenty-one millions." (It is believed to be at present,
31, little if anything under twenty-four millions.) " The precise accuracy of such an
imate cannot of course be relied on. The witness by whom it was made thought that
amount of deposits could not be less than sixteen millions, nor exceed twenty-five
lions, and took an intermediate sum as the probable amount. Another witness, who
been connected for many years with different banks in Scotland, and has had expence of their concerns at Stirling, Edinburgh, Perth, Aberdeen, and Glasgow, stated
t more than one half of the deposits in the banks with which he had been connected were in
is from ten pounds to two hundred pounds. Being asked what class of the com-
nity it is that makes the small deposits, he gave the following answer, from which it
ears that the mode of conducting this branch of the banking business in Scotland has
g given to that country many of the benefits derivable from the establishment of
ing banks.

Question. What class of the community is it that makes the smallest deposits?
Answer. They are generally the labouring classes in towns like Glasgow: in
ntry places, like Perth and Aberdeen, it is from servants and fishermen, and that
s of the community, who save small sums from their earnings, till they come
e a bank deposit. There is now a facility for their placing money in the Pro-
nt Banks, which receive money till the deposit amounts to ten pounds. When
mes to ten pounds, it is equal to the minimum of a bank deposit. The system of
king in Scotland is an extension of the Provident Bank system. Half-yearly or
ly those depositors come to the bank, and add the savings of their labour, with the
rest that has accrued upon the deposits from the previous half year or year, to the
cipal; and in this way it goes on without being at all reduced, accumulating (at
pound interest) till the depositor is able either to buy or build a house, when it
es to be one, or two, or three hundred pounds, or till he is able to commence busi-
as a master in the line in which he has hitherto been a servant. A great part of the
ositors of the bank are of that description, and a great part of the most thriving of our
ers and manufacturers have arisen from such beginnings."

he loans or advances made by the Scotch banks are either in the shape of discounts
pon cash credits, or, as they are more commonly termed, cash accounts.
his species of account does not differ in principle from an over-drawing account at a
ate banker's in England. A cash credit is a credit given to an individual by a banking
pany for a limited sum, seldom under 100l. or 200l., upon his own security, and that
vo or three individuals approved by the bank, who become sureties for its payment.
individual who has obtained such a credit is enabled to draw the whole sum, or any
of it, when he pleases; replacing it, or portions of it, according as he finds it con-
ent; interest being charged upon such part only as he draws out. " If a man bor-

rows five thousand pounds from a private hand, besides that it is not always to be found when required, he pays interest for it whether he be using it or not. His bank credit costs him nothing, except during the moment it is of service to him; and this circumstance is of equal advantage as if he had borrowed money at a much lower rate of interest." (*Hume's Essay on the Balance of Trade.*) This, then, is plainly one of the most commodious forms in which advances can be made. Cash credits are not, however, intended to be a *dead loan;* the main object of the banks in granting them is to get their notes circulated, and they do not grant them except to persons in business, or to those who are frequently drawing out and paying in money.

The system of cash credits has been very well described in the Report of the Lords Committee of 1826, on Scotch and Irish banking. " There is also," say their lordships, " one part of their system, which is stated by all the witnesses (and, in the opinion of the committee, very justly stated) to have had the best effects upon the people of *Scotland*, and particularly upon the middling and poorer classes of society, in producing and encouraging habits of frugality and industry. The practice referred to is that of cash credits. Any person who applies to a bank for a cash credit, is called upon to produce two or more competent sureties, who are jointly bound; and after a full inquiry into the character of the applicant, the nature of his business, and the sufficiency of his securities, he is allowed to open a credit, and to draw upon the bank for the whole of its amount, or for such part as his daily transactions may require. To the credit of the account he pays in such sums as he may not have occasion to use, and interest is charged or credited upon the daily balance, as the case may be. From the facility which these cash credits give to all the small transactions of the country, and from the opportunities which they afford to persons, who begin business with little or no capital but their character, to employ profitably the minutest products of their industry, it cannot be doubted that the most important advantages are derived to the whole community. The advantage to the banks who give these cash credits arises from the call which they continually produce for the issue of their paper, and from the opportunity which they afford for the profitable employment of part of their deposits. The banks are indeed so sensible, that in order to make this part of their business advantageous and secure, it is necessary that their cash credits should (as they express it) be frequently operated upon, that they refuse to continue them unless this implied condition be fulfilled. The total amount of their cash credits is stated by one witness to be five millions, of which the average amount advanced by the banks may be one third."

The expense of a bond for a cash credit of 500*l.* is 4*l.* stamp duty, and a charge of 10*s.* 6*d.* per cent. for filling it up.

According to a demi-official return given in the Commons' Report already referred to, the total number of notes in circulation in Scotland, in the early part of 1826, amounted to 3,309,082, of which 2,079,344 were under 5*l.*, and 1,229,838, 5*l.* and upwards.

The Scotch banks draw on London at 20 days' date. This is denominated the par of exchange between London and Edinburgh.

Most of the great Scotch banks, such as the Bank of Scotland, the Royal Bank, &c. have established branches in other towns besides that where the head office is kept.

By the act 9 Geo. 4. c. 65., to restrain the negotiation in England of Scotch or Irish promissory notes and bills under 5*l.*, it is enacted, that if any body politic or corporate, or person, shall, after the 5th of April, 1829, publish, utter, negotiate, or transfer, in any part of England, any promissory or other note, draft, engagement, or undertaking, payable on demand to the bearer, for any sum less than 5*l.*, purporting to have been made or issued in Scotland or Ireland, every such body politic or corporate, or person, shall forfeit for every such offence not more than 20*l.* nor less than 5*l.*

Nothing contained in this act applies to any draft or order drawn by any person on his or her banker, or on any person acting as such banker, for the payment of money held by such banker or person for the use of the person by whom such draft or order shall be drawn.

ᴛᴇ I. — The following Table contains an Account of the Number of Banks in ᴿotland ; the Names of the Firms or Banks ; Dates of their Establishment ; Places of ᴇ Head Offices ; Number of Branches ; Number of Partners ; and the Names of their ᴼndon Agents. (Extracted principally from the Appendix, p. 19. to the Commons' ᴇport of 1826, on Scotch and Irish Banking.)

Names of Firms or Banks.	Date.	Head Office.	No. of Branches.	No. of Partners.	London Agents.
ᴮank of Scotland - -	1695	Edinburgh	16	Charter	Coutts and Co.
ᴿoyal Bank of Scotland -	1727	Ditto	1	Ditto	Bank of England, and ditto.
ᴮritish Linen Company -	1746	Ditto	27	Ditto	Smith, Payne, and Co.
ᴬberdeen Banking Company	1767	Aberdeen	6	80	Glyn and Co.
ᴬberdeen Town and Coun. Bk.	1825	Ditto	4	446	Jones, Loyd, and Co.
ᴬrbroath Banking Company	1825	Arbroath	2	112	Glyn and Co.
ᶜarrick and Co. or Ship Bank	1746	Glasgow	None	3	Smith, Payne, and Co.
ᶜom. Bank. Comp. of Scotland	1810	Edinburgh	31	521	Jones, Loyd, and Co.
ᶜommercial Banking Comp.	1778	Aberdeen	None	15	Kinloch and Sons.
ᴰundee Banking Company -	1777	Dundee	None	61	Kinloch and Sons.
ᴰundee New Bank - -	1802	Ditto	1	6	Ransom and Co.
ᴰundee Commercial Bank -	1825	Ditto	None	202	Glyn and Co.
ᴰundee Union Bank - -	1809	Ditto	4	85	Glyn and Co.
ᴱxchange and Deposit Bank	—	Edinburgh	—	1	—
ᶠalkirk Banking Company -	1787	Falkirk	1	5	Remington and Co.
ᴳreenock Banking Company	1785	Greenock	3	14	Kay and Co.
ᴳlasgow Banking Company -	1809	Glasgow	1	19	Ransom and Co., Glyn and Co.
ᴴunters and Co. - - -	1773	Ayr	3	8	Herries and Co.
ᴸeith Banking Company -	1792	Leith	4	15	Barnett and Co.
ᴺational Bank of Scotland -	1825	Edinburgh	8	1,238	Glyn and Co.
ᴹontrose Bank - - -	1814	Montrose	2	97	Barclay and Co.
ᴾaisley Banking Company -	1783	Paisley	4	6	Smith, Payne, and Co.
ᴾaisley Union Bank - -	1788	Ditto	3	4	Glyn and Co.
ᴾerth Banking Company -	1766	Perth	5	147	Barclay and Co.
ᴾerth Union Bank - -	—	Ditto	—	69	Remington and Co.
ᴿamsay's, Bonar's, and Co. -	1738	Edinburgh	None	8	Coutts and Co.
ᴿenfrewshire Banking Comp.	1802	Greenock	5	6	Kay and Co.
ˢhetland Bank - - -	—	Lerwick	—	4	Barclay and Co.
ˢir Wm. Forbes and Co. -	—	Edinburgh	—	7	Barclay & Co., Coutts & Co.
ˢtirling Banking Company -	1777	Stirling	2	7	Kinloch and Sons.
ᵀhistle Bank - - -	1761	Glasgow	None	6	Smith, Payne and Co.

Private Banking Companies in Edinburgh who do not issue Notes.

Names of Firms or Banks.	Date.	Head Office.	No. of Branches.	No. of Partners.	London Agents.
ᴹessrs. Kinnear, Smith, & Co.	1830*	Edinburgh	None	None	Smith, Payne, and Co.
ᴿobert Allan and Son -	1776	Ditto	None	None	Bosanquet and Co.
ᴶames Inglis and Co. - -		Ditto	None	None	Bosanquet and Co.

ᴇ II. — An Account of the Number of Licences taken out by Country Bankers ˢcotland for the Years ending the 10th October, 1824, 1825, 1826, and 1827 ; ᶜifying such as have been given to Firms carrying on Business in more Places than ⁻.

	1824.	1825.	1826.	1827.
ᵇer of Licences issued to Bankers who issue Notes ᵒne place only - - - - -	10	13	9	9
to Bankers who issue Notes at two different ᶜes - - - - - -	10	12	12	6
to Bankers who issue Notes at three different ᶜes - - - - - -	6	6	12	6
to Bankers who issue Notes at four or more ᶜes - - - - -	52	52	56	60
	78	83	89	81

ᵐp Office, Edinburgh, 4th March, 1828.   Tʜᴏᴍᴀs Pᴇɴᴅᴇʀ, Compt.
       Certified.

ᵢs firm was established last year by the junction of two long established and highly respectable ᵀhomas Kinnear and Sons, and Donald Smith and Co.

TABLE III. — Statement of the Number of Persons convicted of Forgery of all Instruments connected with the Chartered and other Banks of Scotland; whether of Bank Notes or Post Bills, Bills of Exchange, or otherwise; in each Year, from 1791 to 1829 inclusive; particularising the Capital Convictions upon which Execution took place, and the Cases of mitigated Punishment.

Years.	For Forging.	For Uttering.	Total Number Convicted.	Number where Pains of Law restricted, and Sentence short of Death pronounced.	Number on whom Capital Sentence pronounced.	Number whose Sentences were mitigated by His Majesty.		Number executed.
						Pardoned.	Commuted.	
1791	2	1	3	2	1	1	-	1
1792	2	-	2	2	—	—	—	—
1793	—	—	—	—	—	—	—	—
1794	—	—	—	—	—	—	—	—
1795	-	1	1	1	—	—	—	—
1796	—	—	—	—	—	—	—	—
1797	-	1	1	-	1	-	-	1
1798	—	—	—	—	—	—	—	—
1799	—	—	—	—	—	—	—	—
1800	-	1	1	-	1	-	-	1
1801	—	—	—	—	—	—	—	—
1802	1	-	1	1	—	—	—	—
1803	—	—	—	—	—	—	—	—
1804	1	-	1	1	—	—	—	—
1805	2	-	2	-	2	-	-	2
1806	-	2	2	-	2	-	2	—
1807	1	-	1	1	—	—	—	—
1808	—	—	—	—	—	—	—	—
1809	1	-	1	1	—	—	—	—
1810	1	-	1	1	—	—	—	—
1811	2	-	2	1	1	-	1	—
1812	—	—	—	—	—	—	—	—
1813	3	3	6	5	1	-	-	1
1814	1	4	5	3	2	-	-	2
1815	2	-	2	2	—	—	—	—
1816	2	-	2	1	1	-	-	1
1817	1	2	3	2	1	-	-	1
1818	1	2	3	2	1	-	1	—
1819	4	3	7	6	1	-	1	—
1820	3	1	4	4	—	—	—	—
1821	2	9	11	7	4	-	2	2
1822	2	3	5	5	—	—	—	—
1823	-	10	10	5	5	-	3	2
1824	3	10	13	12	1	—	-	1
1825	1	8	9	9	—	—	—	—
1826	3	20	23	23	-	1	—	—
1827	2	25	27	25	2	-	1	1
1828	4	27	31	31	—	—	—	—
1829	2	17	19	19	—	—	—	—
	49	150	199	172	27	2	11	16

Edinburgh,
18th June, 1830.

Certified by   JA. ANDERSON,
Depute Clerk of Justiciary

V. BANKS (IRISH).

" In no country, perhaps," says Sir Henry Parnell, " has the issuing of
per money been carried to such an injurious excess as in Ireland.   A national
nk was established in 1783, with similar privileges to those of the Bank of
ngland, in respect to the restriction of more than six partners in a bank ; and the
jury that Ireland has sustained from the repeated failure of banks may be mainly
ributed to this defective legislative regulation.   Had the trade of banking been left
free in Ireland as it is in Scotland, the want of paper money that would have arisen
th the progress of trade would, in all probability, have been supplied by joint stock
mpanies, supported with large capitals, and governed by wise and effectual rules.
" In 1797, when the Bank of England suspended its payments, the same privilege
s extended to Ireland ; and after this period the issues of the Bank of Ireland were
idly increased.   In 1797, the amount of the notes of the Bank of Ireland in circula-
n was 621,917l. ; in 1810, 2,266,471l. ; and in 1814, 2,986,999l.
" These increased issues led to corresponding increased issues by the private banks, of
ich the number was fifty in the year 1804.   The consequence of this increase of paper
s a great depreciation of it ; the price of bullion and guineas rose to ten per cent.
ove the mint price ; and the exchange with London became as high as 18 per
nt., the par being 8¼.   This unfavourable exchange was afterwards corrected ; not by
y reduction in the issues of the Bank of Ireland, but by the depreciation of the
itish currency in the year 1810, when the exchange between London and Dublin
led again at about par.
" The loss that Ireland has sustained by the failure of banks may be described in a
y words.   It appears by the Report of the Committee on Irish Exchanges, in 1804,
t there were at that time in Ireland fifty registered banks.   Since that year, a great
ny more have been established ; but *the whole have failed,* one after the other, involv-
the country from time to time in immense distress, with the following exceptions :
first, a few that withdrew from business ;   secondly, four banks in Dublin ; thirdly,
ee at Belfast ; and, lastly, one at Mallow.   These eight banks, with the new Provin-
l Bank, and the Bank of Ireland, are the only banks now existing in Ireland.
" In 1821, in consequence of eleven banks having failed nearly at the same time, in
preceding year, in the south of Ireland, government succeeded in making an
ngement with the Bank of Ireland, by which joint stock companies were allowed to
established at a distance of fifty miles (Irish) from Dublin, and the Bank was per-
ted to increase its capital 500,000l.   The act of 1 and 2 Geo. 4. c. 72. was
nded on this agreement.
" But ministers having omitted to repeal in this act various restrictions on the trade
banking that had been imposed by 33 Geo. 2. c. 14., no new company was
ned.   In 1824, a party of merchants of Belfast, wishing to establish a joint stock
ipany, petitioned parliament for the repeal of this act of Geo. 2. ; and an act was
ordingly passed in that session, repealing some of the most objectionable restrictions
t (the 5 Geo. 4. c. 73.).
" In consequence of this act, the Northern Bank of Belfast was converted into a joint
k company, with a capital of half a million, and commenced business on the 1st of
uary, 1825.   But the remaining restrictions of 33 Geo. 2., and certain provisions
tained in the new acts of 1 and 2 Geo. 3. and 5 Geo. 4., obstructed the progress of
company, and they found it necessary to apply to government to remove them ; and
ill was accordingly introduced, which would have repealed all the obnoxious clauses
he 33 Geo. 2., had it not been so altered in the committee as to leave several of them
orce.   In 1825, the Provincial Bank of Ireland commenced business, with a capital
wo millions ; and the Bank of Ireland have of late established branches in all the
cipal towns in Ireland.
The losses that have been sustained in Ireland by abusing the power of issuing
er have been so great, that much more is necessary to be done, by way of protecting
public from future loss, than the measure proposed last session (1826) by ministers,
olishing small notes ; and the measure already adopted, of allowing joint stock comes to be established in the interior of the country.   As the main source of the evil
sists in the interference of the law in creating a national bank with exclusive privi-
s, the first step that ought to be taken for introducing a good system into Ireland is
getting rid of such a bank, and opening the trade of banking in Dublin.   The next
sure should be the requiring of each bank to give security for the amount of paper
is issued ; for after the experience of the ignorance with which the Irish banks have
ducted their business, and the derangement of the natural course of the trade by the
existence of the Bank of Ireland, it would be unwise to calculate upon a sound
m of banking speedily supplanting that which has been established.

" Under the circumstances in which Ireland is placed, nothing would so much contri
bute to her rapid improvement in wealth, as the introducing of the Scotch plan of cas
credits, and of paying interest on deposits.   By cash credits the capital which nov
exists would be rendered more efficient, and the paying of interest on small deposit
would lead to habits of economy, and to the more rapid accumulation of new capital.

" The charter of the Bank of Ireland has still to run till the year 1838 ; but as th
charter of the Bank of England expires in 1833, unless measures are taken for gettin
rid of that of the Bank of Ireland in 1833, each part of the United Kingdom will afte
that year have a separate system of banking."— (*Observations on Paper Money, &c., by
Sir Henry Parnell,* pp. 171—177.)

The capital of the Bank of Ireland at its establishment in 1783 amounted t
600,000*l.* ; but it has been increased at various periods; and has, since 1821, amounte
to 3,000,000*l.*   At present no bank having more than six partners can be establishe
any where within 50 Irish miles of Dublin ; nor is any such bank allowed to draw bill
upon Dublin for less than 50*l.*, or at a shorter date than six months.   This enactmen
seems to amount to a virtual prohibition of the drawing of such bills.   The Bank o
Ireland draws on London at 20 days' date.   She neither grants cash credits, no
allows any interest on deposits.   She discounts at the rate of 5*l.* per cent.

The Provincial Bank and the Northern Banking Company grant cash credits, an
allow interest on deposits.

It appears from the statements given in the Report of the Commons' Committee o
1826, that the average value of the notes and post bills of the Bank of Ireland of 5*l
and upwards in circulation, during the five years ending with 1825, amounted t
3,646,660*l.* Irish currency ; and that the average value of the notes and post bills unde
5*l.* in circulation during the same period amounted to 1,643,828*l.* Irish currency.   Th
average value of the notes of all descriptions issued by the other banking establishment
in Ireland, in 1825, amounted to 1,192,886*l.*

In 1828, the currency of Ireland was assimilated to that of Great Britain.   Previousl
to that period, the currency of the former was 8⅓ per cent. less valuable than that of th
latter.

TABLE I. — An Account of the Number of Licences taken out by Country Bankers i
Ireland, for the Years ending 10th October, 1824, 1825, 1826, and 1827 ; specifyin
such as have been given to Firms carrying on Business in more Places than one.

Year.	Total Number of Licences taken out.	Number of Firms.	Number issued to Firms carrying on Business at more Places than one.	Number of Firms.
Ended 10th October, 1824 -	20	11	11	2
— 10th October, 1825 -	38	10	31	3
— 10th October, 1826 -	31	6	28	3
— 10th October, 1827 -	34	7	31	4

Note. — One of the firms carrying on business at more places than one in 1827 ob
tained two licences, and has since merged in a joint stock company.   One obtaine
fourteen, another eleven ; and the last obtained four, which is the highest numb
required to be taken out since the 2d of July, 1827, by firms carrying on business
several places.

Stamp Office, Dublin,   J. S. COOPER,
    March 4. 1828.   Compt. Gen.

LE II.—Account of the Number of Bank of Ireland Notes in Circulation, including Bank Post Bills, in each Half Year, commencing with the Half Year ending 1st January, 1797, to 1st January, 1819, inclusive.

		£	s.	d.			£	s.	d.
97 January 1	-	733,763	3	1	1809 January 1	-	3,002,699	1	8
July 1	-	785,101	9	1	July 1	-	3,144,677	4	3
98 January 1	-	1,081,512	18	1	1810 January 1	-	3,170,064	17	1
July 1	-	1,245,214	17	11	July 1	-	3,171,607	13	3
99 January 1	-	1,363,710	17	9	1811 January 1	-	3,331,892	16	0
July 1	-	1,557,737	12	4½	July 1	-	3,472,781	11	9½
00 January 1	-	1,928,381	4	1½	1812 January 1	-	3,616,476	13	10
July 1	-	2,317,235	6	9	July 1	-	3,763,229	11	7½
01 January 1	-	2,350,133	8	7½	1813 January 1	-	3,957,920	3	10½
July 1	-	2,323,901	19	11	July 1	-	4,199,474	16	4½
02 January 1	-	2,431,152	16	1	1814 January 1	-	4,165,906	12	7½
July 1	-	2,587,187	9	2½	July 1	-	4,281,449	17	11
03 January 1	-	2,662,405	5	6	1815 January 1	-	4,528,041	7	1
July 1	-	2,617,144	10	4½	July 1	-	4,434,455	0	4
04 January 1	-	2,798,767	15	7	1816 January 1	-	4,179,549	4	6½
July 1	-	2,859,977	13	7½	July 1	-	4,193,853	11	4½
05 January 1	-	2,817,697	7	3	1817 January 1	-	4,277,018	15	2½
July 1	-	2,778,635	12	4	July 1	-	4,304,040	11	7½
06 January 1	-	2,560,271	12	3	1818 January 1	-	4,387,155	5	4½
July 1	-	2,517,581	8	11	July 1	-	4,413,463	8	0
07 January 1	-	2,693,796	7	1½	1819 January 1	-	4,477,019	2	5
July 1	-	2,789,544	16	6					
08 January 1	-	2,746,717	5	2					
July 1	-	2,798,835	10	9½					

E III.—An Account of the Average Amount of Bank of Ireland Notes, including Bank Post Bills, issued during the Six Years ending with 1825.

Irish Currency.

		£	s.	d.	£	s.	d.
Notes and Bills	of 5l. and upwards	2,894,777	5	2½			
—	under 5l.	1,314,806	15	9			
					4,209,584	0	11½
—	of 5l. and upwards	3,501,119	10	11			
—	under 5l.	1,710,603	3	8			
					5,211,792	14	7
—	of 5l. and upwards	3,618,111	1	6½			
—	under 5l.	1,552,321	2	1			
					5,170,432	3	7½
—	of 5l. and upwards	3,528,625	6	11			
—	under 5l.	1,588,764	7	3			
					5,117,389	14	2
—	of 5l. and upwards	3,890,337	8	7½			
—	under 5l.	1,732,118	5	10½			
					5,622,455	14	6
—	of 5l. and upwards	4,446,994	19	9			
—	under 5l.	1,964,354	8	3			
					6,411,349	8	4

(*Commons' Report of* 1826, p. 29.)

en it was proposed in 1826 to suppress the small notes of Scotland and Ireland, ⸱ as those of England, the directors of the Provincial Bank of Ireland presented ⸱ memorial to the Treasury in opposition to the measure. As this memorial con- ⸱ good deal of authentic information, in respect not only of the condition of the ⸱cial Bank, but also of the banking system of Ireland, we have thought it right to ⸱ a place here.

" The Memorial of the Directors of the Provincial Bank of Ireland to the
                                    Treasury;

" SHEWETH,

" That the society or copartnership denominated the Provincial Bank of Ireland was
established by deed of settlement, of date 1st August, 1825, under the authority of an
act passed in the last session of parliament, intituled, ' An Act for the better Regulation
Copartnerships of certain Bankers in Ireland;' in the preamble of which it is stated to be
'expedient to make further provision for the regulation of such societies and copartnerships
*and to encourage the further introduction of British capital into banking establishments in
Ireland.*'

" That under the encouragement thus held out by the wise and liberal policy of the legislature, a capital of two millions, divided into twenty thousand shares, was subscribed
by the shareholders of this society or copartnership, chiefly in London.

" That the names of the shareholders have been duly registered at the stamp office in
Dublin, and amount in number nearly to one thousand, composed almost entirely of persons of wealth and respectability; and that the security to the public for the obligations
of the Provincial Bank of Ireland, whether arising from the issue of notes, or from deposits, is thus of the most ample and satisfactory nature.

" That your memorialists, on the faith of the continuance of the existing laws for regulating the circulation of bank notes in Ireland, have, at a very great expense, provided
the means of supplying the population of that country with a circulating medium
founded on the soundest principles of banking, which have hitherto been scarcely known
or acted upon in that part of the kingdom.

" That the distinguishing features of the system adopted by the memorialists, are as
follow :—

" 1. The establishment of branches in every principal town throughout Ireland, at a
greater distance than fifty miles from Dublin, from the space within which circle your
memorialists are excluded by the existing privileges of the Bank of Ireland.

" 2. The notes of the Provincial Bank *are all payable on demand at the branches where
they are respectively issued, and convertible into gold there, at the will of the holders, differing in
this respect from the notes of the Bank of Ireland, which are convertible into gold at Dublin only.*

" 3. The issues of notes by the Provincial Bank are made only on securities founded
on real transactions arising out of the industry of the people in the pursuit of commerce
and agriculture; and the rate of interest which it charges to those dealing with it is
under that which the law allows.

" 4. The Provincial Bank *allows interest at the rate of two per cent. on money deposited*
—a practice but partially known in the north of Ireland, and altogether new in by far the
greater part of the country.

" That on these principles, your memorialists conceive the currency of Ireland will,
in so far as depends on them, be preserved in a sound and healthy state; and that while
the necessary stimulus to trade and agriculture, of which the want has been so much felt
in Ireland, is thus supplied by the 'introduction of British capital into this banking
establishment,' all danger of excess of its paper circulation is guarded against; first, by
its convertibility into gold at so many places; secondly, by the inducement which the interest allowed on deposits holds to every one to return to the Bank all surplus money not
wanted for immediate purposes; thirdly, by the exchange of notes with other banks,
which, according to the custom prevalent in Scotland, is regularly made, and which in fact
is more frequently made by your memorialists than is done in Scotland, as it takes place
every day; and, lastly, by the effect on the exchange with Britain, and consequent demand
for gold which would 'instantly be produced by any such excess; this last check being
one of instant operation in the case of your memorialists, through whose establishment
a considerable part of the business of rent and commercial remittances is now carried on.

" That the system thus laid down has been commenced, and has, for the last six months
been in actual operation in Ireland, with every appearance of success which could have
been anticipated either by the legislature in enacting the law under which this banking
society has been formed, or by the shareholders in raising its capital.

" That of the branches intended to be established by your memorialists, five have been
already opened, viz., Cork, Limerick, Clonmel, Londonderry, Sligo; and that nine more
are in progress, houses having been engaged, officers appointed, notes prepared, and other
arrangements made for commencing business without delay.

" That 300,000*l.* of the capital stock of the society has been already called up; and
that intimation has been given to the shareholders, that further calls will be made progressively as the branches come into operation.

" That when the aforesaid act, authorising this and similar societies to be formed,
passed, it must have been obvious that the intentions of the legislature could not possibly
be carried into effect, unless the shareholders of such societies or copartnerships were to
be permitted to derive the fair and legitimate profits which belong to banking.

" That the fair profits of banking, when conducted by a public company, and on the
eral principles which your memorialists have adopted, arise in a considerable degree
m the circulation of notes; *and that without such profit, the expenses of conducting their
siness, unless they should happen to possess exclusive privileges, would necessarily be so
eat as to oblige them to relinquish such undertakings.*

" That it is a well known fact, which the experience of your Memorialists, since the
siness of the Provincial Bank was commenced, most amply confirms, that two thirds of
e circulation of notes in Ireland consist in notes of one pound, and other denominations
der five pounds' value; and of these, much the greater part are notes of one pound
ly.

" That this circulation of small notes necessarily arises from the peculiarities which
end four of the chief branches of industry in Ireland; viz. the linen manufacture, the
sing of corn, the production of butter, and rearing of pigs. That although each of
ese branches is, in the aggregate, of very considerable magnitude, yet, from the very
eat number of persons engaged in them, the produce which one individual brings to
arket is so very small that, without a circulating medium adapted to the circumstances,
e trade could not be carried on.

" That, from the facts above stated, it is of the utmost importance to Ireland that the
erchants and traders who deal in its produce should be supplied with that species of
culating medium which is adapted to the wants of the people, and which can only be
pplied, under proper regulation, by societies or co-partnerships such as your memorial-
s represent.

" That notwithstanding the state of things here mentioned, which can be proved to
e satisfaction of the Legislature, if need be, the Memorialists are given to understand
t the measure which is now before Parliament for restraining the issue of notes under
e pounds in England is, at no great distance of time, to be extended both to Scotland
d Ireland; and if the Memorialists are rightly informed, it is the intention of Govern-
nt to propose that its operation in Ireland shall take effect sooner than in Scotland.

" That in these circumstances your Memorialists feel it to be their duty to represent
the most earnest manner to His Majesty's Government, the great hardship, if not in-
tice, with which the proposed measure will press against the Provincial Bank of
land, which has been so recently established under the sanction of the Legislature,
en expressly for the benefit of Ireland, by encouraging the introduction of British
ital into that country, and which without such sanction and encouragement never
uld have been established; for if this measure be carried into effect, the Provincial
nk must instantly be deprived of any sufficient means of reimbursing itself for the
vy expense to which it has been subject in preparing that very relief to Ireland which
was the object of Parliament to administer, and the country must in consequence be
ied the advantages which would be conferred on it by its permanent establishment:
should the paper of the Provincial Bank be withdrawn, a monopoly would be given
hat of the Bank of Ireland, which, though issued locally at the branches of that Bank,
onvertible at Dublin only.

" That this measure is altogether uncalled for in Ireland, where there is not the
llest complaint of an excessive issue of paper, nor any overtrading, or inordinate
it of speculation. It is not only uncalled for, but universally deprecated as being
gnant with the most serious mischief, and calculated to crush the rising spirit of intry in that country, by taking from the manufacturers and others the means of em-
ying the population, and so to produce ruin to persons engaged in trade and agricul-
e, and amongst the lower classes discontent, disorder, and rebellion.

That your Memorialists trust, &c.''

We agree with the authors of this Memorial, in thinking that there were no reasons
icient to justify the suppression of small notes either in Scotland or Ireland, as contem-
ed in 1826. But after the general destruction of banks that has repeatedly taken
e in Ireland, and the wide-spread ruin that their bankruptcy has occasioned, it does
m most extraordinary, to say the least of it, that no steps, or none of a decided charac-
should have been taken to guard against the recurrence of such calamities. We have
ady shown that they can only be completely prevented by obliging every banker, or
pany of bankers, issuing notes, to give security for their payment. Other schemes
palliate the mischiefs that have already resulted, and will certainly continue to re-
, from the present system, but the one now proposed would obviate them entirely:
while it is easy of adoption, and effectual to its object, it would entail no real hard-
on those carrying on the business of banking, nor drive a single individual from the
e that ought ever to have been in it. It would leave no room for fraud or deception.
establishment for the issue of notes could exist, under the proposed plan, unless it
e set on foot by individuals possessed of adequate capital. Adventurers speculating
he funds of others, and sharpers anxious only to get themselves indebted to the

public, would not then find, as they have hitherto often done, that banking was a field on which they could advantageously enter. (See *ante*, p. 85., and the reference there made.)

VI. Banks (Foreign).

To attempt giving any detailed account of the principal foreign banks would very far exceed our limits; we shall, therefore, only notice a few of the more celebrated: —

The *Bank of Venice* seems to have been the first banking establishment in Europe. It was founded so early as 1171, and subsisted till the subversion of the republic in 1797. It was essentially a deposit bank; and its bills bore at all times a premium or *agio* over the current money of the city.

The *Bank of Amsterdam* was established in 1659. It was a deposit bank; and payments were made by writing off sums from the account of one individual to those of another. According to the principles on which the bank was established, it should have had at all times in its coffers bullion equal to the full amount of the claims upon it. But the directors privately lent about 10,500,000 florins to the states of Holland and Friesland. This circumstance transpired when the French invaded Holland, and caused the ruin of the bank. (See my edition of the *Wealth of Nations*, vol. ii. p. 333.) A new bank, denominated the *Bank of the Netherlands*, was established in 1814. It is formed on the model of the Bank of England; and was to enjoy for twenty-five years the exclusive privilege of issuing notes. The original capital of five millions of florins was doubled in 1819. The king holds *one tenth* of the shares. The affairs of the bank are managed by a president, secretary, and five directors, who are chosen every six months, but may be indefinitely re-elected.

The *Bank of Hamburgh* is a deposit bank, and its affairs are managed according to a system that ensures the fullest publicity. It receives no deposits in coin, but only in bullion of a certain degree of fineness. It charges itself with the bullion at the rate of 442 schillings the mark, and issues it at the rate of 444 schillings; being a charge of $\frac{4}{9}$ths, or nearly $\frac{1}{2}$ per cent. for its retention. It advances money on jewels to $\frac{3}{4}$ths of their value. The city is answerable for all pledges deposited with the bank; they may be sold by auction, if they remain a year and six weeks without any interest being paid. If the value be not claimed within three years, it is forfeited to the poor. The Bank of Hamburgh is universally admitted to be one of the best managed in Europe.

The *Bank of France* was founded in 1803. The exclusive privilege of issuing notes payable to bearer was granted to it for forty years. The capital of the bank consisted at first of 45,000,000 fr., but it was subsequently increased to 90,000,000 fr. divided into 90,000 shares or *actions* of 1,000 fr. each. Of these shares, 67,900 are in the hands of the public; 22,100, being purchased up by the bank, form part of her capital. The notes issued by the bank are for 1,000 and 500 fr. The dividend varies from 4 to 5 per cent. , and there is besides, a *reserve* retained from the profits, which is vested in the 5 per cents. A bonus of 200 fr. a share was paid out of this reserve to the shareholders in 1820. The reserve in possession of the bank in 1828, amounted to 6,623,000 fr. No bills are discounted that have more than three months to run. The customary rate of discount is 4 per cent., but it varies according to circumstances. The discounts in 1827, amounted to 621 millions fr. The bank is obliged to open a *compte courant* for every one who requires it; and performs services for those who have such accounts, similar to those rendered by the private banks of London to their customers. She is not allowed to charge any commission upon current accounts, so that her only remuneration arises out of the use of the money placed in her hands by the individuals whose payments she makes. This branch of the business is said not to be profitable. There are about 1600 accounts current at the bank; and of the entire expenses of the establishment, amounting to about 900,000 fr. a year, *two thirds* are said to be incurred in this department. The bank advances money on pledges of different kinds, such as foreign coin or bullion, government or other securities, &c. It also undertakes the care of valuable articles, as plate, jewels, bills, title-deeds, &c. The charge is $\frac{1}{8}$ per cent. of the value of each deposit for every period of six months or under.

The administration of the bank is vested in a council general of twenty members, viz. seventeen regents, and three censors, who are nominated by 200 of the principal proprietors. The king appoints the governor and deputy governor. The first must be possessed of 150, and the latter of 50 shares. A *Compte Rendu* is annually published, and a report by the censors, which together give a very full exposition of the affairs of the bank. The institution is flourishing, and enjoys unlimited credit. (For further details with respect to the Bank of France, see *Storch, Cours D'Economie Politique*, Paris, 1823, tom. iv. pp. 168—180, and the *Comptes Rendus* of the different years.)

Banks have also been established at Berlin, Copenhagen, Vienna, and Petersburgh. Those who wish for detailed information with respect to these establishments, may consult the work of M. Storch, to which we have just referred. In the 4th volume, there

admirable account of the paper money of the different continental states. The ob-
we have in view will be accomplished by laying before our readers the following
ils with respect to the *Commercial Bank* of Russia, established in 1818 : — " This
: receives deposits in gold and silver, foreign as well as Russian coin, and in bars
ingots. It has a department for transferring the sums deposited with it on the plan
e Hamburgh Bank. It discounts bills, and lends money on deposits of merchandise
Russian produce or origin. Its capital consists of 30 millions of bank note rubles.
administered by a governor and four directors appointed by government, and four
tors elected by the commercial body of Petersburgh. The property in the bank is
cted against all taxation, sequestration, or attachment; and it is enacted, that sub-
of countries with which Russia may be at war shall be entitled at all times to re-
back their deposits without any reservation. It is also declared, that at no time
the bank be called upon for any part of its capital to assist the government. All
sits must be made for six months at least, and be repayable at or before that period,
not be less than 500 rubles : sums so deposited to pay ¼ per cent. The deposits, if in
ingots, or foreign specie, are estimated in Russian silver coin, and so registered in
ttestation ; and if not demanded back within 15 days of the expiration of six months,
e necessary premium paid for the prolongation, the owner loses the right of claim-
is original deposit, and must take its estimated value in Russian silver coin. No
are discounted that have less than eight days or more than six months to run. The
of discount is 6 per cent. No interest is allowed on money deposited in the bank,
s notice be given that it will be allowed to lie for a year, and three months' notice
ven of the intention to draw it out, when *six* per cent. interest is allowed." (*Kelly's*
ist, vol. i. p. 303.) This bank has branches at Archangel, Moscow, Odessa,
, &c.

e *Bank of the United States* was incorporated in 1816. Its capital is 35 millions
llars, divided into 350,000 shares of 100 dollars each. Seven millions were sub-
ed by the United States, and the remaining 28 millions by individuals, companies,
rations, &c. The bank issues no note for less than five dollars ; all its notes are
ole in specie on demand. It discounts bills and makes advances on bullion at the
of 6 per cent. The management is under twenty-five directors ; five of whom, being
rs are annually appointed by the president of the United States. Seven directors,
ding the president, constitute a board.

e principal office of the bank is in Philadelphia ; but in January, 1830, it had
y-two subordinate offices, or branch banks, established in different parts of the
n. Subjoined is a state of the affairs of the Bank of the United States, 1st April,
: —

Notes discounted	32,138,270·39 dollars
Domestic bills discounted	10,506,882·54
Funded debt held by the bank	11,122,530·90
Real estate	2,891,890·75
Funds in Europe, equal to specie	2,789,498·54
Specie	9,043,748·97
Public deposits	8,905,501·87
Private deposits	7,704,256·87
Circulation	16,083,894·00

(*American Almanac for* 1831, p. 153.)

e establishment of the Bank of the United States has been of material service, by
ing a currency of undoubted solidity, readily accepted in all parts of the Union. At
riod when it was organised, nothing could be in a less satisfactory condition than
aper currency of the United States ; in fact, with the exception perhaps of England
reland, they have suffered more than any other country from the abuse of banking.
14, all the banks south and west of New England stopped payment ; and it
rs, from the official returns, that in all, no fewer than 165 banks stopped payment
en the 1st of January, 1811, and the 1st of July, 1830 ! Most of these banks were
stock companies. At present there are no strictly private banking companies in
nited States. They are *all* incorporated by law, with a fixed capital, to the extent
ich, in most cases, but not uniformly, the stockholders are only liable. They all
notes of five dollars ; but the issue of notes of a lower value has been forbidden in
ylvania, Maryland, and Virginia. The banks of the New England States and
others are now in the habit of regularly publishing statements of their affairs ; but
sight they afford into the real situation of the banks is not nearly so great as is
only supposed. They give the aggregate of bills discounted, and of the advances
urities, &c. ; but they convey no information as to the validity or convertibility of
bills and securities, nor with respect to many other circumstances of great import-
Those best acquainted with the state of the country and the banks, seem to be of

opinion that the latter are still very defective ; an opinion from which we feel convince
that no one who investigates the subject will see any reason to dissent.

The following is an account of the number and capital of the banking establishmen
existing in the United States on the 1st of January, 1830 : —

States.	No. of Banks.	Capital.
		Dollars.
Massachusetts - -	66	20,420,000
Maine - - -	18	2,050,000
New Hampshire - -	18	1,791,670
Vermont - - -	10	432,625
Rhode Island - -	47	6,118,397
Connecticut - -	13	4,485,177
New York - -	37	20,083,353
New Jersey - -	18	2,017,009
Pennsylvania - -	33	14,609,963
Delaware - - -	4	830,000
Maryland - - -	13	6,250,495
District of Columbia -	9	3,875,794
Virginia - - -	4	5,571,100
North Carolina - -	3	3,195,000
South Carolina . -	5	4,631,000
Georgia - - -	9	4,203,029
Louisiana - - -	4	5,665,980
Alabama - - -	2	648,503
Mississippi - -	1	950,600
Tennessee - - -	1	737,817
Ohio - - -	11	1,454,386
Michigan - . -	1	10,000
Florida - - -	1	75,000
	328	
Delaware - - -	1	
	329	
Ditto - - - -	1	
	330	110,101,898

For further information with respect to the banks of the United States, see
Report, 12th February, 1820, of the secretary of the treasury (W. H. Crawford, Es
to congress, and the pamphlet of Albert Gallatin, Esq. on the currency and banki
system of the United States, Philadelphia, 1831.   The foregoing table is extract
from the latter.

VII. Banks for Savings,

Are banks established for the receipt of small sums deposited by the poorer class
persons, and for the accumulation of such sums at compound interest.   They are ma
aged by individuals, who derive no benefit whatever from the deposits.   All monies p
into any Savings Bank established according to the provisions of the act 9 Geo.
c. 92., are ordered to be paid into the Banks of England and Ireland, and vested in Ba
annuities or exchequer bills.   The interest payable to depositors is not to exceed 2¼d.
cent. *per diem*, or 3*l*. 8*s*. 5¼*d*. per cent. *per annum*.   No depositor can contribute m
than 30*l*., exclusive of compound interest, to a Savings Bank in any one year; and
total deposits to be received from any one individual are not to exceed 150*l*. ; and wh
ever the deposits, and compound interest accruing upon them, standing in the name
any one individual, shall amount to 200*l*., no interest shall be payable upon such dep
so long as it shall amount to 200*l*   Since the establishment of this system in 18
down to January 1831, the sums received from depositors, and the interest accru
upon them, amounted to 20,760,228*l*., of which the depositors had received, in princi
and interest, 5,648,838*l*. ; leaving, at the period in question, a balance due to the de
sitors of 15,111,890*l*.   The Commissioners for the Reduction of the National D
have the disposal of the sums vested in the public funds on account of Savings Bank

The principle and object of these institutions cannot be too highly commended.
the metropolis, and many other parts of England, public banks do not receive small

sits, and upon none do they pay any interest. And even in Scotland, where the
ablic banks allow interest upon deposits, they do not generally receive less than 10l.
ut few poor persons are able to save so large a sum, except by a lengthened course of
onomy. The truth, therefore, is, that until Savings Banks were established, the poor
re every where without the means of securely and profitably investing those small sums
ey are not unfrequently in a condition to save; and were consequently led, from the
fficulty of disposing of them, to neglect opportunities for making savings, or if they
d make them, were tempted, by the offer of high interest, to lend them to persons of
ubtful characters and desperate fortunes, by whom they were, for the most part,
uandered. Under such circumstances, it is plain that nothing could be more import-
t, in the view of diffusing habits of forethought and economy amongst the labouring
sses, than the establishment of Savings Banks, where the smallest sums are placed in
rfect safety, are accumulated at compound interest, and are paid, with their accumu-
ions, the moment they are demanded by the depositors. The system is yet only in
infancy; but the magnitude of the deposits already received, sets its powerful and
utary operation in a very striking point of view.

We subjoin a copy of the rules of the St. Pancras Savings Bank, which may be taken
a model for similar institutions, inasmuch as they have been drawn up with great care,
d closely correspond with the provisions in the act 9 Geo. 4. c. 92.

1. *Management.*—This Bank is under the Management of a President, Vice-Presi-
nts, Trustees, and not less than Fifty Managers, none of whom are permitted to
:ive any benefit whatsoever, directly or indirectly, from the Deposits received, or the
oduce thereof. One or more of the Managers attend when the Bank is open for
siness.

2. *Superintending Committee.* — A Committee of not less than Ten Managers, Three
whom form a quorum, is empowered to superintend, manage, and conduct the
eral business of this Bank; to add to their number from among the Managers;
fill up vacancies in their own body, and to appoint a Treasurer or Treasurers, Agent
Agents, Auditors, an Actuary and Clerks, and other Officers and Servants, and to with-
w any such appointments, and to appoint others, should it be considered necessary
to do. — The proceedings of this Committee are regularly laid before the General
etings of the Bank.

3. *Elections.* — The Superintending Committee is empowered to add to the num-
of Managers, until they amount to One Hundred and Twenty, exclusively of the
esident, Vice-Presidents, and Trustees. And any vacancy of President, Vice-Presi-
ts, and Trustees, are to be filled up at a General Meeting.

4. *General Meetings.* — A General Meeting of the President, Vice-Presidents,
ustees, and Managers of this Bank shall be held once a year, in the month of Fe-
ary. The Superintending Committee shall lay before every such Meeting a Report
he Transactions of the Bank, and State of the Accounts. The Superintending Com-
tee for the succeeding year shall be elected at such General Meeting; and failing
h Election, the former Committee shall be considered as re-appointed.

, *Special Meetings.* — The Superintending Committee are authorised to call Special
eral Meetings when they think proper; and also, on the requisition of any Ten
nagers, delivered in writing to the Actuary, or to the Manager in attendance at
Bank; and of such Meeting seven days' notice shall be given.

, *Liability of Trustees, Managers, Officers, &c.* — No Trustee or Manager shall
personally liable except for his own acts and deeds, nor for any thing done by him
irtue of his office, except where he shall be guilty of wilful neglect or default; but
Treasurer or Treasurers, the Actuary, and every Officer entrusted with the receipt or
:ody of any sum of money deposited for the purposes of this Institution, and every
:er, or other person, receiving Salary or Allowance for their services from the
ds thereof, shall give good and sufficient security, by Bond or Bonds, to the Clerk
he Peace of the County of Middlesex, for the just and faithful execution of such
e of trust.

, *Investment and Limitation of Deposits.* — Deposits of not less than *One Shilling,*
not exceeding *Thirty Pounds* in the whole, exclusive of Compound Interest, from
one Depositor, or Trustee of a Depositor, during each and every year ending on the
of November, will be received and invested, pursuant to 9 Geo. 4. c. 92. s. 11.,
the same shall amount to *One Hundred and Fifty Pounds* in the whole; and
n the principal and interest together shall amount to *Two Hundred Pounds,* then
nterest will be payable on such Deposit, so long as it shall continue to amount to that
But Depositors, whose accounts amounted to, or exceeded, *Two Hundred Pounds,*
e passing of the said Act, on the 28th July, 1828, will continue to be entitled to
rest and Compound Interest thereon.

Interest to be allowed to Depositors.—In conformity with the 24th clause of the
:o. 4. c. 92., an Interest at the rate of two-pence farthing per cent. per day, being

3l. 8s. 5¼d. per cent. per annum (*the full amount authorised by the said Act*), will be allowed to Depositors, and placed to their accounts as a Cash Deposit, in the month of *November* in each year.   Depositors demanding payment of the whole amount of their Deposits in this Bank, will be allowed the Interest due on such Deposits up to the day on which notice of withdrawing shall be given, but no interest will be allowed, in any case, on the fractional parts of a pound sterling.

9. *Description and Declaration.* — Every person desirous of making any Deposit in this Bank, shall, at the time of making their first Deposit, and at such other times as they shall be required so to do, declare their residence, occupation, profession, or calling, and sign (either by themselves, or, in case of infants under the age of seven years, by some person or persons to be approved of by the Trustees or Managers, or their officer), a declaration that they are not directly or indirectly entitled to any Deposit in, or benefit from, the funds of any other Savings Bank in England or Ireland, nor to any sum or sums standing in the name or names of any other person or persons in the Books of this Bank.   And in case any such declaration shall not be true, every such person (or the person on whose behalf such declaration may have been signed) shall forfeit and lose all right and title to such Deposits, and the Trustees and Managers shall cause the sum or sums so forfeited to be paid to the Commissioners for the Reduction of the National Debt; but no Depositor shall be subject or liable to any such forfeiture, on account of being a Trustee on behalf of others, or of being interested in the funds of any Friendly Society legally established.

10. *Trustees on Behalf of others.* — Persons may act as Trustees for Depositors whether such Persons are themselves Depositors in any Savings Bank or not, provided that such Trustee or Trustees shall make such declaration on behalf of such Depositor or Depositors, and be subject to the like conditions in every respect, as are required in the case of persons making Deposits on their own account, and the receipt and receipts of such Trustee or Trustees, or the survivor of them, or the Executors or Administrators of any sole Trustee, or surviving Trustee, with or without (as may be required by the Managers) the receipt of the person on whose account such sum may have been deposited shall be a good and valid discharge to the Trustees and Managers of the Institution.

11. *Minors.* — Deposits are received from, or for the benefit of, Minors, and are subject to the same regulations as the Deposits of persons of twenty-one years of age and upwards.

12. *Friendly and Charitable Societies.* — Friendly Societies, legally established previous to the 28th of July, 1828, may deposit their funds through their Treasurer Steward, or other Officer or Officers, without any limitation as to the amount.   But Friendly Societies formed and enrolled after that date, are not permitted to make Deposits exceeding the sum of 300*l.*, principal and interest included; and no interest will be payable thereon, whenever the same shall amount to, or continue at the said sum of 300*l.* or upwards.

Deposits are received from the Trustees or Treasurers of Charitable Societies, not exceeding 100*l.* per annum, provided the amount shall not at any time exceed the sum of 300*l.*, exclusive of Interest.

13. *Deposits of Persons unable to attend.* — Forms are given at the Office, enabling persons to become Depositors who are unable to attend personally; and those who have previously made a deposit, may send additional sums, *together with their Book*, by any other person.

14. *Depositors' Books.* — The Deposits are entered in the Books of the Bank at the time they are made, and the Depositor receives a Book with a corresponding entry therein, which Book must be brought to the Office every time that any further sum is deposited also when notice is given for withdrawing money, and at the time the repayment is to be made, so that the transactions may be duly entered therein.

15. *Withdrawing Deposits.* — Depositors may receive the whole or any part of their Deposits on any day appointed by the Managers, not exceeding *fourteen* days after notice has been given for that purpose; but such Deposits can only be repaid to the Depositor personally, or to the bearer of an Order under the hand of the Depositor, signed in the presence of either the Minister or a Churchwarden of the Parish in which the Depositor resides, of a Justice of the Peace, or of a Manager of this Bank.

☞ *The Depositor's Book must always be produced when notice of withdrawing is given*

16. *Money withdrawn may be re-deposited.* — Depositors may withdraw any sum or sums of money, and re-deposit the same at any time or times within any one year, reckoning from the 20th day of November, provided such sum or sums of money re-deposited and any previous deposit or deposits which may have been made by such Depositor in the course of the year, taken together, shall not exceed, at any time in such year, the sum of 30*l.*, additional principal money bearing interest.

17. *Return or Refusal of Deposits.* — This Bank is at liberty to return the amount the Deposits to all or any of the Depositors, and may refuse to receive Deposits in any case, where it shall be deemed expedient so to do.

3. *Deposits of a Deceased Depositor exceeding 50l.* — In case of the death of any Detor in this Bank, whose Deposits, and the Interest thereon, shall exceed in the whole sum of *Fifty Pounds*, the same shall only be paid to the Executor or Executors, Adistrator or Administrators, on the production of the Probate of the Will, or Letters dministration.

. *Deposits of a Deceased Depositor not exceeding Fifty Pounds.* — In case a Depo- in this Bank shall die, whose Deposits, including Interest thereon, shall not exceed sum of Fifty Pounds, and that the Trustees or Managers shall be satisfied that no was made and left, and that no Letters of Administration will be taken out, they be at liberty to pay the same to the relatives or friends of the deceased, or any or r of them, or according to the statute of distribution, or require the production of ers of Administration, at their discretion. And the Bank shall be indemnified by such payments from all and every claim in respect thereof by any person whater.

. *Certificate.* In all cases wherein Certificates shall be required of the Amount of osits in this Bank belonging to Depositors therein, for the purpose of obtaining, free amp duties, a Probate of Will, or Letters of Administration, such Certificate shall gned by a Manager, and countersigned by the Actuary for the time being, as a true ct from the Ledger of the Institution.

. *Arbitration of Differences.* — In case any dispute shall arise between the Trustees anagers of this Bank, or any person or persons acting under them, and any indial Depositor therein, or any Trustee of a Depositor, or any person claiming to be Executor, Administrator, or Next of Kin, then, and in every such case, the matter dispute shall be referred to the Barrister at Law appointed by the Commissioners he Reduction of the National Debt, under the authority of the 9 Geo. 4. c. 92. ; and whatever award, order, or determination shall be made by the said Barrister, be binding and conclusive upon all parties, and shall be final, to all intents and oses, without any appeal.

UMMARY OF SAVINGS BANKS, &c. IN ENGLAND, WALES, AND IRELAND.

England there were, on the 20th November, 1829, three hundred and seventy-one Savings Banks: of these, eight have made no return, the remaining Banks contain,

Depositors.		Amount.			Average Amount of each Deposit.		
£		£	s.	d.	£	s.	d.
Under 20 - - -	179,989	1,309,117	14	4	7	5	5½
50 - - -	99,609	3,062,011	12	0½	30	14	9¼
100 - - -	48,218	3,436,143	14	2½	71	5	3
150 - - -	16,601	2,000,044	15	6½	120	9	6½
200 - - -	7,114	1,200,825	3	7¼	168	15	11¼
Above 200 - - -	4,755	1,153,694	0	6½	242	14	2¼
	356,287	12,161,837	0	3¾	34	2	8¼
Friendly Societies ..	4,217	700,418	3	9½	166	1	10½
Charitable ditto -	1,349	122,336	15	2¼	90	13	8¾
Accounts - - -	361,853	12,984,591	19	3½	35	17	8

Wales there were, on the 20th November, 1829, thirty-two Savings Banks. Four have made no return; the remaining Banks contain,

Depositors.		Amount.			Average Amount of each Deposit.		
		£	s.	d.	£	s.	d.
Depositors - - -	15,926	496,737	18	9	31	3	9½
Friendly Societies -	200	34,136	0	0	170	13	7¼
Charitable ditto -	48	6,586	10	6¾	137	4	4½
Accounts - - -	16,174	537,460	9	3¾	33	4	7¼

In *Ireland* there were, on the 20th November, 1829, sixty-five Savings Banks. Seven have made no return; the remaining Banks contain,

Depositors.		Amount.			Average Amount of each Deposit.		
		£	s.	d.	£	s.	d.
Depositors - - -	31,530	864,854	0	2¾	21	2	1½
Friendly Societies -	132	12,570	7	7¾	95	4	7¼
Charitable ditto -	287	35,444	8	3¾	123	10	0
Accounts - -	31,919	912,868	16	2¼	28	12	0

Grand Total in England, Wales, and Ireland, on the 29th November, 1829 : —

Savings Banks.	Accounts.	Amount.			Average amount of each Deposit.		
		£	s.	d.	£	s.	d.
487	409,954	14,434,921	4	9½	35	4	2¾

(*Abridged from "History of Savings Banks," by John Tidd Pratt, Esq.*)

BANKRUPT AND BANKRUPTCY. In the general sense of the ter bankrupt is equivalent to insolvent, and is applied to designate any individu unable to pay his debts. But in the law of England bankrupts form that p: ticular class of insolvents who are engaged in trade, or who " seek their living buying and selling," and who are declared, upon the oath of one or more of th creditors, to have committed what the law has defined to be an *act of bankrupt* At present, however, we shall merely lay before the reader a few observatio with respect to the principles and leading provisions embodied in the law as bankruptcy and insolvency; referring the reader to the article INSOLVENCY a BANKRUPTCY, for a detailed statement of these and the other provisions in th law.

" All classes of individuals, even those who have least to do with industrious und takings, are exposed to vicissitudes and misfortunes, the occurrence of which m render them incapable of making good the engagements into which they have enter and render them bankrupt or insolvent. But though bankruptcy is most frequent perhaps, produced by uncontrollable causes, it is frequently also produced by t thoughtlessness of individuals, or by their repugnance to make those retrenchme which the state of their affairs demands; and sometimes also by fraud or bad fai Hence it is, that the laws with respect to bankruptcy occupy a prominent place in judicial system of every state in which commerce has made any progress, and cre been introduced. They differ exceedingly in different countries and stages of societ and it must be acknowledged that they present very many difficulties, and that it is possible, perhaps, to suggest any system against which pretty plausible objections n not be made.

" The execrable atrocity of the early Roman laws with respect to bankruptcy is w known. According to the usual interpretation of the law of the twelve tables, wh Cicero has so much eulogised[*], the creditors of an insolvent debtor might, after so preliminary formalities, cut his body to pieces, each of them taking a share proportio to the amount of his debt; and those who did not choose to resort to this horrible tremity, were authorised to subject the debtor to chains, stripes, and hard labour; to sell him, his wife, and children, to perpetual foreign slavery *trans Tyberim !* T law, and the law giving fathers the power of inflicting capital punishments their children, strikingly illustrate the ferocious and sanguinary character of the e Romans.

" There is reason to think, from the silence of historians on the subject, that no fortunate debtor ever actually felt the utmost severity of this barbarous sentence; the history of the republic is full of accounts of popular commotions, some of wh

[*] Fremant omnes, licet! dicam quod sentio; bibliothecas, mehercule, omnium philosophorum r mihi videtur duodecim tabularum libellus; siquis legum fontes et capita viderit et authoritatis por et utilitatis ubertate superare. — *De Oratore*, lib. i.

l to very important changes, that were occasioned by the exercise of the power given
creditors of enslaving their debtors, and subjecting them to corporal punishments.
he law, however, continued in this state till the year of Rome 427, 120 years after the
omulgation of the twelve tables, when it was repealed. It was then enacted, that the
rsons of debtors should cease to be at the disposal of their creditors, and that the
ter should merely be authorised to seize upon the debtor's goods, and sell them by
ction in satisfaction of their claims. In the subsequent stages of Roman jurispru-
nce, further changes were made, which seem generally to have leaned to the side of
e debtor; and it was ultimately ruled, that an individual who had become insolvent
thout having committed any fraud, should, upon making a *cessio bonorum*, or a surrender
his entire property to his creditors, be entitled to an exemption from all personal
nalties. (*Terasson, Histoire de la Jurisprudence Romaine*, p. 117.)
" The law of England distinguishes between the insolvency of persons engaged in
de, and that of others. The former can alone be made bankrupts, and are dealt
th in a comparatively lenient manner. ' The law,' says Blackstone, ' is cautious of
couraging prodigality and extravagance by indulgence to debtors; and therefore it
ows the benefit of the laws of bankruptcy to none but actual traders, since that set
men are, generally speaking, the only persons liable to accidental losses, and to an
bility of paying their debts without any fault of their own. If persons in other situa-
ns of life run in debt without the power of payment, they must take the consequences
their own indiscretion, even though they meet with sudden accidents that may
luce their fortunes; for the law holds it to be an unjustifiable practice for any person
t a trader to encumber himself with debts of any considerable value. If a gentle-
n, or one in a liberal profession, at the time of contracting his debts has a sufficient
id to pay them, the delay of payment is a species of dishonesty, and a temporary
ustice to his creditors; and if at such time he has no sufficient fund, the dishonesty
l injustice are the greater: he cannot, therefore, murmur if he suffer the punishment
has voluntarily drawn upon himself. But in mercantile transactions the case is far
erwise; trade cannot be carried on without mutual credit on both sides: the con-
cting of debts is here not only justifiable, but necessary; and if, by accidental cala-
ies, as by the loss of a ship in a tempest, the failure of brother traders, or by the
payment of persons out of trade, a merchant or trader becomes incapable of dis-
rging his own debts, it is his misfortune and not his fault. To the misfortunes,
refore, of debtors, the law has given a compassionate remedy, but denied it to their
lts; since at the same time that it provides for the security of commerce by enacting
t every considerable trader may be declared a bankrupt, for the benefit of his cre-
rs as well as himself, it has also, to discourage extravagance, declared that no one
ll be capable of being made a bankrupt but only a trader, nor capable of receiving
full benefit of the statutes but only an *industrious* trader.' (*Commentaries*, book ii.
. 31.)
" After the various proceedings with respect to bankruptcy have been gone through,
othing be discovered to impeach the honesty of the debtor, he is allowed a cer-
ate or discharge, provided *three out of five* of his creditors both in number and
ie agree to sign it. The bankrupt is then entitled to a reasonable allowance out
his effects; which is, however, made to depend partly on the magnitude of his
dend. Thus, if his effects will not pay half his debts, or 10s. in the pound, he is
to the discretion of the commissioners and assignees, to have a competent sum
wed him, not exceeding 3 per cent. upon his estate, or 300l. in all; but if his estate
10s. in the pound, he is to be allowed 5 per cent., provided such allowance do not
eed 400l.; 12s. 6d. then 7½ per cent. under a limitation as before of its not
eeding 500l.; and if 15s. in a pound, then the bankrupt shall be allowed 10 per cent.
n his estate, provided it do not exceed 600l.
According to our present law, when a person not a trader becomes insolvent, he may,
r being actually imprisoned at the suit of some of his creditors for fourteen days,
ent a petition to the court to be relieved; and upon surrendering his entire property,
s, unless something fraudulent be established against him, entitled to a discharge.
ile, however, the certificate given to the bankrupt relieves him from all future claims
account of debts contracted previously to his bankruptcy, the discharge given to an inent only relieves him from imprisonment; in the event of his afterwards accumulating
property, it may be seized in payment of the debts contracted anterior to his in-
ency. This principle was recognised in the *cessio bonorum* of the Romans, of which
insolvent act is nearly a copy.
It may be questioned, however, notwithstanding what Blackstone has stated, whether
e be any good ground for making a distinction between the insolvency of traders
other individuals. There are very few trades so hazardous as that of a farmer, and
should he become insolvent, he is not entitled to the same privileges he would have
yed had he been the keeper of an inn, or a commission agent! The injustice of this

distinction is obvious; but, without dwelling upon it, it seems pretty clear that certificates should be granted indiscriminately to all honest debtors. Being relieved from all concern as to his previous incumbrances, an insolvent who has obtained a certificate is prompted to exert himself vigorously in future, at the same time that his friends are not deterred from coming forward to his assistance. But when an insolvent continues liable to his previous debts, no one, however favourably disposed, can venture to aid him with a loan; and he is discouraged, even if he had means, from attempting to earn any thing more than a bare livelihood; so that, while creditors do not, in one case out of a hundred, gain the smallest sum by this constant liability of the insolvent, his energies and usefulness are for ever paralysed.

" The policy of imprisoning for debt seems also exceedingly questionable. Notwithstanding the deference due to the great authorities who have vindicated this practice, I confess I am unable to discover any thing very cogent in the reasonings advanced in its favour. Provided a person in insolvent circumstances intimate his situation to his creditors, and offer to make a voluntary surrender of his property to them, he has, as it appears to me, done all that should be required of him, and ought not to undergo any imprisonment. If he had deceived his creditors by false representations, or if he conceal or fraudulently convey away any part of his property, he should of course be subjected to the pains and penalties attached to swindling; but when such practices are not alleged, or cannot be proved, sound policy, I apprehend, would dictate that creditors ought to have no power over the persons of their debtors, and that they should be entitled only to their effects. The maxim, *carcer non solvit*, is not more trite than true. It is said, that the fear of imprisonment operates as a check to prevent persons from getting into debt; and so no doubt it does. But then it must, on the other hand, be borne in mind, that the power to imprison tempts individuals to trust to its influence to enforce payment of their claims, and makes them less cautious in their inquiries as to the condition and circumstances of those to whom they give credit. The carelessness of tradesmen, and their extreme earnestness to obtain custom, are, more than any thing else, the great causes of insolvency; and the power of imprisoning merely tends to foster and encourage these habits. If a tradesman trust an individual with a loan of money or goods, which he is unable to pay, he has made a bad speculation. But why ought he, because he has done so, to be allowed to arrest the debtor's person? If he wished to have perfect security, he either should not have dealt with him at all, or dealt with him only for ready money : such transactions are, on the part of tradesmen, perfectly voluntary ; and if they place undue confidence in a debtor who has not misled them by erroneous representations of his affairs, they have themselves only to blame.

" It would really, therefore, as it appears to us, be for the advantage of creditors were all penal proceedings against the persons of honest debtors abolished. The dependence placed on their efficacy is deceitful. A tradesman ought rather to trust to his own prudence and sagacity to keep out of scrapes, than to the law for redress : he may deal upon credit with those whom he knows; but he should deal for ready money only with those of whose circumstances and characters he is either ignorant or suspicious. By bringing penal statutes to his aid, he is rendered remiss and negligent. He has the only effectual means of security in his own hands; and it seems highly inexpedient that he should be taught to neglect them, and put his trust in prisons.

" It is pretty evident, too, that the efficacy of imprisonment in deterring individual from running into debt has been greatly overrated. Insolvents who are honest, mus have suffered from misfortune, or been disappointed in the hopes they entertained o being able, in one way or other, to discharge their debts. The fear of imprisonmen does not greatly influence such persons; for when they contract debts, they have n doubt of their ability to pay them. And though the imprisonment of *bonâ fide* insolvents were abolished, it would give no encouragement to the practices of those wh endeavour to raise money by false representations; for these are to be regarded a swindlers, and ought as such to be subjected to adequate punishment.

" But the regulations with respect to bankruptcy and insolvency differ radically i other important respects. An individual cannot be subjected to the insolvent law, ex cept by *his own act*, that is, his petitioning for relief from actual imprisonment for debt and, on the other hand, an individual cannot be made a bankrupt and subjected t the bankrupt law, except by the act of *another*, that is, of a petitioning creditor,* as h is called, swearing that the individual in question is indebted to him, and that h believes he has committed what is termed an act of bankruptcy. These differences coupled with the refinements introduced into other branches of the law, give rise to ver extraordinary results.

" While the law of England gives the creditor an unnecessary degree of power ove the debtor's person, it does not give him sufficient power over his property. I

* One creditor, whose debt is to the amount of upwards of 100*l.*; or two, whose debts amount to 150*l.* or three, whose debts amount to 200*l.*

respect, indeed, it is so very defective, that one is almost tempted to think it had
intended to promote the practices of fraudulent debtors.   The property of persons
ected to the bankrupt laws, as well as those who *choose to subject themselves* to the
vent laws, is placed at the disposal of assignees or trustees for the benefit of their
tors ; but when a person possessed of property, but not subject to the bankrupt
, contracts debts, if he go abroad, or live within the rules of the King's Bench or the
t, or remain in prison without petitioning for relief (in neither of which cases can
e subjected to the insolvent laws), he may most probably continue to enjoy the in-
e arising from that property without molestation.

It is true, the law says that the creditors shall be authorised to seize the debtors'
s *and goods*, a description which an unlearned person would be apt to conclude was
idantly comprehensive ; but the law is so interpreted, that neither funded property,
ey, nor securities for money, is considered goods.   If the debtor have a copyhold
e, it cannot be touched in any way whatever ; if his estate be freehold, the creditor
after a tedious process, receive the rents and profits, but no more, during the life-
of his debtor.   Should the debtor die before judgment against him in a court has
obtained, then, unless the debt be on bond, the creditor has no recourse upon the
left by the debtor, whatever may be its tenure :   nay, though his money borrowed
ote or bill has been laid out in buying land, the debtor's heir takes that land wholly
arged of the debt !' "—(*Lord Brougham's Speech on the State of the Law*, p. 100.)

In consequence of this preposterously absurb system, an individual known to have
ge income, and enjoying a proportionally extensive credit, may, if he go to Paris or
sels, or confine himself within the rules of the King's Bench or Fleet, defraud his
tors of every farthing he owes them, without their being entitled to touch any part
s fortune.   All owners of funded, monied, and copyhold property, have a licence
them to cheat with impunity ; and the only wonder is, not that some do, but that
t number more do not, avail themselves of this singular privilege.   In point of fact,
fore, the power of imprisonment is operative only on the really necessitous — on
from whom it can extract little or nothing.   The rich debtor is seldom subjected
operation ; he resorts, before a writ can be executed against him, either to the
inent or the rules, and then laughs at the impotent wrath of those he has defrauded,
perhaps ruined.   That such a system of law should be suffered to exist in a com-
al country, and so little outcry be raised against it, is truly astonishing, and
ngly exemplifies the power of habit in reconciling us to the most pernicious abies.   Can any one wonder at the frequency of fraudulent bankruptcy, when it is
fostered and encouraged ?

A reform of the bankrupt law on the principles already mentioned, seems, thereto be imperiously called for.   Its evils were forcibly stated by Mr. Brougham
Lord Brougham) in his masterly ' Speech on the State of the Law.'   He has
pointed out the remedial measures necessary to be adopted to render this important
tment of commercial jurisprudence consistent with the obvious principles of justice
ommon sense.   ' Let the whole,' says he, ' of every man's property, real and per-
—his real, of what kind soever, copyhold, leasehold, freehold ; his personal, of
ver nature, debts, money, stock, chattels — be taken for the payment of all his
equally, and, in case of insolvency, let all be distributed rateably ; let all he pos-
be sifted, bolted from him unsparingly, until all his creditors are satisfied by
ent or composition ; but let his person only be taken when he conceals his goods,
s merited punishment by fraudulent conduct.' — (pp. 106—110.)   Where these
ires adopted, and a certificate given to every man who has been divested of his
rty for behoof of his creditors, and against whom no charge of fraud has been
ished, there would be little room for improvement in the principles of the law of
uptcy." — (See my *Principles of Political Economy*, 2d ed. pp. 264—274.)

RCALAO, or BACALAO, the Spanish name for cod.

RCELONA, the capital of Catalonia, and the principal town of Spain, on
lediterranean, in lat. 41° 22′ N. and long. 2° 10′ E. It is a strongly fortified,
uilt city.   The population is supposed to amount to about 100,000.   Cata-
is the most industrious of all the Spanish provinces ; and several valuable
xtensive manufactories have been established at Barcelona : but neither its
factures nor commerce are at present in a flourishing condition.   Its prin-
exports are brandy and wine, cork-bark, wrought silks, wool, fruits, &c.
mports are corn, sugar, salt fish, (the greater part of which is furnished
English,) spices, hides, cotton wool and cotton goods, linens, hardware,
nware, &c.   In 1820, 3,838 vessels entered the port of Barcelona ; of which
e ships of war, 3,625 Spanish traders, and 206 foreigners.   In 1821, the
number of ships entering the port amounted to 2,570 ; of which 106 were

foreigners, and the remainder Spaniards. The principal part of the Spanish vess
in both years were coasters, many of them of very small burden. — (*Bulletin e
Sciences Géographiques*, vii. p. 56.) In 1828, 40 British ships, of the burden
5,262 tons, entered Barcelona.

Money.—Accounts are kept in *libras* of 20 *sueldos*, 240 *dineros*, or 480 *mallas*. T
libra is likewise divided into *reales de plata Catalan*, of 3 *sueldos* each ; and into *rea
ardites*, of 2 *sueldos* each. Hence, 6⅔ of the former, or 10 of the latter = 1 *libra Catalo
The *libra Catalan* is = 2s. 4d. sterling nearly.

The *peso dúro*, or hard dollar, is valued at 37½ *sueldos* Catalan; eight such doll
making 15 *libras*.

Weights and Measures.—There are endless discrepancies amongst the weights a
measures in the different Spanish provinces, and there is a very great discrepancy
the accounts of the authors who have written upon them. The following statemes
are taken from Nelkenbrecher : —

The quintal is divided into 4 *arrobas*, or 104 lib. of 12 oz. to the pound. The pou
= 6174 Eng. grains = 4 kilog. = 8325·6 as of Holland. 100 lib. of Barcelona
88·215 lib. avoirdupois.

The yard, named *cana*, is divided into 8 *palmos*; of 4 *quartos*, and is = 21 incl
very nearly. Hence, 100 canas = 53·499 metres = 77·5 yards of Amsterdam = 58·5
English yards.

The *quartera*, or measure for grain, is divided into 12 *cortanes* and 48 *picolins*. 1
quarteras = 23·536, or 23½ Winchester quarters.

The *carga*, or measure for liquids, is divided into 12 *cortanes* or *arrobas*, 24 *cortarin*
and 72 *mitadellas*. It is = 32·7 English wine gallons. 4 cargas = 1 *pipe*. The pi
of Majorca oil contains 107 cortanes.

For an account of the imports and exports of Spain, see CADIZ.

BARILLA (Du. *Soda*; Fr. *Soude, Barille*; Ger. *Soda, Barilla*; It. *Barrigl*
Por. *Solda, Barrilha*; Rus. *Socianka*; Sp. *Barrilla*; Arab. *Kali*), carbonate
soda (see ALKALIES), is found native in Hungary, Egypt, and many other countrie
It is largely used by bleachers, manufacturers of hard soaps, glass-makers, &
The barilla of commerce consists of the ashes of several marine and other pla
growing on the sea-shore. The best, or Alicant barilla, is prepared from t
Salsola Soda, which is very extensively cultivated for this purpose in the *huerta*
Murcia, and other places on the eastern shores of Spain. (*Townsend's Trav
in Spain*, vol. iii. p. 195.) The plants are gathered in September, dried, a
burned in furnaces heated so as to bring the ashes into a state of imperfect fusio
when they concrete into hard, dry, cellular masses of a greyish blue colo
Sicily and Teneriffe produce good barilla, but inferior to that of Alicant and C
thagena. Kelp, which is a less pure alkali, is formed by the incineration of t
common sea-wrack. See KELP.

The Saracens established in Spain seem to have been the first who introduc
the manufacture of barilla into Europe. They called the plants employed in
preparation *kali*; and this, with the Arabic article *al* prefixed, has given rise
the modern chemical term alkali.

Of 213,299 cwts. of barilla imported into Great Britain in 1828, 134,529 cw
came from Spain, 51,571 from Teneriffe, and 23,909 from Sicily. The values
these species are, for the most part, in the proportion of about 12, 9, and 1
that is, if Spanish barilla fetch 12*l.* a ton, Teneriffe barilla will fetch 9*l.* and Sici
10*l.* Prime quality in barilla is to be distinguished by its strong smell when wett
and by its whitish colour. Particular attention should be paid to have as li
small or dust as possible. The duties on barilla have recently been very c
siderably reduced. See TARIFF.

BARK, the outer rind of plants. There is an immense variety of ba
known in commerce, as cinnamon, Peruvian bark, oak bark, quercitron, &c. 1
term " bark " is, however, generally employed to express either Peruvian ba
or oak bark ; and it is these only that we shall describe in this place.

1. *Peruvian or Jesuit's Bark.* — (Fr. *Quiquina*; Ger. *Kron-china*; Du. *China-b*
Sp. *Quina, Quinquina*; Lat. *Quinquina, Cortex Peruvianus.*) There are t
principal species of this bark known in commerce, which have been elaborately
scribed by Dr. A. T. Thomson, from whose valuable account the following particu
are selected : —

The first species is the *pale* bark of the shops. It is the produce of the *Cincl
lancifolia*, and is the original cinchona of Peru. It is now very scarce. It is impo
in chests covered with skins, each containing about 200 lbs., well packed, but gene

ixed with a quantity of dust and other heterogeneous matter.   It consists of pieces eight
ten inches long, some of them being scarcely one tenth of an inch thick, singly and
ubly quilled, or rolled inwards; the quills, generally, being in size from a swan's quill
an inch and a half.   It is internally of a pallid fawn or cinnamon hue; but approxi-
ates, on being moistened, to the colour of a pale orange.   When in substance it has
arcely any odour; but during decoction the odour is sensible, and agreeably aromatic.
he taste is bitter, but not unpleasant, acidulous, and austere.

The second species, or red bark, is obtained from the *Cinchona oblongifolia,* growing on
e Andes.   It is imported in chests containing from 100 to 150 lbs. each.   It consists
variously sized pieces, most of them flat, but some partially quilled or rolled.   The
ternal part is woody, and of a rust red colour: it has a weak peculiar odour; and its
ste is much less bitter, but more austere and nauseous, than that of the other barks.

The third species, or yellow bark of the shops, is obtained from the *Cinchona cordifolia,*
owing in Quito and Santa Fé.   It is imported in chests containing from 90 to 100
s. each, consisting of pieces eight or ten inches long, some quilled, but the greater
rt flat.   The interior is of a yellow colour, passing to orange.   It has nearly the same
our in decoction as the pale; the taste is more bitter and less austere, and it excites no
ringent feeling when chewed.   The goodness decreases when the colour varies from
ange yellow to pale yellow; when of a dark colour, between red and yellow, it should
rejected.

It is needless to add, that bark is one of the most valuable medical remedies.   The
dians were unacquainted with its uses, which seem to have been first discovered by the
suits.   It was introduced into Europe in 1632, but was not extensively used till the
ter part of the seventeenth century.   According to M. Humboldt, the Jesuits' bark
nually exported from America amounts to from 12,000 to 14,000 quintals.   Of
se 2,000 are furnished by Santa Fé, and 110 by Loxa; Peru furnishing the remainder,
ich is shipped at Callao, Guayaquil, &c.

2. *Oak-bark* (Fr. *Ecorce de la Chene;* Ger. *Eichenrinde;* It. *Corteccia della Quer-*
; Lat. *Quercús cortex*).   The bark of the common oak is a powerful astringent, and
preferred to all other substances for tanning leather.   The bark of the larch is now,
wever, used for the same purpose.   The import of oak-bark is very considerable; but
ing to the cork-tree being a species of oak (*Quercus Suber,*) bark for tanning and
k-bark are usually mixed together in the parliamentary returns.   The latter, how-
r, does not amount to a tenth part of the whole quantity imported.   The imports of
h sorts amounted, in 1828, to 807,888 cwts., which is about the average importa-
n.   Of this quantity, no less 589,749 cwts. were brought from the Netherlands
olland and Belgium), 81,097 cwts. from Germany, &c.   Cork-bark is almost en-
ly imported from Italy, Spain, and Portugal; the imports from them being, in the
ve-mentioned year, Italy 81,035 cwts., Spain 12,935 cwts., and Portugal 5,029 cwts.
e quality of bark varies according to the size and age of the tree, the season when it is
ked, &c., so much, that the price varies, at this moment, from about 5*l.* to about 10*l.*
ton.   The duty, which is 13*s.* 4*d.* a ton, produced in 1829, in Great Britain,
981*l.* 0*s.* 8*d.* of nett revenue.

Quercitron is the bark of a species of oak-tree (*Quercus tinctoria*).   It is not used, at
st in this country, for tanning, but for imparting a yellow dye to silk and wool.   It
rincipally imported from North America.   The price varies, at present, according to
quality, from about 9*s.* to 13*s.* a cwt.   The imports usually amount to from 18,000
4,000 cwts.   The duty of 20*s.* a ton produced 1,138*l.* of nett revenue in 1829.

We are indebted for the discovery and application of the useful properties of quer-
on to Dr. Bancroft.   The doctor obtained a patent for his invention in 1775; but
American war breaking out soon after, deprived him of its advantages.   In consi-
ation of this circumstance, parliament passed, in 1785, an act (25 Geo. 3. c. 38.)
uring to him the privileges conveyed by his patent for fourteen years.   At the ex-
tion of the latter period, the House of Commons agreed to extend the doctor's pri-
ge for an additional seven years; but the House of Lords rejected the bill.   Like
many discoverers, Dr. Bancroft profited but little by his invention, though it has been
great use to the arts and manufactures of the country.   (See *Bancroft on Permanent*
urs, vol. ii. p. 112., and the *Report of the Committee of the House of Commons on*
nts, Appendix, p. 175.)

k bark, the produce of Europe, is not to be imported into the United Kingdom for home consump.
   except in British ships, or in ships of the country of which it is the produce, or in ships of the
   try from which it is imported, on pain of forfeiting the goods, and 100*l.* by the master of the vessel.
   d 8 Geo. 4. c. 58.)

BARLEY (Fr. *Orge;* Ger. *Gerstengraupen;* Du. *Ryg;* It. *Orzo;* Sp. *Cebada;*
s. *Fatschmea;* Lat. *Hordeum;* Arab. *Dhourra*), a species of grain cultivated
very country in Europe.   It is used largely as food; but still more largely,
aps, in the manufacture of malt liquors and spirits.   It is too well known

to require any description. For accounts of its price, and of the regulations with respect to its importation and exportation, see Corn Laws.

Pearl barley, Scotch barley, &c. is barley stripped of the husk, and used in the making of broths, drinks, &c.; pearl barley is the finest.

BARLEY-SUGAR (Fr. *Sucre d'orge;* Ger. *Gerstenzucker;* It. *Pennito;* Sp. *Alfenique;* Lat. *Alphenix*), a preparation of sugar, candied with orange or lemon peel.

BARRATRY, in navigation, is, in its most extensive sense, any fraudulent or unlawful act committed by the master or mariners of a ship, contrary to their duty to their owners, and to the prejudice of the latter. It appears to be derived from the Italian word *barratrare,* to cheat. It may be committed by running away with a ship, wilfully carrying her out of the course prescribed by the owners, delaying or defeating the voyage, deserting convoy without leave, sinking or deserting the ship, embezzling the cargo, smuggling, or any other offence whereby the ship or cargo may be subjected to arrest, detention, loss, or forfeiture.

It is the practice, in most countries, to insure against barratry. Most foreign jurists hold, that it comprehends every fault which the master and crew can commit, whether it arise from fraud, negligence, unskilfulness, or mere imprudence. But in this country it is ruled, that no act of the master or crew shall be deemed barratry, unless it proceed from a *criminal* or *fraudulent* motive.

" Barratry can only be committed by the master and mariners by some act contrary to their duty, in the relation in which they stand to the owners of the ship. It is, therefore, an offence against them, and consequently an owner himself cannot commit barratry. He may, by his fraudulent conduct, make himself liable to the owner of the goods on board, but not for *barratry.* Neither can barratry be committed against the owner, *with his consent ;* for though he may be liable for any loss or damage occasioned by the misconduct of the master to which he consents, yet this is not barratry. Nothing is more clear than that a man can never set up as a crime, an act done by his own direction or consent." — (*Marshall on Insurance,* book i. c. 12. § 6.)

When, therefore, the owner of a ship is also the master, no act of barratry can be committed ; for no man can commit a fraud against himself.

It is a maxim in law, that fraud shall not be presumed, but must be clearly proved ; and it is a rule in questions of insurance, that he who charges barratry must substantiate it by conclusive evidence.

It is not necessary, to render an act barratrous, that it should be committed with a criminal intent as respects the owners, in order to injure them, or to benefit the captain or crew. It may even be committed with a view to promote the owner's interests; for *an illegal act* done without the authority or privity of the owners, and which proves detrimental to them, is barratry, whatever be the motives in which it originated. Lord Ellenborough, in an able judgment, has laid it down as clear law, " that a breach of duty by the master in respect of his owners, with a fraudulent or criminal intent, or *ex maleficio,* is barratry ; that it makes no difference whether this act of the master be induced by motives of advantage to himself, malice to the owner, or *a disregard of those laws which it was his duty to obey ;* and that it is not for him to judge or suppose, in cases not entrusted to his discretion, that he is not breaking the trust reposed in him, when he endeavours to advance the interests of his owners by means which the law forbids, and which his owners also must be taken to have forbidden."

The circumstance of the owners of ships being permitted to insure against the barratry of the master and mariners can hardly fail, it may be not uncharitably presumed, of rendering them less scrupulous in their inquiries with respect to their character than they would otherwise be. Perhaps, therefore, it might be expedient to prohibit such insurances, or to lay some restrictions upon them. They were, indeed, expressly forbidden by the ordinance of Rotterdam ; and Lord Mansfield, whose authority on all points connected with the law of insurance is so deservedly high, seems to have thought that it would be well to exclude barratry entirely from policies, and to cease " making the underwriter become the insurer of the conduct of the captain whom he does not appoint, and cannot dismiss, to the owners who can do either." But though it were expedient to prevent the owner from making an insurance of this sort, nothing can be more reasonable than that third parties, who freight a ship, or put goods on board, should be allowed to

are against such a copious source of loss. For a further discussion of this ject, see the article MARINE INSURANCE; and *Marshall on Insurance*, book i. 2. § 6., and *Park on Insurance*, c. 5.

Owners, masters, or seamen, who wilfully cast away, burn, or destroy ships, to prejudice of freighters or insurers, incur the penalty of death. See SEAMEN.

BARREL, a cask or vessel for holding liquids, particularly ale and beer. merly the barrel of beer in London contained only 32 ale gallons = 32½ Imial gallons: but it was enacted by 43 Geo. 3. c. 69., that 36 gallons of beer uld be taken to be a barrel; and by the 6 Geo. 4. c. 58. it is enacted, that never any gallon measure is mentioned in any excise law, it shall always be med and taken to be a standard Imperial gallon. At present, therefore, the el contains 36 Imperial gallons.

BARWOOD, a red dyewood brought from Africa, particularly from Angola, the river Gaboon. The dark red which is commonly seen upon British dana handkerchiefs, is for the most part produced by the colouring matter of vood, saddened by sulphate of iron. (*Bancroft on Colours.*) The imports of vood in 1829, amounted to 246 tons 15 cwt. It fetches at present (May 1) about 11*l.* a ton (duty 7*s.* included) in the London market.

BASKETS (Fr. *Corbeilles;* Ger. *Körbe;* Du. *Bennen;* It. *Paniere;* Sp. *Ca-as, Canastos, Cestas, Cestos;* Rus. *Korsinii;* Pol. *Kosze*), are made of rushes, aters, or the twigs of willows, osiers, sallows, or some other slender bodies, rwoven.

BAST, or straw hats or bonnets. See HATS.

BATAVIA, a city of the island of Java, the capital of the Dutch possessions in East Indies, and the largest port of trade in the Oriental Islands, in lat. 6° 8′ S. long. 106″ 54′ E. Batavia is situated in the north-west part of the island, n extensive bay. The harbour, or rather road, lies between the main land several small uninhabited islands, which, during the boisterous or north-western soon, afford sufficient shelter and good anchorage. Ships of from 300 to 500 anchor at the distance of about a mile and a half from shore. A small river through the town, which is navigable for vessels of from 20 to 40 tons, from ea to the distance of a couple of miles inland, and from which a number of ls, branching off into different parts of the town, afford great conveniences for . The climate, at one time so notorious for its insalubrity, has been greatly oved within the last few years, by the filling up of useless canals, the ling of dead walls, and the removal of unnecessary fortifications. The popu-n, which is increasing, may be estimated at 60,000, the bulk of which consists atives of the island itself, of the neighbouring islands, and of Chinese. Besides e, there are a considerable number of the mixed race professing the Christian ion, and some Arabs and natives of Hindostan. The Europeans, as usual in East, form but a small portion of the population. Among the principal mer-ts are Dutch, English, Americans, French, and Germans. The island of forming the most important portion of the Dutch possessions in the east, being, in fact, one of the finest colonies in the world, it may not be out of to mention a few particulars respecting it. It contains an area of 50,000 e miles, with a population of six millions of inhabitants, or 120 to the square The annual revenue of the Dutch government, which possesses about two s of the island, amounts to about 3,000,000*l.* sterling; and the military force ents to about 15,000; of which not less than 8,000 are European troops, about one third of the whole European force in British India, which has a lation of 90,000,000, and an area of between 1,200,000 and 1,300,000 square of territory.

e staple products of the island are rice, a variety of pulses, vegetable oils, co, sugar, and coffee. The production of indigo, cocoa, tea, and raw is making some progress. The tin exported from Batavia is brought Banca, the copper from Japan, the finer spices from the Moluccas, and the er from Sumatra.

1828 the exports from Batavia in quantity and value were as follow:—

	Piculs of 136 lb. each.	Cents.	Florins.	Cen
Coffee - - -	416,171	96	8,024,039	9
Mace - - - -	600	43	96,078	6
Cloves - - - -	1,832	8	229,107	
Nutmegs - - -	1,647	81	221,121	4
Rice - - - -	419,499		1,194,486	3
Tin - - - -	19,554		866,521	3
Sugar * - - -	25,869	75	456,084	1
Birds' Nests - -			521,392	1
Piece Goods -			499,470	9
Java Tobacco -			401,002	2
Pepper - - -	8,226		151,537	
Rattans - - -	31,301		141,506	
Salt - - - -	24,930		119,890	
Japan and Sandal Wood -	7,240		96,474	9
Indigo * - - -	188	88	94,342	
Arrack - - -	Leaguers 533		86,362	
Hides - - -			52,140	
Turmerick - -	5,412		42,038	
Horses 384 (to the Isle of France) -			35,975	
Tortoiseshell - -	37	95	57,941	
Japan Camphor -	489		43,200	
Articles not specified -			2,859,336	
Treasure - - -			1,209,294	1
			17,499,341	1

In the same year the imports were as follow: —

	Piculs of 136 lb. each.	Cents.	Florins.	Cen
Cotton Manufactures, Netherlands -			2,940,685	3
English - -			1,819,435	3
French - -			18,679	
Woollen ditto Netherlands -			246,545	
English and French			16,861	
Provisions from England only - -			522,342	
Brandy and Geneva - - -			322,606	
Wines - - - -			1,154,868	
Opium, Levant - -	559	66	717,529	
Bengal - - -	110		314,300	
Lead - - - -	2,891		76,612	
Copper, Europe - - -	354		45,110	
Japan - - -	11,631		988,635	
Steel from the Netherlands - -	726	95	22,963	
England - - -	404		12,625	
Sweden - - -	186		5,812	
Iron from Sweden - - -	3,200		23,275	
England - - -	4,593		45,050	
Netherlands - -	9,033		138,003	
Cotton Piece Goods, Bengal and Madras			787,917	
Cotton Yarn from the Netherlands -	99	16	1,146	
Ditto English - -	243	10	41,430	
Gambir, (Terra Japonica) - -			477,854	
Rattans - - - -			223,667	
Tripang (Holothurion) - -			380,964	
Silk and Cotton Piece Goods, Chinese manufacture - - -			366,701	
Marine Stores - - -			264,226	
Articles not specified - - -			3,383,596	5
Treasure - - - -			2,616,707	2
			17,976,094	5

* The quantity of sugar exported in 1829 had risen to 80,000 piculs, and the ind
to 1,200 lbs.

each. It is for the year 1828.

IMPORTS.

From	Merchandise.	Treasure.	Total.
the Netherlands	6,459,852 22	1,001,913	7,461,765 22
England	2,166,515		2,166,515
France	139,302		139,302
Hamburgh	59,932	16,830	76,762
Gibraltar	18,275	89,250	107,525
Sweden	30,384		30,384
U. S. of America	805,161 27	697,210	1,002,371 27
Cape of Good Hope	1,624		1,624
Isle of France	21,051		21,051
Persian Gulf	1,510		1,510
Bengal	737,424 02	10,200	747,624 02
Siam	131,004		131,004
Cochin China	4,909		4,909
China	585,566 88	5,408	590,974 88
Macao	65,628		65,628
Manilla	29,989 47		29,989 47
Japan	1,067,231		1,067,231
New Holland	7,613	2,550	10,163
Eastern Archipelago	3,526,415 44	798,346 25	4,319,761 69
Florins	15,359,387 30	2,616,707 25	17,976,094 55

EXPORTS.

To	Merchandise.	Treasure.	Total.
the Netherlands	9,188,929 87	279,601	9,398,530 87
England	200,962 50	165,750	366,712 50
France	102,628	7,650	110,278
Hamburgh	85,174		85,174
Sweden	23,652		23,652
U. S. of America	120,880		120,880
Cape of Good Hope	1,970		1,970
Isle of France	88,547	62,523	151,070
Mocha	28,481		28,481
Persian Gulf	112,957 55		112,957 55
Bombay	3,055		3,055
Bengal	77,497	2,040	79,537
Siam	77,451 22½	22,785	100,236 22½
Cochin China	21,883		21,883
China	1,474,486 55	87,167 05	1,561,653 60
Macao	78,361	15,536	98,897 85
Manilla	35,240	37,500	72,740
Japan	291,263 71	22,050	313,318 71
New Holland	75,083	1,377	76,460
Eastern Archipelago	271,544 56½	505,314 25	4,776,858 81½
Florins	16,290,046 97	1,209,294 15	17,499,341 12

I

The exports and imports under different flags were as follow : —

IMPORTS.			EXPORTS.		
Netherlands - -	12,843,901	88	Netherlands - -	11,986,049	26½
English - - -	1,928,743		English - - -	2,312,449	24½
American, (U. States)	1,715,306	27	French - - -	166,025	50
Chinese - - -	472,093	50	American, (U. States)	1,324,570	34½
Siamese - - -	314,802	94½	Siamese - - -	314,802	94½
Native - - -	473,088	73	Chinese - - -	951,133	97
Various other Flags -	228,168	22½	Portuguese - -	103,822	85
			Various other Foreign	334,487	
Florins	17,976,094	55	Florins	17,499,341	12

In 1828, the number of ships and amount of tonnage entering inwards and clearing outwards under different flags were as follow : —

OUTWARDS.			INWARDS.		
Flag.	Number of Vessels.	Tonnage in Lasts.	Flag.	Number of Vessels.	Tonnage in Lasts.
Netherlands -	843	45,689	Netherlands -	801	45,684
English - -	68	14,778½	English - -	54	10,799½
French - -	9	861½	French - -	8	692½
Hamburgh -	1	137	Hamburgh -	1	137
Danish - -	1	85	Danish - -	1	85
Swedish - -	1	66	Swedish - -	1	66
Russian - -	1	153	Russian - -	1	153
Spanish - -	2	420	Spanish - -	3	505
Portuguese -	4	962½	Portuguese -	4	962½
American - -	19	3,116	American - -	14	2,087
Chinese - -	8	805	Chinese - -	8	805
Siamese - -	7	308	Siamese - -	9	497½
Other Asiatic -	26	813	Other Asiatic -	55	804
	1,026	68,194¼		960	63,278

(*Note.* Taking the last at 2 tons, the quantity of tonnage which cleared outward will be 136,388½, and inwards 126,556 tons.

Port Regulations. — The following is the substance of the port regulations of Batavia : — 1st. The commander of a ship arriving in the roads, is not to land himself, or permit any of his crew or passengers to land, until his vessel be visited by a boat from the guard-ship. — 2d. The master, on landing, is first to wait on the master attendant, and afterwards report himself at the police office. — 3d. A manifest of the whole cargo must be delivered at the Custom-house within four and twenty hours of the ship's arriving in the roads. — 4th. The master of a vessel must lodge the ship's papers with the master attendant when he first lands, which are duly delivered up to him when he receives his port clearance from the same authority. — 5th. No goods can be shipped or landed after sunset, under a penalty of 500 florins. — 6th. No goods can be shipped on Sunday without a special permission from the water fiscal, which, however, is never refused on application. — 7th. No muskets or ammunition can be imported; but the prohibition does not extend to fowling pieces exceeding 100 florins value.

With respect to the tariff, all foreign woollens and cottons being the manufacture of countries to the westward of the Cape of Good Hope, under whatever flag imported, pay an *ad valorem* duty of 26¼ per cent., that is, a duty upon the wholesale price at Batavia, not in bond. With the exception of wines, spirit and opium, which pay a rated duty, all other articles, if imported under a foreign flag, pay an *ad valorem* duty rated on the invoice value of 16$\frac{38}{100}$ per centum ; and under the Netherland flag, of about 6 per cent. Cottons and woollens the manufacture of the Netherlands, if accompanied by a certificate of origin, are duty free

xport duty is a specific one. Coffee, if exported on a foreign bottom to a
 country, pays 5 florins per picul; if on a foreign bottom to a port in the
rlands, 4 florins; and if on a Netherland bottom to a Netherland port, 2
. Sugar, if exported on a foreign bottom to a foreign country, pays 1 florin
cul; but if exported in a Netherland bottom to a Netherland port, it is duty
 Rice, on whatever bottom exported, and to whatever country, pays a duty
orins per coyang of 27 piculs.

ods are received in *entrepôt* not only at Batavia, but at the ports of Sama-
Sourabaya, and Anjier in Java, and Rhio in the Straits of Malacca, on
nt of a duty of one per cent. levied on the invoice value.

ney. — Accounts are kept at Batavia, in the florin or guilder, divided into
nes, or 100 parts, represented by a copper coinage or doits. The florin is a
oin made expressly for India, but of the same value as the florin current in
etherlands. It is usually estimated at the rate of twelve to the pound ster-
ut the correct par is 11 florins 58 centimes per pound. Doubloons, and the
of continental India, are receivable at the Custom-house at a fixed tariff; the
sh dollar, for example, at the rate of 100 for 260 florins.

ghts. — The Chinese weights are invariably used in commercial transactions
tavia, and throughout Java and the other Dutch possessions in India.
 are the picul, and the cattie, which is its hundredth part. The picul is com-
 estimated at 125 Dutch, or 133¼lbs. avoirdupois, but at Batavia it has
long ascertained and considered to be equal to 136lbs. avoirdupois. See
g van den Handel, Scheepvaart en Inhomende, en Vitgaande Regten op Java,
oor J. Kruseman, Batavia, 1829. Evidence of Gillian Maclaine, Esq. taken
 the select committee of the House of Commons on the affairs of the East
Company, 1831.

TTEN, a name in common use for a scantling of wood about one inch
nd three wide, sometimes more and sometimes less.

ZAAR, a name used in the East to designate markets, or buildings in which
s articles of merchandise are exposed for sale. Bazaars are now met with
t large cities of Europe. There are several in London, of which the one
o-square is the most considerable.

ELLIUM (Arab. *Aflatoon*), a gum resin, semi-pellucid, and of a yellowish
 or dark brown colour according to its age, unctuous to the touch, but brittle;
however, softening between the fingers; in appearance it is not unlike myrrh,
tterish taste, and moderately strong smell. Two kinds have been distin-
d: the *opocalpasum* of the ancients, which is thick like wax; and the com-
ark sort. It is found in Persia and Arabia, but principally in the latter;
t is met with in India is of Arabic origin. The tree which produces it has
en clearly ascertained. — (*Dr. Ainslie's Materia Indica.*)

ACONS, in commerce and navigation, public marks or signals to give
ng of rocks, shoals, &c. No man is entitled to erect a lighthouse, beacon,
ithout being empowered by law. The Trinity House Corporation are au-
ed to set up beacons in whatever places they shall think fit; and any per-
ho shall wilfully remove or run down any buoy, beacon, &c. belonging
 Trinity House, or to any other corporation, individual, or individuals,
; authority to establish it, shall, besides being liable to the expense of re-
g the same, forfeit a sum of not less than 10*l.* nor more than 50*l.* for every
ffence. — 6 Geo. 4. c. 125. § 91.

ADS (Fr. *Rosaires;* Ger. *Rosenkränze;* Du. *Paternosters;* It. *Corone;*
ronas), the small globules or balls used as necklaces, and made of different
als; as pearl, steel, amber, garnet, coral, diamonds, crystal, glass, &c.
n Catholics use beads in rehearsing their Ave Marias and Paternosters.
beads or bugles are exported in large quantities to Africa.

ANS (Fr. *Féves;* Da. *Bönner;* Du. *Boonen;* Ger. *Bohnen;* It. *Fave;*
avas; Rus. *Boobü;* Sp. *Habas;* Sw. *Bönor;* Lat. *Fabœ*), a well-known
ble of the pulse species, largely cultivated both in gardens and fields.

AVER. See SKINS.

ECII, *fagus sylvatica*, a forest tree to be met with every where in England.
 is only one species, the difference in the wood proceeding from the dif-
e of soil and situation. A considerable quantity of beech is grown in the
rn parts of Bucks. It is not much used in building, as it soon rots in

damp places; but it is used as piles in places where it is constantly wet. I*
manufactured into a great variety of tools, for which its great hardness and u*
form texture render it superior to all other sorts of wood; it is also extensiv*
used in making furniture.

BEEF, as every one knows, is the flesh of the ox. It is used either fresh
salted. Formerly it was usual for most families, at least in the country, to sup*
themselves with a stock of salt beef in October or November, which served *
their consumption until the ensuing summer; but in consequence of the u*
versal establishment of markets where fresh beef may be at all times obtained, *
practice is now nearly relinquished, and the quantity of salted beef made use
as compared with fresh beef is quite inconsiderable. Large supplies of sal*
beef are, however, prepared at Cork and other places for exportation to the E*
and West Indies. During the war, large supplies were also required for victu*
ling the navy. The vessels engaged in the coasting trade, and in short voyages, *
only fresh provisions.

The English have at all times been great consumers of beef; and at this mom*
more beef is used in London, as compared with the population, than any wh*
else. For further details with respect to the consumption of beef, &c., *
CATTLE.

BEER. See ALE AND BEER.

BELL-METAL (Fr. *Metal de Fonte ou de Cloches;* Ger. *Glockengut;* Du. *Kl*
spys; Sp. *Campanil;* Rus. *Koloklnaja mjed*), a composition of tin and copp*
usually consisting of three parts of copper and one of tin. Its colour
greyish white; it is very hard, sonorous, and elastic. Less tin is used for chu*
bells than for clock bells; and in very small bells, a little zinc is added to *
alloy. — (*Thomson's Chemistry.*)

BENZOIN. See BALSAM.

BERGEN, the first commercial city of Norway, situated at the bottom *
a deep bay, in lat. 60° 10′ N., long. 7° 14′ E.; population about 15,000. C*
fish, salted or dried, is one of the principal articles of export; when dried, i*
called stock-fish, and goes chiefly to Italy and Holland. The cod fishery e*
ploys several thousand persons during the months of February and March; *
the annual exports from Bergen amount to about 12,000 barrels. The herr*
fishery, which used to be very successfully carried on upon the coasts of N*
way, has, for a good many years, been comparatively unproductive. Considera*
quantities of iron, copper, tar, pitch, and skins, are also exported. Timber, ho*
ever, forms the great natural wealth of the country, and it is the principal arti*
sent to England. Norway timber is not so large as that brought from the Pr*
sian ports, nor so free from knots; but, being of slower growth, it is more comp*
and less liable to rot. The planks are either red or white fir or pine: the
wood is produced from the Scotch fir; the white wood, which is in the high*
estimation, from the spruce fir: each tree yields three pieces of timber 11 or *
feet in length; and is 70 or 80 years of age before it arrives at perfection. *
planks or deals of Bergen are, however, a good deal inferior to those of Ch*
tiania. (*Coxe's Travels in the North of Europe,* 5th ed. vol. v. p. 28.) The
ports into Bergen principally consist of grain from the Baltic; and salt, hardw*
coffee, sugar, &c. from England.

The monies, weights, and measures of Norway continue, notwithstanding
junction with Sweden, to be the same as those of Denmark; for which, see
PENHAGEN.

For some details with respect to the imports into England from Norway,
CHRISTIANIA.

BERRIES (*baccæ*), the fruits or seeds of many different species of pla*
The berries quoted in London Price Currents are bay, juniper, Turkey, *
Persian.

1. **Bay berries** (Fr. *Baies de Laurier;* Ger. *Lorbeeren;* It. *Bacchi di Lauro;*
Bayas), the fruit of the *Laurus nobilis.* This tree is a native of the South of Eur*
but is cultivated in this country, and is not uncommon in our gardens. The berry
an oval shape, fleshy, and of a dark purple colour, almost black; it has a s*
fragrant odour, and an aromatic astringent taste. Bay berries, and the oil obtaine*
boiling them in water, are imported from Italy and Spain. (*Thomson's Dispensator*

2. *Juniper berries* (Fr. *Genèvrier;* Dut. *Sevenboom;* It. *Ginepro;* Sp. *Embro*), the fru*

e common juniper (*Juniperus communis*). They are round, of a black purple colour,
d require two years to ripen. They have a moderately strong, not disagreeable, but
culiar smell, and a warm, pungent, sweetish taste, which, if they be long chewed, or
eviously well bruised, is followed by a considerable bitterness. They are found in
is country; but most of those made use of here are imported from Holland, Germany,
d Italy. They should be chosen fresh, not much shrivelled, and free from
ouldiness, which they are apt to contract in keeping. On distillation with water,
ey yield a volatile essential oil, very subtile and pungent, and in smell greatly resem-
ng the berries. The peculiar flavour and diuretic qualities of Geneva depend prin-
ally on the presence of this oil. English gin is said to be, for the most part, flavoured
h oil of turpentine.—(*Lewis's Mat. Med. Thomson's Dispensatory*).
The duty on juniper berries is 11s. 1d. a cwt., being *fully* 100 *per cent. on their price
bond.* The oppressiveness of this duty seems to be the principal reason why turpen-
e, which in point of flavour and all other respects is so inferior, is used in preference
juniper berries in the preparation of gin. In 1829, the duty produced 6,964l. 14s.,
owing that about 12,650 cwt. of berries had been entered for home consumption.
ere the duty reduced to 2s. or 2s. 6d., we believe that it would be decidedly more
oductive, at the same time that it would materially improve the beverage of a large
portion of the people.
Italian juniper berries fetch at present (May 1831), in the London market, from 20s.
21s. a cwt., duty included; and German and Dutch ditto, from 25s. to 27s.
3. *Turkey yellow berries,* the unripe fruit of the *Rhamnus infectorius* of Linnæus.
ey are used as a dye-drug, in preparing a lively but very fugitive yellow, for topical
lication in calico-printing. Considerable quantities of them are exported from
onica, to which they are brought from Thessaly and Albania. An inferior sort is
duced in France.—(*Bancroft on Colours*). The duty on Turkey berries is 14s.;
d their price, duty included, in the London market is (May 1831) 40s. a cwt.
4. *Persian yellow berries* are said by the merchants to be of the same species as the
rkey yellow berries. The colours which they yield are more lively and lasting.
ey are high priced, fetching (duty 14s. included) from 130s. to 160s. a cwt.
therto the imports have not been very considerable.

BERYL, called by the jewellers *Aqua marina.* This stone, as its name implies,
most commonly green of various shades, passing into honey-yellow, smalt,
d sky blue. The colours are usually pale, the lustre shining vitreous: it is
mmonly transparent, but sometimes only translucent. It is harder than the
erald. It is found in many parts of the world; amongst others, at Cairngorm,
d elsewhere, in Scotland. — (*Ure's Dictionary,* and *Thomson's Chemistry.*)
'hose only which are of good colour and sufficient depth are manufactured;
y have a pretty, lively effect, if in good proportion and well polished. Large
nes, from one to three and four ounces, are not uncommon, but from their
k are only in request as specimens for the cabinet: smaller stones suitable for
klaces may be bought at low prices, within the reach of every description of
chasers: ring stones may be had at a few shillings each; and larger, for brooches
seals, from 1l. to 5l. and often lower." — (*Mawe on Diamonds, &c.* 2d edit.)

BETEL-NUT, or ARECA, the fruit of the Areca palm, or pepper vine, which
ws luxuriantly and with little care in the India islands, the Malay peninsula, &c.
t it is only on the western coast of Sumatra that betel-nut is in such abund-
e as to form an article of export. It is insipid to the taste, and gently nar-
ic. The betel-nut of commerce is of two kinds — that which is dried carefully
hout being split, and that which is split and more hastily dried. The first is
most valuable. It is principally carried to China and Bengal. Mr. Crawfurd
nks that it might be imported into Europe, and used with advantage in the
ing of cottons. The natives of the Indian islands are passionately fond of
el-nut. " Persons of all ranks, from the prince to the peasant, are unceasingly
ticating it; and seem to derive a solace from it, which we can scarce
erstand, and they cannot explain."—(*Eastern Archipelago,* vols. i. p. 102.
. 414.)

BEZOAR (Arab. *Faduj;* Hind. *Zeher-morah;* Pers. *Padzehr Kanie*), a con-
ion found in the stomach of an animal of the goat kind; it has a smooth glossy
ace, and is of a dark green or olive colour: the word bezoar, however, has
ly been extended to all the concretions found in animals; — such as the *hog-
ar,* found in the stomach of the wild boar in India; the *bovine-bezoar,* found
he gall-bladder of the ox, common in Nepaul; and the *camel-bezoar,* found in
gall-bladder of the camel: this last is much prized as a yellow paint by the

Hindoos. The finest bezoar is brought to India from Borneo and the sea-ports of the Persian Gulf; the Persian article is particularly sought after, and is said to be procured from animals of the goat kind, *capra gazella*. Many extraordinary virtues were formerly ascribed to this substance, but without any sufficient reason. — (*Dr. Ainslie's Materia Indica.*)

BILL OF EXCHANGE. See EXCHANGE.

BILL OF HEALTH, a certificate or instrument signed by consuls or other proper authorities, delivered to the masters of ships at the time of their clearing out from all ports or places suspected of being particularly subject to infectious disorders, certifying the state of health at the time that such ships sailed. A *clean* bill imports, that at the time that the ship sailed no infectious disorder was known to exist. A *suspected* bill, commonly called a touched patent or bill, imports that there were rumours of an infectious disorder, but that it had not actually appeared. A *foul* bill, or the absence of clean bills, imports that the place was infected when the vessel sailed. See QUARANTINE.

BILL OF LADING, is a written document subscribed by masters of ships, acknowledging the receipt of goods on board, and promising to deliver them at a certain specified place, in the like good order and condition as at the place of shipment, (" the act of God, the King's enemies, fire, and all and every other dangers and accidents of the seas, rivers, and navigation, of whatever nature and kind soever, save risk of boats, as far as ships are liable thereunto, excepted.") Bills of lading are made out in sets of three or four; three of them being on stamped paper : one of them should be remitted by the first post after signing to the person to whom the goods are consigned, a second being sent to him by the ship; a third is to be retained by the shipper of the goods; and a fourth, on unstamped paper, is to be given to the master for his government.

Form of a Bill of Lading.

W. B.   } SHIPPED, in good order, by *A. B.* merchant, in and upon the good ship called
No. 1. *a*. 10. }   whereof *C. D.* is master, now riding at anchor in the river Thames, and boun for Alicant, in Spain, ten bales, containing fifty pieces of broad cloth, marked and numbere as *per* margin ; and are to be delivered, in the like good order and condition, at Alicar aforesaid, (*the act of God, the king's enemies, fire, and all and every other dangers an accidents of the seas, rivers, and navigation, of whatever nature and kind soever, sav risk of boats, so far as ships are liable thereunto, excepted*,) unto *E. F.* merchant, there, to his assigns, he or they paying for the said goods   *per* piec freight, with primage and average accustomed. In witness whereof, I, the said master o the said ship, have affirmed to three bills of lading, of this tenour and date ; the one o which bills being accomplished, the other two to stand void. And so God send the good shi to her destined port in safety ; Amen.
London,   **C. D.**, *Master*.
10th May, 1831.

The difference between a bill of lading and a charterparty is, that the first i required and given for a single article, or more, laden on board a ship that ha sundry merchandise shipped on sundry accounts ; whereas a charterparty is mos commonly a contract for the whole ship. When a bill of lading is given togethe with a charterparty, it is to be considered merely as evidence of the shipment o the goods. Bills of lading ought to be signed within twenty-four hours afte delivery of the goods on board. But, upon delivery of the goods, the master, o person officiating for the master in his absence, is to give a common receipt fo them, which is to be delivered up on the master signing the bill of lading.

" Where several bills of lading of the same date, but of different imports, hav been signed, no reference is to be had to the time when they were first signed b the captain; but the person who first gets one of them by a legal title from th owner or shipper, has a right to the consignment And where such bills of ladin, though different upon the face of them, are constructively the same, and the ca tain has acted *bona fide*, a delivery according to such legal title will discharge hi from them all."—(*Park on Insurance*, c. 20.)

By stat. 6 Geo. 4. c. 94. § 2. any person in possession of any bill of ladin shall be deemed the true owner of the goods specified in it, so as to make a sal or pledge by him of such goods or bill of lading valid.

The stamp-duty on a bill of lading of or for any goods to be exported or ried coastwise, is 3*s*.

BILL OF SALE, a contract under seal, by which an individual conveys passes away the right and interest he has in the goods or chattels named in th bill. The property of ships is transferred by bill of sale. See REGISTRY.

ILL OF SIGHT. When a merchant is ignorant of the real quantities or qualities
ny goods assigned to him, so that he is unable to make a perfect entry of them,
ust acquaint the collector or comptroller of the circumstance; and they are
orised, upon the importer or his agent making oath that he cannot, for want
ll information, make a perfect entry, to receive an entry by *bill of sight*, for the
ages, by the best description which can be given, and to grant warrant that
same may be landed and examined by the importer in presence of the officers;
within three days after any goods shall have been so landed, the importer
make a perfect entry, and shall either pay down the duties, or shall duly
chouse the same.— (6 *Geo.* 4. c. 105. § 23.)

default of perfect entry within three days, such goods are to be taken to the
's warehouse; and if the importer shall not, within one month, make perfect
y, and pay the duties thereon, or on such parts as can be entered for home
together with charges of moving and warehouse rent, such goods shall be
for payment of the duties.— § 24.

he East India Company are authorised, without the proof-before mentioned,
nter goods by bill of sight, and to make perfect entry, and pay the duties
in three months.— § 25.

LL OF STORE, is a licence granted by the Custom-house, to mer-
ts, to carry such stores and provisions as are necessary for a voyage, free
ty.

the act 6 Geo. 4. c. 107., returned goods may be entered by bill of store,
llows :—

m 5th January, 1826, it shall be lawful to re-import into the United Kingdom, from any place, in a ship
country, any goods (except as herein-after excepted) which shall have been legally exported from the
d Kingdom, and to enter the same by bill of store, referring to the entry outwards, and exportation
f; provided the property in such goods continue in the person by whom or on whose account the
have been exported; and if the goods so returned be foreign goods which had before been legally
ted into the United Kingdom, the same duties shall be payable thereon as would, at the time of
e-importation, be payable on the like goods, under the same circumstances of importation as those
which such goods had been originally imported; or such goods may be warehoused upon a first
ation thereof; provided always, that the several sorts of goods enumerated or described in the list
ing shall not be re-imported into the United Kingdom for *home use*, upon the ground that the same
een legally exported from thence, but that the same shall be deemed to be *foreign* goods, whether
ally such or not, and shall also be deemed to be imported for the first time into the United King-
viz.

Goods exported, which may not be re-imported for Home Use :—

rn, grain, meal, flour, and malt; hops, tobacco, tea.
ods for which any bounty or any drawback of excise had been received on exportation, unless
pecial permission of the commissioners of customs, and on repayment of such bounty or such
wback.
l goods for which bill of store cannot be issued in manner herein-after directed, except small rem-
s of British goods, by special permission of the commissioners of customs, upon proof to their
faction that the same are British, and had not been sold. — § 31.

person in whose name any goods so re-imported were entered for exportation, shall deliver to the
er, at the port of exportation, an exact account signed by him of the particulars of such goods, referring
ntry and clearance outwards, and to the return inwards of the same, with the marks and numbers
packages both inwards and outwards; and thereupon the searcher, finding that such goods had
gally exported, shall grant a bill of store for the same; and if the person in whose name the goods
ntered for exportation was not the proprietor thereof, but his agent, he shall declare upon oath on
ll of store the name of the person by whom he was employed as such agent; and if the person to
such returns are consigned shall not be such proprietor and exporter, he shall declare upon oath on
ll of store the name of the person for whose use such goods have been consigned to him; and the
oprietor, ascertained to be such, shall make oath upon such bill of store to the identity of the goods
rted and so returned, and that he was at the time of exportation and of re-importation the proprie-
uch goods, and that the same had not during such time been sold or disposed of to any other per-
d such affidavits shall be made before the collectors or comptrollers at the ports of exportation and
ortation respectively, and thereupon the collector and comptroller shall admit such goods to entry
of store, and grant their warrant accordingly. — § 32.

LLINGSGATE, a market for fish, contiguous to the custom-house in Lon-
It is held every lawful day, and was established in 1699 by stat. 10. &
ill. 3. c. 24. Every person buying fish in Billingsgate market, may sell the
in any other market place or places within the city of London or elsewhere,
ail, with this condition, that none but fishmongers be permitted to sell in
shops or houses. No person or persons shall purchase at Billingsgate any
ity of fish to be divided by lots or in shares amongst any fishmongers or other
ns, in order to be afterwards put to sale by retail or otherwise; nor shall
shmonger engross, or buy in the said market, any quantity of fish, but what
e for his own sale or use, under the penalty of 20*l.* No person is to have
possession, or expose to sale, any spawn of fish, or fish unsizeable, or out
son. — (36 *Geo.* 3. c. 118.) The minimum size of the lobsters to be sold at
zsgate is fixed by statute. See LOBSTER.

fish of foreign taking or curing, or in foreign vessels, is to be imported into

I 4

the United Kingdom, under penalty of forfeiture, except turbots and lobste
stock-fish, live eels, anchovies, sturgeon, botargo, and caviare. Fresh fish
British taking, and imported in British ships, and turbot however taken or i
ported, may be landed without report, entry, or warrant. — (6 *Geo.* 4. c. 107.)

For some further remarks with respect to this subject, see FISH.

BIRCH (Fr. *Bouleau;* Du. *Berke;* Ger. *Birke;* It. *Betulla;* Lat. *Betula*
Pol. *Brzoza;* Rus. *Bereza;* Sp. *Abedul, Betulla*), a forest tree met with
where in the north of Europe. It is applied to various purposes. In Laplan
Norway, and Sweden, the long twigs of the birch are woven into mats and twist
into ropes; the outer bark forms an almost incorruptible covering for house
and the inner bark is used, in periods of scarcity, as a substitute for bread. Russ
leather is prepared by means of the empyreumatic oil of the birch. It is
excellent wood for the turner, being light, compact, and easily worked. Its dur
bility is not very great. It is sometimes used in the manufacture of herring barre

BIRDLIME (Ger. *Vogelleim;* Du. *Vogellym;* Fr. *Glu;* It. *Pania;* Sp.*Lig*
Port. *Visco;* Rus. *Ptitschei Klei;* Pol. *Lep*), exudes spontaneously from certa
plants, and is obtained artificially from the middle bark of the holly. Its colo
is greenish, its flavour sour, and it is gluey, shining, and tenacious. The natu
is more adhesive than the artificial birdlime. — (*Thomson's Chemistry.*)

BIRDS' NESTS (Ger. *Indianische Vogelnester;* Du. *Indiaansche Vog*
nestjes; Fr. *Nids de Tunkin;* It. *Nidi di Tunchino;* Sp. *Nidos de la China;* Jav
Susu; Malay, *Sarungburung*), the nests of a species of swallow peculiar to t
Indian islands (*Hirundo esculenta*), very much esteemed in China. In shape th
nest resembles that of other swallows; it is formed of a viscid substance; and
external appearance, as well as consistence, is not unlike fibrous, ill-concoct
isinglass. Esculent nests are principally found in Java, in caverns that are mo
frequently, though not always, situated on the sea-coast. Many conflicting sta
ments have been made as to the substance of nests; some contending that th
are formed of sea-foam or other marine products, and others that they are e
borated from the food of the bird, &c. But these are points as to which nothi
satisfactory is known.

We borrow from Mr. Crawford's valuable work on the Eastern Archipelago, (v
iii. pp. 432 — 437.) the following authentic and curious details as to the traffic in ti
singular production : —" The best nests are those obtained in deep damp caves, a
such as are taken before the birds have laid their eggs. The coarsest are those obtain
after the young have been fledged. The finest nests are the whitest, that is, those tak
before the nest has been rendered impure by the food and *fæces* of the young birds. Th
are taken twice a-year, and, if regularly collected, and no unusual injury be offered
the caverns, will produce very equally, the quantity being very little, if at all, improv
by the caves being left altogether unmolested for a year or two. Some of the cave
are extremely difficult of access, and the nests can only be collected by persons acc
tomed from their youth to the office. The most remarkable and productive caves
Java, of which I superintended a moiety of the collection for several years, are those
Karang bolang, in the province of *Baglen,* on the south coast of the island. Here
caves are only to be approached by a perpendicular descent of many hundred feet,
ladders of bamboo and rattan, over a sea rolling violently against the rocks. When
mouth of the cavern is attained, the perilous office of taking the nests must often be p
formed with torch light, by penetrating into recesses of the rock where the slightest
would be instantly fatal to the adventurers, who see nothing below them but the turl
lent surf making its way into the chasms of the rock.

" The only preparation which the birds' nests undergo is that of simple drying, with
direct exposure to the sun, after which they are packed in small boxes, usually of hal
picul. They are assorted for the Chinese market into three kinds, according to th
qualities, distinguished into *first* or *best,* *second,* and *third* qualities. Caverns that are
gularly managed, will afford in 100 parts 53$\frac{3}{10}$ parts of those of the first quality, 35 p
of those of the second, 11$\frac{7}{10}$ parts of those of the third.

" The common prices for birds' nests at Canton are, for the first sort no less than 3,
Spanish dollars the picul, or 5*l.* 18*s.* 1$\frac{1}{2}$*d.* per pound; for the second. 2,800 Spani
dollars per picul; and for the third, 1,600 Spanish dollars. From these prices
is sufficiently evident, that the birds' nests are no more than an article of exp
sive luxury. They are consumed only by the great; and, indeed, the best
is sent to the capital for the consumption of the court. The sensual Chinese
them, under the imagination that they are powerfully stimulating and tonic; bu
is probable that their most valuable quality is their being perfectly harmless.

ople of Japan, who so much resemble the Chinese in many of their habits, have no taste
r the edible nests; and how the latter acquired a taste for this foreign commodity is no
ss singular than their persevering in it. Among the western nations there is nothing
rallel to it, unless we except the whimsical estimation in which the Romans held some
ticles of luxury, remarkable for their scarcity rather than for any qualities ascribed to
em."

Mr. Crawfurd estimates the whole quantity of birds' nests exported from the Archi-
lago at 242,400 lbs. worth 284,290*l.* " The value," he observes, " of this immense
operty to the country which produces it, rests upon the capricious wants of a single
ople. It is claimed as the exclusive property of the sovereign, and every where forms
valuable branch of his income, or of the revenue of the state. This value, however,
of course not equal, and depends upon the situation and the circumstances connected
th the caverns in which the nests are found. Being often in remote and sequestered
uations, in a country so lawless, a property so valuable and exposed is subject to the
rpetual depredation of freebooters, and it not unfrequently happens that an attack upon
s the principal object of the warfare committed by one petty state against another.
such situations, the expense of affording them protection is so heavy, that they are
cessarily of little value. In situations where the caverns are difficult of access to
angers, and where there reigns enough of order and tranquillity to secure them from
ernal depredation, and to admit of the nests being obtained without other expense
n the simple labour of collecting them, the value of the property is very great.
e caverns of *Karang-bolang*, in Java, are of this description. These annually afford
10 lbs. of nests, which are worth, at the Batavia prices of 3,200, 2,500, and 1,200
anish dollars the picul, for the respective kinds, nearly 139,000 Spanish dollars; and
whole expense of collecting, curing, and packing, amounts to no more than 11 per
t. on this amount. The price of birds' nests is of course a monopoly price, the
antity produced being by nature limited, and incapable of augmentation. The value
he labour expended in bringing birds' nests to market is but a trifling portion of their
ce, which consists of the highest sum that the luxurious Chinese will afford to pay
them, and which is a tax paid by that nation to the inhabitants of the Indian islands.
ere is, perhaps, no production upon which human industry is exerted, of which the
t of production bears so small a proportion to the market price."

BISMUTH (Ger. *Wismuth*; Du. *Bismuth, Bergsteen*; Fr. *Bismuth*; It. *Bis-
ttc*; Sp. *Bismuth, Piedra inga*; Rus. *Wismut*; Lat. *Bismuthum*), a metal of a
dish white colour, and almost destitute of taste and smell. It is softer than
per; its specific gravity is 9 822. When hammered cautiously, its density is
siderably increased; it breaks, however, when struck smartly by a hammer,
, consequently, is not malleable, neither can it be drawn out into wire; it
lts at the temperature of 476°. — (*Thomson's Chemistry.*)

Bismuth is used in the composition of pewter, in the fabrication of printers'
es, and in various other metallic mixtures. With an equal weight of lead, it
ns a brilliant white alloy, much harder than lead, and more malleable than
muth, though not ductile; and if the proportion of lead be increased, it is
dered still more malleable. Eight parts of bismuth, five of lead, and three of tin,
stitute the fusible metal, sometimes called Newton's, from its discoverer, which
ts at the heat of boiling water, and may be fused over a candle in a piece of
paper without burning the paper. One part of bismuth, with five of lead,
three of tin, forms pewterers' solder. It forms the basis of a sympathetic
" — (*Dr. Ure.*)

BITUMEN (Ger. *Judenpech*; Du. *Jodenlym*; It. *Asfalto*; Sp. *Asfalto*; Port.
halto*; Rus. *Asfalt*; Lat. *Asphaltum, Bitumen judiacum*). This term includes
nsiderable range of inflammable mineral substances, burning with flame in the
n air. They differ in consistency, from a thin fluid to a solid; but the solids
for the most part liquefiable at a moderate heat. They are, 1. *Naphtha;*
ne, white, thin, fragrant, colourless oil, which issues out of white, yellow, or
k clays in Persia and Media. This is highly inflammable. Near the vil-
of Amiano, in the state of Parma, there exists a spring which yields this
stance in sufficient quantity to illuminate the city of Genoa, for which pur-
e it is employed. With certain vegetable oils, naphtha is said to form a good
ish. 2. *Petroleum* is much thicker than naphtha, resembling in consistence
mon tar. It has a strong disagreeable odour, and a blackish or reddish
wn colour. During combustion, it emits a thick black smoke, and leaves a
e residue in the form of black coal. It is more abundant than the first-
tioned variety, from which it does not seem to differ, except in being more

inspissated. It occurs, oozing out of rocks, in the vicinity of beds of coal, or floating upon the surface of springs. In the Birman empire, near Rainanghong is a hill containing coal, into which 520 pits have been sunk for the collection of petroleum, the annual produce of the hill being about 400,000 hogsheads. It i used by the inhabitants of that country as a lamp oil, and, when mingled with earth or ashes, as fuel. In the United States it is found abundantly in Kentucky, Ohio, and New York, where it is known by the name of *Seneca* or *Genesee* oil. It is used as a substitute for tar, and as an external application for the cure of rheumatism and chilblains. 3. *Maltha* is a bitumen still less fluid than petroleum from which it differs in no other respect. It is very abundant at Puy de la Pege in France, where it renders the soil so viscid that it adheres strongly to the foot of the traveller. It is also found in Persia, and in the Hartz. It is employed like tar and pitch on cables, and in calking vessels : it is used, as well as petroleum, to protect iron from rusting, and sometimes forms an ingredient in black sealing-wax. 4. *Elastic bitumen* yields easily to pressure, is flexible and elastic It emits a strong bituminous odour, and is about the weight of water. On exposure to the air it hardens, and loses its elasticity. It takes up the traces of crayons in the same manner as caoutchouc, or Indian rubber, whence it has obtained the name of *mineral caoutchouc.* It has hitherto been found only in the lead mines of Derbyshire. 5. *Compact bitumen,* or *asphaltum* (see ASPHALTUM), is of a shining black colour, solid, and brittle, with a conchoidal fracture. Its specific gravity varies from 1 to 1·6. Like the former varieties, it burns freely and leaves but little residuum. It is found in India, on the shores of the Dead Sea, in the Palatinate, in France, in Switzerland, and in large deposits in sandstone in Albania; but nowhere so largely as in the island of Trinidad, where it forms a lake three miles in circumference, and of a thickness unknown. A gentle heat renders it ductile, and, when mixed with grease or common pitch, it is used for paying the bottoms of ships, and is said to protect them from the teredo of the West Indian seas. The ancients employed bitumen in the construction of their buildings. The bricks of which the walls of Babylon were built were, it is said (*Herodotus,* lib. i. § 179.) cemented with hot bitumen, which gave them unusual solidity. — (*Ure's Dictionary. Conversations Lexicon. Ainslie's Mat Indica.*)

BLACKING (Ger. *Schuhschwärze, Wichse*; Du. *Schoenzwartzel*; Fr. *Noir (d cordonnier)*; It. *Nero da ugner le scarpe*; Sp. *Negro de zapatos*). A factitiou article, prepared in various ways, used in the blacking of shoes. Considerabl quantities are exported.

BLACK-LEAD (Du. *Potloot*; Fr. *Mine de plomb noir, Plomb de mine, Po telot*; Ger. *Pottloth, Reissbley*; It. *Miniera di piombo, Piombaggine, Corezolo* Lat. *Plumbago*; Sp. *Piedra mineral de plomo*), or plumbago, a mineral of dark steel grey colour, and a metallic lustre; it is soft, and has a greasy feel ; i leaves a dark coloured line when drawn along paper. It is principally employe in the making of pencils; it is also employed in the making of crucibles, in rubbin bright the surface of cast-iron utensils, and in diminishing friction, when inter posed between rubbing surfaces. The finest specimens of this mineral are foun in the celebrated mine of Borrowdale, in Cumberland. This mine has bee worked since the days of Queen Elizabeth, and is said to be the only one whic supplies plumbago of sufficient purity to be made into pencils. — (*Thomson' Chemistry.*)

BLACK-LEAD PENCILS (Du. *Potlootpennen*; Fr. *Crayons noirs*; Ge *Bleystifte*; It. *Lapis nero*; Por. *Lapis negro*; Ru. *Karanaschü*; Sp. *Lapis negro* are formed of black-lead encircled with cedar.

BLOOD-STONE (Ger. *Blutsein*; Fr. *Pierre sanguine à crayon*; It. *Sanguigno* Sp. *Piedra sanguinaria*; Lat. *Hœmatites*), or the *lapis hœmalatites*, a species calcedony, is a mineral of a reddish colour, hard, ponderous, with long pointe needles. It is found among iron ore in great abundance. These stones are be chosen of the highest colour, with fine striæ or needles, and as much like ci nabar as possible. Goldsmiths and gilders use it to polish their works. It is al used for trinkets.

BLUBBER (Ger. *Thran, Fischtran*; Du. *Thraan*; It. *Olio di pesce*; S *Grassa, Aceite de pescado*; Rus. *Salo worwannoe, Worwan*; Lat. *Oleum piscinum* the fat of whales and other large sea-animals, of which is made train oil. T

ber is the *adeps* of the animal: it lies under the skin, and over the muscular
: it is about six inches in thickness, but about the under lip it is two or three
thick. The whole quantity yielded by one of these animals, ordinarily
unts to 40 or 50, but sometimes to 80 or more cwt. Formerly train oil was
ufactured from the blubber in the seas round Spitzbergen, and other places
re whales were caught; but the practice is now to bring the blubber home in
s, and to prepare the oil afterwards.

s enacted by the 6 Geo. 4. c. 107. § 44., that before any blubber, train oil, spermaceti oil, head matter,
ale fins, shall be entered as being entirely the produce of sea-animals caught by the crews of ships
out in the United Kingdom, or the islands of Jersey, Guernsey, Sark, and Man, the master of the ship
ting such goods shall make oath, and the importer also shall make oath, to the best of his knowledge
elief, that the same are the produce of fish or creatures living in the sea, taken and caught wholly
crew of such ship, or by the crew of some other ship (naming it) fitted out in the United King-
or in one of the islands of Guernsey, Jersey, Alderney, Sark, or Man (naming which).
ore blubber, train oil, &c. can be entered as from a British possession, a certificate must be obtained
the custom-house officer at such British possession, or in default of such officer being there, from
rincipal inhabitants, notifying that oath had been made before him or them that such blubber, &c.
he produce of fish or creatures living in the sea, and had been taken by British subjects usually
ng in some part of his Majesty's dominions; and the importer is to make oath, to the best of his
edge and belief, to the same effect.

gauging of casks of oil and blubber is dispensed with since 1825. They are to be passed at the
f 126 gallons the pipe, and 63 gallons the hogshead.

OATS are open vessels, commonly wrought by oars, and of an endless va-
of shapes, according to the purposes to which they are to be applied.

s ordered by statute 6 Geo. 4. c. 108., that every boat belonging to or attached to any other vessel,
ave painted on the outside of the stern of such boat, the name of the vessel and place to which she
s, and the master's name within side of the transum, in white or yellow Roman letters, two inches
on a black ground, under pain of forfeiture. Boats *not belonging* to vessels, are to be painted with
ame of the owner and place to which they belong, under penalty of forfeiture. All boats having
sides or bottoms, or secret places for the purpose of concealing goods, or having any hole, pipe, or
device for the purpose of running goods, are to be forfeited.

ulations of Watermen on Thames.— From Chelsea Bridge towards Windsor, 3d. per half mile for
s.

the water directly between Windsor and Crawley's Wharf, Greenwich (excepting the Sunday
, for one person 3d., two persons 1½d. each, exceeding two persons 1d. each.
r from ships westward of Greenwich, for one person 2d., exceeding one person 1d. each; and, where
tance to the ship does not exceed the distance across the river, the fare across the river shall be

r from ships eastward of Greenwich, at the rate of 6d. per half mile.
r from vessels for passengers, for one person 4d., exceeding one person 3d. each, with not exceeding
f luggage for each. After this at the rate of 1s. per cwt.
ermen detained by passengers to be paid for time or distance, at the option of the watermen.

	s. d.		s. d.
Time for a Pair of Oars.—First hour ...	2 0	Each succeeding hour	1 0
hour	1 6	For the day	12 0

st from 7 A.M. to 5 P.M. between Michaelmas and Lady Day; and from 6 A.M. to 6 P.M. from
Day to Michaelmas.

SCULLER'S FARES.
The Bridges &c. stand in the following order.

Bridge	Nine Elms	Shadwell Dock Stairs
ark Bridge	Red House, Battersea	Kidney ditto
iars Bridge	Swan Stairs, Chelsea	Limehouse Hole ditto
oo Bridge	Chelsea Bridge	Ditto, Torrington Arms
nster Bridge	Iron Gate	Deptford, George Stairs
th Stairs	Union Stairs	Ditto, Low-Water Gate
all Bridge	King Edward ditto	Greenwich, Crawley's Wharf.

fare from either of the above places to the next is 3d., and so on in proportion.

Passage Boats.— Oars' Fare 8 Passengers.   Sculler's Fare 6 Passengers.

	each		each		each
	s. d.	London Bridge to	s. d.	London Bridge to	s. d.
Bridge to		Brentford	1 3	Walton-upon-Thames	1 9
Bridge	0 6	Isleworth	1 3	Shepperton	2 0
worth	0 7	Richmond	1 3	Weybridge	2 0
....	0 8	Twickenham	1 6	Laleham	2 0
Elms	0 8	Tide-end Town	1 6	Chertsey	2 0
ersmith	0 9	Kingston	1 6	Staines	2 6
ck	0 9	Hampton Court	1 9	Datchet	3 0
....	1 0	Hampton Town	1 9	Windsor	3 0
ke	1 0	Sunbury	1 9		
d	0 6	Blackwall	0 9	Gravesend	1 6
ich	0 6	Woolwich	1 0		

full boat load of luggage, same as for eight passengers.
alf a load, same as for four passengers.
ties.— Taking more than fare, not exceeding 2l.
rman to have a list of fares in his boat, and on not permitting the passenger to examine it, the
er is discharged from paying his fare, not exceeding 5l.
ing to take a passenger, or not answering when called by the number of his boat, not exceeding 5l.
cessarily delaying a passenger, not exceeding 5l.
ing to permit any person to read the name and number of his boat, or to tell his Christian or sur-
r the number of his boat, *on being paid his fare*, or making use of any abusive language, not
ng 5l.

and By-laws made by the Court of Aldermen, 15th April, 1828.— Letting his boat remain at any
while wilfully absent, or not being ready to take a passenger into his boat, not exceeding 1l.

Refusing to give his name or number, or that of any other waterman, not exceeding 1l.

Obstructing any other waterman in taking in or landing a passenger, or obstructing a passenger, exceeding 1l.

Towing or being towed by any other boat without the consent of all the passengers, not exceeding 5

Agreeing to take any lesser sum than the rate allowed, and afterwards demanding more than the s agreed for, not exceeding 2l.

Only two boats to be placed aboard any steam-boat at the same time in turn. Waterman, previous taking turn as aforesaid, to lie with his boat upon his oars at least one boat's length distant from any oth boat lying alongside, and shall not approach nearer, until after the former boat shall have proceeded t boats' length, not exceeding 5l.

The offices of Harbour-masters are in Little Thames Street, St. Catharine's; and Canal Off Blackwall.

BOHEA, a species of tea. See TEA.

BOMBAY, the second port of commerce in British India, and, after Calcut and Canton, the greatest commercial emporium in the East. Lat. 18° 56′ I long. 72º 57′ E. The town and harbour of Bombay are situated on the sout eastern extremity of a small barren island on the west coast of India, compos chiefly of two ranges of whinstone rocks, running parallel with each other at t distance generally of about three miles. The island was ceded by the Portugue to the English in 1661, as the dower of Queen Catherine, wife of Charles I and taken actual possession of in 1664; so that it has been in our occupati near 170 years, and constitutes by far the oldest of our possessions in the ea In 1668, it was transferred by the crown to the East India Company, by lette patent, in free and common soccage, on payment of the annual rent of 1 It is the only portion of British India held by such a tenure. Notwithstandi this, the greater part of the island is private property, and even the small part it which belongs to the Company has been acquired by purchase. In the ye 1716, the population of Bombay amounted only to 16,000 souls. In 1816, o complete century afterwards, a census of it was taken, which gave the followi result : —

British, not military - - - - - - - -	1,840
Ditto military and marine - - - - - - -	2,460
Native Christians, Armenians, and descendants of Portuguese	11,500
Jews - - - - - - - - - -	800
Mohammedans - - - - - - - - -	28,000
Hindoos - - - - - - - - - -	103,800
Parsees - - - - - - - - - -	13,550
Total	**161,550**

The number of houses was then 20,786, giving eight residents to each house. T above enumeration of the population does not include temporary sojourners fr the neighbouring continent, and foreigners resorting to the place for trade, who numerous, and estimated as high as 60,000. Adding this floating population, a the accession to the resident inhabitants which must have followed the increa commerce of Bombay, it will not be overrating the whole if we estimate at present at 250,000. The fort stands on the south-east extremity the island, on a narrow neck of land, immediately over the harbour. The fo fications are extensive, and on the sea side very strong. Bombay is the o considerable British possession in India in which the rise and fall of the t is so considerable as to admit of the construction of extensive wet docks. ordinary spring tides, the rise is about fourteen feet, but occasionally as high seventeen. The capacious docks that have been constructed by the East In Company are their property, being for the most part under the direction of Parsees, who, excepting the Chinese, are the most industrious and intellig people of the East. The expense of repairing ships in them is enormous. M chant vessels of great size, or from 1000 to 1200 tons burden, for the cot trade to China, have been built in these docks. Frigates and line-of-ba ships have also been occasionally constructed in them, sometimes under the clusive direction of Parsee artificers. Ships built at Bombay, on account of timber being brought from a great distance, are very costly; but being, contrar the practice of other parts of India, entirely constructed of teak, they are most durable vessels in the world, requiring little repair, and often running 1 and sixty years. Being for the most part built by natives, without any v strict application of the rules of art, they are commonly, though not alw heavy sailers.

Monies. — Accounts are here kept in rupees; each rupee being divided into 4 quar-
rs, and each quarter into 100 reas. The rupee is also divided into 16 annas, or 50
ce. An urdee is 2 reas; a doreea, 6 reas; a dooganey, or single pice, 4 reas; a
ddea, or double pice, 8 reas; a paunchea is 5 rupees; and a gold mohur, 15 rupees.
f these the annas and reas only are imaginary monies. The coins of Bombay are
: mohur, or gold rupee, the silver rupee, and their divisions; also the double and
igle pice, the urdee, and doreea, which are copper coins with a mixture of tin or lead.
ie following is the assay and sterling value of the present gold and silver coinage of
ombay : —

	Gross Weight. grs. dec.	Pure Metal. grs. dec.	Sterling Value. sh. dec.
Gold Mohur	179·0	164·68	29·18
Silver Rupee	179·0	164·68	2·48

In the East India Company's financial accounts rendered to Parliament, the Bombay
pee is reckoned at 2s. 3d. The charge for coinage in the Bombay Mint is 2½ per
nt. for gold, and 3 per cent. for silver, including the charges for refining. The
achinery for this Mint was sent out from England a few years ago, and is complete,
t very costly. At Bombay there are no banks, as at Madras and Calcutta, and paper
oney is unknown in mercantile transactions.

Weights and Measures. — The weights and measures used at Bombay are as follow :—

Gold and Silver Weight.

	gr.
1 Wall =	4·475
40 Walls = 1 Tola =	179

Pearl Weight.

	gr.
1 Tucka =	0·208
13¾ Tuckas = 1 Ruttee =	3
24 Ruttees = 1 Tank =	72

Commercial Weight.

	Avoirdupois. lb. oz. dr.
1 Tank =	0 0 2·488
Tanks = 1 Seer =	0 11 3·2
Seers = 1 Maund =	28 0 0

These weights are used for all heavy
ds, excepting salt.

Grain Measure.

	lb. oz. dr.
Tipprees = 1 Seer =	0 11 3·2
Seers = 1 Paily =	2 12 12·8

		lb. oz. dr.
7 Pailies	= 1 Parah =	19 9 9·6
8 Parahs	= 1 Candy =	156 12 12·8

Salt Measure.

		cubic inches.
10½ Adowlies	= 1 Parah =	1607 61
100 Parahs	= 1 Anna =	160761
16 Annas	= 1 Rash =	2572176

The Anna weighs 2½ tons, and the Rash
40 tons.

Liquor Measure.

(Spirits, and Country Arrack.)

The Seer weighs 60 Bombay Rupees,
and equals 1 lb. 8 oz. 8½ dr.; and 50 Seers
make the Maund.

Long Measure.

	English inches.
16 Tussoos = 1 Hath =	18
24 Tussoos = 1 Guz =	27

All the foregoing standards are likewise divided into halves, quarters, &c. The pre-
ing weights and measures are generally used in Bombay; but it sometimes occurs in
cantile transactions, that calculations are made in pounds and maunds, which last
ght is reckoned at 40, 40½, 41, 43¼, and 44 seers; and sometimes in Surat candies
0, 21, and 22 maunds.

Shipping, Commerce, &c. — At Bombay there is an insurance society with a
ital of 20 lacs of rupees, or about 200,000l. sterling; and there are also private
derwriters who insure separately on ships. In 1820, and we believe the
mber continues about the same, there were forty-five registered ships belonging
this port engaged in the trade to China and Europe, the aggregate burden of
ich amounted to about 20,000 tons, giving at an average 450 tons to each ship.
ese are for the most part navigated by Indian seamen or Lascars, those of
mbay being accounted by far the best in India, the master and superior officers
ie being Englishmen. Besides this class of large vessels, there is a numerous
s of native craft, under various forms and names. In 1820, they were com-
ed to amount in all to near 47,000 tons, of from 2 to 175 tons each. These
sels, besides furnishing the town with firewood, hay, straw, &c. from the
ghbouring continent, navigate coastways from Cape Comorin to the Gulph of
ch, and sometimes cross the sea to Muscat and the Arabian Gulph. During
eight fair months, that is, from October to May, the largest sized vessels
orm five or six trips to Damaun, Surat, Cambay, Broach, Jumbosier, and
ich, bringing from these ports, where they sometimes winter, and where many
their owners reside, cotton, ghee, oil, pulse, wheat, cotton cloths, timber, fire-
d, putchok, mawah, &c.; and return to the northern ports laden with the

produce of Europe, Bengal, and China. The capital employed in this trade, in the minor articles of commerce, exclusive of·cotton, has been estimated to amount to a million and a half sterling.

The island of Bombay, itself a small and sterile spot, affords no produce for exportation; indeed, hardly yields a week's consumption of corn for its inhabitants. Neither is the neighbouring territory fruitful, nor does the whole presidency of Bombay, although computed to contain about seventy thousand square miles and from ten to eleven millions of inhabitants, yield, with the exception of cotton and rice, any of the great colonial staples, such as coffee, sugar, and indigo; a circumstance, no doubt, to be ascribed to the impolitic restraints upon British settlement and capital hitherto imposed by law, and acted upon with peculiar rigour at this and the sister presidency of Madras, in contradistinction to the greater latitude afforded under that of Bengal. Bombay is, notwithstanding, a great emporium for the exports and imports of foreign countries. Its principal trade is carried on with the countries on the Gulphs of Cambay, Persia, and Arabia, with Calcutta, China, Great Britain, and other European countries, and the United States of America. From the countries on the Gulph of Cambay it receives cotton wool, and grain; and from the Persian and Arabian Gulphs, raw silk of Persia, copper from the same country, and also pearls, galls, coffee, gum-arabic, bdellium, copal, myrrh, olibanum, and assafœtida, with dates and other dried fruits, horses and bullion. Its exports to Arabia and Persia consist of grain, raw sugar from China and Bengal, British cotton manufactures, woollens and metals, pepper, and other spices. From Calcutta, Bombay receives raw silk, sugar, indigo, and grain, and exports to it oak timber, coir, or the fibre of the cocoa-nut husk, with cocoa-nuts and sandal-wood. The trade between Bombay and Calcutta has declined since the abolition of the restrictive system in 1815 gave to Bombay a wider intercourse with foreign countries. Previously to the opening of the trade, Calcutta was the *entrepôt* from which many of the productions of the neighbourhood of Bombay used to find a market in distant countries. In 1813 and 1814, according to the custom-house returns of Calcutta the value of the imports into it from Bombay amounted to 400,000*l.* sterling; in 1819 and 1820, to 360,000*l.*; and in 1827 and 1828, to 200,000*l.* The exports from Calcutta to Bombay in the first-named year amounted to 280,000*l.*, and in 1827, to only half that amount. The greatest branch of the trade of Bombay used to be that with China; but it has considerably declined of late years. The principal article of export is cotton wool, to which opium has been added, since we obtained possession of the province of Malwa. The minor articles are pepper, sandal-wood, Arabian gums, salt fish, fish maws, and sharks' fins. The imports consist of alum, camphor, cassia, nankeens, rhubarb, tea, raw sugar, vermilion and other paints, with a considerable quantity of bullion. In 1828 and 1829 the number of ships which cleared out from Bombay for Canton was 36, of the burthen of 25,731 tons; but the number which entered from thence was only 30, of the burthen of 17,534 tons; many of the ships which cleared out having made intermediate voyages, after discharging their cargoes at Canton.

The principal export from Bombay to Great Britain is cotton wool, after which follow pepper, cardamoms, Arabian gums and drugs, and Persian raw silk. The chief imports are cotton fabrics and cotton twist, for both of which Bombay is, after Calcutta, the greatest mart in India, woollens, iron, copper, spelter, glass ware, &c. &c. Bombay trades with France and Hamburgh, but not to any considerable amount. Neither is her trade with the United States of America of much importance. The following statements, drawn up from papers laid before parliament in 1830 and 1831, show the whole amount of the trade carried on by Bombay, including Surat, with Great Britain, foreign Europe, and America, in the years 1813 and 1814, and 1828 and 1829. (*See opposite side.*)

In some of the intermediate years between 1814 and 1829 there was some trade between Bombay, Portugal, and the Brazils, but not very considerable. will appear from these statements that the present imports into Bombay from Great Britain amount to above 780,000*l.*, and the exports to near 840,000*l.*; the first having increased since the opening of the free trade by half a million sterling or above 180 per cent., and the latter by somewhat more than that amount.

IMPORTS INTO BOMBAY AND SURAT.

	1813 and 1814.			1828 and 1829.		
	Merchandise.	Bullion.	Total.	Merchandise.	Bullion.	Total.
	£	£	£	£	£	£
om Great Britain.	275,716	110	275,826	781,248	—	781,248
— France........	—	—	—	63,291	—	63,291
— Hamburgh ...	—	—	—	7,329	—	7,329
— America......	—	—	—	1,461	—	1,461
otal, Bombay, &c.	275,716	110	275,826	853,394	—	853,394

EXPORTS FROM BOMBAY AND SURAT.

	1813 and 1814.			1828 and 1829.		
	Merchandise.	Bullion.	Total.	Merchandise.	Bullion.	Total.
	£	£	£	£	£	£
Great Britain.	135,342	169,811	305,154	694,654	139,113	833,767
France.........	—	—	—	5,995	—	5,995
Hamburgh ...	—	—	—	—	—	—
America.......	—	—	—	—	—	—
Total	135,342	169,811	305,154	700,649	139,113	839,762

k Regulations. — At daylight the wickets of the gates are opened, and at seven o'clock the sentry Half an hour after sunset the gates are shut, the wicket of the centre gate being left open till the g gun be fired. No boats, saving those belonging to the Company's marine department, or his ty's navy, are permitted to come to the dock-yard stairs ; but must use the piers expressly con- d for their accommodation. No meat, stores, or baggage for the merchant shipping, of any tion, are to be passed through the dock-yards. After the firing of the evening gun, nobody belong- the ships in the harbour, below the rank of a commissioned officer, is to be allowed to land or enter ck-yard, without the express permission of the master attendant, or other constituted authorities. s' crews are not to be permitted to quit their boat at the stairs, after the hour of shutting the gates. craft are not to deliver firewood or any other lading within the limits of the yard, without the ntendent's sanction. The ships and vessels in dock are not to land any lumber whatever on the No cargo of any description is to be landed in or passed through the yard, from or to any ship in without the superintendent's permission in writing. No fire or light is allowed on board any ship el in dock, without the authority of the superintendent, to whom the purposes for which either e required, must be stated in writing.

ee *Horsburgh's East India Directory. Hamilton's East India Gazetteer,* 1828. *Bombay Calendar and Register. Kelly's Cambist. Wilson's Review of the rnal Commerce of Bengal, under head, " Coast of Malabar." Papers relating Finances of India, and the Trade of India and China ; printed by order of the e of Commons,* 1830, 1831. *Evidence of James Ritchie, Esq., before the Select ittee of the House of Commons,* 1831.)

MBAZINE, a kind of silk stuff, originally manufactured at Milan, and e sent into France and other countries. Now, however, it is nowhere factured better, or in larger quantities, than in this kingdom.

NES of cattle and other animals are extensively used in the arts, in forming es for knives, and various other purposes. So long as bones are preserved a highly nutritious jelly may be obtained from them.

nes have latterly been employed, particularly in Lincolnshire and York- as a manure for dry soils, with the very best effect. They are commonly d and drilled in, in the form of powder, with turnip seed. Their effect is lerably increased when they have undergone the process of fermentation. uantities employed are usually about 25 bushels of dust, or 40 bushels of to the acre. They first began to be imported from the continent to Hull 1800. They are principally brought from the Netherlands and Germany, ccupy about 40,000 tons of small vessels belonging to these countries. uskisson estimated the real value of those annually imported for the se of being used as manure at 100,000*l.*; and he contended, that it was not

too much to suppose, that an advance of between 100,000*l.* and 200,000*l.*
pended on this article occasioned 500,000 additional quarters of corn to
brought to market.—(*Loudon's Encyclopædia of Agriculture*, 2d edit. *No.*49'
Mr. Huskisson's Speech, May 7. 1827.)

There are no means of distinguishing between the bones imported for mant
and for other purposes. In the year 1829, the declared value of the bor
imported amounted to 72,063*l.* 16*s.* 7*d.*, and in 1830 it amounted to 66,76
10*s.* 1*d.*

BOOK, BOOKS, (Ger. *Bücher;* Du. *Boeken;* Da. *Böger;* Sw. *Böcker;* l
Livres; It. *Libri;* Sp. *Libros;* Port. *Livros;* Rus. *Knigi;* Pol. *Ksiaski, Ksieg*
Lat. *Libri,*) a written or printed treatise or treatises on any branch of scien
art, or literature, composed in the view of instructing, amusing, or persuadi
the reader.

Copyright is the right which the authors of books or treatises claim to t
exclusive privilege of printing, publishing, and selling them.

Books are sometimes blank, as account books; but these enjoy no peculiar p
vileges, and do not come within the scope of our inquiries.

Books are divided into the following *classes*, according to the mode in which t
sheets of the paper on which they are printed or written, are folded : viz. *fo*
when the sheet is folded into two leaves; *quarto*, when folded into *four; octo*
when folded into *eight ; duodecimo*, when the sheet is folded into *twelve*, &c.
making these classifications, no attention is paid to the *size* of the sheet.

I. *Progress and present State of the Law as to the Copyright of Books.*—It l
been doubted whether, in antiquity, an author had any exclusive right to a wo
or whether, having once published it, he could restrain others from copying
and selling copies. We incline to think that he could. The public sale of cop
of works is often referred to in the classics ; and in such a way as warrants the
ference that they were productive to the author, which could not have been t
case had every one been permitted to copy them at pleasure. Terence, in c
of his plays (*Prol. in Eunuch.* l. 20.), says, *Fabulam, quam nunc acturi sum*
postquam ædiles emerunt; but why should the magistrates have bought it, had
been free to every one to copy it? Martial, in one of his epigrams, says —

> Sunt quidam, qui me dicunt non esse poëtam :
> Sed qui me vendit, bibliopola, putat.   Mart. lib. xiv. Ep. 19

This evidently conveys the idea that he had assigned the right to sell his bo
to a single person, who profited by it. Passages to the same effect may be fou
in Horace (*De Arte Poetica*, line 345.), Juvenal (*Sat.* 7. line 83.), &c.

It would have been singular, indeed, had it been otherwise. Of all the spec
of property a man can possess, the fruits of his mental labours seem to be m
peculiarly his own. And though it may, we think, be shown, that many seri
inconveniences would result from giving the same absolute and interminable p
perty over ideas that is given over material objects, these inconveniences co
hardly have been perceived in antiquity.

It will also be observed, that in antiquity a copyright was of much less va
than in modern times. Books could then only be multiplied by copying th
with the pen ; and if any one chose privately to copy a work, or to buy it
another, it must have been very difficult to hinder him ; but when printing l
been introduced, the greater cheapness of books not only extended the dem
for them in far greater proportion, and consequently rendered copyrights more
luable, but it also afforded the means of preventing their piracy. Printing is
a device by which a few copies of a book can be obtained at a cheap rate. l
productive of cheapness only when it is employed upon a large scale, or whe
considerable impression is to be thrown off. And hence after its invent
piracy could hardly be committed in secret : the pirated book had to be brou
to market; the fraud was thus sure to be detected, and the offending p
might be prosecuted and punished.

For a considerable time after the invention of printing, no questions seen
have occurred with respect to copyrights. This was occasioned by the e
adoption of the licensing system. Governments soon perceived the vast imp
ance of the powerful engine that had been brought into the field ; and they en
voured to avail themselves of its energies by interdicting the publication of
works not previously licensed by authority. During the continuation of

stem, piracy was effectually prevented. The licensing act (13 and 14 Chas. 2. 2.), and the previous acts and proclamations to the same effect, prohibited e printing of any book without consent of the owner as well as without a li- nce. In 1694, the licensing act finally expired, and the press then became really e. Instead, however, of the summary methods for obtaining redress for any vasion of their property enjoyed by them under the licensing acts, authors re now left to defend their rights at *common law ;* and as no author or book- ller could procure any redress for a piracy at common law, except in so far as could *prove damage,* property in books was virtually annihilated ; it being in st cases impossible to prove the sale of one printed copy out of a hundred. nder these circumstances, applications were made to parliament for an act to pro- t literary property, by granting some speedy and effectual method of preventing e sale of spurious copies. In consequence, the statute 8 Anne, c. 19., was ssed, securing to authors and their assignees the exclusive right of printing their oks for fourteen years certain, from the day of publication, with a contingent irteen years, provided the author were alive at the expiration of the first term. rsons printing books protected by this act, without the consent of the authors their assignees, were to forfeit the pirated copies, and one penny for every sheet the same. Such books as were not entered at Stationers' Hall were excluded m the benefit of this act.

It had been customary, for some time previous to this period, for the libraries the Universities of Oxford and Cambridge, &c. to get a copy of most books ered at Stationers' Hall ; and the act of Anne made it imperative that one y of all works entitled to its protection should be delivered to the following aries : viz. the Royal Library, now transferred to the British Museum ; the li- ries of Oxford and Cambridge ; the libraries of the four Scotch Universities ; library of Sion College, London ; and that of the Faculty of Advocates in inburgh ;—in all, *nine* copies.

The act of Anne did not put to rest the questions as to copyrights. The authors tended that it did not affect their natural ownership ; and that they or their ignees were entitled to proceed at *common law* against those who pirated their ks after the period mentioned in the statute had expired. The publishers of rious editions resisted these pretensions, and contended that there was either right of property at common law in the productions of the mind ; or that, sup- ing such a right to have existed, it was superseded by the statute of Anne. re was some difference of opinion in the courts as to these points ; but Lord nsfield, Mr. Justice Blackstone, and the most eminent judges, were favourable he claims of the authors. However, it was finally decided, upon an appeal to House of Lords in 1774, that an action could not be maintained for pirating a yright after the term specified in the statute.—(*Godson on the Law of Patents Copyrights,* p. 205.)

The act of Queen Anne referred only to Great Britain ; but in 1801, its provi- s were extended to Ireland ; the penalty, exclusive of forfeiture, on printing or orting books without consent of the proprietor, was also increased from 1*d.* to a sheet. In return for this concession, two additional copies of all works en- d at Stationers' Hall were to be delivered ; one to Trinity College, Dublin, and to the King's Inns, Dublin.

very one must be satisfied that fourteen years exclusive possession is far too t a period to indemnify the author of a work, the composition of which has ired any considerable amount of labour and research ; though twenty-eight s is, perhaps, all things considered, as proper a period as could be fixed upon. v, the grand defect of the statute of Anne consisted in its making the right he exclusive possession for twenty-eight years contingent on the fact of a per- having lived a day more or less than fourteen years after the publication of work. This was making the enjoyment of an important right dependent on a e accidental circumstance over which man has no control. Could any thing nore oppressive and unjust than to hinder an author from bequeathing that pro- y to his widow and children, that would have belonged to himself had he been ? Nothing, indeed, as it appears to us, can be more obvious than the justice xtending all copyrights to the same period, whether the authors be dead or not. ut though the extreme hardship, not to say injustice, of the act of Queen e had been repeatedly pointed out, its provisions were continued down to

1814, when the existing copyright act, 54 Geo. 3. c. 156., was passed. This act extended the duration of all copyrights, whether the authors were dead or alive, to twenty-eight years certain; with the further provision, that if the author should be alive at the end of that period, he should enjoy the copyright during the residue of his life. We subjoin the principal clauses of this statute.

Having recited the acts 8 Anne, c. 19. and 41 Geo. 3. c. 107., it enacts, that so much of the said several recited acts as requires that any copies of any books which shall be printed or published, or reprinted and published with additions, shall be delivered by the printers thereof to the warehouse-keeper of the said company of stationers, for the use of any of the libraries in the said act mentioned, and as requires the delivery of the said copies by the warehouse-keeper for the use of the said libraries, and as imposes any penalty on such printer or warehouse-keeper for not delivering the said copies, shall be repealed.

And that eleven printed copies of the whole of every book, and of every volume thereof, upon the paper upon which the largest number or impression of such book shall be printed for sale, together with all maps and prints belonging thereto, which from and after the passing of this act shall be printed and published, on demand thereof being made in writing to or left at the place of abode of the publisher or publishers thereof, at any time within twelve months next after the publication thereof, under the hand of the warehouse-keeper of the company of stationers, or the librarian or other person thereto authorised by the persons or body politic and corporate, proprietors or managers of the libraries following; *videlicet*, the British Museum, Sion College, the Bodleian Library at Oxford, the Public Library at Cambridge, the Library of the Faculty of Advocates at Edinburgh, the Libraries of the Four Universities of Scotland, Trinity College Library and the King's Inns Library at Dublin, or so many of such eleven copies as shall be respectively demanded, shall be delivered by the publishers thereof respectively, within one month after demand made thereof in writing as aforesaid, to the warehouse-keeper of the said company of stationers; which copies the said warehouse-keeper shall receive for the use of the library for which such demand shall be so made; and he is hereby required, within one month after any such book or volume shall be so delivered to him, to deliver the same for the use of such library. And if any such publisher or warehouse-keeper shall not observe the directions of this act, he and they so making default shall forfeit, besides the value of the said printed copies, the sum of 5*l.* for each copy not so delivered or received together with the full costs of suit; to be recovered by action in any court of record in the United Kingdom.—§ 2.

Provided always, that no such copy shall be so demanded or delivered, &c. of the second, or of any subsequent edition of any such book, unless the same shall contain additions or alterations; and in case any edition after the first shall contain any addition or alteration, no printed copy thereof shall be demanded or delivered, if a printed copy of such additions or alterations only, printed in an uniform manner with the former edition of such book, be delivered to each of the libraries aforesaid : Provided also, that the copy of every book that shall be demanded by the British Museum shall be delivered of the best paper on which such work shall be printed. — § 3.

And whereas by the said recited acts it is enacted, that the author of any book, and the assigns of such author, should have the sole liberty of printing and reprinting such book for the term of 14 years, &c.; and it was provided, that after the expiration of the said term of 14 years, the right of printing or disposing of copies should return to the authors thereof, if they were then living, for another term of 14 years. And whereas it will afford further encouragement to literature, if the duration of such copyright were extended; Be it enacted, that the author of any book or books composed, and not printed and published, or which shall hereafter be composed, and be printed and published, and his assigns, shall have the sole liberty of printing and reprinting such book or books, for the full term of *twenty-eight years*, to commence from the day of first publishing the same; and also, if the author shall be living at the end of that period, for the residue of his natural life : and if any bookseller or printer, or other person whatsoever, in any part of the United Kingdom of Great Britain and Ireland, in the Isles of Man, Jersey, or Guernsey or in any other part of the British dominions, shall, from and after the passing of this act, within the times granted and limited by this act, print, reprint, or *import*, or shall cause to be printed, &c. any such book, without the consent of the author, or other proprietor of the copyright, first had in writing or knowing the same to be so printed, &c. without such consent shall sell, publish, or expose to sale or cause to be sold, &c., or shall have in his possession for sale, any such book, without such consent first had and obtained; such offender shall be liable to a special action at the suit of the author or other proprietor of such copyright; and every such author or other proprietor may, in such special action recover damages, with double costs; and every such offender shall also forfeit such book, and every sheet of such book, and shall deliver the same to the author or other proprietor, to be made waste paper of, and shall also forfeit the sum of 3*d.* for every sheet thereof either printed or printing, or published or exposed to sale; the one moiety thereof to any person who shall sue for the same. — § 4.

And in order to ascertain what books shall be from time to time published, the publishers of every book demandable under this act shall, within one calendar month after the day on which any such book shall be first sold, published, advertised, or offered for sale, within the bills of mortality, or within three calendar months in any other part of the United Kingdom, enter the title to the copy of every such book and the names and place of abode of the publisher, in the register book of the company of stationers in London (for every of which several entries the sum of 2*s.* shall be paid, and no more), under a penalty of the sum of 5*l.*, together with eleven times the price at which such book shall be sold or advertised; to be recovered, together with full costs of suit, by persons authorised to sue, and who shall first sue for the same : Provided, that in the case of magazines, reviews, or other periodical publications, it shall be sufficient to make such entry in the register book of the said company within one month next after the publication of the first number or volume : provided, that no failure in making any such entry shall in any manner affect any copyright, but shall only subject the person making default to the penalty aforesaid under this act. — § 5.

Provided always, that if any publisher shall be desirous of delivering the copy of such book or volume on behalf of any of the said libraries, at such library, it shall and may be lawful for him to deliver the same at such library; and such delivery shall be held as equivalent to a delivery to the said warehouse-keeper.

And if the author of any book, which shall not have been published 14 years at the time of passing this act, shall be living at the said time, and if such author shall afterwards die before the expiration of the said 14 years, then the personal representative of the said author, and the assigns of such personal representative, shall have the sole right of printing and publishing the said book for the further term of 14 years after the expiration of the first 14.

And if the author of any book which has been already published shall be living at the end of 28 years after the first publication, he or she shall, for the remainder of his or her life, have the sole right of printing and publishing the same.

Actions and suits shall be commenced within 12 months next after such offence committed, or be void and of no effect. — §§ 7, 8, 9, 10.

Musical compositions, engravings, maps, sculptures, models, &c. enjoy a similar protection.

he great practical difficulty in interpreting the copyright acts, is in distin-
hing between an original work and a copy made, *animo furandi*, from one
ady in existence. The following is a summary of Mr. Godson's remarks on
subject : —

The identity of a literary work consists entirely in the *sentiments* and *language*.
same conceptions, clothed in the same words, must necessarily be the same compo-
n; and whatever method is taken of exhibiting that composition to the ear or the
by *recital*, or by *writing*, or by *printing*, in any number of copies, or at any period of
the property of another person has been violated ; for the new book is still the
ical work of the real author.

Thus, therefore, a transcript of nearly all the sentiments and language of a book is
ring piracy. To copy part of a book, either by taking a few pages *verbatim*, when
entiments are not new, or by imitation of the principal ideas, although the treatises
her respects are different, is also considered to be illegal.

Although it was held by Ellenborough C. J. that a variance in *form* and *manner*
variance in *substance*, and that any material alteration which is a *melioration* cannot
nsidered as a piracy ; yet a piracy is committed, whether the author attempt an ori-
work, or call his book an abridgment, if the principal parts of a book are servilely
d or unfairly varied.

But if the main design be not copied, the circumstance that part of the composition
ne author is found in another is not of itself piracy sufficient to support an action.
an may fairly adopt part of the work of another ; he may so make use of another's
rs for the promotion of science, and the benefit of the public : but having done so,
uestion will be, Was the matter so taken used fairly with that view, and without
may be termed the *animus furandi ?*

In judging of a quotation, whether it is fair and candid, or whether the person who
s has been swayed by the *animus furandi*, the quantity taken, and the *manner* in
it is adopted, of course, must be considered.

If the work complained of be *in substance* a copy, then it is not necessary to show
ntention to pirate ; for the greater part of the matter of the book having been pur-
d, the intention is apparent, and other proof is superfluous. A piracy has undoubt-
peen committed.

But if only a *small portion* of the work is quoted, then it becomes necessary to show
t was done *animo furandi*, with the intention of depriving the author of his just
d, by giving his work to the public in a cheaper form. And then the *mode* of doing
omes a subject of inquiry ; for it is not sufficient to constitute a piracy, that part
e author's book is found in that of another, unless it be nearly the whole, or so
as will show (being a question of fact for the jury) that it was done with a bad
, and that the matter which accompanies it has been *colourably* introduced."—
15—217.)

If a work be of such a libellous or mischievous nature as to affect the *public morals*,
nat the author cannot maintain an action at law upon it, a court of equity will not
ose with an injunction to protect that which cannot be called property. Even if
be a doubt as to its evil tendency, the Lord Chancellor will not interfere."—(God-
. 212.)

Expediency of limiting Copyrights to Twenty-eight Years. — It is argued by
that copyrights should be made perpetual ; that were this done, men of
and learning would devote themselves much more readily than at present
e composition of works requiring great labour ; inasmuch as the copyright of
works, were it perpetual, would be an adequate provision for a family. But
ubt much whether these anticipations would be realised. Most books or
scripts are purchased by the booksellers, or published upon the pre-
ion that there will immediately be a considerable demand for them ; and
prehend that when copyrights are secured for eight and twenty years
n, very little more would be given for them were they made perpetual.
an annuity, or the rent or profit arising out of any fixed and tangible pro-
with respect to which there can be no risk, is sold, if the number of years
ich it is to continue be considerable, the price which it is worth, and
it fetches does not differ materially from what it would bring were it per-
. But the copyright of an unpublished work is, of all descriptions of pro-
in which to speculate, the most hazardous ; and the chances of reaping
gent advantages from it, at the distance of eight and twenty years, would
rth very little indeed.

ose who write books, and those who publish them, calculate on their ob-
g a ready and extensive sale, and on their being indemnified in a few years.

Very few authors, and still fewer booksellers, are disposed to look forward to distant a period as eight and twenty years for remuneration. They are mos all sanguine enough to suppose that a much shorter term will enable them reap a full harvest of fame and profit from the publication; and we doubt mu whether there be one case in a hundred, in which an author would obtain larger sum for a perpetual copyright, than for one that is to continue for t period stipulated in the late act.

But while the making of copyrights perpetual would not, as it appears to be of any material advantage to the authors, there are good grounds for thinki that it would be disadvantageous to the public. Suppose an individual ca culates a table of logarithms to five or seven places; if his computations be corre no improvement can be made upon them, to the extent at least to which they g but is he or his assignees to be entitled, in all time to come, to prevent oth individuals from publishing similar tables, on the ground of an invasion of priva property? Such a pretension could not be admitted without leading to the me mischievous consequences; and yet there is no real ground (though the cou have attempted to make one) on which the claim in question and others of t same description, could be resisted, were copyrights made perpetual, and plac in all respects on the same footing as other property. We, therefore, are clea of opinion that good policy suggests the limitation of the exclusive right printing and publishing literary works to such a reasonable period as may secu to authors the greater part of the profit to be derived from their works; and th this period being expired, they should become public property.

Perhaps the period of twenty-eight years might be advantageously extend to thirty-five or forty; but we are satisfied that more injury than benefit wo result to literature, by extending it beyond that term. In France, copyrights co tinue for twenty years after the death of the author. In most of the Germ states they are perpetual; but this hardly indemnifies the authors for the e with which spurious copies may be obtained from other states.

III. *Taxes on Literature.* — These taxes have been carried to such an extent England as to be in the highest degree injurious. They are at once impoli oppressive, and unjust: impolitic, because they tend to obstruct the growth diffusion of knowledge; oppressive, because they very frequently swallow up entire reward of the labours of the most deserving persons; and unjust, beca they are not proportioned to the value of the article on which they are laid, a are, indeed, much oftener paid out of capital than out of profit.

These taxes consist of the duty on paper (see PAPER), the duty on adverti ments (see ADVERTISEMENTS), and the eleven copies given to the public librar The following statements, drawn up by a very competent authority (Mr. Rees the firm of Longman, Rees, and Co.), show the mode in which they oper They refer to an octavo volume of 500 pages, printed like the Comparative V of England and France, or the Introduction to the second edition of M'Culloc Principles of Political Economy, and sold by retail for twelve shillings a copy

Estimate of the cost of such a volume, when 500, 750, and 1000 copies printed, showing what part of this cost consists of taxes.

Five Hundred Copies.			Cost.			Duty.		
			£	s.	d.	£	s.	c
Printing and corrections - - - -			88	18	0	0	0	
Paper - - - - - -			38	10	0	8	12	
Boarding - - - - -			10	0	0	3	3	
Advertising - - - -			40	0	0	20	0	
			177	8	0	31	16	

	£	s.	d.
11 Copies to public libraries.			
14 Copies (say) to author.			
475 Copies for sale at 8s. 5d.	199	17	11
Deduct cost - -	177	8	0
Profit to author and publisher, commission, and interest on capital, *when all are sold.*	22	9	11

	Cost.			Duty.		
Seven Hundred and Fifty Copies.	£	s.	d.	£	s.	d.
Printing and corrections - - -	95	6	0	0	0	0
Paper - - - - -	57	15	0	12	19	4
Boarding - - - - -	15	0	0	4	15	7
Advertising - - - - -	50	0	0	25	0	0
	218	1	0	42	15	11

11 Copies to public libraries.
14 Copies to author.

	£	s.	d.
725 Copies for sale at 8s. 5d.	305	2	5
Deduct cost - -	218	1	0
Profit to author and publisher, commission, and interest on capital, *when all are sold.*	87	1	5

	Cost.			Duty.		
One Thousand Copies.						
Printing and corrections - - -	102	14	0	0	0	0
Paper - - - - -	77	0	0	17	5	9
Boarding - - - - -	20	0	0	6	7	5
Advertising - - - - -	60	0	0	30	0	0
	259	14	0	53	13	2

11 Copies to public libraries.
14 Copies to author.

	£	s.	d.
975 Copies for sale at 8s. 5d.	410	6	3
Deduct cost - -	259	14	0
Profit for author, &c. &c., *when all are sold.*	150	12	3

The following statement shows the operation of the duties on a pamphlet of sheets, or eighty pages, of which 500 copies are printed.

				Cost.			Duty.		
Pamphlet, Five Hundred Number.	£	s.	d.	£	s.	d.	£	s.	d.
Printing - - - -	14	14	0	19	19	0	0	0	0
Extras - - -	5	5	0						
Paper - - - - -				6	0	0	1	0	0
Stitching - - - - -				0	12	6	0	0	0
Stamp office duty - - -				0	15	0	0	15	0
Advertising (say) - - -				15	0	0	7	10	0
				42	6	6	9	5	0

25 Copies for author and public libraries.
475 Copies for sale, 25 for 2l. 14s. 51 6 0

Profit to author and publisher, interest, &c., after *all are sold.*	8	19	6

These statements set the oppressive operation of the taxes on literature in a very striking point of view. Where the edition is an average one of 750 copies, the duties amount to about a *fifth*, or *twenty per cent.* of the cost of the edition; and

whether the edition consist of 500, 750, or even 1000 copies, *the duties invariabl*,
amount to more than the entire remuneration of the author.

It is essential, however, to bear in mind that the previous statements shov
only how the duties affect books when the *entire impression is sold off at the ful*
publication price; but this *seldom happens.* Excluding pamphlets, it ma
be truly affirmed, that, at an average, the original impression of half the book
printed is hardly ever sold off, except at a ruinous reduction of price. Now
if we suppose, in the previous example of an edition of 750 copies, that only 62!
instead of 725 were sold, the result would be that only 44*l.* 19*s.* 5*d.* woul
remain as profit to the author and publisher, and as a compensation for interest
the risk of bad debts, &c. Were only 525 copies sold, the cost would not be mor
than balanced; and there would be nothing whatever to remunerate the autho
for his labour, or the bookseller for the use of his capital. Were only 42.
copies sold, government would have received 42*l.* 15*s.* 11*d.* of duty from a specula
tion by which the author had lost all his labour, and the bookseller 40*l.* 4*s.* o
his capital! The mere possibility of such a supposition being realised, would b
a sufficient ground for a revision of the duties; but, in point of fact, such cases
instead of being merely possible or rare, are *of every day occurrence!*

There is a radical difference between the demand for books, or food for th
mind, and food for the body. The latter is always sure, under any circumstances
to command a sale. The demand for it is comparatively constant; it cannot b
dispensed with. If a tax is laid on malt, hats, or shoes, it will, perhaps
somewhat lessen the demand for these articles; but the quantities of then
brought to market, in future, will sell for such an advanced price as wil
leave the customary rate of profit to their producers. But with books th
case is altogether different. The taste for them is proverbially capricious; s
much so, that the most sagacious individuals are every day deceived in thei
anticipations as to the success of new works, and even as to the sale o
new editions. But if a book do not take, it is so very ruinous an affair, that
publisher is glad to dispose of the greater part of an impression at a fourth o
fifth part of its regular price; and is often, indeed, obliged to sell it as *waste pape*
to the trunkmaker or the tobacconist.

On a late investigation into the affairs of an extensive publishing concern, it wa
found, that of 130 works published by it in a given time, *fifty had not paid thei*
expenses. Of the eighty that did pay, thirteen only had arrived at a second edi
tion; but in most instances these second editions had not been profitable. I
general it may be estimated, that of the books published, a *fourth* do not pay thei
expenses; and that only *one in eight or ten can be reprinted with advantage.* A
respects pamphlets, we know we are within the mark, when we affirm that no
one in fifty pays the expenses of its publication!

Now, when such is the fact, can any thing be more glaringly unjust than to im
pose the same duty on all works before they are published? In a *very few* case!
such duty may fall principally on the buyers, and be only a reasonable deductio
from the profits of the author and publisher; but in a vast number more it swa
lows them up entirely; and in very many cases there are no profits for the dut
to absorb, so that it *falls wholly on the capital of the unfortunate author or pu*
lisher. Were the judges of the courts of law to decide cases by a throw of th
dice, there would be quite as much of reason and justice in their decisions,
there has been in the proceedings of our finance ministers as to taxes on liter
ture. If books *must* be taxed, let publishers be put under the *surveillance* of th
excise; let them be obliged to keep an account of the books they sell, and l
them be taxed accordingly; but do not let the loss arising from an unsuccessf
literary speculation — and more than half such speculations are unsuccessful — b
aggravated to a ruinous degree by the pressure of a system of taxation, tha
which there is nothing, even in Algiers, more unequal or oppressive.

The reduction of the advertisement duty will do something to lessen this inju
tice. But the relief is most inadequate. It acknowledges, without correcting tl
evil. Instead of being reduced, the advertisement duty ought to have been e
tirely repealed. It only amounts to about 170,000*l.* year; and there cannot be
doubt that the loss of revenue occasioned by its repeal, and by the repeal of ha
the paper duty, would, at no distant period, be made up by the greater produ
tiveness of the remaining duty on paper, resulting from its greater consumptio

advertisement duty presses very severely on all sorts of works, but particu-
on pamphlets: it may, indeed, be said to have utterly destroyed the latter
of publications, in so far at least as they are a source of profit.

ut we object altogether to the imposition of taxes on books previously to
being published. It is not possible, for the reasons already stated, that
taxes can be otherwise than *unjust*. This objection to them might, indeed,
emoved by imposing the duties according to the number and value of the
es actually sold. Still such duties must, however imposed, by raising the
of books, and preventing the diffusion of knowledge among the poorer and
instructed classes, be in the utmost degree injurious; at the same time that
can never be rendered considerably productive. They seem, in fact, to have
quality that taxes ought not to have, and hardly one that they should

.

ne delivery of *eleven* copies to public libraries, is exceedingly burdensome upon
nore expensive class of works, of which small impressions only can be printed;
n copies of such works would in many instances be a very fair profit for the
or; and the obligation to make such a sacrifice has frequently, indeed, caused
publication to be abandoned. A tax of this sort would not be tolerable even
it imposed for a public purpose; but such is not the object of its imposition.
igh called *public*, the libraries which receive the eleven copies are, with the
ption of the British Museum, private establishments, belonging to par-
ar corporations or institutions, and *accessible only to their members*. Why,
an author produces a book, should he be compelled to bestow copies
on the lawyers of Edinburgh and Dublin, and on the Universities? On what
iple can these bodies pretend to demand from him a portion of his property?
aps it might be expedient, in order to insure the preservation of every work,
copies of it should be deposited, one in London, one in Edinburgh, and one
ublin. Even this would be calling upon authors to make a considerable sa-
e for the public advantage. But to call upon them to sacrifice *ten* copies, ex-
ve of that given to the British Museum, for the benefit of so many *private*
utions, is a proceeding utterly at variance with every principle of justice.
e law of other countries is, in this respect, far preferable to ours. In Ame-
Prussia, Saxony, and Bavaria, only *one* copy of any work is required from
uthor; in France and Austria, *two* copies are required; and in the Nether-
, *three*. The governments of the most despotical states treat authors better
they have hitherto been treated by the legislature of England.

Book Trade of Great Britain.—London is the great centre of the British book
; the number of new publications that issue from its presses being far greater than
at appear in the rest of the empire. Within the course of the last forty years,
er, many very important works have been published at Edinburgh: but the latter,
l as those that appear at Oxford, Cambridge, Glasgow, &c., are principally dis-
of by the London trade. The booksellers of Edinburgh, and of all the provincial
, have agents in London to whom they consign a certain number of copies of every
they publish; and to whom, also, they address their orders for copies of such new or
orks as they have occasion for. The London booksellers, who act as agents for
in the country, are in the habit of regularly despatching parcels to their corre-
ents on the last day of each month, with the magazines and other monthly publica-
but if any new work of interest appears in the interim, or orders be received from
untry that cannot be conveniently deferred to the end of the month, a parcel is im-
tely forwarded by coach. The booksellers of Edinburgh and Dublin act as agents
ose of London, and supply the Scotch and Irish country trade with the metropolitan
ations.

price of new works is fixed by the publishers, who grant a deduction to the
dealers of from 20 to 25 per cent on the price of *quartos*, and from 25 to 30
nt. on that of *octavos*, and those of smaller size. The credit given by the pub-
to the retailers varies from seven to twelve months; a discount being allowed
ompt payment at the rate of 5 per cent. per annum.

m enquiries we have made, we believe it may be laid down that about 1,500 volumes
publications (exclusive of reprints, pamphlets, and periodical publications not in
es) are annually produced in Great Britain: and, estimating the average impres-
each volume at 750 copies, we have a grand total of 1,125,000 volumes; the value
ich, if sold at an average publication price of 9s. a volume, would be 506,250l.
umber of reprinted volumes, particularly of school books, is very great; and if
e we add the reviews, magazines, pamphlets, and all other publications, exclusive

of newspapers, the total *publication value* of the new works of all sorts, and new copi
of old works, that are annually produced, may be estimated at about 750,000*l.*

The old book trade carried on in Great Britain is very extensive, and employs ma
dealers. The price of old books depends very much on their condition; but, indepen
ently of this circumstance, it is very fluctuating and capricious; equally good copi
of the same works being frequently to be had in some shops for half or a third of wh
they can be bought for in others.

V. *Regulations as to Importation of Works.*—For the duties, see TARIFF. To preve
foreign books and maps, the property of individuals, from being charged with duty mo
than once, the proprietor shall, on each importation subsequent to the original one, ma
oath that the duties were paid when they were first imported, or that he purchased the
in this country in a fair way of trade; that they are the identical books or maps he e
ported from this kingdom, and that they are now brought back for his private use, a
not for sale.—(Treasury Order, 3d, and Customs Order, 8th October, 1818.)

No books, first composed, written, or printed in the United Kingdom, imported f
sale, except books not reprinted in the United Kingdom within twenty years, or bei
parts of collections, the greater part of which had been composed or written abroa
shall be imported into the United Kingdom, under forfeiture thereof.—(6 Geo. 4.
107. § 52.)

Books first composed or written, or printed and published, in the United Kingdc
and reprinted in any other country or place, may not be entered to be warehoused.
(§ 53.)

The permission to import English works reprinted abroad for private use, is limited
a *single copy* of each work, brought as a part of a passenger's baggage, for the priva
use of the parties themselves.—(Treasury Order, 29th June, 1830.)

VI. *Book Trade of France.*—The activity of the French press has been very great
increased since the downfall of Napoleon. The Count Daru, in a very instructive wo
Notions Statistiques sur la Librairie, published in 1827, estimated the number of print
sheets, exclusive of newspapers, produced by the French press in 1816, at 66,852,88
and in 1825, at 128,011,483! and we believe that the increase from 1825 down to t
present period has been little if any thing inferior. The quality of many of the wor
that have recently issued from the French press is also very superior; and it may
doubted whether such works as the *Biographie Universelle,* the new and enlarged editi
of the *Art de vérifier les Dates,* in 38 vols. octavo, and the two octavo editions of *Bayl
Dictionary,* could have been published in any other country. The greater number
new French works of merit, or which it is supposed will command a considerable sa
are immediately reprinted in the Netherlands, or Switzerland, but principally in t
former. To such an extent has this piratical practice been carried, that it is stated in
Requête presented by the French booksellers to government in 1828, that a single boc
seller in Brussels had, in 1825 and 1826, and the first six months of 1827, reprint
318,615 volumes of French works! Having nothing to pay for copyright, these cou
terfeit editions can be afforded at a lower price than those that are genuine. This i
very serious injury to French authors and publishers, not only by preventing the sale
their works in foreign countries, but from the ease with which spurious copies may
introduced into France.

All the French booksellers are *brevetés,* that is, licensed, and sworn to abide by cert
prescribed rules. This regulation is justly complained of by the publishers, as bei
vexatious and oppressive; and as tending to lessen the number of retail booksellers
the country, and to prevent that competition that is so advantageous.

The discount allowed by the French publishers to the retail dealers is not regulat
as in England, by the size of the volumes, but by the subjects. The discount on
sale of books of history, criticism, and general literature, is usually about 25 per cen
in the case of mathematical and strictly scientific works, it is seldom more than 1C
15 per cent.; while upon romances, tales, &c. it is often as high as 50 or 60 per cen

VII. *German Book Trade.*—"This trade is very much facilitated by the book fair
Leipsic; the Easter fair being frequented by all the booksellers of Germany, and by th
of some of the neighbouring countries, as of France, Switzerland, Denmark, Livo
&c., in order to settle their mutual accounts, and to form new connections. The G
man publisher sends his publications to the keeper of assortments *à condition,* that is,
commission, for a certain time, after which the latter pays for what have been sold,
may return the remainder. This is not so favourable for the publisher as the custor
the French and English book trades, where the keepers of assortments take the q
tity they want at a fixed rate. In the German book trade, it is the custom for al
every house, either in the country or abroad, which publishes or sells German books
have its agent at Leipsic, who receives and distributes its publications. A., of Riga,
publishes a book calculated for the German trade, has his agent B., in Leipsic, to w
he sends, free of expense, a number of copies of his publication, that he may distri

e new work to all the booksellers with whom he is connected, from Vienna to Ham-
rgh, and from Strasburgh to Königsberg, each of whom has his agent in Leipsic.   In-
uctions are also given as to the number of copies to be sent to each.   B. delivers those
pies in Leipsic to the agents, who send them every week, or more or less frequently, by
e post or by carriers, at the expense of the receiver.   C., of Strasburgh, who finds that
has not received copies enough, writes for an additional number of copies to his agent
, of Leipsic : D. gives this order to B., who delivers the number wanted to D., to be
ansmitted to C.   This arrangement is advantageous to the German book trade, as well
to Leipsic.   The dealer receives every thing from Leipsic ; and as a great number
packets, with books from all parts of Germany, arrive there for him every week, he
can have them packed together and sent at once.   The carriage is thus much
s than if the packets were sent to him separately from the different places ; and the
ole business is simplified.   The booksellers are also enabled to agree with ease on a
tain discount per cent.   No such intimate connection of the booksellers has yet been
med in any other country.   The German booksellers rarely unite, as is the practice
England, in undertaking the publication of extensive works."—(*German Conversation*
ricon, American edition.)
The literary deluge which commenced in Germany in 1814, still continues to in-
ase.   For the 2,000 works which were then about the annual complement, we have
w nearly 6,000.   The catalogue of the last Leipsic fair (Michaelmas 1830) contains
44 articles, of which 2,764 are actually published ; and if these are added to the 3,162
nounced in the Easter catalogue, the number of books published in 1830 will amount
5,962.   The number published in 1829 was 5,314 ; in 1828, 5,654 ; in 1827, 5,108 ;
viously to which, the number had never exceeded 5,000.   Magazines and popular
cyclopædias have increased in the same proportion ; and the public has shown as
at a desire to read, as the learned have to write.   Private libraries are diminishing,
ile the public ones are daily increasing. — (*Foreign Quarterly Review*, No. XIV.
651.)

BOOK-KEEPING, the art of keeping the accounts and books of a merchant.
ok-keeping by double entry means that mode or system in which every entry
louble, that is, has both a debtor and a creditor.   It is called also the Italian
thod, because it was first practised in Venice, Genoa, and other towns in Italy,
ere trade was conducted on an extensive scale at a much earlier date than in
gland, France, or other parts of Europe.   This method, however familiar to
rchants and book-keepers, seems intricate to almost all who have not practised
nor is the dryness and difficulty of the task much lessened by the printed
rks on the subject, which, having been compiled more by teachers than by
ctical merchants, contain a number of obsolete rules and unnecessary details.
e most effectual mode of giving clearness and interest to our remarks will be,
t, to state a few mercantile transactions, and then to explain the nature of the
ounts and entries which result from them.
he Journal of a mercantile house ought to open, at the beginning of each year, with
enumeration of their assets and debts, as follows.

| o of | SUNDRIES Drs. to STOCK. | £ | s. | d. |
ger.	For the following, being the Assets of the house.			
	CASH ; amount at the Bankers' this day (1st Jan.) - -	2,550	0	0
	EXCHEQUER BILLS ; amount in hand - -	5,310	0	0
	BILLS RECEIVABLE ; in hand, as per Bill book -	7,300	15	0
	THREE AND A HALF PER CENT. STOCK, 6000*l*., valued at 90*l*.			
	per 100*l*. Stock - - - - -	5,400	0	0
	DEBENTURE ACCOUNT ; drawbacks receivable at the Custom-			
	house - - - - -	513	0	0
	SHIP AMELIA ; our three eighths of that vessel - -	3,000	0	0
	ADVENTURE IN IRISH LINEN ; amount in hand, computed at			
	cost price - - - - -	2,467	0	0
	JAMES BAILEY & Co., Liverpool ; due by them - -	1,350	10	0
	THOMAS WATSON & Co., Dublin ; do. - - -	3,530	12	0
	WILLIAM SPENCE & Co., Plymouth ; do. - -	970	0	10
		£32,391	17	10

Folio of Ledger.	STOCK Dr. to SUNDRIES. For the Debts of the house, as follows : —	£	s.	d.
6	To BILLS PAYABLE ; amount of acceptances at this date	2,350	10	0
3	To INSURANCE ; amount of premiums due to underwriters	1,880	15	0
9	To MORRIS PITMAN, Trinidad ; balance due to him	1,370	5	0
4	To JAMES FORBES, Demerara ; do.	720	5	0
7	To SIMON FRAZER, London ; do.	960	15	0
2	To JAMES ALLAN & Co., Kingston, Jamaica ; do.	1,150	10	0
8	To GEORGE AND WILLIAM FOX, Falmouth ; do.	320	15	0
		8,753	15	0
	Balance, being the present capital of the house	23,638	2	10
		£32,391	17	10

Let the transaction to be first explained be an order for goods from a correspondent abroad. A house in Jamaica sends instructions to the house at home to buy and ship quantity of manufactured articles, suited to the Jamaica market, as follows : —

Order from JAMES ALLAN & Co., of Kingston, Jamaica, to HENRY BARCLAY & Co.,
of London.

I. A. *Linen ;* Lint Strelitz Osnaburghs, 14 bales, about 6d. ⅌ yard.
& Co.   Best Tow Strelitz do., 9 bales, 4d. or 4½d.
            Best White Platillas, 1 case.
            Linen Tick assorted, ¾ths width, 9d., 1s., 1s. 3d. ; 10 pieces each, cut
                up in 22 yard lengths.
        Woollens ; 5 bales Penistones, ¾ths wide, best Indigo blue, 1s. a yard.
        Cottons ; 50 pieces stout Calico, 28 yards each, ¾ths wide, 4d. a yard.
            50 do.   do.   do.   ⅞ths, superior, 5d. a yard.
            100 do.   stout Calico Shirting, ⅞ths wide, superior, 6d. a yard.
        Hats ; 4 dozen Gentlemen's superfine Black, 20s. each.
            2 do.   do.   Drab, 20s. each.
            1 do. Youths' do.   Black, 15s. each.
            20 do. Felt Hats, for Negroes, 22s. ⅌ dozen.
        Shoes ; 10 dozen prime Calf-skin Shoes, full size, 65s. ⅌ dozen.
            10 do.   Youths'   do.   52s. ⅌ dozen.
            5 do.   Gentlemen's dress do., 72s. ⅌ dozen.

This order the London merchant divides among six, seven, or more wholesale dealers according to their respectives lines of business. Each dealer, or tradesman, as he is commonly called, provides his portion of the order in the course of the fortnight, three weeks, or month, allowed him by the merchant ; and when the goods are packed and ready to ship, he sends in his account, or bill of parcels, thus : —

Messrs. HENRY BARCLAY & Co.

London, 20th February, 1831.

Bought of SIMON FRAZER.

I. A. & Co. No. 8.		£	s.	d.
	10 pieces best Tow Strelitz Osnaburghs, 146 yards each, at 4d. ⅌ yard	24	6	10
	Inside Wrapper, 16 yards, at 3d.	0	4	0
	Cord, bale, and press packing	0	10	0
		24	0	10
	Then follow, stated in like manner, the particulars of 8 bales, No. 9. to 16., both inclusive, amounting to	212	4	2
		£236	5	0

London, 20th February, 1831.

Messrs. Henry Barclay & Co.

Bought of J. Borradaile & Co.

		£	s.	d.	£	s.	d.
Case, 1 dozen and 2 Youths' Hats and Bands, at							
15s. each - - - - -		10	10	0			
Case (small) - - - - -		0	4	0			
					10	14	0
Case, 9 dozen Felt Hats for Negroes, at 22s. ℔ dozen		9	18	0			
Case (large) - - - - -		0	16	0			
					10	14	0
Do. the same - - - - - -					10	14	0
					£32	2	0

...e merchant, having received the whole of the bills of parcels, fixed on a vessel, and ...d for the freight, proceeds to make an entry at the Custom-house, and to ship the ...s. That done, the next step is to prepare the Invoice, or general account of the ...nent, as follows : —

...ce of Goods shipped by Henry Barclay & Co., in the *Rawlins*, J. Thomson, ...m London to Kingston in Jamaica, on account and risk of Messrs. James Allan ...Co. of Kingston.

A.			£	s.	d.	£	s.	d.
Co.								
1.	Puncheon strong Calf-skin Shoes, ℔ J. John-							
	son's bill of parcels - -		93	7	0			
2.	Do. do. ℔ do. -		94	16	4			
3.	French Calf-skin Shoes, ℔ do. -		23	9	0			
5, 6.	3 Trunks do. ℔ do. -		67	3	7			
						278	15	11
7.	Case Linen Tick assorted, ℔ J. Wilson's bill of parcels					42	0	0
16.	9 Bales best Tow Osnaburghs, 10 pieces each, ℔ Simon							
	Frazer's bill of parcels - - -					236	5	0
7.	1 Case White Platillas, ℔ Molling & Co.'s bill of parcels					41	0	8
24.	7 Cases the same, ℔ do. - -					287	4	8
38.	14 Bales Lint Osnaburghs, ℔ J. Mackenzie's bill of							
	parcels - - - -					367	10	0
.	1 Case Youths' Hats and Bands, ℔ J. Borradaile & Co.'s							
	bill of parcels - - - -					10	14	0
41.	2 Cases Felt Hats, do. ℔ do. -					21	8	0
						1,284	18	3
	Entry; Duty on part at ½ ℔ Cent. ; Bond	£	s.	d.				
	and Debenture - - -	4	8	0				
	Cartage, Wharfage, and Shipping Charges -	7	9	6				
	Freight and Primage 38l. 7s. ; Bills of Lad-							
	ing 3s. 6d. - - - -	38	10	6				
	Insurance on 1,500l. at 40s.							
	℔ 100l. - - £30 0 0							
	Policy Duty - - 3 18 9							
		33	18	9				
	Commission, 5 ℔ Cent. on 1,335l. -	66	15	0				
	Do. ½ ℔ Cent. on 1,500l. insured -	7	10	0				
						158	11	9
	Errors excepted.					£1,443	10	0

At 6 Months' Credit ; due 6th September.

London, 6th March, 1830.   Henry Barclay & Co.

...s invoice, being sent out by the vessel to Messrs. Allan & Co., conveys to them a ...er of particulars in a short space ; viz. the mark, the numbers, the value, and the ...ts of each package. In former times it was the practice to make an invoice ...ong, inserting in it a literal copy of each bill of parcels, but it has now become

usual to make each tradesman deliver a duplicate of his account, to be sent abroad w
the goods; in which case the invoice may be, like the above, little more than a summa
of the bills of parcels. This method has two advantages: it saves time at the countin
house of the exporter; and it affords to his correspondent an assurance, that no more
charged to him than has been actually paid for the articles.

An invoice ought to be made out with the utmost care, for it is a document of gr
importance in several respects: first, between the exporting merchant and his cor
spondent abroad; and next, when in the hands of the latter it may and generally de
form a voucher for calculating the import duty, as well as for the sales effected to
tailers or other dealers.

The sum insured by the exporting merchant generally exceeds the amount of the
voice by two per cent., because the recovery of a loss from insurers involves a charge
fully that amount. It is thus necessary to cover not only the price of the goods a
the charges of shipping, insurance, and freight, but such farther sum as may enable
shipper, in case of loss, to carry to the credit of his correspondent the amount of
invoice, clear of any deduction.

JOURNAL ENTRIES resulting from the foregoing Invoice.

Folio of Ledger.	JAMES ALLAN AND Co. Drs. to SUNDRIES. For Goods shipped to them in the *Rawlins*, Thomson, for Jamaica.	£	s.	c
1	To JAMES JOHNSON; Amount of Shoes, ⅌ his bills of parcels	278	15	1
1	To JOHN WILSON; Linen Tick ⅌ do. -	42	0	
1	To SIMON FRAZER; Tow Osnaburghs ⅌ do. -	236	5	
1	To JOHN MACKENZIE; Lint Osnaburghs ⅌ do. -	367	10	
2	To JAMES BORRADAILE & Co.; Hats ⅌ do. -	32	2	
2	To MOLLING & Co.; for Platillas ⅌ do. -	328	5	
3	To FREIGHT ACCOUNT; Freight, Primage, and Bills of Lading - - - - -	38	10	
3	To INSURANCE; Premium, and Policy - -	33	18	
3	To CHARGES; Entry Outward, Duty, and Shipping Charges	11	17	
3	To PROFIT AND LOSS; for Commissions - -	74	5	
		£1,443	10	

The preceding invoice, being for account of a mercantile house, who sell again
dealers, comprises a variety of articles: as a farther specimen, we subjoin two s
invoices, for account of sugar planters, and confined to articles consumed on their estat

INVOICE of Plantation Stores, shipped by HENRY BARCLAY & Co., in the *Advent*
J. Williamson, Master, for Kingston, Jamaica, by order of Mr. JAMES THOMS
Planter, and for his account and risk.

I. T. 1. to 6.		£	s.
	6 Bales Lint Osnaburghs, ⅌ bill of parcels from James Anderson - - £240 0 0		
	Then follow, in like manner, the Mark, Number, and Contents of various other packages of Plantation Stores, (Hats, Shoes, Nails, &c.) composing the Shipment; amounting in all to - - - - -	2,352	10
	CHARGES. £ s. d. Custom-house Entry, and Shipping Charges - 2 12 6 Freight, Primage, and Bills of Lading - 18 7 6 Commission on 2,374*l.* at 2½ ⅌ Cent. - 59 7 0		
		80	7
	Insurance on 2,550*l.* at 2*l.* ⅌ Cent. - - 51 0 0 Policy Duty - - - 6 10 0 Commission, ½ ⅌ Cent. - - 12 15 0		
		70	5
		£2,503	2

                         Errors excepted.

London, 2d October, 1830.   HENRY BARCLAY & Co.

voice of 60 Barrels Herrings, shipped by HENRY BARCLAY & Co. of London, in the *Barclay*, James Ferrier, bound to Barbadoes, by order, and for account and risk of JOHN HENDERSON, Esq., Planter, and consigned to him at Bridgetown, Barbadoes.

London, 18th Feb. 1824.

. H.	60 Barrels prime White Herrings, deliverable at Bridgetown, Barbadoes, free of Charges, at 21s. ℔ Barrel -	£63 0 0

This invoice is very short; the agreement having been, that the herrings should be livered at a fixed price, all charges included.

ACCOUNT OF SALES.—We come now to a transaction of a different kind; to the sale goods imported from abroad. A merchant in England receives from a correspondent, ether in India, the West Indies, or North America, notice of a shipment of sugar, fee, rice, or other produce, about to be made to England, with instructions to effect surance on the computed value. This is the first step in the transaction; on the aral of the vessel the goods are entered, landed, and warehoused; and a broker is structed to report on the state and prospects of the market. On a sale taking place, account is made out and forwarded to the correspondent abroad, as follows: —

ccount SALE of 7 Hhds. Sugar, by the *Ceres*, from Trinidad, for Account of MORRIS PITTMAN, Esq., of Trinidad.

	£	s.	d.	M. P. 1. to 7.	7 Hogshds. Cwt. qrs. lbs.	£	s.	d.
nsurance on 175l. at 60s. ℔ 100l. - £5 5 0					7 Hogshds. weighing 87 3 21			
Policy - 0 10 6					Deduct draft 0 0 14			
	5	15	6					
reight of 79 cwt. 25 lbs. at 6s. ℔ cwt. - -	23	15	4		87 3 7			
rimage, Pierage, and Trade - - -	0	9	7		Deduct tare 9 3 7			
uty on 79 cwt. 25 lbs. at 27s. ℔ cwt.	106	19	0		Nett 78 0 0 at 60s. ℔ cwt.	234	0	0
Entry - -	0	6	0					
ock Dues - - -	2	12	10					
andwaiters, and Entry -	0	16	0					
arehouse Rent, 19 weeks	1	15	2					
ampling - -	0	3	6					
nsurance from Fire	0	6	0					
terest on Freight and Duty - -	1	12	3					
rokerage, 1 ℔ Cent. -	2	6	9					
ommission, 2 ℔ Cent. -	4	13	4					
℔ Cent. on 175l. insured	0	17	6					
	152	8	9					
ett Proceeds, due 2d May, 1830 - -	81	11	3					
	£234	0	0			£234	0	0

Errors excepted.

London, 2d April, 1831. HENRY BARCLAY & Co.

Ve have here on one side of the account the quantity and value of the goods sold; he other, the various charges attending the bringing home, the warehousing, and the of the articles.

he quantity of goods accounted for in an account sale must be the same as in the ice; if it be less, whether through damage at sea, through waste, or any other cause, extent of the deficiency should be explicitly stated. By the "overtaker" in the owing sale is meant the additional barrel or package required for the coffee taken out uch of the tierces as have been opened on account of breakage or other damage. llowances of Weight. - The tare is the weight of the cask, and differs, of course, in ost every package: but trett (see the following sale) is a fixed allowance of 5lb. per e in the case of coffee, intended, like draft in the case of sugar, to insure good weight e buyer, and to enable him to do the same to those who purchase again from him.

ACCOUNT SALE of 20 Tierces Coffee, ℔ *Vittoria*, from Demerara, for Account of JAMES FORBES, Esq., Demerara.

CHARGES.	£	s.	d.			Gross Weight. Cwt. qrs. lbs.	Tare. Cwt. qrs. lbs.	£	s.	d.
Insurance on 20 Tierces at 35*l.* a Tierce, 700*l.* at 50*s.*; Policy, 36*s.* 9*d.* - - -	19	6	9	I. F. No. 1 to 20.	5 Tierces 5 Do. 4 Do.	30 1 7 32 2 5 24 2 4	3 2 15 4 0 5 2 3 16			
Freight on 114 Cwt. at 7*s.* 6*d.* ℔ Cwt. - £42 15 0						87 1 16	10 2 8			
Primage, Pierage, and Trade - -	1	7	6				Trett 0 2 14			
	44	2	6				11 0 22			
Dock Dues - - - -	10	9	1							
Landwaiters, Entry, and part of bond - - -	1	2	6			Deduct 11 0 22				
Insurance from Fire - -	0	19	6							
Public Sale Charges - - -	1	7	6			Nett 76 0 22 at 121*s.* 6*d.* ℔ cwt.	}	462	17	9
Brokerage, 1 ℔ Cent. - -	6	16	7							
Commission, 2½ ℔ Cent. on 676*l.*	16	18	0			Gross Weight. Cwt. qrs. lbs.	Tare. Cwt. qrs. lbs.			
Commission, ½ ℔ Cent. on 700*l.* insured - - -	3	10	0		3 Tierces 3 Do.	17 1 1 19 3 15	2 0 9 2 1 15			
	104	12	5			37 0 16	4 1 24	–		
Nett Proceeds, due 3d May, 1831 -	571	13	1				Trett 0 1 1			
	£676	5	6				4 2 25			
						Deduct 4 2 25				
						Nett 32 1 19 at 120*s.* ℔ cwt.		194	9	4
						Gross Weight. Cwt. qrs. lbs.	Tare. Cwt. qrs. lbs.			
					Overtaker	5 1 9	0 3 9 Trett 0 0 11			
							0 3 20			
						Deduct 0 3 20				
						Nett 4 1 17 at 117*s.* ℔ cwt.		25	15	0
								683	2	1
						Discount, 1 ℔ Cent.		6	16	7
						Gross Proceeds	£676	5	6

London, 3d *April*, 1831.   Errors excepted.   HENRY BARCLAY & Co.

Freight is charged on the weight of the produce only; not of the produce and package together. This allowance is of old standing, and is to be traced less to the reason of the case, than to the competition prevailing among shipmasters.

JOURNAL ENTRIES, resulting from the preceding accounts of Sale.

Folio of Ledger.	June 1831.	£	s.	d.
4	THOMAS KEMBLE & Co. Drs. to SUNDRIES.			
2	To SUGAR ℔ *Ceres.*			
	Proceeds of 7 Hhds., M. P. 1. to 7., sold by them at one month's credit, from 2d April - - -	234	0	0
4	To COFFEE ℔ *Vittoria.*			
	Proceeds of 20 Tierces, I. F. 1. to 20., sold at one month's credit, from 3d April - - - -	676	5	6
		910	5	6
2	SUGAR ℔ CERES Dr. to SUNDRIES.			
3	To INSURANCE ACCOUNT; for Premium and Policy - -	5	15	6
3	To FREIGHT ACCOUNT; for Freight, Primage, and Pierage	24	4	11
4	To CUSTOMS INWARD; Duty and Entry - - -	107	5	0
3	CHARGES; Dock Dues, 52*s.* 10*d.*; Warehouse Rent, 35*s.* 2*d.*; Landwaiters, 16*s.*; Sampling, 3*s.* 6*d.*; and Fire Insurance, 6*s.*	5	13	6
4	To THOMAS KEMBLE & Co.; Brokerage, 1 ℔ Cent. -	2	6	9
3	To PROFIT AND LOSS; for Commissions - £5 10 10 Interest on Freight and Duty - - 1 12 3	7	3	1
4	To MORRIS PITTMAN; Proceeds due 2d May, 1831 -	81	11	8
		234	0	0

		£	s.	d.
	Coffee ꝑ Vittoria Dr. to Sundries.			
To Insurance; for Premium and Policy - - -		19	6	9
To Freight Account; Freight, Primage, and Pierage -		44	2	6
To Charges; Dock Dues, Landwaiters, Insurance from Fire, and Public Sale Charges - - - -		13	18	7
To Thomas Kemble & Co. ; Brokerage - - -		6	16	7
To Profit and Loss; for Commissions - - -		20	8	1
To James Forbes; Nett Proceeds due 3d June, 1830 -		571	13	1
		£676	5	7

We have thus given an example of the transactions which form a great part of the business of our merchants ; the export of manufactured goods, and the import and sale of produce received in return. Our next illustration shall be of a merchant's cash-book: the following is an example of the entries for a month : —

CASH.					PAID.					Cr.		
		£	s.	d.	1830.					£	s.	d.
Balance at the Banker's - -		2,550	0	0	Mar.2	By Bills payable, paid No. 261. to James Harding - -				145	10	0
Ship *Amelia*, received of James Jobs, for Freight - -		175	3	0	4	By George and William Fox, paid their Balance of Account -				320	15	0
Bills receivable, received Payment No. 251. on J. Henderson -		200	0	0	6	By John Smith & Sons, paid J. Jackson for their Account - -				98	0	0
James Bailey & Co., received payment of their Draft at Sight on Bainbridge -		152	10	0	7	By Bills payable, paid No. 269. to J. Stewart - - -				300	0	0
William Spence & Co., received Balance of their account -		970	0	10	18	By Interest paid, Discount on Harrison & Co., 2 months -				6	1	10
Debenture Account, received Drawback on Tobacco shipped by *Plover* - -		15	8	0		By J. Johnson, paid his Bill of Parcels By John Wilson do. By Simon Frazer do.				278 42 236	15 0 5	11 0 0
Bills receivable, discounted at the Bankers, Harrison & Co., due 15 March -		730	10	0		By John Mackenzie do. By James Borradaile & Co. do. By Molling & Co. do.				367 32 328	10 2 5	0 0 4
Profit and Loss, received 5 ꝑ Cent. Discount, on paying with ready money, the Accounts per contra, not till six months hence, from					31	By Charges paid, Postage, and petty Disbursements this month, per Petty Cash Book - - -				15	2	6
James Johnson £13 19 0 John Wilson 2 2 0 Simon Frazer 11 16 0 John Mackenzie 18 7 6 James Borradaile&Co. 0 16 0 Molling & Co. 16 8 3					—	By Balance, carried to next month				2,686	13	0
		63	8	9								
		£4,857	0	7						£4,857	0	7

These transactions, when put into the Journal form, stand thus : —

March, 1830. CASH Dr. to SUNDRIES. Received this Month.			£	s.	d.
To Ship Amelia. 3d. Freight from James Jacobs - -			175	3	0
To Bills Receivable. 6th. Received Payment of J. Anderson, due this day - - - £200 0 0 18th. Discounted Harrison and Co., due 9th May - - - 730 10 0			930	10	0
To James Baily & Co. 9th. Received their Draft on Bainbridge, due			152	10	0
To William Spence & Co. 15th. Received Balance of their Account			970	0	10
To Debenture Account. 15th. Drawback on Tobacco by the *Plover* - -			15	8	0
To Profit and Loss. 18th. Received Discount on sundry Accounts, per Cash Book - - - - - -			63	8	9
			£2,307	0	7

Folio of Ledger.	SUNDRIES Drs. to CASH.			£	s.	
	Paid this Month as follows :					
6	BILLS PAYABLE.					
	2d. Paid No. 261. - -	- £145	10	0			
	7th. Do. 269. - -	- 192	15	0			
					338	5	
4	CUSTOMS INWARD.					
	23d. Paid Duty on Sugar, ℗ *Ceres*, 79 cwt.					
	25 lbs., at 27s. ℗ cwt. - -	106	19	0			
	Entry - - -	0	6	0			
					107	5	
8	SIMON FRAZER.					
	18th. Paid his Bill of Parcels - -	236	5	0			
1	26th. Paid J. Jackson for his Account -	98	0	0			
					334	5	
8	INTEREST ACCOUNT.					
	18th. Paid Discount on Harrison & Co. -	-			6	1	1
1	JAMES JOHNSON.					
	18th. Paid his Bill of Parcels -	-	-		278	15	1
1	JOHN WILSON.					
	18th. Paid his Bill of Parcels -	-	-	-	42	0	
1	JOHN MACKENZIE.					
	18th. Paid his Bill of Parcels -	-	-	-	367	10	
2	JAMES BORRADAILE & Co.					
	18th. Paid his Bill of Parcels -	-	-	-	32	2	
2	MOLLING & Co.					
	18th. Paid their Balance of Account -	,,	-		328	5	
8	GEORGE AND WILLIAM FOX.					
	24th. Paid their Balance of Account -	-	-		320	15	
3	CHARGES.					
	31st. Paid Postage, and petty Disbursements this Month				15	2	
					£2,170	7	

The above shows, that for all sums received the account of cash is made debtor, the parties paying the same are made creditors ; while for all sums paid the cash credited and the parties receiving them are made debtors.

We are next to state the mode of entering bill transactions.

BILLS RECEIVABLE. — We have seen by the Balance sheet that several corresponde are indebted to the house. The debts of correspondents abroad may be reduced remitting either bills, specie, or merchandise for sale : from correspondents in Engla bills are almost the only mode of remitting. When bills come to hand, the rule i enter each in the bill book, with a minute statement of the date, term, sum, and o particulars, thus : —

No.	Received.	From whom.	Drawn by.	Date.	Term.	Drawn on.	To order of.	Due.	Sum.	Ho
630	8 Mar.	Jas. Bailey & Co.	W. Adams	Belfast, 1 Mar.	2 months date.	T. Jones, Dublin	A. Williams	1—4 May	L.350	Rai
631	10 do.	T. Watson & Co	J. Jacobs	Cork, 3 do.	1 do.	J. Adams, London	G. Wilson	3—6 April	135	Smi
632	12 do.	W. Spence & Co.	T. Johnson	Falmouth, 5 do.	2 do.	T. Allan, Liverpool	D. Jones	5—8 May	260	Ove

The JOURNAL ENTRIES for these bills are as follows : —

Folio of Ledger.	BILLS RECEIVABLE Dr. to SUNDRIES.			£	s.
	For the following remitted this Month :				
7	To JAMES BAILEY & Co.				
	No. 630. on T. Jones, Dublin, due 4th May -	-		350	0
7	To T. WATSON & Co.				
	No. 631. on J. Adams, London, due 6th April -	-		135	0
7	To WILLIAM SPENCE & Co.				
	No. 632. on T. Allan, Liverpool, due 8th May	-		260	0
				£745	0

Bills Payable. — The entries under this head are, of course, wholly different from the preceding, being for acceptances of the house given on account of sums owing by it to correspondents. Each acceptance is entered in the book of bills payable, thus : —

o.	Drawn by	Place and Date.	To order of	On Account of	Term.	When accepted.	Due.	Sum.
1	J. Allan & Co.	Jamaica, 15 Jan.	J. Jones	J. Allan & Co.	90 days' sight	12 March	10—13 June	L.175 10 0
2	G. & W. Fox	Falmouth, 7 Mar.	J. Thomson	G. & W. Fox	15 days' date	14 do.	22—25 Mar.	73 15 0
3	J. Clark	Hull, 5 Mar.	G. Barclay	J. Smith & Sons	1 months' date	16 do.	5—8 ditto	132 10 0

The Journal entries for these bills are as follow : —

Folio of Ledger.			
	SUNDRIES Drs. to BILLS PAYABLE.		
	For the following Bills accepted.		£ s. d.
2	James Allan & Co. No. 151. their Draft, due 13th June -		175 10 0
8	G. & W. Fox. No. 152. their Draft, due 25th March -		73 15 0
1	Simon Frazer. J. Clark's Draft, on his Account, due 8th March		132 10 0
			£381 15 0
	————— MAY, 1830. —————		
	CASH Dr. to THOMAS KEMBLE & Co.		
1	27th. Received from them Proceeds of Sugar		
	℔ Ceres - - -	234 0 0	
	Less their Brokerage - - -	2 6 9	
			231 13 3
4	30th. Received Coffee ℔ Vittoria - -	676 5 6	
	Less Brokerage - - -	6 16 7	
			669 8 11
			£901 2 2

The preceding entries, few as they are compared to the monthly transactions of a house of business, are sufficient to show the nature of a Journal as well as of the subsidiary books, (for cash, bills, invoices, and account sales,) from which it is composed. The Journal, being a complete record of the business of the house, is very varied and comprehensive in its nature, and may be termed an index to every book of consequence in a counting-house. But while in the cash book every payment or receipt is entered on the day it takes place, and in the bill book every bill is registered on the day it comes to hand, or is accepted, the Journal entries, being completed only at the end of the month, admit of being combined to a considerable extent, so as to exhibit a number of transactions in collective sums. Thus all the acceptances of the house paid in the course of the month appear in the Journal entry of Bills Payable Dr. to Cash : they are arranged in this entry as they fall due, after which the whole are added into one sum, which sum alone needs be carried to the Ledger. In like manner, all bills receivable, whether discounted, or kept by the house till they fall due, are collected under the head of Bills Receivable Dr. to Cash, summed up together, and carried to the Ledger in one sum ; a point of great importance, as we shall see presently, in facilitating the balance of the Ledger.

We proceed to give a specimen of the Ledger : the whole of the Journal entries in the preceding pages, when posted into the Ledger, will stand thus :—

Dr.		STOCK.				Cr.	
Fo.		£ s. d.	1831.	Fo.		£ s. d.	
1	To Sundries -	8,753 15 0	Jan. 1	1	By Sundries -	32,391 17 10	

Dr.		CASH.				Cr.	
1	To Stock - -	2,550 0 0	Mar. 31		By Sundries -	2,170 7 7	
4	To Sundries - -	2,307 0 7					
15	To T. Kemble & Co.	901 2 2					

Dr.			EXCHEQUER BILLS.			Cr
	Fo.		£ s. d.	1831.	Fo.	£ s.
1831. Jan. 1	1	To Stock - -	5,310 0 0			

Dr.			THREE AND A HALF ⅌ CENT. STOCK.			Cr
Jan. 1	1	To Stock - -	5,400 0 0			

Dr.			JAMES JOHNSON, London.			Cr
Mar. 1	4	To Cash - -	278 15 11	Mar. 6	9	By J. Allan & Co. 278 15

Dr.			JOHN WILSON, London.			Cr
Mar. 1	4	To Cash - -	42 0 0	Mar. 6	9	By J. Allan & Co. 42 0

Dr.			SIMON FRASER, London.			Cr
Mar. 26	4	To Cash - -	334 5 0	Jan. 1	2	By Stock - - 960 15
31	5	To Bills Payable	132 10 0	Jan. 6	9	By J. Allan & Co. 236 5

Dr.			JOHN MACKENZIE, London.			Cr
Mar. 8	4	To Cash - -	367 10 0	Mar. 6	9	By J. Allan & Co. 367 10

Drs.			JAMES BORRADAILE & Co., London.			Crs
Mar. 1	4	To Cash - -	32 2 0	Mar. 6	9	By J. Allan & Co. 32 2

Drs.			MOLLING & Co., London.			Cr
Mar. 1	4	To Cash - -	328 5 4	Mar. 6	9	By J. Allan & Co. 328 5

Drs.			J. ALLAN & Co., Kingston, Jamaica.			Cr
Mar. 6	9	To Sundries -	1,443 10 0	Jan. 1	2	By Stock - - 1,150
31	11	To Bills Payable -	175 10 0			

Dr.			SUGAR BY THE CERES.			Cr
April 2	11	To Sundries -	234 0 0	April 2	11	By T. Kemble & Co. 234

r.

FREIGHT ACCOUNT. Cr.

Fo.		£	s.	d.	1831.	Fo.		£	s.	d.
					Mar. 6	9	By J. Allan & Co.	38	10	6
					April 2	11	By Sugar ℗ Ceres -	24	11	11
					May 3	13	By Coffee ℗ Vittoria	44	2	6

INSURANCE ACCOUNT. Cr.

					Jan. 1	2	By Stock - -	1,880	15	0
					Mar. 6	9	By J. Allan & Co.	33	18	9
					April 2	11	By Sugar ℗ Ceres -	5	16	6
					May 3	13	By Coffee ℗ Vittoria	19	6	9

CHARGES. Cr.

4	To Cash - -	15	2	6	Mar. 6	9	By J. Allan & Co.	11	17	6
					April 2	11	By Sugar ℗ Ceres -	5	13	6
					May 3	13	By Coffee ℗ Vittoria	13	18	7

PROFIT AND LOSS. Cr.

					Mar. 6	9	By J. Allan & Co.	74	5	0
					Mar. 8	4	By Cash - -	63	8	9
					April 2	11	By Sugar ℗ Ceres -	7	3	1
					May 3	13	By Coffee ℗ Vittoria	20	8	1

CUSTOMS INWARD. Crs.

4	To Cash - -	107	5	0	April 2	11	By Sugar ℗ Ceres -	107	5	0

COFFEE PER VITTORIA. Cr.

13	To Sundries -	676	5	6	April 3	11	By T. Kemble & Co.	676	5	5

MORRIS PITMAN, Trinidad. Cr.

					Jan. 1	2	By Stock - -	1,370	5	0
					April 2	11	By Sugar ℗ Ceres -	81	11	3

JAMES FORBES, Demerara. Cr.

					Jan. 1	2	By Stock - -	720	5	0
					May 3	13	By Coffee ℗ Vittoria	571	13	1

THOMAS KEMBLE & Co., London. Crs.

1	To Sundries -	910	5	6	April 7	11	By Sugar ℗ Ceres -	2	6	9
					30	13	By Coffee ℗ Vittoria	6	16	7
					May 30	15	By Cash - -	901	2	2
								910	5	6

L 2

Dr.   BILLS RECEIVABLE.

1831.	Fo.				£	s.	d.	1831.	Fo.				£
Jan. 1	1	To Stock	-		7,300	15	0	Mar. 1	4	By Cash	-	-	980
Mar. 3	5	To Sundries	-		745	0	0						

Dr.   BILLS PAYABLE.

Mar. 7	4	To Cash	-	-	338	5	0	Jan. 1	2	By Stock	-	-	2,359
								Mar. 3	5	By Sundries	-		381

Dr.   SHIP AMELIA.

Jan. 1	1	To Stock	-	-	3,000	0	0	Mar. 1	4	By Cash	-	-	175

Dr.   ADVENTURE IN IRISH LINEN.

Jan. 1	1	To Stock	-	-	2,467	0	0						

Drs.   JAMES BAILEY & Co., Liverpool.

Jan. 1	1	To Stock	-	-	1,350	10	0	Mar. 3	4	By Cash	-	-	152
								Mar. 9	5	By Bills Receivable			350

Drs.   THOMAS WATSON & Co., Dublin.

Jan. 1	1	To Stock	-	-	3,530	12	0	Mar. 3	5	By Bills Receivable			135

Drs.   WILLIAM SPENCE & Co., Plymouth.

Jan. 1	1	To Stock	-	-	970	0	10	Mar. 3	4	By Cash	-	-	970
								Mar. 5	5	By Bills Receivable			260

Drs.   GEORGE AND WILLIAM FOX, Falmouth.

Mar. 4	4	To Cash	-	-	320	15	0	Jan. 1	2	By Stock	-	-	320
Mar. 6		To Bills Payable	-		73	15	0						

Dr.   DEBENTURE ACCOUNT.

Jan. 1	1	To Stock	-	-	513	0	0	Mar. 5	4	By Cash	-	-	15

Dr.   INTEREST ACCOUNT.

Mar. 8	4	To Cash	-	-	6	1	10						

The Ledger is thus a register of all the entries in the Journal; and a register so arranged as to exhibit on one side all the sums at Debtor; on the other all those at creditor. It is kept in the most concise form, the insertions in it hardly ever exceeding a line each, or containing more than the title of the entry in the Journal. On opening a page in the Ledger, a person unacquainted with book-keeping is apt to consider its brevity unsatisfactory; and it was formerly the practice to add in each line a few explanatory words. Thus the entries in the account of Simon Fraser, which in our preceding page are briefly

		£	s.	d.
March 26.	To Cash - - - -	334	5	0
31.	To Bills Payable - - -	132	10	0

would, at an earlier date in the practice of book-keeping, have been expanded to

		£.	s.	d.
March 18.	To Cash paid for goods per Rawlins - -	236	5	0
26.	To ditto paid J. Jackson for his account - -	98	0	0
31.	To Bills Payable, paid J. Clark's draft for his account	132	10	0

This method is still followed in some counting-houses, and such explanatory additions are certainly conducive to clearness; but they are practicable only in a house of limited business: wherever the transactions are numerous and varied, they should be left out of the ledger for two reasons; they increase greatly the labour of the book-keeper, and they never can be so full or circumstantial as to supersede the account current book.

The same Ledger may continue in use from one to five years, according to the size of the book, or the extent of the transactions of the house. On opening a new ledger, it is proper to place in succession accounts of the same class or character: thus — Stock account ought to be followed by that of the Three per cent. consols, Exchequer bills, or other property belonging to the house; and if the business be with the West Indies, it is fit that accounts with Jamaica should be placed near those with Demerara, Trinidad, and other sugar colonies.

Balancing the Ledger. — This important operation is performed by adding up the debtor and Creditor side of every account in the Ledger, ascertaining the difference or balance in each, and carrying that balance, as the case may be, to the Debtor or Creditor column in the balance sheet. On closing, for example, a few of the preceding ledger accounts, we find them to stand thus: —

Debtors.				Creditors.			
	£	s.	d.		£	s.	d.
Cash - - -	3,587	15	2	Simon Fraser - -	730	5	0
James Allan & Co. -	468	10	0	Freight Account -	107	4	11

And so on with every account except Stock, which, having no entries in the current year, is left out of the balance. Exclusive of Stock, the total at the Debtor side of the balance sheet ought to agree exactly with the total at the Creditor side; and if it do not, it is a rule in all well regulated counting-houses to follow up the examination perseveringly, until they are made to agree. The apparent difference may not exceed a few shillings or a few pence; still the search is continued, because the smallest discrepancy shows the existence of error, and to an extent perhaps greatly beyond the fraction in question. It often happens indeed, that, as the examination proceeds, the difference undergoes a change from a smaller to a larger amount, and without increasing the difficulty of discovering the error, which is as likely to have occurred in the case of a large as of a small sum. Differences, when in round sums, such as 10*l.*, 100*l.*, or 1000*l.*, generally lie in the addition; fractional sums frequently in the posting. All this, however, is uncertain; for the error or errors may be in any month in the year, and in any of the thousand entries and upwards which have been made in the course of it. Hence the necessity of examining the whole; and young book-keepers are often obliged to pass week after week in the tedious labour of revising, adding, and subtracting. On the other hand, there are sometimes examples of the balance being found on the first trial; but such cases are rare, and occur only to careful and experienced book-keepers. The only effectual means of lessening the labour and perplexity of balancing the Ledger, is to exercise great care in every stage of the book-keeping process; as well in making the additions in the Journal, as in posting from the Journal into the Ledger, and casting up the Ledger accounts; and, lastly, in adding up the balance sheet, which is generally of formidable length.

Accuracy in addition is one of the main requisites in a clerk, and particularly in a book-keeper. Of the extent to which it may be attained by continued practice, those only can judge who have experienced it themselves, or have marked the ease and correctness with which clerks in banking-houses perform such operations. They are in the habit of striking a daily balance which comes within small compass; but a merchant's balance, comprising the transactions of a year, extends commonly over a number of folio pages. It is advisable, therefore, to divide each page into portions of ten lines each, adding such portions separately. This lessens the risk of error, as it is evidently easier to add five or six such portions in succession, than to do at once a whole folio containing fifty or sixty sums.

Another important point towards agreeing a balance, is to limit carefully the number of Ledger entries; in other words, to comprise as much as possible in those aggregate sums in the Journal which are posted in the Ledger. Thus, in the case of the monthly entries for bills, whether receivable or payable, while the inner column of the Journal contains the amount of each specific bill — the final column, that which is carried to the Ledger—should, and generally does, comprise a number of bills in one sum. Entries in the cash book, which generally form so large a proportion of the transactions of the month, are carried by some book-keepers directly from the cash book into the Ledger without an intermediate arrangement in the journal form. In some lines of business this plan may answer; but as a general rule it is better to take the trouble of journalising the cash, thereby comprising in 30 or 40 ledger entries the transactions of the month which, when posted separately, would exceed 100. The time required for re-writing or rather re-casting them, will, in most cases, be amply made good, by exhibiting the cash in a proper form, and by facilitating the balance of the Ledger at the close of the year.

We have said the close of the year, because, in nine mercantile houses out of ten, that is the period for striking a balance. In some branches of trade, however, the case is otherwise. Thus, among West India merchants, the 30th of April is the time of balancing, because at that season the sales of the preceding crop are, in general, completed, and those of the current year not yet begun.

Arrears in book-keeping ought to be most carefully avoided — calculated as they are to engender mistakes, and to produce loss from delay in adjusting accounts. The practice of balancing the Ledger every six months, and of transmitting as often account current to the correspondents and connections of merchants, will, it is to be hoped become general. It is, however, hardly practicable in cases where, as too often happen in the lesser mercantile establishments, the book-keeper is charged with a share of the active management. Exemption from interruption, and removal from the bustle of current business, are main requisites to accuracy and despatch in accounts. In examining, or as it is called, collating the books, the book-keeper requires not only a retired apartment, but the assistance of a clerk, for the purpose of calling them over. A similar arrangement for another purpose—we mean for composing the Journal, the book-keeper dictating from the subsidiary books to a clerk whose writing forms the draught or rough copy of the Journal, has as yet been seldom adopted; although, when properly applied, it is highly conducive both to accuracy and expedition.

A Ledger must, of course, have an index; but it is very brief, containing merely the titles of the accounts and a reference to the page, as follows: —

	Folio		Folio
Allan & Co., James - - - 2	Bailey & Co., James - - 7
Amelia, Ship - - - 6	Bills Payable - - - 6

The Subsidiary Books. — In former times, when business in this country was conducted by most persons on a very limited scale, the accounts of a number of merchants or rather of those dealers whom we should now think it a compliment to call merchants were often kept on a plan somewhat like that at present followed by our shopkeepers The merchant or his chief clerk kept a daily record of transactions, whether sales, purchases, receipts, or payments, in a diary, which was called a Waste-book, from the rude manner in which the entries or rather notices in it were written, being inserted, one by one soon after the transactions in question took place. From this diary the Journal and Ledger were posted; and book-keeping by double entry being in those days days understood by few one person frequently kept the books of several merchants, passing one or two days in the week at the house of each, and reducing these rough materials into the form of regular entries. In process of time, as transactions multiplied and mercantile business took a wider range, separate books were more generally required for particular departments, such as bill book for all bills of exchange, and a cash book for all ready money transactions. This had long been the case in the large mercantile towns of Italy and Holland; and above a century ago it became a general practice in London and Bristol, which were then the only places of extensive business in England. But in English, as in foreign countries houses, the bill book and even the cash book were long considered as little more than

...oranda of details ; not as books of authority, or as fit documents for Journal entries: ...hat purpose the diary only was used. In time, however, the mode of keeping these ...idiary books improved, and merchants became aware, that when cash or bill transac- ...s were properly entered in them, the Journal might be posted from them as well as ...1 the diary.

...imilar observations are applicable to the other subsidiary books, viz. an invoice book ...goods shipped, and an account of sales book for goods received and sold. When from ...gradual improvement in the management of counting-houses these books were kept ...manner to supply all that was wanted for Journal entries, the use of the diary was ...ensed with for such entries also. And at last it was found, that in all well regulated ...ting-houses the books kept for separate departments of the business were sufficient ...he composition of the Journal, with the exception of a few transactions out of the ...lar course, which might be easily noted in a supplementary book called a Petty ...nal, or a book for occasional entries. The consequence was, that the diary or waste ..., formerly the groundwork of the Journal and Ledger, became excluded from every ...regulated counting-house. This has long been the case, and the name of waste ...would have been forgotten, were it not found in the printed treatises on book- ...ing which have appeared from time to time, and have been generally composed by ...ers in schools or academies, who, unacquainted with the actual practice of mer- ...ts, were content to copy and reprint what they found laid down in old systems of ...-keeping.

...he subsidiary books required in a counting-house are, the ...ash book ; ...ook of Acceptances of the house, or Bills Payable ; ...ook of Bills Receivable, or bills on other merchants which are or have been in pos- ...on of the house ; ...ought book, or book for Bills of Parcels ; ...voice book, or register of goods sold or exported ; ...ccount of Sales book ; ...surance Policy book, containing copies of all policies of insurance ; ...etty Journal, or book for such occasional entries as do not belong to any of the ...ding.

...ch are the authorities from which it is now customary, in every well regulated ...e, to compose the Journal. Their number indicates a repartition or subdivision to ...siderable extent of counting-house work, and nowhere is such repartition produc- ...f greater advantage. How much better is it to enter all bills receivable in one ...all bills payable in another, and all cash transactions in a third, than in any way ...end these very distinct entries. The effect of this subdivision is to simplify the ...al entries in a manner highly conducive to accuracy and despatch ; and to present ...means of checking or examining them, that many transactions may be stated, and ...count extended over a number of folios, without a single error.

...e use of most of the subsidiary books is sufficiently pointed out by their names ; ...may be well to add a few remarks on the "Bought book," or receptacle for the ...nts of goods purchased. A bill of parcels is the name given to the account of ...supplied by a manufacturer, tradesman, or dealer, to a merchant. Such accounts ...become numerous, and it is evidently of consequence to adopt the best method of ...ng them. In former times it was the practice to fold them up in a uniform size, ...fter writing on the back the names of the respective furnishers, to put them away ...dles. But wherever the purchases of a merchant are extensive and the bills of ...s numerous, the better mode, after arranging them alphabetically, is to paste them ...large book, generally a folio, made of blue or sugar loaf paper : this book ...e its pages numbered, and to have an alphabetical index. Any single bill of ...s may thus be referred to with the same ease as we turn to an account in a Ledger ; ...he of these folios may be made to hold a very great quantity of bills of parcels ; ...ny as would form a number of large bundles when tied up on the plan of former

...k of Bills Payable. — The notice, or, as it is termed, advice of bills payable ...ight, generally comes to hand before the bills themselves. As the time of the ...l of the latter is uncertain, the better plan is not to enter them from the advice ...; the other bills payable, but to appropriate a space of ten or twelve pages at the ...ing or end of the book of bills payable, and to insert there the substance of the ...received.

...re are a few books in every counting-house which do not form part of the vouchers ...terials for the Journal ; viz.

...Account Current book, containing duplicates of the accounts furnished by the ...to their different correspondents and connections ;

L 4

The Letter book, containing copies of all letters written to the correspondents connections of the house;

The Petty Cash book, or account of petty disbursements, the sum of which is enter once a month in the cash book;

The Order book, containing copies of all orders received;

The Debenture book, or register of drawbacks payable by the Custom-house.

It was formerly a practice in some houses for the book-keeper to go over the lett book at the end of each month, that he might take note of any entries not supplied the subsidiary books. This, however, is now unnecessary, these books, when careful kept, containing, in one shape or other, every transaction of the house.

The Principle of Double Entry. — From these explanations of the practice of boo keeping, we must call the attention of our readers to a topic of more intricacy — origin of the present system, and the manner in which it was adopted. To record transactions of a merchant in a Journal or day book was an obvious arrangement, a to keep a Ledger or systematic register of the contents of the Journal was a natu result of his business, particularly when conducted on credit. Such, in a rude for are the books of our shopkeepers, who enter their sales and purchases in a day bo and in their Ledger carry the former to the Dr. of their customers, the latter to the C of the wholesale dealers who supply them with goods. By making at the end of year a list of the sums due to him by his customers, and of those due by him wholesale dealers, a shopkeeper may, after adding to the former the value of his sto on hand, make out an approximative statement of his debts and assets. Now, th which in this manner is done indirectly and imperfectly, it is the object of double en to do with method and certainty. The shopkeeper makes out a list of Debtors on o side and of Creditors on the other, but he cannot make them balance because his entr have been single; that is, they have had no counterpart. On making a purchase of c tons from Messrs. Peel of Manchester, or of woollens from Messrs. Gott of Lee he merely enters the amount to their credit, but he makes no one Dr. to them, beca the goods are not sold; and to introduce an imaginary account would be too great a finement for a plain, practical man. But a person accustomed to double entry wou without any effort of thought, make "Printed Calicoes" Dr. to Messrs. Peel, a "Kerseymeres" Dr. to Messrs. Gott, for the respective amounts; after which, as sales proceeded, he would make the buyers Drs. to these accounts for the amount their purchases.

We thus perceive that the intricacy in the application of double entry was not w the personal so much as with the nominal accounts. Let us refer to the country wh book-keeping was first studied, and take as an example the case of Doria, a merch in Genoa, shipping, in a former age, silk, of the value of 200*l.*, bought from Flori Piedmont, to Henderson & Co., silk manufacturers, in England, on the terms charging, not an additional price, but a commission of 5 per cent. with interest u reimbursed his advance. In entering the transaction, Doria's book-keeper would, matter of course, make Hendersons debtors to Flori 200*l.*, for the cost of the silk; he might not so readily find a creditor for the 10*l.* commission, or the 7*l.* inte eventually due on the advance. The custom in this primitive era of book-keep probably was, to introduce the firm of the house into their books, making Henders debtors to Doria for the 10*l.* and 7*l.*; but as the practice of book-keeping improv it was found preferable to avoid inserting, on any occasion, the firm of the house, and substitute nominal accounts, such as, commission, interest, bills payable, bills receival These, attention and practice rendered in time familiar to the book-keeper, who lear to open his Journal at the beginning of a year by making the parties who owed balar to the house debtors, not to the firm by name, but to Stock; and those to whom house was indebted, creditors by Stock. As the transactions of the year proceeded, made those to whom money was paid debtors, not to the firm of the house, but to ca and those for whose account bills were accepted debtors to bills payable; so that bo keeping by double entry assumed its present form gradually and almost imperceptibl

What are the advantages of this method compared to that of single entry? Firs supplies a test of accuracy, inasmuch as the entries on the debtor side of the Ledger be equal to those on the creditor side, their respective totals ought, as a matter of cours balance. After going through this proof, personal accounts of whatever length may settled with confidence; while in a general account, such as Kerseymeres or Printed Calic the value sold and the value remaining on hand may be ascertained by merely balan the account in the Ledger, without the repeated references to the sales book that w otherwise be required. Without double entry a dealer could hardly estimate his prop unless he took stock; but with it an extraction of the Ledger balances fulfils that ob and stock-taking, however proper as a test of the honesty of servants, becomes q unnecessary as a means of calculation. In short, in regard to any person in t

hether merchant, dealer, or manufacturer, double entry forms the connecting link of
s accounts, and affords a ready solution of any inquiry as to the appropriation, increase,
diminution of his capital.

This advantage may fortunately be obtained without any great sacrifice of time or
our. Of the books of dealers, manufacturers, and retailers, nine parts in ten may
ntinue to be kept by single entry ; for the addition of a few pages of double entry in
e form of a summary, at the end of the month or quarter, will be sufficient to exhibit
e result of a great extent of transactions.

Nominal Accounts. — Of these our limits permit us to notice only two ; Profit and
ss, and Merchandise. The former contains on the creditor side all the entries of com-
ssions earned, and gains obtained on particular adventures ; while the debtor side
hibits the losses incurred, whether by bad debts or by unsuccessful purchases. Every
use keeping regular books must have a Profit and Loss account, but a Merchandise
count is altogether optional. Those who have such a head in their Ledger are accus-
med to make it Dr. to the dealers or furnishers from whom they make purchases,
d to credit it in return by the correspondents or connections to whom they make sales.
many houses, however, there is no such intermediate account; the parties to whom the
ods are sent being made Drs. at once to the furnishers of the goods, as in the case
the shipment to Jamaica stated in our preceding pages.

A merchant, before estimating his profits, ought to charge interest on each head of
estment. His clear profit cannot be ascertained without it; and the practice of
arging it is a lesson to him to hold no property that does not afford, at least, interest
his advances.

Mercantile books and accounts must be kept in the money of the country in which
partners reside. A house in Rotterdam composed of English partners necessarily
p their accounts in Dutch money, although their transactions may be chiefly with
gland. Farther, books, it is obvious, can be kept in only one kind of money; and
en a merchant in England receives from a distant country accounts, which cannot at
time be entered in sterling for want of a fixed exchange, these accounts should be
ed in a separate book, until the exchange being ascertained, they can be entered in
Journal in sterling.

A book-keeper will do well to avoid all such puzzling distinctions, as " J. Johnson,
account with him ;" and "J. Johnson, his account proper ;" on the plain ground
t every account in the Ledger ought to be the general account of the person whose
ne it bears.

Errors Excepted. — This expression is merely a proviso, that if any mistakes be dis-
ered in the account in question, they shall be open to correction.

Accounts Current. — An account current generally contains all the transactions of the
se with one of its correspondents during a given time, generally six or twelve
iths. The following is an example : —

essrs. James Allan & Co., Jamaica, in Account Current with Henry Barclay & Co., London.

Drs.	£ s. d.	Days to 31 Dec.	Inter-est.		Crs.	£ s. d.	Days to 31 Dec.	Inter-est.
				1831.				
To Balance of last Account	867 10 0	184	1595	Aug.10	By Proceeds of 20 Tierces Coffee ₩ *Louisa*, due Sept. 10	410 0 0	112	459
To your Draft to J. Smith, due Aug. 13	128 0 0	140	179		By your Remittance on J. Austin, due Oct. 10	350 0 0	82	287
To Invoice of Goods ₩ Amelia, due Oct. 9	752 0 0	83	624	Sept. 15	By Proceeds of 17 hhds. Sugar, ₩ *Hercules*, due Oct. 15	238 0 0	77	173
To Cash paid J. Harvey on your account	75 10 0	82	62	Sept. 20	By Cash received from J. Johnson on your account	260 0 0	102	265
To Insurance on Produce shipped by you in the *Ann*, Nokes, £1,400, at 2 Guineas perCent. £29 8 0 Policy 3 10 0	32 18 0			Dec. 31	Balance of Interest carried to Dr. Balance of Account carried to your Dr. in new Account	621 8 7		1,276
Postage and Petty Charges during this half year	1 15 0							
To Commission, ½ ₩ Cent. on £203, paid Do. on £260, received on your account	4 6 0							
To Balance of Interest this half year, 1,276 divided by 73, is	17 9 7							
	£1,879 8 7		2,460			£1,879 8 7		2,460

Errors excepted.

ondon, *31st December,* 1831.   Henry Barclay & Co.

154 BOOTS AND SHOES. — BORAX.

We have here on the Dr. side all the payments made or responsibilities incurred for the correspondents in question, and ou the Cr. side the different receipts on their account. The interest for the half year, the commission on receipts and payments, the postage and petty charges, being then added, the account may be closed and the balance carried to next year. Copies of accounts current ought to be sent off as soon as possible after the day to which they are brought down ; and with that view they ought to be written out from the Ledger before the close of the year or half year, particularly as the entries for interest and commission can be made only after they are written out. The whole ought then to be copied into the account current book.

But in some counting-houses the account current book, instead of being copied from the Ledger and Journal, is posted, like the latter, from the bill book, the cash book, the invoice book, and the account of sales book. It is then considered a check on the Journal and Ledger ; and from the comparative ease with which it is posted, may be completed and made use of before the latter are fully brought up. This is certainly an advantage in houses where, from pressure on the book-keeper, the Journal and Ledger are in arrear, but such ought never to be the case for any length of time ; while as to the former point — that of forming a check on the Journal and Ledger — the fact is, that these books, from the mode in which they are kept, are much more likely to be correct than the account current book.

Printed Works on Book-keeping. — To the publications of old date by teachers have succeeded, in the present age, several treatises on book-keeping by accountants. Some of these are of very limited use, being directed more to recommend a favourite practice of the author in some particular branch of book-keeping, than to convey a comprehensive view of the system. The only works on the subject entitled to that character are two : one by the late Benjamin Booth, published above thirty years ago ; the other by Mr. Jones, an accountant in London, printed so lately as the present year. Booth was a man of ability, who had experience both as a merchant and a book keeper, having passed one part of his life in London, the other in New York. The reader of his work finds a great deal of information in short compass, without being perplexed either by superfluous detail or by fanciful theory.*

The form of Mr. Booth's Journal and Ledger is similar to what we have given in the preceding pages, and to the practice of our merchants for more than a century : it was by much the best work on book-keeping, until Mr. Jones devised several improvements calculated to lessen the risk of error in both Journal and Ledger. One of these improvements is the use of two columns for figures in each page of the Journal, one for the Drs., the other for the Crs. : by inserting each sum twice, the book-keeper obtains the means of proving the Journal additions page by page. The posting from the Journal to the Ledger is also simplified and rendered less subject to error by the use of these columns. In regard to the great task of balancing the Ledger, Mr. Jones's plan is to do it quarter by quarter, making use of a separate book, called a balance book, in which are inserted the totals on each side of the Ledger accounts at the end of three months. By these means the agreement of the general balance is made a matter of certainty after completing the additions. Other parts of Mr. Jones's book, viz. his *formulæ* for books on the single entry plan, and for the accounts of bankers, contain suggestions of evident utility. His volume consists of two parts : the printed part (120 pp.) containing the treatise, with directions ; and the lithographed part (140 pp.) giving copious examples in two sets of books, one kept by single, the other by double entry. If, on re-impression, the author were to divide the work, and to sell the single entry part separately from the double entry, the price of each might be moderate, and a great service would be rendered to the mercantile public.

BOOTS and **SHOES**, the external covering for the legs and feet, too well known to require any description. For an account of the value of the boots and shoes annually produced in Great Britain, see LEATHER.

BORAX, or **TINCAL** (Arab. *Buruk ;* Pers. *Tunkar*), one of the salts of soda. This salt is obtained in a crystallised state from the bottom of certain lakes in Thibet. It is found dissolved in many springs in Persia, and may be procured of a superior quality in China. It is also said to be found in Saxony and South America ; but it is more abundant in Thibet than any where else. When dug up it is in an impure state, being enveloped in a kind of fatty matter. It is then denominated tincal ; and it is not till it has been purified in Europe that it takes the name of borax. The process followed in its purification was for a long time known only to the Venetians and Hollanders. Borax is white, transparent, rather greasy in its fracture, its taste is styptic, and it conveys

* The title of the book is " A Complete System of Book-keeping, by Benjamin Booth." London, 1799, thin 4to. Printed for Grosvenor and Chater, and for the late J. Johnson, St. Paul's Churchyard.
Mr. Jones's book is entitled " The Science of Book-keeping exemplified." 4to. London, 1831. *4l.*

p of violets to a green. It readily dissolves in hot water, and swells and
bles in the fire. It is of great use as a flux for metals. The duty on borax
per pound on refined, and 3d. per ditto on unrefined) produced, in 1829,
4l. 14s. 6d. — (*Thomson's Chemistry, Ure's Dictionary, &c.*)

ORDEAUX, a large and opulent commercial city of France, situated on
Garonne, about 75 miles from its mouth, in lat. 44° 50½′ N., long. 0° 34′
Population about 100,000. The commerce of Bordeaux is very exten-
. The Garonne is a noble river, with depth of water sufficient to enable the
est ships to come up to the city, laying open, in conjunction with the Dor-
e and their tributary streams, a large extent of country. The commerce of
deaux is greatly promoted by the famous canal of Languedoc, which com-
icates with the Mediterranean. By its means Bordeaux is enabled to furnish
south of France with colonial products at a cheaper rate than Marseilles.
es, brandies, and fruits, are the staple articles of export; but the merchants
y themselves more particularly to the wine trade. Most part of their other
ness is confined to dealing upon commission; but this they conduct almost
riably on their own account. The reason they assign for this is, that the
ulties attending the purchase, racking, fining, and proper care of wines, so
o render them fit for exportation, are so very great, as to make it almost
ssible to conduct the business on any thing like the ordinary terms so as to
fy their employers. Colonial products, cotton, &c., form the principal articles
nportation.

oney is the same at Bordeaux as in other parts of France. All accounts are kept
ancs, the par of exchange being 25 fr. 20 cent. the pound sterling. See Ex-
GE.

ights and Measures.—With the exception of wines and brandies, the new or de-
system is of general application in Bordeaux, both in wholesale and retail oper-
s. See WEIGHTS and MEASURES.
ine is still sold by the ton of 4 hogsheads. The hogshead contains 30 veltes.
andy by the 50 veltes.
irits of wine by the velte.
e *velte* is an old measure of which 50 are equal to 3 $\frac{8}{10}$ hectolitres.
l is sold by weight (per 50 kilog.) 50 - - 81¾ imperial gallons.

ticles of Import.—The number of ships which arrived from countries out of Eu-
during the years 1827 and 1828 was as follows: —

		1827.	1828.
French Colonies	West Indies - -	58	61
	East Indies - -	16	10
	Senegal - -	8	10
	Hayti - -	0	12
United States of America	- -	33	38
Cuba and Spanish America	- -	71	71
East Indies, China, &c.	- -	12	20
		198	222

e ships in the European and coasting trade are not given; but the returns from
onsul show, that in 1828, 83 British ships, carrying 13,265 tons, entered Bor-

following is a note of the leading articles imported by the ships, not of Europe,
from the ship brokers' reports. There is no official account published by the
ms.

1827.	1828.			1827.	1828.	
16,094	22,748	hogshds	Cocoa	130	51	hogshds.
5,073	4,783	boxes		1,202	525	casks
312	346	tierces		34,424	12,229	sacks
1,540	1,608	casks	Pimento	1,996	342	bales
5,717	39,317	sacks	Pepper	25,498	21,698	do.,scks, &pckges
2,273	1,949	hogshds				
4,800	3,490	casks	Cinnamon	149	0	cases & serons
736	663	tierces				
38,661	27,540	sacks or bales		2,635	2,374	bundles 3 to 5 lbs

	1827.	1828.			1827.	1828.	
Cloves	543	323	casks	Raw Silk	46	0	{ cases bales
	2,997	227	bales				
Do. bruised	614	434	do.	Wool, Cash-mere }	6	0	bales
Vanilla	52	45	chests	Do. Peru	3	616	do.
Indigo	4,144	5,693	do.	Tufia (new Rum) }	1,031	460	punch
	1,143	1,568	serons				
Lac Dye	0	210	chests	Guinea BlueCloth }	122	490	bales
Campeachy & other Dye Woods }	118	152	{ parcels, quantits. unknwn.	American Hides }	47,116	15,738	single
Cochineal	1,243	·2,926	serons		109	0	bales
Anatto	680	666	casks				
Gums (difft. kinds) }	9,423	15,151	{ do., bales, & sacks	Ox Horns	10,000	21,700	
				Chinchilla	216	0	dozen
				Raw Skins	55	80	bales
Quercitron	340	116	casks	Tobacco	4,594	4,616	{ hogsh & bal
Quino	4,793	250	serons				
Bablap	512	208	bales	Cigars	170,000	80,000	
Jalap	252	717	serons		466	685	boxes
Sarsaparilla	290	230	{ do. and bales	Rattans	1,604	10,370	packe
				Quicksilver	2,739	1,990	bottle
Saltpetre	9,467	8,713	sacks	Tin, Peru & Banca }	9,759	804	bars
Saffron	0	110	bales	Lead	0	11,583	salon
Tea	670	99	chests	Copper	4,400	3,240	do.or
Rice	2,520	4,806	casks	Platina	5	10	packa
White & Yellow Wax }	460	680	{ do., scks,&c.	Gold	735	29	ingot
Curcuma	1,130	2,034	sacks		8,250	2,517	doubl
Ivory	28	70	teeth,&c.	Silver	105	51	chests
Mother of Pearl }	602	0	canisters		25	40	ingot
Cotton	9,429	7,068	{ bales & serons		23	11	{ boxes sacks
					1,559,569	3,784,231	dolla

In addition to the articles above specified, there were also received for re-exportat
considerable quantities of bar iron, utensils, and tools, from England, Spain,
Sweden; zinc from Germany; and linens from England, Holland, and Germany:
consumption, lead, tin plates, coal (as ballast), arsenic, litharge, minium, &c. fr
England; lead, steel, olive oil, liquorice paste, saffron, and saffrarum from Spa
steel from Germany; olive oil from Italy; fish, glue, and tallow, from Russia; tim
from Baltic ports; cheese, stock-fish, &c. from Holland.

Exports.— It is impossible to procure even approximative information regarding
quantities of the several articles of exportation. No reports are published by the C
toms, nor do they allow extracts of the entries outwards to be taken.

The following is a list of the species of articles exported from Bordeaux to the
ferent parts of the world:—

To Martinique and Guadaloupe — Provisions, flour, wine, brandy, and a small qu
tity of manufactured goods.

To Bourbon — Wines, provisions, cattle, furniture, coarse and fine hardwares,
fumery, silk, cotton, and linen stuffs, stationery, fashionable articles, &c.

To the United States — Wines, brandy, almonds, prunes, verdigrease, and a trif
quantity of manufactured goods.

To Spanish America, Cuba, &c. — Wines, brandy, silks, cloths, stationery, fashi
jewellery, perfumery, saddlery, &c.

To the South Seas — Wines, brandy, liqueurs, and all sorts of manufactured articl

To the East Indies and China — Wines, brandy, furniture, silver, &c.

To England — Wines, brandy, liqueurs, fruits, tartar, cream of tartar, plums, ch
nuts, walnuts, loaf-sugar to Guernsey and Jersey, clover seed, anatto, corn, flour, s
raw and dressed, corkwood and corks, vinegar, turpentine, resins, &c.

To the North of Europe — Wines, brandy, spirits of wine, tartar, cream of ta
colonial produce, loaf-sugar, molasses, &c.

Wine.—This forms the great article of export from Bordeaux. The estimated
duce of the department of the Gironde in wines of all kinds, and one year with anot
is from 220.000 to 250,000 tons; the disposal of which is, approximatively, as
lows:—

Consumed in the department	-	- about	50,000 tons
Expedited to the different parts of France		-	125,000 —
Converted into brandy	- - -	- -	25,000 —
Exported to foreign countries	- -	- -	50,000 —
			250,000 tons.

The exports to foreign countries are as follow :—

To England	- -	1,500 to 2,000 tons
Holland	- -	12,000 15,000 —
The North of Europe	27,000	34,000 —
America and India	1,000	1,200 —
		41,500 to 52,200 tons

The red wines are divided into three great classes, each of which is subdivided into
eral sorts.

Class 1. embraces the Medoc wines,
2.   Grave, and St. Emilion,
3.   common, or cargo wines.

The *first class* is composed of the " grands crus," the "crus bourgeois," and the " crus
linaires."

The " grands crus " are further distinguished as *firsts, seconds,* and *thirds.*

The *firsts* are the wines of Château Margaux, Lafitte, Latour, and Haut Brion. The
ter is properly a *Grave* wine, but it is always classed amongst the first Medocs.

The *seconds* are the wines of Rauzan, Leoville, Larose, Mouton, Gerse, &c.

The *thirds*, wines which are produced by the vineyards touching those above named,
l which differ little in quality from them.

The quantity of " grands crus " wine of the above descriptions does not exceed 3,000
s, and sells at from 1,600 fr. to 3,500 fr. per ton *on the lees.*

The " crus bourgeois " consists of the superior Margaux, St. Julien, Pauillac, St.
tephe, &c. : quantity estimated about 2,000 tons, and prices on the lees 800 fr. to
00 fr. per ton.

The " crus ordinaires," sell at 300 fr. to 700 fr. according to the year and the qua-
. Quantity, 25,000 to 35,000 tons.

The whole produce of *Medoc* is therefore about 40,000 tons.

The " grands crus " and " crus bourgeois " require four years' care and preparation
ore delivery for use, or for exportation ; and this augments their price from 30 to 35
cent.

The *second class* is composed of the red wines of *Grave* and *St. Emilion*, which are in
ater quantity, and amongst them some of a very superior quality, that are generally
ght for mixing with Medoc. The first quality of these wines sells from 800 fr. to
0 fr. per ton. The second qualities — Queyries, Montferrand, Bassans, &c.—300 fr.
00 fr.

The *third class* consists of the common or cargo wines, the greater part of which is
sumed in the country, or converted into brandy. The portion exported is sent off
year of its growth. Prices from 160 fr. to 250 fr. per ton.

The white wines of the first "crus," such as Haut-Barsac, Preignac, Beaumes, Sau-
e, &c., are only fit for use at the end of four or six years, and for exportation at
end of one or two years more. Prices on the lees vary from 800 fr. to 1500 fr.
ton.

The "grand crus," of white *Grave*, St. Briés, Carbonieux, Dulamon, &c., sell, in
d years, from 500 fr. to 800 fr.

nferior white wines 130 fr. to 400 fr. per ton.

The expenses of all kinds to the wine grower of Medoc, for the cultivation, gathering,
making his wine, and the cask, are estimated to amount, in the most favourable years,
0 fr. per hogshead, or 200 fr. per ton.

The merchants in general purchase up the finest *crus* as soon as sufficiently advanced
dge of their character ; or more frequently they are bought up for a series of years,
ther good or bad. They are transported to their cellars or "chays," in Bordeaux,
ituated and protected by surrounding houses, as to preserve a tolerably equable tem-
ture throughout the year; and in these they ripen, and undergo all the different
esses of fining, racking, mixing, &c., considered necessary to adapt them to the
rent tastes of the foreign consumers.

is pretty generally the practice to adapt the wines for the English market by a
tiful dose of the strong, full-bodied, and high flavoured wines of the Rhone ; such
ermitage, Côte Rotie, and Croze — especially the first, by which means they are

hardly cognizable by the Medoc flavour. Perhaps the principal reason for keeping these wines so long before they are used, is to give them time to acquire a homogeneous flavour, destroyed by the mixture of several different qualities. The wines shipped under the titles of Château Margaux, Lafitte, and Latour, are also mixed with the wines of the surrounding vineyards, which, from the nature of the soil, and proximity, cannot be greatly different. Other good wines are also said to enter largely into the composition of these celebrated *crus;* and those of a superior year are employed to bring up the quality of one or two bad years, so that it is easy to conceive, that the famous wines of 1811 and of the years 1815, 1819, and 1825, are not speedily exhausted. Some houses pretend to keep their wines pure; but the practice of mixing is, at any rate, very general.

The purchase of the wines, whether from the grower or merchant, is always effected through a broker. There are a few of them who have acquired a reputation for accuracy in dissecting the different flavours, and in tracing the results of the wines by certain measures of training, or treatment.

England takes off nearly half the highest priced wines, and very little of any other quality. Except in Bordeaux itself, there is but a very moderate portion of the superior Medoc consumed in France. The capital even demands only second, third, and fourth rate wines.

The Dutch, who are the largest consumers of Bordeaux wine, go more economically to work. They send vessels to the river in the wine season, with skilful supercargoes, who go amongst the growers, and purchase the wines themselves, cheaper even than a broker would do. They live on board the ship, take their own time to select, and wait often for months before their cargo is completed; but they attain their object, getting a supply of good sound wine, and at as low a rate, with all charges of shipping included, as the wine merchants can deliver it into their stores in Bordeaux. They never purchase old wine; they take only that newly made, which, being without the support of stronger bodied wines, must be consumed in the course of two or three years. They follow the same system at Bayonne, where two or three ships go annually for the white wines of Jurancon, &c.

The cargo wines are so manufactured that it is hardly possible to know of what they are composed. They are put free on board for 2*l.* per hogshead and upwards, according as they are demanded. They are such as will not bear exposure in a glass when shipping: the tasters have a small flat silver cup expressly for them. These wines are principally shipped to America and India, and some at a higher price to the north of Europe.

The principal wine merchants have agents in London, whose business is more particularly to introduce their wines to family use; and it is to that end they pay them from 300*l.* to 800*l.* for travelling expenses and entertainments, besides allowing 3 per cent., or more, on the amount of sales. They generally look out for individuals for their agents of good address, and some connection amongst the upper classes.

Brandies, and Spirits of wine. The quantity distilled in the neighbourhood of Bordeaux is estimated at about

	18,000 pieces, of 50 veltes each.	
Ditto, in the Armagnac - -	20,000	ditto
Ditto, in the Marmauduis -	8,000	ditto
	46,000 pieces, ordinary proof.	

Of this quantity, France takes off about

	23,000 pieces for consumption.	
England - -	2,500	ditto
United States -	10,000	ditto
India -	2,500	ditto
North of Europe -	5,000	ditto
	43,000 pieces, part of which of greater strength, or spirits of wine.	

Languedoc produces annually about 40,000 pieces, of 80 veltes each, the greater part of which comes to Bordeaux to be forwarded to the different ports of the north of France, or to foreign countries.

France consumes about two thirds of the above quantity; the remaining one third goes to the north of Europe.

The prices of brandy are from 130 fr. to 150 fr. per 50 veltes, ordinary proof; spirit of wine, from 4 fr. to 5 fr. per velte.

It is at the port of Formay, on the Charente, that the greatest shipments of brandy take place to England. Cognac, from which the brandy takes its name, and where the

ge distilleries, is a few leagues up the river. The quantity exported is far greater
chat is made at Cognac — the two leading distillers there (Martel, and Henessey)
; great quantities from the small cultivators. The greater part of the wines made
Angoulême, and thence down toward the sea, are of inferior quality, and fit only for
g brandy ; and so little do the prices vary, that the proprietors look upon it nearly
same light as gold. When they augment their capital by savings or profits, it
loyed in keeping a larger stock of brandy, which has the further advantage of
the interest of their capital by its improved value from age. England is said to
upwards of 6,000 pieces annually from Charente.

Bordeaux, as at Paris and Marseilles, there is a constant gambling business in
argains of spirits of wine. It is in the form of spirits of wine that nearly all
ndy consumed in France is expedited; as in this form there is a great saving
iage.

fruits exported consist almost entirely of prunes and almonds. The latter come
ally from Languedoc.

policy of the Spanish government toward her American colonies during the last
rs has been the cause of a great many very wealthy Spaniards settling in Bor-
; and their number has been still further increased by the Spaniards expelled from
o, who do not choose to employ their fortunes in their native country, or find
facilities for employing them in Bordeaux. These are in possession of the
part of the Spanish-American trade of this port, and are viewed with a very
eye by the old merchants. They have also contributed greatly to beautify
y, by employing their wealth in building, which they have done to a consider-
xtent. They have also reduced the rate of interest, and contributed to the
es of discounting bills: the Spanish houses generally discount long bills at 1½ or
ent. lower than the Bank.

deaux possesses some iron founderies, cotton factories, sugar refineries, glass
&c., but labour and living are too high to admit of its becoming a considerable ma-
uring city.

king Establishments. — There is only one banking company in Bordeaux — the
eaux Bank;" it enjoys perfect confidence, and is of great service to the mercan-
erests of the town, but is said not to be very profitable to the shareholders.

notes, payable to bearer on demand, of this bank, are of 500 and 1,000 fr., and
te freely in the town and amongst the proprietors of the surrounding country ; but,
are only convertible into cash in Bordeaux, their circulation is limited. The
t issued and in circulation at this date (1st November, 1829) is from 9 to 10
s of francs.

rate of discount is fixed by the directors, as well as the number of names which
o guarantee each bill presented for discount. The rate has been as low as 4, but
esent 5 per cent.

n bills are presented, not having the required number of names, they take, in
tee of them, public stock bonds or other effects — advancing to the extent of
f their current value.

Bank advances ¾ths of the value of gold and silver in ingots, or in foreign money,
ed with them, at the rate of 5 per cent. per annum. It also accepts in de-
iamonds, plate, and every kind of valuable property, engaging to re-deliver the
i the state received, for ¼ per cent. per quarter, or 1 per cent. per annum.
se who have accounts current with the Bank may have all their payments made,
ney received by the Bank, without fee. It allows no interest on balances, and
nakes advances either on *personal security* or on mortgage.

exchange or *money brokers* of Bordeaux follow a kind of business pretty similar
London private bankers. They receive, negotiate, and pay bills and orders, of
ouses as have accounts open with them, charging and allowing an interest on
es, which varies from 3½ to 4½ per cent. according to circumstances. They
¼ per cent. for negotiating bills, and ⅛ per cent. on all the payments they make.
re are besides, numerous capitalists who employ their spare funds in discounting
They prefer bills at long dates, and take from 3 to 6 per cent. discount, according
confidence they have in the paper presented.

re are not wanting individuals who guarantee, with their names, every sort of
oresented, taking from 5 to 60 per cent. for the risk.

omary Mode of Payment, and Length of Credit. — Colonial produce, spices, dye-
and metals, are usually sold for cash, with 3 per cent. discount. Corn, flour,
, and several other articles, are sold for net cash, without discount.
es are generally bought of the cultivators at 12 and 15 months' credit, or 6 per
iscount. When they change hands amongst the merchants, the practice is to sell
n, allowing 3 or 5 per cent. discount.

The usage is generally established in Bordeaux, to consider all paper having less thirty days to run *as cash;* and with such all payments are made, where there is n express stipulation to be paid in coin.

The following Tares are allowed on paying the Duties at the Custom-house.

Muscovado sugars	None	Coffee, in casks	12
Clayed, in casks	15 p. ct.	in sacks	3
in cases	12 p. ct.		

The importer has always the privilege of taking the real weight of the package tare.

The following are the Tares allowed on selling.

Clayed sugar, in casks	13 p. ct.	Tobacco	12
White ditto in cases	13 p. ct.	Whale and cod oil	18
Brown ditto ditto	15 p. ct.	Logwood	1
Muscovado	17 p. ct.	Green tea, in cases	20lb.
Coffee and pepper, in casks	net tare	Black ditto	22 di
in bags under 100lbs.	2lbs. p. bag	Half cases	14 di
150lbs.	3 ditto	Indigo	net
over ditto	4 ditto	4 p. ct. tret.	
in bales	7 ditto	16 p. ct. tare.	
Cotton, in round bales	4 p. ct.	Potashes	12
Cotton, in square bales	6 p. ct.		

*** The instructive details with respect to the trade of Bordeaux given above, so superior to what are to be found in any other publication, were obligingly communic by Mr. Buchannan, of the house of James Morrison and Co., who acquired his inf ation on the spot.

Operation of the French commercial System on the Trade of Bordeaux, &c. —The tra this great city has suffered severely from the short-sighted, anti-social policy o French government. This policy was first broadly laid down, and systematically a upon, by Napoleon; and we believe it would not be difficult to show that the priva it entailed on the people of the Continent powerfully contributed to accelerate downfall. But those by whom he has been succeeded, have not hitherto seen the e diency of returning to a sounder system; on the contrary, they have carried, in s respects at least, the "continental system" to an extent not contemplated by Napol Notwithstanding the vast importance to a country like France, of supplies of iron hardware at a cheap rate, that which is produced by foreigners is excluded, thou might be obtained for half the price of that which is manufactured at home. A sin line of policy has been followed as to cotton yarn, earthenware, &c. And in ord force the manufacture of sugar from the beet-root, oppressive duties have been laid, only on foreign sugar, but even on that imported from the French colonies. The o ation of this system on the commerce and industry of the country has been most chievous. By forcing France to raise, at home, articles for the production of which has no natural or acquired capabilities, the exportation, and consequently the growt those articles in the production of which she is superior to every other country, has very greatly narrowed. All commerce being bottomed on a fair principle of recipro a country that refuses to import must cease to export. By excluding foreign produc by refusing to admit the sugar of Brazil, the cottons and hardware of England iron of Sweden, the linens of Germany, and the cattle of Switzerland and Wirtember France has done all that was in her power to drive the merchants of those countries f her markets. They are not less anxious than formerly to obtain her wines, bran and silks; inasmuch, however, as commerce is merely an exchange of products, an France will accept very few of the products belonging to others, they cannot, anxious soever, maintain that extensive and mutually beneficial intercourse with they would otherwise carry on: they sell little to her, and their purchases are, of cou proportionally diminished.

This, indeed, is in all cases the necessary and inevitable effect of the prohib system. It never fails to lessen exportation to the same extent that it lessens importat so that, when least injurious, it merely substitutes one sort of industry for another — production of the article that had been obtained from the foreigner, in the place of production of that which had been sent to him as an equivalent. See COMMERCE.

France is not only extremely well situated for carrying on an extensive interco with foreign countries, but she is largely supplied with several productions, which, she to adopt a liberal commercial system, would meet with a ready and advantag sale abroad, and enable her to furnish equivalents for the largest amount of imp The superiority enjoyed by Amboyna in the production of cloves is not more dec

an that enjoyed by France in the production of wine. Her claret, burgundy, cham-
gne, and brandy, are unrivalled; and furnish, of themselves, the materials of a vast
mmerce. Indeed, the production of wine is, next to the ordinary business of agri-
lture, by far the most extensive and valuable branch of industry in France. It is
imated by the landholders and merchants of the department of the Gironde, in the
mirable *Petition et Mémoire à l'Appui*, presented by them to the Chamber of Deputies
1828, that the quantity of wine annually produced in France amounts, at an average,
about forty millions of hectolitres, or 1,060 millions of gallons; that its value is not
s than from 800 to 1,000 millions of francs, or from thirty-two to forty millions ster-
g; and that upwards of *three millions* of individuals are employed in its production.
some of the southern departments, it is of paramount importance. The population
the Gironde, exclusive of Bordeaux, amounts to 432,839 individuals, of whom no
ver than 226,000 are supposed to be directly engaged in the cultivation of the vine.
Here, then, is a branch of industry in which France has no competitor, which even
w affords employment for about a tenth part of her population, and which is suscepti-
of indefinite extension. The value of the wines, brandies, vinegars, &c. exported
m France, at an average of the three years ending with 1790, amounted to about
y-one millions of francs, or upwards of *two* millions sterling. The annual exports of
ne from Bordeaux only, exceeded 100,000 tons; and as the supply of wine might be
reased to almost any amount, France has, in this single article, the means of carrying
the most extensive and lucrative commerce. " Le gouvernement Français," says
Chaptal, in his work *Sur l'Industrie Française*, " doit les plus grands encourage-
nts à la culture des vignes, soit qu'il considère ses produits relativement à la consom-
tion interieure, soit qu'il les envisage sous le rapport de notre commerce avec l'étranger,
it il est en effet la base essentielle."

But instead of labouring to extend this great branch of industry, government has
sented to sacrifice it to the interests of the iron-founders, and the planters of Marti-
ue and Guadeloupe! We do not, indeed, imagine that they were at all aware that
h would be the effect of their policy. Theirs is only one instance, among myriads
t may be specified, to prove that ignorance in a ministry is quite as pernicious as bad
entions. The consideration, apparently not a very recondite one, that, notwithstand-
the bounty of nature, wine was not gratuitously produced in France, and could not,
refore, be exported except for an equivalent, would seem never to have occurred to
ministers of Louis and Charles X. But those whose interests were at stake, did not
to apprise them of the hollowness of their system of policy. In 1822, when the
ject for raising the duties on sugar, iron, linens, &c. was under discussion, the mer-
nts of Bordeaux, Nantes, Marseilles, and other great commercial cities, and the
e-growers of the Gironde, and some other departments, presented petitions to the
ambers, in which they truly stated, that it was a contradiction and an absurdity to
mpt selling to the foreigner, without, at the same time, buying from him; and ex-
sed their conviction, that the imposition of the duties in question would be fatal to
commerce of France, and would consequently inflict a very serious injury on the
e-growers and silk manufacturers. These representations did not, however, meet
a very courteous reception. They were stigmatised as the work of ignorant and
rested persons. The Chambers approved the policy of ministers; and in their
ur to extend and perfect it, did not hesitate deeply to injure branches of industry on
ch several millions of persons are dependent, in order that a few comparatively in-
ificant businesses, nowise suited to France, and supporting 100,000 persons, might
olstered up and protected !

he event has shown that the anticipations of the merchants were but too well
ded. There is a discrepancy in the accounts laid before the late *Commission
quête* by government, and those given in the above-mentioned *Petition et Mémoire
ppui* from the Gironde. According to the tables printed by the Commission, the
rt of wine from France is, at this moment, almost exactly the same as in 1789.
, however, plain that, had there not been some powerful counteracting cause in
ation, the export of wine ought to have been very greatly augmented. The United
es, Russia, England, Prussia, and all those countries that have at all times been the
t importers of French wines, have made prodigious advances in wealth and popu-
n since 1789; and, had the commerce with them not been subjected to injurious
ictions, there is every reason to think that their imports of French wine would have
much greater now than at any former period.

ut the truth is, that the accounts laid before the Commission are entitled to ex-
ely little credit. In so far as respects the export of wine from Bordeaux, which
always been the great market for this species of produce, the statements in the
oire à l'Appui are taken from the Custom-house returns. Their accuracy may,
fore, be depended upon, and they show an extraordinary falling off. Previously to

M

the Revolution, the exports amounted to 100,000 tons a year (*Peuchet, Statistiqu* *Elémentaire*, p. 138.); but since 1820, they have only been as follows: —

Tons.		Tons.
1820, 61,110.	1824,	39,625.
1821, 63,244.	1825,	46,314.
1822, 39,955.	1826,	48,464.
1823, 51,529.	1827,	54,492.

It is also stated (*Mémoire,* p. 33.), that a large proportion of these exports has bee made on speculation; and that the markets of Russia, the Netherlands, Hamburgh, &c are glutted with French wines, for which there is no demand. " Dans ce moment, (25th April, 1828,) it is said in the *Mémoire*, " il existe en consignation, à Hambourg 12,000 à 15,000 barriques de vin pour compte des propriétaires du departement de l Gironde, qui seront trop heureux s'ils ne perdent que leur capital."

This extraordinary decline in the foreign demand has been accompanied by a corre sponding glut of the home market, a heavy fall of prices, and the ruin of a great numbe of merchants and agriculturists.   It is estimated, that there were, in April 1828, n fewer than 600,000 tons of wine in the Gironde, for which no outlet could be found and the glut, in the other departments, is said to have been proportionally great.   Th fall in the price of wine has reacted on the vineyards, most of which have become quit unsaleable; and a total stop has been put to every sort of improvement.   Nor hav matters been in the least amended during the current year · on the contrary, they seem to be gradually getting worse.   Such is the poverty of the proprietors, that wine is now frequently seized, and sold by the revenue officers in payment of arrears of taxes; and it appears, from some late statements in the *Mémorial Bordelais* (a newspaper published at Bordeaux), that the wine so sold, has not recently fetched more, at an average, than about two thirds of the cost of its production !

Such are the effects that the restrictive system of policy has had on the wine trade o France, — on a branch of industry which, as we have already seen, employs *thre millions* of people.   It is satisfactory, however, to observe, that the landowners and mer chants are fully aware of the source of the misery in which they have been involved They know that they are not suffering from hostile or vindictive measures on the par of foreigners, but from the blind and senseless policy of their own government; tha they are victims of an attempt to counteract the most obvious principles — to mak France produce articles directly at home, which she might obtain from the foreigner i exchange for wine, brandy, &c. at a third or a fourth part of the expense they now cost *They cannot export, because they are not allowed to import.*   Hence they do not ask fo bounties and prohibitions; on the contrary, they disclaim all such quack nostrums; an demand, what can alone be useful to them, and beneficial to the country, a free com mercial system.

" Considéré en lui même," say the landowners and merchants of the Gironde, " l systeme prohibitif est *la plus déplorable des erreurs.*   La nature, dans sa variété infinie a departi à chaque contrée ses attributs particuliers; elle a imprimé sur chaque sol s veritable destination, et c'est par la diversité des produits et des besoins, qu'elle a voul unir les hommes, par un lien universel, et operer entre eux ces rapprochements, qui or produit le commerce et la civilisation.

" Quelle est la base du systeme prohibitif? Une véritable chimère, qui consiste essayer de vendre à l'étranger sans acheter de lui.

" Quelle est donc la consequence la plus immediate du systeme prohibitif, ou, e d'autres termes, du monopole? C'est que le pays qui est placé sous son empire ne pe vendre ses produits à l'étranger.   Le voilà donc refoulé dans lui même; et à l'imposs bilité de vendre ce qu'il a de trop, vient se joindre la nécessité de payer plus cher ce q lui manque.

" Notre industrie ne demandoit, pour fructifier, ni la faveur d'un monopole, ni cet foule d'artifices et des secours dont bien d'autres ont imposé le fardeau au pays.   U sage liberté commerciale, une économie politique fondée sur la nature, en rapport av sa civilisation, en harmonie avec tous les interêts véritables : telle etoit son seul besoi Livrée à son essor naturel, elle se seroit étendue d'elle même sur la France de 18 comme sur celle de 1789; elle auroit formé la plus riche branche de son agricultur elle auroit fait circuler et dans son sol natal, et dans tout le sol du royaume, une se de vie et de richesse; elle auroit encore attiré sur nos plages le commerce du monde; la France, au lieu de s'ériger avec effort en pays manufacturier, auroit reconquis, par force des choses, une superiorité incontestable comme pays agricole.

" Le systeme contraire a prevalu.

" La ruine d'un des plus importants départements de la France; la détresse d départements circonvoisins; le dépérissement général du Midi; une immense popu tion attaquée dans ses moyens d'existence; un capital enorme compromis; la persp

de ne pouvoir prelever l'impôt sur notre sol appauvri et depouillé; un préjudice
ense pour tous les départements dont nous sommes tributaires; un décroissement
le dans celles de nos consommations qui profitent au Nord; la stagnation générale
ommerce, avec tous les désastres qu'elle entraine, toutes les pertes qu'elle produit,
us les dommages ou matériels, ou politiques ou moraux, qui en sont l'inévitable
; enfin, l'anéantissement de plus en plus irréparable de tous nos anciens rapports
merciaux; les autres peuples s'enrichissant de nos pertes et développant leur systeme
nerciale sur les débris du nôtre;

Tels sont les fruits amers du systeme dont nous avons été les principales victimes."
ich is the well authenticated account, laid before the Chamber of Deputies, by 12,563
owners and merchants, of Gironde, of the *practical* operation and real effect of that
system of policy, which, extraordinary as it may seem, has been held up for imitation
e parliament of England!

ie effect of this system upon the silk trade of France, the most important branch
r *manufacturing* industry, and one in which she had long the superiority, is similar,
nardly less destructive. Her prohibitions have forced others to manufacture for
selves, so that the foreign demand for silks is rapidly diminishing. It is stated, in
vations Addressées à la Commission d'Enquéte, by the delegate of the Chamber of
merce of Lyons, that the silk manufacture is in the worst possible state. " Ce qui
surtout exciter," he observes, " la sollicitude du gouvernement, et le décider à
r dans nos vues, c'est *l'état déplorable, alarmant, de la fabrique de Lyon :* les quatre
es de 1824 à 1827 offrent sur les quatre années precedentes un deficit qui excéde
mille kilog. pour les seules expeditions d'Allemagne; l'année 1828, et l'année
ante, 1829, nous donnent une progression décroissante plus effrayante encore."
l.) It is further stated, in a Report by the manufacturers of Lyons, that there
26,000 looms employed in that city in 1824, while at present there are not more
15,000. The competition of Switzerland and England has been chiefly instru-
al in producing these effects. At Zurich, where there were only 3,000 looms em-
d in 1815, there are now more than 5,000; and at Eberfeld, where there were none
15, there are now above 1,000. Switzerland is said to have in all 10,000 looms
oyed at this moment in the manufacture of plain broad silks.

sides the injury done to the wine trade of France by her anti-commercial system,
s been much injured by the *octrois*, and other duties laid on wine when used for
consumption. These, however, have been modified since the accession of Louis
ppe; and it is reasonable to suppose, that the experience that has been afforded of
inous effects of the prohibitive system, and the more general diffusion of correct
with respect to the real sources of wealth, will at no distant period cause the
ion of such changes in the commercial legislation of France, as may render it
conducive to her interest, and more in accordance with the spirit of the age. If
ere hostile to France, we should wish her to continue the present system; but we
m being actuated by any such feelings. We are truly anxious for her prosperity,
r sake and our own; for, unless she be surrounded by Bishop Berkeley's wall of
whatever contributes to her prosperity must, in some degree, redound to the ad-
ze of her neighbours.

Vere such narrow and malignant politics to meet with success," said Mr. Hume,
g in the middle of last century, and when the prosperity of others was generally
ed with an evil eye, " we should reduce all our neighbouring nations to the same
f sloth and ignorance that prevails in Morocco and the coast of Barbary. But
vould be the consequence? They could send us no commodities; they could take
from us: our domestic commerce itself would languish for want of emulation,
le, and instruction; and we ourselves should soon fall into the same abject con-
to which we had reduced them. I shall, therefore, venture to acknowledge, that
ly as a man, but as a British subject, I pray for the flo rishing commerce of Ger-
Spain, Italy, and even France itself. I am, at least, certain that Great Britain,
l those nations, would flourish more, did their sovereigns and ministers adopt
nlarged and benevolent sentiments towards each other." — (*Essay on the Jealousy
de.*)

a more ample exposition of the nature and effects of the French commercial
i, the reader is referred to an article in the 99th Number of the Edinburgh Re-
contributed by the author of this work. Most of the foregoing statements are
from that article.

STON, a commercial city of the United States, the capital of Massachusetts,
ie largest town of New England, situated in lat 42 22' N., long. 70 59' W.
ation about 62,000. The harbour, which is excellent, has water of sufficient
to admit the largest vessels at all periods of the tide, and is accessible
hout the year. The exports consist principally of wheat, flour, and other

agricultural products, timber, fish and fish oil, coarse manufactured goods, &
The imports consist principally of cotton and woollen goods, silks, sugar, t
coffee, tobacco, wine, brandy, spices, hardware, &c.   Salem, near Boston, carr
on an extensive trade with India and China; and Nantucket, situated on a lit
island of the same name opposite to the coast of Massachusetts, is one of t
ports that are most largely engaged in the whale fishery.   There are sixty-
banks in Massachusetts, of which seventeen are at Boston.   According to t
Report on the state of those banks in January 1830, their capital stock paid
amounted to 20,420,000 dollars; bills in circulation, 4,747,784 do.; spec
987,210 do.   The rate of dividend varies from 2½ to 4 per cent.   The register
enrolled, and licensed tonnage belonging to Boston in 1828 amounted to 176,
tons, of which 45,779 tons were employed in the coasting trade, and 9,450 in t
fisheries.   The total value of the articles imported into Massachusetts in the y
ending 30th September, 1829, was 12,520,744 dollars, and the total value of
exports, during the same year, was 8,254,937 do.   In 1828, 13 British ships,
the burden of 3,793 tons, entered Boston.   In Massachusetts, and throughc
New England, the dollar passes at 6s., so that the pound sterling = 1l. 6s.
Boston currency.   See NEW YORK.   Weights and measures same as those
England.

BOTARGO, called in Provence *Bouargues*, a sausage made on the shores
the Mediterranean and the Black Sea, of the roe of the mullet.   The best con
from Tunis and Alexandria.

BOTTLES (Du. *Bottels*; Fr. *Bouteilles*; Ger. *Bouteillen*; It. *Bottig
Fiaschi*; Rus. *Bulülki*; Sp. *Botellas*; Sw. *Bouteiller*), vessels for holding liqui
They are made of glass, and are too well known to require any description.   Th
are exported in considerable quantities.

BOTTOMRY and RESPONDENTIA. — Bottomry, in commercial navi
tion, is a mortgage of the ship.   The owner or captain of a ship is, under cert
circumstances, authorised to borrow money, either to fit her out so as to ena
her to proceed on her voyage, or to purchase a cargo for the voyage, pledging
keel, or bottom of the ship (a part for the whole) in security for payment.
bottomry contracts it is stipulated, that if the ship be lost in the course of
voyage, the lender shall lose his whole money; but if the ship arrive in safety
her destination, the lender is then entitled to get back his principal, and the
terest agreed upon, however much that interest may exceed the legal ra
(*Black. Com.* book ii. cap. 30.)   The extraordinary hazard run by the lenders
money on bottomry, who in fact become adventurers in the voyage, has been he
in all countries, as justifying them in stipulating for the highest rate of interes

When the loan is not on the ship, but on the goods laden on board, whi
from their nature, must be sold or exchanged in the course of the voyage,
borrower's personal responsibility is then the principal security for the perfor
ance of the contract, which is therefore called *respondentia*.   In this consists
principal difference between bottomry and respondentia.   The one is a loan up
the ship, the other upon the goods.   The money is to be repaid to the lend
with the *marine interest*, upon the safe arrival of the ship, in the one case; and
the goods, in the other.   In all other respects, these contracts are nearly
same, and are governed by the same principles.   In the former, the ship
tackle, being hypothecated, are liable, as well as the person of the borrower;
the latter, the lender has, in general, only the personal security of the borrow

This contract, which *must always be in writing*, is sometimes made in the fo
of a deed poll, called a bill of bottomry, executed by the borrower; sometin
in the form of a bond or obligation, with a penalty.   But whatever may be
form, it must contain the names of the lender and the borrower, those of the s
and the master; the sum lent, with the stipulated marine interest; the voy
proposed, with the commencement and duration of the risk which the lende
to run.   It must show whether the money is lent upon the ship, or upon go
on board, or on both; and every other stipulation and agreement which the
ties may think proper to introduce into the contract.   (See the *Forms* at the
of this article.)

" It is obvious," says Lord Tenterden, " that a loan of money upon bottom
while it relieves the owner from many of the perils of a maritime adventure,
prives him also of a great part of the profits of a successful voyage; and, th

re, *in the place of the owners' residence*, where they may exercise their own dgment upon the propriety of borrowing money in this manner, the master of e ship is, by the maritime law of all states, precluded from doing it, so as to nd the interest of his owners without their consent. With regard to a *foreign untry*, the rule appears to be, that if the master of a vessel has occasion for oney to repair or victual his ship, or for any other purpose necessary to enable n to complete the enterprise in which she is engaged; whether the occasion ses from any extraordinary peril or misfortune, or from the ordinary course of e adventure; he may, if he cannot otherwise obtain it, borrow money on bot- nry at marine interest, and pledge the ship, and the freight to be earned in the yage, for repayment at the termination of the voyage. When this is done, the ners are never personally responsible. The remedy of the lender is against e master of the ship." — (*Law of Shipping*, part ii. c. 3.)

In bottomry and respondentia bonds the lender receives the whole of his prin- al and interest, or nothing; *he is not answerable for general or particular aver- e;* * nor will any loss by capture, if subsequently recaptured, affect his claim. this respect our law differs from that of France (*Code de Commerce*, art. 330.) d most other countries: the lenders on bottomry bonds being there subject average, as our underwriters upon policies of insurance. No loss can void a tomry contract, unless a total loss, proceeding from a peril of the sea, during e voyage, and within the time specified by the contract. If the loss happen ough any default or act of the owners or master, to which the lender was t privy, he may still recover.

There is no restriction by the law of England as to the persons to whom ney may be lent on bottomry or at *respondentia*, except in the single case of ns on the ships of foreigners trading to the East Indies, which are forbidden the 7 Geo. 1. stat. 1. c. 21. § 2.

Bottomry contracts were well known to the ancients. At Athens the rate of erest was not fixed by law; but the customary rate seems to have been about per cent. But when money was lent for a voyage, upon the security of the p and cargo, the interest on account of the superior risk encountered by the der was in most cases much higher. In voyages to the Taurica Chersonesus l Sicily, it was sometimes as high as 30 per cent. — (*Anacharsis' Travels*, vol. iv. 369. Eng. trans.) By the Rhodian law, the exaction of such high interest as sual in bottomry was declared to be illegal, unless the principal was really osed to the dangers of the sea. — (*Boeckh's Public Economy of Athens*, vol. i. 77. Eng. trans.) This principle was adopted by the Romans, who gave to tomry interest the name of *nauticum fœnus;* and has been transferred from Roman law into all modern codes.

Formerly," says Mr. Serjeant Marshall, " the practice of borrowing money on tomry and respondentia was more general in this country than it is at present. e immense capitals now engaged in every branch of commerce render such s unnecessary; and money is now seldom borrowed in this manner, but by masters of foreign ships who put into our ports in need of pecuniary assistance efit, to pay their men, to purchase provisions, &c. Sometimes officers and ers belonging to ships engaged in long voyages, who have the liberty of trad- to a certain extent, with the prospect of great profit, but without capitals of r own to employ in such trade, take up money on respondentia to make their stments; but even this, as I am informed, is now not very frequently done his country."

he term bottomry has sometimes been incorrectly applied to designate a con- t, by the terms of which the ship is not pledged as a security, but the repay- t of money, with a high premium for the risk, is made to depend upon the ess of the voyage. This, however, is plainly a loan upon a particular adven- , to be made by a particular ship, and not a loan upon the ship, and, of course, lender has only the personal security of the borrower for the due perform- e of the contract. And it seems that loans have sometimes been made in this ner, and probably also with a pledge of the ship itself, to an amount exceed- the value of the borrower's interest in the ship; and such a contract is still l in this country in all cases, except the case of ships belonging to British

Ir. Sergeant Marshall doubts this; but it was so decided by the Court of King's Bench in *Joyce v. mson*, B. R. Mich. 23 Geo. 3.

subjects bound to or from the East Indies; as to which it is enacted (19 *Geo.* &
c. 37. § 5.),

" That all sums of money lent on bottomry or at respondentia upon any ship or ships belonging
his Majesty's subjects, bound to or from the East Indies, shall be lent only on the ship, or on the me
chandise or effects laden, or to be laden, on board of such ship, and shall be so expressed in the conditio
of the bond, and the benefit of salvage shall be allowed to the lender, his agents or assigns, who alon
shall have a right to make assurance on the money so lent; and no borrower of money on bottomry
at respondentia as aforesaid, shall recover more on any assurance than the value of his interest o
the ship, or in the merchandises and effects laden on board of such ship, exclusive of the money so bor
rowed; and in case it shall appear that the value of his share in the ship, or in the merchandises an
effects laden on board, doth not amount to the full sum or sums he hath borrowed as aforesaid, such bor
rower shall be responsible to the lender for so much of the money borrowed, as he hath not laid out o
the ship, or merchandises laden thereon, in the proportion the money not laid out shall bear to the who
money lent, notwithstanding the ship and merchandises be totally lost."

Lord Tenterden says that this statute was introduced for the protection of th
trade of the East India Company; and its rules must be complied with in the cas
of bottomry by the *masters* of ships trading to the East Indies.

For a farther discussion of this subject, see *Abbott on the Law of Shipping*,
part ii. c. 3.; *Marshal on Insurance*, book ii.; and *Park on Insurance*, c. 21.

I. *Form of a Bottomry Bond.*

KNOW ALL MEN by these presents, That I, *A. B.* commander and two-thirds owner of the shi
Exeter, for myself, and *C. D.* remaining third-owner of the said ship, am held and firmly bound un
E. F. in the penal sum of *two thousand pounds* sterling, for the payment of which well and truly to b
made unto the said *E. F.* his heirs, executors, administrators, or assigns, I hereby bind myself, my heir
executors and administrators, firmly by these presents. *In witness* whereof I have hereunto set my han
and seal, this 14th day of *December*, in the year of our Lord 1796.

WHEREAS the above bound *A. B.* hath taken up and received of the said *E. F.* the full and just sum
one thousand *pounds* sterling, which sum is to run at respondentia on the block and freight of the shi
Exeter, whereof the said *A. B.* is now master, from the port or road of *Bombay* on a voyage to the po
of *London*, having permission to touch, stay at, and proceed to all ports and places within the limits
the voyage, at the rate or premium of *twenty-five per cent* (25 per cent) for the voyage. In consideratio
whereof usual risks of the seas, rivers, enemies, fires, pirates, &c. are to be on account of the said *E.*
And for the further security of the said *E. F.* the said *A. B.* doth by these presents mortgage and assig
over to the said *E. F.* his heirs, executors, administrators, and assigns, the said ship *Exeter*, and h
freight, together with all her tackle, apparel, &c. And it is hereby declared, that the said ship *Exet*
and her freight is thus assigned over for the security of the respondentia taken up by the said *A. B.* an
shall be delivered to no other use or purpose whatever, until payment of this bond is first made, with th
premium that may become due thereon.

Now THE CONDITION of this obligation is such, that if the above bound *A. B.* his heirs, executors,
administrators, shall and do well and truly pay, or cause to be paid, unto the said *E. F.* or his attorneys
London, legally authorised to receive the same, their executors, administrators, or assigns, the full an
just sum of 1,000*l.* sterling, being the principal of this bond, together with the premium which shall b
come due thereupon, at or before the expiration of *ninety* days after the safe arrival of the said ship
Exeter, at her moorings in the river *Thames*, or in case of the loss of the said ship *Exeter*, such an avera
as by custom shall have become due on the salvage, then this obligation to be void and of no effect, othe
wise to remain in full force and virtue. Having signed to three bonds of the same tenor and date, th
one of which being accomplished, the other two to be void and of no effect.

A. B. for self } (L. S.)
and *C. D.** }

Signed, sealed, and delivered, where no stamped } G. H.
paper is to be had, in the presence of } I. K.

* In this bond the occasion of borrowing the money is not expressed, but the money was in reali
borrowed to refit the ship, which being on a voyage from *Bengal* to *London* was obliged to put back
Bombay to repair. See *The* EXETER, *Whitford*, 1 Rob. A. R. 176. The occasion therefore of borrowir
the money gave the lender the security of the entire interest of the ship. But this bond, although e
pressed to be executed by the master for himself and the other part-owner, would not bind the other par
owner personally, *unless he had by a previous deed authorised the master to execute such a bond for hir*
(*Abbot on the Law of Shipping*, part iii. c. 1. § 2.)

II. *Form of a Bottomry Bill.*

TO ALL MEN TO WHOM THESE PRESENTS SHALL COME. I, *A. B.* of *Bengal*, marine
part-owner and master of the ship, called the *Exeter*, of the burthen of five hundred tons and upwar
now riding at anchor in *Table-Bay*, at the *Cape of Good Hope*, send greeting:

WHEREAS I, the said *A. B.* part-owner and master of the aforesaid ship, called the *Exeter*, now in pr
secution of a voyage from *Bengal* to the port of *London*, having put into *Table-Bay* for the purpose
procuring provision and other supplies necessary for the continuation and performance of the voya
aforesaid, am at this time necessitated to take up upon the adventure of the said ship, called the *Exete*
the sum of *one thousand pounds* sterling moneys of *Great Britain*, for setting the said ship to sea, a
furnishing her with provisions and necessaries for the said voyage, which sum *C. D.* of the *Cape of Go
Hope*, master attendant, hath at my request lent unto me, and supplied me with, at the rate of *twelve hu
dred and twenty pounds* sterling for the said *one thousand pounds*, being at the rate of *one hundred an
twenty-two pounds* for every *hundred pounds* advanced as aforesaid, during the voyage of the said sh
from *Table Bay* to *London*. Now KNOW YE, that I, the said *A. B.* by these presents, do, for me, my e
cutors and administrators, covenant and grant to and with the said *C. D.* that the said ship shall, with t
first convoy which shall offer for *England* after the date of these presents, sail and depart for the port
London, there to finish the voyage aforesaid. And I, the said *A. B.* in consideration of the sum of
thousand *pounds* sterling unto me in hand paid by the said *C. D.* at and before the sealing and deliver
these presents, do hereby bind myself, my heirs, executors and administrators, my goods and chattels, a
particularly the said ship, the tackle and apparel of the same, and also the freight of the said ship, wh
is or shall become due for the aforesaid voyage from *Bengal* to the port of *London*, to pay unto the s
C. D. his executors, administrators, or assigns, the sum of *twelve hundred and twenty pounds* of law
British money, within thirty days next after the safe arrival of the said ship at the port of *London* fr
the same intended voyage.

AND I, the said *A. B.* do, for me, my executors and administrators, covenant and grant to and with
said *C. D.*, his executors and administrators, by these presents, that I, the said *A. B.* at the time of sea

elivering of these presents, am a true and lawful part-owner and master of the said ship, and have
r and authority to charge and engage the said ship with her freight as aforesaid, and that the said
with her freight, shall at all times after the said voyage, be liable and chargeable for the payment of
id *twelve hundred and twenty pounds*, according to the true intent and meaning of these presents.
D lastly, it is hereby declared and agreed by and between the said parties to these presents, that in
the said ship shall be lost, miscarry, or be cast away before her arrival at the said port of *London*
the said intended voyage, that then the payment of the said *twelve hundred and twenty pounds* shall
e demanded, or be recoverable by the said *C. D.* his executors, administrators, or assigns, but shall
and determine, and the loss thereby be wholly borne and sustained by the said *C. D.* his executors
dministrators, and that then and from thenceforth every act, matter, and thing herein mentioned
e part and behalf of the said *A. B.* shall be void; any thing herein contained to the contrary not-
tanding.

IN WITNESS whereof the parties have interchangeably set their hands and seals to four
bonds of this tenor and date, one of which being paid, the others to be null and void.

At the *Cape of Good Hope*, this 15th day of *November*, in the year of our Lord
one thousand eight hundred and thirty.

tness, { *E. F.*
{ *G. H.*   *A. B.*   (L. S.)
{ *I. K.*

OUNTY, a term used in commerce and the arts, to signify a premium paid
overnment to the producers, exporters, or importers of certain articles, or to
e who employ ships in certain trades.

Bounties on Production are most commonly given in the view of encou-
g the establishment of some new branch of industry; or they are intended to
r and extend a branch that is believed to be of paramount importance. In
er case, however, is their utility very obvious. In all old settled and wealthy
tries, numbers of individuals are always ready to embark in every new under-
g, if it promise to be really advantageous, without any stimulus from govern-
: and if a branch of industry, already established, be really important and
ble for the country, it will assuredly be prosecuted, to the necessary extent,
ut any encouragement other than the natural demand for its produce.

ounties on Exportation and Importation. — It is enacted by the 6 Geo. 4. c. 107., that a merchant or
er claiming a bounty or drawback on goods exported, must make oath that they have been actually
ed, and have not been relanded, and are not intended to be relanded, in any part of the United
om, or in the Isle of Man (unless entered for the islands of Faro or Ferro : is further enacted, that if any goods cleared to be exported for a bounty or drawback, shall not be
xported to parts beyond the seas, or shall be relanded in any part of the United Kingdom, or in the
s of Faro or Ferro, or shall be carried to the islands of Guernsey, Jersey, Alderney, Sark, or Man,
aving been duly entered, cleared, and shipped for exportation to such islands,) such goods shall be
ed, together with the ship or ships employed in relanding or carrying them; and any person by
or by whose orders or means such goods shall have been cleared, relanded, or carried, shall forfeit
equal to treble the value of such goods. — (§§ 82—90.)

Policy of Bounties. — It was formerly customary to grant bounties on the
rtation of various articles; but the impolicy of such practice is now very
ally admitted. It is universally allowed that bounties, if they be given at all,
d be given only to the exporters of such commodities as could not be ex-
d without them. But it is plain that, by granting a bounty in such cases, we
tax the public, in order to supply the foreigner with commodities at less
they cost. A. has a parcel of goods which he cannot dispose of abroad for
han 110*l.*; but they will fetch only 100*l.* in the foreign market; and he
s and gets a bounty of 10*l.* to enable him to export them. Such is the mode
ich bounties on exportation uniformly operate; and to suppose that they
e a means of enriching the *public*, is equivalent to supposing that a shop-
r may be enriched by selling his goods for less than they cost!

t however injurious to the state, it has been pretty generally supposed that
ies on exportation are advantageous to those who produce and export the
s on which they are paid. But the fact is not so. A trade that cannot be
d on without the aid of a bounty, must be a naturally disadvantageous one.
e, by granting it, individuals are tempted to engage or continue in businesses
are necessarily very insecure, and are rarely capable of being rendered
ive; at the same time that they are prevented, by trusting to the bounty,
making those exertions they naturally would have made, had they been
d to depend entirely on superior skill and industry for the sale of their
ce. The history of all businesses carried on in this country by the aid of
es, proves that they are hardly less disadvantageous to those engaged in
than to the public.

truth of these remarks has been acknowledged by government. The
y on the exportation of corn was repealed in 1815; and the bounties on the
ation of linen and several other articles ceased in 1830.

M 4

4. *Bounties on Shipping* have principally been paid to the owners of vess
engaged in the fishery, and their influence will be treated of under the artic
HERRING FISHERY, and WHALE FISHERY.

For an account of the bounties that still exist, see the article TARIFF.

BOX-WOOD (Ger. *Buchsbaum;* Du. *Palmhout;* Fr. *Buis;* It. *Busso, Bos
Bossolo*), the wood of the box-tree (*Buxus sempervirens*), growing wild in seve
places in Great Britain. This tree was greatly admired by the ancient Roma
and has been much cultivated in modern times, on account of the facility w
which it is fashioned into different forms. Box is a very valuable wood. It
of a yellowish colour, close-grained, very hard, and heavy; it cuts better than a
other wood, is susceptible of a very fine polish, and is very durable. In con
quence, it is much used by turners, and mathematical and musical instrume
makers. It is too heavy for furniture. It is the *only* wood used by the engrav
of wood-cuts for books; and provided due care be exercised, the number of i
pressions that may be taken from a box-wood cut is very great. In France, bo
wood is extensively used for combs, knife-handles, and button-moulds; and son
times, it has been said, as a substitute for hops in the manufacture of beer. T
value of the box-wood sent from Spain to Paris is reported to amount to ab
10,000 fr. a year. In 1815, the box-trees cut down on Box-hill, near Dorki
in Surrey, produced upwards of 10,000*l.* They are now, however, become v
scarce in England. The duty on box-wood is oppressive, being 5*l.* a ton
brought from a foreign country, and 1*l.* a ton if from a British possession.
1829, this duty produced 1,526*l.* 15*s.* 3*d.* Turkey box-wood sells in the Lond
market for from 9*l.* to 14*l.* a ton, duty included.

BRAN, the thin skins or husks of corn, particularly wheat, ground, and se
rated from the corn by a sieve or boulter.

BRANDY (Ger. *Brantewein;* Du. *Brandewyn;* Fr. *Eau de vie, Brandev
It. *Aquarzente;* Sp. *Aguardiente;* Port. *Aguardente;* Rus. *Wino;* Lat. *Vin
adustum*), a spirituous and inflammable liquor, obtained by distillation fr
wine and the husks of grapes. It is prepared in most of the wine countries
Europe; but the superiority of French brandy is universally admitted. T
latter is principally distilled at Bordeaux, Rochelle, Cognac, the Isle
Rhé, Orleans, Nantes, and in Poitou, Touraine, and Anjou. That of Cognac
in the highest estimation.

Wines of all descriptions, but chiefly those that are strong and harsh (*pousse
are used in' the manufacture of brandy. The superior vintages, and those t
have most flavour, are said to make the worst brandy. It is naturally cl
and colourless. The different shades of colour which it has in commerce, ar
partly from the casks in which it is kept, but chiefly from the burnt sugar, sa
ders-wood, and other colouring matter intentionally added to it by the deal
It is said that the burnt sugar gives mellowness to the flavour of the liquor, a
renders it more palatable.

The art of distillation is believed to have been first discovered by the Arabia
From a passage in the *Testamentum Novissimum* of the famous Raymond Lu
who flourished in the thirteenth century, it would appear that the production
brandy and alcohol from wine was familiar to his contemporaries.—(p. 2. edit.
gent. 1571.) But the practice does not appear to have been introduced i
France till 1313.—(*Le Grand d'Aussi Vie privé de François*, iii. p. 64.) When f
introduced, brandy or burnt wine (*vinum adustum*) appears to have been u
principally as an antiseptic and restorative medicine; and the most extravag
panegyrics were bestowed on its virtues. It was described as a sovereign rem
in almost all the disorders of the human frame; it was commended for its effic
in comforting the memory, and strengthening the reasoning powers; it was
tolled, in short, as the elixir of life, and an infallible preservative of youth a
beauty! — (*Henderson's Hist. of Wine*, p. 24.) Dr. Henderson says that the ex
rience of later times has shown how little this eulogy was merited; but in this
is contradicted by Burke, who maintains, with equal eloquence and ingenuity, t
" the *alembic* has been a vast benefit and blessing." — (*Thoughts and Detail
Scarcity*, p. 41.)

Brandy has always formed a very prominent article in the exports of Fran
few ships sailing from Bordeaux, Rochelle, or Nantes, without taking a cer
quantity of it on board. The following is an account of the exportation

andy from France during the three years ending with 1789, and the fourteen
ars ending with 1828. (*Enquête sur les Fers*, p. 39.)

Years.				Hectolitres.
1787	-	-	-	305,638
1788	-	-	-	221,499
1789		-	-	234,500

Years.		Hectolitres.	Years.		Hectolitres.
1815	- -	154,160	1822	- -	230,186
1816	- -	137,398	1823	- -	310,059
1817	- -	61,697	1824	- -	317,347
1818	- -	99,402	1825	- -	259,937
1819	- -	231,652	1826	- -	194,110
1820	- -	253,349	1827	- -	273,574
1821	- -	153,408	1828	- -	403,207

Which, as the hectolitre is equal to 26·42 wine gallons, shows that the export-
on in 1828 was equivalent to 10,252,728 gallons.

Duties on Brandy in Great Britain and Ireland— Quantities consumed. — In nothing,
haps, has the injurious operation of oppressive duties been so strikingly exemplified
in the case of brandy. At the latter end of the seventeenth century, when the duty
brandy did not exceed 9*l.* a ton, the imports into England amounted to about 6,000
s, or 1,512,000 gallons — (*Historical and Political Remarks on the Tariff of the late
aty,* 1786, p. 113.); whereas at present, notwithstanding our vast increase in wealth
population since the period referred to, we do not import as much brandy as we did
n ! Nor is this extraordinary circumstance to be ascribed to any preference on the
t of the public to other beverages, but is wholly owing to the exorbitant duties with
ich brandy is loaded. The price of brandy in bond varies, at this moment, accord-
to quality, from 3*s.* to 5*s.* a gallon (imperial measure), while the duty is no less than
. 6*d.* Had the imposition of such a duty taken away the taste for brandy, it would
e been comparatively innocuous. But it has done no such thing. Its only effect
been to convert a trade, that might otherwise have been productive of the most ad-
tageous results, into a most prolific source of crime and demoransation. The tempt-
n to smuggle, occasioned by the exorbitancy of the duty, is too overpowering to be
nteracted by the utmost penalties of the law. All along the coasts of Kent and
sex, and the districts most favourably situated for *running spirits,* almost the whole
he labouring population are every now and then withdrawn from their ordinary em-
yments, to engage in smuggling adventures. The efforts of the revenue officers to
e foreign brandy and geneva have in innumerable instances been repelled by force.
ody and desperate contests have, in consequence, taken place. Many individuals
, but for this fiscal scourge, would have been industrious and virtuous, have become
, predatory, and ferocious; they have learned to despise the law, to execute summary
geance on its officers; and are influenced by a spirit that has been, and may be,
ed to the most dangerous purposes.
either can it be truly said that this miserable system is upheld for the sake of re-
ue. On the contrary, it is easy to show that, besides the other mischievous effects it
ils on the public, it occasions the loss of at least a million a year. In 1786, Mr. Pitt,
a wise and politic measure, took 50 per cent. from the duty on brandy and geneva;
duty on the latter has been for a lengthened period the same as that on brandy)
instead of being diminished, the revenue was increased. In 1790, when the duty
rrandy and geneva was 5*s.* the wine gallon, the quantity retained for home consump-
was 2,225,590 gallons. During the three years ending with 1803, when the duty
9*s.* 2*d.*, the quantities of brandy and geneva retained for home consumption
unted, at an average, to about 2,700,000 gallons; but during the three years
ing with 1818, when the duty had been increased to 18*s.* 10*d.* the wine gallon, the
ntities retained did not exceed 850,000 gallons, while the quantities actually
red for home consumption were considerably less ! Since then the consumption
increased with the increasing wealth of the country; but, at this moment, the
ntity consumed in Great Britain is fully 900,000 gallons less than in 1790 ! Nothing,
efore, can be more palpably erroneous than to contend that the revenue is improved by
resent system. Have we not seen the revenue derived from coffee trebled, by reducing
duty from 1*s.* 7*d.* to 6*d.* ? Have we not seen the revenue derived from British
ts greatly increased, by reducing the duty from 5*s.* 6*d.* to 2*s.* the wine gallon ?
where is the ground for supposing that the result would be different, were the
es on brandy equally reduced ? But the experience afforded by Mr. Pitt's measure,
786, is decisive as to this point. He quadrupled the consumption and increased the

revenue, by taking a half from the duty when it was a good deal less oppressive than
now?   Were a similar reduction made at present, does any one doubt that a similar re
sult would follow ?   Smuggling and adulteration would immediately cease ; our trad
with France would be very greatly extended ; and the revenue would gain, not merely
by a direct increase of duty, but indirectly by a very great diminution of the expens
of collection.

But the effect of the increase of the duties on brandy in Ireland has been still mor
extraordinary.   At an average of the three years ending with 1802, when the duty wa
7s. 3¾d. the wine gallon the average annual consumption of brandy in Ireland amounte
to 208,064 gallons, producing a nett revenue of 77,714l.   Now, mark the consequence
of *trebling* the duties.   The consumption during the last three years, notwithstandin
the population is more than doubled, did not amount, at an average, to 8,000 gallons
producing about 9,000l. a year of revenue !   Dr. Swift has shrewdly remarked, tha
in the arithmetic of the customs two and two do not always make four, but sometime
only one.   But here we have threefold duties, with between an eighth and a nint
part of the revenue, and a twenty-fifth part of the consumption !

It is surely impossible that such a system — a system evincing in every part a degre
of ignorant rapacity, to be paralleled only by that of the savages, who to get at the frui
cut down the tree — should be permitted for a much longer period to disgrace our fisca
code.   Those only who are anxious for the continuance of smuggling, with all its con
sequent crime and misery, can be hostile to a reduction of the duty on brandy.   By fixin
it at 10s. the gallon, neither the consumption of British spirits nor rum would be sensibl
affected.   The middle classes would, however, be able to use brandy, on occasion
when, perhaps, at present, they use nothing ; its clandestine importation would be pre
vented ; those engaged in smuggling would be obliged to have recourse to industriou
pursuits; and the manufacture of the abominable compounds, that are now so frequentl
substituted in its stead, would be put an end to.   It is not easy, indeed, to suggest an
measure that would be productive of so much advantage, and be attended with fewe
inconveniences.

In most of the public accounts, the imports of brandy and geneva are blended to
gether.   It would appear, too, from the note to the following account, that there are n
means of accurately distinguishing them, except since 1814.   The reader will find, i
the article SPIRITS, the account (No. 340. Sess. 1829), on which most of the previou
statements have been founded, of the quantities of brandy and geneva entered for hom
consumption, and the rates of duty upon them, in each year since 1789.   The followin
account shows the consumption of brandy, and rates of duty on it, since 1814 : —

An Account of the Number of Gallons (Imperial Measure) of Foreign Brandy entere
for Home Consumption in Great Britain and Ireland, the Rates of Duty affectin
the same, and the entire nett Produce of the Duty each Year since 1780.

Years.	Quantities retained for Home Consumption.			Net Produce of Duty (Customs and Excise).			Rates of D per Imper Gallon (Cus and Exci	
	Gt. Britain.	Ireland.	United Kingdom.	Great Britain.	Ireland.	United Kingdom.	Gt. Brit.	Ir
	Imper. Gal.	Imper. Gal.	Imper. Gal.	£ s. d.	£ s. d.	£ s. d.	£ s. d.	£
1814	500,592	7,169	507,761	581,056 1 1	6,618 12 4	587,674 13 5	1 2 6¼	0
1815	656,555	5,160	661,715	740,747 12 1	4,702 6 1	745,449 18 2	—	
1816	657,062	5,275	662,337	742,304 8 0	4,124 19 5	746,429 7 5	—	
1817	634,017	3,875	637,892	716,734 0 6	3,248 4 4	719,982 4 10	—	
1818	531,583	6,232	537,815	599,586 0 4	5,287 10 1	604,873 10 5	—	
1819	787,422	7,080	794,502	890,068 19 8	6,090 17 10	896,159 17 6	1 2 7½	
1820	842,864	6,025	848,889	956,275 16 9	5,219 8 6	961,495 5 3	—	
1821	914,630	6,001	920,631	1,034,327 17 0	5,173 19 2	1,039,501 16 2	—	
1822	1,001,607	7,308	1,008,915	1,132,416 3 5	6,414 1 10	1,138,830 5 3	—	
1823	1,083,104	17,118	1,100,222	1,225,481 19 7	14,330 1 8	1,239,812 1 3	—	1
1824	1,226,715	984	1,227,699	1,387,204 2 8	1,207 9 8	1,388,411 12 4	—	
1825	1,321,327	3,550	1,324,877	1,489,768 11 4	4,177 3 9	1,493,945 15 1	—	
1826	1,473,243	7,371	1,480,614	1,656,499 6 7	8,397 15 3	1,464,897 1 10	1 2 6	1
1827	1,313,217	7,271	1,320,488	1,471,501 12 4	8,232 5 0	1,479,733 17 4	—	
1828	1,327,929	7,556	1,335,485	1,490,793 4 2	8,629 19 10	1,499,423 4 0	—	
1829	1,301,450	8,529	1,309,979	1,460,764 17 6	9,686 17 8	1,470,451 15 2	—	
1830	(See Note below.)		1,285,967	- - -	- - -	1,443,018 5 8	—	

Note. — In consequence of the destruction of the official records by fire, no separate account can
rendered of the consumption of brandy and geneva, or the revenue derived therefrom, for the ye
prior to 1814.

The trade accounts of Great Britain and Ireland having been incorporated from the commenceme
of 1830, the particulars required by the above order for that year are stated for the United Kingdc
only.

Inspector General's Office,   WILLIAM IRVING,
Custom-House, London;   Inspector General of Imports and Expo
4th May, 1831.

egulations as to Importation, &c. — Brandy, geneva, and other foreign spirits, must be imported in casks containing not less than 40 gallons, or in cases containing not less 36 reputed quart bottles, under penalty of forfeiture. — (6 *Geo.* 4. c. 107.) They : also be imported in ships of 70 tons burden or upwards, and are not to be ex-d from a bonded warehouse except in a vessel of like tonnage, under pain of for-re. — (*Ibid.*)

it spirits in packages under the legal size may be entered by special permission of ommissioners of customs, provided the same are *bonâ fide* for private use, and larly inserted in the manifest and report, and consigned to the person for whose use are intended ; and provided the application and proof be made by such person, and y an agent. — (*Min. Customs,* 11 *July,* 1826.)

ckages containing 36 reputed quart bottles may be removed from Guernsey to a housing port in England, to be bonded for exportation only, on the parties giving ity for the due delivery of such packages to the proper officers.

randy is not to be imported except in British ships, or in ships of the country or place hich it is the product, or from which it is imported, on pain of forfeiture thereof, 00*l.* by the master of the ship. — (6 *Geo.* 4. c. 109.)

andy may be exported to Mexico, Chili, or Peru, in casks containing not less than llons each. — (*Treas. Ord.* 17 *December,* 1827.)

andy and geneva may be bottled in bonded warehouses, for exportation to British ssions in the East Indies, under the same conditions as wine and rum. See SPIRITS.

RASS (Ger. *Messing* ; Du. *Messing, Missing, Geelkoper* ; Fr. *Cuivre jaune,* on ; It. *Ottone* ; Sp. *Laton, Azofar* ; Rus. *Selenoi mjed* ; Lat. *Orichalcum, halcum*) is a factitious metal, made of copper and zinc in certain propor-. It is of a beautiful yellow colour, more fusible than copper, and not so o tarnish. It is malleable, so ductile that it may be drawn out into wire, s much tougher than copper. Its density is greater than the mean density e two metals. By calculation it ought to be 7·63 nearly, whereas it is lly 8·39 ; so that its density is increased by about one tenth. The ancients ot seem to have known accurately the difference between copper, brass, and ve. They considered brass as only a more valuable kind of copper, and fore used the word *æs* to denote either. They called copper *æs cyprium,* vards *cyprium* ; and this in process of time was converted into *cuprum.* Dr. on has proved that it was to brass they gave the name of *orichalcum.* Brass lleable when cold, unless the proportion of zinc be excessive ; but when d it becomes brittle. It may be readily turned upon the lathe ; and, indeed, s more kindly than any other metal.

ere is a vast variety in the proportions of the different species of brass used nmerce ; nor is it easy to determine whether the perfection of this alloy ds on any certain proportions of the two metals. In general, the extremes e highest and lowest proportions of zinc are from 12 to 25 parts in the 100. me of the British manufactories, the brass made contains one third its t of zinc. In Germany and Sweden the proportion of zinc varies from ifth to one fourth of the copper. The ductility of brass is not injured the proportion of zinc is highest. This metal is much used in the escape-wheels, and other nicer parts of watch-making : and bars of brass, very lly made, fetch for this purpose a high price.

e use of brass is of very considerable antiquity. Most of the ancient ge-relics are composed of various mixtures of brass with tin and other metals, re rather to be denominated bronzes. The best proportion for brass guns is be 1,000 pounds of copper, 990 pounds of tin, and 600 pounds of brass, in 12 hundred weight of metal. The best brass guns are made of malleable , not of pure copper and zinc alone ; but worse metals are used to make closer and sounder, as lead and pot-metal. — (*Thomson's Chemistry, Ency. nica, &c.*)

AZILETTO, an inferior species of Brazil wood brought from Jamaica. ne of the cheapest and least esteemed of the red-dye woods.

AZIL NUTS, or *Chestnuts of Brazil,* the fruit of the Juvia (*Bertholletia*), a majestic tree growing to the height of 100 or 120 feet, abounding on nks of the Orinoco, and in the northern parts of Brazil. The nuts are ular, having a cuneiform appearance, with sutures at each of the angles ; ell is rough and hard, and of a brownish ash colour. The kernel resembles an almond, but is larger, and tastes more like a common hazel nut ; it

contains a great deal of oil, that may be obtained by expression or otherwi
These nuts do not grow separately, or in clusters, but are contained, to t
number of from 15 to 50 or more*, in great ligneous pericarps or outer she
generally of the size of a child's head.   This outer shell is very hard and stro
so that it is rather difficult to get at the nuts, which are closely packed in ce
inside.   The natives are particularly fond of this fruit, and celebrate the harv
of the juvia with rejoicings; it is also very much esteemed in Europe.   The n
brought to this country and the Continent are chiefly exported from Para, a
form an article of considerable commercial importance.—(*Humboldt's Pers. N
vol. v. p. 538. Eng. trans.*)

BRAZIL WOOD (Fr. *Bois de Brésil ;* Ger. *Brasilienholz ;* Du. *Brasilienho*
It. *Legno del Brasile, Verzino ;* Sp. *Madera del Bresil ;* Port. *Pao Brasil*).   It h
been commonly supposed that this wood derived its name from the country
which it is principally produced.   But Dr. Bancroft has conclusively shown t
woods yielding a *red dye* were called Brazil woods long previously to the d
covery of America; and that the early voyagers gave the name of Brazil to th
part of that continent to which it is still applied, from their having ascertain
that it abounded in such woods. —(See the learned and excellent work, *Phi
sophy of Colours*, vol. ii. pp. 316—321.)

It is found in the greatest abundance, and is of the best quality, in the provin
of Pernambuco, where it is called *Pao da rainha*, or Queen's wood; but it is a
found in many other parts of the Western Hemisphere, and in the East Indi
The tree is large, crooked, and knotty; the leaves are of a beautiful red, and e
hale an agreeable odour.   Its botanical name is *Cæsalpinia Brasiletto ;* but it
called by the natives *ibiripitanga*.   Notwithstanding its apparent bulk, the bark
so thick, that a tree as large as a man's body with the bark, will not be so thi
as the leg when peeled.   When cut into chips, it loses the pale colour it befc
had, and becomes red; and when chewed, has a sweet taste.   It is used for varic
purposes by cabinet-makers, and admits of a beautiful varnish : but its princi
use is in dyeing red; and though the colour is liable to decay, yet, by mixing w
it alum and tartar, it is easily made permanent; there is also made of it, by me
of acids, a sort of liquid lake or carmine, for painting in miniature.

Brazil wood has been for many years past a royal monopoly ; its exportati
except on account of government, being prohibited under the severest penalti
Owing to the improvident manner in which it has been cut down by the gove
ment agents, it is now rarely found within several leagues of the coast.
deed, we are assured that many of the planters have privately cut down the tr
on their estates, and used the timber as fire-wood, that they might not expe
themselves to annoyance from the arbitrary and vexatious proceedings of th
functionaries.   The quantity of Brazil wood imported into this country is
inconsiderable.   Its price in the London market, exclusive of the duty (5*l.*
ton), varies from 25*l.* to 40*l.* per ton. — (*Dr. Bancroft in loc. cit. Ency. Metr
Modern Traveller*, vol. xxix. p. 87. *Malte Brun*, vol. v. p 525. Eng. ed. &c.)

BREAD, the principal article in the food of most civilised nations, consists
a paste or dough formed of the flour or meal of different sorts of grain mi
with water, and baked.   When stale dough or yeast is added to the fresh dou
to make it swell, it is said to be *leavened ;* when nothing of this sort is added, i
said to be *unleavened*.

1. *Historical Sketch of Bread*. — The President de Goguet has endeavour
with his usual sagacity and learning, to trace the successive steps by which i
probable men were led to discover the art of making bread — (*Origin of La
&c.* vol. i. pp. 95—105. Eng. trans.); but nothing positive is known on the s
ject.   It is certain, however, from the statements in the sacred writings, t
the use of unleavened bread was common in the days of Abraham —(*Gen.* c. x
v. 8.) ; and that leavened bread was used in the time of Moses, for
prohibits eating the Paschal lamb with such bread. —(*Exod.* c. xii. v.
The Greeks affirmed that Pan had instructed them in the art of making bre
but they no doubt were indebted for this art, as well as for their kno
ledge of agriculture, to the Egyptians and Phœnicians, who had early settle

---

* Humboldt says he had most frequently found from 15 to 22 nuts in each pericarp ; but De Laet,
gave the first and most accurate description of this fruit, says that the pericarp is divided int
compartments, each of which incloses from eight to twelve nuts.   (See *Humboldt in loc. cit.*)

eir country. The method of grinding corn by hand mills was practised in Egypt
d Greece from a very remote epoch; but for a lengthened period the Romans
d no other method of making flour, than by beating roasted corn in mortars.
ae Macedonian war helped to make the Romans acquainted with the arts and
finements of Greece; and Pliny mentions, that public bakers were then, for the
st time, established in Rome. — (*Hist. Nat.* lib. 18. cap. 11.). The conquests of
e Romans diffused, amongst many other useful discoveries, a knowledge of the
 of preparing bread, as practised in Rome, through the whole south of Europe.
The use of yeast in the raising of bread seems, however, from a passage of
iny (lib. 18. cap. 7.) to have been practised by the Germans and Gauls before
was practised by the Romans; the latter, like the Greeks, having leavened
eir bread by intermixing the fresh dough with that which had become stale.
ae Roman practice seems to have superseded that which was previously in use
France and Spain; for the art of raising bread by an admixture of yeast was
t practised in France in modern times, till towards the end of the seventeenth
ntury. It deserves to be mentioned, that though the bread made in this way was
cidedly superior to that previously in use, it was declared, by the faculty of
dicine in Paris, to be prejudicial to health; and the use of yeast was prohibited
der the severest penalties! Luckily, however, the taste of the public concur-
g with the interest of the bakers, proved too powerful for these absurd regula-
ns, which fell gradually into disuse; and yeast has long been, almost every-
aere, used in preference to any thing else in the manufacture of bread, to the
olesomeness and excellence of which it has not a little contributed.

The species of bread in common use in a country depends partly on the taste
the inhabitants, but more on the sort of grain suitable for its soil. But the
eriority of wheat to all other farinaceous plants in the manufacture of bread
so very great, that wherever it is easily and successfully cultivated, wheaten
ad is used to the nearly total exclusion of most others. Where, however, the
l or climate is less favourable to its growth, rye, oats, &c. are used in its stead.
very great change for the better has, in this respect, taken place in Great
tain within the last century. It is mentioned by Harrison, in his description
England (p. 168.), that in the reign of Henry VIII. the gentry had wheat
icient for their own tables, but that their *household* and poor neighbours were
ally obliged to content themselves with rye, barley, and oats. It appears from
household book of Sir Edward Coke, that, in 1596, rye bread and oatmeal formed
onsiderable part of the diet of servants even in great families, in the southern
nties. Barley bread is stated in the grant of a monopoly by Charles I., in
6, to be the usual food of the ordinary sort of people.—(*Sir F. M. Eden on
Poor*, vol. i. p. 561.) At the revolution, the wheat produced in England and
les was estimated by Mr. King and Dr. Davenant to amount to 1,750,000
rters. — (*Davenant's Works*, vol. ii. p. 217.) Mr. Charles Smith, the very
 informed author of the Tracts on the Corn Trade, originally published in
8, states, that in his time wheat had become much more generally the food of
 common people than it had been in 1689; but he adds (2d ed. p. 182.
d. 1766.), that notwithstanding this increase, some very intelligent inquirers
e of opinion, that even then not more than *half* the people of England fed
vheat. Mr. Smith's own estimate, which is very carefully drawn up, is a little
er; for taking the population of England and Wales, in 1760, at 6,000,000,
upposed that

3,750,000	were consumers of wheat.
739,000	barley.
888,000	rye.
623,000	oats.

Ir. Smith further supposed that they individually consumed, the first class,
uarter of wheat; the second, 1 quarter and 3 bushels of barley; the third,
arter and 1 bushel of rye; and the fourth, 2 quarters and 7 bushels of oats.
bout the middle of last century, hardly any wheat was used in the northern
ties of England. In Cumberland, the principal families used only a small
tity about Christmas. The crust of the goose-pie, with which almost every
 e in the county is then supplied, was, at the period referred to, almost uni-
 ly made of barley meal. — (*Eden on the Poor*, vol. i. p. 564.)
very one knows how inapplicable these statements are to the condition of

the people of England at the present time. Loaf-bread is now universally made use of in towns and villages, and almost universally in the country. Barley is no longer used, except in the distilleries and in brewing; oats are employed only in the feeding of horses; and the consumption of rye bread is comparatively inconsiderable. The produce of the wheat crops has been, at the very least, *trebled* since 1760. And if to this immense increase in the supply of wheat we add the still more extraordinary increase in the supply of butchers' meat (see art. CATTLE), the fact of a very signal improvement having taken place in the condition of the population, in respect of food, will be obvious.

But great as has been the improvement in the condition of the people of England since 1760, it is but trifling compared to the improvement that has taken place, since the same period, in the condition of the people of Scotland. At the middle of last century, Scotch agriculture was in the most depressed state; the tenants were destitute alike of capital and skill; green crops were almost wholly unknown; and the quantity of wheat that was raised was quite inconsiderable. A field of eight acres sown with this grain, in the vicinity of Edinburgh, in 1727 was reckoned so great a curiosity that it excited the attention of the whole neighbourhood! — (*Robertson's Rural Recollections*, p. 267.) But even so late as the American war, the wheat raised in the Lothians and Berwickshire did not exceed a third part of what is now grown in them; and taking the whole country at an average, it will be a moderate estimate, to say that the cultivation of wheat has increased in a *tenfold* proportion since 1780. At that period no loaf-bread was to be met with in the country places and villages of Scotland; *oat cakes* and *barley bannocks* being universally made use of. But at present the case is widely different. The upper and also the middle and lower classes in towns and villages use only wheaten bread, and even in farmhouses it is very extensively consumed. There is, at this moment, hardly a village to be met with, however limited its extent, that has not a public baker.

In many parts of England it is the custom for private families to bake their own bread. This is particularly the case in Kent, and in some parts of Lancashire. In 1804, there was not a single public baker in Manchester; and their number is still very limited.

2. *Regulations as to the Manufacture of Bread.* — Owing to the vast importance of bread, its manufacture has been subjected in most countries to various regulations, some of which have had a beneficial and others an injurious operation.

a. *Assize of Bread.* — From the year 1266, in the reign of Henry III., down to our own days, it has been customary to regulate the price at which bread should be sold according to the price of wheat or flour at the time. An interference of this sort was supposed to be necessary, to prevent that monopoly on the part of the bakers which it was feared might otherwise take place. But it is needless, perhaps, to say that this apprehension was of the most futile description. The trade of a baker is one that may be easily learned, and it requires no considerable capital to carry it on; so that were those engaged in the business in any particular town to attempt to force up prices to an artificial elevation, the combination would be immediately defeated by the competition of others; and even though this were not the case, the facility with which bread may be baked at home would of itself serve to nullify the efforts of any combination. But the assize regulations were not merely useless, they were in many respects exceedingly injurious: they rendered the price of flour a matter of comparative indifference to the baker; and they obliged the baker who used the finest flour, and made the best bread, to sell at the same rate as those who used inferior flour, and whose bread was decidedly of a worse quality. But these considerations, how obvious soever they may now appear, were for a long time entirely overlooked. According, however, as the use of loaf-bread was extended, it was found to be impracticable to set assizes in small town and villages; and notwithstanding the fewness of the bakers in such places gave them greater facilities for combining together, the price of bread was almost uniformly lower in them than in places where assizes were set. In consequence, partly of this circumstance, but still more of the increase of intelligence as to such matters, the practice of setting an assize was gradually relinquished in most places; and in 1815 it was expressly abolished, by an act of the legislature (55 *Geo.* 3. c. 99.), in London and its environs. In other places, though the power to set an assize still subsists, it is seldom acted upon, and has fallen into comparative disuse.

b. *Regulations as to the Weight, and Ingredients to be used in making Bread.* — According to the assize acts, a sack of flour weighing 280 lbs. is supposed capable of being baked into 80 quartern loaves; one fifth of the loaf being supposed to consist of water

salt, and four fifths of flour. But the number of loaves that may be made from a
of flour depends entirely on its goodness. Good flour requires more water than
flour, and old flour than new flour. Sometimes 82, 83, and even 86 loaves have
made from a sack of flour, and sometimes hardly 80.

nder the assize acts, bakers are restricted to bake only three kinds of bread, viz.
ten, standard wheaten, and household; the first being made of the finest flour, the
nd of the whole flour mixed, and the third of the coarser flour. The loaves are
ed into peck, half-peck, and quartern loaves; the legal weight of each, when baked,
, the peck loaf 17 lbs. 6 oz., the half-peck 8 lbs. 11 oz., and the quartern 4 lbs.
 avoirdupois.

w, however, it is enacted, that within the city of London, and in those places in
ountry where an assize is not set, it shall be lawful for the bakers to make and sell
made of wheat, barley, rye, oats, buckwheat, Indian corn, peas, beans, rice, or
oes, or any of them, along with common salt, pure water, eggs, milk, barm, leaven,
o or other yeast, and *mixed in such proportions as they shall think fit.*—(3 *Geo.* 4.
6. § 2. and 1 & 2 *Geo.* 4. c. 50. § 2.)

is also enacted, by the same statutes, that bakers in London, and in the country,
s, in all places ten miles from the Royal Exchange where an assize is not set, *may
and sell bread of such weight and size as they think fit,* any law or assize to the con-
notwithstanding. But it is at the same time enacted, that such bread shall always
ld by avoirdupois weight of 16 ounces to the pound, and in no other manner, under
nalty for every offence of not more than 40s.; except, however, French or fancy
, or rolls, which may be sold without previously weighing the same.

kers or sellers of bread are bound to have fixed, in some conspicuous part of their
a beam and scales, with proper weights for weighing bread; and a person pur-
ng bread may require it to be weighed in his presence. Bakers and others sending
read in carts, are to supply them with beams, scales, &c., and to weigh the bread if
red, under a penalty of not more than 5l.—(3 *Geo.* 4. c. 106. § 8.)

kers, either journeymen or masters, using alum or any other unwholesome ingre-
, and convicted on their own confession, or on the oath of one or more witnesses,
feit not exceeding 20l. and not less than 5l. if beyond the environs of London,
ot exceeding 10l. nor less than 5l. if within London or its environs. Justices
owed to publish the names of offenders. The adulteration of meal or flour is
hable by a like penalty. Loaves made of any other grain than wheat, without the
nd its liberties, or beyond ten miles of the Royal Exchange, to be marked with a
Roman M.; and every person exposing such loaves without such mark shall
 not more than 40s. nor less than 10s. for every loaf so exposed.—(1 & 2 *Geo.* 4.
§ 6.)

y ingredient or mixture found within the house, mill, stall, shop, &c. of any
, mealman, or baker, which after due examination shall be adjudged to have been
t there for the purpose of adulteration, shall be forfeited; and the person within
 premises it is found punished, if within the city of London and its environs, by a
y not exceeding 10l. nor less than 40s. for the first offence, 5l. for the second
e, and 10l. for every subsequent offence.—(3 *Geo.* 4. c. 106. § 14.) And if
ut London and its environs, the party in whose house or premises ingredients for
ration shall be found, shall forfeit for every such offence not less than 5l. and not
than 20l.—(1 & 2 *Geo.* 4. c. 5. § 8.)

ers in London and its environs are not to sell, or expose to sale, any bread, rolls,
es, nor bake or deliver any meat, pudding, pie, tart, or victuals of any sort, on
ys, except between the hours of *nine* in the morning and *one* in the afternoon,
 penalty of 10s. for the first offence, 20s. for the second offence, and 40s. for
subsequent offence.—(3 *Geo.* 4. c. 106. § 16.)

ers in the country are prohibited from selling, &c. any bread, &c., or baking or
ring any meat, &c. on Sundays, any time after half past one o'clock of the after-
f that day, or during the time of divine service, under penalty of 5s. for the first
e, 10s. for the second, and 20s. for the third and every subsequent offence.—
o. 3. c. 36. § 12.)

re are several regulations in the acts now in force with respect to the sale, &c. of
 where an assize is set; but as the practice of setting an assize is nearly relin-
d, it seems unnecessary to recapitulate them. The weight of the assize bread has
y been mentioned, and the principle on which its price is fixed.

hwithstanding the prohibition against the use of alum, it is believed to be very
lly employed, particularly by the bakers of London.—" In the metropolis," says
homson (*Suppl. to Ency. Brit.* art. *Baking*), "where the goodness of bread is
ted entirely by its whiteness, it is usual with those bakers who employ flour of an
r quality, to add as much alum as common salt to the dough; or, in other words,
antity of salt added is diminished a half, and the deficiency supplied by an equal

weight of alum.   This improves the look of the bread, rendering it much whiter a
firmer."

There are believed to be about 1700 bakers in London, Westminster, &c.   The tra
which they carry on is in general but limited, and it is not reckoned a very advantage
line of business.

BREMEN, one of the free Hanseatic cities, situated on the river Weser,
miles from its mouth, in lat. 53° 4¾' N., long. 8° 48' E.   Population about 46,0
Small ships, drawing 7 feet water, come up to the town; but larger ships lo
and unload at Vegesack, the port of Bremen, 13 miles down the river.
situation on the Weser renders Bremen the principal emporium of Hanov
Brunswick, Hesse, and other countries traversed by that river.   The charges
the buying, selling, and shipping of goods are very moderate.   The principal e
ports are linens, grain, oak bark, glass, smalts, hams, hides, rags, wool and wooll
goods, wine, &c.   The linens are mostly the same as those from Hambur
Wheat is not so good as that from the Baltic.   The imports consist of cof
sugar, and other colonial products; wines, raw cotton, cotton stuffs and ya
hardware, earthenware, brandy, tallow, tar, oil, tea, &c.

Money.—Accounts are kept here in thalers, or rix-dollars, of 72 groots or grotes;
grote being divided into 5 swares.   The Bremen rix-dollar current is worth 3s.
sterling; and the par of exchange is 1l. sterling = 6 rix-dollars, 22 grotes, 4 swares.

Weights and Measures. — The commercial pound = 2 marks = 16 ounces = 32 lo
= 7,690 English grains.   Hence, 100 lbs. of Bremen = 109·8 avoirdupois, or 49.8
kilog.   A load or pfundschwer = 300 lbs., but carriers reckon it at 308 lbs.   A cent
= 116 lbs.; a shippound = 2½ centners, or 290 lbs.; a waage of iron = 120 lbs.; a sto
of flax = 20 lbs.; a stone of wool = 10 lbs.   A ton of butter great measure = 300 lb
and a ton of do. small measure = 220 lbs.

The dry measures are

4 spints	=	1 viertel
4 viertels	=	1 scheffel
10 scheffels	=	1 quart
4 quarts	=	1 last.

The last = 80·70 bushels Winchester measure, or 10·087 quarters; that is, 10 quar
and ⁷⁄₁₀ bushel.   A barrel of salt = 3½ scheffels.   A last of coals = 2 chaldrons Ne
castle measure.

The liquid measures are

8⅝ quarts	=	1 viertel
5 viertels	=	1 anker
4 ankers	=	1 tierce
1½ tierce	=	1 oxhoft.

The oxhoft = 58 English wine gallons.   Wine is sometimes sold by the ahm o
ankers = 37¾ Eng. wine gallons.   A barrel of whale oil = 6 steckan, or 216 lbs. r
= 31½ Eng. wine gallons.   A ship last of herrings, salt, and coals = 12 barrels.
The Bremen foot = 11·38 Eng. inches: hence, 100 Bremen feet = 94⅘ Eng. di
The Bremen ell is 2 feet; and 100 ells of Bremen = 63⅓ Eng. yards.
The usual tares are, on sugar in casks and Brazil chests, 17 per cent.; on Havan
boxes, 70 lbs.; tobacco, 90 lbs. per hogshead; cotton, 4 per cent.; tea (green) 20
per quarter chest; ditto (black), 20 lbs. per quarter chest.   All other articles, suc
East India indigo, rice, coffee, spices, &c. real tare.

During the year 1829, 881 ships entered the port of Bremen.   Of these 110 w
from Britain, 66 from the United States of America, 45 from the West Indies,
from South America, 37 from France, 80 from Russia, 66 from Denmark and H
stein, 41 from Prussia, 78 from Hamburgh, 131 from the ports of Hanover,
from the Netherlands, &c.   The principal articles imported during the same year w
coffee 13½ millions of pounds, sugar 17 millions, tobacco 14 millions, rice 5 milli
cotton 1½ million.   The imports of wine amounted to about 15,000 oxhofts. —(*Bull*
des Sciences Géographiques, tom. xxiii. p. 262.)

BRIBE.   Any person offering a bribe, recompence, or reward, to any off
of the customs to induce him to neglect his duty, whether the same be accep
or not, to forfeit 500l. — (6 *Geo.* 4. c. 106. § 29.)

BRICKS AND TILES, well known articles used in the building and co
ing of houses.   They are made of baked clay and sand.   Their manufactur
placed under the control of the excise; and it is ordered by 17 Geo. 3. c.
that all bricks made in England for sale shall be 8½ inches long, 2½ inches th
and 4 wide; and all pantiles 13½ inches long, 9½ inches wide, and ½ an inch thi
on pain of forfeiting, for bricks or tiles made of less dimensions when burnt
follows, viz. 20s. for every 1,000 of bricks, and 10s. for every 1,000 of panti

d proportionally for a greater or less number. It is also provided, that the size the sieves or screens for sifting or screening sea-coal ashes to be mixed with ick earth in making bricks, shall not exceed ¼ of an inch between the meshes. akers of bricks and tiles must give notice, under a penalty of 100l., to the cise, of their intention to begin the manufacture. Tiles used in draining land e exempted from the duties.

Account of the Rates of Duty on, and Quantities of the different Species of BRICKS produced in England and Wales in 1827, 1828, and 1829.

Species.	Rates of Duty.	Quantity. 1827.	Quantity. 1828.	Quantity. 1829.
Common	5s. 10d. per 1,000	1,092,447,058	1,068,400,330	1,099,744,701
Large	10s. per do.	2,683,046	2,645,425	2,540,360
Polished	12s. 10d. per do.	8,150,750	7,769,075	7,295,366
Large Polished .	2s. 5d. per 100	98,550	122,810	110,275
	Totals	1,103,379,404	1,078,937,640	1,109,690,702

. Account of the Rates of Duty on, and Quantities of the different Species of BRICKS produced in Scotland in 1827, 1828, and 1829.

Species.	Rates of Duty.	Quantity. 1827.	Quantity. 1828.	Quantity. 1829.
Common	5s. 10d. per 1,000	20,071,337	24,281,032	24,741,582
Large	10s. per do.	255,850	406,439	396,187
Polished	12s. 10d. per do.	3,375	1,850	6,522
	Totals	20,330,562	24,689,321	25,144,291

. Account of the Rates of Duty on, and Quantities of the different Species of TILES produced in England and Wales in 1827, 1828, and 1829.

Species.	Rates of Duty.	Quantity. 1827.	Quantity. 1828.	Quantity. 1829.
Plain	5s. 8d. per 1,000	55,793,384	47,255,675	45,822,700
Pan, or Ridge	12s. 10d. per do.	26,547,787	23,666,373	22,849,815
Paving (small)	2s. 5d. per 100	5,002,859	4,375,298	4,536,504
Do. (large)	4s. 10d. per do.	1,161,377	1,112,855	1,127,073
Other Tiles	4s. 10d. per 1,000	295,750	340,875	272,625
	Totals	88,801,157	76,751,076	74,608,717

Account of the Rates of Duty on, and Quantities of the different Species of TILES produced in Scotland in 1827, 1828, and 1829.

Species.	Rates of Duty.	Quantity. 1827.	Quantity. 1828.	Quantity. 1829.
Plain	5s. 8d. per 1,000	Nil.	Nil.	1,300
Pan, or Ridge	12s. 10d. per do.	2,947,940	3,026,122	2,854,453
Paving (small)	2s. 5d. per 100	56,267	44,302	66,686
Do. (large)	4s. 10d. per do.	17,825	30,799	29,760
Other Tiles	4s. 10d. per 1,000	—	875	600
	Totals	3,022,032	3,102,098	2,952,799

Nett Produce of the Duties in 1829.

		£	s.	d.			£	s.	d.
England	Bricks	319,051	14	5	Scotland	Bricks	6,714	0	0
	Tiles	34,830	7	5		Tiles	1,922	12	0

Total nett amount of revenue from bricks and tiles in Great Britain, 362,518l. 13s. 10d.
There were, in 1830, 5,369 brick and tile manufacturers in England and Wales, and 104 in Scotland. *

The entire duties on bricks and tiles are drawn back upon exportation. Sufficient security must be given before their shipment, that they shall be shipped and exported, and not re-landed in Great Britain. (24 Geo. 3. sess. 2. c. 24. § 16.)

If bricks or tiles shipped for drawback be re-landed, the bricks or tiles so re-landed shall, over and above the penalty in the bond, be forfeited.—(§ 17.)

Return of the Number of TILES made in the Year 1830, in Great Britain ; stating the Number of each Kind, and the Rate of Duty charged per Thousand on each ; also the Gross Amount of Duty for the Year, and Amount paid for Drawback on Tiles exported ; distinguishing each Country, and the Number of Tiles exported.

	Plain.	Rate of Duty.	Pan, or Ridge.	Rate of Duty.	Small Paving.	Rate of Duty.	Large Paving.	Rate of Duty.	All other.	Rate of Duty.	Gross Am Du
		s. d.		s. d.		s. d.		s. d.		s. d.	£
England	41,707,915	5 8 ₩1000	20,603,450	12 10 ₩1000	3,972,507	2 5 ₩100	1,036,300	4 10 ₩100	399,675	4 10 ₩1000	32,438
Scotland.......	3,250	—	2,638,942	—	57,330	—	19,370	—	1,750	—	1,810
Great Britain	41,711,165	—	23,242,392	—	4,029,837	—	1,055,670	—	401,425	—	34,249

	Number of TILES exported.					
	Plain.	Pan, or Ridge.	Small Paving.	Large Paving.	All other.	Amount of Drawback.
						£ s. d.
England	17,000	734,742	126,909	143,073	1,424	975 9 5
Scotland	—	52,000	7,900	750	—	44 14 6
Great Britain	17,000	786,742	134,809	143,823	1,424	1,020 3 11

Note. — Bricks and tiles made in Ireland are not subject to excise duty.

BRIMSTONE. See SULPHUR.

BRISTLES (Fr. *Soies ;* Ger. *Borsten ;* Du. *Borstels ;* It. *Setole ;* Sp. *Cerdas Setas ;* Pol. *Szezeciny ;* Rus. *Schtschetina ;* Lat. *Setæ*), are the strong glossy hairs growing on the back of the hog and the wild boar. They are very extensively used by brushmakers, shoemakers, sadlers, &c., and form a considerable article of import. Russia is the great mart for bristles ; those of the Ukraine being held in the highest estimation. Of the total quantity imported in 1828 amounting to 1,748,921 lbs., Russia furnished 1,483,404 lbs., and Prussia (Königsberg) 209,182 lbs. The duty, which varies from 2½d. to 3½d. a pound, produced in the same year 26,822l. 16s. 8d. nett.

BROCADE (Du. *Brokade ;* Fr. *Brocade ;* Ger. *Brokat ;* It. *Broccato ;* Rus. *Partscha ;* Sp. *Brocado*), a stuff made of silk variegated with gold and silver.

BROKERS, are persons employed as middlemen to transact business or negotiate bargains between different merchants or individuals. They are sometimes licensed by public authority, and sometimes not.

Brokers are divided into different classes ; as bill or exchange brokers, stock brokers, ship and insurance brokers, pawnbrokers, and brokers simply so called, or those who sell or appraise household furniture distrained for rent. Exclusive too, of the classes now mentioned, the brokers who negotiate sales of produce between different merchants usually confine themselves to some one department or line of business ; and by attending to it exclusively, they acquire more intimate knowledge of its various details, and of the credit of those engaged in it, than could be looked for on the part of a general merchant ; and are consequently able, for the most part, to buy on cheaper and to sell on dearer terms than those less familiar with the business. It is to these circumstances—to a sense of the advantages to be derived from using their intervention in the transacting of business — that the extensive employment of brokers in London and all other large commercial cities is wholly to be ascribed.

* (Compiled from the Parliamentary Papers, No. 194. sess. 1830, and No. 354. sess. 1831.)

he number of brokers in London is unlimited; but by the statute 8 & 9 Will. 3.
. they are to be licensed by the lord mayor and aldermen, under such restrictions
limitations as they may think fit to enact. By the 57 Geo. 3. c. 60. brokers
g without being duly admitted are made liable in a penalty of 100*l.* The fee on
ssion is fixed by the same act at 5*l.*, and there is besides an annual payment also
.

e following are some of the regulations established by the mayor and aldermen
ant to the act of Will. 3. : — That every person shall, upon his admission,
an oath truly and faithfully to execute and perform the office of broker between
and party, in all things pertaining to the duty of the said office, without fraud or
sion, to the best and utmost of his skill and knowledge; — that he shall in all
reveal the name of his principal; and neither deal in goods on his own account,
arter and sell again, or make any gain in goods beyond the usual brokerage; and
he shall regularly register all the contracts, &c. into which he enters.
okers grant a bond under a penalty of 500*l.* for the faithful performance of the
s sworn to in the oath of admission.
medal is delivered to the broker, with his named engraved thereon, which he may
ce, if required, as evidence of his qualification.
velve persons professing the Jewish religion are permitted to act as brokers within
ity, under the same regulations, and receive the silver medal accordingly. This
l is transferable; and sold generally at from 800*l.* to 1,500*l.*, exclusive of the
se of transfer, which is uncertain. Upon the decease of any of the holders of
nedal without its having been transferred, the appointment falls to the lord mayor
e time being; and for it the sum of 1,500*l.* has not unfrequently been given. —
tefiore's Com. Dict. art. Brokers.)
goods in the city of London be sold by a broker, to be paid for by a bill of ex-
e, the vendor has a right, *within a reasonable time*, if he be not satisfied with the
iency of the purchaser, to annul the contract, provided he intimate his dissent as
as he has an opportunity of inquiring into the solvency of the purchaser. In a
of this sort (*Hodgson* v. *Davies*, 2 Camp. N. P. C. 536.), Lord Ellenborough
at first, rather inclined to think that the contract concluded by a broker must be
te, unless his authority were limited by writing, of which the purchaser had
. But the special jury said, that "unless the name of the purchaser has been
usly communicated to the seller, if the payment is to be by bill, the seller is
s understood to reserve to himself the power of disapproving of the sufficiency
purchaser, and annulling the contract." Lord Ellenborough allowed that this
was reasonable and valid. But he clearly thought that the rejection must be
ated as soon as the seller has had time to inquire into the solvency of the purchaser.
ury found, in the case in question, that *five* days was not too long a period for
g the necessary inquiries.
kers, Bill, — propose and conclude bargains between merchants and others in
rs of bills and exchange. They make it their business to know the state of the
nge, and the circumstances likely to elevate or depress it. They sell bills for those
g on foreign countries, and buy bills for those *remitting* to them: and, from their
edge of the mutual wants of the one class as compared with those of the other,
of the principal brokers are able to fix the rate of exchange at a fair average,
it would not be possible to do if the merchants directly transacted with each
Their charge as brokerage is 2*s.* per cent.
hose," says Mr. Windham Beawes, "who exercise the function of bill brokers,
to be men of honour and capable of their business; and the more so, as both the
and fortune of those who employ them may, in some measure, be said to be in
ands; and, therefore, they should avoid babbling, and be prudent in their office,
consists in one sole point, that is, *to hear all and say nothing*; so that they ought
to speak of the negotiations transacted by means of their intervention, or relate
report which they may have heard against a drawer, nor offer his bills to those
ve spread it."
kers, Stock, — are employed to buy and sell stock in the public funds, or in the funds
t stock companies. Their business is regulated by certain acts of parliament,
ch, among other things, it is enacted, that contracts in the nature of wagers, or
ts apparently framed for the sale or purchase of stock, but really intended only
le the parties to speculate on contingent fluctuations of the market, without any
eing actually sold, shall be void, and those engaging in them subjected to a penalty
. —(7 *Geo.* 2. c. 8., made perpetual by 10 *Geo.* 2. c. 8.) And by the same act,
e contracting to sell stock of which he is not actually possessed, or to which he
entitled, forfeits 500*l.* Brokers not keeping a book in which all contracts are
ly inserted, are liable in a penalty of 50*l.* for each omission; half to the king,
f to those who sue for it. The charge for brokerage on all public funds, except

exchequer bills and India bonds, is 2s. 6d. per cent. ; on these it is 1s. per cent.
transaction with respect to the purchase and sale of stock in the public funds ca
concluded except by the intervention of a licensed broker, unless by the parties themse

Brokers, Ship and Insurance. — The chief employment of this class of brokers
the buying and selling of ships, in procuring cargoes on freight, and adjusting the t
of charterparties, settling with the master for his salary and disbursements, &c.
charge as shipbrokers, is about 2 per cent. on the gross receipts. When they a
insurance brokers, they charge 5 per cent. on the premium, exclusive of a disc
allowed them on settling with the underwriter. The merchant looks to the broke
the regularity of the contract, and a proper selection of underwriters. To him also
underwriters look for a fair and candid disclosure of all material circumstances affec
the risk, and for payment of their premiums. From the importance of their emp
ment, ship and insurance brokers ought to be, and indeed generally are, person
respectability and honour, in whom full confidence may be reposed. A ship brok
not within the various acts for the regulation and admission of brokers. — (*Gibbor*
Rule, C. P. 27 June, 1827.)

Brokers, Custom House. — It is enacted by the 6 Geo. 4. c. 107. that no person s
be authorised to act as an agent for transacting business at the Custom-house, in
port of London, relative to the entry or clearance of any ship, &c., unless author
by licence of the commissioners of customs, who are to require bond with one su
for 1,000l., for the faithful conduct of such person and his clerks. This regulation
not, however, apply to the clerk or servant of any person or persons transacting b
ness at the Custom-house on his or their account. The commissioners may ex
this regulation to other ports.

Brokers, Pawn. See PAWNBROKERS.

Brokers, simply so called, in their character of appraisers and sellers of goods
trained for rent, are regulated by 57 Geo. 3. c. 93., which enacts, that no *such pe*
making any distress for rent, where the sum due does not exceed 20l., shall take n
than the following sums ; viz.

							£	s.	d.
For levying	-	-	-	-	-	-	0	3	0
For men keeping possession, per day			-	-	-	-	0	2	0
Advertisements, if any	-	-	-	-	-	-	0	10	0
Catalogues, sale, commission, &c. in the pound on the net produce							0	1	0
Stamp duty, lawful amount.									

Appraisements, whether by one broker or more, 6d. per pound on the value of the go
under a penalty of treble the amount of the money unlawfully taken, with costs, t
recovered summarily before a justice of the peace.

In France, the brokers who deal in money, exchange, merchandise, insurance,
stock, are called *agents de change,* and their number, at Paris, is limited to *sixty.*
company of *agents de change* is directed by a chamber of syndics (*chambre syndic*
chosen annually by the company. They are severally obliged to give bonds to
amount of 125,000 fr. for the prevention of abuses. They are also obliged to k
books; are restricted to a charge of from ⅛ to ¼ per cent. ; and are interdicted from
rying on, or having any interest in, any commercial or banking operations. — (See
de Commerce, § 74. &c.)

In the United States, brokers are not licensed, nor do they give bonds.

BROKERAGE, the commission, or per centage, paid to brokers on the sal
purchase of bills, funds, goods, &c. See FACTORAGE.

BRONZE (Ger. *Stückgut, Stükmetall;* Du. *Stückgoed;* It. *Bronzo;* Sp. *M*
de Canones; Lat. *Metallum tormentorum*) "a mixed metal, consisting chiefl
copper, with a small proportion of tin, and sometimes other metals. It is u
for casting statues, cannon, bells, and other articles, in all of which the prop
tions of the ingredients vary." — (*Dr.* Ure.)

BROOMS (Ger. *Besen;* Fr. *Balais;* It. *Scope, Granate;* Sp. *Escobas;* F
Metlii) are principally made of birch or heath. Vast quantities are manu
tured in Southwark, for the supply of the London market.

BRUSHES (Ger. *Bürsten;* Fr. *Brosses;* It. *Setole, Spazzole;* Sp. *Bro*
Cepillos, Escobillas; Rus. *Schtschetki*), well-known implements, made of bris
and manufactured of various forms.

BUBBLES, a familiar name applied generally to fraudulent or unsubstan
commercial projects, which hold out hopes of rapid gain for the purpose of
riching the projectors at the expense of sanguine and ignorant adventurers;
particularly used to designate those projects the funds for which are raised by
sale of shares or subscription to a transferable stock. In consequence of

schief produced by the gambling in transferable shares of bubble companies
the time of the South Sea project, 1719 and 1720, the stat. 6. Geo. 1. c. 18. re-
ing that several undertakings or projects had been contrived and practised,
ich "manifestly tended to the common grievance, prejudice, and inconvenience
great numbers of his Majesty's subjects in their trade and commerce," and
scribing, among other practices of the time, the ordinary mode of raising money
shares and subscriptions to a pretended transferable stock, enacted, that
e undertakings and attempts so described, and public subscriptions, assign-
nts, and transfers for furthering them, and particularly the raising or pretend-
; to raise transferable stocks without authority of charter or act of parliament,
uld be deemed illegal and void, and prohibited them under severe penalties.
me decisions limited the operation of, and finally the stat. 6 Geo. 4. c. 91. alto-
her repealed, these enactments and prohibitions. The projectors of bubbles,
refore, are now punishable only when they can be deemed guilty of frauds or
spiracies at common law; and there is no other check on the adventurers
n the loss and troublesome liabilities under the law of partnership, in which
ticipation in these projects often involves them.

BUCKRAM (Fr. *Bougran*; Ger. *Schettre, Steife Leinwand*; It. *Tela collata
ommata*; Rus. *Kleanka*; Sp. *Bucaran*), a sort of coarse cloth made of
np, gummed, calendered, and dyed several colours.

BUCKWHEAT (Fr. *Blé Sarrasin, Blé noir*; Ger. *Buchweizen, Heidekorn*; It.
ano Saraceno, Faggina, Fraina*; Sp. *Trigo Saraceno, Trigo negro*; Pol. *Tatarca,
yka, Pohanca*; Rus. *Gretscha*; Lat. *Fagopyrum*) is principally cultivated, in order
t it may be cut when young and green, and employed as fodder for cattle;
en allowed to ripen the grain is usually employed to feed pigeons and poultry.
en ripe it is of a deep yellow colour, the seeds bearing a great resemblance
beech-mast: it will grow on the poorest soils. Buckwheat has been cultivated
his country from the latter part of the sixteenth century. Its native country
unknown, but supposed to be Asia. Beckmann has a very learned dissertation
its introduction and early culture in Europe. — (See *Hist. of Invent.* vol. i. art.
ckwheat.) The average quantity of buck-wheat imported, is about 10,000
rters. The duty is the same as on barley. See CORN LAWS.

BUENOS AYRES, a city of South America, on the south side of the La
ta, about 200 miles from its junction with the sea, in lat. 34° 36½ S., long. 57°
W. Population very differently estimated; but said (*Bulletin des Sciences
graphiques*, vol. xx. p. 152.) to amount to 81,000. The La Plata is one of
largest rivers of the world, traversing a vast extent of country, of which it is
great outlet. Unluckily, however, it is of very difficult navigation, being
low, infested with rocks and sand-banks, and exposed to sudden and violent
ts of wind. There is no harbour at Buenos Ayres, or none worthy of the name.
ps can only come within two or three leagues of the town: there they unload
r goods into boats; from which they are received at the landing places into
s that convey them to the town, which is about a quarter of a league distant.
ps that want careening repair to the bay of Barragon, a kind of port about ten
ues to the S. E. of the city; and there also the outward bound ships wait for
r cargoes. All the timber used in the construction of houses, and in the
ding and repairing of vessels, comes down the river from Paraguay in rafts.
principal articles of export consist of hides and tallow, of which vast quan-
s are sent to England, the United States, Holland, Germany, &c.; besides
e there are exported bullion and viccunna wool from Peru, copper from
i, salt beef, wheat and other grain, &c. The imports principally consist of cot-
and woollen goods from England, hardware and earthenware from ditto, linens
Germany, spices, wines, salt fish, machinery, furniture, &c.: the finest tobacco,
rs, wax, &c. are brought from the interior; as is Paraguay tea, an article in
siderable demand in South America. The inland trade carried on between
nos Ayres, and Peru, and Chili, is very considerable; and its trade by sea
foreign countries is daily becoming of more importance. In 1828, sixty-four
ish ships, of the burden of 12,746 tons, entered the port; the total number
oreign vessels that annually enter it being from 300 to 400. The commerce
uenos Ayres will no doubt continue to increase according as the vast countries
ted on the La Plata, now in a great degree unoccupied, are settled.
Ionies, weights, measures, &c. same as those of Spain; for which, see CADIZ.

BUFF (Ger. *Büffel, Büffelhäute;* Du. *Buffelsleér, Buffelshuiden;* Fr. *Buffle, Peau de buffles, et Peaux passées en buffles;* It. *Bufalo, Cuojo di bufalo*), a sort of leather prepared from the skin of the buffalo, dressed with oil, after the manner of chamois. The skins of elks, oxen, and other like animals, when prepared after the same manner as that of buffalo, are likewise called *buffs.* It is used in making sword-belts and other articles, where great thickness and firmness are required.

BUGLES, small glass beads of different colours. They are in considerable demand in Africa, to which thay are mostly exported.

BULLION, uncoined gold and silver in the mass. See GOLD, and SILVER.

BUOY, a short piece of wood, or a close-hooped barrel, made of various shapes, and fastened by a rope so as to float directly over a ship's anchor, that the men who go in the boat to weigh the anchor may know where it lies.

Buoy is also a piece of wood or cork, sometimes an empty cask, strong and well closed, swimming on the surface of the water, and fastened by a chain or cord to a rock, a large stone, &c. serving to mark the dangerous places near a coast, as rocks, shoals, wrecks of vessels, anchors, &c.

By the 1 & 2 Geo. 4. c. 75. § 11. it is enacted, that if any person or persons shall wilfully cut away, cast adrift, remove, alter, deface, sink, or destroy, or in any way injure or conceal, any buoy, buoy-rope, or mark belonging to any ship or vessel, or which may be attached to any anchor or cable belonging to any ship or vessel, whether in distress or otherwise, such person or persons offending shall upon conviction be adjudged guilty of felony, and shall be liable to be transported for any term not exceeding seven years, or to be imprisoned for any number of years, at the discretion of the court.

BURDEN of a ship. See TONNAGE.

BURGUNDY. See WINE.

BURGUNDY PITCH, the produce of various species of fir. It is obtained by making incisions through the bark, when the pitch flows out and concretes in the form of flakes. The greatest quantity is collected in the neighbourhood of Neufchatel, whence it is brought to us packed in casks. A fictitious sort is made in England, and found in the shops under the title of *common* Burgundy pitch it may be distinguished by its friability, want of viscidity, and unctuosity.

BUSHEL, a measure of capacity for dry goods, as grain, fruit, dry pulse, &c containing four pecks, or eight gallons, or one eighth of a quarter.

The Winchester bushel contains 2150·42 cubic inches, while the imperial bushel contains 2218·192. Hence, to convert Winchester bushels into imperial, multiply by the fraction $\frac{2150\cdot42}{2218\cdot192}$ or ·969447, or approximately deduct $\frac{1}{30}$th, and $\frac{1}{200}$th; and if great accuracy be required, $\frac{1}{7000}$th, and $\frac{1}{20000}$th more. To convert prices per Winchester bushel into prices per imperial bushel, multiply by the fraction $\frac{2218\cdot192}{2150\cdot42}$, or 1·0315157.

By 5 Geo. 4. c. 74. § 7. the bushel shall be the standard measure of capacity for *coals, culm, lime, fish, potatoes,* or *fruit,* and all other goods and things commonly sold by heaped measure. The bushel shall contain eighty pounds, avoirdupois, of distilled water, being made round, with a plain and even bottom, and being nineteen inches and a half from outside to outside. Sections 7. and 8. direct the mode in which the bushel shall be used for heaped measure. See WEIGHTS and MEASURES.

The standard measure of capacity, by this act, as well for liquids as for dry goods not measured by heaped measure, shall be the *gallon,* containing ten pounds avoirdupois weight of distilled water weighed in air at the temperature of 62° of Fahrenheit's thermometer, the barometer being at thirty inches; and such measure shall be the imperial standard gallon (containing 277,274 cubic inches); and all measures shall be taken in parts or multiples, or certain proportions, of the said imperial standard gallon; and the quart shall be the fourth part, and the pint shall be an eighth of such standard gallon; and two such gallons shall be a peck, and eight such gallons shall be a bushel, and eight such bushels a quarter of corn or other dry goods not measured by heaped measure.

BUSS, a small sea-vessel, used by us and the Dutch in the herring fishery, commonly from 50 to 60 tons burden, and sometimes more. A buss has two small sheds or cabins; one at the prow, and the other at the stern: that at the prow serves for a kitchen, See FISHERY.

BUTLERAGE. See PRISAGE.

BUTT, a vessel or measure of wine, containing two hogsheads, or 126 wine gallons.

BUTTER (Dan. *Smör;* Du. *Boter;* Fr. *Beurre;* Ger. *Butter;* It. *Burro, Butirro,* Lat. *Butyrum;* Pol. *Maslo;* Por. *Manteiga;* Rus. *Masslo Korowe;* Sp. *Manteca,* Sw. *Smör*), as every one knows, is a fat, unctuous, and, in temperate climates, pretty firm substance, obtained from milk, or rather from cream, by the process of churning.

he various circumstances attending the introduction and use of butter in an-
ity have been investigated by Beckmann with great learning and industry.
conclusion at which he arrives is, " that butter was not used either by the
eks or Romans in cooking or the preparation of food, nor was it brought upon
tables by way of dessert, as is every where customary at present. We never
it mentioned by Galen and others as a food, though they have spoken of it
oplicable to other purposes. No notice is taken of it by Apicius; nor is there
thing said of it in that respect by the authors who treat of agriculture, though
have given us very particular information with respect to milk, cheese, and
This, as has been remarked by others, may be easily accounted for, by the
ents having accustomed themselves to the use of good oil; and in the like
ner butter is very little employed at present in Italy, Spain, Portugal, and
southern parts of France."—(*History of Inventions*, vol. ii. p. 413. Eng. ed.)
utter is very extensively used in this and most other northern countries: that
ngland and Holland is reckoned the best. In London, the butter of Epping
Cambridge is in the highest repute: the cows which produce the former, feed
ng summer in the shrubby pastures of Epping Forest; and the leaves of the
, and numerous wild plants which there abound, are supposed to improve
lavour of the butter. It is brought to market in rolls from one to two feet
, weighing a pound each. The Cambridgeshire butter is produced from cows
feed one part of the year on chalky uplands, and the other on rich meadows
ns: it is made up into long rolls like the Epping butter, and generally salted
ured before being brought to market; the London dealers, having washed it,
wrought the salt out of it, frequently sell it for Epping butter.
he butter of Suffolk and Yorkshire is often sold for that of Cambridgeshire,
hich it is little inferior. The butter of Somersetshire is thought to equal that
pping: it is brought to market in dishes containing half a pound each; out of
h it is taken, washed, and put into different forms, by the dealers of Bath and
tol. The butter of Gloucestershire and Oxfordshire is very good; it is made
half pound packs or prints, packed up in square baskets, and sent to the
lon market by waggon. The butter of the mountains of Wales and Scotland,
the moors, commons, and heaths of England, is of excellent quality when it is
erly managed; and though not equal in quantity, it often is confessedly superior,
at produced by the richest meadows.—(*Loudon's Ency. of Agriculture.*)
nsiderable quantities of butter are made in Ireland, and it forms a prominent
e in the exports of that country: generally, it is very inferior to that of Britain;
his is a consequence rather of the want of cleanliness and attention, than of
nferiority in the milk. Some of the best Irish butter brought to London,
being washed and repacked, is sold as Dorsetshire and Cambridge butter.
e salt butter of Holland is superior to that of every other country; large
ities of it are annually exported. It forms about three fourths of all the
n butter we import.
e production and consumption of butter in Great Britain is very great. The
umption in the Metropolis may, it is believed, be averaged at about one
ound per week for each individual, being at the rate of 26 lbs. a year;
upposing the population to amount to 1,450,000, the total annual con-
tion would, on this hypothesis, be 37,700,000 lbs., or 16,830 tons: but to
ay be added 4,000 tons, for the butter required for the victualling of ships
ther purposes, making the total consumption, in round numbers, 21,000
or 47,040,000 lbs., which at 10*d.* per lb. would be worth 1,960,000*l.*
e average produce per cow of the butter dairies is estimated by Mr. Marshall
lbs. a year; so that, supposing we are nearly right in the above estimates,
280,000 cows will be required to produce an adequate supply of butter for
ondon market.

consumption of butter in London has sometimes been estimated at 50,000 tons;
according to Mr. Marshall's statement, of the accuracy of which no doubt can
ertained, would require for its supply upwards of 666,000 cows! Further com-
ry on such a statement would be superfluous.

following is an Account of the Total Quantity (in Hundred Weights) of BUTTER
ed into Great Britain from Foreign Countries and Ireland, in each Year, from
nuary 1801, to 5th January 1830; distinguishing the Quantity from Ireland,
the Isles of Jersey, Guernsey, and Man, from Holland and the Netherlands,

and from all other Foreign Countries; and stating the Rate and Amount of I
in each Year paid thereon.

Years.	Quantities of Butter imported into Great Britain from Ireland.	Quantities of Butter imported into Great Britain from all Parts (except Ireland). From the Isles of Jersey, Guernsey, Alderney, and Man.	From Holland and the Netherlands.	From Germany and other Foreign Countries.	Total from all Parts, except Ireland.	Amount of Duty received in Great Britain on Foreign Butter. £	s.	d.	Rates of Duty on Foreign Butter.
	Cwts.	Cwts.	Cwts.	Cwts.	Cwts.	£	s.	d.	s. d.
1801	186,821	339	71,206	43,583	115,130	86	4	7	2 9 ℔ cwt., and 3*l.* ℔ centum ad valorem.
1802	254,248	99	84,100	8,819	93,018	-	-	-	2 9 ℔ cwt., and 3*l.* 12*s.* ℔ cen- centum ad valorem, (from 12th May)
1803	246,388	26	53,682	50,411	104,120	3	11	11	3 6¾ ℔ cwt. (from 5th July)
1804	196,037	59	100,685	25,989	126,734	960	10	5	3 11½ ℔ cwt. (from 1st June)
1805	242,441	56	64,616	32,169	96,843	4	10	2	4 0$\frac{9}{20}$ ℔ cwt. (from 5th April)
1806	261,911	143	66,544	18,968	85,657	244	12	4	4 3$\frac{37}{60}$ ℔ cwt. (from 10th May)
1807	314,386	61	68,315	18,970	87,346	2	12	1	—
1808	312,408	46	73,727	5,816	79,590	0	0	6	—
1809	317,676	36	44,061	32,185	76,283	0	19	0	4 4 ℔ cwt. (from 5th July)
1810	311,551	611	5,956	26,676	33,244	-	-	-	—
1811	353,791	359	- -	2,451	2,810	-	-	-	—
1812	311,475	27	22,415	3,451	25,894	196	4	4	—
1813	351,832	- -	the records were destroyed by fire						5 1¾ ℔ cwt. (from 15th April)
1814	315,421	1,864	96,560	17,373	115,798	7,397	13	8	—
1815	320,655	944	106,885	17,470	125,300	32,301	10	8	—
1816	280,586	327	61,753	2,062	64,143	48,737	11	5	£1 ℔ cwt. (from 5th April)
1817	305,662	258	20,279	152	20,690	20,540	10	4	—
1818	352,538	1,917	66,232	15,544	83,694	83,550	10	1	—
1819	429,614	1,256	62,498	2,295	66,050	65,836	16	4	—
1820	457,730	275	65,986	2,295	68,557	68,578	15	9	—
1821	413,088	190	99,345	16,291	115,827	115,980	12	4	—
1822	377,651	291	108,501	9,627	118,420	118,263	13	10	—
1823	466,834	387	101,549	20,394	122,331	122,164	14	10	—
1824	431,174	305	132,093	28,255	160,654	160,854	10	2	—
1825	425,670	394	160,048	118,975	279,418	263,861	19	6	—
1826	* - -	131	136,779	59,288	196,200	202,130	8	8	—
1827	- -	366	142,658	68,117	211,141	209,427	1	3	—
1828	- -	493	145,647	55,532	201,673	195,850	7	9	—
1829	-	445	116,233	31,485	148,164	147,997	4	1	—

But in B ping, ping amity Majes mitte under rity o Coun of the 3. c. 8 July, tinue quent six n the ra the treaty and f tinue in Co 25th 1814.

N. omitt *lbs.* f count are a the totals

* No account can be furnished of the quantities of butter imported from Ireland for the years s quent to 1825, the records of the trade between Great Britain and Ireland having been discontinu consequence of the regulations adopted for the purpose of giving effect to the law which placed th tercourse between the two countries on the footing of a coasting traffic.

Inspector General's Office, Custom House, London.
30th April 1830.

WILLIAM IRVING,
Inspector General of Imports and Ex

The average contract prices of the butter furnished to Greenwich Hospital 1800 to 1828, both inclusive, have been as follows: —

Years.	Prices ℔ lb.	Years.	Prices ℔ lb.	Years.	Prices ℔ lb.
	s. d.		s. d.		s.
1800 -	0 11⅛	1813 - -	1 3	1821 - -	0 8
1805 - -	0 11⅜	1814 -	1 2	1822 -	0 7
1806 -	0 11½	1815 - -	1 2	1823 - -	0 7
1807 - -	1 0⅛	1816 -	0 9½	1824 -	0 8
1808 -	1 0¼	1817 - -	0 8¾	1825 - -	0 10
1809 - -	1 1	1818 -	0 11	1826 -	0 [illegible]
1810 -	1 1⅜	1819 - -	0 11	1827 - -	0 8
1811 - -	1 2½	1820 -	0 9½	1828 -	0 [illegible]
1812 -	1 3½				

(*Parl. Papers,* Nos. 54. and 72. sess. 1830.

n order to obviate the practice of fraud in the weighing and packing of butter, different statutes have
n passed, particularly the 36 Geo. 3. c. 86., and 38 Geo. 3. c. 73., the principal regulations of which are
joined. It is very doubtful, however, whether they have been productive of any good effect. It
ght be proper, perhaps, to order the weight of the butter, exclusive of the vessel, and the dairyman's
seller's name, to be branded on the inside and outside of each vessel; but most of the other regu-
ions, especially those as to the thickness of the staves, and the weight of the vessels, seem to be
once vexatious and useless.

very cooper or other person who shall make any vessel for the packing of butter, shall make the same
good well-seasoned timber, tight and not leaky, and shall groove in the heads and bottoms thereof;
every vessel made for the packing of butter shall be a tub, firkin, or half-firkin, and no other.

very tub shall weigh of itself, including the top and bottom, not less than 11 lbs. nor more than 15 lbs.
irdupois; and neither the top nor the bottom of any such tub shall exceed in any part five eighths of
inch in thickness.

very firkin shall weigh at least 7 lbs. including the top and the bottom, which shall not exceed four
nths of an inch thick in any part.

alf-firkins to weigh not less than 4 lbs. nor more than 6 lbs. including the top and the bottom, which
ll not exceed the thickness of three eighths of an inch in any part; upon pain that the cooper or every
er person making any such vessel, in any respect contrary to the preceding directions, shall forfeit
ry such vessel and 10s.

very cooper, &c. shall brand every cask or vessel before going out of his possession, on the outside,
h his name, in legible and permanent letters, under penalty of 10s., together with the exact weight or
e thereof.

very dairyman, farmer, or seller of butter, or other person packing the same for sale, shall pack it in
sels made and marked as aforesaid, and in no other, and shall properly soak and season every such
sel; and on the inside, and on the top on the outside, shall brand his name at length, in permanent
legible letters; and shall also, with an iron, brand on the top on the outside, and on the bouge or
y of every such cask, the true weight or tare of every such vessel, when it shall have been soaked and
soned; and also, shall brand his name at length, on the bouge or body of every such vessel, across two
erent staves at least, and shall distinctly, and at length, imprint his Christian and surname upon the
of the butter in such vessel when filled, on pain of forfeiting 5l. for every default thereof.

very tub of butter shall contain, exclusive of the tare, of good and merchantable butter 84 lbs.; every
in 56 lbs.; every half-firkin 28 lbs.; and no old or corrupt butter shall be mixed, or packed in any
sel whatever, with any butter that is new and sound; nor shall any butter made of whey be packed or
ced with butter made of cream, but the respective sorts shall be packed separately, and the whole
sel shall, throughout, be of one sort and goodness; and no butter shall be salted with any great salt,
all butter shall be salted with small salt, nor shall more salt be intermixed with the butter than is
dful for its preservation, under penalty of 5l. for offending against any of these regulations.

o change, alteration, fraud, or deceit, shall be practised by any dealers or packers of butter, either
h respect to the vessel or the butter so packed, whether in respect to quantity or otherwise, under a
alty of 30l. to be imposed on every person engaged in the offence.

very cheesemonger, dealer in butter, or other person, who shall sell any tubs, firkins, or half-firkins
butter, shall deliver, in every such cask or vessel respectively, the full quantity appointed by this act,
in default thereof, shall be liable to make satisfaction to the person who shall buy the same for what
ll be wanting, according to the price for which it was sold, and shall be liable to an action for recovery
he same, with full costs of suit.

o cheesemonger, dealer in butter, &c. shall repack for sale any butter, under penalty of 5l. for every
firkin, or half-firkin, so repacked.

othing in this act shall extend to make any cheesemonger, dealer in butter, or other person, liable to
penalties for using any of the tubs, firkins, or half-firkins, after the British butter used in such
els shall have been taken thereout, for the repacking for sale of any foreign butter, who shall, before
o repack such foreign butter, entirely cut or efface the several names of the original dairyman, farmer,
eller of butter, from every such vessel, leaving the name and tare of the cooper, and the tare of the
nal dairyman, farmer, or seller, thereon; and, after the names are so effaced, shall, with an iron,
d his Christian and surname, and the words *foreign butter*, upon the bouge of every such vessel,
ss two staves at least, to denote that such butter is foreign butter.

rsons counterfeiting or forging any such names or marks, shall for every such offence forfeit 40l.

malties not exceeding 5l. to be determined by one justice, upon the evidence of one witness, and the
le shall go to the informer.

malties above 5l. to be recovered by action of debt, or information in the courts at Westminster, and
whole to the informer.

othing to extend to the packing of butter in any pot or vessel which shall not be capable of contain-
more than 1¼ lbs.

eviously to 1826, no butter could be sold in any public market in Ireland, or exported from it, with-
being previously examined and branded by a public inspector; but compliance with this regulation is
anger compulsory, but is left to the discretion of the parties.

is enacted by statute 4 Will. 3. c. 7., that every warehouse-keeper, weigher, searcher, or shipper of
er and cheese, shall receive all butter and cheese that shall be brought to him for the London cheese-
gers, and ship the same without undue preference; and shall have for his pains 2s. 6d. for every
; and if he shall, make default, he shall, on conviction before one justice, on oath of one witness, or
ession, forfeit for every firkin of butter 10s., and for every weigh of cheese 5s., half for the use of the
and half to the informer.

d every such person shall keep a book of entry of receiving and shipping the goods, on pain of 2s. 6d.
very firkin of butter and weigh of cheese.

e master of a ship refusing to take in butter or cheese before he is full laden (except it be a cheese-
ger's own ship sent for his own goods) shall forfeit for every firkin of butter refused 5s., and for every
n of cheese 2s. 6d.

is act does not extend to any warehouse in Cheshire or Lancashire.

Butter made in hot countries is generally liquid. In India it is denominated
, and is mostly prepared from the milk of buffaloes: it is usually conveyed
uppers, or bottles made of hide, each of which contains from ten to forty
ons. Ghee is an article of considerable commercial importance in many parts
ndia.

he Arabs are the greatest consumers of butter in the world. Burckhardt tells
hat it is a common practice among all classes to drink every morning a coffee
full of melted butter or ghee! and they use it in an infinite variety of other
s. The taste for it is universal; and the poorest individuals will expend half
r daily income that they may have butter for dinner, and butter in the morn-

ing. Large quantities are annually shipped from Cosseir, Souakin, and Massouah
on the west coast of the Red Sea, for Djidda and other Arabian ports. — (*Burckhardt's Travels in Nubia*, p. 440. *Travels in Arabia*, vol. i. p. 52.)

BUTTONS (Du. *Knoopen;* Fr. *Bouton;* Ger. *Knöpje;* It. *Bottoni;* Rus. *Pogo-
wizü;* Sp. *Botones*) are well known articles, serving to fasten clothes, &c. They
are manufactured of an endless variety of materials and forms.

It might have been supposed, that the manufacture of such an article as this would have been left to
be carried on according to the views and interests of those concerned, individuals being allowed to select
any sort of button they pleased. Such, however, has not been the case; and various statutes have been
passed, pointing out the kind of buttons to be worn, and the way in which they are to be made! Most of
these regulations have luckily fallen into disuse, but they still occupy a place in the statute book, and
may be enforced. The following are amongst the more prominent of these regulations : —

No person shall make, sell, or set upon any clothes, or wearing garments whatsoever, any buttons made
of cloth, serge, drugget, frieze, camblet, or any other stuff of which clothes or wearing garments are
made, or any buttons made of wood only, and turned in imitation of other buttons, on pain of forfeiting
40*s.* per dozen, for all such buttons. — (4 *Geo.* 1. c. 7.)

No tailor shall set on any buttons, or button-holes, of serge, drugget, &c. under penalty of 40*s.* for
every dozen of buttons or button-holes so made or set on.

No person shall use or wear, on any clothes, garments, or apparel whatsoever, except velvet, any
buttons or button-holes made of or bound with cloth, serge, drugget, frieze, camblet, or other stuffs
whereof clothes or woollen garments are usually made, on penalty of forfeiting 40*s.* per dozen, under a
similar penalty. — (7 *Geo.* 1. c. 22.)

To prevent the frauds which it is alleged had taken place in the manufacture of gilt and plated
buttons, an act, 36 Geo. 3. c. 6., was passed, which regulates what shall be deemed gilt and what plated
buttons ; and imposes penalties on those who order as well as on those who make any buttons with the
words " gilt " or " plated " marked upon them, except they be gilt and plated as the act directs. Inasmuch as this statute goes to obviate a fraud, it is, perhaps, expedient ; but no apology can be made for
the regulations previously alluded to, which are at once vexatious and absurd.

The importation of buttons from abroad was prohibited in the reign of Charles II. But the 6 Geo. 4.
c. 107. § 52. repealed this prohibition, and they may now be imported, for home consumption, on paying
an *ad valorem* duty.

C.

CABBAGE, a biennial plant (*Brassica,* Lin.), of which there are many
varieties. It is too well known to require any particular description: it is extensively cultivated in the vicinity of London. Sour crout, or properly *sauer kraut,*
is a very favourite dish in Germany: it consists of a fermented mass of salted
cabbage.

CABLES are strong ropes or chains, principally used in the anchoring or
mooring of ships.

1. *Rope cables* are in Europe principally manufactured of hemp; but in the East
they are very frequently made of *coir* or the fibrous part of the cocoa-nut, and in some
places, particularly on the Red Sea, of the coating of the branches of the date-tree. Hemp
cables are formed of three principal strands, every strand of three ropes, and every rope
of three twists. The twists have more or fewer threads according to the greater or less
thickness of the cable. All vessels have ready for service three cables, which are usually
designated the *sheet* cable, the *best-bower* cable, and the *small-bower* cable ; but besides
these, most ships have some spare cables. The ordinary length of a cable is from 100 to
120 fathoms. The following are the existing regulations as to the manufacture of hemp
cables and cordage.

No person shall make or sell any cordage for shipping in which any hemp is used, called short chuckings,
half clean, whale line, or other toppings, codilla, or any damaged hemp, on pain of forfeiting the same
and also treble the value thereof.

Cables, hawsers, or ropes, made of materials not prohibited by this act, and whose quality shall be
inferior to clean Petersburgh hemp, shall be deemed inferior cordage, and the same shall be distinguished
by marking on the tally, *staple* or *inferior.* Manufacturers making default herein forfeit for every hundred
weight of cordage, 10*s.*

Manufacturers are to affix their names and manufactory to new cordage before sold, under the like
forfeiture ; and putting a false name is a forfeiture of 20*l.*

Persons making cables of old and overworn stuff, containing above seven inches in compass, shall forfeit
four times the value.

Vessels belonging to British subjects, having on board foreign-made cordage, are to make entry thereof
on entering into any British port, on penalty of 20*s.* for every hundred weight. But this is not to extend
to cordage brought from the East Indies, nor to materials at present used by any vessels built abroad
before this act. — (25 *Geo.* 3. c. 56.)

2. *Iron cables.* — The application of strong iron chains or cables to the purposes of
navigation is a late and an important discovery, for which we are indebted to Captain
Samuel Brown, R.N. It is singular, indeed, that this application should not have been
made at a much earlier period. On rocky bottoms, or where coral is abundant, a
hempen cable speedily chafes, and is often quite destroyed in a few months, or perhaps
days. A striking instance of this occurred in the voyage of discovery under the orders
of M. Bougainville, who lost *six* anchors in the space of nine days, and narrowly escaped
shipwreck ; a result, says that able seaman, which would not have happened, " *si no*

ons été munis des quelques chaînes de fer. C'est une précaution que ne doivent jamais
er tous les navigateurs destinés à de pareils voyages."—(*Voyage autour du Monde,*
7. 4to ed.) The work from which this extract is taken was published in 1771; and
t was not till nearly *forty* years after, that any attempt was made practically to profit
o judicious a suggestion. The difficulties in the way of importing hemp from 1808
14, and its consequent high price, gave the first great stimulus to the manufacture
on cables.

on cables are constructed in different ways (see *Ency. Metrop.*); but they are
rmly tried by a machine, which strains them by a force greater than the absolute
gth of the hempen cable they are intended to replace. By this means the risk of
ent from defective links is effectually obviated; and there are exceedingly few
nces in which an iron cable has broken at sea. Their great weight also contri-
s to their strength, inasmuch as the impulse of the ship is checked before the cable
ought nearly to a straight line, or that the strain approaches to a maximum. Bolts
heckles are provided at every fathom or two fathoms, by striking out which the ship
if necessary, be detached from her anchors with less difficulty than a hempen cable
e cut.

en in their most defective form, iron cables are a great deal stronger than those of
; and as to durability, no sort of comparison can be made. No wonder, therefore,
they should be rapidly superseding the latter; which are now almost wholly laid
in the navy, and, to a great extent, also, in the merchant service.

ACAO, or, as it is commonly, but incorrectly, written in this country, *Cocoa*
and Sp. *Cacao;* Ger. *Kakao*), the seed, or nuts, of the cacao tree (*theobroma*
), growing in the West Indies, and in many parts of South America. It is
by Mr. Bryan Edwards, to bear some resemblance, both in size and shape,
young *blackheart cherry.* The nuts are contained in pods, much like a
mber, that proceed immediately from all parts of the body and larger
hes; each pod contains from 20 to 30 nuts, of the size of large almonds,
compactly set. The shell of the nut is of a dark brown colour, brittle,
thin; the kernel is, both internally and externally, brownish, divided into
al unequal portions, adhering together, but separating without much diffi-
; it has a light agreeable smell, and an unctuous, bitterish, rather rough, and
iar, but not ungrateful taste. The nuts should be chosen full, plump, and
ng, without any mustiness, and not worm-eaten. They yield, by expression,
at deal of oil; but they are cultivated only that they may be employed in
reparation of the excellent beverage cacao, and the manufacture of choco-
of which they form the principal ingredient. The finest cacao is said to
at of Socomusco. The principal importations are, however, derived from
araccas and Guayaquil, particularly the former. The price of the cacao
e Caraccas is, also, at an average, from 30 to 40 per cent. more valuable
that of Guayaquil.

Humboldt estimated the consumption of cacao in Europe, in 1806, at 23 millions
nds, of which from 6 to 9 millions were supposed to be consumed in Spain. The
ction of cacao had been languishing in the Caraccas for several years previously to
mmencement of the disturbances in South America; and latterly the cultivation
or other of the great staples of cotton, sugar, and coffee, seems to have been every
gaining the ascendancy. — (*Humboldt, Pers. Narrative*, vol. iv. pp. 236—247.
Trans.)

y little cacao is consumed in England; a result which we are inclined to ascribe
oppressiveness of the duties with which it has been loaded, and not to its being
able to the public taste. It is now many years since Mr. Bryan Edwards declared
e ruin of the cacao plantations, with which Jamaica once abounded, was the effect
e *heavy hand of ministerial exaction.*" — (*Hist. West Indies*, vol. ii. p. 363.) And
ountable as it may seem, this pressure has not been materially abated since. At
oment (May, 1831) Trinidad and Grenada cacao is worth in bond, in the London
t, from 24s. to 65s. a cwt., while the duty is no less than 56s., being nearly 100
nt. upon the finer qualities, and no less than 230 per cent. upon those that are
r! The duty of 7l. a cwt. on foreign cacao is of course completely prohibitory.
se duties were intended to discourage the consumption of cacao, they certainly
ad the desired effect; but if they were intended to produce revenue, their failure
en signal and complete. In 1829, the cacao entered for home consumption in
Britain amounted to only 393,715 lbs., producing a revenue of 9,742l.; not one
part, we venture to say, of what the revenue would amount to, were the duty
d from 56s. to 10s. or 12s. a cwt.

Cacao nut *husks and shells* are allowed to be imported under a duty of 18s. 8d. a cw
None of them are imported into Great Britain; but, in 1829, 244,118 lbs. were import
into Ireland, and in some of the immediately preceding years the quantity imported v
a good deal larger.   They are brought not only from the West Indies, but fr
Gibraltar and other places, being the refuse of the chocolate manufactories carried on
them.   Such, with chocolate made of flour and soap (see CHOCOLATE), are the substitu
to which the exorbitancy of the duties force us to resort!

Cacao cannot be entered as being the produce of some British possession in America, or of the Maurit
until the master of the ship by which it is imported delivers to the collector or comptroller a *certifica*
and make oath that the goods are the produce of such places. — (6 *Geo.* 4. c. 107. § 35.)   Neither shall t
be deemed to be the produce of such places, unless they be imported direct from thence. — (7 *Geo.* 4. c.
Permits are no longer required for the removal of cacao. — (9 *Geo.* 4. c. 44. § 5.)

CADIZ, the principal commercial city of Spain, situated on the Atlan
lat. 36° 32′ N., long. 6° 17¼′ W.   It is a well-built, strongly fortified city, hav
one of the finest ports in Europe.   Population about 70,000.   The trade to t
Spanish colonies used to be confined to Cadiz, and its commercial importan
has declined since their emancipation.   It was recently made a free port; that
a port where goods may be bonded without paying duty.   The exports cons
principally of wine, particularly the white wines of Xeres in the vicinity, bran
oranges and other fruits, oil, wool, quicksilver, &c.   The imports consist chie
of cotton wool and cotton goods, sugar from the Havannah, hemp, and flax, dr
fish, linens, spices, hides, cacao, bullion, coffee, hardware, earthenware, &c.
1828, 184 British ships (tonnage not stated) entered Cadiz.

Money. — The monies, weights, and measures, used at Cadiz are those of Cast
Accounts are kept by the *real* (of old plate), of which there are 10⅝ in the *peso du*
or hard dollar : and as the dollar = 4s. 3¾d., the real = 4¾d.   A real is divid
into 16 *quintos*, or 34 *maravedis*.   The *ducado de Plata*, or ducat of Plate, is wo
11 reals.

Weights and Measures. — The ordinary quintal is divided into 4 *arrobas*, or 100
of 2 marcs each : 100 lbs. Castile = 101½ lbs. avoirdupois.   The yard, or *vara* = '
English yard, or 100 varas = 92⅔ English yards.   The *cahiz*, or measure for corn
divided into 12 *fanegas*, or 144 *celeminas*, or 576 *quartillas* ; 100 cahiz's = 19·7 Win
quarters, and 5 fanegas = 1 quarter.   The *cantaro*, or *arroba*, the measure for liqui
is divided into 8 *axumbres*, and 32 *quartillos*.   There are two sorts of arrobas,
greater and the lesser : they are to each other as 32 to 25 ; the former being equa
4¼ English wine gallons, the latter to 3¾ do.   A *moyo* of wine = 16 arrobas.
botta = 30 arrobas of wine, or 38½ of oil.   A *pipe* = 27 arrobas of wine, or 34½
oil.   Hence the botta = 127½ English wine gallons, and the pipe 114¾ do.

In 1826, the Spanish government published what they termed the *Balanza Merca*
or an account of the commodities imported into, and exported from, Spain during
year.   It is a very defective document ; but as it is the best that can be obtained, i
subjoined.   The values of the articles only are given.   We have converted the su
into English money.

Note of the most considerable Articles of Importation into Spain in 1826.

	Europe, Asia, Africa, and United States of America.	From Spanish American Colonies, inclusive of the Philippines.		Europe, Asia, Africa, and United States of America.	From S nish Ar can Colo inclusi the Ph pine
	£	£		£	£
Sugar - - -	7,640	437,550	Hides - - -	120,600	4,9
Cocoa - - -	104,400	90,425	Cotton Wool - -	166,970	7,
Indigo - - -	4,770	69,030	Ditto Yarn - -	63,660	
Spices, Cinnamon £95,420			Ditto Manufactures -	430,080	
Cloves 40,100			Woollen ditto - -	91,030	
Pepper - 67,500			Hemp and Flax - -	165,760	
	204,020		Linen Manufactures -	222,870	
Wood of kinds - -	167,560	21,440	Ditto Thread - -	12,970	
Rice - - 102,270			Silk Manufactures -	106,170	
Wheat - - 8,110			Iron and Brass ditto -	108,700	
	110,380		Gold and Silver, in Coin and		
Salt Fish - -	200,560		Bars - -	81,880	15,
Coffee - - -		75,830	Earthenware - -	19,700	
Olive Oil - -	18,130		Copper - - -	12,400	2,
Butter - - 57,560			Tin - - -	11,630	
Cheese - - 17,660			Crystal and Glass Ware -	37,000	
	75,210				

Note of the most considerable Articles of Exportation from Spain in 1826.

	To Europe, Asia, Africa, and United States of America.	To Spanish American Colonies, inclusive of the Philippines.			To Europe, Asia, Africa, and United States of America.	To Spanish American Colonies, inclusive of the Philippines.
	£	£			£	£
Vines - - -	137,550	51,790		Raw Silk - -	28,890	
Fruits, Almonds £24,355				Indigo - -	11,240	
Filberts - 29,165		3,030		Silk Manufactures -	218,930	74,590
Lemons & Oranges 36,240				Wool - - -	161,650	
Raisins - 59,905				Woollen Manufactures -	12,020	
Grapes, Olives, and				Corkwood and Corks -	34,640	
Figs - 2,410				Leeches - -	19,080	
	148,075	2,645		Paper of all kinds - -	20,220	17,500
Brandy - - -	107,715	13,156		Gut, Fishing £18,480		
Olive Oil - -	7,170	6,030		for Guitars 2,500		
Saffron - - -	14,610	2,800			20,980	16,905
Lead - - -	215,360			Thread Lace - -	10,285	
Ditto Ore - -	7,765			Cast Iron - -	16,626	
Quicksilver - -	66,300			Garbanzos, Beans, & Wheat	3,980	3,600
Barilla - - -	79,290			Flour - - -		49,290

CAJEPUT OIL, the volatile oil obtained from the leaves of the cajeput tree
(*Melaleuca Leucadendron*, Lin.). This tree is common in Amboyna and other
eastern islands. The oil is obtained by distillation from the dried leaves of the
taller of two varieties. It is prepared in great quantities in Banda, and sent to
Holland in copper flasks. As it comes to us it is of a green colour, very limpid,
lighter than water, of a strong smell resembling camphor, and a strong pungent
taste. It burns entirely away without leaving any residuum. It is often adulterated with other essential oils, coloured with resin of milfoil. In the genuine
the green colour depends on the presence of copper; for, when rectified, it is
colourless. — (*Conversations Lexicon*, Amer. ed.)

CALABAR SKIN (Da. *Graaverk*; Fr. *Petit-gris*; Ger. *Grauwerk*; It. *Vaor*,
io; Rus. *Bjelka*; Sp. *Gris pequeno*; Sw. *Gravàrk*), the Siberian squirrel skin,
of various colours, used in making muffs, tippets, and trimmings for cloths.

CALABASH, a light kind of vessel formed of the shell of a gourd, emptied
and dried. The Indians both of the North and South Sea put the pearls they
are fished in calabashes, and the natives of Africa do the same by their gold
dust. They also are used as a measure in Africa.

CALAMANCO (Du. *Kallemink, Kalmink*; Fr. *Calmande, Calmandre*; It. *Du-
ante*; Rus. *Kolomenka*; Sp. *Calmaco*; Sw. *Kalmink*), a sort of wollen stuff,
manufactured in England, and the Netherlands; it has a fine gloss, and being
chequered in the warp, the checks appear only on the right side.

CALAMANDER-WOOD, is the name given to a beautiful species of wood
brought from Ceylon. It is so hard that common edge tools cannot work it, and
must be rasped and almost ground into shape. It is singularly remarkable for
variety and admixture of colours. The most prevailing is a fine chocolate,
now deepening almost into absolute black, now fading into a medium between
brown and cream colours. It arrests the eye from the rich beauty of the intermingled tints, not from any undue showiness. It takes a very high polish; and
wrought into chairs, and particularly into tables. Sir Robert Brownrigg, late
governor of Ceylon, has the doors of the dining-room of his seat in Monmouth-
shire made of calamander. It is scarce in Ceylon, and is not regularly imported;
that that is in Great Britain has been imported by private gentlemen, returning
from the colony, for their own use. It is by far the most beautiful of all the
fancy woods. The nearer it is taken from the root of the tree, the finer it is.
Milburn's Orient. Com. Lib. of Entertaining Knowledge, Vegetable Substances,
279.)

CALCUTTA, the principal city of the province of Bengal, the capital of the
British dominions in India, and the greatest emporium to the eastward of the
Cape of Good Hope; lat. 22° 23' N., long. 88° 28' E.

It is 100 miles distant from the sea, being situated on the eastern bank of the river
Hoogly, or western branch of the Ganges, the only one navigable to any considerable
distance. In 1717, Calcutta was a petty native village of paltry huts, with a few hundred inhabitants. Little more than a century later, or in 1822, the following were the
returns of the population; viz.

Christians	-	-	-	13,138
Mohammedans	-	-	-	48,162
Hindoos	-	-	-	118,203
Chinese	-	-	-	414
				179,917

A great part, however, of what may be fairly considered the population of Calcutta consisting of labourers, mechanics, and persons engaged in trade, reside at night in the suburbs, or neighbouring villages; coming into the town early in the morning to their respective employments. These have been estimated by the magistrates, on tolerably good data, at 100,000; and allowing for the increase of inhabitants which is admitted to have taken place within the last nine years, the existing population may be estimated at about 300,000. The town, excluding suburbs, extends to about four miles and a half along the bank of the river, with an average breadth inland of about a mile and a half. Fort William lies on the left bank of the river, immediately before reaching the town, in approaching it from the sea. It is a strong and a regular fortification, but so extensive that it would require a garrison of 10,000 men for its effectual defence. Calcutta possesses great natural advantages for inland navigation; all sorts of foreign produce being transported with great facility on the Ganges and its subsidiary streams to the north-western quarters of Hindostan, over a distance of at least 1000 miles, while the productions of the interior are received by the same easy channels.

The principal merchants and traders of Calcutta consist of the following classes; viz. British and other Europeans, Portuguese born in India, Armenians, Greeks, Jews, Persians from the coast of the Persian Gulf, commonly called Moguls, Parsees, Mohammedans of Hindostan, and Hindoos; the latter usually either of the Braminical or mercantile castes, and natives of Bengal. In 1813, the total number of adult male British subjects, in the Bengal provinces (the great majority being in Calcutta), engaged in trade or agriculture, was 1,225; in 1830, it was 1,707. This is the statement given by the printed register; but it is probably much underrated, particularly for the last year. The native Portuguese and Armenian merchants have of late greatly declined in wealth and importance. On the other hand, the Persian merchants have increased in number and wealth, several of them being worth 250,000*l.* sterling. The large fortunes of the Hindoo merchants have been much broken down of late years by litigation in the courts, and naturally through the law of equal co-parcenary among brothers. To counterbalance this, there has been, since the opening of the free trade in 1814, a vast augmentation of the number of inferior merchants, worth from 20,000*l.* to 50,000*l.* sterling. There are very few Hindoo merchants at present whose wealth exceeds half a million sterling.

The principal foreign business is conducted by the English merchants; but the other parties also, either in partnership with the English, or on their own account, speculate largely to Europe, America, and especially to China. The brokers known under the name of Sircars and Baboos are all Hindoos. The general rates of agency-commission are as follow:—

1. On the sale or purchase of ships, vessels, houses, and lands - - - - 2½ per cent.
2. On the sale, purchase, or shipment of bullion - - - - - - ¼ do.
   Do. of jewellery, diamonds, or other precious stones - - - - - 2 do.
   Do. of indigo, lac-dye, country piece goods, silk, opium, cochineal, coral, spices, coffee, copper, tin, and tutenague - - - 2½ do.
   Do. of all other kinds of goods - - - - - - - - 5 do.
3. On goods or treasure, &c. consigned, and afterwards withdrawn or sent to auction; and on goods consigned for conditional delivery to others - - - - ½ commission
4. On all advances of money for the purposes of trade, whether the goods are consigned to the agent or not, and where a commission of 5 per cent. is not charged - - 2½ per cent.
5. On ordering goods, or superintending the fulfilment of contracts, where no other commission is derived - - - - - - - - - - 2½ do.
6. On guaranteeing bills, bonds, or other engagements, and on becoming security for administrations of estates, or to government or individuals for contracts, agreements, &c. 2½ do.
7. On delcredere, or guaranteeing the responsibility of persons to whom goods are sold - { ½ per cent. per mensem
8. On acting for the estates of persons deceased, as executors or administrators - - 5 per cent.
9. On the management of estates for others, on the amount received - - - 2½ do.
10. On procuring freight, or advertising as the agent of owners or commanders; on the amount of freight, whether the same passes through the hands of the agent or not - 5 do.
11. On chartering ships for other parties - - - - - - - 2½ do.
12. On making insurance, or writing orders for insurance - - - - - ¼ do.
13. On settling insurance losses, total or partial, and on procuring returns of premium - 1 do.
14. On effecting remittances, by bills of the agent or otherwise, or purchasing, selling, or negotiating bills of exchange - - - - - - - - 1 do.
15. On debts, when a process at law or arbitration is necessary - - - - 2½ do.
    And if recovered by such means - - - - - - - 5 do.
16. On bills of exchange returned noted or protested - - - - - 1 do.
17. On the collecting of house-rent - - - - - - - 2½ do.
18. On ships' disbursements - - - - - - - - 2½ do.
19. On negotiating loans on respondentia - - - - - - 2½ do.
20. On letters of credit granted for mercantile purposes - - - - - 2 do.
21. On purchasing or selling government securities, and on each exchange of the same, in the transfer from one loan to another - - - - - ¼ do.

n delivering up government securities, or depositing the same in the treasury   -   ½ per cent.

n all advances not punctually liquidated, the agent to have the option of charging a second commission, as upon a fresh advance, provided the charge does not occur twice same year.

t the option of the agent on the amount debited or credited within the year, including interest, and excepting only items on which a commission of 5 per cent. has been charged -   -   -   -   -   -   -   -   -   -   1   do.

B. This charge not to apply to paying over a balance due on an account made up to a ular period, unless where such balance is withdrawn without reasonable notice.

oney.—Accounts are kept here in imaginary money called rupees, either current or ., with their subdivisions, annas and pice: 12 pice make 1 anna; 16 annas 1 rupee; 16 rupees 1 gold mohur. To this currency must all the real specie be converted, e any sum can be regularly entered in a merchant's books. The Company keep accounts in Sicca rupees, which bear a batta (premium) of 16 per cent. over the nt. The coins current are gold mohurs, with their subdivisions halves and quar- Sicca rupees, halves and quarters; annas, pice, and half pice. The two last are of er. There are two mints under the Bengal presidency: that at Calcutta; and that rruckabad, in the north-western provinces. The first is probably the most splendid lishment of the kind in the world; the original cost of the machinery, supplied by rs. Bolton and Watt of Birmingham, having exceeded 300,000*l.* Gold money is d at Calcutta only; but silver, which is now, and has always been, the standard of ., equally at both mints. The following statement shows the present weight, fine- and sterling value of the coins, reckoning the value of gold at 3*l.* 17*s.* 10½*d.* tandard ounce, and silver at 5*s.* 2*d.*

	Grains pure.	Grains alloy.	Grains Gross Weight.	Value.	
				£ s. d.	
d Mohur - -	187·651	17·059	204·710	1 13 2¼	2·25
a Rupee - -	175·923	15·993	191·916	0 2 0½	6·25
ruckabad Rupee -	165·215	15·019	180·234	0 1 11½	8·25

e charge for coining silver at the Calcutta mint is 2 per cent. if the bullion be andard fineness; but, where it differs, a proportional charge of from one quarter e half per cent. is made for refining.

her sorts of rupees are met with in Bengal, differing in fineness and weight, though denominations be the same. From this, and from the natives frequently punching in the rupees, and filling them up with base metal, and their fraudulently diminishing eight of the coin after coming from the mint, the currencies of the different provinces different values. This defect has introduced the custom of employing *shroffs* or mo- hangers, whose business is to set a value upon the different currencies, according ry circumstance, either in their favour or their prejudice. When a sum of rupees ught to one of these shroffs, he examines them piece by piece, and arranges them ling to their fineness; then by their weight; he then allows for the different legal upon Siccas and Sounats; and this done, he values in gross, by the rupees current, the whole are worth; so that the rupee current is the only thing fixed, by which s valued.

urrent rupee is reckoned at 2*s.*, and a Sicca rupee of account commonly at 2*s.* 6*d.* means 100,000; and a crore 100 lacs, or 10,000,000. The following are the s of account, premising that the lowest denomination is represented by a small h shell, a species of cypræa, chiefly imported as an article of trade from the Lac- e and Maldive islands, and current as long as they continue entire.

wries - -	- 1 Gunda.	
do. -	- 1 Current Rupee.	
ndas - -	- 1 Punn.	
nns or 12 Pice	- 1 Anna.	
nas - -	- 1 Cahaun.	
nas -	- 1 Sicca Rupee.	
ca Rupees -	- 1 Gold Mohur.	

There are two maunds in use, viz. the factory maund, which is 74 lbs. 10 oz. 10·666 drs. avoirdupois; and the bazar maund, which is 10 per cent. better, viz. 82 lbs. 2 oz. 2.133 drs.

ghts.—The great weights are maunds, chittacks, and siccas or rupee weights, ivided:—

5 Siccas	=	1 Chittack.
6 Chittacks	=	1 Seer.
0 Seers	=	1 Maund.

Liquid Measure.

5 Sicca weight	=	1 Chittack.
4 Chittacks	=	1 Pouah, or Pice.
4 Pouahs	=	1 Seer.
40 Seers	=	1 Maund.
5 Seers	=	1 Pussaree, or Measure.
8 Measures	=	1 Bazar Maund.

Gold and Silver.

4 Punkhos	=	1 Dhan or grain.
4 Dhans	=	1 Rutty.
6¼ Rutties	=	1 Anna.
8 Rutties	=	1 Massa.
10 Massas	=	{ 1 Sicca weight =179⅜ grs. troy, or 6·5705 drs. avoirdupois.
100 Rutties	=	1 Tolah.
12½ Massas	=	1 Tolah.
16 Annas	=	1 Tolah.
166¼ Rutties	=	1 Mohur.
13·28 Massas	=	1 Mohur.
17 Annas	=	1 Mohur.

The tolah is equal to 224.588 grs. troy.

Grain Measure.

4 Khaonks	=	1 Raik, or 9¹/₁₂ lbs. avoird.
4 Raikes	=	1 Pallie.
20 Pallies	=	1 Soallie.
16 Soallie	=	1 Khahoon = 40 bz. mds.

Long Measure.

3 Barley Corns, or Jows (barley) }	=	1 Finger.
4 Fingers	=	1 Hand.
3 Hands	=	1 Span.
2 Spans	=	{ 1 Cubit or Ar = 18 inche
4 Cubits	=	1 Fathom.
1000 Fathoms	=	{ 1 Coss = mile 1 fur. poles 3½ yds

Square Measure.

5 Cubits or Hauts in length × 4 in breadth }	=	{ 1 Chittack, 45 feet (En square.)
16 Chittacks	=	1 Cottah.
20 Cottahs	=	{ 1 Biggah = 14,440 sq.
3½ Biggahs	=	{ 1 English st tute acre.

The course of exchange by which the customs of Calcutta are at present regulated as follows : —

Monies and Coins.

			Sic. Rup.	An.	Pice.
Great Britain - -	Pound Sterling	=	10	0	0
Cape of Good Hope -	Rix-dollar (2s.)	=	1	0	0
Madras - - -	100 Rupees	=	93	1	8
Bombay - - -	100 ditto	=	94	13	0
Ceylon - - -	Rix dollar	=	0	14	0
China - - -	1 Tale	=	3	5	4
Burmah - - -	125 Tickals	=	100	0	0
Manilla - - -	Spanish Dollar	=	2	4	0
Portugal - - -	1,000 Reas	=	2	12	0
France - - -	24 Francs	=	10	0	0
Holland - - -	2½ Florins	=	2	4	0
Hamburgh and Copenhagen	1½ Marc Banco	=	1	0	0
Leghorn - - -	100 Pezzas	=	202	8	0

BANKS, BANKING. — The paper currency of Calcutta is supplied by the follow banks : —

Bank of Bengal. — This is the only bank in Calcutta that has a charter. Its cap is 50 lacks ; divided into 500 shares of 10,000 sicca rupees each, of which the E India Company hold 300 shares. The shares are now at a premium of 5,000 to 6, rupees. It is managed by nine directors ; three appointed by government, and elected by the proprietors : time of service, for the latter, three years. The secret to government in the financial department, the accountant-general, and the sub-t surer, are the ex-officio government directors. The bank secretary and treasurer is a civil servant. This bank possesses peculiar advantages, but has not been so usefu the public as it might have been. Its notes are received at all the public offices, payment of revenue by the collectors in all the districts below Benares ; and, c sequently, its circulation, averaging 80 to 100 lacks, extends over a very large and wealthiest portion of our Indian territory. The government being such consider shareholders, too, it is generally supposed by the natives that the Bengal Bank is and parcel thereof ; and it enjoys, therefore, the same credit. But other circumsta have operated against the usefulness, which, with the advantages alluded to, it m have been supposed, would have certainly attended it.

1. The government required a deposit in their treasury of 20 lacks of rupee Company's paper, as security for the notes received at the public offices and the dis treasuries. To this extent, therefore, their means applicable to commercial purpose rather to the assistance of the commercial community, were crippled.

2. By their charter, they were required to issue their notes in the proportion of third of specie to two thirds of paper — in other words, for every 90 rupees of n issued, they kept 30 rupees cash in their strong box.

3. Their rules for granting accommodation on personal credit were so severe, the public rather avoided applications to them, if they could obtain discounts elsewh

d, consequently, the business of the Bengal Bank was almost entirely confined to the
anting of loans on the security of the Company's paper. In 1826, 1827, and 1828,
en the Burmese war, and the financial arrangements of the government, occa-
ned a great demand for money, the amount of discounts of mercantile paper in Cal-
tta did not exceed 10 or 12 lacks of rupees, whilst loans secured by Company's paper
se to 60 and 70 lacks.

The inconvenience of this system having been felt, the government of Calcutta has
ommended an alteration: and we understand the capital is to be increased to 75 lacks;
• proportion of one third of specie to be reduced to one fourth; the deposit of 20
ks of Company's paper at the treasury to be done away; and greater facilities to be
orded to the mercantile community in obtaining accommodation.

As soon as this alteration is carried into effect, there will, unquestionably, be a great
provement in the money market in Calcutta.

Bank of Hindostan — the oldest establishment in India of this description. The
culation of its notes is confined entirely to Calcutta and the immediate neighbourhood,
no private notes are receivable at the collectors' treasuries. The amount of its issues
s been very fluctuating; sometimes not exceeding 2 or 3 lacks, and at others reaching
20 or 25 lacks, according to the state of the market. On two occasions this bank
st successfully supported very severe runs upon it. One in 1819; when, in
sequence of some forgeries, the proprietors issued a notice to the public, pointing
ir attention to the mode of distinguishing the genuine from the forged notes. Some
l-disposed persons gave to this notice a false character, and spread reports among the
ives, that, unless the notes were brought in by a certain day, they would not be paid.
e consequence was an immediate run, which brought in all, or nearly all, the notes
n outstanding — about 18 lacks; which, being cashed without difficulty, and the real
dency of the notice in question explained, were issued again within a few hours.
e second occasion was in January 1830, when the failure of Messrs. Palmer & Co.
ead the greatest alarm among the inhabitants of Calcutta. The Bank of Hindostan
t the demand with the utmost promptness, to the extent of about 20 lacks of notes.

The Commercial Bank. — This bank was established in 1819, by ten or twelve gentle-
n, European and native, connected with the mercantile houses: but some dying, and
ers leaving India, it discontinued the issue of notes in 1829-30. During the
iod of its operation, its circulation was from 15 to 20 lacks of rupees.

The Calcutta Bank — established, in 1824, by Messrs. Palmer & Co.; but it' dis-
tinued the issue of notes in 1829, previous to the failure of that firm. Its issues
raged from 10 to 15 lacks of rupees.

The Union Bank. — This establishment was founded in 1829, upon the same prin-
e, only enlarged, as the Commercial Bank. Its capital is 50 lacks of rupees, con-
ng of 1,000 shares of 5,000 each; and they are held by all classes of the community.
• main object of this establishment was to fill up the space in the money market, left
ant as it were by the restrictions imposed on the Bank of Bengal by its charter; but
ing been started only a few months prior to the failure of Messrs. Palmer & Co.,
s not yet been able to effect its intentions to their full extent, from its notes not
g generally circulated; and it is possible the proposed alterations in the Bengal
k may, in some measure, limit its operations. There is no doubt, however, but
it will be a favourite establishment; and, if it should obtain a charter, will get
t of the banking business of Calcutta; its rules being well adapted for facilitating
mercial transactions, and sustaining commercial credit and confidence.

he rates of discount at these several establishments, of course, vary from time to
e, with the state of the money market; but the private banks do their business a
le lower than the Bank of Bengal. The last rates quoted were, at the Union Bank,

6 per cent. per annum on notes at 3 months,
5   ditto   2 ditto,
4   ditto   1 ditto;

Bank of Bengal,
    Discount on private bills at 3 months, 6 per cent. per annum,
    Ditto   govern. bills *   ditto   4   ditto,
    Interest on loans, on deposit   ditto   5   ditto;

Pilotage. — The navigation of the river Hoogly from the Sand Heads to Calcutta, a
nce of about 130 miles, is naturally dangerous and intricate; but rendered com-
tively safe by a skilful and excellent, though very costly, pilot establishment.
• consists of twelve vessels, being brigs of between 150 and 200 tons burden, capable
naintaining their stations in the most boisterous season, which extends from April
ctober inclusive; 12 branch pilots, 24 masters, 24 first mates, 24 second mates,

---

This partiality to the government bills is objected to. The Union Bank makes no distinction.

and between 70 and 80 volunteers. Each branch pilot has a salary of 70*l.* a month
each master 27*l.*, first mates 15*l.*, and second mates and volunteers 6*l.* each.   The fol
lowing table exhibits the rates of pilotage: —

Table of Rates of full and broken Pilotage, chargeable to Ships and Vessels, inwar
and outward of the River Hoogly.

Draught of Water.	Full Pilotage inward.	Additional Pilotage outward.	Inward Proportion.	Outward Proportion.
Feet.	£	£	*From Sea.*	*From Calcutta.*
9 to 10	10		To Saugor..... 4 12ths	To Moyapore, or
10 11	12	} 1	To Kedgeree.. 6 12ths	Fulta 2 12ths
11 12	14		To Culpee..... 8 12ths	To Fulta harb. 3 12ths
12 13	16			
			To Culpee harb. 9 12ths	To Culpee ... 4 12ths
13 14	18	} 2	To Fulta, or	To Kedgeree.. 6 12ths
14 15	21		Moyapore . 10 12ths	To Saugor 8 12ths
15 16	25		To Calcutta, full pilotage	To Sea, full pilotage
16 17	30	} 4		
17 18	35			
18 19	40			
19 20	45	} 6		
20 21	50			
21 22	55			
22 23	60			

Note. — All foreign vessels pay the same pilotage as those under British colours
By broken pilotage is meant the proportion of full pilotage between the differen
stages, or places of anchorage.   All ships, the property of foreigners, as well Asiati
as European, are subject to the charge termed "lead money;" it being indispensabl
necessary that the pilot should have with him a leadsman in whom he can confide.

Detention money, at the rate of 4*s.* per diem, from British and foreign vessels, i
charged by persons of the pilot service kept on board ships at anchor by desire c
the commander or owner.

In the river before Calcutta, and in other parts, there are chain moorings, of whic
the charges are as follow : —

Burthen of Ships.	April to October, 7 Months.	November to March, 5 Months.
	£ s. d.	£ s. d.
500 tons and upwards -	Per diem - 0 16 0	Per diem - 0 12 0
Under 500 tons -	Ditto - - 0 14 0	Ditto - - 0 10 0

Hire of the chain moorings at Diamond harbour 1*l.*, per diem.   The lowest charge
a ship requiring the accommodation of the chain moorings at either of the places abov
mentioned, is for ten days; and using them longer, a further charge is made at th
established rate per diem for every day exceeding ten.   The charge for transporting
ship from her moorings, into any of the docks at Kidderpore, Howrah, or Sulkea, c
from any of the docks to her moorings, is fixed at 50 rupees ; and no higher charge fc
such service is authorised.   Besides pilotage, every ship is chargeable with the hire of
row-boat to accompany her ; viz. for a boat of the first class 24*s.*, of the second class 18*s.
and of the third class 14*s.*   Of late years a lighthouse has been erected at Kedgeree, fc
which the charge on British or American flags is at the rate of 3*d.* per ton per annum
Ships proceeding to Calcutta must land their gunpowder at the powder magazine
Moyapore ; the charge is at the rate 1½*d.* per ton for each voyage.   The whole pil
establishment and the care of the navigation of the Hoogly is under the managemer
of government, and is directed by a marine board, with a master attendant and harbo
master.

There are several dry docks at Calcutta, in which vessels of any size may be built
repaired.   Ships built at Calcutta are of inferior durability to those constructed
Bombay, in consequence of the framework being always of the inferior woods of t
country ; and the planks, sheathing, upperworks, and decks alone, of teak ; which last
furnished almost entirely from Pegu.

In 1824, the number of registered ships belonging to the port of Calcutta was 12
of the burden of 44,366 tons ; being at an average about 370 tons for each.   T

st class of vessels carry near 800 tons; but ships drawing so much water are
 for the navigation of the Hoogly. Not being able to load at Calcutta, they are
ged to receive part of their cargo at Diamond harbour, about 34 miles further
n the river. The most convenient sized ship for trade between Calcutta, and
ope, and America, is from 300 to 400 tons.

uties, &c. — At Calcutta there are two distinct Custom-houses; the one for the sea,
he other for the inland duties. Our business is with the first only. The export and
rt duties and drawbacks are regulated by an ordinance of the year 1825, and are the
 for every port under the government of Bengal; or, as it is technically called, the
idency of Fort William. The tariff is regulated by three schedules, stating re-
ively the rates of duty chargeable on goods imported by sea, the drawbacks allowed
e-exports, and the rates of duty chargeable and drawbacks allowed on exported
es being the produce and manufacture of the country. The duty on goods and
handise imported by sea is imposed *ad valorem*, or according to their market value
e time of importation, except when otherwise specially provided. The value of
ich goods and merchandise must be stated on the face of the application to clear
ame from the Custom-house presented by the importer, consignee, or proprietor of
 goods, or his known agent or factor, who must subjoin to such application a de-
tion of the truth of the same, according to a prescribed form.

e following schedule contains the import duties. No duty is charged on any
e produce or manufacture of the country, if exported in a British vessel, and
rarely when exported in a foreign vessel. The inland duties vary from 10 to 2½
ent., a drawback of *two thirds* of which is usually allowed when the articles on
h they are charged are exported in British vessels, and of *one third* when they are
ted in foreign vessels. The drawbacks allowed on re-exports of foreign articles
ted in British vessels vary from half to two thirds and three fourths of the import
; on re-exports in a foreign vessel, they are commonly from half to two thirds and
eighths.

s of Duty chargeable on Goods imported by Sea into Calcutta, or any Port or
Place belonging to the Presidency of Fort William.

Enumeration of Goods.	Imported on a British Bottom.	Imported on a Foreign Bottom.
Goods, the Produce or Manufacture of the United Kingdom.		
ullion and Coin - - -	Free - -	Free.
orses - - -	Free - -	Free.
arine Stores - - -	Free - -	2½ per cent.
etals, wrought and unwrought	Free - -	2½ ditto.
pium - - -	24 Rs. a seer of 80 Sa. Wt.	48 Rs. a seer of 80 Sa. Wt.
ecious Stones and Pearls -	Free	Free.
lt - - -	3 Rs. a md. of 82 Sa. Wt. per seer -	6 Rs. a maund of 82 Sa. Wt. per seer.
irituous Liquors - -	10 per cent.	20 per cent.
bacco - - -	4 As. a md. of 80 Sa. Wt. per seer -	8 Annas a maund of 80 Sa. Wt. per seer.
ines - - -	10 per cent. -	20 per cent.
oollens - - -	Free - -	2½ ditto.
ticles not included in the above eleven items -	2½ per cent. -	5 ditto.
oods, the Produce of Foreign Europe, of the United States of America.		
rrack at a fixed valuation of 30l. per ask of 126 gallons -	10 per cent. -	20 per cent.
llion and Coin - -	Free - -	Free.
rses - - -	Free - -	Free.
ium - - -	24 Rs. a seer of 80 Sa. Wt.	48 Rs. a seer of 80 Sa. Wt.
ecious Stones and Pearls -	Free	Free.
t - - -	3 Rs. a md. of 82 Sa. Wt. per seer -	6 Rs. a maund of 82 Sa. Wt. per seer.
rits - - -	10 per cent.	20 per cent.
bacco - - -	4 As. a maund of 80 Sa. Wt. a seer -	8 Annas a maund of 80 Sa. Wt. per seer.
nes - - -	10 per cent.	20 per cent.
ticles not included in the above nine tems -	5 ditto -	10 ditto.
ds, the Produce or Manufacture of s other than the United Kingdom, n Europe, or the United States of ica.		
spice - - -	10 per cent. -	20 per cent.
e Wood - - -	7½ ditto -	15 ditto.

Enumeration of Goods.	Imported on a British Bottom.	Imported on a Foreign Bottom.
3. Altah	7½ per cent.	15 per cent.
4. Alum	10 ditto	20 ditto.
5. Ambergris	7½ ditto	15 ditto.
6. Arrack, Batavia	55 Sa. Rs. per Leager	110 Sa. Rs. per Leager.
7. Arrack, from Foreign Territories in Asia	30 Sa. Rs. per Leager	60 Sa. Rs. per Leager.
8. Arsenic, white, red, or yellow	10 per cent.	20 per cent.
9. Asafœtida	10 ditto	20 ditto.
10. Awl Root, or Morinda	7½ ditto	15 ditto.
11. Beads, Malas, or Rosaries	7½ ditto	15 ditto.
12. Beetle Nut (customs)	7½ ditto	15 ditto.
Ditto (Town duty)	5 ditto	10 ditto.
13. Benjamin, or Loban	7½ ditto	15 ditto.
14. Brandy, from Foreign Territories in Asia	30 ditto	60 ditto.
15. Brass, wrought and unwrought	10 ditto	20 ditto.
16. Brimstone	10 ditto	20 ditto.
17. Brocades, and Embroidered Goods	7½ ditto	15 ditto.
18. Buhera, or Myrobolan	10 ditto	20 ditto.
19. Buckum, or Sapan Wood	7½ ditto	15 ditto.
20. Bullion and Coin	Free	Free.
21. Calizeerah, or Nigellah	7½ per cent.	15 per cent.
22. Camphire	10 ditto	20 ditto.
23. Canvas, — excepting Canvas made of Sunn or Hemp, or other material, the growth or manufacture of places subject to the Government of the East India Company, which is exempted from charge of duty on importation by Sea	5 ditto	10 ditto.
24. Cardamums	7½ ditto	15 ditto.
25. Carriages and Conveyances	7½ ditto	15 ditto.
26. Cassia	10 ditto	20 ditto.
27. Chanks	7½ ditto	15 ditto.
28. Cherayta	10 ditto	20 ditto.
29. China Goods, or Goods from China, not otherwise enumerated in this table	7½ ditto	15 ditto.
30. Cloves	10 ditto	20 ditto.
31. Cochineal, or Crimdanah	7½ ditto	15 ditto.
32. Coffee	7½ ditto	15 ditto.
33. Coir, the produce of places not subject to the Government of the East India Company in India	5 ditto	10 ditto.
34. Coin and Bullion	Free	Free.
35. Columbo Root	10 per cent.	20 per cent.
36. Coosoom Fool, or Safflower	7½ ditto	15 ditto.
37. Copal, or Kahroba	10 ditto	20 ditto.
38. Copper, wrought and unwrought	10 ditto	20 ditto.
39. Coral	10 ditto	20 ditto.
40. Cordage,—excepting cordage made of Sunn, Hemp, or other material, the produce of places subject to the Government of the East India Company, which shall be exempt from the charge of duty on importation by Sea	5 ditto	10 ditto.
41. Crimdana, or Cochineal	7½ ditto	15 ditto.
42. Dhye Flower	7½ ditto	15 ditto.
43. Elephants' Teeth	7½ ditto	15 ditto.
44. Embroidered Goods and Brocades	7½ ditto	15 ditto.
45. Frankincense, or Gundiberoza	7½ ditto	15 ditto.
46. Galbanum	10 ditto	20 ditto.
47. Galingall	7½ ditto	15 ditto.
48. Ghee (customs)	5 ditto	10 ditto.
Ditto (Town duty)	10 ditto	20 ditto.
49. Gin, from Foreign Territories in Asia	30 ditto	60 ditto.
50. Goopee Muttee, or Yellow Ochre	10 ditto	20 ditto.
51. Goomootoo, Sunn, and Hemp	Free	Free.
52. Gum Arabic	10 per cent.	20 per cent.
53. Gundiberoza, or Frankincense	7½ ditto	15 ditto.
54. Hemp, Sunn, or Goomootoo	Free	Free.
55. Hurrah, or Myrobolan	10 per cent.	20 per cent.
56. Horses	Free	Free.
57. Hurshinghar Flower	7½ per cent.	15 per cent.
58. Hurtaul, or Orpiment, or Yellow Arsenic	10 ditto	20 ditto.
59. Iron, wrought or unwrought	10 ditto	20 ditto.
60. Ivory	7½ ditto	15 ditto.
61. Juttamunsee, or Spikenard	10 ditto	20 ditto.
62. Kullinjun	7½ ditto	15 ditto.
63. Lead, pig, sheet, milled, and small shot	10 ditto	20 ditto.
64. Loadh	7½ ditto	15 ditto.
65. Loban, or Benjamin	7½ ditto	15 ditto.
66. Mace	10 ditto	20 ditto.
67. Madder, or Munjeet	7½ ditto	15 ditto.
68. Mahogany, and all other sorts of Wood used in Cabinet-work	7½ ditto	15 ditto.

Enumeration of Goods.	Imported on a British Bottom.	Imported on a Foreign Bottom.
Mastick	10 per cent.	20 per cent.
Minium, or Red Lead	10 ditto	20 ditto.
Morinda, or Awl Root	7½ ditto	15 ditto.
Munjeet, or Madder	7½ ditto	15 ditto.
Musk	7½ ditto	15 ditto.
Myrobolans, viz. Buhera, Hurrah, and Ownla	10 ditto	20 ditto.
Myrrh	10 ditto	20 ditto.
Nutmegs	10 ditto	20 ditto.
Oils, Vegetable or Animal (customs)	7½ ditto	15 ditto.
Ditto ditto (Town duty)	5 ditto	10 ditto.
Oil Seeds (customs)	7½ ditto	15 ditto.
Ditto (Town duty)	5 ditto	10 ditto.
Oils, perfumed or essential, or Otter and Fooleyl Teyl	7½ per cent.	15 ditto.
Opium, Foreign	24 Rs. per seer of 80 Cal. Sa. Wt.	48 Rs. per seer of 80 Cal. Sa. Wt.
Orpiment, or Yellow Arsenic, or Hurtaul	10 per cent.	20 per cent.
Otter, or Essential Oils	7½ ditto	15 ditto.
Ownla, or Myrobolan	10 ditto	20 ditto.
Pepper, black and white	10 ditto	20 ditto.
Piece Goods — Cotton, Silk, and partly Cotton and partly Silk, the Manufacture of the Honourable Company's Territories in India	2½ ditto	5 ditto.
Ditto ditto ditto, when not the Manufacture of the Honourable Company's Territories in India	7½ ditto	15 ditto.
Pimento, or Allspice	10 ditto	20 ditto.
Pipe Staves	7½ ditto	15 ditto.
Precious Stones and Pearls	Free	Free.
Prussian Blue	10 per cent.	20 per cent.
Putcha Paut	7½ ditto	15 ditto.
Quicksilver	10 ditto	20 ditto.
Rattans	7½ ditto	15 ditto.
Red Sandal Wood	7½ ditto	15 ditto.
Red Lead, or Minium	10 ditto	20 ditto.
Rose Water	7½ ditto	15 ditto.
Rum, from Foreign Territories in Asia	30 ditto	60 ditto.
Saffron	10 ditto	20 ditto.
Safflower, or Coosoom Fool	7½ ditto	15 ditto.
Sago	7½ ditto	15 ditto.
Salt, Foreign	3 Rs. per md. of 82 Sa. Wt. per seer	6 Rs. per md. of 82 Sa. Wt. per seer
Sandal Wood, red, white, or yellow	7½ per cent.	15 per cent.
Sapan, or Buckum Wood	7½ ditto	15 ditto.
Senna	10 ditto	20 ditto.
Soonamookey Leaf	10 ditto	20 ditto.
Spikenard, or Jattamunsee	10 ditto	20 ditto.
Spirituous Liquors, not otherwise described in this table	10 ditto	20 ditto.
Steel, wrought or unwrought	10 ditto	20 ditto.
Storax	10 ditto	20 ditto.
Stones (Precious) and Pearls	Free	Free.
Sugar, wet or dry, including Jaggery and Molasses (customs)	5 per cent.	10 per cent.
Ditto ditto (Town duty)	5 ditto	10 ditto.
Sulphur, or Brimstone	10 ditto	20 ditto.
Sunn, Hemp, and Goomootoo	Free	Free.
Tape	7½ per cent.	15 per cent.
Taizepaut, or Malabathrum Leaf	10 ditto	20 ditto.
Tea	10 ditto	20 ditto.
Teak Timber	Free	Free.
Thread	7½ per cent.	15 per cent.
Tin and Tin Ware	10 ditto	20 ditto.
Tobacco (customs)	4 As. per md. of 80 Sa. Wt. per seer	8 As. per md. of 80 Sa. Wt. per seer.
Ditto (Town duty)	10 per cent.	20 per cent.
Toond Flower	7½ ditto	15 ditto.
Tugger Wood	7½ ditto	15 ditto.
Turmeric (customs)	5 ditto	10 ditto.
Ditto (Town duty)	5 ditto	10 ditto.
Tutenague	10 ditto	20 ditto.
Ugger, or Aloe Wood	7½ ditto	15 ditto.
Vermilion	10 ditto	20 ditto.
Verdigrease	10 ditto	20 ditto.
Wax and Wax Candles	10 ditto	20 ditto.
Wines and Spirits, not otherwise provided for	10 ditto	20 ditto.
Wood of all sorts used in Cabinet-work	7½ ditto	15 ditto.
Yellow Ochre, or Goopee Mattee	10 ditto	20 ditto.
Articles not enumerated above	5 ditto	10 ditto.

The following table exhibits the amount of the import and export trade of Calcutta and the countries with which it is conducted, for the years 1813–14, and 1827–28 the official values being corrected from the judicious calculations of Mr. Horace Wilson

	Imports.		Exports.	
	1813–14.	1827–28.	1813–14.	1827–28.
	£	£	£	£
Great Britain - - -	537,677	1,899,175	1,196,340	3,042,028
France - - - - -	- - -	138,392	- - -	268,630
Denmark - - - -	- - -	- - -	- - -	- - -
Sweden - - - -	- - -	7,949	- - -	9,147
Hamburgh - - -	- - -	7,391	- - -	- - -
Holland - - -	- - -	- - -	- - -	- - -
Mediterranean - - -	- - -	- - -	- - -	- - -
Spain - - - -	- - -	- - -	36,544	- - -
Portugal - - -	16,991	8,711	57,043	19,386
Brazil - - - -	1,932	8,057	33,117	43,766
Independent States of S. Amer.	- - -	16,232	- - -	- - -
United States - - -	- - -	45,461	- - -	168,754
Burman Empire - - -	47,095	35,089	41,492	98,915
Singapore, &c. - - -	74,811	36,598	221,609	113,807
Sumatra, &c. - - -	43,454	21,616	39,139	5,561
Java - - - -	31,598	50,637	58,628	77,502
China - - - -	181,576	217,066	928,649	1,469,034
Manilla - - - -	21,262	3,948	858	16,354
Australia - - - -	2,499	22,546	27,397	13,554
Madras, &c. - - -	61,189	42,093	217,316	87,496
Ceylon - - - -	5,982	21,931	25,893	6,192
Bombay, &c. - - - -	110,754	43,465	282,738	149,326
Arabian and Persian Gulfs -	60,624	126,680	280,795	225,342
Maldive and Laccadive Isles -	17,361	10,127	16,988	5,692
Mauritius - - - -	30,989	34,198	80,785	114,930
Mosambique - - -	1,936	- - -	1,358	- - -
Cape of Good Hope -	5,735	2,386	3,071	17,286
	1,253,472	2,799,756	3,549,768	5,952,710
Corrected value, including Company's	1,574,707	2,799,756	5,388,624	8,284,759
Treasure corrected - - - -	547,992	1,352,996	4,275	440,256
Total - - £	2,122,699	4,152,753	5,392,899	8,725,015

According to this statement the import trade has increased, in the course of 14 year nearly 100 per cent., and the export by about 60 per cent. While the trade with Grea Britain and China has greatly augmented, the transit trade, chiefly owing to the resto ation of the Dutch and French colonies, has decreased.

The great staples of import into Calcutta are British cotton manufactures and cotto twist, iron, copper, spelter, tin, lead, woollens, glass and earthenware, wines and bee pepper, timber, and bullion; and the exports, indigo, sugar, saltpetre, cotton wool, ra silk, cotton and silk piece goods, opium, lac-dye and shell-lac, grain, munjeet, madder, &c.

he value of bullion imported and exported in 1813–14, and 1827–28, is exhibited
e following table : —

	Bullion Imported.		Bullion Exported.	
	1813–14.	1827–28.	1813–14.	1827–28.
	£	£	£	£
eat Britain - - -	3,275	7,362	- - -	416,569
ance - - -	- - -	92,854	- - -	1,350
nmark - - -	- - -	- - -	- - -	- - -
lland - - -	- - -	- - -	- - -	- - -
editerranean - - -	- - -	- - -	- - -	- - -
ain - - -	- - -	- - -	- - -	- - -
rtugal - - -	- - -	11,092	- - -	- - -
azil - - -	13,864	107,500	- - -	- - -
dependent States of S. Amer.	- - -	2,025	- - -	- - -
ited States - - -	- - -	172,121	- - -	- - -
rman Empire - -	4,893	212,425	- - -	- - -
gapore, &c. - - -	60,970	16,882	- - -	- - -
matra, &c. - -	23,056	3,496	3,375	- - -
va - - - -	18,540	48,633	- - -	- - -
ina - - - -	351,930	641,802	- - -	8,177
nilla - - -	2,780	1,454	- - -	- - -
stralia - - -	- - -	6,908	- - -	225
dras, &c. - -	17,332	6,187	- - -	- - -
vlon - - - -	- - -	- - -	900	- - -
nbay, &c. - -	9,800	15	- - -	- - -
bian and Persian Gulfs -	55,624	86,021	- - -	101
cadive and Maldive Isles -	225	- - -	- - -	- - -
uritius - - - -	12,076	3,375	- - -	21,675
sambique - - -	1,165	- - -	- - -	- - -
e of Good Hope - -	- - -	- - -	- - -	- - -
	575,536	1,420,160	4,275	448,098
ected value, including Company's -	£547,992	1,352,996	4,275	440,256

e two annexed statements exhibit the quantities and value of all merchandise and
n imported into and exported from Calcutta, in the year 1829–30.   The reader
bear in mind that the value of indigo is taken at the fixed Custom-house rate of
pees per maund, whereas its real price was 250 nearly ; and that, where maunds
entioned, they are taken at 82 lbs. avoirdupois, except the article of indigo, which
xoned at 74 lbs. 10 oz.

Account of all Merchandize imported into Calcutta, during the Official
Year 1829–30.

es of Merchandise Imported.	Quantities Imported.		Amount Value in Sa. Rs.		
			Sicca Rup.	An.	Pice.
Beer, and Porter -	{ 683 butts, 6,418 hhds., 12 barrels, and 2,621 dzs. }		355,557	8	0
onds - -	Bz. Mds.	4,737 24 6	32,078	0	0
s - - -	—	573 34 8	5,124	0	0
n - -	—	26,786 13 9	76,932	0	0
atto - -	—	21 38 12	334	0	0
eed - -	—	239 15 8	3,384	0	0
mony - -	—	34 12 0	307	0	0
thecaries' Drugs and edicines - -	} -	- -	77,644	14	1
arel - -	- -	- -	8,234	12	0
nic - -	—	333 34 8	4,132	0	0
fœtida - -	—	118 24 8	893	0	0
nnah or Quince Seed -	—	312 30 13	6,388	1	6

O 4

Species of Merchandise Imported.	Quantities Imported.			Amount Value in Sa. Rs	
	Mds.	Ss.	Ch.	Sicca Rup.	An. P
Beads of sorts, and false Pearls - -	-	-	-	101,832	7
Beetlenut - -	Bz. Mds. 18,748	6	2	54,124	7
Books and Pamphlets -	-	-	-	226,743	14
Boots and Shoes - -	-	-	-	15,811	11
Brass Leaf - -	-	-	-	5,877	2
Brimstone - -	— 8,112	30	7	22,057	7
Buffalo Horns - -	193,167 in Number		-	12,882	1
Cabinet and Upholstery Wares - -	-		-	7,635	8
Camphor - -	Bz. Mds. 1,917	31	10	74,256	6
Canvas - - -	1,728 bolts -		-	28,842	4
Cardamums - -	Bz. Mds. 475	12	0	44,637	7
Carriages and Conveyances	-	-	-	32,591	4
Cassia - - -	— 708	32	14	14,409	1
Cheese - - -	-	-	-	58,985	15
China Root - -	— 254	30	1	750	8
Cloves - - -	— 5,826	38	15	155,297	14
Cochineal - -	— 117	15	15	45,715	13
Cocoa Nuts - -	-	-	-	44,718	11
Do. Shells - -	-	-	-	3,185	0
Do. Kernels - -	-	-	-	38,327	6
Do. Oil - -	— 434	7	10	4,867	3
Coffee - - -	— 8,707	33	5	116,318	14
Colours for Painters, including Oil and Varnish	-	-	-	330,466	5
Confectionery and Fruits -	-	-	-	90,278	5
Copperas - - -	— 1,016	6	10	3,370	1
Coral (Real) - -	139,007 Sicca weight		-	92,732	12
Do. (False) - -	-	-	-	21,940	13
Cordage and Coir - -	-	-	-	31,626	10
Corks - - -	-	-	-	20,708	13
Corrosive Sublimate -	Bz. Mds. 14	19	4	2,850	6
Cotton (Raw) - -	— 3,647	19	3	45,463	12
Cotton Piece Goods (white)	952,543 pieces, 125,835 yds. 1,974 pairs and 491 doz.			4,054,912	0
Do. do. (printed)	169,431 pieces and 16,722 doz.			868,655	0
Cotton Twist and Yarn -	1,626,003 lbs. -		-	1,453,571	13
Cotton for Sewing -	38 boxes and 16,044 lbs.		-	22,495	11
Cubebs - - -	Bz. Mds. 138	36	11	4,481	5
Cutch - - -	— 3,236	24	14	7,369	6
Dammer - -	— 233	17	10	515	15
Dates (wet and dry) -	— 25,508	4	12	54,259	12
Dragon's Blood - -	— 3	20	0	112	8
Earthenware of all sorts -	-	-	-	142,726	9
Earth Oil - -	57 hhds. -		-	1,804	12
Elephants' Teeth -	Bz. Mds. 83	2	12	7,752	14
Empty Bottles of all sorts	47 packages and 94,198 doz.			104,542	0
Engravings, Drawings, and Paintings -	-	-	-	21,786	11
Galingal - -	Bz. Mds. 587	37	8	4,784	10
Gall Nuts - - -	— 1,862	15	8	31,006	10
Gambier - - -	— 847	30	10	1,697	15
Gauzabhau Bugloss, or Ox Tongue - -	— 463	8	4	4,287	1
Ghee - - -	— 1,122	36	0	18,024	10
Glass Ware - -	-	-	-	181,256	10
—— Window - -	-	-	-	102,385	3
—— Plate - -	-	-	-	7,350	3

Species of Merchandise Imported.	Quantities Imported.			Amount Value in Sa. R		
	Mds.	Ss.	Ch.	Sicca Rup.	An.	Pice.
Glass, Pier (framed) -	-	-	-	3,645	8	0
Gold Leaf -	-	-	-	1,850	3	9
Gum Arabic -	Bz. Mds. 475	18	0	3,048	15	9
—— Bdellium -	— 1,169	37	8	3,666	13	0
—— Benzoin -	— 410	28	13	10,223	12	0
—— Copal -	— 653	8	0	10,087	0	6
—— Myrrh -	— 113	22	0	983	7	3
—— Olibanum -	— 304	4	4	1,684	15	3
Guns and Pistols -	-	-	-	81,109	0	0
Gunpowder -	-	-	-	10,146	0	0
Haberdashery, Millinery, and Lace -	-	-	-	287,849	15	8
Hams -	-	-	-	24,901	0	0
Hardware and Cutlery -	-	-	-	382,795	14	8
Hats and Caps -	-	-	-	51,961	12	9
Hides and Skins (untanned) -	-	-	-	24,985	12	0
Hops -	— 53	19	12	2,139	12	0
Hosiery and Gloves -	-	-	-	110,592	11	3
Indigo -	5	25	5	570	10	0
Lace and Thread, of Gold and Silver -	-	-	-	50,693	10	6
Lametta -	16,664 corge	-	-	48,031	9	6
Leather of all sorts (tanned and dressed) -	-	-	-	24,993	0	0
Mace -	Bz. Mds. 96	10	9	12,777	2	6
Marble -	-	-	-	22,192	0	3
Marine Stores -	-	-	-	82,626	9	9
Metals (unwrought)						
Copper -	— 107,418	0	5	4,182,379	8	0
Spelter -	— 99,795	6	0	487,228	2	0
Tin (Block) -	— 18,288	30	14	384,746	10	7
Tin Plates -	1,401 boxes	-	-	33,615	9	6
Lead and Shot -	{ sundry kegs & Bz. Mds. } 20,930	2	11	143,152	0	0
Steel -	Bz. Mds. 6,745	8	12	63,361	7	0
Iron -	— 132,803	27	7	497,557	2	4
Quicksilver -	— 1,160	0	0	138,586	11	0
Metals (wrought)						
Iron Machinery, Chain Cables, &c. -	-	-	-	464,157	5	9
Mixed Piece Goods -	1,145 pieces and 40 yrds.	-	-	17,821	5	9
Mother of Pearl Shells -	Bz. Mds. 551	3	0	2,602	1	0
Nutmegs -	— 338	39	8	41,988	6	9
Oilman's Stores, Grocery, &c. -	-	-	-	132,103	8	0
Oil Cloth -	-	-	-	12,989	0	0
Pepper (Black) -	— 85,293	1	8	668,039	13	3
(Long) -	— 3,466	29	7	31,296	3	6
Perfumery -	-	-	-	54,030	12	9
Pitch, Tar, and Resin -	3,095 barrels	-	-	15,071	9	6
Plate, Plated Ware, Jewellery, and Watches -	-	-	-	277,585	4	9
Precious Stones and Pearls -	-	-	-	85,068	11	6
Provisions -	-	-	-	16,865	1	9
Rattans and Canes -	-	-	-	23,691	5	0

Species of Merchandise Imported.	Quantities Imported.			Amount Value in Sa. Rs.		
	Mds.	Ss.	Ch.	Sicca Rup.	An.	Pice
Saddlery and Whips	-	-	-	106,931	1	6
Sago	Bz. Mds. 2,651	38	2	10,621	6	6
Salt (alimentary)	— 5,125	30	0	15,376	8	0
Sandal Wood	— 6,866	38	14	68,063	4	0
Sandal Wood Oil	— 18	1	11	7,620	9	9
Sapan Wood	— 21,203	10	6	61,804	4	9
Segars and Cheroots	-	-	-	93,703	6	9
Senna Leaf	1,302	7	0	6,122	2	6
Silk Manufactures	{ 25,568 ps. 829 yds., 10,102 ells, and 212 doz. }			493,940	0	7
Silk (raw China)	Bz. Mds. 48	28	0	14,610	0	0
Snuff	-	-	-	2,466	6	0
Soap and Candles	-	-	-	19,492	1	9
Spirits, &c. *viz.*						
Brandy	137,233½ gall. and 12,654 doz.			413,775	7	6
Gin	9,682 ga. 3,226 doz., & 1,290 ca.			57,149	8	0
Rum	621½ gall. and 38½ doz.			1,930	11	6
Whisky	437 — 1,284½ —			9,703	0	0
Cherry and Raspberry Brandy	} 442 dozens			6,256	5	6
All other Liquors	289 gallons and 725 dozens			7,476	4	3
Stationery and Cards	-	-	-	250,687	11	0
Stick Lac	Bz. Mds. 1,354	1	0	9,942	13	0
Sugar Candy	{ 1,546 whole and 2,616 half tubs }			50,156	10	2
Tea	-	-	-	181,208	0	6
Timber. *See* Wood.						
Tobacco	Bz. Mds. 2,251	31	6	17,103	8	0
Tortoise Shell	— 25	34	0	24,816	0	0
Turmeric	— 5,104	21	8	17,258	12	3
Wax	— 329	28	8	12,779	10	6

Wines, *viz.*	Butts.	Pipes.	Hhds.	Qr. Cks.	Brls.	Doz.	Sicca Rup.	An.	Pice
Sherry	210	11	113	38	0	18108	405,567	9	9
Madeira, Sercial, and Malmsey	7	130	36	22	0	321	104,804	2	9
Port	0	10	0	0	0	8774	110,131	2	9
Claret	0	0	121	46	0	43502	412,988	7	6
Burgundy	0	0	0	0	0	772	10,870	5	0
Champagne	0	0	0	0	0	4941	78,138	9	0
Teneriffe and Lisbon	0	121	4	0	692	8	21,142	14	0
All others	0	10	49	23	0	4045	47,810	15	3

Species of Merchandise Imported.	Quantities Imported.			Amount Value in Sa. Rs.		
Wood, *viz.*						
Mahogany	-	-	-	9,549	7	3
Boards, Planks, and Oars	-	-	-	8,334	0	0
Teak Timbers of sorts	-	-	-	135,285	0	0
Woollens	{ 67 bales, and 52 cases (contents not described), and 14,761 pieces, 7,835 yds. 1,187 dozens, and 24,000 sheets }			911,585	3	9
All other Articles	-	-	-	349,683	12	0
Total Value of Merchandise imported - - Sa. Rs.				22,959,162	9	9

Account of all Goods Exported from Calcutta on Private Account during the Year 1329-30.

cies of Merchandise Exported.	Quantities Exported.				Amount Value in Sa.. Rs.		
		Mds.	Ss.	Ch.	Sicca Rup.	An.	Pice.
rax, refined - -	Bz. Mds.	1,221	6	5	23,829	0	0
. unrefined or Tincal -	—	1,368	15	4	23,338	3	0
mphire - -	—	255	35	0	13,966	9	0
nvas, Hemp, or Cordage	- -				121,401	6	6
stor Oil - -	69 doz. and	3,213	9	11	53,487	13	3
ffee - - -	—	4,757	18	7	76,393	1	6
ton - -	—	1,028	33	4	8,712	3	3
ephants' Teeth -	—	203	34	8	17,571	13	3
ur - -	723 bags and 206 barrels				10,290	3	0
l Nuts - -	Bz. Mds.	1,648	35	15	27,979	2	9
ee - - -	—	420	18	9	8,248	11	6
ger - -	—	1,461	24	8	4,463	2	9
GRAIN, viz.							
e - - -	—	1,192,180	0	0	1,710,399	7	9
eat - -	—	105,428	0	0	154,968	6	0
dy - -	—	6,850	36	8	8,897	14	9
in and Dholl -	—	31,532	12	8	40,821	15	0
GUM LAC, viz.							
Dye - -	—	5,183	1	3	263,111	15	9
ll Lac - -	—	10,193	9	5	187,589	4	9
d Lac - -	—	72	32	0	737	11	9
k Lac - -	—	1,350	22	10	10,797	1	3
GUM RESINS, viz.							
bic - -	—	697	34	12	6,396	2	0
al - -	—	286	16	8	2,980	1	0
zoin - -	—	556	0	7	12,520	7	11
banum - -	—	11	11	0	45	1	6
anum - -	—	292	21	0	1,522	7	7
rh - -	—	33	30	0	512	12	6
icea - -	—	65	22	0	327	0	0
nies, &c. - -	723 bales (contents not described) and 1,213,940 in number				121,559	13	3
es and Skins (Raw) of sorts - -	456,570 in number				140,699	0	0
s' Lard - -	Bz. Mds.	2,370	20	6	37,617	15	0
n Tips - -	32,400 in No. &	2,967	27	4	13,031	11	0
go - -	Fy. Mds.	96,167	39	6	C. H. value of 100 rupees per Md. 9,616,800	0	0
er of Pearl Shells -	Bz. Mds.	413	16	12	2,323	11	9
jeet - -	—	1,443	16	7	9,618	6	3
m - -	9111½ chests				11,479,846	9	0
er (Long) -	Bz. Mds.	1,903	30	0	20,956	12	9
(Black) -	—	2,060	17	10	15,605	15	9
PIECE GOODS.							
on, White, Country -	509,592 pieces, 835 doz. & 685 corge				1,068,069	3	9
British - -	108,561 pieces, and 5,419 doz.				531,222	10	3
Coloured, Country -	189,071 — 1,495 —				303,849	13	3
British - -	60,190 — 24,713 —				420,437	2	9
d, of sorts -	107,929 — 433 —				455,403	1	3
isions (Salt) -	- -				35,637	0	0
huck - -	Bz. Mds.	290	23	0	3,138	3	6
(Bengal) -	3,698 gallons	-	-	-	3,698	0	0
- -	Bz. Mds.	1,092	10	13	6,456	8	11
wer - -	—	2,455	21	13	58,596	4	0

Species of Merchandise Exported.	Quantities Exported.			Amount Value in Sa. R
	Mds.	Ss.	Ch.	Sicca Rup. An. P
Sal Ammoniac - -	Bz. Mds. 903	19	8	13,866 14
Saltpetre - -	— 246,399	17	15	969,708 12
Silk (Raw) - -	— 4,109	11	13	1,092,646 0
Silk Piece Goods -	311,313 pieces and 24,150 doz.			1,380,548 3
Soap (Country) - -	Bz. Mds. 445	21	8	3,716 0
Sugar - -	— 245,817	22	13	1,963,646 10
Tin (Block) re-exported to Great Britain - -	— 10,415	27	13	241,477 14
Tincal. — See Borax -				
Tortoise Shell - -	— 25	35	6	25,402 14
Turmeric - -	— 11,905	20	13	45,422 0
Wax and Wax Candles -	— 8	20	2	4,550 2
Woollens, including Shawls, &c. - -	25,393 pieces -		-	404,862 0
All other Articles exported	- -	-	-	266,262 15
Do. re-exported - -	- -	-	-	787,058 1
Total Official Value of Exports				34,285,281 1

BULLION and SPECIE Imported and Exported from 1st May, 1829, to 30th April, 18

IMPORTS.		EXPORTS.	
Quarters.	Amount. Value in Sa. Rs.	Quarters.	Amount Value in Sa.
1st Quarter -	2,638,601 6 6	1st Quarter -	254,086 4
2d Do. - -	1,807,466 15 3	2d Do. -	360,181 0
3d Do. - -	3,168,036 0 9	3d Do. -	674,766 11
4th Do. - -	1,577,816 10 0	4th Do. -	351,287 4
Total Imports	9,191,921 0 6	Total Exports	1,640,321 7

HONOURABLE COMPANY'S EXPORTS.

An Account of the actual Quantity of Merchandise Exported from Calcutta during Official Year 1829–30; i. e. from the 1st May, 1820, to 30th April, 1830.

(Abstracted from the Custom House Books.)

Species of Merchandise.	Quantities Imported.	Amount Value in
Cotton - -	36,018 bales, Bz. Mds. 139,486 37 13	1,158,142
Silk - - -	7,078 do. — 12,446 32 12	At 7 Rs. per See registered, 3,485,109
Cotton Piece Goods -	138 do. 9,549 pieces - -	50,918
Silk Piece Goods -	473 boxes, 103,823 pieces -	696,339
Indigo - -	9,928 chests, Fy. Mds. 36,093 12 1	At 100 Rs. per M the fixed rate, 3,609,335
Saltpetre - -	31,190 bags Bz. Mds. 57,223 15 6	342,013
Sugar - -	64,490 do. — 156,672 25 2	1,332,682 1
Rice - -	— 50,264 0 0	66,624
Wheat, Grain, & Dholl	— 5,210 0 0	9,086
Carpets - -	538 pieces	24,202 1
Gunnies - -	2,864 bales, containing 449,400 in number, no value given.	
All other Articles of which value is specified - -	- - - - -	42,383
Besides many other items, of which no particulars of value are noted.		

The following is an account of the arrivals and departures respectively in the years
13-14, and 1827-28 : —

Under	ARRIVALS.				DEPARTURES.			
	1813—14.		1827—28.		1813—14.		1827—28.	
	Ships.	Tons.	Ships.	Tons.	Ships.	Tons.	Ships.	Tons.
English Colours -	246	94,234	251	97,882	237	96,534	255	100,236
French do. -	—	—	25	8,147	—	—	25	7,798
Swedish do. -	—	—	3	595	—	—	1	335
Dutch do. -	—	—	3	1,028	—	—	4	1,096
Danish do. -	—	—	—	—	—	—	—	—
Portuguese do. -	13	3,747	4	1,500	15	4,217	3	1,275
Spanish do. -	2	724	1	320	2	781	1	320
American do. -	1	75	10	2,788	—	—	11	3,254
Arabian do. -	—	—	19	7,257	—	—	22	8,419
Russian do. -	—	—	—	—	—	—	—	—
Dhonies do. -	343	56,280	370	55,500	345	57,600	370	55,500
Indian do. -	—	—	—	—	—	—	—	—
Total	605	155,060	686	175,017	599	159,132	692	178,233

This article has been compiled from the following authorities : — *Milburn's Oriental
Commerce; A Review of the external Commerce of Bengal, by Horace Hayman Wilson,
. 1830; Bell's Review of the external Commerce of Bengal, 1830; Colbrooke's
History of the Commerce and Husbandry of Bengal; The Bengal Directory; Kelly's
Cambist; Parliamentary Papers relating to the Finances of India and the Trade of
India and China, 1830; Evidence of Thomas Bracken, Esq., taken before the Select
Committee of the House of Commons, on the Affairs of India, 1831, and private Commu-
nications from the same; private communications from Raja Ram Mohun Roy, since
his arrival in England.*

CALICO (Ger. *Kattun;* Du. *Katoen;* Dan. *Kattun;* Sw. *Cattun;* Fr. *Coton,
Toile de Coton;* It. *Tela Bambagina, Tela dipinta;* Sp. *Tela de Algodon;* Port.
Pano de Algodao; Rus. *Wüboika;* Pol. *Bawelnika*), cloth made of cotton; so
called from Calicut, on the Malabar coast, whence it was first imported. In
England, all white or unprinted cotton cloths are denominated calicoes ; but in
United States this term is applied to those only that are printed.

Historical Notice of the Art of Calico Printing. — This art, though apparently one
of the most difficult, has been practised from a very remote era. Herodotus mentions
(l. 1. § 202.), that a nation on the shores of the Caspian were in the habit of painting the figures of animals on their clothes, with a colour formed from the leaves of
trees bruised and soaked in water ; and he adds, that this colour was not effaceable,
but was as durable as the clothes themselves. It is difficult to imagine that the colours
could have been so permanent, had not those using them been acquainted with the use
of mordants. There is, however, a passage in Pliny (*Hist. Nat.* lib. 35. § 11.), which,
though in some respects obscure, shows that the ancient Egyptians were fully acquainted
with the principle of calico-printing. " They paint," says he, " the clothes, not with
colours, but with drugs (*sorbentibus medicamentis*) that have no colour. This being
done, they immerse them in a vat full of boiling dye, and leave them there for a little :
when they take them out, they are painted of various colours. It is extraordinary, seeing
that there is only one colour in the vat (*unus in cortina color*), that a variety of colours
should be produced by the operation of the drugs." Pliny further states, that the
colours were so adhesive they could not be washed out; and that clothes were the
stronger for being dyed. A similar process is known to have been followed in India
from the earliest times. The chemical and mechanical inventions of modern ages have
been the cause of vast improvements in this ingenious and beautiful art; but the passage
just quoted shows distinctly that we have, in this instance, been only perfecting and
improving processes practised in the remotest antiquity.

Calico Printing in this Country — Duties on Calicoes. — In Great Britain the printing
of cottons has formed, for a considerable period, a very important and valuable business.
It has been calculated that there are not less than 230,000 individuals employed in, and
dependent upon, the print trade for subsistence, receiving the annual sum of 2,400,000l.
in wages.

This important and valuable business may be truly said to have grown up amongst us in
spite of repeated efforts for its suppression. To prevent the use of calicoes from in-

terfering with the demand for linen and woollen stuffs, a statute was passed in 1721 imposing a penalty of 5*l.* upon the weaver, and of 20*l.* upon the seller, of a piece of calico! Fifteen years after, this extraordinary statute was so far modified, that calicoes manufactured in Great Britain were allowed to be worn, " provided the warp thereof was entirely of linen yarn." This was the law with respect to calicoes till after the inventions of Sir Richard Arkwright introduced a new era into the history of the cotton manufacture, when its impolicy became obvious to every one. In 1774 a statute was passed, allowing printed goods, wholly made of cotton, to be used, upon paying a duty of 3*d.* a yard (raised to 3½*d.*, in 1806); and enacting some regulations as to the marks to be affixed to the ends of the pieces, the stripes, &c.

This act continued in force down to the present year (1831); but, though an improvement upon the old law, it was much, and justly, complained of. Its injustice and injurious operation were very forcibly pointed out by Mr. Poulett Thomson, in his excellent speech on taxation. " It is a matter of surprise to me," said the Right Hon Gent., "that this most impolitic impost should have been allowed to continue, especially when it was declared by the committee of 1818 to be *partial and oppressive,* and that its repeal was most desirable:' who, indeed, can examine it, and not feel the truth of this observation? Is it credible, that in order to raise a nett revenue of 599,669*l.,* a gross tax should be imposed of 2,019,737*l.?* and yet this was the return, according to the paper on your table, for 1828. And these figures are still far from showing the real cost of the collection of this tax;—that must be taken upon the gross produce and supposing the rate of the collection for the excise to be 5 per cent., which is less than it really is, you have a cost of 20 per cent. on the nett produce of this tax, for charges. In addition to this, from all the inquiry I have been able to make, the increased cost to the manufacturer is fully 5 per cent. upon the whole quantity made; so that you have thus two sums, each of 100,000*l.,* levied on the public, for the sake of exacting a duty of 600,000*l.* But the revenue is again, in this case, far from being the measure of the injury you inflict. The inequality of the tax constitutes its chief objection. The duty is levied upon the square yard, at 3½*d.* per yard. Thus, the price of calico which sells for 6*d.,* duty paid, contributes equally with that which is worth 5*s.* yard. You levy an onerous and oppressive tax of 100 or 150 per cent. upon the poor who are the purchasers of inferior cottons; whilst the rich, who buy only the finest kinds, pay but 10 or 15 per cent."

It is due to Mr. Thomson to state, that, not satisfied with giving this forcible exposition of the inequality and injurious operation of the duty on printed goods, one of his first measures, on coming into office, was to propose its repeal.

The following tables exhibit the quantity of printed cloths produced in Great Britain the quantity exported, and the amount of revenue and drawback thereon, during each of the three years ending with the 5th of January, 1830.

I. Return of the Number of Square Yards of Calicoes, Muslins, Linens, and Stuffs made either of Cotton or Linen, printed, painted, stained, or dyed, in Great Britain (except such as shall have been dyed of one Colour throughout), with the Amount of Excise Duties collected thereon in England and Scotland, in the three Years ended 5th January, 1830; distinguishing the Number of Square Yards and Amount of Duty collected thereon in each Year. (*Parl. Paper,* No. 335. Sess. 1830.)

	Number of Yards.			Amount of Duty.		
	Foreign Calicoes.	Linens and Stuffs.	Calicoes and Muslins.	£	s.	d.
England - -	37,397	1,376,779	115,598,924	1,706,986	8	9
Scotland - -	- -	31,965	22,863,883	333,897	15	8
Year ended 5th January, 1828 }	37,397	1,408,744	138,462,807	2,040,884	3	11
England - -	26,028	1,654,457	112,472,500	1,665,110	12	
Scotland - -	- -	23,252	25,971,724	379,093	8	0
Year ended 5th January, 1829 }	26,028	1,677,709	138,444,224	2,044,204	0	
England - -	22,338	1,704,761	102,234,454	1,516,431	14	10
Scotland - -	- -	8,755	26,105,550	380,833	12	9
Year ended 5th January, 1830 }	22,338	1,713,516	128,340,004	1,897,265	7	

Return of the Total Number of Square Yards of printed Calicoes, Muslins, Linens, and Stuffs, exported from England and Scotland, in the three Years ended 5th January, 1830; the Amount of Drawbacks paid or allowed thereon; distinguishing each Year the Quantities and Amount of Drawbacks allowed to Foreign Parts from the Quantities and Drawbacks paid or allowed on the like Articles on the Removal coastwise to Ireland.

	Exported to Foreign Countries.					Exported to Ireland.			
	Number of Yards.		Amount of Drawback.			No. of Yds. Linens, Stuffs, Calicoes, and Muslins.	Amount of Drawback.		
	Foreign Calicoes.	Linens, Stuffs, Calicoes, and Muslins.	£	s.	d.		£	s.	d.
...land - -	20,707	81,173,155	1,184,379	2	7	3,268,707	47,668	12	10
...land - -	-- --	8,751,365	127,624	1	5	700,462	10,215	1	5
Year ended } Jan. 1828	20,707	89,924,520	1,312,003	4	0	3,969,169	57,883	14	3
...land - -	6,688	82,602,528	1,204,815	5	4	6,197,326	90,377	13	5
...land - -	-- --	7,440,349	108,505	1	9	1,122,479	16,369	9	8
Year ended } Jan. 1829	6,688	90,042,877	1,313,320	7	1	7,319,805	106,747	3	1
...land - -	3,672	81,445,424	1,187,852	17	4	5,169,683	75,391	4	2
...land - -	-- --	8,417,009	122,748	0	11	869,358	12,678	2	9
Year ended } Jan. 1830	3,672	89,862,433	1,310,600	18	3	6,039,041	88,069	6	11

...the 34 Geo. 3. c. 23. it is enacted, that the inventor designer, or printer of any ...and original pattern for printing linens, cottons, calicoes, or muslins, shall have ...le right of printing and reprinting the same for three months, to commence from ...ay of first publishing.

CALOMEL. Chloride of mercury; frequently called mild muriate of mer...; and sometimes, but less properly, submuriate of mercury.

CAMBRIC, or CAMBRICK (Ger. *Kammertuch*; Du. *Kameryksdoek*; Fr. *...ray Batiste*; It. *Cambraja*; Sp. *Cambrai*; Port. *Cambraia*; Rus. *Kamertug*), ...cies of very fine white linen, first made at Cambray, in French Flanders, ...ce it derives its appellation. It is now produced, of an equally good quality, ...eat Britain.

CAMEL (Fr. *Chameau*; It. and Sp. *Camelo*; Ger. *Kæmel*; Arab. *Djimel*; *Camelus*; Greek καμηλος), is indigenous to Arabia, and we only mention ...his place on account of its extreme importance in the commerce of the

...e camel is, certainly, by far the most useful of all the animals over which the in...nts of Asia and Africa have acquired dominion. These continents are intersected ...t tracts of burning sand, the seats of desolation and drought, so as, apparently, to ...e the possibility of any intercourse taking place between the countries that they ...te. "But as the ocean, which appears at first view to be placed as an insuperable ...between different regions of the earth, has been rendered, by navigation, subser...to their mutual intercourse; so, by means of the camel, which the Arabians ...tically call *the Ship of the Desert*, the most dreary wastes are traversed, and the ...s which they disjoin are enabled to trade with one another. Those painful ...ys, impracticable by any other animal, the camel performs with astonishing despatch. ...heavy burdens of six, seven, and eight hundred pounds weight, they can continue ...narch during a long period of time, with little food or rest, and sometimes without ...water for eight or nine days. By the wise economy of Providence, the camel seems ...d of purpose to be the beast of burden in those regions where he is placed, and ...his service is most wanted. In all the districts of Asia and Africa, where deserts ...ost frequent and extensive, the camel abounds. This is his proper station, and ...d this the sphere of his activity does not extend far. He dreads alike the ex...of heat and cold, and does not agree even with the mild climate of our temperate ...—(*Robertson's Disquisition on Ancient India*, Note 53.)

The first trade in Indian commodities of which we have any account (Genesis xxxvii. 2 was carried on by camels; and they still continue to be the instruments employed in conveyance of merchants and merchandise throughout Turkey, Persia, Arabia, Egy Barbary, and many contiguous countries. The merchants assemble in considera numbers, forming themselves into an association or *caravan*, (see CARAVAN,) for th mutual protection against the attacks of robbers, and the dangers incident to a jour through such rude and inhospitable countries. These caravans are often very lar and usually consist of more camels than men. The capacity of the camel to end fatigue, and the small supply of provisions that he requires, is almost incredit " His ordinary burden," says Volney, "is 750 lbs. ; his food, whatever is given him straw, thistles, the stones of dates, beans, barley, &c. With a pound of food a d and as much water, he will travel for weeks. In the journey from Cairo to Suez, wh is forty or forty-six hours, they neither eat nor drink; but these long fasts, if of repeated, wear them out. Their usual rate of travelling is very slow, hardly above t miles an hour: it is in vain to push them; they will not quicken their pace; bu allowed some short rest, they will travel fifteen or eighteen hours a day." — (*Voyage Syrie*, tom. ii. p. 383.)

The Arabians regard the camel as a sacred animal, the gift of Heaven, without wh aid they could neither subsist, nor trade, nor travel. Its milk is their ordinary foo they also eat its flesh, especially that of the young camel, which they reckon excelle its hair, which is renewed every year, is partly manufactured into stuffs for their clot and furniture, and partly sent abroad as a valuable article of merchandise; and even fæces serve them for fuel. Blest with their camels, the Arabs want nothing, and nothing. In a single day they can traverse fifty leagues of the desert, and interpose trackless sands as an impenetrable rampart between them and their foes. — (See the mirable description of the camel in Buffon.)

CAMELS' HAIR (Ger. *Kameelhaar*; Fr. *Poil de chameau, Laine de chevrc* It. *Pelo di camello*; Sp. *Pelo ó lana de cámello*).

The hair of the camel imported into this country is principally used in the ma facture of fine pencils for drawing and painting. In the East, however, it is an i portant article of commerce, and is extensively used in the arts. It serves for fabrication of the tents and carpets of the Arabs, and for their wearing apparel. Cl is also manufactured of it in Persia and other places. The most esteemed hair cor from Persia. It is divided into three qualities; black, red, and grey. The blac the dearest, and the grey is only worth half the red. Considerable quantities of cam hair are exported from Smyrna, Constantinople, and Alexandria. It is used in manufacture of hats, particularly by the French. — (*Rees's Cyclopædia*, art. *Camelus*

CAMLET, or CAMBLET (Ger. and Du. *Kamelot*; Fr. *Camelot*; It. *Ciambellot* Sp. *Camelote*; Rus. *Kamlot*), a plain stuff, manufactured on a loom, with t treadles, as linens are. There are camlets of various colours and sorts: so wholly of goats' hair; others, in which the warp is of hair, and the woof half h and half silk; others again, in which both the warp and the woof are of wo and lastly, some, of which the warp is of wool and the woof of thread; so are striped, some watered, and some figured.

CAMOMILE (Fr. *Camomille*; It. *Camomilla*; Sp. *Manzanilla*; Port. *Ca milla, Macella*; Lat. *Chamomilla*), a well-known plant, whose flowers are u for medical purposes. Most of what is brought to the London market is gro about Mitcham, in Surrey.

CAMPHOR, or CAMPHIRE (Ger. *Kampfer*; Du. *Kamfer*; Fr. *Camph* It. *Canfora*; Sp. *Alcanfor*; Rus. *Kamfora*; Lat. *Camphora*; Arab. and P *Kâfoor*; Mal. *Kaafur*), is obtained from various plants. Most of that impor into Europe comes from Sumatra and Borneo, and is the produce of the *Dr balanops Camphora.* It is imported in chests, drums, and casks; and is in sm granular, friable masses, of a dirty white or greyish colour, very much res bling in appearance half refined sugar. When pure, camphor has a strong, culiar, fragrant, penetrating odour; and a bitter, pungent, aromatic taste.

Camphor is obtained in Sumatra in concrete masses from the heart of the tree; not above one tree in 300 contains this valuable substance, which is daily becom scarcer. China and Japan camphor is obtained by boiling the roots and smaller bran of the tree, cut into small pieces, in large iron kettles with conical heads, into wh the camphor rises.

" The camphor of Sumatra and Borneo is divided in commerce into three sorts, acc ing to quality; the relative values of which to each other may be estimated in the pro tions of 25, 14, and 4. The price of this article depends upon the factitious value w

e Chinese attach to it, and its limited production in nature. A pound avoirdupois of the
st kind usually sells in China at the exorbitant price of about 18$\frac{7}{10}$ Spanish dollars, or
4s. 4$\frac{1}{2}$d. ; while the camphor of Japan, which does not apparently differ from it, and
equally esteemed every where else, sells for the 78th part of this amount, or costs no
•re than 1s. 1d. per lb. The best camphor is purchased at Barus, in Sumatra, always the
porium of the commodity, and which strangers usually affix to its name, at about 8 Span.
.lars per catty, or 27s. per lb."—(*Crawfurd's Eastern Archipelago*, vol. iii. p. 418.)
Camphor when refined is in thin hollow cakes of a beautiful virgin whiteness, and, if
•osed to the air, totally evaporates. Great care is therefore requisite in packing cam-
or, to prevent serious loss.

. drawback is allowed upon the exportation of any camphor refined in the United Kingdom, upon oath
¡g made that it was produced solely from unrefined camphor which had paid the customs duty upon
ortation. — (6 *Geo.* 4. c. 111. § 8.)

CAMWOOD, a red dye-wood, first brought to Europe from Africa by the
rtuguese. It is principally obtained from the vicinity of Sierra Leone. The
ouring matter which it affords differs but little from that of ordinary Nicaragua
od, either in quality or quantity; and it may be employed with similar mor-
ts. (*Bancroft on Colours*. See also *Dampier*, vol. ii. part ii. p. 58.) Camwood
it present worth, in the London market, from 17*l*. to 18*l*. a ton, duty (15*s*.
on) included. In 1828, 475 tons of camwood were imported; but the imports
1829 only amounted to 119 tons.—(*Parl. Paper*, No. 661. Sess. 1830.)

CANAL, CANALS. — A canal is an artificial channel, filled with water, and
•t at the desired level by means of locks or sluices, forming a communication
ween two or more places.

Historical Sketch of Canals. — The comparative cheapness and facility with which goods
y be conveyed by the sea, or by means of navigable rivers, seems to have suggested,
. very early period, the formation of canals. The best authenticated accounts of
ient Egypt represent that country as intersected by canals conveying the waters of
Nile to the more distant parts of the country, partly for the purpose of irrigation,
| partly for that of internal navigation. The efforts made by the old Egyptian mo-
chs, and by the Ptolemies, to construct a canal between the Red Sea and the Nile
well known; and evince the high sense which they entertained of the importance
his species of communication. — (*Ameilhon, Commerce des Egyptiens*, p. 76.)
Greece was too small a territory, too much intersected by arms of the sea, and sub-
ded into too many independent states, to afford much scope for inland navigation.
empts were, however, made to cut a canal across the isthmus of Corinth; but they
not succeed.

The Romans did not distinguish themselves in canal navigation. Their aqueducts,
stupendous ruins of which still attest the wealth and power of their founders, were
nded to convey water to some adjoining city, and not for the conveyance of vessels
roduce.

n China, canals, partly for irrigation, and partly for navigation, have existed from a
' early period. The most celebrated amongst them is the Imperial or Grand Canal,
ning a communication between Pekin and Canton, being about 1660 miles long.
locks are constructed with very little skill; and as the vessels are generally dragged
nen, the navigation is extremely slow. The canals are mostly faced with stone;
the bridges across them are said to be very ingeniously contrived.

he Italians were the first people in modern Europe that attempted to plan and
ute canals. They were principally, however, undertaken for the purpose of irri-
on; and the works of this sort executed in the Milanese and other parts of Lom-
ly, in the eleventh, twelfth, and thirteenth centuries, are still regarded as models,
excite the warm admiration of every one capable of appreciating them. In 1271,
Navilio Grande, or canal leading from Milan to Abbiate Grasso and the Tesino,
rendered navigable. — (*Young's Travels in France, &c.* vol. ii. p. 170.)

'o country in Europe contains, in proportion to its size, so many navigable canals as
kingdom of the Netherlands, and particularly the province of Holland. The con-
ction of these canals commenced as early as the twelfth century, when, owing to its
ral and convenient situation, Flanders began to be the *entrepôt* of the commerce
een the north and south of Europe. Their number has since been astonishingly
eased. " Holland," says Mr. Phillips, in his *History of Inland Navigation*, " is
sected with innumerable canals. They may be compared in number and size to
public roads and highways: and as the latter with us are continually full of
hes, chaises, wagons, carts, and horsemen, going from and to the different cities,
s, and villages; so on the former, the Hollanders, in their boats and pleasure barges,
. treckschuyts and vessels of burden, are continually journeying and conveying
modities for consumption or exportation from the interior of the country to the

great cities and rivers. An inhabitant of Rotterdam may, by means of these canals breakfast at Delft or the Hague, dine at Leyden, and sup at Amsterdam, or return home again before night. By them, also, a most prodigious inland trade is carried on between Holland and every part of France, Flanders, and Germany. When the canals are frozen over, they travel on them with skaits, and perform long journeys in a very short time; while heavy burdens are conveyed in carts and sledges, which are then as much used on the canals as on our streets.

" The yearly profits produced by these canals are almost beyond belief; but it is certain, and has been proved, that they amount to more than 250,000l. for about forty miles of inland navigation, which is 625l. per mile, the square surface of which miles does not exceed two acres of ground; a profit so amazing, that it is no wonder other nations should imitate what has been found so advantageous.

" The canals of Holland are generally sixty feet wide and six deep, and are carefully kept clean; the mud, as manure, is very profitable; the canals are generally levels, of course locks are not wanted. From Rotterdam to Delft, the Hague, and Leyden, the canal is quite level, but is sometimes affected by strong winds. For the most part the canals are elevated above the fields or the country, to enable them to carry off the water, which in winter inundates the land. To drain the water from Delftland, a province not more than sixty miles long, they employ 200 windmills in spring time to raise it into the canals. All the canals of Holland are bordered with dams or banks of immense thickness, and on these depends the security of the country from inundation; of course it is of great moment to keep them in the best repair; to effect which there is a kind of militia, and in every village is a magazine of proper stores and men, whose business it is to convey stones and rubbish in carts to any damaged place. When a certain bell rings or the waters are at a fixed height, every man repairs to his post. To every house or family there is assigned a certain part of the bank, in the repair of which they are to assist. When a breach is apprehended, they cover the banks all over with cloth and stones."

The first canal executed in France was that of Briare, to form a communication between the Seine and Loire, commenced in the reign of Henry IV., and completed in that of his successor Louis XIII. The canal of Orleans, which joins the above, was commenced in 1675. But the most stupendous undertaking of this sort that has been executed in France, or indeed on the continent, is the canal of Languedoc. It was projected under Francis I.; but was begun and completed in the reign of Louis XIV. It reaches from Narbonne to Toulouse; and was intended to form a safe and speedy means of communication between the Atlantic Ocean and the Mediterranean. It is sixty-four French leagues long and six feet deep; and has in all 114 locks and sluices. In its highest part it is 600 feet above the level of the sea. In some places it is conveyed by bridges of great length and strength over large rivers. It cost upwards of 1,000,000l.; and reflects infinite credit on the engineer, Riquet, by whom it was planned and executed.

But this splendid and successful effort has not been so much followed as might have been expected, and France is still very inadequately furnished with canals. Several causes have conspired to produce this effect; the principal of which seems to be the system adopted in France, of carrying on all public works at the expense of government and under the control of its agents. No scope has been given to the enterprise of individuals or associations; and, before either a road or a canal can be constructed plans and estimates must be made out and laid before the minister of the interior, by whom they are referred to the prefect of the department, and then to the *Bureau des Ponts et des Chaussés*; and supposing the project to be approved by these, and the other functionaries consulted with respect to it, the work must after all be carried on under the superintendence of some public officer. In consequence of this preposterous system very few works of this description have been undertaken as private speculations. And while many of those that have been begun by government remain unfinished and comparatively useless, those that have been completed have, as was to be expected, rarely proved profitable. There are some good remarks on this subject in the valuable and instructive work of M. Dupin, on the *Forces Commerciales* of Great Britain.

Various canals have been undertaken and completed in Russia, Prussia, Spain, and other continental states. (For some remarks on the inland navigation of Russia, see PETERSBURGH.)

Owing partly to the late rise of extensive manufactures and commerce in Great Britain, but more, perhaps, to the insular situation of the country, no part of which is very distant from the sea, or from a navigable river, no attempt was made, in England to construct canals till a comparatively recent period. The efforts of those who first began to improve the means of internal navigation, were limited to attempts to deepen the beds of rivers, and to render them better fitted for the conveyance of vessels. S

as 1635, a Mr. Sandys, of Flatbury, Worcestershire, formed a project for render-
the Avon navigable from the Severn, near Tewksbury, through the counties of
wick, Worcester, and Gloucester, " that the towns and country might be better
lied with wood, iron, pit-coal, and other commodities." This scheme was ap-
ed by the principal nobility and landowners in the adjoining counties; but the
war having broken out soon after, the project was abandoned, and does not seem
ve been revived. After the restoration, and during the earlier part of last century,
us acts were at different times obtained for cheapening and improving river
ation. For the most part, however, these attempts were not very successful.
current of the rivers gradually changed the form of their channels; the dykes
other artificial constructions were apt to be destroyed by inundations; alluvial
-banks were formed below the weirs; in summer the channels were frequently too
o admit of being navigated, while at other periods the current was so strong as to
er it quite impossible to ascend the river, which at all times, indeed, was a laborious
xpensive undertaking. These difficulties in the way of river navigation seem to
suggested the expediency of abandoning the channels of most rivers, and of
ng parallel to them artificial channels, in which the water might be kept at the
er level by means of locks. The act passed by the legislature in 1755, for im-
ng the navigation of Sankey brook on the Mersey, gave rise to a lateral canal of
description, about 11¼ miles in length, which deserves to be mentioned as the
st effort of the sort in England.
it before this canal had been completed, the celebrated Duke of Bridgewater,* and
qually celebrated engineer, the self-instructed James Brindley, had conceived a
of canalisation independent altogether of natural channels, and intended to afford
reatest facilities to commerce, by carrying canals across rivers and through moun-
wherever it was practicable to construct them.†
e Duke was proprietor of a large estate at Worsley, seven miles from Manchester,
ich were some very rich coal-mines, that had hitherto been in a great measure
s, owing to the cost of carrying coal to market. Being desirous of turning his
to some account, it occurred to his Grace that his purpose would be best ac-
lished by cutting a canal from Worsley to Manchester. Mr. Brindley, having
consulted, declared that the scheme was practicable; and an act having been ob-
l, the work was immediately commenced. " The principle," says Mr. Phillips,
down, at the commencement of this business, reflects as much honour on the
undertaker as it does upon his engineer. It was resolved that the canal should
rfect in its kind; and that, in order to preserve the level of the water, it should
e from the usual construction of locks. But in accomplishing this end many
lties were deemed insurmountable. It was necessary that the canal should be
l over rivers, and many large and deep valleys, where it was evident that such
dous mounds of earth must be raised, as would scarcely, it was thought by
ers, be completed by the labour of ages; and, above all, it was not known from
source so large a supply of water could be drawn, even on this improved plan,
uld supply the navigation. But Mr. Brindley, with a strength of mind peculiar
self, and being possessed of the confidence of his great patron, contrived such
able machines, and took such methods to facilitate the progress of the work,
e world soon began to wonder how it could be thought so difficult.
hen the canal was completed as far as Barton, where the Irwell is navigable for
vessels, Mr. Brindley proposed to carry it over that river by an aqueduct 39
bove the surface of the water in the river. This, however, being considered
ld and extravagant project, he desired, in order to justify his conduct towards
ble employer, that the opinion of another engineer might be taken, believing
e could easily convince an intelligent person of the practicability of the design.
tleman of eminence was accordingly called, who, being conducted to the place
it was intended that the acqueduct should be made, ridiculed the attempt; and,
he height and dimensions were communicated to him, he exclaimed — ' I have
heard of castles in the air, but never was shown before where any of them were
rected.' This unfavourable verdict did not deter the Duke from following the
n of his own engineer. The aqueduct was immediately begun; and it was
on with such rapidity and success as astonished those who, but a little before,
t it impossible."
re the canal from Worsley to Manchester had been completed, it occurred to

is truly noble person expended a princely fortune in the prosecution of his great designs; and, to
his resources, restricted his own personal expenses to 400l. a year! He died at the early age of
having shortened his life by the toils and anxiety of mind inseparable from such great enter-
But his projects have been productive of great wealth to his successors; and have promoted, in no
degree, the wealth and prosperity of his country.
re is a good account of Brindley in *Aikin's Biographical Dictionary.*

the Duke and his engineer that it might be practicable to extend it by a branch, whi
running through Chester parallel to the river Mersey, should at length terminate
that river, below the limits of its artificial navigation; and thus afford a new, saf
and cheaper means of communication between Manchester and its vicinity and Liv
pool. The execution of this plan was authorised by an act passed in 1761. T
canal, which is above 29 miles in length, was finished in about five years. It w
constructed in the best manner, and has proved equally advantageous to its nol
proprietor and the public.

"When the Duke of Bridgewater," says Dr. Aikin, "undertook this great desi
the price of carriage on the river navigation was 12s. the ton from Manchester to Liv
pool, while that of land carriage was 40s. the ton. The Duke's charge on his ca
was limited, by statute, to *six* shillings; and together with this vast superiority in chea
ness, it had all the speed and regularity of land carriage. The articles conveyed by
were, likewise, much more numerous than those by the river navigation; besid
manufactured goods and their raw materials, coals from the Duke's own pits we
deposited in yards at various parts of the canal, for the supply of Cheshire; lin
manure, and building materials were carried from place to place; and the markets
Manchester obtained a supply of provisions from districts too remote for the ordina
land conveyances. A branch of useful and profitable carriage, hitherto scarcely kno
in England, was also undertaken, which was that of passengers. Boats, on the mo
of the Dutch treckschuyts, but more agreeable and capacious, were set up, which,
very reasonable rates and with great convenience, carried numbers of persons daily
and from Manchester along the line of the canal."—(*Aikin's Description of the Coun
round Manchester*, p. 116.)

The success that attended the Duke of Bridgewater's canals stimulated public spiri
individuals in other districts to undertake similar works. Mr. Brindley had ea
formed the magnificent scheme of joining the great ports of London, Liverpool, Brist
and Hull, by a system of internal navigation: and, though he died in 1772, at t
early age of 56, he had the satisfaction to see his grand project in a fair way of bei
realised. The Trent and Mersey, or, as it has been more commonly termed, the Gra
Trunk Canal, 96 miles in length, was begun in 1766 and completed in 177
It stretches from near Runcorn on the Mersey, where it communicates with the Du
of Bridgewater's canal, to Newcastle-under-Line; thence southwards to near Titc
field; and then north-westerly, till it joins the Trent at Wilden Ferry, at the nor
western extremity of Leicestershire. A water communication between Hull a
Liverpool was thus completed: and by means of the Staffordshire and Worcestersh
Canal, which joins the Grand Trunk near Haywood in the former, and the Severn ne
Stourport in the latter, the same means of communication was extended to Brist
During the time that the Grand Trunk Canal was being made, a canal was undertak
from Liverpool to Leeds, 130 miles in length; another from Birmingham to t
Staffordshire and Worcestershire Canal, joining it near Wolverhampton; and one fr
Birmingham to Fazeley and thence to Coventry. By canals subsequently undertak
a communication was formed between the Grand Trunk Canal and Oxford, and c
sequently with London, completing Brindley's magnificent scheme. In 1792,
Grand Junction Canal was begun, which runs in a pretty straight line from Brentfo
on the Thames, a little above the metropolis, to Braunston in Northamptonshi
where it unites with the Oxford and other central canals. It is about 90 miles
length. There is also a direct water communication, by means of the river I
navigation, the Cambridge Junction Canal, &c., between London and the Wash.
addition to these, an immense number of other canals, some of them of very gr
magnitude and importance, have been constructed in different parts of the country;
that a command of internal navigation has been obtained, unparalleled in any Europ
country, with the exception of Holland.

In Scotland, the great canal to join the Forth and Clyde was begun in 1768, bu
was suspended in 1775, and was not resumed till after the close of the American w
It was finally completed in 1790. It is on a larger scale than any of the Engl
canals; being upwards of *eight* feet deep. It is 35 miles long; and, where high
is 160 feet above the level of sea.

The Union Canal joins the Forth and Clyde Canal near Falkirk, and stretches the
to Edinburgh. It was completed in 1822; but has not answered the views of
projectors, who have not hitherto received any dividend.

The Crinan Canal, across the peninsula of Kintyre, is 9 miles long, and 12
deep, admitting vessels of 160 tons burden.

The Caledonian Canal is the greatest undertaking of the sort attempted in the emp
It stretches across the island from a point near Inverness to another near Fort Willi
It is chiefly formed by Loch Ness, Loch Oich, and Loch Lochy. The total lengt

canal, including the lakes, is 58¾ miles; but the excavated part is only 21½ miles. the summit it is 96½ feet above the level of the Western Ocean. It has been nstructed upon a very grand scale, being 20 feet deep, 50 feet wide at bottom, and 2 at top; the locks are 20 feet deep, 172 long, and 40 broad. Frigates of 32 is and merchant ships of 1,000 tons burden may pass through it. This canal was ened in 1822. It was executed entirely at the expense of government, from the igns and under the superintendence of Thomas Telford, Esq., on whose skill and ents as an engineer it reflects the highest credit. The entire cost has been 986,924*l.* would, however, appear to have been projected without due consideration, and pro- es to be a very unprofitable speculation. During the year 1829, the total revenue the canal, arising from tonnage dues and all other sources, amounted to only '75*l.* 6*s.* 4*d.*, while the ordinary expenditure, during the same year, amounted to 78*l.* 0*s.* 1½*d.* ! It is, therefore, very doubtful whether the revenue derived from it will r be able to defray the expense of keeping it in repair, without allowing any thing the interest of capital.

The following is a detailed account of the various items of expenditure on account of Caledonian Canal, from 20th October, 1803, to 1st May, 1830 : —

	£	s.	d.
nagement and travelling expenses - - - -	36,691	12	10¾
iber, and carriage thereof - - - - -	72,317	1	10¼
chinery, cast iron works, tools, and materials -	128,886	4	7¾
arries and masonry - - - - -	200,014	4	10¾
pping - - - - - - -	11,719	1	6
uses and other buildings - - - -	5,559	10	6
our and workmanship (day-work) - - - -	54,209	1	1¾
our and workmanship (measure-work) - -	418,551	16	8½
rchase of land, and payments on account of damages -	47,956	12	9¾
chase and hire of horses and provender - -	3,638	12	2¾
idental expenses - - - - -	2,820	18	10
idmaking - - - - -	4,579	3	6¾
Total cost - -	986,924	1	6½

ome other canals have been projected and completed in different parts of Scot-
l.

'arious canals have been undertaken in Ireland of which the Royal Canal, stretch in a Dublin to Mullingar, and the Grand Canal, stretching from Dublin to Banagher, re it joins the Shannon, are the principal. They were projected by private asso-ions; but their funds having proved inadequate for their completion, they obtained e advances of public money. Neither of these canals has succeeded; and the iter part of the money expended upon them has been, in fact, little better than lost. scale on which they were constructed was far too expensive. The intercourse be-en the parts of the country through which they pass was so very limited as scarcely istify the construction even of the cheapest canal. The entire tolls and duties of orts, received for the use of the Royal Canal, amounted, in 1820 to 9,645*l.*, and in 9 to 12,234*l.* ; a sum hardly adequate to defray the repair of a work that cost more a million sterling !

Utility of Canals. — The utility of canals, when judiciously contrived, and opening asy communication between places capable of maintaining an extensive intercourse a each other, has never been better set forth than in a work published in 1765, en-l "A View of the Advantages of Inland Navigation," &c. But the following ex-: from Macpherson's *Annals of Commerce* (anno 1760) contains a brief, and at same time eloquent, summary of the principal advantages resulting from their truction. " They give fresh life to established manufactures, and they encourage stablishment of new ones, by the ease of transporting the materials of manufacture provisions ; and thence we see new villages start up upon the borders of canals in s formerly condemned to sterility and solitude. They invigorate, and in many es create, internal trade, which, for its extent and value, is an object of still more ortance than foreign commerce, and is exempted from the many hardships and dan-of a maritime life and changes of climate. And they greatly promote foreign e ; and consequently enrich the merchants of the ports where they, or the navigable s they are connected with, terminate, by facilitating the exportation of produce from, the introduction of foreign merchandise into, the interior parts of the country, h are thus placed nearly on a level with the maritime parts; or, in other words, nterior parts become coasts, and enjoy the accommodations of shipping. The price

of provisions is nearly equalised through the whole country; the blessings of Providence are more uniformly distributed; and the monopolist is disappointed in his schemes of iniquity and oppression, by the ease wherewith provisions are transported from a considerable distance. The advantages to agriculture, which provides a great part of the materials, and almost the whole of the subsistence, required in carrying on manufacture and commerce, are pre-eminently great. Manure, marl, lime, and all other bulky articles, which could not possibly bear the great expense of cartage, and also corn and other produce, can be carried at a very light expense on canals; whereby poor lands are enriched, and barren lands are brought into cultivation, to the great emolument of the farmer and landholder, and the general advantage of the community, in an augmented supply of the necessaries of life and materials of manufactures, coals (the importance of which to a manufacturing country, few people, not actually concerned in manufactures, are capable of duly appreciating), stone, lime, iron ore, and minerals in general, as well as many other articles of great bulk in proportion to their value, which had hitherto lain useless to their proprietors by reason of the expense, and, in many cases impossibility, of carriage, are called into life, and rendered a fund of wealth, by the vicinity of a canal; which thus gives birth to a trade, whereby, in return, it is maintained. The cheap, certain, and pleasant conveyance of travellers by the treckshuyts in Holland has been admired by all who have been in that country; and it must be owing to the universal desire in this country of flying over the ground with the greatest possible rapidity, that a mode of travelling so exceedingly easy to the purse and the person is so little used here. Neither ought we entirely to forget, among the advantages of canals, the pleasure afforded to the eye and the mind by a beautiful moving landscape of boats, men, horses, &c. busied in procuring subsistence to themselves, and in diffusing opulence and convenience through the country. And, in a word, we have now the experience of about forty years to establish as a certain truth, what was long ago said by Dr. Adam Smith, that 'navigable canals are among the greatest of all improvements."

3. *Profit of Canals.* — It is a well-known fact that canals, at an average, and allowing for the length of time that must elapse from the first outlay of capital before they yield any return, are not very productive. When, indeed, they connect places that have an extensive intercourse, and when no very extraordinary difficulties have to be surmounted in their construction, they most commonly yield very large profits; but, generally speaking, this does not appear to be the case; and, on the whole, they seem to have been more beneficial to the public than to their projectors.

It is customary to insert clauses in the acts authorising canals to be cut, limiting the charge which the proprietors shall be entitled to impose upon the goods conveyed by them. But we think that the dividend ought also to be limited; and that it should be stipulated that whatever a moderate toll yielded over and above defraying this dividend, and providing for the repair of the canal, should be accumulated as a fund in order to buy up the stock of the canal, so that the toll may ultimately be reduced to such a sum as may suffice merely to meet the necessary repairs. We are not aware that any good objection could be made to a plan of this sort; and had it been adopted in this country there are several instances in which it would have been very advantageous for the public.

When the canal of Languedoc was completed, the most likely method, it was found of keeping it in constant repair, was to make a present of the tolls to Riquet the engineer. "These tolls constitute," says Dr. Smith, "a very large estate to the different branches of the family of that gentleman; who have, therefore, a great interest to keep the work in constant repair. But had these tolls been put under the management of commissioners, who had no such interest, they might, perhaps, have been dissipated in ornamental and unnecessary expenses, while the most essential parts of the work were allowed to go to ruin." Dr. Smith ought, however, to have mentioned that Riquet advanced *a fourth* part of the entire sum laid out upon the canal (*Dutens Navigation Intérieure de la France*, tom. i. p. 119, &c.); and that officers were appointed by the Crown to see that the tolls were not rendered oppressive, and the canal kept in good order. At the Revolution most part of the property of the canal was confiscated; but at the restoration of the Bourbons in 1814, such parts of the confiscated property as had not been sold were restored to the successors of M. Riquet, who have at this moment the principal management of the canal.

The following authentic particulars, extracted from the list of Mr. Edmunds, Broker (9 Change Alley, Cornhill, 4th June, 1831) give an account of the number of shares in the principal British canals, the cost or sum actually expended upon each share, the dividend payable upon it, its selling price at the abovementioned date, and the period when the dividends are payable : —

No. of Shares	Names of Canals.	Amount of Share.	Average Cost per Share.	Price per Share.	Div. per Annum.	Dividend Payable.
		£ s.	£ s. d.	£ s. d.	£ s. d.	
482	Ashby-de-la-Zouch	100 0	113 0 0	80 0 0	4 0 0	Ap. Oct.
766	Ashton and Oldham		113 0 0	100 0 0	5 0 0	Ap. Oct.
720	Barnsley	160 0		220 0 0	10 0 0	Feb. Aug.
260	Basingstoke	100 0		5 0 0		
—	Ditto Bonds	100 0				April.
000	Birmingham (⅛th sh.)	17 10		250 0 -	12 10 0	Ap. Oct.
000	Birmingham and Liverpool Junction	100 0	95 0 0 pd	60 0 dis.		
477	Bolton and Bury	250 0		106 0 0	6 0 0	January.
005	Brecknock and Abergavenny	150 0		105 0 0	6 0 0	Jan. July.
500	Bridgewater and Taunton	100 0	100 0 0 pd	55 0 0		
—	Calder and Hebble			490 0 0		
600	Carlisle	50 0	21 10 0 pd			
400	Chelmer and Blackwater	100 0		106 0 0	5 0 0	January.
500	Chesterfield	100 0		170 0 0	8 0 0	
500	Coventry	100 0		795 0 0	44 0 0	May, Nov.
351	Crinan	50 0		2 0 0		
460	Cromford	100 0		420 0 0	19 0 0	Jan. July.
46	Croydon	100 0	31 2 10	1 17 6		
0l.	Ditto Bonds	100 0		50 0 0	5 0 0	
0l.	Derby	100 0	110 0 0	130 0 0	6 0 0	Jan. July.
50	Dudley	100 0		52 0 0	2 15 0	Mar. Sept.
75	Ellesmere and Chester	133 0	133 0 0	72 0 0	3 15 0	September.
1	Erewash	100 0		700 0 0	70 0 0	
7	Forth and Clyde	100 0	400 10 0	600 0 0	27 0 0	June, Dec.
00	Glamorganshire	100 0	172 13 4	290 0 0	13 12 8	Ma. Jun. / Sep. Dec.
60	Gloucester and Berkeley O. S.	100 0		14 0 0		
	Ditto Optional Loan	60 0				
00	Grand Junction	100 0		243½ 241½	13 0 0	Jan. July.
21	Grand Surrey	100 0		40 0 0		Apr. Oct.
0l.	Grand Loan			97 0 0	5 0 0	Jan. July.
9½	Grand Union	100 0		21 0 0	1 0 0	1st Oct.
96	Grand Western	100 0	89 0 0 pd	8 0 0		
49	Grantham	150 0	150 0 0	195 0 0	10 0 0	May.
00	Hereford and Gloucester	100 0				
38	Huddersfield	100 0	57 6 6	15 10 0	0 10 0	September.
48	Ivel and Ouse Beds	100 0	100 0 0 pd	115 10 0	5 0 0	Jan. July.
28	Kennet and Avon	100 0	39 18 10	25 10 0	1 5 5	September.
50	Kensington	100 0	100 0 0 pd	10 0 0		
9½	Lancaster	100 0	47 6 8	18 0 0	1 0 0	April.
7½	Leeds and Liverpool	100 0		395 0 0	20 0 0	May, Nov.
3½	Ditto (New)				16 0 0	May, Nov.
5	Leicester		140 0 0	218 0 0	17 0 0	Jan. July.
	Ditto		90 0 0		13 10 0	Jan. July.
97	Leicester and Northampton	100 0	83 10 0	74 0 0	4 0 0	Jan. July.
70	Loughborough		142 17 0	2100 0 0	180 0 0	Jan. July.
00	Macclesfield	100 0	100 0 0 pd	60 0 0		
50	Melton Mowbray	100 0		200 0 0	9 0 0	July.
00	Mersey and Irwell	100 0		600 0 0	40 0 0	June.
01	Monkland	100 0		90 0 0		
09	Monmouthshire	100 0	100 0 0	225 0 0	12 0 0	Jan. July.
00	Montgomeryshire	100 0		80 0 0	4 0 0	Mar. Aug.
00	North Walsham and Dilham	50 0	50 0 0 pd	10 0 0		January.
47	Neath		107 10 0	300 0 0	18 0 0	Aug. Feb.
00	Nottingham	150 0		250 0 0	12 0 0	Apr. Oct.
30	Nutbrook	109 0			6 2 0	
22	Oakham	130 0		32 0 0	2 0 0	May.
36	Oxford	100 0		500 0 0	32 0 0	Mar. Sept.
00	Peak Forest	100 0	48 0 0	65 0 0	3 0 0	June, Dec.
20	Portsmouth and Arundel	50 0	50 0 0	10 0 0		
18	Regent's	100 0	33 16 8	18 0 0	0 13 6	July.
39	Rochdale	100 0	85 0 0	70 0 0	4 0 0	May.
00	Shrewsbury	125 0		250 0 0	11 0 0	May, Nov.
00	Shropshire	125 0		140 0 0	8 0 0	June, Dec.
50	Somerset Coal	50 0		160 0 0	10 10 0	Jan. July.
00	Ditto Lock Fund	12 10		13 0 0	5 10 p. ct.	June, Dec.
00	Stafford and Worcester	140 0	140 0 0	710 0 0	36 0 0	Feb. Aug.
47	Stourbridge	145 0		220 0 0	11 0 0	Jan. July.
	Stratford-on-Avon		79 9 8	35 0 0	1 5 0	August.
0	Ditto Bonds					
3	Stroudwater	150 0		480 0 0	23 0 0	May, Nov.
00	Swansea	100 0		200 0 0	15 0 0	November
00	Tavistock	100 0		105 0 0		
5	Thames and Medway	100 0	30 4 3	4 0 0		
4	Ditto New	3 10	2 15 0 pd			
—	Ditto 1st Loan		56 0 0		2 10 0	
—	Ditto 2d Loan		40 0 0		2 0 0	
—	Ditto 3d Loan		100 0 0		5 0 0	
—	Ditto 4th Loan		100 0 0		5 0 0	June.
0	Thames and Severn, New			30 0 0	1 10 0	June.
00	Ditto Original			25 0 0	1 10 0	Jan. July.
50	Trent and Mersey (½)	50 0		620 0 0	37 10 0	May, Nov.
	Warwick and Birmingham	100 0 / 50 0		240 0 0	12 0 0	May, Nov.
00	Warwick and Napton	100 0		210 0 0	12 0 0	May, Nov.
5	Wey and Arun	110 0	110 0 0	32 0 0		May.
00	Wilts and Berks			5 0 0	0 4 0	June.
5	Wisbeach	105 0	105 0 0	40 0 0		February.
00	Worcester and Birmingham			87 10 0	3 0 0	February.
00	Wyrley and Essington	125 0		115 0 0	6 0 0	February.

American Canals. — The United States are justly distinguished by the spirit w
which they have undertaken, and the perseverance they have displayed, in executing
most gigantic plans for improving and extending internal navigation.   Besides ma
others, of great, though inferior, magnitude, a canal has been formed connecting
Hudson with Lake Erie.   This immense work is 363 miles long, 40 feet wide at
surface, 28 feet wide at the bottom, and 4 feet deep.   The locks, 81 in number, exc
sive of guard locks, are 90 feet long and 14 feet wide, the average lift of each being
feet ; they are constructed of stone, and finished, like the rest of the canal, in a substan
and handsome manner.   The rise and fall along the entire line is 661 feet.   T
great work was opened on the 8th of October, 1823, but was not finally completed
1825.   It cost nearly 1,800,000*l.* sterling, and was executed at the expense of the st
of New York.   It has completely answered the views of the projectors ; and will rem
an example to the other states ; fully justifying the encomiums that have been bestov
upon it.

Besides Erie Canal, the state of New York has completed Champlain Canal, stretch
from the Hudson, near Albany, to the lake of that name, and two smaller ones.   T
length, cost, and revenue of these canals are as follow : —

	Length.	Cost.	Tolls, 1829.
Erie Canal - -	363 miles	9,027,456·05 dollars	707,883·49 dolla
Champlain ditto - -	63	1,179,871·95	87,171·03
Oswego ditto - -	38	525,115·37	9,439·44
Cayuga and Seneca ditto, -	20	214,000·31	8,643·49
	484	10,946,443·68	813,137·45
Navigable feeders - -	8		
Total miles -	492		

Tolls on the above canals in 1830 : —

Erie and Champlain Canals - -	1,029,932·29 dollars.
Oswego ditto - - - -	12,100·60
Cayuga and Seneca ditto - - -	11,901·87
	1,053,934·76

Various canals have been completed in other parts of the Union, and some v
extensive ones are now in progress in New York and the other states. — (*New I
Annual Register for* 1831, p. 125.)

The British government have expended a very large sum upon the Rideau River
Canal, stretching from Kingston, on Lake Ontario, to the Ottawa, or Grand Riv
but this work was undertaken as much in the view of improving the military defer
of Canada, as of promoting its commerce.   It is doubtful whether it will be spee
completed.   The expense appears to be enormous, and the benefits contingent
doubtful.

Great, however, as have been the advantages derived from the formation of canal
is probable that they are now about to be partially, at least, superseded by the n
recent invention of rail-roads.   The reader will find some observations on the comp
tive advantages of canals and rail-roads, as means of communication, under the art
RAIL-ROADS.

** We cannot quit the subject of canals without directing the attention of our rea
to the magnificent six-sheet Map of the Canals and Rail-roads of Great Britain, publis
by J. Walker, Esq. of Wakefield.   This map, which is equally correct and beauti
is a truly national work, and well deserves the public patronage.   " An Historical
count of the Navigable Rivers and Canals, &c. of Great Britain," in 4to, is attache
it by way of index.   This last is an accurate and a useful publication.

CANARY SEED.   See SEED.

CANDLE (Ger. *Lichter, Kerzen ;* Du. *Kaarzen ;* Fr. *Chandelles ;* It. *Cande
Sp. and Port. *Velas ;* Rus. *Swjetschi ;* Lat. *Candela*), a taper of tallow, wax
spermaceti, the wick of which is commonly of several threads of cotton s
and twisted together.

Dr. Ure gives the following table, as containing the result of certain exp
ments he had made, in order to determine the relative intensity of the light,
the duration of different sorts of tallow candles.

mber in a Pound.	Duration of a Candle.	Weight in Grains.	Consumption per Hour, in Grains.	Proportion of Light.	Economy of Light.	Candles equal one Argand.
mould,	5 h. 9 m.	682	132	12¼	68	5·7
dipped,	4 36	672	150	13	65½	5·25
mould,	6 31	856	132	10½	59½	6·6
do.	7 2½	1160	163	14¾	66	5·0
do.	9 36	1787	186	20¼	80	3·5
rgand oil ame.			512	69·4	100	

" A Scotch mutchkin," says Dr. Ure, " or one eighth of a gallon of good seal , weighs 6010 gr., or 13 1/10 oz. avoirdupois, and lasts in a bright Argand ap 11 hours 44 minutes. The weight of oil it consumes per hour is equal to r times the weight of tallow in candles 8 to the pound, and 3¼ times the ight of tallow in candles 6 to the pound. But its light being equal to that of of the latter candles, it appears from the above table, that 2 lbs. weight of value 9d. in an Argand, are equivalent in illuminating power to 3 lbs. of low candles, which cost about 2s. The larger the flame in the above candles, greater the economy of light."

Until the present year, 1831, when it was repealed, candles had been, for a gthened period, subject to an excise duty; and their consumption had, in sequence, been pretty exactly ascertained.

Account of the Rates of Duty separately charged on Tallow, Wax and Spermaceti Candles, the Number of Pounds' Weight of each sort produced, and the total annual Net Revenue derived from Candles, in Great Britain, in each Year since 1800. — Parl. Paper, No. 468. Sess. 1830.)

	Pounds' Weight of Candles.						
ars.	Tallow.	Rate of Duty per lb.	Wax.	Rate of Duty per lb.	Spermaceti.	Rate of Duty per lb.	Net Revenue.
		d.		d.		d.	£ s. d.
00	65,618,885	1	533,900	3½	41,488	3½	269,593 10 5
01	66,402,684	—	549,385	—	47,011	—	275,660 12 10
02	68,721,071	—	501,594	—	42,987	—	285,909 11 4
03	73,466,589	—	553,098	—	33,125	—	307,069 8 10
04	72,504,879	—	537,351	—	33,817	—	303,475 8 9
05	78,339,528	—	557,936	—	51,891	—	329,921 0 4
06	75,595,585	—	602,474	—	81,971	—	317,384 15 8
07	80,479,945	—	595,182	—	118,258	—	337,527 19 5
08	77,824,853	—	590,159	—	111,956	—	328,607 13 6
09	68,156,653	—	575,081	—	108,589	—	265,567 19 2
10	75,789,441	—	633,660	—	104,208	—	317,811 16 10
11	77,903,144	—	633,942	—	103,469	—	328,891 18 0
12	79,746,767	—	653,064	—	118,269	—	336,103 5 6
13	73,280,627	—	618,672	—	131,304	—	307,965 16 6
14	78,060,469	—	668,280	—	159,375	—	324,534 17 0
15	82,903,123	—	653,841	—	220,978	—	350,113 10 7
16	84,106,963	—	591,263	—	250,611	—	353,985 10 4
17	83,794,223	—	645,230	—	243,027	—	353,738 18 0
18	82,646,964	—	693,194	—	164,395	—	349,540 5 8
19	87,536,031	—	675,875	—	153,260	—	369,701 12 11
20	88,352,461	—	692,705	—	193,463	—	373,455 14 5
21	93,816,346	—	697,196	—	165,647	—	395,911 8 7
22	98,311,801	—	682,241	—	179,208	—	415,609 15 3
23	102,461,879	—	694,194	—	180,401	—	433,537 15 8
24	109,810,900	—	759,751	—	179,454	—	466,042 16 1
25	114,187,550	—	851,370	—	208,377	—	485,014 8 9
26	110,102,643	—	705,615	—	201,790	—	467,069 12 1
27	114,939,578	—	713,655	—	226,277	—	487,318 3 4
28	117,342,157	—	748,293	—	270,263	—	497,770 2 9
29	115,156,808	—	746,052	—	308,683	—	489,059 1 9

CANDLE, *Sale or Auction by Inch of*, is when a small piece of candle being lighted the by-standers are allowed to bid for the merchandise that is selling: but th moment the candle is out, the commodity is adjudged to the last bidder.

CANDLESTICKS (Ger. *Leuchter ;* Du. *Kandelaars ;* Fr. *Chandeliers ;* It. *Can dellieri ;* Sp. *Candeleros ;* Rus. *Podsweschnikü*) are of silver, brass, iron, bronze tin japanned, or copper plated, made of different patterns and sorts. The bes plated candlesticks are manufactured at Sheffield; the common sort of plate ones, as also brass, japanned, &c. are made at Birmingham.

CANELLA ALBA (Fr. *Canelle blanche ;* Ger. *Weisser Zimmet ;* It. *Canell bianca ;* Sp. *Canella blanca ;* Lat. *Canella alba*), the inner bark of the *canella alba* a tree growing in the West Indies. It is brought to this country packed in cask and cases, in long pieces, some rolled in quills and others flat; the quilled sort i considerably thicker than cinnamon, and the flat nearly a quarter of an inch i thickness. The quilled pieces are yellow on both sides; the flat pieces ar yellow on the outside and pale brown within. The odour of both kinds, wher fresh broken, is aromatic, something like a mixture of cloves and cinnamon, anc the taste slightly bitter and extremely warm and pungent.

CANES. See BAMBOO, RATTANS.

CANNON, CANNONS (Du. *Kanonen ;* Fr. *Canons ;* Ger. *Kanonen ;* It. *Can noni ;* Pol. *Dziala ;* Por. *Canhoes ;* Rus. *Puschki ;* Sp. *Canones ;* Sw. *Kanon*), kind of long hollow engines for throwing iron, lead, or stone balls by the force of gunpowder. They are commonly made of iron, but frequently also of mixture of copper, tin, and brass. They are either cast hollow, or cast soli and then bored; those made in the latter way being very superior. Bras cannons, or cannons made of mixed metal, are said not to be so well calculate for hard service, or quick and continued firing, as those made of iron. The pro portions of the ingredients used in making the former do not differ materially i different countries, though they rarely coincide. To 240 lbs. of metal fit for casting we commonly put 68 lbs. of copper, 52 lbs. of brass, and 12 lbs. of tin. To 4,200 lbs of metal fit for casting, the Germans put $3,687\frac{3}{41}$ lbs. of copper, $204\frac{11}{41}$ lbs. o brass, and $307\frac{36}{41}$ lbs. of tin. Others, again, use 100 lbs. of copper, 6 lbs. of brass and 9 lbs. of tin; and others, 100 lbs. of copper, 10 lbs. of brass, and 15 lbs. o tin.

It seems to be the general opinion that cannon were first made use of in 1336 or 1338 but Don Antonio de Capmany has produced some statements, which render it almos certain that some sort of artillery was used by the Moors in Spain so early as 1312. — (*Questiones Criticas*, p. 181, &c.) Cannons were certainly used by the English i 1347 at the siege of Calais, and by the Venetians at Chioggia in 1366, and in thei wars with the Genoese in 1379 and 1380. The Turks employed them at the sieges o Constantinople, in 1394 and 1453. When first introduced, they were for the most par very heavy and unwieldy, and threw balls of an enormous size : they were, howeve owing to their frequently bursting, about as dangerous to those using them as to thei opponents. There is a valuable article on the construction and history of cannons i *Rees's Cyclopædia ;* but it was published previously to the appearance of Capmany work referred to above.

CANTHARIDES, OR SPANISH FLY (Fr. *Cantharides, Mouches d'E pagne ;* Ger. *Spanische Fliegen ;* It. *Cantarelle ;* Lat. *Cantharis ;* Rus. *Hischpansk muchi ;* Sp. *Cantaridas*). This insect is found on a variety of shrubs in Spai Italy, France, &c. Those used in this country are imported partly from Sicil but principally from Astracan, packed in casks and small chests. The best a of a lively fresh colour, a small size, and not mouldy. They are frequent adulterated with the *Melolontha vitis ;* but this is distinguishable by its form which is squarer than the cantharis, and by its black feet. If they be proper dried and protected from the air, they may be kept for a very long perio (*Thomson's Dispensatory.*)

CANTON, one of the greatest emporiums in the East, ranking, as a po of trade, immediately after, or, perhaps, before Calcutta, situated in the provin of Quantong, in China; being the only place in that empire frequented t European traders : lat. 23° 7′ N., lon. 113° 14′ E.

Canton stands on the eastern bank of the Pekiang River, which flows from the interi in a navigable stream of 300 miles to this city, where it is rather broader than t Thames at London bridge; falling, after an additional course of 80 miles, into t

ıern sea of China. Near its junction with the sea it is called by foreigners Bocca
ıs. The town is surrounded by walls about 5 miles in circumference, on which
ɔannon are mounted; but its fortifications could oppose no effectual resistance to
ɔpean troops and artillery.

lthough Canton is situated nearly in the same parallel of latitude as Calcutta, yet
ɔ is a considerable difference in their temperature; the former being much the
ɔst, and requiring fires during the winter months. The suburbs may be frequented
Juropeans, but they are not permitted to enter the gates of the Tartar city; which
ɔver, in its architecture and exterior appearance, entirely resembles the suburbs.
ɔ streets of Canton are very narrow, paved with little round stones, and flagged close
ɔ sides of the houses. The front of every house is a shop, and those of particular
ɔts are laid out for the supply of strangers; China-street (named by seamen Hog-
ɔ being appropriated to Europeans; and here the productions of almost every part
ɔe globe are to be found. One of the shopkeepers is always to be found sitting
ɔe counter, writing with a camels' hair brush, or calculating with his swanpan, on
ɔh instrument a Chinese will perform operations in numbers with as much celerity
ɔe most expert European arithmetician. This part of Canton being much fre-
ɔted by the seamen, every artifice is used by the Chinese retailers to attract their
ɔtion; each of them having an English name for himself painted on the outside of
ɔop, besides a number of advertisements composed for them by the sailors in their
ɔpeculiar idiom. The latter, it may be supposed, are often duped by their Chinese
ɔds, who have, in general, picked up a few sea-phrases, by which the seamen are
ɔced to enter their shops : but they suit each other extremely well; as the Chinese
ɔrs possess an imperturbable command of temper, laugh heartily at their jokes with-
ɔnderstanding them, and humour the seamen in all their sallies.

ɔe foreign factories extend for a considerable way along the banks of the river, at
ɔistance of about 100 yards. They are named, by the Chinese, hongs, and resemble
ɔ courts, or closes, without a thoroughfare, which generally contain four or five
ɔate houses. They are built on a broad quay, and have a broad parade in front.
ɔ promenade is railed in, and is generally called Respondentia Walk ; and here the
ɔpean merchants, commanders, and officers of the ships, meet after dinner and
ɔ the cool of the evening. The English hong, or factory, far surpasses the others
ɔgance and extent, and before each the national flag is seen flying. The neigbour-
ɔof the factories is occupied with warehouses for the reception of European goods,
ɔ Chinese productions, until they are shipped. In 1822, during a dreadful con-
ɔtion that took place at Canton, the British factories and above 10,000 other houses
ɔdestroyed ; on which occasion the East India Company's loss was estimated at
ɔ million sterling, three fifths in woollens.

ɔr the space of four or five miles opposite to Canton, the river resembles an exten-
ɔloating city, consisting of boats and vessels ranged parallel to each other, leaving
ɔrow passage for vessels to pass and repass. In these the owners reside with
ɔfamilies ; the latter of whom, in the course of their lives, but rarely visit the shore.
ɔ the business at Canton with Europeans is transacted in a jargon of the English
ɔage. The sounds of such letters as B, D, R, and X, are utterly unknown in
ɔ. Instead of these they substitute some other letter, such as L for R, which
ɔons a Chinese dealer in rice to offer for sale in English a very unmarketable commo-
ɔ The name mandarin is unknown among the Chinese ; the word used by them to
ɔ a person in authority being quan. Mandarin is a Portuguese word derived
ɔthe verb *mandar*, to command.

ɔcorrect estimate of the population of Canton has ever been formed, but it is
ɔ to be very great. The total population of China is estimated in native works
ɔd authority, translated by M. Klaproth, at 141,470,000, and the revenue at
ɔ,912l.

ɔnies. — Accounts are kept here in tales, mace, candarines, and cash ; the tale
ɔ divided into 10 mace, 100 candarines, or 1,000 cash. There is but one kind of
ɔ made in China, called cash, which is not coined but cast, and which is only used
ɔnall payments : it is composed of 6 parts of copper and 4 of lead; it is
ɔ, marked on one side, and rather raised at the edges, with a square hole in the
ɔe. These pieces are commonly carried, like beads, on a string or wire. A tale
ɔ silver should be worth 1,000 cash ; but, on account of their convenience for
ɔn use, their price is sometimes so much raised that only 750 cash are given for
ɔe.

ɔeign coins, however, circulate here, particularly Spanish dollars ; and for small
ɔ they are cut into very exact proportions, but afterwards weighed ; for which
ɔe merchants generally carry scales, called dotchin, made somewhat after the plan
ɔ English steelyards.

The tale is reckoned at 6s. 8d. sterling in the books of the East India Compan
but its value varies, and is generally computed according to the price paid per ounce i
Spanish dollars in London. The tables given for this proportional value may be c
culated in pence sterling, by the multiplier 1·208. Thus, if the price of the Spani
dollar be 60d. per ounce, the value of the tale will be 60 × 1·208 = 72·48d.; if
66d., the value of the tale will be 79·728d.; and for any other price in the same pr
portion.

Fineness of Gold and Silver.—The fineness of gold and silver is expressed by dividi
the weight into 100 parts, called toques or touch; similar to the modern practice
France. Thus, if an ingot be 93 touch, it is understood to contain 7 parts of allo
and 93 of pure metal, making in the whole 100.

The fineness of the precious metals, expressed in these decimal proportions, may
converted into English proportions by the following analogies. Suppose gold is 91·
touch, say, as 100 : 91·66 :: 12 : 11, the standard, and *vice versâ;* and to conv
standard silver into touch, say, as 240 : 222 :: 100 : 92·5, the touch of sterling silv
Pure gold or silver without alloy is called by the Chinese sycee; and sometimes, wh
of less purity, the metal is accepted as sycee.

Silver Ingots are used as money, and weigh from ½ to 100 tales, their value bei
determined by their weight. These ingots are of the best sort of silver; that is, abo
94 touch.

Gold Ingots. — Gold is not considered as money, but as merchandise: it is sold
regular ingots of a determined weight, which the English call shoes of gold: t
largest of these weigh 10 tales each; and the gold is reckoned 94 touch, though it m
be only 92 or 93.

Weights. — Gold and silver are weighed by the catty of 16 tales; the tale is divid
into 10 mace, 100 candarines, or 1,000 cash. 100 tales are reckoned to weigh 120 o
16 dwt. troy, which make the tale equal to 579·8 English grains, or 37·566 gramme

The principal weights for merchandise are the pecul, the catty, and the tale; t
pecul being divided into 100 catties, or 1,600 tales.

	lb.	oz.	dwt.	
1 Tale weighs, avoirdupois - -	0	1	5·333	= 1⅓ oz.
16 Tales, or 1 Catty - -	1	5	5·333	= 1⅓ lb.
100 Catties, or 1 Pecul - -	133	5	5·333	= 133⅓ lbs.

Hence the pecul weighs 60·472 kilogrammes, or 162 lbs. 0 oz. 8 dwt. 13 gr. troy.

The above weights are sometimes otherwise denominated, especially by the nativ
thus, the catty is called gin; the tale, lyang; the mace, tchen; the candarine, fivan; :
the cash, lis.

There are no commercial measures in China, as all dry goods and liquids are s
by weight. In delivering a cargo, English weights are used, and afterwards turn
into Chinese peculs and catties.

Long Measure. — That used in China is the covid or cobre; it is divided into
punts, and is equal to 0·3713 metres, or 14·625 English inches.

The Chinese have four different measures answering to the foot, viz.

	Metres.	Eng. Inches.
The foot of the mathematical tribunal	= 0·333	= 13·125
The builders' foot, called congpu	= 0·3228	= 12·7
The tailors' and tradesmen's foot	= 0·3383	= 13·33
The foot used by engineers	= 0·3211	= 12·65

The li contains 180 fathoms, each 10 feet of the last-mentioned length; there
the li = 1897½ English feet; and 192½ lis measure a mean degree of the merid
nearly: but European missionaries in China have divided the degree into 200 lis, e
li making 1,826 English feet; which gives the degree 69·166 English miles, or 11·
French myriametres.

Hong, or Security Merchants. — In Canton, as in every other port of the Chir
empire, a limited number of persons, denominated *hong,* or *security* merchants,
established; and every foreign ship must, on her arrival, get one of these mercha
to become security for the import and export duties payable on the inward and outw
cargoes, and for the conduct of the crew. It may be supposed, perhaps, that difficulties
occasionally experienced before such security is obtained: but such is not really the ca
not the least hesitation has ever been evinced by a hong merchant about securing a sh
The Americans, who have had as many as *forty* ships in one year at Canton, have ne
met with a refusal. The captain of a merchant ship may resort to any hong merch
he pleases, and, by way of making him some return for his becoming security,
generally buys from him 100l. or 200l. worth of goods. Individuals, are, howeve
perfect liberty to deal with any hong merchant, whether he has secured their shi

t, or with any *outside merchant;* that is, with any Chinese merchant not belonging
the hong. So that, though there are only eight or ten hong merchants at Canton,
re is, notwithstanding, quite as extensive a choice of merchants with whom to deal
that city, as in either Liverpool or New York.

Trade with the Indian Islands, &c. — In his evidence before the Select Committee of
House of Commons, Mr. Crawfurd has given the following instructive details with
pect to the native foreign trade of China : —

Jative Foreign Trade of China.—"The principal part of the junk trade is carried on by the four contiguous
vinces of Canton, Fokien, Chekiang, and Kiannan.
No foreign trade is permitted with the island of Formosa ; and I have no means of describing the ex-
t of the traffic which may be conducted between China, Corea, and the Leechew Islands. The
owing are the countries with which China carries on a trade in junks ; viz. Japan, the Philippines, the
-loo Islands, Celebes, the Moluccas, Borneo, Java, Sumatra, Singapore, Rhio, the east coast of the
ayan peninsula, Siam, Cochin-China, Cambodia, and Tonquin. The ports of China at which this
le is conducted are Canton, Tchao-tcheou, Nomhong, Hoeltcheon, Suheng, Kongmoon, Changlim,
Hainan, in the province of Canton ; Amoy and Chinchew, in the province of Fokien ; Ningpo and
g-haig, in the province of Chekiang ; and Soutcheon, in the province of Kiannan. The following
y be looked upon as an approximation to the number of junks carrying on trade with the different
ces already enumerated ; viz.

	Junks.
Japan 10 junks, two voyages	20
Philippine Islands	13
Soo-loo Islands	4
Borneo 13, Celebes 2	15
Java	7
Sumatra	10
Singapore 8, Rhio 1	9
East Coast of Malay Peninsula	6
Siam	89
Cochin China	20
Cambodia	9
Tonquin	20
	— Total 222.

This statement does not include a great number of small junks belonging to the island of Hainan,
ch carry on trade with Tonquin, Cochin China, Cambodia, Siam, and Singapore. Those for Siam
unt yearly to about 50, and for the Cochin Chinese dominions to about 43 ; these alone would bring
total number of vessels carrying on a direct trade between China and foreign countries to 307. The
e with Japan is confined to the port of Ningpo, in Chekiang, and expressly limited to 10 vessels ; but
e distance from Nangasaki is a voyage of no more than four days, it is performed twice a year.
With the exception of this branch of trade, the foreign intercourse of the two provinces Chekiang and
nnan, which are famous for the production of raw silk, teas, and nankeens, is confined to the Philip-
Islands, Tonquin, Cochin China, Cambodia, and Siam ; and none of this class of vessels, that I am
re of, have ever found their way to the western parts of the Indian Archipelago. The number of these
ing with Siam is 24, all of considerable size ; those trading with the Cochin Chinese dominions 16,
of considerable size ; and those trading with the Philippines 5 ; making in all 45, of which the average
ten does not fall short of 17,000 tons. I am the more particular in describing this branch of the
ese commerce, as we do not ourselves at present partake of it, and as we possess no direct means of
ining information in regard to it. All the junks carrying on this trade with Siam, are owned in the
r country and not in China ; and I am not sure how far it may not also be so in the other cases. I do
oubt but that a similar commerce will, in the event of a free trade, extend to Singapore ; and that
gh this channel may eventually be obtained the green teas of Kiannan, and the raw silks of
ciang.
Besides the junks now described, there is another numerous class, which may be denominated the
ial shipping of the Chinese. Wherever the Chinese are settled in any numbers, junks of this descrip-
are to be found ; such as in Java, Sumatra, the Straits of Malacca, &c. ; but the largest commerce of
description is conducted from the Cochin Chinese dominions, but especially from Siam, where the
ber was estimated to me at 200. Several junks of this description from the latter country come
ially to Singapore, of which the burden is not less than from 300 to 400 tons.
The junks which trade between China and the adjacent countries, are some of them owned and built
ina ; but a considerable number also in the latter countries, particularly in Siam and Cochin China.
ose carrying on the Siamese trade, indeed, no less than 81 out of the 89, of considerable size, were
sented to me as being built and owned in Siam. The small junks, however, carrying on the trade of
an, are all built and owned in China.
The junks, whether colonial or trading direct with China, vary in burden from 2,000 peculs to 15,000,
rry dead weight from 120 to 900 tons. Of those of the last size I have only seen three or four, and
were at Siam, and the same which were commonly employed in carrying a mission and tribute yearly
Siam to Canton. Of the whole of the large class of junks, I should think the average burden will not
errated at 300 tons each, which would make the total tonnage employed in the native foreign trade
ina between 60,000 and 70,000 tons, exclusive of the small junks of Hainan, which, estimated at 150
each, would make in all about 80,000 tons.
The junks built in China are usually constructed of fir and other inferior woods. When they arrive
mbodia, Siam, and the Malayan Islands, they commonly furnish themselves with masts, rudders, and
en anchors, of the superior timber of these countries. The junks built in Siam are a superior class of
s, the planks and upper works being invariably teak. The cost of ship-building is highest at the port
noy in Fokien, and lowest in Siam. At these places, and at Chang-lim in Canton, the cost of a junk
00 peculs, or 476 tons burden, was stated to me, by several commanders of junks, to be as
rs : —

At Siam	7,400 dollars.
Chang-lim	16,000
Amoy	21,000

ik of the size just named has commonly a crew of 90 hands, consisting of the following officers,
es the crew ; a commander, a pilot, an accountant, a captain of the helm, a captain of the anchor, and
tain of the hold. The commander receives no pay, but has the advantage of the cabin accommodation
ssengers, reckoned on the voyage between Canton and Singapore worth 150 Spanish dollars. He is
he agent of the owners, and receives a commission, commonly of 10 per cent. on the *profits* of such

share of the adventure, generally a considerable one, in which they are concerned. The pilot receives for the voyage 200 dollars of wages, and 50 peculs of freight out and home. The helmsman has 15 pecul. of freight and no wages. The captains of the anchor and the hold have 9 peculs of freight each; and the seamen 7 peculs each. None of these have any wages. The officers and seamen of the colonial junks are differently rewarded. In a Siamese junk, for example, trading between the Siamese capital and Sincapore of 6,000 peculs burden, the commander and pilot had each 100 dollars for the voyage, with 12 peculs of freight a piece. The accountant and helmsman had half of this allowance, and each seaman had 13 dollars with 5 peculs of freight.

" In construction and outfit, Chinese junks are clumsy and awkward in the extreme. The Chinese are quite unacquainted with navigation, saving the knowledge of the compass : notwithstanding this, as their pilots are expert,.their voyages short, and as they hardly ever sail except at the height of the monsoons, when a fair and steady seven or eight knots' breeze carries them directly from port to port, the sea risk is very small. During thirteen years' acquaintance with this branch of trade, I can recollect hearing of but four shipwrecks ; and in all these instances the crews were saved.

" The construction and rigging of a Chinese junk may be looked upon as her proper registry, and they are a very effectual one ; for the least deviation from them would subject her at once to foreign charges and foreign duties, and to all kinds of suspicion. The colonial junks, which are of a more commodious form and outfit, if visiting China, are subjected to the same duties as foreign vessels. Junks built in Siam or any other adjacent country, if constructed and fitted out after the customary model, are admitted to trade to China upon the same terms as those built and owned in the country. If any part of the crew consist of Siamese, Cochin Chinese, or other foreigners, the latter are admitted only at the port of Canton ; and if found in any other part of China, would be seized and taken up by the police exactly in the same manner as if they were Europeans. The native trade of China conducted with foreign countries is not a clandestine commerce, unacknowledged by the Chinese laws, but has in every case at least the express sanction of the viceroy or governor of the province, who, on petition, decides the number of junks which shall be allowed to engage in it ; and even enumerates the articles which it shall be legal to export and import. At every port, also, where such a foreign trade is sanctioned, there is a hong or body of security merchants as at Canton ; a fact which shows clearly enough that this institution is parcel of the laws or customs of China, and not a peculiar restraint imposed upon the intercourse with Europeans.

" The Chinese junks, properly constructed, pay no measurement duty, and no kumsha or present ; duties, however, are paid upon goods exported and imported, which seem to differ at the different provinces. They are highest at Amoy, and lowest in the island of Hainan. The Chinese traders of Siam informed me that they carried on the fairest and easiest trade, subject to the fewest restrictions in the ports of Ningpo and Siang-hai, in Chekiang, and Southeon in Kiannan. Great dexterity seems every where to be exercised by the Chinese in evading the duties. One practice, which is very often followed, will afford a good example of this. The coasting trade of China is nearly free from all duties and other im- posts. The merchant takes advantage of this ; and intending in reality to proceed to Siam or Cochin China, for example, clears a junk out for the island of Hainan, and thus avoids the payment of duties. When she returns she will lie four or five days off and on at the mouth of the port, until a regular bargain be made with the Custom-house officers for the reduction of duties. The threat held out in such cases is to proceed to another port, and thus deprive the public officers of their customary perquisites. I was assured of the frequency of this practice by Chinese merchants of Cochin China, as well as by several commanders of junks at Singapore. From the last-named persons I had another fact of some consequence, as connected with the Chinese trade ; viz. that a good many of the junks, carrying on trade with foreign ports to the westward of China, often proceeded on voyages to the northward in the same season. In this manner they stated that about 20 considerable junks, besides a great many small ones, proceeded annually from Canton to Souchong, one of the capitals of Kiannan, and in wealth and commerce the rival of Canton where they sold about 200 chests of opium at an advance of 50 per cent. beyond the Canton prices. Another place where the Canton junks, to the number of five or six, repair annually, is Chinchew, in the province of Shanton, within the Gulf of Pechely, or Yellow Sea, and as far north as the 37th degree of latitude."—(*Appendix, Report of* 1830, p. 298).

A Chinese ship or junk is seldom the property of one individual. Sometimes 40, 50, or even 100 different merchants purchase a vessel, and divide her into as many different compartments as there are partners ; so that each knows his own particular part in the ship, which he is at liberty to fit up and secure as he pleases. The bulk heads, by which these divisions are formed, consist of stout planks, so well caulked as to be completely water-tight. A ship thus formed may strike on a rock, and yet sustain no serious injury : a leak springing in one division of the hold will not be attended with any damage to articles placed in another ; and, from her firmness, she is qualified to resist a more than ordinary shock. A considerable loss of stowage is, of course, sustained, but the Chinese exports generally contain a considerable value in small bulk. It is only the very largest class of junks that have so many owners ; but even in the smallest class the number is very considerable.

British Trade with China. — The foreigners carrying on the principal intercourse with China are the British, Americans, French, Dutch, Danes, Swedes, Portuguese, Spaniards, Siamese, and Cochin Chinese. The British and American commerce is very extensive. The British trade is divided into two branches : that carried on between China and Great Britain, or the Company's trade ; and that carried on between China and the British possessions in India, which is, with a trifling exception, in the hands of private individuals. The following is the tonnage employed by the East India Company in their trade between Canton and England, in the two years ending 1815-16 and 1827-28 : —

1814-15	-	- 29,231		1826-27	-	- 28,571
1815-16	-	- 27,002		1827-28	-	- 27,868

e invoice value of the Company's trade between China and England, in the same , stood as follows : —

ears.	IMPORTS into China from England.			EXPORTS from China to England.	Total Imports and Exports.	Average.
	Merchandise.	Treasure.	Total.	Merchandise.		
	£	£	£	£	£	£
4–15	860,093	127,695	987,788	1,967,978	2,955,766	} 3,620,782½
5–16	926,920	1,127,513	2,054,433	2,231,366	4,285,799	
6–27	764,418	—	764,418	2,264,726	3,029,144	} 2,859,912
7–28	709,261	—	709,261	1,981,419	2,690,680	

e exports by the East India Company and their officers from England to China, st of woollens, copper, iron and lead, glass and earthenware, and jewellery. The ving is an enumeration of the principal articles, with their value, or amount, in vo years 1813-14 and 1828-29 ; with the exception of woollens, which are after-s given : —

	1813-14.		1828-29.	
	Quantity.	Value.	Quantity.	Value.
		£		£
tons and printed Calicoes	Bales -	35,191	Pieces 29,950	68,543
ton Twist - -	Cases -	- -	Bales 50	955
per - - -	Tons -	- -	- -	35
ss and Earthenware -	- -	6,710	- -	598
als ; viz. Iron -	Tons 1,539	26,166	Tons 1,886	18,180
Lead -	— 250	7,249	— 1,000	17,792
Tin -	— 620	49,500		
ches - - -	- -	- -	- -	3,216
other Articles except } Woollens - - }	- -	38,393	- -	14,779
		£163,209		£124,098

ollens forming the principal export of the Company, and a branch of their mo-y on which they still insist, we give the particulars in detail.

	1813-14.		1828-29.	
	Quantity.	Amount.	Quantity.	Amount.
		£		£
erfine Spanish } Stripe Cloth - }	Cloths 6,123	162,238	Cloths 12,000	132,136
r Cloth - -	— 1,662	29,916	— 3,000	26,597
ster Cloth - -	— 804	15,812	— 600	6,688
g Ells - -	Pieces 179,520	423,359	Pieces 120,000	204,000
rior Long Ells -	— 11,780	38,415		
ble Camlets -	— 2,700	24,891	— 2,000	14,387
le Camlets -	— 7,800	59,598	— 6,000	35,679
nd Single Camlets	— 9,500	60,570	— 4,000	20,066
eys - -	— 3,940	14,812		
ossed Long Ells -	— 800	2,361		
nia Cloth - -	— 11	188		
	Total	£832,160	Total	£459,553

n this statement it will appear that the whole export trade of the East India ny to the Chinese empire in 1813-14 amounted to little short of 1,000,000l.

sterling, and in 1828-29 to only 583,651*l.*, a decrease of between 400,000*l.* and 500,00 a result which strikingly contrasts with the results of the free trade between Great Bri and India in the same period.

Since the year 1824-25 the East India Company have exported nothing from Ch except tea. Previously they exported raw silk, amounting, at an average of the years ending with that just mentioned, to about 90,000 lbs. a year. The follow are statements of the species, quantities, and prime cost, of the teas exported to G Britain and the Canadas, in the years 1824-25 and 1828-1829.

	Teas Exported to England.				Teas Exported to the North Americ Colonies.			
	1824—25.		1828—29.		1824—25.		1828—29.	
	Quantity.	Average Prime Cost per Pound.	Quantity.	Average Prime Cost per Pound.	Quantity.	Average Prime Cost per Pound.	Quantity.	Aver Prime per Pou
	lbs.	*s.* *d.*	*lbs.*	*s.* *d.*	*lbs.*	*s.* *d.*	*lbs.*	*s.* *d.*
Bohea	3,589,804	0 9·301	4,198,964	0 9·512	87,340	0 9·301	100,385	0 9·
Congou	18,773,989	1 3·397	16,951,171	1 2·587	81,733	1 3·600	914,616	1 0·
Campoi	214,153	1 6·427	507,881	1 7·461			19,768	1 9·
Souchong	269,456	1 10·501	183,493	1 10·870	51,312	1 3·067		
Pekoe	33,973	1 11·569			3,539	2 0·594	146,753	1 6·
Twankay	3,791,405	1 4·460	5,471,633	1 3·810	579,120	1 3·831	10,195	1 4·
Hyson Skin	178,596	1 5·526	154,767	1 4·238	163,929	1 3·309		
Young Hyson					173,347	2 2·038	33,284	2 6·
Hyson	666,562	2 7·094	1,149,371	2 2·263	38,830	2 4·730	4,953	2 6·
Gunpowder								
	27,517,938		28,617,280		1,179,150 27,517,938		1,229,954 28,617,280	
Whole Exports to Britain and America in the Year 1824—25					28,697,088	In 1828—29	29,847,234	

N. B. For full details with respect to the tea trade, see art. TEA.

Company's Factory at Canton. — The Company's business in China is carried on an establishment of public officers, consisting of twelve supercargoes and as ma writers, promoted according to seniority; the former being paid by a commission chie derived from the monopoly sales of tea in England, and the latter by fixed salari both having lodging and a public table furnished to them at the Company's expen The three senior supercargoes, called the select committee, constitute the governing bo and have the whole control, not only of the Company's trade, but politically of British interests in China. The whole charges of the Company's establishment China, in 1826-27, amounted to 166,362*l.*, and the following year to 144,212*l.*, and 1828-29 to 138,526*l.* We give the particulars for the last named year.

Twelve supercargoes	£53,121
Twelve writers	10,226
Persons filling professional and other distinct offices	8,857
Rents and repairs of private apartments	16,782
Rent of factory, port charges, and other expenses	49,440

The Company's business is wholly conducted with the hong merchants, to the exc sion of the unlicensed or outside merchants, as they are called. The select commit divides amongst such of the solvent hong merchants as it pleases the whole amount the Company's export and import cargoes, and the business is done by a kind of bart a sytem long banished among the free traders in China. In 1813-14, the registe tonnage employed by the East India Company in their trade with China, includ such ships only as returned to England with cargoes, was 23,971 tons; in 1820-21 was 27,815 tons; and in 1827-28, 27,868 tons. The ships employed by the East Ir Company in the China trade are commonly from 1,000 to between 1,400 and 1, tons burden, the greater proportion being from 1,300 to 1,400 tons. For ships ta up for six entire voyages the lowest rate of freight, at present, is 21*l.*, and the high 26*l.* 10*s.* per ton, per voyage. The Company, however, occasionally engage pri ships to bring tea home from China at from 10*l.* to 11*l.* per ton.

Besides the Company's trade between England and China, they import from Ii cotton and sandal wood, but chiefly the former, to the extent of 300,000*l.* sterling. annum; but export nothing. The tea, to a small extent, is paid for beyond what proceeds of the import cargoes will yield, chiefly in bills drawn on the governor gen of India; that is, by the territorial revenue of India.

Trade between India and China. — The trade between China and British Indi of more value and importance than the Company's trade between China and G

itain. It is chiefly conducted from Calcutta and Bombay, to a much smaller extent
m Madras, and latterly to a considerable amount from Singapore. The following
tement, including three separate years, exhibits the staple articles of this trade, their
antity, and value in China.

Description of Articles.	1817—18.		1822—23.		1827—28.	
	Quantity.	Value.	Quantity.	Value.	Quantity.	Value.
	lbs.	£	lbs.	£	lbs.	£
otton	46,629,900	1,310,920	23,317,826	459,187	35,981,554	696,016
pium	360,000	590,220	793,744	1,865,800	1,520,108	2,248,699
in	807,044	25,480	929,803	29,362	401,527	12,076
epper	2,734,480	71,960	2,738,603	53,536	1,895,516	19,952
etel-Nut	1,508,220	7,940	7,195,965	43,284	4,229,400	14,310
ll other Articles	-	209,800	-	202,480	-	178,075
tal Value imported to Canton and Macao	-	£2,216,320	-	£2,653,649	-	£3,169,128

B. The Spanish dollar in this table is converted into English money at the rate of 4s., which, for
e time back, has been about its exchangeable value. Its mint price is 4s. 3¾d.

The greatest article of import from India to Canton used to be cotton wool; but
 branch of trade has lately declined, probably owing to large importations of manu-
tured cottons and twist from Great Britain. Opium is at present the greatest branch
this commerce; and it will be seen, on comparing the first and last years of the pre-
ing table, that the quantity and value of the imports of opium had been quadrupled,
ore, in a period of ten years. The subsequent table shows the importations of the dif-
nt kinds of opium throughout the entire year 1828-29. In this year there is a
her augmentation, making the total value of the imports above two millions and a
 sterling, which exceeds by half a million sterling the whole exports of the East
ia Company in tea, and is within a fraction of the total amount of their exports
 imports in China.

Opium is strictly contraband in China; but is, notwithstanding, smuggled with great
 and safety. The trade was, at first, conducted at Whampoa, about 15 miles below
ton. The vexatious conduct of the Chinese mandarines drove the trade to the
d of Macao, where it increased; and from whence it was once more driven by the
tions of the Portuguese. It then took refuge in the bay of Lintin. Here the
m is kept on board ships, commonly called receiving ships, of which there are
uently not less than twelve quietly lying at anchor, without danger or molest-
.

he opium is sold by the resident European or American agents; and, on an order
 these for its delivery, it is handed over to the smugglers who come alongside the
s at night to receive it; putting the naval force, Custom-house establishment, and
e of the empire, at defiance.

unt of the Imports of the different Sorts of Opium into China, during the Year
1828—29.

	Patna.			Benares.			Malwa.			Total.	
	Chests.	Price.	Value in Dollars.	Chests.	Price.	Value in Dollars.	Chests.	Price.	Value in Dollars.	Chests.	Value in Dollars.
April	317	1,000	317,000	104	960	99,840	291	1,250	363,750	712	780,590
May	471	985	463,935	156	940	146,640	341	1,100	375,100	963	985,675
June	371	915	339,465	89	875	77,875	778	830	645,740	1,238	1,063,080
July	529	950	502,550	120	910	109,200	1,014	900	912,600	1,668	1,524,350
August	498	1,040	517,920	96	1,015	97,440	651	1,025	674,450	1,252	1,289,810
September	410	960	393,600	68	930	63,240	627	1,000	627,000	1,105	1,083,840
Coast of China	98	980	96,040	79	935	73,320	30	1,050	31,500	200	194,860
October	396	925	366,300	52	885	46,020	775	980	759,500	1,223	1,171,820
November	424	920	390,080	102	890	90,780	734	940	689,960	1,260	1,170,820
December	360	885	318,600	35	850	29,750	486	890	432,540	881	780,890
January	341	900	306,900	29	850	24,650	315	975	307,125	685	638,675
February	220	930	204,600	59	890	52,510	601	1,000	601,000	880	858,110
March	309	890	275,010	148	840	124,320	390	980	382,200	847	781,530
ao during the ason	87	950	82,650	0	0	0	131	965	126,415	218	209,065
Total	4,831		4,574,650	1,130		1,029,585	7,171		6,928,880	13,132	12,533,115

he exports from China to India consist of sugar for the western parts of India
Chinaware, nankeens, cassia, camphor, &c.; but the amount of these is very
ng, and the returns are chiefly made in bills and bullion. Estimating the exports,

Q

at the same value as the imports, their joint amount in 1827-28 would be 6,338,236l., above a million more than double the amount of the Company's trade.

The following is an account of the tonnage employed in the free trade between Indi and China : —

	Cleared from the Ports of British India for Canton.								
	Calcutta.		Madras & Ports subordinate.		Bombay.		Total.		Average
	Ships.	Tons.	Ships.	Tons.	Ships.	Tons.	Ships.	Tons.	Tons.
In the Year 1817—18	36	17,762	2	2,400	19	17,300	57	37,472	} 38,618
— 1818—19	30	16,128	2	2,767	24	20,850	76	39,745	
— 1827—28	27	17,079	5	5,122	37	27,690	69	49,891	} 45,771
— 1828—29	16	11,544	4	4,376	36	25,731	56	41,651	

	Cleared from Canton for the Ports of British India.								
	Calcutta.		Madras & Ports subordinate.		Bombay.		Total.		Average
	Ships.	Tons.	Ships.	Tons.	Ships.	Tons.	Ships.	Tons.	Tons.
In the Year 1817—18	29	15,701	4	2,101	14	9,206	47	27,008	} 24,258
— 1818—19	22	10,568	2	848	15	10,095	39	21,511	
— 1827—28	18	6,159	10	5,342	30	16,748	58	28,249	} 28,265
— 1828—29	14	5,928	7	4,810	30	17,544	51	28,282	

The free traders of India, or country traders as they are more frequently termed, d business indiscriminately, both with the hong and outside merchants. Cargoes of cotto are most frequently sold to the former, who rarely venture to deal in opium.

American Trade with China. — The American intercourse with China commence shortly after the termination of the revolutionary war, and has since gone on rapidl increasing, so as to constitute one of the most valuable branches of the trade of th United States. The following statement shows its amount from 1804-5 to 1826-27 :-

An Account of the Value of Imports into, and Exports from, the Port of Canton, b the Subjects of the United States of America, in the following Years : —

Years.	Ships.	Imports into China.			Exports from China.	Total Value Imports and Exports.			Average
		Sale Value Merchandise.	Number of Dollars.	Total Value.	Total Value.		£	£	£
		Dollars.	Dollars.	Dollars.	Dollars.	Dollars.			
1804—5	34	658,818	2,902,000	3,555,818	3,842,000	{ 7,397,818 } or at 4s. 4d.	1,602,861		
1805—6	42	1,150,358	4,176,000	5,326,358	5,127,000	10,453,358	2,264,894	} 7,245,034	1,811,2.
1806—7	37	982,362	2,895,000	3,877,362	1,294,000	8,171,362	1,770,461		
1807—8	33	909,090	3,032,000	3,940,090	3,476,000	7,416,090	1,606,819		
1808—9	8	409,850	70,000	479,850	808,000	1,287,850	279,034		
1809—10	37	1,021,600	4,723,000	5,744,600	5,715,000	11,459,600	2,482,913		
1810—11	16	568,800	2,330,000	2,898,800	2,973,000	5,871,800	1,272,233	} 5,034,294	1,678,0
1811—12	25	1,257,810	1,875,000	3,132,810	2,771,000	5,903,810	1,279,158		
1812—13	8	837,000	616,000	1,453,000	620,000	2,073,000	449,166		
1813—14 1814—15	9	451,500	—	451,500	572,000	1,023,500	221,758		
1815—16	30	605,500	1,922,000	2,527,500	4,220,000	6,747,500	1,461,958		
1816—17	38	1,064,600	4,545,000	5,609,600	5,703,000	11,312,600	2,451,063	} 11,044,112	2,761,0
1817—18	39	1,475,828	5,601,000	7,076,828	6,777,000	13,853,828	3,001,662		
1818—19	47	2,603,151	7,414,000	10,017,151	9,041,755	19,058,906	4,129,429		
1819—20	43	1,861,961	6,297,000	8,158,961	8,182,015	16,340,976	3,540,545		
1820—21	26	Value not stated for this year.							
1821—22	45	3,074,741	5,125,000	8,199,741	7,058,741	15,258,482	3,306,004		
1822—23	40	2,046,558	6,292,840	8,359,398	7,523,492	15,862,890	3,436,960	} 22,020,243	3,145,7
1823—24	34	2,217,126	4,096,000	6,313,126	5,677,149	11,990,275	2,597,893		
1824—25	43	2,437,545	6,524,500	8,962,045	8,501,121	17,463,166	3,783,686		
1825—26	42	2,050,831	5,705,200	7,756,031	8,752,562	16,508,593	3,576,862		
1826—27	26	2,002,549	1,841,168	3,843,717	4,363,788	8,207,505	1,778,293		

In the last year of this statement the trade was scarcely half the amount of the preceding it. In the following year (1827-28) the imports rose to 6,238,788 dollars, the exports to 6,559,925 Spanish dollars. The causes which have contributed to reta the progress of the American commerce since 1818-19 are chiefly the return of Dutch and French to the China trade, and the resolution of the East India Compa to furnish the Canadas with teas which had hitherto been furnished to them by Americans. The principal articles carried by the Americans to China are bulli furs, Turkey opium, English woollens and cottons, and ginseng. The following is a sta

 of the furs imported into Canton in the three years ending 1806-7 and 1826-27.
e consist of sea otter, seal, beaver, rabbit, fox, land otter, sable, and musk rat

	Average.			Average.
1804-5 - - 270,132		1824-25 - - 100,794		
1805-6 - - 195,406	254,829	1825-26 - - 65,958	80,109
1806-7 - - 298,949		1826-27 - - 73,575		

appears from this statement that there has been a great decline in the quantity of
imported by the Americans; a fact to be ascribed, not to any decline of the taste for
article on the part of the Chinese, but to the enhanced price of the skins owing to
increased scarcity. This seems to have induced the Americans to seek for sub-
es; and to this circumstance, and the monopoly of the East India Company, may
cribed their importation of British woollens into China, which commenced about
ear 1817-18.
e following is a statement of the quantities of woollens and cottons imported by
into Canton in 1824-25 and 1826-27 : —

		Imports by the Americans.		
		1824—25.		**1826—27.**	
		Quantities.	Value.	Quantities.	Value.
		Pieces.	Dollars.	Pieces.	Dollars.
mlets - - -		4,338	121,464	3,272	104,704
mbazets - - -		672	9,448	1,800	27,000
oths - - -		10,257	430,794	14,064	421,920
irtings - - -		7,612	64,602	21,567	150,969
ndkerchiefs - -		27,123	54,246	27,090	40,635
ng Ells - - -		7,842	78,420	8,040	80,400
mbric - - -		3,250	10,574	4,592	11,480
intz - - -		4,161	24,966	8,104	56,728
		Total	794,514	Total	893,836

ppears from the evidence laid before the House of Commons, that one London
has shipped, since 1818, to the extent of 762,118*l.* worth of woollens and cottons,
Liverpool house to the extent of 744,257*l.* worth, making a total between them
ve 1,506,000*l.*, on account of American houses. The increase of this trade may
ged of from the exports in four years by the house of Baring and Co., according
following statement given to the Committee of the House of Lords by Mr.
one of its partners : —

norandum of Shipments to China, on Account of Americans, by the House of Baring & Co.				
	1827.	1828.	1829.	1830.
	£	£	£	£
n - -	35,580	24,740	34,600	6,029
lens - -	16,930	31,070	97,720	41,641
- - -	3,280	3,440	5,920	—
er - - -	3,120	—	—	—
ksilver -	4,500	—	—	—
neal - -	3,280	—	—	—
m - -	13,370	39,000	—	83,699
and Iron -	—	—	500	947
- - -	—	—	2,670	—
India Cotton, Raw	—	—	6,060	—
e - -	—	—	—	36,301
ies - -	2,830	—	—	1,214
	£82,440	£98,250	£147,470	£169,831

commodities exported by the Americans from China are teas, nankeens, raw
ought silks, sugar, cassia, and camphor, with minor articles. The quantity of
orted from 1815-16 to 1826-27, in each year, was as follows : —

1815—16	*lbs.* 7,245,280	1821—22	*lbs.* 9,312,267
1816—17	8,954,100	1822—23	12,142,400
1817—18	9,622,130	1823—24	10,152,267
1818—19	11,988,649	1824—25	13,741,467
1819—20	10,193,003	1825—26	12,802,534
1820—21	Not distinguished.	1826—27	8,577,566

The American exports from China are divided into two branches; those destined
the United States of American and those destined for the Continent of Europe,
Sandwich Islands, &c.   Their proportion to each other may be judged of from
following statement of their respective values:—

	For the United States.	For the Continent of Europe.
1821—22	Spanish Dollars 6,344,596	Spanish Dollars 714,145
1822—23	——— 7,139,582	——— 383,910
1823—24	——— 5,223,243	——— 453,906
1824—25	——— 7,916,444	——— 584,677
1825—26	——— 8,067,706	——— 684,856
1826—27	——— 4,219,323	——— 144,465

It will appear, from the average of the six last years given in the table of exp
and imports, that their joint amount has exceeded 3,000,000*l.* sterling per annu
which exceeds the whole trade of the East India Company, at an average of the
years ending with 1827-28, by 285,000*l.*   On the other hand, the trade of the E
India Company and that of the Americans taken together falls short of the coun
trade, or that between India and China, by between 300,000*l.* and 400,000*l.* sterling
Respecting the extent of the Portuguese, Spanish, French, Swedish, Danish,
Dutch trades, we have no data to lay before the reader on which reliance coul
placed; but they are inconsiderable and fluctuating, compared with the branches alre
described.   The Dutch trade is the largest; but even with the assistance of protect
duties in Holland, the Dutch are unable to withstand the enterprise and activity of A
rican competition.   The Portuguese trade, particularly that between the possession
Portugal on the continent of India, was considerable during the war, but has since gre
declined.   A nation of more enterprise than the Portuguese would, with the advan
which they have in the possession of the convenient station of Macao, be abl
carry on the Chinese trade with superior success.   The Spanish flag is very little
in China, notwithstanding the neighbourhood of the Philippine Islands, which af
many commodities in request in the Chinese markets, and that the Spaniards are
only European people allowed openly to trade with the busy and commercial por
Amoy, in the province of Fokien.
     Exclusive of the trade of the European nations just mentioned, and of the tr
with the Philippine and Eastern Islands, Tonquin, Cochin-China, Camboja, S
and the coasting trade with other ports and places of the empire, it will be seen
these statements, that three branches only of the Canton trade; viz. those of the
India Company, the country trade of India, and the American trade, amoun
12,343,917*l.*   The entire trade of Calcutta in 1827-28 amounted to 12,877,7
This certainly justifies us in ranking Canton as the second place of trade in the E
but we are not sure that it ought not to be considered as decidedly the first.
     Port Charges. — The Chinese measure a ship from the centre of the fore-mast to
centre of the mizen-mast for the length, and close abaft the main-mast from the out
taking the extreme, for the breadth.   They then multiply the length by the brea
and dividing the product by ten, the result is deemed the measurement.   At
Custom-house, ships are classed under three denominations, viz. first, second, and
rates: all ships of 74 cubits long *and upwards,* and 23 broad and upwards, b
reckoned in the first class, pay at the rate of 7 tales 7 mace 7 candarines and 7
per cubit upon the tonnage, as ascertained by the previously described process;
of from 71 to 74 cubits long, and 22 to 23 broad, are reckoned in the second class,
pay per cubit 7 tales 1 mace 4 candarines 2 cash; and all ships of from 71 t
cubits *and under* in length, and from 22 to 20 cubits *and under* in breadth, pay a
rate of 5 tales per cubit.
     Not only, however, are the charges on small vessels rendered comparatively hig
this mode of fixing the tonnage duty, but every vessel is, besides, subject to a ch
called a kumshaw or present, amounting to 1,950 tales; and which is the same wh
the vessel carry 100 or 1,000 tons.   While, therefore, the port duties at Canto

ips of 400 or 500 tons burden and upwards are very moderate, they are very heavy
small ships: and hence small country ships frequently lie off Linting Flora, or
arge Bay, till some of the large European ships come in sight, when they shift their
rgoes on board the latter. They are commonly carried up to Canton for 1 per cent.,
which means the duties and kumshaw are both saved. Chinese junks are exempted
m the port dues.

Vessels of all sorts, importing rice into Canton, are exempted from the kumshaw
d all port duties: and it is not unusual for American ships to stop at Linting; and
tting their specie on board other ships that are going up to Whampoa, to go to
anilla and fetch a cargo of rice, and return while the outward cargo for them is
ting ready at Canton; saving, by this means, the payment of all port charges.

Rates of Pilotage paid by the Company's ships frequenting Canton are usually as
ows: —

				Dollars.	
Inwards:	From Lema Islands to Macao	-	-	30	
	From Macao to Whampoa	-	-	40	
	Kumshaw or present to pilot	-	-	5	
	Ten boats lying on second bar	-	-	10	
				— 85	
Outwards:	Pilot going on board at Whampoa	-	-	16	
	Ten boats on second bar	-	-	10	
	Pilot coming on board	-	-	20	
	Four boats lying on bar below	-	-	4	
	Balance of pilotage to Macao	-	-	4	
	Kumshaw	-	-	5	
				— 59	

Captain Coffin, the commander of an American ship of about 400 tons register
ling to China, informed the late committee of the House of Commons, that the
le charges of every description falling upon his ship, in entering and clearing out
n Canton, including measurement duty, kumshaw, pilotage, *victualling of the ship*,
consul's fee, amounted to between 7,000 and 8,000 dollars. — (*First Report, Evi-
ce*, p. 124.)

The Chinese, considered as traders, are eminently active, persevering, and intelli-
t. They are, in fact, a highly commercial people; and the notion that was once
y generally entertained of their being peculiarly characterised by a contempt of
merce and of strangers, is as utterly unfounded as any notion can possibly be.
iness is transacted at Canton with great despatch; and it is affirmed, by all the
esses examined before the parliamentary committees, that there is no port in the
d, Liverpool and New York not excepted, where cargoes may be sold and bought,
aded and loaded, with more business-like speed and activity.

he fears, whether real or pretended, of disturbances arising from a want of dis-
ne in the crews of private ships, have been proved to be altogether futile; and, in
t of fact, the Americans and other private traders have never experienced the
atest inconvenience from any tumults between their sailors and the natives.

argoes are all weighed on board, and the duties paid by the purchaser.

he resident foreigners at Canton engaged in trade are English, Americans, Portu-
e, Parsees, and Mohammedans of Bombay. The Dutch, French, and Americans,
each consuls; and the English agents have consular or vice consular commissions
German and Italian states, which are merely nominal, but serve to prevent their
lsion by the East India Company, who are vested by law with powers to send
out of China. The usual commission charged by English agents is 5 per cent.
ales, and 2½ per cent. on remittances and produce: the usual commission charged
he Americans is 3 per cent. After the sailing of the last ship of the season, the
gn agents, including the Company's supercargoes, are obliged by the Chinese laws
it Canton for the remainder of the year. They reside at the Portuguese settle-
t of Macao; but this regulation has been considerably relaxed of late years.

rovisions and refreshments of all sorts are abundant at Canton, and, in general, of
xcellent quality; nor is the price exorbitant. Every description of them, dead or
, is sold by weight. It is a curious fact, that the Chinese make no use of milk,
r in its liquid state, or in the shape of curds, butter, or cheese. Among the de-
ies of a Chinese market are to be seen horse flesh, dogs, cats, hawks, and owls.
country is well supplied with fish from the numberless canals and rivers by which
intersected; and the inhabitants breed also great numbers of gold and silver fish;
h are kept in large stock ponds, as well as in glass and China vases.

he perusal of the following price current, reduced to English weights and money,
give the reader a tolerable notion of the extent, variety, and prices of the Canton
et. Articles not the produce of China, but brought there by the junks *en entrepôt*,
narked with an asterisk.

IMPORTS.

	£	s.	d.		£	s.	d.	
Amber - -	1	4	0	and	2	2	1½	
Asafœtida -	0	0	1¾					
Biche de Mer -	0	0	3¼	-	0	0	3½	
—— very superior -	0	1	1					
Bees' Wax - -	0	0	8½	-	0	0	9	
Betel Nut, New -	0	0	1	-	0	0	1¼	
Birds'-nests -	3	17	10	-	6	0	3½	
Black Wood or Ebony - -	0	0	0¾					
Camphor, Malay -	2	2	1¼	-	3	17	10	
Cloves, Molucca -	0	0	9	-	0	0	10¾	
—— Mauritius -	0	0	5½	-	0	0	6½	
Cochineal - -	0	9	0¼	-	0	12	0¼	per lb.
Copper, South American -	0	0	8¾	-	0	0	9¼	
—— Do. at Linting for exportation	0	0	9¾					
—— Do. Japan -	0	0	9	-	0	0	9¾	
Coral Fragments -	0	0	10¾	-	0	1	6	
Cotton Yarn - -	0	0	10¾	-	0	1	9½	
Cotton, Bombay Old Ts., Old Ts. 2*d.* and 2½d. New	0	0	2½	-	0	0	3¼	
—— Bengal -	0	0	3	-	0	0	3¼	
—— Madras -	0	0	3¼					
Cotton Goods, Brit.								
—— Chintzes, 28 yds.	0	18	0,	-	1	4	0	
—— Long Cloths, 40 yds. -	1	0	0	-	1	2	0	
—— Muslins, 34 to 40 yds. - -	0	10	0	-	0	12	0	per piece.
—— Cambrics, 12 yds. - -	0	6	0	-	0	8	0	
Henry Monteith's Bandanas -	0	8	0	-	0	10	0	
Cow Bezoar -	4	10	2¼					
Cudbear - -	0	0	9	-	0	0	9½	
Cutch, Pegu -	0	0	1¼	-	0	0	1½	
Cuttings, Scarlet -	0	2	4¾	-	0	2	8½	
Elephants' Teeth -	0	1	9½	-	0	2	6½	
Fishmaws - -	0	1	2½	-	0	2	1¼	
Flints - -	0	0	0¼					
Gambier - -	0	0	0¼	-	0	0	0½	per lb.
Ginseng, Crude -	0	0	9	-	0	1	6	
Iron, Bar - -	0	0	1					
—— Rod - -	0	0	1¼	-	0	0	1½	
Lead - -	0	0	1½	-	0	0	1¾	
Mace - -								
Myrrh - -	0	0	5½	-	0	0	10¾	
Nutmegs - -	0	1	6	-	0	1	7¾	
Olibanum - -	0	12	0	-	1	0	0	
Opium, Patna - —— Benares -	166	0	0	-	167	0	0	
—— Damaun Malwa - -	108	0	0	-	109	0	0	per chest.
—— Company's do.	112	0	0	-	113	0	0	
—— Turkey -	0	19	10	-	-	-	-	per lb.
Orsidue, per 100 sheets - -	1	0	0	-	1	4	0	
Pepper, Malay -	0	0	2½	-	0	0	2¾	
Putchuck - -	0	0	4	-	0	0	4¼	
Quicksilver -	0	1	11½	-	0	1	11¾	
Rattans - -	0	0	0¾	-	0	0	1	
Rice - -	0	0	0½	-	0	0	0¾	
Rose Maloes -	0	1	3¼					
Saltpetre at Whampoa -	0	0	2					per lb.
—— Do. Linting -	0	0	3	-	0	0	3½	
Salt Fish - -	0	0	1½	-	0	0	1¾	
Sandal Wood -	0	0	3½	-	0	0	4¾	
Sapan Wood -	0	0	0¾					
Sharks' Fins -	0	0	5½	-	0	0	6½	
Smalts - -	0	0	4½	-	0	0	10	
Steel, Swedish, in Kits - -	1	12	0	-	1	16	0	per cwt.
Woollens, Broad-cloth - -	0	6	5	-	0	6	9½	per yd.
—— Camlets, English - -	4	8	0	-	4	16	0	
—— Dutch, Narrow 4*l.* 8*s.* and 4*l.* 16*s.*; Broad -	6	16	0	-	7	0	0	per piece.
—— Long Ells, do.	1	8	0	-	1	12	0	
Skins, Beaver -	0	17	0	-	1	4	0	
—— Fox - -	0	2	9½					
—— Rabbits -	0	1	7¾	-	0	2	0	each.
—— Seal - -	0	6	0					
—— Sea Otter -	10	0	0	-	12	0	0	
—— Land Otter -	0	16	0	-	1	4	0	
Spelter - -	0	0	1½	-	-		-	per lb.
Tin Plates - -								
Tin - -	0	0	6	-	0	0	6½	per lb.

EXPORTS.

	£	s.	d.		£	s.	d.	
Alum - -	0	0	0¾	and	-		-	
Aniseed, Star -	0	0	4½	-	0	0	4¾	p
—— Oil of -	0	7	6¼		-		-	
Bamboo Canes -	2	8	0		-		-	per
Brass Leaf - -								
Camphor at Macao 8¼*d.* and 8½*d.*; here - -	0	0	10	-	0	0	10¾	
Cassia at Macao 3¼*d.* and 3½*d.*; here - -	0	0	4¼	-	0	0	4½	
—— Buds -	0	0	6	-	0	0	6½	
China Root - -	0	0	1¼					
* Cubebs - -								
Dragon's Blood -	0	2	4¾	-	0	3	0	p
Galangal - -	0	0	1¾					
* Gamboge -	0	2	6½	-	0	2	8½	
Glass Beads -	0	0	9	-	0	0	9¼	
Hartall - -	0	0	4¼	-	0	0	4½	
* Mother of Pearl Shells - -	0	0	7¾	-	0	0	8	
Musk - -	10	10	6¼	-	13	10	8	
Nankeens, Company's, 1st -	16	0	0	-	16	8	0	
—— 2d do. 1st sort 13*l.* 12*s.* to 14*l.*; 2d - -	12	8	0	-	13	0	0	1
—— 3d do. do. -	9	12	0	-	11	0	0	
—— Blue - -	14	0	0	-	16	0	0	
—— Small - -								
Oil of Cassia -	0	4	6					
Rhubarb - -	0	1	11	-	0	2	1¼	
Silk, Raw, Nankin Taysan -	0	9	10½	-	0	10	2¼	
—— Ditto Tsatlee -	0	10	9½	-	0	10	11½	
—— Canton -	0	8	2¼	-	0	10	5¾	
Sugar, Raw -	0	0	2					
—— Pingfa -	0	0	2½					
Sugar Candy, Chinchew -	0	0	4½	-	0	0	4¾	
———— Canton, 1st sort - -								
———— 2d sort - -	0	0	2¾	-	0	0	3	P
Tea, Bohea - -								
—— Congou -	0	0	8¾	-	0	0	10	
—— Campoy -								
—— Souchong -	0	0	8	-	0	0	11	
—— Peko - -								
—— Ankoi -								
—— Hyson - -								
—— Do. Skin -	0	0	4½	-	0	0	7	
—— Do. Young -								
—— Gunpowder -								
—— Twankay -	0	0	7½	-	0	0	10	
* Tortoise Shell -								
Turmerick - -	0	0	3					
Tutenague - -	0	0	6½					
Vermilion - -								
White Lead -	0	0	5		-		-	
Whanghees, scarce		-	-		-		-	

N. B. In converting the weights and moneys o[f the] original price current, the Picul has been take[n as a] round number at 133 lbs. avoird.; the Tale at 5*s.* and the Spanish dollar at 4*s.* It should be obse[rved] that the quotation for teas refers to the dead sea[son,] and before the fresh teas have come into the ma[rket.]

compiling this article we have made use of *Hamilton's East India Gazetteer*, ~burgh's Directory, Singapore Chronicle, Parliamentary Papers* relating to the Finances ~dia and the Trade of India and China*, 1829 and 1830, *Reports of the Lords' Commons' Committees of* 1830, *Kelly's Cambist, Milburn's Orient. Commerce, Canton ~ter*, 1830 and 1831.

~ANVAS (Fr. *Toile à voile* ; Ger. *Segeltuch* ; It. *Canevazza, Lona* ; Rus. *Pa- ~oe polotno, Parussina* ; Sp. *Lona*), unbleached cloth of hemp or flax, ~ly used for sails for shipping.

~asters of ships are required to make entry, upon oath, of all foreign made on board their respective ships, and shall pay the duty thereon, under for- ~re of the sails, whether they be in use or not. It has been the practice for a ~iderable period to grant bounties on the exportation of canvas, or sail-cloth ; ~, however, are finally to cease on the 1st of January next, 1832. By an act ~d in the reign of Geo. 2. new sails were ordered to be stamped with the ~r's name and place of abode ; but this regulation was repealed by the 10 Geo. ~43. § 9.

~AOUTCHOUC. " This substance, which has been improperly termed elastic and vulgarly, from its common application to rub out pencil marks on ~, *India rubber*, is obtained from the milky juice of different plants in hot ~tries. The chief of these are the *Jatropha elastica*, and *Urceola elastica*. ~juice is applied in successive coatings on a mould of clay, and dried by the ~r in the sun ; and when of a sufficient thickness, the mould is crushed, and ~ieces shaken out. Acids separate the caoutchouc from the thinner part of ~uice at once, by coagulating it. The juice of old plants yields nearly two ~s of its weight ; that of younger plants less. Its colour, when fresh, is ~wish white, but it grows darker by exposure to the air. The elasticity of ~ubstance is its most remarkable property : when warmed, as by immersion ~t water, slips of it may be drawn out to seven or eight times their original ~h, and will return to their former dimensions nearly. Cold renders it stiff ~igid, but warmth restores its original elasticity. Exposed to the fire, it ~as, swells up, and burns with a bright flame. In Cayenne it is used to give ~as a candle." — (*Dr. Ure*).

~outchouc when imported is, most commonly, in the form of small bottles ; ~being the shape of the clay moulds on which it has been spread. They ~t off ; and the edges, being softened by heat, are again joined.

~PERS (Fr. *Capres* ; Ger. *Kappern* ; Du. *Kappers* ; It. *Cappari* ; Sp. *Alca- ~s* ; Rus. *Kaperszü* ; Lat. *Capparis*), the pickled buds of the *Capparis spinosa*, shrub, generally growing out of the joints of old walls and the fissures of ~, in most of the warm parts of Europe. Capers are imported into Great ~n from different parts of the Mediterranean ; the best from Toulon in ~e. Some small salt capers come from Majorca, and a few flat ones from Lyons. The duty of 6*d.* per lb. on capers produced, in 1829, 1,096*l.* 2*s.* 7*d.* ~howing that 43,845 lbs. had been entered for home consumption.

~PE-TOWN, the capital of the British territory in South Africa ; lat. 33° ~, long. 18° 23¼' E. It lies at the head of the Table Bay, on the west side Cape of Good Hope. The town was founded by the Dutch in 1650 ; and ~ned, with the territory subject to it, in their possession, till it was taken by ~ritish in 1795. It was restored to the Dutch by the treaty of Amiens ; but again captured by the British in 1806, it was finally ceded to us in 1815. ~treets are laid out in straight lines, crossing each other at right angles ; many ~m being watered by canals, and planted on each side with oaks. The popu- amounts to about 6,000 whites and persons of colour, and 10,000 blacks. ~, *Gazet.*) The town is defended by a castle of considerable strength. ~Bay is capable of containing any number of ships ; but it is exposed to the ~ly winds, which, during the months of June, July, and August, throw in a swell, that has been productive of many distressing accidents. This, in ~s the great drawback upon Cape-Town, which in all other respects is most ~ably fitted for a commercial station. At the proper season, however, or ~: the prevalence of the easterly monsoon, Table Bay is perfectly safe ; while ~eapness and abundance of provisions, the healthiness of the climate, and all its position, render it a peculiarly desirable resting place for ships bound ~from India, China, Australia, &c.

The district subject to Cape-Town is of very great extent, and contains every vari
of soil, from the richest level land to the wildest mountain, and tracts destitute of e
the appearance of vegetation. The climate fluctuates between the two extremes of r
and drought. On the whole, its advantages and disadvantages seem to be pretty equ
balanced; and the prospects which it holds out to the industrious emigrant, if not v
alluring, are certainly not discouraging.

Large quantities of corn of a very good description are produced in the immed
neighbourhood of Cape-Town; but its free exportation is restrained; none being allow
to be sent abroad, except a specified quantity decided upon by government after
investigation into the state of the crops! This restriction, Mr. Thompson tells
(*Travels in Southern Africa*, p. 395.), has neither produced regular prices nor aver
scarcity. It has, however, been in no common degree injurious to the colony; an
is really surprising that systems of policy universally condemned in England should
allowed to exert a pernicious influence over any of our colonies. The Mauritius
Rio Janeiro are the principal markets for the corn of the Cape.

Large quantities of wine, and of what is called brandy, are produced at the Cape;
with the exception of Constantia, they are very inferior. Objections have been mad
the duties recently imposed on Cape wines; but, as it appears to us, without any g
foundation. The real effect of allowing their importation at a comparatively low d
is not to occasion their direct consumption, but to cause them to be employed as a c
venient means of adulterating others; so that, besides being injurious to the rever
such reduction of duty promotes fraudulent practices, and detracts from the comfort
the public.

Considerable quantities of hides and skins are exported. They are principally brou
from Algoa Bay, on the eastern side of the colony; and the trade has increased very
during the last four or five years. Aloes are very abundant, and are largely expor
Argol also forms an item in the list of exports; as do dried fruits, and some o
articles.

The exports to the Cape consist of woollens, cottons, hardware, earthenware, furnit
haberdashery, soap, paper, books, and portions of most articles used in this coun
Piece goods and teak timber are imported from India, tea from China, sugar f
India and the Mauritius, &c.

The trade between the colonists and the independent natives is subjected to var
restraints, of which it is not always very easy to discover the policy. The sale of g
powder and fire-arms to the natives has been prohibited; a regulation which might l
been a judicious one, had they not been able to obtain them from any one else.
the Americans have begun to trade at Natal, on the eastern coast, and have liber
supplied the natives with these and various other articles; so that by keeping up
regulation in question we merely exclude ourselves from participating in what migh
an advantageous trade.

According to the Custom-house accounts, the real or declared value of the ex
from the *United Kingdom* to the Cape of Good Hope, in 1829 and 1830, were:—

British and Irish Produce and Manufactures.	1829.	1830.
	£.	£.
Cotton Manufacture - - - -	82,017	123,54
Linens - - - - -	12,542	16,48
Cotton Manufactures - - - -	31,152	38,10
Other Articles; viz. Apparel, Hops, Household ⎫ Furniture, Soap, Candles, Iron, Leather, &c. - ⎭	131,790	151,90
	257,501	330,03
Foreign and Colonial Merchandise (Official Value)	36,424	77,96
Total Exports	£293,925	£408,0(

Official value of imports into the United Kingdom from the Cape of Good H
1829, 238,134*l.*; 1830, 171,498*l.*

During 1830, 23 ships, of the burden of 4,276 tons, entered British ports inv
from the Cape; and 38 ships, of the burden of 7,737 tons, cleared outwards for the C
According to the official returns, the population of the Cape colony, in 1829, cons
of —

Whites.		Slaves.			
Male.	Female.	Male.	Female.		
45,087	41,317	18,312	13,754	Total	118,470.

Regulations as to Trade. — It is enacted by the 6 Geo. 4. c. 111., that all goods, the produce or manufac-
e of the Cape of Good Hope, or the territories or dependencies thereof, are to be subject (on importation
o England) to the same duties as are imposed on the like articles, the produce or manufacture of the
tish possession within the limits of the East India Company's charter, except when any other duty is
ressly laid on them. — § 12.

he 6 Geo. 4. c. 114. enacts, that it shall be lawful for his Majesty, by any order in council to be issued
m time to time, to give such directions and make such regulations touching the trade and commerce
nd from any British possessions in Africa, as to his Majesty in council shall appear most expedient
salutary ; and if any goods be imported or exported in any manner contrary to such order of his
esty in council, the same shall be forfeited, together with the ship importing or exporting the same.—
.

t shall not be lawful for any person to re-export, from any of his Majesty's possessions abroad, to any
eign place, any coals, the produce of the United Kingdom ; and no such coals shall be shipped at any
uch possessions, to be exported to any British place, until the exporter or the master of the exporting
el shall have given bond, with one sufficient surety, in double the value of the coals, that such coals
ll not be landed at any foreign place. — § 85.

t shall be lawful for the shipper of any wine, the produce of the Cape of Good Hope or of its depend-
ies, which is to be exported thence, to go before the chief officer of customs and make and sign an
davit before him that such wine was really and *bonâ fide* the produce of the Good Hope or of its de-
dencies ; and such officer is hereby authorised and required to administer such affidavit, and to grant
rtificate thereof, setting forth in such certificate the name of the ship in which the wine is to be
orted, and the destination of the same. — § 78.

Duties. — A duty of 3¼ per cent. is charged on the importation of all articles of the
wth, production, or manufacture of Great Britain, or of the British plantations in the
st Indies.

A duty of 10 per cent. is charged on the importation (by British vessels) of all articles
he growth, production, or manufacture of foreign Europe, America, or the eastward
he Cape, to be levied according to the declaration of the value by the importer. No
tement or deduction whatever admitted, except of the duties and landing charges
able on the importation thereof.

An additional duty of 1s. 6d. per gallon is charged on the importation of arrack, rum,
, liqueurs, whisky, or other spirituous liquors, *brandy excepted.*

No tea may be landed, unless the permission of the East India Company's agent be
obtained.

No ammunition may be landed or shipped, unless the permission of government be
obtained.

Money. — Accounts are either kept in pounds, shillings, pence, and farthings, or in
dollars, schillings, and stivers.

1 Stiver	=	⅜ of a Penny.
6 Stivers	=	2¼ Pence, or 1 Schilling.
8 Schillings	=	18 Pence, or 1 Rix-dollar.

he commissariat department grant bills on the Treasury at a premium of 1½ per

Weights and Measures. — The weights made use of in the Cape are derived from the
dard pound of Amsterdam ; and those assized are from 50 lbs. down to 1 loot, or the
y-second part of a pound, which is regarded as unity.

Liquid Measure.

16 Flasks	=	1 Anker.
4 Ankers	=	1 Aum.
4 Aums	=	1 Leaguer.

Corn Measure.

4 Schepels = 1 Muid.
10 Muids = 1 Load. 107 sche-
= 82 Winch. bushels, or 4 schepels
Imp. bush. very nearly.

The muid of wheat weighs, at an average,
about 110 lbs. Dutch, being somewhat over
196 lbs. English.

Cloth and Long Measures.

12 Rhynland Ins.	=	1 Rhynland Ft.
27 ditto	=	1 Dutch Ell.
144 ditto	=	1 Square Foot.
144 Square Feet	=	1 Rood.
600 Roods	=	1 Morgen.

Colonial Weights and Measures compared with those of England.

Weights.

100 lbs. Dutch	=	nearly 109 lbs. English avoirdupois.
100 lbs. English	=	nearly 92 lbs. Dutch.

Wine or Liquid Measure.

1 Flask	=	$\frac{19}{32}$ Old Gallon, or	4·946	Imperial Gallons.
1 Anker	=	9½ ditto,	7$\frac{9}{10}$	ditto.
1 Aum	=	38 ditto,	31$\frac{2}{3}$	ditto.
1 Leaguer	=	152 ditto,	126$\frac{7}{11}$	ditto.
1 Pipe	=	110 ditto,	91$\frac{7}{11}$	ditto.

rt dues upon all vessels entering the Cape for purposes of trade, 4½d. per ton ; to
ure refreshments, or for any purpose other than trading, 2¼d. per ton.

CAPITAL, in political economy, is that portion of the produce existing in a country, which may be made directly available, either to the support of human existence, or to the facilitating of production.—(*Principles of Political Economy,* 2d ed. p. 97.) But in commerce, and as applied to individuals, it is understood of the sum of money which a merchant, banker, or trader, adventures in any undertaking, or which he contributes to the common stock of a partnership. It signifies likewise the fund of a trading company, or corporation; in which sense the word *stock* is generally added to it. Thus we say the *capital stock* of the Bank, &c. The profit derived from any undertaking, is estimated by the *rate* which it bears to the capital that was employed.

CAPSICUM. See PEPPER.

CARAVAN, an organised company of merchants, or pilgrims, or both, who associate together in many parts of Asia and Africa, that they may travel with greater security through deserts and other places infested with robbers; or where the road is naturally dangerous. The word is derived from the Persian *kervan,* or *cârvân,* a trader or dealer.—(*Shaw's Travels in the Levant,* p. 9. 4to ed.

Every caravan is under the command of a chief or aga (*caravan-bachi*), who has frequently under him such a number of troops or forces, as is deemed sufficient for its defence. When it is practicable, they encamp near wells or rivulets; and observe a regular discipline. Camels are used as a means of conveyance, almost uniformly, in preference to the horse or any other animal, on account of their wonderful patience of fatigue, eating little, and subsisting three or four days or more without water. There are generally more camels in a caravan than men. See CAMEL.

The commercial intercourse of Eastern and African nations has been principally carried on, from the remotest period, by means of caravans. During antiquity, the products of India and China were conveyed either from Suez to Rhinoculura, or from Bussorah, near the head of the Persian Gulf, by the Euphrates to Babylon, and thence by Palmyra, in the Syrian desert, to the ports of Phœnicia on the Mediterranean, where they were exchanged for the European productions in demand in the East. Sometimes however, caravans set out directly from China, and, occupying about 250 days in the journey, arrived on the shores of the Levant after traversing the whole extent of Asia (*Gibbon,* vol. vii. p. 93.) The formation of caravans is, in fact, the only way in which it has ever been possible to carry on any considerable internal commerce in Asia or Africa. The governments that have grown up in those continents have seldom been able, and seldomer indeed have they attempted, to render travelling practicable or safe for individuals. The wandering tribes of Arabs have always infested the immense deserts by which they are intersected; and those only, who are sufficiently powerful to protect themselves, or sufficiently rich to purchase an exemption from the predatory attacks of these freebooters, can expect to pass through territories subject to their incursions without being exposed to the risk of robbery and murder.

Since the establishment of the Mohammedan faith, religious motives, conspiring with those of a less exalted character, have tended to augment the intercourse between different parts of the Eastern world, and to increase the number and magnitude of the caravans. Mohammed enjoined all his followers to visit, once in their lifetime, the Caaba or square building in the temple of Mecca, the immemorial object of veneration amongst his countrymen; and in order to preserve continually upon their minds a sense of obligation to perform this duty, he directed that, in all the multiplied acts of devotion which his religion prescribes, true believers should always turn their faces towards the holy place. In obedience to a precept so solemnly enjoined and sedulously inculcated large caravans of pilgrims used to assemble annually in every country where the Mohammedan faith is established; and though, owing either to a diminution of religious zeal, or the increasing difficulties to be encountered in the journey, the number of pilgrims has of late years declined greatly, it is still very considerable. Few, however, of the pilgrims are actuated only by devotional feelings. Commercial ideas and objects mingle with those of religion; and it redounds to the credit of Mohammed that he granted permission to trade during the pilgrimage to Mecca; providing at the same time for the temporal as well as the lasting interests of his votaries. " It shall be no crime in you, if ye seek an increase from your Lord *by trading during the pilgrimage.*" — (*Sale's Koran,* c. 2. p. 36. ed. 1764.)

The numerous camels of each caravan are loaded with those commodities of every country which are of easiest carriage and readiest sale. The holy city is crowded during the month of Dhalhajja, corresponding to the latter part of June and the beginning of July, not only with zealous devotees, but with opulent merchants. A fair or market is held in Mecca and its vicinity, on the twelve days that the pilgrims are allowed to remain

at city, which used to be one of the best frequented in the world, and continues to
ell attended.

Few pilgrims," says Burckhardt, "except the mendicants, arrive without bringing
productions of their respective countries for sale : and this remark is applicable as
to the merchants, with whom commercial pursuits are the main object, as to those
are actuated by religious zeal; for, to the latter, the profits derived from selling a
rticles at Mecca diminish, in some degree, the heavy expenses of the journey. The
grebyns (pilgrims from Morocco and the north coast of Africa) bring their red
ets and woollen cloaks; the European Turks, shoes and slippers, hardware,
oidered stuffs, sweetmeats, amber, trinkets of European manufacture, knit silk
s, &c.; the Turks of Anatolia bring carpets, silks, and Angora shawls; the
ans, cashmere shawls and large silk handkerchiefs; the Afghans, tooth-brushes,
1 Mesouak Kattary, made of the spongy boughs of a tree growing in Bokhara,
s of a yellow soapstone, and plain coarse shawls manufactured in their own
try; the Indians, the numerous productions of their rich and extensive region;
eople of Yemen, snakes for the Persian pipes, sandals and various other works in
er; and the Africans bring various articles adapted to the slave trade. The pil-
are, however, often disappointed in their expectations of gain; want of money
s them hastily sell their little adventures at the public auctions, and often obliges
to accept very low prices." — (*Travels in Arabia*, vol. ii. p. 21.)

e two principal caravans which yearly rendezvous at Mecca, are those of Damascus
Cairo. The first is composed of pilgrims from Europe and Western Asia; the
d of Mohammedans from all parts of Africa.

e Syrian caravan is said by Burckhardt to be very well regulated. It is always
panied by the pacha of Damascus, or one of his principal officers, who gives the
l for encamping and starting by firing a musket. On the route, a troop of horse-
ide in the front, and another in the rear to bring up the stragglers. The different
s of pilgrims, distinguished by their provinces or towns, keep close together. At
torches are lighted, and the daily distance is usually performed between three
k in the afternoon and an hour or two after sunrise on the following day. The
uins or Arabs, who carry provisions for the troops, travel by day only, and in
ce of the caravans; the encampment of which they pass in the morning, and are
ken in turn and passed by the caravan on the following night, at their own resting
The journey with these Bedouins is less fatiguing than with the great body of
ravan, as a regular night's rest is obtained; but their bad character deters most
ms from joining them.

every watering-place on the route is a small castle and a large tank, at which the
water. The castles are garrisoned by a few persons, who remain the whole year
rd the provisions deposited there. It is at these watering-places, which belong to
douins, that the sheikhs of the tribe meet the caravan, and receive the accustomed
for allowing it to pass. Water is plentiful on the route; the stations are no
more distant than eleven or twelve hours' march; and in winter, pools of rain
are frequently found. Those pilgrims who can travel with a litter, or on com-
us camel-saddles, may sleep at night, and perform the journey with little incon-
ce : but of those whom poverty, or the desire of speedily acquiring a large sum
ney, induces to follow the caravan on foot, or to hire themselves as servants, many
the road from fatigue. — (*Travels in Arabia*, vol. ii. p. 3—9.)

caravan which sets out from Cairo for Mecca is not generally so large as that
mascus; and its route along the shores of the Red Sea is more dangerous and
ng. But many of the African and Egyptian merchants and pilgrims sail from
Cosseir, and other ports on the western shore of the Red Sea, for Djidda, whence
rney to Mecca is short and easy.

Persian caravan sets out from Bagdad; but many of the Persian pilgrims are
the habit of embarking at Bussorah, and coming to Djidda by sea.

commerce carried on by caravans, in the interior of Africa, is widely extended
considerable value. Besides the great caravan which proceeds from Nubia to Cairo,
joined by Mohammedan pilgrims from every part of Africa, there are caravans
have no object but commerce, which set out from Fez, Algiers, Tunis, Tripoli,
her states on the sea-coast, and penetrate far into the interior. Some of them
many as 50 days to reach the place of their destination; and as their rate of
ing may be estimated at about 18 miles a day at an average, the extent of their
ys may easily be computed. As both the time of their outset and their route is
, they are met by the people of the countries through which they travel, who
vith them. Indian goods of every kind form a considerable article in this traffic;
lange for which, the chief commodity the inhabitants have to give is slaves.

ee distinct caravans are employed in bringing slaves and other commodities from
1 Africa to Cairo. One of them comes direct from Mourzouk, the capital of

Fezzan, across the Libyan desert; another from Senaar; and the third from Darf
They do not arrive at stated periods, but after a greater or less interval, according to
success they have had in procuring slaves, ivory, gold dust, drugs, and such ot
articles as are fitted for the Egyptian markets. The Mourzouk caravan is said to
under the best regulations. It is generally about 50 days on its passage; and seld
consists of less than 100, or of more than 300, travellers. The caravans from Sen
and Darfur used formerly to be very irregular, and were sometimes not seen in Eg
for two or three years together; but since the occupation of the former by the troops
Mohammed Ali, the intercourse between it and Egypt has become comparatively f
quent and regular. The number of slaves imported into Egypt by these caravans
said to amount, at present, to about 10,000 a year. The departure of a caravan fr
Darfur is looked upon as a most important event; it engages for a while the attenti
of the whole country, and even forms a kind of era. — (*Browne's Travels in Afr*
2d ed. p. 278.) A caravan from Darfur is considered large, if it has 2,000 camels a
1,000 slaves. Many of the Moorish pilgrims to Mecca cross the sea from Souakin a
Massouah to the opposite coast of Arabia, and then travel by land to Mecca; a
Burckhardt states, that of all the poor pilgrims who arrive in the Hedjaz, none bea
more respectable character for industry than those from Central Africa.

Caravans are distinguished into *heavy* and *light*. Camels loaded with from 500
600 lbs.* form a heavy caravan; light caravans being the term applied to design
those formed of camels under a moderate load, or perhaps only half loaded. The me
daily rate at which heavy caravans travel is about 18½ miles, and that of light carav
22 miles.

No particular formalities are required in the formation of a caravan. Any dealer
at liberty to form a company and make one. The individual in whose name it is rais
is considered as the leader, or *caravan-bachi*, unless he appoint some one else in his pla
When a number of merchants associate together in the design, they elect a chi
and appoint officers to decide whatever controversies may arise during the journe
For further details with respect to caravans, see the *Modern Part of the Universal H
tory*, vol. xiv. pp. 214—243.; *Robertson's Disquisition on Ancient India*, Note 54
Rees's Cyclopædia, art. *Caravan*, most of which is copied from Robertson, though with
a single word of acknowledgment; and *Burckhardt's Travels in Arabia*, vol. ii. pass

CARAVANSERA, a large public building or inn appropriated for the reception a
lodgment of the caravans. Though serving in lieu of inns, there is this radical diff
ence between them,—that, generally speaking, the traveller finds nothing in a caravans
for the use either of himself or his cattle. He must carry all his provisions and nec
saries with him. They are chiefly built in dry, barren, desert places; and are mos
furnished with water brought from a great distance and at a vast expence. A well
water is, indeed, indispensable to a caravansera. Caravanseras are also numerous
cities; where they serve not only as inns, but as shops, warehouses, and even exchang

CARAWAY-SEED (Fr. *Carvi, Cumin des près*; Ger. *Keummel, Brodkümm*
It. *Carvi*), is a small seed, of an oblong and slender figure, pointed at both en
and thickest in the middle. It is to be chosen large, new, and of a good colc
not dusty, and of a strong agreeable smell. It is extensively cultivated in seve
parts, particularly in Essex.

CARBUNCLE (Ger. *Karfunkel;* Fr. *Escarboukle;* It. *Carbonchio;* Sp. C
bunculo; Lat. *Carbunculus*), a precious stone of the ruby kind, of a very i
glowing blood-red colour; probably a variety of the garnet. It was hig
esteemed by the ancients.

CARD (Fr. *Cardes;* Ger. *Kardätschen, Karden, Wollkratzen;* It. *Cardi;* F
Bardü; Sp. *Cardas*), an instrument, or comb, for arranging or sorting the hair
wool, cotton, &c. Cards are either fastened to a flat piece of wood, and wrough
the hand, or to a cylinder, and wrought by machinery.

CARDAMOMS (Fr. *Cardamomes;* Ger. *Kardamom;* It. *Cardamomi;* Sp. k
damomos; Hind. *Gujarati elachi*), seed capsules produced by a plant, of which th
are different species growing in India, Cochin China, Siam, and Ceylon.
capsules are gathered as they ripen; and when dried in the sun, are fit for s
The small capsules, or lesser cardamoms, are produced by a particular specie
the plant, and are the most valuable. They should be chosen full, plump,
difficult to be broken; of a bright yellow colour; a piercing smell; with an ac
bitterish, though not very unpleasant taste; and particular care should be ta
that they are properly dried. They are reckoned to keep best in a body, and
therefore packed in large chests, well jointed, pitched at the seams, and other
properly secured; as the least damp greatly reduces their value.

* This is the burden of the small camel only. The large ones usually carry from 750 lbs. to 1,000

The best cardamoms are brought from the Malabar coast. They are produced in the ↑esses of the mountains, by felling trees, and afterwards burning them; for wherever ↑ ashes fall in the openings or fissures of the rocks, the cardamom plant naturally ↑ings up. In Soonda Balagat, and other places where cardamoms are planted, the ↑it or berry is very inferior to that produced in the way now mentioned. The Malabar ↑damom is described as a species of bulbous plant, growing three or four feet high. ↑e growers are obliged to sell all their produce to the agents of government, at prices ↑ed by the latter, varying from 550 to 700 rupees the candy of 600 lbs. avoirdupois: ↑ it is stated that the contractor often puts an *enhanced value on the coins* with which ↑ pays the mountaineers; or makes them take in exchange tobacco, cloths, salt, oil, ↑el-nut, and such necessary articles, at prices which are frequently, no doubt, estimated ↑ve their proper level. Such a system ought assuredly to be put an immediate end Not more than *one hundredth* part of the cardamoms raised in Malabar are used in country. They are sent in large quantities to the ports on the Red Sea and the ↑rsian Gulf, to Sind, up the Indus, to Bengal, Bombay, &c. They form a universal ↑redient in curries, pillaus, &c. The market price, at the places of exportation on the ↑labar coast, varies from 800 to 1,200 rupees the candy. — (*Milburn's Orient. Com-* ↑ce, and the valuable evidence of T. H. Baber, Esq., before the Lords' Committee of ↑0, p. 216.)

↑Malabar cardamoms are worth at present (May 1831), from 4s. 6d. to 5s. a pound ↑he London market, duty (2s.) included. Ceylon cardamoms are worth, in bond, 2s. lb.

↑CARDS, OR PLAYING CARDS (Du. *Kaarten, Speelkarden;* Fr. *Cartes à* ↑er; Ger. *Karten, Spiel karten;* It. *Carte da giuoco;* Rus. *Kartü;* Sp, *Carras,* ↑ipes;* Sw. *Kort*). The only thing necessary to be noticed in this place with ↑oect to cards, is the regulations as to their manufacture, sale, and the payment ↑he duty.

↑t is regulated by the 9 Geo. 4. c. 18., that an annual licence duty of 5s. shall be ↑d by every maker of playing cards and dice. The duty on every pack of cards is 1s. ↑ is to be specified on the ace of spades. Cards are not to be made in any part of ↑at Britain, except the metropolis; nor in Ireland, except in Dublin and Cork; under ↑nalty of 100l. Cards are to be enclosed in wrappers, with such marks as the com- ↑sioners of stamps may appoint. Before licence can be had, bond must be given to ↑amount of 500l., for the payment of the duties, &c. Selling or exposing to sale any ↑k of cards not duly stamped, subjects a licensed maker to a penalty of 50l.; and any ↑else to a penalty of 10l. Any person having in his possession, or using, or permit- ↑to be used, any pack of cards not duly stamped, to forfeit 5l. Second-hand cards ↑ be sold by any person, if sold without the wrapper of a licensed maker; and in ↑s containing not more than 52 cards, including an ace of spades duly stamped, and ↑osed in a wrapper with the words " *Second-hand Cards* " printed or written in dis- ↑: characters on the outside: penalty for selling second-hand cards in any other ↑ner, 20l. The gross revenue derived from cards in Great Britain, in 1828, amounted ↑7,365l. 5s. 6d.: the drawbacks and other payments out of which amounted to ↑4l. 9s., leaving 14,500l. 16s. 6d. of nett revenue.

↑urn of the Number of Packs of Playing Cards charged with Duty, in the Years ↑ded 5th January, 1827, and 5th January, 1830; stating the Rate of Duty and ↑mount collected. — (*Parl. Paper,* No. 274. Sess. 1830.)

	Number of Packs.	Rate of Duty.		Amount Collected.		
		s.	d.	£	s.	d.
↑'ear ended 5th January, 1827 -	146,406	2	6	18,300	15	0
↑'ear ended 5th January, 1830 -	310,854	1	0	15,542	14	0

↑ARMEN, of the City of London, are constituted a fellowship by act of ↑mon council. The rates which they are allowed to charge, and the regulations ↑which they are to be guided, are settled at the quarter sessions. In other ↑ects they are subjected to the rule of the president and governors of Christ's ↑pital, to whom the owner of every cart pays an annual licence duty of 17s. 4d. ↑men are to help to load and unload their carts; and if any carman exacts more than the regular ↑upon due proof, before the Lord Mayor, or any two magistrates, he shall suffer imprisonment for ↑ace of 21 days. ↑any person shall refuse to pay any carman his hire, according to the regular rates, upon complaint ↑the president of Christ's Hospital, or a justice of the peace, may compel payment. ↑rchants or other persons may choose what cart they please, except such as stand for wharf-work,

tackle-work, crane-work, at shops and merchant's houses, which are to be taken in turn; and every car-man standing with his empty cart next to any goods to be loaded, shall, upon the first demand, load th same for the accustomed rates; and if any person shall cause a carman to attend at his house, shop, ware-house, or cellar, with his loaded cart, the carman being willing to help to unload the same, he shall pa the carman after the rate of twelve-pence for every hour after the first half-hour for his attendance.

Every licensed carman is to have a piece of brass fixed upon his cart, upon which is to be engraven certain number; which number, together with the carman's name, is registered in a register kept at Christ Hospital; so that, in case of any misbehaviour, the party offended, by taking notice of the number of th cart, may search for it in the register, and the name will be found.

Carmen not conforming to these rules, or working without a numbered piece of brass fixed on the car may be suspended from their employment.

Carmen riding upon the shafts of their carts, or sitting within them, not having some person on foo to guide the horses, shall forfeit 10s.

CARMINE (Ger. *Karmin;* Du. *Karmyn;* Fr. *Carmine;* It. *Carminio;* Lat *Carminum*), a powder of a very beautiful red colour, bordering upon purple, an used by painters in miniature. It is a species of *lake*, and is formed of finel pulverised cochineal, in the manner described by Dr. Ure. It is very high priced

CARNELIAN (Du. *Karneol;* Fr. *Cornaline, Sarde;* Ger. *Karniol;* It. *Corna-lina;* Lat. *Carneolus, Sardus;* Rus. *Seredolik;* Sp. *Cornerina*), a sub-species of chal-cedony; colour blood-red, passing into flesh-red, reddish white, yellow, reddish brown. It is tolerably hard, and susceptible of a very good polish.

CARPET, CARPETS (Ger. *Teppiche;* Du. *Tapyten, Vloer-tapyten;* Fr. *Tapis,* It. *Tappeti;* Sp. *Alfombras, Alcatifas, Tapetes;* Rus. *Kowrü, Kilimi*). Persian and Turkish carpets are the most esteemed. In England, carpets are principally manufactured at Kidderminster, Wilton, Cirencester, Worcester, Axminster, &c. and in Scotland, at Kilmarnock. Those made at Axminster are believed to be very little, if anything, inferior to those of Persia and Turkey.

CARRIAGES. See COACHES.

CARROT (*Daucus Carota*, Lin.), a biennial plant, a native of Britain. Though long known as a garden plant, its introduction into agriculture has been com-paratively recent.. The uses of the carrot in domestic economy are well known It is extensively cultivated in Suffolk, whence large quantities are sent to the London market. Horses are said to be remarkably fond of carrots.

CARRIERS, are persons undertaking for hire to carry goods from one place to another.

Proprietors of carts and wagons, masters and owners of ships, hoymen, lighter-men, bargemen, ferrymen, &c. are denominated common carriers. The master of a stage coach who *only carries passengers for hire,* is not liable for goods; but if h undertake to carry *goods and passengers,* then he is liable for both as a commo carrier. The post-master general is not a carrier in the common acceptation o the term, nor is he subjected to his liabilities.

1. *Duties and Liabilities of Carriers.* — Carriers are bound to receive and carry th goods of all persons, for a reasonable hire or reward; to take proper care of them i their passage; to deliver them safely, and in the same condition as when they wer received (excepting only such losses as may arise from *the act of God or the king enemies*); or in default thereof to make compensation to the owner for whatever loss c damage the goods may have received while in their custody, that might have been pre vented.

Hence a carrier is liable though he be robbed of the goods, or they be taken from hir by irresistible force; and though this may seem a hard rule, yet it is the only one tha could be safely adopted; for if a carrier were not liable for losses unless it could b shown that he had conducted himself dishonestly or negligently, a door would be opene for every species of fraud and collusion, inasmuch as it would be impossible, in mos cases, to ascertain whether the facts were such as the carrier represented. On the sam principle a carrier has been held accountable for goods accidentally consumed by fir while in his warehouse. In delivering the opinion of the Court of King's Bench on case of this sort, Lord Mansfield said — " A carrier, by the nature of his contrac obliges himself to use all due care and diligence, and is answerable for any neglec But there is something more imposed upon him by custom, that is, by the common law *A common carrier is in the nature of an insurer.* All the cases show him to be so. Th makes him liable for every thing except the act of God and the king's enemies; that i even for *inevitable accidents,* with those exceptions. The question then is, *What is th act of God?* I consider it to be laid down in opposition to the act of *man;* such lightning, storms, tempests, and the like, which could not happen by *any human inte vention.* To prevent litigation and collusion, the law presumes negligence except i those circumstances. An armed force, though ever so great and irresistible, does n excuse; the reason is, for fear it may give room for collusion, which can never happ

respect to the act of God. We all, therefore, are of opinion, that there should be
ment for the plaintiff." — (*Forward* v. *Pittard*, 1 *T. R.* 27.)

carrier is not obliged to have a new carriage for every journey; it is sufficient if he
ide one that, without any extraordinary accident, may be fairly presumed capable of
rming the journey.

carrier may be discharged from his liability by any fraud or concealment on the
of the individual employing him, or of the bailor; as if the latter represent a parcel
ntaining things of little or no value, when, in fact, it contains things of great value.
when the carrier has not given a notice limiting his responsibility, and when he
no questions with respect to the parcel to the bailor, the latter need not say any
with respect to it; and though the bailor should represent the thing delivered to
arrier as of no value, yet *if the latter know it to be otherwise*, he will be responsible
e event of its being lost or damaged. If the bailor deliver goods imperfectly
ed, and the carrier *does not perceive it*, he is not liable in the event of a loss occurring;
f the defect in the package were such that the carrier could not but perceive it, he
d be liable. On this principle a carrier was made to answer for the loss of a grey-
d that had been improperly secured when given to him.

carrier may refuse to admit goods into his warehouse at an unseasonable time, or
e he is ready to take his journey; but he cannot refuse to do the ordinary duties
nbent on a person in his situation.

is felony, if a carrier open a parcel and take goods out of it with intent to steal them;
t has been decided, that if goods be delivered to a carrier to be carried to a specified
, and he carry them to a different place and dispose of them for his own profit, he
lty of felony : but the embezzlement of goods by a carrier, without a felonious
g, merely exposes to a civil action.

carrier, wagonman, carman, or wainman, with their respective carriages, shall
on Sundays, under a penalty of 20s. — (3 *Cha.* 1. c. 1.)

carrier is always, unless there be an express agreement to the contrary, entitled to
ard for his care and trouble. In some cases his reward is regulated by the legis-
, and in others by a special stipulation between the parties; but though there be
gislative provision or express agreement, he cannot claim more than a *reasonable*
ensation.

Limitation of Responsibility. — Until the act of last session, a carrier might, by
ss stipulation, giving *public notice* to that effect, discharge his liability from all
by robbery, accident, or otherwise, except those which arose from *misfeazance and*
negligence (from which no stipulation or notice could exempt him), and provided
tice did not contravene the express conditions of an act of parliament.

tices generally bore, that the carrier would not be responsible for more than a certain
usually 5*l.*) on any one parcel, the value of which had not been declared and paid
cordingly; so that a person aware of this notice, entering a box worth 1,000*l.*
t declaring its value, or entering it as being worth 200*l.*, would, should it be lost,
got in the first case only 5*l.*, and in the latter only 200*l.*, unless he could have
that the carrier had acted fraudulently or with gross negligence. But, to avail
f of this defence, the carrier was bound to show that the bailor or his servant was
nted with the notice at the time of delivering the goods. No particular manner
ng notice was required. It might be done by express communication, by fixing
n a conspicuous place in the carrier's office, by insertion in the public papers or
te, by the circulation of handbills, &c.; it being in all cases a question for the jury
de whether the bailor was really acquainted with the notice of the limitation; since,
vere not, he was entitled to recover, whatever efforts the carrier may have made to
h it. Thus, a notice stuck up in a carrier's warehouse, where goods were delivered,
no avail against parties who could not read; neither was it of any avail against
vho could read, and who had seen it, *unless they had actually read it*. On this
le it was held, that a notice in a newspaper is not sufficient, even when it was
that the bailor read the newspaper, unless it could also be proved that he had
e notice itself.

se attempts to limit responsibility gave rise to a great deal of litigation and uncer-
; and to obviate the inconveniences thence arising, the important statute of last
, 1 Will. 4. c. 68., was passed. This act declares, that carriers *by land* shall not
le for the loss of certain articles specified in the act, when their value exceeds 10*l.*,
the *nature and value* of such articles be stated at the time of their delivery to the
, and an increased charge paid or agreed to be paid upon the same. It is further
d, that no publication of any notices by carriers shall have power to limit their
sibility at common law for all other articles except those specified in the act; but
act is of great importance, we subjoin it.

and after the passing of this act, no mail contractor, stage coach proprietor, or other common
y land for hire, shall be liable for the loss of or injury to any article or articles or property of the

description following, viz. gold or silver coin of this realm or of any foreign state, or any gold or silve
a manufactured or unmanufactured state, or any precious stones, jewellery, watches, clocks, or ti
pieces of any description, trinkets, bills, notes of the governor and company of the Banks of Engl
Scotland, and Ireland respectively, or of any other bank in Great Britain or Ireland, orders, notes
securities for payment of money, English or foreign, stamps, maps, writings, title deeds, painti
engravings, pictures, gold or silver plate or plated articles, glass, china, silks in a manufactured or un
nufactured state, and whether wrought up or not wrought up with other materials, furs, or lace, or
of them, contained in any parcel or package which shall have been delivered, either to be carried for
or to accompany the person of any passenger in any mail or stage coach or other public conveyance, w
the value of such article or articles or property aforesaid contained in such parcel or package shall exc
the sum of 10*l.*, unless at the time of the delivery thereof at the office, warehouse, or receiving hous
such mail contractor, &c. the value and nature of such article or articles or property shall have b
declared by the person or persons sending or delivering the same, and such increased charge as her
after mentioned, or an engagement to pay the same, be accepted by the person receiving such parce
package. — § 1.

When any parcel or package containing any of the articles above specified shall be so delivered, anc
value and contents declared as aforesaid, and such value shall exceed the sum of 10*l.*, it shall be la
for such mail contractors, stage coach proprietors, and other common carriers, to demand and receiv
increased rate of charge, to be notified by some notice, affixed in legible character in some public
conspicuous part of the office, warehouse, or other receiving house, where such parcels or packages
received by them for the purpose of conveyance, stating the increased rates of charge required to be
over and above the ordinary rate of carriage, as a compensation for the greater risk and care to be ta
for the safe conveyance of such valuable articles; and all persons sending or delivering parcels or pack
containing such valuable articles as aforesaid at such office shall be bound by such notice, without furt
proof of the same having come to their knowledge. — § 2.

Provided always, that when the value shall have been so declared, and the increased rate of cha
paid, or an engagement to pay the same shall have been accepted as hereinbefore mentioned, the per
receiving such increased rate of charge or accepting such agreement shall, if required, sign a receipt
the package or parcel, acknowledging the same to have been insured, which receipt shall not be liabl
any stamp duty; and if such receipt shall not be given when required, or such notice as aforesaid s
not have been affixed, the mail contractor, stage coach proprietor, or other common carrier as afores
shall not have or be entitled to any benefit or advantage under this act, but shall be liable and respons
as at the common law, and be liable to refund the increased rate of charge. — § 3.

And be it enacted, that from and after the first day of September now next ensuing, no public no
or declaration heretofore made or hereafter to be made shall be deemed or construed to limit or in a
wise affect the liability at common law of any such mail contractors, stage coach proprietors, or ot
public common carriers as aforesaid, for or in respect of any articles or goods to be carried and conve
by them; but that all and every such mail contractors, stage coach proprietors, and other common carr
as aforesaid, shall, from and after the said first day of September, be liable, as at the common law
answer for the loss of any injury (*so in the act*) to any articles and goods in respect whereof they may
be entitled to the benefit of this act, any public notice or declaration by them made and given cont
thereto, or in anywise limiting such liability, notwithstanding. — § 4.

And be it further enacted, that for the purposes of this act every office, warehouse, or receiving be
which shall be used or appointed by any mail contractor, or stage coach proprietor, or other such com
carrier for the receiving of parcels to be conveyed as aforesaid, shall be deemed and taken to be
receiving house, warehouse, or office of such mail contractor, stage coach proprietor, or other com
carrier; and that any one or more of such mail contractors, stage coach proprietors, or common carr
shall be liable to be sued by his, her, or their name or names only; and that no action or suit commen
to recover damages for loss or injury to any parcel, package, or person, shall abate for the want of joi
any co-proprietor or co-partner in such mail, stage coach, or other public conveyance by land for hir
aforesaid. — § 5.

Provided always, and be it further enacted, that nothing in this act contained shall extend or be
strued to annul or in anywise affect any special contract between such mail contractor, stage coach
prietor, or common carrier, and any other parties, for the conveyance of goods and merchandises. —

Provided also, and be it further enacted, that where any parcel or package shall have been delivere
any such office, and the value and contents declared as aforesaid, and the increased rate of charges
paid, and such parcels or packages shall have been lost or damaged, the party entitled to recover dam
in respect of such loss or damage shall also be entitled to recover back such increased charges so pa
aforesaid, in addition to the value of such parcel or package. — § 7.

Provided also, and be it further enacted, that nothing in this act shall be deemed to protect any
contractor, stage coach proprietor, or other common carrier for hire, from liability to answer for lo
injury to any goods or articles whatsoever, arising from the felonious acts of any coachman, guard, b
keeper, porter, or other servant in his or their employ, nor to protect any such coachman, guard, b
keeper, or other servant, from liability for any loss or injury *occasioned by his or their own pers
neglect or misconduct.* — § 8.

Provided also, and be it further enacted, that such mail contractors, stage coach proprietors, or c
common carriers for hire, shall not be concluded as to the value of any such parcel or package by
value so declared as aforesaid, but that he or they shall in all cases be entitled to require, from the p
suing in respect of any loss or injury, proof of the actual value of the contents by the ordinary
evidence; and that the mail contractors, stage coach proprietors, or other common carriers as afore
shall be liable to such damages only as shall be so proved as aforesaid, not exceeding the declared v
together with the increased charges as before mentioned. — § 9.

And be it further enacted, that in all actions to be brought against any such mail contractor, &c.
defendant or defendants may pay the money into court. — § 10.

It will be observed, that carriers continue, notwithstanding this act, liable, as be
for the felonious acts of their servants, and their own misfeazance or gross neglige
It is not possible, however, to lay down any general rule as to the circumstances w
constitute this offence. Differing as they do in almost every case, the question, w
raised, must be left to a jury. But it has been decided, that the *misdelivery* of a pa
or its *non-delivery within a reasonable time*, is a misfeazance that could not be defe
by any notice on the part of the carrier limiting his responsibility. In like manner,
sending of a parcel by a different coach from that directed by the bailor, the remo
it from one carriage to another, are misfeazances. Where a parcel is directed
person at a particular place, and the carrier, knowing such person, delivers the parc
another who represents himself as the consignee, such delivery is gross neglige
Leaving parcels in a coach or cart unprotected in the street is also gross negligence

At common law, there is no distinction between carriage performed by sea or la

t by the 7 Geo. 2. c. 15. and 26 Geo. 3. c. 86., corrected and amended by the
Geo. 3. c. 159., it is enacted, that ship-owners are not to be liable for any loss or
mage happening to goods on board through the fraud or neglect of the master, without
ir knowledge or privity, further than the value of the vessel and the freight accruing
ring the voyage. See OWNERS.

3. *Commencement and Termination of Liability.* — A carrier's liability commences
m the time the goods are actually delivered to him in the character of carrier. A
livery to a carrier's servant is a delivery to himself, and he will be responsible. The
livery of goods in an inn-yard or warehouse, at which other carriers put up, is not a
livery so as to charge a carrier, unless a special notice be given him of their having
en so delivered, or some previous intimation to that effect.

A carrier's liability ceases, when he vests the property committed to his charge in the
nds of the consignee or his agents, by actual delivery; or when the property is resumed
the consignor, in pursuance of his right of stopping it *in transitu.* It is in all cases
 duty of the carrier to deliver the goods. The leaving goods at an inn is not a suffi-
nt delivery. The rule in such cases, in deciding upon the carrier's liability, is to
sider whether any thing remains to be done by the carrier, as such; and if nothing
ains to be done, his liability ceases, and conversely.

A carrier has a lien upon goods for his hire. Even if the goods be stolen, the rightful
ner is not to have them without paying the carriage.

For further details as to this subject see *Jeremy on the Law of Carriers,* passim;
tty's *Commercial Law,* vol. iii. pp. 369—386.; and *Burn's Justice of the Peace,* tit.
rriers. There are some excellent observations with respect to it in *Sir William Jones's
ay on the Law of Bailments.* For an account of the regulations as to the conveyance
passengers in stage coaches, see COACHES, STAGE.

CARTS. Every cart, &c. for the carriage of any thing to and from any place,
ere the streets are paved, within the bills of mortality, shall contain six inches
the felly; and no person shall drive any cart, &c. within the limits aforesaid,
ess the name of the owner, and number of such cart, be placed in some con-
cuous part thereof, and his name entered with the commissioners of hackney-
ches, under penalty of 40s.; and any person may seize and detain such cart
the penalty be paid. — (18 Geo. 2. c. 33.) On changing property, the name of
new owners shall be affixed, and entry shall be made with the commissioners
hackney-coaches. The entry of all carts within five miles of Temple-bar is
ctly enjoined by the 24 Geo. 3. sess. 2. c. 27.

CASH, in commerce, means the ready money, bills, drafts, bonds, and all im-
liately negotiable paper in an individual's possession.

CASH-ACCOUNT, in book-keeping, an account to which nothing but cash
arried on the one hand, and from which all the disbursements of the concern
drawn on the other. The balance is *the cash in hand.* When the credit side
re than balances the debt, or disbursement side, the account is said to be *in
h;* when the contrary, to be *out of cash.*

Cash-account, in banking, is the name given to the account of the advances
de by a banker in Scotland, to an individual who has given security for their
ayment. See BANKS (SCOTCH).

CASHEW-NUTS (Ger. *Akajunüsse, Westindische Anakarden;* Du. *Catsjoe-
ten;* Fr. *Noix d'acajou;* It. *Acaju;* Sp. *Nueces d'acaju;* Port. *Nozes d'acaju),*
produce of the *Anacardium occidentale.* They are externally of a greyish or
wnish colour, of the shape of a kidney, somewhat convex on the one side, and
ressed on the other. The shell is very hard; and the kernel, which is sweet
of a very fine flavour, is covered with a thin film. Between this and the shell
dged a thick, blackish, inflammable oil, of such a caustic nature in the fresh
s, that if the lips chance to touch it, blisters immediately follow. The kernels
used in cooking, and in the preparation of chocolate.

CASSIA. There are three species of cassia in the market; the *Cassia Fistula,
Cassia buds; Cassia Senna;* and *Cassia Lignea.*

Cassia Fistula (Fr. *Casse;* Ger. *Rhonkasie;* It. *Polpa di Cassia;* Lat. *Cassiæ
a; Arab. Khyar Sheber)* is a tree which grows in the East and West Indies, and
pt (*Cassia Fistula,* Lin.). The fruit is a woody, dark brown pod, about the thickness
e thumb, and nearly two feet in length. Those brought to this country come prin-
lly from the West Indies, packed in casks and cases; but a superior kind is brought
 the East Indies, and is easily distinguished by its smaller smooth pod, and b-·
greater blackness of the pulp.

R

2. *Cassia Senna* (Fr. *Séné;* Ger. *Sennablater;* It. *Senna;* Sp. *Sen;* Lat. *Cassia Senna;* Arab. *Suna*), which yields the senna of commerce, is an annual plant, a native of Upper Egypt, and Bernou in Central Africa. The senna, after being collected in Upper Egypt, is packed up in bales, and sent to Boullac, where it is mixed with other leaves, some of which are nearly equally good, while others are very inferior. After being mixed, it is repacked in bales at Alexandria, and sent to Europe. A good deal of senna is imported from Calcutta and Bombay, under the name of East India senna; but it is imported in the first instance from Arabia. — (*Thomson's Dispensatory.*) Senna is very extensively used in medicine. The total quantity imported in 1828, amounted to 219,280 lbs., of which 73,373 lbs. were again exported. Of the imports, 28,834 lbs. were brought at second-hand from Italy; 72,367 lbs. came directly from Egypt; and 107,153 lbs. from the East Indies. The present duty, which is 1s. 3d. per lb., produced, in 1829, 7,587l. 11s. 9d.; so that the quantity entered for home consumption in that year must have been 121,400 lbs.

3. *Cassia Lignea,* or *Cassia Bark* (Fr. *Casse;* Ger. *Cassia;* Port. *Cassia Lenhosa;* Arab. *Seleekeh;* Hind. *Tuj;* Malay, *Kayŭ-legi*), the bark of a tree (*Laurus Cassia,* Lin.) growing in China, Sumatra, Borneo, the Malabar coast, Philippine Islands, &c. It grows to the height of 50 or 60 feet, with large spreading horizontal branches. The bark resembles that of cinnamon in appearance, smell, and taste, and is very often substituted for it: but it may be readily distinguished; it is thicker in substance, less quilled, breaks shorter, and is more pungent. It should be chosen in thin pieces; the best being that which approaches nearest to cinnamon in flavour· that which is small and broken should be rejected. The best is imported from China, but great part of that which is met with in India, is brought from Borneo, Sumatra, and Ceylon. Malabar cassia is thicker and darker coloured than that of China, and more subject to foul packing: each bundle should be separately inspected. — (*Ainslie's Materia Indica; Milburn's Orient. Com.*)

Of 549,535 lbs. of cassia lignea imported in 1828, 486,905 lbs. were brought from the East India Company's territories, and Ceylon; 25,066 lbs. from Sumatra and Java; and 37,561 lbs. from the Philippine Islands. The greater part of the cassia lignea imported into Great Britain, is again re-exported. The duty on that entered for home consumption in 1829, produced 2,015l. 12s. 4d.

CASTOR (Fr. *Castoreum;* Ger. *Kastoreunt;* It. *Castoro;* Sp. *Castoreo*), the produce of the beaver. In the inguinal region of this animal are found four bags a large and a small one on each side: in the two large ones, there is contained a softish, greyish yellow, or light brown substance, which, on exposure to the air becomes dry and brittle, and of a brown colour. This is castor. It has a heavy but somewhat aromatic smell, not unlike musk; and a bitter, nauseous, and sub acrid taste. The best comes from Russia; but of late years it has been very scarce; and all that is now found in the shops, is the produce of Canada. The goodness of castor is determined by its sensible qualities; that which is black is insipid, inodorous, oily, and unfit for use. Castor is said to be sometimes counterfeited by a mixture of some gummy and resinous substances; but the fraud is easily detected, by comparing the smell and taste with those of real castor. — (*Thomson's Dispensatory.*)

CASTOR-OIL (Fr. *Huile du Ricin;* Ger. *Rizinusohl;* It. *Olio di Ricino;* Sp. *Ricinsoel*), the expressed oil of the seeds of the *Ricinus communis.* This plant is a native of the West Indian islands, and South America, and of several parts of Asia and Africa. In the West Indies, the oil is sometimes separated by boiling the decorticated seeds in water: in this case it is deeper coloured, more acrid and more liable to become rancid; generally, also, more active as a purgative. — (*Brande's Pharmacy.*)

CATECHU (Fr. *Cachou;* Ger. *Kaschu;* Hind. *Cut;* Mal. *Gambir*), a brown astringent substance, formerly known by the name of *Terra Japonica,* because supposed to be a kind of earth. It is, however, a vegetable substance obtained from two plants; viz. the *Mimosa,* or more correctly the *Acacia catechu,* and the *Uncaria Gambir.* The first of these is a tree of from 20 to 30 feet high, found in abundance in many of the forests of India, from 16° of lat. up to 30°. The place most remarkable for its production, are the Burman territories; a large province on the Malabar coast, called the Concan; and the forests skirting the northern part of Bengal, under the hills which divide it from Nepaul. The catechu is obtained from this tree by the simple process of boiling the heart of the wood for a few hours, when it assumes the look and consistency of tar. The substance harden by cooling; is formed into small balls or squares; and being dried in the sun, is f

he market. The price to the first purchaser in the Concan, is about 15s. a
According to Dr. Davy, who analyzed it, the specific gravity of Concan
chu is 1·39; and that of Pegu, 1·28. The taste of this substance is astringent,
ng behind a sensation of sweetness: it is almost wholly soluble in water.
ll the astringent substances we know, catechu appears to contain the largest
ion of tannin. According to Mr. Purkis, 1 lb. is equivalent to 7 or 8 lbs. of
bark for tanning leather. From 200 grs. of Concan catechu, Dr. Davy
ured 109 of tannin, 68 of extractive matter, 13 of mucilage, and 10 of earths
other impurities: the same quantity of Pegu catechu afforded 97 grs. of tannin,
f extract, 16 of mucilage, and 14 of impurities. The Uncaria Gambir is a
dent shrub, extensively cultivated in all the countries lying on both sides of
Straits of Malacca; but chiefly in the small islands at their eastern extremity.
catechu is in this case obtained by boiling the leaves, and inspissating the
; a small quantity of crude sago being added, to give the mass con-
ncy: it is then dried in the sun, and being cut like the Concan catechu
small squares, is ready for use. There is a great consumption of this article
ghout all parts of India as a masticatory; it forms an ingredient in the
ound of betel-pepper, areca-nut, and lime, which is in almost universal
Catechu may be purchased at the Dutch settlement of Rhio, or at
cca, in the Straits of Singapore, at the rate of about 10s. a cwt. The quan-
f it, under the corrupted name of cutch, imported yearly into Calcutta from
, at an average at the five years ending with 1828–29, was about 300 tons,
ost not exceeding 9s. per cwt. From Bombay a considerable quantity is an-
y imported into China. The quantity of catechu, under the name of Gambir,
ced in Rhio by the Chinese settlers, is equal to about 4,600 tons a year,
2,000 of which are exported for the consumption of Java; the rest being sent
iina, Cochin-China, and other neighbouring countries.
techu, particularly from Singapore, has lately been imported in considerable
ities for trial in our tanneries; but with a heavy duty of 3l. per cwt., equal
times the prime cost: we fear the speculation is not likely to succeed.—
Ainslie's Materia Indica; Ure's Dictionary; Singapore Chronicle; Buchanan's
ey through Mysore, Canara, and Malabar; Bell's Review of the external
erce of Bengal.

AT'S EYE, a mineral of a beautiful appearance, brought from Ceylon. Its
rs are grey, green, brown, red, of various shades. Its internal lustre is shin-
ts fracture imperfectly conchoidal, and it is translucent. From a peculiar
f light, arising from white fibres interspersed, it has derived its name. The
h call the appearance *chatoyant.* It scratches quartz, is easily broken, and
s the blowpipe. It is set by the jewellers as a precious stone.

TTLE, a collective term applied to designate all those quadrupeds that
sed either as food for man, or in tilling the ground. By *neat* or *horned cattle,*
ant the two species included under the names of the ox (*Bos*), and the
o (*Bubulus*); but as the latter is hardly known in this country, it is the
r only that we have here in view.

e raising and feeding of cattle and the preparation of the various products which
ield, have formed, in all countries emerged from the savage state, an important
of industry.
vould be quite inconsistent with the objects and limits of this work, to enter into
tails with respect to the different breeds of cattle raised in this or other countries.
are exceedingly various. In Great Britain they have been vastly improved, both
weight of carcase, the quality of the beef, and the abundance of the milk, by the
rdinary attention that has been given to the selection and crossing of the best
, according to the objects in view. This sort of improvement began about the
e of last century, or rather later, and was excited and very much forwarded by
ll and enterprise of two individuals — Mr. Bakewell of Dishley, and Mr. Culley
thumberland. The success by which their efforts was attended roused a spirit of
ion in others; and the rapid growth of commerce and manufactures since 1760
occasioned a corresponding increase in the demand for butcher's meat, im-
systems of breeding, and improved breeds, have been very generally intro-

the improvement in the size and condition of cattle has not been alone owing to
cumstances now mentioned. Much of it is certainly to be ascribed to the great
ement that has been made in their feeding. The introduction and universal

extension of the turnip and clover cultivation has had, in this respect, a most astonishi influence, and has wonderfully increased the food of cattle, and consequently the supp of butcher's meat.

It was stated in the First Report of the Select Committee of the House of Commons Waste Lands (printed in 1795), that cattle and sheep had, at an average, increased in s and weight about *a fourth* since 1732; but there are strong grounds for supposing t the increase had been much more considerable than is represented by the committ According to an estimate of Dr. Davenant in 1710, the average weight of the *nett* c case of black cattle was only 370 lbs., of calves 50 lbs., and of sheep only 28 lbs.; b according to Sir F. M. Eden (*Hist. of the Poor*, vol. iii. Appen. p. 88.) and Mr. Mi dleton (*Agric. of Middlesex*, 2d ed. p. 541.), the weight of the carcase of bullocks kill in London is now, at an average, 800 lbs., calves 140 lbs., sheep 80 lbs., and lam 50 lbs., including offal; and deducting the latter, the nett weight of the carcases nearer a half than a fourth greater than the weight assigned by Davenant.

Consumption of Butcher's Meat in London. — The number of head of cattle, sheep a lambs, sold in Smithfield market each year since 1732, has been as follows: —

Years.	Cattle.	Sheep.	Years.	Cattle.	Sheep.	Years.	Cattle.	Sheep.	Years.	Cattle.	Sheep.
1732	76,210	514,700	1757	82,612	574,960	1782	101,176	728,970	1807	134,326	924,0
1733	80,169	555,050	1758	84,252	550,930	1783	101,840	701,610	1808	144,042	1,015,2
1734	78,810	566,910	1759	86,439	582,260	1784	98,143	616,110	1809	137,600	989,2
1735	83,894	590,970	1760	88,594	622,210	1785	99,047	641,470	1810	132,155	962,75
1736	87,606	587,420	1761	82,514	666,010	1786	92,270	665,910	1811	125,012	966,40
1737	89,862	607,330	1762	102,831	772,160	1787	94,946	668,570	1812	133,854	953,63
1738	87,010	589,470	1763	80,851	653,110	1788	92,829	679,100	1813	137,770	891,24
1739	86,787	568,980	1764	75,168	556,360	1789	93,269	693,700	1814	135,071	870,88
1740	84,810	501,020	1765	81,630	537,000	1790	103,708	749,660	1815	124,948	962,84
1741	77,714	536,180	1766	75,534	574,790	1791	101,164	740,360	1816	120,439	968,56
1742	79,601	503,260	1767	77,324	574,050	1792	107,348	760,859	1817	129,888	1,044,71
1743	76,475	468,120	1768	79,660	626,170	1793	116,848	728,480	1818	138,047	963,23
1744	76,648	490,620	1769	82,131	642,910	1794	109,448	719,420	1819	135,226	949,90
1745	74,188	563,990	1770	86,890	649,090	1795	131,092	745,640	1820	132,933	947,99
1746	71,582	620,790	1771	93,573	631,860	1796	117,152	758,840	1821	129,125	1,107,23
1747	71,150	621,780	1772	89,503	609,540	1797	108,377	693,510	1822	142,043	1,340,16
1748	67,681	610,060	1773	90,133	609,740	1798	107,470	753,010	1823	149,552	1,264,99
1749	72,706	624,220	1774	90,419	585,290	1799	122,986	834,400	1824	163,615	1,239,79
1750	70,765	656,340	1775	93,581	623,950	1800	125,073	842,210	1825	156,985	1,130,31
1751	69,589	631,890	1776	98,372	671,700	1801	134,546	760,560	1826	143,460	1,270,53
1752	73,708	642,100	1777	93,714	714,870	1802	126,389	743,470	1827	138,363	1,335,10
1753	75,252	648,440	1778	97,360	658,540	1803	117,551	787,490	1828	147,698	1,288,46
1754	70,437	631,350	1779	97,352	676,540	1804	113,019	903,940	1829	158,313	1,240,34
1755	74,290	647,100	1780	102,383	706,850	1805	125,043	912,410	1830	159,907	1,287,0
1756	77,257	624,710	1781	102,543	743,330	1806	120,250	858,570			

Down to 1820, this table is extracted from papers laid before Parliament; sir 1820, it is made up from returns procured, for this work, from the Chamberlain's offi

The number of *fatted calves*, exclusive of sucklers, of which no account is taken, s annually in Smithfield from 1821 inclusive, has been as follows: —

1821	21,768	1826	22,118
1822	24,255	1827	20,729
1823	22,739	1828	20,832
1824	21,949	1829	20,879
1825	20,958	1830	20,300

Obtained from the clerk of the market, 17th May, 1831.

The contract prices of butcher's meat per cwt. at Greenwich Hospital, since 18 have been as follow: —

	£	s.	d.		£	s.	d.
1820	3	10	4½	1825	2	19	6½
1821	2	18	10	1826	2	17	8
1822	1	19	5¼	1827	2	15	4½
1823	2	2	7¼	1828	2	10	7¼
1824	2	2	8¼				

(*Parl. Paper*, No. 72. Sess. 1830.)

We suspect, from what we have heard from practical men of great experience, the weight assigned by Sir F. M. Eden and Mr. Middleton to the cattle sold in Sm field is a little beyond the average. It must also be observed, as already stated, th is the *gross* weight of the carcase, or the weight of the animal under deduction of bl and refuse; and therefore to get the *nett* weight, we have farther to deduct the offal the hide, tallow, entrails, feet, &c. We have been informed that the following quanti may be deducted from the carcase weights, in order to obtain the nett weights of different animals, viz.; from neat cattle 250 lbs. each, calves 35 lbs., sheep 24 l lambs 12 lbs. If these estimates be nearly right, we should be able, provided we k

respective numbers of sheep and lambs, to estimate the total quantity of butcher's
at furnished for London by Smithfield market, exclusive of hogs and pigs.   Sheep
d lambs are not, however, distinguished in the returns ; but it is known that the former
e to the latter nearly as 9 to 1 ; so that we may estimate the average gross weight of
e sheep and lambs at about 70 lbs., and their average nett weight at about 50 lbs.
e account for 1830 will then stand as under : —

umber and Species of Animals.	Gross Weight.	Offal.	Nett Weight.	Butcher's Meat.
	lbs.	lbs.	lbs.	lbs.
159,907 Cattle -	800	250	550	87,948,850
1,287,070 Sheep and Lambs - -	70	20	50	64,353,500
20,300 Calves -	140	35	105	2,131,500
			Total	154,434,850

This quantity, estimated at the average price of 6d., would cost 3,860,871l. ; at 8d. it
lld cost 5,147,828l.

A part of the cattle sold at Smithfield go to supply the towns in the vicinity ; but, on
other hand, many cattle are sold in the adjoining towns, and slaughtered for the use
London, of which no account is taken.   We have reason to think that the latter
antity rather exceeds the former ; but, supposing that they mutually balance each
er, the above quantity of 154,434,850 lbs. may be regarded as forming the annual
ply of butcher's meat at present required for London ; exclusive, however, of hogs,
s, suckling calves, &c., and exclusive also of bacon, hams, and salted provisions
ught from a distance.   The quantities thus omitted from the account are very con-
rable ; nor can there, we apprehend, be any doubt that, with the addition of such
ts of the offal as are used for food, they may be considered as more than balancing
butcher's meat required for the *victualling of ships*.   On this hypothesis, therefore, it
l follow, assuming the population of the metropolis to amount to 1,450,000, that the
ual consumption of butcher's meat by each individual, young and old, belonging to
s, at an average, very near 107 lbs.

his, though not nearly so great as has been sometimes represented*, is, we believe, a
er consumption of animal food than takes place any where else by the same number
ndividuals.   According to M. Chabrol, the consumption of butcher's meat in Paris
ounts to between 85 lbs. and 86 lbs. for each individual.   At Brussels the consump-
is a little greater, being supposed to average 89 lbs. each individual ; being rather
e than 3 lbs. above the mean of Paris, and 18 lbs. under the mean of London.

Jumber of Head of Cattle in Great Britain. — It would, on many accounts, be very
rable to be able to form an accurate estimate of the number and value of the stock
attle in Great Britain, and of the proportion annually killed and made use of ; but
ng to the little attention that has been paid to such subjects in this country, where
y sort of statistical knowledge is at the very lowest ebb, there are no means of ar-
ng at any conclusions that can be depended upon.   The following details may not,
ever, be unacceptable.

rthur Young has given, both in his *Eastern* and *Northern Tours*, estimates of the
ber and value of the different descriptions of stock in England.   The greatest dis-
ancy, unaccompanied by a single explanatory sentence, exists between them ; but
e can be no doubt that the following estimate (*Eastern Tour*, vol. iv. p. 456.), though
aps, rather under the mark, is infinitely nearer the truth than the other, which is
t twice as great : —

Number of Draught cattle - - -	684,491
Cows - - -	741,532
Fatting cattle - - -	513,369
Young cattle - -	912,656
Total - -	2,852,048

ow, taking this number at the round sum of 3,000,000, and adding a third to it for
ncrease since 1770, and 1,100,000 for the number of cattle in Scotland (*General*

* r. Middleton (*Agriculture of Middlesex*, p. 643.) estimates the consumption of animal food in London,
sive of fish and poultry, at 23¼ lbs. a year for every individual !   And he farther estimates the total
ge annual expense incurred by each inhabitant of the metropolis, for *all* sorts of animal food, at
! To make any comments on such conclusions would be worse than useless ; but the fact of their
met with in a work, otherwise of considerable merit, is one of the many proofs, everywhere to be
ith, of the low state of statistical knowledge in this country.

Report of Scotland, iii. *Addenda*, p. 6.), we shall have 5,100,000 as the total head of cattle of all sorts in Great Britain. The common estimate is, that about a *fourth* part of the entire stock is annually slaughtered; which, adopting the foregoing statement, gives 1,275,000 head for the supply of the kingdom; a result which all that we have heard inclines us to think is very near the mark.

Dr. Colquhoun estimated the total head of cattle in England and Wales only, in 1812, at 5,500,000; but he assigns no data for his estimate, which is entitled to very little attention.

According to the reports of the inspectors of hides and skins, the following are the numbers of cattle, calves, and sheep, slaughtered in Liverpool, Manchester, Leeds, and Sheffield, from 1815 to 1820 inclusive: —

	Cattle.	Calves.	Sheep.
Liverpool - -	74,671	100,329	457,268
Manchester - -	95,054	96,574	489,557
Leeds - - -	22,976	34,598	317,642
Sheffield - - -	30,097	28,455	184,859
Totals	222,798	259,956	1,449,326

(*Appen. to Agric. Report of* 1821, p. 267.)

In estimating the weights of the animals killed at these towns, a lower standard must be adopted than that which we have taken for London; first, because the largest and finest cattle are brought to the metropolis; and secondly, because a very large proportion of the calves are sucklers, which are excluded from the London accounts. These considerations have not been sufficiently attended to by the framers of the estimate in the report now quoted. Sheep, in the above table, means, no doubt, sheep and lambs.

We subjoin an account, from the *Bulletin des Sciences Géographiques* (vol. xxiii. p. 12.) of the number of head of cattle in the following countries. Except, however, in so far as respects Prussia and the other German states, it cannot, we suspect, be much depended upon: —

France -	- 6,681,000	Austria	-	- 4,689,000
Netherlands -	- 1,893,000	German Confederation		12,000,000
Prussia -	- 4,355,000	Spain	-	- 1,000,000
Hungary -	- 2,395,000			

Laws as to Cattle. — No salesman, broker, or factor, employed in buying cattle for others, shall buy for himself in London, or within the bills of mortality, on penalty of double the value of the cattle bought and sold. — (31 *Geo.* 2. c. 40.).

Cattle not to be driven on Sunday, on penalty of 20s. — (3 *Cha.* 1. c. 1.)

Any person unlawfully and maliciously killing, wounding, or maiming any cattle, shall be guilty of felony, and, upon conviction, may be, transported, at the discretion of the court, beyond seas for life, or for any term not less than seven years, or be imprisoned for any term not exceeding four years, and kept to hard labour; and, if a male, may be once, twice, or thrice publicly or privately whipped, if the court shall think fit so to order. — (7 & 8 *Geo.* 4. c. 30.)

Persons wantonly and cruelly abusing, beating, or ill-treating cattle, may, upon being convicted before a justice of such offence, be fined in any sum not exceeding 5l. and not below 10s.; and upon non-payment of fine, may be committed to the house of correction for any time not exceeding three months.

Complaint must be made within ten days after the offence. Justices are instructed to order compensation to be made, not exceeding 20s., to persons vexatiously complained against. — (3 *Geo.* 4. c. 71.)

CAVIARE (Fr. *Caviar*, *Cavial*; Ger. *Kaviar*; It. *Caviario*, *Caviale*; Sp. *Caviario* Pol. *Ikra*; Rus. *Ikra*; Lat. *Caviarium*), the spawn or roe of sturgeon: it is either salted, dried, and made into small cakes, or is in its natural state packed up in kegs. It is in great repute in Russia, on account of the three Lents in that country. The sturgeon is found at the mouth of most of the rivers of Russia, particularly those which fall into the Caspian Sea. The sturgeon caught at the mouth of the Wolga near Astrachan, is of a very large size.

CAYENNE PEPPER, OR GUINEA PEPPER. See PEPPER.

CEDAR (Ger. *Zeder*; Du. *Ceder*; Fr. *Cedre*; It. and Sp. *Cedro*; Rus. *Kedr* Lat. *Cedrus*). The cedar of Lebanon, or great cedar (*Pinus Cedrus*), is famous in Scripture: it is a tall, majestic looking tree. "Behold," says the inspired writer "the Assyrian was a cedar in Lebanon with fair branches, and with a shadowing shroud, and of an high stature; and his top was among the thick boughs. His height was exalted above all the trees of the field, and his boughs were multiplied, and his branches became long. The fir trees were not like his boughs and the chesnut trees were not like his branches; nor any tree in the garden of God was like unto him in beauty." — (*Ezekiel*, xxxi. 3. 5. 8.) The cedar grows to a very great size. The timber is resinous, has a peculiar and

erful odour, a slightly bitter taste, a rich yellowish brown colour, and is
subject to the worm. Its durability is very great; and it was on this
unt (*propter æternitatem*, Vitruvius, lib. ii. § 9.) employed in the construc-
of temples, and other public buildings, in the formation of the statues of the
, and as tablets for writing upon. In the time of Vitruvius, cedars were
:ipally produced in Crete, Africa, and some parts of Syria.—(*loc. cit.*) Very
are now found on Lebanon; but some of those that still remain are of
ense bulk, and in the highest preservation. Cedar exceeds the oak in
hness, but is very inferior to it in strength and stiffness. Some very fine
·s have been produced in England.

1ere are several other kinds of timber that are usually called cedar : thus, a species
press is called white cedar in America; and the cedar used by the Japanese for
1ing bridges, ships, houses, &c., is a kind of cypress, which Thunberg describes as
utiful wood, that lasts long without decay. The *Juniperus Oxycedrus* is a native of
1, the south of France, and the Levant; it is usually called the brown berried
. The Bermudian cedar (*Juniperus Bermudiana*), a native of the Bermuda and
ma Islands, is another species that produces valuable timber for many purposes;
as internal joiners' work, furniture, and the like. The red cedar, so well known
its being used in making black lead pencils, is produced by the Virginian cedar
perus Virginiana), a native of North America, the West India islands, and Japan.
ree seldom exceeds 45 feet in height. The wood is very durable, and, like the
of Lebanon, is not attacked by worms. It is employed in various ways, but
ipally in the manufacture of drawers, wardrobes, &c., and as a cover to pencils. The
al wood is of a dark red colour, and has a very strong odour. It is of a nearly
·m texture, brittle, and light. — (See *Tredgold's Principles of Carpentry ; Lib. of
·taining Knowledge, Veget. Substances ; Rees's Cyclop.*, &c.)

e duty on cedar (3*l.* 16*s.* a ton from a foreign country, and 10*s.* from a British
sion) produced 525*l.* 4*s.* 10*d.* in 1830. The price varies, duty included, from
7*s.* a foot.

ERTIFICATES, in the customs. No goods can be exported by certificate,
·t foreign goods formerly imported, on which the whole or a part of the cus-
paid on importation is to be drawn back. The manner of proceeding is
1ted by the 6 Geo. 4. c. 107. § 62. &c. The person intending to enter out-
s such goods, is to deliver to the collector or comptroller of the port where
1ods were imported or warehoused, two or more bills, specifying the parti-
s of the importation of such goods, and of the entry outwards intended to be
; and the officers, if they find such bills to agree with the entry inwards, are
1e a *certificate* of such entry, with the particulars necessary for the com-
on of the drawback upon the goods, the names of the person and ship by
1 and in which the goods are to be exported, &c. The merchant then enters
1ods outwards, as in the common way of exportation. The cocket granted
this occasion is called a *certificate cocket*, and differs a little in form from
·on over-sea cockets. Notice of the time of shipping is to be given to the
1er. Some time after the departure of the vessel, the exporter may apply
e drawback. The collector and comptroller then make out on a proper
a debenture, containing a distinct narration of the transaction, with the ex-
· or merchant's oath that the goods are really and truly exported beyond
1nd not re-landed, nor intended to be re-landed ; and also with the searcher's
:ate of the quantity and quality of the goods at the time of shipping. The de-
·e being thus duly made out and sworn to, the duties to be repaid are in-
1, the merchant's receipt taken below, and the money paid.

ificates of origin, subscribed by the proper officers of the places where the
were shipped, are required, to entitle the importers of sugar, coffee, cocoa-
spirits, and mahogany (except mahogany from Jamaica), from any British
tion, to get them entered as such. A similar certificate is required in the
·f blubber, (see BLUBBER,) and in the case of flax, wood, hemp, bark, &c.,
New South Wales; wine from the Cape of Good Hope; sugar from the
of the East India Company's charter, &c. See CUSTOMS.

AIN, *in surveying*, a measure of length, composed of a certain number of
1ade of iron wire, serving to take the distance between two or more places.
·r's chain contains 100 such links, each measuring $7\frac{92}{100}$ inches, consequently
to 66 feet, or 4 poles.

ALDRON, a dry English measure. 36 coal bushels make a chaldron, and
R 4

21 chaldrons a score.   The coal bushel is 19½ inches wide from the outside, a
8 inches deep.   It contains 2,217·6 cubic inches; but when heaped, 2,815
making the chaldron 58.65 cubic feet.   There are 12 sacks of coal in a chaldro
and if 5 chaldrons be purchased at the same time, the seller must deliver 63 sack
the three sacks additional are called the *ingrain*.   Coals are also sold by the t
of 20 cwt. avoirdupois.   The Newcastle chaldron of coals is 53 cwt., and is ju
double the London chaldron.   See Coal.

CHAMBER OF COMMERCE, is an assembly of merchants and traders, whe
affairs relating to trade are treated of.   There are several establishments
this sort in most of the chief cities of France; and in this country, chambers
this kind have been erected for various purposes.

Chamber of Assurance, in France, denotes a society of merchants and othe
for carrying on the business of insuring; but in Holland it signifies a court
justice, where causes relating to insurances are tried.

CHAMPAGNE, one of the most esteemed and celebrated of the Fren
wines.   See Wine.

CHANKS, or CHANK-SHELLS, common conch shells are fished up
divers in the Gulf of Manar, on the coast opposite Jaffnapatam, in Ceylon,
about two fathoms water; and at Travancore, Tuticoreen, and other place
Large fossil beds of chanks have also been found.   They are of a spiral form, and for
a considerable article of trade in India, where they are in extensive demand all ov
the country.   They are sawn into narrow rings or bracelets, and are worn as orn
ments for the arms, legs, fingers, &c., by the Hindoo women; many of them are al
buried with the bodies of opulent and distinguished persons.   Those which, fro
being taken with the fish, are called green chanks, are most in demand.   The wh
shank, which is the shell thrown upon the beach by strong tides, having lost
gloss and consistency, is not worth the freight up to Calcutta.   The value of t
green chank depends upon its size.   A chank opening to the right, called in Calcu
the right-handed chank, is so highly prized, as sometimes to sell for 400, or 5(
or even 1,000 rupees.—(*Bell's Commerce of Bengal, and private communications*

The fishery of chanks is monopolised by government, who most commonly let
banks for about 4,000*l.* a year.   Sometimes, however, they are fished by the servants
government on its account.   But as the fishermen of the coast, and those belonging
the little islands where they are found, cannot be prevented from taking chanks,
better plan, as it appears to us, would be to give every one leave to fish them; bu
lay a somewhat heavier duty on their exportation.   We have been assured by those w
acquainted with the circumstances, that this would be advantageous to all parties,
especially to government.

CHARCOAL (Fr. *Charbon de bois;* Ger. *Reine Kohle;* It. *Carbone di legr*
Sp. *Carbon de lena;* Lat. *Carbo ligni*), a sort of artificial coal, consisting of wo
burned with as little exposure to the action of the air as possible.   " It was c
tomary among the ancients to *char* the outside of those stakes which were to
driven into the ground, or placed in water, in order to preserve the wood fr
spoiling.   New-made charcoal, by being rolled up in clothes which have contrac
a disagreeable odour, effectually destroys it.   When boiled with meat beginning
putrefy, it takes away the bad taint: it is, perhaps, the best tooth-powder kno
When putrid water at sea is mixed with about ⅑ of its weight of charcoal pow
it is rendered quite fresh; and a much smaller quantity of charcoal will serv
the precaution be taken to add a little sulphuric acid previously to the water.
the water-casks be charred before they are filled with water, the liquid rema
good in them for years: this precaution ought always to be taken for long
voyages.   The same precaution, when attended to for wine casks, will be fo
very much to improve the quality of the wine."—(*Thomson's Chemistry.*)

CHARLESTON, a city and sea-port of the United States, in South Carol
in lat. 32° 47′ N., long. 79° 54′ W.: population 30,500.   The harbour is spaci
and convenient; but it has a bar at its mouth, through which, however, there
two channels, one of them having 16 feet of water at ebb-tide.   The exports p
cipally consist of cotton, which is the staple production of the state, rice, lum
pitch, tar, turpentine, &c.   The imports are cotton, woollen, and silk goods, h
ware, sugar, coffee, tea, wine, spices, &c.   The registered, enrolled, and licensed
nage belonging to Charleston, in 1828, amounted to 32,445 tons, of which 19
tons were employed in the coasting trade.   The total value of the articles impo

o South Carolina, in the year ending 30th September, 1829, was 1,139,618
llars; the total value of the exports during the same year being 8,175,586 dollars.
1828, 51 British ships, carrying 16,611 tons, entered Charleston. In South
rolina, the dollar is worth 4s. 8d. currency; so that 1l. sterling $=$ 1l. 0s. $8\frac{8}{9}d.$
rrency. Weights and measures same as in England. For further details, see
w YORK.

CHART (Ger. Seekarten; Du. Zeekarten; Fr. Cartes marines; It. Carte marine;
, and Port. Cartas de marear), is properly applied to a projection of some part
the sea, as the term Map is to a portion of the land; wherefore charts are
netimes denominated "Hydrographical Maps." They are distinguished into
'eral kinds, as plain, globular, and Mercator charts.

CHARTERPARTY, is the name given to a contract in writing, between the
ner or master of a ship and the freighter, by which the former hires or lets the
p, or a part of the ship, under certain specified conditions, for the conveyance
he goods of the freighter to some particular place or places. Generally, how-
r, a charterparty is a contract for the use of the whole ship: it is in com-
rcial law, what an indenture is at common law.

No precise form of words, or set of stipulations, is requisite in a charterparty. The
ns subjoined to this article are those most commonly in use; but these may, and,
eed, in many cases must be varied, to suit the views and intentions of the parties.
A charterparty is generally under seal: but sometimes a printed or written instru-
t is signed by the parties, called a memorandum of a charterparty; and this, if a
nal charterparty be not afterwards executed, is binding. The stamp in either case is
same.

Charterparties, when ships are let or hired at the place of the owners' residence, are
erally executed by them, or some of them; but when the ship is in a foreign port, it
t necessarily be executed by the master, and the merchant or his agent, unless the
ters have an agent in such port, having proper authority to act for them in such
ters.

A charterparty made by the master in his name, when he is in a foreign port in the
al course of the ship's employment, and, therefore, under circumstances which do
afford evidence of fraud; or when it is made by him at home, under circumstances
ch afford evidence of the expressed or implied assent of the owners, is binding upon
latter. But, according to the law of England, no direct action can be maintained
n the instrument itself against the owners, unless it be signed and sealed by them, or
ss they authorise the master (or agent, as the case may be,) to enter into the contract,
unless it be distinctly expressed in the charterparty that he acts only as agent.
When a ship is chartered by several owners to several persons, the charterparty should
xecuted by each, or they will not be liable to an action for non-performance. But
e charterparty be not expressed to be made between the parties, but runs thus —
his charterparty indented witnesseth, that C., master of the ship W., with consent of
nd B., the owners thereof, lets the ship to freight to E. and F.," and the instru-
t contains covenants by E. and F. to and with A. and B.; in this case A. and B.
bring an action upon the covenants expressed to be made with them; but unless
seal the deed, they cannot be sued upon it. This, therefore, is a very proper
.

he general rule of law adopted in the construction of this, as of other mercantile
uments, is, that the interpretation should be liberal, agreeable to the real intention of
arties, and conformable to the usage of trade in general, and of the particular trade
hich the contract relates.

he charterparty usually expresses the burden of the ship; and by the famous French
nance of 1681, it is required to do so. According to Molloy (Book 2. c. 4. § 8.),
ship be freighted by the ton, and found of less burden than expressed, the payment
be only for the real burden; and if a ship be freighted for 200 tons, or thereabouts,
ddition of thereabouts (says the same author) is commonly reduced to five tons more
ss; but it is now usual to say so many tons "register measurement."
he usual covenant, that the ship shall be seaworthy, and in a condition to carry the
s, binds the owners to prepare and complete every thing to commence and fulfil the
ge. But though the charterparty contained no such covenant, the owner of the
l would be, at common law, bound, as a carrier, to take care that the ship should be
perform the voyage; and even though he should give notice, limiting his respon-
ty from losses occasioned to any cargo put on board his vessel, unless such loss
ld arise from want of ordinary care, &c., he would be liable if his ship were not sea-
hy. See SEAWORTHY.

all maritime transactions, expedition is of the utmost consequence; for even by a

short delay, the object or season of a voyage may be lost; and therefore, if either party be not ready by the time appointed for the loading of the ship, the other may seek another ship or cargo, and bring an action to recover the damages he has sustained.

The manner in which the owner is to lade the cargo is, for the most part, regulated by the custom and usage of the place where he is to lade it, unless there be any express stipulation in the charterparty with respect to it. Generally, however, the owner is bound to arrange the different articles of the cargo in the most proper manner, and to take the greatest care of them. If a cask be accidentally staved, in letting it down into the hold of the ship, the master must answer for the loss.

If the owner covenants to load a full and complete cargo, the master must take as much on board as he can do with safety, and without injury to the vessel.

The master must not take on board any contraband goods, whereby the ship or cargo may be liable to forfeiture and detention; nor must he take on board any false or colourable papers; but he must take and keep on board all the papers and documents required for the protection and manifestation of the ship and cargo by the law of the countries from and to which the ship is bound, by the law of nations in general, or by any treaties between particular states.

If the master receive goods at the quay or beach, or send his boat for them, his responsibility commences with the *receipt* in the port of London. With respect to goods intended to be sent coastwise, it has been held, that the responsibility of the wharfinger ceases by the delivery of them to the mate of the vessel *upon the wharf*. As soon as he receives the goods, the master must provide adequate means for their protection and security; for even if the crew be overpowered by a superior force, and the goods taken while the ship is in a port or river within the country, the master and owners are liable for the loss, though they may have committed neither fraud nor fault. This may seem a harsh rule; but it is necessary, to put down attempts at collusive or fraudulent combinations.

The master must, according to the terms of the charterparty, commence the voyage without delay, as soon as the weather is favourable, but not otherwise.

Sometimes it is covenanted and agreed upon between the parties, that a specified number of days shall be allowed for loading and unloading, and that it shall be lawful for the freighter to detain the vessel a farther specified time, on payment of a daily sum as *demurrage*. (See DEMURRAGE.) If the vessel be detained beyond both periods, the freighter is liable to an action on the contract. The rate of demurrage mentioned in the charterparty will, in general, be the measure of the damages to be paid; but it is not the absolute or necessary measure; more or less may be payable, as justice may require, regard being had to the expense and loss incurred by the owner. When the time is thus expressly ascertained and limited by the terms of the contract, the freighter is liable to an action for damages, if the thing be not done within the time, *although this may not be attributable to any fault or omission on his part;* for he has engaged that it shall be done — (*Abbot on the Law of Shipping*, part iii. c. 1.)

If there has been any undertaking or warranty to sail with convoy, the vessel must repair to the place of rendezvous for that purpose; and if the master neglect to proceed with convoy, he will be answerable for all losses that may arise from the want of it.

The owners or master should sail with the ship for the place of her destination with all due diligence, and by the usual or shortest course, unless in cases of convoy, which the master must follow as far as possible. Sometimes the course is pointed out in the charterparty. A *deviation* from the usual course may be justified for the purpose of repairs, or for avoiding an enemy or the perils of the seas, as well as by the sickness of the master or mariners, and the mutiny of the crew.

By an exception in the charterparty, not to be liable for injuries arising from the act of God and the king's enemies; the owner or merchant is not responsible for any injury arising from the sea or the winds, unless it was in his power to prevent it, or it was occasioned by his imprudence or gross neglect. " The question," said Lord Mansfield, in an action brought by the East India Company, " is, whether the owners are to pay for the damage occasioned by the storm, the act of God; and this must be determined by the intention of the parties, and the nature of the contract. It is a charter of freight. The owners let their ships to hire, and there never was an idea that they insure the cargo against the perils of the sea. What are the obligations of the owners which arise out of the fair construction of the charterparty? Why, that they shall be liable for damage incurred by their own fault, or that of their servants, as from defects in the ship, or in proper stowage, &c. If they were liable for damages occasioned by storms, they would become insurers." The House of Lords confirmed this doctrine by deciding (20th May 1788) that the owner is not liable to make satisfaction for damage done to goods by storm.

The charterer of a ship may lade it either with his own goods, or, if he have not sufficient, may take in the goods of other persons, or (if not prevented by a clause to the

: in the charterparty) he may wholly underlet the ship to another. For further
ls, see *Abbot on the Law of Shipping*, part iii. c. 1.; *Chitty's Commercial Law*, vol. iii.
&c.; and the articles BILL OF LADING, FREIGHT, MASTER, &c. in this Dictionary.

Forms of Charterparties.

ie following is one of the most usual forms of a charterparty:—

5 charterparty, indented, made, &c., between A. B., &c. mariner, master, and owner, of the good
r vessel, called, &c. now riding at anchor, &c. of the burthen of 200 tons, or thereabouts, of the one
ind C. D. of, &c., merchant, of the other part, witnesseth, that the said A. B., for the consideration
after mentioned, hath granted, and to freight letten, and by these presents doth grant, and to
e let, unto the said C. D., his executors, administrators, and assigns, the whole tonnage of the hold,
heets, and half-deck of the said ship or vessel, called, &c., from the port of London, to, &c., in a voyage
nade by the said A. B. with the said ship, in manner hereinafter mentioned, (that is to say,) to sail
he first fair wind and weather that shall happen after, &c. next, from the port of London, with the
and merchandise of the said C. D., his factors or assigns, on board, to, &c. aforesaid, (the act of
he king's enemies, fire, and all and every other dangers and accidents of the seas, rivers, and navi-
, of whatever nature and kind, in so far as ships are liable thereto, during the said voyage always
ted,) and there unlade and make discharge of the said goods and merchandises; and also shall there
nto and on board the said ship again, the goods and merchandises of the said C. D., his factors or
s, and shall then return to the port of London with the said goods, in the space of, &c. limited for
id of the said voyage. In consideration whereof, the said C. D. for himself, his executors, and
istrators, doth covenant, promise, and grant, to and with the said A. B., his executors, adminis-
, or assigns, by these presents, that the said C. D., his executors, administrators, factors, or assigns,
nd will well and truly pay, or cause to be paid, unto the said A. B., his executors, administrators,
gns, for the freight of the said ship and goods, the sum of, &c. (or so much per ton,) within twenty-
ys after the said ship arrived, and goods returned, and discharged at the port of London aforesaid,
e end of the said voyage; and also shall and will pay for demurrage, (if any shall be by default of
he said C D, his factors or assigns,) the sum of, &c. per day, daily, and every day, as the same shall
lue. And the said A. B., for himself, his executors, and administrators, doth covenant, promise,
ant, to and with the said C. D., his executors, administrators, and assigns, by these presents, that
d ship or vessel shall be ready at the port of London to take in goods by the said C. D., on or before,
xt coming. And the said C. D., for himself, his, &c. doth covenant and promise, within ten days
he said ship or vessel shall be thus ready, to have his goods on board the said ship, to proceed on in
d voyage; and also, on arrival of the said ship at, &c., within, &c. days to have his goods ready to
board the said ship, to return on the said voyage. And the said A. B., for himself, his executors,
ministrators, doth further covenant and grant, to and with the said C. D., his executors, adminis-
, and assigns, that the said ship or vessel now is, and at all times during the voyage shall be, to the
ideavours of him, the said A. B., his executors and administrators, and at his and their own
costs and charges, in all things made and kept stiff, stanch, strong, well-apparelled, furnished,
ovided, as well with men and mariners sufficient and able to sail, guide, and govern the said ship,
l all manner of rigging, boats, tackle, and apparel, furniture, provision, and appurtenances, fitting
cessary for the said men and mariners, and for the said ship during the voyage aforesaid. In
s, &c.

e great variety of circumstances under which different voyages are made produce
esponding diversity in charterparties. The charterparty of which the following
ipy, affords a good example of the more complex species of these instruments.

this day mutually agreed between Mr. T. B. Rann, owner of the good ship or vessel called the
id, William Henniker, master, of the measurement of 472 tons, or thereabouts, now in the river
s, and Mr. David Thomson, of the firm of Messrs. Thomson, Passmore, and Thomson, of Mauritius,
ints, that the said ship, being tight, staunch, and strong, and every way fitted for the voyage, shall,
convenient speed, sail and proceed to Calcutta, with leave to take convicts out to New South
and from thence troops, merchandise, or passengers, to the aforementioned port of Calcutta, with
touch at Madras on her way thither, if required on owner's account, or so near thereunto as she
ifely get, and there load, from the factors of the said merchants at Calcutta, a full and complete
f rice, or any other lawful goods which the charterer engages to ship, and proceed with the same
Louis, in the Isle of France, and deliver the same free of freight; afterwards load there a full
mplete cargo of sugar in bags, or other lawful merchandise of as favourable tonnage, which the
er engages to ship, not exceeding what she can reasonably stow and carry over and above her
apparel, provisions, and furniture; and, being so loaded, shall therewith proceed to London, or so
ereunto as she may safely get, and deliver the same on being paid freight, viz. for such quantity
equal to the actual quantity of rice, or other goods, that may be shipped at Calcutta, at the rate
2s. 6d. per ton of 20 cwt. nett, shipped there; and should the vessel deliver more nett sugar in the
London than the quantity of rice, or other goods, actually shipped in Calcutta, the owners to be
the excess at the regular current rate of freight for sugar which other vessels, loading at the
ne at Port Louis, receive; the tonnage of the rice, wheat, or grain, to be reckoned at 20 cwt. nett
; that of other goods at the usual measurement (the act of God, the king's enemies, fire, and all
ry other dangers and accidents of the seas, rivers, and navigation, of whatever nature and kind
during the said voyage, always excepted). The freight to be paid on unloading and right delivery
argo, as is customary in the port of London. Ninety running days are to be allowed the said
it (if the ship is not sooner despatched) for loading the ship at Calcutta, discharging the cargo at
uis, and loading the cargo there; the said lay days to commence on the vessel being ready to
cargo, the master giving notice in writing of the same at Calcutta, and to continue during the
there; and from the time of her arrival at Port Louis, and being ready to discharge, till the final
at that port, and to be discharged in the port of London with all possible despatch; and 20 days
urrage over and above the said laying days, at 12l. per day. Penalty for non-performance of this
int, 4,000l. The cargo to be brought to and taken from alongside at the expense and risk of
chants. The necessary cash for the disbursements of the vessel at Calcutta, not exceeding 350l.,
vanced by the charterer's agents; they taking the master's drafts on the owner for the same, at
lar current rate of exchange, and at three months' sight; and if the said bill be not regularly
I and paid when due, the same to be deducted from the freight payable by this charterparty. The
be disbursed at Port Louis by the chartering agents; sum not to exceed 300l., free of commission;
amount to be deducted from the freight at the final settlement at the port of London. Captain
hip goods without consent. In the event of the ship being prevented, by damage or any other
eaching the Mauritius on or before the 1st day of January, 1831, the charterer or his agents shall
perty to employ the vessel for one or two voyages to Calcutta, at the rate of 2l. per ton of rice, or
ods, delivered at Mauritius. Fifty running days, to load and discharge, to be allowed on each
it being understood that the charterer or his agents shall load the ship, as before agreed, either
id of the first or second voyage, as the case may be. The freight on the intermediate voyages (if

any) to be paid on delivery of the cargo, in cash, or by bills on London at usance, at the option of master. The vessel to be addressed, both at Calcutta and Isle of France, to the agents of the charte In witness whereof, the said parties have hereunto set their hands and seals, at London, the 2d da December, 1829.

Signed, sealed, and delivered, }
in the presence of   }   (Signed)   THOS. B. RANN, (L.S.)
(Signed)   E. FORSYTH.   D. THOMSON,   (L.S.)

Stamp Duty on Charterparties. —The statute 55 Geo. 3. c. 184. enacts, that any chart party, or any agreement or contract for the charter of any ship or vessel, or a memorandum, letter, or other writing, between the captain, master, or owner of any sh or vessel, and any other person, for or relating to the freight or conveyance of a money, goods, or effects, on board of such ship or vessel, shall be charged with a d of 1*l.* 15*s.*

And when the same, together with any schedule, receipt, or other matter, put indorsed thereon, or annexed thereto, shall contain 2,160 words or upwards, then every entire quantity of 1,080 words contained therein over and above the first 1,0 words, there shall be charged a further *progressive* duty of 1*l.* 5*s.*

CHAY, or CHOY ROOT, the roots of a small biennial, rarely trienni plant, growing spontaneously in light, dry, sandy ground near the sea; and exte sively cultivated, especially on the coast of Coromandel. The cultivated ro are very slender, and from 1 to 2 feet in length, with a few lateral fibres; but t wild are shorter, and supposed to yield one fourth part more of colouring matt and of a better quality. The roots are employed to dye the durable reds which the Indian cotton yarn and chintzes have been long famous, and which c only be equalled by the Turkey red.

Chay root forms a considerable article of export from Ceylon. Only a particular of people are allowed to dig it. It is all bought up by government, who pay t diggers a fixed price of 75 or 80 rix-dollars a candy, and sell it for exportation at ab 175 rix-dollars. — (*Bertolacci's Ceylon,* p. 270.)

This root has been imported into Europe, but with no success. Dr. Bancroft s pects it may be injured by the long voyage; but he adds, that it can produce no eff which may not be more cheaply produced from madder. It is a very bulky article, a is consequently burdened with a very heavy freight. — (*Permanent Colours,* vol. pp. 282—303.)

CHECKS, CHEQUES, or DRAFTS, are orders addressed to some pers generally a banker, directing him to pay the sum specified in the check to t person named in it, or bearer, on demand. The following is the usual form:—

£100.   *London, 30th June,* 1831.

              Pay Mr. A. B. or bearer, One Hundred Pounds, on
      account of
   Messrs. Jones, Loyd, and Co.   C. D.

In point of form, checks nearly resemble bills of exchange, except that they *uniformly payable to bearer,* and should be drawn upon a regular banker, though t latter point is not essential. They are assignable by delivery only; and are paya instantly on presentment, without any days of grace being allowed. But by custom of London, a banker has until five of the afternoon of the day on wh a check is presented for payment, to return it; so that where a check was retur before five, with a memorandum of "cancelled by mistake" written under it was held a refusal to pay. If a check upon a banker be lodged with anot banker, a presentment by the latter at the clearing-house is sufficient. Checks usually taken conditionally as cash; for unless an express stipulation be made the contrary, if they be presented in due time and not paid, they are not a p ment. It is difficult to define what is the due or reasonable time within wh checks, notes, or bills, should be presented. A man, as Lord Ellenborough observed, is not obliged to neglect all other business that he may immediately sent them: nevertheless it is the safest plan to present them without any avoida delay; and if received in the place where payable, they had better be preser that day, or next at furthest. If a check be not presented within a reasona time, the party on whom it is drawn will be justified in refusing to pay it; the holder will lose his recourse upon the drawer. Checks drawn on bank residing ten miles or more from the place where they are drawn, must be c stamp of the same value as a bill of exchange of an equal amount; but che

wn on a banker, acting as such within ten miles of the place where they are
ued, may be on plain paper.—(*Chitty on Commercial Law*, vol. iii. p. 591.;
oolrych on Commercial Law, c. 3. § 2. &c.)

CHEESE (Ger. *Käse;* Du. *Kaas;* Fr. *Fromage;* It. *Formaggio, Cacio;* Sp.
eso; Rus. *Sur;* Lat. *Caseus*), the curd of the milk separated from the whey,
d pressed or hardened. It has been used as an article of food from the earliest
es: vast quantities of it are consumed in Great Britain, and in most countries
Europe.

There is an immense variety of cheeses, the qualities of which depend principally on
richness and flavour of the milk of which they are made, and partly on the way in
ich they are prepared. England is particularly celebrated for the abundance and
ellence of its cheese. Cheshire and Gloucestershire are, in this respect, two of its
st famous counties ; the cheese produced in the former has been estimated at 11,500
s a year. There are two kinds of Gloucester cheese, double and single ; the first is
de of the milk and cream, the latter of the milk deprived of about half the cream.
ey are of various sizes, from 20 to 70 and even 80 lbs. ; but they generally run from
to 60 lbs. A great deal of cheese is also made in that part of Shropshire which
ders upon Cheshire, and in North Wiltshire. The former goes under the name of
eshire cheese : the latter was, till lately, called Gloucestershire cheese ; now it receives
appellation from the county where it is made. A strong cheese, somewhat resem-
g Parmesan, is made at Chedder in Somersetshire. The celebrated rich cheese,
led Stilton, is made in Leicestershire, principally in the villages round Melton Mow-
y. It is not reckoned sufficiently mellow for cutting unless it be two years old ;
is not saleable unless it be decayed, blue, and moist. A rich cheese is also made
Leigh in Lancashire. The other cheeses made in England, which have acquired a
uliar name, either from the quantity made, or from the quality, are the Derbyshire,
tenham, and Southam cheeses. The two last are new milk cheeses, of a peculiarly fine
our : the places where they are made are in Cambridgeshire. Bath and York are
arkable for their cream cheeses. The county of Warwick, and Banbury in Oxford-
e, are also remarkable for cheeses; the former for the quantity made in it, about
)00 tons being annually sent to London, besides a very large supply to Birmingham.
bury cheese is distinguished for its richness.

cotland is not celebrated for its cheese : the best is called Dunlop cheese, from a
sh in Ayrshire, where it was originally manufactured. Dunlop cheeses generally
gh from 20 to 60 lbs. each ; and are, in all respects, similar to those of Derbyshire,
pt that the latter are smaller.

urmeric, marigolds, hawthorn buds, &c. were formerly used to heighten and im-
ve the colour of cheese ; but arnotto (see the word) is decidedly the best ingredient
can be employed for that purpose, and is at present used in Cheshire and Glou-
ershire to the exclusion of every thing else. An ounce of genuine arnotto will co-
a hundred weight of cheese.

arge quantities of very good cheese are produced in Holland. In the manufacture
Gouda cheese, which is reckoned the best made in Holland, muriatic acid is used in
lling the milk instead of rennet. This renders it pungent, and preserves it from
s.

armesan cheese, so called from Parma in Italy, where it is manufactured, is merely
m-milk cheese, which owes its rich flavour to the fine herbage of the meadows along
Po, where the cows feed. The best Parmesan cheese is kept for three or four years,
none is ever carried to market till it be at least six months old.

wiss cheese, particularly that denominated Gruyere, from the bailiwick of that
e in the canton of Fribourg, is very celebrated. Gruyere cheeses are made of
med, or partially skimmed milk, and are flavoured with herbs. They generally
h from 40 to 60 lbs. each, and are packed for exportation in casks containing ten
ses each.

ccording to Mr. Marshall, the average yearly produce of cheese from the milk of a
in England, is from 3 to 4 cwt., or more than double the weight of the butter.

or further details, see *Loudon's Ency. of Agriculture* ; art. *Dairy* in *Supp. to Ency.*
; *Stevenson's* art. *on England,* in the *Edinburgh Ency.*, &c.

he imports of cheese, in 1828, amounted to 217,991 cwts., almost the whole of
h came from the Netherlands. The quantity re-exported was but inconsiderable.
duty of 10s. 6d. a cwt. on imported cheese produced, in 1829, 87,115l. 17s. 9d. ;
ving, that the quantity entered for home consumption must have amounted to very
166,000 cwt.

he contract price of the cheese furnished to Greenwich Hospital, in the under-
tioned years, has been as follows : —

Years.	Prices per lb.	Years.	Prices per lb.	Years.	Prices per lb.	Years.	Prices per lb.
	d.		*d.*		*d.*		*d.*
1730	$3\frac{1}{4}$	1795	$5\frac{1}{4}$	1812	$8\frac{1}{2}$	1821	6
1740	$3\frac{1}{4}$	1800	$6\frac{1}{4}$	1813	$8\frac{3}{4}$	1822	5
1750	$3\frac{1}{4}$	1805	$7\frac{1}{4}$	1814	$8\frac{3}{4}$	1823	4
1760	$3\frac{1}{2}$	1806	$7\frac{1}{8}$	1815	8	1824	$4\frac{1}{4}$
1770	$3\frac{3}{4}$	1807	$7\frac{1}{2}$	1816	$6\frac{1}{2}$	1825	$5\frac{1}{4}$
1775	$3\frac{1}{4}$	1808	$7\frac{7}{8}$	1817	$5\frac{1}{2}$	1826	$6\frac{1}{2}$
1780	$3\frac{3}{8}$	1809	8	1818	6	1827	$5\frac{1}{4}$
1785	$3\frac{3}{4}$	1810	$8\frac{1}{8}$	1819	8	1828	$5\frac{1}{4}$
1790	4	1811	$8\frac{1}{4}$	1820	7		

(*Parl. Papers,* No. 54. Sess. 1829; No. 72. Sess. 1830.)

It is not possible to form any estimate of the value of the cheese annually consume in Great Britain. Dr. Colquhoun states that the butter and cheese consumed in th United Kingdom must be worth at least 5,000,000*l.* a year, exclusive of the milk o which they are made; but he assigns no grounds for this statement; which we ar inclined to think is very greatly exaggerated. See BUTTER.

CHERRIES, the fruit of a tree (*Prunus Cerasus,* Lin.) too well known t require any description. They derive their name from Cerasus, a city of Pontus whence the tree was brought by Lucullus, about half a century before the Chris tian era. It soon after spread into most parts of Europe, and is supposed to hav been carried to Britain about a century after it came to Rome. The principa supplies of cherries for the London market are brought from the cherry orchard in Kent and Herts. The wood of the cherry is close, takes a fine polish, and i not liable to split.—(*Rees's Cyclopædia; Loudon's Ency. of Agric.* &c.)

CHESNUT, a forest tree (*Fagus Castanea*) growing abundantly in most part of the southern countries of Europe. It was at one time very common in England and is still frequently met with. It is long lived; grows to an immense size; an is very ornamental. The wood is hard and compact; when young, it is tough an flexible; but when old, it is brittle and often shaky. The chesnut contains only very small proportion of sap-wood; and hence the wood of young trees is found t be superior to even the oak in durability. It is doubtful whether the roof o Westminster Hall be of oak or chesnut; the two woods being, when old, very lik each other, and having been formerly used almost indifferently in the constructio of buildings. A good deal of chesnut has been planted within the last thirt years.—(*Tredgold's Principles of Carpentry.*)

CHESNUTS (Fr. *Chataignes;* Ger. *Kastanien;* It. *Castagne;* Sp. *Castanas*) the fruit of the chesnut tree. Chesnuts grow in this country, but are ver inferior both in size and perfection to those imported from the south of Europe In some parts of the Continent they are frequently used as a substitute for bread and form a large proportion of the food of the inhabitants. This is particularly the case in the Limousin, in Corsica, and in several districts of Spain and Italy The inhabitants of the Limousin are said to prepare them in a peculiar manner which deprives them of their astringent and bitter properties. Chesnuts im ported from Spain and Italy are frequently kiln-dried, to prevent their germina tion on the passage. In this country they are principally served up roasted a desserts. In 1829, the duty of 2*s.* a bushel on chesnuts produced 2,044*l.* 14*s* showing that 20,447 bushels had been entered for home consumption.

CHETWERT, a measure of corn in Russia, equal to $5\frac{13}{20}$ Winchester bushel so that 100 chetwerts $=74\frac{1}{2}$ Winchester quarters.

CHILLIES, "are long, roundish, taper pods, divided into two or three cell full of small whitish seeds. When this fruit is fresh, it has a penetrating acri smell; to the taste it is extremely pungent, and produces a most painful burnin in the mouth. They are occasionally imported dry, and form the basis of Cay enne pepper; put in vinegar when ripe, they are an acceptable present in Europ In Bengal, the natives make an extract from chillies, which is about the co sistence and colour of treacle."—(*Milburn's Orient. Commerce.*)

CHINA-ROOT (Ger. *Chinawurzel;* Du. *Chinawortel;* Fr. *Squine, Esquine* Sp. *Raiz China, Cocolmeca;* Arab. *Rhubsinie*), the root of a species of climb (*Smilax China,* Lin.). It comes from the West Indies as well as from China; but th

, the latter is best. It is oblong and thick-jointed, full of irregular knobs, of
ddish brown colour on the outside, and a pale red within; while new it will
short, and look glittering within; if old, the dust flies from it when
en, and it is light and kecky. It should be chosen large, sound, heavy, and of
e red colour internally. It is of no value if the worm be in it.—(*Milburn's
nt. Commerce.*)

HINAWARE. See Porcelain.

HINTS or CHINTZ (Fr. *Indiennes*; Ger. *Zitze*; It. *Indiane*; Rus. *Siz*; Sp.
s, *Zaraza*), fine printed calico, first manufactured in the East Indies, but
largely manufactured in Europe, particularly in Great Britain. See Calico.

HIP HATS (Fr. *Chapeaux de copeaux*; Ger. *Spahnhüte*; It. *Cappelli di
lo e di stele*; Sp. *Sombreros de viruta*). The best straw or chip hats are im-
d from Leghorn. Those made in this country are, though much improved,
very inferior to those of Italy.

1828, we imported 384,072 straw hats, of which 330,987 were from Italy,
19,242 from France. The duty that year produced 76,746*l.* 13*s.* 11*d.*; last
the duty produced 48,281*l.* 4*s.* 11*d.*

HOCOLATE (Du. *Chocolade*; Fr. *Chocolat*; Ger. *Schokolate*; It. *Cioccolata*;
Chocolate; Rus. *Schokolad*; Sp. *Chocolate*), a kind of cake or confection,
ared principally from the cacao-nut. The nuts are first roasted like coffee;
being next reduced to powder and mixed with water, the paste is put into
oulds of the desired shape, in which it speedily hardens, being, when taken
nd wrapped in paper, fit for the market. Besides cacao-nut, the Spaniards
anilla, sugar, maize, &c., in the preparation of chocolate. This article, which
ebrated for its nutritious qualities, is but little used in Great Britain; a cir-
tance that seems to be principally owing to the very heavy duties with which
been loaded. The importation of chocolate formerly to be prohibited;
hough this prohibition no longer exists, yet, as the duties on it are propor-
ly much heavier than upon cacao, we manufacture at home almost all that
quired for our consumption. British chocolate is said to be very largely
erated with flour and Castile soap.—(See *Edwards's West Indies*, vol. ii.
4. ed. 1819; and the art. Cacao.) The quantity of chocolate brought from
d, entered for home consumption in the United Kingdom, in 1830, only
nted to 1,324½ lbs., producing 160*l.* of revenue.

like easy to convey and employ as an aliment, it contains a large quantity of
ve and stimulating particles in a small compass. It has been said with truth, that
rica, rice, gum, and *shea* butter, assist man in crossing the deserts. In the New
l, chocolate and the flour of maize have rendered accessible to him the table-lands of
des, and vast uninhabited forests."—(*Humboldt's Pers. Nar.* vol. iv. p. 234. Eng.
)

RISTIANIA, the capital of Norway, situated at the bottom of a gulf or
n the province of Aggerhuus; in lat. 59° 55½′ N., long. 10° 48¾′ E. Popula-
bout 9,000. Christiania is about 30 miles from the open sea; the navigation
bay is somewhat difficult, but it is sufficiently deep for the largest vessels,
six or seven fathoms water close to the quay. The trade of the town is
lerable. The principal exports are planks and deals, tar, soap, iron, copper,
, bark, dried fish, alum, &c. The deals of Christiania have always been in
igh estimation. This depends partly on the quality of the timber; but
it is said, on the skilful sawing of the plank, or on its uniform thickness,
e exact parallelism of its sides. The saw mills used in the cutting of the
, are licensed to cut a certain quantity only. The proprietors are bound
lare on oath that they have not exceeded the stipulated amount; if they do,
ivilege is taken away, and the mill destroyed. It is difficult to believe that
gulation can be more vexatious or absurd.—(*Coxe's Travels in the North of
e*, 5th ed. vol. iv. p. 28.). In 1828, we imported from Norway, principally
Christiania and Bergen, 5,170 battens and batten ends; 11,229 deals and
nds; 3,721 masts, yards, &c. under 12 inches diameter; and 13,506 loads
ber, 8 inches square or upwards. We also imported in the same year, from
y, 10,355 undressed goat-skins, 29,527 cwt. of oak bark, and 155,487 lbs.
lts, being about one fourth part of the total quantity of smalts imported.
nports into Christiania are grain, tobacco, colonial products, hardware, salt,
me species of manufactured goods.

The *monies, weights,* and *measures* of Norway continue, notwithstanding
junction with Sweden, to be the same as those of Denmark; for which,
COPENHAGEN.

A standard Christiania deal is 11 feet long, 1¼ inch thick, and 9 inches broa
and 51¼ such deals make a load.

Timber. — Freight of deals from Norway to England is calculated at the rate
single deals, the standard measure of which for Christiania and all the southern po
of Norway, except Dram (a small town on the Drammen, about 20 miles S. \
of Christiania), is 11 feet long, and 1¼ inch in thickness. A single deal from Dr
is reckoned 10 feet long, and 1½ inch thick.

Battens. — Three battens make two deals, retaining their own length and thickne
Half deals are only counted as deal ends, if they run under 6 feet; but if they r
6 or 7 feet long, then two half deals are counted a deal, retaining their own thickness

Ends of Deals. — Four ends of deals, although 5 feet long, make but a deal 11 f
long, retaining their thickness, which the owners and captains of ships think unreaso
able; but as the freighters of ships seldom wish to have this assortment, which co
monly run from 3 to 5 feet, and are taken on board as stowage, consequently for t
advantage of the ship and not the freighter, the ship ought to bear the burden.

Ends of Battens, called *Larwick Palings.* — No less than six ought to be counte
single deal, 11 feet long and 1¼ of an inch thick.

Pale-boards, when they have their proper length, are 7 feet long; three pale-boar
are counted a single deal.

Staves for hogsheads take up much room; in consequence of which more than t
cannot be computed a single deal.

The width of deal is never noticed in the calculation of freight: a good deal oug
to run 9 inches within the sap, which not a twentieth part of a cargo does at presen
but, though some may be above 9 inches wide, many are only 8, therefore one m
make up for the other.

Timber, or *Hewn Goods,* cannot be exactly computed according to the contents
deals, because it cannot be stowed in a ship in the same manner as deals; the freig
is, therefore, agreed for by the lump, or according to the number of deals which t
vessel may have taken on board on a former occasion.

One hundred deals = 120.

A ton = 40 solid feet of timber, cut to a square.

One load of balk, or timber = 50 solid feet.

Two loads of timber are reckoned for 150 deals.

The several bills of lading contain together an exact account of the cargo which t
captain has received on board his ship, consequently binding him to deliver according
their contents: when, therefore, the deals are mentioned as usual 9 and 10 feet, and
and 12 feet, he cannot insist on more freight than half of the length, according to
description.

One thousand Norway standard deals are reckoned equal to a keel of coals, whic
21 tons.

Bowsprits pay duty as masts; capravens are above 12 and under 18 inches in circu
ference at the middle, and without bark. Clapboard is exported in whole pieces a
unquartered. Deals from Germany pass as Norway deals; spruce deals are upwa
of 20 feet in length; deals from Norway, above 7 feet long, are counted as wh
deals; above 5 feet, and not above 7 feet in length, are accounted as half deals,
two of them pass as one whole deal.

The difference between the Christiania and Dram standard being nearly ₁₁th part,
freights to Dram ought to be varied proportionally. It has sometimes happened t
ships both for Christiania and Dram have been in company, and those for Christia
have got up loaded, and sailed, before the others for Dram have got over Dr
stroom, which runs very strong down in the spring of the year. — (*Rordansz' Europ
Commerce.*)

CIDER, OR CYDER (Da. *Cider;* Du. *Cider, Appeldrank;* Fr. *Cidre;* C
Zider, Apfelwein; It. *Cidro;* Rus. *Sidor;* Sp. *Sidra*), the juice of apples expres
and fermented. The produce of the duty on cider and perry (the expressed
fermented juice of pears) amounted in 1828 to 37,220*l.;* which, as the duty
10*s.* a barrel, shows that the quantity produced must have amounted to 74,
barrels, exclusive of what might be clandestinely manufactured. The per
supposed to have amounted to about a fourth part of this quantity. The d
was repealed in 1830.

CIGARS. See TOBACCO.

CINNABAR (Ger. *Zinnober;* Du. *Cinaber, Vermilioen;* Fr. *Cinnabre;* It. *Cina-*; Sp. *Cinabrio;* Rus. *Kinowar;* Lat. *Cinnabrium.*)

1. *Native Cinnabar* — a mineral substance, red, heavy, and brilliant. It is ~~fou~~nd in various places, chiefly in quicksilver mines, being one of the ores of that ~~me~~tal. The cinnabar of the Philippine Islands is said to be of the highest colour; ~~tha~~t of Almaden, in Spain, is the richest. The best native cinnabar is of a high ~~col~~our, brilliant, and free from earthy or stony matter.

2. *Artificial Cinnabar.* — " When two parts of mercury and one of sulphur are ~~tri~~turated together in a mortar, the mercury gradually disappears, and the whole ~~ass~~umes the form of a black powder, formerly called *Ethiops mineral.* When this ~~mi~~neral is heated red hot it sublimes; and if a proper vessel be placed to receive ~~it,~~ a cake is obtained of a fine red colour. This cake was formerly called cinna-~~ba~~r; and when reduced to a fine powder, is well known in commerce under the ~~na~~me of *vermilion.*" — (*Thomson's Chemistry.*)

CINNAMON (Du. *Kaneel;* Fr. *Cannelle;* Ger. *Zimmet, Kanehl;* It. *Canella;* ~~La~~t. *Cinnamomum, Canella;* Por. *Canella;* Sp. *Canela;* Pers. and Hind. *Darchinie;* ~~Ar~~ab. *Darsini;* Malay, *Kaimanis;* Greek, Κιναμον), the bark of the cinnamon ~~tre~~e (*Laurus Cinnamomum*), a native of Ceylon, where it grows in great abun-~~dan~~ce; but it is also found in China, and in Borneo, and many of the Eastern ~~Isla~~nds. It is said, also, to be met with in Peru; but it nowhere arrives at such ~~per~~fection as in Ceylon. It is brought home in bags or bales weighing 92½ lbs. ~~eac~~h; and in stowing it, black pepper is mixed with the bales to preserve the cin-~~nam~~on. According to Mr. Milburn, the best cinnamon is thin and rather pliable: it ~~oug~~ht to be about the substance of royal paper, or somewhat thicker. It is of a ~~ligh~~t colour, rather inclinable to yellow, bordering but little upon brown: it pos-~~ses~~ses a sweetish taste; has a very pleasant fragrant odour; and is not so ~~pun~~gent but that it may be borne on the tongue without pain, and is not suc-~~cee~~ded by any after taste. It should be rejected if it be hard, or thick as a half-~~cro~~wn piece, if it be very dark-coloured or brown, or if it be so hot that it cannot ~~be~~ borne. Particular care should be taken that it is not false packed, or mixed ~~wit~~h cinnamon of an inferior sort. — (*Oriental Commerce.*)

~~T~~he cultivation of cinnamon in Ceylon is restricted to a few gardens in the neigh-~~bour~~hood of Columbo; the production and sale of the article being wholly monopolised ~~by g~~overnment. Upon the transference of the island from the East India Company ~~to t~~he king's government, the former agreed to pay 60,000*l.* a year, for 400,000 lbs. or ~~4~~12⅓ bales of cinnamon, to which quantity the exports were to be limited; and sub-~~sequ~~ently the Company agreed to increase this payment to 101,000*l.* a year. But this ~~agre~~ement was afterwards broken off; and, at present, government either sell the cin-~~nam~~on on the spot, or send it, which is commonly done, to England. The revenue ~~deri~~ved by the Ceylon treasury from cinnamon in 1826, is said to have amounted to ~~49,8~~31*l.* 4*s.* 1*d.*; but it sometimes exceeds this sum, and sometimes it is less. The ~~expe~~nses attending its cultivation and management are very heavy; and when these are ~~dedu~~cted, little, if any thing, remains as a nett surplus. In 1827 three years' stock ~~of c~~innamon had accumulated in London, and the treasury was obliged to advance ~~40,~~000*l.* to the colonial agent on its account. In this instance we have copied, with-~~out~~ improving, the worst part of the Dutch colonial policy. So much is this the case, ~~that~~ we have been assured, by those well acquainted with the facts, that the quantity ~~of ci~~nnamon burned by order of government in Ceylon is, in most years, greater than ~~wha~~t is required for the home consumption of the empire! The whole system is, in ~~fact~~, a disgrace to the country. The enforcement of the monopoly has occasioned the ~~mos~~t violent interference with private property, the creation of numberless imaginary ~~offen~~ces, and the multiplication of punishments. The natural cost of cinnamon does not, ~~we be~~lieve, exceed 6*d.* or 8*d.* per lb.; and supposing that every one were allowed to cul-~~tivat~~e it, and that a duty of 3*d.* or 4*d.* was laid on its exportation, it might be sold in ~~Engl~~and, in bond, for 1*s.* or 1*s.* 2*d.* per lb. Were the price so reduced, the consumption ~~woul~~d be vastly extended, at the same time that the colonial revenue would be propor-~~tiona~~lly augmented. It is the high price of spices, — a price caused, not by their scarcity, ~~but th~~e difficulty of their production, but by the odious monopolies to which they have ~~been~~ subjected, — that has made them be regarded as luxuries suitable only for the rich. ~~Wer~~e they supplied under a system of free competition, a very short period only would ~~elap~~se before they came into general use. The distinction, at least in a culinary point ~~of vi~~ew, between spices, and salt, and sugar, is more imaginary than real; and there are ~~but f~~ew dishes that are improved by the latter, that would not also be improved by the ~~form~~er.

But though we should be insensible to such considerations, justice to the people of Ceylon requires that an end should be put to this oppressive system. Their energies have been weighed down by the vexatious restraints to which almost every branch of industry carried on amongst them is subjected. Such, indeed, has been their pernicious influence, that notwithstanding the magnitude of the island, the fertility of its soil, and the advantage it enjoys in the possession of cinnamon and other valuable productions, the revenue collected in it hardly amounts to 250,000l. a year, and it is a constant and heavy drain upon England. (See COLUMBO.)

The imports of cinnamon in 1827 were unusually large, amounting to 10,800 bales; in 1828 and 1829 they averaged 5,000 bales, but last year they fell off to 3,900 bales, or (the bale being equal to 92½ lbs.) 360,750 lbs. The following table shows the quantities retained for home consumption, the rates of duty, and the nett amount of the duties in each year, since 1810. The effect of the reduction of the duty, in 1829, is very striking.

Years.	Quantities retained for Home Consumption in the United Kingdom.	Nett Amount of Duty received thereon.			Rates of Duty charged thereon.	Years.	Quantities retained for Home Consumption in the United Kingdom.	Nett Amount of Duty received thereon.			Rates of Duty charged thereon.
	lbs.	£	s.	d.	Of the East Indies.		lbs.	£	s.	d.	Of the East Indies.
1810	12,793	5,609	7	3	2s. per lb. and 2l. 13s. 4d. per cent. ad valorem.	1819	13,077½	1,637	1	1	(From April 10.) 2s. 6d. per lb.
1811	8,748	3,715	16	7	do.	1820	10,618½	1,331	3	6	do.
1812	13,416	4,081	10	1	do.	1821	12,002	1,503	18	2	do.
					(From April 15.)	1822	14,507½	1,816	19	0	do.
1813	Records destroyed	-			2s. 4½d. per lb. and 3l. 3s. 4d. per cent. ad valorem.	1823	14,225	1,767	8	7	do.
						1824	13,766½	1,723	16	4	do.
						1825	14,098½	1,766	0	2	do.
1814	9,565	8,977	3	11	(From April 10.) 2s. 6d. per lb.	1826	14,155½	1,782	14	9	do.
1815	9,355	1,175	17	7	do.	1827	14,451½	1,807	19	7	do.
1816	9,863	1,235	14	1	do.	1828	15,696½	1,773	16	9	do.
1817	10,689	1,324	0	9	do.						(From June 21.) 6d. per lb. from British possessions.
1818	11,981	1,424	18	11	do.	1829	45,921	1,342	8	4	

In the London market cinnamon is divided into four sorts : — the first is worth, at present (May 1831), duty included, from 8s. 2d. to 9s. 2d. per lb. ; the second 7s. to 8s. 2d. ; and the third and fourth from 4s. 2d. to 6s. 6d.

CINQUE PORTS. These are ancient trading towns, lying on the coast of Kent and Sussex, which were selected from their proximity to France, and early superiority in navigation, to assist in protecting the realm against invasion, and invested with certain privileges by royal charter.

" The ports so privileged, as we at present account them, are Dover, Sandwich, Romney, Hastings, Hythe, and the two ancient towns of Winchelsea and Rye ; although the two latter places appear to have been originally only members. The services which they were appointed to perform were either honorary, viz. assisting at the coronation and sending members to parliament ; or auxiliary to the defence of the realm, as furnishing a certain supply of vessels and seamen, on being summoned to that service by the king's writ.

" In process of time the Cinque Ports grew so powerful, and, by the possession of warlike fleet, so audacious, that they made piratical excursions in defiance of all public faith ; on some occasions they made war, and formed confederacies as separate independent states. It seems, however, that these irregularities were soon suppressed, when the government was strong, and sufficiently confident to exert its powers. So long as the mode of raising a navy by contributions from different towns continued, the Cinque Ports afforded an ample supply ; but since that time their privileges have been preserved, but their separate or peculiar services dispensed with. Their charters are traced to the time of Edward the Confessor ; they were confirmed by the Conqueror, and by subsequent monarchs. William the Conqueror, considering Dover Castle the key of England, gave the charge of the adjacent coast, with the shipping belonging to it, to the constable of Dover Castle, with the title of Warden of the Cinque Ports ; an office resembling that of the Count of the Saxon coast (Comes littoris Saxonici) on the decline of the Roman power in this island. The lord warden has the authority of admiral in the Cinque Ports and its dependencies, with power to hold a court of admiralty ; he has authority to hold courts both of law and equity ; is the general returning officer of all the ports — parliamentary writs being directed to him, on which he issues his precepts ; and, in many respects, he was vested with powers similar to those possessed by the heads of counties palatine. At present the efficient authority, charge, or patronage of the lord warden

ery great ; the situation is, however, considered very honourable, and the salary is
l.   He has under him a lieutenant and some subordinate officers ; and there
aptains at Deal, Walmer, and Sandgate Castles, Archcliff Fort, and Moats Bul-

There is an exclusive jurisdiction in the Cinque Ports (before the mayor and jurats
e ports) into which exclusive jurisdiction the king's ordinary writ does not run ;
s, the court cannot direct their process immediately to the sheriff, as in other cases.
e Cinque Ports the process is directed to the constable of Dover Castle, his deputy,
utenant.   A writ of error lies from the mayor and jurats of each port to the lord
en of the Cinque Ports, in his Court of Shepway, and from the Court of Shepway to
ing's Bench ; a memorial of superiority reserved to the crown at the original creation
 franchise ; and prerogative writs, as those of habeas corpus, prohibition, certiorari,
nandamus, may issue, for the same reason, to all these exempt jurisdictions, because
rivilege that the king's writ runs not must be intended between party and party, and
 can be no such privilege against the king." — (*Chitty's Commercial Law*, vol. ii.
)

TRON (Ger. *Succade;* Da. *Sukkat;* It. *Confetti di cedro;* Sp. *Acitron verde;*
itronat verd), an agreeable fruit, resembling a lemon in colour, smell, and
.   The principal difference lies in the juice of the citron being somewhat
cid, and the yellow rind being somewhat hotter, and accompanied with a
derable bitterness.—(*Lewis's Mat. Med.*)   It is imported, preserved and
ed, from Madeira, of the finest quality.

VET (Ger. *Zibeth;* Du. *Civet;* Fr. *Civette;* It. *Zibetto;* Sp. *Algalia*), a per-
taken from the civet cat.   It is brought from the Brazils, Guinea, and the
or of Africa.   When genuine, it is worth 30*s.* or 40*s.* an ounce.

ARET, one of the best French wines.   See the articles BORDEAUX,
.

EARING-HOUSE, the place where the operation termed clearing is car-
n.

EARING, " among *London Bankers*, is a method adopted by them for ex-
ing the drafts on each other's houses, and settling the differences.   Thus,
f-past 3 o'clock, a clerk from each banker attends at the clearing-house,
 he brings all the drafts on the other bankers, which have been paid into
ouse that day, and deposits them in their proper drawers (a drawer being
ed to each banker); he then credits their accounts separately with the
es which they have against him, as found in the drawer.   Balances are then
 from all the accounts, and the claims transferred from one to another, until
re so wound up and cancelled, that each clerk has only to settle with two
ee others, and their balances are immediately paid.

uch drafts as are paid into a banker's too late for clearing, are sent to the
s on which they are drawn, to be *marked*, which is understood as an engage-
that they will be paid the next day." — (*Kelly's Cambist.*)   For an account
 saving of money effected by this device, see *antè*, p. 61.   The technical
tions carried on at the clearing-house, have been described by Mr. Gilbart,
Practical Treatise on Banking, pp. 16—20.

OCK, CLOCKS (Ger. *Uhren, Grosse Uhren, Wianduhren;* Du. *Uuren,*
erken, Horologien; Fr. *Horloges;* It. *Orologgi, Oriuoli;* Sp. *Relojes;* Rus.
ü), a kind of machine, put in motion by a gravitating body, and so con-
ed as to divide, measure, and indicate the successive portions of time with
reat accuracy.   Most clocks mark the hour by striking or chiming.   It is a
useful instrument, and is extensively employed for domestic and philo-
al purposes.   Clocks are made of an endless variety of materials and models,
to suit the different uses to which they are to be applied, and the different
 of their purchasers.   Their price consequently varies from a few shillings
re than 100*l.*   The Germans and Dutch are particularly celebrated for their
n the manufacture of wooden clocks; while the English, French, and
ese, especially the former, have carried the art of making metallic clocks, so
eep time with the greatest precision, to a high degree of perfection.

history of the invention, introduction, and successive improvements in the manu-
 of clocks, has been carefully investigated by some very learned and industrious
ries (see *Beckmann's Hist. of Inventions*, vol. i. pp. 419—462. Eng. ed. ; and
Cyclopædia) ; but, notwithstanding these researches, the subject is still involved in

considerable obscurity. It seems, however, that the middle of the fourteenth cent. may be regarded as the epoch when clocks, having weights suspended as a mov. power, and a regulator, began to be introduced. The period when, and the individ. by whom, the pendulum was first applied to clockwork, have been subjects of mu. contention. Galileo and Huygens have disputed the honour of the discovery. " whoever may have been the inventor, it is certain that the invention never flourished it came into the hands of Huygens, who insists, that if ever Galileo thought of suc. thing, he never brought it to any degree of perfection. The first pendulum clock m. in England was in the year 1662, by one Fromantel, a Dutchman." — (*Hutton's Ma Dictionary.*)

The clock manufacture is of considerable importance and value. It is carried on a great extent in London.

The *ad valorem* duty of 25 per cent. on foreign clocks produced, in 1830, 6,438*l.* ne It is principally derived from the wooden clocks brought from Holland and German.

Clockmakers are obliged to engrave upon the dial-plate of all clocks made by them, their name, the place of their residence. No outward or inward box, case, or dial-plate of any clock or watch, w. the maker's name engraved thereon, shall be exported without the movement or machinery being in with such box or case, under pain of forfeiture. — (6 *Geo.* 4. c. 107. § 99.) It is illegal to import, or enter to be warehoused, any clock or watch impressed with any mark purporting to represent any le British mark, or not having the name of some foreign maker visible on the frame, and also on the face not being in a complete state. — (9 *Geo.* 4. c. 76. § 4.)

It is said, however, not to be an uncommon practice among the less reputable portion of the trade engrave their names and " London " on foreign clocks and watches, and to sell them to the public English work. The fraud may be detected by referring to any respectable watchmaker.

By a Treasury order of the 4th Sept. 1828, clocks and watches for private use, though not marked in manner now specified, may be admitted on payment of the duty, on the parties making affidavit of t. entire ignorance of the law in question.

Persons hired by, or in the employment of, clock and watch makers, who shall fraudulently embez. secrete, sell, &c. any metal, material, or precious stone, with which he may happen to be entrusted, sh. upon trial and conviction before a justice of the peace, forfeit 20*l.* for the first offence; and for the seco. and every subsequent offence, he shall forfeit 40*l.*; and, in default of payment, is to be committed to house of correction. — (27 *Geo.* 2. c. 7. § 1.) See WATCH.

CLOTH. See WOOL, LINEN, &c.

CLOVER (Ger. *Klee;* Du. *Klaver;* Fr. *Trefle, Luzerne;* It. *Trifoglio;* Trebol;* Rus. *Trilistnik;* Lat. *Trifolium*), a very important species of grass. So of the species in cultivation are annual; others biennial or triennial; and oth. perennial. The seed used formerly to be principally imported from Holland; that which is raised in this country is now said to be of a superior quality. (*Loudon's Encyclopædia of Agriculture.*) Culture for seed is, however, very p. carious, and of uncertain profit.

CLOVES (Ger. *Näglein, Gewürznelken;* Du. *Kruidnagelen;* Fr. *Clous girofle, Girofles;* It. *Chiovi di garofano, Garofani, Garoffoli;* Sp. *Clavos de espe. Clavillos;* Rus. *Gwosdika;* Arab. *Kerenful;* Malay, *Chankee*), the fruit, or rat. cups of the unopened flowers, of the clove tree, or *Caryophyllus aromaticus.* clove tree is a native of the Moluccas, where it was originally found; but pla. have since been carried to Cayenne and other places, where they succeed to. ably well. Cloves are shaped like a nail; whence the name from the French c. nail. They are imported from the Dutch settlements; the best in chests, and. inferior kind in bags. The best variety of the Amboyna cloves is smaller and blac. than the other varieties, very scarce, and, as a mark of pre-eminence, is term. the Royal clove. Good cloves have a strong, fragrant, aromatic odour; and a h. acrid, aromatic taste, which is very permanent. They should be chosen la. sized, perfect in all parts; the colour should be a dark brown, almost approach. to black; and when handled, should leave an oily moisture upon the fing. Good cloves are sometimes adulterated by mixing them with those from wh. oil has been drawn; but these are weaker than the rest, and of a paler colour; . whenever they look shrivelled, having lost the knob at the top, and are light . broken, with but little smell or taste, they should be rejected. As cloves rea. absorb moisture, it is not uncommon, when a quantity is ordered, to keep th. beside a vessel of water, by which means a considerable addition is made to th. weight. — (*Thomson's Dispensatory; Milburn's Oriental Commerce.*)

From the expulsion of the English from Amboyna, in 1623, the Dutch hav. few short intervals only excepted, enjoyed the exclusive possession of the Mol. cas, or Clove Islands. In their conduct as to the clove trade, they have exhib. a degree of short-sighted rapacity, which has been, we believe, seldom equa. even in the annals of monopoly. Their object has not been to encourage growth and trade of cloves, but to confine both within the narrowest lin. They have preferred deriving a large profit from a stunted and petty trade,

derate profit from a trade that might have afforded employment for a very
ge amount of capital; and to prevent their narrow and selfish projects from
ng counteracted by the operations of the natives, they have subjected them to
: most revolting tyranny. " That they might," says Mr. Crawfurd, " regulate
l control production and price just as they thought proper, the clove trees
re extirpated every where but in Amboyna, the seat of their power; and the
rounding princes were bribed, by annual stipends, to league with them for the
struction of their subjects' property and birthright. This plan was begun abou t
, year 1551. The contracts are still in force, and an annual fleet visits the
rounding islands to suppress the growth of cloves, which, in their native
intry, spring up with a luxuriance which these measures of Satanic rigour, and
sacrilege towards bountiful nature, can scarce express. By the plan on which
clove trade is now conducted, a plan carried into effect through so much
quity and bloodshed, the country of spices is rendered a petty farm, of which
natural owners are reduced to the worst condition of predial slavery; and
great monopoliser and oppressor is that government, whose duty it should
'e been to insure freedom, and afford protection. Human ingenuity could
dly devise a plan more destructive of industry, more hostile to the growth of
lic wealth, or injurious to morals, than this system framed in a barbarous
; and it reflects disgrace upon the character of a civilised people to persevere
it.

It is curious to remark how the monopolisers, in carrying the details of this
tem into effect, at once impose upon the natives, and deceive themselves. The
inal price paid to the natives is actually above the natural price of the com-
lity, but they are cheated in the details. The cultivator brings his produce
he public stores, where it is subjected at once to a deduction of one fifth for
ment of the salaries of the civil and military officers. The price of the
ainder is fixed at the rate of 9·6 Spanish dollars the pecul: but before pay-
it is made, another deduction of one fifth is made; one half of which is for the
fs or *rajas*, and the other for the native *elders*, who are overseers of the forced
ure. The real price, therefore, paid to the grower is 8 Spanish dollars per
il, or 3¼d. per lb. avoirdupois, instead of 11$\frac{52}{100}$ Spanish dollars per pecul,
¼d. per lb., which is pretended to be given.

When cloves have been sold on the spot, the price usually exacted has been
ut 64 Spanish dollars the pecul, or eight times the price paid to the cultivator.
average price in Holland, previously to the war of the French revolution, may
aken at 6s per lb., or 177$\frac{78}{100}$ Spanish dollars per pecul, being 2,122 per cent.
ance on the real cost of the commodity in the place of its growth. When
ight direct to England, they have cost at an average 3s. 8d. the lb., making
$\frac{64}{100}$ Spanish dollars per pecul, an advance on the natural export price of 1,258
cent." — (*Eastern Archipelago*, vol. iii. pp. 388–390).

he duty on cloves was considerably reduced in 1819; and there has, in con-
ience, been a decided increase in the consumption of the article; though not
·ly so great as it would have been, had it been supplied under a more liberal
em. The cloves at present entered for home consumption in Great Britain,
unt to about 60,000 lbs. a year, of which a part comes from Cayenne. But the
ivation of the clove in Cayenne depends entirely on the existence of the
ent system in the Moluccas. The superiority which the latter enjoy over
y other place in the production of cloves is so very great, that were anything
freedom given to those engaged in their culture, they would very speedily
ide every other from the market. It is not to be imagined, that so liberal and
ligent a government as that of Holland, can much longer continue insensible
e disgrace of supporting a system like the present, and to the many advan-
s that would result from its abolition.

ibjoined is an account of the quantity of cloves entered for home consumption
year since 1810; of the nett amount of duty received therefrom, and the
s of duty.

Years.	Quantities retained for Home Consumption in the United Kingdom.	Nett Amount of Duty received thereon.			Rates of Duty charged thereon.		
					Of the East Indies.	Of the British Possessions in America.	Of the Foreign Possession in America.
	lbs.	£	s.	d.			
1810	35,584	10,197	19	10	4s. 8d. per lb. and 2l. 13s. 4d. per cent. ad valorem.	2s. per lb.	4s. 8d. per lb.
1811	28,977	8,370	1	1	- do. -	- do. -	- do.
1812	35,552	8,547	19	10	- do. -	- do. -	- do.
1813	Records destroyed				From 15 April 5s. 6¼d. per lb. and 3l. 3s. 4d. per cent. ad valorem.	2s. 4½d. per lb.	5s. 6½d. per lb.
1814	31,975	9,540	9	3	From 10 April 5s. 7½d. per lb.	2s. 4½d. per lb.	5s. 6½d. per lb.
1815	50,462	5,708	3	9	- do. -	- do. -	31l. 13s. 4d. per cen ad valorem, equal about 1s. 6d. per lb.
1816	16,470	1,867	6	10	- do. -	- do. -	- do.
1817	73,973	6,390	13	6	- do. -	- do. -	- do.
1818	18,281	1,777	5	3	- do. -	- do. -	- do.
1819	34,254¾	3,354	4	7	From 5 July 2s. per lb.	2s. per lb.	3s. per lb.
1820	36,554½	3,657	0	5	- do. -	- do. -	- do.
1821	32,933	3,285	9	2	- do. -	- do. -	- do.
1822	49,765½	5,026	16	8	- do. -	- do. -	- do.
1823	57,780½	5,747	14	4	- do. -	- do. -	- do.
1824	60,323¼	6,035	10	0	- do. -	- do. -	- do.
1825	45,261	4,543	9	10	- do. -	- do. -	- do.
					Of British Possessions.		Of Foreign Possessions.
1826	52,701½	5,279	4	9	- 2s. per lb. -		- 3s. per lb. -
1827	85,990¾	8,602	1	9	- - do. - -		- - do. - -
1828	61,216¼	6,148	19	2	- - do. - -		- - do. - -
1829	48,637¾	4,875	13	2	- - do. - -		- - do. - -

The price of cloves, exclusive of the duty, in the London market, is, at presen (July 1831), as follows:—

Amboyna, Bencoolen, &c. - - 1s. to 2s. 4d. per lb.
Bourbon, Cayenne, &c. - - - - - 9d. to 1s. 0d. per lb.

Cloves, Oil of, is procured from cloves by distillation. When new, it i of a pale reddish brown colour, which becomes darker by age. It is extremel hot and fiery, and sinks in water. The kind generally imported from India con tains nearly half its weight of an insipid expressed oil, which is discovered b dropping a little into spirits of wine; and on shaking it, the genuine oil mixes wit the spirit, and the insipid separating, the fraud is discovered.—(*Milburn.*)

COACHES, vehicles for commodious travelling. They have sometimes two and sometimes four wheels. The body of the coach is generally suspended b means of springs upon the framework to which the wheels are attached. The are usually drawn by horses, but recently have been impelled by steam. Th forms and varieties of coaches are almost innumerable.

1. *Historical Notice.* — Beckmann has investigated the early history of coaches wit his usual care and learning. It is certain that a species of coaches were used at Rome but whether they were hung on springs, like those now made use of, is not certain. Afte the subversion of the Roman power, horseback was almost the only mode of travelling About the end of the fifteenth century, however, covered carriages began to be employe by persons of distinction on great occasions. In 1550, there were at Paris only thre coaches: one of which belonged to the queen; another to the celebrated Diana c Poitiers; and the third to a corpulent, unwieldy nobleman, René de Laval, lord of Bo Dauphin. Coaches were seen, for the first time, in Spain, in 1546. They began be used in England about 1580; and were in common use among the nobility in the be ginning of the seventeenth century. — (*Hist. of Invent.* vol. i. pp. 111. 127. Eng. trans.

2. *Manufacture of Carriages.* — This is a department of considerable value and im portance. The best built and handsomest carriages are made in London, where on the trade of a coach currier is carried on; but the carriages made at Edinburgh, an some other places, are also very superior. Down to 1825, a duty was laid on all ca riages made for sale; and it appears from the following account, that in 1812, 1,5 four-wheeled carriages, 1,700 two-wheeled ditto, and 105 taxed carts (small carriag without springs), were made for sale.

3. *Duties on Carriages.* — These duties have been long imposed, and have fluctuat considerably at different periods. The following table shows the number of fou wheeled and other carriages (exclusive of hackney coaches) charged with duties in t years 1812, 1825, and 1828, the rates of duty on each species of carriage, and the pr duce of the duties. — (*Parl. Paper,* No. 686. Sess. 1830.)

	Carriages	Duty (£ s. d.)	Amount of Duty (£ s. d.)	Number of Carriages	Rates of Duty (£ s. d.)	Amount of Duty (£ s. d.)	Number of Carriages	Rates of Duty	Amount of Duty (£ s. d.)
FOUR-WHEELED CARRIAGES. Carriages charged at progressive Rates:									
Persons keeping 1	12,866	12 0 0	154,392 0 0	17,242	6 0 0	103,452 0 0	21,876	The same as for 1825	131,256 0 0
2	2,792	13 0 0	39,296 0 0	3,292	6 10 0	21,398 0 0	5,017	do.	32,610 10 0
3	657	14 0 0	9,198 0 0	693	7 0 0	4,851 0 0	994	do.	6,468 0 0
4	180	15 0 0	2,700 0 0	172	7 10 0	1,290 0 0	944	do.	1,830 0 0
5	60	15 15 0	945 0 0	75	7 17 0	590 12 0	96	do.	756 0 0
6	18	16 8 0	295 4 0	30	8 4 0	246 0 0	36	do.	295 4 0
7	7	17 0 0	119 0 0	-	8 10 0	-	14	do.	119 0 0
8	16	17 12 0	281 12 0	-	8 16 0	-	8	do.	70 0 0
9 and upwards	-	18 3 0	-	10	9 1 0	90 15 0	12	do.	108 18 0
Total	16,596	-	204,926 16 0	21,514	-	131,918 7 6	28,927	-	173,514 0 0
Additional Bodies	143	6 6 0	900 18 0	68	3 3 0	214 4 0	55	-	173 5 0
Carriages let to Hire without Horses	949	12 0 0	2,288 0 0	419	6 0 0	2,514 0 0	472	do.	2,832 0 0
Post Chaises and other Carriages let to Hire with Horses	5,295	10 10 0	55,597 10 0	5,786	5 5 0	30,376 10 0	6,596	do.	34,629 0 0
Public Stage Coaches	1,355	10 10 0	14,227 10 0	2,747	5 5 0	14,421 15 0	2,996	do.	15,729 0 0
TWO-WHEELED CARRIAGES. Drawn by 1 Horse	25,957	6 10 0	168,790 10 0	39,191	3 5 0	127,143 5 0	48,318	do.	157,033 10 0
2 or more Horses	1,329	9 0 0	11,961 0 0	539	4 10 0	2,425 10 0	425	do.	1,912 10 0
Total	27,286	-	180,681 10 0	39,660	-	129,568 15 0	48,743	-	158,946 0 0
Additional Bodies	11	3 3 0	34 13 0	20	1 11 6	31 10 0	14	do.	22 1 0
TAXED CARTS. Without Springs	7,592	1 9 0	11,008 8 0						
With Springs, not metallic	11,549	2 15 0	31,759 15 0						
Total	19,141	-	42,768 3 0						
Duties paid by Coachmakers and by Persons selling Carriages. Four-wheeled Carriages made for Sale	1,531	1 5 0	1,913 15 0						
Two-wheeled do. do.	1,701	0 12 6	1,063 2 6						
Taxed Carts made for Sale	407	0 3 0	61 1 0						
Four-wheeled Carriages sold by Auction, or on Commission	105	1 5 0	131 5 0						
Two-wheeled Carriages do. do.	184	0 12 6	115 0 0						
Taxed Carts do. do.	46	0 3 0	6 18 0						
Total	3,974	-	3,991 1 6						

e 1 Will. 4. c. 35. it is enacted, that for every carriage with four wheels, each being of less dia-
an 30 inches, drawn by a pony or ponies, mule or mules, exceeding 12 hands and not exceeding
high, an annual duty shall be charged of 3l. 5s.
ges with four wheels, drawn by one horse, &c. and no more, are to pay 4l. 10s.
carriage with four wheels, used by any common carrier in the carriage of goods, where such
shall be only occasionally used for the conveyance of passengers for hire, and in such manner

that the Stamp Office duty, or any composition for the same, shall not be payable under any licence fr the Commissioners of Stamps, shall be charged 2l. 10s. per annum.

And where such carriage last mentioned shall have less than four wheels, it shall be charged 1l per annum.

Any carriage with less than four wheels, each of which shall be of less diameter than 30 inches, not let to hire, drawn by a pony or mule not exceeding 12 hands high, shall be exempt from duty.

4. *Hackney Coaches* are coaches stationed in the streets or other public places, a bound to carry such persons as require their services, for certain rates of hire accordi to the distances travelled. They have generally been licensed by authority, and subjec to certain regulations, intended to prevent strangers and others using them fr fraud and imposition. It may be doubted, however, whether these regu tions have had any good effect; and whether the public would not be better acco modated, at least in all large towns, by throwing the business open, and trusting competition to rectify abuses. As respects London, nothing can be said in favour of hackney coach establishment. Speaking generally, the coaches are the dirtiest, m disagreeable vehicles that can well be imagined, and the horses and drivers are but lit superior; forming a striking contrast to the elegance and commodiousness of the priv carriages, the excellence of the horses, and the neatness of the servants. The regul ing system having succeeded so ill, little, certainly, would be lost by giving the oppos system a trial.

Hackney coaches were first established in London in 1625; but they were not th stationed in the streets, but at the principal inns. In the reign of Charles II. th number was considerable. Commissioners for licensing and superintending hackn coaches were established by the act 9 Ann. c. 23.; and successive acts have be passed, specifying the number of coaches that might be licensed, the duties payable government, and the conditions under which licences were to be granted. The to number of hackney coaches, chariots, and cabriolets, actually licensed in the metropo on the 1st of January, 1830, appears, from the following table, to have been 1,265.

Hackney coaches were first established at Edinburgh in 1673; but the numb licensed was inconsiderable till after the American war.

An Account of the Number of Hackney Coaches, Chariots, and Cabriolets, Licen in the Metropolis, in each of the Five Years to 1st January, 1830; showing the Ra of Duty, and the Produce of the Duties. — (*Parl. Paper*, No. 687. Sess. 1830.)

	Number Licensed.	Rates of Duty.	Produce of the Duties, includi Fines.
			£ s.
Years ending 1st January 1826	1,150	{ 2l. per lunar Month each Carriage - }	29,392 12
— 1st January 1827	1,200	do.	30,606 12
— 1st January 1828	1,200	do.	31,333 7
— 1st January 1829	1,265	do.	32,176 17
— 1st January 1830	1,265	do.	32,908 18

5. *Hackney Coach Regulations, Fares, &c.* — The commissioners are authorised to regulate the nur and mode of distinction to be adopted by each carriage; and owners neglecting to comply therewith forfeit licence, and shall forfeit any sum not exceeding 10l. — (55 Geo. 3. c. 159. § 7.)

All coaches are to have check-strings, under a penalty of 5l. Commissioners may appoint inspe of hackney coaches and horses; and may suspend the licence where coaches or horses shall be fo defective as to safety, cleanliness, strength, &c. (39 & 40 Geo. 3. c. 47. § 4.) The usual conditio coaches is such, that it would seem as if this clause might as well be repealed.

The following is an account of the fares, &c., as regulated by the act 48 Geo. 3. c. 87. —

Fares computed by distance : —

Not exceeding	s. d.	Not exceeding	s. d.	Not exceeding	
1 Mile	1 0	2 Miles and half	3 0	4 Miles and half	
1 Mile and half	1 6	3 Miles	3 6	5 Miles	
2 Miles	2 0	3 Miles and half	4 0	5 Miles and half	
		4 Miles	4 6		

And so on for any further distance after the rate of 6d. for every half mile; and an additional 6d every 2 miles completed.

Fares computed by time : —

Not exceeding	s. d.	Not exceeding	s. d.	Not exceeding	
30 Minutes	1 0	1 Hour 40 minutes	4 0	3 Hours	
45 Minutes	1 6	2 Hours	5 0	3 Hours 20 minutes	
1 Hour	2 0	2 Hours 20 minutes	6 0	3 Hours 40 minutes	
1 Hour 20 minutes	3 0	2 Hours 40 minutes	7 0	4 Hours	

And for every further time, 6d. for every 15 minutes.

The *Sunset Hours*, after which coaches are obliged to go on the lighted roads, shall be after between Lady-Day and Michaelmas, and after five between Michaelmas and Lady-Day; and coache charged after such hours beyond the carriage-way pavement, shall, besides the above fares, have th fare to the extremity of such pavement; or if hired at a stand beyond the same, the full fare back to extremity or standing; at the option of the party.

or coaches hired to go into the country in the day-time, and there discharged, additional fares are to taken for their return empty to the pavement or next stand where hired from, as follows : — For 10 es, 5s.; 8 miles, 4s.; 6 miles, 3s.; and 4 miles, 2s. If under 4 miles, nothing.

oachmen are not compellable to take more than four adult persons inside, and a servant out; but if y agree to take more, then 1s. in addition to the fare must be paid for each extra person; and if the ch is hired for the country, and to return, 1s. for such extra person going, and 1s. on his returning.

'isiters of Vauxhall, and other places of public resort, ordering coaches to wait, must pay a reasonable n in hand, to be accounted for when the coach is discharged.

oachmen refusing to go at the above fares, or taking more, to forfeit from 10s. to 3l.

t is lawful to require any hackney coachman to drive for a stated sum of money a distance in the dis-tion of such hackney coachman; and in case such coachman shall exceed that distance, he shall not entitled to demand more than the sum for which he was engaged to drive.

abriolet drivers are subject to the same regulations as the coachmen, and are entitled, in all cases, to thirds of coach fares.

he Hackney Coach Office is at the bottom of Essex Street, Strand. It is open from 10 until 3 o'clock ry day, to hear complaints or other business.

he drivers are also liable to be summoned before the police magistrates; and, in the city, before the d Mayor and Aldermen. Experience however shows, that the most satisfactory course for com-nants is to apply to the office in Essex Street.

. *Stage Coaches* are public conveyances, having two or more wheels, and drawn by ses or impelled by steam, &c. The act 3 Geo. 4. c. 95. § 6. defines a stage coach — y carriage or vehicle used, employed, or let out for the purpose of carrying passengers hire, and travelling at the rate of three or more miles in the hour, without regard to number of wheels, number of horses, or of passengers, or whether the same be an n or close carriage, provided each passenger be charged a separate and distinct ."

The following duties have been imposed on stage coaches *drawn by horses;* those im-led by steam being hitherto exempted from taxation.

	d.
Any carriage or vehicle with two or more wheels, without springs, and drawn by one horse only, for every mile which it shall be licensed to travel	1
Any carriage, &c. without springs, and drawn by two horses only, for every mile, &c.	2
Any carriage, &c. having springs, and drawn by one horse only, for every mile	$1\frac{1}{2}$
Any carriage, &c. drawn by two horses only, having springs, not distinguish-ing between inside and outside passengers, per mile	3
And any such carriage, &c. as last-mentioned, drawn by three or more horses, for every mile	$4\frac{1}{2}$

3 Geo. 4. c. 95. § 2.) A duty of 5l. a year is also imposed on every stage coach; ch, as we have already seen, produced in 1828, 15,729l.

n order to guard against accidents by the overloading of stage coaches, the following lations have been made with respect to the number of passengers, the quantity of gage, &c.

mber of Passengers. — By 50 Geo. 3. c. 48., any stage coach drawn by four horses is allowed to carry utside passengers, exclusive of the coachman, but including the guard; namely, one passenger on the three passengers on the front of the roof, and the remaining six behind; no passenger to sit on the age, or on that part of the roof allotted to it. Stage coaches drawn by two or three horses allowed utside passengers, exclusive of the coachman. And all *long* or *double bodied coaches* shall be per-d to carry eight outside passengers, exclusive of the coachman, but including the guard.

child in the lap, or under seven years of age, shall be accounted one of such number, unless there ore than one; in that case, two shall be counted equal to one grown person.

person paying as an outside passenger shall be permitted to sit as an inside passenger, unless with onsent of the inside passenger next to whom such outside passenger shall be placed.

nere the coach is so constructed as to be peculiarly wide, and being licensed for the purpose, four out-passengers instead of three shall be allowed to sit in front, so that the number of outsides may not d ten in all.

the 21st section, stage coaches carrying *no luggage on the top,* and having obtained a special licence ie purpose, and having the number of inside or outside passengers inscribed on the coach, are per-d to carry *two additional* outside passengers.

7 Geo. 4. c. 33. § 2., persons licensed to use any carriage, or vehicle, for conveying passengers *for* at separate fares, having four wheels and drawn by *one* horse or mule, are not allowed to carry more *six passengers;* or having two wheels and drawn by *one* horse or mule, to carry not more than *four* ngers. Penalty 20l.

l coaches are not allowed to carry more than four inside and four outside passengers; the latter to aced, one beside the driver, and three immediately behind the driver. No passenger is allowed to sit e hinder part of the coach beside the guard; nor is any luggage allowed to be placed on the top of coaches.

ggage. — Not to carry luggage exceeding two feet in height on the roof of any coach drawn by four s; if drawn by two or three, then not to exceed eighteen inches above the roof, on penalty of 10l. ery inch above the space allowed; in default of payment, to be committed to goal for two months: vision on the top, for luggage, to be railed off, or otherwise separated from the other part. Refus- allow any passenger, justice, or constable, to measure the luggage, subjects the offender to a penalty .

encourage the lowering of the height of coaches, it is allowed to carry luggage of a greater height two feet, provided such luggage be not a greater height from the ground, including the height of coach, than ten feet nine inches.

ge coach licences shall specify the number of inside and outside passengers to be carried, which er (mail coaches excepted) shall be inscribed in conspicuous characters on the outside of the coach.

alties on Guards and Drivers. — The driver of any coach, or mail coach, or other carriage, stopping place, shall not quit his horses or the box till a proper person be employed to hold the horses; and

such person shall hold the same till the driver has returned to his box, or till the post-boy, who rides on of the fore-horses, is again mounted, and has, in his hands, the reins : penalty for neglecting to do so, no less than 10s. nor more than 5l. This does not extend to hackney coaches drawn by two horses only.

If the coachman permit any other person, without the consent of a proprietor, or against the conser of a passenger, to drive, or shall quit the box without reasonable occasion, although the reins be left i the hands of a passenger on the box, such coachman shall forfeit any sum not exceeding 10l.

Drivers or guards of mail coaches loitering on the road, or not travelling at the speed fixed by the Pos master-General, unless prevented by the badness of roads, or other unavoidable circumstance, or not dul accounting to their employers for all moneys received by them, shall forfeit not less than 5l.nor more tha 10l. ; in case of non-payment, to be committed to goal for not less than three, nor more than six months

Drivers or guards using abusive or insulting language, or insisting on more than the sum to which the are entitled, shall forfeit not less than 5s. nor more than 10s., or be committed to gaol for one or thre months.

Passengers may require toll-collectors to count the number of passengers, or measure the height of th luggage ; the driver refusing to stop for this purpose, forfeits 5l. If any person, endeavouring to evad such examination, shall descend from the coach previous to its reaching the toll-bar, and re-ascend afte it is past, he shall forfeit 10l.

By the same act, 50 Geo. 3., amended by the 3 Geo. 4. c. 85., if the guard or driver of any stage coach, o any other person employed about the same, shall, by intoxication, or wanton and furious driving, or an other wilful misconduct, injure or endanger any person in their life, limbs, or property, every suc offender shall, on conviction, upon the oath of one or more credible witnesses, before any justice or magis trate, forfeit not less than 5l. nor more than 10l. for each offence ; and in default of payment, be com mitted to the house of correction for not less than three, nor more than six months.

By the 12th section of the 3 Geo. 4., penalties against proprietors may be recovered against any of then who reside in or nearest to the place where the offence has been committed.

By 7 Geo. 4. c. 33. § 17., persons standing or plying for hire at separate fares, with any carriage o vehicle without a licensing plate, are subject to a penalty of 2l?. ; and the carriage and horses may b seized by a constable or other person, and lodged at some public greenyard, or place of safe custody, ti one or more magistrates have adjudged the penalty.

By 9 Geo. 4. c. 49. § 16., so much of 50 Geo. 3. c. 48. as directs the names of *proprietors* of stage coache to be painted on the doors, is repealed ; but this does not repeal that part of the 25 Geo. 3. c. 51. whic requires the names of the *persons licensed* to use such coaches to be painted on the doors, together wit the names of the places from whence they set out, and to which they are going. By the same act, s much of 7 Geo. 4. c 33. as permits informations to be laid by any other person than an officer of stamp for the recovery of any fine, penalty, or forfeiture, relating to the *stamp duties*, is repealed ; and suc informations may be quashed by a justice of peace on payment of costs.

Stage coaches taking up passengers within the paved streets of the metropolis are subject to the regula tions of hackney coaches, under 1 Geo. 1. c. 53.

It has been decided, that the statutes 3 Car. 1. c. 1. and 29 Car. 2. c. 7. do not make the travelling c stage coaches on Sunday illegal ; *Sandeman v. Breach*, 7 B. & C. 96. — (We have taken this judiciou abstract of the laws with respect to stage coaches, from a very useful little work — The Cabinet Lawyer

COAL (Da. *Steenkull;* Du. *Steenkoolen;* Fr. *Charbon de terre;* Ger. *Steinkohlen* It. *Carboni fossili;* Lat. *Lithanthrax;* Port *Carvoes de terra, ou de pedra;* Rus *Ugolj, Kamennoe;* Sp. *Carbones de tierra, Carbones de piedra;* Sw. *Stenkol*). Thi highly important combustible mineral is divided by mineralogists into the three great families of black coal, uninflammable coal, and brown coal ; each of thes being again divided into many subordinate species.

All the common coals, as slate coal, foliated coal, cannel coal, &c. belong t the black coal family. Slate and foliated coal is found in vast quantities in Dur ham and Northumberland, at Whitehaven in Cumberland, in the river distric of the Forth and Clyde, &c. The best Newcastle coal kindles easily ; in burnin it cakes or runs together into a solid mass, emitting a great deal of heat, as wel as of smoke and flame ; it leaves a small quantity of heavy, dark-coloured residuur or ashes. Most of the Scotch coals are what are familiarly called *open burn ing* coals. They do not last so long as the Newcastle coal, yield less heat, do n cake or run together in burning, and usually leave a considerable quantity of ligh white ashes. They make, however, a very pleasant, cheerful fire ; and, for mos household purposes, the best fire is said to be made of a mixture of Scotch an Newcastle coal.

Cannel coal is sometimes met with in the Newcastle pits, in Ayrshire, &c. ; bu the largest beds of it, and of the purest kind, are near Wigan in Lancashire. I burns with a beautiful clear flame, emitting a great deal of light, but not a grea deal of heat. It takes a good polish ; and articles made of it are often passed o for pure jet.

The uninflammable coals are those known by the names of Welsh culm or ston coal, Kilkenny coal, and the *blind* or *deaf* coal of Scotland. These coals are di ficult to kindle, which has given rise to their name ; but when once thoroughl ignited, they burn for a long time : they make a hot, glowing fire, like charcoo without either flame or smoke ; but owing to their emitting noxious vapours, the cannot be used in dwelling houses, though they are in considerable demand amon maltsters, dyers, &c.

Brown or Bovey coal, so called from its being principally found at Bovey nea Exeter, is light, yields but little heat in burning, and is seldom used as fuel.

In all, about *seventy* species of coal are said to be imported into London, which *forty-five* are sent from Newcastle ! Of course, many of them differ fro

other by almost imperceptible degrees, and can only be distinguished by
e thoroughly conversant with the trade.

igin of Coal — Phenomena of Combustion, &c. — Coal beds, or strata, lie among those
avel, sand, chalk, clay, &c., which form great part of the present surface of the earth,
ave been evidently accumulated during remote ages by the agency of "moving water,"
milar to accumulations now in process of formation at the mouths of all great rivers,
n the bottoms of lakes and seas. When these strata had, by long contact and pres-
been solidified into a rocky crust to the earth, this crust, by subsequent convul-
of nature, of which innumerable other proofs remain, has been in various parts
en and heaved up above the level of the sea, so as to form the greater part of our
r habitable land; in some places appearing as lofty mountains, in others as ex-
d plains. In many situations, the fracture of the crust exhibits the edges of the
us distinct strata found in a given thickness of it. When the fracture has the form
precipitous cliff, these edges appear one above another, like the edges of piled
s or books; but often also they are met with in horizontal succession along a plain,
e edges of a pile of books laid down upon a table; or they may be seen surround-
ills of granite, which protrude through them. Coal, and other precious minerals,
first discovered by man at the fractures of the strata above described, and by his con-
d digging of the strata or veins he has gradually formed the vast excavations called
. When it was at last discovered, that, all the world over, the mineral strata occur
g themselves in nearly the same order or succession, so that the exposure anywhere
portion of one stratum is a good indication of the other strata lying near, the oper-
of the miner became of much surer result, and expensive boring through superior
might be prudently undertaken, even where no specimen of the desired but more
y buried substance had yet been seen.

ore the discovery of coal mines, or the invention of cheap means of working them,
was the general fuel of the earth; and in many countries where the arts have not
flourished, it is still the chief fuel. Coal, however, for many purposes, answers
better than wood. Now, coal and wood, although in appearance so different, are
ir ultimate composition very nearly allied. They both have for their basis or chief
dient the substance called by the chemists *carbon,* and for their chief other ingre-
the substance called hydrogen, which, when separated, exists in the form of air
. The hydrogen is easily driven away or volatilised from either coal or wood,
ating in a close place; and when it is caught and preserved, it forms the gas now
o light our streets and public buildings. What remains of coal, after being so
d, is the substance called *coak;* and what remains of wood, similarly treated, is the
nce called *charcoal,* – both being nearly pure carbon, but differing as to the states of
ctness. This kindred nature of coal and wood does not surprise, when the fact is
n, that much of our coal is really transformed wood; many coal mines being evi-
the remains of antediluvian forests, swept together in the course of the terrestrial
es already alluded to, and afterwards solidified to the state now seen. In these
the species of the plants or trees which formed them are still quite evident in
ant specimens, mixed often with the remnants of the animals which inhabited the
t the same time. The extensive peat-mosses now existing on the surface of the
consist chiefly of vegetable remains in an early stage of the kind of change which
ates in the formation of coal.

ubstance which, like coal or wood, cheaply answers the purpose of producing great
d light, is called fuel, and the phenomenon of that production is called combustion.
modern discovery has ascertained that, in every instance, combustion is merely an
ance which accompanies the mutual action, when very intense, of two substances
act of forming an intimate or chemical union. Where that act is less energetic,
at produced is less intense, and there is no light. Thus, water and sulphuric acid
mixing produce great heat, but no light. Water and quicklime produce still
heat; sufficient, it is known, to set fire to a ship in which the mixture unfortu-
occurs. It is an occurrence of the same kind when heat is evolved from an acid
ing a metal; and it is still of the same kind when a mass of coal or wood in a
ate is, with the appearance of combustion, undergoing solution in the oxygen of
nosphere. In this last case, however, the temperature of the fuel is, by the very
action, raised so much that the fuel becomes incandescent or luminous; an
ance assumed by every substance, whether burning or not, — of a stone, for in-
or piece of metal, — when heated beyond the temperature indicated by 800° of
heit's thermometer. The inferior degrees of such incandescence are called *red*
he superior degrees *white heat.* The reason why any strongly heated body throws
ht, we cannot yet explain. When a quantity of wood or coal has been burned
in a confined portion of air, the whole of the fuel, vanished from view, is held in
a by the air, as salt is held in water, and is again recoverable by the art of the

chemist. The phenomenon of common fire or combustion, then, is merely the f⸱
being chemically dissolved in the air of the atmosphere. If the fuel has nothing vo⸱
tile in it, as is true of pure carbon, and therefore nearly true of coak and charcoal⸱
burns with the appearance of red-hot stones ; but if there be an ingredient, as hydrog⸱
which, on being heated, readily assumes the form of air, that ingredient dilates bef⸱
burning, and in the act produces the more bulky incandescence called flame.

The two great purposes which combustion serves to man are to give light and he⸱
By the former he may be said to lengthen considerably the duration of his natural ⸱
istence ; for he converts the dismal and almost useless night into what, for many en⸱
serves him as well as day : and by the latter, besides converting winter into any clim⸱
which he desires, he is enabled to effect most important mutations on many of the su⸱
stances which nature offers for his use ; and, since the invention of the steam engine,
makes heat perform a great proportion of the work of society. From these consideratic⸱
may be perceived the importance of having fire at command ; and, as the cheapest mea⸱
of commanding fire, of having abundance of coal.

In respect to the natural supply of coal, Britain, among the nations, is most singula⸱
favoured : much of the surface of the country conceals under it continuous and thi⸱
beds of that valuable mineral, — vastly more precious to the country than would ha⸱
been mines of the precious metals, like those of Peru and Mexico ; for coal, since a⸱
plied to the steam engine, is really hoarded power, applicable to almost any purpose whi⸱
human labour directed by ingenuity can accomplish. It is the possession of her cc⸱
mines which has rendered Britain, in relation to the whole world, what a city is to t⸱
rural district which surrounds it, — the producer and dispenser of the rich products ⸱
art and industry. Calling her coal mines the coal cellars of the great city, there is ⸱
them a known supply which, at the present rate of expenditure, will last for tv⸱
thousand years at least ; and therefore a provision which, as coming improvements in t⸱
arts of life will naturally effect economy of fuel, or substitution of other means to eff⸱
similar purposes, may be regarded as inexhaustible.

The comparative values of the different kinds of fuel have been ascertained, by findi⸱
how much ice a certain quantity of the different kinds, while burning, will melt ; a⸱
thus,

1 lb. of good Coal	- -	melts of ice 90 lbs.
Coke	- -	94 do.
Charcoal of Wood		95 do.
Wood	- -	52 do.
Peat	- -	19 do.
Hydrogen Gas	-	370 do.

The kinds or differences of coal depend on the comparative proportions in them ⸱
carbon and hydrogen, and of earthy impurities totally incombustible. While so⸱
species of coal contain nearly a third of their weight of hydrogen, others have no⸱
fiftieth. The former kinds are flaming coal, pleasing in parlour fires, and fit for
manufacture of gas. The other kinds, some of the Welch stone coal, for instance, v⸱
only burn when in large heaps, or when mixed with more inflammable coal : they h⸱
no flame. When flaming coal is burned where a sufficiency of oxygen cannot p⸱
through or enter above the fire, to combine with and consume the hydrogen as fast a⸱
rises, a dense smoke is given out, consisting of hydrogen and carbon combined in ⸱
proportions which form a pitchy substance. The Welch coal above-mentioned car⸱
little give out smoke as flame, and hence is now much used in great breweries, and⸱
the steam-engine furnaces of towns, where smoke is a serious nuisance.

According to Mr. Kirwan

	Charcoal.	Bitumen.	Earth.	Sp. g⸱
100 Parts Kilkenny Coal yield	97·3	0	3·7	1·52⸱
Comp. Cannel -	75·2	21·68 maltha	3·1	1·23⸱
Swansea - -	73·53	23·14 mixt.	3·33	1·35⸱
Leitrim - -	71·43	23·37 do.	5·20	1·35⸱
Wigan - -	61·73	36·7 do.	1·57	1·26⸱
Newcastle - -	58·00	40·0 do.	—	1·27⸱
Whitehaven -	57·0	41·3	1·7	1·25⸱
Slaty Cannel -	47·62	32·52 mal.	20·0	1·4⸱
Asphalt - -	31·0	68·0 bitumen	—	1·1⸱
Maltha - -	8·0		—	2·0⸱

100 parts of the best English coal give, of coak 63·0 by Mr. Jars.
100 do. - - - - - 73·0 Hielm.
100 do. Newcastle do. - - - 58·0 Dr. Watson.

The foliated or cubical coal, and slate coal, are chiefly used as fuel in private houses ; caking coals, for smithy forges: the slate coal, from its keeping open, answers best giving great heats in a wind furnace, as in distillation on a large scale ; and glance ·l, found in Staffordshire, is used for drying grain and malt. The coals of South Wales ·tain less volatile matter than either the English or the Scotch ; and hence, in equal ·ght, produce a double quantity of cast iron in smelting the ores of this metal. It is ·posed that three parts of good Newcastle coals are equivalent, as fuel, to four parts good Scotch coals.

Consumption of Coal. — Number of Persons engaged in the Trade. — Supply of Coal. — ·e great repositories of coal in this kingdom are in Northumberland and Durham, ·ence London and most part of the South of England are at present supplied ; in Cum- ·land, whence large quantities of coal are exported to Ireland ; and in Staffordshire, ·rbyshire, Lancashire, Yorkshire, Leicestershire, Warwickshire, South Wales, &c. In ·tland, coal is found in the Lothians, Lanarkshire, Renfrewshire, Ayrshire, and ·er counties. In Ireland, coal is both deficient in quantity and inferior in quality ·hat of Great Britain ; and turf forms the great article of fuel.

·Mr. Taylor, an experienced coal owner and coal agent, estimates the annual consump- · of coal in Great Britain, as follows : —

	Tons.
·e annual vend of coals carried coastwise from Durham and Northum- ·erland is - - - - - -	3,300,000
·me consumption, say one fifth - - - - -	660,000
	3,960,000
·ich quantity supplies about 5,000,000 persons ; and supposing the ·hole population of Great Britain to be 15,000,000, this must be ·ebled ; for though these two thirds of population are perhaps less ·ole to afford fuel, yet, taking into consideration the manufacturing ·istricts, and the cheapness of coal in the interior, the estimate will not ·e too high - - - - - -	11,880,000
·sumed by iron works, say 600,000 tons of metal, to produce which ·quires at least four times the quantity of coal in making even pig ·etal, and the extraordinary consumption in the Cornwall, &c. ·ines - - - - - - -	3,000,000
·sumed in Great Britain - - - -	14,880,000
·orted to Ireland, say - - - - -	700,000
Total tons, exclusive of foreign exportation - -	15,580,000

·his estimate does not differ materially form that of Mr. Stevenson (*Edinburgh ·y. art. England*, p. 740.), and Mr. Bakewell, (see *post*) ; and may be regarded ·fficiently accurate.

·r. Buddle, of Wallsend, an extremely well-informed coal engineer, gives the fol- ·ng estimate of the number of persons engaged in the different departments of the trade on the Tyne and Wear, in the conveyance of coal to London, and in the ·don coal trade : —

I hold a paper in my hand stating the number of people employed in the coal trade ·ch department. I would beg to observe, the returns from the Tyne are official ·ments ; from the Wear I have no returns, but it is by an approximate calculation. ·number of persons employed underground on the Tyne are,—men, 4,937 ; boys, ·4 ; together, 8,491 : above ground,—men, 2,745 ; boys, 718 ; making 3,463 ; making ·otal employed in the mines above and below ground, 11,954, which in round ·bers I call 12,000, because I am pretty sure there were some omissions in the ·ns. On the river Wear, I conceive there are 9,000 employed ; making 21,000 ·oyed in digging the coal, and delivering it to the ships on the two rivers. From ·est calculations I have been able to make, it would appear that, averaging the coast- ·essels that carry coals at the size of 220 London chaldrons each vessel, there would ·400 vessels employed, which would require 15,000 seamen and boys. I have made ·nmary. There are, seamen, 15,000 ; pitmen and above-ground people employed at ·ollieries, 21,000 ; keelmen, coal-boatmen, casters, and trimmers, 2,000 : making the number employed in what I call the Northern Coal Trade, 38,000. In London, ·pers, lightermen, and so forth, 5,000 ; factors, agents, &c. on the Coal Exchange, · ;—7,500 in all, in London. Making the grand total in the North country and ·lon departments of the trade, 45,500. This does not, of course, include the persons ·oyed at the outports in discharging the ships there."

In another place, Mr. Buddle states, that "colliers are always paid by the piece," an
consequently their wages, although at the same rate per chaldron, vary according to th
quantity of work they have to do; and it is difficult to form an average, they vary s
very considerably : they have varied from 14s. a week to, in some instances, 40s. Th
colliers can earn up to 5s. or even more per day ; but there is not full employment fo
them ; they have seldom been earning more than half that sum during the last year (1828)
2s. 6d. is the certain wages that they are hired to receive from their employers, whethe
they are employed or not ; that is a tax on the coal owner, during the suspension of hi
colliery from any accident, for he pays them their wages whether they are employed o
not. The men have the option of finding work elsewhere ; but if they cannot do this
they may call upon their master to pay them 14s. per week ; it was 15s. a week till las
year (1828).

We regret that we are unable to lay any estimates before our readers of the numbe
of persons employed in the other branches of the coal trade ; but taking into view the
proportion which the trade on the Tyne and the Wear bears to the trade of Grea
Britain, as shown in Mr. Taylor's statement, we are inclined to think that the tota
number of persons directly engaged in the coal trade may be set down at from 160,000
to 180,000.

The importance of coal as a necessary of life, and the degree in which our superiority
in arts and manufactures depends upon our obtaining supplies of it at a cheap rate,
has naturally attracted a good deal of attention to the question as to the period when
the exhaustion of the coal mines may be anticipated. But the investigations hitherto
made as to the magnitude and thickness of the different coal-beds, and the extent to
which they may be wrought, are too vague and unsatisfactory to afford grounds for
forming anything like a tolerably near approximation to a solution of this question.
But such as they are, they are sufficient to show that *many centuries* must elapse before
posterity can feel any serious difficulties from a diminished supply of coal. According to
Mr. Taylor, whose estimate of the consumption of coal is given above, the coal-fields of
Durham and Northumberland are adequate to furnish the present annual supply for
more than 1,700 years. We subjoin Mr. Taylor's estimate.

ESTIMATE OF THE EXTENT AND PRODUCE OF THE DURHAM AND NORTHUMBERLAND
COAL-FIELDS.

Durham.

Sq. Miles

" From South Shields southward to Castle Eden, 21 miles ; thence westward
to West Auckland, 32 miles ; north-east from West Auckland to Eltring-
ham, 33 miles ; and then to Shields, 22 miles ; being an extent or area of 594

Northumberland.

" From Shields northward, 27 miles, by an average breadth of 9 miles - 243
——— 83

Portion excavated.

Sq. Mile

" In Durham, on Tyne, say - - - . - 39
on Wear - - - - - - - 40
——
79
" In Northumberland, say 13 miles by 2 - - - - 26
— 10
——
73

Tons.

" Estimating the workable coal strata at an average thickness of 12
feet, the contract of one square mile will be 12,390,000 tons, and
of 732 square miles - - - - - - 9,069,480,00
" Deduct one third part for loss by small coal, interceptions by dikes, and
other interruptions - - - - - 3,023,160,00

Remainder 6,046,320,00

" This remainder is adequate to supply the present vend from Newcastle, Sunderlan
Hartley, Blyth, and Stockton, of 3,500,000 tons, for a period of 1,727 years.

" It will be understood that this estimate of the quantity of coal in Durham and Nort
umberland can only be an approximation, especially as the south-eastern coal distri
of Durham is yet almost wholly unexplored ; but the attempt is made, in the hope
satisfying your Lordships that no apprehension need be entertained of this valuab
mineral being exhausted for many future generations.

There is also a considerable extent of coal-field in the northern and south-western
cts of Northumberland; but the foregoing comprises that which is continuous, and
suitable and available for exportation."—(*Lords' Report*, 1829, p. 124.)

. Buckland, the celebrated geologist, considers this estimate as very greatly exag-
ed; but in his examination before the committee of the House of Commons, he
·s and approves a passage of Bakewell's Geology, in which it is stated that the
beds in South Wales are alone sufficient to supply the whole present demand of
and for coal for 2,000 years. The passage is as follows:—

Fortunately we have in South Wales, adjoining the Bristol Channel, an almost
·stless supply of coal and ironstone, which are yet nearly unwrought. It has been
l, that this coal-field extends over about 1,200 square miles; and that there are 23
of workable coal, the total average thickness of which is 95 feet; and the quantity
ined in each acre is 100,000 tons, or 64,000,000 tons per square mile. If from
·e deduct one half for waste, and for the minor extent of the upper beds, we shall
a clear supply of coal equal to 32,000,000 tons per square mile. Now, if we admit
·,000,000 tons from the Northumberland and Durham mines is equal to nearly
hird of the total consumption of coal in England, each square mile of the Welsh
·eld would yield coal for 100 years' consumption; and as there are from 1,000 to
square miles in this coal-field, it would supply England with fuel for 2,000 years,
all our English coal mines are worked out!'

·s, therefore, quite idle either to prohibit, or impose heavy duties on, the export-
of coal, on the ground of its accelerating the exhaustion of the mines. The
·ion of the expensive and destructive process of *screening* (see *post*) will more
·alance any export that is ever likely to take place to foreign countries.

fits of Coal Mining.—Coal Owners' Monopoly, &c.—Instead of the business of
·ining being, generally speaking, an advantageous one, it is distinctly the reverse.
·imes, no doubt, large fortunes have been made by individuals and associations
·ed in this business; but these are rare instances. The opening of a mine is a very
·sive and hazardous operation, and of very uncertain result. Collieries are exposed
·infinite number of accidents, against which no caution can guard. The chances
·losion have, it is true, been a good deal lessened by the introduction of Sir Hum-
Davy's lamp; and some mines are now wrought, that but for the invention of this
·able instrument, must have been entirely abandoned. But besides explosions,
·are still every now and then occurring, from the carelessness of the workmen, and
·contingencies, mines are very liable to be destroyed by *creeps*, or by the sinking of
·of, and by drowning, or the irruption of water from old workings, through fissures
·cannot be seen, and consequently cannot be guarded against. So great, indeed,
·hazard attending this sort of property, that it has never been possible to effect an
·nce on a coal-work, against fire, water, or any other accident.

Buddle, who is intimately acquainted with the state of the coal trade, informed
·mmittee of the House of Lords, that "Although many collieries, in the hands of
·ate individuals and companions, have been perhaps making more than might be
·d a reasonable and fair profit, according to their risk, like a prize in a lottery; yet,
·ade, taking the whole capital employed on both rivers, he should say that certainly
·not been so."—(*First Report*, p. 56.)—Again, being asked, "What have the
·vners, on the Tyne and Wear, in your opinion, generally made on their capital
·yed?" He replied, "According to the best of my knowledge, I should think
· *no means ten per cent. has been made at simple interest, without allowing any extra*
· *for the redemption of capital.*"—(p. 57.)

·ddition to the vast expense attending the sinking of shafts, the erection of steam
·s, &c., and the risk of accidents, the coal, after being brought to the surface, has
·ntly to be conveyed seven or eight miles to the place of shipping; and those whose
·ies are in that situation, have to pay *way-leave* rents, amounting, in some cases,
·. a-year, for liberty to open a communication, or a rail-road, through the pro-
·lying between them and the shore.

·ch has frequently been said of the monopoly of the coal owners on the Tyne and
·ear; but we are satisfied, after a pretty careful investigation of the circumstances,
· such monopoly has ever existed; and that the high price of coal in the metro-
·· to be ascribed wholly to the various duties and charges that have been laid upon
·n the time that it has passed from the hands of the owner, to the time that it is
· in the cellar of the consumer. What means have the coal owners of obtaining
·poly price for their coal? They enjoy no exclusive privileges of any sort; they
·umerous body; and the trade is as open as any other to all capitalists to engage
·he number of places on the east and west coasts, both of England and Scotland,
· southern parts of Wales, from which coals are exported, render it quite visionary
·ose that any general agreement to keep up prices can take place amongst the

various coal proprietors. And though such an agreement were entered into, it is i
possible it could be maintained. The *power* of producing coal greatly exceeds the prese
demand; many new mines have been recently opened, and many others would be broug
into activity were the price artificially enhanced. It is true that the coal owners r
ferred to, having experienced the ruinous effects of throwing a superabundant quant
of coal upon restricted and already glutted markets, have occasionally met together, a
each having named the price he thinks his coal will command, and at which he inten
to sell it, they have proceeded jointly to regulate, according to the probable demand, t
quantity that each shall raise during any particular period. By means of this arrang
ment, the supply and price of coal has been kept, during the time it has existed, co
paratively steady. Common prudence prompts and justifies such an arrangement; b
it also suggests the necessity of reducing the price of coal to the lowest level that w
afford the customary rate of profit. For were the price demanded by the Northe
coal owners raised above this level, new mines would be opened in Durham and Nort
umberland; the imports from the Tees, whence a large supply of excellent coal *is*
present brought to the London market, would be augmented; and fresh competitors, fro
Swansea and other places, would come into the field and undersell them. Governme
should encourage and promote this fair competition; but it ought, at the same time,
do equal justice by all the competitors. It is not to lend assistance to, or remove burde
from, one set of adventurers, which it does not lend to or remove from others. It is
part of its duty to say *how* coals, or any species of produce, shall be carried to mark
It is bound to give every reasonable facility for the opening of new channels or mod
of conveyance between all parts of the country; but it would be glaringly unjust to l
a tax on the coals conveyed by a particular channel, from which those conveyed by ot
channels were exempted.

Mr. Buddle thinks that the aggregate capital employed by the coal owners on t
Tyne amounts to about 1,500,000*l.* exclusive of the craft in the river: and supposi
this estimate to be nearly correct, it will follow, allowing for the value of the ships, th
the total capital employed in the coal trade may be moderately estimated at from *eight*
ten millions; an immense sum to be almost wholly at the risk of the owners, witho
any insurance upon it.

Progressive Consumption of Coal. — Duties and Regulations affecting it, particularly
the Port of London. — There are no mines of coal in either Greece or Italy; and
evidence has been produced to show that the ancients had learned to avail themselves
this most useful mineral. Even in England it does not seem to have been used p
viously to the beginning of the thirteenth century; for the first mention of it occurs
a charter of Henry III., granting licence to the burgesses of Newcastle to dig for co
In 1281, Newcastle is said to have had a considerable trade in this article. About t
end of this century, or the beginning of the fourteenth, coals began to be imported i
London, being at first used only by smiths, brewers, dyers, soap-boilers, &c. T
innovation was, however, loudly complained of. A notion got abroad, that the smo
was highly injurious to the public health; and, in 1316, parliament petitioned the ki
Edward I., to prohibit the burning of coal, on the ground of its being an intolera
nuisance. His Majesty issued a proclamation conformably to the prayer of the petiti
but it being but little attended to, recourse was had to more vigorous measures; a co
mission of oyer and terminer being issued out, with instructions to inquire as to
who burned sea-coal within the city, or parts adjoining, to punish them for the fi
offence, by " pecuniary mulcts;" and upon a second offence, to demolish their furnac
and to provide for the strict observance of the proclamation in all time to come.

But notwithstanding the efforts that were thus made to prohibit the use of coal, a
the prejudice that was long entertained against it; it continued progressively to g
ground. This was partly, no doubt, owing to experience having shown that coal smo
had not the noxious influence ascribed to it, but far more to the superior excelle
of coal as an article of fuel, and the growing scarcity and consequent high price
timber. In the reign of Charles I. the use of coal became universal in London, wh
it has ever since been used to the exclusion of all other articles of fuel. At the rest
ation, the quantity imported was supposed to amount to about 200,000 chaldrons.
1670, the imports had increased to 270,000 chaldrons. At the revolution, they amoun
to about 300,000 chaldrons, and have since gone on increasing with the growing mag
tude and population of the city; being, in 1750, about 500,000 chaldrons; in 1800, ab
900,000 chaldrons; and at present about 1,600,000 chaldrons. — (*Campbell's Polit*
Survey of Great Britain, vol. ii. p. 30.; *Edington on the Coal Trade*, p. 41, &c.)

It might have been supposed, considering that coal is, in this country, a pr
necessary of life, and by far the most important of all the instruments of manufactur
industry, that it would have been exempted from every species of tax; and that ev
possible facility would have been given for its conveyance from the mines to the distr

the South of England, and other places in want of it. But such, we regret to say, not been the case. The coal trade of Great Britain has been for more than a century a half subjected to the most oppressive regulations. From a very early period, the poration had undertaken the task of weighing and measuring the coal brought to ndon; and had been accustomed to charge 8d. a ton for their trouble. In 1613, the ver to make this charge was confirmed to the city by royal charter, it being at the ne time ordered that no coal should be unladen from any vessel till the Lord Mayor given leave. The right to charge this sum according to the chaldron of coal, has ce been confirmed to the city by act of parliament; and as the labouring meters, not-hstanding they have been very well paid, have received only 5d. out of the 8d., the ance of 3d. per chaldron, producing at present about 20,000l. a year, goes to the city isury.

But besides the above, duties for civic purposes have been laid on the coal imported London from the reign of Charles II. downwards. They were originally imposed 1667, after the great fire, in order to assist in the re-building of churches and other lic edifices; and have ever since been continued, to enable the corporation to execute rovements in the city; though it is probable most of our readers will be inclined to k that few improvements could be so great, as a reduction in the price of so very ortant an article as coal. At present, a duty of 10d. per chaldron, denominated the hans' duty, is appropriated, until 1858, to defray the expense of the approaches to don Bridge.

Exclusive of the corporation duties, a duty payable to government was laid on *all* *borne* coal in the reign of William III., which was only repealed *this* year. This y was at once glaringly unjust and oppressive: unjust, inasmuch as it fell only on e parts of the empire to which coals had to be carried by sea; and oppressive, inas-h as it amounted to full *fifty* per cent. upon the price paid to the coal owner for the . It is not very easy to calculate the mischief that this tax has done to the southern nties. We, however, are satisfied that the depressed condition of the peasantry of South, as compared with those of the North, is, in no inconsiderable degree, to be ibed to the operation of the coal tax. This tax, after being long stationary at 5s. a dron, was raised to 9s. 4d. during the late war; but was reduced to 6s. in 1824. : the inequality of the tax was not confined to its affecting those parts only of the ire to which coal had to be carried by sea. Even there its pressure was not equal: for, e it amounted to 6s. a chaldron, or 4s. a ton, in the metropolis and all the South ngland, it only amounted to 1s. 7¼d. a ton on coal carried by sea to Ireland, and s. 8d. on that carried to Wales; while Scotland was for many years entirely ex-ted from the duty.

esides this striking partiality and injustice, various troublesome Custom house lations were required in consequence of distinctions being made between the duties arge and small coal, between those on coal and culm (a species of coal), and coal cinders, and of coal being allowed to be imported duty free into Cornwall, Devon, for the use of the mines. These distinctions are now, however, wholly abolished; no duties exist on coal except those collected in London and a few other ports, and opriated to local purposes.

small supply of coal was of late years brought to London from Staffordshire, by navigation. This coal was charged with a duty of 1s. a chaldron; but this is now repealed.

he regulations to which the sale and delivery of coals have been subjected in the of London, have been, if possible, still more objectionable than the duties imposed em. Instead of being sold by weight, all coals imported into the Thames have been by measure. It is curious to observe the sort of abuses to which this practice has n rise. It is stated by the celebrated mathematician, Dr. Hutton, who, being a e of Newcastle, was well acquainted with the coal trade, that, " If one coal, measur- xactly a cubic yard (nearly equal to *five* bolls), *be broken into pieces of a moderate* *it will measure seven bolls and and a half; if broken very small, it will measure nine* ; which shows that the proportion of the weight to the measure depends upon the of the coals; therefore, *accounting by weight is the most rational method.*" The ers were well aware of this, and insisted upon the coal owners supplying them with coal only; and to such an extent was this principle carried, that all coal for the don market was *screened*, as it is technically termed, or passed over gratings, to ate the smaller pieces. Inasmuch, however, as coals were sold in all their subsequent s by measure, no sooner had they been delivered by the owner, than it was for the est of every one else into whose hands they came before reaching the consumer, eak them into smaller portions. In fact, the profit of many of the retailers in don has arisen chiefly from the increase of measure by the breakage of coal. And Brandling, a very intelligent and extensive coal owner, stated to the Commons' com-

T

mittee, that, in consequence of the breakage, coals are reduced in London to a si₂e
inferior to what they would be, were they put on board *unscreened,* and subjected to n
additional breakage.

The statements now made sufficiently evince the nullity of all the regulations enforcing the sale of coal by correct measures: for even though these regulations had been
enforced, instead of being, as they usually were, wholly neglected, they would have been
of almost no use; inasmuch as any dishonest dealer was as able to cheat, by breaking his
coals a little smaller than usual, as if he had sold them in deficient measures.

The loss occasioned by the useless process of screening has been very great. The
quantity of coal separated by it has amounted in some cases to from 20 to 25 per cent.
of the whole, and the greater part of this residue, containing a portion of the very best
coal, is *burned on the spot.* " I have known," says Mr. Buddle, " at one colliery, as
many as from 90 to 100 chaldrons a day destroyed. If they were not consumed, they
would cover the whole surface, and in the burnings of them they are extremely
destructive; *they destroy the crops a great way round, and we pay large sums for injury done
to the crops, and for damage to the ground.*" — (*First Lords' Rep.* p. 72.) The waste of
coal has been in this way enormous; and the coal owner has been obliged to charge a
higher price upon the coal sold, in order to indemnify himself for the loss of so great
a quantity, and for the mischief he does to others in burning.

The fact, that so monstrous a system should have been persevered in for more than a
century, sets the power of habit in reconciling us to the most pernicious absurdities in a
very striking point of view. Happily, however, the nuisance has been at last abated;
the sale of coal by weight taking away both the temptation to break coal, and the
necessity of screening.

But the abuses that have infected the coal trade were not confined to those that grew
out of the duties, and the sale by measure. They have insinuated themselves into most
departments of the business; and to such an extent have they been carried, that it takes,
at this moment, a larger sum to convey a chaldron of coal from the *pool,* a little below
London Bridge, to the consumers in the city, *than is sufficient to defray the entire cost of
the coal in the North,* including the expense of digging them from the mine, their
conveyance to the shore, landlord's rent, &c.! The following statement shows the various
items that made up the price of coal to the London consumer, in October, 1830, distributed under their proper heads. They have been carefully abstracted from the evidence
before the parliamentary committees.

CHARGES UP TO THE TIME OF ARRIVAL IN THE PORT OF LONDON.	£	s.	d.	£	s.	d.	£	s.	d.
Coal Owner.									
Paid coal owner for coals - - - -				0	14	0			
Deduct river duty paid by him for improvement of Sunderland harbour - - - -				0	0	3			
							0	13	9
Coal Fitter.									
Keel dues, and fittage (including seven miles' water-carriage) - - - - -				0	2	3			
Ship Owner.									
For freight, including insurance of ship and cargo, pilotage, seamen's wages, wear and tear of the ship and materials, discharging ballast, &c. - -				0	8	6⅛			
Municipal Dues.									
River duty, as above - - -	0	0	3						
Pier duty, lights, &c. paid by ship -	0	0	5¼						
				0	0	8¼			
							0	11	5⅝
CHARGES IN THE PORT OF LONDON.									
Government Tax - - - - -				0	6	0			
Municipal Dues.									
Trinity and Nore Lights, tonnage duty, Trinity House for ballast, &c. - - -	0	0	5						
Entries, &c. - - - -	0	0	2¾						
Corporation of London metage - -	0	0	4						
Ditto orphans' dues - - -	0	0	10						
Carried forward - -	0	1	9¾	0	6	0	1	5	2¾

	£	s.	d.	£	s.	d.	£	s.	d.
Brought forward - -	0	1	$9\frac{3}{8}$	0	6	0	1	5	$2\frac{3}{8}$
tto meter's pay and allowance -	0	0	4						
tto market dues - - -	0	0	1						
to Lord Mayor's groundage, &c. -	0	0	$0\frac{1}{2}$						
tto land metage - - -	0	0	6						
tto undertaker - - -	0	0	1						
al-whippers - - - - -	0	1	7						
				0	4	$4\frac{7}{8}$			
Factor.									
torage and del credere commission - -				0	0	$4\frac{1}{8}$			
Merchant.									
yer's commission - - -	0	1	0						
hterage - - - - - -	0	2	0						
tage - - - - -	0	6	0						
dit - - - - -	0	2	0						
otage - - - - -	0	1	3						
d for even money - - -	0	0	3						
(See *Com. Rep.* p. 8.)	0	12	6						
d for discount, *scorage*, and *ingrain* * (see same *Rep.* p. 9.) - -	0	2	$2\frac{1}{8}$						
				0	14	$8\frac{1}{8}$			
							1	5	$5\frac{1}{8}$
g the price paid by the consumer - -							2	10	$7\frac{1}{2}$
is thus apportioned: —									
l owner for coal - - - - -				0	13	9			
owner, &c. for voyage to London - -				0	11	$5\frac{3}{8}$			
ernment duty, corporation charges, and London oal merchant - - - -				1	5	$5\frac{1}{8}$			
							2	10	$7\frac{1}{2}$

these charges but little reduction need be looked for in those incurred in the Tyne and Wear, and in the rate of freight: and as the government duty of 6*s.* aldron has been abolished, the charges that admit of further reduction are the ipal dues, and those attending the delivery of coal to the consumers; and in these, ly, there is ample room for retrenchment.

the items which make up the sum of 4*s.* $4\frac{7}{8}$*d.* of charges in the port of London, of 1*s.* 2*d.* (10*d.* as orphan duty, appropriated to the new bridge, and 4*d.* as coron metage) is a species of public tax. So soon, however, as the term for which the duty is appropriated has expired, it ought to be abolished; and it would be highly ble were some means then also found of indemnifying the corporation for the 4*d.* age claimed by them; inasmuch as the abolition of these duties would not only n a direct saving in the price of coal, but would afford great facilities for its y.†

most important item, in those forming the charges in the port of London, is the fee *coal-whipper*, or coal-heaver—that is, the deliverer of the coals from the ship to the or lighter. This fee is about 1*s.* 7*d.*, and is at least *five* times as great as it ought to

* rage and ingrain were allowances that grew out of the system of selling by measure. As this s now repealed, it is unnecessary to describe them.

† produce of the 4*d.* prescriptive metage, received by the Chamberlain of London, after all expenses cted: —

	£	s.	d.
In the year 1824 - - -	19,088	2	4
1825 - - -	18,340	7	$11\frac{1}{4}$
1826 - - -	18,645	6	$9\frac{3}{4}$
1827 - - -	17,399	1	1
1828 - - -	18,479	8	8
1829 - - -	18,632	14	5

l amount of municipal dues upon coal imported into London, taken in the year 1828, upon an of the three preceding years: —

City metage, 4*d.* per chaldron - -	25,210	2	0
Meters' pay and allowances - -	24,068	11	0
Water baillage, Lord Mayor, &c. -	3,229	3	3
Coal market - - -	6,302	10	6
Orphans' duty - - - - -	63,025	5	0
	£121,835	11	9

be. At Newcastle and Sunderland the filling of a chaldron of coal into the wa
costs from 1¼d. to 1¾d. ; and admitting that to raise coal from the hold is a little m
difficult, still, if 4d. were allowed, it would be a most liberal payment. But the truth
that this item should be struck off altogether. It is occasioned by *a regulation pecu
to the Thames, which prevents the crews of colliers from performing this indispensable p
of their peculiar duty.* In the outports, to which luckily this preposterous regulat
does not extend, the crews act as coal-heavers, and they do so without either asking
obtaining additional wages. And there certainly is no reason whatever for suppos
that the case would be materially different in the port of London, were it not for
regulation referred to. In 1829, the total amount of money paid to the coal-heav
was 107,566l. 13s. ; of which at least 90,000l. may be saved to the citizens, by sim
allowing the crew to perform the function of coal-heavers.

The evidence given by the ship owners and captains before the parliamentary co
mittees establishes, in the fullest manner, all that has now been stated. To discha
a ship when loaded with timber is admitted to be rather more difficult than when sh
loaded with coal. Luckily, however, the masters of all ships other than colliers m
employ, in their discharge, either the crew, or such other labourers as they think
without any sort of interference. And it is proved, that while the cost of dischargin
ship of 300 tons, laden with coal, amounts to about 36l., a ship of the same burd
laden with timber, may be discharged for 9l. or 10l. — (*Com. Rep.* p. 321.) This, c
tainly, is a subject deserving of the immediate attention of parliament.

Besides the charge of 8d. on account of ship metage, there has been a further cha
of 6d. per chaldron on account of land metage. But the new regulations enforc
sale by weight will lead to the abolition of the land as well as the ship meters. Th
inefficiency for all useful purposes was conclusively shown by the witnesses examin
by the parliamentary committees. In fact, the system of metage has rather bee
means of concealing than of discovering fraud.

The duties appropriated to public purposes, those claimed by the city of Lon
as private property, and those required to defray the cost of the coal exchange, and
weighing establishments, &c., are, in future, to be charged in the aggregate at so m
a ton on the coal imported, and paid into the city Chamberlain's office ; accounts of
distribution of the produce of the duty being annually prepared and laid before p
liament.

But the charges on account of the delivery of coal from the ship to the consu
are the most oppressive. They amount in all to no less than 14s. 8½d. ! One item
lighterage, being a sum of 2s. a chaldron paid for conveying the coals from
ship to the wharf. This charge seems to be in no ordinary degree exorbitant. I
mentioned by Mr. Buddle, in his evidence (*First Lords' Rep.* p. 121.), that the T
keelmen, who take the coals from the spouts or staiths, as they are termed, to del
them to the ships, are paid only 1s. 6d. a chaldron, though they have to navigate t
keels from seven to eight miles, and though it be far more difficult to shovel the coals fr
the keels into the port-holes of the ships, than from a lighter to a wharf. Were
charge for lighterage reduced to the same level in the Thames as in the Tyne, it wo
not certainly exceed 8d. or 9d. a chaldron. But before this desirable result can be
complished, this department of the trade must, like all the rest, be thrown op
Here again the trammels of monopoly interfere. At present no individual can ac
a lighterman, who is not free of the Waterman's Company, and who has not served se
years as an apprentice upon the river. Competition is thus wholly excluded, and
charges rendered far higher than they would be under a different system.

The next item in the charge for delivery is 6s. a chaldron for cartage from the w
to the consumer's residence. The best way, perhaps, to judge of the reasonablenes
this charge, is by comparing it with the sums charged for similar work done elsewh
Now, assuming the average weight of the chaldron to be 27 cwt., and the average
tance to which coals are carted one mile and a half, the charge will be 3s. 5¼d. per
per mile ; but in the North, in Durham, Lancashire, &c , it is usual to let the car
of coals, including the loading, by contract, at from 7d. to 8d. a ton on turnpike ro
and 9d. and 10d. on heavy country roads. So that the expense of cartage in Lon
is *four* or *five* times as much as it costs in the North. It seems difficult to account
this difference by the greater expense attending the keep of men, horses, &c. in
metropolis, though that certainly is very heavy. Perhaps a part of it is owing to
system of licensing carts, and regulating the fees of cartage. At all events the su
is one that ought to be investigated.

Exclusive of the charge of 6s. for cartage, there is a further charge of 1s. 6d
shooting, that is, for unloading the wagon into the cellar. Next to the item for w
pers, this is the most outrageous overcharge in this lengthened catalogue of ab

ere are thousands of labourers in London who would be glad to be allowed to per-
m the same work for 3d. or 4d., for which the citizens are obliged to pay 1s. 6d.
deed, we believe it might be done for a good deal less. Mr. Buddle says, " At the
e we pay our wagon-men for filling the wagons, *I believe they would be very glad, for*
, *to heave these same coals out of the cellar again up the hole,*" — (*First Lords' Rep.*
121.) ; — an operation which, every one knows, would be about ten times as trouble-
e as pouring them down.

Such of our readers as may have gone through these statements will, we think, feel
little disposed to differ from the Committee of the House of Lords, who observe, in
Second Report, "that in every stage, from the port of shipment to the coal mer-
nt's wharf, and thence to the consumer's cellar, the regulations under which the
le is conducted *are productive of delay, of an aggravation of expense, and an encou-
ement to fraud !*" — (*Rep.* p. 8.)

The abolition of the metage system, and the sale of coal by weight, will undoubtedly
dicate some of the more flagrant abuses that have infected the trade. But the state-
ts now laid before the reader show that there are other departments that require to be
roughly examined. The exorbitancy of the existing charges for the delivery of coal
n the ships to the wharf, and for carting, shooting, &c. demand that nothing should
eft untried that may have any chance of contributing to their effectual reduction.

New Regulations as to Sale. — A seller's ticket is to accompany all coals sold within
city of London and its environs, *specifying the species of coal and the weight of the
ntity sent.* The coals may be either in bags of a certain fixed size, or in bulk. The
nan is in all cases bound to carry a weighing machine with the coal, which machine
 be made conformably to regulation ; and upon being desired, he is to weigh any one
, or the whole sacks in his wagon, — weighing them first when full, and then when
ty, that the exact weight of the coal may be ascertained. In the event of the weight
g deficient, a penalty is to be imposed on account of every sack so deficient.

n order to save trouble in collecting the duties that still attach to coal in the port of
don, the corporation is authorised to compound with the owner or master of
 ship or vessel importing coal, for the tonnage upon which the duties are to be
. A certificate of such composition, expressing the number of tons of coal,
ers, or culm, agreed to be taken as the cargo of the ship or vessel compounded for,
 be given to the master or owner of the same, and is to be taken as evidence of the
ntity on board.

Then no composition is entered into, the coal is to be weighed in the presence of an
er of the customs *at the port of shipment ;* and the duties are to be paid upon the
ght so shipped.

he shipment of coal in the Tyne is at present regulated by the act 5 Geo. 4. c. 72.,
monly called the *Turn Act.* The object of this act is to make all ships engaged in
rade of the Tyne be loaded in the order which they arrive. It prevents any pre-
nce being given to particular ships ; and renders it nearly impossible for any coal
er to give constant employment to any vessel in the trade which he may wish to
loy. In some respects this act is probably advantageous, but, on the whole, its
y seems very questionable. Why should a coal owner be prevented from employ-
certain ships in preference to others ? Under this act, if more ships engage in the
 than can be profitably employed in it, the loss produced by detention in port, and
ing for a cargo, instead of falling, as it naturally would, were the trade free, on
cular ships, and driving them from the business, falls equally on every ship employed,
depresses the whole trade. There is no regulation of this sort in the Wear.

xportation of Coal. — For a considerable number of years past a duty of 17s. 6d.
aldron has been laid on all large, and of 4s. 6d. a chaldron on all small coal ex-
d. The first of these duties is quite excessive ; and is not to be vindicated, unless
olicy of preventing the exportation of coal were admitted. Inasmuch, however,
nall coal is the only species used in manufactures, no ground could be assigned
rohibiting the exportation of round coal, except the risk of exhausting the mines.
 the statements previously made show the futility of this apprehension. There
ot, therefore, be any reasonable doubt as to the policy of the reduction that has
tly been made in the duty on large coal exported. We believe, indeed, that it
t have been carried a good deal further with advantage to the revenue and to all
s. For the existing duties on coal exported, see TARIFF.

ice of Coal. — The following is an account of the price of coal supplied to Green-
 Hospital in the undermentioned years : —

Years.	Per Chaldron.			Years.	Per Chaldron.			Years.	Per Chaldron.		
	£	s.	d.		£	s.	d.		£	s.	d.
1730	1	4	6	1775	1	10	11½	1820	2	5	9
1735	1	5	0	1780	1	17	3¾	1821	2	6	6
1740	1	9	0	1785	1	14	2½	1822	2	4	6¼
1745	1	10	0	1790	1	14	4¾	1823	2	6	7
1750	1	7	7½	1795	1	19	9	1824	2	3	8
1755	1	8	7½	1800	2	11	7	1825	2	3	2
1760	1	12	8	1805	2	11	8¾	1826	2	0	4
1765	1	12	4½	1810	3	0	8	1827	2	1	5¼
1770	1	9	1½	1815	2	15	6¾	1828	2	0	8¼

(*Parl. Papers*, No. 54. Sess. 1829. No. 72. Sess. 1830.)

In London the *average* price of coal per chaldron in the pool, with the ingrain, in the undermentioned years, was as follows: — 1790, 1*l.* 12*s.* 9¼*d.* ; 1795, 2*l.* 1*s.* 10½*d.* 1800, 2*l.* 12*s.* 3½*d.*

The price in the pool of the undermentioned coals, in the month of May, in the following years, has been —

	£	s.	d.			£	s.	d.	
1807	2	7	6	Adair's Main.	1825	1	15	6	Brown's Wallsend.
1810	2	13	0	Hepburn.	1828	1	15	6	Do.
1815	2	6	6	Do.	1829	1	11	6	Bewicke's Wallsend.
1820	1	17	0	Bell's Wallsend.					(*Com. Report*, 1830, p. 7.)

An Account of the Number of Chaldrons of Coals imported into the County of Cornwall; distinguishing the Quantity entered at each Custom-house, with the Amount of the Duties paid thereon for the Year 1829; also, an Account of the Amount of Drawback paid at each Custom-house of the said County for Coals consumed at the Mines during the same Period.

Names of Ports.	Coals and Cinders.		Culm.	Amount of Duty paid thereon.	Amount of Drawback paid for Coals consumed at the Mills.
	Charged by Weight.	Charged by Measure.			
	Tons.	Chaldrons.	Chaldrons.	£	£
Fowey	8,174	5,739	3,908	3,454	1,724
Falmouth	9,472	1,298	793	2,304	31
Gweek	1,479	1,165	549	659	49
Truro	9,052	16,786	2,488	6,909	3,567
Penzance	5,746	3,916	559	2,338	654
Scilly	762	16	9	157	—
St. Ives	—	43,369	817	13,031	9,146
Padstow	13,029	4,106	1,242	3,869	977
Total	47,714	76,395	10,365	32,721	16,148

Account of the Number of Coal Ships entering the Port of London, and the Delivery of Coals from the same, from the Year 1820 to 1829, both inclusive ; with the Amount of the Government Duty thereon. — (*Compiled from Parl. Papers.*)

Years.	Ships.	Coals, Culm, &c.		Amount of Public Duty received thereon.
		Chaldrons.	Vats.	£
1820	5,922	1,327,825	1	616,774
1821	5,735	1,269,753	1	603,121
1822	5,611	1,199,511	3	576,340
1823	6,464	1,437,251	2	669,407
1824	7,151	1,524,807	3	486,372*
1825	6,668	1,423,823	0	426,891
1826	6,808	1,595,866	1	467,441
1827	6,432	1,462,058	3	416,571
1828	6,823	1,553,461	3	442,898
1829	7,021	1,593,581	2	464,599

* On the 5th of April, 1824, the duty was reduced from 9*s.* 4*d.* to 6*s.* a chaldron.

To other Ports of Great Britain (Coastwise).

Years.	Coals (except Small Coals) and Cinders. Tons.	Small Coals. Chaldrons Imperial Measure.	Culm. Chaldrons Imperial Measure.	Total Quantity sent Coastwise, stated in Tons Weight. Tons.
1819	438,045	18	70,934	3,459,508
1820	437,074	71	105,911	3,947,908
1821	463,974	105	97,396	3,731,908
1822	491,094	427	83,953	3,810,239
1823	534,835	62	92,425	4,372,839
1824	547,939	232	121,091	4,308,571
1825	539,760	25,036	121,357	4,384,433
1826	557,355	78,758	139,360	4,730,307
1827	595,278	103,115	127,026	4,440,318
1828	645,471	75,097	121,201	4,507,935

To Ireland.

Years.	Coals (except Small Coals) and Cinders. Tons.	Coals. Chaldrons Imperial Measure.	Small Coals. Chaldrons Imperial Measure.	Culm. Chaldrons Imperial Measure.	Total Quantity exported to Ireland, stated in Tons Weight. Tons.
1819	156,581	354,439	21	15,168	669,660
1820	119,609	399,743	-	10,946	606,400
1821	140,851	362,600	-	10,441	644,787
1822	156,236	376,943	-	10,486	694,094
1823	166,131	373,333	112	6,415	693,413
1824	162,878	367,815	1,607	11,352	691,429
1825	159,723	368,815	2,368	15,036	695,832
1826	236,052	367,849	119	23,599	779,584
1827	198,857	306,289	30	19,914	650,798
1828	242,944	336,550	486	21,100	740,071

To British Colonies.

Years.	Coals (except Small Coals) and Cinders. Tons.	Coals. Chaldrons Imperial Measure.	Small Coals. Chaldrons Imperial Measure.	Culm. Chaldrons Imperial Measure.	Total Quantity exported to British Colonies, stated in Tons Weight. Tons.
1819	9,895	42,813	1,333	233	71,497
1820	9,191	56,500	1,784	254	90,447
1821	10,521	55,431	2,016	115	90,423
1822	9,741	54,891	18,719	-	111,892
1823	13,606	51,281	3,448	99	89,713
1824	12,211	60,254	2,684	-	99,575
1825	10,527	69,648	5,022	63	114,264
1826	42,490	55,231	2,796	988	123,437
1827	43,963	53,645	3,096	578	123,109
1828	50,563	53,277	2,438	118	128,092

To Foreign Countries.

Years.	Coals (except Small Coals) and Cinders. Tons.	Coals. Chaldrons Newcastle Measure.	Small Coals. Chaldrons Newcastle Measure.	Culm. Chaldrons Newcastle Measure.	Total Quantity exported to Foreign Countries, stated in Tons Weight. Tons.
1819	9,475	22,732	35,712	9	164,375
1820	7,081	20,536	36,509	159	158,672
1821	8,236	23,671	37,509	218	170,941
1822	9,692	22,425	38,892	916	172,754
1823	5,446	16,579	42,599	526	163,662
1824	10,952	18,783	44,349	515	179,617
1825	27,827	15,301	47,671	755	197,234
1826	45,518	9,292	57,565	270	223,919
1827	54,090	11,403	59,867	478	244,292
1828	38,507	11,056	60,315	26	227,709

Aggregate Quantities shipped to all Parts.

Years.	Coals (except Small Coals) and Cinders. Tons.	Coals. Chaldrons Newcastle Measure.	Coals. Chaldrons Imperial Measure.	Small Coals. Chaldrons Imperial Measure.	Small Coals. Chaldrons Newcastle Measure.	Culm. Chaldrons Newcastle Measure.	Culm. Chaldrons Imperial Measure.	Total Quantity shipped to all Parts, stated in Tons Weight. Tons.
1819	613,996	22,732	2,502,997	1,372	35,712	9	86,335	4,365,040
1820	572,955	20,536	2,819,506	1,855	36,509	159	117,111	4,803,427
1821	623,582	23,671	2,664,788	2,121	37,509	218	107,952	4,638,059
1822	666,763	22,425	2,733,534	19,146	38,892	216	99,439	4,788,839
1823	720,018	16,579	3,097,070	3,692	42,599	526	98,939	5,319,627
1824	733,980	18,783	3,015,949	4,523	44,349	515	132,443	5,279,192
1825	737,837	15,301	3,061,817	32,426	47,671	755	136,456	5,291,763
1826	881,415	9,292	3,211,905	81,673	57,565	270	163,247	5,856,547
1827	892,188	11,403	2,899,805	106,240	59,867	478	146,518	5,458,377
1828	977,485	11,056	2,976,093	78,041	60,315	26	142,419	5,003,807

WILLIAM IRVING,
Inspector General of Imports and Exports.

Inspector General's Office,
Custom House, London,
30th May, 1829.

An Account of the several Counties in England and Wales into which Coals have be brought Coastwise during the Year 1829; with the Number of Chaldrons enter and the Amount of Duty thereon, in each respective County.

(*Parl. Paper*, No. 301. Sess. 1830.)

Names of Counties.	Coals and Cinders. Charged by Weight.	Coals and Cinders. Charged by Measure.	Culm.	Amount of Duty pai thereon.
	Tons.	*Chaldrons.*	*Chaldrons.*	£
London	265	1,548,170	3,797	464,59[illegible]
Kent	2,359	173,555	436	52,54[illegible]
Sussex	3,072	118,228	8,441	36,295
Hampshire	2,436	124,404	119	37,81[illegible]
Dorsetshire	676	43,493	3,931	13,281
Devonshire	61,388	96,408	63,323	42,784
Cornwall	47,714	76,395	10,365	32,721
Somersetshire	- -	3,559	17,413	1,52[illegible]
Gloucestershire	1,797	638	7	55[illegible]
Monmouthshire	43	22	224	2[illegible]
Glamorganshire	440	- -	1,488	7[illegible]
Caermarthenshire	103	- -	212	14
Pembrokeshire	7,016	- -	242	59[illegible]
Cardiganshire	9,276	10	12,906	1,09[illegible]
Isle of Anglesea	70,668	56	9,398	6,137
Cheshire	263	- -	- -	22
Lancashire	56	555	- -	178
Cumberland	73	18	- -	20
Berwick-upon-Tweed	- -	146	- -	44
Durham	- -	118	- -	35
Yorkshire	20	25,412	- -	7,634
Lincolnshire	- -	23,985	- -	7,195
Cambridgeshire (Wisbeach)	- -	29,030	- -	8,769
Norfolk	2,010	277,206	- -	83,564
Suffolk	50	62,876	- -	18,874
Essex	590	102,544	- -	30,881
Total	210,315	2,706,828	132,302	847,26[illegible]

Customs Revenue on Coals, Cinders, and Culm.															
Years.	Gross Revenue. On Coals, Cinders, and Culm brought or carried Coastwise, or by Inland Navigation, in the United Kingdom.			Gross Revenue. On Coals, Cinders, and Culm exported to Foreign Parts.			Total Gross Revenue.			Deductions from the Gross Revenue for Drawbacks on Exportation, &c., and Repayments on Over-Entries.			Nett Produce of the Duties on Coals, Cinders, and Culm in the United Kingdom.		
	£	s.	d.	£	s.	d.	£	s.	d.	£	s.	d.	£	s.	d.
1819	957,899	9	10¼	48,861	7	11½	1,006,760	17	9¾	19,891	13	2½	986,869	4	7½
1820	1,086,564	17	3½	48,359	3	9	1,134,924	1	0½	18,928	13	3	1,115,995	7	9½
1821	1,019,865	10	5½	50,911	13	1¼	1,070,777	3	6¾	20,744	9	2½	1,050,032	14	4¼
1822	1,006,506	2	3¾	52,771	4	6¼	1,059,277	6	10	21,425	0	8	1,037,852	6	2
1823	1,145,659	1	3¾	44,020	5	6¾	1,189,679	6	9½	21,911	8	10½	1,167,767	17	11
1824	948,810	16	10	42,821	16	10¾	991,632	13	8¾	23,340	17	3¼	968,291	16	5½
1825	899,918	14	9¾	43,421	1	10	943,339	16	7¾	26,109	11	9½	917,230	4	10½
1826	972,839	19	9¼	40,553	17	8	1,013,393	17	5¼	26,309	19	10	987,083	17	7½
1827	862,526	8	6¼	45,182	9	3	907,718	17	9¼	24,349	8	4½	883,369	9	4¾
1828	922,682	1	4¼	41,423	6	2	964,105	7	6¼	28,017	2	8¼	936,088	4	10

COASTING TRADE, the trade or intercourse carried on by sea betw two or more ports or places of the same country.

It has been customary in most countries to exclude foreigners from all par pation in the coasting trade. This policy began in England in the reign Elizabeth (5 Eliz. c. 5.), or, perhaps, at a more remote era; and was perfe by the acts of navigation passed in 1651 and 1660. A vast number of regulati have been since enacted at different periods. The existing rules with respec it, which have been a good deal simplified, are embodied in the act 6 Ge c. 107., and are as follow:—

efinition of Coasting Trade. — All trade by sea from any one part of the United Kingdom to any other
t thereof, or from one part of the Isle of Man to another part thereof, shall be deemed to be a coasting
e, and all ships while employed therein shall be deemed to be coasting ships; and no part of the
ted Kingdom, however situated with regard to any other part thereof, shall be deemed in law, with
rence to each other, to be parts beyond the seas, in any matter relating to the trade or navigation or
enue of this realm. — § 100.

ords of Treasury to regulate what shall be deemed trading by Sea under this Act. — It shall be lawful
the commissioners of his Majesty's treasury to determine and direct in what cases the trade by water
n any place on the coast of the United Kingdom to another of the same shall or shall not be deemed
ade by sea within the meaning of this act or of any act relating to the customs. — § 101.

oasting Ship confined to Coasting Voyage. — No goods shall be carried in any coasting ship, except such
hall be laden to be so carried at some port or place in the United Kingdom, or at some port or place
he Isle of Man; and no goods shall be laden on board any ships, to be carried coastwise, until all goods
ght in such ship from parts beyond the seas shall have been unladen; and if any goods shall be taken
or put out of any coasting ship at sea or over the sea; or if any coasting ship shall touch at any place
: the sea, or deviate from her voyage, unless forced by unavoidable circumstances; or if the master
ny coasting ship, which shall have touched at any place over the sea, shall not declare the same in
ting under his hand to the collector or comptroller at the port where such ship shall afterwards first
ve; the master shall forfeit 200*l*. — § 102.

*efore Goods be laden or unladen, Notice of Intention, or of Arrival, to be given, and proper Documents
sue.* — No goods shall be laden on board any ship in any port, to be carried coastwise, nor, having
1 brought coastwise, shall be unladen, until notice in writing, signed by the master, shall have been
n to the collector or comptroller, by the master, owner, wharfinger, or agent, of the intention to lade
ls to be so carried, or of the arrival of such ship with goods so brought; nor until proper documents
l have been granted for the lading or for the unlading of such goods; and such goods shall not be
n or unladen, except at such times and places, and in such manner, and by such persons, and under
care of such officers, as are hereinafter directed; and all goods laden to be so carried, or brought to
) unladen, contrary hereto, shall be forfeited. — § 103. *

articulars in Notice. — In such notice shall be stated the name and tonnage of the ship, and the name
he port to which she belongs, and the name of the master, and the name of the port to which she is
nd, or from which she has arrived, and the name of the wharf or place at which her lading is to be
n in or discharged, as the case may be; and such notice shall be signed by the master, owner, wharf-
r, or agent, and shall be entered in a book to be kept by the collector; and every such notice for the
ding of any ship shall be delivered within twenty-four hours after the arrival of such ship, under a
lty of 20*l*., to be paid by the master; and in every such notice for the lading of any ship shall be stated
ast voyage on which such ship shall have arrived at such port; and if such voyage shall have been
parts beyond the seas, there shall be produced, with such notice, a certificate from the proper officer
he discharge of all goods, if any, brought in such ship, and of the due clearance of such ship inwards
1ch voyage. — § 104.

om and to Ireland. — Upon the arrival of any coasting ship at any port in Great Britain from Ireland,
t any port in Ireland from Great Britain, the master shall, within twenty-four hours after arrival,
er such notice, signed by him, to the collector or comptroller; and if such ship shall have on board
goods subject to any duty of excise, or any goods which had been imported from parts beyond the seas,
particulars, with the marks and numbers of the packages, shall be set forth in such notice; and if
e shall be no such goods on board, then it shall be declared in such notice that no such goods are on
d; and the master shall also answer on oath any questions relating to the voyage, as shall be
inded of him by the collector or comptroller; and every master who shall fail to deliver such notice,
truly to answer such questions, shall forfeit 100*l*. — § 105.

ter Notice given of lading Goods, Collector may grant a general Sufferance. — When notice shall
been given to the collector or comptroller at the port of lading, of the intention to lade goods on
1 any coasting ship, such collector or comptroller shall grant a general sufferance for the lading of
s (without specifying the same) on board such ship, at the wharf which shall be expressed in such
rance; and such sufferance shall be a sufficient authority for the lading of any sort of goods, except
if any, as shall be excepted therein: Provided always, that before any sufferance be granted for any
s prohibited to be exported, or subject to any export duty, other than any *ad valorem* duty, the
er or the shipper shall give bond with one surety, in treble the value of the goods, that the same shall
nded at the port for which such sufferance is required, or shall be otherwise accounted for to the
action of the commissioners of customs. — § 106.

aster of coasting Vessel to keep a Cargo Book. — The master of every coasting ship shall keep a cargo
, stating the name of the ship, and of the master, and of the port to which she belongs, and of the
to which bound on each voyage, and in which book shall be entered, at the port of lading, an
int of all goods taken on board, stating the descriptions of the packages, and the quantities and
iptions of the goods therein, and the quantities and descriptions of any goods stowed loose, and the
s of the shippers and consignees, and in which book at the port of discharge shall be noted the days
which any such goods be delivered out of such ship, and also the times of departure from the port
ling, and of arrival at any port of unlading; and such master shall produce such book for the in-
son of the coastwaiter, or other officer, as often as demanded, and who shall be at liberty to make
ote or remark therein; and if such master shall fail correctly to keep such book, or to produce the
, or if at any time there be found on board any goods not entered in the cargo book, or if it be found
iny goods entered as laden, or any goods not noted as delivered, be not on board, the master shall
t 50*l*.; and if, upon examination at the port of lading, any package entered in the cargo book as con-
ig any foreign goods, shall be found not to contain such goods, such package, with its contents, shall
feited; and if, at the port of discharge, any package shall be found to contain any foreign goods which
ot entered in such book, such goods shall be forfeited. — § 107.

*:ount of Foreign Goods, and of Goods subject to Coast Duty, or Export Duty, to be delivered to
:tor.* — Before any coasting ship shall depart from the port of lading, an account, together with a
cate and triplicate of the same, all fairly written and signed by the master, shall be delivered to the
tor or comptroller; and in such account shall be set forth such particulars as are required to be
ed in the cargo book, of all foreign goods, and of all goods subject to coast duty, and of all goods sub-
) export duty, (other than *ad valorem* duty,) and of all corn, grain, meal, flour, or malt, laden on
; and generally whether any other British goods, or no other British goods, be laden on board, or
er such ship be wholly laden with British goods, not being of any descriptions before mentioned;
he collector or comptroller shall select and retain two of such accounts, and shall return the third,
and signed by him, and noting the clearance of the ship thereon, and such account shall be the
nce of the ship for the voyage, and the transire for the goods expressed therein; and the collector
omptroller shall transmit one of such accounts to the collector and comptroller of the port of destin-
; and if such account be false, or shall not correspond with the cargo book, the master shall forfeit
§ 108.

y Customs orders issued at different periods, live fish, chippings of granite, cobble-stones, whin-
, kelp, Kentish rag-stones, flints gathered from the land, pebbles, gravel, and chalk, faggots or
s for bakers' use, hay, straw, fresh meat, soap-ashes for manure, coal-ashes, iron-stone, bones for
:e, and bricks, are exempt from coast regulations.

Transire to be delivered to the Collector before Goods be unladen. — Before any goods be unladen from any coasting ship at the port of discharge, the master, owner, wharfinger, or agent, shall deliver the transire to the collector or comptroller, who shall thereupon grant an order for the uplading of such ship at the wharf specified in such order : provided that if any of the goods on board be subject to any duty of customs or excise payable on arrival coastwise at such port, the master, owner, wharfinger, or agent or the consignee, shall also deliver to the collector or comptroller a bill of the entry of the particulars of such goods, in words at length, together with a copy thereof, in which all sums and numbers may be expressed in figures, and shall pay down all duties of customs, or produce a permit in respect of all duties of excise, which shall be payable on any of such goods, and thereupon the collector and comptroller shall grant an order for the landing of such goods, in the presence or by the authority of the coastwaiter. — § 109.

Collector, in certain Cases, may grant general Transire for Coasting Vessels. — Provided always, that it shall be lawful for the collector and comptroller, in the cases hereinafter mentioned, to grant for any coasting ship a general transire, to continue in force not exceeding one year, for the lading of any goods (except such goods as shall be expressly excepted therein), and for the clearance of the ship in which the goods shall be laden, and for the unlading of the goods at the place of discharge ; (that is to say),
For any ship regularly trading between places in the river Severn, eastward of the Holmes :
For any ship regularly trading between places in the river Humber :
For any ship regularly trading between places in the Firth of Forth :
For any ship regularly trading between places to be named in the transire, and carrying only manure, lime, chalk, stone, gravel, or any earth not being fuller's earth :
Provided always, that such transire shall be written in the cargo book ; also, that if the collector and comptroller shall at any time revoke such transire, and notice thereof shall be given to the master or owner, or shall be given to any of the crew on board, or shall be entered in the cargo book by any officer of customs, such transire shall become void, and be delivered up by the master or owner to the collector or comptroller. — § 110.

Commissioners of Customs to appoint Coal Meters for any Port in the United Kingdom. — For the better ascertaining and collecting of the duties of customs upon coals, culm, or cinders, it shall be lawful for the commissioners of customs to appoint coal meters in the service of the customs, for any port ; and such meters shall measure or weigh all coals, culm, or cinders brought coastwise into such port, and shall give to the collector or comptroller a certificate of the total quantities ; and if any such meter shall give a false certificate, he shall forfeit 100*l.* ; and if any coals, culm, or cinders be landed without the presence or permission of a proper meter, the same shall be forfeited, together with all duties paid thereon : Provided always, that nothing herein shall extend to repeal or in any way affect any right of appointment of meter possessed under any law or charter by any corporate body at the time of the commencement of this act. — § 111.

Coastwaiter, Landingwaiter, or Searcher, may go on board and examine any Coasting Ship. — It shall be lawful in any case, and at all legal times, for the coastwaiter, and also for the landingwaiter, and for the searcher, and for any other officer of customs, to go on board any coasting ship in any port, or at any period of her voyage, and strictly to search any ship, and to examine all goods on board, and all goods being laden or unladen, and to demand all documents which ought to be on board. — § 112.

Times and Places for landing and shipping. — No goods shall be unshipped from any ship arriving coastwise, and no goods shall be shipped, or waterborne to be shipped, to be carried coastwise, but only on days not being Sundays or holidays, and in the day-time, that is to say, from the first day in September until the last day of March betwixt sun-rising and sun-setting, and from the last day of March until the first day of September between seven in the morning and four in the afternoon ; nor shall any such goods be so unshipped, shipped, or waterborne, unless in the presence or with the authority of the proper officer of customs, nor unless at places which shall be appointed by the officer of customs. — § 113.

Goods prohibited or restrained. — Whenever any goods which may be prohibited to be exported by proclamation, or by order in council, shall be so prohibited, it shall be lawful in such proclamation or order to prohibit the carrying of such goods coastwise, and if any spirits or any such goods shall be carried coastwise, or shall be shipped or waterborne to be carried coastwise, contrary hereto, or to any such prohibition or restraint, the same shall be forfeited. — § 114.

Dues of the City of London. — For the purpose of enabling the dues payable to the city on articles imported coastwise to be ascertained and collected, it is enacted, that if all or any of the following goods, viz. firkins of butter, tons of cheese, fish, eggs, salt, fruit, roots eatable, and onions, brought coastwise into the port of the said city, and which are liable to the said dues, be landed or unshipped at or in the said port before a proper certificate of the payment of the said dues shall have been obtained, such goods shall be forfeited, and may be seized by an officer of customs empowered to seize any goods that may be landed without due entry thereof. — (7 & 8 Geo. 4. c. 56. § 15.)

COBALT (Ger. *Kobalt;* Du. *Kobal;* Sw. *Cobolt;* Fr. *Cobalt;* It. *Cobalto* Rus. *Kobolt;* Lat. *Cobaltum*), a mineral of a grey colour, with a shade of red, and by no means brilliant. It has scarcely any taste or smell ; it is rather soft ; its specific gravity is about 8·6. Its oxides are principally employed. They form the most permanent blue with which we are acquainted. The colouring power of oxide of cobalt on vitrifiable mixtures is greater, perhaps, than that of any other metal. One grain gives a full blue to 240 grains of glass. — (*Thomson's Chemistry,* and *Ure's Dictionary.*)

COCCULUS INDICUS, OR INDIAN BERRY (Sans. *Kakamari;* Malay *Tuba-bidgi*), the fruit of the *Menispermum cocculus,* a large tree of the Malabar coast, Ceylon, &c. It is a small kidney-shaped berry, having a white kernel inside of a most unpleasant taste. It is of a poisonous and intoxicating quality, and has been employed to adulterate ale and beer. But its employment in that way is prohibited, under a penalty of 200*l.* upon the brewer, and of 500*l.* upon the seller of the drug, by the 56 Geo. 3. c. 58.

COCHINEAL (Ger. *Koschenilje;* Du. *Conchenilje;* Fr. *Cochenille;* It. *Cocciniglia;* Sp. *Cochinilla, Grana;* Port. *Cochenilha;* Rus. *Konssenel*), an insect (*Coccus cacti*) found in Mexico, Georgia, South Carolina, and some of the West India islands ; but it is in Mexico only that it is reared with care, and forms an important article of commerce. It is a small insect, seldom exceeding the size of a grain of barley ; and was generally believed, for a considerable time after it began to be imported into Europe, to be a sort of vegetable grain or seed

e are two sorts or varieties of cochineal : the best or domesticated, which the
iards call *grana fina*, or fine grain; and the wild, which they call *grana syl-*
z. The former is nearly twice as large as the latter; probably because its
has been improved by the favourable effects of human care, and of a more
us and suitable nourishment derived solely from the *coctus cochenilifer*
g many generations. Wild cochineal is collected six times in the year; but
which is cultivated is only collected thrice during the same period. The
ts are detached from the plants on which they feed by a blunt knife; they
hen put into bags, and dipped in boiling water to kill them, after which they
ried in the sun; and though they lose about two thirds of their weight by
process, about 600,000 or 700,000 lbs. (each pound being supposed to contain
0 insects) are brought annually to Europe. It is principally used in the
of scarlet, crimson, and other esteemed colours. The watery infusion is of
let crimson; the alcoholic of a deep crimson; and the alkaline of a deep
e, or rather violet hue. It is imported in bags, each containing about
s.; and has the appearance of small, dry, shrivelled, rugose berries or seeds,
deep brown, purple, or mulberry colour, with a white matter between the
les. In this state they suffer no change from length of keeping. Dr. Ban-
says that that cochineal is the best, which " is large, plump, dry, and of a
white colour on the surface."

e species of cochineal called *granilla*, or dust, is supposed by Dr. Bancroft
principally formed of *grana sylvestra*. The insects of which it consists are
er than those composing the fine cochineal; and it does not yield more than
rd of the colouring matter that is yielded by the latter. The cochineal
. was introduced into India in 1795; but a very inferior sort only is pro-
l. It has also been introduced into Java and Spain, but with what success
ns to be seen. — (*Thomson's Dispensatory ; Bancroft on Colours*, &c.)

e imports of cochineal usually vary from 1,500 to 1,800 bags, or from 300,000 to
00 lbs. In 1828, the quantity imported amounted to 258,032 lbs.; of which
36 lbs. were brought from Mexico, 44,964 lbs. from the United States, 64,911 lbs.
the British West Indies, and 3,084 lbs. from the East Indies. The exports
g the same year amounted to about 110,000 lbs. The duty on foreign cochineal
duced, in 1826, from 1s. per lb. to 6d.

e price of cochineal fluctuated very much during the war, partly on account of
stacles which it occasionally threw in the way of importation, and partly on ac-
of its being an article of direct government expenditure. In 1814, the price of
st cochineal was as high as 36s. and 39s.; and it has since gone on regularly
ing, without a single rally, till it has sunk to 8s. or 9s. Previously to the war it
ver been under 12s. or 13s. Lac dye has recently been employed to some extent
g scarlet; but notwithstanding this circumstance, the consumption of cochineal,
ned, no doubt, partly by its cheapness, and partly, perhaps, by some change of
n, has been materially increased during the last two years. This, however, has
d any influence on its price; and it would appear, from the long continuance of
ces, without any diminution of imports, that they are still sufficient to remunerate
wers of the article. — (*Tooke on High and Low Prices; Cooke's Commerce of Great*
for 1830; *Parl. Papers*, &c.)

COA. See CACAO.

CO, COKER, OR, more properly, COCOA NUTS (Ger. *Kokosnüsse;*
okosnooten; Fr. and Sp. *Cocos;* It. *Cocchi;* Rus. *Kokos;* Sans. *Narikila*),
it of a species of palm tree (*Cocos nucifera*, Lin.). This tree is common
everywhere within the tropics, and is one of the most valuable in the
It grows to the height of from 40 to 60 feet; it has no branches, but the
are from 12 to 14 feet in length, with a very strong middle rib. The fruit
rly as large as a man's head; the external rind is thin, tough, and of a
ish red colour; beneath this there is a quantity of very tough fibrous matter,
is used in many countries in the manufacture of cordage, and coarse sail-
see COIR); within this fibrous coating is the shell of the nut, which is
globular, very hard, susceptible of a high polish, and used for many domes-
rposes; the kernel is white, in taste and firmness resembling that of a
ut; it is hollow in the interior, the hollow being filled with a milky fluid.
the nut is green, the whole hollow of the shell is filled with fluid, which
eshing, agreeable, and pleasant to the taste. The solid part of the ripe
is extremely nutritious, but rather indigestible. The kernels yield by

expression a great deal of oil, which, when recent, is equal to that of sw
almonds; but it soon becomes rancid, and is then employed by painters.   A t
generally yields about 100 nuts, in clusters near the top of about a dozen ea
The wood of the tree is made into boats, rafters, the frames of houses, and gutt
to convey water.   The leaves are used for thatching buildings; and are wrou
into mats, baskets, and many other things, for which osiers are employed
Europe; so that every part of it is applied to some useful purpose.

If the body of the tree be bored, there exudes from the wound a wh
liquor, called palm wine or toddy.   It is very sweet when fresh; kept a few hou
it becomes more poignant and agreeable; but next day it begins to grow so
and in the space of twenty-four hours is changed into vinegar.   When distill
it produces the best species of Indian arrack; it also yields a great deal of sug
Toddy is obtained from several species of palms, but that of the *Cocos nucifera*
the best.—(See *Ainslie's Materia Indica; Rees's Cyclopædia*, &c.)

An improvement has recently been effected in the preparation of cocoa oil, wh
promises to be of much importance in the arts, by making it available in the manuf
ture of candles and soap, and for various purposes to which it was not previou
applicable.

The palm oil met with in the market is not obtained from the *Cocos-nucifera*,
from another species of palm.   It is chiefly imported from the coast of Guinea.
PALM OIL.

Cocoa nuts are produced in immense quantities in Ceylon, forming, with their p
ducts, — oil, arrack, and coir, — the principal articles of export from that island.   Co
oil is in very extensive use all over India, and large quantities are manufactured in
lower provinces of Bengal.   This latter is said to be superior to that imported fr
Ceylon.

The duty on cocoa nuts is imposed by tale, being 5s. per 120.   Their price in
London market, duty included, varies, at this moment (May 1830), from 10s. to 2
the 120.

COD (Ger. *Kabljau, Bakalau;* Du. *Kabeljaauw, Baukaelja;* Da. *Kabliau, Sk*
torsk, Bakelau; Sw. *Kabeljo, Bakelau;* Fr. *Morue, Cabillaud;* It. *Baccala, B*
calare; Sp. *Bacalao;* Port. *Bacalhão;* Lat. *Gadus*), a species of fish, too w
known to require any description.

"The cod-fish is amazingly prolific.   Leewenhoek counted 9,384,000 eggs i
cod-fish of a middling size; a number that will baffle all the efforts of man to
terminate.   In our seas they begin to spawn in January, and deposit their e
in rough ground, among rocks.   Some continue in roe till the beginning of Ap

"The cod is only found in the northern parts of the world; it is an ocean fi
and never met with in the Mediterranean.   The great rendezvous of the cod-
is on the banks of Newfoundland, and the other sand-banks that lie off the coa
of Cape Breton, Nova Scotia, and New England.   They prefer those situatio
by reason of the quantity of worms produced in these sandy bottoms, which ter
them to resort there for food.   But another cause of the particular atta
ment the fish have to these spots is their vicinity to the polar seas, where th
return to spawn: there they deposit their roes in full security; but want of fo
forces them, as soon as the more southern seas are open, to repair thither
subsistence.   Few are taken to the north of Iceland, but they abound on
south and west coasts.   They are also found to swarm on the coasts of Norw
in the Baltic, and off the Orkney and Western Isles; after which their numb
decrease in proportion as they advance towards the south, when they seem q
to cease before they reach the mouth of the Straits of Gibraltar.

"Before the discovery of Newfoundland, the greater fisheries of cod were
the seas of Iceland, and off our Western Isles, which were the grand resort
ships from all the commercial nations; but it seems that the greatest plenty
met with near Iceland.   The English resorted thither before the year 1415;
we find that Henry V. was disposed to give satisfaction to the king of Denm
for certain irregularities committed by his subjects on those seas.   In the reig
Edward IV. the English were excluded from the fishery, by treaty.   In l
times, we find Queen Elizabeth condescending to ask permission to fish in th
seas, from Christian IV. of Denmark.   In the reign of her successor, howe
no fewer than 150 English ships were employed in the Iceland fishery; wh
indulgence might arise from the marriage of James with a princess of Denma
—(*Pennant's British Zoology.*)

Cod Fishery, British. — The extraordinary abundance of cod-fish on the banks of Newfoundland was first discovered in 1536, and for the last two centuries the fishery has been principally prosecuted on them. A good many vessels are, however, employed on the coasts of Norway and of the Orkney and Shetland Islands, and on the Well-bank, the Dogger-bank, and the Broad-fourteens. The English, Americans, and French are, at present, the nations by whom the fishery on the banks of Newfoundland is principally carried on. The American fishermen are remarkable for their activity and enterprise, sobriety and frugality; and the proximity of their country, and the various facilities which it affords for carrying on the trade, give them advantages with which it is difficult to contend.

Cod is prepared in two different ways; that is, it is either gutted, salted, and then barrelled — in which state it is denominated green or pickled cod, — or it is dried and cured — in which state it is called dried cod. Ready access to the shore is indispensable to the prosecution of the latter species of fishery.

The exports of cod and cod-sounds from Newfoundland and the coasts of Labrador, on account of British subjects, during the three years ending with 1826, were as follow: —

	1824.	1825.	1826.
Dry Cod -	996,976 ...	973,464 ...	928,442 quintals.
Wet do. -	— ...	— ...	—
Sounds and Tongues -	4,168 ...	6,680 ...	6,472 kegs.

The quintal of dried cod is worth from 10s. to 12s.

In 1815, the exports of dried cod amounted to 1,245,808 quintals. Since 1817 they have been nearly stationary. The number of British sailors, including those belonging to the island, to Nova Scotia, the West Indies, &c., at present employed in the Newfoundland fisheries, may amount to from 8,000 to 10,000. The number of men employed in different businesses on shore, subservient to the fishery, is considerably greater.

The vessels, with their tonnage and men, that cleared out from the different ports of the United Kingdom, for Newfoundland and the coasts of Labrador, during the three years ending with 1826, were as follow: —

	Ships.	Tonnage.	Men.
1824 -	313 ...	40,625 ...	2,572
1825 -	322 ...	44,255 ...	2,768
1826 -	282 ...	35,781 ...	2,267

No separate account is kept of the vessels employed in the Newfoundland fishery, except under the general head of the trade with that island; and as the vessels engaged in the other British fisheries neither enter nor clear out at the Custom-house, no account can be given of their number or tonnage.

About eight tenths of the dried fish exported from Newfoundland by British subjects, is sent to Spain, Portugal, Italy, and other continental nations; the rest goes to the West Indies and to Great Britain.

By the act 26 Geo. 3. c. 26. bounties were given, under certain conditions specified in the act, to a certain number of vessels employed in the fishery on the coasts and banks of Newfoundland; but these bounties have entirely ceased several years since. A bounty was, however, paid, down to the 5th of April, 1830, to all persons residing in Great Britain and Ireland, curing, drying, or pickling cod-fish, ling, or hake; the bounty being 4s. a cwt. on the dried cod, &c., and 2s. 6d. a barrel on that which was pickled. A tonnage bounty was at the same time paid on vessels fitted out for the cod, ling, and hake fishery on the coasts of Great Britain and Ireland; but this has also ceased.

The act 5 Geo. 4. c. 51. contains several regulations with respect to the Newfoundland fisheries. Aliens are prohibited from fishing on the coasts, or in the bays or rivers of Newfoundland; excepting, however, the rights and privileges granted by treaty to foreign states at amity with his Majesty.

British subjects may take, cure, and dry fish, occupy vacant places, cut down trees for building, and other things useful for the trade. — § 3.

Certificates shall be granted to vessels clearing out for the fishery; and on arrival at Newfoundland report shall be made of such certificate, and registered; and on leaving the fishery the usual clearance to be obtained. Vessels having on board any goods other than fish, &c. to forfeit the fishing certificate.

Persons throwing out ballast, &c. to the prejudice of the harbours in Newfoundland, shall be subject to penalty. — § 5.

A contract in writing, specifying wages, and how to be paid, must be entered into with seamen and fishermen. — § 7.

A fisherman is prohibited receiving more than three fourths of his wages during service; but the balance due to him is to be paid immediately upon the expiration of the covenanted time of service. No fisherman to be turned off, except for wilful neglect of duty, or other sufficient cause, under a penalty, for each offence, of not less than 5l. nor more than 50l.

In order to fulfil the conditions in any treaty with a foreign state, his Majesty may empower the governor of Newfoundland to remove any works erected by British subjects for the purpose of carrying on the fishery between Cape St. John and Cape Ray, and to compel them to depart to another place.— § 12. Every person so refusing to depart shall forfeit 50l. — § 13.

The governor is empowered to sell or lease places within the island called Ship-rooms. — § 14.

There are no means whatever by which to form any estimate of the number of ship
and boats employed, either regularly or occasionally, in the cod fishery on the coasts o
Great Britain and the adjoining seas; or of the quantity and value of the fish annuall
caught. They must, however, be very considerable.

The Quebec Star of the 28th of November, 1829, gives the following account of th
cod fishery on the coast of Labrador : —

Countries which send out Ships.	Ships.	Men.	Quintals of Fish.	Oil worth
				£
United States - -	1,500	15,000	1,000,000	11,500
Newfoundland - -	400	4,000	350,000	3,500
Nova Scotia - - -	100	800	70,000	700
England, Jersey, &c. - -	80	4,000	240,000	2,400
Lower Canada - -	8	150	5,000	50
New Brunswick, &c. - -	20	160	8,000	80
Totals	2,108	24,110	1,773,000	17,730

We have no means of judging of the general accuracy of this table; but it is obviou
that the number of men given to the British ships is grossly exaggerated: we suspec
too, that the number of these ships is far above the mark. In 1826, only 7 ships
manned by 46 seamen, cleared out of British ports for the coast of Labrador. — (Par
Paper, No. 113. Sess. 1827.)

For the regulations, &c. as to the importation of fish into Great Britain, see FISH.

It is doubtful whether the distant cod fishery may not have passed its zenith. Spain
Italy, and other Catholic countries, have always been the great markets for dried fish
but the observance of Lent is every day becoming less strict; and the demand for drie
fish will, it is most likely, sustain a corresponding decline. The relaxed observance o
Lent in the Netherlands and elsewhere has done more than any thing else to injure th
herring fishery of Holland.

Cod Fishery, American. — The Americans have at all times prosecuted the cod fisher
with great vigour and success. In 1795, the ships they had employed in it carrie
about 31,000 tons; in 1807, they increased to 70,306 tons : they subsequently decline
for several years. During the five years ending with 1824, the American tonnage i
this trade was as follows : —

1820·	-	-	72,049	1823	-	-	78,839
1821	-	-	62,293	1824	-	-	77,627
1822	-	-	69,226				

It is stipulated in the first article of a convention between Great Britain and th
United States, signed at London, 20th of October, 1818, that the subjects of the Unite
States shall have liberty to take all sorts of fish " on that part of the coast of Newfound
land from Cape Ray to the Rameau Islands, on the western and northern coasts o
Newfoundland from Cape Ray to the Quirpon Islands, on the Magdalen Islands, an
also on the coasts, bays, harbours, and creeks, from Mount Joly, on the southern coa
of Labrador, to and through the Straits of Belleisle, and thence northwardly indefinite
along the coast, without prejudice, however, to any of the exclusive rights of the Hud
son's Bay Company ; and that the American fishermen shall also have liberty, for eve
to dry and cure fish in any of the unsettled bays, harbours, and creeks, of the souther
part of the coast of Newfoundland here above described, and of the coast of Labrado
but so soon as the same, or any portion thereof, shall be settled, it shall not be lawful f
the said fishermen to dry or cure fish without previous agreement for such purpose wi
the inhabitants, proprietors, or possessors of the ground. And the United States heret
renounce for ever any liberty heretofore enjoyed or claimed by the inhabitants thereof, t
take, dry, or cure fish, on or within three marine miles of any of the coasts, bays, creek
or harbours, of his Britannic Majesty's dominions in America not included within th
above mentioned limits." The American fishermen are, however, admitted into all bay
&c. for the purpose of shelter, of repairing damages, of purchasing wood, and of obtaini
water, and for no other purpose whatever ; and when there, they are to be placed und
such restrictions as may be necessary to prevent their abusing the privileges hereby r
served to them.

Cod Fishery, French. — France has always enjoyed a considerable share of the c
fishery. The following table shows the extent to which she has carried it since t
peace : —

unt of the Number of Ships, their Crews, and their Destination, cleared out from
ance for the Cod Fishery, in the period from 1816 to 1826, both inclusive.

ears.	Newfoundland, St. Pierre, and Miquelon.		Great Bank of Newfoundland.		Iceland.	
	Ships.	Men.	Ships.	Men.	Ships.	Men.
316	153	5,827	78	1,068	78	1,035
317	139	5,970	105	1,375	104	1,415
318	139	5,638	113	1,470	64	740
319	176	6,851	91	1,248	56	1,612
320	160	5,417	78	1,031	70	849
321	200	7,780	55	522	71	1,096
322	194	8,382	51	670	67	790
323	87	3,505	20	257	68	839
324	182	7,465	46	640	89	1,063
325	137	5,510	30	428	89	1,104
326	213	8,415	47	648	90	1,136

e total number of ships sent out in 1826 was 350, carrying 40,016 tons, and 10,199
In 1829, there were 400 ships sent out.

t notwithstanding the apparent prosperity of this branch of industry, it may be
ed whether it be really so beneficial to France as would at first sight appear. It
ds more upon artificial regulations than upon any thing else. Foreign cod is
led from the French markets by the oppressive duty with which it is loaded; and
mparatively great demand for dried fish in Catholic countries renders this a very
boon to the French fishermen. But it is admitted, that this would not be enough
tain the fishery; and bounties amounting to about 1,500,000 fr. or 60,000l. a
are paid to those engaged in it. — (*Bulletin des Sciences Géographiques*, vol. xxii.
.)

Pierre and Miquelon, small islands on the coast of Newfoundland, belong to the
h. Their right of fishing upon the shores of that island, and upon the great bank,
placed, in 1814, upon the footing on which it stood in 1792.

FFEE (Ger. *Koffe*, *Koffebohnen*; Du. *Koffy*, *Koffiboonen*; Da. *Kaffe*, *Kaffe-
-*; Sw. *Koffe*; Fr. It. and Port. *Caffé*; Sp. *Café*; Rus. *Kofé*; Pol. *Kawa*;
Coffea, *Caffea*; Arab. *Bun*; Malay, *Kāwa*; Pers. *Tochem*, *Kéwéh*; Turk.
e), the berries of the coffee plant (*Coffea Arabica*, Lin.). They are generally
oval form, smaller than a horse-bean, and of a tough, close, and very hard
e; they are prominent on the one side and flattened on the other, having a
y marked furrow running lengthwise along the flattened side; they are
rately heavy, of a greyish or greenish colour, and a somewhat bitterish

torical Notice of Coffee.— The coffee plant is a native of that part of
a called *Yemen*; but it is now very extensively cultivated in the southern
nity of India, in Java, the West Indies, Brazil, &c. We are ignorant of the
e period when it began to be roasted, and the decoction used as a drink,
h the discovery is not supposed to date further back than the early part of
teenth century. No mention of it is made by any ancient writer; nor by any
moderns previously to the sixteenth century. Leonhart Rauwolf, a German
ian, is believed to be the first European who has taken any notice of coffee.
ork was published in 1573, and his account is, in some respects, inaccurate.
: was, however, very accurately described by Prosper Albinus, who had been
ypt as physician to the Venetian Consul, in his works de *Plantis Egypti*,
e *Medicina Egyptiorum*, published in 1591 and 1592.

ublic coffee-house was opened for the first time, in London, in 1652. A
y merchant, of the name of Edwards, having brought along with him from
vant some bags of coffee, and a Greek servant accustomed to make it, his
was thronged with visiters to see and taste this new sort of liquor. And
desirous to gratify his friends without putting himself to inconvenience, he
d his servant to make and sell coffee publicly. In consequence of this
sion, the latter opened a coffee-house in St. Michael's Alley, Cornhill, on
ot where the Virginia coffee-house now stands. Garraway's was the first

coffee-house opened after the great fire in 1666.—(*Mosely on Coffee*, 5th p. 15.)*

M. de la Roque mentions that the use of coffee was first introduced i France in the period between 1640 and 1660; and he further states, that the fi coffee-house for the sale of coffee in France was opened at Marseilles, in 167 and that one was opened at Paris in the following year.—(*Voyage de la Sy* tom. ii. pp. 310—319.)

Some time between 1680 and 1690, the Dutch planted coffee beans they l procured from Mocha, in the vicinity of Batavia. In 1690, they sent a plant Europe; and it was from berries obtained from this plant that the first cof plantations in the West Indies and Surinam were derived.

Progressive Consumption of Coffee in Great Britain. — Influence of the Duties. — 1660, a duty of 4*d*. a gallon was laid on all coffee made and sold. Previously to 17 the duty on coffee amounted to 2*s*. a pound; but an act was then passed, in complia with the solicitations of the West India planters, reducing the duty to 1*s*. 6*d*. a pound which it stood for many years, producing, at an average, about 10,000*l*. a year. In co sequence, however, of the prevalence of smuggling, caused by the too great magnit of the duty, the revenue declined, in 1783, to 2,869*l*. 10*s*. 10½*d*. And it having b found impossible otherwise to check the practice of clandestine importation, the d was reduced, in 1784, to 6*d*. The consequences of this wise and salutary meas were most beneficial. Instead of being reduced, the revenue was immediately raised near *three* times its previous amount, or to 7,200*l*. 15*s*. 9*d*., showing that the consum tion of legally imported coffee must have increased in about *a nine fold proportion !* striking and conclusive proof, as Mr. Bryan Edwards has observed, of the effec heavy taxation in defeating its own object. — (*Hist. of the West Indies*, vol. ii. p. 3 8vo ed.)

The history of the coffee trade abounds with similar and even more striking exam of the superior productiveness of low duties. In 1807, the duty was 1*s*. 8*d*. a pour and the quantity entered for home consumption amounted to 1,170,164 lbs., yieldin revenue of 161,245*l*. 11*s*. 4*d*. In 1808, the duty was reduced from 1*s*. 8*d*. to ? and in 1809 there were no fewer than 9,251,837 lbs. entered for home consumpti yielding, notwithstanding the reduction of duty, a revenue of 245,856*l*. 8*s*. 4*d*. duty having been raised, in 1819, from 7*d*. to 1*s*. a pound, the quantity entered home consumpton, in 1824, was 7,993,041 lbs., yielding a revenue of 407,544*l*. 4*s*. In 1824, however, the duty being again reduced from 1*s*. to 6*d*., the quantity entered home consumption, in 1825, was 10,766,112 lbs., and in 1828 it had increased 16,522,422 lbs., yielding a nett revenue of 425,389*l*. 3*s*. 7*d*.

The consumption of the United Kingdom may, *at present*, be estimated 22,000,000 lbs., producing about 580,000*l*. of revenue.

We subjoin

I. Quantities of the different Sorts of Coffee entered for Home Consumption in United Kingdom, each Year since 1822. —(*Parl. Paper*, No. 272. Sess. 1830.)

	Of the British Plantations.	Of the Foreign Plantations.	East India.	Total of all S
	lbs.	lbs.	lbs.	lbs.
Year ended 5th Jan. 1822	7,386,060	764	206,177	7,593,00
—— 1823	7,494,218	3,416	171,717	7,669,35
—— 1824	8,218,342	881	235,697	8,454,92
—— 1825	7,947,890	1,540	313,513	8,262,94
—— 1826	10,622,376	2,849	457,745	11,082,97
—— 1827	12,409,000	2,753	791,570	13,203,32
—— 1828	14,676,968	1,210	888,198	15,566,37
—— 1829	16,151,239	2,984	973,410	17,127,63
—— 1830	18,495,407	6,197	974,576	19,476,18

* Charles II. attempted, by a proclamation issued in 1675, to suppress coffee-houses, on the grou their being resorted to by disaffected persons who "devised and spread abroad divers false, mali and scandalous reports, to the defamation of his Majesty's government, and to the disturbance o peace and quiet of the nation." The opinion of the judges having been taken as to the legality o proceeding, they resolved, " That retailing coffee might be an innocent trade; but as it was us nourish seditions, spread lies, and scandalise *great men*, it might also be a common nuisance !"

An Account of the Quantity of Coffee entered for Home Consumption in Great Britain, the Rates of Duty thereon, and the Produce of the Duties, each Year since 1789. — (*Parl. Paper*, No. 340. Sess. 1829.)

Years.	Quantities retained for Home Consumption.	Rates of Duty on			Nett Revenue of Customs and Excise.		
		British Plantation.	East India.				
	lbs.	per lb. s. d.	per lb. s. d.	per cent. ad valorem. £ s. d.	£	s.	d.
1789	930,141	0 10¾	2 0½	Nil.	46,286	17	11
1790	973,110	—	—	—	50,799	7	4
1791	1,047,276	—	—	—	57,659	5	11
1792	946,666	—	—	—	48,825	6	2
1793	1,070,438	—	—	—	67,357	11	9
1794	969,512	—	—	—	74,430	4	6
1795	1,054,588	1 5½	2 6⅜	—	65,788	3	7
1796	396,953	—	—	—	30,048	6	11
1797	637,001	1 5½	3 7	—	92,469	3	11
1798	697,487	1 5½	2 7¾	—	78,966	6	9
1799	682,432	1 5½	2 7¾	2 0 0	74,001	2	2
1800	826,590	—	—	—	142,867	11	5
1801	750,861	1 5½	2 7	2 0 0	106,076	2	7
1802	829,435	1 6	2 7½	2 0 0	72,183	2	3
1803	905,532	1 6¾	1 11½	2 16 3	72,093	15	8
1804	1,061,327	1 7½	2 0½	3 2 6	151,388	0	11
1805	1,201,736	1 7½	2 0⅝	3 3 9	120,172	18	7
1806	1,157,014	1 7½	2 0¾	3 7 11	152,759	6	9
1807	1,170,164	—	—	—	161,245	11	4
1808	1,069,691	0 7	0 10	3 7 11	229,738	16	8
1809	9,251,837	0 7	0 10	3 6 8	245,886	8	4
1810	5,308,096	—	—	—	175,567	1	4
1811	6,390,122	—	—	—	212,890	12	10
1812	8,118,734	—	—	—	255,184	7	1
1813	8,788,601	0 7¼	0 10¾	3 19 2	Custom Records destroyed.		
1814	6,324,267	0 7¾	0 11½	Nil.	213,513	18	4
1815	6,117,311	—	—	—	258,762	18	3
1816	7,557,471	—	—	—	290,834	0	11
1817	8,688,726	—	—	—	298,540	5	1
1818	7,967,857	—	—	—	250,106	4	10
1819	7,429,352	1 0	1 6	—	292,154	8	10
1820	6,869,286	—	—	—	340,223	6	7
1821	7,327,283	—	—	—	371,252	5	6
1822	7,404,204	—	—	—	374,596	19	7
1823	8,209,245	—	—	—	416,324	3	9
1824	7,993,040	—	—	—	407,544	4	3
1825	10,766,112	0 6	0 9	—	307,204	14	2
1826	12,724,139	—	—	—	324,667	11	1
1827	14,974,378	—	—	—	384,994	13	2
1828	16,522,423	—	—	—	425,389	3	7

Account of the Quantity of Coffee imported into the United Kingdom from the several British Colonies and Plantations, from the British Possessions in the East Indies, and from Foreign Countries, in the Year ended 5th January, 1831; distinguishing the several Sorts of Coffee, and the Colonies and Countries from which the same was imported. — (*Parl. Paper*, No. 379. Sess. 1831.)

	Coffee imported into the United Kingdom in the Year ended 5th January, 1831.			
	Of the British Plantations.	Of the East Indies and Mauritius.	Of the Foreign Plantations.	Total Quantity imported.
ish Colonies and Plantations in America; viz.	*lbs.*	*lbs.*	*lbs.*	*lbs.*
Antigua	242	.	.	242
Barbadoes	334	.	.	334
Dominica	1,016,631	.	.	1,016,631
Grenada	28,541	.	.	28,541
Jamaica	19,753,603	.	112	19,753,715
Nevis	1,362	.	.	1,362
St. Christopher	44	.	.	44
St. Lucia	113,517	.	.	113,517
St. Vincent	124	.	.	124
Tortola	5	.	.	5
Trinidad	54,502	.	.	54,502
Bahamas	195,637	.	31,432	227,069
Demerara	3,447,426	.	.	3,447,426
Berbice	2,816,909	.	.	2,816,909
ot	.	.	16,939	16,939
a Leone, and the West Coast of Africa	267	.	16,624	16,891
e of Good Hope	.	88	101	189
ritius	.	29,506	.	29,506
Carried forward	27,429,144	29,594	65,208	27,523,946

U

COFFEE.

Table III. — *continued.*

	Coffee imported into the United Kingdom in the Year ended 5th January, 1831.			
	Of the British Plantations.	Of the East Indies and Mauritius.	Of the Foreign Plantations.	Total Quantity imported.
	lbs.	*lbs.*	*lbs.*	*lbs.*
Brought forward	27,429,144	29,594	65,208	27,523,946
British Possessions in the East Indies; viz.				
East India Company's Territories, exclusive of Singapore	-	2,359,229	-	2,359,229
Singapore	-	2,853,408	-	2,853,408
Ceylon	-	803,779	-	803,779
Java	-	973,450	-	973,450
Philippine Islands	-	6,427	-	6,427
China	-	113	-	113
Hayti	-	-	966,609	966,609
Foreign Colonies in the West Indies; viz.				
Cuba	-	-	1,598,528	1,598,528
Porto Rico	-	-	241,687	241,687
United States of America	-	-	33,545	33,545
Columbia	-	-	274,386	274,386
Brazil	-	-	3,242,513	3,242,513
Europe	-	40,199	34,344	74,543
Total	27,429,144	7,066,199	6,456,820	40,952,163

IV. Account of the Quantity of Coffee exported from the United Kingdom, in the Year ended 5th January, 1831; distinguishing the several Sorts of Coffee, and the Countries to which the same was exported. — (*Parl. Paper*, No. 379. Sess. 1831.)

Countries to which exported.	Coffee exported from the United Kingdom in the Year ended 5th January, 1831.			
	Of the British Plantations.	Of the East Indies and Mauritius.	Of the Foreign Plantations.	Total Quantity exported.
	lbs.	*lbs.*	*lbs.*	*lbs.*
Russia	1,216,318	4,924	427,561	1,648,803
Sweden	118,978	6,252	115,597	240,827
Norway	17,818	-	250,617	268,435
Denmark	79,547	196,507	623,194	899,248
Prussia	1,336,090	308,739	592,721	2,037,550
Germany	2,491,614	1,158,654	2,727,363	6,377,631
The Netherlands	335,882	2,432,343	1,579,237	4,345,462
France	451	12,818	43,219	56,488
Portugal, Azores, and Madeira	325	-	364	689
Spain and Canaries	382	218	40	640
Gibraltar	-	252	-	252
Italy	1,350,146	193,952	605,294	2,149,392
Malta	176	-	48,539	48,715
Ionian Islands	-	25,909	105,330	131,239
Turkey	182	140,075	681,435	121,692
Guernsey, Jersey, Alderney, and Man	24,365	1,115	499	25,979
	6,970,274	4,481,758	7,601,010	19,053,049
East Indies and China	20,921	9,323	5,223	35,467
New South Wales, Swan River, and Van Diemen's Land	5,334	4,936	3,404	13,674
Cape of Good Hope	10,263	2,300	765	13,328
Other Parts of Africa	59,021	1,694	16,884	77,599
British North American Colonies	134,562	14,982	19,663	169,207
British West Indies	8,038	3,854	2,005	13,897
Foreign West Indies	1,652	-	9,914	11,566
United States of America	5,539	667,703	3,020	676,366
Mexico	3,153	287	485	3,935
Columbia	665	-	-	665
Brazil	6,760	741	4,336	11,837
States of the Rio de la Plata	2,216	146	640	3,002
Chili	1,802	142	879	2,823
Peru	1,325	-	370	1,695
Total	7,231,530	5,187,866	7,668,598	20,087,994

ccount of the Amount of Duties received on Coffee in the United Kingdom in
Year ended 5th January, 1831; distinguishing each Sort of Coffee, and the Nett
oduce of the Duties on Coffee in the United Kingdom in such Year. — (*Parl.*
per, No. 379. Sess. 1831.)

Year ended 5th January, 1831.	Amount of Duty received on Coffee in the United Kingdom.
	£ s. d.
the British Plantations in America - -	542,417 10 8
Sierra Leone - - - -	56 2 0
the East Indies and Mauritius - - -	37,123 3 0
her Sorts - - - - -	248 3 11
Total Gross Receipt - - -	579,844 19 7
Nett Produce - - -	£579,363 10 7

e introduction of tea and coffee, it has been well remarked, "has led to the mos
erful change that ever took place in the diet of modern civilised nations, — a
e highly important both in a moral and physical point of view. These beverages
the admirable advantage of affording stimulus without producing intoxication, or
f its evil consequences. Lovers of tea or coffee are, in fact, rarely drinkers; and
the use of these beverages has benefited both manners and morals. Raynal ob-
that the use of tea has contributed more to the sobriety of the Chinese than the
st laws, the most eloquent discourses, or the best treatises on morality." —
man, 17th October, 1827.)

ply and Consumption of Coffee. — Owing to the rapidly increasing consumption of
in this country, the Continent, and America, the great value of the article, the
amount of capital and labour employed in its production, and the shipping re-
d for its transport, it has become a commodity of primary commercial importance.
serves particular attention, too, inasmuch as there are few, if any, articles whic
t such variations, not only as to consumption, but also as to growth and price.
are occasioned partly by changes of commercial regulations and duties, and
, also, by the plant requiring four or five years before it comes to bear; so that
pply is neither suddenly increased when the demand increases, nor diminished
it falls off. St Domingo used formerly to be one of the greatest sources of
, having exported, in 1786, about 35,000 tons; and it is supposed that, but for
gro insurrection which broke out in 1792, the exports of that year would have
ted to 42,000 tons. The devastation occasioned by this event caused, for a series
rs, an almost total cessation of supplies. Recently, however, they have again
to increase; and are understood to amount, at present, to about 15,000 or 16,000
year. In Cuba, the exports of coffee have fallen off, within a few years, from
or 25,000 tons to about 14,000 tons; owing partly to an increased consumption
island, and partly to the efforts of the planters having, a little time back, been
directed to the cultivation of sugar. In Java, also, the exports of coffee have, of
een on the decline, while those of sugar have been increasing; but the recent rise
prices of the former, and decline of those of the latter, will, it is probable, speedily
e, there and every where else, a decided re-action from sugar to coffee. In
ca and the other British West India colonies the cultivation of coffee was greatly
ed during the prevalence of the high prices, but the growth has latterly been on
cline. In Brazil it has increased with unprecedented rapidity. So late as 1821,
antity of coffee exported from Rio de Janeiro did not exceed 7,500 tons; whereas
amounts to about 28,000 tons! This extraordinary increase has probably been,
e measure, owing to the continuance of the slave trade; and it remains to be
whether the growth of coffee may not now be checked by the late cessation
abominable traffic. See SLAVE TRADE.
following may, we believe, be regarded as a pretty fair estimate of the annual
of coffee from the principal places where it is produced, and of its annual *con-*
on in those countries into which it is imported from abroad, at the present time: —

Exports.							Tons.
ocha, Hodeida, and other Arabian Ports		-	-		12,000
va - - - - -	-	-		19,000
umatra and other Parts of India	-	-	-		6,000
razil and the Spanish Main	-	-	-		32,000
Carried forward	-	-		69,000

Exports.					Tons.
Brought forward		-		-	69,000
St. Domingo	-	-	-	-	15,000
Cuba	-	-	-	-	14,000
British West India Colonies	-	-	-	-	12,500
Dutch West India Colonies	-	-	-	-	5,000
French West India Colonies and the Isle de Bourbon		-		-	8,000
					123,

Consumption.					Tons.
Great Britain	-	-	-	-	10,000
Netherlands and Holland	-	-	-	-	40,200
Germany and Countries round the Baltic		-		-	32,000
France, Spain, Italy, Turkey in Europe, the Levant, &c.			-		28,500
America	-	-	-	-	18,500
					129,

Of this quantity, the consumption of Great Britain and America amounts to ne
a fourth part, and may be said to have arisen almost entirely since 1807.

Of the entire export of coffee from Arabia, not more, perhaps, than 7,000 or 8,
tons finds its way to the places mentioned above; so that, supposing these estimate
be about correct, it would follow that the supply of coffee is, at present, under
demand; and that a reduction of the stocks throughout Europe, amounting in Janu
last to about 50,000 tons, may be anticipated.   This inference, however, is not altoge
to be depended upon, as we are without the means of arriving at very accurate c
clusions either as to the supply or consumption of coffee.   In the meantime the pr
of the article are (August, 1831) materially on the rise; but whether the advance
be maintained, it is impossible to say.

The consumption of coffee in the United States has been nearly trebled since 1
in which year it amounted to 6,680 tons.   Part of this increase is, no doubt, t
ascribed to the reduction of the duty from 5 to 2 cents per pound, part to the fa
the price of coffee, part to the relative high price of, and high duties on, tea in Ame
and a part, perhaps, to the increase of temperance societies.

Antwerp, Hamburgh, Amsterdam, Rotterdam, &c. are the great continental m
for coffee.   The imports into them, in 1829 and 1830, have been as under : —

Years.	Antwerp.	Hamburgh.	Amsterdam.	Rotterdam.	Bremen.
	Tons.	Tons.	Tons.	Tons.	Tons.
1829	20,950	17,460	9,500	6,000	5,600
1830	21,200	20,250	9,000	4,500	4,960

The price of St. Domingo and Jamaica coffee per cwt., exclusive of the duty, ir
London market, since 1814, has been as follows : —

		s.	s.				s.	
1814	St. Domingo	-	90 to 104	1823	St. Domingo	-	75	to
	Jamaica	-	81 105		Jamaica	-	79	
1815	St. Domingo	-	72 80	1824	St. Domingo	-	58	
	Jamaica	-	61 110		Jamaica	-	50	
1816	St. Domingo	-	74 75	1825	St. Domingo	-	55	
	Jamaica	-	68 102		Jamaica	-	48	
1817	St. Domingo	-	93 98	1826	St. Domingo	-	50	
	Jamaica	-	86 105		Jamaica	-	42	
1818	St. Domingo	-	144 148	1827	St. Domingo	-	37	
	Jamaica	-	134 155		Jamaica	-	30	
1819	St. Domingo	-	128 134	1828	St. Domingo	-	36	
	Jamaica	-	147 165		Jamaica	-	28	
1820	St. Domingo	-	118 120	1829	St. Domingo	-	32	
	Jamaica	-	112 135		Jamaica	-	30	
1821	St. Domingo	-	98 102	1830	St. Domingo	-	34	
	Jamaica	-	85 125		Jamaica	-	32	
1822	St. Domingo	-	95 100	1831	St. Domingo	-	45	
	Jamaica	-	85 135		Jamaica	-	50	

We are indebted for several of the previous details to a valuable little tract c
" *Commerce of Great Britain*," by Mr. Cook of Mincing Lane, published in th
ginning of the present year.

The following extract from the Price Current of Messrs. Trueman and Cook shows
prices of the different sorts of coffee in London on the 23d of June, 1831.   They
ve since advanced; the best Jamaica being now (4th August, 1831,) 85s. and the
t Mocha, 100s.

COFFEE (in Bond.) Duty on British Plantation, 6d. per lb. on Foreign 1s. 3d. per lb.		Triage and ordinary.	Good and fine ordinary.	Middling and good middling.	Fine mid. and fine.
		s. s.	s. s.	s. s.	s. s.
lantation	Jamaica - - Demerara & Berbice -	40 à 45	47 à 50	53 à 62	65 à 75
	Dominica, St. Lucia, &c. Trinidad & Grenada -	38 – 44	46 – 48	none	none
oreign	St. Domingo - -	35 – 38	40 – 42	none	none
	Havannah & Porto Rico	33 – 37	42 – 50	52	—
	Brazil - -	32 – 36	39 – 42	—	—

	Ceylon, Samarang, & Sumatra.	Cheribon. Pale and coly.	Java.		Mocha.
			Yellow.	Brown.	
ast India (in Bond) -	29 à 34	36 à 39	42 à 44	none	60 à 70

Notwithstanding the great reduction of the duties on coffee in 1824, there can be no
bt that they are still too high.   At this moment they amount to 100 per cent. on
price of good coffee, and to full 150 per cent. on the price of inferior sorts.   Were
duties on British plantation coffee reduced to 3d. per lb. and those on Mocha and
t India coffee to 6d. per lb., the consumption would be so much extended, that, in-
d of being diminished, we believe the revenue would be decidedly increased.   The
ease of consumption mentioned above must not, however, be *wholly* attributed to the
iction of the duty: the recent low prices have, no doubt, also had a material effect.
or to 1825, when the duty was 1s. per lb., fine ordinary Jamaica coffee fetched 60s.
w, when the duty is 6d., the same quality, a few months ago, brought only 40s.   The
at reduction in the price of low brown sugar (at least 1½d. per lb.) must also have
sted the consumption of coffee, — the one being so necessary to the extensive use of
other.   The considerable improvement that has lately taken place in the prices of
st India coffee, is likely, unless the duty be further decreased, to lessen the consump-
.   Some qualities have advanced from 32s. to 60s., an improvement of 3d. per lb.
pecies of Coffee. — Roasting, &c. — The coffee of Mocha is generally esteemed
best; then follow the coffees of Jamaica, Dominica, Berbice, Demerara, Bourbon,
a, Martinique and Hayti.   Arabian or Mocha coffee is produced in a very dry
ate, the best being raised upon mountainous slopes and sandy soils.   The most
le soils are not suitable for the growth of very fine coffee.   Mr. Bryan Edwards
rves, that "a rich deep soil, frequently meliorated by showers, will produce a
uriant tree and a great crop; but the beans, which are large, and of a dingy green,
e, for many years, rank and vapid." And the same remark is made by Mr. Craw-
, with respect to the coffee of Java. — (*East Indian Archipelago*, vol. i. p. 487.)
ee is improved by being kept; it then becomes of a paler colour.
Mocha, or, as it is commonly called, Turkey coffee, should be chosen of a greenish light
h hue, fresh and new, free from any mustiness, the berries of a middling size, clean,
mp, and without any intermixture of sticks or other impurities.   Particular care
ild be taken that it is not false packed.   Good West India coffee should be of a
nish colour, fresh, free from any unpleasant smell, the berries small and unbroken.
offee berries readily imbibe exhalations from other bodies, and thereby acquire an
ntitious and disagreeable flavour.   Sugar placed near coffee will, in a short time, so
egnate the berries, as to injure their flavour.   Dr. Moseley mentions, that a few
of pepper, on board a ship from India, spoiled a whole cargo of coffee.
The roasting of the berry to a proper degree requires great nicety : the virtue and
eableness of the drink depend upon it; and both are often injured by the ordinary
od.   Bernier says, when he was at Cairo, where coffee is so much used, he was
ed by the best judges, that there were only two people in that great city who un-
ood how to prepare it in perfection.   If it be under-done, its virtues will not be
rted, and, in use, it will load and oppress the stomach; if it be over-done, it will
a flat, burnt, and bitter taste, its virtues will be destroyed, and, in use, it will heat
ody, and act as an astringent." — (*Moseley*, p. 39.)
egulations with respect to Sale, Importation, &c. — Roasted beans and rye, reduced
wder, have frequently been used to adulterate ground coffee : and the possession
ch substitutes for coffee was formerly an offence punishable by the forfeiture of

the articles and a penalty of 100*l.* But by the act 3 Geo. 4. c. 53., persons who ar
not dealers in coffee may take a licence for roasting and selling corn, peas, beans, o
parsneps, labelling the parcels with the names, and conforming to the various regula
tions prescribed in the act.

Dealers in coffee must take out a licence renewable annually, which, at present, cost
11*s.*

No coffee can be imported in packages of less than 100 lbs. *nett* weight.

No abatement of duties is made on account of any damage coffee may have received

Coffee cannot be entered as being the produce of any British possession in Americ
or of the Mauritius, until the master of the ship in which the coffee is imported de
liver to the collector or comptroller a certificate of its origin, and make oath that th
coffee is the produce of such place. — (*6 Geo.* 4. c. 107. § 35.)

We subjoin two accounts, one *pro forma* of the sale of 100 bags of Brazil coffee, th
other an account of the actual sale by auction of thirteen tierces of Jamaica coffee
They are interesting, as showing in detail the various charges affecting this importan
article.

PRO FORMA ACCOUNT SALES A. B. 100 Bags Brazil Coffee per London, on Account of C. D. & Co.

1831. June 1	Sold E. F. Lots 1 to 5. 100 Bags	Cwt. qrs. lbs. 145 0 0 / 1 3 4 Dft.	£ s. d.	£ s. d
		145 0 24 at 40s.		286 8 7
		Discount 2½ per cent.		7 3 3
		£. s. d.		279 5 5
	Insuring 250l. at 30s. per cent. and Policy	4 10 9		
	Commission ¼ per cent.	1 5 0	5 15 9	
	Dock Rates on 145 cwt. at 1s. 2d. per cwt.	8 9 2		
	Lotting, &c.	0 8 4	8 17 6	
	Warehouse Entry 5s. ; Stamp 4s.		0 9 0	
	Insurance against fire		0 15 0	
	Freight on 145 cwt. at 3s. 3d.	23 11 3		
	Primage 5 per cent.	1 3 6		
	Pierage 6d. per ton gross	0 3 7	24 18 4	
	Brokerage 1 per cent.		2 15 10	
	Commission 2½ per cent.		6 19 7	50 11 0
July 2	To C. D. & Co., paid			£228 14 5
	If the Coffee had been disposed of at public sale, there would have been, of additional charges,			
	Advertising, Printing Catalogues, &c.		0 17 6	
	Lotting and Showing for Sale		0 12 6	
	Auction Duty ¼ per cent.		1 8 7	

ACCOUNT SALES of Thirteen Tierces Coffee per Star, Captain Maim, from Jamaica, on Account of
Mount Pleasant Estate.

M. P.		Sold C. and A. CARLOW & Co. at Public Sale.			
		Gross Wt.	Tare.	Dft.	
		Cwt. qrs. lbs.	Cwt. qrs. lbs.	Cwt. qrs. lbs.	£ s. d.
	Lot 6. 1 Cask Coffee	7 2 19 / 0 3 19	0 3 14	0 0 5	
		6 3 0 Nett	-	- at 78s.	26 6 6
	— 7. 3 Do.	23 0 1	2 1 23	0 0 15	
	— 8. 3 Do.	21 0 25	2 1 10	0 0 15	
		44 0 26 / 5 0 7	4 3 5 / 0 1 2	0 1 2	
		39 0 19 Nett	-	- at 71s. 6d.	140 0 6
	— 9. 2 Do.	15 2 20 / 1 3 5	1 2 23	0 0 10	
		13 3 15 Nett	-	- at 68s.	47 4 ?
	—10. 1 Do.	7 0 7 / 0 3 13	3 0 8	0 0 5	
		6 0 22 Nett	-	- at 65s.	20 2 8
	10			Carried forward - -	233 13 9

Account Sales of Thirteen Tierces of Coffee — *continued.*

	Gross Wt.	Tare.	Dft.	£	s.	d.
Brought forward				233	13	9
10	*Cwt.qrs.lbs.*	*Cwt.qrs.lbs.*	*Cwt.qrs.lbs.*			
Lot 11. 1 Cask Coffee -	7 0 5	0 3 7	0 0 5			
	0 3 12					
6 0 21 Nett . . at 66s.				28	8	4
—12. 2 Do. - -	13 1 10	1 2 23	0 0 10			
	1 3 5					
11 2 5 Nett . . at 63s. 6d.				36	13	1
13 Casks.						
—13. 1 Bag over Sugar damaged	0 1 14	0 0 3	0 0 2			
	0 0 5					
0 1 9 Nett . . at 58s.				0	19	1
—14. 1 Cask Sweepings -	7 3 11	0 3 16	0 0 5			
	0 3 21					
6 3 18 Nett . . at 17s.				5	17	6
				305	11	9
		Discount 1 per cent.		3	1	1
				302	10	8
Amount recovered from Owners of Ship for 1 Bag Sugar damaged - -				0	4	7
				302	6	1

CHARGES.	£.	s.	d.
Insurance on 130l., valuing each Tierce at 10l., at 45s. per cent. } Policy and Commission	4	2	0
Custom-house Entry -	0	5	0
Freight on 91 cwt. 2 qrs. 21 lbs. at 6s. per cwt. ; Primage, Pierage, &c.	28	10	8
*Dock Rate on do. at 1s. 6d. per cwt. ; Lotting 14 Casks at 9d. each ; } 1 Bag, 1d. ; 1 Cask found, 7s. 6d. - -	7	16	1
Advertising and printing Catalogues, 21s. ; Sampling, Lotting, and } Showing for Sale, 15s. - -	1	16	0
Receipt Stamps - -	0	4	6
Brokerage 1 per cent. on 302l. 10s. 8d. - -	3	0	6
Commission 2¼ per cent. on 302l. 10s. 8d. - -	7	11	3
	53	6	0

Errors excepted. Nett Proceeds £249 0 1

London, 1st June, 1831.

* Coffee in bags pays 1s. 2d., and in casks 1s. 6d. per cwt., dock dues.

●INS, are pieces of metal, most commonly of gold, silver, or copper, im-
ed with a public stamp, and frequently made legal tender in payment of
, either to a limited or unlimited extent.

Circumstances which led to the Introduction and Use of Coins.—When the
us metals first began to be used as money, or as standards by which to
re the value of different articles, and the equivalents for which they were
commonly exchanged, they were in an unfashioned state, in bars or ingots,
arties first agreed as to the quantity of metal to be given for a commodity,
e quantity was then ascertained by weight. But it is obvious that a prac-
f this sort must have been attended with a great deal of trouble and
venience. There can, however, be little doubt that the greatest obstacle to
e of unfashioned metals as money, would be found in the difficulty of de-
ing their quality, or the degree of their purity, with sufficient precision.
peration of assaying is one of great nicety and difficulty; and could not be
med in the early ages otherwise than in a clumsy, tedious, and inaccurate
r. It is, indeed, most probable, that when the precious metals were first
as money, their quality would be appreciated only by their weight and
. A very short experience would, however, be sufficient to show the ex-
inexactness of conclusions derived from such loose and unsatisfactory
a; and the devising of some method, by which the fineness of the metal might
ly and correctly ascertained, would very soon be felt as indispensable to
neral use of gold and silver as money. Such a method was not long in
ting itself: it was early discovered, that, to ascertain the purity of the

U 4

metal, and also to avoid the trouble and expense of weighing it, no more v
necessary than to mark each piece with a *stamp*, declaring its weight and finene
This invention was made at a very early period. According to Herodotus, t
Lydians were the first who coined money.—(Lib. i. c. 94.) Other anci
authors say that the art of coining was invented during the period when Satu
and Janus reigned in Italy; that is, in a period antecedent to authentic histo
—(*Goguet de l'Origine des Loix, &c.*, tom. i. p. 267.)

2. *Metal used in the Manufacture of Coins.*—Before the art of metallurgy v
well understood, the baser metals were frequently used as money. Iron was t
primitive money of the Lacedæmonians, and copper of the Romans. But bc
iron and copper deteriorate by being kept; and besides this defect, the rapid i
provement of the arts, by lowering their price, rendered their bulk too great
proportion to their value to permit of their continuing to be used as mon
Copper, indeed, is still used in the form of tokens, convertible into silver in v
small payments. In this country, copper pence and halfpence are rated at abc
72 per cent. above their real value; but as their issue is exclusively in the har
of government, and as they are only legal tender to the extent of *one shilling*
any one payment, this over-valuation is not productive of any bad effect. T
use of copper in other countries is limited in much the same way; gold and sil
being every where the only metals made use of in the manufacture of the co
used in considerable payments.

3. *Standard of Coins.*—By the standard of a coin, is meant the degree
its purity and its weight; that is, the fineness of the metal of which it is ma
and the quantity of metal contained in it.

(1.) *Silver Coins.*—A pound Troy, or 12 ounces, of the metal of which Engl
silver coins are made, contains 11 oz. 2 dwts. pure silver, and 18 dwts. alloy. T
pound is coined into 66 shillings, so that each shilling contains 80·727 grains f
silver, and 87·27 grains standard silver; and the *money pound*, consisting of twer
shillings, contains 1614·545 grains pure silver, and 1745·454 grains standard silv
From 1600 down to 1816, the pound weight of standard silver bullion was coined i
62 shillings. All the English silver coins have been coined out of silver of 11
2 dwts. fine, from the Conquest to this moment, except for the short period of 16 yea
from the 34th Henry 8. to the 2d Elizabeth.

(2.) *Gold Coins.*—The purity of gold is not estimated by the weights commo
in use, but by an Abyssinian weight called a *carat*. The carats are subdivided into fc
parts, called grains, and these again into quarters; so that a *carat grain*, with respec
the common divisions of a pound Troy, is equivalent to 2½ dwts. Gold of
highest degree of fineness, or pure, is said to be 24 carats fine. When gold coins w
first made at the English mint, the standard of the gold put in them was of 23 cai
3½ grains fine, and ½ grain of alloy; and so it continued, without any variation, to
18th Henry 8., who, in that year, first introduced a new standard of gold of
carats fine, and 2 carats alloy. The first of these standards was called the old; and
second the new standard, or crown gold; because crowns, or pieces of the value of t
shillings, were first coined of this new standard. Henry 8. made his gold coins
both these standards under different denominations; and this practice was contin
by his successors until 1633. From that period to the present, the gold of which
coins of this kingdom have been made has been invariably of the *new* standard,
crown gold; though some of the coins made of the old standard, previously to 16
continued to circulate till 1732, when they were forbidden to be any longer curre
(*Liverpool on Coins*, p. 27.)

The purity of our present gold coins is, therefore, 11 parts fine gold and 1 part al
The sovereign, or twenty shilling piece, contains 113·001 grains fine gold, and 123·
grains standard gold. The pound Troy of standard gold is coined into 46 soverei
and 89/123 of a sovereign, or into 46*l*. 14*s*. 6*d*. The mint or standard price of gole
therefore, said to be 46*l*. 14*s*. 6*d*. per lb. Troy, or 3*l*. 17*s*. 10½*d*. an ounce.

The alloy in coins is reckoned of no value. It is allowed, in order to save
trouble and expense that would be incurred in refining the metals, so as to bring th
to the highest degree of purity; and because, when its quantity is small, it has a t
dency to render the coins harder, and less liable to be worn or rubbed. If the quar
of alloy were considerable, it would lessen the splendour and ductility of the me
and would add too much to the weight of the coins.

The standard of the coins of foreign countries may be learned at a glance, by
specting the Table of Coins subjoined to this article.

4.) *Variations of the Standard.* — The value of all sorts of property being estimated, the stipulations in almost all contracts for its purchase, sale, or hire, being made money or coins, it is plain that no change can take place in the value of such money coins without virtually subverting these estimates and contracts, and enriching the ⎡tor portion of society at the expense of the creditor portion, or *vice versâ.* As the ⎡t of producing all commodities is liable to vary from improvements in the arts, the ⎡austion of the present or the discovery of new sources of supply, none can be se-⎡ted to serve as money or coin, that may not vary in its real value. It is believed, ⎡wever, that the precious metals vary less than any material that could be suggested. ⎡d with the exception of the extraordinary fall in their value caused by the discovery ⎡the American mines, it seems to have been remarkably constant at other periods.

But in addition to the fluctuations naturally inherent in the value of coins, arising ⎡m variations in the cost of the metal of which they are made, their standard has been ⎡eatedly changed. Notwithstanding that money or coin, from its being universally ⎡d as a scale by which to compute the value of all commodities, and as the equivalent which they are commonly exchanged, is by far the most important of all the ⎡asures used in society; and should, consequently, be preserved as invariable as pos-⎡e; there is none that has been so frequently altered. The necessities or extravagance ⎡governments have forced them to borrow; and to relieve themselves of the incum-⎡nces thus contracted, they have almost universally had recourse to the disgraceful ⎡edient of degrading the coin; that is, of *cheating* those who lent them money, to the ⎡ent of the degradation, and of enabling every other debtor in their dominions to do ⎡ same.

The ignorance of the public in remote ages facilitated this species of fraud. Had ⎡ names of the coins been changed when the quantity of metal contained in them ⎡ diminished, there would have been no room for misapprehension. But, although ⎡ weight of the coins was undergoing perpetual, and their purity occasional, reductions, ⎡r ancient denominations were almost uniformly preserved: and the people who saw ⎡ same names still remaining after the substance was diminished; who saw coins of a ⎡ain weight and fineness circulate under the names of florins, livres, dollars, and ⎡nds; and who saw them continue to circulate as such, after both their weight and ⎡ degree of their fineness had been lessened; began to think that they derived their ⎡ue more from the *stamp* affixed to them by authority of government, than from the ⎡ntity of the precious metals they contained. This was long a very prevalent opinion. ⎡ the rise of prices which invariably followed every reduction of the standard, and ⎡ derangement that was thereby occasioned in every pecuniary transaction, undeceived ⎡public, and taught them, and their rulers, the expediency of preserving the standard ⎡oney inviolate.

⎡he standard may be reduced by simply raising the denomination of the coin; by ⎡ring, for example, that a half sovereign should pass for a sovereign, and the latter ⎡ a double sovereign, &c. If injustice be resolved upon, this is the least mischievous ⎡ in which it can be perpetrated, inasmuch as it saves all the trouble and expense of ⎡ coinage. But as it renders the fraud obvious and glaring, it has rarely been re-⎡ed to; and most reductions have been effected either by diminishing the weight of ⎡coins, or by increasing the proportion of alloy in the metal of which they are made, ⎡oth.

⎡riginally the coins of all countries seem to have had the same denomination as the ⎡ghts commonly used in them; and contained the exact quantity of the precious ⎡ls indicated by their name. Thus, the *talent* was a weight used in the earliest ⎡d by the Greeks, the *as* or *pondo* by the Romans, the *livre* by the French, and the ⎡d by the English and Scotch; and the coins originally in use in Greece, Italy, ⎡ce, and England, bore the same names, and weighed precisely a talent, a pondo, a ⎡, and a pound. The standard has not, however, been preserved inviolate, either in ⎡ern or ancient times. It has been less degraded in England than any where else; ⎡even here the quantity of silver in a pound sterling is less than the *third* part of a ⎡d weight, — the quantity it contained in 1300. In France, the livre current in 1789 ⎡ained less than *one sixty-sixth* part of the silver implied in its name, and which it ⎡actually contained previously to 1103. In Spain, and some other countries, the ⎡adation has been carried still further. *

⎡om 1296 to 1355, the coins of England and Scotland were of the same weight and ⎡y; but at the last mentioned epoch the standard of Scotch money was, for the first ⎡ sunk below that of England; and by successive degradations the value of Scotch ⎡y, at the union of the crowns in 1600, was only a *twelfth* part of the value of the

⎡r an account of the degradation of the coins of the ancient and modern continental nations, see ⎡icle *Money*, in the Supplement to the Encyclopædia Britannica.

English money of the same denomination. It remained at this point till the union of the kingdoms cancelled the separate coinage of Scotland.

The gold and silver coins of Ireland have been for a considerable period the same as those of Great Britain; but, until 1825, they were nominally rated 8⅓ per cent. higher. This difference of valuation, which was attended with considerable inconveniences, was put an end to by the act 6 Geo 4. c. 79., which assimilated the currency throughout the empire.

The tables annexed to this article contain all the information that can be desired by mercantile men with respect to the weight, fineness, &c. of English and Scotch gold and silver coins from the earliest periods to the present moment.

(5.) *Mint, or Government Valuation of Gold and Silver Coins.* — If both gold and silver coins be made legal tenders, it is obviously indispensable that their value with respect to each other should be fixed by authority; or that it should be declared, that individuals shall be entitled to discharge the claims upon them by payments, either of gold or silver coins, according to some regulated proportion. The practice of making both metals legal tenders was long adopted in England. From 1257 till 1664, the value of gold coins was regulated by proclamation; or, which is the same thing, it was ordered that the gold coins, then current, should be taken as equivalent to certain specified sums of silver. — (*Liverpool on Coins*, p. 128.) From 1664, down to 1717, the relation of gold to silver was not fixed by authority; and silver being then the only legal tender, the value of gold coins fluctuated, according to the fluctuations in the relative worth of the metals in the market. But in 1717, the ancient practice was again reverted to; and it was fixed that the guinea should be taken as the equivalent of 21 shillings, and conversely.

But the value of each of the precious metals is liable to perpetual changes. And hence, how accurately soever their proportional value, as fixed by the mint regulations may correspond with the proportion which they actually bear to each other in the market when the regulation is made, the chances are ten to one that it will speedily cease to express their relation to each other. But the moment that such a change takes place, it becomes the obvious interest of every one who has a payment to make, to make it in the *overvalued* metal; which consequently becomes the sole, or nearly the sole, currency of the country. Hence the reason why the coins of some countries are almost wholly of silver, and others almost wholly of gold. It is estimated, for example, that when it was fixed, in 1717, that the guinea should exchange for 21 shillings, gold was over valued as compared with silver to the extent of 1¹⁰⁄₁₃ per cent.—(*Liverpool on Coins*, p. 85.) and as the real value of silver with respect to gold continued to increase during the greater part of last century, the advantage of paying in gold in preference to silver became more decided, and ultimately led to the universal use of gold in all large pay ments, and to the fusion or exportation of all silver coins of full weight. — (*Liverpool loco cit.*)

In France, a different valuation of the metals has had a different effect. Previously to the recoinage in 1785, the *Louis d'or* was rated in the Mint proportion at only 24 livres, when it was really worth 25 livres 10 sols. Those, therefore, who should have discharged the obligations they had contracted by payments of gold coin instead of silver, would plainly have lost 1 livre 10 sols on every sum of 24 livres. In consequence very few such payments were made; gold was almost entirely banished from circulation and silver became almost the only species of metallic money used in France. — (*Say, Traité d'Economie Politique*, tom. i. p. 393.)

In 1816, however, a new system was adopted in this country; it being then enacted (56 Geo. 3. c. 68.), *that gold coins only should be legal tender in all payments of more than 40 shillings.* The pound of silver bullion, that had previously been coined into 62 shillings, was then also coined into 66 shillings, the additional *four* shillings being retained by government as a *seignorage* or duty (amounting to 6¹¹⁄₁₃ per cent.) upon the coinage. To prevent the silver coins from becoming redundant, government has retained the power to issue them in its own hands. Under these regulations, silver has ceased to be a standard of value, and forms merely a subordinate or subsidiary species of currency or change, occupying the same place in relation to gold that copper occupies in relation to itself. This system has been found to answer exceedingly well.

A good deal of difference of opinion has existed as to whether gold or silver coins are best fitted for being made a legal tender. It does not seem that the one possesses any very striking advantage over the other; none, certainly, that would justify a change after a selection has been made and acted upon for any considerable period.

Down to 1626, a seignorage or duty upon the coinage was usually charged upon the gold and silver coins issued by the Mint; and it may be easily shown that the imposition of such a duty, when it is not carried to an undue height, is advantageous. A coin

e useful than a piece of uncoined bullion of the same weight and purity ; the coinage
ng it for being used as money, while it does not unfit it for being used for any other
pose. When, therefore, a duty or seignorage is laid upon coin, equal to the expense
oinage, it circulates at its real value ; but when this charge is defrayed by the public,
rculates at *less* than its real value, and is consequently either melted down or exported
never there is any demand for bullion in the arts, or any fall in the exchange. It
ideed, true, that were a seignorage to be laid on gold coins, it would be necessary, to
ent an enhancement of the value of the currency, that their weight should be pro-
ionally reduced ; and it is on this account better, perhaps, to let them remain on
present footing. But when a seignorage was laid on the silver coins, in 1816, it was
necessary to take the circumstance now alluded to into consideration ; for as they
e made subordinate to gold, and were intended to serve as change merely, its impo-
n had no tendency to raise the value of the currency, at the same time that it was
ilated effectually to prevent the fusion of the coins, and to yield a small revenue to
rnment.

.) *The Exportation and Importation of Gold and Silver Coins* — was formerly prohi-
; but in 1819 it was enacted (59 *Geo.* 3. c. 49.), that they might be freely exported
imported, without being liable to any charge or duty whatever ; and they may be
rted without being either reported or entered at the Custom-house. This regulation
endered it next to impossible to ascertain the value of the bullion imported.

.) *Forgery of Coin.* — *Issue of forged or spurious Coins.* — The forgery of coin is an
ce that is practised more or less at all periods. The most effectual means of pre-
ng it is to improve the fabric of the genuine coins, to cut the dyes with great deli-
and occasionally to vary the form of the coins. During the lengthened period
1770 down to 1816, the genuine silver coins in circulation were so much worn and
ed, that it was very difficult to distinguish between them and counterfeits, which,
spite of the severest penalties, were thrown into circulation in immense quantities.
since the issue of the new coins, in 1816, forgery has been comparatively rare ; and
mprovement of the coins has done more to prevent the issue of counterfeits than
 have been done by a dozen acts of parliament.

e offence of counterfeiting the king's money was made high treason by statutes of
ard 3. and Elizabeth. The act 8 & 9 Will. 3. c. 26., made perpetual by 7 Anne,
, makes it high treason to mark any coin with letters or grainings, or other marks
ures, like unto those on the edges of money coined in his Majesty's Mint. The
15 Geo. 2. c. 28. makes it high treason to wash, gild, or colour any of the lawful
coins of the realm, so as to make them resemble guineas, half-guineas, &c.
e counterfeiting of foreign coin current in the realm is felony punishable by death.
Mary, st. 2. c. 6. § 2.)
e counterfeiting foreign gold or silver coin *not* current in the realm is a felony that
be punished by transportation for any term of years not exceeding seven. —
Geo. 3. c. 126.) The same statute makes the *importation* of foreign counterfeit
, with *intent to utter* the same, a felony punishable by the like penalty of trans-
ion for seven years. — § 3.
s high treason for any one, not employed in his Majesty's Mints, nor authorised by
ords of the Treasury, to assist in the making or mending of the instruments of
g mentioned in the act (8 & 9 Will. 3. c. 26.), or to have the same in his posses-
r to convey them out of the Mint.
 " uttering of false money, knowing it to be false," subjects the offender, for the
ffence, to six months' imprisonment, and security for two years more ; for the
 offence, the punishment is two years' imprisonment, and security for two years
 and those who offend a third time are adjudged guilty of felony, without the
 of clergy. — (15 *Geo.* 2. c. 28.) The act 37 Geo. 3. c. 126. enacts a similar
ment for the offence of knowingly uttering false or counterfeit foreign coin.
 mere fact of having counterfeit coin in one's possession, with an intent to utter it
d, is not held to be an offence, inasmuch as no criminal *act* has been committed.
e *procuring* of base coin, with intent to utter it, is a misdemeanour ; and the mere
sion of a large quantity of such coin is evidence of having procured it with such
 unless there be other circumstances to induce a suspicion that the holder was the
, — (*Chitty's Black.* vol. iv. p. 99. note 6.)
law as to the counterfeiting of the copper coin of the realm is not very clear. —
hitty's edit. of *Burn's Justice*, vol. i. p. 726.)

TABLES RELATIVE TO THE COINS OF GREAT BRITAIN AND OTHER COUNTRIES.

No. I. English Coins. — Account of the English Silver and Gold Coins; showi their Value, the Seignorage or Profit upon the Coinage, and the Price of the Pou Troy of Standard Gold and Silver, from the Conquest to the present Time. (Th and the next Table, No. II., are taken from Part II. of *Essays on Money, Exchang and Political Economy*, by Henry James.)

A. D.	Anno Regni.	Silver. 1. Fineness of the Silver in the Coins.	2. Pound Weight of such Silver coined into	3. Profit or Seignorage on the Coinage.	4. Equal to the Mint Price for Standard Silver of 11 oz. 2 dwts. fine Troy weight.	Gold. 5. Fineness of the Gold in the Coins.	6. Pound Weight of such Gold coined into	7. Profit or Seignorage on the Coinage.	8. Equal to Mint Pri for Standa Gold of carats fin Troy wt
		oz. dts.	£ s. d.	£ s. d.	£ s. d.	crts. gns.	£ s. d.	£ s. d.	£ s.
1066	Conquest	11 2	1 0 0	....	....	... ...	....	....	....
1280	8 Edward I. ...	— —	1 0 0	0 1 0	1 0 3¼	... ...	....	....	....
1300	28 ———	— —	1 0 3	0 1 2½	....	... ...	....	....	....
1344	18 Edward III..	— —	1 0 3	0 1 3	1 0 3¼	23 3½	13 3 4	0 8 4	12 10
1349	23 ———	— —	1 2 6	0 1 3	1 2 8	— —	14 0 0	0 11 8	13 3
1356	30 ———	— —	1 5 0	0 0 10	1 5 9⅓	— —	15 0 0	0 6 8	14 8
1394	18 Richard II. ..	— —	1 5 0	0 0 10	1 5 9⅓	— —	15 0 0	0 5 0	14 9
1401	3 Henry IV. ...	— —	1 5 0	0 0 10	1 5 9⅓	— —	15 0 0	0 5 0	14 9
1421	9 Henry V......	— —	1 10 0	0 1 0	1 10 11¼	— —	16 13 4	0 5 0	16 2
1425	4 Henry VI. ...	— —	1 10 0	0 1 0	1 10 11½	— —	16 13 4	0 5 10	16 1
1464	4 Edward IV...	— —	1 17 6	0 4 6	1 15 2¼	— —	20 16 8	2 10 0	18 0
1465	5 ———	— —	1 17 6	0 4 6	1 15 2½	— —	22 10 0	1 0 10	21 1
1470	49 Henry VI. ...	— —	1 17 6	0 2 0	1 17 10⅝	— —	22 10 0	0 13 0	21 9
1482	22 Edward IV...	— —	1 17 6	0 1 6	1 18 4¾	— —	22 10 0	0 7 6	21 15
1483	1 Richard III..	— —	1 17 6	0 1 6	1 18 4¾	— —	22 10 0	0 7 6	21 15
1485	1 Henry VII...	— —	1 17 6	0 1 6	1 18 4¾	— —	22 10 0	0 7 6	21 15
1509	1 Henry VIII.	— —	1 17 6	0 1 0	1 18 11¼	— —	22 10 0	0 2 6	22 0
*1527	18 ———	— —	2 0 0	0 1 0¾	1 18 11¼	— —	24 0 0	0 2 8	22 0
—	———	— —	2 5 0	0 1 0	2 4 0	— — {	27 0 0	0 2 9	....
—	———	... ...	....	....	....	22 0 {	25 2 6	0 3 0	24 19
1543	34 ———	10 0	2 8 0	0 8 0	2 4 4¾	23 0	28 16 0	1 4 0	26 8
1545	36 ———	6 0	2 8 0	2 0 0	2 11 9¼	22 0	30 0 0	2 10 0	27 10
1546	37 ———	4 0	2 8 0	4 4 0	2 15 6	20 0	30 0 0	5 0 0	27 10
1547	1 Edward VI...	4 0	2 8 0	4 4 0	2 15 6	20 0	30 0 0	1 10 0	31 7
1549	3 ———	6 0	3 12 0	4 0 0	2 19 2½	22 0	34 0 0	1 0 0	33 0
1551	5 ———	3 0	3 12 0	....	....	... ...	....	....	....
—	———	11 0	3 0 0	....	....	23 3½ {	36 0 0	....	....
—	———	... ...	....	....	....	22 0 {	33 0 0	....	....
1552	6 ———	11 1	3 0 0	0 1 0	2 19 3¼	23 3½ {	36 0 0	0 2 9	....
—	———	... ...	....	....	....	22 0 {	33 0 0	0 3 0	32 17
1553	1 Mary	11 0	3 0 0	0 1 0	2 19 6½	23 3½	36 0 0	0 3 0	33 0
1560	2 Elizabeth	11 2	3 0 0	0 1 6	2 18 6	23 3½ {	36 0 0	0 5 0	....
—	———	... ...	....	....	....	22 0 {	33 0 0	0 4 0	32 16
1600	43 ———	— —	3 2 0	0 2 0	3 0 0	23 3½ {	36 10 0	0 10 0	....
—	———	... ...	....	....	....	22 0 {	33 10 0	0 10 0	33 0
1604	2 James I.	— —	3 2 0	0 2 6	2 19 6	22 0	37 4 0	1 10 0	35 14
1626	2 Charles I.	— —	3 2 0	0 2 0	3 0 0	— —	41 0 0	1 1 5	39 18
†1666	18 Charles II....	— —	3 2 0	0 0 0	3 2 0	— —	44 10 0	0 0 0	44 10
1717	3 George I......	— —	3 2 0	0 0 0	3 2 0	— —	46 14 6	0 0 0	46 14
1816	56 George III...	— —	3 6 0	0 4 0	....	— —	46 14 6	0 0 0	46 14

* 1527—Henry VIII.] The Saxon or Tower pound was used at the mint up to this time, when pound Troy was substituted in its stead. The Tower pound was but 11 oz. 5 dwts. Troy; so that, the Conquest to the 28th of Edward I., twenty shillings in tale were exactly a pound in weight.

† 1666—18 Charles II.] The seignorage on the coinage was at this time given up, and the gold bu brought to the Mint has ever since been coined free of expense. A seignorage of 6 14/31 per cent. was posed on the coinage of silver by 56 Geo. 3.

o. II. ENGLISH COINS. — Account of the Quantity of *Fine* Silver coined into 20s. or the Pound Sterling; the Quantity of *Standard* Silver, of 11 oz. 2 dwts. fine, and 18 dwts. alloy, contained in 20s. or the Pound Sterling, in the different Reigns, from the Time of Edward I. to the Reign of William IV. — A similar Account with respect to Gold. — And an Account of the proportional Value of Fine Gold to Fine Silver, according to the Number of Grains contained in the Coins. — *Calculated in Grains, and* 1000 *Parts Troy weight.*

		Silver.		Gold.		
		1.	2.	3.	4.	5.
. D.	Anno Regni.	Number of Grains of Fine Silver in 20 Shillings, or the Pound Sterling, as coined by the Mint Indentures.	Number of Grains of Standard Silver, 11 oz. 2 dwts. fine in 20 Shillings, or the Pound Sterling, as coined by the Mint Indentures.	Number of Grains of Fine Gold in 20 Shillings, or the Pound Sterling, as coined by the Mint Indentures.	Number of Grains of Standard Gold, 22 carats fine, in 20 Shillings, or the Pound Sterling, as coined by the Mint Indentures.	Proportionate Value of Fine Gold to Fine Silver, according to the Quantity of each Metal contained in the Coins.
		Grains.	*Grains.*	*Grains.*	*Grains.*	*Gold to Silver.*
066	Conquest	4,995·000	5,400·000	....	....	....
280	8 Edward I.	4,995·000	5,400·000	....	....	....
344	18 Edward III.	4,933·333	5,333·333	407·990	445·080	1 to 12·091
349	23 —————	4,440·000	4,800·000	383·705	418·588	1 — 11·571
356	30 —————	3,996·000	4,320·000	358·125	390·682	1 — 11·158
401	3 Henry IV.	3,996·000	4,320·000	358·125	390·682	1 — 11·158
421	9 Henry V.	3,330·000	3,600·000	322·312	351·613	1 — 10·331
464	4 Edward IV.	2,664·000	2,880·000	257·850	281·291	1 — 10·331
465	5 —————	2,664·000	2,880·000	238·750	260·454	1 — 11·158
470	49 Henry VI...........	2,664·000	2,880·000	238·750	260·454	1 — 11·158
482	22 Edward IV.	2,664·000	2,880·000	238·750	260·454	1 — 11·158
509	1 Henry VIII.	2,664·000	2,880·000	238·750	260·454	1 — 11·158
527	18 —————	2,368·000	2,560·000	210·149	229·253	1 — 11·268
543	34 —————	2,000·000	2,162·162	191·666	209·090	1 — 10·434
545	36 —————	1,200·000	1,297·297	176·000	192·000	1 — 6·818
546	37 —————	800·000	864·864	160·000	174·545	1 — 5·000
547	1 Edward VI.	800·000	864·864	160·000	174·545	1 — 5·000
549	3 —————	800·000	864·864	155·294	169·412	1 — 5·151
551	5 —————	400·000	....	....	....	....
—		1,760·000	1,902·702	160·000	174·545	1 — 11·000
552	6 —————	1,768·000	1,911·351	160·000	174·545	1 — 11·050
553	1 Mary.................	1,760·000	1,902·702	159·166	173·636	1 — 11·057
560	2 Elizabeth	1,776·000	1,920·000	160·000	174·545	1 — 11·100
500	43	1,718·709	1,858·064	157·612	171·940	1 — 10·904
504	2 James I.	1,718·709	1,858·064	141·935	154·838	1 — 12·109
626	2 Charles I...........	1,718·709	1,858·064	128·780	140·487	1 — 13·346
666	18 Charles II.........	1,718·709	1,858·064	118·651	129·438	1 — 14·485
717	3 George I.	1,718·709	1,858·064	113·001	123·274	1 — 15·209
816	56 George III........	1,614·545	1,745·454	113·001	123·274	1 — 14·287

III. SCOTCH COINS. — Account of the Number of Pounds, Shillings, and Pennies Scotch, which have been coined out of One Pound Weight of Silver, at different Times; with the Degree of Purity of such Silver, or its Fineness, from the Year 1107 to the Year 1601. — (From *Cardonnel's Numismata Scotiæ*, p. 24.)

O.	Anno Regni.		Purity.	Alloy.	Value of the Money coined out of a lb. weight of Silver.	A. D.	Anno Regni.		Purity.	Alloy.	Value of the Money coined out of a lb. weight of Silver.
			oz. pw.	oz. pw.	£ s. d.				oz. pw.	oz. pw.	£ s. d.
m	Alexander I.	⎫				1451	James II.	15	11 2	0 18	3 4 0
7	David I.	⎬				1456		20	11 2	0 18	4 16 0
	William		11 2	0 18	1 0 0	1475	James III.	16	11 2	0 18	7 4 0
	Alexander II.					1484		24	11 2	0 18	7 0 0
6	Alexander III.	⎬				1488	James IV.	{1}	11 2	0 18	7 0 0
m	John Baliol	⎭				1489		{2}			
6						1529	James V.	16	11 0	1 0	9 12 0
	Robert I.	⎬	11 2	0 18	1 1 0	1544	Mary	3	11 0	1 0	9 12 0
9						1556		14	11 0	1 0	13 0 0
5	David II.	38	11 2	0 18	1 5 0	1565		23	11 0	1 0	18 0 0
7		39	11 2	0 18	1 9 4	1567	James VI.	1	11 0	1 0	18 0 0
m						1571		5	9 0	3 0	16 14 0
	Robert II.	⎬	11 2	0 18	1 9 4	1576		10	8 0	4 0	16 14 0
						1579		13	11 0	1 0	22 0 0
0						1581		15	11 0	1 0	24 0 0
3	Robert III.	4	11 2	0 18	1 12 0	1597		31	11 0	1 0	30 0 0
4	James I.	19	11 2	0 18	1 17 6	1601		35	11 0	1 0	36 0 0

551—5 Edward VI.] The coinage of debased silver money in the 5th year of Edward VI. of 3 oz. ought more properly to be considered as Tokens. The sum of 120,000l. only was so coined. (See 's *Essays*, chap. iv.)

816—56 George III.] The Government having taken the coinage of silver into its own hands, there present no fixed price paid to the public, by the Mint, for standard silver. And supposing the nment to continue the present Mint regulations, and to keep gold at 77s. 10¼d. an ounce, as the of silver varies, the relative value of gold to silver will vary in like proportion.

No. IV. Scotch Coins. — Account of the Number of Pounds, Shillings, and Pennies Scotch, which have been coined out of One Pound Weight of Gold; with the Degree of their Purity, and the Proportion that the Gold bore to the Silver. — (*Cardonnel*, p. 25.)

A. D.	Anno Regni.		Fineness.			Alloy.			Value of the Coin coined out of One Pound of Gold.			Pound of Pure Gold weighed of Pure Silver.			
			oz.	*pw.*	*gr.*	*oz.*	*pw.*	*gr.*	£	*s.*	*d.*	*lb.*	*oz.*	*pw.*	*gr.*
1371, &c.	Robert II.		11	18	18	0	1	6	17	12	0	11	1	17	22
1390, &c.	Robert II.		11	18	18	0	1	6	19	4	0	11	1	17	22
1424	James I.	19	11	18	18	0	1	6	22	10	0	11	1	17	22
1451	James II.	15	11	18	18	0	1	6	33	6	0	9	8	4	14
1456		20	11	18	18	0	1	6	50	0	0	9	8	4	14
1475	James III.	16	11	18	18	0	1	6	78	15	0	10	2	0	20
1484		24	11	18	18	0	1	6	78	15	0	10	5	7	9
1488	James IV.	1	11	18	18	0	1	6	78	15	0	10	5	7	9
1529	James V.	16	11	18	18	0	1	6	108	0	0	10	5	7	9
1556	Mary	14	11	0	0	1	0	0	144	0	0	10	5	8	6
1567	James VI.	10	11	0	0	1	0	0	240	0	0	10	5	8	6
1579		13	10	10	0	1	10	0	240	0	0	11	5	2	20
1597		31	11	0	0	1	0	0	360	0	0	12	0	0	0
1601		35	11	0	0	1	0	0	432	0	0	12	0	0	0
1633	Charles I.	9	11	0	0	1	0	0	492	0	0	13	2	7	11

No. V. Gold Coins of different Countries. — A Table containing the Assays, Weights, and Values of the principal Gold Coins of all Countries, computed according to the Mint Price of Gold in England, and from Assays made both at London and Paris, which have been found to verify each other.*

*** The publishers of this work have purchased the right to publish this table from Dr. Kelly, in the second edition of whose *Cambist* it originally appeared.

		Assay.			Weight.		Standard Weight.			Contents in Pure Gold.	Value in Sterling.	
			car.	*gr.*	*dwt.*	*gr.*	*dwt.*	*gr.*	*mi.*	*grains.*	*s.*	*d.*
Austrian Dominions	Souverain	W.	0	0¼	3	14	3	13	15	78, 6	13	10,92
	Double ducat	B.	1	2¾	4	12	4	20	5	106, 4	18	9,97
	Ducat Kremnitz, or Hungarian	B.	1	3	2	5¾	2	10	3	53, 3	9	5,91
Bavaria	Carolin	W.	3	2	6	5¼	5	5	10	115,	20	4,23
	Max d'or, or Maximilian	W.	3	2¼	4	4	3	14	0	77,	13	7,44
	Ducat	B.	1	2¼	2	5¾	2	19	11	52, 8	9	4,1
Bern	Ducat (double, &c. in proportion)	B.	1	1¾	1	23	2	2	1	45, 9	8	1,48
	Pistole	W.	0	1½	4	21	4	19	0	105, 5	18	7,86
Brunswick	Pistole (double in proportion)	W.	0	1¼	4	21¼	4	19	5	105, 7	18	8,48
	Ducat	B.	1	0½	2	5¾	2	8	9	51, 8	9	2
Cologne	Ducat	B.	1	2	2	5¾	2	9	8	52, 6	9	3,70
Denmark	Ducat current	W.	0	3¾	2	0	1	21	19	42, 2	7	5,6
	Ducat specie	B.	1	2	2	5¾	2	9	8	52, 6	9	3,70
	Christian d'or	W.	0	1	4	7	4	5	16	93, 3	16	6,1
England	Guinea	Stand.			5	9½	5	9	10	118, 7	21	0
	Half-Guinea	Stand.			2	16¾	2	16	15	59, 3	10	6
	Seven Shilling Piece	Stand.			1	19	1	19	0	39, 6	7	0
	Sovereign	Stand.			5	3¼	5	3	5	113, 1	20	0
France	Double Louis (coined before 1786)	W.	0	2	10	11	10	5	6	224, 9	39	9,6
	Louis	W.	0	2	5	5½	5	2	12	112, 4	19	10,7
	Double Louis (coined since 1786)	W.	0	1½	9	20	9	15	19	212, 6	37	7,5
	Louis	W.	0	1½	4	22	4	19	19	106, 3	18	9,7
	Double Napoleon, or piece of 40 francs	W.	0	1¾	8	7	8	3	0	179,	31	8,9
	Napoleon, or piece of 20 francs	W.	0	1¾	4	3½	4	1	10	89, 7	15	10,
	New Louis (double, &c.) the same as the Napoleon.											
Francfort on the Maine	Ducat	B.	1	2½	2	5¾	2	9	14	52, 9	9	4,3
Geneva	Pistole, old	W.	0	2	4	7¼	4	4	18	92, 5	16	4,4
	Pistole, new	W.	0	0½	3	15¾	3	15	4	80,	14	1,9
Genoa	Sequin	B.	1	3½	2	5¾	2	10	6	53, 4	9	5,4
Hamburgh	Ducat (double in proportion)	B.	1	2¼	2	5¾	2	9	14	52, 9	9	4,3
Hanover	George d'or	W.	0	1¼	4	6¼	4	5	3	92, 6	16	4,6
	Ducat	B.	1	3¼	2	5¾	2	10	3	53, 3	9	5,1
	Gold florin (double in proportion)	W.	3	0½	2	2	1	18	6	39,	6	10,
Holland	Double ryder	Stand.			12	21	12	21	0	283, 2	50	1,
	Ryder	Stand.			6	9	6	9	0	140, 2	24	9,
	Ducat	B.	1	2¼	2	5¾	2	9	12	52, 8	9	4,

* The London Assays in this Table were made by Robert Bingley, Esq. F. R. S. the King's Ass Master of the Mint, and those at Paris by Pierre Frederic Bonneville, Essayeur du Commerce, as pu lished in his elaborate work on the coins of all nations.

Specimens of all the foreign coins brought to London for commercial purposes have been supplied this Table from the Bullion-Office, Bank of England, by order of the Bank Directors, and have be selected by John Humble, Esq., the chief Clerk of that office, who also examined the tables in their p gress. It may likewise be added, that the Mint Reports of these commercial coins are chiefly from av age assays; and that all the computations have been carefully verified by different calculators.—(Note Dr. Kelly, to second edition of the *Cambist*, published in 1821.)

		Assay.	Weight.	Standard Weight.	Contents in Pure Gold.	Value in Sterling.
		car. gr.	dwt. gr.	dwt. gr. mi.	grains.	s. d.
TA -	- Double Louis - - -	W. 1 3¼	10 16	9 18 18	215,3	38 1,25
	Louis - - -	W. 1 3	5 8	4 21 16	108,	19 1,37
	Demi Louis - - -	W. 1 2¼	2 16	2 11 3	54,5	9 7,75
AN -	- Sequin - - -	B. 1 3	2 5¾	2 10 0	53, 2	9 4,98
	Doppia or pistole - -	W. 0 1	4 1⅛	4 0 8	88, 4	15 7,74
	40 Lire piece of 1808 - -	W. 0 1¾	8 8	8 4 0	179, 7	31 9,64
ES -	- Six ducat piece of 1783 - -	W. 0 2¼	5 16	5 12 18	121, 9	21 6,89
	Two ducat piece, or sequin, of 1762	W. 1 2¾	1 20¼	1 16 6	37, 4	6 7,42
	Three ducat piece, or oncetta, of 1818	B. 1 3⅜	2 10¼	2 15 1	58, 1	10 3,40
ERLANDS	Gold lion, or 14 florin piece - -	Stand.	5 7¾	5 7 16	117, 1	20 8,69
	Ten florin piece (1820) - -	W. 0 1¾	4 7¾	4 5 15	93, 2	16 5,93
IA -	- Quadruple pistole (double in proportion) - - -	W. 1 0	18 9	17 12 18	386,	68 3,78
	Pistole or doppia of 1787 - -	W. 0 3	4 14	4 10 4	97, 4	17 2,85
	Ditto of 1796 - - -	W. 1 0¼	4 14	4 8 14	95, 9	16 11,67
	Maria Theresa (1818) - -	W. 0 1¾	4 3½	4 1 10	89, 7	15 10,5
MONT	- Pistole coined since 1785 (½, &c. in prop.) - - -	W. 0 1¼	5 20	5 17 0	125, 6	22 2,75
	Sequin (½ in proportion) - -	B. 1 2½	2 5¾	2 9 12	52, 9	9 4,34
	Carlino, coined since 1785 (½, &c. in prop.) - - -	W. 0 1¼	29 6	28 20 0	634, 4	112 3,33
	Piece of 20 francs, called *Marengo* -	W. 2 0	4 3¼	3 18 4	82, 7	14 7,63
ND	- Ducat - - -	B. 1 2½	2 5¾	2 9 12	52, 9	9 4,34
UGAL	- Dobraon of 24,000 rees - -	Stand.	34 12	34 12 0	759,	134 3,96
	Dobra of 12,800 res - -	Stand.	18 6	18 6 0	401, 5	71 0,70
	Moidore or Lisbonnine (½,&c. in prop.)	Stand.	6 22	6 22 0	152, 2	26 11,24
	Piece of 16 testoons, or 1600 rees -	W. 0 0⅝	2 6	2 5 14	49, 3	8 8,70
	Old crusado of 400 rees - -	W. 0 0⅛	0 15	0 14 18	13, 6	2 4,88
	New crusado of 480 rees - -	W. 0 0⅜	0 16¼	0 16 2	14, 8	2 7,43
	Milree (coined for the African colonies 1755) - - -	Stand.	0 19⅝	0 19 15	18, 1	3 2,44
SIA	- Ducat of 1748 - - -	B. 1 2½	2 5¾	2 9 14	52, 9	9 4,34
	Ducat of 1787 - - -	B. 1 2	2 5¾	2 9 6	52, 6	9 3,71
	Frederick (double) of 1769 - -	W. 0 1⅝	8 14	8 9 18	185,	32 8,90
	Frederick (single) of 1778 - -	W. 0 1½	4 7	4 5 4	92, 8	16 5,08
	Frederick (double) of 1800 -	W. 0 2	8 14	8 9 6	184, 5	32 7,84
	Frederick (single) of 1800 - -	W. 0 2	4 7	4 4 13	92, 2	16 3,42
-	- Sequin (coined since 1760) - -	B. 1 3½	2 4½	2 9 0	52, 2	9 2,86
	Scudo of the Republic - -	W. 0 1¾	17 0¼	16 16 6	367,	64 11,43
A -	- Ducat of 1796 - - -	B. 1 2½	2 6	2 10 0	53, 2	9 4,98
	Ducat of 1763 - - -	B. 1 2	2 5¾	2 9 8	52, 6	9 3,71
	Gold ruble of 1756 - -	Stand.	1 0½	1 0 10	22, 5	3 11,78
	Ditto of 1799 - - -	W. 0 0¼	0 18¾	0 18 14	17, 1	3 0,31
	Gold poltin of 1777 - -	Stand.	0 9	0 9 0	8, 2	1 5,41
	Imperial of 1801 - - -	B. 1 2¼	7 17¼	8 6 8	181, 9	32 2,31
	Half imperial of 1801 - -	B. 1 2¼	3 20½	4 3 4	90, 9	16 1,05
	Ditto of 18.8 - -	B. 0 0⅛	4 3½	4 3 12	91, 3	16 1,98
NIA	- Carlino (½ in proportion) - -	W. 0 2¾	10 7½	9 23 16	219, 8	30 8,10
Y	- Ducat of 1784 - - -	B. 1 2	2 5¾	2 9 8	52, 6	9 3,71
	Ducat of 1797 - - -	B. 1 2½	2 5¾	2 9 14	52, 9	9 4,34
	Augustus of 1754 - - -	W. 0 2⅜	4 6⅛	4 3 8	91, 2	16 1,69
	Augustus of 1784 - -	W. 0 1¾	4 6⅛	4 4 12	92, 2	16 3,81
*	- Ounce of 1751 - - -	W. 1 2⅜	2 20½	2 15 8	58, 2	10 3,60
	Double ounce of 1758 - -	W. 1 2	5 17	5 7 14	117,	20 8,48
-	- Doubloon of 1772 (double and single in proportion) - -	W. 0 2¼	17 8½	61 21 16	372,	65 10,05
	Quadruple pistole of 1801 - -	W. 1 1	17 9	16 9 6	360, 5	63 9,62
	Pistole of 1801 - -	W. 1 1	4 8¼	4 2 6	90, 1	15 11,35
	Coronilla, gold dollar, or vintem of 1801 - - -	W. 1 2½	1 3	1 0 18	22, 8	4 0,42
N	- Ducat - - -	B. 1 2	2 5	2 8 12	51, 9	9 2,22
ERLAND	Pistole of the Helvetic Republic of 1800 - - -	W. 0 1½	4 21½	4 19 9	105, 9	18 8,91
S -	- Ducat - - -	B. 1 2	2 5¾	2 9 8	52, 6	9 3,71
Y	- Sequin fonducli of Constantinople of 1773 - - -	W. 2 2½	2 5¾	1 23 6	43, 3	7 7,94
	Sequin fonducli of 1789 - -	W. 2 3¼	2 5¾	1 22 16	42, 9	7 7,11
	Half missier (1818) - -	W. 5 3½	0 18¼	0 13 5	12,16	2 1,82
	Sequin fonducli - -	W. 2 3	2 5	1 22 7	42, 5	7 6,26
	Yermeebeshlek - -	B. 0 3½	2 1¾	3 4 13	70, 3	12 5,30
NY	- Zecchino or sequin - -	B. 1 3¾	3 5¾	2 10 14	53, 6	9 5,83
	Ruspone of the kingdom of Etruria	B. 1 3⅞	6 17¼	7 7 13	161,	28 5,93
D STATES	†Eagle (½ and ¼ in proportion) -	W. 0 0⅜	11 6	11 4 8	246, 1	43 6,66
E -	- Zecchino or sequin (½ and ¼ in proportion) - - -	B. 1 3¼	2 6	2 10 10	53, 6	9 5,83
MBERG	Carolin - - -	W. 3 2	6 3⅛	5 4 0	113, 7	20 1,47
	Ducat - - .	B. 1 2	2 5	2 8 12	51, 9	9 2,22
	Ducat (double and ½ ducat in proportion) - - -	B. 1 2	2 5¾	2 9 8	52, 6	9 3,71
	EAST INDIES.					
NDIA -	Rupee, Bombay (1818) - -	B. 0 0⅛	7 11	7 11 13	164, 7	29 1,78
	Rupee of Madras (1818) - -	Stand.	7 12	7 12 0	165,	29 2,42
	Pagoda, star - -	W. 3 0	2 4¾	1 21 11	41, 8	7 4,77

Much variation is found in the fineness of the Sicilian gold coins.
This value of the American Eagle is taken from average assays of the coins of twelve years.

No. VI. Silver Coins of different Countries. — A Table containing the Ass[ays,] Weights, and Values of the principal Silver Coins of all Countries, compute[d at] the rate of *5s. 2d.* per Ounce Standard, from Assays made both at the London [and] Paris Mints.

		Assay.	Weight.	Standard Weight.	Contents in Pure Silver.	Value Sterlin[g]
		oz. dwt.	*dwt. gr.*	*dwt. gr. mi.*	*grains.*	*s.*
Austria -	Rixdollar of Francis II., 1800 -	W. 1 5	18 1	16 0 4	355, 5	4 1
	Rixdollar of the kingdom of Hungary	W. 1 2	18 1	16 6 1	360, 9	4 2
	Half rixdollar, or florin, *Convention*	W. 1 3	9 0½	8 2 1	179, 6	2 1
	Copftsuck, or 20 creutzer piece -	W. 4 3	4 6½	2 16 3	59, 4	0 8
	17 Creutzer piece - -	W. 4 8	4 0	2 9 18	53, 5	0 7
	Halbe copf, or 10 creutzer piece -	W. 5 5	2 11	1 7 1	28, 8	0 4
Baden - -	Rixdollar - - -	W. 1 4	18 2	16 3 1	358, 1	4 2
Bavaria -	Rixdollar of 1800 (½ in proportion) -	W. 1 4½	17 12	15 13 13	345, 6	4 0
	Copftsuck - - -	W. 4 3	4 6½	2 16 3	59, 4	0 8
Bern - -	Patagon or crown (½ in proportion) -	W. 0 7	18 22	18 7 14	406, 7	4 8
	Piece of 10 batzen - -	W. 1 2	5 3	4 14 17	102, 5	1 2
Bremen -	Piece of 48 grotes - -	W. 2 2	11 0	8 22 1	198,	2 3
Brunswick -	Rixdollar, *Convention* - -	W. 1 3	18 1	16 4 4	359, 2	4 2
	Half rixdollar - - -	W. 1 3	9 0½	8 2 2	179, 6	2 1
	Gulden, or piece of ⅔, fine, of 1764 -	B. 0 16	8 10½	9 1 1	200, 8	2 4
	Gulden, common, of 1764 - -	W. 1 2	9 0	8 2 10	180,	2 1
	Gulden, ditto, of 1795 - -	W. 2 2	11 1½	8 23 7	199, 1	2 3
	Half gulden, or piece of ⅓, of 1764 -	W. 1 2	4 12	4 1 5	90,	1 0
Denmark -	Ryksdaler, specie, of 1798 -	W. 0 13	18 14	17 11 17	388, 4	4 6
	New piece of 4 marks - -	W. 0 12	12 9	11 16 14	259, 8	3 0
	Half ryksdaler - - -	W. 0 13	9 7	8 17 8	194, 2	2 3
	Mark, specie, or ⅙ ryksdaler	W. 3 1	4 0	2 21 12	64, 4	0 7
	Rixdollar, specie, of Sleswig and Holstein (pieces of ⅔ and ⅓ in prop.)	W. 0 12	18 13	17 12 6	389, 4	4 6
	Piece of 24 skillings - -	W. 4 7	5 2½	3 2 10	68, 9	0 9
England -	Crown (*old*) - - -	Stand.	19 8½	19 8 10	429, 7	5 0
	Half-crown - - -	Stand.	9 16¼	9 16 5	214, 8	2 6
	Shilling - - -	Stand.	3 21	3 21 0	85, 9	1 0
	Sixpence - - -	Stand.	1 22½	1 22 10	42, 9	0 6
	Crown (*new*) - - -	Stand.	18 4¼	18 4 7	403, 6	4 8
	Half-crown - - -	Stand.	9 2	9 2 4	201, 8	2 4
	Shilling - - -	Stand.	3 15½	3 15 6	80, 7	0 11
	Sixpence - - -	Stand.	1 19¾	1 19 14	40, 3	0 5
France -	Ecu of 6 livres - - -	W. 0 7	18 18	18 7 16	403, 1	4 8
	Demi ecu - - -	W. 0 7	9 9	9 1 18	201, 5	2 4
	Piece of 24 sous (divisions in prop.) -	W. 0 7	3 20	3 16 19	83, 4	0 11
	Piece of 30 sous (½ in proportion) -	W. 3 8	6 12	4 12 4	100, 2	1 1
	Piece of 5 francs of the Convention	W. 0 10½	16 0	15 5 14	338, 3	3 11
	Piece of 5 francs (Napoleon) of 1808	W. 0 7	16 1	15 12 4	344, 9	4 0
	Piece of 2 francs of 1808 - -	W. 0 7	6 11	6 6 2	138, 8	1 7
	Franc of 1809 - - -	W. 0 7	3 5½	3 3 1	69, 4	0 9
	Demi franc - - -	W. 0 8½	1 15	4 13 6	34, 7	0 4
	Franc (Louis) of 1818, same as franc of 1809 - -					
Geneva -	Patagon - - -	W. 1 0	17 9	15 19 8	351,	4 1
	Piece of 15 sous of 1794 - -	W. 2 6	2 1¼	1 15 1	36, 1	0 5
Genoa - -	Scudo, of 8 lire, of 1796 (½, ¼, &c. in proportion) - -	W. 0 8	21 9	20 14 10	457, 4	5 3
	Scudo of the Ligurian Republic -	W. 0 9½	21 9	20 11 2	454, 3	5 3
Hamburgh -	Rixdollar, specie - -	W. 0 10	18 18	17 21 12	397, 5	4 7
	Double mark, or 32 schilling piece (single in proportion) - -	W. 2 3	11 18	9 11 8	210, 3	2 5
	Piece of 8 schillings - -	W. 3 12	3 8¼	2 6 4	50, 1	0 6
	Piece of 4 schillings - -	W. 4 6	2 2	1 6 12	28, 3	0
Hanover -	Rixdollar, *Constitution* - -	W. 0 9	18 19	18 0 14	400, 3	4 7
	Florin, or piece of ⅔, fine - -	B. 0 16	8 10	9 0 10	200, 3	2
	Half florin, or piece of ⅓, ditto -	B. 0 16	4 4	4 11 4	99, 2	1
	Quarter, or piece of 6 good groschen, ditto - - -	B. 0 16	2 1	2 4 10	48, 6	0
	Florin, or piece of ⅔, base - -	W. 2 1	11 0¾	8 23 15	199, 6	2
Hesse Cassel	Rixdollar, *Convention* - -	W. 1 6	18 1	15 22 6	353,	4
	Florin, or piece of ⅔ (⅓ in proportion)	W. 1 6	9 0½	7 23 3	176, 8	2
	Thaler of 1789 - - -	W. 0 10½	12 7½	11 17 5	259, 7	3
	Ecu, *Convention* (1815) - -	W. 1 6	17 23¾	15 21 2	349, 3	4
	Bon Gros - - -	W. 6 14	1 4	0 11 5	10, 3	0
Holland -	Ducatoon - - -	B. 0 3	20 22	21 4 15	471, 6	5
	Piece of 3 florins - -	W. 0 2	20 7	20 2 12	446, 4	5
	Rixdollar (the assay varies) -	W. 0 16	18 6	16 20 8	375, 9	4
	Half rixdollar - -	W. 0 16	9 0	8 8 8	185, 4	2
	Florin or guilder (½ in proportion) -	W. 0 4½	6 18	6 14 14	146, 8	1
	12 Stiver piece - - -	W. 0 16½	4 12	4 3 18	92, 4	1
	Florin of Batavia - -	W. 0 5½	6 13	6 9 2	141, 6	1
	Rixdollar, or 50 stiver piece of the kingdom of Holland - -	W. 0 5½	17 0	16 13 18	367, 9	4
Lubec - -	Rixdollar, specie - -	W. 0 13	18 8	17 15 12	391, 9	4
	Double mark - - -	W. 2 3	11 18	9 11 8	210, 3	2
	Mark - - -	W. 2 3	5 21	4 17 14	105, 1	1
Lucca - -	Scudo - - -	W. 0 3	17 0	16 18 10	372, 3	4
	Barbone - - -	W. 3 3	1 20¼	1 7 14	29, 3	0
Malta - -	Ounce of 30 tari of Emmanuel Pinto	W. 2 5	19 1½	15 4 14	337, 4	3
	2 Tari piece - - -	W. 2 19	1 2	0 19 2	17, 7	0

		Assay. oz. dwt.	Weight. dwt. gr.	Standard Weight. dwt. gr. mi.	Contents in Pure Silver. grains.	Value in Sterling. s. d.
LAN -	Scudo of 6 lire (½ in proportion) -	W. 0 7	14 20¾	14 9 10	319, 6	3 8,62
	Lira, new - - -	W. 4 10	4 0	2 9 0	52, 8	0 7,37
	Lira, old - - -	W. 0 3	2 10	2 9 4	52, 9	0 7,38
	Scudo of the Cisalpine Republic -	W. 0 7	14 21½	14 10 4	320, 2	3 8,71
	Piece of 30 soldi of ditto -	W. 2 18	4 17	3 11 8	77, 2	0 10,78
DENA -	Scudo of 15 lire, 1739 (double, &c. in proportion) - -	W. 0 14	18 12½	17 8 9	385, 2	4 5,78
	Scudo of 5 lire, of 1782 - -	W. 0 3	5 19	5 17 2	126, 8	1 5,70
	Scudo of 1796 - -	W. 3 3	18 1¾	12 22 12	287, 4	3 4,13
PLES -	Ducat, new (½ in proportion) -	W. 1 0	14 15	13 7 8	295, 4	3 5,24
	Piece of 12 Carlini of 1791 - -	W. 1 0	17 15	16 0 18	356,	4 1,71
	Ditto of 1796 - - -	W. 1 2	17 16¾	15 22 12	353, 9	4 1,41
	Ditto of 1805 (½ in proportion) -	W. 1 2	17 18¼	15 23 18	355, 2	4 1,60
	Ditto of 10 Carlini (1818) - -	W. 1 2	14 18	13 7 0	295, 1	3 5,20
THERLANDS	Ducatoon, old - -	B. 0 4	21 0	21 9 0	474, 6	5 6,27
	Ducatoon of Maria Theresa -	W. 0 14	21 10	20 1 12	445, 5	5 2,20
	Crown (½, &c. in proportion) -	W. 0 14	19 0	17 19 4	395, 2	4 7,18
	5 Stiver piece - - -	W. 6 3	3 4	1 9 18	31, 3	0 4,37
	Florin of 1790 - - -	W. 0 14	5 23½	5 14 9	124, 3	1 5,35
	Florin of 1816 - -	W. 0 7½	6 22	6 16 6	148, 4	1 8,72
	Half florin (with divisions in prop.)	W. 4 5½	5 11	3 9 2	75,	0 10,46
RMA -	Ducat of 1784 - - -	W. 0 9	16 11	15 18 18	350, 6	4 0,95
	Ducat of 1796 (½ in proportion) -	W. 0 5½	16 12¾	16 2 18	357, 9	4 1,97
	Piece of 3 lire - - -	W. 1 4	4 1¼	4 2 2	90, 7	1 0,66
DMONT -	Scudo (1755), ½, &c. in proportion -	W. 0 5½	22 14	22 0 10	488, 9	5 8,26
	Scudo (1770), ½ and ¼ in proportion -	W. 0 5	22 14	22 1 16	490,	5 8,42
	Piece of 2 lire (1714) - -	W. 0 4½	7 20½	7 16 13	170, 8	1 11,85
	5 Franc piece (1801) - -	W. 0 8	16 1½	15 11 12	343, 7	3 11,99
LAND -	Rixdollar, old - - -	W. 1 2	18 1	16 6 0	360, 8	4 2,38
	Rixdollar, new (1794) - -	W. 2 17	15 10½	11 11 6	254, 3	2 11,51
	Florin, or gulden - -	W. 4 2	6 0	3 18 16	84,	0 11,72
RTUGAL -	New crusado (1690) - -	W. 0 4	11 0	10 19 0	239, 2	2 9,40
	Ditto (1718) - -	W. 0 6½	9 8	9 1 0	200, 2	2 3,95
	Ditto (1795) - -	W. 0 7	9 9	9 1 18	201, 6	2 4,15
	Doze vintems, or piece of 240 rees (1799) - - -	W. 0 7	4 16	4 12 10	100, 4	1 2,01
	Testoon (1799) - -	W. 0 7	2 0½	1 22 18	43, 4	0 6,06
	New crusado (1809) - -	W. 0 4	9 3	8 23 0	198, 2	2 4,67
	Seis vintems, or piece of 120 rees (1802) - - -	W. 0 9	2 4½	2 2 8	46, 6	0 6,50
	Testoon (1802) - - -	W. 0 9	2 0	1 22 0	42, 5	0 5,93
	Tres vintems, or piece of 60 rees (1802)	W. 0 9	1 2¼	1 1 4	23, 3	0 3,25
	Half testoon (1802) - -	W. 0 9	0 23	0 22 0	20, 4	0 2,84
TUGUESE OLONIES }	Piece of 8 macutes, of Portuguese Africa - - -	W. 0 9	7 12	7 4 14	159, 8	1 10,31
	Ditto of 6 ditto - -	W. 0 9	5 13	5 7 12	118,	1 4,47
	Ditto of 4 ditto - - -	W. 0 9	3 16	3 12 8	78, 1	0 10,90
SSIA -	*Rixdollar, Prussian currency (½ in proportion) - - -	W. 2 5	14 6½	11 9 0	252, 6	2 11,27
	Rixdollar, *Convention* - -	W. 1 3	18 1	16 4 2	359,	4 2,13
	Florin, or piece of ⅔ - -	W. 2 3	11 2	8 22 8	198, 4	2 3,70
	Florin of Silesia - -	W. 2 2	9 11	7 16 0	170, 3	1 11,78
	Drittel, or piece of 8 good groschen	W. 3 3	5 8¾	3 20 4	85, 3	0 11,91
	Piece of 6 groschen - -	W. 2 8	3 14	2 19 6	62, 3	0 8,69
ME - -	Scudo, or crown (coined since 1753)	W. 0 4	17 1	16 17 13	371, 5	4 3,87
	Mezzo scudo, or half-crown -	W. 0 4	8 12½	8 8 16	185, 7	2 1,93
	Testone (1785) - -	W. 0 5	5 2	4 23 4	110, 3	1 3,40
	Paolo (1785) - - -	W. 0 4	1 17	1 16 4	37, 2	0 5,19
	Grosso, or half paolo (1785) -	W. 0 5	0 20½	0 20 0	18, 5	0 2,58
	Scudo of the Roman Republic (1799)	W. 0 6	17 1	16 13 18	368, 1	4 3,40
SIA - -	Ruble of Peter the Great -	W. 2 7	18 1	14 1 8	312, 1	3 7,56
	Ditto of Catherine I. (1725) -	W. 2 4½	17 11	13 23 0	309, 9	3 7,27
	Ditto of Peter II. (1727) - -	W. 2 12	18 5¾	13 23 4	310,	3 7,28
	Ditto of Anne (1734) - -	W. 1 11	16 14½	14 6 16	317, 2	3 8,29
	Ditto of Elizabeth (1750) - -	W. 1 7	16 12	14 11 16	321, 8	3 8,93
	Ditto of Peter III. (1762) -	W. 2 2	15 10	12 12 0	277, 5	3 2,75
	Ditto of Catherine II. (1780) -	W. 2 4	15 12	12 10 6	275, 9	3 2,52
	Ditto of Paul (1799) - -	W. 0 14	13 12	12 15 10	280, 8	3 3,21
	Ditto of Alexander (1802) -	W. 0 13	13 1½	17 7 2	273,	3 2,12
	Ditto of ditto (1805) - -	W. 0 16	13 12	12 12 12	278, 1	3 2,83
	20 Copeck piece (1767) - -	W. 2 2	3 10¾	2 19 0	62, 6	0 8,74
	Ditto (1784) - - -	W. 2 2	3 3	2 12 18	56, 2	0 7,84
	15 Copeck piece (1778) - -	W. 2 2	2 6	1 19 18	40, 5	0 5,65
	10 Copeck piece - -	W. 2 6	2 1	1 14 16	35, 9	0 5,11
	Ditto (1798) - - -	W. 0 14½	1 9	1 6 16	28, 5	0 3,97
	Ditto (1802) - - -	W. 0 13	1 8½	1 6 11	28, 3	0 3,95
	5 Copeck piece (1801) - -	W. 0 13½	0 16½	0 15 10	15, 3	0 2,13
INIA -	Scudo, or crown (½ and ¼ in prop.) -	W. 0 7	15 2½	14 15 0	324, 7	3 9,34
NY - -	Rixdollar, *Convention* (½ and ¼ in proportion) - -	W. 1 3	18 0	16 3 4	358, 2	4 2,01
	Piece of 16 groschen of Leipsic -	W. 2 2	9 9½	7 14 16	169, 1	1 11,61
	Rixdollar current of Saxe Gotha -	W. 4 4½	18 1	11 4 2	248, 1	2 10,64
	⅙ Thaler of 1804 - -	W. 4 11	3 11	2 0 19	45, 3	0 6,32
	Ditto of 1808 - - -	W. 4 11½	3 5½	1 21 8	42, 1	0 5,87
	Ditto of Jerome Bonaparte of 1809	W. 5 4	3 17	1 23 6	43, 7	0 6,10

* The Prussian coins, having been debased at different periods, vary in theis reports.

		Assay.	Weight.	Standard Weight.	Contents in Pure Silver.	Value in Sterling.
		- oz. dwt.	dwt gr.	dwt. gr. mi.	grains.	s. d.
SICILY - -	Scudo (½ in proportion) - -	W. 1 4	17 14	15 16 6	348, 2	4 0,62
	Piece of 40 grains - -	W. 1 2	5 21	5 7 2	117, 5	1 4,40
SPAIN - -	*Dollar, of late coinage - -	W. 0 8	17 8	16 17 0	370, 9	4 3,79
	Half dollar, ditto - -	W. 0 8	8 16	8 8 10	185, 4	2 1,88
	Mexican peceta (1774) - -	W. 0 8	4 7½	4 3 16	92, 3	1 0,88
	Real of Mexican plate (1775) -	W. 0 8	2 3¾	2 1 20	46, 1	0 6,43
	Peceta provincial of 2 reals of new plate (1775) - -	W. 1 9½	3 18	3 6 0	72, 2	0 10,08
	Real of new plate (1795) -	W. 1 9½	1 21	1 15 0	36, 1	0 5,04
SWEDEN - -	Rixdollar (1762) - -	W. 0 12	18 20	17 19 10	395, 5	4 7,22
	Rixdollar of late coinage - -	W. 0 14½	18 17	17 12 0	388, 5	4 6,28
SWITZERLAND	Ecu, or rixdollar of Lucerne, ½, &c. in proportion (1715) - -	W. 0 14½	17 8½	16 5 8	360, 1	4 2,28
	Old gulden, or florin of Lucerne (1714)	W. 1 19	8 14½	7 2 8	157, 5	1 9,99
	Ecu of 40 batzen of Lucerne (1796)	W. 0 5	19 0	18 13 14	412, 3	4 9,57
	Half ditto - - -	W. 1 2	9 20	8 20 12	196, 7	2 3,46
	Florin, or piece of 40 schillings of Lucerne (1793) - -	W. 1 5	4 22	4 8 14	96, 8	1 1,51
	Ecu of 40 batzen of the Helvetic Republic (1798), ½ in proportion -	W. 0 6	18 23	18 10 14	409, 5	4 9,18
	Ecu of 4 franken (1801) -	W. 0 7	18 23	18 8 12	407, 6	4 9,18
TURKEY - -	Piastre of Selim of 1801 -	W. 5 6	8 6	4 7 8	95, 7	1 1,36
	Piastre of Crim Tartary (1778) -	W. 6 13	10 5	4 2 4	90, 9	1 0,69
	Piastre of Tunis (1787) - -	W. 6 5½	10 0	4 8 6	96, 5	1 1,47
	Piastre (1818) - -	W. 5 14	6 6½	3 1 4	67, 7	0 9,45
TUSCANY -	Piece of 10 paoli of the Kingdom of Etruria (1801) - -	W. 0 4	17 13½	17 5 18	382, 9	4 5,46
	Scudo Pisa of ditto (1803) -	W. 0 2	17 12	17 8 4	385, 0	4 5,76
	Piece of 10 lire ditto (1803) -	B. 0 7	25 6	26 1 12	578, 7	6 8,80
	Lira (1803) - - -	B. 0 7	2 8	2 9 16	53, 4	0 7,45
UNITED STATES	† Dollar (1795), ½, &c. in proportion	W. 0 6½	17 8	16 19 16	373, 5	4 4,15
	Dollar (1798) - -	W. 0 7	17 10½	16 21 6	374, 9	4 4,35
	Dollar (1802) - -	W. 0 10½	17 10	16 14 0	368, 3	4 3,42
	Dollar, an average of 8 years -	W. 0 8½	17 8	16 16 0	370, 1	4 3,68
	Dime, or one-tenth dollar (1796) -	W. 0 4	1 19½	1 18 14	39, 5	0 5,71
	Half dime (1796) - -	W. 0 7	0 21¾	0 21 0	19, 5	0 2,72
VENICE - -	Piece of 2 lire, or 24 creutzers (1800)	W. 8 4½	5 19½	1 12 2	33, 4	0 4,66
	Ditto of 2 lire, called moneta provinciale (1808) - -	W. 8 3	5 13½	1 11 8	32, 8	0 4,58
	Ditto of 2 lire (1802) ½ and ¼ in prop.	W. 8 4	5 6¼	1 8 19	30, 5	0 4,25
WIRTEMBERG	Rixdollar, specie - -	W. 1-3	18 1	16 14 2	359, 1	4 2,14
	Copftsuck - - -	W. 4 2	4 16½	2 16 12	59, 8	0 8,35
	EAST INDIES.					
EAST INDIA -	Rupee Sicca, coined by the East India Company at Calcutta -	B. 0 13	7 11½	7 22 0	175, 8	2 0,54
	Calcutta (1818) - -	Stand.	8 0	8 0 0	175, 9	2 0,56
	Bombay, new, or Surat (1818)	W. 0 0¼	7 11	7 10 4	164, 7	1 11,01
	Fanam, Cananore - -	W. 0 1¼	1 11¾	1 11 10	32, 9	0 4,5
	Bombay, old - -	B. 0 13	1 11¾	1 13 16	35,	0 4,88
	Pondicherry - -	B. 0 5½	1 0¾	1 1 2	22, 8	0 3,18
	Ditto, double - -	W. 0 3	1 18¾	1 18 2	39,	0 5,44
	Gulden of the Dutch East India Company (1820) - -	W. 0 7½	6 22	6 16 6	148, 4	1 8,7

The sterling value of the foreign coins, in the foregoing tables, has been compute from the assays as follows: — Let it be required to assign the value in sterling, of a Frenc double Louis d'or coined since 1786, the assay master's report being as follows:- "Weight, 9 dwt. 20 grs.; assay W. 1½ grs., that is, 0 car. 1½ grs. worse than the Engli standard." We proceed as under: —

From 22 car. 0 gr. the fineness of English standard gold,
Take 0 1½ grs.

Remains 21 2½

Then, as 22 car. : 21 car. 2½ grs. :: 9 dwt. 20 grs. : 9 dwt. 16 grs., the standard go contained in the Louis d'or: and hence, as 1 oz. : 3*l.* 17*s.* 10½*d.* :: 9 dwts. 16 grs. : 1 17*s.* 7½*d.*, the value of the Louis in sterling money and so for any of the other coins.

Ancient Coins. — We subjoin, for the convenience of such of our readers as may any time have occasion to consult works in which reference is made to ancient coins, t following tables of those that were principally current among the Jews, Greeks, a Romans. They were calculated by Dr. Arbuthnot (*Tables of Ancient Coins, Weights, &* 4to ed. Lond. 1754.), and do not differ materially from the tables of Paucton, whc

* This is the coin which is universally circulated under the name of the Spanish dollar.
† The American dollars, and inferior silver pieces of late coinage, vary in fineness from W. 4 dwt. W. 9½ dwt.

ologie (4to. Paris, 1780.) is the most complete and elaborate work that has ever been ...shed with respect to ancient moneys, weights, and measures. At the same time we ...ss we should not be disposed to place much reliance on these tables, and we have ...here stated our reasons for holding this opinion. — (Art. *Money, Supp. to Ency. ...nnica.*)

JEWISH COINS.

...es and Proportions.								Value in Sterling.		
								£	s.	d.
...Gerah	-	-	-	-	-	-	-	0	0	$1\frac{59}{100}$
10	Bekah,	-	-	-	-	-	-	0	1	$1\frac{11}{10}$
20	2	Shekel,	-	-	-	-	-	0	2	$3\frac{3}{8}$
1200	120	50	Maneh, Mina Hebraica,		-	-	-	5	14	$0\frac{3}{4}$
...60,000	6,000	3,000	60	Talent,	-	-	-	342	3	9
...s aureus, or sextula, worth			-	-	-	-	-	0	12	$0\frac{1}{2}$
...s aureus, worth		-	-	-	-	-	-	1	16	6
...nt of gold, worth		-	-	-	-	-	5,475	0	0

GRECIAN COINS.

									s.	d.	qrs.
...epton,	-	-	-	-	-	-	-		0	0	$0\frac{31}{336}$
7	Chalcus,	-	-	-	-	-	-		0	0	$0\frac{31}{48}$
14	2	Dichalcus,	-	-	-	-	-		0	0	$1\frac{7}{24}$
28	4	2	Hemiobolum,	-	-	-	-		0	0	$2\frac{7}{12}$
56	8	4	2	Obolus,	-	-	-		0	1	$1\frac{1}{8}$
112	16	8	4	2	Diobolum,	-	-		0	2	$2\frac{1}{4}$
224	32	16	8	4	2	Tetrobolum,	-	-	0	5	$0\frac{3}{4}$
336	48	24	12	6	3	$1\frac{1}{2}$	Drachma,	-	0	7	3
662	96	48	24	12	6	3	2	Didrachma,	1	3	2
1,324	112	96	48	24	12	6	4	2 Tetradrachma,	2	7	0
1,660	384	120	60	30	15	$7\frac{1}{2}$	$5\frac{2}{3}$	$1\frac{1}{4}$ Pentadrachma,	3	2	3

...hese the drachma and didrachma were of silver; the rest, for the most part, of

...drachma is here, with the generality of authors, supposed equal to the denarius: ...there is reason to believe that the drachma was somewhat the weightier.

	Value in Sterling.		
	£	s.	d.
...recian gold coin was the stater aureus, weighing two Attic drachms, ...alf of the stater argenteus; and exchanging usually for 25 Attic ...mas of silver - - - - -	0	16	$1\frac{3}{4}$
...cording to our proportion of gold to silver it was worth -	1	0	9
...were likewise the stater Cyzicenus, exchanging for 28 Attic ...mas, or - - - - -	0	18	1

...ter Philippicus, and stater Alexandrinus, were of the same value.

...Daricus, according to Josephus, worth 50 Attic drachmas, or	1	12	$3\frac{1}{2}$

...Crœsius, of the same value.

VALUE AND PROPORTION OF THE ROMAN COINS.

								Sterling.
								s.	d.	qrs
Teruncius,			-	-	-	-	-	0	0	0$\frac{77}{10}$
2	Sembella,		-	-	-	-	-	0	0	1$\frac{55}{10}$
4	2	Libella, As,	}	-	-	-	-	0	0	3$\frac{1}{10}$
10	5	2$\frac{1}{2}$	Sestertius,	-	-	-	-	0	1	9$\frac{3}{4}$
20	10	5	2	Quinarius, Victoriatus,	}	-	-	0	3	3$\frac{1}{2}$
40	20	10	4	2	Denarius,	-	-	0	7	3

	£	s.
The Roman gold coin, or aureus, weighed generally double the denarius; its value, according to the proportion of gold to silver, mentioned by Pliny, was - - - - - -	1	4
According to the proportion that now obtains amongst us - -	1	0
According to the decuple proportion mentioned by Livy and Julius Pollux - - - - - -	0	12	1
According to the proportion mentioned by Tacitus, by which the aureus exchanged for 25 denarii, its value - - - -	0	16	

COIR, a species of yarn manufactured out of the husk of cocoa-nuts. husks being steeped in water, the dry dusty substance mixed with the fibre separated. These are afterwards spun into yarn, and manufactured into corda that is deemed by some superior to that made of hemp. The goodness of depends on the fineness of the filaments, and on their being of a bright yell colour. About 3,000,000lbs. weight are annually exported from Ceylon, p cipally to Calcutta, and other ports in the East Indies. It is also prepared in Maldive islands, and many other places; and is very extensively used through the East.—(*Bertolaeci's Ceylon; Bell's Commerce of Bengal*, &c.)

COLOCYNTHIS, COLOQUINTIDA, or BITTER CUCUMBER (*Koloquinten;* Du. *Bitter-appelen;* Fr. *Coloquintes;* It. *Coloquintida;* Sp. *Coloq tidas;* Arab. and Pers. *Hunzil*), the produce of an annual plant (*Cucumis Colo this*, Lin.) growing in Turkey, Nubia, India, and other places, much resemb the cucumber in herbage. When ripe, the fruit is peeled and dried in a sto and in this state is brought to England. It is inodorous, but has an extrem bitter, nauseous taste. It is an exceedingly powerful drastic cathartic. When larger than a St. Michael's orange, and has black acute pointed ends, it is good.—(*Ainslie's Materia Indica.*)

COLONIES.—COLONY TRADE.—*Colonies* are establishments foun in foreign countries by individuals who either voluntarily emigrate from, or torcibly sent abroad by, their mother country. The *colony trade* is the trade ried on between colonies and their parent states.

 I. ESTABLISHMENT OF COLONIES.
 II. INFLUENCE OF THE MONOPOLY OF THE COLONY TRADE.
 III. MAGNITUDE, POPULATION, TRADE, &c. OF BRITISH COLONIES.
 IV. REGULATIONS UNDER WHICH COLONY TRADE IS CONDUCTED. —
  POSAL OF LAND IN THE COLONIES, &c.
 V. FOREIGN COLONIES.

I. ESTABLISHMENT OF COLONIES.

(1.) *Greek Colonies.*—Various motives have, in different countries and led to the formation of colonies.* The Greek colonies of antiquity seem to

---

* Seneca has given, in a few words, a very clear and accurate statement of the different motive induced the ancients to found colonies.—" *Nec omnibus eadem causa relinquendi quærendique pa fuit. Alios excidia urbium suarum, hostilibus armis elapsos, in aliena, spoliatos suis, expulerunt : domestica seditio submovit : Alios nimia superfluentis populi frequentia, ad exonerandas vires, en Alios pestilentia, aut frequens terrarum hiatus, aut aliqua intoleranda infelicis soli ejecerunt : Que fertilis oræ, et in majus laudatæ, fama corrupit : Alios alia causa excivit domibus suis.*"—(Cons Helviam, c. 6.)

en chiefly founded by citizens whom the violence and fury of contending tions forced to leave their native land; but they were sometimes formed the purpose of relieving the mother country of a redundant population, d sometimes also for the purpose of extending the sphere of commercial nsactions, or of providing for their security. The relations between the ther country and the colony depended, in a great measure, on the motives ich led to the establishment of the latter. When a colony was founded by itives, forcibly expelled from their ancient homes; or when it was founded, as s frequently the case, by bodies of voluntary emigrants, who received no istance from, and were in no respect controlled by, the parent state, it s from the first independent: and even in those rarer cases in which the igration was conducted under the superintendence of the parent city, and en the colony was protected by her power and influence, the dependence s, mostly, far from being absolute and complete. The great bulk of the eek colonies were really independent states; and though they commonly re- ded the land of their forefathers with filial respect, though they yielded to its zens the place of distinction at public games and religious solemnities, and e expected to assist them in time of war, they did so as allies only, on fair equal terms, and never as subjects. Owing to the freedom of their institutions, their superiority in the arts of civilised life to the native inhabitants of the ntries among whom they were generally placed, these colonies rose, in a com- atively short period, to a high pitch of opulence and refinement; and many ong them, as Miletus and Ephesus in Asia Minor, Syracuse and Agrigentum Sicily, and Tarentum and Locri in Italy, not only equalled, but greatly sur- sed, their mother cities in wealth and power.

2.) *Roman Colonies.* — The Roman colonies were, for the most part, founded and under the authority of government; being intended to serve both as out- for poor and discontented citizens, and as military stations, or garrisons, to ure the subjection of the conquered provinces over which they were scattered. e most intimate political union was always maintained between them and the her city. Their internal government was modelled on that of Rome; and, le their superior officers were mostly sent from the capital, they were made to tribute their full quota of troops and taxes, to assist in carrying on the con- s in which the Republic was almost constantly engaged.

3.) *Spanish Colonies.* — The early colonies of most modern nations were ded by private adventurers, influenced either by the hope of gain, or by a re to escape from religious persecution, without any wish to relieve the her country of a surplus population, or to bridle subjugated provinces. On r first institution, therefore, the modern colonies approached, though with some ntial variations, more nearly to the Grecian than the Roman model — but period of their freedom was of very limited duration. They were very soon ected to laws and regulations framed in the metropolis, and calculated, as to be supposed, rather to promote its interests than those of the colony. At mewhat, later period, the foundation of colonial establishments was eagerly onised by most European governments, in the view of extending commerce, of enriching the mother country, by securing to her the exclusive possession e market of distant countries; and where, from the thinness of the aboriginal lation, or their inferiority in the arts of civilised life, the colonists were led to amass fortunes with comparative rapidity.

he Spaniards who first resorted to America after its discovery, had no inten- of settling in the country, or of colonising it. The idea that gold and silver e constituted wealth was then universally prevalent; and the bold and enter- ng companions and followers of Columbus, instead of engaging in industrious rtakings, which they neither understood nor relished, sought only to enrich selves by plundering the feeble and defenceless natives of the gold and silver eir possession, and of the abundance of which the most exaggerated accounts immediately spread throughout Europe. When new adventurers arrived on nknown coast, their single inquiry was, whether it abounded in gold. If it they remained, for some time at least, in the country; if not, they immediately ail for some other quarter. *Auri rabida sitis a cultura Hispanos divertit*, is the essive statement of a contemporary writer. — (Petrus Martyrus, in the *Novus* s of Grynæus, p. 511.) The slow progress of the Spanish colonies, after their

first discovery, must principally be ascribed to this cause. The gold and silve
accumulated by the natives were very soon exhausted; and the skill and energ
of the successive swarms of adventurers, who continued to pour into the country
were principally directed to the unproductive and generally ruinous trade o
mining. The few large fortunes that were made in this way, like the large prize
in a lottery, inflamed the cupidity of the multitude, and gave an appearance o
credibility to the fabulous accounts of the excessive productiveness of the mines
After the gambling spirit which had exclusively actuated the early adventurer
had begun to subside, the colonists gradually betook themselves to agricultura
and commercial pursuits: and the vast variety of valuable productions witl
which Mexico and the other Spanish colonies abound, the extreme richness of thei
soil, and their advantageous situation, would, had they been only tolerably wel
governed, have occasioned their rapid increase in wealth and civilisation. Bu
a blind and intolerant despotism paralysed their energies, and fettered an
retarded their progress. All the abuses and defects of the government of ol
Spain were transferred to, and multiplied in, the colonies. The whole propert
of those vast regions was considered as vested in the crown of Spain; and ever
law or regulation, whether of a local or general nature, affecting their government
emanated from the council of the Indies, in which it was supposed the king wa
always present. We cannot stop to describe the sort of regulations to which the
colonists were subjected with any degree of minuteness; but we may notice a few
of them, to furnish the means of judging of their general spirit and probable effect
It was, for example, made a *capital* offence to carry on any intercourse witl
foreigners; and the inhabitants of the different colonies were even forbidden an
intercourse with each other, unless under the strictest and most vexatious regu
lations. There were several articles, such as flax, hemp, and wine, which the
were not permitted to cultivate; at the same time that the crown reserved tc
itself the monopoly of salt, tobacco, gunpowder, and some other less importan
articles. The alcavala, and other oppressive imposts, which had proved destruc
tive of industry in Old Spain, were rigorously levied as well on the exports as o
the imports of the colonies. No situation of power or emolument could be fille
except by a native of Old Spain. The Catholic religion was established, to th
exclusion of every other; and bishops, tithes, and the inquisition, followed in it
train: while, in order still better to consolidate and strengthen the foundations o
this monstrous despotism, the government endeavoured to make the colonist
insensible of their degradation, by proscribing every species of instruction, an
watchfully opposing the introduction and progress of all useful knowledge!

Under such circumstances, we cannot be surprised that the continenta
colonists, among whom the monopoly system was maintained in its greates
purity, should have languished for above two centuries in a state of sluggish in
activity. Though surrounded by all the means of producing wealth, they wer
not generally wealthy. Oppression rendered them indolent; and went far t
deprive them not only of the power, but also of the wish, to emerge from povert
The progress of the colonists, who occupied the West India islands, was nc
quite so slow. It is certain, however, that down to the middle of last centur
Spain reaped no greater advantage from the possession of Cuba, Hispaniola, an
Porto Rico, than England or France from the smallest of its dependencies. I
proof of this we may mention, that the noble island of Cuba, which could withou
difficulty supply all Europe with sugar, did not, in 1750, produce a sufficie
quantity even for the consumption of Old Spain. But the combined influence
an arbitrary and intolerant government, and of a degrading superstition, could n
balance the means of improvement, which the fertility of the soil, and the con
mand thence arising over most of the necessaries and many of the convenienc
of life, gave to the colonists. Owing also to the total incapacity of Old Spain
furnish her Transatlantic provinces with a sufficient supply of the articles she h
forced them to import from Europe, and the consequent extension of the co
traband trade carried on with them by the other European nations, she had be
compelled gradually to relax the severity of her commercial monopoly. A ne
impulse was thus given to the spirit of industry. The colonists began to be mo
sensible of the natural advantages of their situation, and less inclined to subn
to the blind and bigoted policy of the Spanish court. In 1781, a rebellion bro
out in Peru, in consequence of an attempt made by the government to establi

v monopoly in that province, which threatened to end in the total dissolution
e connection between Spain and South America, and was not quelled with-
great difficulty and much bloodshed. But the spirit of liberty, when once
ed, could not be suppressed. It continued to gain ground progressively,
the commencement of the late contest between France and Spain inter-
d the communication with the mother country, and gave the colonists an
rtunity of proclaiming that independence which, after a lengthened and
ly struggle, they happily succeeded in achieving.

.) *British Colonies.* — The English, who, like all the other nations of Europe,
een impressed with mingled feelings of admiration and envy by the extent
importance of the acquisitions made by the Spaniards in the New World,
ily entered with enthusiasm and ardour into the career of discovery. Owing,
ver, to the bull which Ferdinand and Isabella had obtained from the Pope,
eying to them the ample donation of all the countries inhabited by infidels
he Spaniards had discovered, or might discover, the English, to avoid en-
hing on the dominions of their rivals, directed their efforts further to the
.. Several attempts to found colonies on the coast of America were made
e reign of Elizabeth by Sir Humphrey Gilbert, Sir Richard Grenville, Sir
er Raleigh, and others. But in consequence of their ignorance of the
try, the deficiency of their supplies of provisions, the loss of time in fruitless
hes after gold, and the various difficulties incident to the first settlement of
ony, none of these attempts proved successful : and it was not until 1607,
a small body of adventurers founded the first permanent establishment of
nglish in America, at James Town in Virginia. Letters patent were granted
09, by King James, to the principal persons resident in London, by whom
xpense attending the formation of the colony was to be defrayed, incorpo-
 them into a company, and establishing a council in England for the direction
ir proceedings, the members of which were to be chosen by, and removeable
 pleasure of, the majority of the partners of the company; permitting what-
was necessary for the support and sustenance of the colony for the first
years to be exported free of duty; declaring that the colonists and their
ndants were to be secured in all the rights and privileges of Englishmen, the
 as if they had remained at home, or been born in England; and reserving
as the stipulated price of these concessions, and in imitation of the policy of
aniards, *one fifth* part of the gold and silver ore to be found in the colonies,
was to be paid to his Majesty and his successors in all time to come. In
of these powers, the company issued, in 1621, a charter or ordinance,
gave a legal and permanent form to the constitution of the colony. By
harter the supreme legislative authority was lodged, partly in the governor,
eld the place of the sovereign, partly in a council of state named by the
any, and partly in a general council, or assembly composed of the represent-
of the people, in which were vested powers and privileges similar to those
House of Commons. It was not long, however, before the king and the
ny quarrelled. The latter were in consequence divested of all their rights,
by open violence, and partly under colour of law, without compensation,
having expended upwards of 150,000*l.* in founding the colony; and a
or and council of state appointed by the king succeeded to the powers of
appointed by the committee. — (*Robertson's History of America*, book 9th,
; *Jefferson's Notes on Virginia*, p. 179.)

 founders of the colony in Virginia had been actuated solely by the hopes
: but the colonies that were soon after established in New England, were
planted by men who fled from religious and political persecution. The
f government in the New England colonies, though at first modified a good
y the peculiar religious opinions entertained by the colonists, was in its
 principles essentially free. For a considerable period, the colonists
 their own governors, coined money, and exercised most of the rights of
ignty; while the English, wholly engrossed with the contest between free-
nd prerogative at home, had no leisure to attend to their proceedings.
quently to the Restoration, however, the governments of most of the New
d states were established nearly on the same footing as that of Virginia;
indeed, became the favourite model, not only for the constitution of the
s established on the Continent, with the exception of the proprietary

governments of Pennsylvania and Maryland, but also for those that were es
blished in the West India islands.   But under every vicissitude of governm
and fortune, the New England colonists were distinguished by the same ard
and enthusiastic love of liberty that had first induced them to quit their nat
land.   Every thing relating to the internal regulation and administration of
different colonies was determined, in the colonial assemblies, by representati
freely chosen by the settlers. The personal liberty of the citizens was well secu
and vigilantly protected.   And if we except the restraints on their commer
the monopoly of which was jealously guarded by the mother country, the in
bitants of Virginia, Pennsylvania, and New England, enjoyed nearly the sa
degree of freedom, when colonists of England, that they now enjoy as citizens
the powerful republic of North America. Their progress in wealth and populati
was in consequence quite unprecedented in the history of the world.   The wh
population of the colonies had increased in 1776, at the commencement of t
revolutionary war, to above 2,000,000, and the value of the exports fr
Great Britain to them amounted to about 1,300,000*l.* a year !

It is not difficult to discover the causes of the unexampled prosperity and ra
growth of our North American colonies, and generally of all colonies plac
under similar circumstances.   The North American colonists carried with th
a knowledge of the arts and sciences practised by a civilised and polished peop
They had been trained from their infancy to habits of industry and subordinati
They were practically acquainted with the best and wisest form of civil pol
that had been established in Europe; and they were placed in a situation t
enabled them, without difficulty, to remedy its defects, and to try every instituti
by the test of utility.   But the thinness of the aboriginal population, and t
consequent facility of obtaining inexhaustible supplies of fertile and unoccupi
land, must certainly be placed at the head of all the causes which have promot
the rapid increase of wealth and population in the United States, and in all t
other colonies, both of North and South America.   On the first foundation o
colony, and for long after, each colonist gets an ample supply of land of the *b
quality;* and having no rent, and scarcely any taxes, to pay, his industry nec
sarily becomes exceedingly productive, and he has every means, and every moti
to amass capital.   In consequence, he is eager to collect labourers from
quarters, and is both willing and able to reward them with high wages. But th
high wages afford the means of accumulation, and, joined to the plenty and che
ness of the land, speedily change the more industrious labourers into propriet
and enable them, in their turn, to become the employers of fresh labourers ;
that every class participates in the general improvement, and capital and popu
tion advance with a rapidity hardly conceivable in old settled and fully peop
countries.

It has been frequently said, that the establishment of our American and W
India colonies was a device of the supporters of the exclusive or mercan
system — that they founded them in the view of raising up a vast agricultu
population, whose commerce should be confined entirely to an exchange of th
raw products for our manufactured goods.   There is, however, no truth in th
assertions.   On the contrary, the charters granted to the founders of the set
ment in Virginia distinctly *empower the colonists to carry on a direct interco
with foreign states.*   Nor were they slow to avail themselves of this permissi
for they had, so early as 1620, established tobacco warehouses in Middlebu
and Flushing — (*Robertson's America,* book 9th, p. 104.); and the subsequent p
ceedings of the British government, depriving them of this freedom of comme
were the chief cause of those disputes, which broke out, in 1676, in an o
rebellion of ominous and threatening import. — (*Robertson's America,* p. 1
It was not until the colonists had surmounted the difficulties and hardsl
incident to their first establishment, and had begun to increase rapidly in wea
that their commerce became an object of importance, and that regulations w
framed in the view of restricting its freedom, and of rendering it peculiarly adv
tageous to the mother country.   The act of 1650, passed by the republi
parliament, laid the first foundations of the monopoly system, by confining
import and export trade of the colonies exclusively to British or colony b
ships.   But the famous Navigation Act of 1660 (12 Charles 2. c. 18.) w
much farther.   It enacted, that certain specified articles, the produce of

onies, and since well known in commerce by the name of *enumerated* articles, ould not be exported directly from the colonies to any foreign country; but it they should first be sent to Britain, and there unladen (the words of the act , *laid upon the shore*), before they could be forwarded to their final destination. gar, molasses, ginger, fustic, tobacco, cotton, and indigo, were originally enu- rated; and the list was subsequently enlarged by the addition of coffee, hides d skins, iron, corn, lumber, &c. In 1739, the monopoly system was so far axed, that sugars were permitted to be carried directly from the British plant- ons to any port or place southward of Cape Finisterre; but the conditions ler which this indulgence was granted, continued so strict and numerous down 1803, when they were a good deal simplified, as to render it in a great degree gatory—(*Edwards's West Indies*, vol. ii. p. 452. ed. 1819.); and with this excep- n, the oppressive and vexatious restrictions on their direct exportation to eign countries were maintained on most of the other *enumerated* commodities ány importance, down to the recent alterations.

But besides compelling the colonists to *sell* their produce exclusively in the glish markets, it was next thought advisable to oblige them to *buy* such foreign cles as they might stand in need of entirely from the merchants and manu- urers of England. For this purpose it was enacted in 1663, that " no com- dity of the growth, production, or manufacture of Europe, shall be imported the British plantations, but such as are laden and put on board in England, les, or Berwick-upon-Tweed, and in English built shipping, whereof the ter and three fourths of the crew are English." The preamble to this statute, ch effectually excluded the colonists from every market for European pro- e, except that of England, assigns the motive for this restriction to be, " the ntaining a greater correspondence and kindness between the subjects at home those in the plantations; keeping the colonies in a firmer dependence on the her country; making them yet more beneficial to it, in the farther employment increase of English shipping, and the vent of English manufactures and com- lities; rendering the navigation to and from them more safe and cheap; and ing this kingdom a staple, not only of the commodities of the plantations, but of the commodities of other countries and places for their supply; it being usage of other nations to keep their plantation trade exclusively to them- es."

t was also a leading principle in the system of colonial policy, adopted as well England as by the other European nations, to discourage all attempts to manu- ure such articles in the colonies as could be provided for them by the mother ntry. The history of our colonial system is full of efforts of this sort; so essential was this principle deemed to the idea of a colony, that Lord tham did not hesitate to declare, in his place in parliament, that " the British nists of North America had *no* RIGHT *to manufacture even a nail for a horse- !* " — (*Edwards's West Indies*, vol. ii. p. 566.) And when such were the tments made by the legislature, and such the avowed sentiments of a great amentary leader and a friend to the colonies, we need not be surprised at a aration of the late Lord Sheffield, who did no more, indeed, than express the ion of almost all the merchants and politicians of his time, when he affirmed " THE ONLY *use of American colonies or West India islands is* THE MONOPOLY eir consumption, and the carriage of their produce !*"

II. INFLUENCE OF THE MONOPOLY OF THE COLONY TRADE.

is not necessary to enter into any lengthened disquisitions with respect to this part of subject. The rules by which we are to form our judgment upon it, are unfolded in rticle COMMERCE. Here it is sufficient to observe, in the first place, that, though it d be shown that restrictions on the colony trade were really advantageous to the er country, that is not enough to prove that they should be adopted. In dealing with ony, we are not dealing with a foreign country, but with an integral part of our own re. And hence, in order to show that restrictions on the colony trade are advan- us, it must not merely be shown that they are beneficial to the mother country, t must further be shown that they are beneficial, or, at all events, not injurious, to olony. The advantage of one part of the empire is not to be purchased by the ssion of some other part. The duty of government is to promote the prosperity, maintain the equal rights and privileges of all; not to enrich one class, or one nce, at the expense of others.

This principle is decisive of the whole question. Owing to the identity of language manners, and religion, the merchants of the mother country must always have ver great advantages in the colony markets: and if the commodities which they have t sell be about as suitable for them, and as low priced, as those of others, none else will b imported into them; but if they be not, it would plainly be to the injury of the colon to compel her to buy from the mother country what she might procure cheaper fron others. It will immediately be seen that such forced sale could be of no real advantag to the mother country; but whether that were so or not, its mischievous influence upo the colony is manifest. Were Jamaica, for example, obliged to import any article from England which cost her 100,000*l.* a year more than she could procure a similar articl for elsewhere, she manifestly loses this amount; and though it were true that ever shilling of this sum found its way as *extra profit* into the pockets of the merchants o manufacturers of England, that would be no sufficient justification of the policy o such a system. The protection due by a government to its subjects does not depen on the varying degrees of latitude and longitude under which they happen to live. I would not be more glaringly unjust to lay peculiar burdens on the Lothians for the sak of Middlesex, than it is to lay them on Jamaica for the sake of England.

In point of fact, however, the monopoly of the colony trade is of no real use, bu the reverse, to the mother country. If, as has been already observed, she can suppl her colonists with goods as cheaply as they can be supplied by others, she will have n competitors in their markets; and if she cannot do this, the monopoly is really hostil to her interests. Each country has some natural or acquired capabilities that enabl her to carry on certain branches of industry more advantageously than any one else But the fact of a country being liable to be undersold in the markets of her colonie shows conclusively, that instead, of having any superiority, she labours under a disad vantage, as compared with others, in the production of the peculiar articles in deman in them. And hence, in providing a forced market in the colonies for articles that w should not otherwise be able to dispose of, we really engage a portion of the capita and labour of the country in a less advantageous channel than that into which it woul naturally have flowed. We impress upon it an artificial direction; and withdraw it fron those secure and really beneficial businesses in which it would have been employed, t engage it in businesses the existence of which depends only on the continuance of op pressive regulations, and in which we are surpassed by foreigners.

Even were it conceded that the possession of an outlet in the colonies for goods tha could not otherwise be disposed of, was an advantage, it is one that can exist in theor only. Practically it can never be realised. The interests of the colonists, and th dexterity and devices of the smuggler, are too much for Custom-house regulation Cheap goods never fail of making their way through every obstacle. All the tyrannic laws and *guarda costas* of Old Spain did not hinder her colonies from being glutte with prohibited commodities. And we may be assured that the moment a competito appears in the field capable of supplying the Canadians and people of Jamaica wi cottons, woollens, hardware, &c. cheaper than we can supply them, that moment wi they cease to be our customers. All the revenue officers, and all the ships of Eng land, supposing them to be employed for that purpose, would be unable to avert th result.

The consequences of the American war ought to have led to sounder opinions tha those that are still current as to the value of the monopoly of the colony trade. Ha the independence of the United States been in any respect injurious to us? So fa from this, it is certain that it has redounded materially to our advantage. We hav been relieved from the expense and trouble of governing extensive countries at a gre distance from our shores, at the same time that we have continued to reap all the ad vantage that we previously reaped from our intercourse with them. It is visionary t imagine that we could either have succeeded in preventing them from establishir manufactories at home, or in importing products from abroad, had any one been ab to undersell us. Our command of the American market depends, at this moment, c the very same principle — the comparative cheapness of our goods — on which it d pended when we had a governor in every state. So long as we preserve this advantag we preserve the only means by which the monopoly of any distant market can b maintained, and the only means by which such monopoly is rendered of the lea advantage.

But it is not to be supposed that, because restrictions on the trade of colonies can of no real advantage to their mother countries, they are not often very injurious to the and to the colonies. We could not, however anxious, exclude manufactured articl and such foreign goods as are valuable without being very bulky, from our West Ind islands, provided they were offered cheaper by others. But such is not the case w lumber, provisions, &c. They are too bulky to be easily smuggled; and may be, a

d are, very much raised in price by restrictions on their importation. For many
past, all direct intercourse between our West India colonies and the United States
een interdicted; and, in consequence, the planters have been compelled either to
y themselves with lumber, staves, &c. by a distant voyage from Canada, or, which
een by far the most common practice, from the United States, through the cir-
us and expensive channel of St. Thomas and other neutral islands! In papers
by the West India merchants and planters before the House of Commons
120. Session 1831.), they estimate the increased expense they thus incur on
er, staves, flour, shingles, fish, &c, at 15 per cent. of the entire value of these ar-
, or at 187,576l. a year. And it will be observed, that no part of this sum goes into
ckets of any British merchant. It goes wholly to indemnify the Americans and
s for being obliged to bring their products round about by St. Thomas, instead of
: from the States.

is system grew out of the American war; but it is due to Mr. Pitt to state that
eived no countenance from him. On the contrary, he introduced a bill, in 1785,
viving the beneficial intercourse that existed previously to the war, between the
d States and the West India islands. But being opposed by a powerful party in
ment, and by the ship owners and Canada merchants, he was obliged reluctantly
hdraw the bill. The following remarks of Mr. Bryan Edwards on this subject
s applicable at this moment, as they were at the period (1794) when they were
n.

his," says he, "is not a business of selfishness or faction; nor (like many of
questions which are daily moved in parliament merely to agitate and perplex
iment) can it be dismissed by a vote. It will come forward again and again, and
administration in a thousand hideous shapes, until a more liberal policy shall take
; for no folly can possibly exceed the notion that any measures pursued by Great
n will prevent the American states from having, some time or other, *a commercial
urse with our West Indian territories on their own terms.* With a chain of coast
enty degrees of latitude, possessing the finest harbours for the purpose in the
, all lying so near the sugar colonies and the track to Europe, with a country
ding in every thing the islands have occasion for, and which they can obtain no-
else; all these circumstances necessarily and naturally lead to a commercial
urse between our islands and the United States. It is true we may ruin our
colonies, and ourselves also, in the attempt to prevent it; but it is an experiment
God and nature have marked out as impossible to succeed. *The present restrain-
tem is forbidding men to help each other; men who, by their necessities, their climate,
eir productions, are standing in perpetual need of mutual assistance, and able to
it.*" — (*Hist. West Indies,* Preface to 2d ed.)

have also thought fit to interdict the West Indians from the refining, or, as it is
cally termed, the *claying* of sugars. This is one one of the few manufactures that
be advantageously set up in the islands. The process adds considerably to the value
ar; and it might be carried on in the buildings, and by the hands, that are required
the cane, or to prepare the raw or muscovado sugar. Instead, however, of being
d to refine their sugars on the spot, and where it might be done for a third of the
e that is required in England, the planters have been prohibited from engaging
branch of industry; and have been obliged to export all their sugars either raw
shed to England. Nothing can exceed the oppressiveness of such a regulation;
hat is most singular, it has not been enforced, like most regulations of the sort, in
o bolster up any of the leading interests of the country, but merely to give a
us employment to a very small class, that of the sugar refiners, whose natural
ce is in the West Indies. The planters and merchants estimate the loss caused
preposterous regulation at 75,550l. a year.

distillation of spirits from sugar has only been occasionally allowed; but, pro-
the duties were so adjusted as to give no advantage to the planters over the
s of barley, or to the latter over the former, we think the distillers should be, at
es, allowed to distil indiscriminately from sugar, molasses, or grain. It is the
f government to take care that the duties be so arranged as to give no unfair
ge to any party over another; but having done this, it should do nothing more.
hibit distillation from sugar, that a forced market may be opened for grain, or
tion from grain, that a forced market may be opened for sugar, are interferences
e freedom of industry, for which no good reason has been, nor we believe can
gned.

interests of the planters have been sacrificed in many other ways besides those
inted out, in the view of securing some illusory advantage to our merchants and
rners. Perseverance in this line of policy will be the less excusable, as it is in
pposition to the *principle* of the measures introduced by Mr. Robinson (now

Lord Goderich) in 1822, and Mr. Huskisson in 1825; and sanctioned by the le[g]lature. The avowed object of these measures was the subversion of the old colo[ny] system, and the repeal of the vexatious restrictions laid on the trade of the coloni[es] "If we look," said Mr. Robinson, "to the dominions of England in the East[ern] hemisphere, we shall find the restrictive system has been entirely and systematica[lly] abandoned. The whole of the East India Company's territories have never b[een] shackled with the peculiar restrictions of the navigation laws; and who will say t[hat] the interests of commerce and navigation have suffered? or rather, *who will deny [that] they have been materially benefited by the freedom they have enjoyed ?*"—"I propose," s[aid] Mr. Huskisson, in 1825, "to admit a free intercourse between all our colonies a[nd] other countries, either in British ships, or in the ships of those countries, allowing [the] latter to import all articles, the growth, produce, or manufacture of the country to which the ship belongs; and to export from such colonies all articles whatever of th[eir] growth, produce, or manufacture, either to the country from[ ]which such ship came, [or] to any other part of the world; the United Kingdom and all its dependencies o[nly] excepted."

Unluckily, however, the conditions and regulations introduced into the bills we[re] for the most part, in direct contradiction to the principle laid down in the speeches [now] quoted; nor is it easy, indeed, to conceive for what purpose the latter were made, unl[ess] it were to exhibit the impolicy of the former. Among others which will subsequently [be] specified, the act of 1825 imposed the following duties for the express purpose [of se-] curing to Canada and to British ships the supply of the West India islands with f[ood] and lumber.

Table of Duties imposed by 6 Geo. 4. c. 114. on certain Articles of Provision, and[on] Wood and Lumber, not being the Growth, Production, or Manufacture of the Uni[ted] Kingdom, nor of any British Possession, imported or brought into the Bri[tish] Possessions on the Continent of South America, or in the West Indies, the Baha[ma] and Bermuda Islands included.

Provisions, viz.	£	s.	d.		£	s.
Wheat, the bushel -	0	1	0	Shingles, being more than 12		
Wheat Flour, the barrel -	0	5	0	inches in length, the 1,000 -	0	14
Bread or Biscuit, the cwt. -	0	1	6	Staves and Headings, viz.		
Flour or Meal, not of Wheat,				Red Oak, the 1,000 - -	0	15
the barrel - - -	0	2	6	White Oak, the 1,000 -	0	12
Peas, Beans, Rye, Calavances,				Wood Hoops, the 1,000 -	0	5
Oats, Barley, Indian Corn,				White, Yellow, and Pitch Pine		
the bushel - - -	0	0	7	Lumber, the 1,000 feet of 1		
Rice, the 1,000 lbs. nett weight	0	2	6	inch thick - - -	1	1
Live Stock, 10 per cent.				Other Wood and Lumber, the		
Lumber, viz.				1,000 feet of 1 inch thick -	1	8
Shingles, not being more than				Fish, Beef, Pork, prohibited.		
12 inches in length, the 1,000	0	7	0			

The revenue derived from these and the other duties imposed by the act of 18[25] amounted to about 75,000*l*. a year, and the charges of collection to about 68,000*l*. !

The effect of these duties in adding to the prices of the food and lumber impo[rted] by the planters, is exhibited in the following statement of the prices of some of [the] principal of these articles in the United States and the Continent, and in Canada and[the] United Kingdom : —

	£	s.
Herrings (Danish) at the Island of St. Thomas, the barrel -	1	0
Ditto (British) in the Colonies, the barrel - - -	1	1[?]
Mess Beef, in Hamburgh, the barrel - - -	3	0
Ditto, in the United Kingdom, ditto - - -	4	0
Pork, in Hamburgh, the barrel - - -	2	6
Ditto, in the United Kingdom, ditto - - -	3	5
Red Oak Staves, in the United States, per 1,000 - -	4	6
Ditto, at Quebec, per ditto - - - -	7	3
White Oak Staves, in the United States, per ditto - -	6	10
Ditto, at Quebec, per ditto - - - -	10	6
Flour, in the United States, the barrel - - -	1	1
Ditto, at Quebec, ditto - - - -	1	4
Shingles, in the United States, per 1,000 - - -	0	14
Ditto, in Canada, per ditto - - - -	0	15

The United States, who felt themselves aggrieved by the imposition of such oppre[ssive] duties on flour, wheat, and lumber, refused to accede to those conditions of recipr[ocity]

ler which the colonial ports were to be opened to their ships ; and, owing to this cir-
nstance, it was not till the end of last year (1830), when fresh negotiations were
ered into with the United States, and it was agreed to modify some of the duties,
t the West India colonies derived any sensible advantage from the changes, such as
y were, that were made in 1825.

But, notwithstanding the modifications introduced by the act 1 Will. 4. c. 24. (see
t), the duties that continue to be charged on some very important articles, when im-
ted from their natural market, the United States, into the West Indies, are very
ressive. We confess, too, that we have not been able to discover any principle by
ich the imposition even of low duties on these articles can be justified. Jamaica and
other West India colonies may be viewed as immense sugar, rum, and coffee
nufactories, which, though situated at a distance from England, belong to En-
hmen, and are carried on by English capital. But to promote the prosperity of
manufacture without injuring that of others, there are no means at once so
ious, and effectual, as to give those engaged in it every facility for supplying
mselves with the materials necessary to carry it on at the lowest price, and to keep
duties on its produce as low as possible. This is the sound and obvious principle
ought to have been kept steadily in view in legislating for the colonies; but which,
regret to say, has been totally lost sight of. That the system of forcing importation
n Canada may be advantageous to that province, we do not presume to deny ; but
are not to impoverish one part of our dominions that we may enrich another,
re especially when it is certain, as in the present case, that the advantage conferred
ery inferior to the injury inflicted. In a general point of view, the operation of the
sent system is equally pernicious. Sugar is an important necessary of life, and
rs largely into the consumption of every individual in Great Britain. Surely, then,
highly important that every means should be resorted to for reducing its cost; and
ve have excluded foreign sugars from our markets, the only way in which any such
ction can be effected is by abolishing the existing restrictions, and allowing the
ters to furnish themselves with the materials necessary for their manufacture at the
est rate, and to dispose of their produce in the state and at the places they prefer.

he vexatious regulations now alluded to, have been, for the most part, imposed
enefit the mother country at the expense of the colonies. There has, however,
a, in this respect, a reciprocity of injuries. Being obliged to buy whatever they
ted in the markets of the mother country, the colonists early succeeded in obtain-
what, indeed, could not, under the circumstances of the case, be denied to them,
monopoly of these markets for the sale of their peculiar productions. And hence
high discriminating duties on foreign sugars, coffee, timber, &c. Owing to the
great fertility of the colonies of Demerara, Berbice, &c. acquired during the late
the exclusion of foreign sugar has not latterly been so great a burden as it used to
hough it still occasions an enhancement of its price. But there are no palliating
umstances about the discriminating duty on foreign timber. Not satisfied with
ig the Canadians an unfair advantage in the markets of the West Indies, we give
a still more unjustifiable advantage in those of England. It was proved in
ence taken before a committee of the House of Lords, that timber from Canada is
nalf so durable as that from the Baltic, and is, besides, peculiarly liable to dry rot.
not allowed to be used in the building of ships for the navy, and is rejected by all
nore respectable house builders : and yet, under the miserable pretext of giving
loyment to saw mills in Canada, and a few thousand tons of additional shipping,
ctually force the use of this worthless article by imposing a discriminating duty of
ss than 45s. a load on all timber from the North of Europe. A regulation more
letely at variance with every principle of sound policy is not to be found in the
mercial legislation of either Turkey or Spain. It has been shown, by papers laid
e parliament, that were the same duty laid on timber from Canada that is laid on
er from the Baltic, the revenue would gain 1,500,000l. a year, while the durability
ur ships and houses would be doubled. (For a farther discussion of this subject,
TIMBER.)

ese restrictions tend to render the colony trade a source of loss, and of irritation and
st to all parties. In other respects, too, their influence is most pernicious. So
as the colonists are prevented from purchasing lumber, provisions, &c. in the
est markets, and as their trade continues subjected to regulations injurious to their
sts, they are justified in resisting all efforts to make them contribute any thing
derable to the expenses of the armaments required for their protection. "At-
ts," said Lord Palmerston, "have been made in all the West India islands to
e them to contribute to the expenses of the establishments; and they have always
sented that *their means of doing so were crippled by the commercial arrangements of*
other country : they have said, ' *If you will let us trade as we like, and collect our*

own custom duties, and so on, we will do it.' " And no proposal could be fairer. — (*Fi nance Committee, Evidence,* p. 146.)

The expense of the colonies is a very heavy item in the national expenditure — fa more so than is generally supposed. Not only are we subjected, as in the case of timber to oppressive discriminating duties on foreign articles, that similar articles from the co lonies may enjoy the monopoly of our markets, but we have to defray a very large sum on account of their military and naval expenditure. There are no means by which t estimate the precise amount of this expense ; but it is, notwithstanding, abundantl certain, that Canada and the islands in the West Indies cost us annually, in militar and naval outlays, upwards of a *million and a half in time of peace, exclusive of the revenue collected in them.* And if to this heavy expense were added the vast additional sum their defence costs during war, the debtor side of a fairly drawn up colonial budge would attain to a very formidable magnitude ; and one which we apprehend could no possibly be balanced.

In entertaining this opinion we are not singular. "If," said Lord Sheffield, " w have not purchased our experience sufficiently dear, let us derive a lesson of wisdom from the misfortunes of other nations, who, like us, pursued the phantom of foreig conquest and distant colonisation ; and who, in the end, found themselves less populous opulent, and powerful. By the war of 1739, which may be truly called an Ame rican contest, we incurred a debt of upwards of 31,000,000*l.* ; by the war of 1755 w incurred a further debt of 71,500,000*l.* ; and by the war of the revolt we have adde to both these debts nearly 100,000,000*l.* more ! And thus we have expended a fa larger sum in defending and retaining our colonies, than the value of all the merchan dise we have ever sent them. So egregious has our impolicy been, in rearing colonist for the sake of their custom !" — (*On the Commerce of the American States,* p. 240.)

But our object is not to excite unavailing regrets for bygone follies, but to induce th return to a better system. The repeal of the restrictions on the colony trade seems in dispensable, as a preliminary to other reforms. We have already seen that the legislatur has recognised the principle of this repeal ; and until it has taken place, or the existin restrictions been materially modified, we shall neither be able to rid ourselves of the dis criminating duties in favour of colonial products, nor to make the colonies defray an considerable part of the expenditure incurred on their account.

If there be no room for surprise at the complaints so constantly put forth by the Wes Indians, there is very great room for surprise that so few attempts should have bee made to redress the grievances of which they complain. Met in every quarter by th keen and active competition of the Brazilians and Cubans, who have been emancipate from the trammels of monopoly, and permitted freely to resort, whether as buyers c sellers, to every market, the planters in the British colonies could not be otherwise tha depressed. They have been made the victims of an erroneous system of policy ; fo there is nothing in the circumstances under which they are naturally placed, to lead t a belief that their distresses are incurable. Were they permitted freely to supply them selves with such articles as they require, to refine their sugar in the islands, and were th exorbitant duties that are now laid on some of their staple products adequately reduced can any one doubt that their condition would be materially improved ? or that thes measures would not equally redound to the general advantage of the public ?

The colonies being integral parts of the empire, the trade with them should, as far a circumstances will permit, be conducted on the footing of a coasting trade. The sta of the revenue requires that moderate duties should be laid on sugar, coffee, and rum when imported into Great Britain or Ireland ; but the duties on cotton, cacao, and mo other colonial products, might be repealed without injury to the revenue, and with a vantage to all parties. The system we have hitherto pursued has been a radicall different one, and in most respects the reverse of what it ought to have been. B excluding the colonists from the cheapest markets for their food and lumber, we ha artificially raised the cost of their produce ; and then, to protect them from the cons quences of such short-sighted policy, we give them a monopoly of the British market ! is thus that one unjust and vicious regulation is sure to give birth to others ; and th those who depart from sound principle have nothing left but to endeavour to bolster u one absurdity by another. It is time, surely, that an end were put to so ruinous a systen It is as much for the interest as it is the *duty* of England, to remove all restrictions fro the colonists not essential for the sake of revenue : for this is the only means by whic she can provide for their real prosperity, and rid herself of those monopolies that for the heaviest clog upon her industry.

It is deeply to be regretted that the difficult questions as to the present and futu treatment of the black population in the West India islands should be so mixed i with questions of colonial policy. Every one, however, must admit the necessity

ing some fixed and certain rules with respect to the slaves. The constant agitation
question of emancipation, and the excitement kept up here and in the islands, has
in the highest degree injurious to the planters, who have been deprived of that
ity so essential to the successful prosecution of all undertakings. Both parties in
contest seem equally to blame;—the planters, for their evident backwardness in
ing plans effectual to secure the better treatment and moral improvement of the
; and the emancipators, for the intemperate zeal they have evinced in urging for-
schemes of premature emancipation. To render the concession of freedom to the
s a blessing and not a curse, they must be prepared by previous training for its en-
ent. Education must be diffused amongst them; and they must be made to know
though they may be emancipated from the control of individual masters, they are
subjected, for their own sakes, in common with the whites, to the authority of the
To prepare those who have been sunk and brutalised by ages of slavery, for per-
ng the part of free citizens, must, under any circumstances, be an exceedingly
ult task; and especially so in the West India islands, where the slaves form so great
ority of the population. Any thing like precipitation, in a matter of such extreme
cy and difficulty, is sure to be ruinous alike to all parties, and cannot be too
ly deprecated. Hence the necessity of adopting some consistent and uniform
n; and, if possible, of putting an end to these intemperate discussions, which serve
o excite animosities that ought to be allayed, to paralyse the efforts of the planters,
o retard the period when emancipation may be safely conceded.

hope it will not be supposed, from any thing now stated, that we consider the
ation of colonial establishments as, generally speaking, inexpedient. We entertain
ch opinion. It is not to the establishment of colonies, provided they are placed in
tageous situations, but to the trammels that have been laid on their industry, and
terference exercised by the mother countries in their domestic concerns, that we
. Every individual ought to have full liberty to leave his native country; and
ons very frequently occur, when governments may advantageously interfere to
emigrants in foreign countries, and when the soundest policy dictates the propriety
ir supporting and protecting them until they are in a situation to support and pro-
emselves. There can be no question whatever that Europe has been prodigiously
ted by the colonisation of America. The colonists carried the arts, the sciences,
nguage, and the religion of the most civilised communities of the Old World, to
s of vast extent and great natural fertility, occupied only by a few miserable
s. The empire of civilisation has in consequence been immeasurably extended:
hile the experience afforded by the rise and progress of communities placed under
ovel circumstances, has served to elucidate and establish many most important and
nental principles in government and legislation, Europe has been enriched by the
riety of new products America has afforded to stimulate the inventive powers of
, and to reward the patient hand of industry.

whatever may have been the advantages hitherto derived from the colonisation of
ica, they are trifling compared to what they would have been, had the European
left the colonists at liberty to avail themselves of all the advantages of their
on, and avoided encumbering themselves with the government of extensive terri-
3,000 miles distant. Fortunately, however, a new era is, at length, begun — *Novus*
um nascitur ordo! The monopoly of the trade of America is destroyed, and her
ndence achieved. From Canada to Cape Horn, every port is ready to receive
urers from Europe; and a boundless field has, in consequence, been opened for
ception of our surplus population, and for the advantageous employment of
can arts, capital, and skill. The few remains of the old colonial system which
ist, and which are principally to be found in the mercantile policy of this country
ance, cannot be of long duration. Their mischievous operation is no longer
ul; and they will disappear according as the knowledge of sound commercial
les is more generally diffused.

farther information on this subject, we beg to refer our readers to an article on
l Policy, in No. 84. of the Edinburgh Review, to the chapter on *Colonies*, in Sir
Parnell's invaluable work on "Financial Reform," and to the Parliamentary
No. 120. Sess. 1831. This paper, being prepared by a committee of West India
nts and planters, occasionally, perhaps, exaggerates the injury they sustain from
sting regulations; it is, however, a very instructive and valuable document. Some
previous statements are taken from the article in the Edinburgh Review; but
not, on that account, liable to the charge of appropriating the labours of others.

III. MAGNITUDE, POPULATION, TRADE, &c. OF THE BRITISH COLONIES.

vithstanding the loss of the United States, the colonies of Great Britain, ex-
of India, exceed in number, extent, and value, those of every other country.

Previously, indeed, to the breaking out of the late contests, the colonial dominions Spain far exceeded in extent and importance those of any other power. But Cu Porto Rico, and the Philippine Islands, are now all that remain to her. These, inde are very valuable possessions, though inferior to those of England.

(1.) *North American Colonies.* — In North America we possess the provinces of Low and Upper Canada, Nova Scotia, and New Brunswick, with their dependencies. situation and boundaries of these provinces will be more easily learned from the insp tion of the accompanying map, than they could be from any description. The shores Nova Scotia and New Brunswick are washed by the Atlantic Ocean; and the no River St. Lawrence, by its communication with the great American lakes, gives Canada all the benefits of a most extensive inland navigation, and forms a natu outlet for her surplus produce, as well as for the surplus produce of that part of United States which is washed by the lakes. There is every variety in the soil a climate of these regions. In Lower Canada the winter is very severe. The surface the country is covered with snow for nearly half the year. From the beginning December to the middle of April the St. Lawrence is frozen over, and affords a smoo and convenient passage for the sledges by which it then covered. But though seve the climate is far from being unhealthy or disagreeable. The weather is generally cl and bracing; and the labour of artisans, at their out-door employments, is rarely s pended for many days in succession. On the breaking up of the ice in the latter of April, or the beginning of May, the powers of vegetation almost immediately sume their activity, and bring on the fine season with a rapidity that is astonishing t stranger. The highest temperature in Lower Canada varies from 96° to 102° of F renheit; but the purity of the atmosphere abates the oppressive heat that is felt in m countries where the mercury ranges so high; and the weather is, on the whole, decide pleasant. In 1814, it was ascertained that the province of Lower Canada contai about 335,000 inhabitants; at present the number may amount to about 450,000. population is chiefly confined to the banks of the St. Lawrence.

That part of the province of Upper Canada, which stretches from Lake Simcoe a the rivers Trent and Severn, westward to Lake Huron and the St. Clair River, southward to Lake Erie, and part of Lake Ontario, has a soil of extraordinary fertil capable of producing the most luxuriant crops of wheat, and every sort of gra " The climate," says Mr. Bouchette, surveyor-General of Lower Canada, "is particularly salubrious, that epidemic diseases, either among men or cattle, are alm entirely unknown. Its influence on the fertility of the soil is more generally percept than it is in Lower Canada, and is supposed to be congenial to vegetation in a m superior degree. The winters are shorter, and not always marked with such rigou in the latter. The duration of frost is always accompanied with a fine clear sky an dry atmosphere. The spring opens, and the resumption of agricultural labours ta place, from six weeks to two months earlier than in the neighbourhood of Quebec. summer heats rarely prevail to excess, and the autumns are usually very friendly to harvests and favourable for securing all the late crops."—(*Bouchette's Topographical scription of Canada*, p. 595.) The ground on the shores of Lake Ontario and Lake E as far west as the junction of the Thames with the St. Clair Lake, is laid out in townsh and partly settled. But the population is so very thin as not, on an average, to amoun more than *sixteen* persons to a square mile, in settled townships; while the fertility of soil is such, that 120 persons to a square mile would not be a dense population. the north of the River Thames, along the banks of the St. Clair, and the shores of L Huron, round to the River Severn, and thence to the river that joins Lake Nippis and Lake Huron, is a boundless extent of country that is entirely unoccupied. interior of this space has hitherto been but imperfectly explored; but the banks of St. Clair and the shores of Lake Huron afford the finest situations for settleme The soil is in many places of the greatest fertility, the river and lake teem with and every variety of the best timber is found in the greatest profusion. In 1783, settlers in Upper Canada were estimated at only 10,000: in 1825 they amounte upwards of 157,000; and now amount to about 190,000: a miserably small popula for a country that could easily support *many millions* of inhabitants, in a state of greatest comfort.

The winters in the provinces of Nova Scotia and New Brunswick are more se than in Upper Canada, and they are a good deal infested with fogs and mists. their proximity to England, and their favourable situation for the fishing business, them considerable advantages.

In addition to the above, we possess the Hudson's Bay territory — a tract of extent, but situated in an inhospitable climate, and worth very little except as hur grounds. We also possess the large islands of Newfoundland and Cape Breton; the soil is barren. and the climate severe and foggy; so that they are valuable p pally as fishing stations.

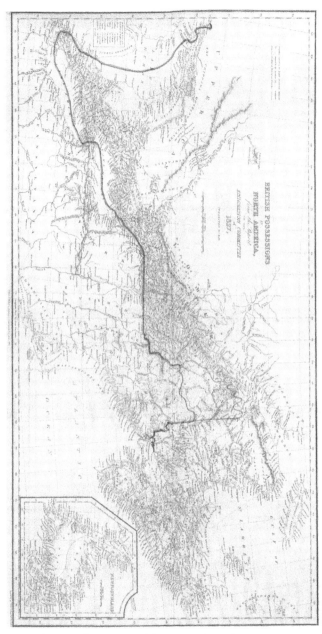

e entire population of the British North America colonies may be estimated, at noment, at about 1,000,000.

formation for Emigrants to Upper Canada, &c. — As Upper Canada is, and no will continue to be, one of the principal places selected by emigrants from this ry, the following authentic information with respect to it, circulated by the Canada any and others, may not be unacceptable : —

rsons desirous of obtaining employment, and having the means of emigrating to Upper Canada, et work at high prices compared with what they have been accustomed to receive in this country cultural labourers. The wages given in Upper Canada are from 2l. to 3l. per month, with board and g. At these wages there is a constant demand for labour in the neighbourhood of York, in Upper a; and there is no doubt that a very great number, beyond those now there, would find employment. ng artisans, particularly blacksmiths, carpenters, bricklayers, masons, coopers, millwrights, and wrights, get high wages, and are much wanted. Industrious men may look forward with confidence mprovement in their situation, as they may save enough out of one season's work to buy land them-in settled townships.

eehold land, of excellent quality, is to be sold at 10s. per acre, payable as follows : — 2s. per acre at the time of making choice of the land in Canada, and the remainder in small annual payments, nterest, which an industrious settler would be able to pay out of the crops.

pper Canada is a British province within a few weeks' sail of this country. The climate is good ; fruits and vegetables common to the English kitchen-garden thrive well ; sugar, for domestic pur-is made from the maple-tree on the land. The soil and country possess every requisite for farming es, and comfortable settlement, which is proved by the experience of the numerous industrious nts now settled there. The samples of Upper Canada wheat have not been exceeded in quality by the British market during the past year. The population of the province, which is rapidly increas-nsists almost exclusively of persons from Great Britain, who have gone there to settle. The taxes y trifling, and there are no tithes. The expense of clearing the land ready for seed is about 4l. per paid for in money ; but if done by the purchasers themselves, they must employ part of their wages, or possess some means of their own. The expense of removing from this country to York, of the principal towns in the Upper Province, adjoining the lands of the Canada Company, is, at nost, as follows, and is frequently done for much less : — Grown persons, men or women, 6l. each for sage, and half-price for children, without provisions for their maintenance during the voyage, with they must furnish themselves ; or, if parties prefer to take their passage to Quebec only, (which done for 3l. from England, children 1l. 10s.), provisions about as much more ; and from Ireland otland for considerably less,) on arrival there, they may be forwarded to the Upper Province by the ny's agents, on the following terms : —

e agents of the Canada Company, on the arrival of emigrants at Quebec or Montreal, will, for the season, convey, at the Company's expense, purchasers who pay a first instalment in London, , or Montreal, of 2s. an acre upon not less than one hundred acres, to the head of Lake Ontario, as in the vicinity of their choicest lands ; and their agents in all parts of the Upper Province will ch emigrants every information and assistance in their power. Should emigrants, on arrival, not n the Company's lands, the money paid by them will be returned, deducting the actual expense of ance to York."

Canada Company sold upwards of eighty thousand acres of land in 1829, 1830, and 1831, in lots of extent, at from 10s. to 14s. per acre.

'ollowing is a copy of a letter from an emigrant in Upper Canada to his relations in this country, ing authentic information for the guidance of emigrants, published by the Canada Company : — ter a passage of nearly eight weeks I landed at Quebec, and made a stay there of upwards of a month ; liking the appearance of the country, which is very mountainous and sterile, I refused several land in the townships of Inverness and Leeds, and came to Montreal, one hundred and eighty igher up the River St. Lawrence, by steam-packet. At Montreal I remained another month, deter-o give every part a fair trial, and to form no opinion without good grounds for it. The land here, h better than that at Quebec, was still not what I had been led to expect. I, therefore, again set finally reached York, the capital of Upper Canada, situated on Lake Ontario, about three hun-les from Montreal. It is from this place that I am now writing, and you will understand that the g remarks have reference to this neighbourhood : —

price of land varies from 5s. to 25s. per acre ; but the medium price in the townships in this neigh-od is 15s., equal to 13s. 6d. sterling money : part is payable in cash at the time of purchase, and the der generally in four or five yearly instalments, with interest at six per cent. The expense of g an acre into cultivation — that is, cutting down and burning the timber — is from 2l. 10s. to 3l. 10s. he wood is of the hard kinds, and not unusually thick. After this process, the only thing that to do, is to sow and harrow in the seed, which is generally wheat — one bushel to the acre. The generally from twenty-five to thirty-five bushels per acre, and is worth, at the present price in ., a bushel, equal to 36s. sterling per quarter ; from 5l. to 8l. 15s. per acre. A second crop, equally ay often be taken ; and the land, then sown with grass seed, will produce excellent hay and pas-arley is not much cultivated ; the produce is equal to that of wheat, but it is not worth more than er bushel. Oats are also a good crop, and sell for 1s. 6d. a bushel. And the white peas equal any at I have seen, both in quantity and quality. Vegetables of all kinds are abundant, and bear good potatoes, turnips, carrots, and cabbage in particular, grow to perfection. Horses cost from 20l. to ir. Some of them are very good, but they might be much improved ; and it would be well worth while to bring out a stout, compact English stud with him. Oxen, from their being better adapted work of a new country, are more used than horses, and of course better attended to. They are ned, thrifty beasts, but not equal in size or appearance to the short horns we have been accus-o see in Yorkshire. From 10l. to 15l. a pair is the price for working oxen, according to the size Cows are sold at from 4l. to 6l. each, and young beasts in proportion. Very little trouble or s required in the raising of cattle in this country, as they are left to browse in the woods, where d plenty of food, and thrive remarkably well. Sheep are not yet numerous, the wooded lands not apted for them ; but as the country becomes more cleared they will increase. Some manufactories are already established, and wool is in good demand at 1s. 8d. a pound. The new Leicester nd its crosses, will be the kind required ; and if imported, would soon repay their cost and s.

ow only remains for me to speak with respect to your plan of coming out to this country. I feel t that every sober and industrious man, however poor he may be, on arriving here, will, in the f a few years, find himself in comfort and independence, if not in affluence. I have met with who came from England ten years ago, without a shilling, and who now possess farms with or eighty acres cleared, eight or ten stacks of corn, besides well-filled barns, horses, horned cattle, ogs, and poultry ; every thing that is wanted to render them contented and happy. I have, on the , met with men who, whatever they may have had originally, are beggars now, and ever will be But these are characters whose disgusting intemperance makes them a disgrace to themselves s to their country, and who must be despised and shunned by all sober men. Many inconveniences suffered, many difficulties overcome, both in the voyage from England and in the first settlement

Y

on lands here. But these once over, an establishment once effected, and I have little doubt that, with ――dence and economy, the emigrant will receive a fair return for his toil and privation.

"14th November, 1830.―Since writing the foregoing letter, my time as been occupied in examin―tract of land belonging to the Canada Company, and which I find to be one in every way likely to ar―my views. It contains 1,200 acres, being composed of six ordinary sized lots, and is situated in the ac―ing township of Vaughan, within twenty miles from this place. The River Humber, a fine clear str―passes through the centre, and offers the advantage of water-power for mills or machinery of any ――On its banks are extensive flats, of the richest alluvial soil; and, beyond these, the land rises to an elev―of 60 or 80 feet, in part covered with hard wood, and in part with very fine pine. The soil of this―vation being dry, it affords excellent building sites, and the situation appears to be very healthy.―settlements are within a short distance on all sides, and very little road-cutting will be required. Aft―favourable a description of this spot, you will be anxious to know the terms on which it may be sec―The price is what I stated as the average price of land in this neighbourhood, 15s., or 13s. 6d. sterlin―acre. One fifth of the money only is required to be paid down; the remainder is divided into five p―and one of these parts made payable yearly. These terms are sufficiently reasonable; and I should――concluded a bargain immediately, because it would be a great advantage to begin upon land at this sea―and have houses built, and a part ready for crop, by the spring. But, as you know, I am yet uncer―whether you, and my other relations, are to join me, and my property is still in England, and will rec―some time before it can be converted into money. These circumstances induced me to decline the―chase for the present; but I am still in hopes of securing it after hearing from you. It would be――desirable for us, if we all determine on coming to this country, to be settled together, and enable―render each other assistance in the heavy works of clearing and building.

"On reaching Quebec, you should proceed immediately, by steam-packet, to Montreal; from then―Prescott, you will travel partly by land, and partly by boats on the River St. Lawrence: but, in all c―prefer the fastest mode of conveyance, notwithstanding the increased expense. From Prescott, a ste―packet will bring you direct to York, where you will hear of me. My expenses from Montreal to――place, with my daughter, amounted to 4l. 10s., but I have since learned that I could have come up for――half that sum. The Canada Company have contracted with the proprietors of the packets and r―boats to have their settlers forwarded at very low rates; and any person is allowed the advantage of―arrangement, on depositing with the agent, at Quebec, a sum sufficient to cover the expenses incurre―the Company. Besides the saving of expense, the passengers, by this means, are secured from all ris―being imposed upon along the route.

"I annex a more particular statement of the present prices of farm produce in this town, and also o―common rate of wages for journeymen of different trades.

　　November, 1830.　　　　　　　　　　　　　　　　(Signed) &c.

" Market Prices.

Wheat, per bushel, 4s. 8d. to 5s., or 37s. 6d. to 40s. per qr.				Tallow, per lb., 4¼d. rough.		
Barley	—	3s. 2d.	—	25s. 4d.	—	Lard — 5d.
Rye	—	3s. 3d.	—	26s.	—	Butter — 9d. Fresh, 7¼d. Salt.
Oats	—	1s. 6d.	—	12s.	—	Cheese — 5d.
IndianCorn—		3s. 9d.	—	30s.	—	Eggs, per dozen, 6d.
Peas	—	3s. 2d.	—	25s. 4d.	—	Geese, per couple, 3s. 9d.
Flour, 25s. per barrel of 196 lbs.						Ducks, per couple, 1s. 10d.
Beef, per lb., 3d., or by the quarter 22s. 6d. per 100 lbs.						Fowls — 1s. 3d.
Mutton — 3¼d.						Turkeys — 3s. 2d.
Pork — 3d., or 25s. per 100 lbs.						Hay, per ton, 2l. 10s.

" Wages. Board not found. — Stone-masons earn from 6s. 3d. to 7s. 6d. a day, or 6s. 3d. to 7s. 6d. per――of work. — Bricklayers, 7s. 6d. to 8s. 9d. a day, or 12s. 6d. to 15s. per 1,000 bricks laid. — Brickma―5s. to 7s. 6d. a day. — Plasterers, 7s. 6d. a day, or 9d. to 10d. per square yard of work. — Carpenters――Joiners, 6s. 3d. a day. — Cabinet-makers, 7s. 6d. a day. — Sawyers, 7s. 6d. a day, or 7s. 6d. per 100 fe―pine, and 8s. 9d. oak. — Painters and Glaziers, 5s. a day. — Coopers, 6s. 3d. to 7s. 6d. a day. — Shipwri―7s. 6d. to 10s. a day. — Blacksmiths, 5s. a day. — Wheelwrights, 5s. a day. — Wagon-makers, 5s. a da―Saddlers, 5s. a day. — Curriers, 5s. a day. — Tailors, 1l. for making a coat, 5s. trowsers, and 5s. waistco―Shoemakers, 22s. 6d. for making a pair of top-boots; 13s. 9d. for a pair of Hessian boots; and 12―Wellington boots. — Labourers and Farm Servants, 3s. 9d. a day; in harvest time, 6s. 3d. — Reapi―acre of wheat, 12s. 6d. — Cradling do. 6s. 3d. — Mowing an acre of hay, 5s. — Ploughing an acre of land, 6―— Harrowing do. 2s. 6d."

We have extracted the previous statement from a valuable pamphlet on Emigra――to Upper Canada, by John William Banister, Esq., London, 1831.

(2.) *West India Colonies.* — In the West Indies we possess Jamaica, Barbadoes, St. Lu――Antigua, Grenada, Trinidad, and some other islands, exclusive of Demerara and ――bice in South America. Jamaica, by far the largest and most valuable of our ins―possessions, is about 120 miles in length and 40 in mean breadth, containing a―2,800,000 acres, of which from 1,100,000 to 1,200,000 are supposed to be in cultiva―Being situated within the tropic of Cancer, the heat in the West Indies is intense,―is moderated by the sea breeze which blows regularly during the greater part of the――The rains make the only distinction of seasons. They sometimes fall with prodig―impetuosity, giving birth to innumerable torrents, and laying all the low country u―water: the trees are green the whole year round: they have no snow, no frost, and――rarely some hail. The climate is very humid; iron rusts and corrodes in a very s―time; and it is this, perhaps, that renders the West Indies so unfriendly to Euro――constitutions, and produces those malignant fevers that are so very fatal. The vege―productions are numerous and valuable; but the sugar cane and the coffee plan―incomparably more important than the others, and constitute the natural riches of―islands.

The West Indies are occasionally assailed by the most dreadful hurricanes, w―destroy in a moment the hopes and labours of the planters, and devastate entire isla―Whole fields of sugar canes are sometimes torn up by the roots, houses are either tha―down or unroofed, and even the heavy copper boilers and stills in the works hav―numerous instances, been wrenched from the ground and battered to pieces. The―pours down in torrents, sweeping before it every thing that comes in its way. The―

ction caused by such dreadful scourges seldom fails to produce a very great scarcity,
not unfrequently famine ; and we are ashamed to have to add, that the severity of
distress has on several occasions been materially aggravated by a refusal on the part
the authorities to allow importation direct from the United States ! * This was the
e at Dominica so late as 1817.

amaica was discovered by Columbus in 1494, and continued in possession of the
niards till 1655, when it was wrested from them by the English. Although it had
s been for more than a century and a half under the power of Spain, such was the
dening influence of her colonial system, that it did not, when we conquered it, con-
1,500 white inhabitants, and these were immersed in sloth and poverty. Of the
ny valuable articles which Jamaica soon after produced in such profusion, many were
n altogether unknown ; and of those that were known, such a supply only was cul-
ted as was required for the consumption of the inhabitants. " The Spanish settlers,"
s said by Mr. Bryan Edwards, " possessed none of the elegances of life ; nor were
y acquainted even with many of those gratifications which, in civilised states, are
sidered necessary to its comfort and convenience. They were neither polished by
al intercourse, nor improved by education ; but passed their days in gloomy languor,
ebled by sloth, and depressed by poverty. They had been for many years in a state
progressive degeneracy, and would probably in a short time have expiated the guilt
eir ancestors, by falling victims themselves to the vengeance of their slaves." — (Hist.
t Indies, vol. i. p. 197. 8vo ed.)

or a considerable number of years after we obtained possession of Jamaica, the
f exports were cacao, hides, and indigo. Even so late as 1772, the exports of sugar
unted to only 11,000 hogsheads. In 1774, they had increased to 78,000 hogs-
ds of sugar, 26,000 puncheons of rum, and 6,547 bags of coffee. The American
was very injurious to the West India settlements ; and they may, indeed, be said to
till suffering from its effects, as the independence of America led to the enactment
hose restrictions on the importation of food, lumber, &c. that have been so very
ful to the planters. In 1780, Jamaica was visited by a most destructive hurricane,
devastation occasioned by which produced a dreadful famine ; and other hurricanes
wed in the immediately succeeding years. But in 1787, a new era of improvement
n. The devastation of St. Domingo by the negro insurrection, which broke out in
2, first diminished, and in a few years almost entirely annihilated, the annual
ly of 115,000 hogsheads of sugar, which France and the Continent had pre-
sly been accustomed to receive from that island. This diminution of supply, by
ing a greatly increased demand for, and a consequent rise in the price of, the sugar
d in the other islands, occasioned an extraordinary extension of cultivation. So
erful in this respect was its influence, that Jamaica, which, at an average of the six
s preceding 1799, had produced only 83,000 hogsheads, exported, in 1801 and
, upwards of 286,000 hogsheads, or 143,000 a year !

he same rise of price, which had operated so powerfully in Jamaica, occasioned a
lar though less rapid extension of cultivation in our other islands, and in Cuba,
o Rico, and the foreign colonies generally. The vacuum caused by the cessation
e supplies from St. Domingo being thus more than filled up, a reaction commenced.
price of sugar rapidly declined ; and notwithstanding a forced market was for a
e opened to it, by substituting it for malt in the distillery, prices did not attain to their
er elevation. On the opening of the continental ports, in 1813 and 1814, they, in-
, rose, for a short time, to an extravagant height ; but they very soon fell again, ining in ruin many of the speculators upon an advance. During the last ten years prices
been uniformly low, and have declined considerably during the last two years. This
f price seems to be entirely owing to the vast extension of the sugar cultivation in
, Brazil, Java, Louisiana, &c., and in Demerara, Berbice, and the Mauritius.
the facility, too, with which sugar may be raised in most of these countries, and
vast extent, there seems little prospect of prices ever again attaining to their old
. It is to no purpose, therefore, to attempt to relieve the distresses of the planters
amaica and our other islands by temporary expedients. The present low prices
not been brought about by accidental or contingent circumstances. And to
le the planters to contend successfully with the active competitors that surround
on all sides, we must place them, at least in so far as we have the means, in a similar
tion, by allowing them to resort for supplies to the cheapest markets, and to send
produce into Europe in such a shape as they may think best.

is stated in a report by a committee of the Assembly of Jamaica, that 15,000 negroes perished be-
the latter end of 1780 and the beginning of 1787, through famine occasioned by hurricanes and the
ition of importation from the United States ! — (Edwards's West Indies, vol. ii. p 515.) Those who
very fond of vituperating " hard hearted economists," as they are pleased to term those who advo-
e repeal of oppressive restrictions, must, we presume, look upon occurrences of this sort as merciful
sations.

The devastation of St. Domingo gave the same powerful stimulus to the growth coffee in the other West India colonies, that it did to the growth of sugar; and owin to the extraordinary increase in the demand for coffee in this and other European cou tries during the last ten years, the impulse has been, in a great measure, kept up. (S COFFEE.) In 1752, the export of coffee from Jamaica amounted to only 60,000 lbs. in 1775, it amounted to 440,000 lbs.; in 1797, it had increased to 7,931,621 lbs.; an last year the exports to England amounted to 19,758,000 lbs.

We have already seen, that when Jamaica was taken from the Spaniards it only con tained 1,500 white inhabitants. In 1673, the population amounted to 7,768 white and 9,504 slaves. It would have been well for the island had the races continued to pre serve this relation to each other; but, unfortunately, the black population has increase more than *five* times as rapidly as the white; the latter having increased only from 7,76 to about 30,000, while the former has increased from 9,504 to 322,421, exclusive persons of colour. It is the immense preponderance of the slave population that rende the question of emancipation so very difficult.

The correspondence of the slaves in Jamaica with their emancipated brethren in Hay or St. Domingo has been prohibited by a provision in the act 6 Geo. 4. c. 114. § 48. – (see *post*).

The real value of the exports to Jamaica amounts to about 2,000,000*l.* a year, bein more than half the amount of the exports to the West India colonies. It shoul however, be observed, that a considerable portion of the articles sent to Jamaica, an some of the other colonies, are only sent there as to an *entrepôt*, being subsequentl exported to the Spanish main. During the ascendancy of the Spanish dominion i Mexico and South America, this trade, which was then contraband, was carried on a very great extent. It is now much fallen off; but the central situation of Jamaic will always secure to her a considerable share of this sort of transit trade.

Barbadoes was the earliest of our possessions in the West Indies. It is the mo easterly of the Caribbee Islands; Bridge Town, the capital, being in long. 58° 35 Barbadoes is by far the best cultivated of all the West India islands. It con tains about 105,000 acres, having a population of about 16,000 whites, 2,700 fre people of colour, and 68,000 slaves. It exports about 21,000 hogsheads of suga of 16 cwt. each. Barbadoes had attained the acmé of its prosperity in the latt part of the seventeenth century, when the white population is said to have amounted about 50,000, though this is probably an exaggeration. But it is only as compared wi itself that it can be considered as having fallen off; for, compared with the other We India islands, its superiority is manifest. It raises nearly as much food as is adequa for its supply.

The islands next in importance are St. Vincent, Grenada, Trinidad, Antigua, & It is unnecessary to enter into any special details with respect to them. Their popul tion and trade being exhibited in the tables annexed to this section.

During the late war, we took from the Dutch the settlements of Demerara, Berbic and Essequibo, in Guiana, which were definitively ceded to us in 1814. The soil these settlements is naturally very rich; and they have, in this respect, a decided a vantage over most of the West India islands. Their advance, since they came into o possession, has been very great. The imports of sugar from them amount to abo *a third* of the imports from Jamaica. The rum of Demerara enjoys a high reput tion; and of the total quantity of rum imported from the British colonies and plan ations in 1830, amounting to 6,751,000 gallons, Demerara and Berbice furnish 2,094,330 gallons. The best samples of Berbice coffee are of very superior qualit but the planters finding the cultivation of sugar more profitable, the imports coffee from Demerara and Berbice have declined of late years. Still, however, t exports during last year amounted to above 6,000,000 lbs. Considerable quantities cotton were formerly exported from Guiana; but the Americans having superior faci ties for its production, the planters have in a great measure ceased to cultivate Cacao, anotto, &c. are produced in considerable abundance.

These statements are sufficient to show the importance of Demerara and Berbic Considering, indeed, their great natural fertility, and the indefinite extent to whi every sort of tropical culture may be carried in them, they certainly form among t most valuable of the colonial possessions we have acquired for many years.

According to the existing regulations, no slaves are allowed to be carried from o British colony to another. And hence, notwithstanding they are in excess in some the islands, it is not permitted to send them to Demerara, where there is the great competition for their services. The policy of this regulation is not very obvious. We it modified, it would have a powerful influence in forwarding the improvement of D merara and Berbice; and would also, we think, forward the period when the slaves the islands might be safely emancipated. Of course, were the export of slaves fr

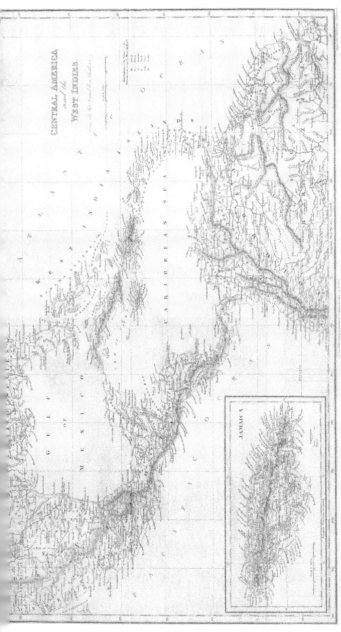

material originally positioned here is too large for reproduction in this
ue. A PDF can be downloaded from the web address given on page iv
is book, by clicking on 'Resources Available'.

islands to the Continent permitted, it would be competent to enact any sort of regu-
.ons that might be deemed necessary to advance their interests.

Exclusive of the above, we possess the settlement of Balize on the Bay of Honduras.
.is is of importance, as affording a means of obtaining abundant supplies of mahogany;
, it is of more importance as an *entrepôt* for the supply of Guatemala with English
nufactured goods.   For accounts of the colonies in Australasia, &c., see COLUMBO,
PE OF GOOD HOPE, PORT LOUIS, SYDNEY, &c.

The following is an account of the quantities of the three great articles of sugar,
'ee, and rum, imported from the British West Indies into the United Kingdom in
year 1830 : —

British Colonies in the West Indies.				Sugar.			Coffee.	Rum.
				Cwts.	qrs.	lbs.	lbs.	Proof Gallons.
ntigua	-	-	-	158,611	1	16	242	155,514
arbadoes	-	-	-	336,881	0	11	334	2,357
ominica	-	-	-	60,063	0	20	1,016,631	36,321
renada	-	-	-	213,160	1	13	28,541	298,933
maica	-	-	-	1,379,347	3	2	19,758,603	3,213,503
ontserrat	-	-	-	20,646	0	17	-	49,075
evis	-	-	-	54,236	1	21	1,362	51,243
. Kitt's	-	-	-	133,452	0	22	44	219,706
. Lucia	-	-	-	86,971	0	10	113,517	12,817
. Vincent	-	-	-	261,551	2	9	124	173,262
obago	-	-	-	93,471	2	4	-	428,810
ortola	-	-	-	17,099	3	7	5	- -
rinidad	-	-	-	204,987	0	10	54,502	12,941
ahamas	-	-	-	-	-	-	195,637	- -
ermudas	-	-	-	894	2	13	-	2,987
emerara	-	-		780,286	2	12	3,447,426	1,859,710
erbice	-	-	-	110,967	2	21	2,816,909	234,618
Total	-	-		3,912,628	2	12	27,428,877	6,751,797

.he duties on West India produce entered for home consumption during the year
, amounted to about 7,500,000*l*.

.he exports from this country to our West Indian colonies consist of coarse cottons,
.s, checks, hats, and other articles of negro clothing ; hardware and earthenware ;
.s, hoops, coal, lime, paint, lead ; Irish provisions, herrings and other salt-fish ; along
.furniture, wine, beer, medicines, and, indeed, almost every article which a great
.ufacturing country can supply to one, situated in a tropical climate, which has very
mechanics, and hardly any manufactures.   Since the depression of West India
.erty, and the opening of the ports on the Spanish main to ships from England, the
.rts to the West Indies have decreased both in quantity and value.   Their declared
.al value amounted, as appears from the following account, in 1829, to 3,612,075*l*.
.e following are the *quantities* of some of the principal articles exported to the West
.n colonies in 1826 : — Cottons, 26,287,447 yards ; linens, 11,655,657 yards ;
.lens, 346,967 yards ; hats, 40,852 dozens ; leather, wrought and unwrought,
.268 lbs. ; earthenware, 1,924,483 pieces ; glass, 523,395 pieces ; hardware and
.ry, 14,396 cwt. ; coals and culm, 32,993 tons ; beef and pork, 12,965 barrels ; soap
.candles, 27,395 cwt., &c. — (*Parl. Paper*, No. 541. Sess. 1827.)
.e articles exported from Canada and the British possessions in North America
.ipally consist of timber and lumber of all sorts ; grain, flour, and biscuit ; furs, dried
.fish-oil, turpentine, &c.   The imports principally consist of woollens, cottons, and
.s ; earthenware, hardware, leather, salt, haberdashery of all sorts, tea, sugar, and
.e, spices, wine, brandy, and rum, furniture, stationery, &c.
.e following are the quantities of some of the principal articles exported from Great
.in to Canada, Nova Scotia, &c. in 1826 : — Cottons, 6,057,417 yards ; woollens,
.16 yards ; linens, 2,232,107 yards ; earthenware, 1,484,912 pieces ; iron and steel,
.ght and unwrought, 6,669 tons ; hardware and cutlery, 15,235 cwt. ; coals and
., 30,723 tons ; salt, 1,095,367 bushels ; beef and pork, 13,203 barrels, &c. — (*Parl.*
., No. 541. Sess. 1827.)
.e are indebted to Mr. Mayer of the Colonial Office for the following tables, the
.complete that have ever been published, of the population and trade of the Ameri-
.nd West Indian colonies.

Y 3

POPULATION OF AMERICAN AND WEST INDIAN COLONIES.

British North American Colonies

British North American Colonies	1806	1825	*1829, or latest Census
	Total. Male and Female	Total. Male and Female	Total. Male and Female
Lower Canada	200,000	423,630	423,630
Upper Canada	70,718	157,541	188,558
New Brunswick	35,000	72,932	72,932
Nova Scotia	65,000	104,000 }	142,548
Cape Breton	2,513	16,000 }	
Prince Edward's Island	9,676	20,000	23,473
Newfoundland	26,505	52,497	60,088
	409,412	846,600	811,229

British West Indian Colonies

British West Indian Colonies	1806 Whites M	Whites F	Free Coloured M	Free Coloured F	Slaves M	Slaves F	Total M&F	1824 Whites M	Whites F	Free Coloured M	Free Coloured F	Slaves M	Slaves F	Total M&F	1829 Whites M	Whites F	Free Coloured M	Free Coloured F	Slaves† M	Slaves† F	Total M&F
Antigua	2,102		2,185		30,282		34,574	1,140	840	1,549	2,346	14,454	16,531	36,860	1,140	840	1,549	2,346	14,066	15,773	35,714
Barbadoes	15,605	*no census*	2,716		68,219		86,540	6,827	7,803	2,258	2,266	36,159	42,657	97,970	7,049	7,910	2,609	2,537	37,691	44,211	102,007
Dominica	921	673	1,263	1,559	11,161	10,922	26,499	487	417	1,406	1,758	7,919	8,635	20,692	435	405	1,604	2,002	7,362	8,030	19,858
Grenada	1,100		813		15,960	16,167	34,044	628	219	1,387	2,104	12,258	13,052	29,648	596	205	1,562	2,924	11,711	12,434	28,732
Jamaica	36,272	*no census*			312,341		348,613	37,152	*no census*			166,595	169,658	373,405	37,152	*no census*			158,254	164,167	359,578
Montserrat	444		402		6,537		7,383	175	213	234	320	3,032	3,473	7,447	157	173	310	504	2,867	3,395	7,496
Nevis	501		603		9,167		10,271	1,140				4,583	4,678	10,401	700		2,000		4,574	4,685	11,959
St. Kitt's	1,610		1,996		19,885		23,491	676	518	1,576	1,996	9,505	10,312	23,425	491	481	3,000		9,198	10,112	23,962
St. Lucia	1,214		1,896		14,967		18,077	1,053			2,083	6,997	7,497	18,647	849	452	1,714	2,004	6,980	7,381	18,351
St. Vincent	1,053		691		24,920		26,664	200	44		1,482	12,007	12,245	26,787	265	57	1,091	1,733	11,583	12,006	27,714
Tobago	583		350		17,347		18,280	207	201	225	360	7,098	7,479	14,485	229	248	477	687	5,872	6,684	14,042
Tortola and Virgin Islands	486		938		7,448		8,872	162	203	283	328	2,975	3,485	7,479	558	203	558	738	2,510	2,889	7,172
Anguilla	-		-		-		3,600	-		150	177	1,279	1,695	3,666	150	177			1,279	1,695	3,666
Trinidad	2,974		7,008		20,761		30,043	2,943	1,853	6,681	7,314	13,052	10,336	41,479	2,308	1,893	7,599	8,357	13,141	10,865	44,163
Bahamas	1,579		1,344		10,093		14,016	2,282	2,278	867	1,332	5,529	5,279	17,567	2,042	2,198	1,396	1,665	4,608	4,660	16,499
Bermudas	4,755		451		4,794		10,000	1,897	2,751	312	410	2,692		10,612	1,564	2,341	308	430	2,308	2,400	9,251
Demerara	2,871		2,980		71,180		77,031	2,609		1,836	1,773	41,924	33,753	80,945	2,100	2,906	2,530	3,880	37,141	32,326	78,833
Berbice	550		240		25,169		25,959	453	108	325	510	13,007	10,349	94,752	1,496	126	463	688	11,284	10,035	23,032
Honduras	225		775		2,595		3,959	156	61	685	737	1,654	811	4,107	174	76	1,422	844	1,329	798	4,643

* When the same numbers are given as in 1825, no later census has been taken.
† The census of the slave population is taken from the last Slave Registry Returns laid before parliament

Imports, Exports (Official Value), and Declared Value

COLONIES.	Imports into the United Kingdom, Official Value. 1806	1825	1829	Exports — British Produce and Manufactures. 1806	1825	1829	Foreign and Colonial Merchandise. 1806	1825	1829	Total Exports. 1806	1825	1829	Exports, Declared Value. 1806	1825	1829
British North American Colonies.	£.	£.	£.	£.	£.	£.	£.	£.	£.	£.	£.	£.	£.	£.	£.
Lower Canada	158160	731855	569451	319632	916058	980176	81868	229405	136915	401301	1145461	1117421		866258	709140
Upper Canada	19568	319559	213812	48666	492051	252224	5189	71995	22698	53855	474044	274922		458604	224393
New Brunswick			61701		927353			1105	22440		928596	277966		234226	243887
Nova Scotia	29720	44548		194714	11014	215596	35881	30560		230595	121119			106622	
Cape Breton		6864		1906	32458		222	6185		1428	38658			38626	
Prince Edward Island		9244													
Newfoundland	178064	290841	243628	211224	270282	306601	77256	46983	67213	288480	317265	373817		351964	339467
Total	353812	1312911	1088622	775642	1859211	1814830	200116	387014	249296	976058	2246283	2064126		1960300	1517059
Settlements of the Hudson's Bay Company	18879	35902	60522	12206	11295	60636	901	2416	7815	13110	13711	67851		20153	64662
British West India Colonies.	£.	£.	£.	£.	£.	£.	£.	£.	£.	£.	£.	£.	£.	£.	£.
Antigua	236647	243991	283500	187902	124479	129793	13624	13051	16864	201526	138533	116657		111620	123101
Barbadoes	406421	558110	389211	497950	304792	316432	65555	12530	24916	562605	322322	369828		301762	293417
Dominica	426683	172460	118191	237263	23755	27476	50110	67840	8077	287373	94427	27478		42207	24583
Grenada	589016	327586	359813	157557	65125	84918	30560	4086	18817	188117	69559	33015		67379	38847
Jamaica	4615075	5736025	3741179	2081883	2594796	2620901	178117	145258	140582	2260000	2739554	2761443		1909607	1084296
Montserrat	49514	37588	40958	23085	8701	7259	340	519	513	23425	12924	8302		10648	7531
Nevis	92971	63358	79328	18510	12608	25771	1031	826	1452	19541	13434	25223		14925	21456
St. Kitt's	218820	131109	199298	91644	55637	72749	11795	4715	4465	103439	59852	97234		54923	71717
St. Lucia	129641	117063	157553	61993	30411	48511	5692	5105	7095	70505	41116	51505		31559	37681
St. Vincent	387802	358992	411548	86665	108229	96185	4656	5349	3406	91321	105578	90891		33372	94005
Tobago	265367	187874	158385	90342	39708	46002	3142	2983	5306	93786	42691	51368		44007	493296
Tortola & Virgin Islands	115579	36550	33943	134309	623	5600	1742	37	66	136051	665	5666		775	4992
Trinidad	268547	463365	694001	335747	300862	318535	35011	29915	49539	370158	923077	361077		230557	258551
Bahamas	41184	25200	17915	191070	105242	193660	18433	2649	22930	209543	107881	158791		37030	29571
Bermudas	2222	12945	4901	24777	92138	6720	2056	5851	3435	34345	506552	94817		35149	620
Demerara	1260208	1492250	1764409	994759	362138	418112	33694	26970	54124	330455	389108	509236		364418	487585
Berbice		2680803	3325051		83317	46485		7443	5102		90920	51587		81553	51215
Honduras	76246	143502	190795	27010	342940	753710	2723	14893	36568	29733	357833	792278		191420	256993
Total	9104647	8495277	9087914	4925680	4600665	5168118	438111	285247	359051	4963791	4835912	5521169		3678120	3612075

Notes for 1806 columns:
- *The real or declared Value of British and Irish (goods exported) was not obtained until after the passing of the Act 53 Geo. 3. c. 98. Anno 1813.*

Number and Tonnage of Vessels to and from the United Kingdom and the Colonies.

COLONIES.	Inwards. Ships 1806	Tons 1806	Ships 1825	Tons 1825	Ships 1829	Tons 1829	Outwards. Ships 1806	Tons 1806	Ships 1825	Tons 1825	Ships 1829	Tons 1829
British North American Colonies.												
Lower Canada	90	21095	732	203886	778	227909	97	22532	662	178786	760	221694
Upper Canada			842	235097					842	210071		
New Brunswick	23	6818	109	25571	121	30146	20	5637	101	24092	460	133469
Nova Scotia	57	12960	35	6795			70	15471	15	3266	126	31738
Cape Breton			32				1	366	16	3351		
Prince Edward Island							6	1672				
Newfoundland	117	16009	126	11447	148	17820	276	35894	316	43590	306	31246
Total	317	56224	1856	189908	1609	431124	470	81472	1815	463155	1652	418147
Settlements of the Hudson's Bay Company			2	746	3	866			2	751	5	1274
British West India Colonies.												
Antigua			33	7395	46	9751			40	8949	43	9367
Barbadoes			72	19048	65	17191			81	21968	82	20887
Dominica			11	1603	12	3011			11	2623	9	2921
Grenada			35	12206	41	85310			33	10189	17	11031
Jamaica			279	86825	286	85310			284	88055	274	82558
Montserrat			5	1039	8	1253			6	1441	4	944
Nevis			5	2069	11	1892			10	2324	8	1996
St. Kitt's			15	4314	24	6924			13	3644	26	6804
St. Lucia			17	3491	22	5290			32	2670	19	4209
St. Vincent			17	6678	32	6594			39	10495	29	12094
Tobago			25	6728	26	6594			22	2816	22	1913
Tortola & Virgin Islands			6	1258	5	1317			2	504	3	606
Trinidad			65	14411	94	22224			57	12938	82	20157
Bahamas			13	2903	7	1360			10	1986	7	1338
Bermudas			3	529	9	620			9	1147	9	2936
Demerara			153	41749	190	55250			143	41477	183	53857
Berbice			98	6053	29	7710			25	5413	23	6070
Honduras			46	11731	42	11184			44	11689	33	8847
Total			861	233840	948	263538			842	232717	918	252992

Note for 1806 shipping columns: *The Fire at the late Custom House destroyed the Records for the Year 1806.*

Money. — What is called West India currency is an imaginary money, and h
different value in different colonies. The value it bears, as compared with ster
money, was supposed to represent the corresponding value of the coins in circulatio
the different islands at the time the proportion was fixed: these coins being for the r
part mutilated, and otherwise worn and defaced, currency is in all cases less valu
than sterling. The following are the values of 100*l.* sterling, and of a dollar, in
currencies of the different islands: —

				Sterling.	Currency.	Dollar.	Currency.
Jamaica	-	-	-	100*l.* =	140*l.*	1 =	6*s.* 8*d.*
Barbadoes	-	-	-	100*l.* =	135*l.*	1 =	6*s.* 3*d.*
Windward Islands (except Barbadoes)			100*l.* =	175*l.*	1 =	8*s.* 3*d.*
Leeward Islands	-	-	-	100*l.* =	200*l.*	1 =	9*s.*

But these proportions are seldom acted upon; the exchange being generally f
10 to 20 per cent. above the fixed par.

By an order in council of the 23d of March, 1825, British silver money is m
legal tender throughout all British colonial possessions, at the nominal value as in E
land; and bills for the same are given on the Treasury of London, of 100*l.* each bill
103*l.* such silver money. By this order, also, the value of the Spanish dollar is fixe
4*s.* 4*d.* British silver money throughout all the colonies where it is current.

The following are the gold coins circulating at Jamaica, with their legal weight
fineness: —

	dwts.	gr. Tr.				Value in Curre
						£ *s.*
Spanish Doubloon - - - -	17	8	-	-	-	5 0
Two Pistole Piece -	8	16	-	-	-	2 10
Pistole - -	4	8	-	-	-	1 5
Half Pistole - -	2	4	-	-	-	0 12
Portuguese Johanes (called Joe) -	18	12	-	-	-	5 10
Half Joe - -	9	6	-	-	-	2 15
Quarter Joe - -	4	15	-	-	-	1 7
Moidore - - -	6	22	-	-	-	2 0
Half Moidore - -	3	11	-	-	-	1 0
English Guinea - - -	5	8	-	-	-	1 12
Half Guinea - - -	2	16	-		-	0 16
Sovereign - - -	5	2	-	-	-	1 12

IV. Regulations under which Colony Trade is conducted. — Disposal of L in the Colonies, &c.

The trade with the colonies in America and the West Indies is principally regul
by the act 6 Geo. 4. c. 114.; but that act has been in some respects materially modi
partly by the 7 & 8 Geo. 4. c. 56., and partly by the act 1 Will. 4. c. 24., which c
into operation on the 15th April, 1831.

Importation and Exportation of Goods confined to free Ports. — No goods shall be imported into
shall any goods, except the produce of the fisheries in British ships, be exported from any of the B
possessions in America by sea, from or to any place other than the United Kingdom, or some oth
such possessions, except into or from the several ports in such possessions called "free ports" enume
or described in the table following. — (6 Geo. 4. c. 114. § 2.)

Table of Free Ports. — Kingston, Savannah le Mar, Montego Bay, Santa Lucia, Antonio, Saint
Falmouth, Maria, Morant Bay, and Annotto Bay, in Jamaica; Saint George in Grenada; Rose
Dominica; Saint John's in Antigua; San Josef in Trinidad; Scarborough in Tobago; Road Harbc
Tortola; Nassau in New Providence; Pitt's Town in Crooked Island; Kingston in Saint Vincent;
Saint George and Port Hamilton in Bermuda; any port where there is a Custom-house in Baha
Bridgetown in Barbadoes; Saint John's, Saint Andrew's, in New Brunswick; Halifax in Nova S
Quebec in Canada; Saint John's in Newfoundland; George Town in Demerara; New Amsterda
Berbice; Castries in Saint Lucia; Basseterre in Saint Kitt's; Charles Town in Nevis; Plymou
Montserrat.

His Majesty may extend the Privileges to other Ports not enumerated. — Provided always, that
Majesty shall deem it expedient to extend the provisions of this act to any port not enumerated, it
be lawful for his Majesty, by order in council, to extend the provisions of this act to such port; and
the day mentioned in such order, all the privileges of this act, and all the provisions therein cont
shall extend to such ports as fully as if the same had been inserted in the said table.* Provided als
nothing herein shall extend to prohibit the exportation of the produce of the fisheries from any p
any of the said possessions in British ships, nor to prohibit the importation or exportation of goo
or from any ports in Newfoundland or Labrador in British ships. — § 3.

Privileges granted to foreign Ships, limited to those Countries which shall grant like Privileges to &
Ships. — And whereas by the law of navigation, foreign ships are permitted to import into any
British possessions abroad, from the countries to which they belong, goods the produce of those cou
and to export goods from such possessions to be carried to any foreign country whatever; it is the
enacted, that the privileges thereby granted to foreign ships shall be limited to the ships of those cou
which, having colonial possessions, shall grant the like privileges of trading with those possessi

* Under this regulation the ports of Pictou and Sydney in Nova Scotia, St. John's in Newfoun
and St. George's in Grenada, have been added to the list of free ports; and by the act 7 & 8 Geo.
Kingston and Montreal in Canada are made free warehousing ports for goods brought by land or
navigation, or imported by sea in British ships.

ish ships, or which, not having colonial possessions, shall place the commerce and navigation of this
ntry, and of its possessions abroad, upon the footing of the most favoured nation, unless his Majesty,
is order in council, shall in any case deem it expedient to grant the whole, or any of such privileges,
e ships of any foreign country, although the conditions aforesaid shall not, in all respects, be fulfilled
uch foreign country. — § 4.

ut nothing in this act, or in any other act passed in the present session, shall extend to repeal an act
eo. 4. c. 77.), intituled " An act to authorise his Majesty, under certain circumstances, to regulate the
es and drawbacks on goods imported or exported in foreign vessels, and to exempt certain foreign
els from pilotage ;" nor to repeal, or in any way alter or affect, an act (5 Geo. 4. c. 1.) to amend the
mentioned act ; and that all trade and intercourse between the British possessions and all foreign
ntries shall be subject to the powers granted to his Majesty by those acts. — § 5.

oreign Ships trading between British Possessions and other Places in America. — Until the expiration
n years, to be computed from the 24th of June, 1822, every foreign ship which, previous to that day,
been engaged in trade between any of the British possessions in America and other places in
erica, shall, for the purposes of this act, be deemed to be a ship of the country to which she had then
nged, if still belonging thereto. — § 6.

oods prohibited or restricted to be imported into Colonies. — The several sorts of goods enumerated in
table following are hereby prohibited to be imported or brought, either by sea or by inland carriage
avigation, into the British possessions in America, or into the island of Mauritius; or shall be so im-
ed or brought only under the restrictions mentioned in such table.

A Table of Prohibitions and Restrictions.

powder, arms, ammunitions or utensils of war, beef and pork, fresh or salted, except into Newfound-
d, prohibited to be imported, except from the United Kingdom, or from some other British pos-
ssion.

prohibited to be imported, except from the United Kingdom, or from some other British possession
America, unless by the East India Company or with their licence.

, dried or salted, and train oil, blubber, fins, or skins, the produce of creatures living in the sea, pro-
ited to be imported, except from the United Kingdom or from some other British possession, or
less taken by British ships fitted out from the United Kingdom, or from some British possession, and
ught in from the fishery, and except herrings from the Isle of Man, taken and cured by the inhabit-
ts thereof.

e, cocoa-nuts, sugar, molasses, and rum, being of foreign production, or the production of any place
thin the limits of the East India Company's charter, except the island of Mauritius, prohibited to be
ported into any of the British possessions on the continent of South America, or in the West Indies,
ept the Bahama and Bermuda islands, or into the island of Mauritius, and may also be prohibited to
imported into the Bahama or the Bermuda islands by his Majesty's order in council.

or counterfeit coin, and books such as are prohibited to be imported into the United Kingdom, pro-
ited to be imported.

d if any goods shall be imported or brought into any of the British possessions in America, or into
sland of Mauritius, contrary to any of the prohibitions mentioned in such table, the same shall be
ted. — § 7.

fee, though British, deemed foreign in certain Cases. — All coffee, cocoa-nuts, sugar, molasses, and
(although the same may be of the British plantations), imported into any of the British possessions
merica into which the like goods of foreign production can be legally imported, shall, upon subsequent
rtation from thence into any of the British possessions in America into which such goods, being of
gn production, cannot be legally imported, or into the island of Mauritius, or into the United King-
be deemed to be of foreign production, and shall be liable, on such importation, to the same duties
e same forfeitures as articles of the like description, being of foreign production, would be liable to
s the same shall have been warehoused under the provisions of this act, and exported from the
house direct to such other British possession, or to the island of Mauritius, or to the United
dom. — § 8.

ties of Importation in America. — There shall be raised, levied, collected, and paid unto his Majesty
everal duties of customs, set forth in figures in the table of duties hereinafter contained, upon goods
rted into any of his Majesty's possessions in America. — § 9.

Table of Duties.

s payable upon spirits, being of the growth, production, or manufacture of the United Kingdom, or
any of the British possessions in America or the West Indies, imported into Newfoundland or
ada.

	£	s.	d.
s imported into Newfoundland, *videlicet,*			
the produce of any of the British possessions in South America or the West Indies; *videlicet,*			
from any of the British possessions in South America or the West Indies, the gallon	0	0	6
imported from the United Kingdom, the gallon	0	1	6
imported from any other place, to be deemed foreign, and to be charged with duty as such.			
the produce of any British possessions in North America, or of the United Kingdom, and imported from the United Kingdom, or from any British possession in America or the West Indies, the gallon	0	1	6
imported from any other place, to be deemed foreign, and to be charged with duty as such.			
imported into Canada ; *videlicet,*			
the produce of any British possession in South America or the West Indies, and imported from the United Kingdom, the gallon	0	0	6
imported from any other place, to be deemed foreign, and be charged with duty as such.			

s payable upon goods, wares, and merchandise, not being of the growth, production, or manufacture
e United Kingdom, or of any of the British possessions in America, or of the island of Mauritius,
rted or brought into any of the British possessions in America or the island of Mauritius by sea or
land carriage or navigation.

	£	s.	d.
very barrel of wheat flour not weighing more than 196 lbs. nett weight	0	5	0
very hundred weight of biscuit or bread	0	1	6
very barrel of flour or meal, not weighing more than 196 lbs., not made from wheat	0	2	6
very bushel of wheat	0	1	0
very bushel of peas, beans, rye, calavances, oats, barley, or Indian corn	0	0	7
for every 100 lbs. nett weight	0	2	6
very 1,000 shingles not more than 12 inches in length	0	7	0
very 1,000 shingles being more than 12 inches in length	0	14	0
very 1,000 red oak staves or headings	0	15	0
very 1,000 white oak staves or headings	0	12	6
very 1,000 feet of white, yellow, or pitch pine lumber of 1 inch thick	1	1	0
ery 1,000 feet of other kinds of wood and lumber	1	8	0

* See *post,* act 1 Will. 4. c. 24.

	£.	s.
For every 1,000 wood hoops - - - - - - - - - - -	0	5
Horses, mules, asses, neat cattle, and all other live stock, for every 100*l.* value - - -	10	0
Spirits; *videlicet*,		
Brandy, geneva, or cordials, for every gallon - - - - - - -	0	1
and further, the amount of any duty payable for the time being on spirits the manufacture of the United Kingdom.		
Wine, imported in bottles, the tun containing 252 gallons - - - - - -	7	7
and further, for every 100*l.* of the true and real value thereof - - - -	7	10
and for every dozen of foreign quart bottles, in which such wine may be imported -	0	1
not in bottles, for every 100*l.* value - - - - - - - -	7	10
Coffee, for every cwt. - - - - - - - - - - -	0	5
Cocoa, for every cwt. - - - - - - - - - - -	0	5
Sugar, for every cwt. - - - - - - - - - - -	0	5
Molasses, for every cwt. - - - - - - - - - -	0	3
Rum, for every gallon - - - - - - - - - - -	0	0
and further, the amount of any duty payable for the time being on coffee, cocoa, sugar, molasses, and rum respectively, being the produce of any of the British possessions in South America or the West Indies.		

The act 7 & 8 Geo. 4. c. 56. § 29. imposes the following duties; viz.—

	£	s.
Silk manufactures, for 100*l.* value - - - - - - - - -	30	0
Cotton manufactures, for 100*l.* value - - - - - - - -	20	0
Salted beef and salted pork, except into Newfoundland, and all salted beef and salted pork imported from Newfoundland, whether of foreign production or not, the cwt. - - -	0	12
Spirits, not otherwise charged with duty, the gallon - - - - - -	0	1
Alabaster, anchovies, argol, aniseed, amber, almonds, brimstone, botargo, boxwood, currants, capers, cascasoo, cantharides, cummin-seed, coral, cork, cinnabar, dates; essence of bergamot, of lemon, of roses, of citron, of oranges, of lavender, of rosemary; emery-stone, flax, fruit, viz. dry, preserved in sugar; wet, preserved in brandy; figs; gum arabic, mastic, myrrh, Sicily, ammoniac; hemp, honey, jalap, iron in bars unwrought, and pig iron, juniper-berries, incense of frankincense, lava and Malta stone for building, lentils, manna; marble, rough and worked; mosaic work, medals, musk, maccaroni, nuts of all kinds; oil of olives, of almonds; opium, orris-root, ostrich feathers, ochres, orange buds and peel, olives, pitch, pickles in jars and bottles, paintings, pozzolana, pumice-stone, punk, Parmesan cheese, pickles, prints, pearls, precious stones (except diamonds), quicksilver, raisins, rhubarb, sausages, senna, scammony, sarsaparilla, saffron, safflower, sponges, tar, tow, turpentine, vermilion, vermicelli, whetstones; for every 100*l.* of the true and real value thereof - - - - - -	7	10
Clocks and watches, leather manufactures, linen, musical instruments, wires of all sorts, books and papers, for every 100*l.* of the true and real value thereof - - -	30	0
Glass and manufactures, soap, refined sugar, sugar candy, tobacco manufactured, for every 100*l.* of the true and real value thereof - - - - -	20	0
Hay and straw, coin and bullion, diamonds, salt, fruit and vegetables fresh, cotton wool, goods the produce of places within the limits of the East India Company's charter; horses of persons travelling into or through the province of Upper Canada, and necessarily used in removing themselves, their families and baggage; cord, wood for fuel and saw logs brought into Upper Canada; herrings taken and cured by the inhabitants of the Isle of Man, and imported direct from thence; any sort of craft, food and victuals, except spirits, and any sort of clothing and implements or materials fit and necessary for the British fisheries in America, imported into the place at or from whence such fishery is carried on, in British ships; rice and Indian corn, and lumber, the produce of any British possession on the west coast of Africa, and imported direct from thence - - - - - - - -	DUTY FREE	
Goods, wares, or merchandise, not being enumerated or described, nor otherwise charged with duty by this act, for every 100*l.* of the true and real value thereof - - -	15	0

And if any of the goods hereinbefore mentioned shall be imported through the United Kingdo (having been warehoused therein, and exported from the warehouse, or the duties thereon, if then pa having been drawn back,) one tenth part of the duties herein imposed shall be remitted in respect of su goods; and if any of the goods herein-before mentioned shall be imported through the United Kingdo (not from the warehouse,) but after all duties of importation for home use thereon shall have been pa thereon in the said United Kingdom, and not drawn back, such goods shall be free of all duties here imposed. — § 9.

But in consequence of the complaints of the West India planters, and of the Americ government, of the operation of these duties, the following act, 1 Will. 4. c. 24., w passed. It enacts,

" That from and after the 15th day of April, 1831, so much of the said acts as imposes any duty in a of the British possessions in America, upon the importation or bringing in of corn or grain unground, of meal or flour not made of wheat, or of bread or biscuit, or of rice, or of live stock, shall be and same is hereby repealed." — § 1.

Repeal of Duties in Canada. — And be it further enacted, that so much of any of the said acts as impo any duty in the provinces of Upper or Lower Canada upon the importation or bringing in of wheat flo or of beef, pork, hams, or bacon, or of wood or lumber, shall be and the same is hereby repealed. — § 2.

Repeal of Duties in New Brunswick, &c. — And be it further enacted, that so much of any of the sa acts as imposes any duty, in New Brunswick, Nova Scotia, or Prince Edward's Island, upon woo lumber, shall be and the same is hereby repealed. — § 3.

Repeal of Duties in the West Indies, &c. — And be it further enacted, that so much of any of the acts as imposes any duty, in the British possessions on the continent of South America or in the W Indies, or in the Bahama or Bermuda Islands, upon wheat flour, or upon beef, pork, hams, or bacon upon wood or lumber, when imported from any of the British possessions in North America, shall be a the same is hereby repealed. — § 4.

Additional Duties on Importation. — And be it further enacted, that upon the importation from a foreign country into the British possessions on the continent of South America or in the West Indies into the Bahama or Bermuda Islands, of the articles mentioned in the following table, there shall be rais levied, collected, and paid unto his Majesty the several temporary additional duties the same as are forth in the said table; (that is to say,)

	£	s.	d.
Staves and Headings, until the First Day of January 1834, - - the 1,000	0	11	9
on and from the First Day of January 1834 to the First Day of January 1836, the 1,000	0	7	9
White or Yellow Pine Lumber, until the First Day of January 1834, the 1,000 Feet of One Inch thick	0	7	0
on and from the First Day of January 1834 to the First Day of January 1836, the 1,000 Feet of One Inch thick	0	5	0

§ 5.

ction of Duties. — And be it further enacted, that the duties imposed by this act shall be raised, collected, and paid unto his Majesty in like manner as if such duties had been imposed by the said *entioned act, and had been set forth in the table of duties therein contained. — § 6.

e remaining clauses of the act 6 Geo. 4. c. 114. are as follow: —

not repealed. — Nothing in this act, or in any other act passed in the present session, shall extend *al*, or in any way to alter or affect an act (18 Geo. 3. c. 12.), intituled " An act for removing all *and* apprehensions concerning taxation by the parliament of Great Britain, in any of the colonies, *ces*, and plantations in North America and the West Indies, and for repealing so much of an act *n* the seventh year of the reign of his present Majesty, as imposes a duty on tea imported from Great *a* into any colony or plantation in America, as relates thereto;" nor to repeal or in any way alter or *any* act now in force, which was passed prior to the last-mentioned act, and by which any duties in the British possessions in America were granted, and still continue payable to the crown ; nor to *or* in any way alter or affect an act of 31 Geo. 3. c. 31., intituled " An act to repeal certain parts of *passed* in the fourteenth year of his Majesty's reign, intituled ' An act for making more effectual *ons* for the government of the province of Quebec in North America, and to make further pro- *for the* government of the said province.'" — § 10.

s imposed by Acts prior to Act 18 Geo. 3. to be applied to Purposes of those Acts. — The duties im- *y* any of the acts passed prior to the said act of 18 Geo. 3. shall be received, accounted for, and *a* for the purposes of those acts : Provided that no greater proportion of the duties imposed by this *ll* be charged upon any article which is subject also to duty under any of the said acts, or subject *duty* under any colonial law, than the amount, if any, by which the duty charged by this act shall *such* other duty : Provided that the full amount of the duties mentioned in this act, whether on *t* of such former acts, or on account of such colonial law, or on account of this act, shall be levied *eived* under the regulations of this act. — § 11.

ncy Weights and Measures. — All sums of money granted by this act, either as duties, penalties, *itures*, in the British possessions in America, shall be deemed to be sterling money, and shall be *the* amount of the value which such nominal sums bear in Great Britain ; and such monies may *ived* according to the proportion of 5s. 6d. the ounce in silver ; and all duties shall be paid in every *the* British possessions in America, according to British weights and measures, and in all cases *uch* duties are imposed according to any specific quantity, or any specific value, the same shall be *to* apply in the same proportion to any greater or less quantity or value ; and all such duties shall *r* the management of the commissioners of customs. — § 12.

s paid by Collector of Customs. — The produce of the duties so received by the powers of this act, *duties* payable under any act prior to 18 Geo. 3, shall be paid by the collector of customs into *ds* of the treasurer or receiver-general of the colony, to be applied to such uses as shall be directed *ocal* legislatures of such colonies ; and the produce of such duties, in the colonies which have no *gislature*, shall be applied in such manner as shall be directed by the commissioners of the treasury.

back on Rum and Spirits. — There shall be allowed upon the exportation from Newfoundland to *of* rum or other spirits, being the produce of the British possessions in South America or the *adies*, a drawback of the full duties of customs paid upon the importation thereof from any of *places* into Newfoundland, provided proof on oath be made to the satisfaction of the collector *nptroller* at the port from whence such rum or spirits shall be exported, that the full duties on im- *n* had been paid, and that a certificate be produced under the hands and seals of the collector *nptroller* at Quebec, that such rum or spirits had been duly landed in Canada : but no drawback *allowed* upon any such rum or spirits unless the same shall be shipped within one year from the *hipment.*—§ 14.

and Cargo to be reported on Arrival. — The master of every ship arriving in any of the British *ons* in America, or the island of Mauritius, or in the islands of Guernsey, Jersey, Alderney, or *nether* laden or in ballast, shall come directly, and before bulk be broken, to the Custom-house *ort* where he arrives, and there make a report upon oath in writing to the collector or comptroller *rrival* and voyage of such ship, stating her name, country, and tonnage, and if British the port *ry*, the name and country of the master, the country of the owners, the number of the crew, and *ny* are of the country of such ship, and whether she be laden or in ballast, and if laden, the marks, *s*, and contents of every package and parcel of goods on board, and where the same was laden, and *nd* to whom consigned, and where any and what goods, if any, had been unladen during the voy- *d* the master shall further answer upon oath all such questions concerning the ship, and the cargo *crew*, and the voyage, as shall be demanded of him by such officer ; and if any goods be unladen *uch* report, or if the master fail to make such report, or make an untrue report, or do not truly *he* questions demanded of him, he shall forfeit 100*l.* ; and if any goods be not reported, such goods forfeited.—§ 15.

outwards of Ship for Cargo. — The master of every ship bound from any British possession in *a*, or the island of Mauritius, or the islands of Guernsey, Jersey, Alderney, or Sark, shall, before *ds* be laden therein, deliver to the collector or comptroller an entry outwards under his hand of *nation* of such ship, stating her name, country, and tonnage, and if British the port of registry, *ne* and country of the master, the country of the owners, the number of the crew, and how many *ne* country of such ship ; and if any goods be laden on board before such entry, the master shall *0l.*, and before such ship depart, the master shall deliver to the collector or comptroller, a content *ng* under his hand of the goods laden, and the names of the shippers or consignees, with the marks *nbers* of the packages, and shall make oath to the truth of such content ; and the master of every *nd* from any British possession in America, or from the island of Mauritius, or from the islands *nsey*, Jersey, Alderney, or Sark, (whether in ballast or laden,) shall before departure come before *ctor* or comptroller, and answer upon oath all such questions as shall be demanded of him by *cer* ; and thereupon the collector and comptroller, if such ship be laden, shall give to the master *ate* of the clearance, containing an account of the total quantities of the several sorts of goods *erein*, or a certificate of her clearance in ballast : and if the ship shall depart without such clear- *if the* master shall deliver a false content, or shall not truly answer the questions demanded of *shall* forfeit 100*l.* — § 16.

undland Fishing Certificates in lieu of Clearance, during the Fishing Season.—Whenever any ship *cleared* out from any port in Newfoundland or in any other part of his Majesty's dominions, for *ries* on the banks of Newfoundland or Labrador, without having on board any article of traffic, *only* provisions, nets, tackles, and things usually employed in the fishery, and for the carrying on *ne*,) the master shall be entitled to demand from the collector a certificate under his hand that *p* hath been specially cleared out for the Newfoundland fishery, and such certificate shall be in the fishing season of the year and no longer ; and upon the first arrival in any port in Newfound- *eport* thereof shall be made by the master to the principal officer of customs ; and all ships having *tificate* so reported, and being actually engaged in the fishery, or in carrying coastwise to be *r* put on board any other ships engaged in the said fishery, any fish, oil, salt, provisions, or other *les*, shall be exempt from all obligation to make any entry at or obtain any clearance from any *house* at Newfoundland, upon arrival at or departure from any of the ports of the said colony *ne* fishing season ; and previously to obtaining a clearance at the end of such season for any other *: any* of such ports, the master shall deliver up the certificate to the principal officer of customs :

Provided always, that in case any such ship shall have on board, during the time the same may be eng
in the said fishery, any goods other than fish, seals, oil made of fish or seals, salt provisions, and c
thing, the produce of or employed in the said fishery, such ship shall forfeit the fishing certificate, ar
subject to the same rules as ships in general are liable to. — § 17.

Entry of Goods to be laden or unladen.—No goods shall be laden or water-borne to be laden on board
ship, or unladen from any ship in any of the British possessions in America, or the island of Maur
or the islands of Guernsey, Jersey, Alderney, or Sark, until entry shall have been made of such g
and warrant granted ; and no goods shall be so laden or water-borne, or so unladen, except at some
at which an officer of customs is appointed, or at some place for which a sufferance shall be grante
the collector and comptroller ; and no goods shall be so laden or unladen except in the presence or
the permission in writing of the proper officer : Provided always, that it shall be lawful for the com
sioners of customs to appoint such other regulations for the carrying coastwise, or for the removing o
goods for shipment, as to them shall appear expedient ; and all goods laden, water-borne, or unladen,
trary to this act, or contrary to any regulations so made, shall be forfeited. — § 18.

Particulars of Entry of Goods inwards and outwards. — The person entering any such goods shal
liver to the collector or comptroller a bill of the entry in words at length, containing the name or
exporter or importer, and of the ship, and of the master, and of the place to or from which bound, a
the place within the port where the goods are to be laden or unladen, and the particulars of the goods
the packages, and the marks and numbers on the packages, and such person shall at the same time
down all duties due upon the goods, and the collector and comptroller shall thereupon grant their wa
for the lading or unlading of such goods. — § 19.

Entry inwards by Bill of Sight. — If the importer shall declare upon oath before the collector or c
troller, that he cannot, for want of full information, make perfect entry, it shall be lawful for the coll
and comptroller to receive an entry by a bill of sight for the packages, by the best description which
be given, and to grant a warrant thereupon, in order that the same may be landed and secured, a
expense of the importer, and may be seen by such importer, in the presence of the officers ; and wi
three days after the goods shall have been so landed, the importer shall make a perfect entry, and
down all duties ; and in default of such entry, such goods shall be taken to the king's warehouse, a
the importer shall not, within one month after such landing, make perfect entry, and pay the du
together with charges of removal and warehouse rent, such goods shall be sold for the payment the
and the overplus, if any, shall be paid to the proprietor.—§ 20.   See BILL OF SIGHT.

Goods subject to ad valorem Duty. — In all cases where the duties are charged, not according to
weight, tale, gauge, or measure, but according to the value thereof, such value shall be ascertained b
declaration of the importer, or his agent, in manner following ; (that is to say,)

" I *A. B.*, do hereby declare, that the articles mentioned in the entry, and contained in the pack
[*here specifying the several packages, and describing the several marks and numbers, as the case ma*
are of the value of   Witness my hand the   d
    A. B.

The above declaration, signed the   day of   in the presence of *C. D.* colle
[*or other principal officer.*]"

Which declaration shall be written on the bill of entry, and shall be subscribed with the hand o
importer, or his agent, in the presence of the collector : Provided, that if upon view and examinatio
the proper officer, it shall appear to him that the said articles are not valued according to the true v
then the importer, or his agent, shall be required to declare on oath before the collector or compt
what is the invoice price ; and such invoice price, with the addition of 10*l.* per cent. thereon, sh
deemed to be the value, in lieu of the value declared by the importer or agent, and upon which the c
shall be charged : Provided also, that if it shall appear to the collector and comptroller, that such ar
have been invoiced below the real value, or if the invoice price is not known, the articles shall in
case be examined by two competent persons, to be nominated by the governor or commander in ch
the colony, and such persons shall declare on oath before the collector or comptroller what is the
value in such colony, and the value so declared on oath shall be deemed to be the true value, and
which the duties shall be charged.—§ 21.

If Importer refuse to pay such Duty, the Goods may be sold. — If the importer of such articles
refuse to pay the duties, it shall be lawful for the collector or chief officer of customs to take and s
the same, with the casks or packages, and to cause the same to be publicly sold within twenty days
such refusal, and at such time and place as such officer shall, by four or more days' public notice, ap
for that purpose, which articles shall be sold to the best bidder ; and the money shall be applied i
first place in payment of the duties, together with the charges occasioned by the said sale, and the
plus, if any, be paid to such importer or proprietor —§ 22.

Goods not entered in Twenty Days. — Every importer of any goods shall, within twenty days aft
arrival of the importing ship, make due entry inwards, and land the same ; and in default, it sh
lawful for the officers of customs to convey such goods to the king's warehouse ; and if the duties b
paid within three months after such twenty days shall have expired, together with all charges of re
and warehouse rent, the same shall be sold, and the produce applied first to the payment of freigh
charges, next of duties, and the overplus, if any, paid to the proprietor.—§ 23.

Goods imported from United Kingdom or British Possessions. — No goods shall be imported int
British possession as being imported from the United Kingdom, or from any other British possessi
any advantage attach to such distinction,) unless such goods appear upon the cockets to have been
cleared outwards at the port of exportation, nor unless the ground upon which such advantage be cl
be stated in such cocket.—§ 24.

Entry not to be valid, if Goods be not properly described in it. — No entry, nor any warrant f
landing of any goods, or for the taking of any goods out of any warehouse, shall be valid, unle
particulars of the goods and packages in such entry shall correspond with the particulars of the goo
packages purporting to be the same in the report of the ship, or in the certificate or other docu
where any is required, by which the importation or entry of such goods is authorised, nor unle
goods shall have been properly described in such entry by the denominations, and with the characte
circumstances, according to which such goods are charged with duty, or may be imported ; and any
taken or delivered out by virtue of any entry or warrant not corresponding, or not properly describi
same, shall be deemed to be goods landed without due entry, and shall be forfeited.—§ 25.

Certificate of Production for Sugar, Coffee, Cocoa-nuts, Spirits, or Mahogany.—Before any sugar,
cocoa-nuts, spirits, or mahogany shall be shipped for exportation in any British possession in Amer
in the island of Mauritius, as being the produce of such possession, the proprietor of the estate,
agent, shall make and sign an affidavit in writing before the collector or comptroller, or before one
of the peace, declaring that such goods are the produce of such estate ; and such affidavit shall se
the name of the estate, and the description and quantity of the goods, and the packages, with the
and numbers thereon, and the name of the person to whose charge the place of shipment they ar
sent ; and if any justice, or other officer, shall subscribe his name to any such affidavit, unless the
shall actually appear before him, and be sworn, such justice or officer shall forfeit 50*l.* ; and the
entering and shipping such goods shall deliver such affidavit to the collector or comptroller, and
oath before him that the goods are the same ; and the master of the ship in which such goods s
laden, shall, before clearance, make oath before the collector or comptroller, that the goods ship
the same ; and thereupon the collector and comptroller shall give to the master a certificate of prod

ing that proof has been made that such goods are the produce of such British possession, and setting
h the name of the exporter, and of the exporting ship, and of the master, and the destination of the
ds; and if any sugar, coffee, cocoa-nuts, or spirits, be imported as being the produce of some other
session, without such certificate of production, the same shall be forfeited; and if any mahogany be so
orted, the same shall be deemed to be of foreign production.—§ 26.

ertificate of Production on Re-exportation from another Colony.—Before any sugar, coffee, cocoa-nuts,
ts, or mahogany, shall be shipped for exportation in any British possession, as being the produce of
e other such possession, or of the island of Mauritius, or shall be so shipped in the said island as being
produce of some British possession, the person exporting shall in the entry outwards state the place
he production, and refer to the entry inwards and landing of such goods, and shall make oath before
collector or comptroller to the identity of the same; and thereupon, if such goods shall have been
imported with a certificate of production, within twelve months prior to the shipping for exportation,
collector and comptroller shall give to the master a certificate of production referring to the certifi-
of production under which such goods had been so imported, and containing the like particulars,
the date of importation. — § 27.

oods brought over Land, or by inland Navigation.—It shall be lawful to bring or import by land, or by
nd navigation, into any of the British possessions in America, from any adjoining foreign country,
goods which might be lawfully imported by sea, and so to bring or import such goods in the vessels,
s, or carriages of such country, as well as in British. — § 28.

essels on the Lakes in America. — No vessel or boat shall be admitted to be British on any of the in-
waters or lakes in America, except such as shall have been built at some place within the British
nions, and shall be wholly owned by British subjects, and shall not have been repaired at any foreign
e to a greater extent than in the proportion of 10s. for every ton at one time: Provided always, that
ing herein shall extend to prevent the employment of any vessel or boat as a British vessel or boat,
h shall have wholly belonged to British subjects before the passing of this act, and which shall not be
ired in any foreign place after the passing of this act. — § 29.

oods must be brought to a Place where there is a Custom-house. — It shall not be lawful so to bring or
rt any goods, except into some port or place of entry at which a Custom-house now is or hereafter
be established : Provided that it shall be lawful for the governor, lieutenant-governor, or person ad-
stering the government of any of the said possessions, with the consent of the executive council, to
nish or increase, by proclamation, the number of ports or places of entry. — § 30.

ties to be collected on Goods imported by Sea. —The duties shall be levied, for all goods so brought or
rted, in the same manner as the duties on like goods imported by sea ; and if any goods shall be
ght or imported contrary hereto, or be removed from the station appointed for the examination of
goods, before all duties shall have been paid, such goods shall be forfeited, together with the vessel,
or carriage, and the horses or other cattle. — § 31.

ties in Canada on American Boats, as in America on British Boats. — The same tonnage duties shall
aid upon all vessels or boats of the United States of America, importing goods into Upper or Lower
ada, as are payable in the United States on British vessels or boats. — § 32.

CONDITIONS WITH RESPECT TO WAREHOUSING IN THE COLONIES.

rts herein mentioned to be free warehousing Ports.— The several ports hereinafter mentioned ; (that
say,) Kingston in Jamaica, Halifax in Nova Scotia, Quebec in Canada, Saint John's in New Bruns-
, and Bridge Town in Barbadoes, shall be free warehousing ports for the purposes of this act ; and it
be lawful for the collectors and comptrollers, by notice in writing under their hand, to appoint such
houses, at such ports as shall be approved of by them, for the free warehousing and securing of goods
in, and also in such notice to declare what sorts of goods may be so warehoused, and also by like
e to revoke or alter any such appointment or declaration : Provided always, that every such notice
be transmitted to the governor, and shall be published in such manner as he shall direct. — (6 Geo. 4.
. § 33.)

ods warehoused without Duty. — It shall be lawful for the importer of goods to warehouse the same
e warehouses so appointed, without payment of duty on the first entry, subject to the conditions
nafter contained. — § 34.

wage of Goods in Warehouses. — All goods so warehoused shall be stowed in such parts or divisions,
n such manner as the collector and comptroller shall direct ; and the warehouse shall be locked in
manner, and shall be opened only at such time, and in the presence of such officers, and under such
as the collector and comptroller shall direct ; and all such goods shall, after being landed upon im-
tion, be carried to the warehouse, or shall, after being taken out of the warehouse for exportation,
rried to be shipped, under such regulations as the collector and comptroller shall direct. — § 35.

d upon Entry of Goods to be warehoused. — Upon the entry of any goods to be warehoused, the im-
r instead of paying down the duties shall give bond with two sureties, to be approved by the collector
mptroller, in treble the duties, with condition for the safe depositing of such goods in the warehouse
oned in such entry, and for the payment of all duties, or for the exportation thereof, according to
rst account taken, and with further condition that no part shall be taken out until cleared upon
and payment of duty, or upon entry for exportation ; and with further condition, that the whole of
goods shall be so cleared, and the duties upon any deficiency, according to such first account, shall
d within two years from the first entry, and if after bond given, the goods or any part shall be sold,
t the original bonder shall be no longer interested in the same, it shall be lawful for the collector
mptroller to admit fresh security to be given by the bond of the new proprietor, with his sureties,
cancel the bond given by the original bonder, or to exonerate him to the extent of the fresh
ty. — § 36.

ds not duly warehoused. — If any goods entered to be warehoused shall not be duly deposited in the
ouse, or shall afterwards be taken out without due entry and clearance, or having been entered and
d for exportation, shall not be duly carried and shipped, or shall afterwards be relanded, except with
ssion of the officer of customs, such goods shall be forfeited. — § 37.

ount of Goods to be taken on landing. — Upon the entry and landing of any goods to be warehoused,
ficer of customs shall take a particular account of the same, and shall mark the contents on each
ge, and shall enter the same in a book ; and no goods so warehoused shall be delivered from the ware-
, except upon due entry, and under care of the proper officers for exportation, or upon due entry
ayment of duty for home use ; and whenever the whole shall be cleared from the warehouse, or
ever further time shall be granted for such goods to remain warehoused, an account shall be made
the quantity upon which the duties have been paid, and of the quantity exported, and of the
ty of the goods still remaining in the warehouse, deducting from the whole the quantity contained
whole packages (if any) which may have been abandoned for the duties ; and if upon such account
shall in either case appear to be any deficiency of the original quantity, the duty payable upon the
nt of such deficiency shall then be paid. — § 38.

ples may be taken. — It shall be lawful for the collector and comptroller, under such regulations as
ee fit, to permit moderate samples to be taken of any goods so warehoused without entry, and with-
yment of duty, except as the same shall eventually become payable, as on a deficiency of the ori-
quantity. — § 39.

ds may be sorted and repacked. — It shall be lawful for the collector or comptroller, under such re-
ons as they see fit, to permit the proprietor to sort, separate, and pack and repack any such goods,
make such alterations therein, or assortments thereof, as may be necessary for the preservation of

such goods, or in order to the sale, shipment, or disposal of the same; and also to permit any parts of su
goods so separated to be destroyed, but without prejudice to the claim for duty upon the whole origin
quantity: Provided always, that it shall be lawful for any person to abandon any whole packages to t
officers for the duties, without being liable to duty upon the same. — § 40.

All Goods to be cleared within Two Years, or sold. — All goods so warehoused shall be cleared, either f
exportation or for home consumption, within two years from the first entry; and if not so cleared, it sh
be lawful for the collector and comptroller to cause the same to be sold, and the produce applied, first
the payment of the duties, next of warehouse-rent and charges, and the overplus (if any) to the pr
prietor: Provided always, that it shall be lawful for the collector and comptroller to grant further tim
if they see fit so to do. — § 41.

Bond on Entry for Exportation. — Upon the entry outwards of any goods to be exported from the war
house, the person entering the same shall give security by bond, in treble the duties of importation, wi
two sureties, to be approved by the collector or comptroller, that the same shall be landed at the place f
which they be entered outwards, or be otherwise accounted for. — § 42.

Power to appoint other Ports. — It shall be lawful for his Majesty in council from time to time to appoi
any port in his Majesty's possessions in America to be a free warehousing port, and every such port so a
pointed shall be a free warehousing port in as ample a manner as any of the ports hereinbefore mentione
— § 43.

Goods from Mauritius liable to same duties and regulations as West India goods. See Port Louis.

DUTCH PROPRIETORS, FORFEITURES, &c.

Dutch Proprietors in Demerara, Essequibo, and Berbice. — It shall be lawful for any of the subjects
the King of the Netherlands, being Dutch proprietors in the colonies of Demerara, Essequibo, and
Berbice, to import in Dutch ships, from the Netherlands into the said colonies, all the usual articles
supply for their estates therein; and also wine imported for the purposes of medicine only, and whi
shall be liable to a duty of 10s. per ton, and no more; and in case seizure be made of any articles so ir
ported, upon the ground that they are not such supplies, or are for the purposes of trade, the proof to tl
contrary shall lie on the Dutch proprietor, and not on the seizing officer: Provided always, that if suf
cient security by bond be given in court to abide the decision of the commissioners of customs upon su
seizure, the goods so seized shall be admitted to entry and released. — § 45.

It shall be lawful for such Dutch proprietors to export the produce of their estates to the United Kin
dom, or to any of his Majesty's sugar colonies in America. — § 46.

What Persons shall be deemed Dutch Proprietors. — All subjects of his Majesty the King of the Nethe
lands, resident in his European dominions, who were at the date of the signature of the convention t
tween his late Majesty George III. and the King of the Netherlands, dated the 12th of August, 1815, pr
prietors of estates in the said colonies, and all subjects of his said Majesty who may hereafter becom
possessed of estates then belonging to Dutch proprietors, and all such proprietors as being then reside
in the said colonies, and being natives of his Majesty's dominions in the Netherlands, may have declare
within three months after the publication of the aforesaid convention in the said colonies, that they wis
to continue to be considered as such, and all subjects of his said Majesty the King of the Netherlan
who may be the holders of mortgages of estates in the said colonies, made prior to the date of the co
vention, and who may under their mortgage deeds have the right of exporting from the said colonies
the Netherlands the produce of such estates, shall be deemed Dutch proprietors under this act; provid
that where both Dutch and British subjects have mortgages upon the same property, the produce to
consigned to the different mortgages shall be in proportion to the debts due to them. — § 47.

No Ship to sail from Jamaica to Saint Domingo, or from Saint Domingo to Jamaica. — No British me
chant ship shall sail from Jamaica to Saint Domingo, nor from Saint Domingo to Jamaica, under the fo
feiture of such ship, together with her cargo; and no foreign ship, which shall have come from, or sh
in the course of her voyage have touched at any place in Saint Domingo, shall come into any port
Jamaica; and if any such ship, having come into any such port, shall continue there for forty-eight hou
after notice shall have been given by the officer of the customs to depart, such ship shall be forfeited; an
if any person shall be landed in the island of Jamaica from on board any ship which shall have con
from or touched at Saint Domingo, except in case of urgent necessity, or unless licence shall have be
given by the governor of Jamaica to land such person, such ship shall be forfeited, together with h
cargo. — § 48.

Colonial Laws repugnant to any Act of Parliament to be void. — All laws, by-laws, usages or customs
any of the British possessions in America, repugnant to this act, or to any act made or hereafter to
made in the United Kingdom, so far as such act shall relate to the said possessions, shall be null and ve
to all intents and purposes. — § 49.

Officers may board Ships hovering on the Coasts. — It shall be lawful for the officers of customs to go
board any ship in any port in any British possession in America, and to search all parts for prohibit
and uncustomed goods, and also to go on board any ship hovering within one league of the coasts, and
either case to stay on board so long as she shall remain in port, or within such distance; and if any su
ship be bound elsewhere, and shall continue so hovering for twenty-four hours after the master shall ha
been required to depart, it shall be lawful for the officer of customs to bring such ship into port, and
examine her cargo, and to examine the master upon oath touching the cargo and voyage, and if there
any goods on board prohibited to be imported, such ship and her cargo shall be forfeited; and if
master shall not truly answer the questions, he shall forfeit 100l. — § 50.

Forfeiture of Vessels, Carriages, &c. removing Goods liable to Forfeiture. — All vessels, boats, and c
riages, and all cattle, made use of in the removal of any goods liable to forfeiture, shall be forfeited, a
every person who shall assist in the unshipping, landing, or removal, or in the harbouring of such goo
or into whose hands the same shall knowingly come, shall forfeit treble value, or the penalty of 100l.
the election of the officers of customs; and the averment in any information that the officer has elec
to sue for the sum mentioned, shall be deemed sufficient proof of such election, without any furtl
evidence. — § 51.

Goods and Vessels liable to Forfeiture may be seized. — All goods, and all ships, vessels, and boats, a
all carriages, and all cattle liable to forfeiture, may be seized by any officer of the customs or navy, or
any person employed by the commissioners of customs; and every person who shall in any way hind
oppose, molest, or obstruct any officer of the customs or navy, or any person so employed, or any pers
acting in his aid, shall forfeit 200l. — § 52.

Writ of Assistance. — Under authority of a writ of assistance granted by the superior or Supreme Co
of Justice, or Court of Vice-admiralty, it shall be lawful for any officer of customs, taking with him a pea
officer, to enter any building or other place in the daytime, and to search for and seize and secure
goods liable to forfeiture under this act; and in case of necessity, to break open doors, chests, or pa
ages; and such writ of assistance, when issued, shall be deemed to be in force during the whole of
reign in which the same shall have been granted, and for twelve months from the conclusion of su
reign. — § 53.

Obstruction of Officers by Force. — If any person shall, by force or violence, assault, resist, oppose, mol
hinder, or obstruct any officer of the customs or navy, or other person employed as aforesaid, or any p
son acting in his aid, such person shall be adjudged a felon, and punished at the discretion of the Co
— § 54.

Goods seized to be secured at the next Custom-house.—All things which shall be seized, shall be delive
into the custody of the collector and comptroller at the Custom-house next to the place where the sa

eized, who shall secure the same in such manner as shall be directed by the commissioners of cus-
— § 55.

ds seized to be sold by Auction. — All things condemned as forfeited shall, under the direction of the
or and comptroller, be sold by public auction; and it shall be lawful for the commissioners of cus-
o direct in what manner the produce shall be applied, or in lieu of such sale, to direct that any of
hings shall be destroyed or shall be reserved for the public service. — § 56.

sdiction for Prosecution of Seizures and Penalties. — All penalties and forfeitures shall be recovered
court of record or of vice-admiralty having jurisdiction in the colony or plantation, and where
shall be no such courts, then in any court of record or of vice-admiralty in some British colony or
tion near : Provided that in cases where a seizure is made in any other colony than that where the
ure accrues, such forfeiture may be prosecuted in any court of record or of vice-admiralty having
ction either in the colony where the forfeiture accrues, or in the colony where the seizure is made,
election of the seizor or prosecutor; and in cases where there shall happen to be no such courts,
the court of record or of vice-admiralty in some British colony near to that where the forfeiture
s, or to that where the seizure is made, at the election of the seizor or prosecutor. — § 57.

may be given for Goods or Ships seized. — If any goods or any ship shall be seized as forfeited, and
ed, it shall be lawful for the judge or judges of any court having jurisdiction to try and determine
izures, with the consent of the collector and comptroller, to order the delivery thereof on security
d, with two sureties, to be approved by such collector and comptroller, to answer double the value
of condemnation. — § 58.

to be commenced in Name of Officers of Customs, &c. — No suit shall be commenced for the reco-
any penalty or forfeiture, except in the name of some superior officer of the customs or navy, or
erson employed as before-mentioned, or of his Majesty's advocate or attorney-general for the place
such suit shall be commenced. — § 59.

probandi to lie on Party. — If any goods shall be seized for nonpayment of duties, or any other
f forfeitnre, and any dispute shall arise whether the duties have been paid, or the same have been
y imported, or lawfully laden or exported, the proof shall lie on the owner or claimer, and not on
cer. — § 60.

n to Thing seized, to be entered in Name of the Owner. — No claim to any thing seized, and re-
into any court for adjudication, shall be admitted, unless entered in the name of the owner, with
dence and occupation, nor unless oath to the property in such thing be made by the owner, or by
orney or agent; and every person making a false oath shall be guilty of a misdemeanor, and
o the pains and penalties for a misdemeanor. — § 61.

'erson to enter Claim, unless Security first given. — No person shall be admitted to enter a claim
ifficient security shall have been given, in the court, in a penalty not exceeding 60l., to pay the
and in default of such security such things shall be adjudged to be forfeited, and be condemned.

nth's Notice of Action to be given to Officers. — No writ shall be sued out against, nor a copy of any
served upon any officer of the customs or navy, or person aforesaid, for any thing done in the
e of his office, until one calendar month after notice in writing; in which notice shall be expli-
ntained the cause of action, the name and abode of the person who is to bring such action, and
ne and abode of the attorney. — § 63.

ns to be brought within Three Months. — Every such action shall be brought within three calendar
after the cause thereof, and tried in the district where the facts were committed, and the defendant
ad the general issue; and if the plaintiff be nonsuited, defender may recover treble costs. — § 64.

following clauses of the act 7 & 8 Geo. 4. have reference to this subject : —

s, the Produce of the West Indies, from one Colony of North America to another. — *Wine in Casks*
ibraltar or Malta. — *Wine in Bottles from the United Kingdom.* — Spirits, the produce of any of
tish possessions in South America or the West Indies, imported into any of the British possessions
h America, shall not be subject to any higher duty than would have been payable if such spirits
n imported from some British possession in South America or the West Indies; and wine in casks
d into the British possessions in North America, from Gibraltar or Malta, shall not be subject to
her duty than would have been payable if such wine had been imported from the United King-
nd wine in bottles having been bottled in the United Kingdom, imported into any of the British
ons in America, from the United Kingdom, shall not be subject to any higher duty, than would
en payable if such wine had been imported in casks; and no duty shall be charged upon the bottles
ng such wine. — § 30.

, &c. from the Canadas deemed Produce of the Canadas. — All masts, timber, staves, wood hoops,
lath wood, and cord wood for fuel, imported from the Canadas into any other British possession
rica, or into the United Kingdom, shall be deemed the produce of the Canadas; and wood of all
ich shall have been warehoused at any warehousing port in any of the British possessions in North
a, and exported from the warehouse, shall, upon importation into any other British possession in
a, be subject only to one fourth part of such duty as would otherwise be charged thereon. —

, &c. brought inland into British Possessions in America, Duty free. — Masts, timber, staves, wood
hingles, lath wood, cord wood for fuel, raw hides, tallow, ashes, fresh meat, fresh fish, and horses,
s, and equipages of travellers, being brought by land or inland navigation into the British posses-
America, shall be so brought duty free. — § 33.

otion to extend only to Duties by Act of Parliament. — Provided that no exemption from duty in
he British possessions abroad does or shall extend to any duty imposed by act of parliament,
nd so far only as any other duty is or shall be expressly mentioned in such exemption. — § 34.

passed on from frontier Ports in the Canadas to warehousing Ports. — Upon the arrival of any
any frontier port in the Canadas, such goods may be entered with the proper officer of the cus-
such port, to be warehoused at some warehousing port in the Canadas, and may be delivered by
cer to be passed on to such warehousing port under bond, to the satisfaction of such officer for
val and re-warehousing of such goods at such port. — § 36.

oused Goods removed to another Port. — Goods warehoused at any warehousing port in any of the
possessions in America, being first duly entered, may be delivered under the authority of the
fficer of customs without payment of any duty, except for any deficiency thereof, for the purpose
val to another warehousing port in the same possession, under bond, to the satisfaction of such
r the arrival and re-warehousing of such goods at such port. — § 37.

Vessels importing prohibited Goods forfeited. — If any goods which are prohibited to be imported
port or place in the British possessions in America, shall be imported, contrary to such prohibi-
ny ship or vessel which is of less burthen than seventy tons, such ship or vessel shall be forfeited;
tonnage of that ship or vessel shall be ascertained in the same manner as the tonnage of British
d ships is ascertained. — § 38.

n Persons may cease to be deemed Dutch Proprietors in Demerara, &c. — Whereas by the said
egulating the trade of the British possessions abroad, certain persons therein described, subjects
ing of the Netherlands, being proprietors of estates or holders of mortgages of estates in the
of Demerara and Essequibo and of Berbice, are deemed to be Dutch proprietors in the said
for certain purposes in the said act mentioned, and it is expedient to permit such persons to re-
such character of Dutch proprietor; it is therefore enacted, that if any such person shall make

and sign a declaration in writing, attested by credible witnesses, setting forth that he is desirous and elected not to be deemed to be a Dutch proprietor, within the meaning of the said act, in respect of such estate or mortgage to be mentioned and named in such declaration, and shall cause such declaration to be delivered to the commissioners of his Majesty's customs, such person shall henceforth be no lo nor again deemed a Dutch proprietor, within the meaning of the said act, in respect of the estate or r gage so mentioned in such declaration ; and such declaration shall have effect in respect to any good produce of any such estate of which such person, so far as relates to those goods, was a Dutch propri although such goods may have been exported from the colony before the delivering of such declar — § 40.

Limiting the Period for the Fulfilment of the Conditions as to the Intercourse of foreign Ships wit British Possessions abroad. — Whereas by the said act for regulating the trade of the British posses abroad, it is, amongst other things, recited, that by the law of navigation foreign ships are permitte import into any of the British possessions abroad, from the countries to which they belong, goods the duce of those countries, and to export goods from such possessions to be carried to any foreign cou whatever, and that it is expedient that such permission should be subject to certain conditions ; and therefore by the said act enacted, that the privileges thereby granted to foreign ships shall be limited to ships of those countries which, having colonial possessions, shall grant the like privileges of trading those possessions to British ships, or which, not having colonial possessions, shall place the commerce navigation of this country and of its possessions abroad upon the footing of the most favoured na unless his Majesty, by his order in council, shall in any case deem it expedient to grant the whole or of such privileges to the ships of any foreign country although the conditions aforesaid shall not i respects be fulfilled by such country : and whereas unless some period be limited for the fulfilmen foreign countries of the conditions mentioned and referred to in the said recited act, the trade and gation of the United Kingdom and of the British possessions abroad cannot be regulated by fixed certain rules, but will continue subject to changes dependent upon the laws from time to time mad such foreign countries ; it is therefore enacted, that no foreign country shall hereafter be deemed to fulfilled the conditions so prescribed as aforesaid in and by the said act, as to be entitled to the privil therein mentioned, unless such foreign country had in all respects fulfilled those conditions within tw months next after the passing of the said act, that is to say, on or before the 5th of July, 1826. — § 4

For ascertaining what foreign Countries are to be deemed entitled to Privileges of British Ships. — the better ascertaining what particular countries are permitted by law to exercise and enjoy the said vileges, it is enacted, that no foreign country shall hereafter be deemed to have fulfilled the before-tioned conditions, or to be entitled to the privileges aforesaid, unless and until his Majesty shall by order or orders by him made by the advice of his privy council have declared that such foreign cou hath so fulfilled the said conditions and is entitled to the said privileges. — § 42.

Act not to affect Orders in Council issued under recited Acts. — Provided, that nothing herein conta extends or shall be construed to extend to make void or annul any order or orders in council heret issued under the authority of the said recited act, or to take away or abridge the powers vested i Majesty by that act, or any of them. — § 43.

The American government having declined complying with those conditions of r procity under which the trade between the United States and the British colonies to be opened by the act 6 Geo. 4. c. 114., it was directed by an order in council, d the 27th of July, 1826, that a duty of 4s. 3d. per ton should be charged upon American vessels entering his Majesty's possessions in the West Indies, as well a addition of 10 per cent. upon the duties imposed by the above-mentioned act on all each of the articles named in it, when imported into the West Indies in American sh

In the course of 1830, however, the negotiations that had been entered into with United States relative to this subject were happily terminated by the Americans ag ing to the conditions of reciprocity above-mentioned ; so that the discriminating d imposed upon the ships and goods under authority of the above-mentioned orde council are wholly repealed.

Subjoined is the circular letter of the American government, and an extract from British order in council, dated 5th November, 1830, relative to this new arrangeme

Circular to the Collectors of Customs.

Treasury Department, Oct. 6. 1830
Sir, — You will perceive by the proclamation of the president herewith transmitted, that from and the date thereof, the act entituled " An act concerning navigation," passed on the 13th of April, an act supplementary therein, passed the 15th of May, 1820 ; and an act entituled " An act to reg the commercial intercourse between the United States and certain British ports," passed on the March, 1823, are absolutely *repealed ; and the ports of the United States are open to British vessel their cargoes, coming from the British colonial possessions in the West Indies, on the continent of America, the Bahama Islands, the Caicos, and the Bermuda or Somer Islands ; also from the islands vinces, or colonies of Great Britain on or near the North American continent, and north or east United States.* By virtue of the authority of this proclamation, and in conformity with the arrange made between the United States and Great Britain, and under the sanction of the president, you a structed to admit to entry such vessels being laden with the productions of Great Britain or her said nies, subject to the same duties of tonnage and impost, and other charges, as are levied on the ves the United States or their cargoes arriving from the said British colonies : you will also grant clear to British vessels for the several ports of the aforesaid colonial possessions of Great Britain, such v being laden with such articles as may be exported from the United States in vessels of the United S and British vessels coming from the said colonial possessions may also be cleared for foreign port places other than those in the said British colonial possessions, being laden with such articles as m exported from the United States in vessels of the United States. I am, &c.

(Signed) S. D. Ingham, Secretary to the Treas

Extract from the British Order in Council, dated 5th November, 1830, relative to the Trade betwee United States and the British West Indies.

" Whereas it hath been made to appear to his Majesty in council, that the restrictions heretofor posed by the laws of the United States upon British vessels navigated between the said States an Majesty's possessions in the West Indies and America, have been repealed ; and that the discrimin duties of tonnage and of customs heretofore imposed by the laws of the said United States upon B vessels and their cargoes entering the ports of the said States from his Majesty's said possessions, hav been repealed, and that the ports of the United States are now open to British vessels and their ca coming from his Majesty's possessions aforesaid. His Majesty doth, therefore, with the advice privy council, and in pursuance and exercise of the powers so vested in him by the act passed in the year of the reign of his said late Majesty, or by any other act or acts of parliament, declare, that th

ted orders in council of the 21st July, 1823, and of the 27th July, 1826, and the said order in council he 16th July, 1827 (so far as such last-mentioned order relates to the said United States), shall be, and same are hereby respectively revoked.

And his Majesty doth further, by the advice aforesaid, and in pursuance of the powers aforesaid, declare the ships of and belonging to the said United States of America may import from the United States esaid into the British possessions abroad, goods the produce of those States, and may export goods n the British possessions abroad, to be carried to any country whatever.

And the Right Honourable the Lords Commissioners of his Majesty's Treasury, and the Right Honour-Sir G. Murray, one of his Majesty's principal secretaries of state, are to give the necessary directions ein, as to them may respectively appertain.

(Signed) " JAMES BULLER."

Connection of the Planter and Home Merchant. — Mode of transacting Business in gland. — The mode of transacting West India business is as follows: — A sugar nter forms a connection with a mercantile house in London, Bristol, Liverpool, or sgow; stipulates for an advance of money on their part; grants them a mortgage on estate; and binds himself to send them annually his crop, allowing them the full e of mercantile commissions. These commissions are 2½ per cent. on the amount sugar sold, and of plantation stores sent out; along with ½ per cent. on all insurances cted. During the war, when prices were high, the amount of those commissions large; but, like other high charges, the result has, in nine cases in ten, been to the ry of those who received them: they led the merchants to undertake too much, and nake too large advances to the planters, for the sake of obtaining their business. that time it was usual to allow a permanent loan at the rate of 3,000l. for the assured signment of 100 hogsheads of sugar; but that *ratio* was very often exceeded by planter, the 3,000l. becoming 4,000l., 5,000l., 6,000l., and, in very many cases, still e, in consequence of unforeseen wants and too sanguine calculations on his part. 'ersons resident in the West Indies are almost always bare of capital, and for obas reasons. A climate of such extreme heat, and a state of society possessing so attractions to persons of education, offer no inducements to men of substance in 'ope to go thither. Those who do go, must trust to their personal exertion and the port of others; and when, after a continued residence in the West Indies, they e made some progress in acquiring a competency, and have become accustomed he climate, they hardly ever consider themselves as settled there for life; their wish hope is to carry their acquisitions so far as to be enabled to pass the remainder of r days comfortably at home. The readiest means, in the view of the planter, of acplishing this is the extension of his undertakings; which he can do only by borrowing ey. Hence a continued demand on his mercantile correspondents at home for fresh nces: the consuming effect of heavy commissions, and of the interest on borrowed ey, is, or rather was, overlooked in his ardent speculations. But when prices rtunately fall, he finds himself 10,000l. or 20,000l. in debt, with a reduced ine. The merchants at home become equally embarrassed, because the case of one is ase of three fourths of their correspondents; and the capital of the merchants, e as it may be, is absorbed and placed beyond their control. The mortgages they are of value only in an ultimate sense: to foreclose them, and to take possession of estates is, in general, a very hazardous course.

ich has been for a number years the state of our West India trade, though at no was the depression so great and general as at present. Perhaps it is impossible to out any means of effectual relief: our planters must not build expectations on doubtful, or rather improbable, events as the stoppage of distillation from malt, insurrection of the negroes in rival countries, such as Cuba or Brazil. Of a bounty xportation it is idle to speak: so that their only rational and substantial ground of seems to be in a further reduction of the duties on sugar, coffee, and rum; and an tion of the duties on imports, and of the restrictions laid on their trade with America other countries.

e sale of West India articles takes place through the medium of produce brokers, in London reside chiefly in Mincing Lane and Tower Street. Samples of sugar 'um are on show in their respective sale rooms during four days of the week, viz. day, Wednesday, Thursday, and Friday, from 11 to 1 o'clock; during which time uigar refiners, wholesale grocers, and other dealers in produce, call in, observe the of the market, and buy what they require. The term of credit is short; only one h for coffee and rum, and two months for sugar. Coffee is generally sold by c auction, sugar and rum by private contract. The broker's commission is usually cent. on the amount; but in the case of coffee, as they guarantee the buyers, charge amounts to 1 per cent. The brokers have no correspondence or connection the planters; they are employed by the merchants; and their sales, though for large nts, being very simple, a brokerage house of consequence generally does the busiof a number of merchants. Neither merchant nor broker see, or are in the least r the necessity of seeing, the bulky packages containing the different articles of ce of which they effect the sales: all is done by sample; the packages remaining

Z

in the bonded warehouse from the time of landing till they are sold; after whic they pass to the premises of the refiner, wholesale grocer, or whoever may be the pu chaser.

The allowances made to the buyer in respect of weight, consist, first of the tare, whic is the exact weight of the cask; and, in the second place, of a fixed allowance of 5 lb per cask in the case of coffee, called trett, and of 2 lbs. per cask on sugar, under th name of draft. (See *Account Sales* of both, in pp. 141, 142.)

The shipping of stores from England to the plantations is also a very simple tran action. West India merchants in London, Liverpool, or Bristol, receive from th planters, in the autumn of each year, a list of the articles required for the respectiv estates: these lists they divide, arrange, and distribute among different wholesa dealers in the course of September and October, with instructions to get them ready ship in a few weeks. November and December are the chief months for the despatch outward bound West Indiamen, as the plantation stores ought, by rights, to arrive abou the end of December, or in the course of January. That is a season of activity, an generally of health, in the West Indies; the comparatively cool months of Novembe and December having cleared the air, and the produce of the fields having become rip and ready to carry. Crop time lasts from January to the end of July, after which th heavy rains put a stop to field work in the islands. Demerara, being so near the Lin experiences less difference in the seasons, and it is customary there to continue makin sugar all the year round.

The arrivals of West Indiamen in England with homeward cargoes begin in Apr and continue till October; after which, with the exception of occasional vessels fro Demerara and Berbice, they cease till the succeeding April. This corresponds wi the time of carrying and loading the crops: for it would be quite unadvisable, on t score of health, as well as of the interruptions to work from the heavy rains, to attem loading vessels in the sugar islands during the autumnal months.

The unloading of West Indiamen in London usually takes place at the West Ind docks; and did so uniformly from the autumn of 1802, when the docks were fir opened, till August, 1823, when the dock monopoly expired. The delays in discharging occasionally complained of during the war, arose from two causes; from the vesse arriving in fleets (in consequence of sailing with convoy, and from the imperfectio inseparable from a new establishment. The latter have been long remedied; and as the former, though at particular seasons, and after a change of wind, the vessels st come close on each other, the crowding in the docks is by no means to be compare to that arising from the arrival of a convoy. Cargoes are discharged very speedily, t time seldom exceeding three days. The dock dues have also been materially reduc since the peace: and the whole exhibits a striking example of the advantage attenda on transacting a mass of business on one spot; an advantage which can be enjoy only in great sea-ports, such as London, Liverpool, or Amsterdam. (See Docks)

The rates of freight during the war were, on sugar from 7s. to 8s. per cwt., and coffee from 10s. to 11s.; whereas they now amount, the former to 4s. and 4s. 6d., a the latter to 6s. The ship owners complain that these freights leave them very lit profit; but in consequence of the speed with which vessels may now be unloaded a cleared at London, it is probable that the practice of making *two* voyages in the seas will become general.

Disposal of Land in the Colonies. — The chief cause of the rapid advancement of colonies placed in rude and thinly peopled countries, has been the facility with whi they have obtained supplies of fertile and unoccupied land. Were the inhabitants o colony so situated, that instead of resorting to new land to obtain increased supplies food, they were obliged to improve the land already in cultivation, their progress wou be comparatively slow, and they would approach to the condition of an old countr and the greater the concentration of the inhabitants, the nearer, of course, would be th approach to that state. On the other hand, several inconveniences result from allowi the colonists to spread themselves at pleasure over unoccupied districts. The inhabita become too much dispersed to be able to lend efficient assistance to each other; a lar extent of roads is necessary, and their construction is a task too great for so thin a pop lation. But the greatest injury that can be done to a colony is the making of gratuito grants of large tracts of land to corporations or individuals, without laying upon the any obligation as to their occupation, or obliging them to contribute their share of expenses necessary on account of public improvements. Wherever such an unw policy has been pursued, as in Lower Canada for example, the consequences have be most injurious. The occurrence of the unoccupied districts obliges the settlers to es blish themselves at inconvenient distances from each other; it prevents, by the want roads, their easy communication; and retards, in a degree not easy to be imagined, advancement of the district. The inconveniences resulting from these grants are, inde

us. They have been loudly complained of by the colonists, and are now almost
rsally admitted.

is not difficult to discover the *principle* of the measures that ought to be adopted
respect to the disposal of unoccupied colonial land. They should be so contrived
prevent too great a diffusion of the colonists, without, however, occasioning their
reat concentration. And it is plain that these advantages may be realised by
g all lands at a moderate price, or by imposing upon them a moderate quit rent.
e price or quit rent were very high, it would, of course, occasion too great a con-
ation, and be an insuperable obstacle to the rapid progress of the colony; while, if
e too low, it would not obviate the inconvenience of too great dispersion. The
: of the price at which land should be sold is, therefore, the only really difficult
to be decided upon. The Americans sell their public lands at 2 dollars an acre;
his is, perhaps, all things considered, as proper a sum as could be selected.
therto we have not followed any fixed plan in the disposal of colonial lands, which
n many instances been bestowed in the most improvident manner. But we are
o observe that a new system is to be adopted, and that lands in the colonies are
n future, to be obtained except by purchase. We, however, are not without appre-
ns that considerable inconvenience will result from the proposed plan of selling
y *auction*. It is easy, no doubt, to fix a minimum upset price; but the market
must entirely depend on the *quantity put up for sale* compared with the number
eans of the buyers. And as the regulation of this quantity must necessarily be
the local authorities, they will, in fact, have the power of fixing the price. A
a of this sort can hardly fail of leading to very great abuses; and will give rise to
ual complaints, even when they are not deserved, of partiality and preference. The
ay, as it appears to us, would be to order competent persons to fix certain prices
all the lands to be located, according to the various circumstances for and against
and to grant specified portions of such lands to all who claimed them, according
amount of capital they proposed to employ in their cultivation. We do not, how-
hink that the maximum price ought in any case to exceed 12s. or 15s. an acre: a
f this magnitude would secure a sufficient degree of concentration, without carry-
e principle so far as to make it injurious.*

regulations proposed to be issued by government with respect to the mode of
ing of the public land in Canada have not yet been published. But it is said in
at notice from the Colonial Office, that " The regulations upon which lands have
o been granted in these colonies are no longer in force; and the principle of sale
tion will, in future, be adopted in all instances, except in those of naval and military
s. Until the details can be further considered, and information on certain points
d from the colonies, no printed form of regulations for the sale of lands can be
by this department. All persons, therefore, who may be ready to proceed, in the
ime, to North America, as settlers, must be prepared to purchase land at an upset
or on a payment of short instalments, instead of receiving it, as heretofore, by grant
t rent, or by instalments payable at distant periods."

understood that the regulations under which lands are in future to be disposed
Canada, will be very similar to those which have recently been adopted for the
l of land in New South Wales and Van Diemen's Land. These we subjoin.

upon which the Crown Lands will be disposed of in New South Wales and Van Diemen's Land.
been determined by his Majesty's government that no land shall, in future, be disposed of in
uth Wales or Van Diemen's Land otherwise than by public sale, and it has therefore been
expedient to prepare for the information of settlers the following summary of the rules which it
a thought fit to lay down for regulating the sales of land in those colonies
division of the whole territory into counties, hundreds, and parishes, is in progress. When that
shall be completed, each parish will comprise an area of about 25 square miles.
the lands in the colony, not hitherto granted, and not appropriated for public purposes, will be
o sale. The price will of course depend upon the quality of the land, and its local situation; but
will be sold below the rate of 5s. per acre.
persons proposing to purchase lands not advertised for sale, must transmit a written application
vernor, in a certain prescribed form, which will be delivered at the Surveyor General's Office to
ns applying, on payment of the requisite fee of 2s. 6d.
se persons who are desirous of purchasing, will be allowed to select, within certain defined limits,
tions of land as they may wish to acquire in that manner. These portions of land will be adver-
sale for three calendar months, and will then be sold to the highest bidder, provided that such
shall at least amount to the price fixed by Article 2.
eposit of 10 per cent. upon the whole value of the purchase must be paid down at the time of
the remainder must be paid within one calendar month from the day of sale, previous to which
haser will not be put in possession of the land: and in case of payment not being made within
ribed period, the sale will be considered void, and the deposit forfeited.
payment of the money, a grant will be made in fee-simple to the purchaser at the nominal quit
pepper corn. Previous to the delivery of such grant, a fee of 40s. will be payable to the colonial
, for preparing the grant, and another fee of 5s. to the registrar of the Supreme Court, for en-

injurious consequences resulting from the late system of granting lands in the colonies have
forcibly pointed out by Mr. Gouger, Mr. Tennant, and others; but the *degree* of concentration
mmend would be ten times more injurious.

7. The land will generally be put up to sale in lots of 1 square mile, or 640 acres; but smaller lots 640 acres may, under particular circumstances, be purchased, on making application to the govern writing, with full explanations of the reasons for which the parties wish to purchase a smaller quanti

8. The crown reserves to itself the right of making and constructing such roads and bridges as ma necessary for public purposes in all land purchased as above; and also to such indigenous timber, st and other materials, the produce of the land, as may be required for making and keeping the said r and bridges in repair and for any other public works. The crown further reserves to itself all min precious metals.

Colonial Office, 20th January, 1831.

Selection of Sites for Colonial Establishments. — Nothing can be more unwise than plan, if so we may call it, hitherto followed in the selection of places at which to fou colonies. The captain of a ship, without any knowledge whatever of the nature of so or the capacities of a country in an agricultural point of view, falls in after a long cru with a river or bay, abounding with fish and fresh water, and surrounded with land *looks* fertile, and is covered with herbage. He forthwith reports all these circumstan duly embellished, to the Admiralty, strongly recommending the situation as an admir one at which to found a colony; and in nine cases out of ten *this* is all the informa that is required in taking a step of such infinite importance! No wonder, theref that many fine schemes of colonisation should have ended only in loss and disappo ment; and that situations which the colonists were taught to look upon as a specie paradise, have proved to be any thing but what they were represented. Botany B though described by Captain Cook as one of the finest places in the world, had to abandoned by the colonists that were sent out to it; as the country round it, instea being favourable for cultivation, is a mere sandy swamp. Is it possible to suppose, the proper inquiries been entered into, that any attempt would have been made establish a colony in so pestilential a climate as that of Sierra Leone? The colony the district of Albany, in the Cape of Good Hope, was founded upon the representati of an individual, who, whatever might be his information in other respects, had not slightest knowledge of agriculture; and the distresses the settlers have had to encoun were the natural consequences of their relying on such authority. The late establishm at Swan River may be adduced as another instance of misplaced or premature confide in the reports of those who were really without the means of forming a correct estin of the various circumstances necessary to be attended to in forming a colony.

We do, therefore, hope that an end will be put to this system, — a system which i no common degree injurious to the public interests, and is highly criminal towards th who embark as colonists. The founding of a colony ought to be looked upon in its point of view — as a great national enterprise. It is not an adventure to be entruste presumptuous ignorance; but should be maturely weighed, and every circumsta connected with it carefully investigated. Above all, the situation in which it is prop to found the colony should be minutely surveyed; and its climate, soil, and capacitie production, deliberately inquired into by competent persons employed for the purp Were this done, government and the public would have the best attainable grounds u which to proceed; and neither party would have much reason to fear those disappo ments, which have hitherto so often followed the exaggerated representations of th to whom the important and difficult task of selecting situations for colonies has l delegated.

V. Foreign Colonies.

1. *Spanish Colonies.* — Spain, whose colonial possessions extended a few years from the frontiers of the United States to the Straits of Magellan, is not, at pres possessed of a foot of ground in the whole American continent. Still, however, colonial possessions are of great value and importance. In the West Indies she is tress of Cuba and Porto Rico; — the former by far the largest and finest of the India islands; and the latter also a very valuable possession. In the East, Spai mistress of the Philippine Islands, which, were they in the hands of an enterpri people, would speedily become of very great commercial importance. (See the Art HAVANNAH, MANILLA.)

2. *Dutch Colonies.* — Java forms the most important and valuable of the D colonial possessions. (See BATAVIA.) In the East they also possess the Molu Bencoolen on the coast of Sumatra, Macassar, and the eastern coast of Celebes, Ba &c. They have several forts on the Gold Coast in Africa; and in the West Indies possess the islands of Curaçoa and St. Eustatius, Saba, and part of St. Martin; an the continent of South America, they are masters of Dutch Surinam. Curaçoa an Eustatius are naturally barren, but they have been both highly improved. Fro being very conveniently situated for maintaining a contraband traffic with the Car and other districts in South America, Curaçoa was formerly a place of great trade, ticularly during war. But since the independence of South America, Curaço ceased in a great measure to be an *entrepôt;* the goods destined for the Continent now. for the most part, forwarded direct to the places of their destination.

That district of Surinam ceded to the British in 1814, comprising the settlements of merara, Berbice, and Essequibo (see *antè*, p. 324.), formed the most valuable portion Surinam, or Dutch Guiana. The district which still belongs to the Dutch lies to the th of Berbice. It contains about 25,000 square miles, and a population of about 000. It is daily becoming of more value and importance.

. *French Colonies.* — Previously to the negro insurrection that broke out in 1792, Domingo was by far the most valuable colony in the West Indies. But this disous event, having first devastated the island, terminated in the establishment of the pendent black republic of Hayti. (See PORT AU PRINCE.) Having also sold nisiana to the Americans, and ceded the Mauritius to the English, without making any acquisitions, the colonial dominions of France are, at this moment, of very limited nt. They consist of Guadeloupe and Martinique, and the small islands of Marie-lante and Deseada, in the West Indies; Cayenne in South America; Senegal and ee in Africa; the Isle de Bourbon in the Eastern Ocean; St. Marie in Madagascar; Pondichery and Chandernagor, with a very small surrounding territory, in the East ies. The following tabular statements show the population, trade, &c. of Martinique, adeloupe, and the Isle de Bourbon: —

Population of Martinique, Guadeloupe, and the Isle de Bourbon, in 1827.

	Whites.	Free Coloured Persons.	Slaves.			Total of Population.
			Male.	Female.	Total.	
rtinique - -	9,937	10,786	—	—	81,182	101,905
adeloupe - -	17,257	16,705	50,564	50,990	101,554	135,516
urbon - -	18,747	6,387	41,340	22,107	63,447	88,581

Trade of France with her Colonies.

Years.	Importation.	Exportation.	Number of Ships employed in Colonial Trade.	Tonnage of Ships.
	Fr.	*Fr.*		
1816	28,107,713	18,618,204	448	92,372
1817	43,147,023	17,067,436	563	114,405
1818	37,518,976	23,518,708	635	141,795
1819	36,048,238	17,635,342	523	122,252
1820	41,871,689	29,898,810	614	154,345
1821	48,766,852	30,237,968	651	154,759
1822	42,375,162	31,948,676	635	154,345
1823	45,240,972	34,862,305	665	155,910
1824	57,065,132	41,787,386	781	190,412
1825	44,417,924	44,100,274	729	184,255
1826	59,069,247	58,889,216	889	224,622
1827	55,370,588	50,817,657	842	214,258

(*Bulletin des Sciences Géographiques*, vol. xxiv. p. 357.)

Danish Colonies. — In the West Indies, these consist of the islands of St. Croix, Thomas, and St. John: of these, St. Croix only is valuable. It is about 81 square s in extent, and contains about 30,000 inhabitants, of whom 2,500 are whites, 1,200 blacks and mulattoes, and the remainder slaves. The soil is fertile, and it is well vated. The principal productions are sugar, rum, and coffee. In India, the Danes ss Tranquebar, near Madras; and Serampoor, near Calcutta. The former contained, 09, about 19,000 inhabitants; but it has greatly improved since the peace both in merce and population. Serampoor is a neat but not very considerable place. It s as an asylum for the debtors of Calcutta, and is the capital station of the mis-ries. The Danes have a few forts on the coast of Guinea.

Swedish Colonies. — The Swedes only possess one colony — the small island of St. holomew in the West Indies. It is only about 25 square miles in extent, but is fertile. It has no springs, nor fresh water of any sort, except such as is supplied e rain. Population between 8,000 and 9,000.

OLUMBO, the modern capital of Ceylon, situated on the south-west coast e island; lat. 6° 55' N., long. 79° 45' E. It is defended by a very strong In 1804, the population was ascertained to amount to about 50,000; and, aps, it may now amount to 60,000. The houses are generally only one story ; they are of stone, clay, and lime; and the town has more of a European arance than any other in India. The inhabitants are principally Cingalese. 321, there were only 32 Europeans in the place qualified to serve on juries. temperature of the air is remarkable for its equality; and though very humid, limate may, on the whole, be esteemed salubrious and temperate. There is, erly speaking, no harbour at Columbo, but only an open roadstead. It

affords secure anchorage from the beginning of October to the end of March when the wind blows off the land to the north-east; but during the six month of the other monsoon, when the wind blows on shore, the coast is not pract cable, and the inhabitants are cut off from all maritime intercourse either wit the rest of the island or with foreign countries. In this respect Columbo very inferior to Trincomalee, the harbour of which is accessible at all times, an is one of the best in India: but the country in the vicinity of Columbo is mor fertile; and it has the command of an internal navigation, stretching in a later direction along the coast, from Chilaw, to the north of the city, to Caltura on th south, a distance of about 70 miles, partly obtained by rivers, and partly by canal Many flat-bottomed boats are employed in this navigation, the families dependen on which reside permanently on board. Nearly all the foreign trade of Ceylo is carried on from Columbo; and it has also a large proportion of the coastin traffic.

Trade, Revenue, &c. — The quantity and estimated value of the principal articl exported from Ceylon in 1825, beginning with cinnamon, the most important of al were as follow, viz.: Cinnamon 403,501 lbs., value 114,418*l.*; arrack 611,218 gallon value 21,500*l.*; coir 5,788 coils, 2,260,109 lbs., value about 10,000*l.*; cocoa-nu 6,933,582, value 7,561*l.*; chanks and chank rings 2,196,008, value 8,219*l.*; timbe value 12,100*l.*; jaggery 309,955 lbs., value 4,946*l.*; coffee 33,922 parrahs, valu 13,883*l.* &c. The total value of the exports in 1825 and 1828 was as under: —

Years.	To Great Britain.	To India and China.	To Foreign States.	Total.
1825	- £97,537 ...	£122,956 ...	£3,895 ...	£224,388
1828	- 149,551 ...	64,189 ...	1,631 ...	215,372*

Of the imports, the principal is rice and other grain, the estimated value of the quan tity imported in 1825 being 158,636*l.*; the next article of importance is cotton cloth almost entirely brought from India, estimated at about 80,000*l.* The imports from Great Britain are very trifling; their entire value in 1828 being only estimated at 29,984 The total imports during that year amounted to 323,933*l.*; of which 269,518*l.* were fro India and China.†

The number and tonnage of the ships entering Ceylon inwards in 1828 were follow: —

Great Britain.		India and China.		Foreign States.		Total.	
No.	Tons.	No.	Tons.	No.	Tons.	No.	Tons.
23	8,765	1,137	41,682	154	9,631	1,314	60,670

manned by 14,794 men.

Ceylon, considered as a colonial dependency, is one of the least valuable in our po session. It appears from the official accounts, that during the fourteen years endi with 1824, the excess of expenditure over revenue in the island amounted to 1,365,452 at the same time that various heavy items of expense are not included in this accoun A part of this excess of expenditure may fairly be ascribed to the nature of the establis ment kept up in the island; which, in point of magnitude and expensiveness, seems be very much beyond what is really required. We are, however, inclined to think th the greater part of the excess is to be ascribed to the poverty and backward state of t colony, arising from the perpetual interference of government with every branch of i dustry. All the restrictive regulations enacted by the Dutch more than a century a are still kept up. The cultivation of cinnamon, the fishery of pearls and chanks, t digging for chaya root, the felling of timber, &c. (see these articles) are all monopolis by government, and are carried on exclusively either by its servants or those whom has licensed. A country where most of the principal branches of industry are subject to such restrictions, cannot be otherwise than languishing. We believe, too, that most these monopolies are not worth to government the expense attending them. In fact, t whole revenue of the island, including land rent, customs, cinnamon monopoly, & seldom exceeds 300,000*l.* a year; but looking at its extent, its fertility, its favourab situation for commerce, and the advantage it enjoys in the possession of cinnamon, c any one doubt that, were it rightly governed, its trade and revenue would be far grea than they are? Nothing is wanted but the adoption of measures calculated to gi freedom and security to industry, and the imposition of moderate duties on imports a exports, to increase them both in a very high degree. Considerable difficulties, no dou stand in the way of any material change; but if the right hon. gentleman now at t head of the government of Ceylon regards the present system in the light which it is

* Add amount of pearl fishery for 1828, 30,612*l.*
† Dr. Colquhoun (2d ed. p. 412.) estimated the exports of Ceylon at 1,500,000*l.* a year, and the imp at 1,000,000*l.* Perhaps a third of the Doctor's estimates are about equally near the mark.

►ped he will do, his firmness and intelligence will enable him to introduce the ne-
►ry changes with comparative facility.

►e population of Ceylon has been very much exaggerated. It has frequently been
►ated as high as two millions ; and even Mr. Bertolacci reckoned it at a million and
►. — (*View of Ceylon*, p. 65.) But it was found, by actual enumeration, that the
►population, including the Candyan provinces, in 1825, amounted to only 754,394.
►rly the population has increased rapidly, in consequence of the prevalence of vac-
►on having checked the ravages of the small pox, that were previously very fatal.
►resent population is, we understand, estimated at about 900,000.

►*neys.* — The rixdollar = 1*s.* 6*d.* ; but accounts are kept in pounds, shillings, and
►, as in England.

►*ights, Measures, &c.* — The weights are divided into ounces, pounds, &c., and are
►me as in Great Britain. The candy or bahar = 500 lbs. avoirdupois, or 461 lbs.
►n Troy weight. The principal dry measures are *seers* and *parrahs.* The former is
►ect cylinder, of the depth and diameter undermentioned : —

	Depth.	Diameter.
Seer - - 4·35 inches.	4·35 inches.

►e parrah is a perfect cube, its internal dimensions being every way 11·57 inches.
►e liquid measure consists of gallons, and their multiples and sub-multiples. 150
►►s = 1 leaguer or legger.
►e bale of cinnamon consists of 92½ lbs. very nearly.
►compiling this article, we have made use of *Hamilton's East India Gazetteer, Ber-
►'s View of Ceylon, &c.* ; but the principal part of our information has been derived
►fficial documents laid before the finance committee.

►*LUMBO ROOT* (Du. *Columbo wortel* ; Fr. *Racine de Colombo* ; Ger. *Co-
►-wurzel* ; It. *Radice di Columbo* ; Port. *Raiz de Columba* ; Sp. *Raiz de Columbo* ;
►mb. *Kalumb*), the root of the plant of that name. It is a staple export of
►ortuguese from Mosambique. It is not cultivated, but grows naturally in
►abundance. It is imported in circular pieces, from ½ inch to 3 inches in
►ter, generally from ¼ to ¾ of an inch thick ; the bark is wrinkled and thick,
►rownish colour without, and a brightish yellow within ; the pith is spongy,
►ish, and slightly striped : when fresh, its smell is rather aromatic ; it is dis-
►bly bitter, and slightly pungent to the taste, somewhat resembling mustard
►as been too long kept. Choose the largest pieces, fresh, and of a good
►·, as free from worms as possible, rejecting that which is small and broken.
►eight is calculated at 16 cwt. to a ton.—(*Milburn's Orient. Com.*)

►MBS (Ger. *Kamme* ; Du. *Kammen* ; Fr. *Peignes* ; It. *Peltini* ; Sp. *Peines* ;
►Grebnü ; Lat. *Pectines*), instruments for combing the hair, sometimes made
►ns of bullocks, or of elephants' and sea-horses' teeth ; sometimes also of
►se-shell, and sometimes of box or holly-wood.

►MMERCE, from *commutatio mercium*, is simply, as its name imports, the
►ige of commodities for commodities.

    I. Origin of Commerce. — Mercantile Classes.
    II. Home Trade.
    III. Foreign Trade.
    IV. Restrictions on Commerce.

I. Origin of Commerce. — Mercantile Classes.

► *The Origin of Commerce* is coëval with the first dawn of civilisation. The
►nt that individuals ceased to supply themselves directly with the various
►s and accommodations they made use of, that moment must a commercial
►ouse have begun to grow up amongst them. For it is only by exchanging
►ortion of the produce raised by ourselves that exceeds our own consumption,
►tions of the surplus produce raised by others, that the division of employ-
►can be introduced, or that different individuals can apply themselves in pre-
►e to different pursuits.

►only, however, does commerce enable the inhabitants of the same village
►sh to combine their separate efforts to accomplish some common object,
►lso enables those of different provinces and kingdoms to apply themselves
►special manner to those callings, for the successful prosecution of which
►rict or country which they occupy gives them some peculiar advantage. This
►ial division of labour has contributed more, perhaps, than anything else to

increase the wealth and accelerate the civilisation of mankind. Were it not it, we should be destitute of a vast number of the necessaries, comforts, and joyments, which we now possess; while the price of the few that would remain us would, in most instances, be very greatly increased. But whatever advant may be derived—and it is hardly possible to exaggerate either their magnitud importance—from availing ourselves of the peculiar capacities of produc enjoyed by others, are wholly to be ascribed to commerce as their real source origin.

We do not mean to say any thing in this article with respect to the pract details connected with the different departments of commerce. These will found under the various titles to which they refer. Our object, at present merely to show the nature and influence of commerce in general, and of restrictions that have sometimes been imposed upon it. We shall begin by deavouring, first of all, to give some account of the nature of the serv performed by those individuals by whom commercial undertakings are usu carried on. In the second place, we shall consider the influence of the *home* tr or of the intercourse subsisting amongst individuals of the same country. In third place, we shall consider the influence of *foreign* trade, or of that intercou which subsists amongst individuals belonging to different countries. After th topics have been discussed, we shall offer a few remarks on what has been terr the restrictive system; or on the principles involved in the regulations enacte different times, in this and other countries, for the government and direction commerce.

(2.) *Mercantile Classes.* — While the exchange of different products is carried by the producers themselves, they must unavoidably lose a great deal of time, experience many inconveniences. Were there no merchants, a farmer wishing sell his crop would be obliged, in the first place, to seek for customers, and dispose of his corn as nearly as possible in such quantities as might suit the mands of the various individuals inclined to buy it; and after getting its price, would next be obliged to send to ten or twenty different and, perhaps, rem places, for the commodities he wanted to get in its stead. So that besi being exposed to a world of trouble and inconvenience, his attention woulc continually diverted from the labours of his farm. Under such a state of thi the work of production, in every different employment, would be meeting perpetual interruptions, and many branches of industry that are successf carried on in a commercial country would not be undertaken.

The establishment of a distinct mercantile class effectually obviates th inconveniences. When a set of dealers erect warehouses and shops for the chase and sale of all descriptions of commodities, every producer, relieved f the necessity of seeking customers, and knowing beforehand where he may a times be supplied with such products as he requires, devotes his whole time energies to his proper business. The intervention of merchants gives a continu and uninterrupted motion to the plough and the loom. Were the class of tra annihilated, all the springs of industry would be paralysed. The numberless ficulties that would then occur in effecting exchanges would lead each partic family to endeavour to produce all the articles they had occasion for: soc would thus be thrown back into primæval barbarism and ignorance. The divis of labour would be relinquished; and the desire to rise in the world and imp our condition would decline, according as it became more difficult to gratif What sort of agricultural management could be expected from farmers who to manufacture their own wool, and make their own shoes? And what sor manufacturers would those be, who were every now and then obliged to leave shuttle for the plough, or the needle for the anvil? A society, without that tinction of employments and professions resulting from the division of lab that is, *without commerce*, would be totally destitute of arts or sciences of any It is by the assistance each individual renders to and receives from his neighbe by every one applying himself in preference to some peculiar task, and combir though probably without intending it, his efforts with those of others, that civi man becomes equal to the most gigantic efforts, and appears endowed with al omnipotent power.

The mercantile class has generally been divided into two subordinate class the wholesale dealers, and the retail dealers. The former purchase the va

ducts of art and industry in the places where they are produced, or are least uable, and carry them to those where they are more valuable, or where they more in demand; and the latter, having purchased the commodities of the olesale dealers, or the producers, collect them in shops, and sell them in such ntities and at such times as may best suit the public demand. These classes lealers are alike useful; and the separation that has been effected between their ployments is one of the most advantageous divisions of labour. The operations he wholesale merchant are analogous to those of the miner. Neither the one the other makes any change on the bodies which he carries from place to e. All the difference between them consists in this,—that the miner carries m from below ground to the surface of the earth, while the merchant carries m from one point to another on its surface. Hence it follows that the value n to commodities by the operations of the wholesale merchant may frequently eed that given to them by the producers. It requires as much labour, or is ut as expensive, to convey a ton of coals from Newcastle to London, as it s to dig them from the mine; and it is certain that far more labour and ex- se are required to convey a piece of timber from Canada to England, than to down the tree. In this respect there is no difference between commerce and culture and manufactures. The latter give utility to matter, by bestowing on ich a shape as may best fit it for ministering to our wants and comforts; and former gives additional utility to the products of the agriculturist and manu- urer, by bringing them from where they are of comparatively little use, or in excess, to where they are of comparatively great use, or are deficient.

f the wholesale merchant were himself to retail the goods he has brought from rent places, he would require a proportional increase of capital; and it would mpossible for him to give that exclusive attention to any department of his ness, which is indispensable to its being carried on in the best manner. It r the interest of each dealer, as of each workman, to confine himself to some business. By this means each trade is better understood, better cultivated, carried on in the cheapest possible manner. But whether carried on by a rate class of individuals or not, it is obvious that the retailing of commodities dispensable. It is not enough that a cargo of tea should be imported from na, or a cargo of sugar from Jamaica. Most individuals have some demand these articles; but there is not, perhaps, a single private person, even in don, requiring so large a supply of them for his own consumption. It is r, therefore, that they must be *retailed;* that is, they must be sold in such ntities and at such times as may be most suitable for all classes of consumers. since it is admitted on all hands, that this necessary business will be best lucted by a class of traders distinct from the wholesale dealers, it is impossible oubt that their employment is equally conducive as that of the others to the ic interest, or that it tends equally to augment national wealth and comfort.

II. HOME TRADE.

he observations already made serve to show the influence of the home trade lowing individuals to confine their attention to some one employment, and to ecute it without interruption. But it is not in this respect only that the lishment of the home trade is advantageous. It is so in a still greater degree s allowing the inhabitants of the different districts of the empire to turn labour into those channels in which it will be most productive. The dif- t soils, different minerals, and different climates of different districts, fit them eing appropriated, in preference, to certain species of industry. A district, Lancashire, where coal is abundant, which has an easy access to the ocean, and nsiderable command of internal navigation, is the natural seat of manufac- . Wheat and other species of grain are the natural products of rich arable ; and cattle, after being reared in mountainous districts, are most advan- ously fattened in meadows and low grounds. Hence it follows, that the itants of different districts, by confining themselves to those branches of stry for the successful prosecution of which they have some peculiar capability, exchanging their surplus produce for that of others, will obtain an incom- ly larger supply of all sorts of useful and desirable products, than they could vere they to apply themselves indiscriminately to every different business. territorial division of labour is, if possible, even more advantageous than its

division among individuals. A person may be what is commonly termed *Jack* •
all trades; and though it is next to certain that he will not be well acquainte
with any one of them, he may nevertheless make some sort of rude efforts in the
all. But it is not possible to apply the same soil or the same minerals to ever
different purpose. Hence it is, that the inhabitants of the richest and most exter
sive country, provided it were divided into small districts without any intercours
with each other, or with foreigners, could not, how well soever labour might b
divided among themselves, be otherwise than poor and miserable. Some of the
might have a superabundance of corn, at the same time that they were wholl
destitute of wine, coal, and iron; while others might have the largest supplies •
the latter articles, with but very little grain. But in commercial countries n
such anomalies can exist. Opulence and comfort are there universally diffuse
The labours of the mercantile classes enable the inhabitants of each district t
apply themselves principally to those employments that are naturally best suite
to them. This superadding of the division of labour among different provinces t
its division among different individuals, renders the productive powers of industr
immeasurably greater; and augments the mass of necessaries, conveniences, an
enjoyments, in a degree that could not previously have been conceived possibl
and which cannot be exceeded except by the introduction of foreign commerce

"With the benefit of commerce," says an eloquent and philosophical write
"or a ready exchange of commodities, every individual is enabled to avail himsel
to the utmost, of the peculiar advantage of his place; to work on the peculi
materials with which nature has furnished him; to humour his genius or dispo
sition, and betake himself to the task in which he is peculiarly qualified to succee
The inhabitant of the mountain may betake himself to the culture of his wood
and the manufacture of his timber; the owner of pasture lands may betake hin
self to the care of his herds; the owner of the clay-pit to the manufacture of h
pottery; and the husbandman to the culture of his fields, or the rearing of h
cattle. And any one commodity, however it may form but a small part in th
accommodations of human life, may, under the facility of commerce, find a mark•
in which it may be exchanged for what will procure any other part, or the whole
so that the owner of the clay-pit, or the industrious potter, without producir
any one article immediately fit to supply his own necessities, may obtain posse
sion of all that he wants. And commerce, in which it appears that commoditi•
are merely exchanged, and nothing produced, is nevertheless, in its effects, ver
productive, because it ministers a facility and an encouragement to every arti
in multiplying the productions of his own art; thus adding greatly to the mass •
wealth in the world, in being the occasion that much is produced."—(*Ferguson
Principles of Moral Science*, vol. ii. p. 424.)

The roads and canals that intersect a country, and open an easy communicatic
between its remotest extremities, render the greatest service to internal commerc
and also to agriculture and manufactures. A diminution of the expense of ca
riage has, in fact, the same effect as a diminution of the direct cost of productio
If the coals brought into a city sell at 20*s.* a ton, of which the carriage amoun
to a half, or 10*s.*, it is plain that in the event of an improved communication, su•
as a more level or direct road, a railway, or a canal, being opened for the co
veyance of the coals, and that they can, by its means, be imported for half t
previous expense, their price will immediately fall to 15*s.* a ton; just as it wou
have done, had the expense of extracting them from the mine been reduced
half.

Every one acquainted with the merest elements of political science is awa
that employments are more and more subdivided, that more powerful machine
is introduced, and the productive powers of labour increased, according as larg
masses of the population congregate together. In a great town like Londo
Glasgow, or Manchester, the same number of hands will perform much more wo
than in a small village, where each individual has to perform several operatio
and where the scale of employment is not sufficiently large to admit of the intr
duction of extensive and complicated machinery. But the great towns with whi
England is studded, could not exist without our improved means of communi
tion. These, however, enable their inhabitants to supply themselves with the bul
products of the soil and of the mines almost as cheap as if they lived in coun
villages; securing to them all the advantages of concentration, with but few of

veniences   Roads and canals are thus productive of a double benefit: for
, by affording comparatively cheap raw materials to the manufacturers, they
them the means of perfecting the divisions of labour, and of supplying pro-
onally cheap manufactured goods; the latter are conveyed by their means,
t an extremely small expense, to the remotest parts of the country.   The
t advantages which they confer on agriculture are not less important.   With-
hem it would not be possible to carry to a distance sufficient supplies of
marl, shells, and other bulky and heavy articles necessary to give luxuriance
e crops of rich soils, and to render those that are poor productive.   Good
  and canals, therefore, by furnishing the agriculturists with cheap and
dant supplies of manure, reduce, at one and the same time, the *cost of*
cing the necessaries of life, and the cost of bringing them to market.
other respects the advantages resulting from improved communications are
bly even more striking.   They give the same common interest to every different
of the most widely extended empire; and put down, or rather prevent, any
pt at monopoly on the part of the dealers of particular districts, by bringing
into competition with those of all the others.   Nothing in a state enjoying
facilities of communication is separate and unconnected.   All is mutual,
ocal, and dependent.   Every man naturally gets into the precise situation
e is best fitted to fill; and each, co-operating with every one else, contributes
e utmost of his power to extend the limits of production and civilisation.
Canals, and Rail Roads.)
h being the nature and vast extent of the advantages derived from the home
  it is obviously the duty of the legislature to give it every proper encourage-
and protection.   It will be found however, on a little consideration, that
uty is rather negative than positive—that it consists less in the framing of
tions, than in the removal of obstacles.   The error of governments in
rs of trade has not been that they have done too little, but that they have
pted too much.   It will be afterwards shown that the encouragement which
en afforded to the producers of certain species of articles in preference to
, has uniformly been productive of disadvantage.   In the mean time it is
ent to observe that the encouragement which a prudent and enlightened
ment bestows on industry, will equally extend to all its branches; and
e especially directed to the removal of every thing that may in any respect
the freedom of commerce, and the power of individuals to engage in different
yments.   All regulations, whatever be their object, that operate either
vent the circulation of commodities from one part of the empire to another,
free circulation of labour, necessarily tend to check the division of employ-
and the spirit of competition and emulation, and must, in consequence,
the amount of produce.   The same principle that prompts to open roads,
struct bridges and canals, ought to lead every people to erase from the
e book every regulation which either prevents or fetters the operations of
erchant, and the free disposal of capital and labour.   Whether the freedom
ernal commerce and industry be interrupted by impassable mountains and
s, or by oppressive tolls or restrictive regulations, the effect is equally per-
s.
  common law and the ancient statute law of England are decidedly hostile
nopolies, or to the granting of powers to any particular class of individuals
ish the market with commodities.   Lord Coke distinctly states " that all
olies concerning trade and traffic are against the liberty and freedom
d by the great charter, and divers other acts of parliament which are good
ntaries upon that charter."—(2 *Inst.* 63.) And he affirms, in another place,
Commercium jure gentium commune esse debet, et non in monopolium et
m paulolorum questum convertendum.   Iniquum est aliis permittere, aliis
e mercaturam."
, notwithstanding this concurrence of the common and statute law of the
y in favour of the freedom of industry, during the arbitrary reigns of the
 of the house of Tudor, the notion that the crown was by its prerogative
d to dispense with any law to the contrary, and to establish monopolies,
e fashionable among the court lawyers, and was acted upon to a very great
.   Few things, indeed, occasioned so much dissatisfaction in the reign of
eth as the multiplication of monopolies; and notwithstanding the opposition

made by the crown, and the court party in parliament, the grievance becam
length so intolerable as to give rise to the famous statute of 1624 (21 Jame
c. 3.), by which all monopolies, grants, letters patent, and licences, for the s
buying, selling, and making of goods and manufactures, not given by an act of
legislature, are declared to be " *altogether contrary to the laws of this realm, v
and of none effect.*"   This statute has been productive of the greatest advanta
and has, perhaps, contributed more than any other to the development
industry, and the accumulation of wealth.   With the exception of the monop
of printing Bibles, and the restraints imposed by the charters of bodies leg
incorporated, the freedom of internal industry has ever since been vigila
protected; full scope has been given to the principle of competition; the wh
kingdom has been subjected to the same equal law; no obstacles have b
thrown in the way of the freest transfer of commodities from one county or pl
to another; the home trade has been perfectly unfettered; and though the pu
have not been supplied with commodities at so low a price as they might h
obtained them for, had there been no restrictions on foreign commerce, they b
obtained them at the lowest price that would suffice to pay the *home produ*
the cost of producing and bringing them to market.   It is to this freedom t
the comparatively flourishing state of industry in Great Britain is mainly to
ascribed.

III. FOREIGN TRADE.

What the home trade is to the different provinces of the same country, fore
trade is to all the countries of the world.   Particular countries produce o
particular commodities, and, were it not for foreign commerce, would be enti
destitute of all but such as are indigenous to their own soil.   It is difficult for th
who have not reflected on the subject, to imagine what a vast deduction wo
be made, not only from the comforts, but even from the necessaries, of every c
mercial people, were its intercourse with strangers put an end to.   It is not,
haps, too much to say that in Great Britain we owe to our intercourse with ot
a full half or more of all that we enjoy.   We are not only indebted to it for the
ton and silk manufactures, and for supplies of wine, tea, coffee, sugar, the preci
metals, &c.; but we are also indebted to it for most of the fruits and vegeta
that we now cultivate.   At the same time, too, that foreign commerce supplie
with an immense variety of most important articles, of which we must other
have been wholly ignorant; it enables us to employ our industry in the mod
which it is sure to be most productive, and reduces the price of almost e
article.   We do not misemploy our labour in raising sugar from the beet-root
cultivating tobacco, or in forcing vines; but we employ ourselves in those dep
ments of manufacturing industry in which our command of coal, of capital,
of improved machinery, give us an advantage; and obtain the articles produ
more cheaply by foreigners, in exchange for the surplus produce of those bran
in which we have a superiority over them.   A commercial nation like Eng
avails herself of all the peculiar facilities of production given by Providenc
different countries.   To produce claret here is perhaps impossible; and at all ev
it could not be accomplished, unless at more than a hundred times the exp
required for its production in France.   We do not, however, deny ourselves
gratification derivable from its use; and to obtain it, we have only to sen
France, or to some country indebted to France, some article in the produc
of which we have an advantage, and we get claret in exchange at the price w
it takes to raise it under the most favourable circumstances.   One country
peculiar capacities for raising corn, but is at the same time destitute of wine,
and tea.   Another, again, has peculiar facilities for raising the latter, but is desti
of the former; and it is impossible to point out a single country which is al
dantly supplied with any considerable variety of commodities of domestic gro
Non omnis fert omnia tellus.   Providence, by giving to each particular nation s
thing which the others want, has evidently intended that they should be mutu
dependent upon one another.   And it is not difficult to see that, *cæteris par*
those must be the richest and most abundantly supplied with every sort of u
and desirable accommodation, who cultivate the arts of peace with the gre
success, and deal with all the world on fair and liberal principles.

" The commerce of one country with another is, in fact," to use the wor
an able and profound writer, " merely an extension of that division of labou

ich so many benefits are conferred upon the human race. As the same
intry is rendered the richer by the trade of one province with another; as its
our becomes thus infinitely more divided and more productive than it could
erwise have been; and as the mutual supply to each other of all the accommo-
ions which one province has, and another wants, multiplies the accommodations
the whole, and the country becomes thus in a wonderful degree more opulent
happy; the same beautiful train of consequences is observable in the world at
e,—that great empire of which the different kingdoms and tribes of men may
regarded as the provinces. In this magnificent empire, too, one province is
ourable to the production of one species of accommodation, and another pro-
e to another: by their mutual intercourse they are enabled to sort and
ribute their labour as most peculiarly suits the genius of each particular spot.
e labour of the human race thus becomes much more productive, and every
ies of accommodation is afforded in much greater abundance. The same
nber of labourers, whose efforts might have been expended in producing a very
gnificant quantity of home-made luxuries, may thus, in Great Britain, produce
antity of articles for exportation, accommodated to the wants of other places,
peculiarly suited to the genius of Britain to furnish, which will purchase for
an accumulation of the luxuries of every quarter of the globe. There is not
eater proportion of her population employed in administering to her luxuries,
onsequence of her commerce; there is probably a good deal less: but their
ur is infinitely more productive: the portion of commodities which the people
reat Britain acquire by means of the same labour, is vastly greater."—(*Mill's
merce defended*, p. 38.)

hat has been already stated is sufficient to expose the utter fallacy of the
ion that has sometimes been maintained, that whatever one nation may gain
er foreign commerce, must be lost by some one else. It is singular, indeed,
such a notion should ever have originated. Commerce *is not directly produc-*
nor is the good derived from it to be estimated by its immediate effects. What
mercial nations give is uniformly the fair equivalent of what they get. In
r dealings they do not prey upon each other, but are benefited alike. The
antage of commerce consists in its enabling labour to be divided, and giving
people the power of supplying themselves with the various articles for which
have a demand, at the lowest price required for their production in those
tries and places where they are raised with the greatest facility. We import
from Portugal, and cotton from America, sending in exchange cloth and
r species of manufactured goods. By this means we obtain two very
rtant articles, which it would be all but impossible to produce at home,
which we could not certainly produce except at an infinitely greater cost.
our gain is no loss to the foreigners. They derive precisely the same sort of
antage from the transaction that we do. We have very superior facilities for
ufacturing, and they get from us cloth, hardware, and other important articles,
e price at which they can be produced in this country, and consequently for
ess than their direct production would have cost them. The benefits resulting
an intercourse of this sort are plainly mutual and reciprocal. Commerce
no advantage to any one people over any other people; but it increases the
th and enjoyments of *all* in a degree that could not previously have been
eived possible.

ut the influence of foreign commerce in multiplying and cheapening con-
ences and enjoyments, vast as it most certainly is, is perhaps inferior to its
ect influence—that is, to its influence on industry, by adding immeasurably
e mass of desirable articles, by inspiring new tastes, and stimulating enter-
and invention by bringing each people into competition with foreigners,
making them acquainted with their arts and institutions.

e apathy and languor that exist in a rude state of society have been uni-
lly remarked. But these uniformly give place to activity and enterprise,
rding as man is rendered familiar with new objects, and is inspired with a
e to obtain them. An individual might, with comparatively little exertion,
sh himself with an abundant supply of the commodities essential to his sub-
ice; and if he had no desire to obtain others, or if that desire, however strong,
not be gratified, it would be folly to suppose that he should be laborious,
tive, or enterprising. But, when once excited, the wants and desires of man

become altogether illimitable; and to excite them, no more is necessary than t
bring new products and new modes of enjoyment within his reach. Now, the su
way to do this is to give every facility to the most extensive intercourse wit
foreigners. The markets of a commercial nation being filled with the various con
modities of every country and every climate, the motives and gratifications whic
stimulate and reward the efforts of the industrious, are proportionally augmente
The husbandman and manufacturer exert themselves to increase their supplies
raw and manufactured produce, that they may exchange the surplus for th
products imported from abroad. And the merchant, finding a ready demand fc
such products, is prompted to import a greater variety, to find out cheape
markets, and thus constantly to afford new incentives to the vanity and ambitio
and consequently to the enterprise and industry, of his customers. The whol
powers of the mind and the body are thus called into action; and the passio
for foreign commodities — a passion which has sometimes been ignorantly censure
— becomes one of the most efficient causes of wealth and civilisation.

Not only, however, does foreign commerce excite industry, distribute the gif
of nature, and enable them to be turned to the best account, but it also distr
butes the gifts of science and of art, and gives to each particular country the mear
of profiting by the inventions and discoveries of others as much as by those of he
own citizens. The ingenious machine invented by Mr. Whitney, of the Unite
States, for separating cotton wool from the pod, by reducing the cost of the ra
material of one of our principal manufactures, has been quite as advantageous t
us as to his own countrymen. And the discoveries and inventions of Watt, Ar
wright, and Wedgwood, by reducing the cost of the articles we send abroad, hav
been as advantageous to our foreign customers as to ourselves. Commerce ha
caused the blessings of civilisation to be universally diffused, and the treasures
knowledge and science to be conveyed to the remotest corners. Its huma
ising influence is, in this respect, most important; while, by making each count
depend for the means of supplying a considerable portion of its wants on th
assistance of others, it has done more than anything else to remove a host of th
most baleful prejudices, and to make mankind regard each other as friends ar
not as enemies. The dread, once so prevalent, of the progress
other nations in wealth and civilisation, is now universally admitted to be as a
surd as it is illiberal. While every people ought always to be prepared to resi
and avenge any attack upon their independence or their honour, it is not to
doubted that their real prosperity will be best secured by their endeavouring
live at peace. "A commercial war, whether crowned with victory or brand
with defeats, can never prevent another nation from becoming more industrio
than you are; and if they are more industrious they will sell cheaper; and cons
quently your customers will forsake your shop and go to their's. This will happe
though you covered the ocean with fleets, and the land with armies. The sold
may lay waste; the privateer, whether successful or unsuccessful, will make poo
but it is the eternal law of Providence that " *the hand of the diligent can alone ma
rich.*" — (*Tucker's Four Tracts*, p. 41. 3d ed.)

Mr. Hume has beautifully illustrated the powerful and salutary influen
of that spirit of industry and enterprise resulting from the eager prosecuti
of commerce and the arts. "Men," says he, "are then kept in perpetu
occupation, and enjoy, as their reward, the occupation itself, as well as tho
pleasures which are the fruits of their labour. The mind acquires new vigou
enlarges its powers and faculties; and, by an assiduity in honest industry, bo
satisfies its natural appetites, and prevents the growth of unnatural ones, whi
commonly spring up when nourished with ease and idleness. Banish those a
from society, you deprive men both of action and of pleasure; and, leaving nothi
but indolence in their place, you even destroy the relish of indolence, whi
never is agreeable but when it succeeds to labour, and recruits the spirits,
hausted by too much application and fatigue.

"Another advantage of industry and of refinements in the mechanical arts,
that they commonly produce some refinements in the liberal; nor can the one
carried to perfection, without being accompanied in some degree with the oth
The same age which produces great philosophers and politicians, renown
generals and poets, usually abounds with skilful weavers and ship-carpenters.
cannot reasonably expect that a piece of woollen cloth will be wrought to perf

in a nation which is ignorant of astronomy, or where ethics are neglected.
spirit of the age affects all the arts; and the minds of men, being once roused
their lethargy, and put into a fermentation, turn themselves on all sides, and
improvements into every art and science. Profound ignorance is totally
hed; and men enjoy the privilege of rational creatures, to think as well as
t, to cultivate the pleasures of the mind as well as those of the body.
The more these refined arts advance, the more sociable do men become; nor
ossible that, when enriched with science, and possessed of a fund of con-
tion, they should be contented to remain in solitude, or live with their fellow
ns in that distant manner which is peculiar to ignorant and barbarous
ns. They flock into cities; love to receive and communicate knowledge; to
their wit or their breeding; their taste in conversation or living, in clothes
·niture. Curiosity allures the wise, vanity the foolish, and pleasure both.
cular clubs and societies are every where formed; both sexes meet in an easy
ociable manner; and the tempers of men, as well as their behaviour, refine
. So that beside the improvements they receive from knowledge and the
arts, it is impossible but they must feel an increase of humanity from the
abit of conversing together, and contributing to each other's pleasure and
ainment. Thus *industry, knowledge*, and *humanity*, are linked together by an
oluble chain; and are found, from experience as well as reason, to be peculiar
more polished, and, what are commonly denominated, the more luxurious
'—(*Essay of Refinement in the Arts*.)
st commercial treatises, and most books on political economy, contain
ened statements as to the comparative advantages derived from the home
reign trade. But these statements are almost always bottomed on the most
eous principles. The quantity and value of the commodities which the in-
nts of an extensive country exchange with each other, is far greater than
antity and value of those they exchange with foreigners: but this is not, as
monly supposed, enough to show that the home trade is proportionally
advantageous. Commerce, it must be borne in mind, is not a direct but an
ct source of wealth. The mere exchange of commodities adds nothing to
hes of society. The influence of commerce on wealth consists in its allow-
ployments to be separated and prosecuted without interruption. It gives
eans of pushing the divisions of labour to the farthest extent; and supplies
nd with an infinitely greater quantity of necessaries and accommodations of
rts, than could have been produced, had individuals and nations been
to depend upon their own comparatively feeble efforts for the supply of
vants. And hence, in estimating the comparative advantageousness of the
and foreign trades, the real questions to be decided are, which of them
outes most to the division of labour? and which of them gives the greatest
us to invention and industry? These questions do not, perhaps, admit of
ry satisfactory answer. The truth is, that both home trade and foreign
are most prolific sources of wealth. Without the former no division of
could be established, and man would for ever remain in a barbarous state.
, perhaps, we may say that it is the most indispensable; but the length to
it could carry any particular country in the career of civilisation, would
ited indeed. Had Great Britain been cut off from all intercourse with
ers, there is no reason for thinking that we should have been at this day
ed beyond the point to which our ancestors had attained during the
rchy! It is to the products and the arts derived from others, and to the
ion inspired by their competition and example, that we are mainly indebted
extraordinary progress we have already made, as well as for that we are
stined to make.
Smith, though he has satisfactorily demonstrated the impolicy of all restric-
on the freedom of commerce, has, notwithstanding, endeavoured to show
is more for the public advantage that capital should be employed in the
trade than in foreign trade, on the ground that the capitals employed in
mer are more frequently returned, and that they set a greater quantity of
in motion than those employed in the latter. But we have elsewhere endea-
to show that the rate of profit which different businesses yield, is the only
their respective advantageousness.—(*Principles of Political Economy*, 2d ed.
—180.) Now, it is quite evident that capital will not be employed in foreign

trade, unless it yield as much profit as could be made by employing it at ho
No merchant sends a ship to China, if it be in his power to realise a larger pr
by sending her to Dublin or Newcastle; nor would any one build a ship, unles
expected that the capital so laid out would be as productive as if it were
ployed in agriculture or manufactures. The more or less rapid return of ca
is a matter of very little importance. If the average rate of profit be 10 per ce
an individual who turns over his capital ten times a year, will make *one*
cent. of profit each time; whereas if he turns it only once a year, he will
the whole 10 per cent. at once. Competition reduces the rate of nett prof
about the same level in all businesses; and we may be quite certain that th
who employ themselves in the departments in which capital is most rap
returned do not, at an average, gain more than those who employ themselve
the departments in which the returns are most distant. No one is a for
merchant because he would rather deal with foreigners than with his own coun
men, but because he believes he will be able to employ his capital more adv
tageously in foreign trade than in any other business: and while he does this
is following that employment which is most beneficial for the public as wel
for himself.

IV. RESTRICTIONS ON COMMERCE.

The statements already made, by explaining the nature and principles of c
mercial transactions, are sufficient to evince the inexpediency of subjecting t
to any species of restraint.* It is obvious, indeed, that restrictions are founde
false principles. When individuals are left to pursue their own interest in t
own way, they naturally resort to those branches of industry which they rec
most advantageous for themselves; and, as we have just seen, these are the
branches in which it is most for the public interest that they should be emplo
Unless, therefore, it could be shown that a government can judge better a
what sort of transactions are profitable or otherwise than private individuals,
regulations cannot be of the smallest use, and may be exceedingly injuri
But any such pretension on the part of government would be universally scoutec
is undeniably certain that a regard to our own interest is, if not an unerring g
to direct us in such matters, at least incomparably better than any other. If
trade with a particular country or in a particular commodity be a losing
or merely a less profitable one than others, it is quite as unnecessary to
an act to prevent it from being carried on, as it would be to interfere
prevent individuals from selling their labour or their commodities below
market price. It appears, therefore, that all regulations affecting the free
of commerce, or of any branch of industry, are either useless or pernicious. 7
are useless, when they are intended to protect the interest of individuals by
venting them from engaging in disadvantageous businesses; and pernicious, v
they prevent them from engaging in those that are advantageous. The
interest of the parties concerned is the only safe principle to go by in
matters. When the acts of the legislature are in unison with it, there is not
to object to in them, save only that they might as well not exist; but when
they are inconsistent with it—that is, whenever they tend to divert capital an
dustry into channels, into which individuals, if left to their own discretion, w
not have carried them—they are decidedly injurious.

No one denies that it is possible to confer, by means of a restrictive regula
an advantage on a greater or less number of individuals. This, however, i
proof that it is advantageous in a public point of view; and it is by its influen
this respect that we are to decide concerning it. If the exclusion of an ar
imported from abroad, in order to encourage its manufacture at home, raise its pr
the home market, that circumstance will, for a while at least, be advantageor
those engaged in its production. But is it not clear that all that is thus gaine
them, is *lost by those who purchase the article?* To suppose, indeed, that
exclusion of commodities that are comparatively cheap, to make room for
that are comparatively dear, can be a means of enriching a country, is equiv
to supposing that a people's wealth might be increased by destroying their
powerful machines, and throwing their best soils out of cultivation.

But it is contended, that though this might be the case in the instan
commodities produced at home, it is materially different when the commodit

ded came to us from abroad. It is said, that in this case the exclusion of
eign produce increases the demand for that produced at home, and consequently
tributes to increase the demand for labour; so that the rise of price it
asions is, in this way, more than balanced by the other advantages which it
ngs along with it. But the fact is, that though the demand for one species of
duce may be increased by a prohibition of importation, the demand for some
er species is sure to be at the same time equally diminished. There is no
glery in commerce. Whether it be carried on between individuals of the same
ntry, or of different countries, it is in all cases bottomed on a fair principle of
iprocity. Those who will not buy need not expect to sell, and conversely.
s impossible to export without making a corresponding importation. We get
hing from the foreigner gratuitously: and hence, when we prevent the im-
tation of produce from abroad, we prevent, by the very same act, the ex-
tation of an equal amount of British produce. All that the exclusion of
ign commodities ever effects, is the substitution of one sort of demand for
ther. It has been said, that " when we drink beer and porter we consume the
duce of English industry, whereas when we drink port or claret we con-
e the produce of the industry of the Portuguese and French, to the obvious
antage of the latter, and the prejudice of our countrymen!" But, how
doxical soever the assertion may at first sight appear, there is not at bottom
real distinction between the two cases. What is it that induces fo-
ners to supply us with port and claret? The answer is obvious: — We
er send directly to Portugal and France an *equivalent in British produce*, or
send such equivalent, in the first place, to South America for bullion, and
a send that bullion to the Continent to pay for the wine. And hence it is
lear as the sun at noon-day, that the Englishman who drinks only French
e, who eats only bread made of Polish wheat, and who wears only Saxon
h, gives, by occasioning the exportation of a corresponding amount of
ish cotton, hardware, leather, or other produce, the same encouragement to
industry of his countrymen, that he would give were he to consume nothing
immediately produced at home. A quantity of port wine and a quantity of
ningham goods are respectively of the same value; so that whether we
ctly consume the hardware, or, having exchanged it for the wine, consume
latter, must plainly, in so far as the employment of British labour is concerned,
together indifferent.

s is absolutely nugatory, therefore, to attempt to encourage industry at home
estraining importation from abroad. We might as well try to promote it by
rdicting the exchange of shoes for hats. We only resort to foreign markets,
we may supply ourselves with articles that cannot be produced at home, or
require more labour to produce them here, than is required to produce the
valent exported to pay for them. It is, if any thing can be, an obvious con-
iction and absurdity to attempt to promote wealth or industry by prohibiting
itercourse of this sort. Such prohibition, even when least injurious, is sure
orce capital and labour into less productive channels; and cannot fail to dish the foreign demand for one species of produce, quite as much as it extends
home demand for another.

is but seldom, however, that a restriction on importation from abroad does
more than substitute one sort of employment for another. Its usual effect
th to alter the distribution of capital, and to increase the price of commo-
s. A country rarely imports any commodity from abroad that may be as
ply produced at home. In the vast majority of instances the articles
ght of the foreigner could not be directly produced at home, without a much
ter outlay of capital. Suppose that we import a million's worth of any com-
ity, that its importation is prohibited, and that the same quantity of produce
ot be raised in this country for less than 1,200,000*l.*, or 1,500,000*l.*: In a
of this sort,— and this is actually the case in ninety-nine out of every
red instances in which prohibitions are enacted, — the prohibition has the
effect on the consumers of the commodity, as if, supposing it not to have
ed, they had been burdened with a peculiar tax of 200,000*l.* or 500,000*l.*
r. But, had such been the case, what the consumers lost would have gone
the coffers of the treasury, and would have afforded the means of repealing
qual amount of other taxes; whereas, under the prohibitory system, the high

A a

price, being occasioned by an increased difficulty of production, is of no advan
tage to any one. So that, instead of gaining any thing by such a measure, th
public incurs a dead loss of 200,000*l.* or 500,000*l.* a year.

We have said that a prohibition of importation may be productive of imme
diate advantage to the home producers of the prohibited article. It is essentia
however, to remark that this advantage cannot continue for any considerabl
time, and that it *must* be followed by a period of distress. Were the importatio
of foreign silks put an end to, that circumstance, by narrowing the supply of sil
goods, and raising their prices, would, no doubt, be, in the first instance, advan
tageous to the manufacturers, by elevating their profits above the common leve
But the consequence would be, that those already engaged in the trade woul
immediately set about extending their concerns; at the same time that not a fe
of those engaged in other employments would enter a business which presente
such a favourable prospect : nor would this transference of capital to the sil
manufacture be stopped, till such an increased supply of silks had been brought t
market as to occasion a glut. This reasoning is not founded upon hypothesi
but upon the widest experience. When a business is carried on under the pro
tection of a restriction on importation, it is limited by the extent of the hom
market, and is incapable of further extension. It is, in consequence, particular
subject to that fluctuation which is the bane of industry. If, owing to a chang
of fashion, or any other cause, the demand be increased, then, as no supplies ca
be brought from abroad, prices suddenly rise, and the manufacture is rapidly ex
tended, until a reaction takes place and prices sink below their usual level : an
if the demand decline, then, as there is no outlet abroad for the superfluous good
their price is ruinously depressed, and the producers are involved in inextricabl
difficulties. The businesses deepest entrenched behind ramparts of prohibitio
and restrictions, such as the silk trade previously to 1825, the West India trad
and agriculture since 1815, have undergone the most extraordinary vicissitudes
and have been at once more hazardous and less profitable than the businesse
carried on under a system of fair and free competition.

A prohibition against buying in the cheapest markets is really, also, a prohibitio
against selling in the dearest markets. There is no test of high or low price, ex
cept the quantity of other produce for which an article exchanges. Suppos
that, by sending a certain quantity of cottons or hardware to Brazil, we might ga
in exchange 150 hhds. of sugar, and that the same quantity, if sent to Jamaic
would only fetch 100 hhds.; is it not obvious, that by preventing the importatic
of the former, we force our goods to be sold for *two thirds* of the price the
would otherwise have brought ? To suppose that a system productive of suc
results can be a means of increasing wealth, is to suppose what is evidently a
surd. It is certainly true that a restrictive regulation, which has been long acte
upon, and under which a considerable quantity of capital is employed, oug
not to be rashly or capriciously repealed. Every change in the public econom
of a great nation ought to be gone about cautiously and gradually. Adequa
time should be given to those who carry on businesses that have been protecte
either to withdraw from them altogether, or to prepare to withstand the fair co
petition of foreigners. But this is *all* that such persons can justly claim. T
persevere in an erroneous and oppressive system, merely because its abando
ment might be productive of inconvenience to individuals, would be a proceedi
inconsistent with every object for which society is formed, and subversive of a
improvement.

It may, perhaps, be supposed that in the event of commodities being importe
from abroad, after the abolition of a protecting regulation, that were previous
produced at home, the workmen and those engaged in their production would
thrown upon the parish. Such, however, is not the case. We may, by givi
freedom to commerce, change the *species* of labour in demand, but it is not po
sible that we should thereby change its *quantity*. If, in consequence of the ab
lition of restrictions, our imports were increased to the amount of four or fi
millions, our exports, it is certain, must be augmented to the same extent :
that whatever diminution of the demand for labour might be experienced in ce
tain departments would be balanced by a corresponding increase in others.

The pressure of taxation has often been alleged as an excuse for restrictic
on commerce, but it is not more valid than the rest. Taxation may be hea

even oppressive; but so long as it is impartially and fairly assessed, it equally *all* branches of industry carried on at home, and consequently affords no ... d whatever for the enactment of regulations intended to protect any parti- business. And to propose to protect *all* branches of industry from foreign ...etition, is, in effect, to propose to put a total stop to commerce; for if no- ... is to be imported, nothing can be exported. The imposition of moderate ... on foreign commodities, for the sake of revenue, is quite another thing. ... of these form among the very best subjects of taxation; and when the ... on them are confined within proper bounds, that is, when they are not so ... as to exert any injurious influence upon trade, or to occasion smuggling ...aud, they cannot fairly be objected to.

... is sometimes contended, by those who assert, on general grounds, that re- ...ions are inexpedient, that it would be unwise, on the part of any country, to ...h them until she had obtained a security that those imposed by her neigh- ... would also be abolished. But the reasons that have been alleged in favour ... statement are not entitled to the least weight. It is our business to buy ... cheapest and sell in the dearest markets, without being, in any degree, in- ...ed by the conduct of others. If they consent to repeal the restrictions ...ave laid on commerce, so much the better. But whatever others may ... line of policy *we* ought to follow is clear and well defined. To refuse, ...ample, to buy claret, brandy, &c. from the French, because they lay absurd ...ctions on the importation of British hardware, cottons, &c., would not be ...aliate upon them, but upon ourselves. The fact that we *do* import French ...and brandy shows that we do export to France, or to some other country ...ich France is indebted, an equivalent, in some sort, of British produce. ...ear of being glutted with foreign products, unless we secure beforehand a ... outlet for our own, is the most unfounded that can be imagined. The ...ner who will take nothing of ours, can send us nothing of his. Though our ... were open to the merchants of all the countries of the world, the exports ...itish produce must always be equal to the imports of foreign produce; and ...but those who receive our commodities, either at first or second hand, could ...ue to send any thing to us.

...es étrangers ne peuvent demander ni désirer rien mieux, que la liberté de ...cheter et de vous vendre chez vous et dans vos colonies. Il faut la leur ...er, non par foiblesse et par impuissance, mais parcequ'elle est juste en ...eme, et qu'elle vous est utile. Ils ont tort sans doute de la refuser chez ...mais cette faute d'ignorance dont, sans le savoir, ils sont punis les premiers, ...pas un raison qui doive vous porter à vous nuire à vous-même en suivant ...emple, et à vous exposer aux suites et aux dépenses d'une guerre pour ...la vaine satisfaction d'user des représailles, dont l'effet ne peut manquer de ...ber sur vous, et de rendre votre commerce plus désavantageux." — (*Le ... de l'Ordre Social*, p. 416.)

...re are some, however, who contend, that though restrictions on importation ...broad be unfavourable to opulence, and the advancement of individuals and ... in arts and civilisation, they may, notwithstanding, be vindicated on other ...ls, as contributing essentially to independence and security. The short ...ecisive answer to this is to be found in the reciprocity of commerce. It ...ot enrich one individual or nation at the expense of others, but confers ...ours equally on all. We are under no obligations to the Portuguese, the ...ns, or any other people with whom we carry on trade. It is not *our* ad- ...e, but *their own*, that they have in view in dealing with us. We give them ... value of all that we import; and they would suffer quite as much incon- ...ce as we should do were this intercourse put an end to. The indepen- ...at which those aspire who would promote it by laying restrictions on ...rce, is the independence of the solitary and unsocial savage: it is not an ...ndence productive of strength, but of weakness. " The most flourishing ... at the moment of their highest elevation, when they were closely con- ...with every part of the civilised world by the golden chains of successful ...rcial enterprise, were, according to this doctrine, in the most perfect state ...lute dependence. It was not till all these connections were dissolved, ...ey had sunk in the scale of nations, that their true independence com- ...! Such statements carry with them their own refutation. There is a

natural dependence of nations upon each other, as there is a natural depende
of individuals upon each other. Heaven has so ordered it. Some soils, so
climates, some situations, are productive exclusively of some peculiar fruits, wh
cannot elsewhere be profitably procured. Let nations follow this as their gu
In a rich and rising community, the opulent capitalists may be as dependent up
the poor labourers, as the poor labourers upon the opulent capitalists. So i
with nations. The mutual dependence of individuals upon each other knits a
binds society together, and leads to the most rapid advancement in wealth
intelligence, and in every kind of improvement. It is the same, but on a
larger scale, with the mutual dependence of nations. To this alone do we c
all the mighty efforts of commerce; and what lights, what generous feelings, a
multiplied means of human happiness, has it not every where spread!" — (N
American Review, No. 57.)

The principles of commercial freedom, and the injurious influence of restric
regulations, were set in a very striking point of view by Dr. Smith, in his gr
work; and they have been since repeatedly explained and elucidated. Perh
however, the true doctrines upon this subject have no where been better sta
than in the petition presented by the merchants of London to the House
Commons on the 8th of May, 1820. This document is one of the most gratify
proofs of the progress of liberal and enlarged views. It was subscribed by all
principal merchants of the metropolis, who have not scrupled to express th
conviction, that the repeal of every *protective regulation* would be for the pu
advantage. Such an address to the legislature, confirming, as it did, the con
sions of science, by the approval of the best informed and most extensive m
chants of the world, had a powerful influence on the legislature. During the
ten years several most important reforms have been made in our commer
system; so that, besides being the first to promulgate the true theory of co
merce, we are now entitled to the praise of being the first to carry it into eff
No doubt our trade is still fettered by many vexatious restraints; but these
gradually disappear, according as experience serves to disclose the benefits res
ing from the changes already made, and the pernicious operation of the restricti
that are still allowed to continue.

The petition now referred to, is too important to be omitted in a work of
sort. It is as follows: —

" To the Honourable the Commons, &c., the Petition of the Merchants of the Ci
London.

" Sheweth,

" That foreign commerce is eminently conducive to the wealth and prosperity
country, by enabling it to import the commodities for the production of which the
climate, capital, and industry of other countries are best calculated, and to expor
payment, those articles for which its own situation is better adapted.

" That freedom from restraint is calculated to give the utmost extension to for
trade, and the best direction to the capital and industry of the country.

" That the maxim of buying in the cheapest market, and selling in the dearest, w
regulates every merchant in his individual dealings, is strictly applicable, as the
rule for the trade of the whole nation.

" That a policy founded on these principles would render the commerce of the w
an interchange of mutual advantages, and diffuse an increase of wealth and enjoym
among the inhabitants of each state.

" That, unfortunately, a policy the very reverse of this has been and is more or
adopted and acted upon by the government of this and every other country; each tr
to exclude the productions of other countries, with the specious and well-meant de
of encouraging its own productions: thus inflicting on the bulk of its subjects, wh
consumers, the necessity of submitting to privations in the quantity or quality of
modities; and thus rendering what ought to be the source of mutual benefit ar
harmony among states, a constantly recurring occasion of jealousy and hostility.

" That the prevailing prejudices in favour of the protective or restrictive system
be traced to the erroneous supposition that every importation of foreign commo
occasions a diminution or discouragement of our own productions to the same ex
whereas it may be clearly shown, that although the particular description of produ
which could not stand against unrestrained foreign competition would be discour
yet, as no importation could be continued for any length of time without a correspor
exportation, direct or indirect, there would be an encouragement for the **purpose of**

ortation, of some other production to which our situation might be better suited; s affording at least an equal, and probably a greater, and certainly a more beneficial, oloyment to our own capital and labour.

That of the numerous protective and prohibitory duties of our commercial code, it y be proved that, while all operate as a very heavy tax on the community at large, y few are of any ultimate benefit to the classes in whose favour they were originally ituted, and none to the extent of the loss occasioned by them to other classes.

That among the other evils of the restrictive or protective system, not the least is the artificial protection of one branch of industry or source of production against ign competition, is set up as a ground of claim by other branches for similar pro- ion ; so that if the reasoning upon which these restrictive or prohibitory regulations founded were followed out consistently, it would not stop short of excluding us n all foreign commerce whatsoever. And the same train of argument, which, with esponding prohibitions and protective duties, should exclude us from foreign trade, ht be brought forward to justify the re-enactment of restrictions upon the inter- ige of productions unconnected with public revenue) among the kingdoms com- ig the union, or among the counties of the same kingdom.

That an investigation of the effects of the restrictive system at this time is peculiarly d for, as it may, in the opinion of your petitioners, lead to a strong presumption, the distress, which now so generally prevails, is considerably aggravated by that m ; and that some relief may be obtained by the earliest practicable removal of such e restraints as may be shown to be most injurious to the capital and industry of the munity, and to be attended with no compensating benefit to the public revenue.

That a declaration against the anti-commercial principles of our restrictive system the more importance at the present juncture ; inasmuch as, in several instances of nt occurrence, the merchants and manufacturers of foreign countries have assailed respective governments with applications for further protective or prohibitory es and regulations, urging the example and authority of this country, against which are almost exclusively directed as a sanction for the policy of such measures. And inly, if the reasoning upon which our restrictions have been defended is worth any g, it will apply in behalf of the regulations of foreign states against us. They insist our superiority in capital and machinery, as we do upon their comparative ex- ion from taxation, and with equal foundation.

That nothing would tend more to counteract the commercial hostility of foreign s, than the adoption of a more enlightened and more conciliatory policy on the part is country.

That although, as a matter of mere diplomacy, it may sometimes answer to hold the val of particular prohibitions, or high duties, as depending upon corresponding essions by other states in our favour, it does not follow that we should maintain our ictions in cases where the desired concessions on their part cannot be obtained. restrictions would not be the less prejudicial to our own capital and industry, ise other governments persisted in preserving impolitic regulations.

That, upon the whole, the most liberal would prove to be the most politic course on occasions.

That independent of the direct benefit to be derived by this country, on every oc- n of such concession or relaxation, a great incidental object would be gained, by ecognition of a sound principle or standard, to which all subsequent arrangements it be referred ; and by the salutary influence which a promulgation of such just s, by the legislature and by the nation at large, could not fail to have on the policy her states.

That in thus declaring, as your petitioners do, their conviction of *the impolicy and ice of the restrictive system*, and in desiring every practicable relaxation of it, they in view only such parts of it as are not connected, or are only subordinately so, the public revenue. As long as the necessity for the present amount of revenue sts, your petitioners cannot expect so important a branch of it as the customs to be up, nor to be materially diminished, unless some substitute less objectionable be sted. But it is *against every restrictive regulation of trade, not essential to the revenue, st all duties merely protective from foreign competition, and against the excess of such s as are partly for the purpose of revenue, and partly for that of protection*, that the r of the present petition is respectfully submitted to the wisdom of parliament. May it therefore, &c."

r examples of the practical working and injurious operation of restrictions, he articles AMSTERDAM, BORDEAUX, COLONY TRADE, CORN LAWS and v TRADE, WOOD, &c., in this Dictionary; the articles on the American f and the French Commercial System in Nos. 96. and 99. of the *Edinburgh w;* the Report of the Committee of Commerce and Navigation, to the

House of Representatives of the United States, 8th February, 1830; and th
Petition and *Memoire à l'Appui*, addressed, in 1828, by the landowners and me
chants of the Gironde to the Chamber of Deputies.

For an account of the doctrines with respect to the *balance of trade*, and th
importation and exportation of the precious metals, see the articles BALANCE O
TRADE, and EXCHANGE.

For an account of the articles exported from and imported into Great Britai
see IMPORTS, and EXPORTS.

COMPANIES. In commerce or the arts, a company is a number of persor
associated together for the purpose of carrying on some commercial or industrio
undertaking. When there are only a few individuals associated, it is mo
commonly called a *copartnery*; the term company being usually applied to larg
associations, like the East India Company, the Bank of England, &c., who cor
duct their operations by means of agents acting under the orders of a board
directors.

Companies have generally been divided into two great classes — exclusive or joi
stock companies, and open or regulated companies.

1. *Exclusive or Joint Stock Companies.* — By an institution of this sort is meant
company having a certain amount of capital, divided into a greater or smaller number
transferable shares, managed for the common advantage of the shareholders by a body
directors chosen by and responsible to them. After the stock of a company of this sc
has been subscribed, no one can enter it without previously purchasing one or mo
shares belonging to some of the existing members. The partners do nothing individuall
all their resolutions are taken in common, and are carried into effect by the directors ar
those whom they employ.

According to the common law of England, all the partners in a joint stock compar
are jointly and individually liable, to the whole extent of their fortunes, for the debts
the company. They may make arrangements amongst themselves, limiting their obli
ations with respect to each other; but unless established by an authority competent
set aside the general rule, they are all indefinitely responsible to the public. Parliame
sometimes limits the responsibility of the shareholders in joint stock companies establishe
by statute, to the amount of the shares they respectively hold. Charters of incorporati
granted by the Crown were also, until lately, supposed necessarily to have this effec
but by the act 6 Geo. 4. c. 96. the Crown is empowered to grant charters of incorporati
by which the members of corporate bodies may be made *individually liable, to such exter
and subject to such regulations and restrictions*, as may be deemed expedient. Her
charters are now frequently granted for the purpose merely of enabling companies to s
and be sued in courts of law, under the names of some of their office-bearers, without
any respect limiting the responsibility of the shareholders to the public. This limitati
cannot be implied in a charter any more than in an act of parliament, and will be he
not to exist unless it be distinctly set forth.

" In a private copartnery, no partner, without the consent of the company, can transf
his share to another person, or introduce a new member into the company. Each memb
however, may, upon proper warning, withdraw from the copartnery, and demand pa
ment from them of his share of the common stock. In a joint stock company, on t
contrary, no member can demand payment of his share from the company; but ea
member may, without their consent, transfer his share to another person, and there
introduce a new member. The value of a share in a joint stock is always the pr
which it will bring in the market; and this may be either greater or less, in any prope
tion, than the sum which its owner stands credited for in the stock of the company."
(*Wealth of Nations*, vol. iii. p.238.)

2. *Utility of Joint Stock Companies.* — Whenever the capital required to carry on a
undertaking exceeds what may be furnished by an individual, it is indispensable, in ore
to the prosecution of the undertaking, that an association should be formed. In all th
cases, too, in which the chances of success are doubtful, or where a lengthened peri
must necessarily elapse before an undertaking can be completed, an individual, thou
ready enough to contribute a small sum in connection with others, would, genera
speaking, be very little inclined, even if he had the means, to encounter the whole
sponsibility of such enterprises. Hence the necessity and advantage of companies
associations. It is to them that we are indebted for those canals by which every part
the country is intersected, for the formation of so many noble docks and warehouses,
the institution of our principal banks and insurance offices, and for many other establi
ments of great public utility carried on by the combined capital and energies of la
bodies of individuals.

3. *Branches of Industry, for the Prosecution of which Joint Stock Companies may*

tageously established. — In order to ensure a rational prospect of success to a com-
the undertaking should admit of being carried on according to a regular systematic
The reason of this is sufficiently obvious. The business of a great association
be conducted by factors or agents; and unless it be of such a nature as to admit
ir duties being clearly pointed out and defined, the association would cease to have
ffectual control over them, and would be, in a great measure, at their mercy. An
dual who manages his own affairs reaps all the advantage derivable from superior
industry, and economy; but the agents, and even directors, of joint stock companies
', in most cases, entirely or principally for the advantage of others; and cannot,
ore, however conscientious, have the same powerful motives to act with energy, pru-
and economy. "Like," says Dr. Smith, "the stewards of a rich man, they are apt
sider attention to small matters as not for their masters' honour, and very easily
hemselves a dispensation from having it. Negligence and profusion, therefore, must
s prevail more or less in the management of the affairs of such a company." It
ot unfrequently happens that they suffer from the bad faith, as well as the careless-
d extravagance, of their servants; the latter having, in many instances, endeavoured
ance their own interests at the expense of their employers. Hence the different
s of companies whose business may be conducted according to a nearly uniform
, — such as dock, canal, and insurance companies, banking companies, &c. — and
whose business does not admit of being reduced to any regular plan, and where
must always be left to the sagacity and enterprise of those employed. All purely
ercial companies, trading upon a joint stock, belong to the latter class. Not one
m has ever been able to withstand the competition of private adventurers; they
subject the agents they employ to buy and sell commodities in distant countries
effectual responsibility; and from this circumstance, and the abuses that usually
ate themselves into every department of their management, no such company has
icceeded, unless when it has obtained some exclusive privilege, or been protected
ompetition.
circumstances now mentioned would seem to oppose the most formidable obstacles
success of the companies established in this country for the prosecution of mining
erica. This business does not admit of being reduced to a regular routine system.
must always depend on the skill and probity of the agents employed at the mines;
must plainly be very difficult, if not quite impossible, for directors resident in
n to exercise any effectual *surveillance* over the proceedings of those who are at so
distance. Hence it is not at all likely that these establishments will ever be so
tive to the undertakers, as if they had been managed by the parties themselves.
Abbé Morellet has given, in a tract published in 1769 (*Examen de la Réponse de*
, pp. 35—38.), a list of fifty-five joint stock companies, for the prosecution of
branches of foreign trade, established in different parts of Europe since 1600,
ine of which had failed, though most of them had exclusive privileges. Most of
hat have been established since the publication of the Abbé Morellet's tract have
imilar fate.
notwithstanding both principle and experience concur in showing how very ill
large association is for the purpose of prosecuting commercial undertakings, there
es in which they cannot be prosecuted except by associations of this sort, and when
be expedient to grant them certain peculiar privileges. When, owing either to
inclination or inability of government to afford protection to those engaged in any
lar department of trade, they are obliged to provide for their own defence and
y, it is obviously necessary that they should have the power to exclude such indias may refuse to submit to the measures, or to bear their due share of the expense,
d for the common protection of all. The Russia Company, the East India Com-
he Levant or Turkey Company, and most of the other great trading companies
have existed in this country, seem principally to have grown out of a real or sup-
necessity of this sort. It was not believed that any safe or advantageous intercourse
ie carried on with barbarous countries without the aid of ships of war, factories,
iters, &c. And as government was not always able or willing to afford this
ce, the traders were formed into companies or associations, and vested with such
r privileges as appeared to be necessary for enabling them to prosecute the trade
t any extrinsic support. "When," says Dr. Smith, "a company of merchants
ke, at their own risk and expense, to establish a new trade with some remote and
us nation, it may not be unreasonable to incorporate them into a joint stock com-
nd to grant them, in case of success, a monopoly of the trade for a certain number
s. It is the easiest and most natural way in which the state can recompense them
irding a dangerous and expensive experiment, of which the public is afterwards
the benefit. A temporary monopoly of this kind may be vindicated upon the
inciples upon which a like monopoly of a new machine is granted to its inventor,

and that of a new book to its author. But upon the expiration of the term, the mono
ought certainly to determine ; the forts and garrisons, if it was found necessary to estab
any, to be taken into the hands of government, their value to be paid to the comp
and the trade to be laid open to all the subjects of the state." — (*Wealth of Nat*
vol. iii. p. 258.)

It may be doubted, however, whether it be really necessary, even in such a case as
now mentioned, to establish a *joint stock company* with peculiar privileges, and whe
the same thing might not be more advantageously effected by the establishment o
open or regulated company.

4. *Open or Regulated Companies.* — The affairs of such companies or associations
managed by directors appointed by the members. They do not, however, possess a c
mon or joint stock.　Each individual pays a fine upon entering into the company,
most commonly an annual contribution : a duty applicable to the business of the comp
is also sometimes charged upon the goods imported and exported from and to the coun
with which they trade.　The sums so collected are applied by the directors to fit
ambassadors, consuls, and such public functionaries as may be required to facilitate c
mercial dealings, or to build factories, maintain cruisers, &c.　The members of s
companies trade upon their own stock, and at their own risk.　So that when the fin
the sum payable on admission into a regulated company is moderate, it is impossible
its members to form any combination that would have the effect of raising their pr
above the common level ; and there is the same keen and close competition amongst t
that there is amongst other classes of traders.　A regulated company is in fact a do
for making those engaged in a particular branch of trade bear the public or poli
expenses incident to it, at the same time that it leaves them to conduct their own busi
with their own capital, and in their own way.

Should, therefore, government at any time refuse, or be unable to afford, that pro
tion to those engaged in any branch of trade which is necessary to enable them to c
it on, their formation into a regulated company would seem to be the most judic
measure that could be adopted ; inasmuch as it would obtain for them that protec
which is indispensable, without encroaching on the freedom of individual enterprise.

The African, the Levant, and some other branches of trade, were for a long time
ducted by open or regulated companies.　These, however, have been recently abolis
the African Company, by the act 1 & 2 Geo. 4. c. 28. ; and the Levant Company, by
act 6 Geo. 4. c. 33.　The Russia Company still exists.　(See RUSSIA COMPANY.)

In so far as relates to protection, it may perhaps be thought, for the reasons give
Dr. Smith, that a joint stock company is better calculated to afford it than a regul
company.　The directors of the latter having, Dr. Smith alleges, no particular inte
in the prosperity of the general trade of the company, for behoof of which, ships of
factories, or forts, have to be maintained, are apt to neglect them, and to apply their w
energies to the care of their own private concerns.　But the interest of the directo
a joint stock company are, he contends, in a great measure identified with those of
association.　They have no private capital employed in the trade ; their profits
depend upon the prudent and profitable management of the common stock ; and it
therefore, it is argued, be fairly presumed that they will be more disposed to attend
fully to all the means by which the prosperity of the association may be best secured.
the other hand, however, it is seldom that the directors of joint stock companies ste
the proper point ; having almost invariably attempted to extend their commercial dea
by force, and to become not only merchants but sovereigns.　Nor is this any thing
what might have been expected, seeing that the consideration and extensive patro
accruing from such measures to the directors is generally of far more importance to
than a moderate increase of the dividends on their stock.　Whenever they have
able, they have seldom scrupled to employ arms to advance their projects ; and inste
contenting themselves with shops and factories, have constructed fortifications, embo
armies, and engaged in war.　But such has not been the case with regulated compa
The businesses under their control have uniformly been conducted in a compara
frugal and parsimonious manner ; their establishments have been, for the most part,
fined to factories ; and they have rarely, if ever, allowed themselves to be seduce
schemes of conquest and dominion.

And hence, considering them as *commercial machines*, it does not really seem that
can be any doubt as to the superiority of a regulated over a joint stock company.
latter has the defect, for which nothing almost can compensate, of *entirely excl
individual enterprise and competition.*　When such a company enjoys any peculiar
lege, it naturally, in pursuing its own interest, endeavours to profit by it, how inju
soever it may be to the public.　If it have a monopoly of the trade with any parti
country, or of any particular commodity, it rarely fails, by understocking the home
foreign markets, to sell the goods which it imports and exports at an artificially enha

e. It is not its object to employ a comparatively large capital, but to make a large
fit on a comparatively small capital. The conduct of the Dutch East India Company
urning spices, that their price might not be lowered by larger importations, is an
mple of the mode in which such associations uniformly and, indeed, almost necessarily

All individuals are desirous of obtaining the highest possible price for what they
e to sell; and if they are protected by means of a monopoly, or an exclusive privilege,
n the risk of being undersold by others, they never hesitate about raising the price of
r products to the highest elevation that the competition of the buyers will allow them;
thus frequently realise the most exorbitant profits.

And yet, notwithstanding these advantages, such is the negligence, profusion, and
ulation, inseparable from the management of great commercial companies, that even
e that have had the monopoly of the most advantageous branches of commerce have
ly been able to keep out of debt. It will be shown in the article East India Company,
that association has lost by its trade; and that, had it not been for the aid derived
n the revenues of India, it must long since have ceased to exist. To buy in one
ket, to sell with profit in another; to watch over the perpetually occurring variations
he prices, and in the supply and demand of commodities; to suit with dexterity and
gment the quantity and quality of goods to the wants of each market; and to conduct
operation in the best and cheapest manner; requires a degree of unremitting vigilance
attention, which it would be visionary to expect from the directors or servants of a
t joint stock association. Hence it has happened, over and over again, that branches
ommerce which proved ruinous to companies, have become exceedingly profitable
n carried on by individuals.

Constitution of Companies. — When application is made to parliament for an act to
rporate a number of individuals into a joint stock company for the prosecution of any
ul undertaking, care ought to be taken not to concede to them any privileges that
be rendered injurious to the public. If a company be formed for the construction
dock, a road, or a canal, it may be necessary, in order to stimulate individuals to
age in the undertaking, to give them some peculiar privileges for a certain number
ears. But if other persons were to be permanently hindered from constructing new
s, or opening new lines of communication, a lasting injury might be done to the
ic. It may be highly expedient to incorporate a company for the purpose of bring-
water into a city; but supposing there were no springs in the vicinity, other than
e to which this company has acquired a right, they might, unless restrained by the
ncorporating them, raise the price of water to an exorbitant height; and make large
ts for themselves at the expense and to the injury of the public. In all cases of this
; and in the case, indeed, of all joint stock companies established for the formation
nals, railroads, &c.; it would be sound policy to limit the rates charged for their
ces, or on account of the water, ships, goods, &c. conveyed by their means, and also
nit the dividends, or to fix a *maximum* beyond which they should not be augmented:
ting, that if the rates charged by the company produce more than sufficient to pay
maximum rate of dividend, and to defray the wear and tear of the aqueduct, canal,
they shall be allowed to reduce them till they only yield this much; and, in the
t of their declining to do so, that the whole surplus above paying the dividend shall
pplied to purchase up the stock of the association, so that ultimately the charges on
unt of dividends may be entirely abolished. Had this principle been acted upon
canals first began to be formed in England, the carriage of goods conveyed by
of the most important lines of communication would now have cost almost nothing;
his desirable result might have been accomplished in the way now suggested, with-
we believe, diminishing in any degree the number of those undertakings. There
ew who, at the time they engage in such enterprises, suppose that they will yield
than 10 or 12 per cent.; and vast numbers will always be disposed to engage in
, if there be any reasonable prospect of their yielding this much. Now, when such
case, is it not the duty of government to provide, in the event of the undertaking
ning in an *unexpected* and *unusual degree profitable*, that the public should derive
advantage from it? This is not a case in which competition can reduce profits to
ommon level. The best, perhaps the only practicable, line for a canal or a railroad
een any two places will be appropriated by those who are first in the field; who
in fact, obtain a natural monopoly of which they cannot be deprived: and hence
dvantage of limiting the charges and dividends: without discouraging enterprise,
rds a security that private individuals shall not reap an unusual and unlooked for
at the expense of the public.

all those cases in which companies are formed for the prosecution of undertakings
may be carried on, with equal advantage to the public, by individuals; or where
are no very considerable difficulties to overcome, or risks to encounter; they ought
joy no privilege whatever, but should be regarded, in every point of view, as if
vere mere individuals.

For accounts of the principal joint stock and regulated companies established in th
country, see the articles BANK OF ENGLAND, DOCKS, EAST INDIA COMPANY, INSURANC
RUSSIA COMPANY, &c. &c.

6. *Companies en Commandite.* — In France there is a sort of companies denominate
societés en commandite. A society of this description consists of one or more partner
liable, without limitation, for the debts of the company ; and one or more partners, *
commanditaires,* liable only to the extent of the funds they have subscribed. A *con
manditaire* must not, however, take any part in the business of the company; if he d
this he loses his inviolability, and makes himself responsible for the debts of the associa
tion. The names of the partners in such societies must be published, and the amou
of the sums contributed by the *commanditaires.*

It has been proposed to introduce partnerships of this sort into this country ; but
seems very doubtful whether any thing would be gained by such a measure. Pa
nerships *en commandite* may be very easily abused, or rendered a means of defraudin
the public. It is quite visionary to imagine that the *commanditaires* can be prevente
from indirectly influencing the other partners : and supposing a collusion to exi
amongst them, it might be possible for them to divide large sums as profit, whe
perhaps, they had really sustained a loss ; and to have the books of the association s
contrived, that it might be very difficult to detect the fraud. This, it is alleged, is b
no means a rare occurrence in France.

7. *Civic Companies, or Corporations.* — Exclusive of the companies previously me
tioned, a number of ancient companies or corporations exist in this and most oth
European countries, the members of which enjoy certain political as well as con
mercial privileges. When the feudal system began to be subverted by the establis
ment of good order and regular government in the towns, the inhabitants were divide
into certain trades or corporations, by which the magistrates and other functionari
were chosen. The members of these trades, or corporations, partly to enhance tl
value of their privileges, and partly to provide a resource, in case of adversity, to then
selves, acquired or usurped the power of enacting by-laws regulating the admissio
of new members, and at the same time set about providing a fund for the support
such as accident or misfortune might reduce to a state of indigence. Hence the orig
of apprenticeships, the refusal to allow any one not a member of a corporation to carry c
any business within the precincts of any town corporate, and the various regulations th
had to be submitted to, and the fees that had to be paid by the claimants for inrolment :
corporations. For a lengthened period these privileges and regulations were very oppre
sive. Within the last century, however, their influence has been progressively diminishin
In France, where the abuses inseparable from the system had attained to a very gre
height, it was entirely swept off by the Revolution : and though corporations still exist
this country, they have been stript of several of their peculiar franchises ; and should no
for the most part, be regarded more, perhaps, in the light of charitable than of politic
institutions. It would be well, however, were they reduced entirely to the form
character ; and were the few political and commercial privileges, which they still enjo
communicated to the rest of the citizens. At their first institution, and for some tin
after, corporations, considered as political bodies, were probably useful : but such
no longer the case ; and in so far as they now possess any special immunities, th
tend to obstruct that free competition that is so advantageous.

The following extract from a Report on the Commerce and Manufactures of the Unit
States, drawn up by Albert Gallatin, Esq., then secretary to the Treasury, and laid befc
congress in 1816, sets the superior advantages resulting from the unrestricted freedom
industry in a very striking point of view. " No cause," says he, " has, perhaps, more pi
moted in every respect the general improvement of the United States, than the absence
those systems of internal restriction and monopoly which continue to disfigure the sta
of society in other countries. No laws exist here, directly or indirectly, confining m
to a particular occupation or place, or excluding any citizen from any branch he may,
any time, think proper to pursue. Industry is, in every respect, free and unfettere
every species of trade, commerce, and profession, and manufacture, being equally op
to all, *without requiring any regular apprenticeship, admission, or licence.* Hence
improvement of America has not been confined to the improvement of her agricultu
and to the rapid formation and settlement of new states in the wilderness ; but I
citizens have extended their commerce to every part of the globe, and carry on w
complete success even those branches for which a monopoly had heretofore been con
dered essentially necessary."

There is in Rees's Cyclopædia, article *Company,* a list of the different Civic Co
panies belonging to the City of London, in which the periods of their incorporati
and various other important particulars with respect to several of them, are specified.

)MPASS (Ger. *Ein Kompass;* Du. *Zeekompas;* Da. *Söekompass;* Sp. *Sjö-
ass;* Fr. *Boussole, Compas de mer;* It. *Bussola;* Sp. *Aguja de marear;* Port.
asso de marear; Rus. *Kompass korabelnüi*), or mariner's compass, an instru-
composed of a needle and card, by which the ship's course is directed. The
e, with little variation, always points towards the north, and hence the mode
ering by the compass.

common opinion is that the compass was invented by Flavio Gioia, a citizen of
ce famous republic of Amalphi, very near the beginning of the fourteenth century.
.obertson has adopted this opinion, and regrets that contemporary historians furnish
ails as to the life of a man to whose genius society is so deeply indebted — (*Hist.
erica,* vol. i. p. 47. 8vo ed.) But though Gioia may have made improvements on
mpass, it has been shown that he has no claim to be considered as its discoverer.
ges have been produced from writers who flourished more than a century before
in which the polarity of the needle, when touched by the magnet, is distinctly
d out. Not only, however, had this singular property been discovered, but also
·lication to the purposes of navigation, long previously to the fourteenth century.
rench writers have been quoted (*Macpherson's Annals of Commerce,* anno 1200;
Cyclopædia*), that seem fully to establish this fact. But whatever doubts
xist with respect to them, cannot affect the passages which the learned Spanish
ary, Don Antonio de Capmany (*Questiones Criticas,* pp. 73—132. , has given
a work of the famous Raymond Lully (*De Contemplatione*), published in 1272.
e place Lully says, " as the needle, when touched by the magnet, naturally
to the north " (*sicut acus per naturam vertitur ad septentrionem dum sit tacta
nete*). This is conclusive as to the author's acquaintance with the polarity of
edle; and the following passage from the same work — " as the nautical needle
mariners in their navigation " (*sicut acus nautica dirigit marinarios in sua naviga-
c.*) — is no less conclusive as to its being used by sailors in regulating their
There are no means of ascertaining the mode in which the needle Raymond
had in view was made use of. It has been sufficiently established (see the
.ties already referred to, and Azuni *Dissertation sur l'Origine de la Boussole,*) that
usual to float the needle, by means of a straw, on the surface of a basin of water;
npmany contends that we are indebted to Gioia for the card, and the method now
·d of suspending the needle; improvements which have given to the compass all
venience, and a very large portion of its utility. But this part of his *Dissertation,*
equally learned and ingenious, is by no means so satisfactory as the other. It is
t to conceive how mariners at sea could have availed themselves of a floating
; but, however this may be, it seems most probable that Gioia had considerably
ed the construction of the compass; and that, the Amalphitans having been the
introduce it to general use, he was, with excusable partiality, represented by them,
bsequently regarded by others, as its inventor.
reader will not consider these details out of place in a work on commerce, which
npass has done so much to extend. " Its discovery," to borrow the language of
acpherson, " has given birth to a new era in the history of commerce and navi-
The former it has extended to every shore of the globe, and increased and mul-
its operations and beneficial effects in a degree which was not conceivable by
·ho lived in the earlier ages. The latter it has rendered expeditious, and com-
ely safe, by enabling the navigator to launch out upon the ocean free from the
of rocks and shoals. By the use of this noble instrument, the whole world has
one vast commercial commonwealth, the most distant inhabitants of the earth
ught together for their mutual advantage, ancient prejudices are obliterated, and
d are civilised and enlightened."— (Vol. i. p. 366.)

MPOSITION, in commerce, commonly implies the dividend or sum paid
insolvent debtor to his creditors, and accepted by them in payment for
ebts.

NEY-WOOL (Ger. *Kaninchenwolle;* Du. *Konynhair;* Fr. *Poil de lapin;* It.
Coniglio;* Sp. *Conejuna*), or the fur of rabbits, principally used by hatters.
erable quantities are imported.

NSTANTINOPLE, the metropolis of the Turkish empire, is situated on
·thern side of the Bosphorus, between the Black Sea and the Sea of Marin lat. 41° N., long. 25° 56′ E. Population variously estimated at from
) to 600,000; but believed, by the best authorities, to be under 400,000.
rt of Constantinople is one of the finest in the world; and is admirably
d for carrying on the most extensive commerce. We are also told by Mr.
on (*Present State of Turkey,* vol. i. p. 82.), that no restriction is laid on

commerce in the Turkish empire, except on the exportation of corn, and o*
articles of provision; and it is only in the capital that this prohibition is rigoro*
enforced. But the wretched policy of the Turks in other respects, the oppres*
and extortion to which husbandmen, and, indeed, every one engaged in any in*
trious employment, is exposed to, and the consequent feeling of insecurity, re*
the freedom of trade of comparatively little importance; and have oversp*
some of the fairest provinces of Europe and Asia with poverty and barbar*
The imports into Constantinople consist of corn, iron, timber, tallow, and *
principally from the Black Sea; and of tin, tin-plates, woollens, cotton st*
and yarn, silks, cutlery, watches and jewellery, paper, glass, furniture, ind*
cochineal, &c. from the different countries of Europe. Corn and coffee are*
ported from Alexandria; but a good deal of Brazil and West India coffee is *
imported, particularly in American bottoms. Sugar is partly imported from*
East, but principally from the West Indies. The exports are very trifling, *
sisting of hides, wool, goats' hair, potashes, wax, and a few other articles,*
principally of bullion and diamonds. Ships carrying goods to Constantino*
either return in ballast, or get return cargoes at Smyrna, Odessa, Salonica, *
on which places they frequently procure bills at Constantinople. Trade is ch*
in the hands of English, French, and other European merchants (denomin*
Franks), and of Armenians and Greeks. Bargains are negotiated on their acc*
by Jew brokers, some of whom are rich.

Money.—Accounts are kept in piastres of 40 paras, or 120 aspers. The Turkish *
has been so much degraded, that the piastre, which a few years ago was worth 2s. *
ling, is now worth little more than 4*d.* A bag of silver (*kefer*) = 500 piastres, and a *
of gold (*kitze*) = 30,000 piastres.

Weights and Measures.—The commercial weights are —

176 Drams	=	1 Rottolo.
2$\frac{3}{11}$ Rottoli	=	1 Oke.
6 Okes	=	1 Batman.
7$\frac{1}{3}$ Batmans	=	1 Quintal or Cantaro = 124·457 (124$\frac{1}{2}$ very nearly) lbs. av

dupois = 56·437 kilogrammes = 116·527 lbs. of Hamburgh. The quintal of cott*
45 okes = 127$\frac{1}{3}$ lbs. avoirdupois.

The pik or pike is of two sorts, the greater and the less. The greater, called *hale*
arschim, used in the measurement of silks and woollens, is very near 28 inches (2*
The lesser, called *endese,* used in the measuring of cottons, carpets, &c. = 27 in*
Hence 100 long piks = 77·498 English yards, and 100 short piks = 75·154 do.
in ordinary commercial affairs, the pik is estimated at $\frac{3}{4}$ of an English yard.

Corn is measured by the *kisloz* or *killow* = 0·941 of a Winchester bushel; 8$\frac{1}{2}$ k*
= 1 quarter. The *fortin* = 4 kisloz.

Oil and other liquids are sold by the *alma* or *meter* = 1 gallon 3 pints English *
measure. The alma of oil should weigh 8 okes.—(*Nelkenbrecher* and *Dr. Kelly.*)

CONSUL, in commerce, an officer appointed by competent authority to r*
in foreign countries, in the view of facilitating and extending the commerce ca*
on between the subjects of the country which appoints him, and those of *
country or place in which he is to reside.

1. *Origin and Appointment of Consuls.*—The office of consul appears to have origi*
in Italy, about the middle of the twelfth century. And soon after, the French and*
Christian nations trading to the Levant began to stipulate for liberty to appoint co*
to reside in the ports frequented by their ships, that they might watch over the*
terests of their subjects, and judge and determine such differences with respect to*
mercial affairs as arose amongst them. The practice was gradually extended to *
countries; and in the sixteenth century was generally established all over Europ*
Martens, Precis du Droit des Gens, § 147.)

British consuls were formerly appointed by the crown, upon the recommendati*
great trading companies, or of the merchants engaged in the trade with a parti*
country or place; but they are now directly appointed by government, without any*
recommendation.

The right of sending consuls to reside in foreign countries depends either up*
tacit or express convention. Hence their powers differ very widely in different s*
In some they exercise a very extensive jurisdiction over the subjects of the state *
appoints them; but the extent of this jurisdiction is not discretionary, and must, *
cases, be regulated either by an express convention between the state appointing*
the state receiving the consul, or by custom. Consuls established in England ha*
judicial power; and the British government has rarely stipulated, in its comm*

ties with civilised countries, for much judicial authority for its consuls. In the
ty between Sweden and the United States of America, ratified on the 24th of July,
8, it is stipulated, " The high contracting powers mutually grant the right of maining consuls, vice-consuls, or agents, in each other's ports and commercial towns,
 shall enjoy full protection and receive every assistance necessary to enable them
y to execute their functions; but it is hereby expressly declared, that in the case of
gal or improper conduct against the laws or government of the country to which any
a consul or vice-consul is sent, he may be punished conformably to the laws, be
rived of his functions, or dismissed by the offended government, the said govern-
t giving an account of the transaction to the other; it being, however, well under-
d, that the archives or documents relative to the affairs of the consulate shall be
ject to no examination, but shall be carefully preserved, being placed under the
s of the said consul, and of the authorities of the place where he shall have resided.
consuls or their substitutes shall, as such, have the right of acting as judges or
ters in all cases of differences which may arise between the captains and crews of
vessels of the nation whose affairs are entrusted to their care. The respective
ernments shall have no right to interfere in these sort of affairs, except in the case
he conduct of the crews disturbing public order and tranquillity in the country in
ch the vessel may happen to be, or in which the consul of the place may be obliged
all for the intervention and support of the executive power, in order to cause his
sion to be respected; it being, however, well understood, that this sort of judgment
rbitration cannot deprive the contending parties of their right of appealing, on their
rn, to the judicial authorities of their country."

Duties of Consuls. — The duties of a consul, in the confined sense in which they
even commonly understood, are important and multifarious. It is his business to
lways on the spot, to watch over the commercial interests of the subjects of the
 whose servant he is; to be ready to assist them with advice on all doubtful occa-
s; to see that the conditions in commercial treaties are properly observed; that
e he is appointed to protect are subjected to no unnecessary or unjustifiable demands
nducting their business; to represent their grievances to the authorities at the place
re they reside, or to the ambassador of the sovereign appointing him at the court on
h the consulship depends, or to the government at home; in a word, to exert him-
to render the condition of the subjects of the country employing him, within the
s of his consulship, as comfortable, and their transactions as advantageous and
re, as possible.

he following more detailed exposition of the duties of a British consul, is taken
Mr. Chitty's valuable work on Commercial Law : —

A British consul, in order to be properly qualified for his employment, should take
to make himself master of the language used by the court and the magistracy of
ountry where he resides, so as to converse with ease upon subjects relating to his
s. If the common people of the port use another, he must acquire that also, that
ay be able to settle little differences without troubling the magistracy of the place
he interposition of their authority; such as accidents happening in the harbour, by
hips of one nation running foul of and doing damage to each other.

He is to make himself acquainted, if he be not already, with the law of nations
reaties, with the tariff or specification of duties on articles imported or exported,
with all the municipal ordinances and laws.

He must take especial notice of all prohibitions to prevent the export or import of
articles, as well on the part of the state wherein he resides, as of the government
oying him; so that he may admonish all British subjects against carrying on an
commerce, to the detriment of the revenues, and in violation of the laws of either.
it is his duty to attend diligently to this part of his office, in order to prevent
gling, and consequent hazard of confiscation or detention of ships, and imprison-
of the masters and mariners. — (*Beawes, Lex Merc.* vol. ii. p. 42.)

t is also his duty to protect from insult or imposition British subjects of every
iption within his jurisdiction. If redress for injury suffered is not obtained, he is
ry his complaint by memorial to the British minister residing at the court on which
onsulship depends. If there be none, he is to address himself directly to the
; and if, in an important case, his complaint be not answered, he is to transmit
emorial to his Majesty's secretary of state. — (*Beawes, Warden,* &c.)

When insult or outrage is offered by a British subject to a native of the place, and
agistrate thereof complains to the consul, he should summon, and in case of dis-
ence may by armed force bring before him the offender, and order him to give im-
te satisfaction; and if he refuse, he resigns him to the civil jurisdiction of the
trate, or to the military law of the garrison; nevertheless *always acting as counsellor
ocate at his trial,* when there is question of life or property.

" But if a British subject be accused of an offence alleged to have been committed at se within the dominion or jurisdiction of his sovereign, it is then the duty of the consul claim cognizance of the cause for his sovereign, and to require the release of the partie if detained in prison by the magistracy of the place on any such accusation broug before them ; and that all judicial proceedings against them do instantly cease ; and may demand the aid of the power of the country, civil and military, to enable him secure and put the accused parties on board such British ship as he shall think fit, th they may be conveyed to Great Britain, to be tried by their proper judges. If, co trary to this requisition, the magistrates of the country persist in proceeding to try tl offence, the consul should then draw up and transmit a memorial to the British minist at the court of that country ; and if that court give an evasive answer, the consul shoul if it be a sea offence, apply to the Board of Admiralty at London, stating the case ; ar upon their representation the secretary for the proper department will lay the matt before the king, who will cause the ambassador of the foreign state, resident in Englan to write to his court abroad, desiring that orders may immediately be given by th government, that all judicial proceedings against the prisoner be stayed, and that he released. — (See *case of Horseman and his crew, Beawes*, vol. ii. p. 422.)

" It is the duty also of a British consul to relieve all distressed British mariners, allow them sixpence daily for their support, to send them home in the first Britis vessels that sail for England, and to keep a regular account of his disbursements, whic he is to transmit yearly, or oftener if required, to the Navy Office, attested by two Britis merchants of the place : this is provided for by positive enactment (1 Geo. 2. s. 2. c. § 12.). He is also to give free passes to all poor British subjects wishing to retu home, directed to the captains of the king's packet boats, or ships of war, requirin them to take them on board. (See SEAMEN.)

" The consul is not to permit a British merchant ship to leave the port where resides without his passport, which he is not to grant until the master and crew there have satisfied all just demands upon them ; and for this purpose he ought to see tl governor's pass of a garrisoned town, or the burgomaster's ; unless the merchant factor to whom the ship was consigned will make himself responsible. — (*Beawes, L Merc.* vol. ii. p. 423.)

" It is also his duty to claim and recover all wrecks, cables, and anchors, belonging British ships, found at sea by fishermen or other persons, to pay the usual salvage, ar to communicate a report thereof to the Navy Board.

" The consuls and vice-consuls of his Majesty are, by express enactment (46 Geo. c. 98. § 9.), empowered to administer oaths in all cases respecting quarantine, in li manner as if they were magistrates of the several towns or places where they respec ively reside. It is also laid down, that a consul is to attend, if requested, all arbitr tions where property is concerned between masters of British ships and the freighte being inhabitants of the place where he resides." — (*Chitty on Commercial Law*, vol. pp. 58—61., and the numerous authorities there quoted.)

Any individual, whether he be a subject of the state by which he is appointed, or another, may be selected to fill the office of consul, provided he be approved and a mitted by the government in whose territory he is to reside. In most instances, howev but not always, consuls are the subjects of the state appointing them.

3. *Emoluments of Consuls. — Cost and Inefficacy of the Establishment. — Improt ments that ought to be made in it.* — The emoluments of our consuls were, until the few years, principally derived from certain fees, depending on the tonnage, length the voyages, &c. of the British ships entering and clearing out of the limits of the consulships. But this mode of remunerating them was materially changed by the 6 Geo. 4. c. 87. The fees payable under this act (see *post*) are but inconsiderabl but the deficiency is amply compensated by the handsome salaries that are now allow by government. We are, however, inclined to think, that, with proper modificatio the old system of paying consuls by means of fees might be advantageously revive and that the public might be relieved from the heavy expense attending the new pla without entailing any serious burden upon trade.

Under the system now followed, our consuls are prohibited from engaging, eit directly or indirectly, in any sort of commercial speculation. But, while we are d posed to approve of this regulation when applied to the consuls resident at ports mu frequented by British ships, as Petersburgh, Hamburgh, Rotterdam, Antwerp, A sterdam, &c., we cannot help considering it as most preposterous, when applied consuls resident at ports with which we have little direct intercourse. The former ha sufficient public business to occupy their time ; but the latter have almost no official dut to attend to ; none certainly that they might not discharge in the most efficient mann though engaged in trade. We confess, too, that we see no good reason why Englishm should be sent as consuls to places not much resorted to by English ships. Individu

ntly qualified to give a sound opinion upon such points have assured us, that some
 respectable inhabitants of such places might easily be selected to fill the office of
1 ; and that they would discharge its duties quite as well as a consul sent from
nd, and at a tenth part of the expense. In fact, this department of our foreign
diture seems to be arranged on the most lavish scale. The consul at Corunna
00l. a year, though, in 1828, only 5 British ships, carrying 418 tons, entered that
the consuls at Fiume and Venice have, the former 400l. to take charge of 4 small
s, carrying 144 tons ; and the latter 1,000l. to take care of 8 vessels, carrying 1,138
the consul at Maracaibo has 1,200l., while only 5 British ships, carrying 413 tons,
the port ; making the consul's emolument equivalent to a duty of nearly 3l. per
A dozen similar instances might be pointed out. At Port-au-Prince, we have
consul-general and a vice-consul ; the former with a salary of 1,250l., and the
with a salary of 500l. a year, though in 1828 only 16 British ships, carrying
tons, entered the port. It seems also very difficult to discover why there should
consul-general as well as a vice-consul at such places as Valparaiso, Buenos
, Lima, &c. Surely, if *a single consul* be able properly to discharge all the duties
nt to the office at Rotterdam and Hamubrgh, he must be far more than able to
m them at Valparaiso and Buenos Ayres.

as, no doubt, been said that the consuls now alluded to ought to be looked upon
rt of political as well as commercial agents. But admitting this to be the case,
ains to be explained why one individual should not suffice for both purposes ; and
ur political resident at Valparaiso should have a larger salary than that of the
can minister at London.

efficiency of our consular establishment is not proportioned to its cost. Consuls
t in foreign countries might and *ought* to be made instrumental in the collection
istical and other information with respect to them. But this very important
of the peculiar duty of a consul has been most strangely neglected by the go-
ent of England. The returns of the prices of foreign corn, and the different
and regulations affecting it, made within the last half dozen years, comprise
all the information of a generally useful kind that has ever been obtained by
itish consuls ; at least, it is about all that has been made public. We do hope
fectual measures will be taken for remedying this defect ; and that it will be
mperative upon our consuls regularly to send home detailed accounts, embodying
authentic information attainable with respect to commercial affairs ; such as
antities and prices of the goods imported into and exported from the places where
side ; the qualities which principally recommend them ; the duties and regula-
y which they are affected ; the improvements that take place in the arts ; the
s in the laws as to trade ; and whatever, in short, may tend to enlighten the
as to the condition of such places. The preparation of these reports for pub-
, and of queries for transmission to the consuls, ought to be one of the most
ant duties of the Board of Trade.

following are the provisions of the act 6 Geo. 4. c. 87. with respect to the
and charges of consuls : —

s to Consuls. — " Whereas the provision which hath hitherto been made for the maintenance
ort of the consuls general and consuls appointed by his Majesty to reside within the dominions
eigns and foreign states in amity with his Majesty, is inadequate to the maintenance and support
consuls general and consuls, and it is expedient to make further and due provisions for that
" it is therefore enacted, that it shall be lawful for his Majesty, by any orders to be issued by the
f his privy council, to grant to all or any of the consuls general or consuls appointed by his
to reside within any of the dominions of any sovereign or foreign state or power in amity with
sty, such reasonable salaries as to his Majesty shall seem meet, and by such advice from time to
lter, increase, or diminish, any such salaries or salary as occasion may require. — (6 *Geo.* 4. c. 87.

on which Salaries shall be granted. — *Leave of Absence.* — Such salaries shall be issued and paid
onsuls general and consuls without fee or deduction ; provided that all such salaries be granted
s Majesty's pleasure, and not otherwise, and be held and enjoyed by such consuls general and
so long only as they shall be actually resident at the places at which they may be so appointed to
nd discharging the duties of such their offices : Provided nevertheless, that in case his Majesty
any order to be for that purpose issued through one of his principal secretaries of state, grant to
consul general or consul leave of absence from the place to which he may be so appointed, such
neral or consul shall be entitled to receive the whole, or such part as to his Majesty shall seem
the salary accruing during such period of absence. — § 2.

s in lieu of Fees formerly paid. —Consuls not to take other than the Fees hereinafter mentioned.—
ries so to be granted shall be taken by the consuls general and consuls as a compensation for all
heretofore granted, and all fees of office and gratuities heretofore taken by them from the masters
anders of British vessels, or from any other person, for any duties or services by such consuls
r consuls done or performed for any such persons ; and no such consuls general or consuls shall,
January, 1826, on account of any thing by him done in the execution of such his
for any service by him rendered to any masters or commanders of British vessels, or to any other
the execution of such his office, to ask or take any fees, recompence, gratuity, compensation, or
r any sum of money, save as hereinafter is excepted. — § 3.

s Fees still allowed to be taken. — It shall be lawful for all consuls general and consuls appointed
ajesty, and resident within the dominions of any sovereign, or any foreign state or power in
th his Majesty, to accept the several fees particularly mentioned in the tables to this present act

annexed, marked with the letters A. and B., for the several things and official acts and deeds particu
mentioned in the said schedules ; and it shall be lawful for his Majesty, by any orders to be by him n
by the advice of his privy council, from time to time, as occasion may require, to diminish, or who.
abolish, all or any of the fees aforesaid, and to establish and authorise the payment of any great
smaller or new or additional fees for the several things mentioned in the said schedules, or for any c
thing to be by any such consul general or consul done in the execution of such his office. — § 4.

Penalty on Consuls demanding more Fees than specified in the Schedule.—In case any consul gene
consul, appointed by his Majesty as aforesaid, shall, by himself or deputy, or by any person autho
thereto in his behalf, ask or accept for any thing by him done in the execution of such his office, or for
service, or duty by him rendered or performed in such his office, for any person whomsoever, any oth
greater fee or remuneration than is specified in the schedule, or than shall be sanctioned and specifi
or by any such order in council, the person so offending shall forfeit and become liable to pay t
Majesty any sum of sterling British money, not exceeding the amount of the salary of such perso
one year, nor less than the twelfth part of such annual salary, at the discretion of the court in which
penalty may be recovered, and shall moreover upon a second conviction for any such offence fo
such his office, and for ever after become incapable of serving his Majesty in the same or the like capa
— § 5.

Table of Fees to be exhibited at Custom-houses. — A printed copy of the tables of fees allowed by this
or which may be sanctioned or allowed by any order to be made in pursuance of this act, by his Ma
in council, shall be exhibited in a conspicuous manner, for the inspection of all persons, in the Cus
house in the port of London, and in all other Custom-houses in the several ports and harbours of
United Kingdom of Great Britain and Ireland ; and printed copies thereof shall, by the collector or c
chief officer of customs in all such ports and harbours, be delivered gratuitously, and without fe
reward, to every master of any vessel clearing out of any such port or harbour, and demanding a
thereof. — § 6.

Table of Fees to be exhibited at Consuls' Offices. — A copy of the schedule or table of fees to this pr
act annexed, or which may be established and authorised by any such order in council, shall be hun
and exhibited in a conspicuous place in the public offices of all consuls general or consuls appointe
his Majesty, in the foreign places to which they may be appointed, for the inspection of all pe
interested therein ; and any consul general or consul omitting or neglecting to exhibit any such co
the schedules in such his public office, or refusing to permit the same to be inspected by any pe
interested therein, shall for every such offence forfeit and pay a sum of British sterling money not ex
ing one half the amount of the salary of such person for one year, nor less than the twelfth part of
annual salary, at the discretion of the court in which such penalty may be recovered. — § 7.

Superannuation. — "And whereas it is expedient that his Majesty should be enabled to grant to
said consuls general and consuls, appointed as aforesaid, allowances in the nature of superannuatic
reward for meritorious public services ;" it is further enacted, that all the regulations containe
50 Geo. 3. c. 117., 3 Geo. 4. c. 113., 5 Geo. 4. c. 1C4., respecting superannuation allowances, are he
extended to the said consuls general and consuls, so far as such regulations can be applied to the c
of such several persons respectively, as fully to all intents and purposes as if the same were repeate
re-enacted in this present act. — § 8.

Allowances during War.—If it shall at any time happen that by reason of any war which may here
arise between his Majesty and any sovereign, or foreign state or power, within the dominions of w
any such consul general or consul shall be appointed to reside, he shall be prevented from residing,
shall in fact cease to reside, at the place to which he may be so appointed, it shall be lawful fo
Majesty, by any order to be issued by the advice of his privy council, to grant to any such consul ge
or consul, who may have served his Majesty in that capacity for any period not less than three year
more than ten years next preceding the commencement of any such war, a special allowance not ex
ing the proportion of their respective salaries to which such consuls general and consuls would be ent
under the provisions of the said act of 3 Geo. 4., in case the period of their respective service had exce
ten years and had not exceeded fifteen years : Provided that in case any such consul general or c
shall have served in such his office for the space of ten years and more, it shall be lawful for his Ma
by any such order in council as aforesaid, to grant to him such a proportion of his salary, which, b
said act is authorised to be granted, as a superannuation allowance, according to the several peric
service exceeding ten years, in the said act. — § 9.

Commencement. — This act shall take effect from the 1st January, 1826, except where any other
mencement is particularly directed. — § 22.

Tables of Fees allowed to be taken by Consuls General and Consuls, by the preceding Ac
6 Geo. 4. c. 87.

Table A. — Certificate of due landing of goods exported from the United Kingdom	2 d
Signature of ship's manifest	2 d
Certificate of origin, when required	2 d
Bill of health, when required	2 d
Signature of muster roll, when required	2 d
Attestation of a signature, when required	1 d
Administering an oath, when required	½ c
Seal of office, and signature of any other document not specified herein, when required	1 c
Table B. — Bottomry or arbitration bond	2 d
Noting a protest	1 c
Order of survey	2 d
Extending a protest or survey	1 c
Registrations	1 c
Visa of passport	½ c
Valuation of goods	1 pe

Attending sales, ½ per cent. where there has been a charge for valuing ; otherwise, 1 per cent.
Attendance out of consular office at a shipwreck, 5 dollars per diem for his personal expenses, ov
above his travelling expenses.

Ditto on opening a will	5 c
Management of property of British subjects dying intestate	2½ pe

The dollars mentioned in the preceding tables are in all cases to be paid by the delivery of c
each of which is to be of the value of 4s. 6d. sterling, and no more, according to the rate of ex
prevailing at the place where such payment is made.

CONTRABAND,

CONTRABAND, in commerce, a commodity prohibited to be export
imported, bought or sold.

CONTRABAND is also a term applied to designate that class of commo
which neutrals are not allowed to carry during war to a belligerent power.

It is a recognised general principle of the law of nations, that ships may s

trade with all kingdoms, countries, and states, in peace with the princes or
horities whose flags they bear; and that they are not to be molested by the
ps of any other power at war with the country with which they are trading,
ess they engage in the conveyance of *contraband* goods. But great difficulty
arisen in deciding as to the goods comprised under this term. The reason of
limitation suggests, however, the species of articles to which it principally
lies. It is indispensable that those who profess to act upon a principle of
trality should carefully abstain from doing any thing that may discover a bias
avour of either party. But a nation who should furnish one of the belligerents
n supplies of warlike stores, or with supplies of any article, without which that
igerent might not be able to carry on the contest, would obviously forfeit her
tral character; and the other belligerent would be warranted in preventing
h succours from being sent, and in confiscating them as lawful prize. All the
t writers on international law admit this principle; which, besides being enforced
ing every contest, has been sanctioned by repeated treaties. In order to
ate all disputes as to what commodities should be deemed contraband, they
e sometimes been specified in treaties or conventions. — (See the references in
npredi *Del Commercio de' Popoli Neutrali*, § 9.) But this classification is not
ays respected during hostilities; and it is sufficiently evident that an article
ch might not be contraband at one time, or under certain circumstances, may
ome contraband at another time, or under different circumstances. It is aded on all hands, even by M. Hubner, the great advocate for the freedom of
tral commerce, (*De la Saisie des Batimens Neutres*, tom. i. p. 193.) that every
g that may be made *directly available* for hostile purposes is contraband, as
s, ammunition, horses, timber for ship-building, and all sorts of naval stores.
greatest difficulty has occurred in deciding as to provisions, which are some-
es held to be contraband, and sometimes not. Lord Stowell has shown that
character of the port to which the provisions are destined, is the principal cir-
stance to be attended to in deciding whether they are to be looked upon as
traband. A cargo of provisions intended for an enemy's port, in which it was
wn that a warlike armament was in preparation, would be liable to arrest and
iscation; while, if the same cargo were intended for a port where none but
chantmen were fitted out, the most that could be done would be to detain it,
ng the neutral the same price for it he would have got from the enemy.
y the ancient law of Europe, a ship conveying any contraband article was
e to confiscation as well as the article. But in the modern practice of the
rts of Admiralty of this and other countries, a milder rule has been adopted,
the carriage of contraband articles is attended only with the loss of freight
expenses, unless when the ship belongs to the owner of the contraband cargo,
hen the simple misconduct of conveying such a cargo has been connected
other malignant and aggravating circumstances. Of these a false destination
false papers are justly held to be the worst. — (5 *Rob. Adm. Rep.* 275.)
ie right of visitation and search is a right inherent in all belligerents; for it
d be absurd to allege that they had a right to prevent the conveyance of con-
nd goods to an enemy, and to deny them the use of the only means by which
can give effect to such right. — (*Vattell*, book iii. c. 7. § 114.) The object of
earch is two-fold: *first*, to ascertain whether the ship is neutral or an enemy,
he circumstance of its hoisting a neutral flag affords no security that it is really
; and *secondly*, to ascertain whether it has contraband articles, or enemies'
erty, on board. All neutral ships that would navigate securely during war
, consequently, be provided with passports from their government, and with
e papers or documents necessary to prove the property of the ship and cargo
Ship's Papers); and they must carefully avoid taking any contraband articles
elligerent property on board. And hence, as Lampredi has observed, a
hant ship which seeks to avoid a search by crowding sail, or by open force,
justly be captured and subjected to confiscation. — (§ 12.)
has, indeed, been often contended that *free ships make free goods* (*que le pavillon
e la marchandise*), and that a belligerent is not warranted in seizing the proof an enemy in a neutral ship, unless it be contraband. The discussion of
important question would lead us into details which do not properly come
n the scope of this work. We may, however, shortly observe that no such
ege could be conceded to neutrals, without taking from belligerents the right,

inseparable from a state of war, of seizing an enemy's property if found in plac
where hostilities may be lawfully carried on, as on the high seas. In fact, we
the principle in question admitted, the commerce of a belligerent power with i
colonies, or other countries beyond sea, might be prosecuted in neutral ships, wi
as much security during war as in peace; so that neutrals would, in this way, b
authorised to render a belligerent more important assistance than, perhaps, the
could have done had they supplied him with troops and ammunition! But it
surely unnecessary to say, that to act in this way is a proceeding altogether.
variance with the idea of neutrality. Neutrals are bound to conduct themselv
in the *spirit of impartiality*; and must not afford such aid or assistance to one part
as may the better enable him to make head against the other. It is their du
" *non interponere se bello, non hoste imminente hostem eripere.*" And yet it
manifest that the lending of neutral bottoms to carry on a belligerent's trade is
direct contradiction to this rule. The ships or cruisers of a particular power m
have swept those of its enemy from the sea, and reduced him to a state of gre
difficulty, by putting a stop to his commerce with foreigners, or with his ow
colonies; but of what consequence would this be, if neutrals might step in to resc
him from such difficulties, by carrying on that intercourse for him which he c
no longer carry on for himself? It is natural enough that such a privilege shou
be coveted by neutrals; but, however advantageous to them, it is wholly subversi
of the universally admitted rights of belligerent powers, as well as of the principles
neutrality; and cannot, therefore, be truly said to be bottomed on any sound princip

In the war of 1756, the rule was laid down by Great Britain, that neutrals a
not to be allowed to carry on a trade during war, that they were excluded fro
during peace; so that, supposing a nation at war with Great Britain had, while
peace, prohibited foreigners from engaging in her colonial or coasting trade, v
should not have permitted neutrals to engage in it during war. This rule has be
much complained of; but the principle on which it is founded seems a sound on
and it may in most cases be safely adopted. The claims of neutrals cannot sure
be carried farther than that they should be allowed to carry on their trade duri
war, as they had been *accustomed* to carry it on during peace, except with plac
under blockade; but it is quite a different thing when they claim to be allowed
employ themselves, during war, in a trade in which they had not previously a
right to engage. To grant them this, would not be to preserve to them the
former rights, but to give them new ones which may be fairly withheld. Suppo
ing, however, that either of the belligerent powers has *force sufficient to prevent a
intercourse between the other and its colonies, or any intercourse between differe
ports of the other*, she might, in the exercise of the legitimate rights of a belligere
exclude neutrals from such trade, even though it had formerly been open
them; because otherwise she would be deprived of the advantage of her super
force; and the neutrals would, in fact, when employed in this way, be acting as t
the most efficient allies of her enemy.

For a full discussion of this important and difficult question, and of the vario
distinctions to which it gives rise, see the work of Hubner (*De la Saisie des Ba
mens Neutres*, 2 tomes, 12mo. 1757.), in which the different arguments in favour
the principle that " the flag covers the cargo" are stated with great perspicui
and talent. The opposite principle has been advocated by Lampredi, in his ve
able treatise *Del Commercio de' Popoli Neutrali*, § 10.; by Lord Liverpool, in
Discourse on the Conduct of Great Britain in respect to Neutrals, written in 175
and above all by Lord Stowell, in his justly celebrated decisions in the Admira
Court. Martens inclines to Hubner's opinion; (see *Precis du Droit des Gens*, liv.
c. 7.).

CONVOY, in navigation, the term applied to designate a ship or ships of w
appointed by government, or by the commander in chief on a particular statio
to escort or protect the merchant ships proceeding to certain ports. Convo
are mostly appointed during war; but they are sometimes, also, appointed duri
peace, for the security of ships navigating seas infested with pirates.

Individuals have not always been left to themselves to judge as to the expediency
sailing with or without convoy. The governments of most maritime states have thou
proper, when they were engaged in hostilities, to oblige their subjects to place themsel
under an escort of this sort, that the enemy might not be enriched by their captu
Acts to this effect were passed in this country during the American war and the

h war. The last of these acts (43 Geo. 3. c. 57.) enacted, that it should not be
for any ship belonging to any of his Majesty's subjects (except as therein pro-
) to depart from any port or place whatever, unless under such convoy as should
pointed for that purpose. The master was required to use his utmost endeavours
tinue with the convoy during the whole voyage, or such part thereof as it should
ected to accompany his ship ; and not to separate therefrom without leave of the
ander, under very heavy pecuniary penalties. And in case of any ship departing
ut convoy contrary to the act, or wilfully separating therefrom, all insurances
ship, cargo, or freight, belonging to the master, or to any other person directing
vy to such departure or separation, were rendered null and void. The customs
s were directed not to allow any ship that ought to sail with convoy to clear out
any place in the United Kingdom for foreign parts, without requiring from the
r, bond with one surety, with condition that the ship should not depart without
y, nor afterwards desert or wilfully separate from it. The regulations of this act
t extend to ships not requiring to be registered, nor to those licensed to sail with-
nvoy, nor to those engaged in the coasting trade, nor to those belonging to the
India Company, &c.

s very common, during periods of war, to make *sailing or departing with convoy*
dition in policies of insurance. This, like other warranties in a policy, must be
performed. And if a ship warranted to sail with convoy, sail without it, the
becomes void, whether this be imputable to any negligence on the part of the
d, or the refusal of government to appoint a convoy.

re are five things essential to a sailing with convoy, viz. *first*, it must be with a
r convoy under an officer appointed by government ; *secondly*, it must be from
ace of rendezvous appointed by government ; *thirdly*, it must be a convoy for the
; *fourthly*, the master of the ship must have sailing instructions from the com-
ng officer of the convoy ; and *fifthly*, the ship must depart and continue with the
till the end of the voyage, unless separated by necessity.

h respect to the third of these conditions we may observe, that a warranty to sail
onvoy generally means a convoy *for the voyage ;* and it is not necessary to add the
"for the voyage" to make it so. Neither will the adding of these words in
nstances, make the omission of them, in any case, the ground of a different con-
on. A warranty to sail with convoy does not, however, uniformly mean a
that is to accompany the ship insured the entire way from the port of departure
port of destination ; but such convoy as government may think fit to appoint
fficient protection for ships going the voyage insured, whether it be for the whole
a part of the voyage.

ing instructions, referred to in the fourth condition, are written or printed direc-
elivered by the commanding officer of the convoy to the several masters of the
nder his care, that they may understand and answer signals, and know the place
ezvous appointed for the fleet in case of dispersion by storm, or by an enemy, &c.
sailing instructions are so very indispensable, that no vessel can have the full
ion and benefit of convoy without them ; hence, when, through the negligence of
ster, they are not obtained, the ship is not said to have sailed with convoy ; and
anty in a policy of insurance to that effect is held not to be complied with. If,
r, the master do all in his power to obtain sailing instructions, but is prevented
btaining them by any insuperable obstacle, as the badness of the weather ; or
be refused by the commander of the convoy ; the warranty in the policy is held
omplied with.

further information as to convoy, see *Abbot on the Law of Shipping*, Part III.
Marshall on Insurance, Book I. c. 9. § 5., and the Act 43 *Geo.* 3. c. 57, &c.

PAIVA. See BALSAM.

PAL, improperly called gum copal, is a valuable and singular kind of resin,
aturally exudes from different large trees, and is imported partly from
ca, and partly from the East Indies. The best copal is hard and brittle,
ded lumps of a moderate size, easily reducible to a fine powder, of a light
yellow colour, beautifully transparent, but often, like amber, containing
f insects and other small extraneous bodies in its substance. Its specific
varies from 1·045 to 1·139. It has neither the solubility in water common
s, nor the solubility in alcohol common to resins, at least in any consider-
gree. It may be dissolved by digestion in drying linseed oil, and other
menstrua. This solution forms a beautiful transparent varnish, which,
roperly applied, and slowly dried, is very hard and very durable. Copal
was first discovered in France, and was long known by the name of *vernis*
It is applied to snuff-boxes, tea-boards, and other utensils. It preserves

and gives lustre to paintings; and contributes to restore the decayed colours of
pictures, by filling up cracks, and rendering the surface capable of reflecting l
more uniformly. Copal is liable to be confounded with *gum-animé*, when the la
is very clear and good. But it is of importance to distinguish between them
the animé, though valuable as a varnish, is much less so than the finest copal;
varnish with the former being darker coloured; and not so hard. Besides the
ternal appearance of each, which is pretty distinct to a practised eye, the solub
in alcohol furnishes a useful test, — the animé being readily soluble in this fl
while the copal is hardly affected by it; copal is also brittle between the te
whereas animé softens in the mouth.—(*Rees's Cyclopædia; Ure's Dictionary,*

Copal in bond is at present (July, 1831) worth, in the London market, fi
10*d.* to 2*s.* per lb. The imports vary from about 20,000lbs. to 60,000lbs.

COPENHAGEN, the capital of Denmark, situated on the east coast of
island of Zealand, in the channel of the Baltic called the Sound; in lat. 55°
N., long. 12° 35′ E. Population about 110,000. Copenhagen is a well-b
handsome city. The entrance to the harbour is narrow, but the water is de
and there is space for the accommodation of several hundred ships. The for
trade carried on here is not very considerable, and has latterly declined. Anch
pitch, and tar, are chiefly imported from Sweden and Norway; flax, hemp, ma
sail-cloth, and cordage, from Russia; West India produce from the Danish W
India islands; tobacco from America; wines and brandy from France; cot
stuffs and yarn, hardware, &c. from England. The exports principally con
of butter and cheese, cattle, wool, hides and skins, grain, (but not in considera
quantities, and the wheat inferior,) &c. The Danes send annually a few vessel
the East Indies and China. In the former, they possess factories at Tranque
near Madras, and at Serampoor near Calcutta.

Money.— Accounts are kept in rixdollars of 6 marcs, or 96 skillings; the rixdc
being formerly worth about 4*s.* 1*d.* sterling. But in 1813, a new monetary sys
was adopted, according to which the new or *rigsbank* dollar is worth 2*s.* 3¼*d.*, b
half the value of the old specie dollar, and ⅝ of the old current dollar. But the mc
generally used in commercial transactions is bank money, which is commonly
heavy discount. The *par* of exchange, estimated by the rigsbank dollar, would
dollars 7⁶⁄₁₀ skillings per pound sterling.

Weights and Measures. — The commercial weights are,

16 Pounds	= 1 Lispound.
20 Lispound	= 1 Shippound.

100 lbs. = 110¼ lbs. avoirdupois = 134 lbs. Troy = 101 lbs. of Amsterdam = 103 lb
Hamburgh.

The liquid measures are

4 Ankers	= 1 Ahm or Ohm.
1½ Ahm	= 1 Hogshead.
2 Hogsheads	= 1 Pipe.
2 Pipes	= 1 Quarter.

The anker = 10 (very nearly) English wine gallons. A *fuder* of wine = 930 pots ;
100 pots = 25½ wine gallons.

The dry measures are

4 Viertels	= 1 Scheffel.
8 Scheffels	= 1 Toende or Ton.
12 Tons	= 1 Last = 47⅓ Winchester bushels.

The last of oil, butter, herrings, and other oily substances, should weigh 224 lbs. ne
The measure of length is the Rhineland foot = 12⅓ inches very nearly. The Da
ell = 2 feet; 100 ells = 68⅔ English yards.

COPPER (Ger. *Kupfer;* Du. *Koper;* Da. *Kobber;* Sw. *Koppar;* Fr. *Cu*
It. *Rame;* Sp. *Cobre;* Port. *Cobre;* Rus. *Mjed, Krasnoi mjed;* Pol. *Miedz;*
Cuprum; Arab. *Nehass;* Sans. *Tamra*), a well known metal, so called fro
having been first discovered, or at least wrought to any extent, in the islar
Cyprus. It is of a fine red colour, and has a great deal of brilliancy. Its
is styptic and nauseous; and the hands, when rubbed for some time on it, ac
a peculiar and disagreeable odour. It is harder than silver; its specific gr
varies according to its state, being, when quite pure, near 9,000. Its malleab
is great: it may be hammered out into leaves so thin as to be blown abou
the slightest breeze. Its ductility is also considerable. Its tenacity is so g
that a copper wire 0·078 inch in diameter is capable of supporting 302·2
avoirdupois without breaking. Its liability to oxidation from exposure to a
damp is its greatest defect. The rust with which it is then covered is known b
name of verdigris, and is one of the most active poisons.—(*Thomson's Chemi*

f we except gold and silver, copper seems to have been more early known
n any other metal. In the first ages of the world, before the method of
rking iron was discovered, copper was the principal ingredient in all domestic
nsils, and instruments of war. Even now it is applied to so many purposes,
o rank next, in point of utility, to iron.

lloys of Copper are numerous and of great value. Those of tin are of most import-
e. Tin added to copper makes it more fusible, less liable to rust or to be corroded
he air and other common substances, harder, denser, and more sonorous. In these
ects the alloy has a real advantage over unmixed copper: but this is in many cases
e than counterbalanced by the great brittleness which even a moderate portion of
imparts; and which is a singular circumstance, considering that both metals are
rately very malleable.

opper alloyed with from 1 to *5 per cent.* of tin is rendered harder than before; its
ur is yellow, with a cast of red, and its fracture granular: it has considerable mal-
ility. This appears to have been the usual composition of many of the ancient edged
s and weapons, before the method of working iron was brought to perfection. The
xos of the Greeks, and, perhaps, the *æs* of the Romans, was nothing else. Even
r copper coins contain a mixture of tin. The ancients did not, in fact, possess (as
been often contended) any peculiar process for hardening copper, except by adding
t a small quantity of tin. An alloy in which the tin is from $\frac{1}{10}$ to $\frac{1}{8}$ of the whole is
l, brittle, but still a little malleable, close grained, and yellowish white. When the tin
much as $\frac{1}{3}$ of the mass, it is entirely brittle; and continues so in every higher propor-
The yellowness of the alloy is not entirely lost till the tin amounts to $\frac{2}{3}$ of the whole.
opper (or sometimes copper with a little zinc), alloyed with as much tin as will make
about $\frac{1}{10}$ to $\frac{1}{8}$ of the whole, forms an alloy, which is principally employed for bells,
s cannon, bronze statues, and various other purposes. Hence it is called *bronze*, or
metal; and is excellently fitted for the uses to which it is applied, by its hardness,
ity, sonorousness, and fusibility. For cannon a lower proportion of tin is com-
ly used. According to Dr. Watson, the metal employed at Woolwich consists of
parts of copper and from 8 to 12 of tin; hence it retains some little malleability,
therefore, is tougher than it would be with a larger portion of tin. This alloy
g more sonorous than iron, brass guns give a louder report than iron guns. A
mon alloy for bell metal is 80 parts of copper and 20 of tin: some artists add to
e ingredients zinc, antimony, and silver, in small proportions; all of which add to
sonorousness of the compound. (See BELL METAL.)

hen, in an alloy of copper and tin, the latter metal amounts to about $\frac{1}{8}$ of the mass,
esult is a beautiful compound, very hard, of the colour of steel, and susceptible of
ry fine polish. It is well adapted for the reflection of light for optical purposes;
is therefore called *speculum metal.* Besides the above ingredients, it usually con-
a little arsenic, zinc, or silver. The application of an alloy similar to the above,
e construction of mirrors, is of great antiquity, being mentioned by Pliny; who
that formerly the best mirrors were reckoned those of Brundisium, of tin and
er mixed (*stanno et ære mistis*). — (*Hist. Nat.* lib. xxxiii. § 9.).

r the alloys of copper with zinc, see the articles BRASS, PINCHBECK. See, also,
son's *Chemistry*; *Rees's Cyclopædia*; *Dr. Watson's Chemical Essays*, vol. iv., &c.
ritish Copper Trade. — Great Britain has various copper mines; particularly those of
wall, Wales, Derbyshire, Devonshire, &c. But, though known long before, they
not wrought with any great degree of spirit till last century. From 1726 to 1735,
Cornwall mines produced, at an average, about 700 tons of pure copper; whereas
g the ten years, from 1766 to 1775, they produced, at an average, 2,650 tons.
ut 1773, new copper mines were opened in Derbyshire; and this was nearly, also,
poch of the discovery of the famous mines of Anglesea. In consequence of the
ly increased quantities that were thus obtained, England, instead of being, as
erly, dependent on foreigners for supplies of copper, became, previously to 1793,
f the principal markets for the supply of others. Notwithstanding the vastly ined demand for copper for the sheathing of ships and other purposes during the
war, the produce of the mines was increased in a corresponding proportion; the
rts having amounted, in 1811, to only 20,000 cwt.

r the following details with respect to the present state of the British copper trade
re indebted to Mr. Pascoe Grenfell, who is very largely engaged in it, and on
e accuracy every reliance may be placed: —

The quantity of copper produced during last year in Cornwall, from ores raised in
county, exceeded *ten thousand* tons of pure metal: and if to this be added what
een produced in Wales, in other parts of England, and in Ireland, the whole
ity of *fine* or *pure* metal produced in the United Kingdom, in 1829, may be fairly
at *twelve thousand* tons.

"The quantity of British copper exported in 1829 amounts, according to an accou recently laid before the House of Commons, to 7,976 tons of fine metal; to whi adding the exports of foreign copper, the total export was 8,817 tons. The copp imported is altogether intended for re-exportation. I cannot state its precise quanti in fine metal, because the greater part of it arrives in a state of *ore*, and I have means of knowing the produce in pure metal of that ore, beyond such part of it may come into my own possession.

"The value of the 12,000 tons of copper produced in the United Kingdom, above stated, at 90*l.* per ton, is 1,080,000*l.*"

Account of the Copper produced from the Mines in Cornwall for the last Thirty Year showing the Quantity of Ore, of Metal or Fine Copper, the Value of the Ores Money, the Average per Centage or Produce, and the Average Standard or Mine Price of fine Copper, made up to the End of June in each Year.

Years.	Quantity of Ores.	Metal or Fine Copper.				Value of the Ores.			Produce of Ores per cent.	AverageStanda Price per Ton.		
		Tons.	*cwt.*	*qrs.*	*lbs.*	£	*s.*	*d.*		£	*s.*	*d.*
1800	55,981	5,187	0	3	7	550,925	1	0	$9\frac{1}{4}$	133	3	6
1801	56,611	5,267	18	3	10	476,313	1	0	$9\frac{1}{4}$	117	5	0
1802	53,937	5,228	15	3	5	445,094	4	0	$9\frac{5}{8}$	110	18	0
1803	60,566	5,616	16	0	21	533,910	16	0	$9\frac{1}{4}$	122	0	0
1804	64,637	5,374	18	1	20	507,840	11	0	$8\frac{3}{8}$	138	5	0
1805	78,452	6,234	5	0	6	862,410	16	0	$7\frac{7}{8}$	169	16	0
1806	79,269	6,863	10	2	13	730,845	6	6	$8\frac{5}{8}$	138	5	0
1807	71,694	6,716	12	1	26	609,002	13	0	$9\frac{3}{8}$	120	0	0
1808	67,867	6,795	13	2	25	495,303	1	6	10	100	7	0
1809	76,245	6,821	13	1	19	770,028	15	6	$8\frac{7}{8}$	143	12	0
1810	66,048	6,682	19	1	27	570,035	8	0	$8\frac{1}{2}$	132	5	0
1811	66,786	6,141	13	3	7	556,723	19	0	$9\frac{1}{8}$	120	12	0
1812	71,547	5,720	7	2	4	549,665	6	6	$9\frac{3}{8}$	111	0	0
1813	74,047	6,918	3	0	6	594,345	10	0	$9\frac{1}{4}$	115	7	0
1814	74,322	6,369	13	3	7	627,501	10	0	$8\frac{1}{2}$	130	12	0
1815	78,483	6,525	6	3	25	552,813	8	6	$8\frac{1}{4}$	117	16	0
1816	77,334	6,697	4	0	17	447,959	17	0	$8\frac{5}{8}$	98	13	0
1817	76,701	6,498	2	0	16	494,010	12	6	$8\frac{1}{2}$	108	10	0
1818	86,174	6,849	7	1	1	686,005	4	6	$7\frac{7}{8}$	134	15	0
1819	88,736	6,804	2	2	7	623,595	4	6	$7\frac{5}{8}$	127	10	0
1820	91,473	7,508	0	3	26	602,441	12	0	$8\frac{1}{8}$	113	15	0
1821	98,426	8,514	19	2	12	605,968	19	6	$8\frac{5}{8}$	103	0	0
1822	104,523	9,140	8	3	20	663,085	13	6	$8\frac{3}{4}$	104	0	0
1823	95,750	7,927	17	2	7	608,033	1	0	$8\frac{1}{4}$	109	18	0
1824	99,700	7,823	15	1	10	587,178	3	6	$7\frac{7}{8}$	110	0	0
1825	107,454	8,226	3	0	21	726,353	12	0	$7\frac{3}{8}$	124	4	0
1826	117,308	9,026	12	3	15	788,971	15	6	$7\frac{5}{8}$	123	3	0
1827	126,710	10,311	14	3	15	745,178	1	0	$8\frac{1}{8}$	106	1	0
1828	130,366	9,921	1	2	11	756,174	16	0	$7\frac{5}{8}$	112	7	0
1829	124,502	9,656	10	3	4	717,334	0	0	$7\frac{3}{4}$	109	14	0

Exports and Imports of Copper, for Ten Years, ending 5th Jan. 1830.

Years ending 5th Jan.	British Copper exported.	Foreign Copper exported.	Foreign Copper imported.
	Tons.	*Tons.*	*Tons.*
1821	6,096	71	72
1822	6,270	167	405
1823	5,680	680	634
1824	5,321	1,092	2,108
1825	5,301	1,240	142
1826	3,926	262	676
1827	4,799	1,061	890
1828	7,171	625	575
1829	6,206	220	398
1830	7,976	841	738

pper ores are abundant in Sweden, Saxony, Russia, &c., and in Persia, Sumatra,
apan. Near Fahlun, in the province of Dalecarlia in Sweden, is an immense
r mine, supposed to have been wrought for nearly 1,000 years. — (*Coxe's Travels
North of Europe*, 5th ed. vol. v. p. 74.)

:opper sheathing and old copper utensils returned to this kingdom from the British plantations,
o old copper stripped off vessels in ports in the United Kingdom, may be admitted to entry, duty
nder the following regulations and conditions, viz. —
Old copper sheathing stripped off a British vessel in a port in a British possession, and brought in
essel, upon the master of the vessel making proof to the fact that the copper had been stripped off
itish port abroad.
ld copper sheathing of British ships stripped off in ports in the British possessions, but *not* brought
ships, upon the production of certificates from the principal officers of this revenue in the said
ons that such copper had been stripped off such vessels in their ports.
ld copper sheathing stripped off any ship in ports in the United Kingdom, upon the fact being
d by the landing waiter superintending the process.
three cases, the old copper to be delivered only to the copper-smith, who may re-copper the vessel
hich the copper was stripped, he making proof to that fact; and
That old worn-out British copper utensils be in all cases delivered when brought from British pos-
abroad in British ships, upon the consignee submitting proof that they had been used on a par-
estate, and are consigned to him on account of the owner of that estate, and that he (the consignee)
elieves them to have been of British manufacture. — *Min. Com. Cus.* 17 Dec. 1828.
above indulgence is extended to British vessels from which the copper may have been stripped in
n port, provided they come to this country to be re-coppered, and bring the old copper with them.
s. *Letter*, 24 *July*, 1829.
er ore may be taken out of warehouses to be smelted, on proper notice being given to the customs
and giving sufficient security, by bond, for returning the computed quantity of fine copper in it.
Geo. 4. c. 58. § 23.)

pper is in extensive demand all over India; being largely used in the dock-yards,
manufacture of cooking utensils, in alloying spelter and tin, &c. The funeral of
Hindoo brings an accession to the demand, according to his station; the relatives
deceased giving a brass cup to every Brahmin present at the ceremony: so that
50, 100, 1,000, and sometimes more than ten times this last number, are dispensed
uch occasions! — (*Bell's Commerce of Bengal.*)

PPERAS, a term employed by the older chemists, and popularly, as
ymous with vitriol. There are three sorts of copperas: the *green*, or sulphate
n; the *blue*, or sulphate of copper; and the *white*, or sulphate of zinc. Of
the first is the most important.

hate of iron is distinguished in common by a variety of names, as Martial vitriol,
h vitriol, &c. When pure it is considerably transparent, of a fine bright, though
y deep, grass green colour; and of a nauseous astringent taste, accompanied with
of sweetness. Its specific gravity is 1·834. It uniformly reddens the vege-
lues. This salt was well known to the ancients; and is mentioned by Pliny,
Nat. lib. xxxiv. § 12.), under the names of *misy*, *sory*, and *calchantum*. It is
de in the direct way, because it can be obtained at less charge from the decom-
n of pyrites on a large scale in the neighbourhood of collieries. It exists in two
one combined oxide of iron, with 0·22 of oxygen, which is of a pale green, not
by gallic acid, and giving a white precipitate with prussiate of potass. The
n which the iron is combined with 0·30 of oxygen, is red, not crystallisable, and
black precipitate with gallic acid, and a blue with prussiate of potass. In the
n sulphate, these two are often mixed in various proportions.
hate of iron is of great importance in the arts. It is a principal ingredient in
; in the manufacture of ink, and of Prussian blue: it is also used in tanning,
g, medicine, &c. Sulphuric acid, or oil of vitriol, was formerly manufactured
lphate of iron. See Acids.
hate of copper, or *blue* vitriol, commonly called Roman or Cyprian vitriol, is of
ant sapphire blue colour, hard, compact, and semi-transparent; when perfectly
ised, of a flattish, rhomboidal, decahedral figure; its taste is extremely nauseous,
and acrid; its specific gravity is 2·1943. It is used for various purposes in the
d also in medicine.
hate of zinc, or *white* vitriol, is found native in the mines of Goslar and other
Sometimes it is met with in transparent pieces, but more commonly in white
ences. These are dissolved in water, and crystallised into large irregular masses,
at resembling fine sugar, having a sweetish, nauseous, styptic taste. Its specific
when crystallised, is 1·912; when in the state in which it commonly occurs in
rce, it is 1·3275. Sulphate of zinc is prepared in the large way from some varieties
ative sulphuret.* The ore is roasted, wetted with water, and exposed to the air.
lphur attracts oxygen, and is converted into sulphuric acid; and the metal, being
ame time oxidized, combines with the acid. After some time the sulphate is
d by solution in water; and the solution being evaporated to dryness, the mass
to moulds. Thus, the white vitriol of the shops generally contains a small por-
iron, and often of copper and lead. — (*Lewis's Mat. Medica*; *Ure's Dictionary*;
yclopœdia; *Thomson's Chemistry*, &c.)

B b 4

COPYRIGHT. See Books.

CORAL (Ger. *Korallen;* Du. *Koraalen;* Fr. *Corail;* It. *Corale;* Sp. and P.
Coral; Rus. *Korallü;* Lat. *Corallium;* Arab. *Besed;* Pers. *Merjān;* Hind. *Moong*
a marine production, of which there are several varieties. It was well known
the ancients, but it was reserved for the moderns to discover its real nature.
is in fact the nidus or nest of a certain species of vermes, which has the sa
relation to coral, that a snail has to its shell. As an ornament, black coral
most esteemed; but the red is also very highly prized. Coral is found in very g
abundance in the Red Sea, the Persian Gulf, in various places in the Mediterrane
on the coast of Sumatra, &c. It grows on rocks, and on any solid submar
body; and it is necessary to its production, that it should remain fixed to
place. It has generally a shrub-like appearance. In the Straits of Messi
where a great deal is fished up, it usually grows to nearly a foot in length, and
thickness is about that of the little finger. It requires eight or ten years to arr
at its greatest size. The depth at which it is obtained is various — from 10
100 fathoms or more; but it seems to be necessary to its production that the r
of the sun should readily penetrate to the place of its habitation. Its value
pends upon its size, solidity, and the depth and brilliancy of its colour; and is
very various, that while some of the Sicilian coral sells for eight or ten guin
an ounce, other descriptions of it will not fetch a shilling a pound. It is hig
prized by opulent natives in India, as well as by the fair sex throughout Euro
The inferior or worm-eaten coral is used in some parts of the Madras coast,
the celebration of funeral rites. It is also used medicinally. Besides the fish
in the Straits of Messina already alluded to, there are valuable fisheries on
shores of Majorca and Minorca, and on the coast of Provence A good dea
Mediterranean coral is exported to India, which, however, draws the largest p
tion of its supplies from the Persian Gulf. The produce of the fishery at Mess
is stated by Spallanzani (*Travels in the Two Sicilies*, vol. iv. p. 308, &c.)
amount to 12 quintals of 250 lbs. each.

The manner of fishing coral is nearly the same every where. That which is n
commonly practised in the Mediterranean, is as follows: — Seven or eight men
in a boat, commanded by the proprietor; the caster throws his net, if we may so
the machine which he uses to tear up the coral from the bottom of the sea; and
rest work the boat, and help to draw in the net. This is composed of two beam
wood tied crosswise, with leads fixed to them to sink them: to these beams is fasten
quantity of hemp, twisted loosely round, and intermingled with some loose netting.
this condition the machine is let down into the sea, and when the coral is pretty stro
entwined in the hemp and nets, they draw it up with a rope, which they unw
according to the depth, and which it sometimes requires half a dozen boats to draw.
this rope happen to break, the fishermen run the hazard of being lost. Before
fishers go to sea, they agree for the price of the coral; and the produce of the fishe
divided, at the end of the season, into thirteen parts; of which the proprietor has f
the caster two, and the other six men one each: the thirteenth belongs to the comp
for payment of boat hire, &c. — (See *Ainslie's Mat. Indica; Rees's Cyclopædia; E*
Metrop.; Bell's Com. of Bengal, &c.)

CORDAGE (Ger. *Tauwerk;* Du. *Touwwerk;* Fr. *Manœuvres, Cordage;*
Caolame; Sp. *Jarcia, Cordaje*), a term used in general for all sorts of cord, whe
small, middling, or great, made use of in the rigging of ships. The manufac
of cordage is regulated by the act 25 Geo. 4. c. 56., which specifies the sor
materials that are to be employed in the manufacture of cables, hawsers,
other ropes, the marks that are to be affixed to them, and the penalties for r
compliance with the respective enactments. — (See CABLE.) Masters
British ships are obliged, on coming into any port in Great Britain or the colo
to make entry on oath of all the foreign cordage on board, paying the dt
thereon. A bounty is allowed by the 6 Geo. 4. c. 113. of 3s. 10d. a cwt
cordage or spun yarn manufactured in the United Kindgom from foreign h
not being the produce of any British plantation, nor of the East Indies,
China, nor imported by the East India Company.

The following table shows how many fathoms, feet, and inches, of a rope of any
not exceeding fourteen inches, make a hundred weight.

At the top of the table, marked inches, fathoms, feet, inches, the first column i
thickness of a rope in inches and quarters; the second, the fathoms, feet, and in
that make up a hundred weight of such a rope. One example will make it plain.

uppose it is required how much of a 7-inch rope will make a hundred weight: d 7, in the third column, under inches, or thickness of the rope, and against it, in fourth column, you will find 9, 5, 6; which shows that, in a rope of seven inches, re will be 9 fathoms 5 feet 6 inches required to make 1 cwt.

Cordage Table.

Inches.	Fathom.	Feet.	Inches.	Inches.	Fathom.	Feet.	Inches.	Inches.	Fathom.	Feet.	Inches.	Inches.	Fathom.	Feet.	Inches.
1	486	0	0	4½	24	0	0	7¾	8	3	6	11	4	0	3
1¼	313	3	0	4¾	21	3	0	8	7	3	6	11¼	3	5	7
1½	216	3	0	5	19	3	0	8¼	7	0	8	11½	3	4	1
1¾	159	3	0	5¼	17	4	0	8½	6	4	3	11¾	3	3	3
2	124	3	0	5½	16	1	0	8¾	6	2	1	12	3	2	3
2¼	96	2	0	5¾	14	4	6	9	6	0	0	12¼	3	2	1
2½	77	3	0	6	13	3	0	9¼	5	4	0	12½	3	2	0
2¾	65	4	0	6¼	12	2	9	9½	5	2	0	12¾	2	7	8
3	54	0	0	6½	11	3	0	9¾	5	0	6	13	2	5	3
3¼	45	5	2	6¾	10	4	0	10	4	5	0	13¼	2	4	9
3½	39	3	0	7	9	5	6	10¼	4	4	1	13½	2	4	0
3¾	34	3	9	7¼	9	1	6	10½	4	2	2	13¾	2	3	6
4	30	1	6	7½	8	4	0	10¾	4	1	8	14	2	2	1
4¼	26	5	3												

ORK (Ger. *Kork;* Du. *Kork, Kurk, Vlothout;* Fr. *Liège;* It. *Sughero, Suvero;* *Corcho;* Port. *Cortica* (*de Sovreiro*); Rus. *Korkowoe derewo;* Lat. *Suber*), the of a tree of the oak species. It grows principally in Italy, Spain, Portugal, on the French side of the Pyrenees. The bark is made into stoppers for les, serves as buoys for nets, and when calcined yields ashes, from which nish black is made. The French cork-wood is the best we import. (See Bark.)

ORN (Ger. *Corn, Getreide;* Du. *Graanen, Koren;* Da. *Korn;* Sw. *Säd, Span-* Fr. *Bleds, Grains;* It. *Biade, Grani;* Sp. *Granos;* Rus. *Chljeb;* Pol. *Zboze;* *Frumentum*), the grain or seed of plants separated from the spica or ear, used for making bread, &c. Such are wheat, rye, barley, oats, maize, peas, ; which see.

ORNELIAN. See Carnelian.

ORN LAWS and CORN TRADE. — From the circumstance of corn ing, in this and most other countries, the principal part of the food of the le, the trade in it, and the laws by which that trade is regulated, are justly ed upon as of the highest importance. But this is not the only circumstance renders it necessary to enter at some length into the discussion of this sub- Its difficulty is at least equal to its interest. The enactments made at rent periods with respect to the corn trade, and the opinions advanced as to policy, have been so very various and contradictory, that it is indispensable bmit them to some examination, and, if possible, to ascertain the *principles* h ought to pervade this department of commercial legislation.

I. Historical Sketch of the Corn Laws.
II. Principles of the Corn Laws.
III. State of the Corn Trade.

I. Historical Sketch of the Corn Laws.

r a long time the regulations with respect to the corn trade were principally ded to promote abundance and low prices. But, though the purpose was ble, the means adopted for accomplishing it had, for the most part, a directly site effect. When a country exports corn, it seems, at first sight, as if nothing do so much to increase her supplies as the prevention of exportation: and in countries that do not export, its prohibition seems to be a prudent measure, alculated to prevent the supply from being diminished, upon any emergency, its natural level. These are the conclusions that immediately suggest them- upon this subject; and it requires a pretty extensive experience, an attention ts, and a habit of reasoning upon such topics, to perceive their fallacy. These,

however, were altogether wanting when the regulations affecting the corn trade began to be introduced into Great Britain and other countries. They were framed in accordance with what were supposed to be the dictates of common sense; and their object being to procure as large a supply of the prime necessary of life as possible, its exportation was either totally forbidden, or forbidden when the home price was above certain limits.

The principle of absolute prohibition seems to have been steadily acted upon, as far as the turbulence of the period would admit, from the Conquest to the year 1436, in the reign of Henry VI. But at the last mentioned period an act was passed, authorising the exportation of wheat whenever the home price did not exceed 6s. 8d. (equal in amount of pure silver to 12s. 10¾d. present money) per quarter, and barley when the home price did not exceed 3s. 4d. In 1463, an additional benefit was intended to be conferred on agriculture by prohibiting importation until the home price exceeded that at which exportation ceased. But the fluctuating policy of the times prevented these regulations from being carried into full effect; and, indeed, rendered them in a great measure inoperative.

In addition to the restraints laid on exportation, it has been common in most countries to attempt to increase the supply of corn, not only by admitting its unrestrained importation from abroad, but by holding out extraordinary encouragement to the importer. This policy has not, however, been much followed in England. During the five hundred years immediately posterior to the Conquest, importation was substantially free; but it was seldom or never promoted by artificial means: and during the last century and half it has, for the most part, been subjected to severe restrictions.

Besides attempting to lower prices by prohibiting exportation, our ancestors attempted to lower them by proscribing the trade carried on by corn dealers. This most useful class of persons were looked upon with suspicion by every one. The agriculturists concluded that they would be able to sell their produce at higher prices to the consumer were the corn dealers out of the way: while the consumers concluded that the profits of the dealers were made at their expense; and ascribed the dearths that were then very prevalent entirely to the practices of the dealers, or to their buying up corn and with-holding it from market. These notions, which have still a considerable degree of influence, led to various enactments, particularly in the reign of Edward VI., by which the freedom of the internal corn trade was entirely suppressed. The *engrossing* of corn or the buying of it in one market with intent to sell it again in another, was made an offence punishable by imprisonment and the pillory; and no one was allowed to carry corn from one part to another without a licence, the privilege of granting which was confided by a statute of Elizabeth to the Quarter Sessions. But as the principles of commerce came to be better understood, the impolicy of these restraints gradually grew more and more obvious. They were considerably modified in 1624; and, in 1663, the engrossing of corn was declared to be legal so long as the price did not exceed 48s. a quarter — (15 *Cha*. 2. c. 7.); an act which, as Dr. Smith has justly observed, has, with all its imperfections, done more to promote plenty than any other law in the statute book. In 1773, the last remnant of the *legislative* enactments, restraining the freedom of the internal corn dealers, was entirely repealed. But the engrossing of corn has, notwithstanding, been since held to be an offence at common law; and, so late as 1800 a corn dealer was convicted of this imaginary crime. He was not, however, brought up for judgment; and it is not very likely that any similar case will ever again occur to the attention of the courts.

The acts of 1436 and 1463, regulating the prices when exportation was allowed and when importation was to cease, continued, nominally at least, in force till 1562, when the prices at which exportation might take place were extended to 10s. for wheat and 6s. 8d. for barley. But a new principle — that of imposing duties on exportation—was soon after introduced; and, in 1571, it was enacted that wheat might be exported, paying a duty of 2s. a quarter, and barley and other grain a duty of 1s. 4d., whenever the home price of wheat did not exceed 20s. a quarter, and barley and malt 12s. At the Restoration, the limit at which exportation might take place was very much extended; but, the duty on exportation was, at the same time, so very high as to be almost prohibitory: the extension was of little or no service to the agriculturists. This view of the matter seems to have been speedily taken by the legislature; for, in 1663, the high duties on exportation were taken off, and an *ad valorem* duty imposed in their stead, at the same time that the limit of exportation was extended. In 1670, a still more decided step was taken in favour of agriculture; an act being then passed which extended the exportation price to 53s. 4d. a quarter for wheat, and other grain in proportion, imposing, at the same time, prohibitory duties on the importation of wheat till the price rose to 53s. 4d., and a duty of 8s. between that price and 80s. But the real effects of this act were not so great as might have been anticipated. The extension of the limit of exportation was rendered comparatively nugatory, in consequence of the continuance of the duties

tation caused by the necessities of the crown; while the want of any proper method
e determination of prices went far to nullify the prohibition of importation.

the accession of William III. a new system was adopted. The interests of
alture were then looked upon as of paramount importance: and to promote them,
aly were the duties on exportation totally abolished, but it was encouraged by the
of a *bounty* of 5s. on every quarter of wheat exported while the price continued
below 48s.; of 2s. 6d. on every quarter of barley or malt, while their respective
did not exceed 24s.; and of 3s. 6d. on every quarter of rye, when its price did
ceed 32s. — (1 *Will. & Mary*, c. 12.) A bounty of 2s. 6d. a quarter was subse-
ly given upon the exportation of oats and oatmeal, when the price of the former did
ceed 15s. a quarter. Importation continued to be regulated by the act of 1670.
ch diversity of opinion has been entertained with respect to the policy of the
y. That it was intended to raise the price of corn is clear, from the words of the
e, which states, "that the exportation of corn and grain into foreign parts, *when
ice thereof is at a low rate in this kingdom*, hath been a great advantage not only to
wners of land, but to the trade of this kingdom in general; therefore," &c. But
ting this to have been its object, it has been contended that the low prices which
led during the first half of last century show that its real effect had been precisely
verse; and that it had, by extending tillage, contributed to reduce prices. It
e afterwards shown that this could not really be the case; and the fall of prices
e sufficiently accounted for by the improved state of agriculture, the gradual con-
ion of farms, the diminution of sheep husbandry, &c., combined with the slow in-
of the population. In point of fact, too, prices had begun to give way thirty years
the bounty was granted; and the fall was equally great in France, where, instead
ortation being encouraged by a bounty, it was almost entirely prohibited; and in
ther continental states. — (For proofs of what is now stated, see the article *Corn*
in the *Supp.* to the *Ency. Brit.*)

tables annexed to this article show that, with some few exceptions, there was,
; the first 66 years of last century, a large export of corn from England. In
the wheat exported amounted to 947,000 quarters; and the total bounties paid
; the ten years from 1740 to 1751 reached the sum of 1,515,000l. But the rapid
se of population subsequently to 1760, and particularly after the peace of Paris,
3, when the commerce and manufactures of the country were extended in an
edented degree, gradually reduced this excess of exportation, and occasionally,
, inclined the balance the other way. This led to several suspensions of the
ions on importation; and, at length, in 1773, a new act was framed, by which
wheat was allowed to be imported on paying a nominal duty of 6d., whenever
ne price was at or above 48s. a quarter, and the bounty* and exportation were
er to cease, when the price was at or above 44s. This statute also permitted the
ation of corn at any price, duty free, in order to be again exported, provided it
the mean time lodged under the joint locks of the king and the importer.

prices when exportation was to cease by this act seem to have been fixed too low;
Dr. Smith has observed, there appears a good deal of impropriety in prohibiting
ation altogether the moment it attained the limit, when the bounty given to force
withdrawn; yet, with all these defects, the act of 1773 was a material improve-
n the former system, and ought not to have been altered unless to give greater
a to the trade.

idea that this law must, when enacted, have been injurious to the agriculturists,
altogether illusory: the permission to import foreign grain, when the home price
a moderate height, certainly prevented their realising exorbitant profits, in dear
at the expense of the other classes; and prevented an unnatural proportion of the
of the country from being turned towards agriculture. But as the limit at
importation at a nominal duty was allowed, was fixed a good deal above the
e price of the reign of George II., it cannot be maintained that it had any
y to reduce previous prices, which is the only thing that could have discouraged
ture: and, in fact, no such reduction took place.

, indeed, true, that, but for this act, we should not have imported so much foreign
n the interval between 1773 and 1791. This importation, however, was not a
ence of the decline of agriculture; for it is admitted that every branch of rural
y was more improved in that period than in the whole of the preceding century;
se entirely from a still more rapid increase of the manufacturing population, and
f the effective demand for corn.

eferring to the tables annexed to this article, it will be seen that, in 1772, the
on the side of wheat imported amounted to 18,515 quarters; and in 1773, 1774,
75, all years of great prosperity, the balance was very much increased. But the

bounty amounted to 5s. on every quarter of wheat; 2s. 6d. on every quarter of barley; 3s. 6d. on
arter of rye; and 2s. 6d. on every quarter of oats.

loss of a great part of our colonial possessions, the stagnation of commerce, and diffic
of obtaining employment, occasioned by the American war, diminished the consu
tion ; and this, combined with unusually productive harvests, rendered the balance h
on the side of exportation, in 1778, 1779, and 1789.   In 1783 and 1784, the crop
unusually deficient, and considerable importations took place; but in 1785, 1786,
1787, the exports again exceeded the imports; and it was not till 1788, when
country had fully recovered from the effects of the American war, and when ma
facturing improvements were carried on with extraordinary spirit, that the imp
permanently overbalanced the exports.

The growing wealth and commercial prosperity of the country had thus, by increas
the population and enabling individuals to consume additional quantities of food, cau
the home supply of corn to fall somewhat short of the demand ; but it must not, th
fore, be concluded that agriculture had not at the same time been very greatly ameliora
" The average annual produce of wheat," says Mr. Comber, " at the beginning of
reign of George III. (1760) was about 3,800,000 quarters, of which about 300,0
had been sent out of the kingdom, leaving about three millions and a half for home c
sumption.   In 1773, the produce of wheat was stated in the House of Commons to
4,000,000 of quarters, of which the whole, and above 100,000 imported, were consur
in the kingdom.   In 1796, the consumption was stated by Lord Hawkesbury to
500,000 quarters per month, or 6,000,000 quarters annually, of which about 180,
were imported ; showing an increased produce in about 20 years of 1,820,000 quart
It is evident, therefore, not only that no defalcation of produce had taken place in c
sequence of the cessation of exportation, as has been too lightly assumed from
occasional necessity of importation, but that it had increased with the augmentatio
our commerce and manufactures." — (Comber on National Subsistence, p. 180.)

These estimates are, no doubt, very loose and unsatisfactory ; but the fact of a g
increase of produce having taken place is unquestionable.   In a report by a commi
of the House of Commons on the state of the waste lands, drawn up in 1797,
number of acts passed for enclosing, and the number of acres enclosed, in the follow
reigns, are thus stated : —

	Number of acts.	Number of acres.
In the reign of Queen Anne -	2	1,439
George I. -	16	17,960
George II. -	226	318,778
George III. to 1797	1,532	2,804,197

It deserves particular notice that from 1771 to 1791, both inclusive, the period du
which the greater number of these improvements were effected, there was no ris
prices.

The landholders, however, could not but consider the liberty of importation gra
by the act of 1773 as injurious to their interests, inasmuch as it prevented prices f
rising with the increased demand.   A clamour, therefore, was raised against that l
and in addition to this interested feeling, a dread of becoming habitually dependen
foreign supplies of corn, operated on many and produced a pretty general acquiesc
in the act of 1791.   By this act, the price when importation could take place from ab
at the low duty of 6d., was raised to 54s. ; under 54s., and above 50s., a middle dut
2s. 6d., and under 50s. a prohibitory duty of 24s. 3d. was exigible.   The bounty c
tinued as before, and exportation without bounty was allowed to 46s.   It was
enacted, that foreign wheat might be imported, stored under the king's lock, and a
exported free of duty ; but, if sold for home consumption, it became liable
warehouse duty of 2s. 6d., in addition to the ordinary duties payable at the tin
sale.

In 1797, the Bank of England obtained an exemption from paying in specie ;
the consequent facility of obtaining discounts and getting a command of capital, w
this measure occasioned, gave a fresh stimulus to agriculture ; the efficacy of which
most powerfully assisted by the scarcity and high prices of 1800 and 1801.   An a
cultural mania now seized the nation ; and as the prices of 1803 would not allow
cultivation of the poor soils, which had been broken up in the dear years, to be
tinued, a new corn law, being loudly called for by the farmers, was passed in 1
This law imposed a prohibitory duty of 24s. 3d. per quarter on all wheat impo
when the home price was at or below 63s. ; between 63s. and 66s. a middle du
2s. 6d. was paid, and above 66s. a nominal duty of 6d.   The price at which
bounty was allowed on exportation was extended to 50s., and exportation wit
bounty to 54s.   By the act of 1791, the maritime counties of England were di
into 12 districts, importation and exportation being regulated by the particular pric
each ; but by the act of 1804 they were regulated, in England, by the aggregate av
of the maritime districts ; and in Scotland by the aggregate average of the four mar

ricts into which it was divided. The averages were taken four times a year, so that
ports could not be open or shut for less than three months. This manner of ascer-
aing prices was, however, modified in the following session; it being then fixed that
portation, both in England and Scotland, should be regulated by the average price of
twelve maritime districts of England.

n 1805 the crop was very considerably deficient, and the average price of that year
about 22s. a quarter above the price at which importation was allowed by the act of
4. As the depreciation of paper, compared with bullion, was at that time only *four*
cent., the high price of that year must have been principally owing to the new law
venting importation from abroad till the home price was high, and then fettering mer-
tile operations; and to the formidable obstacles which the war threw in the way of
ortation. In 1806*, 1807, and 1808, the depreciation of paper was nearly 3 per
t.; and the price of wheat in those years being generally from 66s. to 75s., the im-
tations were but small. From autumn 1808 to spring 1814 the depreciation of the
rency was unusually great, and several crops in that interval being likewise deficient,
price of corn, influenced by both causes, rose to a surprising height. At that time
essel could be laden in any continental port for England without purchasing a
nce, and the freight and insurance were at least five times as high as during peace.
the destruction of Napoleon's anti-commercial system, in the autumn of 1813,
ng increased the facilities of importation, a large quantity of corn was poured into
kingdom; and in 1814, its *bullion* price fell below the price at which importation was
wed.

efore this fall of price, a committee of the House of Commons had been appointed
quire into the state of the laws affecting the corn trade; and recommended in their
ort (dated 11th of May, 1813) a very great increase of the prices at which exportation
allowable, and when importation free of duty might take place. This recommend-
was not, however, adopted by the House; but the fact of its having been made
n the home price was at least 112s. a quarter, displayed a surprising solicitude to
ude foreigners from all competition with the home growers.

he wish to lessen the dependence of the country on foreign supplies formed the sole
nsible motive by which the committee of 1813 had been actuated, in proposing an
ation in the act of 1804. But after the fall of price in autumn 1813, and in the
y part of 1814, it became obvious, on comparing our previous prices with those of the
tinent, that without an alteration of the law in question this dependence would be a
l deal increased; that a considerable extent of such poor lands as had been brought
cultivation, during the high prices, would be again thrown into pasturage; and that
s would be considerably reduced. These consequences alarmed the landlords and
piers; and in the early part of the session of 1814, a series of resolutions were
l by the House of Commons, declaring that it was expedient to repeal the bounty,
ermit the free exportation of corn whatever might be the home price, and to impose
aduated scale of duties on the importation of foreign corn. Thus, foreign wheat
orted when the home price was at or under 64s. was to pay a duty of 24s.; when
under 65s. a duty of 23s.; and so on, till the home price should reach 86s., when
luty was reduced to 1s., at which sum it became stationary. Corn imported from
ada, or from the other British colonies in North America, was to pay half the duties
ther corn. As soon as these resolutions had been agreed to, two bills founded on
— one for regulating the importation of foreign corn, and another for the repeal of
ounty, and for permitting unrestricted exportation — were introduced. Very little
tion was paid to the last of these bills; but the one imposing fresh duties on im-
tion encountered a very keen opposition. The manufacturers, and every class not
tly suported by agriculture, stigmatised it as an unjustifiable attempt artificially to
up the price of food, and to secure excessive rents and large profits to the land-
rs and farmers at the expense of the consumers. Meetings were very generally
and resolutions entered into strongly expressive of this sentiment, and dwelling on
atal consequences which, it was affirmed, a continuance of the high prices would
on our manufactures and commerce. This determined opposition, coupled with
ndecision of ministers, and perhaps, too, with an expectation on the part of some of
andholders that prices would rise without any legislative interference, caused the
arriage of this bill. The other bill, repealing the bounty and allowing an unlimited
om of exportation, was passed into a law.

mmittees had been appointed in 1814, by both Houses of parliament, to examine
nce and report on the state of the corn trade; and, in consequence, a number of

veral impolitic restraints had been for a long time imposed on the free importation and exportation
n between Great Britain and Ireland, but they were wholly abolished in 1806; and the act of that
46 Geo. 3. c. 97.), establishing a free trade in corn between the two great divisions of the empire, was
ly a wise and proper measure in itself, but has powerfully contributed to promote the general
tage.

the most eminent agriculturists were examined. The witnesses were unanimous in th
only, that the protecting prices in the act of 1804 were insufficient to enable the farme
to make good the engagements into which they had subsequently entered, and to contin
the cultivation of the inferior lands lately brought under tillage. Some of them thoug
that 120s. ought to be fixed as the lowest limit at which the importation of wheat free
duty should be allowed: others varied from 90s. to 100s. — from 80s. to 90s. — and
few from 70s. to 80s. The general opinion, however, seemed to be that 80s. wou
suffice; and as prices continued to decline, a set of resolutions founded on this assum
tion were submitted to the House of Commons by Mr. Robinson, of the Board
Trade (now Lord Goderich); and having been agreed to, a bill founded on them wa
after a very violent opposition, carried in both Houses by immense majorities, and final
passed into a law (55 Geo. 3. c. 26.). According to this act all sorts of foreign cor
meal, or flour, might be imported at all times free of duty into any port of the Unite
Kingdom, in order to be warehoused; but foreign corn was not permitted to be importe
for home consumption, except when the average prices of the several sorts of Briti
corn were as follows: viz. wheat, 80s. per quarter; rye, peas, and beans, 53s.; barle
bear, or bigg, 40s.; and oats, 26s.: and all importation of corn from any of the Briti
plantations in North America was forbidden, except when the average home prices we
at or under, wheat, 67s. per quarter; rye, peas, and beans, 44s.; barley, bear or big
33s.; and oats, 22s.

The agriculturists confidently expected that this act would immediately effect a rise
prices, and render them steady at about 80s. But, for reasons which will be afterwar
stated, these expectations were entirely disappointed; and there has been a more ruino
fluctuation of prices during the 16 years that have elapsed since it was passed, than
any previous period of our recent history. In 1821, when prices had sunk very low,
committee of the House of Commons was appointed to inquire into the causes of th
depressed state of agriculture, and to report their observations thereupon. This com
mittee, after examining a number of witnesses, drew up a report, which, though not fr
from error, is a very valuable document. It contains a forcible exposition of th
pernicious effects arising from the law of 1815, of which it suggested several importa
modifications. These, however, were not adopted; and as the low prices, and cons
quent distress of the agriculturists, continued, the subject was brought under the co
sideration of parliament in the following year. After a good deal of discussion a ne
act was then passed (3 Geo. 4. c. 60.), which enacted, that after prices had risen to th
limit of free importation fixed by the act of 1815, that act was to cease and the ne
statute to come into operation. This statute lowered the prices fixed by the act
1815, at which importation could take place for home consumption, to the followir
sums, viz. : —

	For Corn not of the British Possessions in North America.	For Corn of the British Possessions in North Americ
Wheat - - -	70s. per quarter.	59s. per quarter.
Rye, peas, and beans	46s.	39s.
Barley, bear, or bigg	35s.	30s.
Oats - - -	25s.	20s.

But, in order to prevent any violent oscillation of prices from a large supply of gra
being suddenly thrown upon the market, it was enacted, that a duty of 17s. a quart
should be laid on all wheat imported from foreign countries, during the first 3 mont
after the opening of the ports, if the price was between 70s. and 80s. a quarter, and
12s. afterwards; that if the price was between 80s. and 85s., the duty should be 1
for the first 3 months, and 5s. afterwards; and that if the price should exceed 85s.,
duty should be constant at 1s.; and proportionally for other sorts of grain.

This act, by preventing importation until the home price rose to 70s., and then loadi
the quantities imported between that limit and the limit of 85s. with heavy duties, w
certainly more favourable to the views of the agriculturists than the act of 1815. B
unluckily for them, the prices of no species of corn, except barley, were sufficiently hig
while this act existed, to bring it into operation.

In 1825, the first approach was made to a better system, by permitting the impo
ation of wheat from British North America, without reference to the price at home,
payment of a duty of 5s. a quarter. But this act was passed with difficulty, and v
limited to one year's duration.

Owing to the drought that prevailed during the summer of 1826, there was ev
prospect that there would be a great deficiency in the crops of that year; and in or
to prevent the disastrous consequences that might have taken place had importation b
prevented until the season was too far advanced for bringing supplies from the gr
corn markets in the north of Europe, his Majesty was authorised to admit 500,0
quarters of foreign wheat, on payment of such duties as the order in council for

tation should declare. And when it was ascertained that the crops of oats, peas,
ere greatly below an average, ministers issued an order in council, on their own
nsibility, on the 1st of September, authorising the immediate importation of oats
yment of a duty of 2s. 2d. a boll; and of rye, peas, and beans, on payment of a
of 3s. 6d. a quarter. A considerable quantity of oats was imported under this
the timely appearance of which had undoubtedly a very considerable effect in
ating the pernicious consequences arising from the deficiency of that species of
Ministers obtained an indemnity for this order on the subsequent meeting of
ment.
thing could more strikingly evince the impolicy of the acts of 1815 and 1822,
the necessity, under which the legislature and government had been placed, of
g the temporary acts and issuing the orders alluded to. The more intelligent
n of the agriculturists began, at length, to perceive that the corn laws were not
calculated to produce the advantages that they had anticipated; and a conviction
ncreased facilities should be given to importation became general throughout the
·y. The same conviction made considerable progress in the House of Commons;
ch so, that several members who supported the measures adopted in 1815 and 1822,
sed themselves satisfied that the principle of exclusion had been carried too far,
aat a more liberal system should be adopted. Ministers having participated in
sentiments, Mr. Canning moved a series of resolutions, as the foundation of a
orn law, on the 1st of March, 1827. These resolutions were to the effect that
n corn might always be imported, free of duty, in order to be warehoused; and
should always be admissible for home consumption on payment of certain duties.
in the instance of wheat, it was resolved that, when the home price was at or
70s. a quarter, the duty should be a fixed one of 1s.; and that for every shilling
e price fell below 70s., a duty of 2s. should be imposed; so that when the price
69s. the duty on importation was to be 2s., when at 68s. the duty was to be 4s.,
on. The limit at which the constant duty of 1s. a quarter was to take place in
se of barley, was originally fixed at 37s., but it was subsequently raised to 40s.;
ty increasing by 1s. 6d. for every 1s. which the price fell below that limit. The
at which the constant duty of 1s. a quarter was to take place in the case of oats
ginally fixed at 28s.; but it was subsequently raised to 33s., the duty increasing
rate of 1s. a quarter for every shilling that the price fell below that limit. The
n colonial wheat was fixed at 6d. the quarter when the home price was below
and when the price was under that sum, the duty was constant at 5s.; the duties
er descriptions of colonial grain were similar. These resolutions were agreed to
rge majority; and a bill founded on them was subsequently carried through the
of Commons. Owing, however, to the change of ministers, which took place
interim, several peers, originally favourable to the bill, and some, even, who
l in its preparation, saw reason to become amongst its most violent opponents;
lause moved by the Duke of Wellington, interdicting all importation of foreign
ntil the home price exceeded 66s., having been carried in the Lords, ministers
p the bill, justly considering that such a clause was entirely subversive of its
le.
ew set of resolutions with respect to the corn trade were brought forward in 1828,
Charles Grant. They were founded on the same principles as those which had
jected during the previous session. But the duty was not made to vary equally,
Ir. Canning's resolutions, with every equal variation of price; it being 23s. 8d.
he home price was 64s. the imperial quarter; 16s. 8d. when it was 69s.; and 1s.
ren it was at or above 73s. After a good deal of debate, Mr. Grant's resolutions
rried in both Houses; and the act embodying them (9 Geo. 4. c. 60.) is that by
the corn trade is now regulated. An abstract of this act will be found in a
ent part of this article.

II. Principles of the Corn Laws.

ternal Corn Trade. — It is needless to to take up the reader's time by endeavour-
rove by argument the advantage of allowing the free conveyance of corn from
vince to another. Every one sees that this is indispensable, not only to the equal
tion of the supplies of food over the country, but to enable the inhabitants of
stricts that are best fitted for the raising and fattening of cattle, sheep, &c. to
themselves to these or other necessary occupations not directly connected with
luction of corn. We shall, therefore, confine the few remarks we have to make
subject, to the consideration of the influence of the speculations of the corn mer-
n buying up corn in anticipation of an advance. Their proceedings in this respect,
of the greatest public utility, have been the principal cause of that odium to
hey have been so long exposed.

Were the harvests always equally productive, nothing would be gained by storing
supplies of corn; and all that would be necessary would be to distribute the crop equ
throughout the country, and throughout the year. But such is not the order of natu
The variations in the aggregate produce of a country in different seasons, though
perhaps so great as are commonly supposed, are still very considerable; and experie
has shown that two or three unusually luxuriant harvests seldom take place in successi
or that when they do, they are invariably followed by those that are deficient.
speculators in corn anticipate this result. Whenever prices begin to give way in c
sequence of an unusually luxuriant harvest, speculation is at work. The more opul
farmers withhold either the whole or a part of their produce from market; and the m
opulent dealers purchase largely of the corn brought to market, and store it up in
pectation of a future advance. And thus, without intending to promote any one's inte
but their own, the speculators in corn become the great benefactors of the public. T
provide a relief stock against those years of scarcity which are sure at no distant pe
to recur: while, by withdrawing a portion of the redundant supply from immediate c
sumption, prices are prevented from falling so low as to be injurious to the farmers,
at least are maintained at a higher level than they would otherwise have reached; j
vident habits are maintained amongst the people; and that waste and extravagance
checked which always take place in plentiful years, but which would be carried t
much greater extent if the whole produce of an abundant crop were to be consu
within the season.

It is, however, in scarce years that the speculations of the corn merchants are pri
pally advantageous. Even in the richest countries, a very large proportion of
individuals engaged in the business of agriculture are comparatively poor, and are to
without the means of withholding their produce from market, in order to speculate u
any future advance. In consequence the markets are always most abundantly supp
with produce immediately after harvest; and in countries where the merchants enga
in the corn trade are not possessed of large capitals, or where their proceedings
fettered and restricted, there is then, almost invariably, a heavy fall of prices. Bu
the vast majority of the people buy their food in small quantities, or from day to da
they want it, their consumption is necessarily extended or contracted according to
price at the time. Their views do not extend to the future; they have no mean
judging whether the crop is or is not deficient. They live, as the phrase is, from han
mouth; and are satisfied if, in the mean time, they obtain abundant supplies at a ch
rate. But it is obvious, that were there nothing to control or counteract this improvide
the consequence would very often be fatal in the extreme. The crop of one harvest n
support the population till the crop of the other harvest has been gathered in; and if
crop should be deficient—if, for instance, it should only be adequate to afford, a
usual rate of consumption, a supply of nine or ten months' provisions instead of twelv
it is plain that, unless the price were so raised immediately after harvest, as to enf
economy, and put, as it were, the whole nation on short allowance, the most drea
famine would be experienced previously to the ensuing harvest. Those who exar
the accounts of the prices of wheat and other grain in England, collected by Bi
Fleetwood and Sir F. M. Eden, will meet with abundant proofs of the accurac
what has now been stated. In those remote periods when the farmers were gener
without the means of withholding their crops from market, and when the trade of a
dealer was proscribed, the utmost improvidence was exhibited in the consumptio
grain. There were then, indeed, very few years in which a considerable scarcity wa
experienced immediately before harvest, and many in which there was an absolute fan
The fluctuations of price exceeded every thing of which we can now form an idea; the
of wheat and other grain being four or five times as high in June and July, as in
tember and October. Thanks, however, to the increase of capital in the hands of
large farmers and dealers, and to the freedom given to the operations of the corn i
chants, we are no longer exposed to such ruinous vicissitudes. Whenever the de
who, in consequence of their superior means of information, are better acquainted
the real state of the crops than any other class of persons, find the harvest likely t
deficient, they raise the price of the corn they have warehoused, and bid against
other for the corn which the farmers are bringing to market. In consequence of
rise of prices, all ranks and orders, but especially the lower, who are the great consu
of corn, find it indispensable to use greater economy, and to check all improvident
wasteful consumption. Every class being thus immediately put upon short allowa
the pressure of the scarcity is distributed equally throughout the year; and instea
indulging, as was formerly the case, in the same scale of consumption as in seaso
plenty, until the supply became altogether deficient, and then being exposed wit
resource to the attacks of famine and pestilence, the speculations of the corn merc
warn us of our danger, and compel us to provide against it.

t is not easy to suppose that these proceedings of the corn merchants should ever be
rious to the public. It has been said that in scarce years they are not disposed to
g the corn they have purchased to market until it has attained an exorbitant price,
that the pressure of the scarcity is thus often very much aggravated; but there is no
ground for any such statement. The immense amount of capital required to store
any considerable quantity of corn, and the waste to which it is liable, render most
lers disposed to sell as soon as they can realise a fair profit. In every extensive
ntry in which the corn trade is free, there are infinitely too many persons engaged in
enable any sort of combination or concert to be formed amongst them; and though
ere formed, it could not be maintained for an instant. A large proportion of the
ers and other small holders of corn are always in straitened circumstances, more
icularly if a scarce year has not occurred so soon as they expected; and they are con-
ently anxious to relieve themselves, as soon as prices rise, of a portion of the stock
heir hands. Occasionally, indeed, individuals are found, who retain their stocks for
long a period, or until a re-action takes place, and prices begin to decline. But
ead of joining in the popular cry against such persons, every one who takes a dis-
ionate view of the matter will perceive that, inasmuch as their miscalculation must,
er the circumstances supposed, be exceedingly injurious to themselves, we have the
security against its being carried to such an extent as to be productive of any ma-
l injury or even inconvenience to the public. It ought also to be borne in mind, that it
rely, if ever, possible to determine beforehand, when a scarcity is to abate in con-
ence of new supplies being brought to market; and had it continued a little longer,
e would have been no miscalculation on the part of the holders. At all events, it is
n that, by declining to bring their corn to market, they preserved a resource on which,
he event of the harvest being longer delayed than usual, or of any unfavourable con-
ency taking place, the public could have fallen back; so that instead of deserving
e, these speculators are most justly entitled to every fair encouragement and
ction. A country in which there is no considerable stock of grain in the barn
s of the farmers, or in the warehouses of the merchants, is in the most perilous
tion that can easily be imagined, and may be exposed to the severest privations, or
famine. But so long as the sagacity, the miscalculation, or the avarice of merchants
dealers retain a stock of grain in the warehouses, this last extremity cannot take
. By refusing to sell it till it has reached a very high price, they put an effectual
to all sorts of waste, and husband for the public those supplies which they could
have so frugally husbanded for themselves.

e have already remarked that the last remnant of the shackles imposed by statute
he freedom of the internal corn dealer was abolished in 1773. It is true that en-
sing, forestalling, and regrating (see ENGROSSING, &c.), are still held to be offences
mmon law; but there is very little probability of any one being in future made to
er for such ideal offences.

Exportation to Foreign Countries. — The fallacy of the notion so long entertained,
the prevention of exportation was the surest method of increasing plenty at home,
vious to every one who has reflected upon such subjects. The markets of no
try can ever be steadily and plentifully supplied with corn, unless her merchants
power to export the surplus supplies with which they may be occasionally fur-
d. When a country without the means of exporting grows nearly her own average
lies of corn, an abundant crop, by causing a great overloading of the market, and a
y fall of price, is as injurious to the farmer as a scarcity. It may be thought, per-
that the greater quantity of produce in abundant seasons will compensate for its
r price; but this is not the case. It is uniformly found that variations in the
tity of corn exert a much greater influence over prices, than equal variations in the
tity of almost any thing else offered for sale. Being the principal necessary of life,
the supply of corn happens to be less than ordinary, the mass of the people make
great, though unavailing, exertions, by diminishing their consumption of other and
ndispensable articles, to obtain their accustomed supplies of this prime necessary;
at its price rises much more than in proportion to the deficiency. On the other
, when the supply is unusually large the consumption is not proportionally ex-
d. In ordinary years the bulk of the population is about adequately fed; and
gh the consumption of all classes be somewhat greater in unusually plentiful years,
xtension is considerable only among the lowest classes, and in the feeding of horses.
e it is, that the increased supply at market, in such years, goes principally to cause
t, and, consequently, a ruinous decline of prices. These statements are corrobo-
by the widest experience. Whenever there is an inability to export, from what-
:ause it may arise, an unusually luxuriant crop is uniformly accompanied by a very
fall of price, and severe agricultural distress; and when two or three such crops
n to follow in succession, the ruin of a large proportion of the farmers is completed.

If the mischiefs resulting from the want of power to export stopped here, they migh though very great, be borne: but they do not stop here. It is idle to suppose that system ruinous to the producers can be otherwise to the consumers. A glut of th market, occasioned by luxuriant harvests, and the want of power to export, cannot be long continuance: for, while it continues, it can hardly fail, by distressing all classes farmers, and causing the ruin of many, to give a check to every species of agricultur improvement, and to lessen the extent of land in tillage. When, therefore, an unfa vourable season recurs, the re-action is, for the most part, appalling. The supply, bein lessened not only by the badness of the season, but also by a diminution of the quantit of land in crop, falls very far below an average; and a severe scarcity, if not an absolu famine, is most commonly experienced. It is, therefore, clear, that if a country woul render herself secure against famine, and injurious fluctuations of price, she must giv every possible facility to exportation in years of unusual plenty. If she act upon different system,—if her policy make exportation in such years impracticable, or ver difficult,—she will infallibly render the bounty of Providence an injury to her agricu turists; and two or three abundant harvests in succession will be the forerunners scarcity and famine.

3. *Bounty on the Exportation of Corn.* — In Great Britain, as already observed, w have not only been allowed to export for a long series of years, but from the Revolutio down to 1815 a bounty was given on exportation, whenever the home prices were de pressed below certain limits. This policy, however, erred as much on the one hand a restriction on exportation errs on the other. It causes, it is true, an extension of th demand for corn: but this greater demand is not caused by natural, but by artifici means; it is not a consequence of any really increased demand on the part of th foreigner, but of our furnishing the exporters of corn with a bonus, in order that the may sell it abroad below its natural price! To suppose that a proceeding of this so can be a public advantage, is equivalent to supposing that a shopkeeper may get rich b selling his goods below what they cost. (See BOUNTY.)

4. *Importation from Foreign Countries.* — If a country were, like Poland or Russi uniformly in the habit of exporting corn to other countries, a restriction on importatio would be of no material consequence; because, though such restriction did not exis no foreign corn would be imported, unless its ports were so situated as to serve for a *entrepôt.* A restriction on importation is sensibly felt only when it is enforced in country which, owing to the greater density of its population, the limited extent of i fertile land, or any other cause, would, either occasionally or uniformly, import. It familiar to the observation of every one, that a total failure of the crops is a calami that but rarely occurs in an extensive kingdom; that the weather which is unfavourab to one description of soil, is generally favourable to some other description; and tha except in anomalous cases, the total produce is not very different. But what is th generally true of single countries, is always true of the world at large. History fu nishes no single instance of a universal scarcity; but it is uniformly found, that whe the crops in a particular country are unusually deficient, they are proportionally abu dant in some other quarter. It is clear, however, that a restriction on importatio excludes the country which enacts it from profiting by this beneficent arrangemen She is thrown entirely on her own resources. Under the circumstances supposed, sh has nothing to trust to for relief but the reserves in her warehouses; and should the be inadequate to meet the exigency of the crisis, there are apparently no means by whi she can escape experiencing all the evils of scarcity, or, it may be, of famine. country deprived of the power to import is unable to supply the deficiencies of h harvests by the surplus produce of other countries; so that her inhabitants may star amidst surrounding plenty, and suffer the extreme of scarcity, when, but for the restri tions on importation, they might enjoy the greatest abundance. If the restriction be n absolute, but conditional; if, instead of absolutely excluding foreign corn from the hor markets, it merely loads it with a duty, the degree in which it will operate to increa the scarcity and dearth will depend on the magnitude of that duty. If the duty be co stant and moderate, it may not have any very considerable effect in discouraging in portation; but if it be fluctuating and heavy, it will, by falsifying the speculations the merchants, and making a corresponding addition to the price of the corn importe be proportionally injurious. In whatever degree foreign corn may be excluded in yea of deficient crops, to the same extent must prices be artificially raised, and the pressu of the scarcity rendered so much the more severe.

Such would be the disastrous influence of a restriction on importation in a coun which, were there no such obstruction in the way, would sometimes import and som times export. But its operation would be infinitely more injurious in a country whi under a free system, would uniformly import a portion of her supplies. The restricti in this case, has a twofold operation. By preventing importation from abroad, a

g the population to depend for subsistence on corn raised at home, it compels re-
e to be had to comparatively inferior soils; and thus, by increasing the cost of pro-
g corn above its cost in other countries, adds proportionally to its average price.
auses of fluctuation are, in this way, increased in a geometrical proportion; for,
the prevention of importation exposes the population to the pressure of want
ever the harvest happens to be less productive than usual, it is sure, at the same
by raising average prices, to hinder exportation in a year of unusual plenty, until
ome prices fall ruinously low. It is obvious, therefore, that a restriction of this
ust be alternately destructive of the interests of the consumers and producers.
ures the former by making them pay, at an average, an artificially increased price
eir food, and by exposing them to scarcity and famine whenever the home crop
s deficient; and it injures the latter, by depriving them of the power to export in
of unusual plenty, and by overloading the market with produce, which, under a
stem, would have met with an advantageous sale abroad.

e principle thus briefly explained, shows the impossibility of permanently keeping
e home prices by means of restrictions on importation, at the same time that it
s a clue by which we may trace the causes of most of that agricultural distress
has been experienced in this country since the peace. The real object of the
aw of 1815 was to keep up the price of corn to 80s. a quarter; but to succeed in
t was indispensable not only that foreign corn should be excluded when prices
under this limit, but that the markets should never be overloaded with corn pro-
at home: for it is clear, according to the principle already explained, that if the
y should in ordinary years be sufficient to feed the population, it must, in an un-
y abundant year, be more than sufficient for that purpose; and when, in such a
he surplus is thrown upon the market, it cannot fail, in the event of our average
being considerably above the level of those of the surrounding countries, to cause
ous depression. Now this was the precise situation of this country at the end of
r. Owing partly to the act of 1804, but far more to the difficulties in the way of
ation, and the depreciation of the currency, prices attained to an extraordinary
on from 1809 to 1814, and gave such a stimulus to agriculture, that we grew, in
nd 1813, sufficient corn for our own supply. And, such being the case, it is
though our ports had been hermetically sealed against importation from abroad,
e first luxuriant crop must have occasioned a ruinous decline of prices. It is the
ion, not the introduction, of foreign corn that has caused the distress of the agri-
sts; for it is this exclusion that has forced up the price of corn in this country,
ce and average years, to an unnatural level, and that, consequently, renders ex-
on in favourable seasons impossible, without such a fall of prices as is most dis-
s to the farmer. It may be mentioned in proof of what is now stated, that the
e price of wheat in England and Wales, in 1814, was 74s. a quarter, and in 1815,
fallen to 64s. But as these prices would not indemnify the occupiers of the poor
wrought under tillage during the previous high prices, they were gradually relin-
g their cultivation. A considerable portion of them was converted into pasture;
were generally reduced; and wages had begun to decline: but the legislature
prohibited the importation of foreign corn, the operation of this natural principle
stment was unfortunately counteracted, and the price of 1816 rose to 75s. 10d.
se was, however, insufficient to occasion any new improvement; and as foreign
as now excluded, and large tracts of bad land had been thrown out of cultivation,
ply was so much diminished, that, notwithstanding the increase in the value of
prices rose in 1817, partly, no doubt in consequence of the bad harvest of the
s year, to 94s. 9d., and in 1818, to 84s. 1d. These high prices had their natural
They revived the drooping spirits of the farmers, who imagined that the corn
s, at length, beginning to produce the effects anticipated from it, and that the
days of 1812, when wheat sold for 125s. a quarter, were about to return! But
sperity carried in its bosom the seeds of future mischief. The increased prices
rily occasioned a fresh extension of tillage; capital was again applied to the iment of the soil; and this increase of tillage, conspiring with favourable seasons,
e impossibility of exportation, sunk prices to such a degree, that they fell, in
r, 1822, so low as 38s. 1d., the average price of that year being only 43s. 3d.

thus demonstrably certain, that the recurrence of periods of distress, similar to
at have been experienced by the agriculturists of this country since the peace,
be warded off by restricting or prohibiting importation. A free corn trade is the
stem that can give them that security against fluctuations that is so indispensable.
creased importation that would take place, were the ports always open, as soon
considerable deficiency in the crops was apprehended, would prevent prices from
o an oppressive height; while, on the other hand, when the crops were unusually
nt, a ready outlet would be found for the surplus in foreign countries, without

its occasioning any very heavy fall. To expect to combine steadiness of prices
restrictions on importation, is to expect to reconcile what is contradictory and abs
The higher the limit at which the importation of foreign corn into a country like E
land is fixed, the greater will be the oscillation of prices. If we would secure for
selves abundance, and avoid fluctuation, we must renounce all attempts at exclusion,
be ready to deal in corn, as we ought to be in every thing else, on fair and liberal p
ciples.

That the restrictions imposed on the foreign corn trade during the last ten y
should not have been productive of more disastrous consequences than those that h
actually resulted from them, is, we believe, principally to be ascribed to the very g
increase that has taken place in the imports from Ireland. Previously to 1806, w
a perfectly free corn trade between Great Britain and Ireland was for the first t
established, the yearly imports did not amount to 400,000 quarters, whereas they
amount to 2,400,000; and any one who has ever been in Ireland, or is aware of
wretched state of agriculture in it, and of the amazing fertility of the soil, must be s
fied that a very slight improvement would occasion an extraordinary increase in
imports from that country; and it is believed by those best qualified to form an opin
on such a subject, that the settlement of the Catholic question, and the disfranchisem
of the 40s. freeholders, by promoting the public tranquillity, and taking away one of
principal inducements to the pernicious practice of splitting farms, has, in this resp
already had great influence, and that it will eventually lead to the most material
provements. Hence it is by no means improbable, that the growing imports f
Ireland may, at no distant period, reduce our prices to the level of those of the Contin
and even render us an occasionally exporting country. These, however, are contin
and uncertain results; and supposing them to be ultimately realised, the corn laws n
in the mean time be productive of great hardship, and must, in all time to come, ag
vate to a frightful extent the misery inseparable from bad harvests.

Nothing but the great importance of the subject could excuse us for dwelling
long on what is so very plain. To facilitate production, and to make commod
cheaper and more easily obtained, are the grand motives which stimulate the
ventive powers, and which lead to the discovery and improvement of machines
processes for saving labour and diminishing cost; and it is plain that no system of c
mercial legislation deserves to be supported, which does not conspire to promote
same objects: but a restriction on the importation of corn into a country like Engl
which has made a great comparative advance in population and manufacturing indus
is diametrically opposed to these principles. The density of our population is such,
the exclusion of foreign corn forces us to resort to soils of a decidedly less degre
fertility than those that are under cultivation in the surrounding countries; and, in
sequence, our average prices are comparatively high. We have resolved that our pe
should not employ their capital and industry in those branches of manufacturing
commercial industry in which they have a decided advantage over every other coun
but that they should be made to force comparatively barren soils to yield them a sc
return for their outlay. If we could, by laying out 1,000l. on the manufactur
cottons or hardware, produce a quantity of these articles that would exchange for
quarters of American or Polish wheat; and if the same sum, were it expended in
tivation in this country, would not produce more than 300 quarters; the preventio
importation occasions an obvious sacrifice of 100 out of every 400 quarters consume
the empire; or, which is the same thing, it occasions an artificial advance of 25 per
in the price of corn. In a public point of view, the impolicy of such a system is obvi
but it seems, at first sight, as if it were advantageous to the landlords. The advan
is, however, merely apparent. at bottom there is no real difference between the inte
of the landlords and those of the rest of the community. It would be ridiculous, ind
to imagine for a moment that the landlords can be benefited by a system in which
tremendous fluctuations of prices, so subversive of all agricultural prosperity, are
herent; but though these could be got rid of, the result would be the same.
prosperity of agriculture must always depend upon, and be determined by, the prosp
of other branches of industry; and any system which, like the corn laws, is mos
jurious to the latter, cannot but be injurious to the former. Instead of being pul
advantageous, high prices are in *every case* distinctly and completely the reverse.
smaller the sacrifice for which any commodity can be obtained, so much the be
When the labour required to produce, or the money required to purchase, a suffi
supply of corn is diminished, it is as clear as the sun at noon-day that more labo
money must remain to produce or purchase the other necessaries, conveniences,
amusements of human life, and that the sum of national wealth and comforts mu
proportionally augmented. Those who suppose that a rise of prices can ever be a m
of improving the condition of a country might, with equal reason, suppose that it w

improved by throwing its best soils out of cultivation, and destroying its most powerful chines. The opinions of such persons are not only opposed to to the plainest and st obvious scientific principles, but they are opposed to the obvious conclusions of mon sense, and the universal experience of mankind.

Experience of the injurious effects resulting from the corn laws has induced many ; were formerly their zealous advocates to come round to a more liberal way of king. It would, however, be unjust not to mention that there has always been a ;e and respectable party amongst the landlords, opposed to all restrictions on the e in corn; and who have uniformly thought that their interests, being identified 1 those of the public, would be best promoted by the abolition of restrictions on im-:ation. A protest expressive of this opinion, subscribed by ten peers, was entered on Journals of the House of Lords, against the corn law of 1815. This document is ; to have been drawn up by Lord Grenville, who has always been the enlightened bcate of sound commercial principles. Its reasoning is so clear and satisfactory, that ire sure we shall gratify our readers, as well as strengthen the statements previously le, by laying it before them.

Dissentient. — I. Because we are adverse in principle to all new restraints on com-ce. We think it certain that public prosperity is best promoted by leaving uncon-led the free current of national industry; and we wish rather, by well considered 3, to bring back our commercial legislation to the straight and simple line of wisdom, 1 to increase the deviation by subjecting additional and extensive branches of the lic interest to fresh systems of artificial and injurious restrictions.

II. Because we think that the great practical rule, of leaving all commerce unfet-d, applies *more peculiarly*, and on still stronger grounds of justice as well as policy, 1e corn trade than to any other. Irresistible, indeed, must be that necessity which d, in our judgment, authorise the legislature to tamper with the sustenance of the le, and to impede the free purchase of that article on which depends the existence o large a portion of the community.

III. Because we think that the expectations of ultimate benefit from this measure founded on a delusive theory. We cannot persuade ourselves that this law will ever ribute to produce plenty, cheapness, or steadiness of price. So long as it operates at its effects must be the opposite of these. *Monopoly is the parent of scarcity, of dearness, of uncertainty.* To cut off any of the sources of supply, can only tend to lessen its idance; to close against ourselves the cheapest market for any commodity, must ince the price at which we purchase it; and to confine the consumer of corn to the uce of his own country, is to refuse to ourselves the benefit of that provision which vidence itself has made for equalising to man the variations of climate and of seasons.

IV. But whatever may be the future consequences of this law at some distant and rtain period, we see with pain that these hopes must be purchased at the expense of eat and present evil. To compel the consumer to purchase corn dearer at home than ight be imported from abroad, is the immediate practical effect of this law. In way alone can it operate Its present protection, its promised extension of agricul-must result (if at all) from the profits which it creates by keeping up the price of to an artificial level. These future benefits are the consequences expected, but, as onfidently believe, erroneously expected, from giving a bounty to the grower of by a tax levied on its consumer.

V. Because we think the adoption of any permanent law for such a purpose, re-d the fullest and most laborious investigation. Nor would it have been sufficient ur satisfaction, could we have been convinced of the general policy of a hazardous iment. A still further inquiry would have been necessary to persuade us that the nt moment is fit for its adoption. In such an inquiry, we must have had the means tisfying ourselves what its immediate operation will be, as connected with the various iressing circumstances of public difficulty and distress with which the country is unded; with the state of our circulation and currency, of our agriculture and ifactures, of our internal and *external* commerce, and, above all, with the condition eward of the industrious and labouring classes of our community.

On all these particulars, as they respect this question, we think that parliament is st wholly uninformed; on all we see reason for the utmost anxiety and alarm from peration of this law.

Lastly, Because, if we could approve of the principle and purpose of this law, we that no sufficient foundation has been laid for its details. The evidence before us, isfactory and imperfect as it is, seems to us rather to disprove than to support the iety of the high price adopted as the standard of importation, and the fallacious by which that price is to be ascertained. And on all these grounds we are anxious ord our dissent from a measure so precipitate in its course, and, as we fear, so in-is in its consequences."

C c 3

Attempts have sometimes been made to estimate the pecuniary burden which the restrictions on importation entail in ordinary years upon the country. This, however is a subject with respect to which it is not possible to obtain any very accurate data. But supposing the total quantity of corn annually produced in Great Britain and Ireland to amount to 52,000,000 quarters, every shilling that is added to its price by the corn law is equivalent to a tax on corn of 2,600,000*l.*; and estimating the average rise on all sorts of grain at 7*s.* a quarter, the total sum will be 18,200,000*l.* So great a quantity of corn is, however, consumed by the agriculturists themselves as food, in seed, the keep of horses, &c., that not more than a half, perhaps, of the whole quantity produced brought to market. If we are nearly right in this hypothesis, and in the previous esti mates, it will follow that the restrictions cost the classes not engaged in agriculture no less than 9,100,000*l.*, exclusive of their other pernicious consequences. Of this sum *fifth*, probably, or 1,800,000*l.* may go to the landlords as rent; and this is *all* that the agriculturists can be said to gain by the system, for the additional price received by the farmer on that portion of the produce exclusive of rent is no more than the ordinary return for his capital and labour. His profits, indeed, instead of being increased by the system, are really diminished by it; (for proofs of this, see the note on *Corn Laws*, in my edition of the *Wealth of Nations*, vol. iv. pp. 358—361.;) and though the rents of the landlords be, nominally at least, somewhat increased by it, it is, notwithstanding, abun dantly certain that it is any thing but advantageous to them. It would require a far larger sum to balance the injury which fluctuations of price occasion to their tenants and the damage done to their estates by over-cropping when prices are high, than a that is derived from the restrictions.

5. *Duties on Importation.* — A duty may be equitably imposed on imported corn, for two objects; that is, either for the sake of revenue, or to balance any excess of taxes laid on the agriculturists over those laid on the other classes. — (See my edition of *Wealth of Nations*, vol. iv. pp. 363—369.) With respect, however, to a duty imposed for the sake of revenue, it may be doubted whether corn be a proper subject for taxation. But at all events such a duty should be exceedingly moderate. It would be most inexpedien to attempt to add largely to the revenue by laying heavy duties on the prime necessaries of life.

If it be really true that agriculture is more heavily taxed than any other branch of industry, the agriculturists are entitled to demand that a duty be laid on foreign corn when imported, corresponding to the *excess* of burdens affecting them. It has been doubted, however, whether they are in this predicament. But though the question be by no means free from difficulty, we should be disposed to decide it in the affirmative being pretty well satisfied that, owing to the local and other burdens laid on the land those occupying it are really subjected to heavier taxes than any other class. It is dif ficult, or rather, perhaps, impossible, to estimate with any degree of precision what the *excess* of taxes laid on the agriculturists beyond those laid on manufacturers and mer chants may amount to; but we have elsewhere shown, that if we estimate it as making an addition of 5*s.* or 6*s.* to the quarter of wheat, we shall certainly be beyond the mark — (See my edition of the *Wealth of Nations*, vol. iv. p. 369.) However, we should, in a case of this sort, reckon it safer to err on the side of too much protection than of too little; and would not, therefore, object to a fixed duty of 6*s.* or 7*s.* a quarter being laid on wheat, and a proportional duty being laid on other species of grain. Under such a system the ports would be always open. The duty would not be so great as to inter pose any very formidable obstacle to importation. Every one would know beforehand the extent to which it would operate; at the same time that the just rights and interest of the agriculturists, and of every other class, would be maintained unimpaired.

When a duty is laid on the importation of foreign corn, for the equitable purpose of countervailing the peculiar duties laid on the corn raised at home, an *equivalent drawback* ought to be allowed on its exportation. " In allowing this drawback, we are merely returning to the farmer a tax which he has already paid, and which he must have place him in a fair state of competition in the foreign market, not only with the foreign producer, but with his own countrymen who are producing other commodities. It essentially different from a bounty on exportation, in the sense in which the word bounty is usually understood; for, by a bounty, is generally meant a tax levied on the people for the purpose of rendering corn unnaturally cheap to the foreign consumer; whereas what I propose is to sell our corn at the price at which we can really afford to produce it, and not to add to its price a tax which shall induce the foreigner rather purchase it from some other country, and deprive us of a trade which, under a system of free competition, we might have selected."—(*Ricardo on Protection to Agriculture*, p. 53.)

A duty accompanied with a drawback as now stated, would not only be an equitable arrangement, but it would be highly for the advantage of farmers, without being injurious

y one else. The radical defect, as already shown, of the system followed from 1815 to the present moment, in so far, at least, as respects agriculture, is, that it forces ices in years when the harvest is deficient, while it leaves the market to be glutted it is abundant. But while a constant duty of 6s. would secure to the home ers all the increase of price which the regard due to the interests of others should them to realise in a bad year, the drawback of 6s., by enabling them to export in usually plentiful year, would prevent the markets from being overloaded, and from falling to the ruinous extent that they now occasionally do. Such a plan render the business of a corn dealer, and of agriculture, comparatively secure ; and , therefore, provide for the continued prosperity of them both. We are astonished he agriculturists have not taken this view of the matter. If they be really entitled uty on foreign corn, on account of their being heavier taxed than the other classes ir fellow citizens, they must also be entitled to a corresponding drawback. And its of demonstration, that *their* interests, as well as those of the community, would better promoted by such a duty and drawback as we have suggested, than they er be by any system of mere duties, how high soever they may be carried.

principal objection to this plan is, that it would not be possible to levy the duty the home price became very high, and that, consequently, it would be every now en necessary to suspend it. But this objection does not seem to be by any means nidable as it has sometimes been represented. It may, we think, be concluded on ilable grounds, that were the ports constantly open under a moderate fixed duty equivalent drawback, extreme fluctuations of price would be very rare. Suppos-were enacted, that when the home price rises above a certain high level, as 80s., ty should cease, we believe the clause would very seldom come into operation ; and who object that it is not fair to the farmers to deprive them of the full advantage derived from the highest prices, should recollect that in matters of this sort it is vays either possible, or, if possible, prudent, to carry the soundest principles to an e ; and that, generally speaking, the public interests will be better consulted by ng against scarcity and dearth, than by securing, at all hazards, a trifling though vantage to a particular class.

III. STATE OF THE CORN TRADE.

branch of the subject may be conveniently divided into four heads: viz. 1. Quan-corn consumed ; 2. Regulations under which the corn trade is at present con-; 3. Tables showing the prices of the different species of corn, the quantities ed and exported, &c. ; 4. Foreign corn trade.

Quantity of Corn consumed in Great Britain. — Attempts have sometimes been o compute the quantity of corn raised in a country, from calculations founded on mber of acres in tillage, and on the average produce per acre ; but it is plain accurate estimate can ever be framed of the extent of land under cultivation. It etually changing from year to year ; and the amount of produce varies not only he differences of seasons, but also with every improvement of agriculture. This , therefore, is now rarely resorted to ; and the growth of corn is generally esti-from the *consumption.* The conclusions deduced from this criterion must indeed ect to error, as well from variations in the consumption, occasioned by variations price of corn, as from the varying extent to which other food is used. But sup-the prices of corn to be reduced to an average, if the consumption of a consider-mber of persons, of all ranks and orders, and of all ages and sexes, were accurately ined, we should be able, supposing the census of the population to be nearly cor-make a very close approximation to the total consumption of the country. Mr. Smith, the well-informed and intelligent author of the Tracts on the Corn Trade, any curious investigations, with a view to discover the mean annual consumption ; and reducing it to *the standard of wheat*, he found it to be at the rate of about *r for each individual*, young and old. This estimate has been confirmed by a of subsequent researches ; and, among others, by inquiries made during the of 1795 and 1796, by the magistrates of Suffolk, in 42 different parishes, in the ascertaining the average consumption of each family, which they found to cor- very closely with Mr. Smith's estimate. It is also worthy of remark, that cton, the intelligent author of the *Métrologie*, estimates the mean annual average ption in France, when reduced to the standard of wheat, at about 10 bushels for dividual ; and as the French consume considerably more bread, and less animal an the English, this estimate affords a strong proof of the correctness of that of ith.

ng taken the population of England and Wales in 1765 at 6,000,000, Mr. Smith d the consumers of each kind of grain, the quantity consumed by each individual, ce the whole consumed by man, to be as follows : —

Estimated Population of England and Wales.	Average Consumption of each Person.	Consum... by M... Qr...
3,750,000 consumers of wheat, at one quarter each - - -		3,750...
739,000 do. of barley, at 1⅜ do. - - - -		1,016...
888,000 do. of rye, at 1⅛ do. - - - -		999...
623,000 do. of oats, at 2⅞ do. - - - -		1,791...
Consumed by man - - -		7,556...

In addition to this, Mr. Smith estimated the wheat distilled, made into

starch, &c. - - - - -		90...
Barley used in malting, &c. - - - -		3,417...
Rye for hogs, &c. - - - -		31...
Oats for horses, &c. - - -		2,461...
Total of home consumption - -		13,555...
Add excess of exports over imports -		398...
		13,954...
Add seed (one tenth) - -		1,395...

Total growth of all kinds of grain in England and Wales in 1765 - 15,349...

This estimate, it will be observed, does not include either Scotland or Ireland; later inquiries have rendered it probable that Mr. Smith underrated the popula... of England and Wales by nearly a million. The most eminent agriculturists seem to be of opinion that the allowance for seed ought to be stated as high as a *seventh*.

Mr. Chalmers, availing himself of the information respecting the numbers of people furnished under the population act of 1800, estimated the total consumptio... all the different kinds of grain in Great Britain at that epoch at 27,185,300 quar... whereof wheat constituted 7,676,100 quarters. The crops of 1800 and of 1801 being usually deficient, the importation in these years was proportionally great; but exclu... these scarcities, the total average excess of all sorts of grain imported from Ireland... foreign countries into Great Britain over the exports had previously amounted to a... 1,000,000 of quarters, which deducted from 27,185,300, leaves 26,185,300, to whi... we add *one seventh* as seed, we shall have 29,925,057 quarters as the average growt... Great Britain in 1800.

The population of Ireland, as ascertained by the census of 1821, amounted to near 7,000,000, and probably at present exceeds 8,000,000. The greatest portion o... inhabitants are, it is true, supported by the potato, and seldom or never taste bread; we shall perhaps be within the mark, if we estimate the number of those fed on... various kinds of corn at 3,000,000, and the average quantity of the different sor... grain consumed by each individual at 2 quarters. This would give 6,000,000 qua... as the total consumption of Ireland.

But the population of Great Britain has increased, since 1800, from 10,942,00... probably, 16,000,000, or 16,500,000; and both Mr. Western and Dr. Colquhoun... curred in estimating the average consumption of the whole empire, in 1812 and 1... at about 35,000,000 of quarters.

The following is Dr. Colquhoun's estimate: —

Species of Grain.	Estimated Average of the Population of Great Britain and Ireland.	Each Person averaged.	Consumed by Man.	Consumed by Animals.	Used in Beer and Spirits.	Used in various Manufactures.	Total Quart...
		Quarters.	Quarters.	Quarters.	Quarters.	Quarters.	
Wheat - -	9,000,000	1	9,000,000	-	-	170,000	9,17...
Barley -	1,500,000	1¼	1,875,000	210,000	4,250,000	-	6,33...
Oats - -	4,500,000	1½	6,750,000	10,200,000	-	-	16,95...
Rye - -	500,000	1¼	625,000	59,000	-	1,000	68...
Beans and Peas -	500,000	1	500,000	1,360,000	-	-	1,86...
Totals - -	16,000,000		18,750,000	11,829,000	4,250,000	171,000	35,00...

Dr. Colquhoun has made no allowance for seed in this estimate; and there can l... doubt that he has underrated the consumption of oats by at least one half quart... the consumption of each of the 4,500,000 individuals he supposes fed on them... by 2,250,000 quarters. Adding, therefore, to Dr. Colquhoun's estimate 5,50... quarters for seed, and 2,250,000 quarters for the deficiency of oats, it will... it to 42,750,000 quarters; and taking the increase of population since 1813...

ount, it does not appear to us that the annual average consumption of the different ds of grain in the United Kingdom can now be estimated at less than FORTY-FOUR lions of quarters, exclusive of seed, and at FIFTY-TWO millions when it is included. uming this estimate to be correct, and the proportion of wheat to amount to *twelve* lions of quarters, the progressive consumption will be as follows : —

sumption of Wheat and other Grain in the United Kingdom, in a Year, Six Months, a Month, a Week, &c.

		Wheat. Qrs.	Other Grain. Qrs.	Total. Qrs.
A Year	-	12,000,000	40,000,000	52,000,000
Six Months	-	6,000,000	20,000,000	26,000,000
Three Months	-	3,000,000	10,000,000	13,000,000
Six Weeks	-	1,500,000	5,000,000	6,500,000
One Month	-	1,000,000	3,333,333	4,333,333
Two Weeks	-	500,000	1,666,666	2,166,666
One Week	-	250,000	833,333	1,083,333
One Day	-	35,714	119,048	154,762

he total imports of foreign corn in 1818 amounted to 3,522,729 quarters, being the est quantity ever brought into Great Britain in any one year. Now, as this quantity not amount to one fourteenth part of the entire produce, it would seem as if the test importation could have but a very slight influence on prices ; but it has been ady shown that a very large proportion, perhaps a half, of the entire corn produced e empire is never brought to market, but is partly consumed by the agriculturists, partly used as seed and in the feeding of farm horses, &c. Hence, if we are nearly t in this estimate, it follows that an importation of 3,500,000 quarters is really equi- nt to about *one seventh* part of the entire produce brought to market in an average , and must consequently have a material influence in alleviating the pressure of city in a bad year, and in checking the rise of prices.

Regulations under which the Corn Trade of Great Britain is at present conducted. — se regulations are embodied in the act 9 Geo. 4. c. 60., an abstract of which is sub- d : —

tions 1. and 2. repeal the acts 55 Geo. 3. c. 26., 3 Geo. 4. c. 60., and 7 & 8 Geo. 4. c. 58., and so much of ct 6 Geo 4. c. 111. as imposes duties on the importation of buck-wheat and Indian corn.

eign Corn may be imported on Payment of the Duties specified. — And whereas it is expedient that grain, meal, and flour, the growth, produce, and manufacture of any foreign country, or of any sh possession out of Europe, should be allowed to be imported into the United Kingdom for con- tion, upon the payment of duties to be regulated from time to time according to the average price itish corn made up and published in manner herein-after required ; be it therefore enacted, that shall be levied and paid to his Majesty, upon all corn, grain, meal, or flour entered for home con- tion in the United Kingdom from parts beyond the seas, the several duties specified and set forth in ble annexed to this act ; and that the said duties shall be raised, levied, collected, and paid in such he same manner in all respects as the several duties of customs mentioned and enumerated in the of duties of customs inwards annexed to the act 6 Geo. 4. c. 111. — §3. e following is the table referred to : —

If imported from any foreign Country :	£	s.	d.
EAT . — According to the average price of Wheat, made up and published in manner required by law ; *videlicet,*			
—— Whenever such price shall be 62s. and under 63s. the quarter, the duty shall be for every quarter - - - - - - -	1	4	8
—— Whenever such price shall be 63s. and under 64s. the quarter, the duty shall be for every quarter - - - - - - -	1	3	8
—— Whenever such price shall be 64s. and under 65s. the quarter, the duty shall be for every quarter - - - - - - -	1	2	8
—— Whenever such price shall be 65s. and under 66s. the quarter, the duty shal. be for every quarter - - - - - - -	1	1	8
—— Whenever such price shall be 66s. and under 67s. the quarter, the duty shall be for every quarter - - - - - - -	1	0	8
—— Whenever such price shall be 67s. and under 68s. the quarter, the duty shall be for every quarter - - - - - - -	0	18	8
—— Whenever such price shall be 68s. and under 69s. the quarter, the duty shall be for every quarter - - - - - - -	0	16	8
—— Whenever such price shall be 69s. and under 70s. the quarter, the duty shall be for every quarter - - - - - - -	0	13	8
—— Whenever such price shall be 70s. and under 71s. the quarter, the duty shall be for every quarter - - - - - - -	0	10	8
—— Whenever such price shall be 71s. and under 72s. the quarter, the duty shall be for every quarter - - - - - - -	0	6	8
—— Whenever such price shall be 72s. and under 73s. the quarter, the duty shall be for every quarter - - - - - - -	0	2	8
—— Whenever such price shall be at or above 73s. the duty shall be for every quarter - - - - - - -	0	1	0
—— Whenever such price shall be under 62s. and not under 61s. the duty shall be for every quarter - - - - - - -	1	5	8
- - And in respect of each integral shilling, or any part of each integral shilling by which such price shall be under 61s., such duty shall be increased by 1s.			

	£	s.	d.
BARLEY : — Whenever the average price of barley, made up and published in manner required by law, shall be 33s. and under 34s. the quarter, the duty shall be for every quarter	0	12	4
- - - - And in respect of every integral shilling by which such price shall be above 33s., such duty shall be decreased by 1s. 6d., until such price shall be 41s.			
—— Whenever such price shall be at or above 41s., the duty shall be for every quarter	0	1	0
—— Whenever such price shall be under 33s. and not under 32s., the duty shall be for every quarter	0	13	10
- - - - And in respect of each integral shilling, or any part of each integral shilling, by which such price shall be under 32s., such duty shall be increased by 1s. 6d.			
OATS : — Whenever the average price of oats, made up and published in manner required by law, shall be 25s. and under 26s. the quarter, the duty shall be for every quarter	0	9	3
- - - - And in respect of every integral shilling by which such price shall be above 25s., such duty shall be decreased by 1s. 6d., until such price shall be 31s.			
—— Whenever such price shall be at or above 31s., the duty shall be for every quarter	0	1	0
—— Whenever such price shall be under 25s. and not under 24s., the duty shall be for every quarter	0	10	9
- - - - And in respect of each integral shilling, or any part of each integral shilling, by which such price shall be under 24s. such duty shall be increased by 1s. 6d.			
RYE, PEAS, AND BEANS : — Whenever the average price of rye, or of peas, or of beans, made up and published in manner required by law, shall be 36s. and under 37s. the quarter, the duty shall be for every quarter	0	15	6
- - - - And in respect of every integral shilling by which such price shall be above 36s. such duty shall be decreased by 1s. 6d., until such price shall be 46s.			
—— Whenever such price shall be at or above 46s., the duty shall be for every quarter	0	1	0
—— Whenever such price shall be under 36s. and not under 35s., the duty shall be for every quarter	0	16	9
- - - - And in respect of each integral shilling, or any part of each integral shilling, by which such price shall be under 35s., such duty shall be increased by 1s. 6d.			
WHEAT MEAL AND FLOUR : — For every barrel, being 196 lbs., a duty equal in amount to the duty payable on 38½ gallons of wheat.			
OATMEAL : — For every quantity of 181½ lbs., a duty equal in amount to the duty payable on a quarter of oats.			
MAIZE OR INDIAN CORN, BUCK-WHEAT, BEER OR BIGG : — For every quarter, a duty equal in amount to the duty payable on a quarter of barley.			
If the Produce of and imported from any British Possession in North America, or else-where out of Europe.			
WHEAT : — For every quarter	0	5	0
- - - - Until the price of British wheat, made up and published in manner required by law, shall be 67s. per quarter.			
—— Whenever such price shall be at or above 67s., the duty shall be for every quarter	0	0	6
BARLEY : — For every quarter	0	2	0
- - - - Until the price of British barley, made up and published in manner required by law, shall be 34s. per quarter.			
—— Whenever such price shall be at or above 34s., the duty shall be for every quarter	0	0	6
OATS : — For every quarter	0	2	6
- - - - Until the price of British oats, made up and published in manner required by law, shall be 25s. per quarter.			
—— Whenever such price shall be at or above 25s., the duty shall be for every quarter	0	0	6
RYE, PEAS, AND BEANS : — For every quarter	0	3	0
- - - - Until the price of British rye, or of peas, or of beans, made up and published in manner required by law, shall be 41s.			
—— Whenever such price shall be at or above 41s., the duty shall be for every quarter	0	0	6
WHEAT MEAL AND FLOUR : — For every barrel, being 196 lbs., a duty equal in amount to the duty payable on 38½ gallons of wheat.			
OATMEAL : — For every quantity of 181½ lbs., a duty equal in amount to the duty payable on a quarter of oats.			
MAIZE OR INDIAN CORN, BUCK-WHEAT, BEER OR BIGG : — For every quarter, a duty equal in amount to the duty payable on a quarter of barley.			

Regulations to be observed upon shipping Corn from any British Possession out of Europe, &c. — No co grain, meal, or flour shall be shipped from any port in any British possession out of Europe, as being produce of any such possession, until the owner or proprietor or shipper thereof shall have made and s scribed, before the collector or other chief officer of customs at the port of shipment, a declaration writing, specifying the quantity of each sort of such corn, grain, or flour, and that the same was the p duce of some British possession out of Europe to be named in such declaration, nor until such owner proprietor or shipper shall have obtained from the collector or other chief officer of the customs at said port a certificate, under his signature, of the quantity of corn, grain, meal, or flour so declared to shipped; and before any corn, grain, meal, or flour shall be entered at any port or place in the Uni Kingdom, as being the produce of any British possession out of Europe, the master of the ship import the same shall produce and deliver to the collector or other chief officer of customs of the port or plac importation a copy of such declaration, certified to be a true and accurate copy thereof under the hand the collector or other chief officer of customs at the port of shipment before whom the same was ma together with the certificate, signed by the said collector or other chief officer of customs, of the quan of corn so declared to be shipped; and such master shall also make and subscribe, before the collector other chief officer of customs at the port or place of importation, a declaration in writing, that the seve quantities of corn, grain, meal, or flour on board such ship, and proposed to be entered under the aut rity of such declaration, are the same that were mentioned and referred to in the declaration certificate produced by him, without any admixture or addition ; and if any person shall, in any s declaration, wilfully and corruptly make any false statement respecting the place of which any such cc grain, meal, or flour was the produce, or respecting the identity of any such corn, grain, meal, or flo such person shall forfeit and become liable to pay to his Majesty the sum of 100l., and the corn, gra meal, or flour to such person belonging, on board any such ship, shall also be forfeited ; and such forf ures shall and may be sued for, prosecuted, recovered, and applied in such and the same manner in respects as any forfeiture incurred under and by virtue of the said act 6 Geo. 4. c. 111. : Provided alw that the declarations aforesaid shall not be required in respect of any corn, grain, meal, or flour wh shall have been shipped within three months next after the passing of this act. — § 4.

Penalty for importing Malt or ground Corn. — It shall not be lawful to import, from parts beyond seas into the United Kingdom, for consumption there, any malt, or to import, for consumption, Great Britain, any corn ground, except wheat meal, wheat flour, and oatmeal ; or to import, for consu

ny corn ground into Ireland; and that if any such article as aforesaid shall be imported contrary provisions aforesaid, the same shall be forfeited. — § 5.

unt of Corn and Flour imported, &c. to be published in the Gazette monthly. — The commissioners of jesty's customs shall, once in each calendar month, cause to be published in the London Gazette an t of the total quantity of each sort of the corn, grain, meal, and flour respectively, which shall have nported into the United Kingdom; and also an account of the total quantity of each sort of the rain, meal, and flour respectively, upon which the duties of importation shall have been paid in the Kingdom during the calendar month next preceding; together with an account of the total quan each sort of the said corn, grain, meal, and flour respectively remaining in warehouse at the end next preceding calendar month. — § 6.

ion 7. enacts, that if any foreign state shall subject British vessels, goods, &c., to any higher duties rges than are levied on the vessels, &c. of other countries, his Majesty may prohibit the importation from such state.

tly Returns of Purchases and Sales of Corn to be made in the Places herein mentioned. — And is it is necessary, for regulating the amount of such duties, that effectual provision should be made ertaining from time to time the average prices of British corn; be it therefore enacted, that weekly s of the purchases and sales of British corn shall be made in the manner herein-after directed, in lowing cities and towns; (that is to say,) London, Uxbridge, Hertford, Royston, Chelmsford, Col-. Rumford, Maidstone, Canterbury, Dartford, Chichester, Guildford, Lewes, Rye, Bedford, or, Aylesbury, Ipswich, Woodbridge, Sudbury, Huntingdon, Hadleigh, Stowmarket, Bury Saint uls, Beccles, Bungay, Lowestoft, Cambridge, Ely, Wisbeach, Norwich, Yarmouth, Lynn, Thetford, n, Diss, East Dereham, Harleston, Holt, Aylesham, Fakenham, North Walsham, Lincoln, Gains- h, Glanford Bridge, Lowth, Boston, Sleaford, Stamford, Spalding, Derby, Northampton, Leicester, ;ham, Worcester, Coventry, Reading, Oxford, Wakefield, Warminster, Birmingham, Leeds, k, York, Bridlington, Beverley, Howden, Sheffield, Hull, Whitby, New Malton, Durham, Stockton, ;ton, Sunderland, Barnard Castle, Walsingham, Belford, Hexham, Newcastle-upon-Tyne, Mor- lnwick, Berwick-upon-Tweed, Carlisle, Whitehaven, Cockermouth, Penrith, Egremont, Appleby, -in-Kendal, Liverpool, Ulverston, Lancaster, Preston, Wigan, Warrington, Manchester, Bolton, r, Nantwich, Middlewich, Four Lane Ends, Denbigh, Wrexham, Carnarvon, Haverford West, then, Cardiff, Gloucester, Cirencester, Tedbury, Stow-on-the-Wold, Tewkesbury, Bristol, Taunton, Bridgewater, Frome, Chard, Monmouth, Abergavenny, Chepstow, Pont-y-Pool, Exeter, Barn- Plymouth, Totness, Tavistock, Kingsbridge, Truro, Bodmin, Launceston, Redruth, Helstone, ustel, Blandford, Bridport, Dorchester, Sherbourne, Shaston, Wareham, Winchester, Andover, toke, Fareham, Havant, Newport, Ringwood, Southampton, and Portsmouth; and for the purpose collecting and transmitting such weekly returns as aforesaid, there shall be appointed in each of l cities and towns, in manner herein-after directed, a fit and proper person to be inspector of corn — § 8.

inting Comptroller of Corn Returns. — It shall be lawful for his Majesty to appoint a fit and proper to be comptroller of corn returns, for the purposes herein-after mentioned, and to grant to such ller of corn returns such salary and allowances as to his Majesty shall seem meet : Provided always, h person shall be appointed to and shall hold such his office during his Majesty's pleasure, and erwise; and shall at all times conform to and obey such lawful instructions, touching the execution uties of such his office, as shall from time to time be given to him by the Lords of the committee y council appointed for the consideration of all matters relating to trade and foreign plantations.

ns 10, 11, 12. embody the comptroller's oath, enact that he shall execute his office in person and eputy, provide for supplying his place during illness or absence, and authorise him to send and letters relating exclusively to the duties of his office free of postage.

ns 13. and 14. authorise the Lord Mayor and aldermen to appoint an inspector for the city of , who is to do the duty in person, &c.

ns 15, 16. and 17. declare that no person shall be eligible to the office of corn inspector in the city on, who shall be engaged in trade as a miller, maltster, or corn factor, or be anywise concerned in ng of corn for sale, or in the sale of bread made thereof; they also embody the oath the inspector e, and provide for the enrolment of his appointment.

rs in Corn in London to deliver in a Declaration to the Lord Mayor, &c. — Every person who shall a trade or business in the city of London, or within five miles from the Royal Exchange in the as a corn factor, or as an agent employed in the sale of British corn, and every person who shall British corn within the present Corn Exchange in Mark Lane in the said city, or within any other or place which now is or may hereafter be used within the city of London, or within five miles Royal Exchange in the said city, for such and the like purposes for which the said Corn Exchange Lane hath been and is used, shall, before he or they shall carry on trade or business, or sell any manner aforesaid, make and deliver to the Lord Mayor, or one of the aldermen of the city of a declaration in the following words; (that is to say,)

B. do declare, that the returns to be by me made, conformably to an act passed in the ninth year ign of King George the Fourth, intituled [here set forth the title of this act], of the quantities of British corn which henceforth shall be by or for me sold or delivered, shall, to the best of my ge and belief, contain the whole quantity, and no more, of the corn bonâ fide sold and delivered me within the periods to which such returns respectively shall refer, with the prices of such corn, names of the buyers respectively, and of the persons for whom such corn shall have been sold by ctively; and to the best of my judgment the said returns shall in all respects be conformable to isions of the said act."

declaration shall be in writing, and shall be subscribed with the hand of the person so making the id the Lord Mayor or such alderman as aforesaid of the city of London for the time being shall hereby required to deliver a certificate thereof, under his hand, to the inspector of corn returns city of London, to be by him registered in a book to be by him provided and kept for that — § 18.

s in Corn to make Returns to Corn Inspector. — Every such corn factor and other person as afore- is herein-before required to make and who shall have made such declaration as aforesaid, shall r she is hereby required to return or cause to be returned, on Wednesday in each and every week, spector of corn returns for the city of London, an account in writing, signed with his or her own the name of his or her agent duly authorised in that behalf, of the quantities of each respective ritish corn by him or her sold during the week ending on and including the next preceding Tues- n the prices thereof, and the amount of every parcel, with the total quantity and value of each orn, and by what measure or weight the same was sold, and the names of the buyers thereof, and rsons for and on behalf of whom such corn was sold; and it shall and may be lawful for any such of corn returns to deliver to any person making or tendering any such returns a notice in writ- iring him or her to declare and set forth therein where and by whom and in what manner any ish corn was delivered to the purchaser or purchasers thereof; and every person to whom any such all be so delivered shall and he or she is hereby required to comply therewith, and to declare and in such his or her return the several particulars aforesaid. — § 19.

s 20, 21, 22, 23. and 24. authorise the appointment of corn inspectors in the places before-mentioned, ose being employed as such who have within the preceding twelve months been engaged in any

department of the corn trade, or as a miller, or maltster, forbid those who are appointed from engagi
such occupations, prescribe the oath they are to take, and provide for the enrolment of their app
ments, &c.

Dealers in Corn in Cities and Towns to make Declaration. — Every person who shall deal in Br
corn at or within any such city or town as aforesaid, or who shall at or within any such city or tow
gage in or carry on the trade or business of a corn factor, miller, maltster, brewer, or distiller, or who
be the owner or proprietor, or part owner or proprietor, of any stage coaches, wagons, carts, or c
carriages carrying goods or passengers for hire to and from any such city or town, and each and e
person who, as a merchant, clerk, agent, or otherwise, shall purchase at any such city or town any Br
corn for sale, or for the sale of meal, flour, malt, or bread made or to be made thereof, shall, before h
she shall so deal in British corn at any such city or town, or shall engage in or carry on any such tra
business as aforesaid, or shall purchase any British corn for any such purpose as aforesaid, at or w
any such city or town, make and deliver, in manner herein-after mentioned, a declaration in the follo
words ; (that is to say,)

" I *A. B.* do declare, that the returns to be by me made conformably to the act passed in the ninth
of the reign of King George the Fourth, intituled [*here set forth the title of this act*], of the quantities
prices of British corn which henceforward shall by or for me be bought, shall, to the best of my knowl
and belief, contain the whole quantity, and no more, of the British corn *bonâ fide* bought for or b
within the periods to which such returns respectively shall refer, with the prices of such corn, anc
names of the sellers respectively ; and to the best of my judgment the said returns shall in all respec
conformable to the provisions of the said act."

Which declaration shall be in writing, and shall be subscribed with the hand of the person so makin
same, and shall by him or her, or by his or her agent, be delivered to the mayor or chief magistrate,
some justice of the peace for such city or town, or for the county, riding, or division in which the sar
situate, who are hereby required to deliver a certificate thereof to the inspector of corn returns for
such city or town as aforesaid, to be by him registered in a book to be by him provided and kept for
purpose. — § 25.

Inspectors empowered to require such Declaration from Corn Dealers. — It shall and may be lawfu
any inspector of corn returns for the city of London, or for any such other city or town as aforesai
serve upon and deliver to any person buying or selling corn in any such city or town, and who i
within the terms and meaning of this present act specially required to make any such declaration as a
said, a notice in writing under the hand of such inspector, requiring him to make such declaratic
aforesaid ; and any person upon whom such notice shall be served as aforesaid shall and he is hereb
quired to comply with such notice and to make such declaration in such and the same manner l
respects as if he or she had been specially required to make the same by the express provisions of
present act. — § 26.

Corn Dealers to make Returns in Writing to Corn Inspectors. — All persons who are herein-b
required to make and who shall have made such declaration as aforesaid, shall and they are hereb
quired, on the first market day which shall be holden in each and every week within each and every
city or town as aforesaid at or within which they shall respectively deal in corn, or engage in or carr
any such trade or business as aforesaid, or purchase any corn for any such purpose as aforesaid, to re
or cause to be returned, to the inspector of corn returns for such city or town, an account in writing, si
with their names respectively, of the amount of each and every parcel of each respective sort of B
corn so by them respectively bought during the week ending on and including the day next prece
such first market day as aforesaid, with the price thereof, and by what weight or measure the same
so bought by them, with the names of the sellers of each of the said parcels respectively, with the n
of the person or persons, if any other than the person making such return, for or on account of whor
same was so bought and sold ; and it shall and may be lawful for any such inspector of corn returns t
liver, to any person making or tendering any such return, a notice in writing, requiring him or h
declare and set forth therein where and by whom and in what manner any such British corn was deli
to him or her ; and every person to whom any such notice shall be delivered shall and he or she is he
required to comply therewith, and to declare and set forth in such his or her return, or in a sep
statement in writing, the several particulars aforesaid. — § 27.

*Inspector not to include Returns until he has ascertained that the Persons making them have take
Declaration required.* — No inspector of corn returns shall include, in the return so to be made by the
aforesaid to the comptroller of corn returns, any account of sales or purchases of corn, unless such insp
shall have received satisfactory proof that the person or persons tendering such account hath mad
declaration herein-before required, and hath delivered the same to the mayor or chief magistrate or to
justice of the peace of the city or town for which such inspector shall be so appointed to act, or to
justice of the peace for the county, riding, or division in which such city or town is situate. — § 28.

Inspector to enter Returns made to him in a Book, &c. — Every inspector of corn returns shall dul
regularly enter, in a book to be by him provided and kept for that purpose, the several accounts o
quantities and prices of corn returned to him by such persons respectively as aforesaid ; and every
inspector of corn returns for the city of London, and for the several other cities and towns aforesaid,
in each and every week return to the comptroller of corn returns an account of the weekly quantitie
prices of the several sorts of British corn sold in the city or town for which he is appointed insp
according to the returns so made to him as aforesaid, and in such form as shall be from time to tim
scribed and directed by the said comptroller of corn returns ; and the said returns shall be so made t
said comptroller by the inspector of corn returns for the city of London on Friday in each week, a
the inspector of corn returns for the several other cities and towns as aforesaid within three
next after the first market day holden in each and every week in any such city or town — § 29.

Average Prices to be made up and published every Week. — The average prices of all British co
which the rate and amount of the said duties shall be regulated, shall be made up and computed on T
day in each and every week in manner following ; (that is to say,) the said comptroller of corn returns
on such Thursday in each week, from the returns received by him during the week next preceding, e
on and including the Saturday in such preceding week, add together the total quantities of each s
British corn respectively appearing by such returns to have been sold, and the total prices for whic
same shall thereby appear to have been sold, and shall divide the amount of such total prices respec
by the amount of such total quantities of each sort of British corn respectively, and the sum pro
thereby shall be added to the sums in like manner produced in the five weeks immediately precedi
same, and the amount of such sums so added shall be divided by six, and the sum thereby given sh
deemed and taken to be the aggregate average price of each such sort of British corn respectively, f
purpose of regulating and ascertaining the rate and amount of the said duties ; and the said comp
of corn returns shall cause such aggregate weekly averages to be published in the next succeeding Ga
and shall on Thursday in each week transmit a certificate of such aggregate average prices of each
British corn to the collector or other chief officer of the customs at each of the several ports of the U
Kingdom ; and the rate and amount of the duties to be paid under the provisions of this act shal
time to time be regulated and governed at each of the ports of the United Kingdom respectively
aggregate average prices of British corn at the time of the entry for home consumption of any corn,
meal, or flour chargeable with any such duty, as such aggregate average prices shall appear and be
in the last of such certificates as aforesaid which shall have been received as aforesaid by the colle
other chief officer of customs at such port. — § 30.

ow Quantities of Corn are to be computed. — In the returns so to be made as aforesaid to the comp-
er of corn returns, and in the publications so to be made from time to time in the London Gazette, and
e certificate so to be transmitted by the said comptroller of corn returns to such collectors or other
r officers of the customs as aforesaid, the quantities of each sort of British corn respectively shall be
puted and set forth by, according, and with reference to the imperial standard gallon. — § 31.

mptroller may use the present Averages. — Until a sufficient number of weekly returns shall have been
ived by the said comptroller of corn returns under this act, to afford such aggregate average prices of
sh corn as aforesaid, the weekly average prices of British corn published by him immediately before
passing of this act shall by him be used and referred to in making such calculations as aforesaid, in
and the same manner as if the same had been made up and taken under and in pursuance of this
— § 32.

hat shall be deemed British Corn. — All corn or grain, the produce of the United Kingdom, shall be
ned and taken to be British corn for the purposes of this act. — § 33.

ovisions of this Act may be applied to any Town in the United Kingdom. — For the purpose of ascer-
ng the average price of corn and grain sold within the United Kingdom of Great Britain and Ireland,
all and may be lawful for his Majesty, by any order or orders to be by him made, by and with the
ce of his privy council, to direct that the provisions of this act, so far as regards the appointment of
ectors and the making of weekly returns, shall be applicable to any cities or towns within the United
gdom of Great Britain and Ireland which shall be named in any such order or orders in council : Pro-
d always, that the returns so received from such towns shall not be admitted into the averages made
or the purpose of regulating the duties payable upon foreign corn, grain, meal, or flour. — § 34.

ction 35. provides for the continuance in office of the present comptrollers and inspectors.

Returns are untrue, Comptroller to lay a Statement thereof before the Committee of Privy Council. —
e said comptroller of corn returns shall at any time see cause to believe that any return so to be made
oresaid to any such inspector of corn returns for the city of London, or for any other such city or
as aforesaid, is fraudulent or untrue, the said comptroller shall and he is hereby required, with all
enient expedition, to lay before the Lords of the said committee of privy council a statement of the
nds of such his belief; and if, upon consideration of any such statement, the said Lords of the said
mittee shall direct the said comptroller to omit any such return in the computation of such aggregate
ly average price as aforesaid, then and in that case, but not otherwise, the said comptroller of corn
ns shall and he is hereby authorised to omit any such return in the computation of such aggregate
ly average price. — § 36.

ction 37. enacts, that corn dealers having made the declaration previous to this act shall transmit
ns and comply with the rules hereby required.

mptroller to issue Directions respecting Inspection of Books of Inspectors. — The comptroller of corn
ns shall, and he is hereby authorised from time to time, in pursuance of any instructions which he
receive in that behalf from the Lords of the said committee of privy council, to issue to the several
ctors of corn returns any general or special directions respecting the inspection by any person or
ns of the books so directed as aforesaid to be kept by every such inspector of corn returns; and no
inspector as aforesaid shall permit or suffer any person to inspect any such book, or to peruse or
cribe any entry therein, except in compliance with some such general or special directions from the
comptroller of corn returns as aforesaid. — § 38.

py of the last Return to be affixed on Market Place on each Market Day. — Each and every inspector
n returns shall and he is hereby required on each and every market day to put up or cause to be put
the market place of the city or town for which he shall be appointed inspector, or if there shall be
arket place in such city or town, then in some other conspicuous place therein, a copy of the last
n made by him to the comptroller of corn returns, omitting the names of the parties who may have
and bought the said corn; and every such inspector shall also again put up such account on the
ct day immediately following that on which it shall first have been put up, in case the same shall
accident or any other cause have been removed, and shall take due care that the same shall remain
r public inspection until a new account for the ensuing week shall have been prepared and set up. —

tions 40. and 41. relate to the payment of comptrollers and inspectors.

alty on Corn Dealers for not making Declarations or Returns. — If any person who is hereby
red to make and deliver the declaration or declarations herein-before particularly mentioned and set
, or either of them, shall not make and deliver such declaration or declarations at the time, and in
rm and manner, and to the person or persons, herein-before directed and prescribed in that behalf,
person so offending shall forfeit and pay the sum of 20*l.* for each and every calendar month during
h he shall neglect or delay to make and deliver any such declaration; and if any person who is
n-before required to make any return to any such inspector of corn returns as aforesaid shall not
such returns to such inspector, at the time and in the form and manner herein-before directed and
ibed, every such offender shall for such his offence forfeit and pay the sum of 20*l.* — § 42.

tions 43, 44. and 45. regard the recovery and application of penalties, and impose a fine, not exceeding
n any person, lawfully summoned as a witness touching any matter of fact under this act, who
s to attend without reasonable excuse.

ishment for making false Returns. — If any person shall make any false and fraudulent statement
y such return as he is herein-before directed and required to make, or shall falsely and wilfully
le, or procure or cause to be included, in any such return, any British corn which was not truly and
ide sold or bought to, by, or on behalf of the person or persons in any such return mentioned in that
, in the quantity and for the price therein stated and set forth, every such offender shall be and be
ed guilty of a misdemeanor. — § 46.

not to affect the Practice of measuring or Privileges of the City of London. — Nothing in this act
ned shall extend to alter the present practice of measuring corn, or any of the articles aforesaid, to
pped from or to be landed in the port of London, but that the same shall be measured by the sworn
s appointed for that purpose, by whose certificate the searchers or other proper officers of his Ma-
customs are hereby empowered and required to certify the quantity of corn or other articles as
aid so shipped or landed; and that nothing in this act contained shall extend to lessen or take away
ghts and privileges of, or the tolls or duties due and payable to, the mayor and commonalty and
as of the city of London, or to the mayor of the said city for the time being, or to take away the
rges of any persons lawfully deriving title from or under them. — § 47.

itation of Actions. — Actions brought or commenced under this act must be within three months
the matter or thing done. Defendants may plead the general issue; and if judgment be given
t the plaintiff, defendants shall have treble costs. — § 48.

3. Tables showing the Prices of the different Sorts of Grain in Great Britai AND THE QUANTITIES IMPORTED AND EXPORTED, &c.

I. Account of the Prices of Middling or Mealing Wheat per Quarter at Windsor Market, as ascertain by the Audit-Books of Eton College.

Years.	Prices of Wheat at Windsor, 9 Gallons to the Bushel. £ s. d.	Prices of Wheat reduced to the Winchester Bushel of 8 Gallons. £ s. d.	Average of Ten Years according to the Winchester Bushel of 8 Gallons. £ s. d.
1646	2 8 0	2 2 8	
1647	3 13 8	3 5 5¾	
1648	4 5 0	3 15 6¾	
1649	4 0 0	3 11 1¼	
1650	3 16 8	3 8 1¾	
1651	3 13 4	3 5 2¼	
1652	2 9 6	2 4 0	
1653	1 15 6	1 11 6¾	
1654	1 6 0	1 3 1¼	
1655	1 13 4	1 9 7½	2 11 7¾
1656	2 3 0	1 18 2¾	
1657	2 6 8	2 1 5¾	
1658	3 5 0	2 17 9¼	
1659	3 6 0	2 18 8	
1660	2 16 6	2 10 2¾	
1661	3 10 0	3 2 2¾	
1662	3 14 0	3 5 9¼	
1663	2 17 0	2 10 8	
1664	2 0 6	1 16 0	
1665	2 9 4	2 3 10¼	2 10 5¾
1666	1 15 0	1 12 0	
1667	1 16 0	1 12 0	
1668	2 0 0	1 15 6¾	
1669	2 4 4	1 19 5	
1670	2 1 8	1 17 0½	
1671	2 2 0	1 17 4	
1672	2 1 0	1 16 5¼	
1673	2 6 8	2 1 5¾	
1674	3 8 8	3 1 0½	
1675	3 4 8	2 17 5¾	2 0 11¾
1676	1 18 0	1 13 9¼	
1677	2 2 0	1 17 4	
1678	2 19 0	2 12 5¼	
1679	3 0 0	2 13 4	
1680	2 5 0	2 0 0	
1681	2 6 8	2 1 5¾	
1682	2 4 0	1 19 1¼	
1683	2 0 0	1 15 6¾	
1684	2 4 0	1 19 1½	
1685	2 6 8	2 1 5¾	2 1 4¼
1686	1 14 0	1 10 2¾	
1687	1 5 2	1 2 4½	
1688	2 6 0	2 0 10¾	
1689	1 10 0	1 6 8	
1690	1 14 8	1 10 9¾	
1691	1 14 0	1 10 2¾	
1692	2 6 8	2 1 5¾	
1693	3 7 8	3 0 1½	
1694	3 4 0	2 16 10¾	
1695	2 13 0	2 7 1¼	1 19 6¾
1696	3 11 0	3 3 1½	
1697	3 0 0	2 13 4	
1698	3 8 4	3 0 9	
1699	3 4 0	2 16 10¾	
1700	2 0 0	1 15 6¾	
1701	1 17 8	1 13 5¾	
1702	1 9 6	1 6 2¾	
1703	1 16 0	1 12 0	
1704	2 6 6	2 1 4	
1705	1 10 0	1 6 8	2 2 11
1706	1 6 0	1 3 1½	
1707	1 8 6	1 5 4	
1708	2 1 6	1 16 10¾	
1709	3 18 6	3 9 9¼	
1710	3 18 0	3 9 4	
1711	2 14 0	2 8 0	
1712	2 6 4	2 1 2¼	
1713	2 11 0	2 5 4	
1714	2 10 4	2 4 9	
1715	2 3 0	1 18 2¾	2 4 2¼
1716	2 8 0	2 2 8	
1717	2 5 8	2 0 7¼	
1718	1 18 10	1 14 6¼	
1719	1 15 0	1 11 1¼	
1720	1 17 0	1 12 10¾	
1721	1 17 6	1 13 4	
1722	1 16 0	1 12 0	
1723	1 14 8	1 10 10¾	
1724	1 17 0	1 12 10¾	
1725	2 8 6	2 3 1¼	1 15 4¾
1726	2 6 0	2 0 10¾	
1727	2 2 0	1 17 4	
1728	2 14 6	2 8 5¼	
1729	2 6 10	2 1 7½	
1730	1 16 6	1 12 5¼	
1731	1 12 10	1 9 2¼	
1732	1 6 8	1 3 8½	
1733	1 8 4	1 5 2¼	
1734	1 18 10	1 14 6¼	
1735	2 3 0	1 18 2¾	1 15 2
1736	2 0 4	1 15 10¼	
1737	1 18 0	1 13 9¼	
1738	1 15 6	1 11 6¾	
1739	1 18 6	1 14 2¾	
1740	2 10 8	2 5 1½	
1741	2 6 8	2 1 5¾	
1742	1 14 0	1 10 2¾	
1743	1 4 10	1 2 1	
1744	1 4 10	1 2 1	
1745	1 7 6	1 4 5¼	1 12 1
1746	1 19 0	1 14 8	
1747	1 14 10	1 10 11½	
1748	1 17 0	1 12 10¾	
1749	1 17 0	1 12 10¾	
1750	1 12 6	1 8 10¾	
1751	1 18 6	1 14 2¾	
1752	2 1 10	1 17 2¼	
1753	2 4 8	1 19 8½	
1754	1 14 8	1 10 9¾	
1755	1 13 10	1 10 1	1 1 2¾
1756	2 5 2	2 0 1¾	
1757	3 0 0	2 13 4	
1758	2 10 0	2 4 5¼	
1759	1 19 8	1 15 3	
1760	1 16 6	1 12 5½	
1761	1 10 2	1 6 9¾	
1762	1 19 0	1 14 8	
1763	2 0 8	1 16 1¾	
1764	2 6 8	2 1 5¾	
1765	0 14 0	2 8 0	1 19 3¼
1766	2 8 6	2 3 1¼	
1767	3 4 6	2 17 4	
1768	3 0 6	2 13 9¼	
1769	2 5 8	2 0 7	
1770	2 9 0	2 3 6¾	
1771	2 17 0	2 10 8	
1772	3 6 0	2 18 8	
1773	3 6 6	2 19 1½	
1774	3 2 0	2 15 1¼	
1775	2 17 8	2 11 3¼	2 11
1776	2 8 0	2 2 8	
1777	2 15 0	2 8 10¾	
1778	2 9 6	2 4 0	
1779	2 0 8	1 16 1¾	
1780	2 8 6	2 3 1½	
1781	2 19 0	2 12 5½	
1782	3 0 6	2 13 9¾	
1783	3 1 0	2 14 2¾	
1784	3 0 6	2 13 9½	
1785	2 14 0	2 8 0	2 7
1786	2 7 6	2 2 2¾	
1787	2 11 6	2 5 9¾	
1788	2 15 6	2 9 4	
1789	3 3 2	2 16 1¾	
1790	3 3 2	2 16 1¾	
1791	2 15 6	2 9 4	
1792*		2 13 0	
1793		2 15 8	
1794		2 14 0	
1795		4 1 6	2 14
1796		4 0 2	
1797		3 2 0	
1798		2 14 0	
1799		3 15 8	
1800		6 7 0	
1801		6 8 6	
1802		3 7 2	
1803		3 0 0	
1804		3 9 6	
1805		4 8 0	4 1
1806		4 3 0	
1807		3 18 0	
1808		3 19 2	
1809		5 6 0	
1810		5 12 0	
1811		5 8 0	
1812		6 8 0	
1813		6 0 0	
1814		4 5 0	
1815		3 16 0	4 17
1816		4 2 0	
1817		5 16 0	
1818		4 18 0	
1819		3 18 0	
1820		3 16 0	
1821		3 11 0	
1822		2 13 0	
1823		2 17 0	
1824		3 12 0	
1825		4 4 0	3 18
1826		3 13 0	

The Eton Account of Prices commenced in 1595; the accuracy of the returns in the first years can however, be so implicitly relied on, as those quoted above. — Bishop Fleetwood and Sir F. M. Eden h collected, with great industry, almost all the existing information respecting the state of prices in Engl during the last *six hundred* years.

* From this year, inclusive, the account at Eton College has been kept according to the bushel of e gallons, under the provision of the act 31 Geo. 3. c. 30. § 82.

count of the **Average Prices of British Corn per Winchester Quarter**, in England and Wales, since 1792, as ascertained by the Receiver of Corn Returns.

ars.	Wheat £ s. d.	Rye £ s. d.	Barley £ s. d.	Oats £ s. d.	Beans £ s. d.	Peas £ s. d.
92	2 2 11	1 10 8	1 6 9	0 17 10	1 11 7	1 12 8
93	2 8 11	1 15 11	1 11 9	1 1 3	1 17 8	1 18 4
94	2 11 8	1 17 9	1 12 10	1 2 0	2 2 6	2 6 8
95	3 14 2	2 8 5	1 17 8	1 4 9	2 6 8	2 13 4
96	3 17 1	2 7 0	1 15 7	1 1 9	1 18 10	2 3 6
97	2 13 1	1 11 11	1 7 9	0 16 9	1 7 6	1 13 5
98	2 10 3	1 10 11	1 9 1	0 19 10	1 10 1	1 13 11
99	3 7 6	2 3 9	1 16 0	1 7 7	2 4 7	2 5 2
00	5 13 7	3 16 11	3 0 0	1 19 10	3 9 3	3 7 5
01	5 18 3	3 19 9	3 7 9	1 16 6	3 2 8	3 7 8
02	3 7 5	2 3 3	1 13 1	1 0 7	1 16 4	1 19 6
03	2 16 6	1 16 11	1 4 10	1 1 3	1 14 8	1 18 6
04	3 0 1	1 17 1	1 10 4	1 3 9	1 18 7	2 0 10
05	4 7 10	2 14 4	2 4 8	1 8 0	2 7 5	2 8 4
06	3 19 0	2 7 4	1 18 6	1 5 8	2 3 9	2 3 6
07	3 13 3	2 7 6	1 18 4	1 8 1	2 7 3	2 15 11
08	3 19 0	2 12 4	2 2 1	1 13 8	3 0 8	3 6 7
09	4 15 7	3 0 9	2 7 3	1 12 8	3 0 9	3 0 2
10	5 6 2	2 19 0	2 7 11	1 9 4	2 13 7	2 15 9
11	4 14 6	2 9 11	2 1 10	1 7 11	2 7 10	2 11 6
12	6 5 5	3 15 11	3 6 6	2 4 0	3 12 8	3 13 7
13	5 8 9	3 10 7	2 18 4	1 19 5	3 16 5	3 18 6
14	3 14 0	2 4 6	1 17 4	1 6 6	2 6 7	2 10 0
15	3 4 4	1 17 10	1 10 3	1 3 10	1 16 1	1 18 10
16	3 15 10	2 3 2	1 13 5	1 3 6	1 18 4	1 18 4
17	4 14 9	2 16 6	2 8 3	1 12 1	2 12 0	2 11 5
18	4 4 1	2 14 10	2 13 6	1 12 11	3 3 1	2 19 11
19	3 13 0	2 9 0	2 6 8	1 9 4	2 15 5	2 16 0

count of the Average Prices of British Corn per Imperial Quarter, in England and Wales, for Eleven Years, ending December, 1830, each Year, and in Periods of Five Years.

Years.	Wheat. s. d.	Rye. s. d.	Barley. s. d.	Oats. s. d.	Beans. s. d.	Peas. s. d.
1820	67 11	42 0	33 10	24 9	43 4	45 11
1821	56 2	32 1	26 0	19 6	30 11	32 9
1822	44 7	20 11	21 11	18 2	24 6	26 5
1823	53 5	31 11	31 7	22 11	33 1	35 0
1824	64 0	41 5	36 5	24 10	40 1	40 8
ge of the Five Years	57 2	33 8	29 11	22 0	34 4	36 1
1825	68 7	42 4	40 1	25 8	42 10	45 5
1826	58 9	41 2	34 5	26 9	44 3	47 8
1827	56 9	39 0	36 6	27 4	47 7	47 7
1828	60 5	34 2	32 10	22 6	38 4	40 6
1829	66 3	34 10	32 6	22 9	36 8	36 8
ge of the Five Years	62 1	38 3	35 3	25 0	41 11	43 6
1830	64 3	35 10	32 7	24 5	36 1	39 2

The Winchester bushel contains 2150·42 cubic inches, while the Imperial bushel contains 2218·192 ...hes, being about one thirty-second part larger than the former. See BUSHEL, and WEIGHTS AND ...es.

...lowing account of the current prices of *all sorts* of corn in the London market, 22d August, 1831, ...ting, as showing their comparative values, and the estimation in which they are held: —

IV. Current Prices of Grain per Imperial Quarter. London, 22d August, 1831.

		s. s.		s. s.
Wheat, Essex and Kent	red	60 to 72	White	66 to 80
Norfolk and Suffolk	do.	59 — 68	Ditto	65 — 74
Lincolnshire and Yorkshire		57 — 64		62 — 68
Northumberland and Scotch	white	— —	Fine	— —
Irish	red	50 — 53	White	54 — 58
new		36 — 38		— — —
...wheat		34 — 36		
grinding 26 to 30	Distilling	30 — 32	Malting	37 — 40
brown 56 — 62	Pale	57 — 68	Ware	68 — 72
ticks, new 38 — 41	Old	40 — 42	Harrow	42 — 46
grey 37 — 42	Maple	38 — 44	White	41 — 44
Lincolnshire and Yorkshire	feed	23 — 28	Poland	27 — 30
Scotch	Angus	27 — 28	Potato	30 — 32
Irish	white	23 — 24	Black	25 — 27
...d Cakes 10l. 0s. to 11l. 0s. per 1,000				
...akes 6l. 0s. — 6l. 6s. per ton.				

IV. Current Prices of Grain per Imperial Quarter — *continued.*

	Per Sack.		Per Sac...
	s. *s.*		*s.* *s.*
Town-made Flour	52 to 60	Stockton and Yorkshire	48 to 4...
Essex and Kent	50 — 54	West Country	52 — 5...
Norfolk and Suffolk	49 — 52		

			Free.	In Bon...
			s. *s.*	*s.*
Foreign Wheat, Dantzic, Königsberg, &c.			64 to 76	48 to
Saale, Marks, Anhalt, and Magdeburg			55 — 64	40 —
Silesian and Pomeranian			56 — 67	42 —
Mecklenburg and Holstein			54 — 60	— —
Zealand and Brabant			52 — 63	— —
Danish (Friesland none)			50 — 53	— —
Russian	hard 52 to 56	soft	54 — 60	40 —
Spanish, &c.	52 — 56	ditto	54 — 63	40 —
Italian	red 54 — 64	white	62 — 72	40 —
Odessa	hard 52 — 57	soft	52 — 59	39 —
American	red 57 — 61	high mixed	62 — 68	— —
Indian Corn	red and yellow 33 — 35	white	35 — 37	— —
Rye, Baltic	dried — — —	undried	— —	— —
Barley, Sale and Bohemian			30 — 34	— —
Dantzic and Russian, grinding			25 — 28	— —
Pomeranian, Mecklenburg, and Danish			25 — 30	— —
Beans, ticks			38 — 39	28 —
small			42 — 46	28 —
Mediterranean			36 — 38	26 —
Peas, boiling			40 — 43	25 —
hog and grey			36 — 40	
Oats, Dutch brew and thick			25 — 31	20 —
Russian and Prussian, feed			23 — 27	16 —
Mecklenburgh, Danish, and Friesland, feed			22 — 26	15 —
Linseed Cakes	7l. 0s. to 7l. 10s. per ton			
Rape Cakes	5l. 10s. — 6l. 0s.			
Flour, Dantzic	per barrel		31 — 34	— —
American	ditto		32 — 36	23 —
Canadian	ditto		33 — 36	— —

V. Account of the Quantity of Wheat and Wheat Flour exported, and of Foreign Wheat and W... Flour imported, in the following Years (Winchester Measure).

Years.	Wheat and Flour exported.	Foreign Wheat and Flour imported.	Years.	Wheat and Flour exported.	Foreign Wheat and Flour imported.	Years.	Wheat and Flour exported.	For... Whea... Flour port...
England.	*Qrs.*	*Qrs.*	England.	*Qrs.*	*Qrs.*	Gt. Britain.	*Qrs.*	*Q...*
1697	14,699	400	1732	202,058	—	1766	164,939	1...
1698	6,857	845	1733	427,199	7	1767	5,071	49...
1699	557	486	1734	498,196	6	1768	7,433	34...
1700	49,056	5	1735	153,343	9	1769	49,892	4...
1701	98,324	1	1736	118,170	16	1770	75,449	
1702	90,230	—	1737	461,602	32	1771	10,089	9...
1703	166,615	50	1738	580,596	2	1772	6,959	2...
1704	90,313	2	1739	279,542	5,423	1773	7,637	5...
1705	96,185	—	1740	54,390	7,568	1774	15,928	28...
1706	188,332	77	1741	45,417	40	1775	91,037	56...
1707	74,155	—	1742	293,260	1	1776	210,664	2...
1708	83,406	86	1743	371,431	2	1777	87,686	23...
1709	169,680	1,552	1744	231,984	2	1778	141,070	10...
1710	13,924	400	1745	324,839	6	1779	222,261	
1711	76,949	—	1746	130,646	—	1780	224,059	
1712	145,191	—	1747	266,907	—	1781	103,021	15...
1713	176,227	—	1748	543,387	385	1782	145,152	8...
1714	174,821	16	1749	629,049	382	1783	51,943	58...
1715	166,490	—	1750	947,602	279	1784	89,288	21...
1716	74,926	—	1751	661,416	3	1785	132,685	11...
1717	22,954	—	1752	429,279	—	1786	205,466	5...
1718	71,800	—	1753	299,609	—	1787	120,536	5...
1719	127,762	20	1754	356,270	201	1788	82,971	14...
1720	83,084	—	Gt. Britain.			1789	140,014	1...
1721	81,633	—	1755	237,466	—	1790	80,892	22...
1722	178,880	—	1756	102,752	5	1791	70,626	46...
1723	157,720	—	1757	11,545	141,562	1792	300,278	5...
1724	245,865	148	1758	9,234	20,353	1793	76,869	49...
1725	204,413	12	1759	227,641	162	1794	155,048	32...
1726	142,183	—	1760	393,614	3	1795	18,839	31...
1727	30,315	—	1761	441,956	—	1796	24,679	87...
1728	3,817	74,574	1762	295,385	56	1797	54,525	5...
1729	18,993	40,315	1763	429,538	72	1798	59,782	39...
1730	93,971	76	1764	396,857	1	1799	39,362	44...
1731	130,025	4	1765	167,126	104,547	1800	22,013	1,26...

Account specifying the total Quantities of all Sorts of Grain imported into Great Britain, from different Countries, in each Year, from 1801 to 1825, both inclusive; the Average Quantity of all Sorts of Grain, and the Average Quantity of each particular Species of Grain, as Wheat, Rye, Barley, &c., imported in each of the above Years, from each different Country, in Winchester Quarters.

Russia.	Sweden and Norway.	Denmark.	Prussia.	Germany.	The Netherlands.	France and South of Europe.	United States of America.	British North American Colonies.	Other Foreign Countries, Isle of Man, and Prize Corn.	Ireland.
204,656	26,375	7,088	663,584	699,340	351,330	3,223	372,151	67,724	10,074	900
12,870	10,961	3,882	377,984	151,363	103,194	2,032	80,820	75,172	856	467,067
16,448	540	8,619	171,001	161,147	81,758	1,565	109,832	43,245	1,782	343,548
8,215	19,931	31,029	531,564	138,810	170,977	168	4,351	21,214	4,576	316,958
173,874	25,859	52,837	702,605	126,146	72,516	2,794	13,475	2,250	8,511	306,923
57,416	- -	10,284	90,040	108,581	29,949	3,790	79,906	9,801	5,613	466,947
6,183	110	74,049	22,890	141,537	237,523	32,113	250,866	27,693	18,996	463,406
3,664	195	1,800	- -	29,998	18,137	11,736	13,206	21,506	12,236	656,770
14,089	2,348	9,027	2,015	169,655	328,582	30,848	172,878	23,737	20,848	933,658
66,869	87,961	132,287	316,224	255,475	436,286	241,345	98,361	25,938	28,465	632,849
49,597	40,391	45,127	97,886	2,429	- -	5,167	18,097	440	15,934	430,189
128,437	14,919	52,302	9,063	619	2	454	11,524	23,774	17,970	600,268
64,938	71,629	58,872	133,907	125,156	- -	- -	1,093	1	10,112	977,164
9,760	30,926	18,356	186,241	116,861	420,009	170,596	2	3	7,476	812,805
1,443	626	9,250	19,428	35,279	135,778	79,051	45,586	25	6,600	821,192
24,198	660	14,874	94,791	54,157	118,048	1,189	7,209	3	4,077	873,865
405,933	1,166	149,012	414,947	253,403	191,141	35,372	316,364	25,876	8,016	699,809
676,793	2,455	342,213	829,646	571,864	761,874	92,891	187,576	56,617	8,740	1,207,851
543,554	2,255	123,638	323,350	235,076	193,029	218,215	47,654	14,257	6,484	967,861
372,169	13,492	147,595	356,288	218,711	78,813	12,917	91,098	40,898	9,869	1,417,120
28,445	- -	26,778	39,258	51,540	19,964	102	38,488	40,916	12,163	1,822,816
22,040	- -	15,045	28,745	21,528	3,024	741	6,242	23,439	5,000	1,063,089
14,568	- -	6,948	8,743	4,635	3,896	102	4,237	209	10,303	1,528,153
14,500	2,858	106,998	76,780	231,430	132,160	1,395	33,872	891	9,154	1,634,024
26,895	4,284	248,282	217,836	372,839	63,954	499	12,903	95,059	15,227	2,203,962
117,902	14,397	67,847	228,584	171,103	158,078	37,932	80,712	25,627	10,363	865,968
53,377	9,576	16,324	157,359	58,103	56,817	24,649	74,024	24,863	4,836	187,438
9,968	960	1,123	5,689	5,189	1,690	293	2,431	-	1,438	253
7,112	987	18,808	18,718	24,839	9,500	1,097	31	51	2,194	33,331
46,652	2,446	30,672	39,209	75,828	84,269	1,953	3	1	1,703	639,857
785	428	823	7,609	7,144	5,802	9,124	201	697	151	4,922
8	- -	97	- -	- -	- -	816	4,022	15	41	167

Account of the total Importation of all Sorts of Corn and Grain, Meal and Flour, from all Countries except Ireland, during the Six Years ending with the 10th of October, 1830.

	Total of Corn and Grain.			Total of Meal and Flour.		
	From British Possessions out of Europe.	From other Parts.	Total of the Importations from all Parts except Ireland.	From British Possessions out of Europe.	From other Parts.	Total of the Importations from all Parts except Ireland.
	Qrs. bus.	Qrs. bus.	Qrs. bus.	Cwts. qrs. lbs.	Cwts. qrs. lbs.	Cwts. qrs. lbs.
	64,718 5	810,017 7	875,736 4	3,135 2 20	83,878 0 17	87,013 3 9
	41,307 7	1,465,847 1	1,507,155 0	11,053 0 12	31,166 0 9	42,219 0 21
	63,202 4	3,377,107 1	3,440,309 5	12,657 3 24	115,664 1 20	128,322 1 16
	20,565 4	606,215 1	626,780 5	23,603 1 12	124,651 3 20	148,255 1 4
	9,842 3	3,153,267 6	3,163,110 1	6,159 1 10	459,137 0 3	465,296 1 13
	50,108 3	2,171,292 3	2,221,400 7	48,561 3 1	550,208 0 3	598,769 3 4

Account of the Quantities of Wheat, Wheatmeal or Flour, Barley, Oats, Oatmeal, and all other of Grain, imported from Ireland into Great Britain during the Ten Years ending with the 10th of ...ber, 1830, in Imperial Quarters and Cwts.

Wheat.	Barley.	Oats.	Wheatmeal or Flour.	Oatmeal.	Total of Corn and Grain.	Total of Meal and Flour.
Qrs. bus.	Qrs. bus.	Qrs. bus.	Cwts. qrs. lbs.	Cwts. qrs. lbs.	Qrs. bus.	Cwts. qrs. lbs.
501,992 6	94,605 5	1,093,871 0	271,441 2 5	73,070 3 18	1,701,447 7	345,086 3 23
378,417 3	27,982 6	668,772 7	306,987 0 0	20,950 1 20	1,082,225 6	327,937 1 20
357,480 0	24,099 4	943,643 0	408,171 3 8	102,567 1 4	1,332,219 0	510,699 0 12
178,792 4	29,730 0	1,027,533 3	210,703 0 24	98,719 0 16	1,241,987 0	339,422 1 12
346,584 6	119,698 1	1,543,574 5	418,104 2 0	200,960 1 2	2,028,899 7	619,064 3 2
205,150 6	-85,766 4	1,101,655 2	298,756 2 0	177,615 3 6	1,407,831 6	476,372 1 6
249,684 3	64,410 4	1,006,207 0	280,553 1 8	176,143 3 6	1,327,748 6	456,776 0 14
474,597 6	94,998 3	1,917,933 3	631,427 1 12	445,201 1 16	2,507,226 3	1,076,851 1 0
379,105 6	60,018 5	1,417,355 2	597,049 2 4	353,614 3 4	1,872,249 5	952,194 0 8
347,686 4	157,197 4	1,299,714 1	705,575 2 11	390,552 0 2	1,834,032 1	1,096,381 0 13

IX. Account of the total Quarters of Foreign Wheat that have paid Duty for Consumption in the Unit Kingdom, under 9 Geo. 4. c. 60., since that Act came in force in 1828, to 1st July, 1831, and the to Amount of Duty received thereon ; and showing, from the total Quantity of Quarters, and the to Amount of Duty so received thereon, what the Duty was equal to, per Quarter, on the Average, this whole Period : the same Account for Foreign Barley, Rye, Peas and Beans, Wheatmeal and Flo Oatmeal, and Maize or Indian Corn, Buck-wheat, Beer or Bigg : and the same Account for all the the Produce of, and imported from, any British Possession in North America, or elsewhere, out Europe. — (*Parl. Paper*, No. 120. Sess. 1831.)

Species.	Foreign Corn, Meal and Flour.			Corn, Meal and Flour, the Produc of, and imported from, British Possessions out of Europe.		
	Quantities entered for Home Consumption, from 15 July 1828, to 1 July 1831.	Amount of Duty received thereon.	Average Rates of Duty paid on the Total Quantities consumed	Quantities entered for Home Consumption, from 15 July 1828 to 1 July 1831.	Amount of Duty received thereon.	Average Rates of Duty paid on the Total Quantitie consumed
	Quarters.	£	per Qr. s. d.	*Quarters.*	£	per Qr. s. d.
Wheat - - -	4,620,029	1,389,290	6 1	130,481	7,492	1 2
Barley - - -	916,252	198,880	4 4	—	—	—
Oats - - -	1,158,934	320,320	5 6	1,996	53	0 6
Rye - - -	140,639	26,223	3 9	—	—	—
Peas - - -	145,089	54,893	7 7	4,910	507	2 1
Beans - - -	154,416	79,532	10 4	—	—	—
Maize or Indian Corn -	93,791	17,523	3 9	11½	2	3 9
Buck-wheat -	34,034	10,290	6 1	—	—	—
Beer or Bigg -	—	—	—	—	—	—
Total of Corn	7,263,184	2,096,951	-	137,398½	8,054	
	Cwt.		per Cwt.	*Cwt.*		per Cwt.
Wheatmeal and Flour -	1,812,905	156,381	1 9	88,870	2,504	0 7
Oatmeal - -	2¼	1	7 6	521	9	0 4
Total of Meal and Flour	1,812,907¼	156,382	—	89,391	2,513	

X. — Account of the Quantity of Foreign Wheat imported in each Quarter, from the passing of the 9 Geo. 4. c. 60. to the latest Period to which the same can be made up, and the Amount of Duty ceived thereon, and of the Average Rate of Duty paid in each Quarter. — (*Parl. Paper*, No. Sess. 1831.)

Quarterly Periods, ending on	Quantity of imported Wheat entered for Home Consumption in the United Kingdom.			Amount of Duty paid thereon.		Average Rates of Du paid in each Quarte	
	Imported from Foreign Countries.	The Produce of and imported from British Possessions out of Europe.	Total Quantity.	On Wheat imported from Foreign Countries.	On Wheat, the Produce of and imported from British Possessions out of Europe.	On Wheat imported from Foreign Countries.	On Wheat, Produce of imported fr British Pos sions out Europe.
	Qrs. bus.	*Qrs. bus.*	*Qrs. bus.*	£ s. d.	£ s. d.	per Qr.	per Qr
30 Sept. 1828 -	22,536 7	12,216 5	34,753 4	28,705 19 4	3,080 4 7	25s. 6d.	5s. 0d
31 Dec. - -	705,565 5	2,749 2	708,314 7	36,179 2 2	340 16 10	1s. 0d.	2s. 6d
31 March, 1829	562,530 0	29 2	562,559 0	43,589 12 1	7 5 0	1s. 7d.	5s. 0a
30 June -	105,473 7	4,057 6	109,531 5	62,765 18 4	101 10 0	11s. 11d.	0s. 6d
30 Sept.	640,517 2	1,907 5	642,424 7	453,971 18 7	48 3 2	14s. 2d.	0s. 6a
31 Dec.	30,066 4	1,183 7	31,250 3	31,820 3 11	295 9 11	21s. 2d.	5s. 0a
31 March, 1830	506 4	1,727 0	2,233 4	560 1 7	431 15 8	22s. 2d.	5s. 0a
30 June	259,719 4	829 1	260,548 5	272,212 6 6	207 5 5	21s. 0d.	5s. 0a
30 Sept. -	1,231,595 3	42,756 2	1,274,351 5	213,569 0 0	1,059 4 4	3s. 6d.	0s. 6a
31 Dec. -	9,238 2	1,763 0	11,001 2	7,058 14 6	416 14 6	15s. 3d.	4s. 9a
31 March, 1831	357,721 3	54,146 6	391,868 1	18,227 6 6	827 8 1	1s. 0d.	0s. 6a
30 June - -	718,006 5	27,759 6	745,766 3	220,630 5 6	676 15 4	6s. 2d.	0s. 6a
	4,643,477 6	131,126 0	4,774,603 6	1,389,290 9 5	7,492 12 10		
Deduct over Entries - }	23,448 6	645 0	24,093 6				
Total from the passing of Act 9 Geo. 4. c.60. (15 July 1828, to 30 June 1831 - }	4,620,029 0	130,481 0	4,750,510 0				

We have, in the previous parts of this article, sufficiently illustrated the impoli generally speaking, of imposing duties on the importation of corn ; but besides objections that may be made to all duties of this sort, from their tendency to force average prices, and to render exportation in abundant years impossible, the duty existing in this country is liable to some which may be looked upon as peculiar to its From the way in which it is graduated, it introduces a new element of uncertainty

transaction connected with the corn trade; producing a disinclination on the part
merchant to import, and of the foreigner to raise corn for our markets. Suppose
chant commissions a cargo of wheat when the price is at 71s. a quarter; in the
of the price declining only 3s., or to 68s., the duty will rise from 6s. 8d. to 16s. 8d.;
t if the merchant brings the grain to market, he will realise 13s. 8d. a quarter less
e expected, and 10s. less than he would have done had there been no duty, or the
been constant!

nay, perhaps, be said that if, on the one hand, the present scale of duties is injurious
merchant when prices are falling, and when importation is consequently either
essary or of less advantage, it is, on the other hand, equally advantageous to him
prices are rising, and when the public interests require that importation should be
raged: but the prices in the view of the merchant when he gives an order, are
y such as he supposes will yield a fair profit; and if they rise, this rise would, sup-
; the duty to be constant, yield such an extra profit as would of itself induce him
rease his importations to the utmost. If it were possible to devise a system that
diminish the losses of the merchants engaged in unfavourable speculations, by
g a proportional deduction from the extraordinary gains of those whose speculations
ut to be unusually successful, something, perhaps, might be found to say in its
. But the system we have been considering proceeds on quite opposite principles:
ct is not to diminish risks, but to increase them; it adds to the loss resulting from
successful, and to the profit resulting from a successful, speculation!
vould, therefore, seem that if a duty is to be imposed, one that is constant is pre-
to one that fluctuates. When the duty is constant, all classes, farmers as well
chants, are aware of its amount, and can previously calculate the extent of its
ice. But the effect of a duty that fluctuates with the fluctuations of price, can
be appreciated beforehand. Its magnitude depends on contingent and accidental
stances; and it must, therefore, of necessity, prejudice the interests of the farmer
as of the corn dealer.

ppears, from No. X. of the preceding accounts, that the total imports of foreign
during the three years ending with the 1st of July, 1831, amounted to 4,620,029
rs, and that the entire duty received thereon was 1,389,290l., being at the rate of
per quarter. Had the duty been a constant one of 6s., the interests of all parties
have been materially promoted. It is doubtful, whether the quantity imported
have been, on the whole, materially increased; for, though the present system of
frequently checks importation for a lengthened period, yet, on the other hand,
prices rise, and the duties are reduced, every bushel in the warehouses is imme-
entered for home consumption; and the chance, which is every now and then
ing, of getting grain entered under the nominal duty of 1s., probably tempts the
nts to speculate more largely, though at a greater risk to themselves, than they
do under a different system. A moderate duty, accompanied by an equal draw-
esides giving a greater degree of security to the corn trade, would, in this respect,
icularly beneficial to the farmer. Under the present system it is not possible to
, with any thing approaching to accuracy, what may be the range of prices during
ure period, however near; so that the trade of a farmer, which is naturally one of
st stable, has been rendered almost a species of gambling. But were the ports
open under the plan previously suggested, the variations of price would be con-
ithin comparatively narrow limits; and the business of farming would acquire
urity, of which it is, at present, so completely destitute, and which is so indis-
e to its success.

EIGN CORN TRADE. — PRICES AT WHICH FOREIGN CORN MAY BE IMPORTED
INTO ENGLAND. — QUANTITIES THAT MAY BE OBTAINED.

h Corn Trade.—Dantzic is the port whence we have always been accustomed
rt the largest supplies of corn; and it would seem fully established by the data
d by Mr. Jacob, in his tours, that 28s. or 30s. a quarter is the lowest price
ich any considerable quantity of wheat for exportation can be permanently
n the corn-growing provinces in the vicinity of Warsaw: its minimum cost price,
rought to London, according to the data furnished by Mr. Jacob, would be as

	s.	d.
st of wheat, at Warsaw, per quarter - - -	28	0
nveyance to the boats, and charges for loading and stowing, and		
securing it by mats - - - - - -	0	6
eight to Dantzic - - - - - -	5	0
Carried over - - - -	33	6

D d 2

	s.	d.
Brought forward - - -	33	6
Loss on the passage by pilfering, and rain causing it to grow -	3	0
Expenses at Dantzic in turning, drying, screening, and warehousing, and loss of measure - - - - - -	2	0
Profit or commission, as the case may be, to the merchant at Dantzic	1	6
Freight, primage, insurance, and shipping charges, at Dantzic and in London - - - - - - -	8	0
Cost of the wheat to the English merchant - - -	48	0

It ought, however, to be observed, that the premium paid the underwriters doe
cover the risk attending damage from heating or otherwise on the voyage; and it o
farther to be observed, that the freight from Warsaw to Dantzic, and from Dantzic h
is here charged at the lowest rate. Mr. Jacob supposes that an extraordinary dem
for as much wheat as would be equal to *six* days' consumption of that grain in Engl
or for 216,000 quarters, would raise the cost of freight on the Vistula from 30 t
per cent.: and as such a demand could hardly be supplied without resorting t
markets in the provinces to the south of Warsaw, its *minimum cost* to the London
chants could not, under such circumstances, amount, even supposing some of
statements to be a little exaggerated, to less than from 50s. to 53s. or 55s. a quarte

It appears from the consular returns, that the price of wheat, per Winchester qua
in Dantzic, in November and December, 1830, was 35s. 4d. The exports of
from the port during that year were —

	Total Quarters.		Quarters.
Wheat,	404,000	of which for England	311,000
Rye	86,000		7,500
Barley	7,500		2,700
Oats	21,500		21,000

(*Parl. Paper*, No. 72. Sess. 1831)

We subjoin an account, furnished by Mr. Jacob, of the total annual average qua
of wheat and rye exported from Dantzic, in periods of 25 years each, for the 166 y
ending with 1825.

Years.	Wheat. Quarters.	Rye. Quarters.	Total Quarters.
1651 to 1675	81,775	225,312	307,087
1676 — 1700	124,897	227,482	352,379
1701 — 1725	59,795	170,100	229,895
1726 — 1750	80,624	119,771	200,395
1751 — 1775	141,080	208,140	349,220
1776 — 1800	150,299	103,045	253,344
1801 — 1825	200,330	67,511	267,841

" The average of the whole period," Mr. Jacob observes, " gives an annual qua
of wheat and rye, of 279,794 quarters; and this surplus may be fairly consider
the nearest approach that can be made, with existing materials, to what is the
excess of the produce of bread corn above the consumption of the inhabitants,
no extraordinary circumstances occur to excite or check cultivation." — (*Report*, p.

We, however, have been assured by gentlemen well acquainted with the country
versed by the Vistula, that were the free importation of corn under a duty of 6s. c
permitted in England, the exports from Dantzic might be fairly estimated at
350,000 to 450,000 quarters.

Mr. Grade of Dantzic furnished the committee of 1821 with the following
of the average prices of corn at that city, free on board, in decennial periods, from
to 1820: —

Average Price, from ten to ten Years, of the different Species of Corn, free on b
per Quarter, in Sterling Money, at Dantzic.

	Wheat.		Rye.		Barley.		Oats
	s.	d.	s.	d.	s.	d.	s.
From 1770 to 1779 - - -	33	9	21	8	16	1	11
1780 — 1789 - - -	33	10	22	1	17	11	12
1790 — 1799 - - -	43	8	26	3	19	3	12
1800 — 1809 - - -	60	0	34	10	25	1	13
1810 — 1819 - - -	55	4	31	1	26	0	20
Aggregate Average Price of 49 Years -	45	4	27	2	20	10	13

In 1823, 1824, and 1825, prices, owing to the cessation of the demand from
land, were very much depressed; but, during the last three years, they have

vered their former elevation.   In September, 1830, the best high-mixed wheat cost
to 48s. free on board, and the ordinary from 34s. to 37s.
The following is an account of the ordinary charges on 100 quarters of wheat,
ped from Dantzic on consignment, and landed under bond in London. — (*Parl.*
er, No. 333. Sess. 1827. p. 28.)

	£	s.	d.	£	s.	d.
e hundred quarters, supposed cost at Dantzic, free on board, 30s.	-	-	-	150	0	0
eight at 5s. per quarter, and 10 per cent. - - - -	27	10	0			
tage ex Ship, &c., 6s. 6d. per last - - -	3	5	0			
hterage and Landing, 9d. per quarter - - -	3	15	0			
urance on 180l., including 10 per cent. imaginary Profit, at 80s. per cent. ; Policy 5s. per cent. - - -	7	14	0			
anary Rent and Insurance for one week - - -	0	5	0			
rning and Trimming, about - - - -	0	2	0			
livering from Granary, 3d. per quarter - - -	1	5	0			
tage, &c. ex Granary, 2s. per last - - -	1	0	0			
mmission on Sale, 1s. per quarter - - -	5	0	0			
l Credere, 1 per cent. on, suppose, 40s. - - -	2	0	0			
				51	16	0
Total Cost to Importer if sold in Bond				201	16	0
Imaginary Profit 10 per cent. - -				20	3	6
				221	19	6
Would produce, at 44s. 4d. per quarter				£221	13	4

N. B. Loss on re-measuring not considered.

reight and insurance are taken in this statement at an average, being sometimes
er and sometimes lower.

ow, it is obvious from this statement, that even supposing wheat to be put on board
antzic so low as 30s., or 5s. 4d. below its price in December last, it could not be
here, were it burdened with a duty of 6s., for less than 50s. a quarter.   This shows
little foundation there is for the notions so prevalent in this country as to the very
price at which Dantzic wheat might be imported under a free system, or with a
onable duty.

rn Trade of the Elbe, &c.—Next to Dantzic, Hamburgh is, perhaps, the greatest corn
ket in the north of Europe, being a depôt for large quantities of Baltic corn, and for
produce of the countries traversed by the Elbe.   But the excess of wheat exported
Hamburgh over that which is imported, is less than might have been expected, and
unted, at an average of the ten years ending with 1825, to only 48,263 quarters a year.
average price of wheat at Hamburgh, during the six years ending with 1822, was
4d. a quarter.   Bohemian wheat is occasionally forwarded by the river to Ham-
h ; but the charges attending its conveyance from Prague amount, according to
Jacob, to full 17s. a quarter, and prevent its being sent down, except when the
e is comparatively high.   We, however, are inclined to think that Mr. Jacob has
errated the supplies of wheat that might be obtained from Hamburgh, were our
s constantly open under a reasonable duty.   Last year (1830) there were shipped
Hamburgh for British ports, 271,700 quarters of wheat, 1,900 of rye, 18,200 of
y, and 2,800 of oats.   Prices that year were lower than at Dantzic ; but the
ity of the grain is inferior.

r. Jacob mentions, that the quantity of wheat exported from Denmark in the six
ths which followed the abundant harvest of 1824, amounted to only 57,561 quar-
and he doubts whether there were 20,000 quarters in store in that kingdom in
ber, 1825. (*Report*, p. 10.)   Undoubtedly, however, a greater quantity of grain
d be obtained from Denmark, were our ports constantly open ; and perhaps we
t be able, did our prices average about 50s., to import in ordinary years from
00 to 300,000 quarters of wheat from Denmark and the countries intersected by
Veser and the Elbe.

msterdam is merely a depôt, though a very important one, for foreign corn : a small
only of its consumption is supplied from corn of the growth of Holland ; so that
s there are, for the most part, dependent upon the prices at Dantzic and the other
northern markets.

eviously to the late revolution in the Netherlands, there used to be a considerable
e in corn from Antwerp to England.   The wheats, both white and red, are among
nest we receive from the Continent, but are usually rather high.   Beans and peas
lso fine.   Antwerp buck-wheat is the best in Europe.   According to Mr. Jacob,
ost of storing and turning wheat per month at Antwerp does not exceed 1½d. a
ter, or about half what it costs in London.

ench Corn Trade. — It appears, from the accounts given by the Marquis Garnier in
st edition of his translation of the *Wealth of Nations*, that the price of the *hectolitre*

of wheat at the market of Paris amounted, at an average of the nineteen years beginnin
with 1801 and ending with 1819, to 20 fr. 53 cent. ; which is equal to 30 fr. 80 cen
the septier ; or, taking the exchange at 25 fr., to 45s. 6d. the quarter.　Count Chapta
in his valuable work, *Sur l'Industrie Françoise*, (tom. i. p. 226.), published in 1819, est
mates the ordinary average price of wheat throughout France at 18 fr. the hectolitre,
42s. 10d. the quarter.　The various expenses attending the importation of a quarter
French wheat into London may be taken, at a medium, at about 6s. a quarter.　Franc
however, has very little surplus produce to dispose of; so that it would be impossible f
us to import any considerable quantity of French corn without occasioning a great ad
vance of price ; and in point of fact, our imports from France have been at all times qui
inconsiderable.

The mean of the different estimates framed by Vauban, Quesnay, Expilly, Lavoisie
and Arthur Young, gives 61,519,672 septiers, or 32,810,000 quarters, as the total averag
growth of the different kinds of grain in France. — (*Peuchet, Statistique Elémentai*
p. 290.)　We, however, took occasion formerly to observe (*Supp. to Encyc. Brit.* ar
Corn Laws) that there could not be a doubt that this estimate was a great deal too low
and the more careful investigations of late French statisticians fully confirm this remar
It is said that the mean annual produce of the harvests of France, at an average of th
four years ending with 1828, amounted to 60,533,000 hectolitres of wheat, ar
114,738,000 ditto of other sorts of grain ; making in all 175,271,000 hectolitres,
62,221,205 Winch. quarters.　Of this quantity it is supposed that 16 per cent. is co
sumed as seed, 19 per cent. in the feeding of different species of animals, and 2 per cen
in distilleries and breweries. — (*Bulletin des Sciences Géographiques*, tom. xxv. p. 34
This estimate is believed to be pretty nearly accurate ; perhaps, however, it is still rath
under the mark.

The foreign corn trade of France has been regulated during the last few years by
law which forbids exportation, except when the home prices are below certain limits
and restrains and absolutely forbids importation when they are above certain oth
limits.　The prices regulating importation and exportation differ in the three differe
districts into which the kingdom is divided; and it has not unfrequently happened th
corn warehoused in a particular port, where it was either not admissible at all, or n
admissible except under payment of a high duty, has been carried to another port
another district, and admitted duty free !　But by an ordinance dated the 2d of June las
some of the regulations in this law were suspended ; and it is believed that a new la
will speedily be enacted, admitting importation at all times under a graduated duty.

Spanish Corn Trade. — The exportation of corn from Spain was formerly prohibit
under the severest penalties.　But in 1820, grain and flour were both allowed to be free
exported ; and in 1823, this privilege was extended to all productions (*frutos*) the grow
of the soil.　There is now, in fact, no obstacle whatever, except the expense of carriage,
the conveyance of corn to the sea-ports, and thence to the foreigner.　Owing, howeve
to the corn-growing provinces being principally situated in the interior, and to the e
treme badness of the roads, which renders carriage to the coast both expensive and difficu
the exports are comparatively trifling ; the same difficulty of carriage frequently giv
rise to very great differences in the prices of places, in all parts of the country, only a fe
leagues distant.

Corn Trade of Odessa. — Odessa, on the Black Sea, is the only port in southe
Europe from which any considerable quantity of grain is exported.　We believe, indee
that the fertility of the soil in its vicinity has been much exaggerated ; but the whe
shipped at Odessa is principally brought from Volhynia and the Polish provinces to t
south of Cracow, the supplies from which are susceptible of an indefinite increas
Owing to the cataracts in the Dnieper, and the Dniester having a great number
shallows, most part of the corn brought to Odessa comes by land carriage.　The exper
of this mode of conveyance is not, however, nearly so great as might be suppose
The carts with corn are often in parties of 150 ; the oxen are pastured during the nig
and they take advantage of the period when the peasantry are not occupied with
harvest, so that the charge on account of conveyance is comparatively trifling.

Both soft and hard wheat are exported from Odessa ; but the former, which is by
the most abundant, is only brought to England.　Supposing British wheat to sell
about 60s., Odessa wheat, in good order, would not be worth more than 52s. in
London market ; but it is a curious fact, that in the Mediterranean the estimation
which they are held is quite the reverse ; at Malta, Marseilles, Leghorn, &c., Ode
wheat fetches a decidedly higher price than British wheat.

The hard wheat brought from the Black Sea comes principally from Taganrog.
is a very fine species of grain ; it is full 10 per cent. heavier than British wheat, and
less than half the bran.　It is used in Italy for making macaroni and vermicelli, a
things of that sort ; very little of it has found its way to England.

e voyage from Odessa to Britain is of uncertain duration, but generally very long.
essential to the importation of the wheat in a good condition, that it should be made
g the winter months. When the voyage is made in summer, unless the wheat be
superior, and be shipped in exceedingly good order, it is almost sure to heat; and
ometimes, indeed, been injured to such a degree as to require to be dug from the
with pickaxes. Unless, therefore, some means can be devised for lessening the
f damage during the voyage, there is little reason to think that Odessa wheat will
e largely imported into Britain. — (See the evidence of J. H. Lander, Esq. and
ineider, Esq. before the Lords' Committee of 1827, on the price of foreign corn.)
copy the following account from the first-mentioned evidence now referred to:—

it of the **Average Prices of Wheat at Odessa**, with the **Shipping Charges**, reduced into British
ure and Currency; the Rate of Exchange (the whole taken Quarterly for the Years 1814 to 1824,
sive); and the Quantities annually exported.

ter ending	Price per Chetwert in Russian Money.	Charges on Shipping.	Exchange.	Price on board per Quarter.	Quantity exported.	Observations.
	R.	R.	R.	s. d.	Quarters.	
March 31.	20·75	2·75	18·60	33 8		
June 30.	21·50	2·65	18·90	34 1	187,685	
Sept. 30.	17·50	2·50	19·55	27 3		
Dec. 31.	18	2·50	20·50	26 8		
March 31.	24·30	3·55	20·30	36 6		
June 30.	21	2·75	20·10	31 6	372,309	
Sept. 30.	24·80	2·95	20·60	35 11		
Dec. 31.	23·50	3·75	21·20	34 3		
March 31.	32	5·50	22·10	45 3		
June 30.	35·35	3·60	22·60	46 0	801,591	
Sept. 30.	35·80	3·65	23·10	45 7		
Dec. 31.	36·90	3·65	23	47 0		
March 31.	44·75	4·40	22·40	58 6		
June 30.	34·60	3·60	22	46 4	870,893	
Sept. 30.	30	3·30	21·55	41 2		
Dec. 31.	33·60	3·75	20·80	47 11		
March 31.	29·80	3·80	20·55	43 7		
June 30.	22·70	2·85	20·85	32 8	538,513	
Sept. 30.	23·80	2·90	20·40	34 11		
Dec. 31.	21·30	2·80	19·20	33 6		
March 31.	17·20	2·60	19·80	26 8		
June 30.	17·30	2·60	20·85	25 5	627,926	
Sept. 30.	16·30	2·55	21·85	23 1		
Dec. 31.	14	2·45	23·70	18 6		
March 31.	15·30	2·50	24·30	19 7		
June 30.	17	2·60	24·20	21 7	534,199	
Sept. 30.	19·30	2·65	24·40	24 0		
Dec. 31.	23·30	2·75	23·40	29 8		
March 31.	24·50	2·80	23·70	30 9		
June 30.	23·50.	2·75	24·15	29 0	435,305	
Sept. 30.	20·15	2·65	25·25	24 3		
Dec. 31.	19·80	2·65	24·90	24 2		
March 31.	17·25	2·60	24·80	20 8		
June 30.	17·75	2·60	25	21 8	342,752	The present price of wheat is less than the cost of cultiva- tion. The charge on warehousing wheat at Odessa does not exceed 2d. per quarter per month.
Sept. 30.	17·45	2·60	24·65	21 7		
Dec. 31.	15·25	2·50	23·90	19 10		
March 31.	15·20	2·50	24	19 8		
June 30.	15	2·50	24·50	19 2	443,035	
Sept. 30.	12·25	2·35	24·75	15 7		
Dec. 31.	12·70	2·30	24·95	16 0		
March 31.	12·90	2·30	25·40	16 1		
June 30.	13	2·30	25·10	16 3	427,767	
Sept. 30.	13	2·30	25·10	16 3		
Dec. 31.	13	2·30	24·50	16 7		

prices in 1823 and 1824 were, however, unusually depressed. It appears from
ort of the British consul, dated Odessa, 31st December, 1830, that the prices
at during the quarter then terminated, varied from 22s. 4d. to 34s. 6d. a quarter.
; the summer quarter 149,029 quarters of wheat were exported.
entire expense of importing a quarter of wheat from Odessa to London may be
ed at from 16s. to 19s. We borrow, from the valuable evidence of J. Schneider,
ready referred to, the following account, which states in detail the various items
nse. — (See next page.)
price free on board is here estimated at under 16s., being no less than 12s. below
rage price of October and December last, as returned by the consul; but not-
nding, if we add to the cost of the wheat in London, as given in the above state-
s. of duty, and allow 7s. for its supposed inferiority to English wheat, its price
hen thus reduced to the standard of the latter, would be about 47s. 6d. At
(1st August, 1831) Odessa wheat, entered for home consumption, is worth in
idon market from 50s. to 58s.; in bond it is worth from 42s. to 45s.

PRO FORMA INVOICE of 2,000 Chetwerts of Wheat shipped at Odessa for London.			
2,000 Chetwerts Wheat, at 12 Rs. per Chet. - - - - -			Rs. 24,000
CHARGES.			
Measuring when received, at 5 Cops. per Chet. - - -		Rs. 100	
Ditto when shipped 9 — - - - -		180	
Duty 77 — - - - -		1,540	
Carriage to the Mole 18 — - - - -		360	
Lighterage 15 — - - - -		300	
Use of Bags 10 — - - - -		200	
Brokerage, ¼ per cent. - - - - -		120	
			2,800
			Rs. 26,800
Commission, 3 per cent. - - - - -			804
			Rs. 27,600
			£ s.
Exchange at 24 Rs. per £ sterling			£1,150 3
			£ s.
Would produce 1,450 Imperial quarters, to cost per quarter - -			0 15

CHARGES IN LONDON.	£ s. d.	£ s. d.	
Policy Duty on 1,200l. at ¼d. per cent. -	3 0 0		
Insurance on 1,150l. at 2l. 2s. per cent. -	24 3 0		
		27 3 0	
Commission do. ¼		5 15 0	
Freight on 1,453 quarters Wheat, at 12s. per quarter	871 10 0		
Primage 10 per cent. - - -	87 3 7		
Gratification - - - -	10 10 0		
		969 9 7	
Charterparty 1l. ; Custom-house Entries, 10s. - -		1 10 0	
Metage on Ship, at 4s. 3¼d. per last - -		31 3 7	
Lastage - - - - -		1 4 2	
Lighterage of 1,453 quarters at 4d. - -		24 4 4	
Landing, Wharfage, Housing, and Delivering, at 9d. -		54 9 8	
Rent 4 Weeks, at 5s. per 100 quarters per Week -		14 10 7	
Metage, &c. ex Granary - - -		7 5 0	
		£1,136 15 0	
Or per Quarter			0 15
			1 11
Estimated Charge for probable Damage on the Voyage - - -			0 2
Factorage in London - - - - -			0 1
Del Credere, 1 per cent.			£1 14

American Corn Trade. — The prices of wheat at New York and Philadelphia ma
taken, on an average, at from 37s. to 40s. a quarter; and as the cost of importi
quarter of wheat from the United States into England amounts to from 8s. to 12s.,
seen that no considerable supply could be obtained from that quarter, were our p
under 50s. or 52s. It ought also to be remarked, that prices in America are us
higher than in the Baltic; so that but little can be brought from the former, except
the demand is sufficient previously to take off the cheaper wheats of the northern
The usual price of wheat in Canada, when there is a demand for the English mark
about 40s. a quarter; but taking it as low as 35s., if we add to this 10s. a quarter a
expenses of carriage, it will make its cost price in Liverpool 45s.; and being s
wheat, it is not so valuable, by about 6s. a quarter, as English wheat.

We may therefore conclude that, in the event of all restrictions on the importati
foreign corn being abolished, the price for which it could be obtained would n
ordinary years, be less than 48s. a quarter, and would most probably range from 5
55s.

Now, it appears from the official accounts laid before the House of Commons, th
average price of wheat in England and Wales, for the *ten* years ending with
amounted to 58s. 4½d. a quarter; and, lest we should be accused of overstating the
nary importation price of foreign wheat, we shall estimate it at the low rate of only
so that, provided it were burdened, as we have already shown it ought to be, with a
duty of 6s. a quarter, it might still be sold at an average for 52s.: and even on this
reasonable hypothesis, there is no ground whatever to suppose, in the event of the
being thrown open, that prices would be reduced more than 6s. or 6s. 6d. a quarter
the average of the last *ten* years.

We feel pretty confident that the statements now made cannot be controverted
they show, conclusively, how erroneous it is to suppose that the repeal of the ex
corn laws, and the opening of the ports for importation, under a duty of 6s. would
the effect of throwing a large proportion of our cultivated lands into pasture, and ca

inous decline in the price of corn. The average price of wheat in England and les in 1802, 1803, and 1804, years of decided agricultural improvement, was exactly a quarter, being only 8*s.* or 9*s.* above its probable future average price under a free em; while the greater cheapness of labour, and the various improvements that e been made in agriculture since 1804, would enable corn to be raised from the same s at a much less expense in this than in that year. It cannot be justly said that 1823 was by any means an unfavourable year for the farmers; and yet the average e of wheat was then only 51*s.* 9*d.*, being 3*d.* a quarter *less* than its probable lowest age price under the system we have ventured to propose. The landlords and farmers , therefore, take courage. Their prosperity does not depend on restrictive regulations; is the effect of the fertility of the soil which belongs to them, of the absence of all essive feudal privileges, and of the number and wealth of the consumers of their luce. The unbounded freedom of the corn trade would not render it necessary to ndon any but the most worthless soils, which ought never to have been broken up; would, consequently, have but a very slight effect on rent; while it would be in r respects supremely advantageous to the landlords, whose interests are closely iden-d with those of the other classes.

OTTON (Ger. *Baumwolle;* Du. *Katoen, Boomwol;* Da. *Bomuld;* Sw. *Bomull;* *Coton;* It. *Cotone, Bambagia;* Sp. *Algodon;* Port. *Algodão;* Rus. *Chlobtschataja aga;* Pol. *Bawelna;* Lat. *Gossypium, Bombax*), a species of vegetable wool, produce of the *gossypium*, or cotton-tree, of which there are many varieties. found growing naturally in all the tropical regions of Asia, Africa, and America, nce it has been transplanted, and has become an important object of cultiva-, in the southern parts of the United States, and to some extent also in ope.

otton is distinguished in commerce by its colour, and the length, strength, and fine- of its fibre. White is usually considered as characteristic of secondary quality. ow, or a yellowish tinge, when not the effect of accidental wetting or inclement ns, is considered as indicating greater fineness.

here are many varieties of raw cotton in the market, their names being principally ed from the places whence they are brought. They are usually classed under the minations of *long and short stapled.* The best of the first is the *sea-island* cotton, or brought from the shores of Georgia; but its qualities differ so much, that the price e finest specimens is often four times as great as that of the inferior. The superior les of Brazil cotton are reckoned among the long stapled. The *upland* or *bowed* rgia cotton forms the largest and best portion of the short stapled class. All the ns of India are short stapled.

e estimation in which the different kinds of cotton wool are held may be learned from following statement of their prices in Liverpool, on the 1st January last (1831). inferiority of Bengal and Surat cotton is sometimes ascribed to the defective mode hich it is prepared; but Mr. Horace H. Wilson doubts whether it can be grown in a of a better kind. The raw cotton of the Indian islands has hitherto been almost ely consumed on the spot.

Prices of Cotton in Liverpool, 1st *Jan.* 1831.

	d.	*d.*		*d.*	*d.*
Island, stained and saw-ginn'd	6 to	11½	Alabama and Mobile, good	6⅞ —	7⅛
inferior	11½ —	12	Upland, inferior	5⅞ —	6
middling	12¼ —	12½	middling	6 —	6¼
fair, clean, not fine	12½ —	12¾	fair	6⅜ —	6⅝
good, clean, & rather fine	13 —	13½	good fair	6⅝ —	6⅞
fine and clean	13¾ —	20	good	7 —	7⅜
Orleans, inferior	6¼ —	6⅜	Egyptian	8 —	9½
middling	6½ —	6¾	Pernambuco	7½ —	8⅜
fair	6¾ —	7	Bahia	7 —	7½
good fair	7 —	7¼	Maranham	7 —	7⅝
good	7⅜ —	7⅝	Demerara	6½ —	9
very choice gin marks	7¾ —	8	Barbadoes	6½ —	7¼
ama and Mobile, inferior	5¾ —	5⅞	Com. West India	6 —	7
middling	6 —	6⅛	Carthagena	5½ —	5¾
fair	6¼ —	6½	Surat	4½ —	5¾
good fair	6⅝ —	6⅞	Bengal	4 —	5

small quantity of very superior cotton has been imported from New South Wales. e manufacture of cotton has been carried on in Hindostan from the remotest anti-. Herodotus mentions (lib. iii. c. 106.) that in India there are wild trees that pro- a sort of wool superior to that of sheep, and that the natives dress themselves in made of it. (See to the same effect, *Arrian Indic.* c. 16. p. 582.) The manufacture ned no footing worth mentioning in Europe till last century.

Rise and Progress of the British Cotton Manufacture. — The rapid growth and prod
gious magnitude of the cotton manufacture of Great Britain are, beyond all questio
the most extraordinary phenomena in the history of industry. Our command of th
finest wool naturally attracted our attention to the woollen manufacture, and paved th
way for that superiority in it to which we have long since attained: but when w
undertook the cotton manufacture, we had comparatively few facilities for its prosecu
tion, and had to struggle with the greatest difficulties. The raw material was produce
at an immense distance from our shores; and in Hindostan and China the inhabitan
had attained to such perfection in the arts of spinning and weaving, that the lightne
and delicacy of their finest cloths emulated the web of the gossamer, and seemed to s
competition at defiance. Such, however, has been the ascendancy we have derived fro
the stupendous discoveries and inventions of Hargraves, Arkwright, Crompton, Car
wright, and others, that we have overcome all these difficulties—that neither the extrem
cheapness of labour in Hindostan, nor the perfection to which the natives had previous
attained, has enabled them to withstand the competition of those why buy their cotto
and who, after carrying it five thousand miles to be manufactured, carry back the goo
to them. This is the greatest triumph of mechanical genius: and what perhaps is mo
extraordinary, our superiority is not the late result of a long series of successive disc
veries and inventions: on the contrary, it has been accomplished in a very few yea
Little more than half a century has elapsed since the British cotton manufacture was
its infancy; and it *now* forms the principal business carried on in the country, affordi
an advantageous field for the accumulation and employment of millions upon millio
of capital, and of thousands upon thousands of workmen! The skill and genius b
which these astonishing results have been achieved, have been one of the main sources
our power: they have contributed in no common degree to raise the British nation
the high and conspicuous place she now occupies. Nor is it too much to say that it w
the wealth and energy derived from the cotton manufacture that bore us triumphant
through the late dreadful contest, at the same time that it gives us strength to susta
burdens that would have crushed our fathers, and could not be supported by any oth
people.

The precise period when the manufacture was introduced into England is not know
but it is most probable that it was some time in the early part of the 17th century. T
first authentic mention is made of it by Lewis Roberts, in his *Treasure of Traffic*, pu
lished in 1641, where it is stated, " The town of Manchester, in Lancashire, must b
also herein remembered, and worthily for their encouragement commended, who buy t
yarne of the Irish in great quantity, and weaving it, returne the same again into Irela
to sell. Neither doth their industry rest here; for they buy cotton wooll in London th
comes first from Cyprus and Smyrna, and at home worke the same, and perfect it in
fustians, vermillions, dimities, and other such stuffes, and then return it to Londo
where the same is vented and sold, and not seldom sent into forrain parts, who ha
means, at far easier termes, to provide themselves of the said first materials." — (Ori
ed. p. 32.) It is true, indeed, that mention is frequently made by previous writers, a
in acts of the legislature passed at a much earlier period[*], of " Manchester cotton
" cotton velvets," "fustians," &c.; but it is certain that these articles were *wholly co
posed of wool*, and had most probably been denominated cottons from their having be
prepared in imitation of some of the cotton fabrics imported from India and Italy.

From the first introduction of the cotton manufacture into Great Britain down to t
comparatively late period of 1773, the weft, or transverse threads of the web, only, we
of cotton; the warp, or longitudinal threads, consisting wholly of linen yarn, principal
imported from Germany and Ireland. In the first stage of the manufacture, t
weavers, dispersed in cottages throughout the country, furnished themselves as well
they could with the warp and weft for their webs, and carried them to market wh
they were finished: but about 1760, a new system was introduced. The Manches
merchants began about that time to send agents into the country, who employ
weavers, whom they supplied with foreign or Irish linen yarn for warp, and with r
cotton, which was first to be carded and spun, by means of a common spindle or dista
in the weaver's own family, and then used for weft. A system of domestic manufactu
was thus established; the junior branches of the family being employed in the cardi
and spinning of the cotton, while its head was employed in weaving, or in converti
the linen and cotton yarn into cloth. This system, by relieving the weaver from t
necessity of providing himself with linen yarn for warp and raw cotton for weft, and
seeking customers for his cloth when finished, and enabling him to prosecute his e
ployment with greater regularity, was an obvious improvement on the system that h

[*] In an act of 5 & 6 Edw. 6. (1552), entitled, for the true making of WOOLLEN cloth, it is ordered, " 7
all cottons called Manchester, Lancashire, and Cheshire cottons, full wrought for sale, shall be in lengt
&c. This proves incontestibly, that what were then called cottons were made wholly of wool.

previously followed: but it is at the same time clear that the impossibility of
~g any considerable division among the different branches of a manufacture so con-
~d, or of prosecuting them on a large scale, added to the interruption given to the
~r business of the weavers, by the necessity of attending to the cultivation of the
~es of ground which they generally occupied, opposed invincible obstacles to its pro-
so long as it was conducted in this mode.

~ppears from the Custom-house returns, that the total quantity of cotton wool an-
~ imported into Great Britain, at an average of the *five* years ending with 1705,
~nted to only 1,170,881 lbs. The accounts of the imports of cotton from 1720 to
~ have not been preserved; but until the last two or three years of that period the
~facture increased very slowly, and was of very trifling amount. Dr. Percival,
~anchester, who had the best means of being accurately informed on the subject,
~ that the entire value of all the cotton goods manufactured in Great Britain, at the
~ion of his late Majesty in 1760, was estimated to amount to only 200,000*l.* a year,
~he number of persons employed was quite inconsiderable: but in 1767, a most
~ous person, James Hargraves, a carpenter at Blackburn in Lancashire, invented
~*inning jenny.* At its first invention, this admirable machine enabled *eight* threads
~spun with the same facility as one; and it was subsequently brought to such per-
~ as to enable a little girl to work no fewer than from *eighty* to *one hundred and*
~ spindles.

~ jenny was applicable only to the spinning of cotton for weft, being unable to give
~ yarn that degree of firmness and hardness which is required in the longitudinal
~s or warp: but this deficiency was soon after supplied by the invention of the
~*g frame* — that wonderful piece of machinery which spins a vast number of
~s of any degree of fineness and hardness; leaving to man merely to feed the ma-
~with cotton, and to join the threads when they happen to break. It is not difficult
~erstand the principle on which this machine is constructed, and the mode of its
~ion. It consists of two pairs of rollers, turned by means of machinery. The
~ roller of each pair is furrowed or fluted longitudinally, and the upper one is
~d with leather, to make them take a hold of the cotton. If there were only one
~ rollers, it is clear that a carding of cotton passed between them would be drawn
~d by the revolution of the rollers, but it would merely undergo a certain degree
~pression from their action. No sooner, however, has the carding, or *roving*, as it
~nically termed, begun to pass through the first pair of rollers, than it is received
~ second pair, which are made to revolve with (as the case may be) three, four, or
~nes the velocity of the first pair. By this admirable contrivance, the roving is
~ out into a thread of the desired degree of tenuity; a twist being given to it by the
~tion of the spindle and fly of the common flax-wheel to the machinery.

~h is the principle on which Sir Richard Arkwright constructed his famous spin-
~ame. It is obvious that it is radically and completely different from the previous
~ds of spinning, either by the common hand-wheel or distaff, or by the jenny, which
~ a modification of the common wheel. Spinning by rollers was an entirely
~l idea; and it is difficult which to admire most — the profound and fortunate
~y which led to so great a discovery, or the consummate skill and address by which
~so speedily perfected and reduced to practice.*

~e the dissolution of Sir Richard Arkwright's patent, in 1785, the progress of dis-
~ and improvement in every department of the manufacture has been most rapid.
~*ule-jenny* — so called from its being a compound of the jenny and the spinning
~ — invented by Mr. Crompton, and the *power-loom*, invented by the Rev. Mr. Cart-
~, are machines that have had the most powerful influence on the manufacture;
~consequence of their introduction, and of innumerable other inventions and im-
~ents, the prices of cotton cloth and yarn have gone on progressively diminishing.
~ the demand for cottons has been, owing to their extraordinary cheapness, extended
~ill greater degree, the value of the goods produced, and the number of per-
~nployed in the manufacture, are now decidedly greater than at any previous

~rts of Cotton *Wool*; *Countries whence it is imported*; *Prices, &c.* — The following
~ave been partly taken from official documents, and partly from the accounts of
~nts of great experience. We believe they may be relied on as approaching as
~ accuracy as it is possible to attain in such matters.

~an account of the life of Sir Richard Arkwright, see the *Edinburgh Review*, No. 91., and the
~ion of the *Ency. Britannica*.

Account of the Imports and Exports of Cotton Wool to and from Great Britain,
1781 to 1812, both inclusive.

Years.	Imported.	Exported.	Years.	Imported.	Exported.
	lbs.	*lbs.*		*lbs.*	*lbs.*
1781	5,198,778	96,788	1797	23,354,371	609,058
1782	11,828,039	421,229	1798	31,880,641	601,139
1783	9,735,663	177,626	1799	43,379,278	844,671
1784	11,482,083	201,845	1800	56,010,732	4,416,610
1785	18,400,384	407,496	1801	56,004,305	1,860,872
1786	19,475,020	323,153	1802	60,345,600	3,730,480
1787	23,250,268	1,073,381	1803	53,812,284	1,561,053
1788	20,467,436	853,146	1804	61,867,329	503,171
1789	32,576,023	297,837	1805	59,682,406	804,243
1790	31,447,605	844,154	1806	58,176,283	651,867
1791	28,706,675	363,442	1807	74,925,306	2,176,943
1792	34,907,497	1,485,465	1808	43,605,982	1,644,867
1793	19,040,929	1,171,566	1809	92,812,282	4,351,105
1794	24,358,567	1,349,950	1810	132,488,935	8,787,109
1795	26,401,340	1,193,737	1811	91,576,535	1,266,867
1796	32,126,357	694,962	1812	63,025,936	1,740,912

Account of the Imports of Cotton Wool into Great Britain, of the Stocks on han
the 31st December, of the Annual and Weekly Delivery for Consumption,
Amount of the Crops of Cotton in North America, and the Average Price of
lands, each Year from 1814 to 1830, both inclusive. — (From *Mr. Cook's Trac
the Commerce of Great Britain in 1830.*)

	Total Imports into Great Britain.	Stock in the Ports, 31st December.	Total Deliveries for Consumption.	Estimated weekly Consumption.	Amount of Crop in North America.	Aver Price Uplan
	lbs.	*lbs.*	*lbs.*	*lbs.*	*lbs.*	*per*
1814	73,728,000	22,272,000	80,640,000	1,664,000		28.
1815	96,200,000	22,360,000	85,800,000	1,612,000		20
1816	97,310,000	22,355,000	88,631,000	1,709,500	No correct Returns.	18
1817	126,240,000	31,034,000	108,356,000	2,051,400		20
1818	173,960,000	85,800,000	111,800,000	2,132,000		20
1819	137,592,000	88,452,000	108,864,000	2,116,800		13
1820	147,576,000	103,458,000	125,646,000	2,322,000		11
1821	126,420,000	106,800,000	126,420,000	2,476,800	110,940,000	9
1822	141,510,000	76,362,000	144,180,000	2,750,100	121,485,000	8
1823	183,700,000	105,875,000	147,125,000	3,025,000	136,125,000	8
1824	147,420,000	64,428,000	174,174,000	3,166,800	152,880,000	8
1825	244,360,000	123,968,000	169,264,000	3,456,000	169,860,000	11
1826	170,520,000	100,548,000	164,640,000	3,410,400	211,680,000	6
1827	264,330,000	134,244,000	211,167,000	3,801,600	285,120,000	6
1828	222,750,000	120,582,000	217,701,000	4,158,000	213,840,000	6
1829	218,324,000	84,966,000	221,676,000	4,263,000	255,780,000	5
1830	259,856,000	95,360,000	242,000,000	4,768,000	292,040,000	6

In 1786, the supplies of cotton wool were derived from the following sources : —

	lbs.
From the British West Indies - -	5,800,000
French and Spanish Colonies - -	5,500,000
Dutch Colonies - - -	1,600,000
Portuguese Colonie - - -	2,000,000
Smyrna and Turkey - -	5,000,000
	19,900,000

or about 66,000 bales. N. B. The bale or package is of various magnitudes ; but
at an average, be estimated at 300 lbs.

Previously to 1790, North America did not supply us with a single pound weig
raw cotton. After the termination of the American war, cotton began to be culti
in Carolina and Georgia ; and it has succeeded so well, that it now forms one o
staple productions of the United States. American cotton is generally known b
names of *sea island, upland, New Orleans,* and *Alabama.* The first is the finest c
imported into Britain. It grows on small sandy islands contiguous to the sho
Georgia, and on the low grounds bordering on the sea. The *upland* grows at a di
from the coast, and is so very difficult to separate from the seed, that it was for a c
derable period not worth cultivating. But the genius of a Mr. Whitney, who inv
a machine which separates the wool from the seed with the greatest facility, has do
the planters of Carolina and Georgia what the genius of Arkwright did for the n
facturers of Lancashire. Before Mr. Whitney's invention, in 1793, very little u
was produced, and none was exported from the United States. No sooner, how
had his machine been constructed, than the cultivation of this species of cotton be

principal object of the agriculturists of Carolina and Georgia; and the exports have ·reased to upwards of 100,000,000 lbs. New Orleans and Alabama cottons are so ed from the ports whence they are shipped. At present, the exports of all sorts of :on from the United States considerably exceed 230,000,000 lbs. a year.

Brazil, the East Indies, Egypt, &c. are, after the United States, the countries that nish the largest supplies of cotton for exportation.

)f 227,760,000 lbs. of cotton wool imported into the United Kingdom in 1828, ,752,000 lbs. were from the United States, 29,143,000 lbs. from Brazil, 32,187,000 lbs. n the East Indies, 6,454,000 lbs. from Egypt, 5,893,000 lbs. from the British West ies, 726,000 lbs. from Columbia, 471,000 lbs. from Turkey and Continental Greece, — (*Parl. Paper*, No. 267. Sess. 1830.)

The subjoined statement is taken from the circular of George Holt and Co., eminent on brokers at Liverpool, dated 31st December, 1830. It contains some additional ails. In some respects it does not quite coincide with the previous statements; but differences are so very inconsiderable, as to afford a strong proof of its accuracy, as l as that of the details already given.

:ement of the Consumption, Exportation, &c. of Great Britain, for the different sorts of Cotton Wool, from 1824 to 1830, both inclusive.

·erage Weekly Consumption.	1824.	1825.	1826.	1827.	1828.	1829.	1830.
Upland	4,212	3,713	3,783	4,241	4,990	5,304	5,452
Orleans and Tennessee	2,298	2,442	2,713	3,940	4,210	3,788	5,756
Sea Island	754	360	369	673	635	539	460
Total United States	7,264	6,515	6,865	8,854	9,835	9,631	10,668
Brazil	2,890	2,502	1,188	1,815	2,456	3,094	3,602
Egypt	362	891	975	1,142	671	485	508
East India	644	1,096	489	664	738	658	940
Demerara, West India, &c.	473	527	308	502	380	463	284
Total	11,633	11,531	9,825	12,977	14,080	14,331	16,002
:kages annually con-umed	604,900	599,600	510,900	674,800	732,200	745,200	832,100
·erage Weight of Pack-ges consumed in lbs.	273	278	294	297	297	294	298
·ekly Consumption in ·ackages, average 298 ·s.	10,659	10,766	9,694	12,726	14,059	14,143	16,002
·rage Weight of Pack-ges imported in lbs.	266	270	295	303	293	297	300
kages exported	53,600	72,800	95,000	69,100	63,700	118,100	33,400
Weight annually im-orted, in Millions and ·enths	143·7	222·4	171·5	271·1	219·8	221·8	261·2
Weight consumed, do.	165·2	166·8	150·2	197·2	217·9	219·2	247·6
Weight in Ports, 31st ·ec. do.	64·0	107·0	89·0	129.2	112·7	80·8	91·4
Weight in Great ·ritain do.	80·3	115·5	110·9	164·8	147·0	115·5	118·8
·rage Price per lb. of ·plands in Liverpool	8½*d.*	11⅝*d.*	6¾*d.*	6½*d.*	6⅝*d.*	5¾*d.*	6⅝*d.*
do. Pernams	11⅝*d.*	15⅛*d.*	10½*d.*	9⅝*d.*	8⅝*d.*	7¼*d.*	8¼*d.*
do. Surats	6⅝*d.*	8⅜*d.*	5½*d.*	5⅛*d.*	4⅝*d.*	4*d.*	5*d.*

·ral Statement of the Import, Export, and Consumption of Great Britain, in Cotton Wool, for the Year 1830.

	Bags.		Bags.
·k in the Ports, 1st Jan. 1830	289,300	Export to the Continent and Ireland, 7,300 American, 3,600 Brazilian, 21,000 East Indian, 1,500 Egyptian	33,400
·n Dealers' and Spinners' hands England - 110,000; Scotland - 10,000	120,000	Taken for Consumption of England and Scotland from the Ports 807,100; Decrease of Stocks in hands of Dealers and Spinners 25,000	
·rt in 1830	871,500	Consumed in England 748,400 bags, or 14,392 bags per week; Do. Scotland 83,700 do. or 1,610 do. per week	832,100
		Remaining on hand in the Ports, 1st Jan. 1831	320,300
		In Dealers' and Spinners' hands, England - 89,000; Do. do. Scotland 6,000	95,000
	1,280,800		1,280,800

The following is an Account of the Imports of Cotton into the principal Continent Ports in 1829 and 1830, and of the Stocks on hand in these Years.

	Imports.		Stocks.	
	1829.	1830.	1829.	1830.
	lbs.	lbs.	lbs.	lbs.
Havre · · · · ·	53,100,000	57,300,000	5,235,000	13,650,000
Bordeaux · · · ·	2,715,000	2,520,000	450,000	600,000
Marseilles · · ·	14,070,000	20,385,000	2,505,000	3,300,000
Other French Ports ·	2,784,000	7,155,000	600,000	825,000
Trieste · · · ·	10,500,000	12,705,000	1,965,000	2,640,000
Genoa · · · ·	3,300,000	2,511,000	645,000	324,000
Antwerp · · ·	10,200,000	6,465,000	1,740,000	1,470,000
Rotterdam · · ·	7,680,000	4,974,000	1,530,000	1,170,000
Amsterdam · · · ·	3,060,000	1,365,000	1,350,000	732,000
Bremen · · · ·	1,740,000	1,200,000	927,000	570,000
Hamburgh · · ·	11,700,000	6,420,000	3,750,000	2,475,000
Petersburgh · · ·	3,120,000	2,520,000	900,000	900,000
	123,969,000	125,520,000	21,597,000	28,656,000
Bales ·	(413,230)	(418,400)	(71,990)	(95,520)

Present Value of the British Cotton Manufacture. — Amount of Capital, and Numb of Persons employed in it. — It would be very desirable to be able to form a tolerab accurate estimate of the present value of the cotton manufacture, and of the number persons employed in its different departments; but the data on which such estimates a founded being necessarily very loose, it is impossible to arrive at any thing like precisic Perhaps, however, the following calculations are not very wide of the mark.

In 1817, Mr. Kennedy, one of the best informed cotton manufacturers in the empi in a paper published in the Manchester Transactions, estimated the number of perso employed in the *spinning* of cotton in Great Britain at 110,763; the aid they deriv from steam-engines as equal to the power of 20,768 horses; and the number spindles in motion at 6,645,833. Mr. Kennedy farther estimated the number of han of yarn annually produced at 3,987,500,000; and the quantity of coal consumed their production at 500,479 tons. We subjoin Mr. Kennedy's statement for the ye 1817: —

Raw Cotton converted into yarn in the United
   Kingdom · · · - 110,000,000 lbs.
Loss in spinning estimated at $1\frac{1}{2}$ oz. per lb. -   10,312,500
Quantity of yarn produced · · ————————   99,687,500 lt
Number of hanks, taking the average at 40 per lb. · · 3,987,500,0?
Number of spindles employed, each spindle being supposed to pro-
   duce two hanks per day, at 300 working days in the year -   6,645,8?
Number of persons employed in spinning, supposing each to pro-
   duce 120 hanks per day · · · · 110,7?
Horse-power employed, equal in number to · ·· · 20,7?

Four ounces and a half of coal estimated to produce one hank of No. 40.; and 130 lt of coal per day, equal to one horse power.

But the cotton manufacture has increased rapidly since 1817. Mr. Huskisson state in his place in the House of Commons, in March 1824, that he believed the total val of the cotton goods then annually manufactured in Great Britain amounted to the pr digious sum of *thirty-three and a half* millions; and, we believe, we shall be within t mark if we estimate their present value at *thirty-six* millions! If, indeed, we took t increase in the imports of the raw material, as a test of the increase in the value of t manufacture, we should estimate it much higher. But it will be afterwards seen tl the improvements that have been made in the different processes, and the fall in t price of raw cotton, have had so powerful an influence in reducing the price of the goo brought to market, that the augmentation in the *value* of the manufacture, since 18? cannot be estimated at more than we have stated.

The average annual quantity of cotton wool imported, after deducting the expor may be taken at about 220,000,000 lbs. weight. It is supposed, that of this quant about 20,000,000 lbs. are used in a raw or unmanufactured state, leaving a balance 200,000,000 for the purposes of manufacturing, the cost of which may be taken, on average, at 7d. per lb. Deducting, therefore, from the total value of the manufactur goods, or 36,000,000l., the value on the raw material amounting to 6,000,00 (5,833,000l.), there remains 30,000,000l.; which, of course, forms the fund whence t wages of the persons employed in the various departments of the manufacture, the pro of the capitalists, the sums required to repair the wear and tear of buildings, machine

he expense of coals, &c. &c., must all be derived. If, then, we had any means of
aining how this fund is distributed, we should be able, by taking the average of wages
rofits, to form a pretty accurate estimate of the number of labourers, and the quantity
ital employed. But here, unfortunately, we have only probabilities and analogies to
us. It may, however, be confidently assumed, in the first place, that in consequence
extensive employment of highly valuable machinery in all the departments of the
manufacture, the proportion which the profits of capital, and the sum to be set
to replace its wear and tear, bears to the whole value of the manufacture, must be
larger than in any other department of industry. We have heard this proportion
sly estimated, at from a fourth to a half of the total value of the manufactured
exclusive of the raw material; and as the weight of authority seems to be pretty
divided on the subject, we shall take an intermediate proportion. Assuming,
ore, that the profits of the capital employed in the cotton manufacture, the wages
erintendence, &c., the sum required to replace the wear and tear of machinery,
ngs, &c., and to furnish coals, &c., amount together to *one third* of the value of
anufactured goods, exclusive of the raw material, or to *ten* millions; a sum of
millions will remain as the wages of the spinners, weavers, bleachers, &c. engaged
manufacture; and taking, inasmuch as a large proportion of children under six-
ears of age are employed, the average rate of wages at only 24*l.* a year, we shall
dividing 20,000,000 by 24) 833,000 as the total number of persons directly emin the different departments of the manufacture.

should mistake, however, if we supposed that this number, great as it certainly
iprised the whole number of persons to whom the cotton manufacture furnishes
ence, exclusive of the capitalists. Of the sum of 10,000,000*l.* set apart as the
of the capitalists, and the sum required to furnish coal, and to defray the wear
ar of machinery, &c., a large proportion must annually be laid out in paying the
of engineers, machine-makers, iron-founders, smiths, joiners, masons, bricklayers,
It is not easy to say what this proportion may amount to; but taking it at a *third*,
nillions, and supposing the rate of wages of each individual to average 30*l.* a year,
al number employed in the various capacities alluded to will be (3½ millions di-
by 30) 111,000; and a sum of 6⅔ millions sterling will remain to cover the profits
capital employed in the various branches of the manufacture, the expense of
sing materials to repair the different parts of the machinery and buildings as
ear out, coal, &c. The account will, therefore, stand as under: —

	£
value of every description of cotton goods annually manufactured ireat Britain - - - - - - -	36,000,000

naterial, 200,000,000 lbs. at 7*d.* per lb. - -	£6,000,000	
of 833,000 weavers, spinners, bleachers, &c. at 24*l.* ar each - - - - - -	20,000,000	
of 111,000 engineers, machine-makers, smiths, ons, joiners, &c. at 30*l.* a year each - -	3,333,000	
of the manufacturers, wages of superintendence, s to purchase the materials of machinery, coals, &c.	6,666,000	
		36,000,000

capital employed may be estimated as follows: —

employed in the purchase of the raw material - -		6,000,000
employed in payment of wages - - - -		15,000,000
invested in spinning-mills, power and hand looms, workshops, houses, &c. - - - - - -		35,000,000
		£56,000,000

, this sum of 56,000,000*l.*, supposing the interest of capital, inclusive of the
f superintendence, &c. to amount to 8 per cent., will yield a sum of 4,480,000*l.*;
being deducted from the 6⅔ millions profits, &c. leaves about *two* millions to
e materials to repair the waste of capital, the coals necessary in the employment
steam-engines, to effect insurances, and to meet all other outgoings.
aggregate amount of wages, according to the above estimate, is 23,333,000*l.*;
re are not many departments of the business in which wages have to be ad-
more than six months before the article is sold. We, therefore, incline to think
,000,000*l.* is a sufficient allowance for the capital employed in the payment of

If we are nearly right in these estimates, it will follow — allowance being made old and infirm persons, children, &c. dependent on those who are actually employe the various departments of the cotton manufacture, and in the construction, rej &c. of the machinery and buildings required to carry it on — that it must furnish the most moderate computation, subsistence for from 1,200,000 to 1,400,000 pers And for this new and most prolific source of wealth, we are indebted partly and pri pally, as already shown, to the extraordinary genius and talent of a few individu but, in a great degree, also, to that security of property and freedom of indu which give confidence and energy to all who embark in industrious undertaki and to that universal diffusion of intelligence which enables those who carry on work, to press every power of nature into their service, and to avail themselves of ductive capacities of which a less instructed people would be wholly ignorant.

The effect that the sudden opening of so vast and profitable a field for the emp ment of capital and labour has had on the population of the different towns of I cashire and Lanarkshire, the districts where the cotton manufacture is principally ca on, has been most striking. In 1774, for example, the parish of Manchester is mated to have contained 41,032 inhabitants — a number which was swelled, in 183. 187,019, having more than quadrupled in the space of 57 years! The populatic Preston, in 1780, is said not to have exceeded 6,000; whereas it amounts, at presen 33,112. In like manner, the population of Blackburn has increased from 11,98(1801, to 27,091, in 1831; that of Bolton has increased in the same period, from 17,4) 41,195; that of Wigan, from 10,989 to 20,774, &c. But the progress of Liverpo most extraordinary, and can be matched only by the progress of one or two c in the United States. Liverpool is not properly one of the seats of the cotton m: facture; but it is, notwithstanding, mainly indebted to it for the unparalleled rapi of its growth. It is the grand emporium of the cotton district — the port where al all the raw cotton, and the various foreign articles required for the employment subsistence of the persons engaged in the manufacture, are imported, and from whe the finished goods are exported to other countries. It has, therefore, become a p of vast trade, and is now, in that respect, second only to London. In 1700, accor to the best accounts that can be obtained, the population of Liverpool amounte only 5,145; in 1750, it had increased to 18,450; in 1770, it amounted to 34,050. cotton manufacture now began rapidly to extend, and, in consequence, the popula of Liverpool increased, in 1801, to 77,653; in 1821, to 118,972; and, in 183 amounted to 165,175. The progress of population in Lanarkshire and Renfrews has been equally striking. In 1780, the city of Glasgow contained only 42,83; habitants; in 1801, that number had increased to 83,769; and, in 1831, it amou to nearly 203,000. The growth of Paisley is similar. In 1782, it contained, inclu of the Abbey Parish, only 17,700 inhabitants; in 1801, it contained 31,179; in 1 it contained about 46,000; and, at present, it probably contains nearly 60,000.

Since the repeal of the absurd system of Irish protecting duties, in 1823, the cc manufacture has begun to make considerable progress in Ireland. This is prove a statement, laid before the House of Commons, which shows that the number of y of cotton goods, manufactured chiefly from yarn sent from England, exported Ireland to Great Britain, in 1822, amounted to 406,687; in 1823, to 556,646 1824, to 3,840,699; and in 1825, it amounted to no less than 6,418,645; — ha increased in nearly a *twelvefold* proportion in two years, by the abolition of duties were intended to *protect* the industry of Ireland!

Exports of Cotton Goods and Yarn. — Fall of Prices, &c. — For a very long pe the woollen manufacture was the great staple of the country. But the progre improvement in the spinning and manufacturing of cotton, since 1770, being so r more rapid than any that has taken place in the woollen manufacture, the value o former is now vastly greater than that of the latter. It appears, from the accour the declared or real values of the different sorts of exported commodities obtaine the Custom-house, that the exports of cotton goods, including yarn, amount, o average, to about 17,000,000*l.* sterling, or to nearly half the value of the whole m facture; and form of themselves about *two thirds* of the total value of all the fabrics exported from the empire. We subjoin a statement, compiled from p printed by order of the House of Commons, "of the official, and the declared or valuesof the cotton manufactured goods, cotton yar n, woollen, and silk manufact and the totals of all other articles of British produce and manufactures, exp from Great Britain to all parts of the world (except Ireland) in each of the thi years 1814—1826."

ears.	Cotton Manufactures.	Cotton Yarn.	Manufactures. Woollen.	Linen.	Silk.	Total of Wove Fabrics.	Total of all other Articles.
	£	£	£	£	£	£	£
1814	16,690,365	1,119,850	4,931,670	1,524,457	173,348	24,439,684	8,760,896
1815	21,699,505	808,853	7,122,570	1,599,074	224,873	31,445,876	10,266,126
1816	16,335,124	1,380,486	5,586,364	1,559,367	161,874	25,023,215	9,751,305
1817	20,357,147	1,125,257	5,676,920	1,943,194	152,734	29,255,253	9,980,144
1818	21,627,936	1,296,776	6,344,100	2,153,309	167,559	31,589,683	10,373,844
1819	16,876,206	1,585,753	4,602,270	1,547,352	126,809	24,738,390	8,185,185
1820	20,704,600	2,022,153	4,363,973	1,935,186	118,370	29,144,283	8,673,753
1821	21,630,493	1,898,695	5,500,922	2,303,443	136,402	31,478,955	8,715,938
1822	24,566,920	2,353,217	5,943,612	2,594,783	141,007	35,599,539	7,958,950
1823	24,117,549	2,425,419	5,539,789	2,654,098	141,320	34,878,175	8,266,291
1824	27,170,107	2,984,329	6,136,092	3,283,403	159,648	39,733,579	8,296,457
1825	26,597,574	2,897,706	5,929,342	2,709,772	150,815	38,285,209	8,167,812
1826	21,445,565	3,748,526	5,041,585	2,056,760	106,738	32,399,174	7,932,830
1827	29,203,138	3,979,759	5,979,701	2,808,081	173,334	42,144,013	9,132,435
1828	28,989,976	4,485,841	5,720,079	3,118,270	178,871	42,493,037	9,536,113
1829	31,810,436	5,458,985	5,361,997	3,003,394	220,436	45,855,248	9,610,475
1814	17,393,796	2,791,249	6,372,494	1,701,384	530,020	28,788,940	14,658,432
1815	19,124,062	1,674,022	9,338,142	1,777,563	622,120	32,535,905	17,117,340
1816	13,072,757	2,628,448	7,844,855	1,452,667	480,522	25,479,252	14,849,690
1817	14,178,022	2,014,182	7,163,472	1,703,632	408,523	25,467,827	14,869,292
1818	16,643,579	2,385,305	8,143,193	1,949,815	499,175	29,621,067	15,567,182
1819	12,388,833	2,516,783	5,986,807	1,391,245	376,798	22,660,467	11,588,029
1820	13,843,569	2,826,643	5,583,430	1,653,804	374,114	24,278,570	11,290,109
1821	13,786,957	2,307,830	6,461,567	1,981,465	373,938	24,911,759	10,914,223
1822	14,534,253	2,700,437	6,488,523	2,192,772	381,455	26,297,429	9,879,468
1823	13,751,415	2,625,947	5,634,137	2,095,574	350,880	24,457,952	10,233,172
1824	15,240,006	3,135,496	6,011,534	2,442,440	442,582	27,272,059	10,301,359
1825	15,034,138	3,206,729	6,193,775	2,130,705	296,677	26,862,024	11,221,749
1826	10,522,357	3,491,268	4,982,898	1,489,647	168,453	20,652,623	10,195,015
1827	13,956,825	3,545,568	5,277,861	1,895,186	236,092	24,911,532	11,484,807
1828	13,545,638	3,594,945	5,120,226	2,000,033	255,755	24,516,647	11,636,151
1829	13,420,544	3,974,039	4,656,809	1,885,831	267,192	24,204,415	11,008,458

; will be observed, from the above table, that while the *official* value of the cotton ls exported has been rapidly increasing, their *declared* or real value has been about onary, or has rather diminished. This circumstance has given rise to a great deal relevant discussion; and has even been referred to as proving that the manufacture a declining state! But it proves precisely the contrary. — It shows that the decline e price of the raw material, and the improvements in the machinery and processes in the manufacture have been so great, that we are now able to export and sell a profit, (for, unless such were the case, the exportation would very speedily cease,) y double the quantity of cotton goods we exported in 1814, for about the same . Had the table been carried farther back, the result would have been still more ing.

illustration of this view of the matter, we beg to subjoin the following statement e production and cost of the different species of cotton yarn in England, in 1812 1830. It was furnished by Mr. Kennedy, of Manchester, to the committee on the India Company's affairs, so that no doubt can be entertained of its accuracy.

Hanks per day, per spindle. Description of Yarn.	1812.	1830.	Price of Cotton and Waste per lb. 1812.		1830.		Labour per lb.* 1812.		1830.		Cost per lb. 1812.		1830.	
No.			s.	d.	s.	d.	s.	d.	s.	d.	s.	d.	s.	d.
40	2·	2·75	1	6	0	7	1	0	0	7½	2	6	1	2½
60	1·5	2·5	2	0	0	10	1	6	1	0½	3	6	1	10½
80	1·5	2·	2	2	0	11¼	2	2	1	7½	4	4	2	6¾
100	1·4	1·8	2	4	1	1¾	2	10	2	2½	5	2	3	4¼
120	1·25	1·65	2	6	1	4	3	6	2	8	6	0	4	0
150	1·	1·33	2	10	1	8	6	6	4	11	9	4	6	7
200	·75	·90	3	4	3	0	16	8	11	6	20	0	14	6
250	·05	·06	4	0	3	8	31	0	24	6	35	0	28	2

e following table is interesting, from its exhibiting the state of our trade in ght cottons, with the different countries of the world. It sets the importance of arkets of Brazil, Chili, and the other states of South America, as outlets for our ns, in a very striking point of view.

ages are estimated at the same rate, or at 20*d.* a day, for every person employed, men, women, and en, in 1812 and 1830, the saving being entirely in the better application of the labour.

Account of the Export of Cotton Goods and Yarn, in 1829; specifying the Countri to which they were sent, and the Quantity and Value of those sent to each. —(Pa_ Paper, No. 153. Sess. 1831.)

Countries to which Exported.	Cotton Manufactures.		Hosiery, Lace and Small Wares.	Cotton Twist and Yarn	
	Entered by the Yard.		Declared Value.		
	Quantity.	Declared Value.	Declared Value.	Quantity.	Declared Value.
	Yards.	*£*	*£*	*lbs.*	*£*
Northern Europe — Russia - -	2,453,676	94,872	23,146	17,921,369	1,062,22_
Sweden - - -	12,986	538	205	320,660	18,92_
Norway - - - -	574,650	20,543	2,296	16,242	89_
Denmark - - -	352,097	8,439	429	85,161	5,22_
Prussia - - -	17,725	517	405	42,878	3,79_
Germany - - -	41,019,652	1,137,532	279,355	24,055,423	1,585,97_
The Netherlands -	11,399,792	443,705	214,681	7,878,249	673,7_
Southern Europe — France -	509,030	15,462	3,335	19,500	1,48_
Portugal, Proper -	24,701,993	631,125	12,385	159,567	14,08_
———. Azores -	466,326	13,108	521	1,400	6_
———. Madeira -	502,631	14,602	616	12	—
Spain and the Balearic Islands	11,018,689	326,708	12,978	17,620	1,47_
——— Canaries - - -	712,424	21,767	1,206	3,054	23_
Gibraltar - - -	10,242,089	310,723	10,052	21,873	2,19_
Italy and the Italian Islands -	36,808,440	1,081,461	44,849	6,355,154	317,58_
Malta - - - -	4,628,367	105,995	1,869	438,640	21,52_
Ionian Islands - -	96,028	3,141	66	15,100	85_
Turkey and Continental Greece	15,536,350	392,725	1,431	662,538	39,91_
Africa — Egypt (Ports on the Mediterranean) - }	1,875,161	43,410	—	28	_
Western Coast of Africa -	1,910,940	70,104	115	—	—
Cape of Good Hope -	2,520,127	75,310	6,363	3,331	33_
St. Helena - - -	31,597	1,048	173	1	—
Mauritius - - -	1,658,937	53,150	7,845	—	—
Asia — East India Company's Territories, Ceylon and China }	39,733,698	1,267,216	28,395	3,185,689	210,18_
Sumatra, Java, and other Islands of the Indian Seas - }	3,502,163	121,036	447	—	—
Philippine Islands - -	93,279	4,448	—	—	—
New South Wales, Van Diemen's Land, and Swan River - }	476,065	19,067	3,498	4,805	47_
New Zealand and South Sea Islands - - }	2,008	80	—	—	—
America—British Northern Colonies	8,671,237	261,546	16,191	84,760	4,47_
British West Indies -	33,319,295	997,408	52,872	1,230	19_
Hayti - - - -	6,654,839	207,630	3,065	616	14_
Cuba, and other Foreign W. Indies	11,447,514	395,288	11,906	50	—
United States of America -	32,552,162	1,346,023	155,334	30,182	1,99_
States of Central and Southern America; viz. — Mexico - }	6,007,047	204,677	9,441	97,320	6,66_
Columbia - - -	4,277,904	132,526	5,918	—	—
Brazil - - - -	50,077,739	1,437,963	50,369	⌐ 5,300	67_
States of the Rio de la Plata -	15,429,383	485,381	24,657	5,460	50_
Chili - - - -	16,972,286	570,863	22,508	2,735	3_
Peru - - - -	3,465,460	143,798	15,689	800	_
Isles of Guernsey, Jersey, Alderney, Man, &c. - - }	785,510	55,312	17,269	4,554	7_
Total Exported	402,517,196	12,516,247	1,041,885	61,441,251	3,976.8_

Such being the vast extent and importance of the cotton manufacture, the probability our preserving our ascendancy in it becomes a very interesting topic of inquiry.   B it is obvious, that a great deal of conjecture must always insinuate itself into our reasc ings with respect to the future state of any branch of manufacturing industry.   They : all liable to be affected by so many contingent and unforeseen circumstances, that it impossible to predicate, with any thing like certainty, what may be their condition a f years hence. But abstracting from the effect of national struggles and commotio_ which can neither be foreseen nor calculated, we do not think that there is any thing our state, or in that of the different commercial and manufacturing countries of _ world, that should lead us to anticipate that the gloomy forebodings of those who c_ tend that the cotton manufacture of England has reached its zenith, and that it m_ now begin to decline, will be realised.   The natural capabilities we possess for carry_ on the business of manufacturing, are, all things considered, decidedly superior to th_ of any other people.   But the superiority to which we have already arrived, is, perha_ the greatest advantage in our favour.   Our master manufacturers, engineers, and a_ sans, are more intelligent, skilful, and enterprising, than those of any other country ; _ the extraordinary inventions they have already made, and their familiarity with all principles and details of the business, will not only enable them to perfect the proce_

y in use, but can hardly fail to lead to the discovery of others. Our establish-
for spinning, weaving, printing, bleaching, &c. are infinitely more complete and
t than any that exist elsewhere; the division of labour in them is carried to an
parably greater extent; the workmen are trained from infancy to industrious
, and have attained that peculiar dexterity and sleight of hand in the performance
ir separate tasks, that can only be acquired by long and unremitting application
same employment. Why, then, having all these advantages on our side, should
t keep the start we have already gained? Every other people that attempt to
manufactures, must obviously labour under the greatest difficulties as compared
s. Their establishments cannot, at first, be sufficiently large to enable the divi-
f employments to be carried to any considerable extent, at the same time that ex-
ss in manipulation, and in the details of the various processes, can only be at-
by slow degrees. It appears, therefore, reasonable to conclude, that such new
ners, having to withstand the competition of those who have already arrived at a
high degree of perfection in the art, must be immediately driven out of every
t equally accessible to both parties; and that nothing but the aid derived from
tive regulations and prohibitions will be effectual to prevent the total destruction
ir establishments in the countries where they are set up.

VERLETS (Ger. *Bettdecken;* Du. *Beddedekkens;* Fr. *Couvertures;* It.
te da letto;* Sp. *Cobertores;* Rus. *Pokriwalu*), counterpanes or bed-covers.

WHAGE or COWITCH (Hind. *Kiwach*), the fruit or bean of a per-
climbing plant (*Dolichos pruriens,* Lin.). It is a native of India, as well as
eral other eastern countries, and of America. The pod is about 4 or 5 inches
a little curved, and contains from three to five oval and flattish seeds;
utside is thickly covered with short, bristly, brown hairs, which, if in-
usly touched, stick to the skin, and occasion intolerable itching. Syrup
ned with the hairs is prescribed in certain complaints.—(*Ainslie's Materia
.)*

WRIES (Ger. *Kauris;* Du. *Kauris;* Fr. *Coris, Cauris, Bouges;* It. *Cori,
lane;* Sp. *Bucios Zimbos*) are small shells brought from the Maldives, which
urrent as a coin in smaller payments in Hindostan, and throughout exten-
stricts in Africa. They used to be imported into England previously to
olition of the slave trade, in which they were subsequently employed. They
article of trade at Bombay. The best are small, clean, and white, with a
ful gloss upon them; those that are yellow, large, and without lustre, should
cted. The freight is calculated at 20 cwt. to the ton.—(*Milburn's Orient.*

ANBERRIES or RED WHORTLEBERRIES, the fruit of a moss
the *Vaccinium oxycoccus* of Linnæus. The berries are globular, about the
currants; are found in mossy bogs in different parts of Scotland, but not
t numbers: they were once common in Lincolnshire, and the northern parts
folk; but since the bogs have been drained and cultivated, they are rarely
th. Cranberries have a peculiar flavour, and a sharp, acid, agreeable taste;
re easily preserved, and are extensively used in making tarts. They are
undant in North America, and in the northern parts of Russia; the latter
f a superior quality. We import from 30,000 to 35,000 gallons annually.
aid that some very fine ones have recently been brought from New South

APE (Fr. *Crépe;* Ger. *Flohr, Krausflohr;* It. *Espumilla, Soplillo;* Rus.
Sp. *Crespon*), a light transparent stuff, in manner of gauze, made of raw
ummed and twisted on the mill, and woven without crossing. It is princi-
sed in mourning. Crape was originally manufactured in Bologna; but
ade in this country is now deemed superior to any made in Italy.

EAM OF TARTAR. See ARGAL.

EDIT, the term used to express the trust or confidence placed by one
ual in another, when he assigns him money, or other property in loan, or
t stipulating for its immediate payment. The party who lends is said to
edit, and the party who borrows to obtain credit.
in and Nature of Credit.—In the earlier stages of society credit is in a great
e unknown. This arises partly from the circumstance of very little capital
hen accumulated, and partly from government not having the means, or not
sufficiently careful, to enforce that punctual attention to engagements so
nsable to the existence of confidence or credit. But as society advances,

capital is gradually accumulated, and the observance of contracts is enfor
by public authority. Credit then begins to grow up. On the one hand, th
individuals who have more capital than they can conveniently employ, or who
desirous of withdrawing from business, are disposed to lend, or to transfer, a
or the whole of their capital to others, on condition of their obtaining a cer
stipulated premium or interest for its use, and what they consider sufficient
curity for its repayment; and, on the other hand, there are always individual
be met with, disposed to borrow, partly (and among merchants principally
order to extend their business beyond the limits to which they can carry it
means of their own capital, or to purchase commodities on speculation, and pa
to defray debts already contracted. These different classes of individuals mutu
accommodate each other. Those desirous of being relieved from the fatigue
business, find it very convenient to lend their capital to others; while such as
anxious to enlarge their businesses, obtain the means of prosecuting them t
greater extent.

It is plain, that to whatever extent the power of the borrower of a quantit
produce, or a sum of money, to extend his business may be increased, that of
lender must be equally diminished. The same portion of capital cannot be
ployed by two individuals at the same time. If A. transfer his capital to B.
necessarily, by so doing, deprives himself of a power or capacity of product
which B. acquires. It is most probable, indeed, that this capital will be m
productively employed in the hands of B. than of A.; for the fact of A. hav
lent it, shows that he either had no means of employing it advantageously, or
disinclined to take the trouble; while the fact of B. having borrowed it, sh
that he conceives he can advantageously employ it, or that he can invest it s
to make it yield an interest to the lender, and a profit to himself. It is obvi
however, that except in so far as credit contributes, in the way now mentio
to bring capital into the possession of those who, it may be fairly presumed,
employ it most beneficially, it conduces nothing to the increase of wealth.

The most common method of making a loan is by selling commodities on cre
or on condition that they shall be paid at some future period. The price is
creased proportionally to the length of credit given; and if any doubt
entertained with respect to the punctuality or solvency of the buyer, a far
sum is added to the price, in order to cover the risk that the seller or lender r
of not recovering the price, or of not recovering it at the stipulated period. T
is the usual method of transacting where capital is abundant, and confide
general; and there can be no manner of doubt that the amount of property
in Great Britain, the Netherlands, and most other commercial countries, in
way, is infinitely greater than all that is lent in every other way.

When produce is sold in the way now described, it is usual for the buyer
give their bills to the sellers for the price, payable at the period when the cr
is to expire; and it is in the effects consequent to the negotiation of such
that much of that magical influence that has sometimes been ascribed to cred
believed to consist. Suppose, to illustrate this, that a paper-maker, A., sells
printer, B., a quantity of paper, and that he gets his bill for the sum, payab
twelve months after date: B. could not have entered into the transaction ha
been obliged to pay ready money; but A., notwithstanding he has occasion for
money, is enabled, by the facility of negotiating or discounting bills, to give
requisite credit, without disabling himself from prosecuting his business. In a
like this, both parties are said to be supported by credit; and as cases of this
are exceedingly common, it is contended that half the business of the count
carried on by its means. All, however, that such statements really amou
is, that a large proportion of those engaged in industrious undertakings do
employ their own capital, but that of others. In the case in question, the pr
employs the capital of the paper-maker, and the latter employs that of the ba
or broker who discounted the bill. This person had most likely the amou
spare cash lying beside him, which he might not well know what to make of;
the individual into whose hands it has now come, will immediately apply
useful purposes, or to the purchase of the materials, or the payment of the w
of the workmen employed in his establishment. It is next to certain, there
that the transaction will have been advantageous. But still it is essential to
in mind that it will have been so, not because credit is of itself a means of

tion, or because it can give birth to capital not already in existence; but
ause, through its agency, capital finds its way into those channels in which it has
best chance of being profitably employed.

The real advantage derived from the use of bills and bank notes as money con-
s, as has been already shown, in their substituting so cheap a medium of
hange as paper, in the place of one so expensive as gold, and in the facilities
ch they give to the transacting of commercial affairs. If a banker lend A. a
e for 100*l.* or 1,000*l.*, the latter will be able to obtain an equivalent portion of
land or produce of the country in exchange for it; but that land or produce
already in existence. The issue of the note did not give it birth. It was
viously in some one's possession; and it will depend wholly on the circum-
ace of A.'s employing it more or less advantageously than it was previously
loyed, whether the transaction will, in a public point of view, be profitable or
. On analysing any case of this kind, we shall invariably find that all that the
est degree of credit or confidence can do, is merely to change the distribution
capital — to transfer it from one class to another. These transfers are
asionally, too, productive of injurious results, by bringing capital into the hands
spendthrifts: this, however, is not, except in the case of the credit given by
pkeepers, a very common effect; and there can be no doubt that the vast
ority of regular loans are decidedly beneficial.

buses of the present Credit System in Great Britain. — Means of obviating them. —
previous observations refer rather to the credit given to individuals engaged in
iness, who mean to employ the capital which they borrow in industrious under-
ngs, than to that which is given to individuals not so engaged, and who employ
advances made to them in supporting themselves and their families. In neither
is credit of advantage, unless it be granted with due discrimination, and with
rence to the character, condition, and prospects of those receiving it. In this
ntry, however, these considerations have been in a great measure lost sight of,
he granting of credit by shopkeepers and tradesmen of all descriptions. Owing
e competition of such persons, and their extreme eagerness to secure custom-
and the general indolence of opulent persons, which disinclines them to satisfy
y small debt when it is contracted, the system of selling upon credit has become
st universal. Few among us think of paying ready money for any thing; seven
hs of the community are in the constant practice of anticipating their incomes;
there is hardly one so bankrupt in character and fortune as to be unable to find
ers, bakers, butchers, tailors, &c. ready to furnish him upon credit with supplies
e articles in which they respectively deal. We look upon this facility of ob-
ng accommodations as a very great evil. They are not, in one case out of
of any real advantage to the parties receiving them, while they are productive
ery pernicious results. The system tempts very many, and sometimes even
most considerate individuals, to indulge in expenses beyond their means; and
becomes the most fruitful source of bankruptcy, insolvency, and bad faith.
;uarantee themselves from the extraordinary risk to which such proceedings
se them, tradesmen are obliged to advance the price of their goods to a most
bitant height; so that those who are able, and who really mean to pay the
s they contract, are, in fact, obliged to pay those of the hosts of insolvents
swindlers maintained by the present system. Many tradesmen consider
selves as fortunate, if they recover from two thirds to three fourths of the
standing in their books, at the distance of several years.

e extraordinary extent to which the credit practice is carried may be learned
the inquiries of the Parliamentary Committee on Small Debts. It appears
them that hatters, shoemakers, &c., in the metropolis, have often 4,000*l.* and
rds on their books in debts below 10*l.*, and that *five sixths of their book debts
elow that sum!* A large proportion of these debts are irrecoverable; but
g to the artificial enhancement of prices, those that are good are sufficient to
nnify the traders for the loss of the bad.

is not easy, we think, to imagine any system better fitted to generate impro-
ce and fraud. The vast majority of those who become insolvent, or are impri-
d for debt, consist of labourers, artisans, half-pay officers, clerks in public and
' offices, annuitants, &c.—persons whom no prudent shopkeeper would ever
to get permanently into his debt. The following table exhibits some of the
s resulting from this system: —

Number of Persons committed for Debt to the several Prisons of the Metropolis
the Year 1827, and the Sums for which they were committed.—(*Parl. Paper*, No. 7
Sess. 1828.)

	For Sums above 100*l*.	For Sums between 50*l*. & 100*l*	For Sums between 50*l*. & 20*l*.	For Sums under 20*l*.	Total.	In custody Jan. 1. 1828.
King's Bench prison - -	474	354	550	213	1,591	674
Fleet prison - - -	206	141	223	113	683	253
Whitecross-street prison - -	206	273	816	600	1,893	378
Marshalsea prison - -	20	30	166	414	630	102
Horsemonger-lane prison - -	57	58	134	923	1,172	105
Total -	963	856	1,889	2,263	5,969	1,512

It is time, certainly, that something effectual were done to put an end to such
flagrant abuses — to a system that sends 923 persons to a single prison for debt
under 20*l*.! We do not mean to say or insinuate that credit may not frequently
be given to the labouring classes with the best effects : but it is of its abuse that
we complain, of its being indiscriminately granted to every one; to those whom
encourages to continue in a course of idleness and profligacy, as well as to those
industrious and deserving persons to whom it may occasionally be of the greatest
service. To secure the advantages of credit to the public, free from the enormous
evils that result from its abuse, is an object of the highest importance; and few
things, we believe, would do so much to secure it, as the taking from creditors
the power to arrest and imprison for debt. (See BANKRUPTCY.)

It was stated in the House of Commons, (19th February, 1827,) that in the
space of two years and a half, 70,000 persons were arrested in and about London, at
an expense to the parties, it may be estimated, of between 150,000*l*. and 200,000*l*.
In 1827, in the metropolis and two adjoining counties, 23,515 warrants to arrest
were granted, and 11,317 bailable processes were executed. Hence it may be
concluded, that in this single year, within the above limits, no fewer than 12,000 persons were deprived of their liberty, on the mere allegation of others, without any
proof that they owed them a farthing ! Well might Lord Eldon say " that *the law
of arrest is a permission to commit acts of greater oppression and inhumanity than a
to be met with in slavery itself*, and that the redress of such a grievance would not
be attended with any fatal consequences to the country."

We defy any one to show that the law of arrest and imprisonment has a single
good consequence to be placed as a set-off against the intolerable evils of which
it is productive. Tradesmen depend, as is clearly evinced by the above statement,
upon the despotical power which it puts in their hands, to get them out of scrapes
and believe that the fear of being subjected to arrest will stimulate even the most
suspicious portion of their debtors to make payment of their accounts. The records
of our prisons, and of our insolvent and other courts, show how miserably these expectations are disappointed. We believe, indeed, that we are warranted in affirming
that the more respectable classes of shopkeepers and tradesmen are now generally
satisfied that the present system requires some very material modifications. The
law of arrest and imprisonment is, in fact, advantageous to none but knaves and
swindlers, and the lowest class of attorneys, who frequently buy up small accounts
and bills, that they may bring actions upon them, and enrich themselves at the
expense of the poor, by the magnitude of their charges. Such oppressive proceedings are a disgrace to a civilised country. Were the law in question repealed,
credit would be granted to those only who deserved it ; for, generally speaking,
tradesmen, supposing they had nothing to trust to but their own discretion, would
not deal, except for ready money, with those of whose character and situation they
were not perfectly informed; and the difficulty under which all idle and impro-
dent persons would thus be placed of obtaining loans, would do much to wean
them from their vicious courses, and to render them industrious and honest.

The power of taking goods in execution for debts is also one that requires
to be materially modified. At present the household furniture of every man, and
even the *implements used in his trade*, should there be nothing else to lay hold of
may be seized and sold in satisfaction of any petty claim. It seems to us quite
clear that some limits should be set to this power; and that such articles as are
indispensable either to the subsistence or the business of any poor man ought to
be exempted from execution, and, perhaps, distress. The present practice,

ing its victims of the means of support and employment, drives them to de-
and is productive only of crimes and disorders.

t we are disposed to think that by far the most desirable reform that could
fected in this department would be, not only to take away the power of
: and imprisonment, except in the case of *fraudulent* bankruptcy, but *to
away all action for debts under a given sum, as* 40*l.* or 50*l.* The only
tion to this rule should be in the case of *claims for wages,* or labour
under executory contracts. To prevent the measure from being defeated,
ction should be granted on bills under 50*l.*, except upon those drawn
 upon regular bankers. This would be a radical change certainly; but
e fully satisfied that it would be highly advantageous to every class of the
unity, and most of all to labourers, retail dealers, and small tradesmen. It
protect the former from oppression, at the same time that it would tend
fully to render them more provident and considerate; it would teach the
to exercise that discretion in the granting of credit which is so very indis-
ble; and it would be publicly beneficial, by strengthening the moral principle,
aking the contraction of debts for small sums, without the means of paying
at once difficult and disgraceful.

agree entirely in opinion with those who think that it is to no purpose to
pt to remedy the defects now pointed out, by establishing courts of conscience
her devices for facilitating the speedy recovery of small debts. This is be-
g at the wrong end. The object ought not to be to enforce payment of such
 but *to prevent their contraction.* A measure of the sort here proposed
not, as some appear to imagine, annihilate credit. It would, no doubt, an-
e that spurious indiscriminating species of credit, that is as readily granted
spendthrift and prodigal, as to the frugal and industrious individual; but to
me extent that it deprived the former of the means of obtaining accommo-
, it would extend those of the latter. Nothing short of this — nothing but
acing of all small debts beyond the pale of the law — will ever fully impress
men with a conviction of the vast advantages that would result to themselves
heir withdrawing their confidence from courts and prisons, and preventing every
om getting upon their books, of whose situation and circumstances they are
lly aware; nor will any thing else be able completely to eradicate the flagrant
 inherent in the present credit system, and which have gone far to render
blic nuisance.

some valuable remarks and observations on the topics now treated of, see
eatise on the Police, &c. of the Metropolis,* by the author of the " Cabinet
r," pp. 114—134.

EW, the company of sailors belonging to any ship or vessel. No ship is
ed to be a British ship, unless duly registered and navigated as such by a
three fourths of which are British subjects, besides the master.—(6 *Geo.* 4.
 § 12.) The master or owners of any British ship having a foreign seaman
rd not allowed by law, shall for every such seaman forfeit 10*l.*; unless they
ow, by the certificate of the British consul or of two British merchants, or
tisfactorily prove, that the requisite number of British seamen could not be
ed at the place where the foreign seaman was taken on board. It is also
d that the master of every British vessel arriving from the West Indies
eliver, within ten days after arrival, to the Custom-house, a list of the crew
rd at the time of clearing out from the United Kingdom, and of arrival in
est Indies, and of every seaman who has deserted or died during the voyage,
e amount of wages due to each so dying, under a penalty of 50*l.*—(6 *Geo.*
7; 7 *Geo.* 4. c. 148.)

BEBS (Ger. *Kubeben;* Fr. *Cubebes;* It. *Cubebi;* Sp. *Cubebas;* Rus. *Kubebü;*
iper Cubeba;* Arab. *Kebābch;* Malay, *Komoonkoos;* Hind. *Cubab-chinie*), the
e of a tree growing in Java and Nepaul, particularly the former. It is a
ried fruit, like a pepper corn, but somewhat longer. Cubebs have a hot,
t, aromatic, slightly bitter taste; and a fragrant, agreeable odour. They
 be chosen large, fresh, sound, and the heaviest that can be procured. The
y entered for home consumption in 1830 amounted to 18,540 lbs., pro-
a nett revenue of 1,854*l.* 6*s.* Their price in the London market, (July,
in bond, varies from 4*l.* to 4*l.* 4*s.* per cwt.

CUMBER, a tropical plant, of which there are many species, largely
ed in hothouses in England.

CUDBEAR, a purple or violet coloured powder used in dyeing violet, purple, crimson, prepared from a species of lichen (*Lichen tartareus*, Lin.), or crustace moss, growing commonly on limestone rocks in Sweden, Scotland, the nort England, &c. About 130 tons of this lichen are annually exported from Swee It commonly sells in the port of London for about 20*l.* per ton; but to prepa for use it must be washed and dried; and by these operations the weight is c monly diminished a half, and the price, in effect, doubled. Though posses great beauty and lustre at first, the colours obtained from cudbear are so fugacious, that they ought never to be employed but in aid of some other m permanent dye, to which they may give body and vivacity. In this country chiefly used to give strength and brilliancy to the blues dyed with indigo, an produce a saving of that article; it is also used as a *ground* for madder reds, w commonly incline too much to yellow, and are made *rosy* by this addition. name cudbear was given to this powder by Dr. Cuthbert Gordon, who, ha obtained a patent for the preparation, chose, in this way, to connect it with own name.—(*Bancroft, Philosophy of Permanent Colours*, vol. i. pp. 300—304

CUMMIN-SEED (Ger. *Kumin;* Du. *Komyn;* Fr. *Cumin;* It. *Comino, Cum* Sp. *Comino;* Rus. *Kmin, Timon;* Arab. *Kemun*), the seeds of an annual p (*Cuminum Cyminum*, Lin.), a native of Egypt, but extensively cultivated in Si and Malta. They have a strong, peculiar, heavy odour, and a warm, bitter disagreeable taste. They are long and slender.

CURRANTS (Fr. *Raisins de Corinthe;* Ger. *Korinthen;* It. *Uve passe di* into; Lat. *Passulæ Corinthiacæ;* Rus. *Korinka, Opoek;* Sp. *Pasas de Corinto* small species of grape, largely cultivated in Zante and Cephalonia, and in Morea, particularly in the vicinity of Patrass. They are dried in the sun, and packed in large butts. There is a considerable demand for currants; and notw standing the exorbitant duty of 44*s.* 4*d.* a cwt. with which they are loaded, t were 117,860 cwt. imported for home consumption in 1828, producing a reve of 261,300*l.* There can, however, be no doubt that the revenue derived f currants, as well as the consumption, would be very decidedly increased, were duty reduced to 10*s.* or 12*s.* The price of currants in London, exclusive of duty, may, at an average, be taken at from 20*s.* to 26*s.* a cwt.: and as they applicable to many culinary purposes, (making, exclusive of their other uses, w mixed with flour and a little fat, a very agreeable dish,) and might be importee much larger quantities without any material increase of price, nothing but a duction of the present exorbitant duty seems to be required to render the very important commercial article.

No abatement of duties is made on account of any damage received by currants.

Currants, the produce of Europe, are not to be imported for home use except in British ships, ships of the country of which they are the produce, or of the country whence they are import (6 *Geo.* 4. c. 109.)

Currants imported in foreign ships are deemed *alien goods*, and pay town and port duties as sue (6 *Geo.* 4. c. 111.)

A Treasury letter of the 30th March, 1816, directs the following tares to be allowed, with liberty merchant and officers to take the actual tare when either party is dissatisfied.

Currants in casks from Zante	-	13 per cent.
Leghorn	-	10 —
Trieste	-	10 —

CUSTOM-HOUSE, the house or office where commodities are entere importation or exportation; where the duties, bounties, or drawbacks payab receivable upon such importation or exportation are paid or received; and w ships are cleared out, &c.

For information as to the proceedings necessary at the Custom-house on porting or exporting commodities, see the article IMPORTATION and EXPORTAT

The principal British Custom-house is in London; but there are Cus houses subordinate to the latter in all considerable sea-port towns.

CUSTOMS, are duties charged upon commodities on their being imported or exported from a country.

Custom duties seem to have existed in every commercial country. The Athe laid a tax of a fifth on the corn and other merchandise imported from foreign cour and also on several of the commodities exported from Attica. The *portoria*, or cus payable on the commodities imported into, and exported from, the different ports i Roman empire, formed a very ancient and important part of the public revenue. rates at which they were charged were fluctuating and various, and little is now k respecting them. Cicero informs us, that the duties on corn exported from the po Sicily were, in his time, 5 per cent. Under the imperial government, the amou

portoria depended as much on the caprice of the prince as on the real exigencies of state. Though sometimes diminished, they were never entirely remitted, and were ch more frequently increased. Under the Byzantine emperors, they were as high as ‖ per cent. — (*Supp. to Encyc. Brit.*, art. *Taxation*.)

Customs seem to have existed in England before the Conquest; but the king's claim them was first established by stat. 3 Edw. 1. These duties were, at first, principally on wool, woolfels (sheep-skins), and leather when exported. There were also ex-rdinary duties paid by aliens, which were denominated *parva costuma*, to distinguish n from the former, or *magna costuma*. The duties of tonnage and poundage, of ch mention is so frequently made in English history, were custom duties; the first ‖g paid on wine by the ton, and the latter being an *ad valorem* duty of so much a nd on all other merchandise. When these duties were granted to the crown, they e denominated *subsidies ;* and as the duty of poundage had continued for a lengthened od at the rate of 1*s.* a pound, or 5 per cent., a subsidy came, in the language of the oms, to denote an *ad valorem* duty of 5 per cent. The *new subsidy* granted in the n of William III. was an addition of 5 per cent. to the duties on most imported modities.

he various custom duties were collected, for the first time, in a book of rates pub-d in the reign of Charles II. ; a new book of rates being again published in the n of George I. But, exclusive of the duties entered in these two books, many more been imposed at different times; so that the accumulation of the duties, and the plicated regulations to which they gave rise, was productive of the greatest embar-nent. The evil was increased by the careless manner in which new duties were d to the old ; a per centage being sometimes added to the original tax, while at r times the commodity was estimated by a new standard of bulk, weight, number, lue, and charged with an additional impost, without any reference to the duties erly imposed. The confusion arising from these sources was still farther aug-ted by the special appropriation of each of the duties, and the consequent neces-of a separate calculation for each. The intricacy and confusion inseparable from a state of things proved a serious injury to commerce, and led to many frauds and es.

he Customs Consolidation Act, introduced by Mr. Pitt in 1787, did much to remedy e inconveniences. The method adopted was, to abolish the existing duties on all les, and to substitute in their stead one single duty on each article, equivalent to the egate of the various duties by which it had previously been loaded. The resolutions hich the act was founded amounted to about 3,000. A more simple and uniform m was, at the same time, introduced into the business of the Custom-house. These ations were productive of the very best effects; and several similar consolidations since been effected. The last of these took place in 1825, when the various statutes existing relative to the customs, amounting, including parts of statutes, to about were consolidated and compressed into only eleven statutes of a reasonable bulk, drawn up with great perspicuity.* Since then, a few statutes have been passed, nding and changing some of the provisions in the consolidation statutes.

he Board of Customs is not to consist of more than thirteen commissioners, and are to be reduced to eleven as vacancies occur. The Treasury may appoint one nissioner, and two assistant commissioners, to act for Scotland and Ireland.

ficers of customs taking any fee or reward, whether pecuniary or of any other sort, count of any thing done, or to be done, by them in the exercise of their duty, from ne, except by the order or permission of the commissioners of the customs, shall smissed their office ; and the person giving, offering, or promising, such gratuity, &c. shall forfeit 100*l.*

ny officer of customs who shall accept of any bribe, recompence, or reward, to in-him to neglect his duty, or to do, conceal, or connive at any act whereby any of rovisions of the customs laws shall be evaded, shall be dismissed the service, and be red incapable of serving his Majesty in future in any capacity whatever ; and the n offering such bribe, recompence, &c. shall, whether the offer be accepted or not, t 500*l.*

stom duties, like all duties on particular commodities, though advanced in the first nce by the merchant, are ultimately paid by those by whom they are consumed. n a government lays a duty on the foreign commodities which enter its ports, the falls entirely on such of its own subjects as purchase these commodities ; for the gners would cease supplying its markets with them, if they did not get the full of the commodities, exclusive of the tax ; and, for the same reason, when a govern-lays a duty on the commodities which its subjects are about to export, the duty not fall on them, but on the foreigners by whom they are bought. If, therefore,

* 6 Geo. 4. c. 106, 107, 108, 109, 110, 111, 112, 113, 114, 115, and 116.

it were possible for a country to raise a sufficient revenue by laying duties on export commodities, such revenue would be wholly derived from others, and it would be total relieved from the burden of taxation, except in so far as duties might be imposed b foreigners on the goods it imports from them. Care, however, must be taken, in in posing duties on exportation, not to lay them on commodities that may be produced a the same, or nearly the same, cost by foreigners ; for the effect of the duty would the be to cause the market to be supplied by others, and to put an entire stop to their expor ation. But in the event of a country possessing any decided natural or acquired advan tage in the production of any sort of commodities, a duty on their exportation woul seem to be the most unexceptionable of all taxes. If the Chinese chose to act on the principle, they might derive a considerable revenue from a duty on exported teas, whic would fall entirely on the English and other foreigners who buy them. The coal an tin, and perhaps, also, some of the manufactured goods produced in this country, seen to be in this predicament.

The revenue derived from the custom duties in 1590, in the reign of Elizabet amounted to no more than 50,000*l.* In 1613, it had increased to 148,075*l.* ; of whic no less than 109,572*l.* were collected in London. In 1660, at the Restoration, tl customs produced 421,582*l.* ; and at the Revolution, in 1688, they produced 781,98? During the reigns of William III. and Anne, the customs revenue was considerab augmented, the nett payments into the exchequer in 1712 being 1,315,423*l.* Durin the war terminated by the peace of Paris in 1763, the nett produce of the custom revenue of Great Britain amounted to nearly two millions. In 1792, it amounted 4,407,000*l.* In 1815, at the close of the war, it amounted to 11,360,000*l.* ; and la year it amounted to about 18,000,000*l.*, and, including Ireland, to about 19,500,000*l.*

Astonishing, however, as the increase of the customs revenue has certainly been, it not quite so great as it appears. Formerly the duties on some considerable articles, suc as sugar, brandy, wine, &c. imported from abroad, were divided partly into custom duties charged on their importation, and partly into excise duties on their being take into consumption. But these duties have now, with the exception of tea, been tran ferred wholly to the customs; the facilities afforded, by means of the warehousin system, for paying the duties in the way most convenient for the merchant, havin obviated the necessity of dividing them into different portions.

It will be seen from various articles in this work (see BRANDY, GENEVA, SMUGGLIN TEA, TOBACCO, &c.), that the exorbitant amount of the duties laid on many articles im ported from abroad, leads to much smuggling and fraud ; and requires, besides, an extr ordinary expense in many departments of the customs service, which might be total avoided were these duties reduced within reasonable limits. This, however, is tl business of government, and not of those entrusted with the management of the custom and it would be unjust to the latter not to mention that this department has been esse tially improved, during the last few years, both as respects economy and efficiency. T following extracts from a letter to the Right Hon. H. Goulburn, ascribed to the prese chairman of the Board of Customs (R. B. Dean, Esq.), give a brief but satisfacto view of the improvements that have been effected : —

" As regards the department of customs in 1792, the principal officers engaged in t receipt of the duties in the port of London were patent officers.

" The first Earl of Liverpool was collector inwards.

" The late Duke of Manchester, collector outwards.

" The Duke of Newcastle, and afterwards the Earl of Guilford, comptroller inwa and outwards.

" Lord Stowell, surveyor of subsidies and petty customs.

" These noblemen took no part in the official duties, but merely exercised the rig of appointing deputies and clerks.

" Both principals and deputies were remunerated by fees. The patentees receiv the fees denominated patent, and the deputies retained the fees called the fees of usa for their own use. In addition to these fees, both deputies and clerks received fees despatch.

" The same system prevailed throughout the whole department. The salaries of officers were nominal ; and the principal proportion of all official income was deriv from fees. These fees were constantly varying both in rate and amount, and forme continual source of dispute and complaint between the merchant and the officer.

" This system (after having been repeatedly objected to by various commissions inquiry, and finally by the committee of finance in 1797,) was put an end to in the y 1812, by the act 51 Geo. 3. c. 71., by which all patent offices and fees were abolish and compensation allowances granted to the patent officers, and fixed salaries establish

" The additional salaries granted under this arrangement amounted to about 200,00 and the temporary compensation allowances to about 40,000*l.* per annum.

The fees abolished, and from which the public were relieved, amounted to about 00l. per annum.

n addition to the amount of fees from which the public were relieved, various ances made by the crown to officers for quarantine, coal poundage, poundage on es, and many other incidental allowances, which did not appear on the establish-were also abolished, and the salaries of every officer placed at one view upon the ishment.

he effect of these salutary measures has been to give a great apparent increase to s' salaries since 1792; and, upon a mere comparison of the establishment of 1792 830, without the above explanation, it would appear that the pay of the officers en most materially augmented, whereas, in point of fact, the difference is in the of payment; and the incomes of the officers at the present period (as compared 792) are in general less; and, consequently, the public are less taxed for the per-nce of the same duty *now* than in 1792.

n the year 1792, the warehousing system had not been established. Officers were ted at all ages, and there was no system of classification or promotion. The officers out-ports and in London were generally appointed through local influence; and oo often persons who had failed in trade, or had been in menial service, and who ed their situations rather as a comfortable provision for their families than as offices nich efficient services were required. The superintendence and powers of the were cramped and interfered with by circumstances and considerations which ted the enforcement of wholesome regulation. The whole system was so imper-o far back only as 1818, that a special commission was appointed to inquire into partment; and, upon the recommendation of that commission, various regulations een adopted.

he age of admission has been limited; a system of classification and promotion of s, and a graduated scale of salaries established throughout the whole department; y this means, local interference in the promotion of officers has been abolished; endance of officers increased, regulated, and strictly enforced; holidays reduced orty-six in the year to three; viz. Good Friday, the king's birthday, and Christ-ay; useless oaths, and bonds, and forms of documents of various kinds, disconti-increased facility and despatch afforded to the merchant's business; the accounts n the different offices, and returns of all kinds, revised, simplified, and reduced; rious minor regulations of detail established; the whole machinery of the depart-emodelled, and adapted to the trade and commerce of the country.

Ireland the number of officers employed at all the ports, in the year ended the January, 1830, and the salaries and charges, did not much exceed the number and e at the port of Dublin alone in 1818: and, within the space of eleven years, two thirds of the officers employed at the ports in Ireland have been discontinued; mber having been in 1818, 1755; in 1829, 544: and an annual reduction in sa-nd charges has been effected to the extent of 173,724l.; the amount having been 3, 285,115l.; in 1829, 111,391l. (103,813l. of that amount having been reduced n the years 1823 and 1828), upon an expenditure of 285,115l.; and the receipts early equal, in 1827, to those of 1818 and 1823, notwithstanding the total repeal cross Channel duties, amounting to about 340,000l. per annum, subsequent to the eriod.

ready has government relinquished, it may be said, any interference with pro-in the department of the customs, and the road is open to advancement to the ious officer.

fluence is no longer allowed to prevail; and in many cases which have recently d, and in which the patronage of government might have been fairly exercised, een at once abandoned, in order to give way to arrangements by which the services e very intelligent and highly respectable officers, whose offices had been abolished, e again rendered available, with a material saving to the public.

a recent order from the Lords of the Treasury, of the 20th February, 1830, the of the commissioners, and of other officers, have been prospectively reduced, and ns given to revise the whole establishment in the spirit of that order, with a view y possible reduction."

e are very great improvements, certainly, and reflect much credit on the govern-nd on the Board by whom its efforts have been zealously seconded; but we are, standing, satisfied that very great reductions may still be made in the cost of the hment. These, however, are not to be effected by reducing the salaries of the which, if any thing, are now too low; but by lessening the demand for their , by reducing and simplifying the duties. The coast guard and coast blockade ter is under the orders of the Admiralty), costing together above 400,000l. a year, e wholly dispensed with, were it not for the exorbitant duties on brandy, gin, and

tobacco — duties which seem to be intended only to encourage smuggling ; and whic is quite certain would be three times as productive as they are at this moment, were reduced to *one third* of their present amount. The duties on a great variety of s articles might also be entirely repealed, without any sensible loss of revenue, and great advantage to commerce: and were these alterations effected, and the proceedings respect to the entry and clearing out of ships and goods adequately simplified, a *great saving* might be made in this department, and the services of a large numbe those now employed in it might be dispensed with.

In Scotland, separate Custom-houses seem to be multiplied to an absurd ex Within these few years, indeed, a very considerable change for the better was eff in the Scotch Custom-house ; but it is still susceptible of, and ought to be subjected great curtailment.

The reader will find, in the accounts of most imported articles of any consequ given in this work, statements of the customs duty paid on their importation. It be gratifying, however, to have them all brought together in one point of view, a the following table : —

Account of the Gross Receipt and Nett Produce of the Revenue of Customs in the United dom, in the Year ending the 5th January, 1831 ; distinguishing the Amount collected on each A usually producing 1,000*l.* or more per Annum, and also the Amount of Payments out of the Receipt during the said Year, for Drawbacks and Bounties of the nature of Drawbacks, and for A ances on Over-Entries, Damages, &c.

List of Articles.	Gross Receipt.	Payments out of the Gross Receipt.		Nett Produ
		Drawbacks and Bounties of the nature of Drawbacks.	Re-payments on Over-Entries, Damaged Goods, &c.	
	£　s.　d.	£　s.　d.	£　s.　d.	£　s
Acid, Boracic - - -	5,295　8　11	-	14　5　0	5,282
Alkanet Root - - -	2,651　14　7	0　7　6	-	2,651
Almonds - - -	18,610　8　4	145　0　3	191　7　8	18,274
Aloes - - -	4,235　7　3	24　18　6	-	4,210
Angelica - - -	520　1　3	-	-	520
Annotto - - -	1,246　6　11	-	-	1,246
Apples, not dried -	4,261　5　6	-	30　19　0	4,230
Argol - - -	2,055　2　9	-	15　11　0	2,039
Arrow Root or Powder	2,223　17　6	-	20　3　8	2,203
Ashes, Pearl and Pot	4,939　15　5	4　2　3	4　18　8	4,930
Bacon and Hams -	2,180　14　0	-	16　0　9	2,164
Balsams - - -	5,357　2　1	-	24　6　0	5,269
Barilla and Alkali -	65,862　1　2	17,825　15　2	36　0　11	48,000
Bark, Oak and Cork Tree -	35,157　4　4	-	131　9　0	35,025
Bark Quercitron -	1,398　13　11	-	2　1　5	1,396
Baskets - - -	843　3　6	-	-	843
Beef, salted - - -	301　18　8	-	9　19　10	291
Beer, Spruce - -	7,735　17　4	-	3　5　11	7,732
Books - - -	11,865　4　4	-	54　10　2	11,810
Boots, Shoes, and Calashes	3,496　2　1	-	0　12　0	3,495
Borax - - -	1,628　13　9	-	2　10　0	1,626
Boxes of all sorts -	3,849　15　5	-	85　1　6	3,764
Brimstone - - -	6,652　17　4	-	24　1　1	6,628
Bristles - - -	27,062　11　10	-	80　0　10	26,982
Bugles - - -	2,746　16　4	-	-	2,746
Butter - - -	102,881　18　10	-	129　15　2	102,752
Canes of all sorts -	3,729　13　0	-	-	3,729
Cantharides - - -	2,760　12　6	57　1　0	-	2,703
Capers - - -	1,722　2　6	-	0　11　6	1,721
Cassia Lignea - -	1,324　5　11	-	0　10　0	1,323
Cheese - - -	55,093　12　9	-	222　13　4	54,870
Chinaware, Porcelain, and Earthen-ware	7,132　17　6	-	105　15　10	7,027
Cinnamon - - -	709　5　0	-	-	709
Clocks - - -	6,500　16　2	-	152　9　1	6,348
Cloves - - -	6,061　9　7	-	-	6,061
Cochineal, Granilla and Dust	4,480　8　11	-	15　1　6	4,465
Cocoa, Cocoa Nut, Husks and Shells, and Chocolate	13,650　6　5	-	28　13　2	13,621
Coffee - - -	579,844　19　7	323　11　0	157　18　0	579,363
Coral Beads - -	2,758　18　2	-	0　7　11	2,758
Cordage and Cables -	162　17　5	-	17　0　6	145
Cork, unmanufactued -	15,982　9　11	-	42　0　1	15,240
Corks, ready made -	799　8　0	-	0　7　0	799
Corn, Grain, Meal and Flour, (including Buck-Wheat)	798,082　6　7	-	7,972　8　11	790,109
Cotton Manufactures, not otherwise described	3,414　7　4	-	13　14　6	3,400
Cream of Tartar -	2,671　5　4	-	17　7　3	2,653
Cubebs - - -	1,854　6　0	-	-	1,854
Currants - - -	263,124　10　4	1,057　16　4	396　8　10	261,670
Dye and Hard Woods : viz.				
Box wood -	1,819　14　7	-	5　0　0	1,814
Cedar, under 8 inches square	525　6　6	-	0　1　8	525

List of Articles.	Gross Receipt.	Drawbacks and Bounties of the nature of Drawbacks.	Repayments on Over-Entries, Damaged Goods, &c.	Nett Produce.
	£ s. d.	£ s. d.	£ s. d.	£ s. d.
Fustic Logwood - - -	1,214 9 7	- -	12 14 4	1,201 15 3
Logwood - - -	2,012 3 8	- -	17 2 6	1,995 1 2
Mahogany - - -	59,977 6 6	- -	87 9 1	59,889 17 5
Nicaragua - - -	1,102 12 1	- -	7 18 3	1,094 13 10
Rosewood - - -	10,491 19 4	- -	1 9 6	10,490 9 10
gs - - -	18,519 1 4	- -	13 6 8	18,505 14 8
phants' Teeth - -	3,721 7 2	- -	32 10 6	3,688 16 8
broidery and Needle-work -	4,863 7 7	- -	135 0 0	4,728 7 7
ence of Bergamot and Lemons -	3,087 17 11	- -	- -	3,087 17 11
thers for Beds - -	4,579 5 2	- -	18 18 8	4,560 6 6
—— Ostrich - -	1,062 8 9	- -	- -	1,062 8 9
s - - -	21,118 6 8	131 9 0	137 0 2	20,849 17 6
h, Anchovies - -	1,441 3 9	- -	9 12 0	1,431 11 9
- Eels - -	924 16 6	- -	- -	924 16 6
- Oysters - -	514 17 6	- -	- -	514 17 6
x and Tow, or Codilla of Hemp and Flax -	3,993 19 4	- -	28 0 2	3,965 19 2
wers, Artificial (not of Silk) -	777 7 10	- -	0 15 0	776 12 10
s - - -	31,957 2 11	16 8 0	4 11 0	31,936 3 11
ger, Dry - -	3,623 13 7	4 8 10	59 5 11	3,559 18 10
ss; viz. Bottles, Green or Common -	11,494 10 7	- -	11 6 10	11,483 3 9
—— of all other sorts -	5,703 19 6	- -	53 18 9	5,650 0 9
ins, Guinea - -	1,809 16 0	- -	- -	1,809 16 0
pes - -	1,641 0 3	- -	0 1 0	1,640 19 3
n, Animi and Copal -	3,068 17 9	- -	14 11 11	3,054 5 10
—— Arabic - -	6,383 17 11	- -	- -	6,383 17 11
—— Lac of all sorts -	5,992 14 8	- -	4 10 6	5,988 4 2
—— Senegal - -	4,501 18 7	- -	44 0 9	4,457 17 10
—— Tragacanth -	1,412 15 0	3 0 0	- -	1,409 15 0
r, Horse - -	213 4 3	- -	0 7 0	212 17 3
- Human - -	846 9 8	- -	0 6 0	846 3 8
r or Goats' Wool, Manufactures of	4,814 0 0	- -	15 17 0	4,798 3 0
s of Chip and Straw -	48,417 16 3	- -	136 11 4	48,281 4 11
np - - -	80,828 7 9	5,752 14 1	756 17 3	74,318 16 5
es, not Tanned - -	42,534 8 11	- -	384 11 9	42,149 17 2
—— Tanned - -	1,254 4 2	- -	1 5 0	1,252 19 2
ns, Horn Tips and Pieces -	1,414 16 10	- -	12 15 1	1,402 1 9
ses - -	1,150 12 0	- -	1 0 0	1,149 12 0
p - - -	3,639 16 5	27 9 0	- -	3,612 7 5
go - - -	34,348 5 7	- -	86 1 5	34,262 4 2
in Bars - -	19,554 12 11	- -	56 17 3	19,497 15 8
of all other sorts -	1,245 1 8	- -	7 14 2	1,237 7 6
glass - -	3,426 9 3	- -	6 15 7	3,419 13 8
e of Lemons, Limes, & Oranges	2,192 4 9	- -	0 3 1	2,192 1 8
e, Thread - -	5,680 6 4	- -	24 0 7	5,656 5 9
uered Ware - -	643 11 6	- -	- -	643 11 6
l, Black - -	1,100 19 7	- -	21 15 0	1,079 4 7
her Gloves - -	2,323 8 9	- -	0 9 9	2,322 19 0
—— Manufactures of, except -	19,488 1 7	- -	29 3 0	19,458 18 7
oots, Shoes, and Gloves -	795 13 2	- -	4 5 0	791 8 2
ons and Oranges -	59,564 8 6	- -	318 12 6	59,245 16 0
ns, Foreign - -	20,726 14 10	- -	27 5 4	20,699 9 6
orice Juice - -	21,195 12 2	- -	3 6 3	21,192 5 11
e - - -	2,205 3 3	- -	- -	2,205 3 3
der and Madder Root -	17,652 11 9	- -	39 2 6	17,613 9 3
na - - -	1,156 11 3	10 8 9	- -	1,146 2 6
of Russia - -	5,652 7 5	- -	14 10 5	5,637 17 0
of other sorts -	1,152 4 5	- -	10 9 11	1,141 14 6
sses - -	160,429 14 5	- -	746 7 6	159,683 6 11
cal Instruments -	1,980 16 3	- -	15 9 0	1,965 7 3
h - - -	1,222 5 0	15 18 3	- -	1,206 6 9
negs - -	15,183 5 1	- -	25 5 0	15,158 0 1
, Chestnuts -	1,467 1 6	- -	41 6 5	1,425 15 1
Small - -	13,561 2 0	- -	3 15 0	13,557 7 0
Walnuts - -	1,615 5 6	- -	5 5 0	1,610 0 6
astor - -	4,235 10 10	- -	12 18 0	4,222 12 10
hemical and Perfumed, of all ther sorts -	7,831 8 7	- '	- -	7,831 8 7
live - - -	71,879 11 9	- -	98 16 1	71,780 15 8
alm - - -	22,468 5 1	- -	40 6 10	22,427 18 3
rain, Spermaceti, and Blubber	4,657 1 8	- -	10 10 3	4,646 11 5
m - - -	954 11 11	- -	- -	954 11 11
al and Orchelia -	4,543 4 0	14 8 0	0 16 0	4,528 0 0
r - - -	353 12 5	- -	- -	353 12 5
- for Hangings -	1,927 19 2	- -	2 9 6	1,925 9 8
er of all sorts -	1,495 5 0	- -	19 6 3	1,475 18 9
xes - -	100,498 9 10	- -	6 7 0	100,492 2 10
ces - -	3,454 15 1	- -	49 2 1	3,405 13 0
nto - - -	7,267 11 3	- -	18 2 11	7,249 8 4
- - -	742 3 6	- -	4 5 4	737 18 2
ng of Chip or Straw -	6,689 9 10	- -	- -	6,689 9 10
s, dried - -	548 3 3	- -	2 9 1	545 14 2

| List of Articles. | Gross Receipt. | Payments out of the Gross Receipt. | | Nett Produce |
		Drawbacks and Bounties of the nature of Drawbacks.	Repayments on Over-Entries, Damaged Goods, &c.	
	£ s. d.	£ s. d.	£ s. d.	£ s.
Prints and Drawings - -	1,921 3 2	- -	2 7 2	1,918 16
Prunes - - -	7,558 14 11	- -	19 8 10	7,539 6
Quicksilver - - -	4,959 18 6	2 9 6	5 14 0	4,951 15
Quills, Goose - -	4,253 16 7	- -	0 17 6	4,252 19
Radix, Ipecacoanhœ -	868 16 10	28 17 4	64 0 0	775 19
Rags, &c. for Paper - -	2,335 10 3	- -	22 16 7	2,312 13
Raisins - - -	159,965 13 8	949 14 2	469 4 5	158,546 15
Rapeseed and other Oil Cakes	2,767 18 10	- -	36 17 9	2,731 1
Rhubarb - - -	4,324 2 10	0 4 0	-	4,323 18 1
Rice - - -	9,214 5 0	4,954 13 11	18 9 5	4,250 1
—— in the Husk -	25,856 11 1	-	-	2,856 11
Sago - - -	1,623 13 0	-	-	1,623 13
Saltpetre - - -	3,714 4 6	-	23 6 2	3,690 18
Sarsaparilla - - -	6,202 16 0	187 11 8	65 4 5	5,949 19 1
Scammony - -	2,366 8 8	11 17 6	66 16 4	2,287 13 1
Seeds of all sorts (including Tares)	135,123 11 3	0 4 0	340 8 7	134,782 18
Senna - - -	9,072 13 9	12 0 10	33 12 7	9,027 0
Ships' Hulls and Materials -	1,553 9 5	-	137 9 10	1,415 19
Shumac - - -	5,330 8 5	-	53 19 10	5,276 8
Silk, Raw - - -	15,749 17 8	-	98 18 6	15,650 19
—— Waste, Knubs and Husks	216 17 3	-	2 2 4	214 14
—— Thrown - -	73,551 0 8	36,690 8 7	2 2 0	36,858 10
—— Manufactures, East India	21,141 15 4	-	70 10 0	21,071 5
—————— not East India	136,388 2 2	-	1,136 4 5	135,251 17
Skins (not being Furs) -	17,498 11 0	-	301 14 2	17,196 16 1
Smalts - - -	9,327 17 1	-	16 1 6	9,311 15
Soap, Hard and Soft -	1,337 14 6	-	0 15 5	1,336 19
Spelter - - -	9,388 0 6	-	22 14 0	9,365 6
Spirits, Foreign, Rum -	1,599,941 16 0	-	496 9 1	1,599,445 6 1
————— Brandy -	1,432,724 8 7	-	720 3 1	1,432,004 5
————— Geneva -	34,718 7 4	-	50 0 2	34,668 7
————— of all other sorts	11,064 10 9	-	54 14 4	11,009 16
Spirits of the Manufacture of Guernsey and Jersey - }	2,832 8 7	-	7 14 6	2,824 14
Sponge - - -	3,502 5 6	-	19 10 0	3,482 15
Stones, viz. Burrs for Millstones	1,602 19 11	-	0 4 6	1,602 15
—— Marble Blocks -	1,961 11 1	-	148 11 0	1,813 0
Succades - - -	1,325 2 4	-	7 10 9	1,317 11
Sugar - - -	6,063,321 16 6	1,286,753 4 10	9,226 11 1	4,767,342 0
Tallow - - -	180,947 3 11	-	416 5 1	180,530 18 1
Tamarinds - - -	1,189 5 0	-	9 17 2	1,179 7
Tar - - -	8,756 4 9	-	112 10 7	8,643 14
Timber; — viz. { Balks and Ufers, under 5 inches square }	1,208 1 11	-	11 0 7	1,197 1
Battens and Batten Ends	111,305 10 4	5 16 8	481 4 9	110,818 8
Deals and Deal Ends -	568,651 5 10	55 14 6	8,063 13 5	560,531 17
Firewood - -	3,930 15 3	-	30 15 1	3,900 0
Fir Quarters - -	3,083 7 3	-	5 8 2	3,077 19
Knees of Oak - -	1,160 18 11	-	4 4 6	1,156 14
Lathwood - -	30,912 14 6	-	307 10 9	30,605 3
Masts and Spars -	12,051 9 11	-	57 17 7	11,993 12
Oak Plank - -	6,219 1 4	-	6 7 0	6,212 14
Oars - - -	808 9 4	-	3 9 10	804 19
Staves - - -	47,181 14 0	-	509 2 10	46,672 11
Teak - - -	11,104 0 11	-	22 13 4	11,081 7
Timber, Fir, 8 inches square or upwards }	542,227 1 8	33,878 12 1	15,294 12 8	493,053 16
—— Oak, - ditto	23,821 16 2	-	85 7 3	23,736 8
—— of other sorts, ditto	6,305 5 4	-	187 5 9	6,117 19
Wainscot Logs -	8,309 9 8	-	36 15 8	8,272 14
Tobacco and Snuff - -	2,938,050 10 10	13,719 6 9	66 10 2	2,924,264 13
Tortoise Shell - -	825 9 0	-	7 19 10	817 9
Toys - - -	3,624 18 5	-	47 5 0	3,577 13
Turpentine, common -	57,739 1 10	-	50 2 0	57,688 19
Valonia - - -	11,664 8 2	-	288 3 10	11,376 4
Verdigris - - -	3,894 2 6	-	19 6 0	3,874 16
Vermicelli and Macaroni -	2,246 4 3	-	34 11 0	2,211 13
Vinegar - - -	1,435 2 10	-	7 7 10	1,427 15
Water, Cologne, in flasks -	4,290 3 1	-	18 12 0	4,271 11
Wax, Bees - - -	5,901 14 10	-	8 12 4	5,893 2
Wines of all sorts - -	1,575,438 6 9	50,165 3 7	1,095 4 11	1,524,177 18
Wool, Cotton - -	360,637 6 1	-	649 5 8	359,988 0
—— Sheep and Lambs -	120,623 6 9	-	202 18 9	120,420 8
Woollen Manufactures, not otherwise described, including Carpets }	9,844 2 4	-	27 6 0	9,816 16
Yarn, Cotton - - -	1,147 9 4	-	6 8 0	1,141 1
—— Linen, Raw - -	971 3 7	-	8 19 5	962 4
Yellow Berries - -	1,609 15 10	-	0 7 0	1,609 8
Zaffar - - -	805 13 5	-	8 6 1	797 7
All other Merchandise -	97,420 9 8	122 0 4	1,151 2 2	96,147 7
Total Duties Inwards, carried forward - }	19,749,137 2 6	1,453,006 13 2	56,870 5 10	18,239,260 3

List of Articles.	Gross Receipt.	Payments out of the Gross Receipt.		Nett Produce.
		Drawbacks and Bounties of the nature of Drawbacks.	Repayments on Over-Entries, Damaged Goods, &c.	
	£ s. d.	£ s. d.	£ s. d.	£ s. d.
s and Culm exported -	63,889 17 6	- -	327 1 4	63,562 16 2
h Sheep and Lambs' Wool, } oollen Yarn, &c. exported - }	1,866 3 6	- -	- -	1,866 3 6
, ditto - - -	25 4 7	- -	- -	25 4 7
entage Duty on British Goods ;ported - - -	63,357 17 7	- -	1,193 9 10	62,164 7 9
otal Duties Outwards, carried } forward - - }	129,139 3 2		1,520 11 2	127,618 12 0
and Culm, Coastwise -	979,197 5 6	19,948 4 5	949 11 4	958,299 9 9
- ditto -	36,813 2 11	716 2 6	523 11 11	35,573 8 6
otal Duties Coastwise, carried } forward - - }	1,016,010 8 5	20,664 6 11	1,473 3 3	993,872 18 3
s Inwards - brought forward	19,749,137 2 6	1,453,006 13 2	56,870 5 10	18,239,260 3 6
Outwards - ditto	129,139 3 2	- -	1,520 11 2	127,618 12 0
Coastwise - ditto	1,016,010 8 5	20,664 6 11	1,473 3 3	993,872 18 3
	20,894,286 14 1	1,473,671 0 1	59,864 0 3	19,360,751 13 0
and Dock Duty -	47,201 13 0	- -	290 11 7	46,911 1 5
s collected at the Isle of Man	23,613 3 2	- -	- -	23,613 3 2
tances from the Plantations, luding Receipts of Plantation } zures - - - }	17,107 10 0	- -	- -	17,107 10 0
us Charge on Account of } nes and Seizures, exclusive } Legal Expenses - }	- -	- -	9,697 0 10	—
ds of Goods sold for the Duties	16,609 3 8	- -	84 6 0	16,524 17 8
of Legal Quays, Warehouse } nt, Wharfage, &c. &c. }	24,788 17 10	- -	41 0 0	24,747 17 10
ds of Surcharges, Sale of Old } res, &c. &c. - }	12,781 6 7	- -	13,776 6 10	—
	21,036,388 8 4	1,473,671 0 1	83,753 5 6	19,478,964 2 9
it received in reimbursement } Sums advanced out of the stoms Revenue of Ireland, } vy and Army Half Pay, Pen- ns, &c. in the Year 1829	48,136 11 4	- -	- -	48,136 11 4
Total - £	21,084,524 19 8	1,473,671 0 1	83,753 5 6	19,527,100 14 1

ector General's Office, Custom House, London, }
March 25th, 1831. }
William Irving,
Inspector General of Imports and Exports.

charges of collection on the customs revenue of the United Kingdom during the ear were —

	Great Britain.	Ireland.
	£ s. d.	£ s. d.
Civil Department - -	770,724 8 6½	146,751 9 2
Harbour Vessels - -	5,292 7 1¾	139 16 3
Cruisers - -	101,662 15 8½	10,575 7 0¾
Preventive Water Guard -	135,632 3 10¼	113,326 4 9¾
Land Guard ' -	11,084 12 8½	
	£1,024,396 7 11½	£270,792 17 3½

ector General of Imports and Exports.— Miserable Attempt at Economy in this De- nt. — The office of inspector general of imports and exports was established in The accounts of the trade and navigation of the country, annually laid before ent, are furnished by this Office ; and, owing to the improved manner in which ccounts are now made out, and the practice of giving statements of the quantities principal articles exported and imported, and the declared or real value of the they have become of great public importance. It is singular, however, that after existed for about 135 years, and being gradually brought to a high pitch of per- this office was last year rendered nearly useless by a pitiful attempt to save the f a couple of clerks! Previously to last year, the accounts of the trade and of the two great divisions of the empire were exhibited separately and jointly ; if any one, for example, wished to know the quantity of sugar entered for home ption in 1829, in Great Britain and in Ireland, he would have found the results ly stated ; and in the same way for the produce of any article or tax. Nothing,

it is plain, could be more desirable than an arrangement of this sort; which, ind
considering the entirely different situation of the two great divisions of the empire, is
only one capable of affording the means of drawing any useful conclusions.   But
year, ministers, in order to accomplish the miserable object already alluded to, had
the accounts consolidated into one mass (*rudis et indigesta moles*); so that it became
possible to tell what was the consumption of any article, or the produce of any tax, ei
in Great Britain or in Ireland, the only information communicated being the ger
result as to the United Kingdom ! Nothing more absurd was ever imagined.   On
principle that Ireland is taken into the same average with Great Britain, we m
take in Canada; for there is decidedly less difference between the condition and h
of the people of Canada and those of Britain, than there is between those of the Bri
and Irish.   But this measure was not objectionable merely from its confounding s
dissimilar elements, and laying a basis for the most absurd and unfounded inferen
it rendered all the previous accounts in a great measure useless; and would, ha
been persevered in, have effectually deprived statesmen and statisticians of some of
very best means of instituting a comparison between the past and future state of I
divisions of the empire.   Happily, however, this abortive attempt at economy has I
relinquished.   The moment Mr. Poulett Thomson attained to office, he took meas
for the restoration of that system which had been so unwisely abandoned; and every
in any degree conversant with matters of finance, commerce, or statistics, will agree
us in thinking that the Right Hon. Gentleman could have rendered few more accept
services.   The public accounts for 1830, the only ones made out on the new system
a disgrace to the country.   They ought to be withdrawn, and replaced by others.

CUTLERY, a term used to designate all manner of sharp and cutting ins
ments made of iron or steel, as knives, forks, scissors, razors, shears, scythes,
Sheffield is the principal seat of the cutlery manufacture; but the knives
other articles made in London are said to be of superior quality.

The act 59 Geo. 3. c. 7. gives the manufacturers of cutlery made of *wrought* steel, the privilege of n
ing or stamping them with the figure of a hammer; and prohibits the manufacturers of any artic
cutlery, edge tools, or hardware, *cast or formed in a mould*, or manufactured otherwise than by mea
a hammer, from marking or impressing upon them the figure of a hammer, or any symbol or devi
sembling it, on pain of forfeiting all such articles, and 5*l.* for every dozen.   A penalty of 10*l.* per d
exclusive of forfeiture, is also imposed upon every person having articles of cutlery in his possessio
the purpose of sale, marked with the words *London*, or *London made*, unless the articles so marked
been really manufactured within the city of London, or a distance of 20 miles from it.

CYPRESS, a forest tree of which there are many varieties, the species
nominated the evergreen cypress (*Cupressus sempervirens*) and the white c
(*Cupressus Thyoides*) being the most celebrated.

The cypress is indigenous in the southern parts of Europe, in several part
Asia, and in America.   It grows to a great size, and is a most valuable specie
timber.   It is never attacked by worms; and exceeds all other trees, even
cedar, in durability.   Hence the Athenians, when desirous to preserve the
mains of their heroes and other great men, had them enclosed in cypress coff
and hence, also, the external covering of the Egyptian mummies is made of
same enduring material.   The cypress is said to live to a great age; and this
cumstance, combined with its thick dark green foliage, has made it be rega
as the emblem of death and the grave.

In his Geography and History of the Western States of America, Mr. Timothy I
has given the following account of the cypress trees found in the southern parts o
valley of the Mississippi : — " These noble trees rear their straight columns from a I
cone-shaped buttress, whose circumference at the ground is, perhaps, three times th
the regular shaft of the tree.   This cone rises from 6 to 10 feet, with a regular and s
taper, and from the apex of the cone towers the perpendicular column, with little t
after it has left the cone, from 60 to 80 feet clear shaft.   Very near its top it begi
throw out multitudes of horizontal branches, which interlace with those of the adjo
trees, and, when bare of leaves, have an air of desolation and death, more easil
than described.   In the season of vegetation the leaves are short, fine, and of a ver
so deep, as almost to seem brown, giving an indescribable air of funereal solemnity t
singular tree.   A cypress forest, when viewed from the adjacent hills, with its numbe
interlaced arms covered with this dark brown foliage, has the aspect of a scaffoldi
verdure in the air.   It grows, too, in deep and sickly swamps, the haunts of fever,
quitoes, moccasin snakes, alligators, and all loathsome and ferocious animals,
congregate far from the abodes of man, and seem to make common cause with n
against him.   The cypress loves the deepest, most gloomy, inaccessible swamps;
south of 33°, is generally found covered with sable festoons of long moss, han
like shrouds of mourning wreaths, almost to the ground.   It seems to flourisl

n water covers its roots for half the year.   Unpromising as are the places and
umstances of its growth, no tree of the country where it is found is so extensively
ful.   It is free from knots, is easily wrought, and makes excellent planks, shingles,
timber of all sorts.   It is very durable, and incomparably the most valuable tree in
southern country of this valley." — (Vol. i. p. 62.)

D.

)AMAGED GOODS. — Goods, with the exceptions under-mentioned, receiv-
damage during the voyage, will be allowed an abatement of duty proportionally
the damage received, provided a claim for such abatement be made to the Board
Customs (if in London), or to the collector and comptroller (if in the out-
s), within four days from the time of the first examination of the goods, and
le they are in the custody of the officers.   Satisfactory proof must be given
the damage was received after the goods had been shipped.   If the officers
not estimate the damage, or if the importer is dissatisfied with their estimate,
may appoint two indifferent merchants, who shall estimate the damages upon
—(6 Geo. 4. c. 107.)   Should such goods be afterwards exported for draw-
, a like abatement will be made.   No abatement of duties is made on account
damage done to coffee, currants, figs, lemons, oranges, raisins, tobacco, and
e.

MAR, a kind of indurated pitch or turpentine exuding spontaneously from
ous trees indigenous to most of the Indian islands.   Different trees produce
rent species of resin, which are designated according to their colour and con-
nce.   " One is called *Damar-batu* in Malay, or *Damar-selo* in Javanese, which
ns hard or stony rosin; and another in common use *Damar-puteh*, or white
n, which is softer.   The trees which produce the damar yield it in amazing
ntity, and generally without the necessity of making incisions.   It exudes
ugh the bark; and is either found adhering to the trunk or branches in large
ss, or in masses, on the ground, under the trees.   As these often grow near
sea-side, or on the banks of rivers, the damar is frequently floated away, and
cted in distant places as drift.   It is exported in large quantities to Bengal
China; and is used for all the purposes to which we apply pitch, but princi-
in paying the bottoms of ships.   By a previous arrangement, almost any
ntity may be procured at Borneo, at the low rate of half a dollar per picul."—
wfurd, East. Archip. vol. i. p. 455.; vol. iii. p. 420.)

AMASK (Ger. *Damasten Tafelzeug;* Du. *Damaskwerk;* Fr. *Venise;* It. *Tela*
schina; Sp. *Tela adamascada;* Rus. *Kamtschatnüä salfftki*), a species of table
.   See LINEN.

ANTZIC, situated on the Vistula, near its mouth, in West Prussia, in lat. 54°
., lon. 18° 38′ E.   Population about 60,000.   Next to Petersburgh, Dantzic
e most important commercial city in the north of Europe.   It owes its dis-
ion in this respect to its situation; the Vistula giving it the command of a
internal navigation, and rendering it the *entrepôt* where the surplus proof West Prussia, and Poland as far as Hungary, are exchanged for those
rted from the foreigner.   The exports of wheat from Dantzic are greater than
any other port in the world.   There are four sorts of wheat distinguished
; viz. *white, high-mixed, mixed,* and *red,* according as the white or red predo-
tes.   The quality of Dantzic wheat is for the most part excellent; it being,
gh small in the berry, and not so heavy as many other sorts, remarkably thin
ied, and yielding the finest flour.   The white Polish wheat exported here is
est in the Baltic.   Rye is also very superior, being both clean and heavy; and
xports are very large.   The exports of barley and oats are comparatively in-
iderable, and the qualities but indifferent.   Very fine white peas are exported.
n is conveyed down the Vistula to Dantzic from Cracow and Warsaw in flat-
med boats, and is in most cases exposed to the weather, and to all sorts of
ing and depredation.

here are," says Mr. Jacob, " two modes of conveying wheat to Dantzic by the Vistula.   That which
near the lower parts of the river, comprehending Polish Russia, and part of the province of Plock,
Masovia, in the kingdom of Poland, which is generally of an inferior quality, is conveyed in covered
with shifting boards that protect the cargo from the rain, but not from pilfering.   These vessels are

long, and draw about 15 inches water, and bring about 150 quarters of wheat. They are not, howev so well calculated for the upper parts of the river. From Cracow, where the Vistula first becomes na gable, to below the junction of the Bug with that stream, the wheat is mostly conveyed to Dantzic in op flats. These are constructed on the banks, in seasons of leisure, on spots far from the ordinary reach the water, but which, when the rains of autumn, or the melted snow of the Carpathian mountains in t spring, fill and overflow the river, are easily floated.

"Barges of this description are about 75 feet long, and 20 broad, with a depth of 2¼ feet. They a made of fir, rudely put together, fastened with wooden treenails, the corners dovetailed and secu with slight iron clamps, — the only iron employed in their construction.

"A large tree, the length of the vessel, runs along the bottom, to which the timbers are secured. T roughly cut keelson rises 9 or 10 inches from the floor, and hurdles are laid on it, which extend to t sides. They are covered with mats made of rye straw, and serve the purpose of dunnage; leaving belo space in which the water that leaks through the sides and bottom is received. The bulk is kept from t sides and ends of the barge by a similar plan. The water which these ill constructed and imperfec caulked vessels receive, is dipped out at the end and sides of the bulk of wheat.

"Vessels of this description draw from 10 to 12 inches water, and yet they frequently get agrou in descending the river. The cargoes usually consist of from 180 to 200 quarters of wheat.

"The wheat is thrown on the mats, piled as high as the gunwale, and left uncovered, exposed to all inclemencies of the weather, and to the pilfering of the crew. During the passage, the barge is carr along by the force of the steam, oars being merely used at the head and stern, to steer clear of the sa banks, which are numerous and shifting, and to direct the vessel in passing under the several bridg These vessels are conducted by six or seven men. A small boat precedes with a man in it, who is emplo sounding, in order to avoid the shifting shoals. This mode of navigating is necessarily very slow ; a during the progress of it, which lasts several weeks and even months, the rain, if any fall, soon cau the wheat to grow, and the vessel assumes the appearance of a floating meadow. The shooting of the fib soon forms a thick mat, and prevents the rain from penetrating more than an inch or two. The ma bulk is protected by this kind of covering, and when that is thrown aside, is found in tolerable conditic

"The vessels are broken up at Dantzic, and usually sell for about two thirds of their original cost. T men who conduct them return on foot.

"When the cargo arrives at Dantzic or Elbing, all but the grown surface is thrown on the land, spre abroad, exposed to the sun, and frequently turned over, till any slight moisture it may have imbibed dried. If a shower of rain falls, as well as during the night, the heaps of wheat on the shore are thro together in the form of a steep roof of a house, that the rain may run off, and are covered with a lin cloth. It is thus frequently a long time after the wheat has reached Dantzic, before it is fit to be plac in the warehouses.

"The warehouses (speichers) are very well adapted for storing corn. They consist generally of sev stories, three of which are in the roof. The floors are about 9 feet asunder. Each of them is divided perpendicular partitions, the whole length, about 4 feet high, by which different parcels are kept distin from each other. Thus the floors have two divisions, each of them capable of storing from 150 to 2 quarters of wheat, and leaving sufficient space for turning and screening it. There are abundance windows on each floor, which are always thrown open in dry weather to ventilate the corn. It is usua turned over three times a week. The men who perform the operation throw it with their shovels as hi as they can, and thus the grains are separated from each other, and exposed to the drying influence the air.

"The whole of the corn warehouses now left (for many were burnt during the siege of 1814), a capable of storing 500,000 quarters of wheat, supposing the quarters to be large enough to fill each of two divisions of the floors with a separate heap; but as of late years it has come down from Poland smaller parcels than formerly, and of more various qualities, which must of necessity be kept distinct, present stock of about 280,000 quarters is found to occupy nearly the whole of those warehouses whi are in repair, or are advantageously situated for loading the ships. Ships are loaded by gangs of port with great despatch, who will complete a cargo of 500 quarters in about three or four hours."—(Fi Report.)

The expense of granary rent, turning, and fire insurance, is only 1 guilder p last year per month, or 1⅙ penny sterling per quarter per month. (For an account the exports and prices of wheat and other grain at Dantzic, see the artic CORŇ LAWS and CORŇ TRADE.)

Timber, both fir and oak, is another principal article of export, especially stave which are superior to those from North America; the sizes are pipe, hogshea and barrel staves. Of all kinds of oak wood articles there are three qualitie crown, first brack, and second brack, or bracks brack : fir timber is not so mu exported here as at Memel, where it may be had cheaper, but the quality Dantzic is rather better. Ashes are largely exported to Holland and France, whe they are justly considered as better than those of America. The best quality calcined potashes is prepared similar to that of Hungary; the inferior qualities calcined are called Polish : of blue potashes the best quality is crown ; t inferior kinds are brack-kant and ocras.

Weed-ashes used for bleaching linen, &c. are frequently exported. White a grey feathers of very superior quality, linens, wax, bristles, hemp and flax, hid tallow, pitch, spruce beer, &c. are also exported : a kind of cordial, called Dant liquor, is much esteemed on the continent.

The imports into Dantzic consist of sugar, coffee, wine, oil, brandy, spices, cc per, lead, furs, cottons and cotton yarn, woollens, hardware, silks, indigo, d woods, &c. Few comparatively of the ships that frequent Dantzic belong to Amber is found all along the coast of West Prussia.

Money. — Accounts are kept in guldens, guilders, or florins of 30 groschen. T rixdollar = 3 florins ⚊ 90 groschen = 270 schillings = 1620 pfenings. The flc or guilder = 9d. sterling, and the rixdollar = 2s. 3d. sterling. The *par* of excha is, therefore, 26⅔ florins per pound sterling.

ights and Measures. — The commercial weights are,

32	Loths	= 1 Ounce.		20	Pounds	= 1 Small Stone.
16	Ounces	= 1 Pound.		33	Pounds	= 1 Large Stone.
16½	Pounds	= 1 Lispound.				

s. = 1 centner; 3 centners = 1 shippound (330 lbs.); 100 lbs. of Dantzic =
lbs. avoirdupois = 46·85 kilog. = 94·7 lbs. of Amsterdam = 96·6 lbs. of Ham-

*liquid measures are, for beer,

5	Quarts	= 1 Anker.		2	Hhds.	= 1 Both.
4	Ankers	= 1 Ahm.		2	Both	= 1 Fuder.
1½	Ahm	= 1 Hhd.		2	Fuder	= 1 Last = 620⅔ Eng. wine gallons.

e measure, which is less than beer measure, the ahm = 39¾ Eng. gallons. The
= 2 ahms.

last of corn = 3¾ malters = 60 scheffels = 240 viertels = 960 metzen; and
s 4,680 lbs. Dantzic weight in rye. The scheffel = ·547 of a hectolitre = 1·552
ester bushel. Hence the last of 60 scheffels = 11 quarters 3 bushels; the last
scheffels = 10 quarters 7 bushels.

Dantzic foot = 11·3 Eng. inches, or 100 Dantzic feet = 94.16 Eng. feet.
l is two feet Dantzic measure. (There is a slight discrepancy as to the values
ussian weights and measures between Dr. Kelly and Nelkenbrecher; those now
are from the former.)

planks, deals, and pipe staves, are sold by the shock of 60 pieces; wheat, rye,
e sold by the last of 56½ scheffels.

re are two great fairs at Dantzic; one commencing on the 5th of August, and the
n the 24th of December.

subjoin an account of the vessels that entered and were despatched from the
an ports in the year 1828.

Names of Ports.	Total of Vessels entered and despatched.	Tonnage calculated by the last of 4,000 lbs.	Foreign Vessels comprised in the previous Columns.	
			Number.	Tonnage.
, entered	869	99,193	650	72,845
despatched	875	99,301	651	72,117
, entered	623	43,675	476	26,205
despatched	638	46,292	466	25,577
c, entered	1,050	101,234	650	45,564
despatched	1,072	105,669	653	46,447
munde, entered	52	1,801	5	193
despatched	54	1,862	5	193
walde, entered	57	2,008	19	647
despatched	55	1,700	19	647
g, entered	86	2,512	9	225
despatched	85	2,469	9	225
munde, entered	809	50,446	247	14,974
despatched	727	53,320	259	14,972
st, entered	79	5,149	26	1,017
despatched	113	7,159	29	1,303
walde, entered	168	11,728	50	2,548
despatched	171	11,694	48	2,220
nd, entered	302	18,655	120	6,095
despatched	326	19,706	126	6,266
Entered	4,095	336,401	2,260	169,313
Despatched	4,116	349,172	2,255	169,967
Totals	8,211	685,573	4,515	339,280

countries to which the greater number of the foreign vessels that entered and were
hed from the Prussian ports, in 1828, belonged, may be learned from the follow-
ement: —

Names of Countries to which the Foreign Vessels belonged.	Total of Vessels entered and despatched.	Tonnage.
Great Britain, entered	823	93,498
despatched	814	92,593
Netherlands, entered	614	33,958
despatched	607	33,398
Denmark, entered	303	14,367
despatched	286	14,398
Sweden, entered	114	7,246
despatched	113	7,157
Hanover, entered	193	9,421
despatched	203	10,044

Then follow Norway, the Hanse Towns, and Oldenburg. Only 11 vessels f Russia, 7 from North America, and 2 from France, entered the Prussian ports in 1 There was not a single vessel from Spain or Portugal.

The total number of native vessels belonging to the different Prussian ports, in 1 was 623, and their tonnage 70,731. Of this number 73 vessels, carrying 15,386 belonged to Dantzic. The number of vessels built in Prussia, in 1825, was 19 1826, 54; and, in 1827, 47. — (*Bulletin des Sciences Géographiques*, tome xxi. p. 1?

Remarks on the Timber shipped at Dantzic. — The pipe staves (as has been obser are of three sorts; crown, brack, and bracks brack. The gauge for crown is 4½ in broad, 1¾ thick, and 64 inches in length, which they must be at least; but they are pected to be larger in every respect.

Pipe staves are from 64 to 68 inches long; 6, 5, and 4½, at least, broad; and 1½ inch to 3 inches thick.

Brandy staves are at least 54 to 58 inches long, as thick and broad as pipe staves.

Hogshead staves are 42 to 45 inches long, as thick and broad as pipe staves, all I lish measure.

The quality is ascertained by marks, to distinguish each sort, as follows: —

Crown pipe staves, stamped at the end, K.	Hogshead Bracks brack, II.
Ditto Brack, in the middle, I.	Ditto Brandy hogshead crown, at the
Ditto Bracks brack, II.	B. K.
Hogshead crown, at the end, O. K.	Ditto Brack, in the middle, ✕.
Ditto Brack, in the middle, I.	Ditto Bracks brack, ✕ ✕.

Oak planks are assorted in the same manner. Crown plank is marked in the mid C. Brack, in the end and middle, B. Bracks brack, B. B.

To distinguish 1½ from 2, and 2½ from 3 inches; the 1½ are marked with I, 2½ ✕.

At the end, in rough strokes, with coloured paint, brack is yellow, bracks brack w' crown red.

A last of hemp, flax, &c. is 6 shippound, or 60 great stone Prussian weight; a of salt is 18 barrels, or 6,000 lbs., equal to about 95¾ bushels of Liverpool.

DATES (Ger. *Datteln;* Fr. *Dattes;* It. *Datteri;* Sp. *Datiles*), the fruit of palm tree (*Phœnix dactylifera*, Lin.). This tree is abundant in Egypt, Barb Arabia, Persia, and the adjacent countries, particularly on the confines of desert, and wherever there is sufficient moisture. It is a tall majestic tree; repeated references are made to it in the sacred writings (Ecclus. xxiv. 1 and in the Koran. Mohammed, in one of his sayings, beautifully compares upright and generous man to the palm tree. " He stands erect before his L? in his every action he follows the impulse received from above, and his whole is devoted to the welfare of his fellow-creatures." But the veneration in wl the palm tree is held in the East is to be ascribed more to its utility than to beauty. Dates form the principal part of the subsistence of the inhabitant many parts of Arabia and Barbary, and they are held in the highest estima wherever they are met with. " They are," says Burckhardt, " by far the r essential article of food to the lower classes of Medina; their harvest is expe with as much anxiety, and attended with as much general rejoicing, as the vin in the south of Europe; and if the crop fails, which often happens, as those t are seldom known to produce abundantly for three or four successive years, eaten up by the locusts, universal gloom overspreads the population, as if a fa? were apprehended."—(*Travels in Arabia*, vol. ii. p. 214.)

There is an endless variety of dates. Generally, however, they may be descr as being somewhat in the shape of an acorn, but usually larger, consisting of a fleshy substance, including and freely separating from an oblong stone or kernel, ha a furrow on the one side. Their taste is agreeably sweet, accompanied with a s astringency. The new fruit is called by the Arabs *ruteb*. When the dates are all? to remain on the tree till they are quite ripe, and have become soft and of a high colour, they are formed into a hard solid paste or cake called *adjoue*. This is for by pressing the ripe dates forcibly into large baskets, each containing about 2 " In this state," says Burckhardt, " the Bedouins export the adjoue: in the m? it is cut out of the basket, and sold by the pound. It forms part of the daily of all classes of people: in travelling it is dissolved in water, and thus affo? sweet and refreshing drink. During the monsoon, the ships from the Persian bring adjoue from Bussorah to Djidda for sale in small baskets, weighing abou lbs. each; this kind is preferred to every other. Ships bound from Arabia for ?

with them a considerable quantity of adjoue, which is readily disposed of amongst Mohammedans of Hindostan."—(*Travels in Arabia*, vol. i. p. 57.)

he Arabians and Egyptians use the leaves of the tree in the preparation of bags and ets; the boughs, the outer and inner bark of the trunk, and the fleshy substance at root of the leaves, where they spring from the trunk, have all their respective uses; besides this, the kernels of the fruit, notwithstanding their hardness, are used as for cattle; they are soaked for two days in water, when they become softened, are given to camels, cows, and sheep, instead of barley: they are said to be h more nutritive than that grain. There are shops at Medina in which nothing is sold but date kernels; and the beggars are continually employed in all the main ets in picking up those that are thrown away.—(*Burckhardt*, vol. ii. p. 212.)

ll the refinements of Arabian cookery are exhausted in the preparation of dates; and Arabs say that a good housewife will daily supply her lord, for a month, with a dish ates differently dressed.

alm trees are raised by shoots; and Dr. Shaw mentions that they arrive at their ur in about thirty years, and continue so seventy years afterwards, bearing yearly en or twenty clusters of dates, each of them weighing 15 or 20 lbs.: after this d they begin to decline.—(*Travels in the Levant*, p. 142. 4to. ed.)

he best dates imported into Great Britain are said to come from Tunis, but they are commonly brought from Smyrna and Alexandria. They should be chosen large, sh, not much wrinkled, of a reddish yellow colour on the outside, with a whitish brane betwixt the flesh and the stone. Those that are dry and hard are of little e.

EALS or **DEAL BOARDS** (Ger. *Dielen;* Du. *Deelen;* Da. *Dæler;* Sw. or; Fr. *Planches minces;* It. *Tavole, Piane;* Rus. *Doski;* Pol. *Tarcice*), a thin kind planks, much used in carpentry: they are formed by sawing the trunk of a tree longitudinal divisions, of more or less thickness, according to the purposes are intended to serve. They are imported from Dantzic, Petersburgh, Narva, many other ports in the Baltic, and from North America; but those from stiania, the capital of Norway, are the best, and bring the highest price. They distinguishable from those produced in the contiguous provinces of Norway; superiority is said to depend principally on the more perfect operation of ng them.

Russian standard deal is 12 feet long, 11 inches wide, and 1½ inch thick; feet of 1½ inch plank make a load.

Christiania standard deal is 11 feet long, 9 inches wide, and 1¼ inch thick. e is another standard of Norway deals at Dram, 10 feet long, 9 inches wide, 1½ thick. (See CHRISTIANIA.)

EBENTURE, a term used at the Custom-house to signify the *certificate* cribed by the customs officers, and given to the exporter of goods on which a ty or drawback is allowed, bearing that the exporter has complied with the red regulations, and that he is entitled to such bounty or drawback.

enacted by 6 Geo. 4. c. 107. § 81., that no drawback or bounty shall be allowed upon the exportation goods, unless entered in the name of the real owner thereof, or of the person who had actually pur-1 and shipped the same, in his own name and at his own risk, on commission.

n owner or commission merchant shall make oath on the debenture that the goods have been ly exported, and are not to be relanded in any part of the United Kingdom, &c.; and if such owner mmission merchant shall not have purchased the right to such drawback or bounty, he shall declare his hand in the entry, and in his oath upon the debenture, the person who is entitled thereto; and me of such person shall be inserted in the cocket, and in the debenture, and his receipt on the latter e the discharge of such drawback or bounty.—§ 82.

these and the other clauses in the act relating to debentures, see IMPORTATION and EXPORTATION. entures must be stamped as follows:—

	£.	s.	d.
Where value to be received does not exceed 100*l.*	0	5	0
Exceeding 100*l.* and not exceeding 200*l.*	0	10	0
Exceeding 200*l.* and not exceeding 500*l.*	1	0	0
Exceeding 500*l.*	2	0	0

entures or certificates for bounty on the exportation of linens or sailcloth exempted from duty.

ELFT or DELF (Ger. *Fayence, Unächtes Porzellän, Halbporzellan;* Du. porcelyn; Fr. *Faience;* It. *Maiolica;* Sp. *Loza de Fayanza, China imitada*), rse species of porcelain originally manufactured at Delft, whence its name. now rarely used in this country.

EMURRAGE, in commercial navigation, is an allowance made to the master wners of a ship by the freighter, for detaining her in port longer than the d agreed upon for her sailing. It is usually stipulated in charterparties ills of lading, that a certain number of days, called running or working days, be allowed for receiving or discharging the cargo, and that the freighter may

detain the vessel for a further specified time, or as long as he pleases, on paymen
of so much *per diem* for such overtime. When the contract of affreightment ex
pressly stipulates that so many days shall be allowed for discharging or receivin
the cargo, and so many more for overtime, such limitation is interpreted as a
express stipulation on the part of the freighter, that the vessel shall in no even
be detained longer, and that if detained he will be liable for demurrage. Th
holds even in cases where the delay is not occasioned by any fault on the freighter
part, but is inevitable. If, for example, a ship be detained, owing to the crowde
state of the port, for a longer time than is allowed by the contract, demurrage
due; and it is no defence to an action for demurrage, that it arose from po
regulations, or even from the unlawful acts of the Custom-house officers. De
murrage is not, however, claimable for a delay occasioned by the hostile detentio
of the ship, or the hostile occupation of the intended port; nor is it claimab
for any delay wilfully occasioned by the master, or owners, or crew of the vesse
The claim for demurrage ceases as soon as the ship is cleared out and ready fo
sailing, though she should be detained by adverse winds, or tempestuous weathe
— (*Chitty's Commercial Law*, vol. iii. pp. 426—431.)

DENARIUS, a Roman coin, estimated by Dr. Arbuthnot to have bee
worth 7¾d.; but its value differed at different periods.

DENIER, a small French coin, of which there were twelve to a sol.

DIAMOND (Ger. Du. Da. and Fr. *Diamant*; Sw. *Demant*, *Diamant*; It. S
and Port. *Diamante*; Rus. *Almas*; Pol. *Dyamant*; Lat. *Adamas*), a preciou
stone, which has been known from the remotest ages. Pliny has described
(Hist. Nat. lib. 37. § 4.); but his account is, in many respects, inaccurate. It
found in different parts of Asia, particularly in Golconda and Visapour; it is als
found in Brazil, on which, indeed, Europe may be said to be at present entire
dependent for supplies of diamonds. Hitherto, however, it has not been me
with any where except within the tropics. It is the most beautiful and mo
valuable of all the precious stones. Its most common colours are white and gre
of various shades. It occurs also red, blue, brown, yellow, and green. Th
colours are commonly pale. It is always crystallised, but sometimes so impe
fectly that it might pass for amorphous. It is the hardest body in nature. Extern
lustre from splendid to glimmering; internal always splendid. It is brittle; i
specific gravity is 3·5. When rubbed it becomes positively electric, even befo
it has been cut by the lapidary, which is not the case with any other gem.—
(*Thomson's Chemistry*.)

According to Mr. Milburn (*Orient. Com.*), the colour should be perfectly cry
talline, resembling a drop of clear spring water, in the middle of which you w
perceive a strong light playing with a great deal of spirit. If the coat be smoo
and bright, with a little tincture of green in it, it is not the worse, and seldo
proves bad; but if there be a mixture of yellow with the green, then beware of it
it is a soft, greasy stone, and will prove bad.

Tests of Diamonds. — *Cutting, &c.* — To ascertain whether any specimen is a tr
diamond or not, a fine file may be used; and if the surface of the stone be the le
abraded or scratched by its action, it is not a diamond. The difference will also appe
upon close examination without this instrument; the rays of light easily pass throu
other gems, but in the diamond they are refracted to the surface, which occasions
superior brilliancy. If the specimen under examination be very minute, it may
placed between two half crowns, or other flat metallic surfaces, and pressed with
thumb and finger; if a diamond, it will not be injured, but, if otherwise, it will bre
and fall to powder. On account of the extreme hardness of the diamond, the art
cutting and polishing it was for a long time unknown in Europe. But, in 1456, a you
man of the name of Louis Berghen, a native of Bruges, is said to have constructe
polishing wheel for the purpose, which was fed with diamond powder instead of cor
dum, which the Chinese and Hindoos had been long accustomed to employ. Bergh
was led to this discovery by observing the action produced by rubbing two rough d
monds together. Diamonds are cut into brilliants and rose diamonds; the for
being, for the most part, made out of the octahedral crystals, and the latter from
spheroidal varieties. — (*Joyce's Practical Mineralogy; Rees' Cyclopædia, &c.*)

" *Commercial Value of Diamonds.* — In the great or wholesale trade there is but li
fluctuation in the price of those diamonds which may be termed *stones in general
mand*. I will begin with brilliants from 1 grain to 2½ grains each. — Such brillia
double cut, and what may be termed fine, are worth from 7l. to 8l. per carat. Ne

, may take 10 per cent. less for cash; but this is the general average price for a 10, 20, or 50 carats of well-made stones, if the quality be good.

rilliants, from 2 grains to 3, may be bought in lots, at from 7*l.* 7*s.* to 8*l.* per carat. o be understood, that diamonds in a lot are never all quite free from faults; hence may arise a difference of 10 per cent. in the price. Stones of 3 grains, if fine erfect, are always in demand, at 8*l.* or 9*l.* per carat.

rilliants, from 3 grains to 4, if very fine and well proportioned, are worth from 9*l.* per carat. Those of a carat each, if very fine and well selected, are worth 10*l.* Three years ago I offered 12*l.* each for 8, and could not obtain them.

rilliants, from 5 grains to 6, if pure, are worth from 13*l.* to 14*l.* ; if perfectly nd of the full weight of 6 grains, they are worth from 17*l.* to 18*l.* each: I have, ch, paid 20*l.*

rilliants, of 2 carats each, are worth from 27*l.* to 30*l.* Stones of this weight, if roportioned, are considered of a fine size, and well calculated for pins, or the of clusters; indeed, well proportioned diamonds, from 6 grains to 2 carats each, vays in demand, and are retailed at from 20*l.* to 35*l.* each, according to their de- f perfection, or as the retailer may think fit to charge them.

or brilliants of 3 carats, if fine and well formed, from 70*l.* to 80*l.* may be ob- . Stones of this size, and larger, are more liable to capricious fluctuations of than the smaller ones before named, being chiefly required for the centre stones of e necklaces.

rilliants of 4 carats, if fine, are worth from 100*l.* to 130*l.* I have sold stones, cut, a little *off colour*, of this weight, at 80 guineas. I possessed one of 17 grains, ly white, having a surface as large as that of a 7 carat stone ought to be; it was, uently, very thin, but being much in request, on account of its great *spread*, or , it was sold for 160*l.*

illiants of 5 carats are not frequently met with in general trade, and are valuable e; as the dealers exact more if they know that such stones are wanted, than they in the regular course of business. The prices may be said to vary from 180*l.* to

illiants of 6 carats, as before stated, are not common: they are suitable for centre of expensive necklaces, and single stone rings; if perfect and well shaped, they 230*l.* to 250*l.* or more.

or estimating the value of peculiarly fine diamonds, there is no fixed standard. diamonds, selected as fine, and well formed for cutting, may be estimated as : — Square the weight of the stone, multiply the product by 2, and the result will value in pounds sterling. Brilliants, if fine, may be estimated by squaring the in carats, and multiplying the product by 8, which will give the amount in sterling.

a very large property, both in this kingdom and in other countries of Eu- is vested in diamonds, it may be interesting to be informed, that not only ce of these gems has for several years been, upon the whole, gradually but that it is likely to continue on the advance. At the present time, indeed, r the last few years, there has been a dull sale of diamonds in England, nor coronation occasion a demand worth notice; but on the Continent the trade has eady, and rough diamonds have been constantly rising in price. That this ad- vill be progressive, may be assumed from the fact, that the best diamond ground own, the Serro do Frio in Brazil, has assuredly passed the zenith of its prosperity. over the greater part of what is yet reserved, and still remains to be worked, and ive that there would be no difficulty in calculating the length of time in which sent number of workmen may reduce it to a state of exhaustion, like that of the ed Golconda. The average annual produce of future years may be estimated mount obtained from that portion which has been already worked. Brazil may to furnish Europe with 25,000 or 30,000 carats *per annum* of rough diamonds; if reduced to brilliants, may make an influx into the market of 8,000 or 9,000 nnually." — (*Mawe's Treatise on Diamonds*, 2d ed. pp. 9—14. and p. 60.)

rule stated by Mr. Mawe, and adopted by the jewellers, for estimating the value onds (multiply the square of the weight in carats by 2, and the product is the pounds sterling), can only hold in the case of those that are of a small size, or weigh more than 20 carats. The value of the largest diamonds, which are ex- ly rare, (*non nisi regibus, et iis admodum paucis cognitus*, Pliny,) can, it is clear, upon nothing but the competition of the purchasers. The diamond belonging mperor of Brazil is the largest in the world. It is still uncut, and weighs 1,680 so that, according to the jewellers' rule, it must be worth the enormous sum 4,800*l.* ! It may, however, be doubted, whether his Imperial Majesty would y disinclination to part with it for the odd sum of 644,800*l.* The famous

diamond belonging to the emperor of Russia, which the jewellers tell us is w
4,804,000*l*., did not cost 150,000*l*.

Diamonds are not used exclusively as articles of ornament or luxury. They
frequently employed with great advantage in the arts. " Bad, discoloured diamon
says Mr. Mawe, " are sold to break into powder, and may be said to have a more
tensive sale than brilliants, with all their captivating beauty. In many operation
art they are indispensable; the fine cameo and intaglio owe their perfection to
diamond, with which alone they can be engraved. The beauty of the onyx would
remain dormant, had not the unrivalled power of the diamond been called forth to
artist's assistance. The carnelian, the agate, or cairngorm, cannot be engraved by
other substance; every crest or letter cut upon hard stone is indebted to the diamo
This is not all; for without it blocks of crystal could not be cut into slices for spe
cles, agate for snuff-boxes, &c."

Diamonds may be landed without report, entry, or warrant. — (6 *Geo.* 4. c.
§ 2.)

The carat grain used in weighing diamonds is different from the Troy grain, 5 diam
grains being only equal to 4 Troy grains.

DIAPER (Ger. *Drell;* Du. *Drel;* Fr. *Linge ouvré;* It. *Tela tessuta a op*
Sp. *Manteles alemaniscas ;* Rus. *Salfetotsschnoe*), a sort of fine flowered li
commonly used for table-cloths, napkins, &c., brought to the finest perfectio
the manufactories in the north of Ireland, in Germany, and Scotland.

DICE (Ger. *Würfel;* Du. *Taarlingen;* Fr. *Dés (à jouer);* It. *Dadi;* Sp. *Da*
Rus. *Kosti*), cubical pieces of bone or ivory, marked with dots on each sid
their faces, from one to six, according to the number of faces. The regulat
as to the manufacture and sale of dice are the same as those with respect to ca
which see. Every pair of dice is to pay a duty of 20*s*. All pieces of ivory, b
or other matter, used in any game, having letters, figures, spots, or other m
denoting any chance, marked thereon, to be adjudged dice; and if more than
chances are signified on any one piece, then such piece to be charged with the
duty of a pair of dice.— (9 *Geo.* 4. c. 18.)

DIMITY (Fr. *Basin;* It. *Dobletto;* Sp. *Dimite*), a species of cross-barred
entirely composed of cotton, similar in fabric to fustian.

DISCOUNT, is an allowance paid on account of the immediate advance
sum of money not due till some future period. It is usually said to be of
kinds; viz. discount of bills, and discount of goods; but they are essentially
same.

When a bill of exchange is presented at a banker's for discount, it is the practi
calculate the simple interest for the time the bill has to run, including the days of g
which interest is called the *discount ;* and this being deducted from the amount of
bill, the balance is paid over to the presenter of the bill. This is the method follo
by the Bank of England, the London and provincial bankers, and by commercial
in general. But it is, notwithstanding, inaccurate. The true discount of any sun
any given time is such a sum as will in that time amount to the interest of the sum
discounted. Thus, if interest be *five* per cent., the proper discount to be received fo
immediate advance of 100*l.* due twelve months hence is not 5*l.*, but 4*l.* 15*s.* 2½*d.*
this sum will, at the end of the year, amount to 5*l.*, which is what the 100*l.* w
have produced. Those, therefore, who employ their money in discounting, make s
what more than the ordinary rate of interest upon it; for a person discounting
due at the end of a year, advances, supposing interest to be 5*l.* per cent., only 95*l.*
that, as this 95*l.* produces 100*l.* at the period in question, the interest received has r
been 5*l.* 5*s.* 3*d.* per cent.

The rule for calculating discount on correct principles is as follows:

> As the amount of 100*l.* for the given rate and time
> Is to the given sum or debt;
> So is 100*l.* to the present worth, or
> So is the interest of 100*l.* for the given time
> To the discount of the given sum.

Mr. Smart has calculated, on this principle, a table of the discount of 1*l.* for any
ber of days, at 2, 2½, 3, 3½, &c. to 10 per cent., to eight decimal places. But the si
interest of the sum being the only thing looked to in practice, such tables are h
ever referred to.

Bills in the highest credit are discounted on the lowest terms; the discoun
creasing according to the suspicions entertained of the punctuality or solvency c
parties subscribing the bills. During the war, the rate of interest, or, which i

e thing, of discount, was comparatively high; but since 1818, the rate of discount
n good bills has seldom been above 4, and has often been as low as 3 and even 2½
cent.

)iscount on merchandise takes place when, after making a purchase of goods at an
ed on term of credit, the buyer finds means to make his payment before the ex-
tion of that term, receiving from the seller a discount or allowance, which is com-
ly a good deal above the current rate of interest. The discount on goods varies, of
rse, according to the interest of money. During the late war, the loans to government
e so large, and the facility of investing money was such, that the discount on goods
often as high as 5 per cent. for six, and 10 per cent. for twelve months. Now, how-
, the discount on goods has fallen, with the fall in the rate of interest, to 7 or 7½ per
:. for twelve months; being about double the current interest arising from funded
perty, or the discount of good mercantile bills.

ong credits and discounts upon goods have, for a lengthened period, been usual in
;land. This arose from a variety of causes, but principally, perhaps, from the mag-
de of our exports to the United States of America, Russia, and other countries
re there was a great demand for capital; but in whatever causes it originated, it has
rly been carried to what seems to be an injurious extent.—(See CREDIT.) In France
Germany, the manufacturers, in general bare of capital, are obliged to stipulate with
merchants for short credits. In Holland, the *usage* of the exporting merchants has
a to pay either in ready money, or at so short a date as to put discounting out of the
;tion, the manufacturer setting at once the lowest price on his goods.

IVIDEND, the name given to the payment made to creditors out of the
te of a bankrupt, and to the annual interest payable upon the national debt,
other public funds.

)JIDDA, a town of Arabia, on the Red Sea, about 21 miles from Mecca, of
:h it is the sea-port, in lat. 21° 29′ N., lon. 39° 15′ E. It is well built; the
ets are unpaved, but spacious and airy; the houses high, and constructed, for
most part, of madrepores and other marine fossils. The supply of water is
rty, and its quality indifferent. Small vessels approach close to the quays;
large vessels are obliged to anchor in the roads, about two miles off, loading
unloading by means of lighters. The entrance to the roads is difficult, and
ild not be attempted without a pilot. Djidda is a place of considerable com-
cial importance. It is the *entrepôt* in which is centred the greater part of
commerce between India, Egypt, and Arabia. Many of its merchants possess
: capitals; some of them as much as from 150,000*l.* to 200,000*l.* The trade
)ffee brought from Mocha, and other ports in Yemen, is the most consider-
, but it is said also to be the most hazardous. The returns are principally
e in cash. The trade with India and the Gulf of Persia is safer than the
e trade, and is very considerable. Djidda has also a good deal of intercourse
the ports of Cosseir, Souakin, and Massouah, on the opposite coast of the
Sea. The imports from the last two principally consist of slaves, gold,
cco, dhourra or barley, hides, butter (of which immense quantities are made
)f in Arabia), mats, &c.; in return for which the Africans receive Indian
is suitable for their markets, dresses and ornaments for their women, dates
:ch are not produced in any part of Nubia), iron, &c. The principal article of
rt from Cosseir is wheat; and not only Djidda, but the whole Hedjaz, or
/ Land of Arabia, is almost entirely dependent upon Egypt for corn. Coffee
e principal article sent in return. Business is transacted at Djidda with ease
expedition. The number of ships belonging to the port is estimated at 250.
ng to the scarcity of timber, none of them are built at Djidda; those beng to it being either purchased at Bombay or Muscat, or at Mocha, Ho-
a, or Suez. For a considerable period each year, before and after the feast
amadhan, when pilgrims come from all quarters to visit Mecca, the town is
iged with strangers, and a great deal of mercantile business is transacted.
la is at present, and has been for a number of years, under the government of
ammed Ali, pacha of Egypt. The moneys, weights, and measures of the
country (for which see ALEXANDRIA), are now generally used in Djidda, the
nerce of which has been much improved and extended in consequence of the
arative security and good order enforced by the pacha. (We have gleaned
details from the different works of Burckhardt, particularly from his *Tra-
n Arabia*, vol. i. pp. 1—100.)

)CKS are artificial basins for the reception of ships. The term has been

supposed by some to be derived from the Greek δεκομαι, to receive; but it obviously no other than the Teutonic *dock*, originally perhaps derived from *dekke* to cover, inclose, or protect.

Docks are of two sorts—*wet* and *dry*. Wet docks are generally constructe with gates to retain the water. Ships are admitted at high water; and the gate being shut, they are kept constantly afloat. A dry dock is intended for th building, repairing, or examination of ships. The ships to be repaired or examine are admitted into it at high water; and the water either ebbs out with the recedin sea, or is pumped out after the gates are shut.

Utility of Docks. — The construction of wet docks has done much to facilitate an promote navigation. A large vessel, particularly if loaded, could not be allowed t come to the ground, or to lie on the beach, without sustaining considerable injury, an perhaps being destroyed ; and even the smaller class of vessels are apt to be strained, an otherwise hurt, if they are left dry, unless the ground be very soft. Hence, when larg vessels have to be loaded or unloaded where there are no docks, and where the wate close to the shore or quay is not sufficiently deep, the work can only be carried on durin a particular period of each tide ; it being necessary, in order to keep the vessel afloat, th she should leave the shore with the ebbing tide. Attempts have sometimes been mad to obviate this inconvenience, by running jetties or piers to such a distance into the se that there might always be a sufficient depth of water at their heads : but this can onl be done in peculiar situations; and it requires that the ship's position should be fre quently changed. It is in most cases, too, impossible properly to protect the cargoes c ships loading or unloading at quays, or on the beach, from depredation. Previously t the construction of the wet docks on the Thames, the property annually pillaged fro ships was estimated to amount to 500,000*l.* a year, though this is probably much exag gerated.

DOCKS AND DOCK CHARGES.

I. *Docks on the Thames.* — It is singular that, notwithstanding the obvious utili of wet docks, and the vast trade of the metropolis, there was no establishment of th sort on the Thames till nearly a century after a wet dock had been constructed at L verpool. The inconvenience arising from the crowded state of the river, at the perio when fleets of merchantmen were accustomed to arrive, the insufficient accommodatio afforded by the legal quays and sufferance wharfs, the necessity under which many shi; were placed of unloading in the river into lighters, and the insecurity and loss of pr perty thence arising, had been long felt as almost intolerable grievances : but so powerf was the opposition to any change, made by the private wharfingers and others interest in the support of the existing order of things, that it was not till 1793 that a plan w projected for making wet docks for the port of London ; and six years more elapse before the act for the construction of the West India docks was passed.

The West India Docks were the first, and continue to be the most extensive, of the gre warehousing establishments formed in the port of London. Their construction com menced in February, 1800, and they were partially opened in August, 1802. Th stretch across the isthmus joining the Isle of Dogs to the Middlesex side of t Thames. They originally consisted of an import and export dock, each communicatin by means of locks, with a basin of five or six acres in extent at the end next Blackwa and with another of more than two acres at the end next Limehouse ; both of the basins communicate with the Thames. To these works the West India Dock Compa have recently added the South Dock, formerly the City Canal, which runs parallel to t Export Dock. This canal was intended to facilitate navigation, by enabling ships to avo the circuitous course round the Isle of Dogs. It was, however, but little used for th purpose, and is now appropriated for the wood trade. The Export Dock, or that appr priated for ships loading outwards, is about 870 yards in length, by 135 in width ; so th its area is near 25 acres : the North or Import Dock, or that appropriated for ships enteri to discharge, is of the same length as the Export Dock, and 166 yards wide ; so that contains nearly 30 acres. The South Dock which is appropriated both to import or expo vessels, is 1183 yards long, with an entrance to the river at each end ; both the locks, well as that into the Blackwall basin, being 45 feet wide, or large enough to admit shi of 1,200 tons burthen. At the highest tides, the depth of water in the docks is feet ; and the whole will contain, with ease, 600 vessels of from 250 to 500 tons. T separation of the homeward bound ships, which is of the utmost importance for p venting plunder, and giving additional security to the revenue and the merchant, w for the first time, adopted in this establishment. The Import and Export Docks parallel to each other, being divided by a range of warehouses, principally appropria to the reception of rum, brandy, and other spirituous liquors. There are sma warehouses and sheds on the quays of the Export and South Docks, for the reception

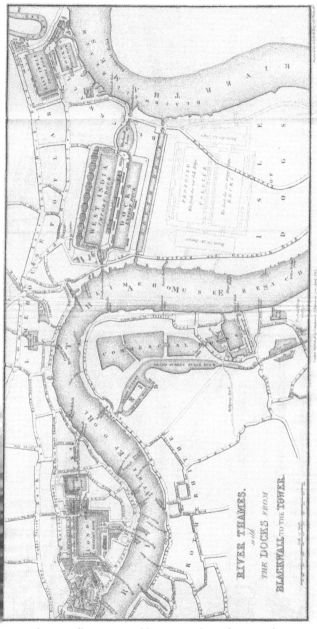

The material originally positioned here is too large for reproduction in this volume. A PDF can be downloaded from the web address given on page iv of this book, by clicking on 'Resources Available'.

ds sent down for exportation. The warehouses for imported goods are on the noith and each end of the Import Dock. They are well contrived, and of great extent, g calculated to contain 160,000 hhds. of sugar, exclusive of coffee and other pro-luce. There have been deposited, at the same time, upon the quays, under the ls, and in the warehouses belonging to these docks, 148,563 barrels or casks of sugar, 75 barrels and 433,648 bags of coffee, 35,158 pipes of rum and Madeira wine, 21 logs of mahogany, 21,350 tons of logwood, &c. The whole area occupied by docks, warehouses, &c., extends in all to about 295 acres; and the most effectual autions are adopted for the prevention of fire and pilfering.

his spacious and magnificent establishment was formed by subscription, and the le property now vests in the West India Dock Company, the affairs of which are aged by twenty-one directors, as a body corporate. The right of voting is vested hose shareholders only who hold 500l. of the Company's stock. The Company's tal is 1,380,000l.

he West India docks have proved a most successful undertaking, and very beneficial he original shareholders. All West India ships frequenting the Thames were ged to use them for a period of twenty years from their completion. The dividend he Company's stock was limited to 10 per cent.; and, after making dividends to ull amount, with the exception of the first half year, in 1819, they had an accumu-l fund of near 400,000l. But having then diminished their charges, at the suggestion e committee of the House of Commons on the foreign trade of the country, most of the surplus fund was appropriated to the payment of the dividend. Latterly Company have been obliged, in consequence of the competition of the other Com-s, to make a further deduction from their charges; and their revenue having sustained responding diminution, the dividend has been reduced to 6 per cent.

he nearest dock gate at Limehouse is about three miles from the Exchange; and the r, next Blackwall, about half a mile more. This distance has the disadvantage not of materially increasing the expense of cartage, but of being inconvenient to the hants and others using the docks. On the other hand, however, ships entering the t India docks avoid a considerable extent of troublesome, if not dangerous, naviga-that must be undertaken by those bound for the St. Katharine's and London s.

s AND ORDERS to be observed by Masters, Pilots, and other Persons having the Charge of Ships, sels, Lighters, or Craft, coming into, lying in, and going out of, the West India Docks, pursuant n Act relative to these Docks of the present Year of the Reign of his Majesty King William the arth.

Company's Moorings. — The moorings in the river, within 200 yards of each of the entrances at wall, and that into Limehouse basin, and within 150 yards of the Limehouse entrance of the South are reserved for the exclusive use of vessels entering into, or which have recently come out of the Not more than 9 ships can be permitted to make fast at each mooring chain.
ry master or person in charge of any ship, lighter, barge, boat, or other vessel, of any description ever, lying within the above distance, shall immediately remove the same, when so required by the masters or their assistants. Penalty 5l. for every hour which such vessel may remain.
ts shall not attempt to place ships inside the buoys, if other ships have previously brought up, but ring them to their berths in due succession on the outside, unless they shall be expressly ordered dock-master to take a berth inside the tier for the convenience of docking.
parties creating obstructions will be prosecuted, and the penalties will be rigidly enforced.
els about to enter the Docks, &c. — Signals. — The red flag on the flag-staff at the entrance, is the for ships to prepare. A blue flag will be kept flying the whole time proper for docking; when the s reached high water mark, that flag will be struck, and all ships must immediately haul off and or.
laration Book. — When ships have brought up properly at the moorings, an officer will deliver the any's regulations; and the commander or pilot of every vessel exceeding 100 tons, must certify in claration book her draught of water; that she is provided with all necessary and sufficient warps, and tackle, to remove and moor her in safety; and that her anchors are (or shall be before the moorings) so secured and stowed as not to endanger the works, the ships therein, or the vessel

aring Ships for Admission. — Every master or pilot, in charge of a ship, should lose no time in g the following preparations, viz. her anchors to be properly secured and stowed; her sails all ; all quarter boats lowered down, guns unloaded, gunpowder put out, fires extinguished, and ther precautions taken as the dock-master may direct: when these preparations are completed, a ust be hoisted at the fore, as a signal that the ship is ready.
ships are required to send down top-gallant-yards and strike top-gallant masts, and to have their mizen booms rigged close in, bomkins, martingales, and all out-riggers unshipped, if time will , and at all events immediately after entering. Vessels will, however, be exempted from striking yards and top-masts, upon the master certifying that the same may be safely dispensed with, and ng to be answerable for all consequences; and before being placed at the quay, the yards must be well up, and the yard-arms lashed close in to the rigging.
king Tickets and Order of Admission. — In fixing the order of admission, and issuing the docking , regard will be had to the state of the tides, and the size and draught of water of each vessel, as the time of arrival: the largest ships must necessarily be taken in when the tides are highest, gh they may have arrived subsequent to smaller vessels. Loaded vessels must always have the nce over light ships.
ets will be withheld, and no ship can be admitted, if neither the master nor pilot is on board. The g ticket will only remain in force for the tide for which it is granted.
he proper time for the admission of each ship, notice will be given by hoisting her ticket number pier head, provided she has made the signal for being properly prepared.
ny vessel shall attempt to gain admittance before her number is hoisted, the owners, and the , pilot, or other person in charge, must be responsible for all consequences of such misconduct.

Entering. — When a ship's number is hoisted, she must drop up to the entrance, and be read good and sufficient warps to send to *each* pier, when ordered by the dock-master. If the ship sh then come to the entrance, she shall forfeit her turn.

When within the piers, proper ropes will be sent on board to guide and check the vessel throu lock : the master and pilot will be held responsible for making these, as well as the ship's properly fast on board : the vessel must be hauled ahead by the latter, and they are on no account cast off, unless ordered by the dock-master, until the ship is in the basin.

Every pilot must bring his boat into the basin, or South Dock, as it is a most essential part of hi to moor the ship.

No ship's boats can be admitted into the Import Dock except such as are conveniently stowed on All other boats must be sent out of the docks. The hatches of all loaded ships are to be locked and the keys delivered to the officer appointed to receive the same.

The boats of ships in the South Dock which cannot be securely stowed on deck, must be hauled the north bank, or secured afloat in such manner as the dock-master may direct, after the s moored. Ships, however, which are not lying at a jetty, will be allowed to employ one boat duri legal hours of business, which boat must be chained by the Company's officers to the north bank a as that time has expired.

Any boats found afloat in any of the docks or basins, contrary to these regulations, will be remov the dock-master, and will be detained until the charges occasioned by such removal shall be paid.

Import Dock. — No person whatever can be allowed to remain in this dock after the established of business : nor nor can any person be permitted to have access to vessels therein, excepting the o master, or chief officer, without a pass.

Passes will be given on the application of the captain or chief mate, to admit the ship's apprer or other persons, to prepare the ship for discharging, or to do any other work which may be unavoi necessary ; but, to prevent the abuses which sometimes occur, it is strongly recommended that the pany's labourers be employed.

Ships Discharging. — Previously to any ships being quayed, the decks must be cleared, and thing prepared to begin working out the cargo. If, through want of proper tackle, or any neglect, be not in readiness to take her turn, another will be quayed in the mean time.

The master must deliver a correct list of all articles of baggage or presents to the Company's at the baggage warehouse, with proper directions for the delivery thereof. Masters are partic cautioned against signing blank manifests, or allowing themselves to be influenced by the i tunity of brokers ; and it is most desirable that one broker only should be appointed for each ship.

An officer of the revenue is authorised to forward all despatches for the departments of governm packets so addressed will, therefore, be delivered into his charge, unless the Company receive directions to the contrary.

Packages of bullion or specie (whether cargo or private property) must be delivered by the c under his own responsibility ; the delivery of goods overside will also rest with him ; and he mus such steps as he may think necessary, to prevent detention from the non-attendance of craft a want of sufficient hands to stow them, or to protect his owners in respect to their freight, and a any claim for damage or plunder which take place before they reach their destination.

Leaky ships may be lightened in the Blackwall basin ; they may also be hauled in to discharge quay in the morning, and put into the basin at night ; the master or owner must, in such case an engagement to pay the expense of such extra labour, and to be answerable for all damage tha arise therefrom.

When a ship is finally discharged and moored in the Export Dock, or either of the basins, purpose of going out to the river, all the services provided for in the import rate are completed.

For the more expeditious discharge of vessels, or despatch in re-loading, every assistance will be in clearing the decks, or stiffening them ; coopering water casks, and shipping them when filled ; ing the hold after discharge ; shipping and stowing the outward cargo, under the directions of the officers ; and any other services which can be reasonably required. — Should the Company's mo machinery be desired, it will be lent upon application to the principal dock-master. — The foll charges will be made for such services : —

For labourers hired to work under the directions of the commanding officer of the ship, each man per day, of the regulated hours of attendance (and not less than ¼ day to be charged.

Overtime will be charged in proportion) - - - - - Articles loaded, shipped, or struck down by the dock cranes or jiggers, under 2 tons, per ton - Two tons, and under 5 tons (and not less than 1 ton to be charged) - - ditto - Moveable machinery lent, each jigger with its gear, per day - - - - The use of the floating engine for washing ships, including the attendance of the man in charge, (and not less than one day to be charged) per day - - - - -

Export and South Docks. — All vessels entering or lying in these docks are in charge of the m and owners ; and it is the duty of the pilots, or officers and crews, to transport their respective v under their own responsibility, as directed by the dock-master, to or from the river, and to or fro part of the docks or basins.

Light ships on entering from the river must be provided with sufficient hands to dock and tra them, and should move in due time into the dock ; otherwise they will be removed by the dock-m and the owners charged with the expense.

Vessels discharging their inward cargoes in these docks will be regarded as privileged ships, transporting within the docks will be performed by the dock-master, assisted by the crew, gratuit but unless there are sufficient crews on board to assist in transporting the outward bound ships, th not be moved.

Whenever assistance is required by other vessels, it will be furnished by the dock-master on t lowing terms, viz. —

A boat with warp and two hands - 10s. 0d.
Ditto and four hands - 13s. 0d.

And for every additional hand employed, either on board or in the boats, 6d. per hour.

The warps are only lent in aid of the ship's warps.

Ships taking in cargoes will be moored at the quays in due rotation. Light ships not taking in shall be moored in either of the docks or basins, as the dock-masters may judge convenient.

While ships are lying at, or moving to or from the quay, all out-riggers should be got in and snug ; and sails are by no means to be loose while so moving.

No ship must be removed from her berth without notice being given to the dock-master, and his as to the time of removal being obtained.

Craft must be fastened to the ships from which they are receiving, or to which they may be de goods : the charge upon craft which shall not be *bona fide* so engaged, will be the same as the re sloops and craft coastwise, and, as usual, not less than one week's rent will be charged. To obvi doubt as to the time for which they may be fairly entitled to exemption, 24 hours will be allowe the time of entering the dock, for receiving goods, and 24 hours after being loaded or discharg going out of the docks.

Convenient receptacles on the quays and craft are provided, wherein all dust, ashes, &c. in deposited, and which shall be cleared by the persons appointed by the Company, and by no one els

essel shall be permitted to take in ballast after daylight, or before daybreak.

' provisions or stores cannot be permitted to pass the gates without an order signed by the captain
er.

epair or caulking can be permitted without the special permission of the Court of Directors, to
application should be made through the principal dock-master.

Jetties. — Ships landing cargoes in the South Dock, or taking in goods by land, shall have the pre-
use of the jetties.

s which are fitting out, but have not commenced loading, shall be accommodated as far as possible;
ch ships must be removed to make room for vessels about to discharge or take in cargo by land.

ther respects, preference will be given to ships intended for sale, over those which are merely laying
d as between ships which are similarly circumstanced, the priority of their entering the dock shall
ine the preference.

and Candle. — Vessels in these docks shall be considered as forming three classes, viz. —
essels actually discharging, having their crews on board, or loading outwards.
'essels rigging or fitting out, but which shall not have commenced taking in goods.
Vessels for sale or laying up.

ach of these classes special licences will be granted. Every such licence will express the place in
fire may be kept, and the circumstances under which it may be used; upon the slightest infringe-
t the conditions, the penalty prescribed by law will be rigidly enforced.

y application for a licence must be made by the master or owner, specifying the names and ca-
of the persons in charge of the ship, and engaging to be responsible for their attention to the regu-

ing and shutting the Gates. — The gates of the Export and South Docks will be opened at 6 o'clock
morning and shut at 8 o'clock in evening, from the 1st of March to the 10th of November; and
he 11th of November to the last day of February, opened at 8 in the morning and shut at 7
evening.

ins and mates may be furnished with tickets upon applying at the Police Office, at the Import
which will entitle them to admission till 9 o'clock p. m., but no person whatever can be allowed to
after the hour for closing the gates.

ls about to leave the Docks. — Export vessels should be hauled out in sufficient time to be at the
Locks, at Blackwall, at low water, or two hours before high water at the latest; to prevent the
nience of hauling down the Blackwall basin or South Dock during the time that other vessels
airing admission, which must have the preference.

ls can only be let out after high water, upon the special request of the officers in charge of them.
going into the river must use their own ropes, as they are out of the dock-master's charge when
' the outer gates.

ce. — Two true copies of the manifest of the cargo must be delivered into the General Office, at
st India Dock House, within 12 hours after every vessel shall enter the docks, or after the cargo
ve been reported at the Custom-house, which shall first happen. Penalty for refusal or neglect,
n not exceeding 5l.

anifests will be required for ships discharging by their own crews.

ips can receive their rotation, or be allowed to break bulk, until their cargoes are duly entered;
h cargoes will be landed in due succession, according to the strict order in which the manifests
vered at the General Office, after being certified by the Company's officer at the Custom-house,
ch entries being completed.

h manifest, or bill of lading, or copy, shall be false; or if any bill of lading be uttered by any
-and the goods expressed therein shall not have been *bond fide* shipped on board such ship;
y bill of lading uttered or produced by any master, shall not have been signed by him; or any
by shall not have been received or made by him previously to his leaving the place where the
pressed in such bill of lading, or copy, were shipped; penalty 100l. — (6 *Geo.* 4. c. 107. §. 10.)

s *of Attendance* are, from 10th of May to 9th of November inclusive, 8 in the morning to 4 in the
n; from 10th of November to 9th of May inclusive, 9 in the morning to 4 in the afternoon; and
to be no intermission of business during these hours.

olidays are to be kept, except Sundays, Christmas-day, Good Friday, fast days appointed by
oclamation, and the King's or Queen's birthdays.

cases not specified or provided for in the foregoing rules and orders, application must be made
rincipal dock-master, Charles C. Parish.

oregoing regulations approved and confirmed by the Court of Directors of the West India Dock
y.

st India Dock House, Aug. 26. 1831.   H. LONGLANDS, Secretary.

entering the West India docks are permitted to retain their crews on board, when required by
ers; and the directors have fitted up the ship Waterloo, in the South Dock, for the accommo-
f junior officers and apprentices, while their ships are discharging their cargoes in the Import

aptains, officers, and crews of ships are requested not to give either wine, spirits, or grog, to the
of the Company, as, by so doing, they expose them to the certain and immediate forfeiture of
uations.

e, perquisite, or reward, of any kind or denomination whatsoever, is to be taken by the Company's
or any persons who shall be employed in the service of the Company, for any act done within the
Penalty, forfeiture of the sum taken, and any sum not exceeding 5l. for each offence.

*nda for the Information of the Consignees and Proprietors of Goods imported in Ships which dis-
charge their Cargoes in the West India Docks.*

p is allowed to break bulk until her cargo is duly entered; it is, therefore, important that con-
should give directions for the entry of their respective consignments at the Custom-house as soon
ip is reported.

ge and presents may be cleared at the baggage warehouse, at the docks, after examination by the

riginal bills of lading must be deposited when required, except where a part of the goods are
t to be placed under the East India Company's care: in that case, the original bill must be
d, and a true copy thereof deposited. Should the original bill have been previously delivered
st India House, a certified copy must be obtained from the accountant-general of the Honourable
y.

ular attention is necessary to the regularity of the indorsements, as the Company's officers cannot
bill of lading, on which the authority from the shipper to the holder is not deduced by a complete
arate chain of indorsement.

bill of lading should be specially indorsed, so as clearly to designate the party to whose order the
are to be delivered.

cases of informality in bills of lading, from want of indorsement, &c., or of their being lost, appli-
ust be made to the court by letter, stating the circumstances, and enclosing any documents which
w the title to the goods. In every such case, the applicant must engage to indemnify the Com-
bond or otherwise, as the court may direct.

When bills of lading are produced, which are at variance with the manifest as to the original consi, the Company will not pass any delivery order founded thereon until three clear days shall have elaps

The delivery of goods afloat will be the act of the captain or officer in charge of the vessel. The prietor should, however, give notice to the West India Dock Company that it is not his intention to them landed; but such notices will not be required where the goods are placed under the care of the India Company.

No order can be received until the manifest of the cargo, duly certified by the captain, has been sited at the West India Dock House; but the orders of the importers of all goods intrusted to the India dock Company's management may then be passed, according to circumstances.

To facilitate passing orders before the charges due upon the goods can be ascertained, the Company open deposit accounts, upon requests from the merchants, as hereinafter noticed.

When parties, holding orders for delivery from the quays, wish the goods housed in their own na or in the names of other parties, they must lodge the order, indorsed to that effect, and warrants w granted accordingly.

All merchandise warehoused under the care of the West India Dock Company is deliverable, ir ordinary course of business, by warrant, with the exception of Muscovado sugar, wood*, returned m factures, and articles imported in bulk, of which the weight or measure is liable to increase or dec from natural causes, and goods which are not to be warehoused, or are intended for immediate shipp In the latter case, the importers must state on their orders that "warrants are not required."

All goods intrusted to the management of the East India Company, although deposited in the India docks, will be delivered in the usual course of the Honourable Company's business, by East warrants.

That the course of business, as respects the West India Dock Company, may be fully understoo attention of importers and purchasers of produce is particularly requested to the following memorand

The West India Dock *Warrants* for goods which are usually sold without lotting, will be made ou such quantities as have been found generally convenient to the importers. Warrants or cheque smaller quantities, or single packages, may, however, be granted, on paying for the extra number a rates herein fixed.

For goods which are lotted, made merchantable, &c., the warrants will be made out as soon a operations are performed. When directions from the importer are required, notice will be given o landing accounts. It is desirable that particular and early attention should be paid to such notices; that the importers of cotton, pepper, or other articles which usually require being made merchant should lodge a general order, directing that operation to be performed to all their importations.

The first warrants of the West India Dock Company will be issued to the order of the importe their assigns (provided there is no stop upon the goods for freight or otherwise), upon payment o prime rates or landing charges.

Such payments must include all charges to the time of housing, and those for lotting or making chantable for the importer; but, if the goods are deliverable by warrant, are not to include rent. Ch accruing subsequently, and the rent, must be paid by the holders of the warrants before delivery o goods. The proprietors of goods may, however, clear the rent and incidental charges to any desired and have new warrants or cheques accordingly.

When the assignment or removal of part of the goods only is intended, the warrants or cheques sl be divided at the Dock-house in London as hereafter provided.

If the delivery of the whole of the contents is directed, and the goods are not removed within two a new warrant or cheque for the remainder of the parcel must be taken out.

In the case of casks of liquids used to fill up others, the warrant must be lodged; and the proprietor either have a new warrant for the remainder, or it may be delivered (if not required again to be us the same way) to his order.

When the holders of warrants or cheques are desirous of assigning part of their contents, wi delivery, reweighing, rehousing, &c., new documents will be given in exchange, on lodging the orig duly indorsed. The indorsement should specially direct the manner in which the contents are divided, and state the names of the parties in whose favour the new warrants or cheques are to be is in the following form:— "Please to divide the within;" or, when part is to be delivered— "Deliv bearer (state how many packages), and grant new , one for (state how many packages), in fa of ; one for," &c.

Warrants may be exchanged or divided without assigning the goods, when desired by the holder, a same rate of charge.

The charges for dividing or issuing new documents are—

For each new warrant granted, containing	s.	d.	For each new warrant granted, containing s
1 or 2 packages or quantities	0	1	26 to 30 packages or quantities
3 or 4	0	2	31 to 35
5 or 7	0	3	36 to 40
8 to 10	0	4	41 to 45
11 to 15	0	5	46 and upwards
16 to 20	0	6	For every new cheque granted
21 to 25	0	7	

If, from the nature of the contract between the seller and buyer, reweighing, &c. may be necessar warrants must be deposited, indorsed with directions to that effect; and new warrants will be issued taining the landing weights and reweights, as soon as the operations are completed.

When any alterations, such as repacking, &c., are to be made (except when preparatory to imm delivery), the warrants must be lodged; and others, representing the goods, correctly issued in the manner.

The warrants must likewise be lodged on giving orders to vat; and when immediate shipment intended, new warrants will be issued.

In the three last-mentioned cases, the charges for performing the operations include the expense new warrants.

When warrants or cheques are lost or mislaid, the Company require that they should be advertis the Public Ledger; the paper containing the advertisement, and an engagement to indemnify the pany, by bond or otherwise, to be enclosed with the application for duplicates. The new documen to be issued (unless the original shall be found and delivered up) until seven clear days shall have c from the date of notice by advertisement. Upon notice of the loss, the goods will be stopped; ar original document can, on no account, be acted upon. When East India warrants are lost, the should be given to the Honourable Company's warehouse keeper.

Irregularities in the indorsements lessen the security of the proprietors of goods, and render the ments incomplete as authorities. The attention of the holders is therefore particularly called t point, to prevent the impediments which must otherwise arise to the regular despatch of business.

Any attempt to remove such impediments, by indorsing any warrant, order, or cheque, withou authority, even although no fraud may be intended, will be invariably noticed in the most serious m by the directors of the West India Dock Company.

* Warrants will be granted, however, at the desire of the proprietor, for dye-wood imported fro East Indies, or any article that can be separated into distinct and corresponding parcels, on his payi expenses of making such allotment.

rms on which persons may be authorised to sign for others, may be obtained in the General Office at Dock-house; and as no signature but that of the party named on the warrant, delivery order, or ue, can be acted upon, when goods are made deliverable to order, persons so authorised should adhere e following form:—" For (name or firm). "(Signature of the person authorised)."

posit Accounts may be opened with such deposits as the merchants think proper. When the ce is reduced below 10*l.*, a further deposit must be made; 10*l.* being the smallest sum which can be ived at a time.

rties having deposit accounts with the Company, must transmit a note of advice, on the proper form, each deposit; and it will be necessary that they should invariably state, on their orders or warrants, m the charges are to be paid by; thus—

   Charges to the (date), to our account."   (Signature.)

·, "Charges to be paid by the holder."   (Signature.)

· opening such accounts, the business of merchants with the Company, particularly where goods are rent, is much facilitated. The proper forms and pass books may be obtained on application at the k-house.

ders for Extra Work. — The charges for repacking, or preparing for exportation, and all work not rised in these tables, will be fixed from time to time, with reference to the cost of labour and mate-

No such work, however, can be done but by the order of the proprietors of goods, or parties duly orised by them. The warrants or other documents must, therefore, be produced, to show their ority.

e charges under this head must be paid by the parties giving the order or clearing the goods.

ods prepared for Shipment. — When goods housed in the import warehouses are prepared for ship-, and are not taken away within the fixed number of days, they will be rehoused at the expense of roprietor; and the charge for such rehousal, and any additional rent which may have accrued, must id before delivery.

e time allowed to elapse before restowing mahogany, and other measured wood, is four days; dye-s, and all other goods, seven clear days. When the export vessel loads in the docks, the time will tended to the date of her departure.

Dock Rates. — *Import Vessels, when discharged by the Company.*

	Per Ton Reg.
	s. d.
laden entirely, or in part, with hogsheads and tierces of sugar or molasses - - 2 0	
laden entirely with chests or bags of sugar, coffee, spirits, wine, oil, tallow; iron, copper, ss, lead, spelter, or other metal, in pigs, bars, rods, plates, or similar pieces; rice, tobacco, or er goods, packed in bales, bags, serons, cases, chests, or similar packages, or brought loose, luding wood in planks or billets, such as dye-wood, staves, &c. - - 1 0	
laden entirely, or in part, with mahogany, timber, or other wood, in logs - - 2 0	

e foregoing rates include docking, mooring, and removing within the docks, (if not leaky, or other-requiring extra labour,) until placed in the Export Dock, or taken to the river; unloading and ring the cargoes, (except on delivery overside, in which case any cooperage or mending will be an charge,) and the use of the docks for any period not exceeding eight weeks from the date of discharge.

Wood laden, from Europe or the North American Colonies, when discharged by the Company.

	Per Ton Reg.
	s. d.
entirely with deals, planks, staves, or wood in billets - - 1 6	
principally with ditto, and bringing hard wood or pine timber; for every load of hard wood of pine timber, 6*d.* in addition - - 1 6	
entirely with hard wood or pine timber - - - - 2 0	

e foregoing rates include docking, mooring, and removing within the docks, until discharged; un-g the cargoes, and the use of the docks for any period not exceeding eight weeks from the date of al discharge.

Ships discharging or loading by their own Crews, or laying up.

	Per Ton Reg.
	s. d.
RT Dock. —Vessels discharging by their own crews in the Export Dock; the use of the docks any period not exceeding four weeks from the day of entering - - 0 9	
which have not discharged in the docks; for any period not exceeding four weeks from the e of entering - - - - - - 0 6	
ls from any port in the United Kingdom, or European port outside the Baltic, between the th Cape and Ushant, with cargoes for trans-shipment, or delivery on board ships, or landing, remaining beyond three weeks - - - - 0 6	
and craft coastwise, with bricks for delivery on board ships, not remaining beyond one week 0 3	
els which have re-entered, after having been out for repair, are to pay the dock rent of 1*d.* r ton register per week only from the expiration of the time allowed under the rate in-rred at the vessel's previous entry.	
rent, for remaining over the periods above specified, per week - - 0 1	
Dock. — Vessels entering to lay up, immediately after their discharge in the Import Dock, ng paid the rates for the use of that dock, first six weeks - - Free.	
s to discharge by their own crews, for any period not exceeding six weeks from the date of ring - - - - - - 0 9	
vessels, which have not discharged in either of the docks, for any period not exceeding six ks from the date of entering - - - - 0 6	
s in short trades, as described under the head *Export Dock*, not remaining beyond three weeks 0 6	
and craft coastwise, with bricks for delivery on board ships, not remaining beyond one week 0 3	
els which enter, after having left either dock for repair, are to pay the dock rent of ¾*d.* per register per week only, from the expiration of the time allowed, under the rate incurred their previous entry.	
rent, for remaining over the periods above specified, per week - - 0 0¾	
boats to lay up, for any period not exceeding four weeks, per ton builders' measurement - 0 6	
ent, after the first four weeks, per ton per week, builders' measurement - 0 1	

foregoing rates do not include the expense of docking, mooring, unmooring, and removing.

Ships taking in Cargoes from the Import Warehouses.

els intending to load from the import warehouses will be allowed one week for that purpose, on nt of 6*d.* per ton on the gross weight shipped. If they remain longer, a dock rent of 1*d.* per ton r per week will be charged in addition. If any vessel which shall enter the docks for this purpose t take in goods, she will be charged 1*d.* per ton register per week for the time she remains.

s from the Export or South Docks will be allowed to go into the Import Dock to load, as soon as ds they intend to take are prepared for shipment, paying 6*d.* per ton on the gross weight of the in addition to the rate for the use of those docks.

following conditions must be observed:—

ne taking the ship in and out of dock, or to and from the quay, to be performed by the master and s directed by the dock-masters.

2. The goods to be taken from the slings, and to be stowed away by the crew, under the orders of t master.

3. If a sufficient crew be not on board to receive and stow away the goods as delivered, or to transpc the vessel, a further number of men shall be provided by the Company *, at the charge of 3*s.* per man p day, to work under the direction and responsibility of the master and his officers.

4. The vessel to be hauled into the basin or Export Dock after the usual hours of business, by her ov officers and crew, and to continue in their charge.

Goods sent by land carriage for such vessels will be shipped in either of the docks, on payment of t usual charges.

To prevent delay in loading export vessels, the shippers should pay up the rent and charges upon t goods; or, where the amount cannot be ascertained without weighing, &c., make a deposit to cover t same.

Supply of Water for Shipping.	*s.*	*d.*
If received in boats or craft, at Blackwall basin, per tun - - -	1	0
If taken to the ship by the Company's servants, per ditto - - -	1	6
If filled by ditto into casks or tanks on shipboard, per ditto - - -	2	3

TABLE FOR GOODS IMPORTED.

The Prime Rate includes all expenses for landing, wharfage, weighing or gauging at landing, coope ing, marking, sampling, housing, weighing for actual delivery, and delivering; furnishing landing a delivery weights or gauges, surveying and furnishing certificates of damage, and rent for twelve wee from the date of the ship's commencement of discharge.

This rate will be charged on all goods imported from the East or West Indies, the Mauritius, Mexic or South America, and upon wood, spirits or wine, and tobacco, from whatever place of importatio unless notice be given, by the importers, of their desire to have them placed under the landing rate, their intention to remove them without housing or piling. If such notice is given before housing piling, the rate in the second column will be discharged.

The Landing Rate includes landing, wharfage, and housing, or delivering from the quay, and furnishi landing accounts.

This rate will attach to all other merchandise than as above specified, which may be imported; to Ea India cotton, to hides and skins, hair, horns and tips, to manufactures returned, and to every descripti of goods relanded, or removed in bond or coastwise into the docks, unless the importers signify their wi that they should be warehoused under the prime or consolidated rates.

The Rates for Unhousing and Loading, or Unloading and Housing, when not otherwise specifie are each one third of the landing rate; and that for unhousing, wharfage, and shipping, is the whole ra as stated in the second column. When the prime rate has not been paid, those charges will be made, t gether with reasonable charges for coopering, sampling, and other operations contingent on housing.

The Charges for Weighing and Rehousing are each one third of the rate in the second column. F repiling or weighing wood, one fourth of that rate is charged.

Goods sold from the Landing Scale, or not intended to be warehoused, will be allowed four clear da from the final weighing of the parcel for removal; in default of which, they will be housed or piled. intended for immediate trans-shipment, they may remain on the quay, subject to the same regulations goods prepared for shipment, paying rent as if housed at landing.

Warehouse Rent, on goods to which the prime rate does not attach, will be charged from the date the ship's breaking bulk; but when goods sold from the landing scale are housed, the rent will be charg from the final weighing of the parcel.

A week's rent will be charged for all fractions of a week.

Before the transfer by the Company, or delivery of any goods can take place, the charges on the quant to be transferred or delivered must be paid either to the collector, at the General Office in London, or the comptroller, at the General Office at the docks.

Rates on Goods imported.

N. B. All sorts of goods may be imported into and warehoused at the West India docks, on about same terms as at the other docks. We have given, under the head *London Docks*, a table of the dc dues, &c. on most articles commonly imported, which may be applied, with very trifling modificatio either to the West India or St. Katharine's docks. The following table includes merely the dock charg on the importation, warehousing, &c. of the principal articles of West India produce: —

		Prime Rate.		Landing Rate.		Rent per Week.		
	Nett ℔	*s.*	*d.*	*s.*	*d.*	*Gross* ℔	*s.*	*d.*
Annotto - - - -	ton	20	0	7	0	ton - -	0	7
baskets and packages under 1 cwt.		3	0	1	7½	ton - -	0	7
Arrow Root - - -	ton	16	8	5	0	ton - -	0	7
Canella Alba - - -	cwt.	1	6	0	6	cwt. - -	0	0¾
Chocolate - - -	box	3	3	0	9	box - -	0	2
Cochineal - - - -	cwt.	2	0	0	9	cwt. - -	0	1
Cocoa and Coffee, casks -	cwt.	1	6	0	6	ton - -	0	6
bags - - - -	cwt.	1	2	0	6	ton - -	0	6
Cotton Wool, press packed -	cwt.	0	9	0	3	ton - -	0	4
not press packed - -	cwt.	1	0	0	4½	ton - -	0	5
Ginger, casks - - -	cwt.	1	6	0	6	ton - -	0	6
bags - - - -	cwt.	1	2	0	6	ton - -	0	6
preserved, see Succades.								
Jalap - - - -	cwt.	1	0	0	5¼	ton - -	0	7
Indian Rubber - -	hhd. or pipe	4	6	1	6	hhd. or pipe -	0	4
	case	2	6	1	0	case 1 to 2 cwt.	0	1
	barrel	1	3	0	6	barrel - -	0	0½
Ipecacuanha - - - -	cwt.	1	0	0	5¼	ton - -	0	7
Molasses - - - -	cwt.	0	7	0	3	pun. - -	0	2½
						hhd. or tierce -	0	1½
						barrel or keg -	0	0¾
Mother o'Pearl, Shells - -	ton	16	6	7	6	ton - -	0	4
Ware - - - -	chest	5	0	1	6	chest - -	0	2
	box	3	0	1	0	box - -	0	1
Piccaba - - - - -	cwt.	1	0	0	6	ton - -	0	4
Pickles, cases -	doz. bottles	0	9	0	2¼	doz. bottles -	0	0½
barrels - - -	gallon	0	1¼	0	0½	barrel - -	0	1

* No labourers or lumpers are allowed to be employed in discharging or loading ships in the Im Dock, except those employed by the Company.

Rates on Goods imported — continued.

		Prime Rate.		Landing Rate.		Rent per Week.		
	Nett per	*s.*	*d.*	*s.*	*d.*	*Gross per*	*s.*	*d.*
Pimento, casks - - cwt.		1	6	0	6	ton - -	0	6
bags - - cwt.		1	2	0	6	ton - -	0	6
Snake Root - - - cwt.		2	0	0	9	barrel or ½ bale	0	1
						trc. or bale -	0	2
						hhd. - -	0	3
Succades, under 28 lbs. - package		0	6	0	3	cwt. - -	0	0½
28 lbs. to 1 cwt. - package		1	6	0	6	cwt. - -	0	0½
1 cwt. and upwards - - cwt.		1	0	0	6	cwt. - -	0	0½
Sugar, casks - - cwt.		0	8	0	3	ton - -	0	5
chests above 5 cwt., or baskets cwt.		0	6	0	3	ton - -	0	4
chests under 5 cwt., or bags cwt.		0	5	0	3	ton - -	0	3
Candy - - cwt.		1	0	0	4½	cwt. - -	0	0½
Tobacco. See *London Docks*, p. 458.								
Wood. See separate table, p. 450.								

	Prime Rate.		Landing Rate.		Rent and Superintendence per Week, to be charged prospectively from 21st of June, 1831, inclusive, and to apply only to the Stock then on hand, and to all Importations prior to the 1st of June, 1832.						
	s.	*d.*	*s.*	*d.*	Per	‡ First 6 Months.		Next 6 Months.		After 12 Months.	
Nett per						*s.*	*d.*	*s.*	*d.*	*s.*	*d.*
* and Wine, in casks - 100 galls.	†10 0		3	6	Butt - -	0	7	0	6	0	4½
and Geneva - - -	*8	0			Pun. or ½ butt	0	5	0	4	0	3
ch cask intended to be laid up is					Hhd. - -	0	2½	0	2	0	1½
d to have at least six iron hoops, or					Qr. cask or brl.	0	2	0	1½	0	1½
hen usual in any particular trade;											
eficient of the regular number, the					For casks of a different description, or exceeding the usual sizes, imported from any particular port, a proportionate rent will be charged.						
nal hoops to be supplied at 6d. each.											
casks, when requisite, to be charged											
tion.											
n the Spirits or Wines are imported										*s.*	*d.*
s made of proper Oak, the Com-					For cooper's care and attendance after the first 12 weeks, per cask - 0 1						
ngages to be responsible for de-											
es in *measure*, which shall exceed											
llon per cask for each year, or											
of a year, the goods remain in											
but the Company will not be an-											
e for deficiencies arising from the											
eing made of other and inefficient											
s.											
- - - doz. quarts.	0	9	0	3	Case of 6 dozen quarts - 0 2						
id up in store for ripening ditto	0	9	—		Case of 3 ditto - 0 1						
					Case of 6 ditto, per quarter - 1 0						
					Case of 3 ditto ditto - 0 6						

Racking Spirits into Vats and Refilling.

	s.	*d.*
ousing, racking, the use of the vat (remaining one night), refilling and bunging up, per lons, drawn from the vat	2	8
aining in the vat more than one night, per 100 gallons ditto, each additional night -	1	0
r reducing the strength, per pun. - - - - - -	1	0

REFINED SUGAR.		Wharfage & Porterage.		Rent per Week.	
		s.	*d.*	*s.*	*d.*
r Shipment.					
Bastard - - hogshead - - - -		1	2	0	4
Refined - - ditto - - - -		1	0	0	3
16 cwt. and upwards, vat -		1	8	0	6

	s.	*d.*
nded for Exportation.		
Housing, weighing, unhousing, wharfage, and shipping, each per hogshead -	0	6
Ditto per vat 16 cwt. and upwards - - -	0	10
Rent per week, per ton - - - -	0	5

CRUSHING SUGAR. — The following charges include all expenses for receiving, delivering, pering, and rent, for one week; viz.

	s.	*d.*			*s.*	*d.*
rushed by hand, partly, per ton -	16	0	Crushed by the mill, per ton -		16	0
— rough — -	18	0	Rent per week - - -		0	5
— fine -	21	0				

‡ Reckoning from the commencement of the ship's discharge.

Rates on Dye Woods.

Dyers' Wood, &c.		Prime Rate, viz. Landing, Wharfage, Piling, 12 Weeks' Rent, & Delivering.		Landing, Wharfage, Weighing, and Delivering.		Rent pe Week, a the firs 12 Mont
		s.	*d.*	*s.*	*d.*	*s.*
Bar Wood						
Box Wood						
Brazil Wood, large						
Cam Wood						
Cocus Wood						
Ebony	Ton	6	6	4	6	0
Fustic	under cover	7	0	—		0
Lignum Vitæ						
Logwood						
Nicaragua, large						
Quassia						
Sanders Wood						
Braziletto	Ton	8	0	5	6	0
Brazil Wood, small	—	8	0	5	6	0
Fustic, young	—	8	0	5	6	0
Nicaragua Wood, small	—	8	0	5	6	0
Sapan	—	8	0	5	6	0
Sassafras	—	8	0	5	6	0
Sandal	—	8	0	5	6	0
Other Wood, charged with duty, at per ton.						
Mahogany, Cedar, Jacaranda, Rose Wood, Satin Wood, Tulip, Zebra, &c.	—	7	0	5	0	0

Special Charges.   *s. d*

Rummaging mahogany, timber, and other measured wood, as usual, per ton or load - 1 0
Delivering into decked vessels - - - - - - - - 0 6

2. *London Docks.* — These were the next undertaking of this sort set on foot in Thames. They are situated in Wapping, and were principally intended for the recep of ships laden with wine, brandy, tobacco, and rice. The western dock covers a s of above 20 acres; and the new or eastern dock covers about 7 acres. The tobacco d lies between the above, and exceeds 1 acre in extent, being destined solely for the re tion of tobacco ships. The entire space included within the outer dock wall is 71 a and 3 roods. The warehouses are capacious and magnificent. The great tob warehouse, on the north side of the tobacco dock, is the largest, finest, and most c venient building of its sort in the world. It is calculated to contain 24,000 h of tobacco, and covers the immense space of near *five* acres! There is also a very l tobacco warehouse on the south side of the tobacco dock. These warehouses are wh under the management of the officers of customs; the Dock Company having noth whatever to do with them, save only to receive the rent accruing upon the tob deposited in them. The vaults are under the tobacco and other warehouses, and stowage for 65,000 pipes of wine and spirits. These docks were opened in 1805. ships bound for the Thames, laden with wine, brandy, tobacco, and rice (except s from the East and West Indies), were obliged to unload in them for the spac twenty-one years: but this monopoly expired in January, 1826; and the use of docks is now optional.

The only entrances to the London docks were, until lately, by the basins at mitage and Wapping. Recently, however, another entrance has been completed old Shadwell dock, through what was formerly, Milkyard, to the eastern dock. new entrance is three fourths of a mile lower down than Wapping entrance, and most material improvement.

The capital of the Company amounts to 3,238,310*l.* 5*s.* 10*d.* A considerable po of this vast sum, and of a further sum of 700,000*l.* borrowed, was required for the chase of the houses, about 1,300 in number, that occupied the site of the docks. present dividend is 3 per cent., and a 100*l.* share is worth about 60*l.* The Boa Directors consists of twenty-five members, of whom the Lord Mayor, as conservat the River Thames, is one.

REGULATIONS TO BE OBSERVED BY THE MASTERS, AND CHARGES TO BE PAID, BY VESSELS USIN LONDON DOCKS.

1. *Regulations.* — You are required to deliver at the superintendent's office, within twelve hou your vessel has entered the dock, or reported at the Custom-house (which shall first happen), a tru of the manifest, or report of the cargo, signed by yourself.

The decks are to be speedily cleared of such articles as may impede the discharge; and either yo the mate, or some person duly authorised by the owners, must remain on board during the time oc in loading or unloading.

The Company, with the consent of the chief officer of the customs, are authorised to forbid the br bulk, or landing any part of the cargo, until the whole thereof shall have been entered.

If the speedy unloading of your ship be obstructed by the entries not having been passed forty-eight hours from the date of your report, the Company will, on the application of yourself or cause a warehousing entry to be passed, at the expense of the consignee of the goods; or land go entered within seven clear days from the date of the report.

The Company are authorised to employ a sufficient number of persons to discharge, or assist charging, the cargo, at the expense of the vessel, whenever they shall see occasion.

ur crew may discharge the cargo; and if you require additional hands, the Company's warehouse-
ers will supply any number of labourers, at 3s. 6d. per day each, to work under your direction and
onsibility; but you are not at liberty to employ lumpers in the dock.

ostracts of cargoes will be supplied to the owners, for the purpose of making up freight accounts, on
cation at the comptroller's office, at the following rates: viz.

	s.	d.
If containing 10 marks or under - - - - -	2	0
11 to 20 marks - - - - -	3	6
21 and upwards, 2d. each mark or parcel.		

tices to detain goods for freight are to be lodged at the superintendent's office, and must specify the
unt claimed on each parcel. Goods delivered overboard into craft cannot be detained for freight.

ater will be supplied from the reservoir, at 1s. per 220 gallons, delivered into your boats, on application
e dock-master.

entering the dock or basin, or when removing in the docks, you are to peak your lower and top-sail
s. Main, spanker, jib, and steering-sail booms, are all to be run close in.

ur vessel must neither have her sails loose after sunset, be so placed as to obstruct the entrances to
lock or basin, nor be moored to the Company's buoys or rings with iron chains; and, on leaving the
, must not ride by the transporting buoy, nor within 200 yards of the entrance.

you have tobacco on board, or intend loading tobacco, you are to strike your lower yards and top-
s, and brace the top-sail yards fore and aft upon the cap (if required), before entering the tobacco

ter discharging your cargo, you are not to lie at the quays without special leave, but are to haul off
diately to the buoys, and to strike your yards and top-masts, between the 1st of October and the 1st
oril; as also when going out to refit.

es, lights, or smoking, are not permitted on board before seven o'clock A.M. from the 30th of Sep-
er to the 25th of March; or before five o'clock A.M. from the 26th of March to the 29th of Sep-
er.

es and lights must be wholly extinguished at four o'clock P.M., when a bell is rung as notice for that
se; except coal fires, and lights in lanterns, which may be used in the cabin until eight o'clock in the
ng, (or in the cabouse until six o'clock, from Lady-day to Michaelmas-day,) provided permission in
ng be previously obtained from the superintendent or dock-master.

es are not allowed on the deck if you have combustibles on board.

ch, tar, rosin, turpentine, oil, or other combustible matter, is not allowed to be heated or boiled,
r on board ship or craft, or on the premises of the Company. Permission may be had from the ac-
ant's office for heated pitch to be brought in. Fires and lights must be wholly extinguished on
 whilst it is being used.

e-arms are not to be brought into the dock loaded, or loaded whilst in the dock. Gunpowder is not
 brought into the dock on any account.

last can be taken on board of, or delivered from, your vessel, whilst in the dock, by permission from
countant's office; and to prevent any part from falling into the water, canvass must be nailed to the
 f the vessel.

t or filth must on no occasion be thrown overboard; nor is the scraping of ship-sides, bottoms, or
asts permitted, except in the basin, where the top-gallant yards may be crossed the day previous to
vessel going into the river.

 are to keep charge of your own boats; and are responsible, together with the owner of your ship,
y damage done by lightermen, boatmen, bargemen, or other persons in your employ.

r vessel being about to leave the dock, should pass into the basin the day before, in order to insure
assage out the following tide; but cannot be removed from the dock to the basin on Sundays; nor
 eight o'clock in the morning, or after four o'clock in the afternoon, on other days.

gs are to be secured as the constables shall direct.

s are not to be rung on board ship.

Tonnage Rates. — Vessels are not permitted to leave the dock until the tonnage dues and other ex-
s have been paid; for which purpose the register must be produced at the superintendent's office, if
h, or a certificate of admeasurement by the proper officer of the customs, if foreign; when a pass
 granted, which must be lodged with the dock-master on leaving the dock.

st Class. — Vessels trading *coastwise* between the port of London and any port or place in the United
dom, for every register ton of th vessel, 6d.; and rent, after the expiration of six weeks, 1d. per
er ton per week. If with part of their cargoes, for every ton of goods landed, 1s.; for every ton of
shipped or trans-shipped, 6d.; and rent, after the expiration of one week, 1d. per register ton per

nd-Class. — Vessels *arriving* from any port in Denmark, Norway, Lapland on the southern side of
orth Cape; Holstein, Haml ro', Bremen, or any other port of Germany without the Baltic; the Ne-
nds, France (within Ushant), Guernsey, Jersey, Alderney, Sark, or Man, with liberty to reload for
 those ports*, for every register ton of the vessel, 6d.; and rent, after the expiration of six weeks,
r register ton per week.

els *loading* for any of those places, not having previously discharged their cargoes in the docks, for
register ton of the vessel, 6d.; and rent, after the expiration of four weeks, 1d. per register ton per

rd Class. — Vessels *arriving* from the East or West Indies, Cape of Good Hope, or South America,
iberty to reload; for every register ton of a vessel from the East Indies (including the discharge of
rgo), 1s.; for every register ton of a vessel from the West Indies (including the discharge and
ing of the cargo), 2s.; for every register ton of a vessel from the Cape of Good Hope, or South
ica (not including the discharge of the cargo), 6d.; and rent, after the expiration of six weeks from
ischarge of the vessel, 1d. per register ton per week.

els *loading* for either of those places, not having previously discharged their cargoes in the docks;
ry register ton of the vessel, 9d.; and rent, after the expiration of four weeks, 1d. per register ton
ek.

rth Class. —Vessels *arriving* from all other ports or places whatsoever (with the exceptions enume.
below), with liberty to reload; for every register ton of the vessel, 9d.; and rent, after the expiration
weeks, 1d. per register ton per week.

els *loading* for any of those places, not having previously discharged their cargoes in the docks; for
register ton of the vessel, 9d.; and rent, after the expiration of four weeks, 1d. per register ton per

ptions. — Vessels from Spain, laden with cork or wool; for every register ton of the vessel, 6d.; and
ter the expiration of three weeks, 1d. per register ton per week.

els to or from the whale fisheries; for every register ton of the vessel, 1s.; and rent, after the ex.
n of six weeks, 1d. per register ton per week; for every tun of oil delivered into craft, 6d.

els (excepting coasters, for which see first class,) landing part of their cargoes; for every ton of
landed, 1s.; for every ton of goods trans-shipped, 6d.; and rent, from entering the dock, 1d. per
r ton per week.

port vessels in the first and second classes are allowed to load for any other port or place whatso.
n payment of the same dues and rent as import vessels in the fourth class.

Vessels loadihg part of their cargoes for any place in Europe or Africa; for every ton of goods from t quays or by craft, 6*d.*; and rent, after the expiration of one week, 1*d.* per register ton per week.

Light vessels entering the docks to lie up; entrance, *one guinea*; rent of the vessel, 1*d.* per register t per week; and on leaving the docks light, *one guinea.*

Vessels which enter the docks light, and load out, pay dues according to their ports of destinati instead of those on light vessels.

Whenever required, the Company will discharge the cargo of a vessel upon the following terms; v From the Cape of Good Hope or South America, per register ton, 6*d.*; casks, bales, general merchandi wine, brandy, or jars of oil, from other places, for every register ton, 9*d.*; tallow or cotton, for ev register ton, 6*d.*; hemp, barilla, or valonea in bulk, for every register ton, 1*s.*; hemp and tallow, as th respective proportions bear to the register tonnage; for every ton of hemp, 1*s.*; for every ton of tallo 6*d.*; provided the entries for the goods be all made previously to the ship breaking bulk.

Vessels which leave the docks for repairs are not charged rent while absent.

3. *Memoranda.* — Registers of ships inwards and outwards are kept in the superintendent's office.

The wicket gates at the north west principal entrance, and at Wapping, are opened and closed as und

From 21st March	to 21st May,	both inclusive,	opened at	6 o'clock,	closed at	7 o'clock.
22d May	21st Aug.		—	6	—	8	—
22d Aug.	21st Sept.		—	6	—	7	—
22d Sept.	1st Nov.		—	7	—	6	—
2d Nov.	20th Feb.		—	7	—	5	—
21st Feb.	20th March,		—	7	—	6	—

Visitors are not admitted on Sundays.

No person is permitted to quit a vessel after the wicket gate is closed.

The hours for the commencement of business, and opening and closing the barrier gate, are,

From 25th March	to 29th Sept.,	both inclusive,	opened at	8 o'clock,	closed at	4 o'clock.
30th Sept.	24th March,		—	9	—	4	—

Explanation of the following Table of Rates and Charges on Goods imported into the London Docks.

The consolidated rate is charged upon the nett weight, and includes landing, wharfage, and housing, piling on the quay, coopering, sampling, weighing for delivery, delivery, and twelve weeks' rent from t date of the ship's report; which may be paid on each mark separately.

The import rate is charged upon the gross weight, and includes landing, wharfage, and housing, or pili on the quay, or loading from the landing scale, and furnishing the landing weights or tales; to be p before the delivery of any part of an entry can take place.

The charges for reweighing, rehousing, unhouisng and loading, or repiling, are each one third of t import rate; those for unhousing or unpiling, wharfage, and shipping, the same as the import rate; wh not otherwise specified.

TABLE OF RATES AND CHARGES ON GOODS IMPORTED INTO THE LONDON DOCKS.

Goods Imported.	Import Rate.		Rent. Per Week.		Rent. Quantities, &c.
Per	s.	d.	s.	d.	Per
Alkanet Root - - cwt.	0	5½	0	1	cwt.
Almonds, from Africa, ton	4	6	0	4	ton
in boxes and barrels, cwt.	0	6	2	0	100 boxes
			1	3	100 half boxes
			0	2	brl. 2 cwt. 2 qrs. to 3 cwt.
			0	0½	quarter barrel
Shell - cwt.	0	9	0	2	large bale
			0	1½	small bale
			0	1	half bale or seron ¾ to 1½ cwt.
Aloes, in gourds - ton	8	0	0	3	score gourds
Or a consolidated rate of 24*s.* per ton nett.					
in chests or casks - ton	6	0	0	1	package under 3 cwt.
Or a consolidated rate of			0	1½	do. 3 and under 5 cwt.
20*s.* per ton nett.			0	2	do. 5 and under 8 cwt.
			0	3	do. 8 cwt. and upwards.
Alum - - ton	3	6	0	3	ton
Amber and Beads - cwt.	2	0	0	1	box or case
Ambergris, in boxes or kegs, package	1	0	0	3	package
Anchovies - - cwt.	0	9	2	6	100 brls. or double brls.
			1	3	100 kegs
			0	0½	cask under 1½ cwt.
Angelica Root - ton	5	0	0	1	barrel
			0	2	tierce
			0	3	hogshead
Annatto - - ton	7	0	0	1	cask or case under 3 cwt.
in baskets or small packages - cwt.	1	7½	0	2	cask 3 to 8 cwt.
			0	0½	mat or basket 1 cwt. and under
Anniseed - cwt.	0	3	0	6	ton
Star - cwt.	0	4½	0	6	ton
Antimony - - ton	5	0	0	4	ton
Apples - basket or barrel	0	6	0	0½	basket or barrel
tierce	1	0	0	1½	tierce
hogshead	1	6	0	3	hogshead
Argol - ton	5	0	0	4	in casks
			1	6	100 cases under 2 cwt.
			2	6	100 bags or cases 2 cwt. and under 4 cwt.
Arrow Root - ton	5	0	0	6	ton
Or a consolidated rate of 16*s.* 8*d.* per ton.					
Arsenic - - ton	5	0	0	4	ton
Asafœtida - - cwt.	0	3¾	0	0½	cwt.
Ashes, from America, ton	3	0	0	0½	cask
Russia - - ton	3	0	0	2	cask
Odessa - ton	3	0	0	3	ton
Unhousing, wharfage, and shipping, 2*s.* per ton.					
Asphaltum - - ton	5	0	0	6	ton
Bacon - - hogshead	1	6	0	3	hogshead
bale	0	9	0	1	bale
side	0	3	2	1	100 sides

Goods Imported.	Import Rate.		Rent. Per Week.		Rent. Quantitie
Per	s.	d.	s.	d.	Per
Baggage, including delivery and one week's rent.					
Presents, samples, parcels of papers, and other small articles, package	0	6	0	1	package
Cases - - package	1	0	0	1	package
Trunks, boxes, bundles of bedding, and wearing apparel - package	1	9	0	1	package
Middle-sized ditto, and chests - - package	2	6	0	2	package
Larger packages in proportion.					
Bags, empty - score	0	2	0	6	100 bundles
Balsam Capivi, in jars, cwt.	1	1½	0	0½	jar
in barrels - - cwt.	0	6	0	1	barrel 2 cwt.
			0	1½	barrel above
Peru, in jars - cwt.	1	1½	0	0½	jar
Cooper's attendance at landing and delivery is a separate charge.					
Canada - - package	1	6	0	1	package
Bamboos, see *Canes*.					
Bark, Oak, in bags or loose - - ton	5	0	0	4	ton
in casks - - ton	3	0	0	4	ton
in cases about 1 cwt. 2 qrs. - - cwt.	0	6	0	1	case
Jesuits' or Peruvian, cwt.	1	0	0	1	chest
			0	0¾	half chest or
			0	0½	half seron
Barilla, loose - - ton	3	6	0	2	ton
Unhousing, wharfage, and shipping, 3*s.* per ton.					
Filling and weighing, 2*s.* per ton.					
in serons - - ton	3	3	0	2	ton
Unhousing, wharfage, and shipping, 2*s.* 6*d.* per ton.					
Beads, Jet, or other kinds, ton	5	0	0	9	ton
Beans, in bags - bag	0	6	0	1	bag
Beef and Pork - tierce	0	8½	4	0	100 tierces
barrel	0	5¼	3	0	100 barrels
Berries, Juniper ton	8	0	2	6	100 bags und
			5	0	100 bags 2 t
Yellow or Bay ton	5	0	0	4	ton
Biscuits - - cwt.	0	3	0	2	puncheon
			0	0½	bag or barre
Bones - - 1,000	3	0	0	2	1,000
in bags - - bag	0	6	0	0¼	bag
Books - - cwt.	1	0	0	2	bale or box
			0	3	package or
Boracic Acid - ton	5	0	0	4	ton
Borax, rough or refined, ton	5	0	0	10	ton
Bottles, empty Glass, gross	3	0	0	1	gross

Imported.	Import Rate.		Rent. Per Week.		Rent. Quantities, &c.
Per	*s.*	*d.*	*s.*	*d.*	*Per*
ton	5	0	0	2	ton
oose - ton	3	6	0	2	ton
, wharfage, and					
, 3*s.* per ton.					
l weighing, 2*s.*					
cases - ton	3	3	0	3	in casks
, wharfage, and			8	4	100 cases of about 2 cwt.
, 2*s.* 6*d.* per ton			4	2	100 boxes about 1 cwt.
			2	1	100 boxes about 56 lbs.
ackages above					
- ton	5	0	0	6	ton
5 cwt. - ton	6	8¼	0	6	ton
- case	1	6	0	2	case
box	1	0	0	1	box
- ton	1	0	0	1½	case or barrel 2 cwt.
			0	2	case 3 to 5 cwt.
- ton	5	0	0	9	ton
- package	1	6			
small package	1	0			
arcels not ex-					
ng 5*l.* in value	0	4			
- ton	5	0	4	0	100 casks 2 cwt.
			2	0	100 tubs
			2	0	100 firkins
ton	7	6	0	4	ton
- cwt.	0	6	0	4	ton
- package	2	6	0	4	package
small package	1	6	0	3	small package
- cwt.	0	10½	0	2	bale or case
- cwt.	0	6	0	1	case under 3 cwt.
			0	2	case 3 cwt. and upwards
on Rattan, 1,000	1	6	0	1½	1,000
lidated rate of r 1000.					
- 1,000	4	0	0	3	1,000
ndles, 25 each 100	6	3	1	6	100
- cwt.	1	0	0	3	case or cask under 4 cwt.
			0	4	case or cask 4 and under 8 cwt.
			0	6	case or cask 8 cwt. and upwards
- cwt.	0	3	0	6	butt
			0	4	puncheon
			0	3	hogshead
			0	1	barrel
package	1	6	0	2	package
small package	1	0	0	1	small package
- cwt.	0	6	0	1½	chest
- bale	2	0	0	4	bale
ballot	1	4½	0	2	ballot
- hogshead	0	6	0	1	hogshead
barrel	0	3	0	0½	barrel
- cwt.	0	4½	1	0	ton
- cwt.	0	4½	1	0	ton, in chests
dated rate of			5	0	100 bags
cwt. nett.					
- cwt.	0	4½	1	3	ton
- cwt.	0	3	0	0½	cwt.
or small box	0	8½	0	1	keg or small box
case or chest	1	0	0	2	case or chest
- package	0	6	0	1	package
rriages, with					
- each	7	6	1	0	each
- each	10	6	1	6	each
ton	5	0	0	6	ton
ton	4	0	1	0	ton
- cwt.	0	6	0	1	tub or case
			1	6	100 small do.
- bushel	0	2½	4	0	100 sacks
			2	0	100 bags
			4	2	100 barrels
- cwt.	0	4½	0	7	ton
- cwt.	0	6	0	0½	cwt.
r Porcelain, case	1	6	0	3	case
small case	1	0	0	2	small case
box	1	0	0	1	box
- box	0	9	0	2	box
- cwt.	2	4½	0	10	ton
- cwt.	1	8¼	0	3	bale containing 3 bdles.
			0	4	case or cask containing 4 bundles
- pipe	1	6	0	4	pipe
hogshead	1	0	0	3	hogshead
e *Succades.*					
- chest	2	0	0	2	chest
case or large bale	2	0	0	3	case or large bale
pieces, ordinary ditto	1	6	0	2	ordinary bale
es, small do.	1	0	0	1½	small bale
- cwt.	0	8¼	0	1	cwt.
ated rate of wt.					
- ton	5	0	0	5	ton
- cwt.	0	9	0	2	bag or barrel
ated rate of					
.	-	-	4	2	100 bags
e, all kinds, cwt.	0	6	0	6	ton
- cwt.	0	6	0	4½	cwt.
- ton	6	0	0	3	ton
- 100	2	0	0	1	100
ated rate of)).					

Goods imported.	Import Rate.		Rent. Per Week.		Rent. Quantities, &c.	
Per	*s.*	*d.*	*s.*	*d.*	*Per*	
Coloquintida - - cwt.	0	8¼	0	1	case or cask under 1 cwt.	
			0	2	case or cask 1 and under 3 cwt.	
			0	3	case or cask 3 cwt. and upwards.	
Columbo Root - cwt.	0	6	0	0½	cwt.	
Copper - - ton	5	0	0	2	ton	
Wharfage and shipping, when piled on the quay, 3*s.* 4*d.* per ton						
Or a consolidated rate on old copper of 10*s.* per ton.						
Copperas - - ton	5	0	0	6	ton	
Coquilla Nuts - 1,000	2	3	0	2	1,000	
Coral, Fragments - cwt.	0	7½	0	3	case or cask	
Beads - - case	1	6	0	2	case	
box	1	0	0	1	box	
Cordage, Small - ton	5	0	0	4	ton	
Cork - - ton	6	0	0	7	on quay	
Unhousing, wharfage, and shipping, 4*s.* per ton.			1	0	under cover	
Corks - - cwt.	2	0	0	1	bag 1 cwt.	
			0	0½	bag 56 lbs.	
			0	2	hogshead	
Cornelians and Beads, chest	1	6	0	2	chest	
box	1	6	0	1	box	
Corpses - - each	15	0				
Cotton Goods - bale	1	6	0	2	bale	
box or case	1	0	0	1½	box or case	
trunk	0	9	0	1	trunk	
Cotton Wool, press-packed cwt.	0	3	0	4	ton	
not press-packed - cwt.	0	4½	0	5	ton	
Cotton Yarn - - cwt.	0	5¼	0	1	bale	
			0	0½	ballot	
Cowries - - ton	5	0	0	3	ton	
Cows - - each	10	0				
Cranberries - - keg	0	6	0	1	keg	
barrel	0	9	0	1	barrel	
Cream of Tartar - ton	5	0	0	3	cask above 13 cwt.	
			0	2	cask under 13 cwt.	
Cubebs - - cwt.	0	6	0	0¾	cwt.	
Cummin Seed - - cwt.	0	6	0	0¼	cwt.	
					Unhousing and Loading. *s.* *d.*	
Currants, 23 cwt. and upwards - - butt	4	6	0	6	1 0	
13 to 23 cwt. - butt	3	0	0	4	0 8	
9 to 15 cwt. - pipe	2	3	0	3	0 6	
5 to 9 cwt. - carotel	1	6	0	2	0 4	
Deals, see *Wood Goods.*						
Deer - each	5	0				
Diamonds - - package	1	6	0	3	package	
Dragons' Blood - cwt.	0	6	0	0½	cwt.	
Dripstones - each	0	9	0	0½	each	
Eau de Cologne - case	1	6	0	4	case	
small case	1	0	0	2	small case	
Elephants' Teeth, see *Ivory.*						
Emery Stone, see *Stone.*						
Essences - - case	2	0	0	4	case	
under 2 cwt., small case	1	6	0	2	small case	
Extract from Oak Bark cwt.	0	3	0	1	cask about 4 cwt.	
			0	1½	cask above 6½ cwt.	
Rhatania - - cwt.	0	9	0	1	cwt.	
Jesuits' Bark - cwt.	0	9	0	1	cwt.	
Fans - - - case	1	0	0	1½	case	
box	1	0	0	1	box	
Feathers, Beds - cwt.	0	10½	0	1	small bale	
			0	1½	bag 1½ and under 2 cwt.	
			0	2	bag 2 and under 3 cwt.	
			0	3	bale 3 and under 5 cwt.	
from Ireland - -	-		0	2	bale	
Ostrich and Vulture, package	1	6	0	2	package	
			Unhsg and Loadg		Rent per Week.	
Figs, 3 qrs. to 1 cwt. 1 qr., chest	0	3	0	0½	2 0	100 chests
about 56 lbs. ½ chest	0	3	0	0½	1 3	100 ½ chests
¼ chest — 28 lbs. score	2	6	0	6	1 5	ton
drums - score	2	6	0	6		
½ and ¼ drums score	1	6	0	6		
⅛ drums - - score	1	6	0	6		
tapnets - score	1	6	0	6		
			Rent per Week.			
Fish, Cod - - ton	4	6	1	6	100 barrels or bales	
Herrings, Mackerel - barrel	0	3	1	6	100 barrels	
Salmon tierce	0	6	3	0	100 tierces	
Stock, or Sturgeon, 1,000	6	0	0	4	1,000 stock	
			1	0	100 kegs sturgeon	
			2	6	100 brls. stock or sturg.	
Roes - barrel	0	9	3	0	100 barrels	
Flax (including weighing), ton	4	6	0	1	ton	
Unhousing, wharfage, and shipping, 4*s.* per ton.						
Flour - ton including delivery by land or water.	4	9	1	9	100 bags, small cases or barrels	
from France - -	-	-	2	6	100 ditto	
Forest Seeds, Nuts and Acorns barrels	0	9	0	1	rrel	

Goods Imported.	Import Rate.		Rent. Per Week.		Rent. Quantities, &c.
Per	s.	d.	s.	d.	Per
Frankincense - - chest	0	8½	0	1	chest
Fruit, see *the Species of Fruit.*					
Furniture, very large case	4	6	0	4	large case
ordinary case	3	0	0	3	ordinary
middling case	2	0	0	2	middling case
small case	0	6	0	1	small case
Furs, see *Skins.*					
Galangal - - cwt.	0	6	0	0½	cwt.
Galls - - - cwt.	0	3¾	0	3	hogshead
			0	1½	sack
			0	1	bag about 2 cwt.
Gamboge - - cwt.	0	6	0	0½	cwt.
Gentian Root - - ton	5	0	0	2	cask under 3 cwt.
			0	3	cask 3 and under 5 cwt.
			0	4	cask 5 cwt. and upwards
Ginger - - cwt.	0	6	0	6	ton
Ginseng Root - - ton	5	0	0	1	barrel
Glass - - cask or chest	1	6	0	3	cask or chest
case	1	0	0	2	case
box	1	0	0	1	box
Glue - - ton	5	0	0	4	ton
Granilla - - cwt.	0	9	0	2	barrel
Grapes - - box	0	6	5	0	100 boxes
jar	0	3	2	6	100 jars
Grease - ton	5	0	0	3	ton
Greaves - - ton	4	6	0	3	ton
Guinea Grains - ton	5	0	0	1	cask or case under 3 cwt.
			0	2	cask or case 3 and under 5 cwt.
			0	3	cask or case 5 cwt. and upwards
			5	0	100 bags under 2 cwt.
Gum, loose or in hogsheads, ton	5	0	0	4	ton
in serons or bags - ton	4	6	0	4	ton
in cases or chests - cwt.	0	6	0	1½	chest
			0	0½	barrel
Guns, Carronades, 6 cwt. and upwards - each	2	0			no rent if taken away in 14 days
Hair, Horse, Ox, or Cow, cwt.	0	4½	0	1	bale under 3 cwt.
			0	1½	bale 3 and under 5 cwt.
			0	2	bale 5 cwt. and upwards
			0	0½	cwt. loose
Human - - cwt.	1	0	0	2	bale
Hams - - hogshead	2	0	0	3	hogshead
tierce	1	6	0	1	tierce
basket	0	6	0	1	basket
loose - - each	0	0¼	0	0¼	each
Hats, Chip or Leghorn, single case of 10 or 20 doz.	0	6	0	1	single case
small tub or case under 40 doz.	1	0	0	2	small tub or case
large tub or case of 40 doz.	2	0	0	4	large tub or case
60 doz.	3	0	0	4	large tub or case
Hemp (including weighing), ton	4	6	0	4	ton
Unhousing, wharfage, and shipping, 4*s.* per ton.					
press-packed - - ton	3	0	0	4	ton
Hellebore Root - cwt.	0	6	0	6	ton
Hides, about 4 cwt. 2 qrs., bale	1	6	0	1½	bale
in casks - - - pipe	1	6	0	10	100 hides
Losh - chest or bale	2	0	0	3	bale
Horse - - bale	2	8¼	0	3	bale
Ox and Cow, salted or dry, Buenos Ayres - each	0	1½	0	10	100
if with short horns, each	0	2	2	0	100
Brazil and Cape, dry, 100	9	0	0	8	100
Horse, African, or East India - - each	0	0¾	0	6	100
Horse from Hambro', dry, 100	7	6	0	8	100
bundle of 2 hides	0	3	0	10	100 hides
Honey - - cwt.	0	6	0	1	barrel
			0	0½	keg or jar
Hops - - cwt.	0	4½	0	2	bag
			0	1	pocket
Horns and Horn Tips, cwt.	0	6	0	6	1,000 horns
counting horns 2*s.* per 1,000			0	1½	1,000 tips
tips 9*d.* per 1,000					
Harts' and Stags', 100 pair	3	0	0	3	100 pair
Horses - - each	12	6			
Jalap - - - cwt.	0	10½	0	1	bale about 3 cwt.
			0	0¾	bale about 1½ cwt.
Jewellery - - package	1	6	0	3	package
box	1	6	0	2	box
Indian Rubber, hogshead or pipe	1	6	0	4	hogshead or pipe
1 to 2 cwt. case	1	0	0	1	case
barrel	0	6	0	0½	barrel
Indian Corn - - bag	0	3	0	0½	bag
Indigo, see *St. Katharine's Dock Charges.*					
Ink - - - cwt.	0	6	0	2	cask
Inkle - - - cwt.	1	0	0	1½	case
			0	1	box or keg
Ipecacuanha - - cwt.	0	5¼	0	1	cask or case under 3 cwt.
			0	1½	cask or case 3 to 5 cwt.
Iron (including weighing), ton	3	4	0	1	ton
When shipped from landing scale (including delivery) - - ton	4	2	none		if shipped within one week from the last day of landing
Unpiling, wharfage, and shipping, without weighing, 2*s.* 6*d.* per ton.					

Goods Imported.	Import Rate.		Rent. Per Week.		Rent. Quantiti
Per	s.	d.	s.	d.	Per
Iron Ore - - ton	3	0	0	2	ton
Steam Engines, Boilers, Cylinders, and other heavy Machinery, ton	7	6	0	1	ton
If discharged from the vessel into craft, without landing or weighing - - ton	6	0			
Isinglass - - cwt.	0	4½	0	6	ton
Ivory - - - cwt.	0	4½	0	1	cwt.
Or a consolidated rate of 1*s.* 6*d.* per cwt.					
Kelp - - - ton	3	6	0	2	ton
Filling and weighing, 2*s.* per ton.					
Knives - - package	1	6	0	2	case
			0	1	barrel
			0	0½	box
Lac Dye and Lake - chest	1	0	0	1	chest
Or a consolidated rate, including all operations incident on taring, raising, re-packing, stowing, and attendance whilst on show, nailing down, lotting and piling away, 8s. per chest.					
Lace - - case or box	2	6	0	6	case or box
Lacquered Ware - chest	1	6	0	2	chest
box	1	0	0	1	box
Lard - - cwt.	0	2¼	0	4	ton
Lead - - ton	2	6	0	1	ton
Unpiling, wharfage, and shipping, 1*s.* 8*d.* per ton.					
Ore - - - ton	3	0	0	2	ton
Black - - ton	3	9	0	3	ton
Leather, Tanned, loose, ton	5	0	0	9	ton
bale	1	6	0	2	bale
Lemons, see *Oranges.*					
Lexia - ton	5	0	0	4	ton
Limes - - barrel	0	8½	0	1	barrel
Lime Juice 100 gallons	2	1	0	4	puncheon
			0	2	hogshead
Laying up to gauge, and cooper's attendance at landing and delivery, form a separate charge.					
Linen, German - bale	2	3	0	4	bale
half bale	1	3	0	2	half bale
quarter bale	0	8¼	0	1	quarter bale
loose or in bags - roll	0	1½	1	0	100 rolls
chest	2	6	0	4	chest
half chest	1	3	0	2	half chest
quarter chest	0	8¼	0	1	quarter chest
Russia - - bale	1	2¼	0	2	bale
½ bale containing 10 pieces, or boarded bale	0	9	0	1	half bale
quarter bale	0	7½	0	1	quarter bale
Crash - - bale	1	2¼	0	3	bale
half bale	1	2¼	0	2	half bale
quarter bale	0	7½	0	1	quarter bale
Sail Cloth - bolt or roll	0	1½	1	0	100 bolts or
Mats, 2 pieces - each	0	3	2	0	100 mats (2
Irish - - case or bale	1	6	0	3	case or bale
box or bundle	0	9	0	2	box or bund
sample box	0	6	0	1	sample box
Linseed - bushel	0	2¼	2	6	100 barrels
Cakes - - ton	3	6	0	3	ton
Liquorice - cwt.	0	3¾	0	1	case or barre
Root - cwt.	0	6	1	0	loose, ton
			0	1	bale under
Mace - - cwt.	0	8¼	0	1½	chest
Or a consolidated rate of 3*s.* per cwt.					
Madder - - ton	3	4½	0	6	ton, unsizea
			0	3	ordinary cas
Roots - cwt.	0	4½	0	1	bale under 3
			0	1½	bale 3 cwt. under 5 c
			0	2	bale 5 cwt. a
Maiden Hair - bale	1	0	0	1	bale
Manna - cwt.	0	3¾	0	1	chest or cas
Marbles - - ton	5	0	0	4	ton
Marble Baths - - each	6	0	0	6	each
Mortars - - ton	5	0	0	6	ton
Sculptured Works of Art: import rate according to the size and value	-	-	0	3	case
			0	2	small case
Rough, in cases - cwt.	0	6	0	2	case
					Delivered into Craft, p Ton of 25 Palms or 1 Cubic Feet s. d.
Blocks, under 2 tons, ton	6	0	0	3	3 0
above 2 tons - ton	10	0	0	3	5 0
above 10 tons - ton	20	0	0	3	10 0
Mastic - cwt.	0	4½	0	1	case or che
Mats - - - 100	1	8¼	0	6	100 bundle
Indian - - chest	1	0	0	2	chest
box	0	9	0	1	box
Melting Pots - - cask	4	0	0	4	cask
Minerals - - case	1	0	0	2	case
Mohair Yarn - - cwt.	0	7½	0	1	bale
Molasses, see *West India Dock Charges.*					

…s Imported.	Import Rate.	Rent. Per Week.	Rent. Quantities, &c.
Per	s. d.	s. d.	Per
…ck or Iceland, ton	7 6	0 9	ton, in bags
		1 6	100 casks about 84 lbs.
		3 0	100 casks above 2 cwt.
Pearl, Shells, ton	7 6	0 4	ton
- - chests	1 6	0 2	chest
box	1 0	0 1	box
in bales - cwt.	0 6	0 0½	cwt.
…les - - cwt.	0 9	0 0¾	cwt.
- - chest	1 6	0 2	chest
box	1 0	0 1	box
…ns - - cwt.	0 4½	0 0¼	cwt.
- - cwt.	0 6	0 0½	cwt.
- - cwt.	0 3	0 0½	barrel or bag
- - chest	1 3	0 1	chest
…ose - - ton	3 6	0 3	ton
…and weighing, 2s. …n.			
- - cwt.	0 4½	0 2	chest
- bushel	0 2¼	4 0	100 sacks
barrel	0 4½	0 1	barrel
bag or sack	0 4½	2 0	100 bags
- bushel	0 2¼	1 0	100 bushels
…ica - - cwt.	0 4½	0 0¼	cwt.
- - ton	5 0	0 4	ton
- - ton	3 9	0 4	ton
- - cask	1 0	0 1	cask
- - cwt.	0 6	0 3	puncheon or hhd.
		1 3	ton, in jars or duppers
		0 2	tierce
		0 1	barrel under 2 cwt.
		0 1½	barrel above 2 cwt.
		0 0½	case 12 bottles
…al - - cwt.	0 11½	0 4	large case
		0 2	small case under 2 cwt.

	Per Tun of 252 Imp. Gals. Olive in casks.	Fish.	Newfoundland.
	s. d.	s. d.	s. d.
…wharfage, and …up to gauge -	4 6	3 6	2 4
…attendance, if de… from the quay -	2 0	2 0	2 0
…g and filling up …e) - -	1 0	1 0	1 0
…or housing - -	1 6	1 6	1 2
…attendance at …g, and at delivery …he vault -	1 0	1 0	
…ng and loading -	1 6	1 6	1 6
…ng, wharfage, and …ng - -	4 6	3 6	3 6
…week - -	0 6	0 4	0 3
—Fourteen Days …d from final day …ing previous to …mmencement of …out the Company …liberty to house …after gauging, …detained by writ… …er previously.			

	Impt. Rate.	Per Week.	
…jars			
…n jars - cwt.	0 8¼	0 3	common jar
…s - - cwt.	0 8¼	0 2	half jar
…rs - - cwt.	0 6	0 6	large jar
…alf chest of 30 bottles	0 6	0 2½	score ½ chests
…Cocoa Nut, ton	3 9	0 4	ton
…casks, for every …t. above 30 cwt.	0 9		
- - ton	6 0	0 6	ton
…e *Linseed-Cakes.*			
…see *Gum*, in cases			
gallon	0 0¼	0 3	tierce
		0 2	barrel 30 gallons
		0 1	½ barrel
		0 0½	¼ barrel
…g about 4 gallons, keg	0 3	0 0¼	keg
bushel	0 6	0 1	basket or barrel
- cwt.	0 10½	0 1½	chest under 4 cwt.
…d Lemons, chest	0 7½	0 1	chest
box	0 5½	0 0½	box
…cases case	1 0	0 1½	case
…ds - cwt.	0 4½	0 2	tierce
		0 3	hogshead
…eed - cwt.	0 5¼	0 1	bale under 4 cwt.
		0 1½	bale 4 and under 6 cwt.
…, in casks above		0 2	bale 6 to 10 cwt.
- - cwt.	0 2¼	0 3	hogshead
…under 10 cwt.			
cwt.	0 3	0 2	tierce
		0 1	barrel
		0 1	seron
- - package	1 6	0 3	large case
		0 2	small case
…s - package	2 0	0 4	package
small package	1 0	0 4	small package
		0 2	bottle
- each	10 0		
…lk - quarter	0 10	0 1	quarter

Goods Imported.	Import Rate.	Rent. Per Week.	Rent. Quantities, &c.
Per	s. d.	s. d.	Per
Paper - - cwt.	0 6	0 2	bale or chest
		0 1	half bale
		1 8	100 bundles
Pearl Barley - - keg	0 3	0 0¼	keg
parcel	0 6	0 0½	parcel
Peas - tierce or barrel	0 9	0 1	tierce or barrel
bag	0 4½	2 6	100 bags
Pepper (unsifted) - ton	5 0	0 6	ton
Or a consolidated rate, in bags - 13s. ton			
Long - - - cwt.	0 4½	0 7	ton
Cayenne - - cwt.	0 4½	0 7	ton
Piano Fortes - - each	4 6	0 6	each
Piccaba - - cwt.	0 6	0 4	ton
Pickles - dozen bottles	0 2¼	0 0½	dozen bottles
Pictures, large bale or case	4 6	0 6	large bale or case
middling bale or case	3 0	0 4	middling bale or case
small bale or case	1 6	0 3	small bale or case
Piece Goods - - bale	1 3	0 1½	bale
Pill Boxes - large vat	4 6	0 6	large vat
small vat	3 0	0 4	small vat
Pimento - - cwt.	0 4½	0 3	hhd. 8 cwt. and upwards
		0 2	tierce 3 & under 8 cwt.
		0 1	barrel under 3 cwt.
		0 6	ton, in bags
Or a consolidated rate, in bags - 1s. 2d. cwt. in casks - 1s. 6d. cwt.			
Pitch - - ton	2 6	3 0	100 barrels
Plaster of Paris - ton	3 0	0 2	ton
Plums, Portugal, in boxes, dozen	0 9	1 0	100 boxes
Porcelain - case	1 6	0 3	case
small case	1 0	0 2	small case
Potatoes - - bag	0 6	0 1	bag
barrel	0 9	0 1	barrel
Potash, see *Ashes.*			
Preserves, consolidated rate, under 28 lbs. - 6d. 28 to 112 lbs. - 1s.			

	Import Rate.	Unhsg and Loadg.	Rent per Week.	
Prunes or French Plums, about 8 cwt., hhd. or pun.	1 6	0 6	0 2	hhd. or pun.
5 to 7 cwt. - barrel	1 0	0 3	0 1½	barrel
2 to 5 cwt. - ½ barrel	0 9	0 2	0 1	half barre
under 2 cwt. ¼ barrel	0 6	0 2	4 2	100
about 1 cwt. - chest	0 3	0 0½	2 0	100
about 56 lbs. ½ chest	0 3	0 6 score	1 3	100
about 28 lbs. - ¼ chest	0 1½	0 6 score	1 0	100
⅛ boxes and small packages - - score	1 6	0 6	1 0	100

	Import Rate.	Rent per Week.	
Prussiate of Potash - ton	4 6	0 4	ton
Quicksilver, in bottles, bott.	0 3	0 0¼	bottles
containing 1 skin - case	0 6	0 0½	case
Quills - - vat	4 6	0 4	vat
small vat	3 0	0 3	small vat
hogshead or barrel	1 6	0 3	hogshead or barrel
case	2 0	0 3	case
bale	0 6	0 2	bale
Radix Senekæ - barrel	0 6	0 0½	barrel
Rags or Old Ropes - ton	3 0	0 3	ton

	Import Rate.	Unhsg and Loadg.	Rent per Week.	
Raisins, 12 to 20 cwt., butt	3 0	0 8	0 4	butt
9 to 12 cwt. - pipe	2 3	0 6	0 3	pipe
5 to 9 cwt. - carotel	1 6	0 4	0 2	carotel
2 cwt. 2 qrs. to 4 cwt. 2 qrs. barrel	0 9	0 2	0 0¾	barrel
1 cwt. 2 qrs. to 2 cwt. 2 qrs. - ½ barrel	0 6	0 2	0 0½	half barre
under 1cwt. 2 qrs., ¼ bar.	0 3	0 0½	2 0	100
Weighing do. 1s. score.				
Cape, casks under 3 cwt., cask	0 9		0 0¾	cask
3 to 5 cwt., cask	1 6		0 2	cask
boxes about 60 lbs., score	3 0	- -	1 8	100
Denia and Valencia, boxes - - score	2 6	0 6	1 3	100
Weighing do. 8d. score.				
¼ and ½ boxes - score	1 6	0 6	1 0	100
frails or baskets score	1 8	0 5	1 0	100
Weighing do. 6d. score.				
¼ and ½ frails or baskets, score	1 0	0 4	1 0	100
Malaga, boxes - score	2 0	0 6	1 0	100
¼ and ½ boxes - score	1 6	0 6	0 10	100
Weighing do. 8d. score.				
Smyrna, drums - score	2 6	0 6	1 0	100
¼ and ½ drums - score	1 6	0 6	1 0	100

	Import Rate.	Rent per Week.	
Rhatania Extract - cwt.	0 9	0 1	cwt.
Root - cwt.	0 10½	0 0½	cwt.
Rhubarb - - cwt.	0 8¼	0 2	case or cask
Rice - - cwt.	0 2¼	0 1	tierce or barrel
		2 0	100 bags
Or a consolidated rate of, in casks 13s. 4d. ton in bags - 16d. 0s. to			

Goods Imported.	Per	Import Rate. s.	d.	Rent. Per Week. s.	d.	Quantities, &c. Per
Roots, Sassafras	cwt.	0	9	0	2	cask or case
Rosin	ton	2	6	0	6	loose
				3	0	100 barrels
Rugs	bale	1	6	0	3	bale
	half bale	1	0	0	1½	half bale
Rushes	load	1	6	0	3	load
for polishing	bundle	0	1½	1	0	100 bundles
Saffron	cwt.	2	0	0	2	bale or case
Safflower	ton	5	0	0	6	ton
Sago	cwt.	0	6	0	6	ton
Sal Ammoniac	ton	5	0	0	6	ton
Salep	package	1	6	0	2	package
Saltpetre	ton	3	6	0	3	ton
Salts	cwt.	0	3	0	4	ton
Sarsaparilla	cwt.	2	0	0	2	bale
				0	10	100 bundles
Scaleboards	100 bundles	3	0	0	4	100 bundles
Scammony	cwt.	3	0	0	0½	drum
Seed (except Cummin and Aniseed), in bags	ton	3	9	0	0½	bag
in casks	ton	4	6	0	3	ton
Seed Lac	cwt.	0	9	0	0½	cwt.
Senna	cwt.	0	4½	0	1½	bale or case under 5 cwt.
				0	2	bale or case 5 to 7 cwt.
				0	3	bale or case 10 cwt.
Shellac	cwt.	0	9	0	0½	cwt.
Ships' Stores warehoused, consolidated rate, 2 cwt. and upwards	cwt.	1	6	0	1	package
under 2 cwt.	package	1	0	0	0½	package
under 28 lbs.	package	0	6	0	0¼	package
If Liquids	gallon	0	1	0	5	tun
Shot	ton	3	0	0	1½	ton
Shurf	ton	5	0	0	2	ton
Silk, Raw	cwt.	0	8½	0	2	bale above 2 cwt.
				0	1½	bale under 2 cwt.
Manufactured	case	1	0	0	1½	case
	small case	0	9	0	1	small case
Skins, Calf or Kip, about 4 cwt.	large bale	1	6	0	1½	large bale
about 2 cwt.,	mid. bale	1	0	0	0½	middling or small bale
	small bale	0	9			
salted, wet	dozen	0	4½	0	4	120
Mogadore, loose, dry, salted	dozen	0	3	0	0½	dozen
salted, including weighing	dozen	0	4	0	0½	dozen
Weighing and loading, 1*d.* per dozen each charge.						
Cat or Fitch, cask or	case	1	6	0	3	cask or case
Chinchilli, bale, cask, or	case	1	6	0	3	bale, cask, or case
Deer - puncheon,	hogshead, or bale	1	6	0	2	pun. hhd. or bale
	case or pack	1	0	0	1	case or pack
	bundle	0	9	0	0½	bundle
Dog Fish	bale	0	9	0	1	bale
Elk	120	3	0	0	4	120
Goat, Trieste, bale about	8 cwt.	2	0	0	3	bale
Hambro', bale of 100	skins and under	1	0	0	1	bale
	bale above 100 skins	1	6	0	1½	bale
Mogadore - bale of 60	skins	0	6	0	1	bale
	bale of 30 skins	0	3	0	0½	bale
Hare and Coney	bale	1	6	0	3	bale
Ireland	bale	1	2	0	1	bale
Kangaroo	dozen	0	0½	0	2	bale
Kid or Lamb - hogshead,	puncheon or bale	1	6	0	3	hhd. pun. or bale
	tierce	1	0	0	2	tierce
	barrel	0	6	0	1	barrel
	large bundle	1	0	0	2	large bundle
	ordinary bundle	0	9	0	1	ordinary bundle
	small bundle	0	6	0	1	small bundle
Lamb, Hambro', or Copenhagen, under 200 skins	bale	1	0	0	1	bale
above 200 skins	bale	1	6	0	1½	bale
Leopard, Lion, and Tiger,	each	0	1½	0	0½	each
Neutra	bale	1	6	0	2	bale
	small bale	1	0	0	1	small bale
Quebec or Hudson's Bay,	case, bale, or puncheon	1	6	0	2	case, bale, or puncheon
	large bundle	1	0	0	2	large bundle
	ordinary bundle	0	9	0	1	ordinary bundle
	small bundle or keg	0	6	0	1	small bundle or keg
Seal	pipe	2	0	0	3	pipe
	puncheon or hogshead	1	6	0	2	puncheon or hogshead
	barrel	1	0	0	1	barrel
loose	120	1	6	0	3	120
South Seas, wigs	120	1	9	0	6	120
middlings	120	1	9	0	4	120
smalls and pups	120	1	6	0	3	120
Greenland, loose	120	1	6	0	2	120
Sheep, Hambro'	bale	1	6	0	2	bale
Sheep or Goat, Cape	bale, 100 skins	2	0	0	2	bale
	50 skins	1	0	0	1	bale
	25 skins	0	6	0	0½	bale
loose dry	dozen	0	3	0	3	120
salted	dozen	0	4½	0	4	120
India, loose	120	1	0	0	2	120
4 cwt.	bale	2	0	0	3	bale

Goods Imported.	Per	Import Rate. s.	d.	Rent. Per Week. s.	d.	Quantities Per
Skins, — *continued.*						
Swan - bale containing	150 skins	1	6	0	2	bale
Vicienia, loose	120	1	6	0	3	120
Smalts	cwt.	5	0	0	5	ton
Snake Root	ton	0	9	0	1	½ bale or barre
				0	2	tierce
				0	2	bale
				0	3	hogshead
Soap	cwt.	0	4½	0	1	case under 6 c
Soy	chest	1	0	0	2	chest
Spectacles	case	1	0	0	1	case
Spelter	ton	3	0	0	1	ton
Wharfage and shipping, 2*s.* per ton, when piled on the quay.						
Sponge	cwt.	0	9	0	2	case or bale un
				0	3	large case or c
Squills	ton	5	0	0	3	ton
dried	case	1	0	0	1½	case
Starch	ton	5	0	0	6	ton
Steel	ton	4	6	0	2	ton
Stick Lac	cwt.	0	9	0	0½	cwt.
Sticks, Walking	1,000	5	0	0	2	1,000
Stock Fish, see *Fish.*						
Stone, Burr	each	0	1½	0	9	100
Emery	ton	3	6	0	1	ton
Filling and weighing, 2*s.* per ton.						
Lithographic	ton	5	0	0	6	ton
Pumice	ton	7	6	0	8	ton
				0	4	ton in bricks
Turkey	cwt.	0	3	0	1	cask 3 to 5 cw
Sugar, see *West India Dock Charges.*						
Sumach	ton	3	9	0	2	ton
Tallow, in casks (including weighing)	ton	3	0	0	1	cask
If sold from the landing scale	ton	2	3			
also to the buyer	ton	1	0			
(with rent from the last day of landing), if not delivered within three days on a duty paid or sight entry.						
Unhousing, wharfage, and shipping, 2*s.* per ton.						
in skins	ton	3	9	0	3	
Cape or American, packages under 5 cwt.	ton	5	0	0	0½	package under
				0	1	package above
Tamarinds	cwt.	0	3	0	1	cask under 3 c
				0	1½	cask 3 and und
				0	2	cask 5 and unc
				0	3	cask 8 cwt. and
Tapes	bale	1	6	0	2	bale
Tapioca	cwt.	0	8½	0	0½	barrel
Tar -	barrel of 32 gallons	0	3	3	0	100 barrels
Tares	quarter	1	0	0	1	quarter
Working out and delivering into craft, 3*d.* per qr.						
Terra, Japonica	ton	5	0	0	3	ton
Sienna	ton	5	0			
Verde	ton	5	0			
Umbra	ton	3	6			
Thread	bale	1	6	0	2	bale
Timber, see *Wood.*						
Tin	ton	3	0	0	1	ton
Tobacco, a consolidated rate, see page 458.						
Tongues, about 2 doz.,	bale	0	6	0	1	bale
loose	dozen	0	3	0	0½	dozen
Tortoiseshell	cwt.	0	6	0	2	barrel or case
Tow, in bales	cwt.	0	4½	0	1	bale 4 cwt. an
				0	1½	bale above 4 a 6 cwt.
				0	2	bale 6 cwt. and
Toys -	large case or vat	4	6	0	6	large case or v
	middling case or vat	3	0	0	4	middling case
	small case or vat	2	0	0	3	small case or v
Trees, Live Plants, &c.	large case	1	6	0	1	large case
	small case	1	0	0	1	small case
Turmeric	cwt.	0	3	2	6	100 bags under
				0	6	ton, bags abov
				0	0½	chest 1 cwt. 2
Turpentine	ton	2	6	3	6	100 tierces
				3	0	100 barrels
Delivery by land or water, 1*s.* 8*d.* per ton.				5	0	100 casks, fror
Twine	cwt.	0	4½	0	1	mat or bundle
Valerian	bale	1	6	0	2	bale
Valonia	ton	4	6	0	3	ton
Filling and weighing, 2*s.* per ton.						
Vanelloes	cwt.	1	6	0	1½	case
Verdigris	ton	5	0	0	6	ton
Vermilion	cwt.	2	4½	0	1	barrel
Vermicelli, case under 1 cwt.	cwt.	1	0	0	0½	box under 56
case above 1 cwt.	cwt.	0	6	0	1	case 56 lbs. ar cwt.
				0	2	case 2 and unc
				0	4	case 4 and unc
				0	6	case 6 cwt. an

Left table

Imported.	Import Rate. s. d.	Rent Per Week. s. d.	Quantities, &c.
Per			*Per*
uncheon of 100			
gallons	2 1	0 4	puncheon
hogshead	1 2	0 2	hogshead
tierce	1 0	0 2	tierce
quarter cask	0 6	0 1½	quarter cask
tendance, if de- from the quay, a 1s.; hhd. 9d.;			
including at- at delivery, a 2s.; hhd. 1s. ce 1s.			
- bushel	0 2½	4 0	100 sacks
		2 0	100 bags
ral, dozen bottles	0 3	0 0½	dozen bottles
- ton	5 0	0 6	ton
- ton	7 6	0 9	ton
- ton	7 6	0 4	ton
- ton	7 6	0 6	ton

	Landing, Wharfage, Housing, and Delivering. In a Ship. s. d.	In a Barge. s. d.	Rent per 100 Qrs. per Week. s. d.	
Grain, &c. qr.	0 9	0 6	5 0	Rent commences from the last day of landing.
Grain, &c. qr.	0 8	0 6	4 0	

porter- landing, qr. 0 2
delivery, qr. 0 2
ch time 100 qrs. 2 6 100 qrs. 6 6
g to be n skreen-
00 sacks 0 6
er heavy - qr. 0 5 - qr. 0 4½
in bags, al charge alfpenny cutting shooting
empty packing es, bdle. 0 1 hipping, bdle. 0 1 t and deliver- craft, 3d. per

	Import Rate. s. d.	Rent per Week. s. d.	Quantities, &c.
- cwt.	0 3	0 0½	cask 3 to 5 cwt.
		0 0½	case or cask 1 cwt.
ooms -			
100 bundles	3 0	0 3	100 bundles
loose, 1,000	3 0	0 4	loose, 1,000
bale	1 10½	0 3	bale
half bale	1 0	0 1½	half bale
quarter bale	0 9	0 1	quarter bale
hth of a bale	0 6	0 0½	one eighth of a bale
d - 100	1 6	0 2	100
, see consoli- page 458.			
page 458.			
- cwt.	0 2½	0 0½	cwt.
d. or Lamb,			
- cwt.	0 4½	0 0¾	bale under 3 cwt.
		0 1	bale 3 to 4 cwt.
		0 1½	bale 4 to 6 cwt.
		0 2	bale 6 cwt. and upwards

Right table

Goods Imported.	Import Rate. s. d.	Rent Per Week. s. d.	Quantities, &c.
Wool,—*continued.*			*Per*
Or a consolidated rate of 5s. per bale of about 4 cwt.			
Australian - cwt.	0 4½	0 0¾	bale under 3 cwt.
		0 1	bale 3 to 4 cwt.
		0 1½	bale 4 to 6 cwt.
		0 2	bale 6 cwt. and upwards
Or a consolidated rate of 4s. per bale of about 2½ cwt., including landing, wharfage, housing, and 12 weeks' rent from the date of the ship breaking bulk, landing weights, original warrants, certificate of damage, or survey after landing, mending at landing, taring, loting, sampling, unpiling for show, showing, repiling, mending, and filling in, re-weighing, and any other usual operation performed by order of the importer.			
Unhousing and loading by land, or direct into ship or lighter, and mending, 8d. per bale, of about 2½ cwt.			
Goats' - cwt.	0 6	0 1	bale about 2 cwt.
		0 2	bale above 2 cwt.
Hair or Beards cwt.	0 10½	0 2	case
Spanish - cwt.	0 4½	0 1	bale 2 cwt. 2 qrs.
		0 0¾	bale about 2 cwt.
		0 0½	bale about 1 cwt.
Or a consolidated rate of 4s. per bale of about 2 cwt. and 3s. per half bale, including the same operations as to Australian wool.			
Unhousing, &c. 6d. per bale, 4d. per half bale.			
Vigonia - cwt.	0 4½	0 3	bale
Woollen Cloth, see *Cloth.*			
Wood. For consolidated rate on Staves, Deals, &c. see page 458.			
Barwood - ton	4 0	0 1	
Boxwood - ton	4 0	0 1	
Brazil, large - ton	4 0	0 1	
Camwood - ton	4 0	0 1	
Cedar, Pencil - ton	4 0	0 1	
Cocus-wood - ton	4 0	0 1	ton; if under cover, 2d. per ton
Ebony - ton	4 0	0 1	
Fustic, large - ton	4 0	0 1	
Lignum Vitæ, large - ton	4 0	0 1	
Mahogany Logs under 2 tons - ton	4 0	0 1	
Nicaragua, large - ton	4 0	0 1	
Sanders-wood - ton	4 0	0 1	
Unhousing or unpiling, wharfage, and shipping, 2s. 6d. per ton.			
Brazilletto - ton	5 0	0 2	ton
Brazil-wood, small - ton	5 0	0 2	ton
Fustic, young - ton	5 0	0 2	ton
Maple - ton	4 6	0 2	ton
Nicaragua, middling, - ton	5 3	0 2	ton
Unpiling, &c. 3s. 9d.			
Nicaragua, small - ton	5 6	0 2	ton
Sassafras - ton	5 0	0 4	ton
Sapan - ton	5 0	0 2	ton
Unhousing or unpiling, wharfage, and shipping, 5s. per ton.			
Logwood, see consolidated rate, page 458.			
Jaccaranda Rosewood Tulip Zebra - ton	5 6	0 1	ton
		0 1½	ton, if under cover.
Unhousing or unpiling, wharfage, and shipping, 3s. 9d. per ton.			
Unpiling and loading, 1s. 6d. per ton.			
Cedar, N. S. Wales Beef and other Logs of the same denomination. - ton	4 6	0 1½	ton
		0 2	ton, if under cover
Unpiling, wharfage, and shipping, 2s. 6d. per ton. Loading 1s. 8d. per ton.			
Yarn, in vats - ton	5 0	0 4	ton
above 1 ton additional for every cwt.	0 3		
in bales - cwt.	0 4½	0 1½	bale
Zaffres ton	5 0	0 5	ton
Zinc, see *Spelter.*			

Consolidated Rates on Wood Goods. — Transferring, One Penny per Load.

Goods Imported.	Per	Landing, Wharfage, Piling, Delivery, and One Quarter's Rent. s.	d.	Landing, Wharfage, and Delivery. s.	d.	Rent per Quarter after the first Quarter. s.	d.
Staves,							
From America,							
pipe	1,200	24	0	12	0	5	0
hogshead	—	20	0	10	0	4	0
barrel or heading	—	14	0	7	0	3	0
barrel logs	—	88	0	44	0	14	8
double barrel	—	44	0	22	0	7	4
From Quebec,							
pipe logs - - 3 to 4 inches thick	—	120	0	60	0	20	0
double pipe - 2 to 2½ —	—	64	0	32	0	10	8
single - - 1 to 1½ —	—	36	0	18	0	6	0
hogshead logs 3 to 4 —	—	100	0	50	0	16	8
double hogshead 2 to 2½ —	—	50	0	25	0	8	4
single - - 1 to 1½ —	—	30	0	15	0	5	8
barrel logs 3 to 4 —	—	88	0	44	0	14	0
double barrel 2 to 2½ —	—	44	0	22	0	7	4
single - - 1 to 1½ —	—	26	0	13	0	4	4
heading logs 3 to 4 —	—	88	0	44	0	14	8
double heading 2 to 2½ —	—	44	0	22	0	7	4
single - - 1 to 1½ —	—	26	0	13	0	4	4
From Hambro' and Dantzic,							
pipe	—	40	0	20	0	15	0
hogshead	—	37	6	18	9	12	6
barrel	—	35	6	17	9	10	0
heading	—	32	0	16	0	10	0
thin pipe 1 to 1½ inch thick,	—	27	0	13	6	10	6
hogshead - - - —	—	25	0	12	6	10	0
barrel and heading —	—	20	0	10	0	8	0
sorting, per 1,200	5s.						
Deals, - - standard hundred of	120						
Russia and Prussia Deals and Deal Ends, 1½ inch thick and 12 feet long	—	12	6	6	3	4	0
Swedish Deals from ports in the Baltic, 2½ and 3 inches thick, 14 feet long	—	20	0	12	6	7	0
1½ and 2 — 14 —	—	16	8	8	4	5	6
Quebec, Norway, and Swedish Deals from ports in the North Sea, 2½ and 3 in. thick, 10 and 12 ft. long	—	16	0	8	0	5	6
to 14 —	—	19	0	9	6	6	6
to 16 —	—	22	0	11	0	7	6
to 18 —	—	25	0	12	6	8	6
to 20 —	—	28	0	14	0	9	6
Battens from all ports, 2½ and 3 in. thick, 10 and 12 ft. long	—	12	0	6	0	4	0
to 14 —	—	14	3	7	0	4	9
to 16 —	—	16	6	8	3	5	6
to 18 —	—	18	9	9	0	6	3
to 20 —	—	21	0	10	6	7	0
2½ and 3 inch half Deals	—	9	0	4	6	3	0

Goods Imported.	Per	Landing, Wharfage, Piling, Delivery, and One Quarter's Rent. s.	d.
Battens from all ports, — *continued.*			
Deal ends - standard hundred of	120	7	0
Batten ends	—	5	0
Pailing boards	—	6	0
Deck Deals,			
3 in. thick, 30 to 40 feet long	each	1	0
2½ — 30 to 40 —	—	0	10
2 — 30 to 40 —	—	0	8
3 — 20 to 30 —	—	0	9
2½ — 20 to 30 —	—	0	7½
2 — 20 to 30 —	—	0	6
Dunnage Boards	—	12	6
Norway Timber and Balks	load	6	0
Spars under 6 and above 4 inches	120	40	0
Rickers, under 4 inches, and 24 feet long and upwards	—	25	0
under 24 feet long	—	12	0
Handspikes	—	6	0
Uffers, under 24 feet long	—	25	0
from 24 to 32 —	—	40	0
32 feet long and upwards	—	66	0
Sparholtz and 10 ells to add one third to the Rates on Uffers.			
Oars under 24 feet long	—	12	6
from 24 to 32 —	—	20	0
32 feet long and upwards	—	30	0
Lancewood Spars	—	30	0
Gun Stocks	—	6	0
Lathwood under 5 feet long	fathom	9	0
from 5 to 8 —	—	12	0
Fir Staves	—	15	0
Treenails, large, above 2½ feet long	1,200	20	0
small, under 2½ —	—	10	0
Wainscot Logs, 7 feet long	each	0	9
14 —	—	2	0
Clap Boards 3 —	—	0	3
6 —	—	0	6
Oak and other Timber	load	10	0
Deal Plank and Boards	—	7	0
Firewood	fathom	7	0
Spokes, American	1,200	20	0
Teakwood, Planks of	load	7	6

Charges on Cigars and Tobacco.

Cigars.	Chests containing from 500 to 600 lbs.	Boxes containing above 300 and not exceeding 400 lbs.	above 200 and not exceeding 300 lbs.	abo an exc 20
	s. d.	s. d.	s. d.	s.
Import rate; including landing, wharfage, housing, weighing *gross*; and examining, or sampling, one side	8 0	4 6	2 9	2
both sides	10 0	5 6	3 9	3
Unpacking, weighing nett, repacking, (when in bundles*,) and coopering	10 6	5 0	2 9	2
* If loose, an extra charge is made. Garbling, or sorting, is also an extra charge.				
Examining, or resampling, one side	4 0	2 0	1 0	1
both sides	6 0	3 0	2 0	2
Unhousing, wharfage, and shipping	3 0	2 6	2 0	1
Ditto, and loading	1 0	1 0	0 9	0
Transferring	0 2	0 2	0 2	0
Boxes or chests, not of the above specified weights, are charged in proportion.				

Tobacco.	s. d.
Landing charges and coopering, weighing, sampling, and making merchantable at landing scale, per 100 lbs. nett	0 6
On delivery for exportation, including coopering, per 100 lbs. nett	0 2½
Ditto, if resampled, ditto	0 3
Unhousing and loading, per hogshead	1 0
Resampling ditto	2 0

1 hogshead - - -
2 ditto - - - - -
3 ditto - - - -
any quantity exceeding 3 hogsheads, 2*d.* per hogshead additional.
transfer, per hogshead - -

Rates on Wines and Spirits.

Consolidated Rate on Wines, when delivered from the Quay within six working Days after Ga

	Pipe. s. d.	Hhd. s. d.	Third. s. d.	Quarter Cask. s. d.	Double Aum. s. d.
Home consumption	3 6	1 9	1 6	1 2	2 6
Exportation or coastwise, and shipping	4 8	2 4	2 1	1 7	3 4

ıe consolidated rate on wines in oak casks landed under a warehousing entry, with the standard ber of iron hoops, (see *note*,) is chargeable on the sixth working day after gauging, (unless previously ined on the quay by a written order,) and comprises landing, wharfage, housing, cooper's attend- , coopering, thirteen weeks' rent from the day the vessel began working, and delivery from the :.

	Pipe.	Hhd.	Third.	Quarter Cask.	Double Aum.	Single Aum.
	s. d.	s. d.	s. d.	s. d.	s. d.	s. d.
rt, Lisbon, Sherry, Malaga, Spanish red, and Rhenish wine	15 3	7 8	6 6	5 1	11 6	5 9
deira, Teneriffe, Cape, and Sicilian	14 6	7 3	6 0	4 10		
ret and other French wines	- -	8 9	7 0	5 6		
nt after three months	0 4	0 2	0 2	0 1½	0 3	0 2
to twelve months	0 5	0 2½	0 2½	0 2	0 4	0 2½

te. — The standard number of iron hoops is as follows; viz. port and Lisbon pipes, ten; sherry butts, ; Spanish red, brandy, and geneva puncheons, six; double aums, hogsheads, and smaller casks, six. e casks be landed with a less number, the charge is 4½*d.* per hoop.

Consolidated Rates on Spirits landed under a Warehousing Entry, exclusive of Rent.

	Pun.	Hhd.	Third.
	s. d.	s. d.	s. d.
ndy and geneva	8 6	4 3	3 6
nt from the day the vessel begins landing — first year	0 4	0 2	0 2
— second year	0 5	0 2½	0 2½

te. — When any quantity not exceeding one fifth of an entry is required to be delivered or trans- l, the "consolidated rate" is to be paid on one fifth: when any further quantity is to be delivered ansferred, the "consolidated rate" must be paid on the whole.

sizeable casks in proportion, at the rate of 210 gallons for 2 pipes or 4 hogsheads.

e company engage to make good the following deficiencies, from whatever cause arising, if the casks f oak timber, but not otherwise; provided they be claimed within six months of delivery, and ished by the customs gauge at landing and delivery, viz. —

ceeding one gallon on each cask, for any period not exceeding one year: two gallons, if more than and not exceeding two years: and in like proportion for each succeeding year.

nes and spirits landed under a dock order, are charged with the consolidated rate, if not taken away ained on the quay by a written order, within six working days after landing.

nes and spirits landed under a prime entry, cannot be housed until the whole of the duty has been but are chargeable with quay rent and watching, after the sixth working day from the landing, ably to the table.

	s. d.
ne in cases, in lieu of rent for three months, and all other charges (except tasting), on ondition that the proprietors make their election prior to the second day after xamination; the Company being responsible for all deficiencies, per dozen bottles	1 4
to, on which the consolidated rate is not charged:	
Import rate, per dozen bottles	0 3
Examining and coopering, ditto	0 3
Smaller cases than 3 dozen, per case, extra	0 1
Rent per week, per dozen bottles	0 0½
ne and spirits, in cases, when landed for immediate exportation, including delivery and e week's rent, per dozen	0 3

Rates on Wines and Spirits, where those in the foregoing Tables do not apply, viz.

	Pipe or Pun.	Hhd.	Third.	Quarter Cask.	Double Aum.	Single Aum.
	s. d.	s. d.	s. d.	s. d.	s. d.	s. d.
ding	1 0	0 6	0 4	0 3	0 8	0 4
arfage	0 8	0 4	0 3	0 3	0 6	0 3
per's attendance at landing and loading	1 0	0 6	0 6	0 4	0 8	0 6
ing up to gauge in numerical order	0 3	0 1½	0 1	0 1	0 2	0 1
ding	0 8	0 4	0 4	0 3	0 6	0 4
sing	1 0	0 6	0 4	0 3	0 8	0 4
ousing and loading	1 4	0 8	0 6	0 6	1 0	0 6
er's attendance at landing and housing	1 6	0 10	0 8	0 8	1 3	0 8
per's attendance at delivery from vault	1 0	0 6	0 6	0 4	0 9	0 4
ousing, wharfage, and shipping	2 0	1 0	1 0	0 9	1 6	0 9
ping from the quay	0 8	0 4	0 4	0 3	0 6	0 3
ging off	1 6	0 9	0 9	0 9	1 0	0 9
mming and replacing wood hoops	2 0	1 0	1 0	0 9	1 6	1 0
ing	0 10	0 5	0 5	0 4	0 6	0 4
hoops, each	0 8	0 8	0 8	0 6	0 8	0 6
es of lead, — 9*d.*						
ts, — 1*d.*						
ies, — 6*d.*						
ning and turning	0 3	0 1½	0 1½	0 1	0 2	0 1
sing, and porters' work	1 6	0 9	0 9	0 6	1 0	0 6
g ditto	1 6	0 9	0 9	0 6	1 0	0 6
ing*	2 6	1 3	1 0	0 10	1 6	1 0
king out for coopering and filling	0 6	0 3	0 3	0 2	0 4	0 3
for delivery and laying up again	1 0	0 6	0 6	0 4	0 8	0 4
ing, per cask 6*d.*						
r rent, for the first three months, per week	0 4	0 2	0 2	0 1½	0 3	0 1½
after three months	0 5	0 2½	0 2½	0 2	0 4	0 2

cking in the vaults is not charged until the expiration of six months from the period of the "con- ed rate" attaching; those for exportation excepted.

Casks, when necessary, are supplied by the Company at the market price; and the proceeds of racked casks, when sold, are paid to the proprietor, after deducting expenses.

	Pipe or Pun.	Hhd.	Third.	Quarter Cask.	Double Aum.	Single Aum.
	s. d.	s. d.	s. d.	s. d.	s. d.	s. d.
Fining - - - - -	0 6	0 6	0 6	0 6	0 6	0 6
Racking from the lees - - - -	3 6	2 0	1 9	1 6	2 6	1 9
Racking and repairing casks - -	15 0	12 6	10 6	9 0	12 6	9 0
Bark hoops - - - - -	1 9	1 4	1 4	1 0	1 6	1 0
Painting casks - - - - -	4 0	2 6	2 0	1 9	3 0	2 0
Spirits brought forward for inspection or re-dipping - - - - -	1 0	0 6	0 6	0 4		
Tasting* in store, each time - - -	0 2	0 2	0 2	0 2	0 2	0 2
Ditto, at public sale - - - -	0 1	0 1	0 1	0 1	0 1	0 1
Sampling in vault, or second sampling on the quay - - - - - -	0 6	0 6	0 6	0 6	0 6	0 6

N. B. No charge for tasting is made to the proprietor, or clerk (if fully authorised to sign all orders) when not accompanied by another person.

Quay Rent, if detained by Order beyond the Sixth Working Day after Gauging or Examination.

	Pipe, Butt, or Puncheon.	Double Aum, Hogshead, or Third.	Single Aum, or Quarter Cask.	Cases of Wine. — (Dozens.)		
				One to Three.	Four to Six.	Seven and upwards.
	s. d.	s. d.	s. d.	s. d.	s. d.	s. d.
Per day, each - - -	0 4	0 2	0 1½	0 1	0 1½	0 2

Watching, per Night, if detained by Order beyond the Sixth Working Day after Gauging or Examination. If Cases of Wine are intended to be detained on the Quay, Notice must be given on the Day of Examination.

	Pipe, Butt, or Puncheon.	Double Aum, Hogshead, or Third.	Single Aum, or Quarter Cask.	Cases of Wine. — (Dozens.)		
				One to Three.	Four to Six.	Seven and upwards
	s. d.	s. d.	s. d.	s. d.	s. d.	s. d.
1 to 5 - - - - -	0 4	0 3	0 2	0 1½	0 2	0 3
6 to 10 - - - - -	0 6	0 4	0 3	0 2	0 3	0 4
11 to 20 - - - -	1 0	0 8	0 6	0 4	0 6	0 8
21 to 30 - - - -	1 6	1 0	0 10	0 8	0 10	1 0
31 to 40 - - - -	2 0	1 6	1 4	1 0	1 4	1 6
41 to 50 - - - -	2 6	2 0	1 8	1 4	1 8	2 0

	Per Certificate
	£ s. d.
Surveys and certificates thereof, as follows :	
On 1 to 5 casks - - - - - - -	0 2 6
6 to 20 ditto - - - - - -	0 5 0
21 and upwards - - - - - -	0 7 6
An entire cargo - - - - - -	1 1 0
Duplicate or copy of certificate - - - -	0 1 0

Scotch and Irish Spirits.

	Per Pun.
	s. d.
Landing, wharfage, loading, laying up to gauge, cooper's attendance, and weighing when required - - - - - -	4 0
Rent, to commence 21 days after the date of the ship's report, per week - -	0 4

Bottling Wine.	Magnum.	Quarts.	Pints
	s. d.	s. d.	s. d.
Consolidated rate for bottling wine, per dozen, including removing, housing, fining, bottling, corking, straw, packing, sealing, marking, nailing down, weighing, bagging the lees, and rent on the empty bottles - - -	1 6	1 0	0 9
Unhousing, wharfage, and shipping, per dozen - - - -	0 4	0 3	0 2
Rent, to commence the day after bottling, per six dozen per week - -	0 6	0 3	0 2

RATES ON GOODS SENT TO THE LONDON DOCKS FOR EXPORTATION.

If goods be not shipped at the expiration of three weeks, rent is charged upon them. Goods enumerated in the following table, are charged by the package, see *post.*

Goods for Exportation.	Wharfage and Shipping.	Rent after Three Weeks.		Goods for Exportation.	Wharfage and Shipping.	Rent after Three	
		Per Week.	Quantities, &c.			Per Week.	Quanti
	Per	s. d.	s. d.	Per		Per	s. d.	s. d.	Per
Acids - middling case	3 0	0 9	middling case	Baggage, ordinary package	0 6	0 2½	ordinary pac
small case	2 0	0 6	small case	large ditto	2 0	0 6	large packag
Alum - ton	2 6	0 6	ton	Intermediate sizes will be charged in proportion, and rent one fourth of the rate for wharfage and shipping.			
Anchors or Grapnels, ton	3 4	0 3	ton				
Annatto - small basket	0 4	0 1	small basket				
Anniseed, under 1 cwt. chest	0 6	0 1½	chest				

* Tasting not permitted without a written order.

[Goods for E]xportation.	Wharfage and Shipping.		Rent after Three Weeks. Per Week.		Rent after Three Weeks. Quantities, &c.
Per	s.	d.	s.	d.	Per
ut 2 qrs., roll	0	2	2	6	100 rolls
- chest	1	0	0	3	chest
chest or seron	0	8	0	2	half chest or seron
- - each	0	2	0	5	score
	0	6	0.	1	
ccording to } - each }	to		to		} each
	1	0	0	3	
k tierce	0	6	8	0	100 tierces
barrel	0	4	6	0	100 barrels
- kilderkin	0	4	0	1	kilderkin
barrel	0	4	0	1½	barrel
hogshead	0	8	0	2	hogshead
: or puncheon	1	4	0	4	butt or puncheon
asks, doz. bott.	0	1	0	0½	dozen bottles
bottles, or					
, doz. bottles	0	2	0	0½	dozen bottles
- - ton	3	4	0	10	ton
- firkin	0	4	0	0¾	firkin
barrel	0	6	0	1	barrel
small cask	0	8	0	1½	small cask
to 7 cwt. cask	1	0	0	2	cask
ut 8 cwt. cask	1	2	0	2½	cask
9 cwt. cask	1	4	0	3	cask
11 cwt. cask	1	6	0	4	cask
20 cwt. cask	3	0	0	6	cask
Glass, con-					
om 15 to 20					
- crate	0	8	0	2	crate
9 dozen, crate	1	0	0	2½	crate
dozen, crate	1	4	0	3	crate
) dozen, crate	2	0	0	4	crate
- - bag	0	4	0	0½	bag
- 1,200	7	6	0	6	1,200
by the crew,					
1,200	2	6	0	6	1,200
4,000 dollars,					
case or cask	1	6			
- firkin	0	1	3	0	100 firkins
quarter cask	0	2	6	0	100 quarter casks
- ton	3	4	0	8	ton
- ton	3	4	0	3	ton
- chest	0	8	0	1½	chest
exceeding 56					
lbs. box	0	2	0	0½	box
to 1 cwt. box	0	4	0	1	box
on Rattan,					
1,000	1	0	0	3	1,000
2 tons, each	3	0			
2 tons, each	6	0			
- bolt	0	1	1	3	100 bolts
	2	0	0	3	
ng to size, } each }	to		to		} each
	5	0	0	6	
- chest	0	8	0	2	chest
- ½ ditto	0	4	0	1	half chest
- barrel	0	6	0	1	barrel
half barrel	0	4	0	0¾	half barrel
or Mahogany					
each	0	2	0	0½	each
ndle contain-					
- -	0	4	0	0½	bundle
proportion.					
wheels, each	6	0	0	10	each
wheels, each	5	0	0	6	each
- - ton	2	6	0	6	ton
- - cwt.	0	3	0	0½	cwt.
cwt. basket	0	4	0	1	basket
2 qrs. basket	0	2	0	0½	basket
- single bale	0	8	0	2	single bale
double bale	1	0	0	3	double bale
lts, package	1	6	0	4	package
lts, package	2	6	0	8	package
	1	0	0	2	
g to size, } each }	to		to		} each
	2	0	0	4	
small bag	0	4	0	1	small bag
2 cwt. bag	0	8	0	2	bag
6 cwt. cask	2	0	0	6	cask
iots, each	10	0	1	0	each
- hogshead	1	6	0	3	hogshead
- bag	0	6	}		
small bag	0	4	} 1	0	ton
4 cwt. bale	0	8	}		
5 cwt. bale	1	0	}		
chaldron	4	0	1	0	chaldron
- ton	3	4	0	8	ton
, 4 to 6 cwt.					
ton	3	4	0	4	ton
5 cwt. case	1	4	}		
8 cwt. case	2	0	} 0	6	ton
10 cwt. case	2	6	}		
cwt. bottom	0	4	1	0	ton
cwt. bottom	0	8	1	0	ton
cwt. bundle	0	8	0	1	bundle
- ton	5	0	1	0	ton
- ton	3	4	0	8	ton
- ton	4	0	1	0	ton
lbs. - bag	0	4	0	1	bag
cwt. cask	0	6	0	1½	cask
ia - bale	0	8	0	1½	bale
- bale	1	0	0	2	bale
cwt. 2 qrs.					
bale	0	8	0	2	bale
- ton	3	4	0	6	ton
- butt	2	0	0	6	butt
cwt. 2 qrs.					
chest	0	8	0	2	chest
s. to 5 cwt.					
chest	1	0	0	3	chest

Goods for Exportation.	Wharfage and Shipping.		Rent after Three Weeks. Per Week.		Rent after Three Weeks. Quantities, &c.
Per	s.	d.	s.	d.	Per
Earthenware, large or small					
crate	0	8	0	2	crate
Fish, loose - - ton	5	0	0	8	ton
Flax - - - ton	3	0	0	8	ton
1 cwt. 2 qrs. bag	0	4	0	0¾	bag
Flour - - barrel	0	4	0	10	score barrels
Ginger - - ton	5	0	1	0	ton
Glass - box or half box	0	4	0	1	box or half box
crate	0	8	0	2	crate
quarter crate	0	8	0	1	quarter crate
tierce	1	0	0	3	tierce
Plate small case	0	8	0	2	small case
middling case	1	4	0	4	middling case
large case	2	0	0	6	large case
Grindstones, for every six					
inches in diameter -	0	2	0	0½	
Gum - - seron	0	6	0	1	seron
Guns, ordinary sized chest	1	0	0	2	ordinary chest
large chest	1	4	0	3	large chest
Hams, loose - - each	0	1	0	5	score
Hardware, 5 to 7 cwt. cask	1	0	0	2½	cask
8 to 9 cwt. cask	1	4	0	3	cask
9 to 11 cwt. cask	1	6	0	4	cask
12 to 14 cwt. cask	2	0	0	5	cask
15 to 17 cwt. cask	2	6	0	6	cask
	2	6	0	6	
Harps or Harpsichords, } according to size, each }	to		to		} each
	5	0	0	9	
Hats, ordinary-sized case	1	0	0	3	ordinary case
Hay - - 3 trusses	0	4	0	3	score trusses
Hemp - - ton	3	0	0	8	ton
Hemp Screws - each	0	4	0	1	each
Herrings - barrel	0	4	0	0½	barrel
Hides or Skins, East India,					
5 to 7 lbs. 100	2	0	0	6	100
10 to 12 lbs. each	0	0½	0	6	100
Ox and Cow - 100	6	0	1	6	100
Hops - - bag	1	4	0	4	bag
pocket	0	8	0	2	pocket
Horn, Tips and Plates,					
hogshead	1	4	0	4	hogshead
Horses - - each	10	0			
India Rubber - barrel	0	6	0	1½	barrel
Indigo - seron	0	6	0	1½	seron
about 3 qrs. half chest or					
box	0	6	0	1½	half chest or box
chest	0	8	0	2	chest
Iron, Bars and unmanu-					
factured - - ton	2	6	0	3	ton
Hoops - 1 cwt. bundle	0	4	}		
3 qrs. bundle	0	3	} 0	6	ton
2 qrs. bundle	0	2	}		
Pots - 100	4	0	0	9	100
Tier - 1 cwt. bundle	0	4	0	0½	bundle
Heavy manufactured Ma-					
chinery, Mill Work,					
&c. &c., pieces above 1					
ton - - ton	6	0	0	6	ton
under 1 ton ton	5	0	0	6	ton
Scrap, loose - ton	4	0	0	6	ton
in bags - ton	3	0	0	6	ton
Ivory - - cwt.	0	3	0	1	cwt.
Lac Dye, about 1 cwt. 2 qrs.					
chest	0	8	0	2	chest
Lace - package	1	0	0	6	package
Laths - - bundle	0	1	1	6	100 bundles
Lead, in pigs - ton	2	0	0	3	ton
Black - - 40 lbs. cask	0	2	0	0½	cask
Shot, Bars, or Rolls, ton	3	4	0	3	ton
Logwood - - ton	2	3	0	6	ton
Mace and Nutmegs, small					
cask	0	8	0	2	small cask
Mangles - - each	5	0	0	6	each
Manure, about 1 ton, cask	2	6	0	4	cask
Melting Pots - - ton	5	0	0	6	ton
Millstones, about 1 ton each	4	0	0	6	each
Mineral Brown (in turpen-					
tine casks) - 3 cwt. barrel	0	6	0	6	ton
Molasses - - puncheon	1	2	0	3	puncheon
Mother o'Pearl Shells, ton	5	0	0	8	ton
Musk box	0	8	0	2	box
Mustard - - keg	0	4	0	1	keg
not exceeding 28 lbs. keg	0	2	0	0½	keg
Nails - - 2 qrs. keg	0	2	3	0	100 kegs
1 cwt. 2 qrs. keg	0	4	0	0¾	keg
1 cwt. 2 qrs. to 2 cwt.					
- cask	0	6	0	1	cask
Nankeens, not exceeding					
1 cwt. case or chest	0	6	0	1½	case or chest
Negro Clothing, puncheon	1	0	0	3	puncheon
Nutria Skins - 4 cwt. bale	0	8	0	2	bale
5 cwt. bale	1	0	0	3	bale
Oakum 2 qrs. bundle	0	2	0	0½	bundle
Oil Cake - - ton	3	6	0	6	ton
Oil - - - tun	3	6	0	8	tun
under 3 gallons, jug	0	2	}		
3 to 7 gallons, jug	0	4	} 0	0½	gallon
8 to 10 gallons, jug	0	6	}		
11 to 12 gallons, jug	0	8	}		
Paint, in small kegs - ton	8	0	1	0	ton
in casks containing do., ton	3	4	0	6	ton
Paper - - small bale	0	6	0	1½	small bale
Pearl Barley, 1 cwt. barrel					
or keg	0	4	0	1	barrel or keg
Pepper - ton	5	0	1	0	ton
Piano Fortes, Grand, each	4	0	1	0	each
Cabinet - - each	3	0	0	9	each
Square - - each	2	0	0	6	each
Pickles - - small box	0	4	0	0¾	small box

Goods for Exportation.	Wharfage and Shipping.	Rent after Three Weeks. Per Week.	Quantities, &c.
Per	s. d.	s. d.	Per
Pipes, empty - each	0 4	0 1	each
Pitch - - barrel	0 4	6 0	100 barrels
Plants, abt. 5 cwt. package	1 6	0 4	package
middling package	1 0	0 3	middling package
small package	0 8	0 2	small package
Potatoes, abt. 1 cwt. basket	0 3	0 0½	basket
3 bushels sack	0 6	0 1	sack
Quicksilver - iron bottle	0 2	0 0½	each
Rags - - 3 cwt. bag	0 4	0 1	bag
Rigging - - cwt.	0 4	0 0¾	cwt.
Rosin - barrel	0 4	6 0	100 barrels
Safflower, under 2 cwt. 2 qrs. - - bale	0 8	0 2	bale
above 2 cwt. 2 qrs. bale	1 0	0 3	bale
Saltpetre, rough, in bags, ton	3 0	0 6	ton
Refined, under 1 cwt. barrel	0 4	0 0½	barrel
1 to 2 cwt. - - cask	0 6	0 1	cask
10 cwt. - - cask	1 2	0 3	cask
Seed, Clover - - bale	0 8	0 1½	bale
Seedlac, 2 cwt. to 2 qrs. bag	0 8	0 2	bag
Sheep - - each	0 6		
Shellac, in bags or bundles, ton	5 0	1 0	ton
Skins - 18 to 20 cwt. cask	3 0	0 7	cask
15 cwt. cask	2 6	0 6	cask
vat	1 6	0 6	vat
hogshead	1 2	0 4	hogshead
tierce	1 0	0 3	tierce
Goat and Mogadore, about 2 cwt. 2 qrs. - bale	0 4	0 1½	bale
Soap, 56 lbs. and under, small box	0 2	0 0½	small box
57 and under 112 lbs. box	0 4	0 1	box
under 3 cwt. - chest	0 8	0 2	chest
3 to 5 cwt. - chest	1 0	0 3	chest
Spelter - - ton	2 0	0 4	ton
Spirits, see *Wines*.			
Starch, 1 cwt. - - box	0 6	0 1	box
under 1 cwt. - box	0 4	0 1	box
Staves, Wine Hogshead, pack	0 2	0 0½	pack
Pipe, Leager, or Sugar Hogshead - pack	0 4	0 0½	pack
Steel, in bars - - ton	3 4	0 4	ton
in bundles, 1 cwt. bundle	0 4	0 6	ton
Straw - - truss	0 1	0 3	score trusses
Sugar - - mat or bag	0 4	0 0½	mat or bag
4 or 5 cwt. mat or bask.	0 8	0 1	mat or basket
boxes or chests - ton	3 4	0 5	ton
Bastard, not ex. 2 cwt. 2 qrs. - - barrel	0 5	0 1	barrel
under 8 cwt. - tierce	0 9	0 2	tierce
12 and under 14 cwt. cask	1 6	} 0 5	ton
14 cwt. and upwards, cask	2 0	}	
Refined - - hogshead	1 2	0 3	hogshead
12 to 14 cwt. - cask	1 6	0 4	cask
14 to 18 cwt. - cask	2 0	0 6	cask
18 to 24 cwt. - cask	2 6	0 7	cask

Refined, packed in Hogsheads or Vats, to be housed for Exportation.	Per Hhd.	Per Vat, 16 cwt. & upwards.
Housing - -	0 6	1 0
Weighing or re-weighing	0 6	1 0
Unhousing, wharfage, and shipping - - -	1 8	3 0
Rent - per week	0 3	0 6

Goods for Exportatiou.	Wharfage and Shipping.	Rent after Thre[e Weeks.] Per Week.	Quanti[ties, &c.]
Per	s. d.	s. d.	Per
Tallow - ton	2 6	0 6	ton
Tar - - barrel	0 4	6 0	100 barrels
Tea - - chest	1 0	0 3	chest
half chest	0 8	0 2	half chest
quarter chest	0 6	0 1½	quarter ch
small box	0 4	0 1	small box
Tiles, Welch, abt. 1 ft. sq. 100	2 0	0 6	100
Tin - - box	0 4	0 0½	box
barrel	0 6	0 1	barrel
Turmeric - - ton	4 0	1 0	ton
Varnish - - barrel	0 6	0 1	barrel
Vermilion, 2 to 3 cwt. chest or package	2 0	0 4	chest or pa
Vinegar - - puncheon	1 4	0 4	puncheon
hogshead	0 8	0 2	hogshead
barrel or half hogshead	0 6	0 1½	barrel or ha
* Vitriol, Carboys - gallon	0 4	0 1	gallon
Whalebone - 5 cwt. bale	1 0	0 4	bale
Wheels, according to size, each	0 4 to 1 0	0 1 to 0 2	pair
Wine, bottled, in casks, dozen bottles	0 1	0 0½	dozen bott
in cases - dozen bottles	0 2	0 0½	dozen bott
Spirits, pipe, puncheon, or butt	2 0	0 6	pipe, punc
hogshead	1 0	0 3	hogshead
No charge is made for wharfage of wines and spirits landed at the docks, and carted to the Export Quay, except for "striking and shipping," viz.			
Pipe, butt, and puncheon - - 8*d*.			
Hogshead - 4*d*.			
Wire, Iron, 1 cwt. 2 qrs. bundle	0 6	0 1	bundle
Wood - - ton	2 3	0 3	ton
When not cleared the same day as sent down, piling is charged.			
Wood Hoops - bundle	0 1	0 3	score bund
truss	0 2	0 5	score bund
Wool, English, 3 cwt. to 3 cwt. 2 qrs. - bale	0 9	0 2½	bale
3 cwt. 2 qrs. to 5 cwt. bale	1 0	0 3	bale
Spanish - 1 cwt. bag	0 5	0 1	bag
2 cwt. bag	0 8	0 2	bag
2 cwt. 2 qrs. bag	0 9	0 2½	bag
German, under 4 cwt. bag	0 8	0 2	bag
4 to 6 cwt. bag	1 0	0 3	bag
6 cwt. and upwards, bag	1 4	0 4	bag

WHEN CHARGED BY THE PACKAGE.

Goods for Exportation.	Wharfage and Shipping.	Rent after Three Weeks. Per Week.	Quantities, &c.
	s. d.	s. d.	
Bags, small each	0 4	0 1	each
Bales, small each	0 8	0 2	each
middling - each	1 0	0 3	each
large, 5 and under 7 cwt. each	1 4	0 3	each
7 and under 8 cwt., each	1 6	} 0 0½	cwt.
8 and under 12 cwt. each	2 0	}	
12 and under 14 cwt. each	2 6	}	
14 and under 16 cwt. each	3 0	}	
16 cwt. and upwards	4 0	}	
E. I. Goods, single each	0 8	0 2	each
double - each	1 4	0 .	each
Barrels - each	0 6	0 1½	each
Baskets, small - each	0 2	0 ½	each
middling each	0 4	0 1	each
large - - each	0 6	0 1½	each
Bottles or Jars, 1 to 3 gallons, each	0 2	} 0½	gallon
4 to 7 gallons - each	0 4	}	
7 to 10 gallons - each	0 6	}	
11 to 12 gallons - each	0 8	}	
Boxes, ordinary sized, each	0 6	0 1½	each
small - each	0 4	0 1	each
Bundles, large - each	1 0	0 3	each
middling - each	0 9	0 2½	each
small - each	0 6	0 1½	each

Goods for Exportation.	Wharfage and Shipping.	Rent after Th[ree Weeks.] Per Week.	Quan[tities, &c.]
	s. d.	s. d.	
Cases, small - each	0 8	0 2	each
middling - each	1 0	0 3	each
large, 5 cwt. - each	1 4	0 3	each
6 cwt. - each	1 6	0 0½	cwt.
extra large, 6 to 8 cwt. each	2 0	} 0 0½	cwt.
9 to 12 cwt. each	2 6	}	
above 12 cwt. - each	3 0	}	
Casks, small - each	0 8	0 2	each
middling or tierce, each	1 0	0 3	each
Chests, small - each	0 8	0 2	each
middling each	1 0	0 3	each
large - each	1 4	0 4	each
Hogsheads, not exceeding 8 or 9 cwt. - each	1 2	0 3	each
Jars, see *Bottles*.			
Kegs - each	0 4	0 1	each
small - each	0 2	0 0½	each
Pipes - - each	1 4	0 4	each
Portmanteaus, ordinary sized - each	0 6	0 1½	each
Other sizes will be charged in propo tion, and rent one fourth of the rate for wharfage and shipping.			
Puncheons - each	1 4	0 4	each
Trunks - - each	0 6	0 1½	each
Trusses - - each	1 0	0 1½	each

Goods not included in the foregoing tables, pay in proportion to the rates therein contained, a[ccording] to weight or size.

* N. B. — " Persons sending to the dock, for shipment, aqua fortis, oil of vitriol, or other go[ods of a] dangerous quality, and neglecting to distinctly mark, or state, the nature of such goods on the [outside] of the package, or otherwise give due notice thereof to the superintendent, are subject to a penalty[…]" See act 9 Geo. 4. c. 116. § 132.

East India Docks. — These docks, situated at Blackwall, were principally intended the accommodation of the ships employed by the East India Company. There are docks; one for ships unloading inwards, and one for those loading outwards. The ort Dock contains about 18 acres, and the Export Dock about 9 acres. The entrance n, which connects the docks with the river, contains about 2¾ acres; the length of entrance lock is 210 feet, the width of the gates 48 feet clear. Having to receive els of great burthen, the depth of water in the East India docks is never less than cet. Most of the merchandise imported into these docks is conveyed, without loss me, to warehouses in the city; so that the extent of warehouses belonging to them mparatively small.

he discharging of ships in the Import Dock is wholly performed by the servants of Company; and the regulations as to fire, cooking, &c. are stricter than in the other s. The principal are subjoined.

e gates of the Import Dock are, from the 1st of March to the 1st of October inclusive, to be open usiness at and from the hour of 7 in the morning until the hour of 3 in the afternoon; and from the November to the last day of February inclusive, at and from the hour of 8 in the morning until the of 3 in the afternoon, during which hours there is to be no intermission or cessation of business; either before nor after the thus regulated hours of business, can visitors, or any other description of ns resorting to the docks, and not belonging to the authorised establishments, be permitted to remain ard the ships, or within the Import Dock.

e gates of the Export Dock and basin will, from the 1st of March to the 1st of November, be opened usiness at the hour of 6 in the morning, and continue open until, and be shut at, the hour of 7 in the ng, and continue so shut until the hour of 6 in the morning; and from the 1st of November to the March, will be opened for business at the hour of 7 in the morning, and continue open until, and ut at, the hour of 5 in the evening, and continue so shut until the hour of 7 in the morning; and no n shall have access to the dock, basin, or premises, during the period they are ordered to be closed, the dock and revenue officers, and watchmen, and such persons as may be permitted to attend ular duties by the dock officers.

shipwright's work, or repairs (beyond caulking the upper deck), may be performed within the Dock any's premises, except in special cases, with the express permission of the Court of Directors; but ers' and joiners' work will be permitted as heretofore in the outer dock and basins. Pitch-pots will e permitted to be heated within the dock walls, or work done by candle-light, either by joiners or tradesmen.

prevent danger from fire, stoves or cooking-places will not be allowed to be used on board the ships sels, in either docks or basins; but candles will be permitted on special occasions, on application to ock-master, who will grant a written permission for the purpose. Any person offending against this ation will be subject to a penalty of 5*l*.

oking tobacco, or any other herb, is prohibited within the docks and premises, or on board any ship sel within them, under a penalty not exceeding 5*l*.

person shall be suffered to remain on board the ships in the Export Dock or basin during the night, ting ship-keepers, and apprentices of the respective ships, to whom a ticket of permission will be ed, on application to the dock-master. Any person evading this regulation shall forfeit 40*s*. for each e.

e East India docks are at the greatest distance from town. The Company's tea other goods are conveyed to the warehouses in the city in locked wagons of a liar description.

e capital of the Company is under 500,000*l*., and the dividend is 4 per cent. A share of the Company's stock is at present worth about 64*l*. The management is ded to thirteen directors, four of whom must be directors of the East India Com-, and they must each hold at least twenty shares of the Company's stock.

RATES *charged on Ships from the East Indies using the East India Docks.*

rate for receiving and unloading ships or vessels under 800 tons, in the East India docks, and for e of the same for 28 days from the date of the final discharge, is 1*s*. 6*d*. per ton register.

ock rent, if the 28 days be exceeded, 1*d*. per register ton per week, which is also the rate for light ships laying up in the dock.

rate for such ships and vessels as are loaded outwards by the Dock Company will be 2*s*. per ton r, should the packages or articles laden not exceed 2 tons each by measurement or weight; but on s exceed 2 tons, and up to 10 tons, 3*s*. per ton additional will be charged on the quantity laden; es or articles exceeding 10 tons the Dock Company decline lading, except by special agreement. ate for ships and vessels loaded by their owners will be 1*s*. per ton register only, for the use and modation of the dock. Ships and vessels loading outwards to be allowed 28 days for the purpose, heir commencement of receiving cargo.

ock rent, if the 28 days be exceeded, 1*d*. per register ton per week.

ters, or other vessels, loading from the import warehouses, will be charged 6*d*. per ton on the gross they take on board; to be allowed one week for such purpose.

ock rent, if the one week be exceeded, 1*d*. per register ton per week.

. — These docks receive no other than ships or vessels in the East India trade, or coasters to load he warehouses.

RATES *charged for Wharfage, Storehouses, &c., and for sundry Work done by the East India Dock Company.*

age of guns above 20 cwt.		2*s*. 6*d*. each
above 15 cwt. and under 20 cwt.	2*s*. 0*d*.
above 10 cwt. and under 15 cwt.	1*s*. 6*d*.
nder 10 cwt.	-	1*s*. 0*d*.
f gun carriages belonging to the		
of the above scale, 1*s*. 3*d*., 1*s*. 9*d*. & 6*d*.		
f anchors	-	0*s*. 3*d*. per cwt.
f kentledge	-	1*s*. 6*d*. per ton.
of other articles deposited on		
wharfs or quays	-	2*s*. 6*d*.

These rates of wharfage are for the season the ship may remain at home; or for a period not exceeding twelve months: if the twelve months be exceeded, the same rate of charge will be made as if a new season had been commenced, and this rate of wharfage be considered an annual charge. N. B. — By the present existing agreement between the East India Company and the Dock Company, the guns and anchors of ships whilst in the Company's service are free of wharfage.

Landing guns from craft, and stowing them on skids, 2d. per cwt. — Ditto carriages of guns, ab
10 cwt., 1s.; under ditto, 6d. each. — Shipping of ditto into craft, the same rate. — Getting guns on bo
ship, and mounting them, 2s. 6d. per ton. — Getting on board gun carriages, of guns above 10 cw
6d. each; under ditto, 4d. each. — Landing anchors from craft and placing them at racks, 3d. per c
— Shipping off ditto into craft, the same rate. — Placing anchors for unstocking or for stocking, 1
per cwt. — Discharging kentledge from ships, and stacking it on the wharf, 1s. 2d. per ton. — Discha
ing ditto from ships into craft, 1s. per ton — Shipping off kentledge from the wharf, and stowing it
the hold, 1s. 2d. per ton. — Shipping off ditto into craft, 10d. per ton. — Discharging shingle or sto
ballast into craft or on the quay, 1s. 3d. per ton. — Water supplied to outward-bound ships, as well
what is used for seasoning their casks, 1s. per ton imperial measure.

Admission of loaded waggons, conveying
cargo, or passengers' baggage, in lieu of
wharfage - - - 5s. 0d. each } N. B. Ships' stores, and commanders' and office
Ditto of carts, with ditto, ditto - 2s. 6d. } baggage, admitted free to outward bound ships
Ditto of trucks, with ditto, ditto - 1s. 0d.

Storehouses (for ships' stores) may be hired at 1l. 1s. per week; if rented annually, large storehouses
a year — smaller ditto, 35l. a year; or if taken permanently, large storehouses, 35l. a year — smal
ditto, at 30l. a year.

Use of the rigging shed for fitting rigging, viz.
For ships of 800 tons and upwards - 5l. 5s. }
Ditto from 500 to 800 tons - 4l. 4s. } N.B. Time for this operation limited to 1 month
Ditto from 300 to 500 tons - 3l. 3s. }
Ditto under 300 tons - - 2l. 2s. }

Every ship using the docks, outwards or homewards, and making fast alongside the hulk, of 500 t
burthen, or upwards, to pay 1l. 1s., and ships and vessels under that burthen, 10s. 6d. for every 24 hou
for the first three days; should this period be exceeded, to pay for every 24 hours beyond the sam
5l. 5s., unless such detention is caused by special circumstances, such as the bye-laws provide for.
The charge for any description of labour or service performed by the Dock Company, and not specified
this table, will be made on moderate terms.
Note. — In loading ships outward, the Dock Company engage to get on board all goods and stores fr
craft, or the wharf, without extra charge, except the following, viz. kentledge, anchors, guns and c
riages, sails, standing and running rigging, booms, and boats.

Charges for Masting or Dismasting at the Mast-Building.

	Main Mast.	Fore Mast.	Mizen Mast.	Bowspri
	£ s. d.	£ s. d.	£ s. d.	£ s. d
For ships of 1,000 to 1,500 tons - - 10 0 0	9 0 0	4 0 0	5 0
Ditto 800 — 1,000 - 7 10 0	7 0 0	3 10 0	4 0
Ditto 650 — 800 - 5 0 0	4 10 0	2 10 0	2 10
Ditto 500 — 650 - 4 0 0	3 10 0	2 0 0	2 0
Ditto 300 — 500 - 3 10 0	3 0 0	1 15 0	1 15
Ditto under 300 - 2 10 0	2 5 0	1 10 0	1 10

For putting on and taking off Tops.

	Main.	Fore.	Mizen
	£ s. d.	£ s. d.	£ s.
For ships of 1,000 to 1,500 tons - 1 0 0	1 0 0	0 12
Ditto 800 — 1,000 - - - 0 16 0	0 16 0	0 10
Ditto 500 — 800 - 0 12 6	0 12 6	0 8
Ditto under 500 - - - in proportion.		

The prices of the above tables are for each operation, which includes the use of masting-fall and slir
N. B. Owners of ships may purchase not less than half a fall, at 15 per cent. under the ready mo
cost price.

4. *St. Katharine Docks.* — The Company for the construction of these docks was inc
porated by the act 6 Geo. 4. c. 105. (local), and they were partially opened on the 2
of October, 1828. They are situated immediately below the Tower, and are consequen
the most contiguous of any to the city, the Custom-house, and other places where bu
ness is transacted. The capital raised by shares amounts to 1,352,800l.; but an ad
tional sum of 800,000l. has been borrowed, on the security of the rates, for the completi
of the works, and the purchase of a freehold property possessing river frontage from
Tower to the corner of Lower East Smithfield, of the value of upwards of 100,00
but not required for the immediate purpose of the act. A portion of this property
been appropriated as a steam packet wharf, where passengers embark and land with
the aid or risk of boat conveyance. The purchase of the numerous houses that stood up
the ground occupied by the docks proved, as in the case of the London docks, a he
item of expense. The space included within the outer wall is about 24 acres, nea
11 of which are water. There are two docks, communicating by a basin. The l
leading from the river is 180 feet long, and 45 broad: it is so constructed, that sh
of upwards of 600 tons burthen may pass in and out three hours before high water
that outward bound ships have the opportunity of reaching Blackwall before the t
begins to recede. Ships of upwards of 800 tons register are docked and undoc
without difficulty, and the depth of water at the entrance exceeds that of any other
dock in the port of London. Vessels are also docked and undocked by night as wel
by day, an advantage peculiar to this establishment. A clear channel of not less t
300 feet in width is at all times to be kept in the pool; and vessels drawing 18
water may lie afloat at low water at the principal buoy off the dock entrance. The w
houses and vaults are upon a very large scale; far more so than one might be dispo
to infer from the extent of water. The warehouses are exceedingly well contrived
commodious; and, owing to their being built partly on pillars (within which, wh

the quay work of the other docks is transacted), close to the water's edge, goods are
d direct from the hold of the vessel, without its being necessary, as in the West
and London docks, to land them on quays; so that there is in this way a great
g both of room, time, and labour. The whole establishment is exceedingly com-
and reflects the greatest credit on the public spirit, enterprise, and skill, of those
om it was projected and executed.

lations to be observed, and Charges to be paid, by Vessels using the St. Katharine Docks. — " Prior
ssel entering, the sails should be furled, yards topped and secured, jib-booms, running bowsprits,
gers, and spanker-boom run in, spritsail yard fore and aft, all boats lowered down, davits topped up,
ders ready at the bows, anchors stowed on the forecastle, guns, if any, unloaded and run in, and
rder removed from on board : the vessel should also be provided with good and sufficient hawsers,
nd tackle, to make fast, moor, and remove her with safety.
gunpowder or loaded gun is permitted to be brought into the docks, or allowed to remain on ship-
herein, under a penalty of 5l.
e docking and undocking, mooring, unmooring, moving and removing, dismantling, &c. will be
under the control and direction of the dock-masters, and no rope must be cast off or slackened
hauling in or out, without the dock-master's orders.
sters or other persons in charge of vessels or craft about to enter or depart the docks, or during the
transporting within the same, must cause fenders to be hung over the sides, and at the bows, and
enjoin the crews to be cautious in the use of staffs or boat-hooks, so that no damage be done to
ds of the docks, lock, or works.
e boat afloat, only, is allowed for the use of each ship whilst in the docks, nor are sails permitted
ose after sunset.
opy of the manifest of every vessel entering the docks must be lodged at the Manifest Office in
g room at the dock-house, within twelve hours from the time of entering the basin; it should
, whether the vessel is fully laden, or not, and denote, as far as possible, the goods at hand, and
ver it can be ascertained) what goods are to be delivered overside, or are to be stopped for freight,
ether the cargo is to be unloaded by the servants of the Dock Company, also whether any survey
red to be held. Whenever a survey of goods on shipboard is required, notice should be given by
ter or person in charge, to the wharfinger at the quay where the vessel is berthed. The Dock Com-
lank form of manifest may be obtained from the dock-master, or upon application at the Mani-
ce. If the master or person in charge of any vessel or craft has reason to believe that part of
o has sustained damage on board, he should notify the same upon the manifest or lighter-note.
s desirable that the vessel's register, or certificate of admeasurement, should be produced to the
the Manifest Office at the time of lodging the manifest, as it will obviate the necessity of doing so
me of paying the tonnage dues.
h a view to despatch in the charge of the cargoes of vessels entering the docks, the Company
hority, under the act of parliament, to enter and land such goods as shall not have been entered
customs order for landing lodged with the proper officer at the docks, with 48 hours from the date
hip's report.
enever parties are desirous of communicating with a vessel which shall be lying in a part of the
here she cannot be approached without a boat, and such vessel shall not be provided with one at
, upon application, in the first instance, to the lockman stationed with a boat at the West Dock
the dock-master, or the foreman at the lock, the parties will be put on board in one of the boats
ock Company, free of expense.
ds *landed* and lodged in the custody of the Dock Company, remain subject to freight upon *due*
Such notice to stop goods for freight must be lodged at the Manifest Office, or at the Cargo Ledger
n the long room, dock-house.
en goods have been entered by the Company under the 10th section of the 10th Geo. 4. c. 1., the
r masters of the vessel may lodge an order at the Manifest Office that such goods are not to be de-
without the production of the bill of lading.
ts and fires are only allowed on board ships or craft in the docks during the under-mentioned
nd times : viz.

From 22d September to 20th March, between 7 o'clock A. M. and 4 o'clock P. M.
    21st March to 21st September,   —   6   —   4   —
                        both inclusive.

dock-master, however, has authority to grant permission for fires in cabouses, or in the forecastle
ouse on deck, until 6 o'clock in the evening from Lady-day to Michaelmas (inclusive) ; and until
in the evening from Michaelmas to Lady-Day, and for a CANDLE IN A LANTERN, and COAL-FIRES
ABIN until 8 o'clock in the evening, throughout the year ; such permission to be subject to revo-
circumstances shall render it necessary.
ll will be rung at the first-mentioned hours, as a notice when lights and fires are allowed to be
and at 4 and 8 o'clock, for their being extinguished.
den funnels to the chimneys, or cabouses, must be securely lined with tin, copper, or iron : smok-
pes or segars will not be allowed *upon land* within the Company's premises, nor smoking, fires,
of any kind *upon the deck* of any vessel whilst in the act of discharging combustibles.
bustibles in the custody of the owners thereof, are not to be allowed to remain on the quays,
r deck of any ship, lighter, barge, boat, or other vessel, beyond two hours after notice of removal,
y combustible matter should be melted or heated on board of vessels or craft, or on any part
emises within the dock walls, but a place has been provided for such purpose on the west pier-

ds are not permitted to be landed, unshipped, delivered, loaded, or received, except at such places
cks as shall be assigned for that purpose by the Company.
discharge of the cargo will be effected by the servants of the Dock Company, if desired by the
master ; but no person is allowed to be employed in the unloading or loading of vessels within
s, except the crews thereof, and the servants of the Dock Company, or in any work and labour to
rmed within the dock premises, whether on board or on shore, without special permission from
rintendent in writing (stowers on board of ships loading outwards excepted).
e unloading is required to be effected by the Dock Company, after the manifest is lodged, notice
given to the superintendent or wharfinger, so soon as that mode of delivery has been determined

e vessel is not provided with proper or sufficient tackle to effect the delivery of the cargo with
atch, machinery may be obtained for that purpose from the Dock Company upon a moderate
ut should any unnecessary delay take place in the discharge by the crew, the Dock Company are
d by the Dock Act to send assistance on board to accelerate unloading, and to charge the expense
ners of the vessel.
master or mate, or some person appointed by the former or by the owners, is by law required to
n board, during the whole of the time the vessel is in the act of discharging or loading, and must
writing, to the wharfinger, whenever the final delivery inwards cannot be completed without

" When ballast is taken on board, canvass or tarpauling must be nailed to the ship's side, so as to prevent any dirt or ballast from falling into the dock.

" The responsibility of the ship owner, with respect to the cargo, continues in all cases whilst the goods are in the vessel's hold, and also as respects any injury sustained from imperfect or careless hooking or slinging, except when the goods are landed and the discharge wholly effected by the Dock Company.

" The Dock Company will in no case be responsible for goods received by lighter into a vessel, or discharged from a vessel into a lighter.

" Vessels, when ready for clearing, will hoist their colours.

" If any ship, lighter, craft, or vessel, shall be left in the docks or basin without any person on board, the master, or other person having the command, or the owner, will be liable to a penalty.

" No baggage, wearing apparel, or uncustomable goods, are permitted to be removed from the dock without a written application from the captain or mate of the vessel to, and a pass from, the warehouse keepers or wharfingers, which baggage and wearing apparel will be searched by the customs previous to passing the gates.

" Bells must not be rung, nor fire-arms discharged, on board vessels lying in the docks.

" Dirt-bins are provided at convenient places at the back of the quays, in which dirt and rubbish brought on shore from on board ship must be deposited ; a penalty will be incurred for placing, causing or permitting to be placed, dirt or rubbish on any part of the Company's premises, except as aforesaid, or for throwing or letting any fall into the docks.

" Caulking or scraping of ships' decks, sides, or masts, is not allowed, — nor are any repairs to the hull of vessels permitted in the docks, except such as shall be permitted in writing by the dock-master. Permission will be given for vessels to lie at one of the buoys of the Company in the river to caulk or scrape, upon application to the dock-master.

" No fire will be allowed on board a vessel, near the place where carpenters or joiners shall be at work.

" No persons will be allowed to remain on the quays, &c. after dark, or land from a vessel to which they belong, or pass inwards or outwards after the hour of finally closing the wicket-gate at the principal entrance in East Smithfield ; the periods and times for which are as follow : —

From 21st March to 21st May, open at 6 A. M. shut at 7 P. M.
— 22d May — 21st August — 6 — 8 —
— 22d August — 21st Sept. — 6 — 7 —
— 22d Sept. — 20th March — 7 — 6 —
} *all inclusive.*

Permission may, however, be obtained for ingress or egress, at all times, in case of *illness or accident,* on application to the superintendent of the police, who resides in the dock-house. The constable, watchman, or firemen on duty, will show the parties where they are to apply.

" Tickets of admission, during the hours before specified, for the female part of the families of masters or mates of vessels lying in dock, may be obtained on application at the Superintendent's Office any time during hours of business ; but such tickets must be delivered up to the dock-master on the vessel quitting the docks. — Female passengers entering the docks on board ship, must, if desirous of quitting or returning landside, be furnished with a note, signed by the master or person in charge of the vessel on board of which they have entered, certifying the fact ; to be produced at the gate, and to be lodged with the gate-keeper.

" No visiters admitted on Sundays or holidays, except upon business.

" Free access on board of vessels and craft in the docks is at all times to be allowed to the officers, stables, firemen, watchmen, and other servants of the Dock Company. It is requested that dogs may be tied up after dark.

" Tonnage-dues and charges on vessels should, if possible, be paid the day previous to their quitting the docks, and notice given to the dock-master (whenever practicable) prior to the intended departure. Accounts of charges, &c. will be obtained at the Manifest Office, and the amount thereof must be paid to the collector, — upon the production of the receipt to the clerk in such office, a ship's pass will be granted, which must be deposited with the dock-master on the vessel quitting the docks.

" For the accommodation of ship owners, and despatch of business, deposit accounts may be opened with the Company, upon application to the Deposit Ledger clerk, in the Collector's Office.

" Freight-books will be supplied to ship owners, captains, or brokers, on application at the Manifest Office."

The hours of attendance for the transaction of public business by the revenue within the docks, are as under : —

From 1st March to 31st October, both inclusive, at 8 o'clock A.M. until 4 o'clock P.M.
— 1st November to last day of February, both inclusive, at 9 o'clock A.M. until 4 o'clock P.M.

Table of Tonnage Rates chargeable on Vessels entering the St. Katharine Docks, to discharge Cargoes, or to load Outwards.

VESSELS INWARDS.				
On *Vessels laden, arriving from*	s. d.		*Privilege.*	Rent after expiration of Privilege, One Penny per Ton Register per Week. * See remarks during absence on repairs in annexed Table.
Any Port of the United Kingdom, Isle of Man, Jersey, Guernsey, Alderney, or Sark, or other European Ports outside the Baltic, between the North Cape and Ushant - -	0 6	Per Ton Register.	Use of the Docks for Six Weeks from the Date of Entrance, with liberty to Load Outwards, and quit the Docks for Repairs, and re-enter.	
Any other Port - - -	0 9			

For partial Remission as to Ships from Spain or Portugal laden with Wool or Cork, and Ships laden with Provisions or Corn, see annexed Table.

RATES FOR DISCHARGING CARGOES TO BE LANDED BY THE COMPANY.		
First Class. — Cargoes, consisting either in the whole or in part, of hogsheads or tierces of Sugar, including Ship-cooperage or mending - - - - -	s. d. 1 6	Per Ton Register
Second Class. — Cargoes, consisting of Sugar, in bags or chests, or other Goods, (not being Tallow, Hemp, Corn, Wood Goods, Pitch, Tar, Hay, or Straw,) contained in casks, bales, serons, chests, cases, bags, baskets, mats, bundles, or similar packages : also, Spelter, or Metal in pigs, bars, rods, plates		
From the East Indies, Cape, and South America	0 6	
From any other place - - -	0 9	} Per Ton Register
Third Class. — Cargoes consisting of Hemp only, or Merchandise in bulk	1 0	
Do. do. Tallow only - - -	0 6	
Mixed Cargoes of { Hemp - - - -	1 3	Per Ton of Goods. Charge in no case to exceed the Register Tonnage of Vessel.
Tallow - - - -	0 6	
Ashes - - - -	0 6	
Do. do. Part being in bulk, on the latter -	1 0	

Provided customary Ship-cooperage or mending shall be found necessary, in the *second* or *third* Class, three pence per ton register will be added to the rates for discharging.

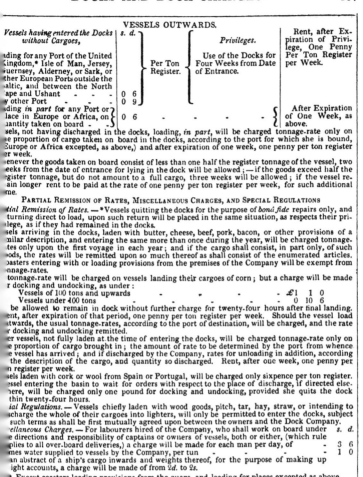

VESSELS OUTWARDS.

Vessels having entered the Docks without Cargoes,	s. d.		Privileges.	Rent, after Expiration of Privilege, One Penny Per Ton Register per Week.
		Per Ton Register.	Use of the Docks for Four Weeks from Date of Entrance.	
...ading for any Port of the United Kingdom,* Isle of Man, Jersey, Guernsey, Alderney, or Sark, or other European Ports outside the Baltic, and between the North ...ape and Ushant - - -	0 6			
...y other Port - - - -	0 9			
...ading *in part* for any Port or ...lace in Europe or Africa, on ...uantity taken on board - -	0 6			After Expiration of One Week, as above.

...sels, not having discharged in the docks, loading, *in part*, will be charged tonnage-rate only on ...e proportion of cargo taken on board in the docks, according to the port for which she is bound, ...Europe or Africa excepted, as above,) and after expiration of one week, one penny per ton register ...er week.

...enever the goods taken on board consist of less than one half the register tonnage of the vessel, two ...eeks from the date of entrance for lying in the dock will be allowed ; —if the goods exceed half the ...egister tonnage, but do not amount to a full cargo, three weeks will be allowed ; if the vessel re...ain longer rent to be paid at the rate of one penny per ton register per week, for such additional ...me.

PARTIAL REMISSION OF RATES, MISCELLANEOUS CHARGES, AND SPECIAL REGULATIONS

...tial Remission of Rates. — *Vessels quitting the docks for the purpose of *bonâ fide* repairs only, and ...turning direct to load, upon such return will be placed in the same situation, as respects their pri...lege, as if they had remained in the docks.

...sels arriving in the docks, laden with butter, cheese, beef, pork, bacon, or other provisions of a ...milar description, and entering the same more than once during the year, will be charged tonnage...tes only upon the first voyage in each year ; and if the cargo shall consist, in part only, of such ...ods, the rates will be remitted upon so much thereof as shall consist of the enumerated articles. ...oasters entering with or loading provisions from the premises of the Company will be exempt from ...nnage-rates.

...tonnage-rate will be charged on vessels landing their cargoes of corn ; but a charge will be made ...r docking and undocking, as under : —

Vessels of 100 tons and upwards - - - -	£1 1 0
Vessels under 100 tons - - - - -	0 10 6

...be allowed to remain in dock without further charge for twenty-four hours after final landing. ...ent, after expiration of that period, one penny per ton register per week. Should the vessel load ...twards, the usual tonnage-rates, according to the port of destination, will be charged, and the rate ...r docking and undocking remitted.

...er vessels, not fully laden at the time of entering the docks, will be charged tonnage-rate only on ...e proportion of cargo brought in ; the amount of rate to be determined by the port from whence ...e vessel has arrived ; and if discharged by the Company, rates for unloading in addition, according ...the description of the cargo, and quantity so discharged. Rent, after one week, one penny per ...n register per week.

...els laden with cork or wool from Spain or Portugal, will be charged only sixpence per ton register. ...essel entering the basin to wait for orders with respect to the place of discharge, if directed else...here, will be charged only one pound for docking and undocking, provided she quits the dock ...thin twenty-four hours.

...ial Regulations. — Vessels chiefly laden with wood goods, pitch, tar, hay, straw, or intending to ...scharge the whole of their cargoes into lighters, will only be permitted to enter the docks, subject ...such terms as shall be first mutually agreed upon between the owners and the Dock Company.

...ellaneous Charges. — For labourers hired of the Company, who shall work on board under s. d. ...e directions and responsibility of captains or owners of vessels, both or either, (which rule ...plies to all over-board deliveries,) a charge will be made for each man per day, of - 3 6 ...mes water supplied to vessels by the Company, per tun - - - - - 1 0 ...an abstract of a ship's cargo inwards and weights thereof, for the purpose of making up ...ight accounts, a charge will be made of from 2d. to 2s.

* Except coasters loading provisions from the quays, and loading for places excepted as above.

...routine to be followed by merchants and others transacting business at the St. Katharine docks ...lar to that followed at the West India and London docks. The landing and consolidated rates on ...mported and warehoused embrace the same particulars as at the other docks. We subjoin a table ...s on some of the principal articles of merchandise, imported and landed at the St. Katharine docks.

...ates on some of the principal Articles of Merchandise imported and landed at the St. Katharine Docks.

...of Goods and ...ages.	Landing Rate.		Rate of Rent per Week.	Description of Goods and Packages.	Landing Rate.		Rate of Rent per Week.
	Per s. d.	s. d.	Per		Per s. d.	s. d.	Per
...ton	3 0	0 3 / 0 2 / 0 0½	cask, from Black Sea / do. from other parts / of Russia / do. from America	Butter, Foreign, Friesland or Holstein. Landing, wharfage, and housing, or loading, and furnishing landing weights to the import...ers · ½ cask / the like · cask	0 3 / 0 3	4 0 / 2 0	100 / 100	No rent or watching will be charged if taken away from the quay within 6 working days from the period of the importing ship breaking bulk.
...wharfage, and 2s. per ton. ...ton	3 6	0 2		Loading from the warehouse, 1d. per cask. Weighing on delivery, if required, and furnishing delivery weights to the buyer, 1d. per cask.				Watching on the quays, after the expiration of one week, per night, on any number of casks or firkins,
...weighing, 2s. ...delivery). ...wharfage, and 3s. per ton. ...ests, mats, or ...ton	3 3	0 2		Emb…den or Holland. Landing, wharfage, and housing, or loading, and furnishing landing weights	0 3	2 0	100	s. d. Not exceeding 25 0 6
...wharfage, and 2s.6d. per ton. ...se ton	3 6	0 2		Loading from the warehouse, ¼d. per firkin. Weighing on delivery, when required, ¼d. per firkin.				26 and not exceeding 50 · 0 9 51 — 75 · 1 0 76 — 100 · 1 6
...weighing, 2s. ...delivery). ...wharfage, and 3s. per ton. ...ases, - ton	3 3	0 3 / 0 1 / 0 0½ / 0 0½	ton, in casks / case about 2 cwt. / box about 1 cwt. / do. about 56 lbs.	Irish - score firkins Weighing upon delivery, cask or firkin 1d.	3 0	2 0	100.	On any number above 100 in like proportion.
...wharfage, and ...6d. per ton. ...kages, ...pwards, ton ... ton	5 0 / 6 8¼	0 6						And see further under the head of *Provisions.*

Description of Goods and Packages.	Landing Rate.		Rate of Rent per Week.		
Per	s.	d.	s.	d.	Per
Unhousing, wharfage, and shippg. cask or firk. 1½d.					
Cables, Chain - ton	7	6	} 0	4	
Rope - - ton	10	0			
Calicoes, White - bale	1	3	0	1½	
Casks landed empty, or Cask Cases. If not delivered within 6 days (including delivery).					
butt, pipe, or pun.	0	8			
double aum	0	6	} 0	1	
single aum, hhd., or third pipe	0	4			
half aum and quarter cask	0	3	} 0	0½	
half quarter casks	0	2			
If taken away within 6 days, half the above charge and no rent.					
Oil Casks in same proportion.					
Wine or Spirits, small ullages, including turning over contents, storing, and delivery, each	1	0	0	1	
Clover and Lucern Seed, in bags ton	3	9	} 0	3½	
in casks - ton	4	6			
Cochineal - - cwt.	0	9	0	1½	
Or a Consolidated Rate of 2s. per cwt. nett.					
Dust - - bag	0	3	0	0½	
Codilla of Hemp or Flax, ton	5	3			
if sold from landing scale			} 0	4	
to importer - ton	4	3			
to buyer - ton	1	0			
Coffee - - cwt.	0	6	0	6	
Or a Consolidated Rate, in casks, 1s. 6d. per cwt. nett in bags, 1s. 2d. do. do.					
Coir, unwrought, press-packed - ton	3	0			
Rope - - ton	5	0	} 0	4	
Yarn - - ton	5	0			
Cordage, small - ton	5	0	0	4	
Old, see *Rags* and *Old Rope and Junk*.					
Corn, viz. Wheat, Barley, Peas, Horse or Pigeon Beans, Tares, Rye, Linseed, and other heavy Grain, landing, wharfage, housing, and deliver. qr.	0	9	4	9	100 quarters. Risk from fire for account of the proprietors.
Oats and light Grain, landing, wharfage, housing, and delivering, qr.	0	8	3	10	100 quarters, do. do.
Corn and grain delivered overside, worked out by Company, per qr. 3d.					
Flax - - ton	4	6			
if sold from landing scale			} 0	4	
to importer - ton	3	6			
to buyer - ton	1	0			
Unhousing, wharfage, and shipping, 4s. per ton.					
Flour, including deliv. ton	4	9	0	2½	
Weighing on delivery, if required, per barrel or chest, 1d.					
Hemp - - ton	4	6			
if sold from landing scale,					
to importer - ton	3	6	} 0	4	
to buyer - ton	1	0			
Unhousing, wharfage, and shipping, 4s. per ton.					
press-packed - ton	3	0	0	4	
Consolidated Rate on E. I. press-packed, 10s. per ton.					
Horses, Mares, or Geldings (landed by machine) each	12	6			
Indigo, (not East India) cwt.	0	7½	0	1	seron
Or a Consolidated Rate of 1s. 3d. per cwt.					
East India, in chests, chest	1	0	0	1½	
Or a Consolidated Rate, including also all operations incident on taring, raising, repacking, stowing, and attendance whilst on show, nailing down, lotting, and piling away, of 15s. per chest.					
Iron (in bars, &c.) - ton	3	4	} 0	1	No Rent will be charged if shipped from the quays within 14 days from the period of the ship breaking bulk.
if landed for transit, and not weighed - ton	2	6			
Unpiling, wharfage, and shipping (without weighing,) 2s. 6d. per ton.					
When shipped from landing scale, including delivery - ton	4	2			
Ore - - ton	3	0	0	2	
Steam-engines, Boilers, Cylinders, and other heavy Machinery, ton	7	6	0	1	
Do. discharged from vessel and deposited in craft, without landing or weighing - ton	6	0			

Description of Goods and Packages.	Landing Rate.		Rate of Rent per		
Per	s.	d.	s.	d.	Per
Kelp - - ton	3	6	0	2	
Filling and weighing, 2s. per ton (on delivery).					
Lead - - ton	2	6	0	1	
Unpiling, wharfage, and shipping, 1s. 8d. per ton.					
Old and Ore ton	3	0	0	2	
Black - - ton	3	9	0	3	
Linen, German - bale	2	3	0	4	
half bale	1	3	0	2	
quarter bale	0	8½	0	1	
loose or in bags roll	0	1½	1	0	100
chest	2	6	0	4	
half chest	1	3	0	2	
quarter chest	0	8½	0	1	
Russia - - bale	1	2½	0	2	
boarded bale or ½ bale, containing ten pieces	0	9	0	1	
quarter bale	0	7½	0	1	
Crash - - bale	1	2½	0	3	
half bale	0	9	0	2	
quarter bale	0	7½	0	1	100
Sail Cloth - bolt or roll	0	1½	1	0	100
Mats, 2 pieces each	0	3	2	0	
Irish - case or bale	1	6	0	3	
box or bundle	0	9	0	2	
sample box, each	0	3	0	1	
Linseed, see *Corn*.					
Cakes (landed direct from the importing ship) ton	3	6	0	3	
Mats - - 100	1	8½	0	6	100 bundles
Indian - chest	1	0	0	2	
box	0	9	0	1	
East India, as dunnage, 100	0	9	0	3	
			{ 0	2½	puncheon
Molasses - - cwt.	0	3	{ 0	1½	hogshead or ti
Or a Consolidated Rate of 7d. per cwt. nett.			{ 0	0½	barrel or keg
Oil, Bay - - cask	1	0	0	1	
			{ 0	3	puncheon or b
			{ 0	2	tierce
			{ 0	1½	barrel 2 cwt. &
Castor - - cwt.	0	6	{ 0	1	do. under 2 cw
			{ 0	0½	case of 12 bot
			{ 0	3	case of 6 doze
			{ 1	3	ton, in jars or
Chemical or perfumed, cwt.	0	11½	{ 0	4	large case
			{ 0	2	small do.
* Olive, in casks - tun	5	0			† Fourteen
if not housed, landing and					lowed from fi
wharfage - tun	3	4	} 0	7†	landing, with
to buyer, on delivery, tun	1	8			ing. No char
laying up to guage, tun	1	8			if cleared from
Cooper's attendance at landing, searching, filling up, and deliv. from quay, 2s. 6d. per tun.					within that pe
Do. do. at landing, housing, unhousing, and delivery, 3s. 6d. per tun.					
large jars, cwt.	0	6	0	6	
common jars, cwt.	0	8½	0	3	each
half jars, cwt.	0	8½	0	2	do.
case containing 30 quart					do.
bottles, case	1	0	3	0½	
Salad, ½ chest of 30 bottles	0	6	0	2½	score cases
Palm or Cocoa Nut, in					score ½ chests
casks not above 30 cwt., ton	3	9	} 0	4	
in casks above 30 cwt., ton	4	6			
* Fish - tun	4	6			† Fourteen
if not housed, landing					lowed from f
and wharfage - tun	3	0	} 0	5†	landing, with
to buyer, on delivery, tun	1	6			ing. No cha
laying up to gauge, tun	1	6			if cleared fro
Cooper's attendance at landing, searching, filling up, and delivery, 2s. 6d. per tun.					within that p
Wharfage and shipping, 3s. per tun.					
Unhousing, wharfage, and shipping, 3s. 6d. per tun.					
Seed - - ton	4	6	0	4	
Oranges and Lemons, chest	0	7½	0	1	
box	0	5½	0	0½	
case	1	0	0	1½	
Buds - - cwt.	0	4½	{ 0	3	hogshead
			{ 0	2	tierce
Peel - - cwt.	0	6	{ 0	3	bale of 5 cwt.
			{ 0	1½	do. of 2½ cwt
Trees - large package	2	6	0	4	
small package	1	6	0	2	
Flower Water - gallon	0	1½	0	1	case
Paddy, in bulk - quarter	0	10	0	1	
Pepper (unsifted) - cwt.	0	3	0	6	ton
Or a Consolidated Rate of 9d. per cwt. nett.					
Or a Consolidated Rate (including ordinary sifting and bagging) of 2s. 3d. per cwt. nett.	-	-	0	1	bag of 317 lb
Long or Cayenne - cwt.	0	4½	0	7	ton
Pimento, in casks - cwt.	0	6	} 0	6	ton
in bags - cwt.	0	4½			
Or a Consolidated Rate in casks, 1s. 6d. per cwt. in bags, 1s. 2d. do.					

* The charges on these oils will be calculated at per tun of 252 imperial gallons, to meet the custom of the trade and the revenu proprietor shall give notice prior to the final landing, the goods will be housed upon the expiration of 14 days from final day of la

Description of Goods and Packages.	Landing Rate.	Rate of Rent per Week.		Description of Goods and Packages.	Landing Rate.	Rate of Rent per Week.
	s. d.	s. d.	Per		s. d.	s. d. Per
French Plums, ., hhd. or pun.	1 6	0 2		Skins, Seal · pipe	2 0	0 3
· · barrel	1 0	0 1½		puncheon or hhd.	1 6	0 3
· ½ barrel	0 9	0 1		barrel	1 0	0 3
t. · ¼ barrel	0 6	0 0½ 100	0 6	loose · 120	1 6	
· · ¼ chest	0 3	2 0 100	0 2	Sheep or Goat, Cape,		
· · ¼ chest	0 3	1 3 100	0 2	100 skins · bale	2 0	0 2
· ¼ chest	0 1½		chest	75 do. · bale	1 6	0 1½
d small pack-		1 0 100	0 6	50 do. · bale	1 0	0 1
· · score	1 6		score	25 do. · bale	0 5	0 0½
n bottles, bottle	0 3	0 1½		loose, dry · doz.	0 3	0 1
arrels · cwt.	0 9	0 1		loose, salted, doz.	0 4½	0 4 120
containing			Weigh-ing.	Sheep, Hambro' · bale	1 6	0 2 120
one skin	0 6	0 0½		Soap · · ton	3 0	0 1 case under 6 cwt.
20 cwt. butt	3 0	0 4	1 0	0 8	Spelter · · ton	3 0	0 1
wt. · pipe	2 3	0 3	0 9	0 6	Wharfage and shipping, 2s. per ton, when piled on the quay.		
vt. · carotel	1 6	0 2	0 6	0 4	Spirits, see Wines and Spirits.		
cwt., ½ barrel	0 9	0 0½	0 3	0 2	Straw, Leghorn, un-manufactured,		
cwt., ½ barrel	0 6	0 0½	0 2	0 2	1 cwt. and under 2, case	1 0	0 2
cwt., ¼ barrel	0 3	2 0	1 0	0 0½	2 cwt. and under 3, case	1 6	0 3
alencia, boxes,				3 cwt. and upwards, case	2 0	0 4
· score	2 6	1 3	0 6	Sugar, in casks · cwt.	0 3	0 5 ton
oxes · score	1 6	1 0	0 6	chests or baskets 5 cwt.		
askets · score	1 8	1 0	0 6	or above · cwt.	0 3	0 4 ton
ils or baskets,				chests, baskets, or bags,		
· score	1 0	1 0	0 4	under 5 cwt. · cwt.	0 3	0 3 ton
es · score	2 0	1 0	0 8	Or a Consolidated Rate,		
oxes · score	1 6	0 10	0 8	in casks, cwt. nett, 8d.		
ums score	2 6	1 0	0 10	in chests or baskets, 5 cwt. and upwards,		
ums · score	1 6	1 0	0 6	cwt. nett, 6d.		
r 3 cwt. cask	0 9	0 0½	0 3	in chests, baskets, or bags.		
to 5 cwt. cask	1 6	0 2	0 3	under 5 cwt. · cwt.		
60 lbs. score	3 0	0 4	0 8	nett, 5d.		
· cwt.	0 2½	0 4 ton		Candy · · cwt.	0 4½	0 0½
olidated Rate				Sunn, press-packed · cwt.	3 0	0 4
per ton nett.				Or a Consolidated Rate of 10s. per ton nett.		
· ton	3 6	0 3		Tallow, in casks · ton	3 0	
Thrown, cwt.	0 8½	0 2 bale of 2 cwt. & upwards	if sold from the landing scale, to the im-porter · ton	2 3	0 1 cask
		0 1½ bale under 2 cwt.	to the buyer · ton	1 0	
tured · case	0 9	0 1		Unhousing, wharfage, and shipping, 2s. per ton.		
small case				in skins · · ton	3 9	0 3
ip, 150 skins,						
· bale	1 6					
· bale	1 3	0 3 120 skins	American or Cape, pack-ages under 5 cwt., ton	5 0	0 0½ package under 3 cwt.
· bale	0 9					0 1 package 3 cwt. and above
do. · doz.	0 4*	0 4 120 skins	Turpentine · · ton	2 6	3 6 100 tierces
or loading,						3 0 100 barrels
			Delivery by land or water, 1s. 8d. per ton.		5 0 100 casks from France
loose · doz.	0 4½	0 4 120 skins	Whalebone and Whalefins, ton	7 6	0 4
dry salted,						
· doz.	0 3	0 0½			Conso-lidated Rate.)	Land-ing Rate.	Rate of Rent per Week.
arge cask or bale	1 6	0 2			s. d.	s. d.	s. d.
ing do. do.	1 0	0 1		Wool, Sheep or Lamb, German, about 4 cwt. bale	5 0	0 4½	0 2 bale, 6 cwt. & up.
ck or bundle 120	3 0	0 4		cwt.			0 1½ do. 4 to 6 cwt.
· bale	0 9	0 1		Unhousing and loading by land or water, and mending at delivery, when charged under Consolidated Rate, per bale of about ½ cwt. 1s.			0 1 do. 3 to 4 do.
ale, case, or cask	1 6	0 6					0 0¾ do. 3 and under
do. do.	1 0	0 3					
do. do.	0 9	0 2		Australian, about 2½ cwt. bale	4 0	0 4½	0 2 bale 6 cwt. & up.
tore, above							0 1½ do. 4 to 6 cwt.
· bale	1 6			Unhousing and loading as above stated, per bale of about 2½ cwt. 8d.			0 1 do. 3 to 4 do.
to 100, bale	0 9	0 2 120 skins				0 0¾ do. 3 and under
60 do., bale	0 5			Spanish, about 2 cwt. bale	4 0	0 4½	0 1 bale 2½ cwt. & up.
under, bale	0 3			half bale	3 0		0 0¾ do. 1½ to 2½ cwt.
dozen	0 2	0 2 120 skins		cwt.			0 0½ do. under 1½ do.
y, above 300				Unhousing and loading, as above stated, per bale of about 2 cwt. 6d. per half bale, 4d.			
· bale	1 6	0 3					
under, bale	1 0	0 2		Vigonia · · cwt.		0 4½	0 3 bale
large cask	2 0	0 6		Goats' · · cwt.		0 6	0 2 do. 2 cwt. & up.
iddling do.	1 0	0 4		Hair or Beards · cwt.		0 10½	0 1 do. un · e2
small do.	0 3	0 3					0 2 case
dozen	0 4½	0 4 bale					
or Goat,							
· bale	1 6	0 3					
large bale	1 6	0 3					
iddling do.	1 0	0 2					
small do.	0 9	0 1½					
or Tiger,							
each	0 1½	0 0½					
hhd.	1 6	0 4					
barrel	1 0	0 3					
n skins, bale	1 6	0 4					
do. bale	1 0	0 3					
do. bale	0 9	0 2					
50 skins, bundle	0 6	0 t					

ommercial Docks. — Exclusive of the previously mentioned docks, which are all
north side of the river, there are on the south side the Commercial Docks, opposite
est end of the West India docks. These docks are of large extent; the space
d within the outer wall being about 49 acres, of which nearly 38 acres are water.
e principally intended for the reception of vessels with timber, corn, and other
ommodities. They have but little accommodation for warehousing; and their
ments are not constructed so as to entitle them to bond all goods. The Surrey
Company also admit vessels to be docked in the basin of their canal.

onsolidated rate, besides including the customary charges, (except delivery,) also embraces mending at landing,
ing merchantable, lotting, unpiling for show, showing, re-piling, mending, filling in, re-weighing, and any other
tions performed by order of the importer.

LONDON PORT DUES; AND CHARGES ON ACCOUNT OF LIGHTS, PILOTAGE, &c. IN THAMES.

The improved accommodations afforded by the docks, have materially contribute increase the commerce of the metropolis. Previously to 1825, the charges of all on ships entering the Thames were exceedingly heavy; and well-founded compl were made to government of their injurious operation. Since then, however, the ferent dock monopolies have expired; and a very great reduction has been made ir charges on account of the docks, which, as already seen, are now very moderate ind Exclusive of the dock dues, the port charges on ships entering inwards or clea outwards from London, are as follow: —

	Ton Bur £.
Antwerp — Brabant — Bremen — Denmark — Flanders, or any other part of the Netherlands — France, within Ushant — Germany, any part of, bordering on or near the Germanic Ocean — Guernsey, Jersey, Alderney, and Sark — Hamburgh — Holland, or any other of the United Provinces — Holstein, Ireland, Lapland, on this side of the North Cape — Man, Isle of — Norway - - - - -	0
Baltic Sea, any country or places within — Courland — Finland — Lapland, beyond the North Cape — Livonia — Poland — Prussia — Russia, without or within the Baltic Sea — Sweden	0
America, North, any of the British colonies or provinces in — America, any of the United States of — Azores, any of — Canary Islands, any of — Florida — France, between Ushant and Spain — Madeira Islands, any of — Portugal — Spain, without the Mediterranean — Louisiana - - -	0
Africa — America, South — China — East India — France, within the Mediterranean — Gibraltar — Greenland — Mediterranean or Adriatic Sea, any country, island, port, or place within, or bordering on, or near — Mexico — Pacific Ocean, any country, island, port, or place within, or bordering on, or near — Spain, within the Mediterranean — West Indies, and any other country, island, port, or place, to the southward of 25 degrees of north latitude -	0
Vessels trading coastwise between the port of London and any port or place in Great Britain, the Orkneys, Shetland, or the western islands of Scotland, for every voyage in and out -	0

Exemptions. — Any vessel coming to or going coastwise from the port of London, or to any part of Britain, unless such vessel shall exceed 45 tons.

Any vessel bringing corn coastwise, the principal part of whose cargo shall consist of corn.

Any fishing-smacks, lobster, and oyster-boats, or vessels for passengers.

Any vessel or craft, navigating the River Thames above and below London-bridge, as far as Grav only.

And any vessel entering inwards or outwards in ballast.

These rates were imposed by the acts 39 Geo. 3. c. 69., 43 Geo. 3. c. 124., &c. improving the port of London, and particularly for making a navigable canal acros Isle of Dogs. This canal has, however, been sold, as already mentioned, under auth of the 10 Geo. 4. c. 130., to the West India Dock Company, for 120,000l.; and sum, in addition to the produce of the rates above mentioned, amounting to from 35, to 40,000l. a year, will, it is believed, speedily pay off all the sums, to provide for w the rates were imposed. Whenever this is done, the rates in question ought to c and the shipping frequenting the river to be relieved from this charge.

The charges for lights and pilotage are, however, by far the most oppressive. show the nature and amount of these and other charges, we subjoin the follo statement of the various charges actually incurred (in 1831) by an American sh 482 tons, drawing 18 feet water, from the period of her taking a pilot on board i Channel, including the expense of discharging at the London docks, down to the p of her discharging the pilot on her outward voyage.

		£	s.
* Reporting, Appointing, &c.	-	2	1(
Tonnage Duty Inwards 5d., and Entry	-	10	1!
Do. do. Outwards	-	10	
Putting a Pilot on board	£ 4 0 0		
Pilotage Inwards to London Docks	17 0 6		
Do. Outwards to Sea	17 0 6		
		38	
Boat and Men up the River and down	-	10	
Lights Inward	27 13 8		
Do. Outwards	27 13 8		
*Trinity Duty and Certificates	3 1 2		
		58	
† Dock Duty, 9d. per Ton	18 1 6		
Do. do. if discharged by the Company	18 1 6		
		36	
* Clearing Outwards	-	2	
		£168	

		£	s.	d.
Trinity Lights	£15 6 2			
Foreland and Ness	8 7 0			
Ramsgate and Dover	4 0 6			
		27	13	8
Trinity Duty	2 0 2			
Broker	1 1 0			
		3	1	2

The usual Brokerage is 2½ per Cent. on Freight Inwards, and 5½ Outwards.

* These are brokers' charges, exclusive of brokerage on freight inwards and outwards.
† The dock duty of 9d. entitles a ship to lie one month; and the charge for discharging may be entirely if the ship discharges by her own crew.

t will be seen, that of the total charges incurred by this ship, in the Channel and river, amounting to 168*l.* 9*s.* 6*d.*, lights and pilotage amounted to no less than *l.* 9*s.* 6*d.* Such a charge seems to be out of all proportion to the other items of expense; we know of nothing that calls louder for inquiry and revision than the Trinity-House lations. We have been assured that the charges referred to might, without in wise impairing the efficiency of the pilotage and lighthouse establishments, be ced from a third to a half. But, in the event of its not being possible to effect material reductions by adopting more economical arrangements, the injurious oper- of these enormous charges is such, that it would be good policy to defray a con- rable portion of the lighthouse expenses out of the ordinary revenue of the country, out throwing them entirely on the shipping. It is highly desirable that expert ts, brilliant lights, and every other means, should be afforded to render navigation and speedy. But, to secure these advantages, it is indispensable that the charges heir account should be moderate, which, in the Thames at least, they certainly are When the charges are excessive, navigators are tempted to resort to less secure, at the same time, less expensive channels. In point of fact, repeated instances occurred of very valuable foreign ships being lost, from the disinclination of their manders to subject themselves to the heavy charges in our ports. A striking in- ce in confirmation of what is now stated, may be found in the able pamphlet of Sir Hall, the Secretary of the St. Katharine Docks, on the Navigation Laws. " The ch ship Vreede, Captain Schuler, from the Texel for Batavia, with passengers, eeded down Channel; on her arrival off the Isle of Wight, she encountered h weather and contrary winds, which obliged her to put back : on her arrival off geness, the master laid the vessel to; he was entreated, however, by the passengers officers to run her into the Downs, where she might have anchored in safety, but he refused, *alleging in excuse the very heavy charges he should be subject to for light other dues :* in the night, the vessel having drifted to the northward of Dungeness, wind suddenly veered to S. S. E., by which she became embayed, was driven on e at Dymechurch, near Hythe, in Kent; only 12 persons being saved out of that were on board !" — (p. 41.)

system productive of such results is not more disgraceful to the humanity than it urious to the commercial interests of the country ; for, by making foreigners shun orts, it not only prevents that intercourse of good offices which is so advantageous, t lessens the demand for our commodities, and contributes to increase the trade of burgh, Rotterdam, &c. by diminishing ours. We know that we are only echoing pinions of all mercantile men, when we affirm that nothing would contribute more omote the trade of the metropolis than the effectual reduction of the oppressive, apparently exorbitant, charges in question.

e necessity of inquiry into this subject will appear still more evident, if we take account the fact, that the dues for several lighthouses are collected for behoof of *te individuals,* who have obtained grants or leases of the same from the crown, not rmed by any act of parliament. Some of these leases constitute a very valuable rty for the lessees ; who have obtained, generally without any sacrifice on their a right to enrich themselves at the expense and to the injury of the trade of the try. If no other means can be devised of putting a stop to so great an abuse, let ensation be made to the leaseholders, and let the charges be reduced to the lowest necessary to keep up the lights. For further and more minute details with respect s subject, see LIGHTHOUSE, and PILOTAGE.

nount of Shipping, &c. belonging to the Port of London. — According to the official nts, there are in all, belonging to this port, about 2,700 vessels (exclusive of boats ther vessels not registered), the ascertained burthen of which is about 573,000 tons ! customs duty collected in it amounts to above above *ten millions sterling,* being than half the entire customs revenue of the United Kingdom. So vast an amount pping and commerce was never previously concentrated in any single port. — Lon- nay be truly said to be *universi orbis terrarum emporium.* May her prosperity be ting as it is great !

Liverpool Docks. — The first wet dock in the British empire was constructed at pool, in pursuance of an act of parliament obtained in 1708. At this period pool was but an inconsiderable town ; and the accommodation she has derived her docks is one of the circumstances that has done most to promote her extra- ary increase in commerce, population, and wealth. A second wet dock was d about the middle of last century ; and since that period many more have been ucted, some of them on a very magnificent scale, and furnished with all sorts of niences. At this moment several new docks are in progress. The following table the annual amount of the Liverpool dock duties since 1757, the number of vessels ng the docks since that period, and the tonnage of the same since 1800. It ex- an increase of commerce unequalled in any other port.

Amount of Dock Duties at the Port of Liverpool, from the Year 1757, ending 24th June each Year.

Year.	No. Vessels.	£	s.	d.	Year.	No. Vessels.	£	s.	d.
1757	1,371	2,336	15	0	1779	2,374	4,957	17	10
1758	1,453	2,403	6	3	1780	2,261	3,528	7	9
1759	1,281	2,372	12	2	1781	2,512	3,915	4	11
1760	1,245	2,330	6	7	1782	2,496	4,249	6	3
1761	1,319	2,382	0	2	1783	2,816	4,840	8	3
1762	1,307	2,526	19	6	1784	3,098	6,597	11	1
1763	1,752	3,141	1	5	1785	3,429	8,411	5	3
1764	1,625	2,780	3	4	1786	3,228	7,508	0	1
1765	1,930	3,455	8	4	1787	3,567	9,199	18	8
1766	1,908	3,653	19	2	1788	3,677	9,206	13	10
1767	1,704	3,615	9	2	1789	3,619	8,901	10	10
1768	1,808	3,566	14	9	1790	4,223	10,037	6	2¼
1769	2,054	4,004	5	0	1791	4,045	11,645	6	6
1770	2,073	1,142	17	2	1792	4,483	13,243	17	8½
1771	2,087	4,203	19	10	1793	4,129	12,480	5	5
1772	2,259	4,552	5	4	1794	4,265	10,678	7	0
1773	2,214	4,725	1	11	1795	3,948	9,368	16	4
1774	2,258	4,580	5	5	1796	4,738	12,377	7	7
1775	2,291	5,384	4	9	1797	4,528	13,319	12	8
1776	2,216	5,064	10	10	1798	4,478	12,057	18	3
1777	2,361	4,610	4	9	1799	4,518	14,049	15	1
1778	2,292	4,649	7	7					

Year.	No. Vessels.	Tonnage.	£	s.	d.	Year.	No. Vessels.	Tonnage.	£	s.	d.
1800	4,746	450,060	23,379	13	6	1806	4,676	507,825	44,560	7	3
1801	5,060	459,719	28,365	8	2¼	1807	5,791	662,309	62,831	5	10
1802	4,781	510,691	28,192	9	10	1808	5,225	516,836	40,638	10	4
1803	4,791	494,521	28,027	13	7	1809	6,023	594,601	47,580	19	3
1804	4,291	448,761	26,157	0	11	1810	6,729	734,391	65,782	1	0
1805	4,618	463,482	33,364	13	1	1811	5,616	611,190	54,752	18	5

Year	No. Vessels.	Tonnage.		£	s.	d.	£	s.	d.
1812	4,599	446,788		20,260	3	5	44,403	7	11
			Duties on Goods	24,143	4	6			
1813	5,341	547,426		24,134	18	8	50,177	13	9
			Duties on Goods	26,042	14	6			
1814	5,706	548,957		28,630	11	3	59,741	2	4
			Duties on Goods	31,110	11	1			
1815	6,440	709,849		36,310	1	9	76,915	8	8
			Duties on Goods	40,605	6	11			
1816	6,888	774,243		43,765	6	3	92,646	10	9
			Duties on Goods	40,881	4	6			
1817	6,079	653,425		35,186	8	0	75,889	16	4
			Duties on Goods	40,703	8	4			
1818	6,779	754,690		43,842	16	6	98,538	8	
			Duties on Goods	54,695	11	9			
1819	7,849	867,318		50,042	7	8	110,127	1	1
			Duties on Goods	60,084	14	0			
1820	7,276	805,033		44,717	17	10	94,412	11	10
			Duties on Goods	49,694	14	0			
1821	7,810	839,848		43,131	6	2	94,556	9	
			Duties on Goods	51,425	2	11			
1822	8,136	892,902		47,229	10	4	102,403	17	
			Duties on Goods	55,174	7	0			
1823	8,916	1,010,819		52,837	5	5	115,783	1	
			Duties on Goods	62,945	16	1			
1824	10,001	1,180,914		60,878	9	7	130,911	11	
			Duties on Goods	70,033	1	11			
1825	10,837	1,223,820		59,446	7	8	128,691	19	
			Duties on Goods	69,245	12	0			
1826	9,601	1,228,318		60,411	9	11	131,000	19	
			Duties on Goods	70,589	9	1			
1827	9,592	1,225,313		61,601	0	6	134,472	14	
			Duties on Goods	72,871	13	9			
1828	10,703	1,311,111		62,969	7	10	141,369	15	
			Duties on Goods	78,400	7	9			
1829	11,383	1,387,957		66,128	18	10	147,327	4	
			Duties on Goods	81,198	6	1			
1830	11,214	1,411,964		68,322	9	11	151,329	17	
			Duties on Goods	83,007	7	11			

Dock Office, Liverpool, 24th June, 1830.

The following dues are payable upon all vessels entering inwards, or clearing out-wards at the port of Liverpool, for dock rates and harbour lights : —

	s.
From between the Mull of Galloway and St. David's Head, Isles of Man and Anglesea, the ton	0
From between the Mull of Galloway and Duncan's Bay Head, Orkney Isles, and islands on the western coast of Scotland; between St. David's Head and the Land's End, the Scilly Islands, and the east coast of Ireland, from Cape Clear to Malling Head, the ton	0
From the east and southern coast of Great Britain, between Duncan's Bay Head and the Land's End, the Islands of Shetland, the west coast of Ireland, from Cape Clear to Malling Head, including the islands on that coast, the ton	0

	s.	d.

Europe, north of Cape Finisterre, and westward of the North Cape, and without the
gat and Baltic Sea, the islands of Guernsey, Jersey, Alderney, Sark, the Faro Isles,
nd, the ton - - - - - - - - - 1 3
within the Cattegat and Baltic, the whole of Sweden, the White Sea, eastward of the
h Cape, Europe, south of Cape Finisterre, without the Mediterranean, Newfoundland,
nland, Davis's Straits, Canaries, Western Islands, Madeira, and Azores, the ton - 1 7
he east coast of North America, the West Indies, east coast of South America, north
o Plata, the west coast of Africa, and islands north of the Cape of Good Hope, all
within the Mediterranean, including the Adriatic, the Black Sea, and Archipelago, the
ls of St. Helena, Ascension, and Cape de Verd Islands, the ton - - - 2 3
outh America, south of Rio Plata, the Pacific Ocean, Africa and Asia, eastward of the
of Good Hope, the ton - - - - - - - - 3 4
Vessels remaining longer than six months in dock, to pay in addition to the above
per month - - - - - - - - - 0 2

sels arriving at or clearing from the said port, are to pay the said rates from or for the most distant
r place from or for which they shall trade; but vessels arriving from any parts in ballast do not
ockage on entering inwards; and should such vessels proceed to sea again in ballast, then only one
f the dock rates are due, with the whole of the lights; but taking a cargo outwards subjects such
s to full dock dues.

New vessels built in Liverpool are subject only to half the above rates on the first outward
nce.

Liverpool docks are all constructed upon the estate of the corporation, and are
ed by commissioners appointed by parliament. The warehouses belong to
uals, and are private property. None of them belong to the dock estate. Most
n are, of course, situated in the immediate vicinity of the docks. The discharging
ading of vessels in Liverpool is all done by a class of men called *lumpers*. Indi-
s who follow this business engage to discharge a ship for a specific, or *lump* sum,
guineas, perhaps, up to 20, according to the size and description of cargo, having
quisite number of common labourers (chiefly Irishmen) to do the work; the
being master and superintendent: these labourers are generally paid day wages,
netimes the job is a joint concern among the whole.

West India ship of 500 tons would be discharged by lumpers for 15l. to 20l.: a
ship of the same burthen for 4l. to 6l. By discharging is merely meant putting
cargo on the quay; the proprietors of the goods employ their own porters to
load, and warehouse the property: they likewise employ their own coopers,
cooperage is required.

ill be seen that the system of managing business of this sort in Liverpool, is
different from the plan followed in London, at least in the East India docks,
all these operations are performed by the Dock Company.

expense of loading a West India ship of 500 tons *outwards* would not be half as
s that of discharging inwards, because they very seldom take a full cargo *outwards*.
erage does not, perhaps, exceed *a third*. Hence the total expense of a West
ship of 500 tons, coming into and going out of the port of Liverpool, may be
ed as follows:—

	£	s.	d.
Pilotage inwards - - - -	8	11	0
Boat hire, warping, &c. - -	0	10	6
Lumpers discharging - - -	17	10	0
Labourers' hire for loading - -	5	10	0
Pilotage outwards - - -	3	8	0
Boat hire assisting out - - -	0	10	6
	£36	0	0

these, there is the charge for the various lighthouses in St. George's Channel,
annot be called an expense peculiar to Liverpool. It has been already stated
ds both inwards and outwards have, for some years, paid *dockage*. The charge
tain rate per *package*, and is paid by the *proprietors* of the goods. *Town dues*
levied on goods inwards and outwards, at a certain rate per package. But the
the corporation to enforce payment of town dues (from which the *freemen* of
ugh are exempted) is at present disputed by the merchants, and the question of
about to be tried in the Courts of Westminster.

29 there belonged to Liverpool 805 registered vessels, of the burthen of 161,780
The gross customs duty collected in the port during the same year amounted to
mous sum of 3,308,347l.!

ollowing statement, extracted from Priestley and Co.'s *Price Current*, Liverpool,
ary, 1831, gives some details with respect to the trade of this great and growing
m :—

Statement of the Imports of some of the principal Articles into Liverpool, with the Stocks remaini[ng] hand at the Close of the undermentioned Years.

	Packages and Quantities.	Imports, Jan. 1. to Dec. 31.			Stocks on hand, Dec. 3[1]		
		1828.	1829.	1830.	1828.	1829.	18[30]
Ashes, American	barrels	18,500	15,700	22,500 {	pot.6,300	6,800	8..
					prl.4,200	1,200	..
Cocoa	barrels and bags	2,600	400	880	3,700	2,000	5..
Coffee	casks	6,200	7,900	7,800	6,500	6,000	4..
	barrels and bags	7,000	5,000	7,300	6,100	7,400	6..
Cotton	bags, &c.	630,000	641,200	792,350	295,500	203,250	258..
Dyewoods, Fustic	tons	4,800	5,100	3,900	1,200	1,900	1..
Logwood	tons	7,200	4,500	6,200	3,100	1,660	2..
Nicaragua Wood	tons	1,000	500	850	2,200	1,600	1..
Barwood	tons	110	250	650	45	60	
Flour, American and Canadian	barrels	20,400	160,000	300,500	6,000	24,650	140..
Ginger, West India	barrels and bags	1,300	450	500	2,300	1,050	1..
East India	bags and pockets	1,400	2,000	400	......	1,800	
Hides, Ox and Cow	number	280,000	426,200	396,500	22,000	97,700	76..
East India ditto	number	8,500	16,800	23,700	......	......	6..
Horse, B. A. &c.	number	29,500	88,000	89,200	13,000	35,000	10..
Indigo	serons	360	500	960	130	140	
East India	chests	2,220	2,050	1,430	900	500	
Mahogany	logs	6,850	5,850	6,150	280,000	uncert.	567..
Molasses	puncheons	13,500	13,800	9,500	3,000	5,750	1..
Palm Oil	casks	16,450	25,500	27,000	......	......	
	tons	5,600	8,310	9,900	730	2,150	1..
Pepper, East India	bags and pockets	9,700	4,840	4,400	5,800	4,600	4..
Pimento	barrels and bags	2,350	3,860	3,500	2,300	2,500	4..
Rice American	casks	4,100	4,700	1,100	500	2,000	
East India	bags	20,000	50,000	31,200	12,000	14,000	10..
Rum	puncheons	11,000	11,700	12,000	8,000	10,700	11..
Saltpetre	bags and boxes	33,000	28,000	31,000	3,550	2,300	5..
Sugar, British Plantation	hhds. and tierces	46,000	43,700	42,000	11,000	11,000	10..
East India	bags and boxes	18,500	29,800	46,300	2,000	8,000	23..
Havannah	boxes	1,850	......	......	......	......	
Brazil	chests	550	750	860	90	80	
Other Foreign	casks	150	100	50	......	......	
Tar	barrels	59,500	30,000	42,500	24,500	11,000	12..
Tallow	casks	15,500	17,400	13,500	2,800	5,500	2..
	serons	......	......	......	......	......	
Tobacco	hogsheads	5,980	4,900	8,090	9,200	6,400	7..
Turpentine	barrels	58,600	59,000	51,000	18,500	13,000	8..

*** We have been indebted for most of the previous statements with respect to L[iver]pool, to our excellent friend, Hugh Mure, Esq., of the great commercial house of Cro[p] Benson, and Co.

III. *Bristol Docks.* — These were formed in pursuance of the act 43 Geo. 3. c. by changing the course of the rivers Avon and Frome, and placing gates or loc[ks] each extremity of the old channel. The accommodation thus obtained is very exten[sive] The warehouses at Bristol, as at Liverpool, are not in any way connected with docks. They all belong to private individuals.

Bristol, as a port, used to be inferior only to London; but now she ranks far b[elow] Liverpool, and probably is second to Hull. However, she still enjoys a very exte[nsive] trade, particularly with the West Indies and Ireland. The custom duties collecte[d at] Bristol amount to about 1,200,000*l.* About 320 vessels belong to the port, of the bu[rden] of about 50,000 tons.

The produce of the dock duties on tonnage and goods, since 1820, has be[en] follows: —

	Tonnage Rates.			Rates on Goods.		
	£	s.	d.	£	s.	d.
Years ending 30th April, 1821	10,469	19	6	7,237	7	6
1822	10,530	11	2	8,062	5	3
1823	10,747	19	2	7,746	7	7
1824	12,395	6	4	7,990	7	2
1825	13,424	4	10	9,409	11	0
1826	14,863	10	0	9,438	14	3
1827	13,934	1	8	7,775	12	0
1828	15,292	0	2	8,396	16	2
1829	15,833	4	6	8,871	13	0

The charges on ships entering Bristol are very heavy. They are as follow: —

For every vessel on entering into the port of Bristol, except barges or other vessels passing or g[oing] or from the Bath River Navigation, or Kennet and Avon Canal, or re-shipping or discharging th[at which] goes to be again laden, and pass or go up the said navigation or canal, but not discharging any their cargoes at the quays of Bristol for sale, the several rates or duties, according to the register t[on] of such vessels following, *viz.*

Per Ton.

	£ s. d.
Class. — For every vessel trading from Africa, Honduras, Surinam, and other ports in ᵗh America, the United States of America, the East and West Indies, all the ports within ᵉ Straits of Gibraltar, and the Southern Whale Fishery	0 3 0
ᵈ Class. — For every vessel trading from the British Colonies, Portugal, Prussia, Russia, ᵃin without the Straits, and Sweden	0 2 0
ᵈ Class. — For every vessel trading from Flanders, France without the Straits, Germany, ᵘernsey, Holland, Jersey, Norway, Poland, and Zealand	0 1 0
ᵗh Class. — For every vessel trading from Ireland, the Isle of Man, and Scotland	0 0 8
Class. — For every vessel employed as a coaster, except as aforesaid, not including vessels ᵐm Cardiff, Newport, and other ports to the eastward of the Holmes, at each entering into ᵉ said port	0 0 6
vessels from Cardiff, Newport, and other ports to the eastward of the Holmes (except as ᵃresaid), being market boats or vessels, having one third part at least of the lading consisting coal, scruff, tin, iron, tin plates, grain, copper, bricks, stones, coal, tar, slate, bark, timber, wood, and not exceeding 75 tons burthen, each voyage	0 5 0
— if exceeding 75 tons burthen, each voyage	0 7 6
all other vessels from Cardiff, Newport, and other ports to the eastward of the Holmes (ex- ᵗt as aforesaid), if under 40 tons burthen, each voyage	0 7 6
— if of 40 tons and under 75 tons burthen, each voyage	0 12 6
— if 75 tons, and under 100 tons burthen, each voyage	0 16 0
— if 100 tons burthen or upwards, each voyage	1 1 0

ᵗhe following is an estimate of the various expenses incurred by a West India ship ⁰0 tons, entering and discharging at Bristol : —

ᵛards. — Anchorage, moorage, and lights, about 6d. per ton. — Dock dues, 3s. per do. — Pilotage, ᵒ 25l. — Warner, 12. 1s. — Mayor and quay-wardens' fees, 2l. 5s. — Cranage about 30l. — Labour dis- ᵍing, 30l. to 40l. — Coopers' charges, from 50l. to 100l. The two last items depend greatly on the con- ᵗ the cargo is in.

ᵗwards. — Lights, about 4d. per ton. — Pilotage, 15l. to 20l.

V. *Hull Docks.* — There are three considerable docks in Hull; occupying, inclusive ᵉir basins, an area of 26 acres. They are capable of affording accommodation for ᵗ 312 ships of the average size of those that frequent the port. Hull is the next port ᵉ empire, after Bristol, or perhaps Liverpool ; for, although the customs duty col- ᵈ in Hull be inferior to that of Bristol, it having amounted in 1829 to only 740,868l., ᵃas a larger amount of shipping. In 1829, there belonged to this port 579 regis- ᵈ vessels, of the aggregate burthen of 72,248 tons.

ᵉ Hull dock dues amounted, in 1824, to 18,776l. 6s. 3d. ; in 1825, to 25,861l. 16s. ; ²26, to 19,089l. 16s. ; and in 1827, to 22,381l. 9s. 9d.

ᵉ dock and harbour dues are as follow : —

Per Ton.

	s. d.
within the Baltic	1 3
ᵃrk, Sweden, Norway below Elsinore, or any place in Germany, Holland, Flanders, France, ᵉe eastward of Ushant, Ireland, Guernsey, and Jersey	0 10
ᵃrd of Ushant, without the Straits of Gibraltar	1 3
Indies, North and South America, Africa, Greenland, eastward of the north cape of Norway, ᵃin the Straits of Gibraltar	1 9

Goole Docks. — The port of Goole, situated on the Ouse, a little above its junction the Humber, about 22 miles more inland than Hull, promises to prove a very ᵃidable rival to the latter. Six or seven years ago, Goole was but an insignificant ᵉt. It communicates by means of canals with Liverpool, Manchester, Leeds, ᵉfield, &c. Though so remote from the sea, vessels drawing 15 or 16 feet of water Goole in safety. It has two wet docks and a basin. The first, or *ship dock,* is ᵉet long by 200 in breadth. The second, or *barge dock,* is 900 feet long by 150 and is intended for the accommodation of the small craft which ply upon the ᵇ and rivers. The warehouses at Goole are extensive and convenient; and it has ᵃdmitted to the privileges of a bonding port.

Leith Docks. — Leith has two wet docks, constructed in the very best manner, ᵃining more than 10 acres of water-room, and capable of accommodating 150 such ᵃas frequent the port. There are also three dry docks contiguous to the wet docks. ᵉ total expense of these docks seems to have amounted to 285,108l. sterling. Ex- ᵛe improvements are at present going forward at the harbour of Leith; but the ᵞ for this purpose has not been furnished by individuals, but by government, and is much reason to doubt whether the expenditure will be profitable.

ᵉ customs duty collected at Leith in 1829, amounted to 444,411l. ; the number of ᵉered vessels belonging to the port is 263, and their burthen 26,362 tons.

ᵒck *Rates* at Leith were as follow : —

Per Ton.

	s. d.
ᵉry ship or vessel, from any port between Buchanness and Eymouth, including the great ᵈ and the river Clyde, as far down as Greenock, coming by the canal	0 4
from any other port in Great Britain and Ireland	0 8
from Norway, Sweden, Denmark, Holstein, Hamburgh, Bremen, Holland, and Flanders, is, without the Baltic, and no further south than Dunkirk	0 10½
from the Baltic, all above the Sound, Onega, Archangel, Jersey or Guernsey, Portugal, ᵃce, and Spain, without the Straits of Gibraltar, Newfoundland, Madeira, or western islands	1 1½
from within the Straits of Gibraltar, or from America	1 4
from the West Indies, Asia, Africa, or the Cape de Verd Islands	1 8
from Greenland, or Davis's Straits	2 0
But if such ship or vessel shall make a second voyage, she shall be credited in the charge for such second voyage	4

For all ships and vessels (excepting those from Greenland or Davis's Straits) remaining in the dock above three calendar months, for each after-month, for any part thereof   -   -   - 0
For all foreign vessels from any of the before-mentioned ports or places, the aforesaid respective rates, and one half more.
For all loaded vessels not breaking bulk, and for all vessels in ballast which do not take in goods, coming into the present harbour, provided they do not make use of any of the docks, nor remain in the harbour above four weeks, one half of the aforesaid rates or duties.
For every ship or vessel going from the port of Leith to any other port in the Frith of Forth, to take in a part of a cargo, and return to Leith, upon her return   -   -   - 0
No ship or vessel shall be subjected in payment of the aforesaid rates and duties for more than ei voyages in any one year.

Flag, or Light Dues. — Every vessel, of whatever burthen, from foreign ports   -   - 2
—— of 40 tons burthen and upwards, to pay for each coasting voyage   - 2
Beacon and anchorage, per ton   -   -   -   -   -   - 0
This duty is only charged upon four fifths of the register tonnage.

DOG (Fr. *Chien;* Ger. *Hund;* It. *Cane;* Lat. *Canis familiaris*). Of th quadruped, emphatically styled "the friend and companion of man," the are a vast variety of species. But to attempt to give any description of an anin so well known, would be quite out of place in a work of this description ; and v mention it for the purpose only of laying the following account before our reade and a remark or two with respect to it.

An Account of the Number of Dogs entered, and for which Duty was paid in Great Britain, in the Y ending 5th April, 1829 ; distinguishing the Number of Packs of Hounds, and the Number of ea Description of Dog, the Rate of Duty on each, and the aggregate Amount paid.

Description of Dogs.	Rates of Duty.			Total Number.	Amount of Duty.
	£	s.	d.		£
Greyhounds - - - - -	1	0	0	19,995	19,995
Pointers, Hounds, Setting Dogs, Spaniels, Terriers, Lurchers, or any other Dogs, where persons keep two or more Dogs - - - - -	0	14	0	114,500	80,150
Other Dogs ; persons keeping one only - - -	0	8	0	218,590	87,436
Total, exclusive of Packs of Hounds - -	-	-	-	353,085	187,581
Packs of Hounds - - - - - -	36	0	0	69	2,484

" Many dogs are exempted, either as belonging to poor persons, or as sheep dogs on small farms.
" From the number of persons compounding for their taxes, it is impossible to ascertain the num of dogs kept ; the account is, therefore, made out of the number assessed."

Cuvier, the great French naturalist, says, " The dog is the most complete, t most remarkable, and the most useful conquest ever made by man : every species l become our property ; each individual is altogether devoted to his master, assumes l manners, knows and defends his goods, and remains attached to him until dea and all this proceeds neither from want nor constraint, but solely from true gratitu and real friendship. The swiftness, the strength, and the scent of the dog h created for man a powerful ally against other animals, and were, perhaps, necessary the establishment of society. He is the only animal which has followed man throu every region of the earth."—(*Menageries, Lib. of Useful Knowledge.*)

But while we admit the truth of this statement, we must, at the same time, press our conviction that the unnecessary multiplication of dogs, particularly in la cities, is a very great nuisance : coming, as they often do, into the possession of th who are without the means of providing for them, they are frequently left to wan about in the streets ; and from ill usage, want of food and of proper attention, are a during hot weather, to become rabid. In several districts of the metropolis the nuisa has attained to a formidable height ; and it is singular, considering the numerous fa occurrences that have taken place, that no effort should have been made to have it abat It has grown to its present excess, partly from too many exemptions being gran from the duty, and partly from a want of care in its collection. Hence, to obviate evils alluded to, the best and simplest plan would be to charge the tax indiscriminat upon *all* dogs, other than greyhounds, pointers, &c. (the duty on which might rem as at present), with the exception only of those employed by shepherds, drovers, butch and small farmers. To facilitate and insure the collection of the tax, it would proper to enact, that every dog should be furnished with a collar marked with the own name and address, as also with the designation of the Excise Office at which the dog entered as paying duty or as being exempted ; the police being ordered to destroy dogs found without such collars. Those wandering in the streets with collars, without masters, might be seized ; and if, upon intimation given to their masters, t were not relieved, they also might be destroyed. Were some such regulations ena and carried into effect, the revenue would be at least doubled ; and while we sho

additional security against the occurrence of so dreadful a malady as *hydrophobia,* ⸴uld lose none of the services rendered by this valuable animal.

⸴WN (Ger. *Dunen, Flaumfedern;* Du. *Dons;* Fr. *Duvet;* It. *Penna matta,* ⸴ni;* Sp. *Flojel, Plumazo;* Rus. *Puch;* Lat. *Plumæ*), the fine feathers from ⸴easts of several birds, particularly those of the duck kind. That of the eider ⸴is the most valuable. These birds pluck it from their breasts and line their ⸴with it. Mr. Pennant says that it is so very elastic, that a quantity of it ⸴ing only ¾ of an ounce, fills a larger space than the crown of the greatest hat. ⸴found in the nest is most valued, and termed *live down;* it is much more ⸴: than that plucked from the dead bird, which is comparatively little esteemed. ⸴ider duck is found on the western islands of Scotland, but the down is prin- ⸴⸴ imported from Norway and Iceland.

⸴AGONS' BLOOD. See BALSAM.

⸴AWBACK, a term used in commerce to signify the remitting or paying ⸴f the duties previously paid on a commodity on its being exported.

⸴rawback is a device resorted to for enabling a commodity affected by taxes to be ⸴ed and sold in the foreign market on the same terms as if it had not been taxed at ⸴t differs in this from a bounty,—that the latter enables a commodity to be sold ⸴for *less* than its natural cost, whereas a drawback enables it to be sold exactly at ⸴ural cost. Drawbacks, as Dr. Smith has observed, " do not occasion the export- ⸴f a greater quantity of goods than would have been exported had no duty been ⸴d. They do not tend to turn towards any particular employment a greater share ⸴capital of the country, than what would go to that employment of its own accord, ⸴ly to hinder the duty from driving away any part of that share to other employ- ⸴ They tend not to overturn that balance which naturally establishes itself among ⸴various employments of the society; but to hinder it from being overturned by ⸴ty. They tend not to destroy, but to preserve, what it is in most cases advantageous ⸴serve—the natural division and distribution of labour in the society."—(Vol. ii. ⸴.)

⸴e it not for the system of drawbacks, it would be impossible, unless when a ⸴⸴ enjoyed some very peculiar facilities of production, to export any commodity ⸴s heavier taxed at home than abroad. But the drawback obviates this difficulty; ⸴ables merchants to export commodities loaded at home with heavy duties, and to ⸴m in the foreign market on the same terms as those fetched from countries where ⸴e not taxed.

⸴t foreign articles imported into this country may be warehoused for subsequent ⸴tion. In this case they pay ⸴o duties on being imported; and, of course, get no ⸴ck on their subsequent exportation.

⸴etimes a drawback exceeds the duty or duties laid on the article; and in such ⸴e *excess* forms a real bounty of that amount, and should be so considered.

⸴nacted by the act 6 Geo. 4. c. 107., that no drawback of excise shall be allowed upon any goods ⸴r exportation, unless the person claiming such drawback shall have given due notice to the ⸴excise, and shall have obtained and produced to the searcher, at the time of clearing such goods, ⸴document under the hand of the officer of excise, describing the goods for which such drawback ⸴laimed; and if the goods to be cleared and shipped correspond in all respects with the goods de- ⸴a such document, and such goods shall be duly shipped and exported, the searcher is bound, if ⸴ to certify such shipment upon such document, and shall transmit the same to the officer of ⸴ § 69.

⸴shipped for any drawback or bounty, and not agreeing with the shipping bill, or with the indorse- ⸴the cocket, shall be forfeited. — § 71.

⸴wback shall be allowed upon the exportation of any goods, unless such goods be shipped within ⸴rs after the payment of the duties inwards thereon. And no debenture for any drawback or ⸴pon the exportation of any goods, shall be paid after the expiration of two years from the ship- ⸴ch goods; and no drawback shall be allowed upon any goods which, by reason of damage or decay, ⸴e become of less value for home use than the amount of such drawback; and all goods so damaged ⸴all be cleared for drawback shall be forfeited; and the person who caused such goods to be so ⸴all forfeit 200*l.*, or treble the amount of the drawback, at the option of the commissioners of ⸴— § 85.

⸴wback or bounty shall be allowed upon goods exported and cleared as being press-packed, unless ⸴ities and qualities of the same be verified by oath of the master packer thereof, or, in case of his ⸴ble absence, by oath of his foreman. — § 88.

⸴ds cleared for drawback or bounty, or from any warehouses, shall be carried to be put on board ⸴exportation, except by a person authorised for that purpose by licence of the commissioners of ⸴— § 89. — (See IMPORTATION and EXPORTATION.)

E.

EARNEST, in commercial law, is the sum advanced by the buyer of go
in order to bind the seller to the terms of the agreement.   It is enacted by
seventeenth section of the famous statute of frauds, 29 Cha. 2. c. 3., that '
contract for the sale of any goods, wares, and merchandises, for the prices of
sterling or upwards, shall be allowed to be good, except the buyer shall acc
part of the goods so sold, and actually receive the same, or give somethin,
earnest to bind the bargain, or in part payment, or that some note or memoranc
in writing of the said bargain be made and signed by the parties to be chai
by such contract, or their agents thereunto lawfully authorised."

As to what amounts to sufficient earnest, Blackstone lays it down, " tha
any part of the price is paid down, if it is but a penny, or any portion of
goods is delivered by way of earnest, it is binding."   To constitute earnest,
thing must be given as a token of ratification of the contract, and it should
expressly stated so by the giver.— (*Chitty's Commercial Law*, vol. iii. p. 289.)

EARTHENWARE (Ger. *Irdene Waaren;* Du. *Aardegoed;* Fr. *Vaisselle*
terre, Poterie; It. *Stoviglie, Terraglia;* Sp. *Loza de barro;* Rus. *Gorschetsch*
possudü; Pol. *Gliniana naczynia*), or crockery, as it is sometimes termed, c
prises every sort of household utensil made of clay hardened in the fire.
manufacture is, in England, of very considerable importance; and the impr
ments that have been made in it since the middle of last century have contrib
powerfully to its extension, and have added greatly to the comfort and convenie
of all classes.

" There is scarcely," it has been well observed, " any manufacture which is so in
esting to contemplate in its gradual improvement and extension, as that of earthenw
presenting, as it does, so beautiful a union of science and art, in furnishing us with
comforts and ornaments of civilised life.   Chemistry administers her part, by inv
gating the several species of earths, and ascertaining as well their most appropriate c
binations, as the respective degrees of heat which the several compositions require.
has studied the designs of antiquity, and produced from them vessels even more ex
site in form than the models by which they have been suggested.   The ware has '
provided in such gradations of quality as to suit every station from the highes
the lowest.   It is to be seen in every country, and almost in every house, through
whole extent of America, in many parts of Asia, and in most of the countries of Eu
At home it has superseded the less cleanly vessels of pewter and of wood,
by its cheapness, has been brought within the means of our poorest housekeep
Formed from substances originally of no value, the fabrication has induced labou
such various classes, and created skill of such various degrees, that nearly the whole v
of the annual produce may be considered as an addition made to the mass of nati
wealth.   The abundance of the ware exhibited in every dwelling-house is suffi
evidence of the vast augmentation of the manufacture, which is also demonstrated by
rapid increase of the population in the districts where the potteries have been establish
—(*Quarterly Review.*)

For the great and rapid extension of the manufacture we are chiefly indebted t
late Mr. Josiah Wedgwood; whose original and inventive genius enabled him to i
many most important discoveries in the art; and who was equally successful in brin
his inventions into use.   The principal seat of the manufacture is in Staffordshire, w
there is a district denominated the Potteries, comprising a number of villages, and i
pulation which is supposed to amount, at this moment, to about 60,000, by fa
greater proportion of which is engaged in the manufacture.   There are no auth
accounts of the population of this district in 1760, when Mr. Wedgwood bega
discoveries; but the general opinion is, that it did not at that time exceed 20,000.
village of Etruria, in the Potteries, was built by Mr. Wedgwood.   The manufactur
been carried on at Burslem, in the same district, for several centuries.

The canals by which Staffordshire is intersected, have done much to accelerat
progress of the manufacture.   Pipe-clay from Dorsetshire and Devonshire, and
from Kent, are conveyed by water carriage to the places where the clay and coal abo
and the finished goods are conveyed by the same means to the great shipping j
whence they are distributed over most parts of the globe.

It is estimated that the value of the various sorts of earthenware produced at the
teries may amount to about 1,500,000*l.* a year; and that the earthenware produc
Worcester, Derby, and other parts of the country, may amount to about 750,

e ; making the whole value of the manufacture 2,250,000*l.* a year. The consumption
old at the Potteries is about 650*l.* a week, and of coal about 8,000 tons a week.
he earthenware manufacture has increased considerably since 1814, but it is not
ible to state the exact ratio. It has been estimated at ⅔ for the porcelain, ⅔ for
best earthenware, and at ¼ or ⅓ for the common or cream-coloured ware. The
es of the different sorts of earthenware are said to have fallen 20 per cent. during
last fifteen years. Wages have not fallen in the same proportion ; but we are assured
a workman can, at the present day, produce about *four* times the quantity he did in
). (This article has been prepared from information obtained at the Potteries,
gingly communicated by James Loch, Esq. M. P.)
he real value of the earthenware exported from Great Britain to foreign countries,
ng the three years ending with 1829, according to the declarations of the exporters,
as follows : —

1827	-	-	-	£437,812	17	8
1828	-	-	-	499,743	6	6
1829	-	-	-	461,710	5	7

he foreign demand for earthenware has increased considerably since 1815. The ex-
 to South America, Cuba, and other *ci-devant* Spanish colonies, have been largely
ased. But, notwithstanding this increase, the United States continues to be by far
est market for British earthenware. Of the entire value exported in 1829, amount-
to 461,710*l.*, the exports to the United States amounted to no less than 196,690*l.*
markets next in importance are Brazil, the British North American and West In-
colonies, Germany, the Netherlands, Cuba, &c. We have been assured that it is
ssary to add one fourth to the declared value of the exports, to get their true value.

AST INDIA COMPANY, a famous association, originally established for
ecuting the trade between England and India, which they acquired a right to
 on exclusively. Since the middle of last century, however, the Company's
ical have become of more importance than their commercial concerns.

I. Historical Sketch of the East India Company.
II. Trade with India.
III. Extent, Population, Revenue, &c. of British India.

I. Historical Sketch of the East India Company.

e persevering efforts of the Portuguese to discover a route to India, by sailing
 Africa, were crowned with success in 1497. And it may appear singular, that,
ithstanding the exaggerated accounts that had been prevalent in Europe, from the
test antiquity, with respect to the wealth of India, and the importance to which
mmerce with it had raised the Phœnicians and Egyptians in antiquity, the Vene-
in the middle ages, and which it was then seen to confer on the Portuguese, the
should have been allowed to monopolise it for nearly a century after it had been
d into a channel accessible to every nation. But the prejudices by which the
e of most European states were actuated in the sixteenth century, and the pe-
circumstances under which they were placed, hindered them from embarking
that alacrity and ardour that might have been expected in this new commercial
. Soon after the Portuguese began to prosecute their discoveries along the coast
rica, they applied to the pope for a bull, securing to them the exclusive right to
ossession of all countries occupied by infidels, they either had discovered,
ight discover, to the south of Cape Non, on the west coast of Africa, in 27° 54′
latitude : and the pontiff, desirous to display, and at the same time to ex-
his power, immediately issued a bull to this effect. Nor, preposterous as such
ceeding would now appear, did any one then doubt that the pope had a right
ue such a bull, and that all states and empires were bound to obey it. In con-
nce, the Portuguese were, for a lengthened period, allowed to prosecute their
ests in India without the interference of any other European power. And it
ot till a considerable period after the beginning of the war, which the blind and
 bigotry of Philip II. had kindled in the Low Countries, that the Dutch
tors began to display their flag on the Eastern Ocean, and laid the foundations
ir Indian empire.

e desire to comply with the injunctions in the pope's bull, and to avoid coming
ollision, first with the Portuguese, and subsequently with the Spaniards, who had
ered Portugal in 1580, seems to have been the principal cause that led the En-
o make repeated attempts, in the reigns of Henry VIII. and Edward VI., and
rly part of the reign of Elizabeth, to discover a route to India by a north-west
th-east passage ; channels from which the Portuguese would have had no pretence

for excluding them. But these attempts having proved unsuccessful, and the pop
bull having ceased to be of any effect in this country, the English merchants and na
gators resolved to be no longer deterred by the imaginary rights of the Portuguese fro
directly entering upon what was then reckoned by far the most lucrative and adva
tageous branch of commerce. Captain Stephens, who performed the voyage in 158
was the first Englishman who sailed to India by the Cape of Good Hope. The voya
of the famous Sir Francis Drake contributed greatly to diffuse a spirit of naval ente
prise, and to render the English better acquainted with the newly opened route to Indi
But the voyage of the celebrated Mr. Thomas Cavendish was, in the latter respect, t
most important. Cavendish sailed from England in a little squadron, fitted out at
own expense, in July, 1586; and having explored the greater part of the Indian Ocea
as far as the Philippine islands, and carefully observed the most important and chara
teristic features of the people and countries which he visited, returned to Englan
after a prosperous navigation, in September, 1588. Perhaps, however, nothing co
tributed so much to inspire the English with a desire to embark in the Indian trade,
the captures that were made, about this period, from the Spaniards. A Portugue
East India ship, or carrack, captured by Sir Francis Drake, during his expedition
the coast of Spain, inflamed the cupidity of the merchants by the richness of her carg
at the same time that the papers found on board gave specific information respectir
the traffic in which she had been engaged. A still more important capture, of the sar
sort, was made in 1593. An armament, fitted out for the East Indies by Sir Walt
Raleigh, and commanded by Sir John Borroughs, fell in, near the Azores, with t
largest of all the Portuguese carracks, a ship of 1,600 tons burthen, carrying 700 m
and 36 brass cannon; and, after an obstinate conflict, carried her into Dartmouth. S
was the largest vessel that had then been seen in England; and her cargo, consisting
gold, spices, calicoes, silks, pearls, drugs, porcelain, ivory, &c., excited the ardour
the English to engage in so opulent a commerce.

In consequence of these and other concurring causes, an association was formed
London, in 1599, for prosecuting the trade to India. The adventurers applied to t
queen for a charter of incorporation, and also for power to exclude all other Engli
subjects, who had not not obtained a licence from them, from carrying on any species
traffic beyond the Cape of Good Hope or the Straits of Magellan. As exclusi
companies were then very generally looked upon as the best instruments for prosecuti
most branches of commerce and industry, the adventurers seem to have had little di
culty in obtaining their charter, which was dated 31st December, 1600. The C
poration was entitled "The Governor and Company of Merchants of London tradi
into the East Indies:" the first governor (Thomas Smythe, Esq.) and 24 direct
were nominated in the charter; but power was given to the Company to elect a depu
governor, and, in future, to elect their governor and directors, and such other offi
bearers as they might think fit to appoint. They were empowered to make bye-law
to inflict punishments, either corporal or pecuniary, provided such punishments were
accordance with the laws of England; to export all sorts of goods free of duty fo
years; and to export foreign coin, or bullion, to the amount of 30,000l. a year, 6,00
of the same being previously coined at the mint; but they were obliged to returr
months after the completion of every voyage, except the first, the same quantity
silver, gold, and foreign coin that they had exported. The duration of the charter v
limited to a period of 15 years; but with and under the condition that, if it were
found for the public advantage, it might be cancelled at any time upon 2 years' no
being given. Such was the origin of the British East India Company, — the most
lebrated commercial association either of ancient or modern times, and which has n
extended its sway over the whole of the Mogul empire.

It might have been expected that, after the charter was obtained, considerable eag
ness would have been manifested to engage in the trade. But such was not the ca
Notwithstanding the earnest calls and threats of the directors, many of the adventur
could not be induced to come forward to pay their proportion of the charges incid
to the fitting out of the first expedition. And as the directors seem either to h
wanted power to enforce their resolutions, or thought it better not to exercise it, t
formed a subordinate association, consisting of such members of the Company as w
really willing to defray the cost of the voyage, and to bear all the risks and losses
tending it, on condition of their having the exclusive right to whatever profits mi
arise from it. And it was by such subordinate associations that the trade was condu
during the first 13 years of the Company's existence.

The first expedition to India, the cost of which amounted, ships and cargoes inclu
to 69,091l., consisted of 5 ships, the largest being 600 and the smallest 130 tons burth
The goods put on board were principally bullion, iron, tin, broad cloths, cutlery, g
&c. The chief command was entrusted to Captain James Lancaster, who had alre

n India. They set sail from Torbay on the 13th of February, 1601. Being
mperfectly acquainted with the seas and countries they were to visit, they did not
at their destination, Acheen in Sumatra, till the 5th of June, 1602. But though
s, the voyage was, on the whole, uncommonly prosperous. Lancaster entered
ommercial treaties with the kings of Acheen and Bantam; and having taken on
a valuable cargo of pepper and other produce, he was fortunate enough, in his
ome, to fall in with and capture, in concert with a Dutch vessel, a Portuguese
k of 900 tons burthen, richly laden. Lancaster returned to the Downs on the
of September, 1603. — (*Modern Universal History*, vol. x. p. 16.; *Macpherson's
erce of the European Powers with India*, p. 81.)

: notwithstanding the favourable result of this voyage, the expeditions fitted out
years immediately following, though sometimes consisting of larger ships, were
t an average, materially increased. In 1612, Captain Best obtained from the
at Delhi several considerable privileges; and, amongst others, that of establishing
ry at Surat; which city was, henceforth, looked upon as the principal British
in the west of India, till the acquisition of Bombay.

establishing factories in India, the English only followed the example of the
guese and Dutch. It was contended, that they were necessary to serve as *depôts*
goods collected in the country for exportation to Europe, as well as for those
ed into India, in the event of their not meeting with a ready market on the
of the ships. Such establishments, it was admitted, are not required in civilised
ies; but the peculiar and unsettled state of India was said to render them in-
sable there. Whatever weight may be attached to this statement, it is obvious
ctories formed for such purposes could hardly fail of speedily degenerating into a
of forts. The security of the valuable property deposited in them furnished a
s pretext for putting them in a condition to withstand an attack, while the agents,
warehousemen, &c. formed a sort of garrison. Possessing such strong holds,
ropeans were early emboldened to act in a manner quite inconsistent with their
er as merchants; and but a very short time elapsed before they began to form
s for monopolising the commerce of particular districts, and acquiring territorial
on.

ugh the Company met with several heavy losses during the earlier part of their
with India, from shipwrecks and other unforeseen accidents, and still more from
tility of the Dutch, yet, on the whole, the trade was decidedly profitable. There
wever, be little doubt, that their gains, at this early period, have been very much
rated. During the first 13 years, they are said to have amounted to 132 per
But then it should be borne in mind, as Mr. Grant has justly stated, that the
s were seldom accomplished in less than 30 months, and sometimes extended to
years: and it should further be remarked, that on the arrival of the ships at
the cargoes were disposed of at long credits of 18 months or 2 years; and that
requently even 6 or 7 years before the concerns of a single voyage were finally
d.—(*Sketch of the History of the Company*, p. 13.) When these circumstances are
nto view, it will immediately be seen that the Company's profits were not, really,
means so great as has been represented. It may not, however, be uninstructive
rk, that the principal complaint that was then made against the Company did
ceed so much on the circumstance of its charter excluding the public from any
a an advantageous traffic, as in its authorising the Company to export gold and
f the value of 30,000*l.* a year. It is true that the charter stipulated that the
ny should import an equal quantity of gold and silver within 6 months of the
tion of every voyage: but the enemies of the Company contended that this
on was not complied with; and that it was, besides, highly injurious to the public
, and *contrary to all principle*, to allow gold and silver to be sent out of the king-
The merchants and others interested in the support of the Company could not
ert the reasoning of their opponents, without openly impugning the ancient
f absolutely preventing the exportation of the precious metals. They did not,
r, venture to contend, if the idea really occurred to them, that the exportation of
to the East was advantageous, on the broad ground of the commodities purchased
ing of greater value in England. But they contended that the exportation of
to India was advantageous, because the commodities thence imported were
e-exported to other countries from which a much greater quantity of bullion
ained than had been required to pay for them in India. Mr. Thomas Mun, a
of the East India Company, and the ablest of its early advocates, ingeniously
es the operations of the merchant in conducting a trade carried on by the export-
gold and silver to the seed time and harvest of agriculture. "If we only
says he, "the actions of the husbandman in the seed time, when he casteth
uch good corn into the ground, we shall account him rather a madman than a

I i

husbandman. But when we consider his labours in the harvest, which is the en his endeavours, we find the worth and plentiful increase of his actions." — (*Tre by Foreign Trade*, p. 50. ed. 1664.)

We may here remark, that what has been called the *mercantile system* of poli economy, or that system which measures the progress of a country in the care wealth by the supposed balance of payments in its favour, or by the estimated exce the value of its exports over that of its imports, appears to have originated in the cuses now set up for the exportation of bullion. Previously to this epoch, the polic prohibiting the exportation of bullion had been universally admitted; but it now b to be pretty generally allowed, that its exportation might be productive of advan provided it occasioned the subsequent exportation of a greater amount of raw or m factured products to countries whence bullion was obtained for them. This, v compared with the previously existing prejudice — for it hardly deserves the nan system — which wholly interdicted the exportation of gold and silver, must be allowe be a considerable step in the progress to sounder opinions. The maxim, *ce n'est q premier pas qui coute*, was strikingly verified on this occasion. The advocates of East India Company began gradually to assume a higher tone, and, at length, be contended that bullion was nothing but a commodity, and that its exportation o to be rendered as free as that of any other commodity. Nor were these opinions fined to the partners of the East India Company. They were gradually comm cated to others; and many eminent merchants were taught to look with suspicio several of the then received dogmas with respect to commerce, and were, in cc quence, led to acquire more correct and comprehensive views. The new ideas mately made their way into the House of Commons; and, in 1663, the statutes proh ing the exportation of foreign coin and bullion were repealed, and full liberty giv the East India Company and to private traders to export them in unlimited quantit

But the objection to the East India Company, or rather the East India trade, o ground of its causing the exportation of gold and silver, admitted of a more direct conclusive, if not a more ingenious, reply. How compendious soever the ancient i course with India by the Red Sea and the Mediterranean may appear to have bee was attended with very great expense. The productions of the remote parts of brought to Ceylon, or the ports on the Malabar coast, by the natives, were there pt board the ships which arrived from the Arabic gulf. At Berenice they were lar and carried by camels 250 miles to the banks of the Nile. They were there embarked, and conveyed down the river to Alexandria, whence they were despatch different markets. The addition to the price of goods by such a multiplicity of ations must have been considerable; more especially as the price charged on operation was fixed by monopolists, subject to no competition or control. But the passage to India by the Cape of Good Hope was discovered, its various commo being purchased at first hand in the countries of which they were the growth and m facture, the price was proportionally reduced. Mr. Mun, in a tract published in estimates the quantity of Indian commodities imported into Europe, and their cost bought in Aleppo and in India, as follows: —

Cost of Indian commodities consumed in Europe when bought in Aleppo (or andria).   £

	£
6,000,000 lbs. pepper cost, with charges, &c. at Aleppo, 2s. per lb.	600,000
450,000 lbs. cloves, at 4s. 9d. - - -	106,875
150,000 lbs. mace, at 4s. 9d. - - -	35,626
400,000 lbs. nutmegs, at 2s. 4d. - - -	46,666
350,000 lbs. indigo, at 4s. 4d. - - -	75,833
1,000,000 lbs. Persian raw silk, at 12s. - - -	600,000
	£1,465,000

But the same quantities of the same commodities cost, when bought in the Indies, according to Mr. Mun, as follows: —   £

	£
6,000,000 lbs. pepper, at 2½d. per lb. - - -	62,500
450,000 lbs. cloves, at 9d. - - - -	16,875
150,000 lbs. mace, at 8d. - - - -	5,000
400,000 lbs. nutmegs, at 4d. - - -	6,666
350,000 lbs. indigo, at 1s. 2d. - - - -	20,416
1,000,000 lbs. raw silk, at 8s. - - -	400,000
	£511,458

Which being deducted from the former, leaves a balance of 953,542l. 13s. 4d. supposing that the statements made by Mr. Mun are correct, and that allowa

e for the difference between the freight from Aleppo and India, the result would
cate the saving which the discovery of the route by the Cape of Good Hope occa-
ed in the purchase of the above-mentioned articles. — (*A Discourse of Trade from*
gland to the East Indies, by T. M., original edit. p. 10. This tract, which is very
ce, is reprinted in Purchas's Pilgrims.)

n the same publication (p. 37.), Mr. Mun informs us that, from the beginning of the
npany's trade to July, 1620, they had sent seventy-nine ships to India; of which
ty-four had come home safely and richly laden, four had been worn out by long ser-
in India, two had been lost in careening, six had been lost by the perils of the sea,
twelve had been captured by the Dutch. Mr. Mun further states, that the exports
ndia, since the formation of the Company, had amounted to 840,376*l*.; that the pro-
e brought from India had cost 356,288*l*., and had produced here the enormous sum
,914,600*l*.; that the quarrels with the Dutch had occasioned a loss of 84,088*l*.; and
the stock of the Company, in ships, goods in India, &c., amounted to 400,000*l*.
he hostility of the Dutch, to which Mr. Mun has here alluded, was long a very for-
able obstacle to the Company's success. The Dutch early endeavoured to obtain the
isive possession of the spice trade, and were not at all scrupulous about the means
hich they attempted to bring about this their favourite object. The English, on
part, naturally exerted themselves to obtain a share of so valuable a commerce;
as neither party was disposed to abandon its views and pretensions, the most violent
iosities grew up between them. In this state of things, it would be ridiculous to
ose that unjustifiable acts were not committed by the one party as well as the other;
gh the worst act of the English appears venial, when compared with the conduct
he Dutch in the massacre at Amboyna in 1622. While, however, the Dutch
pany was vigorously supported by the government at home, the English Company
with no efficient assistance from the feeble and vacillating policy of James and
les. The Dutch either despised their remonstrances, or defeated them by an ap-
nt compliance; so that no real reparation was obtained for the outrages they had
mitted. During the civil war, Indian affairs were necessarily lost sight of; and the
ch continued, until the ascendancy of the republican party had been established, to
triumphant in the East, where the English commerce was nearly annihilated.
it notwithstanding their depressed condition, the Company's servants in India laid
oundation, during the period in question, of the settlements at Madras and in Bengal.
ission to build Fort St. George was obtained from the native authorities in 1640.
558, Madras was raised to the station of a Presidency. In 1645, the Company
n to establish factories in Bengal; the principal of which was at Hooghly. These
, for a lengthened period, subordinate to the presidency at Madras.

o sooner, however, had the civil wars terminated, than the arms and councils of
well retrieved the situation of our affairs in India. The war which broke out
een the long parliament and the Dutch, in 1652, was eminently injurious to the
. In the treaty of peace, concluded in 1654, it was stipulated that indemnification
d be made by the Dutch for the losses and injuries sustained by the English mer-
s and factors in India. The 27th article bears, " That the Lords, the states-ge-
of the United Provinces, shall take care that justice be done upon those who were
kers or accomplices in the massacre of the English at Amboyna, as the republic of
and is pleased to term that fact, provided any of them be living." A commission
t the same time appointed, conformably to another article of the treaty, to inquire
he reciprocal claims which the subjects of the contracting parties had upon each
for losses sustained in India, Brazil, &c.; and, upon their decision, the Dutch
he sum of 85,000*l*. to the East India Company, and 3,615*l*. to the heirs or executors
sufferers at Amboyna. — (*Bruce's Annals*, vol. i. p. 489.)

e charter under which the East India Company prosecuted their exclusive trade to
, being merely a grant from the crown, and not ratified by any act of parliament,
nderstood by the merchants to be at an end when Charles I. was deposed. They
confirmed in this view of the matter, from the circumstance of Charles having him-
ranted, in 1635, a charter to Sir William Courten and others, authorising them to
with those parts of India with which the Company had not established any regular
ourse. The reasons alleged in justification of this measure, by the crown, were,
the East India Company had neglected to establish fortified factories, or seats of
to which the king's subjects could resort with safety; that they had consulted
own interests only, without any regard to the king's revenue; and, in general, that
ad broken the condition on which their charter and exclusive privileges had been
d to them." — (*Rym. Fœdera*, vol. xx. p. 146.)

urten's association, for the foundation of which such satisfactory reasons had been
ed, continued to trade with India during the remainder of Charles's reign; and
ner had the arms of the commonwealth forced the Dutch to desist from their de-

predations, and to make reparation for the injuries they had inflicted on the English
India, than private adventurers engaged in great numbers in the Indian trade, and carri
it on with a zeal, economy, and success, that monopoly can never expect to rival. It
stated in a little work, entitled *Britannia Languens*, published in 1680, the author
which has evidently been a well-informed and intelligent person, that during the yea
1653, 1654, 1655, and 1656, when the trade to India was open, the private traders i
ported East Indian commodities in such large quantities, and sold them at such reduc
prices, that they not only fully supplied the British markets, but had even come in
successful competition with the Dutch in the market of Amsterdam, "and very mu
sunk the actions (shares) of the Dutch East India Company."—(p. 132.) This c
cumstance naturally excited the greatest apprehensions on the part of the Dutch Co
pany; for, besides the danger that they now ran of being deprived, by the acti
competition of the English merchants, of a considerable part of the trade which th
had previously enjoyed, they could hardly expect that, if the trade were thrown open
England, the monopoly would be allowed to continue in Holland. A striking pro
of what is now stated is to be found in a letter in the third volume of *Thurlow's St*
Papers, dated at the Hague, the 15th January, 1654, where it is said, "that the me
chants of Amsterdam have advice that the Lord Protector intends to dissolve the E.
India Company at London, and to declare the navigation and commerce of the E
Indies free and open; which doth cause great jealousy at Amsterdam, *as a thing th*
will very much prejudice the East India Company in Holland."

Feeling that it was impossible to contend with the private adventurers under a syste
of fair competition, the moment the treaty with the Dutch had been concluded,
Company began to solicit a renewal of their charter; but in this they were not or
opposed by the free traders, but by a part of themselves. To understand how this ha
pened, it may be proper to mention that Courten's association, the origin of which h
been already noticed, had begun, in 1648, to found a colony at Assuda, an island n
Madagascar. The Company, alarmed at this project, applied to the council of state
prevent its being carried into effect; and the council, without entering on the questi
of either party's rights, recommended to them to form a union; which was according
effected in 1649. But the union was, for a considerable time, rather nominal than rea
and when the Dutch war had been put an end to, most of those holders of the Compan
stock who had belonged to Courten's association joined in petitioning the council
state that the trade might in future be carried on, not by a joint stock, but by a *regula*
company; so that each individual engaging in it might be allowed to employ his ow
stock, servants, and shipping, in whatever way he might conceive most for his own a
vantage. — (*Petition of Adventurers*, 17th Nov. 1656; *Bruce's Annals*, vol. i. p. 518.

This proposal was obviously most reasonable. The Company had always found
their claim to a monopoly of the trade on the alleged ground of its being necessary
maintain forts, factories, and ships of war in India; and that as this was not done
government, it could only be done by a company. But, by forming the traders w
India into a regulated company, they might have been subjected to whatever rules w
considered most advisable; and such special duties might have been laid on the comm
dities they exported and imported, as would have sufficed to defray the public expen
required for carrying on the trade, at the same time that the inestimable advantages
free competition would have been secured; each individual trader being left at liberty
conduct his enterprises, subject only to a few general regulations, in his own way a
for his own advantage. (See COMPANIES.)

But notwithstanding the efforts of the petitioners, and the success that was clea
proved to have attended the operations of the private traders, the Company succeeded
obtaining a renewal of their charter from Cromwell in 1657. Charles II. confirm
this charter in 1661; and at the same time conferred on them the power of making pe
or war with any power or people *not of the Christian religion;* of establishing fortifi
tions, garrisons, and colonies; of exporting ammunition and stores to their settleme
duty free; of seizing and sending to England such British subjects as should be fou
trading to India without their leave; and of exercising civil and criminal jurisdiction
their settlements, according to the laws of England. Still, however, as this charter v
not fully confirmed by any act of parliament, it did not prevent traders, or interlop
as they were termed, from appearing within the limits of the Company's territories.
energy of private commerce, which, to use the words of Mr. Orme, "sees its drift w
eagles' eyes," formed associations at the risk of trying the consequence at law, being s
at the outset, and during the voyage, since the Company were not authorised to sto
seize the ships of those who thus attempted to come into competition with them. He
their monopoly was by no means complete; and it was not till after the Revolut
and when a free system of government had been established at home, that, by a sing
contradiction, the authority of parliament was interposed to enable the Company wh
to engross the trade with the East.

addition to the losses arising from this source, the Company's trade suffered
ly, during the reign of Charles II., from the hostilities that were then waged with
>utch, and from the confusion and disorders caused by contests among the native
es; but in 1668, the Company obtained a very valuable acquisition in the island of
>ay. Charles II. acquired this island as part of the marriage portion of his
Catharine of Portugal; and it was now made over to the Company, on condition
ir not selling or alienating it to any persons whatever, except such as were subjects
> British crown. They were allowed to legislate for their new possession; but it
njoined that their laws should be consonant to reason, and "as near as might be"
ible to the practice of England. They were authorised to maintain their dominion
ce of arms; and the natives of Bombay were declared to have the same liberties as
il born subjects. The Company's western presidency was soon after transferred
Surat to Bombay.

1664, the French East India Company was formed; and ten years afterwards they
ie foundation of their famous settlement at Pondicherry.

. the reign of Charles II. is chiefly memorable in the Company's annals, from its
the era of the commencement of the tea trade. The first notice of tea in the
any's records is found in a despatch, addressed to their agent at Bantam, dated
anuary, 1667–8, in which he is desired to send home 100 lbs. of tea, "the best he
t." — (*Bruce's Annals*, vol. ii. p. 210.) Such was the late and feeble beginning
tea trade; a branch of commerce that has long been of vast importance to the
i nation; and without which, it is more than probable that the East India Company
long since have ceased to exist, at least as a mercantile body.

1677, the Company obtained a fresh renewal of their charter; receiving at the same
n indemnity for all past misuse of their privileges, and authority to establish a mint
ibay.

·ing the greater part of the reigns of Charles II. and James II., the Company's
at home were principally managed by the celebrated Sir Josiah Child, the ablest
ercial writer of the time; and in India, by his brother Sir John Child. In 1681,
siah published an apology for the Company, under the signature of Φιλοπατρις — "A
se wherein is demonstrated that the East India Trade is the most National of all
n Trades:" in which, besides endeavouring to vindicate the Company from the ob-
s that had been made against it, he gives an account of its state at the time. From
count it appears that the Company consisted of 556 partners; that they had from
36 ships, of from 775 to 100 tons, employed in the trade between England and
and from port to port in India (p. 23.); that the custom duties upon the trade
ited to about 60,000*l.* a year; and that the value of the exports, "in lead, tin, cloth,
iffs, and other commodities of the production and manufacture of England,"
ited to about 60,000*l.* or 70,000*l.* a year. Sir Josiah seems to have been struck,
vell might, by the inconsiderable amount of the trade; and he therefore dwells
advantages of which it was indirectly productive, in enabling us to obtain sup-
f raw silk, pepper, &c. at a much lower price than they would otherwise have
. But this, though true, proved nothing in favour of the Company; it being
iitted fact, that those articles were furnished at a still lower price by the inter-
or private traders.

'osiah Child was one of the first who projected the formation of a territorial empire
a. But the expedition fitted out in 1686, in the view of accomplishing this pur-
·roved unsuccessful; and the Company were glad to accept peace on the terms
by the Mogul. Sir John Child, having died during the course of these
tions, was succeeded in the principal management of the Company's affairs in
y Mr. Vaux. On the appointment of the latter, Sir Josiah Child, to whom he
is advancement, exhorted him to act with vigour, and to carry whatever instruc-
e might receive from home into immediate effect. Mr. Vaux returned for answer
should endeavour to acquit himself with integrity and justice, and that he would
ie laws of his country the rule of his conduct. Sir Josiah Child's answer to this
curious; — "He told Mr. Vaux roundly that he expected his orders were to he
es, and not the laws of England, which were a heap of nonsense, compiled
v ignorant country gentlemen, who hardly knew how to make laws for the
overnment of their own private families, much less for the regulating of
ies and foreign commerce."—(*Hamilton's New Account of the East Indies*, vol. i.

ig the latter part of the reign of Charles II., and that of his successor, the num-
orivate adventurers, or interlopers in the Indian trade, increased in an unusual
The Company vigorously exerted themselves in defence of what they conceived
eir rights; and the question with respect to the validity of the powers conferred
i by their charter was at length brought to issue, by a prosecution carried on at

their instance against Mr. Thomas Sandys, for trading to the East Indies without licence.   Judgment was given in favour of the Company in 1685.   But this dec was ascribed to corrupt influence; and instead of allaying, only served to increas clamour against them.   The meeting of the Convention Parliament gave the Comp opponents hopes of a successful issue to their efforts; and had they been united, might probably have succeeded.   Their opinions were, however, divided — part b for throwing the trade open, and part for the formation of a new company on a mo beral footing.   The latter being formed into a body, and acting in unison, the stru against the Company was chiefly carried on by them.   The proceedings that took p on this occasion are amongst the most disgraceful in the history of the country. most open and unblushing corruption was practised by all parties.—" *It was, in fa trial which side should bribe the highest, public authority inclining to one or other as th resistible force of gold directed.*"—(*Modern Universal History*, vol. x. p. 127.)   Gov ment appears, on the whole, to have been favourable to the Company; and they obta a fresh charter from the crown in 1693.   But in the following year the trade was tually laid open by a vote of the House of Commons, "That all the subjects of E land had an equal right to trade to the East Indies, unless prohibited by act of parliam 1698.   Matters continued on this footing till 1698.   The pecuniary difficulties in which gov ment was then involved, induced them to apply to the Company for a loan of 2,000,(for which they offered 8 per cent. interest.   The Company offered to advance 700,(at 4 per cent.; but the credit of government was at the time so low, that they prefe accepting an offer from the associated merchants, who had previously opposed the C pany, of the 2,000,000*l.* at 8 per cent., on condition of their being formed into a new exclusive company.   While this project was in agitation, the advocates of free trade not idle, but exerted themselves to show that, instead of establishing a new Company old one ought to be abolished.   But however conclusive and unanswerable, their a ments, having no adventitious recommendations in their favour, failed of making impression.   The new Company was established by authority of the legislature; an the charter of the old Company was not yet expired, the novel spectacle was exhibit two legally constituted bodies, each claiming an exclusive right to the trade of the possessions!

Notwithstanding all the pretensions set up by those who had obtained the new c ter during their struggle with the old Company, it was immediately seen that they as anxious as the latter to suppress every thing like free trade.   They had not, in obvious, been actuated by any enlarged views, but merely by a wish to grasp at monopoly which they believed would redound to their own individual interest. public, in consequence, became equally disgusted with both parties; or if there were difference, it is probable that the new Company was looked upon with the greatest sion, inasmuch as we are naturally more exasperated by what we conceive to be dup and bad faith, than by fair undisguised hostility.

At first the mutual hatred of the rival associations knew no bounds.   But they not long in perceiving that such conduct would infallibly end in their ruin; and while one was labouring to destroy the other, the friends of free trade might step i procure the dissolution of both.   In consequence, they became gradually reconciled in 1702, having adjusted their differences, they resolved to form themselves into company, entitled, *The United Company of Merchants of England trading to the Indies.*

The authority of parliament was soon after interposed to give effect to this agreer The United Company engaged to advance 1,200,000*l.* to government without int which, as a previous advance had been made of 2,000,000*l.* at 8 per cent., made the sum due to them by the public 3,200,000*l.*, bearing interest at 5 per cent.; and go ment agreed to ratify the terms of their agreement, and to extend the charter to the of March, 1726, with three years' notice.

While those important matters were transacting at home, the Company had acq some additional possessions in India.   In 1692, the Bengal agency was transf from Hooghly to Calcutta.   In 1698, the Company acquired a grant from one c grandsons of Aurengzebe, of Calcutta and two adjoining villages; with leave to cise judiciary powers over the inhabitants, and to erect fortifications.   These were after constructed, and received, in compliment to William III., then king of Eng the name of Fort William.   The agency at Bengal, which had hitherto been subs only, was now raised to the rank of a Presidency.

The vigorous competition that had been carried on for some years before the coa of the old and new Companies, between them and the private traders, had occasio great additional importation of Indian silks, piece goods, and other products, and a reduction of their price.   These circumstances occasioned the most vehement comp amongst the home manufacturers, who resorted to the arguments invariably made

such occasions by those who wish to exclude foreign competition; affirming that
ufactured India goods had been largely substituted for those of England; that
English manufacturers had been reduced to the cruel necessity either of selling
ing, or of selling their commodities at such a price as left them no profit; that great
bers of their workmen had been thrown out of employment; and last of all, that
an goods were not bought by British goods, but by gold and silver, the exportation of
h had caused the general impoverishment of the kingdom ! The merchants and others
rested in the India trade could not, as had previously happened to them in the con-
ersy with respect to the exportation of bullion, meet these statements without attack-
the principles on which they rested, and maintaining, in opposition to them, that it
for the advantage of every people to buy the products they wanted in the cheapest
ket. This just and sound principle was, in consequence, enforced in several petitions
ented to parliament by the importers of Indian goods; and it was also enforced in se-
able publications that appeared at the time. But these arguments, how un-
erable soever they may now appear, had then but little influence; and in 1701,
ct was passed, prohibiting the importation of Indian manufactured goods for home
umption.

or some years after the re-establishment of the Company, it continued to prosecute
orts to consolidate and extend its commerce. But the unsettled state of the Mogul
ire, coupled with the determination of the Company to establish factories in every
enient situation, exposed their affairs to perpetual vicissitudes. In 1715, it was re-
d to send an embassy to Delhi, to solicit from Furucksur, an unworthy descendant
urengzebe, an extension and confirmation of the Company's territory and privileges.
ress, accident, and the proper application of *presents*, conspired to ensure the success
e embassy. The grants or patents solicited by the Company were issued in 1717.
were in all thirty-four. The substance of the privileges they conferred was, that
ish vessels wrecked on the coasts of the empire should be exempt from plunder;
the annual payment of a stipulated sum to the government of Surat should free the
ish trade at that port from all duties and exactions; that those villages contiguous
adras, formerly granted and afterwards refused by the government of Arcot,
d be restored to the Company; that the island of Diu, near the port of Masuli-
, should belong to the Company, paying for it a fixed rent; that in Bengal all
ersons, whether European or native, indebted or accountable to the Company,
d be delivered up to the presidency on demand; that goods of export or import,
ging to the English, might, under a *dustuck* or passport from the president of Cal-
, be conveyed duty free through the Bengal provinces; and that the English
d be at liberty to purchase the lordship of thirty-seven towns contiguous to Cal-
, and in fact commanding both banks of the river for ten miles south of that city. —
nt's *Sketch of the Hist. of the East India Company*, p. 128.)

e important privileges thus granted were long regarded as constituting the great
er of the English in India. Some of them, however, were not fully conceded;
vere withheld or modified by the influence of the emperor's lieutenants, or sou-
rs.

1717, the Company found themselves in danger from a new competitor. In the
e of that year some ships appeared in India, fitted out by private adventurers from
ad. Their success encouraged others to engage in the same line; and in 1722, the
aturers were formed into a Company under a charter from his imperial Majesty.
Dutch and English Companies, who had so long been hostile to each other, at
laid aside their animosities, and joined heartily in an attempt to crush their new
etitors. Remonstrances being found ineffectual, force was resorted to; and the
s of the Ostend Company were captured, under the most frivolous pretences, in the
seas and on the coasts of Brazil. The British and Dutch governments abetted
lfish spirit of hostility displayed by their respective Companies. And the emperor
in the end, glad to purchase the support of Great Britain and Holland to the prag-
sanction, by the sacrifice of the Company at Ostend.

ough the Company's trade had increased, it was still inconsiderable; and it is very
alt, indeed, when one examines the accounts that have from time to time been pub-
of the Company's mercantile affairs, to imagine how the idea ever came to be en-
ned that their commerce was of any considerable, much less paramount, import-

At an average of the ten years ending with 1724, the total value of the British
factures and other products annually exported to India, amounted to only 92,410l.
d. The average value of the bullion, annually exported during the same period,
nted to 518,102l. 11s. 0d.; making the total annual average exports 617,513l.
d.; — a truly pitiful sum, when we consider the wealth, population, and industry
countries between which the Companys' commerce was carried on; and affording
smallness a strong presumptive proof of the effect of the monopoly in preventing
owth of the trade.

In 1730, though there were three years still unexpired of the Company's charter vigorous effort was made by the merchants of London, Bristol, and Liverpool, to preve its renewal.   It has been said that the gains of the Company, had they been exac known, would not have excited any very envious feelings on the part of the merchant but being concealed, they were exaggerated; and the boasts of the Company as to t importance of their trade contributed to spread the belief that their profits were en mous, and consequently stimulated the exertions of their opponents.   Supposing, ho ever, that the real state of the case had been known, there was still enough to justify utmost exertions on the part of the merchants: for the limited profits made by t Company, notwithstanding their monopoly, were entirely owing to the misconduct their agents, which they had vainly endeavoured to restrain; and to the waste insepara from such unwieldy establishments.

The merchants, on this occasion, followed the example that had been set by the p titioners for free trade in 1656.   They offered, in the first place, to advance t 3,200,000l. lent by the Company to the public, on more favourable terms.   And in t second place, they proposed that the subscribers to this loan should be formed into *regulated* company for opening the trade, under the most favourable circumstances to classes of their countrymen.

It was not intended that the Company should trade upon a joint stock, and in th corporate capacity, but that every individual who pleased should trade in the way private adventure.   The Company were to have the charge of erecting and maintaini the forts and establishments abroad; and for this, and for other expenses attending wh was called the enlargement and preservation of the trade, it was proposed that th should receive a duty of 1 per cent. upon all exports to India, and of 5 per cent. up all imports from it.   For ensuring obedience to this and other regulations, it was to enacted, that no one should trade to India without licence from the Company.   And was proposed that thirty-one years, with three years notice, should be granted as duration of their peculiar privilege.

" It appears from this," says Mr. Mill, " that the end which was proposed to be a swered, by incorporating such a company, was the preservation and erection of forts, buildings, and other fixed establishments, required for the trade of India.   T Company promised to supply that demand which has always been held forth as pecul to the India trade, as the grand exigency which, distinguishing the traffic with In from all other branches of trade, rendered monopoly advantageous in that peculiar ca how much soever it might be injurious in others.   While it provided for this real pretended want, it left the trade open to all the advantages of private enterprise, priv vigilance, private skill, and private economy,—the virtues by which individuals thrive a nations prosper.   And it gave the proposed Company an interest in the careful discha of its duty, by making its profits increase in exact proportion with the increase of trade, and, of course, with the facilities and accommodation by which the trade was p moted.

" Three petitions were presented to the House of Commons in behalf of the p posed Company, by the merchants of London, Bristol, and Liverpool.   It was urg that the proposed Company would, through the competition of which it would be p ductive, cause a great extension of the trade; that it would produce a larger exporta of our own produce and manufactures to India, and reduce the price of all Ind commodities to the people at home; that new channels of traffic would be opened Asia and America, as well as in Europe; that the duties of customs and excise wo be increased; and that the waste and extravagance caused by the monopoly would entirely avoided." — (*Mills's India*, vol. iii. p. 37.)

But these arguments did not prevail.   The Company magnified the importanc their trade; and contended, that it would be unwise to risk advantages already reali for the sake of those that were prospective and contingent.   They alleged that, if trade to India were thrown open, the price of goods in India would be so much hanced by the competition of different traders, and their price in England so m diminished, that the freedom of the trade would certainly end in the ruin of all had been foolish enough to adventure in it.   To enlarge on the fallacy of these st ments would be worse than superfluous.   It is obvious that nothing whatever cc have been risked, and that a great deal would have been gained, by opening the t in the way that was proposed.   And if it were really true that the trade to I ought to be subjected to a monopoly, lest the traders by their competition should each other, it would follow that the trade to America — and not that only, but e branch both of the foreign and home trade of the empire — should be surrendere exclusive companies.   But such as the Company's arguments were, they seemed s factory to parliament.   They, however, consented to reduce the interest on the due to them by the public from 5 to 4 per cent., and contributed a sum of 200,0

e public service. On these conditions it was agreed to extend their exclusive
ges to Lady-day, 1766, with the customary addition of three years' notice.

about 15 years from this period, the Company's affairs went on without any very
nent changes. But, notwithstanding the increased importation of tea, the con-
ion of which now began rapidly to extend, their trade continued to be compara-
insignificant. At an average of the 8 years ending with 1741, the value of the
h goods and products of all sorts, exported by the Company to India and China,
ited to only 157,944l. 4s. 7d. a year! And during the 7 years ending with 1748,
mounted to only 188,176l. 16s. 4d. And when it is borne in mind that these
s included the military stores of all sorts, forwarded to the Company's settlements
ia and at St. Helena, the amount of which was, at all times, very considerable,
, appear exceedingly doubtful whether the Company really exported, during the
period from 1730 to 1748, 150,000l. worth of British produce as a legitimate
itile adventure! Their trade, such as it was, was entirely carried on by shipments
lion; and even its annual average export, during the 7 years ending with 1748,
mounted to 548,711l. 19s. 2d. It would seem, indeed, that the Company had
l no perceptible advantage from the important concessions obtained from the
l emperor, in 1717. But the true conclusion is, not that these concessions were of
alue, but that the deadening influence of monopoly had so paralysed the Company,
ey were unable to turn them to account; and that, though without competitors,
ith opulent kingdoms for their customers, their commerce was hardly greater than
rried on by some single merchants.

732, the Company were obliged to reduce their dividend from 8 to 7 per cent.,
:h rate it continued till 1744.

opposition the Company had experienced from the merchants, when the question
ie renewal of their charter was agitated, in 1730, made them very desirous to
the next renewal in as quiet a manner as possible. They therefore proposed, in
when 23 years of their charter were yet unexpired, to lend 1,000,000l. to govern-
at 3 per cent., provided their exclusive privileges were extended to 1780, with the
notice. And as none were expecting such an application, or prepared to oppose
consent of government was obtained without difficulty.

the period was now come, when the mercantile character of the East India Com-
-if, indeed, it could with propriety be, at any time, said to belong to them—was to
ised by their achievements as a military power, and the magnitude of their con-
For about two centuries after the European powers began their intercourse with
the Mogul princes were regarded as amongst the most opulent and powerful of
hs. Though of a foreign lineage—being descended from the famous Tamerlane,
ur Bec, who overran India in 1400—and of a different religion from the great
f their subjects, their dominion was firmly established in every part of their ex-
empire. The administration of the different provinces was committed to officers,
nated soubahdars or nabobs, who were entrusted with powers in their respective
nents, similar to those enjoyed by the Roman prætors. So long as the em-
retained any considerable portion of the vigour and bravery of their hardy
rs, the different parts of the government were held in due subordination,
e soubahdars yielded a ready obedience to the orders from Delhi. But the
rs were gradually debauched by the apparently prosperous condition of their
Instead of being educated in the council, or the camp, the heirs of almost un-
d power were brought up in the slothful luxury of the seraglio; ignorant of
affairs; benumbed by indolence; depraved by the flattery of women, of eunuchs,
slaves; their minds contracted with their enjoyments, their inclinations were
by their habits; and their government grew as vicious, as corrupt, and as worth-
themselves. When the famous Kouli Khan, the usurper of the Persian
invaded India, the effeminate successor of Tamerlane and Aurengzebe was
prepared to oppose, and too dastardly to think of avenging the attack. This
signal for the dismemberment of the monarchy. No sooner had the invader
wn, than the soubahdars either openly threw off their allegiance to the emperor,
only a species of nominal or mock deference to his orders. The independence
oubahdars was very soon followed by wars amongst themselves; and, being well
f the superiority of European troops and tactics, they anxiously courted the
and support of the French and English East India Companies. These bodies,
espoused different sides according as their interests or prejudices dictated, began
on to turn the quarrels of the soubahdars to their own account. Instead of
ontented, as hitherto, with the possession of factories and trading towns, they
to the dominion of provinces; and the struggle soon came to be, not which of
ve princes should prevail, but whether the English or the French should become
ires of India.

But these transactions are altogether foreign to the subject of this work; nor c
any intelligible account of them be given without entering into lengthened stateme
We shall only, therefore, observe that the affairs of the French were ably conducte
La Bourdonnais, Dupleix, and Lally, officers of distinguished merit, and not less
brated for their great actions than for the base ingratitude of which they were the vict
But though victory seemed at first to incline to the French and their allies, the En
affairs were effectually retrieved by the extraordinary talents and address of a single
vidual; — Colonel, afterwards Lord Clive, was equally brave, cautious, and enterpris
not scrupulous in the use of means; fertile in expedients; endowed with wonderfu
gacity and resolution; and capable of turning even the most apparently adverse circ
stances to advantage. Having succeeded in humbling the French power in the vic
of Madras, Clive landed at Calcutta in 1757, in order to chastise the soubahdar, S
jah ul Dowlah, who had a short while before attacked the English factory at that p
and inhumanly shut up 146 Englishmen in a prison, where, owing to the excessive
and want of water, 123 perished in a single night. Clive had only 700 European tr
and 1,400 Sepoys with him when he landed; but with these, and 570 sailors furnishe
the fleet, he did not hesitate to attack the immense army commanded by the soubah
and totally defeated him in the famous battle of Plassey. This victory threw the w
provinces of Bengal, Bahar, and Orissa, into our hands; and they were finally
firmed to us by the treaty negotiated in 1765.

Opinion has been long divided as to the policy of our military operations in In
and it has been strenuously contended, that we ought never to have extended our
quests beyond the limits of Bengal. The legislature seems to have taken this vie
the matter; the House of Commons having resolved, in 1782, " That to pu
schemes of conquest and extent of dominion in India are measures repugnant to
wish, the honour, and the policy of this nation." But others have argued, and a
rently on pretty good grounds, that having gone thus far, we were compelled to adva
The native powers, trembling at the increase of British dominion, endeavoured, v
too late, to make head against the growing evil. In this view they entered into
binations and wars against the English; and the latter having been uniformly v
rious, their empire necessarily went on increasing, till all the native powers have
swallowed up in its vast extent.

The magnitude of the acquisitions made by Lord Clive powerfully excite
attention of the British public. Their value was prodigiously exaggerated; a
was generally admitted that the Company had no legal claim to enjoy, during the w
period of their charter, all the advantages resulting from conquests, to which
fleets and armies of the state had largely contributed. In 1767, the subject was
up by the House of Commons; and a committee was appointed to investigate the v
circumstances of the case, and to calculate the entire expenditure incurred by the p
on the Company's account. During the agitation of this matter, the right of the
pany to the new conquests was totally denied by several members. In the end, how
the question was compromised by the Company agreeing to pay 400,000l. a year fo
years; and in 1769, this agreement, including the yearly payment, was further exte
for five years more. The Company, at the same time, increased their dividend, w
had been fixed by the former agreement at 10, to 12½ per cent.

But the Company's anticipations of increased revenue proved entirely visionary.
rapidity of their conquests in India, the distance of the controlling authority at h
and the abuses in the government of the native princes, to whom the Company had
ceeded, conspired to foster a strong spirit of peculation among their servants. A
of every sort were multiplied to a frightful extent. The English, having obtaine
rather enforced, an exemption from those heavy transit duties to which the native tr
were subject, engrossed the whole internal trade of the country. They even w
far as to decide what quantity of goods each manufacturer should deliver, and wl
should receive for them. It is due to the directors to say, that they exerted them
to repress these abuses. But their resolutions were neither carried into effect by
servants in India, nor sanctioned by the proprietors at home; so that the abuses, ir
of being repressed, went on acquiring fresh strength and virulence. The resour
the country were rapidly impaired: and while many of the Company's servan
turned to Europe with immense fortunes, the Company itself was involved in det
difficulties; and so far from being able to pay the stipulated sum of 400,000l. a y
government, was compelled to apply, in 1772, to the treasury for a loan!

In this crisis of their affairs, government interposed, and a considerable chang
made in the constitution of the Company. The dividend was restricted to 6 per
till the sum of 1,400,000l., advanced to them by the public, should be paid.
further enacted, that the Court of Directors should be elected for four years, six me
annually, but none to hold their seats for more than four years at a time; that no

to vote at the Courts of Proprietors who had not possessed his stock for twelve
ths; and that the amount of stock required to qualify for a vote should be increased
n 500*l.* to 1,000*l.* The jurisdiction of the Mayor's Court at Calcutta was in future
fined to small mercantile cases; and, in lieu of it, a new court was appointed, con-
ng of a chief justice and three principal judges appointed by the crown. A supe-
ty was also given to Bengal over the other presidencies, Mr. Warren Hastings being
ed in the act as governor-general of India. The governor-general, councillors, and
es, were prohibited from having any concern whatever in trade; and no person
ling in the Company's settlements was allowed to take more than 12 per cent. per
um for money. Though strenuously opposed, these measures were carried by a
e majority.

t this period (1773) the total number of proprietors of East India stock, with their
ifications as they stood in the Company's books, were as follow:—

	Proprietors.	Stock.		
		£	s.	d.
nglishmen, possessing 1,000*l.* stock and upwards -	487	1,018,398	19	11
oreigners, possessing 1,000*l.* stock and upwards -	325	890,940	17	0
nglishmen, possessing 500*l.* stock and upwards -	1,246	634,464	1	8
oreigners, possessing 500*l.* stock and upwards -	95	50,226	0	0
Total - -	2,153	£2,594,029	18	7

otwithstanding the vast extension of the Company's territories, their trade continued
e apparently insignificant. During the three years ending with 1773, the value of
ntire exports of British produce and manufactures, including military stores exported
he Company to India and China, amounted to 1,469,411*l.*, being at the rate of
803*l.* a year; the annual exports of bullion during the same period being only
33*l.*! During the same three years, 23 ships sailed annually for India. The
, indeed, seems to be, that but for the increased consumption of tea in Great
ain, the Company would have entirely ceased to carry on any branch of trade with
East; and the monopoly would have excluded us as effectually from the markets
dia and China, as we should have been, had the trade reverted to its ancient channels,
the route by the Cape of Good Hope ceased to be frequented.

1781, the exclusive privileges of the Company were extended to 1791, with three
' notice; the dividend on the Company's stock was fixed at 8 per cent.; three
hs of their surplus revenues, after paying the dividend, and the sum of 400,000*l.*
ple to government, was to be applied to the public service, and the remaining fourth
e Company's own use.

1780, the value of British produce and manufactures exported by the Company to
a and China amounted to only 386,152*l.*; the bullion exported during the same
was 15,014*l.* The total value of the exports during the same year was 12,648,616*l.*;
ing that the East India trade formed only *one thirty-second* part of the entire foreign
of the empire!

e administration of Mr. Hastings was one continued scene of war, negotiation, and
ue. The state of the country, instead of being improved, became worse; so much
at in a council minute by Marquis Cornwallis, dated the 18th of September, 1789,
distinctly stated, "*that one third of the Company's territory is now a jungle for wild
.*" Some abuses in the conduct of their servants were, indeed, rectified; but,
thstanding, the nett revenue of Bengal, Bahar, and Orissa, which, in 1772, had
nted to 2,126,766*l.*, declined, in 1785, to 2,072,963*l.* This exhaustion of the
ry, and the expenses incurred in the war with Hyder Ally and France, involved
ompany in fresh difficulties. And being unable to meet them, they were obliged,
83, to present a petition to parliament, setting forth their inability to pay the
ated sum of 400,000*l.* a year to the public, and praying to be excused from that
ent, and to be supported by a loan of 900,000*l.*

l parties seemed now to be convinced that some further changes in the constitution
e Company had become indispensable. In this crisis Mr. Fox brought forward his
us India bill; the grand object of which was to abolish the Courts of Directors and
rietors, and to vest the government of India in the hands of seven commissioners
nted by parliament. The coalition between Lord North and Mr. Fox had ren-
the ministry exceedingly unpopular; and advantage was taken of the circum-
e to raise an extraordinary clamour against the bill. The East India Company
atised it as an invasion of their chartered rights; though, it is obvious, that from
inability to carry into effect the stipulations under which those rights were con-
to them, they necessarily reverted to the public; and it was as open to parliament
islate upon them as upon any other question. The political opponents of the
nment represented the proposal for vesting the nomination of commissioners in

the legislature, as a daring invasion of the prerogative of the crown, and an insidio
attempt of the minister to render himself all-powerful, by adding the patronage
India to that already in his possession. The bill was, however, carried through th
House of Commons; but, in consequence of the ferment it had excited, and th
avowed opposition of his Majesty, it was thrown out in the House of Lords. Th
event proved fatal to the coalition ministry. A new one was formed, with Mr. Pitt
its head; and parliament being soon after dissolved, the new minister acquired a decisi
majority in both Houses. When thus secure of parliamentary support, Mr. Pitt broug'
forward his India bill, which was successfully carried through all its stages. By th
bill a Board of Control was erected, consisting of six members of the privy counc
who were " to check, superintend, and control all acts, operations, and concerns, whi
in anywise relate to the civil or military government, or revenues of the territories a
possessions of the East India Company." All communications to or from Indi
touching any of the above matters, were to be submitted to this Board; the directo
being ordered to yield obedience to its commands, and to alter or amend all instructio
sent to India as directed by it. A secret committee of three directors was formed, wi
which the Board of Control might transact any business it did not choose to submit
the Court of Directors. Persons returning from India were to be obliged, under ve
severe penalties, to declare the amount of their fortunes; and a tribunal was appoint
for the trial of all individuals accused of misconduct in India, consisting of a jud
from each of the Courts of King's Bench, Common Pleas, and Exchequer; five mer
bers of the House of Lords, and seven members of the House of Commons; the la
being chosen by lot at the commencement of each session. The superintendence of a
commercial matters continued, as formerly, in the hands of the directors.

During the administration of Marquis Cornwallis, who succeeded Mr. Hasting
Tippoo Saib, the son of Hyder Ally, was stripped of nearly half his dominions; t
Company's territorial revenue was, in consequence, greatly increased; at the same tin
that the permanent settlement was carried into effect in Bengal, and other importa
changes accomplished. Opinion has been long divided as to the influence of the
changes. On the whole, however, we are inclined to think that they have been decided
advantageous. Lord Cornwallis was, beyond all question, a sincere friend to the peop
of India ; and laboured earnestly, if not always successfully, to promote their interes
which he well knew were identified with those of the British nation.

During the three years ending with 1793, the value of the Company's exports
British produce and manufactures fluctuated from 928,783*l*. to 1,031,262*l*. But th
increase is wholly to be ascribed to the reduction of the duty on tea in 1784, and t
vast increase that, consequently, took place in its consumption. — (See article TEA
Had the consumption of tea continued stationary, there appear no grounds for thinki
that the Company's exports in 1793 would have been greater than in 1780 ; unless
increase had taken place in the quantity of military stores exported.

In 1793, the Company's charter was prolonged till the 1st of March, 1814. In t
act for this purpose, a species of provision was made for opening the trade to India
private individuals. All his Majesty's subjects, residing in any part of his Europe
dominions, were allowed to export to India any article of the produce or manufact
of the British dominions, except military stores, ammunition, masts, spars, corda
pitch, tar, and copper: and the Company's civil servants in India, and the free mercha
resident there, were allowed to ship, on their own account and risk, all kinds of Indi
goods, except calicoes, dimities, muslins, and other piece goods. But neither the m
chants in England, nor the Company's servants or merchants in India, were allowed
export or import except in Company's ships. And in order to ensure such conveyan
it was enacted, that the Company should annually appropriate 3,000 tons of shippi
for the use of private traders; it being stipulated that they were to pay, in time
peace, 5*l*. outwards, and 15*l*. homewards, for every ton occupied by them in the Co
pany's ships ; and that this freight might be raised in time of war, with the approbati
of the Board of Control.

It might have been, and, indeed, most probably was, foreseen that very few Brit
merchants or manufacturers would be inclined to avail themselves of the privilege
sending out goods in Company's ships ; or of engaging in a trade fettered on all si
by the jealousy of powerful monopolists, and where, consequently, their superior ju
ment and economy would have availed almost nothing. As far, therefore, as they w
concerned, the relaxation was more apparent than real, and did not produce any use
result.* It was, however, made use of to a considerable extent by private mercha

---

* In his letter to the East India Company, dated March 21. 1812, Lord Melville says: " It will no
denied that the facilities granted by that act (the act of 1793) have not been satisfactory, at least to
merchants either of this country or of India. They have been the source of constant dispute, and
have even entailed a heavy expense upon the Company, without affording to the public any adeq
benefit from such a sacrifice." — (*Papers published by E. I. Comp.* 1813, p. 84.)

ia; and also by the Company's servants returning from India, many of whom
ed a part, and some the whole of their fortune, in produce fit for the European
ts.

financial difficulties of the East India Company led to the revolution which
lace in its government in 1784. But, notwithstanding the superintendence of the
of Control, its finances have continued nearly in the same unprosperous state as
. We have been favoured, from time to time, with the most dazzling accounts of
e that was to be immediately derived from India; and numberless acts of parlia-
ave been passed for the appropriation of surpluses that never had any existence
in the imagination of their framers. The proceedings that took place at the
l of the charter, in 1793, afford a striking example of this. Lord Cornwallis
en concluded the war with Tippoo Saib, which had stripped him of half his
ions: the perpetual settlement, from which so many benefits were expected to be
, had been adopted in Bengal; and the Company's receipts had been increased,
sequence of accessions to their territory, and subsidies from native princes, &c., to
ds of *eight* millions sterling a year, which, it was calculated, would afford a future
surplus, after every description of charge had been deducted, of 1,240,000*l.*
undas (afterwards Lord Melville), then president of the Board of Control,
himself of these favourable appearances, to give the most flattering representation
Company's affairs. There could, he said, be no question as to the permanent and
increase of the Company's surplus revenue; he assured the House that the
es had all been framed with the greatest care; that the Company's possessions
a state of prosperity till then unknown in India; that the abuses, that had
y insinuated themselves into some departments of the government, had been
out; and that the period was at length arrived, when India was to pour her
treasures into the lap of England! Parliament participated in these brilliant an-
ons, and in the act prolonging the charter it was enacted, 1st, That 500,000*l.* a year,
surplus revenue should be set aside for reducing the Company's debt in India to
00*l.*; 2dly, That 500,000*l.* a year should be paid into the exchequer, to be appro-
for the public service as parliament should think fit to order; 3dly, When the
lebt was reduced to 2,000,000*l.*, and the bond debt to 1,500,000*l.*, *one sixth* part
surplus was to be applied to augment the dividends, and the other *five sixths* were
aid into the Bank, in the name of the commissioners of the national debt, to be
lated as a *guarantee fund*, until it amounted to 12,000,000*l.*; and when it
that sum, the dividends upon it were to be applied to make up the dividends on
tal stock of the Company to 10 per cent., if, at any time, the funds appropriated
purpose should prove deficient, &c.

one of these anticipations has been realised! Instead of being diminished, the
ny's debts began immediately to increase. In 1795, they were authorised to add
mount of their floating debt. In 1796, a new device to obtain money was fallen
Mr. Dundas represented that as all competition had been destroyed in consequence
war, the Company's commerce had been greatly increased, and that their mer-
capital had become insufficient for the extent of their transactions. In conse-
of this representation, leave was given to the Company to add *two millions* to
pital stock by creating 20,000 new shares; but, as these shares sold at the rate
each, they produced 3,460,000*l.* In 1797, the Company issued additional
the extent of 1,417,000*l*; and, notwithstanding all this, Mr. Dundas stated
louse of Commons, on the 13th of March, 1799, that there had been a deficit in
ious year of 1,319,000*l.*

ng the administration of the Marquis Wellesley, which began in 1797-8 and
ted in 1805-6, the British empire in India was augmented by the conquest of
patam and the whole territories of Tippoo Saib, the cession of large tracts by
ratta chiefs, the capture of Delhi, the ancient seat of the Mogul empire, and
other important acquisitions; so that the revenue, which had amounted to
00*l.* in 1797, was increased to 15,403,000*l.* in 1805. But the expenses of
nent, and the interest of the debt, increased in a still greater proportion than the
; having amounted, in 1805, to 17,672,000*l.* leaving a deficit of 2,269,000*l.* In
wing year the revenue fell off nearly 1,000,000*l.*, while the expenses continued
he same. And there was, at an average, a continued excess of expenditure,
g commercial charges, and a contraction of fresh debt, down to 1811-12.

ithstanding the vast additions made to their territories, the Company's commerce
m continued to be very inconsiderable. During the five years ending with 1811,
rts to India by the Company, exclusive of those made on account of individuals
ships, were as under: —

	£				£
1807	952,416		1810	- -	1,010,815
1808	919,544		1811	- -	1,033,816
1809	866,153				

The exports by the private trade, and the *privilege* trade, that is, the commanders
officers of the Company's ships, during the above mentioned years, were about as l:
During the five years ending with 1807-8, the annual average imports into Ind
British private traders, only, amounted to 305,496*l*. — (*Papers published by the
India Company*, in 1813, 4to. p. 56.)

The Company's exports include the value of the military stores sent from (
Britain to India. The ships employed in the trade to *India and China*, during the s
five years, varied from 44 to 53, and their burthen from 36,671 to 45,342 tons.

For some years previously to the termination of the Company's charter in 1813
conviction had been gaining ground among all classes, that the trade to the East
capable of being very greatly extended ; and that it was solely owing to the wa
enterprise and competition, occasioned by its being subjected to a monopoly, that it
confined within such narrow limits. Very great efforts were, consequently, mad
the manufacturing and commercial interests to have the monopoly set aside, an
trade to the East thrown open. The Company vigorously resisted these pretensi
and had interest enough to procure a prolongation of the privilege of carrying on a
clusive trade to China to the 10th of April, 1831, with three years' notice ; the govern
of India being continued in their hands for the same period. Fortunately, how
the trade to India was opened, under certain conditions, to the public. The prin
of these conditions were, that private individuals should trade, directly only, wit
presidencies of Calcutta, Madras, and Bombay, and the port of Penang ; that the ve
fitted out by them should not be under 350 tons burthen ; and that they should abs
unless permitted by the Company or the Board of Control, from engaging in the
rying trade of India, or in the trade between India and China. And yet, in despi
these disadvantages, such is the energy of individual enterprise as compared
monopoly, that the private traders gained an almost immediate ascendancy over
East India Company, and in a very short time more than *trebled* our trade with Ind

In the report of the committee of the House of Lords on the foreign trade of
country, printed in May, 1821, it is stated, that " the greatly increased consumptio
British goods in the East, since the commencement of the free trade, cannot b
counted for by the demand of European residents, the number of whom does
materially vary ; and it appears to have been much the greatest in articles calcu
for the general use of the natives. That of the cotton manufactures of this cou
alone is stated, since the first opening of the trade, to have been augmented from
to *five* fold (it is now augmented from *fifty* to *sixty* fold). The value of
merchandise exported from Great Britain to India, which amounted, in 181‡
870,177*l*., amounted *, in 1819, to 3,052,741*l*. ; and although the market appears
to have been so far overstocked as to occasion a diminution of nearly one half in
exports of the following year, that diminution appears to have taken place more i
articles intended for the consumption of Europeans than of natives ; and the tra
now stated to the committee by the best informed persons to be reviving. When
amount of population, and the extent of the country over which the consumpti
these articles is spread, are considered, it is obvious that any facility which can,
sistently with the political interests and security of the Company's dominions, be
to the private trader, for the distribution of his exports, by increasing the numb
ports at which he may have the option of touching in pursuit of a market, cannot f
promote a more ready and extensive demand."

II. Trade with India.

1. *Regulations under which the Trade is at present conducted.* — In consequence of the recommend
in the report now quoted, the act 4 Geo. 4. c. 80. was passed, which made some modifications in t
53 Geo. 3. c. 155. for the renewal of the charter. The former laid open the entire trade, direct and circu
of the East, in all articles except tea, and with all countries except China, to every one licensed b
Company or the Board of Control. The following are the principal regulations, in the two act
alluded to, that have reference to trade.

The act 53 Geo. 3. c. 155. enacts, that from and after the 10th day of April, 1814, the right of tr
trafficking, and adventuring in, to, and from all ports and places within the limits of the Com
charter, save and except the dominions of the emperor of China, should be open to all his Majesty
jects, in common with the said united Company, subject to certain regulations and provisions, &c.
the further term hereby limited ; it is therefore enacted, that the territorial acquisitions mentioned
said act of the parliament of Great Britain of 53 Geo. 3, together with such territorial acquisition
obtained upon the continent of Asia, or in any islands situate to the north of the equator, as are ‖
the possession, and under the government, of the said united Company, with the revenues thereof r‖
ively, shall remain and continue in their possession, subject to such powers and authorities f
superintendence, direction, and control over all acts, operations, and concerns, which relate to th
or military government or revenues of the said territories, and to such further and other powers, ‖
tions, and restrictions, as have been already made or provided by any act or acts of parliament
behalf, or are made and provided by this act, for a further term, to be computed from the said 10
of April, 1814, until the same shall be determined by virtue of the proviso hereinafter contai
§ 1.

Exclusive Trade with China, &c. — The sole and exclusive right of trading and using the busin
merchandise, in, to, and from the dominions of the emperor of China, and the whole, sole, and ex

---

* This is the amount of the Company's exports only, and the sum is not quite accurate, see p‖

: of trading in tea, in, to, and from all islands, ports, and places between the Cape of Good Hope and Straits of Magellan, in such manner as the same rights are now lawfully exercised or enjoyed by the united Company, by virtue of any act or charter now in force, so far as the same, or any of them, are rce, and not repealed by, or repugnant to, this act, shall continue and be in force during the further hereby granted to the said Company: subject to such alterations therein as may be made by any of nactments, &c. contained in this act. — § 2.

clusive Trade may cease at any time, upon three years' notice to be given by parliament, after 0th day of April, 1831, and upon payment made to the East India Company, of any sum or sums of •y, which may, upon the expiration of the said three years, become payable to the said Company.— § 3.

t to determine the Corporation, &c. — Nothing in the last proviso, or in any act or charter contained, extend to determine the corporation of the united East India Company, or to preclude the said pany, or their successors, from carrying on at all times after such determination of their exclusive as aforesaid, a free trade in, to, and from the East Indies, with all or any part of their joint stock de, goods, merchandise, estates, and effects, in common with other the subjects of his Majesty trading , and from the said parts. — § 4.

ps in Private Trade not to go within certain Limits without a Licence from the Directors. — No vessel ged in private trade under the authority of this act shall proceed to any place within the limits of the oany's charter situate on the continent of Asia, from the River Indus to the said town of Malacca sive, or in any island under the government of the Company lying to the north of the equator, or said Company's factory of Bencoolen or its dependencies, without a *licence* to be granted for that ose from the Court of Directors of the Company; and no such vessel, unless *specially* authorised ereinafter mentioned, shall proceed to any place within the limits last mentioned, except to of the principal settlements of Fort William, Fort St. George, Bombay, and Prince of Wales's d: and when any application shall be made to the Court of Directors for a licence on behalf of such vessel about to proceed from the United Kingdom to anj of the Company's principal settle- s, the Company shall forthwith issue their licence for that purpose, according to such form as shall fter be settled by the Court of Directors, with the approbation of the Board of Commissioners •e affairs of Indies: and when any application shall be made to the Court of Directors for a licence ally authorising any such vessel to proceed to any place upon the continent of Asia, from the River s to the town of Malacca inclusive, or in any island under the government of the Company lying to orth of the equator, except the Company's principal settlements, or to the Company's factory of Ben- n or its dependencies, the Court of Directors shall, within fourteen days from the receipt thereof, s they shall think fit to comply therewith, transmit the same to the Board of Commissioners for the s of India, together with any representation which the court may think proper to make upon the ct of such application; and in case the Board of Commissioners shall think fit to direct the Court of tors to issue any such licence, the Court of Directors shall forthwith issue the same, upon such con- s as the Court of Directors with the approbation of the Board of Commissioners shall from time to think fit: Provided, that in all cases in which the Board of Commissioners shall direct the Court of tors to issue any such licence, which they shall have declined to issue without such direction, the l circumstances inducing them to give such direction shall be recorded in the books of the Board. —

ties. — All goods, wares, and merchandise, of or belonging to the said Company, exported or imported or into any ports or places under their government in the East Indies, or other places within the of their charter, shall be subject to the payment of the like rates, customs, and duties of import and t, as the goods, wares, and merchandise of the same kinds or sorts, exported or imported in private under the authority of this act, are or shall be subject or liable to be charged with. — § 24.

ties imposed in India. — No new or additional imposition of any duty or tax upon the export, import, nsmit of any goods, wares, or merchandise whatsoever, made by authority of the governor-general, vernor in council, of any of the said Company's presidencies or settlements in the East Indies, or aforesaid, shall be valid or effectual, until the same shall have been sanctioned by the Court of Di- s, with the approbation of the Board of Commissioners. — § 25.

ectors refusing Permission to any Persons to proceed to the East Indies. — When any application •e made to the Court of Directors, for or on behalf of any person or persons desirous of proceeding East Indies, for permission so to do, the said court shall, unless they shall think fit to comply there- transmit every such application, within one month from the receipt thereof, to the Board of Com- oners for the affairs of India; and, in case the commissioners shall not see sufficient objection thereto, l be lawful for them to direct that such person or persons shall, at his, or their own special charge, mitted to proceed to any of the said principal settlements of the Company; and that such person or s shall be furnished by the Court of Directors with a certificate or certificates, signifying that such or persons hath or have so proceeded with the cognizance and under the sanction of the Court of tors. — § 33.

nothing herein contained shall extend to restrict the Court of Directors from offering such repre- ions to the Board of Commissioners, respecting persons so applying for permission to proceed to the ndies, as the court may at any time think fit; and all persons who shall proceed to the East Indies upon their arrival at any place within the limits of the united Company's government, be subject to h rules and regulations as now are, or hereafter may be, in force within those limits. — §§ 34, 35.

ernments in India may declare Certificates and Licences void. — But if any person, having obtained ficate or licence from the Court of Directors, authorising him to proceed to the East Indies, shall time so conduct himself, as in the judgment of the governor-general, or governor of the pre- y within which such person shall be found, to have forfeited his claim to the countenance and ion of the governor of such presidency, it shall be lawful for such governor-general, or governor, er, to declare that the certificate or licence so obtained by such person shall be void, from a day so amed, and such person may be sent forthwith to the United Kingdom: Provided nevertheless, that no whose certificate or licence shall have been so vacated, shall be subject or liable to any prosecution ding, or being found in the East Indies, until two months after notice of such order having been to such person, by delivery of a copy thereof, or by leaving the same at the last place of his abode, •ublication of such order in the Gazette of the presidency where such order shall be made. — § 36.

•censed Persons trading illegally. — If any of the subjects of his Majesty, of or belonging to any of jesty's dominions situate without the East Indies and limits of the said Company's charter, other ıch as shall be licensed by the said united Company, or otherwise thereunto lawfully authorised, at any time before the determination of the term hereby granted to the said Company, directly or tly sail to, visit, haunt, frequent, trade, traffic, or adventure to, in, or from the East Indies or parts id, or go, sail, or repair thereto, or be found therein, in any other manner than is prescribed or l by the provisions of this act, and the terms and conditions of any licence or certificate to be granted ue thereof, all such persons shall be deemed and taken to have unlawfully traded and trafficked and they, with all ships and vessels found in their custody, or engaged or concerned in such un- trade or traffic, and the owners, masters, and crews thereof, and all goods, merchandise, treasure, ects, shipped or laden thereon, or taken out of the same, or found in the custody of any such person ons, shall be subject and liable to all the pains, penalties, forfeitures, disabilities, and methods of are contained in any act or acts now in force for the purpose of securing to the said Company the d exclusive right of trading to the East Indies, and other parts within the limits of their charter, the continuance of such sole and exclusive right, and of restraining clandestine and illicit trade in, from the East Indies and parts aforesaid. — § 40.

The act 4 Geo. 4. c. 80., already referred to, enacts, that it shall be lawful for any of his Majesty's su
jects, in ships or vessels registered and navigated according to law, to carry on trade and traffic in a
goods, wares, or merchandise, except tea, as well directly as circuitously, between all ports and plac
belonging either to his Majesty, or to any prince, state, or country at amity with his Majesty, and all po
and places whatsoever situate within the limits of the charter of the Company, except the dominions
the emperor of China; and also from port to port and from place to place within the same limits, exce
China; under such rules and restrictions as are hereinafter mentioned. — § 2.

Company's Trade. — And it shall be lawful for the Company to carry on any trade and traffic which h
Majesty's other subjects may carry on under the authority of this act. — § 3.

Places without Limits of Charter, &c. — Nothing herein shall extend to permit the importation into t
United Kingdom, or into any colony or possession of his Majesty without the limits of the charter of t
East India Company, of any goods, wares, and merchandise, the produce of countries without such lim
which cannot now be legally imported, nor to permit the exportation from the United Kingdom, or fr
such colonies or possessions, to any countries without such limits, of any goods, which cannot now be
gally carried to such countries. — § 4.

Restrictions on Military Stores. — It shall not be lawful for any persons to carry any military stores
any place upon the continent of Asia, between the River Indus and the town of Malacca on the peninsu
of Malacca inclusively, or to the said Company's factory of Bencoolen, save only the said united Compar
or such as shall obtain their licence in writing, or a licence in writing under their authority. — § 5.

Ships trading without Limits to be entered. — It shall not be lawful for any ship or vessel, other th
of the said Company, to proceed from any port or place without the limits of the Company's charter,
any port or place on the continent of Asia, between the River Indus and the town of Malacca inclusi
other than the said Company's principal settlements of Fort William, Fort St. George, Bombay, a
Prince of Wales's Island, until after such ship or vessel shall have been admitted to entry at some one
the said four principal settlements, without a special licence in writing from the Court of Directors. —

Applications for Licence. — When any application shall be made to the said Court of Directors fo
licence, especially authorising any ship or vessel to proceed to any place or places upon the continent
Asia, from the River Indus to the said town of Malacca, other than the said four principal settlemer
the said Court of Directors shall, within fourteen days, unless they think fit to comply therewith, transr
the same to the Board of Commissioners for the affairs of India, together with any representation whi
the said court may think proper to make upon the subject of such application; and in case the said Boa
of Commissioners shall think fit to direct the said Court of Directors to issue such licence, the said Cou
of Directors shall forthwith issue the same, upon such terms as the said Board of Commissioners sh
think fit: Provided always, that in all cases in which the said Board of Commissioners shall direct the sa
Court of Directors to issue any such licence, which they shall have declined to issue without such dir
tion, the special circumstances inducing them to give such directions shall be recorded in the books of
said Board. — § 7.

Additional Ports considered as Settlements. — It shall be lawful for the said Court of Directors, w
the consent of the commissioners for the affairs of India, to declare that any other ports or places
the continent of India, between the Indus and the town of Malacca, or in any island in the East Indi
seas under the government of the said Company or of his Majesty, shall be considered, for the purpo
of this act only, as one of the principal settlements of the Company. — § 8.

Tea Trade. — Nothing herein shall authorise any of his Majesty's subjects, other than the Company,
persons licensed by them, to carry on trade or traffic with the dominions of the emperor of China, or
export or import from or to any ports or places within or without the limits of the Company's chart
any tea, or in any other manner to trade or traffic in tea. — § 9.

Ports for Importation of Indian Goods. — It shall not be lawful to import any goods, wares, or m
chandise, from any port or place within the limits aforesaid, into any port of the United Kingdom, exc
only such as shall be provided with warehouses, together with wet docks or basins, or such other securit
as shall in the judgment of the Commissioners of the Treasury be fit for the deposit of all such goods,
well as for the collection of all duties thereon, and shall have been duly declared so to be, by the order
his Majesty in council, or by order of the lord-lieutenant in council in Ireland: Provided always, that
copies of all such orders shall have been published three times in the London and Dublin Gazette; a
copies of all such orders shall be laid before both houses of parliament in the session next after. — § *

List of Persons and Arms to be made out. — It shall not be lawful for any ship or vessel, other than
ships of the Company, to clear out from any port or place belonging to his Majesty, or to any prince, sta
or country in amity with his Majesty, where any consul or vice-consul shall be resident, for any port
place under the government of his Majesty or of the said Company, situate more to the northward th
11 degrees of south latitude, and between the 64th and 150th degrees of east longitude from London, un
the master shall have made out and exhibited to the collector of customs, or to his Majesty's consu
vice-consul, (as the case may be,) a true list in such form as has been settled in virtue of former acts,
shall from time to time be settled by the Court of Directors, with the approbation of the Board of Co
missioners for the affairs of India, specifying the names, capacities, and descriptions of all persons embar
or intended to be embarked on board, and all arms; and when any such vessel shall have been admi
to entry, the master shall in like manner make out and exhibit to the principal officer of customs a t
list, in form to be settled as aforesaid, specifying the names, capacities, and descriptions of all person
board, or who shall have been on board such vessel from the time of the sailing thereof to the time o
rival, and of all arms on board, or which shall during that time have been on board, and the several ti
and places at which such of the said persons as may have died or left such ship or vessel, or such of
said arms as may have been disposed of, have been disposed of. — § 11.

Whale Fishery Ships. — Ships and vessels clearing out for the southern whale fishery shall be sub
to such and the same restrictions as the ships and vessels of his Majesty's subjects generally engage
trade under the authority of this act are hereby made subject to. — § 12.

Trade with Malta, &c. — All goods and commodities imported under the authority of this act into
island of Malta or its dependencies, or into the port of Gibraltar, from any ports or places within the lir
of the Company's charter, may be re-exported from the said island, port, or places, to the United Ki
dom, and imported into any of the ports where such goods and commodities may be lawfully imported
like manner as if such goods and commodities were imported directly from the place of their grov
production, or manufacture; any thing in 3 Geo. 4. c. 43., or in any other act, to the contrary notw
standing. — § 13.

Duties on Importation into America. — And after the passing of this act there shall be raised, lev
collected, and paid, upon the importation of any goods, wares, and merchandise, the produce or ma
facture of any country within the limits of the Company's charter, into his Majesty's possession
America and the West Indies, from any port or place not being a port or place in the United Kingd
the same duties which are payable on such goods, if imported into such possessions from the Un
Kingdom; and the same shall be raised, levied, collected, paid, and received under the managemer
the commissioners of customs in England, and applied as the duties authorised by 3 Geo. 4. c. 45. —

False Lists of Passengers, &c. — And if any commander or other officer of any ship or vessel enga
in trade under the authority of this act, shall knowingly take on board, or connive at the taking on bo
any persons, or exhibit any false or incomplete list of persons embarked or intended to be embarked,

---

* The ports of London, Liverpool, Bristol, Hull, Dublin, Cork, Belfast, Leith, Greenock, and Port G
gow, have been declared proper places for the importation of East Indian goods.

the said act of the 53 Geo. 3., or this act, every such commander or officer shall forfeit for every 100l., to be recovered in the same manner as penalties imposed by the said act of 53 Geo. 3.; one rt of which penalty shall belong to such person as shall inform or sue, and the other half to the ny; and if the Company shall inform or sue, then the whole shall belong to the said Company. —

rs not deemed British Seamen. — No Asiatic sailors, Lascars, or natives of any of the territories the limits of the charter of the Company, although born in territories under the government of esty, or the East India Company, shall at any time be deemed to be British sailors, within the g of any act relating to the navigation of British ships, for the purpose of entitling any ship to be to be a British ship navigated according to law, and to have the privileges and advantages of ships having the master and three fourths of the mariners British subjects: Provided also, that it lawful for his Majesty, by proclamation, upon or after the commencement of any hostilities, to all merchant ships or any other trading vessels, and all privateers, to be manned wholly, or in any portions as shall be specified in any such proclamation, with such Asiatic sailors, Lascars, or during such periods as shall be specified in such proclamation. — § 20.

h Seamen proportioned to Tonnage. — And "as Lascars and other natives of the East are not to be equal in strength and use to European or other seamen, and the requiring the proportion fourths of British seamen in ships having as part of the crew Lascars and natives of the East ompel such ships to carry a larger number of British seamen than other ships, or to employ a number of Lascars and natives of the East than would be sufficient to make a proper crew," it is , than any ship duly registered, manned in part with Lascars or natives of India, which shall be ded by a British master, and navigated by four British seamen, as part of the crew, for every 100 her registered burthen, and so in proportion for any part of 100 tons, shall be deemed to be navi-ccording to law as to the crew of any such ship, although the number of such British seamen shall qual to the proportion of three fourths of the whole crew. — § 21.

's licensed to sail without due Proportion of British Seamen. — And "as it may not always be pos-procure the due proportion of British seamen at ports in India, for vessels sailing from India," it ed, that it shall be lawful for any of the governments of the East India Company in India, or for ernor or lieutenant-governor of any colony, territory, or island belonging to his Majesty, within ts of the said charter, on application made by the owner or commander of any ship, and after ascertained by due inquiry that a sufficient number of British seamen cannot be procured for the any ship sailing from India, within ten days from such application, to certify the same, and license p to sail with a less proportion of British seamen than required by law; and every such ship, on board such licence, and the proportion of British seamen therein specified, shall be deemed to ated according to law, notwithstanding such deficiency of British seamen. — § 22.

h Seamen not required in Country Trade. — Nothing in this act, or any other act, shall extend to any number of British seamen to be on board as part of the crew of any ship employed in trade ween ports and places within the limits of the charter of the said Company, including the Cape of ope. — § 23.

nor may enact Rules as to Lascars. — It shall be lawful for the governor-general of Fort in Bengal, in council, as soon as may be, to make, ordain, and publish, and from time to time, as may require, to repeal and alter, and newly to make, ordain, and publish such rules and regula-to be observed by masters, officers, and owners of ships trading under the authority of this act, which shall be wholly or in part composed of Asiatic sailors, Lascars, or natives of any of the thin the limits of the charter of the said Company, for the due supply of provisions, clothing, and cessary accommodation of such Asiatic sailors, Lascars, and natives, whilst they shall be on board, st absent from the places to which they shall belong, and until they shall be carried back to the which they may belong, or from whence they may have been brought, and for the conveyance uch Asiatic sailors, Lascars, or natives, within a reasonable time to be fixed by such rules or re-s. — § 25.

Lascars to be exhibited, &c. — The master of every ship trading under the authority of this act, ter the passing of this act shall arrive at any port in the United Kingdom, and which shall have , or during any part of her voyage shall have had on board, either as part of her crew or in any aracter, or for any other reason, any Asiatic sailor, Lascar, or native of places within the limits arter of the said Company, before such ship shall be admitted to entry, shall make out and exhibit incipal officers of the customs, a true list and description of every such Asiatic sailor, Lascar, or vhich shall then be, or who, during any part of her voyage, shall have been, on board such ship, ue account of what shall have become of every such Asiatic sailor, Lascar, and native, who may n and shall not then be on board. — § 27.

ies under this Act as to Lascars. — For every breach or non-observance of any rule or regulation de in pursuance of this act, which shall have happened, and for every omission to make out and such list, description, account, or statement, the master and all the owners of the ship on board y such Asiatic sailor, Lascar, or native, shall be or shall have been, shall forfeit 10l. for every ailor, Lascar, or native, in respect of whom such breach, non-observance, omission, or defect e happened. — § 28.

acy of Lascars. — If any Asiatic sailor, Lascar, or native, shall at any time be convicted of an act cy under any of the laws in force, it shall be lawful for the justices, before whom such conviction e place, to direct that he shall be shipped on board any ship bound to the place, or as near as may place to which he shall belong, or from which he shall have been brought, and the commander shall be willing to take charge of him, at the expense of the persons liable under any rule or re-to be made as before-mentioned, or of any other person being otherwise willing to defray the d it shall be lawful for the commander of any such ship to keep and detain him on board for the r which he shall be shipped. — § 31.

sed Lascars to be supported. — If any Asiatic sailor, Lascar, or native, having been brought to ed Kingdom on board any ship not being a ship of war in the service of his Majesty, shall, after ng of this act, be found within the United Kingdom in distress for want of food, clothing, or other es, it shall be lawful for the said Company to supply necessary and reasonable relief to such per-to maintain them until they shall be sent on board some ship bound for some place within the resaid; and also to advance the money necessary to procure such persons proper and sufficient their homes; and all such sums as the said Company shall pay for such relief or maintenance, e home, shall become a joint and several debt due to the said Company from the commander or such ship on board whereof such persons shall have been brought into the kingdom, and shall rable as so much money paid to and for the use of such owners in any of the courts of the United or in the East Indies, if the owner shall reside there: and in all such actions and suits, where ompany shall recover, they shall be entitled to full costs. — § 34.

regulations as to manifests, entry, &c. of East India commodities, in the article IMPORTATION.

2. Company's Stock, General Courts, Courts of Directors, Committees, &c.

ny's Stock — forms a capital of 6,000,000l., into which all persons, natives or foreigners, males s, bodies politic or corporate (the Governor and Company of the Bank of England only excepted), erty to purchase, without limitation of amount. Since 1793, the dividends have been 10½ per which they are limited by the act of 1813.

K k

General Courts. — The proprietors in general court assembled are empowered to enact bye-
declare dividends, and in other respects are competent to the complete investigation, regulation
control of every branch of the Company's concerns; but, for the more prompt despatch of busines
executive detail is vested in a Court of Directors   A General Court is required to be held once i
months of March, June, September, and December, in each year. No one can be present at a Ge
Court unless possessed of 500*l.* stock; nor can any person vote upon the determination of any que
who has not been in possession of 1,000*l.* stock for the preceding twelve months, unless such stock
been obtained by bequest or marriage. Persons possessed of 1,000*l.* stock are empowered to give a
vote; 3,000*l.* are a qualification for two votes; 6,000*l.* for three votes; and 10,000*l.* and upwards fo
votes. The number of proprietors on the Company's books in 1825, were 2,003; of these, 1,494 were
lified to give single votes; 392, two votes; 69, three votes; and 48, four votes. Upon any special occa
nine proprietors, duly qualified by the possession of 1,000*l.* stock, may, by a requisition in writing
Court of Directors, call a General Court; which the directors are required to summon within ten
or, in default, the proprietors may call such court by notice affixed upon the Royal Exchange.
such courts the questions are decided by a majority of voices; in case of an equality, the determin
must be by the treasurer drawing a lot. Nine proprietors may, by a requisition in writing, dem
ballot upon any question, which shall not be taken within twenty-four hours after the breaking up
General Court.

Court of Directors. — The Court of Directors is composed of twenty-four members, chosen
among the proprietors, each of whom must be possessed of 2,000*l.* stock; nor can any director, after
chosen, act longer than while he continues to hold stock. Of these, six are chosen on the second
nesday in April in each year, to serve for four years, in the room of six who have completed such se
After an interval of twelve months, those who had gone out by rotation are eligible to be re-elect
the ensuing four years. No person who has been in the Company's civil or military service in I
eligible to be elected a director until he shall have been a resident in England two years after quitti
service. The directors choose annually, from amongst themselves, a chairman and a deputy chai
They are required by bye-laws to meet once in every week at least; but they frequently meet ofter
occasion requires. Not less than thirteen can form a court. Their determinations are guided
majority; in case of an equality, the question must be decided by the drawing of a lot by the treas
upon all questions of importance, the sense of the court is taken by ballot. The Company's officers
at home and abroad, receive their appointments immediately from the court; to whom they are re
sible for the due and faithful discharge of the trust reposed in them. The patronage is, neverthel
arranged, as that each member of the court separately participates therein.

Statement of the Committees into which the Court of Directors is divided, with the Number of Me
in each, and the Duties they have to perform.

Name of Committees.	How each Committee is composed.	Duties of each Committee in London.
Secret.	Of three members, the chairman, deputy, and senior committee.	To receive and consider all communications of a par larly private and delicate nature, in the political de ment, both with his Majesty's ministers and the I government, and also with the Board of Control, it may be deemed inexpedient, at least in the first inst to render liable to general discussion. This comm may justly be termed the cabinet council of the Com Its functions, indeed, are specially defined and regu by act of parliament: its meetings are of course depe on the occurrence of matters requiring the comm attention; not stated or constant.
Correspondence.	Of the two chairs, and nine senior directors.	With the exception of the few matters which, for s reasons, are confined to the secret committee, on this devolve the whole of the political system and arrange of the Indian empire, together with some of its comm transactions, all communications with his Majesty's sters, the Board of Control, and the various departme the Indian executive. The suggestion, approval, or ch of political measures, and especially a revision of all actions, civil and military, together with the princi rangement of the home and foreign establishments the destination of ships to their respective voyages, this committee prepared for the decision of the Co Directors.
Treasury.	Same eleven members as the last.	To superintend the whole of the payments and re of the Company in this country.
Government Troops and Stores.	The same.	To regulate all matters relating to those subjects be the Company in this country.
Lawsuits.	The same.	To manage all lawsuits in behalf of the Company the aid of their legal advisers, and subject to the re of the court.
Military Funct.	The same eleven as above, and also three of the junior directors.	To pass and examine all accounts, petitions, and r rials, from invalid or disabled military officers on the pany's establishment, and what is called Lord Clive's and report the same to the Court of Directors.
Accounts.	Of eight members, including the chairs and six first junior directors.	To pass and examine all accounts, compare and rev pecuniary demands on the Company, as bills of exch and generally to ascertain that all disbursements ar perly vouched and made up.
Buying.	Of the same eight members as the last.	To provide and inspect the price, quality, and con of the various articles composing the Company's ments, especially woollens.
House (Committee)	Of the same eight members as the last.	To take the charge and management of the East House, and the departments thereunto attached, a repairs, alterations, &c. in the building.
Warehouses.	Of the same eight members as the last.	By them the whole of the investments, and genera whole of the commercial affairs of the Company, at and abroad, are transacted, discussed, and prepared ultimate decision of the Court of Directors.
Private Trade.	Of nine members, including the two chairs and seven last junior directors.	Their duty is to superintend the private trade through the Company's hands, to prepare and se freight accounts for the same; also to examine ships nals, and to superintend the direction of all craft car by the Company's shipping.

...me of Committees.	How each Committee is composed.	Duties of each Committee in London.
...ping.	Of the same nine members as the last.	They arrange the hiring of ships, examination of officers, the regulation of all troops, and other persons proceeding to India; also the trade of freight and war contingencies, and all points relating to charterparties.
...l College.	Of twelve members, including the two chairs, and six senior and four jun. directors.	To superintend the concerns of that establishment.
...tary Seminary.	Of thirteen members, including the two chairs and five of the senior directors.	Ditto ditto ditto.

...8. The chairman and deputy chairman are, by virtue of their office, members of all committees. ...etters and papers on the subject of the Company's affairs are read in court, and referred to the con...ation of a committee, according to their contents. The reference upon ordinary occasions is for the ...nittee [to give such directions therein as they may think fit; but in more important matters, the ...nittee is required to examine the facts, and report an opinion thereon, for the ultimate determination ...e court.

...llowances on Goods sold by the East India Company. — The allowances made on weighable goods, sold ...e Company's warehouses in London, are chiefly *draft* and *supertare.*
...e draft is 1 lb. on every package, or quantity of upwards of 28 lbs.; besides which, a two-ounce weight ...ced with the other weights to give the scale a turn in favour of the buyer. If in weighing the beam ...n, that is, if the scale containing the goods do not preponderate, 1 lb. is struck from the weight: this ...d is also allowed by the customs and excise; but not the two-ounce weight, except by the excise, and ...n tea only.
...taring goods, that is, in weighing the packages, the scale in which the weights are placed is allowed ...ponderate.
...making an average tare, if the mean of the packages tared should prove a fraction, the next whole ...er above it is taken. Thus, if the average or mean be 28¾ lbs., the allowance is 29 lbs. This is al...d on all goods by the customs and excise, as well as by the Company.
...all goods (tea excepted) 1 lb. is allowed by the Company, but not by the customs or excise, on ...ges that tare 28 lbs. or upwards; and if the tare is taken at an average, and there be a fraction, it is ...ised to a pound, as per example; viz. —

Actual average tare	-	-	28¾ lbs.
Fraction wanting	-	-	¼
			29
Supertare	-	-	1
Tare allowed	-	-	30 lbs.

...Quarter Chests of Tea. — If on averaging those tares they turn out even pounds, no further allow...s made, unless the chest weigh gross 8¼ lbs. or upwards; in which case 1 lb. for supertare is allowed ...h package; but if there be a fraction, the fraction wanting only is allowed. Thus, if the average ...e 22 lbs., the allowance is 23 lbs.; and it is the same if the average tare be 22¾ lbs.
...Half Chests of Tea. — If on averaging those tares they turn out even pounds, 1 lb. is allowed for ...are on each package; and if there be a fraction, it is reckoned a pound as before. Thus, if the ...ge tare be 36 lbs., the allowance is 37 lbs.; and if 36¼ lbs., the allowance is 38 lbs.
...hole Chests of Tea. — If on averaging those tares they turn out even pounds, 2 lbs. are allowed on ...ackage for supertare; but if there be a fraction, 1 lb. only and the fraction wanting are allowed. ...if the average tare be 66 lbs., the allowance is 68 lbs.; and it is the same if the average tare is 66¾ lbs.
...*. — The foregoing allowances on tea are also made by the excise; but the customs allow only the ...for a fraction as before stated.
...ilks. — Bengal and China raw silks are weighed in new Hessen bags in the following manner: — ...rge Bengal bag, containing about 300 lbs., is tared upon the average at 6 lbs.; and 2 lbs. more are al...for supertare. The small Bengal bag, containing about 150 lbs, is tared on the average at 3 lbs.; and ...ore is allowed for supertare. The China silk bag, containing about 100 lbs., is tared on the average ...; and 1 lb. is allowed for supertare. Thus, the allowance on the large Bengal bag is 8 lbs.; on the ...4 lbs.; and on the China bag, 3 lbs. The two-ounce weight is invariably put into the scale, and the ...aft is also allowed; but this pound draft, not being allowed by the customs, is charged with duty to ...yers by the Company. — (See *Kelly's Cambist,* vol. i. p. 235.)

Distinction of Castes in India. — *Inaccuracy of the Representations as to the Inhabit*...*eing unalterably attached to ancient Customs and Practices.* — *Extensive and growing* ...*nd for English Goods.* — *Obstacles to the Extension of the Trade; how they may be* ...*ed.* — *Trade conducted by the Company at a heavy Loss.* — We have taken occasion, ...e preceding sketch of the history of the East India Company, repeatedly to notice ...mall extent of the trade carried on by its agency. It has been contended, however, ...his is to be ascribed, not to the deadening influence of monopoly, but to the ...iar state of the people of India. A notion has long been prevalent in this quar...the world, that the Hindoos are a race unsusceptible of change or improvement ...y sort; that every man is brought up to the profession of his father, and can ...e in none else; and that, owing to the simplicity and unalterableness of their ...s, they never can be consumers, at least to any considerable extent, of foreign ...odities. " What is now in India, has always been there, and is likely still to ...ue." — (*Robertson's Disquisition,* p. 202.) The Hindoos of this day are said to ...e same as the Hindoos of the age of Alexander the Great. The description of them ...by Arrian has been quoted as applying to their actual situation. It is affirmed ...hey have neither improved nor retrograded; and we are referred to India as to ...ntry in which the institutions and manners that prevailed three thousand years ago ...ill be found in their pristine purity! The President de Goguet lays it down distinctly,

in his learned and invaluable work on the origin of laws, arts, and sciences, that India " every trade is confined to a particular caste, and can be exercised only by the whose parents professed it." — (*Origin of Laws, &c.* Eng. trans. vol. iii. p. 24.) I Robertson says, that " *the station of every Hindoo is unalterably fixed ; his destiny is irr vocable ; and the walk of life is marked out, from which he must never deviate.*" — (*Disq sition on India,* p. 199.) The same opinions are maintained by later authorities. D Tennant says, that " the whole Indian community is divided into four great classe and each class is stationed between certain walls of separation, which are impassable the purest virtue, and most conspicuous merit." — (Quoted by *Mr. Rickards,* p. 6.) Th unalterable destiny of individuals has been repeatedly assumed in the despatches an official papers put forth by the East India Company ; and has been referred to on occasions by them and their servants, as a proof that the depressed and miserable co dition of the natives is not owing to misgovernment, or to the weight of the burdens la upon them ; and that it is in vain to think of materially improving their condition, or making them acquainted with new arts, or giving them new habits, so long as the insti tution of castes, and the prejudices to which it has given rise, preserve their ascendan unimpaired.

But notwithstanding the universal currency which the opinions now referred to ha obtained, and the high authority by which they are supported, they are, in all the mo essential respects, entirely without foundation ! The books and codes of the Hindoo themselves, and the minute and careful observations that have recently been made Indian society, have shown that the influence ascribed to the institution of castes by th ancients, and by the more early modern travellers, has been prodigiously exaggerate In the first part of his excellent work on India, Mr. Rickards has established, partly references to the authoritative books of the Hindoos, and partly by his own observation and those of Mr. Colebrook, Dr. Heber, and other high authorities, that the vast m jority of the Hindoo population may, and, in fact, does engage in all sorts of emplo ments. Mr. Rickards has farther shown, that there is nothing in the structure Indian society to oppose any serious obstacle to the introduction of new arts, or t spread of improvement ; and that the causes of the poverty and misery of the peop must be sought for in other circumstances than the institution of castes, and the natu of Hindoo superstition.

The early division of the population into the four great classes of priests (Brahmin soldiers (Cshatryas), husbandmen and artificers (Vaisyas), and slaves (Sudras), w maintained only for a very short period. The Hindoo traditions record that a par intermixture of these classes took place at a very remote epoch ; and the mixed bro thence arising were divided into a vast variety of new tribes, or castes, to whom, speaki generally, no employments are forbidden.

" The employments," says Mr. Rickards, " allowed to these mixed and impure castes, may be said to every description of handicraft, and occupation, for which the wants of human society have create demand. Though many seem to take their names from their ordinary trade or profession, and some h duties assigned them too low, and disgusting, for any others to perform, but from the direst necessi yet no employment, generally speaking, is forbidden to the mixed and impure tribes, excepting thre the prescribed duties of the sacerdotal class ; viz. teaching the *Vedas,* officiating at a sacrifice, and rece ing presents from a pure-handed giver ; which three are exclusively *Brahminical.*"

Mr. Colebrook, who is acknowledged on all hands to be one of the very high authorities, as to all that respects Indian affairs, has a paper in the fifth volume of Asiatic Researches on the subject of castes. In this paper, Mr. Colebrook states th the *Jatimala,* a Hindoo work, enumerates *forty-two* mixed classes springing from intercourse of a man of inferior class with a woman of a superior class, or in the *inve* order of the classes. Now, if we add to these the number that must have sprung fr intermixture in the *direct* order of the classes, and the hosts further arising from continued intermixture of the mixed tribes amongst themselves ; we shall not certai be disposed to dissent from Mr. Colebrook's conclusion, " that the sub-divisions of th classes have further multiplied distinctions to an *endless variety.*"

Mr. Colebrook has given the following distinct and accurate account of the p fessions and employments of the several classes at the present day. It forms a curi commentary on the " irrevocable destiny " of Dr. Robertson, and the " impassable wal of Dr. Tennant.

" A *Brahman,* unable to subsist by his duties, may live by the duty of a soldier ; if he cannot get a sistence by either of these employments, he may apply to tillage and attendance on cattle, or ga competence by traffic, avoiding certain commodities. A *Cshatrya* in distress, may subsist by all t means ; but he must not have recourse to the highest functions. In seasons of distress a further lati is given. The practice of medicine, and other learned professions, painting, and other arts, work for wa menial service, alms, and usury, are among the modes of subsistence allowed both to the *Brahman* Cshatrya. A *Vaisya,* unable to subsist by his own duties, may descend to the servile acts of a *Sudra* : a *Sudra,* not finding employment by waiting on men of the higher classes, may subsist by handicr principally following those mechanical operations, as joinery and masonry, and practical arts, as pain and writing, by which he may serve men of superior classes ; and although a man of a lower class general restricted from the acts of a higher class, the *Sudra* is expressly permitted to become a trade a husbandman.

sides the particular occupation assigned to each of the mixed classes, they have the alternative of
ng that profession, which regularly belongs to the class from which they derive their origin on
ther's side; those at least have such an option, who are born in the direct order of the classes. *The
lasses are also permitted to subsist by any of the duties of a Sudra, that is, by menial service, by
rts, by commerce, and agriculture.* Hence it appears, THAT ALMOST EVERY OCCUPATION, THOUGH
RLY IT BE THE PROFESSION OF A PARTICULAR CLASS, IS OPEN TO MOST OTHER CLASSES; and that the
ons, far from being rigorous, do in fact reserve only the peculiar profession of the *Brahman*, which
in teaching the *Veda*, and officiating at religious ceremonies."
have thus," says Mr. Rickards, by whom this passage has been quoted, "the highest existing
ty for utterly rejecting the doctrine of the whole Hindoo community 'being divided into four
' and of their peculiar prerogatives being guarded inviolate by 'impassable walls of separation.' It
lear, that the intermixture of castes had taken place, to an indefinite extent, at the time when
rma Sastra was composed, which Sir William Jones computes to be about 880 years B. C.; for the
lasses are specified in this work, and it also refers, in many places, to past times, and to events
course of time only could have brought about. The origin of the intermixture is therefore lost
emotest and obscurest antiquity; and having been carried on through a long course of ages, a he-
eous mass is every where presented to us, in these latter times, without a single example in any
ar state, or kingdom, or separate portion of the Hindoo community, of that quadruple division of
which has been so confidently insisted upon.
ve myself seen carpenters of five or six different castes, and as many different bricklayers, em-
n the same building. The same diversity of castes may be observed among the craftsmen in dock-
nd all other great works; and those, who have resided for any time in the principal commercial
India, must be sensible, that every increasing demand for labour, in all its different branches and
of old and new arts, has been speedily and effectually supplied, in spite of the tremendous insti-
f castes; which we are taught to believe forms so impassable an obstruction to the advancement
n industry."

difficult to suppose that the directors of the East India Company should not have
arly aware of the fallacy of the opinions as to the fixedness of Indian habits. So
wever, as we know, they have not, in this instance, evinced any acquaintance with
coveries of their servants. On the contrary, in all the discussions that took place
spect to the opening of the trade in 1814, the Company invariably contended that
ease of trade to India could be expected. In a letter of the chairman and deputy
an to the Right Honourable Robert Dundas, dated 13th of January, 1809, it is
that the small demand for foreign commodities in India "results from the nature
Indian people, their climate, and their usages. The articles of first necessity their
untry furnishes, more abundantly and more cheaply than it is possible for Europe
ply them. The labour of the great body of the common people only enables them
ist on rice, and to wear a slight covering of cotton cloth; they, therefore, *can pur-
one of the superfluities we offer them.* The comparatively few in better circum-
restricted, like the rest, by numerous religious and civil customs, of which all
narkably tenacious, find few of our commodities to their taste; and their climate,
milar to ours, renders many of them unsuitable to their use; so that a commerce
n them and us cannot proceed far upon the principle of supplying mutual wants.
except woollens, in a very limited degree, for mantles in the cold season, and
on a scale very limited, to be worked up by their own artisans for the few
they need, hardly any of our staple commodities find a vent among the Indians;
er exports which Europe sends to India being chiefly consumed by the European
ion there, and some of the descendants of the early Portuguese settlers, all of
taken collectively, form but a small body, in view to any question of national
rce." — (*Papers published by authority of the East India Company*, 1813, p. 21.)
volume from which we have made this extract contains a variety of passages to
e effect. So confident, indeed, were the Company that they had carried the trade
a to the utmost extent of which it was capable, that it is expressly stated, in reso-
passed in a General Court held at the India House, on the 26th of January, 1813,
o large or sudden addition can be made to the amount of British exports to India
a;" that the Company had suffered a loss in attempting to extend this branch of
ide; that the warehouses at home were glutted with Indian commodities for
here was no demand; and that to open the outports to the trade would be no
an "a ruinous transfer of it into new channels, to the destruction of immense and
stablishments, and the beggary of many thousands of industrious individuals."
ily, however, these representations were unable to prevent the opening of the
nd the result has sufficiently demonstrated their fallacy. The enterprise and
of individuals has vastly increased our exports to India—to that very country
he Company had so confidently pronounced was, and would necessarily continue
icapable of affording any additional outlet for our peculiar products!
ommercial accounts for 1812 and 1813 were unfortunately destroyed by the fire
ustom-house. The trade to India was opened on the 10th of April, 1814; and
ear the declared or real value of the products exported from Great Britain to
tries eastward of the Cape of Good Hope, excepting China, by the East India
y, was 826,558*l*., and by the private traders, 1,048,132*l*. In 1817, the Com-
xports had declined to 638,382*l*., while those of the private traders had increased
,333*l*.; and in 1828, the former had sunk to only 488,601*l*., while the latter had
d to 3,979,072*l*., being more than double the total exports to India, as well by
pany as by private traders, in 1814!

The Company state, and no doubt truly, that they have lost a very large sum in tempting to extend the demand for British woollens in India and China, which, withstanding, continues very limited. But in their efforts to force the sale of wool they seem to have forgotten that we had attained to great excellency in the manufac of cotton stuffs, the article principally made use of as clothing in Hindostan; and notwithstanding the cheapness of labour in India, the advantage we derived from superior machinery might enable us to offer cotton stuffs to the natives at a lower than they could afford to manufacture them for. No sooner, however, had the been opened to private adventurers, than this channel of enterprise was explored; the result has been, that, instead of bringing cottons from India to England, the for has become *one of the best and most extensive markets for the cottons of the la* We question, indeed, whether, in the whole history of commerce, another equally stri example can be produced of the powerful influence of competition in opening new and almost boundless fields for the successful prosecution of commercial enterprise.

In 1814, the first year of the free trade to India, the exports of cotton amounte 817,000 yards, of which only about 170,000 yards were exported by the Company! progress of the trade will be seen in the following statement: —

Account of the Quantities of printed and plain Cotton Stuffs exported to all Par the East except China, and of the declared Values of those exported by the East I Company and the Private Trade, since 1814.

	Quantity of British Cotton Manufacture exported.		Value of British Cotton Manufacture exporte		
Years.	Printed.	Plain.	By the East India Company.	By Private Trade.	Total.
	Yds.	*Yds.*	*£*	*£*	*£*
1814	604,800	213,408	17,778	91,702	109,480
1815	866,077	489,399	4,948	137,462	142,410
1816	991,147	714,611	372	160,162	160,534
1817	2,848,705	2,468,024	35	422,779	422,814
1818	4,227,665	4,614,381	349	700,543	700,892
1819	3,713,601	3,414,060	181	461,087	461,268
1820	7,602,245	6,724,031	1,605	832,513	834,118
1821	9,979,866	9,910,736	6,108	1,078,332	1,084,440
1822	9,670,651	13,830,016	5,281	1,139,776	1,145,057
1823	9,867,523	15,133,862	-	1,128,468	1,128,468
1824	9,153,550	14,551,876	13,092	1,100,385	1,113,477
1825	10,682,207	16,487,422	2,798	1,034,073	1,058,871
1826	14,985,370	28,840,788	2,960	991,059	994,019
1827	12,969,365	32,047,485	786	1,613,731	1,624,517

And, during the last three years, there has been a considerable increase of the qu exported.

The demand for several other articles of British manufacture has recently incre though not in the same unprecedented manner as cotton, with considerable rap Notwithstanding all that has been said as to the immutability of Hindoo habits, th is not to be denied, that a taste for European products and customs is rapidly spre itself over India. And the fair presumption is, that it will continue to gain g according as education is more diffused, and as the natives come to be better acqua with our language, arts, and habits. The authenticity of Dr. Heber's statements c be called in question; and there are many passages in different parts of his journa might be quoted in corroboration of what has now been stated. Our limits, how will only permit us to make a very few extracts.

" Nor have the religious prejudices, and the unchangeableness of the Hindoo habits, been less e rated. Some of the best informed of their nation, with whom I have conversed, assure me, that ha most remarkable customs of civil and domestic life are borrowed from their Mahommedan conqu and *at present there is an obvious and increasing disposition to imitate the English in every thing*, has already led to very remarkable changes, and will, probably, to still more important. The w natives now all affect to have their houses decorated with Corinthian pillars, and filled with Engli niture; they drive the best horses and the most dashing carriages in Calcutta; many of them English fluently, and are tolerably read in English literature; and the children of one of our friend one day dressed in jackets and trowsers, with round hats, shoes and stockings. In the Bengalee papers, of which there are two or three, politics are canvassed with a bias, as I am told, incl whiggism; and one of their leading men gave a great dinner, not long since, in honour of the S revolution: among the lower orders the same feeling shows itself more beneficially in a growing of caste." — (Vol. ii. p. 306.)

" To say that the Hindoos or Mussulmans are deficient in any essential feature of a civilised po an assertion which I can scarcely suppose to be made by any who have lived with them; their m are at least as pleasing and courteous as those in the corresponding stations of life among ourselves houses are larger, and, according to their wants and climate, to the full as convenient as ours; th chitecture is at least as elegant; nor is it true that in the mechanic art they are inferior to the run of European nations. Where they fall short of us, (which is chiefly in agricultural implemen the mechanics of common life,) they are not, so far as I have understood of Italy and the south of surpassed in any degree by the people of those countries. Their goldsmiths and weavers prod beautiful fabrics as their own; and it is so far from true that they are obstinately wedded to their terns, that they show an anxiety to imitate our models, and do imitate them very successfully. Th built by native artists at Bombay are notoriously as good as any which sail from London or Liv The carriages and gigs which they supply at Calcutta are as handsome, though not as durable, a

ng Acre. In the little town of Monghyr, 300 miles from Calcutta, I had pistols, double-barrelled , and different pieces of cabinet work, brought down to my boat for sale, which in outward form (for ow no further) nobody but perhaps Mr. ———— could detect to be of Hindoo origin ; and at i, in the shop of a wealthy native jeweller, I found brooches, ear-rings, snuff-boxes, &c. of the latest ls (so far as I am a judge), and ornamented with French devices and mottos."—(Vol. ii. p. 382.)

s Bishop Heber penetrated into the interior of India, he found the same taste as in utta, for European articles and for luxuries, to prevail every where among the natives, Benares, he writes as follows : —

ut what surprised me still more, as I penetrated further into it, were the large, lofty, and handsome ing-houses, the beauty and apparent richness of the goods exposed in the bazaars, and the evident of business. Benares is in fact a very industrious and wealthy, as well as a very holy city. It is the mart where the shawls of the north, the diamonds of the south, and the muslins of Dacca and the rn provinces centre ; and it has very considerable silk, cotton, and fine woollen manufactories of its while English hardware, swords, shields, and spears, from Lucknow and Monghyr, and *those Euro- luxuries and elegancies which are daily becoming more popular in India*, circulate from hence gh Bundlecund, Gorruckpoor, Nepaul, and other tracts which are removed from the main artery of ανges."—(Vol. i. p. 289.)

roceeding still further into the interior of the country, and when at Nusseerabad, nt above 1,000 miles from Calcutta, the bishop continues his journal in the same n ; viz.

uropean articles are, at Nusseerabad*, as might be expected, very dear ; the shops are kept by a and two Parsees from Bombay : they had in their list all the usual items of a Calcutta warehouse. h cotton cloths, both white and printed, are to be met with commonly in wear among the people of untry, and may, I learned to my surprise, be bought best and cheapest, as well as all kinds of hard- crockery, writing-desks, &c., at Pallee, a large town and celebrated mart in Marwar, on the edge of sert, several days' journey west of Joudpoor, where, till very lately, no European was known to have ated."—(Vol. ii. p. 56.)

s to the character of the Hindoos, their capacity, and even anxious desire for im- ement, the bishop's testimony is equally clear and decided ; and as this is a point re-eminent importance, the reader's attention is requested to the following state- s : —

n the schools which have been lately established in this part of the empire, of which there are at at nine established by the Church Missionary, and eleven by the Christian Knowledge Societies, some unexpected facts have occurred. As all direct attempts to convert the children are disclaimed, the ts send them without scruple. But it is no less strange than true, that there is no objection made use of the Old and New Testament as a class-book ; that so long as the teachers do not urge them what will make them lose their caste, or to be baptized, or to curse their country's gods, they readily it to every thing else ; and not only Mussulmans, but Brahmins, stand by with perfect coolness, and sometimes with apparent interest and pleasure, while the scholars, by the road side, are reading the of the creation and of Jesus Christ."—(Vol. ii. p. 290.)

earing all I had heard of the prejudices of the Hindoos and Mussulmans, I certainly did not at all to find that the common people would, not only without objection, but with the greatest thankful- end their children to schools on Bell's system ; and they seem to be fully sensible of the advantages red by writing, arithmetic, and, above all, by a knowledge of English. There are now in Calcutta, e surrounding villages, twenty boys' schools containing 60 to 120 each ; and twenty-three girls', f 25 or 30."—(Vol. ii. p. 300.)

the same holy city (Benares) I visited another college, founded lately by a wealthy Hindoo banker, trusted by him to the management of the Church Missionary Society, in which, besides a gramma- nowledge of the Hindoostanee language, as well as Persian and Arabic, the senior boys could pass examination in English grammar, in Hume's History of England, Joyce's Scientific Dialogues, the he globes, and the principal facts and moral precepts of the Gospel ; most of them writing beautifully Persian, and very tolerably in the English character, and excelling most boys I have met with in uracy and readiness of their arithmetic."—(Vol. ii. p. 388.)

e different nations which I have seen in India, (for it is a great mistake to suppose that all India led by a single race, or that there is not as great a disparity between the inhabitants of Guzerat, , the Dooab, and the Deckan, both in language, manners, and physiognomy, as between any four s in Europe,) have of course, in a greater or less degree, the vices which must be expected to at- arbitrary government, a demoralising and absurd religion, and (in all the independent states, and e of the districts which are partially subject to the British) a laxity of law, and an almost universal nce of intestine feuds and habits of plunder. Their general character, however, has much which emely pleasing to me ; they are brave, courteous, intelligent, and most eager after knowledge and ement, with a remarkable talent for the sciences of geometry, astronomy, &c., as well as for the painting and sculpture. In all these points they have had great difficulties to struggle with, both e want of models, instruments, and elementary instruction ; the indisposition, or rather the horror, ined, till lately, by many among their European masters, for giving them instruction of any kind ; w from the real difficulty which exists of translating works of science into languages which have esponding terms."—(Vol. ii. p. 409.)

en if our space permitted, it would be unnecessary to add to these extracts. The nd circumstances now mentioned, must, we think, satisfy every one that there is g in the nature of Indian society, in the institution of castes as at present existing, he habits and customs of the natives, to hinder them from advancing in the career lisation, commerce, and wealth. " It may safely be asserted," says Mr. Hamilton, with so vast an extent of fertile soil, peopled by so many millions of tractable and rious inhabitants, Hindostan is capable of supplying the whole world with any s of tropical merchandise ; the production, in fact, being only limited by the d." We subjoin —

---

* Nusseerabad, near Ajmere, in the heart of the Rajepoot country

An Account of the Value of the Imports and Exports between Great Britain and all Places Eastward the Cape of Good Hope (excepting China); distinguishing the Private Trade from that of the E India Company, in each Year, from 1813 to the latest Period to which the same can be made up.

Years.	Value of Imports into Great Britain, from all Places Eastward of the Cape of Good Hope (except China), according to the Prices at the East India Company's Sales in the respective Years.			Value of Exports from Great Britain to all Places Eastward of the Cape of Good Hope (except China), according to the Declarations of the Exporters.		
	By the East India Company.	Private Trade.	Total Imports.	By the East India Company.	Private Trade.	Total Exports.
	£	£	£	£	£ :	£
1814	4,208,079	4,435,196	8,643,275	826,558	1,048,132	1,874,690
1815	3,016,556	5,119,611	8,136,167	996,248	1,569,513	2,565,761
1816	2,027,703	4,402,082	6,429,785	633,546	1,955,909	2,589,455
1817	2,323,630	4,541,956	6,865,586	638,382	2,750,333	3,388,715
1818	2,305,003	6,901,144	9,206,147	553,385	3,018,779	3,572,164
1819	1,932,401	4,683,367	6,615,768	760,508	1,586,575	2,347,083
1820	1,757,137	4,201,389	5,958,526	971,096	2,066,815	3,037,911
1821	1,743,733	3,031,413	4,775,146	887,619	2,656,776	3,544,395
1822	1,092,329	2,621,334	3,713,663	606,089	2,838,354	3,444,443
1823	1,587,078	4,344,973	5,932,051	458,550	2,957,705	3,416,255
1824	1,194,753	4,410,347	5,605,100	654,783	2,841,795	3,496,578
1825	1,462,692	4,716,083	6,178,775	598,553	2,574,660	3,173,213
1826	1,520,060	5,210,866	6,730,926	990,964	2,480,588	3,471,552
1827	1,612,480	4,068,537	5,681,017	805,610	3,830,580	4,636,190
1828	1,930,107	5,135,073	7,065,180	488,601	3,979,072	4,467,673

Note. — The records of the year 1813 were destroyed by fire.

The principal obstacle in the way of extending the commerce with India, does not consist in any indisposition on the part of the natives to purchase our commodities, but in the difficulty under which they are placed of furnishing equivalents for them. This however, is rather a factitious than a real difficulty. It results more from the discriminating duties laid on several articles of Indian produce, than from their being, in any respect, unsuitable for our markets. Instead of admitting all the articles raised in the different dependencies of the empire for home consumption on the same terms, we have been accustomed to give a marked preference to those raised in the West Indies. We confess, however, that we are wholly unable to discover any grounds on which to vindicate such preference. The protection which every just government is bound to afford to all classes of its subjects, cannot vary with the varying degrees of latitude and longitude under which they happen to live. And as no one denies that the inhabitants of Bengal are, as well as those of Demerara or Jamaica, liege subjects of the British crown, it does seem quite at variance with every fair principle, to treat them worse than the West Indians, by imposing higher duties on their produce when brought to markets.

The preference in favour of West Indian commodities was at one time more considerable than at present; but the following statement shows that it is still very considerable. — (See Table I. next page.)

Since this table was printed, the duties on both East and West India sugars have been reduced, the former to 32s. a cwt., and the latter to 24s. But were the duties on the former reduced to the same level as the latter, and Englishmen allowed to employ themselves in the manufacture of sugar in India, as they are allowed to employ themselves in the manufacture of indigo, the probability is, that the imports of it would, in a few years, be greatly extended, and that it would become an article of great commercial importance.

Besides being unfairly assessed, the duties on several important articles of East India produce are most oppressive in their amount. On black pepper, for example, the price of which may be reckoned at from 3d. to 4d. per lb., the duty is no less than 1s. lb., or about 400 per cent.! — (See Pepper.) Rhubarb, the price of which varies from 6d. to 4s. per lb., is loaded with an equal duty of 2s. 6d. Unrefined borax, an article extensively used in the potteries, and in the smelting of metals, pays a duty of no less than 50 per cent.; and shell-lac, made from the refuse of lac-dye, is charged with a duty of 20 per cent. *ad valorem*, while lac-dye is charged with a duty of only 5 cent.!

We subjoin a statement of the prices, in bond, in London, of the principal articles of East India produce, on the 1st of January last (1831); the duties on such articles and the rate per cent. of the duties. — (See Table II. next page.)

There is another grievance affecting the East India trade, which calls loudly for redress. Goods from America, the West Indies, or any where except the East Indies may be conveyed from one warehousing port to another without payment of the duties But with East India goods a different rule has been established. There are only *two* ports in the empire in which East India goods may be received and warehoused — *antè*, p. 496.); and whenever it becomes necessary to remove these goods to any o

Table I.

...ount of every Article imported from British Possessions East of the Cape of Good Hope, on which
...er Duty of Customs is charged on Import into the United Kingdom, than is charged on the same
...le imported from British Possessions in any other Parts of the World : showing, in three parallel
...ns, the different Rates and the Excess of Duty on each Article ; also, the Amount of Duty levied
...ch of these Articles in the Year 1829, and the Quantity on which the same was levied.

Rates of Duty charged.			Quantities charged with Duty in the Year 1829.		Amount of Duty received in the Year 1829.	
On Importations from British Possessions within the Limits of the East India Company's Charter (except Mauritius).	On Importations from other British Possessions.	Excess of Duty charged on Importations from British Possessions within the Limits of the East India Company's Charter.	Imported from British Possessions within the Limits of the East India Company's Charter (except Mauritius).	Imported from other British Possessions, and charged with a lower Rate of Duty.	On Importations from British Possessions within the Limits of the East India Company's Charter (except Mauritius).	On Importations from other British Possessions, charged with a lower Rate of Duty.
					L. s. d.	L. s. d.
9d. per lb.	6d. per lb. if the produce of and imported from Mauritius, or any British possession in America.	3d. per lb.	Lbs. 974,869	Lbs. 18,499,350	36,557 11 9	462,389 6 11
30s. per gal.	20s. per gal. if the produce of Mauritius, or any British possession in America.	10s. per gal.	Gallons. 26⅝	Gallons. 220¼	40 5 8	220 2 6
15s. per gal. 5d. per lb.	8s. 6d. per gal. ditto ditto 3d. per lb. if the produce of Mauritius, or any British possession in America.	6s. 6d. per gal. 3d. per lb.	619 5/12 Lbs. 3,843½	3,379,845 1/12 Lbs. 44,305	464 11 3 96 1 9	1,436,459 5 2 553 16 3
37s. per cwt.	27s. per cwt. if the produce of and imported from Mauritius, or any British possession in America.	10s. per cwt.	Cwt. qrs.lbs. 118,425 0 12	Cwt. qrs.lbs. 4,196,337 2 9	219,083 8 9	5,665,155 9 6
6d. per lb.	2d. per lb. if the produce of and imported from Mauritius, or any British possession in America, or on the west coast of Africa.	4d. per lb.	Lbs. 983	Lbs. 164,380	24 11 6	1,369 16 8
6s. per lb.	2s.9d. per lb. if the produce of and imported from Mauritius, or any British possession in America.	3d. per lb.	Lbs. 36	Lbs. 28,401	5 8 0	3,905 2 9
30s. per load.	10s. per load, if the growth of any British possession in Africa.	1l. per load.	Loads feet. 117 48 8/12	Loads feet. 16,437 46	176 19 4	8,218 18 2
20 per cent. ad valorem.	5 per cent. ad valorem, if the growth of Mauritius, or any British possession in America.	15 per cent. ad valorem	Declared Value. L. s. d. 883 7 4	Declared Value. L. s. d. 6,763 19 5	176 13 5	338 6 5
			Total Amount of Duty -		L. 256,625 11 5	7,578,610 4 4

Table II.

Goods.	Prices.				Per	Duties.	Duty, Rate per Cent.	
	from		to				from	to
	£ s. d.		£ s. d.					
...	2 10 0		10 0 0		cwt.	1s. 3d. per lb.	70	280
...tida	0 15 0		2 0 0		—	10d. —	233	622
...in, 1st	none.							
2d	15 0 0		20 0 0		—}	2s.	{ 56	74
3d	3 0 0		6 0 0		—}		{ 186	373
...	0 5 0		0 6 0		—	2l. per ton	33	40
...refined	2 15 0		2 16 0		—	6d. per lb.	100	102
...unrefined, or Tincal	2 16 0		2 18 0		—	3d. —	48	50
...or	4 10 0		4 15 0		—	1d. —	9	10
...ons, Ceylon	0 0 9		0 1 4		—}	2s. —	{ 150	266
Malabar	0 3 0		0 4 6		—}		{ 44	66
...Buds			4 0 0		—	1s. —	-	140
...Lignea	3 0 0		3 10 0		—	6d. —	80	93
...on	0 8 0		0 9 6		lb.	6d. —	5	6
Bourbon	0 0 10		0 1 2		—	2s. —	171	240
Amboyna	0 1 6		0 2 2		—	2s. —	92	133
Indicus			1 0 0		cwt.	2s. 6d. —	-	1,400
...al	0 1 1		0 1 2		lb.	4d. —	28	30
...Mocha	3 5 0		4 0 0		cwt.	9d. —	105	128
...Java, brown	nil.					1s. —		
Cheribon	1 11 0		1 18 0		—}	1s. —	{ 295	361
Sumatra	1 10 0		1 15 0		—}		{ 320	373
Bengal	0 0 4½		0 0 5		lb.	4d. per cwt.	{ 5s.6d.	5s.7d.
Madras,	0 0 4½		0 0 5¾		}		{ 5s.6d.	5s.8d.
Surat	3 10 0		4 0 0		cwt.	2s. per lb.	280	320
...s Blood	2 0 0		15 0 0		—	1s. 8d. —	62	465
...	0 4 0		0 5 0		—	15s. per ton	15	19
...	2 10 0		3 5 0		—	5s. per cwt.	7	10
...	5 0 0		16 0 0		—	1s. 8d. per lb.	58	187
...e	1 0 0		1 4 0		—	11s.6d. per cwt.	47	57
Bengal	1 10 0		5 0 0		—	1s. 3d. per lb.	140	406
...mmoniac								

Table II. — *continued.*

Goods.	Prices. from £ s. d.	Prices. to £ s. d.	Per	Duties.	Duty Rate per from
Gum Animi	6 0 0	12 0 0	cwt.	6d. per lb.	23
Arabic	2 10 0	2 15 0	—	6s. per cwt.	10
Lac: Lac Dye, fine D.T.	-	0 3 0	lb. ⎰	‖ ‖	
other marks, good	0 1 6	0 2 0	—		
middling	0 1 0	0 1 6	— ⎱		
ordinary	0 0 6	0 1 0	—		
Shell-lac, dark	4 0 0	5 0 0	cwt. ⎰		
orange	6 0 0	7 0 0	— ⎱		
Hemp	-	20 0 0	ton	free.	
Hides, Buffalo	0 0 3	0 0 5	lb.	per cwt. 2s. 2d. wet	4
Ox and Cow, dry	0 0 3	0 0 4	—	2s. 4d. dry	6
Indigo	-	0 4 0		3d. per lb.	-
Mace	0 4 0	0 5 6		3s. 6d. —	63
Mother-of-Pearl Shells, China	4 5 0	4 10 0	cwt.	-	-
Bombay	2 10 0	3 0 0			
Musk	1 0 0	2 10 0	oz.	5s. per oz.	19
Myrrh	5 0 0	12 0 0	cwt.	1s. 8d. per lb.	77
Nutmegs, 1st	0 3 6	0 4 0	lb. ⎰	2s. 6d. —	62
2d	0 2 10	0 3 2	⎱		
Nux Vomica	0 7 0	0 8 0	cwt.	2s. —	233
Oils, of Aniseed	0 0 4	0 0 5	oz.	4s. —	60
Cassia	0 0 3½	0 0 4	—	1s. per oz.	300
Cinnamon	0 10 0	0 12 0	—	1s. —	8
Cloves	0 0 6	0 0 8	—	2s. —	300
Mace	0 0 1	0 0 2	—	2s. 6d. —	1,200
Nutmegs	0 1 0	0 1 8	—	2s. 6d. —	150
Olibanum	0 10 0	2 6 0	cwt.	2l. per cwt.	87
Pepper, black	0 0 3	0 0 4½	lb. ⎰	1s. per lb.	{ 266 150
white	0 0 4½	0 0 8	⎱		
Rhubarb, common	0 0 6	0 3 0	— ⎰	2s. 6d. —	{ 83 62
fine Dutch, trimmed	0 2 6	0 4 0	⎱		
Rice, Patna	0 15 0	1 0 0	cwt. ⎰		
Bengal, white	0 14 0	0 18 0	—	1s. per cwt.	5
yellow	0 10 0	0 12 0			
Java	-	0 10 0		15s. —	-
Rum, Bengal	-	0 1 9	gallon.	1l. per gallon	-
Safflower	2 0 0	9 0 0	cwt.	2s. 6d. per cwt.	1
Sago, common	0 6 0	0 12 0	—	1s. —	8
pearl	2 10 0	1 10 0	—	10s. —	33
Sal Ammoniac	2 15 0	3 10 0	—	3d. per cwt.	40
Saltpetre	1 15 0	1 17 0	—	6d. per cwt.	1
Sapan Wood	0 5 0	0 10 0	—	15s. per ton	7
Sanders ditto, red	0 12 0	0 15 0	—	1s. —	4
Seeds, Aniseed, Star	-	4 0 0	—	3s. per cwt.	-
Silk, Bengal	0 12 9	0 14 6	lb. ⎰	1d. per lb.	19 13
China	0 11 6	0 17 6	—		
Persian	0 12 0	0 12 6	⎱		
Sugar, Bengal, white	1 7 0	1 13 0	cwt. ⎰	1l. 12s. per cwt.	{ 94 118
middling white	1 5 0	1 7 0	⎱		
low ditto and brown	1 1 0	1 3 0	— ⎱		139
China and Siam, white	1 2 0	1 5 0	— ⎱	3l. 3s. per cwt.	250
yellow	0 16 0	1 3 0	⎱	Duty paid.	270
Mauritius, fine	2 11 0	2 14 0	—		80
yellow	2 6 0	2 10 0	— ⎱	1l. 4s. per cwt.	84
brown	2 0 0	2 4 0	—		120
Teeth, Elephants'	19 0 0	23 0 0	—	20s. per cwt.	4
Terra Japonica	1 5 0	1 15 0	—	3s. —	8
Turmeric, Bengal	0 12 0	0 14 0	—	2s. 4d. —	16
Java	0 12 0	0 15 0	— ⎰	10s. —	66
China	0 18 0	1 2 0	⎱		
Tortoiseshell	1 10 0	2 5 0	lb.	6d. per lb.	1
Vermilion	0 2 6	0 3 0	—	1s. —	33

place, not privileged to receive India goods, the whole duties have to be paid ; s‖
if a merchant found it expedient to convey 1,000*l.* worth of pepper from London or
to Newcastle, Portsmouth, &c., to supply the demand of these places, he would,
he could make such transfer, have to advance about 4,000*l.* as duty ! This is s
oppressive regulation. There is not, and there never was, any good reason for pre
ing East India goods from being removed, under bond, from one port to another
goods are allowed to be bonded. Many considerable advantages would result
permitting this to be done. It would distribute East India goods more equall
the country ; and country dealers would be able to lay in and keep up sufficient
with a far less outlay of capital than at present. Such a measure, coupled, as it
to be, with an adequate reduction of the duties, would materially extend the co‖
of all classes at home.

According to the revenue accounts, printed in the next section, it would seer

revenue of India had been almost always inadequate to defray the expenditure, and the debt of the Company has been incurred to supply this deficiency. But this ‑lusion has been disputed by some very high authorities *, who contend, that the ‑nue of India has, speaking generally, always sufficed to defray the expenses justly ‑geable upon it; and that the debt of the East India Company has originated entirely ‑eir commercial operations, which have, notwithstanding their monopoly of the tea ‑e, been, for the most part, disadvantageous. This conclusion has been stoutly ‑ed by the Company, and their servants, examined before the late committees on ‑an affairs; and, if any thing more than the mere inspection of the Company's ac‑ ‑ts were required, to convince every one of the erroneous principles on which they ‑made up, it would be the fact, that gentlemen of the greatest experience in business ‑accounts differ by many millions in the results they deduce from the same statements! the fact is, as was stated by Mr. Rickards before the Lords' committee, that the ‑pany have never furnished to the public any account, drawn out on fair mercantile ‑iples, of their commercial transactions; nor is there any thing in their accounts to ‑y a merchant that they have actually realised any mercantile profit. — (*Lords' Re‑* *of* 1830, *Appendix*, p. 331.)

‑ithout presuming to say positively which of the parties is right or wrong in this ‑roversy, the probabilities are all adverse to the Company. We take it for granted, they have conducted their affairs as well as any similar association placed under ‑ike circumstances could have done. But whatever may be the Company's merits, ‑ affairs must, of necessity, be conducted, like those of all other great companies, ‑ding to a system of routine, and with a plentiful alloy of carelessness and abuse. ‑ indeed, quite visionary to suppose that the servants of such bodies can have the ‑ powerful motives to exert all their energies, or to conduct the business entrusted ‑eir charge in the same frugal and parsimonious manner as private individuals ‑ng on their own account, and reaping all the advantages of superior industry, ‑omy, and enterprise. Branches of commerce, productive only of loss when ma‑ ‑d by the former, have, in innumerable instances, become extremely lucrative ‑ent they were placed in the hands of the latter. Monopoly has always been, and ever continue to be, the parent of indolence and profusion. " By the establish‑ ‑," says Dr. Smith, "of the commercial monopoly of the East India Company, the subjects of the state are taxed very absurdly in two different ways: first, by the price of goods, which, in the case of a free trade, they could buy much cheaper; secondly, by their total exclusion from a branch of business which it might both be ‑enient and profitable for many of them to carry on. It is for the most worthless ‑ purposes, too, that they are taxed in this manner. It is merely to enable the Com‑ ‑ to support the negligence, profusion, and malversation of their servants, whose ‑derly conduct seldom allows the dividend to exceed the ordinary rate of profit ‑des which are altogether free, and frequently sinks it much lower." — (*Wealth of* ‑ns, vol. iii. p. 257.)

‑e admissions of the directors go far to confirm the accuracy of these statements. They ‑" of being enabled to show with precision *the extent of pecuniary sacrifices to which* ‑ubmit, in order to *extend the consumption of British staples.*" — (*Fourth Report of* ‑ *Appendix*.) And Mr. Tucker, one of the directors, admits in his work on Indian ‑ce, published in 1825, that " *the* EXPORTS *to India and China* NEVER PRODUCED A ‑T GENERALLY, *or for a continuance*" — (p. 191.); and then he goes on to tell us ‑" *it has long been matter of doubt whether the Company's trade from India has been* ‑*led with a profit!*" — (p.192.) We believe, however, that there is not the least room ‑ doubt" upon the subject; and that, taking every thing into account, the Company ‑always traded at a heavy loss. Their mercantile transactions have been at once ‑ and unprofitable. Their monopoly of the tea trade, and the other advantages ‑a they have enjoyed, would have enabled individuals to realise a profit of 100 per ‑; and yet they, who divide only 10½ per cent., are overwhelmed with debt! — Can ‑more convincing proof be required of the paralysing effects of monopoly, of its ‑ncy to shut up what would otherwise be the most productive channels of commerce, ‑ fetter and restrict the mutually beneficial intercourse that would naturally take among nations?

‑cording to accounts recently laid before parliament, (printed the 30th of June, ‑) the Company incurred a total loss by their trade with India in the year 1829-30 ‑ less than 585,940*l.* But they say that a large part of this loss is apparent only, ‑g from the accounts having been made up according to an arbitrary rate of ex‑ ‑e fixed by the Board of Control; and that had they been made up according to ‑ercantile or actual rate of exchange, the loss would have been *only* 234,164*l.*

‑rticularly by Mr. Rickards; whose opinion, from the high station he filled in India, his intelli‑ ‑candour, and great experience in commercial affairs, is entitled to very great weight.

According to the same accounts, corrected as above, the Company claim to have gain 924,517*l.* by the trade to China. So that, if we deduct from this sum the divide (650,000*l.*) of 10½ per cent. on the Company's commercial capital of 6,000,000*l.*, a the loss as above (254,164*l.*), their nett surplus profit will be only 40,353*l.* !

Such, according to the Company's own showing, is the result of their trade for la year, during which they admit *they sustained no loss at sea.* And can any one, in whose hands such a statement may come, and who is aware that a large proportion their consignments to China consists of Indian produce — some of it obtained from t' natives at prices fixed by the Company's servants — and that their tea, when brought England, is sold at an enormous advance as compared with its price in Hamburgh, N York, &c. (see Tea);' doubt their total unfitness to act as a commercial body? It is the last degree problematical, whether the Company's profits on their trade last ye really enabled them to pay the dividend; but it is beyond all question, that priva merchants, enjoying equal opportunities, would have realised most enormous gains.

III. Extent, Population, Revenue, &c. of British India.

1. *Extent, Population, &c. of British Dominions in Hindostan, and of the Tributary a Independent States.* — We copy the following table from the second edition of Mr. H milton's *Gazetteer.* It must, however, be regarded as an approximation only, inasmu as no means exist of coming at correct conclusions; but the talents of the writer, a his perfect acquaintance with the subject, warrant the belief that it is as accurate as can be made with the present imperfect means of information.

Table of the relative Area and Population of the Modern States of Hindostan.

	British Square Miles.	Population.
Bengal, Bahar, and Benares -	162,000	39,000,000
Additions in Hindostan since A. D. 1765 - - -	148,000	18,000,000
Gurwal, Kumaon, and the tract between the Sutuleje and Jumna -	18,000	500,000
Total under the Bengal Presidency - - -	328,000	57,500,000
Under the Madras Presidency - - -	154,000	15,000,000
Under the Bombay Presidency - - -	11,000	2,500,000
Territories in the Deccan, &c. acquired since 1815, consisting of the Peshwa's Dominions, &c., and since mostly attached to the Bombay Presidency - - - - - -	60,000	8,000,000
Total under the British Government - -	553,000	83,000,000
British Allies and Tributaries.		
The Nizam - - - - -	96,000	10,000,000
The Nagpoor Raja - - - -	70,000	3,000,000
The King of Oude - - - -	20,000	3,000,000
The Guicowar - - - -	18,000	2,000,000
Kotah, 6,500; Boondee, 2,500; Bopaul, 5,000 - -	14,000	1,500,000
The Mysore Raja - - - -	27,000	3,000,000
The Satara Raja - - - -	14,000	1,500,000
Travancore, 6,000; Cochin, 2,000 - -	8,000	1,000,000
Under the Rajas of Joudpoor, Jeypoor, Odeypoor, Bicancere, Jesselmere, and other Rajpoot chiefs, Holcar, Ameer Khan, the Row of Cutch, Bhurtpoor, Macherry, and numerous other petty chiefs, Seiks, Gonds, Bheels, Coolies, and Catties, all comprehended within the line of British protection - - -	283,000	15,000,000
Total under the British Government and its Allies - -	1,103,000	123,000,000
Independent States.		
The Nepaul Raja - - - -	53,000	2,000,000
The Lahore Raja (Runjeet Singh) - - -	50,000	3,000,000
The Ameers of Sinde - - -	24,000	1,000,000
The Dominions of Sindia - -	40,000	4,000,000
The Cabul Sovereign east of the Indus - -	10,000	1,000,000
Grand Total of Hindostan - - -	1,280,000	134,000,000

India beyond the Ganges. — British Acquisitions in 1824 and 1825.

	Sq. Miles.	Populatio
Countries south of Rangoon, consisting of half the province of Martaban, and the provinces of Tavoy, Ye, Tenasserim, and the Mergui Isles - - - -	21,000	51,000
The province of Arracan - - - -	11,000	100,000
Countries from which the Burmese have been expelled, consisting of Assam and the adjacent petty states, occupying a space of about - - - - -	54,000	150,000
Total - -	77,000	301,000

1805, according to official returns transmitted, the total number of British-born
·ts in Hindostan was 31,000. Of these, 22,000 were in the army as officers and
·es ; the civil officers of government of all descriptions were about 2,000 ; the free
ants and mariners who resided in India under covenant, about 5,000 ; the officers
·actitioners in the courts of justice, 300 ; the remaining 1,700 consisted of adven-
who had smuggled themselves out in various capacities. Since the date above
·ned, no detailed reports have been published : but there is reason to believe that
·ow (1828) the total number of British subjects in Hindostan does not exceed
·) ; the removal of the restrictions on the commercial intercourse having, contrary
·ectation, added very few to the previous number.
· army required for the protection of these extensive provinces, and for the retain-
·m under due subordination, although it presents a formidable grand total, probably
·ot amount to the fifth of the number maintained by the Mogul sovereigns and
·unctionaries, when that empire was in its zenith ; yet, even under the ablest of the
·rs, commotions in some quarter of their ill-subdued territories were unceasing.
·ritish system in India has always been to keep the troops in a constant state of
·ation for war ; but never to enter into unprovoked hostilities, or engage in any
·s except those rendered necessary by the principle of self-defence. At present,
·he exception of the Russian, the British military force is probably the largest
·g army in the world. In 1796 it amounted to 55,000 ; in October, 1826, it
·ed 300,000 men, viz. Artillery, 15,782 ; Native cavalry, 26,094 ; Infantry,
·2 ; Engineers, 4,575 ; King's troops, 21,934 ; — Grand total 302,797 men. Of
·the irregulars of all descriptions amounted to 82,937 men.
·s formidable army is distributed throughout Hindostan under the orders of the
·ie government, promulgated through its political agents. Commencing from the
·tations in the Doab of the Ganges, at Ajmeer is one corps ; another at Neemutch ;
·· at Mow ; all supplied from the Bengal army. These are succeeded by the
·t subsidiary forces, the field corps at Mulligaum, and the Poonah division, fur-
chiefly by the Bombay army. The circle is further continued by the field force
·southern Maharatta country ; the Hyderabad and Nagpoor subsidiaries, composed
·dras troops ; and the detachments from the Bengal establishment, forming the
·lda and Saugur divisions, from whence the cordon terminates in Bundelcund.
·s the general outline, liable, of course, to temporary modifications, and occasional
· in the selection of stations. At present, with the exception of a tract 35 miles
·n each side of Aseerghur, there is an unbroken line of communication through
·tish territory from Bombay to Calcutta.
·lirect and authoritative control, the dominion of the British government extends
·urther than that possessed by any prior dynasty, whether Patan or Mogul ; yet
·er, so long as they abstained from persecution, had nothing to apprehend from
·gion of the Hindoos ; and history proves that the commotions which agitated the
·imedan monarchies chiefly arose from their own internal dissensions and national
·s. Neither does it appear that any prior conquerors ever employed disciplined
·f their own countrymen in defence of their own sovereignty, although they had
·end with one very numerous tribe — the Hindoo ; while the British, more advan-
·ly situated, have two to put in motion against each other, and in process of time
·se up a third. Each foreign invader certainly favoured his own countrymen ;
·vas by bestowing on them places and high appointments, which excited envy,
· essentially strengthening his domination. Besides, therefore, total abstinence
·ersecution, the British government, in a powerful corps entirely European, and
·distinguished from the natives by colour, language, and manners, possesses a
· and consistence much beyond any of the prior Mohammedan dynasties. —
·ion's East India Gazetteer, 2d edit. vol. i. pp. 656 — 659.)
·venue and Expenditure of the East India Company. — The far greater part of the
· of India is at present, and has always been, derived from the soil. The land
·n held by its immediate cultivators generally in small portions, with a perpetual
·nsferable title ; but they have been under the obligation of making an annual
·t to government of a certain portion of the produce of their farms, which might
·ased or diminished at the pleasure of the sovereign ; and which has, in almost
··, been so large, as seldom to leave the cultivators more than a bare subsistence.
·the Mohammedan government, the *gross* produce of the soil was divided into
·r nearly equal shares, between the ryots or cultivators and the government.
·ret we are not able to·say that the British government has made any material
·ns from this enormous assessment. Its oppressiveness, more than any thing
· prevented our ascendancy in India, and the comparative tranquillity and good
·e have introduced, from having the beneficial effects that might have been

anticipated. The cultivators throughout Hindostan are proverbially poor ; and til
amount of the assessment they are at present subject to be effectually reduced, they ca
be otherwise than wretched. They are commonly obliged to borrow money to buy
seed and carry on their operations, at a high interest, on a species of mortgage ove
ensuing crop. Their only object is to get subsistence — to be able to exist in the s
obscure poverty as their forefathers. If they succeed in this, they are satisfied.
Colebrooke, whose authority on all that relates to India is so deservedly high, men
that the quantity of land occupied by each ryot or cultivator in Bengal is comm
about six acres, and rarely amounts to twenty-four ; and it is obvious that the abstra
of half the produce raised on such patches can leave their occupiers nothing more
the barest subsistence for themselves and their families. Indeed, Mr. Colebrooke
us that the condition of ryots subject to this tax is generally inferior to that of a l
labourer, who receives the miserable pittance of two annas, or about three pence, a
of wages.

Besides the land revenue *, a considerable revenue is derived in India from the m
polies of salt and opium, the sale of spirituous liquors, land and sea customs, post-ol
&c. Of these monopolies, the first is, in all respects, decidedly the most objection.
Few things, indeed, would do more to promote the improvement of India, than the
abolition of this monopoly. An open trade in salt, with moderate duties, would,
can be no doubt, be productive of the greatest advantage to the public, and of a l
increase of revenue to government. The opium monopoly, though less objectior
than the last, is, notwithstanding, very oppressive. It interferes with the industry o
inhabitants ; those who are engaged in the cultivation of opium being obliged to sell
produce at prices arbitrarily fixed by the Company's agents. It would be worse
useless to waste the reader's time, by pointing out in detail the mischievous effec
such a system ; they are too obvious not to arrest the attention of every one. The
duce of these and the other branches of Indian taxation is specified in the subjo
table, which we have carefully compiled from the official accounts.

Account of the Territorial Revenues of the East India Company during the Official Year 1827-

Description.	Bengal.	Madras.	Bombay.	Penang	Malacca.	Singapore.	Saint Helena	London	To
	£	£	£	£	£	£	£	£	£
Land Rent	8,252,797	3,519,745	1,965,093	21,893	4,881	18,559	1,064	—	13,78
Liquors (Nett)	485,422	257,638	—	—	—	—	—	—	74
Opium (Monopoly)	2,051,620	—	—	—	—	—	—	—	2,05
Tobacco (do)	—	85,482	—	—	—	—	—	—	8
Salt (Partial Monopoly)	2,389,600	346,192	19,936	—	—	—	—	—	2,7
Farms and Licences (Nett)	—	56,252	225,650	—	—	—	66	—	29
Mint	38,1?9	4,332	5,440	—	—	—	—	—	
Post Office	91,833	32,043	12,584	—	—	—	—	—	1
Stamps	327,709	56,261	5,161	—	—	—	—	—	3
Bank, Madras (Nett)	—	9,162	—	—	—	—	—	—	
Customs — Sea	126,859	—	65,698	—	—	—	2,216	—	1
Inland	—	439,870	109,209	—	—	—	—	—	5
Do. unspecified	831,794	—	219,784	—	—	—	—	—	1,0
Sundries	308,355	392,355	—	—	—	—	—	—	7
Revenue	14,777,909	5,326,191	2,628,555	21,893	4,881	18,559	3,346	—	22,7
General (Board, Repayment by)	—	—	—	3,617	—	—	—	—	
Marine (Pilotage)	38,486	7,802	18,383	367	—	—	—	—	
Judicial (Fines and Fees)	106,287	13,845	17,890	5,039	—	—	52	—	1
Total Civil Revenue	14,921,982	5,347,838	2,664,825	30,916	4,881	18,559	3,398	—	22,9
Military (Repayments)	—	—	—	373	—	—	—	—	
Buildings (do.)	—	—	—	49	—	—	—	—	
Total Receipts	14,921,982	5,347,838	2,664,835	31,338	4,881	18,559	3,398	—	22,
Interest	—	—	—	—	—	—	—	—	
Gross Revenue & Receipts	14,921,982	5,347,838	2,664,825	31,338	4,881	18,559	3,398	—	22,9
Nett Surplus Revenue over Expenditure	1,479,273	—	—	—	—	—	—	—	

* For an account of the land revenue of India, of the various modes in which it is assessed,
influence on the condition of the inhabitants, we beg to refer to Mr. Rickards's work on Indi
various important and difficult questions with respect to Indian taxation are there treated wit
learning and sagacity, and placed in the most luminous point of view.

Account of the Territorial Charges of the East India Company during the Official Year 1827—28.

Description.	Bengal.	Madras.	Bombay.	Penang.	Malacca.	Singapore.	Saint Helena.	London.	Total.
	£	£	£	£	£	£	£	£	£
d Rent (Collection, ensions, &c.)	1,608,480	702,677	642,551	3,000	500	1,500	—	—	2,958,708
iors (Charges of Collection not specified.)									
um (Cost and harges)	658,254	—	—	—	—	—	—	—	658,254
acco (do.)	—	31,843	—	—	—	—	—	—	31,843
(do.)	808,322	74,419	—	—	—	—	—	—	882,741
ns and Licences (Charges of Collection not specified.)									
t (Charges on)	51,786	20,406	3,637	—	—	—	—	—	75,829
Office (do.)	89,075	29,339	18,848	—	—	—	—	—	137,262
ips (do.)	81,690	9,437	—	—	—	—	—	—	91,127
k (Charges not specified.)									
oms—Sea(Charges Collection)	—	23,445	14,867	—	—	—	—	—	38,312
nland (do.)	—	28,587	3,037	—	—	—	—	—	31,624
eneral unspecified	126,808	—	25,605	—	—	—	—	—	152,413
ries	140,849	363,854	136,944	—	—	—	—	—	641,647
ge under Revenue ard	3,565,264	1,284,007	845,489	3,000	500	1,500	—	—	5,699,760
ges under General do.	1,102,824	353,659	474,781	100,014	12,825	36,637	46,808	—	2,127,548
ges under Marine	117,745	18,781	212,862	6,000	1,000	3,000	—	—	359,388
ges under Judicial	1,150,394	371,751	305,446	12,000	2,000	6,000	—	—	1,847,591
s Amount of Civil arges	5,936,227	2,028,198	1,838,578	121,014	16,325	47,137	46,808	—	10,034,287
Military do.	5,245,737	3,697,520	2,051,810	49,255	8,030	11,341	75,172	—	11,338,865
dings both Civil d Military do.	548,492	81,877	163,088	4,833	1,186	4,606	1,989	—	786,071
ge in India	11,730,456	6,007,595	4,033,476	175,102	25,541	63,084	123,969	—	22,159,223
rest on Debt	1,712,253	179,025	27,230	2,024	—	—	—	—	1,920,532
ecified	—	—	—	—	—	—	—	2,060,141	2,060,141
s Charge or Excess of Expenditure er Revenue	13,442,709	6,186,620	4,060,706	177,126	25,541	63,084	123,969	2,060,141	26,139,896
	—	838,782	1,395,881	145,788	20,660	44,525	120,571	2,060,141	3,147,975

e territorial revenues at the disposal of the East India Company have, for a length-period, equalled those of the most powerful monarchies. At present they are er than those of either Russia or Austria, being inferior only to those of Great in and France! Still, however, the Company's financial situation is the very se of prosperous. Vast as their revenue has been, their expenditure appears, in instances, to have been still larger; and at this moment their debts amount to no han 54,973,452*l*.

e subjoined abstract is drawn up from an account intended to exhibit a statement e Company's affairs on the 1st of January, 1813.

Stock of the East India Company, 1st January, 1831.

	£	£
Merchandise, stores, &c., and debts due to the Company in India	25,821,587	
nmoveable stock, consisting of buildings, fortifications, &c. in India	10,870,132	36,691,719
Merchandise, debts, and other moveable stock in England	11,164,955	
uildings, ships, &c.	1,208,020	12,372,975
Total stock		£49,064,694

Debts owing by the East India Company, 1st January, 1831.

	£	£
ebt in India		32,213,759
ebt in England, bearing interest	6,595,900	
onds at the Bank	800,000	13,916,431
ills not due, arrears of duties, &c. &c.	6,520,531	
Total debts due by the Company		£46,130,190

From this account it would appear that the assets then in possession of the Compa exceeded the claims upon it by nearly *three* millions. It is clear, however, that reliance can be placed on this, or any similar statement. In the first place, debts d to the Company, and arrears of tribute, a large portion of which can never be realise form a very important item in the credit side of this account; and secondly, the for houses, warehouses, &c. belonging to the Company in India and England, may be es mated at any sum; but if an attempt were made to sell them, where could a purchas be found to buy them, even at a third part of the price at which they are here set dow All, therefore, that this account proves, is that the claims upon the Company in 18 amounted to 46,000,000*l.*; but it leaves it exceedingly doubtful whether they had rea 25,000,000*l.* worth of available property to set against them.*

The following is an account of the Company's affairs, 1st May, 1828, to which, how ever, the previous remarks are strictly applicable: —

	£
Total Territorial and Political Debts, abroad and at home - - -	54,973,452
Do. - - - Credits - do. - - -	26,934,663
Balance deficient in the Territorial and Political Branch	28,038,789
Total Commercial Debts, abroad and at home - - £ 1,710,458	
Do. - Credits do. - - 23,442,327	
Balance in favour in the Commercial Branch - -	21,731,869
Balance deficient - -	6,306,920
Add, the amount of the Company's Home Bond Debt, as above - -	3,795,892
Total Balance deficient, including the Home Bond Debt - -	£10,102,812

The following account shows the balance between the revenue and expenditure of o Indian dominions, from 1809-10 to 1827-28:—

An Account of the Total annual Revenues and Charges of the British Possessions in India under East India Company, from 1809-10 to 1827-28: showing also the Nett Charge of Bencoolen, Prince Wales Island, and St. Helena; the Interest paid on account of Debts in India; and the Amount Territorial Charges paid in England. — (Abstracted from the *Parl. Paper*, No. 22. Sess. 1830.)

					Territorial Charges paid in England.			General
Years.	Total Gross Revenues of India.	Total Charges in India.	Nett Charge of Bencoolen, Prince of Wales Island, and St. Helena.	Interest on Debts.	Cost of Political Stores.	Other Territorial Payments chargeable on the Revenue. (Pensions, &c.)	Total.	Surplus Revenue.
	£	£	£	£	£	£	£	£
1809-10	16,464,391	13,775,577	203,361	2,159,019	190,128	867,097	1,057,225	- -
1810-11	16,679,198	13,909,983	199,663	2,196,691	217,703	901,688	1,119,391	- -
1811-12	16,605,616	13,220,967	168,288	1,457,077	154,998	922,770	1,077,768	681,516
1812-13	16,450,774	13,659,429	201,349	1,491,870	193,784	1,184,976	1,378,768	- -
1813-14	17,228,711	13,617,725	209,957	1,537,434	64,257	1,148,156	1,212,413	651,182
1814-15	17,231,191	14,182,454	204,250	1,502,217	129,873	1,064,223	1,194,596	147,677
1815-16	17,168,195	15,081,587	225,558	1,584,157	81,903	1,199,952	1,281,885	- -
1816-17	18,010,135	15,129,839	205,372	1,719,470	194,374	1,071,176	1,265,550	- -
1817-18	18,305,265	15,844,964	219,793	1,753,018	81,941	1,094,701	1,176,642	- -
1818-19	19,392,002	17,558,615	210,224	1,665,928	130,162	1,150,378	1,280,540	- -
1819-20	19,172,506	17,040,848	142,049	1,940,327	265,055	1,150,391	1,415,446	- -
1820-21	21,292,036	17,520,612	220,043	1,902,585	228,058	1,072,106	1,300,164	348,632
1821-22	21,753,271	17,555,688	207,816	1,932,835	202,735	1,175,149	1,377,884	679,068
1822-23	23,190,934	18,083,482	154,761	1,694,731	204,147	1,354,960	1,559,107	1,528,853
1823-24	21,238,623	18,902,511	257,276	1,652,449	395,276	758,590	1,153,866	- -
1824-25	20,705,152	20,410,929	279,277	1,460,433	414,181	1,166,078	1,580,259	- -
1825-26	21,096,960	22,346,365	214,285	1,575,941	740,798	1,076,504	1,817,232	- -
1826-27	23,327,753	21,424,894	207,973	1,749,068	1,111,792	1,318,102	2,429,894	- -
Estimate 1827-28	22,819,229	21,088,051	312,983	1,912,725	805,016	1,255,125	2,060,141	- -

But, however much this account of the financial concerns of our Eastern empire r be at variance with the exaggerated ideas entertained respecting it, as well by a la proportion of the people of England as by foreigners, it will excite no surprise in mind of any one who has ever reflected on the subject. It is due, indeed, to the direct to state, that though they have occasionally acted on erroneous principles, they h always exerted themselves to enforce economy in every branch of their expenditure, to impose and collect their revenues in the best and cheapest manner. But though have succeeded in repressing many abuses, it would be idle to suppose that they sh ever entirely succeed in rooting them out. How can it be imagined, that strangers

* The committee of the House of Commons, appointed in 1810, deducted about a half from the acc which the Company exhibited of their assets in 1810.

ia, conscious that they are armed with all the strength of government, placed
no real responsibility, exempted from the salutary influence of public opinion,
g no exposure through the medium of the press, and anxious only to accumulate
ne, should not occasionally abuse their authority? or that they should manage the
icated and difficult affairs of a vast empire, inhabited by a race of people of whose
age, manners, and habits, they are almost wholly ignorant, with that prudence,
ny, and vigilance, without which it were idle to expect that any great surplus
ie could ever be realised?

priety of prohibiting the Company from engaging in Commercial Transactions. — We
to doubt that, during the next or following session of parliament, measures will be
for throwing open the trade to China, as well as that to India, to private adven-
We should, however, be inclined to go farther than this; and conceive that it
ily necessary not only that the trade to all places eastward of the Cape of Good
should be laid open to individual enterprise, but that the Company should be
ited from engaging, either directly or indirectly, in any sort of commercial adven-
In making a suggestion of this sort, we are actuated by no feelings of hostility
Company. Though we regard them, and every association of the same kind, as
unfit to prosecute any sort of commercial undertaking either with advantage to
lves or the public, we are very far from being prepared to advocate the abolition
r territorial rights and privileges. Indeed, we have no hesitation in subscribing to
ills's statement, " that there is no government which has on all occasions shown
ch of a disposition to make sacrifices of its own interests to the interests of the
whom it governed, and which has, in fact, made so many and important sacrifices,
East India Company." But we are, at the same time, thoroughly convinced
e circumstance of the Company being engaged in commerce has had a very pre-
l influence over their proceedings as rulers of India; and that nothing would do
ch to promote the good government of their subjects, as well as their own
ary interests, as an abandonment on their part of all commercial pursuits.* A
ry which carries a sword in one hand and a ledger in the other, which maintains
and retails tea, is a contradiction; and, if it traded with success, would be a pro-
The agents of such a body stand on a very different footing from private traders.
ate adventurer is compelled to be courteous; he must accommodate himself to
its and wishes of those with whom he deals, and must labour to conciliate their
and esteem. Armed with no extrinsic powers, supported by no imposing
ins, and appearing amongst them for purely commercial purposes, he excites
jealousy nor apprehension, while the advantages derived from his intercourse
him a kind and hospitable reception. Acts of violence and aggression have
ss been sometimes committed by private traders; but they have been, and must
ie to be, of very rare occurrence. Each private trader is a guaranty for the
ile conduct of every one else. It is for the interest of the whole that their com-
pursuits should not be interrupted by the violence or misconduct of individuals,
y never fail to do all in their power to repress them. But it is obvious that the
s of a great joint stock association like the East India Company, must come into
ket under the influence of very different feelings and interests. Appearing in
ble and irreconcileable character of soldiers and merchants, they feel themselves
l from the necessity of treating the natives in a kind and conciliatory manner.
ius of their power, they must be more than men if they do not occasionally place
nfidence in force rather than in address. Instead of rising to wealth by slow
, and by the fair and honest exercise of their industry, the agents of monopolists
commonly resorted to more compendious processes; and, what is worse, they
iil to identify their own arbitrary and unjustifiable proceedings with the honour
rest of the nation to which they belong, and pervert the power placed in their
o insure the success of their schemes. Their mercantile is always sunk in their
character; and, with various capacity and fluctuating fortune, they generally
te the grand object of enriching themselves by means of extortion instead of fair
ite profits.

dia, a commercial resident, with a large establishment of servants under him,
them intended for coercive purposes, is stationed in all the considerable towns;
ias been stated, and by no less authority than the Marquis Wellesley, that the
on of a wish from the Company's resident is always received as a command by the
anufacturers and producers. How, then, is it possible for the private trader to
rly into competition with persons possessing such authority, and often instructed
their purchases on any terms? Mr. Tucker admits that the Company's invest-
a India during the last ten years may, in some instances, be said to have been forced;

this point the valuable evidence of Sir Charles Forbes, before the Commons' committee, 18th
1831.

that is, the goods bought by them have sometimes been compulsorily obtained from
natives, and sometimes purchased at a higher price than they would have brought
market frequented only by regular merchants.   But the truth is, that it is not in
nature of things that the Company's purchases can *ever* be fairly made; the na
cannot deal with their servants as they would deal with private individuals; an
would be absurd to suppose that agents authorised to make purchases on account
government, and to draw on the public treasury for the means of payment, she
generally evince the prudence and discretion of individuals directly responsible in t
own private fortunes for their transactions.

" From the influence," says Mr. Rickards, " of the resident on the one hand, and
pecuniary want of the manufacturers on the other, it is quite clear that they may be
in perpetual bondage to the Company's service.   And when we thus see the indust
the country subject to the entire direction of the ruling authority; supported for the v
part, and often irregularly, by advances from the public revenues; and all competi
the soul and essence of commerce, far removed from this feeble and delicate fabric,
its very touch were ruin; who but the most prejudiced can possibly see or expect p
perity under such a system?   It is completely subversive of every principle on w
both experience and theory would teach us to found any rational hope of public go

It is the interference of the Company's agents, and that only, that renders the t
to India more than ordinarily hazardous.   Whenever it is known that they are in
market as purchasers, the commodity in demand, whether it be indigo, cotton,
pepper, or saltpetre, immediately rises 10, 20, or 30 per cent.; so that all the comb
tions and calculations of the private traders are in a moment overset.   In illustratio
this we may mention, that a few years ago, the Company having sent out large order
the purchase of Bengal indigo, the local government, aware how prices would rise v
it was known the Company were in the market, employed Mr. Palmer (late Pa
and Co.) secretly to purchase for them; but Mr. Palmer's purchases very soon excee
what were known to be his private wants, it was first suspected, and afterwards as
tained, that he was buying for the Company, when prices immediately rose from 19
230 or 240 rupees per maund.   The correspondents of the private merchants, who
received orders to purchase indigo, were of course compelled to pay the same enha
price.   No sooner, however, had the indigo got to England, than the price fell bac
its natural level, most of it being sold at a very heavy loss.

The only argument put forward by the Company in defence of their Indian trac
that otherwise they would not be able to realise the surplus revenue of India in Engl
But if we may believe their accounts, such surplus revenue has rarely existed, and c
not, therefore, be very difficult to realise.   Although, however, it had been ten t
greater than it really has been, the Company might have got it paid over to them
without the slightest inconvenience, supposing they had had nothing to do with tr
What is to prevent them from buying bills upon London?   This is what a pr
individual in Calcutta would do, who wished to make a remittance to England; an
the Company do the same, they may remit 1,000,000*l.* with less trouble than they
remit 10,000*l.*   It is well known to every mercantile man in London, that they a
this moment selling indigo, that cost them a rupee, or 2*s.* in India, for 1*s.* 2*d.*; incu
a loss upon the remittance of no less than FORTY *per cent. !*   Now, mark how easil
heavy loss might have been avoided.   In September, 1829, the Bengal govern
advertised that they would advance on cargoes to England, *two thirds* of their ascert
value, for good bills in favour of the Board of Trade, at six months' sight, and 1*s.*
the rupee; the advance being guaranteed by the cargo being placed in the hands c
Company till the bills were paid : and it is a fact, that most of these bills were pa
presentation, six months before they were due, and some months before the arriv
England of the goods on which the advance was made.   Here, then, is a large r
tance made to the Company in the most expeditious way possible, and without
incurring the smallest loss, or even risk : whereas in their simultaneous attempt to
revenue by importing Indian produce, they have incurred a loss of some hundre
thousands of pounds; at the same time that, by glutting the market with indigo
have done serious injury to the private trader.   Need another word be said, to sho
extreme absurdity of such a proceeding, and the advantage to all parties of preve
its repetition ?

EBONY (Ger. *Ebenholz;* Du. *Ebbenhout;* Fr. *Ebéne;* It. *Ebano;* Rus
enowoederewo; Lat. *Ebenus*), a species of wood brought principally from the
It is exceeding hard and heavy, of great durability, susceptible of a very
polish, and on that account used in mosaic and other inlaid work.   Ther
many species of ebony.   The best is that which is jet black, free from vein
rind, very compact, astringent, and of an acrid pungent taste.   This specie.
nominated by botanists *Diospyrus Ebenus*), is found principally in Madag

Mauritius, and Ceylon. The centre only of the tree is said to be valuable.
826, 2,002,783 lbs. of ebony, of the estimated value of 9,017*l*. 7*s*. 6½*d*. were
orted from the Mauritius. Besides the black, there are red, green, and yellow
nies; but the latter are not so much esteemed as the former. Cabinet-makers
in the habit of substituting pear-tree and other woods dyed black, in the place
genuine ebony; these, however, want its polish and lustre, though they hold
better. The price of ebony varies, in the London market, from 5*l*. to 20*l*. a
The quantities imported are but inconsiderable.

EL (*Anguilla muræna* of Linnæus), a fish, the appearance of which is too
known to require any description. It is a native of almost all the waters of
ope, frequenting not only rivers but stagnant pools. Eels are, in many places,
emely abundant. In some of the rivers in Jutland 2,000 have been taken by
gle sweep of the net, and 60,000 have been taken in the Garonne by one net
day. Several ponds are appropriated in England to the raising of eels; and
e quantities are taken in the Thames, and other British rivers. They are in
siderable estimation as an article of food.

GGS (Fr. *Œufs;* Lat. *ova*), are too well known to require to be described.
y differ in size, colour, taste, &c. according to the different species of birds
lay them. The eggs of hens are those most commonly used as food; and
a an article of very considerable importance in a commercial point of view.
t quantities are brought from the country to London and other great towns.
e the peace they have also been very largely imported from the Continent.
this moment, indeed, the trade in eggs forms a considerable branch of our
merce with France, and affords constant employment for a number of small
els!

he following is an official account of the number of eggs imported during 1826,
', 1828, and 1829, specifying the countries whence they were brought, and
·evenue accruing thereon: —

Countries from which imported.	1826.	1827.	1828.	1829.
	Number.	*Number.*	*Number.*	*Number.*
len - - - - - - -	- -	- -	1,640	- -
mark - - - - - -	9,042	1,140	2,610	300
ssia - - - - - -	- -	- -	840	- -
many - - - - - -	7,200	9,020	- -	80
ted Netherlands - - - -	2,524,410	3,088,698	5,447,280	6,749,759
ace - - - - - -	59,507,899	63,109,618	60,043,026	56,370,479
res - - - - - -	- -	180	- -	- -
e of Good Hope - - -	5			
of Guernsey, Jersey, Alderney, and } an, Produce (Duty Free) - - }	718,086	456,802	609,930	671,435
of Guernsey, Jersey, Alderney, and } an, Produce (Foreign) - - }	493,985	220,674	348,447	573,419
l of the Importations into the United } ngdom - - - - - }	63,260,627	66,886,132	66,453,773	64,165,472
	£ *s. d.*	£ *s. d.*	£ *s. d.*	£ *s. d.*
unt of Duty received - - -	21,726 10 2	23,071 4 1	22,920 8 3	22,189 2 10
Rates of Duty charged -	- - 10*d*. per 120 during the whole period.			

appears from this official statement, that the eggs imported from France
nt to about 60,000,000 a year; and supposing them to cost, at an average, 4*d*. a
1, it follows that the people of the metropolis and Brighton (for it is into
that they are almost all imported) pay the French above 83,000*l*. a year for
and supposing that the freight, importers' and retailers' profit, duty, &c. raise
price to the consumer to 10*d*. a dozen, their total cost will be 213,000*l*.

'OO. See GOMUTI.

.EMI, a resin obtained from the *Amyris elem fera*, a tree growing in different
of America, Turkey, &c. It is obtained by wounding the bark in dry
aer, the juice being left to thicken in the sun. It is of a pale yellow colour,
transparent; at first softish, but it hardens by keeping. Its taste is slightly
and warm. Its smell, which is, at first, strong and fragrant, gradually di-
hes. It used to be imported in long roundish cakes, wrapped in flag leaves,
is now usually imported in mats and chests. — (*Thomson's Chemistry*.)

EPHANTS' TEETH (Du. *Olyfanttanden;* Fr. *Dents d'éléphant;* Ger. *Ele-
enzalme;* It. *Denti di liofante;* Sp. *Dientes de elefante*), or tusks, of which

each animal has two, are of a yellowish, brownish, and sometimes a dark colc
on the outside, internally white, and hollow towards the root.　Ceylon, varic
parts of India, Mosambique and other African countries, Siam, &c. produce the
The best are large, straight, and white, without flaws; not very hollow in t
stump, but solid and thick.　The most esteemed come from Africa, being of
closer texture, and less liable to turn yellow, than those from the East Indies.

The trade in London thus divide them : —

First sort, weighing 70 lbs. or upwards ; second sort, weighing 56 lbs. to 60 lbs. ; third sort, weigh
38 lbs. to 56 lbs. ; fourth sort, weighing 28 lbs. to 37 lbs. ; fifth sort, weighing 18 lbs. to 27 lbs.

All under 18 lbs. are called *scrivelloes*, and are of the least value.　In purchasing elephants' teeth, th
that are very crooked, hollow, and broken at the ends, or cracked and decayed in the inside, should be
jected ; and care taken that lead or any other substance has not been poured into the hollow.　The frei
is rated at 16 cwt. to the ton. — (*Milburn's Orient. Com.*)

The price of elephants' and sea-horse teeth in the London market, August, 1831, was as follows : —

	£	s.	d.	£	s.	d.	
70 lbs. or 1st, per cwt. - - -	24	0	0	to 29	4	0	⎫
56 — 2d, — - . - -	21	0	0	— 24	10	0	⎪
38 — 3d, — - . - -	19	0	0	— 22	0	0	⎬ £1 duty
28 — 4th, — - . - -	15	0	0	— 17	0	0	⎪ per cwt.
18 — 5th, — - - -	14	0	0	— 16	0	0	⎭
Scrivelloes - - - -	12	0	0	— 24	0	0	
Sea Horse, per lb. - - -	0	2	0	— 0	10	0	£3 4s. per do.

ELM (*Ulmus*), a forest tree common in Great Britain, of which there a
several varieties.　It attains to a great size, and lives to a great age : its trunk
often rugged and crooked, and it is of slow growth.　The colour of the heart-wo
of elm is generally darker than that of oak, and of a redder brown.　The sap-wo
is of a yellowish or brownish white, with pores inclined to red.　It is in gene
porous, and cross-grained, sometimes coarse-grained, and has no larger septa.
has a peculiar odour.　It twists and warps much in drying, and shrinks ve
much both in length and breadth.　It is difficult to work, but is not liable to sp
and bears the driving of bolts and nails better than any other timber.　In Scotla
chairs and other articles of household furniture are frequently made of elm-woo
but in England, where the wood is inferior, it is chiefly used in the manufactu
of coffins, casks, pumps, pipes, &c.　It is appropriated to these purposes becau
of its great durability in water, which also occasions its extensive use as piles a
planking for wet foundations.　The naves of wheels are sometimes made of el
It is said to bear transplanting better than any other large tree. — (*Tredgol
Principles of Carpentry*, pp. 201—203. &c.)

ELSINEUR, a town in Zealand, about 22 miles north of Copenhagen, in l
56° 2¼′ N., lon. 12° 37¾′ E.　Population about 7,000.　Adjacent to Elsineur is
castle of Cronenberg, which commands the entrance to the Baltic by the Sou
All merchant ships passing to and from the Baltic are obliged to heave to in E
neur roads for the purpose of paying toll, guaranteed to the king of Denmark
treaties entered into with all European nations.　The first treaty negotiated
England with reference to this subject is dated in 1450.　The Sound duties h
their origin in an agreement between the king of Denmark on the one part, a
the Hanse Towns on the other, by which the former undertook to construct lig
houses, landmarks, &c. along the Cattegat, and the latter to pay duty for
same.　The duties have since been varied at different periods.　Ships of wa
exempted from the payment of duties.　Most maritime nations have consuls r
dent at Elsineur.

The *moneys, weights,* and *measures* of Elsineur are the same as those of Copenha;
(which see,) except that the rixdollar is divided into 4 *orts* instead of 6 marcs : thus
skillings make 1 ort ; and 4 orts 1 rixdollar.

In paying toll, however, at the passage of the Sound, the moneys are distinguished into three diff
values ; namely, specie, crown, and current.

Specie money is that in which the duties of the Sound were fixed in 1701.

Crown money was the ancient currency of Denmark, in which the toll is sometimes reckoned.

Current money is the actual currency of the country.

The proportion between these denominations is as follows : —

Eight specie rixdollars = 9 crown rixdollars ; 16 crown rixdollars = 17 current rixdollars : there
to reduce specie money into crown money, add one eighth ; and for the reverse operation, subtrac
ninth.

To reduce crown money into current money, add one sixteenth ; and for the reverse operation, sub
one seventeenth.

Hence, also, 128 specie rixdollars are worth 144 crown rixdollars, or 153 current rixdollars ; and t
fore specie money is 12½ per cent. better than crown money, and 19 17/32 per cent. better than cu
money.

.Houses in the Baltic charge the Sound duties in the invoices, and have their own agents at Elsine
clear all the merchandise shipped by them.　If this be not the case, the merchants at Elsineur then
upon the owners or agents where the goods are directed or addressed.

hts. — A shippound from the Baltic, of 10 stone, is calculated as 300 lbs. Danish ; a Russian berko-
s 300 lbs. ; a pud, as 30 lbs. Danish ; a centner from the Baltic, as 110 lbs. ; and a cwt. English, as
Danish.

Corn Measure of different Places reduced to Danish Lasts, for paying the Sound Dues.

	Three lasts will	Grypswalde		Four lasts reck-	Riga		
	be reckoned in	Wismar		oned as five.	Königsberg		
	the Sound as	Anclam			Dantzic		
lde	four lasts.	Rostock, five lasts for six.			Elbing		The same as
	Three lasts will	Stettin		Six lasts for	Memel		the Dutch.
	be reckoned in	Warnemunde		seven.	Revel		
	the Sound as	Winemunde			Petersburgh		
	four lasts.	Lubeck, seven lasts for eight.			Oesel		

	Lasts.			Lasts.
ussian chetwerts	1	Ten muids from Havre		12
of twenty-eight muids French salt, from Ro-		Seven moyos from Cadiz, Lisbon, &c.		12
	13	Four hundred Dutch marts (measures)		7
from Bordeaux	12	One English chaldron, two weighs, two tons, or eighty	
raziers from Dunkirk	1	bushels		1

d Measure. — A tonneau of French wine is considered as four oxhofts, or twenty-four ankers.
e of Spanish or Portuguese wine, as two oxhofts.
y Spanish arrobas, or twenty-five Portuguese almudes, as a regular pipe.
y Spanish arrobas, or forty-eight pots of oil, as a regular both (pipe) ; a hogshead of brandy, as six
a tierce, as four ankers ; an anker, five velts, or forty Danish pots.

Duties payable at the Sound on the principal Articles commonly passing through.

A.	Rixd. St.	F.	Rixd. St.
er, the eight hogsheads, at four and a half	0 36	Feathers, the shippound	0 6
, the 100 lbs.	0 9	Femambuco wood, 1,000 lb.	0 30
e shippound	0 12	Figs, the eighteen baskets, 800 lbs.	0 48
the 100 lbs.	0 9	Fish, cod, the last, twelve barrels	0 12
y, the shippound	0 12	stock, the last, twelve shippound, or 1,000 fish	0 30
nd locks, the schock of sixty	1 0	salmon, the barrel	0 5
he last of twenty-two barrels		salted herrings, the barrel	0 2
ries' drugs, the lispound valued at thirty-six		red herrings, the last of twenty straes, or 20,000	0 12
dollars	0 18	Flannels, the eight pieces of twenty-five ells each	0 10
e shippound	0 12	Flax, dressed, the shippound	0 36
ditto	0 12	undressed, as Petersburg, Narva, twelve hogsheads;	
eed, the last of twelve barrels, or twelve ship-		Marienburg, all fine sorts podilla, racketzer, and	
nd	0 6	paternoster, the four shippound	1 0
he last of twelve barrels, or twelve shippound	1 0	coarse, half clean, Farken, Rassets, Memels, and	
		Marienburg, the six shippound	1 0
B.		tow, the five shippound	0 18
e shippound	0 9	Flounders, dry, the 20,000	0 12
single piece	0 3	Flour of wheat, the 200 lbs.	0 9
uble ditto	0 6	barley or rye, the last of twelve barrels	0 12
at, of oak, the piece	0 3	Frieze, the piece	0 6
of fir, four ditto	0 6		
, ditto, twenty ditto	0 13	G.	
es, the 200 lbs.	0 9	Galls, or gum, the 200 lbs.	0 9
d, the last of twelve barrels	0 36	Glass for windows, English, French, Lubeck, and	
bread of wheat, four barrels	0 6	Dantzic, the eight chests	0 30
ad of rye, four barrels	0 4	Venice, drinking ditto, the chest	0 9
nted, the 100 lbs. valued at thirty-six rixdoll.	0 18	bottles, the tan, four hogsheads, and thirty schocks	0 30
rass wire, the shippound	0 24	the two pipes	0 10
ht, the 100 lbs. valued at thirty-six rixdollars	0 18	quart bottles, 100 dozen, fifty rixdollars	0 24
, the last of twelve shippound	1 0	Gloves, Russia, or Courland, the 250 pair	0 9
rench or Spanish, the hogshead	0 24	leather, the dozen, value two rixdollars	1 0
he barrel	0 6	Gunpowder, the 100 lbs.	0 6
sh, the ohm	0 24		
od, the 500 lbs.	0 15	H.	
e shippound, valued at thirty-six rixdollars	0 18	Haberdashery ware, the 100 lbs. valued at thirty-six rix-	
barrel	0 5	dollars	0 18
		Hair, camels' or coneys', the 50 lbs.	0 50
C.		Handspikes, the 500	0 8
rdage, or cable yarn, the shippound	0 6	Hats, felt, the cask	0 12
he eight pieces	0 15	beaver, the dozen, value forty-eight rixdollars	0 24
e pipe, or two hogsheads	0 18	castor, the dozen, ditto	0 12
playing or for wool, the ten dozen	0 6	Hemp, the shippound	0 8
s, cinnamon, cloves, or cochineal, the 100 lbs.	0 54	tow, the ten shippound	0 36
e four pieces	0 10	Hides, elks, harts, bucks, or Russia, the decker	0 9
cambrics, the four pieces	0 15	salted, elks, harts, bucks, or Russia, the decker	0 6
es, the eight pieces	0 18	dry, elks, harts, bucks, or Russia, the five deckers	0 18
wood, the 500 lbs.	0 18	Russia, the shippound	0 36
eds, the 100 lbs.	0 9	Honey, the hogshead	0 7
e shippound, valued at thirty-six rixdollars	0 9	Hops, the shippound	0 6
shippound	0 4	Horses, the pair	0 36
the thirty-six sacks	0 36		
hogshead	0 12	I. J.	
, the 100 lbs. valued at thirty-six rixdollars	0 18	Indigo, the 100 lbs.	0 36
k, the piece	0 9	Iron wire, or pans, the 100 lbs.	0 4
short cloths, or double dozens, the two		stoves, plates or pots, the shippound	0 6
s	0 9	bars, bats, bolts, hoops, anchors, and guns, the	
or long cloths, or dozens, the four pieces	0 24	shippound	0 4
200 lbs.	0 21	wrought, the 100 lbs. valued at twenty-four rix-	
e shippound	0 6	dollars	0 12
t, the 100 lbs. valued at thirty-two rixdoll.	0 36	old, the shippound	0 3
nirty bundles	0 6	Ostermunds, the shippound	0 6
alamine, or cream of tartar, the shippound	0 18	Isinglass, the 100 lbs.	0 9
, the 100 lbs.	0 22	Juniper berries, the 200 lbs.	0 9
y, the last of twenty barrels			
eas, oats, or buckwheat, the last of twelve		K.	
s	0 18	Kerseys, the eight pieces	0 10
he last of twelve barrels	0 12		
last of twenty barrels	1 0	L.	
the last of twenty barrels	1 8	Lace, silk, or ferret, the 4 lbs.	0 10
and currants, the 200 lbs.	0 6	thread, wool, cotton, or hair, the 10 lbs.	0 6
od or timber, twenty-five pieces	0 0	gold and silver, the lb.	0 5
		Lemons, the twelve chests, or 36,600	0 24
D.		pickled, the pipe or hogshead	0 18
silk, the piece	0 12	Lead, fodder, ton, or six shippound	0 24
ne four pieces	0 10	shot, the 100 lbs.	0 4
, the eight pieces	0 10	red or white, the 100 lbs.	0 2
k or fir, above twenty feet, the schock	1 0	Leather, Russia or Scotch, the decker	0 9
rn, under twenty feet	0 24	Spanish, Cordovan, Turkey, and buff, the decker	0 12
	0 36	sems, the ten decker	0 36
a, 10 to 14 feet, the 1,000	0 36	Baxanes, the ten decker	0 18
illing, the twenty pieces	0 30	tanned or sole, the 100 lbs.	0 9
hippound	0 36	alumed or white, the 500 pieces	0 18
e two pieces	0 9	Lignumvitæ, the 100 lbs.	0 9
		Linseed, the last of twenty four barrels	0 36
E.		Linen, calicoes, the sixteen pieces	0 30
t of twelve barrels	0 30	flax, the twenty pieces	0 30
euth, each	0 36	Holland, Silesia, and Westphalia, the four pieces	0 10

	Rixd. St.

Linen, tow, linen, crocus, Dantzic tow, ditto the forty
pieces ⋯ 0 0
hemp, black tow, the eighty pieces ⋯ 0 30
canvass, the eight pieces ⋯ 0 30
damask, the twelve pieces ⋯ 0 30
drilling, the twenty pieces, or 500 arsheens ⋯ 0 30
from Petersburgh, all sorts, forty pieces, or 2,000
arsheens ⋯ 0 30
Logwood, the 800 lbs. ⋯ 0 30

M.

Mace, the 50 lbs. ⋯ 0 18
Masts, fifteen palms and upwards, the piece ⋯ 0 24
small ⋯ 0 1
for boats, the schock ⋯ 1 24
Mats from Petersburgh, the 1,000 ⋯ 0 15
Mohair, the 50 lbs. ⋯ 0 30
Mustard seed, the last of twelve barrels ⋯ 0 30

N.

Nails, Holland or Lubeck, the centner ⋯ 0 4
tree nails for ships, the 40,000 ⋯ 0 36
Nutmegs, ditto ⋯ 0 18
Nuts, the last of twenty barrels or sacks ⋯ 0 12

O.

Oars, great, the schock ⋯ 0 12
small, ditto ⋯ 0 8
Oil, olive, of Seville or Portugal, the pipe ⋯ 0 36
rape, linseed, hemp, the last of eight aulns ⋯ 0 36
train, the last of eight hogsheads, or twelve barrels ⋯ 0 36
Olibanum, the 100 lbs. ⋯ 0 9
Olives, the pipe, or two hogsheads ⋯ 0 18
Oranges, the twelve chests, or 3,600 ⋯ 0 24

P.

Paper, the eight bales, or eighty reams ⋯ 0 30
Pepper, the 100 lbs. ⋯ 0 12
Pewter, the shippound ⋯ 0 24
Pitch, great band ⋯ 0 18
small ⋯ 0 -9
Plates of tin, the four casks or shippound ⋯ 0 12
Pladding, the 1,000 ells, or forty pieces ⋯ 0 50
Prunes, the 400 lbs. ⋯ 0 9
Prunelloes, the 100 lbs. ⋯ 0 9

Q.

Quicksilver, the 50 lbs. ⋯ 0 36

R.

Rapeseed, the last of twenty-four barrels ⋯ 0 36
Raisins, the 400 lbs. or thirty-six baskets ⋯ 0 36
Resin, the shippound ⋯ 0 6
Ribbons of silk, or ferrets, the 4 lbs. ⋯ 0 10
gold or silver, the 2 lbs. ⋯ 0 10
Rice, the 200 lbs. ⋯ 0 9

S.

Saffron, the 2 lbs. ⋯ 0 9
Salt, Spanish, French, and Scotch, the last of eighteen
barrels, or eight bushels ⋯ 0 24
Lunenburg, the last of twelve bushels ⋯ 0 36
Saltpetre, the shippound ⋯ 0 6
Says, double, the two pieces ⋯ 0 9
single, or English, the four pieces ⋯ 0 6
Sail cloth, the eight pieces ⋯ 0 30
Sarsaparilla, ditto ⋯ 0 9
Shumac, the 400 lbs. ⋯ 0 9
Silk, sewing, ferret, wrought lace, the 4 lbs. ⋯ 0 10
raw, the 100 lbs. ⋯ 0 50
stuffs, the 100 lbs. ⋯ 0 15
with gold and silver, the piece ⋯ 0 18
Skins, beaver, the five deckers ⋯ 0 24
otter, the piece ⋯ 0 6
Russia, dry, wolf and fox, the five deckers ⋯ 0 18
goat, the twenty deckers ⋯ 0 36
calf, the ten deckers ⋯ 0 12
cat and sheep, the 500 pieces ⋯ 0 18

Skins, black rabbit, or lamb, the 1,000 pieces ⋯
grey rabbit, or kid, the 2,000
marten, the forty
hare, the bale valued at seventy-two rixdollars
Soap, white, the 100 lbs.
green, the last of twelve barrels
Spars, great, the twenty-five pieces
small, the 1,000
Starch, the 300 lbs.
Staves, pipe, hogshead, and barrel, the great hundred
of forty-eight schocks
Steel, the 100 lbs.
Stones, Poland, the 1,000 feet of 500 ells
Stockings of silk, the dozen, or 12 lbs.
kersey, woollen, or worsted, for children, the 100
pair
worsted, floret, and sayet, the 50 pair
woollen, for children, the 200 pair
Sturgeon, the last of twelve barrels
Stuffs, woollen, the eight pieces
Succade, the 50 lbs.
Sugar candy, or confectionary, the 100 lbs.
loaves, powder, or Muscovado, the 200 lbs.
Sword blades, the 50
hilts, ditto
Sweetwood, the 100 lbs.

T.

Tallow, the shippound
Tarras, the last, six shippound, or twelve barrels
Tar, great band, the last of twelve barrels
small band, the last of ditto
Thread, white and coloured, the 50 lbs.
gold and silver, the lb.
Tin, the shippound
Tobacco, the 100 lbs.
Treacle, the pipe or two hogsheads
Turpentine, the shippound

V.

Verdigris, the 100 lbs.
Vermilion, ditto
Velvet, fine, the piece
with thread, the two pieces
Vinegar of wine, the hogshead
beer, ale, or cider, the two hogsheads

W.

Wax, the shippound
Wainscot boards, the schock
Wine, Bordeaux, the ton, or four hogsheads, at fifty-
two rixdollars
Picardin, Hoogland, Muscat, and Frontignac, the
two hogsheads
Spanish or Portuguese, the pipe
Italian and Levant
Rhemish, the ohm
Wire, iron, or brass, the shippound
steel, the 100 lbs.
gold and silver, the lb.
Wool, beaver, the 50 lbs.
Spanish, or fine, the four shippound
coarse, or Scotch, the six shippound
flock, or cutting wool, the two shippound
Scotch, shirts, the forty pieces
shifts, the eight pieces
Wood shovels, the ten schocks
dishes or trays, the five schocks
plates, the five schocks
nails, the 20,000

Y.

Yarn, cotton, the 50 lbs.
linen, the shippound, or forty schocks
tow, the four shippound
sail, the shippound
all sorts of woollen, the 50 lbs.

Memorandum respecting the mode of preventing certain Overcharges of Sound Duties on Goods ship
the Baltic.

There have been many complaints of the Sound duty being overrated on goods which, as they
noticed in the tariff, are chargeable *ad valorem*, (1 per cent. in the case of the English, Dutch, and S
1¼ per cent. in the case of other nations;) this charge being solely regulated by the value expre
the cockets, the only documents by which the Custom-house officers at the Sound are governe
originates in the shippers of goods finding it expedient occasionally to give a nominal value to merch
not liable to an export duty in England, far exceeding the real value, in order to provide for a
shipment of the same species of goods in the same vessel (which entry can alone be considered as ex
of the intention to ship goods to that extent). It is, therefore, suggested to the shippers of merc
for the Baltic, that, besides the above-mentioned nominal value, they should cause the *real valu*
goods actually shipped to be inserted on the reverse of the cocket, as there is every reason to beli
this real value will then become the criterion by which the Sound duty will be calculated. For i
supposing a cocket to run thus —

" Know ye that Parkinson and Co. have entered British cottons, value 10,000*l.* sterling, to be
per the Newland, Francis Hunter, master, for St. Petersburgh :"

The indorsement should be —

" P. 1. a 10. Ten bales cambrics, value 4,794*l.* 5*s.* sterling, shipped on board the Newland,
Hunter, for Petersburgh."

(Signed by)   Parkinson and

(Or by the signing Custom-house officer)

The Sound duty will then probably be charged not on 10,000*l.*, but on 4,794*l.* 5*s.* Should, how
latter entry be wanting, the first sum will be the only criterion by which to calculate the Sou
and in case of overcharge, no restitution need be hoped for. — (*Rordanz, European Commerce.*)

:turn of the Number of Ships which have passed *The Sound* during each of the Years 1827, 1828, and
 9; distinguishing the respective Nations to which the same belonged. — (*Parl. Paper*, No. 249.
 s. 1830.)

Nations.	1827.	1828.	1829.
·itish · · · · · ·	5,099	4,426	4,790
anoverian · · · · ·	457	570	592
anes · · · · · ·	856	903	861
vedes · · · · · ·	1,389	1,324	1,132
orwegians · · · ·	879	1,063	1,176
ussians · · · · ·	2,038	2,222	2,185
ussians · · · · ·	384	407	359
nited Netherlands · ·	814	1,066	1,120
ecklenburghers · · ·	555	657	629
amburghers · · · ·	35	26	44
ıbeckers · · · · ·	99	122	103
emeners · · · · ·	55	60	63
nericans · · · · ·	191	221	181
rtuguese · · · · ·	11	8	6
ench · · · · · ·	103	128	181
aniards · · · · ·	—	—	10
ldenburghers · · · ·	25	42	47
lians · · · · ·· ·	—	2	2
Total · ·	13,000	13,247	13,475

MBARGO, an order issued by the government of a country to prevent the
ng of ships.

MBROIDERY (Fr. *Broderic*; Ger. *Stickerey*; It. *Ricamo*; Rus. *Schitje*; Sp.
lado), figures wrought with gold, or silver, or silk thread, upon cloth, stuffs, or
'in.

MERALD (Du. *Smaragd*; Fr. *Emeraude*; Ger. *Smaragd*; It. *Smeraldo*; Lat.
·*ragdus*; Rus. *Isumrud*; Sp. *Esmeralda*), a precious stone of a beautiful green
ur of various depths. The purest specimens come from the East Indies and
.. It is of various sizes, but usually small; great numbers being found of $\frac{1}{10}$
a inch in diameter, and a few the size of a walnut. Crystal tinged with green
ry often substituted for the inferior sorts of emeralds. Its specific gravity is
2·6 to 2·77.

MERY (Fr. *Emeril, Emeri*; Ger. *Smirgel*; Du. *Ameril, Smergel*; It. *Smer-
Smeregio*; Sp. *Esmeril*; Rus. *Nashdak*; Lat. *Smiris*). This mineral is brought
·ritain from the isle of Naxos, where it exists in large quantities. It occurs
in Germany, Italy, and Spain. It is always in shapeless masses, and mixed
other minerals. Colour intermediate between greyish black and bluish grey.
ific gravity about 4. Lustre glistening and adamantine. Emery is extensively
in the polishing of hard bodies. Its fine powder is obtained by trituration.
'homson's Chemistry.)

NTRY, BILL OF. See IMPORTATION.

RMINE (Ger. *Hermelin*; Fr. *Hermine, Ermine*; Rus. *Gornostai*), a species
·eazel (*Mustela candida*, Lin.), abundant in all cold countries, particularly
ia, Norway, Lapland, &c., and producing a most valuable species of fur.
ımmer the ermine is of a brown colour, and is called the *stoat*. It is in
·r only that the fur has that beautiful snowy whiteness and consistence so
a admired.

STRICH or ESTRIDGE (Fr. *Duvet d'autruche*; It. *Penna matta di strozzo*;
Plumazo de avestrux; Lat. *Struthionum plumæ molliores*), is the fine soft down
a lies immediately under the feathers of the ostrich. The finest is used as a
itute for beaver in the manufacture of hats, and the coarser or stronger sort
ployed in the fabrication of a stuff which resembles fine woollen cloth. We
ly import estridge from the Levant, Italy, and other parts of the Medi-
iean.

JPHORBIUM (Ger. *Euphorbiengummi*; Lat. *Euphorbium*; Fr. *Euphorbe*;
. *Akal-nafzah*), the produce of a perennial plant, a native of Africa,
of many parts of India, &c. It is a concrete gum resin; is inodorous;
first chewed has little taste, but it soon gives a very acrid burning impression
e tongue, palate, and throat, which is very permanent, and almost insupport-
It is imported in scrons containing from 100 to 150 lbs. It is in small,
v, forked pieces, often mixed with seeds and other impurities. — (*Thomson's
nsatory.*)

XCHANGE. In commerce, this term is generally used to designate that
:s of mercantile transactions, by which the debts of individuals residing at a
·ce from their creditors are cancelled without the transmission of money·

Among cities or countries having any considerable intercourse together, the deb
mutually due by each other approach, for the most part, near to an equality.   The
are at all times, for example, a considerable number of persons in London indebted
Hamburgh; but, speaking generally, there are about an equal number of persons
London to whom Hamburgh is indebted.   And hence, when A. of London has a pa
ment to make to B. of Hamburgh, he does not remit an equivalent sum of money to t
latter; but he goes into the market and buys a *bill* upon Hamburgh, that is, he buys
order from C. of London addressed to his debtor D. of Hamburgh, requesting him
pay the amount to A. or his order.   A., having indorsed this bill or order, sends it
B., who receives payment from his neighbour D.   The convenience of all parties
consulted by a transaction of this sort.   The debts due by A. to B, and by D. to C
are extinguished without the intervention of any money.   A. of London pays C. of dit
and D. of Hamburgh pays B. of ditto.   The debtor in one place is substituted for t
debtor in another; and a postage or two, and the stamp for the bill, form the whole e
penses.   All risk of loss is obviated.

A bill of exchange may, therefore, be defined to be an order addressed to some pers
residing at a distance, directing him to pay a certain specified sum to the person in who
favour the bill is drawn, or his order.   In mercantile phraseology, the person who dra
a bill is termed the *drawer;* the person in whose favour it is drawn, the *remitter;* t
person on whom it is drawn, the *drawee;* and after he has accepted, the *acceptor.* The
persons into whose hands the bill may have passed previously to its being paid, are, fro
their writing their names on the back, termed *indorsers;* and the person in whose po
session the bill is at any given period, is termed the *holder* or *possessor.*

The negotiation of *inland* bills of exchange, or of those drawn in one part of Gre
Britain and Ireland on another, is entirely in the hands of bankers, and is conduct
in the manner already explained. — (See *antè,* p. 60.)   Bills drawn by the merchants
one country upon another are termed *foreign* bills of exchange, and it is to their neg
tiation that the following remarks principally apply.

I. *Par of Exchange.* — The *par* of the currency of any two countries means, among me
chants, the equivalency of a certain amount of the currency of the one in the curren
of the other, *supposing the currencies of both to be of the precise weight and purity fixed
their respective mints.*   Thus, according to the mint regulations of Great Britain a
France, 1*l.* sterling is equal to 25 fr. 20 cent., which is said to be the par between Lo
don and Paris.   And the exchange between the two countries is said to be at par wh
bills are negotiated on this footing; that is, for example, when a bill for 100*l.* drawn
London is worth 2,520 fr. in Paris, and conversely.   When 1*l.* in London buys a b
on Paris for more than 25 fr. 20 cent., the exchange is said to be in favour of Lond
and against Paris; and when, on the other hand, 1*l.* in London will not buy a bill
Paris for 25 fr. 20 cent., the exchange is against London and in favour of Paris. — S
table of the par of exchange at the end of this article.

II. *Circumstances which determine the Course of Exchange.* — The exchange is affect
or made to diverge from par, by two classes of circumstances: *first,* by any discrepar
between the actual weight or fineness of the coins, or of the bullion for which the su
stitutes used in their place will exchange, and their weight or fineness, as fixed by t
mint regulations; and, *secondly,* by any sudden increase or diminution of the bills dra
in one country upon another.

1. It is but seldom that the coins of any country correspond exactly with their m
standard; and when they diverge from it, an allowance corresponding to the differe
between the actual value of the coins, and their mint value, must be made in determin
the *real* par.   Thus, if while the coins of Great Britain corresponded with the mint stand
in weight and purity, those of France were either 10 per cent. worse or debased be
the standard of her mint, the exchange, it is obvious, would be at *real* par when it w
nominally 10 per cent. against Paris, or when a bill payable in London for 100*l.*
worth in Paris 2,772 fr. instead of 2,520 fr.   In estimating the real course of excha
between any two or more places, it is always necessary to attend carefully to this circ
stance; that is, to examine whether their currencies be all of the standard weight
purity, and if not, how much they differ from it.   When the coins circulating i
country are either so worn or rubbed as to have sunk considerably below their r
standard, or when paper money is depreciated from excess or want of credit, the excha
is at real par only when it is against such country to the extent to which its coins
worn or its paper depreciated.   When this circumstance is taken into account, it wil
found that the exchange during the latter years of the war, though apparently very m
against this country, was really in our favour.   The depression was nominal only; b
occasioned by the great depreciation of the paper currency in which bills were paid.

2. Variations in the actual course of exchange, or in the price of bills, arising f
circumstances affecting the currency of either of two countries trading together, are *nom
only*: such as are *real* grow out of circumstances affecting their trade.

en two countries trade together, and each buys of the other commodities of pre-
the same value, their debts and credits will be equal, and, of course, the *real*
ige will be at par.   The *bills* drawn by the one will be exactly equivalent to those
by the other, and their respective claims will be adjusted without requiring the
r of bullion or any other valuable produce.   But it very rarely happens that the
reciprocally due by any two countries are equal.   There is almost always a balance
on the one side or the other; and this balance must affect the exchange.   If the
lue by London to Paris exceeded those due by Paris to London, the competition
London market for bills on Paris would, because of the comparatively great
at of payments our merchants had to make in Paris, be greater than the competition
is for bills on London; and, consequently, the real exchange would be in favour
is and against London.

cost of conveying bullion from one country to another forms the limit within
the rise and fall of the *real* exchange between them must be confined.   If 1 per
ufficed to cover the expense and risk attending the transmission of money from
n to Paris, it would be indifferent to a London merchant whether he paid 1 per
remium for a bill of exchange on Paris, or remitted money direct to that city.   If
mium were less than 1 per cent., it would clearly be his interest to make his pay-
by bills in preference to remittances: and that it could not exceed 1 per cent. is
s; for every one would prefer remitting money, to buying a bill at a greater pre-
han sufficed to cover the expense of a money remittance.   If, owing to the breaking
hostilities between the two countries, or to any other cause, the cost of remitting
from London to Paris were increased, the fluctuations of the *real* exchange
n them *might* also be increased.   For the limits within which such fluctuations
nge, correspond in all cases with the cost of making remittances in cash.

ctuations in the *nominal* exchange, that is, in the value of the currencies of
es trading together, have no effect on foreign trade.   When the currency is
ated, the premium which the exporter of commodities derives from the sale of
l drawn on his correspondent abroad, is only equivalent to the increase in the
f the goods exported, occasioned by this depreciation.   But when the premium
reign bill is a consequence not of a fall in the value of money, but of a deficiency
supply of bills, there is no rise of prices; and in these circumstances the unfa-
le exchange operates as a stimulus to exportation.   As soon as the *real* ex-
diverges from *par*, the mere inspection of a price current is no longer sufficient
late the operations of the merchant.   If it be unfavourable, the premium
the exporter will receive on the sale of his bill must be included in the
e of the profit he is likely to derive from the transaction.   The greater that pre-
the less will be the difference of prices necessary to induce him to export.   And
n unfavourable *real* exchange has an effect exactly the same with what would be
ed by granting a bounty on exportation equal to the premium on foreign bills.

for the same reason that an unfavourable *real* exchange increases exportation, it
ionally diminishes importation.   When the exchange is really unfavourable, the
f commodities imported from abroad must be so much lower than their price at
s not merely to afford, exclusive of expenses, the ordinary profit of stock on their
t also to compensate for the premium which the importer must pay for a foreign
ie remit one to his correspondent, or for the discount, added to the invoice price,
orrespondent draw upon him.   A less quantity of foreign goods will, there-
it our market when the *real* exchange is unfavourable; and fewer payments
to be made abroad, the competition for foreign bills will be diminished, and the
hange rendered proportionally favourable.   In the same way, it is easy to see
vourable *real* exchange must operate as *duty* on exportation, and as a *bounty* on
tion.

thus that fluctuations in the *real* exchange have a necessary tendency to correct
ves.   They can never, for any considerable period, *exceed* the expense of trans-
bullion from the debtor to the creditor country.   But the exchange cannot
e either permanently favourable or unfavourable to this extent.   When fa-
e, it corrects itself by restricting exportation and facilitating importation; and
ifavourable, it produces the same effect by giving an unusual stimulus to export-
d by throwing obstacles in the way of importation.   The true PAR forms the
f these oscillations; and although the thousand circumstances which are daily
rly affecting the state of debt and credit, prevent the ordinary course of exchange
ing almost ever precisely at *par*, its fluctuations, whether on the one side or the
e confined within certain limits, and have a constant tendency to disappear.

natural tendency which the exchange has to correct itself, is powerfully assisted
perations of the bill-merchants.

nd, for example, might owe a large excess of debt to Amsterdam, yet, as the
e amount of the debts *due* by a commercial country is generally balanced by

the amount of those which it has to receive, the deficiency of bills on Amsterda
London would most probably be compensated by a proportional redundancy of
on some other place. Now, it is the business of the merchants who deal in bil
the same way as of those who deal in bullion or any other commodity, to buy them w
they are cheapest, and to sell them where they are dearest. They would, therefore,
up the bills drawn by other countries on Amsterdam, and dispose of them in Lon
and by so doing, would prevent any great fall in the price of bills on Amsterda
those countries in which the supply exceeded the demand, and any great rise in (
Britain and those countries in which the supply happened to be deficient. In the
between Italy and this country, the bills drawn on Great Britain amount almost
riably to a greater sum than those drawn on Italy. The bill-merchants, howeve
buying up the excess of the Italian bills on London, and selling them in Holland,
other countries indebted to England, prevent the *real* exchange from ever beco
very much depressed.

III. *Negotiation of Bills of Exchange.* — Bills of exchange are either made pay
at *sight*, at a certain specified time *after sight* or *after date*, or at *usance*, which
usual term allowed by the custom or law of the place where the bill is payable. G
rally, however, a few days are allowed for payment beyond the term when the
becomes due, which are denominated *days of grace*, and which vary in different count
In Great Britain and Ireland, *three* days' grace are allowed for all bills except
payable at sight, which must be paid as soon as presented. The following is a stateme
the usance and days of grace for bills drawn upon some of the principal commercial c

[m|d. m|s. d|d. d'.s. d|a. respectively denote *months after date, months after sight,
after date, days after sight, days after acceptance.*]

London on	Usance.	Days of Grace.	London on	Usance.	Days of Grace.	London on	Usance	Da of Gra
Amsterdam	1 m|d.	6	Geneva	30 d|d.	5	Vienna †	14 d|a.	
Rotterdam	1 m|d.	6	Madrid	2 m|s.	14	Malta	30 d|d.	15
Antwerp	1 m|d.	6	Cadiz	60 d|d.	6	Naples	3 m|d.	
Hamburgh	1 m|d.	12	Bilboa	2 m|d.	14	Palermo	3 m|d.	
Altona	1 m|d.	12	Gibraltar	2 m|s.	14	Lisbon	30 d|s.	
Dantzic	14 d'a.	10	Leghorn	3 m|d.	0	Oporto	30 d|s.	
Paris*	30 d|d.	10	Leipsic	14 d|a.	0	Rio Janeiro	30 d|d.	
Bordeaux	30 d'd.	10	Genoa	3 m|d.	30	Dublin	21 d|s.	
Bremen	1 m'd.	8	Venice	3 m|d.	6	Cork	21 d|s.	
Barcelona	60 d d.	14						

In the dating of bills the new style is now used in every country in Europe, wit
exception of Russia.

In London, bills of exchange are bought and sold by brokers, who go round
principal merchants and discover whether they are buyers or sellers of bills. A f
the brokers of most influence, after ascertaining the state of the relative suppl
demand for bills, suggest a price at which the greater part of the transactions of th
are settled, with such deviations as particular bills, from their being in very high c
credit, may be subject to. The price fixed by the brokers is that which is publish
Wettenhall's list ; but the first houses generally negotiate their bills on ½, 1, 1½,
per cent. better terms than those quoted. In London and other great commercial
a class of middlemen speculate largely on the rise and fall of the exchange, buying
when they expect a rise, and selling them when a fall is anticipated.

It is usual, in drawing foreign bills of exchange, to draw them in sets, or dupli
lest the first should be lost or miscarry. When bills are drawn in sets, each must
tain a condition that it shall be payable only while the others remain unpaid : thu
first is payable only, "second and third unpaid ; " the second, "first and third bein
paid," and the third, " first and second unpaid."

All bills of exchange must be drawn upon stamps as under : —

Inland Bills and Notes. — Not exceeding Two Months after Date, or Sixty Days after Sight.				Exceeding Two Months, &c.
£ s.	£ s.	£ s. d.		£ s. d.
If - 2 0 and not above	5 5 . .	0 1 0		0 1 6
Above 5 5 —	20 0 . .	0 1 6		0 2 0
— 20 0 —	30 0 . .	0 2 0		0 2 6
— 30 0 —	50 0 . .	0 2 6		0 3 6
— 50 0 —	100 0 . .	0 3 6		0 4 6
— 100 0 —	200 0 . .	0 4 6		0 5 0
— 200 0 —	300 0 . .	0 5 0		0 6 0
— 300 0 —	500 0 . .	0 6 0		0 8 6
— 500 0 —	1,000 0 . .	0 8 6		0 12 6
— 1,000 0 —	2,000 0 . .	0 12 6		0 15 0
— 2,000 0 —	3,000 0 . .	0 15 6		1 5 0
— 3,000 0	.	1 5 0		1 10 0

* In France no days of grace are allowed on bills payable à vue.
† In Austria, bills payable at sight, or on demand, or at less than seven days after sight or date,
allowed any days of grace.

omissory notes from 2l. to 100l. inclusive, are not to be drawn payable to bearer on demand, (excepting
crs' *re-issuable* notes, which require a different stamp.) — But notes for any sum exceeding 100l. may
awn either payable to bearer on demand, or otherwise. — (See *ante*, p. 64.)

reign Bills of Exchange. — Foreign bill, drawn in but payable out of Great Britain, if drawn singly,
ame duty as an inland bill.

	s.	*d.*					*s.*	*d.*
gn bills of exchange, drawn in sets,			Exceeding £ 500 and not exceeding £1,000				5	0
every bill of each set, if the sum does			— 1,000 — 2,000				7	6
exceed £ 100	1	6	— 2,000 — 3,000			10	0
eding £100 and not exceeding £200	3	0	— 3,000 . . .			15	0
— 200 — 500	4	0						

o one acquainted with the fundamental rules of arithmetic can have any difficulty
ever in estimating how much a sum of money in one country is worth in another, acing to the state of the exchange at the time. The common arithmetical books abound
amples of such computations. But in conducting the business of exchange, a direct
ttance is not always preferred. When a merchant in London, for example, means to
arge a debt due by him in Paris, it is his business to ascertain not only the state of
lirect exchange between London and Paris, and, consequently, the sum which he
t pay in London for a bill on Paris equivalent to his debt, but also the state of
exchange between London and Hamburgh, Hamburgh and Paris, &c.; for it
lently happens, that it may be more advantageous for him to buy a bill on Ham-
h, Amsterdam, or Lisbon, and to direct his agent to invest the proceeds in a bill
Paris, rather than remit directly to the latter. This is termed the ARBITRATION
xchange. An example or two will suffice to show the principle on which it is con-
ed.

us, if the exchange between London and Amsterdam be 35s. Flemish (old coinage) per pound sterling,
etween Paris and Amsterdam 1s. 6d. Flemish per franc, then, in order to ascertain whether a direct or
ect remittance to Paris would be most advantageous, we must calculate what would be the value of
ranc in English money if the remittance were made through Holland; for if it be less than that
ing from the direct exchange, it will obviously be the preferable mode of remitting. This is deter-
l by stating, as 35s. Flem. (the Amsterdam currency in a pound sterling) : 1s. 6d. Flem. (Amsterdam
ncy in a franc) : : 1l. : 10d. the proportional, or *arbitrated* value of the tranc. — Hence, if the English
y, or bill of exchange, to pay a debt in Paris, were remitted by Amsterdam, it would require 10d. to
arge a debt of a franc, or 1l. to discharge a debt of 24 francs : and, therefore, if the exchange between
on and Paris were at 24, it would be indifferent to the English merchant whether he remitted directly
ris, or indirectly *via* Amsterdam; but if the exchange between London and Paris were *above* 24, a
direct remittance would be preferable; while, if, on the other hand, the direct exchange were less
24, the indirect remittance ought as plainly to be preferred.

uppose," to borrow an example from Dr. Kelly (*Universal Cambist*, vol. ii. p. 137.), " the exchange
ndon and Lisbon to be at 68d. per milree, and that of Lisbon on Madrid 500 rees per dollar, the arbi-
price between London and Madrid is 34d. sterling per dollar; for as 1,000 rees : 68d. : : 500 rees

But if the direct exchange of London on Madrid be 55d. sterling per dollar, then London, by
ting directly to Madrid, must pay 35d. for every dollar; whereas, by remitting through Lisbon, he
ay only 34d.; it is, therefore, the interest of London to remit indirectly to Madrid through Lisbon.
e other hand, if London draws directly on Madrid, he will receive 35d. sterling per dollar; whereas,
wing indirectly through Lisbon, he would receive only 31d.; it is, therefore, the interest of London
w directly on Madrid. Hence the following rules : —

Where the certain price is given, draw through the place which produces the lowest arbitrated
and remit through that which produces the highest.

Where the uncertain price is given, draw through that place which produces the highest arbitrated
and remit through that which produces the lowest."

ompound arbitration, or when more than three places are concerned, then, in order to find how
a remittance passing through them all will amount to in the last place, or, which is the same thing,
the arbitrated price between the first and the last, we have only to repeat the different statements
same manner as in the foregoing examples.

s, if the exchange between London and Amsterdam be 35s. Flem. for 1l. sterling; between Amster-
nd Lisbon 42d. Flem. for 1 old crusade; and between Lisbon and Paris 480 rees for 3 francs; what
arbitrated price between London and Paris ?

ne first place, as 35s. Flem. : 1l. : : 42d. Flem. : 2s. sterling, = 1 old crusade.

nd, as 1 old crusade, or 400 rees : 2s. sterling : : 480 rees : 2s. 4¾d. sterling, = 3 francs.

rd, as 2s. 4¾d. sterling : 3 francs : : 1l. sterling : 25 francs, the arbitrated price of the pound sterling
n London and Paris.

s operation may be abridged as follows : —

		1l. sterling.
1l. sterling	=	35s. Flemish.
3½ shillings Flem.	=	1 old crusade.
1 old crusade	=	400 rees.
480 rees	=	3 francs.

$$\text{Hence } \frac{35 \times 400 \times 3}{480 \times 3\frac{1}{2}} = \frac{4{,}200}{168} = 25 \text{ francs.}$$

abridged operation evidently consists in arranging the terms so that those which would form the
s in continued statements in the Rule of Three are multiplied together for a common divisor,
e other terms for a common dividend. The ordinary arithmetical books abound with examples of
erations.

following account of the manner in which a very large transaction was actually conducted by
t remittances, will sufficiently illustrate the principles we have been endeavouring to explain.
04, Spain was bound to pay to France a large subsidy; and, in order to do this, three distinct
s presented themselves : —

o send dollars to Paris by land.

remit bills of exchange directly to Paris.

authorise Paris to draw directly on Spain.

first of these methods was tried, but it was found too slow and expensive; and the second and
lans were considered likely to turn the exchange against Spain. The following method by the
t, or circular exchange, was, therefore, adopted.

rchant, or *banquier*, at Paris, was appointed to manage the operation, which he thus conducted :—
se London, Amsterdam, Hamburgh, Cadiz, Madrid, and Paris, as the principal hinges on which

the operation was to turn; and he engaged correspondents in each of these cities to support the circulat Madrid and Cadiz were the places in Spain from whence remittances were to be made; and dollars we of course, to be sent to where they bore the highest price, for which bills were to be procured on Paris on any other places that might be deemed more advantageous.

The principle being thus established, it only remained to regulate the extent of the operation, so as to issue too much paper on Spain, and to give the circulation as much support as possible from business. With this view, London was chosen as a place to which the operation might be chiefly direc as the price of dollars was then high in England; a circumstance which rendered the proportional excha advantageous to Spain.

The business was commenced at Paris, where the negotiation of drafts issued on Hamburgh and A sterdam served to answer the immediate demands of the state; and orders were transmitted to th places to draw for the reimbursements on London, Madrid, or Cadiz, according as the course of excha was most favourable. The proceedings were all conducted with judgment, and attended with comp success. At the commencement of the operation, the course of exchange of Cadiz on London was 36 but, by the plan adopted, Spain got 39¾d., or above 8 *per cent.* by the remittance of dollars to Lond and considerable advantages were also gained by the circulation of bills through the several places on Continent. — (*Kelly's Cambist*, vol. ii. p. 168.; *Dubost's Elements of Commerce*, 2d ed. p. 218.)

LAW OF BILLS OF EXCHANGE.

The chief legal privileges appertaining to bills are, first, that though only a simple contract, yet th are always presumed to have been originally given for a good and valuable consideration; and, second they are assignable to a third person not named in the bill or party to the contract, so as to vest in assignee a right of action, in his own name; which right of action, no release by the drawer to the accept nor set-off or cross demand due from the former to the latter, can affect.

All persons, whether merchants or not, being legally qualified to contract, may be parties to a bill. no action can be supported against a person incapable of binding himself, on a bill drawn, indorsed, or cepted by such incapacitated person; at the same time the bill is good against all other competent part thereto.

Bills may be drawn, accepted, or indorsed by the party's agent or attorney verbally authorised for purpose. When a person has such authority, he must either write the name of his principal, or state writing that he draws, &c. as agent: thus, " per procuration, for A. B."

Where one of several partners accepts a bill drawn on the firm, for himself and partners, or in his o name only, such acceptance binds the partnership if it concern the trade. But the acceptance of one several partners on behalf of himself and partners, will not bind the others, if it concern the accep only in a separate and distinct interest; and the holder of the bill, at the time he become so, was aware that circumstance. If, however, he be a *bonâ fide* holder for a sufficient consideration, and had no su knowledge at the time he first became possessed of the bill, no subsequently acquired knowledge of misconduct of the partner in giving such security will prevent him from recovering on such bills agai all the partners.

Although no precise form of words is required to constitute a bill of exchange or promissory note, it is necessary that it should be *payable at all events*, and not depend on any contingency; and that it made for the payment of money only, and not for payment of money and performance of some other a as the delivery of a horse, or the like.

If, however, the event on which the payment is to depend must inevitably happen, it is of no impo ance how long the payment may be in suspense; so a bill is negotiable and valid if drawn payable weeks after the death of the drawer's father, or payable to an infant when he shall become of age.

Any material alteration of a bill after it has been drawn, accepted, or indorsed, such as the date, su or time of payment, will invalidate it: but the mere correction of a mistake, as by inserting the words " order " will have no such effect.

The negotiability of a bill depends on the insertion of sufficient operative words of transfer; such as making it payable to A. or order, or to A. or bearer generally.

Although a bill is presumed to have been originally drawn upon a good and valuable consideration, in certain cases a want of sufficient consideration may be insisted on in defence to an action on a Certain considerations have been made illegal by statute; as for signing a bankrupt's certificate, for mo won at gaming, or for money bet on a usurious contract. But with respect to gaming, it is held, th bill founded on a gambling transaction is good in the hands of a *bonâ fide* holder; and by 58 Geo. 3. c. a bill or note in the hands of an innocent holder, although originally founded on a usurious contract not invalid.

In general, if a bill is fair and legal in its origin, a subsequent illegal contract or consideration on indorsement thereof, will not invalidate it in the hands of a *bonâ fide* holder.

A bill cannot be given in evidence in a court of justice, unless it be duly stamped, not only with a sta of the proper value, but also of the proper denomination.

Acceptance of a Bill. — An acceptance is an engagement to pay a bill according to the tenour of the ceptance, which may be either *absolute* or *qualified*. An *absolute* acceptance is an engagement to pa bill according to its request, which is done by the drawee writing " Accepted" on the bill, and subscri his name; or writing " Accepted" only; or merely subscribing his name at the bottom or across the A *qualified* acceptance is when a bill is accepted conditionally; as when goods conveyed to the dra are sold, or when a navy bill is paid, or other future event which does not bind the acceptor till the tingency has happened.

An acceptance may be also partial; as to pay 100*l.* instead of 150*l.*, or to pay at a different time or p from that required by the bill. But in all cases of a conditional or partial acceptance, the holder sho if he mean to resort to the other parties to the bill in default of payment, give notice to them of partial or conditional acceptance.

In all cases of presenting a bill for acceptance, it is necessary to present the bill at the house where drawee lives, or where it is made payable. By 1 & 2 Geo. 4. c. 78., all bills accepted payable at a bank or other place are to be deemed a general acceptance; but if they are accepted payable at a banker's " o and not otherwise or elsewhere," it is a qualified acceptance, and the acceptor is not liable to pay the except in default of payment when such payment shall have been first demanded at the banker's. drawee is entitled to keep the bill twenty-four hours when presented for acceptance. The acceptan an inland bill must be *in writing on the face of the bill*, or, if there be more parts than one, on one of parts; nothing short of this constitutes a valid acceptance.

If a bill is made payable a certain time *after sight*, it must, in order to fix the time when it is paid, be presented for acceptance, and the date of the acceptance should appear thus: " Accepted, 1st, 1831."

Due diligence is the only thing to be considered in presenting any description of bill for acceptance; such diligence is a question depending on the situation of the parties, the distance at which they live, the facility of communication between them.

When the drawee refuses to accept, any third party, after protesting, may accept for the honour of bill generally, or for the drawee, or for the indorser; in which case the acceptance is called an accept *supra protest.*

The drawers and indorsers are discharged from liability, unless due notice of non-acceptance when sented for acceptance, or non-payment at the time the bill becomes due, is given. These notices mu given with all due diligence to all the parties to whom the holder means to resort for payment. Gener

foreign and inland bills, notice is given next day to the immediate indorser, and such indorser is
a day, when he should give fresh notice to the parties who are liable to him.

e may be sent by the post, however near the residence of the parties may be to each other; and
the letter containing such notice should miscarry, yet it will be sufficient; but the letter containing
ice should be delivered at the General Post-office, or at a receiving-house appointed by that office,
he bellman in the street. In all cases of notice, notice to one of several parties is held to be notice
and if one of several drawers be also the acceptor, it is not necessary to give notice to the other
s.

the non-acceptance or non-payment of a bill, the holder, or a public notary for him, should pro-
that is, draw up a notice of the refusal to accept or pay the bill, and the declaration of the holder
sustaining loss thereby. Inland bills need not be protested; in practice they are usually only noted
acceptance; but this, without the protest, is wholly futile, and adds nothing whatever to the
e of the holder, while it entails a useless expense on those liable to pay.

sement of Bills. — An indorsement is the act by which the holder of a negotiable instrument
rs his right to another person, termed the indorsee. It is usually made on the back of a bill, and
e in writing; but the law has not prescribed any set form of words as necessary to the ceremony,
general the mere signature of the indorser is sufficient.

.lls payable to order or to bearer for 1*l.* and upwards are negotiable by indorsement; and the
r of them for a good consideration, before they are payable, gives a right of action against all the
nt parties on the bill, if the bills in themselves are valid; but a transfer after they are due will
ice the indorser in the situation of the person from whom he takes them.

may be transferred either by delivery only, or by indorsement and delivery: bills payable to order
isferred by the latter mode only; but bills payable to bearer may be transferred by either mode.
insfer by delivery, the person making it ceases to be a party to the bill; but on a transfer by indorse-
e is to all intents and purposes chargeable as a new drawer.

l originally transferable may be restrained by restrictive words; for the payee or indorsee, having
olute property in the bill, may, by express words, restrict its currency by indorsing it " Payable to
nly," or " to A. B. for his use," or any other words clearly demonstrating his intention to make a
ive and limited indorsement. Such special indorsement precludes the person in whose favour it
from making a transfer, so as to give a right of action against the special indorser, or any of the
nt parties to the bill.

king bills to account or discount, it is important well to examine all special indorsements. Lord
len has decided that a person who discounts a bill indorsed " Pay to A. B. or order *for my use,*"
ts it subject to the risk of having to pay the money to the special indorser, who so limited the ap-
n *for my use*; thus a party may be liable to pay the amount of the bill twice over, unless he
sly ascertains that the payment has been made conformably to the import of the indorsement.
the payment of part, a bill may be indorsed over for the residue.

ntment for P yment. — The holder of a bill must be careful to present it for payment at the time
ie, or the drawer and indorsers will be exonerated from their liability; even the bankruptcy, in-
/, or death of the acceptor will not excuse a neglect to make presentment to the assignees or
r; nor will the insufficiency of a bill in any respect constitute an excuse for non-presentment:
entment should be made at a reasonable time of the day when the bill is due; and if by the known
of any trade or place bills are payable only within particular hours, a presentment must be within
urs. If a bill has a qualified acceptance, the presentment should be at the place mentioned in
alified acceptance, or all the parties will be discharged from their obligations.

ll fall due on Sunday, Good Friday, Christmas Day, or any public fast or thanksgiving day, the
ment must be on the day preceding these holidays. By 7 & 8 Geo. 4. c. 15., if a bill or note be pay-
the day preceding these holidays, notice of the dishonour may be given the day following the
and if Christmas Day fall on Monday, notice may be given on Tuesday.

however, payable at usance, or at a certain time after date or sight, or after demand, ought not to
ited for payment precisely at the expiration of the time mentioned in the bills, but at the ex-
of what are termed *days of grace.* The days of grace allowed, vary in different countries, and
ways to be computed according to the usage of the place where the bill is due.—(See *antè*, p. 5ᴜ2.)
ourgh, and in France, the day on which the bill falls due makes one of the days of grace; but no
se.

is payable on demand, or when no time of payment is expressed, no days of grace are allowed;
are payable instantly on presentment. On bank post bills no days of grace are claimed; but on a
ble at sight the usual days of grace are allowed from the sight or demand.

nt of a bill should be made only to the holder; and it may be refused unless the bill be produced
ered up. On payment, a receipt should be written on the back; and when a part is paid, the same
e acknowledged upon the bill, or the party paying may be liable to pay the amount a second time
fidc indorser.

ssory Notes and Checks. — The chief distinction between promissory notes and bills of exchange
he former are a direct engagement by the drawer to pay them according to their tenor, without
vention of a third party as drawee or acceptor. Promissory notes may be drawn payable on de-
a person named therein, or to order, or to bearer generally. They are assignable and indorsable;
l respects so nearly assimilated to bills by 3 & 4 Ann. c. 9., that the laws which have been stated
g upon the latter, may be generally understood as applicable to the former. In *Edis* v. *Bury*
en decided, in case an instrument is drawn so equivocally as to render it uncertain whether it
of exchange or promissory note, the holder may treat it as either against the drawer.

ssory notes, bills, drafts, or undertakings in writing, being made negotiable or transferable for a
than 20*s.*, are void, and persons uttering such are subject to a penalty not exceeding 20*l.* recover-
re a justice of peace.

sue of any promissory note payable to bearer on demand for a less sum than 5*l.* by the Bank of
or any licensed English banker, is prohibited; and by 9 Geo. 4. c. 65. it is provided, that no cor-
or person shall utter or negotiate, in England, any such note which has been made or issued in
Ireland, or elsewhere, under a penalty not exceeding 20*l.* ncr less than 5*l.* But this does not ex-
ny draft or order on bankers for the use of the drawer.

ssory notes for any sum exceeding 100*l.* may be drawn payable to bearer on demand or otherwise;
from 2*l.* to 100*l.* inclusive are not to be drawn payable to bearer on demand, except bankers
le notes, which require a different stamp.

t or *draft* is as negotiable as a bill of exchange, and vests in the assignee the same right of action
ie assignor. As to the presentation of checks, &c. (see CHECK.)

rson making, accepting, or paying any bill, draft, order, or promissory note, not duly stamped, is
penalty of 50*l.*; for post-dating them, 100*l.*; and for not truly specifying the place where un-
drafts are issued, 100*l.*: and any person knowingly receiving such unstamped draft, 20*l.*; and the
nowingly paying it, 100*l.*; besides not being allowed such sum in account.

concluding this article on mercantile paper, it may not be improper to introduce one or two
with regard to acceptances, and accommodation paper, and proceedings in case of the loss of

man should not put his name as acceptor to a bill of exchange without well considering whether
e means of paying the same when due, as otherwise he may be liable not only to the cost of the
inst himself, but also to the costs of the actions against the other parties to the bill: the shrewd

tradesman is generally anxious to get the acceptance of his debtor at a short date, well knowing [that it] not only fixes the amount of the debt, but it is more speedily recoverable by legal procedure than a[...] debt.

Secondly, Traders who wish to support their respectability, and desire to succeed in business, sho[uld be] cautious in resorting to the destructive system of cross-accommodation acceptances: it seldom ends [...] and usually excites suspicion as to the integrity of the parties; it being an expedient often adopt[ed by] swindlers to defraud the public. Independent of the expense in stamps and discounts, and frequen[t] noting, interest, and law expenses, the danger attending such accommodation is sufficient to deter [...] the practice. Suppose, for instance, A. and B. mutually accommodate each other to the amount of 1[...] the acceptances being in the hands of third persons: both A. and B. are liable to such third persons [to the] extent of 2,000l. each; and should A. by any unforeseen occurrence be suddenly rendered unable to [meet] his acceptances, the holders of the whole, as well the acceptances of A. as the acceptances of B., will [look] to B. for payment; and it may so happen, that although B. could have provided for his own share [of] accommodation paper, he may be unable to provide for the whole, and may thus become insolvent.

Thirdly, In case of the loss of a bill, the 9 & 10 Will. 3. c. 17. provides, that if any inland bill be l[ost or] missing within the time limited for its payment, the drawer shall, on sufficient security given to inde[mnify] him if such bill be found again, give another bill of the same tenor with the first.

Lastly, It is of great importance to bankers and others taking bills and notes, that they should have knowledge of the parties from whom they receive them; otherwise, if the instrument turn out to [have] been lost or fraudulently obtained, they may, without equivalent, be deprived of their security, [and] action by the owner to recover possession. Lord Tenterden has decided, "if a person take a bill, n[or] any other kind of security, under circumstances which ought to excite suspicion in the mind [of a] reasonable man acquainted with the ordinary affairs of life, and which ought to put him on his gua[rd to] make the necessary inquiries, and he do not, then he loses the right of maintaining possession of t[he in]strument against the rightful owner." — (*Guildhall, Oct. 25. 1826.*)

I. Table containing the VALUE OF THE MONIES of Account of different Places (expressed in Pence [and] Decimals of Pence), according to the Mint Price both of Gold and Silver in England: th[e] 3l. 17s. 10½d. per oz. for Gold, and 5s. 2d. per oz. for Silver. — (*Kelly's Cambist*, ii. p. 149.)

Place	Currency	Value in Silver (d.)	Value in Gold (d.)
Aix-la-Chapelle,	Rixdollar current	31, 40	31, 43
Amsterdam,	Rixdollar banco (agio at 4 per cent.)	52, 54	variable
	Florin banco	21,	ditto
	Florin current	20, 72	ditto
	Pound Flemish current	124, 32	ditto
Antwerp	Pound Flemish (money of exchange)	123, 25	123, 87
	Florin (money of exchange)	20, 54	20, 64
	Pound Flemish current	105, 65	106, 18
	Florin current	17, 60	17, 70
Barcelona	Libra Catalan	28, 14	26, 70
Basil	Rixdollar, or ecu of exchange	47, 27	47,
	Rixdollar current	42, 45	42, 20
Berlin	Pound banco	47, 25	variable
	Rixdollar current	36,	ditto
Berne	Ecu of 3 livres	42, 64	42, 90
	Crown of 25 batzen	35, 53	35, 75
Bremen	Rixdollar current	37, 80	variable
	Rixdollar in Carls d'or	—	39, 68
Cassel	Rixdollar current	37, 80	variable
Cologne	Rixdollar specie of 80 albuses	31, 38	ditto
	Rixdollar current of 78 albuses	30, 60	ditto
Constantinople,	Piastre, or dollar	9, 45	uncer.
Dantzic	Gulden or florin	9,	9,
Denmark	Rixdollar specie	54, 72	—
	Rixdollar crown money	48, 37	—
	Rixdollar Danish currency	41, 27	44, 88
England	Pound sterling	240,	240,
Florence	Lira	8, 12	8, 53
	Ducat, or crown current	56, 84	59, 71
	Scudo d'or, or gold crown	—	63, 97
France	Livre Tournois	9, 58	9, 38
	Franc (new system)	9, 70	9, 52
Francfort	Rixdollar convention money	37, 80	37, 65
	Rixdollar Muntze, or in small coins	31, 50	—
Germany	Rixdollar current	37, 80	variable
	Rixdollar specie	50, 4	ditto
	Florin of the Empire	25, 20	ditto
	Rixdollar Muntze	31, 50	ditto
	Florin Muntze	21,	ditto
Geneva	Livre current	16, 13	16, 13
	Florin	4, 60	4, 84
Genoa	Lira fuori banco	8,	7, 83
	Pezza, or dollar of exchange		
	Scudo di cambio, or crown of exchange	45, 92	45, 50
Hamburgh	Mark banco (at a medium)	18, 22	variable
	Pound Flemish banco	136, 65	ditto

Place	Currency	Value in Silver (d.)
	Mark current	14,
	Pound Flemish current	111,
Hanover	Rixdollar (in cash)	42,
	Rixdollar (gold value)	39,
Königsberg,	Gulden or florin	12,
Leghorn	Pezza of 8 reals	46,
	Lira moneta buona	8,
	Lira moneta lunga	7,
Leipsic	Rixdollar convention money	37,
	Rixdollar in Louis d'ors or Fredericks	—
Malta	Scudo or crown	21,
Milan	Lira Imperiale	10,
	Lira corrente	7,
	Scudo Imperiale	60,
	Scudo corrente	42,
Modena	Lira	3,
Munich	Gulden or florin	21,
Naples	Ducat of 1818	41,
Parma	Lira	2,
Persia	Toman of 100 mamoodis	287,
Poland	Gulden or florin	6,
Portugal	Milree	—
	Old Crusade	—
Riga	Rixdollar Alberts	52,
	Rixdollar currency (agio at 40 per cent.)	37,
Rome	Scudo or crown	52,
	Scudo di stampa d'oro	79,
Russia	Ruble	—
Sardinia	Lira	18,
Sicily	Ounce	123,
	Scudo or crown	49,
Spain	Real of old plate	4,
	Real of new plate	5,
	Real of Mexican plate	6,
	Real Vellon	2,
	Dollar of old plate, or of exchange	39,
Sweden	Rixdollar	55,
Switzerland	Franc (new system)	22,
Trieste	Florin, Austrian currency	25,
	Lira, Trieste currency	4,
	Lira di piazza	4
Turin	Lira	11
Valencia	Libra	39
Venice	Lira piccola (in the old coins)	5
	Lira piccola (in the coins introduced by the Austrians)	4
Vienna	Florin	25
Zante	Real	4
Zurich	Florin, money of exchange	25
	Florin current	23

AR OF EXCHANGE between England and the following Places, viz. Amsterdam, Hamburgh, Paris, drid, Lisbon, Leghorn, Genoa, Naples, and Venice, the same being computed from the intrinsic ue of their principal Coins, by comparing Gold with Gold, and Silver with Silver, according to their nt Regulations, and to Assays made at the London and Paris Mints —(Presented by Dr. Kelly to the mmittee of the House of Lords, on the Expediency of the Bank's resuming Cash Payments.)

	Gold.		Silver.				Explanations.
			Old Coinage.		New Coinage.		
	Mint Regulations.	Assays.	Mint Regulations.	Assays.	Mint Regulations.	Assays.	Moneys of Exchange.
sterdam, banco	36 8	36 6,8	37 3	37 10,5	35 0	35 6,5	Schillings and pence Flemish per pound sterling. Agio 2 per cent.
Do. current	11 4,5	11 3,8	11 8,5	11 11,8	10 14,6	10 17,6	Florins and stivers per pound sterling.
nburgh -	34 3,5	34 1,5	35 1	35 1,3	32 11	32 11,5	Schillings and pence Flemish banco per Pound sterling.
s - -	25 20	25 26	24 73	24 91	23 23	23 40	Francs and cents. per pound sterling.
rid - -	37·3	37·2	39·2	39·0	41·7	41·5	Pence sterling for the piastre or dollar of exchange.
on - -	67·4	67·5	60·41	58·33	64·30	62·69	Pence sterling per milree.
horn - -	49·1	49·0	46·46	46·5	49·60	49·5	Pence sterling per pezza of exchange.
oa - -	45·5	45·5	46·46	48·9	49·4	52·0	Pence sterling per pezza fuori banco.*
les - -	41·22	- -	41·22	- -	43·9	- -	Pence sterling per ducat (new coinage of 1818).
ice - -	46.3	46·0	47·5	49·0	44·6	46·1	Lire piccole per pound sterl.

An Account of the COURSE OF EXCHANGE, London, 19th of August, 1831, with some Explanatory Statements.

Course of Exchange.		Explanatory Statements.
sterdam, 3 Ms. -	12 2	that is, London receives 12 florins 2 stivers for 1*l*.
werp -	12 2½	— receives 12 ditto 2½ ditto for 1*l*.
nburgh, Mcs. Bco.	13 11	— receives 13 marcs 11 schillings banco for 1*l*.
s, 3 Ms. -	25 45	— receives 24 francs 45 cent. for 1*l*.
ncfort - -	149¾	— receives 149¾ batzen for 1*l*.
rsburgh, p. ru. 3 Us.	10	— gives 10 pence sterling for 1 ruble bank money.
na, eff. Flo. 2 Ms. -	9 58	— receives 9 florins 58 creutzers for 1*l*.
rid, 3 Ms. - -	36¾	— gives 36¾ pence sterling for 1 dollar.
horn - -	48¼	— gives 48¼ ditto for 1 pezza of 8 reals.
oa -	25 45	— receives 25 lire Italiane 45 cent. for 1*l*.
ice - - -	46	— receives 46 lire piccoli for 1*l*.
les - -	39½	— gives 39½ pence sterling for 1 ducato di regno.
on, 30 days' sight -	46½	— gives 46½ ditto for 1 milree.
Janeiro, ditto -	19½	— gives 19½ ditto for 1 ditto.

further and more ample elucidations, see the articles on the great trading towns in this Dic- y.

XCHEQUER BILLS. See FUNDS.

XPECTATION, of life. See INSURANCE.

XPORTATION, in commerce, the act of sending or carrying commodities one country to another. See IMPORTATION and EXPORTATION.

XCISE, the name given to the duties or taxes laid on such articles as are uced and consumed at home. Custom duties are those laid on commodities imported into or exported from a country.

cise duties were introduced into England by the Long Parliament in 1643; being aid on the makers and venders of ale, beer, cider, and perry. The royalists soon followed the example of the republicans; both sides declaring that the excise should ntinued no longer than the termination of the war. But it was found too ctive a source of revenue to be again relinquished; and when the nation had been tomed to it for a few years, the parliament declared, in 1649, that "the impost of was the most easy and indifferent levy that could be laid upon the people." It laced on a new footing at the Restoration; and notwithstanding Mr. Justice Black- says, that "from its first original to the present time its very name has been odious people of England"— *Com.* book i. c. 3.); it has continued progressively to gain d; and is at this moment imposed on a variety of most important articles, and fur- nearly half the entire public revenue of the kingdom.

counts are given of the different duties and regulations affecting the articles subject excise laws, under these articles. We shall, therefore, content ourselves at present giving, from the parliamentary returns,

e currency of Genoa has consisted, since 1826, of *Lire Italiane* of exactly the same weight and s as francs; so that the par of exchange with Genoa is now the same as with Paris.

An Account of the Gross and Nett Produce of the Excise Duties in Great Britain the Year ending 5th January, 1830.

Articles.	Gross Receipt. £ s. d.	Drawbacks, and Bounties of the Nature of Drawbacks. £ s. d.	Allowances. £ s. d.	Repayments on over-Entries, Damaged Goods, &c. £ s. d.	Nett Produce. £ s.
Auctions	244,490 6 10	- - -	- -	3,935 2 6¼	240,555 4
Beer	3,110,570 7 10	54,906 17 8½	160 0 0	49 14 2	3,055,453 15
Bricks and Tiles	373,027 17 1½	6,107 19 2¾	- -	3,489 12 4	363,430 5
Candles	496,696 6 2	5,939 6 5½	- -	6 3 9	490,750 15
Cider and Perry	25,000 8 5¾	- - -	- -	17 1 10½	24,983 6
Glass	852,738 10 10¾	217,570 8 2	534 16 7¼	765 5 2½	633,868 0
Hides and Skins	363,930 17 2¼	14,172 1 9½	- -	6 5 0	349,752 10
Hops	245,024 13 8½	2,233 13 10	- -	132 19 0	242,658 0
Licences	711,829 5 5½	- - -	- -	942 11 9¾	710,886 13
Malt	3,834,480 13 0	22 17 8¼	293,118 6 10½	3,707 8 1¾	3,537,632 0
Paper	701,629 7 2¼	29,183 5 8½	17,406 13 3	44 14 0	654,994 14
Printed Goods	1,942,918 8 6	1,390,534 9 4	- -	113 6 9½	552,270 12
Soap	1,357,688 0 6½	112,729 13 10½	93,015 19 6½	32 11 9	1,151,909 15
Spirits, British	3,310,960 9 1¼	- - -	- -	7,495 14 0	3,303,464 15
Starch	85,696 17 3	1,409 6 8¾	16,879 1 4½	48 14 2	67,359 15
Stone Bottles	4,166 18 3¼	646 11 2¼	- -	- -	3,520 7
Sweets and Mead	2,455 8 8	- - -	- -	- -	2,455 8
Tea	3,321,722 2 6	- - -	- -	- -	3,321,722 2
Vinegar	21,895 12 10	- - -	- -	- -	21,895 12
Consolidated Duties	21,006,922 11 6¼	1,835,456 11 8¾	421,114 17 7½	20,787 4 6¼	18,729,563 17
Payments in Scotland exceeding the Excise Receipt, on the following Articles:					
Hops	- - -	12 5 4	- -	} Deduct -	673 0
Starch	- -	- - -	660 14 8½		
					18,728,890 17
Fines and Forfeitures	7,117 7 7	- - -	- -	- -	7,117 7
Total - £	21,014,039 19 1¼	1,835,468 17 0¾	421,775 12 4	20,787 4 6¼	18,736,008 5

The total charges attending the collection of the excise revenue of Great Brit during the same year amounted to 1,003,471*l.* 6*s.* 5¼*d.*, being at the rate of 4¾ cent. upon the gross receipt.

The duties on beer, candles, cider and perry, hides and skins, and printed goo have since been repealed.

Account of the Gross and Nett Produce of the Revenue of Excise in Ireland, for Year ending 5th January, 1830.

Articles.	Gross Receipt. £ s. d.	Drawbacks, and Bounties of the Nature of Drawbacks. £ s. d	Repayments and Allowances on Overcharges, &c. £ s. d.	Nett Produc £ s.
Auctions	11,283 2 9	- -	275 7 6	11,007 15
Cider and Perry	31 17 2¼	- -	- -	31 17
Glass	24,432 12 8	5,094 4 7	- -	19,338 8
Hides and Skins	47,586 19 4½	1,131 11 5	- -	46,455 7
Licences	134,872 1 7½	- -	367 17 0	134,504 4
Malt	277,561 5 4	836 18 6¾	51 5 7	276,673 1
Paper	27,235 12 7½	1,032 11 1½	- -	26,203 1
Spirits (home-made)	1,484,198 6 3¾	3,310 13 2	396 6 2	1,480,486 6
Sweets and Mead	210 8 6	- -	- -	210 8
Vinegar	646 5 8½	- -	- -	646 5
	2,008,053 12 0¾	11,405 18 10¼	1,090 16 3	1,995,556 16
Late Collectors' Balances	1,158 3 1½	- -	- -	1,158 3
Profits made by Returns of Money	25 15 4	- -	- -	25 15
Repayments of Advances for Army and Navy Half-pay	21,903 2 9	- -	- -	21,903 2
Fines and Seizures	7,005 7 11	-	- -	7,005 7
Total - £	2,038,146 1 2¼	11,405 18 10¼	1,090 16 3	2,025,649 6

The total charges for collecting the excise revenue in Ireland during the year 1 amounted to 222,588*l.* 8*s.* 6*d.*, being at the rate of very near 11 per cent. (10*l.* 18*s.* on the gross receipt.

The prejudice in the public mind to which Blackstone has alluded, against the excise duties, see depend more on the regulations connected with their imposition, than on the oppressive extent to w they have sometimes been carried. The facilities of smuggling, and the frauds that might be comm upon the revenue, unless a very strict watch were kept, have led to the enactment of several rather s regulations. The officers have been empowered to enter and search the houses of such individuals as in exciseable commodities at any time of the day, and in most instances also of the night. And the ceedings in cases of transgression are of such a nature, that persons may be convicted in heavy pen

summary judgment of two commissioners of excise, or two justices of the peace, without the inter-
of a jury.

he more easily levying the revenue of excise. England and Wales are divided into about fifty-six
ons, some of which are called by the names of particular counties, others by the names of great
where one county is divided into several collections, or where a collection comprehends the con-
parts of several counties. Every such collection is subdivided into several districts, within which
a supervisor; and each district is again subdivided into out-rides and foot-walks, within each of
here is a gauger or surveying officer.

aws with respect to the general management of the excise were consolidated by the 7 & 8 Geo. 4.
om which the following particulars are selected : —

nissioners. — Four commissioners constitute a Board. They are to be subject, in all things relating
peculiar duty, to the orders of the Treasury. They may appoint collectors and other subordinate
, and give them such salaries and allowances as the Treasury shall direct : but they are not allowed
ase the number of inferior officers without the permission and approval of the Treasury. No
r of the House of Commons can be a commissioner of excise.

rs of Excise. — No officer of excise is to vote or interfere at any election of a member of parliament,
ain of forfeiting 500l., and being rendered incapable of ever holding any office or place of trust
is Majesty.

rson holding any office of excise is to deal in any sort of goods subject to the excise laws.

erson bribing or offering to bribe any officer of excise shall forfeit 500l.; and every officer accept-
. bribe, or doing, conniving at, or permitting any act or thing whereby any of the provisions of
se laws may be evaded or broken, shall forfeit 500l., and be declared incapable of ever after serving
esty in any capacity whatever. But if any of the parties to such illegal transactions shall inform
the other, before any proceedings thereupon shall have been instituted, he shall be indemnified
the penalties and disabilities imposed for such offences.

s and Powers of Officers. — It is lawful for any officer to enter any building or other place, used
ying on any trade subject to the excise, either by night or by day (but if by night, in the presence
staple or peace officer), to inspect the same, &c. And upon an officer making oath that he has
suspect that goods forfeited under the excise acts are deposited in any private house or place,
missioners of excise, or one justice of the peace, may grant warrant to the officer to enter such
place (if in the night, in the presence of a constable,) to search for and seize such forfeited goods.
nen Books may be left by the officers on the premises of persons subject to the excise laws; and
who shall remove or deface such books shall be liable to a penalty of 200l.

ring Goods to avoid Duty. — Goods fraudulently removed or secreted, in order to avoid the duty,
feited; and every person assisting in such removal shall forfeit and lose treble the value of such
r 100l., at the discretion of the commissioners.

scting Officers. — All persons who shall oppose, molest, &c. any officer of excise in the execution
ty, shall respectively, for every such offence, forfeit 200l.

rs violently resisted in making any seizure may oppose force to force; and in the event of their
g, maiming, or killing any person, when so opposed, they shall be admitted to bail, and may plead
ral issue.

es, mayors, bailiffs, constables, &c. are required to assist excise officers; and any constable, or
icer, who, on notice and request, declines going with an excise officer, is to forfeit 20l. for every
ence.

nts of Goods seized. — No claim shall be entered for goods seized, except in the real names of the
ors of such goods. Claimants are bound with two sureties in a penalty of 100l. to pay the expenses
; and in default thereof the goods are to be condemned.

dings in Courts of Law. — All penalties under the excise laws may be sued for and recovered in
ts of Exchequer at Westminster, Edinburgh, or Dublin respectively, according as the offence
e taken place in England, Scotland, or Ireland; provided that the proceedings within the courts
e within three years after the commission of the offence.

ations for the recovery of penalties against the excise laws in London may be heard and adjudged
hree or more of the commissioners of excise; and in other places such informations may be ex-
efore one or more justices of the peace, and may be heard and adjudged by any two or more such

tion of Penalties. — Justices are authorised, if they shall see cause, except when there is a special
to the contrary, to mitigate any penalty incurred for any offence committed against the excise
ne fourth part thereof; but it is lawful for the commissioners of excise, when they see cause,
mitigate, or entirely remit, such penalty.

ution of Penalties. — All penalties and forfeitures incurred under the excise acts are to be distri-
alf to his Majesty, and half to the officer or person who shall discover, inform, or sue for the
On proof being made of any officer acting collusively in making a seizure, the commissioners
t his share to be forfeited.

and Affirmations. — Persons wilfully taking or making any false oath or affirmation as to any
nnected with the excise laws shall, upon being convicted of such offence, suffer the pains and
incident to wilful and corrupt perjury; and those procuring or suborning such persons to swear
falsely shall, upon conviction, be liable to the pains and penalties incident to subornation of

against Excise Officers. — No writ, summons, or process, shall be sued out or served upon, nor
action be brought, raised, or prosecuted, against any officer of excise for any thing done under
e excise laws, until after the expiration of one calendar month next after notice in writing has
vered to such officer, specifying the cause of such action, and the name and place of abode of the
whose name it is to be brought. No action shall lie against any excise officer for any thing done
excise laws, unless it be brought within three months after the cause of action shall have arisen.
ent be given against the plaintiff, and in favour of the defendant, the latter shall, in every such
ve treble costs awarded to him.

Certificates, &c. — By the 41 Geo. 3. c. 91. it is enacted, that if any one shall forge, counterfeit,
ngly give any forged certificate required to be granted by any officer of excise, he shall be guilty
and being convicted, shall be transported for seven years.

viduals carrying on any business subjected to the control of the excise, must take out licences
annually on the 5th of July. — (See Licences.)

h individuals are also obliged to make entries of every building, place, vessel, or utensil, as the
be, in the name of the real owner, with the officer of excise in whose survey such building,
shall be situated. Individuals found employed in unentered excise manufactories are severally
a penalty of 30l. for the first offence; and in the event of any such offender refusing or neglect-
such penalty, he is to be committed to the house of correction or other prison for three calendar
o be kept to hard labour, and not to be liberated until the fine of 30l. has been paid, or the term of
aths has expired: and if found guilty of a second offence, the fine is to be 60l.; and in the event
being paid, the imprisonment is to be for six months. — (7 & 8 Geo. 4. c. 53. § 33.)
are usually necessary for the removal of exciseable commodities. — (See Permits.)

'ORTS, the articles exported, or sent beyond seas. See Imports and
rs.

M m

F.

FACTOR. — A factor is an agent employed by some one individual or induals, to transact business on his or their account. He is not generally reside
the same place as his principal, but, usually, in a foreign country. He is author
either by letter of attorney or otherwise, to receive, buy, and sell goods
merchandise ; and, generally, to transact all sorts of business on account o
employers, under such limitations and conditions as the latter may choose to
pose. A very large proportion of the foreign trade of this and most other coun
is now carried on by means of factors or agents.

Factors and brokers are, in some respects, nearly identical, but in others the
radically different. " A factor," said Mr. Justice Holroyd, in a late case, " differ
terially from a broker. The former is a person to whom goods are sent or consig
and he has not only the possession of, but, in consequence of its being usual to ad
money upon them, has also a special property in them, and a general lien upon
When, therefore, he sells in his own name, it is within the scope of his authority ;
it may be right, therefore, that the principal should be bound by the consequenc
such sale. But the case of a broker is different : he has not the possession of the g
and so the vendor cannot be deceived by the circumstance ; and, besides, the empl
a person to sell goods as a broker does not authorise him to sell in his own name.
therefore, he sells in his own name, he acts beyond the scope of his authority ; an
principal is not bound."

A factor is usually paid by a per centage or commission on the goods he sells or
If he act under what is called a *Del credere* commission, that is, *if he guarant
price of the goods sold on account of his principal*, he receives an additional per cent
indemnify him for this additional responsibility. In cases of this sort the factor s
in the vendee's place, and must answer to the principal for the value of the goods
But where the factor undertakes no responsibility, and intimates that he acts on
account of another, it is clearly established that he is not liable in the event o
vendee's failing.

The sound maxim, that the principal is responsible for the acts of his agent, pre
universally in courts of law and equity. In order to bind the principal, it is nece
only that third parties should deal *bonâ fide* with the agent, and that the conduct o
latter should *be conformable to the common usage and mode of dealing.* Thus, a
may sell goods upon credit, that being in the ordinary course of conducting merc
affairs : but a stock-broker, though acting *bonâ fide*, and with a view to the ben
his principal, cannot sell stock upon credit, *unless he have special instructions to that
that being contrary to the usual course of business.

A sale by a factor creates a contract between the owner and buyer ; and this rule
even in cases where the factor acts upon a *del credere* commission. Hence, if a
sell goods, and the owner *give notice to the buyer to pay the price to him*, and not
factor, the buyer will not be justified in afterwards paying the factor, and the
may bring his action against the buyer for the price, unless the factor has a lien the
But if no such notice be given, a payment to the individual selling is quite suffic

If a factor buy goods on account of his principal, where he is accustomed so
the contract of the factor binds the principal to a performance of the bargain ; a
principal is the person to be sued for non-performance. But it is ruled, that if a
enter into a charterparty of affreightment with the master of a ship, the contract o
him only, unless he lade the vessel with his principal's goods, in which case the
cipal and lading become liable, and not the factor. Where a factor, who is auth
to sell goods in his own name, makes the buyer debtor to himself ; then, though
not answerable to the principal for the debt, if the money be not paid, yet he has a
to receive it, if it be paid, and his receipt is a sufficient discharge ; the factor m
such a case, enforce the payment by action, and the buyer cannot defend hims
alleging that the principal was indebted to him in more than the amount.

" Where a factor," said Lord Mansfield, " dealing for a principal, but conc
that principal, delivers goods in his own name, the person contracting with him
right to consider him, to all intents and purposes, as the principal ; and though t
principal may appear, and bring an action on that contract against the purchaser
goods, yet that purchaser may set off any claim he may have against the factor, in a
to the demand of the principal."

Merchants employing the same factor run the joint risk of his actions, althoug
are strangers to each other : thus, if different merchants remit to a factor differen

:oods, and the factor sell them as a single lot to an individual who is to pay one :ty of the price down and the other at six months' end ; if the buyer fail before the nd payment, each merchant must bear a proportional share of the loss, and be con- to accept his dividend of the money advanced. — (*Beawes, Lex Merc.*)

factor employed, without his knowledge, in negotiating an illegal or fraudulent saction, has an action against his principal. On this ground it was decided, that erchant who had consigned counterfeit jewels to his factor, representing them to be iine, should make full compensation to the factor for the injury done to him by g concerned in such a transaction, as well as to the persons to whom the jewels had sold.

he office of a factor or agent being one of very great trust and responsibility, those undertake it are bound, both legally and morally, to conduct themselves with the st fidelity and circumspection. A factor should take the greatest care of his prin- 's goods in his hands : he should be punctual in advising him as to his transactions is behalf, in sales, purchases, freights, and, more particularly, bills of exchange : hould deviate as seldom as possible from the terms, and never from the *spirit and ir of* the orders he receives as to the sale of commodities : in the execution of a mission for purchasing goods, he should endeavour to conform as closely as prac- le to his instructions as to the quality or kind of goods : if he give more for them he is authorised, they may be thrown on his hands ; but he is bound to buy them s much less as he possibly can. After the goods are bought, he must dispose of according to order. If he send them to a different place from that to which he directed, they will be at his risk, unless the principal, on getting advice of the trans- n, consent to acknowledge it.*

factor who sells a commodity under the price he is ordered, may be obliged to make the difference, unless the *commodity be of a perishable nature and not in a condition r to be kept*. And if he purchase goods for another at a fixed rate, and their price g afterwards risen, he fraudulently takes them to himself, and sends them some- e else, in order to secure an advantage, he will be found, by the custom of mer- ts, liable in damages to his principal.

a factor, in conformity with a merchant's orders, buys with his money, or on his , a commodity he is directed to purchase, and, without giving advice of the trans- n, sells it again at a profit, appropriating that profit to himself, the merchant may er it from him, and have him amerced for fraud.

a factor buy, conformably to his instructions, goods of which he is *robbed*, or which some unavoidable injury, he is discharged, and the loss falls on the principal. But goods be *stolen* from the factor, he will not be so easily discharged ; for the fact eir having been abstracted by *stealth*, and not by *violence*, raises a strong presumption e had not taken that reasonable care of them which was incumbent upon him. owever, he can prove that the goods were lodged in a place of security, and that he ot been guilty of positive negligence, nor exercised less care towards them than ds his own property, he will not be held responsible even for a theft committed by rvants. — (*Jones on Bailments*, 2d ed. p. 76. ; *Chitty on Commercial Law*, vol. iii. 8.)

a factor, having money in his hands belonging to his principal, neglect to insure a nd goods, according to order, he must, in the event of the ship miscarrying, make the damage ; and if he make any composition with the insurers after insurance, ut orders to that effect, he is answerable for the whole insurance. A principal,

---

Whoever," says Dr. Paley, " undertakes another man's business, makes it his own ; that is, promises loy upon it the same care, attention, and diligence, that he would do if it were actually his own ; for ws that the business was committed to him with that expectation. And he promises nothing nan this. Therefore, an agent is not obliged to wait, inquire, solicit, ride about the country, toil, y, whilst there remains a possibility of benefiting his employer. If he exert as much activity, and h caution, as the value of the business in his judgment deserves ; that is, as he would have thought nt if the same interest of his own had been at stake ; he has discharged his duty, although it should rds turn out, that by more activity, and longer perseverance, he might have concluded the busi- th greater advantage." — (*Moral and Pol. Phil.* c. 12.)

e seems to be a good deal of laxity in this statement. It is necessary to distinguish between those executing a commission, render their services for the particular occasion only, without hire, and ho undertake it *in the course of business*, making a regular charge for their trouble. If the bestow on it that ordinary degree of care and attention which the *generality of mankind* bestow lar affairs of their own, it is all, perhaps, that can be expected : but the latter will be justly cen- if they do not execute their engagements on account of others with that care and diligence which vident and attentive father of a family" uses in his own private concerns. It is their duty to hemselves proportionably to the exigency of the affair in hand ; and neither to *do* any thing, how soever, by which their employers may sustain damage, nor omit any thing, however inconsi- hich the nature of the act requires. Perhaps the best general rule on the subject is, to suppose a r agent bound to exert that degree of care and vigilance that may *be reasonably expected of him rs*. At all events, it is clear he is not to be regulated by his own notions of the "value of the s." A man may neglect business of his own, or not think it worth attending to ; but he is not, re, to be excused for neglecting any similar business he has undertaken to transact for others. — are some very good observations on this subject in *Sir William Jones's Essay on Bailments*, 2d ed, d *passim.*)

at the end of a very long letter, directed his agent thus: "Observe the premium on t
value is also to be insured." But the agent, not noticing this sentence, neglected
insure the premium; and, being sued, was held liable for the omission.

If goods are remitted to a factor, and he makes a false entry of them at the Custo
house, or land them without entry, and they are, in consequence, se ред or forfeited,
is bound to make good the damage to his principal: but if the factor make his em
according to invoice or letters of advice, and these proving erroneous, the goods
seized, he is discharged.

It is now a settled point, that a factor has a lien on goods consigned to him, not o
for incidental charges, but as an item of mutual account for the balance due to him
long as he remains in possession. If he be surety in a bond for his principal, he
a lien on the goods sold by him on account of such principal, to the amount of the s
he is bound for.

It being the general rule of law "that property does not change while *in transitu*,"
in the hands of a carrier, a consignment made *before* the bankruptcy of a consignor,
not arriving till *after*, remains the property of the consignor, except, indeed, where
delivery is made *by the order*, and upon the account of the consignee, and is a compl
alienation from the consignor. In the case, therefore, of a consignment to a factor,
property remains the consignor's, and passes into the hands of *his* assignees. Whe
factor has a lien on goods, he has a right to the price, though received after the ban
ruptcy.

Where general or unlimited orders are given to a factor, he is left to buy and sell
the best conditions he can. And if detriment arise to a principal from the proceedir
of a factor acting under such authority, he has no redress, unless he can show that
acted fraudulently or with *gross negligence*.

A factor or broker acting against the interest of his principal cannot even receive
commission. If he pay money an account of his principal, without being authoris
he cannot recover it back.

An agent cannot delegate his rights to another so as to bind the principal, unl
expressly authorised to nominate a sub-agent.

For further information as to the general powers and liabilities of factors and ager
see *Beawes's Lex Mercatoria*, art. *Factors, Supercargoes*, &c.; *Chitty's Commercial L
vol. iii. c. 3.*; *Woolrych on Commercial Law*, pp. 317—329. &c. See also the arti
BROKERS.

The law with respect to the effect of the transactions of factors or agents on th
parties, was placed on its present footing by the act 6 Geo. 4. c. 94. Under the l
that previously obtained, it was held, that a factor, as such, had no authority to *ple
but only to *sell* the goods of his principal; and it was repeatedly decided that a p
cipal might recover back goods on which a *bonâ fide* advance of money had been m
by a third party, without his being bound to repay such advance; and notwithstand
this third party was wholly ignorant that the individual pledging the goods held th
as a mere factor or agent. It used also to be held, that *bonâ fide* purchasers of go
from factors or agents not vested with the power of sale, might be made liable to
the price of the goods a second time to the real owner.

The extreme hardship and injurious influence of such regulations is obvious. I
the business of a principal to satisfy himself as to the conduct and character of
factor or agent he employs; and if he make a false estimate of them, it is more eq
table, surely, that he should be the sufferer, than those who have no means of know
any thing of the matter. The injustice of the law in question, and the injury it
to the commerce of the country, had frequently excited attention; and was very a
set forth by Lord Liverpool, in his speech in the House of Lords, on moving the sec
reading of the new bill.

"Those of their Lordships who were acquainted with commercial transactions, would know that m
was frequently advanced on goods, without its being possible for the person advancing the money to
any further acquaintance with the transactions, than that the factor was in actual possession of the g
It then became a question, putting fraud out of view, if the factor became a bankrupt, or in any c
way failed to execute his engagements, whether the loss should fall on the principal who had consi
these goods, or on the *pledgee* who had advanced money on them. It had been of late ruled, that i
factor were intrusted only to dispose of the property, the loss must fall on the pledgee. He meant to
tend, that this was contrary to equity, and contrary to analogy; that it was disapproved of by high au
rity, and was contrary to the law in every country of the world, except this and the United Stat
America, which had drawn their law from this country. It was contrary to equity, he thought, tha
pledgee, who had advanced his money without any fraud, but on the *bonâ fide* possession of the g
should suffer. He had placed no confidence, but the principal who had appointed the factor had p
confidence. He could limit him in his operations as he pleased — he could give him any kind of ins
tions — he might qualify his power — he was bound to take precautions before placing confidence
he was in all respects more liable to suffer from his faults than the pledgee. The latter knew nothi
the power of the factor, he saw only the goods, and advanced his money on what was a sufficient see
for repayment. On every principle of natural equity, therefore, the loss ought to fall, not on the pl
but on the principal. He knew that this view was connected with one very important question — th
possession and title; but it was not possible for transactions to go on, unless the possession was adm
as the title to the goods. If this were an indifferent question, or a question involving only a few cas

not have called on their Lordships to legislate on this subject; but all the commercial interests of ntry were connected with it. And he might say he believed that two thirds of the whole com- of the country was carried on by consigning goods to a factor, and leaving it to his discretion to of them to the greatest advantage, sending them to market when he pleased, and raising money n when he could not send them to market. Bills of exchange, exchequer bills, and money bills of escription, were subject to this rule. If a person consigned exchequer bills to a second person, parted with them, the third party who obtained them was held to have a right to them. Com- proceedings were of as much importance as money proceedings, and he could not see why they not receive the same security. It might be asked, perhaps, when this was felt to be so great an y it was not altered before; but it seemed to be one of those things which had grown up gradually, ich did much mischief before they became extensively known. The first decision, he believed, established the law as it now stood, was delivered in 1742; and he knew that Lord Chief Justice ad said, he could not explain the origin of that decision. He supposed it might have been dictated fraud. That decision, the Lord Chief Justice maintained, was at variance with the best interests nerce, and had grown out of circumstances he could not explain. From the time of the first , the decisions had not been numerous, till of late years. He did not doubt but the judges had according to the law as it was established by these precedents; but in doing that, they had ex- their regret that these precedents had been established. Here his Lordship read an extract from s delivered by the late Lord Chief Justice Ellenborough, and a late judge, Mr. Le Blanc, expressing gret, in deciding cases according to these precedents, that they had been established. He inferred ese opinions, that these judges, though they had felt themselves obliged to decide in this way, sup- at that the law was contrary to the general analogy of our laws, and to the principles of justice. He me to the last consideration, the law of this country being in this respect different from the law of r countries, except the law of the United States of America. In all other countries, the law was sed to be what he wished to establish it by the bill before their Lordships. When there was no e of fraud, it was held, that the man, advancing money on goods held by a factor, should not or his faults, but that the person who confided in the factor must be the sufferer. This was also in Scotland. He had understood, too, that the evils of the law were felt in America, and that had been taken for bringing it before the congress, with a view to assimilate the law of America to of other countries. If the question were examined by the principles of equity, by analogy with ses, by the authority of those who decided in our courts, or by the practice of other countries, it e found that the reasons were strong in favour of the bill. It was of great importance in com- transactions, that our law should be like the laws of other countries. It was not the same with relative to real property — to our local law, if he might so call it; but when the bill was founded y and analogy, he thought it was an additional reason in its favour, that it assimilated our com- law to the commercial law of other countries. He did not know if he had made himself under- r if he had sufficiently explained the object of the bill; but the measure was founded in justice, oped to have their Lordships' consent to it." The noble Earl concluded by moving the second of the bill.

he new law, all persons intrusted with and in possession of goods are supposed, the contrary be made distinctly to appear, to be their *owners*, so far, at least, that ay pledge them or sell them to third parties. The following are the principal of this important act, 6 Geo. 4. c. 94.

s or *Agents having Goods or Merchandise in their Possession, shall be deemed to be the true* — Any person intrusted, for the purpose of consignment or of sale, with any goods, wares, or dise, and who shall have shipped such in his own name, and any person in whose name any ares, or merchandise shall be shipped by any other person, shall be deemed to be the true owner, to entitle the consignee to a lien thereon in respect of any money or negotiable security advanced consignee for the use of the person in whose name such goods, wares, or merchandise shall be or in respect of any money or negotiable security received by him to the use of such consignee, manner as if such person was the true owner; provided such consignee shall not have notice by of lading, or otherwise, before the time of any advance of such money or negotiable security, or receipt of money or negotiable security in respect of which such lien is claimed, that such person ng in his own name, or in whose name any goods, wares, or merchandise shall be shipped by any s not the actual and *bonâ fide* owner, any law, usage, or custom to the contrary thereof notwith- : Provided also, that the person in whose name such goods, wares, or merchandise are so shipped aken, for the purposes of this act, to have been intrusted therewith for the purpose of consign- of sale, unless the contrary thereof shall be made to appear by bill of discovery, or be made to evidence by any person disputing such fact. — § 1.

s in *Possession of Bills of Lading to be the Owner, so far as to make valid Contracts.* — From the 1st of October, 1826, any person intrusted with any bill of lading, India warrant, dock war- ehouse keeper's certificate, wharfinger's certificate, warrant or order for delivery of goods, shall d to be the true owner, so far as to give validity to any contract or agreement thereafter to be nto by such person so intrusted, with any person, body politic or corporate, for the sale of the s, wares, and merchandise, or for the deposit or pledge thereof as a security for any money or e instrument advanced or given by such person, body politic or corporate, upon the faith of such ts; provided such person, body politic or corporate, shall not have notice by such documents or , that such person so intrusted is not the actual and *bonâ fide* owner. — § 2.

rson to acquire a *Security upon Goods in the Hands of an Agent for an antecedent Debt, beyond nt of the Agent's Interest in the Goods.* — In case any person, body politic or corporate, shall, act, accept any such goods, in deposit or pledge from any such person so intrusted, without aforesaid, as a security for any debt or demand due from such person so intrusted, to such person, tic or corporate, before the time of such deposit, then such person, body politic or corporate, so such goods in deposit or pledge, shall acquire no further interest in the said goods, or any such , than was possessed, or might have been enforced by the said person so intrusted, at the time of sit or pledge; but such person, body politic or corporate, so accepting such goods in deposit or all acquire, possess, and enforce such right, title, or interest, as might have been enforced by such intrusted. — § 3.

s *may contract with known Agents in the ordinary Course of Business, or out of that Course, if Agent's Authority.* — From and after the 1st of October, 1826, it shall be lawful for any person, ic or corporate, to contract with any agent, intrusted with any goods, or to whom the same may ned, for the purchase of such goods, and to receive the same of and pay for the same to such d such contract and payment shall be binding upon the owner, notwithstanding such person, c or corporate, shall have notice that the person making and entering into such contract, or on alf such contract is made, is an agent; provided such contract and payment be made in the rse of business, and that such person, body politic or corporate, shall not have notice that such ot authorised to sell the said goods, or to receive the said purchase money. — § 4.

may accept and take Goods in Pledge from known Agents. — From and after the passing of this ll be lawful for any person, body politic or corporate, to accept any such goods, or any such as aforesaid, in deposit or pledge from any factor or agent, notwithstanding such person, body corporate, shall have notice that the person making such deposit or pledge is a factor or agent;

but then and in that case such person, body politic or corporate, shall acquire no further interest said goods, or any such document, than was possessed or might have been enforced by the said fac agent, at the time of such deposit or pledge; but such person, body politic or corporate, shall ac possess, and enforce such right, title, or interest as was possessed and might have been enforced b factor or agent. — § 5.

Right of the true Owner to follow his Goods while in the Hands of his Agent or of his Assignee i of Bankruptcy. — Nothing herein contained shall be deemed to deprive the true owner or propri such goods from demanding and recovering the same from his factor or agent, before the same shal been so sold, deposited, or pledged, or from the assignees of such factor or agent, in the event of hi or their bankruptcy; nor to prevent such owner or proprietor from demanding or recovering of and any persons, bodies politic or corporate, the price agreed to be paid for the purchase of such goods, s to any right of set-off on the part of such persons, bodies politic or corporate, against such factor or a not (nor) to prevent such owner or proprietor from demanding or recovering of and from such pe bodies politic or corporate, such goods, so deposited or pledged, upon repayment of the money, restoration of the negotiable instrument so advanced or given on the security of such goods, by suc sons, bodies politic or corporate, to such factor or agent; and upon payment of such further sum, restoration of such other negotiable instrument (if any) as may have been advanced or given b factor or agent, to such owner or proprietor, or on payment of a sum equal to the amount of such i ment; nor to prevent the said owner or proprietor from recovering of and from such persons, politic or corporate, any balance remaining in their hands, as the produce of the sale of such goods deducting thereout the amount of the money or negotiable instrument so advanced or given upc security thereof: Provided always, that in case of the bankruptcy of any such factor or agent, the or proprietor of the goods so pledged and redeemed shall be held to have discharged *pro tanto* the de by them to the estate of such bankrupt. — § 6.

Agents fraudulently pledging the Goods of their Principals. — The 7 & 8 Geo. 4. c. 29. § 51. " That if any factor or agent intrusted, for the purpose of sale, with any goods or merchandise, trusted with any bill of lading, warehouse keeper's or wharfinger's certificate, or warrant or order delivery of goods or merchandise, shall, *for his own benefit, and in violation of good faith*, depc pledge any such goods or merchandise, or any of the said documents, as a security for any money gotiable instrument borrowed or received by such factor or agent, at or before the time of making deposit or pledge, or intended to be thereafter borrowed or received, every such offender shall be gu a misdemeanor, and, being convicted thereof, shall be liable, at the discretion of the court, to be ported beyond the seas for any term not exceeding fourteen years, nor less than seven years, or to such other punishment by fine or imprisonment, or by both, as the court shall award; but no such or agent shall be liable to any prosecution for depositing or pledging any such goods or merchand any of the said documents, in case the same shall not be made a security for, or subject to the paym any greater sum of money than the amount which, at the time of such deposit or pledge, was just and owing to such factor or agent from his principal, together with the amount of any bill or bills change drawn by or on account of such principal, and accepted by such factor or agent."

This provision does not extend to partners not being privy to the offence; nor does it take aw remedy at law or equity which any party aggrieved by any offence might have been entitled to a such offender. And no one shall be liable to be convicted by any evidence whatever as an offender a this act, in respect of any act done by him, if he shall, at any time previously to his being indict such offence, have disclosed such acts, on oath, in consequence of any compulsory process of any c law or equity, in any action, suit, &c. which shall have been *bonâ fide* instituted by any party agg or if he shall have disclosed the same in any examination or deposition before any commissio bankrupt. — § 52.

FACTORAGE, or COMMISSION, the allowance given to factors b merchants and manufacturers, &c. who employ them: it is a per centage o goods they purchase, or sell, on account of their principals; and varies in diff countries, and as it refers to different articles. It is customary for facto observed in the previous article, to insure the debts due to those for whom sell for an additional, or *del credere*, commission, generally averaging from 2 per cent. Factorage or commission is also frequently charged at a certair per cask, or other package, measure, or weight, especially when the factor is employed to receive or deliver: this commission is usually fixed by special a ment between the merchant and factor.

Factorage, Brokerage, and Commission Table.

Amt.	At ⅛ per Ct.	At ¼ per Ct.	At ⅜ per Ct.	At ½ per Ct.	At ⅝ per Ct.	At ¾ per Ct.	At ⅞ per Ct.	At 1
L.	L. s. d.	L. s. d.	L. s. d.	L. s. d.	L. s. d.	L. s. d.	L. s. d.	L.
1	0 0 0¼	0 0 0½	0 0 0¾	0 0 1	0 0 1½	0 0 1¾	0 0 2	0
2	0 0 0½	0 0 1	0 0 1¾	0 0 2¼	0 0 3	0 0 3½	0 0 4	0
3	0 0 0¾	0 0 1¾	0 0 2¾	0 0 3½	0 0 4½	0 0 5½	0 0 6¼	0
4	0 0 1	0 0 2½	0 0 3¾	0 0 4¾	0 0 6	0 0 7	0 0 8½	0
5	0 0 1½	0 0 3	0 0 4½	0 0 6	0 0 7½	0 0 9	0 0 10½	0
6	0 0 1¾	0 0 3½	0 0 5½	0 0 7	0 0 9	0 0 10¾	0 1 0¾	0
7	0 0 2	0 0 4	0 0 6¼	0 0 8½	0 0 10½	0 1 0¾	0 1 2¾	0
8	0 0 2½	0 0 4¾	0 0 7	0 0 9¾	0 1 0	0 1 2¼	0 1 4¾	0
9	0 0 2½	0 0 5¼	0 0 8	0 0 10¾	0 1 1½	0 1 4	0 1 6¾	0
10	0 0 3	0 0 6	0 0 9	0 1 0	0 1 3	0 1 6	0 1 9	0
20	0 0 6	0 1 0	0 1 6	0 2 0	0 2 6	0 3 0	0 3 6	0
30	0 0 9	0 1 6	0 2 3	0 3 0	0 3 9	0 4 6	0 5 3	0
40	0 1 0	0 2 0	0 3 0	0 4 0	0 5 0	0 6 0	0 7 0	0
50	0 1 3	0 2 6	0 3 9	0 5 0	0 6 3	0 7 6	0 8 9	0
60	0 1 6	0 3 0	0 4 6	0 6 0	0 7 6	0 9 0	0 10 6	0
70	0 1 9	0 3 6	0 5 3	0 7 0	0 8 9	0 10 6	0 12 3	0
80	0 2 0	0 4 0	0 6 0	0 8 0	0 10 0	0 12 0	0 14 0	0
90	0 2 3	0 4 6	0 6 9	0 9 0	0 11 3	0 13 6	0 15 9	0
100	0 2 6	0 5 0	0 7 6	0 10 0	0 12 6	0 15 0	0 17 6	1
200	0 5 0	0 10 0	0 15 0	1 0 0	1 5 0	1 10 0	1 15 0	2
300	0 7 6	0 15 0	1 2 6	1 10 0	1 17 6	2 5 0	2 12 6	3
400	0 10 0	1 0 0	1 10 0	2 0 0	2 10 0	3 0 0	3 10 0	4
500	0 12 6	1 5 0	1 17 6	2 10 0	3 2 6	3 15 0	4 7 6	5
600	0 15 0	1 10 0	2 5 0	3 0 0	3 15 0	4 10 0	5 5 0	6
700	0 17 6	1 15 0	2 12 6	3 10 0	4 7 6	5 5 0	6 2 6	7
800	1 0 0	2 0 0	3 0 0	4 0 0	5 0 0	6 0 0	7 0 0	8
900	1 2 6	2 5 0	3 7 6	4 10 0	5 12 6	6 15 0	7 17 6	9
1,000	1 5 0	2 10 0	3 15 0	5 0 0	6 5 0	7 10 0	8 15 0	10
2,000	2 10 0	5 0 0	7 10 0	10 0 0	12 10 0	15 0 0	17 10 0	20
3,000	3 15 0	7 10 0	11 5 0	15 0 0	18 15 0	22 10 0	26 5 0	30
4,000	5 0 0	10 0 0	15 0 0	20 0 0	25 0 0	30 0 0	35 0 0	40
5,000	6 5 0	12 10 0	18 15 0	25 0 0	31 5 0	37 10 0	43 15 0	50
10,000	12 10 0	25 0 0	37 10 0	50 0 0	62 10 0	75 0 0	87 10 0	10[illegible]

Factorage, Brokerage, and Commission Table — *continued.*

Amt.	At 1½ per Ct.	At 2 per Ct.	At 2½ per Ct.	At 3 per Ct.	At 4 per Ct.	At 4½ pr Ct.	At 5 per Ct.
L.	*L. s. d.*	*L. s. d.*	*L. s. d.*	*L. s. d.*	*L. s. d.*	*L. s. d.*	*L. s. d.*
1	0 0 3½	0 0 4¾	0 0 6	0 0 7	0 0 9½	0 0 10¾	0 1 0
2	0 0 7	0 0 9½	0 1 0	0 1 2¼	0 1 7	0 1 9½	0 2 0
3	0 0 10¾	0 1 2¼	0 1 6	0 1 9½	0 2 4¾	0 2 8¼	0 3 0
4	0 1 2¼	0 1 7	0 2 0	0 2 4¾	0 3 2¼	0 3 7	0 4 0
5	0 1 6	0 2 0	0 2 6	0 3 0	0 4 0	0 4 6	0 5 0
6	0 1 9½	0 2 4¾	0 3 0	0 3 7	0 4 9½	0 5 4¾	0 6 0
7	0 2 1	0 2 9½	0 3 6	0 4 2½	0 5 7	0 6 3½	0 7 0
8	0 2 4¾	0 3 2¼	0 4 0	0 4 9½	0 6 4¾	0 7 2¼	0 8 0
9	0 2 8¼	0 3 7	0 4 6	0 5 4¾	0 7 2¼	0 8 1	0 9 0
10	0 3 0	0 4 0	0 5 0	0 6 0	0 8 0	0 9 0	0 10 0
20	0 6 0	0 8 0	0 10 0	0 12 0	0 16 0	0 18 0	1 0 0
30	0 9 0	0 12 0	0 15 0	0 18 0	1 4 0	1 7 0	1 10 0
40	0 12 0	0 16 0	1 0 0	1 4 0	1 12 0	1 16 0	2 0 0
50	0 15 0	1 0 0	1 5 0	1 10 0	2 0 0	2 5 0	2 10 0
60	0 18 0	1 4 0	1 10 0	1 16 0	2 8 0	2 14 0	3 0 0
70	1 1 0	1 8 0	1 15 0	2 2 0	2 16 0	3 3 0	3 10 0
80	1 4 0	1 12 0	2 0 0	2 8 0	3 4 0	3 12 0	4 0 0
90	1 7 0	1 16 0	2 5 0	2 14 0	3 12 0	4 1 0	4 10 0
100	1 10 0	2 0 0	2 10 0	3 0 0	4 0 0	4 10 0	5 0 0
200	3 0 0	4 0 0	5 0 0	6 0 0	8 0 0	9 0 0	10 0 0
300	4 10 0	6 0 0	7 10 0	9 0 0	12 0 0	13 10 0	15 0 0
400	6 0 0	8 0 0	10 0 0	12 0 0	16 0 0	18 0 0	20 0 0
500	7 10 0	10 0 0	12 10 0	15 0 0	20 0 0	22 10 0	25 0 0
600	9 0 0	12 0 0	15 0 0	18 0 0	24 0 0	27 0 0	30 0 0
700	10 10 0	14 0 0	17 10 0	21 0 0	28 0 0	31 10 0	35 0 0
800	12 0 0	16 0 0	20 0 0	24 0 0	32 0 0	36 0 0	40 0 0
900	13 10 0	18 0 0	22 10 0	27 0 0	36 0 0	40 10 0	45 0 0
1,000	15 0 0	20 0 0	25 0 0	30 0 0	40 0 0	45 0 0	50 0 0
2,000	30 0 0	40 0 0	50 0 0	60 0 0	80 0 0	90 0 0	100 0 0
3,000	45 0 0	60 0 0	75 0 0	90 0 0	120 0 0	135 0 0	150 0 0
4,000	60 0 0	80 0 0	100 0 0	120 0 0	160 0 0	180 0 0	200 0 0
5,000	75 0 0	100 0 0	125 0 0	150 0 0	200 0 0	225 0 0	250 0 0
10,000	150 0 0	200 0 0	250 0 0	300 0 0	400 0 0	450 0 0	500 0 0

ACTORY, a place where merchants and factors reside, to negotiate busi- for themselves and their correspondents on commission. We have factories e East Indies, Turkey, Portugal, Russia, &c.

AIRS AND MARKETS. These institutions are very closely allied. A as the term is now generally understood, is only a greater species of market rring at more distant intervals. Both are appropriated to the sale of one or species of goods, the hiring of servants, or labourers, &c.; but fairs are, in cases, attended by a greater concourse of people, for whose amusement us exhibitions are got up.

Origin of Fairs. — Institutions of this sort are of far greater service in the earlier s of society than at a more advanced period. The number of shops, and the com- ties in them, are then comparatively limited; so that it is for the advantage of all, airs should be established, and dealers induced to attend them. For this purpose us privileges have been annexed to fairs, and numerous facilities afforded to the sal of property in them. To give them a greater degree of solemnity, they were ally, both in the ancient and modern world, associated with religious festivals. ost places, indeed, they are still held on the same day with the wake or feast of the to whom the church is dedicated; and till the practice was prohibited, it was cus- y to hold them in churchyards! — (*Jacob's Law Dict.* art. *Fair.*) But since the h of towns, and the opportunities afforded for the disposal and purchase of all sorts oduce at the weekly or monthly markets held in them, the utility of fairs has very diminished, and they have lost much of their ancient splendour. Not a few of might, indeed, be advantageously abolished; but there are some that are still well led, and are really serviceable.

Establishment of Fairs. — No fair can be holden without grant from the crown, rescription which supposes such grant. And before a patent is granted, it is usual e a writ of *ad quod damnum* executed and returned, that it may not be issued to ejudice of a similar establishment already existing. The grant usually contains se that it shall not be to the hurt of another fair or market; but this clause, if ed, will be implied in law: for if the franchise occasion damage either to the king ubject, in this or any other respect, it will be revoked; and a person, whose ancient s prejudiced, is entitled to have a *scire facias* in the king's name to repeal the patent. If his Majesty grant power to hold a fair or market in a particular the lieges can resort to no other, even though it be inconvenient. But if no be appointed, the grantees may keep the fair or market where they please, or where they can most conveniently.

Times of holding Fairs and Markets. — These are either determined by the letters appointing the fair or market, or by usage. The statute 2 Edw. 3. c. 15. enacts, e duration of the fair shall be declared at its commencement, and that it shall not ntinued beyond the specified time. By statute 5 Edw. 3. c. 5., any merchant goods after the stipulated time is to forfeit double the goods sold.

Effect of Sales in Fairs and Markets. — A *bonâ fide* sale made in a fair or open t, in general, transfers the complete property of the thing sold to the vendee; so

that, however vicious or illegal the title of the vendor may be, the vendee's is go
against every one except the king. But the sale, in order to come within this rule, m
take place *on the market day, and at the place assigned for the market.* The city
London is said to be a market overt every day of the week except Sunday; every sh
being a market overt for such things as the shopkeeper professes to deal in. The p
perty of goods may, however, be changed, and effectually transferred to the buyer, b
bonâ fide sale in a shop out of London, whether the shopkeeper be the vendor or vend
if the goods are of the kind in which he trades. A wharf in London is not within
custom, and is not a market overt for articles brought there. But a sale in a mar
will not be binding, if it be such as carries with it a presumption of fraud: as,
example, if it take place in a back room, or secret place; if the sale be covinous, a
intended to defraud the real owner; or if the buyer know that the vendor is not the r
owner of the goods, &c. It is very difficult to transfer the property of horses, ev
when they are sold in an open market, without the consent of the real owner. — (
HORSES.)

5. *Court of Pié Poudre.* — To every fair or market there is incident, even withe
any express words in the grant, a court of *pié poudre*, in allusion to the dusty feet
the suitors. The steward or mayor may preside. It has cognizance of all questic
as to contracts made in the market, respecting goods *bought and delivered there,* &
Formerly *pié poudre* courts were held at every considerable fair; but they are n
entirely laid aside.

6. *Clerk of the Market.* — Owners and governors of fairs are to take care that ev
thing be sold according to just weights and measures. And for that and other purpo
they may appoint a clerk of the fair or market, who is to mark and allow all su
weights, &c.; charging 1*d.* for sealing and marking a bushel, $\frac{1}{2}$*d.* for marking a h
bushel or peck, and $\frac{1}{4}$*d.* for marking a gallon, pottle, quart, pint, &c., under pena
of 5*l.* — (22 *Cha.* 2. c. 8.)

7. *Tolls.* — Being a matter of private benefit to the owners of fairs or markets, a
not incident to them, tolls are not exigible unless specially granted in the pate
but the king may by a new grant authorise a reasonable toll to be taken. If the
granted be excessive, the patent will be void. It is a general rule, unless changed b
contrary custom obtaining time out of mind, that no toll be paid for any thing brou
to a fair or market, before the same is sold, and that it shall then *be paid by the buyer*

The owner of a house next to a fair or market is not allowed to open his shop dur
such fair or market, without paying *stallage* (toll for having a stall); on the ground
if he take the benefit of the market, he ought to pay the duties thereon. This regula
has been a good deal complained of.

The owners of fairs and markets are required by statute (2 & 3 Ph. and M. c.
to appoint a person in a special open place to take the toll. The most important
of this person's duty has reference to his entering the horses sold with three distingu
ing marks, and the names, &c. of those who buy and sell them. — (See HORSES.)

An action lies against any one who refuses to pay the customary toll.

For further information as to fairs and markets, see *Chitty on Commercial Law,* vo
c. 9.

Among the principal British fairs are : — Stourbridge fair, near Cambridge. Bri
two fairs. Exeter. West Chester. Edinburgh. Weyhill and Burford fair,
for sheep. Pancras fair, in Staffordshire, for saddle-horses. Bartholomew fair
London. St. Faith's, in Norfolk, for Scotch cattle. Yarmouth fishing-fair, for
rings; the only fishing-fair in Great Britain, and now much decayed. Ipswich shi
fair. Woodborough-hill, in Dorsetshire, for west-country manufactures, as kers
druggets, &c. Two cheese-fairs at Chipping Norton. One ditto at Nottingh
Howden and Boroughbridge fairs, for Holderness cows and Yorkshire hunters. H
castle, in Lincolnshire, for horses of all kinds; and Harborough, in Leicestershire
Scotch cattle, to be fed on the Essex and Norfolk marshes for the supply of the Lon
markets in winter. Falkirk, for cattle and sheep.

Among the principal French fairs are those of St. Germains, Lyons, Rhe
Chartres, Rouen, Bordeaux, Troyes, Bayonne, Dieppe, &c. The most noted Ger
fairs are those of Frankfort; Leipsic, famous for the vast number of its new pub
ations; and Nuremberg. The German fairs are celebrated not only on account of
great trade, but the vast concourse of princes, nobility, and people, who come to t
from all parts to partake of the diversions. Dr. Bright gives, in his "Travels in 1
gary" (pp. 201—223.), a very interesting account of the fairs held at Debretzin
Pesth. There are also other fairs much resorted to: as, Zurich, in Switzerland;
in the Milanese; Dantzic; Riga, in Livonia, &c. An annual fair has recently
established at Warsaw; and there has long been one at Archangel. But the
important fair in the Russian dominions, or, perhaps, in Europe, is held at Nis

gorod. This city is situated at the confluence of the Oka with the Wolga, in
5° 16′ N., lon. 44° 18′ E. It is the great emporium of the internal trade of
a ; communicating by an inland navigation with the Baltic, the Black Sea, and
aspian. The fair was formerly held at Makarief, 84 versts distant. It gene-
asts from 6 weeks to 2 months, and is well known all over the East of Europe.
azaars erected for the accommodation of those who attend this fair, form, accord-
Dr. Lyall, the finest establishment of the kind in the world. The sale of iron
n articles usually amounts to above 10,000,000 roubles ; the furs to 36,000,000 ;
ages to 1,300,000. Captain Cochrane is of opinion, that " the fair, in point of va-
second to none in Europe; the business done being estimated at nearly 200,000,000
s." The stationary population of the place amounts to from 15,000 to 16,000 :
ring the fair it is said to amount to 120,000, or 150,000 ; among whom may be
Chinese, Persians, Circassians, Armenians, Tâtars, Bucharians, Jews, " and a
en of almost every European nation." Nor are theatrical exhibitions, shows of
easts, and other Bartholomew-fair amusements, wanting to add to the attractions
scene. — (See *Modern Traveller*, a work of very great merit, art. *Russia*, p. 305.)
irs held at Porto Bello, Vera Cruz, and the Havannah, in Spanish America, used
much frequented, but are now comparatively deserted. The most important fair
Eastern world is that held at Mecca, during the resort of pilgrims in the
of Dhalhajja. It used to be frequented by many thousands of individuals of
ks and orders, brought together from the remotest corners of the Mohammedan
; and though the numbers attending it have declined of late years, the concourse
very great.

THOM, a measure of length, 6 feet, chiefly used for measuring the length
lage, and the depth of water and mines.

ATHERS, BED-FEATHERS (Fr. *Plumes, Plumes à lit;* Ger. *Federn, Bettferden;*
edveern, Pluimen; It. *Piume;* Sp. *Plumas*), make a considerable article of
erce ; particularly those of the ostrich, heron, swan, peacock, goose, and
poultry; for plumes, ornaments of the head, filling of beds, quills, &c.
arsest part of the ostrich plumage is generally denominated *hair*, to which
s a resemblance, and is used in the manufacture of hats. Many parts of
Britain supply feathers for beds, and an inferior sort is brought from Ire-
Eider down is imported from the north of Europe; the ducks that supply
g inhabitants of Greenland, Iceland, and Norway. The cider duck breeds
islands on the west of Scotland, but not in sufficient numbers to form a
ble branch of trade to the inhabitants. Hudson's Bay furnishes very fine
s. The down of the swan is brought from Dantzic, as well as large quan-
f superior feathers.

bed-feathers imported in 1828 amounted to 3,103 cwt., yielding 6,826*l.*
duty. The duty on ostrich feathers during the same year produced 962*l.*

DLE, OR VIOLIN (*Fiddles;* Ger. *Violinen, Geigen;* Du. *Vioolen;* Fr. *Vio-*
:. *Violini;* Sp. *Violines;* Rus. *Sskripizii*), a musical instrument, too well known
any particular description. The finest toned violins are those made in
they are usually called Cremonas, from the name of the town where those
ents were formerly manufactured in the highest perfection. Fifty or sixty
have not unfrequently been given for a Cremona violin.

S (Ger. *Feigen;* Du. *Vygen;* Fr. *Figues;* It. *Fichi;* Sp. *Higos;* Lat. *Fici,*
; Arab. *Teen*), the fruit of the fig tree, a native of Asia, but early introduced
rope. It flourishes in Turkey, Greece, France, Spain, Italy, and Northern
and even sometimes ripens its fruit in the open air in this country. Figs,
ipe, are, for the most part, dried in ovens to preserve them ; and then
very closely in the small chests in which we import them. The best come
urkey; those of Kalamata, in the Morea, are said to be the most
s. — (*Thomson's Dispensatory.*)

figs form a very considerable article of commerce in Provence, Italy, and Spain ;
affording, as in the East, a principal article of sustenance for the population. In
figs are chiefly exported from Andalusia and Valencia; but they are more or
ndant in every province. In the northern parts of France there are many fig
particularly at Argenteuil.

belong to that class of articles, the duties on which might be reduced, not only
any loss, but with very great advantage to the revenue. They are extensively
he tables of the opulent ; and would, there is no doubt, be extensively used by

the middle classes, were their price lower. The importation, even with the present du
21s. 6d., is about 20,000 cwt. ; and as this duty is full 100 per cent. upon their pri
bond, it may be fairly concluded, that were it reduced to 8s. or 10s. a cwt., the qua
imported would very soon be trebled, or more.

No abatement of duty is made on account of any damage received by figs.

FILE, FILES (Da. *File;* Du. *Vylen;* Fr. *Limes;* Ger. *Feilen;* It. *Lime*)
instrument of iron or forged steel, cut in little furrows, used to polish or sm
metals, timber, and other hard bodies.

FIR. See PINE.

FIRE-ARMS. Under this designation is comprised all sorts of guns, fow
pieces, blunderbusses, pistols, &c. The manufacture of these weapons is of
siderable importance ; employing at all times, but especially during war, a
number of persons.

In consequence of the frequent occurrence of accidents from the bursting of insufficient barrel
legislature has most properly interfered, not to regulate their manufacture, but to prevent all persons
using or selling barrels that have not been regularly *proved* in a public proof-house. The first act fo
purpose was passed in 1813, but it was soon after superseded by a fuller and more complete on
55 Geo. 3. c. 59. This statute imposes a fine of 20l. on any person *using,* in any of the progressive
of its manufacture, any barrel not duly proved ; on any person *delivering* the same, except through a
house ; and on any person *receiving,* for the purpose of making guns, &c. any barrels which have not
through a proof-house. These penalties to be levied on conviction before two justices ; with like pen
to be similarly levied, on persons counterfeiting the *proof-marks.*

FIRE-WORKS. By 9 & 10 Will. 3., all sorts of fire-works are declared
a common nuisance ; and the *making, causing to be made, giving, selling,* or *off*
for sale, any squibs, rockets, serpents, or *other fire-works,* or any cases or in
ments for making the same, is made subject to a penalty of 5l. to be recovere
conviction before a justice of the peace. Casting or firing any such fire-w
or permitting the same to be cast or fired, *from* any house or place, and ca
or firing the same *into* any house, shop, street, highway, or river, is subjected
penalty of 20s. to be recovered in like manner ; and if not immediately paid
party to be imprisoned and kept to hard labour for any time not exceedi
month. But the statute provides, that it shall be lawful for the master,
tenant, or commissioners of his Majesty's ordnance, or those authorised by t
to give orders for making any fire-works, to be used according to such orders

FIRKIN, a measure of capacity, equal to 9 ale gallons, or $7\frac{1}{2}$ imperial ga
or 2,538 cubic inches. — (See WEIGHTS and MEASURES.)

FIRLOT, a dry measure used in Scotland. The Linlithgow wheat firlot
the imperial bushel as ·998 to 1 ; and the Linlithgow barley firlot is to the imp
bushel as 1·456 is to 1. — (See WEIGHTS and MEASURES.)

FISH (Ger. *Fische;* Du. *Visschen;* Da. and Sw. *Fisk;* Fr. *Poissons;* It. *P*
Sp. *Pescados;* Port. *Peixes;* Rus. *Rüb;* Pol. *Ryby;* Lat. *Pisces*), a term
in natural history to denote every variety of animal inhabiting seas, rivers, l
ponds, &c. that cannot exist for any considerable time out of the water. B
a commercial point of view, those fishes only are referred to, that are caug
man, and used either as food or for some other useful purpose. Of these, he
salmon, cod, pilchard, mackerel, turbot, lobster, oyster, whale, &c. are amon
most important. — (See the different articles under these titles.)

The supply of fish in the seas round Britain is most abundant, or rather
inexhaustible. " The coasts of Great Britain," says Sir John Boroughs, " doe
such a continued sea harvest of gain and benefit to all those that with diligence doe l
in the same, that no time or season of the yeare passeth away without some app
meanes of profitable employment, especially to such as apply themselves to fishing ; v
from the beginning of the year unto the latter end, continueth upon some part or
upon our coastes ; and these in such infinite shoales and multitudes of fishes are o
to the takers, as may justly move admiration, not only to strangers, but to thos
daily are employed amongst them." — " That this harvest," says Mr. Barrow, " ri
gathering at all seasons of the year — without the labour of tillage, without expe
seed or manure, without the payment of rent or taxes—is inexhaustible, the extraord
fecundity of the most valuable kinds of fish would alone afford abundant proof.
enumerate the thousands, and even millions of eggs, which are impregnated i
herring, the cod, the ling, and indeed in almost the whole of the esculent fish, woul
but an inadequate idea of the prodigious multitudes in which they flock to our sl
the shoals themselves must be seen, in order to convey to the mind any just not
their aggregate mass." — (For an account of the shoals of herrings, see HERRING.)

But notwithstanding this immense abundance of fish, and notwithstanding the bo
that have been given by the legislature to the individuals engaged in the fishery,

been profitable to those by whom it has been carried on, nor has it made that pro-
s that might have been expected. —(See HERRING FISHERY.) There is but little
consumed in the interior; and even in most sea-port towns the consumption is not
great. In London, indeed, immense quantities of fish are annually made use of;
there can be little doubt that the consumption would be much greater, were it not
he abuses in the trade, which render the supply comparatively scarce, and, in most
nces, exceedingly dear. All fish brought to London is sold in Billingsgate market;
in consequence of this restriction, the salesmen of that market have succeeded in
lishing what is really equivalent to a monopoly; and are, in a great measure, enabled
egulate both the supply and the price. This is an abuse that calls loudly for coron; and the most effectual way in which it could be obviated would be by opening
tional markets in Westminster and Southwark, and giving every possible facility to
shermen supplying them with fish. But no encouragement other than the removal
bstacles of this sort to the introduction of fish into general use, ought to be given
e fishery. It will be seen, in our articles on the herring and whale fisheries, that the
ty system has been attended with vast expense, without leading to any useful result.
r. Barrow, in a valuable article on the fisheries in the *Supplement to the Encyclo-
a Britannica*, has estimated the value of the entire annual produce of the foreign and
stic fisheries of Great Britain at 8,300,000*l.* But it is admitted by every one who
vs any thing of the subject, that this estimate is very greatly exaggerated. We doubt
h, whether the entire value of the fisheries can be reckoned so high as *four* millions.

ulations as to Importation. — Fresh fish, British taken, and imported in British ships, may be landed
United Kingdom without report, entry, or warrant. — (6 Geo. 4. c. 107. § 2.)
sh fish of every kind, of British taking, and imported in British ships; and fresh lobsters and tur-
however taken, or in whatever ship imported; and cured fish of every kind, of British taking and
, imported in British ships; shall be imported *free of all duties*, and shall not be deemed to be in-
in any charge of duty imposed by any act hereafter to be made on the importation of goods generally;
ed that before any *cured fish* shall be entered free of duty, as being of such taking and curing, the
r of the ship importing the same shall make oath before the collector or comptroller, that such fish
tually caught, taken, and cured wholly by his Majesty's subjects. — § 42.
of foreign taking or curing, or in foreign vessels, except turbots and lobsters, stockfish, live eels,
vies, sturgeon, botargo, and caviare, prohibited to be imported on pain of forfeiture. — § 52.

LAX (Ger. *Flachs;* Du. *Vlasch;* Fr. *Lin;* It. and Sp. *Lino;* Rus. *Len, Lon;*
Len; Lat. *Linum*), an important plant that has been cultivated from the
est ages in Great Britain and many other countries; its fibres being manu-
red into thread, and its seed crushed for oil. Generally, however, we have
in the habit of importing a large proportion of our supplies. The premiums
by the legislature to force the cultivation of flax, have had very little effect;
ct being, as Mr. Loudon has stated, that its culture is found to be, on the
e, less profitable than that of corn. When allowed to ripen its seed, it is
f the most severe crops.

e principal sorts of flax imported into this country are, Petersburgh, Narva, Riga,
, Pernau, Liebau, Memel, Oberland, and Dutch flax. The Petersburgh and
a flax are nearly of the same quality, the latter being but little inferior to the
r. Both sorts come to us in bundles of twelve, nine, and six heads. The Riga
eems to deserve the preference of any imported from the Baltic. It is the growth
e provinces of Marienburg, Druania, Thiesenhausen, and Lithuania. The best
nburg is called simply Marienburg (M), or Marienburg clean; the second quality,
M); and the third, *risten dreyband* (RD): of the three other provinces, the first
y bears the name of *rakitzer;*—as *Druania rakitzer* (DR), *Thiesenhausen rakitzer*
, and *Lithuania rakitzer* LR). The cut flax of these three provinces is the second
y: and to the third quality belong, the *badstub*, and *badstub* cut (B and BG); the
oster (PN); and *hafs three band* (HD). *Badstub and paternoster* is the refuse of
kitzer flax, and the *three band* again the refuse of the former sorts, and consequently
rdinary. The Revel and Pernau consists of Marienburg, *cut, risten, hafs three*
and *three band*. The Liebau and Memel growths are distinguished by the de-
ation of *four* and *three band*. These two sorts, as well as the Oberland flax, come
Königsberg, Elbing, &c. and are little esteemed in the British markets.
nders or Dutch flax is well dressed, and of the finest quality.
x is extensively cultivated in Egypt. Of late years, some of the Italian ports
used to be supplied from Russia, have been fully supplied on lower terms from
ndria.
en flax is brought to the principal Russian ports whence it is shipped, it is classified
ing to its qualities, and made up in bundles by sworn inspectors (*brackers*) ap-
d by government for the assortment of that and all other merchandise. These
naries are said to perform their task with laudable impartiality and exactness. A
is attached to every bundle of assorted flax, containing the names of the inspector
ner, the sort of flax, and the period when it was selected or inspected. — (See

Hemp.) Good flax should be of a fine bright colour, well separated from the to codilla, or coarser portion of the plant; and of a long, fine, and strong fibre. In pu chasing flax, it is usual to employ agents wholly devoted to this peculiar business.

Of 876,189 cwt. of flax and tow imported into Great Britain in 1828, 643,153 cw were brought from Russia; 130,529 cwt. from the Netherlands; 59,447 cwt. fro Prussia; 39,210 cwt. from France; 1,466 cwt. from Italy; and about 2,300 cwt. fro New South Wales, &c. The whole of this quantity was retained for home consumptic The duty was recently reduced, and is now only 1d. a cwt.

Flax, the produce or manufacture of Europe, not to be imported for home consumption, except British ships, or in ships of the country of which it is the produce, or of the country from which it is ported. — (6 Geo. 4. c. 109.)

Flax imported in foreign ships to be deemed *alien goods*, and to pay town and port dues as such. (6 Geo. 4. c. 111.)

We subjoin an account of the charges on the importation of the different sorts of flax from Petersbu and Riga.

Charges at Petersburgh on 12 Head Flax, per ton.

Circa, 16 Bobbins = 63 Poods = 1 ton.

	Rub.	Cop.
Duty, 540 cop. per bercovitz	34	2
Quarantine duty, 1 per cent.	0	34
Additional duty, 10 per cent.	3	40
	R. 37	76
Custom-house charges, 4 per cent.	1	51
Receiving and weighing, 40 cop. per bobbin	6	40
Bracking, 1 rub. per bercovitz	6	30
Binding, 75 cop. per ditto	4	72
Lighterage and attendance to Cronstadt, 8 rub. per 60 poods	8	40
Mats	8	0
Brokerage, 60 cop. per ton	0	60
Fixed charges	R. 73	69

Brokerage, ½ per cent.
Commission and extra charges, 3 per cent.
Stamps, ¼ per cent.
Brokerage on bills, ¼ per cent. } ½ per cent.
are charges varying according to the price paid.

Riga flax is bought at so much per shippound. 6¾ shippound = 1 ton.

The charges of importation are the same, or nearly so, as on Petersburgh flax.

Charges here, per ton, taking the price at 45*l.*

	L.	s.
Insurance, 12s. 6d. per cent. and policy, during the summer, for best risks	0	6
Sound dues	0	5
Freight, say 52s. 6d. per ton in full	2	12
Customs	0	1
Landing charges	1	11
Discount, 3½ per cent. (being sold at 9 months' credit)	1	13
Brokerage, ½ per cent.	0	4
	L. 5	15
Loss by tare, 2 per cent.	0	18
	L. 6	13

9 Head Flax.

26 Bobbins = 63 Poods = 1 ton. Ru. C
Fixed charges at Petersburgh amount to . . 80
The other charges same as on 12 head; the charges of import may be called the same as on 12 head also, the difference being only on the value; which makes the insurance, discount, and brokerage, of less amount. The increase of fixed charges at Petersburgh is owing to the larger number of bobbins to the ton.

6 Head Flax.

47 Bobbins = 63 Poods = 1 ton. Ru. C
Fixed charges, per ton 91
Other charges, *vide supra*.

FLAXSEED, or LINSEED (Fr. *Lin, Graine de Lin;* Ger. *Leinsaat;* D *Lynzaad;* It. *Linseme;* Sp. *Linaza;* Port. *Linhaca;* Pol. *Siemie, Iniane;* R *Semja lenjanoe;* Lat. *Lini semen*), the seed of flax. It contains a great deal of which it yields by expression; and is cultivated either that it may be used sowing, or sent to the crushing mills to be converted into oil.

As the quality of the crop depends much on the seed employed, a good deal of care is quisite in selecting the best. Generally speaking, it should be chosen of a bright, brown colour, oily to the feel, heavy, and quite fresh. Dutch seed is in the highest estimati for sowing; it not only ripens sooner than any other that is imported, but produ larger crops, and of the quality that best suits our principal manufactures. Ameri seed produces fine flax, but the produce is not so large as from Dutch seed. British fl seed is sometimes used instead of Dutch; but the risk of the crop misgiving is so mu greater, "that those only who are ignorant of the consequences, or who are compel from necessity, are chargeable with this act of ill-judged parsimony." — (*Loudon's En of Agriculture.*) Crushing seed is principally imported from Russia, but considera quantities are also brought from Italy and Egypt. Of 2,052,258 bushels of lins imported in 1829, 1,505,861 were brought from Russia, 79,611 from Prussia, 33, from the Netherlands, 199,607 from Italy, 156,373 from Egypt, 68,710 from the Uni States, &c. The duty is 1s. a quarter, and the price at this moment (August, 18 varies from 35s. to 47s. a quarter.

FLOTSAM, JETSAM, AND LAGAN. In order to constitute a legal wre the goods must come to land. If they continue at sea, the law distinguishes th by the foregoing uncouth and barbarous appellations: *flotsam* is when the go continue swimming on the surface of the waves; *jetsam* is when they are s under the surface of the water; and *lagan* is when they are sunk, but tied t cork or buoy to be found again. — (*Blackstone*, book i. c. 8.) Foreign liqu brought or coming into Great Britain or Ireland, as derelict, flotsam, &c. are pay the same duties and receive the same drawbacks as similar liquors regul imported.

FLOUR (Ger. *Feines mehl, Semmelmehl;* Du. *Bloem;* Fr. *Fleur de farine; Fiore;* Sp. *Flor*), the meal of wheat-corn, finely ground and sifted. There three qualities of flour, denominated *firsts, seconds,* and *thirds,* of which the fir the purest. See Corn Laws and Corn Trade.

OT, a measure of length, consisting of 12 inches. See WEIGHTS and
URES.

RESTALLING, the buying or contracting for any cattle, provision, or
andise, on its way to the market, or dissuading persons from buying their
there, or persuading them to raise the price, or spreading any false rumour,
ntent to enhance the value of any article. Several statutes had from time
e been passed prohibiting forestalling under severe penalties. But as more
ed views upon such subjects began to prevail, the impolicy of these statutes
e obvious. They were consequently repealed in 1772. But forestalling is
unishable at common law by fine and imprisonment. It is doubtful, how-
whether any jury would now convict an individual accused of such practices.
ealth of Nations, vol. ii. p. 409.)

ANKINCENSE. See ROSIN.

EIGHT, the sum paid by the merchant or other person hiring a ship, or
f a ship, for the use of such ship or part, during a specified voyage or for
ified time.

freight is most commonly fixed by the charterparty — (see CHARTERPARTY), or
lading — (see BILL OF LADING) ; but in the absence of any formal stipulations on
ject, it would be due according to the custom or usage of trade.
he case of a charterparty, if the stipulated payment be a gross sum for an entire
r an entire part of a ship, for the whole voyage, the gross sum will be payable
;h the merchant has not fully laden the ship. And if a certain sum be stipulated
ry ton, or other portion of the ship's capacity, for the whole voyage, the payment
e according to the number of tons, &c. which the ship is proved capable of con-
, without regard to the quantity actually put on board by the merchant. On the
and, if the merchant have stipulated to pay a certain sum per cask or bale of
the payment must be, in the first place, according to the number of casks and
ipped and delivered ; and if he have further covenanted to furnish a complete
or a specific number of casks or bales, and failed to do so, he must make good
s which the owners have sustained by his failure.
1 entire ship be hired, and the burthen thereof be expressed in the charterparty,
merchant bind himself to pay a certain sum for every ton, &c. of goods which
lade on board, but does not bind himself to furnish a complete lading, the
can only demand payment for the quantity of goods actually shipped. But if
chant agree to load a full and complete cargo, though the ship be described as
burthen than she really is, the merchant must load a full cargo, according to the
then of the ship, and he will be liable for freight according to what ought to be

delivery of goods at the place of destination is in general necessary to entitle the
o freight ; but with respect to living animals, whether men or cattle, which may
tly die during the voyage, without any fault or neglect of the persons belonging
hip, it is ruled, that if there be no express agreement whether the freight is to be
the lading, or for the transporting them, freight shall be paid as well for the
for the living : if the agreement be to pay freight for the *lading*, then death cer-
annot deprive the owners of the freight ; but if the agreement be to pay freight
sporting them, then no freight is due for those that die on the voyage, because as to
e contract is not performed. These distinctions have been made in the civil law,
e been adopted into the modern systems of maritime law.
ght is most frequently contracted to be paid either by the whole voyage, or by the
or other time. In the former case the owners take upon themselves the chance
oyage being long or short : but in the latter the risk of the duration falls upon
chant : and if no time be fixed for the commencement of the computation, it
in from the day on which the ship breaks ground and commences her voyage,
continue during the whole course of the voyage, and during all unavoidable
ot occasioned by the act or neglect of the owners or master, or by such circum-
as occasion a suspension of the contract for a particular period. Thus, the
will be payable for the time consumed in necessary repairs during a voyage,
l it do not appear that the ship was insufficient at the outset, or that there was
roper delay in repairing her.
e absence of an express contract to the contrary, the entire freight is not earned
e whole cargo be ready for delivery, or has been delivered to the consignee accord-
ie contract for its conveyance.
consignee receive goods in pursuance of the usual bill of lading, by which it is
d that he is to pay the freight, he, by such receipt, makes himself debtor for the
and may be sued for it. But a person who is only an agent for the consignor,

and who is known to the master to be acting in that character, does not make him
personally answerable for the freight by receiving the goods, although he also enters t
in his own name at the Custom-house.

In some cases freight is to be paid, or rather an equivalent recompence made to
owners, although the goods have not been delivered at the place of destination,
though the contract for conveyance be not strictly performed. Thus, if part of the c
be thrown overboard for the necessary preservation of the ship and the remainder of
goods, and the ship afterwards reaches the place of destination, the value of this pa
to be answered to the merchant by way of general average, and the value of the fr
thereof allowed to the owner. So, if the master be compelled by necessity to sell a
of the cargo for victuals or repairs, the owners must pay to the merchant the price w
the goods would have fetched *at the place of destination;* and, therefore, are allowe
charge the merchant with the money that would have been due if they had been
veyed thither.

When goods are deteriorated during a voyage, the merchant is entitled to a com
sation, provided the deterioration has proceeded from the fault or neglect of the ma
or mariners; and of course he is not answerable for the freight, unless he accept the go
except by way of deduction from the amount of the compensation. On the other h
if the deterioration has proceeded from a principle of decay naturally inherent in
commodity itself, whether active in every situation, or in the confinement and close
of a ship, or from the perils of the sea, or the act of God, the merchant must bear
loss and pay the freight; for the master and owners are in no fault, nor does their
tract contain any insurance or warranty against such an event. In our West I
trade, the freight of sugar and molasses is usually regulated by the weight of the c
at the port of delivery here, which, in fact, is in every instance less than the weig
the time of the shipment; and, therefore, the loss of freight occasioned by the lea
necessarily falls upon the owners of the ship by the nature of the contract.

Different opinions have been entertained by Valin, Pothier, and other great author
as to maritime law, with respect to the expediency of allowing the merchant to abar
his goods for freight, in the event of their being damaged. This question has not
judicially decided in this country. "The only point," says Lord Tenterden, "inter
to be proposed by me as doubtful, is the right to abandon for freight alone at the po
destination: and in point of practice, I have been informed that this right is never cla
in this country."—(*Law of Shipping,* part iii. c. 7.)

Freight being the return made for the conveyance of goods or passengers to a parti
destination, no claim arises for its payment in the event of a total loss; and it is
down by Lord Mansfield, that "in case of a total loss with salvage, the merchant
either take the part saved, or abandon."—(*Abbott,* part iii. c. 7.) But after the merc
has made his election, he must abide by it.

It often happens that a ship is hired by a charterparty to sail from one port to ano
and thence back to the first—as, for example, from London to Leghorn, and from
horn back to London—at a certain sum to be paid for every month or other peri
the duration of the employment. Upon such a contract, *if the whole be one entire vo*
and the ship sail in safety to Leghorn, and there deliver the goods of the merchant
take others on board to be brought to London, but happen to be lost in her r
thither, nothing is due for freight, although the merchant has had the benefit o
voyage to Leghorn: but, *if the outward and homeward voyages be distinct,* freight w
due for the proportion of the time employed in the outward voyage. "If," said
Mansfield, in a case of this sort, "there be *one entire voyage out and in,* and the sh
cast away on the homeward voyage, no freight is due; no wages are due, becaus
whole profit is lost; and by express agreement the parties may make the outwar
homeward voyage one. Nothing is more common than two voyages: *wherever the
two voyages, and one is performed,* and the ship is lost on the homeward voyage, fi
is due for the first."—(*K. B. Trin. Term,* 16 Geo. 3.)

It frequently happens that the master or owner fails to complete his contract, eith
not delivering the whole goods to the consignee or owner, or by delivering them
place short of their original destination; in these cases, if the owner or consignee
goods *derive any benefit from their conveyance,* he is liable to the payment of freig
cording to the proportion of the voyage performed, or *pro ratâ itineris peracti:* and th
contracts of this nature be frequently entire and indivisible, and the master or ow
the ship cannot, from their nature, sue thereon, and recover a rateable freight,
ratâ itineris; yet he may do so upon a fresh *implied* contract, for as much as he de
to have, unless there be an express clause in the original charterparty or contract
contrary. A fresh implied contract is inferred from the owner's or consignee's accep
of the goods. Many difficulties have, indeed, arisen in deciding as to what shall ar
to an acceptance: it is not, however, necessary actually to receive the goods; accep

be made by the express or implied directions, and with the consent, of the owner or
ignee of the goods, but not otherwise.

sometimes happens that the owner of the ship, who is originally entitled to the
ght, sells or otherwise disposes of his interest in the ship; where a chartered ship is
before the voyage, the vendee, and not the vendor or party to whom he afterwards
gns the charterparty, is entitled to the freight. But where a ship has been sold *during*
voyage, the owner, with whom a covenant to pay freight has been made, is entitled
e freight, and not the vendee. A mortgagee who does not take possession, is not
led to the freight.

he time and manner of paying freight are frequently regulated by express stipulations
charterparty, or other written contract; and when that is the case, they must be reed; but if there be no express stipulation contrary to or inconsistent with the right
n, the goods remain as a security till the freight is paid; for the master is not bound
liver them, or any part of them, without payment of the freight and other charges
spect thereof. But the master cannot detain the cargo on board the vessel till these
ents be made, as the merchant would, in that case, have no opportunity of examin-
he condition of the goods. In England, the practice is, when the master is doubtful
yment, to send such goods as are not required to be landed at any particular wharf,
public wharf, ordering the wharfinger not to part with them till the freight and
charges are paid. No right of lien for freight can exist, unless the freight be
ed; if the freighter or a stranger prevent the freight from becoming due, the ship-
r or master's remedy is by action of damages.

r further information and details with respect to this subject, see the art. CHARTER-
r, in this Dictionary; *Abbott* (Lord Tenterden) *on the Law of Shipping*, part iii.
; *Chitty's Commercial Law*, vol. iii. c. 9.; *Molloy de Jure Maritimo*, book ii. c. 4.,

RUIT (Ger. *Obst, Früchte;* Du. *Ooft;* Fr. *Fruit;* It. *Frutta, Frutte;* Sp.
a; Rus. *Owoschtsch;* Lat. *Fructum*). This appellation is bestowed by com-
ial men upon those species of fruit, such as oranges, lemons, almonds, raisins,
ants, apples, &c. &c. which constitute articles of importation from foreign
tries.

ULLERS' EARTH (Ger. *Walkererde;* Du. *Voläarde;* Fr. *Terre à foulon;* It.
a da purgatori; Sp. *Tierra de batan;* Rus. *Schiffernaia;* Lat. *Terra fullonum*),
cies of clay, of a greenish white, greenish grey, olive and oil green, and some-
s spotted colour. It is usually opaque, very soft, and feels greasy. It is used by
s to take grease out of cloth before they apply the soap. The best is found
ckinghamshire and Surrey. When good, it has a greenish white, or greenish
colour, falls into powder in water, appears to melt on the tongue like butter,
nunicates a milky hue to water, and deposits very little sand when mixed
boiling water. The remarkable detersive property on woollen cloth depends
e alumina, which should be at least one fifth of the whole, but not much
than one fourth, lest it become too tenacious. — (*Thomson's Chemistry;*
son's Mineralogy.)

JNDS (PUBLIC), the name given to the public funded debt due by govern-

e practice of borrowing money in order to defray a part of the war expenditure
, in this country, in the reign of William III. In the infancy of the system, it
ustomary to borrow upon the security of some tax, or portion of a tax, set apart
and for discharging the principal and interest of the sum borrowed. This dis-
e was, however, very rarely effected. The public exigencies still continuing, the
were, in most cases, either continued, or the taxes were again mortgaged for fresh

At length the practice of borrowing for a fixed period, or, as it is commonly
d, upon *terminable* annuities, was almost entirely abandoned, and most loans were
upon *interminable* annuities, or until such time as it might be convenient for
ment to pay off the principal.

the beginning of the funding system, the term fund meant the taxes or funds
priated to the discharge of the principal and interest of loans; those who held
ment securities, and sold them to others, selling, of course, a corresponding claim
some fund. But after the debt began to grow large, and the practice of borrow-
on interminable annuities had been introduced, the meaning attached to the term
was gradually changed; and instead of signifying the security upon which loans
dvanced, it has, for a long time, signified the principal of the loans themselves.

ing partly, perhaps, to the scarcity of disposable capital at the time, but far more
supposed insecurity of the Revolutionary establishment, the rate of interest paid
ernment in the early part of the funding system was, comparatively, high. But

as the country became richer, and the confidence of the public in the stability of gover ment was increased, ministers were enabled to take measures for reducing the intere first in 1716, and again in 1749.

During the reigns of William III. and Anne, the interest stipulated for loans w very various. But in the reign of George II. a different practice was adopted. I stead of varying the interest upon the loan according to the state of the money mark at the time, the rate of interest was generally fixed at *three* or *three and a half* per cent the necessary variation being made in the principal funded. Thus, suppose governme were anxious to borrow, that they preferred borrowing in a 3 per cent. stock, and th they could not negotiate a loan for less than $4\frac{1}{2}$ per cent. ; they effected their object giving the lender, in return for every 100*l*. advanced, 150*l*. 3 per cent. stock ; that they bound the country to pay him or his assignees 4*l*. 10*s*. a year in all time to com or, otherwise, to extinguish the debt by a payment of 150*l*. In consequence of the pr valence of this practice, the principal of the debt now existing amounts to nearly *t fifths* more than the sum actually advanced by the lenders.

Some advantages are, however, derivable, or supposed to be derivable, from t system. It renders the management of the debt, and its transfer, more simple a commodious than it would have been, had it consisted of a great number of fun bearing different rates of interest : and it is contended, that the greater field for spec lation afforded to the dealers in stocks bearing a low rate of interest, has enabl government to borrow, by funding additional capitals, for a considerably less payme on account of interest than would have been necessary had no such increase of capi been made.

Were this a proper place for entering upon such discussions, it would be easy to sh that the advantages now referred to are really of very trifling importance ; and that method of funding by an increase of capital has been a most improvident one, and m injurious to the public interests. But it would be quite foreign from the objects of t work to enter into any examination of such questions : our readers will, however, fi them fully investigated in an article in the 93d No. of the Edinburgh Review. He we have merely to consider funded property, or government securities, as transfera or marketable commodities. The following is an account of the progress of the tional debt of Great Britain, from the Revolution to the present time : —

	Principal.	Interest.
	£	£
Debt at the Revolution in 1689 - - - -	664,263	39,855
Excess of debt contracted during the reign of William III. above debt paid off - - - -	15,730,439	1,271,087
Debt at the accession of Queen Anne in 1702 - -	16,394,702	1,310,942
Debt contracted during Queen Anne's reign - -	37,750,661	2,040,416
Debt at the accession of George I. in 1714 - -	54,145,363	3,351,358
Debt paid off during the reign of George I. above debt contracted -	2,053,125	1,133,807
Debt at the accession of George II. in 1727 -	52,092,238	2,217,551
Debt contracted from the accession of George II. till the peace of Paris in 1763, three years after the accession of George III. -	86,773,192	2,634,500
Debt in 1763 - - - - - -	138,865,430	4,852,051
Paid during peace - - - - - -	10,281,795	380,480
Debt at the commencement of the American war in 1775 -	128,583,635	4,471,571
Debt contracted during the American war - -	121,267,993	4,980,201
Debt at the conclusion of the American war in 1784 -	249,851,628	9,451,77:
Paid during peace, from 1784 to 1793 - - -	10,501,380	243,27:
Debt at the commencement of the French war in 1793 -	239,350,148	9,208,49:
Debt contracted during the French war -	608,932,329	24,645,97:
Total Funded and Unfunded Debt, 5th January, 1817, when the English and Irish Exchequers were consolidated -	£848,282,477	£33,854,46:

Since 1817, a deduction has been made of about *sixty* millions from the principa the debt, and about *five* millions from the annual charge on its account. This dimi tion has been principally effected by taking advantage of the fall in the rate of inte since the peace, and offering to pay off the holders of different stocks, unless they sented to accept a reduced payment ; and had it not been for the highly objection practice, already adverted to, of funding large capitals at a low rate of interest, the sa in this way might have been incomparably larger. We subjoin

DEBT.

	Capital of Unredeemed Debt. £	s.	d.
Great Britain.			
Debt due to the South Sea Company, at 3 per cent.	3,662,784	8	6½
Old South Sea Annuities - - — -	3,501,870	2	7
New South Sea Annuities - - — -	2,489,830	2	10
South Sea Annuities, 1751 - - — -	527,100	0	0
Debt due to the Bank of England - — -	14,686,800	0	0
Bank Annuities created in 1726 - — -	876,049	19	0
Consolidated Annuities - - — -	348,828,660	15	6¼
Reduced Annuities - - — -	123,771,890	19	2
Total bearing Interest at 3 per cent. -	498,344,986	7	7¾
Annuities at 3½ per cent., anno 1818 - -	12,804,559	2	2
Reduced Annuities, do. - - - -	64,250,381	1	11
New 3½ per cent. Annuities - - -	138,680,967	5	3
4*l*. per cent. Annuities, created 1826 - -	10,806,966	0	0
New 5 per cent. Annuities - - -	467,712	19	11¾
Great Britain -	725,355,572	16	11½
Ireland.			
Irish Consolidated Annuities, at 3 per cent. -	2,455,317	13	6
Irish Reduced Annuities, do. - - -	150,228	17	10
3½*l*. per cent. Debentures and Stock - -	14,173,495	7	1
Reduced 3½ per cent. Annuities - - -	1,289,703	17	10
New 3½ per cent. Annuities - - -	11,425,247	18	8
Debt due to the Bank of Ireland, at 4 per cent. -	1,615,384	12	4
New 5 per cent. Annuities - - - -	6,661	1	0
Debt due to the Bank of Ireland, at 5 per cent. -	1,015,384	12	4
Ireland -	32,131,424	0	7
Total United Kingdom -	757,486,996	17	6½
Exchequer Bills outstanding - - -	32,079,483	6	5½
Total Funded and Unfunded Debt -	£789,566,480	4	0

CHARGE.

		In Great Britain. £	s.	d.	In Ireland. £	s.	d.	Total Annual Charge. £	s.	d.
Due to the Public Creditor.	Annual Interest on Unredeemed Capital	22,956,770	13	4½	1,134,979	14	5½			
	Long Annuities, expire 1860 - -	1,193,089	9	7	—					
	Annuities per 4 Geo. 4. c. 22., do. 1867 -	585,740	0	0	—					
	Annuities per 10 Geo. 4. c. 24., expire at various periods - - -	775,914	5	0	—					
	Annuities to the Trustees of the Waterloo Subscription Fund, per 59 Geo. 3. c. 34., expire 5 July, 1831 - - -	7,300	0	0	—					
	Life Annuities, per 48 Geo. 3. c. 142. and 10 Geo. 4. c. 24. - - -	669,361	9	0	—					
	Life Annuities payable at the Exchequer. English - -	23,455	8	2¾	—					
	Life Annuities payable at the Exchequer. Irish - - -	35,476	18	7	7,038	0	9			
Interest of Funded Debt - - - - -		£26,247,108	3	9½	1,142,017	15	2	27,389,125	18	11¾
Management of Debt - - - - - -		-	-	-	-	-	-	275,179	3	4
Annual Charge on Account of Public Funded Debt -		-	-	-	-	-	-	27,664,305	2	3¾
Interest on Exchequer Bills - - - - -		-	-	-	-	-	-	793,031	1	8
Total Charge on Account of Funded and Unfunded Debt - - - - - -		-	-	-	-	-	-	£28,457,336	3	11¾

We shall now subjoin some account of the different funds or stocks forming public debt.

I. FUNDS BEARING INTEREST AT THREE PER CENT.

1. *South Sea Debt and Annuities.* — This portion of the debt, amounting, on the of January last, to 10,181,584*l.*, is all that now remains of the capital of the once far or rather infamous, South Sea Company. The Company has, for a considerable past, ceased to have any thing to do with trade: so that the functions of the dire are wholly restricted to the transfer of the Company's stock, and the payment o dividends on it; both of which operations are performed at the South Sea House not at the Bank. The dividends on the Old South Sea annuities are payable o 5th of April and 10th of October; the dividends on the rest of the Company's are payable on the 5th of January and 5th of July.

2. *Debt due to the Bank of England.* — This consists of the sum of 14,686,800*l.* by the Bank to the public at 3 per cent.; dividends payable on the 5th of April 10th of October. This must not be confounded with the Bank capital of 14,553,C on which the stockholders divide. The dividend on the latter has been 8 per cent. 1823. — (See *antè*, p. 76.)

3. *Bank Annuities created in* 1726. — The civil list settled upon George I. 700,000*l.* a year; but having fallen into arrear, this stock was created for the pu of cancelling exchequer bills that had been issued to defray the arrear. "The ca is irredeemable; and being small, in comparison with the other public funds, and a in which little is done on speculation, the price is generally at least 1 per cent. than the 3 per cent. consols." — (*Cohen's* edit. of *Fairman on the Funds*, p. 40.)

4. *Three per Cent. Consols, or Consolidated Annuities.* — This stock forms by the largest portion of the public debt. It had its origin in 1751, when an act passed, consolidating (hence the name) several separate stocks bearing an intere 3 per cent. into one general stock. At the period when the consolidation took p the principal of the funds blended together amounted to 9,137,821*l.*; but by the ing of additional loans, and parts of loans, in this stock, it amounted on the 5 January last (1831) to the immense sum of 348,828,660*l.*!

The consolidated annuities are distinguished from the 3 per cent. reduced annu by the circumstance of the interest upon them never having been varied, and b dividends becoming due at different periods. This stock is, from its magnitude the proportionally great number of its holders, the soonest affected by all those cir stances which tend to elevate or depress the price of funded property. And, on account, it is the stock which speculators and jobbers most commonly select for operations. Dividends payable on the 5th of January and 5th of July.

5. *Three per Cent. Reduced Annuities.* — This fund was established in 1757. I sisted, as the name implies, of several funds which had previously been borrowe higher rate of interest; but, by an act passed in 1749, it was declared that such ho of the funds in question as did not choose to accept in future of a reduced inter 3 per cent. should be paid off, — an alternative, which comparatively few embr The debts that were thus reduced and consolidated, amounted, at the establishment fund, to 17,571,574*l.* By the addition of new loans, they now amount to 123,771, Dividends payable on the 5th of April and 10th of October.

II. FUNDS BEARING MORE THAN THREE PER CENT. INTEREST.

1. *Annuities at* 3½ *per Cent.*, 1818. — This stock was formed in 1818, partly by scription of 3 per cent. consolidated and 3 per cent. reduced annuities, and partly subscription of exchequer bills. It was made redeemable at par any time afte 5th of April, 1829, upon six months' notice being given. Dividends payable c 5th of April and 10th of October. The capital of this stock amounts to 12,804,5

2. *Reduced* 3½ *per Cent. Annuities.* — This stock was created in 1824, by the tr of a stock bearing interest at 4 per cent. (Old 4 per Cents.). It is redeemable at sure. Dividends payable 5th of April and 10th of October. Amount on the January last, 64,250,381*l.*

3. *New* 3½ *per Cent. Annuities.* — This stock was formed by the act 11 G c. 13., out of the stock known by the name of "New 4 per Cents.," amounti the 5th of January, 1830, to 144,331,212*l.* The holders of this 4 per cent. stoc their option either to subscribe it into the new 3½ per cent. annuities, or into 5 per cent. stock at the rate of 100*l.* 4 per cents. for 70*l.* 5 per cents. Dissenti be paid off. Only 467,713*l.* new 5 per cent. stock was created under this arrange The sum required to pay dissentients was 2,610,000*l.* The new 3½ per cent. that was thus created, amounted on the 5th of January last to 138,680,967*l.* Div payable 5th of January and 5th of July.

4. *Four per Cent. Annuities*, created 1826. — By virtue of the act 7 Geo. 4. eight millions of exchequer bills were funded, at the rate of 107*l.* 4 per cent. an

every 100*l.* bills. In 1829 (10 Geo. 4. c. 31.), three additional millions of ex-
quer bills were funded in this stock, at the rate of 101*l.* 10*s.* stock for every 100*l.*
. Dividends payable 5th of April and 10th of October. Amount, 5th of January
10,806,966*l.* A considerable sum has been transferred from this stock for the
hase of annuities under the 10 Geo. 4. c. 24.

New 5 per Cent. Annuities. — See above, 3. *New* 3½ *per Cent. Annuities.*

III. Annuities.

Long Annuities. — These annuities were created at different periods, but they all
re together in 1860. They were chiefly granted by way of premiums or douceurs
e subscribers to loans. Payable on the 5th of April and 10th of October.

Annuities per 4 *Geo.* 4. *c.* 22. — This annuity is payable to the Bank of England,
s commonly known by the name of the " Dead Weight" annuity — (see *antè,* p. 75.).
pires in 1867. It is equivalent to a *perpetual* annuity of 470,319*l.* 10*s.*

Annuities per 48 *Geo.* 3. *and* 10 *Geo.* 4. *c.* 24. — These acts authorised the
missioners for the reduction of the national debt, to grant annuities for terms of
s, and life annuities; accepting in payment either money or stock according to rates
fied in tables to be approved by the Lords of the Treasury. No annuities are
ted on the life of any *nominee* under fifteen years of age, nor in any case not ap-
ed by the commissioners. Annuities for terms of years not granted for any period
than *ten* years. These annuities are transferable, but not in parts or shares.
se for terms of years, payable 5th of January and 5th of July; and those for lives,
f April and 10th of October.

he annuities for terms of years granted under the above acts, amounted, on the
of October, 1830, to 772,758*l.*, being equal to a *perpetual* annuity of 491,058*l.* The
nnuities amounted, at the same period, to 666,411*l.*, being equal to a *perpetual*
ity of 266,071*l.* — (*Parl. Paper,* No. 174. Sess. 1831.)

sh *Debt.* — It seems to be unnecessary to enter into any details with respect to the
c debt of Ireland. The various descriptions of stock of which it consists, and their
nt, are specified above. The dividends on the Irish debt are paid at the Bank of
nd; and in order to accommodate the public, stock may be transferred, at the plea-
of the holders, from Ireland to Great Britain, and from the latter to the former.

chequer Bills, are bills of credit issued by authority of parliament. They are
rious sums, and bear interest (at present at the rate of 1½*d.* per diem, per 100*l.*)
ding to the usual rate at the time. The advances of the Bank to government are
upon exchequer bills; and the daily transactions between the Bank and govern-
are principally carried on through their intervention. Notice of the time at which
nding exchequer bills are to be paid off is given by public advertisement. Bankers
investing in exchequer bills to any other species of stock, even though the interest
r the most part comparatively low; because the capital may be received at the
ury at the rate originally paid for it, the holders being exempted from any risk of
ation. Exchequer bills were first issued in 1696, and have been annually issued
ince. The amount outstanding, and *unprovided for,* on the 5th of January, 1831,
7,278,400*l.*

ia Stock and India Bonds, are always quoted in the lists of the prices of the public
The stock on which the East India Company divide is 6,000,000*l.*; the dividend
ich has been, since 1793, 10½ per cent. India bonds are generally for 100*l.* each;
ear at present 2½ per cent. interest, payable 31st of March and 30th of September.
ting them, the interest due down to the day of sale is, with the premium, added to the
nt of the bills; the total being the sum to be paid by the purchaser. The premium,
is, consequently, the only variable part of the price, is influenced by the circumstances
influence the price of stocks generally — the number of bonds in circulation, &c.
e price of stocks is influenced by a variety of circumstances. Whatever tends to
or to increase the public confidence in the stability of government, tends, at the
time, to lower or increase the price of stocks. They are also affected by the state
revenue; and, more than all, by the facility of obtaining supplies of disposable
, and the interest which may be realised upon loans to responsible persons.
1730 till the rebellion in 1745, the 3 per cents. were never under 89, and were
in June, 1737, as high as 107. During the rebellion they sunk to 76; but in
rose again to 100. In the interval between the peace of Paris, in 1763, and the
ng out of the American war, they averaged from 80 to 90; but towards the close
war they sunk to 54. In 1792 they were, at one time, as high as 96. In 1797,
ospects of the country, owing to the successes of the French, the mutiny in the
nd other adverse circumstances, were by no means favourable; and, in conse-
e, the price of 3 per cents. sunk, on the 20th of September, on the intelligence
ring of an attempt to negotiate with the French republic having failed, to 47⅝,
the lowest price to which they have ever fallen.

The following is a statement of the prices of the different descriptions of British fu
during the week commencing 16th August, 1831: —

	Tuesday.	Wednes.	Thursday.	Friday.	Saturday.	Mond
Bank Stock, dividend 8 per Cent. -	198¾ 9¼	199½ 9	199¼	199½ 9	198¾ 9	198¾
3 per Cent. Reduced - - -	82¼ ⅝	82¼ 2	82¼ 2	82 ½	82¼ ¼	82⅝
3 per Cent. Consols - -	81⅝ ¾	81¾ ⅝	81⅝ ½	81½ ⅞	82 1⅜	82
3½ per Cent Annuities, 1818 - -	90¼ ⅛	90⅛ ¼	90⅛	89⅝ ⅞		
3 per Cent. Annuities, 1726 - -						
3½ per Cent. Reduced - - -	90 ¼	90⅛ ¼	90 89¾	89⅞ 90⅛	90¾ ⅛	90½
New 3½ per Cent. Annuities - -	89½ ½	89⅝ ½	89⅜ ⅛	89⅝ ½	89½ ⅝	89⅝
New 4 per Cent. Annuities, 1826 -	99⅝ ⅞	- -	99½ ¾	99¾ ⅝	100⅛ 100	100¼
New 5 per Cent. - - -						
Long Annuities, expire 5 Jan. 1860 -	17 1-16	17 1-16 17	17 16-15	17 16⅛	16 17 1-16	17 1-
India Stock, dividend 10½ per Cent. -	- -	198 7½	- -	199	199	
South Sea Stock, dividend 3½ per Cent.	- -	- -	90⅝ ⅝	91		
Do. Old Annuity, dividend 3 per Cent.	- -	- -	80½			
Do. New Annuity, dividend 3 per Cent.						
3 per Cent. Annuities, 1751 - -						
India Bonds 2½ per Cent. - -	1*s.* pm.	par. 1*s.* pm.	2*s.* pm.	11*s.* 7*s.* pm.	1*s.* pm.	1*s.* pm.
Exchequer Bills 1½*d.* 1,000*l.* - -	8*s.* 9*s.* pm.	9*s.* 10*s.* p.	9*s.* 11*s.* pm.	11*s.* 9*s.* p.	8*s.* pm.	8*s.* 9*s.*
3 per Cent. Consols for Acct., Aug. 26.	81¾ ⅞	81¾ ⅝	81⅝ ⅞	81½ ⅞	82 1⅞	81⅞
Commissioners purchased Reduced, at						
Do. Consols - - - - -						
Do. 3½ per Cent. Annuities, 1818 -	90¼	90¼	90⅛	89⅞		
Do. 3½ per Cent. Reduced Annuities	90⅛	94¼	90¼	89⅞		

Agreements for the sale of stock are generally made at the Stock Exchange, which frequented by a set of middlemen called *jobbers*, whose business is to accommodate buyers and sellers of stock with the exact sums they want. A jobber is generally p sessed of considerable property in the funds; and he declares a price at which he w either sell or buy. Thus, he declares he is ready to buy 3 per cent. consols. at 85½, to sell at 85⅝; so that, in this way, a person willing to buy or sell any sum, howe small, has never any difficulty in finding an individual with whom to deal. The jobbe profit is generally ⅛ per cent., for which he transacts both a sale and a purcha He frequently confines himself entirely to this sort of business, and engages in no ot sort of stock speculation.

We borrow the following details from Dr. Hamilton's valuable work on the Natio Debt: —

"A bargain for the sale of stock being agreed on, is carried into execution at the Transfer Office, at Bank, or the South Sea House. For this purpose the seller makes out a note in writing, which cont the name and designation of the seller and purchaser, and the sum and description of the stock t transferred. He delivers this to the proper clerk*, and then fills up a receipt, a printed form of wh with blanks, is obtained at the office. The clerk in the mean time examines the seller's accounts, ar he find him possessed of the stock proposed to be sold, he makes out the transfer. This is signed in books by the seller, who delivers the receipt to the clerk; and upon the purchaser's signing his accepta in the book, the clerk signs the receipt as witness. It is then delivered to the purchaser upon paym of the money, and thus the business is completed.

"This business is generally transacted by brokers, who derive their authority from their employer powers of attorney. Forms of these are obtained at the respective offices. Some authorise the broke sell, others to accept a purchase, and others to receive the dividends. Some comprehend all these obje and the two last are generally united. Powers of attorney authorising to sell must be deposited in proper office for examination one day before selling: a stockholder acting personally, after granting a l of attorney, revokes it by implication.

"The person in whose name the stock is invested when the books are shut, previous to the paymer the dividends, receives the dividend for the half year preceding; and, therefore, a purchaser during currency of the half year has the benefit of the interest on stock he buys, from the last term of paym to the day of transfer. The price of stock, therefore, rises gradually, *cæteris paribus*, from term to te and when the dividend is paid, it undergoes a fall equal thereto. Thus the 3 per cent. consols shoul higher than the 3 per cent. reduced by ¾ per cent. from 5th of April to 5th of July, and from 10th of Oct to 5th of January; and should be as much lower from 5th of January to 5th of March, and from 5th of to 10th of October; and this is nearly the case. Accidental circumstances may occasion a slight deviat

"The dividends on the different stocks being payable at different terms, it is in the power of the st holders to invest their property in such a manner as to draw their income quarterly.

"The business of speculating in the stocks is founded on the variation of the price of stock, whi probably tends in some measure to support. It consists in buying or selling stock according to the v entertained, by those who engage in this business, of the probability of the value rising or falling.

"This business is partly conducted by persons who have property in the funds. But a practice also vails among those who have no such property, of contracting for the sale of stock on a future day at a agreed on. For example, A. may agree to sell B. 10,000*l.* of 3 per cent. stock, to be transferred in 20 for 6,000*l.* A. has in fact no such stock; but if the price on the day appointed for the transfer be onl he may purchase as much as will enable him to fulfil his bargain for 5,800*l.*, and thus gain 200*l.* by transaction: on the other hand, if the price of that stock should rise to 62, he will lose 200*l.* The bus is generally settled without any actual purchase of stock, or transfer; A. paying to B. or receiving him the difference between the price of stock on the day of settlement, and the price agreed on.

"This practice, which amounts to nothing else than a wager concerning the price of stock, is not tioned by law; yet it is carried on to a great extent: and as neither party can be compelled by l implement these bargains, their sense of honour, and the disgrace attending a breach of contract, ar principles by which the business is supported. In the language of the Stock Exchange, the buyer is a *Bull*, and the seller a *Bear*, and the person who refuses to pay his loss is called a *Lame Duck*; ar names of these defaulters are exhibited in the Stock Exchange, where they dare not appear afterwa

* The letters of the alphabet are placed round the room, and the seller must apply to the clerk has his station under the initial of his name. In all the offices there are supervising clerks who j witnessing the transfer.

ese bargains are usually made for certain days fixed by a committee of the Stock Exchange, called
days, of which there are about eight in the year; viz. one in each of the months of January,
ry, April, May, July, August, October, and November; and they are always on Tuesday, Wed-
Thursday, or Friday, being the days on which the commissioners for the reduction of the national
ke purchases. The settling days in January and July are always the first days of the opening of
k books for public transfer; and these days are notified at the Bank when the consols are shut to
for the dividend. The price at which stock is sold to be transferred on the next settling day, is
he price *on account*. Sometimes, instead of closing the account on the settling day, the stock is
on to a future day, on such terms as the parties agree on. This is called a *continuation*.
the business, however, which is done in the stocks *for time*, is not of a gambling nature. In a
so extensive commerce as London, opulent merchants, who possess property in the funds, and are
ng to part with it, have frequently occasion to raise money for a short time. Their resource in
e is to sell for money, and buy for account; and although the money raised in this manner costs
an the legal interest, it affords an important accommodation, and it may be rendered strictly legal
verable."— (Third ed. pp. 314—317.)

ould be foreign to the object of this work to enter upon any examination of the
rative advantages and disadvantages of the funding system. Perhaps, on the
the latter preponderate; though it is not to be denied that the former are very
erable. The purchase of funded property affords a ready method of investment;
neither the Bank of England, nor any of the London private banks, allows interest
eposits, it is plain that, were it not for the facilities given by the funds, individuals,
to employ their savings in some branch of business, would derive no advantage
em, unless they resorted to the hazardous expedient of lending upon private credit.
tland, where the public and private banks are universally in the habit of allowing
t upon deposits, the advantages of funded investments are not quite so obvious,
probably as great; for it may be doubted whether the banks could afford interest,
ther, indeed, they could be conducted at all, without the aid of the funds.
subjoined account of the number of dividend warrants issued in the half year
with January, 1830, is a very important document. The large number (83,609)
lers of sums not producing above 5*l.* of half yearly dividend, is principally to be
d to the circumstances already mentioned as peculiar to the banking system of the
olis; and there can be little doubt that their number would be materially dimi-
were the Scotch system adopted in its stead. In one respect the subjoined
is fallacious. The number of persons having a direct interest in the funds is
reater than it represents. The dividends upon the funded property belonging to
uitable and other insurance companies, the Scotch and other banks, &c. are paid
ngle warrants, as if they were due to so many private individuals; whereas
e, really, paid to these individuals only because they act as factors or trustees for
umber more. It is consequently quite absurd to pretend, as is sometimes done,
v interference with funded property would affect only 275,000 individuals out of
ation of 25,000,000. Any attack upon the dividends would really be destructive,
ely of the interests of those to whom dividend warrants are issued, but of *all* who
upon them: it would destroy our whole system of insurance and banking, and
ead the country with bankruptcy and ruin. Not only, therefore, is every proposal
nvasion of the property of the fundholders bottomed on injustice and robbery,
ould, were it acted upon, be little less ruinous to the community than to the pe-
lass intended to be plundered.

of the Total Number of Persons to whom a Half Year's Dividend on Three per Cent. Consols
due on 5th January last; specifying the Number respectively of those whose Dividend for the
ar did not exceed 5*l.*, 10*l.*, 50*l.*, 100*l.*, 200*l.*, 300*l.*, 500*l.*, 1,000*l.*, 2,000*l.*, and the Number of those
Dividend exceeded 2,000*l.*; a like Account of Dividends on Three per Cent. Reduced, payable
October last; a like Account of the Dividends on Three and a Half per Cents., payable on 10th
last; a like Account of Dividends on Four per Cents., payable on 10th October last; a like Ac-
f the Dividends on Long Annuities, payable on 10th October last; a like Account of the Divi-
n New Four per Cents., payable on 5th January last; and a like Account of the Dividends on
er Cent. Annuities, Anno 1726, payable on 5th Janury last; with a Total of the Number of
under each Head.— (*Parl. Paper*, No. 41. Sess. 1830.)

	Dividends payable.	Not exceeding									Exceeding 2,000*l.*	Total.
		5*l.*	10*l.*	50*l.*	100*l.*	200*l.*	300*l.*	500*l.*	1,000*l.*	2,000*l.*		
Consoli-	Jan. 5. 1830	26,596	12,779	30,651	9,326	6,163	2,192	1,421	820	239	82	90,269
nuities - Reduced	Oct. 10. 1829	10,078	4,653	11,460	3,491	2,110	775	455	222	85	32	33,361
s - - ent. Re-	ditto	6,933	4,381	10,365	2,978	1,613	428	291	124	39	15	27,167
nuities - ent. An-	ditto	222	186	489	192	155	53	40	32	7	7	1,383
18 - - Annui-	ditto	1,269	735	1,486	430	266	80	71	29	8	5	4,379
ties - r Cent.	ditto	9,077	4,008	9,210	1,985	1,017	339	209	95	20	2	25,962
- - Annui-	Jan. 5. 1830	29,307	15,403	33,451	7,874	3,857	1,037	589	233	52	18	91,821
- -	ditto	127	82	195	40	28	8	1	Nil.	Nil.	Nil.	481
Totals -	-	83,609	42,227	97,307	26,316	15,209	4,912	3,077	1,555	450	161	274,823

The following table has been calculated, in order to show in which of the public f
money may be invested, so as to yield the greatest interest. It gives the prices, diff
by 1 per cent. from 50 to 94 for 3 per cents, &c., at which they all must be, to yiel
same interest; so that supposing the 3 per cents. to be at 80, a sum invested in the
in the 3½ per cents., will yield the same interest, provided the latter be at 93½ : i
3½ per cents. be *below* this sum, it will of course be more advantageous, in so far at
as interest is concerned, to invest in them than in the 3 per cents. ; while, if the
above 93½, it will be less advantageous.

To get the *true value* of the different funds at any particular period, in order to
pare them accurately together, it is necessary to deduct from each the amount of int
accruing upon it from the payment of the last dividend. — (For farther details, see
p. 77. and p. 179.)

Table showing the Prices the different Funds must be at to produce an equal Interest; and also
annual Interest produced by 100*l*. Sterling, invested at any of those Prices.

3 per Cent. Price.	3½ per Cent. Price.	4 per Cent. Price.	5 per Cent. Price.	Interest.	3 per Cent. Price.	3½ per Cent. Price.	4 per Cent. Price.	5 per Cent. Price.	Inte
£	£ s. d.	£ s. d.	£ s. d.	£ s. d.	£	£ s. d.	£ s. d.	£ s. d.	£
50	58 6 8	66 13 4	83 6 8	6 0 0	72	84 0 0	96 0 0	120 0 0	4
51	59 10 0	68 0 0	85 0 0	5 17 7	73	85 3 4	97 6 8	121 13 4	4
52	60 13 4	69 6 8	86 13 4	5 15 4	74	86 6 8	98 13 4	123 6 8	4
53	61 16 8	70 13 4	88 6 8	5 13 2	75	87 10 0	100 0 0	125 0 0	4
54	63 0 0	72 0 0	90 0 0	5 11 1	76	88 13 4	101 6 8	126 13 4	3
55	64 3 4	73 6 8	91 13 4	5 9 0	77	89 16 8	102 13 4	128 6 8	3
56	65 6 8	74 13 4	93 6 8	5 7 1	78	91 0 0	104 0 0	130 0 0	3
57	66 10 0	76 0 0	95 0 0	5 5 3	79	92 3 4	105 6 8	131 13 4	3
58	67 13 4	77 6 8	96 13 4	5 3 5	80	93 6 8	106 13 4	133 6 8	3
59	68 16 8	78 13 4	98 6 8	5 1 8	81	94 10 0	108 0 0	135 0 0	3
60	70 0 0	80 0 0	100 0 0	5 0 0	82	95 13 4	109 6 8	136 13 4	3
61	71 3 4	81 6 8	101 13 4	4 18 4	83	96 16 8	110 13 4	138 6 8	3
62	72 6 8	82 13 4	103 6 8	4 16 9	84	98 0 0	112 0 0	140 0 0	3
63	73 10 0	84 0 0	105 0 0	4 15 2	85	99 3 4	113 6 8	141 13 4	3
64	74 13 4	85 6 8	106 13 4	4 13 8	86	100 6 8	114 13 4	143 6 8	3
65	75 16 8	86 13 4	108 6 8	4 12 3	87	101 10 0	116 0 0	145 0 0	3
66	77 0 0	88 0 0	110 0 0	4 10 10	88	102 13 4	117 6 8	146 13 4	3
67	78 3 4	89 6 9	111 13 4	4 9 6	89	103 16 8	118 13 4	148 6 8	3
68	79 6 8	90 13 4	113 6 8	4 8 2	90	105 0 0	120 0 0	150 0 0	3
69	80 10 0	92 0 0	115 0 0	4 6 11	91	106 3 4	121 6 8	151 13 4	3
70	81 13 4	93 6 8	116 13 4	4 5 8	92	107 6 8	122 13 4	153 6 8	3
71	82 16 8	94 13 4	118 6 8	4 4 6	93	108 10 0	124 0 0	155 0 0	3

FURS, in commerce, the skins of different animals, covered, for the most
with thick fine hair, the inner side being converted by a peculiar process i
sort of leather. Furs, previously to their undergoing this process, are denomin
peltry.

Beaver fur, from its extensive use in the hat-manufacture, is a very important
mercial article. That made use of in this country is almost entirely brought
North America. It is gradually becoming scarcer and dearer, being now obtair
only in considerable quantities from the most northerly and inaccessible districts.
fur of the middle-aged or young animal, called cub-beaver, is most esteemed.
the finest, most glossy, and takes the best dye. Fitch, or the fur of the fitchet or polec
principally imported from Germany: it is soft and warm, but the unpleasant s
which adheres to it depresses its value. Marten and mink (a diminutive species of o
are principally imported from the United States and Canada. The fur of the musqua
musk rat, a diminutive species of beaver, is imported in vast quantities from our
sessions in North America ; which also supply us with considerable quantities of otter s
Neutria skins are principally brought from Buenos Ayres. The more valuable fu
ermine, sable, &c., come principally from Russia.

FUR TRADE. We are indebted for the following details with respect t
fur trade, to one of the most extensive and intelligent fur merchants of Lon

" Though practically engaged in the fur trade, I fear I shall be able to say little with regard t
already known to you ; but were I to write on the subject, I should divide the trade into two, or
three classes.

" 1. The first class would comprise articles of necessity, among which I should principally num
immense variety of lamb skins, varying so widely from each other in size, quality, colour, and valu
to most persons, they would appear as the produce of so many different species of animals. Thes
skins are produced in all parts of the globe, and are every where consumed ; but they form, in par
an essential part of the dress of thousands among the lower classes in Russia, Poland, East Prussi
gary, Bohemia, and Saxony. In Russia and other cold climates, the skins of various other anim
be considered as articles of actual necessity.

" 2. The second class would in a measure form part of the first, as it also comprises furs which
habit and fashion have now become articles of necessity. I should here enumerate all those c
skins commonly called *hatting furs*. Few who are not acquainted with this branch of the fur tr
form an idea of its extent. It spreads, of course, over all parts of the globe where hats are wo
requires very superior judgment and considerable capital to conduct it successfully. The furs ne
for hat making are beaver, musquash, otter, neutria, hare, and rabbit; but each of these may
divided into twenty different sorts or classes.

Neutria, or nutria, is comparatively a new article. It began first to be imported in large quantities
: 1810, from the Spanish possessions in South America. — (See NUTRIA.) The skin is used for
ent purposes, being either dressed as a peltry or cut (shorn) as a hatting fur; and if well manu-
red and prepared, it bears some resemblance to beaver fur, and is used for similar purposes.
. Under the third and last class I should bring all those furs, which, though continually sold and
in immense quantities, must still be considered mere articles of fashion, as their value varies
ding to the whims and fancies of different nations. There are, however, exceptions among these;
nany furs may be considered as standard articles, since they are always used, though their price is
influenced by changes of fashion.

This class comprises an endless variety of furs, as under it may be brought the skins of most
als in existence, almost all of them appearing occasionally in the trade.
urs being entirely the produce of nature, which can neither be cultivated nor increased, their value
not depend upon fashion alone, but depends materially on the larger or smaller supplies received.
weather has great influence on the quality and quantity of furs imported from all quarters of the
; and this circumstance renders the fur trade more difficult, perhaps, and precarious than any other.
uality, and consequently the price, of many furs will differ every year. It would be completely im-
le to state the value of the different articles of furs, the trade being the most fluctuating imaginable.
ve often seen the same article rise and fall 100, 200, and 300 per cent. in the course of a twelve-
h; nay, in several instances, in the space of one month only.
mong the furs which always rank very high (though, like all the rest, they change in value), may be
led the Siberian sable, and the black and silver fox. These articles are at all times comparatively
scarce, and command high prices.
he chief supplies of peltries are received from Russia (particularly the Asiatic part of that empire),
om North America. But many other countries produce very beautiful and useful furs; and though
e most indebted to Asia and America, Europe furnishes a very considerable quantity. Africa and
alia are of little importance to the fur trade, as, from their situation, they furnish but few arti-
and consume still less. From the former we draw leopard and tiger skins (the most beautiful of
pecies), while the only production of the latter is the kangaroo; this, however, is never used as a
ing chiefly consumed by leather dressers and tanners for the sake of its pelt.
esides numerous private traders, there are several fur companies of very old standing, who in various
ries do a great amount of business. Among these, the Hudson's Bay Company (in London)
ves to be mentioned first, not only from the extent of their business, but because it is one of the
chartered companies in England.
he American Fur Company (in New York) stands next. They chiefly trade to London, whither
end the produce of the United States and other parts of North America.
he third company is the Russian American (in Moscow.) They trade to the Russian possessions on
stern coast of North America, whence they draw their supplies, which are chiefly consumed in Russia.
he fourth and last company of any consequence is the Danish Greenland Company (in Copenhagen).
do but a very limited business; exposing their goods for sale once a year in Copenhagen.
he principal consumption of the furs which I should bring under the head of the third class, is in
, Turkey, and Russia, and among the more civilised countries of Europe, particularly in England.
any consumes a considerable quantity. The consumption of America is comparatively little. In
a none but the Egyptians wear fur. In Australia none is consumed.
latting furs are used throughout Europe (with the exception of Turkey and Greece), and in
ca, but by far the principal trade in these articles is carried on in London and New York.
ost of the companies sell their goods by public sale, and the principal fur fairs are held at Kiachta
e borders of China); Nishnei Novogorod, between Moscow and Casan in Russia; and twice a year
osic. — (See FAIRS.)
is a remarkable feature of the fur trade, that almost every country or town which produces and
s furs, imports and consumes the fur of some other place, frequently the most distant. It is but
that an article is consumed in the country where it is produced, though that country may con-
urs to a very great extent."

e following details with respect to the North American fur trade may not be
eresting: —

is trade was first practised by the early French settlers at Quebec and Montreal; and
ted then, as now, in bartering fire-arms, ammunition, cloth, spirits, and other articles
nand among the Indians, for beaver and other skins. In 1670, Charles II. established
udson's Bay Company, to which he assigned the exclusive privilege of trading
he Indians in and about the vast inlet known by the name of Hudson's Bay. The
any founded establishments at Forts Churchill and Albany, Nelson River, and
places on the west coast of the bay. But the trade they carried on, though said
a profitable one, was of very limited extent; and their conduct on various occasions
how thoroughly they were "possessed with that spirit of jealousy which prevails
he degree in all knots and societies of men endued with peculiar privileges." —
pean Settlements, vol. ii. p. 268.) Mr. Burke has, in the same place, expressed
tonishment that the trade has not been thrown open. But as the Company's
r was never confirmed by any act of parliament, all British subjects are lawfully
d to trade with those regions; though, from the difficulties attached to the trade,
rotection required in carrying it on, and the undisguised hostility which private
s have experienced from the agents of the Company, the latter have been allowed
nopolise it with but little opposition. In 1783-4, the principal traders engaged
fur trade of Canada formed themselves into an association known by the name
North-West Company, having their chief establishment at Montreal. This new
ny prosecuted the trade with great enterprise and very considerable success.
ourse of their proceedings in their adventurous undertakings has been minutely
bed by Mr. Mackenzie, one of the agents of the Company, in his "Voyage from
eal through the Continent of America." This gentleman informs us, that some
se engaged in this trade are employed at the astonishing distance of upwards of
miles north-west of Montreal! A very numerous caravan, if we may so call it,
t every year for Le Grande Portage, on Lake Superior, where they meet those
ave wintered in the remoter establishments, from whom they receive the furs col-

lected in the course of the season, and whom they, at the same time, furnish with fre
supplies of the various articles required in the trade. Fort Chepeywan, on the Lake
the Hills, in long. 110° 26′ W., used to be one of the most distant stations of the serva
of the North-West Company; but many of the Indians who traded with the fort ca
from districts contiguous to, and sometimes even beyond, the Rocky Mountains.

The competition and success of the North-West Company seem to have roused
dormant energies of the Hudson's Bay Company. The conflicting interests and pr
tensions of the two associations were naturally productive of much jealousy and ill-wi
Under the auspices of the late Earl of Selkirk, who was for a considerable period at
head of the Hudson's Bay Company, a colony was projected and founded on the Re
River, which runs into Lake Winnipec. The North-West Company regarded t
establishment as an encroachment upon their peculiar rights; and the animosities ther
arising led to the most violent proceedings on the part of the servants of both compani
At length, however, the more moderate individuals of each party began to perceive t
their interests were not materially different; and the rival companies, wearied and i
poverished by their dissensions, ultimately united under the name of the *Hudson's B*
Fur Company, which at present engrosses most of the fur trade of British America. T
most important part of the trade is still carried on from Montreal in the way describ
by Mr. Mackenzie.

The *North American Fur Company*, the leading directors of which reside in the c
of New York, have long enjoyed the principal part of the Indian trade of the gr
lakes and the Upper Mississippi. But with the exception of the musk rat, most of
fur-clad animals are exterminated in the vicinity of the lakes. The skins of racoo
are of little value; and the beaver is now scarce on this side the Rocky Mountains. T
further north the furs are taken, the better is their quality.

There are no means of obtaining any very accurate accounts of the extent and value of the Ameri
fur trade; but the following statements throw considerable light on the subject.

In Mr. Gray's " Letters from Canada " we have the following account of the quantity and value of
furs and peltries exported from Quebec in 1808 : —

		Number.		£	s.	d.			£	s.	d.
Beaver	- - -	126,927	at	0	18	9	- -	-	118,994	1	3
Marten	- -	9,530	—	0	3	4	-	-	1,588	6	8
Otters	- - -	7,230	—	1	0	0	-	-	7,230	0	0
Mink	- - -	9,108	—	0	2	0	-	-	910	16	0
Fishers	- - -	3,866	—	0	4	0	-	-	773	4	0
Foxes	- - -	1,038	—	0	5	0	-	-	259	10	0
Bears and cubs	-	1,268	—	1	5	0	-	-	1,622	10	0
Deers	- - -	103,875	—	0	3	4	- -	-	17,312	10	0
Cased and open cat	5,718	—	0	3	4	- -	-	953	0	0
Racoons	- - -	123,307	—	0	2	0	-	-	12,330	14	0
Musk rats	- -	6,513	—	0	1	6	- -	-	488	9	6
Wolf	- - -	18	—	0	7	6	-	-	6	15	0
Elk	- - -	662	—	0	15	0	-	-	496	10	0
Wolverines	- -	39	—	0	5	0	-	-	9	15	0
Seals	- - -	10	—	0	4	0	-	-	2	0	0
Buffalo	- - -		-	1	0	0			1	0	0
							Total value	-	£ 162,979	1	5

In 1826, the exports of furs and peltries from Quebec were, 7,510 beaver, 39,619 marten, 600 hare,
fisher (sable), 6,433 racoon, 3,782 bear and cub, 1,698 otter, 15,028 musk rat, 4,218 mink, 362 lynx,
fox, 187 cat, 5,459 deer, 4 wolf, 17 wolverine, and 14 buffalo. The value of these is not given. We
join

An Account of the principal Furs imported in 1829, the Countries whence they were brought, and
Quantity furnished by each Country.

	Bear.	Beaver.	Fitch.	Marten.	Mink.	Musquash.	Neutria.	Ott
	No.	No.	No.	No.	No.	No.	No.	N
Prussia - -	—	—	5,351	—	—	—	—	
Germany - -	—	28	219,738	13,461	1,159	—	1,578	—
Netherlands -	—	—	37,378	471	—	—	2,365	—
France - -	—	—	16,272	6,782	—	—	—	—
British North American Colonies -	2,377	72,199	—	84,779	23,026	1,068,903	—	13,
United States -	10,166	4,200	—	46,415	53,173	1,101	73,822	1,
Buenos Ayres -	—	—	1	29	3	—	540,422	
All other places -	40	—	1	29	3	12	—	
Total -	12,583	76,427	278,740	151,937	77,361	1,070,016	618,187	14,

Of these imports, the beaver, fitch, marten, and neutria skins were mostly retained for home consum
the bear and otter skins were almost wholly re-exported to Germany and the Netherlands; and nearly a
musquash skins were re-exported, chiefly to the United States. — (*Parl. Paper*, No. 153. Sess. 1831.

The official value of the skins and furs imported in 1829, was 389,909*l.* The revenue derived from
in the same year amounted to 32,641*l.*; and that derived from skins, not being furs, amounted to 10

China is one of the best markets for furs. The Americans began, with their characteristic activi
send furs to Canton very soon after their flag had appeared in the Eastern seas in 1784; and they sti
secure the trade to a considerable extent, though it has rapidly declined within the last three or four
The Americans procure the furs intended for the China markets, partly from the American Fur
pany already alluded to, and partly from Canada; but they have also been in the habit of sending ou

north-west coast of America, who, having purchased large quantities of skins from the natives,
em direct to Canton. Recently, however, this trade has been materially diminished, in consequence,
, of the regulations of the Russian government, who do not permit the American traders to cruise
orth as they did formerly.

STIAN (Ger. *Barchent;* Du. *Fustein;* Fr. *Futaine;* It. *Fustagno, Frus-*
; Sp. *Fustan;* Rus. *Bumasea;* Pol. *Barchan*), a kind of cotton stuff, wealed
bed on one side.

STIC (Ger. *Gelbholz, Fustick;* Du. *Geelhout;* Fr. *Bois jaune de Bresil;* It.
giallo de Brasilio;* Sp. *Palo del Brasilamarillo*), the wood of a species of
rry (*Morus tinctoria*), growing in most parts of South America, in the United
, and the West India islands. It is a large and handsome tree; and the
, though, like most other dye-woods, brittle, or at least easily splintered, is
nd strong. It is very extensively used as an ingredient in the dyeing of
, and is largely imported for that purpose. Of 7,597 tons of fustic imported
reat Britain in 1828, 2,122 tons were brought from the British West Indies,
itto from Cuba and the foreign West Indies, 1,258 ditto from the United
, 513 ditto from Mexico, 2,532 ditto from Colombia, 242 ditto from Brazil,
small quantity from Hayti. Fustic from Cuba fetches full 35 per cent.
n the London market than that of Jamaica or Colombia. At present, the
f the former varies from 8*l.* 10*s.* to 9*l.* 10*s.* a ton, while the latter varies
l. to 7*l.* a ton.

te, or *young* fustic, is really a species of sumach (*Rhus cotinus*, Lin.), and is
listinct from the *morus tinctoria*, or *old* fustic; the latter being a large Ame-
ree, while the former is a small European shrub. It grows in Italy and the
of France, but is principally exported from Patrass in the Morea. It im-
beautiful bright yellow dye to cottons, &c., which, when proper mordants
d, is very permanent. It is conveniently stowed amongst a cargo of dry
as it may be cut into pieces of any length without injury. In 1828, about
s of this species of sumach were imported. Its price fluctuates considerably.
, 1831, it was worth, in the London market, from 9*l.* to 10*l.* a ton.

G.

LANGAL (Ger. *Galgant;* Du. and Fr. *Galanga;* Rus. *Kalgan;* Lat. *Ga-*
Arab. *Kusttulk;* Chin. *Laundon*), the root of the *galanga*, brought from
and the East Indies in pieces about an inch long, and hardly half an inch
A larger root of the same kind (*Greater Galangal*), an inch or more in
ss, is to be rejected. It has an aromatic smell, not very grateful; and an
ant, bitterish, extremely hot, biting taste. It should be chosen full and
of a bright colour, very firm and sound: 12 cwt. are allowed to a ton.—
s Mat. Med.; Milburn's Orient. Com.)

BANUM, (Fr. *Galbanum;* Ger. *Mutterharz;* It. *Galbano;* Lat. *Galbanum;*
Barzud*), a species of gum resin obtained from a perennial plant growing in
near the Cape of Good Hope, and in Syria and Persia. It is brought to
untry from the Levant in cases or chests containing from 100 to 300 lbs.
The best is in ductile masses, composed of distinct whitish tears aggluti-
ogether by a pale brown or yellowish substance. It is generally much
with stalks, seeds, and other impurities. The separate tears are considered
est. When the colour is dark brown or blackish, it is to be rejected. It
rong peculiar odour, and a bitterish, warm, acrid taste.—(*Thomson's Dis-*
y.*)

LON, a measure of capacity, both for dry and liquid articles, containing 4
By 5 Geo. 4. c. 74. the imperial gallon shall be the standard measure of
, and shall contain 10 lbs. avoirdupois weight of distilled water, weighed
the temperature of 62° of Fahrenheit's thermometer, the barometer being
ches, or 277·274 cubic inches; and all other measures of capacity to be
well for wine, beer, ale, spirits, and all sorts of liquids, as for dry goods,
asured by heaped measure, shall be derived, computed, and ascertained
ch gallon; and all measures shall be taken in parts, or multiples, or certain
ions, of the said imperial standard gallon. The old English gallon, wine
, contained 231 cubic inches; and the old English gallon, ale measure,

contained 282 cubic inches. Hence the imperial gallon is about $\frac{1}{5}$ larger than old wine gallon, and about $\frac{1}{60}$ less than the old ale gallon. By the 6 Ge c. 58. § 6. it is enacted, that from and after the 5th of January, 1826, whenever gallon measure is mentioned in any act of parliament relative to the excise, it be taken and deemed to be a gallon imperial standard measure.—(See WEI and MEASURES.)

GALLS, OR GALL-NUTS (Fr. *Galles, Noix de galle;* Ger. *Gallöpfel, lus;* It. *Galle, Gulluze;* Lat. *Galæ;* Arab. *Afis;* Hind. *Majouphal;* Pers. *M* are excrescences produced by the attacks of a small insect, which dep its eggs in the tender shoots of a species of oak (*quercus infectoria,* I abundant in Asia Minor, Syria, Persia, &c. Galls are inodorous, and a nauseously bitter and astringent taste. They are nearly spherical, and va magnitude from the size of a pea to that of a hazel-nut. When good, are of a black or deep olive colour; their surface is tubercular, and almost pri they are heavy, brittle, and break with a flinty fracture. They are known in merce by the names of *white, green,* and *blue.* The white galls are those w have not been gathered till after the insect has eat its way out of the nidus made its escape. They are not so heavy as the others, are of a lighter colour do not fetch so high a price. The green and blue galls are gathered before insect has escaped; they are heavier and darker than the former, and are sa afford about one third more of colouring matter.

Galls are of great importance in the arts, being very extensively used in dyeing in the manufacture of ink, of which they form one of the principal ingredients. are the most powerful of all the vegetable astringents; and are frequently used great effect in medicine.

The ancients reckoned the gall-nuts of Syria superior to every other, and they retain their pre-eminence. They are principally exported from Aleppo, Tripoli, Sm and Said; those brought from the first come chiefly from Mosul, on the western of the Tigris, about ten days' journey from Aleppo. The real Mosul galls are un tionably the best of any; but all that are gathered in the surrounding country are under this name. Those from Caramania are of a very inferior quality. The met with in India are carried thither from Persia by Arabian merchants.

It is not unusual to dye the whitish gall-nuts blue, in order to increase their v. The fraud is, however, detected by the deeper blue tinge that is thus imparted to t and by their being perforated, and lighter than the genuine blue galls.

The price of galls in bond varies in the London market from 65s. to 85s. a cwt. duty is 5s. a cwt.—(*Rees's Cyclopædia; Bancroft on Colours; Ainslie's Mat. Indica,*

GAMBOGE (Fr. *Gomme gutte;* Ger. *Gummigutt;* It. *Gomma gutta; Gummi guttæ, Cambogia;* Arab. *Ossararewund,*) is a concrete vegetable the produce of two trees, both called by the Indians caracapulli (*Gan gutta,* Lin.), and is partly of a gummy and partly of a resinous nature. brought to us either in the form of orbicular masses, or of cylindrical of various sizes; and is of a dense, compact, and firm texture, and of a bea yellow. It is chiefly imported from Cambaja, in the East Indies, called also bodja, and Cambogia; and hence it has obtained its name. The larger cakes such as are dark coloured, should be rejected. 20 cwt. of gamboge are all to a ton.—(*Ure's Dictionary; Milburn's Orient. Com.*)

GARNET, GARNETS (Fr. *Grenats;* Ger. *Granaten, Granatsteine;* It. *Gra* Lat. *Granati;* Rus. *Granatnoi kamen;* Sp. *Granadas*). There are two spec garnet, the precious and the common. The colour of the first is red; and the name of the mineral, from its supposed resemblance to the flower of the pon nate: passes from Columbine red, to cherry and brown red; commonly crysta External lustre glistening, internal shining, vitreous; transparent, sometimes translucent; specific gravity 4·08 to 4·35. The colour of the common gar of various shades of brown and green. Different colours often appear same mass: translucent; black varieties nearly opaque: specific gravity from to 3·75.—(*Thomson's Chemistry.*) The finest varieties come from India some good specimens have been received from Greenland. When large an from flaws, garnets are worth from 2l. to 5l. or 6l., and even more; but sto this value are of rare occurrence, and always in demand.—(*Mawe on Dia &c.* 2d ed. p. 113.)

GAS COMPANIES, the term usually applied to designate the compan associations established in most large towns for lighting the streets and with gas.

very one must have remarked that most species of coal, when ignited, give out large
titties of gas, which burns with much brilliancy, yielding a great quantity of light
ell as of heat. Dr. Clayton seems to have been the first who attempted, about 1736,
pply this gas to the purposes of artificial illumination; but his experiments were
a very limited scale, and no further attention was paid to the subject till more than
a century afterwards. At length, however, Mr. Murdoch, of Soho, instituted a
s of judicious experiments on the extrication of gas from coal; and, by his ingenuity
sagacity, succeeded in establishing one of the most capital improvements ever made
e arts. Mr. Murdoch found that the gas might be collected in reservoirs, purified,
eyed by pipes to a great distance from the furnace where it was generated; and that
fords, by its slow combustion, when allowed to escape through small orifices, a
tiful and steady light. This great discovery, which places Mr. Murdoch in the
rank among the benefactors of mankind, was first brought into practice at Redruth
ornwall. In 1802, it was applied to light Mr. Murdoch's manufactory at Soho; in
, it was adopted by Messrs. Philips and Lee, of Manchester, in the lighting of their
cotton mill; and is now employed in the lighting of the streets, theatres, and other
ic buildings, factories, &c. of *all* the considerable towns of the empire; and also in
considerable towns of the Continent and America.

as-light is indebted, for its rapid diffusion, not more to its peculiar softness, clearness,
unvarying intensity, than to its comparative cheapness. According to Dr. Thomson
p. to Ency. Brit., art. *Gas Lights*), if we value the quantity of light given by 1 lb.
llow in candles at 1*s.*, an equal quantity of light from coal gas will not cost more
2¾*d.*, being less than a *fourth part* of the cost of the former.

l and other substances have been used in furnishing gas for the purpose of illumin-
, but none of them has answered so well as coal. Most of the oil-gas establishments
been abandoned.

e construction of gas works on a large scale, and the carrying of pipes through the
s and into houses, &c., is very expensive, and requires a large outlay of capital.
e most of the gas lights in the different towns are supplied by joint stock companies.
y of them have turned out to be very profitable concerns.

e subjoined table contains a statement of the most important particulars connected
the principal gas companies; viz. the number of shares in each, the nominal amount
:h share, the sums actually paid up, the market price of shares, the dividend payable
em, &c. (From the circular of Mr. Charles Edmonds, broker, of Change Alley,
hill, 25th June, 1831.)

per res.	Names of Companies.	Amount of Share.	Paid up.		Price per Share.		Dividend per Annum.	Dividends payable.
		£	£	s.	£	s.		
00	Gas Light and Coke Chart. Company	50	50	0	53	10	6 per cent.	May, Nov.
00	Ditto New (Lond.) - -	50	10	0	10	10	6 per cent.	May, Nov.
00	City (Lond.) - -	100	100	0	192	0	10 per cent.	Mar. Sept.
00	Ditto New (Lond.) - -	100	60	0	120	0	10 per cent.	Mar. Sept.
0l.	Imperial (Lond.) - -	50	50	0	43	0	5 per cent.	April, Oct.
00	Ditto Debentures - -	100			87	0	4 per cent.	Jan. July.
00	Phœnix or South London -	50	39	0	42	0	6 per cent.	Feb. Aug.
00	British (London) - -	40	16	0	12	15	5 per cent.	May, Nov.
00	Ditto (Country) - -	20	18	0	10	15	4 per cent.	May, Nov.
	Ditto Debentures - -	100			100	0	5 per cent.	Jan. July.
00	Independent - -	30	30	0	38	0	6 per cent.	Mar. Sept.
00	General United Gas Light Company	50	42	0	26	15	4 per cent.	Mar. Sept.
0	Imperial Continental -	20	10	0	1	5	- -	
0	Bradford - -	25	20	0	40	0	8 per cent.	May.
0	Brentford - -	50	50	0	40	0	4 per cent.	Mar. Sept.
0	Bath - -	20	16	0	31	5	7l. 10s. per ct	
0	Barnsley - -	10	10	0	17	0	-	Mar. Sept.
4	Birmingham - -	50	50	0	98	0	10 per cent.	Mar. Sept.
0	Birmingham Staffordshire -	50	42	0	97	0	4l. per share.	April, Oct.
0	Brighton - -	20	20	0	9	0		
0	Brighton New - -	20	18	0	8	0		
0	Bristol - -	20	-	-	40	0	10 per cent.	Feb. Aug.
-	Burnley - -	10	-	-				
0	Canterbury - -	50	-	-	47	10	4 per cent.	January.
0	Cheltenham - -	50	50	0	75	0	6 per cent.	
0	Coventry - -	25	-	-	20	0	5 per cent.	
0	Derby - -	50	50	0	55	0	5 per cent.	
0	Dover - -	50	-	-	50	0	5 per cent.	
0	Dudley - -	20	-	-	12	0	3 per cent.	
0	Exeter - -	50	-	-	70	0	5l.	
0	Great Yarmouth - -	20	18	0	10	5	- -	
0	Guildford - -	25	25	0	24	0	1l.	
4	Halifax - -	25	21	0	36	0	- -	
0	Ipswich - -	10	-	-	12	0	12s.	Mar. Sept.
0	Isle of Thanet - -	25	20	0	2	0 dis.	5 per cent.	
0	Kidderminster - -	50	-	-	53	0	5 per cent.	
0	Leeds - -	100	100	0	195	0	10l.	
0	Leicester - -	50	50	0	65	0	3l. 10s.	January.

Number of Shares.	Names of Companies.	Amount of Share.	Paid up.	Price per Share.	Dividend per Annum.	Dividends payable.
		£	£ s.	£ s.		
220	Lewes	25	25 0	21 0	4 per cent.	January.
500	Liverpool	100	100 0	375 0	10l.	Feb. Aug
200	Maidstone	50	50 0	60 0	5 per cent.	
200	Newcastle-under-Line	25	- -	- -	-	
320	Newport, Isle of Wight	50	- -	13 0	1l.	
542	Northampton	20	- -	- -	-	
320	Nottingham	50	50 0	96 0	8 per cent.	
120	Oxford	150	130 0	- -	-	
3,200	Paisley	50	- -	- -	-	
600	Poplar	50	- -	24 10	-	
600	Portsea Island	50	53 0	45 0	5 per cent.	Jan. July
2,500	Portable	100	20 0	18 10 dis.	-	
10,000	Portable Provincial	100	9 10	7 15 dis.	-	
10,000	Plymouth	50	- -	70 0	5l.	July.
1,000	Ratcliff	100	60 0	38 15	3¾ per cent.	Mar. Sep
480	Rochdale	25	15 0	par	-	
240	Rochester	50	50 0	58 0	3l.	
1,600	Sheffield	25	18 5	58 0	10 per cent.	
1,000	Shrewsbury	10	- -	12 10	12s.	January
144	Stockton	55	- -	- -	-	
294	Warwick	50	- -	48 0	5 per cent.	March.
400	Wakefield	25	- -	- -	2l. 10s.	
100	Warrington	20	- -	27 0	7l. 10s. per ct.	
1,000	Wigan	10	- -	- -	-	
240	Woolwich	50	- -	par	-	
550	Wolverhampton	20	20 0	20 0	-	
600	Worcester ,	20	- -	16 0	4 per cent.	
640	York	25	17 0	16 0 pm.	-	

GENEVA (Du. *Genever;* Fr. *Genièvre;* Ger. *Gaud, Genever;* It. *Acqua Ginepro;* Lat. *Juniperi aqua;* Sp. *Agua de Enebro*), a spirit obtained by distillati from grain, rectified, with the addition of juniper berries. The latter give to t spirit that peculiar flavour by which it is distinguished, and are also said to ren it diuretic. Geneva is a corruption of *genièvre*, the French term for the junip berry.

By far the best geneva is made in Holland, where its manufacture is carried on t very great extent. The distilleries of Schiedam have long been famous, and are at pres in a very prosperous condition. Schiedam geneva is made solely of spirit obtained fr rye and barley, flavoured with juniper berries. It becomes milder, and acquires, a gets old, an oily flavour disliked by the Hollanders; hence nearly the whole of " Schiedam " is exported, principally to the East Indies. There are no fewer than 9 distilleries in Schiedam, 100 in other parts of Holland, and not more than 40 in Belgiu The entire annual produce of the distillery in Holland is estimated at 2,000,000 ank or 20,500,000 wine gallons, of which about two thirds are exported. — (*Cloet, Desc tion Géographique des Pays Bas,* p. 92.)

In nothing, perhaps, has the destructive effect of heavy taxation been so strongly exhibited as in trade in geneva. It appears from the Parl. Paper, No. 248. Sess. 1826, that during the ten years enc with 1786, when the duty on geneva was about 10s. the wine gallon, the average annual consumptio Great Britain amounted to about 80,362 gallons. But in 1786, Mr. Pitt reduced the duties to 5s. a gall and the effect of this wise and politic measure was such, that in the next decennial period the ave imports for home consumption amounted to 444,891 gallons! From 1796 to 1806, the duties fluctu from 7s. 6d. to 14s.; but as the taste for geneva had been formed, and as the duties on other spirits been increased in about the same proportion, the consumption went on increasing, having been, a average of the ten years, as high as 724,351 gallons a year. This was the maximum of consumption. Vansittart soon after began his inauspicious career, and immediately raised the duty from 14s. to 20s. the consequence of this increase being, that in the ten years ending with 1816, the average consump amounted to only 272,898 gallons. Since then the duties have continued stationary, being at this mon 22s. 6d. the imperial gallon, on an article which may be bought in bond for 2s.-3d. or 2s. 6d. ! The du on rum and British spirits having been materially reduced during the last ten years, the consumptic geneva has gone on progressively diminishing, till it now amounts, as appears from the subjoined off statement, to no more than 35,300 gallons; being only *one twentieth* part of what it amounted to during ten years ending with 1806!

In Ireland, the effects of this *felo de se* system have been more injurious than appears from this t During the four years ending with 1803, the books of the Irish Custom-house show that there were, a average, 82,828 gallons of geneva entered for home consumption, producing, at the then duty of 7s. 39,923l. a year; whereas, notwithstanding the vast increase of population, the consumption of gene Ireland, in 1829, was under 2,000 gallons, and the revenue only 2,075!

To make any lengthened commentary on such statements would be useless. Our policy, if we apply this term to so revolting a display of short-sighted rapacity, has had no other effect than to le the public revenue and enjoyments of the people, to injure our trade with Holland, and to foster and mote the ruinous and destructive practice of smuggling. The exorbitant duties on geneva, brandy tobacco, have led to the formation of the coast guard and the preventive water guard, costing toge between 400,000l. and 500,000l. a year; and yet, notwithstanding this enormous outlay, and notwiths ing the innumerable penalties and punishments to which he is exposed, the trade of the smuggler i put down, but is, on the contrary, in a peculiarly flourishing condition; and so it will continue, in de of every thing that can be done for its suppression, till these duties be adequately reduced.

We believe our gin manufacturers have nothing to apprehend from a reduction of the duties on ge to 10s. a gallon. The lower classes, who are the great consumers, prefer English gin to every othe mulant; and were the duties on juniper berries — (see BERRIES) — sufficiently reduced, its quality mig materially improved. But nothing would have so much influence in this respect as the admissi

at a moderate duty. It would also have the beneficial effect of putting an end to the manufacture
ourious compounds sold under its name.
egulations as to the importation, &c. of geneva are similar to those affecting BRANDY; which see.

ount of the Number of Gallons (Imperial Measure) of Geneva entered for Home Consumption in
Britain and Ireland, the Rates of Duty on the same, and the entire nett Produce of the Duty,
Year since 1780.

Quantities retained for Home Consumption			Nett Produce of Duty (Customs and Excise).			Rates of Duty per Imperial Gallon (Customs and Excise)	
Great Britain.	Ireland.	United Kingdom.	Great Britain.	Ireland.	United Kingdom.	Gt. Britain.	Ireland.
Imp.Gall.	Imp.Gall.	Imp.Gall.	£ s. d.	£ s. d.	£ s. d.	£ s. d.	£ s. d.
149,302	6,072	155,374	168,559 13 3	5,581 18 5	174,141 11 8	1 2 6¾	0 17 3¾
124,508	4,446	128,954	139,768 13 3	4,029 8 11	143,798 2 2		
103,973	1,305	105,278	116,967 12 11	1,359 15 8	118,327 8 7		
105,483	2,174	107,657	118,837 19 10	2,612 16 0	120,850 15 10		
113,255	3,032	116,287	127,503 18 11	2,772 3 3	130,275 2 2		
102,523	3,124	105,647	114,799 13 7	2,795 2 9	117,594 16 4	1 2 7½	
105,067	3,383	108,450	114,903 15 2	2,943 17 11	117,847 13 1		
89,443	3,324	92,767	100,965 15 9	2,940 2 10	103,905 18 7		
88,670	2,917	91,587	99,981 16 2	2,523 14 3	102,505 10 5		
82,784	8,164	90,948	93,442 0 0	7,020 14 5	100,462 14 5	- -	1 2 8
19,605	412	90,017	101,089 12 3	472 7 11	101,562 0 2		
83,709	1,000	84,709	94,463 2 1	1,145 17 11	95,609 0 0		
67,079	2,081	69,160	75,553 5 10	2,337 10 11	77,890 16 9	1 2 6	1 2 6
50,760	1,908	52,668	57,204 11 11	2,147 12 6	59,352 4 5		
43,037	2,223	45,260	48,433 9 1	2,500 11 10	50,934 0 11		
35,301	1,845	37,146	39,647 17 2	2,075 12 6	41,723 9 8		
(See Note below.)		30,802	-	-	34,668 7 2		

—In consequence of the destruction of the official records by fire, no separate account can be
of the consumption of geneva, or the revenue derived therefrom, for the years prior to 1814.
ade accounts of Great Britain and Ireland having been incorporated from the commencement of
particulars required by the above order for that year are stated for the United Kingdom only.
tor General's Office, Custom-house,   WILLIAM IRVING,
        London, 4th May, 1831.   Inspector General of Imports and Exports.

NOA, a maritime city of Italy, once the capital of the famous republic of
ame, now the capital of a province of the kingdom of Sardinia, in lat.
' N., lon. 8° 55' E.   Population, 76,000.

ɔa is celebrated for her palaces and public buildings, erected during the period
prosperity.   The harbour is in the form of a semicircle, the diameter of which
t 1,000 fathoms.   It is enclosed by two strong walls, the opening between which
fathoms in width; but the entrance is difficult.   Genoa exports the products of
acent country, such as rice and fruit; and, in particular, olive oil to a great
value; also her own manufactures — silks, damasks, and velvets; for the last of
he has been long celebrated.   Of imports the chief articles are, corn from Sicily
Black Sea, raw silk from Sicily, iron and naval stores from the Baltic, linen
cloth from Germany; tin, lead, hardware, woollens, and cottons, from England.
e are to be added, wool from Spain, wax and cotton from the Levant, and from
ited States different articles of colonial produce.   Stock-fish is here, as in other
c cities, an article of which large quantities are imported.   But the policy of
dinian government is hostile to foreign trade; and the additions that have been
ɔ the duties laid on most of the considerable articles of import since 1815, have
ally depressed the commerce of Genoa. — (Edinburgh Gazetteer, art. Genoa.)

·y. — Accounts were formerly kept at Genoa in lire of 20 soldi, each soldo con-
12 denari; and money was divided into banco and fuori di banco.   But since the
anuary, 1827, the ancient method of reckoning has ceased, and accounts are now
lire Italiane, divided into cents.   The weight and fineness of the new coins
isely the same as those of France: so that the par of exchange = 24·73 lire
nd sterling, if estimated in silver; and 25·20, if estimated in gold.   6 old lire
ɔ are equal to 5 new lire very nearly. — (Manuel de Nelkenbrecher.)

its and Measures. — The pound is of two sorts; the peso sottile = 4,891½ English
and the peso grosso.   The latter is 10 per cent. heavier than the former: hence
aro, of 150 lbs. peso sottile, = 69·89 lbs. avoirdupois; and the cantaro, of 150 lbs.
ɔsso, = 76·875 lbs. avoirdupois.   The latter is used for weighing bulky commo-
he former is used in the weighing of gold and silver, and of all commodities of
lk.

is measured by the mina of 8 quarte or 96 gombette — 1 mina = 3½ Winches-
els nearly.   Salt is sold by the mondino of 8 mine.

juid measure, 100 Pinte   =   1 Barilla.
                2 Barilli   =   1 Mezzarola = 39¼ English wine gallons.   The
f oil = 17 English gallons.

ɡ measures, the palmo = 9·725 English inches.   The canna is of three sorts:
a piccola, used by tradesmen and manufacturers, = 9 palme, or 87·5 English

inches; the canna grossa, used by merchants, = 12 palmi = 116·7 English inc
and the canna used at the Custom-house = 10 palmi = 97·25 English inches.
braccio = 2½ palmi.

Allowances, Tares, &c. — Alum, copper, hemp, hides, iron, lead, rice, and tin in
are sold by the cantaro of 150 lbs. peso sottile, with real tare only.

Bark, cinnamon, cochineal, coffee, indigo, drugs, tobacco, and tea, are sold b
pound, with a trett of 6 lbs. per 106 lbs., besides real tare.

Cotton wool, cod-fish, and stock-fish, are sold by the cantaro sottile, with 4 per
tare. Raw sugars by the 100 lbs., with 6 per cent. trett; ditto from Lisbon, in ch
with 20 per cent. tare; ditto from St. Domingo, in hhds., with 13 per cent. tare;
from Martinique, with 11 per cent. tare; ditto Muscovado, with 14 per cent.
ditto from the Havannah, in boxes, with 14 per cent. tare, and the trett of 6 lb
106 lbs. Loaf sugars have 2 per cent. allowed for paper and string. — (*Kelly's*
list.)

GENTIAN (Ger. *Enzian*; Fr. *Gentiane*; It. *Genziana*; Sp. *Jenciana*; Rus. *En*
Lat. *Gentiana*), the roots of a plant found growing in Switzerland and Austria
Apennines, the Pyrenees, and in North America. Those brought to this cou
come from Germany. They are in pieces of various lengths and thickness, twi
wrinkled on the outside, and covered with a brownish grey cuticle. They
no particular odour; and the taste is intensely bitter, without being nauseou
(*Thomson's Dispensatory.*)

GHEE. See BUTTER.

GIBRALTAR, a famous fortress, situated on a rock or promontory of
same name, near the southernmost extremity of Spain, lat. 36° 6¾′ N., lon. 5
W., and near the narrowest part of the strait joining the Atlantic and Medit
nean. Population about 16,500, exclusive of the troops, which usually am
in time of peace to from 3,000 to 4,000.

The north side of the rock, next the isthmus connecting it with Spain, is almost
pendicular and wholly inaccessible; the east and south sides are so rugged and pre
tous, as to render any attack upon them, even if they were not fortified, next to in
sible; so that it is only on the west side, fronting the bay, where the rock declin
the sea and the town is built, that it can be attacked with the least chance of suc
Here, however, the strength of the fortifications, and the magnitude of the batt
are such, that the fortress seems to be impregnable, even though attacked by an e.
having the command of the sea. It was taken by the English in 1704, but th
tifications were then very inferior to what they are at present. Towards the end c
American war, it was attacked by a most formidable armament fitted out jointl
Spain and France; but the strength of the place, and the bravery of the gar
defeated all the efforts of the combined powers. The bay of Gibraltar is spac
and, being protected from all the more dangerous winds, affords a convenien
tion for ships. Large vessels come close to the quay. Gibraltar is of conside
importance as a commercial station, being a depôt for all sorts of English
modities, with which it supplies the adjacent Spanish provinces, and the coa
Barbary. It is a free port, subject to no duties and few restrictions. The o
value of the articles of British and Irish produce and manufacture exported fro:
United Kingdom for Gibraltar, in 1830, amounted to 988,234*l.*; and the foreig
colonial produce exported to it during the same year amounted to 129,381*l.*
trade with Gibraltar, or any British dependency in the Mediterranean, may be reg
by an order in council; and any goods imported or exported contrary to such
shall be forfeited, together with the ship importing or exporting the same. — (6 G
c. 114. § 73.) THe making of Cadiz a free port has, in some measure, lessene
importance of Gibraltar as an *entrepôt*. The possession of this city is of great
quence to Britain, from its affording a convenient and secure station for the re
ment, repair, and accommodation of our ships of war and merchantmen; and fr
being, in fact, the key of the Mediterranean. The revenue collected in Gil
amounts to about 45,000*l.* a year, which is about equal to defray the public e:
incurred in the town; but the expense annually incurred in Great Britain on ac
of the garrison, in time of peace, amounts to about 200,000*l.* — a small sum con
with the important political and commercial advantages it is the means of securin

Money. — The effective or hard dollar = 4*s.* 4*d.*; the current dollar, being est:
at ¾ hard dollars, = 2*s.* 10¾*d.* Reals and quartos of both hard and current
are the same, being, the former = 4½*d.*, and the latter = 1 1/12*d.*

Accounts are kept in current dollars (pesos), divided into 8 reals of 16 quartos
12 reals currency are a cob or hard dollar, by which goods are bought and sold
3 of these reals are considered equal to 5 Spanish reals vellon.

ibraltar draws on London in effective dollars of 12 reals, and London on Gibraltar
irrent dollars of 8 reals.

he exchange of Gibraltar on Cadiz, and other cities of Spain, is in hard dollars at
r centage, which varies considerably, and mostly in favour of Gibraltar.

'eights and Measures are those of England, excepting the arroba = 25 lbs. English:
1 is sold by the fanega, 5 of which make one Winchester quarter; wine is sold
ie gallon, 100 of which are equal to 109⅔ English wine gallons. — (See *Papers laid
e Finance Committee; Edinburgh Gazetteer; Kelly's Cambist, &c.*)

ILD, OR GUILD, a company of merchants or manufacturers, whence the
of such companies are denominated Gild or Guild Halls.

ILL, a measure of capacity. See WEIGHTS and MEASURES.

IN. English geneva, or gin, is made of spirit obtained from oats, barley, or
, rectified, or re-distilled, with the addition of juniper berries, oil of turpentine,
All the spirits manufactured in England, and most of the Scotch and Irish
ts imported into England, are subjected to the process of rectification. English
s said to be one of the most wholesome spirits. — (See SPIRITS.)

INGER (Ger. *Ingwer;* Du. *Gember;* Fr. *Gingembre;* It. *Zenzero;* Sp. *Jen-
Agengibre;* Rus. *Inbir;* Lat. *Zingiber;* Pers. *Zungebeel;* Arab. *Zingebeel*),
oots of a plant (*Amomum Zingiber*), a native of the East Indies and China,
which was early carried to and succeeds very well in the West Indies. After
oots are dug, the best are selected, scraped, washed, and dried in the sun
great care. This is called *white ginger;* while the inferior roots, which are
led in boiling water before being dried, are denominated *black ginger.* Pre-
ed ginger is made by scalding the green roots, or the roots taken up when
are young and full of sap, till they are tender; then peeling them in cold
r, and putting them into a thin syrup, from which they are shifted into the
n which they come to us, and a rich syrup poured over them. Dried ginger
pungent aromatic odour, and a hot, biting taste. It is imported in bags, each
ining about a cwt. The white brings the highest price, being more pungent
better flavoured. The external characters of goodness in both sorts of dried
r are, soundness or the being free from worm holes, heaviness, and firmness;
ieces that are small, light, and soft, or very friable and fibrous, should be re-
d. The best preserved ginger is nearly translucent; it should be chosen of a
t yellow colour; rejecting that which is dark coloured, fibrous, or stringy. —
burn's Orient. Commerce; Thomson's Dispensatory.*)

11,007 cwt. of ginger imported in 1829, 4,911 cwt. came from the East
s, and 6,081 cwt. from the British West Indies.

INSENG (Du. *Ginseng, Ginsem;* Fr. *Ginseng;* Ger. *Kraftwerzel, Ginseng;
inseng;* Sp. *Jinseng;* Chin. *Yansam;* Tart. *Orhota*), the root of a small plant
ax quinquefolium, Lin.*), growing in China, Tartary, and several parts of North
rica. The latter is what we generally see in England, and is an article of
to China, where it is in the highest estimation. Large quantities used for-
to be exported from this country; but it is now carried direct to China by
mericans. Ginseng for the China market should be chosen in large roots,
l, firm, and of a fresh colour, moderately heavy, not very tough, but such as
nap short, free from worm-holes and dirt. — (*Milburn's Orient. Com.*)

ASS (Ger. and Du. *Glas;* Fr. *Vitre, Verre;* It. *Vetro;* Sp. *Vidrio;* Rus. *Steklo;
Vitrum*), a transparent, brittle, factitious body. It is formed by mixing together
sort of siliceous earth, as fine sand, or pounded flint, with an alkali, such as
potash, or pearl-ash, and subjecting them to a strong heat. By this means
re melted into a transparent, soft, tenacious mass, that may, when hot, be
d into thin plates, bent and shaped in every possible way. When cool, it
nes brittle, and is denominated glass. Litharge, minium, borax, the black
of manganese, &c. are sometimes used in the manufacture of glass, according
purposes to which it is to be applied.

kinds of glass, and their ingredients, are stated by Dr. Ure as follows: —

ere are five distinct kinds of glass at present manufactured: — 1. Flint glass, or glass of lead;
glass, or glass of pure soda; 3. Crown glass, the best window glass; 4. Broad glass, a coarse
glass; 5. Bottle, or coarse green glass.
lint Glass, so named because the siliceous ingredient was originally employed in the form of ground
It is now made of the following composition: —

Purified Lynn sand	-	-	-	100 parts.
Litharge or red lead	-	-	-	60 —
Purified pearl-ash	-	-	-	30 —

" To correct the green colour derived from combustible matter, or oxide of iron, a little black oxid‹ manganese is added, and sometimes nitre and arsenic. The fusion is accomplished usually in abou‹ hours.

" 2. *Plate Glass.* — Good carbonate of soda, procured by decomposing common salt with pearl-ash‹ employed as the flux. The proportion of the materials is,

Pure sand	-	-	-	43·0	
Dry subcarbonate of soda	-	-	25·5	
Pure quicklime	-	-	-	4·0	
Nitre	-	-	-	1·5	
Broken plate glass	-	-	-	25·0 —— 100·0.

About 70 parts of good plate glass may be run off from these materials.

" 3. *Crown, or fine Window Glass.* — This is made of sand vitrified by the impure barilla manufactu‹ by incineration of sea-weed on the Scotch and Irish shores. The most approved composition is,

		By measure.	By weight.
Fine sand purified	-	- 5	200
Best kelp ground	-	- 11	330

" 4. *Broad Glass.* — This is made of a mixture of soap-boilers' waste, kelp, and sand. The first ing‹ dient consists of lime used for rendering the alkali of the soap-boiler caustic, the insoluble matter of kelp or barilla, and a quantity of salt and water, all in a pasty state. The proportions necessarily va 2 of the waste, 1 of kept, and 1 of sand, form a pretty good broad glass. They are mixed together, dri and fritted.

" 5. *Bottle Glass* is the coarsest kind. It is made of soapers' waste and river sand, in proportions wh‹ practice must determine according to the quantity of the waste; some soap-boilers extracting more sa‹ matter, and others less, from their kelps. Common sand and lime, with a little common clay and sea ‹ form a cheap mixture for bottle glass."

1. *Historical Notices with respect to Glass.* — The manufacture of glass is one of ‹ very highest beauty and utility. It is most probable that we are indebted for this wonder‹ art, as we are for the gift of letters, to the Phœnicians. According to Pliny (*Hist. N* lib. 36. c. 26.), glass had been made for many ages, of sand found near the mouth of ‹ small river Belus in Phœnicia. " The report," says he, " is, that the crew of a merch‹ ship laden with nitre (fossile alkali) having used some pieces of it to support the kett‹ placed on the fires they had made on the sand, were surprised to see pieces formed o‹ translucent substance, or glass. This was a sufficient hint for the manufacture. ‹ genuity (*astuta et ingeniosa solertia*) was immediately at work, to improve the proc‹ thus happily suggested. Hence the magnetical stone came to be added, from an id‹ that it contained not only iron but glass. They also used clear pebbles, shells, and foss‹ sand, Indian glass is said to be formed of native crystal, and is on that account super‹ to every other. Phœnician glass is prepared with light dry wood, to which copper a‹ nitre are added, the last being principally brought from Ophir. It is occasionally ting‹ with different colours. Sometimes it is brought to the desired shape by being blov‹ sometimes by being ground on a lathe, and sometimes it is embossed like silver." Sid‹ he adds, is famous for this manufacture. It was there that mirrors were first invent‹ In Pliny's time, glass was made in Italy, of fine sand on the shore between Cumæ a‹ the Lucrine bay.

Glass was manufactured at Rome into various articles of convenience and ornam‹ Pliny mentions that Nero gave 6,000 sesterces (50,000*l.* according to the ordinary meth‹ of reckoning) for two glass cups, each having two handles! These, however, must h‹ been of an immense size and of exquisite workmanship; for glass was then in comm‹ use for drinking vessels, and was used even in the form of bottles in which to k‹ wine. — (*Mart. Epig.* lib. ii. 22. 40., and lib. iv. 86.)

There is no authentic evidence of glass being used in windows previously to the th‹ or fourth century; and then, and for long after, it was used only in churches and ot‹ public buildings. In this country, even so late as the latter part of the sixtee‹ century, glass was very rarely met with. In a survey of Alnwick castle, made‹ 1573, it is stated — " And, because throwe extreme winds, the glasse of the windo‹ of this and other my lord's castles and houses here in the country dooth decay ‹ waste, yt were good the whole leights of everie windowe, at the departure of‹ lordshippe from lyinge at any of his said castels, and houses, and dowring the tyme‹ his lordship's absence, or others lyinge in them, were taken doune and lade up in safe‹ And at sooche time as ather his lordshippe or anie other sholde lye at anie of the s‹ places, the same might then be set uppe of newe, with smale charges, whereas now‹ decaye thereof shall be verie costlie and chargeable to be repayred." — (*North. Ho‹ Book,* xvii.) Sir F. M. Eden thinks it probable that glass windows were not introdu‹ into farm-houses in England much before the reign of James I. They are mentio‹ in a lease in 1615, in a parish in Suffolk. In Scotland, however, as late as 1661,‹ windows of ordinary country houses were not glazed, and only the upper parts‹ even those in the king's palaces had glass; the lower ones having two wooden shutt‹ to open at pleasure, and admit the fresh air. From a passage in Harrison's Descrip‹ of England, it may be inferred that glass was introduced into country houses in the r‹ of Henry VIII. He says, " Of old time," (meaning, probably, the beginning of‹ century,) " our countrie houses instead of glasse did use much lattise, and that n‹ either of wicker or fine rifts of oke in checkerwise. I read also that some of the b‹ sort, in and before the time of the Saxons, did make panels of horne instead of gl‹

them in wooden calmes (casements); but as horne in windowes is now (1584) quite
wne in everie place, so our lattises are also growne into disuse, because glasse is
o be so plentiful, and within verie little so good, cheape, if not better than the other."
is now introduced into the windows of almost every cottage of Great Britain;
this cold, damp climate, it ought rather to be considered as a necessary of life,
s the most elegant and useful of conveniences. What Dr. Johnson has said as to
eserves to be quoted. — " By some fortuitous liquefaction was mankind taught to
e a body at once in a high degree solid and transparent, which might admit the
f the sun, and exclude the violence of the wind; which might extend the sight of
ilosopher to new ranges of existence, and charm him at one time with the un-
d extent of the material creation, and at another with the endless subordination
nal life; and, what is yet of more importance, might supply the decays of nature,
ccour old age with subsidiary sight. Thus was the first artificer in glass employed,
without his own knowledge or expectation. He was facilitating and prolonging
oyment of light; enlarging the avenues of science, and conferring the highest and
asting pleasures; he was enabling the student to contemplate nature, and the
to behold herself."— (Rambler, No. 9.)
ice, for a long time, excelled all Europe in the manufacture of glass, but was sub-
tly rivalled by France. The manufacture was early introduced into England;
vas not carried on to any extent previously to the sixteenth century. The first
'or looking-glasses and coach windows were made in 1673, at Lambeth, by Ve-
artists under the protection of the Duke of Buckingham. The British Plate
Company was incorporated in 1773, when it erected its extensive works at Raven-
near St. Helen's, in Lancashire. The manufacture was at first conducted by
en from France, whence we had previously brought all our plate glass. But
iich is now made at Ravenhead, at Liverpool, and London, is equal or superior
imported from the Continent.
difficult to form any precise estimate of the value of the glass annually produced in
Britain. We believe, however, that it cannot amount to less than 2,000,000l.; and
workmen employed in the different departments of the manufacture exceed 50,000.

ies on Glass. — The glass manufacture is subjected to the excise; and it is difficult to say whether
lations under which the duty is charged, or the duty itself, be most oppressive. The wealth
ilation of the country have more than doubled since 1790; and we are well convinced that, had
manufacture not been interfered with, it would have increased in a still greater ratio. But
f advancing, it has positively declined; and is actually less at this moment than it was forty years
extraordinary a result is wholly to be ascribed to the exorbitant excess to which the duties have
ried. Instead, however, of submitting any remarks of our own in vindication of this view of the
we shall take the liberty of laying before the reader the following extract from the speech deli-
Mr. Poulett Thomson in the House of Commons, 26th of March, 1830 — a speech which combines,
ee rarely exhibited, a familiar knowledge of practical details and of sound scientific principles.
administration of which the Right Hon. Gentleman is a distinguished member, has not yet pro-
repeal of this oppressive tax, is not, we are sure, owing to his colleagues differing in opinion
as to its impolicy, but is wholly to be ascribed to other causes — to the res dura et regni novitas
ficulty of finding a substitute, and the urgency of the claims for relief advanced by others.
gross duty on glass for the year 1828 amounted, in Great Britain (exclusive of Ireland), to 950,103l.,
lett duty to 586,770l.; the difference being either returned or sacrificed in the collection. And
uld entreat the House to remark, that for the sake of such a sum as half a million, a charge of
on nearly a million is incurred. The duty is 6d. per pound on flint, but equal to 7d. from the
its collection; in other words, upwards of 100 per cent.; the glass, when made, selling for 1s. to
his duty, too, is very much reduced from what it was; and here the House will observe an ad-
lustration of the effect of heavy duties on consumption, and consequently on revenue. In 1794,
ear in which the duty was 1l. 1s. 5d. per cwt. for plate and flint, and other kinds in proportion,
ities paying duty were as follow: —

Flint and Plate.	Broad.	Crown.	Bottle.
Cwt. 67,615	20,607	83,940	227,476

s were successively raised to 2l. 9s.; and at last, by Mr. Vansittart, in pursuit of his favourite
1813, to 4l. 18s.! and let us see the result. In 1816 the consumption had declined to

Plate.	Broad.	Crown.	Bottle.
Cwt. 29,600	6,140	55,502	155,595

overnment saw a part of their error, and reduced the duty by one half, still leaving it too high;
the effect. In 1828, the last year for which I have the returns, the consumption rose to

Plate.	Broad.	Crown.	Bottle.
Cwt. 68,134	6,956	90,603	224,864

ever, only about the same as in 1794. It appears, therefore, that notwithstanding the increase
tion and general luxury, the consumption has been kept down by your improvident system, and
now less than it was five and thirty years ago. But here again the duty is far from being the
vil. Let any one turn to the act: he will find thirty-two clauses of regulations, penalties, prohi-
ll vexatious to the manufacturer, and all to be paid for by the public. I have said that the duty
ass is 6d. per pound; the glass, when made, selling for 1s. But the excise officer has the power
ng the duty, either when the glass is in the pot, 3d. per pound, or after it has been turned out, at
glass, when turned out, gaining 100 per cent. It is found more advantageous to the revenue to
duty on glass in the pot, at 3d.; and in this way the duty is raised to 7d. Nor is this all. The
urer is driven by this method into the necessity of producing frequently an article which he does
He makes the fine glass from the middle; the coarser from the top and bottom of the pot.
ntly wants only fine glass, and he would re-melt the flux of the coarser parts if he had not paid
it; but of course he is unable to do so. All the glass manufacturers whom I have consulted,
the whole cost of the excise to the consumer, besides the duty, which is 100 per cent., is 25 per
besides, there is great inconvenience and oppression from the frauds that are daily taking
d observe the effect which is produced upon your trade, both at home and abroad.
nufacturer who has lately travelled through France, the Netherlands, and Germany, has

assured me that our manufacturers could advantageously cope with foreigners, were it not for the ... imposed by the government. Labour is as cheap in this country, our ingenuity is greater, and the ... rials are also as cheap; it is, then, the vexatious onerous duty alone that gives the foreign manufa... the advantage over the English. But the effect of the duty goes further; it operates to prevent a... provement in the article, because, to improve, experiments must be made; but a man with a duty ... per cent. over his head is not very likely to make many experiments. This argument applies esp... with respect to colours. A manufacturer has assured me that he has never been able to produce a ... tiful red, because the duties have prevented his trying the necessary experiments, without his inc... a great risk or loss. Thus a miserable duty, amounting to only 500,000*l.*, and upon which a cha... 10 per cent. is allowed for collecting, is allowed to impede our native industry, and to put a stop to a... provement, and be a source of endless oppression and fraud. I really cannot believe that the legis... will resist such an appeal as the manufacturers of this article could make to them, or refuse to r... them from the gratuitous injury which is inflicted on them.''

We subjoin

An Account of the Amount of Duty received and Drawback paid thereout, from 5th January, 1828, ... January, 1830; distinguishing the Amount of Duty and Drawback upon the several Sorts of ... Glass, Flint, Plate, Bottles, Broad or Spread; and distinguishing also the Amount of Duties p... Ireland, with Drawbacks paid there. — (*Parl. Paper*, No. 302. Sess. 1830.)

	Amount of Duty on					
	Crown Glass.	Flint.	Plate.	Bottles.	Broad or Spread.	Total
	£ s. d.	£ s. d.	£ s. d.	£ s. d.	£ s. d.	£
England - -	416,835 14 6	184,045 5 0	53,090 15 6	129,878 10 8	10,458 0 0	794,308
Scotland -	104,234 18 10	23,328 6 6	-	28,232 6 11	-	155,795
Ireland - -	-	23,612 7 6	-	3,360 0 1	-	26,972
Year ended 5th January, 1829, £	521,070 13 4	230,985 19 0	53,090 15 6	161,470 17 8	10,458 0 0	977,076
England - -	357,424 1 4	177,812 4 0	43,497 9 1	105,653 14 3	10,296 0 0	694,683
Scotland -	64,693 15 7	23,034 14 7	-	25,384 17 10	-	113,113
Ireland - -	-	21,044 7 0	-	2,974 17 6	-	24,019
Year ended 5th January, 1830, £	422,117 16 11	221,891 5 7	43,497 9 1	134,013 9 7	10,296 0 0	831,816
Total Duties in the two Years. £	943,188 10 3	452,877 4 7	96,588 4 7	295,484 7 3	20,754 0 0	1,808,892

	Amount of Drawback.					
	Crown Glass.	Flint.	Plate.	Bottles.	Broad or Spread.	Total
	£ s. d.	£ s. d.	£ s. d.	£ s. d	£ s. d.	£
England - -	143,375 13 3	67,764 0 0	4,547 18 11	63,664 7 10	24 17 8	279,376
Scotland -	62,091 12 3	7,276 1 3	128 12 7	14,560 5 2	-	84,056
Ireland - -	-	4,038 6 8	-	26 9 6	-	4,064
Year ended 5th January, 1829, £	205,467 5 6	79,078 7 11	4,676 11 6	78,251 2 6	24 17 8	367,498
England - -	65,933 19 11	66,816 10 5	1,677 15 1	47,900 9 0	-	182,328
Scotland -	19,345 3 1	7,295 13 10	-	9,716 4 5	-	36,357
Ireland - -	-	5,367 17 10	-	38 7 0	-	5,406
Year ended 5th January, 1830, £	85,279 3 0	79,480 2 1	1,677 15 1	57,655 0 5	-	224,092
Total Drawback in the two Years. £	290,746 8 6	158,558 10 0	6,354 6 7	135,906 2 11	24 17 8	591,590

3. *Regulations as to the Manufacture of Glass.* — The excise regulations with respect to gl... numerous, complex, and enforced under heavy penalties. We can notice only a few of the leadin... lations. All glass makers must take out a licence, renewable annually, which costs 20*l.* for each ... house; and they must make entry at the next Excise Office of all workhouses, furnaces, pots, pot-cha... annealing arches, warehouses, &c., under a penalty of 200*l.* No pot is to be charged without ... *twelve* hours' previous notice, in writing, of the time of beginning, the weight of metal, and species o... on pain of 50*l.* If, after notice given and a gauge taken by the officer, any material or preparation ... into any pot, a penalty of 50*l.* is incurred; but if the manufacture be of flint glass, the penalty ... Manufacturers of flint glass are allowed three hours for beginning to charge their pots after th... specified in their notices. Entries of the quantities made are to be made in writing, upon oath, a... duties paid monthly in London, and every six weeks in the country. Duty upon materials lost or ... is allowed for, upon due proof being made of the fact. Officers at all times, by day and night, are ... access to workhouses, &c., to gauge the materials and mark the pots as they think fit; any atte... obstruct the officers so employed incurs a penalty of 200*l.*: the counterfeiting, altering, or effac... marks made by the officers is visited with a penalty of 500*l.*; a penalty of 200*l.* being also impose... any one procuring or conniving at its being done. Officers are entitled to take samples, not ex... four ounces in all, out of each pot; paying for them, if demanded, ¼*d.* an ounce. The whole of th... intended to be manufactured into common glass bottles is to be worked within sixteen hours ne... the same shall be begun; and when the bottles are deposited in the annealing arches, manufactu... again, in the presence of the officer, to charge each pot with fresh materials, other than broken g... less than 50 lbs. weight; and declarations are to be delivered, in writing, of the number of such bot... penalty of 100*l.*

nufacturers of glass bottles are to affix proper hooks or staples, with scales and weights, to be ap-ed of, in writing, by the surveyor or supervisor, under a penalty of 50*l*.; the using any false or insuffi-scales or weights in the weighing of bottles, incurs a penalty of 100*l*.

tices are not to be given for drawing out bottles, but only between 8 o'clock in the morning and 6 in fternoon.

crown glass, or German sheet glass, or broad or spread window glass, shall be made of greater thick-excluding the centre or bullion and the selvage or rim thereof, than one ninth part of an inch, unless e shall have given that it was intended to manufacture the metal into plate glass, and the duty ate glass be paid thereon. — (See the Statutes in *Burn's Justice*, Marriott's ed. vol. ii. pp. 186—228.)

r an account of the duties on foreign glass imported into Great Britain, and the drawbacks, &c. ed upon the exportation of British made glass, see Tariff.

Exportation of Glass. — It is enacted by stat. 6 Geo. 4. c. 117., that no flint glass shall be entitled to rawback on exportation, if it be not of the specific gravity of 3,000, that of water being 1,000; and if not worth at least 11*d*. a pound for home consumption at the time when it is entered for exportation. int glass entered for exportation, of less specific gravity than 3,000, or of less value than 11*d*. per l, is forfeited, and may be seized by any officer of excise. — §§ 24, 25.

e exporter of glass is to make oath that he believes it to be entirely of British manufacture, and that aties imposed upon it by law have been paid. Persons wilfully taking a false oath in this matter are to the pains and penalties of perjury. — (55 *Geo.* 3. c. 13. § 3.)

urity by bond is to be given (usually for a larger sum and a greater quantity of goods than are ded to be exported), that glass, on the exportation of which a drawback is allowed, shall be shipped n one month after the date of such security; but if the commissioners be satisfied that the shipment glass within the specified time has been prevented by some unavoidable accident, they may grant er time, not exceeding three months, for the shipment thereof. — § 7.

drawback is to be allowed upon the exportation of used, old, or second hand glass. — § 9.

stat. 54 Geo. 3. c. 97. § 6. it is enacted, that no drawback shall be allowed for any regular panes, es, or rectangular figures of spread glass or other window glass, any part of which shall consist of lude the bullion or thick centre part of the table from which such panes, squares, or rectangular s shall have been cut or taken, or any part of the said bullion, unless no side of any such panes, all measure less than 8 inches; nor shall any drawback be allowed for any lozenges, any part of shall consist of or include the bullion or thick centre part of the table from which such lozenges nave been taken, or any part of the bullion, unless no side of any such lozenge shall measure less 3 inches; nor unless the distance between the two obtuse angles of each such lozenge shall measure es at the least; nor shall any drawback be allowed for any lozenges not containing the bullion or centre part of the table from which such lozenges shall have been cut or taken, or any part of the n, unless the distance between the two obtuse angles of every such lozenge shall measure 3¼ inches t; and all window glass, any part whereof shall include or consist of the bullion or thick centre f the table from which the same shall have been cut or taken, and which shall be of any other or of less dimensions than as aforesaid, shall be deemed to be *waste glass;* and if any person shall ngly enter or ship for exportation, in order to obtain any drawback, any panes, squares, or rectan-figures or lozenges of spread window glass, commonly known by the name of *broad glass*, or other w glass, not being spread glass as aforesaid, containing or including the bullion or thick part of ole from which such panes, squares, rectangular figures, or lozenges of spread glass or other window espectively, which shall not be of the dimensions in that behalf aforesaid, such person shall, for every ze containing any such glass so entered or shipped contrary to this act, forfeit 100*l*.

2 Geo. 3. c. 77. § 6. it is enacted, that no glass whatsoever made in Great Britain, or made in Ireland aported into Great Britain, shall be packed for exportation on drawback, in any package made with id space in or between the component parts thereof, but all such glass shall be packed for export-n casks, boxes, or chests only, and in which the exporter shall, previous to the packing of such glass s, have cut or sunk a sufficient number of circular cavities, each thereof not less than ⅓ of an or more than 1¼ inch in diameter to receive the seal directed to be put on such package, and for rpose of protecting such seal from being destroyed, defaced, broken, or damaged; and where any ʾass shall be packed for exportation in any cask, box, or chest, each such cavity shall be cut and one part thereof on the edge of the lid or cover, and the other on the side of such box or chest, so ach such seal may be conveniently placed by the proper officer of excise, part on the wood of such cover, and the residue on the wood of the side of each such box or chest; and no drawback shall be r any glass not packed in a cask, box, or chest as aforesaid, nor for any glass packed in any box or not having a sufficient number of such cavities: Provided that nothing herein shall prohibit the g of whole or half tables of spread glass, or of crown glass, or any common bottles made of common metal, in any crate or other package whatsoever.

dulent Packing. — If any person shall place any brick, stone, or any other heavy substance, other nt glass, or phial glass, or broad glass, or crown glass, in any cask, box, or chest containing flint kc. packing or packed for exportation on drawback, the person so offending shall for each such forfeit 200*l*., and all such glass, brick, stone, or other heavy substance contained therein, shall be ed. — (52 *Geo.* 3. c. 77. § 7.)

person altering or defacing any marks on any cask, box, &c. containing glass for exportation, ex-g the weight and tare of such cask, &c., or the weight of the glass therein, or the time or place of g, or the number of the cask, &c., shall for each offence forfeit 200*l*., with the glass. — § 8.

officers of excise are to brand or mark every cask, box, &c. of glass for exportation with the letters and if any cask, &c. of glass so branded be not put on board within twelve hours after the branding , or if any cask, &c. so branded be found on land after twelve months from the time when such as packed for exportation, the same shall be forfeited. Any person obliterating, defacing, altering, e aforesaid letters, to forfeit 200*l*. — § 9.

5 Geo. 3. c. 108. it is enacted, that no drawback shall be paid for the exportation of any ground shed plate glass made in Great Britain, unless such glass be exported in rectangular plates of e of 6 inches in length by 4 inches in breadth at the least, and unless each plate of such glass be m stains and blisters, and be perfect and fit for immediate use, as and for ground and polished ass; and if any person shall pack or ship for exportation on drawback, any plate of plate glass as and polished plate glass made in Great Britain, which is not plate glass, or has not been ground ished, or which shall be foreign glass, or of less dimension or thickness throughout than aforesaid, be stained, or blistered, or imperfect, or not immediately fit for use as ground and polished plate r any other sort of glass with any ground and polished plate glass, the same, and all the glass there-all be forfeited, and the person so offending shall forfeit for each such package 100*l*.

person packing for exportation on drawback, any unground or unpolished plate glass of less or dimensions in thickness and size than as last aforesaid, or any foul, imperfect, or unmerchantable nd or unpolished plate glass, in any package, with or amongst any other kind of glass, the same, the glass therewith, shall be forfeited, and the person so offending shall forfeit for each such e 100*l*. — (56 *Geo.* 3. c. 108. § 4.)

Geo. 3. c. 39. it is enacted, that if glass shipped for drawback be fraudulently unshipped or re-every person in anywise concerned or assisting in the same shall, over and above all other penal-feit for every such offence 100*l*.; and every person knowingly entering any *broken or waste glass* ortation upon a drawback shall, exclusive of all other pains and penalties, forfeit 100*l*. — § 37.

By 6 Geo. 4. c. 117. it is enacted, that every person shipping or intending to ship, or being about to sh
in Ireland, any plate glass, broad glass, or crown glass, for exportation on drawback, or for the remo
thereof to Great Britain, shall give 24 hours' notice of such intention, and of the place of shipping, to
nearest collector or officer of excise ; and such collector and officer are required thereupon to attend, a
to cause all such glass to be weighed and measured ; and in case such glass has not been charged w
the respective duties under the provisions of this act, and is about to be removed to Great Britain, it sh
be lawful for such collector or officer, and he is required to charge all such glass with duty at the resp
tive rates of duty made payable by this act on such sort or kind of glass respectively ; and upon paym
of such duty, it shall be lawful for such collector or officer to grant a certificate of the payment of su
duty, to accompany such glass upon such removal, and to be produced at the port of entry in G
Britain ; and in case any such glass which shall have been duly charged with the respective duties paya
by this act shall be entered for exportation to foreign parts upon drawback, or be sent and removed
Great Britain, it shall be lawful for such collector or officer upon proof that such duties have been pa
or have been charged and duly secured to be paid, to grant a certificate of the payment of such duty
a certificate that such duty has been charged and is duly secured to be paid, to accompany such glass u
such exportation to foreign parts or such removal to Great Britain, and to be there produced as afc
said ; and if at any time any person shall export or enter for exportation from Ireland, upon drawba
or shall remove or send from Ireland to be brought into Great Britain, or shall bring into Great Brita
any plate glass, broad glass, or crown glass, unaccompanied by such certificate containing such particul
as aforesaid ; or if any person shall refuse to produce such certificate at the port of entry in Great Brita
or shall forge or counterfeit any certificate required in this act, or shall make use of or deliver any fa
or untrue certificate as and for a certificate required by this act; all such glass respectively shall be
feited, and may be seized by any officer of excise, and the person so offending shall forfeit 500l. : F
vided always, that if any plate glass, broad glass, crown glass which, shall have been previously sent
Ireland from Great Britain, on drawback, shall at any time afterwards be sent or removed to Great Brita
the rate of duty to be charged thereon as aforesaid, shall be equal and according to the rate of drawb
now payable thereon respectively when exported to foreign parts — § 7.

GLOVES (Ger. *Handschuhe* ; Fr. *Gants* ; It. *Guanti* ; Sp. *Guantes* ; Rus. *I*
kawizü, Pertschatki, Golizü), well known articles of dress used for covering t
hands, usually made of leather, but frequently also of cotton, wool, silk, &c.

The leather used in the manufacture of gloves is not, properly speaking, tanned, b
prepared by a peculiar process that renders it soft and pliable. Some sorts of leath
gloves admit of being washed, and others not. Woodstock and Worcester, but parti
larly the former, are celebrated for the manufacture of leather gloves of a superior quali
and which affords employment to a great number of women and children, as well as me
The manufacture is also carried on at Stourbridge, Hereford, York, &c. In some pla
gloves are made by machinery. Limerick used to be famous for the manufacture o
sort of ladies' gloves, called chicken gloves. Large quantities of cotton gloves are ma
at Nottingham and Leicester.

The importation of leather gloves and mitts was formerly prohibited, under the severest penal
This prohibition had the effect, by preventing all competition and emulation with the foreigner, to ch
improvement, and to render British gloves at once inferior in quality and high in price. This system v
however, permitted to continue till 1825, when the prohibition was repealed, and gloves allowed to be
ported on payment of duties, which, though high, are not prohibitory. This measure was veheme
opposed ; and many predictions were made of the total ruin of the manufacture ; but in this, as in ev
similar instance, experience has shown that the trade had not been benefited ; but that, on the contr
it had been injured by the prohibition. The wholesome competition to which the manufacturers now
themselves, for the first time, exposed, made them exert all their energies ; and it is admitted or
hands, that there has been a more rapid improvement in the manufacture during the last half dozen y
than in the previous half century. In consequence of the better fabric and lower price of the Eng
gloves, the imports of those of foreign manufacture have recently been materially diminished ; and tl
is, besides, a great increase in the imports of skins used in making gloves. We have no doubt, ind
that if the impulse that has been given to the trade be kept up, by a reduction of the existing dut
foreign gloves, we shall be, at no distant period, as superior in this as we are in most other branche
manufacturing industry.

Leather gloves must be imported in packages, containing each 100 dozen pairs at least, and in vesse
70 tons burthen or upwards, on penalty of forfeiture. — (7 *Geo.* 4. *c.* 48. § 7.)

Account of the Number of Dozen Pairs of Habit Gloves, Men's Gloves, and Women's Gloves and M
imported into the United Kingdom ; the Amount of Duty paid thereon during the Years 1828, 1829,
1830 ; and the Rates of Duty.

Years.	Habit Gloves.		Mens' Gloves.		Women's Gloves and Mitts.		Total Quantity of Leather Gloves and Mitts imported.		Total Receip of Duty on Lea Gloves and Mit
	Dozen.	Pairs.	Dozen.	Pairs.	Dozen.	Pairs.	Dozen.	Pairs.	L. s.
1828	69,564	7	27,668	10	3,025	8	100,259	1	21,653 3
1829	45,679	5	23,635	6	2,781	6	72,096	5	15,510 15
1830	62,925	10	25,013	3	3,187	8	91,126	9	19,488 1
Rates of Duty throughout the whole period -	4s. per doz. pair.		5s. per doz. pair.		7s. per doz. pair.				

Account of the Number of Lamb and Kid Skins entered for Home Consumption in the Nine Years er
with 1828, with an Estimate of the Quantity of Gloves which such Skins would produce, on the
position that from each 120 Skins there would be manufactured 18 Dozen Pairs of Gloves.

Years.	Number of Lamb Skins.	Number of Kid Skins.	Total Lamb and Kid.	Doz. Gloves produced each Year.	Years.	Number of Lamb Skins.	Number of Kid Skins.	Total Lamb and Kid.	Doz. Glo produced each Ye
1820	932,817	286,443	1,219,260	182,889	1825	2,098,553	771,522	2,870,075	430,5
1821	1,202,029	242,996	1,445,025	216,756	1826	1,743,778	575,533	2,319,311	347,8
1822	1,908,651	408,523	2,317,174	347,562	1827	2,749,397	640,863	3,390,260	508,5
1823	1,974,143	497,444	2,471,587	370,728	1828	2,917,476	904,639	3,822,115	573,3
1824	2,201,295	631,995	2,833,290	424,980					

atter account is borrowed from the "Companion to the Almanac" for 1830; to which excellent
ion it was furnished by James Morrison, Esq., M.P.

LD (Ger. *Gold;* Du. *Goud;* Da. and Sw. *Guld;* Fr. *Or;* It. and Sp. *Oro;*
Oiro, Ouro; Rus. *Soloto;* Pol. *Zloto;* Lat *Aurum;* Arab. *Tibr* and *Zeheb;*
Swarna; Malay, *Mās*), the most precious of all the metals, seems to have
:nown from the earliest antiquity. It is of an orange red, or reddish yellow
, and has no perceptible taste or smell. Its lustre is considerable, yielding
o that of platinum, steel, silver, and mercury. It is rather softer than silver.
ecific gravity is 19·3. No other substance is equal to it in ductility and mal-
:y. It may be beaten out into leaves so thin, that one grain of gold will cover
uare inches. These leaves are only $\frac{1}{282000}$ of an inch thick. But the gold
ith which silver wire is covered has only $\frac{1}{12}$ of that thickness. An ounce
l upon silver is capable of being extended more than 1,300 miles in length.
acity is considerable, though in this respect it yields to iron, copper, pla-
and silver. From the experiments of Seckingen it appears, that a gold
·078 inch in diameter, is capable of supporting a weight of 150·07 lbs.
upois without breaking. It melts at 32° of Wedgwood's pyrometer. When
, it assumes a bright blueish green colour. It expands in the act of fusion,
nsequently contracts while becoming solid more than most metals; a cir-
nce which renders it less proper for casting into moulds. — (*Thomson's
try.*)

the quantities of gold produced, and the places where it is produced, see
ous METALS.

MUTI, OR EJOO, a species of palm (*Borassus Gomutus*), growing in the
islands. A valuable product is obtained from this palm, resembling
orse hair; it is found between the trunk and the branches, at the insertion
latter, in a matted form, interspersed with long, hard, woody twigs of the
olour. When freed from the latter, it is manufactured by the natives into
e. Its fibres are stronger and more durable, but less pliant, than those of
:oa-nut, or coir — (see COIR); and is, therefore, fitter for cables and stand-
;ing, but less fit for running rigging.

native shipping of the Eastern islands of all kinds are entirely equipped with
of the gomuti; and the largest European shipping in the Indies use cables of it.
rgoes no preparation but that of spinning and twisting; no material similar to
or pitch, indispensable to the preservation of hempen cordage, being necessary
ubstance that, in a remarkable degree, possesses the quality of resisting alter-
of heat and moisture. The gomuti of Amboyna, and the other Spice islands, is
. That of Java has a coarse ligneous fibre. Gomuti is generally sold in twisted
or yarns, often as low as a dollar a picul, and seldom more than two. Were
an ingenuity applied to the improvement of this material, there seems little doubt
night be rendered more extensively useful. — (*Crawfurd's East. Archip.* vol. iii.

)D HOPE, CAPE OF. See CAPE TOWN.

TENBURGH, in the south-west part of Sweden, near the mouth of
r Gotha-elf, in lat. 57° 41′ N., lon. 11° 57¾′ E. Population about 20,000.
r good and spacious. After Stockholm, Gottenburgh has the most exten-
mmerce of any town in Sweden. Iron and steel, both of which are
it, furnished by the rich mines of Warmeland, form the principal articles
rt; and after them, herrings, linen, timber, tar, train-oil, and alum. Got-
h deals are of an inferior quality. The Swedish government would appear
ll firmly attached to the exploded errors of the mercantile system, rigidly
ig most articles of foreign growth, or loading them with heavy duties.
stem is productive of a double injury; first, by lessening the purchases
eigners would otherwise make of the peculiar products of Sweden; and
y, by encouraging smuggling, and forcing the inhabitants to pay an unnatu-
hanced price for such foreign articles as taste or necessity leads them to
he principal imports are salt and colonial products. It was provided by
igreed to in 1813, that British subjects should have liberty to use, for
years to come, the ports of Gottenburgh and Carlsham, as *entrepôts* for
of merchandise, the produce of Great Britain or her colonies, whether
e be prohibited in Sweden or not, upon paying *one* per cent. ad valorem
upon entrance, and the same upon discharge.

s, *weights,* and *measures,* same as at Stockholm; which see.

GRACE, DAYS OF. See Exchange.

GRAPES (Ger. *Trauben;* Fr. *Raisins;* It. *Grappoli, Grappi;* Sp. *Ubas, F̶ mos;* Lat. *Uvæ*), a well known fruit produced from the vine. France, S̶ Portugal, and Italy, as well as some parts of Germany and Hungary, pro̶ grapes which yield wines of various qualities and flavour, many of them excel̶ We import green grapes from Malaga and some other parts of Spain; the̶ brought packed in jars, and secured from damage by means of saw-dust, plenti̶ strewed in the jars between the layers of fruit. The grapes grown in Great Br̶ in the open air are much smaller, and by no means so luscious, as those of for̶ countries; but those raised in hothouses are quite equal, if not superior, t̶ former. Grapes are imported not only in their natural state, but dried and̶ served, in which latter state they are denominated raisins; which see.

GUAIACUM, or Lignumvitæ (Fr. *Gayac, Bois saint;* Ger. *Pockhaln̶ Guajaco;* Lat. *Guaiacum, lignumvitæ;* Sp. *Guagaco*), the wood of a tree, a n̶ of Jamaica, Hayti, and the warmer parts of America. It is a dark-looking̶ green, growing to from 40 to 50 feet in height, and from 14 to 18 inche̶ diameter. The bark is hard, smooth, and brittle; the wood is externally yello̶ and internally of a blackish brown colour. Lignumvitæ is the weightiest ti̶ with which we are acquainted, its specific gravity being 1·333. It is exceed̶ hard, and difficult to work. It can hardly be split, but breaks into pieces l̶ stone, or crystallised metal. It is full of a resinous juice (*guaiac*), which pre̶ oil or water from working into it, and renders it proof against decay. Its w̶ and hardness make it the very best timber for stampers and mallets; and it i̶ mirably adapted for the sheaves or pulleys of blocks, and for friction rolle̶ castors. It is extensively used by turners.

The *guaiac*, or gum, spontaneously exudes from the tree, and concretes in very̶ tears. It is imported in casks or mats, the former containing from 1 to 4 cwt., the latte̶ nerally less than 1 cwt. each. Its colour differs considerably, being partly brownish, ̶ reddish, and partly greenish; and it always becomes green when left exposed to the̶ in the open air. It has a certain degree of transparency, and breaks with a vit̶ fracture. When pounded, it emits a pleasant balsamic smell, but has scarcely any̶ although when swallowed it excites a burning sensation in the throat. When hea̶ melts, diffusing, at the same time, a pretty strong fragrant odour. Its specific gra̶ 1·229. — (See *Veget. Sub. Lib. of Entert. Knowledge; Thomson's Chemistry, &c.*)

GUERNSEY. For the peculiar regulations to be observed in trading̶ Guernsey, Jersey, &c. see Importation and Exportation.

GUMS, RESINS, GUM-RESINS. In commerce, the term gum is no̶ applied to gums properly so called, but also to resins and gum-resins.̶ though these substances have many properties in common, they are yet suffici̶ distinct.

1. *Gum* is a thick transparent fluid that issues spontaneously from certain spec̶ plants, particularly such as produce stone fruit, as plum and cherry trees. It i̶ adhesive, and gradually hardens by exposure to the atmosphere. It is usually obt̶ in small pieces, like tears, moderately hard and somewhat brittle while cold; so ̶ can be reduced by pounding to a fine powder. When pure, it is colourless; but̶ commonly a yellowish tinge; it is not destitute of lustre; it has no smell; its t̶ insipid; its specific gravity varies from 1·3161 to 1·4317; it readily dissolves in ̶ but is insoluble in alcohol. Gum is extensively used in the arts, particularly in̶ printing, to give consistence to the colours, and to hinder them from spreading.̶ also used in painting, in the manufacture of ink, in medicine, &c.

The only important gums, in a commercial point of view, are *gum Arabic̶ gum Senegal.* Genuine gum Arabic is the product of the *Acacia vera* (which s̶ tree growing in Arabia, and in almost every part of Africa. The best gum is imp̶ from Alexandria, Morocco, Tripoli, &c.; but large quantities of an inferior so̶ imported from the East Indies. Of 8,232 cwt. of gum Arabic imported in̶ 3,746 were brought from the East Indies, 2,520 from Tripoli, Morocco, &c., 1,31̶ Italy and the Italian islands (at second hand from Turkey), and some small qua̶ from other places. The price of gum Arabic in the London market, in bond,̶ at present (Aug. 1831), East India from 35*s.* to 60*s.* per cwt., Turkey from 1̶ 240*s.* per ditto, and Barbary from 46*s.* to 108*s.* per ditto.

Gum Senegal, principally brought from the island of that name on the coast of ̶ is obtained from various trees, but chiefly from two; one called *Vereck,* which yi̶ white gum, the other called *Nebuel,* which yields a red gum, varieties of the̶ *gummifera.* Gum Arabic is very often mixed with gum Senegal. The latter is̶

ure as the former, but it is usually in larger masses, of a darker colour, and more
my and tenacious. It is the sort of gum principally employed by calico printers.
s worth, at present (Aug. 1831), duty (6s.) paid, from 68s. to 73s. a cwt. —
mson's Chemistry, Thomson's Dispensatory, Ainslie's Materia Indica, &c.)

Resins, for the most part, exude spontaneously from trees, though they are often
ined by artificial wounds, and are not uncommonly, at first, combined with volatile
rom which they are separated by distillation. They are solid substances, naturally
te; have a certain degree of transparency, and a colour most commonly inclining
llow. Their taste is more or less acrid, and not unlike that of volatile oils; but
have no smell, unless they happen to contain some foreign body. They are all
ier than water, their specific gravity varying from 1·0182 to 1·1862. They differ
gums in being insoluble in water, whether cold or hot, while they are, with a few
ntions, soluble in alcohol, especially when assisted by heat. When heated, they
; and if the heat be increased, they take fire, burning with a strong yellow flame,
emitting a vast quantity of smoke. Common rosin furnishes a very perfect example
resin, and it is from this substance that the whole genus have derived their name.
n is, indeed, frequently denominated resin. The principal resins are Animi, Elemi,
, Lac, Labdanum, Mastick, Rosin, Sandarach, Tacamahac, &c.; which see, under
respective names. — (Thomson's Chemistry.)

Gum-resins, a class of vegetable substances consisting of gum and resin. They
from resins in this — that they never exude spontaneously from the plant, being ob-
d either by bruising the parts containing them, and expressing the juice, which is
ys in a state of emulsion, generally white, but sometimes of a different colour, or by
ng incisions in the plant, from which the juice flows. The juice, being exposed to the
n of the sun, is condensed and inspissated, till it forms the gum-resin of commerce.
-resins are usually opaque, or, at least, their transparency is inferior to that of resins.
are always solid, and most commonly brittle and have, sometimes, a fatty appear-
When heated, they do not melt as resins do; neither are they so combustible.
, however, commonly softens them, and causes them to swell. They burn with a
. They have almost always a strong smell, which, in several instances, is allia-
. Their taste, also, is often acrid, and always much stronger than that of resins.
are usually heavier than resins. They are partially soluble in water, but the solu-
s always opaque, and usually milky. Alcohol partially dissolves them, the solution
transparent.

e most common gum-resins are Aloes, Ammonia, Euphorbium, Galbanum, Gamboge,
h, Olibanum, Sagapenum, Scammony, &c.; which see, under their respective names.
oudon's Ency. of Agricult.; Thomson's Chemistry.)

JNPOWDER (Ger. Pulver, Schiesspulver; Du. Buskruid; Da. Krudt,
r; Sw. Krut; Fr. Poudre; It. Polvere; Sp. and Port. Polvora; Rus. Poroch;
Proch; Lat. Pulvis pyrius). This well known inflammable powder is com-
d of nitre, sulphur, and charcoal, reduced to powder, and mixed intimately
each other. The proportion of the ingredients varies very considerably;
ood gunpowder may be composed of the following proportions; viz. 76 parts
re, 15 of charcoal, and 9 of sulphur. These ingredients are first reduced to
: powder separately, then mixed intimately and formed into a thick paste
water. After this has dried a little, it is placed upon a kind of sieve full of
through which it is forced. By this process it is divided into grains, the
f which depends upon the size of the holes through which they have been
zed. The powder, when dry, is put into barrels, which are made to turn
on their axis. By this motion the grains of gunpowder rub against each
their asperities are worn off, and their surfaces are made smooth. The
er is then said to be glazed. — (Thomson's Chemistry.)

Thomson, whose learning is equal to his science, has the following remarks with
t to the introduction of gunpowder into warlike operations: — " The discoverer of
mpound, and the person who first thought of applying it to the purposes of war,
known. It is certain, however, that it was used in the fourteenth century. From
archives quoted by Wiegleb, it appears that cannons were employed in Germany
the year 1372. No traces of it can be found in any European author previously
thirteenth century; but it seems to have been known to the Chinese long before
eriod. There is reason to believe that cannons were used in the battle of Cressy,
was fought in 1346. They seem even to have been used three years earlier, at the
f Algesiras; but before this time they must have been known in Germany, as
s a piece of ordnance at Amberg, on which is inscribed the year 1303. Roger
, who died in 1292, knew the properties of gunpowder; but it does not follow that

he was acquainted with its application to fire-arms." — (*Thomson's Chemistry*.)
further particulars as to the introduction of cannon, see that article.

The manufacture and sale of gunpowder is regulated by several statutes. By the 12 Geo. 3. c. 61. i
enacted, that no person shall use mills or other engines for making gunpowder, or manufacture the sa
in any way, except in mills and other places which were *actually in existence* at the time of passing
act, or which, if erected afterwards, have been sanctioned by a licence, under pain of forfeiting the g
powder, and 2*s.* a pound. It is further enacted, that no mill worked by a pestle, and usually terme
pestle-mill, shall be used in making gunpowder, under the above mentioned penalty; and that no m
than 40 lbs. of gunpowder, or materials to be made into gunpowder, shall be made at any one time un
a single pair of mill-stones, on pain of forfeiting all above 40 lbs., and 2*s.* for every pound; nor shall m
than 40 cwt. be dried in any one stove or place at any one time, under forfeiture of all above that quant
and 2*s.* for every pound thereof. The powder mills erected at Battle, Crowhurst, Seddlescombe,
Brede, in Sussex, previously to 1772, are exempted from the above regulations so far as relates to
making of fine fowling powder.

No dealer is to keep more than 200 lbs. of powder, nor any person not a dealer, more than 50 lbs. in
cities of London or Westminster, or within 3 miles thereof, or within any other city, borough, or mar
town, or 1 mile thereof, or within 2 miles of the king's palaces or magazines, or half a mile of any pa
church, on pain of forfeiture, and 2*s.* per lb.; except in licensed mills, or to the amount of 300 lbs. for
use of collieries, within 200 yards of them.

Not more than 25 barrels are to be carried by any land-carriage, nor more than 200 barrels by wa
unless going by sea or coastwise, each barrel not to contain more than 100 lbs.

All vessels, except his Majesty's, coming into the Thames, are to put on shore, at or below Blackw
all the gunpowder they have on board exceeding 25 lbs. Vessels outward bound are not to receive
board more than 25 lbs. of gunpowder previously to their arrival at Blackwall. The Trinity-house h
authority to appoint searchers to inspect ships, and search for gunpowder. All the gunpowder fo
above 25 lbs., and the barrels containing it, and 2*s.* for every lb. above that quantity, are forfeited.
person obstructing an officer searching for concealed gunpowder is liable to a penalty of 10*l.* The pla
of deposit for gunpowder are regulated by the 54 Geo. 3. c. 159.

The exportation of gunpowder may be prohibited by order in council. Its importation is prohibi
on pain of forfeiture, except by licence from his Majesty; such licence to be granted for furnishing
Majesty's stores only. — (6 *Geo.* 4. c. 107.)

The act 1 Will. 4. c. 44. prohibits the manufacture and keeping of gunpowder in Ireland by any per
who has not obtained a licence from the Lord Lieutenant; such licences may be suspended on notice fr
the chief secretary, and any one selling gunpowder during the suspension of such licence shall for
500*l.* Gunpowder makers under this act are to return monthly accounts of their stock, &c. to the ch
secretary. This act, which contains a variety of restrictive clauses, was limited to one year's duration

GUNNY (Hind. *Tāt;* Ben. *Gŭni*), a strong coarse sackcloth manufactured
Bengal for making into bags, sacks, and packing generally, answering at on
the two purposes for which canvass and *bast* are used in Europe. The mate
from which this article is manufactured, is the fibre of two plants of the ger
Corchorus; viz. *Corchorus olitorius,* and *Corchorus capsularis* (Bengali, *pāt*); bo
but particularly the first, extensively cultivated throughout lower Bengal. Besi
a large domestic consumption of gunny, the whole rice, paddy, wheat, puls
sugar, and saltpetre of the country, as well as the pepper, coffee, and other
reign produce exported from Calcutta, is packed in bags or sacks made of t
article. There is also a considerable exportation of manufactured bags, e
commonly capable of containing two maunds, or about 160 lbs. weight, to Pri
of Wales Island, Malacca, Singapore, Java, and Bombay. In 1828–29, the num
exported from Calcutta was 2,205,206, of the value of 166,109 sicca rupees,
about 16,000*l.* sterling, showing the price of each sack to be less than 2*d.* — (*W
lich; Roxburgh; Bell's Review of the External Commerce of Bengal.*)

GYPSUM, OR SULPHATE OF LIME, is found in various parts of the C
tinent, and in Derbyshire and Nottinghamshire. When reduced to a powder,
formed into a paste with water, it is termed *plaster of Paris,* and is much used
forming casts, &c. It is also used for laying floors; and has been advantageo
employed as a manure.

H.

HAIR, HUMAN HAIR (Ger. *Haare, Menschen-haar;* Du. *Hair;* Fr. *Cheve
It. *Capelli umani;* Sp. *Cabellos;* Lat. *Capilli*).

HAIR OF BEASTS (Ger. *Haare, Huhaare;* Du. *Hair;* Fr. *Poil;* It. and Sp. *P
Lat. *Pelles*). "Human hair makes a very considerable article in comme
especially since the mode of peruques has obtained. Hair of the growth
the northern countries, as England, &c., is valued much beyond that of
more southern ones, as Italy, Spain, the southern parts of France, &c. G
hair is well fed, and neither too coarse nor too slender; the bigness rende
it less susceptible of the artificial curl, and disposing it rather to frizzle;
the smallness making its curl of too short duration. Its length shoulc
about 25 inches; the more it falls short of this, the less value it bears.
(*Ency. Brit.*) The hair of horses is extensively used in the manufacture of cl

saddles, &c.; while the hair or wool of beavers, hares, rabbits, &c. is exten-
used in the manufacture of hats, &c.

IR-POWDER (Ger. *Puder;* Fr. *Poudre à poudrer;* It. *Polvere di cipri;*
olvos de peluca*), is used as an ornament for the hair, and generally made
starch pulverised, and sometimes perfumed. A tax of 1*l.* 3*s.* 6*d.* a year is
pon all persons who wear hair-powder. Different statutes prohibit the
of hair-powder with starch or alabaster. And hair-powder makers are
ited having alabaster in their custody.

MS (Ger. *Schinken;* Du. *Hammen;* Fr. *Jambons;* It. *Prosciutti;* Sp. *Jamo-
us. Okorokü*), the thighs of the hog salted and dried. Yorkshire, Hampshire,
ire, and Cumberland, in England, and Dumfries and Galloway in Scotland,
e counties most famous for producing fine hams. Those of Ireland are
ratively coarse and without flavour.—(See BACON.) The hams of Portugal
'estphalia are exquisitely flavoured, and are frequently imported into Great
.

MBURGH, a free Hanseatic city, on the north bank of the river Elbe,
78 miles from its mouth, in lat. 53° 33′ N., lon. 9° 58¼′ W. Population
120,000. Hamburgh is the greatest commercial city of Germany, and,
s, of the Continent. It owes this distinction principally to its ad-
e situation; the Elbe, and the canals which join it, giving it the command
ast internal navigation. It communicates by a canal with the Trave, and,
uently, with Lubeck and the Baltic; avoiding by this means the lengthened
angerous navigation by the Sound. Vessels drawing 14 feet water come
he town at all times; and vessels drawing 18 feet may come safely up with
'ing tides. The largest vessels sometimes load from and unload into lighters
haven. Its trade embraces every article that Germany either sells to or buys
reigners. The exports principally consist of linens, grain of all sorts, wool
ollen cloths, leather, flax, glass, iron, copper, smalts, rags, staves, wooden
and toys, Rhenish wines, &c. Most sorts of Baltic articles, such as
lax, iron, pitch and tar, wax, &c., may generally be bought as cheap at
rgh, allowing for the difference of freight, as in the ports whence they
riginally brought. The imports consist principally of sugar; coffee, which
avourite article for speculative purchases; cotton wool, stuffs, and yarn;
), hides, indigo, wine, brandy, rum, dyewoods, tea, pepper, &c. Being
t from many different places, there is a great variety of quality in the grain
at Hamburgh; but most of the wheat is good red. Some of the barley is
od, and fit for malting. The oats are feed of various qualities.—(See CORN
.)

y. — Accounts are kept at Hamburgh in *marks*, divided into 16 sols or schillings
d the schilling into 12 pfenings lubs.
unts are also kept, particularly in exchanges, in pounds, schillings, and pence
. The pound consisting of 2½ rixdollars, 3¼ thalers, 7½ marcs, 20 schillings
, and 240 grotes Flemish.
moneys in circulation at Hamburgh are divided into *banco* and *current money.*
ner consists of the sums inscribed in the books of the Bank opposite to the
f those who have deposited specie or bullion in the Bank. *Banco* is intrinsi-
rth about 23 per cent. more than *currency*, but the *agio* is constantly varying.
account of the Bank of Hamburgh, see BANKS (FOREIGN).
e coins in circulation at Hamburgh, the rixdollar banco and the rixdollar
are the most common. The weight of the former is not uniform; but
ly estimates it, at a medium, at 391¾ Eng. grains pure silver, = 4s. 6¾d.
rrent rixdollar = 318·3 grains = 3s. 8½d. very nearly. The Hamburgh gold
9s. 4d.
ig the mean value of the rixdollar banco at 54⅔d. sterling, it follows, that 1l.
= 13 marcs, 2⅔ schillings banco, or 1l. sterling = 35s. 1d. Flemish banco. No
r of exchange can, however, be established between London and Hamburgh,
int of the fluctuation of banco. 1l. sterling = 16 marcs 2 schillings Hamburgh
, or 1 marc current = 14⅜d. sterling. — (*Kelly's Cambist, Hamburgh*)

ts and Measures. — The commercial weights are,

2 Loths = 1 Ounce.	8 Lispounds = 1 Centner.
16 Ounces = 1 Pound.	2½ Centners = 1 Shippound.
14 Pounds = 1 Lispound.	

Iamburgh pounds = 106·8 lbs. avoirdupois = 129·8 lbs. Troy = 48·43 kilo-

grammes = 98 lbs. of Amsterdam. A stone of flax is 20 lbs. A stone of wo
feathers is 10 lbs.

In estimating the carriage of goods, the shippound is reckoned at 380 lbs.

The measures for liquids are,

2 Oessels	=	1 Quartier.	5 Eimers	= {	1 Ahm or
2 Quartiers	=	1 Kanen.			4 Ankers.
2 Kanens	=	1 Stubgen.	6 Ahms or }	=	1 Fuder.
2 Stubgens	=	1 Viertel.	24 Ankers }		
4 Viertels	=	1 Eimer.			

The ahm is equal to $38\frac{1}{4}$ and the fuder to $229\frac{1}{2}$ English wine gallons.

A fass of wine = 4 oxhoft = 6 tierces. The oxhoft or hogshead is of variou
mensions. 1 oxhoft French wine = 62 to 64 stubgens, an oxhoft of brandy
stubgens. A pipe of Spanish wine = 96 to 100 stubgens. A ton of beer is 48
gens. A pipe of oil is 820 lbs. nett. Whale oil is sold per barrel of 6 steck
32 Eng. wine gallons.

The dry measures are,

4 Spints	=	1 Himtems.	10 Scheffels	=	1 Wisp.
2 Himtems	=	1 Fass.	2 Wisps	=	1 Last.
3 Fass	=	1 Scheffel.	$1\frac{1}{2}$ Last	=	1 Stock.

The last = $11\frac{1}{3}$ Winchester quarters. A keel of coals yields from 8 to 9 lasts.

The Hamburgh foot = 11·289 English inches. The Rhineland foot, used by
gineers and land-surveyors, = 12·36 inches. The Brabant ell, most commonly
in the measurement of piece goods, = 27·585 inches.

A ton in the lading of a ship is generally reckoned at 40 cubic feet. Of things
are sold by number, a gross thousand = 1,200; a gross hundred = 120; a ring
a common or small thousand = 1,000; a schock = 60; a steige = 20; a gross
dozen.

All merchandise imported or exported by sea, except such as is mentioned hereafter, pays a duty
per cent. currency, ad valorem in banco, which must be paid before the landing of the same. Flour p
addition, an excise duty of 1 marc 8 schillings currency per 100 lbs. when imported; but no other ar
subject to it, except what is paid by the consumer himself. If goods arrive here for immediate re-e
ation, they may be bonded on arrival, and pay no duty. Free of all import duty are corn, books, linen
tin, copper, and coined silver and gold: free of duty, on exportation, are all Hamburgh manufa
goods. The Stade duty levied by the Hanoverian government on merchandise coming or going pay
trifling for most articles — for some, more heavy. The stamp duty on bills and policies is very incor
able. Brokerage on all articles, with a few exceptions, is only paid by the seller, and varies; bu
generally it is five sixths per cent. currency, on the value in currency.

Merchants as well as brokers are prohibited either to allow or to take a higher rate of brokerag
that stipulated in the tariff annexed to law. An abstract of the present tariff of brokerage on the pri
articles of importation is subjoined: —

" Brokerage is exclusively paid by the seller, and amounts to —

" Five sixths per cent. on cotton, cotton twist, cocoa, cochineal, copper, hides, indigo, manufa
goods, nankeens, sugar, and tea *.

" One per cent. on annotto, camphire, cinnamon, cardamons*, cassia*, cloves*, drugs not denomin
deer-skins, dyewoods, ginger*, jalap*, mace*, nutmegs*, pepper, pimento, potashes, Peruvian bark
citron bark, rice*, saltpetre, sarsaparilla*, shellac*, tamarinds*, tobacco in leaves* and tobacco sto
the growth of the United States of America, whale oil*, vinelloes*.

" N. B. — Tobacco stems* of all other origin, segars, and other manufactured tobacco, pay 2 per
all other leaf and roll tobacco*, $1\frac{1}{4}$ per cent.

" One and a half per cent. on wine, brandy, rum, and arrack, if sold in parcels amounting t
marcs banco and upwards.

" Two per cent. on ditto, for sales of and under 3,000 marcs banco.

" In auction, the selling broker is entitled to $1\frac{1}{2}$ per cent. and the purchasing broker to 2 per cent
out regard to the amount."

All articles marked (*) pay the brokerage before-mentioned, if the quantity sold amounts to 60C
banco, or higher; for smaller lots of less than 600 marcs banco, and down to 150 marcs banco, the-
age is paid, with the addition of one half, and under 150 marcs banco, the double is allowed. All
merchandise pays $1\frac{1}{4}$ per cent. at least for sales not exceeding 150 marcs banco.

It is, however, to be observed, that all augmentations in proportion to the amount sold, are on
understood for sales by private contract, and not for those by auction; and even not for such privat
where a broker has made the purchase of a larger quantity of goods above the said amount of 60C
banco, and has afterwards divided it into smaller lots.

All other charges — as lighterage, landing, housing, weighing, delivering, warehouse rent, ins
against fire, &c. — are very moderate.

All merchandise is either sold on 2 or 3 months' credit; or, with a discount of 1 to $1\frac{1}{4}$ per-cent. fo
money: even then no calculation can be made on receiving the money before 8 or 14 days a
delivery. The commission charged on purchase or sale is $2\frac{1}{4}$ per cent.; for guaranty of debt, $1\frac{1}{4}$ p
if sold at 2 or 3 months' credit; and $\frac{1}{2}$ per cent. if sold for ready money, unless the consigner wishes
the risk upon himself.

Conditions of Sale. — Imports. — Coffee is sold per pound in schill. banco, discount 1 per cent
weight is $\frac{1}{2}$ per cent. Tare is as follows: viz. on casks, real weight: on bags of 130 lbs. or less
above 130 lbs. and not above 180 lbs., 3 lbs.; above 180 lbs. and not exceeding 200 lbs., 4 lbs. On
bales of about 300 lbs., $14\frac{1}{2}$ lbs.; if 600 lbs., 30 lbs. On Bourbon single bales, 2 lbs.; on double, 4 lbs

Cotton is sold per lb. in groats Flemish; discount, 1 per cent.; good weight, 1 per cent.; tare o
West Indian and North American, 4 per cent.; on square bales, 6 per cent.; on Bombay and Sura
8 per cent.; on Bourbon bales and Manilla serons, 6 per cent.; on Caraccas and Guiana small
10 per cent. For the regulation of the Stade duty, all packages should be called bags or bales in
of lading.

East India piece goods are sold per piece, in marcs banco; discount, 1 per cent. For saving in th
duty, if more than thirty pieces are in a bale, the number of pieces should not be mentioned in th
lading, but only the number of bales.

›ur is sold per 100 lbs. in marcs currency, uncertain agio; discount, 1 per cent.; good weight, 1 per ; tare, 20 lbs. per barrel.
stic is sold per 100 lbs. in marcs currency; agio, 20 per cent.; discount, 1 per cent.; good weight, 1 ent.; and frequently an allowance in weight is made, if the wood is not very solid.
digo is sold per lb. in schill. Flemish; discount, 1 per cent.; good weight, ½ per cent.; tare, if in s upwards of 120 lbs., 22 lbs.; in half serons less than 120 lbs., 20 lbs.; in chests, real tare.
gwood is sold like fustic.
pper is sold per lb. in groats Flemish; discount, 1 per cent.; good weight, ½ per cent.; tare, if in bales of 300 lbs., 3 lbs.; in double bales, 6 lbs.
ercitron bark is sold per 100 lbs. in marcs currency; agio, 20 per cent.; discount, 2 per cent.; good ht, 1 per cent. To determine the tare, the American tare is reduced to Hamburgh weight.
e is sold per 100 lbs. in marcs currency; agio, 20 per cent.; discount, 1 per cent.; good weight, cent.; tare real; and super-tare for tierces, 4 lbs.; for half tierces, 2 lbs.
m is sold per 30 quarts in rixdoll. currency, agio uncertain.
ar, raw and clayed, is sold per lb. in Flemish groats, with a rebate of 8⅓ per cent.; discount, cent., and sometimes 1½ per cent.; Brazil or Havannah chest, good weight, ¾ per cent.; real tare; tare, 10 lbs. for Brazil, and 5 lbs. for Havannah sugar, per chest. Muscovados in casks, good weight, cent.; tare, if the casks weigh upwards of 1,000 lbs., 18 per cent.; if less, 20 per cent. Clayed sugars, weight, 1 per cent.; tare, 16 per cent. East India sugars, in bags, good weight, ¾ per cent.; tare for , 4 to 5 lbs.; for brown, 6 to 7 lbs.
, per lb. in schill. currency, agio uncertain; discount, 1 per cent; good weight, ½ per cent. Tare hea, in chests of 400 lbs., 70 lbs.; of 150 to 180 lbs., 45 lbs. All black tea, 28 lbs. tare; green, 24 lbs. he regulation of the Stade duty, the nett weight should likewise be mentioned in the bill of lading.
acco. — Leaf tobacco is sold per lb. in schillings currency, agio uncertain; discount, 1½ per cent.; weight, 1 per cent.; tare per cask, 80 lbs. Brazil leaf in serons; tare, 5 per cent. In rolls; canister, kets of about 100 lbs.; good weight, 1 lb. per basket; tare, 14 lbs. if the basket is packed up in linen, 2 lbs. if without linen. Porto Rico rolls, good weight, 1 per cent.; no tare, as the rolls are weighed emselves. Brazil rolls, in serons of 400 to 600 lbs., are sold per lb., in schillings banco; good weight, cent.; tare, 8 lbs. per seron. Tobacco stems, per 100 lbs. in marcs currency, agio uncertain; dis-, 1½ per cent.; good weight, 1 per cent.; tare, if in casks, real weight; if packed up with cords, per cent. according to the thickness of the rope. As there is a great difference in the Stade duty e different sorts of tobacco, it is necessary that, on shipping leaf tobacco, there should be inserted in ll of lading, *Leaf Tobacco*, and the nett weight. With tobacco in rolls, only the number of packages ning roll tobacco and the nett weight, without mentioning the number of rolls, should appear in the lading.

ie ships arriving at Hamburgh in the undermentioned years, have been as follows: —

From the	1827.	1828.	1829.	1830.
East Indies	9	12	8	13
Brazil	83	71	85	82
West Indies	90	115	84	102
United States	40	42	40	23
Mediterranean	46	62	63	61
Spain	21	15	20	20
Portugal	30	18	16	28
France	62	86	61	65
Great Britain	570	529	587	710
Netherlands	346	342	395	375
Baltic	281	292	338	443
Totals	1,578	1,584	1,697	1,922

ORTS. — *Linen Trade.* — Linens are one of the most important articles of export from Hamburgh. are generally sold by the piece; but there are great differences in the dimensions of pieces of differ-nominations. The following table is, therefore, of importance, as it exhibits the various description ns usually met with at Hamburgh, with the length and breadth of the different pieces. It also heir cost on board in sterling, in October, 1830.

Descriptions.	Lgth.	Wdth	Sold.	Cost on Board, in Sterling.							
	Yds.	Yds.		s.	d.		s.	d.		s.	d.
illas royales	35	15/16	per piece.	17	11	to	30	7	to	45	9
wn Silesias	35	15/16	ditto.	14	11	—	18	4	—	22	11
annias	7	15/16	ditto.	3	10	—	7	7	—	9	11
)	7	9/8	ditto.	6	10	—	12	2	—	15	8
las	67½	15/16	ditto.	36	8	—	45	9	—	54	11
s à la morlaix	67½	15/16	ditto.	38	1	—	61	2	—	76	2
dos	43	9/8	ditto.	21	4	—	30	7	—	36	8
e sheetings	50	5/4	ditto.	50	4	—	59	6	—	68	10
lawns	8⅛	15/16	ditto.	8	5	—	18	4	—	27	6
, fig. and worked lawns	8⅛	15/16	ditto.	9	2	—	12	2	—	13	9
ias	21½	7/8	ditto.	10	8	—	13	9	—	15	4
ks, No. 2.	17½	3/4	ditto.	6	3	—	6	10	—	7	7
ed and checked books	43	3/4	per 3 pieces.	13	9	—	16	9	—	18	4
ia rolls	35	8/4	per piece.	8	9	—	15	4	—	16	9
n for coarse bags	35	19/16	ditto.	8	5	—	9	2	—	13	10
burgs	-	-	per 100 dble. ells	32	1	—	76	2	—	85	5
lenburgs	-	-	ditto.	61	2	—	73	4	—	76	2
ia sheeting	36	5/4	per piece.	33	7	—	36	8	—	39	10
ia sailcloth	36	7/8	ditto.	42	8	—	48	10	—	61	2
nsduck	36	3/4	ditto.	20	7	—	27	6	—	30	7

The Platillas and Britannias come principally from Silesia; the Creas from Lusatia, &c. Osnabu made of flaxen, and Teklenburgs of hempen, yarn. Linens are sold with a discount of 1 per cent.

Glass (window) is sold per chest, in marcs currency, agio uncertain; other glass-ware per piece, or hundred, in schillings or marcs currency, with uncertain agio; discount, 1 per cent.

Hares' Wool is sold per 2 lbs. in marcs currency, agio uncertain; discount, 1 per cent.

Hare-skins (German, grey) are sold per 100 pieces, in rixdoll. banco. Russian, grey, per 104 pi rixdoll. banco. White, in marcs currency, agio uncertain; discount, 1 per cent.

Iron is sold per shippound at 280 lbs. in marcs currency, agio uncertain; discount, 1 per cent.

Copper is sold per shippound of 280 lbs. in rixdollars banco; discount, 1 per cent.

The exchange business done at Hamburgh is very great; for besides the business of the place, the merchants in the inland towns have their bills negotiated there.

We subjoin an account of the quantities of some of the principal articles imp into Hamburgh, during each of the four years ending with 30th of September, 1

COFFEE.

Import.	Casks.	Bags.	Mll.lbs.		Mll.lbs.		Mll.lbs.	
1830	8,783	220,332	abt. 34¼	Stock 1. Jan. 24	1. Oct. 21		Of the import this year (1830)	
1829	11,306	199,272	33¼	1.	27	1.	30	nished 11 mll. lbs., St. Thomas an
1828	13,519	246,163	39¼	1.	24	1.	30	4¾ mll. lbs., Domingo 6¾ mll. lb
1827	11,962	248,863	40	1.	13	1.	22	transatlantic ports 3 mll. lbs., Euro

SUGAR.

Import.	Hhds.Musc.	Hhds.refin.	Bxs.Hav.	Tcs.	Chs.Braz.	Bgs.East Ind.	Mll.lbs.		Mll.
1830	1,744	20,681	51,276	1,683	28,545	61,376	abt. 81¼	Stock 1. Jan.	
1829	637	12,997	36,335	1,047	27,561	25,600	62¼	1.	36
1828	3,242	15,603	75,516	4,317	24,347	31,793	79¾	1.	15
1827	1,335	14,797	48,725	1,376	28,979	21,888	70¼	1.	8

The direct supply from Cuba was 49,786 bxs., Bahia 19,027 chs., Rio 4,233 chs., Pernambuco 2,547 ch India 3¾ mll. lbs.

COTTON.

	Import 1830.	Stock 1. Jan.1830.	Stock 1.Oct.1830.	Import 1829.	Stock 1. Jan.1829.	Stoc
United States,	3,662 bales	5,000 bales	1,775 bales	12,760 bales	3,300 bales	7,
Brazil,	3,765	605	930	3,126	780	1,
West India,	5,643	1,835	1,420	4,670	920	1,
East India,	3,027	4,110	690	11,143	4,600	4,
Egyptian,	—	860	815	404	340	
	16,097 bales	24,410 bales	5,630 bales	32,103 bales	9,940 bales	16,

HIDES.

Import.	Pcs.		Pcs.		Pcs.		
1830	77,571	Stock 1. Jan.	10,500	Stock 1. Oct.	18,400	consisting of 8,600 pcs. Buenos-Ayres	
1829	38,808	1.	7,450	1.	4,600	Rio Grande, 1,300 Chili.	

INDIGO.

Import.	Chs.	Ser.		Chs.	Ser.		Chs.	Ser.	
1830	3,971	527	Stock 1. Jan.	1,200	455	Stock 1. Oct.	730	510	Annual average consu
1829	4,119	230	1.	1,015	505	1.	1,340	485	1820 to 1824, 3,368 chs.
1828	4,463	314	1.	745	605	1.	610	565	1825 to 1829, 5,025 ch. 36

TOBACCO.

Import, 2,538 hhds. (of which but 900 hhds. direct from America) 1,175 ser. Domingo, 14,635 bale Porto Rico, 2,420 can. Varinas, 372 bales 5,130 rolls Brazil.

RICE.

Import,	1830	10,148 blls.	3,107 bags,	Stock 1. Jan.	5,800 blls.	3,400 bags,	1. Oct. 5,700 blls.	3,20
	1829	12,314	4,444	1.	8,000	3,300	1. 9,450	4,70
	1828	16,712	1,665	1.	1,800	3.300	1. 8,000	3,70

RUM.

Import, 1830, 3,483 punchs.; 1829, 4,184 punchs.; 1828, 3,481 punchs.; 1827, 2,843 punchs. Present punchs. Jamaica, 1,200 punchs. West India.

PEPPER.

Import, 1830, abt. 680,600 lbs.; 1829, 800,000 lbs.; 1828, 1,100,000 lbs.; 1827, 1,200,000 lbs.; 1826,

PIMENTO.

Import 1830: 7,416 bags; 1829, 9,231 bags; 1828, 4,721 bags; 1827, 9,278 bags; present Stock abt. 320

TEAS.

Import reduced to ¼ bxs.; 1830, 8,799 ¼ bxs.; 1829, 15,177 ¼ bxs.; 1828, 9,123 ¼ bxs.; 1827, 26,424 ¼ first hand. Stock 4,774 ¼ bxs. Black, 4,221 ¼ bxs. Green; of which 7,129 ¼ bxs. of last year's in

We have compiled this article principally from the annual statement (for last year) of Ber Gossler, and Co., and from communications from other merchants.

HANSEATIC LEAGUE, an association of the principal cities in the nor of Germany, Prussia, &c., for the better carrying on of commerce, and for th mutual safety and defence. This confederacy, so celebrated in the early histo of modern Europe, contributed in no ordinary degree to introduce the blessir of civilisation and good government into the North. The extension and protecti of commerce was, however, its main object; and hence a short account of it m not be deemed misplaced in a work of this description.

Origin and Progress of the Hanseatic League. — Hamburgh, founded by Charlemag in the ninth, and Lubeck, founded about the middle of the twelfth century, were earliest members of the League. The distance between them not being very consid able, and being alike interested in the repression of those disorders to which most parts Europe, and particularly the coasts of the Baltic, were a prey in the twelfth, thirteenth, a fourteenth centuries, they early formed an intimate political union, partly in the view

.ining a safe intercourse by land with each other, and partly for the protection of
tion from the attacks of the pirates with which every sea was, at that time, in-
There is no very distinct evidence as to the period when this alliance was con-
ated ; some ascribe its origin to the year 1169, others to the year 1200, and others
year 1241. But the most probable opinion seems to be, that it would grow up
v degrees, and be perfected according as the advantage derivable from it became
bvious. Such was the origin of the Hanseatic League, so called from the old
nic word *hansa*, signifying an association or confederacy.
m of Bremen, who flourished in the eleventh century, is the earliest writer who
en any information with respect to the commerce of the countries lying round
ltic. And from the errors into which he has fallen in describing the northern
stern shores of that sea, it is evident they had been very little frequented and not
nown in his time. But from the beginning of the twelfth century, the progress
merce and navigation in the North was exceedingly rapid. The countries which
along the bottom of the Baltic, from Holstein to Russia, and which had been
ed by barbarous tribes of Sclavonic origin, were then subjugated by the kings of
ark, the dukes of Saxony, and other princes. The greater part of the inhabiting exterminated, their place was filled by German colonists, who founded the
of Stralsund, Rostock, Wismar, &c. Prussia and Poland were afterwards sub-
d by the Christian princes, and the knights of the Teutonic order. So that, in a
atively short period, the foundations of civilisation and the arts were laid in
es whose barbarism had ever remained impervious to the Roman power.
cities that were established along the coast of the Baltic, and even in the interior
countries bordering upon it, eagerly joined the Hanseatic confederation. They
debted to the merchants of Lubeck for supplies of the commodities produced in
vilised countries, and they looked up to them for protection against the bar-
by whom they were surrounded. The progress of the League was in conse-
singularly rapid. Previously to the end of the thirteenth century it embraced
onsiderable city in all those vast countries extending from Livonia to Holland ;
s a match for the most powerful monarchs.
Hanseatic confederacy was at its highest degree of power and splendour during
teenth and fifteenth centuries. It then comprised from sixty to eighty cities,
were distributed into four classes or circles. Lubeck was at the head of the first
nd had under it Hamburgh, Bremen, Rostock, Wismar, &c. Cologne was at
d of the second circle, with twenty-nine towns under it. Brunswick was at the
the third circle, consisting of thirteen towns. Dantzic was at the head of the
circle, having under it eight towns in its vicinity, besides several that were more
The supreme authority of the League was vested in the deputies of the dif-
owns assembled in congress. In it they discussed all their measures ; decided
e sum that each city should contribute to the common fund ; and upon the
s that arose between the confederacy and other powers, as well as those that
ly arose between the different members of the confederacy. The place for the
of congress was not fixed, but it was most frequently held at Lubeck, which
sidered as the capital of the League, and there its archives were kept. Some-
owever, congresses were held at Hamburgh, Cologne, and other towns. They
e every three years, or oftener if occasion required. The letters of convocation
d the principal subjects which would most probably be brought under discussion.
e might be chosen for a deputy ; and the congress consisted not of merchants
t also of clergymen, lawyers, artists, &c. When the deliberations were con-
the decrees were formally communicated to the magistrates of the cities at the
each circle, by whom they were subsequently communicated to those below
und the most vigorous measures were adopted for carrying them into effect.
the burgomasters of Lubeck presided at the meetings of congress ; and during
ss the magistrates of that city had the sole, or at all events the principal, direction
fairs of the League.
es the towns already mentioned, there were others that were denominated con-
d cities, or allies. The latter neither contributed to the common fund of the
nor sent deputies to congress ; even the members were not all on the same
n respect of privileges : and the internal commotions by which it was frequently
, partly originating in this cause, and partly in the discordant interests and
ng pretensions of the different cities, materially impaired the power of the
acy. But in despite of these disadvantages, the League succeeded for a
ed period, not only in controlling its own refractory members, but in making
pected and dreaded by others. It produced able generals and admirals,
oliticians, and some of the most enterprising, successful, and wealthy merchants
rn times.

As the power of the confederated cities was increased and consolidated, they bec
more ambitious.   Instead of limiting their efforts to the mere advancement of
merce and their own protection, they endeavoured to acquire the monopoly of the
of the North, and to exercise the same sort of dominion over the Baltic that the V
tians exercised over the Adriatic.   For this purpose they succeeded in obtaining, p
in return for loans of money, and partly by force, various privileges and immun
from the northern sovereigns, which secured to them almost the whole foreign
merce of Scandinavia, Denmark, Prussia, Poland, Russia, &c.   They exclus
carried on the herring fishery of the Sound, at the same time that they endeavoure
obstruct and hinder the navigation of foreign vessels in the Baltic.   It should, how
be observed that the immunities they enjoyed were mostly indispensable to the sec
of their commerce, in consequence of the barbarism that then prevailed ; and not
standing their attempts at monopoly, there cannot be the shadow of a doubt tha
progress of civilisation in the North was prodigiously accelerated by the influence
ascendancy of the Hanseatic cities.   They repressed piracy by sea and robbery by
which must have broken out again had their power been overthrown before civilis
was fully established ; they accustomed the inhabitants to the principles, and set b
them the example, of good government and subordination ; they introduced am
them conveniences and enjoyments unknown by their ancestors, or despised by them
inspired them with a taste for literature and science ; they did for the people roun
Baltic what the Phœnicians had done in remoter ages for those round the Me
ranean, and deserve, equally with them, to be placed in the first rank amongs
benefactors of mankind.

"In order," as has been justly observed, "to accomplish their purpose of rende
the Baltic a large field for the prosecution of commercial and industrious pursu
it was necessary to instruct men, still barbarous, in the rudiments of industry, a
familiarise them in the principles of civilisation.   These great principles were la
the confederation, and at the close of the fifteenth century the Baltic and the n
bouring seas had, by its means, become frequented routes of communication bet
the North and the South.   The people of the former were enabled to follow the
gress of the latter in knowledge and industry.   The forests of Sweden, Poland
gave place to corn, hemp and flax ; the mines were wrought, and in return the pro
and manufactures of the South were imported.   Towns and villages were erect
Scandinavia, where huts only were before seen : the skins of the bear and the wolf
exchanged for woollens, linens, and silks : learning was introduced ; and printin
hardly invented before it was practised in Denmark, Sweden, &c."

The kings of Denmark, Sweden, and Norway, were frequently engaged in host
with the Hanse towns.   They regarded, and it must be admitted not without
good reason, the privileges acquired by the League in their kingdoms, as so
usurpations.   But their efforts to abolish these privileges served, for more tha
centuries, only to augment and extend them.

"On the part of the League there was union, subordination, and money; wh
the half-savage Scandinavian monarchies were full of divisions, factions, and trou
revolution was immediately followed by revolution, and feudal anarchy was at its h
There was another circumstance, not less important, in favour of the Hanseatic
The popular governments established amongst them possessed the respect and confi
of the inhabitants, and were able to direct the public energies for the good of the
The astonishing prosperity of the confederated cities was not wholly the effect of
merce.   To the undisciplined armies of the princes of the North — armies com
of vassals without attachment to their lords — the cities opposed, besides the in
nobles, whose services they liberally rewarded, citizens accustomed to danger, a
solved to defend their liberties and property.   Their military operations were con
and directed by a council, composed of men of tried talents and experience, de
to their country, responsible to their fellow-citizens, and enjoying their confidenc
was chiefly, however, on their marine forces that the cities depended.   They emp
their ships indifferently in war or commerce, so that their naval armaments were
out at comparatively small expense.   Exclusive, too, of these favourable circumst
the fortifications of the principal cities were looked upon as impregnable ; and a
commerce supplied them abundantly with all sorts of provisions, it need not exc
astonishment that Lubeck alone was able to carry on wars with the surrou
monarchs, and to terminate them with honour and advantage ; and still less th
League should long have enjoyed a decided preponderance in the North." — (L'.
vérifier les Dates, 3ᵐᵉ partie, viii. p. 204.)

The extirpation of piracy was one of the objects which had originally led
formation of the League, and which it never ceased to prosecute.   Owing, howe
the barbarism then so universally prevalent, and the countenance openly given by

ces and nobles to those engaged in this infamous profession, it was not possible
ly to root it out. But the vigorous efforts of the League to abate the nuisance,
gh not entirely successful, served to render the navigation of the North Sea and the
ic comparatively secure, and were of signal advantage to commerce. Nor was this
nly mode in which the power of the confederacy was directly employed to promote
ommon interests of mankind. Their exertions to protect shipwrecked mariners
the atrocities to which they had been subject, and to procure the restitution of
wrecked property to its legitimate owners*, though, most probably, like their
tions to repress piracy, a consequence of selfish considerations, were in no ordinary
ee meritorious; and contributed not less to the advancement of civilisation than to
ecurity of navigation.

ctories belonging to the League. — In order to facilitate and extend their commercial
actions, the League established various factories in foreign countries; the principal
hich were at Novogorod in Russia, London, Bruges in the Netherlands, and
en in Norway.

ovogorod, situated at the confluence of the Volkof with the Imler Lake, was, for a
hened period, the most renowned emporium in the north-eastern parts of Europe.
e beginning of the eleventh century, the inhabitants obtained considerable privi-
that laid the foundation of their liberty and prosperity. Their sovereigns were
st subordinate to the Grand Dukes or Czars of Russia; but as the city and the
guous territory increased in population and wealth, they gradually usurped an
st absolute independency. The power of these sovereigns over their subjects,
s, at the same time, to have been exceedingly limited; and in effect, Novogorod
t rather to be considered as a republic under the jurisdiction of an elective magis-
than as a state subject to a regular line of hereditary monarchs, possessed of
sive prerogatives. During the twelfth, thirteenth, and fourteenth centuries, No-
rod formed the grand *entrepôt* between the countries to the east of Poland and the
eatic cities. Its fairs were frequented by an immense concourse of people from
e surrounding countries, as well as by numbers of merchants from the Hanse
s, who engrossed the greater part of its foreign commerce, and who furnished its
ets with the manufactures and products of distant countries. Novogorod is said
ve contained, during its most flourishing period, towards the middle of the fifteenth
ry, upwards of 400,000 souls. This, however, is most probably an exaggeration.
ts dominions were then very extensive; and its wealth and power seemed so great
vell established, and the city itself so impregnable, as to give rise to a proverb,
can resist the Gods and great Novogorod? *Quis contra Deos et magnam Novogor-*
? — (*Coxe's Travels in the North of Europe*, vol. ii. p. 80.)

t its power and prosperity were far from being so firmly established as its eulogists,
lose who had only visited its fairs, appear to have supposed. In the latter part of
tteenth century, Ivan Vassilievitch, czar of Russia, having secured his domi-
against the inroads of the Tartars, and extended his empire by the conquest of
of the neighbouring principalities, asserted his right to the principality of Novo-
, and supported his pretensions by a formidable army. Had the inhabitants been
ted by the spirit of unanimity and patriotism, they might have defied his efforts;
heir dissensions facilitated their conquest, and rendered them an easy prey.
g entered the city at the head of his troops, Ivan received from the citizens the
r of their liberties, which they either wanted courage or inclination to defend, and
d off an enormous bell to Moscow, that has been long regarded with a sort of
titious veneration as the palladium of the city. But notwithstanding the des-
t to which Novogorod was subject, during the reigns of Ivan and his successors,
inued for a considerable period to be the largest as well as most commercial city
Russian empire. The famous Richard Chancellour, who passed through
gorod in 1554, in his way from the court of the czar, says, that "next unto
w, the city of Novogorod is reputed the chiefest of Russia; for although it be
iestie inferior to it, yet in greatness it goeth beyond it. It is the chiefest and
st mart town of all Muscovy; and albeit the emperor's seat is not there, but at
w, yet the commodiousness of the river falling into the Gulph of Finland, where-
s well frequented by merchants, makes it more famous than Moscow itself."
the scourge of the destroyer soon after fell on this celebrated city. Ivan IV.
discovered, in 1570, a correspondence between some of the principal citizens
e king of Poland, relative to a surrender of the city into his hands, punished
n the most inhuman manner. The slaughter by which the blood-thirsty bar-
sought to satisfy his revenge was alike extensive and undiscriminating. The

eries of resolutions were unanimously agreed to by the merchants frequenting the port of Wisby,
he principal emporiums of the League, in 1287, providing for the restoration of shipwrecked
y to its original owners, and threatening to eject from the "*consodalitate mercatorum*" any city
not act conformably to the regulations laid down.

crime of a few citizens was made a pretext for the massacre of 25,000 or 30,00
Novogorod never recovered from this dreadful blow. It still, however, continued
be a place of considerable trade, until the foundation of Petersburgh, which immediate
became the seat of that commerce that had formerly centred at Novogorod. The
gradation of this ill-fated city is now complete. It is at present an inconsidera
place, with a population of about 7,000 or 8,000; and is remarkable only for its histo
and antiquities.

The merchants of the Hanse towns, or Hansards, as they were then commo
termed, were established in London at a very early period, and their factory here w
of considerable magnitude and importance. They enjoyed various privileges a
immunities; they were permitted to govern themselves by their own laws and regu
tions; the custody of one of the gates of the city (Bishopsgate) was committed
their care; and the duties on various sorts of imported commodities were considera
reduced in their favour. These privileges necessarily excited the ill-will and animosity
the English merchants. The Hansards were every now and then accused of acting wi
bad faith; of introducing commodities as their own that were really the produce
others, in order to enable them to evade the duties with which they ought to have be
charged; of capriciously extending the list of towns belonging to the association; a
obstructing the commerce of the English in the Baltic. Efforts were continua
making to bring these disputes to a termination; but as they really grew out of t
privileges granted to and claimed by the Hansards, this was found to be impossib
The latter were exposed to many indignities; and their factory, which was situated
Thames Street, was not unfrequently attacked. The League exerted themselves vig
ously in defence of their privileges; and having declared war against England, th
succeeded in excluding our vessels from the Baltic, and acted with such energy, th
Edward IV. was glad to come to an accommodation with them, on terms which we
any thing but honourable to the English. In the treaty for this purpose, negotiated
1474, the privileges of the merchants of the Hanse towns were renewed, and the ki
assigned to them, in absolute property, a large space of ground, with the buildings up
it, in Thames Street, denominated the Steel Yard, whence the Hanse merchants ha
been commonly denominated the Association of the Steel Yard; the property of th
establishments at Boston and Lynn was also secured to them; the king engaged
allow no stranger to participate in their privileges; one of the articles bore that
Hanse merchants should be no longer subject to the judges of the English Admira
Court, but that a particular tribunal should be formed for the easy and speedy sett
ment of all disputes that might arise between them and the English; and it was furth
agreed that the particular privileges awarded to the Hanse merchants should be p
lished as often as the latter judged proper, in all the sea-port towns of England, a
such Englishmen as infringed upon them should be punished. In return for th
concessions, the English acquired the liberty of freely trading in the Baltic, a
especially in the port of Dantzic and in Prussia. In 1498, all direct commerce w
the Netherlands being suspended, the trade fell into the hands of the Hanse mercha
whose commerce was in consequence very greatly extended. But, according as
spirit of commercial enterprise awakened in the nation, and as the benefits result
from the prosecution of foreign trade came to be better known, the privileges of
Hanse merchants became more and more obnoxious. They were in conseque
considerably modified in the reigns of Henry VII. and Henry VIII., and were
length wholly abolished in 1597. — (*Anderson's Hist. Com.* Anno 1474, &c.)

The different individuals belonging to the factory in London, as well as those
longing to the other factories of the League, lived together at a common table,
were enjoined to observe the strictest celibacy. The direction of the factory in Lon
was intrusted to an alderman, two assessors, and nine councillors. The latter v
sent by the cities forming the different classes into which the League was divided.
business of these functionaries was to devise means for extending and securing
privileges and commerce of the association; to watch over the operations of
merchants; and to adjust any disputes that might arise amongst the members of
confederacy, or between them and the English. The League endeavoured at all ti
to promote, as much as possible, the employment of their own ships. In pursuanc
this object they went so far, in 1447, as to forbid the importation of English merc
dise into the confederated cities, except by their own vessels. But a regulation of
sort could not be carried into full effect; and was enforced or modified accordin
circumstances were favourable or adverse to the pretensions of the League. Its
existence was, however, an insult to the English nation; and the irritation produce
the occasional attempts to act upon it, contributed materially to the subversion of
privileges the Hanseatic merchants had acquired amongst us.

By means of their factory at Bergen, and of the privileges which had been e

d to or usurped by them, the League enjoyed for a lengthened period the mono-
f the commerce of Norway.

the principal factory of the League was at Bruges in the Netherlands. Bruges
e, at a very early period, one of the first commercial cities of Europe, and the
of the most extensive trade carried on to the north of Italy. The art of navi-
in the thirteenth and fourteenth centuries was so imperfect, that a voyage from
o the Baltic and back again could not be performed in a single season; and
for the sake of their mutual convenience, the Italian and Hanseatic merchants
ined on establishing a magazine or store-house of their respective products in
ntermediate situation. Bruges was fixed upon for this purpose; a distinction
it seems to have owed as much to the freedom enjoyed by the inhabitants, and
erality of the government of the Low Countries, as to the conveniency of its
n. In consequence of this preference, Bruges speedily rose to the very highest
mong commercial cities, and became a place of vast wealth. It was at once
e for English wool, for the woollen and linen manufactures of the Nether-
for the timber, hemp and flax, pitch and tar, tallow, corn, fish, ashes, &c. of the
; and for the spices and Indian commodities, as well as their domestic manufac-
mported by the Italian merchants. The fairs of Bruges were the best frequented
in Europe. Ludovico Guicciardini mentions, in his description of the Low
ies, that in the year 1318 no fewer than five Venetian galleasses, vessels of very
rable burthen, arrived in Bruges in order to dispose of their cargoes at the fair.
anseatic merchants were the principal purchasers of Indian commodities; they
d of them in the ports of the Baltic, or carried them up the great rivers into the
f Germany. The vivifying effects of this commerce were every where felt; the
intercourse opened between the nations in the north and south of Europe
hem sensible of their mutual wants, and gave a wonderful stimulus to the spirit
stry. This was particularly the case with regard to the Netherlands. Manu-
s of wool and flax had been established in that country as early as the age of
nagne; and the resort of foreigners to their markets, and the great additional
t was thus opened for their manufactures, made them be carried on with a
and success that had been hitherto unknown. These circumstances, combined
e free spirit of their institutions, and the moderation of the government, so
promoted every elegant and useful art, that the Netherlands early became the
vilised, best cultivated, richest, and most populous country of Europe.

ne of the Hanseatic League. — From the middle of the fifteenth century, the
f the confederacy, though still very formidable, began to decline. This was
ng to any misconduct on the part of its leaders, but to the progress of that
ment it had done so much to promote. The superiority enjoyed by the League
as much from the anarchy, confusion, and barbarism, that prevailed throughout
doms of the North, as from the good government and order that distinguished
ns. But a distinction of this sort could not be permanent. The civilisation
ad been at first confined to the cities, gradually spread from them, as from so
ntres, over the contiguous country. Feudal anarchy was every where super-
a system of subordination; arts and industry were diffused and cultivated;
authority of government was at length firmly established. This change not
dered the princes, over whom the League had so frequently triumphed, superior
power; but the inhabitants of the countries amongst which the confederated
re scattered, having learned to entertain a just sense of the advantages derivable
nmerce and navigation, could not brook the superiority of the association, or
see its members in possession of immunities of which they were deprived: and
ion to these circumstances, which must speedily have occasioned the dissolution
eague, the interests of the different cities of which it consisted became daily
d more opposed to each other. Lubeck, Hamburgh, Bremen, and the towns in
inity, were latterly the only ones that had any interest in its maintenance. The
Zealand and Holland joined it, chiefly because they would otherwise have been
from the commerce of the Baltic; and those of Prussia, Poland, and Russia,
ame, because, had they not belonged to it, they would have been shut out from
course with strangers. When, however, the Zealanders and Hollanders became
ly powerful at sea to be able to vindicate their right to the free navigation of
ic by force of arms, they immediately seceded from the League; and no sooner
ships of the Dutch, the English, &c. begun to trade directly with the Polish
ssian Hanse Towns, than these nations also embraced the first opportunity of
ing from it. The fall of this great confederacy was really, therefore, a con-
of the improved state of society, and of the development of the commercial
the different nations of Europe. It was most serviceable so long as those for
merchants acted as factors and carriers were too barbarous, too much occu-

pied with other matters, or destitute of the necessary capital and skill, to act in
capacities for themselves.   When they were in a situation to do this, the functio
the Hanseatic merchants ceased as a matter of course; their confederacy fell to pi
and at the middle of the seventh century the cities of Lubeck, Hamburgh, and Bre
were all that continued to acknowledge the authority of the League.   Even to thi
they preserve the shadow of its power; being acknowledged in the act for the
blishment of the Germanic confederation, signed at Vienna, the 8th of June, 181
free Hanseatic cities.   (From an article in No. 13. of the *Foreign Quarterly Re*
contributed by the author of this work.)

HARBOURS and HAVENS.   The anchorage, &c. of ships was regu
by several statutes.   But most of these regulations have been repealed, mod
or re-enacted, by the 54 Geo. 3. c. 149.

This act authorises the Admiralty to provide for the moorings of his Majesty's ships; and prohibi
private ship from fastening thereto.   It further authorises the Admiralty to prohibit the *breaming*
ship or vessel at any place or places on shore they may think fit; and to point out the places
private ships shall deposit the gunpowder they may have on board exceeding 5 lbs. — (§ 6.)   It pro
the use of any fire on board any ship or vessel, that is being breamed, in any port, harbour, or b
between the hours of 11 in the evening and 5 in the morning, from the 1st of October to the 31st of I
inclusive; and between the hours of 11 in the evening and 4 in the morning, from the 1st of April
30th of September inclusive: and it prohibits the melting or boiling of any pitch, tar, tallow, &c.,
250 yards of any of his Majesty's ships, or of his Majesty's dock-yards.   By another section, the keep
guns shotted, and the firing of the same in any port, is prohibited under a penalty of 5s. for ever
kept shotted, and 10s. for every gun discharged. — (§ 9.)   The sweeping or creeping for anchors
within the distance of 150 yards of any of his Majesty's ships of war, or of his Majesty's moorii
prohibited under a penalty of 10l. for every offence. — (§ 10.)   The loading and unloading of ballast
regulated by this statute; but for the provisions with respect to it, see BALLAST.

HARDWARE (Ger. *Kurze waaren*; Du. *Yzerkramery*; Da. *Isenkramv*
Sw. *Järnkram*; Fr. *Clinquaillerie, Quincaillerie*; It. *Chincaglio*; Sp. *Quinquill*
Port. *Quincalharia*; Rus. *Mjelotzchnue towarii*), includes every kind of goods
nufactured from metals, comprising iron, brass, steel, and copper articles of a
scriptions. Birmingham and Sheffield are the principal seats of the British hard
manufactures; and from these, immense quantities of knives, razors, scissars
and plated ware, fire-arms, &c. are supplied, as well for exportation to most
of the world, as for home consumption.

The hardware manufacture is one of the most important carried on in Great Bri
and from the abundance of iron, tin, and copper ores in this country, and our inex
tible coal mines, it is one which seems to be established on a very secure founda
The late Mr. Stevenson, in his elaborate and excellent article on the statistics of
land, in the Edinburgh Encyclopædia, published in 1815, estimated the value of a
articles made of iron at 10,000,000l., and the persons employed in the trade at 200
Mr. Stevenson estimated the value of all the articles made of brass and copp
3,000,000l., and the persons employed at 50,000 : and he further estimated the va
the steel, plating, and hardware manufactures, including the toy trade, at 4,000,000l
the persons employed at 70,000.   So that, assuming these estimates to be nearly co
the total value of the goods produced from different sorts of metals in England
Wales, in 1815, must have amounted to the sum of 17,000,000l., and the person
ployed to 320,000.

There is reason to believe that this estimate, in so far, at least, as respects the va
the manufacture, was at the time rather too high; but at this moment it is most pro
within the mark.   There has been a very great augmentation of the quantity of ba
pig iron produced within the last fifteen years; and the rapid increase of Birmin
and Sheffield, as well as of the smaller seats of the hardware manufacture, shows
has been increased in a corresponding proportion.   We have been assured, by those
acquainted with most departments of the trade, that if to the iron and other hare
manufactures of England be added those of Scotland, their total aggregate value c
now be reckoned at less than 17,500,000l. a year, affording *direct* employment,
various departments of the trade, for at least 360,000 persons.

Account of the real or declared Value of the different Articles of Hardware exported from Great I
to Foreign Countries, during the Year ended 5th of January, 1830.

							£	s.
Brass and copper manufactures	.	.	.	.			810,641	2
Hardwares and cutlery	-	.	.	.	.		1,389,514	19
Iron and steel, wrought and unwrought	-	.	.	.	.		1,155,176	15
Mathematical and optical instruments	-	.	.	.	.		21,612	5
Plate, plated ware, jewellery, and watches	.	-	.	.			177,242	1
Tin and pewter wares (exclusive of unwrought tin)	.	.	.	.			235,021	19
				Total	.		£3,789,209	1

he exports of the same articles during the year ended 5th of January, 1820, were as follows: —

	£	s.	d.
Brass and copper manufactures	653,859	13	5
Hardwares and cutlery	1,149,510	19	7
Iron and steel, wrought and unwrought, (mathematical instruments not specified)	924,448	8	1
Tin and pewter wares (exclusive of unwrought tin)	187,811	10	7
Total	£2,915,630	11	8
Increase of the exports of 1829 over those of 1819	£873,578	10	0

he United States is by far the most important market for hardware and cutlery. Of the total value ,514*l.*) exported in 1829, they took no less than 669,871*l.* The East Indies, West Indies, British North rican colonies, and the United States, are the principal markets for iron and steel.

HARPONEER, the man that throws the harpoon in fishing for whales. By eo. 3. c. 92. § 34., no harponeer, line-manager, or boat-steerer, belonging to any or vessel, fitted out for the Greenland or southern whale fisheries, shall be essed from the said service; but shall be privileged from being impressed so as he shall belong to, and be employed on board, any ship or vessel whatever he fisheries aforesaid.

AT, HATS (Ger. *Hüte;* Du. *Hoeden;* Fr. *Chapeaux;* It. *Cappelli;* Sp. *Som-s;* Rus. *Schlopü*), a well known covering for the head. Hats are made of us sorts of materials. The finest and most valuable are made of the fur of eaver or castor; but the entire hat is now rarely made of so costly a material, eaver fur being only used to cover the outside. *Plated* hats are only slightly red with fur, and sometimes with silk. *Felt* hats are the coarsest species, and nade wholly of wool. Hats are made for women's wear of the above materials, so of chips, straw, or cane. Coarse or felt hats are principally made at New-e-under-Lyne; considerable quantities being exported to the West Indies, sive of those consumed at home. Felt hats are also made at Rudgely, &c.; other sorts of hats at Stockport, Oldham, and Manchester. The finest and hats are, however, manufactured in London, where the business has attained e greatest perfection. The manufacture of hats was first noticed as relating ngland in the fourteenth century, in reference to the exportation of rabbit-to the Netherlands. About a century afterwards (1463), the importation of was prohibited. A duty of 10*s.* 6*d.* a hat was substituted for this absolute bition in 1816, and is still continued.

e hat manufacture is one of very considerable importance and value. The male ation of Great Britain may be supposed to be at present 8,000,000; and taking the ge annual expenditure of each individual on hats at about 5*s.*, which is believed to ry near the mark, we have 2,000,000*l.* as the total value of the hats produced each for home consumption, exclusive of women's hats, which may be estimated at 00*l.* additional.

unt of the real or declared Value of the Hats exported from Great Britain to Foreign Parts during the Year ended with 5th of January, 1830.

	£.	s.	d.
Beaver and felt hats	188,902	6	5
Of all other sorts	16,065	19	9
Total	£204,968	6	2

e West Indies and Brazil are the principal markets to which we send beaver and ts, and next to them the British North American colonies.

AVANNAH, OR HAVANA, situated on the north coast of the noble island ba, of which it is the capital, in lat. 23° 9' N., lon. 82° 16' W. The popu-, exclusive of troops and strangers (which may amount to 25,000), is pro-not far short of 100,000. In 1817, the resident population amounted to 3; viz. 37,885 whites, 9,010 free coloured, 12,361 free blacks, 2,543 coloured , and 21,799 black slaves. The port of Havannah is the finest in the West , or, perhaps, in the world. The entrance is narrow, but the water is deep, ithin it expands into a magnificent bay, capable of accommodating 1,000 hips; vessels of the greatest draught of water coming close to the quays. The es along the entrance to, and on the west side of the bay. The suburb is on the opposite side. The Morro and Punta castles, the former on the and the latter on the west side of the entrance of the harbour, are strongly

fortified, as is the entire city; the citadel is also a place of great strength; a
fortifications have been erected on such of the neighbouring heights as comma
the city or port.   The arsenal and dock-yard lie toward the western angle of t
bay, to the south of the city.   In the city the streets are narrow, inconvenie
and filthy; but in the suburbs, now as extensive as the city, they are wider a
better laid out.   Latterly, too, the police and cleanliness of all parts of the to
have been materially improved.

From its position, which commands both inlets to the Gulf of Mexico, its gr
strength, and excellent harbour, Havannah is, in a political point of view, by far
most important maritime station in the West Indies.   As a commercial city it a
ranks in the first class; being, in this respect, second to none in the New World, N
York only excepted.   For a long period, Havannah engrossed almost the whole forei
trade of Cuba; but, since the relaxation of the old colonial system, various ports, su
for instance, as Matanzas *, that were hardly known thirty years ago, have beco
places of great commercial importance.   The rapid extension of the commerce
Havannah is, therefore, entirely to be ascribed to the freedom it now enjoys, and to
great increase of wealth and population in the city, and generally throughout
island.

The advance of Cuba, during the last half century, has been very great; thou
not more, perhaps, than might have been expected, from its natural advantages, at le
since its ports were freely opened to foreigners, in 1809.   It is at once the largest a
the best situated of the West India islands.   It is about 605 miles in length; but
breadth from north to south no where exceeds 117 miles, and is in many places mu
less.   Its total area, exclusive of that of the numerous keys and islands attached to
is about 31,500 square miles.   The climate is, generally speaking, delightful;
refreshing sea breezes preventing the heat from ever becoming excessive, and fitting
for the growth of a vast variety of products.   Hurricanes, which are so destructive
Jamaica and the Caribbee islands, are here comparatively rare; and, when they do occ
far less violent.   The soil is of very various qualities: there is a considerable extent
swampy marshes and rocks unfit for any sort of cultivation; but there is much soil t
is very superior, and capable of affording the most luxuriant crops of sugar, cof
maize, &c.   The ancient policy, now fortunately abandoned, of restricting the tr
of the island to two or three ports, caused all the population to congregate in th
vicinity, neglecting the rest of the island, and allowing some of the finest land and l
situations for planting to remain unoccupied.   But since a different and more libe
policy has been followed, population has begun to extend itself over all the most fer
districts, wherever they are to be met with.   The first regular census of Cuba was ta
in 1775, when the whole resident population amounted to 170,370 souls.   Since
period the increase has been as follows: — 1791, 272,140; 1817, 551,998; and 18
704,867; exclusive of strangers.   We subjoin a

Classification of the Population of Cuba according to the Censuses of 1775 and 182

				1775.			1827.	
			Male.	Female.	Total.	Male.	Female.	Tota
Whites	.	.	54,555	10,864	95,419	168,653	142,598	311,0
Free Mulattoes	.	.	10,021	9,006	19,027	28,058	29,456	57,5
Free Blacks	.	.	5,959	5,629	11,558	23,904	25,079	48,9
Slaves	.	.	28,774	15,562	44,336	183,290	103,652	286,9
		Total	99,309	71,061	170,370	403,905	300,582	704,4

We readily discover, from this table, that, in the term of fifty-two years, from 1775 to 1827, the incr
of the different classes of the population has been as follows: —

The white male population increased from 54,555 to 168,653, or 209 per cent.
The white female   —   —   40,864 — 142,308, — 248   —
The free mulatto male   —   —   10,021 — 28,058, — 180   —
The free mulatto female   —   —   9,006 — 29,456, — 227   —
The free black male   —   —   5,959 — 23,904, — 301   —
The free black female   —   —   5,629 — 25,076, — 345   —
The slave, (black and }   —   28,774 — 183,290, — 537   —
    mulatto) male   }
The slave (black and }   —   15,562 — 103,652, — 556   —
    mulatto) female   }

A very large part of the rapid increase of the black population is to be ascribe
the continuance of the slave trade; which, unfortunately for the real interests of
island, has been prosecuted of late years to an extent, and with a vigour, unknow

* In 1827, Matanzas had a population of 15,000 souls.   During the same year its imports were v
at 1,387,500 dollars, and its exports at 1,717,347 dollars; and 251 vessels entered, and 251 cleared
its port.   We have looked into our latest Gazetteers, but to no purpose, for any notice of this
Those, indeed, who know that the best of these publications sets down the population of Havannah
25,000, will probably think that this was very unnecessary labour.

rmer period. From 1811 to 1825, there were imported into the island 185,000
n slaves; of which number 116,000 are said to have been entered at the
nah Custom-house, between 1811 and 1820! Since 1825, the imports of slaves
derstood to have increased. And, as it is believed that their numbers were
ated in the census of 1827, perhaps the entire population of the island is, at pre-
ittle, if at all, under 1,000,000. The planters of Cuba derive considerable
ace from free labourers, mostly of an Indian mixed breed, who work for moderate
They are not much employed in the fields, but in other branches of labour;
rticularly in bringing the sugar from the interior to the shipping ports.

rticles principally exported from Cuba are, sugar of the finest quality, coffee, tobacco, bees' wax,
nolasses, &c. Of these, the first is decidedly the most important. The following statements show
hishing increase that has taken place in the exportation of this staple article : —

Account of the Exportation of Sugar from Havannah, from 1760 to 1827.

From 1760 to 1767	13,000	boxes, at 400 lbs.	=	5,200,000 lbs.
1786 — 1790	68,150	—	—	27,260,000 —
1790 — 1800	110,091	—	—	44,036,400 —
1800 — 1810	177,998	—	—	71,199,200 —
1810 — 1820	207,696	—	—	83,078,400 —
1820 — 1825	250,384	—	—	100,153,600 —
In 1826	271,013¾	—	—	108,405,500 —
1827	264,954¼	—	—	105,981,800 —

avannah having ceased to be the only port for the exportation of sugar, as it was in former times,
advert to the trade of the other ports, to obtain a correct account of the whole exports of sugar.
owing are the Custom-house returns for 1827 : —

Exports of sugar from Havannah	.	.	.	.	99,354,137 lbs.
Santiago	.	.	.	.	6,032,763 —
Nuevitas	.	.	.	.	375,275 —
Matanzas	.	.	.	.	30,364,844 —
Trinidad	.	.	.	.	10,361,337 —
Holguin	.	.	.		351,450 —
Jagua	.	.	.	.	12,500 —
Manzanilla	.	.	.	.	120,800 —
			Total	.	146,973,106 —

the Custom-house reports are founded upon the assumption, that
sugar weighs but 15 *arrobas* (375 lbs.), while its true weight is,
ucting the tare, at least 16 *arrobas* (400 lbs.), they add to their
ne sixteenth, (it should be one fifteenth,) viz. : —   .   .   9,135,818 —

Making a total of   .   .   156,158,924 lbs.

, however, only the Custom-house report. Much sugar is said to be smuggled out of the country,
uch we have no data to calculate; we have seen it estimated at one fourth part more, making
e exports nearly 200,000,000 of pounds.
) sugar, coffee is the most valuable production of Cuba. Its cultivation has increased with unted rapidity. In 1800, there were but 80 plantations in the island; in 1817, there were 779; and
here were no fewer than 2,067, of at least 40,000 trees each! In 1804, the exportation from
h was 1,250,000 lbs.; in 1809, it amounted to 8,000,000 lbs.; from 1815 to 1820, it averaged
18,186,200 lbs.; and, in 1827, it amounted to 35,837,175 lbs.! The exports from the other ports
eased with equal rapidity. They amounted, in 1827, to 14,202,406 lbs.; making the total export-
that year 50,039,581 lbs. This, however, is only the Custom-house account; and to it, as in the
agar, considerable additions must be made, to get the true export. In the Custom-house estimates
s are supposed uniformly to weigh 150 lbs., though it is well known that they frequently exceed
. It must, however, be observed, that the low prices that have been obtained for coffee during
ew years have caused a diminution of its growth in Cuba, as well as in most places where it is
ly cultivated; and the exports have in consequence fallen off considerably since 1827; but it is
ed that this check will be permanent.
o differs much in quality; but the cigars of Cuba are esteemed the finest in the world. — (See
)   It is impossible to ascertain either the production or exportation of this commodity. Govern-
eavour to monopolise the trade, but immense quantities are smuggled. The monopoly has,
been highly injurious; and it seems to be the general opinion that, were it abolished, the culture
of tobacco would speedily become of paramount importance.
)0 hhds. of molasses exported in 1827, 38,000 were from Havannah, and 23,000 from Matanzas.
d honey of excellent quality are largely produced in Cuba, and form considerable articles of

ncipal imports consist of corn and grain of all sorts, chiefly from the United States and Spain;
rdware, and earthenware goods, from England; linens from Hamburgh, Bremen, the Nether-
and, &c.; gold and silver from Mexico and South America; indigo and cochineal from ditto;
spirits from France and Spain; lumber, dried fish, and salt provisions, from the United States,
every article, in short, that an opulent community, in a tropical climate, without manufactures,

int of the Value of the Trade between Cuba and other Countries in 1828, as ascertained by the
Customs Returns.

	Imports.	Exports.		Imports.	Exports.
	Dollars.	Dollars.		Dollars.	Dollars.
- - -	6,556,810	3,026,245	Russia - -	85,613	719,582
States -	6,599,096	3,176,964	Portugal - -	159,444	11,548
tic Towns -	1,747,398	1,927,561	Denmark - -	69,335	27,953
1 - -	1,770,085	1,611,820	Sweden - -	21,079	35,985
- - -	1,635,855	754,812	Foreign commerce in		
ands - -	335,507	881,727	ships of Cuba -	431,553	711,479
- - -	123,140	225,740			

The articles of all sorts, and their value, imported into Cuba in 1827, were as follow : —

	Imported.		Re-exported.		Remair
	Dol.	Cts.	Dol.	Cts.	Dol.
Liquors and wines - - - -	1,219,580	0	54,986	5½	1,164,59
Smoked and dried meat - - - -	957,377	1	- -	-	957,37
Spices - - - - - -	94,626	1	- -	-	94,62
Fruit - - - - - -	171,048	0	171,048	0	
Corn, and grain of all kinds - - -	2,921,939	2	81,330	4½	2,840,60
Fat, tallow, grease, &c. - - - -	1,043,223	3½	- -	-	1,043,22
Salt fish - - - - - -	308,817	4	- -	-	308,81
Live stock, vegetables, tea, &c. - - -	342,748	0½	- -	-	342,74
Cotton goods - - - - - -	1,387,686	3½	239,148	4½	1,148,53
Woollens - - - - - -	402,080	0	35,536	1	366,54
Linens - - - - - -	2,508,625	7½	420,185	2½	2,088,44
Furs - - - - - -	451,948	5	36,494	3½	415,45
Silk goods - - - - -	666,860	6½	91,315	4	575,54
Sarsaparilla - - - - -	19,296	3	11,332	0½	7,96
Lumber - - - - - -	543,919	6	- -	-	543,91
Indigo and cochineal - - -	588,778	2	836,056	7	
Gold and silver coin, and bullion - - -	1,158,452	2	1,203,211	2	
Dye-woods - - - - - -	52,977	4	99,369	2½	
Iron, and iron manufactures - - -	605,334	7½	57,486	2½	547,84
Linseed oil, white lead, glassware, earthenware, soap, drugs, paper, stationery, paints, perfumery, gunpowder, ready made clothing, bags, bagging, ropes, tobacco, jewellery, &c. &c. - - - - -	1,907,534	5	224,086	3½	1,683,4
Totals	17,352,855	0	3,561,587	3¾	14,129,6

The total value of all sorts of produce imported into Cuba in 1828, is stated at 19,534,922 dollars that of the exports, 13,114,365 do. Of this trade Havannah participated to the extent of 15,807,395 of imports, and of 9,202,485 do. of exports.

An Account of the Number of Foreign Vessels that entered and cleared from Havannah in 1827, fying the Countries to which such Vessels belonged, and their Tonnage.

	Entered.		Cleared.	
	Number of Vessels.	Tonnage.	Number of Vessels.	Tonna
United States of America - -	785	125,087½	667	103,39
Spain - - - -	57	5,412	80	7,09
England - - - -	71	12,337½	53	8,11
France - - - -	48	9,813½	38	7,47
Denmark - - - -	21	3,458	17	3,01
Bremen - - - -	14	2,769½	13	2,58
Netherlands - - - -	24	4,284	19	3,47
Hamburgh - - - -	12	2,021	13	2,25
Sardinia - - - -	8	1,386½	7	1,31
Tuscany - - - -	6	1,322½	5	1,16
Sweden - - - -	3	442½	2	36
Russia - - - -	2	476	2	47
Sicily - - - -	1	247		
Prussia - - - -	1	224		
	1,053	169,281¼	616	140,7

In 1828, 1,889 foreign vessels, of the burthen of 277,066 tons, entered; and 1,686, of the bur 229,830 tons, cleared from the different ports of Cuba. Of these, 1,100 entered and 987 cleare Havannah; and we believe that the commerce of this great emporium has been considerably aug since.

A customs duty is charged on most articles exported and imported. In 1828, the duties on impo duced 4,194,495 dollars, being equal to an *ad valorem* duty of 18¾ per cent. on the imports of th The duties on exports during the same year produced 1,114,641 dollars, equal to an *ad valorem* 8½ per cent. on their amount. According to the tariff, the duties on most imported articles are either 24 or 30 per cent. *ad valorem*; but all Spanish products imported from the peninsula in bottoms (except flour, which pays 1½ dollar per barrel,) pay only 6 per cent. duty; and when imp foreign bottoms, they pay 12 per cent. less than the duties on corresponding foreign articles. Th ducts make about a third part of the imports. Until lately, the export duty on sugar was much cor of, being so high as 2¾ dollars a box; but in the course of last year it has been reduced to little mo 1 dollar — a reduction which will be of material consequence to the planters. Merchandise that h paid the duties on importation, pays nothing on exportation.

The following is an extract from the Custom-house regulations: — Every master of a vessel is to have, on his arrival, ready for delivery to the boarding officers of the revenue, two manifests, cor a detailed statement of his cargo; and in the act of handing them over, is to write thereon the ho he so delivers them, taking care that they be countersigned by the boarding officers. Within 1 from that time he may make any alteration he pleases in the said manifests, or deliver in new o rected. After the expiration of these 12 hours, no alteration will be permitted. Goods not ma will be confiscated without remedy; and if their value should not exceed 1,000 dollars, masters o will be liable to pay a penalty of double the amount of such non-manifested goods: if they do exc sum, and belong to the master, or come consigned to him, his vessel, freight, and other emolume be forfeited to the revenue. Goods over-manifested will pay duties as if they were on board. G manifested, but claimed in time by a consignee, will be delivered up to the latter; but the master case, will be subject to a fine equal in amount to that of such goods. Gold and silver, not manif either captain or consignee, are liable to a duty of 4 per cent. Goods falling short of the quanti fested, when landed, and not being included in any invoice of a consignee, will render the mast to a penalty of 200 dollars for each package so falling short. Every consignee is obliged to pr invoice or note of goods, within 48 hours after the arrival of a vessel; if not, such goods are 2 per cent. extra duty. The same is the case, if such note do not contain a statement of the n pieces, contents, quantity, weight, and measure. All goods imported in vessels exceeding

en, except perishable provisions, bulky articles, and liquors, may be put in deposit for an indefinite
paying 1 per cent. inward and 1 per cent. outward duty on the value, each year. When entered
ome consumption, they are liable to the corresponding duty. If sold in deposit, the exporter pays
utward duty.

anage Duties. — Spanish vessels, 5 reals per ton. Other nations, 20 reals per ton : in case of arrival
eparture in ballast, none ; arriving in distress, 4 reals per ton, but full duties if the cargo be landed
ken in.

arf Duties. — Spanish vessels, 6 reals per day. Other nations, 10 reals per day for each 100 tons of
register measurement.

nies. — One dollar = 8 reals plate = 20 reals vellon. One doubloon = 17 dollars. The merchants
n 444 dollars = 100*l.*, or 1 dollar = 4*s.* 6*d.* very nearly. There is an export duty of 1 per cent. on
and 2 per cent. on silver.

ights and Measures. — One quintal = 100 lbs., or 4 arrobas of 25 lbs. ; 100 lbs. Spanish = 101¾ lbs.
sh, or 46 kilogrammes. 108 varas = 100 yards ; 140 varas = 100 French ells or aunes ; 81 varas =
rabant ells ; 108 varas = 160 Hamburgh ells. 1 fanega = 3 bushels nearly, or 200 lbs. Spanish. An
a of wine or spirits = 4 1-10th English wine gallons nearly.

Spanish authorities disgraced themselves by the countenance which they gave to piratical banditti
nfested many of the ports of Cuba during the late contest between Spain and her revolted colonies,
n pretence of cruising against the Mexicans and Colombians, committed all sorts of enormities.
ommerce of the United States suffered so much from their attacks, that they were obliged to send a
derable squadron to attack the banditti in their strong holds, and to obtain that redress they had in
ought from the government of the island ; but we are not sure that the nuisance is as yet entirely
d.

ompiling this article we have consulted Humboldt's standard work, the *Essai Politique sur l'Isle
ba ;* the excellent abstract of the *Cuadro Estadístico de Cuba*, published at Havannah in 1829, in
merican Quarterly Review for June, 1830; the *Bulletin des Sciences Géographiques*, tom. xxii p. 333. ;
tt's Notes on Mexico, pp. 279—298. (Eng. ed.) ; and private communications from intelligent British
ants established at Havannah.

AVRE, or HAVRE DE GRACE, a commercial sea-port town of France,
e mouth of the Seine, on the English Channel, in lat. 49° 29′ N., lon.
W. Population 21,000. Havre is strongly fortified. The harbour, which
long pier, is capable of containing 600 or 700 ships, and has water sufficient
mit merchant ships of the largest class. Havre is the principal sea-port of
, most of the colonial and other foreign products destined for the consump-
of that city being imported into it. It has also a considerable trade of its
The principal articles of export are silk and woollen stuffs, lace, gloves,
ets, perfumery, Burgundy, Champagne, and other wines, brandy, books, &c.
les colonial products and spices, the imports principally consist of cotton,
o, tobacco, hides, dye-woods, iron, tin, dried fish, &c. Grain and flour are
times imported and sometimes exported.

nies, weights, and *measures*, are the same as those of the rest of France. — (See
EAUX.)

estimated that the entire value of the different articles imported into Havre, in 1829, amounted to
,000 francs, or about 10,000,000*l.* sterling. Of this sum, the cotton imported was estimated at
000 fr. ; the sugars of the French colonies at 44,000,000 fr., and those of foreign countries at
00 fr.; coffee 14,000,000 fr.; indigo 2,000,000 fr.; tobacco 4,000,000 fr., &c. The customs duties at Havre
the same year amounted to 25,876,535 fr., being nearly 11 per cent. upon the estimated value of the
s. There entered the port in the same year 1,481 French and other ships, coming from foreign
ies and the colonies of France, and 2,995 coasting vessels, including those navigating the river :
ps entered *en relâche* and in ballast. — (*Bulletin des Sciences Géographiques*, xvi. p. 390., and xxiii.
We subjoin

count of the Number and Destination of the French Ships clearing out from Havre in the Six
ending with 1829; and of the Number of the French Ships entering Havre during the same
d, specifying the Countries whence they came.

	French Ships despatched from Havre during the following Years.							French Ships entered Havre during the following Years.					
Destination.	1829.	1828.	1827.	1826.	1825.	1824.	From	1829.	1828.	1827.	1826.	1825.	1824.
tinique	42	49	49	48	52	48	Martinique	66	66	53	53	51	55
daloupe	78	64	55	62	54	65	Guadaloupe	86	82	78	77	58	82
rbon	8	6	5	11	5	4	Bourbon	7	5	4	6	6	8
gal	7	5	5	7	9	9	Senegal	3	11	9	6	6	9
nne	1	—	1	1	1	1	Cayenne	—	1	1	1	3	2
ti	21	18	39	19	34	38	Hayti	22	38	43	45	32	52
il	31	21	26	19	28	26	Brazil	34	33	30	32	38	34
ed States	4	15	14	19	19	13	United States	183	161	215	272	160	191
ico	8	5	11	13	12	3	Mexico	5	6	8	4	6	2
mbia	1	2	3	2	3	2	Colombia	·1	3	3	7	7	4
and Chili	2	2	1	2	3	2	Peru and Chili	1	2	4	3	1-	
annah & St. Jago	8	7	15	10	13	5	Havannah & St. Jago	11	11	13	9	18	13
homas and Fo-							St. Thomas and Fo-						
gn Antilles	5	2	5	4	7	4	reign Antilles	7	10	7	3	4	8
de la Plata	7	6	7	12	18	6	River de la Plata	14	6	1	9	11	9
n Seas	2	4	2	1	—	1	Indian Seas	8	5	1	1	2	1
a	1	2	1	2	—	—	China	2	—	1	1	-	·-
e Fishery	7	5	4	6	5	2	Whale Fishery	6	5	4	6	2	3
	233	213	242	238	263	229		456	445	475	534	405	473

Comparative Table of the Navigation of the Port of Havre during the Years 1829, 1828, 1827, 1826, 1825.

Entered.		1829.		1828.		1827.		1826.		1825.	
		Ships.	Tonnage.	Ships.	Tonnage.	Ships.	Tonnage.	Ships.	Tonnage.	Ships.	Tonnage.
Foreign Navigation out of Europe and in Europe	Foreign	982	186,600	617	120,900	457	98,500	607	126,000	441	79,6
	French	499	105,200	457	92,800	376	82,700	404	82,300	399	79,5
		1,481	291,800	1,074	213,700	833	181,200	1,011	208,300	840	159,1
French Navigation coasting trade comprising that of the River	French	2,995	161,200	2,252	123,100	1,997	106,900	2,371	114,700	2,514	114,8
		4,476	453,000	3,326	336,800	2,830	288,100	3,882	323,000	3,354	274,0
Ships *en rélâche* or in ballast		602	-	640	-	820	-	881	-	866	
Total Ships		5,078	-	3,966	-	3,650	-	4,263	-	4,220	

Sailed.		1829.		1828.		1827.		1826.		1825.	
		Ships.	Tonnage.	Ships.	Tonnage.	Ships.	Tonnage.	Ships.	Tonnage.	Ships.	Tonnage.
Foreign Navigation out of Europe and in Europe	Foreign	970	216,600	309	60,000	175	26,000	196	32,000	228	33,6
	French	344	75,500	296	66,000	371	68,000	281	62,300	213	66,3
		1,314	292,100	605	126,000	546	94,000	577	94,300	541	99,9
French Navigation coasting trade comprising that of the River	French	3,217	168,900	2,146	104,000	1,542	77,000	2,048	110,700	1,982	99,2
		4,531	461,000	2,751	230,000	2,088	171,000	2,525	205,000	2,523	199,1
Ships *en rélâche* or in ballast		503	-	1,020	-	1,320	-	1,683	-	1,634	
Total Ships		5,034	-	3,771	-	3,408	-	4,208	-	4,157	

Trade of France. — We avail ourselves of this opportunity to lay before the reader detailed Statement of the FOREIGN TRADE and NAVIGATION OF FRANCE for 18 since which it has not undergone any material change.

IMPORTS INTO FRANCE FROM ALL COUNTRIES.

Species of Merchandise imported into France.	Number of Articles.	On what the Accounts are founded.	Rates of Valuation according to the Kind of Merchandise.		Quantities of Merchandise imported by both Special and General Commerce.		Value in Francs.		
			Low.	High.	Special.	General.	Customs Duties on the Admission of Merchandise into France	Of both Special and Commerce.	
								Special.	Ge
			Fr. C.	Fr. C.			Francs.	Francs.	F
Silk	10	kilog.	3 0	95 0	670,591	1,427,491	1,099,745	32,307,686	68
Cotton	3	kilog.	1 35	2 50	29,684,345	36,485,080	6,631,354	51,918,941	62
Sugar, raw and clayed	4	kilog.	0 45	0 70	60,317,631	77,956,650	30,160,110	36,963,081	47
Linens	28	kilog.	2 0	160 0	4,448,942	5,297,305	2,985,725	18,162,968	24
Coffee	1	kilog.	1 fr.	19 c.	10,027,597	22,620,904	8,703,335	10,995,525	22
Olive oil for manufactures	1	kilog.	0	70	29,803,557	30,069,746	8,356,864	20,862,490	21
Indigo	1	kilog.	20	50	745,089	994,745	1,044,659	14,881,504	19
Oleaginous fruits	4	kilog.	0 75	0 80	20,691,966	21,060,174	1,138,570	15,519,077	15
Tobacco	1	kilog.	2 fr.	30 c.	3,327,849	6,551,050	51,052	* 7,654,053	15
Wood for building	2	stère.	25 0	30 0	156,995	157,463	} 228,337	12,884,450	13
	1	matrè	0 fr.	50 c.	17,078,546	17,205,534			
	6	piece.	0 10	100 0	21,487	21,820			
Wool	2	kilog.	1 0	5 0	7,256	7,325	} 3,674,183	11,141,447	19
	2	declared value.			11,131,987	12,303,601			
Hides, raw and prepared	12	kilog.	0 75	12 0	4,299,407	5,158,616	} 272,982	8,715,799	16
	2	piece.	0 40	0 75	12,235	12,300			
	4	declared value.			275,155	380,071			
Silks	7	kilog.	64 0	100 0	15,053	83,073	199,645	* 1,750,130	
Copper	11	kilog.	1 0	30 0	4,643,878	4,308,620	163,019	9,520,859	
Precious stones, (diamonds)	4	grain.	0 30	500 0	5,272,966	7,586,467	15,577	8,208,941	
Flax and hemp thread	11	kilog.	1 50	200 0	1,010,815	1,045,648	322,267	7,955,429	
Straw hats	2	piece.	3 0	15 0	656,930	1,077,115	417,117	4,550,373	
Coal	2	kilog.	0 1	0 12	540,448,917	566,277,208	1,917,002	8,098,901	
Lead	3	kilog.	0 25	0 50	13,955,098	15,710,524	826,824	6,277,852	
Iron	13	kilog.	0 5	3 0	16,543,647	22,412,085	2,640,055	4,925,040	
Horses	3	each.	120 0	500 0	15,574	16,926	647,245	3,433,360	

IMPORTS — *continued.*

andise France.	Number of Articles.	On what the Accounts are founded.	Rates of Valuation according to the Kind of Merchandise.		Quantities of Merchandise imported by both Special and General Commerce.		Value in Francs.		
			Low.	High.	Special.	General.	Customs Duties on the Admission of Merchandise into France.	Of both Special and General Commerce.	
								Special.	General.
			Fr. C.	Fr. C.			Francs.	Francs.	Francs.
	4	kilog.	0 20	2 50	514,544	23,801,367	157,146	* 147,707	4,808,718
	3	kilog.	0 10	0 80	6,483,157	6,484,690	633,312	4,279,938	4,284,288
d Pi-	1	kilog.	1 fr. 40 c.		1,882,728	2,915,930	1,317,994	2,635,819	4,082,302
r the	1	kilog.	1	40	2,766,834	2,837,605	1,070,559	3,873,568	8,972,647
	1	kilog.	12	0	205,643	221,577			
	3	piece.	1 35	30 0	9,458	8,463	52,279	3,489,694	3,722,950
d ci-	1	declared value.			870,515	912,413			
	1	kilog.	0 fr. 50 c.		7,112,523	7,231,726	805,857	3,556,261	3,615,863
	3	kilog.	30	0	34,939	119,379	56,827	1,048,170	3,581,370
rains)	4	piece.	0 20	0 30	13,437,217	13,474,073	20,540	3,568,202	3,579,363
	4	kilog.	0 4	0 60	7,181,576	6,925,154	1,032,081	3,715,752	3,486,130
	2	each.	8 0	17 0	209,328	211,157	1,060,523	3,400,608	3,431,700
	1	kilog.	0 fr. 70 c.		4,487,437	4,850,726	703,242	3,141,206	3,395,508
	1	kilog.	8	0	171,467	399,223	102,709	1,371,736	3,193,784
dour	4	litre.	0 6	0 10	10,507,827	35,084,122			
	3	kilog.	0 12	0 0	170,958	574,932	169,379	* 944,178	2,994,147
	1	each.	200 fr. 0 c.		14,358	14,386	789,690	2,871,600	2,877,200
	8	kilog.	7 0	413 0	54,093	119,663	125,755	1,022,841	2,847,037
raw,	1	kilog.	6 fr. 0 c.		167,714	467,327	280,870	1,006,284	2,803,962
	1	kilog.	13	0	191,561	191,109			
	1	declared value.			281,273	280,599	44,150	2,771,566	2,764,925
	4	kilog.	0 fr. 40 c.		6,311,564	6,864,901	685,697	2,524,626	2,745,961
	1	kilog.	0 40	1 35	4,591,969	4,634,966	306,279	2,673,206	2,698,488
	2	kilog.	1 0	4 50	62,018	667,812	110,722	* 231,761	2,629,618
	1	kilog.	3 fr. 0 c.		312,856	823,666	202,086	* 938,568	2,470,998
	1	each.	110 0		21,958	21,958	548,950	2,415,380	2,413,380
ewter	1	kilog.	1 75		1,099,592	1,324,154	68,094	2,136,458	2,494,357
	1	kilog.	0 70		1,655,998	1,656,391	13,011	2,365,711	2,366,273
	1	kilog.	0 90		733,619	2,515,817	708,619	* 660,257	2,264,235
	4	kilog.	0 20	0 35	8,254,193	10,276,001	101,290	1,806,918	2,211,660
	2	kilog.	1 35	1 40	1,251,726	1,257,136	50,484	1,742,608	1,749,735
	2	kilog.	0 60	1 40	873,299	1,248,705	113,881	1,705,477	1,742,277
	1	kilog.	36 fr. 0 c.		31,692	45,685	81,087	1,548,912	1,644,660
for	3	kilog.	0 10	0 17	12,899,039	13,879,254	230,954	1,290,450	1,388,548
	1	kilog.	0 f. 5 c.		26,904,523	26,933,405	29,595	1,345,226	1,346,671
	5	kilog.	10 0	30 0	2,016	26,056			
	6	piece.	22 fr. 0 c.			32,028	8,952	* 26,560	1,344,894
ices	1	kilog.	2 0		146,701	659,049	16,158	* 293,402	1,318,084
	9	kilog.	0 60	32 0	744,391	920,755	181,188	* 782,259	1,273,983
	1	each.	10 fr. 0 c.		126,731	126,738	55,761	1,267,510	1,267,380
	2	declared value.			1,045,293	1,262,900	246,174	1,045,293	1,262,900
stil- seed	3	kilog.	0 40	1 50	814,496	798,103	9,627	1,221,748	1,197,154
ry	2	kilog.	4 50	12 0	160,076	204,456	219,844	951,592	1,168,639
ant.	2	kilog.	7 0	20 0	25,865	65,686	63,636	498,411	1,152,273
	2	declared value.			613,216	1,138,105	53,267	613,216	1,138,105
	2	piece.	3 0	4 0	314,859	352,386	517,006	988,250	1,119,674
	1	stère.	6 f. 0 c.		146,977	147,244			
	1	piece.	0 20		1,173,316	1,173,310	43,677	1,320,307	1,118,126
	3	piece.	2 50	4 0	356,545	376,058	416,068	975,704	1,036,106
es united, and of less value than those above mentioned -							8,590,682	43,014,245	64,441,309
							93,591,369	414,137,001	565,804,228

EXPORTS FROM FRANCE FOR ALL COUNTRIES.

er- ted	Number of Articles.	On what the Accounts are founded.	Rates of Valuation according to the Merchandise.		Quantities of Merchandise exported.		Value in Francs.		
			Low.	High.	Special.	General.	Customs Duties on the Export of Merchandise.	Of both Special and General Commerce.	
								Special.	General.
			Fr. C.	Fr. C.			Francs.	Francs.	Francs.
	12	kilog.	40 0	130 0	964,233	994,958		112,247,016	117,714,671
	10	grain.	0 3	0 30	12,973,081	11,180,572	26,168		
	1	declared value.			941,141	717,521			
rted	6	kilog.	12 0	95 0	33,521	830,316	3,660	* 3,184,495	44,086,597
	14	kilog.	8 0	200 0	1,987,678	1,875,240	2,593	46,026,933	44,021,643
	1	piece.	22 fr. 0 c.		1,906,216	30,976			
nd	15	kilog.	3 0	4378 0	1,354,476	2,007,590	4,530	44,065,873	42,777,679
	1	kilog.	declared value.		853,496	776,228			
	4	litre.	0 20	2 0	103,210,135	103,252,856	312,664	41,510,084	41,639,782
	11	kilog.	7 0	143 0	1,006,969	943,799	1,859	26,927,784	25,705,450

EXPORTS FROM FRANCE FOR ALL COUNTRIES — *continued.*

Species of Merchandise exported from France.	Number of Articles.	On what the Accounts are founded.	Rates of Valuation according to the Merchandise. Low.	High.	Quantities of Merchandise exported. Special.	General.	Value in Francs. Customs Duties on the Export of Merchandise.	Of both Special and General Commerce. Special.
			Fr. C.	Fr. C.			Francs.	Francs.
Brandy - -	1	litre.	0 60	1 50	27,357,412	27,331,984	72,694	22,369,075
Grain - -	18	kilog.	0 6	6 0	58,813,983	73,424,251	123,122	8,674,494
Coffee - -	1	kilog.	1 fr. 20 c.		6,347	7,916,589	8	* 7,616
Cotton - -	4	kilog.	1 80	4 0	22,154	4,841,671	114	* 49,263
Sugar, raw and clayed - -	2	kilog.	0 75	1 10	11,051	9,230,457	16	* 8,685
Hides, raw and prepared -	12	kilog.	0 70	12 0	1,406,684	3,038,024	} 24,477	5,544,926
	2	piece.	0 fr. 70 c.		37,536	29,547		
	16	piece.	0 6	200 0	3,855,003	4,047,325		
	5	kilog.	0 10	1 20	347,328	362,201		
Timber - -	3	métre	0 83	0 85	1,166,817	1,159,902	} 15,927	3,985,399
	3	stère	10 0	60 0	39,658	102,269		
	1	litre.	0 fr. 3 c.		5,722	8,222		
Madder - -	2	kilog.	0 75	1 0	7,758,058	7,612,871	49,471	7,448,991
Leather - -	1	kilog.	24 fr. 0 c.		304,389	277,594	511	7,305,336
Haberdashery -	2	kilog.	6 0	20 0	939,229	886,125	10,698	6,890,936
Wines & liqueurs	2	litre.	1 49	1 50	3,817,619	3,996,911	16,714	5,726,429
Lace and dresses	1	kilog.	20 fr. 0 c.		324,213	261,289	1,091	6,484,260
Gloves - -	1	kilog.	40 0		137,915	127,187	381	5,516,600
Refined sugar -	1	kilog.	1 20		3,789,498	4,114,422	4	4,547,396
Mules and mulets	1	each.	300 0		16,125	16,125	25,705	4,837,500
Volatile oils -	1	kilog.	100 0		38,728	44,702	832	3,872,800
Perfumery -	2	kilog.	0 50	7 30	751,074	560,176	13,833	5,401,197
Hardware -	7	kilog.	1 30	10 0	1,668,542	1,910,736	4,860	3,549,167
Fruits, dried and candied -	2	kilog.	0 75	1 0	4,738,580	4,905,923	12,432	3,704,182
Eggs - -	1	kilog.	0 fr. 80 c.		4,783,856	4,783,762	105,229	3,827,083
Paper - -	5	kilog.	1 0	20 0	1,724,890	1,606,144	16,141	3,960,634
Indigo - -	1	kilog.	20 fr. 50 c.		1,120	173,696	6	* 22,960
Olive oil for table	1	kilog.	2 0		964,390	1,544,187	652	1,928,780
Iron - -	14	kilog.	0 15	3 0	3,230,570	8,640,408	5,494	1,055,626
Clockwork -	1	kilog.	20 0	25 0	170,656	120,131	5,407	4,248,345
Bottles - -	1	litre.	0 fr. 30 c.		8,365,027	8,715,717	} 81,371	3,001,619
	1	kilog.	0 30		1,140,370	1,141,055		
Salt - -	1	kilog.	0 3		96,633,229	97,776,758	10,436	2,898,999
Cochineal -	1	kilog.	30 0		4,546	90,086	25	* 136,380
Different articles produced at Paris -		declared value.			5,692,875	2,608,532	12,793	5,692,875
Porcelain - -	1	kilog.	5 fr. 0 c.		737,425	505,895	7,355	3,687,125
Cacao - -	1	kilog.	1 30		2,434	1,911,117	7	* 3,164
Glass - -	2	kilog.	1 0	2 0	2,370,576	2,165,546	7,650	2,603,660
Toys - -	1	kilog.	70 fr. 0 c.		54,182	33,862	541	3,792,740
Books in French	1	kilog.	5 0		627,363	465,627	6,668	3,136,815
Fruits for distillation, and seed - -	5	kilog.	0 40	2 0	1,534,579	1,558,778	5,494	2,233,968
Plates of metal -	1	kilog.	10 fr. 0 c.		317,076	220,159	9,851	3,170,760
Soap - -	1	kilog.	0 60		2,773,605	3,532,963	171	1,664,164
Butter - -	2	kilog.	1 35	1 50	1,450,443	1,471,777	3,520	1,965,462
Fire-arms -	2	kilog.	15 0	18 0	76,820	124,107	1,868	1,229,886
Cattle - -	1	each.	200 fr. 0 c.		9,330	9,365	10,272	1,866,000
Oleaginous fruits	3	kilog.	0 75	0 80	2,203,384	2,373,167	4,669	1,729,496
Fashions -	1		declared value.		2,299,307	1,842,555	5,983	2,299,307
Prepared cork -	1	kilog.	3 fr. 0 c.		174,581	591,051	414	* 523,743
Horses - -	3	each.	120 0	500 0	4,218	5,468	22,554	1,297,860
Wools - -	3	kilog.	1 0	4 0	161,615	512,257	476	* 321,680
Engravings and lithography -	1		35 fr. 0 c.		52,668	48,153	567	1,843,380
Molasses - -	1	kilog.	0 30		5,730,994	5,601,615	35	1,719,298
Straw hats -	2	piece.	3 50	17 0	179,903	138,161	1,574	2,092,304
Jesuits' bark, &c.	3	kilog.	0 50	8 0	8,793	233,506	23	* 32,746
Meat - -	4	kilog.	0 60	3 0	1,934,620	2,164,776	5,216	1,495,075
Sheep - -	1	cachr.	17 fr. 0 c.		81,763	81,763	22,485	1,389,971
Linseed oil -	1	kilog.	1 0		998,979	1,377,378	2,547	998,979
Gold and silver in leaves, thread, &c.	3	grain.	0 6	3 0	1,810,347	1,430,842	681	2,245,632
Candles - -	1	kilog.	1 fr. 25 c.		1,030,824	1,062,797	384	1,288,530
Cutlery - -	1	kilog.	12 0		101,678	103,799	982	1,220,136
Machinery -	2		declared value.		1,319,303	1,207,810	17,575	1,319,303
Drugs - -	2	kilog.	5 0	10 0	148,795	132,992	2,444	1,339,180
Acids - -	6	kilog.	0 45	3 90	566,477	548,838	11,962	1,164,642
All other articles united -		-	-	-	-	-	292,951	50,488,987
							1,445,437	506,823,737

N. B. By *special* commerce, as distinguished from *general*, is understood all the articles which [...] imports for home consumption, and those which she exports which are the produce of the country [...]

* In the articles marked thus (*) there are slight discrepancies in the accounts, owing to the [...] being obtained from different lines of Custom-houses.

NAVIGATION OF FRANCE WITH ALL COUNTRIES, IN 1827.

Country.	French and Foreign Ships.			Tonnage of Ships.			Crews of Ships.		
	Entered and despatched from French Ports.	Entered.	Despatched.	Entered and despatched from French Ports.	Entered.	Despatched.	Entered and despatched from French Ports.	Entered.	Despatched.
d · {	* 4,172	1,146	3,026	195,189	78,648	116,541	24,570	7,505	17,065
	† 1,895	954	941	120,620	59,472	61,148	17,270	8,351	8,919
States ·	564	348	216	146,139	92,214	53,925	6,731	4,249	2,482
lands ·	775	196	579	77,756	17,067	60,689	3,749	1,223	3,526
ia ·	1,818	1,003	815	74,378	38,313	36,065	10,697	5,840	4,857
ique ·	1,972	1,188	784	95,476	55,373	40,103	14,034	8,576	5,458
a ·	345	162	183	90,113	41,453	48,720	4,983	2,276	2,707
·	62	31	31	13,895	6,429	7,466	744	355	389
oupe ·	345	171	174	86,376	42,660	43,716	4,812	2,320	2,492
·	131	62	69	23,814	10,760	13,054	1,492	669	823
·	139	63	76	30,417	13,543	16,874	1,799	800	999
and Sicily	338	202	136	62,541	37,530	25,011	4,124	2,487	1,637
·	278	171	107	50,585	30,843	19,742	2,668	1,659	1,009
·	86	25	44	14,795	5,294	9,501	925	326	599
·	247	197	50	45,379	37,424	7,955	2,124	1,731	393
tic Towns	248	83	165	33,575	9,596	23,979	1,849	606	1,243
Bourbon	102	49	53	30,033	14,062	15,971	1,788	858	930
nd Porto Rico	154	72	82	33,692	15,890	17,802	1,983	913	1,070
y and Roman } s · }	978	497	481	59,010	31,206	24,804	7,393	3,941	3,452
	127	63	64	25,017	12,352	12,665	1,515	755	760
East Indian } ssions · }	29	11	18	10,763	4,448	6,315	633	285	348
and Norway	150	89	61	36,098	19,719	16,379	2,183	1,078	1,105
·	989	660	329	148,225	100,655	47,570	8,170	5,534	2,636
States ·	21	10	11	6,096	2,923	3,173	411	195	216
·	230	140	90	25,066	14,441	10,625	1,906	1,101	985
nd Cochin-China	63	22	41	7,490	2,439	5,051	593	203	390
·	4	2	2	1,660	1,139	521	112	59	53
ia	40	18	22	7,117	3,181	3,936	469	215	254
West Indian } ssions }	10	4	6	2,573	1,022	1,551	180	84	96
Isles in America	50	23	27	7,676	3,314	4,362	572	257	315
us ·	40	23	17	7,563	4,152	3,411	469	258	211
l ·	43	17	26	12,624	4,601	8,023	661	258	403
·	91	61	30	10,581	6,900	3,681	756	503	253
ast Indian Pos- } s- }	14	9	5	4,001	2,814	1,187	247	171	76
Pierre and } lon · }	12	0	12	1,618	0	1,618	180	0	180
k ·	61	13	48	10,225	1,935	8,290	533	117	416
Ayres ·	8	0	8	1,890	0	1,890	112	0	112
American Isles	5	2	3	732	111	621	51	12	39
ese East In- } Possessions · }	1	0	1	80	0	80	6	0	6
Total ·	16,632	7,789	8,843	1,614,923	828,611	786,312	134,748	65,870	68,878
Countries	15,705	7,358	8,347	1,389,004	723,661	665,343	121,640	59,872	61,768
Colonies	927	431	496	225,939	104,950	120,989	13,103	5,998	7,110
Fisheries ·	11,498	5,264	6,234	222,516	97,851	124,665	82,325	37,230	45,095

de between *France and England.* — Nothing can more strikingly illustrate ...ble effects of commercial restrictions, than the present state of the trade between ...Britain and France. Here we have two countries of vast-wealth and population, ...eighbours, and each possessing many important articles that the other wants, and ...intercourse between them is inconsiderable. At a distant period this was not ...e. Previously to the accession of William III., the import of wine only from ...amounted to about 13,500 tuns a year, our imports of brandy and other articles ...proportionally large. But Louis XIV. having espoused the cause of the exiled ...of Stuart, the British government, not recollecting that the blow they aimed at ...ench would also smite their own subjects, imposed, in 1693, a *discriminating* duty ...a tun on French wine, and in 1697 raised it to no less than 33*l.* a tun ! It is ...te that this excess of duty would have been repealed as soon as the peculiar cir-...nces in which it originated had disappeared, had not the stipulations in the famous ...rcial treaty with ·Portugal, negotiated by Mr. Methuen, in 1703, given it per-...ce. But, according to this treaty, we bound ourselves for the future to charge ...d higher duties on the wines of France imported into England, than on those of ...al; the Portuguese, by way of compensation, binding themselves to admit our

* Ships.   † Packet-boats.

woollens into their markets in preference to those of other countries, at a fixed a
invariable rate of duty.

Though very generally regarded, at the time, as the highest effort of diplomatic sk
and address, the Methuen treaty was, undoubtedly, founded on the narrowest and m
contracted views of national interest; and has, in consequence, proved, in no comm
degree, injurious to both parties, but especially to England.   By binding ourselves
receive Portuguese wines for *two thirds* of the duty payable on those of France, we,
effect, gave the Portuguese growers a monopoly of the British market; at the sa
time that we excluded one of the principal equivalents the French had to offer for
commodities, and provoked them to retaliate.   This, indeed, was no difficult task.
Unhappily, they were but too ready to embark in that course of vindictive policy
which we had set them the example; so that prohibitions on the one side being
mediately followed by counter prohibitions on the other, the trade between the
countries was nearly annihilated!   But the indirect were still more injurious than
direct consequences of this wretched policy.   It inspired both parties with feeli
of jealousy and dislike, and kept them in the frowning attitude of mutual defian
Each envied the other's prosperity; and being disposed to take fire at even fancied
croachments, the most frivolous pretexts were sufficient to engage them in contests t
have filled the whole world with bloodshed and confusion.   But had things been left
their natural course — had an unfettered commercial intercourse been allowed to grow
between the two countries — the one would have formed so near, so vast, and so profita
a market for the produce of the other, that they could not have remained long at v
without occasioning the most extensively ruinous distress, — distress which no gove
ment would be willing to inflict on its subjects, and to which, though the governm
were willing, it is most probable no people would be disposed to submit.   A free tra
between England and France would give these two great nations *one common inter*
It would occasion not only a vast increase of the industry, and of the comfo
and enjoyments, of the people of both countries, but would be the best attaina
security against future hostilities.   "We know," said Mr. Villiers, in his very a
and instructive speech (15th of June, 1830), "that British enterprise will fetch
extremest points on earth in the business of exchange; but here are the shores
France nearer to England than those of Ireland itself — nay, Bordeaux is commercia
nearer to London than it is to Paris; and, but for the lamentable perversion of the g
and dispositions of nature, and of the ingenuity of man — the highways of comme
between these countries — the seas which surround Great Britain and Ireland,. a
wash the shores of France, should literally swarm with vessels, engaged, not only in
interchange of material products, but in diffusing knowledge and stimulating impro
ment; in creating every where new neighbourhoods; in consolidating internatio
dependence; in short, in drawing daily more close the bonds of international peace a
confidence, and thus advancing, while they also served to confirm and secure,
peace, the civilisation, and the happiness of Europe."

The commercial treaty which Mr. Pitt negotiated with France in 1786, was the fi
attempt to introduce a better system into the trade between the two countries; and i
one of the few treaties of this description that have been bottomed on fair and lib
principles.   But the Revolution in France, and the lengthened and bloody wars
which it was followed, totally suppressed that mutually beneficial intercourse which
begun to grow up under Mr. Pitt's treaty; and when peace was again restored,
1815, the French government unwisely resolved to continue the system of Napole
and to exclude most sorts of foreign products for which a substitute could be foun
home!   But the wide spread distress that has resulted from this absurd policy, and
more general diffusion of sounder notions as to the real sources of public wealth, v
it may be confidently predicted, at no distant period, induce the government of Fra
to adopt a less illiberal and irrational system. — (See BORDEAUX.)   The late equalisa
of the wine duties in this country will do much to accelerate this desirable result.
will show the French that we are no longer influenced by the prejudices in which
discriminating system originated; and that we are ready to deal with them on the sa
fair and equal terms as with any one else.   In this respect the measure is entitle
the highest praise; and we have no doubt that it will be the harbinger of other
the same kind — of a reduction of the exorbitant duties on brandy, for example —
here and in France.   The statesman who shall succeed in abolishing the restraint
the commerce of the two countries, will render the most essential service to them b
and not to them only, but to all the world; the farthest parts of which have b
harassed by their wars.   It admits of demonstration, that, under a free system, the t
with France would be incomparably more important and valuable than that with Ru
the United States, or any other country.   And we trust, should another edition of
work be called for, that we shall have to congratulate the public on the opening of
" broad and deep" channel of employment.

following tables, the latest of the sort which have been compiled, give a pretty ›te view of the trade with France. Brandy, wine, madder, and flax, are the prin- ›rticles of import; for the silk, as already remarked, comes chiefly from Italy.— ›achinery and mill-work, horses, hardware, spermaceti, &c. are the principal › of British produce and manufacture exported to France. — Cotton-wool and are the principal colonial articles sent to France from England; but of these t worth while to insert a detailed account.

›ance at the first of the following tables will sufficiently explain the real causes of ›ressed state of the French trade. Brandy worth 237,000*l.* is loaded with the ›us duty of 1,175,000*l.*! Wine worth 105,000*l.* pays a duty of 165,000*l.*; ›ats worth under 3,000*l.* pay a duty of 10,766*l.*; and even upon eggs valued at ›*l.* we impose a duty of 21,114*l.*! This, we believe, is about the *ne plus ultra* of ›apacity: and till these exorbitant and destructive duties be adequately reduced, visionary to expect that the trade with France can be any thing but inconsider- The only thing to be wondered at is, that they have not suppressed it altogether.

›into Great Britain from France, during the Year 1825; with the Customs Duty on each Article.

›nports.	Denominations.	In British Shipping.	In French or other Foreign Shipping.	In British and Foreign Shipping.	Official Value of the Imports.	Amount of Customs Duties received on each Article imported.
					£ s. d.	£ s. d.
›t bit- ›dan -	Cwt. qr. lb.	905 1 20	98 3 5	1,004 0 25	2,282 9 10	2,311 2 8¼
›g -	Lb.	153,807	—	153,807	15,325 0 0	934 8 4
›dried -	Bushels.	23,303⅜	12,188⅝	35,492⅛	3,137 16 3	7,331 18 0
-	Cwt. qr. lb.	625 3 27¾	1,769 2 25¾	2,395 2 25½	19,166 6 5	10,232 3 7
›e and ›-	Decl. value.	655 12 0	5,116 11 6	5,772 3 6	5,772 3 6	1,724 17 7
-	Lb.	46,811	3,783	50,594	648 6 6	3,485 7 0
›then- ›-	Decl. value.	2,140 1 6	5,502 8 0	7,642 9 6	7,642 9 6	3,252 15 0
- -	Lb.	15,021	2	15,023	3,004 12 0	0 7 0
-	Decl. value.	1,760 8 0	11,685 5 0	13,445 13 0	13,445 13 0	4,273 0 7
- -	Lb.	2,142	19,760	21,902	5,475 10 0	0 3 0
-	Lb.	161,186	781,637	942,823	58,926 8 9	0 6 3
›ufac- ›urope	Square yds. / Decl. value.	3,889¼ / 353 19 6	88,533½ / 6,831 6 4	92,422¾ / 7,185 5 10	14,887 3 9	3,422 3 11
›ar -	Cwt. qr. lb.	2,062 2 22	1,124 0 20	3,186 3 14	7,915 18 3	1,292 6 1¾
-	Number.	1,288,680	59,465,664	60,754,344	18,985 14 8	21,114 2 10
- -	Cwt. qr. lb.	32,552 3 23	17,812 0 8	50,365 0 3	88,887 9 1	1,200 16 7¼
›icial -	Decl. value.	494 17 0	4,021 1 0	4,515 18 0	4,515 18 0	1,796 2 1
com.	Quarts.	893,227¾	68,240⅞	961,468⅔	17,231 7 11	15,101 0 0¼
- -	Number.	2,364	54,193	56,557	2,945 13 6	10,766 19 0
- -	Decl. value.	725 17 0	13,252 6 0	13,978 3 0	13,978 3 0	5,591 5 3
tulle -	Square yds.	1,055½	59,837¼	60,892¾	6,089 5 6	5,398 13 0
›brics ›ered ›efs -	Pieces.	8⅝	39,689¼	40,297⅞	19,645 4 3	12,332 14 2
-	Cwt. qr. lb.	7,739 1 25	22,019 2 19½	29,759 0 16½	61,059 9 9	10,484 11 0¼
- -	Cwt. qr. lb.	1,268 0 6	13,389 0 2	14,657 0 8	127,771 8 9	1,894 17 6½
-	Cwt. qr. lb.	11,379 1 19	511 3 11¼	11,891 1 2½	9,092 19 4	13,061 7 6¼
›d cakes	Cwt. qr. lb.	19,291 2 24	24,102 1 2	43,393 3 26	6,509 2 0	392 1 2
- -	Cwt. qr. lb.	7,936 1 24	7,997 0 14	15,933 2 10	8,037 13 11	13,626 10 7
-	Lb.	13,884	785,297	799,181	452,869 4 8	9,096 12 9
- -	Lb.	3,885⅔	164,355¼	168,240⅞	206,232 3 0	23,294 18 10
-	Lb.	144	86,009	86,153	8,615 6 0	788 10 9
›ndrssd.	Number.	92,652	510	93,162	7,763 10 0	1,099 16 2
›ssed -	Number.	17,737	739,865	757,602	13,636 16 9	7,027 0 8
›nned ›essed	Number.	16,106	189,719	205,825	2,058 12 2	1,149 12 7
-	Cwt. qr. lb.	2,554 3 14	1,654 3 14	4,209 3 0	10,524 7 6	877 5 5
›y -	Gallons.	2,017,045¼	1,756¾	2,018,802	237,045 8 5	1,175,166 5 2¼
- -	Decl. value.	1,681 2 0	6,989 13 4	8,670 15 4	8,670 15 4	2,563 0 8
- -	Lb.	168,684½	72,384	241,068½	15,066 15 4	3,817 5 8
-	Gallons.	1,031,835	58,744⅝	1,090,579½	105,805 15 10	165,879 15 8
-	Lb.	329,911	20	329,931	10,654 0 5	1,100 6 1
- -	Lb.	41,813	394,865	436,678	10,916 19 0	1,895 1 1
›ufac- -	Pieces. / Shawls. / Decl. value.	87 / 7 / 432 4 6	201 / — / 6,678 11 6	288 / 7 / 7,110 16 0	8,571 16 0	1,269 5 10
-	Value.	—	—	—	149,750 4 10	59,739 17 10½
				Total - £	1,790,561 2 8	1,605,786 15 1¼

Exports of British and Irish Produce and Manufactures from Great Britain to France, during year 1825.

Species of Exports.	Denominations.	In British Shipping.	In French or other Foreign Shipping.	In British and Foreign Shipping.	Official Value of British and Irish Produce and Manufactures exported.	De of Ir and
					£ s. d.	
Apothecary wares -	Cwt. qr. lb.	12 1 24	766 0 0	788 1 24	1,556 18 7	6
Apparel and slops -	Value.	684 0 0	1,939 0 0	2,623 0 0	2,623 0 0	2
Beer and ale - -	Tuns. hhds. gals.	6 2 60	40 3 50	47 2 47	245 11 0	1
Books, printed -	Cwt. qr. lb.	85 3 20	315 3 16	401 3 8	1,617 15 9	7
Brass and copper ⎱ manufactures - ⎰	Cwt. qr. lb.	52 2 0	220 3 5	273 1 5	1,391 17 4	1
Cabinet and uphol-⎱ stery wares - ⎰	Value.	2,513 0 0	3,671 12 0	6,184 12 0	6,184 12 0	6
Cheese - -	Cwt. qr. lb.	54 0 4	127 2 1	181 2 5	217 17 1	
Coals - -	Tons.	19,785 0 0 0	7,507 5 0 0	27,292 5 0 0	24,534 15 4	6
Cotton manufac. ture; viz.						
calicoes, white ⎱ or plain - ⎰	Yards.	32,560	3,650	36,210	2,263 2 6	1
do. printed, ⎱ stained, or ⎰ dyed - - ⎰	Yards.	43,872	3,320	47,192	3,539 8 0	2
muslins -	Yards.	11,914	16,314	28,228	2,364 6 8	2
fustians, vel-⎱ vets, &c. - ⎰	Yards.	5,696	150	5,846	730 15 0	
lace and pa-⎱ tent net - ⎰	Yards.	3,100	137,796	140,896	4,696 10 8	4
hosiery, tapes, ⎱ and small ⎰ wares - - ⎰	Value.	505 0 0	179 8 0	684 8 0	684 8 0	
Earthenware of all ⎱ sorts - ⎰	Pieces.	7,398	59,147	66,545	166 7 3	
Glass of all sorts -	Value.	194 9 6	587 18 0	782 7 6	782 7 6	
Grindstones - -	Cwt. qr. lb.	407 33 0	280 32 0	688 29 0	1,033 3 4	
Haberdashery and ⎱ millinery - ⎰	Value.	7 0 14	21 2 0	28 2 14	57 5 0	
Hardwares & cutlery	Cwt. qr. lb.	95 0 11	3,098 1 18	3,193 2 1	8,782 3 0	24
Horses - -	Number.	692	90	782	7,812 10 0	38
Iron, pig - -	Tons, cwt. qr. lb.	96 0 0 0	952 8 0 0	1,048 8 0 0	1,048 8 0	5
bar and bolt -	Tons, cwt. qr. lb.	57 5 0 0	1,427 2 3 7	1,484 7 3 7	14,843 18 1	14
cast and wrought.	Tons, cwt. qr. lb.	179 17 3 19	301 8 0 22	481 6 0 13	7,809 15 10	7
Lead and shot -	Tons, cwt. qr. lb.	8 2 2 15	441 4 3 0	449 7 1 15	4,718 7 6	11
Leather and saddlery	Value.	221 0 0	1,096 0 0	1,317 0 0	1,317 0 0	
Linens - -	Yards.	3,628	12,469	16,097	811 7 0	
Litharge of lead -	Cwt. qr. lb.	407 2 25	1,641 1 13	2,049 0 13	922 1 10	
Machinery and ⎱ mill work - ⎰	Value.	6,524 10 0	36,257 0 0	42,781 10 0	42,781 10 0	42
Mathematical and ⎱ optical instru-⎰ ments - - ⎰	Value.	550 0 0	79 0 0	629 0 0	629 0 0	
Musical instruments	Value.	2,345 0 0	1,947 0 0	4,292 0 0	4,292 0 0	
Painters' colours ⎱ and materials - ⎰	Value.	63 16 0	2,043 0 0	2,106 16 0	2,106 16 0	
Perfumery -	Value.	35 10 0	408 0 0	443 10 0	433 10 0	
Pictures - -	Value.	315 0 0	1,142 10 0	1,457 10 0	1,457 10 0	
Plants and seeds -	Value.	110 0 0	539 3 0	649 3 0	649 3 0	
Plate of silver -	Oz. dwts.	25,090 8	2,651 10	27,741 18	12,483 17 1	1
Plated ware - -	Value.	274 10 0	179 8	453 18 0	453 18 0	
Sheep - -	Number.	825	20	845	1,056 5 0	
Skins, seal, dressed ⎱ in Great Britain ⎰	Number.	75	1,144	1,219	152 7 6	
of other sorts, do.	Value.	7 0 0	800 0 0	807 0 0	807 0 0	
Spermaceti -	Cwt. qr. lb.	—	2,999 3 27	2,999 3 27	22,499 18 8	2
Stationery - -	Value.	94 12 0	1,501 3 6	1,595 15 6	1,595 15 6	
Steel, unwrought -	Cwt. qr. lb.	—	1,984 0 5	1,984 0 5	2,827 5 3	
Sugar, British, re-⎱ fined - - ⎰	Cwt. qr. lb.	148 0 13	19 2 26	167 3 5	461 8 8	
Tin, unwrought -	Cwt. qr. lb.	3,134 2 27	11,517 0 14	14,651 3 13	53,479 6 2	6
and pewter wares ⎱ and tin plates - ⎰	Value.	4,072 10 0	7,195 0 0	11,267 10 0	11,267 10 0	1
Toys - -	Value.	20 0 0	1,037 0 0	1,057 0 0	1,057 0 0	
Whalebone -	Cwt. qr. lb.	—	536 0 0	536 0 0	2,680 0 0	
Wool, for hatters, ⎱ prepared in Great ⎰ Britain - - ⎰	Lb.	40	46	86	60 0 0	
sheep's -	Lb.	4,108	10,888	14,996	535 11 5	
Woollens, cloths -	Pieces.	7	50	57	633 0 0	
carpets and ⎱ carpeting ⎰	Yards.	1,221	7,830	9,051	1,583 18 6	
other woollens	Value.	7 0 0	337 6 0	344 6 0	344 6 0	
Woollen or worsted ⎱ yarn - ⎰	Lb.	—	2,399	2,399	128 10 5	
All other articles -	Value.	—	—	—	9,960 12 2	1
				Total - £	279,175 11 7	36

would seem, from the subjoined account, as if the imports into Great Britain from
ce very much exceeded the exports, which amount only to the paltry sum of about
000l. a year. But though the fact were so, it would not, as some appear to suppose,
the shadow of a foundation for the statements of those who contend that the
with France is a losing one. A man carries nothing but money to the baker's
, or the butcher's; and yet it is not said that he is injured by dealing with them, or
he should become baker or butcher for himself. We buy certain articles from
ce, because we find we can procure them from her on more reasonable terms than
any other country; for, were it otherwise, does any one suppose we should send a
e ship to her ports? Whether we carry on our intercoure with the French by
ng them returns in bullion or ordinary products, is of no consequence whatever.
may be assured that bullion is not sent to another country, unless it be more valuable
than here; that is, unless its exportation be for *our* advantage. — (See BALANCE
RADE.) In point of fact, however, we very rarely send any bullion to France;
he proof of this is, that, since the peace, the exchange with Paris has been oftener in
avour than against us. When the bills drawn by the French on us exceed those
raw on them, the balance is usually paid by bills on Holland and Hamburgh,
e there is, at all times, an excess of British produce. It is idle, therefore, to
pt to revive the ridiculous cry as to the disadvantageousness of the French trade,
se the imports from France exceed the exports! The imports into all commercial
ries uniformly exceed the exports; and the fact brought forward as a ground of
aint against the French trade, is the strongest recommendation in its favour.
ps, however, it may be consolatory to those who are so alarmed at the excess of
rts from France, to be told that it is to a great extent apparent only. Large
ities of silk and other produce from Italy come to us through France, and are
ned among the imports from that country, when they are in reality imports from
Taking this circumstance into account, it will be found that the discrepancy
en the exports to and imports from France is immaterial.

nt of the Amount in Official and Real Value of all British Exports to France, in each Year since
; distinguishing those of British from Colonial Produce; also, an Abstract of the Amount in
al Value of all Imports from France in each Year, as far as the same can be made up during that
.—(*Parl. Paper*, No. 189. Sess. 1831.)

ars.	Official Value of Imports into the United Kingdom.	Official Value of Exports from the United Kingdom.			Declared Value of British and Irish Produce and Manufactures exported from the United Kingdom.
		British and Irish Produce and Manufactures.	Foreign and Colonial Merchandise.	Total Exports.	
	£ s. d.	£ s. d.	£ s. d.	£ s. d.	£ s. d.
814	740,226 10 0	577,799 9 7	1,867,913 19 4	2,245,713 8 11	582,702 15 0
815	754,372 8 11	214,823 15 9	1,228,856 5 3	1,443,680 1 0	298,291 10 1
816	417,782 17 2	321,070 4 11	1,313,151 17 8	1,634,222 2 7	407,699 11 4
817	527,865 13 6	596,753 7 0	1,054,261 9 9	1,651,014 16 9	1,003,486 12 7
818	1,162,423 15 7	518,850 19 1	877,912 13 0	1,196,763 12 1	369,503 14 9
819	642,011 14 2	248,078 0 9	734,779 9 10	982,857 10 7	299,493 6 8
820	775,132 5 6	334,086 13 2	829,814 9 6	1,163,901 2 8	390,744 10 3
821	865,616 12 9	382,404 2 4	1,037,100 15 5	1,419,504 17 9	438,265 18 5
822	878,272 15 0	346,810 15 1	839,150 11 4	1,185,961 6 5	437,009 2 5
823	1,115,800 7 0	241,837 12 11	743,574 16 4	985,412 9 3	349,616 4 1
824	1,556,733 17 5	260,498 9 9	864,500 16 4	1,124,999 6 1	338,635 8 11
825	1,835,984 12 0	279,212 3 7	892,402 18 1	1,171,615 1 8	360,709 10 1
826	1,247,426 0 6	426,819 13 9	656,124 10 9	1,082,944 4 6	488,438 6 7
827	2,625,747 11 10	416,726 0 8	133,503 12 6	550,229 13 2	446,951 0 9
828	3,178,825 3 9	448,945 2 7	195,497 9 2	644,442 11 9	498,937 12 0
829	2,086,993 10 10	509,921 1 3	337,896 11 6	847,817 12 9	491,388 3 11
830	2,328,483 14 11	486,284 0 1	181,065 1 5	667,349 1 6	475,884 3 2

AWKERS AND PEDLARS. It is not very easy to distinguish between
rs and pedlars. Both are a sort of itinerant retail dealers, who carry about
wares from place to place; but the former are supposed to carry on business
arger scale than the latter. They are subject to the same regulations.

ulations as to Hawkers and Pedlars. — The legislature has always looked with sus-
upon itinerant dealers; and has attempted, by obliging them to take out licences,
acing them under a sort of surveillance, to lessen their numbers, and to hinder
from engaging in dishonest practices. But the resident dealer has so many advan-
on his side, that these precautions seem to be in a great measure superfluous. It
also be recollected, that before shops were generally established in villages and
districts, hawkers and pedlars rendered material services to country people; and
ow the competition which they excite is certainly advantageous.

e 50 Geo. 3. c. 41., hawkers and pedlars are to pay an annual licence duty of 4l.; and if they travel
orse, ass, or other beast, bearing or drawing burthen, they are subject to an additional duty of 4l.
beast so employed. The granting of licences, and management of the duties, are, by a late act,
nder the control of the commissioners of stamps.

Hawkers and pedlars, unless householders or residents in the place, are not allowed to sell by auc
to the highest bidder: penalty 50l.—half to the informer, the other half to the king. But nothing in
act extends to hinder any person from selling, or exposing to sale, any sort of goods, in any public ma
or fair ; or to hinder a hawker or pedlar from selling in a hired room, where he is not a resident, prov
such sale is not by auction.

Every hawker, before he is licensed, must produce a certificate of good character and reputation, sig
by the clergyman and two reputable inhabitants of the place where he usually resides.

Every hawker must have inscribed, in Roman capitals, on the most conspicuous part of every pack, b
trunk, case, cart, or other vehicle, in which he shall carry his wares, and on every room and shop
which he shall trade, and likewise on every hand-bill which he shall distribute, the words " LICEN
HAWKER." Penalty, in default, 10l. Unlicensed persons wrongfully using this designation forfeit 10

Hawkers dealing in smuggled goods, or in goods fraudulently or dishonestly procured, are punisha
by forfeiture of licence, and incapacity to obtain one in future, besides being liable to all the other pe
ties, forfeitures, &c. applicable to such illegal dealing.

By stat. 6 Geo. 4. c. 80. it is enacted, that any person or persons hawking, selling, or exposing to s
any spirits on the streets, highways, &c., or in any boat or other vessel on the water, or in any pl
other than those allowed in this act, shall forfeit such spirits and 100l. for every such offence. Any p
son may detain a hawker of spirits, and give notice to a peace officer to carry the offender befo
justice.

Hawkers trading without licence are liable to a penalty of 10l. So also, if they refuse to show th
licence on the demand of any person to whom they offer goods for sale, or on the demand of any just
mayor, constable, or other peace officer, or any officer of the customs or excise. By 5 Geo. 4. c.
hawkers trading without a licence are punishable as vagrants.

To forge or counterfeit a hawker's licence incurs a penalty of 300l. To lend or hire a hawker's lice
subjects lender and borrower to 40l. each, and the licence becomes forfeited. But the servant
licensed hawker may travel with the licence of his master.

Hawkers trading without a licence are liable to be seized and detained by any person who may g
notice to a constable, in order to their being carried before a justice of peace. Constables refusin
assist in the execution of the act are liable to a penalty of 10l.

Nothing in the act extends to prohibit persons from selling fish, fruit, or victuals ; nor to hinder
maker of any home manufacture from exposing his goods to sale in any market or fair, in every c
borough, town corporate, and market town ; nor any tinker, cooper, glazier, plumber, harness-men
or other person, from going about and carrying the materials necessary to their business.

A single act of selling, as a parcel of handkerchiefs to a particular person, is not sufficient to consti
a hawker within the meaning of the statutes. — Rex v. Little, B. 613.

By the 52 Geo. 3. c. 108 , no person, being a trader in any goods, wares, or manufactures of Great Brit
and selling the same by wholesale, shall be deemed a hawker ; and all such persons, or their age
selling by wholesale only, shall go from house to house, to any of their customers who sell again by wh
sale or retail, without being subject to any of the penalties contained in any act touching hawkers, j
lars, and petty chapmen.

No person committed under these acts for non-payment of penalties can be detained in custody fo
longer period than three months.

Hawkers exposing their goods to sale in a market town, must do it in the market-place.

Persons hawking tea without a licence are liable to a penalty, under 50 Geo. 3. c. 41. ; and even tho
they had a licence, they would be liable to a penalty for selling tea in an unentered place. — (Chitty's
of Burn's Justice, vol. ii. p. 1113.)

Any person duly licensed to trade as a hawker and pedlar may set up any lawful trade in any p
where he is resident, though he have not served any apprenticeship to the same, and, if prosecuted
may plead the general issue, and have double costs. — (See Chitty's edit. of Burn's Justice, vol
pp. 1102—1124.)

The hawkers' and pedlars' duty produced last year (1830) 33,733l. 9s. 9d. gross revenue ; the charge
collection were 6,123l. 6s. 1d. Whatever, therefore, may be the other advantages of this tax, it can
certainly, be said to be very productive.

HAY (Ger. Hew; Du. Hovi; Fr. Foin; It. Fieno; Sp. Heno; Lat. Fœnu
any kind of grass, cut and dried for the food of cattle. The business of h
making is said to be better understood in Middlesex than in any other part of
kingdom. The great object is to preserve the green colour of the grass as m
as possible, and to have it juicy, fresh, and free from all sort of mustiness.

The sale of hay within the bills of mortality, and 30 miles of the cities of London and Westminste
regulated by the act 36 Geo. 3. c. 88. It enacts, that all hay shall be sold by the load of 36 trusses,
truss weighing 56 lbs., except new hay, which is to weigh 60 lbs. till the 4th of September, and afterw
56 lbs. only ; so that till the 4th of September a load of hay weighs exactly a ton, but thereafter only 18
The clerk of the market is bound to keep a regular book for the inspection of the public, specifying
names of the seller, the buyer, the salesman, and the price of each load. Salesmen and factors are
hibited from dealing on their own account.

There are three public markets in the metropolis for the sale of hay and straw ; Whitechapel, Smith
and the Haymarket. An act (11 Geo. 4. c. 14.) has been obtained, for the removal of the market from
Haymarket to the vicinity of the Regent's Park ; but the removal has not yet taken place.

Straw is sold by the load of 36 trusses, of 36 lbs. each, making in all 11 cwt. 64 lbs.

It is affirmed, we know not with what foundation, that considerable frauds are perpetrated in the s
hay and straw.

HEMP (Ger. Hanf; Du. Hennip, Kennip; Da. Hamp; Sw. Hampa; Fr. Cl
vre; It. Canape; Sp. Canamo; Rus. Konapli, Konopel; Pol. Konope), a valu
plant (the Cannabis Sativa of Linnæus), supposed to be a native of India, but l
since naturalised and extensively cultivated in Italy, and many countries
Europe, particularly Russia and Poland, where it forms an article of prin
commercial importance. It is also cultivated in different parts of America, tho
not in such quantities as to supersede its importation. It is stronger and coa
in the fibre than flax ; but its uses, culture, and management, are pretty much
same. When grown for seed, it is a very exhausting crop ; but when pulled gr
it is considered as a cleaner of the ground. In this country its cultivation is
deemed profitable ; so that, notwithstanding the encouragement it has rece
from government, and the excellent quality of English hemp, it is but little gro

: in some few districts of Suffolk and Lincolnshire.   The quantity raised in
d is also inconsiderable. — (*Loudon's Ency. of Agricult.*)

dingly good *huckaback* is made from hemp, for towels and common tablecloths. Low priced
cloths are a general wear for husbandmen, servants, and labouring manufacturers; the better
· working farmers and tradesmen in the country; and the finer ones, ⅜ wide, are preferred by
ntlemen for strength and warmth. They possess this advantage over Irish and other linens, — that
·our improves in wearing, while that of linen deteriorates. But the great consumption of hemp is
.anufacture of sailcloth and cordage, for which purposes it is peculiarly fitted by the strength of
  English hemp, when properly prepared, is said to be stronger than that of every other country,
.ot excepted; and would, therefore, make the best cordage. It is, however, but little used in that
in the making of sailcloth; being principally made into cloth for the uses already stated.
.has been cultivated in Bengal from the remotest antiquity, but not, as in Europe, for the purpose
manufactured into cloth and cordage. In the Hindoo economy it serves as a substitute for malt ;
·ite intoxicating liquor, called *banga*, being produced from it! This, also, is the use to which it is
n Egypt. —(*Milburn's Orient. Commerce, &c.*)

rice of hemp fluctuated very much during the war. In consequence of difficulties in the way of
·tation, it stood at a very high level from 1808 to 1814. This was the principal circumstance that
·y brought iron cables into use; and the extent to which they are now introduced, has contributed
·ly to diminish the consumption and importation of hemp. —(*Tooke on High and Low Prices*, 2d
·.)

.932 cwt. of undressed hemp imported in 1829, 327,379 were brought from Russia, 26,430 from the
·ies, 14,504 from Italy, 3,604 from Prussia, and some small quantities from a few other places.
·y of 4s. 8d. a cwt. on hemp from a foreign country (that imported from any British possession
·y free), produced during the same year 81,124*l*. 9*s*. 8*d*. But as this duty tends to raise the price
·e, sails, and several species of coarse linen, its abolition would be productive of considerable ad-

·rrow the following particulars with respect to the hemp trade of Petersburgh, from the work of
·isow on the commerce of that city :—

·forms a very important article of export from Petersburgh, and deserves particular notice. It
·d, according to its quality, into *clean hemp*, or firsts ; *out-shot hemp*, or seconds ; *half-clean hemp*,
·; and *hemp codilla.*
·e first three sorts, there are annually exported about 2,000,000 poods, the greatest part in
·and American bottoms. It is brought to Petersburgh, from the interior beyond Moscow, by
·nd its quality depends very much on the country in which it is produced. That brought from
·v is the best; next to this, that produced in Belev; hemp from Gshatsk is considered inferior
·ter.
·n as the hemp is brought down in the spring, or in the course of the summer, it is selected and
·in bundles; both operations being performed by sworn selectors (*brackers*) and binders appointed
·nment for this purpose; and it is a well known fact, that this is done with great impartiality and
·.
·dle of clean hemp weighs from 55 to 65 poods; ditto out-shot, 48 to 55 ditto; ditto half-clean,
·litto. (1 pood = 36 lbs. avoirdupois.)
·g of hemp is paid for at the rate of 2 rubles 50 copecks for *clean*, 2 rubles for *out-shot*, and
·· copecks for *half-clean*, per bundle; one half is paid by the seller, and the other half by the pur-
·nd is charged accordingly by their agents.
·pense of selecting hemp is 50 copecks per bercovitz (or 10 poods), and is the same for every sort.
·bundle of assorted hemp is attached a ticket with the names of the selector, binder, and owner,
·ate and year Every bundle has also affixed to it a piece of lead, stamped on one side with the
·the selector, and on the other with the sort of hemp and the time when it was selected. The
·marks of good hemp are, its being of an equal green colour and free from spills; but its good
·proved by the strength of the fibre, which should be fine, thin, and long. The first sort should
·clean and free from spills; the *out-shot* is less so; and the *half-clean* contains a still greater
·f spills, and is moreover of mixed qualities and colours.
·erfect knowledge of the qualities of hemp and flax can only be acquired by experience and
· agents usually employ men constantly occupied in this business ; by which means they are sure
·g goods of the best quality, and have the best chance of giving satisfaction to their principals ;
·although the hemp is selected by sworn selectors, yet, owing to the quantity of business and the
·h which it must be executed, &c., there are often great differences in the same sorts. The
·re in this way somewhat increased; but this is trifling in comparison of the advantage gained.
· separated, or picked out in cleaning hemp, is called *hemp codilla* ; it is generally made up in
·dles of one pood, which are again, when shipped, bound together in large bundles, each consist-
·ut 30 small ones.
·lar care must be taken to ship hemp and flax in fine dry weather ; if it get wet, it heats and is
·oiled For this reason every vessel taking in hemp or flax is furnished with mats to prevent its
·amp. Hemp, being light and bulky, is, when stowed, forced into the hold by means of winches,
·ders the operation of loading rather slow.
·be taken as a general rule, that the prices of hemp are highest in the months of May, June,
· the early part of August, the demand for this article being then greatest, and the exportation
·America being principally effected at this season. Again, the prices of hemp are lowest in the
· September; the reason of which is, that the less opulent hemp-merchants return at the end of
·n to their own country, in order to make new purchases for the ensuing year; and rather than
·d, sell the remainder of their stock some rubles below the market price. This causes a general
·lthough an unusual demand for the article happening at the same time, or political events or
·occasionally produce a contrary effect. Two large warehouses, called *ambares*, are built in
·gh for the special purpose of housing hemp, where the greatest order is observed.

·of the Total Export of Hemp from Petersburgh during the last Six Years, specifying the
Quantities exported in British, American, and other Foreign Ships.

| In British Ships. | | | | American | Other Foreign Ships. | | | | |
Clean.	Out-shot.	Half-clean.	Total in British Ships.	Total.	Clean.	Out-shot.	Half-clean.	Total in Foreign Ships.	Grand Total.
Poods.	Poods.	Poods.	Poods.	Poods.	Poods.	Poods.	Poods.	Poods.	Poods.
1,098,952	101,613	154,637	1,355,232	336,152	104,144	146,941	99,045	350,130	2,041,514
941,934	73,750	111,975	1,127,659	216,963	185,643	186,105	125,130	496,878	1,841,500
1,011,931	36,959	166,304	1,215,194	288,700	166,963	114,155	128,699	409,817	1,913,711
859,753	106,098	103,744	1,069,601	292,652	192,302	150,130	128,822	471,254	1,833,501
324,719	213,452	95,563	633,734	139,567	38,947	94,937	108,311	242,185	1,015,496
481,000	282,664	187,355	952,943	74,221	43,481	157,629	104,930	306,150	1,323,424

Sixty poods of hemp and 40 poods of codilla make a last at Petersburgh; 63 poods make an Englis — (pp. 47—52.)

We subjoin a statement of the various charges on the exportation of hemp from Petersburgh, a its importation into this country.

Clean Hemp. — 1 Bundle = 63 Poods = 1 ton.

	Rub.	Cop.
Duty, 3 rub. 60 cop. per bercovitz	22	68
Additional duty, 10 per cent.	2	27
Quarantine duty, 1 per cent.	0	22
	R. 25	17
Custom-house charges, 4 per cent.	1	1
Receiving, weighing, and shipping, 3¾ rub. per bundle	3	75
Bracking, 50 cop. per bercovitz	3	15
Binding, 4 cop. per ditto	2	52
Lighterage and attendance to Cronstadt, 8 rub. per bundle	8	0
Rebinding, 2¼ rub. per bundle, ½ charged	1	12
Brokerage, 60 cop. per ton	0	60
	R. 45	32

Brokerage, ½ per cent.

Commission and extra charges, 3 per cent.

Stamps on drafts, ⅛ per cent. }
Brokerage, ⅛ per cent. } ¼ per cent.

Charges of importation per ton, taking the price at 40*l.*

	L.
Insurance, say 1*l.*, and policy	0
Freight, 52*s.* 6*d.* per ton	2
Customs and Russia dues	4
Landing charges	0
Sound dues	0
Discount, 3¾ per cent.	1
Brokerage	0
Per ton	*L.* 10

In the above calculation, no allowance is made for d which, if care be taken to select a good vessel and a season, does not amount to much. The estimates are a the lowest rates of charge. The insurance, indeed, is times as low as 12*s.* 6*d.* per cent., and policy. That, h is only in the very earliest part of the season; it rise per cent. in the autumn.

Out-shot Hemp. — 1 Bundle = 63 Poods = 1 tor

	R
Fixed charges	
Other charges same.	

Half-clean Hemp. — 1½ Bundle = 63 Poods = 1 to

	R
Fixed charges	
Other charges same.	

Riga hemp fetches a higher price than that of Petersburgh. It is divided into three sorts: viz rhine, or clean, out-shot, and pass hemp. The following are the prices of hemp, duty paid, as in the London markets, 11th October, 1831: —

	£.	s.	d.		£.	s.	d.	
Hemp, East India, *d. p.*	0	0	0	to	0	0	0	per
Petersburgh, clean	37	0	0	—	37	10	0	—
Outshot	33	0	0	—	34	0	0	—
Half clean	30	0	0	—	31	0	0	—
Riga Rhine	41	0	0	—	0	0	0	—

Hemp imported in foreign ships deemed alien goods, and pays town and port duties accordir (6 *Geo.* 4. c. 111. § 26.)

Hemp the produce or manufacture of Europe may not be imported into the United Kingdom for consumption, except in British ships, or in ships of the country of which it is the produce, or which it is imported, under penalty of forfeiting the same and 100*l.* by the master of the s (6 *Geo.* 4. c. 109.)

HEMP-SEED (Fr. *Chenevis, Chenevi;* Ger. *Hanfsaat;* It. *Cannapuccia; Semen cannabinum;* Rus. *Konopljanoe Semja*), the seed of hemp. The best h seed is that which is brightest, and will not break when rubbed. It is used e as seed, or for crushing for oil, or as food for fowls. Being loaded with a du 2*l.* per quarter, it is but little imported into this country.

HERRINGS, AND HERRING FISHERY. The herring (*Clupea har* of Linnæus) is a fish too well known to require any description. It is where in high esteem, when fresh; and is also in considerable demand salted.

"Herrings are found from the highest northern latitudes yet known, as low northern coasts of France. They are met with in vast shoals on the coast of Am as low as Carolina. In Chesapeak Bay is an annual inundation of those fish, cover the shore in such quantities, as to become a nuisance. We find them again seas of Kamtschatka; and probably they reach Japan. The great winter rendezv the herring is within the Arctic circle: there they continue for many months, in or recruit themselves after the fatigue of spawning; the seas within that space swa with insect food in a far greater degree than those of our warmer latitudes. This n army begins to put itself in motion in spring. They begin to appear off the Sh Isles in April and May. These are only the forerunners of the grand shoal, comes in June; and their appearance is marked by certain signs, such as the nu of birds, like gannets and others, which follow to prey on them: but when the body approaches, its breadth and depth is such as to alter the appearance of th ocean. It is divided into distinct columns of five or six miles in length, and th four in breadth; and they drive the water before them, with a kind of rippling. times they sink for the space of ten or fifteen minutes, and then rise again to the su and in fine weather reflect a variety of splendid colours, like a field of the most pr gems.

"The first check this army meets in its march southward, is from the Shetland which divide it into two parts: one wing takes to the east, the other to the w shores of Great Britain, and fill every bay and creek with their numbers: the proceed towards Yarmouth, the great and ancient mart of herrings; they the through the British Channel, and after that in a manner disappear. Those whic towards the west, after offering themselves to the Hebrides, where the great stat fishery is, proceed to the north of Ireland, where they meet with a second interr

are obliged to make a second division : the one takes to the western side, and is
ely perceived, being soon lost in the immensity of the Atlantic; but the other, that
es into the Irish sea, rejoices and feeds the inhabitants of most of the coasts that
er on it. These brigades, as we may call them, which are thus separated from the
ter. columns, are often capricious in their motions, and do not show an invariable
hment to their haunts.

This instinct of migration was given to the herrings, that they might deposit their
n in warmer seas, that would mature and vivify it more assuredly than those of the
n zone. It is not from defect of food that they set themselves in motion; for they
e to us full of fat, and on their return are almost universally observed to be lean and
rable. What their food is near the pole, we are not yet informed; but in our seas
feed much on the *oniscus marinus*, a crustaceous insect, and sometimes on their own

They are full of roe in the end of June, and continue in perfection till the beginning
inter, when they deposit their spawn. The young herrings begin to approach the
s in July and August, and are then from half an inch to two inches long. Though
ave no particular authority for it, yet, as very few young herrings are found in our
luring winter, it seems most certain that they must return to their parental haunts
ath the ice. Some of the old herrings continue on our coast the whole year." —
tant's British Zoology.)

e herring was unknown to the ancients, being rarely, if ever, found within the Me-
anean. The Dutch are said to have engaged in the fishery in 1164. The invention
ckling or salting herrings is ascribed to one Beukels, or Beukelson, of Biervliet,
Sluys, who died in 1397. The emperor Charles V. visited his grave, and ordered
gnificent tomb to be erected to his memory. Since this early period, the Dutch
uniformly maintained their ascendancy in the herring fishery; but, owing to the
rmation, and the relaxed observance of Lent in Catholic countries, the demand for
igs upon the Continent is now far less than in the fourteenth and fifteenth centuries.

ortance of the Herring Fishery. — Progress of it in Great Britain. — There is, perhaps, no branch of
ry, the importance of which has been so much overrated as that of the herring fishery. For more
wo centuries, company after company has been formed for its prosecution, fishing villages have been
biers constructed, Boards and regulations established, and vast sums expended in bounties, and yet
hery remains in a very feeble and unhealthy state. The false estimates that have been long current
espect to the extent and value of the Dutch herring fishery, contributed more, perhaps, than any
else to the formation of exaggerated notions of the importance of this business. That the
ders prosecuted it to a greater extent, and with far greater success, than any other people, is, indeed,
rue. There is not, however, the shadow of a ground for believing that they ever employed, as has
een stated, about 450,000 individuals in the fishery and the employments immediately subservient
We question whether they ever employed so many as 50,000. At the time when the Dutch carried
fishery to the greatest extent, the entire population of the Seven United Provinces did not certainly
2,400,000 ; and deducting a half for women, and from a half to two thirds of the remaining 1,200,000
s and old men, it would follow, according to the statement in question, that every able-bodied man
land must have been engaged in the herring fishery! It is astonishing how such ridiculously
rated accounts ever obtained any circulation ; and still more so, that they should have been referred
quoted, without, apparently, any doubt being ever entertained of their authenticity, down to our
nes!* Had they been sifted ever so little, their falsehood would have been obvious; and we should
aved many hundreds of thousands of pounds that have been thrown away in attempting to rival
hich never existed.

uld be impossible, within the limits to which this article must be confined, to give any detailed
t of the various attempts that have been made at different periods to encourage and bolster up the
fishery. In 1749, in pursuance of a recommendation in his Majesty's speech at the opening of
ient, and of a report of a committee of the House of Commons, 500,000*l.* was subscribed for carrying
fisheries, under a corporation called " The Society of the Free British Fishery." The Prince of
was chosen governor of the Society, which was patronised by men of the first rank and fortune in
te. But this Society did not trust entirely to its own efforts for success. The duties were remitted
he salt used in the fisheries ; and besides this reasonable encouragement, a high tonnage bounty
inted upon every buss fitted out for the deep sea fishery. In consequence, many vessels were sent
Dr. Smith has truly stated, not to catch herrings, but to *catch the bounty ;* and to such an extent
s abuse carried, that in 1759, when the tonnage bounty was 50s., the almost incredible sum of
6*d.* was paid as bounty *upon every barrel of merchantable herrings that was produced!*—(*Wealth
ons*, vol. iii. p 386. M'Culloch's ed.) But, notwithstanding this encouragement, such was the waste
smanagement of the Company's affairs, that it was speedily destroyed. Dr. Smith says, that in 1794
a vestige remained of its having ever been in existence.

notwithstanding this ill success, a new company was formed, for nearly the same objects, in 1786,
h George III. was patron. It has had nearly the same fate. " For a season or two, busses were
it by the society ; but if every herring caught had carried a ducat in its mouth, the expense of its
would. scarcely have been repaid. The bubble ended by the society for fishing in the deep sea
ig a kind of building society, for purchasing ground in situations where curers and fishermen find
enient to settle, and selling or letting it in small lots to them, at such advance of price as yields
ng better than fishing profits." — (See an excellent article on the Herring Fishery in the 11th
r of the *Quarterly Journal of Agriculture.*)

US, a fresh attempt was made for the improvement and extension of the fishery. The act 48 Geo. 3.
hed a distinct set of commissioners for the superintendence of all matters connected with the
and authorised them to appoint a sufficient number of fishery officers, to be stationed at the dif-
orts, whose duty is to see that the various regulations with respect to the gutting, packing, &c. of
ings, and the branding of the barrels, are duly carried into effect. In 1809, a bounty of 3*l.* per ton

ry seem to have been first set forth in a treatise ascribed to Sir Walter Raleigh ; and, what is very
', they were admitted by De Witt into his excellent work, the " True Interest of Holland." They
en implicitly adopted by Mr. Barrow, in the article *Fisheries* in the Supplement to the Encyclopæ-
annica.

was granted on all vessels employed in the deep sea herring fishery, of above 60 tons burthen, but pay: only on 100 tons; and in 1820, a bounty of 20s. per ton, which, under certain specified circumstan might be increased to 50s., was granted on all vessels of from 15 to 60 tons, fitted out for the shore herr fishery; and, exclusively of these bounties on the tonnage, a bounty of 2s. a barrel was allowed on herrings cured gutted during the six years ending the 5th of April, 1815, and a bounty of 2s. 8d. a ba on their exportation, whether cured gutted or ungutted. During the eleven years ending the 5th April, 1826, the bounty on herrings cured gutted was 4s. a barrel.

It is stated in the article already referred to, that the cost of a barrel of cured herrings is about 1 the half going to the fisherman for the green fish, the other half to the curer for barrel, salt, and lab The bounty of 4s. a barrel was, therefore, equal to *half* the value of the herrings as sold by the fisherm and to *one fourth* of their value as sold by the curer! In consequence of this forced system, the fish was rapidly increased. The following statement, extracted from the Report of the Commissioners of Fishery Board, dated 1st of October, 1830, shows the progress it has made since 1809: —

Abstract of the Total Quantity of White Herrings cured, branded for Bounty, and exported, in so as the same have been brought under the Cognizance of the Officers of the Fishery, from the 1st of June, 1809, when the System hitherto in force for the Encouragement of the British Her Fishery took place, to the 5th of April, 1830; distinguishing each Year, and the Herrings cured Gut from those cured Ungutted. — (*Parl. Paper*, No. 51. Sess. 1830.)

Periods.	Total Quantity of Herrings Cured.			Total Quantity of Herrings branded for Bounty.	Total Quantity of Herring Exported.		
	Gutted.	Ungutted.	Total.		Gutted.	Ungutted.	Tota
	Barrels.	Barrels.	Barrels.	Barrels.	Barrels.	Barrels.	Barre
Period extending from 1st June 1809 to 5th April 1810 - -	42,548	47,657½	90,185½	34,701	11,063½	24,784½	35,8
Year ended 5th April 1811 - -	65,430	26,397½	91,827½	55,662½	18,880	19,253	38,1
Year — 1812 - -	72,515½	39,004	111,519½	58,430	27,564	35,256	62,8
Year — 1813 -	89,900¾	63,587½	153,488¼	70,027½	40,100½	69,625	109,7
Year — 1814 .	52,931½	57,611	110,542½	38,184½	54,929	83,474½	118,4
Year — 1815 - -	105,372¼	54,767	160,139¼	83,376	68,938	72,367¼	141,3
Year — 1816 - -	135,981	26,670¾	162,651¾	116,436	81,544½	26,143½	107,6
Year — 1817 - -	155,776	36,567½	192,343½	140,018½	115,480½	23,148	138,6
Year — 1818 - -	204,270¼	23,420¾	227,691	183,089¼	148,147½	14,192	162,3
Year — 1819 - -	303,777½	37,116½	340,894	270,022½	212,301½	14,860½	227,1
Year — 1820 - -	347,190½	35,301	382,491½	309,700½	244,096	9,420	253,5
Year — 1821 - -	413,308	28,887¾	442,195¾	363,872	289,445½	5,360	294,8
Year — 1822 - -	291,626½	24,897¾	316,542¼	263,205½	212,890½	2,065½	214,9
Year — 1823 - .	225,037	23,832	248,869	203,110	169,459½	985½	170,4
Year — 1824 - -	335,450	56,740¾	392,190¾	299,631	238,505½	1,125	239,6
Year — 1825 - -	303,397	44,268¼	347,665¼	270,844½	201,882½	134	202,0
Year — 1826 -	340,118	39,115¾	379,233¾	294,422½	217,053¼	20	217,0
Year — 1827 - -	259,171¼	29,324	288,495¼	223,606	165,741	695	166,4
Year — 1828 . -	339,360	60,418	399,778	279,317½	210,766	893	211,6
Year — 1829 - -	300,242½	55,737	355,979½	234,827	202,813½	3,062	205,8
Year — 1830 - -	280,933½	48,623½	329,557	218,418½	177,776	3,878½	181,6

On looking at this table, it is seen that the fishery made no progress under the new system till when the bounty was raised to 4s. This is a sufficient proof of the factitious and unnatural state of business. Its extension, under the circumstances in question, instead of affording any proof of its b in a really flourishing condition, was distinctly the reverse. Individuals without capital, but who obta loans sufficient to enable them to acquire boats, barrels, salt, &c. on the credit of the bounty, entere vast numbers into the trade. The market was most commonly glutted with fish; and yet the tempta held out by the bounty caused it to be still further overloaded. Great injury was consequently do those fish curers who possessed capital; and even the *fishermen* were injured by the system. "Mo the boats employed in the fishery never touch the water but during six weeks, from the middle or en July to the middle of September. They are owned and sailed, not by regular fishermen following vocation only, but by tradesmen, small farmers, farm-servants, and other landsmen, who may have cient skill to manage a boat at that season, but who do not follow the sea except for the six weeks o herring fishery, when they go upon a kind of gambling speculation, of earning a twelvemonth's inc by six weeks' work." — (*Quarterly Journal*, No. 11. p. 653.)

It has been often said, in vindication of the bounty system, that by extending the fishery it extende important nursery for seamen; but the preceding statement shows that such has not been its effect. O contrary, it has tended to depress the condition of the genuine fisherman, by bringing a host of interl into the field; and it has also been prejudicial to the little farmers and tradesmen, by withdrawing attention from their peculiar business, that they may embark in what has hitherto been little less th sort of lottery adventure.

These consequences, and the increasing amount of the sum paid for bounties, at length induced government to adopt a different system; and by an act passed in 1825, the bounty of 2s. 8d. on exp herrings was made to cease in 1826, and 1s. was annually deducted from the bounty of 4s. a barrel pa gutted herrings, till it ceased in 1830. Time has not yet been afforded to learn the full effect of measure. We, however, have not the slightest doubt that it will be most advantageous. The going table shows that there has been a decrease in the last three years in the quantity of her taken and exported; and now that the bounties have entirely ceased, this decrease may, it is bable, continue for a while. But this is not really to be regretted. The supply of herrings will forth be proportioned to the real demand; while the genuine fishermen, and those curers who capital of their own, will no longer be injured by the competition of landsmen, and of persons tradi capital furnished by government.

The repeal of the salt laws, and of the duty on salt, which preceded the repeal of the bounty, mu of signal service to the fishery It is true that salt used in the fisheries was exempted from the duty; in order to prevent the revenue from being defrauded, so many regulations were enacted, and the culties and penalties to which the fishermen were in consequence subjected were so very great, that of them chose rather to pay the duty upon the salt they made use of, than to undertake compliance the regulations.

It is much to be regretted, that when government repealed the bounty, it did not also abolis "Fishery Board," and the officers and regulations it had appointed and enacted. So long as the b existed, it was quite proper that those who claimed it should be subjected to such regulations as go ment chose to enforce; but now that it has been repealed, we see no reason whatever why the f should not be made perfectly free, and every one allowed to prepare his herrings as he thinks best. said, indeed, that were there no inspection of the fish, frauds of all sorts would be practised: th barrels would be ill made, and of a deficient size; that the fish would not be properly packed; th bottom and middle of the barrels would be filled with bad ones, and a few good ones only placed

at there would not be a sufficiency of pickle, &c. But it is obvious that the reasons alleged in
ion of the official inspection kept up in the herring fishery, might be alleged in vindication of a
inspection in almost every other branch of industry. It is, in point of fact, utterly useless. It is
apt, on the part of government, to do that for their subjects, which they can do far better for them-
Supposing the official inspection were put an end to, the merchants and others who buy herrings
urers would themselves inspect the barrels ; and while any attempt at fraud by the curers would
effectually obviated, they would be left at liberty to prepare their herrings in any way that they
without being compelled, as at present, to follow only one system, or to prepare fish in the same
the tables of the poor as well as for those of the rich. So far, indeed, is it from being true that
ection system tends to put down trickery, that there is much reason to think that its effect is
the reverse. The *surveillance* exercised by the officers is any thing but strict ; and the official
often affixed to barrels which, were it not for the undeserved confidence that is too frequently
it by the unwary, would lie on the curer's hands. It is rather a security against the detection
than against its existence.

rand object of the herring fishery "Board" has been to enforce such a system of curing as would
ritish herrings to a level with those of the Dutch. In this, however, they have completely
Dutch herrings generally fetching double, and sometimes even three times the price of British
in every market of Europe. Neither is this to be wondered at. The consumers of Dutch her-
the inhabitants of the Netherlands and of the German towns, who use them rather as a luxury
an article of food, and who do not grudge the price that is necessary to have them in the finest
The consumers of British herrings, on the other hand, are the negroes of the West Indies, and
of Ireland and Scotland. Cheapness is the prime requisite in the estimation of such persons ;
hing can be more entirely absurd, than that a public Board should endeavour to force the fish
adopt such a system in the preparation of herrings as must infallibly raise their price beyond the
those by whom they are bought. Why should not the taste of the consumers be consulted as
this as in any thing else? It would not be more ridiculous to attempt to have all cheese made
me richness and flavour as Stilton, than it is to attempt to bring up all herrings to the standard
utch.

, therefore, hope that a speedy end may be put to this system ; and that our legislators and
will cease to torment themselves with schemes for the improvement of the fisheries. The very
g they can do for them is to let them alone. It is not a business that requires any sort of adventi-
ouragement. Every obstacle to the easy introduction of fish into London and other places ought
to be removed ; but all direct interferences with the fishery are sure to be in the last degree per-

181,654 barrels of herrings exported from Great Britain in the year ending 5th of April, 1830,
nt to Ireland, 67,672 to places out of Europe (chiefly the West Indies), and 24,302 to places in
ther than Ireland.

ES (Ger. *Häute;* Du. *Huiden;* Fr. *Peaux;* It. *Cuoja;* Sp. *Pellejos, Pieles;*
oshi), signify, generally, the skins of beasts ; but the term is more particu-
pplied to those of large cattle, such as bullocks, cows, horses, &c. Hides
er raw or green ; that is, the same as when taken off the carcase, or salted
soned, in which case they are dressed with salt, alum, and saltpetre, to
them from putrefying, or they are cured or tanned. The hides of South
a are in the highest repute, and vast quantities of them are annually im-
into Great Britain. Large quantities are also imported from various parts
Continent ; and from Morocco, the Cape of Good Hope, &c.

unt of the Weight of the Hides imported into the United Kingdom in each of the Five Years
with 1829 ; and the Revenue annually derived from the same ; specifying the Countries whence
les were imported, with the Quantities brought from each.

ries from which imported.	1825.	1826.	1827.	1828.	1829.
nned Hides.	Cwt. qrs.lbs.	Cwt. qrs.lbs.	Cwt. qrs.lbs.	Cwt. qrs.lbs.	Cwt. qrs.lbs.
- - -	4,211 3 12	5,426 1 7	14,792 3 2	14,484 2 21	17,089 0 6
nd Norway -	88 0 9	-	7 0 15	3 0 5	1 0 0
- -	8,625 3 14	9,232 3 3	12,919 0 14	12.338 3 6	4,994 0 11
- - -	3,595 3 24	950 0 9	2,074 3 27	6,775 3 15	2,945 2 20
- - -	34,318 0 20	14,260 2 23	33,386 2 22	38,335 1 23	23,353 3 23
etherlands -	35,337 1 11	12,747 3 24	21,518 0 27	27,289 3 2	19,102 2 26
- -			422 0 8	182 0 16	
Madeira, and ores -	-	283 1 7	-	13 1 19	
the Canaries -	114 1 9	1 2 22			
- - -	4,523 3 22	2,903 2 0	1,259 2 22	1,232 1 7	1,808 1 4
- -		5 1 9			
- - -	93 3 2	1,058 2 13			342 0 0
z. Morocco -	2,187 3 4	10,805 1 6	668 0 17	3 2 4	64 0 13
- Sierra Leone ast to Cape of ope	3,284 3 24	1,228 2 9	3,111 1 27	2,875 2 17	3,696 2 25
- Cape of Good	6,590 2 8	7,520 3 27	12,207 1 3	12,963 1 20	15,844 0 22
es (including the us)	6,379 1 18	2,375 0 8	1,111 1 25	3,322 3 12	3,605 1 19
th Wales and men's Land	166 0 18	518 2 16	1,167 1 7	1,112 3 1	3,161 1 10
a Islands and n Fishery	-	3 3 18	4 0 0	15 3 12	5 2 15
orth American	467 3 21	2,492 0 1	1,092 2 20	1,548 1 22	973 3 24
est Indies -	4,599 0 7	3,775 2 27	4,238 1 13	4,537 0 24	2,922 2 25
Vest Indies -	301 3 5	173 1 11	62 1 15	201 3 23	13 2 15
ates of America	21,142 0 11	12,162 3 26	11,549 0 7	19,627 3 11	20,162 3 7
- - -	2,453 1 17	-	2,474 0 24	73 0 26	67 2 2

Account of the Weight of the Hides imported — *continued.*

Countries from which imported.	1825.	1826.	1827.	1828.	1829.
Untanned Hides.	Cwt. qrs.lbs.	Cwt. qrs.lbs.	Cwt. qrs.lbs.	Cwt. qrs.lbs.	Cwt. q⟨
Guatemala - - -	-	-	1,326 2 4	446 0 8	49
Columbia - - -	734 1 3	651 3 12	1,054 1 20	1,454 2 21	1,197
Brazil - - -	16,912 1 19	16,124 1 22	12,942 2 11	23,547 3 17	3,207
States of the Rio de la Plata	140,788 3 10	79,027 0 11	5,598 3 18	40,605 3 9	156,049
Chili - - -	5,043 0 24	7,949 1 19	6,366 2 15	11,266 1 3	3,434
Peru - - -	936 2 14	2,011 3 13	914 3 7	1,726 1 17	2,312
Guernsey, Jersey, Alderney, and Man, Foreign	775 0 13	130 1 9	284 1 15	134 2 7	10
Guernsey, Jersey, Alderney, and Man, Produce of	157 2 20 & 540 Numb.	36 Number.	118 2 14 & 98 Number.	37 3 27 & 182 Numb.	
Total - - -	303,850 2 23 & 540 Numb.	194,243 3 24 & 36 Number.	152,434 0 15 & 98 Number.	225,975 3 15 & 182 Numb.	286,416

Tanned Hides.	No. of Rus. Hides.	Lbs. of other Hides.	No. of Rus. Hides.	Lbs. of other Hides.	No. of Rus. Hides.	Lbs. of other Hides.	No. of Rus. Hides.	Lbs. of other Hides.	No. of Rus. Hides.	⟨I ⟩
Russia - - -	6,430	10	1,542	-	1,506	-	7,620	-	8,095	
Denmark - - -	-	-	-	-	-	-	-	-	-	
Prussia - - -	-	-	-	-	-	-	-	970	-	
Germany - - -	168	76	408	-	-	-	-	266	104	
Netherlands - - -	-	-	-	305	-	-	-	6,858	-	
France - - -	-	-	-	-	-	-	1	9,030	-	
East Indies (including the Mauritius) - - -	-	-	-	-	3,408					
British West Indies	-	-	-	-	7,559	-	-	31	-	
Brazil - - -	-	-	-	-	172	-	-	53	-	
Guernsey, Jersey, Alderney, and Man, Foreign	-	-	-	-	-	-	-	86,668	⟨8	
Guernsey, Jersey, Alderney, and Man, Produce of	-	53,045	-	62,008	-	92,669	-			
Total - - -	6,598	53,131	1,950	62,313	1,506	103,808	7,621	103,876	8,199	

The *rates of duty* on the hides imported during the above years were the same as those now ch⟨
for which, see TARIFF.

Amount of Duty received on Foreign and Colonial Hides.

	1825.	1826.	1827.	1828.	182⟨
	£ s. d.	£ s. d.	£ s. d.	£ s. d.	£
Untanned Hides - -	43,793 1 2	24,491 14 6	26,319 19 3	34,841 15 0	37,379
Tanned Hides - -	3,155 8 3	1,747 12 4	2,219 8 0	2,512 1 4	2,388
Total - - -	46,948 9 5	26,239 6 10	28,539 7 3	37,353 16 4	39,767

His Majesty is authorised to prohibit, by proclamation or order in council published in the ⟨
Gazette, the importation of any hides or skins, horns or hoofs, or any other part of any cattle or b⟨
order to prevent any contagious distemper from being brought into the kingdom —(6 Geo. 4. c. 107

Hides and skins paying duty by weight, may be delivered from the bonded warehouses, on the⟨
entering an average weight, due care being taken that the lockers actually re-tally and re-weigh th⟨
and skins on delivery ; and in the case of delivery for exportation, to express in cart notes the exa⟨
ber delivered from the warehouse, in order to enable the export officer on the quay to check the qu⟨
and the merchant is to indorse on the cocket and bill the total number and weight shipped, be⟨
vessel is suffered to clear.—(*Customs Order*, 4th Dec. 1824.)

HOGSHEAD, a measure of capacity, containing 63 gallons. A hogsh⟨
equal to half a pipe.

HOLIDAYS, are understood to be those days, exclusive of Sundays, on⟨
no regular public business is transacted at particular public offices. Th⟨
either fixed or variable. They are not the same for all public offices. Thos⟨
at the Bank of England have recently been reduced a full half.

The *variable holidays* are, Ash Wednesday, Good Friday, Easter Mond⟨
Tuesday, Holy Thursday, Whit Monday and Tuesday.

It is enacted by stat. 6 Geo. 4. c. 106. § 13, that no holidays shall be kept by the customs except⟨
mas and Good Friday, the King's birthday, and such days as may be appointed by proclamatio⟨
purpose of a general fast.

The 7 & 8 Geo. 4. c. 53. § 16. enacts, that no holidays shall be kept at the Excise, except Christ⟨
Good Friday, the birthdays of his Majesty and the Prince of Wales, the anniversaries of the Res⟨
of Charles II., and of his Majesty's coronation, and such days as may be appointed by proclamatio⟨
celebration of a general fast, or such days as may be appointed as holidays by any warrant issued⟨
purpose by the Lords of the Treasury.

HONEY (Du. *Honig, Honing;* Fr. *Miel;* Ger. *Honig;* It. *Mele;* Lat.⟨
Rus. *Med;* Sp. *Miel*), a vegetable juice collected by bees. " Its flavour⟨
according to the nature of the flowers from which it is collected. Thus, the⟨
of Minorca, Narbonne, and England, are known by their flavours ; and the⟨
prepared in different parts even of the same country differs. It is separate⟨
the comb by dripping, and by expression : the first method affords the pures⟨

second separates a less pure honey; and a still inferior kind is obtained by
ing the comb before it is pressed. When obtained from young hives, which
not swarmed, it is denominated *virgin honey.* It is sometimes adulterated
flour, which is detected by mixing it with tepid water: the honey dissolves,
e the flour remains nearly unaltered." — (*Thomson's Dispensatory.*)

y stat. 23 Eliz. c. 8. § 4., all vessels of honey are to be marked with the
il letters of the name of the owner, on pain of forfeiting 6s. 8d.; and contain,
arrel 32 gallons, the kilderkin 16 gallons, and the firkin 8 gallons, or forfeit
or every gallon wanting; and if any honey sold, be corrupted with any deceitful
ure, the seller shall forfeit the honey, &c.

OPS (Ger. *Hopfen;* Du. *Hoppe;* Fr. *Houblon;* It. *Luppoli, Bruscandoli;* Sp.
n; Rus. *Chmel;* Lat. *Humulus, Lupulus*). The hop is a perennial rooted
, of which there are several varieties. It has an annual twining stem, which
supported on poles, or trees, will reach the height of from 12 to 20 feet or
. It is a native of Britain, and most parts of Europe. When the hop was
used for preserving and improving beer, or cultivated for that purpose, is not
vn — (see ALE); but its culture was introduced into this country from Flanders
e reign of Henry VIII. Hops are first mentioned in the statute book in
, in an act 5 & 6 Edward 6. c. 5.; and it would appear from an act passed in
(1 Jac. 1. c. 18.), that hops were at that time extensively cultivated in Eng-
Walter Blithe, in his *Improver Improved,* published in 1649 (3d ed. 1653,
0.), has a chapter upon improvement by plantations of hops, which has the
wing striking passage. He observes that "hops were then grown to be a
nal commodity: but that it was not many years since the famous city of Lon-
petitioned the parliament of England against two nuisances; and these were,
castle coals, in regard to their stench, &c., and hops, in regard they would
the taste of drink, and endanger the people: and had the parliament been no
than they, we had been in a measure pined, and in a great measure starved;
a is just answerable to the principles of those men who cry down all devices,
genious discoveries, as projects, and thereby stifle and choak improvements."

ter the hops have been picked and dried, the brightest and finest are put into pockets
e bagging, and the brown into coarse or heavy bagging. The former are chiefly
in the brewing of fine ales, and the latter by the porter brewers. A *pocket* of hops, if
e good in quality, well cured, and tight trodden, will weigh about 1½ cwt.; and a
' hops will, under the same conditions, weigh about 2½ cwt. If the weight of either
ls or falls much short of this medium, there is reason to suspect that the hops are
inferior quality, or have been badly manufactured. The brighter the colour of
the greater is the estimation in which they are held. Farnham hops are reckoned
The expense of forming hop plantations is very great, amounting in some in-
s to from 70l. to 100l. an acre; and the produce is very uncertain, the crop being
ntly insufficient to defray the expenses of cultivation.

hop growers are placed under the *surveillance* of the excise, a duty of 2d. per lb. being laid on all
oduced in this country. A hop planter is obliged to give notice to the excise, on or before the 1st
ust each year, of the number of acres he has in cultivation; the situation and number of his oasts
a for drying; the place or places of bagging, which, with these storerooms or warerooms in which the
es are intended to be lodged, are entered by the officer. No hops can be removed from the rooms
tered, before they have been weighed and marked by a revenue officer; who marks, or ought to
ts weight, and the name and residence of the grower, upon each bag, pocket, or package. Counter-
the officer's mark is prohibited under a penalty of 100l., and defacing it under a penalty of 20l.
er or grower knowingly putting hops of different qualities or values into the same bag or package,
20l. And any person mixing with hops any drug, or other thing, to change or alter the colour or
shall forfeit 5l. a cwt. on all the hops so changed or altered. The malicious cutting or destroying
plantations may be punished by transportation beyond seas for life, or any term not less than seven
or by imprisonment and hard labour in a common goal, for any term not exceeding seven years. —
n's *Ency. of Agriculture;* Stevenson's *Surrey;* Burn's *Justice,* &c.)
duty on hops of the growth of Great Britain produced, in 1830, 153,125l. 18s. 6d.; of which sum the
er district paid 57,345l. 19s. 6d., the Sussex 46,838l. 15s. 8d., and the Canterbury 32,406l. 9s. The
of acres occupied by hop plantations in that year, were 46,726¾; of which there were in the Ro-
district 12,318¾, in Sussex 8,051¼, in Hereford 11,688, and in Canterbury 6,851¼. During the same
ere were 2,852 lbs. of British hops exported. Of foreign hops 8,627 lbs. were imported, and 20,641 lbs,
d. — (*Parl. Paper,* No. 59. Sess. 1831.)
exported from Great Britain are, on being again imported, to be treated as foreign, whether
ly so or not.

RSE (Ger. *Pferd;* Du. *Paard;* Da. *Hest;* Sw. *Häst;* Fr. *Cheval;* It. *Ca-*
Sp. *Caballo;* Rus. *Loschad;* Pol. *Kon;* Lat. *Equus;* Gr. ἵππος), a domestic
iped of the highest utility, being by far the most valuable acquisition made
n among the lower animals.

re is a great variety of horses in Britain. The frequent introduction of
a breeds, and their judicious mixture, having greatly improved the native

stocks. Our race horses are the fleetest in the world; our carriage and cava
horses are amongst the handsomest and most active of those employed for th
purposes; and our heavy draught horses are the most powerful, beautiful, a
docile of any of the large breeds.

Number and Value of Horses in Great Britain. — The number of horses used in Gr
Britain for different purposes is very great, although less so, perhaps, than has been
nerally supposed. Mr. Middleton (*Survey of Middlesex*, 2d ed. p. 639.) estimated
total number of horses in England and Wales, employed in husbandry, at 1,200,0
and those employed for other purposes at 600,000.   Dr. Colquhoun, contrary to his us
practice, reduces this estimate to 1,500,000 for Great Britain; and in this instance
are inclined to think his guess is not very wide of the mark.   The Parliamentary Pa
(No. 688. Sess. 1830, see opposite page), gives an account of the number of the vari
descriptions of horses in England and Wales, which paid duty in 1814, when those us
in husbandry were taxed; and the numbers, when summed up, amount to 1,204,3
But this account does not include stage coach, mail coach, and hackney coach hors
nor does it include those used in posting.   Poor persons keeping only one horse w
also exempted from the duty; as were all horses employed in the regular regiments
cavalry and artillery, and in the volunteer cavalry.   In Mr. Middleton's estimate, alrea
referred to, he calculated the number of post chaise horses, and mail, stage, and hack
coach ditto, at 100,000; but this is an extreme exaggeration, and shows how little
pendence can be placed, in such matters, on conclusions drawn from probabilities or
and without any ascertained data to found upon.   According to a statement we h
procured from the Tax-office, the numbers, as returned for 1828, were,

> " Horses employed in stage coaches, including mail coaches   -   16,006
> Ditto in hackney coaches, in so far as they claimed exemption   -   706
> Volunteer cavalry   -   -   -   -   20,253
> In 1829, the volunteer cavalry were reduced to 10,241."

The duties begin to be charged as soon as horses are used for drawing or riding,
not previously.

On the whole, therefore, it may be fairly estimated that there are in Great Brit
1,500,000 horses employed for various purposes of pleasure and utility. They may, p
bably, be worth at an average from 12*l*. to 15*l*., making their total value from 18,000,0
to 22,500,000*l*. sterling, exclusive of the young horses.

The rates of duty payable at present (1831) on horses, are the same as those specified in the following t
for 1825 and 1828.   A horse *bonâ fide* kept and usually employed for the purpose of husbandry, on a f
of less value than 200*l*. a year, though occasionally used as a riding horse, is exempt from the duty.
husbandry horses, whatever may be the value of the farms on which they are kept, may be rode, fre
duty, to and from any place to which a burthen shall have been carried or brought back; to procure
dical assistance, and to or from markets, places of public worship, elections of members of parliam
courts of justice, or meetings of commissioners of taxes.
  Brood mares, while kept for the sole purpose of breeding, are exempted from all duty.
  Horses may be let or lent for agricultural purposes, without any increase of duty.
  Mules employed in carrying ore and coal are exempted from any duty. — (See the Statutes in *Ch*
edition of *Burn's Justice*, vol. v. tit. *Assessed Taxes.*)
  The facility with which horses may be stolen has led to the enactment of several regulations with
spect to their sale, &c.   The property of a horse cannot be conveyed away without the express conse
the owner.   Hence, a *bonâ fide* purchaser gains no property in a horse that has been stolen, unless
bought in a *fair*, or an *open* market.   It is directed that the keeper of every fair or market shall app
a certain open place for the sale of horses, and one or more persons to take toll there, and keep the
from 10 in the forenoon till sunset.   The owner's property in the horse stolen is not altered by sale
legal fair, unless it be openly ridden, led, walked, or kept standing for *one hour at least, and has bee*
gistered, for which the buyer is to pay 1*d*.   Sellers of horses in fairs or markets must be known to the
takers, or to some other creditable person known to them, who declares his knowledge of them, and en
the same in a book kept by the toll-taker for the purpose.   Without these formalities the sale is void.
owner of a horse stolen may, notwithstanding its legal sale, redeem it on payment or tender of the
any time within six months of the time of the theft. — (*Burn's Justice of the Peace, Chitty's* ed. v
p. 264)
  In order to obviate the facility afforded by means of slaughtering houses for the disposal of stolen ho
it was enacted in 1786 (26 Geo. 3. c. 71.), that all persons keeping places for slaughtering horses, geld
sheep, hogs, or other cattle not killed for butcher's meat, shall obtain a licence from the quarter ses
first producing from the minister and churchwardens, or from the minister and two substantial h
holders, a certificate of their fitness to be intrusted with the management and carrying on of such busi
Persons slaughtering horses or cattle without licence are guilty of felony, and may be whipped an
prisoned, or transported.   Persons licensed, are bound to affix over the door or gate of the place w
their business is carried on. in legible characters, the words " *Licensed for slaughtering Horses, pur*
to an Act passed in the 26th Year of his Majesty King Geo. III." The parishioners entitled to meet in v
are authorised to choose annually, or oftener, inspectors, whose duty it is to take an account and do
tion, &c. of every living horse, &c. that may be brought to such slaughtering house to be killed, and of
dead horse that may be brought to be flayed.   Persons bringing cattle are to be asked an account of
selves, and if it be not deemed satisfactory, they may be carried before a justice. This act does not e
to curriers, fellmongers, tanners, or persons killing aged or distempered cattle, for the purpose of us
curing their hides in their respective businesses; but these, or any other persons, who shall knowin
wilfully kill any sound or useful horse, &c., shall for every such offence forfeit not more than 20*l*., or
less than 10*l*.
  The stealing of horses and other cattle is a capital crime, punishable by death.   The malici
wounding, maiming, killing, &c. of horses and other cattle, is to be punished, at the discretion of the
by transportation beyond seas for life, for any term not less than seven years, or by imprisonment f
term not exceeding four years; and if a male, he may be once, twice, or thrice publicly or pri
whipped, should the court so direct. — (7 & 8 *Geo.* 4. c. 29. § 25. ; 7 & 8 *Geo.* 4. c. 30. § 16.)

:ount of the Number of Horses charged with Duty in 1814, 1825, and 1828, the
s of Duty, and the Produce of the Duties. — (*Parl. Paper*, No. 688. Sess. 1830.)

	1814.			1825.			1828.		
r riding rriages, at pros: g 1	Number of Horses.	Rates of Duty for each Horse.	Amount of Duty.	Number of Horses.	Rates of Duty for each Horse.	Amount of Duty.	Number of Horses.	Rates of Duty for each Horse.	Amount of Duty.
		£ s. d.	£ s. d.		£ s. d.	£ s. d.		{ The same as for 1825. }	£ s. d.
g 1	161,123	2 17 6	463,228 12 0	116,529	1 8 9	167,510 8 9	121,263		174,315 11 3
2	31,842	4 14 6	150,453 9 0	27,418	2 7 3	64,775 0 6	29,551	do.	69,814 4 9
3	12,774	5 4 6	66,744 3 0	10,281	2 12 3	26,859 2 3	10,613	do.	27,726 9 3
4	7,612	5 10 0	41,866 0 0	5,748	2 15 0	15,807 0 0	5,913	do.	16,260 15 0
5	3,670	5 11 6	20,460 5 0	3,190	2 15 9	8,892 2 6	3,088	do.	8,607 16 0
6	3,060	5 16 0	17,748 0 0	2,172	2 18 0	6,298 16 0	2,351	do.	6,817 18 0
7 & 8	3,372	5 19 6	20,147 14 0	2,279	2 19 9	6,808 10 3	2,225	do.	6,647 3 9
9	720	6 1 6	4,374 0 0	585	3 0 9	1,776 18 9	558	do.	1,694 18 6
10 to 12	2,079	6 7 0	13,201 13 0	1,486	3 3 6	4,718 1 0	1,308	do.	4,152 18 0
13 to 16	746	6 7 6	4,755 15 0	520	3 3 9	1,657 10 0	601	do.	1,915 13 9
17	51	6 8 0	326 8 0	34	3 4 0	108 16 0	17	do.	54 8 0
18	144	6 9 0	928 16 0	54	3 4 6	174 3 0	126	do.	406 7 0
19	38	6 10 0	247 0 0	133	3 5 0	432 5 0	128	do.	416 0 0
pwards	1,348	6 12 0	8,896 16 0	1,018	3 6 0	3,359 8 0	1,099	do.	3,626 14 0
otal	228,579	-	813,378 11 6	171,447	-	309,178 2 0	178,841	- -	322,456 17 3
ire	1,454	2 17 6	4,180 5 0	1,702	1 8 9	2,446 12 6	2,001	do.	2,876 8 9
s and	560	2 17 6	1,610 0 0	711	1 8 9	1,022 1 3	780	do.	1,121 5 0
ed in } bond	177,025	1 1 0	185,876 5 0						
ndry, a and	722,863	0 17 6	632,505 2 6						
ndry poses ler 13	35,816	0 3 0	5,372 8 0						
ng to , un- keep- than	38,010	0 3 0	5,701 10 0						
rid- Car- ex- ds	-	-	-	19,121	1 1 0	20,077 1 0	21,923	do.	23,028 12 0
arm-	-	-	-	1,251	1 5 0	1,563 15 0	1,391	do.	1,738 15 0
hers, ly is	-	-	-	2,089	1 8 9	4,296 13 9	3,404	do.	4,893 5 0
are rade rge-	-	-	-	1,085	0 10 6 for the 2d horse.	569 12 6	1,084	do.	569 2 0
the ties, ted	-	-	-	112,989	0 10 6	59,319 4 6	117,609	do.	61,744 14 6
	-	-	-	410	0 10 6	215 5 0	481	do.	252 10 6

Trade in Horses. — The horses of France are not, speaking generally, nearly
ome, fleet, or powerful, as those of England. Latterly, however, the French
n making great efforts to improve the breed of horses, and have, in this view,
king large importations from England. — (See HAVRE.) We subjoin
nt of the Importation and Exportation of Horses into and from France, during the Five Years
ending with 1827.

				Horses.	Mares and Geldings.	Foals.	Totals.	Difference in Favour of Importation.
Exported	-	-	-	1	960	897	1,858	} 5,583
Imported	-	-	-	1,097	2,193	4,151	7,441	
Exported	-	-	-	37	1,001	207	1,245	} 16,881
Imported	-	-	-	2,578	8,921	6,627	18,126	
Exported	-	-	-	69	2,935	350	3,354	} 20,823
Imported	-	-	-	2,234	17,027	4,916	24,177	
Exported	-	-	-	nil.	3,799	624	4,433	} 11,355
Imported	-	-	-	1,181	10,352	4,255	15,788	
Exported	-	-	-	3	3,294	921	4,218	} 11,354
Imported	-	-	-	939	9,197	5,438	15,572	
Exported	-	-	-	110	11,929	3,009	15,108	} 65,996
Imported	-	-	-	8,029	47,690	25,387	81,104	

HORSE DEALERS, persons whose business it is to buy and sell horses

Every person carrying on the business of a horse dealer is required to keep a book, in which h
enter an account of the number of the horses kept by him for sale and for use, specifying the du
which the same are respectively liable ; this book is to be open, at all reasonable times, to the inspec
the officers ; and a true copy of the same is to be delivered quarterly to the assessor or assessors
parish in which the party resides. Penalty for non-compliance, 50l.—(43 Geo. 3. c. 161.) Horse c
are assessed, if they carry on their business in the metropolis, 25l. ; and if elsewhere, 12l. 10s.

An Account of the Number and Amount of Licences* granted to Dealers in Horses within the Citi
within the Liberties of London and Westminster, the Parishes of Saint Mary-le-bone and Saint Pa
in the County of Middlesex, and in the Borough of Southwark, in the County of Surrey, for the
1828, 1829, and 1830 ;—also, A similar Account applicable to other Parts of Great Britain, duri
same Years, so far as the same can be made up.—(Parl. Paper, No. 176. Sess. 1831.)

	Year ended 5th of April, 1828.		Year ended 5th of April, 1829.		Year ended 5th of A 1830.	
	Number of Horse Dealers.	Amount of Duty.	Number of Horse Dealers.	Amount of Duty.	Number of Horse Dealers.	Amount of
		£ s. d.		£ s. d.		£
Cities and Liberties of London and Westminster - - Parishes of St. Mary-le-Bone - St. Pancras Borough of Southwark -	47	1,175 0 0	46	1,137 10 0	45	1,125
Rest of Great Britain	1,085	13,925 0 0	1,106	14,187 10 0	1,095	14,087 1
Totals for Great Britain	1,132	15,100 0 0	1,152	15,325 0 0	1,140	15,212 1

* Horse dealers do not take out licences ; they are required to make returns of their exercise
trade, and are assessed to the duty.

HUNDRED WEIGHT, a weight of 112 lbs. avoirdupois, generally w
cwt.

I. and J.

JALAP, or **JALOP** (Ger. Jalapp; Fr. Jalap; It. Sciarappa; Sp. Jalapa
root of a sort of convolvulus, so named from Xalapa, in Mexico, whence we c
import it. The root when brought to this country is in thin transverse slices,
hard, weighty, of a blackish colour on the outside, and internally of a dark
with black circular striæ. The hardest and darkest coloured is the best;
which are light, spongy, and pale coloured, should be rejected. The odour of
especially when in powder, is very characteristic. Its taste is exceedingly nau
accompanied by a sweetish bitterness.—(Lewis's Mat. Med.; Brande's
macy.)

JAMAICA PEPPER. See Pimento.

JAPANNED WARES (Ger. Japanische ware; Du. Japansch lakwerk
Marchandises de Japon), articles of every description, such as tea-trays, clock
candlesticks, snuff-boxes, &c. covered with coats of japan, whether plain, c
bellished with painting or gilding. Birmingham is the grand staple of this
facture, which is there carried on to a great extent. Pontypool, in Monmout
was formerly famous for japanning; but it is at present continued there on
small scale only. It is prosecuted with spirit and success at Bilston and W
hampton.

JASPER (Ger. Jaspiss; Du. Jaspis; Fr. Jaspe; It. Diaspro; Sp. Jaspe
Jaschma). This stone is an ingredient in the composition of many mountai
occurs usually in large amorphous masses, sometimes in round or angular p
its fracture is conchoidal; specific gravity from 2 to 2·7. Its colours are v
when heated it does not decrepitate: it is usually divided into four species,
minated Egyptian jasper, striped jasper, porcelain jasper, and common jasp
is sometimes employed by jewellers in the formation of seals.

JERSEY. See Guernsey.

JET, or **PITCH COAL** (Du. Git, Zwarte barnsteen; Fr. Jais, Jayet
Gagat; It. Gagala, Lustrino; Lat. Gagus, Gagates), of a black velvet colour,
massive, in plates; sometimes in the shape of branches of trees, but wi
regular woody texture. Internal lustre, shining, resinous, soft; rather
easily frangible; specific gravity 1·3. It is used for fuel, and for making

snuff-boxes. In Prussia it is called black amber, and is cut into rosaries and [k]laces. It is distinguished by its splendid lustre, and conchoidal fracture. *Thomson's Chemistry.*)

[J]ETSAM. See FLOTSAM.

[I]MPORTATION AND EXPORTATION, the bringing of commodities from [abroad, and the] sending them to other countries. A very large portion of the revenue of [th]at Britain being derived from customs duties, or from duties on commodities [impo]rted from abroad; and drawbacks being given on many, and bounties on a [few] articles exported; the business of importation and exportation is subjected to [vario]us regulations, which must be carefully observed by those who would [avoi]d incurring penalties, and subjecting their property to confiscation. The [regu]lations referred to, have been embodied in the act 6 Geo. 4. c. 107., which [we su]bjoined.

GENERAL PROVISIONS.

Goods to be landed, nor Bulk broken, before Report and Entry. — No goods shall be unladen from any [ship ar]riving from parts beyond the seas, at any port in the United Kingdom, or in the Isle of Man, nor shall [bulk b]e broken after the arrival of such ship within four leagues of the coast thereof, before due report [of suc]h ship, and the due entry of such goods, shall have been made, and warrant granted in manner [herein]after directed; and no goods shall be so unladen, except at such times and places, and in such [manne]r, and by such persons, and under the care of such officers, as is and are hereinafter directed; and [if goo]ds not duly reported, or which shall be unladen contrary hereto, shall be forfeited; and if bulk be [broken] contrary hereto, the master shall forfeit 100*l.*; and if, after the arrival within four leagues, any [alterat]ion be made in the stowage of the cargo, so as to facilitate the unlading of any part, or if any part [be remo]ved, destroyed, or thrown overboard, or any package opened, such ship shall be deemed to have [broken] Bulk: Provided always, that the several articles hereinafter enumerated may be landed in the [United] Kingdom without report, entry, or warrant; (that is to say,) diamonds and bullion, fresh [fish, or] British taken and imported in British ships, turbots and lobsters fresh, however taken or im-[ported.] — § 2.

MANIFEST.

British Ships, and all Ships with Tobacco, to have Manifests. — No goods shall be imported into the [United] Kingdom, or into the Isle of Man, in any British ship, nor any tobacco in any ship, unless the [master] shall have on board a manifest of such goods, or of such tobacco, made out and dated and signed [by hi]m at the place where the same or the different parts of the same were taken on board, and authen-[ticated] in the manner hereinafter provided; and every such manifest shall set forth the name and the [tonnag]e of the ship, the name of the master, and of the place to which the ship belongs, and of the place [where] the goods were taken on board, and of the place for which they are destined, and shall contain a [particu]lar account of all the packages on board, with the marks and numbers thereon, and the sorts of [kinds a]nd different kinds of each sort contained therein, to the best of the master's knowledge, and of the [particu]lars of such goods as are stowed loose, and the names of the shippers and consignees, as far as [known] to the master; and to such particular account shall be subjoined a general account of the total [numbe]r of the packages of each sort, describing the same by their usual names, or by such descriptions as [the sa]me can best be known by, and the different goods therein, and also the total quantities of the [differe]nt goods stowed loose: Provided always, that every manifest for tobacco shall be a separate mani-[fest, di]stinct from any manifest for any other goods, and shall, without fail, contain the particular weight [of toba]cco in each hogshead, cask, chest, or case, with the tare of the same; and if such tobacco be the [produc]e of the dominions of the Grand Signior, then the number of the parcels or bundles within any [such h]ogshead, cask, chest, or case, shall be stated in such manifest. — § 3.

[Manifest to b]e produced to Officers in Colonies, &c. — Before any ship shall be cleared out from any place in any [of the] British possessions abroad, or from any place in China, with any goods for the United Kingdom or [the] Isle of Man, the master shall produce the manifest to the collector or comptroller of customs, or [the p]roper officer, who shall certify upon the same the date of the production thereof to him: Provided [always] that in all places within the territorial possessions of the East India Company, the servant of the [Comp]any by whom the last despatches of such ship shall be delivered, shall be the proper officer to [authen]ticate the manifest, and in all places in China the chief supercargo of the said Company. — § 4.

[Manifest to be] produced to Consuls. — Before the departure of any ship from any place beyond the seas, not under [Brit]ish dominions, where any tobacco has been taken on board, the master shall produce the manifest [to the B]ritish consul or chief British officer, if there be any such resident at such place; and such consul [or office]r shall certify upon the same the date of the production thereof. — § 5.

[Goods wa]nting, Master to forfeit 100l. — If any goods shall be imported without such manifest, or if any [goods c]ontained in such manifest be not on board, the master shall forfeit 100*l.* — § 6.

[Mani]fest to be produced within Four Leagues, and Copies delivered to Officers. — The master shall pro-[duce su]ch manifest to any officer of customs who shall come on board his ship, after her arrival within [four lea]gues of the coast, and who shall demand the same for his inspection; and such master shall also [produce] to such officer, who shall be the first to demand it, a true copy of such manifest signed by the [master]; and shall also deliver another copy to any other officer of customs, who shall be the first to [demand] the same within the limits of the port to which such ship is bound; and thereupon such officers [shall cer]tify on such manifest and on such copies, the date of the production of such manifest and of the [delivery] of such copies, and shall transmit such copies to the collector and comptroller of the port to which [such ve]ssel is first bound, and shall return such manifest to the master; and if such master shall not pro-[duce su]ch manifest, or deliver such copy, he shall forfeit 100*l.* — § 7.

REPORT.

[Maste]r, within Twenty-four Hours, and before breaking Bulk, shall report. — The master of every ship [arrivin]g from parts beyond the seas at any port in the United Kingdom or in the Isle of Man, whether [laden o]r in ballast, shall, within twenty-four hours after such arrival, and before bulk be broken, make [a repo]rt of such ship, upon oath, before the collector or comptroller, and such report shall contain an [account] of the particular marks, numbers, and contents of all the different packages or parcels of the [goods o]n board, and the particulars of such goods as are stowed loose, and of the place or places where [such go]ods were taken on board, and of the burthen of such ship, and of the country where such ship was [built, or] if British, of the port of registry, and of the country of the people to whom such ship belongs, [and of t]he name and country of the person who was master during the voyage, and of the number of the [crew, b]y whom such ship was navigated, stating how many are subjects of the country to which such [ship bel]ongs, and how many are of some other country; and in such report it shall be further declared, [whethe]r such ship has broken bulk in the course of her voyage, and what part of the cargo, if any, is [intended] for importation at such port; and what part, if any, is intended for importation at another port [in the U]nited Kingdom, or at another port in the Isle of Man; and what part, if any, is prohibited to be

imported, except to be warehoused for exportation only; and what part, if any, is intended for exp
ation, and what surplus stores or stock remain on board such ship; and if a British ship, v
foreign-made sails or cordage, not being standing or running rigging, are in use on board such sh
and the master who shall fail to make such report, or who shall make a false report, shall fo
100*l.* — § 8.

Packages reported " Contents unknown," may be opened and examined. — If the contents of
package so intended for exportation in such ship to parts beyond the seas, shall be reported by
master as being unknown, it shall be lawful for the officers of customs to open and examine s
package, or to bring the same to the king's warehouse for that purpose; and if there be found
such package any goods which may not be entered for home use, such goods shall be forfeited; a
the goods be such as may be entered for home use, the same shall be chargeable with the dutie
importation; unless in either case the commissioners of customs, in consideration of the sort of s
goods, or the small rate of duty payable thereon, shall see fit to deliver the same for exportation. — §

Master to deliver Manifest; and, if required, Bill of Lading, or Copy. — The master shall, at the tim
making such report, deliver to the collector or comptroller the manifest of the cargo, where a manife
required; and if required by the collector or comptroller, shall produce to him any bills of lading,
true copy thereof; and shall answer upon oath all such questions relating to the ship and cargo, and o
and voyage, as shall be put to him by such collector or comptroller; and in case of failure or refus
produce such manifest, or to answer such questions, or to produce such bill of lading or copy;
such manifest, or bill of lading, or copy, shall be false; or if any bill of lading be uttered by any ma
and the goods expressed therein shall not have been *bonâ fide* shipped on board; or if any bill of lad
uttered or produced by any master, shall not have been signed by him; or any such copy shall not h
been received or made by him previously to his leaving the place where the goods were shipped; in ev
such case such master shall forfeit 100*l.* — § 10.

Part of Cargo reported for another Port. — If any part of the cargo for which a manifest is required
reported for importation at some other port, the collector and comptroller of the port at which s
part of the cargo has been delivered, shall notify such delivery on the manifest, and return the sam
the master. — § 11.

Ships to come quickly to Place of Unlading, but to bring to at Stations for boarding Officers. — E
ship shall come as quickly up to the proper place of mooring and unlading as the nature of the port
admit, and without touching at any other place; and in proceeding to such place shall bring to at stat
appointed by the commissioners of customs for the boarding of ships by the officers of customs; and a
arrival at such place of mooring or unlading, such ship shall not remove, except directly to some o
proper place, and with the knowledge of the officer of customs, on penalty of 100*l.*, to be paid by
master: Provided always, that it shall be lawful for the commissioners of customs to appoint places t
the proper places for the mooring or unlading of ships importing tobacco, and where such ships only s
be moored or unladen; and in case the place so appointed shall not be within some dock surrounded v
walls, if any such ship after having been discharged shall remain at such place, or if any ship not imp
ing tobacco shall be moored at such place, the master shall forfeit 20*l.* — § 12.

Officers to board Ships, and to have free Access to all Parts. — It shall be lawful for the proper offi
of customs to board any ship arriving at any port in the United Kingdom or in the Isle of Man, and fr
to stay on board until all the goods shall have been delivered from the same; and such officers shall h
free access to every part of the ship, with power to fasten down hatchways, and to mark any goods be
landing, and to lock up, seal, mark, or otherwise secure any goods on board; and if any place, or any
or chest, be locked, and the keys be withheld, such officers, if they be of a degree superior to tidesme
watermen, may open any such place, box, or chest, in the best manner in their power; and if the
tidesmen or watermen, or only of that degree, they shall send for their superior officer, who may op
and if any goods be found concealed on board any such ship, they shall be forfeited; and if the off
shall place any lock, mark, or seal upon any goods on board, and such lock, mark, or seal be wil
opened, altered, or broken before due delivery of such goods; or if any of such goods be secretly conv
away; or if the hatchways, after having been fastened down by the officer, be opened; the master s
forfeit 100*l.* — § 13.

National Ships, British and Foreign, having Goods on board, Persons in Charge to deliver an Account,
answer on Oath. — If any ship (having commission from his Majesty, or from any foreign prince or s
arriving as aforesaid at any port, shall have on board any goods laden in parts beyond the seas, the
tain, master, purser, or other person having the charge of such ship, or of such goods, for that voy
shall, before any part of such goods be taken out of the ship, or when called upon so to do by any of
of the customs, deliver an account in writing under his hand, of the quality and quantity of every pac
or parcel of such goods, and of the marks and numbers thereon, and of the names of the shippers
consignees, and shall answer upon oath to the collector or comptroller such questions as shall be requ
of him; and on failure thereof, such captain, master, purser, or other person, shall forfeit 100*l.*; an
such ships shall be liable to such searches as merchant ships are liable to; and the officers of customs
freely enter and go on board all such ships, and bring from thence on shore into the king's w
house any goods found on board; subject nevertheless to such regulations in respect of ships of
belonging to his Majesty, as shall be directed by the commissioners of the treasury of the Ur
Kingdom. — § 14.

Master to deliver List of Crew. — The master of every British ship arriving at any port in the Ui
Kingdom, on her return from any British possessions in America, shall, within ten days, deliver
oath to the collector or comptroller, a list containing the names and descriptions of the crew which
on board at the time of clearing from the United Kingdom, and of the crew on board at the tim
arrival in any of the said possessions, and of every seaman who has deserted or died during the voy
and also the amount of wages due at the time of his death to each seaman so dying; and every m
omitting so to do shall forfeit 50*l.*; and such list shall be kept by the collector for the inspection o
persons interested therein. — § 15.   (N. B. By the 7 Geo. 4. c. 48. this clause is made applicable o
ships arriving from the West Indies.)

ENTRY.

After Fourteen Days, Officer may land Goods not entered, and certain Goods before Fourteen Da
Every importer of goods shall, within fourteen days after the arrival of the ship, make perfect
inwards of such goods, or entry by bill of sight in manner hereinafter provided, and shall within
time land the same; and in default of such entry and landing, it shall be lawful for the officers of cus
to convey such goods to the king's warehouse; and whenever the cargo shall have been discharged,
the exception only of a small quantity of goods, it shall be lawful for the officers of customs to co
such remaining goods, and at any time to convey any small packages of goods to the king's wareh
although such fourteen days shall not have expired, there to be kept waiting the due entry th
during the remainder of such fourteen days; and if the duties due upon any goods so conveyed t
king's warehouse, shall not be paid within three months after such fourteen days shall have ex
together with all charges of removal and warehouse rent, the same shall be sold, and the produ
applied, first, to the payment of freight and charges, next of duties, and the overplus, if any, t
proprietor. — § 16.

Bill of Entry to be delivered. — The person entering any goods inwards (whether for payment of
or to be warehoused upon the first entry, or for payment of duty upon taking out of the warehou
whether such goods be free of duty) shall deliver to the collector or comptroller, a bill of the entry

in words at length, expressing the name of the ship, and of the master, and of the place from
they were brought, and the description and situation of the warehouse, if to be warehoused, and
.e of the person in whose name the goods are to be entered, and the quantity and description of
nd number and denomination of packages ; and in the margin shall delineate the marks and
s of such packages, and shall pay down any duties payable upon the goods mentioned in such
and such person shall also deliver at the same time two or more duplicates, as the case may
of such bill, in which all sums and numbers may be expressed in figures, and the particulars in
l shall be written and arranged in such form, and the number of such duplicates shall be such as
ector and comptroller shall require ; and such bill, being duly signed by the collector and
ller, and transmitted to the landing waiter, shall be the warrant for the landing or delivering
goods. — § 17.

lid unless agreeing with Manifest, Report, and other Documents. — No entry, nor any warrant for
ing of goods, or for taking goods out of any warehouse, shall be valid, unless the particulars in
try shall correspond with the particulars in the report of the ship, and in the manifest, where a
t is required, and in the certificate or other document, where any is required, by which the im-
n or entry is authorised ; nor unless the goods shall have been properly described in such entry
enominations, and with the characters and circumstances according to which such goods are
with duty or may be imported, either to be used in the United Kingdom, or to be warehoused
rtation only ; and any goods taken or delivered out, by virtue of any entry or warrant, not
nding in all such respects, shall be deemed to be goods landed without due entry, and shall
ted. — § 18.

by Number, Measure, or Weight, or ad Valorem. — If the goods in such entry be charged to pay
ording to the number, measure, or weight, such number, measure, or weight shall be stated in
; and if to pay duty according to the value, such value shall be stated in the entry, and shall be
by the declaration of the importer or his agent, written upon the entry and attested by his signa-
d if any person make such declaration, not being the importer or proprietor, nor his agent, such
all forfeit the sum of 100*l.* ; and such declaration shall be made in form following, and shall be
upon the person by or in behalf of whom the same shall be made. — § 19.

t. B., do hereby declare, that I am [the importer, *or* authorised by the importer] of the goods
d in this entry, and that I enter the same [*stating which, if part only*] at the sum of ————
————. Witness my hand the ———— day of ————

" *A. B.*"

undervalued, Officers may detain. — If upon examination it shall appear to the officers of
that such goods are not valued according to the true value thereof, it shall be lawful for such
> detain such goods, and (within five days from the landing thereof, if it be in London, Leith, or
>r within seven days if in any other port, or if in any port in the Isle of Man) to take such goods
se of the crown : and if a different rate of duty shall be charged, according as the value shall be
in the entry to be above or to be below any particular price, and such goods shall be entered so
iable to the lower duty, and it shall appear to the officers that such goods, by reason of their real
e liable to the higher duty, it shall be lawful for such officers to take such goods for the use of
n ; and the commissioners shall thereupon cause the amount of such valuation, together with an
l 10 per cent. thereon, and also the duties paid upon such entry, to be paid to the importer or
r in full satisfaction, and shall dispose of such goods for the benefit of the crown ; and if the
of such sale shall exceed the sums so paid, and all charges incurred by the crown, one moiety of
lus shall be given to the officers who had detained the goods ; and the money retained for the
all be paid into the hands of the collector, with the knowledge of the comptroller, and carried to
as duties of customs. — § 20.

of East India Goods according to Sales. — The value of goods imported by the East India Com-
1 of all goods called " piece goods," being articles manufactured of silk, hair, or cotton, or any
thereof, imported by any person into the port of London, from places within the limits of the
r the Company, shall be ascertained by the gross price at which the same shall have been sold by
t the public sales of the Company ; and such goods shall be landed and secured in such manner
nmissioners shall require, until the duties shall have been paid, or the same shall have been
— § 21.

dia Company to sell Goods. — The East India Company shall openly expose to sale all such
charged to pay duty according to the value, by public auction, in the city of London, within
rs from the importation thereof ; and shall give notice at the Custom-house in London, to the
pointed to attend such sales, of the time and place thereof. — § 22.

Sight, if Goods be not known. — If the importer or his agent, after full conference with him,
are upon oath, before the collector or comptroller, that he cannot for want of full information
erfect entry, it shall be lawful for the collector and comptroller to receive an entry by bill of
the packages, by the best description which can be given, and to grant a warrant that the same
nded, and may be examined by such importer, in presence of the officers ; and within three days
goods shall have been so landed, the importer shall make a perfect entry, and shall either pay
duties, or shall duly warehouse the same, according to the purport of the perfect entry* :
always, that if any sum shall have been deposited upon any entry by bill of sight, on account of
, it shall be lawful for the officers to deliver, in virtue of the warrant for landing the same, any
of goods, the duty on which shall not exceed the sum deposited. — § 23.

ds to be taken to the King's Warehouse, and in One Month sold. — In default of perfect entry,
ch three days, such goods shall be taken to the king's warehouse by the officers ; and if the im-
ll not, within one month after such landing, make perfect entry, and pay the duties thereon, or
arts as can be entered for home use, together with charges of removal and of warehouse rent,
s shall be sold for payment of such duties, (or for exportation, if they cannot be entered for
or shall not be worth the duties and charges,) and for the payment of such charges ; and the
f any, shall be paid to the importer or proprietor. — § 24.

dia Company may enter by Bill of Sight, and make perfect Entry within Three Months. — It shall
for the East India Company, without making the proof before required, to enter by bill of sight,
ed and secured in such manner as the commissioners shall require, any goods imported by them,
ny goods imported by any other person, from places within the limits of the charter of the
with the consent of such person, upon condition to cause perfect entry to be made of such
in three months from the date of the importation ; either to warehouse the same, or to pay the
reon within the times hereinafter mentioned ; (that is to say,) if such goods be charged to pay
ding to the value, then within four months from the sale of the goods ; and if charged to pay
ding to the number, measure, or weight, then to pay one moiety of such duties within six

nacted by 7 Geo. 4. c. 48., that such goods, although landed by bill of sight, shall not be deemed
ied, or to be delivered out of the ship, within the meaning of the said act (6 Geo. 4 c. 107.),
virtue of such perfect entry when the same shall be made ; and that if such perfect entry be
n manner required by the said act for the landing of goods, such goods shall then be deemed to
nded without due entry thereof, and shall be forfeited. — § 5.

taking out a bill of sight, to have to make a deposit of 20*l.* ; and the goods must not be removed,
harge of an officer.

calendar months from the time of importation, and the other moiety within twelve calendar mo
and such goods shall be secured in such places and in such manner as the commissioners shall re
until the same shall have been duly entered, and the duties paid, or until the same shall have be
ported : Provided that it shall be lawful for any other person who shall have imported any good
places within the said limits into the port of London, in like manner to enter such goods by bill of
in his own name, upon giving security by bond, to the satisfaction of the commissioners, with th
conditions as are required of the said Company, for making perfect entries, and for selling at the s
the said Company, all such goods as are called " piece goods," and for the securing and paying of d
provided such goods be entered by such bill of sight, to be warehoused in some warehouse und
superintendence of the said Company, and in which goods imported by the Company may be se
— § 25.

In Default of Payment of Duties, Goods to be sold. — In default of perfect entry within three m
or of due entry or payment of duty within the times hereinbefore required, it shall be lawful f
commissioners to cause any such goods to be sold for the payment of duties, (or for exportation,
cannot be entered for home use,) and for the payment of all charges incurred ; and the overplus,
shall be paid to the proprietor. — § 26.

East India Company to pay Duties to Receiver-General. — The East India Company shall pay in
hands of the receiver-general, every sum due from the Company on account of the duties, at the
when the same shall become due ; and the receiver-general shall give a receipt for the moneys p
account of the collector, which receipt, when delivered to such collector, shall be received by h
cash. — § 27.

Goods damaged on Voyage ; Abatement of Duties. — If any goods rated to pay according to the nu
measure, or weight (except goods hereinafter mentioned), shall receive damage during the voya,
abatement of duties shall be allowed in proportion to the damage received ; provided proof be m
the satisfaction of the commissioners, or any officers acting under their directions, that such dama
received after the goods were shipped abroad, and before they were landed ; and provided claim to
abatement be made at the time of the first examination of such goods. — § 28.

Officers to examine Damage, and state Proportion ; or choose Two Merchants. — The offic
customs shall thereupon examine such goods, with reference to such damage, and may state the p
tion, and may make a proportionate abatement of duties ; but if the officers be incompetent to es
such damage, or if the importer be not satisfied with the abatement made, the collector and comp
shall choose two indifferent merchants, who shall examine the same, and declare upon oath in wha
portion such goods are lessened in their value by such damage, and thereupon the officers of custon
make an abatement of the duties according to the proportion of damage so declared by such merch
and if any of such goods be afterwards exported for drawback, an abatement of the drawback
like proportion shall be made, and declared in the bills of entry, and in the clearance for shipm
§ 29.

No Abatement for certain Goods. — Provided always, that no abatement of duties shall be ma
account of any damage received by coffee, currants, figs, lemons, oranges, raisins, tobacco, and w
§ 30.

*Returned Goods ; if Foreign Goods, Duties to be paid again ; or Goods may be warehoused, and c
Goods may not be returned for Home Use.* — It shall be lawful to re-import into the United Ki
from any place, in a ship of any country, any goods (except as hereinafter excepted) which shal
been legally exported, and to enter the same by bill of store, referring to the entry outwards, and e
ation thereof ; provided the property continue in the person by whom the same have been exp
and if the goods so returned be foreign goods, the same duties shall be payable thereon as those
which such goods had been originally imported ; or such goods may be warehoused as like goods
be warehoused upon a first importation : Provided always, that the several sorts of goods described
table following, shall not be re-imported for home use, upon the ground that the same had been
exported, but the same shall be deemed to be foreign goods, whether originally such or not, and sh
be deemed to be imported for the first time. — § 31. (N. B. The 10 Geo. 4. c. 43. enacts, that re
goods are not to be admitted by bill of store, unless re-imported within *six* years of their expor
otherwise they are to be deemed foreign goods, whether originally so or not.)

A Table of Goods exported, which may not be re-imported for Home Use.

Corn, grain, meal, flour, malt, hops, tobacco, and tea.

Goods for which any bounty or any drawback of excise had been received on exportation, un
special permission of the commissioners of his Majesty's customs, and on repayment of such bo
such drawback.

All goods for which bill of store cannot be issued in manner hereinafter directed, except small re
of British goods by special permission of the commissioners of his Majesty's customs, upon proof
satisfaction that the same are British, and had not been sold.

Bill of Store, by whom may be taken out ; when Entry by Bill of Store to be granted. — The pe
whose name any goods so re-imported were entered for exportation, shall deliver to the searcher
port of exportation, an exact account signed by him of the particulars, referring to the entry and
ance outwards, and to the return inwards, with the marks and numbers of the packages, both inwa
outwards ; and thereupon the searcher, finding that such goods had been legally exported, shall
bill of store for the same ; and if the person in whose name such goods were entered for exportati
not the proprietor thereof, but his agent, he shall declare upon oath on such bill of store the name
person by whom he was employed as agent ; and if the person to whom such returned goods are co
shall not be such proprietor and exporter, but he shall declare upon oath on such bill of store the name
person for whose use such goods have been consigned to him ; and the real proprietor shall ma
upon such bill of store to the identity of the goods exported and so returned, and that he was at th
of exportation and of re-importation the proprietor, and that the same had not during such tir
sold or disposed of ; and such affidavits shall be made before the collectors or comptrollers at the
exportation and of importation ; and thereupon the collector and comptroller shall admit such g
entry by bill of store, and grant their warrant accordingly. — § 32.

Surplus Stores subject as Goods. — The surplus stores of every ship arriving from parts beyond th
in the United Kingdom, or in the Isle of Man, shall be subject to the same duties, and the same
tions, as the like sorts of goods when imported by way of merchandise ; but if it shall appear
collector and comptroller that the quantity or description is not excessive or unsuitable, it shall be
for them to permit such surplus stores to be entered for the private use of the master, purser, or
or of any passenger to whom such surplus stores may belong, on payment of the proper duties, to
warehoused for the future use of such ship, although the same could not be imported by way
chandise. — § 33.

Goods from Plantations. — No goods shall be entered as being of any British possessions in A
(if any benefit attach to such distinction), unless the master shall have delivered to the colle
comptroller a certificate, under the hand of the proper officer of the place where such goods wer
on board, of the due clearance of such ship from thence, containing an account of such goods. —

Certificate of Growth of Sugar, Coffee, Cocoa Nuts, Spirits, and Mahogany, from Plantations. —
any sugar, coffee, cocoa nuts, spirits, or mahogany, shall be entered as being of the produce
British possession in America, or the Island of Mauritius, the master shall deliver to the col

troller a certificate, under the hand of the officer of the place where such goods were taken on
, testifying that proof had been made that such goods are of the produce of some British possession,
g the name of the place, and the quantity and quality, and the number and denomination of
ges, and the name of the ship, and of the master thereof; and such master shall also make oath
e the collector or comptroller, that such certificate was received by him at the place where such
were taken on board, and that the goods so imported are the same. — § 35.

tificate of Sugar from Limits of Charter. — Before any sugar shall be entered as being the produce of
ritish possession in the limits of the East India Company's charter, the master shall deliver to the
tor or comptroller a certificate under the hand and seal of the proper officer at the place where such
was taken on board, testifying that oath had been made before him by the shipper of such sugar,
he same was really and *bonâ fide* the produce of such British possession; and such master shall
lake oath before the collector or comptroller, that such certificate was received by him at the place
e such sugar was taken on board, and that the sugar so imported is the same as is mentioned therein.
6.

tificate of Wine, Produce of the Cape of Good Hope. — Before any wine shall be entered as being the
ce of the Cape of Good Hope, the master of the ship importing the same shall deliver to the collector
mptroller, a certificate under the hand of the proper officer of the Cape of Good Hope, testifying
roof had been made in manner required by law, that such wine is of the produce of the Cape of
Hope, or the dependencies thereof, stating the quantity and sort of such wine, and the number and
nination of the packages containing the same; and such master shall also make oath before the
tor or comptroller that such certificate was received by him at the Cape of Good Hope, and that the
so imported is the same as is mentioned therein. — § 37.

ds of Guernsey, Jersey, &c. Duty free ; with Exceptions. — It shall be lawful to import into the
d Kingdom any goods of the produce or manufacture of the Islands of Guernsey, Jersey, Alderney,
or Man, from the said islands respectively, without payment of any duty ; (except in the cases here-
r mentioned ;) and such goods shall not be deemed to be included in any charge of duties imposed
v act hereinafter to be made on the importation of goods generally from parts beyond the seas : Pro-
always, that such goods may nevertheless be charged with any proportion of such duties as shall
countervail any duties of excise, or any coast duty, payable on the like goods, the produce of the
r the United Kingdom into which they shall be imported : Provided also, that such exemption from
hall not extend to any manufactures of the said islands, made from materials the produce of any
i country ; except manufactures of linen and cotton made in and imported from the Isle of Man.

ter to deliver Certificate of Produce, and make Oath to Certificate. — Before any goods shall be
d as being the produce of the said islands, (if any benefit attach to such distinction,) the master of
ip or vessel importing the same shall deliver to the collector or comptroller, a certificate from the
or, lieutenant-governor, or commander-in-chief of the island from whence such goods were im-
, that proof had been made in manner required by law, that such goods were of the produce of such
stating the quantity and quality of the goods, and the number and denomination of the packages
ing the same; and such master shall also make oath before the collector or comptroller, that such
ate was received by him at the place where such goods were taken on board, and that the goods so
ed are the same as are mentioned therein. — § 39.

ssury may permit Produce of Colonial Fisheries to be imported from Guernsey, &c. — It shall be
for the commissioners of his Majesty's treasury, when and so long as they shall see fit, to permit
ods the produce of the British possessions or fisheries in North America, which shall have been
imported into the islands of Guernsey or Jersey direct from such possessions, to be imported into
ited Kingdom for home use direct from those islands, under such regulations as the said commis-
shall direct; any thing in the law of navigation to the contrary notwithstanding. — § 40.

ls with Stone from Guernsey, &c. not to be piloted. — No vessel arriving on the coast of England
uernsey, Jersey, Alderney, Sark, or Man, wholly laden with stone the production thereof, shall
le to be conducted or piloted by pilots appointed and licensed by the corporation of the Trinity-
of Deptford Strond ; any law, custom, or usage to the contrary notwithstanding. — § 41.

British taking and curing, and Lobsters and Turbots, free of Duty on Importation. — Fresh fish of
ind, of British taking, and imported in British ships, and fresh lobsters and turbots, however
or in whatever ship imported, and cured fish of every kind, of British taking and curing, imported
all duties, and shall not be deemed to be included in any charge of duty imposed by any act here-
be made on the importation of goods generally : Provided always, that before any cured fish shall
red free of duty, as being of such taking and curing, the master of the ship importing the same
ake oath before the collector or comptroller, that such fish was actually caught, taken, and cured
by his Majesty's subjects. — § 42.

he *Regulations as to Blubber*, which occupy three sections, see that article.

rtation direct. — No goods shall be deemed to be imported from any particular place, unless they
orted direct from such place, and shall have been there laden on board the importing ship,
s the first shipment of such goods, or after the same shall have been actually landed at such place.

r may sell Goods sufficient to defray Salvage. — It shall be lawful for the owner or salvor of any
y liable to the payment of duty saved from sea, and in respect of which any sum shall have been
d under any law at the time in force, or in respect of which any sum shall have been paid, or
to be paid, by the owner thereof or his agent, to the salvors, to defray the salvage of the same, to
much of the property so saved as will be sufficient to defray the salvage so awarded, or such other
paid or agreed to be paid ; and that upon the production of an award made in execution of any
v to the commissioners of his Majesty's customs, or upon proof to the satisfaction of the said com-
ers that such sum of money has been paid, or has been agreed to be paid, the said commissioners
by empowered and required to allow the sale of such property aforesaid, free from the payment of
s, to the amount of such sum so awarded, paid, or agreed to be paid, or to the amount of such
m as to the said commissioners shall seem just and reasonable : Provided always, that if such owner
r shall be dissatisfied with any determination of the said commissioners as to the amount of such
y to be sold duty free, it shall be lawful for such owner or salvor to refer any such determination
aid commissioners to the judgment and revision of the High Court of Admiralty, and in that case
e shall be suspended until the decision of such court shall have been had thereon. — § 47.

rn Goods, Derelict, &c. to be subject to same Duties as on Importation. — That all foreign goods,
, jetsam, flotsam, and wreck, brought or coming into the United Kingdom, or into the Isle of
all at all times be subject to the same duties as goods of the like kind imported into the United
n respectively are subject to ; and if any person shall have possession of any such goods, either on
within any port in the United Kingdom, and shall not give notice thereof to the proper officer of
oms within twenty-four hours after such possession, or shall not on demand pay the duties due
, or deliver the same into the custody of the proper officer of the customs, such person shall forfeit
a of 100*l*. ; and if any person shall remove or alter in quantity or quality any such liquors or
or shall open or alter any package containing any such liquors or tobacco, or shall cause any such
e done, or assist therein, before such liquors or tobacco shall be deposited in a warehouse, in the
of the officers of the customs, every such person shall forfeit the sum of 100*l*. ; and in default of
 nent of the duties on such liquors or tobacco within eighteen months from the time when the
ns so deposited, the same may be sold in like manner, and for the like purposes, as goods imported

may in such default be sold : Provided always, that any lord of the manor having by law just claim such liquors or tobacco, or if there be no such lord of the manor, then the person having possession of same, shall be at liberty to retain the same in his own custody, giving bond, with two sufficient suret to be approved by the proper officer of the customs, in treble the value of such goods, for the paymer the duties thereon at the end of one year and one day, or to deliver such goods to the proper off of the customs in the same state and condition as the same were in at the time of taking possess thereof. — § 48.

Goods under Excise Permit Regulations. — And whereas it may be expedient to subject some sort goods imported into the United Kingdom, to certain internal regulations and restraints, after the duties of customs have been paid thereon, and to place such regulations and restraints under the mana ment of the commissioners of excise ; it is therefore enacted, that no goods which are subject to regulations of excise, shall be taken or delivered out of the charge of the officers of customs, (altho the same may have been duly entered with them, and the full duties due thereon may have been pa until such goods shall also have been duly entered with the officers of excise, and permit granted by th for delivery of the same, nor unless such permit shall correspond in all particulars with the warran the officers of the customs : Provided always, that such entry shall not be received by the officers of excise, nor such permit granted by them, until a certificate shall have been produced to them of the ticulars of the goods, and of the warrants for the same, under the hand of the officers of customs shall have the charge of the goods : Provided also, that if upon any occasion it shall appear necessar shall be lawful for the officers of excise to attend the delivery of such goods by the officers of custo and to require that such goods shall be delivered only in their presence ; and it shall be lawful for s officers of excise to count, measure, gauge, or weigh such goods, and examine the same, and proceed in all respects in such manner as they shall be required by any act in force relating to the exc — § 49.

Times and Places for landing Goods. — No goods whatever (except diamonds, bullion, fresh fish, Br taken, and imported in British ships, and turbots and lobsters,) shall be unshipped or landed or put shore, but only on days not being Sundays or holidays, and in the day time, (that is to say,) from the day of September until the last day of March between sun-rising and sun-setting, and from the last of March to the first day of September between 7 in the morning and 4 in the afternoon ; nor s any goods, except as aforesaid, be so unshipped or landed, unless in the presence of the officer of custo and such goods, except as aforesaid, shall be landed at one of the legal quays, or at some wharf, quay place appointed by the commissioners of customs for the landing of goods by sufferance ; and no go except as aforesaid, after having been unshipped, shall be trans-shipped, or after having been put into boat or craft to be landed, shall be removed into any other boat or craft previously to their being c landed, without the authority of the officer of customs. — § 50.

Goods to be unshipped at the Expense of Importer. — The unshipping, carrying, and landing of all go and the bringing of the same to the proper place after landing, for examination, or for weighing, and putting of the same into the scales, and the taking of the same out of the scales, shall be performed by at the expense of, the importer. — § 51.

Restrictions absolute or modified as to Goods imported. — The several sorts of goods enumerated in table following shall either be absolutely prohibited to be imported, or shall be imported only under restrictions mentioned in such table, according to the several sorts of such goods.

A TABLE OF PROHIBITIONS AND RESTRICTIONS INWARDS.

List of Goods absolutely prohibited to be imported.

Arms, ammunition, and utensils of war, by way of merchandise, except by licence from his Majesty, for furnishing his Majesty's public stores only.

Bandstrings, of silk, until the 5th July, 1826.

Beef.

Books ; viz. first composed or written or printed in the United Kingdom, and printed or reprinted in any other country, imported for sale, except books not reprinted in the United Kingdom within twenty years ; or being parts of collections, the greater parts of which had been composed or written abroad.

Brocade of gold or silver } until the 5th July, 1826.
Buttons

Cattle, great ; except 600 head yearly from and of the breed of the Isle of Man, into the port of Chester.

Coin : viz. false money, or counterfeit sterling.

silver, of the realm, or any money purporting to be such, not being of the established standard in weight or fineness.

Cutwork, of silk, until the 5th July, 1826.

Fish of foreign taking or curing, or in foreign vessels ; except turbots and lobsters, stockfish, live eels, anchovies, sturgeon, botargo, and caviare.

Fringe, of silk, until the 5th July, 1826.

Gloves, until the 5th July, 1826.

Gunpowder ; except by licence from his Majesty, such licence to be granted for the furnishing his Majesty's stores only.

Lamb.

Malt.

Mutton.

Pork.

Ribands, laces, and girdles, foreign made, whether who partly of silk, until the 5th July, 1826 ; except rib laces, and girdles, brought by any person as part of dress.

Sheep.

Snuff-work.

Silks, until the 5th July, 1826 ; viz. wrought silks, Bes and stuffs mixed with silks or herbs, of the manufa of Persia, China, or the East Indies.

wrought silks, and silks mixed with gold or silver, or materials.

wrought silks, velvets, crapes and tiffanies, and any work made thereof, whether wholly or partly.

silk stockings, foreign made, except stockings broug any person for his or her private use.

Spirits ; viz. from the Isle of Man.

of a greater strength than one to nine over hydro proof ; except spirits the produce of the British posse or of the Cape of Good Hope.

Swine.

Tobacco-stalks stripped from the leaf, whether manufa or not.

Tobacco-stalk flour.

List of Goods subject to certain Restrictions on Importation.

Bonnets, hats, or platting of bast or straw, chip, cane or horse-hair, proper for making such hats or bonnets ; not being packed in bales or tubs, each of which shall contain 75 dozen of such hats, or 224 lbs. of such platting or other manufacture, at least. *

Cambrics or lawns ; not being in bales, cases, or boxes covered with sackcloth or canvass, each of which shall contain 100 who'e or 200 demi-piece., and except into the port of London, and except by licence from the commissioners of the customs. *

China, goods from : unless by the East India Company, and into the port of London.

China ware, or porcelain ware ; except into the ports of Lon-

don, Plymouth, Bristol, Liverpool, Hull, New Leith, Greenock, Dublin, Cork, and Belfast. *

Coffee ; unless in packages, each of which shall contain 1 weight of nett coffee at least. *

East India, goods of places within the limits of the East Company's charter: unless into such ports as sh approved of by the Lords of the Treasury, and de by order in council to be fit and proper for such in ation.

Hides, skins, horns, or hoofs, or any other part of cat beast, his Majesty may, by order in council, prohi order to prevent any contagious distemper.

Or-Molu ; viz. articles manufactured wholly or pas

* The act 7 Geo. 4. c. 48. § 6. is as follows : — So much of the said act (6 Geo. 4. c. 107.) for the ge regulation of the customs as prohibits the importation of any spirits, on account of the strength the and also so much of the said act as prohibits the importation of beef, or bacon, to be warehouse exportation only, shall be, and the same is hereby repealed ; and also so much of the said act a stricts in any way the importation of bonnets, hats, or platting of bast or straw, chips, cane, or horse and also of cambrics or lawns, and also of coffee, and also of or-molu, and also of chinaware and porce not being the produce of places within the limits of the East India Company's charter ; and also tobacco made up in rolls, being the produce of and imported from the state of Colombia, and in pac containing at least 320 lbs. weight of such rolls of tobacco ; shall be, and the same is hereby repealed.

The act 7 & 8 Geo. 4. c. 56. § 3. repeals so much of the said act 6 Geo. 4. c. 107. as prohibits the im ation of beef or pork salted, not being corned beef or pork ; and also so much of the said act as pro the importation of cattle, sheep, swine, beef, lamb, mutton, or pork, from the Isle of Man, being th duce of that island.

nolu; except into the ports of London, Plymouth,
stol, Liverpool, Hull, Newcastle, Leith, Greenock,
alin, Cork, and Belfast. *

articles; viz. any distinct or separate part of any
cle not accompanied by the other part, or all the other
s of such article, so as to be complete and perfect, if
article be subject to duty according to the value
eof.

t being perfumed or medicinal spirits; viz. all spirits
ess in ships of 70 tons or upwards.

f and from the British plantations, unless in casks
taining not less than 20 gallons, or in cases contain-
not less than three dozen reputed quart bottles.

er spirits, unless in casks containing not less than 40
ons, or in cases containing not less than three dozen
ted quart bottles.

ess from the place of its growth, and by the East
a Company, and into the port of London.

nd snuff; viz. unless in a ship of the burthen of 120
or upwards.

nless in hogsheads, casks, chests, or cases, each of
ch shall contain, of nett tobacco and snuff, at least
bs. weight if from the East Indies, or 450 lbs.
ht if from any other place; and not packed in bags
ackages within any such hogshead, cask, chest, or
nor separated, nor divided in any manner what-
; except tobacco of the dominions of the Turkish
ire, which may be packed in inward bags or pack-

ages, or separated or divided in any manner within the
outward package, provided such outward package be a
hogshead, cask, chest, or case, and contain 450 lbs. nett
at least.

and unless the particular weight of tobacco or snuff in
each hogshead, cask, chest, or case, with the tare of the
same, be marked thereon.

and unless into the ports of London, Liverpool, Bristol,
Lancaster, Cowes, Falmouth, Whitehaven, Hull, Port
Glasgow, Greenock, Leith, Newcastle-upon-Tyne, Ply-
mouth, Belfast, Cork, Drogheda, Dublin, Galway,
Limerick, Londonderry, Newry, Sligo, Waterford, and
Wexford.

but any ship wholly laden with tobacco may come into the
port of Cowes or Falmouth to wait for orders, and there
remain fourteen days, provided due report of such ship
be made by the master with the collector or comptroller
of such port.

Wine; viz. unless in a ship of the burthen of 60 tons or upwards.

and in casks containing not less than 21 gallons, or in cases
containing not less than three dozen reputed quart
bottles, or six dozen reputed pint bottles, except for
private use, and with leave of the commissioners of the
customs.

And all goods from the Isle of Man, except such as be of the
growth, produce, or manufacture thereof.

ture. — And if any goods shall be imported into the United Kingdom contrary to any of the
ons or restrictions mentioned in such table, the same shall be forfeited. — § 52.

ods may be warehoused for Exportation only, although prohibited. — Provided always, that any
whatsoever sort may be imported *to be warehoused* under the regulations of any act for the
sing of goods without payment of duty, or notwithstanding such goods may be prohibited to be
into the United Kingdom to be used therein, *except the several goods* following; (that is to say,)
hibited on account of the package in which they are contained, or the tonnage of the ship in
ey are laden; tea and goods from China in other than British ships, or by other persons than
India Company; gunpowder, arms, ammunition, or utensils of war; dried or salted fish, not
ckfish; beef, pork, or bacon; infected hides, silks, horns, hoofs, or any other part of any cattle
counterfeit coin or tokens; books first composed or written, or printed and published in the
kingdom, and reprinted in any other country or place; copies of prints first engraved, etched,
r designed in the United Kingdom; copies of casts of sculptures or models first made in the
kingdom; clocks or watches impressed with any mark or stamp, appearing to be or to represent
British assay mark or stamp, or purporting, by any mark or appearance, to be of the manufac-
he United Kingdom, or not having the name and place of abode of some foreign maker abroad
the frame and also on the face, or not being in a complete state, with all the parts properly fixed
se. — § 53.

o be entered to be warehoused for Exportation only. — If by reason of the sort of any goods, or
ce from whence, or the country or navigation of the ship in which any goods have been imported,
uch, or be so imported, as that they may not be used in the United Kingdom, they shall not be
except to be warehoused; and it shall be declared upon the entry, that they are entered to be
ed for exportation only. — § 54.

ENTRY OUTWARDS.

l Provision as to the Entry of the Ship. — No goods shall be shipped, or waterborne to be shipped
any ship, in any port in the United Kingdom, or in the Isle of Man, to be carried to parts be-
seas, before due entry outwards of such ship, and due entry of such goods, shall have been made,
t granted, nor before such goods shall have been duly cleared for shipment, in manner hereinafter
and no stores shall be shipped for the use of any such ship bound to parts beyond the seas, nor
goods be deemed or admitted to be such stores, except such as shall be borne upon the victualling
ranted for such ship; and no goods shall be so shipped, or waterborne to be so shipped, except
mes and places, and in such manner, and by such persons, and under the care of such officers, as
after directed; and all goods and stores shipped, or waterborne to be shipped, contrary hereto
rfeited. — § 55.

be cleared on Pain of 100l. — No ship, on board of which any goods or stores shall have been
or parts beyond the seas, shall depart from such port until such ship shall have been duly
utwards for her voyage, in manner hereinafter directed, under forfeiture of 100l. by the master.

ing Bill for Stores. — The master of every ship which is to depart for parts beyond seas,
n application made by him, receive from the searcher a victualling bill for the shipment of such
e shall require, and as shall be allowed by the collector and comptroller for the use of such ship,
to the voyage; and no articles taken on board shall be deemed stores, except such as shall be
n the victualling bill. — § 57.

to deliver Certificate of Clearance of last Voyage, and to make Entry outwards. — The master
hip in which any goods are to be exported to parts beyond the seas, shall, before any goods be
oard, deliver to the collector or comptroller a certificate from the officer, of the clearance in-
oastwise of such ship of her last voyage, specifying what goods, if any, have been reported
r exportation, and shall also deliver to the collector or comptroller an account, signed by the
his agent, of the entry outwards of such ship for her intended voyage, setting forth the name
ge, the name of the place to which she belongs if a British ship, or of the country if a foreign
ame of the master, and the name of the place for which she is bound, if any goods are to be
r the same, and the name of the place in such port at which she is to take in her lading for
ge; and if such ship shall have commenced her lading at some other port, the master shall state
of any port at which any goods have been laden, and shall produce a certificate from the
hat the cockets have been delivered to him; and the particulars of such account shall be written
ged in such form as the collector and comptroller shall require; and such account shall be the
wards of such ship, and shall be entered in a book to be kept by the collector for the information
es interested; and if any goods be taken on board before she shall have been entered outwards,
r shall forfeit 100l.: Provided always, that where it shall become necessary to lade any heavy
oard before the whole of the inward cargo is discharged, it shall be lawful for the collector and
r to issue a stiffening order, previous to the entry outwards. — § 58.

r Goods outwards. — The person *entering outwards* any goods to be exported, shall deliver to
or or comptroller a bill of the entry thereof, written in words at length, expressing the
he ship and of the master, and of the place to which the goods are to be exported, and of the
whose name the goods are to be entered, and the quantities and denominations of the several
shall pay down any duties which may be due upon the exportation; and such person shall also
the same time one or more duplicates of such bill, in which all sums and numbers may be ex-
figures; and the particulars to be contained in such bill shall be written in such manner, and
r of such duplicates shall be such, as the collector and comptroller shall require; and thereupon

R r

the collector and comptroller shall cause a cocket to be written for such goods, making it known tha
goods have been so entered ; and every cocket shall be signed by such collector and comptroller, a
delivered to the person who shall have made such entry, and such person shall keep and be responsi'
the proper use of the same. — § 59.

Goods for Drawback or Bounty. — If any drawback or bounty be allowable upon the exporta
such goods, or any duty be payable thereon, or any exemption from duty claimed, or if such goods
portable only according to some particular rule, or under some restriction, or for some particular pu
or destination, such goods shall be entered and cleared by such denominations or descriptions as are
in the granting of such drawback or bounty, or in the levying of such duty, or granting such exem
or in the directing of such rules, purpose, or destination ; and if the goods are charged to pay du
cording to the value thereof, such value shall be stated in the entry, and shall be affirmed by the de
tion of the exporter or his agent, to be made upon the entry, and attested by his signature ; and i
person shall make such declaration, not being the exporter nor his agent, such person shall forfeit
and such declaration shall be made in manner following, and shall be binding upon the person m
the same. — § 60.

" I, *A. B.*, do hereby declare, that I am the exporter of the goods mentioned in this entry, [or,
am duly authorised by him,] and I do enter the same at the value of ———.

" Witness my hand, the ——— day of ———.

" *A.*

Goods undervalued. — If upon examination it shall appear to the officers of customs that such
are not valued according to the true value, the same may be detained and (within two days) take
disposed of for the benefit of the crown, in like manner as in respect of goods imported ; except th
sum in addition to the amount of the valuation, and the duties paid, shall be paid to the expor
proprietor. — § 61.

For Drawback, or from Warehouse, Duties to be first paid. — The person intending to enter out
any foreign goods for drawback, or any foreign goods to be exported from warehouse, or any fo
goods upon which the duties inwards are required to have been paid before exported, shall first d
to the collector or comptroller two or more bills, as the case may require, of the particulars of th
portation, and of the entry outwards intended to be made ; and thereupon such collector and compt
finding such bills to agree with the entry inwards, shall write off such goods from the same, and
issue a certificate of such entry for warehousing or payment of duties, with such particulars there
shall be necessary for the computation of the drawback, or for the due delivery thereof from the
house, and setting forth in such certificate the destination of the goods, and the person in whose
they are to be entered for exportation, and also the ship in which they are to be exported, if they
be exported from the port where such certificate is issued, but if from another port, then only the
of such other port ; and such certificate, together with two or more bills of the same, as the cas
require, in which all sums and numbers may be expressed in figures, being delivered to the collec
comptroller of the port from which the goods are to be exported, shall be the entry outwards of
goods ; and such collector and comptroller shall thereupon cause a cocket to be written and deliver
such goods in manner before directed. — § 62.

Coals Export Bond to Isle of Man and British Possessions. — No cocket shall be granted for t
portation of any coals to the Isle of Man, or any British possession, until the exporter shall have
security by bond in 40s. the chaldron, with condition that the same shall be landed at the place for '
they shall be exported, or otherwise accounted for to the satisfaction of the commissioners of cus
and also with condition to produce (within such time to be expressed in such bond) a certificate
landing of such coals at such place, under the hand of the collector or comptroller : Provided alway
the bond so to be given shall not be liable to any duty of stamps. — § 63.

Clearance of Goods. — Before any part of the goods for which any cocket shall have been granted
be shipped, or waterborne to be shipped, the same shall be duly cleared for shipment with the sea
and before any goods be cleared for shipment, the particulars of the goods for each clearance sh
endorsed on such cocket, together with the number and denomination or description of the pack
and in the margin of each endorsement shall be delineated the marks and numbers of such pack
and to each shall be subjoined, in words at length, an account of the total quantities of each s
goods, and the total number of each sort of packages, distinguishing such goods, if any, as are
cleared for any bounty, or drawback of excise or customs, and also such goods, if any, as are duly
any duty on exportation, or entitled to exemption from duty, and also such goods, if any, as can o
exported by virtue of some particular authority, or under some particular restriction, or for som
ticular purpose or destination ; and all goods shipped, or waterborne to be shipped, not being duly c
as aforesaid, shall be forfeited. — § 64. *

Cocket endorsed. — The person clearing such goods for shipment, shall, upon each occasion, produ
cocket so endorsed to the searcher, and shall also deliver a shipping bill or copy of such endorse
referring by names and date to the cocket upon which such endorsement is made, and shall obta
order of the searcher for the shipment ; and the particulars to be contained in such endorsemen
in such shipping bill, shall be written in such form as the collector and comptroller shall requ
§ 65.

Coals, &c. for Exportation may be trans-shipped. — It shall be lawful for the searcher and coast
in any port to permit any quantity of coals or of slates, duly entered and cleared for exportation
shipped directly by trans-shipment out of any coasting ship, and without payment of any coas
thereon. — § 66.

Coals brought coastwise may be exported without Payment of Coast Duty. — If any coals shal
been brought from one port of the United Kingdom to another, and the master shall be minded
ceed with such coals to parts beyond the seas, it shall be lawful for such master to enter such sh
such coals outwards for the intended voyage, without first landing the coals, and without paying th
duty ; provided the officers of the customs shall be satisfied that the quantity left on board, added
which may have been landed, does not exceed the quantity set forth in the transire. — § 67.

Export of Free Goods. — Upon the clearance for shipment of any goods, the produce or manufac
the United Kingdom, *not liable to any export duty,* an account, containing an accurate specifica
the quantity, quality, and value, together with a declaration to the truth of the same, signed by
porter, or his agent, shall be delivered to the searcher by the person clearing ; and if such declara
false, the person signing the same shall forfeit 20l ; and it shall be lawful for the searcher to call
invoice, bills of parcels, and such other documents as he may think necessary for ascertaining th
value : provided always, that if such exporter or agent shall make and sign an affidavit befo
collector or comptroller, that the value of the goods cannot be ascertained in time for the shipme
such affidavit shall be delivered to the searcher at the time of clearance, a further time of three
shall be allowed for the delivery of such separate shipping bill, on failure whereof such exporter o
shall forfeit 20l. — § 68.

* A Customs Order of the 6th of August, 1829, directs, that in the case of goods incorrectly enter
outport for bounty or drawback, where the amount overclaimed shall not exceed 5l. and no susp
fraud shall attach, the shipment of the goods may be permitted upon a deposit of double the ov
to abide the Board's directions ; the debenture being withheld till such directions are received.

ds for Excise Drawback. — No drawback of excise shall be allowed upon any goods so cleared, un-
...e person intending to claim such drawback shall have given due notice to the officer of excise, in
... required by law, and shall have produced to the searcher at the time of clearing, a proper document
... the hand of the officer of excise, containing the description of the goods for which such drawback
...e claimed; and if the goods to be cleared and shipped under the care of the searcher shall, upon
...nation, be found to correspond in all respects, and such goods shall be duly shipped and exported,
...archer shall, if required, certify such shipment upon such document, and shall transmit the same to
...ficer of excise. — § 69.

...cer of Excise may attend Examination. — It shall be lawful for the officer of excise to attend at
...examination, and to mark or seal the packages, and to keep joint charge of the same, together with
...archer, until the same shall be finally delivered by him into the sole charge of the searcher, to be
...ed and exported. — § 70.

...ds for Duty, Bounty, or Drawback, brought for Shipment. — If any goods, which are subject to any
...or restriction in respect of exportation, or if any goods, which are to be shipped for any drawback
...nty, shall be brought to any quay, wharf, or other place, to be shipped for exportation, and such
... shall not agree with the endorsement on the cocket, or with the shipping bill, the same shall be
...ed; and if any goods prohibited to be exported be found in any package, such package, and every
... contained therein, shall be forfeited. — § 71.

...rcher may open any Package — It shall be lawful for the searcher to open all packages, and examine
...ds shipped or brought for shipment; and if the goods shall be found to correspond in all respects
...he cocket, such goods shall be repacked at the charge of such searcher, who may be allowed such
...e by the commissioners, if they see fit. — § 72.

...tent of Clearance of Ship to be delivered to Searcher. — Before any ship shall be cleared outwards at
...rt, with any goods shipped on board in such port, the master shall deliver a content of such ship to
...archer, setting forth the name and tonnage of such ship, and the place or places of her destination,
... name of the master; and also an account of the goods shipped on board, and of the packages, and
... marks and numbers, and a like account of the goods on board, if any, which had been reported
...ds for exportation, so far as any of such particulars can be known by him; and also, before the
...nce, the cockets, with the endorsements and clearances thereon, shall be finally delivered by the
...rs to the searcher, who shall file the same, and shall attach with a seal a label to the file, showing
...mber of cockets contained in the file, and shall compare the particulars in the cockets with the
...ulars of the goods in such content, and shall attest the correctness thereof by his signature on the
...nd on the content; and the master shall make oath before the collector or comptroller to the truth
...h content; and shall also answer upon oath to the collector or comptroller such questions concern-
...e ship, the cargo, and the intended voyage, as shall be demanded of him; and thereupon the
...or or comptroller shall clear such ship for her intended voyage, and shall notify such clearance
...e date thereof upon the content, and upon the label to the file of cockets, and upon the victualling
...d also in the book of ships' entries outwards; and shall transmit the content, and the cockets,
...e victualling bill, to the searcher; and the particulars in such content shall be written in such
...r as the collector and comptroller shall require. — § 73.

...of Cockets and Victualling Bill delivered to Master as the Clearance. — The file of cockets and the
...ling bill shall thereupon be delivered by the searcher to the master, at such station within the
...nd in such manner, as shall be appointed by the commissioners; and such file of cockets and
...ling bill shall be kept by the master, as the authority for departing from the port. — § 74.

...Ballast. — If any ship is to depart in ballast, for parts beyond the seas, having no goods on board
... stores borne upon the victualling bill, or any goods reported inwards for exportation, the master
...efore her departure, answer upon oath to the collector or comptroller such questions touching
...parture and destination as shall be demanded of him; and thereupon the collector or comptroller
...lear such ship in ballast, and shall notify such clearance and the date thereof on the victualling
...d also in the book of ships' entries outwards, and such victualling bill shall be kept by the master
...clearance. — § 75.

...of former Cargo reported for Exportation. — If there be on board any goods of the inward cargo
...' for exportation, the master shall, before clearance outwards, deliver to the searcher a copy of the
...inwards, certified by collector and comptroller; and such copy, being found to correspond with
...ds remaining on board, shall be the authority to the searcher to pass such ship with such goods on
... and being signed by the searcher, and filed with the cockets, shall be the clearance of the ship for
...oods. — § 76.

...y Passengers, Master may enter Baggage in his Name. — If any passengers are to depart in any
...r parts beyond the seas, it shall be lawful for the master to pass an entry and to receive a cocket in
...ne for the necessary baggage of all such passengers, and to clear such baggage for shipment in their
... stating the particulars of the packages, and the names of the passengers; and if such ship is
... no other goods than the baggage of passengers, it shall be lawful for such master to enter such
...twards in ballast for passengers only; and if no other goods than baggage be taken on board, the
...all be deemed to be a ship in ballast, notwithstanding such baggage, and shall be described in the
...ce, on the content, and on the label to the cocket, and on the victualling bill, and in the book of
...ntries, as a ship cleared in ballast, except as to the baggage of passengers. — § 77.

...er may enter Goods for private Use of Self and Crew. — If the master and crew of any foreign ship
...s to depart in ballast, shall be desirous to take on board chalk rubbish by way of ballast, to take
...em for their private use any small quantities of goods of British manufacture, it shall be lawful
... master, without entering such ship outwards, to pass an entry in his name, and receive a cocket
...any export duty for all such goods, under the general denomination of British manufactures not
...ted to be exported, being for the use and privilege of the master and crew, and not being of greater
...nan in the proportion of 20l. for the master, and 10l. for the mate, and 5l. for each of the crew,
...ting that the ship is in ballast; and the master shall clear such goods for shipment in behalf of
... and crew, stating in such clearances the particulars of the goods and packages, and the names of
...w who shall take any of such goods under this privilege; and such ship shall be deemed to be a
...ballast, and be cleared as such, and without a content, notwithstanding such goods, or such cocket;
...h clearance shall be notified by the collector or comptroller on the label to the cocket, and on the
...ing bill, and in the book of ships' entries, as a clearance in ballast, except as to the privilege of
...ter and crew. — § 78.

...rs may board any Ship after Clearance. — It shall be lawful for the officers of customs to go on
...ny ship after clearance outwards, within the limits of any port in the United Kingdom or in the
...Man, or within four leagues of the coast, and to demand the file of cockets, and the victualling
...d if there be any goods or stores on board not contained in the endorsements on the cockets, nor
...ictualling bill, such goods or stores shall be forfeited; and if any goods contained in such endorse-
...e not on board, the master shall forfeit 20l. for every package not on board; and if any cocket be
...ime falsified, the person who shall have falsified the same, or who shall have wilfully used the
...all forfeit 100l. — § 79.

...to bring to at Stations. — Every ship departing from any port, shall bring to at such stations within
... as shall be appointed by the commissioners for the landing of officers from such ships, or for
...examination previous to departure. — § 80.

...ture Goods to be entered in Name of real Owner, or of the Commission Merchant. — No drawback
...ty shall be allowed upon the exportation of any goods, unless such goods shall have been entered

R r 2

in the name of the person who was the real owner at the time of entry and shipping, or of the person w
had purchased and shipped the same, in his own name and at his own risk, on commission, according
the practice of merchants, and who shall have continued to be entitled in his own right to such drawb
or bounty, except in the cases hereinafter provided for. — § 81.

Oath to Exportation, and to Property, and to Right to Drawback or Bounty. — Such owner or commiss
merchant shall make oath upon the debenture that the goods have been actually exported, and have
been re-landed, and are not intended to be re-landed in any part of the United Kingdom, nor in the I
of Man, (unless entered for the Isle of Man,) nor in the islands of Faro or Ferro, and that he was the r
owner at the time of entry and shipping, or that he had purchased and shipped the said goods in his o
name, and at his own risk, on commission, and that he continued to be entitled to the drawback or bou
in his own right: Provided always, that if such owner or merchant shall not have purchased the righ
such drawback or bounty, he shall declare under his hand upon the entry, and in his oath upon
debenture, the person who is entitled thereto; and the name of such person shall be stated in the coc
and in the debenture; and the receipt of such person on the debenture shall be the discharge for su
drawback or bounty. — § 82.

Agent may pass Entry, and receive Drawback. — If such owner or merchant shall be resident more th
twenty miles from the Custom-house of the port of shipment, he may appoint any agent to make and p
his entry, and to clear and ship his goods, and to receive for him the drawback or bounty payable on
debenture, provided the name of such agent and the residence of such owner or merchant be subjoine
the name of such owner or merchant in the entry and in the cocket for such goods; and such age
being duly informed, shall make declaration upon the entry, if necessary, and also make oath upon
debenture, to the effect before required of such owner or merchant, and shall answer upon oath s
questions, touching his knowledge of the exportation, and the property in, and of the right to the dr
back or bounty, as shall be demanded by the collector or comptroller; and if any goods be exported t
corporation or company trading by a joint stock, it shall be lawful for them to appoint any person to
their agent for the like purposes. — § 83.

Property of Persons abroad consigned here to an Agent, and exported. — If any goods exported for dr
back be the property of any person residing abroad, having been consigned by the owner to some age
to be exported to parts beyond the seas by such agent, it shall be lawful for such person, (being
consignee in whose name the duties inwards had been paid, or his legal representative,) in like man
as agent for such owner, to enter, clear, and ship such goods, and upon like conditions to receive
drawback. — § 84.

Shipment within Three Years, and Payment within Two Years. — No drawback shall be allowed u
the exportation of any goods, unless such goods be shipped within three years after payment of the du
inwards; and no debenture for any drawback or bounty upon the exportation shall be paid after
expiration of two years from the date of the shipment; and no drawback shall be allowed upon any go
which, by reason of damage or decay, shall have become of less value for home use than the amoun
drawback; and all goods so damaged cleared for drawback shall be forfeited; and the person who cau
such goods to be so cleared shall forfeit 200l., or treble the amount of the drawback, at the election
the commissioners. — § 85.

Issuing and passing Debenture. — For the purpose of computing and paying any drawback or bou
payable upon goods duly exported, a debenture shall, in due time after entry, be prepared by the colle
and comptroller, certifying in the first instance the entry outwards, and so soon as the same shall h
been exported, and a notice containing the particulars of the goods delivered by the exporter to
searcher, the shipment and exportation thereof shall be certified to the collector and comptroller, u
such debenture, by the searcher; and the debenture shall thereupon be computed and passed with
despatch, and be delivered to the person entitled to receive the same. — § 86.

Guernsey, &c. Certificate of Landing. — No drawback or bounty shall be allowed for any goods expo
to Guernsey, Jersey, Alderney, Sark, or the Isle of Man, until a certificate shall be produced from
collector and comptroller, or from the register of certificates, or other chief officer of customs, of the
landing of such goods. — § 87.

Press-packing, and Oath of Packer. — No drawback or bounty shall be allowed for any goods expo
in bales, cleared as being press-packed, unless the quantities and qualities of the goods in each sha
verified by the master packer, or in case of unavoidable absence, by the foreman of such packer, by c
made and subscribed upon the cocket before the collector or comptroller; or if such packer reside m
than ten miles from the port, then by oath made and subscribed upon an account of such goods, befo
magistrate or justice of the peace; and if such bales be not cleared as being press-packed, then
searcher having opened any such bale shall not be required to repack the same at his charge. — § 88.

Licensed Lightermen only to ship Debenture or Warehouse Goods. — No goods cleared for drawbac
bounty, or from the warehouse, shall be carried waterborne, to be put on board any ship for exporta
by any person, unless such person shall be authorised by licence under the hands of the commissione
customs; and before granting such licence, it shall be lawful for the commissioners to require s
security by bond for the faithful conduct of such person, as they shall deem necessary; and after gran
such licence, it shall be lawful for the commissioners to revoke the same, if the person shall be convi
of any offence against the laws of customs or excise: Provided that all such licences, which shall b
force at the time of the commencement of this act, shall continue in force as if the same had been a
wards granted under this act. — § 89.

Warehouse or Debenture Goods not exported, or if re-landed without Entry, forfeited. — If any g
taken from the warehouse to be exported, or any goods cleared to be exported for drawback or bou
shall not be duly exported, or shall be re-landed, (such goods not having been duly re-landed or discha
as short-shipped under the care of the proper officers,) or shall be landed in the islands of Faro or Fe
or shall be carried to the islands of Guernsey, Jersey, Alderney, Sark, or Man, (not having been ente
cleared, and shipped to be exported directly to such island,) the same shall be forfeited, together wit
ship, and any other ship, vessel, boat, or craft, which may have been used in so re-landing, landin
carrying such goods; and any person by whom, or by whose orders, such goods shall have been so tak
cleared, or so re-landed, landed, or carried, shall forfeit treble the value of such goods. — § 90.

Drawback of Duties on Wine allowed for Officers in the Navy. — A drawback of the whole of the d
of customs shall be allowed for wine intended for the consumption of officers of his Majesty's r
on board ships in actual service, not exceeding the quantities in any one year hereinafter mention
(that is to say,)

For every admiral	- - - - - - - - - -	1,260 gallons.
— vice-admiral	- - - - - - - - -	1,050 —
— rear-admiral	- - - - - - - - -	840 —
— captain of the first and second rate	- - - -	630 —
— captain of the third, fourth, and fifth rate	- -	420 —
— captain of an inferior rate	- - - - -	210 —
— lieutenant, and other commanding officer, and for every marine officer	105 —

Provided always, that such wine be shipped only at one of the ports hereinafter mentioned; (that is to
London, Rochester, Deal, Dover, Portsmouth, Plymouth, Yarmouth, Falmouth, Belfast, Dublin,
Leith, or Glasgow. — § 91.

Persons entering such Wine for Drawback. — The person entering such wine, and claiming draw
for the same, shall state in the entry, and declare upon oath on the debenture, the name of the offic

se such wine is intended, and of the ship in which he serves; and such wine shall be delivered
charge of the officers of customs at the port of shipment, to be secured in the king's warehouse
e same shall be shipped under their care; and such officers having certified upon the debenture
ipt of the wine into their charge, the debenture shall be computed and passed, and be delivered to
on entitled to receive the same. — § 92.

rs leaving the Service, Wine to be transferred to others. — If any such officer shall leave the service,
moved to another ship, it shall be lawful for the officers of customs, at the ports before mentioned,
it the transfer of such wine from one officer to another, whether on board the same ship or
or the trans-shipment from one ship to another for the same officer, or the re-landing and ware.
for future re-shipment; and it shall also be lawful for the officers of customs at any port to receive
duties for such wine, and deliver the same for home use: Provided that if any such wine be not
board the ship for which the same was intended, or be unladen from such ship without permission
ficer of the customs, the same shall be forfeited. — § 93.

rs of his Majesty's Ships of War may ship Tobacco for Use of Crew, free of Duty, on giving Bond.
ll be lawful for the purser of any of his Majesty's ships of war in actual service, to enter and ship at
s of Rochester, Portsmouth, or Plymouth, in the proportions hereinafter mentioned, any tobacco
rehoused in his name, or transferred in his name, for the use of the ship; provided such purser
ver to the collector or comptroller a certificate from the captain, stating the name of the purser
number of men belonging to the ship, and shall also give bond, with one surety, in treble the
hat no part shall be re-landed without leave of the officers of customs, or be landed in either of
ds of Guernsey, Jersey, Alderney, Sark, or Man. — § 94.

· removed from one Ship to another, may trans-ship with Permission of Collector. — If any purser
removed from one ship to another, it shall be lawful for the collector and comptroller of the port
ich ships shall be, to permit the trans-shipment of the remains of any such tobacco, for the use of
er ship, upon due entry by such purser, setting forth the time when, and the port at which, such
vas first shipped; and if any such ship shall be paid off, it shall be lawful for the collector and
ter to permit the remains of any such tobacco to be landed, and to be entered by the purser either
ent of duties, or to be warehoused for six months, for the supply of some other ship, or for pay-
all duties within such six months: Provided that all tobacco warehoused for the purpose of so
g his Majesty's ships of war, shall be subject to the provisions of this act made for the warehousing
o generally, as far as the same are applicable, and are not altered by any of the provisions herein
§ 95.

ty of Tobacco allowed. — No greater quantity of such tobacco shall be allowed to any ship of war,
pounds for the lunar month for each of the crew, nor shall any greater quantity be shipped at
than sufficient to serve the crew for six months; and the collector and comptroller shall
a particular account to the commissioners of customs, in order that a general account may be
ll the quantities supplied to and consumed on board each of such ships, under the allowances
anted. — § 96.

nd Places for shipping Goods. — No goods shall be put off from any wharf, quay, or other place,
e waterborne in order to be exported, but only on days not being Sundays or holidays, and in
me, that is to say, from the 1st of September until the last day of March, betwixt sun-rising
setting, and from the last day of March until the 1st day of September, between 7 in the
and 4 in the afternoon; nor shall any such goods be then put off or waterborne for
on unless in the presence or with the authority of the proper officer of customs, nor except
gal quay, or at some wharf, quay, or place appointed by the commissioners of customs by
e. — § 97.

for exporting prohibited Goods. — If any goods liable to forfeiture for being shipped for
on shall be shipped and exported without discovery by the officers of customs, the persons who
e caused such goods to be exported shall forfeit double the value. — § 98.

PROHIBITIONS OUTWARDS.

eral sorts of goods enumerated in the table following, (denominated " A Table of Prohibitions
ictions Outwards,") shall be either absolutely prohibited to be exported, or shall be exported
r the restrictions mentioned in such table.

A Table of Prohibitions and Restrictions Outwards.

watches; viz. any outward or inward box, case, or
te, of any metal, without the movement in or with
ich box, case, or dial plate, made up fit for use,
e clock or watch maker's name engraven thereon.
any metal inferior to silver, which shall be
ixed, wrought, or set upon silk, or which shall
or drawn into wire, or flatted into plate, and
woven, or wrought into, or upon, or mixed
ce, fringe, cord, embroidery, tambour work, or
made in the gold or silver lace manufactory,
on silk, or made into bullion spangles, or pearl, or
er materials made in the gold or silver lace manu-
or which shall imitate or be meant to imitate such
nge, cord, embroidery, tambour work, or buttons;
l any person export any copper, brass, or other
vhich shall be silvered, or drawn into wire, or
ito plate, or made into bullion spangles, or pearl,
her materials used in the gold or silver lace manu-
or in imitation of such lace, fringe, cord, embroi-
mbour work, or buttons, or of any of the materials
making the same, and which shall hold more, or
reater proportion than three pennyweights of fine
the pound avoirdupois of such copper, brass, or
tal,
inferior to silver, whether gilt, silvered, stained,
red, or otherwise, which shall be worked up or
ith gold or silver, in any manufacture of lace,
rd, embroidery, tambour work, or buttons.
itensils; viz. any machine, engine, tool, press,
tensil, or instrument used in or proper for the pre-
working, pressing, or finishing of the woollen,
nen, or silk manufactures of this kingdom, or any
ds wherein wool, cotton, linen, or silk is used, or
of such machines, engines, tools, presses, paper,
or instruments, or any model or plan thereof, or
thereof, except wool-cards, or stock-cards, not
bove 4s. per pair, and spinners' cards, not worth
6d. per pair, used in the woollen manufactures.
tes, engines, tools, or utensils, commonly used in
for the preparing, working up, or finishing of the

calico, cotton, muslin, or linen printing manufactures, or
any part of such blocks, plates, engines, tools, or utensils.
rollers, either plain, grooved, or of any other form or denomination, of cast iron, wrought iron, or steel, for the rolling of iron or any sort of metals, and frames, beds, pillars,
screws, pinions, and each and every implement, tool, or
utensil thereunto belonging; rollers, slitters, frames, beds,
pillars, and screws for slitting mills; presses of all sorts, in
iron and steel, or other metals, which are used with a
screw exceeding one inch and a half in diameter, or any
parts of these several articles, or any model of the before-
mentioned utensils, or any parts thereof; all sorts of
utensils, engines, or machines used in the casting or boring
of cannon or any sort of artillery, or any parts thereof, or
any model of tools, utensils, engines, or machines used in
such casting or boring, or any parts thereof; band stamps,
dog's-head stamps, pulley stamps, hammers and anvils for
stamps; presses of all sorts, called cutting-out presses;
beds or punches to be used therewith, either in parts or
pieces, or fitted together; scoring or shading engines;
presses for horn buttons; dies for horn buttons; rolled
metal, with silver thereon; parts of buttons not fitted up
into buttons, or in an unfinished state; engines for chasing;
stocks for casting buckles, buttons, and rings; die-sinking
tools of all sorts; engines for making button-shanks; laps
of all sorts; tools for pinching of glass; engines for covering of whips; bars of metal, covered with gold or silver,
and burnishing stones, commonly called blood stones,
either in the rough state or finished for use; wire moulds
for making paper; wheels of metal, stone, or wood, for
cutting, roughing, smoothing, polishing, or engraving
glass; punching, pincers, shears, and pipes, used in blow-
ing glass; potters' wheels, and lathes for plain, round, and
engine turning; tools used by saddlers, harness makers, and
bridle makers, viz. candle strainers, side strainers, point
strainers, creasing irons, screw creasers, wheel irons, seat
irons, picking irons, bolstering irons, clams, and head
knives.
frames for making wearing apparel.

A List of Goods which may be prohibited to be exported by Proclamation or Order in Council.

Arms, ammunition, and gunpowder.
Ashes, pot and pearl.
Military stores and naval stores, and any articles (except coppery) which his Majesty shall judge capable of being converted into, or made useful in increasing the quantity of military and naval stores.

Provisions, or any sort of victual which may be used by man.
And if any goods shall be exported, or be waterborne to be exported, from the United Kingdom, contrary to any prohibitions or restrictions mentioned in such respect of such goods, the same shall be forfeited.

COASTING TRADE. — The sections from 100. to 114., both inclusive, refer solely to the coasting trade are inserted under that head.

Construction in general — And in order to avoid the frequent use of numerous terms and expressions in this act, and in other acts relating to the customs, and to prevent any misconstruction of the terms expressions used therein, it is enacted, that the term "ship" shall be construed to mean ship or generally, unless such term shall be used to distinguish a ship from sloops, brigantines, and other of vessels; that the term "master" of any ship shall be construed to mean the person having or the charge or command of such ship; that the term "owners" and the term "owner" of any ship be construed alike to mean one owner, if there be only one, and any or all the owners, if there be than one; that the term "mate" of any ship shall be construed to mean the person next in command such ship to the master thereof; that the term "seaman" shall be construed to mean alike se mariner, sailor, or landsman, being one of the crew of any ship; that the term "British possession be construed to mean colony, plantation, island, territory, or settlement belonging to his Majesty the term "his Majesty" shall be construed to mean his Majesty, his heirs and successors; that the "East India Company" shall be construed to mean the United Company of Merchants of England to the East Indies; that the term "limits of the East India Company's charter" shall be constr mean all places and seas eastward of the Cape of Good Hope to the Straits of Magellan; that the "collector and comptroller" shall be construed to mean the collector and comptroller of the custom the port intended in the sentence; that whenever mention is made of any public officer, the officer tioned shall be deemed to be such officer for the time being; that the term "warehouse" shall construed to mean any place, whether house, shed, yard, timber pond, or other place, in which entered to be warehoused upon importation may be lodged, kept, and secured, without payment of or although prohibited to be used in the United Kingdom; that the term "king's warehouse" be construed to mean any place provided by the crown for lodging goods therein for security customs. — § 115.

The island of Malta and its dependencies shall be deemed to be in Europe. — § 116.

GENERAL REGULATIONS.

Weights, Measures, Currency, Management. — All duties, bounties, and drawbacks shall be paid received in every part of the United Kingdom and of the Isle of Man in British currency, and acc to imperial weights and measures; and in all cases where such duties, bounties, and drawbacks a posed and allowed according to any specific quantity or any specific value, the same shall be deem apply in the same proportion to any greater or less quantity or value; and all such duties, bount drawbacks shall be under the management of the commissioners of the customs. — § 117.

Collector to take Bonds in respect of Goods relating to the Customs. — All bonds relating to the cu required to be given in respect of goods or ships, shall be taken by the collector and comptroller use of his Majesty; and after the expiration of three years from the date, or of the time, if any, therein for the performance of the condition, every such bond upon which no prosecution or su have been commenced shall be void, and may be cancelled and destroyed. — § 118.

Mode of ascertaining Strength of Foreign Spirits. — The same instruments, and the same tabl scales of graduation, and the same methods, as the officers of excise shall by any law be directed in trying the strengths and quantities of spirits, for the purpose of computing and collecting the du excise, shall be used by the officers of customs, in trying the strengths and quantities of spirits imp for the purpose of computing and collecting the duties of customs. — § 119.

Coal Owners to deliver Two Certificates to Collector previous to Clearance. — No ship shall be from any port, either for a *coasting* or a *foreign voyage*, laden with any coals or culm which had no previously brought coastwise into such port, until the fitter, or the coal owner or his agent, sha delivered to the collector or comptroller two certificates under his hand, expressing the total quan coals, culm, and cinders, shipped or intended to be shipped; and the collector or comptroller shall one of such certificates, and shall deliver the other signed by him to the master of the ship; and fitter, coal owner, or agent, who shall refuse to give such certificates, or shall give a false certificat forfeit and pay the sum of 100*l*.; and the master of such ship shall keep such certificate, and prod same to any officer of customs demanding such production, and shall, before bulk be broken, deliv certificate to the collector or comptroller of any port in the United Kingdom to which such coals s carried in such ship. — § 120.

Officers of Customs to take Samples of Goods. — It shall be lawful for the officers of the customs such samples of any goods as shall be necessary for ascertaining the amount of any duties payable same; and all such samples shall be disposed of and accounted for in such manner as the commis of his Majesty's customs shall direct. — § 121.

Time of an Importation and of an Exportation defined. — If upon the first levying or repealing duty, or upon the first granting or repealing of any drawback or bounty, or upon the first permit prohibiting of any importation or exportation, whether inwards, outwards, or coastwise, in the Kingdom or in the Isle of Man, it shall be necessary to determine the precise time at which an ation or exportation of any goods made and completed shall be deemed to have had effect; such t respect of importation, shall be deemed to be the time at which the ship importing such goods had come within the limits of the port at which such ship shall in due course be reported, and such ge discharged; and that such time in respect of exportation shall be deemed to be the time at wh goods had been shipped on board the ship in which they had been exported; and that if such q shall arise upon the arrival or departure of any ship, in respect of any charge or allowance up ship, exclusive of any cargo, the time of such arrival shall be deemed to be the time at wh report of such ship shall have been or ought to have been made; and the time of such departu be deemed to be the time of the last clearance of such ship with the collector or comptroller for the upon which she had departed. — § 122.

Return of Duty overpaid. — If any duty of customs shall have been overpaid, or if, after any customs shall have been charged and paid, it shall appear that the same had been charged un erroneous construction of the law, it shall not be lawful to return any such overcharge, unless th to the same shall have been acknowledged or judicially established, and unless the same be duly within three years from the date of such payment. — § 123.

Tonnage or Burthen of Ships declared. — The tonnage or burthen of every British ship wit meaning of this act, shall be the tonnage set forth in the certificate of registry of such ship, tonnage or burthen of every other ship shall, for the purposes of this act, be ascertained in th manner as the tonnage of British ships is ascertained. — § 124.

Officers may refuse Master of British Ship, unless endorsed on Register — It shall be lawful officers of customs at any port under British dominion where there shall be a collector and com of the customs, to refuse to admit any person to do any act at such port as master of any

unless his name shall be inserted in, or have been endorsed upon, the certificate of registry of such as being the master thereof, or until his name shall have been so endorsed by such collector and ...roller. — § 125.

ifying Document. — If any person shall counterfeit or falsify, or wilfully use when counterfeited ...ified, any entry, warrant, cocket, or transire, or other document for the unlading, lading, enter... ...eporting, or clearing of any ship or vessel, or for the landing or shipping of any goods, stores, ...ge, or article whatever, or shall by any false statement procure any writing or document to be ... for any of such purposes, every person so offending shall for every such offence forfeit the sum of ... Provided always, that this penalty shall not attach to any particular offence for which any other ...ty shall be expressly imposed by any law in force for the time being. — § 126.

...hority of an Agent may be required. — Whenever any person shall make any application to any ... of the customs to transact any business on behalf of any other person, it shall be lawful for such ... to require the person so applying, to produce a written authority from the person on whose be... ...uch application shall be made; and in default of the production of such authority, to refuse to ...ct such business. — § 127.

...ure. — Ship to include Tackle, &c. — Goods to include Package. — Goods restricted deemed prohibited. ... goods, and all ships, vessels, and boats, which by this act, or any act at any time in force relating ... customs, shall be declared to be forfeited, shall and may be seized by any officer of the customs, ...ch forfeiture of any ship, vessel, or boat, shall be deemed to include the guns, tackle, apparel, and ...ure of the same ; and such forfeiture of any goods shall be deemed to include the proper package ...ch the same are contained : Provided always, that all goods, the importation of which is restricted ... on account of the packages or the place from whence the same shall be brought, or otherwise, shall ...med and taken to be prohibited goods ; and if any such goods shall be imported into the United ...om, other than to be legally deposited or warehoused for exportation, the same shall be forfeited. ...8.

...oration of seized Goods, Ships, Vessels, or Boats, to be in the Commissioners of Customs. — In case ...ods, ships, vessels, or boats, shall be seized as forfeited, or detained as undervalued, by virtue of ...t relating to the customs, it shall be lawful for the commissioners of customs to order the same ...estored, in such manner and on such terms as they shall think fit ; and if the proprietor shall ac... ...e terms, he shall not have any action for recompence or damage on account of such seizure or ...ion, and the person making seizure shall not proceed for condemnation. — § 129.

...ission of Forfeitures and Penalties by Commissioners, on Proof of Innocence of Owners and Mas- ... If any ship shall have become liable to forfeiture on account of any goods laden therein or unladen ...rom, or if the master shall have become liable to any penalty on account of any goods laden in such ...r unladen therefrom, and such goods shall be small in quantity or of trifling value, and it shall be ...appear to the commissioners of customs that such goods had been laden or unladen contrary to the ...on of the owners, or without the privity of the master, it shall be lawful for the commissioners to ...such forfeiture, and also to remit or mitigate such penalty, as they shall see reason ; and every ...ure and every penalty or part thereof so remitted shall be void, and no suit or action shall be ...t by any person on account thereof. — § 130.

...s not bringing to at Stations, Masters to forfeit 100l. — If any ship coming up or departing out of ...rt, shall not bring to at the proper stations appointed by the commissioners of customs for the ...ng or landing of officers of customs, the master shall forfeit 100l. — § 131.

...ers may be stationed in Ships in the Limits of any Port. — It shall be lawful for the commissioners ...oms, and for the collector and comptroller of any port, to station officers on board any ship while ... the limits of any port ; and the master of every ship on board of which any officer is so stationed ...rovide such officer sufficient room under the deck, in some part of the forecastle or steerage, for his ...hammock, and in case of neglect or refusal, shall forfeit 100l. — § 132.

...r to charge Rent in King's Warehouse. — Whenever any goods shall be secured in any of the king's ...uses for security of the duties, or to prevent the same from coming into home use, it shall be ... for the commissioners to charge and receive warehouse rent for such goods, for all such time as the ...hall remain in such warehouse, at the same rate as may be payable for the like goods when ...used in any warehouse in which such goods may be warehoused without payment of duty. ...3.

...r to sell Goods not cleared from King's Warehouse. — In case such goods shall not be cleared from ...g's warehouse within three calendar months, (or sooner if of a perishable nature,) it shall be law... ...the commissioners to cause such goods to be publicly sold by auction, for home use or for export... ...s the case may be ; and the produce shall be applied towards the payment of the duties, if sold for ...se, and of the warehouse rent and all other charges ; and the overplus, if any, shall be paid to the ...authorised to receive the same : Provided always, that it shall be lawful for the commissioners ...e any of such goods to be destroyed, as cannot be sold for sufficient to pay such duties and ...s if sold for exportation ; also, if such goods shall have been landed by the officers of customs, and ...ght shall not have been paid, the produce of such sale shall be first applied to the payment of such ...— § 134.

...r to appoint Ports and legal Quays. — It shall be lawful for his Majesty, by his commission out of ...irt of Exchequer, from time to time to appoint any port, haven, or creek in the United Kingdom, ...e Isle of Man, and to set out the limits thereof, and to appoint the proper places within the same, ...gal quays for the lading and unlading of goods : Provided always, that all ports, havens, and creeks, ... respective limits thereof, and all legal quays appointed and set out, and existing as such at the ...ncement of this act, under any law then in force, shall continue to be such as if the same had been ...ed under the authority of this act. — § 135.

...uissioners may appoint Sufferance Wharfs. — It shall be lawful for the commissioners of customs, ...ne to time, by any order under their hands, to appoint places to be sufferance wharfs, for the ...nd unlading of goods by sufferance, to be issued by them, or by the officers under their directions, ...manner and in such cases as they may see fit. — § 136.

...engaged in the Carriage of Letters. — No ship or boat employed ordinarily for the carriage of ...shall import or export any goods without permission of the commissioners of customs, under the ... of 100l., to be paid by the master. — § 137.

...ntice's Indenture to be enrolled with Collector. — No person shall be deemed to be an apprentice ...purposes of an act passed 4 Geo. 4. intituled " An Act for regulating the Number of Apprentices ...ken on board British Merchant Vessels, and for preventing the Desertion of Seamen ;" unless the ...re shall have been enrolled with the collector and comptroller of the port from which such ap... ...shall first go to sea after the date of such indenture, or in default of such enrolment, until the ...all have been enrolled at some port from which the ship in which such apprentice shall afterwards ...a shall be cleared. — § 138.

LICENSED AGENTS.

...ll not be lawful for any person to act *as an agent for transacting business at the Custom-house in* ...*of London*, which shall relate to the entry or clearance of any ship, or of any goods, or of any ..., unless authorised so to do by licence of the commissioners of customs, who are to require bond ...en by every person to whom such licence shall be granted, with one surety, in 1,000l., for the ...conduct of such person and of his clerks : Provided always, that such bond shall not be required ...erson who shall be one of the sworn brokers of the city of London ; and if any person shall act as

such agent, not being so licensed, or if any person shall be in partnership in such agency with any per
not so licensed, such person shall forfeit 100*l.* — § 139.

It shall be lawful for the commissioners of the treasury, by any order under their hands, to revoke
such licence, and after a copy of such order shall have been delivered to such person or to his clerk,
left at his usual place of abode or business, such licence shall be void. — § 140.

Provided always, that nothing herein shall extend to prevent the clerk or servant of any person, o
any persons in co-partnership, from transacting any business at the Custom-house, on account of s
person, without such licence; provided such clerk or servant shall not transact any such business
clerk, servant, or agent to any other person; nor to prevent any officer or clerk in the Long Room f
passing entries under this act. — § 141.

It shall be lawful for any such agent, or agents in co-partnership, to appoint any person without lice
to be his or their clerk in transacting such agency : Provided always, that no person shall be admitte
be such clerk to more than one agent or co-partnership of agents, nor until his name and residence,
the date of his appointment, shall have been endorsed on the licence of such agent, and signed by h
and witnessed by the signature of the collector and comptroller of customs, unless such person s
have been appointed with consent of the commissioners of customs before the commencement of this
— § 142.

And it shall be lawful for the said commissioners of the treasury, by their warrant, to be publishe
the London or Dublin Gazette, to extend the regulations herein-before made relating to agents in the p
of London, to agents at any other port in Great Britain, or at any port in Ireland. — § 143.

IMPORTS AND EXPORTS, the articles imported and exported from
country.

We have explained in another article (BALANCE OF TRADE), the mode in which
value of the imports and exports is officially determined by the Custom-house, and h
shown the fallacy of the common notions as to the advantage of the exports exceedi
the imports.   The scale of prices according to which the official value of the impo
and exports is determined having been fixed so far back as 1698, the account is of
use as showing their true value ; but it is of material importance as showing the fluc
ations in their quantity. We were anxious, had the means existed, to have given accou
of the various articles imported and exported at different periods during the last centu
that the comparative increase or diminution of the trade in each might have been ex
bited in one general view.   Unluckily, however, no means exist for completing such
account.   The tables published by Sir Charles Whitworth, Mr. Macpherson, and othe
specify only the aggregate value of the imports from and exports to particular countri
without specifying the articles or their value of which such imports and exports consist
And on applying at the Custom-house, we found that the fire in 1814 had destroyed
records ; so that there were no means of compiling any complete account of the value
the articles imported or exported previously to that period. We, therefore, have b
obliged to confine ourselves, except as respects the period since 1815, to an attempt
exhibit the amount of the trade with each country for such periods as seemed best cal
lated to show its real progress.   Those selected for this purpose, in the first of the
lowing tables, are periods of peace ; for, during war, the commerce with particu
countries is liable to be extended or depressed so far beyond its natural limits, as
afford no means of judging of its ordinary amount.   The averages given in the ta
(with the exception of 1802), are sufficiently extensive to neutralise the influence of s
extraordinary circumstances (whether arising from bad harvests, the repeal or imposi
of duties, or any other cause), as might materially affect an average for two or three y
only ; and as they extend from 1698 to 1822, they afford a very complete view of the prog
of the foreign trade of Great Britain.   This table was compiled from official docume
by the indefatigable Mr. Cesar Moreau, and may be safely relied on. The tables w
follow, and which show the amount and value of the trade of the empire at the pres
time, are all official, or compiled from official sources.

During the first half of last century, and previously, woollen goods formed the princ
article of native produce exported from Great Britain ; and next to it was hardware
cutlery, leather manufactures, linen, tin and lead, copper and brass manufactures, c
earthenware, provisions, slops, &c.   Corn formed a considerable article in the lis
exports down to 1770 ; since which period the balance of the corn trade has been, wi
few exceptions, very decidedly on the side of importation. Cotton did not begin t
of any importance as an article of export till after 1770 ; but since then the exten
and improvement of the cotton manufacture has been so astonishingly great, that the
ports of cotton stuffs and yarn amount, at this moment, to about *a half* of the en
exports of British produce and manufactures ! — (See *antè,* p. 417.)   The expor
woollen goods has been comparatively stationary.

The principal articles of import during the last half century have consisted of su
tea, corn, timber and naval stores, cotton wool, woods and drugs for dyeing, toba
silk, hides and skins, spices, bullion, &c.   Of the colonial and other foreign prod
imported into England, considerable quantities have always been re-exported.

TRADE OF GREAT BRITAIN.

...t of the *Official Value* of the Import and Export Trade of Great Britain with all Parts of the
...at an Annual Medium of the undermentioned Periods; specifying the separate Amount of the
...ith each Country for such Periods.

	Imports into Great Britain from all Parts, of all Sorts of Products.					Exports from Great Britain to all Parts, of all Sorts of Products.				
	Annual Medium of Five Periods of Peace, viz.					Annual Medium of Five Periods of Peace, viz.				
	1698 to 1701.	1749 to 1755.	1784 to 1792.	In 1802.	1816 to 1822.	1698 to 1701.	1749 to 1755.	1784 to 1792.	In 1802.	1816 to 1822.
	£	£	£	£	£	£	£	£	£	£
and										
- -	1,888,176	2,135,870	3,885,999	5,915,853	4,891,885	3,114,285	4,166,669	4,761,965	15,015,209	17,010,820
- -	1,490,904	1,533,896	2,860,914	3,123,007	3,308,502	1,451,231	3,129,499	3,187,139	7,209,291	8,324,987
,Jer-Man,shery 1801,onian	487,640	746,282	2,433,864	3,839,501	5,143,220	429,353	1,353,804	2,251,081	3,663,237	4,097,630
-	- -	111,863	12,238	119,318	147,961	388,594	641,366	210,938	542,404	2,246,565
and										
-	3,866,790	4,527,911	9,193,015	12,907,679	13,491,568	5,383,463	9,291,338	10,411,025	26,430,141	31,680,002
-	656,031	1,119,148	3,179,136	5,794,906	7,119,152	214,212	714,105	1,795,747	2,929,816	5,919,446
-	17,421	34,279	92,252	168,863	267,869	114,013	213,841	809,546	6,161,179	531,712
-	1,029,780	2,529,998	5,252,349	12,480,870	14,042,949	737,876	2,001,690	5,605,626	10,890,830	17,695,335
	5,569,952	8,211,346	17,716,752	31,442,318	34,921,538	6,449,594	12,220,974	18,621,942	41,411,966	53,126,195
th.										
-	110,446	488,053	1,619,146	2,182,430	2,258,975	60,899	100,354	395,696	1,281,555	2,329,725
-	213,657	187,632	261,823	327,350	132,303	59,454	19,859	70,617	90,515	145,217
rway	77,308	84,507	140,138	155,672	196,517	39,874	87,206	294,108	417,016	422,810
-	181,186	280,633	595,544	1,057,603	688,080	152,909	171,091	117,147	818,269	1,002,881
-	681,169	687,803	552,291	1,192,030	684,741	757,621	1,345,212	1,566,311	8,005,237	8,772,871
-	624,410	407,240	717,057	1,000,768	961,269	2,044,228	2,442,947	2,317,986	4,392,617	4,337,316
h.										
-	86,025	60,962	452,734	424,434	737,560	166,115	437,483	921,492	2,390,103	1,314,079
-	202,909	288,549	645,486	961,711	492,193	345,443	1,121,529	675,348	1,984,344	1,933,154
-	566,527	437,869	724,287	830,937	877,436	580,422	1,198,337	709,179	1,421,204	613,923
-	358,537	578,445	835,862	723,401	894,835	143,549	238,476	759,343	1,950,416	3,699,715
-	276,906	168,071	184,545	182,424	306,678	218,002	133,674	121,877	163,134	764,116
th.										
-	296,402	891,169	986,409	1,923,504	3,267,488	387,544	1,238,161	2,839,484	5,329,490	6,393,956
-	18,617	48,750	221,413	367,935	716,572	18,491	72,984	864,489	1,350,896	1,715,220
h. ies from and	714,761	1,588,183	3,860,674	8,531,175	7,926,215	331,839	664,067	1,862,522	3,925,613	5,030,367
s,	- -	1,896	183,853	1,658,256	2,152,674	- -	26,478	39,131	284,831	4,555,792

...t and *Declared Value* of EXPORTS OF BRITISH AND IRISH PRODUCE AND MANUFACTURES; and
Value of Exports of Foreign and Colonial Merchandise from Great Britain; and *Official*
* Imports into the same, for the following Years.—(*Parl. Paper*, No. 243. Sess. 1830.)

	Exports.			Imports.
	British and Irish Produce and Manufactures from Great Britain	Foreign and Colonial Merchandise from Great Britain.		Into Great Britain.
g 5th Jan.	Official Value. £	Declared Value. £	Official Value. £	Official Value. £
'9	18,556,891	31,252,836	8,760,196	25,122,203
'0	22,284,941	35,903,850	7,271,696	24,066,700
'1	22,831,936	36,929,007	11,549,681	28,257,781
'2	24,501,608	39,730,619	10,336,966	30,435,268
'3	25,195,893	45,102,230	12,677,431	28,308,373
'4	20,042,596	36,127,787	8,032,643	25,104,541
'5	22,132,367	37,135,746	8,938,741	26,454,281
'6	22,907,371	37,234,396	7,643,120	27,334,020
'7	22,963,772	39,746,581	7,717,555	25,554,478
'8	22,963,772	36,394,443	7,624,312	25,326,845
'9	24,179,854	36,306,385	5,776,775	25,660,953
'0	32,916,858	46,049,777	12,750,358	30,170,292
'1	33,299,408	47,000,926	9,357,435	37,613,294
'2	21,723,532	30,850,618	6,117,720	25,240,904
'3	28,447,912	39,334,526	9,533,065	24,923,922
'4	*	*	*	*
'5	32,200,580	43,447,373	19,157,818	32,620,771
'6	41,712,002	49,653,245	15,708,435	31,822,053
'7	34,774,521	40,328,940	13,441,665	26,374,921
'8	39,233,467	40,349,235	10,269,271	29,910,502
'9	41,960,555	45,180,150	10,835,800	35,845,340
'0	39,983,689	34,252,251	9,879,236	29,681,640
'1	37,820,293	35,569,077	10,525,026	31,515,222
'2	40,194,681	35,823,127	10,602,090	29,769,122
'3	43,558,488	36,176,897	9,211,928	29,432,376
'4	43,166,039	34,589,410	8,588,996	34,591,264
'5	48,024,952	37,600,021	10,188,596	36,056,551
'6	46,453,022	38,077,330	9,155,305	42,660,954
'7	40,332,854	30,847,528	10,066,503	36,174,350
'8	51,279,102	36,394,817	9,806,343	43,489,346
'9	52,019,728	36,150,379	9,928,655	43,536,187
'0	55,465,723	35,212,873	10,606,441	42,311,649

...ls destroyed by fire. —From the year ending Jan. 5. 1815, inclusive, British produce and manu-
...ve been included in the returns of Irish produce, &c. from Ireland, and consequently omitted
...nn headed Exports, Foreign, Colonial, and British, under which they had been previously

III. Value of IMPORTS into Great Britain from Foreign Parts, calculated at the *Official Ra[te]*
Valuation. — (This Table, and Nos. IV. V. and VI., are taken from the Finance Accounts for 18[...]

Species of Imports.	1828.			1829.			1830.	
	£	s.	d.	£	s.	d.	£	s.
Almonds of all sorts	28,126	2	6	39,505	15	11	18,718	13
Annotto	40,211	18	6	12,923	5	6	31,833	6
Ashes, Pearl and Pot	168,747	3	5	190,687	9	7	197,623	17
Barilla and Alkali	159,296	0	2	72,093	3	11	56,730	6
Bark, Oak and Cork Tree	158,335	16	2	156,764	1	7	186,913	19
Quercitron	2,847	18	11	6,105	8	8	6,987	9
Borax	7,203	8	6	11,474	9	6	28,226	11
Brimstone	102,705	4	5	132,179	18	0	142,374	3
Bristles	43,271	18	10	32,130	16	8	31,887	2
Butter	291,579	19	9	278,677	19	8	203,950	14
Camphire	4,616	17	0	14,010	13	6	20,201	11
Cassia Lignea	31,194	17	10	41,251	8	0	61,433	14
Cheese	272,625	5	6	314,066	10	10	244,321	8
Cinnamon	253,488	15	0	67,496	12	0	108,847	1
Cloves	63,346	7	6	121,946	10	0	9,017	17
Cochineal and Granilla	255,871	19	6	207,051	17	0	231,837	13
Cocoa	103,264	8	6	36,650	12	3	71,678	1
Coffee	2,945,023	10	6	2,502,666	15	6	2,372,650	16
Copper, unwrought, in Bricks and Pigs	40,904	12	11	19,245	0	0	41,069	13
Cork	45,282	1	9	39,508	11	7	40,379	9
Corn, Grain, Meal, and Flour	1,994,214	5	6	1,673,416	13	6	3,500,432	13
Cortex Peruvianus	48,211	5	0	42,342	15	0	50,581	12
Cotton Manufactures of India	273,097	16	8	344,900	18	10	505,114	7
of Europe, &c.	39,100	7	9	59,328	19	5	25,289	7
Currants	151,766	7	9	171,865	12	7	125,920	1
Dye and Hard Woods, Fustic	35,896	16	10	67,443	13	1	64,579	10
Logwood	194,501	5	10	158,295	19	0	156,023	18
Mahogany	175,903	16	1	183,915	10	1	188,569	12
Elephants' Teeth	20,204	0	8	21,581	15	9	25,913	9
Figs	13,910	14	0	16,932	15	8	13,642	17
Fish, Cod, &c. of Newfoundland	26,942	18	0	76,126	2	1	68,398	11
Flax	1,786,304	12	6	1,736,611	4	5	1,845,582	6
Gum, Animi and Copal	20,924	17	6	15,922	14	2	21,047	3
Arabic	27,074	17	6	11,082	12	3	19,313	8
Lac of all sorts	46,218	7	6	51,696	9	9	50,478	6
Senegal	4,747	5	9	26,595	11	0	16,890	2
Hemp, undressed	463,240	10	2	400,814	15	6	287,864	4
Hides, raw and tanned	423,789	8	9	643,891	11	1	829,436	9
Jalap	7,782	15	0	5,475	10	0	9,497	3
Indigo	801,393	18	4	1,349,315	10	7	876,425	5
Iron, in bars	180,439	3	5	146,984	15	4	147,971	6
Isinglass	22,467	1	0	15,594	14	10	21,544	0
Juniper Berries	21,865	4	0	19,571	2	2	31,113	0
Lead, Pig	32,456	7	4	37,195	2	5	22,628	16
Lemons and Oranges	66,259	12	4	58,336	10	3	55,654	0
Linens, Foreign	67,695	6	0	68,214	8	8	63,686	10
Liquorice Juice	41,121	0	6	28,327	6	8	18,923	2
Mace	14,246	5	0	26,333	18	2	4,275	18
Madder and Madder Roots	451,086	11	5	651,646	16	8	412,826	10
Melasses	261,447	15	9	338,970	2	6	261,574	10
Nutmegs	14,971	4	0	11,780	19	0	7,773	10
Oil, Castor	15,297	16	0	20,831	7	3	38,235	1
of Olives	135,796	2	7	309,802	7	4	152,117	19
Palm	94,296	5	0	126,530	11	1	179,945	17
Train and Blubber	497,328	0	8	426,358	5	0	430,039	11
Pepper	151,641	14	4	83,118	4	7	33,580	13
Pimento	57,891	13	11	59,008	4	7	95,036	9
Pitch and Tar	139,107	8	11	126,255	4	0	60,339	12
Quicksilver	176,652	4	0	53,689	8	0	127,181	9
Rags for Paper	31,407	6	5	34,864	18	6	37,183	9
Raisins	88,109	18	11	136,933	13	11	99,743	8
Rhubarb	57,609	13	9	66,977	16	3	91,800	19
Rice	143,691	14	5	183,888	4	8	215,144	4
Saltpetre	121,117	18	3	126,132	2	1	109,166	8
Seeds, Clover	82,126	13	3	84,465	0	5	27,667	13
Flax and Linseed	259,668	15	3	221,159	11	0	223,737	
Rape	65,762	17	1	55,399	7	7	48,864	
Shumac	23,878	11	10	26,523	0	0	23,227	
Silk, raw and waste	1,524,568	0	8	2,131,975	9	4	1,545,363	
thrown	555,490	4	0	613,312	16	0	254,165	
Manufactures of India	176,209	8	5	131,293	5	7	170,415	
of Europe, &c.	379,665	9	9	545,680	13	11	424,689	1
Skins and Furs	314,093	13	3	410,696	9	2	389,909	1
Smalts	10,074	2	10	10,413	11	10	7,490	
Spelter	299,986	9	4	225,688	4	3	210,952	
Spirits, Brandy	236,788	18	1	341,211	4	3	269,663	
Geneva	19,100	6	3	26,517	5	1	11,860	
Rum	497,207	7	4	540,700	19	6	597,843	
Sugar	5,328,114	7	2	6,311,720	14	2	6,279,555	
Tallow	1,249,800	15	9	1,029,126	6	10	1,145,498	
Tea	3,974,623	15	6	3,267,876	14	0	3,054,439	
Timber, Deals and Deal Ends	56,174	5	3	56,667	18	5	57,745	
Masts and Spars	106,920	3	0	80,597	4	4	84,414	
Staves	43,422	4	4	59,380	19	8	63,290	

Table III. Imports into Great Britain, &c. — (*continued*).

Species of Imports.	Years ending 5th January								
	1828.			1829.			1830.		
	£	s.	d.	£	s.	d.	£	s.	d.
..ber, Fir - - -	330,079	7	6	321,523	9	6	332,794	18	4
and Plank Oak -	50,781	0	6	45,089	2	5	42,392	2	8
of other sorts - -	70,999	4	2	71,143	6	7	75,730	19	0
..cco - - - -	308,645	12	8	231,222	13	2	204,963	0	0
..entine, common - -	144,781	12	2	150,085	1	10	130,163	10	3
, Bees' - - -	38,068	10	7	43,779	10	7	55,169	6	6
..efins - - -	119,162	19	10	134,364	14	11	103,046	8	6
..es - - -	867,545	2	1	1,015,530	12	1	789,679	18	1
, Cotton - - -	8,963,688	3	2	7,483,108	12	6	7,289,145	11	4
Sheep's - - -	883,785	5	7	913,189	10	9	678,195	6	9
..len Manufactures (including } ..rpets)	42,659	17	6	56,884	6	5	55,716	7	5
, Linen, raw - -	181,543	3	4	161,525	15	8	165,580	13	9
..ther Articles - -	1,875,156	18	0	2,087,333	16	2	1,993,186	18	4
..cal Official Value of Imports into } ..reat Britain from Foreign Parts	43,467,747	7	7	43,396,527	5	0	42,311,648	11	5

..alue of the Produce and Manufactures of the United Kingdom, exported from Great Britain to Foreign Parts, calculated at the *Official* Rates of Valuation.

Species of Exports.	Years ending 5th January								
	1828.			1829.			1830.		
	£	s.	d.	£	s.	d.	£	s.	d.
..rel, Slops and Negro Clothing -	3,300	11	7	2,301	13	9	2,925	0	8
and Ammunition -	389,390	6	10	419,486	5	4	387,694	8	9
and Hams - -	261,686	3	8	242,978	5	3	278,637	19	1
..a and Pork, salted -	29,021	13	9	23,465	17	9	27,545	16	1
..and Ale - - -	57,645	13	8	41,314	5	7	57,122	16	2
..s, printed - -	55,504	14	11	61,707	8	10	59,857	13	11
and Copper Manufactures -	17,025	9	3	17,041	5	9	18,241	10	7
..t and Biscuit -	776,895	10	0	675,537	19	0	860,315	4	5
and Cheese - ...	5,549	19	8	8,978	13	5	6,787	14	7
..et and Upholstery Wares -	53,830	11	1	67,249	17	0	64,635	14	9
and Culm - -	56,407	10	7	59,032	18	0	60,640	14	3
..ge - - -	314,202	11	9	302,220	7	6	312,854	19	11
Grain, Meal, and Flour -	63,013	8	6	56,942	10	9	47,800	1	5
..n Manufactures -	27,577	12	9	13,931	10	9	12,514	11	3
Yarn - - -	29,203,138	12	3	28,989,976	7	0	31,810,436	17	10
..enware of all sorts -	3,979,759	16	11	4,485,841	9	4	5,458,958	7	11
..f all sorts - -	91,711	8	1	99,753	0	3	96,928	7	3
of all sorts - -	187,252	1	7	241,989	7	3	184,136	3	9
..rdashery and Millinery -	146,109	9	5	137,413	16	4	128,206	15	6
..wares and Cutlery -	62,216	5	10	44,224	7	8	39,988	19	3
Beaver and Felt -	713,523	10	6	710,595	8	10	765,757	4	6
..f all other sorts -	146,484	5	7	166,312	10	10	165,974	14	10
..s - - -	13,001	16	8	16,964	7	10	13,849	19	6
	8,883	0	5	52,031	7	5	6,242	15	0
..nd Steel, wrought and unwrought	15,642	10	0	15,860	0	0	15,192	10	0
..and Shot	1,581,413	11	5	1,687,366	2	2	1,745,245	17	7
..er, wrought and unwrought -	141,094	2	11	105,565	9	11	72,184	1	7
Saddlery and Harness -	102,115	12	9	94,155	2	10	92,851	10	5
Manufactures -	88,434	19	7	89,205	11	1	82,995	11	7
..nery and Mill-work -	2,808,081	13	7	3,118,270	3	3	3,003,394	17	4
..ematical and Optical Instruments	201,551	17	4	262,094	10	7	250,061	12	7
..al Instruments -	32,339	1	1	19,393	18	10	21,612	5	7
..rain, of Greenland Fishery -	68,393	19	11	56,291	4	3	58,731	13	1
..rs' Colours - -	16,434	6	8	52,769	8	7	63,211	4	11
..rs' Colours - -	124,983	7	2	138,004	13	3	130,820	19	1
Plated Ware, Jewellery, and } ..ches	168,003	12	9	181,703	6	5	175,615	19	7
.. - - -	245,918	8	10	295,646	18	9	349,543	1	5
..tre, British refined -	42,088	15	7	58,098	18	10	39,185	11	9
..of all sorts - -	6,260	13	7	5,611	8	0	8,403	18	2
..Manufactures -	173,534	11	0	178,871	9	2	220,436	3	0
..and Candles -	223,597	18	9	234,036	3	1	199,378	8	4
..nery of all sorts -	193,046	11	1	204,362	7	7	187,438	1	4
, refined - -	1,117,329	11	9	1,229,503	0	1	1,294,773	8	11
..nwrought - -	180,768	8	7	151,308	16	4	121,261	4	4
..nd Pewter Wares, and Tin Plates	299,799	0	6	263,983	1	0	232,241	11	4
..co and Snuff, British manu- } ..ured	1,581	14	5	1,957	4	11	1,756	16	1
..llas and Parasols -	38,010	13	9	41,220	19	0	35,311	18	10
..bone - - -	20,102	18	11	·32,425	11	11	23,064	13	5
..en Manufactures -	5,979,701	9	6	5,720,079	3	7	5,361,997	10	4
..her Articles - -	743,286	8	0	854,135	2	3	810,958	0	0
Official Value of the Produce } Manufactures of the United { ..gdom, exported from Great { ..tain to Foreign Parts - }	51,276,448	4	8	52,029,150	17	1	55,465,723	1	9

V. Value of FOREIGN AND COLONIAL MERCHANDISE, exported from Great Britain to Foreign Parts, ca‥ lated at the *Official* Rates of Valuation.

Species of Exports.	Years ending 5th January								
	1828.			1829.			1830.		
	£	s.	d.	£	s.	d.	£	s.	d.
Annotto	6,935	10	10	3,051	2	6	4,902	6	
Ashes, Pearl and Pot	35,252	14	0	28,369	17	10	32,307	19	
Barilla and Alkali	374	8	7	1,936	7	11	1,348	6	
Cassia Lignea	42,769	10	0	35,632	0	0	79,524	4	
Cinnamon	89,923	0	0	88,634	0	0	96,527	0	
Cloves	10,429	13	9	57,279	1	6	21,714	0	
Cochineal and Granilla	164,098	6	6	177,872	12	6	173,136	15	
Cocoa	113,194	7	3	52,759	6	10	59,833	19	
Coffee	1,841,048	16	0	1,485,537	19	6	1,436,829	5	
Copper, unwrought, in Bricks and Pigs	79,713	2	0	16,626	13	0	91,668	19	
Corn, Grain, Meal, and Flour	119,350	13	3	161,318	8	0	206,606	11	
Cortex Peruvianus	26,017	13	0	28,300	7	0	44,322	9	
Cotton, Manufactures of India	673,371	3	8	594,278	5	2	539,216	6	
of Europe, &c.	14,722	16	10	34,631	6	0	22,066	7	
Currants	6,753	14	4	17,668	0	5	58,137	10	
Dye Woods, Fustic	6,825	3	6	9,692	16	7	19,768	2	
Logwood	99,761	9	0	88,371	8	4	86,965	10	
Fish, Cod, &c. of Newfoundland	34,902	3	0	52,582	8	11	78,024	8	
Flax	13,390	4	3	14,661	1	1	18,020	2	
Hemp	26,160	17	9	22,998	5	6	16,441	8	
Hides, raw and tanned	33,820	19	7	37,006	4	11	142,762	5	
Indigo	591,405	3	10	879,528	13	0	821,642	5	
Iron in Bars	44,988	6	6	38,922	2	4	39,316	11	
Lead, Pig	34,233	13	8	26,772	15	9	25,500	7	
Linens, Foreign	19,095	19	9	45,515	9	2	51,495	15	
Mace	30,179	2	6	35,893	17	0	19,100	14	
Nutmegs	11,501	8	6	10,568	7	0	15,571	14	
Oil of Olives	27,483	14	4	24,384	15	6	38,834	10	
Train	2,730	2	3	4,508	17	7	11,116	4	
Pepper	221,533	18	5	228,644	1	3	160,420	10	
Pimento	60,921	9	0	49,923	19	10	80,566	12	
Raisins	23,283	15	9	24,284	18	1	37,787	0	
Rice	52,310	7	4	51,386	8	1	95,562	6	
Saltpetre, rough	111,542	10	6	166,374	2	3	112,246	15	
Silk, raw, thrown, and waste	38,430	5	3	31,777	10	0	212,065	13	
Manufactures of India	221,614	12	0	148,529	0	5	138,427	3	
of Europe, &c.	19,993	13	9	34,151	17	8	19,132	5	
Skins and Furs	50,472	16	10	43,280	1	10	56,570	3	
Spelter	346,428	14	1	217,157	8	7	198,196	18	
Spirits, Brandy	176,052	14	0	292,415	5	7	184,878	11	
Geneva	69,871	15	4	86,690	0	0	41,260	15	
Rum	486,479	11	10	556,139	16	6	507,214	6	
Sugar	645,255	12	1	923,324	0	2	743,651	18	
Tea	38,249	2	0	38,923	19	0	37,795	13	
Tobacco	240,736	12	2	204,526	4	8	137,996	15	
Wines	268,041	0	2	287,295	12	4	218,076	6	
Wool, Cotton	1,517,946	6	10	1,400,978	13	7	2,216,440	11	
Sheep's	53,359	12	1	59,967	2	4	27,951	8	
Woollen Manufactures (including Carpets)	9,628	0	0	9,971	19	6	5,458	15	
All other Articles	953,661	3	1	992,660	0	6	1,122,038	2	
Total Official Value of Foreign and Colonial Merchandise, exported from Great Britain to Foreign Parts	9,806,247	10	11	9,928,654	13	0	10,606,440	11	

VI. Value of the PRODUCE AND MANUFACTURES OF THE UNITED KINGDOM, exported from Great Br‥ to Foreign Parts, according to the *Real or Declared* Value thereof.

Species of Exports.	Years ending 5th January							
	1828.			1829.			1830.	
	£	s.	d.	£	s.	d.	£	s.
Alum	2,290	7	0	1,640	9	2	1,925	10
Apparel, Slops and Negro Clothing	389,390	6	10	419,486	5	4	387,694	8
Arms and Ammunition	406,312	3	6	335,512	11	7	279,381	16
Bacon and Hams	32,494	17	2	26,547	0	8	30,654	14
Beef and Pork, salted	87,394	11	3	71,684	18	8	98,055	1
Beer and Ale	212,390	18	9	239,268	17	10	241,417	2
Books, printed	106,995	7	0	101,377	17	3	109,435	4
Brass and Copper Manufactures	786,803	7	2	678,531	2	5	810,641	2
Bread and Biscuit	8,068	11	6	11,547	16	3	10,301	6
Butter and Cheese	145,848	7	9	181,397	1	4	157,852	1
Cabinet and Upholstery Wares	56,407	10	7	59,032	18	0	60,640	14
Coals and Culm	154,042	18	8	144,838	6	10	145,879	11
Cordage	127,832	3	8	112,568	16	0	98,542	18
Corn, Grain, Meal, and Flour	70,915	10	5	40,591	15	11	37,564	12
Cotton Manufactures	13,956,825	10	9	13,545,638	0	8	13,420,544	6
Yarn	3,545,568	4	8	3,594,945	17	3	3,974,039	5

le VI. Value of PRODUCE AND MANUFACTURES of the United Kingdom, &c. — *(continued)*.

Species of Exports.	Years ending 5th January								
	1828.			1829.			1830.		
	£	s.	d.	£	s.	d.	£	s.	d.
ware of all sorts - -	437,812	17	8	499,743	6	6	461,710	5	7
all sorts - - -	182,084	5	6	241,324	1	10	186,365	5	8
all sorts - - -	527,110	6	11	492,072	17	6	467,155	8	3
ashery and Millinery - -	499,534	8	6	485,981	9	9	394,442	16	8
res and Cutlery - -	1,390,428	13	8	1,385,616	16	0	1,389,514	19	0
eaver and Felt - -	175,293	2	9	196,905	10	10	188,902	6	5
all other sorts - -	17,112	8	0	23,170	2	2	16,065	19	9
- - -	7,172	14	11	18,641	11	3	4,524	16	0
es - - -	62,131	7	8	65,092	9	0	62,001	9	0
Steel, wrought and unwrought	1,214,948	0	11	1,226,836	8	9	1,155,176	15	0
d Shot - -	256,181	12	9	177,656	10	2	114,524	14	3
, wrought and unwrought -	280,265	14	4	261,735	10	9	254,007	7	1
Saddlery and Harness -	88,434	19	7	89,205	11	1	82,995	11	7
anufactures - - -	1,895,186	12	8	2,000,033	6	11	1,885,831	16	7
ry and Mill Work - -	201,551	17	4	262,094	10	7	250,061	12	7
atical and Optical Instruments	32,339	1	1	19,393	18	0	21,612	5	7
Instruments - -	68,393	19	11	56,291	4	3	58,731	13	1
n, of Greenland Fishery -	18,464	8	9	55,585	7	1	73,749	10	6
Colours - -	124,983	7	2	138,004	13	3	130,820	19	1
lated Ware, Jewellery, and } es	169,449	16	7	181,848	13	4	177,242	1	0
, British refined -	121,039	11	4	151,397	10	3	171,978	2	1
all sorts - -	17,942	17	6	25,917	2	0	17,507	14	8
ne - -	5,886	12	3	4,774	0	5	6,976	13	4
ufactures - - -	236,092	12	1	255,755	16	3	267,192	9	1
Candles - -	227,695	13	6	226,205	17	2	192,738	18	1
y of all sorts - -	193,046	11	1	204,362	7	7	187,438	1	4
fined - -	963,430	13	9	1,038,537	18	9	984,837	15	1
rought - -	187,887	13	0	147,130	16	5	120,105	8	11
Pewter Wares, and Tin Plates	301,753	1	4	266,634	7	6	235,021	19	1
and Snuff, British manu- } d	14,981	15	9	18,415	16	6	15,877	16	0
s and Parasols - -	38,010	13	9	41,220	19	0	35,311	18	10
ne - - -	45,316	10	0	63,582	18	0	40,666	15	6
Manufactures - -	5,277,861	6	2	5,120,220	8	11	4,656,809	18	7
Articles - -	1,027,003	2	3	1,146,792	17	6	1,040,402	8	7
eal or Declared Value of the } ce and Manufactures of the } Kingdom, exported from } Britain to Foreign Parts }	36,396,339	6	8	36,152,798	11	4	35,212,873	8	6

TRADE OF IRELAND.

s into Ireland, according to the *Official* Value, distinguishing each Country, from 1790 to 1822.
(Moreau's Tables of the Trade of Ireland, p. 24.)

	1790.	1800.	1810.	1815.	1816.	1817.	1818.	1819.	1820.	1821.	1822.
	£	£	£	£	£	£	£	£	£	£	£
-	65,139	80,551	18,868	67,778	16,321	46,126	52,775	105,960	42,340	52,120	64,151
-	120,881	58,677	41,640	35,932	11,983	10,291	17,625	21,129	7,135	5,454	7,389
}	98,941	94,347	93,944	70,570	35,299	18,584 {	31,593 / 44	33,200	15,255	8,310	16,885
}	62,419	70,352	32,229	40,608	34,477	20,116	35,577	36,212	17,387	27,805	52,296
}	2,746	13,724	- -	38	708	350	325	396	442	900	
}	65,836	55,645	2,581	44,686	16,143 {	9,528	72,505	47,524 / 3,450	30,101 / 645	40,299 / 900	60,911 / 572
}	415,962	373,306	189,272	259,612	114,931	104,995	210,444	247,861	113,307	135,508	210,204
-	120,541	25,447	1,353	11,876	9,575	9,512	24,669	21,025	13,568	12,833	16,072
-	99,465	114,836	214,030	77,214	54,494	45,871	60,935	53,527	64,686	44,959	40,956
-	214,291	120,934	115,380	103,399	80,911	75,344	87,940	112,823	45,084	112,765	107,376
-	50,554	21,956	27,510	43,806	65,788	29,347	32,216	33,189	22,200	34,678	67,613
	- -	- -	- -	- -	3,000	2,613	12,743	15,341	14,971	4,771	9,519
	484,851	283,173	358,273	236,295	213,772	162,687	218,503	235,903	160,509	210,006	241,536
}	3,135	2,327	12,822	5,139	- -	1,078	1,977	2,965	16,324	24,146	28,182
c.	1,472	9,398	16,626	17,352	14,572	12,116	13,139	9,809	6,478	7,646	6,079
}	2,743,158	3,123,526	4,732,720	4,471,775	3,643,127	4,754,840	5,065,060	5,302,727	4,242,650	5,338,838	5,509,200
}	2,747,765	3,135,251	4,762,168	4,494,266	3,657,699	4,768,034	5,080,176	5,315,499	4,265,452	5,370,630	5,543,461

Table I. Imports into Ireland, &c. — (continued).

Countries.	1790.	1800.	1810.	1815.	1816.	1817.	1818.	1819.	1820.	18
Europe - -	3,648,578	3,791,730	5,309,713	4,990,173	3,986,402	5,035,716	5,509,123	5,799,263	4,539,268	5,71
Asia - - -										
Africa - -	10	- -	6,236	- -	- -	- -	- -	6,669	2,868	
America - -	423,199	828,623	1,245,773	753,335	709,944	642,913	595,768	591,955	657,074	68
British N. Colonies	12,881	24,074	90,157	43,941	50,874	78,977	97,563	138,789	106,510	10
British W. Indies.	226,685	241,521	416,497	454,785	301,052	305,723	261,554	300,871	342,371	38
Total British America -	239,566	265,595	506,654	498,726	351,926	384,700	359,117	439,660	448,881	49
United States	183,633	563,028	641,603	235,480	344,749	258,196	236,651	152,295	208,179	18
Foreign W. Indies, Brazils,&c.	- -	- -	97,516	19,129	13,269	17				
Total Foreign America -	183,633	563,028	739,119	254,609	358,018	258,213	236,651	152,295	208,179	18
Grand Total { Including Gt. Britain.	4,071,794	4,202,126	6,564,578	5,637,117	4,693,745	5,644,175	6,098,720	6,395,972	5,197,192	7,40
Grand Total { Exclusive of Gt. Britain.	1,328,636	1,078,600	1,831,858	1,165,342	1,050,618	889,335	1,033,660	1,093,247	954,542	1,06

Note. — The official value for the years 1790, 1800, and 1810, is stated in Irish currency, and fr[om] to 1822 (year ending 5th January, 1823) in British currency, and the grand total includes the pr[o...] fisheries and prize goods.

II. Exports of Irish Produce and Manufactures from Ireland, according to the *Official* Return[s] 1814 to 1823, both inclusive. — (*Moreau's Tables*, p. 30.)

	To Great Britain only.								
Principal Articles.	1814.	1815.	1816.	1817.	1818.	1819.	1820.	1821.	18
	£	£	£	£	£	£	£	£	£
Raw Material of Manufacture.									
Hides - -	26,007	30,439	63,579	123,959	64,361	13,662	4,061	7,008	24
Flax - -	20,827	27,414	30,672	40,657	35,315	29,703	59,872	63,100	34
Sheep's Wool -	20,082	67,544	21,289	26,425	29,985	2,869	7,468	2,038	10
Feathers -	13,867	14,265	16,790	14,815	18,376	18,174	12,560	20,310	35
Rape Seed -	5,385	4,519	2,314	6,107	4,710	39,732	31,711	19,474	2?
Calf Skins -	9,379	14,470	17,373	20,276	14,981	4,105	6,910	11,809	11
Copper Ore -	1,530	3,046	2,623	2,409	3,970	6,945	8,448	7,601	9
Kelp - -	3,443	4,173	2,471	3,168	6,638	5,144	5,717	5,385	8
Tallow -	338	620	572	5,637	3,597	90	1,340	9	1
Manufactured Articles.									
Linens, plain -	2,435,899	3,342,698	2,606,078	3,074,863	2,754,477	2,153,678	2,480,881	2,800,250	2,65?
coloured -	-	-	-	-	747	1,270	-	45	
Cotton Goods -	703	13,730	1,975	9,358	5,994	37,836	53,483	33,705	6?
Yarn, Cotton -	4,737	5,385	6,613	5,385	3,044	1,230	1,228	1,372	1
Linen -	82,298	65,986	76,176	77,230	58,388	30,599	51,104	56,812	2?
Worsted -	4,170	18	6,655		71	589	-	715	
Spirits -	141,305	87,083	29,440	7,239	1,847	16,745	60,500	51,236	8?
Drapery, new -	739	1,612	1,054	238	442	344	913	1,023	
old -	16,685	55,658	34,099	23,344	13,047	22,434	35,804	23,052	2?
Candles -	18	69	334	19	50	-	100	4	
Glass -	2,365	4,619	3,008	1,569	861	3,500	1,093	1,962	
Soap - -	3,456	1,580	1,238	803	1,203	745	322	562	
Grain, Wheat -	401,677	308,078	195,180	102,118	198,183	280,037	809,296	967,972	78?
Oats -	315,087	322,942	379,432	344,491	567,336	430,403	531,284	620,992	30?
Barley -	9,857	26,417	61,195	26,789	24,222	20,187	91,355	73,320	2
Meal, Wheat -	114,187	91,427	71,175	11,949	33,832	82,698	166,605	253,960	29?
Oat -	11,813	11,762	10,309	8,043	36,756	13,620	12,394	17,848	
Live Stock, Cows & Oxen	92,349	187,980	176,084	250,926	322,178	288,681	215,840	137,573	16?
Hogs -	41,900	117,757	77,186	22,557	22,458	57,008	91,477	96,463	6?
Sheep -	10,819	24,524	31,830	27,196	23,217	18,193	22,301	23,363	3?
Salt Provisions, Butter -	689,836	661,784	596,237	628,045	748,442	849,686	962,809	810,278	74?
Bacon -	301,512	312,489	304,433	247,976	293,197	306,428	360,761	502,402	33?
Pork -	157,242	146,300	82,086	122,610	121,835	120,168	146,727	133,545	9?
Beef -	134,335	97,421	63,802	170,513	130,286	97,519	84,955	76,462	6?
HogsLard -	17,519	20,793	20,249	14,870	20,587	14,040	25,457	30,988	2?
Bread -	430	493	307	203	48	204	80	132	
Tongues -	1,507	922	780	2,210	2,706	2,154	1,385	1,655	
Unnumbered Articles -	131,304	153,769	232,631	145,633		178,102	164,973	181,262	15?
Total Exports from Ireland -	5,108,206	5,196,190	5,109,765	5,561,344	5,700,625	5,150,321	6,531,922	7,067,005	6,09

Observations. — The records of the goods imported into Ireland from Great Britain has be[en dis-] tinued in consequence of the commercial intercourse with that part of the United Kingdom ha[ving been] placed, in 1825, upon the footing of a coasting traffic.

Table II. Exports of Irish Produce, &c. — *(continued)*.

		To all Parts of the World, exclusive of Great Britain.								
...al Articles.	1814.	1815.	1816.	1817.	1818.	1819.	1820.	1821.	1822.	1823.
...erial of Manu-	£	£	£	£	£	£	£	£	£	£
...e.										
- - -	1,670	227	246	413	88	270	22	49	35	1,202
...Wool -			420	228	91	15	560	620	171	206
...s -	1,084	1,320	276	274	149	158	423	235	144	319
...ed -	169	207	586	1,718	1,184	1,077	663	154	959	47
...Ore -				9	- -	38	36	41	- -	67
- - -	267	92	355	294	194	89	132	36	103	245
...ared Articles.										
...plain -	209,860	331,358	201,174	359,146	372,020	155,575	196,529	240,769	200,146	185,234
...coloured -	152	532	6,987	8,297	5,209	6,888	3,827	2,365	5,647	6,728
...oods -	37,569	128,300	143,143	59,179	37,757	16,941	28,017	53,580	101,498	106,468
...otton -	2,160	17	-	176	10	128			42	94
...nen -	- -	110	542	336	467	158	167	- -		
...orsted -						2				
...new -	608	1,483	652	997	4,222	16,030	11,068	6,351	7,156	254
...old -	1,483	13,574	2,734	3,279	1,560	4,176	834	467	1,631	154
- - -	17,060	20,619	28,336	29,551	1,303	1,986	2,141	1,015	2,050	3,091
- - -	8,698	29,603	20,362	19,889	17,273	22,535	21,603	21,802	22,575	17,477
- - -	21,436	20,615	16,620	14,272	9,113	11,194	7,277	4,817	6,048	6,893
...eat -	36,124	114,120	50,335	5,074	8,182	10,395	11,993	10,145	10,703	7,989
...s -	30,253	972	3,666	1,150	3,277	4	- -	19	3,535	2,705
...rley -	45,849	52,589	42,338	9,196	1,595	3,027	2,102	1,743	1,354	1,996
...eat -	102,603	9,465	9,965	1,088	1,586	198	48	2,375	891	723
- - -	750	644	587	753	7,069	8,532	1,215	225	2,974	8,624
...Cows & Oxen	4,585	- -	122	88	4,126	1,146	519	309	959	875
...Hogs -	- -	6	10	2	77	376	88	118	116	66
...Sheep -	- -	- -	- -	14	18	- -	6	50	3	3
...ons, Butter -	157,850	178,133	170,956	152,441	99,812	133,364	128,503	117,419	124,571	107,162
...Bacon -	23,264	14,763	10,799	16,298	4,434	3,912	3,028	4,656	3,987	2,991
...Pork -	71,297	67,916	61,339	61,251	42,026	46,640	50,485	61,977	59,761	49,298
...Beef -	44,177	33,861	33,676	37,186	37,508	16,398	16,174	49,466	26,661	25,004
...HogsLard	9,465	8,901	10,114	8,907	6,688	7,572	6,539	8,458	4,281	5,970
...Bread -	23,079	4,886	7,246	9,105	5,946	4,831	3,049	2,972	2,774	7,953
...Tongues	1,825	1,093	961	1,193	1,222	1,024	678	1,135	1,125	616
...ted Articles -	59,259	92,616	80,671	40,332	60,461	81,140	77,693	71,084	84,954	105,468
...the above }	1,006,572	1,163,991	932,488	851,548	736,325	558,261	577,519	636,852	678,044	659,906

Value of IMPORTS into Ireland from Foreign Parts, calculated at the *Official* Rates of Valuation.
(*Finance Accounts for* 1829.)

	Years ending 5th January								
Species of Imports.	1828.			1829.			1830.		
	£	s.	d.	£	s.	d.	£	s.	d.
..., Barilla, Pearl and Pot - -	53,537	5	1	108,222	8	7	94,244	15	10
...Oak and Cork Tree -	19,100	12	1	21,515	0	8	30,918	2	3
...tone, rough -	12,253	14	2	21,257	7	6	18,245	3	9
...e and Cocoa Shell -	21,371	9	10	37,796	10	3	27,169	17	11
...n Wool -	14,944	15	9	13,272	7	6	9,191	18	3
...as, plain and coloured -	121,859	16	0	67,491	7	11	54,354	18	5
...nd Hard Woods -	24	3	0	668	6	6	653	17	6
...enware and Porcelain -	15,083	12	10	33,108	3	6	32,314	9	0
...Cod -	31	16	2	120	17	0	35	11	1
...Herrings -	24,783	3	2	37,352	16	3	55,129	12	3
...Seed -	191	16	11	203	1	7	720	0	0
- - -	79,828	8	4	48,842	10	1	66,618	4	0
- - -	41,188	18	11	44,334	14	9	29,942	19	8
..., undressed -	21,278	5	11	24,086	16	8	14,455	15	9
...tanned and untanned -	13,242	9	8	16,453	3	1	17,508	4	10
...unwrought -	5,134	1	1	6,564	4	1	8,741	2	7
...er -	16,319	2	5	13,368	10	2	9,735	10	1
...ses -	1,777	1	10	7,779	7	3	8,815	18	11
...es and Lemons -	6,797	5	6	5,923	6	8	6,418	17	9
- - -	12,396	7	10	13,826	4	4	13,108	0	4
...Organzine -	3,426	18	6	3,137	6	2	2,913	9	3
..., Foreign -	6,429	19	4	5,890	11	7	5,412	4	1
- - -	444,319	0	3	510,033	3	10	528,826	2	4
- - -	105,280	8	10	123,265	11	5	143,519	15	9
...r, viz. — Deals and Deal Ends -	30,908	15	2	33,948	9	8	38,338	1	9
...Staves -	4,579	12	0	4,588	6	2	4,440	8	5
...Fir, Oak, and other sorts	128,816	18	10	162,807	13	6	191,278	9	1
...o -	21,920	13	1	11,851	9	8	20,665	18	7
...ntine -	14,505	16	2	4,267	3	9	2,313	3	10
...a -	6,156	15	8	26,137	12	3	21,681	16	1
- - -	70,498	6	7	105,978	7	7	104,024	12	4
...Linen -	15,678	0	0	33,747	0	11	28,292	12	11
...Merchandise -	86,432	0	8	84,438	4	3	81,640	15	11
Official Value of Imports into } ...land from Foreign Parts - }	1,420,027	11	7	1,632,278	5	1	1,669,668	10	6

IV. Value of the PRODUCE AND MANUFACTURES OF THE UNITED KINGDOM, exported from Ireland Foreign Parts, calculated at the *Official* Rates of Valuation. — (*Finance Accounts for* 1829.)

Species of Exports.	Years ending 5th January								
	1828.			1829.			1830.		
	£	s.	d.	£	s.	d.	£	s.	c.
Bacon and Hams - - -	2,566	10	2	1,243	10	2	1,735	3	
Beef, salted - - -	15,260	10	10	11,315	15	5	11,107	15	1.
Beer and Ale - - -	2,457	18	4	1,935	4	5	2,167	15	
Bread - - - -	233	3	5	1,315	18	9	1,088	6	
Butter - - - -	89,267	9	7	92,982	0	5	85,951	0	
Candles - - - -	21,141	13	2	22,280	0	1	21,203	5	
Cordage and Twine - -	2,902	6	4	4,023	0	8	4,316	10	
Corn and Meal, viz.									
Barley - - -	39	14	10	4	12	1	22	5	1
Oats - - -	916	0	1	2,236	5	10	957	9	
Oatmeal - - -	172	1	1	788	7	0	439	15	
Wheat - - -	31	19	9	-	-	-	24	7	
Wheat Flour - -	7	15	1	81	8	4	21	10	
Cotton Goods - - -	416,701	5	8	317,026	13	4	349,774	11	
Cows and Oxen - -	293	10	9	83	1	7	1,179	13	
Earthenware - - -	1,019	11	8	2,472	4	11	£,274	15	
Feathers - - -	102	11	0	176	12	3	225	6	
Fish, Herrings - - -	622	3	1	909	13	11	345	13	
Flax, dressed and undressed -	297	15	6	2	10	9	1	10	
Glass - - - -	7,276	3	6	9,056	3	5	8,166	10	
Horses and Mules - -	2,803	7	9	5,915	1	6	1,922	15	
Lard - - - -	3,525	6	3	4,667	12	3	6,261	1	
Leather, wrought and unwrought, } Saddlery and Harness }	9,718	4	11	8,170	17	6	10,909	5	
Linen, plain - - -	259,393	5	10	191,061	18	5	143,013	10	
coloured - -	959	17	8	309	7	10			
Sail Cloth - -	2,896	7	11	5,442	9	8	3,210	12	
Thread - -	5,365	16	0	8,825	17	0	4,433	5	
Linen and Cotton, mixed Manufacture	2,449	0	1	4,508	10	11	1,457	1	
Pork, salted - - -	33,719	17	9	9,773	6	2	29,586	16	
Potatoes - - -	3,604	8	7	5,789	8	6	4,105	3	
Sheep - - - -	362	15	5	82	3	1	88	12	
Skins, Calf - - -	508	6	2	17	4	7	430	9	
Soap - - - -	7,593	6	4	7,721	3	7	2,852	7	
Spirits - - - -	8,298	13	6	1,605	5	6	821	9	
Tallow - - - -	112	10	8	118	0	5	90	5	
Tongues - - - -	1,843	16	11	1,170	0	0	1,637	6	
Woollen Manufactures - -	9,414	17	6	8,890	0	1	10,493	0	
Other Merchandise - -	28,952	0	3	36,302	14	8	35,002	3	
Total Official Value of the Produce } and Manufactures of the United } Kingdom, exported from Ireland } to Foreign Parts - - }	942,832	3	4	768,304	5	0	747,318	13	

V. Value of FOREIGN AND COLONIAL MERCHANDISE exported from Ireland to Foreign Parts, calcul at the *Official* Rates of Valuation. — (*Finance Accounts for* 1829.)

Species of Exports.	Years ending 5th January							
	1828.			1829.			1830.	
	£	s.	d.	£	s.	d.	£	s.
Coffee - - - -	14	16	8	-	-	-.	1,723	16
Corn, Grain, Meal, and Flour -	615	12	0	2,040	1	5	2,764	12
Fish, Cod, of Newfoundland -	2,935	7	8	461	10	9		
Salt - - - -	692	6	2	747	13	10	515	1
Spirits - - - -	2,128	6	9	2,187	10	2	2,357	5
Tobacco - - - -	6,157	11	4	4,391	9	8	1,969	8
Wine - - - -	8,373	19	2	5,264	16	10	4,003	17
Other Merchandise - -	3,562	12	3	2,797	16	7	2,627	19
Total Official Value of Foreign and } Colonial Merchandise, exported } from Ireland to Foreign Parts - }	24,480	12	0	17,890	19	3	15,962	1

VI. Value of the PRODUCE AND MANUFACTURES OF THE UNITED KINGDOM, exported from Ireland Foreign Parts, according to the *Real or Declared* Value thereof. — (*Finance Accounts for* 1829.)

Species of Exports.	Years ending 5th January							
	1828.			1829.			1830.	
	£	s.	d.	£	s.	d.	£	s.
Bacon and Hams - - -	4,828	11	0	2,262	7	1	3,213	17
Beef, salted - - -	27,177	15	4	20,126	19	6	17,127	5
Beer and Ale - - -	7,599	11	1	6,226	18	10	7,706	17
Bread - - - -	332	18	0	1,505	2	6	1,530	10
Butter - - - -	169,781	4	0	170,977	9	6	135,186	14
Candles - - - -	36,375	12	4	36,010	17	1	31,335	18
Cordage and Twine - -	4,793	1	9	7,083	0	3	7,319	5

Table VI. Value of the Produce, &c. — *continued*.

Species of Exports.	Years ending 5th January								
	1828.			1829.			1830.		
	£	s.	d.	£	s.	d.	£	s.	d.
d Meal, viz.									
ey	53	0	0	16	10	0	11	11	0
	2,068	9	0	3,756	0	0	2,074	3	9
eal	379	15	0	1,405	14	0	1,031	3	6
at	30	5	0	-	-	-	25	0	0
at Flour	9	12	0	95	0	0	40	0	0
oods	133,322	6	1	99,794	0	5	138,974	6	11
d Oxen	148	5	6	68	10	0	639	1	6
ware	1,019	11	8	2,472	4	11	2,274	15	9
s	224	4	0	436	3	9	561	5	8
rrings	687	0	0	1,054	16	0	423	2	0
essed and undressed	778	17	0	6	15	0	4	1	0
nd Mules	7,373	6	6	9,149	3	8	8,714	7	2
	4,883	0	4	11,191	9	0	4,750	0	0
	6,654	12	0	8,701	12	5	9,509	18	11
wrought and unwrought, ry and Harness	14,700	14	4	12,635	6	0	14,680	4	6
ain	225,836	7	10	173,107	19	0½	113,385	5	4
oloured	414	15	0	128	5	10			
ail Cloth	3,450	10	2	6,033	16	18	3,675	16	3
hread	3,213	9	8	5,310	2	4	2,345	0	4
d Cotton, mixed Manufacture	2,449	0	1	4,508	10	11	1,457	1	11
ted	70,017	9	4	21,054	8	8	59,737	13	6
	3,496	12	3	4,206	16	2	3,781	2	3
	189	13	0	108	0	0	61	0	0
lf	488	10	0	25	0	0	497	0	0
	6,920	17	7	6,727	3	3	3,154	9	9
	8,216	6	7	1,281	17	0	659	17	6
	143	2	11	141	0	8	117	11	7
Manufactures	2,703	11	0	1,534	4	0	2,376	7	6
rchandise	5,718	13	1	5,757	13	2	4,440	11	10
	30,037	6	1	35,576	15	4	34,773	17	0
al or Declared Value of the ce and Manufactures of the Kingdom, exported from d to Foreign Parts	786,517	16	6	661,377	13	11½	617,596	5	8

TRADE OF THE UNITED KINGDOM.

unt of the *Official Value* of BRITISH AND IRISH PRODUCE AND MANUFACTURES, and of FO-
COLONIAL PRODUCE AND MANUFACTURES, exported from Great Britain in 1829; distinguishing
al Countries; with the Imports into Great Britain from the same Countries, for the same
d the aggregate Imports into and Exports from Ireland for the same Year. — (*Parl. Paper,*
ess. 1831.)

Countries.	Official Value of Imports.			Official Value of Exports.								
				British and Irish Produce and Manufactures.			Foreign and Colonial Produce and Manufactures.			Total Exports.		
	£	s.	d.	£	s.	d.	£	s.	d.	£	s.	d.
EUROPE :												
	4,180,752	12	5	2,157,251	0	2	997,566	1	11	3,154,817	2	1
	187,711	2	8	54,726	18	3	103,490	0	5	158,216	18	8
	67,859	15	5	95,794	14	3	49,772	17	10	145,567	12	1
	484,611	7	4	158,356	7	7	69,288	7	4	227,644	14	11
	1,295,569	19	1	252,576	3	8	533,590	15	5	786,166	19	1
	1,597,854	1	5	8,384,262	8	1	1,829,101	14	11	10,213,364	3	0
rlands	1,521,085	19	0	2,854,618	19	8	3,019,309	5	1	5,873,928	4	9
	2,066,890	4	8	509,419	4	7	336,746	2	3	846,165	6	10
Azores, and Madeira	373,823	16	8	2,327,862	18	9	60,940	3	1	2,388,803	1	10
the Canaries	1,074,184	17	7	1,555,518	7	0	259,219	13	0	1,814,738	0	0
	26,578	3	8	982,330	5	0	129,163	7	0	1,111,493	12	0
	804,220	9	4	4,007,185	14	11	899,672	17	7	4,906,858	12	6
	20,784	12	2	458,178	17	8	47,180	4	2	505,359	1	10
nds	109,448	12	6	34,254	8	3	4,990	9	11	39,244	18	2
d Continental Greece	431,062	6	2	1,393,054	18	9	83,072	8	5	1,476,127	7	2
Greek Islands	9,657	2	2									
nsey, Jersey, Alder- Man	273,788	9	3	304,352	14	6	98,228	9	3	402,581	3	9
	14,525,883	11	6	25,529,744	1	1	8,521,332	17	7	34,051,076	18	8
AFRICA :												
ts on the Mediterra-	223,177	8	3	132,382	12	9	795	17	2	133,178	9	11
rbary, and Morocco	30,558	3	1	-	-	-	453	0	0	453	0	0
oast of Africa	258,245	2	1	350,336	17	0	161,171	16	4	511,508	13	4
od Hope	232,598	9	6	347,003	5	3	36,424	9	7	383,427	14	10
Islands	-	-	-	93	6	4	-	-	-	93	6	4
	5,813	12	7	30,047	18	0	1,604	4	2	31,652	2	2
rbon	-	-	-	16,137	5	4	1,328	18	11	17,466	4	3
	438,714	9	10	255,522	14	0	24,448	11	5	279,971	5	5

S s

Table I. — *(continued.)*

Countries.	Official Value of Imports.	Official Value of Exports.		
		British and Irish Produce and Manufactures	Foreign and Colonial Manufactures	Total Expe
	£ s. d.	£ s. d.	£ s. d.	£
ASIA : East Indies and China	7,859,883 1 1	5,856,287 5 2	605,841 1 9	6,462,128
New South Wales, Van Diemen's Land, and Swan River	125,720 8 3	257,071 1 5	87,578 3 2	344,649
New Zealand and South Sea Islands	583 0 9	826 7 11	320 4 5	1,146
AMERICA : British Northern Colonies	881,444 4 5	1,774,069 3 6	253,914 18 3	2,027,984
British West Indies -	8,501,442 10 9	4,739,048 0 7	354,076 3 1	5,093,124
Foreign West Indies -	402,457 11 11	1,819,366 1 1	47,528 1 1	1,866,894
United States -	6,103,142 10 3	5,734,926 18 7	248,424 1 7	5,983,351
Mexico -	150,386 14 2	520,402 6 2	124,124 2 1	644,526
Guatemala -	11,464 2 1			
Colombia -	84,595 18 9	499,815 0 3	12,879 1 9	512,694
States of the Rio de la Plata	536,050 19 3	1,289,055 14 10	17,337 19 0	1,306,393
Chili -	61,514 5 11	1,375,742 11 2	12,955 15 0	1,388,698
Peru -	69,839 11 8	376,552 11 1	13,176 4 5	389,728
Brazil -	1,469,015 2 9	4,566,010 4 3	76,314 7 9	4,642,324
The Whale Fisheries -	361,086 8 11	6 0 0	2,173 7 7	2,179
Total Great Britain -	42,333,617 7 9	55,470,447 5 9	10,604,203 6 1	66,074,650
Ireland -	1,669,400 19 3	747,441 5 5	15,964 8 2	763,405
Total United Kingdom £	44,003,018 7 0	56,217,888 11 2	10,620,167 14 3	66,838,056

II. Account of the QUANTITIES of the Principal Articles of Foreign and Colonial Merchandi[se] ported and retained for Home Consumption, and also the Quantity exported in the Year 1828[,] tional Quantities omitted, (No. 267. Sess. 1830.)

Articles.	Quantities imported.	Retained for Home Consumption.	Quanties exported.	Articles.	Quantities imported.	Retained for Home Consumption.
Ashes, pearl and pot, cwt.	155,617	148,808	17,369	Linens, Cambrics, &c. pieces	50,401	49,864
Barilla - - cwt.	213,299	211,859		Ditto, plain and diaper : —		
Bark,oak and cork tree, cwt.	807,888	806,412		Entered by the ell - ells	706,490	—
Brimstone, rough - cwt.	279,850	290,638		Entered by the piece,pieces	10,432	—
Bristles - - lbs.	1,748,921	1,888,807		Entered by the square yard		
Butter - - - lbs.	201,675	195,716		Entered at value - L.	131,296	1,816
Cassia lignea - - lbs.	349,535	55,787	356,320	sq. yds.	5,613	8,271
Cheese - - cwt.	217,991	213,594		Liquorice juice - cwt.	6,628	6,643
Cinnamon, - - lbs.	337,483	15,696	354,536	Mace - - lbs.	42,134	16,094
Cloves - - lbs.	484,368	61,216	152,687	Madder - cwt.	96,064	- 95,651
Cochineal - - lbs.	258,032	147,819	158,109	Madder root - cwt.	66,924	67,243
Cocoa-nuts - - lbs.	1,637,000	354,407	1,478,537	Mahogany - - cwts.	540,707	383,761
Coffee - - lbs.	41,069,731	17,114,635	23,785,980	Nutmegs - - lbs.	58,685	141,002
Copper, unwrought - cwt.	4,811	3,489	2,558	Oil :— Castor - lbs.	217,173	250,480
Cork,unmanufactured, cwt.	47,864	46,793	—	Olive - gallons	2,336,001	1,753,338
Corn :— Wheat - qrs.	715,242	805,849	58,646	Palm - - cwts.	126,553	120,599
Barley - - qrs.	168,672	217,540	4,117	Train — Blubber - tuns	7,671	7,671
Oats - - qrs.	166,423	14,373	6,694	Spermaceti, tuns	3,845	4,038
Rye - - qrs.	29,562	488	886	Not blubber or		
Peas and beans - qrs.	126,299	118,671	2,977	spermaceti, do.	13,212	13,186
Wheat-meal & flour, cwt.	151,038	126,703	58,846	Opium - - lbs.	84,186	20,680
Cortex Peruvianus, or				Pepper - - lbs.	4,987,630	1,927,718
Jesuits' bark - -	338,797	110,678	188,669	Pimento - - lbs.	2,269,545	310,182
Cotton, piece goods of India,		value		Prunes - - cwt.	17,395	7,765
not printed - pieces	967,102	L.43,074	524,372	Quicksilver - lbs.	268,278	212,530
Cottons, printed - sq. yds.	505,708	187,598	338,592	Raisins - - cwt.	201,857	153,228
Currants - - cwt.	163,834	118,399		Rhubarb - - lbs.	107,164	38,967
Dye and hard woods : —				Rice - - - cwt.	172,232	80,137
Fustic - - tons	7,597	6,656		Rice in the husk - bushels	319,258	255,682
Logwood - - tons	14,045	9,295	6,395	Safflower - - cwt.	2,161	5,645
Mahogany - - tons	19,926	18,038		Sago - - cwt.	5,335	5,129
Elephants' teeth - cwt.	3,596	3,531		Saltpetre - - cwt.	204,840	171,769
Figs - - cwt.	27,562	21,133		Sarsaparilla - lbs.	169,518	85,509
Flax and tow, and codilla of				Seeds :— Clover - cwts.	140,327	136,542
hemp, &c. - -	876,189	882,289		Flax and linseed, bushels	1,996,414	1,965,660
Furs :— Bear - number	12,683	8,701	10,463	Rape - - bushels	428,905	454,591
Beaver - number	73,842	68,962		Tares - - bushels	170,491	104,993
Fitch - number	325,448	335,292		Senna - - lbs.	219,280	135,909
Martin - number	204,492	146,040	59,765	Shumac - - cwt.	95,935	100,342
Mink - number	83,019	53,163		Silk :— Raw and waste, lbs.	4,256,423	4,161,979
Musquash - number	1,018,309	296,547	275,814	Thrown - - lbs.	508,818	384,650
Nutria - number	854,995	702,920		Manufactures of Europe,		
Otter - number	13,365	2,033	8,952	lbs.	183,417	169,489
Ginger - - cwt.	14,600	7,374	6,930	India, viz. : —		
Gum :— Arabic - cwt.	5,211	18,166	1,507	Bandanas, Romals, &c.		
Lac-dye - - lbs.	694,148	430,665	48,178	pieces	163,519	69,622
Shellack - - lbs.	497,475	343,409	352,162	Crape in pieces - pieces	539	
Hats, straw - number	384,072	274,906		Crape scarfs, shawls, &c.		lbs. 9,36
Hemp, undressed - cwt.	504,120	480,544		number	21,996	
Hides, untanned - cwt.	225,975	214,735		Taffeties, damasks, &c.		
Indigo - - lbs.	9,913,010	3,064,915	4,588,658	pieces	9,055	lbs. 7,655
Iron in bars - tons	15,495	13,983	2,991	Skins :— Calf and kid, un-		
Lead, pig - tons	2,479	121	1,784	tanned - - cwt.	50,205	49,448
Leather, gloves - pairs	1,203,109	1,189,252		Deer, undressed, number	78,618	23,937
Lemons and oranges : —				Goat, undressed, number	299,305	248,81
Packages not exceeding				Kid, undressed, number	332,020	337,82
5,000 cubic inches	47,831	43,869		dressed - number	566,889	566,70
Ditto above 5,000, and not				Lamb, undressed, number	2,770,112	2,773,30
exceeding 7,300 -	159,582	155,823		Seal, undressed, number	297,928	289,66
Ditto above 7,300, and not				Smalts - - lbs.	496,160	554,09
exceeding 14,000 -	69,719	68,819		Spelter - - cwt.	91,325	10,58

Table II. Account of the QUANTITIES, &c. — (continued.)

Articles.	Quantities imported.	Retained for Home Consumption.	Quantities exported.	Articles.	Quantities imported.	Retained for Home Consumption.	Quantities exported.
Rum, proof gal.	6,323,973	3,277,652	1,799,878	Tin - cwt.	3,386	6	3,258
- proof gal.	2,521,069	1,325,169	1,050,972	Tobacco, unmanufactured lbs.	24,944,148	18,504,510	11,026,010
- proof gal.	389,954	45,259	312,125	Tobacco, manufactured and snuff - lbs.	49,830	49,880	14,911
refined - cwt.	4,968,019	3,601,403	371,446	Turpentine, not worth more than 12s. per cwt. cwt.	504,792	312,734	
- cwt.	1,049,806	1,068,693		Valonia - cwt.	165,526	165,309	
- lasts	12,212	11,235		Wax, bees - cwt.	9,202	4,632	
- lbs.	32,678,767	29,305,757	259,659	Whale-fins - cwt.	17,358	17,072	
Battens and bat-ds - great hunds.	10,753	11,520		Wool, cotton - lbs.	27,760,642	208,987,744	17,396,776
d deal ends great hunds.	49,622	51,782		sheep's - lbs.	30,246,898	31,031,461	879,249
- fathoms	10,495	10,735		Wine: — Cape - gallons	758,916	652,285	24,124
rds, &c. under 12 diameter, number	14,545	13,789		French - gallons	550,948	421,469	161,980
inches and above number	3,958	3,840		Portugal - gallons	3,985,146	3,307,021	325,111
k, 2 inches thick ards - loads	2,449	2,426		Spanish - gallons	3,188,355	2,097,629	546,877
great hundreds	91,222	83,026		Madeira - gallons	452,508	272,977	176,574
- loads	13,061	14,304		Canary - gallons	288,042	137,553	188,948
8 inches square, ards - loads	523,053	544,406		Rhenish - gallons	92,325	86,905	8,075
logs, ditto, loads	4,305	4,663		Other sorts - gallons	321,706	186,537	129,916
				Yarn, linen, raw - cwt.	30,617	30,919	
				Zaffa - lbs.	447,434	446,329	

QUANTITIES and Declared Value of British and Irish Produce and Manufactures exported in 1828.

Articles.	Quantity.	Decl. Value.	Articles	Quantity.	Decl. Value.
		L.			*L.*
lops, and haberdashery	- -	910,090	Lead and shot - tons	10,021	177,983
ammunition	- -	335,761	Leather manufactures - lbs.	1,321,542	273,970
hams - cwt.	8,333	28,809	Saddlery and harness	- -	88,600
ork - barrels	33,451	113,906	Linen manufactures - yards	60,287,814	2,120,276
le - tuns	11,374	245,496	Linen threads, tapes, &c.	- -	60,146
nted - cwt.	4,356	102,874	Machinery and mill work	- -	262,115
copper manufactures - cwt.	126,106	678,786	Painters' colours	- -	138,669
cheese - cwt.	94,623	352,615	Plate, plated ware, jewellery, and watches	- -	181,973
o, and cinders - tons	357,864	145,943	Salt - bushels	8,993,124	154,741
	52,420	119,652	Silk manufactures	- -	255,871
anufactures: — entered by			Soap and candles - lbs.	10,902,713	269,109
d - yards	363,328,431	12,483,249	Stationery of all sorts	- -	208,532
ace, and small wares	- -	1,165,763	Sugar - cwt.	456,844	1,038,569
yarn - lbs.	50,505,751	3,595,405	Tin, unwrought - cwt.	41,427	147,131
re of all sorts - pieces	38,136,479	502,215	Tin and pewter wares	- -	266,651
rings - barrels	134,137	157,532	Wool - lbs.	1,669,389	76,881
red by weight - cwts.	126,895	491,811	Woollen manufactures - pieces	1,820,631	4,397,991
nt value	- -	9,145	Do. - yards	6,816,407	527,476
and cutlery - cwt.	242,272	1,387,204	Woollen hosiery and small wares	- -	201,216
r and felt - dozens	83,114	197,581	All other articles	- -	1,709,192
eel, wrought and unwrought, tons	100,403	1,226,617	Total L.		36,812,756

ses of the Magnitude of British Commerce. — The immediate cause of the rapid
se and vast amount of the commerce of Great Britain, is doubtless to be found in
xtraordinary extension of our manufactures during the last half century. To
e into the various circumstances that have contributed to the astonishing
pment of the powers and resources of industry that has been witnessed in this
ry since Arkwright and Watt began their memorable career, would be alike
istent with our objects and limits. There can be no question, however, that *free-
nd security*, — freedom to engage in every employment, and to pursue our own
st in our own way, coupled with an intimate conviction that acquisitions, when
might be securely enjoyed or disposed of, — have been the most copious sources of
ealth and power. There have only been two countries, Holland and the United
which have, in these respects, been placed under nearly similar circumstances as
nd : and, notwithstanding the disadvantages of their situation, the Dutch have
een, and still continue to be, the most industrious and opulent people of the Con-
— (see AMSTERDAM) ; while the Americans, whose situation is more favourable, are
ing in the career of improvement with a rapidity hitherto unknown. In Great
a we have been exempted for a lengthened period from foreign aggression and in-
commotion ; the pernicious influence of the feudal system has long been at an
he same equal burdens have been laid on all classes ; we have enjoyed the ad-
e of liberal institutions, without any material alloy of popular licentiousness or
ce ; our intercourse with foreign states has, indeed, been subjected to many vexatious
pressive regulations ; but full scope has been given to the competition of the home
ers ; and, on the whole, the natural order of things has been less disturbed amongst
artificial restraints, than in most other countries. But without security, no degree
lom could have been of any material importance. Happily, however, every man
t satisfied, not only of the temporary, but of the *permanent* tranquillity of the
y, and of the stability of its institutions. The plans and combinations of the
ists have not been affected by any misgivings as to what might take place in
Monied fortunes have not been amassed, because they might be more easily
road, in periods of confusion and disorder ; but all individuals have unhesitatingly
d, whenever an opportunity offered, in undertakings of which a remote posterity
ne to reap the benefit. No one can look at the immense sums expended upon

the permanent improvement of the land, on docks, warehouses, canals, &c., or ref
for a moment on the settlements of property in the funds, and the extent of our syst
of life insurance, without being impressed with a deep sense of the vast importance
that confidence which the public have placed in the security of property, and, con
quently, in the endurance of the present order of things and the good faith of governme
Had this confidence been imperfect, industry and invention would have been paralys
and much of that capital, which feeds and clothes the industrious classes, would ne
have existed. The maintenance of this security entire, both in fact and in opinion,
essential to the public welfare. If it be anywise impaired, the colossal fabric of
prosperity will crumble into dust ; and the commerce of London, like that of Cartha
Palmyra, and Venice, will at no very remote period be famous only in history. It
therefore, of the utmost consequence, that in introducing the changes which the wa
and altered circumstances of society require should be made in the frame of our poli
nothing be done to impair, but every thing to strengthen, that confidence and secur
to which we are mainly indebted for the high and conspicuous place we have long oc
pied among the nations of the earth.

IMPRESSMENT, the forcible taking away of seamen from their or
nary employment, and compelling them to serve, against their will, in
Majesty's ships.

1. *Regulations as to Impressment.* — This practice is not expressly sanctioned by any
of parliament ; but it is so indirectly by the numerous statutes that have been pass
granting exemptions from it. According to Lord Mansfield, it is " a power foun
upon immemorial usage," and is understood to make a part of the common law.
sea-faring men are liable to impressment, unless specially protected by custom or statu
Seamen executing particular services for government, not unfrequently get protecti
from the Admiralty, Navy Board, &c. Some are exempted by *local* custom ;
ferrymen are every where privileged from impressment. The statutory exemptions
numerous.

1. *Every ship in the coal trade* has the following persons protected, viz. two able seamen (such as
master shall nominate) for every ship of 100 tons ; and one for every 50 tons for every ship of 100 t
and upwards ; and any officer who presumes to impress any of the above, shall forfeit, to the maste
owner of such vessel, 10l. for every man so impressed ; and such officer shall be incapable of hol
any place, office, or employment, in any of his Majesty's ships of war. — (6 & 7 *Will. 3.* c. 18. § 19.) *
2. *No parish apprentice* shall be compelled or permitted to enter into his Majesty's sea service till
arrives at the age of 18 years. — (2 & 3 *Anne*, c. 6. § 4.)
3. Persons *voluntarily* binding themselves apprentices to sea service, shall not be impressed for th
years from the date of their indentures. But no persons above 18 years of age shall have
exemption or protection from his Majesty's service, if they have been at sea before they became app
tices. — (2 & 3 *Anne*, c. 6. § 15. ; 4 *Anne*, c. 19. § 17. ; and 13 *Geo.* 2. c. 17. § 2.)
4. *Apprentices.* — The act 4 Geo. 4. c. 25. enacts some new regulations with respect to the numbe
apprentices that ships must have on board according to their tonnage ; and grants protection to s
apprentices till they have attained the age of 21 years. — (For the regulations of this act, see APPRENTI
5. *Persons employed in the Fisheries.* — The act 50 Geo. 3. c. 108. grants the following exemptions f
impressment, viz. : —
1st, *Masters of fishing vessels* or boats, who, either themselves or their owners, have, or within
months before applying for a protection shall have had, one apprentice or more under 16 year
age, bound for five years, and employed in the business of fishing.
2dly, All such *apprentices*, not exceeding *eight* to every master or owner of any fishing vessel o
tons or upwards ; not exceeding *seven* to every vessel or boat of 35 tons and under 50 ; not exceedin
to every vessel of 30 tons and under 35 tons ; and not exceeding *four* to every vessel or boat under 30
burthen ; during the time of their apprenticeship, and till the age of 20 years, they continuing, for
time, in the business of fishing only.
3dly, *One mariner,* besides the master and apprentices, to every fishing vessel of 10 tons or upw
employed on the sea-coast, during his continuance in such service.
4thly, *Any landman* above the age of 18, entering and employed on board such vessel, for
years from his first going to sea ; and to the end of the voyage then engaged in, if he so long con
in such service.
An affidavit sworn before a justice of the peace, containing the tonnage of such fishing vessel or
the port or place to which she belongs, the name and description of the master, the age of every app
tice, the term for which he is bound, and the date of his indenture, and the name, age, and descri
of every such mariner and landman respectively, and the time of such landman's first going to sea,
be transmitted to the Admiralty ; who, upon finding the facts correctly stated, grant a separate prote
to every individual. In case, however, " *of an actual invasion of these kingdoms, or imminent da
thereof,*" such protected persons may be impressed ; but except upon such an emergency, any offic
officers impressing such protected persons shall respectively forfeit 20l. to the party impressed, if n
apprentice, or to his master if he be an apprentice. — §§ 2, 3, 4.
6. *General Exemptions.* — All persons above 55 years of age or upwards, and under 18 years. I
person being a foreigner, who shall serve in any merchant vessel, or other trading vessel, or priv
belonging to a subject of the crown of Great Britain ; and all persons, of what age soever, who
use the sea, shall be protected for two years, to be computed from the time of their first using th
(13 *Geo.* 2. c. 17.)
7. *Harponeers,* line managers, or boat steerers, engaged in the southern whale fishery, are also
tected. — (26 *Geo.* 3. c. 50.)
8. *Mariners employed in the herring fishery* are exempted while actually employed. — (48 G
c. 110.)

* In order that these men shall be thus protected, it is necessary for the master *to name them*,
they are impressed ; this is to be done by going before the mayor or other chief magistrate of the
who is to give the master a certificate, in which is contained the names of the particular men who
thus nominates : and this certificate will be their protection.

olicy of Impressment. This practice, so subversive of every principle of justice, is
ted on the alleged ground of its being absolutely necessary to the manning of
·t. But this position, notwithstanding the confidence with which it has been
·p, is not quite so tenable as has been supposed. The difficulties experienced in
·ng sailors for the fleet at the breaking out of a war, are not natural but artifi-
·d might be got rid off by a very simple arrangement. During peace, not
·an a fourth or a fifth part of the seamen are retained in his Majesty's service,
·e commonly required during war; and if peace continue for a few years,
·l number of sailors in the king's and the merchant service is limited to that
·is merely adequate to supply the reduced demand of the former, and the
·y demand of the latter. When, therefore, war is declared, and 30,000 or 40,000
·al seamen are wanted for the fleet, they cannot be obtained, unless by withdraw-
·m from the merchant service, which has not more than its proper complement of
But to do this by offering the seamen higher wages would be next to impossi-
·d would, supposing it were practicable, impose such a sacrifice upon the public,
·i hardly be borne. And hence, it is said, the necessity of impressment; a prac-
·ich every one admits can be justified on no other ground than that of its being
·ely essential to the public safety.
plain, however, that a necessity of this sort may be easily obviated. All,
·that is necessary for this purpose, is merely to keep such a number of sailors in
·esty's service during peace as may suffice, with the ordinary proportion of
·n and boys, to man the fleet at the breaking out of a war. Were this
·here would not be the shadow of a pretence for resorting to impressment;
·practice, with the cruelty and injustice inseparable from it, might be entirely
·d.
·t is said that, though desirable in many respects, the *expense* of such a plan will
·prevent it from being adopted. It admits, however, of demonstration, that in-
·f being dearer, this plan would be actually cheaper than that which is now
·l. Not more than 1,000,000*l.* or 1,200,000*l.* a year would be required to be
·o the navy estimates, and that would not be a real, but merely a nominal advance.
·lence and injustice to which the practice of impressment exposes sailors, operates
·nes to raise their wages, by creating a disinclination on the part of many young
·enter the sea service; and this disinclination is vastly increased during war,
·ages *usually rise to four or five times their previous amount*, imposing a burden on
·imerce of the country, exclusive of other equally mischievous consequences,
·nes greater than the tax that would be required to keep up the peace establish-
·the navy to its proper level. It is really, therefore, a vulgar error to suppose
·pressment has the recommendation of cheapness in its favour; and, though
·o reasonable man would contend that that is the only, or even the principal,
·tance to be attended to. In point of fact, however, it is as costly as it is
·ve and unjust. — (The reader is referred, for a fuller discussion of this in-
·; question, to the note on Impressment in the 4th volume of the *Wealth of*
·)

·EMNITY, is where one person secures another from responsibility against
·ticular event; thus, a policy of insurance is a contract of indemnity against
·ticular loss.

·e one person also becomes bail for another, a bond of indemnity is fre-
·executed; and where a bond or bill of exchange has been lost or mislaid,
·ptor or obligee would not act prudently in paying it, without being secured
·nd of indemnity.

·IAN RUBBER. See CAOUTCHOUC.

·IGO (Fr. *Indigo*; Ger. *Indigo*; Sans. *Nili*; Arab. *Neel*; Malay, *Taroóm*),
·; which yields the beautiful blue dye known by that name. It is obtained
·naceration in water of certain tropical plants; but the indigo of commerce
·t entirely obtained from leguminous plants of the *genus indigofera:* that cul-
·in India being the *Indigofera tinctoria;* and that in America the *Indigofera*
·ie Indian plant has pinnate leaves and a slender ligneous stem; and when
·ully cultivated, rises to the height of three, five, and even six feet.

·ears pretty certain that the culture of the indigo plant, and the preparation of
·, have been practised in India from a very remote epoch. It has been ques-
·ndeed, whether the *indicum* mentioned by Pliny (*Hist. Nat.* lib. xxxv. c. 6.)
·go, but, as it would seem, without any good reason. Pliny states that it was
·from India; that when diluted it produced an admirable mixture of blue and
·lours (*in diluendo misturam purpuræ cæruleique mirabilem reddit*); and he gives
·vhich the genuine drug might be discriminated with sufficient precision. It is

true that Pliny is egregiously mistaken as to the mode in which the drug was
duced; but there are many examples in modern as well as ancient times, to prove
the possession of an article brought from a distance implies no accurate knowled
its nature, or of the processes followed in its manufacture. Beckmann (*Hist. of I.
tions*, vol. iv. art. *Indigo*) and Dr. Bancroft (*Permanent Colours*, vol. i. pp. 241 —
have each investigated this subject with great learning and sagacity; and agree in
conclusion that the *indicum* of Pliny was real indigo, and not, as has been suppos
drug prepared from the *isatis* or woad. At all events, there can be no question th
digo was imported into modern Europe, by way of Alexandria, previously to the disc
of the route to India by the Cape of Good Hope. When first introduced, it was
tumary to mix a little of it with woad to heighten and improve the colour of the la
but, by degrees, the quantity of indigo was increased, and woad was, at last, entire
perseded. It is worth while, however, to remark, that indigo did not make its
into general use without encountering much opposition. The *growers of woad* prev
on several governments to prohibit the use of indigo! In Germany, an imperial
was published in 1654, prohibiting the use of indigo, or "*devil's dye*," and directing
care to be taken to prevent its clandestine importation, "because," says the edict,
trade in woad is lessened, dyed articles injured, and money carried out of the coun
The magistrates of Nuremberg went further, and compelled the dyers of that city to
an oath once a year not to use indigo; which practice was continued down to a la
riod. In 1598, upon an urgent representation of the states of Languedoc, at the so
ation of the woad growers, the use of indigo was prohibited in that province; and
not till 1737, that the dyers of France were left at liberty to dye with such articles
in such a way, as they pleased.—(*Beckmann*, vol. iv. p. 142.) Let not those who
happen to throw their eye over this paragraph, smile at the ignorance of our anc
—*Mutato nomine de te fabula narratur.* How much opposition is made at this m
to the importation of many important articles, for no better reasons than were alleg
the sixteenth century, against the importation of indigo!

Indigo is at present produced in Bengal, and the other provinces subject to the presidency o
name, from the 20th to the 30th degree of north latitude; in the province of Tinnevelly, under th
dras government; in Java; in Luconia, the principal of the Philippine Islands; and in Guatemala, a
Caraccas, in central America. Bengal is, however, the great mart for indigo; and the quantity pro
in the other places is comparatively inconsiderable.

Raynal was of opinion that the culture of indigo had been introduced into America by the Span
but this is undoubtedly an error. Several species of *indigofera* belong to the New World; an
Spaniards used it as a substitute for ink very soon after the conquest.—(*Humboldt, Essai Politique
Nouvelle Espagne*, tom. iii. p. 54. 2d ed.)

For the first twenty years after the English became masters of Bengal, the culture and manufact
indigo, now of such importance, was unknown as a branch of British industry; and the export
but trifling. The European markets were, at this period, principally supplied from America. In
however, the attention of the English began to be directed to this business; and though the pr
pursued by them were nearly the same with those followed by the natives, their greater skill, intell
and capital, gave them immense advantages. In their hands, the growth and preparation of indigo
come the most important employment, at least in a commercial point of view, carried on in the co
The indigo made by the natives supplies the internal demand; so that all that is raised by Europ
exported.

In the Delta of the Ganges, where the best and largest quantity of indigo is produced, the plan
only for a single season, being destroyed by the periodical inundation; but in the dry central and w
provinces, one or two *rattoon* crops are obtained: and owing to this circumstance, the latter are e
to furnish a large supply of seed to the former.

The fixed capital required in the manufacture of indigo consists of a few vats of common mason
steeping the plant, and precipitating the colouring matter; a boiling and drying house; and a d
house for the planter. These, for a factory of ten pair of vats, capable of producing, at an av
12,500 lbs. of indigo, worth on the spot about 2,500*l.*, will not cost above 1,500*l.* sterling. The bu
and machinery necessary to produce an equal value in sugar and rum, would probably cost about
This fact, therefore, without any reference to municipal regulations, affords a ready answer to the
tion which has been frequently put, why the British planters in India have never engaged in the
facture of sugar.

During the nine years which preceded the opening of the trade with India, in 1814, the annual a
produce of indigo in Bengal, for exportation, was nearly 5,600,000 lbs.; but the average produce
four last years of this period scarcely equalled that of the preceding five. But since the ports were
the indigo produced for exportation has increased fully a *third*; the exports during the sixteen
ending with 1829-30, being above 7,400,000 lbs. a year. The following brief statement shows the
this increase, taking the average produce of each four years:—

| 1814
1815
1816
1817 | *lbs.*

- - 7,040,000
 | 1818
1819
1820
1821 | *lbs.*

- - 6,000,000
 | 1822
1823
1824
1825 | *lbs.*

- - 8,000,000
 | 1826
1827
1828
1829 |

- - 9,
 |

It deserves to be remarked, that since the opening of the trade, Indian capitalists have betake
selves to the manufacture of indigo on the European method, and that at present about a fifth pa
whole annual produce is prepared by them.

The culture of indigo is very precarious, not only in so far as respects the growth of the plant fr
to year, but also as regards the quantity and quality of the drug which the same amount of pl
afford even in the same season. Thus, the produce of 1825-26 was 10,750,000 lbs., while the pr
the following year was but 6,700,000 lbs.; the produce of 1827-28 was near 11,000,000 lbs., and
1828-29 only 7,300,000 lbs. The average of these years, that is, about 9,000,000 lbs., may be consi
the present annual produce of Bengal. It is a remarkable fact, that the price of indigo in India
creased in a far greater ratio than the quantity. In 1813-14, the real value of that exported from
was 1,461,000*l.*; but in 1827-28, although the quantity had increased but 20 per cent., the valu
2,920,000*l.*, or was nearly doubled. There has been no corresponding rise in the price in Europe,
the contrary, a decline; and the circumstance is to be accounted for by the restraints placed on

ent of capital in the production of colonial articles suited to the European market, the consequent
lty of making remittances from India, and an unnatural flow of capital to the only great article of
n produce and export that is supposed capable of bearing its application.

gal indigo is principally exported to Great Britain, France, the United States, and the countries on
ersian Gulf; from which last a portion finds its way to the southern provinces of the Russian empire.
a little singular, that it is not used by the Chinese, with whom blue is a favourite colour. Its im-
nce, as an article of commerce, to the United Kingdom, is evident from the fact, that, by its cheap-
nd superior quality, it has nearly driven every other description of indigo from the market; that its
tation, although its price has not by any means fallen in a corresponding degree with the prices
er colonial productions, has nearly doubled; and that within the last ten years the consumption of
ngdom has increased by at least one fourth, having amounted, in 1821, to 1,740,000 lbs. weight, and,
0, to 2,310,000 lbs.

indigo of Bengal is divided into two classes, called in commercial language *Bengal* and *Oude ;* the
eing the produce of the southern provinces of Bengal and Bahar, and the last that of the northern
ces. The first is, in point of quality, much superior to the other. This arose at one time, in a
erable degree, from the practice which prevailed in the northern provinces, of the European planter
asing the wet fæcula from the native manufacturer, and completing the processes of curing and drying
ug. This is at present in a great measure discontinued; and the Oude indigo has, in consequence,
crably improved in quality. Its inferiority is probably more the result of soil and climate, than of
fference in the skill with which the manufacture is conducted.

826, and we are possessed of no later data, the export of indigo from the port of Madras amounted
275 lbs. weight; having increased to this amount in the twenty years from 1806, when it was reck-
t no more than 100,000 lbs. Besides the export from Madras, there is also a considerable one from
ench settlement of Pondicherry ; of which, however, we have no detailed statement. In 1818, the
c of indigo from Manilla amounted to 3,400 quintals, or 367,200 lbs. avoirdupois ; but it is understood
e materially increased since. The export from Batavia, in 1829, amounted to 152,000 lbs. weight,
e production is rapidly increasing. According to the statement now given, the annual exports of
c indigo are as follow : — Bengal, 9,000,000 lbs. ; Madras, 438,275 lbs. ; Manilla, 367,200 lbs. ; Bata-
2,000 lbs. Hence the annual average produce for foreign markets, making allowance for a trifling
ntation in the exports from Madras and the Philippines, is certainly not less than 10,000,000 lbs.
ording to M. Humboldt, the exportation of indigo from Guatemala, in 1825, amounted to 1,800,000 lbs.
is also produced in some of the West India islands, but not in large quantities.

d indigo is known by its lightness or small specific gravity, indicating the absence of earthy impurities ;
mass not readily parting with its colouring matter when tested by drawing a streak with it over a
surface ; but, above all, by the purity of the colour itself. The first quality, estimated by this last
called, in commercial language, *fine blue ;* then follow *ordinary blue, fine purple, purple and violet,*
ry purple and violet, dull blue, inferior purple and violet, strong copper,* and *ordinary copper.*
distinctions refer to the Bengal indigo only, and the Oude is distinguished only into *fine* and *ordi-*
The qualities of Madras and Manilla indigo are nearly the same, and equal to ordinary Bengal.
The indigo of Java is superior to these.

748,281 lbs. of indigo imported into Great Britain in 1829, 5,957,939 lbs. were from India, 212,021 lbs.
he British West Indies, 166,139 lbs. from Guatemala, 76,214 lbs. from Colombia, &c. Of the total
ty imported, 4,500,000 lbs. were again exported.

borrow from Mr. Cook's tract on the Commerce of Great Britain in 1830, the following table, which
very comprehensive view of the state of the crops of indigo in Bengal, and the imports, consump-
d prices of Bengal indigo, during the last twenty years :—

Crops in Bengal.			Yrs.	Total Import from India into Great Britain	Total Deliveries for Export and Home Con.*	Stock in Great Britain 31st of Dec.		Average Prices in London.		
s.	Maunds	Chests		Chests.	Chests.	Chests.		Fine Bengal. per lb.	Ord. Bengal. per lb.	Low Oude. per lb.
								s. d. s. d.	s. d. s. d.	s. d. s. d.
812	70,000	= 19,500	1812	17,200	14,600	29,500	1812	8 0 to 10 6	4 0 to 5 3	3 0 to 3 6
813	78,000	= 22,000	1813	14,300	19,300	24,500	1813	10 0 — 14 0	6 3 — 8 3	4 6 — 5 0
814	74,500	= 21,300	1814	24,200	23,800	24,900	1814	10 0 — 14 6	6 6 — 9 0	4 0 — 5 6
815	102,500	= 27,000	1815	28,900	23,400	30,400	1815	8 0 — 11 0	5 0 — 7 0	3 0 — 4 6
816	115,000	= 29,000	1816	15,500	20,200	25,700	1816	6 6 — 10 0	3 9 — 5 6	2 8 — 3 3
817	87,000	= 23,500	1817	13,500	15,700	23,500	1817	7 6 — 10 0	5 6 — 7 6	4 0 — 6 0
818	72,800	= 19,500	1818	16,600	16,100	24,000	1818	8 0 — 9 6	6 6 — 8 0	5 0 — 6 0
819	68,000	= 17,000	1819	11,500	15,800	19,700	1819	7 6 — 9 0	5 0 — 6 0	3 3 — 4 3
820	72,000	= 19,000	1820	16,500	21,600	14,500	1820	7 0 — 9 0	5 6 — 6 6	3 3 — 4 6
821	107,000	= 25,500	1821	13,000	17,300	9,800	1821	7 6 — 9 6	5 6 — 7 0	4 0 — 5 9
822	72,400	= 19,500	1822	13,500	15,100	8,200	1822	11 0 — 12 6	8 6 — 10 3	4 9 — 6 0
823	90,000	= 24,000	1823	21,700	16,800	13,100	1823	9 6 — 11 0	5 9 — 8 6	3 6 — 4 6
824	113,000	= 28,000	1824	16,300	17,200	12,200	1824	12 0 — 13 6	8 0 — 10 6	5 0 — 6 3
825	79,000	= 22,000	1825	25,300	21,100	16,400	1825	13 0 — 15 0	8 6 — 10 6	4 3 — 5 9
826	144,000	= 41,000	1826	27,800	21,900	22,300	1826	8 0 — 9 6	4 6 — 7 0	2 3 — 3 9
827	90,000	= 25,000	1827	19,000	18,500	22,800	1827	11 6 — 13 6	7 0 — 9 6	3 0 — 4 6
828	149,000	= 42,000	1828	35,800	27,500	31,100	1828	8 0 — 10 0	5 3 — 7 3	2 0 — 2 9
829	98,000	= 26,500	1829	23,200	23,100	31,200	1829	7 6 — 8 6	3 9 — 6 6	2 6 — 3 6
830	141,000	= 40,000	1830	22,120	25,700	37,600	1830	6 6 — 7 6	3 3 — 4 6	2 0 — 2 6

rices of the different sorts of indigo in the London market, 1st of July, 1831, were as under : —

l.) — Duty, if taken for home use, 3d. per lb. if imported from British possessions ; 4d. per lb. if from other places.

	s. d. s. d.		s. d. s. d.
blue and purple - per lb.	6 9 to 7 6	Oude, good and fine - per lb.	2 9 to 3 3
rple and violet . —	6 0 — 6 9	Ordinary and middling - —	1 9 — 2 6
ne violet —	5 9 — 6 3	Madras - -	2 0 — 4 0
rdinary middling violet —	4 6 — 5 3	Caraccas, flores - -	5 9 — 6 3
ne violet and copper —	3 9 — 4 6	sobres -	4 6 — 5 6
od and fine copper —	3 6 — 4 3	cortes -	2 0 — 4 0
iddling and low copper —	3 0 — 3 9	Guatemala, flores -	5 6 — 6 0
nsuming qualities —	2 9 — 4 6	sobres -	4 3 — 5 6
		cortes -	1 9 — 4 0

which have been for home consumption, in 1821, 6,500 chests ; 1822, 6,500 ; 1823, 6,800 ; 1824, 6,900 ;
00; 1826, 5,000 ; 1827, 7,900 ; 1828, 9,800 ; 1829, 7,700 ; 1830, 8,250 chests.—N. B. A chest = 25¼ lbs

Indigo of British possessions, not deemed their produce unless imported from thence.— (7 *Geo.* 4. c.
For further information as to indigo, see *Colebrook's Husbandry of Bengal*, p. 154. ; *Milburn's Or*
Com. ; *Bell's Review of Commerce of Bengal* ; *Wilson's Review of do.* ; evidence of Gillian Maclaine,
East India Committee, 1830–31, &c.

INK (Du. *Ink, Inkt;* Fr. *Encre;* Ger. *Dinte;* It. *Inchiostro;* Lat. *Atramentu* Rus. *Tschernilo;* Sp. *Tinta;* Sw. *Blak.*)

" Every liquor or pigment used for writing or printing is distinguished by the name of ink. Com
practice knows only black and red. Of black ink there are three principal kinds : 1. Indian ink ; 2. Prin
ink ; and, 3. Writing ink. The Indian ink is used in China for writing with a brush, and for painting
the soft flexible paper of Chinese manufacture. It is ascertained, as well from experiment as from inf
ation, that the cakes of this ink are made of lampblack and size, or animal glue, with the additio
perfumes or other substances not essential to its quality as an ink. The fine soot from the flame of a
or candle received by holding a plate over it, mixed with clean size from shreds of parchment or gl
leather not dyed, will make an ink equal to that imported. Good printers' ink is a black paint, sm
and uniform in its composition, of a firm black colour, and possesses a singular aptitude to adhere to p
thoroughly impregnated with moisture.

" Common ink for writing is made by adding an infusion or decoction of the nut-gall to sulphate of i
dissolved in water. A very fine black precipitate is thrown down, the speedy subsidence of which is
vented by the addition of a proper quantity of gum Arabic. Lampblack is the common material to giv
black colour, of which 2½ ounces are sufficient for 16 ounces of the varnish. Vermilion is a good red.
are ground together on a stone with a muller, in the same manner as oil paints. Among the amusing
periments of the art of chemistry, the exhibition of sympathetic inks holds a distinguished place.
these the writing is invisible, until some reagent gives it opacity. These inks have been proposed a
instruments of secret correspondence. But they are of little use in this respect, because the prope
change by a few days' remaining on the paper ; most of them have more or less of a tinge when thorou
dry ; and none of them resist the test of heating the paper till it begins to be scorched." — (*Ure's*
tionary.)

INKLE, a sort of broad linen tape, principally manufactured at Manchester
some other towns in Lancashire.

INSOLVENCY AND BANKRUPTCY. Insolvency is a term in merc
tile law, applied to designate the condition of all persons unable to pay their de
according to the ordinary usage of trade. A bankrupt is an insolvent ; but pers
may be in a state of insolvency without having committed any of the specific
which render them liable to a commission of bankruptcy.

We have, under the article BANKRUPTCY, explained the most important difference
the law as to insolvency and bankruptcy ; and have also briefly stated in that article,
in the article CREDIT, some of the alterations which seem to be imperatively requ
to make these laws more in harmony, than they are at present, with the principle
justice, and more conducive to the interests of commerce and the public advantage.
the present article, therefore, we shall confine ourselves to a summary statement of
proceedings under the existing laws.

Under the bankrupt laws, the creditors have a compulsory authority to sequestrate
entire possessions of their debtor ; under the insolvent laws, the debtor himself
make a voluntary surrender of his property for the benefit of all his creditors. F
this diversity in the initiative process results the greatest diversity in the ultimate op
tion of the bankrupt and insolvent acts. The proceedings under a commission of ba
ruptcy being instituted by the creditors, they lose all future power over the property
person of the insolvent after he has obtained his certificate ; but the proceedings u
the insolvent not having been commenced by the debtor himself, he only, by the
render of his effects, protects his *person* in future from arrest, not the property he
subsequently acquire, from liability to the payment of all his debts in full.

Proceedings under the existing Insolvent Act.— In 1813, a special tribunal, called the " Court for I
of Insolvent Debtors," was appointed for the purpose of receiving the surrender of property and e
for the benefit of the creditors of insolvents. It consists of a chief and two other commissioners, appo
by the crown, and is a court of record, with powers similar to those of the superior courts at West
ster ; but it cannot award costs, unless in particular cases. The court sits twice a week in Portugal-st
and no fees are taken, except those established by the court. The commissioners also severally
circuits, and attend at the towns and places appointed for insolvents in the country to appear :
judicial powers in the provincial towns are the same as those exercised in the metropolis.

I. The first step in the insolvent's proceeding is the *Petition.* Any person in actual custody for any
damages, costs, or money due for contempt of court, may, within fourteen days from his first d
tion, petition the court for his discharge ; stating in such petition the particulars of his arrest, an
amount of his debts, and praying to be discharged not only against the demands of the persons deta
him, but against all other creditors having claims at the time of presenting the petition. Person
actually in custody within the walls of a prison, and during the proceedings thereon, are not entitl
the benefit of the act. In case of sickness, however, and after an order for hearing the petition has
obtained, this condition is not required.

Notice of the time appointed for hearing the petition must be given to all creditors whose debts an
to 5*l.*, and be advertised in the London Gazette.

At the time of subscribing the petition, the insolvent executes an assignment to the provisional ass
of the court, renouncing all title to his property, except wearing apparel, working tools, bedding
such necessaries of himself and family as shall not exceed the value of 20*l.* During confinemen
court may order an allowance for the support of the petitioner.

The filing of a petition is an act of bankruptcy, and, if a commission be issued within two cal
months, vacates the assignment : but this does not stop the proceedings of the court ; and any pro
remaining to the petitioner after obtaining his certificate continues liable as if no commission ha
issued.

The voluntary preference of a creditor, by conveyance of money, goods, bills, or other property,
the filing of the petition, or within three months prior to the imprisonment of the petitioner, bein
in insolvent circumstances, is fraudulent and void.

n fourteen days after the filing of his petition, the insolvent must prepare a schedule of his debts ; is property and income from every source whence he derives benefit or emolument, together with int of all debts owing to him, the names of the debtors, and their places of abode. Lastly, the e must describe the wearing apparel and other articles not exceeding 20*l.* which the petitioner is to retain.

ents guilty of omissions in the schedule, with intent to defraud creditors, or excepting in it neces- an amount exceeding 20*l.*, or persons assisting therein, are guilty of a misdemeanor, subjecting to ment for not more than three years.

e Assignees. — Any time after the filing of the petition, the court appoints assignees from among tors, to whom, on their acceptance of the appointment, an assignment is made of the effects of ner. In case of any real estate, the same, within the space of six months, must be sold by public in such manner and place as the major part in value of the creditors approve : but when any he property is so circumstanced that the immediate sale of it would be prejudicial to the interests risoner, the court may direct the management of such property till it can be properly sold ; he debts can be paid by mortgage in lieu of sale, the court may give directions for that pur-

in possession and disposal of the insolvent, whereof he is *reputed* owner, are deemed his property ; does not affect the assignment of any ship or vessel, duly registered according to the 6 Geo. 4.

ount upon oath before an officer of the court, or justice of peace, must be made up by the as- within every three months at the farthest ; and in case of a balance in hand, a dividend must be i made, of which dividend thirty days' previous notice must be given ; and every creditor is to share in the dividend, unless objected to by the prisoner, assignees, or other creditor, in which court decides.

signees may execute powers which the insolvent might have executed, as the granting of leases, nes, transferring public stock or annuities ; but they cannot nominate to a vacant ecclesiastical

signees, with the consent of one commissioner, and the major part of the creditors in value, may d for any debt due to the prisoner ; or may submit differences connected with the estate of the . to arbitration.

nds payable to creditors, unclaimed for twelve months, are to be paid into court to the credit of e of the insolvent : in default of payment of the dividends by the assignees, their goods may be d ; or, if no distress, they may be imprisoned.

signees, in case the insolvent is a beneficed clergyman or curate, are not entitled to the income nefice or curacy ; but they may obtain a sequestration of the profits for the benefit of creditors. are the assignees entitled to the pay, half-pay, pension, or other emolument, of any person who been in the army, navy, or civil service of the government or East India Company ; but the ay order, subject to the approval of the heads of public offices, a portion of such pay, half-pay, or emoluments, to be set aside towards the liquidation of the debts of the insolvent.

urt may inquire into the conduct of the assignees, on the complaint of the insolvent or any of tors ; and, in case of malversation, award costs against them.

ees who wilfully employ or retain any part of the proceeds of the insolvent's estate, may be with interest, at a rate not exceeding 20*l.* per cent. per annum.

scharge of the Insolvent. — On the day appointed for hearing the petition, any creditor may e discharge of the prisoner ; and, for that purpose, put such questions, and examine such wit- the court shall admit, touching the matters contained in the petition and schedule ; or a creditor are, and the court direct, that an officer of the court shall investigate the accounts of the prisoner, t thereon. In case the prisoner is not opposed, and the court is satisfied with his schedule, it r his immediate discharge from custody ; or it may direct him to be detained in custody for any exceeding six months, to be computed from the time of filing the petition.

the prisoner has destroyed his books, or falsified entries therein, or otherwise acted fraudulently is creditors, or wilfully omitted any thing in his schedule, he may be imprisoned for any term ding *three years* : or where a prisoner has contracted debts fraudulently, by means of a breach or put creditors to unnecessary expense ; or incurred debts by means of any false pretence, or robable expectation, at the time when contracted, of ever paying them ; or shall be indebted for or criminal conversation with the wife, or for seducing the daughter or servant of the plaintiff ; ach of promise of marriage ; or for damages in any action for malicious prosecution, libel, slander, s ; the court may imprison for two years.

charge extends to sums payable by annuity ; the annuitants being admitted as creditors to the he insolvent, at a fair valuation of their interest.

discharge does not extend to any debts due to the crown, nor for any offence against the revenue at suit of any sheriff or other public officer, upon any bail-bond entered into for any person l for such offence ; unless the Treasury certify consent to the discharge.

ats under writ of *capias* or extent, must apply to the Barons of the Exchequer to be discharged. the prisoner is not discharged, the court may, on application for that purpose, order the creditor suit he is detained to pay any sum not exceeding 4*s.* weekly ; and in default of payment, the o be liberated.

ure Liabilities of the Insolvent. — Prior to adjudication on the petition, the insolvent is required a warrant of attorney, empowering the court to enter up judgment against him, in the name of ees, for the amount of the debts unpaid ; and when the insolvent is of sufficient ability to pay t, or is dead, leaving assets for the purpose, the court may permit execution to be taken out e property of the insolvent acquired after his discharge ; and this proceeding may be repeated ole of the debt, with costs, is paid and satisfied.

person, after judgment entered up, is liable to imprisonment for any debt to which the adjudica- court extended.

n insolvent is entitled to the benefit of the act, no execution, except under the judgment before t, can issue against him for debts contracted prior to his confinement ; but he may be proceeded a debt which could not be enforced at the period of his discharge.

lvent, after his discharge, may, on the application of an assignee to the court, be again examined he effects set forth in the schedule ; and if he refuse to appear or answer questions, he may be ed.

rtificated bankrupt, nor any person having had the benefit of the insolvent act, can have it a e within *five years*, unless three fourths in number and value of the creditors consent thereto, appear to the court that the insolvent, since his bankruptcy or discharge, has done his utmost ust demands ; and that the debts subsequently incurred have been unavoidable, from inability to acquire subsistence for himself and family.

women are entitled to the benefit of the insolvent act, and may petition the court on executing ssignment.

lvent act, of which the above is a digest, was continued, by an act of the session of 1830, the . 38., for two years, and " from thence to the end of the next session of parliament." It is im- remark, that the act of Will. 4. prohibits, while the insolvent acts are in force, any debtor from arged on his petition under the 32 Geo. 2. c. 28., commonly called the " Lords' Act."

t object will be to present a brief exposition of the BANKRUPT LAWS.

BANKRUPTCY.—Blackstone defines a bankrupt —" A trader who secretes himse does certain other acts tending to defraud his creditors." But an intention t fraud is not now held to be essential to constitute a bankrupt; who may be either si an insolvent, or a person who is guilty of certain acts tending to defraud his credito

There are, as already observed, some important distinctions, between the bankrup insolvent laws, not only in their application to different descriptions of individuals also in the powers they exercise over the estates of persons subsequently to their **b** brought under their adjudication. The benefits of the insolvent act extend withou tinction to every class of persons actually in prison for debt; the benefits of the ban**k** act extend to traders only. But persons relieved under a commission of bankrupt the first time are for ever discharged from all debts proveable against them, and property from any future liability; whereas, if relieved under the insolvent act, persons only are protected from arrest, while any property they may subsequently ac continues liable to their creditors till the whole amount of their debts is paid in full follows that the insolvent act affords merely a personal relief; while the bankrupt ac charges both person and property, and even returns the bankrupt a certain allowanc of the produce of his assets, proportioned to good behaviour, and the amount c dividend.

Having already treated of insolvency, we shall now proceed to describe the procee under a commission of bankruptcy, as regulated by the act of Lord Brougham, the Will. 4. c. 56., and the 6 Geo. 4. c. 16., which are the last general acts on the su and by which former statutes have been consolidated, and several important improve introduced; leaving, however, untouched, many of the radical defects inherent i branch of the law. The chief points to be considered, are — 1. The persons who become bankrupt; 2. Acts constituting bankruptcy; 3. Proceedings of petiti creditor; 4. New Court of Bankruptcy; 5. Debts proveable under the commiss 6. Official assignees; 7. Assignees chosen by creditors; 8. Property liable t bankruptcy; 9. Examination and liabilities of bankrupt; 10. Payment of a divic 11. Certificate and allowance for bankrupt.

1. *Who may become Bankrupt.* — Generally all persons in trade, capable of making binding con whether natural born subjects, aliens, or denizens, are within the jurisdiction of the bankrupt law the statute expressly includes builders, bankers, brokers, packers, carpenters, scriveners, ship insurers housemen, wharfingers, shipwrights, victuallers; keepers of inns, taverns, hotels, and coffee-houses; printers, bleachers, fullers, callenderers, cattle or sheep salesmen, factors, agents, and all persons w the trade of merchandise by bargaining, bartering, commission, consignment, and otherwise, and persons who seek their living by buying and selling, letting for hire, or by the manufacturing of and commodities. Persons who cannot become bankrupt, are, graziers, farmers, workmen for h bourers, receivers general of taxes, and subscribers to any commercial or trading company establi charter or act of parliament.

A clergyman, unless a trader, cannot be made a bankrupt; nor an attorney, in the common cours profession; nor an infant, nor a lunatic, nor a married woman, except in those cases where she may b and taken in execution for her debts. — (8 *T. R.* 545.)

A single act of buying or selling is not sufficient to make a trader; as a schoolmaster selling bc his scholars only, or a keeper of hounds buying dead horses and selling the skin and bones. — (6 56.) But the quantity of dealing is immaterial, where an intention to deal generally may be infe (1 *Rose*, 84.) A buyer or seller of land, or any interest in land, is not a trader within the ac on this principle it has been decided, that a brick-maker selling bricks made in his own field, owner of a mine selling minerals from his own quarry, is not liable, because such business is carr only as a mode of enjoying the profits of a real estate.— (2 *Wils.* 169.)

Traders having privilege of parliament, are subject to the bankrupt laws, and may be pro against as other traders; but such persons cannot be arrested or imprisoned, except in cases made by the statute.

2. *Acts constituting Bankruptcy.* — In general, any act which is intended to delay or defraud cre is an act of bankruptcy; such as a trader concealing himself from his creditors, leaving the co causing himself to be arrested or his goods taken in execution, or making any fraudulent conve gift, or delivery of his property. A trader keeping house commits an act of bankruptcy, if he general order to be denied. So is closing the door, and not admitting persons till ascertained wh are from window, though no actual denial. — (1 *Bar. & Cres.* 54.) But it is no act of bankru the denial be on Sunday, or at an unseasonable hour of the night, or to prevent interruption at time.

Traders held in prison for any really subsisting debt for the period of 21 days, or who, being arreste their escape out of prison or custody, commit acts of bankruptcy. A penalty due to the crown is cient debt, and the time is computed from the first arrest, where the party lies in prison immediate the day of arrest is included, and the whole of the last day.

Filing a petition, in order to take the benefit of the insolvent act, is an act of bankruptcy, an may be issued any time before the petition is heard by the Insolvent Court, or within two c months.

A trader may make a declaration of his insolvency, signed and attested by an attorney or solicit afterwards to be filed in the Bankrupt Office; and the secretary signing a memorandum thereof, i rity for advertising it in the Gazette. Upon this act of bankruptcy no commission can issue, if no two calendar months after such advertisement, and unless such advertisement be within eight da filing declaration; and no docket can be struck till four days after advertisement, if the commiss be executed in London, and eight if in the country. Such declaration of insolvency being co between bankrupt and creditor, does not invalidate the commission.

The execution by a trader of any conveyance by deed, of all his estate and effects for the bene his creditors, is not an act of bankruptcy, unless a commission be sued out within six months aft vided the deed be attested by an attorney or solicitor, and executed within 15 days after, and thereof within two months be given in the Gazette, and two daily newspapers; or, if the trade more than 50 miles from London, notice may be given in the Gazette, and nearest country newsp

3. *Proceedings of Petitioning Creditors.* — A person being a trader, and having committed a bankruptcy, the next step in the proceeding is to petition the Lord Chancellor to issue

at is issued, unless the petitioning creditor's debt, if one person or one firm, amounts to
if two creditors, to 150l.; if three or more creditors, to 200l. or upwards. The petitioning cre-
must make an affidavit before a Master in Chancery, of the truth of his debt, and give bond in 200l.
ove it, and the act of bankruptcy. If the debt prove insufficient to support a fiat, the Lord
cellor, upon the application of another creditor who has proved a sufficient debt, contracted pos-
to that of the petitioning creditor, may order the bankruptcy to be proceeded in.
e petitioning creditor proceeds at his own cost until the choice of assignees, when his expenses are
out of the first money received under the bankruptcy.
ditors entitled to sue out a fiat against all the partners in a firm, may elect to petition only
st one or more of such partners; and the commission may be superseded as to one or more partners,
ut affecting its validity as to the other partners.
ditors who have sued out a fiat compounding with the bankrupt, or receiving more in the pound
other creditors, forfeit the whole of their debt, and whatever gratuity they received, for the
t of the other creditors, and the Lord Chancellor may either order the commission to be pro-
d in or superseded.

ew Court of Bankruptcy. — Formerly the bankrupt business of the metropolis was transacted by 70
issioners, appointed by the Lord Chancellor. They received no regular commission, but derived their
rity from a letter written to them by the Chancellor, informing them of their appointment. The
proceedings under a town commission, from its issuing to the winding up of the bankrupt's affairs,
managed by these commissioners, who acted by rotation, in lists of five each. In place of these an entire
ourt has been substituted, consisting of a chief judge, with three puisne judges, and six commissioners.
are also two principal registrars, and eight deputy registrars. The secretary of bankrupts is also
ued as one of the officers under the new system.
judges, or any three of them, sit as a Court of Review, to adjudicate in all matters of bankruptcy
nt before them, subject to an appeal to the Lord Chancellor. The six commissioners sit occasionally
n subdivision courts of three commissioners each. The powers of the single commissioner are nearly
me as the old commissioners. The examination of any bankrupt or other person, or of a proof of
nay be adjourned by a single commissioner to a subdivision court; and disputed debts, if all parties
nt, may be tried by a jury. An appeal lies from a single commissioner, or a sub-division court, to
ourt of Review; and a decree of this Court is final, unless appealed against within one month.
London commissioners under the old law had a jurisdiction for 40 miles round London, which is
ued to their successors. Commissions in the country beyond this distance were directed to bar-
, or, if these could not be had, to solicitors, resident near the spot where the commission was to be
ted. Under the new act, the judges of assize name to the Lord Chancellor such barristers and soli-
in the county as they think fit for the office, and if he approve, they are to appoint them permanent
issioners for the execution of all bankruptcy business in the county; and fiats, not directed to the
of Bankruptcy in London, are directed to them.
us now proceed with the powers and duties of the commissioners.
missioners are empowered to summon persons, examine them on oath, and call for any deeds or
ents necessary to establish the trading and act of bankruptcy; and upon full proof thereof, to
e the debtor a bankrupt. Notice of such adjudication must be given in the Gazette, and three
meetings appointed for the bankrupt to surrender; the last of which meetings to be the forty-second
er. A bankrupt refusing to attend at the appointed time may be apprehended; and on refusing to
any question touching his business or property, may be committed to prison.
arrant of the commissioners, persons may break open any house, premises, door, chest, or trunk
bankrupt, and seize on his body or property; and if the bankrupt be in prison or custody, they
ze any property (necessary wearing apparel excepted) in the possession of such bankrupt, or any
erson. Authorised by a justice's warrant, premises may be searched not belonging to the bank-
n suspicion of property being concealed there; and persons suspected to have any of the bank-
roperty in their possession, refusing to obey the summons of commissioners, or refusing to answer
gatories, or to surrender documents, without lawful excuse, may be imprisoned. The wife of the
pt may be examined, or, on refusal, committed.
ns summoned are entitled to their expenses; and those attending, whether summoned or not, to
ne commissioners in their inquiries, are protected from arrest on any civil suit.

bts proveable under Commission. — At the three meetings appointed by the commissioners, and at
ther meeting appointed by them for proof of debts, every creditor may prove his debt by affidavit
s own oath; incorporated bodies by an agent authorised for the purpose; and one partner may
n behalf of the firm. Persons living at a distance may prove by affidavit before a Master in Chancery,
esident abroad, before a magistrate where residing, attested by a public notary, or British minister
ul.
s and servants, to whom the bankrupt is indebted for wages, are entitled to be paid six months'
n full, and for the residue they may prove under the commission.
ntures of apprenticeships are discharged by bankruptcy; but in case a premium has been received,
missioners may direct a portion of it to be repaid for the use of the apprentice, proportioned to the
apprenticeship unexpired.
s upon bill, bond, note, or other negotiable security, or where credit has been given upon valuable
ration, though not due at the time the act of bankruptcy was committed, are proveable under the
sion. Sureties, persons liable for the debts of, or bail for the bankrupt, may prove after having
ch debts, if they have contracted the liability without notice of any act of bankruptcy. Obligee in
ry or respondentia bonds, and assured in policy of insurance, are admitted to claim; and after loss,
e as if the loss or contingency had happened before commission had issued against the obligor or
Annuity creditors may prove for the value of their annuities, regard being had to the original
such annuities. Plaintiffs in any action, having obtained judgment against the bankrupt, may
or their costs.
n there are mutual debts between the bankrupt and a creditor, they may be set off against each
nd the balance, if in favour of the creditor, is proveable against the bankrupt's estate.
est may be proved on all bills of exchange and promissory notes over due at the time of issuing
sion, up to the date of the commission.
ng a debt under the commission, is an election not to proceed against the bankrupt by action; and
the bankrupt be in prison at the suit of a creditor, he cannot prove his debt without first discharg-
bankrupt from confinement: but the creditor is not liable for the costs of the action so relinquished

bt barred by the statute of limitations is proveable under the commission.

icial Assignees. — An important alteration introduced by Lord Brougham's act, particularly to
cial men, is the appointment of official assignees. They are 30 in number, merchants and
resident in the metropolis or vicinity; and are selected by the Lord Chancellor. They are to act
assignees chosen by the creditors. All the real and personal estates of the bankrupt, all the
stock in the public funds, securities and proceeds of sale, are transferred and vested in the official
, subject to the rules, orders, and direction of the Lord Chancellor, or a member of the Court of
ptcy. The official assignee gives security for the trust reposed in him; and is required to deposit
eys, securities, &c. in the Bank of England.
fficial assignee is neither remunerated by a per centage nor a fixed salary, but a sum is paid to

him for his trouble, at the discretion of the commissioners, and proportioned to the estates of the bank
and the duties discharged.

7. *Appointment of Assignees by Creditors.*—The official assignee is empowered to act as the sole assig
of the bankrupt's estates and effects until others are chosen by creditors, which must be at the sec
meeting. Every creditor to the amount of 10*l.*, who has proved his debt, is eligible to vote ; persons ma
authorised by letters of attorney to vote, and the choice is made by the major part in value of the cre
tors : but the commissioners may reject any person they deem unfit ; upon which a new choice mus
made.

When only one or more partners of a firm are bankrupt, a creditor to the whole firm is entitled to v
and to assent to or dissent from the certificate ; but such creditor, unless a petitioning creditor, car
receive any dividend out of the separate estate, until all the other creditors are paid in full.

Assignees may, with consent of creditors declared at any meeting duly summoned, compound or sub
disputes to arbitration, and such reference be made a rule of the Court of Bankruptcy, or they may ce
mence suits in equity, but if one third in value of creditors do not attend such meeting, the same pov
are granted to assignees with the consent, in writing, of commissioners.

Assignees to keep a book of account, where shall be entered a statement of all receipts and paymc
relating to bankrupt's estate, and which may be inspected by any creditor who has proved. Commissio
may summon assignees, with their books and papers, before them ; and if they refuse to attend, may ca
them to be committed till they obey the summons.

An assignee retaining or employing the money of the bankrupt, to the amount of 100*l.* or upwards,
his own advantage, may be charged 20*l.* per cent. interest.

Commissioners at the last examination of bankrupt to appoint a public meeting, not sooner than f
calendar months after issuing commission, nor later than six calendar months from last examination
which 21 days' notice must be given in the *Gazette*, to audit the accounts of the assignee ; which accou
must be delivered on oath, and the commissioners may examine the assignee touching the truth ther

8. *Property liable under Bankruptcy.*—The official assignee is vested with all the real and personal es
of the bankrupt, and with all such property as may be devised to him, or come into his possession, till
time he obtain his certificate. The commissioners may sell any real property of which the bankrup
seised, or any estate tail, in possession, reversion, or remainder, and the sale is good against the bankr
the issue of his body, and against all persons claiming under him after he became bankrupt, or whom
fine, common recovery, or other means, he can cut off from any future interest. All property which
bankrupt has in right of his wife passes to the assignee, except such as is settled for her own sole ben
Any property pledged, or securities deposited, may be redeemed for the benefit of the creditors.

If a bankrupt, being at the time insolvent, convey his lands or goods to his children or others, (ex
upon their marriage, or for a valuable consideration,) or deliver securities, or transfer debts into ot
names, such transactions are void.

A landlord after or out of bankruptcy cannot distrain for more than *one year's rent ;* but he may pr
under the commission for the residue.

The assignee may accept any lease to which the bankrupt is entitled, and his acceptance exonerates
bankrupt from any future liability for rent ; or if the assignee decline the lease, and the bankrupt, wit
14 days after, deliver the lease to the lessor, he is not liable for rent.

In general, all power which the bankrupt might lawfully execute in the sale and disposition of his r
perty for the benefit of himself, may be executed by the assignee for the benefit of creditors.

All contracts, conveyances, and transactions by or with any bankrupt, and all executions and att
ments levied, without notice of an act of bankruptcy for more than two months before the issuing of
commission, are valid. All payments whatever, either *by* or *to* the bankrupt, without notice of an ac
bankruptcy, are protected down to the date of the commission ; and purchasers for valuable consi
ations, *with notice*, cannot be molested, unless a commission issue within twelve months after the ac
bankruptcy.

The circumstance of a commission appearing in the Gazette, and a fair presumption that the pe
to be affected thereby may have seen the same, is deemed sufficient legal notice of an act of bankru
having been committed.

9. *Examination and Liabilities of Bankrupt.*—A bankrupt, not surrendering to the commissioner
fore 3 o'clock upon the forty-second day after notice, or not making discovery of his estate and eff
not delivering up goods, books, papers, &c., or removing or embezzling to the value of 10*l.*, is guil
felony, and liable to a discretionary punishment, from imprisonment to transportation for life. The pe
for surrendering may be enlarged by the Lord Chancellor ; and the commissioners, or assignees, wit
proval of commissioners, may grant an allowance for support of the bankrupt and his family till he
passed his last examination. During his attendance on commissioners, the bankrupt is protected f
arrest.

The bankrupt is required to deliver up his books of account to the assignees upon oath, and to ar
them on reasonable notice ; he may inspect his accounts, assisted by other persons, in presenc
assignees. After certificate is allowed, he is required to attend assignees, in settling accounts, at 5s
day ; and may be committed for non-attendance.

A penalty of 100*l.* is imposed on persons concealing bankrupts' effects, and double the value of the
perty so concealed ; and an allowance of 5*l.* per cent. to persons discovering such concealment, with
further reward as the major part of the creditors may think fit to grant.

The bankrupt, or any other person, wilfully swearing falsely, is liable to the penalties of perjury.

If the bankrupt intend to dispute the commission, he must present a petition to the Court of Re
within two calendar months ; or, if out of the United Kingdom, within twelve.

At any meeting of creditors, after the last examination, the bankrupt or his friends may *tender a
position ;* which, if accepted by nine tenths in number and value of the creditors, at two separate meet
the Lord Chancellor may supersede the commission. In deciding on such offer, creditors under 20
not entitled to vote ; but their debts are computed in value. Persons residing out of England may
by letter of attorney, properly attested ; and the bankrupt may be required to make oath that no u
means have been employed to obtain the assent of any creditor to such arrangement.

10. *Payment of a Dividend.*—Not sooner than four, nor later than twelve calendar months, the
missioners are to appoint a public meeting, of which 21 days' previous notice must be given in the Ga
to make a dividend ; and at which meeting, creditors who have not proved, may prove their debts ; a
such meeting commissioners may order the nett produce of bankrupt's estate to be shared among the
ditors that have proved, in proportion to their debts : but no dividend to be declared unless the acce
of the assignees have been first audited and delivered in as before described.

If the estate is not wholly divided upon a first dividend, a second meeting must be called, not later
18 months from the date of commission ; and the dividend declared at such second meeting to be
unless some suit at law be pending, or some part of bankrupt's property afterwards accrue to the assig
in which case it must be shared among the creditors within two months after it is converted into mo

Assignees having unclaimed dividends to the amount of 50*l.*, who do not, within two calendar m
from the expiration of a year from the order of payment of such dividends, either pay them to the cre
entitled thereto, or cause a certificate thereof to be filed in the Bankrupts' Office, with the names,
the parties to whom due, shall be charged with legal interest from the time the certificate ought to
been filed, and such further sum, not exceeding 20*l.* per cent. per annum, as the commissioners thi
The Lord Chancellor may order the investment of unclaimed dividends in the funds ; and after three
the same may be divided among the other creditors.

tion can be brought against assignees for any dividend; the remedy being by petition to the Lord
lor.

rtificate and Allowance to Bankrupt. — The bankrupt who has surrendered, and conformed in all
) the provisions of the bankrupt laws, is discharged by the certificate from all debts and demands
e under the commission; but this does not discharge his partner, or one jointly bound, or in joint
with him, nor does it bar a debt due to the crown.

ertificate must be signed by four fifths in number and value of creditors who have proved debts
mount of 20l. or upwards; or, after six calendar months from last examination, then either by
ths in number and value, or by nine tenths in number. The bankrupt must make oath the certi-
s obtained without fraud; and any creditors may be heard before it is finally allowed by the Lord
lor. Any contract or security given to obtain signatures to the certificate, is void.

krupt, after obtaining this certificate, cannot be arrested for any debt proveable under commission;
liable to satisfy any debt from which he is discharged, upon any promise, contract, or agreement,
ade in writing.

e a person has been bankrupt before, or compounded with his creditors, or taken benefit of
c act, unless the estate produce 15s. in the pound, the certificate only protects the person of
t from arrest; and any future property he acquires may be seized by assignees for benefit of

produce of bankrupt's estate does not amount to 10s. in the pound, he is only allowed out of the
much as assignees think fit, not exceeding 3 per cent., or 300l. in the whole; if it produce 10s.,
t., not exceeding 400l.; if 12s. 6d. is paid in the pound, 7½ per cent., not exceeding 500l.; if 15s.
und and upwards, 10 per cent., and not exceeding 600l. One partner may receive his allowance,
d, from the joint and his separate estate, though the others are not entitled.

krupt is not entitled to certificate or allowance, if he has lost by gaming or wagering, in one day,
ithin one year next preceding his bankruptcy, 200l.; or 200l. by stockjobbing in the same period;
templation of bankruptcy, has destroyed or falsified his books, or concealed property to amount
r, if any person having proved a false debt under the commission, such bankrupt, being privy
r afterwards knowing the same, has not disclosed it to his assignees within one month after such
ge.

upon request by the bankrupt, the official assignee is required to declare to him how he has dis-
his property, and account to him for the surplus, if any: but before any surplus can be admitted,
aust be paid, first, on all debts proved that carry interest, at the rate payable thereon; and next,
other debts, at the rate of 4l. per cent., to be calculated from the date of the commission.

Number of Persons DISCHARGED FROM PRISON under the Acts for the Relief of Insolvent Debtors.
he constitution of the present Court in 1820; and the Number who have been ordered to be
d in Custody for contravening the Provisions of the Acts for the Relief of Insolvent Debtors. —
Paper, No. 141. Sess. 1831.)

e Court makes no Orders of Detention; and the following Table shows all the Judgments given to the 30th June,
however, including the Cases of Petitions dismissed, and not including any Judgments of the Summer Circuits
n in June last.

	Ordered to be discharged forthwith.				Ordered to be discharged at some future Period.				
Years.	In Lon- don.	On Cir- cuit.	Before Justices.	Total.	In Lon- don.	On Cir- cuit.	Before Justices.	Total.	Total.
1820	830	none.	1,495	2,325	61	none.	96	157	2,482
1821	2,347	none.	2,516	4,863	279	none.	208	427	5,290
1822	2,074	none.	2,499	4,573	161	none.	221	382	4,955
1823	1,811	none.	2,047	3,858	181	none.	202	383	4,241
1824	1,745	318	1,255	3,318	142	18	115	275	3,593
1825	1,955	1,342	73	3,370	126	161	8	295	3,665
1826	2,429	1,865	89	4,383	110	183	5	298	4,681
1827	1,929	1,988	89	4,006	90	128	10	228	4,234
1828	1,913	1,450	112	3,475	127	131	6	264	3,739
1829	2,067	1,580	100	3,747	158	152	10	320	4,067
1830	2,056	1,823	111	3,990	189	191	9	389	4,379
831 to ne 30.	781	749	90	1,620	107	28	2	137	1,757
				43,528				3,555	47,083

II. Account of the Number of COMMISSIONS of BANKRUPTCY issued from 1790 to 1830.

Commis- sions.	Years.	Commis- sions.	Years.	Commis- sions.	Years.	Commis- sions.	Years.	Commis- sions.	Years.	Commis- sions.
747	1797	1,115	1804	1,117	1811	2,500	1818	1,245	1825	1,103
769	1798	911	1805	1,129	1812	2,228	1819	1,499	1826	2,582
934	1799	717	1806	1,268	1813	1,953	1820	1,381	1827	1,368
1,956	1800	951	1807	1,362	1814	1,612	1821	1,238	1828	1,212
1,041	1801	1,199	1808	1,433	1815	2,284	1822	1,094	1829	1,654
879	1802	1,090	1809	1,382	1816	2,731	1823	1,070	1830	302*
954	1803	1,214	1810	2,314	1817	1,927	1824			

JRANCE, a contract of indemnity, by which one party engages, for a
d sum, to insure another against a risk to which he is exposed. The
o takes upon him the risk, is called the *Insurer*, *Assurer*, or *Underwriter*;
party protected by the insurance is called the insured, or assured; the

* January and February only.

sum paid is called the *Premium;* and the instrument containing the contr
called the *Policy.*

I. INSURANCE (GENERAL PRINCIPLES OF).
II. INSURANCE (MARINE).
III. INSURANCE (FIRE).
IV. INSURANCE (LIFE).

I. INSURANCE (GENERAL PRINCIPLES OF).

It is the duty of government to assist, by every means in its power, the effor
individuals to protect their property. Losses do not always arise from accid
circumstances, but are frequently occasioned by the crimes and miscondu
individuals; and there are no means so effectual for their prevention, when
arise from this source, as the establishment of a vigilant system of police,
of such an administration of the law as may be calculated to afford those
are injured a ready and cheap method of obtaining every practicable red
and, as far as possible, of insuring the punishment of culprits. But in despi
all that may be done by government, and of the utmost vigilance on the pa
individuals, property must always be exposed to a variety of casualties from
shipwreck, and other unforeseen disasters. And hence the importance of inqu
how such unavoidable losses, when they do occur, may be rendered least injur

The loss of a ship, or the conflagration of a cotton mill, is a calamity that w
press heavily even on the richest individual. But were it distributed a
several individuals, each would feel it proportionally less; and provided
number of those among whom it was distributed were very considerable, it w
hardly occasion any sensible inconvenience to any one in particular. Henc
advantage of combining to lessen the injury arising from the accidental destru
of property: and it is the diffusion of the risk of loss over a wide surface, a
valuation, that forms the employment of those engaged in insurance.

Though it is impossible to trace the circumstances which occasion those e
that are, on that account, termed accidental, they are, notwithstanding, fou
obey certain laws. The number of births, marriages, and deaths; the propo
of male to female, and of legitimate to illegitimate births; the ships cast a
the houses burned; and a vast variety of other apparently accidental event
yet, when our experience embraces a sufficiently wide field, found to be r
equal in equal periods of time; and it is easy, from observations made upon
to estimate the sum which an individual should pay, either to guarantee hi
perty from risk, or to secure a certain sum for his heirs at his death.

It must, however, be carefully observed, that no confidence can be plac
such estimates, unless they are deduced from a very wide induction. Sup
for example, that it is found, that during the present year one house is
dentally burned, in a town containing a thousand houses; this would afford
little ground for presuming that the *average* probability of fire in that tow
as one to one thousand. For it might be found that not a single house had
burned during the previous ten years, or that ten were burned during each of
years. But supposing it were ascertained, that at an average of ten year
house had been annually burned, the presumption that one to one thousan
the real ratio of the probability of fire would be very much strengthened;
it were found to obtain for twenty or thirty years together, it might be he
all practical purposes at least, as indicating the precise degree of probability

Besides its being necessary, in order to obtain the true measure of the prob
of any event, that the series of events, of which it is one, should be observ
a rather lengthened period; it is necessary also that the events should be
rous, or of pretty frequent occurrence. Suppose it were found, by observi
births and deaths of a million of individuals taken indiscriminately from
the whole population, that the mean duration of human life was forty year
should have but very slender grounds for concluding that this ratio would h
the case of the next ten, twenty, or fifty individuals that are born. Such a
ber is so small as hardly to admit of the operation of what is called the
average. When a large number of lives is taken, those that exceed the m
term are balanced by those that fall short of it; but when the number is
there is comparatively little room for the principle of compensation, and the
cannot, therefore, be depended upon.

is found, by the experience of all countries in which censuses of the popula-
have been taken with considerable accuracy, that the number of male children
is to that of female children in the proportion nearly of twenty-two to
ty-one. But unless the observations be made on a very large scale, this re-
will not be obtained. If we look at particular families, they sometimes con-
wholly of boys, and sometimes wholly of girls ; and it is not possible that the
can be to the girls of a single family in the ratio of twenty-two to twenty-one.
when, instead of confining our observations to particular families, or even
hes, we extend them so as to embrace a population of half a million, these
epancies disappear, and we find that there is invariably a small excess in the
ber of males born over the females.

e false inferences that have been drawn from the doctrine of chances, have
rmly almost proceeded from generalising too rapidly, or from deducing a rate
obability from such a number of instances as do not give a fair average. But
the instances on which we found our conclusions are sufficiently numerous,
seen that the most anomalous events, such as suicides, deaths by accident,
umber of letters put into the post-office without any address, &c. form pretty
ar series, and consequently admit of being estimated *à priori*.

e business of insurance is founded upon the principles thus briefly stated.
ose it has been remarked that of *forty* ships, of the ordinary degree of sea-
iness, employed in a given trade, one is annually cast away, the probability
s will plainly be equal to *one fortieth*. And if an individual wish to insure a
or the cargo on board a ship engaged in this trade, he ought to pay a *pre-*
equal to the one fortieth part of the sum he insures, exclusive of such an
ional sum as may be required to indemnify the insurer for his trouble, and to
him a fair profit. If the premium exceed this sum, the insurer is overpaid ;
f it fall below it, he is underpaid.

surances are effected sometimes by societies and sometimes by individuals,
sk being in either case diffused amongst a number of persons. Companies
d for carrying on the business have generally a large subscribed capital, or
a number of proprietors as enables them to raise, without difficulty, whatever
may at any time be required to make good losses. Societies of this sort do
mit their risks to small sums ; that is, they do not often refuse to insure a
sum upon a ship, a house, a life, &c. The magnitude of their capitals affords
the means of easily defraying a heavy loss; and their premiums being pro-
oned to their risks, their profit is, at an average, independent of such con-
cies.

ividuals, it is plain, could not act in this way, unless they were possessed of
arge capitals ; and besides, the taking of large risks would render the business
zardous, that few would be disposed to engage in it. Instead, therefore, of
ng a large sum, as 20,000*l.*, upon a single ship, a private underwriter or
r may not probably, in ordinary cases, take a greater risk than 200*l.* or 500*l.* ;
t, though his engagements may, when added together, amount to 20,000*l.*,
will be diffused over from forty to a hundred ships; and supposing one or
hips to be lost, the loss would not impair his capital, and would only lessen
ofits. Hence it is, that while one transaction only may be required in getting
insured by a company, ten or twenty separate transactions may be required
ting the same thing done at Lloyd's, or by private individuals. When con-
d in this cautious manner, the business of insurance is as safe a line of
lation as any in which individuals can engage.

establish a policy of insurance on a fair foundation, or in such a way that
emiums paid by the insured shall exactly balance the risks incurred by the
rs, and the various necessary expenses to which they are put, including, of
, their profit, it is necessary, as previously remarked, that the experience of
sks should be pretty extensive. It is not, however, at all necessary, that
party should inquire into the circumstances that lead to those events that
ost commonly made the subject of insurance. Such a research would, indeed,
irely fruitless : we are, and must necessarily continue to be, wholly ignorant
causes of their occurrence.

ppears, from the accounts given by Mr. Scoresby, in his valuable work on
rctic Regions, that of 586 ships which sailed from the various ports of
Britain for the northern whale fishery, during the four years ending with

1817, eight were lost (vol. ii. p. 131.), being at the rate of about one ship ou
every *seventy-three* of those employed. Now, supposing this to be about
average loss, it follows that the premium required to insure against it should
1*l*. 7*s*. 4*d*. per cent., exclusive, as already observed, of the expenses and profit
the insurer. Both the insurer and the insured would gain by entering int
transaction founded on this fair principle. When the operations of the insu
are extensive, and his risks spread over a considerable number of ships, his pr
does not depend upon chance, but is as steady, and may be as fairly calcula
upon, as that of a manufacturer or a merchant; while, on the other hand,
individuals who have insured their property have exempted it from any chanc
loss, and placed it, as it were, in a state of absolute security.

It is easy, from the brief statement now made, to perceive the immense adv
tages resulting to navigation and commerce from the practice of marine insuran
Without the aid that it affords, comparatively few individuals would be fo
disposed to expose their property to the risk of long and hazardous voyages;
by its means insecurity is changed for security, and the capital of the merch
whose ships are dispersed over every sea, and exposed to all the perils of
ocean, is as secure as that of the agriculturist. He can combine his measu
and arrange his plans as if they could no longer be affected by accident.
chances of shipwreck, or of loss by unforeseen occurrences, enter not into
calculations. He has purchased an exemption from the effects of such casualti
and applies himself to the prosecution of his business with that confidence a
energy which a feeling of security can only inspire. " Les chances de la navigat
entravaient le commerce. Le système des assurances a paru; il a consulté
saisons; il a porté ses regards sur la mer; il a interrogé ce terrible élément; i
a jugé l'inconstance; il en a pressenti les orages; il a épié la politique; il a
connu les ports et les côtes des deux mondes; il a tout soumis à des calculs sav
à des théories approximatives; et il a dit au commerçant habile, au navigat
intrépide: certes, il y a des désastres sur lesquels l'humanité ne peut que gé
mais quant à votre fortune, allez, franchissez les mers, déployez votre activit
votre industrie; je me charge de vos risques. Alors, Messieurs, s'il est permis
le dire, les quatre parties du monde se sont rapprochées." — (*Code de Comme
Exposé des Motifs*, liv. ii.)

Besides insuring against the perils of the sea, and losses arising from accid
caused by the operation of natural causes, it is common to insure against ener
pirates, thieves, and even the fraud, or, as it is technically termed, *barratry* of
master. The risk arising from these sources of casualty being extremely fluctua
and various, it is not easy to estimate it with any considerable degree of accura
and nothing more than a rough average can, in most cases, be looked for. In t
of war, the fluctuations in the rates of insurance are particularly great; and
intelligence that an enemy's squadron, or even that a single privateer, is crui
in the course which the ships bound to or returning from any given port usu
follow, causes an instantaneous rise in the premium. The appointment of
voys for the protection of trade during war, necessarily tends, by lessening
chances of capture, to lessen the premium on insurance. Still, however, the
in such periods is, in most cases, very considerable; and as it is liable to cha
very suddenly, great caution is required on the part of the underwriters.

Provision may also be made, by means of insurance, against loss by fire,
almost all the casualties to which property on land is subject.

But notwithstanding what has now been stated, it must be admitted, that
advantages derived from the practice of insuring against losses by sea and
are not altogether unmixed with evil. The security which it affords tend
relax that vigilant attention to the protection of property which the fear o
loss is sure otherwise to excite. This, however, is not its worst effect.
records of our courts, and the experience of all who are largely engaged in
business of insurance, too clearly prove that ships have been repeatedly sunk,
houses burned, in order to defraud the insurers. In despite, however, of
temptation to inattention and fraud which is thus afforded, there can be no d
that, on the whole, the practice is, in a public as well as private point of v
decidedly beneficial. The frauds that are occasionally committed raise, in s
degree, the rate of insurance. Still it is exceedingly moderate; and it is
probable, that the precautions adopted by the insurance offices for the prever

, especially in great towns, where it is most destructive, outweigh the
s of increased conflagration arising from the greater tendency to careless-
d crime.

business of life insurance has been carried to a far greater extent in Great
than in any other country, and has been productive of the most beneficial
Life insurances are of various kinds. Individuals without any very near
tions, and possessing only a limited fortune, are sometimes desirous, or
netimes, from the necessity of their situation, obliged, annually to encroach
ir capitals. But should the life of such persons be extended beyond the
ry term of existence, they might be totally unprovided for in old age; and
ire themselves against this contingency, they pay to an insurance company
iole, or a part of their capital, on condition of its guaranteeing them, as long
live, a certain annuity, proportioned partly, of course, to the amount of
n paid, and partly to their age when they buy the annuity. But though
mes serviceable to individuals, it may be questioned whether insurances of
rt are, in a public point of view, really advantageous. So far as their influ-
xtends, its obvious tendency is to weaken the principle of accumulation; to
ite individuals to consume their capitals during their own life, without
ig or caring about the interest of their successors. Were such a practice
me general, it would be productive of the most extensively ruinous con-
ces. The interest which most men take in the welfare of their families and
affords, indeed, a pretty strong security against its becoming injuriously
nt. There can, however, be little doubt that this selfish practice may be
hened by adventitious means; such, for example, as the opening of govern-
ans in the shape of life annuities, or in the still more objectionable form of
s. But when no extrinsic stimulus of this sort is given to it, there do not
be any very good grounds for thinking that the sale of annuities by pri-
dividuals or associations can materially weaken the principle of accumu-

ily, however, the species of insurance now referred to is but inconsiderable
ed with that which has accumulation for its object. All professional per-
persons living on salaries or wages, such as lawyers, physicians, military
al officers, clerks in public or private offices, &c., whose incomes must, of
terminate with their lives, and a host of others, who are either not pos-
of capital, or cannot dispose of their capital at pleasure, must naturally be
s of providing, so far as they may be able, for the comfortable subsistence
families in the event of their death. Take, for example, a physician or
without fortune, but making, perhaps, 1,000l. or 2,000l. a year by his
s; and suppose that he marries and has a family: if this individual attain
iverage duration of human life, he may accumulate such a fortune as will
for the adequate support of his family at his death. But who can pre-
say that such will be the case? — that he will not be one of the many
ons to the general rule? — And suppose he were hurried into an untimely
is family would necessarily be destitute. Now, it is against such calami-
ntingencies that life insurance is intended chiefly to provide. An individual
d of an income terminating at his death, agrees to pay a certain sum
to an insurance office; and this office binds itself to pay to his family, at
h, a sum equivalent, under deduction of the expenses of management and
fits of the insurers, to what these annual contributions, accumulated at
nd interest, would amount to, supposing the insured to reach the common
rage term of human life. Though he were to die the day after the insur-
been effected, his family would be as amply provided for as it is likely
uld be by his accumulations were his life of the ordinary duration. In all
deed, in which those insured die before attaining to an average age, their
bvious. But even in those cases in which their lives are prolonged be-
e ordinary term, they are not losers — they then merely pay for a security
ey must otherwise have been without. During the whole period, from
when they effect their insurances down to the time when they arrive at
n duration of human life, they are protected against the risk of dying
leaving their families sufficiently provided for; and the sum which they
having passed this mean term is nothing more than a fair compensation
ecurity they previously enjoyed. Of those who insure houses against fire,

T t

a very small proportion only have occasion to claim an indemnity for losses ac
sustained ; but the possession of a security against loss in the event of acc
is a sufficient motive to induce every prudent individual to insure his pro
The case of life insurance is in no respect different. When established
proper footing, the extra sums which those pay whose lives exceed the estin
duration is but the value of the previous security.

In order so to adjust the terms of an insurance, that the party insuring
neither pay too much nor too little, it is necessary that the probable dur
of human life, at every different age, should be calculated with as much acc
as possible.

This probable duration, or, as it is frequently termed, expectation of life, n
the period when the chances that a person of a given age will be alive, are
cisely equal to those that he will be dead. The results deduced from the
servations made to determine this period, in different countries and places,
been published in the form of tables ; and insurances are calculated by refe
to them. Thus, in the table of the expectation of life at Carlisle, framed b
Milne, of the Sun Life Office *, and which is believed to represent the averag
of mortality in England with very considerable accuracy, the probable futur
of a person of thirty years of age, is thirty-four years and four months ;
other words, it has been found by observations carefully made at Carlisle, th
an average, *half* the individuals of *thirty* years of age attain to the age of
four years and four months. If, therefore, an individual of thirty years o
were to insure a sum payable at his death, the insurers who adopt the Carlisle
would assume that he would live for thirty-four years and a third, and v
make their calculations on that footing. If he did not live so long, the ins
would lose by the transaction ; and if he lived longer, they would gain pr
tionally. But if their business be so extensive as to enable the law of av
fully to apply, what they lose by premature death will be balanced by the
ments received from those whose lives are prolonged beyond the ordinary d
of probability ; so that the profits of the society will be wholly independe
chance.

Besides the vast advantage of that security against disastrous continge
afforded by the practice of life insurance, it has an obvious tendency to stren
habits of accumulation. An individual who has insured a sum on his life,
forfeit all the advantages of the insurance, were he not to continue regula
make his annual payments. It is not, therefore, optional with him to save
from his ordinary expenditure adequate for this purpose. He is compelled,
a heavy penalty, to do so ; and having thus been led to contract a habit of s
to a certain extent, it is most probable that the habit will acquire additional str
and that he will either insure an additional sum or privately accumulate.

The practice of marine insurance, no doubt from the extraordinary haz
which property at sea is exposed, seems to have long preceded insurances a
fire and upon lives. We are ignorant of the precise period when it began
introduced ; but it appears most probable that it dates from the end of the
teenth or the beginning of the fifteenth century. It has, however,
contended by Loccenius (*De Jure Maritimo*, lib. ii. c. 1.), Puffendorff (*Dr
la Nature et des Gens*, lib. v. c. 9.), and others, that the practice of marine
ance is of much higher antiquity, and that traces of it may be found in the h
of the Punic wars. Livy mentions, that during the second of these contest
contractors employed by the Romans to transport ammunition and provisi
Spain, stipulated that government should indemnify them against such los
might be occasioned by the enemy, or by tempests, in the course of the voya
(*Impetratum fuit, ut quæ navibus imponerentur ad exercitum Hispaniensem defe
ab hostium tempestatisque vi, publico periculo essent.* — Hist. lib. 23. c. 49.) Ma
(*Lex Mercatoria*, 3d ed. p. 105.), founding on a passage in Suetonius, ascrib
first introduction of insurance to the emperor Claudius, who, in a period of sc
at Rome, to encourage the importation of corn, took upon himself all the
damage it might sustain in the voyage thither by storms and tempests. — (*I
atoribus certa lucra proposuit, suscepto in se damno, si cui quid per tempestates acc
et naves mercaturæ causâ, fabricantibus, magna commoda constitui!.* — c. 18.)

* See *post,* INTEREST AND ANNUITIES.

ɔus to observe that this stipulation gave occasion to the commission of acts of
d, similar to those so frequent in modern times. Shipwrecks were pretended
ave happened, that never took place; old shattered vessels, freighted with
les of little value, were purposely sunk, and the crew saved in boats; large
s being then demanded as a recompence for the loss. Some years after, the
d was discovered, and some of the contractors were prosecuted and punished.
Lib. 25. c. 3.) But none of these passages, nor a similar one in Cicero's
rs (*Ad Fam.* lib. ii. c. 17.), warrant the inferences that Loccenius, Malynes, and
rs have attempted to draw from them. Insurance is a contract between two
es; one of whom, on receiving a certain premium (*pretium periculi*), agrees
ke upon himself the risk of any loss that may happen to the property of the
r. In ancient no less than in modern times, every one must have been de-
s to be exonerated from the chance of loss arising from the exposure of
erty to the perils of the sea. But though, in the cases referred to, the carriers
exempted from this chance, they were not exempted by a contract *propter*
ionem periculi, or by an insurance; but by their employers taking the risk
them themselves. And it is abundantly obvious that the object of the latter in
g this was not to profit, like an insurer, by dealing in risks, but to induce
iduals the more readily to undertake the performance of an urgent public

at with the exception of the instances now mentioned, nothing bearing the
test resembling to an insurance is to be met with till a comparatively recent
d. If we might rely on a passage in one of the Flemish chroniclers quoted
e learned M. Pardessus—(see his excellent work, *Collection des Loix Maritimes*,
i. p. 356.), we should be warranted in concluding that insurances had been
ced at Bruges so early as the end of the thirteenth century: for the chronicler
s that, in 1311, the Earl of Flanders consented, on a requisition from the in-
ants, to establish a chamber of insurance at Bruges. M. Pardessus is not,
ver, inclined to think that this statement should be regarded as decisive. It
dent, from the manner in which the subject is mentioned, that the chronicler
ot a contemporary: and no trace can be found either in the archives of
es, or in any authentic publication, of any thing like the circumstance alluded
The earliest extant Flemish law as to insurance is dated in 1537; and none
e early maritime codes of the North so much as alludes to this interesting
ɔt.

ckmann seems to have thought that the practice of insurance originated in
in the latter part of the fifteenth or the early part of the sixteenth century.
ist. of Invent. vol. i. art. *Insurance.*) But the learned Spanish antiquary,
Antonio de Capmany, has given, in his very valuable publication on the History
'ommerce of Barcelona (*Memorias Historicas sobre la Marina, &c. de Barcelona*,
II. p. 383), an ordinance relative to insurance, issued by the magistrates of that
a 1435; whereas the earliest Italian law on the subject is nearly a century later,
dated in 1523. It is, however, exceedingly unlikely, had insurance been as
practised in Italy as in Catalonia, that the former should have been so much
d the latter in subjecting it to any fixed rules; and it is still more unlikely that
ractice should have escaped, as is the case, all mention by any previous
n writer. We, therefore, agree entirely in Capmany's opinion, that, until
authentic evidence to the contrary be produced, Barcelona should be re-
d as the birthplace of this most useful and beautiful application of the
ne of chances.—(Tomo i. p. 237.)

nowledge of the principles and practice of insurance was early brought into
nd. According to Malynes (*Lex Mercat.* p. 105.), it was first practised
st us by the Lombards, who were established in London from a very remote
. It is probable it was introduced some time about the beginning of the six-
, century; for it is mentioned in the statute 43 Eliz. c. 12.—a statute in
its utility is very clearly set forth—that it had been an *immemorial usage*
g merchants, both English and foreign, when they made any great adventure,
cure insurance to be made on the ships or goods adventured. From this it
easonably be supposed that insurance had been in use in England for at least
ury previous. It appears from the same statute, that it had originally been
to refer all disputes that arose with respect to insurances to the decision of
e and discreet" merchants appointed by the Lord Mayor. But abuses

having grown out of this practice, the statute authorised the Lord Chancellor appoint a commission for the trial of insurance cases; and in the reign of Char II. the powers of the commissioners were enlarged. But this court soon a fell into disuse; and, what is singular, no trace can now be discovered of any of proceedings. — (*Marshall on Insurance*, Prelim. Disc. p. 26.)

Few questions as to insurance seem to have come before the courts at We minster till after the middle of last century. The decisions of Lord Mansfi may, indeed, be said to have fixed, and in a considerable degree formed, the upon this subject. His judgments were not bottomed on narrow views, or on municipal regulations of England; but on those great principles of public just and convenience which had been sanctioned and approved by universal experien His deep and extensive information was acquired by consulting the most inte gent merchants, and the works of distinguished foreign jurists; and by carefu studying the famous French ordinance of 1681, the most admirably digested bc of maritime law of which any country has ever had to boast. Hence, the cc prehensiveness and excellence of his Lordship's decisions, and the respect th have justly commanded in all countries.* In his hands the law of insurance becar in a far greater degree than any other department of English law, a branch of t national or public law of which Cicero has beautifully said, " *Non erit alia Romæ, alia Athenis, alia nunc, alia posthac, sed et omnes gentes et omni tempore i lex et sempiterna, et immortalis continebit, unusque erit communis quasi magister imperator omnium Deus.*" — (*Fragm.* lib. iii. *de Republica.*)

The practices of insurance against fire and upon lives are of much later ori, than insurance against the perils of the sea. The former, however, have been kno and carried on amongst us, to some extent at least, for nearly a century and a h The Amicable Society, for insurance upon lives, was established by charter Queen Anne, in 1706; the Royal Exchange and London Assurance Compar began to make insurances upon lives in the reign of George I.; and the Equita Society was established in 1762. But the advantages of life insurance, and the pr ciples on which the business should be conducted, were then very ill understoc and the practice can hardly be said to have obtained any firm footing amongst till the Equitable Society, by adopting the judicious suggestions of Dr. Pr began its career of prosperity about 1775. Notwithstanding the example of E land, life insurance has made very little progress on the Continent. It was, deed, expressly forbidden by the French ordinance of 1681 (liv. iii. tit. 6. art. I by the regulations as to insurance issued at Amsterdam in 1612 (art. 24.); it is doubtful whether the practice be not inconsistent with the 334th art. of *Code de Commerce*. But we are inclined to think that the want of security, m than any positive regulations, has been the principal cause of the little progres life insurance on the Continent. Of whatever disadvantages our large public d may be productive, it is not to be doubted that the facilities it has afforded making investments, and the punctuality with which the national engagements h been fulfilled, have been the principal causes of the extraordinary extent to wl the business of life and even fire insurance has been carried in this country.

II. Insurance (Marine).

There are few persons who are not acquainted, in some degree, with fire and life surances. The security which they afford to individuals and families is a luxury w nobody, in tolerably comfortable circumstances, is willing to be without. Hence great increase, in our days, of companies professing to afford this security; and h the knowledge, on the part of the public generally, of the nature and principle the engagements into which these companies enter. But marine insurance is a su which is of immediate interest only to merchants and ship owners; unless, indeed should refer to that small portion of the community, who have occasion to tran themselves beyond seas with capital and effects for purposes of colonisation, or t some official situation. Hence the comparative indifference, on the part of the pu as to this subject. The general principles, however, of all insurance are the same; in treating of marine insurance, it will be necessary to notice little beyond such topi are peculiar to that branch of the business.

Individual Insurers or Underwriters. — The first circumstance that cannot fa strike the general inquirer into the practice of marine insurance in this country, is while all fire and life insurances are made at the risk of companies, which include w

* See Emerigon's famous *Traité des Assurances*, tome ii. p. 67.

lves the desirable requisites of security, wealth, and numbers; the great bulk of insurances are made at the risk of individuals. London is the only town in England which there are any public companies for this purpose *; and in London there y four: the two old companies, the *London* and the *Royal Exchange*; and the ablished in 1824, the *Alliance Marine* and the *Indemnity Mutual Marine*. The uals engaged in this branch of the insurance business, about whom we shall say resently, assemble at Lloyd's Coffee-house, over the Royal Exchange.

ibition of Companies. — Till 1824, all firms and companies, with the exception of chartered companies, the Royal Exchange and London, were prohibited by law king marine insurances. Towards the latter end of that year, the prohibition noved, and the business of marine insurance was placed on the same footing as escriptions of business. While the restriction lasted, the two chartered companies little business, that marine insurance might, in fact, be said to be wholly in the f individuals. These companies were so much higher in their premiums, and so nore exclusive in the risks they were willing to undertake, than their individual itors, that even those merchants and ship owners, who would cheerfully have paid ifling consideration to obtain the greater security of a company, were obliged to o individuals. And it was only when the repeal of this absurd restriction was d, that the companies showed, by defending it, that they set any value upon their e. The underwriters at Lloyd's joined them in this opposition; and pamphlets ritten, and speeches made, to demonstrate how much merchants and ship owners suffer, were the law to allow them the free use of their discretion in insuring operty; and how much more conducive to their interests it was, that they should d up to Lloyd's, to pay premiums to individuals rather than companies. But amphlets and speeches are forgotten; and we should be sorry to wound the of their authors, or to trespass on the patience of our readers, by referring to ore particularly.

ation of Companies. — During the autumn of 1824 and spring of 1825, five comprung into existence in London: the two already mentioned, and the *St. Patrick*, riotic, and the *South Devon*. The three last have since been given up, having ruinous concerns to the proprietors. The two former are composed of some of t eminent merchants and ship owners of the city of London, who united for the purpose of providing a more perfect security for their property, and of ascerwhether the insurance business might not be made to yield a fair return to the employed in it. The change thus introduced into the business has had the f rousing the two old companies into activity, and thus may be said to have to the public the opportunity of transacting their business with four substantial es, in addition to individual underwriters, whereas they could previously deal h individuals.

ay be computed that these four companies draw to themselves a fifth of the usiness of the country, leaving the other four fifths to individual underwriters Scotch and Irish companies; the business of the latter being, however, of very extent. It has been inferred by some, that the comparatively limited business ompanies is a convincing proof that individuals are much better adapted to in this department than societies; while by others it has been contended that e share of business, thus speedily attracted to the companies, ought to satisfy dy, when due allowances are made for the difficulties to be combated in through established modes and habits of doing business, that the tendency in ic is practically to confirm what antecedent investigation would suggest, — npanies, while they must necesssarily hold out better security, and greater and punctuality in the settlement of claims, are capable of transacting a given f business with a saving both of labour and expense.

of conducting Business. — We shall now give an account of the existing ents for conducting the business of marine insurance, as well by individuals mpanies.

s. — The individual underwriters meet in a subscription room at Lloyd's. The irs of the subscribers to these rooms are managed by a committee chosen by ribers. Agents (who are commonly styled Lloyd's agents) are appointed in incipal ports of the world, who forward, regularly, to Lloyd's, accounts of the defrom and arrivals at their ports, as well as of losses and other casualties; and, in all such information as may be supposed of importance towards guiding the ts of the underwriters. These accounts are regularly filed, and are accessible e subscribers. The principal arrivals and losses are, besides, posted in two laced in two conspicuous parts of the room; and also in another book, placed in an adjoining room, for the use of the public at large. Many of

* Within these few months a company has been formed at Liverpool.

the merchants of the city of London are subscribers to these rooms; and the tw
companies contribute each 100*l.* per annum, in return for which they are furn
with copies of the daily intelligence.   The two new companies made similar
posals, which were, and, we believe, continue to be, rejected; but this feelin
animosity is unworthy of the subscribers, and will no doubt speedily disappear.

The rooms are open from 10 o'clock in the morning till 5 o'clock in the
noon, but the most considerable part of the business is transacted between 1 a
Those merchants and ship owners who manage their own insurance business, pr
blank policies at the office in Lombard-street, or of their stationers, which they fi
so as to meet the particular object in view, and submit them to those underwriters
whom they are connected; by whom they are subscribed or rejected.   Each pol
handed about in this way until the amount required is complete.   The form c
policy and of a subscription is subjoined to this article.

The premium is not paid to the underwriter in ready money, but is passed to acc
Nor does the underwriter debit the account of the person, to whom he subscri
policy, with the whole amount of the premium, but with the premium less 5 per
Whenever losses occur which more than absorb the premiums on any one accoun
underwriter is called upon to pay the balance.   But should the underwriter's ac
be what is called good, that is, should the premiums exceed the claims, he sends r
during the spring and summer, to collect from his various debtors either the balan
his last year's account, or money on account, according to his judgment; but,
what he receives, he makes an allowance of 12 per cent.   An underwriter, if pru
therefore, before he consents to receive, will not only look to the goodness of his acc
but to the probability of its continuing so.

Insurance Brokers.—Many merchants and ship owners do not transact their ow
surance business.   They give their orders for insurance to others, who underta
for them, and are responsible for its proper management.   These latter person
called insurance brokers; and some of them manage the business of a number of
cipals.   To them, likewise, are transmitted the orders for insurance from the out
and manufacturing towns.   They charge the whole premium to their principals
their profit consists in 5 per cent. upon the premium, 12 per cent. upon the mone
they pay to the underwriters, and $\frac{1}{2}$ per cent. that they deduct from all the claims
they recover from the underwriters.   It is proper to remark, that this is the estab
or regular profit; but competition has occasioned numerous deviations from it
brokers, many of whom consent to divide this profit with the principals who e
them.   The insurance brokers are not unfrequently underwriters also; and as
insurances are considered far more lucrative than others to underwriters, and
brokers have particular facilities, in some respects, of judging of the goodness of
own risks, so likewise have they an inducement to play into one another's hand
they do so accordingly. — (See BROKERS.)

It will at once be seen, that the trouble of effecting insurances at Lloyd's is con
able; that a good deal of time must be consumed; and that merchants and ship ov
therefore, have great inducement to consign their insurance business to brokers.
where the business is transacted with a company, this inducement, if not des
altogether, is, at all events, very much diminished.   Any party having proper
insure, has merely to go to the manager of the company, and state the particul
the risk to be insured; the premium being agreed upon, the manager writes
memorandum for the policy, which the party signs, and he is thus effectually in
The companies procure the stamp and write out the policy, which is ready for d
in four or five days.   The companies, like the underwriters, charge the premiu
5 per cent.   In other respects they vary.

The London Assurance Company allow 11$\frac{1}{4}$ per cent. for prompt payment,
per cent. and three months' credit.

The Royal Exchange Assurance Company allow 12 per cent. upon the pro
balance of each year's premiums, with credit till March for the premiums of th
ceding year, and 5 per cent. for prompt payment.

The Alliance Marine Assurance Company allow 12 per cent. upon the pro
balance of each year's premiums, with credit till March; or 10 per cent. for p
payment.

The Indemnity Mutual Marine Assurance Company allow 12 per cent. up
profitable balance of each year's premiums, with credit till June; or 10 per ce
prompt payment.

Payment of Losses. — Losses are paid at all the offices promptly, and without
tion.   A month's credit is allowed to the underwriters; and another month, and
times two months, are given to the broker, to collect from the underwriters, a
over to his principals.

ubs. — Besides the individual underwriters and companies above noticed, there are , or associations formed by ship owners, who agree, each entering his ships for a in amount, to divide among themselves one another's losses. These clubs are utions of long standing; but, since the alteration of the law in 1824, appear to be e decline. Their formation originated in a twofold reason: 1st, that the under- rs charged premiums more than commensurate with the risk; and, 2dly, that they ot afford adequate protection. To avoid the first of these two evils, instead of g a fixed premium, they pay among themselves the actual losses of their several bers as they occur; and to avoid the second, they lay down certain principles of ment in accordance with their views of indemnity. Each member of one of these gives his power of attorney to the selected manager; and this manager issues a y for each ship, which policy is subscribed by him as attorney for all the members, oremium inserted in the policy being understood to be nominal. These clubs pen to the leading objections that apply to individual underwriters; for the mem- are not collectively, but only individually, liable to those of their number who en to sustain a loss; and the delay of settlement is such, that more than twelve bs have been known to elapse before the payment of a loss has been obtained from e members.

te of Premium. — But little need be said upon the circumstances that influence ate of premium demanded by the insurers. It must be self-evident that premiums vary according to the seasons, the quality of the vessel, the known character of the in, the nature of the commodity, and the state of our political relations. All these, urse, are matters upon which each individual must exercise his own discretion, partly general experience, and partly from particular information; exaggeration of risk, consequent exorbitancy of premium for any length of time, being out of the ion, where so many individual underwriters, in addition to the companies, are in com- on with one another, and where the merchants have the means at hand of effecting insurances abroad. We have already taken notice of the intelligence of which l's is the focus. In addition to this, there are two subscription register books for ing maintained by the principal merchants, ship owners, and underwriters. These profess to give an account of the tonnage, build, age, repairs, and quality of it all the vessels that frequent our ports; and, although exceedingly defective in respects, are material assistants to the insurers who have no means of ascertaining eir own observation the particulars of one hundredth part of the ships they are upon to insure.

CONTRACT OF INSURANCE.

ving thus given a general outline of the mode of transacting business between the rs and insured, and the means used to enable both parties to come, as near as le, to a due estimate of the risk to be insured against, our next step will be to n the nature of the contract, and the bearing of its more important clauses.

s unnecessary to state that the object of those who are engaged in commerce, or in g articles of merchandise from one part of the world to another, is to *buy* at such e that, after paying all the expenses of transport, the *sale* price may leave them a s in the shape of profit. If there were no such contrivance as insurance, mer- would be obliged to calculate upon the probability of the occasional loss of their *ty*, and to regulate their transactions accordingly; but it must be obvious that enter- under such circumstances, would be very much crippled. Now insurance, in as it approaches perfection in guaranteeing the merchant against all loss, except that market, substitutes a fixed charge for uncertain and contingent loss, and enables confine his attention exclusively to price and quality, and to charges of transport; ch latter, of course, the premium of insurance is included. As, however, in prac- isurance is by no means a perfect protection, either to the merchant or ship owner, t all loss that may occur *in transitu*, there is, even after insurance, some contin- s remaining to be taken into consideration; and we do not know that we can do by way of explaining the contract of insurance, than state, as briefly and suc- as possible, what are the losses against which the merchant and ship owner are tected by an insurance effected in this country.

Acts of our own Government. — All losses arising from the acts of our own go- ent. Thus, if an embargo were laid on vessels about to sail for a particular r, and the merchant obliged to unload his goods; or if his goods were condemned destroyed in quarantine; or purposely destroyed at sea by some of our cruisers; t of his loss would be made good by the insurer. The insurer in this country, gh liable for the acts of foreign powers, is not liable for such acts directed against perty of their own subjects. Thus, if French property, insured in this country, onfiscated by the French government, the owner would have no remedy against urer.

2. *Breaches of the Revenue Laws.* — All losses arising from a breach of the reve
laws. It may be observed, that if the owner of the ship, by his act, expose the go
of the merchant to loss, the merchant so injured, although he cannot recover from
insurers, may claim from him. It may also be observed, that if the captain of
vessel, by his act, to which neither the owner of the ship nor the merchant is a pa
expose the ship and cargo to loss, the insurers, in such case, are bound to make g
the loss; the insurers being liable for all damage arising from illegal acts of the c
tain and crew, supposing the owner of the ship not to be accessary. The illegal act
the captain and crew, contrary to the instructions and without the consent of the own
are termed "barratry" in the policy.— (See BARRATRY.)

3. *Breaches of the Law of Nations.* — All losses arising from a breach of the law
nations. Thus, if any port is declared by a foreign power to be in a state of blocka
and such blockade is acknowledged by our government; and if a ship, in defianc
that notification, attempt to break the blockade, and is taken in the attempt; the insu
is not liable to the loss. It will often happen, when a port is under blockade, that
profit is so great upon goods introduced in defiance of the blockade, as to tempt
venturers to break it, and to enable them to afford a very high premium to ins
against the risk. But as policies for such an object are not acknowledged in our co
of law, when effected, they are understood to be *policies of honour*. The same k
of policy is adopted by the underwriters, to protect foreign merchants who prefer
suring in this country against British capture.

4. *Consequences of Deviation.* — All losses subsequent to a deviation from the te
of the policy. Thus, if a merchant, in a policy on produce from the West Indies
London, warrant the ship to sail on or before the 1st of August, and the ship sail a
that day and be lost, the insurer is exonerated. Or, if a merchant insure from Lon
to Lisbon, and the ship call at Havre and is afterwards lost, the insurer is not lia
It will be understood, of course, that the owner of the ship is liable to the merchant
any breach of contract on his part, as well as that the insurer is liable for the barra
of the master; a deviation on the part of the master, not intended for the benefi
the owner, and contrary to his instructions, being considered barratry. Should
owner of the goods neglect to describe accurately the voyage for which he wishes
be insured, the loss would be a consequence of his own negligence.

There is a doctrine connected with barratry which it will here be proper to notice.
captain, owner or part owner of the ship in which he sails, cannot commit an ac
barratry. In other words, the insurers are not, in such a case, liable for an act of
which would otherwise be barratrous. The equity of this doctrine, as far as regards
interests of the captain himself, cannot be called in question; but it is difficult to un
stand why the merchant who ships goods on board such a captain's vessel should no
permitted to insure, among other risks, againt the captain's illegal acts. We have he
that a clause has occasionally been introduced into policies to protect merchants aga
captain-owners, and we do not suppose that our courts of law would refuse to enf
such a clause. Indeed, we cannot discover any reason why every party, saving
captain, should not have the power of insuring against the consequences of illegal
of the captain. We believe, that among the life offices, which protect themselves f
loss by suicide and the hands of justice, there are some which make a distinctio
favour of those who merely hold policies on the lives of others as a collateral secu
The propriety of such a distinction must strike every body.

5. *Unseaworthiness.* — All losses arising from unseaworthiness. Unseaworthi
may be caused in various ways, such as want of repair, want of stores, want of
visions, want of nautical instruments, insufficiency of hands to navigate the vessel
incompetency of the master. It might be supposed, at first sight, that insurance aff
a much less perfect security than it really does, seeing on how many pleas it is poss
for the insurer to dispute his liability; but when it is considered, that the proo
unseaworthiness is thrown upon the defendant, and that the leaning of the cou
almost always in favour of the insured, it will be easy to suppose that no respect
insurers would ever plead unseaworthiness, unless they could make out a case of r
than ordinary strength and clearness. The degree of uneasiness felt by merchants
ship owners at their liability to be involved in loss by cases of unseaworthiness, ma
guessed from the fact, that although the Indemnity Assurance Company at one
precluded themselves from pleading unseaworthiness by a special clause in their po
not only did they obtain no additional premium in consequence thereof, but
did not even obtain a preference over other companies and individuals at the s
premium. At least, this fact must either be admitted as a proof of the absen
uneasiness on this head, or of that inveteracy of habit which seems to lead the
bulk of mankind always, if possible, to continue undeviatingly in those course
which they are accustomed, even where the benefits to be derived from a deviatior
undeniable.

Protraction of the Voyage. — All loss arising from unusual protraction of the
Thus, if a ship meet with an accident in the Baltic, and the repairs detain the
ill the close of the season, when the passage home is rendered impracticable by
till the opening of the ensuing season, no payment is made to the merchant, in
ion of his loss from interest of money, loss of market (if the market fall), or de-
ion in the quality of his goods (unless arising from actual sea damage); nor to the
ner, in mitigation of his loss from the extra wages and maintenance of his crew.
t foreign countries the ship owner is remunerated by the insurers for the wages
intenance of his crew while his ship is detained in consequence of any loss for the
good of which they are liable.

iability for doing Damage to other Vessels. — All loss to which the ship owner is
hen his vessel does damage to others. According to our laws, the owner of
hip not in charge of a pilot, that does damage, by negligence of the master and
o any description of craft or vessel, is liable to make good the same to the extent
e of his own ship and freight: for beyond this he is not liable. The com-
olicy in use among the underwriters at Lloyd's and the companies does not
the ship owner from this loss. But the clubs or associations before men-
almost universally take this risk. Indeed, this is one of the purposes which
e to their formation. But even they limit their liability to the amount of the
so that if a ship insured with them were to run down another, and to sink herself
oncussion, the owner would only receive the value of his own vessel from the
d still be liable to the owner of the other vessel. The Indemnity Company, by
e in their policy, make themselves liable for three fourths of the loss which the
f the vessel insured with them may sustain from damage done by his vessel to
others. If such a case as the one just supposed should occur under their policy,
red would receive the value of his own vessel and three fourths of the loss to be
ood by him to the owner of the other vessel. The policies of this Company ap-
n this respect the nearest of any to perfect protection to the ship owner. But
from running down other vessels, although serious, nay, sometimes ruinous,
occurs; and many ship owners trust so confidently that it will never fall upon
hat they are as well satisfied to be without as with this protection.

erage Clause. — The next description of loss of which we shall treat, against
e insured are not protected, is described in the following clause of the policy:
fish, salt, seed, flour, and fruit, are warranted free from average, unless general,
hip be stranded; sugar, tobacco, hemp, flax, hides, and skins, are warranted free
erage under 5 per cent., unless general, or the ship be stranded; and all other
lso the ship and freight, are warranted free from average under 3 per cent., unless
or the ship be stranded."

anguage employed in this clause, being technical, requires explanation, to render
gible to the general reader. Average is a name applied to certain descriptions
o which the merchant and ship owner are liable. There are two kinds of average,
and particular.

al *Average* comprehends all loss arising out of a voluntary sacrifice of a part of
ssel or cargo, made by the captain for the benefit of the whole. Thus, if a captain
art of his cargo overboard, cut from an anchor and cable, or cut away his masts,
so sustained, being voluntarily submitted to for the benefit of the whole, is dis-
over the value of the whole ship and cargo, and is called " general average."

ular *Average* comprehends all loss occasioned to ship, freight, and cargo, which
so serious a nature as to debar them from reaching their port of destination, and
e damage to the ship is not so extensive as to render her unworthy of repair.
here the goods are saved, but in such a state as to be unfit to forward to their
estination, and where the ship is rendered unfit to repair, are called " partial or
loss." The leading distinction between particular average and salvage loss is,
he first, the property insured remains the property of the insurer — the damage
, or part thereof, as the case may be, and as will be hereafter explained, being
od by the insurer; and in the second, the property insured is abandoned to the
and the value insured claimed from him, he retaining the property so abandoned,
ue.

ular *Average on Goods.*—A few cases illustrative of the method of stating a claim
cular average will best explain the nature of this description of loss, and will
me time show the reader what the practical distinction is between particular
and salvage loss.

roperty insured we shall suppose to be *a ton of hemp*, the cost of which at
rgh is 30*l.*, for which sum it is insured from Petersburgh to London, and
uty, freight, and charges to which the merchant is subject on landing at Lon-
0*l.* We shall likewise suppose that the hemp, on its arrival, is so damaged as not
rth more than half what it would have fetched had it been sound. The in-

surer would then be called upon to make good to the insured 15*l.*, or 50 per cent.
the sum insured. But it does not follow that this payment of 15*l.* would indemni
merchant, or that it would not more than indemnify him, for the loss sustained.

	£ s.	£
If the hemp upon arrival in this country would have fetched in a sound state	50 0	
Less duty, freight, and charges	10 0	
		40
But in its damaged state is only worth	25 0	
Less duty, freight, and charges	10 0	
		15
The merchant's loss by the damage is		£25

Whereas he only receives from the insurer 15*l.* Upon the principle of a salvage loss he wou
receive 15*l.*

	£ s.	£
If the hemp would have fetched in a sound state	20 0	
Less duty, freight, and charges	10 0	
		10
But in its damaged state is only worth	10 0	
Less duty, freight, and charges	10 0	
The merchant's loss by the damage is		£10

Whereas he receives from the insurer 15*l.* Upon the principle of a salvage loss he would receiv

	£ s.	£
If the hemp would have fetched in a sound state	30 0	
Less duty, freight, and charges	10 0	
		20
But in its damaged state is only worth	15 0	
Less duty, freight, and charges	10 0	
		5
The merchant's loss by the damage is		£15

And he receives from the insurer 15*l.* Upon the principle of a salvage loss he would receive 25

It will be observed that the merchant's loss by the damage of his goods varie
the state of the market. It may also be observed, that in general the merchant wi
receive from the insurer the whole amount of the loss that he sustains. Whenev
market is a profitable one (and that it must usually be so will be obvious to every l
whenever, indeed, his market is not a decidedly losing one, his policy does not
him a complete protection.

The argument in favour of this mode of settling claims for particular average—
should be observed that the subject has been discussed, and the principle acknowl
in the courts of law—is, that the insurer's liability is to be guided by the amount
which he has received a premium or consideration; that he is not to be affected l
rise or fall of markets; but that the *gross* market price of the *sound,* and the *gross* m
price of the *damaged* goods, are to be the test by which the rate of damage up
amount insured is to be adjusted; the insurer being liable, besides, for all the extra ch
arising out of the damage.

In the first case stated, the merchant's loss by damage is 25*l.* upon 40*l.*, or 6
cent.; in the second, 10*l.* upon 10*l.*, or 100 per cent.; in the third, 15*l.* upon 20*l.*,
per cent. If the duty, freight, and charges, were diminished in proportion to the
nished value of the goods, the loss in each case would be 50 per cent. upon th
price, as it is 50 per cent. upon the gross price. As far as the duty is concerned, g
ment, upon many articles, will reduce the duty in proportion to the diminution
value of the goods; and if the freight were reduced in a similar manner, the me
would always be indemnified for his loss by the insurer. But the practice with
to freight in this country admits of no such arrangement; freight being paid accord
the quantity delivered.

To make the principle upon which claims for particular average are adj
and its bearing, still clearer, we shall illustrate it by a few more cases. Suppo
packages to be insured at cost price—a cask of rice and a cask of sugar—each we
10 cwt.; the cost of each at the port of shipment 10*l.*, the freight of each 10*s.* pe
at the port of delivery, both articles free from duty, and to arrive at a market wh
more than the cost price is realised: assuming that both packages are damaged
cent. — the rice by loss of quality, the sugar by loss of weight, the statement wil
follows: —

	£ s.	£
10 cwt. of rice, had it arrived sound, would have produced	15 0	
Less freight on 10 cwt. at 10*s.* per cwt.	5 0	
		10
But being damaged, did only produce	7 10	
Less freight on 10 cwt. at 10*s.* per cwt.	5 0	
		2
Merchant's loss		£

						£ s.	£ s.
) cwt. of sugar, if sound, would have produced	-		-		-	15 0	
Less freight on 10 cwt. at 10s. per cwt.	-		-		-	5 0	
							10 0
he barrel being damaged, did only weigh 5 cwt., and produce		-				7 10	
Less freight on 5 cwt. at 10s. per cwt.		-				2 10	
							5 0
Merchant's loss	-		-		-		£5 0

each case the merchant is entitled to recover from his insurer 5l., or 50 per cent., 10l., the sum insured, which, although an indemnity to him for his loss on the sugar, from being so for his loss upon the rice. If the merchant would contrive so to his contract with the ship owner for freight, as to reduce the freight in proportion depreciation in the value of the damaged commodity, he would be completely pro-. The ship owner might on his side protect himself by insurance from loss by :tion of quality, as he now does from loss by reduction of quantity. But we have ly more than once adverted to the difficulty of breaking in upon established prac-

The merchants go on from year to year complaining of the losses to which they bject from this awkward contrivance, while no steps are taken to improve it. To that the principle is equitable as between the merchant and his insurer, we subjoin nore statement, where the damage is taken at 100 per cent. :—

						£ s	£ s.
cwt. of rice, if sound, would have produced	-		-		-	15 0	
Less freight on 10 cwt. at 10s. per cwt.	-		-		-	5 0	
							10 0
:ing totally spoiled, did produce nothing	-		-		-		
The merchant being still liable for the freight		-		-			5 0
Making his loss	-		-		-		£15 0

receives 10l. only from the insurer.

cwt. of sugar, if sound, would have produced	-		-		-	15 0	
Less freight on 10 cwt. at 10s. per cwt.	-		-			5 0	
							10 0
ae barrel being washed out produces nothing	-		-				
The merchant, however, not being liable to pay freight		-					
His loss is only	-		-		-		£10 0

ch he recovers from the insurer.

ill be observed, that in each case the insurer pays 10l., or the full sum upon which he received his m.

ien whole cargoes, or parcels of goods of considerable value, are insured, the clause in licy which protects the insurer from particular average under a certain per centage, n partially set aside. Thus, if a cargo of 500 hogsheads of sugar, valued at 10,000l., damaged to the extent of 460l., the merchant, supposing the protecting clause to n in force, would recover nothing from the insurer, the loss not amounting to 5 per

The additional written clause, by which it is the practice to modify the printed , is as follows:—" Particular average, payable upon each 10 hhds. sugar, 10 and 50 bags coffee, and 10 bags cotton, following numbers, and upon each package nufactured goods, chest of indigo, bag of wool or silk, the same as if separately d." Such clauses may be, and are, introduced ad libitum by mutual consent of in- and insured, the premium or consideration being arranged accordingly.

e protecting clause is considered, on the other hand, by the insurers, exceedingly un-:tory in some respects; and they, as occasion requires, insist upon additional pro-. Thus, saltpetre, hides, cocoa, and tin plates, are generally warranted free from ilar average, unless the ship be stranded; and upon tobacco, it is customary for surers to make themselves liable only to such part of the particular average as ex- 5 per cent., throwing 5 per cent. upon the merchant.

ticular Average on Freight.—The clause, as far as it affects "freight," calls for no ilar comment. Particular average upon freight can only arise, according to prevail- actice, from loss of weight; and whenever the loss of weight amounts to 3 per cent. rards, the ship owner is entitled to recover from his insurer. The ship owner, upon ival of the ship at its port of destination, is entitled to hold the goods as security he freight is paid. If the owner of the goods should prove insolvent, and the should be entirely spoiled by sea damage during the voyage, and the ship owner se his freight, he has no claim upon the insurer; because, although his collateral y is destroyed by a peril of the sea, his right to receive freight remains unimpaired, is against the loss or impairing of this right that the insurer protects him.

icular Average on Ships.—Particular average upon ships is a subject somewhat eset with difficulties. There is scarcely a ship that makes a voyage of any length, es not sustain some damage. The clause in the policy warranting the ship free

from particular average under 3 per cent., unless stranded, protects the insurer from
constant recurrence of petty claims; but, in addition to this, it is the practice to class
damage, that a ship sustains in the prosecution of her voyage, under two heads: ordin
damage, or wear and tear; and extraordinary damage, or particular average. T
splitting of sails, the breaking of anchors and cables, the upsetting of windlasses,
losses that come under the first head. The carrying away of masts and bulwarks, dama
to the copper sheathing and hull, from striking on rocks, come under the second.

When a ship sustains damage, if she be on her first voyage, the whole expense of
repairs is made good by the insurers. But if she be not on her first voyage, it is
established custom that the insurer pays no more than two thirds of the repairs,
owner of the vessel having, as it is thought, an equivalent for the one third which falls up
him, in the substitution of new work for old. Where the nature of the damage is su
as to require that the copper should be stripped off the ship's bottom, the insurer pa
the difference between the price of the old and the new copper on the weight of the
copper stripped off; the excess in weight of the new over the old copper is paid
by the ship owner; and the labour of stripping and replacing the copper is p
for on the principle already mentioned. In any general rule of this kind, it must
obvious that the ship owner will sometimes gain and sometimes lose by an accident.
soon as the ship owner, or his captain, learns that his vessel has met with an accide
or as soon after as possible, he summons regular surveyors to examine his vessel a
report all defects, discriminating between those defects that have arisen from perils
the sea, and those from wear and tear. The first only are made good by the insur
together with all charges, such as surveyors' fees, dock dues, &c. caused by the necess
of undergoing repair. It has been already observed, that when a ship is obliged, in
progress of her voyage, to put into port for the purpose of repair, although the owner
the ship be subjected to great expense for the wages and maintenance of his crew duri
the detention, he can recover no part of this expense from the insurer; the doctrine bei
that the owner of the ship is bound to navigate his vessel, and that the insurer does
undertake to guarantee that the voyage shall be completed within any specific tin
Such is the doctrine, at least, in this country, and the practice is founded upon it; but
all other countries the doctrine and practice are the reverse. For in all other countr
allowance is made to the ship owner for the wages and maintenance of the crew duri
the whole period that the ship is under repair. Where a vessel sustains damage and u
dergoes repair in the progress of her voyage, and is subsequently lost, the insurer
liable both for the particular average and a total loss. Or the owner of the ship m
if he please, insure the amount expended in repair; and then, in the event of subsequ
loss, the insurer is liable for the total loss only, but in the event of subsequent safe arriv
the average is augmented by the charge of insurance.

The operation of the clause warranting the ship free from average under 3 per ce
unless general, or the ship be stranded, may now be clearly seen. If a ship be insu
and valued at 10,000l. and the repairs of the vessel do not, after all the deductions ab
referred to, amount to 3 per cent., there is no claim upon the insurer, unless the ves
shall have been stranded.—(See AVERAGE.)

Stranding.—The term stranded is not well chosen, admitting of more than one c
struction; and the clause of which it forms a part is imperfectly conceived. And
settlements of accounts, when differences arise, the parties who discuss them are m
apt to strive for that interpretation of terms and clauses which is favourable to their
terests, than for that which is best adapted for general purposes. It is commonly
derstood that mere striking the ground and coming off is not a stranding; it be
necessary, in order to fall within that term, that the ship should remain on the groun
rock, as it may happen, and that efforts should be made to float her. Striking on
anchor and leaking dangerously is not a stranding. We shall only adduce two ill
trations, for the purpose of showing how ill adapted this clause is as a means to an e
Corn and other such articles are warranted free from particular average, unless
ship be stranded, because the insurers, considering these articles to be peculiarly s
ceptible of damage, will not consent to take that risk, except on some extraordin
occasion. A ship, laden with corn, makes a very stormy passage from the Balti
London, and damages the whole of her cargo. Upon arrival off our coast she is strand
but got off without straining or sustaining any damage. The insurer is held to be li
for the damage to the corn, under the clause of the policy. On another occasion, a
a very favourable passage to our coast, a ship strikes upon a shoal, but is not strane
sustaining, however, so much damage that she arrives at London with six feet wate
her hold, and her cargo almost wholly spoiled. The insurer is held not to be liable u
the clause of the policy.

General Average.—The insurer is bound to make good all general average wit
exception, however trifling the amount. General average is treated as though altoge

ected with particular average; and damage to the goods not amounting to 3 per
not payable by the insurer, although there may be also a general average, and the
and particular average together may amount to more than 3 or 5 per cent. Ge-
verage is a charge which must be paid by the merchant and ship owner, even if
red; although, when insured, he transfers, as it were, in virtue of his insurance, the
from himself to his insurer. All the elements that can by possibility enter into
average may be classed under four heads: —1. Sacrifice of part of the ship and
2. Sacrifice of part of the cargo and freight; 3. Remuneration of services required
eral preservation; 4. Expense of raising money to replace what has been sacrificed,
remunerate services.

Vhen any part of the ship is sacrificed for the general benefit, the owner is entitled
ve (deducting, of course, his share of contribution) the amount of his outlay in
lacing of such sacrifice; allowance being made, on the principle stated above,
ld work and materials are replaced with new. The deduction of one third, however,
t invariably apply. For instance, one sixth only is taken off the price of an iron
at is slipped from for the general benefit, because iron cables are calculated to
a great number of years; and no deduction is ever made from the price of an-
The charge of replacing the loss may amount to considerably more than the
st, computing the value at the place where the ship was originally fitted. Thus,
of replacing an anchor and cable slipped from in the Downs, is frequently double
e of the anchor and cable at London. But whatever the charge may be, such
forms the basis of settlement.

crifice of the cargo and freight takes place in jettison, or where part of the cargo
overboard to lighten the vessel. Upon arrival in port, after such jettison, the
f the goods jettisoned is entitled to receive (deducting his share of contribution)
e goods would have produced nett to him, supposing them to have arrived sound;
owner of the ship is entitled to receive (deducting his share of contribution) the
to which he would have been entitled upon the safe delivery of the goods.

emuneration of services and other charges. When a ship loses her anchors and
very large sums are frequently awarded to boatmen who venture off to her with
es at the imminent hazard of their lives. A ship disabled at sea is towed into
another, and remuneration for such service is awarded according to the value
he detention occasioned, and the loss sustained. The ship rendering the service
laden with fish or fruit that may be totally spoiled by the detention, or may be
st. A ship captured by the enemy may be re-captured by a man of war or armed
t vessel; here, again, salvage is awarded according to the circumstances of
. All these charges are general average; that is to say, must be distributed over
ight, and cargo. When a ship, with her cargo, is driven on shore, the expense
pting to get her off is general average. If she cannot be got off without dis-
, the expense of discharging is general average; but the expense of getting the
after the cargo has been taken out falls exclusively upon the ship. The ware-
of the cargo, and other expenses incurred for its preservation, are charges exclu-
on the cargo. The expense of reloading is borne by the freight. When a
s into port in distress, the pilotage inwards is general average; the pilotage out-
a charge upon the freight. This distribution of charges has settled into a
well established practice; and upon this principle claims are settled at the offices,
loyd's.

e money required to meet the above charges is sometimes attainable without
If the accident happen near home, and the ship owner be respectable, he
the money, and recovers from the various parties concerned so soon as the
can be made up: or if the accident happen in a foreign port, where the owner of
is well known, the captain's bill upon him will sometimes be received in pay-
the charges incurred. But where such facilities do not exist, the captain is em-
to pledge his ship, freight, and cargo, as security to whoever he may prevail
supply the necessary funds. This pledge is termed a bottomry bond. By it
in admits the receipt of the money, consents to the payment of a premium
aries with the distance of the port of destination, the risk of the voyage, the
ility of the owner, and the necessities of the captain), and assigns the ship,
and cargo, as security for the re-payment of the money advanced and the
d premium. Should the captain consider the bottomry premium demanded of
bitant, or should he deem it preferable in other respects, he may sell a portion of
for the purpose of raising such money as he may stand in need of towards the
on of his voyage. The expense of raising the requisite funds, whether by com-
by bottomry premium, or by loss on the sale of the cargo, is charged to those
r whose interest the money is required. Thus, if a ship, having struck upon a
s into port in distress, and is obliged to unload to repair; supposing the par-

ticular average upon the ship to amount to 500*l*. ; the general average, consisti**
assistance into port and expense of unloading, 200*l*. ; particular charges on freight**
sisting of expense of reloading and pilotage outwards, 100*l*. ; and particular ch**
on cargo, consisting of warehouse rent and repair of packages, 200*l*. ; and the expe**
raising money should be 20 per cent. ; — these sums would be severally increased b**
addition, and would be raised to 600*l*., 240*l*., 120*l*., and 240*l*. — (See Bottomry.)*

It still remains to be inquired in what proportion the general average is to be pa**
the different owners of the cargo, and the owner of ship and freight. Almos**
general averages are adjusted at the ship's port of destination, and the values of the**
and cargo are taken at what they would produce in their actual state upon arrival**
the freight according to what is actually receivable, less the wages of the captain**
crew ; the general average being distributed in proportion to these values. Shoul**
cargo be altogether worthless, it cannot be made to contribute ; and should**
wages of the crew exceed the freight, then the freight is not liable to contribute. **
case of jettison, the party whose property has been sacrificed for the general be**
receives indemnity on the same principle ; the value to which he is entitled being**
his property would have produced *nett*, supposing it to have been sold on the arri**
the vessel — the same value serving for the basis of his proportion of contribution. **
few cases occur, where the general average is adjusted at the port of departure. **
if a ship, outward bound to the British colonies, cut from an anchor and cable i**
Downs, or incur other general average on our own coast, the insurances being p**
pally effected in this country, it is the custom to adjust it on the spot, by which n**
both delay and expense are avoided. On these occasions, the values at the port of**
ment are taken as the basis of contribution. A total loss, subsequently to a ge**
average, does not exonerate the insurer from his prior liability ; and although it is**
tomary with the ship owner, or his agent, specifically to insure the money expende**
average, for the purpose of protecting the insurer against any greater liability than**
per cent., he is not absolutely obliged to do so. When the average funds are rais**
bottomry, the party advancing them takes the ship, freight, and cargo, as securit**
charges a premium to cover the risk of the ship's non-arrival at her port of destin**
And thus, on such an occasion, a subsequent total loss relieves the insurer from a**
bility to average.

The laws and customs by which averages are adjusted vary in different countries**
the insurer in this country is only liable for averages adjusted according to our**
The merchant, however, whose goods arrive at a foreign port, is obliged to submit **
laws of that port. He may thus be a considerable loser ; paying general averag**
cording to one law, and receiving from his insurer according to another. And he**
can be a gainer, because, before he is entitled to recover from his insurer, he**
prove that he has paid to the owner of the ship. This is one of the many inconven**
to which mercantile men are exposed, which cannot be removed without, what it m**
hoped will gradually take place, an assimilation of the commercial laws of dif**
countries.

Proof of Loss. — The policy of insurance is the instrument under which the**
chant and ship owner claim indemnification for all losses that are not speciall**
cepted. The proof that the loss has been sustained must also be exhibited ; s**
the title to the vessel and cargo, and the evidence of the captain and crew to es**
the circumstances out of which the claim arises. If A. were to insure his vessel f**
space of twelve months, and at the expiration of six months were to sell his ship t**
A.'s interest in the vessel having ceased, so also does his insurer's liability ; and B.**
wish to be protected, must make a new insurance. Proof of ownership, therefore**
essential preliminary to the recovery of a claim. In general practice, no difficulty**
from this, because the fact of ownership is sufficiently notorious. The bill of lad**
in most cases, satisfactory proof that the cargo was on board, as well as of the amo**
freight.

Valued and open Policies. — If an insurance for 2,000*l*. be effected upon 100**
of sugar, valued at 20*l*. per hhd., the bill of lading, showing that the vessel had 100**
on board, establishes the interest at 2,000*l*., and the policy is termed a valued **
But if an insurance for 2,000*l*. be effected on 100 hhds. of sugar, and nothing be exp**
as to value, the bill of lading only establishes that 100 hhds. are on board, without**
lishing the amount of interest. The production of the invoice, showing the cost**
goods, is necessary to that end, the policy being termed an open one.

Return of Premium for short Interest. — In a valued policy, when the whole**
property insured does not appear to have been shipped, the difference betwe**
quantity insured and the quantity shipped is termed short interest. Thus, if 2,0**
insured upon 100 hhds. of sugar, valued at 20*l*. per hhd., and 80 hhds. only be sh**
as the insurer's liability does not extend beyond 1,600*l*., so he is obliged to retu**

ium upon 400*l.* to which no risk atfaches. This return of premium is called a
n for short interest.

r Over-Insurance.—In an open policy, where the value shipped is not equal to the
insured, the difference is termed over-insurance. If a merchant, A., make an ince for 5,000*l.* upon goods, without specifying any value, from Calcutta to London,
remium being 60*s.* and the stamp duty 5*s.* per cent., the amount of interest that
hes to the policy is so fixed, that he is neither to gain nor lose by the transaction in
vent of the vessel's loss, supposing his insurance to be sufficient. To entitle him to
er a profit, the profit to be insured must be stipulated in the policy. The expense
surance upon 100*l.* being 3*l.* 5*s.*, it is clear that every 100*l.* insurance covers 96*l.* 15*s.*
al cost; that is to say, protects the merchant from loss to that extent in case of
oss of the vessel. If, then, we assume the invoice of the goods shipped to be 40,000
s, or, at the exchange of 2*s.* per rupee, 4,000*l.*, the interest attaching to the policy
ertained as follows : — If 96*l* 15*s.* cost is insured by 100*l.* insurance, what will
l. cost be insured by? Answer, 4,135*l.* Under such circumstances, although a
exists for 5,000*l.*, the insured is not able to prove interest for more than 4,135*l.* ;
onsequently, the insured being entitled to recover no more than that sum in case of
he insurer is called upon to make a return of premium for over-insurance upon 865*l.*
though we have treated separately of returns for short interest and over-insurance,
ould observe that these terms in practice are used indiscriminately; and, indeed,
nnot say that we perceive much advantage in making the distinction, or preserving
stinctive appellations.

ometimes happens that the property expected in a vessel is not all insured at one time
ne policy. But this makes no difference in the principle of settlement according to
w; although, according to the laws of most other countries, the policies take prece-
of one another according to their dates, the whole short interest falling upon the policy
icies last effected. The foreign law, in this instance, appears to us the more equi-
nd reasonable of the two; and that our reason for thinking so may be intelligible, and
ain assent or meet with refutation, we shall state a case of short interest upon a num-
policies, such as not unfrequently appears. A merchant, A., orders his correspond-
Calcutta to ship for his account a quantity of sugar, not exceeding 1,000 tons, at a
not exceeding 20*l.* per ton. In due time he receives a letter from his correspondent
wledging the receipt of his order, and expressing confident hopes of being able to
ase the quantity, or the greater part of it, at the limits prescribed, and promising to
as he proceeds. A., on receipt of this letter, say on 1st of January, makes
isional insurance for 5,000*l.* upon sugar valued at 20*l.* per ton. Continuing with-
rther advices, and fearing lest his correspondent's letter should have miscarried,
at he might have property afloat uninsured, on the 1st of February, 1st of March,
st of April, he effects similar insurances, thus covering the whole 1,000 tons. He
quently receives advice that his correspondent had not been able to purchase more
alf the quantity ordered, at his limit, and he recovers from his insurers half the
im upon each policy. Now, it was not at all improbable that he might have re-
advice from his correspondent, as he expected, much sooner. And if he had re-
advice in the middle of February, of the shipment of 500 tons, and that the ship
contained them was totally lost in the river Hooghly, the insurers upon the two
licies would have been liable for a total loss. And it appears to us a defective
ement, by which a party, who is at one time exposed to a total loss, should at another
pelled to return half his premium. It is true that the merchant may, if he please,
in his policies, a clause by which the policies shall be made to succeed one another;
should say that the law, in insurance cases, as in the disposal of the property of
ed persons, ought to be the best general disposition, leaving to individuals the right
lification according to particular circumstances.

urn for Double Insurance.—Besides returns for short interest and over-insurance,
re returns for double insurance. They are, in fact, to all intents and purposes, the
hing. Double insurance exists where the party, through forgetfulness, makes an
nce upon his property twice over; or where the shippers and consignees of goods,
ncertain of one another's intentions, effect each an insurance upon them; or where
tain of a vessel in foreign parts, fearing lest his advices should not reach his owner,
an insurance upon it, and the owner at the same time, acting with equal caution,
one also. The observations already made upon returns for short interest, and
he difference between our laws and those of other countries, apply with equal
ere.

have now gone over all the principal topics connected with marine assurance.
who peruse this article with ordinary attention will, we hope, gain a tolerably
nsight into the principles and practice of the business. But a perfectly familiar

acquaintance with it can only be acquired by those who are daily conversant w
its details.*

Duty on Policies of Marine Insurance. — Amount and Expediency of such Duty.
All policies of marine insurance must be on stamped paper, the duties on which are
follows: —

For every 100*l.* insured on a voyage in the coasting trade of the kingdom, where
premium does not exceed 20*s.* per cent., 1*s.* 3*d.*

Where premium does exceed 20*s.* per cent., 2*s.* 6*d.*

For every 100*l.* insured to or from any colonial or foreign port, where the premi
does not exceed 20*s.* per cent., 2*s.* 6*d.*

Where premium does exceed 20*s.* per cent., 5*s.*

For every 100*l.* insured on ships for time, (no ship can be insured for time on
stamp, for a longer period than twelve months,) 5*s.*

This duty has been strongly objected to, and with good reason. Its obvious tenden
is to discourage the coasting trade, by imposing a duty on goods carried by sea, fr
which those carried by land and canals are exempted; and we believe it will be fou
that this unjust preference costs more to the public in the greater carriage of goods se
through its means, by the more expensive channel of inland conveyance, than all t
that portion of the duty which affects coasting vessels produces to the revenue. But
other portion of the tax, or that which affects vessels engaged in the foreign or color
trade, is still more objectionable. It is immaterial to a merchant sending a ship to s
whether he insure her in London, Amsterdam, or Hamburgh; and as policies execut
in the last two cities are either wholly exempted from duties, or subject to such only
are merely nominal, the effect of the duty is to transfer to the Continent a considera
part of the business of marine insurance, that would otherwise be transacted in Lond
That such is the case, is known to every commercial man; and is evident from the fa
that, at an average of the three years ending with 1819, the duties on marine insurar
in Great Britain and Ireland produced 296,059*l.* a year; while, notwithstanding
increase of navigation, they only produced, at an average of the three years ending w
1830, 239,236*l.* a year. Last year (1830) they fell off to 220,007. It is plain, therefo
that this duty is operating most injuriously; that it is driving a valuable branch
business from amongst us; and even though it had no such effect, still it is sufficien
clear that a tax on providence, or on the endeavour to guarantee the safety of prope
at sea, is not one that ought to exist in any country, and least of all in so commercia
country as England. We, therefore, hope that the expediency of continuing this
will early come under the consideration of the legislature; and that it will be ei
unconditionally repealed, or some less objectionable substitute found for it.

Form of a Policy of Insurance executed at Lloyd's.

S. G.

£800.

IN THE NAME OF GOD, Amen. Charles Brown and Co. as well in their own names a
and in the name and names of all and every other person or persons to whom the same c
may, or shall appertain, in part or in all, doth make assurance and cause themselves
them and every of them, to be insured, lost or not lost, at and from St. Petersburgh to
port or ports in the United Kingdom, upon any kind of goods and merchandises, and
upon the body, tackle, apparel, ordnance, munition, artillery, boat and other furnitur
and in the good ship or vessel called the Swift, whereof is master, under God, for this pre
voyage, Bright, or whoever else shall go for master in the said ship, or by whatsoever
name or names the said ship, or the master thereof, is or shall be named or called; begin
the adventure upon the said goods and merchandises from the loading thereof on boar
said ship
upon the said ship, &c.

Stamp
£2.

and so shall continue and endure during her abode there,
the said ship, &c. And further, until the said ship, with all her ordnance, tackle, app
&c. and goods and merchandises whatsoever, shall be arrived at her final port of discharg
above) upon the said ship, &c. until she hath moored at anchor twenty.four hours in
safety; and upon the goods and merchandises, until the same be there discharged and
landed. And it shall be lawful for the said ship, &c. in this voyage, to proceed and sa
and touch and stay at any ports or places whatsoever, without prejudice to this insur
The said ship, &c. goods and merchandises, &c. for so much as concerns the assure
agreement between the assured and assurers in this policy, are and shall be valued at
hundred pounds, being on the captain's one fourth share of said ship, said one fourth
valued at that sum. Touching the adventures and perils which we the assurers are cont
to bear, and do take upon us in this voyage; they are of the seas, men of war, fire, ene
pirates, rovers, thieves, jettisons, letters of mart and countermart, surprisals, takings a
arrests, restraints, and detainments, of all kings, princes and people, of what nation, c
tion, or quality soever, barratry of the master and mariners, and of all other perils, I
and misfortunes, that have or shall come to the hurt, detriment, or damage of the said
and merchandises and ship, &c. or any part thereof; offences against the revenue c
United Kingdom of Great Britain or Ireland excepted. And, in case of any loss or m
tune, it shall be lawful for the assured, their factors, servants, and assignees, to sue, l
and travel for, in, and about the defence, safeguard, and recovery, of the said good
merchandises and ship, &c. or any part thereof, without prejudice to this insurance;
charges whereof we the assurers will contribute, each one according to the rate and qu
of his sum herein assured. And it is agreed by us, the insurers, that this writing, or

* This very valuable article (on Marine Insurance) has been, as the reader will easily perceive
nished by a gentleman thoroughly conversant with the principles and details of the business.

of assurance, shall be of as much force and effect, as the surest writing or policy of assurance, heretofore made in Lombard Street, or in the Royal Exchange, or elsewhere in London. And so we the assurers are contented, and do hereby promise and bind ourselves, each one for his own part, our heirs, executors, and goods, to the assured, their executors, administrators, and assigns, for the true performance of the premises, confessing ourselves paid the consideration due unto us for this assurance by the assured, at and after the rate of five guineas per cent. to return one pound per cent. if the voyage end on the east coast of England.

In Witness whereof, we, the assurers, have subscribed our names and sums assured in London,

N.B. Corn, fish, salt, fruit, flour, and seeds, are warranted free from average, unless general, or the ship be stranded.—Sugar, tobacco, hemp, flax, hides, and skins, are warranted free from average under five pounds per cent. ; and all other goods, also the ship and freight, are warranted free from average under three pounds per cent., unless general, or the ship be stranded.

£ 500.   Joseph White, Five hundred pounds. 1st of Sept. 1831.
£ 300.   Thomas Black by George Green, Three hundred pounds. 1st of Sept. 1831.

Policy by the Indemnity Mutual Marine Assurance Company.

Established 1824.

Whereas William Grey hath represented to us whose hands and seals are hereunto subscribed and affixed, and who are two of the directors of the Indemnity Mutual Marine Assurance Company, that he is interested in, or duly authorised as owner, agent, or otherwise, to make the assurance hereinafter mentioned and described, with the Indemnity Mutual Marine Assurance Company, and hath covenanted or otherwise obliged himself to pay forthwith for the use of the said Company, at the office of the said Company, the sum of sixty-two pounds ten shillings as a premium or consideration, at and after the rate of twenty-five shillings per cent. for such assurance. Now this Policy of Assurance witnesseth, that in consideration of the premises and of the said sum of sixty-two pounds ten shillings, We do for ourselves and each of us, covenant and agree with the said William Grey, his executors, administrators, and assigns, that the capital stock and funds of the said Company shall, according to the provisions of the deed of settlement of the said Company, and the resolutions entered into at two extraordinary general courts of the said Company held on the twenty-ninth day of August, and the twentieth day of September, one thousand eight hundred and twenty-seven, be subject and liable to pay and make good, and shall be applied to pay and make good all such losses and damages hereinafter expressed as may happen to the subject matter of this policy, and may attach to this policy in respect of the sum of five thousand pounds hereby assured, which assurance is hereby declared to be upon

1/250.   250 hhds. of sugar valued at 20l. each, average payable upon each 10 hhds. following landing numbers, the same as if separately insured, laden or to be laden on board the ship or vessel called the Nelly, whereof Turner is at present master, or whoever shall go for master of the said ship or vessel, lost or not lost, at and from Grenada to London, including the risk of crat to and from the vessel, warranted to sail on or before the 1st of August, 1831. And We do covenant and agree, that the assurance aforesaid shall commence upon the said ship, at and from Grenada, and until she hath moored at anchor twenty-four hours in good safety ; and upon the freight and goods or merchandise on board thereof, from the loading of the said goods or merchandise on board the said ship or vessel at London, and until the said goods or merchandise be discharged and safely landed at   And that it shall be lawful for the said ship or vessel to proceed and sail to, and touch, and stay at any ports or places whatsoever, in the course of her said voyage, for all necessary purposes, without prejudice to this assurance. And touching the adventures and perils which the capital stock and funds of the said Company are made liable unto, or are intended to be made liable unto, by this assurance, they are, of the seas, men-of-war, fire, enemies, pirates, rovers, thieves, jettisons, letters of mart and countermart, surprisals, takings at sea, arrests, restraints, and detainments of all kings, princes, and people, of what nation, condition, or quality soever ; barratry of the master and mariners, and of all other perils, losses, and misfortunes, that have or shall come to the hurt, detriment, or damage of the aforesaid subject matter of this assurance, or any part thereof. And in case of any loss or misfortune, it shall be lawful to the assured, their factors, servants, and assigns, to sue, labour, and travel for, in and about the defence, safeguard, and recovery of the aforesaid subject matter of this assurance, or any part thereof, without prejudice to this assurance, the charges whereof the capital stock and funds of the said Company shall bear in proportion to the sum hereby assured. And it is declared and agreed, that corn, fish, salt, fruit, flour, and seed, shall be and are warranted free from average unless general, or the ship be stranded ; and that sugar, tobacco, hemp, flax, hides, and skins, shall be and are warranted free from average under five pounds per centum ; that all other goods, also the ship and freight, shall be and are warranted free from average under three pounds per centum unless general, or the ship be stranded. Provided nevertheless, that the capital stock and funds of the said Company shall alone be liable, according to the provisions of the deed of settlement and the resolutions abovementioned, to answer and make good all claims and demands whatsoever, under or by virtue of this policy ; and that no proprietor of the said Company, his or her heirs, executors, or administrators, shall be in anywise subject or liable to any claims or demands, nor be in anywise charged by reason of this policy beyond the amount of his or her share or shares in the capital stock of the said Company, it being one of the original or fundamental principles of the said Company, that the responsibility of the individual proprietors shall, in all cases, be limited to their respective shares in the said capital stock.

In Witness whereof, We have hereunto set our hands and seals in London, the tenth day of July, 1831.

Sealed and delivered ⎱
  in the presence of ⎰
                  E. F.

A. B.   (L. S.)
C. D.   (L. S.)

III. Insurance (Fire).

Insurance against fire is a contract of indemnity, by which the insurer, in conside of a certain premium received by him, either in a gross sum or by annual payn undertakes to indemnify the insured against all loss or damage he may sustain houses or other buildings, stock, goods, and merchandise, by fire, during a spe period.

Insurances against fire are hardly ever made by individuals, but almost alw: joint stock companies, of which there are several in all the considerable towns throu the empire. Of these, the *Sun*, the *Phœnix*, the *British*, &c. insure at their own and for their own profit: but there are others, which are called *contribution societ* which every person insured becomes a member or proprietor, and participates in the or loss of the concern. The *Hand in Hand*, *Westminster*, &c. are of this descripti

The conditions on which the different offices insure are contained in their *pro₁* which are printed on the back of every policy; and it is in most instances exp conditioned, that they undertake to pay the loss, not exceeding the sum insured, *cording to the exact tenor of their printed proposals."*

Nothing can be recovered from the insurers, in the event of loss, unless the insuring had an interest or property in the thing insured at the time when the insu was effected, and when the loss happened. It often occurs that no one office insure to the full amount required by an individual who has a large property; a such a case the party, to cover his whole interest, is obliged to insure at different o But, in order to prevent the frauds that might be practised by insuring the full va various offices, there is, in the proposals issued by all the companies, an article v declares, that persons insuring must give notice of any other insurance made else upon the same houses or goods, that the same may be specified and allowed by in ment on the policy, in order that each office may bear its rateable proportion of an that may happen; and unless such notice be given of each insurance, to the office : another insurance is made on the same effects, the insurance made without such will be void.

Any trustee, mortgagee, reversioner, factor, or agent, has sufficient interest goods under his custody, to effect a policy of insurance, provided the nature of suc: perty be distinctly specified at the time of executing such policy.

Most of the offices except in their proposals against making good any loss occa: by "invasion," "foreign enemy," "civil commotions," &c.; and under this con the Sun Fire Office was exonerated from the loss occasioned by the disgraceful pr ings of the mob in 1780.

One of the principal conditions in the proposals has reference to the proof of The Sun Fire Office (see *post*), and most other offices, make it a condition, th: individual claiming shall "procure a certificate, under the hands of the ministe churchwardens, and some other respectable inhabitants of the parish or place, no cerned or interested in such loss, importing that they are well acquainted with th racter and circumstances of the person or persons insured or claiming; and do kno verily believe, that he, she, or they, really, and by misfortune, without any fraud c practice, have sustained by such fire the loss or damage, as his, her, or their loss, value therein mentioned." This condition has given rise to a great deal of disc in the courts; but it has been finally decided, that the procuring of the certifica: *condition precedent to the payment of any loss, and that its being wrongfully refused u excuse the want of it.*

The risk commences in general from the signing of the policy, unless there be other time specified. Policies of insurance may be annual, or for a term of years annual premium; and it is usual for the office, by way of indulgence, to allow days after each year for the payment of the premium for the next year in succe and provided the premium be paid within that time, the insured is considered as the protection of the office.

A policy of insurance is not in its nature assignable, nor can it be transferred w the *express consent* of the office. When, however, any person dies, his interest re in his executors or administrators respectively, who succeed or become entitled property, provided such representatives respectively procure their right to be in: on the policy.

(For further details, see *Marshall on Insurance*, book 4.; *Park on Insurance*, c

Insurances are generally divided into *common*, *hazardous*, and *doubly hazardous* distinguishing characteristics of these may be learned from the subjoined propo the Sun Fire Office. The charge for insuring property of the first description usually 1*s.* 6*d.* per cent., the second 2*s.* 6*d.*, and the third 4*s.* 6*d.* These char exclusive of the duty payable to government, of 1*s.* on the policy, and 3*s.* per cent. sum in the policy.

e subjoin a copy of a policy of insurance on a house valued at 1,000*l*., and furni-
plate, books, &c. in the same, valued also at 1,000*l*., executed by the Sun Fire
e, and of the proposals indorsed on the same. The latter correspond in most
culars with those issued by the other offices.

eived, for the insurance of property undermentioned, Xmas 1830, to Xmas 1831.				SUN FIRE OFFICE.	To be paid annually at Xmas.			
	£	s.	d.			£	s.	d.
....	0	0	0		Premium	1	10	0
um	1	10	0		Duty	3	0	0
....	3	0	0					
	£4	10	0			£4	10	0

N°. ———

ʀᴇᴀs A. B. Esq. of No. ——————— Street, has paid the sum of one pound
illings to the Society of the Sun Fire Office in London, and has agreed to pay,
use to be paid, to them, at their said office, the sum of one pound ten shillings
e 25th of December, 1831, and the like sum of one pound ten shillings yearly
e 25th day of December during the continuance of this policy, for insurance
loss or damage by fire, on his now dwelling house only, situate as aforesaid, brick,
housand pounds; household goods, wearing apparel, printed books, and plate therein
one thousand pounds.

Now, ᴋɴᴏᴡ ʏᴇ, That, from the date of these presents, and so long as the said A. B.
duly pay, or cause to be paid, the said sum of one pound ten shillings at the times
lace aforesaid; and the trustees or acting members of the said Society, for the
peing; shall agree to accept the same; the stock and fund of the said Society shall
pject and liable to pay to the said A. B., his executors, administrators, and assigns,
ch his damage and loss which he, the said A. B., shall suffer by fire, not exceeding
each head of insurance, the sum or sums above-mentioned, amounting in the whole
more than two thousand pounds, according to the exact tenor of their printed
sals, endorsed on this policy, and of an act of parliament, of the 55th of George
hird, for charging a duty on persons whose property shall be insured against loss by
Iɴ Wɪᴛɴᴇss whereof, we (three of the trustees or acting members for the said
y) have hereunto set our hands and seals, the 24th day of December, 1830.

C. D.	(ʟ. s.)
E. F.	(ʟ. s.)
G. H.	(ʟ. s.)

d and sealed (being stamped
ording to act of parliament)
he presence of   J. K.

. B. — The interest in this policy may be transferred by indorsement, made and
d at the office, if the trustees or acting members approve thereof, but not other-

(ɪɴᴅᴏʀsᴇᴍᴇɴᴛ ᴏɴ ᴛʜᴇ ᴘᴏʟɪᴄʏ.)

SUN FIRE OFFICE.

office insures against loss or damage by fire, in Great Britain and Ireland, all descriptions of
gs, including mills and manufactories, and goods, wares, and merchandise, in the same; ships in
, or in dock; craft on navigable rivers and canals, and the goods laden on the same; waggons
ig the roads, and their contents; and farming-stock of all descriptions, upon the following terms
iditions : —

Common Insurances.

ildings covered with slates, tiles, or metals, and built on all sides with brick or stone, or separated
-walls of brick or stone, and wherein no hazardous trade or manufacture is carried on, or hazard-
ds deposited.
ods in buildings as above described, such as household goods, plate, jewels in private use, apparel,
ited books; liquors in private use, merchandise, stock and utensils in trade, not hazardous, and
stock.
  6*d*. per cent. per annum, with certain exceptions.

Hazardous Insurances.

ildings of timber or plaster, or not wholly separated by partition-walls of brick or stone, or not
with slates, tiles, or metals, and thatched barns and out-houses having no chimney, nor adjoining
uilding having a chimney; and buildings falling under the description of common insurance, but
a some hazardous trade or manufacture is carried on, such as brewers (without a steam engine),
id biscuit bakers (not sea biscuit bakers), bottlers and packers of wine, spirits, or beer; chemists
a laboratory), inn-holders, maltsters (who make pale malt only), oilmen, soap-boilers, stable-
, and certain others; or in which hazardous goods are deposited, as the stock and utensils in the
ades; and, also, tallow, pitch, tar, hemp, flax, rosin, and turpentine; hay, straw, and all manner
r and corn unthreshed; apothecaries' stock, and oil; and wine and spirituous liquors as mer-
.
ns and craft, with their contents (lime barges, with *their* contents, alone excepted).
  6*d*. per cent. per annum, with certain exceptions.

Doubly Hazardous Insurances.

1. Buildings. — All thatched buildings having chimneys, or communicating with, or adjoining
buildings having one, although no hazardous trade shall be carried on, nor hazardous goods depos
therein: and all hazardous buildings, in which hazardous goods are deposited, or hazardous tr
carried on.

2. Goods. — All hazardous goods deposited in hazardous buildings, and in thatched buildings havin
chimney, nor adjoining to any building having a chimney.

3. Trades — and their stock and utensils, such as maltsters (who make brown malt), and certain oth
also, china, glass, and earthenware, saltpetre, and waggons with their contents.

At 4s. 6d. per cent. per annum, with certain exceptions.

Farming stock on any part of a farm may be insured under general policies, without the average cla
at 1s. 6d. per cent., provided it be insured to a fair average value. This office will not be subject to
loss on hay or corn, occasioned by its own natural heating, but the loss of any other property in co
quence of such fire will be made good; as will losses by fire from lightning.

Insurances may also be made by special agreement on the following risks, and on others of a sim
description, not mentioned under the 2d and 3d heads of insurance, viz. on mills of all kinds, and
stock and utensils in them; also on buildings, containing kiln, steam-engine, stove, or oven, used in
process of any manufacture, and the stock therein; sugar refiners, sea biscuit bakers, distillers, var
makers, chemists' laboratories, theatres, coach painters, colour manufacturers, varnishers, musical ins
ment makers, refiners of saltpetre, spermaceti, wax, and oil, barge and boat builders, carpenters, cab
makers, coach makers, coopers, cork burners, floor-cloth painters, japanners, lampblack makers, le
press printers, machine makers, melters of tallow and of rough fat, candle makers, cart grease mak
rope and sail makers, ship-chandlers, hemp and flax dressers, oil leather dressers, medals, curiosi
pictures, prints, drawings, statuary work, spinners of cotton, flax, lint, and wool, throughout all
operations attending the manufacturing of these materials, from the raw state into thread for the wea
and such other risks as, by reason of the nature of the trade, the narrowness of the situation, or o
dangerous circumstances, may increase the hazard thereof: all which special hazards must be inserte
the policy, to render the same valid and in force.

N. B. — Gunpowder, and buildings in which it is made, cannot be insured on any terms; neither
this office insure writings of any kind, books of accounts, ready money, bonds, bills, or any other s
rities for money.

N. B. — By an act of the 55th of Geo. 3. a duty of 3s. per annum is to be levied on every 100l. of
perty insured against fire.

N. B. — Persons may insure for more years than one, and in such cases there will be a discount allo
of 5 per cent. per annum, compound interest, on the premium and duty for every year except the firs

CONDITIONS.

Art. I. — Any person desirous of effecting insurances upon buildings or goods must furnish the of
or its agents, with a particular description thereof, and of the process of manufacture carried on ther
and if there be any omission or misrepresentation in describing the building or goods, or process of ma
facture, whereby the same may be charged at a different rate of premium than they otherwise woul
this office will not be responsible in case of any loss or damage. And if any alteration be made in
state of the buildings or goods, or process of manufacture, after such insurance shall have been effec
then the insured shall give due notice thereof, in writing, to the office or its agents, or in default of s
notice, such insurance shall become void, and no benefit be derived therefrom.

Art. II. — All policies shall be signed and sealed by three or more trustees or acting members; an
receipts are to be taken for any premiums of insurance, but such as are printed and issued from
office, and witnessed by one of its clerks or agents.

Art. III. — Houses, buildings, and goods in trust, and merchandise on commission (except as afores
may be insured, provided the same are declared in the policy to be in trust or on commission, but
otherwise.

Art. IV. — On bespeaking policies, all persons shall pay the premium to the next quarter day, and f
thence for one year more at least, or shall make a deposit for the same, and shall, as long as the mana
agree to accept the same, make all future payments annually at the said office, within fifteen days
the day limited by their respective policies, upon forfeiture of the benefit thereof.

Art. V. — Any number of houses and out-houses, and household goods, printed books, wearing app
plate, prints, jewels and trinkets in private use, stock in trade, goods in trust, or on commission, ma
insured in one policy.

Art. VI. — Persons insured by this office shall receive no benefit from their policies, if the same ho
or goods, &c. are insured in any other office, unless such insurance, and the amount thereof, be
specified and allowed by indorsement on the policy, in which case this office will pay its rateable pr
tion on any loss or damage.

Art. VII. — When any person dies, the policy and interest therein shall continue to the heir, exec
or administrator, respectively, to whom the right of the property insured shall belong, provided, b
any new payment be made, such heir, executor, or administrator, do procure his or her right
indorsed on the policy at the said office, or the premium to be paid in the name of the said heir, exec
or administrator.

Art. VIII. — Persons changing their habitations or warehouses may preserve the benefit of
policies, if the nature and circumstance of such policy be not altered; but such insurance will be c
force till such removal or alteration is allowed at the office, by indorsement on the policy.

Art. IX. — No loss or damage will be paid on fire happening by any invasion, foreign enemy, civil
motion, or any military or usurped power whatever.

Art. X. — Persons insured sustaining any loss or damage by fire are forthwith to give notice there
the office; and, as soon as possible afterwards, deliver in as particular an account of their loss or da
as the nature of the case will admit of, and make proof of the same by their oath or affirmation, acco
to the form practised in the said office, and by their books of accounts, or such other proper vouche
shall be reasonably required, and procure a certificate, under the hands of the minister and ch
wardens, and some other respectable inhabitants of the parish and place, not concerned or interest
such loss, importing that they are well acquainted with the character and circumstances of the pers
persons insured or claiming; and do know, or verily believe, that he, she, or they, really, and by m
tune, without any fraud or evil practice, have sustained by such fire the loss or damage, as his, he
their loss, to the value therein mentioned. And, till the affidavit and certificate of such, the insur
loss, shall be made and produced, the loss money shall not be payable. And, if there appear any fra
false swearing, or that the fire shall have happened by the procurement, or wilful act, means, or con
ance of the insured or claimants, he, she, or they, shall be excluded from all benefit from their pol
And in case any difference shall arise between the office and the insured, touching any loss or dar
such difference shall be submitted to the judgment and determination of arbitrators indifferently ch
whose award in writing shall be conclusive and binding on all parties.

N. B. — In every case of loss the Company reserves the right of re-instatement in preference t
payment of claims, if it should judge the former course to be more expedient; but when any l
settled and adjusted, the insured will receive immediate payment for the same, without any deducti
discount; and will not be liable to any covenants or calls for contribution to make good losses.

₊ To encourage the removal of goods, in cases of fire, this office will allow the reasonable ch
attending the same, and make good the sufferer's loss, whether destroyed, lost, or damaged, by such rem

unt of Property insured. — *Duty.* — Insurance against fire, though practised in , Holland, and some other countries, is not general any where except in Great . It has been known amongst us for a century and a half, and is now very widely *·*d. It appears from the official account, that the *gross* duty received on policies *-*ance against fire in the United Kingdom, in 1829, amounted to 773,783*l.* ; which, *·*luty is 3*s.* per cent., shows that the property insured was valued at the immense 515,855,333*l.* ! But notwithstanding the magnitude of this sum, it is still true that *·*uildings are not insured up to their full value; even in towns, many are not *·* at all; and in the country it is far from being customary to insure farm-buildings *·*yards. It is difficult to imagine that this can be owing to any thing else than *·*rbitance of the duty. On common risks the duty is no less than 200 per cent. *·*e premium; or, in other words, if a person pay to an insurance office 15*s.* for *z* 1,000*l.* worth of property, he must at the same time pay a duty of 30*s.* to go-*·*nt! On hazardous and doubly hazardous risks, the duty varies from about 120 *·*nd 80 per cent. upon the premium. Such a duty is in the last degree oppressive *·*olitic. There cannot, in fact, be the slightest doubt that, were it reduced, as it *·*o be, to *one third* its present amount, the business of insurance would be very *·*xtended; and as it could not be extended without an increase of security, and lessening the injurious consequences arising from the casualties to which pro-exposed, the reduction of the duty would be productive of the best consequences *·*olic point of view, while the increase of business would prevent the revenue from *·*aterially diminished.

Amount of Duty on Fire Insurances paid by the different English Offices for 1829.

Town.	£	s.	d.	Country — (*continued.*)	£	s.	d.
·	19,466	10	1	Bristol	3,903	7	1
·	20,199	5	1	Bristol (Crown)	1,882	16	7
·	15,812	18	9	Bristol (Union)	2,488	19	9
·	44,822	9	2	Essex (Economic)	2,925	16	10
·	25,566	5	9	Essex and Suffolk	6,444	17	11
·	30,595	16	2	Hertford (Cambridge and Country)	4,866	10	2
·Hand	11,254	10	10	Hants, Sussex, and Dorset	2,689	16	8
·	28,510	19	3	Kent	9,279	4	3
·	7,485	0	5	Leeds and Yorkshire	6,728	3	1
·a	5,378	11	7	Manchester	16,703	17	4
·	65,649	19	10	Newcastle-upon-Tyne	4,948	12	8
·	54,287	9	1	Norwich Equitable	3,491	11	2
·change	49,786	7	4	Norwich Union	61,186	13	4
·	118,856	18	4	Reading	108	3	1
·	16,285	5	4	Salamander	4,800	2	6
·ster	15,461	10	3	Salop	2,637	15	0
				Sheffield	1,804	5	4
Country.				Shields, North and South	743	16	1
·)	1,628	5	6	Suffolk, East	5,639	6	1
·ioucestershire and Pro-}	2,477	10	6	Suffolk, West	6,120	14	3
·				West of England	23,858	4	3
·am	6,186	15	5	Yorkshire	3,231	18	4

IV. INSURANCE (LIFE).

*·*part of the business of life insurance which consists of granting annuities upon treated of under INTEREST AND ANNUITIES; so that we have only to treat, *·*lace, of the insurance of sums payable at the death of the insurers or their *·*s.

*·*se an individual of a given age wishes to insure 100*l.* payable at his death, the *·*remium, or the series of annual premiums, he ought to pay an office for such *·*e, must plainly depend on the expectation of life of such individual, and on the *·*aterest, or nett profit which the insurers may make by investing the premiums. *·*respect to the first of these conditions, or the *expectation of life*, it is usual in *·*g it to have recourse to tables framed from the mortality observed to take *·*particular cities or districts, as in Northampton, Carlisle, &c. — (See INTEREST *·*NUITIES.) But though the actual decrement and expectation of life among an *·*population, at every year of their lives, were accurately determined, it is doubted *·*it would form a fair basis for an insurance office to proceed upon. The general *·*seems to be, that insured lives are decidedly above the average; for insurance *·*variably profess to act on the principle of rejecting bad lives, or of making *·*y a proportional increase of premium; and it may, besides, it is said, be fairly *·*l that persons insuring their lives are of a superior class, and are not, generally *·*, engaged in those manual and laborious occupations that are esteemed most to health. But, on the other hand, the friends of parties whose lives are sup-*·*be bad, and the parties themselves, are most anxious they should be insured: *·* far from being an uncommon practice, for certain individuals to prevail on *·*hom they happen to know, or believe to be bad lives, to insure; and then to get a *·*gnment of the policy in their favour, on their giving the "men of straw" a bonus

for their share in the fraud. At all events, there can be no question that large numb
such lives are perpetually offered for insurance ; and every individual conversant wi
business knows, that in despite of all precautions, policies are very frequently eff
upon them. Mr. Milne, on whose judgment every reliance may be placed, state
tinctly that " all the caution and selection which the offices in general can exerc
necessary to keep the lives insured up to the average goodness of the bulk of the
lation." — (*Ency. Brit.* new ed. art. *Annuities.*) Since the competition among th
ferent offices became so very keen as it has been of late years, there are but few li
bad that they will not be taken by one office or another ; and we doubt, were the r
of their experience made public, whether it would be found that there is much foun
for the opinion as to the superiority of insured lives.

With respect to the second condition in valuing an insurance, or the rate at whic
interest of money may be estimated, it is impossible to arrive at any thing like ac
conclusions. At an average, perhaps, transactions in life insurance may extend
period of 30 years from the time when they are entered into ; and in such a lengt
term the greatest changes may take place in the rate of profit and the rate of in
Mr. Finlaison, of the National Debt Office, appears to think that $4\frac{1}{2}$ per cent.
be taken as the true average rate in this country ; and that $4\frac{1}{4}$ is a rate at which n
need be apprehended. — (*Parl. Paper*, No. 284. Sess. 1829.) But this is not a
on which (as Mr. Finlaison seems to suppose) previous experience can be safe
pended upon in forming engagements for the future ; and were this the proper pla
entering upon such discussions, we think we could assign pretty solid grounds for
cluding that no institution, intended to last for the next half century, would be
ranted in reckoning upon realising more than 3 per cent. upon its investments.
should look upon this as the *maximum*, and of course could expect nothing but r
fall upon any institution founded upon the hypothesis of realising $4\frac{1}{4}$ per cent. of in
At the same time, we would not be understood as laying any undue stress upo
opinion ; and are ready to admit that there must always be more of conjecture t
certainty in such conclusions.

Security being the principal object to be aimed at by every insurance office estab
on sound principles, they would not act wisely, if they did not calculate their prer
considerably higher than may appear necessary to those who look only at what has
place during the last 30 or 40 years. Societies contracting prospective engage
that may extend for half a century or more, are exposed to innumerable unfo
contingencies ; and they would be highly censurable, and altogether unworthy
public confidence, were they so to conduct their affairs, that they might be lia
serious embarrassments from fluctuations in the rate of interest, or an increase o
ness, or any other cause. The success that has hitherto attended the Equitable, and
of the long established offices, must not be taken as any criterion of what may befa
and others during the next 100 years. Mr. Morgan, the able actuary of the Equ
in his account of the rise and progress of that institution, published in 1828, has
factorily shown that its peculiar prosperity has been in a very great degree owing
cumstances which cannot possibly occur again. The premium, for example, c
by the Society, so late as 1771, for insuring 100*l.* on the life of a person aged 9
$4l. 1s. 5\frac{1}{2}d.$, whereas it is now only $2l. 13s. 4d.$; and there was a corresponding
ence in the premiums for the other ages. — (p. 36.) But the excessive magnitude
premiums was not the only extraordinary source of profit enjoyed by this Society
earlier part of its career. We learn from the same unquestionable authority, th
*the insurances made during the first twenty-five years of the Society's existenc
abandoned by the insurers*, in many cases after the premiums upon them had bee
for a considerable number of years, *without any valuable consideration being given fo
by the Society !* — (p. 38.). So copious a source of profit was alone adequate to enri
society ; but such things rarely occur now, — people are become too familiar wi
insurance, and sales of policies are of too frequent occurrence, to allow any of
realise any thing considerable in this way. Now, we ask, can any one who take
facts into view, and couples them with the frugal and cautious management whi
hitherto always distinguished the Equitable Society, be surprised at its success ? a
any thing be more absurd than to appeal to its experience in casting the horosc
the societies that have sprung into existence within the last few years. But, indepen
of these considerations, there are other circumstances sufficient to account for th
success of some of the old offices. Since the close of the American war, a very c
diminution has taken place in the rate of mortality ; the public tranquillity has neith
disturbed by foreign invasion nor intestine commotion ; we have not been once vis
any epidemic disorder ; and the investments in the funds, during the war made a
50 to 60, may now be realised at from 80 to 90. We do not presume to say that c
stances may not be even more advantageous for the insurance offices during tl

century; but we should not, certainly, think very highly of the prudence of those
proceeded to insure on such an assumption. Security, we take leave again to repeat,
life insurance, the paramount consideration. It is, we believe, admitted on all
s, that the premiums were at one time too high; but we doubt whether the ten-
y at present be not to sink them too low. A great relaxation has taken place,
in the most respectable offices, as to the selection of lives. And the advertise-
s daily appearing in the newspapers, and the practices known to be resorted to in
ent quarters to procure business, ought to make every prudent individual consider
what he is about before he decides upon the office with which he is to insure.
active statements, unless where they emanate from individuals of unquestionable
acter and science, ought not to go for much. Life insurance is one of the most
ative of businesses; and offices may for a long time have all the appearance of pro-
y, which are, notwithstanding, established on a very insecure foundation. If a man
e a house or a ship with a society, or an individual, of whose credit he gets doubtful,
ll forthwith insure somewhere else. But life insurance is quite a different affair.
bargain is one that is not to be finally concluded for, perhaps, 50 years; and any
ity on the part of an establishment in extensive business to make good its engage-
s, would be productive of a degree of misery not easy to be imagined.

e insurance companies are divided into three classes. The first class consists of
stock companies, who undertake to pay *fixed* sums upon the death of the individuals
ng with them; the profits made by such companies being wholly divided among
roprietors. Of this class are the Royal Exchange, the Sun, the Globe, &c. The
d class are also joint stock companies, with proprietary bodies; but instead of
taking, like the former, to pay certain specified sums upon the death of the insured,
allow the latter to participate to a certain extent, along with the proprietors, in the
s made by the business. The mode in which this sort of *mixed* companies allot the
granted to the insured, is not the same in all; and in some, the principle on which
lotment is made is not disclosed. The Rock, Alliance, Guardian, Atlas, &c. be-
o this mixed class. The third species of company is that which is formed on the
of mutual insurance. In this sort of company there is no proprietary body dis-
from the insured; the latter share among themselves the whole profits of the con-
after deducting the expenses of management. The Equitable Society, the Amicable,
orwich Life, &c. belong to this class.

e advantage to a person insuring in any one office as compared with another, must
y depend on a comparison between the premiums demanded, the conditions of the
, and, above all, the security which it holds out. It may appear, on a superficial
as if the mutual insurance companies would be in all respects the most eligible
with, inasmuch as they have no proprietors to draw away any share of the profits
the insured. It is doubtful, however, whether this advantage be not more than
ed by disadvantages incident to such establishments. Every one being a partner
concern, has not only his own life insured, but is part insurer of the lives of all
her members; and may in this capacity, should the affairs of the society get into
er, incur some very serious responsibilities. The management, too, of such
es, is very apt to get into the hands of a junto; and to be conducted without the
number of those interested knowing any thing of the matter. There is, also,
erable difficulty, in constituting such societies, in distinguishing clearly between
hts of old and new members: for, supposing a society to be prosperous, it is but
able that those who have belonged to it while it has accumulated a large fund,
object to new entrants participating in this advantage. But the affairs of a
conducted in this way, or making distinctions in the rights of the members
a long series of years, could hardly fail of becoming at last exceedingly com-
d: nor is it, indeed, at all improbable that the conflicting claims of the parties in
f the societies of this sort now in existence, may ultimately have to be adjusted
courts of law, or by an act of the legislature.

posing the premiums demanded by the societies which retain the whole profits to
lves, to be fairly proportioned to the values insured, we should be inclined to
hat they are, on the whole, the most advisable to insure in. The subscribed
of such associations as the Royal Exchange, Sun, Globe, Scottish Union, &c.,
e wealth of the partners (which is all liable, except in the case of the chartered
ies, to the claims of the insured), afford unquestionable security. Individuals
with them know exactly what they are about. They know the precise premiums
ll have to pay, and the exact amount of the sums that will be paid to their assignees
event of their death. They incur no responsibility of any kind whatever. For,
some very unprecedented and unlooked for change should take place in the con-
of the country, they may reckon with certainty on the terms of the policy being
to the letter.

But, as already observed, every thing depends, in matters of this sort, on a compari
of the premium with the advantages to be realised. And where the premiums
believed, either through carelessness, or intentionally, in order to provide for the sa
of the establishment, to be a little too high, it may be more expedient, perhaps, to
with a mixed company. The subscribed capital and fortunes of the proprietary b
afford a guarantee on which the public may depend in dealing with any *respect*
company of this sort; while, by receiving a share of the profits, the insured gain
the flourishing condition of the association, and it is of less consequence to them tho
the premiums should be too high.

It should, however, be borne in mind, that an individual insuring with a mixed co
pany, on condition of his getting a proportion of the profits, becomes a *partner of*
company; and being so, incurs responsibilities. In dealing with such association
the Alliance, the Rock, and a few others, this responsibility can hardly be said
amount to any thing. But there are companies of this class in the field, and hold
out very tempting baits to the unwary, those insured in which may find, at some fu
period, that this responsibility is by no means a light matter.

A highly respectable company of this mixed class, with a large subscribed capital
the Guardian, — inserts in all its policies the following condition, viz. " That the resp
sibility of the individual members shall, in all cases, be limited to their respec
shares." It may be doubted whether this condition be good in law; but if it b
materially affects the security afforded by the Company, which otherwise would ju
claim a place in the very first class of offices. As no one attempts to secure him
against a contingency which he is satisfied cannot happen, the existence of a conditio
this sort implies a doubt, on the part of the proprietary body, of the perfect solidit
the establishment. Such a doubt may be, and we believe really is, very illfound
but the public will, most likely, be inclined to think that the proprietors ought to kn
better than any one else.

The allotment of profit to the insured made by the mixed companies, is someti
effected by a diminution of the premiums, and sometimes by increasing the sum
the policy; and individuals should, in dealing with such societies, select, other thi
being equal, the association with which to insure, according as they wish to insu
larger sum, or to get the premiums reduced.

We subjoin from Mr. Babbage's work on Life Assurance *, the following statem
of the terms of the various mixed companies, as to the division of profits with the insu
They are, for the most part, exceedingly vague. We also subjoin an account of
conditions, in respect of profits, under which new entrants are admitted into
Equitable.

Alliance. — At the periods of participation of the Company in the profits p of its concerns, every p
for the whole term of life, which shall have paid five entire annual premiums, shall, if the allowanc
made in reduction of annual premium, be entitled to such reduction from the original charge as
then, and from time to time, be declared ; but if the allowance be in addition to the amount assured,
addition shall also be continually declared from time to time.
Persons assuring their own lives have the option of declaring, at the time of effecting the assura
whether they will participate in the profits by an addition to their policy, or by a reduction of premi
Atlas. — Persons assuring for the whole term of life for 100*l.* and upwards, in Great Britain and Ire
respectively, will be entitled, at the end of every seventh year, to participate in the surplus premium
be then ascertained by actual valuation.
Asylum. — The directors have power to divide such portion of the profits quinquennially as may
imprudently check the growth of the funds intended for the benefit of the assured.
Crown. — Two thirds of such profits as shall periodically be declared divisible, will be apporti
amongst assurers for the whole term of life, and may be applied to the reduction of the future an
premiums, or to the increase of the sum assured, as may be desired.
Economic. — At present three fourths of the savings and profits divided amongst the assured entitl
participate therein, by additions to their policies, proportioned to their respective contributions, a
order to afford them the immediate benefit of such additions, interest thereon applied annually in re
tion of their premiums.
Equitable. — That in case any prospective addition shall hereafter be ordered to be made to the cl
upon policies of assurance in this Society, such order shall not take effect with respect to any p
granted after the 31st of December, 1816, until the assurances existing in the Society prior in number
date to such policy, and if of the same date, prior in the number thereof, shall be reduced to five thous
but as soon as such reduction shall have been ascertained, in manner hereinafter mentioned, the
policy shall be within the effect and operation of the order for such addition, as to the payments
thereon subsequent to such ascertained reduction : so that if such order should be made to take
generally from the 1st of January, 1820, for the space of ten years then next following, a policy effe
in the year 1817, shall not be within the operation of such order, until the assurances existing pri
the number and date of the policy, as aforesaid, shall have been reduced to five thousand ; but such p
shall be within the operation thereof from the time when the reduction shall have been ascertaine
manner hereinafter mentioned, as to the payments made thereon subsequent to such ascertained redue
And the like as to other cases. And this by-law shall be considered as a part of every such order
shall be virtually incorporated therein, although the same may not be thereby expressly referred to.
That in case any retrospective addition shall hereafter be ordered to be made to claims upon polic
assurance in this Society, such order shall not take effect with respect to any policy granted afte
31st of December, 1816, until the assurances existing in the Society prior in number and date, and if

* This work of Mr. Babbage contains a good deal of useful information, intermixed, however,
not a few errors and mis-statements. It was most ably reviewed in an article in the 90th Num
the Edinburgh Review.

e, prior in the number thereof, shall be reduced to five thousand ; but when the said reduction ve been ascertained in manner hereinafter mentioned, such policy shall be within the effect and n, and entitled to the benefit of such order, with respect to every payment made thereon subse such ascertained reduction ; so that if such order shall be made to take effect generally as to pay-ade before the 1st of January, 1820, a policy effected in the year 1817 shall not be within the d operation thereof, unless the life assured shall exist, and the payments continue to be made, assurances existing in the Society prior to the number and date of the policy, as aforesaid, shall ed to five thousand ; but as soon as such reduction shall have been ascertained, in manner here-ientioned, such policy shall be within the effect and operation of such order for the several pay-ade thereon as aforesaid. And the like as to other cases. And this by-law shall be considered of every such order, and be virtually incorporated therein, although the same may not be thereby referred to.

n inquiry be made on the 1st of April in every year, in order to ascertain the number of assur-ide and existing in the Society ; and when it shall have been ascertained by such inquiry that the es existing prior to the 1st of January, 1817, were, on the 31st of December immediately preced-inquiry, reduced below the number of five thousand, the actuary do report the same to the Court ors, who shall communicate such report to the quarterly general Court, to be holden in the June g ; and that as many of such policies as had been made subsequent to the 31st of December, 1816, h were existing in the Society on the 31st of December immediately preceding such inquiry, be ccording to the priority in their dates and numbers, and if of the same date, according to the n their numbers, to those above mentioned, as shall be sufficient to complete the number to five ; and that the persons holding the policies so added shall be considered thenceforward as entitled dditions as shall be thereafter made in respect of all the payments made subsequent to such ed reduction, and, under the same restrictions, to the same privileges of attending at the general nd of being eligible to the office of director.

fter the vacant numbers in the assurances existing in the Society on the 1st of January, 1817, e been filled up agreeably to the foregoing order, the actuary, on the 1st of April in every suc-year, do ascertain the vacancies which have taken place in the preceding year in the policies con-the five thousand mentioned in the fifth resolution, and report the same to the Court of Directors, communicate such report to the quarterly general Court in the month of June following ; and any policies shall be added, according to the priority of their dates and numbers. and if of the e, according to the priority in their numbers, as shall be sufficient to complete the number to five ; and that the persons holding those policies shall thenceforward be considered as entitled to tions as shall be thereafter made in respect of all payments made subsequent to the 31st of the December, and, under the same restrictions, to the same privileges of attending the general nd being eligible to the office of director.

ed that nothing hereby ordered shall be construed to authorise an addition to the sum assured by y, upon which policy the number of payments required in that respect by the present by-laws of ty shall not have been made.

. Those by-laws require that six annual payments at the least shall have been made before any to a claim can take place ; and when such payments shall have been made, the party will be to be received, in his turn, into the number of persons entitled to additions as aforesaid.

an. —The profits derived by this Company are distributed amongst the several persons connected establishment, according to the contingency or certainty of their contract.

surers derive an immediate benefit by the reduction of the premiums generally taken, with the of a liberal addition to their policies, or a further reduction of the premium, in ten years.

an. — Persons assured for the whole term of life will be entitled at the end of every seven years ate in the profits of the Company, after a deduction of such sum per annum, for the guaranty ital, as the directors may think reasonable ; the extent of which is, however, limited by the deed ent.

re of the profits to be so allowed to the assured, may either be added to the amount of their policies, or the value thereof be applied in reduction of the premiums hereafter to be payable olicies, provided such option be declared in writing within three calendar months next after the shall have been declared ; but if such option be not declared, such share of profits will be added ount of policies.

Every person effecting a policy of assurance at this office, is entitled to a participation in the ally with the proprietors of the Company, after a moderate deduction for the guaranty and the of management.

l. — Upon every policy effected for the whole term of life, the assured will participate in the he Company, by having periodical additions made to the sums insured to the amount of two s of such clear gains and profits.

fe. — At stated periods, the surplus of the fund arising from the premiums of assurance, and amulation beyond what may be thought necessary to answer the expected claims upon the ill be ascertained ; and as large a portion of the savings as may be deemed consistent with the f the institution, will be divided between the proprietors and the assured in the following — One fifth will be transferred to the proprietors' guaranty fund ; and reversionary sums, equi-he remaining four fifths, will be added to the policies of those who shall have been three years r the whole term of life.

Life Association. — The distinguishing principle of this Society is, that the benefits resulting ansactions shall be enjoyed by the members during life, so as to render life assurance as easy to d, as a due regard to security will admit.

and Clerical. — Persons assured for the whole term of life will be entitled to share with the roprietors the general profits of the business, in proportion to the amount of their respective

Union. — The whole of the surplus premiums is added at stated periods to the policies of the n proportion to the sums they have respectively contributed.

m. — A general investigation of the affairs of the Society is to take place every seventh year, fifths of the declared profit of the life department will be appropriated by way of bonus or o be placed to the credit of the policies then in force for the whole term of life, upon the most rinciples of division.

That the said bonus shall be short of the actual surplus profits at the time of making the same, of 5,000l. at least.

bonus so declared shall be divided into three equal parts.

of the said parts shall be added to and consolidated with the subscription capital stock. (This rietors' fund.)

remaining two thirds be allotted to the policies in the manner described in the deed.

sum to which any person assured by the Company may become entitled under any such dis-hall be paid by the Company without interest, at the time when the sum assured by the policy e payable, and not before.

Those who assure with this Company will participate with the proprietors in the profits of the ent, which will be added every seven years to the respective policies.

mpire. — Persons effecting assurances for the whole continuance of life will, at the end of the

first five years, and of every subsequent five years, be entitled to participate in whatever nett surpl⸗
fits it may be declared by the directors expedient to divide.

Two fifths of the aforesaid profits will be divided amongst the said assured, in proportion to th⸗
miums they may respectively have paid, and will, at their option, be either added to the amount ⸗
policies, or applied in reduction of their future premiums.

University. — As it is intended that the capital advanced shall be repaid to the shareholder,
bonus of 100*l.* per cent., one tenth of the profits, when ascertained by a valuation of all existing⸗
will every five years be applied to form a fund for that purpose.

The remaining nine tenths of the profits to be divided between the assured and the shareholder,
proportion of eight parts to the former and one to the latter.

The profit or bonus to the assured to be given either by a diminution of the rate of premium, or⸗
increase of the amount of policy, at the option of the party.

In order to hinder the growth of gambling transactions upon life insurance, i⸗
judiciously enacted, by stat. 14 Geo. 3. c. 48., that

No insurance shall be made by any person or persons, bodies politic or corporate, on the life or ⸗
any person or persons, or any other event or events whatsoever, where the person or persons, for
use or benefit, or on whose account, such policy or policies shall be made, *shall have no interest*
way of gaining or wagering; and that every insurance made contrary to the true intent and m⸗
of this act, shall be null and void to all intents and purposes whatsoever. — § 1.

It shall not be lawful to make any policy or policies on the life or lives of any person or pers⸗
other event or events, *without inserting in such policy or policies, the name or names of the pe⸗
persons interested therein, or for what use, benefit, or on whose account, such policy is so made or*
wrote. — § 2.

In all cases where the insured has an interest in such life or lives, event or events, no greater su⸗
be recovered or received from the insurer or insurers, than the amount or value of the interest
insured in such life or lives, or other event or events. — § 3.

A creditor has an insurable interest in the life of his debtor; but it was decided⸗
case which arose out of a policy on the life of the late Mr. Pitt, that if, after the
of a debtor whose life is insured by a creditor, and before any action is brought ⸗
policy, the debt be paid, no action will lie.

All insurance offices either insert in their policies or refer in them to a decla⸗
signed by the insured, setting forth his age, or the age of the party upon whom⸗
making an insurance; whether he has or has not had the small pox, gout, &c.;
he is not afflicted with any disorder that tends to the shortening of life;" that th⸗
claration is to be the basis of the contract between him and the society; and that, if
be any untrue averment in it, all the monies paid to the society upon account ⸗
insurance shall be forfeited to them. — (See Form, *post.*)

The condition as to the party not being afflicted with any disorder that tends ⸗
shortening of life is vague, and has given rise to a good deal of discussion. ⸗
is now settled that this condition is sufficiently complied with, if the insured b⸗
reasonably good state of health; and though he may be afflicted with some diseas⸗
if it can be shown that this disease does not tend to shorten life, and was not, i⸗
the cause of the party's death, the insurer will not be exonerated: " Such a war⸗
said Lord Mansfield, " can never mean, that a man has not in him the seeds of
disorder. We are all born with the seeds of mortality in us. The only quest
whether the insured was in a *reasonably good state of health,* and such a life as ou⸗
be insured on common terms." — (See *Marshall on Insurance,* book iii.; *Park ⸗
surance,* c. 22.)

Policies of life insurance must be on stamped paper, the duty being as follov⸗
viz.

Where the sum in the policy shall not amount to £	500	......	£ 1	0	0
Where it shall amount to £ 500 and not to	1,000	......	2	0	0
— — 1,000 —	3,000	......	3	0	0
— — 3,000 —	5,000	......	4	0	0
— — 5,000 and upwards		....	5	0	0

We subjoin a statement of the terms and conditions on which the Sun Life Ass⸗
and Equitable Societies transact business, and a copy of one of the policies of the ⸗
upon the life of a person aged 30, insuring his own life for 1,000*l.* The con⸗
of most of the other societies are similar, and may be learned by any one, on ap⸗
either at the head offices in town, or at their agents' in the country. The pre⸗
demanded by all the offices are exhibited in the annexed table.

Sun Life. — An assurance for a term of years, or for the whole continuance of life, is a contrac⸗
part of the office to continue the assurance during that term, on the payment of a certain annual pr⸗
but the assured may drop it, whenever the end is answered for which the assurance was made.

The person whose life is proposed for assurance, is required to appear either before the manage⸗
office in London, or before an agent in the country; in default of which, the non-appearance f⸗
be paid when the assurance is effected; which, when the term is one year, is 10*s.* for eve⸗
assured. When the term exceeds one year, but does not exceed seven years, it is 15*s.* for every 10⸗
when the term exceeds seven years, the fine is 1 per cent.

Reference to be made to two persons of repute, to ascertain the identity of the person appearin⸗

Any premium remaining unpaid more than fifteen days after the time stipulated in the poli⸗
policy becomes void; but the defaulter producing satisfactory proof to the managers, of the heal⸗
person on whose life the assurance was made, and paying the said premium within three calendar ⸗
together with the additional sum of 10*s.* upon every 100*l.* assured by such policy, then such ⸗
revived, and continues in force.

Conditions of Assurance made by Persons on their own Lives.

assurance to be void, if the person whose life is assured shall depart beyond the limits of Europe; die upon the seas (except in any whole-decked vessel or steam boat in passing between any one part United Kingdom of Great Britain and Ireland, including the islands of Guernsey, Jersey, Alderney, ark, and any other part thereof; or in passing between any port of the said United Kingdom, and rt on the continent of Europe between Hamburgh and Bordeaux, both inclusive); or shall enter r engage in any military or naval service whatsoever, without the previous consent of the Society; l die by suicide, duelling, or the hands of justice; or shall not be, at the time the assurance is made, d health.

Conditions of Assurance made by Persons on the Lives of others.

party on whose behalf the assurance is made, must be interested in the life of the other to the full t assured thereon.

assurance to be void, if the person whose life is assured shall depart beyond the limits of Europe; ie upon the seas (except in any whole-decked vessel or steam-boat in passing between any one part United Kingdom of Great Britain and Ireland, including the islands of Guernsey, Jersey, Alder- nd Sark, and any other part thereof; or in passing between any port in the said United Kingdom, y port on the continent of Europe between Hamburgh and Bordeaux, both inclusive); or shall into or engage in any military or naval service whatsoever, without the previous consent of the So- or shall not be, at the time the assurance is made, in good health.

arances on the lives of persons engaged in the army or navy, or going beyond the limits of Europe, e made by special agreement.

claims are paid within three months after certificates (according to the required forms) of the death rial of the deceased are approved by the managers.

Form of a Proposal for Assurance.

and rank or profession, of the life to be assured, residence,
birth,
birth,
t birthday,

ce to a medical practitioner, to ⎞
ain the present and ordinary ⎪
of health of the person whose ⎬
proposed to be assured, ⎪
ver had gout or asthma, or any fit or fits? ⎠
ever been afflicted with rupture?
ever exhibited any symptom of consumption of the

icted with any disorder tending to shorten life?
ad the small-pox or the cow-pox?
r the person whose life is proposed to be assured, in-
o appear at the office?
name or behalf the policy is desired?
proposal, ⎞
notices ⎬
ent to ⎠

Declaration to be made and signed by or on behalf of a son making an Assurance on his or her own Life.

he parish of
unty of
                day of
residing at
unty of
irous of making an assurance with the managers for
Life Assurance Society, in the sum of £
a for the continuance of my own life, for the term of
                Do hereby declare, that my age does
ed   years; that I have   had the *

that I have   had the gout,   asthma, rupture,   nor any fit or fits, and that I am not afflicted with any   disorder which tends to the shortening of life; and this declaration is to be the basis of the contract be- tween me and the Society; and if any untrue averment is contained in this declaration, in setting forth my age, state of health, profession, occupation, or circumstances, then all mo- nies which shall have been paid to the said Society, upon ac- count of the assurance so made by me, shall be forfeited. Dated the   day of   18

Form of Declaration to be made and signed by or on behalf of a Person who proposes to make an Assurance on the Life of another.

I
now resident at
in the county of   being
desirous of assuring with the Sun Life Assurance Society, the sum of £   for the term of
on the life of   born in the parish o
            in the county of   on the
            day of   in the year
and now resident at   in the county of
Do declare that I have an interest in the life of the said
£   to the full amount of the said sum of
            that to the best of my knowledge and
belief the age of the said   does not exceed
            years; that he has had the *   that
he   had the gout,   asthma,   rupture, nor any fit or fits, and that   he is not afflicted with any disorder tending to shorten life; and this declaration is to be the basis of the contract between me and the said Society; and if there be any untrue averment therein, all monies which shall have been paid to the Society upon account of the assur- ance made in consequence thereof, shall be forfeited. Dated the   day of   18

* Insert small-pox or cow-pox, as the case may require.

by the Sun Life Assurance Society for 1,000l., on the Life of A. B., aged Thirty, insuring his own Life.

SUN LIFE ASSURANCE SOCIETY.

s POLICY OF ASSURANCE WITNESSETH, that, whereas A. B. Esq. of Square, London, being desirous of making an assurance upon his own or the whole duration thereof, and having subscribed, or caused to be ibed, and delivered into this office, a declaration setting forth his ordinary esent state of health, wherein it is declared that the age of the said A. B. t then exceed thirty years; and having paid to the managers for the Sun ssurance Society, at their office in Cornhill, in the city of London, the f twenty-four pounds eleven shillings and eight pence sterling, as a con- tion for the assurance of the sum under-mentioned for *one year*, from the eth day of October, 1831.

v KNOW ALL MEN BY THESE PRESENTS, that in case the said assured appen to die at any time within the term of *one year*, as above set forth, ock and funds of this Society shall be subject and liable to pay and make o the executors, administrators, or assigns, of the said assured, within nonths after the demise of the said assured shall have been duly certified managers aforesaid, at their said office, the sum of one thousand pounds g, of lawful money of Great Britain.

hereby agreed that this policy may continue in force from *year* to *year*,

until the expiration of the term first above-mentioned, provided that the s[...]
assured shall duly pay, or cause to be paid, to the managers, at their said off[...]
on or before the nineteenth day of October next ensuing, the sum of twenty-f[...]
pounds eleven shillings and eight pence sterling, and the like sum annually, on[...]
before the day aforesaid; which annual payments shall be accepted, at every su[...]
period, as a full consideration for such assurance.

And it is hereby further agreed that the assurance by this policy shall be [...]
tended during peace, to the risk of the above-named A. B. Esq. dying upon [...]
sea in any whole-decked vessel or steam-boat, in passing between any one p[...]
of the United Kingdom of Great Britain and Ireland, including the islands [...]
Guernsey, Jersey, Alderney, and Sark, and any other part thereof; or in pass[...]
between any port in the said United Kingdom, and any port on the continent[...]
Europe between Hamburgh and Bordeaux, both inclusive.

PROVIDED, NEVERTHELESS, that should the said assured depart beyond [...]
limits of Europe, die upon the seas (except as above stated), or engage in [...]
military or naval service whatsoever, within the term for which this policy [...]
granted; or should the assurance have been obtained through any misrep[...]
sentation of the age, state of health, or description of the assured, or should [...]
said assured die by duelling, suicide, or the hands of justice; then this poli[...]
and every thing appertaining thereto, shall cease, be void, and of none effect.

IN WITNESS WHEREOF, we, three of the managers for the said Society, h[...]
hereunto set our hands and seals, this twentieth day of October, 1831.

Signed, sealed, and delivered,
being first duly stamped.

J. K.

C. D. (L. s.
E. F. (L. s.
G. H. (L. s.

The following tabular statement shows the premiums demanded by the principal
insurance societies, for insuring 100*l.* at every different age from 15 to 60, for the w[...]
term of life.

Age	Alliance and Sun	Amicable	Asylum	British Commer.	Crown	Economic	Equitable	Eagle Male	Eagle Female	European	Gua
	L. s. d.	L. s. d.	L. s. d.	L. s. d.	L. s. d.	L. s. d.	L. s. d.	L. s. d.	L. s. d.	L. s. d.	L.
15	1 13 8	1 15 6	1 6 10	1 10 0	1 15 9	1 10 8	1 18 7	1 18 9		1 13 7	1 1
16	1 13 6	1 16 6	1 7 6	1 11 0	1 16 7	1 11 5	1 19 7	1 19 8		1 14 5	1 1
17	1 14 3	1 17 6	1 8 3	1 12 0	1 17 5	1 12 3	2 0 8	2 0 5		1 15 4	1 1
18	1 15 1	1 18 6	1 9 0	1 13 0	1 18 3	1 13 0	2 1 8	2 1 4		1 16 2	1 1
19	1 16 0	1 19 6	1 9 9	1 14 0	1 19 1	1 13 10	2 2 8	2 2 3		1 17 1	2
20	1 16 11	2 0 6	1 10 7	1 15 0	1 19 11	1 14 7	2 3 7	2 3 2	1 12 7	1 18 1	2
21	1 17 11	2 1 6	1 11 5	1 16 0	2 0 10	1 15 5	2 4 6	2 4 2	1 13 5	1 19 0	2
22	1 18 11	2 2 6	1 12 3	1 17 0	2 1 9	1 16 3	2 5 4	2 5 3	1 14 4	1 19 11	2
23	2 0 1	2 3 6	1 13 2	1 18 0	2 2 9	1 17 2	2 6 3	2 6 4	1 15 4	2 0 10	2
24	2 1 3	2 4 6	1 14 1	1 19 0	2 3 9	1 18 1	2 7 1	2 7 5	1 16 5	2 1 10	2
25	2 2 6	2 5 6	1 15 1	2 0 0	2 4 10	1 19 0	2 8 1	2 8 7	1 17 6	2 2 9	2
26	2 3 9	2 6 6	1 16 1	2 1 0	2 5 10	2 0 0	2 9 1	2 9 9	1 18 8	2 3 9	2
27	2 5 2	2 7 6	1 17 1	2 2 0	2 6 11	2 1 0	2 10 1	2 11 0	1 19 9	2 4 10	2
28	2 6 7	2 8 6	1 18 2	2 3 0	2 8 1	2 2 0	2 11 1	2 12 3	2 0 9	2 5 10	2
29	2 7 11	2 9 6	1 19 3	2 4 0	2 9 2	2 3 1	2 12 3	2 13 7	2 1 8	2 6 11	2
30	2 9 2	2 10 6	2 0 5	2 5 0	2 10 4	2 4 3	2 13 5	2 15 0	2 2 6	2 8 1	2
31	2 10 6	2 11 6	2 1 7	2 6 0	2 11 6	2 5 5	2 14 7	2 16 6	2 3 4	2 9 3	2
32	2 11 10	2 12 6	2 2 10	2 7 0	2 12 9	2 6 8	2 15 9	2 18 0	2 3 10	2 10 6	2
33	2 13 4	2 14 0	2 4 0	2 8 0	2 14 0	2 8 0	2 17 1	2 19 9	2 4 4	2 11 10	2
34	2 14 11	2 15 6	2 5 7	2 9 0	2 15 4	2 9 5	2 18 5	3 1 6	2 4 10	2 13 2	2
35	2 16 8	2 17 0	2 7 1	2 10 0	2 16 9	2 10 11	2 19 10	3 3 4	2 5 6	2 14 7	2
36	2 18 5	2 18 6	2 8 8	2 11 0	2 18 2	2 12 6	3 1 4	3 5 5	2 6 2	2 16 0	3
37	3 0 4	3 0 0	2 10 4	2 12 0	2 19 10	2 14 2	3 2 10	3 7 7	2 7 0	2 17 6	3
38	3 2 4	3 1 6	2 12 1	2 16 6	3 1 2	2 15 11	3 4 6	3 9 10	2 7 10	2 19 1	3
39	3 4 5	3 3 0	2 13 11	2 18 0	3 2 10	2 17 9	3 6 2	3 12 4	2 8 10	3 0 9	3
40	3 6 6	3 5 0	2 15 10	3 0 0	3 4 7	2 19 9	3 7 11	3 15 0	2 9 10	3 2 6	3
41	3 8 7	3 7 0	2 17 10	3 2 0	3 6 5	3 1 10	3 9 9	3 17 9	2 10 11	3 4 3	3
42	3 10 9	3 9 0	2 19 11	3 4 0	3 8 4	3 4 1	3 11 8	4 1 0	2 12 0	3 6 3	3
43	3 12 11	3 11 0	3 2 1	3 6 0	3 10 6	3 6 6	3 13 8	4 4 4	2 13 3	3 8 3	3
44	3 15 3	3 13 0	3 4 4	3 8 0	3 12 8	3 9 0	3 15 9	4 7 11	2 14 7	3 10 5	3
45	3 17 8	3 15 0	3 6 10	3 10 0	3 15 0	3 11 9	3 17 11	4 11 8	2 16 0	3 12 7	3
46	4 0 5	3 17 6	3 9 7	3 12 0	3 17 6	3 14 7	4 0 2	4 15 9	2 17 6	3 15 0	3
47	4 3 3	4 0 0	3 12 7	3 14 6	4 0 1	3 17 8	4 2 7	5 0 0	2 19 1	3 17 5	4
48	4 6 6	4 2 6	3 16 1	3 17 0	4 2 11	4 0 11	4 5 1	5 4 6	3 0 9	4 0 0	4
49	4 10 2	4 5 0	3 19 10	3 19 6	4 5 10	4 4 4	4 7 10	5 9 6	3 2 6	4 2 8	4
50	4 14 2	4 8 0	4 3 10	4 6 0	4 8 11	4 8 0	4 10 8	5 14 7	3 4 4	4 5 6	4
51	4 18 9	4 11 0	4 8 0	4 10 0	4 12 1	4 11 11	4 13 6	6 0 3	3 6 3	4 8 6	4
52	5 3 6	4 14 0	4 12 4	4 13 2	4 15 3	4 16 1	4 16 5	6 6 6	3 8 4	4 11 7	4
53	5 8 7	4 17 0	4 16 10	4 15 6	4 18 6	5 0 6	4 19 7	6 12 9	3 10 8	4 15 0	4
54	5 14 1	5 0 0	5 1 7	5 1 0	5 1 11	5 5 3	5 2 10	6 19 3	3 13 0	4 18 7	5
55	5 19 11	5 3 6	5 6 5	5 5 0	5 5 7	5 10 3	5 6 4	7 7 2	3 15 8	5 2 6	5
56	6 6 4	5 7 6	5 11 5	5 9 6	5 9 6	5 15 7	5 10 1	7 15 1	3 18 6	5 6 8	5
57	6 13 2	5 11 6	5 16 7	5 13 2	5 13 6	6 1 3	5 14 0	8 3 6	4 1 7	5 11 2	5
58	7 0 5	5 15 6	6 1 11	5 18 0	5 18 0	6 7 4	5 18 2	8 12 7	4 5 0	5 15 8	5
59	7 7 9	6 0 0	6 7 5	6 2 4	6 2 4	6 13 9	6 2 6	9 2 4	4 8 7	6 0 7	6
60	7 14 11	6 5 0	6 13 0	6 7 2	6 7 2	7 0 7	6 7 8	9 13 0	4 12 4	6 5 8	6

Tabular statement — *continued.*

London, Birchin Lane.	London Life for Members.	Norwich.	Pelican.	Promoter.	United Empire.	University.	West of England.	Scot. Wid. Fund.	Scottish Union.
L. s. d.	L. s. d.	L. s. d.	L. s. d.	L. s. d.	L. s. d.	L. s. d.	L. s. d.	L. s. d.	L. s. d.
1 16 8		1 14 9	1 11 11	1 7 11	1 14 10	1 16 8	1 14 9	1 16 5	1 11 6
1 17 9		1 15 9	1 12 9	1 8 8	1 15 9	1 17 9	1 15 9	1 17 6	1 12 5
1 18 9		1 16 9	1 13 6	1 9 5	1 16 9	1 18 8	1 16 8	1 18 6	1 13 6
1 19 8		1 17 8	1 14 4	1 10 1	1 17 8	1 19 7	1 17 6	1 19 7	1 14 7
2 0 7		1 18 6	1 15 3	1 10 11	1 18 7	2 0 7	1 18 6	2 0 7	1 15 8
2 1 4		1 29 6	1 16 1	1 11 8	1 19 6	2 1 5	1 19 3	2 1 6	1 16 9
2 2 2	2 4 6	2 0 6	1 16 10	1 12 6	2 0 5	2 2 4	2 0 0	2 2 5	1 17 9
2 3 0	2 5 6	2 1 3	1 17 7	1 13 5	2 1 3	2 3 1	2 0 10	2 3 3	1 18 10
2 3 11	2 6 6	2 2 0	1 18 4	1 14 4	2 2 1	2 4 0	2 1 3	2 4 1	1 19 10
2 4 8	2 7 0	2 2 9	1 19 2	1 15 5	2 3 0	2 4 9	2 2 6	2 4 11	2 0 10
2 5 7	2 8 0	2 3 8	2 0 1	1 16 5	2 3 11	2 5 9	2 3 3	2 5 10	2 1 10
2 6 6	2 9 0	2 4 8	2 1 3	1 17 6	2 4 11	2 6 8	2 4 0	2 6 10	2 2 10
2 7 6	2 10 0	2 5 8	2 2 7	1 18 8	2 5 11	2 7 7	2 5 0	2 7 10	2 3 10
2 8 6	2 11 0	2 6 8	2 3 11	1 19 11	2 7 0	2 8 7	2 6 0	2 8 11	2 4 11
2 9 8	2 12 6	2 7 9	2 5 2	2 1 1	2 8 1	2 9 8	2 7 0	2 10 0	2 6 1
2 10 7	2 13 6	2 8 10	2 6 4	2 2 2	2 9 2	2 10 9	2 8 0	2 11 1	2 7 3
2 11 9	2 14 6	2 10 0	2 7 7	2 3 3	2 10 4	2 11 11	2 9 0	2 12 3	2 8 5
2 13 0	2 16 0	2 11 1	2 8 10	2 4 5	2 11 6	2 13 0	2 10 3	2 13 6	2 9 9
2 14 2	2 17 0	2 12 3	2 10 3	2 5 8	2 12 9	2 14 3	2 11 6	2 14 9	2 11 1
2 15 7	2 18 6	2 13 6	2 11 9	2 7 1	2 14 1	2 15 6	2 12 9	2 16 1	2 12 5
2 16 9	3 0 0	2 14 10	2 13 5	2 8 7	2 15 6	2 16 11	2 13 10	2 17 6	2 13 10
2 18 2	3 1 6	2 16 2	2 15 1	2 10 1	2 16 11	2 18 4	2 15 3	2 19 0	2 15 4
2 19 8	3 3 0	2 17 6	2 16 10	2 11 8	2 18 4	2 19 9	2 16 8	3 0 6	2 16 11
3 1 3	3 4 6	2 19 0	2 18 9	2 13 5	2 19 11	3 1 4	2 18 0	3 2 0	2 18 6
3 3 0	3 6 0	3 0 6	3 0 8	2 15 2	3 1 6	3 2 11	2 19 6	3 3 9	3 0 2
3 4 7	3 8 0	3 2 0	3 2 8	2 17 0	3 3 2	3 4 7	3 1 3	3 5 6	3 1 11
3 8 0	3 10 0	3 3 6	3 5 2	2 18 10	3 4 10	3 6 4	3 2 10	3 7 3	3 3 9
3 10 0	3 12 0	3 5 2	3 7 8	3 0 8	3 6 8	3 8 1	3 4 6	3 9 3	3 5 8
3 12 0	3 14 0	3 7 0	3 10 4	3 2 6	3 8 8	3 10 0	3 6 4	3 11 3	3 7 8
3 13 11	3 16 0	3 9 0	3 13 1	3 4 6	3 10 8	3 12 0	3 8 3	3 13 4	3 9 8
3 16 1	3 18 0	3 11 0	3 16 1	3 6 7	3 12 10	3 14 1	3 10 3	3 15 6	3 11 10
3 18 3	4 0 0	3 13 8	3 18 8	3 8 11	3 15 3	3 16 2	3 12 2	3 17 9	3 14 1
4 0 5	4 2 6	3 16 3	4 1 6	3 11 5	3 17 9	3 18 6	3 14 6	4 0 3	3 16 6
4 2 10	4 5 0	3 19 6	4 4 8	3 14 2	4 0 7	4 1 4	3 16 9	4 2 9	3 19 0
4 5 6	4 8 0	4 2 9	4 8 2	3 17 3	4 3 6	4 4 4	3 19 3	4 5 6	4 1 7
4 8 6	4 11 0	4 6 0	4 12 2	4 0 8	4 6 6	4 7 6	4 1 8	4 8 4	4 4 3
4 13 6	4 14 0	4 9 8	4 16 7	4 4 7	4 9 9	4 10 9	4 4 3	4 11 2	4 8 1
4 16 6	4 17 0	4 13 3	5 1 3	4 8 8	4 13 0	4 14 1	4 6 9	4 14 2	4 12 2
4 19 6	5 0 6	4 17 0	5 6 4	4 13 1	4 16 5	4 17 8	4 9 9	4 17 4	4 16 5
5 2 9	5 5 0	5 1 0	5 11 7	4 17 10	5 0 6	5 1 4	4 12 9	4 12 9	5 0 11
5 6 3	5 9 6	5 5 6	5 17 4	5 2 9	5 4 8	5 5 4	4 15 9	4 15 9	5 5 9
5 10 0	5 14 0	5 9 6	6 3 7	5 8 4	5 8 6	5 9 7	4 19 0	5 7 11	5 10 9
5 14 0	5 19 0	5 13 6	6 10 4	5 14 2	5 12 6	5 14 0	5 2 6	5 11 11	5 16 1
5 18 3	6 4 0	5 17 6	6 17 5	6 0 4	5 17 0	5 18 2	5 6 6	5 16 1	6 1 9
6 2 9	6 9 6	6 2 6	7 4 6	6 6 9	6 1 9	6 2 8	5 10 6	6 0 7	6 7 10
6 7 3	6 15 0	6 7 3	7 11 7	6 12 10	6 7 0	6 7 4	5 14 9	6 5 4	6 14 3

...owing offices require the same premiums as the Equitable; viz. Albion, Atlas, Globe, Imperial,
. London Life Association (for persons not members), Palladium, Provident, Rock, Royal Ex-
. nion, Westminster.

...ollowing are the premiums demanded by the Sun Life Assurance Society, for
. es on joint lives and survivorships.

...s.—A Table of Annual Premiums payable during the Joint Continuance of Two Lives, for
assuring One Hundred Pounds, to be paid as soon as either of the Two shall drop.

Age next Birthday.	Annual Premium.	Age next Birth-day.	Age next Birthday.	Annual Premium.	Age next Birth-day.	Age next Birthday.	Annual Premium.
	£ s. d.			£ s. d.			£ s. d.
10	2 7 5	20	35	3 17 3	35	45	5 7 5
15	2 11 0		40	4 6 1		50	6 1 11
20	2 14 6		45	4 16 1		55	7 6 5
25	2 19 4		50	5 11 7		60	9 0 6
30	3 5 3		55	6 16 8			
35	3 11 11		60	8 11 1	40	40	5 5 8
40	4 1 1					45	5 13 10
45	4 11 5	25	25	3 9 6		50	6 7 9
50	5 7 2		30	3 14 10		55	7 11 8
55	6 12 5		35	4 0 11		60	9 5 5
60	8 6 11		40	4 9 6			
			45	4 19 3	45	45	6 1 0
15	2 14 5		50	5 14 7		50	6 13 11
20	2 17 9		55	6 19 7		55	7 16 11
25	3 2 5		60	8 13 11		60	9 9 8
30	3 8 3						
35	3 14 9	30	30	3 19 10	50	50	7 5 6
40	4 3 10		35	4 5 6		55	8 7 4
45	4 14 0		40	4 13 10		60	9 18 11
50	5 9 8		45	5 3 2			
55	6 14 11		50	5 18 3	55	55	9 8 2
60	8 9 6		55	7 3 1		60	10 18 11
			60	8 17 5			
20	3 0 11				60	60	12 8 10
25	3 5 4	35	35	4 10 9			
30	3 10 11		40	4 18 6			

Survivorship.—A Table of Annual Premiums payable during the Joint Continuance of the Two [Lives] for assuring One Hundred Pounds, to be paid at the Decease of one Person, A., provided anoth[er] be then living.

Age of A., the Life to be assured.	Age of B., the Life against which the Assurance is to be made.	Annual Premium.	Age of A., the Life to be assured.	Age of B., the Life against which the Assurance is to be made.	Annual Premium.	Age of A., the Life to be assured.	Age of B., the Life against which the Assurance is to be made.	Annual Premium.
		£ s. d.			£ s. d.			£ s. d.
10	10	1 3 9	30	10	2 2 5	50	10	4
	20	1 4 7		20	2 2 1		20	4
	30	1 2 10		30	1 19 11		30	4
	40	1 1 6		40	1 18 6		40	4
	50	1 0 0		50	1 15 0		50	3 19
	60	0 18 5		60	1 12 2		60	3
	70	0 16 11		70	1 9 10		70	2 11
	80	0 15 7		80	1 7 4		80	2
20	10	1 9 11	40	10	2 19 7	60	10	7
	20	1 10 6		20	2 19 6		20	7
	30	1 8 10		30	2 15 4		30	7
	40	1 6 7		40	2 12 10		40	7
	50	1 4 7		50	2 6 2		50	6 1
	60	1 2 8		60	2 0 6		60	6
	70	1 0 9		70	1 16 3		70	5
	80	0 19 3		80	1 13 6		80	4 1

From the specimens of premiums in the two preceding tables, the reader will easily judge of th[e] portional premium for any combination of two ages not inserted in them.

Instead of a gross sum payable at the decease of A. provided B. be then living, a **reversionary a[nnuity]** on the remainder of the life of B. after the decease of A. may be insured by the payment of an annu[al pre-] mium during the joint continuance of the two lives ; which annual premium may be learnt by app[lying] at the office.

Equitable Assurance Society. — The following is the

A Table of annual Premiums payable during the Continuance of Two Joint Lives for assur[ing One] Hundred Pounds, to be paid when either of the Lives shall drop.

Age.	Age.	L. s. d.	Age.	Age.	L. s. d.	Age.	Age.	L. s. d.	Age.	Age.	L. s. d.	Age.	Age.	L. s. d.
10	10	2 17 1	15	35	4 3 1	20	67	9 13 9	30	60	7 15 0	45	45	5 6
	15	3 1 1		40	4 10 4	25	25	4 0 10		67	9 18 1		50	6 1
	20	3 5 7		45	4 19 5		30	4 5 0	35	35	4 19 0		55	7 7
	25	3 9 3		50	5 11 3		35	4 10 3		40	5 5 6		60	8
	30	3 13 9		55	6 6 1		40	4 17 4		45	5 18 10		67	10
	35	3 19 6		60	7 6 0		45	5 6 2		50	6 5 0	50	50	7
	40	4 6 10		67	9 9 5		50	5 17 10		55	6 19 2		55	8
	45	4 15 11	20	20	3 13 11		55	6 12 6		60	7 18 6		60	8 1
	50	5 7 10		25	3 17 5		60	7 12 5		67	10 1 2		67	10
	55	6 2 8		30	4 1 9		67	9 15 9	40	40	5 11 9	55	55	8
	60	7 2 9		35	4 7 3	30	30	4 8 11		45	5 19 9		60	9
	67	9 6 3		40	4 14 6		35	4 14 1		50	6 10 8		67	11
15	15	3 5 0		45	5 3 6		40	5 0 11		55	7 4 5	60	60	10
	20	3 9 6		50	5 15 4		45	5 9 6		60	8 3 4		67	12
	25	3 13 1		55	6 10 2		50	6 1 0		67	10 5 6	67	67	13
	30	3 17 6		60	7 10 2		55	6 15 5						

An addition of 22 per cent. *computed upon the premium,* is charged upon military persons ; and [por]tion of *eleven per cent.* on officers on half-pay, officers in the militia, fencibles, and the like lev[ied] on persons not having had the small-pox, or having had the gout.

Persons preferring the payment of a gross sum or single premium upon an assurance for any [given] term, are chargeable in a due proportion to the annual premium for such term.

Every person making any assurance with the Society, pays 5s. in the name of entrance mon[ey ;] if the sum assured exceeds 100l., the entrance money is charged after the rate of 5s. for every 100[l.]; if the person upon whose life an assurance is proposed, does not appear before the directors, the e[ntrance] money is charged after the rate of 1l. for every 100l.

following are the premiums demanded by the Equitable Society for insuring 100l., or an equivalent ty on the contingency of one life's surviving the other.

Ages. Life to be assured	Ages. Life against which the Assurance is to be made.	Premium.	Annuity equivalent to 100l. to be paid from the Death of the Life assured, during the Remainder of the other Life.	Ages. Life to be assured	Ages. Life against which the Assurance is to be made.	Premium.	Annuity equivalent to 100l. to be paid from the Death of the Life assured, during the Remainder of the other Life.
		£ s. d.	£ s. d.			£ s. d.	£ s. d.
	10	1 8 6	5 14 6	40	50	2 12 10	9 16 6
	20	1 9 1	6 14 10		60	2 9 4	12 14 3
	30	1 8 3	7 14 11		70	2 5 11	18 5 6
	40	1 7 8	9 5 6		80	2 1 10	29 19 10
	50	1 6 11	11 13 0				
	60	1 6 0	15 13 5	50	10	4 0 11	5 1 4
	70	1 4 11	23 13 0		20	4 1 10	5 16 2
	80	1 3 4	40 10 8		30	4 0 1	6 12 2
	10	1 16 6	5 6 11		40	3 17 10	7 16 9
	20	1 17 0	6 4 1		50	3 13 10	9 12 8
	36	1 15 9	7 0 6		60	3 7 7	12 6 8
	40	1 14 8	8 4 11		70	3 1 6	17 11 5
	50	1 13 6	10 1 9		80	2 15 0	28 12 6
	60	1 12 1	13 0 7				
	70	1 10 6	18 12 8	60	10	5 16 9	4 19 3
	80	1 8 3	30 9 6		20	5 18 1	5 12 10
	10	2 5 5	5 5 8		30	5 16 3	6 7 7
	20	2 6 0	6 2 9		40	5 14 0	7 10 10
	30	2 4 6	6 19 6		50	5 10 7	9 8 0
	40	2 2 9	8 3 8		60	5 2 4	12 5 6
	50	2 0 11	10 0 6		70	4 9 10	17 5 8
	60	1 18 10	13 0 0		80	3 17 11	27 19 10
	70	1 16 7	18 12 10				
	80	1 13 9	30 9 3	67	10	8 1 0	4 17 8
	10	2 19 2	5 3 6		20	8 2 9	5 10 5
	20	2 19 10	5 19 9		30	8 0 10	6 4 0
	30	2 18 2	6 16 8		40	7 18 7	7 5 5
	40	2 15 11	8 1 0		50	7 15 6	9 0 6
					60	7 8 8	12 0 3
					70	6 10 8	17 1 8
					80	5 8 9	27 5 11

stated by Mr. Morgan, in his Account of the Equitable Society already referred to, that the r of insurances in that institution for terms of years does not much exceed *one hundredth part* of or the whole period of life; and that the business of the office at present is almost wholly confined assurance of persons on *their own lives* — those on the lives of *others*, whether for terms or for ance, being, in consequence of the commission money allowed to agents and attorneys, engrossed new offices. — (*Account of the Equitable Society*, p. 53.)

TEREST AND ANNUITIES. Interest is the sum paid by the borrower sum of money, or of any sort of valuable produce, to the lender, for its use.

e rate of interest, supposing the security for and facility of re-possessing the prin- or sum lent, to be equal, must obviously depend on what may be made by the yment of capital in industrious undertakings, or on the rate of profit. Where are high, as in the United States, interest is also high; and where they are com- vely low, as in Holland and England, interest is proportionally low. In fact, the f interest is nothing more than the *nett* profit on capital: whatever returns are ob- by the borrower, beyond the interest he has agreed to pay, really accrue to him ount of risk, trouble, or skill, or of advantages of situation and connection.

besides fluctuations in the rate of interest caused by the varying productiveness ustry, the rate of interest on each particular loan must, of course, vary according supposed solvency of the borrowers, or the degree of risk supposed to be incurred lender, of either not recovering payment at all, or not recovering it at the stipu- erm. No person of sound mind would lend on the personal security of an indi- of doubtful character and solvency, and on mortgage over a valuable estate, at the ate of interest. Wherever there is risk, it must be compensated to the lender by er premium or interest.

yet, obvious as this principle may appear, all governments have interfered with justment of the terms of loans; some to prohibit interest altogether, and others to tain rates which it should be deemed legal to charge, and illegal to exceed. The ice against taking interest seems to have principally originated in a mistaken view e enactments of the Mosaical law — (see *Michaelis on the Laws of Moses*, vol. ii. 7—353. Eng. ed.), and, a statement of Aristotle, to the effect that as money did not e money, no return could be equitably claimed by the lender! But whatever ave been the origin of this prejudice, it was formerly universal in Christendom; still supported by law in all Mohammedan countries. The famous reformer, , was one of the first who saw and exposed the absurdity of such notions — (see an from one of his epistles in *M'Culloch's Political Economy*, 2d ed. p. 510.); and uses caused by the prohibition, and the growing conviction of its impolicy, soon d to its relaxation. In 1554, a statute was passed, authorising lenders to charge cent. interest. In 1624, the legal rate was reduced to 8 per cent.; and in the f Queen Anne it was further reduced to 5 per cent., at which it still continues.

It is enacted, by the statute (12 Ann. c. 16.) making this reduction, that " all pers⋯ who shall receive, by means of any corrupt bargain, loan, exchange, chevizance, or ⋯terest of any wares, merchandise, or other thing whatever, or by any deceitful way ⋯ means, or by any covin, engine, or deceitful conveyance for the forbearing or giving ⋯ of payment, for one whole year for their money or other thing, above the sum of 5l. ⋯ 100l. for a year, shall forfeit for every such offence, the *treble* value of the monies, ⋯ other things, so lent, bargained," &c.

It is needless to waste the reader's time by entering into any lengthened arguments ⋯ show the inexpediency and mischievous effect of such interferences. This has been d⋯ over and over again. It is plainly in no respect more desirable to limit the rate of ⋯ terest, than it would be to limit the rate of insurance, or the prices of commodities. A⋯ though it were desirable, it cannot be accomplished. The real effect of all legislat⋯ enactments having such an object in view, is to increase, not diminish the rate of intere⋯ When the rate fixed by law is less than the market or customary rate, lenders and b⋯ rowers are obliged to resort to circuitous devices to evade the law; and as these devi⋯ are always attended with more or less trouble and risk, the rate of interest is prop⋯ tionally enhanced. During the late war it was not uncommon for a person to be payi⋯ 10 or 12 per cent. for a loan, which, had there been no usury laws, he might have ⋯ for 6 or 7 per cent. Neither is it by any means uncommon, when the rate fixed by ⋯ is more than the market rate, for borrowers to be obliged to pay more than they rea⋯ stipulated for. It is singular that an enactment which contradicts the most obvious p⋯ ciples, and has been repeatedly condemned by committees of the legislature, should s⋯ be allowed to preserve a place in the statute book.

Distinction of Simple and Compound Interest. — When a loan is made, it is usual ⋯ stipulate that the interest upon it should be regularly paid at the end of every year, ⋯ year, &c. A loan of this sort is said to be at simple interest. It is of the essence ⋯ such loan, that no part of the interest accruing upon it should be added to the princi⋯ to form a new principal; and though payment of the interest were not made whe⋯ becomes due, the lender would not be entitled to charge interest upon such unp⋯ interest. Thus, suppose 100l. were lent at simple interest at 5 per cent. payable at ⋯ end of each year, the lender would, at the end of three or four years, supposing him ⋯ have received no previous payments, be entitled to 15l. or 20l., and no more.

Sometimes, however, money or capital is invested so that the interest is not paid at ⋯ periods when it becomes due, but is progressively added to the principal; so tha⋯ every term a new principal is formed, consisting of the original principal, and the s⋯ cessive accumulations of interest upon interest. Money invested in this way is sai⋯ be placed at *compound interest.*

It appears not unreasonable, that when a borrower does not pay the interest he ⋯ contracted for, at the period when it is due, he should pay interest upon such inter⋯ This, however, is not allowed by the law of England; nor is it allowed to make a loa⋯ compound interest. But this rule is often evaded, by taking a new obligation for ⋯ principal with the interest included, when the latter becomes due. Investments at c⋯ pound interest are also very frequent. Thus, if an individual buy into the funds, ⋯ regularly buy fresh stock with the dividends, the capital will increase at compound ⋯ terest; and so in any similar case.

Calculation of Interest. — Interest is estimated at so much per cent. per annum, o⋯ dividing the principal into 100 equal parts, and specifying how many of these parts ⋯ paid yearly for its use. Thus, 5 per cent, or 5 parts out of 100, means that 5l. are ⋯ for the use of 100l. for a year, 10l. for the use of 200l. and 2l. 10s. for the use of ⋯ for the same period, and so on.

Suppose, now, that it is required to find the interest of 210l. 13s. for three years a⋯ half at 4 per cent. simple interest. In this case we must first divide the princi⋯ 210l. 13s. into 100 parts, 4 of which will be the interest for one year; and this b⋯ multiplied by 3½ will give the interest for three years and a half. But instead of ⋯ dividing by 100 and then multiplying by 4, the result will be the same, and the pro⋯ more expeditious, if we first multiply by 4 and then divide by 100. Thus,

£	s.					
210	13		Principal.			
	4		Rate per cent.			
1,00)8,42	12(	£	s.	d.		
20		8	8	6¼		One year's interest
8,52				3½		
12						
6,24		25	5	6¾		Three years' interest
4		4	4	3		Half a year's interest
96		£29	9	9¾		Three and a half years' interest

most superfluous to observe, that the same result would have been obtained by
lying the product of the principal and rate by the number of years, and then
g by 100.
ce, to find the interest of any sum at any rate per cent. for a year, multiply the
the rate per cent., and divide the product by 100.
ind the interest of any sum for a number of years, multiply its interest for one
y the number of years; or, without calculating its interest for one year, multiply
ncipal by the rate per cent. and that product by the number of years, and divide
product by 100.
n the interest of any sum is required for a number of days, they must be treated
ional parts of a year; that is, we must multiply the interest of a year by them, and
oy 365.
ose that it is required to find the interest of 210*l.* for 4 years 7 months and 25
4½ per cent: —

Interest for 4 years	=	£37·8000
6 months = ½ of 1 year	=	4·7250
1 month = ⅙ of 6 months =		·7875
25 days =		·6472
		£43·9597 = £43. 19*s.* 2¼*d.*

Principal.
Rate per cent.

·5 Interest for one year.
4

30 Ditto for four years.

erest for 25 days is $\frac{9 \cdot 45 \times 25}{365} = \cdot6472$; that is, it is equal to the interest for a
ltiplied by the fraction $\frac{25}{365}$. Division by 100 is performed by cutting off two
o the right.
attempts have been made to contrive more expeditious processes than the above
lating interest. The following is the best: —
ose it were required to find the interest upon 172*l.* for 107 days at 5 per cent.?
orms what is called in arithmetical books a double rule of three question, and
e stated as follows: —

days. £ £ days.
× 365 : 5 :: 172 × 107 : 2*l.* 10*s.* 4¾*d.* the interest required.

to find the interest of any sum for any number of days at any rate per cent.,
the sum by the number of days, and the product by the rate, and divide by
(365 × 100); the quotient is the interest required.
the rate is 5 per cent., or 1/20th of the principal, all that is required is to divide
uct of the sum multiplied by the days by 7,300 (365, the days in a year, multi-
20).
er cent. interest being found by this extremely simple process, it is usual in
to calculate 4 per cent. interest by deducting ⅕th; 3 per cent. by deducting
per cent. by dividing by 2; 2 per cent. by taking the half of 4, and so on.
culating interest upon accounts current, it is requisite to state the number of
ween each receipt, or payment, and the date (commonly 31st of December) to
e account current is made up. Thus, 172*l.* paid on the 15th of September,
interest to the 31st of December, 107 days. The amount of such interest
n, be calculated as now explained, or by the aid of tables. The reader will find,
rticle BOOKKEEPING, (p. 153.), an example of interest on an account current
d as above, without referring to tables.
0th of June is, after the 31st of December, the most usual date to which ac-
urrent are made up, and interest calculated. In West India houses the 30th of
the common date, because at that season the old crop of produce is generally
and the new begins to arrive.
f great importance, in calculating interest on accounts current, to be able
find the number of days from any day in any one month to any day in any
onth. This may be done with the utmost ease by means of the following

Table for ascertaining the Number of Days from any one Day in the Year to any other Day.

	Jan.	Feb.	March	April	May	June	July	Aug.	Sept.	Oct.	Nov.	Dec.	Jan.	Feb.	March	April	May	June	July	Aug.	Sept.	Oct.
1	32	60	91	121	152	182	213	244	274	305	335	17	48	76	107	137	168	198	229	260	29
2	33	61	92	122	153	183	214	245	275	306	336	18	49	77	108	138	169	199	230	261	29
3	34	62	93	123	154	184	215	246	276	307	337	19	50	78	109	139	170	200	231	262	29
4	35	63	94	124	155	185	216	247	277	308	338	20	51	79	110	140	171	201	232	263	29
5	36	64	95	125	156	186	217	248	278	309	339	21	52	80	111	141	172	202	233	264	29
6	37	65	96	126	157	187	218	249	279	310	340	22	53	81	112	142	173	203	234	265	29
7	38	66	97	127	158	188	219	250	280	311	341	23	54	82	113	143	174	204	235	266	29
8	39	67	98	128	159	189	220	251	281	312	342	24	55	83	114	144	175	205	236	267	29
9	40	68	99	129	160	190	221	252	282	313	343	25	56	84	115	145	176	206	237	268	29
10	41	69	100	130	161	191	222	253	283	314	344	26	57	85	116	146	177	207	238	269	29
11	42	70	101	131	162	192	223	254	284	315	345	27	58	86	117	147	178	208	239	270	30
12	43	71	102	132	163	193	224	255	285	316	346	28	59	87	118	148	179	209	240	271	30
13	44	72	103	133	164	194	225	256	286	317	347	29		88	119	149	180	210	241	272	30
14	45	73	104	134	165	195	226	257	287	318	348	30		89	120	150	181	211	242	273	30
15	46	74	105	135	166	196	227	258	288	319	349	31		90		151		212	243		30
16	47	75	106	136	167	197	228	259	289	320	350										

By this table may be readily ascertained the number of days from any given day in the year to a[ny]
For instance, from the 1st of January to the 14th of August (first and last days included), there
days. To find the number, look down the column headed January, to number 14, and then look a[long]
a parallel line to the column headed August, you find 226, the number required.

To find the number of days between any other two given days, when they are both after the 1st [Ja]
nuary, the number opposite to the first day must, of course, be deducted from that opposite to the
Thus, to find the number of days between the 13th of March and the 19th of August, deduct fro[m]
the number in the table opposite to 19 and under August, 72, the number opposite to 13 and under
and the remainder, 159, is the number required, last day included.

In leap years, *one* must be added to the number after the 28th of February.

For the mode of calculating discount, or of finding the present values of sum
at some future date, at simple interest, see DISCOUNT.

In counting-houses, interest tables are very frequently made use of. Such public
have, in consequence, become very numerous. Most of them have some peculiar r
mendation; but in the great requisites of simplicity of arrangement and comprehe
ness, we have seen none better adapted for general use, than those recently publish
Mr. Laurie.

When interest, instead of being simple, is compound, the first year's or term's in
must be found, and being added to the original principal, makes the principal
which interest is to be calculated for the second year or term; and the second
or term's interest being added to this last principal makes that upon which interes
be calculated for the third year or term; and so on for any number of years.

But when the number of years is considerable, this process becomes excee
cumbersome and tedious, and to facilitate it tables have been constructed, whi
subjoined.

The first of these tables (No. I.) represents the amount of 1*l.* accumulat
compound interest, at 3, 3½, 4, 4½, and 5 per cent. every year, from 1 year to 70
in pounds and decimals of a pound. Now, suppose that we wish to know how
500*l.* will amount to in 7 years at 4 per cent. In the column marked 4 per cer
opposite to 7 years, we find 1·315,932*l.*, which shows that 1*l.* will, if invested a
cent. compound interest, amount to 1·315,932 in 7 years; and consequently 500
in the same time and at the same rate, amount to 500 × 1·315,932*l.* or 657·966.
is, 657*l.* 19*s.* 4*d.*

For the same purpose of facilitating calculation, the present value of 1*l.* d
number of years hence, not exceeding 70, at 3, 3½, 4, 4½, and 5 per cent. compou
terest is given in the subjoined table, No. II. The use of this table is precisely
to the foregoing. Let it, for example, be required to find the present worth o
due 7 years hence, reckoning compound interest at 4 per cent. Opposite to 7
and under 4 per cent., we find ·75991,781*l.*, the present worth of 1*l.* due at the
7 years; and multiplying this sum by 500*l.*, the product, being 379·9589*l.*, c
19*s.* 2*d.*, is the answer required.

ANNUITIES.

Certain Annuities. — When a sum of money is to be paid yearly for a certain ~~b~~er of years, it is called an annuity. The annuities usually met with are either for ~~a~~n number of years, which are called *certain annuities ;* or they are to be paid so ~~~~as one or more individuals shall live, and are thence called *contingent annuities.*

~~~~ the amount of an annuity at any given time, is meant the sum to which it will ~~~~amount, supposing it to have been regularly improved at compound interest during ~~~~tervening period.

~~~~ the present value of an annuity for any given period, is meant the sum which, if ~~~~down at this moment, and improved at compound interest, will produce at the ~~~~d given an amount sufficient to pay each year's annuity.

~~~~umbers III. and IV. of the subjoined tables represent the amount and present ~~~~ of an annuity of 1*l.*, reckoning compound interest at $2\frac{1}{2}$, 3, $3\frac{1}{2}$, 4, $4\frac{1}{2}$, 5, and 6 ~~~~ent., from one year to 70. They, as well as the others, are taken from "Tables ~~~~terest, Discount, and Annuities, by John Smart, Gent. 4to. London, 1726." ~~~~ are carried to eight decimal places, and enjoy the highest character, both here and ~~~~ Continent, for accuracy and completeness. The original work is now become ~~~~carce.

~~~~e uses of these tables are numerous; and they are easily applied. Suppose, for ~~~~ple, it were required to tell the amount of an annuity of 50*l.* a year for 17 years ~~~~er cent. compound interest?

~~~~posite to 17 (Table III.) in the column of years, and under 4 per cent., is ~~~~751,239, being the amount of an annuity of 1*l.* for the given time at the given ~~~~er cent.; and this multiplied by 50, gives 1184·8756195 or 1184*l.* 17*s.* 6*d.* the ~~~~nt required.

~~~~opose now that it is required, what sum one must pay down to receive an annuity ~~~~*l.* to continue for 17 years, compound interest at 4 per cent.?

~~~~posite to 17 years (Table IV.) and under 4 per cent. is 12·16566,886, the present ~~~~ of an annuity of 1*l.* for the given time and at the given rate per cent.; and this ~~~~plied by 50 gives 608·283443, or 608*l.* 5*s.* 8*d.* the present value required.

~~~~en it is required to find the *time* which must elapse, in order that a given sum ~~~~ved at a specified rate of compound interest may increase to some other given ~~~~divide the latter sum by the former, and look for the quotient, or the number ~~~~st to it, in table No. I. under the given rate per cent., and the years opposite to it ~~~~e answer — Thus,

~~~~what time will 523*l.* amount to 1087*l.* 5*s.* 7*d.* at 5 per cent. compound interest? ~~~~ide 1087·2794 &c., by 523, and the quotient will be 2·0789, &c., which under 5 ~~~~nt. in Table I. is opposite to 15 years, the time required.

~~~~it had been required to find the time in which a given annuity, improved at a ~~~~ rate of compound interest, would have increased to some given sum, the question ~~~~ have been answered by dividing, as above, the given sum by the annuity; and ~~~~g for the quotient (not in table No. I., but) in table No. III. under the given ~~~~er cent., it would be found on a line with the time required. Thus,

~~~~owes 1,000*l.* and resolves to appropriate 10*l.* a year of his income to its discharge: ~~~~t time will the debt be extinguished, reckoning compound interest at 4 per cent.? ~~~~0 divided by 10 gives 100, the number in table No. III. under 4 per cent., and ~~~~t to this quotient is 99·8265, &c. opposite to 41 years, the required time. Had ~~~~te of interest been 5 per cent., the debt would have been discharged in somewhat ~~~~han 37 years. This example is given by Dr. Price (*Annuities,* 6th ed. vol. ii. ~~~~.); and on this principle the whole fabric of the sinking fund was constructed. ~~~~e abstract truth of the principle there cannot, indeed, be a doubt. But every ~~~~lepends on the increasing sums annually produced being immediately invested on ~~~~ne terms; and this, when the sum is large, and the period long, is altogether ~~~~ticable.

~~~~ersionary annuities are those which do not commence till after a certain number of ~~~~or till the occurrence of some event, as the death of an individual, &c.

~~~~ present value of a reversionary annuity is found by deducting from the value of ~~~~uity for the whole period, the value of an annuity to the term at which the ~~~~onary annuity is to commence. Thus,

~~~~at is the present value of an annuity of 50*l.* to continue for 25 years, commencing ~~~~ars from the present time, interest at 4 per cent.?

~~~~ording to table No. IV., the value of an annuity of 1*l.* for 25 years at 4 per cent. ~~~~2207,995, and that of 1*l.* for 7 years is 6·00205,467, which being deducted from ~~~~er, leaves 9·62002,528, which multiplied by 50 gives 481*l.*, the answer required.

~~~~oosing the annuity, instead of being for 25 years, had been a perpetuity, it would ~~~~een worth 1,250*l.*, from which deducting 300*l.* 2*s.*, the value of an annuity for ~~~~ at 4 per cent , there remains 949*l.* 18*s.* the value of the reversion.

For a selection of problems that may be solved by tables of annuities certain,
Smart's Tables, pp. 92—100.

2. *Life Annuities.* — A statement of the principles on which life annuities are ca
lated, is given in the article on INSURANCE (GENERAL PRINCIPLES OF). There
considerable discrepancy in the sums at which different authors, and different insura
offices, estimate the present value of life annuities payable to persons of the same
This does not arise from any difference in the mode of calculating the annuities,
from the different estimates which they form of the *expectation of life;* that is, the
period when, of a given number of persons alive at a certain age, the *half will be d*
It is upon this expectation (the value of which can only be learned by multiplied
careful observations on the rate of mortality), that all calculations of the value of
annuities are founded; and hence the importance of having it determined with
greatest possible accuracy. It is, however, to be regretted, that governments, who a
have the means of ascertaining the rate of mortality by observations made on a la
scale, have been singularly inattentive to their duty in this respect. And until a
few years since, when Mr. Finlaison was employed to calculate tables of the valu
annuities from the ages of the nominees in public tontines, and of individuals on wh
lives government had granted annuities, all that had been done in this country to la
solid foundation on which to construct the fabric of life insurance, had been the w
of a few private persons, who had, of course, but a limited number of observation
work upon.

The celebrated mathematician, Dr. Halley, was the first who calculated a tabl
mortality, which he deduced from observations made at Breslaw, in Silesia. In 1
Mr. De Moivre published the first edition of his tract on *Annuities on Lives.* In orde
facilitate the calculation of their values, Mr. De Moivre assumed the annual decrem
of life to be equal; that is, he supposed that out of 86 (the utmost limit of life on
hypothesis) persons born together, one would die every year till the whole were exti
This assumption agreed pretty well with the true values between 30 and 70 y
of age, as given in Dr. Halley's table; but was very remote from the truth in
earlier and later periods. Mr. Thomas Simson, in his work on *Annuities and Revers*
originally published in 1742, gave a table of mortality deduced from the London b
and tables founded upon it of the values of annuities. But at the period when this t
was calculated, the mortality in London was so much higher than in the rest of
country, that the values of the annuities given in it were far too small for general
In 1746, M. Deparcieux published, in his *Essai sur les Probabilités de la Durée de la*
Humaine — a work distinguished by its perspicuity and neatness — tables of mort
deduced from observations made on the mortuary registers of several religious ho
and on lists of the nominees in several tontines. In this work, separate tables
first constructed for males and females, and the greater longevity of the latter rend
apparent. M. Deparcieux's tables were a very great acquisition to the science; and
decidedly superior to some that are still extensively used. Dr. Price's famous
on Annuities, the first edition of which was published in 1770, contributed power
to direct the public attention to inquiries of this sort; and was, in this respect, of
great utility. Of the more recent works, the best are those of Mr. Baily and
Milne, which, indeed, are both excellent. The latter, besides all that was previo
known as to the history, theory, or practice of the science, contains much new
valuable matter; and to it we beg to refer such of our readers as wish to enter fully
the subject.

The table on which Dr. Price laid the greatest stress, was calculated from the b
registers kept at Northampton and some adjoining parishes. There can be no d
however, as well from original defects in the construction of the table, as from
improvement that has since taken place in the healthiness of the public, that the mort
represented in the Northampton table is, and has long been, decidedly above the av
rate of mortality in England. Mr. Morgan, indeed, the learned actuary of the
table Society, contends that this is not the case, and that the Society's experience s
that the Northampton table is still remarkably accurate. But the facts Mr. Mc
has disclosed in his *View of the Rise and Progress of the Equitable Society* (p. 42.),
lished in 1828, are quite at variance with this opinion: for he there states, that the dea
persons insured in the Equitable Society, from 50 to 60 years of age, during the t
years previously to 1828, were 339; whereas, according to the Northampton
they should have been 545! And Mr. Milne has endeavoured to show (Art. *Ann*
new ed. of *Ency. Brit.*) that the discrepancy is really much greater.

The only other table used to any extent in England for the calculation of life a
ties, is that framed by Mr. Milne from observations made by Dr. Heysham on th
of mortality at Carlisle. — It gives a decidedly lower rate of mortality than the
ampton table; and there are good grounds for thinking that the mortality wh
represents is not very different from the actual rate throughout most parts of Eng

it cannot be supposed that a table founded on so narrow a basis should give a
y fair view of the average mortality of the entire kingdom.

rder to exhibit the foundations on which tables of life annuities and insurance
en founded in this and other countries, we have given, in No. V. of the following
the rate of mortality that has been observed to take place among 1,000 children
gether, or the numbers alive at the end of each year, till the whole become ex-
n England, France, Sweden, &c., according to the most celebrated authorities.*
te of mortality at Carlisle, represented in this table, is less than that observed any
lse : the rates which approach nearest to it are those deduced from the observations
referred to, of M. Deparcieux, and those of M. Kerseboom, on the holders of
uities in Holland.

rder to calculate from this table the chance which a person of any given age
attaining to any higher age, we have only to divide the number of persons alive
higher age, given in that column of the table selected to decide the question,
umber of persons alive at the given age, and the fraction resulting is the chance.
ave added, by way of supplement to this table, Mr. Finlaison's table (No. VI.) of
of mortality among 1,000 children born together, according to the decrement
bserved to take place among the nominees in government tontines and life annui-
his country, distinguishing males from females. The rate of mortality which this
hibits is decidedly less than that given in the Carlisle table ; but the lives in the
re the average of the population, while those in the former are all picked. The
es in tontines are uniformly chosen among the healthiest individuals ; and none
se who consider their lives as good ever buy an annuity. Still, however, the table is
rious ; and it sets the superiority of female life in a very striking point of view.

s VII. and VIII. give the *expectation of life*, according to the mortality observed
hampton and Carlisle ; the former by Dr. Price, and the latter by Mr. Milne.

next table, No. IX., extracted from the Second Report of the Committee of
se of Commons on Friendly Societies, gives a comparative view of the results
of the most celebrated tables of mortality, in relation to the rate of mortality,
ectation of life, the value of an annuity, &c. The coincidence between the re-
luced from M. Deparcieux's table, and that for Carlisle, is very striking. And
r the information on these subjects laid before the reader as complete as the nature
vork will admit, we have given tables (Nos. X.—XV.) of the value of an annuity
a single life, at every age, and at 3, 4, 5, 6, 7, and 8 per cent., according to the
opton and Carlisle tables ; we have also given tables of the value of an annuity
two equal lives, and on two lives differing by five years, at 3, 4, 5, and 6 per
cording to the same tables. It is but seldom, therefore, that our readers will
to resort to any other work for the means of solving the questions that usually
practice with regard to annuities ; and there are not many works in which they
so good a collection of tables. We subjoin one or two examples of the mode of
e tables of life annuities.

ose it were required, what ought a person, aged 45, to give, to secure an annuity
year for life, interest at 4 per cent., according to the Carlisle table ?
le No. XI., under 4 per cent., and opposite 45, is 14·104, the value of an annuity
hich being multiplied by 50, gives 705·2, or 705l. 4s., the value required. Ac-
to the Northampton table, the annuity would only have been worth 555l. 4s
alue of an annuity on two lives of the same age, or on two lives differing by five
ay be found in precisely the same way.

questions in *reversionary* life annuities admit of an equally easy solution. Thus,
it is required to find the present value of A.'s interest in an estate worth 100l. a
ling to him at the death of B., aged 40, interest 4 per cent., according to the
table ?
alue of the perpetuity of 100l. a year, interest 4 per cent., is 2,500l. ; and the
an annuity of 100l. on a person aged 40, interest at 4 per cent., is 1,507l. 8s.,
ducted from 2,500l., leaves 992l. 12s., the present value required.

son, aged 30, wishes to purchase an annuity of 50l. for his wife, aged 25, pro-
e survive him ; what ought he to pay for it, interest at 4 per cent., according to
isle table ?
alue of an annuity of 1l. on a life aged 30, is 16·852 ; from which subtracting
of an annuity of 1l. on two joint lives of 25 and 30, 14·339, the difference,
50 = 125·650, or 125l. 13s., the sum required.

e solution of the more complex cases of survivorship, which do not often occur
ce, recourse may be had to the directions in Mr. Milne's treatise on Annuities,
r works of that description. To attempt explaining them here would lead us
ils quite inconsistent with the objects of this work.

———

able was originally given in Mr. Baily's work on Annuities, and was reprinted in the Second
he Committee of the House of Commons on Friendly Societies.

TABLES OF INTEREST AND ANNUITIES.

I. Table showing the Amount of £1. improved at Compound Interest, at 2½, 3, 3½, 4, 4½, 5, per Cent., at the End of every Year, from 1 to 70.

Years.	2½ per Cent.	3 per Cent	3½ per Cent.	4 per Cent.	4½ per Cent.	5 per Cent.	6 per
1	1·02500,000	1·03000,000	1·03500,000	1·04000,000	1·04500,000	1·05000,000	1·060
2	1·05062,500	1·06090,000	1·07122,500	1·08160,000	1·09202,500	1·10250,000	1·123
3	1·07689,062	1·09272,700	1·10871,787	1·12486,400	1·14116,612	1·15762,500	1·191
4	1·10381,289	1·12550,881	1·14752,300	1·16985,856	1·19251,860	1·21550,625	1·262
5	1·13140,821	1·15927,407	1·18768,631	1·21665,290	1 24618,194	1·27628,156	1·338
6	1·15969,342	1·19405,230	1·22925,533	1·26531,902	1·30226,012	1·34009,564	1·418
7	1·18868,575	1·22987,387	1·27227,926	1·31593,178	1·36086,183	1·40710,042	1·503
8	1·21840,290	1·26677,008	1·31680,904	1·36856,905	1·42210,061	1·47745,544	1·593
9	1·24886,297	1·30477,318	1·36289,735	1·42331,181	1·48609,514	1·55132,822	1·689
10	1·28008,454	1·34391,638	1·41059,876	1·48024,428	1·55296,942	1·62889,463	1·790
11	1·31208,666	1·38423,387	1·45996,972	1·53945,406	1·62285,305	1·71033,936	1·898
12	1·34488,882	1·42576,089	1·51106,866	1·60103,222	1·69588,143	1·79585,633	2·012
13	1·37851,104	1·46853,371	1·56395,606	1·66507,351	1·77219,610	1·88564,914	2·132
14	1·41297,382	1·51258,972	1·61869,452	1·73167,645	1·85194,492	1·97993,160	2·260
15	1·44829,817	1·55796,742	1·67534,883	1·80094,351	1·93528,244	2·07892,818	2·396
16	1·48450,562	1·60470,644	1·73398,604	1·87298,125	2·02237,015	2·18287,459	2·540
17	1·52161,826	1·65284,763	1·79467,555	1·94790,050	2·11337,681	2·29201,832	2·692
18	1·55965,872	1·70243,306	1·85748,920	2·02581,652	2·20847,877	2·40661,923	2·854
19	1·59865,019	1·75350,605	1·92250,132	2·10684,918	2·30786,031	2·52695,020	3·025
20	1·63861,644	1·80611,123	1·98978,886	2·19112,314	2·41171,402	2·65329,771	3·207
21	1·67958,185	1·86029,457	2·05943,147	2·27876,807	2·52024,116	2·78596,259	3·399
22	1·72157,140	1·91610,341	2·13151,158	2·36991,879	2·63365,201	2·92526,072	3·603
23	1·76461,068	1·97358,651	2·20611,448	2·46471,555	2·75216,635	3·07152,376	3·819
24	1·80872,595	2·03279,411	2·28332,849	2·56330,417	2·87601,383	3·22509,994	4·048
25	1·85394,410	2·09377,793	2·36324,498	2·66583,633	3·00543,446	3·38635,494	4·291
26	1·90029,270	2·15659,127	2·44595,856	2·77246,979	3·14067,901	3·55567,269	4·549
27	1·94780,002	2·22128,901	2·531 6,711	2·88336,858	3·28200,956	3·73345,632	4·822
28	1·99649,502	2·28792,768	2·62017,696	2·99870,332	3·42969,999	3·92012,914	5·11
29	2·04640,739	2·35656,551	2·71187,798	3·11865,145	3·58403,649	4·11613,560	5·418
30	2·09756,758	2·42726,247	2·80679,370	3·24339,751	3·74531,813	4·32194,238	5·743
31	2·15000,677	2·50008,035	2·90503,148	3·37313,341	3·91385,745	4·53803,949	6·088
32	2·20375,694	2·57508,276	3·00670,759	3·50805,875	4·08998,104	4·76494,147	6·453
33	2·25885,086	2·65233,524	3·11194,235	3·64838,110	4·27403,018	5·00318,854	6·840
34	2·31532,213	2·73190,530	3·22086,033	3·79431,634	4·46656,154	5·25334,797	7·251
35	2·37320,519	2·81386,245	3·33359,045	3·94608,899	4·66734,781	5·51601,537	7 686
36	2·43253,532	2·89827,833	3·45026,611	4·10393,255	4·87737,846	5·79181,614	8·14
37	2·49334,870	2·98522,668	3·57102,543	4·26808,986	5·09686,049	6·08140,694	8·636
38	2·55568,242	3·07478,348	3·69601,132	4·43881,345	5·32621,921	6·38547,729	9·15
39	2·61957,448	3·16702,698	3·82537,171	4·61636,599	5·56589,908	6·70475,115	9 70
40	2·68506,384	3·26203,779	3·95925,972	4·80102,063	5·81636,454	7·03998,871	10·285
41	2·75219,043	3·35989,893	4·09783,381	4·99206,145	6·07810,094	7·39198,815	10·90
42	2·82099,520	3·46069,589	4·24125,799	5·19278,391	6·35161,548	7·76158,755	11·55
43	2·89152,008	3·56451,677	4·38970,202	5·40049,527	6·63743,818	8·14966,693	12·25
44	2·96382,805	3·67145,227	4·54334,160	5·61651,508	6·93612,290	8·15715,028	12·98
45	3·03790,328	3·78149,584	4·70233,855	5·84117,568	7·24824,843	8·98500,779	13 76
46	3·11385,086	3·89504,372	4·86691,110	6·07482,271	7·57441,961	9·43425,818	14·59
47	3·19169,713	4·01189,503	5·03728,404	6·31781,562	7·91626,849	9·90597,109	15·46
48	3·27148,956	4·13225,188	5·21358,898	6·57052,824	8·27145,557	10·40126,965	16·39
49	3·35327,680	4·25621,944	5·39606,459	6·83334,937	8·64367,107	10·92133,313	17 37
50	3·43710,872	4·38390,602	5·58494,686	7·10668,335	9·03263,627	11·46759,978	18·42
51	3·52303,644	4·51542,320	5·78039,930	7·39095,068	9·43910,490	12·04076,977	19 52
52	3·61111,235	4·65088,590	5·98271,527	7·68658,871	9·86386,463	12·64280,826	20·69
53	3·70139,016	4·79041,247	6·19210,824	7·99405,226	10·30773,853	13·27494,868	21·93
54	3·79392,491	4·93412,485	6·40883,202	8·31381,435	10·77158,677	13·93869,611	23·25
55	3·88877,303	5·08214,859	6·63314,114	8·64636,692	11·25630,817	14·63563,092	24·65
56	3·98599,236	5·23461,305	6·86530,108	8·99222,160	11·76294,204	15·36741,246	26·12
57	4·08564,217	5·39165,144	7·10508,662	9·35191,046	12·29216,993	16·13578,308	27·69
58	4·18778,322	5·55340,098	7·35428,215	9·72598,688	12·84531,758	16·94257,224	29 85
59	4·29247,780	5·72000,301	7·61164,203	10·11502,636	13·42355,687	17·78970,085	31·19
60	4·39978,975	5·89160,310	7·87809,090	10·51962,741	14·02740,793	18·67918,589	32·98
61	4·50978,449	6·06835,120	8·15382,408	10·94041,251	14·65864,129	19·61314,519	34·96
62	4·62252,910	6·25040,173	8·43920,793	11·37802,901	15·31828,014	20·59380,245	37·06
63	4·73809,233	6·43791,379	8·73458,020	11·83315,017	16·00760,275	21·62349,257	39 28
64	4·85654,464	6·63105,120	9·04029,051	12·30647,617	16·72794,487	22·70466,7.0	41 64
65	4·97795,826	6·82998,273	9·35670,068	12·79873,522	17·48070,239	23·83990,056	44 14
66	5·10240,721	7·03488,222	9 68418,520	13·31058,463	18·26733,400	25·03189,559	46 79
67	5·22996,739	7·24592,868	10·02313,168	13·84311,201	19·08936,403	26·28349,036	49 6
68	5·36071,658	7·46330,654	10·37394,129	14·39683,649	19·94838,541	27·59766,488	52·5
69	5·49473,449	7·68720,574	10·73702,911	14·97270,995	20·84606,276	28·97754,813	55 73
70	5·63210,286	7·91782,191	11·11282,596	15·57161,835	21·78413,558	30·42642,553	59 07

ble showing the PRESENT VALUE of £1. receivable at the End of any given Year, from 1 to 70, reckoning Compound Interest at 2½, 3, 3½, 4, 4½, 5, and 6 per Cent.

2½ per Cent.	3 per Cent.	3½ per Cent.	4 per Cent.	4½ per Cent.	5 per Cent.	6 per Cent.
0·97560,976	0·97087,379	0·96618,357	0·96153,846	0·95693,780	0·95238,095	0·94339,623
·95181,440	·94259,591	·93351,070	·92455,621	·91572,995	·90702,948	·88999,644
·92859,941	·91514,166	·90194,270	·88899,636	·87629,660	·86383,760	·83961,928
·90595,064	·88848,705	·87144,223	·85480,419	·83856,154	·82270,247	·79209,366
·88385,429	·86260,878	·84197,317	·82192,711	·80245,105	·78352,616	·74725,817
·86229,687	·83748,426	·81350,064	·79031,453	·76789,574	·74621,540	·70496,054
·84126,524	·81309,151	·78599,096	·75991,781	·73482,846	·71068,133	·66505,711
·82074,657	·78940,923	·75941,156	·73069,020	·70318,513	·67683,936	·62741,237
·80072,836	·76641,673	·73373,097	·70258,674	·67290,443	·64460,892	·59189,846
·78119,840	·74409,391	·70891,881	·67556,417	·64392,768	·61391,325	·55839,478
·76214,478	·72242,126	·68494,571	·64958,093	·61619,874	·58467,929	·52678,753
·74355,589	·70137,988	·66178,330	·62459,705	·58966,386	·55683,742	·49696,936
·72542,038	·68095,134	·63940,415	·60057,409	·56427,164	·53039,135	·46883,902
·70772,720	·66111,781	·61778,179	·57747,508	·53997,286	·50506,795	·44230,096
·69046,556	·64186,195	·59689,062	·55526,450	·51672,044	·48101,710	·41726,506
·67362,493	·62316,694	·57670,591	·53390,818	·49446,932	·45811,152	·39364,628
·65719,506	·60501,645	·55720,378	·51337,325	·47317,639	·43629,669	·37136,442
·64116,594	·58739,461	·53836,114	·49362,812	·45280,037	·41552,065	·35034,379
·62552,772	·57028,603	·52015,569	·47464,242	·43330,179	·39573,396	·33051,301
·61027,094	·55367,575	·50256,588	·45638,695	·41464,286	·37688,948	·31180,473
·59538,629	·53754,928	·48557,090	·43883,360	·39678,743	·35894,236	·29415,540
·58086,467	·52189,250	·46915,063	·42195,539	·37970,089	·34184,987	·27750,510
·56669,724	·50669,175	·45328,563	·40572,633	·36335,013	·32557,131	·26179,726
·55287,535	·49193,374	·43795,713	·39012,147	·34770,347	·31006,791	·24697,855
·53939,059	·47760,556	·42314,699	·37511,680	·33273,060	·29530,277	·23299,863
·52623,472	·46369,473	·40883,767	·36068,923	·31840,248	·28124,073	·21981,003
·51339,973	·45018,906	·39501,224	·34681,657	·30469,137	·26784,832	·20736,795
·50087,778	·43707,675	·38165,434	·33347,747	·29157,069	·25509,364	·19563,014
·48866,125	·42434,636	·36874,815	·32065,141	·27901,502	·24294,632	·18455,674
·47674,269	·41198,676	·35627,841	·30831,867	·26700,001	·23137,745	·17411,013
·46511,481	·39998,714	·34423,035	·29646,026	·25550,241	·22035,947	·16425,484
·45377,055	·38833,703	·33258,971	·28505,794	·24449,991	·20986,617	·15495,740
·44270,298	·37702,625	·32134,271	·27409,417	·23397,121	·19987,254	·14618,622
·43190,534	·36604,490	·31047,605	·26355,209	·22589,589	·19035,480	·13791,153
·42137,107	·35538,340	·29997,686	·25341,547	·21425,444	·18129,029	·13010,522
·41109,372	·34503,243	·28983,272	·24366,872	·20502,817	·17265,741	·12274,077
·40106,705	·33498,294	·28003,161	·23429,685	·19619,921	·16443,563	·11579,318
·39128,492	·32522,615	·27056,194	·22528,543	·18775,044	·15660,536	·10923,885
·38174,139	·31575,355	·26141,250	·21662,061	·17966,549	·14914,797	·10305,552
·37243,062	·30655,684	·25257,247	·20828,904	·17192,870	·14204,568	·09722,219
·36334,695	·29762,800	·24403,137	·20027,792	·16452,507	·13528,160	·09171,905
·35448,483	·28895,922	·23577,910	·19257,493	·15744,026	·12883,962	·08652,740
·34583,886	·28054,294	·22780,590	·18516,820	·15066,054	·12270,440	·08162,962
·33740,376	·27237,178	·22010,231	·17804,635	·14417,276	·11686,133	·07700,908
·32917,440	·26443,862	·21265,924	·17119,841	·13796,437	·11129,651	·07265,007
·32114,576	·25673,652	·20546,787	·16461,386	·13200,392	·10599,668	·06853,781
·31331,294	·24925,877	·19851,968	·15828,256	·12633,810	·10094,921	·06465,831
·30567,116	·24199,880	·19180,645	·15219,476	·12089,771	·09614,211	·06099,840
·29821,576	·23495,029	·18532,024	·14634,112	·11569,158	·09156,391	·05754,566
·29094,221	·22810,708	·17905,337	·14071,262	·11070,965	·08720,373	·05428,836
·28384,606	·22146,318	·17299,843	·13530,059	·10594,225	·08305,117	·05121,544
·27692,298	·21501,280	·16714,824	·13009,672	·10138,014	·07909,635	·04831,645
·27016,876	·20875,029	·16149,589	·12509,300	·09701,449	·07532,986	·04558,156
·26357,928	·20267,019	·15603,467	·12028,173	·09283,683	·07174,272	·04300,147
·25715,052	·19676,717	·15075,814	·11565,551	·08883,907	·06832,640	·04056,742
·25087,855	·19103,609	·14566,004	·11120,722	·08501,347	·06507,276	·03827,115
·24475,957	·18547,193	·14073,433	·10693,002	·08135,260	·06197,406	·03610,486
·23878,982	·18006,984	·13597,520	·10281,733	·07784,938	·05902,291	·03406,119
·23296,568	·17482,508	·13137,701	·09886,282	·07449,701	·05621,230	·03213,320
·22728,359	·16973,309	·12693,431	·09506,004	·07128,901	·05353,552	·03031,434
·22174,009	·16478,941	·12264,184	·09140,423	·06821,915	·05098,621	·02859,843
·21633,179	·15998,972	·11849,453	·08788,868	·06528,148	·04855,830	·02697,965
·21105,541	·15532,982	·11448,747	·08450,835	·06247,032	·04624,600	·02545,250
·20590,771	·15080,565	·11061,591	·08125,803	·05978,021	·04404,381	·02401,179
·20088,557	·14641,325	·10687,528	·07813,272	·05790,594	·04194,648	·02265,264
·19598,593	·14214,879	·10326,114	·07512,760	·05474,253	·03994,903	·02137,041
·19120,578	·13800,853	·09976,922	·07223,809	·05238,519	·03804,670	·02016,077
·18554,223	·13398,887	·09639,538	·06945,970	·05012,937	·03623,495	·01901,959
·18099,242	·13008,628	·09313,563	·06678,818	·04797,069	·03450,948	·01794,301
·17755,358	·12629,736	·08998,612	·06421,940	·04590,497	·03286,617	·01692,737

680

III. Table showing the Amount of an Annuity of £1. per Annum, improved at Compound Intere[st] 2½, 3, 3½, 4, 4½, 5, and 6 per Cent. at the end of each Year, from 1 to 70.

Years.	2½ per Cent.	3 per Cent.	3½ per Cent.	4 per Cent.	4½ per Cent.	5 per Cent.	6 per Cent.
1	1·00000,000	1·00000,000	1·00000,000	1·00000,000	1·00000,000	1·00000,000	1·00000,0
2	2·02500,000	2·03000,000	2·03500,000	2·04000,000	2·04500,000	2·05000,000	2·06000,0
3	3·07562,500	3·09090,000	3·10622,500	3·12160,000	3·13702,500	3·15250,000	3·18360,0
4	4·15251,562	4·18362,700	4·21494,287	4·24646,400	4·27819,112	4·31012,500	4·37461,6
5	5·25632,852	5·30913,581	5·36246,588	5·41632,256	5·47070,973	5·52563,125	5·63709,2
6	6·38773,673	6·46840,988	6·55015,218	6·63297,546	6·71689,166	6·80191,281	6·97531,8
7	7·54743,015	7·66246,218	7·77940,751	7·89829,448	8·01915,179	8·14200,845	8·39383,7
8	8·73611,590	8·89233,605	9·05168,677	9·21422,626	9·38001,362	9·54910,888	9·89746,7
9	9·95451,880	10·15910,613	10·36849,581	10·58279,531	10·80211,423	11·02656,432	11·49131,5
10	11·20338,177	11·46387,931	11·73139,316	12·00610,712	12·28820,937	12·57789,254	13·18079,4
11	12·48346,631	12·80779,569	13·14199,192	13·48635,141	13·84117,879	14·20678,716	14·97164,2
12	13·79555,297	14·19202,956	14·60196,164	15·02580,546	15·46403,184	15·91712,652	16·86994,1
13	15·14044,179	15·61779,045	16·11303,030	16·62683,768	17·15991,327	17·71298,285	18·88213,7
14	16·51895,284	17·08632,416	17·67698,636	18·29191,119	18·93210,937	19·59863,199	21·01506,5
15	17·93192,666	18·59891,389	19·29568,088	20·02358,764	20·78405,429	21·57856,359	23·27596,9
16	19·38022,483	20·15688,130	20·97102,971	21·82453,114	22·71933,673	23·63749,177	25·67252,8
17	20·86473,045	21·76158,774	22·70501,575	23·69751,239	24·74170,689	25·84036,636	28·21287,9
18	22·38634,871	23·41443,577	24·49969,130	25·64541,288	26·85508,370	28·13238,467	30·90565,2
19	23·94600,743	25·11686,884	26·35718,050	27·67122,940	29·06356,246	30·53900,391	33·75999,1
20	25·54465,761	26·87037,449	28·27968,181	29·77807,858	31·37142,277	33·06595,410	36·78559,1
21	27·18327,405	28·67648,572	30·26947,068	31·96920,172	33·78313,680	35·71925,181	39·99272,6
22	28·86285,590	30·53678,030	32·32890,215	34·24796,979	36·30337,795	38·50521,440	43·39229,0
23	30·58442,730	32·45288,370	34·46041,373	36·61788,858	38·93702,996	41·43047,512	46·99582,7
24	32·34903,798	34·42647,022	36·66652,821	39·08260,413	41·68919,631	44·50199,888	50·81557,7
25	34·15776,393	36·45926,432	38·94985,669	41·64590,830	44·56521,014	47·72709,882	54·86451,2
26	36·01170,803	38·55304,225	41·31310,168	44·31174,463	47·57064,460	51·11345,376	59·15638,2
27	37·91200,073	40·70963,352	43·75906,024	47·08421,441	50·71152,361	54·66912,645	63·70576,5
28	39·85980,075	42·93092,252	46·29062,734	49·96758,299	53·99333,317	58·40258,277	68·52811,1
29	41·85629,577	45·21885,020	48·91079,930	52·96628,631	57·42303,316	62·32271,191	73·63979,8
30	43·90270,316	47·57541,571	51·62267,728	56·08493,776	61·00706,966	66·43884,750	79·05818,6
31	46·00027,074	50·00267,818	54·42947,098	59·32833,527	64·75238,779	70·76078,988	84·80167,7
32	48·15027,751	52·50275,852	57·33450,247	62·70146,868	68·66624,524	75·29882,936	90·88977,8
33	50·35403,445	55·07784,128	60·34121,005	66·20952,743	72·75622,628	80·06377,083	97·34516,4
34	52·61288,531	57·73017,652	63·45315,240	69·85790,853	77·03025,646	85·06695,937	104·18575,4
35	54·92820,744	60·46208,181	66·67401,274	73·65222,487	81·49661,800	90·32030,734	111·43477,9
36	57·30141,263	63·27594,427	70·00760,318	77·59831,387	86·16396,581	95·83632,271	119·12086,6
37	59·73394,794	66·17422,259	73·45786,930	81·70224,642	91·04134,427	101·62813,884	127·26811,8
38	62·22729,664	69·15944,927	77·02889,472	85·97033,628	96·13820,476	107·70954,579	135·90420,5
39	64·78297,906	72·23423,275	80·72490,604	90·40914,973	101·46442,398	114·09502,308	145·05845,8
40	67·40255,354	75·40125,973	84·55027,775	95·02551,572	107·03032,306	120·79977,423	154·76196,5
41	70·08761,737	78·66329,753	88·50953,747	99·82653,635	112·84668,759	127·83976,294	165·04768,3
42	72·83980,781	82·02319,645	92·60737,128	104·81959,780	118·92478,854	135·23175,109	175·95064,4
43	75·66080,300	85·48389,234	96·84862,928	110·01238,171	125·27640,402	142·99333,864	187·50757,2
44	78·55232,308	89·04840,911	101·23833,130	115·41287,698	131·91384,220	151·14300,558	199·75803,7
45	81·51613,116	92·71986,139	105·78167,290	121·02939,206	138·84996,510	159·70015,586	212·74351,9
46	84·55403,443	96·50145,723	110·48403,145	126·87056,774	146·09821,353	168·68516,365	226·50812,4
47	87·66788,529	100·39650,095	115·35097,255	132·94539,045	153·67263,314	178·11942,183	241·09861,5
48	90·85958,243	104·40839,598	120·38825,659	139·26320,607	161·58700,163	188·02539,292	256·56452,8
49	94·13107,199	108·54064,785	125·60184,557	145·83373,431	169·85935,720	198·42666,257	272·95840,0
50	97·48434,879	112·79686,729	130·99791,016	152·66708,368	178·50302,828	209·34799,570	290·33590,9
51	100·92145,751	117·18077,331	136·58283,702	159·77376,703	187·53566,455	220·81539,548	308·75605,
52	104·44449,395	121·69619,651	142·36323,631	167·16471,771	196·97476,946	232·85616,526	328·28142,
53	108·05560,629	126·34708,240	148·34594,958	174·85130,642	206·83863,408	245·49897,352	346·97830,
54	111·75699,645	131·13749,488	154·53805,782	182·84535,868	217·14637,261	258·77392,220	370·91700,
55	115·05092,136	136·07161,972	160·94688,984	191·15917,302	227·91795,938	272·71261,831	394·17202,
56	119·43069,440	141·15375,782	167·58003,099	199·80553,994	239·17426,755	287·34824,922	418·82234,
57	122·42568,676	146·38838,156	174·44533,207	208·79776,154	250·93710,959	302·71566,168	444·95168,
58	127·51132,893	151·78003,280	181·55091,869	218·14967,200	263·22927,953	318·85144,477	472·64879,
59	131·69911,215	157·33343,379	188·90520,085	227·87565,888	276·07459,710	335·79401,700	502·00771,
60	135·99158,995	163·05343,680	196·51688,288	237·99068,524	289·49795,397	353·58371,785	533·12818,
61	140·39137,970	168·94503,991	204·39497,378	248·51031,265	303·52536,190	372·26290,375	566·11587,
62	144·90116,419	175·01339,110	212·54879,786	259·45072,516	318·18400,319	391·87604,893	601·08282,
63	149·52369,830	181·26379,284	220·98800,579	270·82875,416	333·50228,333	412·46985,138	638·14719,
64	154·26178,563	187·70170,662	229·72258,599	282·66190,433	349·50988,608	434·09334,395	677·43666,
65	159·11833,027	193·33275,782	238·76287,650	294·96838,050	366·23783,096	456·79801,115	719·08286,
66	164·09625,853	201·16274,055	248·11957,218	307·76711,572	383·71853,335	480·63791,170	763·22783,
67	169·19869,574	208·19762,277	257·80376,238	321·07780,035	401·98586,735	505·66980,729	810·02150,
68	174·42866,313	215·44355,145	267·82689,406	334·92091,236	421·07523,138	531·95329,765	859·62279,
69	179·78937,971	222·90685,800	278·20083,535	349·31774,886	441·02361,679	559·55096,254	912·20016,
70	185·28411,421	230·59406,374	288·93786,459	364·29045,881	461·86967,955	588·52851,066	967·93216,

le showing the PRESENT VALUE OF AN ANNUITY of £1. per Annum, to continue for any given nber of Years, from 1 to 70, reckoning Compound Interest at 2½, 3, 3½, 4, 4½, 5, and 6 per Cent.

per Cent.	3 per Cent.	3½ per Cent.	4 per Cent.	4½ per Cent.	5 per Cent.	6 per Cent.
·97560,976	0·97087,379	0·96618,357	0·96153,846	0·95693,780	0·95238,095	0·94339,623
·92742,415	1·91346,969	1·89969,427	1·88609,467	1·87266,775	1·85941,043	1·83339,267
85602,356	2·82861,135	2·80163,698	2·77509,103	2·74896,435	2·72324,803	2·67301,195
76197,421	3·71709,840	3·67307,921	3·62989,522	3·58752,570	3·54595,050	3·46510,561
64582,849	4·57970,719	4·51505,237	4·45182,233	4·38997,674	4·32947,667	4·21236,378
50812,536	5·41719,144	5·32855,302	5·24213,686	5·15787,248	5·07569,207	4·91732,432
·34939,060	6·23028,295	6·11454,398	6·00205,467	5·89270,094	5·78637,340	5·58238,144
17013,717	7·01969,219	6·87395,553	6·73274,468	6·59588,607	6·46321,276	6·20979,381
97086,553	7·78610,892	7·60768,651	7·43533,161	7·26879,049	7·10782,167	6·80169,227
75206,393	8·53020,284	8·31660,532	8·11089,578	7·91271,818	7·72173,493	7·36008,705
51420,871	9·25262,410	9·00155,103	8·76047,671	8·52891,692	8·30641,422	7·88687,457
25776,460	9·95400,398	9·66333,433	9·38507,376	9·11858,078	8·86325,164	8·38384,393
98318,497	10·63495,532	10·30273,848	9·98564,785	9·68285,242	9·39357,299	8·85268,295
69091,217	11·29607,312	10·92052,027	10·56312,293	10·22282,528	9·89864,094	9·29498,392
38137,773	11·93793,507	10·51741,089	11·11838,744	10·73954,573	10·37965,804	9·71224,898
05500,266	12·56110,201	12·09411,681	11·65229,561	11·23401,505	10·83776,956	10·10589,526
71219,772	13·16611,845	12·65132,058	12·16566,886	11·70719,143	11·27406,625	10·47725,968
35336,363	13·75351,306	13·18968,172	12·65929,698	12·15999,180	11·68958,690	10·82760,347
97889,134	14·32379,909	13·70983,741	13·13393,940	12·59329,359	12·08532,086	11·15811,648
58916,228	14·87747,484	14·21240,330	13·59032,635	13·00793,645	12·46221,034	11·46992,121
18454,857	15·41502,412	14·69797,420	14·02915,995	13·40472,388	12·82115,271	11·76407,661
76541,324	15·93691,662	15·16712,483	14·45111,534	13·78442,476	13·16300,258	12·04158,171
33211,048	16·44360,837	15·62041,047	14·85684,167	14·14777,489	13·48857,388	12·30337,897
88498,583	16·93564,210	16·05836,760	15·24696,314	14·49547,837	13·79864,179	12·55035,752
42437,642	17·41314,766	16·48151,459	15·62207,995	14·82820,896	14·09394,457	12·78335,615
95061,114	17·87684,239	16·89035,226	15·98276,918	15·14661,145	14·27518,530	13·00316,618
46401,087	18·32703,145	17·28536,450	16·32958,575	15·45130,282	14·64303,362	13·21053,413
96488,865	18·76410,820	17·66701,884	16·66306,322	15·74287,351	14·89812,726	13·40616,428
45354,991	19·18845,456	18·03576,700	16·98371,464	16·02188,853	15·14107,358	13·59072,101
03029,259	19·60044,132	18·39204,541	17·29203,330	16·28888,854	15·37245,103	13·76483,115
39540,741	20·00042,847	18·73527,576	17·58849,356	16·54439,095	15·59281,050	13·92908,599
94917,796	20·38876,550	19·06886,547	17·87355,150	16·78889,086	15·80267,667	14·08404,338
29188,093	20·76579,175	19·39020,818	18·14764,567	17·02286,207	16·00254,921	14·23022,961
2378,628	21·13183,665	19·70068,423	18·41119,776	17·24675,796	16·19290,401	14·36814,114
4515,734	21·48722,004	20·00066,109	18·66461,323	17·46101,240	16·37419,429	14·49824,636
5625,107	21·83225,247	20·29049,381	18·90828,199	17·66604,058	16·54685,171	14·62098,713
5731,811	22·16723,541	20·57052,542	19·14257,880	17·86223,979	16·71128,734	14·73678,031
4860,304	22·49246,156	20·84108,736	19·36786,424	18·04999,023	16·86789,271	14·84601,916
3034,443	22·80821,510	21·10249,987	19·58448,484	18·22965,572	17·01704,067	14·94907,468
9277,505	23·11477,195	21·35507,234	19·79277,389	18·40158,442	17·15908,635	15·04629,687
6612,200	23·41239,995	21·59910,371	19·99305,181	18·56610,949	17·29436,796	15·15801,591
2050,083	23·70135,917	21·83488,281	20·18562,674	18·72354,976	17·42320,758	15·24454,331
6644,569	23·98190,211	22·06268,870	20·37079,494	18·87421,009	17·54591,198	15·30617,294
0384,945	24·25427,389	22·28279,102	20·54884,129	19·01838,306	17·66277,331	15·38318,202
5302,386	24·51871,251	22·49545,026	20·72003,970	19·15634,742	17·77406,982	15·45583,209
5416,962	24·77544,904	22·70091,812	20·88465,356	19·28837,074	17·88006,650	15·52436,990
5748,255	25·02470,780	22·89943,780	21·04293,612	19·41470,884	17·98101,571	15·58902,821
7315,371	25·26670,660	23·09124,425	21·19513,088	19·53560,655	18·07715,782	15·65002,661
7136,947	25·50165,689	23·27656,449	21·34147,200	19·65129,813	18·16872,173	15·70757,227
6231,168	25·72976,397	23·45561,787	21·48218,462	19·76200,778	18·25592,546	15·76186,063
4615,774	25·95122,716	23·62861,630	21·61749,521	19·86795,003	18·33897,663	15·81307,607
2308,072	26·16623,996	23·79576,454	21·74758,193	19·96933,017	18·41807,298	15·86139,252
9324,948	26·37499,025	23·95726,043	21·87267,493	20·06634,466	18·49340,284	15·90697,407
5682,877	26·57766,043	24·11329,510	21·99295,667	20·15918,149	18·56514,556	15·94997,554
4397,928	26·77442,761	24·26405,323	22·10861,218	20·21802,057	18·63347,196	15·99054,296
485,784	26·96541,370	24·40971,327	22·21981,940	20·33303,404	18·69854,473	16·02881,412
961,740	27·15093,563	24·55044,760	22·32674,943	20·41438,664	18·76051,879	16·06491,898
840,722	27·33100,546	24·68642,281	22·42956,676	20·49223,602	18·81954,170	16·09898,017
137,290	27·50583,035	24·81779,981	22·52842,957	20·56673,303	18·87575,400	16·13111,336
865,649	27·67556,364	24·94473,412	22·62348,997	20·63802,204	18·92928,953	16·16142,770
3039,657	27·84035,304	25·06737,596	22·71489,421	20·70624,119	18·98027,574	16·19002,613
572,836	28·00034,276	25·18587,049	22·80278,289	20·77152,267	19·02883,404	16·21700,579
778,377	28·15567,258	25·30035,796	22·88729,124	20·83399,298	19·07508,003	16·24245,829
369,148	28·30547,823	25·41097,388	22·96854,927	20·89377,319	19·11912,384	16·26647,008
457,706	28·45289,149	25·51784,916	23·04668,199	20·95097,913	19·16107,033	16·28912,272
056,298	28·59504,028	25·62111,030	23·12180,959	21·00572,165	19·20101,936	16·31049,313
176,876	28·73304,881	25·72087,951	23·19404,768	21·05810,685	19·23906,606	16·33065,390
831,099	28·86703,768	25·81727,489	23·26350,739	21·10823,622	19·27530,101	16·34967,349
030,341	28·99712,396	25·91041,053	23·33029,556	21·15620,691	19·30981,048	16·36761,650
785,698	29·12342,132	26·00039,664	23·39451,497	21·20211,187	19·34267,665	16·38454,387

V. Table of the PROBABLE DURATION OF HUMAN LIFE ; showing the Number of Persons alive at the ... of every Year, from 1 to 100 Years of Age, out of 1,000 born together, in the different Places, and a... ing to the Authorities undermentioned.

Ages.	England.			France.			Sweden.	Vienna.	Berlin.	Switzer-land.	Silesia.	Holl...
	Simpson. London.	Price. Northampton.	Hegsham. Carlisle.	Deparcieux, Annuitants, &c.	Buffon. Part Population.	Duvillard. Whole Population.	Wargentin. Whole Population.	Susmilch.	Susmilch.	Muret. Pays de Vaud.	Halley. Breslaw.	Kersboom.
1	680	743	846	745	731	768	780	542	633	811	769	80
2	548	625	778	709	632	672	730	471	528	765	638	76
3	492	582	725	682	591	625	695	430	485	735	614	73
4	452	553	700	662	557	599	671	400	434	715	585	70
5	426	536	680	647	540	583	656	377	403	701	563	68
6	410	521	668	634	523	573	644	357	387	688	546	6
7	397	509	659	624	511	566	634	344	376	677	532	66
8	388	499	654	615	501	560	625	337	367	667	523	6
9	380	492	649	607	494	556	618	331	361	659	515	64
10	373	487	646	600	489	551	611	327	356	653	508	6
11	367	483	643	595	486	547	606	322	353	648	502	6
12	361	478	640	590	482	543	602	318	350	643	497	6
13	356	474	637	585	479	538	597	314	347	639	492	6
14	351	470	634	581	476	534	594	310	344	635	488	6
15	347	465	630	578	472	529	590	306	341	631	483	6
16	343	461	626	574	468	524	586	302	338	626	479	60
17	338	457	622	570	464	519	582	299	335	622	474	60
18	334	452	618	565	459	514	578	295	332	618	470	59
19	329	446	613	561	455	508	574	291	328	614	465	59
20	325	441	609	556	449	502	570	288	324	610	461	58
21	321	434	605	551	445	496	565	284	320	606	456	57
22	316	428	601	545	438	490	560	280	315	602	451	57
23	310	421	596	540	432	484	555	276	310	597	446	56
24	305	415	592	534	430	478	531	273	305	592	441	56
25	299	409	588	529	419	471	546	269	297	587	436	5
26	294	402	584	523	414	465	541	265	293	582	431	54
27	288	396	579	517	408	458	535	261	287	577	426	5
28	283	389	575	512	402	452	530	256	281	572	421	5
29	278	383	570	506	398	445	525	251	275	567	415	5
30	272	376	564	500	388	438	519	247	269	563	409	5
31	266	370	559	495	384	432	513	243	264	558	403	4
32	260	364	553	490	377	425	507	239	259	553	397	4
33	254	357	547	484	371	418	501	235	254	548	391	4
34	248	351	542	479	366	411	495	231	249	544	384	4
35	242	344	536	474	355	404	488	226	243	539	377	4
36	236	338	531	460	339	397	482	221	237	533	370	4
37	230	331	525	464	341	390	477	216	230	527	363	4
38	224	325	519	459	334	383	471	211	223	520	356	4
39	218	318	514	454	330	376	465	205	216	513	349	4
40	212	312	508	449	314	369	459	199	209	506	342	4
41	207	305	501	444	310	362	453	194	203	500	335	4
42	201	299	499	439	302	355	445	189	197	494	328	4
43	194	292	487	434	297	348	437	185	192	488	321	4
44	187	285	480	429	292	341	430	181	187	482	314	4
45	180	279	473	424	279	334	422	176	182	476	307	4
46	174	272	466	419	273	327	414	171	177	469	299	3
47	167	265	459	413	269	320	407	165	172	461	291	3
48	159	259	452	408	262	312	400	159	167	451	283	3
49	153	252	456	402	258	305	392	153	162	441	275	3
50	147	245	440	396	242	297	385	147	157	431	267	3
51	141	238	434	390	239	289	376	142	152	422	259	3
52	135	231	428	384	233	282	367	137	147	414	250	3
53	130	224	421	378	229	274	358	133	142	406	241	3
54	125	217	414	371	224	265	319	128	137	397	232	3
55	120	210	407	363	212	258	340	123	132	388	224	3
56	116	203	400	355	207	249	331	117	127	377	216	3
57	111	196	392	346	202	240	322	111	121	364	209	3
58	106	189	384	338	194	232	312	106	115	348	201	2
59	101	182	375	329	190	223	303	101	109	331	193	2
60	96	175	364	319	168	214	293	96	103	314	186	2
61	92	168	352	309	165	204	282	91	97	299	178	2
62	87	161	340	299	157	195	271	87	92	286	170	2
63	83	154	327	288	150	186	259	82	88	274	163	2
64	78	147	314	278	144	176	247	77	84	262	155	2
65	74	140	302	267	135	166	285	72	80	250	147	2
66	70	133	289	256	126	157	224	67	75	236	140	2
67	65	126	277	245	197	147	212	62	70	220	132	2
68	61	119	265	234	100	137	200	57	65	202	124	1
69	56	113	251	222	106	129	187	52	60	184	117	1
70	52	106	240	211	90	118	175	48	55	168	109	1
71	47	99	228	199	86	108	162	44	51	153	101	1
72	43	92	214	187	75	99	149	40	47	140	93	1
73	39	85	200	175	70	89	135	36	43	129	85	
74	35	78	184	162	63	80	121	33	39	119	77	
75	32	71	168	148	52	72	108	30	35	109	69	

Table V. Probable Duration of Human Life, &c. — (continued.)

England			France			Sweden.	Vienna.	Berlin.	Switzerland.	Silesia.	Holland.
Simpson. London.	Price. Northampton.	Higham. Carlisle.	Deparcieux. Annuitants, &c.	Buffon. Part Population.	Duvillard. Whole Population.	Wargentin. Whole Population.	Susmilch.	Susmilch.	Muret. Pays de Vaud.	Halley. Breslaw.	Kersboom. Life Annuitants.
28	65	152	134	47	63	96	27	32	98	61	114
25	58	136	120	42	56	84	24	29	85	53	103
22	52	121	106	36	48	75	21	26	71	55	92
19	46	108	94	34	41	65	18	23	58	38	82
17	40	95	81	23	35	56	16	20	46	32	72
14	35	84	70	21	29	47	14	18	36	26	62
12	30	73	59	18	24	38	12	16	29	22	53
10	25	62	49	15	19	31	10	14	24	18	45
8	20	53	40	12	15	24	8	12	20	15	38
7	16	45	33	10	12	19	7	10	17	12	31
6	12	37	26	8	9	14	6	8	14	9	25
5	9	30	21	7	7	11	5	7	11	6	19
4	7	23	16	5	6	8	4	6	9	4	14
3	5	18	12	4	5	6	3	5	7	2	10
2	4	14	8	3	4	5	2	4	5	1	7
1	3	10	5	3	3	3	1	3	4		5
	2	8	3	2	3	3		2	3		4
	1	5	1	2	2	2		1	2		2
	1	4	1	1	2	1			1		1
		3			1	1					
		2			1	1					
		2									
		1									
		1									

...ble of the PROGRESSIVE DECREMENT OF LIFE among 1,000 Infants of each Sex, born together, ...ding to Mr. Finlaison's Observations on the Mortality of the Nominees in the Government ...ines and Life Annuities in Great Britain.

Females.	Age.	Males.	Females.	Age.	Males.	Females.	Age.	Males.	Females.	Age.	Males.	Females.	Age.	Males.	Females.
1,000	17	860	870	34	696	748	51	552	616	68	322	443	85	56	117
981	18	854	863	35	687	740	52	542	608	69	305	428	86	44	103
967	19	846	856	36	679	732	53	531	601	70	288	412	87	34	89
955	20	837	848	37	670	724	54	520	593	71	270	395	88	24	76
945	21	827	841	38	662	716	55	508	585	72	253	377	89	17	64
935	22	816	854	39	653	708	56	495	576	73	235	358	90	11	52
926	23	804	827	40	644	700	57	482	568	74	218	339	91	7	41
919	24	793	820	41	636	693	58	468	559	75	202	319	92	4	30
913	25	782	813	42	627	685	59	454	549	76	185	298	93	3	21
908	26	771	805	43	619	677	60	440	539	77	171	277	94	1	14
903	27	761	798	44	610	669	61	426	529	78	156	255	95		8
899	28	751	791	45	602	661	62	413	519	79	141	233	96		5
895	29	742	784	46	594	654	63	399	508	80	125	210	97		2
892	30	732	777	47	586	646	64	385	496	81	110	189	98		1
887	31	723	770	48	578	638	65	370	484	82	95	168	99		
883	32	714	763	49	570	631	66	355	471	83	81	149	100		
876	33	705	755	50	561	623	67	339	457	84	68	132			

...able showing the EXPECTATION OF LIFE at every Age, according to the Observations made at Northampton.

Age.	Expect.	Age.	Expect.	Age.	Expect.	Age.	Expect.	Age.	Expect.	Age.	Expect.
0	25·18	17	35·20	33	26·72	49	18·49	65	10·88	81	4·41
1	32·74	18	34·58	34	26·20	50	17·99	66	10·42	82	4·09
2	37·79	19	33·99	35	25·68	51	17·50	67	9·96	83	3·80
3	39·55	20	33·43	36	25·16	52	17·02	68	9·50	84	3·58
4	40·58	21	32·90	37	24·64	53	16·54	69	9·05	85	3·37
5	40·84	22	32·39	38	24·12	54	16·06	70	8·60	86	3·19
6	41·07	23	31·88	39	23·60	55	15·58	71	8·17	87	3·01
7	41·03	24	31·36	40	23·08	56	15·10	72	7·74	88	2·86
8	40·79	25	30·83	41	22·56	57	14·63	73	7·33	89	2·66
9	40·36	26	30·33	42	22·04	58	14·15	74	6·92	90	2·41
10	39·78	27	29·82	43	21·54	59	13·68	75	6·54	91	2·09
11	39·14	28	29·30	44	21·03	60	13·21	76	6·18	92	1·75
12	38·49	29	28·79	45	20·52	61	12·75	77	5·83	93	1·37
13	37·83	30	28·27	46	20·02	62	12·28	78	5·48	94	1·05
14	37·17	31	27·76	47	19·51	63	11·81	79	5·11	95	0·75
15	36·51	32	27·24	48	19·00	64	11·35	80	4·75	96	0·50
16	35·85										

VIII. Table showing the EXPECTATION OF LIFE at every Age, according to the Observations mad[e] Carlisle.

Age.	Expect.	Age.	Expect.	Age.	Expect.	Age.	Expect.	Age.	Expect.	Age.	Expect.
0	38·72	18	42·87	36	30·32	53	18·97	70	9·18	87	3·71
1	44·68	19	42·17	37	29·64	54	18·28	71	8·65	88	3·59
2	47·55	20	41·46	38	28·96	55	17·58	72	8·16	89	3·47
3	49·82	21	40·75	39	28·28	56	16·89	73	7·72	90	3·28
4	50·76	22	40·04	40	27·61	57	16·21	74	7·33	91	3·26
5	51·25	23	39·31	41	26·97	58	15·55	75	7·01	92	3·37
6	51·17	24	38·59	42	26·34	59	14·92	76	6·69	93	3·48
7	50·80	25	37·86	43	25·71	60	14·34	77	6·40	94	3·53
8	50·24	26	37·14	44	25·09	61	13·82	78	6·12	95	3·53
9	49·57	27	36·41	45	24·46	62	13·31	79	5·80	96	3·46
10	48·82	28	35·69	46	23·82	63	12·81	80	5·51	97	3·28
11	48·04	29	35·00	47	23·17	64	12·30	81	5·21	98	3·07
12	47·27	30	34·34	48	22·50	65	11·79	82	4·93	99	2·77
13	46·51	31	33·68	49	21·81	66	11·27	83	4·65	100	2·28
14	45·75	32	33·03	50	21·11	67	10·75	84	4·39	101	1·79
15	45·00	33	32·36	51	20·39	68	10·23	85	4·12	102	1·30
16	44·27	34	31·68	52	19·68	69	9·70	86	3·90	103	0·83
17	43·57	35	31·00								

IX. Table giving a COMPARATIVE VIEW of the Results of the undermentioned Tables of Mortality Relation to the following Particulars.

	By Dr. Price's Table, founded on the Register of Births and Burials at Northampton.	By the First Swedish Tables, as published by Dr. Price; for both Sexes.	By Mr. De Parcieux's Table, founded on the Mortality in the French Tontines, prior to 1745.	By Mr. Milne's Table, founded on the Mortality observed at Carlisle.	By Mr. Griffith Davies's Table, founded on the Experience of the Equitable Life Insurance Office.	By Mr. Finlaison's Tables, founded on Experience of the Gov[ern]ment Life Annuit[ie]s	
						According to his First Investiga-tion, as men-tioned in his Evidence in 1825.	Accord[ing] to his Se[cond] Investi[ga]-tion, as [men]-tioned [in] his Evid[ence] in 18[9]
						Mean of both Sexes.	Mean both Se[xes]
Of 100,000 persons aged 25, there would be alive at the age of 65	34,286	43,137	51,033	51,335	49,330	£53,470	53,95[ ]
Of 100,000 persons aged 65, there would be alive at the age of 80	28,738	23,704	29,873	31,577	37,267	38,655	37,35[ ]
Expectation of life at the age of 25 years	30·85	34·58	37·17	37·86	37·45	38·35	38·5[ ]
Expectation of life at the age of 65 years	10·88	10·10	11·25	11·79	12·35	12·81	12·5[ ]
Value of an annuity on a life aged 25, interest being at 4 per cent.	£15·438	£16·839	£17·420	£17·645	£17·494	£17·534	£17·6[ ]
Value of an annuity on a life aged 65, interest being at 4 per cent.	£7·761	£7·328	£8·039	£8·307	£8·635	£8·896	£8·7[ ]
Value of a deferred annuity commencing at 65, to a life now aged 25, interest at 4 per cent.	£0·55424	£0·65842	£0·85452	£0·88823	£0·88723	£0·99078	£0·98[ ]

Note.—In all the tables above mentioned, it is to be observed that the mortality is deduced from an e[qual] or nearly equal number of each sex; with the single exception of Mr. Davies's table, founded on the [ex]-perience of the Equitable, in which office, from the practical objects of life insurance, it is eviden[t the] male sex must have composed the vast majority of lives subjected to mortality. But as it is agreed o[n all] hands that the duration of life among females exceeds that of males, it follows that the results of [Mr.] Davies's table fall materially short of what they would have been, if the facts on which he has reas[oned] had comprehended an equal number of each sex. The tables have not, in all cases, been computed [at 4] per cent., the rate allowed by government.

e showing the VALUE OF AN ANNUITY ON A SINGLE LIFE, according to the Northampton Table of Mortality.

er Cent.	4 per Cent.	5 per Cent.	Age.	3 per Cent.	4 per Cent.	5 per Cent.	Age.	3 per Cent.	4 per Cent.	5 per Cent.
6·021	13·465	11·563	33	16·343	14·347	12·740	65	8·304	7·761	7·276
8·599	15·633	13·420	34	16·142	14·195	12·623	66	7·994	7·488	7·034
9·575	16·462	14·135	35	15·938	14·039	12·502	67	7·682	7·211	6·787
0·210	17·010	14·613	36	15·729	13·880	12·377	68	7·367	6·930	6·536
0·473	17·248	14·827	37	15·515	13·716	12·249	69	7·051	6·647	6·281
0·727	17·482	15·041	38	15·298	13·548	12·116	70	6·734	6·361	6·023
0·853	17·611	15·166	39	15·075	13·375	11·979	71	6·418	6·075	5·764
0·885	17·662	15·296	40	14·848	13·197	11·837	72	6·103	5·790	5·504
0·812	17·625	15·210	41	14·620	13·018	11·695	73	5·794	5·507	5·245
0·663	17·523	15·139	42	14·391	12·838	11·551	74	5·491	5·230	4·990
0·480	17·393	15·043	43	14·162	12·657	11·407	75	5·199	4·962	4·744
0·283	17·251	14·937	44	13·929	12·472	11·258	76	4·925	4·710	4·511
0·081	17·103	14·826	45	13·692	12·283	11·105	77	4·652	4·457	4·277
9·872	16·950	14·710	46	13·450	12·089	10·947	78	4·372	4·197	4·035
9·657	16·791	14·588	47	13·203	11·890	10·784	79	4·077	3·921	3·776
9·435	16·625	14·460	48	12·951	11·685	10·616	80	3·718	3·643	3·515
9·218	16·462	14·334	49	12·693	11·475	10·443	81	3·499	3·377	3·263
9·013	16·309	14·217	50	12·436	11·264	10·269	82	3·229	3·122	3·020
8·820	16·167	14·108	51	12·183	11·057	10·097	83	2·982	2·87	2·797
8·638	16·033	14·007	52	11·930	10·849	9·925	84	2·793	2·708	2·627
8·470	15·912	13·917	53	11·674	10·637	9·748	85	2·620	2·543	2·471
8·311	15·797	13·833	54	11·414	10·421	9·567	86	2·461	2·393	2·328
8·148	15·680	13·746	55	11·150	10·201	9·382	87	2·312	2·251	2·193
7·983	15·560	13·658	56	10·882	9·977	9·193	88	2·185	2·131	2·080
7·814	15·438	13·567	57	10·611	9·749	8·999	89	2·015	1·967	1·924
7·642	15·312	13·473	58	10·337	9·516	8·801	90	1·794	1·758	1·723
7·467	15·184	13·377	59	10·058	9·280	8·599	91	1·501	1·474	1·447
7·289	15·053	13·278	60	9·777	9·039	8·392	92	1·190	1·171	1·153
7·107	14·918	13·177	61	9·493	8·795	8·181	93	0·839	0·827	0·816
6·922	14·781	13·072	62	9·205	8·547	7·966	94	0·536	0·530	0·524
6·732	14·639	12·965	63	8·910	8·291	7·742	95	0·242	0·240	0·238
6·540	14·495	12·854	64	8·611	8·030	7·514	96	0·000	0·000	0·000

e showing the VALUE OF AN ANNUITY ON A SINGLE LIFE, according to the Carlisle Table of Mortality.

Cent.	4 per Cent.	5 per Cent.	Age.	3 per Cent.	4 per Cent.	5 per Cent.	Age.	3 per Cent.	4 per Cent.	5 per Cent.
085	16·556	13·995	36	18·183	15·856	13·987	70	7·123	6·709	6·336
501	17·728	14·983	37	17·928	15·666	13·843	71	6·737	6·358	6·015
683	18·717	15·824	38	17·669	15·471	13·695	72	6·373	6·026	5·711
285	19·233	16·271	39	17·405	15·272	13·542	73	6·044	5·725	5·435
693	19·592	16·590	40	17·143	15·074	13·390	74	5·752	5·458	5·190
846	19·747	16·735	41	16·890	14·883	13·245	75	5·512	5·239	4·989
867	19·790	16·790	42	16·640	14·694	13·101	76	5·277	5·024	4·792
801	19·766	16·786	43	16·389	14·505	12·957	77	5·059	4·825	4·609
677	19·693	16·742	44	16·130	14·308	12·806	78	4·838	4·622	4·422
512	19·585	16·669	45	15·863	14·104	12·648	79	4·592	4·394	4·210
327	19·460	16·581	46	15·585	13·889	12·480	80	4·365	4·183	4·015
143	19·336	16·494	47	15·294	13·662	12·301	81	4·119	3·953	3·799
957	19·210	16·406	48	14·986	13·419	12·107	82	3·898	3·746	3·606
769	19·082	16·316	49	14·654	13·153	11·892	83	3·672	3·534	3·406
582	18·956	16·227	50	14·303	12·869	11·660	84	3·454	3·329	3·211
404	18·837	16·144	51	13·932	12·566	11·410	85	3·229	3·115	3·009
232	18·723	16·066	52	13·558	12·258	11·154	86	3·033	2·928	2·830
058	18·608	15·987	53	13·180	11·945	10·892	87	2·873	2·776	2·685
879	18·488	15·904	54	12·798	11·627	10·624	88	2·776	2·683	2·597
694	18·363	15·817	55	12·408	11·300	10·347	89	2·665	2·577	2·495
504	18·233	15·726	56	12·014	10·966	10·063	90	2·499	2·416	2·339
504	18·095	15·628	57	11·614	10·625	9·771	91	2·481	2·398	2·321
98	17·951	15·525	58	11·218	10·286	9·478	92	2·577	2·492	2·412
385	17·801	15·417	59	10·841	9·963	9·199	93	2·687	2·600	2·513
365	17·645	15·303	60	10·491	9·663	8·940	94	2·736	2·650	2·569
42	17·486	15·187	61	10·180	9·398	8·712	95	2·757	2·674	2·596
12	17·320	15·065	62	9·875	9·137	8·487	96	2·704	2·628	2·555
081	17·154	14·942	63	9·567	8·872	8·258	97	2·559	2·492	2·428
61	16·997	14·827	64	9·246	8·593	8·016	98	2·388	2·332	2·278
456	16·852	14·723	65	8·917	8·307	7·765	99	2·131	2·087	2·045
48	16·705	14·617	66	8·578	8·010	7·503	100	1·683	1·653	1·624
54	16·552	14·506	67	8·228	7·700	7·227	101	1·228	1·210	1·192
10	16·390	14·387	68	7·869	7·380	6·941	102	0·771	0·762	0·753
075	16·219	14·260	69	7·499	7·049	6·643	103	0·324	0·321	0·317
433	16·041	14·127								

XII. Table showing the VALUE OF AN ANNUITY ON THE JOINT CONTINUANCE OF TWO LIVES OF AGES, according to the Northampton Table of Mortality.

Ages.	3 per Cent.	4 per Cent.	5 per Cent.	Ages.	3 per Cent.	4 per Cent.	5 per Cent.	Ages.	3 per Cent.	4 per Cent.
1 & 1	9·490	8·252	7·287	33 & 33	12·079	10·902	9·919	65 & 65	5·471	5·201
2 — 2	12·789	11·107	9·793	34 — 34	11·902	10·759	9·801	66 — 66	5·231	4·982
3 — 3	14·191	12·325	10·862	35 — 35	11·722	10·612	9·680	67 — 67	4·989	4·760
4 — 4	15·181	13·185	11·621	36 — 36	11·539	10·462	9·555	68 — 68	4·747	4·537
5 — 5	15·638	13·591	11·984	37 — 37	11·351	10·307	9·427	69 — 69	4·504	4·312
6 — 6	16·099	14·005	12·358	38 — 38	11·160	10·149	9·294	70 — 70	4·261	4·087
7 — 7	16·375	14·224	12·596	39 — 39	10·964	9·986	9·158	71 — 71	4·020	3·862
8 — 8	16·510	14·399	12·731	40 — 40	10·764	9·820	9·016	72 — 72	3·781	3·639
9 — 9	16·483	14·396	12·744	41 — 41	10·565	9·654	8·876	73 — 73	3·548	3·421
10 — 10	16·339	14·277	12·669	42 — 42	10·369	9·491	8·737	74 — 74	3·324	3·211
11 — 11	16·142	14·133	12·546	43 — 43	10·175	9·326	8·599	75 — 75	3·114	3·015
12 — 12	15·926	13·966	12·411	44 — 44	9·977	9·161	8·457	76 — 76	2·926	2·833
13 — 13	15·702	13·789	12·268	45 — 45	9·776	8·990	8·312	77 — 77	2·741	2·656
14 — 14	15·470	13·604	12·118	46 — 46	9·571	8·815	8·162	78 — 78	2·550	2·470
15 — 15	15·229	13·411	11·960	47 — 47	9·362	8·637	8·008	79 — 79	2·338	2·271
16 — 16	14·979	13·212	11·793	48 — 48	9·149	8·453	7·849	80 — 80	2·122	2·068
17 — 17	14·737	13·019	11·630	49 — 49	8·930	8·266	7·686	81 — 81	1·917	1·869
18 — 18	14·516	12·841	11·483	50 — 50	8·714	8·080	7·522	82 — 82	1·719	1·681
19 — 19	14·316	12·679	11·351	51 — 51	8·507	7·900	7·366	83 — 83	1·538	1·510
20 — 20	14·133	12·535	11·232	52 — 52	8·304	7·723	7·213	84 — 84	1·416	1·387
21 — 21	13·974	12·409	11·131	53 — 53	8·098	7·544	7·056	85 — 85	1·309	1·339
22 — 22	13·830	12·293	11·042	54 — 54	7·891	7·362	6·897	86 — 86	1·218	1·195
23 — 23	13·683	12·179	10·951	55 — 55	7·681	7·179	6·735	87 — 87	1·141	1·124
24 — 24	13·534	12·062	10·858	56 — 56	7·470	6·993	6·571	88 — 88	1·103	1·030
25 — 25	13·383	11·944	10·764	57 — 57	7·256	6·805	6·404	89 — 89	1·036	1·015
26 — 26	13·230	11·822	10·667	58 — 58	7·041	6·614	6·234	90 — 90	0·938	0·922
27 — 27	13·074	11·699	10·567	59 — 59	6·826	6·421	6·062	91 — 91	0·769	0·756
28 — 28	12·915	11·573	10·466	60 — 60	6·606	6·226	5·888	92 — 92	0·591	0·583
29 — 29	12·754	11·445	10·362	61 — 61	6·386	6·030	5·712	93 — 93	0·569	0·365
30 — 30	12·589	11·313	10·255	62 — 62	6·166	5·831	5·533	94 — 94	0·203	0·201
31 — 31	12·422	11·179	10·146	63 — 63	5·938	5·626	5·347	95 — 95	0·060	0·060
32 — 32	12·252	11·042	10·034	64 — 64	5·709	5·417	5·158	96 — 96	0·000	0·000

XIII. Table showing the VALUE OF AN ANNUITY ON THE JOINT CONTINUANCE OF TWO LIVES OF AGES, according to the Carlisle Table of Mortality

Ages.	3 per Cent.	4 per Cent.	5 per Cent.	Ages.	3 per Cent.	4 per Cent.	5 per Cent.	Ages.	3 per Cent.	4 per Cent.
1 & 1	14·079	11·924	10·299	36 & 36	14·477	12·919	11·627	70 & 70	4·556	4·367
2 — 2	16·155	13·671	11·793	37 — 37	14·231	12·724	11·470	71 — 71	4·217	4·050
3 — 3	18·030	15·260	13·162	38 — 38	13·981	12·525	11·309	72 — 72	3·904	3·755
4 — 4	19·065	16·147	13·932	39 — 39	13·727	12·322	11·144	73 — 73	3·631	3·497
5 — 5	19·815	16·801	14·507	40 — 40	13·481	12·125	10·984	74 — 74	3·400	3·279
6 — 6	20·156	17·112	14·789	41 — 41	13·254	11·945	10·839	75 — 75	3·231	3·119
7 — 7	20·280	17·242	14·917	42 — 42	13·036	11·772	10·701	76 — 76	3·068	2·966
8 — 8	20·261	17·251	14·942	43 — 43	12·822	11·602	10·566	77 — 77	2·927	2·833
9 — 9	20·146	17·179	14·898	44 — 44	12·600	11·426	10·425	78 — 78	2·784	2·698
10 — 10	19·963	17·049	14·803	45 — 45	12·371	11·243	10·278	79 — 79	2·610	2·543
11 — 11	19·748	16·891	14·684	46 — 46	12·128	11·047	10·119	80 — 80	2·459	2·390
12 — 12	19·538	16·737	14·568	47 — 47	11·870	10·837	9·947	81 — 81	2·283	2·222
13 — 13	19·327	16·582	14·450	48 — 48	11·591	10·607	9·756	82 — 82	2·155	2·079
14 — 14	19·115	16·425	14·331	49 — 49	11·279	10·345	9·535	83 — 83	1·978	1·929
15 — 15	18·908	16·272	14·215	50 — 50	10·942	10·059	9·291	84 — 84	1·825	1·782
16 — 16	18·719	16·134	14·112	51 — 51	10·579	9·748	9·023	85 — 85	1·657	1·619
17 — 17	18·542	16·007	14·018	52 — 52	10·215	9·434	8·751	86 — 86	1·509	1·476
18 — 18	18·365	15·880	13·925	53 — 53	9·849	9·117	8·474	87 — 87	1·389	1·359
19 — 19	18·182	15·748	13·827	54 — 54	9·480	8·796	8·192	88 — 88	1·328	1·301
20 — 20	17·993	15·610	13·724	55 — 55	9·103	8·465	7·900	89 — 89	1·248	1·223
21 — 21	17·797	15·466	13·616	56 — 56	8·721	8·128	7·600	90 — 90	1·088	1·066
22 — 22	17·588	15·310	13·497	57 — 57	8·334	7·783	7·293	91 — 91	1·050	1·028
23 — 23	17·372	15·148	13·372	58 — 58	7·954	7·444	6·988	92 — 92	1·120	1·096
24 — 24	17·148	14·978	13·240	59 — 59	7·605	7·131	6·705	93 — 93	1·226	1·199
25 — 25	16·916	14·800	13·101	60 — 60	7·295	6·854	6·456	94 — 94	1·302	1·273
26 — 26	16·681	14·620	12·960	61 — 61	7·044	6·630	6·257	95 — 95	1·383	1·353
27 — 27	16·437	14·431	12·811	62 — 62	6·804	6·417	6·067	96 — 96	1·424	1·394
28 — 28	16·196	14·244	12·663	63 — 63	6·563	6·202	5·875	97 — 97	1·395	1·366
29 — 29	15·976	14·075	12·530	64 — 64	6·308	5·974	5·669	98 — 98	1·375	1·349
30 — 30	15·784	13·930	12·419	65 — 65	6·047	5·738	5·456	99 — 99	1·294	1·272
31 — 31	15·591	13·784	12·308	66 — 66	5·774	5·490	5·230	100 — 100	0·991	0·976
32 — 32	15·392	13·632	12·191	67 — 67	5·486	5·228	4·990	101 — 101	0·687	0·679
33 — 33	15·180	13·469	12·064	68 — 68	5·188	4·954	4·737	102 — 102	0·387	0·383
34 — 34	14·954	13·294	11·926	69 — 69	4·877	4·666	4·471	103 — 103	0·108	0·107
35 — 35	14·720	13·111	11·780							

Table showing the VALUE OF AN ANNUITY on the Joint Continuance of two Lives, when the DIFFER-
ENCE OF AGE IS FIVE YEARS, according to the Northampton Table of Mortality.

Ages.	3 per Cent.	4 per Cent.	5 per Cent.	Ages.	3 per Cent.	4 per Cent.	5 per Cent.	Ages.	3 per Cent.	4 per Cent.	5 per Cent.
& 6	12·346	10·741	9·479	32 & 37	11·775	10·659	9·716	62 & 67	5·503	5·285	4·986
— 7	14·461	12·581	11·100	33 — 38	11·591	10·508	9·591	63 — 68	5·265	5·017	4·786
— 8	15·300	13·319	11·755	34 — 39	11·404	10·354	9·463	64 — 69	5·025	4·798	4·585
— 9	15·809	13·775	12·165	35 — 40	11·213	10·196	9·331	65 — 70	4·782	4·573	4·378
— 10	15·974	13·933	12·315	36 — 41	11·021	10·037	9·198	66 — 71	4·540	4·349	4·169
— 11	16·110	14·068	12·447	37 — 42	10·828	9·877	9·062	67 — 72	4·298	4·124	3·960
— 12	16·137	14·111	12·498	38 — 43	10·634	9·716	8·927	68 — 73	4·059	3·901	3·752
— 13	16·089	14·089	12·492	39 — 44	10·437	9·550	8·787	69 — 74	3·825	3·683	3·547
— 14	15·957	13·992	12·421	40 — 45	10·235	9·381	8·643	70 — 75	3·599	3·471	3·347
— 15	15·762	13·841	12·302	41 — 46	10·033	9·210	8·497	71 — 76	3·386	3·270	3·159
— 16	15·538	13·664	12·158	42 — 47	9·829	9·037	8·350	72 — 77	3·175	3·070	2·971
— 17	15·308	13·480	12·009	43 — 48	9·623	8·862	8·200	73 — 78	2·963	2·869	2·780
— 18	15·086	13·303	11·864	44 — 49	9·414	8·683	8·046	74 — 79	2·743	2·659	2·580
— 19	14·870	13·130	11·723	45 — 50	9·204	8·503	7·891	75 — 80	2·526	2·448	2·381
— 20	14·660	12·961	11·585	46 — 51	8·997	8·326	7·737	76 — 81	2·325	2·258	2·195
— 21	14·457	12·799	11·452	47 — 52	8·790	8·147	7·582	77 — 82	2·131	2·077	2·013
— 22	14·265	12·646	11·327	48 — 53	8·579	7·965	7·424	78 — 83	1·947	1·899	1·838
— 23	14·082	12·500	11·209	49 — 54	8·366	7·780	7·262	79 — 84	1·792	1·751	1·750
— 24	13·908	12·361	11·096	50 — 55	8·151	7·593	7·098	80 — 85	1·645	1·608	1·573
— 25	13·741	12·229	10·989	51 — 56	7·910	7·409	6·936	81 — 86	1·510	1·478	1·447
— 26	13·584	12·105	10·890	52 — 57	7·730	7·225	6·774	82 — 87	1·385	1·356	1·329
— 27	13·433	11·987	10·796	53 — 58	7·518	7·039	6·609	83 — 88	1·284	1·259	1·235
— 28	13·280	11·866	10·699	54 — 59	7·304	6·850	6·442	84 — 89	1·187	1·164	1·145
— 29	13·124	11·743	10·600	55 — 60	7·088	6·659	6·272	85 — 90	1·074	1·054	1·038
— 30	12·966	11·618	10·499	56 — 61	6·870	6·465	6·100	86 — 91	0·921	0·902	0·892
— 31	12·805	11·489	10·396	57 — 62	6·651	6·270	5·925	87 — 92	0·755	0·738	0·734
— 32	12·641	11·359	10·289	58 — 63	6·427	6·070	5·744	88 — 93	0·561	0·554	0·547
— 33	12·474	11·225	10·181	59 — 64	6·201	5·867	5·561	89 — 94	0·377	0·373	0·369
— 34	12·304	11·088	10·069	60 — 65	5·970	5·658	5·372	90 — 95	0·179	0·177	0·175
— 35	12·131	10·948	9·954	61 — 66	5·737	5·447	5·180	91 — 96	0·000	0·000	0·000
— 36	11·955	10·805	9·837								

able showing the VALUE OF AN ANNUITY on the Joint Continuance of two Lives, when the DIF-
FERENCE OF AGE IS FIVE YEARS, according to the Carlisle Table of Mortality.

Ages.	3 per Cent.	4 per Cent.	5 per Cent.	Ages.	3 per Cent.	4 per Cent.	5 per Cent.	Ages.	3 per Cent.	4 per Cent.	5 per Cent.
6	16·828	14·269	12·331	34 & 39	14·290	12·773	11·508	67 & 72	4·580	4·386	4·207
7	18·087	15·341	13·258	35 — 40	14·048	12·581	11·354	68 — 73	4·297	4·123	3·961
8	19·100	16·214	14·019	36 — 41	13·812	12·394	11·204	69 — 74	4·035	3·878	3·731
9	19·584	16·644	14·402	37 — 42	13·579	12·209	11·056	70 — 75	3·804	3·661	3·528
10	19·874	16·913	14·649	38 — 43	13·346	12·024	10·907	71 — 76	3·568	3·439	3·319
11	19·935	16·989	14·731	39 — 44	13·107	11·833	10·753	72 — 77	3·353	3·237	3·127
12	19·889	16·975	14·736	40 — 45	12·868	11·641	10·598	73 — 78	3·152	3·047	2·948
13	19·771	16·900	14·689	41 — 46	12·630	11·450	10·444	74 — 79	2·952	2·857	2·767
14	19·606	16·785	14·606	42 — 47	12·389	11·256	10·287	75 — 80	2·790	2·704	2·623
15	19·410	16·643	14·500	43 — 48	12·139	11·053	10·121	76 — 81	2·618	2·540	2·467
16	19·208	16·495	14·389	44 — 49	11·868	10·830	9·937	77 — 82	2·471	2·400	2·333
17	19·014	16·354	14·284	45 — 50	11·580	10·591	9·737	78 — 83	2·318	2·255	2·194
18	18·820	16·213	14·178	46 — 51	11·271	10·332	9·519	79 — 84	2·155	2·099	2·045
19	18·622	16·068	14·069	47 — 52	10·955	10·065	9·292	80 — 85	1·993	1·943	1·895
20	18·423	15·922	13·959	48 — 53	10·628	9·787	9·054	81 — 86	1·834	1·790	1·747
21	18·230	15·781	13·853	49 — 54	10·284	9·492	8·799	82 — 87	1·704	1·664	1·626
22	18·036	15·639	13·746	50 — 55	9·924	9·181	8·528	83 — 88	1·606	1·569	1·535
23	17·838	15·493	13·636	51 — 56	9·550	8·855	8·242	84 — 89	1·496	1·464	1·433
24	17·633	15·341	13·520	52 — 57	9·172	8·524	7·950	85 — 90	1·335	1·307	1·279
25	17·421	15·182	13·398	53 — 58	8·797	8·194	7·657	86 — 91	1·255	1·229	1·203
26	17·204	15·019	13·272	54 — 59	8·439	7·876	7·375	87 — 92	1·245	1·218	1·192
27	16·977	14·846	13·137	55 — 60	8·098	7·574	7·106	88 — 93	1·272	1·245	1·219
28	16·747	14·507	13·000	56 — 61	7·788	7·299	6·860	89 — 94	1·266	1·240	1·214
29	16·524	14·500	12·867	57 — 62	7·480	7·025	6·615	90 — 95	1·217	1·191	1·167
30	16·311	14·339	12·742	58 — 63	7·175	6·752	6·370	91 — 96	1·210	1·185	1·161
31	16·097	14·176	12·615	59 — 64	6·875	6·482	6·127	92 — 97	1·230	1·205	1·181
32	15·875	14·006	12·482	60 — 65	6·589	6·225	5·895	93 — 98	1·262	1·238	1·215
33	15·648	13·830	12·344	61 — 66	6·323	5·986	5·678	94 — 99	1·234	1·212	1·191
34	15·424	13·657	12·206	62 — 67	6·054	5·743	5·458	95 — 100	1·072	1·055	1·038
35	15·209	13·492	12·078	63 — 68	5·779	5·493	5·230	96 — 101	0·851	0·839	0·828
36	14·989	13·321	11·944	64 — 69	5·490	5·229	4·988	97 — 102	0·568	0·562	0·555
37	14·764	13·146	11·806	65 — 70	5·193	4·956	4·737	98 — 103	0·254	0·252	0·249
38	14·531	12·964	11·651	66 — 71	4·882	4·667	4·469				

The Northampton table (No. VII.), by underrating the duration of life, was a very advantageous guide for the insurance offices to go by in insuring lives; but to whatever extent it might be beneficial to them in this respect, it became equally injurious when it adopted it as a guide in the selling of annuities. And yet, singular as it may seem, some of the insurance offices granted annuities on the *same* terms that they insured lives; perceiving that, if they gained by the latter transaction, they must obviously lose by former. Government also continued for a lengthened period to sell annuities according to the Northampton tables, and without making any distinction between male and female lives! A glance at the tables of M. Deparcieux ought to have satisfied them that the were proceeding on entirely false principles. But, in despite even of the admonitions some of the most skilful mathematicians, this system was persevered in till within the *two* years! We understand that the loss thence arising to the public may be moderate estimated at 2,000,000*l.* sterling. Nor will this appear a large sum to those who recollect that, supposing interest to be 4 per cent., there is a difference of no less than 1£ in the value of an annuity of 50*l.* for life, to a person aged 45, between the Northampt and Carlisle tables.

INVOICE, an account of goods or merchandise shipped by merchants for the correspondents abroad, in which the peculiar marks of each package, with other particulars, are set forth. — (See examples, *antè*, pp. 139, 140.)

IPECACUANHA (Fr. *Ipecacuanha;* Ger. *Amerikanische brechwurzel;* It. *I coacanna;* Port. *Cipo de camaras, Ipecacuanha;* Sp. *Ipecacuana, Raiz de oro),* root of a perennial plant (*Cephaëlis ipecacuanha*), growing in Brazil and other part of South America. It is, from its colour, usually denominated *white, grey* or *coloured,* and *brown.* Little of the first variety is found in the shops. The grey a brown varieties are brought to this country in bales from Rio Janeiro. Both in short, wrinkled, variously bent and contorted pieces, which break with a resin fracture. The grey is about the thickness of a small quill, full of knots and de circular fissures, that nearly reach down to a white, woody, vascular cord that r through the heart of each piece; the external part is compact, brittle, and lo smooth : the brown is smaller, more wrinkled, of a blackish brown colour on outside, and whitish within : the white is woody, and has no wrinkles. The ent root is inodorous; but the powder has a faint, disagreeable odour. The tast bitter, sub-acrid, and extremely nauseous. In choosing ipecacuanha, the lar roots, which are compact and break with a resinous fracture, having a whitish g somewhat semi-transparent appearance in the outside of the cortical part, wit pale straw-coloured medullary fibre, are to be preferred. When pounded, i cacuanha forms the mildest and safest emetic in the whole Materia Med Though probably employed in America from time immemorial, it was not in duced into Europe till the time of Louis XIV., when one Grenier, a Fre merchant, brought 150 lbs. of it from Spain, with which trials were made at Hôtel Dieu. Helvetius first made known its use in dysentery, for which L XIV. munificently rewarded him by a douceur of 1,000*l.* sterling.—(*Thoms Dispensatory; Thomson's Chemistry.*)

IRON (Dan. *Jern;* Du. *Yzer;* Fr. *Fer;* Ger. *Eisen;* It. *Ferro;* Ferrum, Mars;* Pol. *Zelazo;* Por. *Ferro;* Rus. *Scheleso;* Sp. *Hierro;* Jern;* Gr. Σίδηρος; Sans. *Loha;* Arab. *Hedeed;* Pers. *Ahun*), is the n abundant and most useful of all the metals. It is of a bluish white colour; when polished, has a great deal of brilliancy. It has a styptic taste, and emi smell when rubbed. Its hardness exceeds that of most other metals; and it ma rendered harder than most bodies by being converted into steel. Its specific gra varies from 7·6 to 7·8. It is attracted by the magnet or loadstone, and is itself substance which constitutes the loadstone. But when iron is perfectly pure retains the magnetic virtue for a very short time. It is malleable in every ten rature, and its malleability increases in proportion as the temperature augmen but it cannot be hammered out nearly as thin as gold or silver, or even as cop Its ductility is, however, more perfect; for it may be drawn out into wire as at least as a human hair. Its tenacity is such, that an iron wire 0·078 of an in diameter, is capable of supporting 549·25 lbs. avoirdupois without breaking

Historical Notice. — Iron, though the most common, is the most difficult of all metals to obtain in a state fit for use; and the discovery of the method of workin seems to have been posterior to the use of gold, silver, and copper. We are wh ignorant of the steps by which men were led to practise the processes required to fu and render it malleable. It is certain, however, that it was prepared in ancient Eg

me other countries, at a very remote epoch; but it was very little used in Greece
er the Trojan war. — (See the admirable work of *M. Goguet* on the *Origin of Arts, &c.* vol. i. p. 140.)

ics of Iron. — There are many varieties of iron, which artists distinguish by parti-
ames; but all of them may be reduced under one or other of the three following
: *cast* or *pig iron, wrought* or *soft iron,* and *steel.*

Cast or *pig iron* is the name given to this metal when first extracted from its ores.
es from which iron is usually obtained are composed of oxide of iron and clay.
ject of the manufacturer is to reduce the oxide to the metallic state, and to
e all the clay with which it is combined. This is effected by a peculiar process;
iron, being exposed to a strong heat in furnaces, and melted, runs out into moulds
d for its reception, and obtains the name of cast or pig iron.

cast iron thus obtained is distinguished by manufacturers into different varieties,
colour and other qualities. Of these the following are the most remarkable: —

hite cast iron, which is extremely hard and brittle, and appears to be composed
ngeries of small crystals. It can neither be filed, bored, nor bent, and is very
reak when suddenly heated or cooled.

rey or *mottled* cast iron, so called from the inequality of its colour. Its texture
lated. It is much softer and less brittle than the last variety; and may be cut,
nd turned on the lathe. Cannons are made of it.

ack cast iron is the most unequal in its texture, the most fusible, and least cohe-
the three.

rought or *soft iron* is prepared from cast iron by a process termed a refine-
r finery. The wrought iron manufactured in Sweden is reckoned the finest in
ld.

eel consists of pieces of wrought iron hardened by a peculiar process. The
iron imported into this country is mostly used in the manufacture of steel. (See
— (*Thomson's Chemistry.*)

of Iron. — To enumerate the various uses of iron would require a lengthened
tion. No one who reflects for a moment on the subject, can doubt that its dis-
and employment in the shape of tools and engines has been of the utmost
nce to man, and has done more, perhaps, than any thing else, to accelerate his
in the career of improvement. Mr. Locke has the following striking observ-
n this subject: —" Of what consequence the discovery of one natural body, and
rties, may be to human life, the whole great continent of America is a convincing
; whose ignorance in useful arts, and want of the greatest part of the conve-
of life, in a country that abounded with all sorts of natural plenty, I think may
uted to their ignorance of what was to be found in a very ordinary, despicable
I mean the mineral of iron. And whatever we think of our parts or improvements
art of the world, where knowledge and plenty seem to vie with each other; yet
ne that will seriously reflect upon it, I suppose it will appear past doubt, that,
use of iron lost among us, we should in a few ages be unavoidably reduced to
ts and ignorance of the ancient savage Americans, whose natural endowments
visions came no way short of those of the most flourishing and polite nations;
e who first made use of that one contemptible mineral, may be truly styled the
arts and author of plenty." — (*Essay on the Understanding,* book iv. c. 12.)

facture of Iron in Great Britain. — Iron mines have been wrought in this
from a very early period. Those of the Forest of Dean, in Gloucestershire,
vn to have existed in the year 1066. In consequence of the great consumption
r which they occasioned, they were restrained by act of parliament in 1581.
ter this, Edward Lord Dudley invented the process of smelting iron ore with
instead of wood fuel; and it is impossible, perhaps, to point out an instance of
nvention that has proved more advantageous. The patent which his Lordship
ined in 1619, was exempted from the operation of the act of 1623 (21 Jac. 1.
etting aside monopolies: but though in its consequences it has proved of im-
lue to the country, the works of the inventor were destroyed by an ignorant
nd he was well nigh ruined by his efforts to introduce and perfect his process;
it till about a century after, that it was brought into general use. In the early
ast century, well founded complaints were repeatedly made of the waste and
on of woods caused by the smelting of iron; and the dearth and scarcity of fuel
thus occasioned, led, about 1740, to the general adoption of Lord Dudley's
or using pit-coal, which was found to be in every respect superior to that pre-
use. — (*Report of Committee of the House of Commons on Patents,* p. 168, &c.)
is period the progress of the manufacture has exceeded the most sanguine
ons. In 1740, the quantity of pig iron manufactured in England and Wales
l to about 17,000 tons, produced by 59 furnaces. The quantities manufactured
dermentioned epochs, in Great Britain, have been as follow: —

```
1750  -   22,000 tons.
1788  -   68,000  —   produced by  85 furnaces.
1796  -  125,000  —        —       121   —
1806  -  250,000  —        —       169   —
1820  -  400,000  —        —       unknown.
1827  -  690,000  —        —       284   —
```

The quantities produced in 1827, in the different districts, were as follow:—

```
Staffordshire  -  216,000 tons, produced by 95 furnaces.
Shropshire     -   78,000  —         —       31   —
South Wales    -  272,000  —         —       90   —
North Wales    -   24,000  —         —       12   —
Yorkshire      -   43,000  —         —       24   —
Derbyshire     -   20,500  —         —       14   —
Scotland       -   36,500  —         —       18   —
   Totals      -  690,000              284
```

About three tenths of this quantity of iron is used as cast iron, and is consumed cipally in Great Britain and Ireland; the exports not exceeding 17,000 tons, sent c to France and the West Indies. The other seven tenths is converted into wr iron, being formed into bars, bolts, rods, &c. The exports of the different so iron amount at present to about 110,000 tons, which, at 10*l.* a ton, would be 1,100,000*l.*

In 1767, the iron exported from Great Britain amounted to only 11,000 tons. an average of the three years ending with 1806, the exports amounted to 28,000 being little more than a *fourth part* of their present amount!

Supposing the total quantity of pig iron at present produced in Great Brita amount to 700,000 tons a year, and to be worth at an average 6*l.* a ton, its total will be equal to 4,200,000*l.*; and the additional labour expended in forming th iron into bar iron, that is, into bars, bolts, rods, &c., may probably add about 1,200 more to its value; making it worth in all about 5,400,000*l.*

The increase of the iron manufacture has not only led to its exportation in large quantities, but has reduced our imports of foreign iron for home consumptior about 34,000 tons, which they amounted to at an average of the five years ending 1805, to about 13,000 tons, consisting principally of Swedish iron, which is subseq manufactured into steel. The following is

An Account of the British Iron (including unwrought Steel) exported from Great Britain in the Year
*** Quarters of a Hundred Weight and Pounds are omitted in the printing of this Table, but th taken into account in the summing up. — (*Parl. Paper,* No. 45. Sess. 1830.)

Countries to which exported.	Bar Iron.	Bolt and Rod Iron.	Pig Iron.	Cast Iron.	Iron Wire.	Wrought; viz.			
						Anchors and Grapnells.	Hoops.	Nails.	Of all o Sorts ex Ordnan
	Tons. cwt.	*Tons. cwt.*	*Tons. cwt.*	*Tons. cwt.*	*Tns.cwt*	*Tons. cwt.*	*Tons. cwt.*	*Tons. cwt.*	*Tons.*
Russia - -	- -	0 6	- -	1 18	1 13	- -	- -	- -	24
Sweden - -	- -	1 0	- -	12 19	- -	0 18	- -	- -	30
Norway - -	11 0	6 5	- -	13 4	- -	5 16	5 2	0 11	22
Denmark - -	432 14	76 7	157 0	4 19	2 4	13 15	220 3	1 4	108
Prussia - -	74 3	36 19	32 0	8 0	1 5	1 0	64 3	2 6	16
Germany - -	2,956 10	490 2	202 5	167 17	50 3	49 2	418 0	70 0	909
Kingdom of the Netherlands	3,686 14	144 15	1,585 7	248 7	64 0	100 19	1,148 2	5 1	648
France - -	2,093 6	98 5	3,952 10	104 6	11 12	142 6	735 2	- -	196
Portugal, Azores, and Madeira	2,324 0	1,776 15	5 0	71 2	4 2	9 13	1,092 14	78 5	215
Spain, and the Canaries -	578 5	66 10	5 0	195 9	9 0	143 10	1,221 19	12 13	187
Gibraltar - -	223 12	0 15	- -	21 11	12 0	48 11	116 0	30 19	18
Italy - -	8,662 7	1,358 9	749 7	395 1	3 0	22 8	807 12	1 8	513
Malta - -	847 17	91 1	- -	16 12	- -	1 3	96 4	1 1	20
The Ionian Islands -	29 15	- -	- -	101 2	- -	- -	- -	0 3	12
Turkey, and the Levant -	4,587 7	42 5	- -	8 17	- -	46 19	14 0	0 7	117
Asia - -	11,721 14	1,156 1	142 12	697 15	2 12	171 7	931 14	511 2	2,561
Africa - -	2,518 2	24 15	- -	546 14	3 10	73 18	428 15	165 8	437
British North American Colonies	3,216 12	385 9	465 0	686 0	1 2	108 11	450 0	1,131 3	1,250
British West Indies -	706 0	62 6	70 5	2,084 5	11 16	51 1	1,085 10	1,156 2	2,273
Foreign West Indies -	1,338 6	122 0	30 0	1,101 19	1 17	84 19	284 17	443 2	146
United States of America -	7,006 8	387 15	1,319 0	476 6	146 5	34 10	211 10	138 7	1,257
The Brazils - -	876 15	15 16	35 0	995 9	- -	46 17	120 10	591 6	366
Mexico, and States of South America	1,314 9	85 5	20 0	257 12	1 8	30 10	37 6	97 12	116
Guernsey, Jersey, Alderney, and Man -	972 4	66 4	161 10	72 6	1 9	65 11	43 0	89 18	220
Total - -	56,178 9	6,475 12	8,931 16	8,219 16	329 2	1,253 13	9,532 9	4,528 4	11,673

The declared value of the above exports was 1,162,931*l.*

:cline of Prices. — Prospects of the Manufacture. — The extraordinary increase that *...*aken place in the iron manufacture since 1823, is mainly to be ascribed to the high *...*s of 1824 and 1825, when pig iron met with a ready sale at from 12*l.* to 14*l.* a ton. *...*in consequence partly of the failure of most of the projects as to railroads and other *...*c works that were then set on foot, and partly and principally of the vast additional *...*ies that the extension of the manufacture threw upon the market, the price of iron *...*, in 1826, to 8*l.* or 9*l.* a ton; and has since gone on gradually declining, notwith-*...*ing the increase of exportation, till it is now only worth from 4*l.* 10*s.* to 5*l.* a ton! *...*effect of the decline has been to introduce the severest economy into every depart-*...*of the manufacture; and to make every device that promised a reduction of *...*e be eagerly grasped at. Still, however, it is very doubtful, should the present low *...*s continue, whether the manufacture can be carried on to its present extent. The *...*lent opinion in the trade seems to be, that, supposing prices not to rise, a consider-*...*number of the furnaces now in blast will have to be laid aside.

*...*ON-WOOD (Ger. *Eisenholz;* Du. *Yserhout;* Fr. *Bois de fer;* It. *Legno di* *...*; Sp. *Palo hierro;* Lat. *Sideroxylon, Lignum ferreum*), a species of wood of a *...*sh cast, so called on account of its corroding as that metal does, and its being *...*rkably hard and ponderous, even more so than ebony. The tree which pro-*...*s it grows principally in the West India islands, and is likewise very common *...*uth America, and in some parts of Asia, especially about Siam.

*...*INGLASS (Ger. *Hausenblase, Hausblase;* Fr. *Colle de poisson, Carlock;* It. *...*di pesce;* Rus. *Klei rübüi, Karluk*), one of the purest and finest of the animal *...*. It is a product, the preparation of which is almost peculiar to Russia. It *...*de of the air-bladders and sounds of different kinds of fish which are found *...*e large rivers that fall into the North Sea and the Caspian. That prepared *...*the sturgeon is generally esteemed the best; next to that the beluga; but *...*ass is also prepared from sterlets, shad, and barbel, though not so good. The *...*s usually rolled in little ringlets; the second sort is laid together like the *...*s of a book; and the common sort is dried without any care. When fine, it *...*a white colour, semi-transparent, and dry. It dissolves readily in boiling water, *...*s used extensively in cookery. It is also used for stiffening silk, making *...*ng plaster, &c. The price varies at present (October, 1831) from 5*s.* to 15*s.* *...*.—(See *Thomson's Chemistry;* and *Tooke's View of Russia*, 2d ed. vol. iii. *...*3.)

*...*LE OF MAN. See MAN, ISLE OF.

*...*ICE OF LEMONS, LIMES, OR ORANGES. The 9th section of the *...*Geo. 4. c. 111. is as follows:—For ascertaining the degrees of specific gravity *...*rength, according to which the duty on the juice of lemons, limes, and *...*es, shall be paid, it is enacted, that the degrees of such specific gravity or *...*th shall be ascertained by a glass citrometer, which shall be graduated in *...*:s in such manner, that distilled water being assumed as unity at the tempe-*...*of 60° by Fahrenheit's thermometer, every degree of the scale of such *...*eter shall be denoted by a variation of $\frac{4}{1000}$ parts of the specific gravity of *...*vater.

*...*NIPER BERRIES. See BERRIES.

*...*JRY, the name given to the teeth or tusks of the elephant, and of the *...*s or sea-horse. We have given, in a previous article (ELEPHANTS' TEETH), *...*t notice of this valuable article; but the following details as to its supply *...*onsumption may not be unacceptable.

*...*e duty of 1*l.* per cwt. on elephants' teeth produced, in 1830, 3,721*l.*, show-*...*at the quantity consumed amounted to as many hundred weights, or to *...*2 lbs. The average weight of an elephant's tusk may be taken at about *...*, so that 6,946 tusks must have been required to furnish this supply of *...*— a fact which supposes the destruction of 3,473 male elephants! But the *...*ction is really much greater; and would probably amount to, at least, *...*:n 5,000 and 6,000 elephants. If to the quantity of ivory required for *...*Britain, we add that required for the other countries of Europe, America, *...*sia, the slaughter of this noble animal will appear immense; and it may *...*xcite surprise, that the breed has not been more diminished. The western *...*astern coasts of Africa, the Cape of Good Hope, Ceylon, India, and the *...*ies to the eastward of the Straits of Malacca, are the great marts whence *...*:s of ivory are derived. The imports from Western Africa into Great *...*, in 1829, amounted to 2,194 cwt.; in 1825, the Cape furnished 919 cwt.;

and the usual imports from India, including Ceylon, &c., are about 1,000 c
—(Different *Parl. Papers.*) The Chinese market is principally supplied w
ivory from Malacca, Siam, and Sumatra.

The chief consumption of ivory in England is in the manufacture of hand
for knives; but it is also extensively used in the manufacture of musical a
mathematical instruments, chess-men, billiard-balls, plates for miniatures, to
&c. Ivory articles are said to be manufactured to a greater extent, and w
better success, at Dieppe, than in any other place in Europe. But the preparat
of this beautiful material is much better understood by the Chinese than by a
other people. No European artist has hitherto succeeded in cutting concent
balls after the manner of the Chinese; and their boxes, chess-men, and ot
ivory articles, are all far superior to any that are to be met with any where els

There is a great discrepancy in the value of the tusks of the walrus; so
fetching (in bond) only 3*l.* per cwt., and others no less than 30*l.* Genera
speaking, they are in about the same estimation as the tusks of the elephant.
is singular, however, that while the duty on the latter is only 1*l.* per cwt., that
the former should be 3*l.* 4*s.* It is impossible to imagine even the shadow c
ground for any such absurd distinction. The hunting of the walrus is sur
entitled to as much encouragement as the hunting of the elephant.

There are some details with respect to the consumption, supply, and manu
ture of ivory, in the very interesting volume on the Elephant (pp. 121—12
published under the auspices of the Society for the Diffusion of Useful Knowled
But this part of the work is much less complete than most of the others.

K.

KELP, is a substance composed of different materials, of which the fo
or mineral alkali, or, as it is commonly termed, soda, is the chief. This ingredi
renders it useful in the composition of soap, in the manufacture of alum, and in
formation of crown and bottle glass. It is formed of marine plants; which, being
from the rocks with a hook, are collected and dried on the beach to a certain
tent; they are afterwards put into kilns prepared for the purpose, the heat
which is sufficient to bring the plants into a state of semi-fusion. They are th
strongly stirred with iron rakes; and when cool, condense into a dark blue
whitish mass, very hard and solid. Plants about three years old yield the lar
quantity of kelp. The best kelp has an acrid caustic taste, a sulphurous od
is compact, and of a dark blue greenish colour. It yields about 5 per cent. o
weight of soda.—(*Barry's Orkney Islands*, p. 377.; *Thomson's Dispensatory.*)

The manufacture of kelp is, or rather *was*, principally carried on in the Western Isla
and on the western shores of Scotland, where it was introduced from Ireland, about
middle of last century. Towards the end of the late war, the kelp shores of the islan
North Uist let for 7,000*l.* a year. It has been calculated that the quantity of kelp
nually manufactured in the Hebrides only, exclusive of the mainland, and of the Ork
and Shetland isles, amounted, at the period referred to, to about 6,000 tons a year;
that the total quantity made in Scotland and its adjacent isles amounted to about 20
tons. At some periods during the war, it sold for 20*l.* a ton; but at an average of
twenty-three years ending with 1822, the price was 10*l.* 9*s.* 7*d.* — (Art. *Scotl*
Edinburgh Encyclopædia.)

Unluckily, however, the foundations on which this manufacture rested were altoge
factitious. Its existence depended on the maintenance of the high duties on barill
salt. Inasmuch, however, as kelp could not be substituted, without undergoing a
expensive process, for barilla, in a great many departments of industry in which the
of mineral alkali is indispensable, it became necessary materially to reduce the
duty laid on barilla during the war. The ruin of the kelp manufacture has
ascribed to this reduction; but though barilla had been altogether excluded from
markets, which could not have been done without great injury to many most impo
manufactures, the result would have been perfectly the same, in so far as kelp is
cerned, unless the high duty on salt had also been maintained. It was the repeal c
latter that gave the kelp manufacture the *coup de grace.* The purification of kelp
to render it fit for soap-making, is a much more troublesome and expensive process
the decomposition of salt; and the greatest quantity of alkali used, is now obtaine

er method. Had the duty on salt not been repealed, kelp might still have been
ctured, notwithstanding the reduction of duty on barilla.
manufacture is now almost extinct. Shores that formerly yielded the proprietors
f 200*l.* to 500*l.* a year, are now worth nothing. The price of kelp since 1822
n, at an average, about 4*l.* a ton; but it is daily declining; and the article will
on cease to be produced.
result, though injurious to the proprietors of kelp shores, and productive of tem-
distress to the labourers employed in the manufacture, is not to be regretted. It
ot have been obviated, without keeping up the price of some of the most im-
necessaries of life at a forced and unnatural elevation. The high price of kelp
asioned by the exigencies of the late war; which, besides obstructing the supply of
forced government to lay high duties on it and on salt. The proprietors had not
ige of a ground for considering that such a state of things would be permanent;
right in profiting by it while it lasted; but they could not expect that govern-
as to subject the country, during peace, to some of the severest privations occa-
y the war, merely that *they* might continue to enjoy an accidental advantage.

NTLEDGE, the name sometimes given to a ship's ballast.

RMES (Ger. *Scharlachbeeren;* Du. *Grein, Scharlakenbessen;* It. *Grana,*
s, *Cremese, Cocchi;* Sp. *Grana Kermes, Grana de la coscoja*), an insect
Ilicis, Lin.) of the same species as the true Mexican cochineal, found
e *quercus ilex,* a species of oak growing in Spain, France, the Levant, &c.
the discovery of America, kermes was the most esteemed drug for
scarlet, and had been used for that purpose from a very remote period.
nn inclines to think that it was employed by the Phœnicians, and that it
even the famous Tyrian purple. — (*Hist. of Invent.* vol. ii. p. 197. Eng.
rom the name of *coccum* or *coccus,* cloth dyed with kermes was called
n, and persons wearing this cloth were said by the Romans to be *coccinati.*
rt. lib. i. Epig. 97. lin. 6.) It is singular, however, notwithstanding its exten-
in antiquity, that the ancients had the most incorrect notions with respect
ature of kermes; many of them supposing that it was the grains (*grana*)
of the *ilex.* This was Pliny's opinion; others after him considered it in
e light, or as an excrescence formed by the puncture of a particular kind
ike the gall-nut. It was not till the early part of last century that it was
nd satisfactorily established that the kermes is really nothing but an insect,
g the appearance of a berry in the process of drying. The term kermes is
an origin. The Arabians had been acquainted with this production from
est periods in Africa; and having found it in Spain, they cultivated it ex-
y as an article of commerce, as well as a dye-drug for their own use. But
e introduction of cochineal, it has become an object of comparatively
mportance. It is still, however, prepared in some parts of Spain. Cloths
h kermes are of a deep red colour; and though much inferior in brilliancy
scarlet cloths dyed with real Mexican cochineal, they retain the colour
nd are less liable to stain. The old tapestries of Brussels, and other places
ers, which have scarcely lost any thing of their original vivacity, though
s old, were all dyed with kermes. The history of this production has
ated with great learning by Beckmann (*Hist. of Invent.* vol. i. pp. 171—
ed. trans.); and by Dr. Bancroft (*Permanent Colours,* vol. i. pp. 393—409.)

) (Fr. *Gomme de Kino;* Ger. *Kinoharz;* It. *Chino*), a gum, the produce of
t grow in the East and West Indies, Africa, Botany Bay, &c. The kino
nd in the shops, is said by Dr. A. T. Thomson, to come from India, and to
oduce of the *nauclea gambir.* The branches and twigs are bruised and boiled
. The decoction is then evaporated until it acquire the consistence of an ex-
ich is kino. It is imported in chests containing from 1 to 2 cwt.; and on the
the lid of each chest is a paper, inscribed with the name of John Brown, the
nd year of its importation, and stating that it is the produce of Amboyna.
dorous, very rough, and slightly bitter when first taken into the mouth;
erwards impresses a degree of sweetness on the palate. It is in small,
deep brown, shining, brittle fragments, which appear like portions of a
tract broken down; being perfectly uniform in their appearance. It is
lverised, affording a powder of a lighter brown colour than the fragments.
ay be doubted whether the inspissated juice of the *nauclea gambir* ought
nsidered as kino. Dr. Ainslie says that Botany Bay kino is the only kind
een in an Indian bazaar. The tree which yields it grows to a great height;

it flows from incisions made into the wood of the trunk.—(*Thomson's Dis[tory; Ainslie's Materia Indica.*)

KNIVES (Ger. *Messer;* Du. *Messen;* Fr. *Couteaux;* It. *Coltelli;* Sp. *Cuch* Rus. *Noshi*), are well known utensils made of iron and steel, and employed t with; they are principally manufactured in London, Salisbury, Sheffield, and mingham. Knives are made for a variety of purposes, as their different de nations imply; such as table-knives, oyster-knives, pruning-knives, pen-knives Although England at present excels every part of the world in the manufactu knives, as in most branches of cutlery, they are said not to have been made fo in this country previously to 1563.—(*Macpherson's Hist. Com. Anno* 1563.) now form a very considerable article of export.

KÖNIGSBERG, the capital of East Prussia, in lat. 54° 43′ N., lon. 20° 3 Population about 68,000. Königsberg is situated on the Pregel; but ships ing more than 7 feetwater are obliged to unload part of their cargoes at P before entering into Fresh Bay (Frische Haf), into which the Pregel flows. nigsberg has a considerable command of internal navigation, and is the prin emporium of a large extent of country. Wheat, rye, and other species of are the chief articles of export. The wheat is somewhat similar to that of Da but of inferior quality, being larger in the berry, and thicker skinned. The r thin, and also the barley, with few exceptions, and light. Peas are of a remar large, fine quality. Oats are common feed, with a slight admixture of tares as these last answer in some degree the purpose of beans, the value of the o rather enhanced than otherwise by the circumstance. More tares are sh here than from any other port in the Baltic. The prices of all sorts of grai usually lower at Königsberg than at the neighbouring Prussian ports. Whe September, 1830, varied from 33s. to 47s. 2d. per Winch. quarter. Hemp, linseed, tallow, wax, and bristles, are also largely exported. The bristles a best in the Baltic. Timber, deals, and staves, are as good as at Memel, bu rather scarce. The imports are coffee, sugar, cotton stuffs and yarn, hard dye-woods, spices, tobacco, coals, rum, &c. Salt is a government monopoly person being allowed to import it, but he must either sell it to governmen price fixed by them, or export it again.

Moneys, Weights, and *Measures,* same as at Dantzic.

L.

LAC, or GUM-LAC (Ger. *Lack, Gummilack;* Fr. *Lacque, Gomme la* It. *Lacca, Gommalacca;* Sp. *Goma laca;* Rus. *Laka, Gunmilak;* Arab. Hind. *Lak'h;* Sans. *Lākshā*), a substance, which has been improperly called produced in Bengal, Assam, Pegu, Siam, &c., on the leaves and branches of trees, by an insect (*chermes lacca*). The trees selected by the insect on wh deposit its eggs, are known by the names of the bihar tree (*Croton lacci* Lin.), the pepel (*Butea frondosa*), bott, and coosim trees, &c. After bein posited, the egg is covered by the insect with a quantity of this peculiar sub or lac, evidently intended to serve, in the economy of nature, as a nidus an tection to the ovum and insect in its first stage, and as food for the mag its more advanced stage. It is formed into cells, finished with as much a honeycomb, but differently arranged. Lac yields a fine red dye, which, t not so bright as the true Mexican cochineal, is said to be more perma and the resinous part is extensively used in the manufacture of sealing wa hats, and as a varnish.

Lac, when in its natural state encrusting leaves and twigs, is called *stick lac* collected twice a year; and the only trouble in procuring it is in breaking do leaves and branches, and carrying them to market. When the twigs or sticks are or only partially covered, the lac is frequently separated from them, as it always to be when shipped for Europe, to lessen the expense of freight. The best stick of a deep red colour. When held against the light it should look bright, and broken should appear in diamond-like points. If it be not gathered till the have left their cells, it becomes pale, and pierced at the top; and is of little use as though probably better for a varnish.

15

ac dye, *lac lake*, or *cake lac*, consists of the colouring matter extracted from the stick Various processes have been adopted for this purpose. It is formed into small e cakes or pieces like those of indigo. It should, when broken, look dark-coloured, ng, smooth, and compact; when scraped or powdered, it should be of a bright red r, approaching to that of carmine. That which is sandy, light coloured, and spongy, which, when scraped, is of a dull brickdust colour, should be rejected.

twithstanding the continued fall in the price of cochineal, the use of lac dye has extending in this country. The annual consumption may at present amount to 600,000 lbs., having trebled since 1818. The finest qualities of lac dye are seldom with for sale in Calcutta, being generally manufactured under contract for the pean market.

hen stick lac has been separated from the twigs to which it naturally adheres, and ely pounded, the native silk and cotton dyers extract the colour as far as it con-ntly can be done by water. The yellowish, hard, resinous powder which remains, g somewhat of the appearance of mustard seed, is called *seed lac*. When liquefied e, it is formed into cakes, and denominated *lump lac*. The natives use the latter in ng bangles, or ornaments in the form of rings, for the arms of the lower class of es; the best *shellac* being used in manufacturing these ornaments for the superior s.

llac is produced from seed lac, by putting the latter into bags of cotton cloth, and ng it over a charcoal fire, when the lac melts, and being strained through the bag, sinous part, which is the most liquefiable, is obtained in a considerable degree of ; it is formed into thin sheets or plates. Thin, transparent, or amber-coloured c is best; avoid that which is thick, dark, or speckled: it should always, when n, be amber-coloured on the edge; that which has a dark brown fracture, however should be rejected. When laid on a hot iron, shellac, if pure, will instantly catch nd burn with a strong but not disagreeable smell. It used to be principally em-l in this country in the manufacture of sealing wax, and as a varnish; but within few years it has begun to be very extensively used in the manufacture of hats. c has advanced rapidly in price during the last three or four years; a circumstance has had a considerable effect in accelerating the fall in the price of lac dye; the ity of the latter being necessarily increased in consequence of the greater demand e former.

Bengal, lac is chiefly produced in the forests of Sylet and Burdwan. The finest said to be obtained from the stick lac of Siam and Pegu; but the shellac or resin-rt obtained from the latter, is inferior to that produced from Sylet stick lac. It e obtained in almost any quantity.

unt of the Quantities of Lac Dye or Lac Lake, Shellac and Seed Lac, and Stick Lac, imported into Great Britain since 1814. — (*Parl. Paper*, No. 22. Sess. 1830, p. 86.)

Years.	Lac Dye or Lac Lake.	Shellac and Seed Lac.	Stick Lac.	Years.	Lac Dye or Lac Lake.	Shellac and Seed Lac.	Stick Lac.
	lbs.	lbs.	lbs.		lbs.	lbs.	lbs.
1814	278,899	110,670	44,439	1822	872,967	282,621	18,429
1815	598,592	575,629	32,677	1823	525,231	366,321	15,517
1816	269,080	587,153	4,200	1824	592,197	571,684	427
1817	384,909	633,256	254,005	1825	535,505	708,687	13,521
1818	249,387	839,977	562,051	1826	760,729	443,589	90,596
1819	178,088	531,549	40,478	1827	729,242	499,813	8,835
1820	439,439	845,539	342,340	1828	689,205	681,971	
1821	640,864	718,063	58,880				

t of the Deliveries of Lac Dye for Home Consumption and Exportation, with the Stocks on hand on the 1st of January, at London and Liverpool, from 1818 to 1830, both inclusive.

| Years. | Deliveries of Lac Dye. | | | | Stock, 1st Jan. | |
| | London. | | Liverpool. | | London. | Liverpool. |
	Hom. Con.	Export.	Hom. Con.	Export.		
	lbs.	lbs.	lbs.	lbs.	Chts.	Chts.
1818	180,385	24,607				
1819	150,650	22,137				
1820	224,101	41,495				
1821	259,892	71,854				
1822	313,506	26,455	46,758	- -	6,462	
1823	333,277	13,106	75,472	- -	5,647	
1824	422,852	51,473	57,573	- -	7,413	
1825	310,519	63,111	57,867	- -	7,630	
1826	355,853	70,100	33,329	- -	7,690	170
1827	358,002	68,673	93,298	1,020	8,595	250
1828	360,694	49,642	67,015	6,395	9,397	380
1829	402,055	28,103	57,021	336	9,778	350
1830	462,934	78,900	112,995	1,167	9,800	490
1831	- -	- -	- -	- -	8,750	260

The finest lac dye is distinguished by the mark D.T. ; the second by J.Mc.R. ; the third by C.E., In October (1831) the prices of the different species of lac in bond in the London market were follows :—

Lac Dye	D.T.	2s. 6d. to 3s. 0d. per lb.		Stick Lac	-	- 1l. 15s. to 2l. 10s. per
—	J.Mc.R.	1 5 — 1 6 —		Shellac, Liver	5 0 — 5 15 —
—	C.E.	1 0 — 1 2 —		— D.T.	- 6 0 — 0 0 —
—	Low and Mid.	0 9 — 1 0 —		— Orange	- 6 0 — 7 0 —
Seed Lac	3l. 10s. — 4l. 15s. per cwt.			— Block	- 5 10 — 5 15 —

In 1823, D.T. lac dye was as high as 8s. 3d. and 8s. 6d. per lb. The duties are 5 per cent. on lac seed lac, and stick lac; and 20 per cent on shellac. It is difficult to discover on what principle she which is prepared, as we have already seen, from the refuse of lac dye, is charged with *four* times duty laid upon the latter. — (*Dr. Bancroft on Permanent Colours*, vol. ii. pp. 1—60.; *Ainslie's Mat. M Milburn's Orient. Com.*; and private information.)

LACE (Du. *Kanten;* Fr. *Dentelle;* Ger. *Spitzen;* It. *Merletti, Pizzi; R Krushewo;* Sp. *Encajes*), a plain or ornamented net work, tastefully compose many fine threads of gold, silver, silk, flax, or cotton, interwoven, from *Laci* Latin, the guard hem or fringe of a garment.

The origin of this delicate and beautiful fabric is involved in considerable obscu but there is no doubt it lays claim to high antiquity. In Mr. Hope's Costumes of Ancients, many beautiful lace patterns are pourtrayed on the borders of the dresse Grecian females; and from the derivation of the word *"lace,"* it is probable it not unknown to the Romans. It is supposed that Mary de' Medici was the first v brought lace into France, from Venice, where, and in the neighbouring states of Ital is understood to have been long previously worn; but we find that in England, so ea as 1483, " laces of thread, and laces of gold, and silk and gold," were enumerated am the articles prohibited to be imported. — (1 *Rich.* 3. c. 10.) It is, therefore, fai presume that this manufacture had begun in England *prior* to that period, as this many subsequent acts were passed — (19 Hen. 7. c. 21.; 5 Eliz. c. 7.; 13 & 14 Car c. 13.; 4 & 5 W. & M. c. 10., &c.) — for the encouragement and protection our home manufacture; but it may equally be concluded, that as *pins* (which are in pensable in the process of lace making) were not used in England till 1543, the ma facture of lace must have been vulgar in fabric, and circumscribed in its extent. Tradi says that the lace manufacture was introduced into this country by some refugees fr Flanders, who settled at or near Cranfert, now a scattered village on the west sid Bedfordshire, and adjoining Bucks; but there is no certain evidence that we are indet to the Flemings for the original introduction of this beautiful art, although from th we have undoubtedly derived almost all the different manufactures relating to dress. have, however, imitated many of their lace fabrics, and greatly improved our manu ture at various periods, from the superior taste displayed in the production of this art in the Low Countries. In 1626, Sir Henry Borlase founded and endowed the free sch at Great Marlow, for 24 boys, to read, write, and cast accounts; and for 24 girls, knit, spin, and make *bone lace* — (*Lewis's Topography*); so that there is reason to s pose that at this time the manufacture had commenced in Buckinghamshire, which degrees extended to the adjoining counties of Bedford and Northampton. In 1640, lace trade was a flourishing interest in Buckinghamshire — (*Fuller's Worthies*, and diffe Itineraries); and so greatly had it advanced in England, that by a royal ordinance France, passed in 1660, a mark was established upon the thread lace *imported from country* and from Flanders, and upon the point lace from Genoa, Venice, and o foreign countries, in order to secure payment of the customs duties. — (*Universal tionary.*)

Pillow Lace,—the original manufacture,—is worked upon a hard stuffed pillow, with flax, or cotton threads, according to a parchment pattern placed upon it, by means of p bobbins, and spindles, which are placed and displaced, twisting and interweaving threads, so as to imitate the pattern designed. This manufacture has been long purs in almost every town and village in the midland counties, particularly in Buckingh shire, Bedfordshire, and Northamptonshire, besides at Honiton and Tiverton, in De and various other places in the west of England. The principal places where it is n in the Netherlands are, Antwerp, Brussels, Mechlin, Louvaine, Ghent, Valencien and Lisle. It is also made at Charleville, Sedan, Le Compté de Bourgoyne, Li Dieppe, Havre de Grace, Harfleur, Pont l'Evesque, Gosors, Fescamp, Caen, A Bapaume, &c. in France, and at various places in Spain, Portugal, and Italy. can form no estimate of the number of persons employed on the Continent; but in B sels alone not less than 10,000 are said to be engaged in this manufacture. — (*E Metrop.*) In England and Ireland, besides the laws passed at different times to courage and protect the manufacture, associations were formed in various places, the view of exciting a spirit of emulation and improvement, by holding out premi for the production of the best pieces of bone lace; and although smuggling of for lace was carried on to a great extent, (in 1772, 72,000 ells of French lace were seize

t of Leigh, and lodged in the king's warehouse there, besides numerous other
s,) the British manufacture advanced in an unparalleled degree. — (*Gentleman's*
1751, vol. xxi. p. 520.; vol xlii. p. 434.) It is imagined that the first lace ever
n this country was of the sort called *Brussels point*, the net work made by bone
s on the pillow, and the pattern and sprigs worked with the needle. Such ap-
p have been the kind worn by the nobility and people of high rank, as is evident
different portraits now in existence painted by Vandyke, in the time of Charles I.,
erwards by Sir Peter Lely and Sir Godfrey Kneller, in the succeeding reigns of
II., Queen Anne, and George I. About a century since, the *grounds* in use were
Mechlin, and what the trade termed the *wire ground*, which was very similar, if not
al, with the *modern* Mechlin, the principal article in the present French manufac-
The laces made in these grounds were singularly rich and durable; the designs
old *Mechlin*, resembled the figures commonly introduced in ornamental carving.
n 70 and 80 years ago, a great deterioration was occasioned by the introduction
Trolly ground, which was exceedingly coarse and vulgar, the figures angular, and
her in the worst taste conceivable. An improvement, however, took place about
1770, when the ground, which is probably the most ancient known, was re-
ced; this was no other than the one still in partial use, and denominated the *old*
ground. About 1777, or 1778, quite a *new* ground was attempted by the inhabitants
ingham and its neighbourhood, which quickly superseded all the others; this was
t *ground*, which had (as is supposed) been imported from the Netherlands. From
appearance of this ground may be dated the origin of the modern pillow lace trade;
as not until the beginning of the present century that the most striking improve-
were made; for during the last quarter of the eighteenth century, the article,
certainly much more light and elegant from the construction of the ground, was
ly poor and spiritless in the design. Soon after the year 1800, a freer and bolder
s adopted; and from that time to 1812, the improvement and consequent success
onishing and unprecedented. At Honiton, in Devon, the manufacture had ar-
that perfection, was so tasteful in the design, and so delicate and beautiful in the
nship, as not to be excelled even by the best specimens of Brussels lace. During
war, veils of this lace were sold in London at from 20 to 100 guineas; they are
d from 8 to 15 guineas. The effects of the competition of machinery, however,
out this time felt; and in 1815, the broad laces began to be superseded by the
nufacture. The pillow lace trade has since been gradually dwindling into insig-
e, and has at length sunk into a state which, compared with its condition
s back, is truly deplorable. It is difficult to form an estimate of the
of persons employed in pillow lace making during its prosperity; but in a pe-
om the makers in Buckingham and the neighbourhood, presented to her present
in 1830, it was stated that 120,000 persons were dependent on this trade; but
aber has since been materially diminished.

agham *Lace.*—A frame-work knitter of Nottingham, named Hammond, about the
8, was the first who made lace by machinery. Dissipated in habits, and destitute of
employment, or credit, the idea struck him while looking at the broad lace on his
p, that he could fabricate a similar article by means of his stocking frame. — (*Gra-*
nson on Hosiery, Lace, &c., p. 295., now in the press.) He tried and succeeded.
machine ostensibly for lace (introduced at Nottingham about the same period, by
nd Harvey, of London) was called a pin machine, for making single press *point*
itation of the Brussels ground. This machine, although lost here, is still used
e to a great extent in manufacturing the net called *tulle*. This was the age of
nts; and workmen at their leisure hours employed themselves in forming new
n the hand, in the hope of perfecting a complete hexagon, which had hitherto
l their efforts to discover. In 1782, the warp frame was introduced, which is
se for making *warp lace*; and in 1799, after many attempts, the *bobbin net* ma-
s invented; but this frame was not completely successful till 1809, when Mr.
at, of Tiverton, from an improved variation of the principle, obtained a patent
ars. Steam power was first introduced by Mr. John Lindley, in 1815-16; but
ome into active operation till 1820. It became general in 1822-23; and a great
was at this period given to the trade, owing to the expiration of Mr. Heathcoat's
e increased application of power, and the perfection to which the different hand
d by this time been brought. A temporary prosperity shone on the trade; and
s individuals — clergymen, lawyers, doctors, and others — readily embarked capi-
empting a speculation. Prices fell in proportion as production increased; but the
was immense; and the Nottingham lace frame became the organ of general sup-
ing and supplanting, in plain nets, the most finished productions of France and
erlands.

illiam Felkin, of Nottingham, the author of a very able tract on this subject,

considers that the amount of capital and the number of hands employed in the b
net trade may be thus estimated. — (Published September, 1831.)

In spinning and doubling the yarn, principally in Manchester, including 55 factories—
860,000 spindles and other machinery, and the stocks on hand -   -   -
In the manufacture of bobbin net, including 22 factories, principally for power machines—
1,000 power looms averaging 10-4ths wide, 3,500 hand machines averaging 8-4ths wide—
the stocks on hand of power and hand machine owners, and the capital employed in embroidering, preparing, &c.   -   -   -   -   -   1,

                    Total capital employed   -   -   - £2,9

The number of hands employed may be also estimated thus : —
In Manchester, spinning ; adults   -   -   -   -   - 3,500
                         children   -   -   -   -   - 4,000

In Manchester and Nottingham, doubling ; adults and children   -   -   -

In power net making ; adults   -   -   -   -   - 1,500
                      youths   -   -   -   -   - 1,000
                      children   -   -   -   -   - 500

                                                                          3,000
                      women, mending   -   -   -   - 2,000
In hand machine working, chiefly adults, including children winding and mending   - 13,000

In embroidering, mending, pearling, finishing, &c. in almost every village round
Nottingham, in Glasgow, Ireland, London, Devon, Somerset, and Norfolk, women
and children   -   -   -   -   -   -   -   -

                    Total number of persons receiving wages   -   - 2

The population of Nottingham and the surrounding villages in 1811, when
bobbin net manufacture commenced, was 47,000 ; the present number is 79,000.
the hosiery and the point net trade are understood to have declined in the mean
and no other branch materially advanced or sprung up, this large increase may
be attributed to the bobbin net manufacture.

By comparing the value of 1,600,000 lbs. of Sea Island cotton worth 130,000l.
25,000 lbs. of raw silk worth 30,000l. (which is considered to be used annually i
manufacture), with the manufactured value of the same, worked into 23,400,000 s
yards of bobbin net, the estimated value of which is 1,891,875l., the great na
utility of this trade will be at once evident.   A clear surplus of more than a p
sterling is realised upon every pound avoirdupois of the raw material, being distri
over the trade in rent, profit, and wages ; in other words, about twelve time
value of the original cost ; and this is altogether independent of the profits arising
embroidery, in itself a most extensive and important branch.   About half o
production is supposed to be exported, chiefly to Hamburgh, the Leipsic and Fra
fairs, Antwerp and the rest of Belgium, to France (contraband), Italy, Sicily
North and South America.   Three eighths are sold unembroidered, and the rema
eighth embroidered in this country.   But in an embroidered and finished state, the
of the article is much further enhanced ; and it is estimated that by the operations o
trade, which had no existence 20 years ago, 130,000l. worth of raw cotton bec
when manufactured, finished, and embroidered, worth 3,820,000l. sterling.

The English manufacture from machinery is now confined to *point net, warp ne
bobbin net,* so called from the peculiar construction of the machines by which the
produced.   There were various other descriptions made ; viz. *two-plain net, squ
tuck knotted net,* the *fish mesh net,* and the *platted* or *Urling's net ;* but they are no
continued.—(*Gravenor Henson.*)   Nottingham is the *depôt* of the lace trade ; a
supplies, collected from all the surrounding villages, and even from the more d
counties where it is manufactured, are thence distributed to the four quarters o
world.

Present Condition of the Lace Trade, Wages, &c. — We are grieved to say th
manufacture, not only of pillow but also of Nottingham lace, is at this moment in
of great depression.   The growth of the latter has been the means of destroyi
former ; but as the new manufacture is by far the most valuable, the change, t
severely felt by many thousands of poor persons in Bucks, Bedford, and other coun
in a national point of view, decidedly advantageous.   The depression in the Notti
lace trade seems to be the result of its previous prosperity ; which, besides contri
to the extraordinary increase in the powers of production, has attracted too much

---

* Mr. Felkin, who is very extensively engaged in the trade, and well acquainted with all its
ments, has been at great pains, in forming these estimates, to make them as correct as possible.
possible, however, to attain to perfect accuracy in such matters ; and we cannot help thinking
number of persons said to be employed in embroidering, mending, &c. is somewhat exaggerated.
three fourths of this number are said to be children, it is not really so great as it appears to be.

oo many hands to the trade So long as the demand kept pace with the supply, men were kept in full employment, wages and profits were good, and the stocks and small. But of late years the supply has been a question of *quantity* rather of *quality*, and prices have consequently suffered a great depression. Lace, having ne a common ornament, easily accessible to all classes, has lost its attractions in shionable circles, by which it was formerly patronised, so that very rich lace is no r in demand. And many articles of dress, which, in our drawing-rooms and ooms, lately consisted of the most costly and tasteful patterns in lace, are now superseded, or made of a different manufacture.

e wages of the *power loom* workmen have fallen, within the last two years, from . to 18s. per week—(*Felkin*,p. 3.); and, in the same period, machines have increased ighth in number, and one sixth in capacity of production. The tendency of this se in power machinery is still further to depreciate the wages of the *hand machine* men (already below the standard of the power loom weaver); and the increased and ulating production, beyond a proportionate demand, renders it hopeless to expect mmediate amelioration in their condition. Many of the *embroiderers* in Nottingham present unemployed; and even for the most splendid and beautiful specimens of idery (some of which have occupied six weeks, working six days a week and four-hours a day) the young women have not earned more than 1s. a day. The de-d condition of the embroiderers is believed to be owing in no inconsiderable degree competition of the Belgians, who have acquired a superiority in *this* department it is not easy to account for. The condition of the *pillow lace* workers is still more rable. Many have now abandoned that pursuit for straw plaiting, which offers a certain, though not a much more profitable, employment; but those who still on in the fabrication of thread lace, working from twelve to fourteen hours a annot obtain more, on the average, than *two shillings and sixpence a week* for their s and unremitting labour. Ten years ago they could, with greater ease, earn week, working only eight hours a day.

health of the power-machine workman is, on the whole, understood to be good; ctories are neither hot nor confined; and the hands have only to superintend, not the machines. Hand machine labour is much heavier; but as it is the custom to by "*shifts*," the men are seldom more than six hours a day at the frame. It is, er, believed, that the gradual depression of wages, requiring increased exertion, end to deteriorate the general health of this class, particularly of those em-d in wide machines. The embroidery frame is, perhaps, the most destructive. 'orkers, in general, commence at a tender age; and, from constantly leaning over ame, while their bodies remain in a state of inactivity, they are frequently distorted r persons, and become the victims of pulmonary disease. Notwithstanding the ary habits of the pillow lace workers, their general health is understood to be than that of the lace embroiderers; but, in both these employments, the hours of are too long for children. They are, however, purely domestic employments, the superintendence of parents; but as the existence of the latter depends on antity of labour they can bring into operation, their necessities place filial con-ions beyond the reach of legislative, or even social, interference.

most celebrated foreign laces are —

Brussels, the most valuable. There are two kinds: *Brussels ground*, having a n mesh formed by platting and twisting four threads of flax to a perpendicular mesh; *Brussels wire ground*, made of silk — meshes partly straight and partly . The pattern is worked separately, and set on by the needle.

Mechlin; a hexagon mesh formed of three flax threads twisted and platted to a dicular line or pillar. The pattern is worked in the net.

Valenciennes; an irregular hexagonal formed of two threads, partly twisted and at the top of the mesh. The pattern is worked in the net similar to Mechlin

Lisle; a diamond mesh, formed of two threads platted to a pillar.

Alençon (called Blond); hexagon of two threads, twisted similar to Buckingham considered the most inferior of any made on the cushion.

Alençon Point; formed of two threads to a pillar, with octagon and square meshes tely.

French nets made by machinery, are —

Single Presspoint, called, when not ornamented, *tulle*, and when ornamented, ; made of silk; is an inferior net, but is attractive from the beautiful manner in t is stiffened.

Trico Berlin; so called from being invented at Berlin, and the stitch being removed eedles from its place of looping; is fanciful and ornamented in appearance, but demand in England.

3. *Fleur de Tulle,* made from the warp lace machine; mesh of two descripti●
which gives a shaded appearance to the net.

4. *Tulle Anglois* is double pressed point lace.

5. *Bobbin Net,* ⎱ principally made by English emigrants, who have settled
6. *Warp Net,* ⎰ France.

** We are indebted for this learned and very excellent article to Mr. Robert Sl●
of Fore Street, London.

LACK, a word used in the East Indies to denote the sum of 100,000 rupe●
which, supposing them standards, or siccas, at 2*s.* 6*d.,* amounts to 12,5●
sterling.

LADING, BILL OF. See BILL OF LADING.

LAGAN. See FLOTSAM.

LAMB-SKINS (Ger. *Lammsfelle ;* Fr. *Peaux d'agneaux ;* It. *Pelli agnelli●*
Sp. *Pieles de corderos*). The price of lamb-skins varies according to the finen●
brilliancy, and colour of the wool. Black lamb-skins are more generally esteem
than those of any other colour. English lamb-skins are seldom to be met w●
perfectly black ; but since the introduction of Merino sheep into this country, ma
of the white fleeces have, in point of quality, arrived at a pitch of perfect●
which justly entitles them to be ranked with some of the best fleeces in Spain

LAMP (Ger. *Lampen ;* Fr. *Lampes ;* It. *Lucerne ;* Sp. *Lamparas ;* R●
Lampadii), an instrument used for the combustion of liquid inflammable bod●
for the purpose of producing artificial light.

It.is unnecessary to give any description of instruments that are so well known. We may, howe●
remark that the discovery of Sir H. Davy, who, by covering the flame with wire gauze, succeede●
producing a lamp that may be securely used in coal mines charged with inflammable gas, is one of
most ingenious and valuable that has ever been made. The following extracts from a communica●
of Mr. Buddle, one of the ablest and best informed coal engineers in the kingdom, evince the g●
importance of Sir Humphry Davy's invention.

" Besides the facilities afforded by this invention, to the working of coal-mines abounding in fire-da
it has enabled the directors and superintendents to ascertain, with the utmost precision and expedi●
both the presence, the quantity, and correct situation of the gas. Instead of creeping inch by inch ●
a candle, as is usual, along the galleries of a mine suspected to contain fire-damp, in order to ascer●
its presence, we walk firmly on with the safe-lamps, and, with the utmost confidence, prove the ac
state of the mine. By observing attentively the several appearances upon the flame of the lamp, i●
examination of this kind, the cause of accidents which happened to the most experienced and cau●
miners is completely developed ; and this has hitherto been in a great measure matter of mere ●
jecture.

" It is not necessary that I should enlarge upon the national advantages which must necessarily r●
from an invention calculated to prolong our supply of mineral coal, because I think them obvio●
every reflecting mind ; but I cannot conclude without expressing my highest sentiments of admira●
for those talents which have developed the properties, and controlled the power, of one of the ●
dangerous elements which human enterprise has hitherto had to encounter."

LAMP-BLACK (Ger. *Kienruss ;* Fr. *Noir de fumée ;* It. *Nero di fumo, Ne●*
fumo ; Sp. *Negro de humo*). " The finest lamp-black is produced by collec●
the smoke from a lamp with a long wick, which supplies more oil than car●
perfectly consumed, or by suffering the flame to play against a metalline co●
which impedes the combustion, not only by conducting off part of the heat,
by obstructing the current of air. Lamp-black, however, is prepared in a m●
cheaper way, for the demands of trade. The dregs which remain after the eli●
tion of pitch, or else small pieces of fir-wood, are burned in furnaces of a pecu●
construction, the smoke of which is made to pass through a long horizontal ●
terminating in a close-boarded chamber. The roof of this chamber is mad●
coarse cloth, through which the current of air escapes, while the soot remai●
— (*Ure's Dictionary.*)

LAND-WAITER, an officer of the Custom-house, whose duty it is, u●
landing any merchandise, to taste, weigh, measure, or otherwise examine
various articles, &c., and to take an account of the same. They are like●
styled searchers, and are to attend, and join with, the patent searchers, in
execution of all cockets for the shipping of goods to be exported to for●
parts ; and, in cases where drawbacks or bounties are to be paid to the merc●
on the exportation of any goods, they, as well as the patent searchers, ar
certify the shipping thereof on the debentures.

LAPIS LAZULI. See ULTRAMARINE.

LAST, an uncertain quantity, varying in different countries, and with res●
to different articles. Generally, however, a last is estimated at 4,000 lbs. ;
there are great discrepancies.

The following quantities of different articles make a last, viz. : 14 barrels of pitch, tar, or a●
12 dozen of hides or skins ; 12 barrels of cod-fish, potash, or meal ; 20 cades, each of 1,000 herrings, ●
1,000 ten hundred, and every 100 five score ; 10½ quarters of cole seed ; 10 quarters of corn or rape

parts of England 21 quarters of corn go to a last; 12 sacks of wool; 20 dickers (every dicker of leather; 18 barrels of unpacked herrings; 10,000 pilchards; 24 barrels (each barrel contain.)s.) of gunpowder; 1,700 lbs. of feathers or flax.

is sometimes used to signify the burthen or lade of a ship.

'H, LATHS (Du. *Latten*; Fr. *Lattes*; Ger. *Latten*; It. *Correnti*; Rus· long, thin, and narrow slips of wood, nailed to the rafters of a roof or in order to sustain the covering. Laths are distinguished into various according to the different kinds of wood of which they are made, and the it purposes to which they are to be applied. They are also distinguished, ng to their length, into 5, 4, and 3 feet laths. Their ordinary breadth is in inch, and their thickness ¼ of an inch. Laths are sold by the bundle, is generally called a hundred: but seven score, or 140, are computed in the d for 3 feet laths; six score, or 120, in such as are 4 feet; and for those are denominated 5 feet, the common hundred, or five score.

VN (Ger. and Fr. *Linon*; It. *Linone, Rensa*; Sp. *Cambray clarin*), a sort r or open worked cambric, which, till of late years, was exclusively manu- d in France and Flanders. At present, the lawn manufacture is established land, and in the north of Ireland, where articles of this kind are brought a degree of perfection, as nearly to rival the productions of the French emish manufactories. In the manufacture of lawns, finer flaxen thread is an in that of cambric.

ARETTO. See QUARANTINE.

D (Ger. *Bley, Blei*; Du. *Lood, Loot*; Fr. *Plomb*; It. *Piombo*; Sp. Rus. *Swinetz*; Pol. *Olow*; Lat. *Plumbum*; Arab. *Anuk*; Hind. *Sisa*; urb), one of the most useful metals. It is of a bluish white colour, en newly melted is very bright, but it soon becomes tarnished by exposure air. It has scarcely any taste, but emits on friction a peculiar smell. It aper or the fingers of a bluish colour. When taken internally, it acts as a It is one of the softest of the metals: its specific gravity is 11·35. It malleable, and may be reduced to thin plates by the hammer; it may also n out into wire, but its ductility is not very great. Its tenacity is so hat a lead wire $\frac{1}{128}$ inch diameter is capable of supporting only 18·4 lbs. breaking. It melts at 612°. — (*Thomson's Chemistry*.)

d is a metal of much importance, as, from its durability, it is extensively used onstruction of water-pipes and cisterns, as a covering for flat surfaces or tops of s, &c. &c. Its salts, which are poisonous, are used in medicine to form external applications, and frequently not a little by the disreputable wine- t, to stop the process of acetous fermentation. Wine thus poisoned, may, , be readily distinguished; a small quantity of the bicarbonate of potassa pro- white precipitate, and sulphuretted hydrogen a black one. Pure wine will not ed by either of these tests. "The oxide of lead enters into the composition glass, which it renders clearer and more fusible: it is also used in glazing earthen vessels; hence the reason that pickles kept in common red pans become s. Lead with tin, and a small quantity of some of the other metals, forms with antimony it forms the alloy of which printing types are made." — (*Joyce's ineralogy*.)

ad mines of Great Britain have been wrought from a very remote era. Pre- o 1289, however, it would seem that those of Derbyshire only had been ex- But in the year now mentioned, lead mines were discovered in Wales; and being ascertained that the ore of these mines produced some silver, increased was paid to their working. The produce of the lead mines at present in Great Britain cannot be accurately ascertained. Mr. Stevenson supposes gland, *Edin. Ency.*) that the lead mines of Derbyshire annually produce 5,000 tons, but they seem to be on the decline. Those on the borders of Cumber- Northumberland are supposed to yield, at an average, from 11,000 to 12,000 he total produce of the Scotch lead mines is estimated at 65,000 bars; which, ar is 1 cwt. 1 qr. 2 lbs., is equal to 4,120 tons. — (*General Report of Scotland*, Addenda, p. 7.) Some of the most productive of the Welsh lead mines have en wrought out, or have been rendered unserviceable from inundations. Sub-

An Account of the Exports and Imports of Lead and Lead Ore, &c. for Ten Years, ending 5th Ja

| | Exports. | | | | | | | | Imports |
| | Pig and Rolled Lead and Shot. | Litharge. | Red Lead. | White Lead. | Lead Ore. | Total British Lead and Lead Ore. | Foreign Lead in Pig. | Foreign Lead Ore. | Lead. |
Years.									
	Tons.	Tons.	Tons.	Tons.	Tons.	Tons.	Tons.	Tons.	Tons.
1821	18,800	395	229	603	252	19,779	4	- -	4
1822	15,646	573	242	652	287	17,400	- -	- -	- -
1823	13,784	576	441	574	455	15,830	69	12	72
1824	11,044	816	280	549	225	12,914	298	9	369
1825	10,833	586	338	885	350	12,991	749	- -	712
1826	8,616	831	338	616	139	10,560	3,655	- -	6,163
1827	10,222	901	408	629	249	12,409	1,847	- -	913
1828	13,275	1,140	534	1,012	256	16,217	2,282	- -	2,164
1829	10,001	1,545	382	1,133	195	13,256	1,785	- -	2,450
1830	6,832	463	382	750	220	8,647	1,700	- -	1,533

An Account of British Lead and Lead Ore exported from the United Kingdom from 1st January, 1st January, 1831; distinguishing the Countries to which it was sent. (Quarters and pounds om the Columns, but allowed for in the summing up.)

Countries to which Exported.	Pig and Rolled Lead and Shot.		Litharge.		Red Lead.		White Lead.		Lead Ore.		Brit an
	Tons.	cwt.	Tons. cwt.		Tons. cwt.		Tons. cwt.		Tons. cwt.		Ton
Russia	1,086	8	64	14	11	0					1,16
Sweden	55	7	10	11	5	8	32	14			10
Norway	55	1	0	8	0	8	19	12			7
Denmark	210	3	21	17	23	0	116	0			37
Prussia	146	2	12	0	6	7	28	14			19
Germany	270	10	116	6	122	6	79	7			58
Netherlands	314	2	69	0	81	4	6	6	120	0	59
France	44	10	60	0	7	11	4	0			11
Portugal, Azores, and Madeira	430	0	25	7	48	6	61	3			56
Spain and the Canaries	55	18	1	11	0	13	3	18			6
Gibraltar	17	5					4	17			5
Italy	82	16	84	11	46	0	0	7	45	10	25
Malta	18	0	1	16	3	15					2
Ionian Islands	46	6			0	16	4	15	14	15	5
Turkey and the Levant	50	12									5
Isles Guernsey, Jersey, Alderney, and Man	206	11	0	19	0	14	8	5			21
East Indies and China	1,849	19			78	18	132	14			2,06
New South Wales, Van Diemen's Land, and Swan River	143	3	0	12	0	6	5	2			14
Cape of Good Hope	133	8			3	5	11	10			14
Other parts of Africa	139	4			4	8	3	3	14	10	16
British North American Colonies	516	10	0	8	53	10	69	12			64
British West Indies	483	10			0	19	27	12			53
Foreign West Indies	87	18					2	0			8
United States of America	171	12					34	5			20
Brazil	747	18	19	12	21	3	5	2			79
Mexico	3	4									
Colombia	7	15									
Chili	21	10					0	7			2
Peru	6	19									
States of La Plata	39	19			0	3	0	12			4
Total	7,442	7	489	18	520	7	662	2	194	5	9,30

Price of Lead per Ton in Great Britain since 1800.

Years.	Price per Ton.	Average for Ten Years.	Years.	Price per Ton.	Average for Ten Years.	Years.	Price per Ton.	Ave Ten
	£ s. d.	£ s. d.		£ s. d.	£ s. d.		£ s. d.	£
1800	19 16 0		1810	28 16 0		1820	21 10 6	
1801	22 8 6		1811	24 0 6		1821	22 10 0	
1802	24 16 6		1812	23 3 6		1822	22 7 0	
1803	27 15 6		1813	25 14 0		1823	22 5 0	
1804	28 0 0		1814	26 11 0		1824	21 0 0	
1805	27 11 0		1815	20 16 0		1825	25 6 0	
1806	35 12 6		1816	16 5 0		1826	19 0 0	
1807	30 3 6		1817	18 5 0		1827	18 7 0	
1808	30 1 0		1818	27 5 6		1828	17 0 0	
1809	31 3 0	27 14 6	1819	22 11 0	23 6 6	1829	14 5 0	20

LEAD, BLACK, or PLUMBAGO. See BLACK LEAD.

LEAD, RED, or MINIUM. See MINIUM.

LEAGUE, a measure of length, containing more or fewer geometrical according to the customs of different countries. (See WEIGHTS and MEAS

LEAKAGE, in commerce, an allowance in the customs, granted to imp of wine, for the waste and damage the goods are supposed to receive by ke — (See *Warehousing Act*, § 38.; in art. WAREHOUSING SYSTEM.)

LEATHER (Ger. *Leder*; Du. *Leder, Leêr*; Da. *Læder*; Sw. *Läder* *Cuir*; It. *Cuojo*; Sp. *Cuero*; Rus. *Kosha*; Lat. *Corium*), the skins of v quadrupeds dressed in a particular manner for the use of manufacturers, business it is to make them up, according to their different employments.

The leather manufacture of Great Britain is of very great importance, and rank third or fourth on the list; being inferior only in point of value and extent to t

n, wool, and iron, if it be not superior to the latter. Sir F. M. Eden, in his work on
rance, estimated the value of the different articles manufactured of leather in 1803,
,000,000l; and there is reason to think that this statement was not very wide of the
. The total quantity of all sorts of leather tanned, tawed, dressed, and curried, in
t Britain, may at present be estimated at about 50,000,000 lbs.; which, at 1s. 8d. per lb.
4,166,000l. as the value of the leather only. Now, supposing, as is sometimes done, the
of the leather to amount to *one third* of the value of the finished articles produced
it, that would show the value of the manufacture to be about 12,500,000l.: but if,
ers contend, the value of the leather does not exceed *one fourth* part of the value of
ished articles, then the value of the manufacture must exceed 16,000,000l. We,
ver, are inclined to think that we shall be nearer the truth, if we take the smaller
and estimate the value of the manufacture at 12,500,000l. To get the number
rsons employed, we have first to deduct from this sum, 4,000,000l. for the material,
leaves 8,500,000l. as the aggregate amount of profits, wages, &c. And setting
20 per cent. as profit, rent of workshops, compensation for capital wasted, &c., we
a sum of 6,800,000l. remaining as wages: and supposing those employed as shoe-
s, saddlers, glovers, &c. to make at an average 30l. a year each, the entire number
h persons will amount to 226,000.

s, however, does not give the total number of persons employed in the leather
inasmuch as it excludes the tanners, curriers, &c. employed in dressing and pre-
g the leather. But if from the value of the prepared leather, 4,000,000l., we
t 1,000,000l. for the value of the hides, and 2,000,000l. for tanners' and curriers'
, including the expense of lime, bark, pits, &c., we shall have 1,000,000l. left as
. Now, as the wages of tanners, curriers, leather dressers, &c. may, we believe,
en at 35l. a year at an average, we shall have 28,300 as the number employed in
departments. And adding these to the persons employed in manufacturing the
, we have a grand total of 254,300 persons employed in the various departments
business.

se who may be inclined to suspect these estimates of exaggeration, would do
o reflect on the value of the shoes annually manufactured. It is generally sup-
that the expenditure upon shoes may be taken, at an average of the whole popu-
at 10s. each individual, young and old; which, supposing the population to
t to 16 millions, would give EIGHT millions for the value of shoes only; but
the value of the shoes at only 8s. 6d. each individual, it gives 6,800,000l. for the
t. Mr. Stevenson (art. *England, Edin. Ency.*) supposes that the value of the
ry, harness, gloves, &c. may be assumed to be at least equal to that of the shoes;
believe this is too high, and have taken it at 1,100,000l. below the value of the
In estimating the value of the entire manufacture at 12,500,000l., we incline to
hat we are as near the mark as it is easy to come in such investigations.

peaking of the leather manufacture, Dr. Campbell has the following striking ob-
ons: — "If we look abroad on the instruments of husbandry, on the implements
a most mechanic trades, on the structure of a multitude of engines and machines;
e contemplate at home the necessary parts of our clothing—breeches, shoes, boots,
— or the furniture of our houses, the books on our shelves, the harness of our
and even the substance of our carriages; what do we see but instances of human
ry exerted upon leather? What an aptitude has this single material in a variety
imstances for the relief of our necessities, and supplying conveniences in every state
ge of life? Without it, or even without it in the plenty we have it, to what diffi-
should we be exposed?"—(*Political State of Great Britain*, vol. ii. p. 176.)

her was long subject to a duty; the manufacture being, in consequence, neces-
onducted under the *surveillance* of the excise. In 1812, the duty, which had
sly amounted to 1½d. per lb., was doubled; and continued at 3d. per lb. till July
when it was again reduced to 1½d. per lb. The reduced duty produced a nett
e of about 360,000l. It is clear, however, that either the duty ought not to
een reduced in 1822, or that it ought to have been totally repealed. The con-
e of any part of the duty rendered it necessary to continue all the vexatious
ions required to insure the collection of the revenue, while the reduction of 1½d.
cost of preparing a pound of leather was so trifling as hardly to be sensible.
owever, unnecessary to enter into any discussion to show the extreme inexpe-
of laying any duty on an article so indispensable to the labouring class, and
rosecution of many branches of industry, as leather; and still less to show the
iency of subjecting so very important and valuable a manufacture to a vex-
ystem of revenue laws, for the sake of only 360,000l. a year. Luckily, how-
ese have become matters of history. The leather duties were totally abolished
; and as the manufacture is now relieved from every sort of trammel and re-
its rapid increase may be confidently expected. It is to be hoped that no future
y may arise to occasion the re-imposition of the leather duty.

Account of the Number of Pounds' Weight of Leather charged with Duties of Excise in Engl
in 1824—1829.

| 1824 | - | 53,429,539 | 1826 | - | 44,927,216 | 1828 | - | 50,233,6 |
| 1825 | - | 52,274,957 | 1827 | - | 47,616,316 | 1829 | - | 46,200,9 |

The quantity annually charged with duty in Scotland during the same period was, a'
average, about 6,000,000 lbs.

The quantity of wrought and unwrought leather exported in 1829, amounte
1,338,937 lbs., of the declared value of 268,380*l.* The value of the saddlery and har
exported during the same year was 83,303*l.* Nearly two thirds of the leather expos
is sent, principally in the shape of shoes, to the British West Indian and North Amerr
colonies.

LEDGER, the principal book of accounts kept by merchants and tradesm
wherein every person's account is placed by itself, after being extracted from
Journal. — (See BOOK-KEEPING.)

LEGHORN, a city and sea-port of Italy, in Tuscany, in lat. 43° 33′ N., B
10° 16¾′ E. Population about 50,000. Leghorn has a good roadstead, an or
harbour protected by a fine mole 600 paces in length, and a small inner harb
or basin. The outer harbour is large, but rather shallow. The lazaretto is s
to be the finest in Europe. The comparative security and freedom which
reigners have long enjoyed in Tuscany, still more than its advantageous situati
render Leghorn the greatest commercial city of Italy. Its exports are m
the same as those from the other Italian ports, consisting principally of a
and manufactured silk, oil, marble, rags, brimstone, anchovies, fruits, che
wine, &c. Leghorn platting for straw hats is the finest in the world; and c
siderable quantities are exported to Great Britain. The imports are exceedir
numerous, comprising almost all sorts of commodities, with the exception of th
which Italy produces. Sugar, coffee, tobacco, cotton, corn, spices, dried f
dye-woods, rice, iron, tin, &c. are among the most prominent articles. SI
with corn on board may unload within the limits of the lazaretto, without be
detained to perform quarantine; a circumstance which has contributed to m
Leghorn one of the principal *depôts* for the wheat of the Black Sea. H
wheat, particularly from Taganrog, is in high estimation here, and in the ot
Italian ports. It is particularly well fitted for making vermicelli, macaroni, &

Money. — Accounts are principally kept in *pezze da otto reali* (or dollars of 8 reali),
pezza being divided into 20 soldi or 240 denari. The *lira* is another money of acco
chiefly used in inferior transactions; it also is divided into 20 soldi and 240 den
1 pezza = 5¾ lire.

The monies of Leghorn have two values; the one called *moneta buona,* the other
neta lunga. The former is the effective money of the place. Moneta buona is conve
into moneta lunga, by adding ¹⁄₃, and the latter is reduced to the former by subtractin
The lira of account = 8½*d.* sterling very nearly; hence the pezza = 3*s.* 10¾*d.* very nea

The principal silver coins are, the Francescone, or Leopoldo, of 10 *paoli,* or 6⅔ lir
4*s.* 6*d.* sterling very nearly. The piece of 5 lire = 3*s.* 4·4*d.,* and the lira = 7·
sterling.

Weights and Measures. — The pound by which gold and silver and all sorts of v
chandise are weighed, is divided into 12 ounces, 96 drachms, 288 denari, and 6,912 gr
It is = 339·542 French grammes, or 5,240 English grains. Hence 100 lbs. of Leg
= 74·864 lbs. avoirdupois; but in mercantile calculations it is usual to reckon 100
of Leghorn = 77 lbs. avoirdupois; this, perhaps, has arisen from taking the tares
other allowances, as to which there is a good deal of uncertainty, into account. I
it is found that the English cwt. seldom renders more than 140 or 142 lbs. at Legh
though it is = 150 lbs.; in the instances of logwood, tobacco, and a few others, it doe
render more than 135 lbs. The quintal, or centinajo = 100 lbs. The cantaro is gene
150 lbs.; but a cantaro of sugar = 151 lbs.; that of oil = 88 lbs.; of brandy = 120 l
of stock fish, and some other articles =, 160 lbs. The rottolo = 3 lbs.

Corn is sold by the stajo = 6913 bushels. The moggio = 24 staja = 2 quarter
bushels Winchester measure.

The liquid measures are — 2 Mezzette = 1 Boccale.

                2 Boccali   = 1 Fiasco.

              20 Fiaschi   = 1 Barile = 12 English wine gallons.

The barile of oil is 16 fiaschi, of two boccali each, = 8½ wine gallons; it weighs a
66 lbs. avoirdupois. A large jar of oil contains 30 gallons; a small one 15; and a
with 30 bottles = 4 gallons.

The long measure is the braccio, which is divided into 20 soldi, 60 quattrini, or
denari; it contains 22·98 English inches. 155 bracci = 100 English yards. The c
of four bracci = 92 English inches.

ls in general are bought and sold for silver money ; between which, and the mo-
which bills of exchange are bought, there is a difference of 7 per cent. (agio)
silver, *i. e.* 107 dollars in silver are equal to 100 in gold.

goods bought or sold (unless it be in effective money, where there is no discount)
, generally speaking, a discount of 3 per cent. ; on all cotton manufactures, 4
t.

ges on sales, including commission, are generally from 6 to 8 per cent. ; on fish,
per cent.

IONS (Ger. *Limonen*; Du. *Limoenen*; Fr. *Limons, Citrons*; It. *Limoni*;
iones; Port. *Limões*; Rus. *Limonü*; Arab. *Lémōn*), the fruit of the lemon-
'itrus Medica, Var. ß. C.). It is a native of Assyria and Persia, whence it
ught into Europe; first to Greece, and afterwards to Italy. It is now cul-
in Spain, Portugal, and France, and is not uncommon in our green-
. Lemons are brought to England from Spain, Portugal, and the Azores,
in chests, each lemon being separately rolled in paper. The Spanish
are most esteemed.

ION JUICE, OR CITRIC ACID (Ger. *Zitronensaft*; Fr. *Jus de limon*;
o Sugo di limone; Sp. *Jugo de limon*), the liquor contained in the lemon.
be preserved in bottles for a considerable time by covering it with a thin
of oil; thus secured, great quantities of the juice are exported from
different parts of the world; from Turkey, also, where abundance of
are grown, it is a considerable article of export, particularly to Odessa. The
ry of the antiscorbutic influence of lemon juice is one of the most valuable
ever been made. The scurvy, formerly so fatal in ships making long voyages,
lmost wholly unknown ; a result that is entirely to be ascribed to the regular
ce of lemon juice served out to the men. The juice is also frequently admi-
t as a medicine, and is extensively used in the manufacture of punch.

ION PEEL (Ger. *Zitronenshalen, Limonschellen*; Fr. *Lames d'écorce de*
It. *Scorze de limone*; Sp. *Cortezas de citra*). The outward rind of lemons
, aromatic, and slightly bitter, — qualities depending on the essential oil it
. It is turned to many uses; and when well candied, constitutes a very
eserve. In Barbadoes, a *liqueur*, known under the name of *Eau de*
, is manufactured from lemon peel, which the inhabitants have the art of
ng in a manner peculiar to themselves. Both the liqueur and the con-
e in high repute, especially in France.

TER. (See POST OFFICE.)

TER OF CREDIT, a letter written by one merchant or correspondent to
, requesting him to credit the bearer with a certain sum of money. Advice
should always follow the granting of a letter of credit; a duplicate of it
nying such advice. It is prudent, also, in giving advice, to describe the
f the letter, with as many particulars as possible, lest it fall improperly
er hands.

TERS OF MARQUE AND REPRISAL, "are grantable by the law of
whenever the subjects of one state are oppressed and injured by those of
and justice is denied by that state to which the oppressor belongs."
Com. Law, vol. iii. p. 604.) Before granting letters of marque, government
ed by the 5 Hen. 5. c. 7., to require that satisfaction be made to the
grieved ; and in the event of such satisfaction not being made within a
le period, letters of marque and reprisal may be issued, authorising the
d party to attack and seize the property of the aggressor nation, without
f being condemned as a robber or pirate. Such letters are now only
the owners or captains of privateers during war, or when war has been de-
upon. They may be revoked at the pleasure of the sovereign ; and when
s terminate, they cease to have any effect.

NCES, in commercial navigation. All vessels, with the exceptions under-
d, must be licensed by the commissioners of customs.

ered by the 6 Geo. 4. c. 108. § 23. that the licence shall contain the proper description of the
names of the owners, with their places of abode, and the manner and the limits within which
ssel is to be employed ; and, if armed, the numbers and description of arms, and the quantity of
n, together with any other particulars the commissioners may direct. And by § 24. it is or-
before such licence shall be issued or delivered, or shall have effect, the owners of such vessel
ecurity by bond, of two sufficient housekeepers, in treble the value of such vessel (not ex-
any case the sum of 3,000*l*. for a square-rigged vessel), that the same shall not be employed in
ation, landing, removal, &c. of any prohibited or uncustomable goods, nor in the exportation
s prohibited to be exported, nor in relanding any goods contrary to law, &c. ; nor shall be

Z z

employed otherwise than mentioned in the licence, and within the limits therein mentioned. V licence has been obtained, it is to be taken to the collector or other proper officer, when the vessel i to depart, who is required to register it; and in default of this registration it is void. Masters o are obliged to produce their licence to any officer of the navy or marines on full pay, and to any of customs or excise.—(§ 27.) The counterfeiting, erasing, or falsifying licences, is visited with a of 500*l.*

A licence is not required, except for arming, for any vessel of the burthen of 200 tons or upwar for any square-rigged vessel, or any vessel or boat propelled by steam, which is not of greater leng in the proportion of 3 feet 6 inches to 1 foot of breadth; and no greater or other security s required on account of any licence to be issued under the above act, than in the sum of 1,000*l.*, or single value of the vessel or boat for which such licence is to be issued, if such value be less than and by the sole bond of such owner or owners of such vessel or boat. —(7 *Geo.* 4. c. 48. § 12.)

No licence is required for any vessel, boat, or lugger, belonging to the Royal Family, or in the se his Majesty, or any whale boat, or boat solely employed in the fisheries, or any boat belonging square-rigged vessel in the merchant service, or any life boat, or row boat used in towing vessels, ing to any licensed pilot, nor any boat used solely in rivers or inland navigation on account of such ship, boat, or lugger, not being licensed as aforesaid.—(6 *Geo.* 4. c. 108. § 22.)

Licences are not required for boats used in fishing in the North and West islands of Scotland; such boats be employed in smuggling, the owners are to be liable in a penalty equal to the v such boats, in addition to any other penalties to which they may be liable.—(10 *Geo.* 4. c. 43. § 10.)

Licences, in the excise, are required in order that individuals may engage in o businesses.

An Account of the Businesses that cannot be carried on in Great Britain without Excise Licences Sums charged for such Licences, of the Number of Licences granted for carrying on such Busi the Year ended 5th of January, 1830, and of the Total Amount of Revenue derived therefrom.

Businesses.	Sums charged for Licences.	Number of Licences granted.		Businesses.	Sums charged for Licences.	Number cences gr
		For a Year.	For Periods less than a Year.			For a Year.
	Per Ann. L. s. d.				*Per Ann.* L. s. d.	
AUCTIONS.				PAPER.		
Auctioneers	5 0 0	3,373	375	Makers of paper, pasteboard, or scaleboard	4 0 0	627
BEER.				Printers, painters or stainers of paper	4 0 0	81
Common brewers of strong beer, not exceeding 20 brls.	0 10 0	2,854		PRINTED GOODS.		
Exceeding 20 — 50	1 0 0	4,871	42	Printers, painters or stainers of calicoes, linens, cottons, or stuffs	20 0 0	197
— 50 — 100	1 10 0	6,997				
— 100 — 1,000	2 0 0	11,526	123	(Repealed in 1831.)		
— 1,000 — 2,000	3 0 0	297	1	SOAP.		
— 2,000 — 5,000	7 10 0	249		Makers of soap	4 0 0	287
— 5,000 — 7,500	11 5 0	63		SPIRITS.		
— 7,500 — 10,000	15 0 0	24		Distillers	10 0 0	264
— 10,000 — 20,000	30 0 0	32		Rectifiers	10 0 0	111
— 20,000 — 30,000	45 0 0	5		Dealers in spirits, not being re-tailers	10 0 0	3,522
— 30,000 — 40,000	60 0 0	2		Retailers of spirits, whose premises are rated under 10*l.* per annum	2 2 0	25,464
exceeding 40,000	75 0 0	12		At 10*l.*, and under 20*l.* per ann.	4 4 0	21,676
Beginners	0 10 0	29	15	20*l.* — 25*l.*	6 6 0	3,379
(And a surcharge according to the quantity brewed.)				25*l.* — 30*l.*	7 7 0	2,043
Brewers of table beer only, not exceeding 20 brls.	0 10 0	22	4	30*l.* — 40*l.*	8 8 0	3,641
Exceeding 20 — 50	1 0 0	8		40*l.* — 50*l.*	9 9 0	2,296
— 50 — 100	1 10 0	13		50*l.* per ann. or upwards	10 10 0	4,176
exceeding 100	2 0 0	111		Makers of stills in Scotland	0 10 0	21
Retail brewers of strong beer	5 5 0	1,279	353	Persons, not being distillers or rectifiers, using stills in Scotland	0 10 0	27
Dealers only in strong beer	3 3 0	1,024	235	STARCH.		
Retailers of beer, cider, or perry, whose premises are rated at a rent under 20*l.* per annum	1 1 0	52,688	3,345	Starch makers	5 0 0	29
Ditto at 20*l.* or upwards*	3 3 0	15,694	181	SWEETS AND MEAD.		
CANDLES.				Makers of sweets or made wines, mead or metheglin	2 2 0	18
Makers of wax or spermaceti candles	5 0 0	15	2	Retailers of ditto	1 1 0	741
Ditto other than ditto	2 0 0	2,706	136	TOBACCO.		
(Repealed in 1831.)				Manufacturers of tobacco and snuff, not exceeding 20,000 lbs.	5 0 0	263
COFFEE.				Exceeding. Not exceeding.		
Dealers in coffee, cocoa nuts, chocolate, tea, or pepper	0 11 0	88,643	10,330	20,000 lbs. 40,000 lbs.	10 0 0	72
GLASS.				40,000 60,000	15 0 0	30
Glass makers, for every glass-house	20 0 0	124	6	60,000 80,000	20 0 0	21
HIDES.				80,000 100,000	25 0 0	7
Tanners	5 0 0	1,533	34	exceeding 100,000	30 0 0	46
Tawers	2 0 0	678	30	Beginners	5 0 0	2
Dressers of hides or skins in oil	4 0 0	72	4	(And a surcharge according to the quantity made.)		
Curriers	4 0 0	2,011	156	Dealers in tobacco and snuff	0 5 0	127,005
Makers of vellum or parchment	2 0 0	77	5	VINEGAR.		
(Repealed from 5th July, 1830.)				Makers of vinegar or acetous acid	5 0 0	54
MALT.				WINE.		
Maltsters or makers of malt not exceeding 50 qrs.	0 7 6	2,339	8	Retailers of foreign wines, having a licence to retail beer, but not spirits	4 4 0	48
Exceeding 50 — 100	0 15 0	1,285		Ditto, having licences to retail beer and spirits	2 2 0	20,186
— 100 — 150	1 2 6	1,240		Dealers in foreign wine, not being retailers	10 0 0	1,834
— 150 — 200	1 10 0	1,255		PASSAGE VESSELS.		
— 200 — 250	1 17 6	869		On board which exciseable liquors and tobacco are sold, to be consumed by the passengers on the voyage	1 0 0	270
— 250 — 300	2 5 0	749				
— 300 — 350	2 12 6	533				
— 350 — 400	3 0 0	396				
— 400 — 450	3 7 6	351				
— 450 — 500	3 15 0	275				
— 500 — 550	4 2 6	218				
exceeding 550	4 10 0	1,423				
Beginners	0 7 6	55				
(And a surcharge according to the quantity brewed.)						
Not exceeding 5 qrs.	0 2 6	2,286				

Total amount of revenue, 711,871*l.* 4*s.*

* It was enacted by the 1 Will. 4. c. 51. s. 7., that from the 10th of October, 1830, brewers should pay their duty according to the malt used by them in brewing; and that every brewer shall be deemed to have brewed *one* beer for every *two bushels* of malt used by him.

RNCES, in the stamps, are required by those engaged in the professions and businesses mentioned
: —

	Per Annum.					Per Annum.		
	L.	s.	d.			L.	s.	d.
okers, in London and Westminster, or				and under 2 ounces, or any quantity of silver ex-				
a twopenny post limits	-	15	0	0	ceeding 5 pennyweights and under 50 ounces, in			
other place - - -	-	7	10	0	one piece - - - - -	-	2	6	0
ers (not being auctioneers) -	-	0	10	0	Ditto of greater weight, and every pawnbroker taking			
to exercise the faculty of -	-	30	0	0	in or delivering out pawns of such plate, and every			
ons trading in gold or silver plate, in which				refiner of gold or silver - -	-	5	15	0
uantity of gold exceeding 2 pennyweights,				Gold or silver lace is not deemed plate.			

GHT-HOUSE, a name for a tower situated on a promontory, or eminence
e sea coast, or on rocks in the sea, for the reception of a light for the guid-
of ships at night. There are also floating lights, or lights placed on board
ls moored in certain stations, and intended for the same purposes as those
iore. The 8 Eliz. c. 13. empowers the corporation of the Trinity-house to
beacons, &c. to prevent accidents to ships; and though the act does not
ssly mention light-houses, it has been held to extend to them. Light-houses
also been erected, though not recently, by private individuals, under the
rity of letters patent sanctioned by act of parliament. The duties for the
rt of light-houses are payable by stat. 4 & 5 Anne, c. 20., and 8 Anne, c. 17.;
ich Custom-house officers are prohibited from making out any cocket or
discharge, or taking any report outwards for any ship, until the duties for
urpose are paid, and the master shall have produced a light-bill testifying
ceipt thereof. It is lawful for every person authorised by the Trinity-house,
on board any foreign ship to receive the duties, and for non-payment to
in the tackle of the ship; and in case of delay of payment for three days
listress, the receivers of the said duties shall cause the same to be appraised
o persons, and proceed to sell the distress.

the light-houses, floating lights, &c., exclusive of harbour lights, from the
Islands, on the coast of Northumberland, round by Beachy Head and the
s End, to the extremity of North Wales, belong to the Trinity-house, with
ception of about a dozen lights, viz. Tynemouth, Spurn (shore), Winterton
)rford, Harwich, Forelands, Dungeness, Longships, Smalls, Skerries, &c.
lights are partly public and partly private property. The duties on their
nt are, for the most part, payable to the Trinity collectors.

rules and regulations as to lights may be altered by the Trinity-house, with
it of the privy council. We subjoin a copy of the existing instructions issued
Corporation to their collectors, and of the fees demanded by them from the Bri-
d foreign vessels passing the different lights under their care, specifying such

TRINITY-HOUSE, LONDON.

UCTIONS to   for the collection of the duties payable to the Corporation of
house, at the port of

ou are to demand and receive from the master or agent of every ship or vessel which hath passed,
ut to pass, in any direction, the several lights belonging to this Corporation, the respective tolls
ies as particularly set forth in the table hereunto annexed; observing nevertheless, the regulation
d in the 3d article, and also that British vessels, and such foreign vessels as are or shall be privi-
respect to charges as British vessels, are exempt from payment of duties to this Corporation,
avigated *wholly in ballast*.

u are to take care to rate all British vessels, of every class or description, to the full amount of
gister tonnage, except for those particular lights, for the duties to which colliers and coasters are
ble per vessel only. Foreign vessels are to be charged to the full amount of their tonnage, as
ued by the officer of his Majesty's customs.

u are to observe that neither British nor foreign vessels are to be charged with the duties on
of a passage which may have taken place, or may be thereafter contemplated, being from one
port to another foreign port, unless in the prosecution of such voyages they shall actually arrive
at a port or roadstead in Great Britain.

he duties are to be collected from all British ships at the ports in Great Britain where they load
er their cargoes. No collection is therefore to be made from any British ship which may happen
at your port on her passage to another port in Great Britain; but you are to observe that this
ot to be applied in respect of vessels touching at your port in their passages to ports not in Great

'ou are to charge all vessels belonging to the following states with the same duties in every respect
h vessels : — The vessels of those states are in fact to be considered, so far as respects charges
account of this Corporation, as British ships, until further orders; viz. Portugal, Brazil, United
f America, the kingdom of the Netherlands, Hanover, Sweden, Norway, Russia, Hamburgh,
Lubeck, Denmark, and Prussia ; to which are to be added vessels belonging to the Duchies of
rgh and Mecklenburgh, as well as those belonging to the kingdom of France, which have been
itted to the privilege of reciprocity in respect of charges ; but as that privilege is granted to
those states under some limitations, it is necessary you should particularly observe the directions
d in the recitals of the orders in council and treaty hereunder given *, whereby you will perceive
els of those states are still liable, in certain cases, to the foreign rate of duty.

urgh Vessels. — Extract of his Majesty's order in | and with the advice of his privy council, is pleased to order,
ated 19th October, 1824 : — "His Majesty, by virtue | and it is, hereby ordered, that from and after the date of this
ers vested in him by the acts above recited, and by | order, Oldenburgh vessels entering the ports of the United

LIGHT-HOUSE.

6th. All vessels belonging to the United Kingdom, and trading between Great Britain and Irel..[cut] are to be deemed and charged as coasting vessels, in respect of all light and other duties payable to... Corporation.

7th. You are to give your receipt on a light-bill, to the master of evrey ship or vessel who shall pay any of the herein-after mentioned tolls or duties, expressing (plainly and fully) his name, the name of vessel, and the place to which she belongs, her voyage and tonnage, the money paid, and time of ... ment. You are to insert all those several particulars in the counterpart of each light-bill, which coun.. part is to be signed by the master or his agent, and the books returned, containing the same, to ... House, at the end of every .... You are to take care that none of the blank light-bills w.. shall be lodged with you fall into improper hands, or be wasted. You are in all cases to require the ... duction of the light bill for the duties last paid; and you are not to admit or allow that the master o.. vessel hath paid elsewhere without seeing the light-bill, duly signed by the collector for the port at w... it may be alleged the duties have been paid; and whenever you shall be satisfied that the duties for ... ship or vessel have been paid at any other port or place, you are to note the same in your book, and ... in your accounts in the column prepared for that purpose, expressing the several particulars as in y... light-bills, with the time and place of payment. Books, containing each a number of blank light-b... will be furnished you from this House, on your application, whenever required. You are to kee.. exact account of all monies which you shall from time to time collect; and, before you fill up your l... bills, to enter the same distinctly in a book to be provided by yourself for that purpose, wherein al.. particulars which are herein-before directed to be expressed in your light bills, are to be entered; — ... which you are, *within fourteen days* after the 1st of January, the 1st of April, the 1st of July, and th... of October (to which periods you are to make up your accounts), to send a copy on the printed form ... nished from this House, together with the balance of your collection, after a deduction of .... in the pound for your care, trouble, and ordinary expenses therein, to the secretary of the Corporatio... this House.

By command of the Corporation,
(Signed) **J. HERBERT**, Secreta..

A Table of Lights, &c., the Duties for which are payable to the Corporation of Trinity-house, Lo... with the Rate of Duty for each.

Lights.	Duties.			
	Foreign Vessels, not privileged as Vessels in respect of Charges, per Ton.	British Oversea Traders, and Foreign privileged Vessels, per Ton.	Coasters, per Ton.	Colliers Coastwise per Ton.
East Coast. (*No.* 1.)				
Ferns - - 3 Light-houses -	3 Halfpence	3 Farthings	3 Farthings	3 Farthings
Flambro' - 1 Light-house -	1 Halfpenny	1 Farthing	1 Farthing	1 Farthing
Well - - 1 Floating light	1 Halfpenny	1 Farthing	1 Farthing	1 Farthing
Spurn - - 1 Floating light	1 Halfpenny	1 Farthing	1 Farthing	1 Farthing
Foulness - 1 Light-house -	1 Farthing	1 Farthing	1 Farthing	1 Farthing
Haisbro' { 2 Light-houses } { 1 Floating light }	1 Halfpenny	1 Farthing	1 Farthing	1 Farthing
Gatt Buoys - - -	½ Farthing	½ Farthing	½ Farthing	½ Farthing
Lowestoft { 2 Light-houses } { 1 Floating light }	1 Halfpenny	1 Farthing	1 Farthing	1 Farthing
Sunk - - 1 Floating light	1 Penny	1 Halfpenny	1 Halfpenny	1 Farthing
Channel Lights. (*No.* 2.)				
Goodwin - 1 Floating light	1 Penny	1 Halfpenny	1 Shilling per vessel	½ Farthing per to..
Owers - - 1 Floating light	1 Penny	1 Halfpenny	1 Shilling per vessel	1 Shilling per vess..
Needles - { 1 Light-house } { 2 Light-houses } { at Hurst - }	1 Penny	1 Halfpenny	1 Shilling per vessel	1 Shilling per vess..
Portland - 2 Light-houses -	1 Penny	1 Halfpenny	1 Shilling per vessel	1 Shilling per vess..
Caskets - 3 Light-houses -	1 Penny	1 Halfpenny	6 Pence per vessel	6 Pence per vesse..
Edystone 1 Light-house -	1 Penny	1 Halfpenny	2 Shillings per vessel	2 Shillings per ves..
Lizard - 2 Light-houses -	1 Penny	1 Halfpenny	2 Shillings per vessel	2 Shillings per ves..
Scilly - 1 Light-house -	1 Halfpenny	1 Farthing	1 Shilling per vessel	1 Shilling per vess..
Bristol and St. George's Channels. (*No.* 3.)				
Flatholm - 1 Light-house -	3 Halfpence	3 Farthings	1 Farthing per ton	* No. 3.
Caldy - - 1 Light-house -	2 Pence	1 Penny	- - - -	* No. 3.
Lundy - - 1 Light-house -	1 Halfpenny	1 Farthing	1 Farthing per ton	1 Farthing per to..
Milford - 2 Light-houses -	1 Penny	1 Halfpenny	1 Shilling per vessel	1 Shilling per vess..
Bardsey - 1 Light-house -	1 Farthing	1 Farthing	1 Farthing per ton	1 Farthing per to..
South Stack 1 Light-house	1 Halfpenny	1 Farthing	1 Farthing per ton	1 Farthing per to..

REFERENCES.

No. 1. EAST COAST. — These duties (with the exception of those for the Spurn floating light) are payable by all vessels once only for the whole voyage out and home; but a single passage subjects them to the payment of the full duties.

Spurn Floating Light. — The duties for this light are to be collected only from such foreign and British oversea traders as actually enter the river Humber, and are payable in those cases for each time of passing. Coasters and colliers are subject

thereto for each time of passing coastwise, if laden; b.. otherwise.

No. 2. CHANNEL LIGHTS. — The duties for the lights e.. rated in this part of the above table are payable for eac.. of passing.

No. 3. BRISTOL AND ST. GEORGE'S CHANNELS. — The du.. for the lights in this district are payable for each time of p.. with the exception of the Bardsey light, as hereunder ..[cut] but the following directions must be attended to, viz :—

Flatholm Light. — Coasters between the Land's End ..

Kingdom of Great Britain and Ireland, in ballast or laden, direct from any of the ports of Oldenburgh, or departing from the ports of the said United Kingdom, together with the cargoes on board the same, such cargoes consisting of articles which may be legally imported or exported, shall not be subject to any other or higher duties or charges whatever than are or shall be levied on British vessels entering or departing from such ports."

Mecklenburgh Vessels. — The purport of the order in council granting the privilege of reciprocity to Mecklenburgh vessels, is precisely the same as the foregoing order in respect of Oldenburgh vessels, and is dated the 14th June, 1825.

French Vessels. — Extract from a convention of commerce and navigation between his Majesty and the King of France, dated 26th January, 1826 : — "That from and after the 5th

day of April, 1826, French vessels coming from or de.. for the ports of France, or, if in ballast, coming from ... parting for any place, shall not be subject, in the ports ... United Kingdom, either on entering into or departin.. the same, to any higher duties of tonnage, harbour, light.. pilotage, quarantine, or other similar or corresponding ... of whatever nature or under whatever denomination ... those to which British vessels, in respect of the same v.. are or may be subject on entering into or departing fro.. ports."

* Observe that colliers are to be charged by the nu.. tons expressed in their registers, and not by the chaldro.. colliers bound to or from foreign parts are to pay the s.. other British ships bound foreign, to all the lights in th.. table.

ad (market boats and fishing vessels excepted) are
er vessel.
ght. — The duties for this light are payable by such
as may put into any port, place, or roadstead, be-
Worm's Head and St. Gowen's Head.
ght. — Duties payable only by vessels on their voyage
ports in the Bristol Channel, or to or from any ports
ward of a line drawn from Hartland Point to St.
ead.
Light. — Duties for foreign vessels and British over-
are payable once only for the whole voyage out and
coasters, and colliers coastwise, each time of passing,
at not otherwise.

South Stack Light. — British or Irish ships and vessels to or from Liverpool, Chester, and ports to the northward thereof, to any other ports to the northward of the Calf of Man (at the south part of the Isle of Man), or to the eastward of Holyhead, with all other vessels bound to or from Liverpool and ports adjacent, to any other ports whatsoever, sailing in or out of the North Channel, viz. " by Fairhead on the coast of Ireland, and the Mull of Cantire, on the coast of Scotland," are not subject to pay the duties to the said light. This exemption, however, is confined and restricted to ships and vessels of the United Kingdom, navigating within the limits above described.

N. B. By the term "each time of passing" is to be understood once for the outward, and once for the inward passage.

believe no good objection can be made to the performance of their peculiar and
nt duties by the Trinity-house; but it is admitted on all hands, that the expense
lights under their care is a very heavy burden on shipping, and that its reduction
be of the greatest importance. We have given, in another place (see *antè*, p. 470.),
nent of the various public charges paid on account of an American ship of 482
rthen, from the time of her taking a pilot on board in the Channel, including her
s in the London docks, to the time of her dismissing the pilot on the outward

The entire sum is 168*l*. 9*s*. 6*d*. ; and of this, the charge on account of lights
s to no less than 58*l*. 8*s*. 6*d*. ! Such a charge seems to be out of all proportion
ther items (with the exception of pilotage), and to be most oppressive. As this
onged to the United States, with which we have entered into a reciprocity treaty,
the same duty as is paid by British ships of the same burthen. Had she be-
to a country whose vessels are not so privileged, the charge on account of lights
ave been about double.

pears from the statements in the Parliamentary Reports on the Coal Trade, that
t-house dues payable by a collier of 204 tons, from Newcastle to London, amount
6d. per voyage; which, supposing she make twelve voyages a year, is equiva-
n annual tax of 37*l*. 10*s*. — (*Lords' Report*, 1829, p. 64.)

generally believed that a very great reduction might be made from these heavy
without either reducing the number or brilliancy of the lights; and we do
eive that any one can doubt that such is really the case, who looks into the fol-
ccount : —

the Gross Receipt of all Tolls upon Vessels passing the Light-houses at Winterton and Orford,
th April, 1826, to 1st January, 1829; of the Light-houses at Dungeness, from 28th June, 1828,
nuary, 1829; of the Light-houses at the North and South Forelands, and at Flamborough Cliff, for
rs 1827 and 1828; stating the Amount of Expense for Maintenance of the said Lights, under
Heads, and of the Nett Proceeds thereof, and how disposed. — (*Parl. Paper*, No. 164.
30.)

Dates.	Gross Receipts.	Expense of Collecting.	Expense of Maintenance.	Nett Proceeds.	How disposed.
	£ s. d.	£ s. d.	£ s. d.	£ s. d.	
Since 13th April, 1826, up to 1st Jan. 1827 -	13,272 13 4	1,542 2 10	1,637 6 9	10,094 3 9	
From 1st Jan. 1827, to 1st Jan. 1828 -	16,389 12 1	1,883 7 1	844 17 5	13,661 7 7	One half paid to the crown, the other half to the lessee.
From 1st Jan. 1828, to 1st June, 1828 -	6,322 14 11	1,705 14 6	363 4 1	11,913 17 8	
From 1st June, 1828, to 1st Jan. 1829 -	8,225 12 4		565 11 0		
From 28th June, 1828, to 1st Jan. 1829 -	5,286 0 0	667 12 7	443 4 7	4,175 2 10	
- - - 1827	10,688 0 6	1,222 15 4	278 17 4½	8,186 7 9½	Paid to Greenwich Hospital.
- - - 1828	11,199 10 7	1,301 15 3½	1,369 16 9½	8,527 18 6½	
- - - 1827	591 18 5	65 17 11	1, 90 17 3	435 3 3	The whole paid to the lessee.
- - - 1828	654 4 11	73 11 8	81 11 9	499 1 6	
				57,493 2 1	

we have a nett revenue, after the expense of collection and maintenance is de-
arising from *six* light-houses, of not less than 28,500*l*. a year. Had this large
a appropriated to the keeping up of light-houses on less frequented parts of the
collection might not, perhaps, have been liable to much objection ; but not
nce of it is so expended. With the exception of the 8,500*l*. a year which goes
wich Hospital, the residue, of about 20,000*l*. a year, is divided in nearly equal
between the crown and *private* individuals ! We believe, however that our
will agree with us in thinking, that of all the pernicious modes of raising a
hat have ever been imagined, the imposition of duties on light-houses is about
worst. It is of quite as much importance for the promotion of trade and na-
that the charges on account of these establishments should be kept as low as
as that the establishments should be multiplied. We should be sorry to see
ue of so noble an institution as Greenwich Hospital impaired ; but surely it
erived from other and more appropriate sources than duties on lights. We are
ainted with the nature of the leases under which the lessees of the Winterton

and Orford, Dungeness, and other lights, receive incomes larger than those pai
secretary of state; but if they do not expire within some reasonable term, or canr
otherwise equitably got rid of, they ought to be purchased up at their fair value, ar
charges on account of the lights reduced to the lowest sum necessary to keep then
or if any surplus be collected, it should go to the support of other lights.

The expense of collecting the light duties, as stated in the above account,
quite enormous — in most cases exceeding, and in one case amounting to
than double, the expense of keeping up the lights! We understand, too, that the T
corporation allowances are quite as high; being, in some instances, no less than *tu
five* per cent. upon the sums levied! The magnitude of these allowances has
justly objected to; and there can be no doubt that they encourage the vexatious
tions to which all ships, but particularly those belonging to foreigners, are frequ
exposed. It seems difficult to discover any reason why the maintenance of light-h
and the expense of collecting the dues on their account, should be greater here th
Scotland; and yet it is believed to be from *three* to *five* times as much. Unless
discrepancies be satisfactorily explained, the existence of some very serious abuse i
department will be more than suspected. But, as was already observed, the entire s
is one that ought to be thoroughly sifted and examined. Lights and pilotage are d
ments in which lavish expenditure is less excusable, and the severest economy mo
dispensable, than almost any others.

For some account of the Trinity Corporation, see that article.
The charges for the undermentioned lights are as follow: —

	Foreign Ships.	British Ships.		Foreign Ships.	British Ships
Forelands	2d. per ton	1d. per ton	Smalls (St. George's Channel	2d. per ton	1d.
Harwich	2d. —	1d. —	Ditto (ditto) (coasting)	2d. —	0½d
Hunston	1d. —	0½d. —	Spurn(shore)mouth of Humber	1d. —	0½d
Longships (off Land's End)	1d. —	0½d. —	Tynemouth	3s. per ves.	1s.
Mumbles (near Swansea)	0½d. —	0½d. —	Ditto (additional)	0½d. pr.ton	0½d.
Skerries(St. George's Channel)	2d. —	1d. —			

Scotch or Northern Lights, are under the management of a set of parliamentary commissio
The charges are,

	Foreign Ships.	British Ships.		Foreign Ships.	Brsetish Ships
Vessels sailing on the coast of Scotland within a line drawn from DunottarCastle on the north to St Abb's Head on the south	5d. per ton	2½d. per ton	Without the above limits	4d. per ton	2d.
			Isle of Man light	0½d. —	0½d.

Irish Lights. — It appears from the Parliamentary Paper, No. 118. Sess. 1831, that the light du
lected in Ireland during last year (1830) amounted to 10,678*l.* The rates of charge are as follow: —
Foreign vessels, ½*d.* per ton for each light passed; except harbour lights, which are only charge
vessels entering the ports within which they are situated.
British and Irish, ¼*d.* per ton (⅛*d.* if in ballast) for each light, except as above.
With a duty of 2s. on every entry, cocket, or warrant, when from foreign ports, but not otherw

LIMA, the capital of Peru, on the west coast of South America, in lat.
S., lon. 77° 7¼ W. Population variously estimated; but may probably a
to from 50,000 to 60,000.

Callao, the port of Lima, is about 6 miles distant from the latter. The harbo
to the north of a projecting point of land, in the angle formed by the small uninh
island of San Lorenzo. Previously to the emancipation of Peru, and the other *ci*-
Spanish provinces in the New World, Lima was the grand *entrepôt* for the trade
the west coast of South America; but a considerable portion of the foreign trade o
is now carried on through Buenos Ayres, and the former is also in the habit of i
ing European goods at second hand from Valparaiso and other ports in Chili.
exports from Lima consist principally of copper and tin, silver, cordovan leathe
soap, vicunna wool, quinquina, &c. The imports consist principally of woolle
cotton stuffs, and hardware, from England; silks, brandy, and wine, from Spa
France; stock-fish from the United States, indigo from Mexico, Paraguay herl
Paraguay, spices, quicksilver, &c. Timber for the construction of ships and ho
brought from Guayaquil. The official value of the different articles of British p
and manufacture exported to Peru in 1829, amounted to 376,552*l.*, besides 1
of foreign and colonial merchandise. The official value of the imports into Gre
tain from Peru during the same year was 69,839*l.*

Moneys, Weights, and *Measures,* same as those of Spain; for which, see CADIZ.

LIME (Ger. *Kalk*; Fr. *Chaux*; It. *Calcina, Calce*; Sp. *Cal*; Rus. *Iswest*
of those earthy substances which exist in every part of the known world.
found purest in limestone, marble, and chalk. None of these substances i
but becomes so when burned in a white heat. Lime is employed princip
mortar in building, and as a manure to fertilise lands. Vast quantities of
used for these purposes. Lime and limestones may be carried and landed
wise without any customs document whatever.

ME (Fr. *Citronier;* Ger. *Citrone;* Hind. *Neemboo*), a species of lemon (*Citrus
ica,* var. δ C.), which grows in abundance in most of the West Indian islands,
is also to be met with in some parts of France, in Spain, Portugal, and
ughout India, &c. The lime is smaller than the lemon, its rind is usually
er, and its colour, when the fruit arrives at a perfect state of maturity, is a
right yellow. It is uncommonly juicy, and its flavour is esteemed superior
at of the lemon; it is, besides, more acid than the latter, and to a certain
e acrid.

NEN (Ger. *Linnen, Leinwand;* Du. *Lynwaat;* Fr. *Toile;* It. *Tela, Panno
Sp. Lienza, Tela de lino;* Rus. *Polotno*), a species of cloth made of thread
x or hemp.

e linen manufacture has been prosecuted in England for a very long period; but
h its progress has been considerable, particularly of late years, it has not been so
as might have been anticipated. This is partly, perhaps, to be ascribed to the
s that have been made to bolster up and encourage the manufacture in Ireland and
nd, and partly to the rapid growth of the cotton manufacture — fabrics of cotton
g to a considerable extent supplanted those of linen.

1698, both houses of parliament addressed his Majesty (William III.), represent-
at the progress of the woollen manufacture of Ireland was such as to prejudice
f this country; and that it would be for the public advantage, were the former dis-
ged, and the linen manufacture established in its stead. His Majesty replied, "I
lo all that in me lies to *discourage the woollen manufacture in Ireland,* and encourage
en manufacture, and to promote the trade of England!" We may remark, by
ay, that nothing can be more strikingly characteristic of the illiberal and erroneous
s that were then entertained with respect to the plainest principles of public
my, than this address and the answer to it. But whatever the people of Ireland
think of their sovereign deliberately avowing his determination to exert himself to
a manufacture in which they had begun to make some progress, government had
ficulty in prevailing upon the legislature of that country to second their views, by
iting the exportation of all woollen goods from Ireland, except to England, where
itory duties were already laid on their importation! It is but justice, however,
parliament and government of England, to state that they have never discovered
ckwardness to promote the linen trade of Ireland; which, from the reign of Wil-
II. downwards, has been the object of regulation and encouragement. It may,
l, be doubted whether the regulations have been always the most judicious that
have been devised, and whether Ireland has really gained any thing by the forced
ion of the manufacture. Mr. Young and Mr. Wakefield, two of the highest
ities as to all matters connected with Ireland, contend that the spread of the linen
acture has not really been advantageous. And it seems to be sufficiently esta-
l, that though the manufacture might not have been so widely diffused, it would
een in a sounder and healthier state had it been less interfered with.

Rates of Bounty on Irish Linens exported to Foreign Parts.

the year 1780 to the 5th July 1805:

		d.
lain linen of the breadth of 25 inches or more, and		
———— under the value of $4\frac{8}{13}d$. per yard - - -	-	$0\frac{6}{13}$ per yard.
———— of the value of $4\frac{8}{13}d$. and under 6d. per yard -	-	$0\frac{12}{13}$ —
———— of the value of 6d. and not exceeding 1s. 6d. per yard - - - - - -	}	$1\frac{5}{13}$ —
hecked or striped linen, not exceeding 1s. 6d. and not under $6\frac{8}{13}d$. per yard - - - - -	}	$0\frac{8}{13}$ —
iaper, sheeting, and other linen upwards of one yard in breadth, and not exceeding 1s. 6d. the square yard in value - -	}	$1\frac{5}{13}$ —
il cloth - - - - - -	-	2 per ell.

the 5th July 1805 to the 5th January 1825:

		d.
lain linen of the breadth of 25 inches or more, and		
———— under the value of 5d. per yard -	-	$0\frac{1}{2}$ per yard.
———— of the value of 5d. and under 6d. per yard -	-	1 —
———— of the value of 6d. and not exceeding 1s. 6d. per yard - - - - - -	}	$1\frac{1}{2}$ —
hecked or striped linen, not exceeding 1s. 6d. and not under $6\frac{8}{13}d$. per yard - - - -	}	$0\frac{1}{2}$ —
iaper, sheeting, and other linen upwards of one yard in breadth, and not exceeding 1s. 6d. the square yard in value - -	}	$1\frac{1}{2}$ —
il cloth - - - - -	-	2 per ell.

From 5th January 1825 to 5th January 1826, $\frac{9}{10}$ths of the rates immediately preced[ing]
From 5th January 1826 to 5th January 1827, $\frac{8}{10}$ths   ditto   ditto.
From 5th January 1827 to 5th January 1828, $\frac{7}{10}$ths   ditto   ditto.
From 5th January 1828 to 5th January 1829, $\frac{6}{10}$ths   ditto   ditto.
From 5th January 1829 to 5th January 1830, $\frac{5}{10}$ths   ditto   ditto.
     The bounty has now ceased entirely.

An Account of the Quantity and Value of the Linens exported from Ireland in each Year, from 17[ ] 1829, both inclusive.

Years.	To Great Britain.	To Foreign Parts.	Total.	Amount of Bounty pa[id] Ireland, on Linen expo[rted] to Foreign Parts		
	Yards.	Yards.	Yards.	£	s.	d.
1800 - -	31,978,039	2,585,829	34,563,868			
1801 - -	34,622,898	3,299,021	37,921,919			
1802 - -	33,246,943	2,368,911	35,615,854			
1803 - -	35,097,936	2,486,662	37,584,598	12,059	14	10
1804 - -	39,837,101	3,303,528	43,140,629	10,545	2	2
1805 - -	40,707,267	2,976,286	43,683,553	12,224	19	4
1806 - -	35,245,280	3,880,961	39,126,241	15,668	4	6
1807 - -	38,461,276	2,603,427	41,064,703	10,323	14	9
1808 - -	41,958,719	2,033,367	43,992,086	6,740	16	0
1809 - -	33,018,884	4,179,988	37,198,872	20,094	7	6
1810 - -	32,584,545	4,313,725	36,898,270	16,448	19	5
1811 - -	29,889,683	1,545,064	31,434,747	7,556	16	4
1812 - -	33,320,767	2,524,686	35,845,453	11,548	3	4
1813 - -	35,096,356	3,927,231	39,023,587	15,252	11	2
1814 - -	39,539,443	3,463,783	43,003,226	17,221	14	11
1815 - -	37,986,359	5,496,206	43,482,565	17,430	17	5
1816 - -	42,330,118	3,399,511	45,729,629	19,082	6	4
1817 - -	50,288,842	5,941,733	56,230,575	21,524	15	4
1818 - -	44,746,354	6,178,954	50,925,308	28,848	6	5
1819 - -	34,957,396	2,683,855	37,641,251	16,177	8	5
1820 - -	40,318,270	3,294,948	43,613,218	11,928	9	11
1821 - -	45,519,509	4,011,630	49,531,139	18,218	19	5
1822 - -	43,226,710	3,374,993	46,601,703	17,112	9	5
1823 - -	48,066,591	3,169,006	51,235,597	17,765	5	1
1824 - -	46,466,950	3,026,427	49,493,377	17,114	13	1
1825 - -	52,559,678	2,553,587	55,113,265	12,015	9	4
1826 - -	{ The exportations to Great Bri-	2,726,297	- -	10,249	17	5
1827 - -	tain cannot be ascertained for	4,284,566	- -	12,114	0	4
1828 - -	these years, the cross-channel trade having been assimilated	3,214,911	- -	9,194	7	1
1829 - -	by law to a coasting traffic.	2,386,223	- -	6,886	1	1

Of these exports more than twelve thirteenths have been to Great Britain. The total average [ ] during the three years ending with 1825, was 51,947,413 yards, of which 49,031,073 came to this cou[ntry,] the exports to *all* other parts being only 2,916,340. Since 1825, the trade between Ireland and Great Bri[tain] has been placed on the footing of a coasting trade, so that linens are exported and imported without [ ] specific entry at the Custom-house.

In 1727, a Board of Trustees was established in Scotland for the superintendence and improveme[nt of] the linen manufacture. It is not easy to suppose that the institution of this Board could of itself have [been] of any material service; but considerable bounties and premiums being at the same time given on the [pro-] duction and exportation of linen, the manufacture rapidly increased. Still, however, it has not incr[eased] so fast as cotton and some others, which have not received any adventitious support; so that it is [ ] doubtful whether the influence of the bounty has been so great as it would, at first sight, appear to [have] been. The regulations as to the manufacture, after having been long objected to by those concerned, [were] abolished in 1822; and the bounties are now in the course of being withdrawn. We subjoin

An Account of the Quantity and Value of the Linen Cloth manufactured and stamped for Sale in [Scot-] land during the Ten Years ending with 1822, being the latest period to which it can be made up.

Years.	Yards.	Value.			Average Price per Yard.	Years.	Yards.	Value.		
		£	s.	d.	d.			£	s.	d.
1813	19,799,146½	977,382	1	7½	11$\frac{10}{19}$	1818	31,283,100½	1,253,528		0½
1814	26,126,620¼	1,253,574	16	10½	11$\frac{6}{12}$	1819	29,334,428¼	1,157,923	4	11
1815	32,056,015¼	1,403,766	15	2	10$\frac{6}{12}$	1820	26,259,011¼	1,038,708	18	5¼
1816	26,112,045½	1,026,674	1	11¾	9½	1821	30,473,461¼	1,232,038	15	4¼
1817	28,784,967¼	1,092,689	2	8¼	9$\frac{1}{12}$	1822	36,268,530½	1,396,295	19	11¾

The exports of linen from the United Kingdom seem to be about equal to the imports from Irelan[d into] Great Britain. During the year 1825, the last in which an account was kept of the linen trade be[tween] Ireland and Great Britain, there were exported from the United Kingdom, of British linen, 35,9[ ] yards, the real or declared value of which was 1,309,616*l*.; and of Irish linen, 16,087,146 yards, th[e real] or declared value of which was 918,585*l*.; amounting together to 52,080,184 yards, worth 2,228,001*l*.

The bounties paid during the same year on the British linen exported amounted to 209,516*l.* 6s. [ ] being between a *sixth* and a *seventh* part of the entire value of the exports! The bounty on the Iris[h linen] exported the same year was 87,549*l.* 16s. 3¾*d.*, being about a *tenth* part of the value of the exports!

This, we believe, is one of the most glaring instances of the abuse of the system of bounties. W[e have ac-] tually persisted, for more than a century, in endeavouring to force a trade in linens by enabli[ng our] merchants to sell them abroad for less than they cost. Were the various sums expended on this manuf[acture] added together, we believe it would be found that the interest accruing upon them would fall little [ ] all, short of the entire value of the linens we now export.

During 1825, the imports of Irish linen into Great Britain amounted to 52,560,000 yards, the de[clared] value of which was 2,893,018*l.* Of these, 38,784,908 yards were retained for home consumption.

mand for foreign linens in Great Britain is but trifling. During 1825, the real or declared value
entered for home consumption only amounted to 2,301*l.* 12*s.* 4*d.*—(The previous details are derived
Parl. Paper, No. 413. Sess. 1826.)

, the exports of linen from the United Kingdom amounted to 57,698,372 yards, of the declared
1,953,607*l.*, exclusive of 52,037*l.*, the value of the thread and small wares exported. The exports
land direct to foreign countries were about one seventeenth part of the whole. The United
he West Indies, and South America, have always been the best markets for British linens. Of
quantity exported in 1829, 18,367,599 yards were destined for the United States, 11,854,207 yards
ritish West Indies, 5,700,962 yards for Brazil, 6,822,637 yards for Spain, &c.
are no means by which to form any accurate estimate of the entire value of the linen manufacture
Britain and Ireland. Dr. Colquhoun estimated it at 15,000,000*l.*, but he assigns no grounds for
ate, which we look upon as very much exaggerated. Perhaps 10,000,000*l.* is as much as it can
valued at. And setting aside a third part of this sum as the value of the raw material, and 20
as profits and return for wear and tear of capital, coal, &c., we shall have 4,667,000*l.*, to be di-
wages among those employed in the manufacture. And supposing each individual to earn, at an
15*l.* a year, the total number employed would be 311,000. It may be thought, perhaps, that 15*l.*
' an estimate for wages; and such, no doubt, would be the case, were not Ireland taken into the
But as very many persons are there either wholly or partly employed in the manufacture at very
s, we believe it will be found that 15*l.* is not far from the mean rate.
flax was spun by the distaff or rock and spindle, more recently by the hand-wheel, and now it is
y spun by machinery or flax mills, driven by water or steam. This last species of spinning has
perseded the hand-wheel; at least, it is now rarely used except in the preparation of yarn for the
d finer fabrics.
rson, native or foreigner, may, without paying any thing, set up in any place, privileged or not,
or not, any branch of the linen manufacture; and foreigners practising the same, shall, on taking
of allegiance, &c., be entitled to all the privileges of natural born subjects. — (15 *Cha.* 2. c. 15.)
s affixing stamps to foreign linens in imitation of the stamps affixed to those of Scotland or Ire-
ll forfeit 5*l.* for each offence; and persons exposing to sale or packing up any foreign linens as
facture of Great Britain or Ireland, shall forfeit the same, and 5*l.* for each piece of linen so ex-
ale or packed up. — (17 *Geo.* 2. c. 30.)
rson stealing to the value of 10*l.* any linen, woollen, silk, or cotton goods, whilst exposed during
of the manufacture in any building, field, or other place, shall, upon conviction, be liable at the
of the court to be transported beyond seas for life, or for any term not less than seven years, or
risoned for any term not exceeding four years, and if a male, to be once, twice, or thrice publicly
ly whipped, as the court shall think fit. — (7 & 8 *Geo.* 4. c. 29. § 14.)

UORICE, or LICORICE (Ger. *Sussholz*; Fr. *Règlisse, Racine douce;* It.
a, *Logorizia, Liquirizia;* Sp. *Regaliz, Orozuz*). This root grows wild in
arts of France, Italy, Spain, and Germany. It is cultivated in several parts
and; the London market being chiefly supplied from Mitcham, in Surrey.
t is from the thickness of a goose-quill to that of the thumb, long, thin,
of a pale yellow colour, and juicy. The taste is sweet and mucilaginous.
g up for use in November, when three years old. The price of the best
said by Mr. Stevenson, in the Agricultural Survey of Surrey, to be about
t. — (*Thomson's Dispensatory.*)

UORICE JUICE, the inspissated juice of the common liquorice root, is
imported in rolls or cakes from Spain.

ON, the capital of Portugal, situated on the north bank of the river
in lat. 38° 42¼′ N., lon. 9° 8⅓′ W. Population about 230,000. The
, or rather road, of Lisbon is one of the finest in the world; and the quays
nce convenient and beautiful. Lisbon possesses about three fourths of
ign trade of Portugal. But the energies of the nation are oppressed by
ootism and intolerance of the government; industry of every sort is
d; manufactures can hardly be said to exist; and commerce is confined
omparatively narrow bounds. Lisbon used to be the grand *entrepôt* for
e of Brazil; but she has no longer any claim to that distinction. The
from Lisbon to England are wines, particularly Lisbon and calcavella;
lemons, and other fruits, which, however, are very inferior to those of
orkwood, and some silk and wool. The imports from England are cot-
ollens, and other British manufactured goods, watches and trinkets,
e, copper, lead, provisions from Ireland, &c. To the north of Europe
ends wine, salt of a very superior quality, fruits, and some colonial pro-
etting back hemp, flax, iron, timber and deals, dried fish, pitch, tar,
and Russian linens, and grain. A smuggling trade is carried on with
sugar, tobacco, spices, &c.

- Accounts are kept in rees, 1,000 of which = 1 milree. In the notation of accounts the milrees
ed from the rees by a crossed cypher (⊕), and the milrees from the millions by a colon : thus,
) 500 = 2,700 milrees and 500 rees.
ado of exchange, or old crusado, = 400 rees; the new crusado = 480 rees; the testoon = 100
he vinten or vintem = 20 rees.
piece of 6,400 rees = 35*s.* 11*d.* sterling; the gold crusado = 2*s.* 3*d.*; and the milree, valued in
d. sterling. It appears, however, from assays made at the London mint in 1812 on modern
dos, that the average value of the milree in *silver* may be estimated at 60*d.* or 5*s.* sterling.
and Measures. — The commercial weights are, 8 ounces = 1 marc; 2 marcs = 1 pound or
pounds = 1 arroba; 4 arrobas = 1 quintal; 100 lbs. or arratels of Portugal = 101·19 lbs. avoir-
·895 kilog. = 94·761 lbs. of Hamburgh = 92·918 lbs. of Amsterdam.
cipal measure for corn, salt, &c., is the moyo, divided into 15 fanegas, 60 alquiéres, 240 quartos,
, &c. The moyo = 23·03 Winchester bushels.

The principal liquid measure is the almude, divided into 2 potes, 12 canadas, or 48 quartellos: 18 des = 1 baril; 26 almudes = 1 pipe; 52 almudes = 1 tonelada. The almude = 4·37 English wine ga and the tonelada = 227½ ditto.

A pipe of Lisbon is estimated by the Custom-house (British) at 140 gallons; and this pipe is suppⁱ be 31 almudes. A pipe of port is 138 gallons, divided into 21 almudes of Oporto.

Of measures of length, 2 pes = 3 palmos = 1 covado, or cubit; 1⅔ cavados = 1 vara; 2 varas = 1 The pe or foot = 12·944 English inches; 100 feet of Portugal = 107⅜ English feet; the var. English inches.

For freight a last is reckoned at 4 pipes of oil or wine, 4 chests of sugar, 4,000 lbs. of tobacco, 3, of shumac.

But from one place in Portugal to another, a tonelada is reckoned at 52 almudes of liquids, or 54 des of dry goods.

Coffee is sold per arroba; cotton, indigo, and pepper, per lb.; oil, per almude; wine, per pipe; co alquiére; salt, per moyo.

Grain, seed, fish, wool, and timber, are sold on board.

Weights and long measures are the same throughout Portugal; but there is a great discrepancy measures of capacity. The almude and alquiére at the principal places, are in English measure as foll.

Lisbon		Almude	= 4·37 gall. Eng. wine meas.	Faro		Alquiére	= 3¾ gall. Winch. m
—		Alquiére	= 3·07 — Winch. meas.	Figuiera		Almude	= 5¼ — wine mea
Oporto		Almude	= 6⅔ — wine meas.	—		Alquiére	= 3¼ — Winch. m
—		Alquiére	= 3⅞ — Winch. meas.	Vianna		Almude	= 6⅔ — wine mea
Faro		Almude	= 4⅔ — wine meas.	—		Alquiére	= 3¾ — Winch. m

(*Kelly's Cambist*, vol. i. art. *List*

LITERARY PROPERTY. See Books.

LITHARGE (Ger. *Glötte, Glätte;* Du. *Gelit;* Fr. *Litharge;* It. *Litargirio Almartaga, Litarjirio;* Rus. *Glet;* Lat. *Lythargyrium*), an oxide of lead in an i. fect state of vitrification. Most of the lead met with in commerce cor silver, from a few grains to 20 ounces or more in the fodder: when the quan sufficient to pay the expense of separation, it is *refined;* that is, the me exposed to a high heat, passing at the same time a current of air over the su. the lead is thus oxidised and converted into *litharge,* while the silver, rem. unchanged, is collected at the end of the process. — (*Thomson's Chemistry* Litharge is used for various purposes in the arts, by potters, glassm. painters, &c.

LOADSTONE (Ger. *Magnet;* Du. *Magneet;* Fr. *Aimant;* It. *Calamita Iman;* Rus. *Magnit;* Lat. *Magnes*). M. Haüy observes, that the ores in v. the iron contains the least oxygen without being engaged in other combina. form natural magnets; and he calls the *loadstones* of commerce, which are ¡ in considerable masses in Germany, Sweden, Norway, Spain, Italy, China, the Philippine Isles, Corsica, and Ethiopia, *oxidulated iron.* The loadsto characterised by the following properties: — A very strong action on the ma. needle. Specific gravity 4·2457. Not ductile. Of a dark grey colour, v. metallic lustre. Primitive form, the regular octahedron. Insoluble in nitric This singular substance was known to the ancients; and they had remark. peculiar property of attracting iron; but it does not appear that they we. quainted with the wonderful property whic'. it also has, of turning to th. when suspended, and left at liberty to move freely. Upon this remarkabl. cumstance the mariner's compass depends, — an instrument which gives us. infinite advantages over the ancients. It is this which enables the marin. conduct their vessels through vast oceans out of the sight of land, in any direction; and this directive property also guides the miners in their subterr. excavations, and the traveller through deserts otherwise impassable. The n. loadstone has also the quality of communicating its properties to iron and and when pieces of steel properly prepared are touched, as it is called, l. loadstone, they are denominated artificial magnets. — (See Compass.)

LOBSTER (Fr. *Ecrévisse;* Lat. *Cancer*), a fish of the crab species, of vast quantities are consumed in London.

The minimum size of lobsters offered for sale is fixed by 10 & 11 Will. 3. c. 24., at *eight* inches f. tip of the nose to the end of the middle fin of the tail. No lobsters are to be taken on the coasts · land between the 1st of June and 1st of September, under a penalty of 5l. The Scilly Islands Land's End abound in lobsters, as well as several places on the Scotch shores, particularly about M. But the principal lobster fishery is on the coast of Norway; whence it is believed upwards of 1 lobsters are annually imported into London. Those of Heligoland are, however, esteemed the be. are of a deeper black colour, and their flesh is firmer than those brought from Norway. Foreign turbots and lobsters may be imported either in British or foreign vessels free of duty.

LOCK, Locks (Ger. *Schlösser;* Du. *Sloten;* Fr. *Serrures;* It. *Serrature Cerraduras, Cerrajos;* Rus. *Samki*), a well known instrument. A great deal and delicacy is required in contriving and varying the wards, springs, bolts, & adjusting them to the places where they are to be used, and to the various sions of using them. From the various structure of locks, accommodated t different intentions, they acquire various names, as stock-locks, spring-lock

s, &c. Of these the spring-lock is the most considerable, both for its
ency and its structure. It is now usually inserted within the timber of a
, instead of being screwed to it; and when so placed, has received the name
rtise lock. Wolverhampton is particularly noted for the skilfulness of its
miths. Some of the locks made there partake of the nature of clockwork,
re of a very minute size. The great desideratum in making locks is to con-
t them so that they may not be opened by any key except their own, nor
t of being picked.

)GWOOD (Fr. *Bois de Campèche*; Ger. *Kampescholz*; Du. *Campecheout*;
°*alo de Campeche*), the wood of a tree (*Hæmatoxylon Campechianum*, Lin.),
ive of America, and which attains the greatest perfection at Campeachy, and
e West Indies. It thrives best in a wet soil, with a large proportion of clay.
logwood tree is like the whitethorn, but a great deal larger. The wood is
compact, heavy, and of a deep red colour internally, which it gives out both
ter and alcohol. It is an article of great commercial importance, being ex-
ely used as as a dyewood. It is imported in logs that are afterwards chip-
Of 14,045 tons of logwood imported in 1828, 7,039 tons were brought from
*ritish West Indies, 6,198 tons from Mexico, and 683 tons from the United
s. Jamaica logwood is at present (May, 1831) worth in the London market
6l. to 6l. 10s. a ton; Honduras is worth about the same; and Campeachy
20s. a ton additional. (The logwood tree, and the adventures of those that
formerly engaged in cutting it, are described by Dampier, see his *Voyages*,
, part 2. p. 56. ed. 1729.)

borrow from the learned and able work of Dr. Bancroft, the following curious
with respect to the use of logwood in this country: — " Logwood seems to have
first brought to England soon after the accession of Queen Elizabeth: but the
s and beautiful colours dyed from it proved so fugacious, that a general outcry
t its use was soon raised; and an act of parliament was passed in the 23d year of
ign, which prohibited its use as a dye under severe penalties, and not only au-
d but directed the *burning* of it, in whatever hands it might be found within the
; and though this wood was afterwards sometimes clandestinely used (under the
d name of blackwood), it continued subject to this prohibition for nearly 100
or until the passing of the act of 13 & 14 Chas. 2.; the preamble of which
es, that the ingenious industry of modern times hath taught the dyers of England
of fixing colours made of logwood, *alias* blackwood, so as that, by experience,
e found as lasting as the colours made with *any other sort of dyeing wood whatever;*
a this ground it repeals so much of the statute of Elizabeth as related to logwood,
ves permission to import and use it for dyeing. Probably the solicitude of the
o obtain this permission, induced them to pretend that their industry had done
more than it really had, in fixing the colours of logwood; most of which, even at
ne, are notoriously deficient in regard to their durability."— (*On Permanent
*, vol. ii. p. 340.)

UIS D'OR, a French gold coin first struck in the reign of Louis XIII. in
equal to 24 livres French, or 1l. sterling.

GGER, a sort of vessel, usually heavily built, and rigged with a square sail.
rench employ luggers as privateers; but there are not many of this descrip-
' ships in our service.

M.

CE (Ger. *Macis, Muskatenblüthe*; Du. *Foelie, Foely, Muscaatbloom*; Fr.
Fleur de muscade; It. *Mace*; Sp. *Macio*; Port. *Maxcis, Flor de noz mos-*
Lat. *Macis*), a thin, flat, membranous substance, enveloping the nutmeg; of
 reddish yellow, saffron-like colour, a pleasant aromatic smell, and a warm,
h, pungent taste. Mace should be chosen fresh, tough, oleaginous, of an
ely fragrant smell, and a bright reddish yellow colour— the brighter the
The smaller pieces are esteemed the best. The best mode of packing is
s, pressed down close and firm, which preserves its fragrance and con-

luction is met with on the coast of Malabar, so like mace, that at first it is not easy to be distin-
but it has not the least flavour of spiciness, and when chewed has a kind of resiny taste.
. of mace are allowed to a ton. — (*Milburn's Orient. Com.*)

Account of the Quantity of Mace retained for Home Consumption, the Rates of Duty on it, and total Revenue derived therefrom, since 1810.

Years.	Quantities retained for Home Consumption in the United Kingdom.	NettAmount of Duty received thereon.	Rates of Duty charged thereon.	Years.	Quantities retained for Home Consumption in the United Kingdom.	NettAmount of Duty received thereon.	Rates of Duty ch thereon.
	Lbs.	*£ s. d.*	Of the East Indies.		*Lbs.*	*£ s. d.*	Of the East I
1810	5,136	2,707 4 0	{ 7s. 8d. per lb. and { 2l. 13s. 4d. per centum ad valorem.	1818	10,836	4,966 10 3	{ (From 10 Ap { 9s. 2d. per
1811	7,949	4,057 1 10	- - ditto.	1819	15,352½	3,526 14 5	{ (From 5 July { 3s. 6d. per
1812	11,907	5,433 2 2	- - ditto.	1820	12,193	2,174 7 0	- - ditt
1813	Records destroyed	-	{ (From 15 April) { 9s. 1½d. per lb. and { 3l. 3s. 4d. per centum ad valorem.	1821	11,572½	1,805 6 5	- - ditt
				1822	13,4·8	2,361 0 10	- - ditt
				1823	14,318½	2,484 10 4	- - ditt
				1824	16,878½	2,967 3 1	- - ditt
1814	5,490	3,259 14 11	{ (From 10 April) { 9s. 2d. per lb	1825	14,851½	2,601 15 1	- - ditt
				1826	15,600½	2,719 17 6	- - ditt
1815	7,834	3,592 14 7	- - ditto.	1827	16,760½	2,962 18 9	- - ditt
1816	6,499	2,984 4 5	- - ditto.	1828	16,094½	2,829 10 4	- - ditt
1817	8,642	3,960 15 9	- - ditto.	1829	14,254½	2,548 15 4	- - ditt

MADDER (Ger. *Färberöthe;* Du. *Mee;* Fr, *Alizari, Garance;* It. *Robbia; Granza, Rubia;* Rus. *Mariona, Krap;* Hind. *Munjith*), the roots of a plant (. *bia tinctorium*), of which there are several varieties. They are long and slen varying from the thickness of a goose-quill to that of the little finger. They semitransparent, of a reddish colour, have a strong smell, and a smooth b Madder is very extensively used in dyeing red; and though the colour whic imparts be less bright and beautiful than that of cochineal, it has the advantage being cheaper and more durable. It is a native of the south of Europe, / Minor, and India; but has been long since introduced into and successfully c vated in Holland, Alsace, Provence, &c. Its cultivation has been attempte England, but without any beneficial result. Our supplies of madder were, f lengthened period, almost entirely derived from Holland (Zealand); but la quantities are now imported from France and Turkey.

Dutch or Zealand madder is never exported except in a prepared or manufact state. It is divided by commercial men into four qualities, distinguished by the te *mull, gamene, ombro,* and *crops.* The roots being dried in stoves, the first specie mull, consists of a powder formed by pounding the very small roots, and the hus bark of the larger ones. It is comparatively low priced, and is employed for dy cheap dark colours. A second pounding separates about a third part of the la roots; and this, being sifted and packed separately, is sold here under the nam gamene, or gemeens. The third and last pounding comprehends the interior, pure, bright part of the roots, and is sold in Holland under the name of *kor kraps,* but is simply denominated crops. Sometimes, however, after the mull has been separated entire residue is ground, sifted, and packed together under the name of *onberoofd* ombro. It consists of about one third of gamene, and two thirds of crop. Prep madder should be kept dry. It attracts the moisture of the atmosphere, and is inj by it.

The Smyrna or Levant madder (*Rubia peregrina*), the alizari or lizary of the mo Greeks, is cultivated in Bœotia, along the border of lake Copais, and in the plai Thebes. It also grows in large quantities at Kurdar near Smyrna, and in Cyp The madder of Provence has been raised from seeds carried from the latter in 1 Turkey madder affords, when properly prepared, a brighter colour than that of Zeal It is, however, imported in its natural state, or as roots: the natives, by whom chiefly produced, not having industry or skill sufficient to prepare it like the Zealan by pounding and separating the skins and inferior roots; so that the finer colou matter of the larger roots being degraded by the presence of that derived from former, a peculiar process is required to evolve that beautiful Turkey red which highly and deservedly esteemed. — (*Thomson's Chemistry; Bancroft on Colours,* v pp. 221—278. : see also *Beckmann, Hist. of Invent.* vol. iii. art. *Madder.*)

In France, madder is prepared nearly in the same manner as in Zealand. following instructive details as to its cultivation, price, &c. in Provence, were oblig furnished to us by an English gentleman intimately acquainted with such subjects, visited Avignon in the autumn of 1829.

" This town (Avignon) is the centre of the madder country, the cultivation of which was intr here about the middle of the 18th century, and, with the exception of Alsace, is still confined (in F to this department (Vaucluse). The soil appears to be better adapted for its cultivation here tha where else, and it has long been the source of great wealth to the cultivators. Of late years, howeve prices have fluctuated so much, that many proprietors have abandoned, or only occasionally cul

so that the crop, which was formerly estimated to average 500,000 quintals, is now supposed not d from 300,000 to 400,000.

root is called *alizari*, and the powder (made from it) *garance*. The plant is raised from seed, ires three years to come to maturity. It is, however, often pulled in 18 months without injury ality, the quantity only is smaller. A rich soil is necessary for its successful cultivation; and e soil is impregnated with alkaline matter, the root acquires a red colour — in other cases it is The latter is preferred in England, from the long habit of using Dutch madder, which is of ur; but in France the red sells at two francs per quintal higher, being used for the Turkey

calculated that when wheat sells at 20 fr. per hectolitre, *alizari* should bring 35 fr. per poids de table), to give the same remuneration to the cultivator. That is, wheat 63s. per Eng. and *alizari* 34s. per Eng. cwt. The price has, however, been frequently as low as 22 fr. al.

es undergo a revolution every seven or eight years, touching the minimum of 22, and rising as 00 fr. As in every similar case, the high price induces extensive cultivation, and this generally its full effect four or five years after. The produce of Alsace, which is inferior both in quan- quality to that of Vaucluse, is generally sold in the Strasburg market.

and employs both the root and the powder, according to the purpose for which they are The Dutch madder is more employed by the woollen dyers, and the French by the cotton d printers.

aking purchases of *garance*, it is essential to employ a house of confidence, because the quality ntirely upon the care and honesty of the agent. The *finest* is produced from the roots after ned and stripped of their bark. The *second* by grinding the roots without cleaning. A *third* g the bark of the *first* while grinding; and so on to any degree of adulteration.

price of *alizari* in the country, which was only 25 fr. in July, is now (November, 1829) at 36 fr., ected to be at 40 fr. very shortly. The crop being deficient both here and in Holland, and the of its being also deficient next year, added to the small quantity existing in England, give believe that the price will reach 60 fr. before many months, and will continue to advance or two more.

quintals above mentioned are of 100 lbs. *poids de table* — the weight in general use over the France, and even at *Marseilles*. This weight is different in the different provinces, varying to 25 per cent. lighter than the *poids métrique*. At Avignon 124 lbs. p. de table = 50 kilog., tly 126 lbs. are equal to 1 cwt. Eng. At the exchange of 25·50, the cwt. costs (including 11s. for uty, and all charges till delivered in London or Liverpool) 61s. or 60s. The selling price is England at 62s. only.

nsidered that only one sixth or one seventh of the present crop remains for sale.

does not deteriorate by keeping, provided it be kept dry.

	Fr.		Fr.
simulé. —			
quintal of roots in the country	35	The English cwt. costs therefore	58·85
in do.	2	All expenses till on board at Marseilles	3
	37		F. 61·85
		Besides commission.	
gives 85 per cent. powder, conse-			
l quintal powder	= 43·50		
	2		
	1		
	2·50		
	F. 46·75		

ccount of East Indian madder, or munjeet, see MUNJEET.

ports of madder have not materially varied for a considerable period. Of 70,017 cwt. of madder imported in 1829, 38,579 were brought from Holland, and 31,352 from France. During ear the imports of madder root amounted to 33,541 cwt., of which 14,592 were brought from ,007 from Turkey and Greece, 2,376 from Holland, and 2,135 (munjeet) from India. The madder from Great Britain are trifling.

y on madder is 6s. per cwt. on prepared, and 1s. 6d. per do. on roots; and its price, duty paid, don market, October 1831, was as under: —

				£ s. d.	£ s. d.	
adder, Dutch Crops	-	-	-	4 0 0 to	4 10 0	per cwt.
Ombro	-	-	-	3 5 0 —	3 15 0	—
Gamene	-	-	-	2 3 0 —	3 12 0	—
Mull	-	-	-	1 0 0 —	2 2 0	—
French	-	-	-	0 0 0 —	4 5 0	—
Spanish	-	-	-	2 16 0 —	3 9 0	—
adder Roots, Turkey	-	-	-	2 10 0 —	2 12 0	—
French	-	-	-	2 8 0 —	2 9 0	—

s not to be imported for home consumption except in British ships, or in ships of the country t is the produce, on which it is imported, under forfeiture of the same, and 100l. by the he vessel. — (6 Geo. 4. c. 109.; 7 & 8 Geo. 4. c. 56.)

EIRA. See WINE.

RAS, the principal emporium on the coast of Coromandel, or western the Bay of Bengal, in lat. 13° 5′ N., lon. 80° 21′ E. It is the seat of ent of the second presidency of the British possessions in India, having a territory of 154,000 square miles, with a population, according to a nsus, of 15,000,000, paying a gross annual revenue of above 5,000,000l. The town is situated in the Carnatic province — a low, sandy, and rather ountry. It is without port or harbour, lying close upon the margin en roadstead, the shores of which are constantly beat by a heavy esides these disadvantages, a rapid current runs along the coast; and it is e sphere of the hurricanes or typhoons, by which it is occasionally visited. respect, indeed, it is a very inconvenient place for trade, and its commerce uently greatly inferior to that of either Calcutta or Bombay. It has been sion of the English 192 years, being founded by them in 1639. In 1823,

the number of houses was ascertained to be 26,786; which, allowing si
habitants to each, makes the total population about 160,000. Fort Saint G
is a strong and handsome fortification lying close to the shore. The Black
of Madras, as it is called, stands to the north and eastward of the fort, from v
it is separated by a spacious esplanade. Here reside the native, Armenian
Portuguese merchants, with many Europeans unconnected with the governi
Like most other Indian towns, it is irregular and confused, being a mixtu
brick and bamboo houses. Madras, like Calcutta and Bombay, is subje
English law; having a Supreme Court of Judicature, the judges of whicl
named by the crown, and are altogether independent of the local government
the East India Company.

In Madras roads, large ships moor in from 7 to 9 fathoms, with the flagstaff
fort bearing W. N. W. 2 miles from shore. From October to January is gen
considered the most unsafe season of the year, in consequence of the prevalence, d
that interval, of storms and typhoons. On the 15th of October the flagstaff is s
and not erected again until the 15th of December; during which period, a ship cc
into the roads, or, indeed, any where within soundings on the coast of Corom
(reckoned from Point Palmyras to Ceylon), vitiates her insurance, according to the
ditions of the policies of all the insurance offices in India. In the fort there is a light-
90 feet above the level of the sea, and which may be seen from the deck of a large ship
miles' distance, or from the mast-head at a distance of 26 miles. The cargo boats
for crossing the surf, called *Massula* boats, are large and light; made of very thin p
sewed together, with straw in the seams, instead of caulking, which it is supposed :
render them too stiff. When within the influence of the surf, the coxswain stan
and beats time in great agitation with his voice and feet, while the rowers work thei
backwards, until overtaken by a strong surf curling up, which sweeps the boat
with frightful violence. Every oar is then plied forward with the utmost vigour t
vent the wave from taking the boat back as it recedes; until at length, by a few succ
surfs, the boat is thrown high and dry upon the beach. The boats belonging to sh
the roads sometimes proceed to the back of the surf, and wait for the country boats
the beach to come to them. When it is dangerous to have communication wil
shore, a flag is displayed at the beach-house, which stands near the landing-place
caution.

The fishermen and lower classes employed on the water, use a species of fl
machine of a very simple construction, named a catamaran. It is formed of
three logs of light wood, 8 or 10 feet in length, lashed together, with a small piece of
inserted between them to serve as a stem-piece. When ready for the water, the
generally two men, who with their paddles impel themselves through the surf, to
letters, or refreshments in small quantities, to ships, when no boat can venture out.
wear a pointed cap made of matting, where they secure the letters, which take no da
The men are often washed off the catamaran, which they regain by swimming,
interrupted by a shark. Medals are given to such catamaran men as distinguish
selves by saving persons in danger.

The following are the established rates of port charges at Madras:—

Lighthouse Dues.

	Rs. a. p.
All British and foreign ships	25 0 0
Country ships	11 0 0
Snow, brig, ketch, and schooner	7 0 0
Sloop and cutter	5 0 0
Large dhonies	5 0 0
Small dhonies	2 0 0

Anchorage Dues.

	S. Roads. Rs. a. p.	N. Roads. Rs. a. p.
British ships, and ships under foreign, European, or American colours	38 0 0	0 0 0
Country ships, from 900 to 500 tons	35 0 0	0 0 0
— 500 to 300 —	28 0 0	0 0 0
— 300 to 200 —	21 0 0	0 0 0
— 200 to 100 —	17 0 0	0 0 0
— 100 to 50 —	14 0 0	0 0 0
— 50 to 10 —	10 0 0	0 0 0
Native craft, from 400 to 300 —	0 0 0	21 0 0
— 300 to 200 —	0 0 0	17 0 0
— 200 to 100 —	0 0 0	14 0 0
— 100 to 50 —	0 0 0	10 0 0
— 50 to 20 —	0 0 0	3 0 0
— 20 to 10 —	0 0 0	1 0 0

Boat Hire.

	S. Roads. Rs. a. p.
Ordinary trips	1 3 0
Do. do. for an accommodation boat	5 0 0
Transhipments	0 12 0
Return trips	0 10 0
Monsoon trips	2 3 0
Do. do. for an accommodation boat	10 0 0
Do. transhipments	1 8 0
Do. return trips	1 3 0
Deep water trips	2 3 0
Extra hire on Sundays	0 9 0
A boat load of water	3 0 0
Sand ballast exclusive of boat hire	0 5 0
Tarpaulin hire	0 4 0

Catamaran Hire.

Small catamarans, to all ships on anchoring
— snow, brig, and ketch, do.
— sloop and cutter, do.
— dhonies and large boats, do.
— carrying letters to ships
— carrying provisions or parcels
Large catamarans, for landing or shipping a European cable of 13 to 16 inches
for do. do. 17 to 22 —
for do. an anchor of 16 to 29 cwt.
for do. do. 30 to 50 —

Port Regulations. — A notification shall be sent to the collector of the customs, through th
attendant, to the commanders of all ships coming into the roads, requiring them to transmit a
full manifest of all goods and merchandises laden on board, according to a printed form; which
being delivered to the collector, he shall, if he so thinks fit, require it to be verified by an aff
oath; which forms being observed, permits are granted for the landing of the goods, under a
signature.

articles are to be shipped or landed, without a permit, or after 6 o'clock P. M. Any merchan-
ttempted to be landed without the prescribed forms, or that were not inserted in the manifest, are
to double duty; and, where a fraudulent intention shall appear, to confiscation. All goods (except
count of the East India Company) shall be shipped or landed at the ghaut opposite to the Custom-
or pay double duty. All goods (except belonging to the Company), on being landed, shall be
ht to the Custom-house; and when required to be passed, a written application, in the following
must be made to the collector. No other form will be attended to. — ' To the Collector of the Cus-
Please to permit the undermentioned goods to pass the Custom-house, on account of, Sir, your
nt servant, ———.'

e.	No. and Nature of Packages.	Name of Ship.	Under what Colours.	Whence Imported.	Sort of Goods.	Quantity of Goods.	Rates.	Total Value.
					N.B. These are to be left blank, and filled up from the tariff, by which the duties are regulated.			

s exported in British vessels, or in those belonging to the native inhabitants of India, are exempt
uty, but must nevertheless pass through the Customs books, and their value be computed at the
rices.

y goods are shipped, or attempted to be shipped, without permission obtained from the Customs,
must be applied for according to the following form, they are liable to a duty of 6 per cent. or
ent., according to the country of the ship. — ' To the Collector of the Customs. Please to permit
lermentioned goods to pass the Custom-house, on account of, Sir, your obedient servant, ———.'

	No. and Nature of Packages.	Name of Ship.	Under what Colours.	Whither bound.	Sorts of Goods.	Rates of Manufactures and Produce.	Quantity of Goods.	Rates.
						These are to be filled up from the tariff.		

collector of customs is allowed a commission of 5 per cent. on the amount of the duty collected
s imported or exported, and upon the amount of the duty computed on goods imported or exported
duty; and where goods become liable to be charged with the additional duty, 5 per cent. is also
he collector on such duty.

clearances cannot be granted to ships clearing outwards, until true and complete manifests of
goes have been lodged with the collector of customs, and a certificate produced from the boat
ter (the chief officer over the boats regularly kept for hire) that he has no demand.

port charges for clearance on every vessel, except paddy boats, is 1 pagoda 24 fanams. For
addy boat, 20 fanams. For every bale imported or exported in foreign vessels (except Americans),
a.

annot employ your own boat to unload your vessel without the permission of the master atten-
nd you can, in no case, let out your boat for hire to another vessel, under any pretence whatever.
es of boat hire are according to your distance from the shore; double charge being made, if em-
on a Sunday. A load of ballast consists of 120 baskets of sand, according to a fixed size, at the
price of 3½ fanams. A boat load of water is 4 butts; the price 55 fanams 40 cash.

ms. — The export and import duties at Madras are the same as at Calcutta; which see.

es. — There is a considerable variety of coins in circulation in Madras and its vicinity. Of the gold
he principal are star or current pagodas = 7s. 5¼d.; commonly, however, valued at 8s. The gold
ew coinage, is worth, according to the mint price of gold in England, 1l. 9s. 2·42d. The Arcot
ilver) and the new silver rupee are very nearly of the same value, being respectively worth 1s. 11¼d.
.1½d. The East India Company and the European merchants keep their accounts at 12 fanams
ee; 80 cash = 1 fanam, and 42 fanams = 1 pagoda. Copper pieces of 20 cash, called pice, and of
cash, called dodees and half dodees, are also current; these are coined in England, and the value
d on each.

ercial Weights. — Goods are weighed by the candy of 20 maunds; the maund is divided into
0 pollams, or 3,200 pagodas; the vis is divided into 5 seers. The candy of Madras is 500 lbs. avoir-
Hence the pagoda weighs 2 oz. 3 grs.; and the other weights are in proportion. These weights
en adopted by the English; but those used in the Jaghire (the territory round Madras belonging
ompany), as also in most other parts of the Coromandel coast, are called the Malabar weights, and
llows: — The gursay (called by the English garce) contains 20 baruays or candies; the baruay,
angus or maunds; the maund, 8 visay or vis, 320 pollams, or 3,200 varahuns. The varahun
2¾ English grains: therefore, the visay is 3 lbs. 3 dr.; the maund, 24 lbs. 2 oz.; the baruay, 482½
d the gursay, 9,645½ lbs. avoirdupois, or 4 tons 6 cwt. nearly.

res of Capacity. — The garce, corn measure, contains 80 parahs, or 400 marçals; and the marçal,
s, or 64 ollucks. The marçal should measure 750 cubic inches, and weigh 27 lbs. 2 oz. 2 dr. avoir-
f fresh spring water: hence, 43 marçals = 15 Winch. bushels; and therefore the garce = 17½
quarters nearly. When grain is sold by weight, 9,256½ lbs. are reckoned for 1 garce, being 18
4¾ maunds.

ng. — There is but a single banking establishment at Madras, which is entirely a government
as the directors consist of the superior officers of government; and the ministerial officers are
salaries. This bank issues notes, receivable as cash at the public treasuries, within the town
as; it receives deposits and grants discounts. The accumulated profits of the bank, from its first
on in 1806, amounted to 690,226l., being at the rate of about 31,000l. a year; but as the Indian
s here reckoned at the rate of 8 shillings the pagoda, which is much above both the mint price
value in exchange, the real profits are considerably smaller.

ntile Establishments. — At Madras there are but three principal European mercantile establish-
houses of agency, with seven of an inferior class. There are two American houses, and one
able native house of business. The daubashes, or native brokers of Madras, are expert, intelli-
l sometimes knavish. Among the native merchants there are few men of wealth, and the con-
this respect, with Calcutta and Bombay, is striking. The degree of liberality exercised by the
e governments, and the prosperity of the different portions of the British territory in India, may
implied by the proportion of British settlers to be found in them. Tried by this test, the Madras
s will be found eminently wanting, as will be seen by the following brief table: —

3	-	Bengal	-	1,225	Madras	-	187	Bombay	-	469
0	-	———	-	1,707	———	-	134	———	-	308

Insurance. — There is but one insurance company, called the India Insurance Society ; but there agents of the Calcutta companies, who effect insurance on shipping.

Agency and Commission. — The general rates of agency, commission, and warehouse rent, a follow : —

1. On the total sum of a debit or credit side of an account, at the option of the agent, excepting items on which a commission of 5 per cent. is chargeable, 1 per cent.
2. On effecting remittances, or purchasing, selling, or negotiating bills of exchange, 1 per cent.
3. On subscriptions to government loans, purchasing, selling, transferring, or exchanging public securities, ½ per cent.
4. On delivering up public securities, or lodging them in any of the public offices, ½ per cent.
5. On receiving and delivering private commissions of wines, cattle, and merchandise, 2½ per cent.
6. On collecting rents, 2½ per cent.
7. On purchase of lottery tickets and amount of prizes, 1 per cent.
8. On the sale of lottery tickets from the other settlements, 2½ per cent.
9. On letters of credit granted, 2½ per cent.
10. On the management of estates, as executors, administrators, or attorneys, 5 per cent.
11. On debts, when a process at law or arbitration is necessary, 2½ per cent.
   And if recovered by such means, 5 per cent.
12. On bills of exchange, notes, &c. dishonoured, 1 per cent.
13. On overdue debts collected for absentees, 2½ per cent.
14. On becoming security for individuals to government, 1 per cent.
15. On all sales or purchases of goods, 5 per cent.
   With the following exceptions : —
   On houses, lands, and ships, 2½ per cent.

On diamonds, pearls, and jewellery, 2½ per cent.
On treasure and bullion, 1 per cent.
On all goods and merchandise withdrawn, shippe delivered to order, half commission.
On all other descriptions of property for sale, if witho or otherwise disposed of by the owners, half con sion.
On goods transferred to auction or commission sale half commission.
16. On retail sales, 10 per cent.
17. On guaranteeing sales, bills, bonds, contracts for goo other engagements, 2½ per cent.
18. On ships' disbursements, 2½ per cent.
19. On advertising as the agents of owners or command ships for freight or passengers ; on the amount of f and passage money, whether the same shall pass th the agent's hands or not, 5 per cent.
20. On effecting insurance, or writing orders for insu ½ per cent.
21. On settling losses, partial or general, and returns of mium, 1 per cent.
22. On procuring money on respondentia, wherever pa 2 per cent.
23. On making up goods to order, and taking risk of adva 10 per cent.
24. On giving orders for the provision of goods, where a mission is not chargeable on sale or shipment, cent.
25. On attending the delivery of contract goods, 2 per ce

Exports and Imports. — Madras trades with Great Britain and other European countries, the U States, the South American States, China, the Eastern islands, the Burman empire, Calcutta, and lon. In speaking of the trade of Madras, it is to be observed that it comprehends, for the most part, trade of the whole coast of Coromandel. The principal articles of import are rice and other grain, ch from Bengal ; cotton piece goods, iron, copper, spelter, and other British manufactures ; raw silk Bengal and China, with betel or areca nut, gold dust, tin, and pepper, from the Malay countries; rice and pepper from the coast of Malabar, with teak timber from Pegu. The exports consist of and printed cottons, cotton wool, indigo, salt, pearls of Ceylon, chank shells, tobacco, soap, natron, dyeing drugs, and a little coffee produced on the table land of Mysore, and of which the quantity i creasing. The great staples of sugar, rice, opium, saltpetre, and lac-dye, of such importance in Be are unknown as exports at Madras.

The following is a statement of the value of the trade of Madras, and its subordinate ports, with Eu and America, in the years 1813-14 and 1828-29 : —

	1813-1814.						1828-1829.			Export	
	Imports.			Exports.			Imports.				
	Merchandise.	Bullion.	Total.	Merchandise.	Bullion.	Total.	Merchandise.	Bullion.	Total.	Merchandise.	Bullion
	Ma. Rs.	*Ma. Rs.*	*Ma. Rs.*	*Ma. Rs.*	*Ma. Rs.*	*Ma. Rs.*	*Ma. Rs.*	*Ma. Rs.*	*Ma. Rs.*	*Ma. Rs.*	*Ma. Rs*
Great Britain	2,717,492	-	2,717,492	4,208,946	156,187	4,365,133	3,354,825	25,156	3,379,981	3,507,741	732,663
United States of America	-	-	-	-	-	-	3,819	7,055	10,874	20,953	-
Portugal	71,128	2,625	73,753	98,462	-	98,462	-	-	-	128,006	-
France	-	-	-	-	-	-	388,593	1,000	389,493	-	-
Brazils	1,228	-	1,228	-	-	-	-	-	-	62,906	-
South American States	-	-	-	-	-	-	-	-	-	-	-
Total -	2,789,848	2,625	2,792,473	4,307,408	156,187	4,463,595	3,747,137	32,211	3,780,348	3,719,606	732,663

Taking the Madras rupee at its British mint value of 1s. 11d. nearly, the joint exports and impo 1813-14 were 695,373l. ; and those of 1828-29, 788,959l. ; showing an increase, in 15 years, of no more 93,586l., or about 13 per cent., — a striking contrast with the great augmentation which has taken in the same period in the trade of Calcutta and Bombay. The exports, it will be seen by the table, even fallen off. The causes which have led to this state of things deserve some explanation. Th silks, nankeens, camphor, and cassia of China, which, on account of the monopoly, could not be di sent from Canton to Europe, were formerly brought by the country ships to Madras, and there re-shi They are now more conveniently, and in much larger quantity, brought for the same purpose to S pore. But the chief causes which have contributed to retard the external commerce of Madras, a vexatious restraints on industry, and the heavier taxation, which prevail under that presidency under those of Bengal and Bombay. The land tax, instead of being fixed in perpetuity, as in Beng temporary and fluctuating ; and hence, neither British nor native industry is applied with any vig the improvement of the productions of the soil. Inland duties prevail every where, and fresh on not only exacted when goods pass from one province to another, but often when passing from to town, or even from village to village. These imposts are, at the same time, farmed to a very c class of persons. Of the value of the trade between Madras and China we have no statement : b tonnage employed in the export trade, at an average of the five years ending with 1817-18, was 3,677 and at an average of the five years ending with 1826-27, 3,078 tons. The import tonnage in the periods amounted respectively to 683 tons and to 2,989 tons ; the disparity in this case being acco for, from its having lately become usual for country ships returning in ballast from China, to at Madras for cargoes of salt to be conveyed to Bengal on behalf of the monopoly. For many ages, a mercial intercourse of considerable extent appears to have prevailed between Madras and other p the Coromandel coast, and the Malay countries, chiefly those situated within the straits of Malacca the west coast of Sumatra and the island of Java. This is still carried on in native vessels to the of 50 or 60 annually, mostly brigs or ketches, clumsily constructed, but equipped and navigated o European model. A few British owned vessels also occasionally engage in it. In this trade, the e from Madras and its subordinate ports consist chiefly of piece goods and salt. British fabrics have years interfered with the former, and the salt of Siam with the latter, so that the trade is on the de The principal foreign trade of Pegu, at one time, was carried on with Madras ; but within the last 30 it has been, in a great measure, transferred to Calcutta. There is still, however, a trade of some ar carried on in vessels owned both by Europeans and natives. The exports from Madras to Pegu c chiefly of piece goods, tobacco, and cocoa nuts ; the returns being made in teak timber, horses, orp stick lac, bullion, sapphires and rubies. The largest branch of the trade of Madras is with Calcutt

the imports from Madras, and other parts of the Coromandel coast, into Calcutta, amounted to
ces 1,874,941, and the exports to sicca rupees 2,377,934, or jointly to about 425,287l. sterling. In
which is the latest statement we possess, the imports amounted to sicca rupees 887,221, and the ex-
sicca rupees 1,235,015, or jointly to about 212,222l.; showing a falling off to the extent of a half of
e. The disproportion, in this case, between the imports and exports, is to be accounted for by the
, in the public accounts, of all salt imported on account of the monopoly, and which has amounted
about 10,000 tons. The great impediment to the intercourse between the Bengal and Madras
s is the salt monopoly, the quantity of salt taken annually being restricted by the government of
This limits the consumption of salt in Bengal, where it is naturally dear, and, by compelling the
ts of Madras to grow corn on poor lands, precludes the export of the cheap rice of Bengal. The
overnments, instead of having improved of late years in liberality, have really drawn tighter
s of monopoly. The effect of this upon the export of corn from Bengal to Madras has been re-
. In 1806-7, when the salt of Madras was admitted into Calcutta with some liberality, the
grain to the Coromandel coast amounted to 2,635,658 maunds, or about 470,000 quarters;
in 1823-24, a year of scarcity in the Madras provinces, it amounted to only 1,591,326 maunds,
284,000 quarters. The trade between Calcutta and the Coromandel coast is carried on both in
a and native vessels. The latter are of the same description, but not so well equipped, as those
c between the Coromandel coast and the Malay islands. In 1810, the number which cleared out
cutta for Madras and its subordinate ports, was no less than 367, their burthen being estimated
tons. Since then, their numbers have declined; being, in 1821, only 103 vessels, of the burthen
tons. The European tonnage employed in this trade is extremely fluctuating. In 1807, a year
rdinary scarcity in the Madras provinces, the registered tonnage which cleared out from Cal-
the Coromandel coast amounted to 93,236 tons, which conveyed 6,000,000 quarters of rice.
r the tonnage amounted to only 6,261 tons. In 1812, another year of scarcity, it was 15,068 tons;
21, a year of plenty, it was but 2,642 tons. These striking facts show the vast importance of a
in corn to the countries in question.—(In compiling this article, we have made use of *Hamilton's
on of Hindostan; Hamilton's East India Gazetteer*, 2d ed. 1828; *Phipp's Guide to the
e of Bengal; Papers relative to the Trade with India and China*, printed by order of the House
ons, and Evidence taken before the Parliamentary Committee, in 1829, 1830, and 1831; *Madras
, for 1831; Kelly's Cambist*, 2d ed.; and *Horsburgh's Directory*, an accurate and useful work.)

GNESIA (Fr. *Magnesie;* Ger. *Gebraunte Magnesia;* It. *Magnesia*), one
rimitive earths having a metallic basis. It is not found native in a state
y, but is easily prepared. It is inodorous and insipid, in the form of a
ht, white, soft powder, having a specific gravity of 2·3. It turns to green
e delicate vegetable blues; is infusible; and requires for its solution 2,000
water at 60°.

HOGANY, the wood of a tree (*Swietenia Mahogani*) growing in the West
nd Central America. There are two other species of Swietenia found in
Indies, but they are not much known in this country.

ny is one of the most majestic and beautiful of trees: its trunk is often 40 feet in length, and 6
meter; and it divides into so many massy arms, and throws the shade of its shining green
r so vast an extent of surface, that few more magnificent objects are to be met with in the
world. It is abundant in Cuba and Hayti, and it used to be plentiful in Jamaica; but in the
d most of the larger trees, at least in accessible situations, have been cut down. The principal
ns into Great Britain are made from Honduras and Campeachy. That which is imported from
s is called Spanish mahogany; it is not so large as that from Honduras, being generally in logs
26 inches square and 10 feet long, while the latter is usually from 2 to 4 feet square and 12 or
g, but some logs are much larger. Mahogany is a very beautiful and valuable species of wood:
s a red brown, of different shades, and various degrees of brightness; sometimes yellowish
ten very much veined and mottled, with darker shades of the same colour. The texture is
nd the annual rings not very distinct. It has no larger septa; but the smaller septa are often
e, with pores between them, which in the Honduras wood are generally empty, but in the
ood are mostly filled with a whitish substance. It has neither taste nor smell, shrinks very
warps or twists less than any other species of timber. It is very durable when kept dry, but
st long when exposed to the weather. It is not attacked by worms. Like the pine tribe, the
est on dry rocky soils, or in exposed situations. That which is most accessible at Honduras
a moist low land, and is, generally speaking, decidedly inferior to that brought from Cuba and
ng soft, coarse, and spongy; while the other is close-grained and hard, of a darker colour, and
strongly figured. Honduras mahogany has, however, the advantage of holding glue admir-
and is, for this reason, frequently used as a ground on which to lay veneers of the finer sorts.
qualities of mahogany bring a very high price. Not long since, Messrs. Broadwood, the dis-
piano-forte manufacturers, gave the enormous sum of 3,000l. for three logs of mahogany!
the produce of a *single tree*, were each about 15 feet long and 38 inches square: they were
neers of 8 to an inch. The wood was particularly beautiful, capable of receiving the highest
l when polished, reflecting the light in the most varied manner, like the surface of a crystal;
he wavy form of the pores, offering a different figure in whatever direction it was viewed.
mahogany generally introduce an augur before buying a log; but, notwithstanding, they are
e to decide with much precision as to the quality of the wood, so that there is a good deal of
he trade. The logs for which Messrs. Broadwood gave so high a price, were brought to this
th a full knowledge of their superior worth. Mahogany was used in repairing some of Sir
eigh's ships at Trinidad, in 1597; but it was not introduced into use in England till 1724
ng of mahogany at Honduras takes place at two different seasons; after Christmas, and towards
r. The negroes employed in felling the trees are divided into groups of from 10 to 50. The
t about 12 feet from the ground, and are floated down the rivers.
5 tons of mahogany imported in 1829, 13,285 came from the British West Indies (including
and 4,939 from Hayti. The duty on foreign mahogany is 7l. 10s. a ton, whereas Honduras
pays only 2l. 10s., and Jamaica mahogany 4l. The effect of such a duty must obviously be to
onsumption of the inferior in preference to the superior article. Last year the duty produced
ee *Tredgold's Principles of Carpentry*, p. 204.; *Library of Entertaining Knowledge*, volume on
es and Fruits; and *Edwards's West Indies*, vol. iv. p. 258. ed. 1819, &c.)
y from Honduras, imported into any free warehousing port in the British possessions in the
s or America, in a ship cleared out from Balize, and then warehoused as having been so im-
cleared, may be exported from the warehouse and imported into the United Kingdom, as if it
ported direct in a British ship, provided it be stated in the ship's clearance that the mahogany
warehoused and exported.—(9 Geo. 4. c. 76. § 13.)
y not to be entered as being the produce of any British possession, unless the master of the ship
he same deliver to the collector or comptroller a *certificate*, and make oath that the goods are
of such place.—(See *ante*, p. 332.)

3 A

MAIZE, or INDIAN CORN (Fr. *Bled de Turquie;* Ger. *Türkisch Mays;* Du. *Turksch koorn;* It. *Grano Turco o Siciliano;* Sp. *Trigo de Indias, de Turquia*), the only species of corn cultivated in America before its disc The ear of maize yields a much greater quantity of corn than any of our corn one ear or spike generally consisting of about 600 grains, which are placed together in rows, to the number of 8 or 10, and sometimes 12. The grain usually yellow, but they are sometimes red, blueish, greenish, or olive col and sometimes striped and variegated. There are three or four varieties of in different parts of America. That of Virginia is very tall and robust, gr to 7 or 8 feet high; that of New England is shorter and lower; and the In further up the country have a still smaller sort in common use. The sta maize is joined like the sugar cane; it is very soft and juicy, and the juice is and saccharine. The straw of maize is an excellent fodder; and the grain bread corn, is much liked by some; but though it abounds in mucilage, it co little or no gluten, and is not likely to be much used by those who can pr wheaten or even rye bread. For the imports of maize, duties, &c., see LAWS AND TRADE.

MALAGA, a city and seaport of Spain, in the kingdom of Granada, 36° 43½' N., lon. 4° 25' W. Population about 55,000. Malaga has a harbour, defended by a fine mole 700 yards in length. The great articles c port are wine and oil; raisins and grapes, almonds and figs, lemons, or lead, and shumac, are also exported. Malaga wine is in considerable estim and large quantities are sent abroad; when old, it fetches a very high price: g are shipped in jars: the raisins are, large sun raisins and goroons, ship casks of 100 lbs. weight; lexias, in barrels of 112½ lbs. and baskets of 56 muscatels and blooms of different qualities, in boxes of 25 lbs.: almonds ar are not much exported; the former being cheaper at Valencia, and the latt being equal to those of Turkey: oranges are finer at Seville and Cadiz. L are shipped in boxes of 1,000; shumac in bags of 100 lbs.; and lead in to 20 cwt. The imports consist principally of German linens, nails and board Sweden, cheese from Holland, butter from Holland and Ireland, dried fish Newfoundland, and grain.

Money. — Accounts are kept in reals of 34 maravedis vellon. For the coins, and their value, Malaga, see CADIZ.

Weights and Measures. — The weights are the same as those of Cadiz. The arroba, or cantar English wine gallons; the regular pipe of Malaga wine contains 35 arrobas, but is reckoned onl a bota of Pedro Ximenes wine = 53¼ arrobas; a bota of oil is 43, and a pipe 35 arrobas; th weighs about 860 lbs. avoirdupois: a carga of raisins is 2 baskets, or 7 arrobas; a cask contains a though only called 4 arrobas: as a last for freight are reckoned — 4 botas or 5 pipes of wine 4 bales of orange peel; 5 pipes of Pedro Ximenes wine or oil; 10 casks of almonds (each about English); 20 chests of lemons and oranges; 22 casks of almonds (of 8 arrobas each); 44 casks o (of 4 arrobas each); 88 half casks of raisins; 50 baskets or 160 jars of raisins.

MALMSEY. See WINE.

MALT (Ger. *Maly;* Du. *Mout;* Fr. *Mal, Blédgermé;* It. *Malto;* Sp. *retonada ó entallecida;* Rus. *Solod;* Lat. *Maltum*). The term malt is applied to nate grain which, being steeped in water, is made to germinate to a certain e after which the process is checked by the application of heat. This evolv saccharine principle of the grain, which is the essence of malt. The proce lowed in the manufacture is very simple. Few changes have been made in it is carried on at this moment very much in the same manner that it was c on by our ancestors centuries ago. Rice, and almost every species of grai been used in malting; but in Europe, and especially in England, malt is pr almost wholly from barley. It is the principal ingredient in the manufact beer, and is not employed for any other purpose.

Duties on, and Consumption of, Malt. — *Influence of the Reduction of the Duty Opening of the Trade.* — Owing to malt liquor having early become the favourite be of the people of England, the manufacture of malt has been carried on amongst a lengthened period, on a very large scale. Instead, however, of increasing w increasing wealth and population of the country, it has been nearly stationary last hundred years. This apparently anomalous result is probably in some mea be accounted for by the increased consumption of tea and coffee, which are almost universal use; but there cannot be a question that it is mainly owing exorbitant duties with which malt, and the ale or beer manufactured from it, hav loaded, and to the oppressive regulations imposed on the manufacture of malt sale of beer. The effect of these duties and regulations was to impose a tax of ab on the malt and beer made from a bushel of barley; which, taking the average p

y at from ∙ʻs. to 5s. a bushel, was equivalent to an *ad valorem* duty of from 140 to
∙er cent. ! The exorbitancy of the duty was not, however, its most objectionable
∙e. It was about equally divided — one half being assessed directly on malt, and the
on beer : but the beer duty affected only beer brewed by public brewers, or for sale,
lid not affect that which was brewed for private use ; and as rich families brewed
∙e beer they made use of, the consequence of this distinction was, that the beer duty
holly on the lower and middle classes, who did not brew any beer ; or, in other
∙, the poor man was compelled to pay twice the duty on the malt he made use of
∙as paid by the rich man ! That such a distinction should ever have been made,
∙mitted to for any considerable period, is certainly not a little astonishing. Origin-
however, the distinction was not so great as it afterwards became ; and being
∙sed by slow degrees, the force of habit reconciled the parliament and the country
gross inequality and oppressiveness of the tax. But the public attention being at
∙ forcibly attracted to the subject, and the effect of the exorbitant duties on malt
∙eer in increasing the consumption of ardent spirits having been clearly pointed out,
Edinburgh Review, No. 98. art. 4.,) the beer duty was repealed in 1830. This
∙re of substantial justice and sound policy reflects the greatest credit on the admi-
∙ion of the Duke of Wellington ; which is also entitled to the public gratitude for
∙ put an end to the licensing system, and established, for the first time, a really
∙ade in beer.

∙ period that has elapsed since this measure was carried, is too limited to allow of
∙ving any specific details as to its effects. We understand, however, that the con-
∙ion of malt during the current year has been very greatly increased ; and that the
∙ations of those who contended that the repeal of the beer duty, if combined with
∙trade in beer, would be no loss to the revenue, are in a fair way of being realised.
∙lamour that has been raised against the measure, on account of its supposed
∙ice in increasing drunkenness, is, we firmly believe, wholly without foundation.
∙measure has increased, as it certainly has done, the consumption of beer, it has at
∙ne time equally diminished the consumption of gin ; and it is surely superfluous
∙, that this is a most beneficial change. It is true that, when the measure first came
∙eration, a great number of new public houses were opened for the sale of beer ;
∙is circumstance, which seems to have occasioned no common alarm among the
∙and magistrates in different parts of the country, has not been productive of any
∙inconvenience whatever, though it has occasioned a good deal of loss to the parties.
∙ll newly opened lines of business, the trade of beer selling has been completely
∙ne ; and a very considerable number of the beer shops have been already shut up.
∙ not," as Dr. Smith has sagaciously remarked, "the multiplication of ale-houses
∙casions a general disposition to drunkenness among the common people ; but that
∙tion, arising from other causes, necessarily gives employment to a multitude of
∙uses." — (*Wealth of Nations*, vol. ii. p. 146.) The way to eradicate this disposition
∙iving a better education to the poor, and inspiring them with a taste for less gro-
∙ enjoyments. All that the fiscal regulations and police enactments intended to
∙e sobriety have ever done, is to make bad worse, to irritate and disgust, to make the
∙classes more enamoured of that which they conceive is unjustly withheld from
∙and to stimulate them to elude and defeat the law.

∙following tables show the consumption of malt in England and Wales from 1787
∙o the present year 1831, and in the whole kingdom from 1821. They show that
∙sumption of malt had been about stationary for nearly half a century, notwith-
∙g the population had been more than doubled in that period, and that the wealth
∙lasses had been materially increased. In point of fact, however, the consumption
∙n stationary for a much longer period — for *more than an entire century !* For
∙ars from the accounts given by the very well informed Mr. Charles Smith, in
∙ts on the Corn Trade (2d ed. p. 199.), that the quantity of malt that paid duty in
∙d and Wales, at an average of the ten years ending with 1723, was 3,542,000
∙s a year ; and that the annual average during the next ten years was 3,358,071
∙s. The beer duties being, in effect, as much a part of the malt duty as if they
∙n laid directly on malt, it is indispensable that they should always be taken into
∙t, before drawing any conclusions as to the influence of the duty. Ample in-
∙on with respect to them will be found in the article ALE AND BEER ; but to save
∙uble of reference, the whole is brought, as far as respects the last ten years, into
∙nt of view in the subjoined table, No. II.

I. An Account of the Total Quantity of Malt made in England and Wales in each Year, from 178[?] 1820, both inclusive, the Rates of Duty, and the Total Amount of the Duty.

Years ended 5th July.	Malt.	Rate of Duty.	Total Amount of Duty.	Years ended 5th July.	Malt.	Rate of Duty.	Total Amount of D[uty]
	Qrs. Bls.	s. d.	£ s. d.		Qrs. Bls.	s. d.	£ s.
1787	3,409,104 7	10 6	1,789,780 1 2	1804	2,602,724 7	34 8	5,772,412 9
1788	3,358,580 1	- -	1,764,264 11 3	1805	2,792,923 1	- -	4,841,066 15
1789	3,031,314 2	- -	1,591,439 19 7	1806	3,435,990 0	- -	5,955,716 0
1790	2,833,697 3	- -	1,487,691 2 5	1807	3,114,020 3	- -	5,397,635 6
1791	3,489,876 2	12 6	2,138,908 14 1	1808	2,800,787 3	- -	4,854,698 2
1792	3,582,671 6	{ 12 6 } { 10 6 }	2,142,950 12 10	1809	2,851,598 7	- -	4,942,771 7
				1810	3,035,401 4	- -	5,261,362 12
1793	3,056,604 5	- -	1,604,717 8 6	1811	3,349,760 5	- -	5,806,251 15
1794	3,194,768 1	- -	1,677,253 13 2	1812	2,332,336 5	- -	4,042,716 16
1795	3,086,695 7	- -	1,620,515 6 8	1813	2,797,741 7	- -	4,849,419 5
1796	3,517,758 4	- -	1,846,823 4 3	1814	3,263,785 5	- -	5,657,228 8
1797	3,865,427 3	- -	2,029,349 7 5	1815	3,384,004 0	- -	5,865,606 18
1798	3,570,431 6	- -	1,769,476 13 4	1816	3,281,929 3	- -	5,688,677 11
1799	3,698,955 5	- -	2,083,701 14 0	1817	2,142,002 4	18 8	1,999,002 6
1800	1,810,089 3	- -	950,296 18 5	1818	3,307,866 5	- -	3,087,342 3
1801	2,320,868 2	- -	1,218,455 16 7	1819	2,793,282 3	- -	2,607,063 11
1802	3,792,297 6	18 8	2,642,040 6 11	1820	3,066,894 3	28 0	4,675,506 8
1803	3,809,900 2	- -	3,555,906 18 0				

II. An Account of the Number of Quarters of Malt charged with Duty, the Amount of the said D[uty,] the Rate per Quarter in each Year; also, the Number of Quarters of Malt used by Brewers [and] Victuallers; the Number of Barrels of Strong, Intermediate, and Table Beer, separately; the Am[ount] of Duty on Beer, and the Rate of Duty per Barrel for each sort of Beer, in each Year, from 5th Jan[uary,] 1821, to 5th January, 1830; stated throughout in the Imperial Measure.—(Parl. Paper, No. 223. Sess. [?])

Years ended 5th January.	England.								
	Malt.				Beer.				
	Quarters charged with Duty.	Rate per Quarter.	Amount of Duty.	Quarters used by Brewers and Victuallers.	Strong, at 9s. 10d. per Barrel.*	Table, at 1s. 11½d. per Barrel.*	Intermediate, at 4s. 11d. per Barrel.	Amo[unt] D[uty]
			£ s. d.		Barrels.	Barrels.	Barrels.	£
1821	2,985,530	28s. 10½ $\frac{6}{21}$d.	4,311,446 2 6	No account has been kept of the quantities used during these years.	5,666,817	1,518,695	- -	2,838,14[?]
1822	3,267,304		4,718,360 10 0		5,969,891	1,528,575	- -	2,987,3[?]
1823	3,336,064	From 25 Feb. 1822, 20s. 8d.	3,624,242 8 0		6,306,981	1,570,043	- -	3,153,6[?]
1824	3,105,644		3,203,502 17 6		6,395,835	1,483,045	7,018	3,190,9[?]
1825	3,451,922		3,560,693 0 0		6,660,968	1,544,048	15,660	3,326,2[?]
1826	3,696,592		3,813,072 7 6		7,014,395	1,606,899	6,160	3,495,5[?]
1827	3,416,996		3,586,084 19 8		6,697,133	1,603,653	7,707	3,268,6[?]
1828	3,137,042		3,241,610 6 6		6,403,309	1,532,308	17,158	3,131,6[?]
1829	3,814,727		3,941,884 19 1		6,570,310	1,530,419	62,617	3,222,8[?]
1830	2,928,500		3,026,126 6 [?]		5,961,048	1,380,469	55,498	2,923,1[?]

	Scotland.								
		From Barley.	From Bear or Bigg.						
1821	147,776	28s. 10½ $\frac{6}{21}$d	{ 28s. 10½ $\frac{6}{21}$d. From 5 July, 1820, 24s. 9$\frac{3}{21}$d. }	212,282 6 6	No account as above.	123,114	207,983	- -	80,9[?]
1822	163,207	- -	{ From 5 July, 1821, 22s. 8½ $\frac{3}{21}$d. }	231,605 9 3	78,406	128,939	219,546	- -	85,6[?]
1823	175,396	{ From 25 Feb. 1822, 20s. 8d.	14s. 5$\frac{20}{21}$d. From 5 July, 1822, 15s. 9$\frac{3}{21}$d. }	183,071 16 7	78,607	128,107	227,478	- -	85,[?]
1824	202,073	- -	- -	198,695 15 10	75,100	119,292	226,332	- -	80,[?]
1825	348,576	- -	- -	335,505 8 1	74,979	118,813	239,956	- -	81,[?]
1826	490,730	- -	- -	462,144 6 6	85,430	133,903	264,035	- -	91,[?]
1827	340,819	- -	16s.	339,104 8 10	72,956	122,158	271,335	- -	79,[?]
1828	339,259	- -	- -	335,488 18 11	79,481	112,067	241,293	- -	72,[?]
1829	483,394	- -	- -	478,507 15 2	82,577	118,943	247,443	- -	76,[?]
1830	464,120	- -	- -	457,587 12 4	75,305	111,071	229,384	- -	71,[?]

	Ireland.				
1821	224,208	28s. 10½ $\frac{6}{21}$d.	319,683 14 0	165,130	
1822	243,664	From 5 April, 1822, 20s. 8d.	347,424 0 0	150,640	
1823	219,548	- -	275,612 14 0	174,466	
1824	213,364	- -	216,752 2 6	187,268	
1825	271,249	- -	268,330 0 0	170,695	Note. — No return can be
1826	349,656	- -	344,600 10 0	167,124	of the quantity of beer brew[ed]
1827	300,821	- -	315,029 15 2	176,349	Ireland, the same not being s[ubject]
1828	225,849	- -	232,899 12 10	189,076	to excise duty.
1829	301,192	- -	311,191 19 0	175,331	
1830	251,579	- -	259,869 17 2	167,175	

* From the year 1827, the rate of duty per barrel for strong beer was—common brewers, 9s. ; victu[allers,] 9s. 10d. : table beer, common brewers, 1s. 9½d, ; victuallers, 1s. 11½d. ; the same also for Scotland.

Account of the Number of Bushels of Malt made, and the Amount of Duties thereon, in each ‑‑ion of Excise in the United Kingdom, from 5th January, 1830, to 5th January, 1831. — (Parl. No. 58. Sess. 1831.)

Collections.	Number of Bushels Malt.	Amount of Duty.
		£ s. d.
England:		
‑le	195,466	25,247 13 10
	556,570	71,890 5 10
	1,254,223	162,003 16 1
	365,860	47,256 18 4
‑dge	1,138,827	147,098 9 9
‑ury	355,870	45,966 10 10
	415,674	53,691 4 6
‑y	202,876	26,204 16 4
‑and	699,853	90,397 13 7
	279,031	36,041 10 1
	675,658	87,272 9 10
	217,644	28,112 7 0
	159,292	20,575 4 4
	930,776	120,225 4 8
	148,509	19,182 8 3
‑er	312,376	40,348 11 4
‑m	928,621	119,946 17 7
	365,357	47,191 18 11
	329,879	42,609 7 5
	198,674	25,662 1 2
	1,031,356	133,216 16 4
	156,011	20,151 8 5
‑ight	290,835	37,566 3 9
‑r	201,417	26,016 7 3
	1,319,067	170,379 9 9
‑d	799,214	103,231 11 0
	830,250	107,240 12 6
‑l	9,198	1,188 1 6
	561,336	72,505 18 0
‑ter	—	—
‑ugh	354,465	45,785 1 3
‑e	221,755	28,643 1 11
‑ton	536,887	69,347 18 1
‑berland	115,413	14,907 10 3
‑h	58,269	7,526 8 3
	1,085,570	140,219 9 2
	447,586	57,813 3 10
	227,942	29,442 10 2
‑c	592,998	76,595 11 6
	329,529	42,564 3 3
	492,971	63,675 8 5
	522,097	67,437 10 7
	555,536	71,756 14 8
	146,998	18,987 4 10
	381,715	49,304 17 1
	558,004	72,075 10 4
‑ge	1,369,772	176,928 17 8
	1,075,879	138,967 14 1
	389,357	50,291 18 11
	439,109	56,718 4 11
‑ast	275,820	35,626 15 0
‑iddle	200,939	25,954 12 5
‑orth	180,146	23,268 17 2
‑est	154,978	20,017 19 10
‑n	180,049	23,256 6 7
	148,979	19,243 2 5
	162,822	21,031 3 6
‑c	288,731	37,294 8 5
	452,692	58,472 14 4
‑ollections	26,876,724	3,471,576 17 0
	24,179	3,123 2 5
‑otal	26,900,903	3,474,699 19 5

Collections.	Number of Bushels Malt.	Amount of Duty.
		£ s. d.
Scotland :		
Aberdeen	224,096	22,850 18 10
Ayr	235,109	29,771 18 3
Argyle, North	29,072	2,988 10 2
—— South	305,781	30,774 3 0
Caithness	67,430	6,745 12 6
Dumfries	48,230	6,172 1 6
Elgin	193,354	22,183 19 11
Fife	200,321	25,874 15 11
Glasgow	616,963	77,652 6 9
Haddington	280,151	36,186 4 8
Inverness	135,206	17,291 13 9
Linlithgow	203,222	25,885 10 3
Montrose	112,277	14,365 5 6
Perth	245,291	31,592 12 1
Stirling	746,765	96,423 13 4
Edinburgh	458,678	58,892 0 4
Total	4,101,946	505,651 6 9
Ireland :		
Armagh	94,616	11,836 11 8
Athlone	38,336	4,951 14 8
Clonmell	74,111	9,572 13 5
Coleraine	38,014	4,662 16 2
Cork	307,774	39,754 2 10
Drogheda	65,227	8,425 3 1
Dundalk	124,358	16,055 19 11
Foxford	36,600	4,727 10 0
Galway	54,303	7,011 14 4
Kilkenny	206,587	26,684 3 1
Limerick	76,263	9,850 12 9
Lisburn	91,252	11,623 10 0
Londonderry	44,872	5,369 10 5
Mallow	76,830	9,916 16 11
Maryborough	75,843	9,796 7 9
Naas	46,709	6,016 13 0
Sligo	36,715	4,659 5 2
Tralee	6,388	825 2 4
Waterford	91,955	11,877 10 0
Wexford	277,301	35,818 0 11
Dublin	95,552	12,210 3 1
Total	1,959,606	251,646 1 11
Totals.		
England	26,900,903	3,474,699 19 5
Scotland	4,101,946	505,651 6 9
Ireland	1,959,606	251,646 1 11
United Kingdom	32,962,455	4,231,997 8 1

of Malt, per Winchester Quarter, at Greenwich Hospital, from 1730 to 1828. — (Parl. Papers, No. 54. Sess. 1830; No. 72. do.)

Prices.	Years.	Prices.	Years.	Prices.
20s. 6d.	1800	84s.	1823	59s. 11d.
27s. 3¼d.	1805	85s. 7d.	1824	62s. 1d.
24s.	1810	84s. 5d.	1825	71s. 10¼d.
24s. 9d.	1815	69s. 7½d.	1826	65s. 1d.
28s. 3d.	1820	68s. 8¼d.	1827	64s. 10d.
31s. 1d.	1821	61s. 11d.	1828	61s. 7d.
35s. 6d.	1822	52s. 8½d.		

‑ns as to the Manufacture of Malt. — These are embodied in the acts 7 & 8 Geo. 4. c. 52., and ‑17. The former act is exceedingly complex : it has no fewer than *eighty-three* clauses ; and ‑ons embodied in it, though frequently repugnant to common sense, are enforced by 106 penal‑ting in all to the enormous sum of 13,500l.! Under such a statute, it was hardly possible for ‑nest and cautious maltster to avoid incurring penalties. Such, indeed, is the nature of this ‑e is almost tempted to believe, in looking into it, that if its framers had any object more than

another at heart, it was to condense into it whatever was most contradictory and absurd in the statutes that had previously been passed for the collection of the malt duty and the oppression trade! But it was not in the nature of things that such a law could be allowed to exist for any considerable period. It was not only loudly and universally condemned by the maltsters, but by all the intelligent officers of excise. In consequence, the 11 Geo. 4. c. 17. was passed. This latter statute entitled to very considerable praise; it repeals a good many of the penalties, and some of the vexatious and useless regulations, in the former; so that the business may now be carried on with security to the revenue, and with infinitely less risk and annoyance on the part of the manufac. The existing regulations principally refer to the gauging of the cisterns, the wetting of the ma emptying of the cisterns, the gauging of the malt when in the couch frames, the payment of the &c. But as no one would think of undertaking the business of a maltster without having a copy acts in his possession, it would be quite unnecessary for us, even if our limits permitted, to gi abstract of these acts. The licence duty on maltsters, and the number of maltsters who took out l in 1829, distributed into classes according to the extent of their business, will be found specified article LICENCES (EXCISE).

Malt may not be imported into the United Kingdom for home use under pain of forfeiture; but be warehoused for exportation. — (6 Geo. 4. c. 107. § 52.)

MALTA, an island in the Mediterranean, nearly opposite to the southern e mity of Sicily, from which it is about 54 miles distant. Valetta, the capi situated on the north coast of the island, in lat. 35° 50′ N., lon. 14° 1 Malta is about 20 miles long, and 10 or 12 broad. The island of Gozo, ab fourth part of the size of Malta, lies to the north-west of the latter, at about 4 distance; and in the strait between them is the small island of Cumino. In the resident population of Malta amounted to 99,623; and including troop strangers, the total population amounted to 102,853. The population of at the same period, was 16,883. The entire revenue collected in Malta am to about 100,000*l.* a year; and the expenditure, exclusive of that incurred in land on account of the island, amounts to about 120,000*l.*

After the capture of Rhodes by the Turks, the emperor Charles V. made a present of Malt knights of St. John of Jerusalem, in whose possession it remained till 1798, when it was taker French. It was taken from the latter by the English in 1800; and was definitively ceded t 1814.

The island consists mostly of a rock, very thinly covered with soil, a good deal of which has been b at an immense expense, from Sicily: but being cultivated with the utmost care, it produces ex fruits, particularly the celebrated Maltese oranges, corn, cotton, with small quantities of indigo, and sugar. The principal dependence of the inhabitants is on their cotton, which they manufact a great variety of stuffs, some of which are highly esteemed. The corn raised in the island sufficient to feed the inhabitants for more than five or six months. The trade in corn use monopolised by government; but though the monopoly has been abandoned, duties on importatio ing, like those in this country, indirectly as the price, have been imposed, partly for the sake of r and partly for the protection of agriculture! There are some good springs of fresh water. V partly supplied by water brought by an aqueduct a distance of about 6 miles, and partly by the rai collected in cisterns.

Valetta, the principal town in Malta, stands on a narrow peninsula, between two most exceller and is defended by almost impregnable fortifications. The harbour on the south-east side of the cit the Grand Port, is the largest: it runs about two miles into the heart of the island; and the wate deep and well sheltered, it affords the best anchorage for the largest ships. " This beautiful divided into five distinct harbours, all equally safe, and each capable of containing an immense nu shipping. The mouth of the harbour is scarcely a quarter of a mile broad, and is commanded side by batteries that would tear the strongest ship to pieces before she could anchor. The harbou north-west side of the city (Port Marsamusceit), though it is used only for fishing, and as a quarantine, would, in any other part of the world, be considered as inestimable. It is likewise d by very strong works; and in the centre of the basin there is an island (peninsula) on which a castle and a lazaretto. The fortifications of Malta are, indeed, a most stupendous work. All the catacombs of Rome and Naples are a trifle to the immense excavations that have been made in th island. The ditches of a vast size are all cut out of the solid rock: these extend for a great man and raise our astonishment to think that so small a state has ever been able to make them."—(Br *Tour through Sicily and Malta*, letter 15.) Since the island came into our possession, the fortis have been considerably strengthened.

PORT CHARGES.

	Vessels under the	
	British and Ionian Flag.	Foreign Flag.
	L. s. d.	*L. s. d.*
Anchorage and lighthouse. — For every 5 tons, or any part thereof, as f.r as 300 tons	0 1 0	0 1 6
For every additional 5 tons, or any part thereof	0 0 0	0 0 0
Water. — For every passenger and individual of the crew	0 0 5	0 0 5
Pilotage. — For every vessel exceeding 60 tons burthen	0 2 1	0 2 1
Hospital. — For each individual composing the crew	0 4 2	
Ballast. — For every 5 tons, or any part thereof	0 0 4	0 0 4
Bill of health. — For the master of a Speronara	0 0 8	0 0 8
For every other person of the crew of ditto	0 0 5	0 0 5
For the master of any other vessel	0 0 10	0 0 10
For every other person of the crew of ditto	0 0 7	0 0 7
Powder magazine. — On powder belonging to the vessel, for each barrel for a month	0 0 10	0 0 10
On ditto imported or lodged on trans't, for each of the first three months ad valorem per 100*l.*	1 0 0	1 0 0
For every succeeding month	0 5 0	0 5 0

Exceptions.

1. Merchant vessels entering either of the harbours main therein 5 days, without being subject to the of any port charges, water (if required) excepted; they neither discharge nor take on board goods, pass their baggage, during such period of their stay.

2. Vessels clearing out, having taken on board fo ation a quantity of Malta wrought stone, not less th cent. on their respective registered tonnage, are from the payment of ballast dues.

3. Pilotage not to be paid oftener than once in a nor hospital dues more frequently than once in six r cases where vessels make more than one voyage du spaces of time respectively.

4. Maltese and Ionian vessels are not subject to th dues.

Charges on Ships in Quarantine at Malta.

For every vessel arriving with a clean bill of health not exceeding 50 tons　　　　(entrance fee)
above 50 and not exceeding 100 tons　ditto
above 100 and not exceeding 150 tons　ditto
above 150 and not exceeding 200 tons　ditto
above 200　　　　　　　　ditto

For every vessel (in addition to the above respective rates) for guards and guard boats (per day)

Vessels arriving with a foul bill of health to pay dou ble the above rates respectively.

Vessels waiting for orders, or convoy, to pay either ac cording to the above rates or (per day)

central position, excellent port, and great strength of Malta, make it an admirable naval station for
pair and accommodation of the men-of-war and merchant ships frequenting the Mediterranean;
nder its possession of material importance to the British empire. It is also of considerable con-
ice, particularly during war, as a commercial *depôt*, where goods may be safely warehoused, and
which they may be sent, when opportunity offers, to any of the ports of the surrounding countries.
ilities are greater in this respect than those enjoyed by Gibraltar. The duties on importation are
oderate, being calculated, with the exception of those on corn, to amount to about 1 per cent. *ad*
n on British manufactured goods, and 2 per cent. on those imported by foreigners. Goods ware-
' pay no duty; but a store rent of ¼ per cent. for the first 3 months, and ½ per cent. for every 3
s afterwards, is levied on all goods lodged in the government warehouses, according to their value.
icial value of the British produce and manufactures exported to Malta in 1829, was 458,179*l.*;
, with 47,180*l.* worth of colonial and foreign merchandise, make the total export 505,359*l.* The im-
uring the same year amounted to only 20,784*l.*

ry. — In 1825, British silver money was introduced into Malta; the Spanish dollar being made
nder at the rate of 4*s.* 4*d* ; the Sicilian dollar at 4*s.* 2*d.* ; and the scudo of Malta at 1*s.* 8*d.*

hts and Measures. — The pound or rottolo, commercial weight, = 30 oncia = 12,216 English grains.
100 rottoli (the cantaro) = 174¼ lbs. avoirdupois, or 79·14 kilog. Merchants usually reckon the
 at 175 lbs.

salma of corn, stricken measure, = 8·221 Winchester bushels : heaped measure is reckoned 16 per
nore. The caffiso, or measure for oil, contains 5¼ English gallons = 20·818 litres. The barrel is
 the caffiso. The Maltese foot = 11¼ English inches = ·2836 métres. The canna = 8 palmi =
nglish inches = 2·079 métres. Merchants usually convert Malta measure into English in the proof 3¼ palmi to a yard, or 2⅔ yards to 1 canna.

on London are usually drawn at 30 and 60 days' sight. The deputy commissary general is obliged
t, at all times, bills on the treasury here for British silver payable to him, at the rate of 100*l.* bill
ry 103*l.* silver, receiving at the same time Spanish dollars at a fluctuating rate of exchange.
Majesty is authorised, by the act 6 Geo. 4. c. 114. § 73., to make such regulations touching the
nd commerce to and from any of the British possessions within the Mediterranean sea, as may seem
xpedient ; and any goods imported or exported contrary to such regulations shall be forfeited, to-
ore the ship importing or exporting the same. — (See *Brydone's Tour in Sicily and Malta, Papers*
'ore the Finance Committee, Kelly's Cambist, &c.)

N (ISLE OF), is, as every one knows, situated in the Irish sea at about
ual distance from England, Scotland, and Ireland. It is about 30 miles long,
0 or 12 broad. The interior is mountainous, and the soil no where very pro-
e. This island used to be one of the principal stations of the herring
y ; but for a considerable period it has been comparatively deserted by the
g shoals, — a circumstance which is not to be regretted ; for the fishery, by
rawing the attention of the inhabitants from agriculture and manufactures,
ading them to engage in what has usually been a gambling and unproductive
ess, has been, on the whole, injurious to the island. The steam packets from
ow to Liverpool touch at the Isle of Man ; which has, in consequence, begun
 largely frequented by visiters from these cities, and other parts of the
, whose influx has materially contributed to the improvement of Douglas
her towns.

feudal sovereignty of Man was formerly vested in the Earls of Derby, and more re-
in the Dukes of Athol, — a circumstance which accounts for the fact of the duties
t commodities consumed in the island having been, for a lengthened period, much
han those on the same commodities when consumed in Great Britain. This dis-
n, which still subsists, has produced a great deal of smuggling, and been in no ordi-
egree injurious to the revenue and trade of the empire. During the present century,
, the clandestine trade of Man has been confined within comparatively narrow
 but to accomplish this, a considerable extra force of Custom-house officers and
e cruisers is required, and the intercourse with the island has to be subjected to
 restraints. Nothing, as it appears to us, can be more impolitic than the con-
e of such a system. The public has, at a very heavy expense, purchased all the
rights of the Athol family ; and having done so, it is certainly high time that an
re put to the anomalous absurdity of having a considerable island, lying, as it
n the very centre of the empire, and in the direct line between some of the prin-
ading towns, with different duties on many important articles ! It might be
ry, perhaps, to make some compensation to the inhabitants for such a change ;
s might be done, with advantage to them and without expense to the public, by
ng and improving the internal regulations and policy of the island, which are
uch in need of amendment. We do not, indeed, imagine that the island would
 thing by the proposed alteration ; for the temptation which the present system
ut to engage in smuggling enterprises diverts the population from the regular
s of industry, and, along with the herring lottery, is the principal cause of that
 for which the Manx are so notorious. We subjoin an

Abstract of 6 Geo. 4. c. 151. — *An Act for regulating the Trade of the Isle of Man.*

t came into force on the 5th of January, 1826.

payable on the Importation of Goods into the Isle of Man. — There shall be levied, upon im-
 into the Isle of Man of the several goods specified below, the following duties. — § 2.

A Table of the Duties of Customs payable on Goods, Wares, and Merchandise, imported into the I[sle] of Man.

	L.	s.	d.		L.
Coals, from the United Kingdom, the chaldron, W. M.	0	0	3	Wood, from foreign parts; viz. deal boards, for every 100l. value	10
Coffee - - - the lb.	0	0	4	timber - - for every 100l. value	10
Hemp, from foreign parts, for every 100l. value	10	0	0	Goods, wares, and merchandise, imported from the United Kingdom, and entitled to any bounty or drawback of excise on exportation from thence, and not hereinbefore enumerated or charged with duty - for every 100l. value	5
Hops, from the United Kingdom - the lb.	0	0	1¼		
Iron, from foreign parts for every 100l. value	10	0	0		
Spirits; viz. foreign brandy - the gallon	0	4	6		
foreign geneva the gallon	0	4	6		
rum of the British plantations - the gallon	0	3	0	Goods, wares, and merchandise, imported from the United Kingdom, and not hereinbefore charged with duty - for every 100l. value	2
Sugar, muscovado - - the cwt.	0	1	0		
Tea; viz. bohea - - the lb.	0	1	0	Goods, wares, and merchandise, imported from any place from whence such goods may be lawfully imported into the Isle of Man, and not herein-before charged with duty, for every 100l. value	15
green - - the lb.	0	1	0		
Tobacco - - the lb.	0	1	0		
Wine; viz. French - the tun of 252 gallons	16	0	0		
any other sort - the tun of 252 gallons	12	0	0		

Except the several goods, wares, and merchandise following, and which are to be imported into the of Man duty free : —

Flax, flax seed, raw or brown linen yarn, wood ashes, weed ashes, flesh of all sorts; also corn, grain, or meal of all sorts, when importable; any of which goods, wares, or merchandise may be imported into the said isle from any place in any ship or vessel.
Any sort of white or brown linen cloth, hemp, hemp seed, horses, black cattle, sheep; all utensils and instruments fit and necessary to be employed in manufactures, in fisheries, or in agriculture; bricks, tiles, all sorts of young trees, sea shells, lime, soapers' waste, packthread, small cordage for nets, salt, boards, timber, woods, hoops, being the growth, production, or manufacture of the United Kingdom, and imported from thence in British ships.

Iron in rods or bars, cotton, indigo, naval stores, and a[ll sorts] of wood commonly called lumber (viz. deals of all timber, balks of all sizes, barrel boards, clap boards, boards, or pipe hold, white boards for shoemakers, and cant spars, bow staves, capravan, clap holt, wood, headings for pipes and for hogsheads, and for hoops for coopers, oars, pipe and hogshead staves, staves, firkin staves, trunnels, speckled wood, sweet small spars, oak plank, and wainscot), being of the gr[owth,] production, or manufacture of any British colony or ation in America or the West Indies, and imported fr[om the] United Kingdom in British ships.

British Goods to appear upon the Cockets. — No goods shall be entered in the Isle of Man, as being growth, produce, or manufacture of the United Kingdom, or as being imported from thence, except goods as shall appear upon the cocket to have been duly cleared at some port in the United Kingdo[m] be exported to the said isle. — § 3.

Goods importable only under Licence. — The several sorts of goods enumerated in the schedule he[re]after contained, denominated "Schedule of Licence Goods," shall not be imported into the Isle of nor exported from any place to be carried to the Isle of Man, without licence of the commissione[rs of] customs first obtained ; nor in greater quantities in the whole, in any one year, than the quan[tity] specified in the said schedule ; and such goods shall not be so exported nor so imported, except from [the] places set forth in the said schedule, and according to the rules subjoined thereto ; (that is to say,)

Schedule of Licence Goods.

Wine - -	110 tuns.	Coffee - -	8,000 lbs.
Foreign brandy -	10,000 gallons.	Tobacco -	60,000 lbs.
Foreign geneva -	10,000 gallons.	Mucovado sugar -	6,000 cwt.
From the United Kingdom, or from any place from		Playing cards	4,000 pack[s]
whence the same might be imported into the United		From England.	
Kingdom for consumption therein.		Refined sugar	
		From the port of Liverpool.	400 cwt.
Rum, of the British plantations	60,000 gallons.	And such additional quantities of any of such several	
From Great Britain.		goods as the commissioners of his Majesty's treasury	
Bohea tea - -	50,000 lbs.	from time to time, under any special circumstances [of ne-]	
Green tea - -	5,000 lbs.	cessity, direct from such ports respectively ;	

Subject to the Rules following :

(1.) All such goods to be imported into the port of Douglas, and by his Majesty's subjects, in British ships of the burthen of 50 tons or upwards :
(2.) Such tobacco to be shipped only in ports in England, where tobacco is allowed to be imported and warehoused without payment of duty :
(3.) Such wine to be imported only in casks or packages containing not less than a hogshead each, or in cases containing not less than three dozen reputed quart bottles or six dozen reputed pint bottles each :
(4.) Such brandy and geneva to be imported only in casks containing 100 gallons each, at least :
(5.) Such brandy and geneva not to be of greater strength than 1 to 9 over hydrometer proof :
(6.) Such goods, when exported from Great Britain, may be so excepted from the warehouse in which they may have been secured without payment of duty :
(7.) If the duties of importation have been paid in the United Kingdom on such goods, a full drawback of such duties shall be allowed on the exportation :
(8.) Upon the exportation from Liverpool of such refined

sugar, the same bounty shall be allowed as would be all[owed] on exportation to foreign parts :
(9.) Upon exportation from the United Kingdom of an[y] goods from the warehouse, or for drawback, or for bou[nty,] much of the form of the bond, or of the oath, or of an[y] document required in the case of exportation of such [goods] generally to foreign parts, as is intended to prevent the la[nding] of the same in the Isle of Man, shall be omitted :
(10.) No drawback, or bounty to be allowed, nor expor[ted] cane. lled, until a certificate of the due landing of the g[oods at] the port of Douglas be produced from the collector and tro ler of the customs at that port :
(11.) If any goods be laden at any foreign port or pla[ce, the] species and quantity of such goods, with the marks, nu[mbers] and denominations of the casks or packages contain[ing the] same, shall be endorsed on the licence, and signed by the consul at the port of lading, or if there be no British con[sul by] two known British merchants :
(12.) Upon importation into the port of Douglas of a[ny such] goods, the licence for the same shall be delivered up [to the] collector or comptroller of that port. — § 4.

Application for Licence. — Every application for licence to import such goods shall be made in w[riting] and delivered, between the 5th of May and 5th of July in each year, to the collector or comptroller [of the] port of Douglas ; and such application shall specify the date and name, residence and occupation, [of the] person applying, and the description and quantity of each article for which such licence is required [; and] all such applications with such particulars shall be entered in a book at the Custom-house at the p[ort of] Douglas, open for public inspection during the hours of business ; and on the 5th of July in each [year] such book shall be closed ; and within fourteen days thereafter, the collector and comptroller shall [make] out and sign a true copy of such entries, specifying the applicants resident and the applicants not res[ident] in the said isle, and transmit such copy to the governor and lieutenant-governor of the said isle. —

Governor to allot Quantities. — Within fourteen days after the receipt of such copy, the gover[nor or] lieutenant-governor shall allot the whole quantity of each article, in the first place, among the appli[cants] resident in the said island, in case the whole quantity shall not have been applied for by residents ; [and] shall allot the quantity not so applied for among the non-resident applicants, in such proportions [and] cases as he shall judge most equitable ; and shall cause a report thereon to be drawn up in writi[ng, and] sign and transmit the same to the Lords Commissioners of the Treasury of the United Kingdom, and [shall] cause a duplicate of such report so signed to be transmitted to the commissioners of customs. — § 6.

Commissioners of Customs to grant Licences. — Upon receipt of such duplicate report, the commiss[ioners] of customs shall grant licences to continue in force for any period until the 5th of July next ensui[ng of] the importation of the quantities allowed by law to be imported, with their licence, according to the [allot-] ments in such report, and dividing the whole portion allotted to any one applicant into several lic[ences] as they shall be desired and see fit ; and such licences shall be transmitted without delay to the col[lector] and comptroller of Douglas, to be by them delivered to the applicants, after taking bond for the [due...] under the provisions of this act. — § 7.

Delivery of Licences, Bond to be given. — Previous to the delivery of any such licences, the
and comptroller of Douglas shall take bond, with sufficient security, for the importation of the
r which the licences are granted, on or before the 5th of July succeeding the delivery of such
with such conditions, and for the forfeiture of such sums, not exceeding the whole amount of
yable in Great Britian on articles similar to those specified in such licences, as the commissioners
as shall think fit : Provided always, that if any person to whom such licence shall be granted,
have given such bond prior to the 5th of January next after the granting such licence, it shall be
: the governor or lieutenant-governor, if he see fit, to transfer such licence to any other person
a be desirous to take up the same, and able to give such bond ; and such transfer shall be notified
cement on the licence signed by such governor or lieutenant-governor. — § 8.

feiting Licence. — If any person shall counterfeit or falsify any licence, or shall knowingly make
y such licence so counterfeited or falsified, such person shall forfeit 500*l.* — § 9.

d Goods not to be re-exported. — It shall not be lawful to re-export from the Isle of Man any
ich have been imported with licence as aforesaid ; and it shall not be lawful to carry any such
stwise from one part of the said isle to another, except in vessels of 100 tons burthen, and in the
kages in which such goods were imported ; and it shall not be lawful to remove any wine from
of the said isle to another by and except (*sic* in act) in such packages or in bottles. — § 10.

. Goods. — It shall not be lawful to export from the Isle of Man to any part of the United King-
goods which are of the growth, produce, or manufacture of any foreign country. — § 11.

nported or exported contrary to Law, forfeited. — If any goods shall be imported into or exported
Isle of Man ; or carried coastwise ; or shall be water-borne, or brought to any wharf or other
a intent to be water-borne, to be so exported or carried ; or shall be removed by land within the
ontrary to any of the directions of this act ; the same and the packages shall be forfeited, toge-
all ships, vessels, or boats, and all cattle and carriages used therein ; and every person offending
it for every such offence 100*l.*, or the full amount of all duties which would be payable in respect
goods for home consumption in the United Kingdom, at the election of the commissioners of
— § 12.

rohibited. — The several sorts of goods enumerated in the schedule hereinafter contained, deno-
" Schedule of Prohibitions," shall not be imported into the Isle of Man. — § 13.

Schedule of Prohibitions.

e produce or manufacture of places within the
e United East India Company's charter ; except
ited Kingdom :
n, cotton cloth, glass manufactures, woollen manu-
ss *bond fide* laden in and imported directly from
ingdom :

British distilled spirits :
All goods prohibited to be imported into the United Kingdom
to be used or consumed therein, on account of the sort or description of the same.

g the Quantity of Spirits, Tea, and Tobacco, for the Use of Seamen. — If any decked vessel bound
sle of Man to any part of Great Britain or Ireland, shall have on board, for the use of the sea-
spirits exceeding the quantity of ½ a gallon for each seaman, or any tobacco exceeding 1 lb.
aman, or any tea exceeding 2 lbs. for the whole of the seamen on board ; or if any open boat,
n the Isle of Man to any port of Great Britain or Ireland, shall have on board for the use of
a any spirits exceeding 1 quart for each seaman, or any tobacco exceeding ½ a lb. for each seaman,
a exceeding 1 lb. for the whole of the seamen on board such boat, all such foreign spirits,
d tea respectively, together with the casks or packages containing the same, and also every
l or boat, together with all the guns, furniture, ammunition, tackle, and apparel thereof, shall
d. — § 14.

nent of Duties. — The duties of customs shall be levied under the direction and control of the
ners of customs, and, except the necessary charges of levying the same, shall be brought and
he receipt of the exchequer distinctly from all other branches of the public revenue, and shall
onsolidated fund : Provided always, that any of the collectors of customs of the said isle shall,
to such directions as shall be given for that purpose by the commissioners of customs, retain
or sums in their hands as may be sufficient to defray the necessary expenses attending the
t of the said Isle of Man and the administration of justice there, and other charges incurred
isle, which have heretofore been or may hereafter be deemed proper charges to be deducted
f the duties, and also for the purpose of defraying any bounties that may be due upon herrings
the inhabitants of the said isle ; and upon the amount of the said expenses, charges, and
ing ascertained, the said commissioners are to direct the same to be paid out of the said monies
, to such persons as may be entitled to receive the same. — § 15.

all be provided and kept, by the receiver-general or collector of the duties of customs in the
a, books, in which the duties of customs payable within the isle shall be entered separate and
nct heads. — § 16.

receiver-general or collector shall, as soon after the expiration of each quarter (ending on the
uary, the 5th of April, the 5th of July, and the 10th of October in each year), as the same can
ake out an account of the gross produce of the duties in the preceding quarter, and shall
duplicate of such account to the commissioners of the treasury, and another duplicate to the
the exchequer, and another to the Duke of Athol, or to the person entitled for the time being
uity out of the said consolidated fund, to be calculated on any amount of such duties ; and if
ceiver general shall refuse or neglect to make out such account, or to transmit such duplicates,
ce of one month after the same can be done, such receiver shall forfeit 200*l.*, and a further sum
every month succeeding for which he shall neglect to make out such account, to be recovered
t at Westminster ; and every such penalty shall go to the use of the said Duke of Athol, or
entitled to as aforesaid. — § 17.

GANESE (Ger. *Braunstein, Glasseise ;* Du. *Bruinsteen ;* Fr. *Manganèse,*
, Savon du verre ; It. *Manganesia ;* Sp. *Manganesia ;* Lat. *Magnesia nigra,*
sium), a metal which, when pure, is of a greyish white colour, like cast
l has a good deal of brilliancy. Its texture is granular ; it has neither
smell ; it is softer than cast iron, and may be filed ; its specific gravity is
very brittle, and can neither be hammered nor drawn out into wire. Its
s unknown. When exposed to the air, it attracts oxygen with consider-
lity. It soon loses its lustre, and becomes grey, violet, brown, and at last
These changes take place still more rapidly if the metal be heated in an
sel. Ores of manganese are common in Devonshire, Somersetshire, &c.
of manganese, known in Derbyshire by the name of *black wadd*, is re-
for its spontaneous inflammation with oil. Oxide of manganese is of
ble use ; it is employed in making oxymuriatic acid, for forming bleaching
It is also used in glazing black earthenware, for giving colours to

enamels, and in the manufacture of porcelain. It is the substance generally
by chemists for obtaining oxygen gas. — (*Thomson's Chemistry*, &c.)

MANGEL WURTZEL, or FIELD BEET (Fr. *Betteraves;* Ger. *Ma*
Wurzel; It. *Biettola*), a mongrel between the red and white beet. It has been a
deal cultivated in France, Germany, and Switzerland, partly as food for cattl
partly to be used in distillation, and in the extraction of sugar. Its culture in
Britain is very recent; and Mr. Loudon questions whether it has any advan
over the turnip for general agricultural purposes. The preparation of the
exactly the same as for turnips, and immense crops are raised on strong clays.
produce per acre is about the same as that of the Swedish turnip; it is a;
almost entirely to the fattening of stock, and the feeding of milch cows. —
don's Ency. of Agriculture.)

MANNA (Fr. *Manne;* Ger. *Mannaesche;* It. *Manna*), the concrete ju
the *fraxinus ornus,* a species of ash growing in the south of Europe. The
exudes spontaneously in warm dry weather, and concretes into whitish tears
the greater part of the manna of commerce is obtained by making incisions i
tree, and gathering the juice in baskets, where it forms irregular masses of
dish or brownish colour, often full of impurities. Manna is imported in c
principally from Sicily and Calabria. The best is in oblong pieces or f
moderately dry, friable, light, of a whitish or pale yellow colour, and in son
gree transparent: the inferior kinds are moist, unctuous, and brown. It
slight peculiar odour, and a sweet taste, with some degree of bitterness no
pleasant, and leaving a nauseous impression on the tongue. — (*Thomson's D*
satory.)

MANIFEST, in commercial navigation, is a document signed by the m
containing the name or names of the places where the goods on board have
laden, and the place or places for which they are respectively destined ; the
and tonnage of the vessel, the name of the master, and the name of the pla
which the vessel belongs ; a particular account and description of all the pac
on board, with the marks and numbers thereon, the goods contained in
packages, the names of the respective shippers and consignees, as far as suc
ticulars are known to the master, &c. A separate manifest is required f
bacco. The manifest must be made out, dated, and signed by the captain,
place or places where the goods, or any part of the goods, are taken on boa
(See IMPORTATION AND EXPORTATION.)

MANILLA, the capital of Luconia, the largest of the Philippine Island
the principal settlement of the Spaniards in the East, in lat. 14° 38′ N., lon
50′ E. Population about 40,000, of whom from 1,200 to 1,500 may b
ropeans. Manilla is built on the shore of a spacious bay of the same nai
the mouth of a river navigable for small vessels a considerable way int
interior. The smaller class of ships anchor in Manilla roads, in 5 fathom
north bastion bearing N. 37° E., the fishery stakes at the river's mouth N.
distant about a mile ; but large ships anchor at Cavita, about 3 leagues t
southward, where there is a good harbour well sheltered from the W. and
winds. The arsenal is at Cavita, which is defended by fort St. Philip, the str
fortress on the islands. The city is surrounded by a wall and towers, and
of the bastions are well furnished with artillery.

Though situated within the tropics, the climate of the Philippines is suffi
temperate ; the only considerable disadvantage under which they labour in this r
being that the principal part of the group comes within the range of the typ
The soil is of very different qualities ; but for the most part singularly fertile.
are rich in mineral, vegetable, and animal productions. It is stated in a sta
account of the Philippines, published at Manilla in 1818 and 1819, that the
population of the islands amounted to 2,249,852, of which 1,376,222 belon
Luconia. There were, at the period referred to, only 2,837 Europeans in the
and little more than 6,000 Chinese. The natives are said to be the most activ
and energetic, of any belonging to the Eastern Archipelago. " These people,"
most intelligent navigator, "appear in no respect inferior to those of Europe.
cultivate the earth like men of understanding ; are carpenters, joiners, smiths, gold
weavers, masons, &c. I have walked through their villages, and found them kir
pitable, and communicative ; and though the Spaniards speak of and treat the
contempt, I perceived that the vices they attributed to the Indians, ought rath
imputed to the government they have themselves established." — (*Voyage de M*
Perouse, c. 15.)

e principal articles of export consist of indigo, sugar, rice, sapan wood, birds'
tripang or *biche de mer*, dried beef, hides, ebony, gold dust, &c. The principal
es of import are stuffs for clothing, iron, hardware, furniture, fire-arms and
unition, &c.

e Singapore Chronicle of the 13th of March, 1828, gives an account of the imports
nd exports from Manilla in 1827, from which it appears that the former consisted
8,233 dollars in merchandise and 110,399 in treasure, and the latter of 937,701
s in merchandise and 156,078 in treasure. Part of this trade is exhibited in the
ving statement : —

	Imports.	Exports.		Imports.	Exports.
	Sp. Doll.	Sp. Doll.	Value of the cargoes of	Sp. Doll.	Sp. Doll.
ue of the cargoes of					
Spanish vessels - -	250,501	385,080	Brazilian vessels - -	26,645	5,051
English do. -	106,011	90,933	Hamburgh do. - -	33,765	8,150
French do. -	49,752	132,928	Danish do. - -	- -	10,106
American do. -	127,372	196,657	Dutch do. - -	5,132	21,711

the same year there entered the port of Manilla 34 Spanish ships, 7 English,
nch, 13 American, 1 Brazilian, 2 Dutch, &c.

subjoin from the same authority

An Account of the Quantities of the Principal Articles exported from Manilla in 1827.

f the 1st quality	169,878		Horns, buffalo -		3,808 catties.
2d —	79,677	285,684 piculs.	Cloth, of the country -		24,983 pièces.
3d —	36,132		Soap, of the country -		1,043 piculs.
1st —	1,106		Canvass, of the country -		111 pièces.
2d —	2,816	5,066 do.	Honey, of the country -		2,145 catties.
3d —	1,144		Birds' nests, fine, 1st quality	263	
fined -	68		2d —	402	855 do.
refined, 1st quality	25,400		3d —	490	
2d —	2,800	28,239 do.	common 1st —	173	
3d —	91		2d —	3,669	6,319 do.
ot spun	5,062		3d —	2,477	
rope	303	5,365 do.	Birds of Paradise -		40 do.
leaned -	1,785 do.		Pepper -		13,464 do.
purified -	1,087 do.		Mats -		16,051 pièces.
ns -	13,765 catties.		Hats, straw	976	1,031
ner, 1st quality	74,155		rattans	5,677	6,653
2d —	95,169	248,778 do.	Tallow -		2,190 catties.
3d —	78,804		Sapan wood -		48,535 piculs.
4th —	650		Cheroots -		1,889 aroles.
- -	250 piculs.		Dried flesh, deer	7,595	
14 quintals.			cow	2,325	39,724 catties.
shell, 1st quality	2,515		buffalo	29,804	
2d —	3,844	7,484 catties.	Isinglass -		519 piculs.
3d —	1,125		Rice, cleaned	8,512	
- -	2,336 piculs.		in ear	5,847	
gh	110		Cocoa nut oil -		1,875 tinagas.
lies	1,200	1,310 lbs.	Snails, dried -		4,639 cavanes.
s'	3,252		Cocoas -		161 do.
alo	21,053	24,325 skins.	Ebony, 2d quality	4,015	
r -	20		twisted	9,326	13,341 piculs.
ned -	6,300 do.				

increase of the trade of Manilla since 1827 has been fully a half. It appears
ne *Registro Mercantil,* published at Manilla, that the imports, during 1830, con-
of 1,562,522 dollars in merchandise and 178,063 dollars of treasure. The
for the same year were, merchandise 1,497,621 dollars, and treasure 81,952
The customs revenue in 1830 was 228,061 dollars. Of the foreign vessels
g Manilla last year, 29 were American, 22 English, 8 French, 4 Dutch, 3
uese, and the remainder Indian.

sidering the great fertility and varied productions of the Philippines, and their
rly favourable situation for carrying on commerce, the limited extent of their
even with its late increase, may excite surprise. This, however, is entirely a
ience of the wretched policy of the Spanish government, which persevered until
cently in excluding all foreign ships from the ports of the Philippines—confining
le between them and Mexico and South America to a single ship ! Even ships
lers from China were excluded. " Provisions," says La Perouse, " of all kinds
the greatest abundance here, and extremely cheap ; but clothing, European
re, and furniture, bear an excessively high price. The want of competition,
r with prohibitions and restraints of every kind laid on commerce, *render the pro-
s and merchandise of India and China at least as dear as in Europe !*" Happily,
r, this miserable policy, the effects of which have been admirably depicted by
la Perouse, has been materially modified during the last few years. The
of the late war destroyed for ever the old colonial system of Spain ; and the
f all nations are now freely admitted into Manilla and the other ports in the
ines. An unprecedented stimulus has, in consequence, been given to all sorts of
y ; and its progress will, no doubt, become more rapid, according as a wider
nce and acquaintance with foreigners makes the natives better aware of the
ges of commerce and industry, and disabuses them of the prejudices of which
ve been so long the slaves.

Monies, Weights, and *Measures,* used at Manilla, are nearly the same as in Spain.
CADIZ.) They have, however, this difference, — that they estimate weight by

15

piastres : 16 piastres are supposed to = 1 lb. Spanish weight, though they are not q¹
so much; 11 ounces or piastres = 1 tale of silk; 22 ounces = 1 catty; 8 ounces
1 marc of silver; and 10 ounces = 1 tale of gold. 16 piastres or ounces = 15¼ our
avoirdupois ; 100 catties = 1 picul = 133½ lbs. avoirdupois.

MARBLE (Ger. Rus. and Lat. *Marmor ;* Du. *Marmer ;* Fr. *Marb*
It. *Marmo ;* Sp. *Marmol*), a genus of fossils, composed chiefly of lime ; bein
bright and beautiful stone, moderately hard, not giving fire with steel, ferment
with, and soluble in, acid menstrua, and calcining in a slight fire.

The colours by which marbles are distinguished are almost innumerable. Some are quite black ; otl
again, are of a snowy white ; some are greenish ; others greyish, reddish, bluish, yellowish, &c. ; v
some are variegated and spotted with many different colours and shades of colour. The finest
modern marbles are those of Italy, Blankenburg, France, and Flanders. Great quantities of very b
tiful marble have been lately discovered at Portsoy in Banffshire, and at Tiree and other places in
Western Isles. Kilkenny, in Ireland, has abundance of beautiful black marble intermixed with v
spots, called *Kilkenny marble*. Derbyshire abounds in this mineral. Near Kemlyn-bay, in Angl
there is a quarry of beautiful marble, called *verde di Corsica*, from its also being found in Corsica.
colours are green, black, white, and dull purple, irregularly disposed. Italy produces the most v
able marble, and its exportation makes a considerable branch of its foreign commerce. The black
the milk-white marble, of Carara, in the duchy of Massa, are particularly esteemed.
The marbles of Germany, Norway, and Sweden, are very inferior, being mixed with a sort of s
limestone.
Marble is of so hard, compact, and fine a texture, as readily to take a beautiful polish. That
esteemed by statuaries is brought from the island of Paros, in the Archipelago : it was employe
Praxiteles and Phidias, both of whom were natives of that island ; whence also the famous Arunde
marbles were brought. The marble of Carara is likewise in high repute among sculptors.
The specific gravity of marble is from 2,700 to 2,800. Black marble owes its colour to a slight mix
of iron.

MARITIME LAW. By maritime law is meant the law relating to harbou
ships, and seamen. It forms an important branch of the commercial law of
maritime nations. It is divided into a variety of different departments ; such
those with respect to harbours, to the property of ships, the duties and right
masters and seamen, contracts of affreightment, average, salvage, &c. The rea
will find those subjects treated of under their respective heads.

Sketch of the Progress of Maritime Law.—The earliest system of maritime law was c
piled by the Rhodians, several centuries before the Christian era. The most celebra
authors of antiquity have spoken in high terms of the wisdom of the Rhodian la
luckily, however, we are not wholly left, in forming our opinion upon them, to the va
though commendatory statements of Cicero and Strabo. — (*Cicero pro Lege Man*
Strab. lib. 14.) The laws of Rhodes were adopted by Augustus into the legislatio
Rome ; and such was the estimation in which they were held, that the emperor Ant
nus, being solicited to decide a contested point with respect to shipping, is reporte
have answered, that it ought to be decided by the Rhodian laws, which were of p
mount authority in such cases, unless they happened to be directly at variance with s
regulation of the Roman law. (" *Ego quidem mundi dominus, lex autem maris leg*
Rhodia, qua de rebus nauticis præscripta est, judicetur, quatenus nulla nostrarum le
adversatur. Hoc idem Divus quoque Augustus judicavit.") The rule of the Rhodian
with respect to average contributions in the event of a sacrifice being made at sea for
safety of the ship and cargo, is expressly laid down in the Digest (lib. xiv. tit. 2.) ;
the more probable conclusion seems to be, that most of the regulations as to mari
affairs embodied in the compilations of Justinian have been derived from the s
source. The regulations as to average adopted by all modern nations, are borrow
with hardly any alteration, from the Roman, or rather, as we have seen, from the I
dian law !—a conclusive proof of the sagacity of those by whom they had been origi
framed. The only authentic fragments of the Rhodian laws are those in the Dig
The collection entitled *Jus Navale Rhodiorum*, published at Bâle in 1561, is now
mitted by all critics to be spurious.

The first modern code of maritime law is said to have been compiled at Amalph
Italy, — a city at present in ruins ; but which, besides being early distinguished fo
commerce, will be for ever famous for the discovery of the Pandects, and the supp
invention of the mariner's compass. The Amalphitan code is said to have been
nominated *Tabula Amalphitana*. But if such a body of law really existed, it is sing
that it should never have been published, nor even any extracts from it. M. Pardo
has shown that all the authors who have referred to the Amalphitan code and asse
its existence, have copied the statement of Freccia, in his book *De Subfeudis*. — (*Colle*
des Lois Maritimes, tome i. p. 145.) And as Freccia assures us that the Amalphitan
continued to be followed in Naples at the time when he wrote (1570), it is difficu
suppose that it could have entirely disappeared ; and it seems most probable, as no¹
peculiar to it has ever transpired, that it consisted principally of the regulations
down in the Roman law, which, it is known, preserved their ascendancy for a lo
period in the south of Italy than any where else.

besides Amalphi, Venice, Marseilles, Pisa, Genoa, Barcelona, Valencia, and
⸱wns of the Mediterranean, were early distinguished for the extent to which they
commerce and navigation. In the absence of any positive information on the
⸱, it seems reasonable to suppose that their maritime laws would be principally
⸱d from those of Rome, but with such alterations and modifications as might be
⸱ requisite to accommodate them to the particular views of each state. But whe-
⸱his or in some other way, it is certain that various conflicting regulations were
⸱hed, which led to much confusion and uncertainty; and the experience of the
⸱niences thence arising, doubtless contributed to the universal adoption of the
⸱o del Mare as a code of maritime law. Nothing certain is known as to the origin
⸱code. Azuni (Droit Maritime de l'Europe, tome i. pp. 414—439., or rather
⸱odice Ferdinando, from whose work a large proportion of Azuni's is literally
⸱d), contends, in a very able dissertation, that the Pisans are entitled to the glory
⸱g compiled the whole, or at least the greater part, of the Consolato del Mare. On
⸱r hand, Don Antonio de Capmany, in his learned and excellent work on the
⸱ce of Barcelona (Antiguo Commercio de Barcelona, tomo i. pp. 170—183.), has
⸱ured to show that the Consolato was compiled at Barcelona; and that it contains
⸱s according to which the consuls, which the Barcelonese had established in foreign
⸱o early as 1268, were to render their decisions. It is certain that the Consolato
⸱nted for the first time at Barcelona, in 1502; and that the early Italian and
⸱ editions are translations from the Catalan. Azuni has, indeed, sufficiently
⸱that the Pisans had a code of maritime laws at a very early period, and that
⸱of the regulations in it are substantially the same as those in the Consolato.
⸱oes not appear that the Barcelonese were aware of the regulations of the Pisans,
⸱he resemblance between them and those in the Consolato is more than accidental;
⸱not fairly be ascribed to the concurrence that can hardly fail to obtain among
⸱ormed persons legislating upon the same topics, and influenced by principles
⸱ctices derived from the civil law.

⸱ardessus, in the second volume of his excellent work already referred to, appears
⸱been sufficiently disposed, had there been any grounds to go upon, to set up a
⸱ favour of Marseilles to the honour of being the birthplace of the Consolato;
⸱andidly admits that such a pretension could not be supported, and unwillingly
⸱to Capmany's opinion. — " Quoique François," says he, " quoique portée par
⸱mens de reconnoissance, qu'aucun évènement ne sauroit affoiblir, à faire valoir
⸱qui est en faveur de Marseilles, je dois reconnaître franchement que les pro-
⸱l'emportent en faveur de Barcelone." — (Tome ii. p. 24.)

⸱⸱ whichever city the honour of compiling the Consolato may be due, there can
⸱ubt that its antiquity has been greatly exaggerated. It is affirmed, in a pre-
⸱e different editions, that it was solemnly accepted, subscribed, and promulgated,
⸱⸱ of maritime law, by the Holy See in 1075, and by the kings of France and other
⸱s at different periods between 1075 and 1270. But Capmany, Azuni, and
⸱s, have shown in the clearest and most satisfactory manner that the circumstances
⸱o in this preface could not possibly have taken place, and that it is wholly un-
⸱f the least attention. The most probable opinion seems to be, that it was com-
⸱d began to be introduced, about the end of the 13th or the beginning of the
⸱tury. And notwithstanding its prolixity, and the want of precision and clear-
⸱correspondence of the greater number of its rules with the ascertained principles
⸱e and public utility, gradually led, without the intervention of any agreement,
⸱option as a system of maritime jurisprudence by all the nations contiguous to
⸱terranean. It is still of high authority. Casaregis says of it, though, perhaps,
⸱gly, " Consulatus maris, in materiis maritimis, tanquam universalis consuetudo
⸱m legis inviolabiliter attenda est apud omnes provincias et nationes." — (Disc. 213.

⸱ollection of sea laws next in celebrity, but anterior, perhaps, in point of time,
⸱nominated the Roole des Jugemens d'Oleron. There is as much diversity of
⸱us to the origin of these laws, as there is with respect to the origin of the Con-
⸱The prevailing opinion in Great Britain has been, that they were compiled by
⸱of Queen Eleanor, the wife of Henry II., in her quality of Duchess of Guienne;
⸱they were afterwards enlarged and improved by her son Richard I., at his return
⸱Holy Land: but this statement is now admitted to rest on no good foundation.
⸱: probable theory seems to be, that they are a collection of the rules or practices
⸱at the principal French ports on the Atlantic, as Bordeaux, Rochelle, St. Malo,
⸱y contain, indeed, rules that are essential to all maritime transactions, wherever
⸱ be carried on; but the references in the code sufficiently prove that it is of
⸱igin. The circumstance of our monarch's having large possessions in France
⸱iod when the Rules of Oleron were collected, naturally facilitated their intro-

duction into England; and they have long enjoyed a very high degree of autho
this country. "I call them the laws of Oleron," said a great civilian — (Sir *I*
Jenkins, Charge to the Cinque Ports,) "not but that they are peculiarly enough Er
being long since incorporated into the customs and statutes of our admiralties; b
equity of them is so great, and the use and reason of them so general, that they are k
and received all the world over by that rather than by any other name." M
however, has more correctly, perhaps, said of the laws of Oleron, that "they
obtained any other or greater force than those of Rhodes formerly did; that is, the;
esteemed for the reason and equity found in them, and applied to the case emerge;
(*De Jure Maritimo et Navali*, Introd.)

A code of maritime law issued at Wisby, in the island of Gothland, in the Balti
long enjoyed a high reputation in the North. The date of its compilation is unce
but it is comparatively modern It is true that some of the northern jurists conten
the Laws of Wisby are older than the Rules of Oleron, and that the latter are chiefly c
from the former! But it has been repeatedly shown that there is not so much
shadow of a foundation for this statement. — (See *Pardessus, Collection*, &c., t
pp. 425—462.; *Foreign Quarterly Review*, No. 13. art. *Hanseatic League.*) The
of Wisby are not certainly older than the latter part of the 14th or the beginning
15th century; and have obviously been compiled from the Consolato del Mai
Rules of Oleron, and other codes that were then in use. Grotius has spoken of
laws in the most laudatory manner : — "*Quæ de maritimis negotiis,*" says he, " ;
Gothlandiæ habitatoribus placuerunt, tantum in se habent, tum equitatis, tum pruden
omnes oceani accolæ eo, non tanquam proprio, sed velut gentium jure, utantur." —
legomena ad Procopium, p. 64.)

Besides the codes now mentioned, the ordinances of the Hanse towns, issued ir
and 1614, contain a system of laws relating to navigation that is of great autl
The judgments of Damme, the customs of Amsterdam, &c. are also often quotee

But by far the most complete and well digested system of maritime jurispru
that has ever appeared, is that comprised in the famous *Ordonnance de la Marine*
by Louis XIV. in 1681. This excellent code was compiled under the directi
M. Colbert, by individuals of great talent and learning, after a careful revision
the ancient sea laws of France and other countries, and upon consultation with tl
ferent parliaments, the courts of admiralty, and the chambers of commerce, of the di
towns. It combines whatever experience and the wisdom of ages had shown to l
in the Roman laws, and in the institutions of the modern maritime states of E
In the preface to his treatise on the Law of Shipping, Lord Tenterden says, "
reader should be offended at the frequent references to this ordinance, I must r
him to recollect that those references are made to the maritime code of a great co;
cial nation, which has attributed much of its national prosperity to that code: ;
composed in the reign of a politic prince ; under the auspices of a wise and enlig!
minister ; by laborious and learned persons, who selected the most valuable princi;
all the maritime laws then existing ; and which, in matter, method, and style, is
the most finished acts of legislation that ever was promulgated."

The ordinance of 1681 was published in 1760, with a detailed and most ela
commentary by M. Valin, in two volumes 4to. It is impossible which to admir;
in this commentary, the learning or the sound good sense of the writer. Lord Ma
was indebted for no inconsiderable portion of his superior knowledge of the pri;
of maritime jurisprudence to a careful study of M. Valin's work.

That part of the *Code de Commerce* which treats of maritime affairs, insurance,
copied, with very little alteration, from the ordinance of 1681. The few chang
have been made are not always improvements.

No system or code of maritime law has ever been issued by authority in Great P
The laws and practices that now obtain amongst us in reference to maritime ;
have been founded principally on the practices of merchants, the principles laid d;
the civil law, the laws of Oleron and Wisby, the works of distinguished jurisco
the judicial decisions of our own and foreign countries, &c. A law so construci
necessarily been in a progressive state of improvement; and, though still suscep!
material amendment, it corresponds, at this moment, more nearly, perhaps, th;
other system of maritime law, with those universally recognised principles of justi
general convenience by which the transactions of merchants and navigators ough;
regulated.

The decisions of Lord Mansfield did much to fix the principles, and to impr;
perfect the maritime law of England. It is also under great obligations to Lord S

* A translation of the laws of Oleron, Wisby, and the Hanse towns, is given in the third c
Malyne's Lex Mercatoria ; but the edition of them in the work of M. Pardessus, referred to in
is infinitely superior to every other.

decisions of the latter chiefly, indeed, respect questions of neutrality, growing out
e conflicting pretensions of belligerents and neutrals during the late war ; but the
iples and doctrines which he unfolds in treating those questions, throw a strong and
y light on most branches of maritime law. It has occasionally, indeed, been alleged,
d the allegation is probably, in some degree, well founded, — that his Lordship has
ded too much to the claims of belligerents. Still, however, his judgments must be
ded, allowing for this excusable bias, as among the noblest monuments of judicial
m of which any country can boast. " They will be contemplated," says Mr. Ser-
Marshall, " with applause and veneration, as long as depth of learning, soundness
gument, enlightened wisdom, and the chaste beauties of eloquence, hold any place
e estimation of mankind." — (*On Insurance*, Prelim. Disc.)

e " Treatise of the Law relative to Merchant Ships and Seamen," by the present
Justice of the Court of King's Bench, does credit to the talents, erudition, and
lity of its noble and learned author. It gives, within a brief compass, a clear
dmirable exposition of the most important branches of our maritime law ; and may
nsulted with equal facility and advantage by the merchant or general scholar, as
e lawyer. Mr. Serjeant Marshall has entered very fully into some, and has
ed upon most points of maritime law, in his work on Insurance ; and has discussed
with great learning and sagacity. The works of Mr. Justice Park, Mr. Holt, and
others, are also valuable. Of the earlier treatises, the Lex Mercatoria of Malynes
ar the best ; and, considering the period of its publication (1622), is a very extra-
ry performance.

utes with respect to Importation and Exportation, Navigation, &c. — The preceding
ks refer merely to the principles, or leading doctrines, of our maritime law.
, however, have often been very much modified by statutory enactments ; and the
ive multiplication of acts of parliament suspending, repealing, or altering parts of
acts, has often involved our commercial and maritime law in almost inextricable
ion ; and been most injurious to the public interests. No one, indeed, who is
etty conversant with the subject, would readily imagine to what an extent this
has sometimes been carried. From the Revolution down to 1786, some hundreds
s were passed, each enacting some addition, diminution, or change, in the duties,
acks, bounties, and regulations, previously existing in the customs. In consequence
stoms laws became so intricate and unintelligible, that hardly one merchant in
uld tell the exact amount of duty affecting any article ; or the course to be
ed either in entering or clearing out vessels ; being obliged to leave it entirely to
erks of the Custom-house to calculate the amount of duties, and to direct him
proceed so as to avoid forfeiting the goods and the ship ! and yet, so powerful
influence of habit in procuring toleration for the most pernicious absurdities,
is monstrous abuse was allowed to go on increasing for 50 years after it had been
nced as intolerable. Mr. Pitt has the merit of having introduced something like
into this chaos. Under his auspices, all the separate customs duties existing
were repealed, and new ones substituted in their stead ; consisting, in most
es, of the equivalents, so far at least as they could be ascertained, of the old duties.
rying this measure into effect, the House of Commons passed no fewer than
resolutions. The regulations as to entries and clearances were also sim-

advantages resulting from this measure were very great ; but during the war
y new duties and regulations were passed, that the necessity for a fresh consolid-
ecame again very urgent, and was effected in 1819. It was not, however, in the
s department only, or in the mere article of duties, that the merchant and ship-
were bewildered by the multiplicity of statutory regulations. There was not a
branch of the law regulating their transactions that escaped the rage for legislation.
usly to 1822, no fewer than 113 statutes had been passed relating to the fisheries ;
makers and buyers of sails and cordage were supposed to be familiar with the
obscure and contradictory regulations embodied in the *twenty-three* acts of
ent relating to these articles ! But the enormity of the abuse will be rendered
pparent, by laying before the reader the following extract from the Report of the
Committee on Foreign Trade in 1820.
fore," say their Lordships, " your committee proceed to advert to the points
ave been the principal objects of their inquiry, they are anxious to call the atten-
the House to the excessive accumulation and complexity of the laws under which
merce of the country is regulated, with which they were forcibly impressed in
y earliest stage of their proceedings. These laws, passed at different periods,
ny of them arising out of temporary circumstances, amount, as stated in a recent
ation of them, to upwards of *two thousand*, of which no less than 1,100 were in
1815 ; and many additions have been since made. After such a statement, it

will not appear extraordinary that it should be matter of complaint to the British m
chant, that, so far from the course in which he is to guide his transactions being p
and simple — so far from being able to undertake his operations, and to avail himsel
favourable openings, as they arise, with promptitude and confidence — he is freque
reduced to the necessity of resorting to the services of professional advisers, to ascert
what he may venture to do, and what he must avoid, before he is able to embark in
commercial adventures with the assurance of being secure from the consequences of
infringement of the law.   If this be the case (as is stated to your committee) with
most experienced among the merchants, even in England, in how much greater a deg
must the same perplexity and apprehension of danger operate in foreign countries ;
on foreign merchants, whose acquaintance with our statute book must be suppose
be comparatively limited, and who are destitute of the professional authority which
merchant at home may at all times consult for his direction ?   When it is recollect
besides, that a trivial unintentional deviation from the strict letter of the acts of par
ment may expose a ship and cargo to the inconvenience of seizure, which (whe
sustained or abandoned) is attended always with delay and expense, and freque
followed by litigation ; it cannot be doubted that such a state of the law must h
the most prejudicial influence both upon commercial enterprise in the country,
upon our mercantile relations and intercourse with foreign nations; and perhaps
service more valuable could be rendered to the trade of the empire, nor any meas
more effectually contribute to promote the objects contemplated by the House, in
appointment of this committee, than an accurate revision of this vast and confused m
of legislation ; and the establishment of some certain, simple, and consistent princi
to which all the regulations of commerce might be referred, and under which the tr
actions of merchants engaged in the trade of the United Kingdom might be conduc
with facility, safety, and confidence." — (*Report*, p. 4.)
Since this report was printed, a very considerable progress has been made in simpl
ing and clearing up the statute law on the principles laid down in it.   The law a
shipping and navigation has been particularly improved.   The principles laid dow
the famous navigation acts of 1650 and 1660 were, indeed, sufficiently distinct and
vious ; but when these acts were passed, there were above 200 statutes in existe
many of them antiquated and contradictory, which they did not repeal, except in so
as the regulations in them might be inconsistent with those in the new acts.
besides these, a number of statutes were passed almost in every session since 1
explaining, limiting, extending, or modifying in one way or other, some of the provis
of the navigation acts ; so that ultimately there were questions perpetually arising, a
which it was very difficult to discover the precise law.   On such occasions recourse
often had to the courts ; and the good sense and equity which generally character
their decisions mitigated the mischievous consequences resulting from the uncertain
the statute law, and even gave it the appearance of consistency.   Latterly, however,
uncertainty has been well nigh removed.   One of the bills introduced by Mr. Wa
for the improvement of the navigation laws repealed above *two hundred* statutes ! and
new acts substituted in the place of those that were repealed, are drawn up with laud
brevity and clearness.   The principal are — the 6 Geo. 4. c. 109. for the encourager
of British shipping and navigation, which may be called the present navigation law
Navigation Laws); the 6 Geo. 4. c. 110. for the registry of British vessels —
Registry); the 6 Geo. 4. c. 107., containing the regulations with respect to importa
and exportation—(see Importation and Exportation) ; and the act 6 Geo. 4. c.
for regulating the trade with the British possessions abroad—(see Colonies and Co
Trade).   Mr. Hume, formerly of the customs, now of the Board of Trade, had
principal share in the compilation of these acts, which do honour to his sagacity,
dustry, and talents for arrangement.
But we are gradually relapsing into the confusion whence we so lately esca
Every session gives birth to more or fewer acts making certain changes or modifica
in those referred to above.   Where these changes apply only to some particular e
gency, without affecting the general principles or rules laid down in the statutes,
can be no doubt that they should be embodied in separate acts ; but where any m
fication or alteration is to be made in the principles of the law, the better way,
appears to us, would be to introduce it directly into the leading act on the subje
re-enacting it in an amended or altered form.   In no other way is it possible to pre
that unity and clearness which are so very desirable.   The multiplication of statu
a very great evil, not only from the difficulty of ascertaining the exact degree in \
one modifies another, but from its invariably leading to the enactment of contrad
clauses.   The property and transactions of merchants ought not to depend upo
subtleties and niceties of forced constructions, but upon plain and obvious rules,
which there can be no mistake.   It would, however, be idle to expect that such

r be deduced from the conflicting provisions of a number of statutes: those in
e statute are not always in harmony with each other.

RK, or MARC, a weight used in several parts of Europe, for various
dities, especially gold and silver. In France, the mark was divided into
= 64 drachms = 192 deniers or pennyweights = 4,608 grains. In Hol-
he mark weight was also called Troy weight, and was equal to that of
. When gold and silver are sold by the mark, it is divided into 24

und, or *livre, poids de marc*, the weight most commonly used in retail dealings throughout
reviously to the Revolution, was equal to two marcs, and consequently contained 16 oz. =
: 384 den. = 9,216 grs. One kilogramme is nearly equal to two livres. — Subjoined is a table of
ds de marc, from 1 to 10, converted into kilogrammes. Any greater number may be learned by
multiplication and addition.

es.		Kilog.	Livres.		Kilog.	Livres.		Kilog.
	=	0·4895	5	=	2·4475	8	=	3·9160
	=	0·9790	6	=	2·9370	9	=	4·4056
	=	1·4685	7	=	3·4265	10	=	4·8951
	=	1·9580						

RK, a term sometimes used among us for a money of account, and in
ther countries for a coin. The English mark is two thirds of a pound
, or 13s. 4d.; and the Scotch mark is two thirds of a pound Scotch. The
bs, or Lubeck mark, used at Hamburgh, is a money of account, equal to
erling.

KET, a public place in a city or town, where provisions are sold. No
is to be kept within seven miles of the city of London; but all butchers,
rs, &c. may hire stalls and standings in the flesh-markets there, and sell
d other provisions. Every person who has a market is entitled to receive
the things sold in it; and, by ancient custom, for things standing in the
though not sold; but those who keep a market in any other manner
is granted, or extort tolls or fees where none are due, forfeit the same.
Fairs.)

SEILLES, a large commercial city and sea-port of France, on the Me-
ean, in lat. 43° 17¾′ N., lon. 5° 22¼′ E. Population 116,000. The
of Marseilles is in the centre of the city. It is completely sheltered
winds; but the water is not sufficiently deep to admit the largest class
. The *lazaretto* is spacious and convenient. Marseilles is a city of great
y, and has long enjoyed a very extensive commerce. It is the grand enfor the trade between France and the countries bordering on the Medi-
n. It exports colonial products, light woollens, silk, &c. to the Levant.
, the exports consist of all kinds of colonial produce, woollens, linens,
oil, hardware, and lead. The exports to England consist of brandy,
e, madder, wines, verdigrise, soap, and oil, preserved fruits, gloves, silks,
shawls, capers, anchovies, syrups, essences, perfumery, &c. The prin-
ports are, wheat from the Black Sea and the coast of Africa, sugar and
sh, raw cotton, indigo, pepper, iron, lead, dye-woods, hides, &c. Mar-
a free port; that is, goods may be warehoused free of duty for a speci-
od.

ies, *Weights*, and *Measures* of Marseilles are the same as those of the rest of France. — (See
)
874 French ships, carrying 87,886 tons, entered Marseilles; the foreign vessels entering the
being 1,174, carrying 102,487 tons.

TER, in commercial navigation, the person intrusted with the care and
n of the ship.

uation of master of a ship is so very important, that in some countries no one
pointed to it, who has not submitted to an examination by competent persons,
in his fitness for properly discharging its duties. (See the famous French
nce of 1681, tit. ii. art. 1., and the Ordonnance of the 7th of August, 1825.
r specifies the various subjects on which candidates shall be examined, and the
conducting the examination.) But in this country the owners are left to their
etion as to the skill and honesty of the master; and although he is bound to
d any damage that may happen to the ship and cargo by his negligence or
ness, he cannot be punished as a criminal for mere incompetence.
e is qualified to be the master of a British ship, unless he be a natural born
ubject, or naturalised by act of parliament, or a denizen by letters of deniza-
have become a subject of his Majesty by conquest, cession, &c., and have taken

3 B

the oaths of allegiance ; or a foreign seaman who has served three years, in time of
on board of his Majesty's ships.

" The master is the confidential servant or agent of the owners; and in confo
to the rules and maxims of the law of England, *the owners are bound to the perfor*
of every lawful contract made by him relative to the usual employment of the shi
(*Abbott* (now Lord Tenterden) *on the Law of Shipping*, part ii. c. 2.)

From this rule of law, it follows that the owners are bound to answer for a bre
contract, though committed by the master or mariners against their will, and w
their fault. — (*Id.*)   Nor can the expediency of this rule be doubted.   The ov
by selecting a person as master, hold him forth to the public as worthy of tru
confidence.   And in order that this selection may be made with due care, and th
opportunities of fraud and collusion may be obviated, it is indispensable that they s
be made responsible for his acts.

The master has power to hypothecate, or pledge, both ship and cargo for nec
repairs executed in foreign ports during the course of the voyage ; but neither the
nor cargo can be hypothecated for repairs *executed at home.*

The master has no lien upon the ship for his wages, nor for money advanced b
for stores or repairs.   In delivering judgment upon a case of this sort, Lord Mar
said—" As to wages, there is no particular contract that the ship should be a pledge ;
is no usage in trade to that purpose ; nor any implication from the nature of the de
On the contrary, the law has always considered the captain as contracting pers
with the owner ; and the case of the captain has, in that respect, been disting
from that of all other persons belonging to the ship. This rule of law may have its f
ation in policy, for the benefit of navigation ; for, as ships may be making profi
earning every day, it might be attended with great inconvenience, if, on the chang
captain for misbehaviour, or any other reason, he should be entitled to keep th
till he is paid. Work done for a ship in England is supposed to be done on the pe
credit of the employer : in foreign parts the captain may hypothecate the ship.
defendant might have told the tradesmen, that he only acted as an agent, and tha
must look to the owner for payment."

The master is bound to employ his whole time and attention in the service
employers, and is not at liberty to enter into any engagement for his own bene
may occupy any portion of his time in other concerns ; and therefore, if he do s
the price of such engagement happen to be paid into the hands of his owners, the
retain the money, and he cannot recover from them. — (*Abbott*, part ii. c. 4.)

During war, a master should be particularly attentive to the regulations as to s
under convoy ; for, besides his responsibility to his owners or freighters, he may b
secuted by the Court of Admiralty, and fined in any sum not exceeding 500*l.*, a
prisoned for any term not exceeding one year, if he wilfully disobey the s
instructions, or lawful commands of the commander of the convoy ; or des
without leave. — (43 *Geo.* 3. c. 160.)

Wilfully destroying or casting away the ship, or procuring the same to be d
the master or mariners, to the prejudice of the owners, freighters, or insurers ; r
away with the cargo ; and turning pirates ; are capital offences punishable by de
(7 & 8 *Geo.* 4. c. 29., and antecedent statutes.)

After the voyage has been commenced, the master must proceed direct to the p
his destination, without unnecessarily stopping at any intermediate port, or de
from the shortest course.   No such deviation will be sanctioned, unless it has beer
sioned by stress of weather, the want of necessary repair, avoiding enemies or
succouring of ships in distress, sickness of the master or mariners, or the mutiny
crew. — (*Marshall on Insurance*, book i. c. 6. § 3.)   To justify a deviation, the
sity must be real, inevitable, and imperious ; and it must not be prolonged one m
after the necessity has ceased.   A deviation without such necessity vitiates all ins
upon the ship and cargo, and exposes the owners to an action on the part of the frei
If a ship be captured in consequence of deviation, the merchant is entitled to
from the owners the prime cost of the goods, with shipping charges ; but he
entitled to more, unless he can show that the goods were enhanced in value beye
sum above mentioned.

If a merchant ship has the misfortune to be attacked by pirates or enemi
master is bound to do his duty as a man of courage and capacity, and to make
resistance that the comparative strength of his ship and crew will allow.

By the common law, the master has authority over all the mariners on board the
it being their duty to obey his commands in all lawful matters relating to the na
of the ship, and the preservation of good order.   But the master should, in al
use his authority with moderation, so as to be the father, not the tyrant, of hi
On his return home he may be called upon, by action at law, to answer to a ma

ither beat or imprisoned during the course of the voyage; and unless he show
ient cause for chastising the mariner, and also that the chastisement was reasonable
noderate, he will be found liable in damages. Should the master strike a mariner
ut cause, or use a deadly weapon as an instrument of correction, and death ensue,
ill be found guilty, according to the circumstances of the case, either of man-
hter or murder. — (*Abbott*, part ii. c. 4.)

e master may by force restrain the commission of great crimes; but he has no
iction over the criminal. His business is to secure his person, and to deliver him
o the proper tribunals on his coming to his own country. — (See art. SEAMEN.)

by shipwreck, capture, or other unavoidable accident, seamen, subjects of Great
in, be found in foreign parts, his Majesty's governors, ministers, consuls, or two or
British merchants, residing in such parts, may send such seamen home in ships of
or in merchant ships homeward bound in want of men; and if such ships cannot
und, they may send them home in merchant ships that are fully manned, but no
merchant ship shall be obliged to take on board more than *four* such persons for
100 tons burthen: and the master, upon arrival, and producing to the Navy
a certificate from the governor, minister, consul, &c. where he shipped the men,
is own affidavit of the time he maintained them, shall receive 1s. 6d. *per diem* for
ch seamen above his own complement of men. — (53 Geo. 3. c. 85.) A subsequent
e (58 Geo. 3. c. 38.) inflicts a penalty of 100l. on any master of a merchant
who shall refuse to take on board or bring home any seafaring man, a subject of
Britain, left behind in any foreign country, upon being required to do so by the
tent authorities.

master of a ship forcing any man on shore when abroad, or refusing to bring
uch of the men he carried out with him as are in a condition to return, shall,
conviction of such offence, be imprisoned for such term as the court shall award.
Geo. 4. c. 31.)

penalty of 20l. is imposed on every master of a vessel, who, having, on account of
ss, left any seafaring man at any foreign port or place, shall neglect or refuse to
an account of the wages due, and to pay the same. — (58 Geo. 3. c. 58.)

law makes no distinction between carriers by land and carriers by water. The
of a merchant ship is, in the eye of the law, a carrier; and is, as such, bound to
asonable and proper care of the goods committed to his charge, and to convey
o the place of their destination, *barring only the acts of God and the king's enemies.*
act which may be provided against by ordinary care, renders the master respon-
He would not, for example, be liable for damage done to goods on board in
uence of a leak in the ship occasioned by the violence of the tempest, or other
t; but if the leak were occasioned by rats he would be liable, for these might
een exterminated by ordinary care, as by putting cats on board, &c. On the
rinciple, if the master run the ship in fair weather against a rock or shallow
to expert mariners, he is responsible. If any injury be done to the cargo by
er or careless stowage, the master will be liable.

master must not take on board any contraband goods, by which the ship and
arts of the cargo may be rendered liable to forfeiture or seizure. Neither must
on board any false or colourable papers, as these might subject the ship to the
capture or detention. But it is his duty to procure and keep on board all the
and documents required for the manifestation of the ship and cargo, by the law
countries from and to which the ship is bound, as well as by the law of nations in
, or by treaties between particular states. These papers and documents cannot
ensed with at any time, and are quite essential to the safe navigation of neutral
uring war. — (See SHIPS' PAPERS.)

customary in bills of lading to insert a clause limiting the responsibility of the
and owners, as follows: — " *The act of God, the king's enemies, fire, and every
ngers and accidents of the seas, rivers, and navigation, of whatever nature and kind
save risk of boats, as far as ships are liable thereto, excepted.*" When no bill of
s signed, the master and owners are bound according to the common law.

most difficult part of the master's duty is when, through the perils of the sea,
cks of enemies or pirates, or other unforeseen accidents, he is prevented from
ing his voyage. If his own ship have suffered from storms, and cannot be re-
within a reasonable time, and if the cargo be of a *perishable nature*, he is *at liberty*
oy another ship to convey it to the place of destination. He may do the same
ip have been wrecked and the cargo saved, or if his own ship be in danger of
, and he can get the cargo transferred to another*; and in *extreme cases* he is at

___

most celebrated maritime codes, and the opinions of the ablest writers, have differed considerably
e points. According to the Rhodian law (Pand. l. 10. § 1.) the captain is released from all his en-
s, if the ship, by the perils of the sea, and without any fault on his part, become incapable of pro-

liberty to dispose of the cargo for the benefit of its owners. But, to use the word Lord Chief Justice Tenterden, " the disposal of the cargo by the master is a ma that requires the utmost caution on his part. He should always bear in mind that his *duty to convey it to the place of destination.* This is the purpose for which he been intrusted with it, and this purpose he is bound to accomplish by every reasona and practicable method. What, then, is the master to do, if, by any disaster happen in the course of his voyage, he is unable to carry the goods to the place of destinati or to deliver them there? To this, as a general question, I apprehend no answer be given. Every case must depend upon its own peculiar circumstances. The cond proper to be adopted with respect to perishable goods, will be improper with respec a cargo not perishable : one thing may be fit to be done with fish or fruit, and ano with timber or iron : one method may be proper in distant regions, another in the nity of the merchant ; one in a frequented navigation, another on unfrequented sho The wreck of the ship is not necessarily followed by an impossibility of sending forw the goods, and does not of itself make their sale a measure of necessity or expedien much less can the loss of the season, or of the proper course of the voyage, have this eff An unexpected interdiction of commerce, or a sudden war, may defeat the advent and oblige the ship to stop in her course ; but neither of these events doth of itself al make it necessary to sell the cargo at the place to which it may be proper for the to resort. In these and many other cases, the master may be discharged of his obli tion to deliver the cargo at the place of destination ; but it does not therefore follow he is authorised to sell it, or ought to do so. What, then, is he to do? In genera may be said, *he is to do that which a wise and prudent man will think most conducive to benefit of all concerned.* In so doing, he may expect to be safe, because the merch will not have reason to be dissatisfied ; but what this thing will be, no general rules teach. Some regard may be allowed to the interest of the ship, and of its owners ; the interest of the cargo must not be sacrificed to it. Trans-shipment for the plac destination, if it be practicable, is the first object, because that is in furtherance of original purpose : if that be impracticable, return, or a safe deposit, may be expedi A disadvantageous sale (and almost every sale by the master will be disadvantageou the last thing he thould think of, because it can only be justified by that necessity w supersedes all human laws." — (*Law of Shipping,* part iii. c. 3.)

The master of a ship is liable for goods of which she is robbed in part ; and reason, as Lord Mansfield stated, is, lest room should be given for collusion, and master should get himself robbed on purpose, in order that he might share in the s The master is, however, entitled to indemnify himself out of the seamen's wages losses occasioned by their neglect.

If any passenger die on board, the master is obliged to take an inventory of his effe and if no claim be made for them within a year, the master becomes proprietor of goods, but answerable for them to the deceased's legal representatives. Bedding furniture become the property of the master and mate ; but the clothing must be bro to the mast head, and there appraised and distributed among the crew.

If a master die, leaving money on board, and the mate, becoming master, improv money, he shall, on allowance being made to him for his trouble, account both for i est and profits.

No master is to proceed on any voyage for parts beyond the seas without previc coming to an agreement, *in writing,* with his mariners, for their wages. If he do s shall forfeit, for every mariner so taken without a written agreement, 5*l.* — (2 Ge c. 36. § 1.)

The master of every vessel is required by the 2 Geo. 2. c. 36. to keep a reg account of the penalties and forfeitures due to Greenwich Hospital in consequen the mariners' disobedience, to deduct the same from their wages, and to pay the am thereof to the collector of the Greenwich Hospital duty, within three months after deduction, upon pain of forfeiting treble the value thereof to the use of the said pital.

Masters of vessels laden with coals are directed by 6 Geo. 4. c. 107. § 12

ceeding on her voyage. The laws of Oleron (art. 4.), and those of Wisby (arts. 16. 37. 55.), say th captain *may hire another ship ;* harmonising in this respect with the present law of England. The f French ordinance of 1681 (tit. *Du Frêt,* art. 11.), and the *Code de Commerce* (art. 296.), *order the cap hire another ship ;* and if he cannot procure one, freight is to be due only for that part of the which has been performed (*pro ratâ itineris peracti*). Valin has objected to this article, and state practically it meant only that the captain must hire another ship if he would earn the whole f Emerigon (tom. i. p. 428.) holds that the captain, being the agent not only of the owners of the sh also of the shippers of the goods on board, is bound, in the absence of both, to use his best endeavo preserve the goods, and to do whatever, in the circumstances, he thinks will most conduce to the i of all concerned ; or what it may be presumed the shippers would do, were they present. This, seems to be the best and wisest rule, has been laid down by Lords Mansfield and Tenterden, as above, and may be regarded as the law of England on this point.

e to any officer of customs demanding its production, a copy of the certificate
lly delivered to them by the fitters or vendors, and to deliver the certificate to the
r or comptroller of the port to which the coals are carried.

the duty of the master, as respects Custom-house regulations, see the articles
ATION AND EXPORTATION, QUARANTINE, SMUGGLING, &c.; and for a further dis-
of this important subject, see the excellent work of *Lord Tenterden on the Law*
ing, part iii. c. 3. &c.; *Chitty on Commercial Law*, vol. iii. cap. 8. &c.; and the
CHARTERPARTY, FREIGHT, &c. in this Dictionary.)

STICH, OR MASTIC (Ger. *Mastix*; Du. *Mastik*; Fr. *Mastic*; It. *Mas-*
p. *Almastica*, *Almaciga*; Arab. *Arāh*). This resinous substance is the
e of the *Pistacia lentiscus*, a native of the Levant, and particularly abundant in
nd of Chios. It is obtained by making transverse incisions in the trunks
nches of the trees, whence the mastic slowly exudes. About 1,500 cwt. are
y exported from Chios, part of which is brought to this country packed in
The best is in the form of dry, brittle, yellowish, transparent tears; it is
inodorous, except when heated, and then it has an agreeable odour;
, it is almost insipid, feeling at first gritty, and ultimately soft; its virtues
ing. — (*Ainslie's Materia Indica; Thomson's Dispensatory.*)

TE, of a merchant ship, the vice master, or second in command. The
kes an account of all goods received on board, and usually passes a receipt
same, prior to the bills of lading being signed; and he likewise takes an
of the delivery of all goods from on board the ship. He commands in
nce of the master, and shares the duty with him when at sea.

nate of a ship of war is generally appointed by the master. The number
officers, whether in ships of war or merchantmen, is always in propor-
the size of the vessel. A first rate man-of-war has six; an East India-
same number; a frigate of 20 guns, and a small merchantman, only one;
intermediate vessels in proportion to their respective sizes. On board a
war, the regulation of the watch, the keeping the log-book, examining the
glasses, adjusting the sails, and attending to the cables, stowage, ballast,
visions, are duties incumbent on the mates. All the assistants of the
s on board are denominated mates; the surgeon, the gunner, carpenter,
in, cook, &c. have their respective mates.

RITIUS. By the act 6 Geo. 4. c. 111. § 12., the island of Mauritius is
to be one of his Majesty's sugar colonies, and is placed, in all respects,
e same footing as the sugar colonies in the West Indies. — (See PORT

D, OR METHEGLIN (Ger. *Meht, Meth*; Du. *Meede, Meedrank*;
romel; It. *Idromele*; Sp. *Aguamiel*; Rus. *Lipez*), the ancient, and, for
time, the favourite drink of the northern nations. It is a preparation
y and water. Manufacturers of mead for sale must take out an annual

L (Ger. *Mehl*; Du. *Meel*; Fr. and It. *Farine*; Sp. *Farina*; Rus.
Lat. *Farina*), the edible part of wheat, oats, rye, barley, and pulse of
kinds, ground into a species of coarse flour.

ALS, are pieces of metal, generally in the form of a coin, and impressed
ne peculiar stamp, intended to commemorate some individual or action.
are of very different prices — varying according to their rarity and pre-
, the fineness of the metal, the beauty of the workmanship, &c.

ITERRANEAN PASS. The nature of this sort of instrument has been
by Mr. Reeves, in his Treatise on the Law of Shipping, as follows : —
he treaties that have been made with the Barbary states, it has been agreed,
ubjects of the King of Great Britain should pass the seas unmolested by the
f those states; and for better ascertaining what ships and vessels belong to
bjects, it is provided, that they shall produce *a pass*, under the hand and seal
rd High Admiral, or the Lords Commissioners of the Admiralty. In pursuance
reaties, passes are made out at the Admiralty, containing a very few words,
n parchment, with ornaments at the top, through which a scolloped inden-
ade : the *scolloped tops* are sent to Barbary; and being put in possession of their
he commanders are instructed to suffer all persons to pass who have passes
fit these scolloped tops. The protection afforded by these passes is such, that
which traverse the seas frequented by these rovers, ever fail to furnish them-
th them, whether in the trade to the East Indies, the Levant, Spain, Italy, or

any part of the Mediterranean; and from the more particular need of them i
latter, they, no doubt, obtained the name of *Mediterranean passes*. For the acco
dation of merchants in distant parts, blank passes, signed by the Lords of the Adm
are lodged with the governors abroad, and with the British consuls, to be gran
those who comply with the requisites necessary for obtaining them. As this pi
security is derived wholly from the stipulations made by the crown with a f
power, the entire regulation and management of it has been under the directi
his Majesty, who, with the advice of his privy council, has prescribed the term
conditions on which these passes shall be granted. Among others are the f
ing: — They are to be granted for none but British built ships, or ships made
navigated with a master and three fourths of the mariners British subjects, or f
protestants made denizens. Bond is to be given in the sum of 300*l.* if the ve
under 100 tons, and in 500*l.* if it is of that or more, for delivering up the pass
12 months, unless in the case of ships trading from one foreign port to another
such passes need not be returned in less than 3 years.

" It has been found expedient, at the conclusion of a war, and sometimes du
peace, to recall and cancel all passes that have been issued, and to issue others in
form. This has been done for two reasons. First, That these useful instrumer
various means, either accidental or fraudulent, came into the hands of foreigners
under cover of them, carried on in security a trade which otherwise would belo
British subjects, and which had been purchased by the crown, at the expense of
ing up this sort of alliance. Secondly, That the Barbary states complained,
adhering to the rule of fitting the other part of the indenture to the passes, the
obliged to suffer ships to pass that did not belong to British subjects."

The act 52 Geo. 3. c. 143. makes the forging of a Mediterranean pass felony without the be
clergy. The 9 Geo. 4. c. 76. enacts, that no Mediterranean pass shall be issued for the benefit
person as being an inhabitant of Malta or of Gibraltar, but not being a person entitled to be an o
a British registered ship, unless such person shall have resided at Malta or Gibraltar, respe
upwards of 15 years previously to the 10th of October, 1827.
Mediterranean passes are either granted for one voyage, or are attached to the ship's certi
registry, and are in force so long as the said certificate. A stamp duty of 2*l.* is charged on each
issued. When issued in the Colonies, they continue in force for 12 months to colonial ships, and
voyage to British ships supplied with them. The duty on such passes is 5*s.* We subjoin

An Account of the Amount paid by Ships for the Mediterranean Pass; stating the Number of
granted, the aggregate Amount received in the Years 1828-9, and to what Purpose the sa
applied. — (*Parl. Paper*, No. 132. Sess. 1830.)

No. of Passes.	For what Time in Force.	Stamp Duty on each.	Aggregate Charge on each.	
	1828.	£ s. d.	£ s. d.	£
220 - -	One voyage - - - - - -	2 0 0	2 10 0	55
342 - -	Attached to the ship's certificate of registry, and in force so long as the said certificate -	2 0 0	5 5 0	1,79
200 - -	Issued in the Colonies, and in force for 12 months to colonial ships, and for one voyage to British ships supplied with them - -	0 5 0	2 0 0	40
				2,74
	Deduct stamp duties -			1,17
			£	1,57
	1829.			
200 - -	One voyage - - - - - -	2 0 0	2 10 0	5
330 - -	Attached to the ship's certificate of registry, and in force so long as the said certificate -	2 0 0	5 5 0	1,79
250 - -	Issued in the Colonies, and in force for 12 months to colonial ships, and for one voyage to British ships supplied with them - -	0 5 0	2 0 0	50
				2,74
	Deduct stamp duties -			1,00
			£	1,68

The foregoing fees for Mediterranean passes, after deducting the sums paid for stamps, ha
applied as all other fees are, in aid of the sum voted on the navy estimate for the contingent
of the Admiralty Office.

MEMEL, a commercial town of East Prussia, in lat. 55° 42¼′ N
21° 5⅛′ E. Population 6,500. Being situated near the junction of t
denominated the *Currische haf* with the Baltic, Memel is the principal *entr*
the country traversed by the Niemen, and has, consequently, an extensive
trade. The harbour is large and safe, but the entrance to it is encumbere
sand banks, and is rather shallow and dangerous, so that ships drawing
18 feet water usually load and unload a part of their cargoes in the roads.
forms the principal article of export; for though that of Dantzic be con
better, it is generally cheaper and more abundant at Memel. It comes pri

the estates of Prince Radzivil, and is floated down the river in rafts. The
quality of all sorts of wood articles is called crown. Large quantities of hemp
flax are also exported, as are bristles, hides, linseed (the finest for crushing
ght to England), wax, pitch and tar, &c. The exports of grain are sometimes
considerable. The wheat of Lithuania is reckoned the best. All flax and hemp
ed from Memel must be *bracked*, or assorted by sworn selectors. — (See FLAX,
HEMP.) The imports consist principally of coffee, sugar, spices, dye-woods,
co, rum, cotton stuffs and yarn, cutlery, &c. Merchants at Memel generally
their bills to Königsberg to be sold, charging their correspondents with 1 per
for bank commission, postages, &c. The navigation generally closes about
atter end of December, and opens about the middle of March.

e *Monies, Weights,* and *Measures* of Memel are the same as those of Dantzic;
a see.

unt of the Ships despatched from Memel; distinguishing those loaded with Grain, Wood, &c.;
from 1814 to 1824.

s.	With Grain and Seeds.		With Wood, &c.		British Ships.	Prussian Ships.	Ships of other Nations.	Total.	
	Ships.	Lasts.	Ships.	Lasts.				Ships.	Lasts.
4	101	5,050	424	52,740	-	-	-	525	57,790
5	29	1,490	411	46,510	132	205	103	440	48,000
5	100	5,500	348	39,893	132	134	182	448	45,393
7	141	11,303	475	62,404	300	101	215	616	73,707
3	141	8,491	665	85,985	413	141	252	806	94,476
9	129	5,989	546	66,836	268	153	254	675	72,825
0	125	8,607	523	60,189	267	152	229	648	68,796
1	23	997	509	62,892	325	97	110	532	63,889
2	2	82	636	84,829	421	146	121	688	84,911
3	6	305	644	79,544	332	185	133	650	79,649
4	10	545	866	104,250	420	327	129	876	104,795
5 to ept.	-	-	-	-	508	181			

umber of lasts of the British, Prussian, and other ships, and the quantity of wheat, rye, and seed,
ot be obtained separately. A ship's or rye last is equal to about 1½ ton British measurement.
. No. 7. to *Mr. Jacob's First Report on the Agriculture of North of Europe.*)

RCURY, OR QUICKSILVER (Fr. *l'if argent;* Ger. *Quicksilber;* It. Ar-
vivo; Sp. *Azogue;* Rus. *Rtut;* Lat. *Hydrargyrum;* Arab. *Zibākh;* Hind.
; Sans. *Pārada*). This metal was known in the remotest ages, and seems
e been employed by the ancients in gilding, and separating gold from other
, just as it is by the moderns. Its colour is white, and similar to that of
; hence the names of *hydrargyrum, argentum vivum, quicksilver,* by which it
en known in all ages. It has no taste or smell. It possesses a good deal
liancy; and when its surface is not tarnished, it makes a very good mirror.
ecific gravity is 13·568. It differs from all other metals in being always
inless when subjected to a degree of cold equal to — 39°, when it becomes
    The congelation of mercury was first observed in 1759. — (*Thomson's*
try.)

cury is found in various parts of the world. Among the principal mines are
f Almaden, near Cordova, in Spain; Idria, in Carniola; Wolfstein and Morsfield,
Palatinate; Guancavelica, in Peru, &c. " Most of the ores of mercury are readily
uished from those of any other metal; in the first variety, globules of the metal are
tached to or just starting on the surface, which is at once a sufficient criterion,
y being unlike every other metal; in the second, by the fine white colour, and
on of the blow-pipe, which sublimes the mercury and leaves the silver behind;
d, by its beautiful deep red tint, varying from cochineal to scarlet red, excepting
e termed hepatic cinnabars, which are generally of a lead grey; the fourth, by its
olour, its partial solubility in water, and its complete volatilisation by heat, emitting
ame time an arsenical odour. Before the blow-pipe, these varieties burn with a
me and sulphurous odour, leaving more or less residue behind them, and which
nsist of earthy matter, as silex and alumina, together with the oxides of iron and
" — (*Joyce's Chem. Min.*)

cury is often adulterated by the admixture of lead, bismuth, zinc, and tin. When
al quickly loses its lustre, is covered with a film, or is less fluid and mobile than
r does not readily divide into round globules, there is reason to suspect its purity.
. stated by Dr. A. T. Thomson, in his Dispensatory — a work generally
ished for its accuracy — that most of the mercury used in this country is brought
ermany. But whatever may have been the case formerly, this is not certainly
present. On the contrary, of 635,905 lbs. of quicksilver imported in 1829, only

5,505 lbs. were brought from Germany; 574,136 lbs. were brought direct from Sp
and 56,137 lbs. from Gibraltar: of the latter, a part was derived from Carniola, ar
part from Spain; only 162,816 lbs. were retained for home consumption in 1829, of
total quantity imported. — (*Parl. Paper*, No. 153. Sess. 1831.)

There are two sulphurets of mercury; the black or *ethiops mineral*, and the red or
nabar. When mercury and sulphur are triturated together in a mortar, the former
dually disappears, and the whole assumes the form of a black powder, denomin
ethiops mineral. If this powder be heated red hot, it sublimes; and on a proper ve
being placed to receive it, a cake is obtained of a fine red colour, which is called
nabar. This cake, when reduced to powder, is well known in commerce by the na
of *vermilion*. Cinnabar may be prepared in various other ways.

Calomel, or protochloride of mercury (*mercurius dulcis*), is the most useful of all
preparations obtained from it. It is in the form of a dull white, semi-transparent m
having a specific gravity of 7·176. It is more generally employed, and with better ef
than almost any other remedy in the whole range of the materia medica.

Besides its uses in medicine, mercury is extensively employed in the amalgamatio
the noble metals, in water-gilding, the making of vermilion, the silvering of look
glasses, the making of barometers and thermometers, &c.

MILE, the usual measure of roads in England, being 8 furlongs, or 1,760 ya

MILK (Fr. *Lait;* It. *Latte;* Lat. *Lac*), a fluid secreted by the female of
those animals denominated *mammalia*, and evidently intended for the nourishn
of her offspring. The milk of every animal has certain peculiarities which dis
guish it from all other milk. But the animal whose milk is most used by m
and with which, consequently, we are best acquainted, is the cow. The exte
character of all milk is that of a white opaque fluid, having a sweetish taste, ar
specific gravity somewhat greater than that of water. When allowed to ren
at rest, it separates into two parts; a thick whitish fluid called *cream*, collec
in a thin stratum over its surface, and a more dense watery body remaining bel
Milk which has stood for some time after the separation of the cream, beco
acescent, and then coagulates. When the coagulum is pressed gently, a ser
fluid is forced out, and there remains the caseous part of the milk, or pure che

Butter, one of the most valuable animal products, is solidified cream, and is obta
artificially by churning. — (See **Butter.**)

Milk has always been a favourite food of most European nations, and especially o
British. *Lacte et carne vivunt*, says Cæsar of our ancestors; and the same articles
continue to form a large part of our subsistence. Mr. Middleton estimates (*Agricult
Survey of Middlesex*, 2d ed. p. 419.), that, in 1806, no fewer than 8,500 milch cows
kept for the supply of London and its environs with milk and cream; and he estim
the average quantity of milk obtained from each cow at *nine quarts* a day, or 3,285 qu
a year, leaving, every deduction being taken into account, 3,200 quarts for market
produce.

If Mr. Middleton be well founded in these estimates, we may reasonably calc
the number of cows that are at present kept in London and its environs at 9,000,
their annual produce at 28,800,000 quarts of milk. Now, as milk is sold by the reta
at 4*d.* a quart after the cream is separated from it, and as the cream is usually so
3*s.* a quart, and there is reason to suspect that a good deal of water is intermixed
the milk, we believe we should not be warranted in estimating that the milk, as obta
from the cow, is sold at less than 6*d.* a quart, which gives 720,000*l.* as the total pri
the milk consumed in the city and its immediate vicinity. If to this sum were a
the further sums paid for cheese and butter, the magnitude of the entire sum paid in
metropolis for milk, and the various products derived from it, would appear astonis

MILLET (Ger. *Hirse;* Fr. *Millet, Mil;* It. *Miglio, Panicastrello;* Sp. I
Lat. *Milium, Panicum miliaceum*). There are three distinct species of millet;
Polish millet, the common or German millet, and the Indian millet. It is cultiv
as a species of grain; and is sometimes employed to feed poultry, and as a subst
for rice. The Indian millet grows to a large size; but the autumns in Englan
seldom dry and warm enough to allow of its being cultivated here. — (*Lou
Ency. of Agriculture.*)

MILL-STONES (Ger. *Mühlstcine;* Fr. *Pierres meulières;* It. *Mole Ma
Sp. *Muelas de molino;* Rus. *Schernowoi kamen*), the large circular stones, w
when put in motion by machinery, grind corn and other articles. The dia
of common mill-stones is from 5 to 7 feet, and their thickness varies from 12
inches. These stones have been principally imported from Rouen and other
of France; the burr-stones of that country being supposed more durable tha

Mill-stones are, however, found at Conway, in North Wales, and in some f Scotland, which are said to equal any imported from foreign countries. mill-stones usually last 35 or 40 years.

ING COMPANIES. By this designation is commonly meant the asso- s formed in London, a few years ago, for working mines in Mexico and America.

mania for mining concerns, which began in London in 1824, after the opening ico and other parts of Spanish America to our intercourse, was such as to form a ible, and, we are sorry to add, disgraceful, æra in our commercial history. Now madness is past, we have difficulty in conceiving how men in the habit of sober ion could have been led to entertain such romantic expectations, and to pay gh premiums for shares in distant and uncertain undertakings. We may, there- excused for appropriating a page or two to the history of an infatuation hardly to that which led to the South Sea and Mississippi schemes.

mining companies formed at the outset had, in some degree, a basis for ble expectation, their directors having made contracts for a number of valuable n Mexico, — for those which are described by Humboldt as having been the f fortune to many hundred Mexican families. This applied to the Real del Company, whose mines are situated in the mountainous district of that name; to glo-Mexican Company, whose mines are at Guanaxuato, the greatest mining in Mexico; and to the United Mexican Company, whose contracts, though far ly spread, comprise several of the most valuable mines at Zacatecas, Sombrerete, uato, and other parts.

of these associations was formed in London in the beginning of 1824, and during ng and summer of that year their stock or shares bore only a small premium; rds the winter there took place a progressive rise of premium, to the surprise of of the directors; as it arose less from favourable intelligence of the mines (for unts from Mexico merely reported the arrival of the English agents at their e districts), than from a blind ardour and spirit of speculation in the public, — which, seeing nothing tempting in our own funds, or in those of continental directed itself to distant objects, and particularly to Spanish America. It ap- s if our countrymen were about to reap an immediate harvest; to lay their hands asure which had been hid for ages. America, it was said, had been discovered, ense, above three centuries; but this was the true discovery, — the effectual its resources. Every new contract for a mine in Mexico produced a rise in s of the companies, as if this fresh undertaking must necessarily be a source of And the result was, that in January, 1825, the premium on the shares of each mpanies mentioned above, exceeded cent. per cent., although no clear or definite uld be given for the advance. It must not, however, be imagined that this ice was occasioned solely by the competition of those who intended to continue tock, and to trust to the dividends made by the company for a return. That the case in the first instance, is, speaking generally, true. But others, actuated ifferent views, speedily entered the field. A peculiar combination of circum- at the head of which must be placed an almost incredible degree of ignorance on the part of a considerable portion of the public, spread a spirit of gambling ll classes. Many who were most eager in the pursuit of shares, intended only hem for a few days or weeks, to profit by the rise which they anticipated would e, by selling them to others more credulous or bold than themselves. The e of one set of speculators confirmed that of others. Meanwhile the public y, or rather its indiscriminating rapacity, was liberally administered to. Com- r company was formed without any previous contract; in other words, without dation whatever! The plan was to fix on a district in America understood to nines; to form a company bearing the name of such district; to obtain a first from the shareholders, and to send out agents, or commissioners as they were o survey the district and engage mines. Such was the case of most of those he names of districts in South America, which are subjoined to the present t: it was the case also of the Hispaniola or St. Domingo Company, which was n the faith of the accounts given by Dr. Robertson of mines wrought in that me three centuries ago! And yet lawyers, clergymen, and even the nobles of were candidates for shares in these miserable bubbles, in the hope of finding , luckily, most of them were disappointed) some dupe to buy their shares at a *

who may be desirous of seeing the extent to which the public credulity was practised upon 1825, may consult a pamphlet published by H. English, broker, in 1827, which contains an all the joint stock companies formed and projected in these memorable years. It presents a rdinary picture. There were in all 74 mining companies formed and projected! The num-

As the year 1825 proceeded, the mining mania gradually declined, from a f
off, not in the prospects of the companies, but in the supply of money in Lo
Speculative merchants had made immense importations of cotton, silk, wool, ti
and other articles; money was, of course, wanted to pay for these; the banks were dra
discounts became difficult; mining shares and South American stock were br
to sale; and the holders found, to their cost, that the public had recovered its s
The panic in December, 1825, took place: the shares of the three principal comp
some of which had been at a premium of 500 per cent., fell to par; that is, 10
money, and no more, could be got for 100l. of the company's stock! This price
maintained a considerable time, because most of the parties interested cont
to have a favourable impression of the issue of their undertakings. Demands,
ever, were made for more money to meet the expenditure abroad: the shareh
felt all the pressure of these demands after their incomes at home had bee
duced by the change of times; and in the course of the years 1826 and 1827 m
shares progressively declined, so that 100l. of their stock fetched only 20l. or 2
money. The bubble companies were entirely destroyed, and the few only rem
who had some foundation to go upon.

Even these would have been relinquished, or have shrunk into very small d
sions, had not the directors had the power of enforcing further payments, by f
ing, in default of such, whatever had been previously paid by the subscribers.
usage was, that on becoming a shareholder each person subscribed the Deed of the
pany, engaging to pay, when called on, such instalments or sums to account (gen
10l. on each share) as should be required by the directors, until completing the
ment of the 100l. Now, a shareholder who had advanced so much as 60l. c
naturally consented to pay 10l. from time to time, rather than incur the forfeiture
that he had advanced. Those who held only a few shares felt this in a less degree
to the holders of a number of shares, the grievance was most serious. They rais
money with great difficulty; often selling at a heavy loss their family property, c
vailing on relations to make them advances, to their great inconvenience, and, as
can yet be seen, with very little prospect of a return from the mines; — a mem
lesson of the caution that should be exercised before signing any engagement
nature of a company deed. Resentment would be excited against the director
they not been, in general, the heaviest sufferers: their regulations required th
hold a certain number of shares (perhaps 20 or 30); but in their blind confidenc
frequently held 200 or 300, and drew on themselves a proportional sacrifice; in s
cases, the loss of their whole property.

The managers of the companies formed in the outset are chargeable with ign
only: they trespassed not knowingly, but from want of information. There h
then been no communication between this country and Spanish America; the mo
enforced by Old Spain had prevented it. Of the Spaniards settled in Mexic
driven from it by the civil wars and consequent emancipation of the country, n
almost none, found their way to this country; they repaired to Cuba, to the so
France, or to Spain. Nor were our printed accounts of the country entitled to
confidence: Humboldt's Travels formed the chief authority; but their illustrious a
though generally cautious, seems, in this instance, to have placed too much conf
in vague exaggerated statements. Our merchants knew generally that silver
formed a main branch of the productive industry of Mexico, and had enriched very
families originally in humble circumstances; but they had no idea of the ex
injury sustained by the mines during the civil war, nor of the amount of exper
required to bring them into a working state: nor were they aware how little use
formation they could expect from the natives; the working of the mines, like
operation requiring skill and intelligence, having been superintended by natives
Spain, who had either fallen in the civil war, or been expelled by the laws
against them after the Mexicans had succeeded in the contest. The agents of ou
panies thus found on the spot only native Mexicans, — men without education o
rience in business, and, it must be added, without any due sense of the importance
dour or probity. They urged our countrymen to drain the mines, not by machin
which they had no idea, but by animal power, the use of which was of advantage
Mexican landholders, by employing their horses, and creating a great consump
maize, — the principal grain of that country, as wheat is in England, and rye in th
of Germany. Then, as to the last and most important stage in the business of
— the mode of extracting the silver from the ore, — the Mexicans, wholly unacq
with the improvements made in Germany during the last half century, recom

ber and quality of the other schemes were similar. It is due to Mr. Baring to say that he denot
evil when in progress; and warned the unthinking multitude of the ruin they were bringing up
selves; but to no purpose.

gamation, — a process conducted by them in a very rude manner, and which, in
qualities of silver ore, fails to extract the whole, or any thing like the whole, of the
The object of the Mexicans, in short, was merely to cause English capital to be
ated among them; thus giving employment to their people for a time, and bringing
ines into an improved state, — in which state they (the Mexicans) might hope to
e them after our countrymen should have exhausted their resources, or have be-
weary of their contracts.

tuated by these views, the Mexicans pressed one undertaking after another on the
s of the companies, who, of themselves, were too eager to enter on them. All the
anies fell into errors of the same kind, viz. engaging with too many mines, and
cting them for a time as if their funds were to have no end. They reckoned on
g, as they proceeded, a fund in the produce of the mines; but that produce, though
erable in quantity, seldom yielded the expected result, owing to the very imperfect
d of extracting the silver from the ore, as well as to the various disadvantages
ant on the vast distance of those undertakings from this country. These disad-
ges were ill supplied by the agents of the companies on the spot. Mining in
nd is not conducted on a scale of such extent as to afford any great choice of
ntendents for mines abroad: it was necessary, in such appointments, to waive the
ication of mining knowledge, and to be satisfied with men of fair character and
d ability in their respective professions, however different from mining. Hence
pointment, as agents, of several officers, *naval and military, on the half pay list*;
whatever might be their personal merits, had habits very different from those that
ere required. The habits of mercantile men were more suitable; but a merchant
mployed in business was not likely to relinquish or suspend it; and in those who
dle age are not fully employed, it is not uncharitable to ascribe it to faults of their
such as vacillation, want of exertion, or deficient judgment. This suffices to
t for the disappointments of the companies in a very material point — the conduct
ir commissioners or agents abroad; for, of the whole number, it would be diffi-
point out above two or three who were entitled to the praise of judicious manage-
The same applied to most of the inferior *employés*, — to the practical miners, the
and the mechanics.

ther cause of the absorption of the capital of the companies was the expense of
ing the requisite machinery from the coast of Mexico to the mining districts,
are generally at a great distance in the interior. That country has few practicable
draught carriages are almost unknown, and burdens are carried on the backs of
and horses: add to this, that Mexico being under-peopled, labour is nearly as
s in the United States of North America; and the mechanical arts being in a
r unknown, all skilled workmen, such as carpenters, blacksmiths, and working
ers, were sent from England at a heavy expense.

were the chief causes of the failure of the Mexican mining companies; and several
e may be referred to one radical disadvantage — the non-existence of silver mines
land. We have, in Cornwall and in North Wales, considerable mines of tin and
, while in the northern counties we have mines of lead; but of silver we have
at deserve the name. How much better had it been that our countrymen had
with a consciousness that Germany is the only country in Europe, or indeed in
ilised world, in which the treatment of silver ore is conducted on scientific prin-
The Saxons at Freyberg succeed in extracting a profit from ore of very inferior
, often worth only a fourth or fifth part of the ore raised at present in abundance
Mexicans for account of our companies, but which, wrought by their crude, in-
t, and expensive process, fails to afford any thing like a satisfactory return.
seems no reason to doubt that the German process may be applied to silver
Mexico as in Europe: the difficulties arise, not from difference in the quality of
, but from the want of experienced smelters, and the general backwardness of the
ns in mechanics. A German mining company established in Mexico has not
ucceeded; but they have had to contend with the same difficulties as the English
ies, with the additional disadvantage of insufficient capital; so that their methods
t had a fair trial.

out pretending to anticipate the result of these remote speculations, we shall
e with a brief notice of the considerations on both sides of the question. The
stances adverse to the success of mining companies in America, conducted for
t of parties in England or in any part of Europe, are —
he various disadvantages of distant management. These are so many and so
, as to admit of only one corrective, — selling the ore as soon as raised, and trans-
to individuals, for their own account, the extraction of the metal, as is done in
ll, and, in a somewhat different manner, in Saxony. The ores also ought to be
y paying the workmen, not fixed wages, but a tribute or portion of the proceeds.

2. The half civilised state of the inhabitants, their unsettled political condition, the probability of changes of the parties in power. For this there seems no reme except the ascendancy of an eminent political leader like Washington, or a close con tion with one of the great powers of Europe.

3. The high price of labour; the ignorance of the natives as to mechanics, and more as to science. Hence the necessity of having artisans and confidential supe tendents from Europe at a heavy expense.

On the other hand, the circumstances in favour of such undertakings are —

1. The abundance of silver ore, which is far greater than in any part of Europe.

2. The former success of mining in Mexico, under a system extremely rude expensive, compared to that which is now followed in Germany.

3. The probability of continued peace in Europe, and of an abundance of mor capital; so that the failure of the present companies would not involve a relinquishm of their enterprises, any more than the failure of the first New River Company, ab two centuries ago, implied an abandonment of their project. Succeeding adventu might come forward, and pursue the same object on a more judicious plan, and more ample funds.

English Mining Companies connected with America, which are still carried on.

United Mexican.	Anglo-Mexican.	Brazilian (two companies).
Real del Monte.	Mexican.	Colombian.
Bolanos.		

The amount of capital invested by these companies is about 5,000,000l. sterling.

Mining Companies connected with America, formed in 1825, but long since dissolved.

Anglo-Chilian.	Famatina.	Peruvian.
Anglo-Peruvian.	General South American.	Potosi La Par.
Bolivar.	Gold Coast (Africa).	Rio de la Plata.
Chilian.	Haytian.	Tlalpuxahua.
Chilian and Peruvian.	Pasco Peruvian.	United Pacific.
Castello.		

The sums raised by these companies were not large; in general only 5 per cent. on their pro capital.

There were also various companies formed in 1825, for mining in England: they were to the numb 30 and upwards; but they proved in general abortions, with the exception of the British Iron Com (with works chiefly in Staffordshire), which has drawn a large sum from its shareholders.

The following extract from the Share List for July 1831, published by Mr. Edmonds, broker, giv account of the existing mining companies; the number of shares in each; the sums paid on acc of such shares; and their selling price, &c. It is an instructive commentary on the prospectuses prices of 1825.

Number of Shares.	Mining Companies.		Average Cost.			Price per Share.		Divid. per Annum.	Divi pay
			£	s.	d.	£	s.	£ s.	
14,000	Anglo-Mexican	- - -	100l. sh.	100	0 0 pd.	21	0		
2,000	Bolanos - - -	-	150l. sh.	150	0 0 pd.	160	0	6 0	
10,000	Bolivar - - -	-	50l. sh.	17	0 0 pd.				
10,000	Brazilian (issued at 5l. premium)		35l. sh.	25	0 0 pd.	46	0	3 6	
6,000	Brazilian - -	-	25l. sh.	5	0 0 pd.	4	10		
6,000	Brazilian (National)	-	25l. sh.	15	0 0 pd.	7	0 pm		
20,000	British Iron - -	-	50l. sh.	48	15 0 pd.	7	0		
10,000	Colombian (issued at 5l. premium)		100l. sh.	45	0 0 pd.	6	0		
20,000	General Mining -	-	20l. sh.	8	0 0 pd.	7	0		
10,000	Hibernian - -	-	50l. sh.	10	0 0 pd.	4	5		
1,000	Real del Monte Mines, Mexico		400l. sh.	400	0 0 pd.	28	0		
30,000	United Mexican -	-	40l. sh.	39	10 0 pd.	7	15		
	Ditto Scrip	- -	-	2	0 0 pd.	1	0		
	United Mexican ditto (New)		- -	8	8 0 pd.				
20,000	Mining Company, Ireland	-	25l. sh.	5	10 0 pd.	6	0		
5,000	Brazilian St. John del Rey	-	20l. sh.	7	10 0 pd.	4	6		
14,000	Ditto Cocaes -	-	- -	5	0 0 pd.	4	10		
2,800	English Mining Company	-	25l. sh.	12	10 0 pd.	19	0	4 0	
6,155	Mexican Company -	-	100l. sh.	40	0 0 pd.	33	15 dis.		

MINIUM, or RED OXIDE OF LEAD, a tasteless powder of an int red colour, often inclining to orange, and very heavy; its specific gravity b 8·94. It is extensively used in the arts.

MOCHA, the principal port in the Red Sea frequented by Europeans, in part of Arabia called Yemen, about 40 miles to the north of the Strait of Ba mandeb, lat. 13° 19′ N., lon. 43° 20′ E. Population variously estimated ; may, perhaps, amount to from 5,000 to 7,000. It is encircled with walls, an differently fortified. Its appearance from the sea is imposing.

Mocha is situated on the margin of a dry sandy plain. It is built close to the s between two points of land which project and form a bay. Vessels drawing fro to 12 feet water may anchor within this bay at about a mile from the town; but ships anchor without the bay in the roads, in 5 or 7 fathoms water — the grand mo

E. S. E., and the fort to the south of the town S. by E. distant about two
rom shore.   The great article of export from Mocha is coffee, which is univer-
lmitted to be of the finest quality.   It is not possible to form any very accurate
e of the quantity exported ; but we believe it may be taken at 10,000 tons, or
. more.   The greater portion is sent to Djidda and Suez ; but there is a large ex-
Bombay, and other parts of India, whence some is sent to Europe : occasionally,
r, the exports from Mocha and Hodeida, direct for Europe, are very consider-
Besides coffee, the principal articles of export are, dates, adjoue or paste made
s, myrrh, gum Arabic, olibanum, senna (*cassia senna*), sharks' fins, tragacanth,
nd hides of the rhinoceros, balm of gilead, ivory, gold dust, civet, aloës, sagape-
c.   The principal articles of import are, rice, piece goods, iron and hardware,
he ivory, gold dust, and civet, met with at Mocha, are brought from the opposite
Abyssinia ; whence are also brought slaves, ghee, &c.
greater part of the foreign trade of Mocha is transacted by the Banians ; and it is
fer to deal with them than with either Turks or Arabs.   Europeans pay a duty of
nt. *ad valorem* on all goods imported by them from Europe, India, or China ; the
ng levied on the amount of the sales.   The buyer pays brokerage, cooley and boat
l kinds of foreign goods are sold on credit, and the payment is made in three instal-
r at a certain day, according as may have been agreed on.   Coffee is always paid for
money.   On the sale of other goods, the produce of the country, a credit is given ;
ly money be paid, a discount is allowed at the rate of 9 per cent.   When goods are
ing, the master must furnish the Custom-house officer with a manifest, or account
narks, numbers, and contents of each package.   He then opens two or three
ken at random ; and if they correspond with the account delivered, no further
tion is made ; but if they do not correspond, the whole bales are opened, and
uty is charged upon the excess.   The quantities being thus ascertained, their
learned from the account of sales rendered by the seller, and the duty charged
gly.   In this respect there is nothing to object to at Mocha ; but a good deal of
. is practised in the exaction of port charges, presents, &c., which may, however,
ed by proper firmness.   The port charges on ships, or *three mast* vessels, may
to about 400 Mocha dollars, and those on brigs to about half as much.   Pro-
re plentiful and cheap ; but water is dear : that in the vicinity being brackish
holesome, whatever is used for drinking, by all but the poorest persons, is
from Mosa, about 20 miles off.   Fish are abundant and cheap, but not very good.
. — The current coins of the country are carats and commassees : 7 carats =
ssee ; 60 commassees = 1 Spanish dollar ; 100 Spanish dollars = 12½ Mocha

s and Measures.—The commercial weights are —

s = 1 Rottolo = 1 lbs. 2 oz. avoird.	10 Maunds = 1 Frazel = 30 lbs. avoird.
s = 1 Maund = 3 lbs. avoird.	15 Frazels = 1 Bahar = 450 lbs. avoird.

also a small maund of only 30 vakias : 1 Mocha bahar = 16½ Bombay maunds ;
bahar = 13 Surat maunds = 15·123 seers.   Grain is measured by the kellah,
ich = 1 tomand, about 170 lbs. avoirdupois.   The liquid measures are 16 va-
nusseah ; 8 nusseahs = 1 cuda, about 2 English wine gallons.   The long
are the guz = 25 English inches ; the hand covid = 18 inches, and the long
l = 27 inches.
piling this article, we made use of *Milburn's Oriental Commerce*, and *Elmore's*
.   Niebuhr has given a plan of the port of Mocha in his *Voyage en Arabie*,
348. ed. Amst. 1776.   He has also given some details as to its trade in his
n de l'Arabie, p. 191.   But the best account we have seen of Mocha is in Ha-
Account of the East Indies (vol. i. pp. 40—52.), an accurate and valuable
Burckhardt did not visit Mocha ; which is much to be regretted.

ADORE, a sea-port town on the west coast of Morocco, lat. 31° 50′ N.,
0′ W.   Population about 10,000.   It is indifferently fortified ; the country
mediate vicinity is low, flat, sandy, and unproductive.   Water is scarce
er dear ; being either rain water collected and preserved in cisterns, or
from a river about 1½ mile distant.   The port is formed by a small island
he southward of the town ; but as there is not more than 10 or 12 feet
it at ebb tide, large ships anchor without, the long battery bearing E.
½ mile.   The city of Morocco derives its most considerable supplies of
n articles from Mogadore, from which it is distant about four days' jour-
avan travelling).   The principal imports are, English woollen and cotton
d hardware, German linens, tin, copper, earthenware, mirrors, glass, sugar,
aper, and a variety of other articles.   The exports principally consist of

sweet and bitter almonds, gum Arabic, and other gums, bees' wax, cow
calf skins, ivory, ostrich feathers, gold dust, olive oil, dates, &c.

Money. — Accounts are kept in nutkeels of 10 ounces; the ounce being divided into 4 blankeels, a
blankeel into 24 fluce. From their proportion to the Spanish dollar, the blankeel may be valued
the ounce at 4*d.*, and the nutkeel or ducat at 3*s.* 4*d.*

Weights and Measures. — The commercial pound is generally regulated by the weight of 20 S
dollars; and, therefore, 100 lbs. Mogadore weight, or the quintal, = 119 lbs. avoirdupois. The
pound for provisions is 50 per cent. heavier, or 1 lb. 12¼ oz. avoirdupois.

The corn measures are for the most part similar to those of Spain, but there are considerable
pancies.

The cubit or canna = 21 English inches, is the principal long measure.

The most ample details with respect to the trade of Mogadore, and the trade and productions of M
in general, may be found in Jackson's Account of Morocco, c. 6, 7. and 13.; see also Kelly's Cambi

MOHAIR (Ger. *Mohr;* Fr. *Moire;* It. *Moerro;* Sp. *Mue, Muer*), the h
a variety of the common goat, famous for being soft and silvery white. It i
found any where but in Angora. The hair is commonly brought ready sp
Europe; and being woven into camlets and other manufactures, is afterward
ported, sometimes to the very places whence the yarn was originally brough

MOLASSES, or MELASSES (Fr. *Syrop de Sucre, Melasses;* Ger. S
It. *Mielazzo di zucchero;* Sp. *Miel de azucar, Chancaca;* Port. *Melasso, Á
liquido;* Rus. *Patoka sacharnaja*), the uncrystallisable part of the juice o
sugar cane, separated from the sugar during its manufacture. It is of a bro
black colour, thick, and viscid; has a peculiar odour, and a sweet empyreu
taste. It is used for various purposes. About 8 gallons of proof spirit m
obtained from a cwt. of molasses as now imported; but that which is imp
into Great Britain is principally converted into a coarse, soft species of
denominated *bastards*. It is sometimes used in preparing the coarser s
preserves, and as a sweet. On the Continent it is extensively used in the
paration of tobacco. The duty on molasses imported into Great Britain for
consumption is 10*l.* a ton, or 10*s.* a cwt.; and the subjoined Parliamentary I
shows that the importation has rapidly increased during the last few years.
Sugar.)

Years ended 5th January.	Quantities of Molasses imported into Great Britain from the British West Indies.			Quantities of British Plantation Molasses exported from Great Britain to Foreign Parts.			Rates of Duty when entered for Home Consumption.	Nett Produce of the Duty on Molasses in Great Britain.		
	Cwt.	*qrs.*	*lbs.*	*Cwt.*	*qrs.*	*lbs.*	*Per Cwt.*	*L.*	*s.*	*d.*
1821	36,900	2	17	3,799	0	26	10*s.*			
1822	56,287	0	11	886	3	20	—			
1823	73,646	0	7	736	3	16	—			
1824	183,385	3	11	824	1	4	—			
1825	233,158	1	10	1,739	1	25	—	119,511	19	8
1826	347,524	1	2	740	2	15	—	165,624	15	10
1827	388,396	3	22	5,488	1	23	—	138,987	4	3
1828	391,157	3	6	928	1	3	—	205,296	12	1
1829	502,476	2	12	439	3	27	—	188,984	5	1
1830	384,259	0	10	2,311	2	16	—	192,405	2	6

MONEY. When the division of labour was first introduced, comm
were directly bartered for each other. Those, for example, who had a sur
corn, and were in want of wine, endeavoured to find out those who were
opposite circumstances, or who had a surplus of wine and wanted corn, an
exchanged the one for the other. It is obvious, however, that the pow
changing, and, consequently, of dividing employments, must have been sub
to perpetual interruptions, so long as it was restricted to mere barter. A.
produce to market, and B. is desirous to purchase it; but the produce bel
to B. is not suitable for A. C., again, would like to buy B.'s produce, bu
already fully supplied with the equivalent C. has to offer. In such cases—an
must be of constant occurrence wherever money is not introduced—no
exchange could take place between the parties; and it might be very d
to bring it about indirectly. *

The extreme inconvenience attending such situations must early have
themselves on the attention of every one. Efforts would, in consequer
made to avoid them; and it would speedily appear that the best or rather th
way in which this could be effected, was to exchange either the whole or a
one's surplus produce for some commodity of known value, and in general de
and which, consequently, few persons would be inclined to refuse to accep

* The difficulties that would arise on such occasions, and the devices that would be adopted
come them, have been very well illustrated by Colonel Torrens, in his work on the " Prod
Wealth," p. 291.

alent for whatever they had to dispose of. After this commodity had begun
: employed as a means of exchanging other commodities, individuals would
ne willing to purchase a greater quantity of it than might be required to pay
he products they were desirous of immediately obtaining; knowing that
d they, at any future period, want a further supply either of these or other
es, they would be able readily to procure them in exchange for this uni-
lly desired commodity. Though at first circulating slowly and with diffi-
, it would, as the advantages arising from its use were better appreciated,
to pass freely from hand to hand. Its value, as compared with other things,
l thus come to be universally known; and it would at last be used not only
e common medium of exchange, but as a standard by which to measure the
of other things.

w this commodity, whatever it may be, is *money.*

infinite variety of commodities have been used as money in different countries
eriods. But none can be advantageously used as such, unless it possess several
eculiar qualities. The slightest reflection on the purposes to which it is applied,
indeed, be sufficient to convince every one that it is indispensable, or, at least,
lingly desirable, that the commodity selected to serve as money should, (1) be
le into the smallest portions; (2) that it should admit of being kept for an inde-
period without deteriorating; (3) that it should, by possessing great value in small
be capable of being easily transported from place to place; (4) that one piece of
, of a certain denomination, should always be equal, in magnitude and quality, to
other piece of money of the same denomination; and (5) that its value should be
ratively steady, or as little subject to variation as possible. Without the *first* of
ualities, or the capacity of being divided into portions of every different magni-
nd value, money, it is evident, would be of almost no use, and could only be
ged for the few commodities that might happen to be of the same value as its
ible portions, or as whole multiples of them: without the *second*, or the capacity
g kept or hoarded without deteriorating, no one would choose to exchange comes for money, except only when he expected to be able speedily to re-exchange
oney for something else: without the *third*, or facility of transportation, money
not be conveniently used in transactions between places at any considerable dis-
without the *fourth*, or perfect sameness, it would be extremely difficult to appre-
e value of different pieces of money: and without the *fifth* quality, or comparative
ess of value, money could not serve as a standard by which to measure the value
er commodities; and no one would be disposed to exchange the produce of his
y for an article that might shortly decline considerably in its power of pur-
.

union of the different qualities of comparative steadiness of value, divisibility,
ity, facility of transportation, and perfect sameness, in the precious metals,
ess, formed the irresistible reason that has induced every civilised community to
them as money. The value of gold and silver is certainly not invariable, but,
ly speaking, it changes only by slow degrees; they are divisible into any number
s, and have the singular property of being easily re-united, by means of fusion,
t loss; they do not deteriorate by being kept; and, from their firm and com-
xture, they are very difficult to wear. Their cost of production, especially that
, is so considerable, that they possess great value in small bulk, and can, of
be transported with comparative facility; and an ounce of pure gold or silver,
om the mines in any quarter of the world, is precisely equal, in point of quality,
ounce of pure gold or silver dug from the mines in any other quarter. No
, therefore, when all the qualities necessary to constitute money are possessed in
ent a degree by the precious metals, that they have been used as such, in civil-
cieties, from a very remote era. " They became universal money," as M. Turgot
erved, " not in consequence of any arbitrary agreement among men, or of the
tion of any law, but by the nature and force of things."
n first used as money, the precious metals were in an unfashioned state, in bars
ts. The parties having agreed about the quantity of metal to be given for a
dity, that quantity was then weighed off. But this, it is plain, must have been
s and troublesome process. Undoubtedly, however, the greatest obstacle that
e experienced in early ages to the use of gold and silver as money, would be
o consist in the difficulty of determining the degree of their purity with suffi-
ecision; and the discovery of some means by which their weight and fineness
e readily and correctly ascertained, would be felt to be indispensable to their ex-
use as money. Fortunately, these means were not long in being discovered.
rication of coins, or the practice of impressing pieces of the precious metals

with a stamp indicating their weight and purity, belongs to the remotest antiqu
— (*Goguet, De l'Origine des Loix, &c.* tome i. p. 269.) And it may safely be affirm
that there have been very few inventions of greater utility, or that have done mor
accelerate the progress of improvement.

It is material, however, to observe that the introduction and use of coined mo
make no change whatever in the *principle* on which exchanges were previously c
ducted. The coinage saves the trouble of weighing and assaying gold and silver,
it does nothing more. It declares the weight and purity of the metal in a coin ;
the *value* of that metal or coin is in all cases determined by precisely the same princi
which determine the value of other commodities, and would be as little affected
being recoined with a new denomination, as the burthen of a ship by a change of
name.

Inaccurate notions with respect to the influence of coinage seem to have given ris
the opinion, so long entertained, that coins were merely the *signs* of values ! But
clear that they have no more claim to this designation than bars of iron or copper, sa
of wheat, or any other commodity. They exchange for other things, because they
desirable articles, and are possessed of real intrinsic value. A draft, check, or bill,
not improperly, perhaps, be regarded as the sign of the money to be given for it.
that money is nothing but a commodity ; it is not a sign — it is the thing signified.

Money, however, is not merely the universal equivalent, or *marchandise bannale*,
by the society : it is also the *standard* used to compare the values of all sorts of produ
and the stipulations in the great bulk of contracts and deeds, as to the delivery and
posal of property, have all reference to, and are commonly expressed in, quantitie
money. It is plainly, therefore, of the utmost importance that its value should be
served as invariable as possible. Owing, however, to improvements in the arts,
exhaustion of old mines and the discovery of new ones, the value of the precious me
is necessarily inconstant ; though, if we except the effects produced in the sixtee
century by the discovery of the American mines, it does not appear to have varie
much at other times as might have been anticipated. Great mischief has, howe
been repeatedly occasioned by the changes that have been made in most countrie
the weight, and sometimes also in the purity, of coins ; and since the impolicy of t
changes have been recognised, similar, and perhaps still more extensive, disorders
sprung from the improper use of substitutes for coins. It is, indeed, quite obvi
that no change can take place in the value of money, without proportionally affec
the pecuniary conditions in all contracts and agreements. Much, however, of th
fluence of a change depends on its direction. An increase in the value of mon
uniformly more prejudicial in a public point of view than its diminution ; the la
though injurious to individuals, may sometimes be productive of national advantage
such can never be the case with the former. — (See my *Principles of Political Econo*
2d ed. pp. 500—504.)

No certain estimate can ever be formed of the quantity of money required to con
the business of any country ; this quantity being, in all cases, determined by the v
of money itself, the services it has to perform, and the devices used for economisin
employment. Generally, however, it is very considerable ; and when it consists wh
of gold and silver, it occasions a very heavy expense. There can, indeed, be no d
that the wish to lessen this expense has been one of the chief causes that have le
civilised and commercial nations to fabricate a portion of their money of some
valuable material. Of the various substitutes resorted to for this purpose, paper
all respects, the most eligible. Its employment seems to have grown naturally o
the circumstances incident to an advancing society. When government becomes s
ciently powerful and intelligent to enforce the observance of contracts, individuals
sessed of written promises from others, that they will pay certain sums at certain spe
periods, begin to assign them to those to whom they are indebted ; and when the
scribers are persons of fortune, and of whose solvency no doubt can be entertained,
obligations are readily accepted in payment of debts. But when the circulatio
promises, or bills, in this way, has continued for a while, individuals begin to perceiv
they may derive a profit by issuing them in such a form as to fit them for being re
used as a substitute for money in the ordinary transactions of life. Hence the orig
bank notes. An individual in whose wealth and discretion the public have confid
being applied to for a loan, say of 5,000*l.*, grants the applicant his bill or note, payab
demand, for that sum. Now, as this note passes, in consequence of the confi
placed in the issuer, currently from hand to hand as cash, it is quite as useful
borrower as if it had been gold ; and supposing that the rate of interest is
cent., it will yield, so long as it continues to circulate, a revenue of 250*l.* a year
issuer. A banker who issues notes, coins, as it were, his credit. He derives the
revenue from the loan of his written promise to pay a certain sum, that he could

e loan of the sum itself, or of an equivalent amount of produce! And while he
creases his own income, he, at the same time, contributes to increase the wealth
public. The cheapest species of currency being substituted in the place of that
s most expensive, the superfluous coins are either used in the arts, or are exported
ange for raw materials or manufactured goods, by the use of which both wealth
oyments are increased. Ever since the introduction of bills, almost all great
cial transactions have been carried on by means of paper only. Notes are also
a very great extent in the ordinary business of society; and while they are
exchangeable at the pleasure of the holder for coins, or for the precise quantities
or silver they profess to represent, their value is maintained on a par with the
f these metals; and all injurious fluctuations in the value of money are as effec-
voided as if it consisted wholly of the precious metals.

ommon mercantile language, the party who exchanges money for a commodity
to buy; the party who exchanges a commodity for money being said to sell.
unless where the contrary is distinctly mentioned, always means the value of a
lity estimated or rated in money. (For a further account of metallic money, see
le COIN; and for an account of paper money, see the article BANKS.)

OPOLY. By this term is usually meant a grant from the crown, or
ompetent authority, conveying to some one individual, or number of indi-
the sole right of buying, selling, making, importing, exporting, &c. some
amodity, or set of commodities. Such grants were very common previously
ccession of the House of Stuart, and were carried to a very oppressive and
s extent during the reign of Queen Elizabeth. The grievance became at
o insupportable, that notwithstanding the opposition of government, which
upon the power of granting monopolies as a very valuable part of the pre-
, they were abolished by the famous act of 1624, the 21 Jac. 1. c. 3. This
ares that all monopolies, grants, letters patent for the sole buying, selling,
ing of goods and manufactures, shall be null and void. It excepts patents
een years for the sole working or making of any new manufactures within
n, to the true and first inventors of such manufactures, provided they be
trary to law, nor mischievous to the state. It also excepts grants by act
ament to any corporation, company, or society, for the enlargement of
nd letters patent concerning the making of gunpowder, &c. This act
ly secured the freedom of industry in Great Britain; and has done more,
to excite a spirit of invention and industry, and to accelerate the progress
h, than any other in the statute book.

OCCO, OR MAROQUIN (Ger. *Saffian*; Fr. *Maroquin*; It. *Marrocchino*;
rroqui; Rus. *Safian*), a fine kind of leather prepared of the skins of goats,
d from the Levant, Barbary, Spain, Flanders, &c. It is red, black, green,
&c. It is extensively used in the binding of books.

JEET, a species of *rubia tinctorum*, or madder, produced in Nepaul and
s districts of India. That which is brought to England, is imported from
, and is cultivated in the high lands about Natpore in Purneah. The
long and slender, and when broken appear of a red colour. It is used
g; the red which it produces being, though somewhat peculiar, nearly the
that produced by European madder. Dr. Bancroft says that the colour
imparts to cotton and linen is not so durable as that of madder; but that
ol or woollen cloth its colour is brighter and livelier; and, when proper
s are used, nearly, perhaps quite, as permanent.—(*Permanent Colours*, vol.
.) The best munjeet is in pieces about the bigness of a small quill, clean
, breaking short, and not pipy or chaffy. Its smell somewhat resembles
root.

very bulky article, as compared with its value, the freight adds greatly to its cost. This seems
rincipal reason of its being so very little used in Great Britain, that the entire imports, during
years ending with 1828, amounted to only 3,962 cwt. In 1824, 4,023 cwt. were imported; this
mportation being accounted for by the then comparatively low rate of freight.—(*Parl. Paper*,
ss. 1830.) The brokers estimate that 4*l*. per ton of freight is equal to 11*s*. 1*d*. per cwt. on
f the article; 5*l*. per ton being equal to 13*s*. 10*d*.; 6*l*. to 16*s*. 7*d*.; and 7*l*. to 19*s*. 4*d*.; and as
f munjeet in bond varies from 20*s*. to 25*s*. a cwt, it is plain it cannot be imported in any
e quantity, except when freights are very much depressed. It is mostly imported in small
undles of 600 or 800 to the ton; but sometimes it is packed in bales like cotton.

(Fr. *Musc*; Ger. *Bisam*; Du. *Muskus*; It. *Muschio*; Sp. *Almizele*; Rus.
Arab. and Pers. *Mishk*), is obtained from a species of deer (*moschus mos-
inhabiting the Alpine mountains of the east of Asia. The musk is found
bag under the belly. Musk is in grains concreted together, dry, yet slightly

unctuous, and free from grittiness when rubbed between the fingers or ch
It has a peculiar, aromatic, and extremely powerful and durable odour; the
is bitterish and heavy; and the colour deep brown, with a shade of red.
imported into England from China, in caddies containing from 60 to 100 oz.
but an inferior kind is brought from Bengal, and a still baser sort from R
The best is that which is in the natural follicle or pod. Being a very high
article, it is often adulterated. That which is mixed with the animal's bloo
be discovered by the largeness of the lumps or clots. It is sometimes mixe
a dark, highly coloured, friable earth; but this appears to the touch to be of a
crumbling texture, and is harder as well as heavier than genuine musk. 2
of musk are allowed to a ton. It is not permitted to be brought home
China ships belonging to the East India Company, but may be imported in o
— (*Thomson's Dispensatory; Milburn's Orient. Com.*)

MUSLIN (Ger. *Musselin, Nesseltuch;* Du. *Neteldoek;* Fr. *Mousselin*
Moussolina; Sp. *Moselina;* Rus. *Kissea*), is derived from the word *mous*
mouseln, a name given to it in India, where large quantities are made. It is
thin sort of cotton cloth, with a downy nap on the surface. Formerly all m
were imported from the East; but now they are manufactured in immense q
ties at Manchester, Glasgow, &c., of a fineness and durability which rival th
India, at the same time that they are very considerably cheaper.—(See Cor

MUSTARD (Ger. *Mustert, Senf;* Fr. *Moutarde;* It. *Mostarda;* Sp.
taza; Rus. *Gortschiza;* Lat. *Sinapis;* Arab. *Khīrdal;* Hind. *Rāi*), a pl
which there are several species, some of them indigenous in Great Britain.
extensively cultivated in the neighbourhood of York, and throughout other
of the North Riding. It is manufactured in the city of York, and is after
sold under the name of Durham mustard. Two quarters an acre is reck
good crop. Mustard is extensively used as a condiment, and is of consid
importance in the materia medica.

MYROBALANS, are dried fruits of the plum kind, occasionally b
from Bengal and other parts of India. There are said to be 5 different species.
vary from the size of olives to that of gall-nuts; have an unpleasant, bitt
austere taste; produce, with iron, a strong, durable, black dye and ink; an
alum, a very full, though dark, brownish yellow. They are used in calico pr
and medicine by the Hindoos. They have also been employed, though to a
paratively trifling extent, in the arts, and in pharmacy, in Europe; but th
now discarded from our Pharmacopœias. — (*Lewis's Mat. Med.; Bancr*
Permanent Colours, vol. i. p. 351.)

MYRRH (Ger. *Myrrhen;* Du. *Mirrhe;* Fr. *Myrrhe;* It. and Sp. *N*
Lat. *Myrrha;* Arab. *Murr*), a resinous substance, the produce of an unl
tree growing in Arabia and Abyssinia. It is imported in chests, each con
from 1 to 2 cwt. Abyssinian myrrh comes to us through the East Indies,
that produced in Arabia is brought by the way of Turkey. It has a peculiar,
fragrant, odour, and a bitter aromatic taste. It is in small irregularly shaped
which can hardly be called tears. Good myrrh is translucent, of a reddish
colour, brittle, breaking with a resinous fracture, and easily pulverised. Its s
gravity is 1·36. When it is opaque, mixed with impurities, and either white
a dark colour approaching nearly to black, with a disagreeable odour, it sho
rejected.—(*Thomson's Dispensatory.*)

N.

NAILS (Ger. *Nägel, Spiker;* Du. *Spykers;* Fr. *Clovis;* It. *Chiodi, Chiovi,*
Sp. *Clavos;* Rus. *Gwosdi*), are small spikes of iron, brass, &c., which, being
into wood, serve to bind several pieces together, or to fasten something upo
There is scarcely a town or village in Great Britain in which *nails* are not
but the principal seats of this useful branch of the iron manufacture are
mingham, Wolverhampton, Dudley, Sheffield, and a small district in Derl
The consumption of nails is immense; and the aggregate value of those a
produced is very large.

ANKEEN, or NANKING (Ger. *Nanking;* Du. *Nankings linnen;* Fr. *Toile ankin;* It. *Nanquino;* Sp. *Nanquina*), a species of cotton cloth closely woven. es its name from Nanking, in China, where the reddish thread of which the is made was originally spun. This manufacture has been carried to great ction in the East Indies, where vast quantities of white, pink, and yellow eens are made. At Manchester, and in other parts of Great Britain, these es are imitated with success; though it must be admitted that British eens are still inferior to those of India; the latter being not only more le, but holding their colour longer, than the British. The nankeens imported England by the East India Company come under the general denomination ece goods; their qualities are various, and there is generally abundance of in the market. Nankeens are mostly used in England in the making of ers and waistcoats for men's wear during summer, and for ladies' pelisses, In some of the more southern parts of Europe, the warmer countries of and America, and the British settlements in Africa, nankeen is worn by sexes the whole year round, and constitutes the chief part of their attire.

NTES, a large commercial city and sea-port of France, on the Loire, about les from its mouth, in lat. 47° 13′ N., lon. 1° 22¾′ W. Population 72,000. vessels only come up to the city; those of a larger size load and unload in ads of Paimbœuf, about 20 miles lower down the river. In consequence extensive inland navigation, Nantes has a pretty considerable foreign com-, particularly with the West Indies. The exports principally consist of y, wine, and vinegar, silk, woollen and linen goods, wheat, rye, and other ltural products, &c. The principal imports are sugar, coffee, and other al products, cotton, indigo, timber, hemp, &c. Nantes is a considerable ôt for the commerce of salt. The quantity imported, in 1828, was ,922 kilog. During the time that the slave trade was carried on, Nantes ore extensively engaged in it than any other French port.

ies, Weights, and Measures, same as in the rest of France. — (See BORDEAUX.)

—2¼ per cent. on coffee in bags, real on ditto in hhds, casks, &c.; 6 per cent. on cottons; real on 17 per cent. on Brazil muscovado sugar, 19 per cent. on Martinique and Guadeloupe ditto, 13 per ditto clayed.

PLES, a very large city and sea-port in the south of Italy, the capital of ngdom of the same name, in lat. 40° 50¼′ N., lon. 14° 15¾′ E. Population 345,000. Naples is well situated for commerce; but the spirit of the ment and of the public institutions has been adverse to its growth. The Naples is celebrated for its picturesque views; but the harbour is small, entirely artificial, being formed by a mole projecting into the sea. The s consist principally of the products of the adjacent country, as silk, oil, wool, raisins, figs, brimstone, &c. Oil (commonly called Gallipoli oil, from oli, a town in the Terra d'Otranto, whence large quantities of it are ex-) is the principal article of export from the kingdom of Naples. A great of wines are exported from Naples; those of Pozzuoli are shipped in the st quantities. The price depends entirely on the abundance of the vintage: small quantity comes to England. Oak and chestnut staves, and red and argol, are shipped from Naples. The imports into England, in 1828, of il from Italy and the Italian islands, amounted to 1,858,033 gallons. The s consist partly of colonial produce, and partly of raw and manufactured from the north of Europe, England, France, &c. The importation of salt-to Naples is very great. The Neapolitans are not so particular as to its as the Tuscans, and some of the other Italians.

y. — Accounts are kept at Naples in ducati di regno of 100 grani. According ew monetary system introduced in 1818, the unit of coins is the silver ducat = . sterling. The ducat = 10 carlini; and there are coins of 1, 2, 6, and 12 car-róportion. Coins of a less value than 1 carlino are in copper. The smallest ece is the oncetta = 10s. 3½d. sterling.

ts and Measures. — The commercial weights are the cantaro and rottolo. The grosso = 100 rottoli = 196½ lbs. avoirdupois. = 89·105 kilog. = 184 lbs. of rgh = 180·4 lbs. of Amsterdam. The cantaro piccolo = 106 lbs. avoirdupois ilog.

y measure, the carro of corn contains 36 tomoli. The tomolo = 1·45 Winch.

In wine measure, the carro is divided into 2 botti, or 24 barili, or 1,440 cara
The carro = 264 English wine gallons. The regular pipe of wine or brandy =
English gallons.

In oil measure, the salma is divided into 16 staja, 256 quarti, or 1,536 misure
The salma at Naples = 12¾ English wine gallons; at Gallipoli it is from 3 to 4
cent. less; at Bari it is a little larger.

In long measure, the canna is divided into 8 palmi, or 96 onzie, and is = 6 feet
inches English. Hence the palmo = 10·38 English inches.

Eleven salma are allowed to a ship's last. — (*Nelkenbrecher ; Dr. Kelly.*)

Most articles of export are purchased for ready money ; on most import articles
4 months' credit are generally given, and in some cases more. The charges on s
including commission, are usually from 6 to 8 per cent.

Customary Tares. — Sugar, Brazil large chests, 20 per cent. ; Brazil small ch
18 per cent. ; Havannah boxes, 14 per cent. ; Havannah casks, 12 per cent. Al
n casks, 10 per cent. Cocoa, in casks, 6 per cent. and the weight of the ca
Pepper, in bags, 2 rot. per bag. Indigo, in serons, 32 lbs. per seron. Coffee, in b
3 rot. per bag ; in casks, weight of casks. Other articles *real* tare.

NAVIGATION LAWS.

These laws form an important branch of Mari
Law. In this country they are understood to comprise the various acts that h
been passed, defining British ships, the way in which such ships are to be man
the peculiar privileges enjoyed by them, and the conditions under which for
ships shall be allowed to engage in the trade of the country, either as impo
or exporters of commodities, or as carriers of commodities from one part of
country to another.

Sketch of the History and Principles of the Navigation Laws. — The origin of
Navigation Laws of England may be traced to the reign of Richard II., or perhap
a still more remote period. But as no intelligible account of the varying and cor
dictory enactments framed at so distant an epoch could be compressed within any rea
able space, it is sufficient to observe, that, in the reign of Henry VII., two of the l
ing principles of the late navigation law were distinctly recognised, in the prohibi
of the importation of certain commodities, unless imported in ships belonging to Eng
owners, and manned by English seamen. In the early part of the reign of Eliza
(5 Eliz. c. 5.), foreign ships were excluded from our fisheries and coasting trade.
republican parliament gave a great extension to the navigation laws, by the act of l
which prohibited all ships, of all foreign nations whatever, from trading with the p
ations in America, without having previously obtained a licence. These acts were, l
ever, rather intended to regulate the trade between the different ports and depende
of the empire, than to regulate our intercourse with foreigners. But in the follow
year (9th of October, 1651) the republican parliament passed the famous *Act of N
gation.* This act had a double object. It was intended not only to promote our
navigation, but also to strike a decisive blow at the naval power of the Dutch, who
engrossed almost the whole *carrying trade* of the world, and against whom various
cumstances had conspired to incense the English. The act in question declared,
no goods or commodities whatever, of the growth, production, or manufacture of
Africa, or America, should be imported either into England or Ireland, or any of
plantations, except in ships belonging to English subjects, and of which the master
the greater number of the crew were also English. Having thus secured the in
trade of Asia, Africa, and America, to the English ship owners, the act went o
secure to them, as far as that was possible, the import trade of Europe. For this
pose, it further enacted, that no goods, of the growth, production, or manufacture o
country in Europe, should be imported into Great Britain, except in British ship
*in such ships as were the real property of the people of the country or place in whic
goods were produced, or from which they could only be, or most usually were, expo*
The latter part of the clause was entirely levelled against the Dutch, who had but
native produce to export, and whose ships were principally employed in carrying
produce of other countries to foreign markets. Such were the leading provisions of
famous act. They were adopted by the regal government which succeeded Crom
and form the basis of the act of the 12th Car. 2. c. 18., which continued, to a
recent period, to be the rule by which our naval intercourse with other countries
mainly regulated ; and has been pompously designated the *Charta Maritima* of Engl

In the statute 12 Car. 2. c. 18., the clause against importing foreign commo
except in British ships, or in ships belonging to the country or place where the
were produced, or from which they were exported, was so far modified that the pro
tion was made to apply only to the goods of Russia and Turkey, and to certain ar
since well known in commerce by the name of *enumerated* articles, leave being

ne given to import all other articles in ships of any description. But this modi-
was of very little importance; inasmuch as the enumerated articles comprised all
aat were of most importance in commerce, as timber, grain, tar, hemp and flax,
s, wines, spirits, sugar, &c. Parliament seems, however, to have very speedily
ound to the opinion that too much had been done in the way of relaxation; and
4th of Charles II. a supplemental statute was passed, avowedly with the intention of
g some evasions of the statute of the preceding year, which, it was affirmed, had
actised by the Hollanders and Germans. This, however, seems to have been a
etence, to excuse the desire to follow up the blow aimed, by the former statute,
arrying trade of Holland. And such was our jealousy of the naval and com-
greatness of the Dutch, that, in order to cripple it, we did not hesitate totally to
e all trade with them; and, to prevent the possibility of fraud, or of clandestine
ect intercourse with Holland, we went so far as to include the commerce with
herlands and Germany in the same proscription. The statute of the 14th Car. 2.
ed all importation from these countries, of a long list of enumerated commodities,
hy circumstances, or in any vessels, whether British or foreign, under the penalty
e and confiscation of the ships and goods. So far as it depended on us, Hol-
Netherlands, and Germany, were virtually placed without the pale of the com-
world! And though the extreme rigour of this statute was subsequently modi-
principal provisions remained in full force until the late alterations.

olicy, if not the motives which dictated these statutes, has met with very general
It has been said, and by no less an authority than Dr. Smith, that national
y did, in this instance, that which the most deliberate wisdom would have re-
ded. "When the act of navigation was made," says he, "though England and
were not actually at war, the most violent animosity subsisted between the two
It had begun during the government of the long parliament, which first framed
and it broke out soon after in the Dutch wars during that of the Protector and
es II. It is not impossible, therefore, that some of the regulations of this famous
have proceeded from national animosity. They are as wise, however, as if they
een dictated by the most deliberate wisdom. National animosity at that par-
me aimed at the very same object which the most deliberate wisdom would have
nded,—the diminution of the naval power of Holland, the only naval power which
danger the security of England. The act of navigation *is not favourable to
ommerce, or to the growth of that opulence which can arise from it.* The interest
on in its commercial relations to foreign nations is, like that of a merchant with
• the different people with whom he deals, to buy as cheap and to sell as dear
le. But the act of navigation, by diminishing the number of sellers, must
ly diminish that of buyers; and we are thus likely not only to buy foreign
arer, but to sell our own cheaper, than if there was a more perfect freedom of
As defence, however, is of much more importance than opulence, the act of
n is, perhaps, the wisest of all the commercial regulations of England."—
Wealth of Nations, vol. ii. p. 293.)

, however, be very fairly doubted, whether, in point of fact, the navigation law
ffects here ascribed to it, of weakening the naval power of the Dutch, and of
g that of this kingdom. The Dutch were very powerful at sea for a long
er the passing of this act; and it seems natural to conclude, that the decline of
itime preponderance was owing rather to the gradual increase of commerce and
n in other countries, and to the disasters and burdens occasioned by the ruinous
he Republic had to sustain with Cromwell, Charles II. and Louis XIV.,
e mere exclusion of their merchant vessels from the ports of England. It is
t to say, that this exclusion was altogether without effect. The efforts of the
procure a repeal of the English navigation law show that, in their apprehen-
erated injuriously on their commerce.* It is certain, however, that its influ-
is respect has been greatly over-rated in this country. *Excessive taxation,* and
avigation law, was the principal cause of the fall of profits, and of the decline
actures, commerce, and navigation, in Holland. "Les guerres," says the well-
author of the *Commerce de la Hollande,* "terminées par les traités de Nimegue,
ck, d'Utrecht, et enfin la dernière par le traité d'Aix-la-Chapelle, ont succes-
obligé la République de faire usage d'un grand crédit, et de faire des em-
ormes pour en soutenir les frais. Les dettes ont surchargé l'état d'une somme
d'intérêts, qui ne pouvoient être payés que par *une augmentation excessive*
dont il a fallu faire porter la plus forte partie par les consommations dans un
a qu'un territoire extrêmement borné, et par conséquent par l'industrie. Il a

reaty of Breda, agreed upon in 1667, between the States General and Charles II., the latter
o procure the repeal of the navigation law. But the subject was never agitated in either
rliament.

donc fallu faire enchérir infiniment la main d'œuvre. Cette cherté de la main-d'
a non seulement restraint presque toute sorte de fabrique et d'industrie à la conso
tion intérieure, mais elle a encore porté un coup bien sensible au commerce de
partie accessoire et la plus précieuse du commerce d'économie : car cette cherté a
la construction plus chere, et augmenté le prix de tous les ouvrages qui tiennen
navigation, même de tous les ouvrages des ports et des magasins. Il n'étoit pas po
que l'augmentation du prix de la main-d'œuvre ne donnât, malgré tous les effo
l'économie Hollandoise, un avantage seusible aux autres nations qui voudroient se
au commerce d'économie et à celui de frêt." — (Tome ii. p. 211.)

This extract, which might, were it necessary, be corroborated by others to the
effect from all the best Dutch writers, show that it is not to our navigation law,
the restrictive regulations of other foreign powers, but to the abuse of the funding sy
and the excess of taxation, that the decline of the commercial greatness and ma
power of Holland was really owing. Neither does it appear that the opinion
tained by Dr. Smith and others, that the navigation law had a powerful influen
augmenting the naval power of this country, rests on any better foundation. The
of the nation for naval enterprise had been awakened, the navy had become excee
formidable, and Blake had achieved his victories, before the enactment of this f
law. So far, indeed, is it from being certain that the navigation act had, in this re
the effect commonly ascribed to it, that there are good grounds for thinking it had
cisely opposite effect, and that it operated rather to diminish than to increase our m
tile navy. It is stated in Roger Coke's *Treatise on Trade*, published in 1671 (p.
that this act, by lessening the resort of strangers to our ports, had a most injurious
on our commerce; and he further states that we had lost, within two years of the
ing of the act of 1650, the greater part of the Baltic and Greenland trades. — (p
Sir Josiah Child, whose treatise was published in 1691, corroborates Coke's state
for, while he decidedly approves of the navigation law, he admits that the Englisl
ping employed in the Eastland and Baltic trades had decreased at least *two thirds*
its enactment, and that the foreign shipping employed in these trades had proporti
increased. — (*Child's Treatise on Trade*, p. 89. Glasg. edit.) Exclusively of thes
temporary authorities, it may be worth while to mention, that Sir Matthew D
an extensive and extremely well informed merchant, condemns the whole principle
navigation act; and contends, that instead of increasing our shipping and seamen,
diminished them both; and that, by rendering the freight of ships higher than it
otherwise have been, it had entailed a heavy burden on the public, and been one
main causes that had prevented our carrying on the fishery so successfully as the
— (*Essay on the Causes of the Decline of Foreign Trade*, p. 60. ed. 1756.)

There does not seem to be any very good grounds on which to question these
ments; and they are at all events sufficient to show, that the assertions of thos
contend that the navigation laws had a prodigious effect in increasing the number
ships and sailors, must be received with very great modification. But, suppose
that has been said by the apologists of these laws were true to the letter; sup
were conceded, that, when first framed, the Act of Navigation was extremely poli
proper; — that would afford but a very slender presumption in favour of the policy
porting it in the present day. Human institutions are not made for immortality
must be accommodated to the varying circumstances and exigencies of society.
situation of Great Britain and the other countries of Europe has totally change
1650. The envied wealth and commercial greatness of Holland have passed
we have no longer any thing to fear from her hostility: and "he must be
strangely influenced by antiquated prejudices and bygone apprehensions, who can
tain any of that jealousy from which the severity of this law principally origi
London has become, what Amsterdam formerly was, the grand emporium of th
mercial world — *universi orbis terrarum emporium.* And the real question whic
presents itself for our consideration is, not, what are the best means by which v
rise to naval greatness? but — what are the best means of preserving that undi
pre-eminence in maritime affairs to which we have attained?

Now, it does not really seem that there can be much difficulty in deciding this qu
Navigation and naval power are the children, not the parents — the effect, not th
— of commerce. If the latter be increased, the increase of the former will foll
matter of course. More ships and more sailors become necessary, according as tl
merce between different and distant countries is extended. A country, circum
like Great Britain in the reign of Charles II., when her shipping was compa
limited, might perhaps be warranted in endeavouring to increase its amount, by
ing foreign ships from which harbours. But it is almost superfluous to add, that
by any such regulations, but solely by the aid of a flourishing and widely extende
merce, that the immense mercantile navy we have now accumulated can be supp

t it is extremely easy to show, that to have continued to enforce the provisions of
d navigation law, in the present state of the world, would have been among the
efficient means that could have been devised for the destruction of our commerce.
wealth and power to which Britain has attained, has inspired other nations with the
envious feelings that the wealth of Holland formerly generated in our minds.
id of ascribing our commercial and manufacturing superiority to its true causes,—
comparative freedom of our constitution, the absence of all oppressive feudal pri-
s, the security of property, and the fairness of our system of taxation, —our foreign
contend that it has been entirely owing to our exclusive system ; and appeal to our
ple to stimulate their respective governments to adopt retaliatory measures, and to
t them against British competition. These representations have had the most
ous operation. In 1787, the American legislature passed an act, copied to the
etter from our navigation law, with the avowed intention of its operating as a re-
iry measure against this country. The northern powers threatened to act on the
principle; and would have carried their threats into effect, but for timely conces-
on our part. The same engines by which we laboured to destroy the trade of
nd were thus about to be brought, by what we could not have called an unjust
ation, to operate against ourselves. Nor can there be a doubt that, had we con-
d to maintain our illiberal and exclusive system, and refused to set a better example
ers, and to teach them the advantage of recurring to sounder principles, we should
un a very great risk of falling a victim to the vindictive spirit which such short-
d and selfish policy would have generated.

these reasons, it seems difficult to question the policy of the changes that have
ly been effected in the navigation laws, partly by the bills introduced by Mr. (now
Wallace in 1821, and Mr. Huskisson in 1825, and partly by the adoption of what
en called the *Reciprocity System*. Under the existing law (6 Geo. 4. c. 109., see
the intercourse with all European countries in amity with Great Britain is placed
same footing. The memorials of our former animosity, and of our jealousy of
osperity of certain of our neighbours, have thus been abolished ; and the same law
ceforth to regulate our commerce with the Continent. This uniformity, besides
greater scope to mercantile operations, and extending our traffic with some of our
pulent neighbours, removes a great source of embarrassment and litigation ; at the
ime that it detracts considerably from that selfish character which had been be-
on the Continent, and not without considerable reason, to be the animating prin-
f our commercial system.

distinction between enumerated and non-enumerated goods is still kept up under
w regulations ; but, instead of confining the importation of the former into the
Kingdom, either to British ships, or ships belonging to the country or place
the goods were produced, or from which they originally were exported, the new
ions permit that they may be imported either in British ships, in ships of the
y of which the goods are the produce, or in ships of the country or place from
they are imported into England. This is a very important alteration. Under
law, when a number of articles, the products of different countries, but all of
itable for importation into England, were found in a foreign port, they could not
orted except in a British ship, or separately in ships belonging to the different
es whose produce they were. This was obviously a very great hardship on the
er, without being of any real advantage to our own ship owners. When the
merchant had vessels of his own, it was not very probable he would permit them
in unoccupied, and freight a British vessel ; and there were very few ports of any
ance in which foreign bottoms might not be found, in which the articles could be
imported. The real effect of the old law was not, therefore, to cause the employ-
f British ships, but to oblige foreigners to assort their cargoes less advantageously
ey might otherwise have done, and thus to lessen their intercourse with our mar-
The new law obviates this inconvenience ; while, by restricting the importation
opean goods to ships of the built of the country of which the goods are the
, or to those of the built of the country or port from which the goods are shipped,
ich are *wholly owned* by the inhabitants of such country or port, it is rendered very
for the people of a particular country to become the carriers of the produce of
ountries to our markets.

her new regulation is of such obvious and unquestionable utility, that it is sur-
it was not long ago adopted. By the old law, all articles, the produce of Asia,
or America, could only be imported directly in a British ship from the place of
oduction. This law had already been repealed in so far as respected the United
whose ships were allowed to import their produce directly into this country ; but
maintained with respect to Asia, Africa, and South America. And hence,
h a British ship happened to find, in South American, African, or Asiatic ports,

articles, the produce of one or more of the other quarters of the globe, suitable for markets, and with which it might have been extremely advantageous for her to comp her cargo, she was prohibited from taking them on board, under penalty of forfeiture confiscation, not only of the goods, but also of the ship. This regulation has been pealed; and it is now lawful for British ships to take on board all articles, the importa of which is not prohibited, on meeting with them in any Asiatic, African, or Ameri port. Lord Wallace originally intended to extend this principle to European ports to make it lawful for British ships to import all non-prohibited articles from wher they might find them. But it was supposed by some, that foreign ships might be n cheaply navigated than ours; and that foreigners, taking advantage of this circumstal would import the Asiatic, African, and American products required for our consump into the contiguous continental ports, and would consequently restrict the employmel British ships to their carriage thence. We believe that these apprehensions were, great measure, visionary. But the law is so contrived as to avoid even the possibilit danger on this head: such of the products of Asia, Africa, and America, as are requ for home consumption, being, with a few trifling exceptions, inadmissible from Euro and only admissible when they are imported in British ships, or in ships of the countr place of which the goods are the produce, and from which they are brought. The exceptions to this rule are articles from Asiatic and African Turkey imported f the Levant, and bullion.

Besides the restrictive regulations already alluded to, it had been a part of our po to encourage the employment of our shipping by imposing higher duties on commod imported into our harbours in foreign vessels, than were imposed on them when ported in British vessels; and it had also been customary to charge foreign vessels higher port and light-house duties, &c. This system was always loudly complaine by foreigners; but we had little difficulty in maintaining it, so long as the state of manufactures enabled us to disregard the retaliatory measures of other powers. But extraordinary increase that took place, since the commencement of the late war, in manufactures for foreign consumption, and the necessity under which we were, in sequence, placed, of conciliating our customers abroad, led to the adoption of the procity system. This system was first introduced into the trade with the United St After the North American colonies had succeeded in establishing their independe they set about framing a code of navigation laws on the model of those of this cour Among other regulations of a restrictive character, it was enacted, that all foreign ve trading to the United States should pay half a dollar, which was afterwards raised dollar, per ton duty, beyond what was paid by American ships; and further, that g imported in foreign vessels should pay a duty of 10 per cent. over and above what payable on the same description of goods imported in American vessels.

This law was avowedly directed against the navigation of Great Britain; though, was bottomed on the very same principles as our navigation laws, we could not op complain of its operation. Under these circumstances, it would have been sound p to have at once proposed an accommodation; and instead of attempting to meet re tion by retaliation, to have offered to modify our navigation law, in so far as Amel shipping was concerned, on condition of the Americans making reciprocal modifica in our favour. A different course was, however, followed. Various devices were f upon to counteract the navigation system of the Americans, without in any degre laxing our own: but they all failed of their object; and at length it became obvio every one that we had engaged in an unequal struggle, and that the real effect of policy was, to give a bounty on the importation of the manufactured goods of countries into the United States, and thus gradually to exclude both our manufac and ships from the ports of the Republic. In consequence, the conviction of the n sity of making concessions gained ground progressively; and it was ultimately fixe the commercial treaty agreed upon between Great Britain and the United States in that in future equal charges should be imposed on the ships of either country in the of the other, and that equal duties should be laid upon all articles, the produce of th country, imported into the other, whether such importation were effected in the shi the one or the other.

The new states of South America were naturally anxious to establish a comm marine; and, to forward their views in this respect, they contemplated enacting na tion laws. But this intention was frustrated by the interference of the British go ment, who, without stipulating for any peculiar advantage, wisely offered to admit ships into our ports on a fair footing of reciprocity, or on their paying the same ch as our own ships, on condition that they admitted British ships into their ports similar footing. Commercial treaties framed on this sound and liberal principle since been entered into with most of these states.

The principle of the reciprocity system having been thus conceded in the case

rse with the United States, whose commercial marine is second only to that of
Britain, it was not possible to refuse acting on the same principle in the case of
uropean countries as might choose to admit our ships into their ports on a footing
lity.* The first demand of this sort was made on the part of the Prussian
nent, by whom an order in council was issued on the 20th of June, 1822, which
rge additions to the port dues charged on all ships belonging to those nations
did not admit Prussian ships on a footing of reciprocity. The real object of this
as to injure the navigation of this country; and it was speedily found that it had
red effect, and that its operation on British shipping was most pernicious.

r these circumstances, the British merchants and ship owners applied to our
nent for relief. "We were assailed," said Mr. Huskisson, "with representations
quarters connected with the shipping and trade of the country, against the
harges imposed upon British ships in the ports of Prussia. In such circum-
what course did his Majesty's government take? We felt it to be our duty, in
instance, to communicate with the Prussian minister in this country; and our
at Berlin was, I believe, also directed to confer with the Prussian government
ubject. I myself had a conference with the Prussian minister at this court, and
ecollect the substance of his reply to me: — ' You have,' he said, ' set us the
, by your port and light charges, and your discriminating duties on Prussian
nd we have not gone beyond the limits of that example. Hitherto, we have
the increase of our port and tonnage charges to ships only; *but it is the intention
overnment next year,*' (and of this he showed me the written proof,) ' *to imitate
more closely, by imposing discriminating duties on the goods imported in your ships.*
ect is a just protection of our own navigation; and so long as the measure of
ection does not exceed that which is afforded in your ports to British ships, we
ee with what reason you can complain.'

inst such a reply what remonstrance could we, in fairness, make to the Prussian
ent? We might have addressed ourselves, it may be said by some, to the
feelings of that government; we might have pleaded long usage in support of
iminating duties; we might have urged the advantages which Prussia derived
trade with England. Appeals like these were not forgotten in the discussion;
were of little avail against the fact stated by the consul at Dantzic, — that the
ship owners were all going to ruin.'

others it may be said, "Your duty was to retaliate, by increasing your own port
and discriminating duties, on Prussian shipping.' I have already stated gene-
reasons against the policy of this latter course. We were not prepared to begin
of commercial hostility, which, if followed up on both sides to its legitimate
nces, could only tend to reciprocal prohibition. In this state of things, more
y, as I contend, we entered upon an amicable negotiation with the Prussian
ent, upon the principle of our treaty with the United States, — that of abolish-
oth sides, all discriminating duties on the ships and goods of the respective
in the ports of the other.

ing concluded an arrangement with Prussia upon this basis, we soon found it
to do the same with some other of the northern states. Similar conventions
ordingly entered into with Denmark and Sweden. Reciprocity is the found-
all those conventions: but it is only fair to add, that they contain other stipu-
r giving facility to trade, and from which the commerce of this country, I am
, will, in the result, derive considerable advantage." — (*Mr. Huskisson's Speech,
, 1826, on the State of the Shipping Interest.*)

ear and satisfactory statement shows conclusively that the establishment of the
y system, with respect to which so violent a clamour was raised, was not a
of choice, but of necessity. In the state in which our manufactures are now
e could not afford to hazard their exclusion from a country into which they are
imported to a very large extent. So long as the Prussians, Swedes, Danes,
to submit to our system of discriminating duties on foreign ships, and on the
ported in them, without retaliating, it was no business of ours to tell them that
m was illiberal and oppressive. But when they found this out without our
em; and when they declared, that unless we modified our restrictions, they
taliate on our commerce, and either entirely exclude our commodities from
kets, or load those that were imported in British ships with prohibitory duties;
have been justified, had we refused to come to an accommodation with them?
to sacrifice the substance to the shadow? To turn away some of our very best
, because they chose to stipulate that the intercourse between them and us

fourth section of the act 6 Geo. 4. c. 1. it is enacted, that his Majesty may, by an order in
it the ships of foreign states into our ports, on payment of the like duties that are charged on
els, provided that British ships are admitted into the ports of such foreign states, on payment
uties that are charged on their vessels.

should be conducted either in their ships or in ours, as the merchants might think
Our government had only a choice of difficulties; and they wisely preferred adop
system which has preserved free access for the English manufacturer to the mark
Prussia, and to the English ship owners an equal chance with those of Prussia of
employed in the traffic between the two countries, to a system that would event
and at no distant period, have put an end to all intercourse between the two cou
and which had already subjected it to great difficulties.

It was said by the ship owners, and others opposed to the late alterations, th
Prussians can build, man, and victual ships at a cheaper rate than we can do; an
the ultimate effect of the reciprocity system would, consequently, be to give them
cided superiority in the trade. But admitting this statement to be true, still, f
reasons already given, it is pretty evident that the policy we have pursued was,
the circumstances of the case, the best. Had we refused to establish the recip
system, we must have submitted to be entirely excluded from the markets of the l
States, Prussia, &c. In grasping at what was beyond our reach, we should thu
lost what we were already in possession of. We should not only have injured ou
owners by getting them forcibly excluded from the ports of many great comm
states, but we should have done an irreparable injury to our manufacturers, — a
which, without undervaluing the ship owners, is of incomparably more importanc
they. Although, therefore, no doubt could be entertained with respect to the
ments of the ship owners as to the comparative cheapness of foreign shipping, that
be no good objection to the measures that have been adopted. But these state:
though probably in some respects true, were certainly much exaggerated. In co
ing the cost of British and foreign shipping, it is usual to estimate it by the ton
but this is a very false criterion; for, while foreign ships are accurately measure
ships are measured so that a vessel of 150 tons register generally carries 220 ton
mixed cargo, and a vessel registered at 400 tons seldom carries less than 600.
difference be taken into account, it will be found that the Prussians, and other no
nations, from whom the greatest danger was apprehended, have no considerable adva
in the cheapness of their ships; and it is generally admitted that ships built in the
on the Baltic will not last the time, nor bear the wear and tear, that ships built
country or France will do. The wages of American seamen are higher than ours
it is stated by those engaged in the shipping trade, that the wages paid by the no
ship owners are about as high as in England, and that their crews are larger in p
tion to the burthen of the ship. The difference in the cost of victualling must be
terial; for, in all distant voyages, our ships procure provisions and stores of all se
the same rate as the foreigner.* On the whole, therefore, it would appear th
alarm with respect to the apprehended decay of our shipping was in a great de
not entirely, imaginary. And while the late modifications in the navigation law
imperiously required by a just regard to our manufacturing and commercial int
there are no good grounds for thinking that they will be injurious to our shippin

*Abstract of an Act entitled for the Encouragement of British Shipping and Navigatio
6 Geo. 4. c. 109.*

This act shall come into and be and continue in full force and operation, from and after the 5t
January, 1826, and shall constitute and be the law of navigation of the British empire. — § 1.
Importation of enumerated Goods for Home Use. — The several sorts of goods herein-after enur
being the produce of Europe, viz. masts, timber, boards, salt, pitch, tar, tallow, rosin, hemp, f
rants, raisins, figs, prunes, olive oil, corn or grain, pot ashes, wine, sugar, vinegar, brandy, and
shall not be imported into the United Kingdom, to be used therein, except in British *ships*, or in
the country of which the goods are the produce, or in ships of the country from which the g
imported. — § 2.†

---

* See on this subject an able pamphlet, entitled " Observations on the Warehousing System a
gation Laws," by Sir John Hall, Secretary to the St. Katherine's Dock Company. The following
from the evidence of Mr. Edward Solly, before the Lords' Committee of 1820, seems to be conc
to the accuracy of the statements in the text : — " I," said he, " was formerly a considerable e
Prussian ships, and therefore I had a good deal of experience in Prussian shipping, and I can s
that Prussian ships cannot compete with English ships in time of peace: the English ships a
gated cheaper than Prussian ships; the Prussian vessels are more heavily masted and rigged, and
a greater complement of men, whilst the English ship is manned mostly by apprentices; the
ships require less ballast; the economy of shipping is better understood and practised in them :
greater activity of the captain and crew; they are insured in clubs at the average rate of 5 ;
while the Prussian ships cannot get the same insurance done for 12 ; and as to the outfit, the p
and other necessaries for the ship, both parties have their choice where they will lay in th.
whether in a Prussian or an English port — if provisions are cheap in the Prussian port, the
captain lays in his stock of provisions there. Generally, I am of opinion that British ships
cheaper than those of any other nation."—(*Evidence*, p. 14.)

† The act 7 and 8 Geo. 4. c. 56. § 16. enacts, that after the 1st of January, 1828, so much of
act (6 Geo. 4. c. 109.) as restricts the importation of rosin, pitch, vinegar, sugar, pot ashes, and sa
the produce of Europe, shall be repealed ; and in lieu thereof, the several sorts of goods here
enumerated, viz wool, shumac, madders, madder roots, barilla, brimstone, bark of oak, cork,
lemons, linseed, rape seed, and clover seed, being the produce of Europe, shall not be imported
United Kingdom, to be used therein, except in British ships or in ships of the country from w
goods are imported ; and this restriction shall be complied with, and enforced in like manner,
same were contained in the said act.

ls, *the Produce of Asia, Africa, or America.* — Goods, the produce of Asia, Africa, or America, not be imported from Europe into the United Kingdom, to be used therein, except the goods -after mentioned. — § 3.

the produce of places in Asia or Africa within the s of Gibraltar, or of the dominions of the emperor orocco, imported from places in Europe within the s of Gibraltar.
he produce of places within the limits of the East In-ompany's charter, which (having been imported into

Gibraltar or Malta in British ships) may be imported from Gibraltar or Malta.
Goods taken by way of reprisal by British ships.
Bullion, diamonds, pearls, rubies, emeralds, and other jewels or precious stones.

ls, the produce of Asia, Africa, or America, *shall not be imported* into the United Kingdom, to be herein, *in foreign ships,* unless they be the ships of the country in Asia, Africa, or America, ch the goods are the produce, and from which they are imported, except the goods herein-after ned. — § 4.

he produce of the dominions of the Grand Signior, in c Africa, which may be imported from his dominions ope, in ships of his dominions.
and mohair yarn, the produce of Asia, which may be

imported from the dominions of the Grand Signior in the Levant seas, in ships of his dominions.
Bullion.

ided always, that all manufactured goods shall be deemed to be the produce of the country of they are the manufacture. — § 5.

oods shall be imported into the United Kingdom from the islands of Guernsey, Jersey, Alderney, r Man, except in British ships. — § 6.

rts. — No goods shall be exported from the United Kingdom to any British possession in Asia, or America, nor to the islands of Guernsey, Jersey, Alderney, Sark, or Man, except in British - § 7.

wise Ships. — No goods shall be carried coastwise, from one part of the United Kingdom to , except in British ships. — § 8.

oods shall be carried from any of the islands of Guernsey, Jersey, Alderney, Sark, or Man, to er of such islands ; nor from one part of any such islands to another part of the same island, in British ships. — § 9.

en British Possessions. — No goods shall be *carried from* any British possession in Asia, Africa, rica, to any other of such possessions, nor from one part of any of such possessions to another the same, except in British ships. — § 10.

oods shall be *imported into* any British possessions in Asia, Africa, or America, in any foreign nless they he ships of the country of which the goods are the produce, and from which the goods orted. — § 11.

ip British, unless registered and navigated as such. — No ship shall be admitted to be a British nless duly registered and navigated as such ; and every British register ship (so long as the shall be in force, or the certificate retained) shall be navigated during the whole of every (whether with a cargo or in ballast), in every part of the world, by a master who is a British and by a crew whereof three fourths at least are British seamen ; and if such ship be employed asting voyage from one part of the United Kingdom to another, or in a voyage between the Kingdom and the islands of Guernsey, Jersey, Alderney, Sark, or Man, or from one of the said to another of them, or from one part of either of them to another of the same, or be employed in on the coasts of the United Kingdom or of any of the said islands, then the whole of the crew British seamen. — § 12.

ssels under Fifteen Tons Burthen admitted in Navigation upon Rivers, &c. — Provided always, British built boats or vessels under 15 tons burthen, wholly owned and navigated by British although not registered as British ships, shall be admitted to be British vessels, in all navigation vers and upon the coasts of the United Kingdom, or of the British possessions abroad, and not ng over sea, except within the limits of the respective colonial governments within which the ng owners reside ; and all British built boats or vessels wholly owned and navigated by British not exceeding the burthen of 30 tons, and not having a whole or a fixed deck, and being d solely in fishing on the banks and shores of Newfoundland, and of the parts adjacent, or on the ad shores of the provinces of Canada, Nova Scotia, or New Brunswick, adjacent to the Gulf of rence, or on the north of Cape Canso, or of the islands within the same, or in trading coastwise he same limits, shall be admitted to be British boats or vessels, although not registered, so long as ats or vessels shall be solely so employed. — § 13.

ras Ships to be as British, in Trade with United Kingdom. — All ships built in the British nts at Honduras, and owned and navigated as British ships, shall be entitled to the privileges h registered ships in all direct trade between the United Kingdom and the said settlements ; the master shall produce a certificate, under the hand of the superintendent of those settle-hat satisfactory proof has been made before him that such ship (describing the same) was built aid settlements, and is wholly owned by British subjects : Provided also, that the time of the e from the said settlements for every voyage shall be endorsed upon such certificate by such endent. — § 14.

f any Foreign Country. — No ship shall be admitted to be a ship of any particular country, e be of the build of such country ; or have been made prize of war to such country ; or have eited to such country under any law made for the prevention of the slave trade, and condemned rize or forfeiture by a competent court of such country ; or be British built ; (not having been f war from British subjects to any other foreign country ;) nor unless she be navigated by a ho is a subject of such foreign country, and by a crew of whom three fourths at least are subjects ountry ; nor unless she be wholly owned by subjects of such country usually residing therein, or e dominion thereof : Provided, that the country of every ship shall be deemed to include all ich are under the same dominion as the place to which such ship belongs. — § 15.

and Seamen not British. — No person shall be qualified to be a master of a British ship, or to be seaman, within the meaning of this act, except natural born subjects, or persons naturalised parliament, or made denizens by letters of denization ; or except persons who have become abjects by virtue of conquest or cession, and who shall have taken the oath of allegiance, or the idelity required by the treaty or capitulation ; or persons who shall have served on board of any sty's ships of war in time of war for the space of three years : Provided always, that the natives within the limits of the East India Company's charter, although under British dominion, shall a the ground of being such natives, be deemed to be British seamen : Provided always, that every ept ships required to be wholly navigated by British seamen) which shall be navigated by one eaman, if a British ship, or one seaman of the country of such ship, if a foreign ship, for every of the burthen of such ship, shall be deemed to be duly navigated, although the number of men shall exceed one fourth of the whole crew. — § 16.

ers having served Two Years — It shall be lawful for his Majesty, by proclamation, during war, e that foreigners having served two years on board any of his Majesty's ships of war in time of , shall be British seamen within the meaning of this act. — § 17.

Ship not to depart without British Crew. — No British registered ship shall be suffered to depart port in the United Kingdom, or any British possession in any part of the world, (whether with a n ballast,) unless duly navigated : Provided, that any British ships, trading between places in may be navigated by British negroes ; and that ships trading eastward of the Cape of Good

Hope, within the limits of the East India Company's charter, may be navigated by Lascars, or natives, within those limits. — § 18.

Excess of Foreign Seamen. — If any British registered ship shall at any time have, as part of the in any part of the world, any foreign seaman not allowed by law, the master or owners shall for such foreign seaman forfeit 10*l*. : Provided always, that if a due proportion of British seamen cann procured in any foreign port, or in any place within the limits of the East India Company's charte if such proportion be destroyed during the voyage by any unavoidable circumstance, and the master produce a certificate of such facts, under the hand of any British consul, or of two British mercha there be no consul, or from the British governor of any place within the limits of the East India pany's charter; or, in the want of such certificate, shall make proof of the truth of such facts to satisfaction of the collector and comptroller of the customs of any British port, or of any person a rised in any other part of the world to inquire into the navigation of such ship; the same shall be de to be duly navigated. — § 19.

Proportion of Seamen may be altered by Proclamation. — If his Majesty shall, at any time, b royal proclamation, declare that the proportion of British seamen shall be less than the propo required by this act, every British ship navigated with the proportion of British seamen require such proclamation shall be deemed to be duly navigated, so long as such proclamation shall rema force. — § 20.

Goods prohibited only by Navigation Law may be imported for Exportation. — Goods of any sort, o produce of any place, not otherwise prohibited than by the law of navigation herein-before conta may be imported into the United Kingdom from any place in a British ship, and from any plac being a British possession in a foreign ship of any country, and however navigated, to be wareho for exportation only, under the provisions made for warehousing of goods without payment of duty the first entry. — § 21.

Goods imported contrary to Law of Navigation. — If any goods be imported, exported, or ca coastwise, contrary to the law of navigation herein-before contained, all such goods shall be forfeited the master shall forfeit 100*l*. — § 22.

NEW ORLEANS, the capital of Louisiana, one of the United States, situ on the eastern bank of the Mississippi, about 105 miles from its mouth, in lat. 57′ N., lon. 90° 8′ W. Population probably about 60,000. The new built streets broad, intersecting each other at right angles; and the houses are mostly of br It is the grand emporium of all the vast tracts- traversed by the Mississippi, Missouri, and their tributary streams, enjoying a greater command of inte navigation than any other city either of the Old or New World. Civilisa has hitherto struck its roots, and begun to flourish, only in some comparati small portions of the immense territories of which New Orleans is the sea-p and yet it appears, from the official accounts printed by order of congress, during the year ending the 30th of September, 1829, the value of the na American produce exported from this city amounted to 10,898,183 dollars, w the value of that exported from New-York only amounted to 12,036,561. respect to imports, the case is materially different; the value of those of New leans, in the year just mentioned, being only 6,857,209 dollars, or not more a *fifth* part of those of New-York. It is believed by many, seeing how ra settlements are forming in the "West," that New Orleans must, at no distant period, exceed every other city of America, as well in the magnitude o imports as of its exports; and considering the boundless extent and extra nary fertility of the uncultivated and unoccupied basins of the Mississippi Missouri, the anticipations of those who contend that New Orleans is dest to become the greatest emporium, not of America only, but of the world, wil appear very unreasonable. Steam navigation has been of incalculable servi this port, and, indeed, to the whole of central America. The voyage up Mississippi, that used formerly to be so difficult and tedious, is now performe commodious steam packets with ease, celerity, and comfort. " There have counted," says Mr. Flint, " in the harbour, 1,500 flat boats at a time. Steam are arriving and departing every hour; and it is not uncommon to see 50 together in the harbour. A forest of masts is constantly seen along the *levée* cept in the sultry months. There are often 5,000 or 6,000 boatmen from the u country here at a time; and we have known *thirty* vessels advertised togethe Liverpool and Havre. The intercourse with the Havannah and Vera Cr great, and constantly increasing."—(*Geography and History of the Western S* vol. i. p. 557.) From 1811, when the first steam boat was launched on Mississippi, down to the beginning of 1830, no fewer than 336 steam boats been built for the navigation of this river, the Missouri, Ohio, &c., of w 213 were employed at the latter period. Vessels of the largest burthen navigate the river several hundreds of miles above New Orleans. The Bar Louisiana has a capital of 4,000,000 dollars, the State Bank has one of 2,00 dollars; and exclusive of these, and other establishments of the same kind Bank of the United States has here a branch. A large proportion of the fo trade of New Orleans is carried on in foreign bottoms; and as a shipping por ranks far below several of the other ports of the Union. The total of the regist enrolled, and licensed tonnage belonging to New Orleans in 1828, amount

tons; of which 27,598 tons were employed in the coasting trade, and 20,360 steam navigation. The depth of water in the river opposite to New Orleans medium, about 70 feet; and it maintains soundings of 30 feet till within a its confluence with the sea. Besides three or four of inferior consequence, ssissippi has four principal passes or outlets. In the south-east, or main : Balize, the water on the bar at ordinary tides does not exceed 12 feet; the rise of tides in the Gulf of Mexico is not more than 2 or 2½ feet, vessels y much water cannot make their way from the ocean to New Orleans.— 's View of the United States, p. 467.)

unhealthiness of the climate is the great drawback on New Orleans. obably arises from the low and marshy situation of the city and surround- ntry, which is under the level of the Mississippi, being protected from in- n only by an artificial levée or mound, varying from 5 to 30 feet in height, ending along the bank of the river a distance of 100 miles. The unhealthy includes July, August, and September; during which period the yellow ten makes dreadful havoc, particularly among the poorer class of immi- rom the North and from Europe. Latterly great efforts have been made rove the health of the city, by supplying it abundantly with water, the streets, removing wooden sewers, and replacing them with others e, &c. Many places, where water used to stagnate, have been filled up; ge tracts of swampy ground contiguous to the town have been drained. such works will no doubt be prosecuted on a still larger scale, according increase of commerce and population, it is to be hoped that the ravages may be materially abated, though the situation of the city excludes any ong expectation of its ever being rendered quite free from this dreadful

join an account of the quantities of some of the principal articles brought from the interior to ans during the six years ending with 1829. These, of course, form also the principal articles of

Articles.					1824.	1825.	1826.	1827.	1828.	1829.
ssorted	-	-	-	hhds.	349	1,210	470	1,533	3,097	2,868
-	-	-	-	pieces	4,562	6,191	5,299	2,795	5,972	13,472
-	-	-	-	kegs	1,868	2,130	2,926	4,561	3,860	3,995
-	-	-	-	barrels	732	1,242	1,203	1,792	5,622	5,405
x	-	-	-	do.	295	503	560	603	770	795
obes	-	-	-	lbs.	12,609	18,411	7,740	13,412	19,987	15,210
-	-	-	-	bales	142,575	206,993	251,983	337,934	298,042	269,571
-	-	-	-	do.	1,501	3,737	3,030	11,171	4,365	5,557
al	-	-	-	barrels	4,727	3,420	729	1,827	498	6,849
ars	-	-	-	do.	57,351	72,563	143,373	79,973	89,876	91,882
-	-	-	-	do.	100,929	140,546	129,094	131,096	152,593	157,323
-	-	-	-	kegs	18,210	34,373	51,053	85,865	115,535	110,206
-	-	-	-	pigs	45,454	58,479	86,242	106,405	183,712	146,203
oil	-	-	-	barrels	191	622	708	1,723	2,637	2,940
ns	-	-	-	packs	3,863	4,820	11,693	4,169	3,160	6,215
as	-	-	-	do.	163	396	161	253	155	159
-	-	-	-	hhds.	2,573	18,409	19,385	21,704	30,224	29,432
-	-	-	-	do.	647	1,332	1,862	6,442	648	4,239

Cotton in Bales, from New Orleans, Savannah, Charleston, and Mobile, for Nine Months in 1829 and in 1830, ending June 30.

Years.	New Orleans.	Savannah.	Charleston.	Mobile.
1829	207,868	205,959	108,752	58,780
1830	302,852	199,803	186,067	71,518
	510,720	405,762	294,819	120,298

onies, Weights, and Measures, see NEW YORK.

SPAPERS. Publications in Numbers, consisting commonly of single nd published at short and stated intervals, conveying intelligence of pass- s.

ance and Value of Newspapers in a Commercial Point of View. — It is foreign rposes of this work to consider the moral and political effects produced by rs: of the extent of their influence there is no doubt even among those who ely as to its effect. Their utility to commerce is, however, unquestionable. rtisements they circulate, though these announcements are limited in Great r a heavy duty, the variety of facts and information they contain as to the d demand of commodities in all quarters of the world, their prices, and the s by which they are affected, render newspapers indispensable to commercial

men, supersede a great mass of epistolary correspondence, raise merchants in r
places towards an equality, in point of information, with those in the great mart
wonderfully quicken all the movements of commerce.   But newspapers them
have become a considerable commercial article in Great Britain.   In the year
the produce of the stamp duty, deducting the discount, levied on newspaper
410,980*l*. 6*s*. 6*d*.   The gross produce of the sale must have been more than
this sum, without allowing for the papers sold at a higher price than 7*d*.; so tl
consumption of newspapers must have amounted, in that year, to nearly 1,00(
sterling.

Newspapers, in London, are sold by the publishers to newsmen or newsve
by whom they are distributed to the purchasers in town and country.   The new
who are the retailers, receive, for their business of distribution, a regulated allo\
The papers which are sold to the public at 7*d*., which form the great mass of L
newspapers, are sold to the newsmen in what are technically called quires.   Eacl
consists of 27 papers, and is sold, to the newsmen, for 13*s*.; so that the newsman'\
profit on 27 papers is 2*s*. 9*d*.   In some instances, where newspapers are sent
post, ½*d*. additional on each paper is charged by the newsmen to their count\
tomers.   Some of the clerks at the post-office, called clerks of the roads, ar
siderable news agents.   The stamp duty on a newspaper is, at present, nominal\
but a discount is allowed on those papers which are sold at a price not exceedir
of 20 per cent., which reduces the stamp duty actually paid to 3⅛*d*.   Each paper
sold to the newsman at a little less than 5¾*d*., the sum which is received by the
paper proprietors for paper, printing, and the expenses of their establishment
small fraction more than 2⅛*d*. for each copy.   Advertisements form a considerable
of profit to newspapers; and without this source, some of the most widely circul\
them could not support their great expenditure.   Each advertisement is charged, \
distinction on account of length, with a government duty of 3*s*. 6*d*.   The r\
derived from advertisements in Great Britain, in 1830, was 157,482*l*. 7*s*. 4*d*.
have no means of ascertaining exactly the portion of this sum derived from news
as distinguished from other publications, but we believe we should under esti\
by taking it at three fourths of the whole.   The charges of newspapers for advertis
are proportioned to their length, and to the character of the newspaper itself.   Tl
received for them may be taken, inclusive of the duty, at 300,000*l*.

Newspaper stamps are obtained at the Stamp Office, where the paper is sent
stationers to be stamped.   The stamps are paid for before the paper is returned.
duty on advertisements, which is also under the management of the commissio
stamps, is paid monthly; and, for securing these payments, the printer and two \
become bound in moderate sums.

The London newspapers have become remarkable for the great mass and va\
matter which they contain, the rapidity with which they are printed and circulate
the accuracy and copiousness of their reports of debates.   These results are o\
by a large expenditure and considerable division of labour.   The reports of parli
ary proceedings are obtained by a succession of able and intelligent reporter
relieve one another at intervals of three quarters of an hour, or occasionally le
newspaper cannot aim at copious and correct reports with less than 10 repor
the House of Commons; and the expense of that part of a morning news
establishment alone exceeds 3,000*l*. per annum.

Regulations as to Newspapers. — The 38 Geo. 3. c. 78. enacts, that no person shall print or ĵ
newspaper, until an affidavit has been delivered at the Stamp Office, stating the name and places
of the printer, publisher, and proprietor; specifying the amount of the shares, the title of the pap
description of the building in which it is intended to be printed.   A copy of every newspape
delivered, within six days, to the commissioners of stamps, under a penalty of 100*l*.

The act 39 G. 3. c. 79. requires that the name of every printer, type-founder, and maker of
presses, shall be entered with the clerk of the peace, under a penalty of 20*l*.; and every persc
types or presses must, if required by a justice of the peace, state to whom they are sold.

A printer is bound to print, upon the front of every page printed on one side only, and \
first and last sheet of every publication containing more than one leaf, his name and place \
He is also required to keep a copy of every work he prints, on which shall be written or pr\
name of his employer; and shall produce the same to any justice, if required, within six month

Persons publishing papers without the name and abode of the printer may be apprehended, ar
before a magistrate; and a peace officer, by warrant of a justice of peace, may enter any place
for printing presses or types suspected to be kept without the notice required by the act, and r
them off, together with all printed papers found in the place.

The 1 Geo. 4. c. 9. enacts, that all periodical pamphlets or papers, published at intervals not €
26 days, containing public news, intelligence, or occurrences, or any remarks thereon, and not c
more than two sheets, or published for less price than 6*d*., shall be deemed newspapers, and shall l
to the same regulations and stamp duties.

Influence of the Tax on Newspapers. — At present it is impossible, without a \
of the stamp laws, to sell newspapers under 7*d*. or 7½*d*.; so that those poorer
who cannot afford so large a sum, or who have no means of getting a news\
company with others, are obliged either to be without one, or to resort to tl

journals that are circulated in defiance of the law. It has been proposed to
e the duty to 2*d.*, which would be a great improvement; but all fixed duties on
apers seem to be essentially objectionable, inasmuch as, by effectually hindering
ee and open circulation of the cheapest sort, they throw their supply into the
of the least reputable portion of the community, who circulate them surrepti-
y, and not unfrequently make them vehicles for diffusing doctrines of the most
rous tendency. The better way, therefore, would be to assess the duty on news-
s on an *ad valorem* principle, making it 25 per cent., perhaps, or 1*d* on a news-
sold at 4*d.*, $\frac{1}{2}d.$ on one sold at 2*d.*, and so on, proportionally to the price. The
tages resulting from such a plan would be many and great. The unjust stigma
ow attaches to low priced papers would be removed; and men of talent and
ple would find it equally advantageous to write in them as in those of a higher

Were such an alteration made, we venture to predict that the present twopenny
s, than which nothing can be conceived more utterly worthless, would, very soon,
perseded by others of a totally different character; so that, in this way, the change
be in the highest degree beneficial. It would also, we apprehend, introduce into
aper compiling, that division of labour, or rather of subjects, which is found in
thing else. Instead of having all sorts of matters crammed into the same journal,
different topic of considerable interest would be separately treated in a low priced
l, appropriated to it only, and conducted by persons fully conversant with its
ples and details. Under the present omnivorous system, individuals who care
g for the theatre are, notwithstanding, unable to procure a paper in which it does
cupy a prominent place; and those who cannot distinguish one tune from another
aily served up to them long dissertations on concerts, operas, oratorios, and so
The proposed system would give the power of selecting. Those who preferred
podrida to any thing else, would be sure of finding an abundant supply; while
who wished for a more select regimen — who preferred one or two separate dishes
nultitude huddled together — would be able, which at present they are not, to
their taste. Neither can there be much doubt that an *ad valorem* duty would be
productive than the present duty; inasmuch as, though it would be less on each
the number of papers would be prodigiously augmented. It also would have
vantage of being easy of collection; for, being a certain portion of the price, no
n could arise with respect to it.

ead, however, of imposing an *ad valorem* duty on newspapers, it has been pro-
o repeal the duty entirely, and to substitute in its stead a post-office duty, similar
charged in the United States. But it appears to us that an *ad valorem* duty is
ble. The imposition of a postage would give rise to a distinction between the
f newspapers in large towns and in the country; increasing it in the latter,
owing to the few facilities afforded for reading in common, it is of importance
price should be as low as possible.

ces of Newspapers. — The history of newspapers, and of periodical literature in
, remains to be written; and were the task executed by an individual of compe-
lity, and with due care, it would be a most interesting work. It appears, from
earches of Mr. Chalmers, that the first newspaper published in modern Europe
s appearance at Venice, in 1536; but the jealousy of the government would not
f its being printed; so that, for many years, it was circulated in manuscript!
ld seem that newspapers were first issued in England by authority, in 1588,
the alarm occasioned by the approach of the *Armada* to our shores; in order, as
ted, by giving real information, to allay the general anxiety, and to hinder the
nation of false and exaggerated statements. From this æra, newspapers, of one
ther, have, with a few intermissions, generally appeared in London; sometimes at
and sometimes at irregular intervals. During the civil wars, both parties had
wspapers. The earliest newspaper published in Scotland made its appearance
he auspices of Cromwell, in 1652. The Caledonian Mercury was, however,
of the Scotch newspapers of native manufacture; it made its appearance at
gh, under the title of *Mercurius Caledonius*, in 1660; but its publication was
er interrupted. In 1715, a newspaper was, for the first time, attempted in
v.

Daily Courant, the first of the daily newspapers published in Great Britain,
s appearance at London in the early part of the reign of Queen Anne. — (See
of *Ruddiman*, pp. 102—121.)

the Stamp Office it appears that the number of newspapers sold annually in
d, during the 3 years ending with 1753, was 7,411,757; in 1760, 9,464,790;
, 14,035,639; in 1792, 15,005,760.

An Account of the Aggregate Number of Stamps issued for Newspapers in each of the undermenti[oned] Years; distinguishing the Numbers in England, Scotland, and Ireland.

Years.	England.	Scotland.	Great Britain.	Years.	England.	Scotland.	Great Britain.	Ireland.*
1801	15,090,805	994,280	16,085,085	1814	24,931,910	1,376,093	26,308,003	
1802	14,264,289	967,750	15,232,039	1815	23,075,985	1,309,523	24,385,508	
1803	15,888,921	1,060,210	16,949,131	1816	21,053,627	996,727	22,050,354	
1804	16,921,768	1,156,525	18,078,293	1817	20,946,252	850,816	21,797,068	2,480,401
1805	17,610,069	1,172,200	18,782,269	1818	21,015,429	1,048,900	22,064,329	2,654,212
1806	19,218,984	1,313,709	20,532,793	1819	21,904,834	1,143,615	23,048,449	2,782,903
1807	20,097,602	1,337,259	21,434,861	1820	25,177,127	1,236,560	26,413,687	2,974,156
1808	20,714,566	1,343,925	22,058,491	1821	23,699,752	1,162,434	24,862,186	2,931,037
1809	22,536,331	1,470,552	24,006,883	1822	22,709,159	1,223,244	23,932,403	3,088,472
1810	22,519,786	1,459,775	23,979,561	1823	23,422,526	1,247,739	24,670,265	3,339,492
1811	22,977,963	1,443,750	24,421,713	1824	24,556,860	1,017,049	25,573,909	3,364,999
1812	23,719,000	1,573,600	25,292,600	1825	25,485,503	1,465,191	26,950,094	3,500,482
1813	24,839,397	1,503,221	26,342,618	1826	25,684,003	1,296,549	26,980,552	3,473,014

* Until 1817 no distinct account was kept of the stamps issued for newspapers in Ireland.

A Return showing the Number of Stamps issued for London Newspapers in the Years 1825, 1826, [1827,] 1828, and 1829.

1825.	1826.	1827.	1828.	1829.
16,910,066	16,631,099	17,242,697	17,735,604	17,996,279

Note. — As a few of the London newspapers are supplied with stamps through stationers (who procure stamps for the provincial newspapers), the total number of stamps issued for the whole [of] London newspapers cannot be furnished.

An Account showing the Number of Stamps issued for the following London Newspapers in the [year] 1829, and the respective Amount of Stamp and Advertisement Duty paid by each in the same Ye[ar]. (*Parl. Paper*, No. 549. Sess. 1826.)

Title of Newspaper.	Number of Stamps.	Stamp Duties paid by each.	Advertise[ment] Duties pai[d] each.
		£ s. d.	£ s.
* Times and Evening Mail	3,275,311	54,588 10 4	16,433
* Morning Herald and English Chronicle	2,000,475	33,341 5 0	7,383 1[ ]
* Morning Chronicle, Observer, Bell's Life in London, and Englishman	2,331,450	38,857 10 0	4,773 1[ ]
* Morning Advertiser and Weekly Register	1,145,000	19,083 . 6 8	5,560
Morning Post	598,500	9,975 0 0	5,854
New Times, afterwards called Morning Journal	366,500	6,108 6 8	1,672
* Public Ledger, British Traveller, and Weekly Times	561,809	9,363 9 8	4,864
Courier	995,200	16,586 13 4	2,629
Globe and Traveller	864,000	14,400 0 0	1,667 1[ ]
Sun	625,000	10,416 13 4	897
* Standard, St. James's Chronicle, London Packet, and London Journal	1,367,000	22,783 6 8	1,790 1[ ]
* County Chronicle and County Herald	192,000	3,200 0 0	996
John Bull	337,500	5,625 0 0	1,181
Bell's Weekly Messenger	566,000	9,433 6 8	
Bell's Weekly Dispatch	780,552	13,009 4 0	
News	253,000	4,216 13 4	
* Sunday Times and Kent and Essex Mercury	407,003	6,783 7 8	990
Farmer's Journal	107,125	1,785 8 4	150
Literary Gazette	70,430	1,173 16 8	463
Examiner	271,044	4,517 8 0	255
Law Advertiser	38,280	638 0 0	13
Cobbett's Weekly Register	176,500	2,941 13 4	17
Atlas	246,200	4,103 6 8	656
Age	256,000	4,266 13 4	734
Record	145,600	2,426 13 4	360
Atkinson's Price Current	450	7 10 0	
Smith's Price Current	2,500	41 13 4	
Althan's Corn Trade Circular	2,400	40 0 0	
Wetenhall's Stock List	3,800	63 6 8	
Commercial Record	3,650	60 16 8	
Price's Price Current	6,000	100 0 0	

In the instances marked thus (*) the papers mentioned being the property of one person, in whos[e name] the stamps are taken out, the number used and amount of duty received for each of such papers [cannot] be distinguished.

of the Produce of the Duties on Newspapers and Advertisements during each of the last Twenty Years, in England, Scotland, and Ireland. — (*Parl. Papers*, Nos. 405, 406. Sess. 1830.)

rs ed n.	Newspapers.									Advertisements.								
	England.			Scotland.			Ireland.			England.			Scotland.			Ireland.		
	L.	*s.*	*d.*	*L.*	*s.*	*d.*	*L.*	*s.*	*d.*	*L.*	*s.*	*d.*	*L.*	*s.*	*d.*	*L.*	*s.*	*d.*
1	328,413	10	11	21,288	7	8	In those years there was no separate account kept of stamps issued for newspapers in Ireland.			113,546	19	1	15,041	8	0	15,723	11	7
2	335,095	6	0	21,054	13	9				114,195	11	5	14,397	9	0	20,479	5	3
3	345,902	1	8	22,948	6	8				115,875	18	3	14,448	6	0	20,915	5	10
4	362,241	4	4	21,921	19	7				114,111	12	10	14,623	7	0	21,253	3	11½
5	363,600	0	0	20,158	7	7				106,575	9	8	13,410	3	0	19,759	17	6
6	363,414	3	5	20,281	12	10½				110,941	6	6	14,017	7	0	20,475	16	1½
7	350,893	15	8	16,612	2	4				118,202	3	4	15,353	8	6	18,498	7	5
8	349,104	4	0	14,180	5	4	18,885	1	2½	116,352	4	11	16,666	13	0	18,191	12	7
9	350,257	3	0	17,481	13	4	20,210	16	6	119,788	19	4	17,240	6	0	18,535	12	6
0	365,080	11	4	19,060	5	0	21,187	1	11¾	122,227	3	3	16,911	9	6	16,721	1	8½
1	419,618	15	8	20,609	6	8	22,693	10	10	123,772	15	6	16,416	15	0	15,491	0	0
2	394,995	17	4	19,373	18	0	22,346	9	7	125,965	17	5	16,095	2	0	15,102	5	0½
3	378,485	19	8	20,387	8	0	23,556	1	0¼	131,288	12	0	17,030	16	6	13,708	7	3¼
4	390,375	8	8	20,795	13	0	25,448	2	5	125,475	5	7	16,020	11	0	14,524	3	8¼
5	409,281	0	0	22,387	9	4	25,633	13	6½	134,633	19	3½	17,825	17	0	16,426	10	9
6	425,154	10	8	24,419	17	0	26,659	9	3½	144,751	2	6½	18,708	18	0	15,907	15	0
7	429,662	15	2	22,013	6	4	25,187	11	9¼	135,687	7	2	17,779	13	0	15,720	0	0
8	428,629	9	8	29,929	10	4	25,561	3	11¼	133,978	16	11	18,409	14	6	14,379	17	6
9	439,798	8	0	33,556	2	8	27,330	16	8	136,368	17	10	18,939	12	5	15,532	15	0
0	438,667	10	8	42,301	6	0	28,578	16	7¼	136,052	18	10	17,592	5	7	14,985	6	0

ncrease of newspapers in Great Britain, though it is shown by these documents been very considerable, has been materially repressed by the weight of the stamp The circulation of the Parisian daily papers much exceeds that of the London ; a result which can only be ascribed to their greater cheapness.

can Newspapers. — The increase of newspapers in the United States has also greater than in England ; a result, partly, no doubt, to be ascribed to the more crease of population in the Union, but in a far greater degree to freedom from . The total number of newspapers annually issued in the United States is es-at 55,000,000. We believe, however, that the total number issued in Great and Ireland at this moment, notwithstanding the peculiar excitement of the s under 35,000,000 ; so that, making allowance for the difference of population, lividual in America has, at an average, more than twice the supply of news-njoyed by individuals in England. It would be easy to show, were this the lace, that this extraordinary diffusion of these useful vehicles of information and n is attended with the most salutary effects. "From this exuberant supply of and weekly presses, and the low price charged as compared with the English ch newspapers, they are liberally patronised by all classes, and are found in al-ry dwelling and counting-house, and in all hotels, taverns, and shops; and large portion of the public attention. As the paths of honour and promotion open to every one, it follows that political discussion forms the principal the newspapers. There is no country where the press has a more powerful over public opinion." — (*Picture of New-York*, p. 391.)

ing Table contains a Statement of the Number of Newspapers published in the United States at mencement of the Revolutionary War, and the Number of Newspapers and other periodical ublished in the same in 1810 and 1828.

States.	1775.	1810.	1828.	States.	1775.	1810.	1828.
	-	-	29	Georgia	1	13	18
usetts	7	32	78	Florida	-	1	2
npshire	1	12	17	Alabama	-	-	10
	-	14	21	Mississippi	-	4	6
land	2	7	14	Louisiana	-	10	9
cut	4	11	33	Tennessee	-	6	8
k	4	66	161	Kentucky	-	17	23
ey	-	8	22	Ohio	-	14	66
ania	9	71	185	Indiana	-	-	17
	-	2	4	Michigan	-	-	2
	2	21	37	Illinois	-	-	4
f Colombia	-	6	9	Missouri	-	-	5
	2	23	34	Arkansas	-	-	1
rolina	2	10	20	Cherokee Nation	-	-	1
rolina	3	10	16				
				Total	37	358	802

-YORK, the capital of the state of that name; and the commercial is of the United States, in lat. 40° 42⅔′ N., lon. 72° 59¾′ W. It is si- the southern extremity of Manhattan Island, at the point of confluence Hudson river, which separates Manhattan from New Jersey, with East hich separates it from Long Island. New-York bay, or inner harbour, the most capacious and finest in the world; it is completely land-locked, ds the best anchorage. The entrance to the bay through the Nar- extremely beautiful. On each side, the shore, though wooded down to

the water's edge, is thickly studded with farms, villages, and country seats.
the upper end are seen the spires of the city; and in the distance the bold
pitous banks of the Hudson. From New-York to the bar between Sandy
Point and Schryer's Island (the division between the outer bay or harbou
the Atlantic) is about 18 miles. Strong fortifications have been erected a
Narrows, Governor's Island, and other places, for the defence of the cit
shipping. The subjoined wood-cut represents the city and bay of New-
and the surrounding country.

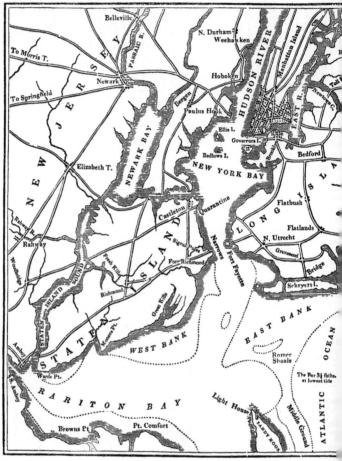

The Hudson river was first explored in 1609, by the famous English navigato
name it bears, then in the service of the West India Company of Holland. In 161
Amsterdam, now New-York, was founded by the Dutch, as a convenient station
fur trade. In 1664, it was taken by the English. The Dutch again recovered po
of it in 1673; but it was retaken by the English in the following year, and co
in their occupation till the termination of the revolutiouary war.

New-York has increased faster than any other city of the United States. I
it contained 6,000 inhabitants. In 1774, previously to the commencement of the
independence, the population amounted to 22,750. During the war, the populati
tinued stationary; but since 1783, its increase has been quite extraordinary. I
the population amounted to 33,131; in 1800, to 60,489; in 1810, to 96,373; :
to 123,706; and in 1830, to above 213,000! Originally the houses were m
wood, and the streets narrow and confined. In these particulars, however, a g
provement has taken place during the last half century; most of the old houses havi

down, and rebuilt with brick. The new streets, which are broad, and intersect each
at right angles, are well paved and lighted. Broadway, the principal street, is one
e largest and finest in the world. Many of the public buildings are commodious
legant. The pools, that were formerly abundant in the city and its vicinity, have
completely filled up ; a measure that has done much to improve the health of the
ation. In respect of cleanliness, however, New-York is not to be compared with
glish town. There is hardly such a thing as a sink or common sewer in the whole
the night soil and filth is collected in pits, of which there is one in every house,
eing conveyed to the nearest quay, is thrown into the water; but as these quays are
of timber, with many projections, a great deal of filth is retained about them,
cing, in hot weather, an abominable stench. The yellow fever, by which New-
is sometimes visited, uniformly breaks out in the lower and dirtiest part of the
and seldom, indeed, extends to the new and more elevated streets. It is now
less prevalent than formerly ; and the general opinion seems to be, that if stones
substituted for timber in the quays, sewers constructed, and proper regulations
ed as to cleanliness, the scourge would entirely disappear.

v-York is indebted, for her wonderful increase, to her admirable situation, which
ndered her the greatest emporium of the New World. Even at ebb tide, there is
t water on the bar ; and the water in the outer and inner bays, and in the river, is
p, that ships of the very largest burthen lie close to the quays, and may proceed to
t distance up the river. The navigation of the bay is but rarely impeded by ice.
reat strength of the tide, and the vicinity of the ocean, keep it generally open, even
the Chesapeake and Delaware bays are frozen over. The influence of the tides is
the Hudson as far as Troy, 160 miles above New-York, affording very peculiar
es for its navigation. These natural advantages have been vastly extended by a
of canalisation, which has already connected the Hudson with Lake Ontario and
Erie ; and which, when completed, will connect it with the Ohio river, and con-
tly with the Mississippi and the Gulf of Mexico ! So prodigious a command of
l navigation is not enjoyed by any other city, with the exception of New Orleans ;
readier access to the port of New-York, the greater salubrity of the climate, and her
n in the most industrious part of the Union, where slavery is abolished, give her
ages over her southern rival, which, it is most probable, will secure her continued
derance.

commerce of New-York is very extensive. The value of the merchandise an-
loaded and unloaded in the port is estimated to amount to from 80,000,000 to
0,000 dollars. The number of vessels in the port in the busy season varies
00 to 750, exclusive of about 50 steam packets. The number of arrivals from
ports amount annually to about 1,500 ; and the coasting arrivals are between
nd 5,000. The total value of the imports into the United States in the year
30th September, 1829, was 74,492,527 dollars ; of which no less than 34,743,307,
ly one half of the whole, were imported into New-York ! The customs revenue
goods paying duties, imported into this city, amounts to about 13,000,000 dol-
nile the total customs revenue of the United States does not exceed 22,000,000
The imports comprise an infinite variety of articles. The principal are cottons,
s, linens, hardware, and cutlery ; earthenware, brass and copper manufactures,
m Great Britain ; silk, wine, brandy, &c. from France and Spain ; sugar and
from the Havannah and Brazil ; with tea, spices, cochineal, indigo, dye-woods,
he value of the exports from New-York in the year ending 30th September,
mounted to 20,119,011 dollars, being between a third and a fourth part of the
ports from the United States. The exports principally consist of wheat, flour, and
; beef, pork, butter, dried fish, and all sorts of provisions ; furs, cotton, tobacco,
manufactured goods, &c. The great excess of the imports into New-York over
orts is accounted for by the fact, that, while mostly all the articles of export from
stern States are shipped at New Orleans, the greater part of the more valuable
brought from abroad, and destined for the consumption of Ohio, Indiana, Illi-
d, in some degree, even Kentucky, are principally imported into New-York.
tonnage of New-York is greater than that of Liverpool, or any other city, with
gle exception of London. The registered tonnage belonging to the port in
mounted to 158,237 tons, and the enrolled and licensed tonnage to 181,167 tons ;
a grand total of 339,404 tons, being between a fifth and a sixth of the whole
of the United States.

Arrivals in New-York from Foreign Ports in 1830.

nuary	-	54	May	-	141	September	-	184
bruary	-	63	June	-	162	October	-	142
arch	-	98	July	-	153	November	-	137
pril	-	127	August	-	130	December	-	119

total of 1,510 ; of which 332 were ships, 28 barques, 714 brigs, 376 schooners, 8 sloops, 1 ketch, and
1,366 were American, 92 British, 7 Spanish, 12 Swedish, 2 Hamburgh, 5 French, 8 Bremen,

6 Haytian, 9 Danish, 2 Brazilian, 2 Dutch, and 1 Portuguese. The number of passengers brought by vessels was 30,224. The arrivals in 1829 were 1,310, passengers 16,064; making an increase in 18 arrivals, 200; passengers, 14,160.

Tonnage entered the Port of New-York in 1830.

							Ton
Registered vessels of the United States, engaged in foreign trade	-	-	284,
Registered vessels of the United States, engaged in the coasting trade	-	-	39,
Licensed vessels of the United States, engaged in the coasting and river trade	-	90,
Licensed for the fisheries	-	-	-	-	-	-	
	Total American tonnage		-	414,
Vessels not of the United States	-	-	-	-	36,
	Total	-	-	-	450,

The above statement is from official returns, except the American registered and licensed vessel gaged in the coasting trade for the last quarter of 1830. Of these an estimate has been made, w however, cannot vary materially from the true amount.

The following were among the articles exported from New-York in 1830:—

Wheat flour	-	-	-	barrels	304,352	Candles, sperm	-	-	boxes
Corn meal	-	-	-	hhds.	9,222	Butter	-	-	firkins
Do.	-	-	-	barrels	9,192	Beef	-	-	barrels
Corn	-	-	-	bushels	174,182	Pork	-	-	do.
Flax seed	-	-	-	tierces	12,099	Lard	-	-	kegs
Hops	-	-	-	bales	1,084	Cheese	-	casks & boxes
Ashes, pot and pearl	-	-	barrels	23,765				
Candles, tallow	-	-	boxes	10,112	Soap	-	-	boxes

Years.	Customs Revenue collected at New-York.	Total Customs Revenue of United States.	Years.	Customs Revenue collected at New-York.	Total Customs Revenue of United Sta
	Dols. cts.	Dols. cts.		Dols. cts.	Dols. c
1825	15,752,100 41	20,098,713 45	1828	13,745,147 21	21,500,600 0
1826	11,525,864 22	23,341,331 77	1829	13,052,676 36	22,681,965 9
1827	13,217,695 89	19,712,283 89	1830 estimated	13,000,000 00	21,756,707 3

Regulations as to Passengers arriving at New-York.— On the arrival of passengers, an entry mu made at the Custom-house of their names, clothes, or implements of trade or profession (all of w are exempt from duty), and an oath taken respecting them; the form of which, and the entry, may b at the office gratis. Cabin passengers make this entry themselves, and pay 20 cents each for a per on exhibiting which to the officer on board, they are allowed to remove their baggage after it has be spected. Only one entry and permit is necessary for a *family*, and only 20 cents demanded, whateve be the number of the family. Remains of sea stores, such as tea, sugar, foreign spirits and wine liable to pay duties; but unless these are of great bulk or quantity, they are generally allowed to free.

An entry is usually made by the master of the vessel, of steerage passengers and their baggage; pay each 20 cents for a permit. When entry is made by any person not the owner, he gives bond for ment of the duties, if any; and if, after entry is made at the Custom-house, and the oath taken, a ticle is found belonging to a passenger, liable to pay duty, *not specified in the entry*, it is forfeited, an person in whose baggage the article is found, subjected in treble the value.

Besides making entry at the Custom-house, it is provided by a law of the State, that every maste vessel arriving from a foreign country, or from any other port of the United States, " shall, with hours after entering his vessel at the Custom-house, make a report in writing, on oath, to the mayo in case of his sickness or absence to the recorder of the said city, of the name, age, and occupation o person who shall have been brought as passenger in such ship or vessel on her last voyage, upon p forfeiting, for every neglect or omission to make such report, the sum of 75 dollars for every alien, a sum of 50 dollars for every other person neglected to be so reported as aforesaid."

The master must also give bond, that none of his passengers shall become chargeable upon the rates of the city for the space of two years. If he permit an alien to come ashore before he gran bond, he subjects himself to a penalty of 500 dollars.

Banks. — There are 15 banks in New-York. Their joint capital is estimated at about 18,000,000 d The following are some of the more important particulars with respect to them :—

	Dollars.
Whole amount of bank capital	-	-	-	17,830,000
Deposits	-	-	-	6,890,937
Circulation	-	-	-	5,547,321
Amount of specie in their vaults	-	-	1,517,004
Profits of the whole banks in 1828	-	-	1,193,000
Supposing their discounts to be at 6 per cent., and to average 60 days, they must have amounted to	119,310,100
Running discounts	-	-	-	19,885,017

Insurance Companies.—There are in New-York *eight* joint stock companies for marine insuran vided into 68,000 shares, with an aggregate capital of 3,050,000 dollars. There are *twenty* joint stoc panies for fire insurance, divided into 179,000 shares, with an aggregate capital of 7,800,000 dollars. is also a company or two for life insurance.

The total tax paid in 1827, by the different incorporated companies in the State of New-York, amount of their capital, was 131,798 dollars.

LINES OF PACKETS.—The establishment of regular lines of packets from New-York, to foreign and also to every principal port in the United States, has produced a new era in the commerce city, and redounded equally to the benefit of the enterprising individuals by whom they were pro and the public. The principal intercourse is carried on with Liverpool. There are about 20 packe employed between these cities, distributed in four *lines*. We are indebted for the following part with respect to these ships, to our esteemed friend Mr. Hugh Mure, of Liverpool.

Statement of the Passages made by the different Ships and Masters employed in the Old Line 1818 to 1827 inclusive, embracing a Period of 10 Years, and comprising 188 complete Voyage

The passages from New-York to Liverpool, during the said period, have averaged	-	24 day
Those from Liverpool to New-York, during the said time, have averaged	-	38
The shortest passage from New-York to Liverpool was made by the ship New-York, Captain Maxwell, in December 1823, being	-	16
The longest passage from New-York to Liverpool was made by the ship Nestor, Captain S. G. Macy, in December 1820 and January 1821, being	-	57

rtest passages from Liverpool to New-York, were made by the ship Amity,
n George Maxwell, in April 1819, and by the ship Colombia, Captain Rogers, in
ry 1824, being   -   -   -   -   -   22   days.
est passage from Liverpool to New-York, was made by the ship Pacific, Captain
r, in December 1827 and January and February 1828, being   -   -   71   days.
ages are not reckoned from land to land, as is sometimes the case; but from one city to the

rate Passages from New-York to Liverpool were as follow:—

sage of 16 days.		8 Passages of 27 days.
— 17	9	— 28
— 18	2	— 29
— 19	4	— 30
— 20	1	— 31
— 21	2	— 32
— 22	3	— 33
— 23	3	— 34
— 24	3	— 35
— 25	1	— 36
— 26	1	— 37

rate Passages from Liverpool to New-York were as follow:—

sages of 22 days.		8 Passages of 43 days.
— 23	4	— 44
— 25	4	— 45
— 26	2	— 46
— 27	1	— 47
— 28	5	— 48
— 29	2	— 49
— 30	2	— 50
— 31	2	— 51
— 32	3	— 52
— 33	1	— 53
— 34	1	— 54
— 35	3	— 55
— 36	2	— 56
— 37	1	— 57
— 38	1	— 59
— 39	2	— 61
— 40	1	— 65
— 41	1	— 70
— 42	1	— 71

ages of the Ships which sailed from New-York to Liverpool, in

eraged 24 days.	July,	averaged 24 days.
— 24	August	— 23
— 23	September	— 25
— 24	October	— 24
— 24	November	— 22
— 25	December	— 24

ages of the Ships which sailed from Liverpool to New-York, in

eraged 42 days.	July,	averaged 40 days.
— 40	August	— 36
— 36	September	— 33
— 34	October	— 37
— 35	November	— 38
— 38	December	— 48

The Passages of the respective Ships have averaged as follows:—viz.

		New-York to Liverpool.	Liverpool to New-York.
Canada	- 15 voyages	21 days.	- 34 days.
Colombia	- 15	22	- 34
Albion	- 9	22	- 36
New-York	- 17	23	- 36
James Cropper	- 17	23	- 37
William Thomson	17	23	- 38
James Monroe	- 16	24	- 38
Manchester	- 8	24	- 38
Florida	- 10	27	- 36
Amity	- 18	25	- 39
New Pacific	- 12	24	- 40
Courier	- 8	23	- 42
Britannia	- 4	24	- 43
Nestor	- 13	26	- 43
Old Pacific	- 4	23	- 50
Orbit	- 5	29	- 46

The Passages of the respective Masters have averaged as follows:—viz.

		New-York to Liverpool.	Liverpool to New-York
J. Stanton	- 3 voyages	- 20 days	- 34 days.
J. Rogers	- 26	22	- 35
J. Bennett	- 10	24	- 34
H. Graham	- 8	23	- 36
C. Marshall	- 17	23	- 37
J. Williams	- 12	22	- 38
W. Thomson	- 5	21	- 39
G. Maxwell	- 22	24	- 37
W. Bowne	- 8	22	- 39
R. Marshall	- 3	24	- 38
W. Lee	- 17	25	- 39
S. G. Macy	- 9	23	- 41
R. R. Crocker	- 14	24	- 41
S. Maxwell	- 10	24	- 41
J. Eldredge	- 2	26	- 39
J. Tinkham	- 14	27	- 39
S. C. Reid	- 1	28	- 39
J. Watkinson	- 6	28	- 42
W. Pease	- 2	34	- 43
J. Macy	- 1	33	- 51

hips for *New-York* sail from Liverpool on the 1st, 8th, 16th, and 24th of each month throughout
And they sail on the same days in each month *from* New-York for Liverpool.
n passage *to* New-York, 35 guineas; from New-York, 30 guineas; which includes provisions,
s, &c., so that the passengers have no occasion to provide any thing except personal apparel.
ships in the whole, varying in size from 500 to 580 tons burthen each, are employed as regular
ween New-York and Liverpool; they are all American property, and built chiefly in New-York,
al workmanship, and fitted up with every convenience for passengers, and in a most expensive
d style. Each ship has a separate cabin for ladies; each state room, in the respective cabins,
modate *two* passengers; but a *whole* state room may be secured for one individual by paying at
1¼ passage, that is, 52½ guineas.
for *Philadelphia* sail from Liverpool on the 8th and 20th of every month throughout the year:
ese ships sail *from* Philadelphia for Liverpool on the 20th of each month; the others do not
rn *direct* from Philadelphia, but go to Charleston, Savannah, &c., to bring cargoes of produce
ol.
ssage same as that to and from New-York.
ps, 9 in number, are all American built and owned, and are from 300 to 500 tons burthen;
m are as splendid as the New-York packets, and all are fitted up with every regard to comfort.
ips for *Boston* sail at specified periods in January, February, and March, and again in June,
August, in each year; but they seldom return *direct* from Boston to Liverpool. The rate of
same as that by the packets for New-York.
of *steerage* passage varies, in the course of the year, considerably; depending on the number of
the number of passengers going at the time. By the packet ships, it fluctuates from 5 to 6
each full-grown person; and children under 14 years are taken at half price. By other ships,
steerage passage varies from 1l. 10s. to 5l.; being sometimes reduced, by competition, so low as
he *average* rate may be taken at 4l. 4s. For these rates, the ship provides nothing but berths,
ater; the passengers provide their own provisions, bedding, &c. The expense of provisions for
n, who might wish to be as economical as possible, for the voyage out to the United States,
e more than from 40s. to 50s.
a passage by the common traders (and many of them are quite equal to the packets in equip-
safety) varies from 15l. to 25l.; no wines being provided by the ships at these rates, but
bedding, malt liquor, and spirits.
of *freight* to New-York, are—

	By Packets.		By other Ships.	
	£ s. d.	£ s. d.	£ s. d.	£ s. d.
per ton measurement of 40 cubic feet - -	2 0 0		1 5 0	to 1 10 0
	1 10 0		0 17 6	— 1 2 6
priced goods - - -	1 0 0 to	1 5 0	0 12 6	— 0 17 6
n of 20 cwt. -	0 10 0 —	0 12 6	0 9 0	— 0 12 6
do. -	1 0 0 —	1 5 0	0 12 6	— 0 15 0
rthenware, per ton of 40 cubic feet -	0 10 0 —	0 12 6	0 8 0	— 0 12 6
of 40 bushels -	0 17 6 —	1 5 0	0 12 6	— 0 15 0

t *and London Packets.*—Nine ships are engaged in this trade. They are fitted out in the same
Liverpool packets. They touch at Cowes.

New-York and Havre Packets. — Twelve ships are engaged in this trade, all fitted up with the g
splendour and attention to comfort. Cabin passage, 140 dollars, including bed, bedding, win
stores of every description.

SALES BY AUCTION.—The practice of selling goods, particularly those imported from abroad, by a
is of long standing in New-York, and is carried to a very great extent. Auctioneers are appoi
the senate, on the nomination of the governor.

Statement of Sales at Auction in the State of New-York, from 1810 to 1830 inclusive, from Retur
by the Auctioneers to the Comptroller.

Years.	Amount of Duties.		Amount of Sales dutiable.		Amount of Sales not dutiable.		Total.	
	Dollars.	*cents.*	*Dollars.*	*cents.*	*Dollars.*	*cents.*	*Dollars.*	*c*
1810	126,404	62	5,602,662	59	510,760	28	6,113,422	
1811	110,220	76	4,393,987	51	342,155	24	4,736,142	
1812	124,236	92	5,203,566	67	425,451	30	5,629,017	
1813	156,481	05	6,001,162	40	1,051,646	40	7,052,808	
* 1814	86,067	76	3,527,155	88	387,631	12	3,914,787	
1815	182,936	57	12,124,054	76	1,037,695	01	13,161,749	
1816	171,907	40	11,349,826	07	765,889	76	12,115,715	
1817	199,123	38	12,472,446	92	726,165	73	13,198,612	
1818	176,032	24	11,873,658	42	1,614,418	83	13,488,077	
1819	141,570	96	9,538,202	51	1,727,356	31	11,265,558	
1820	153,999	86	10,182,967	00	1,833,229	75	12,016,196	
1821	154,543	92	10,527,791	05	1,819,484	72	12,345,275	
1822	180,761	68	12,340,127	54	1,798,880	88	14,139,008	
1823	208,254	01	13,754,821	57	3,117,128	86	16,871,950	
1824	226,218	13	15,716,432	88	3,587,586	48	19,304,019	
1825	285,037	62	19,713,686	67	4,530,600	69	24,244,287	
1826	242,810	06	16,328,198	52	4,722,154	73	21,050,353	
1827	247,808	24	16,401,643	68	3,063,576	64	19,465,220	
1828	257,180	40	17,449,544	64	8,590,116	29	26,039,660	
† 1829	242,552	54	16,536,906	60	8,685,802	29	25,222,708	
1830	218,513	66	15,465,405	99	10,300,705	79	25,766,111	
	3,892,661	78	246,502,249	87	60,638,437	10	307,140,686	

Abstract of the principal Provisions of the Law concerning Auctions.

The duties are —
1. On wines and ardent spirits, foreign or domestic, 2 per cent.
2. On goods imported from beyond the Cape of Good Hope, and sold in packages, bales, &c. as in
1 per cent.
3. On all other articles, subject to duties, 1½ per cent.
The following articles are not subject to duties : —
1. Ships and vessels.
2. Utensils of husbandry, horses, neat cattle, hogs, and sheep.
3. Articles grown, produced, or manufactured in this state, except distilled spirits.
4. All fabrics of cotton, wool, hemp, and flax, manufactured within the jurisdiction of the
States.
Goods are exempted from auction duties —
1. When they belong to the United States or this state.
2. When sold by the authority of a court, or when seized by a public officer on account of any f
or penalty, or under a distress for rent.
3. The effects of a deceased person sold by executors or administrators, or by a person author
surrogate.
4. The effects of a bankrupt or insolvent sold by his assignees, appointed pursuant to law, or by a
assignment for the benefit of all his creditors.
5. Goods damaged at sea and sold within 20 days after being landed, for the owners or insurers.
Any citizen of this state may sell at auction (except in the city of New-York) all such goods a
subject to duties. But in the city of New-York, or where the goods pay duties, the sale must
authorised auctioneer, his partner, or clerk. And any person selling contrary to the said prov
guilty of a misdeameanor.
When an auctioneer cannot attend an auction by *sickness*, by *duty as a fireman*, by *military o
necessary attendance in a court of justice*, or when he is *temporarily* absent from the place for
is appointed, he may employ a partner to attend in his behalf.
He must give bond to the people of this state, with two freehold sureties, conditioned in the p
5,000 dollars, for the payment of the duties imposed by law and accruing on the sales. The pe
selling without executing the bond, is 125 dollars for each article offered for sale.
No auctioneer in any city shall at the same time have more than one house or store for ho
auctions, and shall, before entering on his office, designate in a writing, to be filed with the cle
city, such house or store, and his partner or partners. But goods sold in the packages in which
imported, furniture, and such bulky articles as have usually been sold in warehouses, in the stre
the wharfs, need not be sold in the house or store designated in such writing, if such sales be a
at least two days previously in one or more newspapers.
Auctioneers are to receive 2½ per cent. on the amount of all sales, unless by previous agre
writing ; and for *demanding* or receiving an unlawful commission, shall forfeit 250 dollars, an
the monies so received.
No auctioneer on the same day and at the same place where his public auction shall be held
other person at the same time and place, shall sell at private sale any goods liable to auction dut
penalty of forfeiting their price.
Every auctioneer shall make out in writing a quarterly account, dated on the 1st days of A
October, and January in the year for which he is appointed, stating minutely —
1. The sum for which any goods shall have been sold at every auction held by or for him, from
of his giving bond or from the date of his last quarterly account.
2. The days on which sales were so made, and the amount of each day's sale, designating the s
by himself, or in his presence, and those made in his absence by his partner or clerk, and
of his absence.

---

* The returns of sales for 1814, having been mislaid at the comptroller's office, the amounts a
by estimating the average of the four preceding years in proportion to the duties paid, which a
correct as stated.

† The amount of real estate sold in 1829 (included in the above not dutiable) was 2,131,390 do

amount of all private sales made by himself or his partners, and the times thereof
amount of duties chargeable on all sales made.
y such account shall, withing 20 days after its date, be exhibited, by auctioneers for a city, to the or recorder; and if by an auctioneer for a county, to a county judge, and be verified by oath. partner of an auctioneer and every clerk who has made any sales, shall also swear to his belief in uth and justice of every particular of such account.
state duties (together with the addition of 2½ per cent on the whole amount of them) are to within 10 days after exhibiting such account.
deceit or fraud in violating any provision of the law respecting Auctioneers, is made a misde-r, and subjects the offending party to the payment of *treble* damages to the party injured.

of various Foreign Coins, &c. with their Value in Federal Money.

	Dols.	cts.	m.
h of a dollar	0	06	2½
stareen	0	09	0
te of Spain	0	10	0
ish sixpence	0	11	1
of a dollar	0	12	5
purnois of France	0	18	5
France	0	18	7½
een	0	18	5
lish shilling	0	22	2
of a dollar	0	25	0
nco of Hamburg	0	23	0
n or guilder of the United Netherlands	0	40	0
ar	0	50	0
Bengal	0	50	0
r of Denmark	1	00	0
r of Sweden	1	00	0
dollar	1	00	0
f Russia	1	00	0
f England and France	1	09	0
Portugal	1	24	0
hina	1	48	0
f India	1	84	0
istole	3	66	7
istole	3	77	3
Ireland	4	10	0
erling of Great Britain	4	44	0
uinea	4	60	0
uinea	4	65	7
e	6	00	8
annas	8	00	0
on	14	93	4
as	16	00	0
on of Spain	0	05	0
ibraltar	0	08	5
r of Bremen	0	75	0
Leghorn	0	90	0
Naples	0	80	0
Sicily	2	50	0

Coins of the United States.

Gold Coins.

			L.	s.	d.	
lue 10 dol., wt.	270 grs.	stand. gold	= 2	3	8	sterl.
e, 5 do.	135 do.	do.	= 1	1	10	—
2½ do.	67½ do.	do.	= 0	10	11	—

d gold is 11 parts pure and 1 alloy.

Silver Coins.

l. 10 dimes, wt.	416 grs.	stand. silver	= 4·3·75 —
r, 5 do.	208 do.	do.	= 2·1·87 —
2½ do.	104 do.	do.	= 1·0·93 —
10 cents,	41 3-5ths	do.	= 0·5·46 —
, 5 do.	20 4-5ths	do.	

d silver is 1,485 parts pure, and 179 alloy.
of pure gold is valued at 15 lbs. of pure silver.
the United States decimally divided.—10 mills make) cents 1 dime, 10 dimes 1 dollar, 10 dollars 1 eagle.

educing the Currencies of the different States into each other.

ce the currencies of New Hampshire, Massachusetts, and, Connecticut, and Virginia, into those of New-North Carolina, — to the given sum add 1-3d part Of Pennsylvania, New Jersey, Delaware, and Mary-he given sum add 1-4th thereof. Of South Carolina ia,—from the given sum subtract 2-9ths thereof.
ce New-York and North Carolina into New Hamp-sachusetts, Rhode Island, Connecticut, and Virgi-the given sum deduct 1-4th thereof. Into Pennsyl-w Jersey, Delaware, and Maryland, — from the deduct 1-6th thereof. Into South Carolina, — to ven add 1-16th, then take half of the whole.
ce Pennsylvania, New Jersey, Delaware, and Mary-New Hampshire, Massachusetts, Rhode Island, t, and Virginia,—from the sum given deduct 1-5th nto New York and North Carolina, — to the sum -5th thereof. Into South Carolina and Georgia, — y 3 and 1-9th, and divide the product by 5; or mul-, and divide by 45.
e South Carolina and Georgia into New Hampshire, etts, Rhode Island, Connecticut, and Virginia, — to um add 2-7ths thereof. Into Pennsylvania, New laware, and Maryland, — multiply the given sum divide by 28. Into New-York and North Carolina, e given sum subtract 1-7th, and double the re-

OMMISSIONS,—*Recommended for general Adoption, and by the New-York Chamber of Commerce, when no t subsists to the contrary.*

n Business.—On the sale of merchandise, 5 per cent. urchase of stocks, 1 per cent. — Specie, ½ per cent. e and shipment of merchandise, with funds in hand, *egate amount of costs and charges*, 2½ per cent. — endorsing bills, in all cases, 2½ per cent. —Vessels, rchasing, 2½ per cent. — Procuring freight, 5 per ecting freight on general average, 2½ per cent. — isbursements, with funds in hand, 2½ per cent. — marine insurance, in all cases, when the premium ceed 10 per cent., *on the amount insured*, ½ per cent. e premium exceeds 10 per cent., *on the amount of* per cent. — Collecting dividends on stock, ½ per ecting delayed or litigated accounts, 5 per cent. — Adjusting and collecting insurance losses, 2½ per cent. — Receiving and paying monies, from which no other commission is derived, 1 per cent. — Remittances in bills, in all cases, ½ per cent. — Landing and re-shipping goods from vessels in distress, *on the value*, 2½ per cent. — Receiving and forwarding goods entered at the Custom-house, *on the value*, 1 per cent. — and 2½ per cent. on responsibilities incurred.

On Inland Business.—On the sale of merchandise, 2½ per cent. — Purchase and shipment of merchandise, or accepting for purchase, without funds or property in hand, 2½ per cent. — Sale or purchase of stocks, 1 per cent. — Sale or purchase of specie, ½ per cent. — Sale of bills of exchange with endorsement, ½ per cent. — Sale of bank notes or drafts not current, ½ per cent. — Selling or endorsing bills of exchange, 2½ per cent. — Selling or purchasing vessels, 2½ per cent. — Chartering to proceed to other ports to load, 2½ per cent. — Procuring or collecting freight, 2½ per cent. — Outfits or disbursements, 2½ per cent. —Collecting general average, 2½ per cent. — Effecting marine insurances, in all cases, when the premium does not exceed 10 per cent., *on the amount insured*, ½ per cent. When the premium exceeds 10 per cent., *on the amount of premium*, 5 per cent. — Adjusting and collecting insurance losses, 2½ per cent. — Collecting dividends on stocks, ½ per cent. — Collecting bills, and paying over the amount, or receiving and paying monies from which no other commission is derived, 1 per cent. — Receiving and forwarding goods, *on the value*, ½ per cent. — The same when entered for duty or debenture, 1 per cent. — Remittances in bills, in all cases, ½ per cent.

The above commissions to be exclusive of the guarantee of debts for sales on credit, storage, brokerage, and every other charge actually incurred.— The risk of loss by fire, unless insurance be ordered, and of robbery, theft, and other unavoidable occurrences, if the usual care be taken to secure the property, is in all cases to be borne by the proprietor of the goods. When bills are remitted for collection, and are returned under protest for non-acceptance or non-payment, the same commission to be charged as though they were duly honoured. On consignments of merchandise, withdrawn or re-shipped full commission to be charged to the extent of advances or responsibilities incurred, and half commission on the residue of the value.

RATES OF STORAGE,—*Chargeable per month, as established by the New-York Chamber of Commerce.*

	Cents.
Almonds, in frails or packages, cwt.	6
Alum, in casks or bags, per ton	40
Ashes, pot and pearl, bbl.	8
Beef, bbl.	6
Bottles, quart, in mats, cr. or hmp. gr.	8
Bark, quercitron, in casks, ton	60
Bagging, cotton, loose or in bales, pc.	3
Butter, in firkins of 60 lbs. per fir.	2
Brandy, see Liquors.	
Candles, in boxes of 50 or 60 lbs. box	2
Chocolate, in boxes of 50 lbs. box	2
Cocoa, in bags, per cwt.	2½
in casks, do.	3
Coffee, in casks, do.	2½
in bags, do.	2
Copperas, in casks, per ton	40
Copper, in pigs, do.	20
in sheets or bolts, ton	30
braziers' bottoms, ton	75
Cordage, per ton	50
Cassia, in mats or boxes, per cwt.	10
Cotton, American, in square bales, 300 lbs.	12½
do. in round bales, do.	16
West Indian, in proportion to round.	
East Indian, in bales, per 300 lbs.	9
Cheese, casks, boxes, or loose, cwt.	3
Duck, heavy, per bolt	1½
Ravens or Russia sheeting, piece	0¾
Dry goods, in boxes or bales, 40 cubic feet	40
Fish, pickled, per bbl.	6
dry, in casks or boxes, cwt.	4
in bulk, per cwt.	2½
Figs, in frails, boxes, or drums, cwt.	2½
Flax, per ton	60
Flaxseed, or other dry articles, in tierces of 7 bushels per tierce	10
Flour, or other dry articles, in bbls.	4
Earthenware, in crates of 25 to 30 feet	15
in hhds. of 40 to 50 feet	30
Grain, in bulk, per bushel	1
Ginger, in bags, per cwt.	2
Glass, window, in boxes of 50 feet	1½
Gin, see Liquors.	
Hemp, per ton	75
Hides, dried or salted, per hide	1½
Hardware, in casks of 40 cubic feet	40
Indigo, in seroons or boxes, per cwt.	4
Iron, in bars or bolts, per ton	20
in hoops, sheets, or nailrods, ton	30
Liquors, in puncheons of 120 gallons per puncheon	30
in quarter casks	6¼
in pipes or casks, 120 gallons	30
bottled, in casks or boxes, doz. bottles	1½
Leather, per side	1
Lard, in firkins of 60 lbs.	2
Lead, pig or sheet, per ton	20
dry or gr. in oil, per ton	40

Cents.

Molasses, per hhd. of 110 gallons (other casks in proportion)	30
Nails, in casks, per cwt.	2
Oil, in hhds. or casks, 110 gallons	30
in chests of 30 flasks, per chest	4
bottled, in boxes or baskets, doz.	1½
Pain s, in casks or kegs, per ton	40
Pork, per bbl.	6
Porter, see Liquors.	
Pepper, in bags, per cwt.	2½
Pimento, in casks or bags, cwt.	2½
Rice, in tierces, per tierce	12
in half do., per half do.	8
Rags, in bales, per cwt.	6
Raisins, Malaga, in casks	3
do. in boxes	1
in other packages, per cwt.	2
Rum, see Liquors.	
Saltpetre, in bags, per cwt.	2
in casks, per cwt.	2½
Salt, in bags or bulk, per bushel	1
Shot in casks, per cwt.	37
Soap, in boxes of 50 to 60 lbs.	2
Steel, in bars or bundles, per ton	30
in boxes or tubs, per ton	40
Sugar, raw, in bags or boxes, per cwt.	2
do. in casks, per cwt.	2½
refined, in casks or packages	3
Tallow, in casks or seroons, cwt.	2
Tea, bohea, in whole chests	15
do. in half chests	8
green or black, in quarter chests	4½
in boxes, in proportion to quarter chests.	
Tin, block, per ton	20
in boxes of usual size, per box	1½
Tobacco, in hhds., per hhd.	37½
in bales or seroons, per cwt.	4
manufactured, in kegs of 100 lbs.	2
Wines, see Liquors.	
Woods, for dyeing, under cover, per ton	50
do. in yards	25
Whiting, in hhds. per ton	37½

On articles on which the rate is fixed by weight, it is understood to be on the gross weight; and on liquors, oil, &c. on which the rate refers to gallons, it is understood to be on the whole capacity of the casks, whether full or not. The proprietor of goods is to be at the expense of putting them in store, stowing away, and turning out of store.—All goods taken on storage to be subject to one month's storage; if taken out within 15 days after the expiration of the month, to pay half a month's storage; if after 15 days, a whole month's storage.

RATES OF CARTAGE.

	s.	d.
Ale or beer, per hhd.	2	0
hhd. from 60 to 90 gallons	2	6
Alum or copperas, from 12 to 15 cwt., per hhd.	2	6
from 15 to 20 cwt.	3	0
over 1 ton	4	6
Bar iron, per load	2	0
Boards and plank, per load	2	0
Brandy, pipe over 100 gallons	3	0
Bread, 4 tierces	2	0
Bricks, per load	2	0
handled and piled	2	6
Building or paving stone, load	2	0
Calves, sheep, and lambs	2	6
Cider, cheese, and cocoa	2	0
Clay and sand, 12 bushels	2	0
Coal, half chaldron, per load	2	6
Cocoa, per load	2	0
Coffee, in bags or bbls.	2	0
above 10 cwt., per hhd.	2	6
Cordage, small, per load	2	0
Cotton, per load of 3 bales	2	6
Cut stone, per load	2	6
Dried fish, loose load	2	6
Dye-wood, per load	2	0
Earthenware, loose, per load	2	6
European goods, per load	2	0
Flax, in bales and bundles, load	2	6
Flaxseed, 3 tierces	2	0
Fire-wood, per load	2	0
Flour, in bags, 12 per load	2	0
7 bbls. per load	2	0
Gammons or hams, per load	2	0
Gin, pipe over 100 gallons	3	0
Hay, in trusses, bundles, bales, per load	2	6
loose	6	0
Heading or staves, per load	2	0
Hides, 50 per load	2	6
Hemp, in bales or bundles, per load	2	6
loose, not over 12 cwt.	3	6
Hoops, in bundles	2	0
Hoop-poles, per load	2	6
Hollow-ware, per load	2	6
Household furniture	4	0
Molasses, from 60 to 90 gallons	2	6
from 90 to 140 gallons	3	0
Oil, per load of 3 bbls.	2	0
Oysters, do. shells, &c. load	2	6
Potashes, per load of 3 bbls.	2	0
Paints, common load	2	0
per hhd., from 12 to 15 cwt.	2	6
from 15 to 20 cwt.	3	0
above 20 cwt.	4	6
Pantiles, per load	2	6
Plaster of Paris, ton	2	0
Pork, beef, tar, pitch, and turpentine, 5 bbls.	2	0
Rum, per hhd.	3	0
Salt, 20 bushe's	2	0
Shingles, long cedar, pine, in bundles	2	0
Cyprus, 2,000 (22 inch)	3	0
Stone, paving or building	2	0

Sugar, Havana, 3 boxes	
from 9 to 15 cwt.	
from 15 to 20 cwt.	
above 20 cwt.	
Scantling or timber, per load	
Tea, per load	
Tiles or slate, per load	
Tobacco, in hhds. from 9 to 15 cwt. per hhd.	
from 15 to 20 cwt.	
above 20 cwt.	
Wheat or other grain, per load	
Wine, pipe over 100 gallons	
in 4 quarter casks	
Whiting, common load	
per hhd. 12 to 15 cwt.	
from 15 to 20 cwt.	
above 20 cwt.	

Cables.

For every cable, whole shot of 5 inches in circumference to 7 inches
Do. half shot of like dimensions
Do. whole shot of 7 to 10 inches
Do. half shot of like dimensions
Do. whole shot of 10 and not exceeding 12 inches in circumference
Do. whole shot of 12 and not exceeding 14 inches i circumference
Do. half shot of the dimensions of the two last mer tioned
Do. whole shot of 14 and not exceeding 15 inches
Do. half shot of like dimensions
Do. whole shot of 15 inches
Do. half shot of like dimensions
⁎ *Goods, wares, merchandise, or other articles n herein enumerated, per load*

In all cases where the distance exceeds half a mile, a two miles, half in addition to be allowed.

Rates of Porterage.—For any distance not exceedin mile, 12½ cents; over half a mile, and not exceeding 25 cents; and in that proportion for any greater d For carrying a load upon a hand-barrow, for any dista exceeding half a mile, 25 cents; over half a mile, and ceeding a mile, 44 cents; and in that proportion for any distance.

Handcartmen.—For any distance not exceeding half 18¾ cents; over half a mile, and not exceeding a m cents; and in that proportion for any greater distance.

Harbour Master.

The office of harbour master was created in 1808, lative enactment, with power to regulate and station al in the harbour, or at the wharfs, to accommodate vesse ing to discharge their cargoes, and to decide promptly putes connected with the foregoing subjects. Resisting thority subjects to a fine of 50 dollars and costs, for the of the New-York Hospital.

Fees.—On vessels unloading, 1½ cents per ton. Vess ing foreign duties and tonnage, *double*; which must within 48 hours after arrival. Schooners and sloops coasting trade, 2 dollars. For adjusting any differe specting situation, 2 dollars.

Pilots must register their vessels, names, and places o in his office; and are obliged to put to sea whenever by him. The penalty for refusing is 5 dollars and licence.

Pilots.

There are nine branch and nine deputy pilots, and registered boats.

Rates of Pilotage.—Every pilot who shall take charg vessel to the eastward or southward of the White Buo Eastern Ridge near the bar, and conducts and moor such vessel to a proper mooring, or from the city to the so or eastward of said buoy, is entitled by law to the f rates, to wit :—For vessels of the United States, and th are entitled by treaty to enter upon the same terms as rates, the sums which follow : -Every vessel draw than 14 feet, 1 dol. 50 cts. per foot; do. drawing 14 f less than 18, 1 dol. 75 cts. per foot; do. drawing 18 fee wards, 2 dols. 25 cts. per foot. The same rates of pilota allowed for any vessel that may be piloted any where w Hook, whose master or owner does not wish the sam brought to the city wharfs. Half pilotage only to be al any pilot who shall take charge of a vessel to westwar White Buoy. No pilotage whatsoever to be given to a unless he shall take charge of a vessel to the southwa upper Middle Ground, nor unless such vessel shall tons burthen, provided the usual signal be not given, case half pilotage is to be allowed. Between the Is November and the 1st of April, inclusive, 4 dols. ad to be allowed for vessels of 10 feet water and upw less than 10 feet, 2 dols. One fourth additional to be the pilots who shall take charge of vessels out of sigl light-house. For every day any pilot shall be require main on board, 3 dols. per day. Foreign vessels not by treaty to enter on the same terms as those of th States, to pay one fourth additional to the pilots, ar dols. over and above the foregoing rates of pilotage.

Wardens of the Port.

Vessels and goods arriving in a damaged state, and to be sold at auction for the benefit of underwriters o city of New-York, must be under the inspection of dens, who may be required to certify the cause of the and amount of sale and charges.

Fees.—1½ per cent. on gross amount of sales; and survey on board of any vessel, at any store, or along t or wharfs, 3 dols. on damaged goods : each survey spars, rigging, &c., 5 dols.: each certificate, 1 dol do. of distress of said vessel, 2 dols. 50 cts.; same scr vessels paying foreign duties and tonnage, *double*.

es of Office to the Collector and Naval Officer.

a vessel of 100 tons or upwards, 2 dols. 50 cts.; clear-
essel of 100 tons or upwards, 2 dols. 50 cts.; entry of
der 100 tons, 1 dol. 50 cts.; clearance of a vessel un-
s, 1 dol. 50 cts.; every post entry, 2 dols.; permit to

land goods, 20 cents; every bond taken officially, 40 cents;
permit to load goods, for the exportation for drawback, 30
cents.; debenture, or other official certificate, 20 cents; bill of
health, 20 cents; official document (register excepted) required
by any person, 20 cents.

ve derived these statements partly from the *New-York Annual Register for* 1831, and partly
e Picture of New-York; both accurate and useful publications.

AND NAVIGATION OF THE UNITED STATES, for the year ending 30th of September, 1829. — (From the official Accounts printed by order of Congress.)

ary Statement of the Value of the Exports of the Growth, Produce, and Manufacture, of the
United States, during the Year ending on the 30th Day of September, 1829.

The Sea.	Dollars.	Dollars.	Dollars.
es —			
fish, or cod fisheries		747,541	
ed fish, or river fisheries, herring, shad, salmon, ckerel		220,527	
e (common) oil, and whalebone		495,163	
naceti oil and candles		353,869	
			1,817,100
The Forest.			
nd furs		526,507	
y		114,396	
of wood —			
s, shingles, boards, and other lumber	1,680,403		
ark, and other dye	165,406		
t stores, tar, pitch, rosin, and turpentine	377,613		
s, pot and pearl	817,434		
		3,040,856	
			3,681,759
Agriculture.			
c of animals —			
tallow, hides, and horned cattle	674,955		
r and cheese	176,205		
(pickled), bacon, lard, live hogs	1,493,629		
s and mules	207,858		
	10,644		
le food —		2,563,291	
st, flour, and biscuit	5,972,920		
n corn and meal	974,535		
neal	127,004		
oats, and other small grain and pulse	74,896		
oes	30,079		
s	15,958		
	2,514,370		
		9,709,762	
			12,273,053
			4,982,974
			26,575,311
r agricultural products			123,246
Manufactures.			
l tallow candles		692,691	
, boots, and shoes		356,658	
		35,765	
		270,780	
		132,939	
om grain, beer, ale, and porter		215,494	
ncluding coaches and other carriages)		501,946	
d tobacco		202,396	
		8,417	
oil and spirits of turpentine		30,442	
		7,984	
		223,705	
om molasses		166,740	
fined		50,739	
e		1,759	
der		171,924	
nd brass		129,647	
l drugs		101,524	
			3,301,550
anufactures		1,259,457	
r manufactured articles		542,857	
silver coin		612,886	
			2,415,200
not distinguished in returns —			
actured		309,100	
roduce		221,544	
			530,650
			55,700,193

II. Statistical View of the Commerce of the United States, exhibiting the Value of every Descri[ption of]
Imports from, and the Value of Articles of every Description of Exports to, each Foreign Count[ry; also]
the Tonnage of American and Foreign Vessels arriving from, and departing to, each Foreign C[ountry]
during the Year ending on the 30th Day of September, 1829.

		Commerce.			Navigation.		
			Value of Exports.		Tonnage.		
Countries.	Value of Imports.				American.		F[oreign.]
		Domestic Produce.	Foreign Produce.	Total.	Entered into the U. States.	Departed from U. States.	Enter[ed] into U. Sta[tes.]
	Dollars.	*Dollars.*	*Dollars.*	*Dollars.*	*Tons.*	*Tons.*	*Tons.*
Russia - - -	2,218,995	51,684	334,542	386,226	16,420	2,943	1,0
Prussia - -	22,935	14,411	-	14,411	389	188	
Sweden and Norway -	1,020,910	122,663	126,971	249,634	13,453	2,255	2,0
Swedish West Indies -	283,049	684,523	23,791	708,314	17,969	28,246	8
Denmark - -	32,911	73,597	13,166	86,763	- -	1,043	- -
Danish West Indies -	2,053,266	1,942,010	282,401	2,224,411	43,463	56,738	
Netherlands - -	1,057,854	3,095,857	889,330	3,985,187	24,453	38,372	1,
Dutch East Indies - -	121,348	62,074	176,318	238,392	907	1,985	
West Indies -	438,132	379,874	18,667	398,541	13,325	12,217	9
England - - -	23,892,763	21,281,334	1,767,457	23,048,791	169,207	179,843	61,
Scotland - -	1,024,215	895,315	19,493	914,808	2,275	2,609	9,
Ireland - -	362,511	327,728	366	328,094	6,113	4,833	6,
Gibraltar - -	247,471	301,132	160,130	461,262	5,718	8,701	
British African Ports -	7,787	-	-	-	116		
East Indies -	1,229,569	69,070	477,629	546,699	3,173	3,050	8
West Indies -	240,224	1,463	5,058	6,521	32,777	5,418	
American Colonies -	577,542	2,724,104	40,805	2,764,909	88,492	93,645	4,
Newfoundland - -					125	179	
Hanse Towns, &c. -	2,274,375	1,998,176	1,278,984	3,277,160	12,862	21,962	7,
France on the Atlantic	8,248,921	8,008,923	2,105,573	10,114,496	54,425	73,862	4,
on the Mediterranean -	590,057	886,122	748,777	1,634,899	9,458	18,843	
French West Indies -	777,992	1,056,639	15,768	1,072,407	40,516	65,019	9,
Bourbon - -		10,502	-	10,502			
Hayti - -	1,799,809	814,987	160,171	975,158	21,570	18,164	3,
Spain on the Atlantic -	327,409	545,753	139,732	685,485	7,806	12,719	
on the Mediterranean -	474,120	185,952	45,700	231,652	8,270	4,516	
Teneriffe and other Canaries -	25,283	42,839	23,317	66,156	448	1,714	
Manilla and Philippine Islands-	209,206	10,802	66,430	77,232	2,137	594	
Cuba - - -	4,866,524	3,719,263	1,859,626	5,578,889	99,779	114,599	11,
Other Spanish West Indies -	898,832	209,780	38,900	248,680	19,179	11,051	
Portugal - -	237,351	42,088	628	42,716	23,570	2,397	
Madeira - -	403,056	175,074	15,089	190,163	3,130	6,091	
Fayal and other Azores -	21,302	7,949	78	8,027	731	672	
Cape de Verd Islands -	26,460	68,528	13,477	82,005	1,310	3,268	-
Italy and Malta -	1,409,588	289,755	611,257	901,012	13,311	7,031	
Sardinia - -					345		
Trieste and other Adriatic Ports	191,896	409,288	280,200	689,488	4,432	6,384	-
Turkey, Levant, and Egypt	293,237	27,600	47,384	74,984	2,797	687	
Morocco and Barbary States -	10,710				137		
Mexico - -	5,026,761	495,626	1,835,525	2,331,151	20,352	21,682	3,
Central Republic of America -	311,931	123,631	116,223	239,854	3,435	3,320	
Honduras, Campeachy, &c. -	64,847	12,693	8,229	20,922			
Colombia - -	1,255,310	525,783	241,565	767,348	13,614	8,490	
Brazil - - -	2,535,467	1,510,260	419,767	1,929,927	32,482	40,978	
Cisplatine Republic -	3,076						
Argentine Republic -	912,114	444,716	181,336	626,052	5,860	7,422	
Chili - - -	416,118	890,356	530,778	1,421,134	2,018	9,079	
Peru - - -	1,004,458	91,542	119,615	211,157	5,242	749	
South America, generally -	56,552	147,670	6,175	153,845	310	2,447	
Cape of Good Hope -					- -	165	
China - - -	4,680,847	260,759	1,094,103	1,354,862	8,052	6,351	
West Indies, generally -	3,314	359,496	10,123	369,619	725	10,926	
Asia, generally -	66,191	40,721	232,768	273,489	1,170	3,751	
Europe, generally -	300	102,364	250	102,614	2,392	920	
Africa, generally - -	211,735	108,837	49,516	158,353	2,865	2,369	-
South Seas - -	20,235	45,969	20,991	66,960	10,044	14,312	
North West Coast - -		2,911	4,399	7,310			
Uncertain - -	5,961						
Total -	74,492,527	55,700,193	16,658,478	72,358,671	872,949	944,799	130

Statement of the Commerce of each State and Territory, commencing on the 1st Day of October, 1828, and ending on the 30th Day of September, 1829.

	Value of Imports.			Value of Exports.						
				Domestic Produce.			Foreign Produce.			Total Value of Domestic and Foreign Produce.
	In American Vessels.	In Foreign Vessels.	Total.	In American Vessels.	In Foreign Vessels.	Total.	In American Vessels.	In Foreign Vessels.	Total.	
	Dollars.	Dollars.	Dollars.	Dollars.	Dollars.	Dollars.	Dollars.	Dollars.	Dollars.	Dollars.
	730,473	12,308	742,781	729,106	- -	729,106	8,726	- -	8,726	737,832
	179,889	- -	179,889	98,264	- -	98,264	7,476	- -	7,476	105,740
	205,392	- -	205,392	808,079	- -	808,079	- -	- -	- -	808,079
	12,289,308	231,436	12,520,744	3,896,376	53,375	3,949,751	4,276,423	28,763	4,305,186	8,254,937
	423,811	- -	423,811	337,468	- -	337,468	52,913	- -	52,913	390,381
	309,482	56	309,538	450,985	- -	450,985	6,985	- -	6,985	457,970
	32,771,500	1,971,807	34,743,307	11,125,777	910,784	12,036,561	6,888,900	1,193,550	8,082,450	20,119,011
	785,816	431	786,247	8,022	- -	8,022	- -	- -	- -	8,022
	9,855,715	244,437	10,100,152	2,480,243	136,909	2,617,152	1,384,643	88,140	1,472,873	4,089,935
	24,179	- -	24,179	7,195	- -	7,195	- -	- -	- -	7,195
	4,492,391	311,744	4,804,135	3,237,668	424,605	3,662,273	1,069,590	72,602	1,142,192	4,804,465
	205,921	- -	205,921	891,185	23,100	914,285	13,812	- -	13,812	928,097
	349,610	45,742	395,352	3,476,797	306,696	3,783,493	3,782	156	3,938	3,787,431
	266,550	16,797	283,347	528,595	35,911	564,506	- -	- -	- -	564,506
	778,602	361,016	1,139,618	5,784,789	2,349,887	8,134,676	19,774	21,136	40,910	8,175,586
	273,014	107,279	380,293	4,054,235	926,407	4,980,642	734	- -	734	4,981,376
	129,322	104,398	233,720	1,044,969	634,416	1,679,385	14,573	- -	14,573	1,693,958
	5,167,968	1,689,241	6,857,209	7,992,349	2,905,834	10,898,183	1,353,403	134,474	1,487,877	12,386,060
	46	247	293	2,004	- -	2,004	- -	- -	- -	2,004
	2,957		2,957							
	83,606	70,036	153,642	20,448	17,715	38,163	13,153	4,770	17,923	56,086
	69,325,552	5,166,975	74,492,527	46,974,554	8,725,639	55,700,193	15,114,887	1,543,591	16,658,478	72,358,671

Statement exhibiting a condensed View of the Tonnage of some of the more important Ports of the United States, on the last Day of December, 1828.

Districts.	Registered Tonnage.		Enrolled and Licensed Tonnage.		Total Tonnage of each District.	
	Tons.	95ths.	Tons.	95ths.	Tons.	95ths.
ssamaquoddy, Maine	13,032	67	3,821	52	16,854	23
chias	181	08	5,951	17	6,132	25
enchman's Bay	3,226	79	9,428	53	12,655	37
nobscot	6,364	91	21,634	42	27,999	38
lfast	3,423	37	12,921	16	16,344	53
aldoborough	3,407	65	29,488	32	32,896	02
iscasset	2,661	73	9,549	82	12,211	60
th	19,619	11	16,672	53	36,291	64
rtland	37,060	84	19,889	00	56,949	84
rtsmouth, New Hampshire	19,722	02	6,531	16	26,253	18
wburyport, Massachusetts	12,280	62	14,707	49	26,988	16
ucester	4,219	03	11,890	02	16,109	05
em	34,425	09	13,785	82	48,210	91
rblehead	2,742	84	9,076	11	11,819	00
ston	119,467	59	56,694	59	176,162	23
mouth	12,121	82	16,244	47	28,366	34
w Bedford	36,843	31	13,614	60	50,457	91
rnstaple	1,728	14	28,480	45	30,208	59
ntucket	20,704	48	5,642	83	26,347	36
vidence, Rhode Island	12,289	53	7,962	88	20,252	46
stol	8,330	85	3,259	10	11,590	00
wport	6,732	41	4,831	69	11,564	15
dletown, Connecticut	5,880	45	13,286	36	19,166	81
w London	6,150	75	9,808	34	15,959	14
w Haven	4,416	86	9,024	61	13,441	52
rfield	366	28	11,925	77	12,292	10
w-York	158,237	70	181,167	09	339,404	79
th Amboy, New Jersey	1,101	51	12,051	41	13,152	92
igetown	312	39	18,339	36	18,651	75
at Egg Harbour	28	61	10,108	91	10,137	57
iladelphia, Pennsylvania	66,664	14	37,416	50	104,080	64
imore	65,419	00	40,884	27	106,303	27
ord	231	69	20,428	53	20,660	27
nna	464	38	26,247	93	26,712	36
xandria	5,907	91	10,137	85	16,045	81
folk, Virginia	6,691	00	17,478	93	24,169	93
pahannock	1,802	53	11,794	11	13,596	64
mington, North Carolina	12,334	53	1,717	30	14,051	83
nton	2,668	06	7,527	73	10,195	79
den	4,589	83	6,022	07	10,611	90
rleston, South Carolina	12,871	44	19,573	52	32,445	01
annah, Georgia	6,016	65	4,686	83	10,703	53
ile, Alabama	3,526	07	6,946	90	10,473	02
Orleans	19,397	76	31,708	22	51,105	03
tal tonnage of the United States	812,619	37	928,772	50	1,741,391	87

V. A Comparative View of the Registered, Enrolled, and Licensed Tonnage of the United States from 1815 to 1828, inclusive.

Years.	Registered Tonnage.		Enrolled and Licensed Tonnage.		Total Tonnage.	
	Tons.	*95ths.*	*Tons.*	*95ths.*	*Tons.*	*95ths.*
1815	854,294	74	513,833	04	1,368,127	78
1816	800,759	63	571,458	85	1,372,218	53
1817	809,724	70	590,186	66	1,399,911	41
1818	606,088	64	609,095	51	1,225,184	20
1819	612,930	44	647,821	17	1,260,751	61
1820	619,047	53	661,118	66	1,280,166	24
1821	619,096	40	679,062	30	1,298,958	70
1822	628,150	41	696,548	71	1,324,699	17
1823	639,920	76	696,644	37	1,336,565	68
1824	669,972	60	719,190	87	1,389,163	02
1825	700,787	08	722,323	69	1,423,111	77
1826	737,978	15	796,212	68	1,534,190	83
1827	747,170	44	873,437	34	1,620,607	78
1828	812,619	37	928,772	50	1,741,391	87

TARIFF OF THE UNITED STATES.

The following are the duties charged under the existing law on the principal articles imported into United States : —

Acetate of lead, or white lead, dry or ground in oil, 5 cts. per lb.
Acid, sulphuric, or oil of vitriol, 3 cts. per lb.
Adzes, 35 per cent.
Ale, beer, and porter, imported in bottles, 20 cts. per gallon. otherwise than in bottles, 15 do.
Almonds, 3 cts. per lb.
Alum, 2 dols. 50 cts. per cwt.
Anatomical preparations, free.
Angora goats' wool or hair, do.
Animals, imported for breed, do.
    not do. 15 per cent.
Antimony, regulus of, free.
Antiquities, all collections of, specially imported, do.
    not do. according to materials.
Anvils and anchors, 2 cts. per lb.
    Any articles of the growth or manufacture of the United States, exported to a foreign country, and brought back again, on which no drawback, bounty, or allowance has been made, free.
Anchovies, in bottles, 30 per cent.
    in kegs, 15 do.
Apparatus, philosophical, specially imported by order, for societies, colleges, schools, &c., free.
Apparel, wearing, and other personal baggage in actual use, do.
Apples, pine, 15 per cent.
Aquafortis, 12½ do.
Articles, not free and not subject to any other rates of duty, 15 do.
    all composed wholly or chiefly of gold, silver, pearl, and precious stones, 12½ do.
    manufactured from copper, or of which copper is the principal material, not otherwise enumerated, 25 do.
    imported for the use of the United States, free.
Artificial flowers, 30 per cent.
Arrack, 57 cts. per gallon.
Assafœtida, 15 per cent.
Awl hafts, 30 do.
Axes, 35 do.

B.

Bacon, 3 cts. per lb.
Balsams, all kinds of, 30 per cent.
Bark of cork tree, unmanufactured, free.
Baggage, personal, in the actual use of persons arriving in the United States, do.
Barilla, do.
Baizes, the actual value of which, at the place whence imported, shall not exceed 50 cts. the square yard, shall be deemed to have cost 50 cts. the square yard, and be charged thereon a duty of 45 per cent. ad valorem.
Bandanas, wool, from India, 30 do.
    from any other place, 20 do.
Baskets, wood or ozier, 30 do.
    palm leaf, 15 do.
Beam knives, 25 do.
Beef, 2 cts. per lb.
Bed ticking, flax or cotton, 25 per cent.
Bellows, 25 do.
Bells, 25 do.
Belts, sword, with gold or silver thread, done with the needle, 12½ do.
Binding, quality, carpet, coat, chintz, and woollen, 35 do.
    galloon, of silk and cotton, 25 do.
    entirely of silk, 20 do.
    shoe, leather, 30 do.
Birds, 15 do.
Bitts, bridle, of all descriptions, 35 do.
Black, ivory and lamp, 15 do.
Black lead, unmanufactured, 15 do.
    pencils, 40 do.
Bladders, 15 do.
Blanketing, sold by the yard, 35 do.
Blankets, 35 do.
Blue or Roman vitriol, 4 cts. per lb.
Boards of wood, 30 per cent.
Bobbin wire, 30 do.
Bolting cloths, 15 do.
Bombazines, 33 1-3 do.
Bone, whale, not of the American fisheries, 15 do.
Bonnets for women, not of Leghorn, chip, or grass, 30 do.

Books, specially imported, &c., free.
    all printed previous to the year 1775, and also on all printed in other languages than English, except or Greek, 4 cts. per vol.
    Latin or Greek, when bound, 15 cts. per lb.
      when not do. 13 do.
    all others, when bound, 30 do.
      in sheets or boards, 26 do.
    blank, 30 per cent.
Boots, or bootees, laced, 1 dol. 50 cts. per pair.
Botany, specimens in, free.
Box boards, paper, 3 cts. per lb.
Boxes, Japan dressing, 25 per cent.
Braces, cotton, 25 ; silk, 20 ; worsted, 33 1-3 ; leather,
Brandy, 1st and 2d proof, 53 cts. per gallon.
    3d do., 57 do.
    4th do., 63 do.
    fruits preserved in do., 30 per cent.
Brass, manufactures if not otherwise specified, or of brass is a component material, 25 do.
    in pigs, bars, plates, or old, fit only to be manufa free.
    wire, nails, and handles, 25 per cent.
Bricks, baked or burnt, 15 do.
Bridles, 30 do.
Brimstone or sulphur, free.
Bristles, 3 cts. per lb.
Brown sugar, 3 do.
Brushes, all kinds of, 30 per cent.
Buckram, 25 do.
Bugles (or glass beads), 2 cts. per lb., and in addition valorem duty of 20 per cent.
Bullion, free.
Burlaps, 15 per cent.
Burr stones, not manufactured, free.
Busts, specially imported, do. ; of marble, 30 per cent.
Butter, 5 cts. per lb.
Button moulds, bone or pearl, without shanks, 20 per c
Buttons, made of wool or of which wool is a componen 33 1-3 ; silver and gold, 12½ ; ivory, shell, horn, bo silk, 20 ; iron, steel, pewter, brass, and tin, 25 do.

C.

Cabinet wares, 30 per cent.
Cabinets of coins, free.
Cables and cordage, tarred, 4 cts. per lb. ; untarred, 5 made of grass or bark, 5 do.
Camels' hair pencils, 30 per cent.
Camphor, crude, 8 cts. per lb. ; refined, 12 do.
Candles, tallow, 5 ; spermaceti, 8 ; wax, 6 do.
Cards, playing, 30 cts. per pack ; visiting, 15 cts. per l
Cards, wool and cotton, 25 per cent.
Carpets and carpeting, Brussels, Turkey, and Wilton per square yard ; Venetian and ingrain, 40 do. ; other kinds of wool, flax, hemp, or cotton, or parts o 32 do.
Carpeting of oil cloth, 50 do.
    All other carpets and carpeting, mats and floor-clot of tow, flags, or any other material, 15 cts. per squa
Caps of wool, fur, leather, silk, and lace, 30 per cent. cotton, and hemp, not for women, 25 do.
Cap wire, 30 do.
Carriages, of all descriptions, and parts thereof, 30 do
Casement rod, slit or rolled, 5½ cts. per lb.
Cashmere shawls (real), 15 per cent.
Cast iron vessels not otherwise specified, 1½ ct. per lb.
Castings of iron, on all other, not specified, 1 do.
Castor oil, 40 cts. per gallon.
Casts, specially imported, free ; plaster, not do., 15 pe
Caulking mallets, 30 do.
Chafing dishes, copper, 35 do.
Chairs, 30 do.
Chalk, 15 do.
Champagne wine, 30 cts. per gallon.
Chambray, silk, 20 per cent. ; wool, 40 do.
Charts, specially imported, free.
Cheese, 9 cts. per lb.
Chemical preparations, 15 per cent.
Chinese cassia, 6 cts. per lb.
Chisels, socket, 35 per cent.

and bonnets, 50 per cent.
4 cts. per lb.
e as ale.
ols. per 1,000.
25 cts. per lb.
anufactured, free.
per cent.
eady made, 50 per cent.
of any kind, free.
cts. per lb.
per bushel.
aron, 25 per cent.; copper, 35 do.
per lb.
1 dol. per quintal.
s. per lb.; after Dec. 31. 1831, 1 do.
25 per cent.
ter, 50 do.
ter, 15 do.
n, 15; iron, lead, copper, and brass, 25; wood,
free.
ry preserved in sugar or brandy, 30 per cent.;
do.
heathing ships, free; braziers', 15 per cent.; ves-
.
dols. per cwt.
rns, twine, packthread, and seines, 5 cts. per lb.;
o.
cts. per gallon.
s. per lb.; bark, free.
0 per cent.
0 do.
ng, 5 cts. per square yard.
ufactures of, or which shall be a component part,
t.
that all cotton cloths whatsoever, or cloths of
otton shall be a component material, excepting
s imported directly from China, the original cost
at the place whence imported, with the addition
r cent. if imported from the Cape of Good Hope
lace beyond it, and of 10 per cent. if imported
y other place, shall be less than 35 cts. per square
ill with such addition be taken and deemed to
t 35 cts. per square yard, and shall be charged
y accordingly.
twist, or thread, unbleached and uncoloured, 25

ched and uncoloured cotton yarn, twist, or thread,
nal cost of which shall be less than 60 cts. per
be deemed and taken to have cost 60 cts. per
shall be charged with duty accordingly, 25 per

twist, or thread, bleached or coloured, 25 per cent.
ed or coloured cotton yarn, twist, or thread, the
ost of which shall be less than 75 cts. per lb.,
deemed and taken to have cost 75 cts. per lb.,
harged accordingly, 25 per cent.
from the Cape of Hope, 30 per cent.; from any
ry, 20 do.
s of lead, 40 do.
ts. per lb.
er cent.
es, 40 do.

D.
5 cts. each.
2½ per cent.
and hemp, 25 do.
cially imported, free.
cils, 40 per cent.; knives, 35 do.
, not subject to other rates of duty, 12½ do.
cts. the square yard, and ½ a ct. yearly after 30th
it amounts to 12½ cts. do.
ee.

E.
red, blue, yellow, dry being considered as ochre,
; but if in oil, 1½ do.
20 per cent.
eth, 15 do.
lone with a needle and with thread of gold or
do.
5 do.
4 cts. per lb.
gamot, lemon, lavender, orange, roses, ottar of
ary, thyme, of tyres, and all other essences used
30 per cent.; not used as do., 15 do.

F.
ent.
ich or plumes, 30; bed, 15 do.
, for covering ships' bottoms, 15 do.

r lb.
ept muskets and rifles, 30 per cent.
aught, 1 dol. per quint.; mackarel,1½ dol. per bl.;
.; all other pickled, 1 do.; dry or smoked, 1 dol.
pickled in kegs, 15 per cent.
eries of the United States, or its territories, free.
actual value of which at the place whence im-
not exceed 50 cts. the square yard, shall be
ave cost 50 cts. the square yard, and be charged
a duty of 45 per cent. ad valorem.
factured, 45 dols. per ton; after June 30. 5 dols.
ity.
ures, if not specified, 25 per cent.
50 cts. per cwt.
cial, 30 per cent.
; hats and caps, 30; dressed, 15 do.
ds, undressed, free.
ks for umbrellas or parasols, 30 per cent.
of silk and wool, or cotton and wool, 33 1-3 do.

G.
Gilt ware, 25 per cent.
Gin, 1st proof, 57 cts. per gallon; 2d, 60 do.; 3d, 63 do.;
4th, 67 do.; 5th,|75 do.; above 5th, 90 do.
Gin cases, 30 per cent.; bottles, when imported in the cases,
2½ dols. per gross.
Glass, plain, 2 cts. per lb., and an ad valorem of 20 per cent.;
cut, 3 cts. per lb. and ad valorem of 30 per cent.
Glass bottles and phials not exceeding 6 oz., 1 dol. 75 cts. per
gross; over 6 oz., 2 cts. per lb., and an ad valorem of 20 per
cent.; bottles, black, not exceeding 1 quart, 2 dols. per
gross; over 1 and not exceeding 2, 2½ dols. do.; over 2, and
not exceeding 1 gal., 3 dols. do.
Glass beads, not on strings, 2 cts. per lb. and an ad valorem of
20 per cent.; on strings, 20 do.
Glass, window, not above 8 inches by 10 in size, 3 dols. per 100
square feet; not above 10 by 12, 3½ do.; not above 10 by 15,
4 do.; if above 10 by 15, 5 do.; in plates or sheets uncut,
5 do.
Glue, 5 cts. per lb.
Goats' hair, wool, or raw skins, free.
Gold, dust and coin, do.
Grapes, 15 per cent.
Grass ropes, 5 cts. per lb.
Grindstones, 15 per cent.
Gum, Arabic and Senegal, 12½ per cent.; all others, 15 do.

H.
Hair cloth and seating, 30 per cent.
Hair, human, unmanufactured, 15; manufactured, 30; belts,
15; pencils, 30 do.
Hair powder, not perfumed, 15; perfumed, 30 do.
Hammers, blacksmiths', 2½ cts. per lb.; and others, 25 per
cent.
Hams, 3 cts. per lb.
Hardware generally, 25 per cent.
Harness, 30; furniture, 25 do.
Hatchets, 35 do.
Hats, fur, leather, and silk, 30 do.
—— Leghorn, chip, straw, or grass, 50 do. When the cost
at the place whence imported, with an addition of 10 per
cent., shall be less than 1 dol. each, they shall be taken and
deemed to have cost 1 dol. each.
Hay knives, 40 per cent.
Hemp, unmanufactured, 55 dols. per ton; 5 dols. in addition
after June 30. 1831.
Hempen cloth, 25 per cent.
Hides, raw, free; tanned, 30 per cent.
Hoes, 25 do.
Honey, 15 do.
Hooks, reaping, iron or steel, 40 do.
Hoop iron, 3½ cts. per lb.,
Horns, 15 per cent.
Hose, wool, 35; cotton, 25; silk, 20 do.

I.
Implements of trade of persons arriving in the United States,
free.
India rubber, 15 per cent.
Indigo, till June, 1831, 30 cts. per lb.; from that time an
addition of 10 cts. each year until it amounts to 50 cts.
per lb.
Ingrain and Venetian carpets or carpeting, 40 cts. per square
yard.
Ink and ink powder, 15 per cent.
Instruments, specially imported, free; philosophical, 25 per
cent.; musical, of wood, 30 do.; do. of brass or copper,
25 do.
Iron, anchors, and parts of, 2 cts. per lb.
—— in bars or bolts not manufactured in whole or in part by
rolling, 1 ct. do.
—— in bars and bolts made wholly or in part by rolling,
37 dols. per ton.
—— slabs, blooms, loops, or other form less finished than iron
in bars, or bolts, except pigs or cast iron, shall be rated as
rolled iron in bars and bolts, and pay a duty accordingly.
—— cables or chains, or parts thereof, 3 cts. per lb.
—— cutting knives for cutting hay or straw, scythes, sickles,
reaping hooks, spades, and shovels, 40 per cent.
—— kentledge, 1 ct. per lb.
—— hollow ware, 1½ do.
—— mill cranks and mill irons, of wrought, 4 do.
—— nails, cut or wrought, 5 do.
—— old, 15 per cent.
—— in pigs, 62½ cts. per 112 lbs.
—— round, or braziers' rods of 3-16 to 8-16 of an inch diameter inclusive, and on iron in nail or spike rods slit or rolled,
and on iron in sheets and hoop iron, and on slit or rolled
for band iron, scroll iron, or casement rods, 3½ cts. per lb.
—— screws of, for wood, called wood screws, 40 per cent.
—— screws of, not weighing 25 lbs. and not called wood screws,
25 do.
—— screws of, weighing 25 lbs. or upwards, 30 do.
—— shot, 1 ct. per lb.
—— square wire, used in the manufacture of stretchers for
umbrellas, 12½ per cent.
—— tack, brads, or sprigs, not exceeding 16 oz. per 1,000,
5 cts. per 1,000.
—— tacks, brads, or sprigs, exceeding 16 oz. per 1,000, 5 cts.
per lb.
—— or steel wire, not exceeding No. 14., 6 cts. per lb.; over
No. 14., 10 do.
Ironmongery, 25 per cent.
Isinglass, 15 do.
Ivory, and all manufactures of, 15 do.

J.
Jewellery, gold, set or not set, 12½ per cent.; false or gilt, 25 do.
Juice of lemons, oranges, and limes, 15 do.
Juniper berries, 15 do.

K.
Kaleidoscopes, 25 per cent.
Knobs, iron, steel, copper, or brass, 25 do.

L.

Lace veils, 12½ per cent.
Lampblack, 15 do.
Lamps, except glass, 25 do.
Lapis calaminaris, free.
Lard, 3 cts. per lb.
Laudanum, 15 per cent.
Lead, pigs, bars, or sheets, 3 cts. per lb.; shot, 4 do.; red and white, dry or ground in oil, 5 do.; manufactured into pipes, 5 do.; sugar of, 5 do.; black, 15 per cent.; pencils, 40 do.
Lead, all manufactures of, not otherwise specified, 25 do.
Leaf gold, 15; silver, 12½ do.
Leather, all manufactures of, or of which leather is the material of chief value, 30 do.
Leghorn hats and bonnets, 50 do. (see Hats).
Lemons, lemon juice or peel, 15 do.
Lime, 15 do.
Limes and lime juice, 15 do.
Linen, all manufactures of, not otherwise specified, 25 do.
Lines, fishing, 25 do.
Liquors or cordials, 53 cts. per gal.
Loaf sugar, 12 cts. per lb.
Locks, 25 per cent.
Logwood, free.
Looking glasses not silvered, 2 cts. per lb., and an ad valorem of 20 per cent.; do. glass plates silvered, 20 do.; frames of, gilt on wood, 30 do.
Lump sugar, 10 cts. per lb.

M.

Mace, 1 dol. per lb.; oil of, 15 per cent.
Machinery of iron and brass, 25 do.
Madder and madder root, 12½ do.
Mahogany wood, free.
Malt, 15 per cent.
Manganese, 15 do.
Manufactured tobacco, other than snuff and cigars, 10 cts. per lb.
Manufactures of the United States and its territories, free.
Manufactures of brass, copper, iron, steel, pewter, lead, or tin, not otherwise specified, 25 per cent.
Maps, specially imported, free.
Marble blocks and manufactures, 30 per cent.
Materials for composing dyes not otherwise enumerated, 12½ do.
Mathematical instruments, if of gold or silver, 12½; of ivory or bone, 15; wood, 30; brass, iron, or steel, 25 do.; if specially imported, free.
Matting made of flags, tow, or other materials, 15 cts. per square yard.
Mattresses, 15 per cent.
Medals, specially imported, free; not do. 25 per cent.; silver or gold, 12½ do.
Medical preparations of anatomy, free; other, 15 per cent.
Mercury or quicksilver, and all preparations of it, 15 do.
Mill board paper, 3 cts. per lb.
Mill cranks, if wrought iron, 4 cts. per lb.; mill saws, 1 dol. each.
Millinery of all sorts, except hats, 30 per cent.
Mint, copper in any shape imported for the use of the, free.
Mineralogy, specimens in, do.
Models of machinery and other inventions, do.
Mohair manufactured, 33 1-3 per cent.
Molasses, 5 cts. per gallon.
Morocco skins, 30 per cent.
Moss, all kinds of, 15 do.
Mother of pearl, 15; buttons, 20 do.
Moulds, button, 20 do.
Musk, 15 do.
Muskets, 1½ dol. per stand; barrels, 25 per cent; balls, 25 do.
Mustard, 15 do.

N.

Nail rods, slit, 3½ cts. per lb.
Nails, iron, cut or wrought, 5 cts. per lb.; copper, 4 do.
Nankeens, 25 per cent.
Natural history, specimens in, free.
Needles, 25 per cent.
Nitrate of potash, 3 cts. per lb.
Nitre, refined, 3 cts. per lb.; unrefined, 12½ per cent.
Noyeau, 53 cts. per gallon.
Nut, cocoa, 15 per cent.
Nutmegs, 60 cts. per lb.
Nutria skins, free.

O.

Oakum and junk, 15 per cent.
Oats, 10 cts. per bushel.
Ochre, dry, 1 ct. per lb.; in 'oil, 1½ do.; earth, brown, red, blue, and yellow, to be considered as ochre, 1 do.
Oil, castor, 40 cts. per gal.; hemp seed, linseed, and olive in casks, 25 do.; spermaceti of foreign fisheries, 25 do.
Oil cloths, floor, 50 cts. per square yard; furniture do., 15 do.; other, 25 do.
Oil of vitriol, 3 cts. per lb.
Oil, whale, and others not sperm, of foreign fisheries, 15 cts. per gallon.
Oil, salad, 30 per cent.; palm, 15 do.
Old brass, copper, pewter, or silver, if fit only to be remanufactured, free; iron and junk, do., 15 per cent.
Olives, 30 per cent.
Opium, 15 do.
Oranges, 15 do.
Onions, 15 do.
Ore, specimens, free; not do., 15 per cent.
Orchilli, orchello, or orchelia, 12½ do.
Oznaburgs, 15 do.

P.

Packthread, 5 cts. per lb.
Paint brushes, 30 per cent.
Painters' colours, 15 do.
Paintings, specially imported, free; not do., 15 per cent.
Paints not enumerated and not used principally as dyeing drugs, or materials, 15; do. enumerated and principally used as dyeing drugs or materials, 12½ do.

Paper, antiquarian, demy, drawing, foolscap, imperial, medium, pot, pith, royal, and writing, 17 cts. per lb.; post, folio, and quarto post of all kinds, 20 do.; cartridge, copying, fancy coloured, fullers' boards, sheathing, leaf, paper makers' boards, Morocco, pasteboards, do., sand, or tissue, 15 do.; copper-plate, printers', 10 do.; binders' boards, box boards, mill board, or wrapping, 3 do.
Paper hangings, all, 40 per cent.
Parasols of all kinds, 30 do.
Parchment, 30 do.
Paris white, 1 ct. per lb.
Paste, imitations of precious stones, 15 per cent.; when set in gold or silver, 12½ do.
Pastel or woad, 12½ do.
Pelts, salted, 15 do.
Pencils, black lead, 40; camels' hair and red lead, 15 do.
Penknives, 25 do.
Pens of metal or quills, 25; gold or silver, 12½ do.
Pepper, 8 cts. per lb.; Cayenne, 15 do.
Perfumery, 30 per cent.; do. soap, do.
Persons arriving in the United States, their wearing apparel and their tools and implements of trade, free.
Perry, 53 cts. per gallon.
Pewter, all manufactures of, not otherwise specified, 25 per cent.
Pianofortes, 30 do.
Pickles, 30 do.
Pictures, 15 do.
Pimento, 6 cts. per lb.
Pine apples, 15 per cent.
Pink root, 15 do.
Pins, gold or silver, 12½; all other kinds of, 25 do.
Pipes, clay, for smoking, 15 do.
Pistols, 30 do.
Plaids, Scotch stuff, 25 do.
Plains and paddings, if cost under 33 1-3 cts. per square yard, 14 cts. per do. If cost over 33 1-3 cts. and less than per square yard, they shall be taken and deemed to cost 50 cts. per square yard, and be charged therewith an ad valorem duty of 45 per cent.
Plane irons, free.
Plants, free.
Plaster of Paris, do.
Plate, battered, if only to be manufactured, do.
Plated metal and ware of all kinds, 25 per cent.
Platina, 15 do.
Plats for hats or bonnets, 50 do.
Ploughs, 25 do.
Do. (a plane) 30 do.
Plums, 4 cts. per lb.
Pocketbooks, leather, 30 per cent.
Porcelain, 20 do.
Porter, in bottles, 20 cts. per gal.; not in do., 15 do.
Potatoes, 10 cts. per bushel.
Powder, gun, 8 cts. per lb.
Precious stones, set or not, and all articles composed chiefly of, 12½ per cent.; glass, imitations of, 2 cts. and an ad valorem of 20 per cent.; other imitations, per cent.
Preserves in sugar or brandy, 30; in molasses, 15 do.
Printed music, 15 do.
Printing types, 25 do.
Prints on paper, 15 do.
Prunes, 4 cts. per lb.
Prussian blue, 20 per cent.
Prussiate of potash, 12½ do.

Q.

Quadrants, 25 per cent.
Quercitron bark, 12½ do.
Quicksilver, 15 do.
Quills prepared or manufactured, 25; not do., 15 do.

R.

Rags of any kind of cloth, free.
Raisins, muscatel, and in jars and boxes, 4 cts. per lb.; others, 3 do.
Ratafia, a liquor, 53 cts. per gal.
Rattans, 15 per cent.
Raw silk, 15 do.
Razors, 25 do.
Reaping hooks, 40 do.
Red lead, dry, or ground in oil, 5 cts. per lb.
Regulus of antimony, free.
Rice, 15 per cent.
Rifles, 2½ dols. each.
Roots, bulbous, free.
Rope, grass or bark, 5 cts. per lb.
Rosin, 15 per cent.
Rum, 1st and 2d proof, 53 cts. per gal.; 3d; 57 do.;

S.

Saddlery, silver, 12½ per cent.; metal, 25 do.
Saddles, 30 do.
Sad irons, 25 do.
Salt, 15 cts. per 56 lbs.; after Dec. 31. 10 do.
Saltpetre, refined, 3 cts. per lb.; crude, 12½ per cent.
Salts, Rochelle, 15 per cent.; Glauber, 2 cts. per lb.; 4 do.
Sandal wood, free.
Saws, mill, 1 dol. each; all other, 25 per cent.
Scale beams, 35 do.
Scales, Gunter and other wood, 30 do.
Screws of iron, for wood, called wood screws, 40 cts. 25 lbs. or upwards, 30; not weighing 25 lbs., and those for wood called wood screws, 25 do.
Sculpture, specimens of, specially imported, free; wood, not do., 30 per cent.
Scythes, 40 do.
Seeds, canary and all others, 15 do.
Seines, 5 cts. per lb.
Sheeting, Russia, 25 per cent.
Shoes, of silk, 30 cts. per pair; nankeen, prunelle, 25 do.; for children, 15 do.

and tongs, 25 per cent.
, 12½ do.
. 40 do.
manufactures of, from beyond the Cape of Good Hope,
om any other place, 20 do.
ring, 20 ; hats or caps, 30 ; lace, 12½ do.
aw, free ; tanned, 30 per cent.
oofing, not exceeding 12 inches in length by 6 inches
th, 4 dols. per ton.
xceeding 12 inches and not exceeding 14 inches in
, 5 do.
ceeding 14 inches and not exceeding 16 inches in
, 6 do.
ceeding 16 inches and not exceeding 18 inches in
, 7 do.
ceeding 18 inches and not exceeding 20 inches in
8 do.
ceeding 20 inches and not exceeding 24 inches in
, 9 do.
ceeding 24 inches in length, 10 do.
ohering, all kinds of, 33 1-3 per cent. ; paper, do. do.
blacksmiths', 2½ cts. per lb.
silk, 30 cts. per pair ; leather, 25 do. ; and children's
do.
35 per cent.
cts. per lb.
do.; perfumed, all kinds, 30 per cent.
f iron or steel, 40 do.
rown, dry, 1 ct. per lb. ; ground in oil, 1½ do.
s, gold or silver mounted, 12½ per cent. ; shell do.,
metal do., 25 do.
stilled from grain, 1st proof, 57 cts. per gal. ; 2d, 60
, 63 do. ; 4th, 67 do. ; 5th, 75 do. ; above 5th, 90 do.
stilled from other materials than grain, 1st and 2d
53 ; 3d, 57 ; 4th, 63 ; 5th, 72 ; above 5th, 85 do.
s, 25 per cent.
ron, tin, pewter, or plated, 25 do.
15 do.
f iron or steel, 35 do.
5 do.
specimens of, specially imported, free ; not do., of
r and plaster, 15 per cent. ; brass, bronze, or metal, 25
arble or wood, 30 do.
dol. per 112 lbs. ; do. in bars, do. ; all manufactures
rwise specified, 25 per cent.
, 35 do.
lking, 30 do.
, silk, 20 ; cotton, 25 ; wool or worsted, 35 do.
ecious, set or not, 12½ do.
rr, wrought, 15 do. ; unwrought, free.
d, 25 per cent.
, 20 do.
ves, iron or steel, for cutting straw, 40 do.
s of all kinds, not otherwise specified, 25 do.
wn, 3 cts. per lb. ; white and powdered, 4 do. ; lump,
loaf and candy, 12 do.
lead, 5 do.
f copper or blue vitriol, 4 do.
r brimstone, free.
acid, 3 cts. per lb.
ts, preserved in sugar or brandy, 30 per cent.
d sword blades, 15 do.
est India, 15 do.

T.

ves and forks, 25 per cent.
ads, or sprigs, not exceeding 16 oz. to the 1,000,
1,000 ; exceeding 16 oz. per 1,000, 5 cts. per lb.
ed.
rted in vessels of the United States, direct from
mperial, gunpowder, and gomee, 50 ; hyson and
yson, 40 ; hyson skin, and all other green, 25 ;
; and other black, 25 ; bohea, 12 do., until 31st
.
ted in vessels not of the United States, from any
e, imperial, gunpowder, and gomee, 68 ; hyson and
son, 56 ; hyson skin, and other green, 38 ; souchong,
r black, 34 ; bohea, 14 do., until 31st Dec. 1831.
China, in vessels of the United States, after 31 Dec.
hea, 4 ; souchong, and other black (including Cam-
ngo), 10 ; hyson skin, and other green, 12 ; hyson
ng hyson, 18 ; gomee, gunpowder, and imperial,
any other place than China, in vessels of, or any
an the United States, after 31 Dec. 1831, bohea,
ong, and other black (including Campoi and Congo),
on skin, and other green, 20 ; hyson and young
; gomee, gunpowder, or imperial, 37 do.
per cent.
hants', or other animals', 15 do.
wing, floss, cotton, and shoe, 25 per cent. ; pack,
gs, 15 per cent.
or building, 20 ; marble, 30 do.
, pigs, or blocks, free ; granulated, and grain, 12½
foil, plate or sheets, 15 do.; all manufactures of, or
tin is a component material, not otherwise specified,
medicinal, 15 ; odoriferous, 30 do.
anufactured, other than snuff and segars, 10 cts.
nnanufactured, 15 do.
d sounds, 15 per cent.
ade of persons arriving in the United States, free.
ell, 15 per cent.
, 15 ; of brass, iron, steel, tin, lead, pewter, or
; of wood, 30 do.
per cent.
or zinc, free.
ed, 4 ; untarred, 5 cts. per lb.
ting, 25 per cent.

U.

Umbrellas, 30 per cent ; furniture, metal, 25 do. ; ivory or
bone, 15 do.

V.

Varnishes of all kinds, 15 per cent.
Vegetables of all kinds, not enumerated and not used principally
in dyeing, 15 do.
Veils, lace, 12½ do.
Vellum, 30 do.
Vermicelli, 15 do.
Vessels, copper, 35 do. ; cast iron, not otherwise specified, 1½
ct. per lb.
Vices, 35 per cent.
Vinegar, 8 cts. per gallon.
Vitriol, blue or Roman, 4 cts. per lb. ; oil of, 3 do.

W.

Wafers, 30 per cent.
Walking sticks or canes, 30 do.
Watches, all kinds of, and parts of, 12½ do.
Water colours, 15 do.
Waters, bay, lavender, Cologne, Hungary, and honey, 50 do.
Wax, bees', 15 do.
Wearing apparel in actual use of persons arriving in the
United States, free.
Webbing, silk, 20 per cent. ; worsted, 33 1-3 do. ; all other, 25 do.
Weld, 12½ do.
Whalebone, 15 do.
Wheat, 25 cts. per bushel ; flour, 50 cts. per cwt.
White lead, dry or ground in oil, 5 cts. per lb.
White, Paris, 1 do.
Whiting, 1 do.
Whips, 30 per cent.
Willow sheets, 50 ; for baskets or covering demijohns, 15 do.
Window glass (see Glass).
Wines, Madeira and sherry, in casks, cases, or bottle, 50 cts.
per gallon.
—— of France, Germany, Spain, and the Mediterranean,
when imported in casks, unless specially enumerated, except
the red wine of France and Spain, 15 do.
—— red of France and Spain, when not imported in bottles,
10 do.
—— of all countries, when imported in bottles or cases, unless
specially enumerated, and on wines not enumerated, 30 do.
When wine is imported in bottles, there is a duty charged
on the bottles (see Glass).
Woad or pastel, 12½ per cent.
Wood, unmanufactured, and for dyeing, free ; all manufactures
of, 30 per cent.
Wool, Angora, goats', or camels', free.
—— unmanufactured, 4 cts. per lb., and an ad valorem of
50 per cent.
—— all, imported on the skin, shall be estimated as to weight
and value, and shall pay the rate of duty on other imported
wool.
—— all manufactures of, or of which wool shall be a component part (except carpetings, blankets, worsted stuff goods,
bombazines, hosiery, gloves, mits, caps, and bindings), the
actual value of which, at the place whence imported, shall
not exceed 50 cts. the square yard, shall be deemed to have
cost 50 cts. the square yard, and be charged thereon with a
duty of 45 per cent. ; provided that on all manufactures of
wool, except flannels and baizes, the actual value of which,
at the place whence imported, shall not exceed 33 1-3 cts.
per square yard, 14 cts. per square yard.
—— all manufactures of, or of which wool shall be a component part, except as aforesaid, the actual value of which, at
the place whence imported, shall exceed 50 cts. the square
yard, and shall not exceed 1 dol. the square yard, shall be
deemed to have cost 1 dol. the square yard, and be charged
thereon with a duty of 45 per cent.
—— all manufactures of, or of which wool shall be a component part, except as aforesaid, the actual value of which, at
the place whence imported, shall exceed 1 dol. the square
yard, and shall not exceed 2 dols. 50 cts. the square yard, shall
be deemed to have cost 2 dols. 50 cts. the square yard, and be
charged with a duty thereon of 45 per cent.
—— all manufactures of, or of which wool shall be a component part, except as aforesaid, the actual value of which, at
the place whence imported, shall exceed 2 dols. 50 cts. the
square yard, and shall not exceed 4 dols. the square yard, shall
be deemed to have cost, at the place whence imported, 4 dols.
the square yard, and be charged thereon with a duty of 45
per cent.
—— all manufactures of, or of which wool shall be a component part, except as aforesaid, the actual cost of which, at
the place whence imported, shall exceed 4 dols. the square
yard, 50 per cent.
Woollen hose, 35 ; yarn, 33 1-3 do.

Y.

Yarns, 15 per cent.
Yarn, cotton, bleached or coloured, the original cost of which
shall be less than 75 cts. per lb. shall be deemed and taken
to have cost 75 cts. per lb. and shall be charged with duty
accordingly, 25 per cent.
Yarns, cotton, unbleached and uncoloured, the original cost of
which shall be less than 60 cts. per lb. shall be taken and
deemed to have cost 60 cts. per lb., 25 per cent.

Z.

Zinc, unmanufactured, free ; in sheets or nails, 15 per cent.

The above are the rates of duty imposed on goods imported in American vessels, or in vessels
y treaty to enter the ports of the United States on the same terms as American vessels. Goods
in vessels not so privileged pay 10 per cent. of *additional duty*. Ships from Great Britain,
he Netherlands, Norway, Sweden, the Hanse Towns, &c., enjoy the privilege in question.

Influence of the Tariff on the Commerce of America. — Notwithstanding the unpr
dented progress of the United States in wealth and population, their foreign trade
been nearly stationary for the last 10 years!   And yet, considering the spirit of c
mercial enterprise by which the people, particularly in the New England States
New-York, are animated, and their skill in navigation, it might have been fairly presu
that the growth of their foreign trade would, at least, have kept pace with the
velopment of the internal resources of the country.   That it has not done so, is wh
owing to the policy of government.   Not satisfied with the extraordinary advances
constituents had made in numbers and wealth, Congress seems to have believed that
career might be accelerated by means of Custom-house regulations! — by givin
artificial direction to a portion of the public capital and industry, and turning it
channels into which it would not naturally flow!

No one who has the slightest acquaintance with the condition of America —
knows that she is possessed of boundless tracts of fertile and unappropriated lan
that her population is comparatively thin, and wages high — can doubt for a mor
that agriculture *must*, for a long series of years, be the most profitable species of
ployment in which her citizens can engage.   There can be no question, indeed,
such branches of manufacture as are naturally adapted to her peculiar situat
will gradually grow up and flourish in America, without any artificial encouragem
according as her population becomes denser, and as the advantage which now exis
the side of agriculture becomes less decided.   But to force, by means of duties
prohibitions, the premature growth of manufactures, is plainly to force a portio
the industry and capital of the country into businesses in which it will be
productive.

Such, however, has been the policy of the American legislature.   The expl
sophisms of the mercantile system, though renounced by every statesman in Eur
have acquired a noxious influence in congress, and been put forth with as much
fidence, as if their soundness neither had been, nor could be, questioned!   From
downwards, the object of the American legislature has been to bolster up a man
turing interest, by imposing oppressive duties on most manufactured articles imp
from abroad.   Now, it is obvious, even were the articles produced in America thro
the agency of this plan as cheap as those they have superseded, that nothing woul
gained by it; for, to whatever extent the importation of foreign articles may be d
nished, there must be a corresponding diminution in the exportation of native Ame
products; so that the only result would be the raising up of one species of ind
at the expense of some other species, entitled to an equality of protection.   Bu
" American system" has not been so innocuous.   Instead of the goods manufact
in the States being as cheap as similar ones manufactured in Europe, they are adm
to be, at an average, from 30 to 100 per cent. dearer!   The extent of the pecu
sacrifice that is thus imposed on the Union has been variously estimated by Ame
writers; but we have been assured by those who have the best means of knowing,
it may be moderately estimated at from 50,000,000 to 60,000,000 dollars, or from
11,000,000*l.* to 13,000,000*l.* !   And this immense burden — a burden nearly
times as great as the whole public expenditure of the republic — is incurred f
purpose of public utility, and is productive of nothing but mischief.   The whole
of the scheme is to divert a certain amount of the national capital from the produ
of cotton, wheat, rice, tobacco, &c. (the equivalents sent to foreigners in pay
of manufactured goods), to the direct production of these goods themselves!   A
the latter species of industry is nowise suitable for America, a tax of 13,000,00
year is imposed on the Union, that the manufacturers may be enabled to conti
losing business.   We leave it to others to determine whether the absurdity o
system, or its costliness, be its more prominent feature.

But the pecuniary sacrifice arising out of a policy of this sort is really the leas
of the injury it occasions.   Besides forcing a large proportion of the national c
and industry into comparatively barren channels, it has raised up so many confl
pretensions, and led to such a disunion of interests, as threatens to be, in no cor
degree, injurious to the public tranquillity, and may even seriously endanger the sta
of the Union.   That its influence has not been still more injurious, is solely owi
the smuggling it has occasioned!   With a frontier like that of America, and with
or more of the population hostile to the tariff, it would be worse than absu
suppose that it could be carried into full effect.   But it has enough of influe
render it in the last degree prejudicial — to occasion a great rise in the price of
important articles — to cripple the trade and navigation of the country — and to th
considerable part of it into the hands of foreigners, who carry it on in defiance
law !

We entertain too favourable an opinion of the Americans to suppose that

can be permanent. It has been established in opposition to the wishes of all
najority of congress; is exceedingly unpopular in the southern States, and
y throughout the Union; and has been repeatedly condemned by com-
of the legislature. In an able Report by a committee of the House of
ntatives, dated 8th of February, 1830, it is said: — "We had before us the
t of a long and general peace, and our policy should have been regulated
gly. Our revenue laws should have been restored gradually, but decisively,
condition previously to the war. Our policy unfortunately took another direc-
The tariff of 1816 laid the foundation of all our subsequent errors; and we
w been engaged for 15 years in an unprofitable experiment to effect, what
, non-importation, non-intercourse, and war, failed to accomplish. We have
d, by the mere force of congressional decrees, to resist the natural and salutary
y of our industry to commercial and agricultural pursuits. We have been
sacrificing the commerce, navigation, and capital of New England, merely to
rward new competitors in manufacturing, to embarrass our old and skilful
and to ruin themselves. We have, from session to session, kept trade in such
and uncertainty, that the value of property could never be ascertained till the
nent of congress; and this we have called encouraging and protecting our
! We have wasted millions of our ancient profits of commerce in a visionary
nt to increase our national wealth. In a legislative attempt to make ourselves
npletely independent of foreign nations, we have effectually undermined the
on of that naval power which can alone protect our country from foreign ag-
"

is no exaggeration in this statement; and we shall not do the Americans the
of supposing that they will blindly continue to uphold a system of policy,
on the most erroneous principles, and productive only of the most pernicious
— (Those wishing for further information as to the important subjects now
upon, may consult the Report of the Committee of Commerce and Navigation
ed; Papers as to American Tariffs, printed by order of the House of Commons,
July, 1828; Report by a Committee of the Citizens of Boston and its Vici-
7; Art. 4. in the Edinburgh Review, No. 96., &c.)

ARAGUA or PEACH WOOD (Ger. *Nicaragaholz, Blutholtz;* Du. *Bloed-*
. Bois de sang, Bois de Nicarague; It. *Legno sanguigno;* Sp. *Palo de sangre;*
o sanguinho), a tree of the same genus (*Cæsalpinia*) as the Brazil wood; but
es has not been exactly ascertained. It grows principally in the vicinity of
of Nicaragua, whence its name. It is said by Dr. Bancroft to be almost as
heavy as the true Brazil wood, but it does not commonly afford more than
art, in quantity, of the colour of the latter; and even this is rather less
and less beautiful, though dyed with the same mordants. Nicaragua or
ods differ greatly in their quality as well as price: one sort being so defi-
colouring matter, that six pounds of it will only dye as much wool or
one pound of Brazil wood; while another variety of it will produce
alf the effect of an equal quantity of Brazil wood, and will sell propor-
dear. — (*Bancroft on Colours,* vol. ii. p. 332.)
ondon dealers distinguish Nicaragua wood into three sorts, viz. *large,*
and *small;* the price of the first sort (duty included) being from 14*l.* to 20*l.*
of the second from 8*l.* to 10*l.* per do., and of the third from 7*l.* to 8*l.* per do.
y of 15*s.* a ton on Nicaragua wood produced, in 1829, 641*l.* 12*s.* 10*d.*,
that 855 tons had been entered for home consumption.

EL, a scarce metal, which occurs always in combination with other
rom which it is exceedingly difficult to separate it. When pure, it is of
ite colour resembling silver. It is rather softer than iron: its specific
when cast, is 8·279; when hammered, 8·932. It is malleable, and may
difficulty be hammered into plates not exceeding $\frac{1}{160}$th part of an inch
ess. It is attracted by the magnet; and is not altered by exposure to the
y being kept under water. It is employed in potteries, and in the manu-
porcelain. — (*Thomson's Chemistry.*)

E. See SALTPETRE.

, PROMISSORY. See BANKING, and BANKS.

or HAZEL NUT (Ger. *Haselnüsse;* Fr. *Norsettes, Avelines;* It. *Nac-*
elane; Sp. *Avellanas;* Port. *Avellãas;* Lat. *Avellanæ*), the fruit of different
f coryli, or hazels. The kernels have a mild, farinaceous, oily taste,
to most palates. A kind of chocolate has been prepared from them; and
sometimes been made into bread. The expressed oil of hazel nuts is

3 E

little inferior to that of almonds. We import nuts from different parts of F.
Portugal, and Spain, but principally from the latter. Those brought from I
lona are in the highest estimation. The duty on hazel nuts is 2s. a bushel ; v
as it produces, at an average, about 11,000l. a year, shows that the quanti
ported is about 110,000 bushels.

NUTMEG (Ger. *Muskatennüsse;* Du. *Muskaät;* Fr. *Muscades, Noix musc*
It. *Noce muscada;* Sp. *Moscada;* Arab. *Jowzalteib;* Sans. *Jātiphala; N
Buah-pala*), the fruit of the nutmeg tree (*Myristica Moschata*), a native c
Moluccas, but which has been transplanted to Batavia, Sumatra, Penang
An inferior and long-shaped nutmeg is common in Borneo ; the tree is also me
in Cochin China and New Holland ; but the fruit no where attains to the
perfection as in the Moluccas. Of the several varieties of the tree, that
minated the Queen Nutmeg, which bears a small round fruit, is the best.
kernel, or proper nutmeg, is of a roundish oval form, marked on the outside
many vermicular furrows, within of a fleshy farinaceous substance, varie
whitish and bay. Nutmegs are frequently punctured and boiled, in order t
tain the essential oil ; the orifice being afterwards closed ; but the fraud is
detected by the lightness of the nutmeg. — (*Thomson's Dispensatory; Ai
Materia Indica.*)

Nutmegs should be chosen large, round, heavy, and firm, of a lightish grey
on the outside, and the inside beautifully marbled, of a strong fragrant smell,
aromatic taste, and a fat oily body. They are very subject to be worm-eaten.
best manner of packing them is in dry chunam. The oblong kind, and the smalle
should be rejected. 15 cwt. are allowed to a ton. — (*Milburn's Orient. Com.*)

The dried produce of a nutmeg tree consists of nutmeg, mace (which see), and
Supposing the whole produce to be divided into 100 parts, there are 13¼ of mace,
shell, and 53⅓ of nutmeg. In the ancient commerce, and down to the establishm
the Dutch monopoly, nutmegs were always sold and exported in the shell. The n
whenever the commerce is left to their management, continue the practice, wh
strongly recommended by Mr. Crawford. — (*East Indian Archipelago,* vol. iii. p.

The jealous and miserable policy of the Dutch has reduced the trade in nutme
mere trifle, compared to what it would otherwise have been. They have, in sc
least as it was possible, exerted themselves to exterminate the nutmeg plants every
except in Banda. They bribe the native princes of the surrounding islands to rc
the trees ; and annually send a fleet to see that the work of destruction has been e
and that the bribes have not been bestowed in vain. To engage in an illicit tr
spices is *death* to an inferior person, and *banishment* to a noble ; and yet, notwithst
these tremendous penalties, it is supposed that about 60,000 lbs. of nutmeg
15,000 lbs. of mace, are clandestinely exported each year ! In Banda, the abo
inhabitants have been expatriated, and the island parcelled among settlers from H
under the name of *park keepers.* These persons, who may be turned out of thei
on the most trifling pretext, have about 2,000 slaves, who cultivate and prepare th
megs. The prices paid to the cultivator are all fixed by government ; and it d
to be mentioned, as affording one of the most striking illustrations of the ruinous
of monopoly, that the fixed price which the government is now obliged to pay f
megs is FIVE *times greater than the price at which they bought them when the trade w
Such is a rough outline of that monstrous system, which has reduced what use
one of the most important branches of Eastern commerce so low, that it is un
afford employment for the capital of a single wealthy merchant. We cannot c
how so enlightened and liberal a government as that of Holland should conti
tolerate such scandalous abuses — abuses destructive alike of the rights of tho
jected to its authority in the East, and the commerce and wealth of its subjects at
— (*Modern Universal History,* vol. x. pp. 457—467. 8vo ed. ; and *Crawfurd's
Archipelago,* vol. iii. pp. 394—413.)

Mr. Crawford estimates the produce of the Banda islands at about 600,000
nutmegs, and 150,000 lbs. of mace.

During the period that the English had possession of the Spice islands, nutme
were carried to Penang, Bencoolen, and some of the West India islands. In th
they have altogether failed, at least as far as respects any useful purpose ; but ve
nutmegs, and in considerable quantities, are now raised at Penang and Bencooler
Crawford, however, alleges that the cost of bringing them to market is there s
that the restoration of a free culture in the native country of the nutmeg would i
destroy this unstable and factitious branch of industry. — (*Eastern Archipelago,*
p. 409.)

e duty on nutmegs was reduced, in 1819, from 5s. 5d. to 2s. 6d. per lb.; and the
ities entered for home consumption have since rapidly increased. We subjoin

count of the Quantities of Nutmegs retained for Home Consumption in the United Kingdom, in each Year since 1810, the Nett Amount of Duty received thereon, and the Rates of Duty.

Quantities retained for Home Consumption.	Nett Amount of Duty received thereon.	Rates of Duty charged thereon.	Years.	Quantities retained for Home Consumption.	Nett Amount of Duty received thereon.	Rates of Duty charged thereon.
	£ s. d.				£ s. d.	
9,127	11,166 11 1	{ 4s. 8d. per lb. and 2l. 13s. 4d. per cent. ad valorem.	1818	66,255½	17,944 8 6	(From 10 Apr.)5s.5d.perlb.
0,860	14,462 14 4	- - ditto.	1819	107,575	17,805 18 5	(From 5 July) 2s.6d. per lb.
7,186	11,205 2 9	- - ditto.	1820	90,771½	11,212 8 9	- - ditto.
ecords destroyed.		{ (From 15 April)5s. 6½d. per lb. and 3l. 3s. 4d. per cent. ad valorem.	1821	94,589½	11,721 2 5	- - ditto.
			1822	112,096	14,000 10 6	- - ditto.
			1823	117,767½	14,723 7 9	- - ditto.
			1824	129,702	16,176 19 7	- - ditto.
3,160	14,710 8 3	{ (From 10 April) 5s. 5d. per lb.	1825	99,214½	12,406 13 2	- - ditto.
9,839	16,209 11 1	- - ditto.	1826	101,171½	12,623 13 10	- - ditto.
4,677	14,808 2 8	- - ditto.	1827	125,529	15,707 2 8	- - ditto.
5,747	17,808 1 8	- - ditto.	1828	140,002½	17,514 6 4	- - ditto.
			1829	113,273½	14,114 6 2	- - ditto.

TRIA, or NEUTRIA, the commercial name for the skins of *Myopotamus iensis* (Commerson), the *Coypou* of Molina, and the *Quoiya* of D'Azara. In e, the skins were, and perhaps still are, sold under the name of *racoonda;* England they are imported as *nutria* skins — deriving their appellation, most bly, from some supposed similarity of the animal which produces them, in ap- ace and habits, to the otter, the Spanish name for which is nutria. Indeed, a speaks of the *coypou* as a species of water rat, of the size and colour of ter.

ria fur is largely used in the hat manufacture; and has become, within the last 20 years, an article of very considerable commercial importance. From 600,000 to 0 skins, principally from the Rio de la Plata, are now annually imported into Great . It is also very extensively used on the Continent. Geoffroy mentions *, that ain years, a single French furrier (M. Bechem), has received from 15,000 to skins. — (See Fur Trade.)

coypou or quoiya is a native of South America, very common in the provinces of Buenos Ayres, and Tucuman, but more rare in Paraguay. In size it is less than ver, which it resembles in many points. The head is large and depressed, the all and rounded, the neck stout and short, the muzzle sharper than that of the and the whiskers very long and stiff. There are, as in the beaver, two incisor and eight molar, above and below — twenty teeth in all. The limbs are short. re feet have each five fingers not webbed, the thumb being very small: the hind ve the same number of toes; the great toe and three next toes being joined by a ich extends to their ends, and the little toe being free, but edged with a mem- n its inner side. The nails are compressed, long, crooked, and sharp. The tail, that of the beaver, is long, round, and hairy; but the hairs are not numerous, and the scaly texture of the skin in this part to be seen. The back is of a brownish ich becomes redder on the flanks: the belly is of a dirty red. The edges of the extremity of the muzzle are white.

the beaver, the coypou is furnished with two kinds of fur; viz. the long ruddy ich gives the tone of colour, and the brownish ash-coloured fur at its base, which, down of the beaver, is of such importance in hat making, and the cause of the s commercial value.

habits of the coypou are much like those of most of the other aquatic rodent Its principal food, in a state of nature, is vegetable. It affects the neigh- d of water, swims perfectly well, and burrows in the ground. The female orth from five to seven; and the young always accompany her. coypou is easily domesticated, and its manners in captivity are very mild.

We are indebted for this account of nutria — the first, we believe, that has ap- n any English work — to the kindness of W. J. Broderip, Esq., F. R. S. &c.

X VOMICA (Fr. *Noix Vomique;* Hind. *Kaachla*), the fruit of a species hnos, growing in various places in the East Indies. The fruit is about of an orange, covered with a smooth crustaceous yellow bark, and filled

es du Muséum, vol. vi. p. 82. The figure given is, generally speaking, good; but the tail is too contradicts the description.

with a fleshy pulp, in which are imbedded several orbicular flatted seeds, ab ¾ of an inch in diameter. Nux vomica is inodorous, and has a very bitter, a taste, which remains long on the palate. It is known as a very virulent poi A suspicion has, however, been entertained, that it has been used in po breweries; but its introduction into them is prohibited under heavy penal — (*Thomson's Dispensatory*, &c.)

O.

OAK (Ger. *Eiche*; Du. *Eik*; Da. *Eeg*; Sw. *Ek*; Fr. *Chêne*; It. *Quer* Sp. *Roble, Carballo*; Port. *Roble, Carballo*; Rus. *Dub*; Pol. *Dab*; Lat. *Quer* Arab. *Baalut*). There are several varieties of this valuable tree; but the com English oak claims precedence of every other. The oak timber imported f America is very inferior to that of this country: the oak from the central p of Europe is also inferior, especially in compactness and resistance of cleav The knotty oak of England, the "unwedgeable and gnarled oak," as Shaksp called it, when cut down at a proper age (from 50 to 70 years), is the best tin known. Some timber is harder, some more difficult to rend, and some capable of being broken across; but none contains all the three qualities in great and equal proportions; and thus, for at once supporting a weight, resis a strain, and not splintering by a cannon shot, the timber of the oak is superio every other.

A fine oak is one of the most picturesque of trees: it conveys to the mind as ations of strength and duration, which are very impressive. The oak stands up ag the blast, and does not take, like other trees, a twisted form from the action of winds. Except the cedar of Lebanon, no tree is so remarkable for the stoutness o limbs; they do not exactly spring from the trunk, but divide from it; and thus sometimes difficult to know which is stem and which is branch. The twisted bran of the oak, too, add greatly to its beauty; and the horizontal direction of its bo spreading over a large surface, completes the idea of its sovereignty over all the tre the forest. Even a decayed oak,

" ———————————— dry and dead,
Still clad with reliques of its trophies old,
Lifting to heaven its aged, hoary head,
Whose foot on earth has got but feeble hold,"

— even such a tree as Spencer has thus described, is strikingly beautiful; decay in case looks pleasing. To such an oak Lucan compared Pompey in his decline.

" Qualis frugifero quercus sublimis in agro
Exuvias veteres populi, sacrataque gestans
Dona ducum; nec jam validis radicibus hærens,
Pondere fixa suo est; nudosque per aëra ramos
Effundens, trunco, non frondibus, efficit umbram.
At quamvis primo nutet casura sub Euro,
Tot circum silvæ firmo se robore tollant,
Sola tamen colitur." — (Lib. i. lin. 136.)

The oak is raised from acorns, sown either where the oak is to stand, or in a nu whence the young trees are transplanted.

The colour of oak wood is a fine brown, and is familiar to every one: it is of diff shades; that inclined to red is the most inferior kind of wood. The larger trans septa are in general very distinct, producing beautiful flowers when cut obliq Where the septa are small, and not very distinct, the wood is much the strongest. texture is alternately compact and porous; the compact part of the annual ring bei the darkest colour, and in irregular dots, surrounded by open pores, producing bea dark veins in some kinds, particularly pollard oaks. Oak timber has a particular s and the taste is slightly astringent. It contains gallic acid, and is blackened by co with iron when it is damp. The young wood of English oak is very tough, often c grained, and difficult to work. Foreign wood, and that of old trees, is more brittl workable. Oak warps and twists much in drying; and in seasoning, shrinks ₃¹₀d of its width.

Oak of a good quality is more durable than any other wood that attains a like Vitruvius says it is of eternal duration when driven into the earth; it is extre

in water; and in a dry state it has been known to last nearly 1,000 years. The
mpact it is, and the smaller the pores are, the longer it will last; but the open,
and foxy coloured oak, which grows in Lincolnshire and some other places, is
r so durable.

'es the common British oak (*Quercus robur*), the sessile fruited bay oak
s *sessiliflora*) is pretty abundant in several parts of England, particularly in the
The wood of this species is said by Tredgold to be darker, heavier, harder, and
stic than the common oak; tough, and difficult to work; and very subject to
d split in seasoning. Mr. Tredgold seems disposed to regard this species as
to the common oak for ship-building. But other, and also very high autho-
e opposed to him on this point; and, on the whole, we should think that it is
tly well established, that for all the great practical purposes to which oak timber
d, and especially for ship-building, the wood of the common oak deserves to
rred to every other species. A well-informed writer in the Quarterly Review
ollowing remarks on the point in question: —

: may here notice a fact long known to botanists, but of which our planters and
rs of timber appear to have had no suspicion, that there are two distinct species
a England—the *Quercus robur*, and the *Quercus sessiliflora*; the former of which
close-grained, firm, solid timber, rarely subject to rot; the other more loose
y, very liable to rot, and not half so durable. This difference was noted so
the time of Ray; and Martyn in his *Flora Rustica*, and Sir James Smith in his
ritannica, have added their testimonies to the fact. The second species is sup-
have been introduced some two or three ages back, from the Continent, where
are chiefly of this latter species, especially in the German forests, the timber of
known to be very worthless. But what is of more importance to us is, that
the impostor abounds, and is propagated vigorously, in the New Forest and other
Hampshire; in Norfolk, and the northern counties, and about London; and
out too much reason to believe that the numerous complaints that were heard
r ships being infected with what was called, improperly enough, *dry rot*, were
e the introduction of this species of oak into the naval dock-yards, where, we
nd, the distinction was not even suspected. It may thus be discriminated from
old English oak: — The acorn stalks of the *Robur* are *long*, and its leaves *short*;
the Sessiliflora has the acorn stalks *short*, and the leaves *long*: the acorns of the
row singly, or seldom two on the same footstalk; those of the latter in clusters of
ree close to the stem of the branch. We believe the Russian ships of the Baltic,
ot of larch or fir, are built of this species of oak; but if this were not the case,
osure on the stocks, without cover, to the heat of summer, which though short is
, and the rifts and chinks which fill up with ice and snow in the long winter,
gh to destroy the stoutest oak, and quite suffient to account for their short-lived
"

deal of inquiry and discussion has taken place at different periods as to the supply and con-
f oak timber; but the results have not been very satisfactory. In a Report of the Commis-
Land Revenue, printed in 1812, it is stated that, taking the tonnage of the navy in 1806 at
s, it would require, at 1½ load to a ton, 1,164,085 loads to build such a navy; and supposing the
ration of a ship to be 14 years, the annual quantity of timber required would be 83,149 loads,
f repairs, which they calculate would be about 27,000 loads; making the whole about 110,000
hich, however, the commissioners reckon may be furnished 21,341 loads as the annual average
es; and of the remaining 88,659 loads they think it not unreasonable to calculate on 28,659
sources than British oak. "This," they observe, "leaves 60,000 loads of such oak, as the
hich would be sufficient annually to support, at its present unexampled magnitude, the whole
y, including ships of war of all sorts; but which may be taken as equivalent together to 20
s, each of which, one with another, contains about 2,000 tons, or would require, at the rate of 1½
ton, 3,000 loads; making just 60,000 loads for 20 such ships."
as been supposed that not more than 40 oak trees can stand on an acre of ground, so as to grow
e fit for ships of the line, or to contain each 1½ load of timber: 50 acres, therefore, would be
produce a sufficient quantity of timber to build a 74-gun ship, and 1,000 acres for 20 such ships;
oak requires at least 100 years to arrive at maturity, 100,000 acres would be required to keep
sive supply, for maintaining a navy of 700,000 or 800,000 tons. The commissioners further
t as there are 20,000,000 acres of waste lands in the kingdom, a 200th part set aside for planting
ce furnish the whole quantity wanted for the use of the navy.
g to Mr. Barrow, this calculation is over-rated by about a half. "In the first place," says he,
ed a state of perpetual war, during which the tonnage of the whole navy is considered as more
of what it now actually is; and in the second place, it reckons the average duration of the
ears only, which, from the improvements that have taken place in the construction and pre-
ships of war, with the resources of teak ships built in India, we should not hesitate in assum-
erage of twice that number of years; and if so, the quantity of oak required for the navy will
ike that which the commissioners have stated.
t, however, is certain, that long before the conclusion of the late war a scarcity began to be
lly of the larger kind of timber fit for ships of the line; and so great was this scarcity, that if
eppings had not contrived the means of substituting straight timber for that of different
imensions, before considered to be indispensable, the building of new ships must entirely have

ever, the growth of oak for ship timber was greatly diminished during the war, so as to
alarming scarcity, there is little doubt that from the increased attention paid by individuals
ng plantations, and their great extension, as well as from the measure of allotting off portions
forests to those who had claims on them, and enclosing the remainder for the use of the

public, this country will, in future times, be fully adequate to the production of oak timber equal demand for the naval and mercantile marine." — (*Supp. Ency. Brit.* art. *Navy.*)

The bark of the oak tree is very valuable. It is preferred to all other substances for the pur tanning, and brings a high price. — (See BARK.)

The foreign oak timber imported into Great Britain is principally derived from Canada and I The latter is the most valuable — its price being to the former in the proportion of about 9 to 6; th a load of Prussian oak timber brought 9*l.*, a load of Canada ditto would not bring more than a The quantity imported varies; but may, at an average, amount to about 10,000 loads, of 50 cub each; the greater part from Quebec. Oak plank is almost wholly imported from Prussia. The qu imported during the four years ending with the 5th of January, 1830, were —1827, 5,401 loads; 182 ditto; 1829, 2,253 ditto; and 1830, 1,509 ditto. For further details with respect to the importation its price, duty on, &c., see WOOD.

For further details with respect to this noble and most useful tree, see Tredgold's Principles pentry; art. *Navy*, Supplement to Ency. Brit.; the very interesting work on *Timber Trees and* in the Library of Entertaining Knowledge; Rees's Cyclopædia, &c.

OATS (Ger. *Hafer;* Du. *Haver;* Da. *Havre;* Sw. *Hafre;* Fr. *Avoine Vena, Avena;* Sp. *Avena;* Port. *Avea;* Russ. *Owes;* Pol. *Owies;* Lat. *A* We reckon 25 species of this grain, some of which are said to be indigenou is a very useful grain, and better adapted for northern climates than v rye, or barley. Its culture is chiefly confined to latitudes north of Paris. scarcely known in the south of France, Spain, or Italy; and in tropical cou it is not attended to. In Britain it has long been very extensively cultiv formerly as a bread corn, but at present principally as food for horses. The v denominated *potato oat* is now almost the only one raised on land in a good of cultivation in the north of England and the south of Scotland, and u brings a higher price in the London market than any other variety. It was dentally discovered growing in a field of potatoes in Cumberland in 1788 from the produce of that single stalk has been produced the stock now in g cultivation. — (*Loudon's Ency. of Agriculture.*) See CORN LAWS AND TRADE.

ODESSA, a flourishing sea-port of southern Russia, on the north-west of the Black Sea, between the rivers Dniester and Bug, in lat. 46° 29½′ N 36° 37¾′ E. Population said to amount to 40,000. The foundations of C were laid so lately as 1792, by order of the Empress Catherine, after the pe Jassy. It was intended to serve as an *entrepôt* for the commerce of the R dominions on the Black Sea, and the Sea of Azoff, and has in a great m answered the expectations of its founders. By an imperial ukase, dated February, 1817, it was declared a free port, and the inhabitants exempted taxation for thirty years; since which period its increase has been extremely The bay or roadstead of Odessa is extensive, the water deep, and anchorage the bottom being fine sand and gravel; it is, however, exposed to the south-e wind, which renders it less safe in winter. The port, which is artificial, formed by a mole projecting to a considerable distance into the sea, is calc to contain about 300 ships. It has also the advantage of deep water. A house is erected on the south side of the bay; and there is a convenient laz on the model of that of Marseilles. The want of springs of fresh water greatest disadvantage under which Odessa labours. There are no trees vicinity of the town, which has, in consequence, a bleak and arid appearan

For several years after Odessa was founded, wheat formed almost the only, as forms the principal, article of export. — (For details with respect to the corn t Odessa, see *antè*, pp. 406. 408.) But large quantities of tallow, wool, iron, hides, wax, caviare, potash, salt beef, furs, cordage, sail-cloth, tar, butter, isinglass, &c. a exported. The tallow of Odessa is of a bright yellow straw colour, and is said superior to that of Petersburgh. The following account of the quantity (since and value of the tallow exported from Odessa from 1814 to 1826, both inclusiv the rapid increase in the trade in this article, and its importance, in a very strikin of view : —

Years.	Value of Tallow exported.	Years.	Value of Tallow exported.	Years.	Value of Tallow exported.	Quantity.
	Roubles.		*Roubles.*		*Roubles.*	*Poods.*
1814	84,554	1819	368,792	1824	1,674,566	209,118
1815	72,175	1820	1,137,461	1825	2,687,334	316,157
1816	103,397	1821	1,591,540	1826	2,800,000	331,873
1817	90,318	1822	991,323			
1818	185,110	1823	2,184,762			

This table, says the *Journal d'Odessa* (1827, No. 16.), serves to give some ide means which the south of Russia possesses for carrying on commerce. The ex tallow have increased twentyfold in ten years; materially augmenting the valu

and enriching vast countries, which must have remained comparatively poor, had
is outlet been found for their produce.

e increase in the exportation of wool is also very considerable. Within the last
y years the Merino breed of sheep has been extensively introduced into the govern-
of Taurida, Cherson, and Ekaterinoslov; so that there has been not only a great
se in the quantity, but also a very decided improvement in the quality, of the wool
ted.

e iron shipped at Odessa is principally brought from Siberia, partly by the Volga,
artly by the Don to Taganrog, whence it is conveyed to Odessa. A good deal of
a manufactured state, from the founderies at Tula. Timber for ship-building,
itch and tar, are also brought from Taganrog. In fact, from its not being at the
of any great river, nor having any considerable manufactures, Odessa is not a port
e exportation of what may be termed articles of native growth: but in consequence
convenient situation, and the privileges which it enjoys, it is, as already remarked,
porium where most of the produce of Southern Russia destined for foreign coun-
collected previously to its being exported, and where most of the foreign articles
ed for home consumption are primarily imported. The shallowness of the water
ganrog, and the short period during which the Sea of Azoff is navigable, hinder
vessels of considerable burthen from visiting her port, and occasion the shipment
onsiderable part of the produce brought down the Volga and the Don in lighters
a and Odessa, particularly the latter. A good deal is, however, exported direct
aganrog to the Mediterranean. All the products brought down the Dniester, the
nd the Dnieper, are exported from Odessa; but owing to the difficult navigation
first and last mentioned rivers, most part of the corn brought to Odessa from
a, the Ukraine, &c., is conveyed in wagons drawn by oxen. — (See *antè*, p. 406.)
ssa has a considerable and increasing trade with Redout Kale, at the mouth of
asis, and with several ports on the south coast of the Black Sea. Georgian and
ian merchants are already considerable purchasers at the Leipsic and other Ger-
irs; and civilisation is beginning to strike its roots throughout all the extensive
ies between the Black Sea and the Caspian. It is probable that at no very remote
the Phasis will be frequented by British ships; and that our merchants, without
chantress to aid them, and depending only on the superior cheapness and excellence
goods, will be hospitably received in the ancient Colchis, and bear away a richer
an fell to the lot of Jason and his Argonauts.

incipal trade of Odessa is with Constantinople, Smyrna, and other towns in the Levant, Naples,
, Genoa, Marseilles, &c. " It is generally stated," says Mr. Jacob (Memoir on the Trade of the
a, in the Appendix to the octavo edition of Tracts on the Corn Trade), " that the supply of Con-
ple requires annually 100,000 quarters of Black Sea wheat. The Greek islands scarcely, on the
of years, produce sufficient wheat for their own consumption; and, in some years, require a large
which is furnished partly from the neighbouring continent, and partly from the Black Sea.
Asiatic coasts of the Turkish empire, especially in Anatolia, are nearly in the same predicament.
the market of Smyrna is very favourable for the sale of the corn of Southern Russia. The islands
and Gozo produce only about half as much corn as the 120,000 inhabitants require.
y, though it has greatly declined from its ancient productiveness, has still a quantity of grain to
the less fruitful parts of Italy in most years; and its wheat enters into competition with that of
k Sea, in the ports of Naples, Genoa, and Leghorn.
e are few years in which Tuscany grows a sufficiency of wheat; and its chief port, Leghorn, being
ose in which ships can unload their cargoes of corn, without being detained to perform quaran-
been at all times a place of deposit for the wheat of the Black Sea. A market at some price may
found there, as the capitalists are disposed to purchase; relying on the uncertain productiveness
adjacent country, in which they may realise a profit at no great distance.
a, like Leghorn, is a port where wheat can be unloaded within the bounds of the lazaretto. The
round it yields but little wheat; and at some periods, it enjoys a trade in that article even as far
rland. This internal demand, and the chance of advantageous re-exportation, induces much
corn. There is said to be seldom less than 100,000 quarters in store at the two ports of Genoa and
; and at some periods, a far greater quantity.
, though not having the same advantageous quarantine regulations, and,.consequently, not being
r corn beyond its own demand, from the sterile soil that surrounds it, requires every year a large
on of wheat. That of Sicily and Odessa create a competition in its port; and the government
evenue, by imposing a heavy duty on both.
gh the corn laws of France have kept the ports closed against the introduction of foreign corn for
use, yet it is allowed to be bonded for re-exportation. From the frequent local and partial
which occur on the eastern coast of Spain, at which periods wheat is allowed to be lawfully im-
nd it is said from the facility of its introduction by contraband, when not legally allowed; Mar-
s been a great *depôt* for the wheat of the Black Sea.
thence, as also from Gibraltar, where there is generally some in store, it can easily be trans-
Spain, to Sardinia, to Corsica, to Tunis, to Tripoli, or wherever scarcity has created a beneficial

oasts of Barbary, though often having a surplus of wheat, much of which occasionally assists to
ugal, in some seasons have been affected with most deficient harvests. This was recently the case
rkable degree. Tripoli and Tunis experienced, in the year 1820, a harvest most miserably short,
applied from other countries."

xclusive of wheat, the other articles mentioned as being exported from Odessa,
r way to the different markets in the Mediterranean. Those shipped for Turkey
tallow, sail-cloth, cordage, anchors for ships of war, butter, &c. The exports
and other European countries are similar.

The importation of all foreign articles into the Russian dominions on the Black and the Sea of Azoff is confined to Odessa, Theodosia or Kaffa, and Taganrog. import trade is, however, of inferior importance when compared with the export tr The principal articles are sugar and coffee, dye-woods, wine and brandy, cotton st spices, cutlery, oranges and lemons, lemon juice, oil, tin and tin plates, dried fr paper, silk, specie, &c.

Account of the Value of the Articles imported into and exported from Odessa in the undermenti Years.

		1824.	1825.	1826.	182
Imports by Sea	pro Ro.	6,946,714	5,801,012	6,879,504	10,185
Transit	—	2,413,528	2,256,596	2,487,125	2,344
Total Imports	pro Ro.	9,360,242	8,057,608	9,366,629	12,529
Do. Exports	—	13,039,573	20,029,370	14,711,834	18,479

Account of the Quantities of the principal Articles imported into Odessa in the following Years

		1824.	1825.	1826.	182
Coffee	poods	2,882 33 lbs.	2,615 12¼	2,747 12¾ lbs.	8
Sugar (chiefly refined)	—	9,443 12	5,099 4¼	4,691 24½	7
Oil	—	27,017 19¼	27,649 17¾	25,797 5¼	18
Cotton, raw	—	6,410 36¼	3,801 26	6,478 22	3
Do. twist	—	11,916 7¾	8,831 38¼	6,650 9½	8
Raw silk	—	747 6¼	543 1½	2,973 31½	3
Tea	—	76	337 3¾	486 27½	
Wine	oxhoft	2,485	2,498	2,214	13
	bottles	630	- -	7,084	23
Champagne	—	6,315	8,136	5,166	7
Spices, pepper (value)	Ro.	99,398	128,414	122,732	128
Fruit, for.	—	1,175,015	1,217,024	1,168,905	946
Cotton manufactures	—	568,146	630,752	1,303,566	1,389
Woollen ditto	—	1,093,272	836,892	960,492	1,348
Silk ditto	—	695,764	927,920	534,621	913
Linen ditto	—	137,887	201,395	87,935	122
In the foregoing, are included the following goods received by transit from Radziviloff.					
Coffee	poods	- -	- -	- -	
Sugar	—	7,259 32	2,352 30½	4,038 16½	
Tea	—	76	337 3¾	486 27½	
Wine	oxhoft	- -	- -	19	
	bottles	604	- -	255	
Cotton manufactures	pro Ro.	501,986	512,138	944,120	778
Woollen ditto	—	1,050,625	701,956	828,399	695
Silk ditto	—	427,810	590,653	275,880	419
Linen ditto	—	137,887	201,395	87,935	122

Account of the Quantities of the principal Articles exported from Odessa in the following Years

		1824.	1825.	1826.	18
Wheat	chetwerts	561,465½	712,378	804,763½	1,20
Rye	—	- -	2,200	8,680	3
Barley	—	32	5,305	9,055	
Oats	—	- -	1,506	1,710	
Tallow	poods	209,118	316,157	331,852 33½	19
Hides, raw	—	- -	44,635	40,209 21	3
Potashes	—	7,514 27	9,390	1,611 10	
Cordage	—	41,248 38	49,132	60,484 27	7
Wax	—	5,456 26	8,401	8,178 36½	
Flax	—	- -	82	- -	
Hemp	—	- -	3	- -	1
Copper	—	7,890 31	8,996	10,011 23½	
Iron	—	40,059 31	86,380	78,364 9	7
Linseed	chetwerts	- -	58	80	
Sail-cloth	pieces	880	1,353	712	
Ravenducks	—	382	228	410	
Flems	—	100	2		
Furs, for.	Ro.	360,855	255,632	168,403	10

(From the *Circular of Moberly and Simp*

The *Journal d'Odessa,* for the 9th of February, 1827, gives the subjoined acco the ships entering the port of Odessa in the following years : —

Flags.	1822.	1823.	1824.	1825.	1826.
Russian	61	121	142	116	163
Austrian	144	198	154	212	288
English	52	66	80	96	104
French	22	6	3	3	1
Swedish	12	18			
Sardinian	19	1	21	57	116
Other countries	10				
Turkish	4	6	16	8	10

ıg the late war between Russia and Turkey, the trade of Odessa was much in-
d; but it has again resumed its former activity; and will doubtless continue
ively to increase with the improvement of the vast countries of which it is the
d *entrepôt*. Several American merchantmen appeared, for the first time, in the
Sea, last year.

ınal of commerce was established at Odessa in 1824, the jurisdiction of which extends over all
connected with trade. There is no appeal from its decision, except to the senate. Its insti-
said to have been productive of considerable advantage.
are 12 sworn brokers, approved and licenced by the Tribunal of Commerce, who have depu-
ınted by themselves. They receive ½ per cent. from each party as commission. They are bound
r the various transactions in which they are employed.
unt or loan bank has been established at Odessa, which discounts bills, not having more than
to run, at the rate of 6 per cent. interest; and makes advances upon the security of goods.
tutions for marine insurance, and one for fire insurance, have been established within the
r five years.
rticles of provision are very cheap. Beef may be bought for ¾d. or 1d. per lb.; a quarter of
d.; and poultry at proportionally low prices. Fish costs almost nothing, and is excellent. Water
ensive article; and fire wood is for the most part scarce and dear. Latterly, however, the
s have begun to supply themselves with coal from Bakhmoute in the government of Ekat-
A good deal of English coal has been taken to Odessa as ballast, and sold at a fair price.
n's *Travels in Russia*, p. 262. &c.)

s, *Weights, and Measures*, same as at Petersburgh; which see.
s in the Trade of the Black Sea. — *Depth of Water. — Difficulty of Navigation, &c.*
rade of the Black or Euxine Sea was of great importance in antiquity. The shores
imea, or Taurica Chersonesus, were settled by Milesian adventurers, who founded
ræum and Theodosia. The exports thence to Athens were nearly the same as those
e now sent from Odessa and Taganrog to Constantinople, Leghorn, &c.; viz.
ıber and naval stores, leather, wax, honey, salt fish, caviare, &c., with great num-
laves, the best and most serviceable that were any where to be met with. The
ıs set a very high value upon this trade, which supplied them annually with about
medimni of corn; and to preserve it, they carefully cultivated the alliance of the
ı princes, and kept a garrison at Sestus, on the Hellespont.—(See the authorities
harsis's *Travels*, c. 55.; and in *Clarke's Connexion of the Saxon and English*
p. 54—64.) During the middle ages, the Genoese acquired an ascendancy on
and laboured with pretty considerable success to monopolise its trade. Their
establishment was at Caffa, which was the centre of a considerable com-
But the conquest of Constantinople by the Turks, in 1453, was soon after fol-
the conquest of Caffa, and the total exclusion of European vessels from the
ea, which became in a great measure unknown. This exclusion was maintained
300 years, or till it was opened to the ships of Russia by the treaty of Kai-
ı 1774. The Austrians obtained a similar equality of privileges in 1784; and
French, &c. ships were admitted by the treaty of Amiens. There were, how-
ne restraints still kept up; but these have been abolished by the late treaty
the Turks and Russians in 1829; and for commercial purposes, at least, the
a is now as free as the Mediterranean.
thstanding the number of English and other European ships that have visited
vithin the last twenty years, its geography is still very imperfectly known. A
ems to have been long prevalent, that it was not only stormy, but also infested
erous shoals. Polybius, indeed, contends, that owing to the vast quantities of
eposit brought down by the Danube and other large rivers that fall into the
a, it was gradually filling up, and would become, at no very remote period, an
morass! Dr. Clarke seems to have espoused the same theory. But, how
soever it may appear, extremely little progress has hitherto been made
he consummation described by Polybius. Instead of being shallow, the water
most part remarkably deep; with a bottom, where soundings have been ob-
gravel, sand, and shells. A strong current sets from the Black Sea, through
ıorus, or canal of Constantinople, into the Sea of Marmora, and from the latter
he Dardanelles, which it requires a fresh breeze to stem. This current is said
ibly felt in the Black Sea, 10 or 12 miles from the Bosphorus; and it may
carry off some of the mud brought down by the rivers. — (See *Tournefort's*
: *Levant*, lett. 15, 16.; Art. 9. in No. 1. of the *Journal of the Geographical*
Macgill's Travels in Turkey, vol. i. p. 245.; &c.)
vigation of the Black Sea has been represented, by most modern and all ancient
s exceedingly dangerous. We believe, however, that there is a good deal of
ion in the greater number of the statements on this subject. It is said to be
ly subject to dense fogs, and to currents; but the former are prevalent only at
seasons, and the influence of the latter is not greater than in many other seas
not reputed dangerous. Tournefort, one of the best and most accurate of
considers the navigation of the Black Sea as safe as that of the Mediterranean:
:n de noir, pour ainsi dire, que le nom: les vents n'y soufflent pas avec plus de

furie, et les orages ne sont guères plus frequens que sur les autres mers. — (Tome ii. p
4to ed.) But any sea would be dangerous to the Greek and Turkish pilots, by
the Black Sea is principally navigated. If the progress of navigation were to b
mated by its state amongst them, we should have to conclude that it had been stati
from the era of the Argonauts. They seldom venture to get out of sight of the c
they have neither charts nor quadrants; and hardly even know that one of the poi
the needle turns towards the north! — (Tournefort *in loc. cit.*) There is not ce
much room for wonder at shipwrecks being frequent among vessels so navigated
leaving the Black Sea, the greatest difficulty is in making the Bosphorus. " The
tains," says Mr. Macgill, " are all so much alike, that it is difficult to determine
of them is at the entrance, until you are within a very few miles of the coast: then
a fair wind, you are on a lee shore with a lee current; and if you make a mistak
struction is almost inevitable. The Turks have two light-houses at the entrance
unless you see them before sunset, they are of little use: in the forests, on its bo
great quantities of charcoal are made, and the lights from it bewilder, and often mi
the unhappy mariner." — (Vol. i. p. 245.)

From the vast quantity of fresh water poured into the Black Sea, the saline pa
are so much diluted, that, with a slight frost, the surface becomes covered wit
hence, during a great part of the year, hardly any navigation is attempted. The
that resort to Odessa seldom arrive at that port before the latter end of May; and
whose cargoes are not completed before the end of October, more frequently wait
turn of spring, than adventure to encounter the dangers of an autumnal or
voyage.

At Taganrog the frost commences earlier, and continues longer, than at Odes
that there are scarcely more than four or five months in the year, during which th
of Azoff can be safely navigated.

OIL (Fr. *Huile* ; Ger. *Oel* ; It. *Olie* ; Lat. *Oleum* ; Rus. *Maslo* ; Sp. *A*
The term *oil* is applied to designate a number of unctuous liquors, which,
dropped upon paper, sink into it and make it seem semi-transparent, or g
what is called a greasy stain. These bodies are very numerous, and have b
common use from time immemorial. Chemists have divided them inte
classes; namely, *volatile* and *fixed* oils. We borrow from Dr. Thomas Tho
the following statement with respect to these bodies : —

I. Volatile Oils, called also *essential oils,* are distinguished by the followin
perties : — 1. Liquid, often almost as liquid as water, sometimes viscid ; 2. Very
bustible ; 3. An acrid taste and a strong fragrant odour ; 4. Volatilised at a tempe
not higher than 212° ; 5. Soluble in alcohol, and imperfectly in water ; 6. Eva
without leaving any stain on paper.

By this last test it is easy to discover whether they have been adulterated with
the fixed oils. Let a drop of the volatile oil fall upon a sheet of writing pap
then apply a gentle heat to it : if it evaporates without leaving any stain upon the
the oil is pure ; but if it leaves a stain upon the paper, it has been contaminate
some fixed oil or other.

Volatile oils are almost all obtained from vegetables, and they exist in every
plants ; — the root, the bark, the wood, the leaves, the flower, and even the fruit,
they are never found in the substance of the cotyledons ; whereas the fixed oils,
contrary, are almost always contained in these bodies.

When the volatile oils are contained in great abundance in plants, they are son
obtained by simple expression. This is the case with oil of oranges, of lemo
bergamotte ; but in general they can only be obtained by distillation. The part
plant containing the oil is put into a still with a quantity of water, which is disti
by the application of a moderate heat. The oil comes over along with the wat
swims upon its surface in the receiver. By this process are obtained the oil of
mint, thyme, lavender, and a great many others, which are prepared and emplo
the perfumer : others are procured by the distillation of resinous bodies. Thi
case in particular with oil of turpentine, which is obtained by distilling a kind of
ous juice, called turpentine, that exudes from the juniper.

Volatile oils are exceedingly numerous. They have been long known ; but
use in chemistry is but limited, they have not, hitherto, been subjected to an a
chemical investigation. They differ greatly in their properties from each other
is impossible at present to give a detailed account of each.

1. The greater number of volatile oils are *liquid ;* many, indeed, are as li
water, and have none of that appearance which we usually consider oily. Th
case with the following ; namely, oil of turpentine, oranges, lemons, bergamotte
Others have the oily viscidity. It varies in them in all degrees. This is the ca

ls of mace, cardamom, sassafras, cloves, cinnamon. — Others have the property of
ing solid. This is the case with the oils of parsley, fennel, aniseed, balm.—Others
llise by slow evaporation. This is the case with oil of thyme, peppermint, marjo-
— The oil of nutmegs has usually the consistence of butter This is the case also
he oil of hops and of pepper.

The colour of the volatile oils is as various as their other properties. A great
er are limpid and colourless ; as oils of turpentine, lavender, rosemary, savine,
d : some are yellow ; as spike, bergamotte : some are brown ; as thyme, savory,
wood : others blue ; as camomile, motherwort : others green ; as milfoil, pepper,
parsley, wormwood, cajeput, juniper, sage, valerian : others, though at first
-less, become yellow or brown by age ; as cloves, cinnamon, sassafras.

The odours are so various as to defy all description. It is sufficient to say that
e fragrance of the vegetable kingdom resides in volatile oils. Their taste is acrid,
nd exceedingly unpleasant.

Their specific gravity varies very considerably, not only in different oils, but even
same oil in different circumstances. The following are the specific gravities of
l of the volatile oils, as ascertained by Dr. Lewis :—

il of Sassafras	-	-	1·094	Oil of Tansy	-	-	·946
Cinnamon	-	-	1·035	Carraway seeds	-	-	·940
Cloves	-	-	1·034	Origanum	-	-	·940
Fennel	-	-	·997	Spike	-	-	·936
Dill	-	-	·994	Rosemary	-	-	·934
Pennyroyal	-	-	·978	Juniper berries	-	-	·611
Cummin	-	-	·975	Oranges	-	-	·888
Mint	-	-	·975	Turpentine	-	-	·792
Nutmegs	-	-	·948				

en the volatile oils are heated in the open air, they evaporate readily, and without
ion diffuse their peculiar odours all around ; but there is a considerable dif-
e between the different oils in this respect. When distilled in close vessels, they
so readily assume the form of vapour. Hence they lose their odour, become
in colour, and are partly decomposed. Oils do not seem very susceptible of
ng the gaseous form, unless some other substance, as water, be present.

Fixed Oils are distinguished by the following characters : — 1. Liquid, or easily
e so when exposed to a gentle heat ; 2. An unctuous feel ; 3. Very combustible ;
nild taste ; 5. Boiling point not under 600° ; 6. Insoluble in water, and nearly
lcohol ; 7. Leave a greasy stain upon paper.

se oils, which are called fat or expressed oils, are numerous, and are obtained
from animals and partly from vegetables, by simple expression. As instances,
mentioned whale oil or train oil, obtained from the blubber of the whale and
d ; olive oil, obtained from the fruit of the olive ; linseed oil and almond oil,
d from linseed and almond kernels. Fixed oils may also be extracted from
seeds, hemp seeds, beech mast, and many other vegetable substances.

hese oils differ from each other in several particulars, but have also many parti-
n common.

ixed oil is usually a liquid with a certain degree of viscidity, adhering to the
the glass vessels in which it is contained, and forming streaks. It is never
y transparent ; has always a certain degree of colour, most usually yellowish
nish ; its taste is sweet, or nearly insipid. When fresh, it has little or no

e exist also in the vegetable kingdom a considerable number of bodies which at
nary temperature of the atmosphere are solid, and have hitherto been considered
oils. Palm oil may be mentioned as an example. The various substances
India and Africa as substitutes for butter, and as unguents, may likewise be
ed.

ll the fixed oils hitherto examined are lighter than water : but they differ greatly
e another in specific gravity. The same difference is observable in different
of the same oil. The following table contains the specific gravity of such oils
been examined : —

of Palm	-	-	·968	Oil of Beech nuts	-	-	·923
Hazel nuts	-	-	·941	Ben	-	-	·917
Poppies	-	-	·939	Olives	-	-	·913
Linseed	-	-	·932	Rape seed	-	-	·913
Almonds	-	-	·932	Cacao	-	-	·892
Walnuts	-	-	923 to ·947				

l oil, when in the state of vapour, takes fire on the approach of an ignited body,
ns with a yellowish white flame. It is upon this principle that candles and
urn. The tallow or oil is first converted into a state of vapour in the wick ; it
es fire, and supplies a sufficient quantity of heat to convert more oil into vapour ;
s process goes on while any oil remains. The wick is necessary to present a

sufficiently small quantity of oil at once for the heat to act upon. If the heat w
great enough to keep the whole oil at a temperature of 600°, no wick would
necessary, as is obvious from oil catching fire spontaneously when it has been raise
that temperature.   When oil is used in this manner, either in the open air or in con
with oxygen gas, the only new products obtained are *water* and *carbonic* acid.

The drying oils are used as the vehicle of paints and varnishes. Linseed,
poppy, and hemp-seed oils, belong to this class. These oils in their natural state pos
the property of drying oils, but imperfectly. To prepare them for the use of the pai
and varnish maker, they are boiled for some time in an iron pot, and sometimes b
till they become viscid. When they burn for some time, their unctuous quali
much more completely destroyed than by any method that has been practised.   He
it is followed frequently in preparing the drying oils for varnishes, and always
printers' ink, which requires to be as free as possible from all unctuosity.

Nut oil has been found preferable to all other oils for printers' ink ; though the
colour which it acquires during boiling renders it not so proper for red ink as for bl
Linseed oil is considered as next after nut oil in this respect. Other oils canno
employed, because they cannot be sufficiently freed from their unctuosity. Ink
with them would be apt to come off and smear the paper while in the hands
the bookbinder, or even to spread beyond the mark of the types and stain the p
yellow.

For the regulations with respect to the importation and exportation of train oil,
BLUBBER, and FISHERIES.

OLIBANUM (Fr. *Encens ;* Ger. *Weiranch ;* It. *Olibano ;* Arab. *Looban*
gum resin, the produce of a large tree (*Libanus thurifera*) growing in Arabia
India. It is imported in chests, containing each about 1 cwt., from the Le
and India ; the best comes from the former, and is the produce of Arabia. G
olibanum is in semi-transparent tears, of a pink colour, brittle, and adhesive w
warm ; when burnt, the odour is very agreeable ; its taste is bitterish, and so
what pungent and aromatic ; it flames for a long time with a steady clear li
which is not easily extinguished, leaving behind a *black* (not, as has been sai
whitish) ash. Olibanum is the frankincense (*thus*) of the ancients ; and was
tensively used by them in sacrifices.— (*Plin. Hist. Nat.* lib. xii. c. 14.) It has
been used in the ceremonies of the Greek and Roman churches.—(*Ainslie's
Indica; Thomson's Chemistry ; Kippingü Antiq. Rom.* lib. i. c. 11.)

OLIVE, OLIVES (Ger. *Oliven ;* Fr. *Olives ;* It. *Ulive, Olive ;* Sp. *Aceitu*
Port. *Azeitonas ;* Lat. *Olivæ*), a fruit which yields a large quantity of oil,
produce of the *olea*, olive tree. The wild olive is indigenous in Syria, Gre
and in Africa, on the lower slopes of Mount Atlas. The cultivated species gr
spontaneously in Syria, and is easily reared in Spain and Italy, and the sout
France. It has even been raised in the open air in England, but its fruit is
not to have ripened. The fruit is a smooth oval plum, about ¾ of an inch in le
and ½ an inch in diameter ; of a deep violet colour when ripe, whitish and fl
within, bitter and nauseous, but replete with a bland oil ; covering an ob
pointed, rough nut. Olives intended for preservation are gathered before the
ripe. In pickling, the object is to remove their bitterness, and to preserve them g
by impregnating them with a brine of aromatised sea salt; for this purpose var
methods are employed. The wood of the olive tree is beautifully veined, and
an agreeable smell. It is in great esteem with cabinet-makers, on account of
fine polish of which it is susceptible.

OLIVE OIL (Ger. *Baumöl ;* Fr. *Huile d'olives ;* It. *Olio d'uliva ;* Sp. *A*
de aceitunas ; Lat. *Oleum olivarum*). The olive tree is principally cultivate
the sake of its oil. This is an insipid, inodorous, pale greenish yellow colo
viscid fluid, unctuous to the feel, inflammable, incapable of combining with w
and nearly insoluble in alcohol. It is the lightest of all the fixed oils ; and is
extensively used, particularly in Greece, Italy, Spain, and France, as an artic
food, and in medicine, and the arts.

The ripe fruit is gathered in November, and immediately bruised in a mill, the s
of which are set so wide as not to crush the kernel. The pulp is then subjected t
press in bags made of rushes ; and by means of a gentle pressure, the best, or
oil, flows first ; a second, and afterwards a third, quality of oil is obtained by n
ening the residuum, breaking the kernels, &c., and increasing the pressure. Whe
fruit is not sufficiently ripe, the recent oil has a bitterish taste ; and when too ripe it is
After the oil has been drawn, it deposits a white, fibrous, and albuminous matter

OMNIUM. 797

is deposition has taken place, if it be put into clean glass flasks, it undergoes no
alteration ; the common oil cannot, however, be preserved in casks above a year
alf, or two years. It is sometimes adulterated by the admixture of poppy oil.—
n's Dispensatory.)

est olive oil is said to be made in the vicinity of Aix, in France. That which is
from Leghorn, in chests containing 30 bottles, or 4 English gallons, is also very
 ; it is known in our markets by the name of Florence oil, and is used mostly
ary purposes. Olive oil is the principal article of export from the kingdom of
; and, from its being chiefly exported from Gallipoli, it has acquired that deno-
n. It is principally produced in the provinces of Puglia and Calabria Ultra ;
lian oil is the best, and is preferred by the woollen manufacturers. By far the
oortion of the olive oil brought to England, is imported from Italy, principally
llipoli ; but Spain supplies us with a considerable quantity ; and a few thousand
are obtained from the Ionian Islands.

rice of olive oil, duty paid, in London, in October, 1831, was as follows :—

	£ s. d.	£ s. d.
Florence, ½ chest - - -	1 1 0	to 1 3 0
Lucca, jars, 2½ gallons - -	6 10 0	— 0 0 0
Gallipoli, 252 — - -	46 0 0	— 47 0 0
Sicily, do. - -	44 0 0	— 45 0 0
Spanish, tun - - -	44 0 0	— 0 0 0

duty of 8*l.* 8*s.* a tun (252 gallons) amounts to about 20 per cent., or ⅕ of the
But as olive oil is an article much used in household economy, and of essential
nce in the arts, particularly the woollen manufacture, such a duty seems to be
pressive. Were it reduced to 2*l.* 2*s.* a tun, we believe it would be very little,
less productive than at present, while the fall of price consequent upon such a
n would have many beneficial consequences. Nothing can be more absurd
elevate duties till they become less productive than they would be were they
out when the articles so overtaxed are of great utility, the mischievousness of
ice exceeds its irrationality.

int of the Quantity of Olive Oil entered for Home Consumption, in each Year since 1820 ; dis-
nguishing the Rate of Duty, and stating the Amount of Duty received in each Year.

antities ered for ne Con- nption a the nited gdom.	Amount of Duty received thereon.	Rates of Duty charged.	Years.	Quantities entered for Home Con- sumption in the United Kingdom.	Amount of Duty received thereon.	Rates of Duty charged.
Tuns.	*L. s. d.*	*Per Imp. Tun.* *L. s. d.*		*Imp. Tuns.*	*L. s. d.*	*Per Imp. Tun.* *L. s. d.*
,373	44,706 17 7	{ 18 15 7 in British ships. { 19 19 7 in For. ships.	1827	4,249	35,877 18 10	{ 8 8 0 in any ship (from 5th July).
,162	59,164 10 5	—	1828	6,959	58,580 5 1	{ 9 9 0 in ships of Na- ples and Sicily. { 8 8 0 in other ships.
,699	50,852 12 10	—				
,529	66,295 2 11	{ 8 8 0 in any ship from 5th July.	1829	3,299	45,250 12 0	{ 10 10 0 in ships of Na- ples and Sicily. { 8 8 0 in other ships.
,996	44,288 4 9		1830	8,524	71,878 11 9	
,376	28,366 9 6					

, the produce of Europe, may not be imported into the United Kingdom for home consump-
t in British ships, or in ships of the country of which it is the produce, or from which it is im-
Geo. 4. c. 109.)
imported in foreign ships deemed *alien goods,* and subject to town and port dues accordingly.
c. 111.)
red by a Customs Minute of 23d of July, 1828, that when the actual tare is not taken, ⅓ for tare
, and ⅟ for foot, may be allowed.

IUM, a term used at the Stock Exchange, to express the aggregate value
fferent stocks in which a loan is now usually funded. Thus, in the
,000*l.* contracted for in June, 1815, the omnium consisted of 130*l.* 3 per
luced annuities, 44*l.* 3 per cent. consols, and 10*l.* 4 per cent. annuities,
100*l.* subscribed.

an was contracted for on the 14th of June, when the prices of the above
ere—3 per cent. reduced, 54 ; 3 per cent. consols, 55 ; 4 per cents., 70 :
e parcels of stock given for 100*l.* advanced, were worth —

	£ s. d.
130*l.* reduced, at 54 - - -	70 4 0
44*l.* consols, at 55 - -	24 4 0
10*l.* 4 per cents., at 70 - -	7 0 0
Together - -	£101 8 0

uld be the value of the omnium, or 1*l.* 8*s.* per cent. premium, indepen-
any discount for prompt payment.

ONION (Ger. *Zwiebel;* Fr. *Oignon;* It. *Cipolla;* Sp. *Cebolla;* Rus. *Lu*
bulbous plant (*Allium Cepa*, Lin.) cultivated all over Europe for culinary purp
The Strasburgh, Spanish, and Portuguese varieties are the most esteemed. O
are imported in considerable quantities.

ONYX (Ger. *Onyx;* Fr. *Onix, Onice;* Sp. *Onique;* Lat. *Onyx*). "Any
exhibiting layers of two or more colours strongly contrasted is called an *ony*
banded jasper, chalcedony, &c., but more particularly the latter, when it is m
with white, and stratified with opaque and translucent lines. But the O
onyx is considered a substance consisting of two or more layers or bands o
tinct and different colours. A sard or sardoine, having a layer of white up
would be called an onyx; and according to the number of layers it would b
tinguished as an onyx with three or more bands: some of the antique engra
are upon onyxes of four bands." — (*Mawe's Treatise on Diamonds, &c.*)

OPAL (Ger. *Opal;* Fr. *Opale;* It. *Opalo;* Sp. *Opalo, Piedra iris;* Port. *O*
Lat. *Opalus*), a stone, of which there are several varieties, found in different
of Europe, particularly in Hungary, and in the East Indies, &c. When firs
out of the earth it is soft, but it hardens and diminishes in bulk by expos
the air. The opal is always amorphous; fracture conchoidal; commonly
what transparent. Hardness varies considerably. Specific gravity from
to 2·54. The lowness of its specific gravity in some cases is to be ascri
accidental cavities which the stone contains. These are sometimes fille
drops of water. Some specimens of opal have the property of emitting v
coloured rays, with a particular effulgency when placed between the eye ar
light. The opals which possess this property are distinguished by lapidar
the epithet *Oriental;* and often, by mineralogists, by the epithet *nobilis*. Thi
perty rendered the stone much esteemed by the ancients. — (*Thomson's Chem*
see also *Plin. Hist. Nat.*, lib. 37. c. 6. where there are some very curious
as to this stone.)

Mr. Mawe gives the following statement with respect to the precious opal, or opal *nobilis* :—" Th
of the opal is white or pearl grey, and when held between the eye and the light is pale red, or w
low, with a milky translucency. By reflected light it exhibits, as its position is varied, elegant a
beautiful iridescent colours, particularly emerald green, golden yellow, flame and fire red, violet,
and celestial blue, so beautifully blended, and so fascinating, as to captivate the admirer. When
lour is arranged in small spangles, it takes the name of the harlequin opal. Sometimes it exhib
one of the above colours, and of these the most esteemed are the vivid emerald green and the
yellow. When the stone possesses the latter of these colours, it is called the golden opal.

" The precious opal is not quite so hard as rock crystal; it is frequently full of flaws, which grea
tributes to its beauty, as the vivid iridescent colours which it displays are occasioned by the reflect
refraction of light, which is decomposed at these fissures. It is never cut in facets, but always hem
cal. It is generally small, rarely so large as an almond or hazel nut, though I have seen some sp
the size of a small walnut, for which several hundred pounds were demanded. At present a pre
may be bought at from 1 to 3 or 5 guineas, sufficiently large for a pin or ring stone. It requires gr
and judgment in the cutting, as it is fragile and easily spoiled.

" The opal, in all ages, has been highly esteemed: the history of the Roman senator, who p
death rather than give up his opal ring to the Emperor Nero, is familiar to every one. Am
Eastern nations, the opal ranks higher than in Europe.

" A spurious substance is sometimes sold for black and green opal, and often set in jewellery;
of the size of a small almond, but more commonly not larger than a lentil or pea. This *preciou*
nothing more than the cartilage of the hinge of a large shell. Glass, and even scoria, having a
cent appearance, have also often been sold for opal."—(*Treatise on Diamonds, &c.* 2d ed. pp. 123—

OPIUM (Ger. *Mohnsaft;* Fr. *Opium;* It. *Oppio;* Sp. and Port. *Opio*
Opium; Arab. *Ufyoon;* Hind. *Ufeem;* Turk. *Madjoon*), the concrete juice
white poppy (*Papaver somniferum*), which is most probably a native o
though now found growing wild in the southern parts of Europe, and e
England. Opium is chiefly prepared in India, Turkey, and Persia; but the
poppy is extensively cultivated in France, and other parts of Europe, on a
of its capsules, and of the useful bland oil obtained from its seeds. It h
been cultivated, and opium made, in England; but there is very little prob
of its ever being raised here to any considerable extent.

The poppy is an annual plant, with a stalk rising to the height of three or fo
its leaves resemble those of the lettuce, and its flower has the appearance of
When at its full growth, an incision is made in the top of the plant, from whi
issues a white milky juice, which soon hardens, and is scraped off the plan
wrought into cakes. In India, these are covered with the petals of the plant to
them sticking together, and in this situation are dried, and packed in chests lin
hides and covered with gunny, each containing 40 cakes, and weighing 2 ma
149⅓ lbs.; they are exported in this state to the places where the opium is co
Turkey opium is in flat pieces covered with leaves, and the reddish capsules

s of *rumex*; which is considered an indication of its goodness, as the inferior kinds none of these capsules adhering to them.

cording to Dr. A. T. Thomson, Turkey opium has a peculiar, strong, heavy, tic odour, and a bitter taste, accompanied by a sensation of acrid heat, or biting on ague and lips, if it be well chewed. Its colour when good is a reddish brown, or colour; its texture compact and uniform. Its specific gravity is 1·336. When t is tenacious; but when long exposed to the air, it becomes hard, breaks with a m shining fracture, is pulverulent, and affords a yellowish brown powder.

st Indian opium has a strong empyreumatic smell; but not much of the peculiar tic, heavy odour of the Turkey opium; the taste is more bitter, and equally ous, but it has less acrimony. It agrees with the Turkey opium in other sensible ies, except that its colour is blacker, and its texture less plastic, although it is as te as. Good Turkey opium has been found to yield nearly three times the quantity of ia, or of the peculiar principle of the drug, that is yielded by East Indian opium. um is regarded as bad, when it is very soft, greasy, light, friable, of an in y black colour, or mixed with many impurities. A weak or empyreumatic odour, tly bitter or acrid, or a sweetish taste, or the power of marking a brown or black uous streak when drawn across paper, are all symptoms of inferior opium. — *nsatory.*)

raising of opium is a very hazardous business; the poppy being a delicate plant, arly liable to injury from insects, wind, hail, or unseasonable rain. The produce agrees with the true average, but commonly runs in extremes; while one cul is disappointed, another reaps immense gain: one season does not pay the labour culture; another, peculiarly fortunate, enriches all the cultivators. This circum is well suited to allure man, ever confident of good fortune. — (*Colebrooke's Hus of Bengal*, p. 119.)

England, opium is little used, except as a medicine. The consumption amounts 20,000 lbs. to 25,000 lbs. a year. In 1829, the imports amounted to 48,634 lbs.; ch, 42,804 lbs. were brought direct from Turkey. During the same year, about lbs. were re-exported. Turkey opium in bond was worth, in the London market, ember, 1831, from 17s. to 18s. per lb. The duty is 4s.

mption and Trade of Opium in China. — Opium is pretty extensively used, both as a masticatory moking, in Turkey and India; but its great consumption is in China and the surrounding coun ere the habit of smoking it has become almost universal. The Chinese boil or seethe the crude and by this process the impurities, resinous and gummy matter, are separated, and the remaining only is reserved for use. Thus prepared, the drug loses its ordinary strong and offensive aromatic nd has even a fragrant and agreeable perfume. A small ball of it, inserted in a large wooden some combustible matter, is lighted, and the amateur proceeds to inhale four or five whiffs, lies down and resigns himself to his dreams, which are said to have no inconsiderable resem the sensations produced by inhaling the oxide of azote. Those who do not carry the indulgence s, do not, it is said, experience any bad effects from it.

pplies for the Chinese market are derived from India and Turkey, but principally from the The government of China has issued edict upon edict, forbidding the importation and consump. he drug, but without effect. Most part of the authorities openly connive at the proceedings of gglers, while the few who might be desirous to enforce the law are wholly without the power; so trade is conducted with the greatest facility, and almost perfect security. It was at first carried hampoa, about 15 miles below Canton; next at Macao, whence it was driven by the exactions of uguese; and now the principal *entrepôt* is in the bay of Lintin. The opium is kept on board mmonly called receiving ships, of which there are often 10 or 12 lying together at anchor. s are mostly effected by the English and American agents in Canton, who give orders for the of the opium; which, on producing the order, is handed over to the Chinese smuggler, who comes at night to receive it. Frequently, however, the smuggler purchases the opium on his own paying for it on the spot in silver; it being a rule of the trade, never departed from, to receive y before the drug is delivered. When it is landed, the laws are equally set at defiance in its ice throughout the country; and public smoking houses are said to be every where established! nsumption of opium in China is rapidly extending. During the first ten years of the present the exports from India to China were about 2,500 chests (of 149¼ lbs. each). In 1821-22, after duction of Malwa opium into the markets of Calcutta and Bombay, the exports increased to sts; and, owing, no doubt, to the greatly increased supply and lower price of the article, the xport is supposed to amount to from 12,000 to 13,000 chests, worth about 2,500,000l. — (See *ante*, he whole of this immense trade is in the hands of private individuals; the Company not choosing e in a business prohibited by the Chinese government. The imports of Turkey opium into China ved to amount at present to about 1,500 chests, worth about 212,000l. Smyrna is the principal urkey for the export of opium. — (See SMYRNA.)

tion of Opium in India. — Monopoly. — The cultivation of opium in India is a government mo nd is confined to the provinces of Bahar* and Benares, and Malwa in Central India. Every one e prescribed limits may engage in the opium cultivation; but the drug, when prepared, must all a fixed price to the Company's agents. This price is very far below the price at which it is s sold for exportation; and the circumstance of its being fixed and inadequate deprives the s of most part of the favourable chances in the lottery previously alluded to by Mr. Colebrooke. Ir. C. distinctly tells us (*Husb. Bengal*, p. 118.) that, except in a few situations that are peculiarly e, its cultivation is unprofitable. The peasants engage in it with reluctance; and are tempted e immediate advances the government agents are obliged to make to enable them to carry on ess.

nopoly has sometimes produced a nett revenue of about 1,000,000l. a year. Latterly, however, ue has been materially diminished. This has been occasioned, partly by the conquest of Malwa, npossibility of extending the same sort of monopoly into that province that was established in d Benares, and partly to the introduction of Turkey opium into the Chinese market by the Ame

* The opium of Bahar is known in commerce by the name of Patna opium.

The system under which the Indian opium trade has been conducted, has been the theme of r eulogy, and has been supposed to afford the only example of an *unexceptionable monopoly!* By conf the cultivation of the plant to particular districts, and taking care that the whole produce raised in shall be exported, we prevent, it is said, the use of this deleterious drug from gaining ground in Ir while the high price at which it is sold produces a large revenue to the Company's treasury. It is affir too, that even the interests of the Chinese are consulted by the system; that they obtain the drug state of purity, which would otherwise be adulterated ; and that the high price they are obliged to pay merely acts as a wholesome restraint on their vicious propensity to indulge in what is so very inju We doubt, however, whether there be much foundation for these eulogies. There can be no que. that opium is a very excellent subject for taxation ; and the higher the duty can be raised on it, wit encouraging smuggling, the better. It is not, however, so clear that the monopoly system is the bes of accomplishing this ; and, though the system had been originally a good one, it is no longer possit enforce it. To imagine, indeed, that the illicit cultivation of, and traffic in, opium can be prevented, that it is raised in most parts of the extensive country of Malwa, is altogether ludicrous. As to supposed influence of the monopoly in insuring the purity of the drug, it is sufficient to observe Malwa opium, which is produced under a comparatively free system, has been rapidly improving i quality, and now very often fetches a higher price than the opium of Bahar and Benares, where strictest *surveillance* is kept up. The latter, indeed, has sometimes been nearly unsaleable, from careless way in which it had been prepared, and the extent to which it was adulterated. — (*Craufu the Monopolies of the East India Company*, p. 55.) It is needless, however, to say more on this point, that Turkish opium maintains, in respect of purity and careful preparation, a decidedly higher reput than any produced in India. — (*Thomson's Dispensatory.*)

We doubt, too, whether the use of opium, when taken in moderate quantities, be really so injurio has been represented. That it may, like spirits and wine, be abused, is abundantly certain; but i not been shown that it is more liable to abuse than either of these articles. No one doubts that the nese, by whom it is principally consumed, are a highly industrious, sober, frugal people ; but thou were otherwise, we really do not see that the East India Company are warranted in subjecting a profi article of cultivation in India to the fetters of monopoly, that the morals of the Chinese may be prese It is unnecessary, however, to dwell upon this view of the matter. The Turks and Americans hav scruples of this sort ; and the only effect of the Company's attempting to force up the price of opi an extravagant height, would be to throw a still greater proportion of the trade into the hands of active competitors, to the great injury of the Indian cultivators.

Neither must the interests of the cultivators in India be lost sight of, who are materially injured t existing system. Even were it in other respects proper, their allowances are far too small.

Upon the whole, therefore, we do not see any solid grounds for supposing that this monopoly form exception to the common rule ; and we agree with those who think that the better way would establish the same system, as to the trade in opium, that is established with respect to the spirit tra this country; that is, to allow every one to cultivate it upon taking out a licence, and to lay an e duty on the prepared article. Such a plan would put an end to some most oppressive regulations ; while it would open a new source of wealth to the cultivators, the revenue derived by government v be materially augmented.

Besides the works previously referred to, we have consulted, in compiling this article, *Ainslie's Indica ; Milburn's Orient. Com. ; Bell's Review of the Commerce of Bengal ; Evidence on East I Affairs, before the Parliamentary Committee in 1830 and 1831, &c. &c.*

OPOBALSAM. See BALSAM.

OPOPONAX (Ger. *Opoponax;* Fr. *Opopanax;* It. *Opoponasso;* Sp. *Op naca;* Arab. *Jawesheer*), a gum resin obtained from the *Pastinaca Opopono* species of parsnep. It is a native of the south of Europe, and Asia Minor. stem rises to the height of 4 or 5 feet, with a thick branched yellow coloured The roots being wounded, a milky juice flows from them, which, being drie the sun, is the opoponax of the shops. It is in lumps of a reddish yellow co and white within. Smell peculiar. Taste bitter and acrid. Specific gravity 1 It is imported from Turkey. Being used only to a small extent in medicine, consumption is inconsiderable. — (*Thomson's Chemistry ; Ainslie's Mat. Indic*

OPORTO, OR **PORTO**, a large city and sea-port of Portugal, on the Do about 2 miles from its mouth, in lat. 41° 11¼′ N., lon. 8° 39¼′ W. Popula about 70,000. The harbour is good ; but the bar or entrance at the mouth o river is dangerous, particularly at low water. Oporto is the *entrepôt* of a portion of the kingdom of Portugal, and enjoys a pretty considerable foreign merce. The well known red wine denominated port, from its being entirely shi from this city, forms the principal article of export. The quantity annuall ported amounts to from 40,000 to 60,000 pipes, the greater part of whic brought to Great Britain, where the long continued comparatively high dut French wines has given a preference to port, to which it has no natural c The other exports are oil, fruits, wool, cream of tartar, shumac, leather, &c. imports are corn, rice, beef, and other articles of provision, cotton and wo goods, hardware, drugs, dried fish, hemp, and flax, &c.

For an account of the *Monies, Weights, and Measures* of Oporto, see LISBON.

The Quantity and Value of the Port Wine exported in the four Years, ending with 1819, were as foll

Years.	For Brazil and the Portuguese Possessions.	For Foreign Countries.	Total Pipes.	Value in Crusades.
1816	14,656	21,538	40,764	12,149,000
1817	16,271	29,888	46,159	14,548,000
1818	15,921	35,423	51,344	16,829,000
1819	21,088	21,526	42,614	13,728,000

(*Balbi, Essai Statistique sur le Royaume de Portugal*, tome i. p. 152

NGES (Ger. *Pomeranzen;* Du. *Orangen;* Fr. *Oranges;* It. *Melarance;* ranjas; Rus. *Pomeranezii;* Hind. *Narunge*). The orange tree (*Citrus um*), is a native of India and Persia, and the Eastern islands; but it is now ntly cultivated in the south of Europe and the West Indian islands, and found in our green-houses. Oranges are imported in chests and boxes, separately in paper. The best come from the Azores and Spain; very nes are also brought from Portugal, Italy, Malta, and other places.

orange trade carried on by this country is of very considerable value and import-Oranges are not much more expensive than most of our superior domestic fruits, ey are, perhaps, the most refreshing and wholesome of those of warmer climates. :y on lemons and oranges produced, in 1829, 53,184*l.* It is assessed at the rate *d.* a package, not exceeding 5,000 cubic inches; and, assuming the contents of ge or lemon to amount at an average to 10 cubic inches, there will be 500 in ch package, and the total number imported will have amounted to 212,736,000; the rate of about 13 oranges and lemons for each individual of the population : Britain. It is, however, believed that fully a third of the whole quantity im-s consumed in London and its environs; so that each individual of the metro-y, at a medium, be supposed annually to consume 53 oranges and lemons, in ortion, perhaps, of 50 of the former and 3 of the latter, It is not possible to y estimate of the number of persons employed in the importation and sale of but they must certainly be very great. The policy of charging any duty on seems questionable. They are very apt to spoil; and as no abatement is made duty on account of any damage, its influence on their price is much more con-than might at first be supposed.

HILLA WEED, ORCHELLA, or ARCHIL (Ger. *Orseille;* Fr. ; It. *Oricello, Orcella;* Sp. *Orchilla*), a whitish lichen (*Lichen Orcella*) the isle of Portland; but that which is used is imported from the Canary e de Verd islands, Barbary, and the Levant. From it is obtained the orchal of commerce, which yields a rich purple tincture, fugitive, indeed, emely beautiful. The preparation of orchilla was long a secret, known he Florentines and Hollanders; but it is now extensively manufactured ountry. Archil is generally sold in the form of cakes, but sometimes in noist pulp; it is extensively used by dyers; and in times of scarcity the weed or lichen has sold as high as 1,000*l.* per ton! — (*Thomson's Dis-.*) At this moment (June, 1831) Canary orchilla fetches, in the London from 270*l.* to 290*l.* a ton; while that which is brought from Madeira only 140*l.*, and Barbary not more than from 30*l.* to 45*l.* The total imported in 1829 amounted to 1,813 cwt., or 90½ tons.

OL, see ARGOL.

MENT (Ger. *Operment;* Fr. *Orpiment;* It. *Orpimento;* Sp. *Oropimente;* ipigmentum*), the name usually given to sulphuret of arsenic. When ar-prepared, it is the form of a fine yellow-coloured powder: but it is tive in many parts of the world, particularly in Turkey, the East Indies, emia. Native orpiment is composed of thin plates of a lively gold co-ermixed with pieces of a vermilion red, of a shattery foliaceous texture, soft to the touch like talc, and sparkling when broken. Specific gravity he inferior kinds are of a dead yellow, inclining to green, and want the ppearance of the best specimens. Its principal use is as a colouring ng painters, bookbinders, &c. (*Thomson's Chemistry; Milburn's Orient.*

DEW, ORSIDUE, MANHEIM or DUTCH GOLD (Ger. *Flätter-* . *Klatergoud;* Fr. *Oripean, Oliquant;* It. *Orpello;* Sp. *Oropel*), an infe-of gold leaf, prepared of copper and zinc. It is sometimes called *leaf* t is principally manufactured in Manheim.

ICH FEATHERS, see FEATHERS.

ERS OF SHIPS. Property in ships is acquired, like other personal by fabricating them, or by inheritance, purchase, &c. p is entitled to any of the privileges of a British ship until she be duly as such, and all the provisions in the registry act (6 Geo. 4. c. 110.) be with. — (See REGISTRY.) sh ship may belong either to one individual or to several individuals. It is y the act just cited, that the property of every vessel of which there are more n one, shall be divided into sixty-fourth shares; and that no person shall be

entitled to be registered as an owner who does not, at least, hold one sixty-fourth
It is further provided by the same statute, that not more than *thirty-two* persons sh
owners of any one ship at any one time. Companies or associations holding pr
in ships may choose *three* of their members to act as trustees for them.

Neither the property of an entire ship, nor any share or shares in such ship, c
transferred from one individual to another, except by bill of sale or other instrum
writing ; and before the sale is valid, such bill or instrument must be produced
collector and comptroller, who are to enter the names, residences, &c. of the selle
buyer, the number of shares sold, &c. in the book of registry of such vessel, a
endorse the particulars on the certificate of registry. — (See the clause in the s
art. REGISTRY.)

But though compliance with the directions in the statute accomplishes a con
transference of the property, when the transaction is not in its nature illegal, it gi
sort of security to a transference that is otherwise bad. The purchaser should in al
endeavour to get *possession* of the ship, or of his share in her, as soon as his title
or it is acquired by the registration of the particulars of the bill of sale ; for thou
the formalities of sale have been completed, yet, if the sellers continue as apparent o
in possession of the ship, their creditors may, in the event of their becoming ban
acquire a right to it, to the exclusion of the purchasers. In the case of a sale or
ment for a part only, it is enough if, the sale being completed, the seller ceases to
a part owner. — (*Lord Tenterden on the Law of Shipping*, part i. c. 1.)

Property in ships is sometimes acquired by capture. During war, his Majesty's
and private ships having letters of marque, are entitled to make prizes. But befo
captors acquire a legal title to such prizes, it is necessary that they should be cond
in the admiralty or other court constituted for that purpose. When this is don
captors are considered to be in the same situation, with respect to them, as if the
built or purchased them.

The act 6 Geo. 4. c. 110. has ruled, that no person having the transfer of a
or a share of a ship, made over to him as a security for a debt, shall be deemed an
or part owner, of such ship. And when such transfer has been duly registered a
ing to the provisions of the act, the right and interest of the mortgagee are not to be a
by the bankruptcy of the mortgagor, though he be the reputed owner, or part ow
such ship. — (See REGISTRY.)

In the article MASTERS OF SHIPS is given an account of the liabilities incurred
owners of ships for the acts of the masters. But it has been attempted to enc
navigation by limiting the responsibility of the owners, without, however, deprivi
freighter of a ship of an adequate security for the faithful performance of the co
To effect this desirable object, it has been enacted, that the owner or owners sha
be liable to make good any loss or damage happening *without their fault or pri*
any goods put on board any ship or vessel belonging to such owner or owners,
than the value of such ship or vessel, with all its appurtenances, and the freight
growing due, during the voyage that may be in prosecution, or contracted for,
time when the loss or damage has taken place. — (53 *Geo.* 3. c. 159.)

This limitation was first introduced into our law by the 7 Geo. 2. c. 15. But
previously been adopted in the law of Holland, and in the justly celebrated
ordinance of 1681. In the ordinance of Rotterdam, issued in 1721, it is expres
clared, that " the owners shall not be answerable for any act of the master, done
out their order, any further than their part of the ship amounts to." Independ
however, of this general agreement, the expediency of the limitation appears,
reasons already stated, sufficiently obvious.

It was also enacted in 1786 (26 Geo. 3. c. 60.), that neither the master nor
of any ship or vessel shall be liable to answer for or make good any gold or
diamonds, watches, jewels, or precious stones, lost or embezzled during the co
the voyage, unless the shipper thereof insert in his bill of lading, or declare in
to the master or owners, the true nature, quality, and value of such articles.

The responsibility, at common law, of a *master* or *mariner* is not affected by t
mentioned limitation, even though such master or mariner be owner or part ow
the vessel ; neither does the limitation extend to the owner or owners of any
barge, boat, &c. used solely in rivers or inland navigation, nor to any ship or ves
duly registered according to law.

When several freighters sustain losses exceeding in the whole the value of t
and freight, they are to receive compensation thereout in proportion to their res
losses : and any one freighter, on behalf of himself and the other freighters, or a
owner, on behalf of himself and the other part owners, may file a bill in a c
equity for the discovery of the total amount of the losses, and of the value of t
and for an equal distribution and payment. If the bill be filed by or on behal

wners, the plaintiff must make affidavit that he does not collude with the defend-
and must offer to pay the value of the ship and freight, as the court shall direct.
s usual in most countries, where the part owners of a ship disagree as to her ement, to give those possessed of the greater number of shares power to bind the
. But in this country, while the majority of the owners in value have authority
ploy the ship as they please, the interests of the minority are secured from being
liced by having their property engaged in an adventure of which they disapprove.
his purpose the Court of Admiralty has been in the practice of taking a stipulation
those who desire to send the ship on a voyage, in a sum equal to the value of the
s of those who object to it, either to bring back and restore to them the ship, or to
em the value of their shares. When this is done, the dissentient part owners bear
rtion of the expenses of the outfit, and are not entitled to a share in the profits of
oyage; the ship sails wholly at the charge and risk, and for the profit, of the
. — (*Abbott*, part i. c. 3.)

the statutory enactments as to the sale and transfer of ships, see REGISTRY.

'STER, OYSTERS (Ger. *Austern;* Fr. *Huitres;* It. *Ostriche;* Sp. *Ostras;* Lat.
x).   This well known shellfish is very generally diffused, and is particularly
ful on the British coasts, which were ransacked for the supply of ancient
e with oysters. They differ in quality according to the different nature of
oil or bed. The best British oysters are found at Purfleet; the worst, near
pool. The nursing and feeding of oysters is almost exclusively carried on
Ichester, and other places in Essex. The oysters are brought from the coast
mpshire, Dorset, and other maritime counties, even as far as Scotland, and
n beds or layings in creeks along the shore, where they grow in 2 or 3 years
onsiderable size, and have their flavour improved. There are said to be
200 vessels, from 12 to 40 or 50 tons burthen, immediately employed in
ng for oysters, having from 400 to 500 men and boys attached to them.
uantity of oysters bred and taken in Essex, and consumed mostly in Lon-
s supposed to amount to 14,000 or 15,000 bushels a year. — (*Supp. to Ency.*
rt. *Fisheries.*)

tealing of oysters, or oyster brood, from any oyster bed, laying, or fishery, is larceny, and the
being convicted thereof shall be punished accordingly; and if any person shall unlawfully and
use any dredge, net, &c. for the purpose of taking oysters, or oyster brood, within the limits of
er bed or fishery, every such person shall be deemed guilty of a misdemeanor, and, upon being
d thereof, shall be punished by fine or imprisonment, or both, as the court may award; such fine
xceed 20*l.*, and such imprisonment not to exceed three calendar months. It is provided, that
in the act shall be construed as preventing any one from catching *floating fish* within the limits
oyster fishery, with any net, instrument, or engine adapted to the catching of such fish.—
eo. 4. c. 29. § 36.)

P.

KAGE, SCAVAGE, BAILLAGE, AND PORTAGE, are certain duties
d in the port of London, on the goods imported and exported by aliens, or
izens being the sons of aliens.

ng the dark ages, it was usual to lay higher duties upon the goods imported or
d by aliens, whether in British or foreign ships, than were laid on similar goods
nported or exported by natives. But according as sounder and more enlarged
les prevailed, this illiberal distinction was gradually modified, and was at length
abolished, in so far at least as it was of a public character, by the 24 Geo. 3. c. 16.
t, after reciting that " the several duties and restrictions imposed by various acts of
ent upon merchandise are, by the alterations of the trade now carried on between
gdom and foreign states, in some cases become an unnecessary burden upon
ce, without producing any real advantage to the public revenue, and that it is
nt they should no longer continue," enacts, that the duty commonly called "the
ustoms," imposed by the 12 Car. 2., and all other additional duties imposed by any
n the goods of aliens above those payable by natural born subjects, should be no
ayable.   The act then goes on to provide, that nothing contained in it shall
the duties due and payable upon goods imported into or exported from this
n in any *foreign* ship, nor the duties of *package* and *scavage*, or any duties granted
er to the city of London;" and then follow provisions to prevent the city being
ed of such duties by false entries of aliens' goods in the name of a British sub-
Chitty's Commercial Law, vol. i. p. 160.)

uties thus preserved to the city are not very heavy; but the principle on which
imposed is exceedingly objectionable, and their collection is attended with a

great deal of trouble and inconvenience. Not being levied in other places, they ope to the prejudice of the trade of the metropolis; and if the funds of the corporation not admit of their following the liberal example of the legislature, by voluntarily ab doning this vexatious impost, it would be good policy to give them a compensation relinquishing it.

Tables of Package, Scavage, Baillage, and Portage Duties, payable by Aliens in the Port of Londo

Package Rates inwards for all goods and merchandise imported from ports beyond the seas, belonging to aliens, or denizens being the sons of aliens.

*** The commodities which are marked thus *, are liable to this duty, though British property, if imported in any other than British ships legally navigated.

	s.	d.
Alum - per 112 lbs.	0	2
Andirons. See Brass.		
Annatto - per 100 lbs.	0	4
Apples and pears, per little barrel	0	1¼
*Aquavitæ - per hogshead	0	6
Argol, white or red, per 112 lbs.	0	1½
*Ashes, pot - per 112 lbs.	0	0¾
Babies' heads - per dozen	0	0½
Bacon - per 112 lbs.	0	3
Band-strings - per dozen knots	0	0¼
*Balks, great per 120	1	6
under 8 inches - per 120	0	9
under 5 inches - per 120	0	4
Barilla, or Saphora, per barrel of 2 cwt.	0	4
*Barlings - per 120	0	4
*Barley - per quarter	0	0½
Basket-rods - per dozen bundles	0	4
Bast ropes - per 112 lbs.	0	0½
Battery, bashrones or kettles, per 112 lbs.	0	6
*Beans per quarter	0	0½
Beef - - per barrel	0	1
Bell-metal - per 112 lbs.	0	2
Bermillians. See Fustians.		
Blacking, or lamp-black, per 112 lbs.	0	3
Bottles of all sorts - per dozen	0	0½
*Boards, barrel-boards, per 1,000	0	4
clap-boards - per 120	0	1
pipe-boards - per 120	0	1
Boratoes, or bombazines, viz. narrow, per single piece not above 15 yards	0	2
broad, per single piece not above 15 yards	0	3
Books, unbound per bask or maund	0	8
*Bow-staves - per 120	0	2
Brass andirons, laver-cocks, chafing-dishes, and all other brass or latten wrought, per 100 lbs.	0	3
Brimstone - per 112 lbs.	0	0½
Bristles - per dozen lbs.	0	0½
Buckrams, viz. of Germany, per dozen pieces	0	3
of France, per dozen pieces	0	2
Buftins, Liles, or Mocadoes, viz. narrow, per single piece not above 15 yards	0	1
broad, per single piece not above 15 yards	0	2
Bull-rushes - per load	0	1
Burrs for mill-stones - per 100	0	3
Butter - per 112 lbs.	0	1
Cable ropes for cordage - per 112 lbs.	0	1
Cabinets, viz. great per piece	0	2
small - per piece	0	1
Caddas, or crewel ribbon, per dozen pieces, each of 36 yards	0	1
Candlewick - per 112 lbs.	0	1
Candles of tallow, per dozen lbs.	0	0¼
Capers - per 100 lbs.	0	2
*Capravens - per 120	0	3
Cards, viz. playing, per 12 dozen packs	0	2
wool-cards, per dozen pair	0	0¼
Carpets, viz. Turkey, Persia, East India, and Venice, long - per piece	0	6
of same or like sort, short per piece	0	4
of all other sorts - per piece	0	0½
Cases, viz. for looking-glasses, gilt, from No. 3 to No. 10. per dozen	0	1¼
the same ungilt - per dozen	0	0½
Catlings. See Lutestrings.		
Camlets, mohairs, and Turkey grograms - per 15 yards	0	1½
Cheese - per 112 lbs.	0	1
Cherries - per 112 lbs.	0	1½
Cloth, viz. French walloon, per 20 yards	0	3
scarlet - per yard	0	1
Cochineal, viz. Silvester or Campeachy - per lb.	0	0½
of all other sorts - per lb.	0	1
Combs of box or light wood, per 12 dozen	0	0½
Copper bricks or plates, round or square per 112 lbs.	0	4
Copperas - per 112 lbs.	0	1
Coral, rough or polished, per 2½ lbs.	0	2
Cordage. See Cable ropes.		
Cork - - per 112 lbs.	0	1
for shoemakers, per dozen pieces	0	0¼
Corn. See Barley, Beans, Malt, Oats, Peas, Rye, and Wheat respectively.		
*Deal boards, of all sorts, per 120	1	0
Dogs of earth - per 12 dozen	0	1½
Durance, or durettes, viz. with thread - per 15 yards	0	1½
with silk - per 15 yards	0	2
Drugs, viz. ambergris - per oz.	0	1½
aloes socotorina - per lb.	0	0½
barley hulled - per 112 lbs.	0	1
carraway and cummin-seeds, per 112 lbs.	0	1½
China roots - per 100 lbs.	0	6
civet - - per oz.	0	1
coral. See in C.		
frankincense. See in F.		
gum Arabic. See in G.		
gum ammoniac, per 100 lbs.	0	6
musk - - per oz.	0	1
cods - per dozen	0	1
quicksilver. See in Q.		
Saunders, white or red, per 100 lbs.	0	6
treacle, common, per 100 lbs.	0	2
turpentine, common - per 112 lbs.	0	1
Earthenware, called tiles. See in T.		
Feathers, for beds - per 112 lbs.	0	2
Fish, viz. cod-fish - per 120	0	2
cole-fish - per 120	0	1
eels - per barrel	0	1
quick - per ship load	10	0
herrings, white or red, per last	0	6
ling - per 120	0	6
lub-fish - - per 120	0	2
croplings per 120	0	1
titling - per 120	0	0½
sturgeon - per firkin	0	1
per keg	0	0½
salmon - per barrel	0	1½
*Flax, viz. undressed, per 112 lbs.	0	1½
dressed or wrought - per 112 lbs.	0	4
Flocks - per 112 lbs.	0	2
Frankincense - per 112 lbs.	0	1½
Furs, viz. beavers' skins - per piece	0	0½
beavers' bellies or wombs, per dozen	0	4
budge, tawed or untawed, per 100	0	2
fox skins - per 100	0	4
foyns, without tails, per doz.	0	1½
Fustians, viz. bermillians, per piece, or two half pieces of 15 yards each half piece -	0	2
Naples, fustian, tripe, or velure, per piece of 15 yards	0	2
Galley dishes - per 12 dozen	0	1
Galls - per 112 lbs.	0	2
Glass, viz. for windows, per chest or case	0	3
Venice drinking glasses, per dozen	0	0½
looking-glasses, viz. half-penny ware, per 12 dozen	0	0½
penny ware, per 12 dozen	0	0¼
of steel, small, per dozen	0	0½
large - per dozen	0	1
of crystal, small, under No. 6. - per dozen	0	1
No. 7, 8, 9, 10. per dozen	0	4
middle sort, No. 6. per dozen	0	2
No. 11. and 12. per dozen	1	6
stone plates for spectacles, per dozen	0	0½
plates, or sights, for looking-glasses unfoiled, viz. of crystal, small, under No. 6. per dozen	0	0½
No. 6. - per dozen	0	1
No. 7, 8, 9, 10. per dozen	0	2
No. 11, 12. - per dozen	1	0
Gloves of Spanish leather, per 12 pairs	0	0½
Goats' hair - per 100 lbs.	0	6
Grain for dyers, viz. of scarlet powder - per lb.	0	0½
of Seville, in berries and grains of Portugal or Rotta per lb.	0	0¼
Grocery, viz. almonds per 112 lbs.		
aniseeds - per 112 lbs.		
cinnamon - per 100 lbs.		
cloves - per 100 lbs.		
*currants - per 112 lbs.		
dates - per 112 lbs.		
*figs - per 112 lbs.		
fusses of cloves, per 100 lbs.		
ginger - per 100 lbs.		
liquorice - per 112 lbs.		
mace - per 100 lbs.		
nutmegs - per 100 lbs.		
pepper - per 100 lbs.		
*prunes - per 112 lbs.		
raisins, great, or Malaga, per 112 lbs.		
of the sun - per 112 lbs.		
*sugar, refined, per 112 lbs.		
candy - per 112 lbs.		
Muscovadoes, and white, per 112 lbs.		
St. Thome and Panelles, per 112 lbs.		
Grogram. See Camlets.		
Gunpowder, per barrel of 112 lbs.		
Gum Arabic - per 112 lbs.		
Hair called goats' hair. See in G.		
Hawks of all sorts - per hawk		
Hats, viz. bast or straw hats knotted - per dozen		
plain - per dozen		
wool felts - per dozen		
demi-castors - per piece		
beaver hats - per piece		
*Headings for pipes, hogsheads, or barrels - per 1,000		
Heath for brushes - per 112 lbs.		
*Hemp, viz. undressed - per 112 lbs.		
dressed - per 112 lbs.		
Hides, viz. buff hides, per piece		
cow or horse hides, per dozen		
Honey - per barrel		
Horses and mares - each		
Hops - - per 112 lbs.		
Indigo - - per 100 lbs.		
dust - per 100 lbs.		
Incle, viz. wrought - per 12 lbs.		
rolls - per 12 pieces, 36 yards each		
unwrought per 100 lbs.		
Iron, wrought - per 112 lbs.		
unwrought per ton		
pots - per dozen		
Juice of lemons. See Lemons.		
Lamp-black. See Blacking.		
Latten, viz. shaven latten, per 112 lbs.		
black latten - per 112 lbs.		
Lace, viz. bone lace of thread, per 12 yards		
silk bone lace per 16 oz.		
silk lace of other sorts, per 16 oz.		
Lemons - - per 1,000		
juice of lemons per pipe		
pickled lemons per pipe		
Linseed - per quarter		
Leaves of gold - per 100 leaves		
Lures for hawks - per dozen		
Leather, viz. Brazil leather, per dozen skins		
Leather hangings, gilt, per piece		
for masks - per 12 lbs.		
Lutes - - per dozen		
Lutestrings, viz. catlings - per 144 dozen knots		
minikins, per 12 dozen knots		
Linen, Brabant, Flemish, Embden, viz. British cloth, per 100 ells		
frieze cloth, Ghentish Holland, Isinghams, Overyssels, cloth rows, Cowssield, or Plats cloth - each 30 ells		
calicoes, or dutties, per piece		
cambrics, per piece of 12 ells		
damask, tabling, viz. of Holland - per dozen yards		
of Silesia, per dozen yards		
damask, towelling and napkining, viz. of Holland, per dozen yards		
of Silesia, per doz. yards		
diaper, tabling, viz. of Holland - per dozen yards		
of Silesia, per dozen yards		
diaper, towelling and napkining, viz. of Holland, per dozen yards		
of Silesia, per doz. yards		
French or Normandy canvas and line narrow, Vandales, or Vitry canvass, Dutch		

s. d.
Barras, and Hessen
vass, - per 120 ells 0 2
and spruce canvass,
ngs, pack-duck, Hin-
ngs, Middlegood, Head-
Muscovia, line nar-
Hamburgh cloth, nar-
rish cloth, per 120 ells 0 1
rgh and Silesia cloth,
- per 120 ells 0 3
ies - per bolt 0 1
canvass and line, 1 1-8
oad or more - per
120 ells 0 3
- per piece of 13 ells 0 2
awn - per piece 0 0½
lawn - per piece 0 1½
ns of all sorts - per
106 ells 0 1½
ch - per 120 ells 0 1½
rgh linen, per 30 ells 0 1
or tufted canvass with
l per piece of 15 yards 0 1
tufted, or quilted
s, with silk - per
piece of 15 yards 0 1
- per 112 lbs. 0 1
- per quarter 0 0½
- per 112 lbs. 0 1
vet or satin, per doz. 0 1
above 12 inches, per
mast 0 2
nches - per mast 0 1
ches - per mast 0 0½
d - per ream 0 1
crop and all other
adder - per 112 lbs. 0 2
ler - per 112 lbs. 0 1½
dder - per 112 lbs. 0 0½
our - per 30 cwt. 0 4
See Lutestrings.
- per 12 lbs. 0 1½
ee Camlets.
- per 120 0 4
- per quarter 0 0½
eville, Majorca, Mi-
Provence, Portugal,
ad oil - per tun 2 8
linseed oil - per tun 2 6
of Greenland or
dland - per tun 1 4
- per hogshead 0 4
per 100 bunches 0 1
- per 112 lbs. 0 3
- per 1,000 0 1
- per 112 lbs. 0 1½
- per 100 lbs. 0 1½
dripping or frying
- per 112 lbs. 0 1½
pans - per dozen 0 1½
- per 100 bundles 0 6
er sorts - per
100 reams 1 8
pples.
- per qnarter 0 0½
- per last 0 3
, white or black,
per 100 0 1
hite or black, per
100 0 2
- per 1,000 0 2
- per barrel 0 1½
or stone, covered,
per 100 0 1
stone, uncovered,
casts, containing
to every cast, whe-
one pot or not - 0 2
- per dozen 0 0½
- per 100 lbs. 0 10
- per 100 0 0½
- per quarter 0 1
- per ton 0 8
- per 112 lbs. 0 1
per quarter 0 a½
s - per 12 dozen 0 0½
goods of Muscovy
a, for every 20s. of
es or values on oath 0 1
- per lb. 0 0½
- per 100 lbs. 0 4
- per wey 0 2
- per 112 lbs. 0 1½
able says, or Flan-
ges - per piece 0 3
and milled says,
per piece 0 2
- per 112 lbs. 0 1½
ges, Granados, Na-
ganzine, Pole, and
satin silk, sleeve
and thrown silk,
per 16 oz. 0 1
silk - per 24 oz. 0 1
oret silk, Fillozel,
k, coarse - per
16 oz. 0 0½
lk - per 24 oz. 0 0½
lk, and raw Morea
per 24 oz. 0 0½
- per pair 0 0½
viz. Boratos of
talopher, China,
silk camlet, China
, tabby grograms,
s, narrow tabbies

s. d.
of silk, Towers taffety, per
dozen yards 0 2
silk grograms narrow, silk
say, calimancoes, and Phi-
losellos, broad, per 12 yards 0 3
grograms broad, caffa, or
damask - per 12 yards 0 4
satins of Bolonia, Lukes,
Jeans, others of like making - - per 12 yards 0 6
Bridges, China, and Tur-
key satin, per 12 yards 0 1
sarsnets of Bolonia or Florence - per 12 ells 0 1½
of China - per 12 ells 0 1
Sypers of silk, broad - per
12 yards 0 0½
of silk, narrow - per
24 yards 0 0½
of taffety, ell broad - per
12 yards 0 2
China and Levant, per
12 yards 0 0½
velvets, China velvets - per
12 yards 0 1
all other velvets or
plushes - per 12 yards 0 6
Skins, viz. Cordovan skins, per
dozen 0 2
goats' skins in the hair, per
dozen 0 1
kid skins of all sorts, per 100 0 2
Smalts - - per 100 0 4
*Spars, — boomspars - per 120 0 3
cantspars per 120 0 2
small spars - per 120 0 1
*Spirits, as brandy, &c. for every
20s. of their rates
or values on oath 0 1
Stockings of silk. See Silk.
Stones; dog stones - per last 0 6
marble stones - per ton 0 8
mill stones - per piece 0 6
Quern stone - per last 0 3
Sword blades - per dozen 0 1
*Staves; pipe or hogshead staves,
per 1,000 0 6
barrel staves - per 1,000 0 3
firkin staves per 1,000 0 1½
Steel; long steel, whisp steel,
and such like, per 112 lbs. 0 2
gad steel - per half barrel 0 4
Sturgeon. See Fish.
Succades, wet or dry, per 100 lbs. 0 10
*Syder - per tun 0 4
Tallow - per 112 lbs. 0 1
Tapestry, viz. with hair - per
100 Flemish ells 0 4
with wool - per 100
Flemish e ls 0 6
with caddas - per 100
Flemish ells 1 0
with silk, per 12 Flemish ells 0 2
Tarras - - per barrel 0 0½
Teazels - per 1,000 0 0½
Tykes of all sorts - per tyke 0 1½
Thread, viz. Bridges thread, per
12 lbs. 0 1
Outnal thread - per 12 lbs. 0 1
whited brown or piercing
thread - per 12 lbs. 0 1½
Sisters' thread - per lb. 0 0½
Lyons or Paris thread, per
100 bolts 0 8
Tobacco, viz. Spanish, Varinas,
Brazil tobacco, per 100 lbs. 2 0
St. Christopher's tobacco, or
the like - per 100 lbs. 0 6
Tiles; pantiles or Flanders tiles,
per 1,000 0 2
*Timbers, for every 20s. of their
rates or values on oath 0 1
Tow - per 112 lbs. 0 0½
Tripe. See Fustians.
*Turkey goods, for every 20s. of
rates or values on oath 0 1
Vellure. See Fustians.
Vinegar. See Wine Eager.
Wax - - per 112 lbs. 0 4
*Wainscots - per 100 0 6
Whale fins per dozen fins 0 1
*Wheat - - per quarter 0 1
*Wine, viz. Eager - per tun 0 6
Gascoigne, French wines, all
other wines of the growth
of the French dominions,
per tun 2 0
Rhenish wine - per tun 60 0
Muscadel, and all other
wines - per tun 40 0
Wire; latten and other wire, per
112 lbs. 0 4
Woad; island woad - per ton 1 0
Tholouse woad per 112 lbs. 0 1
Wood, viz. box wood, for every
20s. of the rates or value
on oath 0 1
Brazil, or Pernambuco wood,
per 112 lbs. 0 3
Brazilletto, or Jamaica wood,
per 112 lbs. 0 1
fustic - - per 112 lbs. 0 0½
red or Guinea wood - per
112 lbs. 0 2
sweet wood, West India, per
112 lbs. 0 1

s. d.
Wood, all other sorts, for every 20s.
of the rates or value on oath 0 1
Wool; beaver wool - per lb. 0 1½
cotton wool - per 100 lbs. 0 3
Irish, combed per 100 lbs. 0 4
uncombed - per 112 lbs. 0 2
estridge wool - per 112 lbs. 0 2
Polonia wool - per 112 lbs. 0 3
French wool - per 112 lbs. 0 2
lamb's wool - per 112 lbs. 0 3
Spanish wool - per 112 lbs. 0 4
red wool - - per lb. 0 0½
Yarn; cable yarn - per 112 lbs. 0 1
camel, grogram, or mohair
yarn - per 100 lbs. 1 6
cotton yarn - per 100 lbs. 0 4
Irish yarn, per pack of 480 lbs. 0 6
raw linen yarn, Dutch or
French, per 100 lbs. 0 4
spruce or Muscovia yarn, per
112 lbs. 0 2

All other goods, not mentioned in this table, pay, for scavage duties inwards, after the rate of 1d. in the pound, according as they are expressed or valued in his Majesty's late book of rates; and all others, not expressed therein, pay the same rates, according to their true value.

⁎ All merchants, aliens, and denizens, are to make and deliver to the proper collector of this duty, true and perfect bills of entry of all the goods and merchandise by them imported.

Package Rates Outwards. — For all goods and merchandise to be packed, casked, piped, barrelled, or any ways vesselled, in order to be transported to parts beyond the the seas; although the mayor and commonalty, or their officers, do not pack the said goods when they are ready, and upon reasonable request and notice given.

s. d.
Annatto - per 100 lbs. 0 3
Aquavitæ - per hogshead 0 4
Argol, white or red - per 112 lbs. 0 1½
Ashes; potashes - per 2 cwt. 0 2
soap ashes - per last 0 1
Awl-blades for shoe makers, per
1,000 0 0½
Barilla, or Saphora, per barrel of
2 cwt. 0 4
Beer - per tun 0 6
Birding shot lead per 112 lbs. 0 2
Books - per maund 1 0
Bottles, glass, covered with lea-
ther - - per dozen 0 1
Brimstone - per 112 lbs. 0 1
Brushes - - per dozen 0 0½
Broken glass - per barrel 0 0½
Buttons; brass, steel, copper, or
latten buttons, per 144 doz. 0 1
hair buttons - per 144 dozen 0 1
silk buttons - per 144 dozen 0 0½
thread buttons, per 144 dozen 0 0½
Buckweed - per quarter 0 1
Buckrams of all sorts, per dozen
pieces 0 2
Caps for sailors, Monmouth and
others - per dozen 0 1
Canary seed per bushel 0 0½
Cloaks, old - - per piece 0 0½
Cloths. See Woollen drapery.
Coals. See Sea coal.
Cobweb lawns - each 12 yards 0 1
Cochineal, viz. Silvester or Cam-
pechia - per lb. 0 0½
of all other sorts - per lb. 0 1
Combs, ivory. See Ivory.
Copperas - per 112 lbs. 0 1
Drugs; assafœtida, gum ammoniac, gum lac, olibanum,
and sassafras wood - per
100 lbs. 0 6
cassia fistula - per 100 lbs. 0 8
lignea - per 100 lbs. 0 8
cubebs - per 100 lbs. 0 6
frankincense. See in F.
quicksilver. See in Q.
red lead. See in R.
rhubarb - per lb. 0 1
scammony - per lb. 0 1
wormseed. See in W.
Elephants' teeth - per 100 lbs. 0 4
Estridge feathers, undressed, per
lbs. 0 0½
Filings of iron; swarf, per barrel 0 2
Fish, viz. herrings, full or shotten,
per last 0 6
stockfish of all sorts, per last 0 6
Flasks of horn - per dozen 0 1
Flax, dressed - per 112 lbs. 0 4
undressed - per 112 lbs. 0 2
Frankincense - per 112 lbs. 0 1½
Furs. See Skins.
Fustians, English Millain, per
piece containing 2 half-
pieces of 15 yards each 0 1
Venetian, English make, per
15 yards 0 1
Galls - per 112 lbs. 0 2
Garble, of almonds - per 112 lbs. 0 1
of cloves - per 100 lbs. 0 4
of ginger - per 100 lbs. 0 1

	s.	d.
Garble, of mace, per 100 lbs.	0	9
of pepper - per 100 lbs.	0	3
Glass, broken. See B.		
Glue - - per 112 lbs.	0	1
Glovers' clippings, per maund or bask	0	0½
Gloves, buck's leather - per dozen pairs	0	1
with silk fringe, faced with taffety - per dozen pairs	0	1
lined with coney or lamb skins, or plain, per dozen pairs	0	0½
Grains; scarlet powder, and of Seville in berries, and grain of Portugal or Rota - per 100 lbs.	2	6
French or Guinea, per 100 lbs.	0	4
Grocery, viz. almonds, per 112 lbs.	0	2
almonds, garble. See Garble.		
aniseeds - per 112 lbs.	0	2
cinnamon - per 100 lbs.	1	0
cloves - per 100 lbs.	1	0
cloves, garble. See Garble.		
currants - per 112 lbs.	0	3
dates - per 112 lbs.	0	4
figs - per 112 lbs.	0	0½
ginger - per 100 lbs.	0	9
ginger, garble. See Garble.		
licorice - per 112 lbs.	0	1½
mace - per 100 lbs.	1	6
mace, garble. See Garble.		
nutmegs - per 100 lbs.	1	0
pepper - per 100 lbs.	0	6
pepper, garble. See Garble.		
prunes - per 112 lbs.	0	0½
raisins, great and Malaga per 112 lbs.	0	1
of the sun - per 112 lbs.	0	2
sugar-candy - per 112 lbs.	0	3
of St. Thome and Panelles per 112 lbs.	0	3
of all sorts per 112 lbs.	0	6
Hats; beaver hats - per piece	0	2
demi-castors per piece	0	1
felt hats, plain - per dozen	0	1½
lined or faced, per dozen	0	2
Hair; coney hair - per 100 lbs.	0	4
of goats or kids, per 100 lbs.	0	4
ox or cow-tail hair, - per 112 lbs.	0	0½
Hemp - - per 112 lbs.	0	1½
Hides, India. See India.		
Horns; ink-horns - per 12 dozen	0	0½
horns of lanterns, - per 1,000 leaves	0	2
tips of horns - per 1,000	0	1
Hops - - per 112 lbs.	0	2
Indigo of all sorts - per 100 lbs.	1	0
dust - per 100 lbs.	0	6
India hides - per 100 lbs.	1	6
Irish rugs - per piece	0	1
Iron, unwrought - per ton	0	6
wrought per 112 lbs.	0	1
spurs - per dozen pairs	0	1
Ivory combs - per dozen lbs.	0	2
Knives, viz. London knives, ordinary - per small gross	0	3
Sheffield knives per sm. gross	0	1½
shoemakers' paring knives per small gross	0	0½
Lace, viz. bone lace of thread per dozen yards	0	0½
silk lace - per 16 oz.	0	1½
Lamperns per 1,000	0	1½
Lead - - per fother	0	8
Lead. See Birding shot.		
Lemons, pickled per pipe	0	3
Lemon juice per pipe	0	6
Linseed - - per quarter	0	1
Linen, calico - per piece	0	0½
cambrics, per 2 half-pieces of 13 ells	0	1½
damask tabling, all sorts, per dozen yards	0	2
towelling and napkining, all sorts, per doz. yards	0	1
diaper tabling, all sorts, per dozen yards	0	1
towelling and napkining, all sorts, per dozen yards	0	0½
lawns - per piece of 13 ells	0	1½
linen cloth, called Brabant, Embden, Flemish, Frieze, Ghentish, Holland, Isinghams, Overyssels, and Rouse cloth - - 30 ells	0	2
French and Normandy canvass - - per 120 ells	0	3
Dutch Barras, Hessens, Vitry, canvass - per 120 ells	0	3
canvass, tufted or quilted with copper, silk, or thread, or such like - per 15 yards	0	1
linen shreds - per maund	0	2
Madder, all but mull madder, per 112 lbs.	0	2
Molasses - per hogshead	0	4
Mustard seed - per 112 lbs.	0	0½
Nails, viz. chair nails, brass or copper - per 1,000	0	0½
copper nails, rose nails, and saddlers' nails - per 10,000	0	0½
Ochre, red or yellow, per 112 lbs.	0	1
Onion seed per 112 lbs.	0	4
Orchal per 112 lbs.	0	1

	s.	d.
Ox bones - - per 1,000	0	1
guts - - per barrel	0	2
Oils; Seville, Majorca, Minorca, Provence, Portugal, linseed, or rape oil - per tun	1	4
train or whale oil - per tun	0	8
Paper; printing and copy paper, per 100 reams	1	6
Pewter - per 112 lbs.	0	4
Points of thread. See in T.		
Rape seed - per quarter	0	1
Rape cakes - per 1,000	0	0½
Red lead - per 112 lbs.	0	1
Red earth - per 112 lbs.	0	0½
Rice - per 112 lbs.	0	1
Rosin - - per ton	0	6
Rugs, Irish. See Irish.		
Saffron - - per lb.	0	1
Salt - - per wey	0	2
Saltpetre - per 112 lbs.	0	2
Sea-horse teeth - per 100 lbs.	0	10
Sea coals - per chaldron	0	4
Shot. See Birding shot lead.		
Shumac - per 112 lbs.	0	2
Silk, raw, of all sorts, per 16 oz.	0	1
nubs of husks, the 100, containing 21 oz. to the lb.	0	4
British thrown - per 16 oz.	0	1
Silver, called quicksilver - per 100 lbs.	0	8
Skins and furs, viz. badger skins, per 100	0	6
beaver skins - per 100	2	6
cat skins - per 100	0	4
calf skins - per 100	0	8
coney skins, grey, tawed, seasoned, or stag - per 120	0	2
coney skins, black - per 120	0	2½
elk skins - per piece	0	0½
fitches - per timber	0	1
fox skins - per 100	0	8
jennet skins, black, seasoned, or raw - - per skin	0	0½
kid skins - per 100	0	2
lamb skins, tawed, or in oil, per 120	0	6
mawkins, tawed or raw, per 120	0	4
otter skins - per 100	0	8
rabbit skins per 100	0	1
sheep skins - per 120	0	6
sheep pelts - per 100	0	3
squirrel skins - per 1,000	0	3
Slip - - per barrel	0	1
Soap, viz. hard Castile per 112 lbs.	0	2
per barrel	0	3
Spectacles without cases, per 12 dozen	0	0½
Stockings, viz. children's stockings - per dozen pairs	0	0½
kersey or leather, per dozen pairs	0	1
silk stockings - per pair	0	0½
worsted stockings, per dozen pairs	0	2
woollen knit stockings, per dozen pairs	0	1½
Stuffs, viz. buffins, per piece, broad of 14 yards	0	2
per piece, narrow of 14 yards	0	1
Bridgewaters per piece	0	2
Carrels - per piece	0	1
Carmelians, per piece of 25 yards	0	2
Camlets or grograms - per piece of 14 or 15 yards	0	2
Damosellos or damasins, per piece	0	2
Durants - per piece	0	1
dimity, per piece of 30 yards	0	1
Floramedos - per piece	0	1
figurettos - per piece	0	2
hangings of Bristol or striped stuff - - per piece	0	4
linsey woolsey - per piece	0	1½
Lisles, broad or narrow, per piece not above 15 yards	0	2
Mocadus, single or tufted, per piece of 14 yards	0	1
double, per piece of 28 yards	0	2
mohairs, per piece not above 15 yards	0	1½
miscellany, per piece of 30 yards	0	1
Perpetuans yard broad, per piece	0	2
ell broad per piece	0	2½
paragon, or parapus, per piece	0	2
Pyramides, or marinuff, the narrow piece	0	1
the broad piece	0	2
rashes of all sorts, per piece about 24 yards	0	4
says; Hounscot says, or milled, per piece	0	3
of all other sorts, per piece	0	2½
serges, single, per yard broad of 12 yards	0	2
double, per yard broad of 24 yards	0	3
See also Woollen drapery.		
Succades, wet or dry, per 100 lbs.	0	8
Swarf. See Filings of iron.		
Tallow - per 112 lbs.	0	1

Tapestry, viz. with hair, per 10
Flemish e
with wool, per 100 Flemish e
with gaddis, per 100 Flem
e
with silk, per 12 Flemish e
Taffety, ell broad, per dozen yar
silk tuff tuffety, broad, p
dozen yar
narrow, per dozen yar
Thread, whited brown or c
loured - per dozen lb
Tiffany - per dozen yar
Tobacco, Spanish - per 100 lb
of all other sorts, per 100 lb
Tin, wrought - per 112 lb
unwrought - per 112 lb
Thread points - per great gro
Vellures, British, per single pie
per double pie
Vinegar of wine - per t
Waistcoats, viz. of kersey or fla
nel - per doz
of woollen, knit - per doz
of worsted, knit - per pie
wrought with crewel, p
pie
wrought with silk, per pie
Wax; British wax - per 112 l
British hard wax, per 100 l
Wine; French wine - per t
Muscadel and Levant win
per b
Sacks, Canaries, Madeir
Romney, and Hullocks, p
butt or p
Wood; box wood - per 112 l
Brazil wood per 112 l
ebony wood - per 112 l
fustic wood per 112 l
red wood - per 112 l
Wools; cotton wool, per 100 l
estridge wool - per 112 l
French wool per 112 l
Spanish wool - per 112 l
Woollen drapery, viz. baize,
single pie
per double pie
Minikins baize - per pie
broad cloth, per short piece
24 yar
per long piece of 32 yar
cottons of all sorts - p
100 go
Devonshire dozens per pie
Frizadoes - per pie
kerseys of all sorts, per pie
list of cloth - per 1,000 yar
northern dozens, single,
pie
double - per pie
Spanish cloth, British m
ing - per 20 yar
Penistones - per pie
Wormseed - per 100 l
Yarn; cotton yarn - per 100 l
grogram or mohair yarn,
100 l
raw linen yarn, of all s
per 100 l

All other goods, not mention
preceding table, pay, for
duties, after the rate of
pound, according as they are
or valued in his Majesty's la
rates: and all other, not
therein, shall pay the same
cording to their true value.
entry in the packer's book,
bills to each entry outward
strangers pay the labouring
making up their goods at
charge, as they have always c
they pay the water-side porte
ing to the package office, su
duties for landing and ship
goods as they have usually p
these 12 years past.

Baillage Duties Outwards. -
surveying or delivering of all
merchandise, in order to be ex
parts beyond the seas, and oth

Beer - - per
Canvass - per 120
Cloths. See Drapery.
Coals - - per chald
Cochineal. See Dyeing comm
Drapery of woollens or wors
viz. broad cloth, per p
kerseys of all sorts, per p
Perpetuanas - per p
stuffs per single p
per double p
Dyeing commodities, viz. Co
neal - per 100
indigo - per 100
wood, of all sorts, for
per 112
Fur. See Skins.
Fustians, British making, p
y
Flax or hemp - per 11
Grocery; viz. cloves, mace,
megs, or cinnamon, pe
100

	s.	d.
er or ginger, per 100 lbs.	0	2
ns - per piece or frail	0	0½
f the sun, per 112 lbs.	0	1
See Flax.		
See Dyeing commodities.		
wrought - - per ton	0	6
ght per 112 lbs.	0	1
ns - per 1,000	0	0½
per fother	0	6
See Canvass.		
See Tin.		
per lb.	0	0½
per wey	0	2
per 112 lbs.	0	2
w or thrown silk, per 16		
oz.	0	0½
d furs, viz. beaver skins		
per 100	1	6
r skins - per 100	0	6
skins, black - per 120	0	2½
ins - per 100	0	4
kins - per 100	0	8
kins - per 100	0	8
s - per timber	0	1
ins - per 120	0	6
or lamb skins, per 120	0	2
rel skins - per 1,000	0	1
See Drapery.		
wter - per 112 lbs.	0	2
per 112 lbs.	0	2
dyers. See Dyeing com-		
dities.		
all sorts per 112 lbs.	2	0
merchandise, liquid or dry, not		
rly rated in this table, pay bail-		
es outwards, with their bulk, as		
iz.		
cket or fardle, contain-	s.	d.
etween 15 and 20 cloths,		
er goods to that pro-		
n - - -	1	6
ary pack, truss, or far-		
ontaining, in bigness,		
10 to 12 cloths, 12 or		
baize, or to the like		
tion in friezes, cottons,		
er goods - -	1	0
ntaining 3 or 4 cloths,		
baize, or the like pro-		
n in other goods -	0	6
eat maund, or great		
et - - -	0	8
maund, or basket,		
hing 300 weight or un-		
- - -	0	4
r or coffer, weighing		
weight or under -	0	3
pipe - -	0	4
al or puncheon -	0	2
- - -	0	1
- - -	0	8

	s.	d.
For drum fat - -	0	4
bale - -	0	6
a great chest or great case -	0	8
small chest or case, of 3 cwt.		
or under	0	4
small box - -	0	2
great trunk - -	0	6
small trunk, not above 2 cwt.	0	3
bag or sack - -	0	4
seron - -	0	3

Portage Duties. — The packers' water-side porters' table of duties for landing strangers' goods, and of the like duties or rates to be paid unto them for shipping out their goods.

	s.	d.
For a butt of currants -	1	4
a carateel of currants -	0	8
a quarterole of currants -	0	4
a bag of currants -	0	4
pieces of raisins the ton	1	8
a barrel of raisins -	0	4
all sorts of puncheons -	0	6
a barrel of figs -	0	2
tapnets and frails of figs, ton	1	8
Brazil, or other wood for dye-		
ing - the ton	1	8
iron - the ton	1	2
copperas - the ton	1	2
oil, wine, or vinegar, the ton	1	2
hemp and flax the last	1	8
loose flax and tow, the cwt.	0	2
a great bag of tow -	0	8
a small bag of tow -	0	4
a great bag of hops -	0	8
a pocket or little bag of hops	0	4
packs, trusses, or maunds		
per piece	0	8
great chest - -	0	8
a small chest - -	0	4
all cases, barrels, or bales		
per piece	0	4
a bale of madder -	0	8
a bale of ginger or shumac,		
containing 4 cwt. -	0	8
a faggot of steel -	0	4
any serons - per piece	0	4
fat of pot ashes -	0	8
a last of soap ashes -	1	0
a last of pitch or tar	1	0
a last of fish -	1	0
wainscots - per 120	5	0
clapboards - per 120	1	8
deal boards - per 120	1	4
a great mast - -	5	0
a middle mast - -	2	6
a small mast - -	1	3
great balks - per 120	5	0
middle balks - per 120	3	4
small balks - per 120	1	3
a mill stone - -	5	0
a dog stone - -	2	6
a wolf stone - -	2	0

	s.	d.
For a yard stone - -	0	3
a grind stone - -	1	0
a step stone or grave stone -	0	8
quern stones - the last	1	0
emery stones - the ton	1	0
10 cwt. of Holland cheese -	1	2
rosin - the ton	1	2
woad - the ton	1	2
a chest of sugar -	0	6
half wainscots - per 120	2	6
raw hides - per 120	5	0
boom spars - per 120	0	6
small spars - per 120	0	4
ends of boom spars - per 120	0	9
a horse, gelding, or mare -	2	6
alum - - the ton	1	8
heath for brushes per 112 lbs.	0	1
iron pots - the dozen	0	3
rings of wire, loose, the ring	0	0½
pipe staves - per 1,000	2	6
Rhenish wine - the aum	0	6
burr stones - per 100	2	6
half packs of teazels - the		
piece	0	4
wicker bottles - the dozen	0	0½
stone pots - per 100	0	1
loose fish - per 100, landing	0	3
a barrel of salmon -	0	2
a barrel of stub eels -	0	2
a bundle of basket rods -	0	0½
a ton of cork - -	1	8
a thousand of ox bones -	1	0
a thousand tips of horns -	0	6
a thousand shank bones -	1	0
brimstone - the ton, loose	1	5
a fother of lead - -	1	2
rims of sieves - per load	1	0
a load of fans - -	1	0
a load of bull rushes -	0	4
100 reams of paper, loose	1	0
a barrel of tarras - -	0	2
a barrel of tin - -	0	2
a keg of sturgeon -	0	0½
iron backs for chimneys - per		
piece	0	1
one cwt. of elephants' teeth -	0	1
copper and iron plates - per		
piece	0	0½
100 small barrels of blacking	1	0
a dozen of scales - -	0	1
a hundred of oars - -	2	6
every 20 sugar flags -	0	4
a barrel of shot - -	0	4
a bundle of canes - -	0	1
a cage of quails - -	0	4
a cage of pheasants -	0	4
a cage of hawks - -	0	4
a winch of cable yarn -	0	4
a firkin of shot - -	0	2
All other goods not mentioned in this table pay portage duties as other goods do of like bulk or like condition herein expressed.		

CKETS. See New York, Passengers, and Post-office.

LM OIL (Ger. *Palmol;* Fr. *Huile de palme, Huile de Senegal;* It. *Olio di* Sp. *Aceite de palma*) is obtained from the fruit of several species of palms, ecially from those growing on the west coast of Africa, to the south of do Po, and in Brazil. When imported, the oil is about the consistence er, of a yellowish colour, and scarcely any particular taste: by long keeping mes rancid; loses its colour, which fades to a dirty white; and in this state e rejected. It is sometimes imitated with hog's lard, coloured with turmeric, ented with Florentine iris root. The inhabitants of the coast of Guinea palm oil for the same purposes that we do butter. — (*Lewis's Mat. Med.;* n's Dispensatory.)

st all the palm oil made use of in this country is brought from the western coast a, south of the Rio Volta.

of the Quantities of Palm Oil entered for Home Consumption in the United Kingdom, the Amount of Duty received thereon, and the Rate of Duty, each Year since 1821.

s.	Quantities entered for Home Consumption.	Amount of Duty received thereon.	Rates of Duty charged.	Years.	Quantities entered for Home Consumption.	Amount of Duty received thereon.	Rates of Duty charged.
	Cwt.	L. s. d.	Per Cwt.		Cwt.	L. s. d.	Per Cwt.
	100,059	12,289 11 6	2s. 6d.	1826	94,268	11,783 10 3	2s. 6d.
	69,857	8,429 9 8	ditto	1827	98,070	12,356 10 4	ditto
	73,666	9,045 5 1	ditto	1828	120,599	15,084 15 8	ditto
	74,614	9,373 2 0	ditto	1829	175,393	21,952 0 5	ditto
	84,996	10,632 17 4	ditto	1830	179,658	22,468 5 1	ditto

ce of palm oil (duty paid) varies from 30*l.* to 31*l.* a ton.

IPHLET, a small book, usually printed in the octavo form, and stitched. acted by 10 Ann. c. 19. § 113., that no person shall sell, or expose to sale, any pamphlet, without and place of abode of some known person, by or for whom it was printed or published, written thereon, under a penalty of 20*l.* and costs.

It is enacted by the 55 Geo. 3. c. 185., that a duty of 3s. shall be charged upon every sheet containing one copy of every pamphlet published. That a printed copy of every such pamphlet containing more one sheet shall (if within the bills of mortality in *six*, and if without them in *fourteen* days) be brought the head collector of stamps, and the duty paid thereon. If such copy be not delivered and duty the property of the pamphlet to be forfeited, and 20l. of penalty. And it is enacted, that every book taining one whole sheet, and not exceeding 8 sheets in octavo or any lesser page, or not exceedir sheets in quarto, or 20 sheets in folio, shall be deemed a pamphlet; as are all parts or numbers of book or literary work of the above dimensions.

It may be safely affirmed that no more vexatious and unproductive tax than the pamphlet duty existed. The following table shows that as a source of revenue it is utterly contemptible:—

Account of the Amount of Stamp Duties on Pamphlets during each of the last Ten Years, in Eng Scotland, and Ireland.—(*Parl. Paper*, No. 610. Sess. 1830.)

Years ended 5 Jan.	England			Years ended 5 Jan.	England			Scotland			Irelanc
	£ s. d.				£ s. d.			£ s. d.			£ s.
1821	753 13 9			1826	679 9 7			42 12 0			2 3
1822	977 16 9			1827	971 18 1			33 6 0			8 2
1823	712 8 7			1828	1,551 0 3			83 2 0			13 9
1824	757 15 7			1829	861 12 9			122 5 0			16 19
1825	1,034 2 9			1830	1,028 8 9			101 8 0			19 18

But though no source of revenue, the pamphlet duty is a very productive sourc litigation ; there being, at an average, about *fifty* prosecutions a year for the penal 20l. ! We cannot, indeed, imagine for what purpose such an absurd duty could be impc unless it were to create employment for attorneys. Its existence is a disgrace to country. The duties on paper and advertisements have effectually destroyed pampl as a source of profit. We have been assured by the first practical authorities, that more than *one* in *twenty*, perhaps not so many, of the pamphlets published, pay expenses !

PAPER (Ger. and Du. *Papier; Fr. Papier;* It. *Carta;* Sp. *Papel;* Rus. *maga;* Lat. *Charta*). This highly useful substance is, as every one knows, flexible, of different colours, but most commonly white, being used for writing printing upon, and for various other purposes. It is manufactured of veget matter reduced to a sort of pulp. The term paper is derived from the G πaπυpoς (*papyrus*, see *post*.), the leaves of a plant on which the ancients use write. Paper is made up into *sheets, quires,* and *reams;* each quire consistin 24 sheets, and each ream of 20 quires.

Historical Sketch of Paper. — Difference between Ancient and Modern Paper. I often been a subject of wonder with those learned and ingenious persons who written concerning the arts of the ancient world, that the Greeks and Romans, alth they possessed a prodigious number of books, and approached very near to printir the stamping words and letters, and similar devices, should not have fallen upon art ; the first rude attempts at typography being sufficiently obvious, though much and contrivance be necessary to bring the process to the perfection in which it now vails. They ought rather, perhaps, to have wondered that the more civilised natio antiquity did not discover paper, which must precede the invention of printing, as be easily shown. The rocks, pillars of stone or of marble, and especially the wa edifices, supply fixed surfaces, upon which, were we unprovided with more conve tablets, much valuable information might be preserved ; and were all our public many of our private buildings thickly covered with inscriptions, the memory of d historical facts, and other matters of importance, might be handed down to post Men wrote thus in very remote ages ; and the old usage is still retained in r instances, particularly in our churches and cemeteries. In very remote ages, als read that they were accustomed to write upon portable surfaces of various kinds : a it were possible to deprive us of our ordinary means of fixing and communicating thoughts, modern ingenuity would speedily invent again numerous expedients v have long been superseded ; and we should have recourse to plates of metal of va dimensions, sometimes, probably, as thin as foil ; to slices of soft, light wood, not th than those of which band-boxes are sometimes made ; to cloth, leather, and the These materials would often be primed, like the canvass of painters, that they r more readily receive, and more plainly show, the ink or paint that formed the chara It is evident that, in the course of time, large libraries might be gradually compos books constructed in this manner ; and the whole amount of human learning migh be very considerable. The substances which we have enumerated are all som costly: it would be desirable, therefore, to find one that was cheaper ; and we s doubtless direct our attention very early to that which has served the office of pa all times, and is used as such in some countries of the East at this day, — we me leaves of trees. Some of the palms, and other vegetables, that are natives of hot cou furnish the Orientals with books that are not incommodious : the leaves of the indig

f Great Britain are not so well suited for the purpose; but by care in the selec-
d skill in the preparation, some might certainly be chosen, which would, in some
be fit to receive writing. Leaves, when they are dry, are commonly apt to
the direction of the fibres : it has commonly been found expedient, therefore, to
ers at the back in an opposite direction; and by thus crossing the fibres at right
the texture is strengthened; and when it has been pressed and polished, the page
nseemly and inconvenient than might have been supposed. Such, in the main,
structure of the ancient paper. In Sicily, and in other countries on the shores
Mediterranean sea, but principally in Egypt and in the Nile, or rather in the
nd ditches that communicate with that river, grows, in the nineteenth century
death of the last of the Ptolemies, as of old under that illustrious dynasty, and
eir predecessors the Pharaohs, a lofty and most stately reed or rush, the *Cyperus*
of modern botanists. It has been introduced into the hothouses of some of
nical gardens, where it may be seen conspicuous with its long, drooping, and
plume. A description of the various purposes to which the ancients applied
ul plant would fill a volume: we shall speak of that only from which it has
n immortality of renown. The inner bark was divided with a needle into very
s; these were placed side by side longitudinally, and the edges were glued to-
similar layers were glued across these behind, at right angles, to give the page
site strength; and the sheets were pressed, dried, polished, and otherwise prepared

Ancient writers have described the process, and especially Pliny (*Hist. Nat.*
c. 11, 12, 13.). From that naturalist, and the notes of Hardouin and his other
ators, it may be fully traced; and Mr. Bruce has collected the authorities, and
d his own observations, in the 7th vol. of the 8vo edition of his Travels. That
le person even attempted to make paper from the papyrus; in which, however,
t very successful; and he imputes his failure to the erroneous directions of Pliny;
ms not to have occurred to him, that, had he endeavoured, trusting to written
s, without experience and traditional art, to make modern paper, or even a pair
he would, most probably, have been equally infelicitous. Alexandria was the
t of this valuable manufacture; but in later periods much was also made at
here an article of superior beauty was produced. Pliny enumerates the various
paper that were composed, from the coarsest, which was used, like our brown
r packing, to the most expensive and the finest. The consumption of paper
considerable; it seems to have been tolerably cheap; and since the principal
made at Alexandria, it was an important article in the commerce of that city—
g employment for many workmen and much capital. Flavius Vopiscus relates,
e third century the tyrant Firmus used to say there was so much paper there,
rge a quantity of the glue or size that was used in preparing it, that he could
an army with it — " *Tantum habuisse de chartis, ut publicè sæpe diceret, exercitum
sse papyro et glutino.*" We may doubt whether the value of the paper which
e city now contains would do the like. Learned men have discussed the anti-
his manufacture. It is not improbable that an earlier date ought to be assigned
is commonly given : nor ought we rashly to conclude that it was unknown at
lar period, because it is not mentioned in a poem of that time; for the poet
celebrate the achievements of gods and heroes, and not to compose an En-
ia, or a Dictionary of all the arts and sciences. Ancient paper was white,
urable, and well adapted in all respects for writing; but it was not suited for
r : by reason of the closeness of the grain, it would not receive the ink from
more kindly than shavings of wood, &c.; and so brittle was its texture, that
have shivered into pieces under the press. Nor did it resemble modern paper
cture; it was, in truth, an inartificial mass: leaves, or rather strips of bark
nivea virentium herbarum"), being pasted together by the edges, others were
s them behind; whereas the paper which we now use is, perhaps, the most
extraordinary of human inventions. If a cistern or other vessel be filled with
id with lime or clay, and the earth allowed to subside slowly, the water being
d, or drawn off gently, and the sediment left to dry, the calcareous or argilla-
osit will represent faithfully the formation of paper; and it will be smooth,
equal thickness throughout; for an equal portion of the earth of which it
was suspended in the troubled water over each point in the bottom where
odged. In making paper, the water is turbid with the pulp or paste of tri-
gs, and the suspended pulp is not suffered to subside slowly; but a sieve or
wire gauze is dipped equally into the cistern, and is raised gently to the surface,
ed in a level position, which facilitates the passage of the water through the
le the fibres of rag are in some degree interwoven by it, and remaining on
e of the sieve form the sheet of paper. This is pressed between felts, to
e water, and to render its texture closer; it is dried and sized, and undergoes

various operations, which it is unnecessary to enumerate, as we seek only to
that the result of this wonderful invention is as much an aqueous deposit
earthy sediment at the bottom of a cistern, although it is obtained more ra
Modern paper has nothing in common with the ancient, save that vegetable
is the basis of both.   The application of rotary motion has effected wonders in
of the arts; nor have the results been less astonishing in the paper-mill: inst
dipping the sieves or frames into the cistern of turbid water, a circular web, a
towel of woven wire, revolves under the vessel, receives the deposit, conv
away, and, by an adjustment of marvellous delicacy, transfers it uninjured, alt
as frail as a wet cobweb, to a similar revolving towel of felt; thus an endles
of paper is spun, as long as the machine continues to move, and the water cl
with pulp is supplied.   We are unable to pursue the process, however intere
for we desire merely to explain the general principle according to which our
is constructed.   It is to this admirable material that we owe the invention of pri
which could not subsist without it: its pervious and spongy texture imbibes and
the ink, and its toughness resists the most violent pressure; and, in a well-bound
under favourable circumstances, its duration is indefinite, and, for all practical pu
eternal!   It is true that legal documents are sometimes printed on parchment, w
less liable to be torn, or injured by rubbing, and the luxury of typography occasi
exhibits a few impressions of a splendid work upon vellum, and that these two subs
were known to the ancients: but they are necessarily expensive, and the cost of
far exceeds the price of the best penmanship; so that it would be altogether unpro
to cast types, to construct presses, and to incur the various and heavy charges
establishment for printing, unless we possessed a cheaper material.

We owe the introduction of paper into Europe to the Arabians or Moors.   Th
some uncertainty as to the precise era of its first appearance; and we are unable to
the origin of the precious invention, or even to imagine by what steps men were
it.   We cannot conceive how any one could be tempted to pound wet rags in a n
to stir the paste into a large body of water, to receive the deposit upon a sieve, to
and to dry it.   The labour of beating rags into pulp by the hand would be as ho
as it would be tedious and severe.   It is true that paper was originally made of cot
a substance less obstinate than linen rags, which are now commonly used.   At p
the fresh rags are torn in pieces by a powerful mill: formerly it was the prac
suffer them to rot; to place them in large heaps in a warm and damp situation,
allow them to heat and ferment, and to remain undisturbed until mushrooms be
grow upon them; so that, being partially decayed, it might be less difficult to tr
them.   Nevertheless the invention of paper is a mystery.   The Chinese possess t
of making paper and of printing; but we know not how long they have had the
whether the Mohammedans learned the former from them.   The illiterate inhal
of some of the islands in the South Seas were able to compose a species of paper,
they used in fine weather for raiment, of the bark of trees.   The basis of paper
the vegetable fibre, it has been made of various substances, as straw, as well as of

Manufacture of Paper in England.   The application of paper to the purpo
writing and printing, and the fact of its being indispensable to the prosecution
latter, render its manufacture of the highest utility and importance.   But, e
a commercial point of view, its value is very considerable.   France, Hollan
Genoa had, for a lengthened period, a decided superiority in this department.
finest and best paper being made of linen rags, its quality may be supposed to d
in a considerable degree, on the sort of linen usually worn in the country whe
manufactured; and this circumstance is said to account for the greater whiteness
Dutch and Belgian papers, as compared with those of the French and Italia
still more the Germans.   The rags used in the manufacture of writing paper in
Britain are collected at home; but those used in the manufacture of the best p
paper are imported, principally from Italy and Hamburgh. —(See Rags.)   We
however, that it was owing rather to the want of skill than, as has sometimes be
posed, to the inferior quality of the linen of this country, that the manufacture o
was not carried on with much success in England, till a comparatively recent
During the 17th century, most part of our supply was imported from the Cor
especially from France.   The manufacture is said to have been considerably impr
the French refugees who fled to this country in 1685.   But it is distinctly stated i
British Merchant" (vol. ii. p. 266.), that hardly any sort of paper, except brow
made here previously to the Revolution.   In 1690, however, the manufacture o
paper was attempted; and within a few years most branches were much improve

---

* We are indebted for this valuable historical sketch to our learned friend, T. J. Hogg, Esq.,
at law.   The reader may resort, for further information as to the history of paper, to the articl
Rees's Cyclopædia.

it is supposed that there were about 300,000 reams of paper annually produced in Britain, which was equal to about two thirds of the whole consumption. In 1783, due of the paper annually manufactured was estimated at 780,000l. At present, s making a sufficient quantity of most sorts of paper for our own use, we an export about 100,000l. worth of books. We still, however, continue to import n descriptions of paper for engraving from France, and a small supply of paper ngs. The duty on both amounts to about 2,800l. a year.

1813, Dr. Colquhoun estimated the value of paper annually produced in Great n at 2,000,000l. : but Mr. Stevenson, an incomparably better authority upon ubjects, estimates it at only half this sum. From information obtained from those ed in the trade, we incline to think that the total annual value of the paper ma ure in the United Kingdom, exclusive of the duty, may at present amount to 1,100,000l. or 1,200,000l. There are about 700 paper mills in England, and 70 to 80 in Scotland. The number in Ireland is but inconsiderable. But of mills, we believe there have been lately from a third to a fourth part unemployed. : 25,000 individuals are supposed to be directly engaged in the trade : and, s the workmen employed in the mills, the paper manufacture creates a con ble demand for the labour of millwrights, machinists, smiths, carpenters, iron rass founders, wire-workers, woollen manufacturers, and others, in the machinery paratus of the mills. Some parts of these are very powerful, and subject to strain; and other parts are complicated and delicate, and require continual tion. Owing to this, the manufacture is of much greater importance, as a source ployment, than might at first be supposed, or than it would seem to be considered ernment, who have loaded it with an excise duty amounting to more than *three* s much as the total wages of the work-people employed!

ring the present century, so remarkable for improvements in the arts, this ma ure has been signally promoted, notwithstanding the excise regulations, by the tion of machinery to the conversion of pulp into paper. The first idea of this ted in France: a model of the machinery was brought to this country by a dot, which, though very far from giving assurance of success, was yet sufficient uce English capitalists and engineers, particularly Mr. Donkin, to follow up eme ; and in the course of a few years they have brought it to a high degree fection. Mr. Dickinson, one of the most intelligent mechanists and extensive nanufacturers in England, has invented a machine of a different construction same purpose, and has also introduced various subsidiary improvements into nufacture. — The result is all but miraculous. — By the agency of a great deal plicated machinery, so admirably contrived as to produce the intended effect with g precision and in the very best manner, a process, which in the old system of naking occupied about *three* weeks, is performed in as many minutes! A con s stream of fluid pulp is, within this brief space of time, and the short distance of , not only made into paper, but actually dried, polished, and every separate sheet nd the edges, and rendered completely ready for use! The paper manufactured wonderful combination of intelligence and power is, at once, moderate in price, most purposes superior in quality to that which was formerly made by hand. mple before the reader, though not the finest that is made, will warrant what stated.

on Paper — Excise Regulations. It is difficult to say whether the duty on or the regulations under which that duty is collected, be the more objectionable. iting, coloured, or wrapping paper, card-boards, and pasteboards, are deno 1st class paper, and pay 3d. per lb. duty (28s. a cwt.); unless *manufactured f tarred ropes, without the tar being previously extracted*, in which case the paper minated 2d class, and pays 1½d. per lb. (14s. a cwt.). Mill-boards and scale made of the same materials as 2d class paper, pay 2¼d. per lb. (21s. a cwt.) duty. luty on the various descriptions of 1st class paper varies from about 25 or 30 per the finest, to about 200 per cent. on the coarsest! A duty so oppressive has led to mission of very great frauds, which all the vigilance of the officers, and the endless cation of checks and penalties, have been unable to prevent; the real effect of serable devices being to injure the honest manufacturer, and to give those of a : character greater facilities for carrying on their fraudulent schemes. But ut of view for a moment the oppressiveness of the duty, can any thing be more rously absurd, than to interdict the manufacturer of wrapping paper (for it is to : the regulation applies) from using any other material than *tarred ropes!* If ust be a duty on paper, let it be assessed upon the finished article on an *ad* principle; but do not let the plans and combinations of the manufacturer be d with. Were it not for the existing regulation, wrapping paper of equal and better appearance than v hat is now manufactured, might be made of much

less costly materials. Since the peace, and the very general introduction of iron cat
tarred ropes have advanced considerably in price; but as the use of *any other mate*
whatever would occasion an increase of 14*s.* a cwt. of duty, advantage cannot be ta
of this circumstance; so that the excise regulation, without putting one sixpence into
pockets of government, obliges the public to pay an increased price for an infe
article! Neither is this its only effect: a good deal of the refuse thrown out in sort
rags, which might be used in the manufacture of coarse wrapping paper, is at pres
sold by the manufacturers for about 3*s.* a cwt.; while a good deal that might be use
the same way cannot be sold at all, but is absolutely lost. It is plain, therefore,
this regulation has a twofold operation: first, in adding to the cost of wrapping paper
compelling it to be made from a comparatively expensive article; and secondly, in add
to the expense of fine paper, by preventing the refuse of the rags used in its manufact
from being beneficially employed.

The other regulations in the excise acts (34 Geo. 3. c. 20. and 42 Geo. 3. c. 94.
to paper, are of a piece with that now brought under the reader's notice. Every s
of the manufacture must be conducted under the *surveillance* of the excise; and
provisions as to entries, folding, weighing, sorting, labelling, removing, &c. are not o
exceedingly numerous, but are in the last degree vexatious, at the same time that c
pliance with them is enforced under ruinous penalties. That this is not an exaggera
statement will be obvious from the following extracts from the statements of ma
facturers, given in Mr. Poulett Thomson's admirable speech on the taxation of
empire, 26th of March, 1830.

"We are bound," says a manufacturer on whose accuracy and honour I (Mr. P. Thomson) can
"to give 24 or 48 hours' notice (according to the distance the exciseman lives), before we can change
paper, and to keep it in our mills for 24 hours afterwards before we send it to market, unless it has
re-weighed by the supervisor; to have the different rooms in our manufactories lettered; to have
engines, vats, chests, and presses numbered; and labels pasted on each ream: should we lose one
the penalty is 200*l.* I generally write a request for 500 labels to the excise at one time; and should
person get into my mill, and steal or destroy them, the penalty would be 100,000*l.* I believe there i
any kind of paper pays more than 20*s.* per ream duty. If the penalty were 40*s.*, it would be quite
ficient to answer every purpose for the security of the revenue. We are obliged, also, to take out a y
licence; and a mill with 1 vat pays as much as one that has 10."

Another says, " It is no slight aggravation of the evil, that the laws are so scattered and confused
render it almost impossible for any body to have a knowledge of them; and frequently what is a grea
noyance to an honest man, is no check to a rogue. It is true the excise laws are seldom, or per
never, acted upon to their utmost rigour; but still they confer almost unlimited power, on those who
the administering of them, over the property of all who come under their influence; and I am persu
that they never could have existed, if they had affected the whole of the community."

It is singular that nothing should hitherto have been done to amend regulation
justly complained of. In point of fact, they are good for nothing but the oppressio
the trade. It has not been shown that their maintenance is indispensable to enabl
duty to be assessed and collected; but if such be the case, it is, of itself, a suffic
ground for the repeal of the duty. Our condition is not, fortunately, such as to rec
that one of the most important manufactures carried on in the empire should be
jected to a system of oppressive regulations for the sake of 700,000*l.* a year.

But, though it were possible to assess and collect the duty so as to pre
fraud, without interfering with the manufacture, we should very much doubt,
sidering the purposes to which paper is applied, the policy of subjecting it to
duty whatever. Printers, stationers, bookbinders, type-founders, artists, copper
and lithographic printers, card-makers, paper-stainers, and paper-hangers, &c.
all injured by the duty on paper. But the greatest evil of all is its influence i
creasing the price, and hindering the publication, of books. " This places a
obstacle in the way of the progress of knowledge, of useful and necessary arts, a
sober, industrious habits. Books carry the productions of the human mind ove
whole world, and may be truly called the raw materials of every kind of science an
and of all social improvement." — (See the admirable work of *Sir H. Parnell* or
nancial Reform, 3d ed. p. 30.)

At all events, the existing duties, varying as they do from 30 to 200 per cent. *a*
lorem, are quite exorbitant; nor can there be a doubt that they would be more pro
tive, were they adequately reduced, and assessed on reasonable principles. But, as we
shown in the art. Books, it is not possible to lay a duty on the paper intended to be
in printing, without committing injustice. No one can foretell, with any thing appr
ing to certainty, whether a new book, or even a new edition of an old book, will sell
the fact is, that *one third* of the books, and *nineteen twentieths* of the pamphlets publi
do not pay their expenses. Now, we ask whether, under such circumstances, any
can be more obviously unjust, more utterly subversive of every fair principle, tha
imposition of the same heavy taxes upon *all* publications, — upon those that do no
as well as upon those that do? Upon a successful work, the duty may only be a re
able deduction from the profits of the author and publisher; but when (as i
case with 1 out of 3 books, and 19 out of 20 pamphlets) the work does not sell,

…rofits from which to defray the duty, which has, of course, to be paid entirely …e capital of the author or publisher! Such is the encouragement given to lite-…such the facilities afforded to the diffusion of useful information, by the popular …ient of England! All other businesses meet with very different treatment. …in gin or brandy, for example, may lodge their goods in bonded warehouses, …not obliged to pay any duty upon them until they are sold for home consump-…it such privilege is denied to the bookseller, though the article in which he deals …usand times more capricious. He must pay the duty on the whole impression …book, before bringing a single copy of it to market; so that he not unfrequently …ty upon 1,000 volumes, though unable to sell above 150 or 200, except as waste …Even this is not the whole injury done him: for upon an advertisement an-…g the sale of a sixpenny pamphlet, as heavy a duty is charged as if it announced …of an estate worth 100,000l.!

…are but two ways of putting an end to this scandalous injustice; viz. either by …repealing the paper duty, or by putting publishers under the *surveillance* of the …nd assessing the duty on works according to the number sold at the publication …The former would be the simpler method; but if the state of the finances will …v of the sacrifice of the paper duty, there are no insuperable difficulties in the …he latter alternative. And were it adopted, and the duties reduced and sim-…*ustice* would be done to authors and publishers, and a very great stimulus given …per manufacture, without any loss of revenue.

…t of the Quantities of Paper charged with Duty in England, Scotland, and Ireland, in 1829.

…ies of Paper.	England.	Scotland.	Ireland.	Total.
…ass	38,619,721 lbs.	6,085,995 lbs.	1,501,462 lbs.	46,207,178 lbs.
…Class	11,555,311 —	1,079,800 —	577,734 —	13,212,845 —
…rds, &c.	25,895 cwt.	4,185 cwt.	254 cwt.	30,234 cwt.

…ss revenue collected during the same year, in Great Britain and Ireland, amounted to …s. 9¾d.; the drawbacks payable upon paper exported, and the expense of collection, amounted …s. 1d.; leaving 681,197l. 15s. 8¾d. of nett revenue.

…CEL, a term indifferently applied to small packages of wares, and to large …oods. In this latter sense, 20 hogsheads of sugar or more, if bought at one …in a single lot, are denominated " a parcel of sugar."

…CELS, BILL OF, an account of the items making a parcel.

…CHMENT (Ger. *Pergament;* Fr. *Parchemin;* It. *Cartapecora;* Sp. *Per-*…the skin of sheep or goats prepared in such a manner as to render it …r writing upon, covering books, &c. It is an important article in French …e: besides being largely exported, the home consumption is very con-…The name is derived from Pergamus, the city where it is said to have …manufactured.

…IAL LOSS. See INSURANCE (MARINE).

…NERSHIP, the association of two or more individuals for carrying on …incss or undertaking in common; each deriving a certain share of the …nd bearing a corresponding share of the loss arising therefrom.

…rm partnership is usually applied to those smaller associations in which the …personally conduct their joint affairs: the term company being applied to …it associations conducted by directors and servants appointed by the body of …ers to act for them; the latter having no direct concern in the management of …of the company. — (See COMPANIES.)

…vantages of partnerships are obvious. — Many businesses could not be success-…ied on without a larger command of capital than usually belongs to an indi-…nd most of them require the combination of various species of talent. An in-…nay have capital sufficient to undertake a particular business; but he may not …ghly versed in any of its details, or he may be familiar with certain parts of it …ith others; so that it might be for his advantage to assume one or more indi-…his partners, supposing them to be without capital, provided they possessed …nd other qualifications required in prosecuting the business. Associations of …enable capital and talent to derive all the assistance that each is capable of …the other. And as the gains of each partner usually consist of a certain …of the total profits made by the company, each has the most powerful motive …imself for the benefit of the concern. It is not, indeed, to be denied, that …s of this sort are occasionally productive of mischievous consequences. The …erest requires that the whole partners in a firm should be bound by the acts of …f their number; so that the folly or fraud of a single partner may entail very …nsequences upon those associated with him. Generally, however, this is not

an evil of frequent occurrence; and there can be no question that, both in a priva
public point of view, partnerships are highly beneficial.

To enter into any thing like a full discussion of the law of partnership woul
far exceed our limits. We shall, therefore, merely state a few of those leading
ciples with respect to it, as to which it is of importance that mercantile men, ar
public generally, should be well acquainted.

Formation of Partnerships. — The mere consent of the partners fixed and certifi
acts or contracts, is quite sufficient to constitute a private copartnership; so t
two or more merchants, or other persons, join together in trade, or in any s
business, with a mutual, though it may be unequal, participation in the profit an
of the concern, they are in every respect to be considered as partners. No part
form of words or proceeding is necessary to constitute a partnership. It may b
tered into either by an express written agreement, or by a merely verbal one.
former ought in almost all cases to be preferred. The contract of copartnery s
state the parties to it, the business to be carried on, the space of time the partn
is to continue, the capital each is to bring into the business, the proportion in
the profit and loss are to be divided, the manner in which the business is to be cond
the mode agreed upon for settling accounts at the dissolution of the partnership, to,
with the special covenants adapted to the circumstances of each particular case.

To constitute a partnership, there must be a participation in uncertain profi
losses. And the true criterion to determine, when money is advanced to a t
whether the lender is to be looked upon as a partner or not, is to ascertain wheth
*premium or profit be certain and defined, or casual, indefinite, and depending up
accidents of trade.* In the former case it is a loan; in the latter it is a partne
The mere participation in the profits of any business or adventure, without a p
pation in the losses, constitutes a partnership, so far as to render the individual s
ticipating liable to third parties for the engagements of the concern, though as be
the parties themselves it may be no partnership. Thus, if a clerk or other s
stipulate for a share of the profits of any business as *a reward for his labour*, he be
responsible to third parties as a partner, and no private arrangement can cancel h
bility.

If an individual, by his own act or inadvertence, allow himself *to appear to the
as a partner*, he is precluded from disputing the fact, even though he have no inte
the profits. A partner who withdraws from a firm is liable on account of the rem
partners continuing his name in the firm, though without his consent, unless he ta
necessary precautions (see *post.*) to show that he has ceased to belong to it.

If there be no express stipulation as to the management of partnership proper
majority decide as to the disposition and management of the joint affairs of the
or, if there be but two parties in a firm, one may manage the concern as he thi
provided it be within the rules of good faith, and warranted by the circumstances
case. The general duty of a partner is to keep in view at all times, and in all
actions, the interest and welfare of the partnership, by acting honestly and upright
as a prudent man would conduct his own affairs.

Liability of Partners as to third Parties. — It may be laid down as a general rul
partners, whether actual, ostensible, or dormant, are bound by the act of their p
made in the course of and with reference to the partnership business, and in the r
course of dealing by the firm; and though the general rule of law be, that no
liable upon any contract, except such are privy to it, yet this is not contravened
liability of partners, as they are supposed virtually present at and sanctioning th
ceedings they singly enter into in the course of trade, or as being each vested
power enabling them to act at once as principals and as the authorised agent c
copartners. It is for the advantage of partners that they are thus held liable;
credit of their firm is in consequence greatly enhanced, and facility is given to al
dealings, even when they reside in different parts of the country, or of the worl
due regard to the interest of strangers is at the same time observed; for wh
individual deals with one of several partners, he relies upon the credit of the
firm, and therefore ought to have his remedy against the whole individuals wh
pose it.

Unless, however, the act of one partner relate to and be connected with the p
ship trade, and in the *course of dealing by the firm*, such acting partner only
bound; for it is only by acting in the course of their particular trade or line of b
that an implied authority is delegated by partners to each other; and it is only
transactions that third parties have a right to rely upon the partnership funds.
a partnership, credit must be given to the firm itself, and not to one only of its p
One of them may even, in furtherance of the objects of the firm, enter into a c
with some third party; but if such contract be made *exclusively and solely upon t*

individual partner, it will only bind him, and not the firm. The presumption, of w, however, always is, that a contract with one of the partners in reference to the ess of the firm has been entered into upon the credit of the whole ; and this pre-ion is not to be rebutted except by very clear evidence. One partner cannot, as except in bankruptcy, bind another by *deed*.

e authority of a partner is revocable ; and it is now fully established, that a *dis-r* of the authority of the partners in any particular transaction will preclude him binding his copartners. Even during the subsistence of the partnership, one er may to a certain degree limit his responsibility ; and if there be any particular ation or bargain proposed, which he disapproves of, he may, by giving distinct to those with whom his partners are about to contract that he will not be con-t in it, relieve himself from all consequences. Such notice would rebut his *primâ* ability. The partnership would be suspended *quoad* this transaction. Thus, if ner draw, accept, or endorse a bill or note, he will, in all ordinary cases, thereby the firm liable. But, to use the words of Lord Ellenborough, " it is not essential artnership that every partner should have such power ; they may stipulate among lves that it shall not be done ; and if a third party *having notice of this* will take ecurity from one of the partners, he shall not sue the others upon it, in breach of ipulation, nor in defiance of notice previously given to him by one of them, that not be liable for any bill or note signed by the others," — (*Galway* v. *Matthew,* t, 264.) ; and so in other cases.

wever small the share a partner may have in a concern, he is liable for the *whole* of ots contracted by the firm ; and must seek his remedy in a rateable contribution his partners. Should one party enter into a smuggling or other illegal transaction partnership account, the other partners are liable to the duties and the penalty ; e crown may proceed against the real delinquent alone, or against all the partners. seller, or newspaper proprietor, is answerable for the acts of his agent or co-, not only civilly, but also *criminally*.

olution of Partnerships. — A partnership may be dissolved by the effluxion or ex-of the time during which it was originally agreed that it should continue. When tnership is formed for a single dealing or transaction, the moment that is com-it is at an end. Partnerships may also be dissolved by death, agreement, bank-outlawry, &c. A court of equity will interfere to dissolve a partnership, in cases a partner so misconducts himself as to be injurious to the firm, or to defeat the or which the partnership was formed ; or when a partner becomes insane, or is in state of mind as to render him permanently incapable of transacting the peculiar s of the firm ; or where a partnership is formed for an impracticable purpose. , in all cases, where even a partnership may be dissolved without the interference art of equity, it may be most prudent, if the dissolution be opposed by one of the s, to file a bill, praying a dissolution and account, and an injunction against using tnership name.

n a partnership is dissolved by agreement, or one of the partners withdraws from ic notice of the dissolution must be given in the London Gazette ; and *a specific inti-of the circumstance must be sent to* ALL *individuals accustomed to deal with the firm.* such intimation has not been sent, the individual withdrawing from the firm may e liable to third parties after he has ceased to have any thing to do with it. A t partner, whose name has never been announced, may withdraw from a firm with-ing the dissolution of partnership publicly known.

n the joint debts of the firm are paid, and the property duly distributed among ners, the dissolution may be said, in a general sense, to be accomplished. If any the firm be guilty of a breach of duty, in misapplying the effects before the con-finally wound up, the proper course is to apply to the Court of Chancery to a manager.

in a reasonable time after the death of one partner, the survivors must account epresentatives of the deceased ; and if not willing to do so, a court of equity will them. In taking partnership accounts at the death of a partner, they must com-vith the last stated account ; or, if there be none such, with the commencement artnership ; and they must end with the state of the stock at the time of the s death, and the proceeds thereof until it be got in.

otice is necessary to third parties of the death of a partner ; the partnership is dis-nd all liabilities for subsequent acts cease. The surviving parties are to be sued r the partnership liabilities and obligations, for which they are liable to the full But they are not liable for the separate debts of the deceased partner, unless, ment of all the joint debts, they have a surplus of the partnership effects in their

a dissolution by death, if the joint effects be insufficient to pay the partnership

debts, the separate estate of the deceased partner, if he have any, is liable for the ficiency.

The statements now made will probably be sufficient to give our readers a toler distinct notion of the formation of partnerships; and of the more important rights, du liabilities, &c. arising out of such institutions. Those who wish to go deeper inte subject, may consult the treatises of Watson and Montague on the Law of Part ship; Chitty's Commercial Law, vol. iii. pp. 225—269.; Woolrych on Commercial pp. 298—317. &c.

PASSENGERS, in commercial navigation, are individuals conveyed for from one place to another on board ship. Passage ships are those pecul appropriated to the conveyance of passengers.

Regulations as to the Conveyance of Passengers. — The conveyance of passengers between Britain and Ireland is regulated by the act 4 Geo. 4. c. 88., which provides, that no vessel employ the conveyance of passengers, of less than 200 tons burthen, shall carry more than 20 persons a sengers, unless a licence to that effect has been obtained from the Custom-house. A licensed ve not to take, exclusive of the crew, more than 5 adult persons, or 10 children under 14, or 15 ch under 7 years of age, for every 4 tons burthen; and if such vessels be partly laden with goods or v not to take more than the above proportion of passengers for every 4 tons that remain unladen. Pe for carrying more than *twenty* without licence, 50*l.*; and for a licensed vessel carrying more tha above proportion for each 4 tons burthen, 5*l.* for each passenger. Merchant vessels of not more tha tons not to carry more than 10 persons, or of not more than 200 tons not more than 20 persons, ur penalty of 5*l.* each person.

The conveyance of passengers to North America is regulated by the 9 Geo. 4. c. 21. This act pro that no ship shall sail from the United Kingdom for any port or place in his Majesty's possessions continent or islands of North America, with more than *three* persons on board for every 4 tons registered burthen of such ship, the master and crew being included; and no ship to carry passer unless of the height of 5½ feet, at least, between decks: 2 children under 14, or 3 under 9, or 1 under 12 months with its mother, to be reckoned as one person. Good and wholesome provisions provided, at the rate of 50 gallons of pure water for every person on board, and 50 lbs. of bread, bi oatmeal, or bread-stuffs, for every passenger. Ships that have their full complement of passenge prohibited from carrying any part of their cargo or stores between decks. Before clearing out the n is to deliver to the collector a list of the passengers, specifying as accurately as may be their n ages, professions or occupations, and the name of the port or place at which each is contracted landed. Masters of ships compelling passengers to land at any other place than that agreed upon forfeit to every such passenger so landed a sum of 20*l.* Masters who take a greater number of passe than allowed by law, or do not provide the requisite quantity of water and provisions, or stow an any part of the cargo between decks, or furnish false lists to the collector, shall be deemed guilt misdemeanor. A bond for 1,000*l.*, with one good and sufficient surety, shall be given by the mas every ship clearing out for British North America with passengers on board, that such ship is seaw and that all and every the rules and regulations of this act will be well and truly performed. Such may be without a stamp. This act does not extend to Post-office ships, nor to the Bahama island to the West Indies.

It is enacted by the 9 Geo. 4. c. 47., that the master of any packet or vessel employed in carryir sengers from one part of the United Kingdom to another is to be licensed by the commissioners of to retail foreign wine, strong beer, cider, perry, spirituous liquors, and tobacco. Such licence annually renewed, and to be transferable by endorsement. Duty to be paid by the owners on obt such a licence, 1*l.* Penalty for selling wines, &c. without a licence, for every offence 10*l.*

It is enacted by 9 Geo. 4. c. 76., that every *steam vessel* which is of the registered tonnage of 1 shall be deemed to be a vessel of 200 tons at least.

The act 6 Geo. 4. c. 116., which regulated the conveyance of passengers to foreign parts, was re by 7 & 8 Geo. 4. c. 19.

In some respects passengers may be considered as a portion of the crew. They be called on by the master or commander of the ship, in case of imminent d either from tempest or enemies, to lend their assistance for the general safety; and i event of their declining, may be punished for disobedience. This principle has bee cognised in several cases; but as the authority arises out of the necessity of the it must be exercised strictly within the limits of that necessity. — (*Boyce* v. *Ba* 1 Campbell, 58.) A passenger is not, however, bound to remain on board the sl the hour of danger, but may quit it if he have an opportunity; and he is not requi take upon himself any responsibility as to the *conduct* of the ship. If he incu responsibility, and perform extraordinary services in relieving a vessel in distress, entitled to a corresponding reward. The goods of passengers contribute to ge average. — (*Abbott on the Law of Shipping*, part iii. c. 10.)

Return of the Number of Persons who have emigrated from the United Kingdom to any of the Co of Great Britain, in each Year since 1820; distinguishing the Colonies to which they have emig — (*Parl. Paper*, No. 650. Sess. 1830.)

Years.	British North American Colonies.	British West Indies.	Cape of Good Hope.	New South Wales, Van Diemen's Land, and Swan River.	Total.
	No. of Persons.	No. of Persons.	No. of Persons.	No. of Persons.	No. of Persons.
1821	12,470	1,772	404	320	14,966
1822	11,282	1,423	192	875	13,772
1823	8,133	1,911	184	543	10,771
1824	7,311	1,353	119	780	9,563
1825	8,741	1,082	114	485	10,422
1826	12,818	1,913	116	903	15,750
1827	12,648	1,156	114	715	14,633
1828	12,084	1,211	135	1,056	14,486
1829	13,907	1,251	197	2,016	17,371

egoing statement, founded upon special returns transmitted from the various ports of the United
by the local officers of customs, exhibits the number of persons of both sexes, and of all ages,
emigrated to the Colonies in each of the last ten years, so far as the same can be ascertained.
rs report that they have not the means of distinguishing males from females, or adults from
in these returns; and in some cases they state that the distinction cannot be drawn with accu-
een emigrants and passengers of other descriptions.
regulations as to the landing of passengers in New-York, see NEW-YORK.

ENT, a privilege from the crown granted by letters patent (whence the
conveying to the individual or individuals specified therein, the sole right
, use, or dispose of, some new invention or discovery, for a certain specified

er to grant patents seems to exist at common law; but it is limited and defined by the famous
Jac. 1. c. 3., which enacts, "That any declaration before-mentioned shall not extend to any
ent and grants of privilege for the term of 14 years or under, thereafter to be made, of the sole
r making of any manner of new manufactures within this realm, to the *true and first* inventor
tors of such manufactures, which others at the time of making such letters patent and grants
ase, so as also they be not contrary to the law, nor mischievous to the state, by raising prices of
es at home, or hurt of trade, or generally inconvenient. The said 14 years to be accounted from
f the first letters patent, or grant of such privilege thereafter to be made; but that the same
such force as they should be, if that act had never been made, and none other."

of Patents. — The law with respect to patents is unavoidably incumbered with
lifficulties. The expediency of granting patents has been disputed; though, as
l seem, without any sufficient reason. Were they refused, the inducement to
scoveries would, in many cases, be very much weakened; at the same time that
plainly be for the interest of every one who made a discovery, to endeavour,
e, to conceal it. And notwithstanding the difficulties in the way of conceal-
y are not insuperable; and it is believed that several important inventions have
, from the secret dying with their authors. On the other hand, it is not easy
as to the term for which the patent, or exclusive privilege, should be granted.
ve proposed that it should be made perpetual; but this would be a very great
to the progress of improvement, and would lead to the most pernicious results.
the term of 14 years, to which the duration of a patent is limited in England,
er a one as could be suggested. It may be too short for some inventions, and
for others; but, on the whole, it seems a pretty fair average.

:ation. — Previously to the reign of Queen Anne, it was customary to grant
ithout any condition, except that they should be for really new inventions. But
on was then introduced into all patents, and is still retained, declaring that if
tor do not, by an instrument under his hand and seal, denominated a specifi-
irticularly describe and ascertain the nature of his invention, and in what manner
is to be performed, and also cause the same to be enrolled in Chancery within
time (generally a month), the letters patent, and all liberties and advantages
thereby granted, shall utterly cease and become void. This was a very ju-
gulation. It secures the invention from being lost; and the moment the patent
very one is in a situation to profit by it.

f granting a Patent. — Letters patent are obtained upon petition and affidavit
wn, setting forth that the petitioner has, after great labour and expense, made
discovery, which he describes, and which he believes will be of great public
ıd that he is the first inventor. The petition is referred to the attorney or
general, who is separately attended by the applicant and all competitors, if
ny. They explain their projects to him, and he decides on granting or with-
he patent. When the inventions of two or more conflicting applicants
he rejects all the applications. It would seem that to decide upon such diffi-
ions in mechanics as are often agitated in applications for patents, a familiar
e of the principles and practical application of mechanical science would be
ible. But in the law, as it now stands, such knowledge is not deemed neces-
e legal officers of the crown are the sole judges as to what patents should
not be granted; their award is *final;* and they are subject to no responsibility,
ı the common remedies against public officers by impeachment, indictment,
ne of which would be entertained, unless a corrupt motive were established.
roval by the law officers, the grant is made out, sealed, and enrolled.
ring the authority under which patents are granted, can any one wonder at
r that have been overturned in the courts of justice? or at the litigation to
have given rise?

: of Patents. — Separate patents have to be taken out for England, Scot-
Ireland, if it be intended to secure the privilege in the three kingdoms.
se of stamps, fees, &c. is in all cases very heavy. It varies according to the
f the invention, the opposition (if any) to the patent being granted, &c. Ac-
Mr. Farey, it may be estimated at 120*l.* for England, 100*l.* for Scotland, and
Ireland. — (See his very valuable evidence in the *Commons' Report on*
17.),

3 G

Conditions as to Patents. — The *novelty* and *utility* of the invention are essential
validity of a patent ; if it can be shown to have been in use previously to the gr
the patent, or to be of no utility, it will be void. It must also be for something vend
something " material and useful made by the hands of man." — (*Lord Kenyon,*
R. 99.) A philosophical principle only, neither organised, nor capable of being
no ground for a patent ; because it is an element and rudiment of science, and
till applied to some new production from these elements, cannot, with justice to
inventors, be applied to the exclusive use of any one of them. In all patents th
required, in the words of Lord Tenterden, " something of a *corporeal or substantial n*
something that *can be made* by man from the matters subjected to his art and skill.
the least some *new mode of employing practically his art and skill.*" — (*Godson on th*
of Patents, p. 81.) Previously to Lord Tenterden, it had been ruled that a new p
or method was not the subject of a patent. But his Lordship having suggested that
word manufacture (in the statute) may, perhaps, extend to a *new process* to be c
on by known implements, or elements acting upon known substances, and ultim
producing some other known substance, &c." — (*Godson,* p. 83.) — this principle
terpretation has now been adopted.

A patent for a machine, each part of which was in use before, but in which the
bination of the different parts is *new,* and a *new result* is obtained, is valid. But, in
to its being valid, the specification must clearly express that it is in respect of suc
combination or application, and of that only ; and not lay claim to original invent
the use of the materials.

A patent may be granted for an addition to an old invention. But the patent
be *confined to the addition* or improvement, that the public may purchase it without
incumbered with other things. If the patent include the whole, it will be void ;
property in the addition or improvement can give no right to the thing that has
improved. — (*Godson,* p. 71.)

A valid patent may be obtained for an invention " *new in this realm,*" though
have been previously practised in a foreign country.

A patent is void, if it be for several distinct inventions, and *any one of them*
originality.

The specification must be prepared with *great care.* It should set forth the inv
fully and correctly. The terms used must be clear and unambiguous ; no necessa
scription must be omitted, nor what is unnecessary be introduced ; and the inv
must be described in the *best and most improved state* known to the inventor.
one of these conditions be not complied with, the patent will be void. Any inac
or defective statement, *were it even inserted through inadvertency,* will vitiate the

Caveat. — It is not unusual for inventors who have not brought their inventi
perfection, and who are afraid lest they be anticipated by others, to lodge a caveat
offices of the attorney and solicitor general ; that is, an instrument by which no
requested to be given to the person who enters it, whenever any application is ma
a patent for a certain invention therein described in general terms. The ent
caveat is, therefore, nothing more than giving information that an invention is
completed ; so that if any other person should apply for a patent for the same thi
preference may be given to him who entered it.

An injunction may be obtained for the infringement of a patent, in the same
for a violation of the copyright acts.

Patents have been sometimes extended by act of parliament beyond the term
years, on the ground that that term was too short properly to reward the inventor

Account of the Number of Patents granted in the Eight Years ending with

1821	-	108	1824	-	181	1827	-	1
1822	-	113	1825	-	249	1828	-	1
1823	-	138	1826	-	131			

Total number of patents in force in May, 1829, 1,855.

The reader will find a great deal of curious and instructive information with
to patents, in the Report of the Committee of the House of Commons on that
(No. 332. Sess. 1829), particularly in the evidence and papers laid before the com
by Mr. Farey. The treatise on the Law of Patents and Copyrights, by Mr.
is clear and able.

PATRAS, or PETRASSO, a sea-port in the north-west corner of the
at the entrance of the Gulf of Lepanto, in lat. 38° 33′ N., lon. 21° 43′ E.
lation variously estimated, from 5,000 to 10,000. Patras has a more ex
trade than any other port in Greece. The principal exports are cu
fustic (young), cotton, oil, valonia, &c. The currants are of a very superi
lity. The fruit is larger, and freer from sand and gravel, than that of the

ds. They are shipped in various sized casks; and as these casks are always
led in the weight of the fruit, they are made of heavier wood and stronger
necessary. Morea currants are preferred in most countries except England;
ere the currants of Zante have the preference. Large quantities of fustic are
ed from Patras. The cotton of the Morea, and of the Levant generally, is
inferior; but it is, notwithstanding, always in demand. Valonia is a consider-
article of export. In addition to the above, dried fruits of various kinds,
ds, small nuts, galls, and a variety of drugs, may be had at Patras, and other
of the Morea. The imports consist principally of cottons and woollens, iron
ardware, fish, coffee, sugar, &c.

nies, Weights, and Measures. — Accounts are kept in piastres of 80 aspers. The
sh coins are current here; for which, see CONSTANTINOPLE.
e quintal is divided into 44 okes, or 132 lbs. Hence, 100 lbs. of Patras = 88 lbs.
upois. Silk weight is ⅛ heavier.
ack of currants weighs 140 lbs. of the common weight, or about 123 lbs. avoirdu-

staro corn measure = 2⅛ Winch. bushels.
long pic, or pik, used in measuring linens and woollens, = 27 English inches.
ort pic, used in measuring silks, = 25 ditto.

TTERNS, are specimens or samples of commodities, transmitted by manu-
ers to their correspondents, or carried from town to town by travellers, in
of orders. Patterns, if not exceeding 1 ounce weight, shall be charged
only an additional penny of postage, provided they be sent under cover,
at the sides, and without any letter or writing, except the name of the person
g the same, the place of his abode, and the price of the article or articles.
Geo. 3. c. 88.)

WNBROKERS AND PAWNBROKING. A pawnbroker is a species
ker, who advances money, at a certain rate of interest, upon security of
deposited in his hands; having power to sell the goods, if the principal
nd the interest thereon, be not paid within a specified time.

dvantages and Disadvantages of Pawnbroking. — The practice of impledging or
g goods, in order to raise loans, is one that must necessarily always exist in
d societies, and is, in many cases, productive of advantage to the parties. But
ractice that is extremely liable to abuse. By far the largest proportion of the
e borrowers of money on pawn consist of the lowest and most indigent classes;
re the lenders not subjected to any species of regulation, advantage might be
as, indeed, it is frequently (in, in despite of every precaution,) of their neces-
subject them to the most grievous extortion. But, besides those whose wants
them to resort to pawnbrokers, there is another class, who have recourse to them
r to get rid of the property they have unlawfully acquired. Not only, therefore,
nbrokers instrumental in relieving the pressing and urgent necessities of the
ut they may also, even without intending it, become the most efficient allies of
and swindlers, by affording them ready and convenient outlets for the disposal
ill-gotten gains. The policy of giving legislative protection to a business so
abuse, has been doubted by many. But though it were suppressed by law, it
always really exist. An individual possessed of property which he may neither
nor willing to dispose of, may be reduced to a state of extreme difficulty; and in
ase, what can be more convenient or advantageous for him than to get a loan
deposit of such property, under condition that if he repay the loan, and the in-
on it, within a certain period, the property will be returned? It is said, indeed,
facilities of raising money in this way foster habits of imprudence; that the
ort for aid to a pawnbroker almost always leads to a second; and that it is im-
so to regulate the business as to prevent the ignorant and the necessitous from
undered. That this statement, though exaggerated, is to a certain extent true,
an deny. On the other hand, however, the capacity of obtaining supplies on
of goods, by affording the means of meeting pressing exigencies, in so far tends
nt crime, and to promote the security of property; and it would seem as if the
redeem property in pawn would be one of the most powerful motives to in-
nd economy. At the same time, too, it must be borne in mind, that it is not
do what you will, to prevent those who are poor and uninstructed from borrow-
l that they must, in all cases, obtain loans at a great sacrifice, and be liable to
sed upon. But the fair presumption is, that there is less chance of any improper
ge being taken of them by a licensed pawnbroker, than by a private and irrespon-
ividual. Although, however, the business had all the inconveniences, without

any portion whatever of the good which really belongs to it, it would be to no pur
to attempt its suppression. It is visionary to imagine that those who have property
submit to be reduced to the extremity of want, without endeavouring to raise money u
it. Any attempt to put down pawnbroking would merely drive respectable per
from the trade, and throw it entirely into the hands of those who have neither prop
nor character to lose. And hence the object of a wise legislature ought not to b
abolish what must always exist, but to endeavour, so far at least as is possible, to fr
from abuse, by enacting such regulations as may appear to be best calculated to pro
the ignorant and the unwary from becoming the prey of swindlers, and to facilitate
discovery of stolen property.

2. *Obligations under which Pawnbrokers should be placed.* — For this purpose it se
indispensable that the interest charged by pawnbrokers should be limited; that
should be obliged to give a receipt for the articles pledged, and to retain them f
reasonable time before selling them; that the sale, when it does take place, should b
public auction, or in such a way as may give the articles the best chance for being
at a fair price; and that the excess of price, if there be any, after deducting the amc
advanced, and the interest and expenses of sale, should be paid over to the original ow
of the goods. To prevent pawnbrokers from becoming the receivers of stolen go
they should be liable to penalties for making advances to any individual unable to
a satisfactory account of the mode in which he became possessed of the property b
desirous to pawn; the officers of police should at all times have free access to their
mises; and they should be obliged carefully to describe and advertise the property
offer for sale.

3. *Law as to Pawnbrokers.* — It may appear singular that pawnbrokers should ha
have been named in any legislative enactment till after the middle of last century.
was enacted by the 30 Geo. 2. c. 24., that a *duplicate* or receipt should be given
goods pawned; and that such as were pawned for any sum less than 10*l.* might be
covered any time within *two* years, on payment of the principal and interest; but
rate of interest was not fixed. This defect was supplied by the 25 Geo. 3. c.
but the act 39 & 40 Geo. 3. c. 99. contains the latest and most complete regulat
on the subject.

Every person exercising the trade of a pawnbroker must take out a licence, renewable annuall
days at least before the end of the year, for which he shall pay, within the cities of London and V
minster, and the limits of the twopenny post, 15*l.*, and everywhere else 7*l.* 10*s.* No person shall
more than one house by virtue of one licence; but persons in partnership need only take out one li
for one house, All persons receiving goods by way of pawn or pledge for the repayment of money
thereon, at a higher rate of interest than 5 per cent., to be deemed pawnbrokers.

Upon every pledge on which there shall have been lent not exceeding 2*s.* 6*d.*, interest may be cha
at the rate of ½*d.* per month,

£ s. d.		£ s. d.		£ s. d.		£ s. d.	
If 0 5 0	.	0 0 1 per month.		If 0 17 6	-	0 0 3½ per month.	
0 7 6	-	0 0 1½	—	1 0 0	-	0 0 4	—
0 10 0	-	0 0 2	—	2 0 0 and not exceeding			
0 12 6	-	0 0 2½	—	2 2 0	-	0 0 8	—
0 15 0	-	0 0 3	—				

And for every sum exceeding 40*s.* and not exceeding 10*l.*, at the rate 3*d.* in the pound, by the cal
month, including the current month; and so in proportion for any fractional sum.

Pawnbrokers are to give farthings in exchange.

Persons applying to redeem goods pawned within 7 days after the first calendar month aft
same shall have been pledged, may redeem the same without paying any thing for the first 7 days
upon applying before the expiration of 14 days of the second calendar month, shall be at liberty to r
such goods, upon paying the profit payable for one calendar month and the half of another; and
cases where the parties so entitled, and applying as aforesaid, after the expiration of the first 14 day
before the expiration of the second month, the pawnbroker is allowed to take the interest of the
second month; and the same regulations and restrictions shall take place in every subsequent mon

When goods are pawned for more than 5*s.*, the pawnbroker, before advancing the money, shall
diately enter in his books a description of the pawn, the money lent thereon, the day of the mon
year, the name of the person pawning, and the name of the street, and number of the house, if num
where such person resides, and use the letter L, if the person be a lodger, and the letters H K
housekeeper; and also the name and abode of the owner of the party offering such pledge; and
money lent shall not exceed 5*s.* such entry shall be made within four hours after the goods shal
been pawned; and the pawnbroker shall, at the time of taking the pawn, give to the person so pa
a duplicate, corresponding with the entry in the book, which the party pawning shall take in all
and the pawnbroker shall not receive any pledge, unless the party so pawning shall receive
duplicate.

Rates payable for Duplicates.

	£ s. d.			£ s. d.
If under 5*s.*	- - gratis		If 20*s.* and under 5*l.*	- 0 0 2
5*s.* and under 10*s.*	0 0 0½		And upwards -	- 0 0 4
1(*s.* and under 20*s.*	0 0 1			

The duplicate to be produced to the pawnbroker before he shall be compelled to re-deliver the res
goods and chattels, except as herein-after excepted.

The amount of profits on duplicates shall be added on pledges redeemed, and such duplicate sh
kept by the pawnbroker for one year.

Persons pawning other people's goods without their consent, may be apprehended by the war
one justice, and convicted in a penalty not exceeding 5*l.* nor less than 20*s.* and the full value of the
pawned; and if the forfeiture be not immediately paid, the justice shall commit the party to the h
correction, to be kept to hard labour for 3 calendar months; and if within 3 days before the expir
the commitment the forfeiture shall not be paid, the justice may order the person to be publicly w

rfeitures shall be applied towards making satisfaction to the party injured, and defraying the
t if the party injured shall decline to accept such satisfaction and costs, or if there be any over-
forfeitures or overplus shall be paid to the poor of the parish.
forging or counterfeiting duplicates may be seized and delivered to a constable, who shall con-
before a justice; and, upon conviction, such person shall be committed to the house of correction
me not exceeding 3 calendar months.
offering pledges, not giving a satisfactory account of themselves, or the means by which they
ossessed of such goods, or wilfully giving any false information, or if there shall be reason to
at such goods are stolen, or illegally obtained, or if any person not entitled to redeem goods in
l endeavour to redeem the same, they may be seized and delivered to a constable, to be carried
ustice; and if there should appear ground for a second examination, they shall be committed to
on gaol or house of correction, to be dealt with according to law; or where such proceedings
uthorised by the nature of the offence, the party shall be committed for any time not exceeding
months.
buying or taking in pledge unfinished goods, linen, or apparel, intrusted to others to wash or
ll forfeit double the sum lent, and restore the goods.
fficers are empowered to search for unfinished goods which shall be come by unlawfully.
goods are unlawfully pawned, the pawnbroker is to restore them; and their houses may be
during the hours of business, by a warrant from a magistrate, for the discovery of such

producing notes or memorandums are to be deemed the owners of the property.
duplicates are lost, the pawnbroker, upon affidavit made by the owner of such loss before a
, shall deliver another duplicate.
awned are deemed forfeited at the end of a year; but, on notice from persons having goods in
nonths further are to be allowed beyond the year for redemption; such notice to be given
twelvemonth is expired.
ds pawned may be sold at the expiration of *one* whole year; and all goods so forfeited, on which
and not exceeding 10*l.* shall have been lent, shall be sold by public auction, and not otherwise;
uch sale being twice given, at least 3 days before the auction, in a public newspaper, upon pain
ng to the owner of the goods not more than 5*l.* nor less than 2*l.*
ures, prints, books, bronzes, statues, busts, carvings in ivory and marble, cameos, intaglios,
aathematical, and philosophical instruments, and china, shall be sold by themselves, and with-
goods, four times only in every year; viz. on the first *Monday* in *January, April, July,* and
every year.
okers are not to purchase goods while in their custody, nor take in pledges from persons under
of age, or intoxicated; nor take in any goods before 8 in the forenoon or after 8 in the
tween *Michaelmas-day* and *Lady-day,* or before 7 in the forenoon or after 9 in the evening
remainder of the year, excepting only until 11 on the evenings of *Saturday,* and the evenings
Good Friday and *Christmas-day* and every fast or thanksgiving day.
unt of the sale of pledges for more than 10*s.* is to be entered by pawnbrokers in a book, and the
o be paid to the owner of the goods pawned, if demanded within *three years* of the sale, under
10*l.* and treble the sum lent.
okers are to place in view the table of profits; and their name and business is to be placed over
n penalty of 10*l.*
okers injuring goods, or selling them before the time specified, shall, upon application to a
, be compelled to make satisfaction for the same; and if the satisfaction awarded shall be equal
d the principal and profit, the pawnbroker shall deliver the goods pledged to the owner, with-
baid any thing for principal or profit.
okers shall produce their books before a magistrate; or, refusing so to do, shall forfeit a sum
ing 10*l.* nor less than 5*l.*
kers offending against this act, shall forfeit for every offence not less than 40*s.* nor more

een held by the court of King's Bench, that a pawnbroker has no right to sell unredeemed
ter the expiration of a year from the time the goods were pledged, if, while they are in his
the original owner tender him the principal and interest due.—(*Walter* v. *Smith,* 22d January,
a motion for a new trial, Lord Tenterden said, "I am of opinion, that if the pledge be not
t the expiration of a year and a day, (and no notice given that 3 months further are to be
its redemption,) the pawnbroker has a right to expose it to sale so soon as he can consistently
rovisions of the act; but if at any time *before the sale has actually taken place,* the owner of
ender the principal and interest, and expenses incurred, he has a right to his goods, and the
r is not injured; for the power of sale is allowed him merely to secure to him the money which
anced, together with the high rate of interest which the law allows to him in his character of
r."

the present state of the law with respect to pawnbrokers. On the whole, the
as seem to be judiciously devised. Perhaps, however, the rate of interest on
osits might be advantageously lowered. The law allows interest at the rate of
aonth to be charged on loans of 2*s.* 6*d.,* which is at the rate of 20 per cent.:
ame sum of ½*d.* per month is exigible from all smaller loans; and as very
aot exceed 1*s.* 6*d.,* and even 6*d.,* the interest on them is exceedingly oppressive.
there is a great deal of trouble with respect to such loans; but still, consider-
ast number of advances under 2*s.* 6*d.,* it would seem that the interest on them
somewhat reduced. Perhaps, too, it might be advisable, still better to
mpliance with the provision of the statute, to enact that no one should be
s a pawnbroker without producing sufficient security for a certain sum to be
n the event of his knowingly or wilfully breaking or evading any of the pro-
the statute. This would prevent (what Dr. Colquhoun says is not an
n practice) swindlers from becoming pawnbrokers, in order to get the means
stolen goods. — (*Treatise on the Police of the Metropolis,* 2d ed. p. 156.)
d be a useful regulation to oblige pawnbrokers to insure against losses by fire.
chief has been occasioned by the neglect of this precaution.

An Account of the Number of Pawnbrokers Licensed in the Metropolis, and in the Country, w
Rates respectively charged on their Licences, and the Duty received on the same, in each of th
Years ending 5th January, 1830. — (*Parl. Paper*, No. 681. Sess. 1830.)

Years ending		Taken out at the Head Office, London.			Taken out in the Country.		
		Rate of Duty.	Number.	Duty.	Rate of Duty.	Number.	Duty.
		£ s.		£ s.	£ s.		£ s.
5th January -	1826	15 0	261	3,915 0	15 0 }	- -	7,040 0
		7 10	8	60 0	7 10 }		
—	1827	15 0	267	4,005 0	15 0 }	- -	7,223 0
		7 10	5	37 10	7 10 }		
—	1828	15 0	274	4,110 0	15 0 }	- -	7,904 10
		7 10	7	52 10	7 10 }		
—	1829	15 0	411	6,165 0	15 0	16	240 0
		7 10	6	75 0	7 10	1,596	11,970 0
—	1830	15 0	295	4,425 0	15 0	47	705 0
		7 10	7	52 10	7 10	1,038	7,785 0

The produce of each rate of duty not being distinguished in the distributors' accounts u
year ending 5th January, 1829, the number of licences cannot be given prior to that date
country.

4. *Notices of Pawnbroking in Italy, France, &c.* — The practice of advancing
to the poor, either with or without interest, seems to have been occasionally follo
antiquity. — (*Beckmann*, vol. iii. p. 14. 1st Eng. ed.) But the first public est
ments of this sort were founded in Italy, under the name of *Monti di Pietà*,
fourteenth and fifteenth centuries. As it was soon found to be impossible t
cure the means of supporting such establishments from voluntary contributi
bull for allowing interest to be charged upon the loans made to the poc
issued by Leo X. in 1521. These establishments, though differing in many re
have universally for their object, to protect the needy from the risk of being
dered by the irresponsible individuals to whom their necessities might oblige th
resort, by accommodating them with loans on comparatively reasonable terms.
though their practice has not, in all instances, corresponded with the profession
have made, there seems no reason to doubt that they have been, speaking genera
essential service to the poor.

From Italy these establishments have gradually spread over the Continent.
Mont de Piété, in Paris, was established by a royal ordinance in 1777; and afte
destroyed by the Revolution, was again opened in 1797. In 1804, it obtained a mo
of the business of pawnbroking in the capital. Loans are made, by this establis
upon deposit of such goods as can be preserved, to the amount of *two thirds*
estimated value of all goods other than gold and silver, and to *four fifths* of the v
the latter. No loan is for less than 3 francs (*2s. 6d.*). The advances are mac
year, but the borrower may renew the engagement. Interest is fixed at the rate
per cent. per month.

The *Mont de Piété* receives annually about 1,200,000 articles, upon which it a
from 20,000,000 to 21,000,000 francs; it has generally from 600,000 to 6
articles in its possession. The expense of management amounts to from 60
centimes for each article; so that a loan of 3 francs never defrays the expe
occasions, and the profits are wholly derived from those that exceed 5 francs.
average, the profits amount to about 280,000 francs, of which only about 155,
derived from loans upon deposit, about 125,000 being the produce of other fund
disposal of the company.

The articles in pawn are returned in the proportion of $\frac{18}{23}$ in number and $\frac{17}{23}$ in
Are continued in pawn by a prolongation of the loan - $\frac{3}{22}$ - - $\frac{5}{23}$

Hence are preserved to their proprietors, of articles }
pawned - - - - - } $\frac{21}{22}$ in number and $\frac{22}{23}$ in
Are sold, subject (as in England) to a claim for surplus }
any time during 3 years - - } $\frac{1}{22}$ - - $\frac{1}{23}$

$\frac{22}{22}$ - - $\frac{23}{23}$

(*Bulletin des Sciences Géographiques*, Avril, 1

There are no means of making a statement of this sort with respect to Londo
were it possible to make it, the proportion of forfeited pledges would be found,
no doubt, much greater.

In some respects, particularly the lowness of interest upon small loans,
greater vigilance exercised with respect to the reception of stolen goods, the
Piété has an advantage over the pawnbroking establishments in this country.
be doubted, however, whether it is, on the whole, so well fitted to attain its obje

tion of the loans to 3 francs would be felt to be a serious grievance here, and it
ardly be otherwise in France; nor is it to be supposed, that the servants of a great
: establishment will be so ready to assist poor persons, having none but inferior
s to offer in security, as private individuals anxious to get business.   And such,
nt of fact, is found to be the case, not in Paris only, but in all those parts of the
ent where the business of pawnbroking is confined to a few establishments.   And
it would seem that, were the modifications already suggested adopted, our system
l be the best of any.

ARL-ASH.   See POTASH.

ARLS (Du. *Paarlen;* Fr. *Perles;* Ger. *Perlen;* It. *Perle;* Lat. *Margaritæ;*
 Shemtschug, Perlü; Sp. *Perlas;* Arab. *Looloo;* Cyng. *Mootoo;* Hind.
 e), are well known globular concretions found in several species of shell
but particularly the mother of pearl oyster (*Concha margaritifera,* Lin.).
s should be chosen round, of a bright translucent silvery whiteness, free from
and roughness.   Having these qualities, the largest are of course the most
 le.   The larger ones have frequently the shape of a pear; and when these
 :herwise perfect, they are in great demand for ear-rings.   Ceylon pearls are
 esteemed in England.

ue, &c. of Pearls. — Pearls were in the highest possible estimation in ancient Rome,
re an enormous price.   (*Principium culmenque omnium rerum pretii, margaritæ*
— Plin. Hist. Nat., lib. ix. c. 35.)   Their price in modern times has very much
d; partly, no doubt, from changes of manners and fashions; but more, probably,
he admirable imitations of pearls that may be obtained at a very low price.   Ac-
g to Mr. Milburn, a handsome necklace of Ceylon pearls, smaller than a large
osts from 170*l.* to 300*l.*; but one of pearls about the size of peppercorns may be
' 15*l.*: the pearls in the former sell at a guinea each, and those in the latter at
s. 6*d.*   When the pearls dwindle to the size of small shot, they are denominated
arls, and are of little value.   They are mostly sent to China.   One of the most
able pearls of which we have any authentic account was bought by Tavernier, at
in Arabia, a fishery famous in the days of Pliny, for the enormous sum of
0*l.*!   It is pear-shaped, regular, and without blemish.   The diameter is ·63 inch
argest part, and the length from 2 to 3 inches.

h difference of opinion has existed among naturalists with respect to the produc-
pearls in the oyster; but it seems now to be generally believed that it is the result
se, and is formed in the same manner as bezoar — (see BEZOAR); pearls, like it,
ng of successive coats spread with perfect regularity round a foreign *nucleus.*   In
ie Chinese throw into a species of shell fish (*mytilus cygneus,* or swan muscle),
' opens, 5 or 6 very minute mother of pearl beads strung on a thread; and in the
of a year they are found covered with a pearly crust, which perfectly resembles
pearl. — (*Milburn's Orient. Com.; Ainslie's Mat. Indica,* &c.)

Fisheries. — The pearl oyster is fished in various parts of the world, particularly on the west
:eylon; at Tuticoreen, in the province of Tinnevelly, on the coast of Coromandel; at the Bahreen
in the Gulf of Persia; at the Sooloo Islands; off the coast of Algiers; off St. Margarita, or Pearl
1 the West Indies, and other places on the coast of Colombia; and in the bay of Panama, in the
a.   Pearls have sometimes been found on the Scotch coast, and in various other places.
earl fishery of Tuticoreen is monopolised by the East India Company, and that of Ceylon by
ent.   But these monopolies are of no value; as in neither case does the sum for which the fishery
al the expenses incurred in guarding, surveying, and managing the banks.   It is, therefore, suf-
obvious that this system ought to be abolished, and every one allowed to fish on paying a moderate
ity.   The fear of exhausting the banks is quite ludicrous.   The fishery would be abandoned as
ble long before the breed of oysters had been injuriously diminished; and in a few years it would
ductive as ever.   Besides giving fresh life to the fishery, the abolition of the monopoly would put
' some very oppressive regulations, enacted by the Dutch more than a century ago.
hery at the Bahreen Islands is the most productive in the world.   The annual produce is seldom
s than 60,000 Bussorah tomands (90,000*l.*), and often much more.   It generally commences in
1 lasts about 2 months.   It is principally carried on by Persians, and the divers are all Persians.
may engage in the fishery; the government being paid a certain proportion of the produce as a
is is an incomparably better plan than that followed at Ceylon.
hery at Algiers was farmed by an English association in 1826, but we are ignorant of their

arl fisheries on the coast of Colombia were at one time of very great value.   In 1587, upwards of
pearls are said to have been imported into Seville.   Philip II. had one from St. Margarita, which
250 carats, and was valued at 150,000 dollars.   But for many years past the Colombian pearl
have been of comparatively little importance.   During the mania for joint stock companies, in
were formed; — one, on a large scale, for prosecuting the pearl fishery on the coast of Colombia;
er on a smaller scale, for prosecuting it in the bay of Panama and the Pacific.   Both were aban-
1826.
st fishery ground is said to be in from 6 to 8 fathoms water.   The divers continue under water
nute to a minute and a half, or at most two minutes.   They have a sack or bag fastened to
in which they bring up the oysters.   The exertion is extremely violent; and the divers are un-
nd short lived.

. SHELLS, commonly called *mother of pearl shells,* are imported from the East
and consist principally of the shells of the pearl oyster from the gulf of Persia

and other places; but the shells of other species of oyster are also in considerable
mation.   On the inside, the shell is beautifully polished, and of the whiteness and w
of pearl itself: it has the same lustre on the outside, after the external laminæ have l
removed.   Mother of pearl shells are extensively used in the arts, particularly in ir
work, and in the manufacture of handles for knives, buttons, toys, snuff boxes,
The Chinese manufacture them into beads, fish, counters, spoons, &c. ; giving the
finish to which European artists have not been able to attain.   Shells for the Euro|
market should be chosen of the largest size, of a beautiful pearly lustre, thick and e
and free from stains.   Reject such as are small, cracked or broken, or have lump
them.   When stowed loose as dunnage, they are sometimes allowed to pass fre
freight.   The quantity imported during the three years ending with 1828, amounte
an average, to 289,834 lbs. a year. — (*Milburn's Orient. Com.*, &c.)

PEAS (Ger. *Erbsen;* Fr. *Pois;* It. *Piselli, Bisi;* Sp. *Pesoles, Guisantes;* l
Goroch).   The pea is the most esteemed legume in field cultivation.   It is
well known to require any description in this place.   The varieties are
merous, and new ones may be easily procured.   It is very extensively
tivated in Kent, and to a considerable extent over the whole country.—(Fo|
account of the laws regulating the importation, &c. of peas, see CORN L
AND CORN TRADE.)

PECK, a dry measure for grain, pulse, &c.   The standard, or imperial p|
contains 2 gallons, or 554·55 cubic inches.   Four pecks make a bushel, ar
bushels a coomb. — (See WEIGHTS AND MEASURES.)

PELLITORY, the root of a perennial plant (*Anthemis pyrethrum*), a nativ
the Levant, Barbary, and the south of Europe.   The root is long, tapering, al
the thickness of the finger, with a brownish cuticle.   It is imported packe|
bales, sometimes mixed with other roots, from which, however, it is e|
distinguished.   It is inodorous.   When chewed, it seems at first to be insipid,
after a few seconds it excites a glowing heat, and a pricking sensation on
tongue and lips which remains for 10 or 12 minutes.   The pieces break w|
short resinous fracture; the transverse section presenting a thick brown l
studded with black shining points, and a pale yellow radiated inside.   It is
in medicine as a stimulant. — (*Thomson's Dispensatory.*)   The price varies,
cluding the duty (6*d.*), from 2*s.* to 2*s.* 6*d.* per lb.

PENCILS (Ger. *Pinsel;* Du. *Pinseelen;* Fr. *Pinceaux;* It. *Pennelli;* Sp.
celes), the instruments used by painters in laying on their colours.   They a|
various kinds, and made of various materials; some being formed of the bri|
of the boar, and others of camel's hair, the down of swans, &c.

PENCILS, BLACK LEAD.   See BLACK LEAD PENCILS.

PENKNIVES (Ger. *Federmesser;* Fr. *Canifs;* It. *Temperini;* Sp. *Corta
mas*), small knives, too well known to need any particular description, use
making and mending pens.   The best and most highly ornamented penknive
manufactured at London and Sheffield.

PENNY, formerly a silver, but now a copper, coin.   This was the first s
coin struck in England by our Saxon ancestors, being the 240th part of
pound; so' that its weight was about 22½ grains Troy.

PENS (Fr. *Plumes à écrire;* Ger. *Schreibfedern;* It. *Penne da scrivere;*
Pera Stwoli), well known instruments for writing, usually formed of the qui|
the goose, swan, or some other bird.   Sometimes, however, they are ma|
gold, silver, and steel.   The latter are occasionally contrived so as to cont
considerable quantity of ink, which they allow to flow out by slow degree
that the writer saves the time lost in dipping his pen in the inkstand.

PENNYWEIGHT, a Troy weight, being the 20th part of an ounce, conta
24 grains.

PEPPER (Fr. *Poivre;* Ger. *Pfeffer;* Du. *Peper;* It. *Pepe;* Sp. *Pimienta;*
Perez; Lat. *Piper*), the berry or fruit of different species of plants having an
matic, extremely hot, pungent taste, used in seasoning, &c.   The following
of pepper are met with in commerce: —

I. BLACK PEPPER (Fr. *Poivre;* Ger. *Schwarzen pfeffer;* It. *Pepe negro*,
Pimienta; Hind. *Gol-mirch;* Malay, *Lada;* Jav. *Mariha*), the fruit of a
(*Piper nigrum*) cultivated extensively in India, and the Eastern islands.
quires the support of other trees, to which it readily adheres.   It climbs t
height of 20 feet; but is said to bear best when restrained to the height of 12

s to produce at about the third year, and is in perfection at the seventh;
es in this state for 3 or 4 years; and declines for about as many more,
ceases to be worth keeping. The fruit grows abundantly from all the
s, in long small clusters of from 20 to 50 grains; when ripe, it is of a bright
ʝur. After being gathered, it is spread on mats in the sun, when it loses
colour, and becomes black and shrivelled as we see it. The grains are
ed from the stalks by hand rubbing. That which has been gathered at the
period shrivels the least; but if plucked too soon, it will become broken
sty in its removal from place to place. The vine produces two crops in
r; but the seasons are subject to great irregularities.

er should be chosen of a pungent aromatic odour, an extremely hot and
ste, in large grains, firm, sound, and with few wrinkles — for of these it
has some. Reject that which is shrivelled, or small grained, or which on
bbed will break to pieces.

int of quality the pepper of Malabar is usually reckoned the best; but there
aterial difference between it and that of Sumatra, and the other islands. In
ket of Bengal, where they meet on equal terms, the produce of Malabar is
y about 2 per cent. higher than the other. In Europe, there is generally
nce of 0½d. per lb. in favour of Malabar; but in China they are held in
timation.

pepper sold ground, is said to be often adulterated with burnt crust of

HITE PEPPER is of two sorts, common and genuine: the former is made
hing the grains of the common black pepper, by steeping them for a while
, and then gently rubbing them, so as to remove the dark outer coat. It
than the other, and is much prized by the Chinese; but very little is im-
nto England. Genuine white pepper is merely the blighted or imperfect
icked from among the heaps of black pepper. It is, of course, very

AYENNE PEPPER is the produce of several varieties of the *capsicum*,
al plant, a native of both the Indies. The best, which is brought home
West Indies ready prepared, is made from the *capsicum baccatum* (bird
It has an aromatic, extremely pungent, acrimonious taste, setting the
it were on fire, and the impression remaining long on the palate. It is
es adulterated with muriate of soda; and sometimes with a very dele-
ubstance, the red oxide of lead; but this fraud may be detected by its
nd by chemical tests.

ONG PEPPER. This species does not differ much, except in shape, from
non or black pepper. It is the produce of a perennial, a native of Ma-
Bengal. The fruit is hottest in its immature state; and is therefore ga-
hile green, and dried in the sun. It is imported in entire spikes, which
t 1½ inch long. It has a weak aromatic odour, an intensely fiery pungent
d a dark grey colour. The root of long pepper is a favourite medicine
e Hindoos.

antities of the last three species of pepper imported are quite inconsi-
compared with the quantity of black pepper. — (*Milburn's Orient. Com.*;
Mat. Indica; *Thomson's Dispensatory*, &c.)

in Pepper. — *Consumption of, and Duties on, in England.* — Pepper is exten-
d, all over Europe and the East, as a condiment. It was originally imported
ountry by way of the Levant (see *antè*, p. 482.); and for many years after the
ent of the East India Company, it formed the most important article of their
In nothing has the beneficial effect of opening the Indian trade been so
ally displayed as in the instance of pepper. The private traders have resorted
arkets, and discovered new sources of supply which had hitherto been wholly
d; so that there has been not only a very great increase in the quantity of
ught to Europe, but also a very great fall in its price, which does not now
hird of what it amounted to in 1814!
antities in the following table are taken from p. 186. of the *Parliamentary*
. 22. Sess. 1830; and the prices from Mr. Cook's valuable tract on the *Com-*
Great Britain in 1830.

Account of the Total Quantity of Pepper imported from the East Indies into Great Britain, with i in Bond in London, each Year, from 1814 to 1830, both inclusive.

Years.	Pepper.	Prices.	Years.	Pepper.	Prices.
	Lbs.	*Per lb.*		*Lbs.*	*Per lb.*
1814	5,762,649	11*d.* to 13*d.*	1823	5,955,326	5*d.* to 6½*d.*
1815	12,719,858	9½ — 9¾	1824	8,801,634	5½ — 6
1816	11,985,014	7 — 7½	1825	5,396,217	4⅞ — 5⅝
1817	4,087,062	8 — 8½	1826	13,103,416	4 — 4½
1818	6,134,721	7¼ — 7¾	1827	9,067,766	3¼ — 3¾
1819	5,390,643	6⅛ — 6¼	1828	4,978,102	3¼ — 3⅞
1820	787,947	6⅝ — 6¾	1829	- - -	2⅞ — 3½
1821	845,100	7¼ — 7½	1830	- - -	2¾ — 4
1822	7,211,376	5 — 6¼			

Pepper is one of the most grossly over-taxed articles in the British tariff. Unti the duty was 2*s.* 6*d.* per lb. — a duty so exorbitant, that one would be inclined to it had been imposed in order to put a total stop to the use of the article. In 18 duty on pepper from a British possession was reduced to 1*s.* per lb.; but even this as compared with the price of the article (2¾*d.* to 4*d.* per lb.), is quite eno amounting to no less than from 420 to 300 per cent.! It will be seen from th joined table that the reduction of the duty, in 1823, has increased the consumptio about 1,400,000 lbs. to 1,940,000 lbs. a year; and were the duty reduced, as it ou be, to 2*d.*, or at most 3*d.* per lb., so that pepper might become accessible to the classes, to whom its free use would be of infinite importance, we have not the sl doubt that in a very short period the consumption would amount to 5,000,0 6,000,000 lbs. There would either be no loss of revenue by such a measure, o worth mentioning; and it is not to be endured that the bulk of the people sho deprived of so useful a commodity, and the trade of the country seriously inju keeping up oppressive duties, which serve no purpose whatever, unless it be to keep a remembrance of the ignorance and rapacity of those by whom they were imposed have already shown (see *antè*, p. 504.) the difficulties under which the dealers in labour, in consequence of the absurd regulations as to the warehousing of comm from India.

Account of the Quantity of all Sorts of Pepper retained for Home Consumption in the United K the Rates of Duty thereon, and the Total Revenue derived from the same, in each Year since (*Parl. Paper*, No. 604. Sess. 1830.)

Years.	Quantities retained for Home Consumption.	Nett Amount of Duty received thereon.			Rates of Duty charged thereon. Common Pepper. East India.	Cayenne Pepper. East India.	Cayenne Pepper. Other.	Long Pepper.
	Lbs.	£	*s.*	*d.*			*Per lb.*	*Per lb.*
1810	1,117,982	88,293	8	4	1*s.* 8*d.* per lb., and 2*l.* 13*s.* 4*d.* per cent. *ad valorem.*	4*s.* per lb., and 2*l.* 13*s.* 4*d.* per cent. *ad valorem.*	4*s.*	8*d.*
1811	1,132,086	90,547	1	6	ditto	ditto	ditto	ditto
1812	1,183,489	101,209	10	6	ditto	ditto	ditto	ditto
1813	Records destroyed.				From Ap. 15. 1*s.* 11¾*d.* per lb., and 3*l.* 3*s.* 4*d.* per cent. *ad valorem.*	4*s.* 9*d.* per lb., and 3*l.* 3*s.* 4*d.* per cent. *ad valorem.*	4*s.* 9*d.*	9½*d.*
1814	941,569	95,668	4	10	From 10th April, 1*s.* 10½*d.* per lb.	5*s.* per lb.	ditto	10*d.*
1815	1,099,423	103,025	11	10	ditto	ditto	ditto	ditto
1816	1,065,702½	99,390	19	1	ditto	ditto	ditto	ditto
1817	1,218,750¾	113,887	6	7	ditto	ditto	ditto	ditto
1818	1,457,383	125,093	15	6	ditto	ditto	ditto	ditto
1819	1,302,027	119,271	7	1	From 5th July, 2*s.* 6*d.* per lb.	2*s.* 6*d.* per lb.	2*s.* 6*d.*	2*s.*
1820	1,404,021¼	174,063	2	9	ditto	ditto	ditto	ditto
1821	1,256,532¼	156,208	2	3	ditto	ditto	ditto	ditto
1822	1,446,400½	179,586	11	4	ditto	ditto	ditto	ditto
1823	1,368,983	170,627	6	8	From 10th October, 2*s.* 6*d.* per lb. on all sorts.			
1824	1,447,030½	180,816	3	5	ditto			
1825	850,087¼	106,221	15	0	ditto			
1826	2,529,027	126,517	4	8	From 5th January, 1*s.* per lb. if from British possessions.			
1827	1,949,931½	97,496	5	11	ditto			
1828	1,927,718½	96,467	12	5	ditto			
1829	1,933,641	96,725	19	2	ditto			

Supply of Pepper. — The following instructive details with respect to the supply of pepper from the Singapore Chronicle. We believe they were contributed by John Crawfurd, Esq. — th there can be no more competent authority as to such subjects.

Of all the products of the Eastern islands, and of the countries immediately in their neighbou demand among strangers, black pepper is the most important, both in value and quantity.

The pepper countries extend from about the longitude of 96° to that of 115° E., beyond wh is to be found; and it reaches from 5° S. latitude to about 12° N., where it again ceases. these limits we have Sumatra, Borneo, the Malayan peninsula, and certain countries lying or coast of the Gulf of Siam.

The whole produce of the island of Sumatra is estimated not to fall short of 168,000 piculs, c each; the south-west coast being said to produce 150,000, and the north-east coast 18,000 piculs

The pepper ports on the north-east coast of Sumatra are Lankat and Delli, with Sardang.

oduce 15,000 piculs, and the latter 3,000 annually. The cultivation is carried on by the Batta in the interior.

orts on the south-west coast, and the amount of their produce, as given in a recent estimate, are w: viz. port and district of Trumah, 40,000; district of Pulo Dua, 4,000; ditto of Cluat, 30,000; om Tampat Tuan to Susu, 33,000; port of Susu, 1,000; Kualla Batta, 20,000; Analabu, 2,000; s to the north of Analabu, 20,000; making in all, 150,000 piculs.

it is of importance to remark, that the culture and production are extremely fluctuating.

ng the last pepper season, there obtained cargoes on the west coast of Sumatra, 27 American ships, ry traders, 4 large French ships, besides the ships belonging to the East India Company, which lly take away 500 tons. Nearly the whole of this trade is in the hands of Europeans or Americans; per finds its way to Europe, to America, and in a small proportion to China.

north-east coast of Sumatra, from Pedier down to the Carimons, is estimated, as already men-to produce 18,000 piculs. Prince of Wales Island is the principal *depôt* for this, from whence eatest part is exported to India and China. The produce of Prince of Wales Island itself is 15,000 piculs.

he islands at the mouth of the Straits of Malacca and Singapore, Bingtang, on which Rhio is l, and adjacent islands, produce 10,000 piculs; and Lingga about 2,000. A large proportion of brought to Singapore, which exported last year about 21,000 piculs; some part to Bengal and but principally to Europe direct, in free traders.

west coast of the Malayan peninsula produces no pepper, with the exception of about 4,000 piculs d by the territory of Malacca.

he east coast of the peninsula, the production of pepper is very considerable. The ports of Patmi lantan — chiefly the latter — yield about 16,000 piculs annually, and Tringanu about 8,000. A of this is brought to Singapore and Penang; but we believe the greater proportion goes direct to n junks, of which 3 large ones frequent Tringanu annually, and 1 Calantan. The Americans, too, nally visit these ports. In the year 1821, three vessels of considerable burthen obtained cargoes. east coast of the Gulf of Siam, from the latitude of 10½° to that of 12½° N., affords an extensive of pepper. This coast is scarcely known, even by name, to the traders of Europe. The principal re are Chantibun, Fungyai, Pongsom, and Kampot; the two first being under the dominion of nd the latter under that of Kamboja. The whole produce is estimated at not less than 60,000 40,000 of which are brought at once to the capital of Siam as tribute to the king, and the whole way to China in junks. It remains only to estimate the produce of the island of Borneo. The roduce of Borneo is estimated at about 20,000 piculs; of which a large share is carried to China n junks, some by Portuguese vessels; and about 7,000 piculs are now annually brought by the raft of the country itself to Singapore in the course of that free trade, which is happily flourish-his settlement. The data which have been stated, will enable us to estimate the whole production Malayan archipelago, including that of the peninsula of Malacca, and that of the east coast of the Siam, at 308,000 piculs; and as there is no other part of the world that affords pepper, excepting ern coast of the peninsula of India, and this affords but 30,000 piculs, or less than one tenth part the places we have enumerated produce, we have, accordingly, at one view, the whole produc-he earth, being 338,000 piculs, or 45,066,666 lbs. avoirdupois. The average price of pepper has ely about nine Spanish dollars a picul; so the whole value drawn into India from Europe, China, New World, on account of this single commodity, is 3,042,000 dollars. The quantity given in this it may appear enormous; but if meted out to the whole population of the globe, or to one thou-lions of people, it would be found that the average annual consumption of an individual would to no more than 323 grains.

RCH, a long measure, 16½ feet in length. — (See WEIGHTS AND MEASURES.)

RMIT, a licence or instrument, granted by the officers of excise, authorising noval of goods subject to the excise duties.

acted by the 11 Geo. 3. c. 30., that no person shall demand or receive a permit for the removal y, arrack, rum, spirits, and strong waters, coffee, tea, and cocoa nuts, without the special direc-*riting* of the person out of whose stock they are to come, on pain of forfeiting 50*l.*; and in de-payment, to be imprisoned three months. Persons taking out a permit, and not removing the thin the prescribed period, nor returning the permit to the officer, forfeit *treble* the value of the entioned in such permit. By the 57 Geo. 3. c. 123., persons selling, lending, or making use of for any other purpose than that for which it was granted, forfeit 500*l.* By the 6 Geo. 4. c. it is enacted, that any retailer of spirits sending out more than *one gallon* without a lawful per-r rectifier, compounder, or dealer, receiving into his stock any spirits without a permit; or any boatman, or other person, assisting in the removal or transportation of any spirits without a per-ll forfeit 200*l.* over and above every other penalty, together with all such spirits; the packages, rses, &c. employed in the removal of such goods, shall also be forfeited, and may and *shall* be any officer of excise. The 9 Geo. 4. c. 44. § 5. dispenses with the necessity of a permit for the of coffee and cocoa. The commissioners of excise provide frames or moulds for making the d for permits, which has the words "Excise Office," visible in the substance of it. It is a ca-nce to make such frames, or to have them in one's possession without a lawful excuse.

RRY, a fermented liquor made from pears, in the same manner as cider ples. The pears best fitted for producing this liquor are exceedingly harsh t; but it is itself pleasant and wholesome. — (See CIDER.)

ERSBURGH, the modern metropolis of the Russian empire, situated at fluence of the river Neva with the eastern extremity of the Gulf of Fin-lat. 59° 56¼′ N., lon. 30° 18¾′ E. Population (including military) 425,000. ersburgh Gazette, 10—22 Jan. 1829.)

flourishing emporium was founded by Peter the Great, whose name it bears, In the same year, the first merchant ship that ever appeared on the Neva from Holland; and the czar, to mark his sense of the value of such visiters, he captain and crew with the greatest hospitality, and loaded them with presents. , 16 ships arrived at Petersburgh; in 1730, the number had increased to 180; rapid has been the progress of commerce and civilisation in Russia since that hat at present from 1,200 to 1,500 ships annually enter and clear out from rgh!

nuch to be regretted, that, although favourable to commerce, the situation of rgh is, in other respects, far from being good. The ground on which it stands

is low and swampy; it has on different occasions sustained great injury from inu[n]
tions; and the country round is, generally speaking, a morass and forest, so that al[l]
every thing required for the subsistence of the inhabitants must be brought from a
tance. No one less bold and daring than Peter the Great would have though[t]
selecting such a situation for the metropolis of his empire; and none possessed of
power and resolution would have succeeded in overcoming the all but insuperable
stacles which the nature of the country opposed to the completion of his giga[ntic]
schemes.

Cronstadt, situated on a small island about 20 miles below Petersburgh, may
some measure, be considered as the port of the latter. Almost all vessels bound
Petersburgh touch here; and those drawing above 8 feet water generally load and unl[oad]
at Cronstadt; the goods being conveyed from and to the city in lighters, the charge
which vary according to the demand at the time. The merchants' harbour at Crons[tadt]
is fitted to contain about 600 ships; but it is exposed to the westerly winds. Crons[tadt]
is strongly fortified, and is the principal station of the Russian fleet. Vessels bound
Petersburgh must pass by the narrow channel to the south of the island, commande[d by]
the fortifications of Cronstadt on the one side, and of Cronslot on the other.

Petersburgh has the most extensive foreign trade of any city in the north of Eur[ope.]
This arises from its being the only great maritime outlet on the Gulf of Finland,
from its vast and various communications with the interior of the country. Few c[oun-]
tries have such an extent of internal navigation as Russia. By means partly of riv[ers]
and partly of canals, Petersburgh is connected with the Caspian Sea. Goods are [con-]
veyed from the latter to the capital, through a distance of 1,434 miles, without [once]
landing them! The iron and furs of Siberia, and the teas of China, are receive[d at]
Petersburgh in the same way; but owing to the great distance of those countries, [and]
the short period of the year during which the rivers and canals are navigable, they [are]
3 years in their transit. Immense quantities of goods are also conveyed during wi[nter]
upon the ice, in sledges, to the different ports, to be ready for shipping when the se[ason]
sets in.

Principal Articles of Export and Import. — The principal articles of export are ta[llow,]
hemp and flax, iron, copper, grain, particularly wheat; deals and masts, pota[sh,]
bristles, linseed and hemp seed, linseed and hemp seed oils, furs, leather; fox, hare,
squirrel skins; canvass and coarse linen, cordage, caviare, wax, isinglass, tar, &c.
low, both for candles and soap, is more largely exported from this than from any [other]
port in the Baltic, and is an article of great commercial importance. — (See Tall[ow.)]
The hemp is of good quality, though inferior to that of Riga: it is assorted, accor[ding]
to its quality, into *clean hemp*, or firsts; *outshot hemp*, or seconds; and *half clean h[emp*,]
or thirds. The first sort should be quite clean and free from spills; the second is [not]
so; and the third, or *half clean*, contains a still greater portion of spills, and is be[sides]
of mixed qualities and colours. Russian flax is much esteemed for the length [of its]
fibre; it is naturally brownish, but becomes very white after the first bleaching. [Three]
qualities are distinguished; viz. 12 head, 9 head, and 6 head. — (See Hemp, and F[lax.)]
Iron is of very good quality, and is preferable to that from the other Russian p[orts;]
there are two kinds, old and new sable; the former is the best. Leather is la[rgely]
exported; it is divided into many different sorts. — (See the details with respect to [it in]
the art. Russia Leather.) The grain trade between this country and Petersb[urgh]
has, within the last 3 years, become of considerable importance; and Russia will, [pro-]
bably, continue henceforth to be one of the principal sources of supply to this cou[ntry.]
The *Russian wheat*, so called to distinguish it from the *azemaia* or soft wheat, an[d the]
kubanka or hard wheat, is the lowest description of wheat shipped from Petersburg[h. It]
is very small grained, and dingy coloured; being, though sound, unfit for the man[ufac-]
ture of fine bread. The azemaia is of a larger, though still not a large grain, and [of a]
colour, and has of late been extensively imported into England. The kubanka, or [hard]
wheat, is a large semi-transparent grain. Its hardness has nothing of the flinty cha[racter]
of the Spanish hard wheat, which it most resembles. When first brought to Lo[ndon]
the millers objected to it, on account of the difficulty experienced in grinding it; [but it]
is now much esteemed. All the Russian wheats are well calculated for keeping, [either]
in granary, or when made into bread: but the kubanka has this quality in a peculi[ar de-]
gree; and is in great demand for mixing with other wheats that are old, stale, or [in bad]
condition. A shipment of 100 chetwerts of wheat in Petersburgh is found, whe[n de-]
livered here, to yield about 72 imperial quarters. The principal imports are suga[r, es-]
pecially from the Havannah (the importation of refined sugar was prohibited in 1[837);]
coffee, but not in large quantities; madder, indigo, cochineal, and dye-woods; [dye-]
stuffs, and yarn, — the latter being by far the principal article sent from this coun[try to]
Russia; woollens, oil, spices, salt, wine, lead, tin, coal, fine linen from Hollan[d and]
Silesia, &c.

l as has been the increase of Russian commerce, its progress has been materially
l by restrictions on importation. Considering the immense variety of valuable
productions with which Russia abounds, the thinness of the population, and the
and ignorance of the great bulk of the people, nothing can be more absurd than the
to render them, by dint of Custom-house regulations, rivals of the English and
as in manufacturing industry! However, it must be confessed, that in enacting
ions and restrictions, they are only following a line of policy which we have not
rely abandoned, though it has been quite as injurious to us as it can be to them.
hoped that sound commercial principles were beginning to get an ascendancy
sburgh, inasmuch as the ukase of the 26th of March, 1880, materially modified
of the previous restrictions. But very recently a new ukase has made its appear-
acting a considerable increase of duties on several articles. It is, we are afraid,
ear, that the Russian government has profited little by the admirable work of
ch (*Cours d'Economie Politique*), though written for the special use of the
emperor of Russia, and his brother the Grand Duke Michael, and published by
the late emperor.

tion of Goods. — At Petersburgh, Riga, and other Baltic ports, when goods are
from the interior to be shipped, they are inspected and classified according to
alities, by officers (*brackers*) appointed by government for that purpose, and
the faithful performance of their duty. All sorts of timber, linen and canvass,
hemp, linseed and hemp seed, ashes, wax, &c. are subject to such inspection.
e generally divided into three qualities; *Krohn* (crown) or superior, *Brack* or
, and *Bracks-Brack* or inferior. This classification is said to be, in most cases,
ch considerable fairness. A factor or commission agent in Russia, instructed
on account of his correspondent in England or Holland, a specified quantity of
ription of produce subject to the official visit, is not liable to any action in the
the article being found upon delivery to be of inferior quality, provided he pro-
ertificate to show that it had been officially inspected or *bracked*. But a factor
rty, should any article delivered to him be manifestly defective, to name one or
r *brackers* to decide whether the article be merchantable or not.

and Foreign Merchants, &c. — Every Russian carrying on trade must be a
and have his name registered in the burghers' book; he thus acquires an un-
reedom of trade. All whose names are in the burghers' books, are either
a who have property within the city, or members of a guild. There are three
Those belonging to the first must possess from 10,000 to 50,000 roubles: these
w foreign trade, are not liable to corporal punishment, and may drive about
a carriage drawn by two horses. Those belonging to the second guild declare
es possessed of from 5,000 to 10,000 roubles; they are confined to inland trade.
l of from 1,000 to 5,000 roubles entitles its owner to admission into the third
ich comprises shopkeepers and petty dealers. The rates paid by the members
guilds amount to 1 per cent. upon their declared capital, the "statement of
eft to the conscience of every individual." Burghers are not obliged to serve
ny, but may provide a substitute, or pay a fine. The *guests*, or foreign mer-
ho enrol themselves in the city register on account of their commercial affairs,
vileges nearly similar to those enjoyed by the members of the first guild.
out native Russians are allowed to engage in the internal trade of the country:
e a foreigner, who imports goods into Russia, must sell them to Russians only,
e port where they arrive. A few foreigners, indeed, settled in Russia, and
nnections with the natives, do carry on a trade with the interior; but it is con-
aw, and the goods are liable to be seized.
erchants engaged in foreign trade are mostly foreigners, of whom the English
incipal. The peculiar privileges formerly enjoyed by the latter are now nearly
and their rights, in common with those of other foreigners, are merely those
The English Factory is, at present, little more than a society formed of
the principal English merchants, several of whom, however, do not belong
power extends to little else than the management of certain funds under its

se and Sale of Commodities, &c. — Owing to the scarcity of capital in Russia,
produce of the country, are frequently paid in advance; and foreign goods are
monly sold upon credit. From the month of November till the shipping season
he Russians who trade in flax, hemp, tallow, bristles, iron, &c., either come
to Petersburgh, or employ agents to sell their goods to foreigners, to be de-
cording to agreement, in May, June, July, or August. The payments are
rding to the circumstances of the sellers and buyers: sometimes the buyer pays
amount, in the winter months, for the goods which are to be delivered in the
autumn; and sometimes he pays a part on concluding the contract, and the

remainder on delivery of the goods. The manufacturers and dealers in linens u come to Petersburgh in March, and sell their goods for ready money.

Foreign goods were formerly almost entirely sold at a twelvemonth's credit, and at a still longer term; but of late years several articles, as coffee and sugar, are so ready money : still, however, the great bulk of foreign goods for the supply of t terior is sold on credit. Most of the Russians who buy goods on credit of forei for the use of the interior, have no other connection or trade with Petersburgh merely coming there once or twice a year to make purchases; which having accompl they set off with the goods, and the foreigner neither sees nor hears of them aga the bills become due.

It is obvious, from this statement, that experience and sagacity are no where mo quisite in a merchant than here. He has nothing, in fact, but his own knowledge native dealers to depend upon. And it is highly creditable to the Russians, that forei do not hesitate to trust them with immense sums on such a guaranty. A foreign chant, carrying on business in Russia, must also be acquainted with the customary and obligations of contracts; the mode of making payments; the many form that incumber, and sometimes turn aside, the course of justice; the spirit, still mor the letter, of the tariff and the Custom-house regulations; the privileges claimed crown, and the different orders; with a variety of other particulars, which attentiv able men may learn on the spot, and no where else.

" Another circumstance connected with the British trade is too curious to be passed in silence. mercantile house in Petersburgh employs certain men, called in the language of the countr *schicks*, who are the counting-house men, and employed by every merchant to collect payment to receive money, as well as in many instances to pay it in very considerable sums. This is an im part of their trust. There being no bankers in Russia, every mercantile house keeps its own ca as the payments between merchants, and for bills of exchange, are made entirely in bank note higher value than 5, 10, 25, 50, and 100 roubles—most of them in so tattered a state as to require hours to count over a sum of 2,000*l*. or 3,000*l*.—this business is performed by artelschicks; a few instances have occurred of loss by their inattention, either in miscounting the notes, in takin notes, or, where they are much torn, in receiving parts of different bank notes.

" These artelschicks are also employed to superintend the loading and unloading the different o they receive the most valuable into the warehouse, where they are left solely under their care; and warehouses not merely merchandise, but often large quantities of dollars, are deposited. These P are mostly natives of Archangel and the adjacent governments, of the lowest class; are often slave rally of the crown : and the only security of the merchant arises in some degree from the natur tance of the Russian to betray confidence reposed in him; but in a much greater from their asso which is called an artel.

" An artel consists of a certain number of labourers, who voluntarily become responsible, as a t the honesty of each individual. The separate earnings of each man are put into the common monthly allowance is made for his support; and at the end of the year the surplus is equally divid number varies in different associations from 50 to 100; and so advantageous is it considered to b one of these societies, that 500 and even 1,000 roubles are paid for admission. These societies bound by any law of the empire, or even written agreement; nor does the merchant restrain the any legal obligation; yet there has been no instance of their objecting to any just claim, or of pr an individual whose conduct had brought a demand on the society."—(*Coxe's Travels in Russia*, p. 315.)

Few Russian merchants engage in foreign trade. It is carried on principally reign bottoms, of which by far the largest proportion are English. Marine insu are generally effected in London or Amsterdam; there being no establishment i department of business in Russia. An insurance company against fire has bee blished in Petersburgh, and enjoys several privileges. It is a joint stock co divided into actions, or shares. It has been very successful; and its shares a very high premium. No insurance on houses or goods in Russia, made in a country, can be legally recovered; no official documents of loss being allowed to nished for such a purpose.

Money.—Accounts are kept at Petersburgh, and throughout Russia, in bank roubles of 100 formerly, accounts were kept in silver money; but by an order of government, the practice of accounts in bank note roubles has been enforced since 1811, to the exclusion of the other.

The only gold coin at present struck is the half imperial or 5 rouble piece = 15s. 8*d.* sterling ver The silver rouble is worth 3s. 2¾*d.* sterling very nearly; and is declared, by a ukase issued in 18 worth 360 copecks : this would give the value of the paper rouble at nearly 11*d.*; but it fluctu the exchange. For an account of the Commercial Bank of Russia, see *antè*, p.99.

Weights and Measures.—The Russian weights are the same for gold, silver, and merchandis are—

3 Soltnicks	= 1 Loth.		40 Pounds	= 1 Pood.
32 Loths	= 1 Pound.		10 Poods	= 1 Berkovitz.

The Russian pound contains, according to Dr. Kelly, 6318·5 English grains. Hence, 100 lbs. R 90·26 lbs. avoirdupois = 40·93 kilog. The pood = 36 lbs. 1 oz. 11 drs , but among merchants it is = 36 lbs. According to Nelkenbrecher, 100 lbs. Russian = 90·19 lbs. avoirdupois = 40·9 kilog. = of Amsterdam = 84·444 of Hamburgh.

The principal measure for corn is the chetwert, divided into 2 osmins, 4 pajocks, 8 chetweri garnitz. The chetwert = 5·952 Winchester bushels. Hence, 100 chetwerts = 74·4 English quarte

In liquid measure,					
11 Tsharky	= 1 Krashka.		6 Ankers	= 1 Oxhoft.
8 Krashka	= 1 Wedro.		2 Oxhoft	= 1 Pipe.
40 Wedro	= 1 Sorokovy.		In long measure,	
The wedro = 3¼ English wine gallons.			16 Wershok	= 1 Arsheen.
13½ Bottles	= 1 Wedro.		3 Arsheen	= 1 Sashen.
3 Wedros	= 1 Anker.		500 Sashen	= 1 Verst.

n = 7 English feet; 1 arsheen = 28 English inches. 100 Russian feet = 114½ English feet. The ›r Russian mile, = 5 furlongs 12 poles. The English inch and foot are used throughout Russia, , however, in the measuring of timber. — (*Kelly's Cambist*, art. *Russia*; *Nelkenbrecher*, *Manuel* *sel.*)

king freight to England, a ton is 63 poods of hemp, flax, tallow, iron, copper, and ashes; 44 poods :les, isinglass, leather, and wax; 5 dozen of deals; 3,500 hare skins; 8 chetwerts of wheat or lin- and 60 pieces of sail-cloth.

following charges have been fixed by the merchants of Petersburgh: —

	Per cent.		Per cent.
ssion on sales and purchases - -	2	Ditto for procuring freight outwards - -	2
charges on all goods - - -	1	For clearances - - 40 roub.	
ssion and extra charges for goods deli-		Dues to be paid to the church, 10 roub. each vessel.	
l up - - -	2	Clearing of ships, each vessel	
age on sales and purchases .. -	⅛	of or under 25 lasts - - 40 —	
n bills - - - -	¼	— 25 to 50 do. - 60 —	
n freight, per ton, 60 copecks.		— 50 — 75 do. - 80 —	
- - - -	⅜	— 75 — 100 do. - 100 —	
s on duty, paid inwards - - -	4	— 100 — 150 do. - 150 —	
tto paid outwards - -	4	— 150 or above - 200 —	
ssion for collecting freight, or average			
rds - - -	3		

Tare on Goods exported, as fixed by the Custom-house.

	Per cent.		Per cent.
ods.		*Moist Goods.*	
rrels or chests - - -	10	Pressed caviare - - - - -	15
:ks - - - - -	2	Soap - - -	3
ts, or sacks made of mats - -	3	Meat and salt fish - - -	20
ept Muscovy leather, of which is de-		Tallow - - -	10
ıcted - - - - -	5	Honey - - - -	17
		Treacle - - - -	10
		All other moist goods - -	17

Tare on Goods imported.

	Per cent.		Per cent.
ods.		In double sacks - - -	4
rels or chests - - -	10	In mats - - - - -	3
sels of glass or earthenware -	20	In sacks and mats together - -	5
ks - - -	2	In baskets - - - -	5

Goods imported. — The following are some of the tares specified in the tariff: —

	Per cent.	
in casks - - -	17	Cochineal must be weighed in the sacks after
of Italy, in flasks and straw -	20	being taken from the casks; for every sack
of France, in flasks and earthenware	40	of from 4 to 7 poods - - - 2 lbs.
in barrels - - -	36	sacks of from 2 to 3½ poods - - 1 —
·erally on all moist goods in barrels -	17	Indigo in serons; every seron of from 5½ to
in glass and earthenware -	20	7 poods - - - - - 34 —
'aneous Goods.		half serons, 2½ to 4 poods - - 20 —
wist in bales - - - - -	6	of Guatemala - - 20 per cent.
in chests and barrels -	15	in boxes - - - - 20 —

rawn in Russia, and payable after date, are allowed 10 days' grace; but if payable at sight, 3 days ındays and holidays are included in both cases. The Julian calendar, or old style, is still re- roughout Russia. This is 12 days later than the new style; and in leap-years, 13 days, after the ' February.

rade of Petersburgh is exhibited in the following tables: —

unt of the Quantities of the Principal Articles of Foreign Produce imported into Petersburgh in each of the Four Years ending with 1829.

:les.	1826.	1827.	1828.	1829.	Articles.	1826.	1827.	1828.	1829.
- poods	31,867	96,524	52,125	52,754	Sugar, raw - poods	704,268	767,226	1049374	1384607
- —	14,055	17,020	21,096	26,181	Tin in bars - —	12,618	25,079	26,781	26,905
- —	5,757	4,730	4,415	6,900	foil - - —	159	168	231	255
: —					plates, to 450				
ıbrics,					leaves in a box —	400	324	1,900	2,740
'elvet-					Tobacco leaf - —	14,652	23,433	18,113	30,850
:s, &c. pcs.	267,229	237,347	194,352	195,622	Twist, cotton - —	346,349	360,780	433,848	524,111
·rn - doz.	3,851	14,871	13,885	11,391	Wines, Spanish and				
- barrels	24,538	28,985	39,776	20,770	Portuguese - pipes	5,168	4,297	3,725	1,123
- poods	16,980	19,649	17,682	18,435	French - hhds.	8,271	12,789	10,503	7,835
ron —	6,346	8,860	8,421	10,639	Rhenish aums	570	826	558	642
- —	98,283	235,378	251,184	149,108	in bottles bottl.	87,310	100,241	87,132	58,070
- —	11,137	20,514	8,115	18,826	Champagne —	230,400	409,174	288,898	234,465
- doz.	48,621	41,170	38,139	28,658	Rum, French brandy,				
ıges, chests	42,461	28,828	44,505	36,073	arrack, shrub, &c. ank.	1,233	4,822	9,896	11,261
- poods	51,855	67,490	69,182	46,039	Wood, mahogany poods	140,631	48,882	110,058	14,080
dinary —	124,560	91,607	198,151	231,794	Nicaragua —	45,744	98,997	69,666	57,753
- reams	13,548	9,655	11,150	2,924	Woollens, as flannel,				
- poods	766,279	776,462	613,492	992,813	shalloon, toilinet,				
rk —	42,798	20,389	33,728	30,254	baize, barracan,				
k pieces	126,735	165,677	116,387	60,020	&c. - - pieces	5,839	8,779	20,433	10,572
- poods	12,611	20,757	42,224	23,669	Woollen cloths - —	5,745	7,396	6,055	5,336
- —	182,763	443,721	520,820	901,167	kerseymere —	1,067	990	665	243
- —		15,910	2,006	17,858	carpets - —	356	589	224	420
- —	7,745	31,537	3,517	4,596	shawls - —	8,688	7,950	8,909	10,375
kinds,					stockings - doz.	1,114	1,096	1,361½	1,143
levan-					camlet - pcs.	29,093	29,778	24,289	28,480
serge,					coverlets - —	3,346	989	1,828	4,156
- pieces	17,508	30,744	17,320	15,335	Wool, raw - poods	1,647	854	705	992
poods	556	24,493	22,119	11,422	yarn - - —	2,418	1,069	1,305	1,078
- pieces	2,314	3,050	415	784					

II. Official Account of the Values of the Imports into and Exports from Petersburgh, with the Prod
the Customs Duty thereon, in each Year since 1800.

Years.	Imports.	Exports.	Duties.	Years.	Imports.	Exports.	Dutie
	Roubles.	Roubles.	Roubles.		Roubles.	Roubles.	Roubl
1800	20,070,935	32,255,354	4,931,506	1816	90,204,829	77,766,729	13,908,
1801	27,074,118	31,110,996	5,684,229	1817	118,743,838	100,704,113	20,986,
1802	24,735,783	30,695,561	6,312,509	1818	151,258,904	100,675,732	23,163,
1803	22,846,472	31,893,082	7,079,395	1819	111,106,315	84,998,642	20,623,
1804	21,008,478	29,565,661	6,972,520	1820	168,256,897	105,085,920	29,747,
1805	20,478,047	30,151,653	6,085,222	1821	135,420,718	100,631,673	25,707,
1806	18,710,234	28,997,388	5,230,300	1822	104,166,738	97,932,490	21,656,
1807	18,114,443	28,945,545	4,982,461	1823	105,969,720	104,070,326	22,386,
1808	1,452,223	5,875,896	918,056	1824	120,423,890	97,729,518	27,012,
1809	5,159,798	20,314,406	2,277,908	1825	115,146,068	121,174,898	30,056,
1810	10,058,485	25,798,279	3,204,847	1826	120,188,634	91,591,514	31,633,
1811	25,472,332	39,838,862	5,562,332	1827	126,666,415	116,794,217	34,503,
1812	41,739,114	59,626,165	10,023,966	1828	131,480,572	107,207,647	36,658,
1813	80,613,958	55,173,681	15,475,972	1829	149,135,403	107,428,928	41,184,
1814	75,169,453	92,768,886	11,905,177	1830	144,899,905	111,255,171	
1815	65,961,238	107,989,493	10,684,924				

III. Quantities of Goods cleared for Exportation at the Petersburgh Custom-house during each of t
Years ending with 1830.

Goods.	1827.	1828.	1829.	1830.	Goods.	1827.	1828.	1829.
Bristles,					Manufactures,			
cut, - poods	-	- -	- -	855	ravens-			
Okatka —	-	- -	25	3,776	duck - pieces	79,108	55,577	30,096
1st sort —	37,473	33,037	31,033	26,925	sailcloth —	62,117	62,130	38,408
2d sort —	26,974	29,219	21,065	16,886	diaper,			
Suchoi —	- -	- -	- -	13,074	broad, - arsh.	686,656	1,725,068	1,565,161
Cantharides —	526	841	371	676	narrow - —	129,689	27,549	8,326
Caviare - —	459	5,627	2,672	608	linen,			
Copper - - —	152,671	85,359	207,959	180,581	broad - —	9,780	640	26,091
Cordage, new —	96,063	120,642	81,403	55,951	narrow - —	5,000	10,315	60,087
old —	31,294	49,524	66,554	56,036	drillings - —	192,478	263,763	227,455
Down, eider-					crash —	588,005	707,758	834,288
down - lbs.	14	15	46		Meal, rye			
goose-					meal - chtwt.	10,943	366	403
down, poods	58	110	123	183	Oil, aniseed			
goat's					oil - poods	78	131	110
down —	593	2,950	1,810	5,414	hemp-seed			
Feathers - —	6,467	11,269	10,500	9,281	oil - —	197,354	238,247	410,512
Flax, 12 head —	570,243	486,091	105,470	126,519	linseed oil - —	74	66	47
9 — —	} 84,922	108,344	{ 158,701	252,265	Potashes - —	505,369	380,455	445,627
6 — —			73,396	120,149	Quills - - thous.	6,854	21,713	20,851
codilla —	40,036	73,140	82,423	94,653	Rhubarb poods	396	145	1,006
yarn - —	23,857	16,770	17,250	18,266	Seeds, ani-			
Furs, er-					seed - - —	1,216	870	5,460
mine - pieces	- -	12	2	2	cumin-seed —	3	85	1,737
squirrel - —	709	1,547	1,999	1,455	hemp-			
Galls - - poods	23	25	424	469	seed - chtwt.	- -	197	119
Grain,					linseed - —	92,630	146,030	163,610
barley - chtwt.	4,108	½	6,638	1,513	worm-			
oats - —	65,567	10,092	12,216	8,609	seed - poods	281	1,105	969
rye - —	14,711	53,310	99,909	126,094	Skins, calf - —	2,148	2,754	2,837
wheat - —	1,825	37,756	300,630	243,556	dressed - pieces	14,509	1,697	59
Glue - poods	537	2,980	2,908	1,690	badger - —	- -	383	63
Gum am-					cat - —	- -	150	816
moniac —	23	134	49	61	ermine - —	21,360	29,480	26,200
galbanum —	78	15	3	42	hare grew - —	} 131,593	175,220 {	43,653
Hair, ox and					white —			25,800
cow hair —	1,891	140	691	2,176	sable - —	110	40	30
goats' hair —	- -	- -	1,016	1,033	squirrel - —	166,900	118,750	230,260
Hemp, clean —	1,418,093	1,287,429	416,846	533,363	Soap - - poods	8,167	8,468	7,966
outshot —	191,144	303,480	414,258	532,731	Sole leather —	563	854	670
half clean —	313,129	244,658	209,677	303,716	Sundry goods			
codilla —	16,020	7,674	3,549	26,039	not specified			
yarn —	1,185	743	998	191	in the pre-			
Hides, raw,					sent list, per			
cow —	39,579	72,573	57,341	71,965	value - - R°	1,252,969	1,280,695	1,466,251
horse —	121	4,194	24,385	39,749	Tails, squir-			
ox - —	21,146	33,082	23,993	27,044	rel - - pieces	51,665	610,118	771,140
red - —	32,250	31,081	33,117	22,908	Tallow - poods	3,574,017	3,646,814	3,975,758
white - —	231	1,060	928	1,396	can-			
dressed, pieces	- -	93	52	285	dles - —	21,438	28,229	38,04
Horse					Wax, white - —	1,863	2,107	1,76
manes, poods	10,743	14,668	13,495	10,901	yellow - —	5,343	6,832	12,72
tails - —	7,354	10,526	10,810	8,496	candles —	251	412	36
Iron in bars —	921,282	829,035	1,062,439	658,784	Wood,			
blocks —	8,595	15,875	6,996	992	battens - pieces	15,060	34,905	32,84
sheets —	13,453	33,096	2,909	1,856	beams - —	159	30	87
old - —	27,620	32,242	40,199	22,134	deals - —	931,793	815,798	996,09
Isinglass - —	4,833	3,634	4,473	3,175	lathwood —	118,098	89,150	105,12
Samovy —	1,903	1,854	2,075	1,041	Wool, sheep's			
Liquorice - —	1,119	2,111	2,224	1,923	wool - poods	21,764	15,172	3,99
Manufactures,					woollen			
Flems - pieces	75,654	71,363	39,712	65,327	yarn - - —	255	201	44

IV. Ships cleared out from Petersburgh during the Six Years ending with 1830.

Years.	1825.	1826.	1827.	1828.	1829.	1830.
Flags.	Ships.	Ships.	Ships.	Ships.	Ships.	Ships.
British	801	483	753	749	831	753
American	76	57	64	66	62	46
Other Nations	411	405	415	475	605	684
Total	1,288	945	1,232	1,290	1,498	1,483

wing regulations for the importation of foreign rictly enforced : —
s imported must be accompanied by the following
eclaration of the captain, according to the form he Custom-house.
station from the Russian consul, and, where there from the Custom-house of the place, of the quantity of the goods, and a declaration that they are not manufacture, or property of an enemy's country. lading of all goods, in which the weight, measure, of each package must be specified. In case the g are not exactly after this regulation, the goods pay as a fine. In case more is found than specified in ding, the surplus is confiscated; if less is found, the paid on the quantity specified. Of wine, it is not

sufficient to specify the number of pipes or hogsheads only, but also their contents in gallons, &c. Of lemons, the number in each box must be specified. Of manufactured goods, the measure of each piece must be specified, and the number of pieces in each bale. It is indifferent whether the gross or the nett weight be specified. If the packages be all of the same weight, measure, or contents, a general specification will do, as for example,— 100 casks alum, of 17 lispound each. Of dye-woods, the weight of the whole need only be mentioned. Of goods of small bulk, as pepper, &c., it is sufficient to state the weight of every 5 or 10 bales, but with specification of the numbers. There must not be any erasures or blots in the bill of lading. All goods not accompanied by these documents, or where the documents are not according to the above regulations, will be sent back.
Bills of lading may be made out either to some house, or to order.

iling this article, we have consulted *Storch's Picture of Petersburgh*, c. 9.; *Schnitzler, Essai istique Générale de la Russie*, pp. 133—157.; *Ricard, Traité Général du Commerce*, ed. 1781, 268—317.; *Tooke's View of Russia*, book 12.; *Coxe's Travels in the North of Europe*, 8vo ed. 283—358. &c.; but we have derived our principal information from the private communications Russian merchants.

TER (Ger. *Zinn, Zinngeisserzinn*; Fa. *Etain*; It. *Stagno*; Sp. *Estano*, Rus. *Olowo*), a factitious metal used in making plates, dishes, and other c utensils. It is a compound, the basis of which is tin. The best sort of tin alloyed with about $\frac{1}{20}$th or less of copper, or other metallic bodies, experience of the workmen has shown to be the most conducive to rovement of its hardness and colour, such as lead, zinc, bismuth, and y.

are three sorts of pewter, distinguished by the names of plate, trifle, and er. The first was formerly much used for plates and dishes; of the re made the pints, quarts, and other measures of beer; and of the leywine measures and large vessels. — (*Dr. Ure.*)

ADELPHIA, a large city and sea-port of the United States, in Pennnear the confluence of the rivers Delaware and Schuylkill, in lat. 39° lon. 75° 10′ W. Population 168,000. Vessels of the largest burthen to the city. The exports principally consist of wheat and wheat flour, In, and other agricultural products, lumber, coal and iron, various species actured goods, &c. The principal imports are cotton, woollen, and silk ugar, coffee and tea, wines, brandies, spices, &c. The manufactures of hia are various and extensive. There were in this city, in January, 1831, , whose united capitals are said to have amounted to 6,803,933 dollars; es in circulation being 2,537,053 ditto, and specie 1,184,240 ditto. The s on bank stock vary from 5 to 10 per cent. In point of shipping, Philas the fourth port of the United States; being in this respect inferior only York, Boston, and Baltimore; but with the latter she is nearly on a level, stered, enrolled, and licensed tonnage belonging to Philadelphia, in 1828, d to 104,080 tons, of which 33,446 were employed in the coasting trade. value of the articles imported into Pennsylvania, in the year ended 30th nber, 1829, was 10,100,152 dollars; the total value of the exports during year being 4,089,935 dollars. In Pennsylvania, the dollar is worth 7s. 6d, ; so that 1l. sterling = 1l. 13s. 4d. currency. — (See NEW-YORK.)
and Measures same as those of England.

PHORUS, a substance of a light amber colour, and semi-transpawhen carefully prepared, nearly colourless and transparent. When e time, it becomes opaque externally, and has then a great resemblance wax. It may be cut with a knife, or twisted to pieces with the fingers. luble in water; its specific gravity is 1·77. When exposed to the re it emits a white smoke, and is luminous in the dark. When heated takes fire, and burns with a very bright flame. When phosphorus is in oxygen, the light and heat are incomparably more intense; the zzling the eye, and the latter cracking the glass vessel. — (*Thomson's*)

PIASTRES, or DOLLARS, Spanish and American silver coins in
extensive circulation.   Value, at an average, about 4s. 3d. sterling. —
Coins.)

PILCHARDS (Ger. *Sardellan*; Du. *Sardynen*; Fr. *Sardines*; It. *Sardine*
Sardinas; Rus. *Sardelii*; Lat. *Sardinæ*), are fishes closely resembling the co
herring, but smaller, and at the same time thicker and rounder.   They are
swimming in vast shoals, particularly on the coasts of Cornwall and D
where they are taken in great numbers from the month of July to Septe
both inclusive.   It is a saying of the Cornish fishermen, that the pilchard
least fish in size, most in number, and greatest for gain, that they take from th
—(*Postlethwaite*; art. Fishery.)

In St. Ives' bay, on the 5th of October, 1767, as many were taken as filled 7,000 hhds., each con
35,000 fish !   But though still considerable, the fishery has since declined very considerably.   The
foreign export and winter consumption, are laid upon the shore in large stacks or piles, with layer
between each row.   Here they are suffered to lie for 20 or 30 days, during which time a vast disc
pickle, mixed with blood and oil, takes place; all of which is carefully preserved in pits, and sol
farmers for manure.   The fish are then carefully washed with salt water, dried, and packed in hog
in which state they are sent abroad.   The average value of the pilchards taken annually on the
Cornwall is supposed to be from 50,000l. to 60,000l.   They are principally exported to the Medite
and the West Indies.   A bounty was formerly given on their exportation; but that is now repea

PILOTS and PILOTAGE.   The name of pilot or steersman is applied
to a particular officer, serving on board a ship during the course of a voyag
having the charge of the helm and the ship's route; or to a person taken on
at any particular place, for the purpose of conducting a ship through a river
or channel, or from or into a port.

It is to the latter description of persons that the term pilot is now usually ap
and pilots of this sort are established in various parts of the country by ancient c
of incorporation, or by particular statutes.   The most important of these corpo
are those of the Trinity-house, Deptford Strond; the fellowship of the pilots of
Deal, and the Isle of Thanet, commonly called the *Cinque Port pilots;* and the T
houses of Hull and Newcastle.   The 5 Geo. 4. c. 73. established a corporation
regulation and licensing of pilots in Liverpool.

The principle of the law with respect to pilots seems to be, that where the ma
bound by act of parliament to place his ship in charge of a pilot, and does so accor
the ship is not to be considered as under the management of the owners or their se
and they are not to be liable for any damage occasioned by the mismanagement
ship, unless it be proved that it arose from the negligence or misconduct of the
or men . but when it is in the election or discretion of the master to take a pilot
and he thinks fit to take one, the pilot so taken is to be considered as the servant
owners, who are to be responsible for his conduct. — (*Abbott on the Law of Sh*
part ii. c. 5.)

The statute of 6 Geo. 4. c. 125. has consolidated the laws with respect to
censing, employment, &c. of pilots.   It is of great length; but all its provisions
material importance may be embraced under the following heads : —

1. *Appointment of Pilots.*— The corporation of the Trinity-house of Deptford Strond are re
appoint and license fit and competent persons, duly skilled, to act as pilots for the purpose of con
all ships or vessels navigating the Thames, the Medway, and the several channels, creeks, a
thereof, between Orfordness and London Bridge, as also from London Bridge to the Downs, and
Downs westward as far as the Isle of Wight, and in the English Channel from the Isle of Wig
London Bridge; and all ships and vessels sailing as aforesaid (except as herein-after mentioned
conducted and piloted within the aforesaid limits by such pilots, and by no other persons whomso

No person shall be licensed by the said corporation as a pilot, who has not served as mate for th
on board of, or been for one year in the actual command of, a square rigged vessel of not less tha
register tonnage, as to licences for the *North Channel* upwards, and not less than 150 tons reg
nage, as to licences for the *North Channel*, *Queen's Channel*, *South Channel*, or other channe
wards, or who shall not have been employed in the pilotage or buoyage service of the said corpor
seven years, or who shall not have served an apprenticeship of five years to some pilot vessel
under the act passed in the 52d year of the reign of George III. or under this act; and tha
son so licensed shall take charge as a pilot of any ship or vessel drawing more than 14 feet wate
rivers Thames or Medway, or any of the channels leading thereto or thereupon, until such per
have acted as a licensed pilot for three years, and shall have been, after such three years, on n
nation, approved of in that behalf by the said corporation, on pain of forfeiting 10l. for every such
and the person employing or permitting such pilot to take charge of such ship or vessel is also
10l. — § 3.

Every pilot licensed by the corporation of the Trinity-house of Deptford Strond is to pay an annu
of 3l. 3s., and 6d. in the pound upon his earnings; which sums are to be applied to the uses of t
fund of the said corporation. — § 4.

The said corporation are further authorised to appoint competent persons, not more than *five*, nor
three, at such ports and places as they may think fit, (except within the liberty of the Cinque Ports
other ports and places as may have been specially provided for by act of parliament, or by charte
appointment of pilots,) to be called sub-commissioners of pilotage, who are to take the following

" I, A. B., do swear, that I will diligently and impartially examine into the capacity and skill
                        in the art of piloting ships and vessels into the roadstead, port, or harbour,
the coasts following; *widelicet* [here describe the limits within which the person examined is in

ilot], and will make true and speedy return thereof to the corporation of Trinity-house of Deptford
, without favour, affection, fee, or reward, other than such fee or reward as is allowed by the by-
regulations duly established in that behalf. So help me God."

pon the recommendation of such sub-commissioners, the Trinity-house corporation may grant
s to pilots. — § 5.

es of the appointment of pilots are to be put up in writing at the Trinity-house, and Custom-house,
, and at the Custom-houses of the ports for which they are licensed, and are to be published in the
 Gazette. — § 7.

erson shall take charge of any ship or vessel as a pilot belonging to the *Cinque Ports*, before he be
ed by the master and two fellows, or by four wardens of the society or fellowship of pilots of Dover,
nd the Isle of Thanet, touching his abilities, and shall be approved and admitted into the said
by the Lord Warden of the Cinque Ports, or his lieutenant; and any person presuming to act as
belonging to the said society or fellowship, without having been so examined, approved, and ad-
shall for the first offence forfeit 10*l.*, for the second 20*l.*, and for every other offence 40*l.* — § 15.

erson licensed by the aforesaid society or fellowship is to take charge of any ship or vessel drawing
an 11 feet 6 inches water, until he has acted as a pilot for three years; nor of a vessel drawing more
feet water, till he has acted as a pilot for five years; nor of a vessel drawing more than 17 feet
till he has acted as a pilot for seven years; when he is to be again examined, and if he shall be ap-
of and licensed upon such second examination, he may take charge of ships of any draught of
— § 16.

umber of *Cinque Port* pilots used to be fixed at 140; but during peace, no more than each alternate
 is to be filled up, unless the number be reduced below 120. — § 24.

odies politic and corporate, and all persons authorised to appoint or license pilots for any port or
England, shall, upon any such appointment being made, forthwith transmit to the Trinity-house,
, and to the commissioners of customs, London, the Christian name and surname, age, and place
ence, of every pilot so appointed, distinguishing the limits in which he is to act, and by whom ap-
. And the said bodies politic, &c. are to transmit lists, corrected up to the 31st day of December in
ar, either on that day, or within a month after, to the said Trinity-house, and commissioners of
oms, of the names and residences of all the pilots within their respective jurisdictions; stating all
rations that may have been made within the year in the rates of pilotage charged, and in the rules
lations for governing pilots within their respective districts. — § 35.

ommissioners of the customs are to transmit to their principal officers, at the different ports, the
nd places of residence of all the pilots residing within the limits of each port, as far as they are
ted with the same; and every pilot is to be furnished with copies of all proclamations and orders
il respecting the performance of quarantine. — § 36.

ticular description of the person of every pilot is to be written upon the back of his licence. And
n shall take charge of any ship or vessel, or in any manner act as a pilot, or receive any com-
 for acting as a pilot, until his licence shall have been registered by the principal officers of the
house of the place at or nearest to which such pilot shall reside (which officers are hereby
 to register the same without fee or reward), nor without having his licence at the time of his so
 his personal custody, and producing the same to the master of any ship or vessel, or other person,
ll be desirous of employing him as a pilot, or to whom he shall offer his services, on pain of
 a sum not exceeding 30*l.*, nor less than 10*l.*, for the first offence; and for the second or any
nt offence, a sum not exceeding 50*l.*, nor less than 30*l.*; and upon further pain, as to any person
as aforesaid, of forfeiting his licence, or being suspended from acting as a pilot, by and at the
n of the corporation or other authority from which such pilot's licence was derived, either for the
ond, or any subsequent offence. — §§ 65, 66.

ernment of Pilots. — All persons licensed to act as pilots by the Trinity-house, are subject to the
ent of the said corporation, which is empowered to make by-laws, rules, &c., specifying what sums
aid by such pilots to the sub-commissioners of pilotage for their examination, and for granting,
ing, or confirming their licences from time to time, and annexing such reasonable penalties and
es for the breach of such by-laws as to them shall seem expedient. But no such by-laws, regu-
&c. shall have any force till they have been examined, sanctioned, and approved, by the chief
 the court of King's Bench, or the chief justice of the court of Common Pleas.— § 11. (*N.B.*—The
 of the Trinity-house, Deptford Strond, sanctioned by Lord Tenterden, are annexed to this

of any proposed by-laws are to be transmitted to the privy council and the commissioners of
three months before they are submitted to any chief justice for approval; and the commissioners
stoms are to cause such proposed by-laws to be hung up in the several Custom-houses of the
ports of Great Britain, for the inspection of all parties having an interest therein. And when
laws shall have been sanctioned, they shall be hung up in the several Custom-houses within
s of which the pilots respectively shall be licensed, and also at the Trinity-house in London. —

nque Port pilots are to be subject to the rules and regulations framed by the Lord Warden of the
s, or his deputy, with the assent of the majority of the commissioners of *Loadmanage* (master
ens of the fellowship of pilots of Dover, Deal, and the Isle of Thanet). The privy council may,
amend, correct, or enlarge such rules or regulations, if they shall appear to them, upon the
ation of any person having an interest therein, to be in any material point erroneous, insufficient,
ve. — §§ 21, 22.

inity-house corporation are authorised and required to establish, vary, and alter from time to
ircumstances may require, the rates of pilotage performed by pilots licensed by the said corpora-
rding to the size and draught of water of the vessels, the distance piloted, the detention and re-
ty of the pilot, and such other circumstances as they may think fit to take into account. Tables
rates are to be hung up at the several Custom-houses of the ports to which they apply; and no
 less rates, or other reward or emolument for such pilotage, shall, under any pretence whatever,
ded, solicited, paid, received, or offered, on pain of forfeiting 10*l.* for every such offence, as well
arty offering as by the party accepting or soliciting the same. Ships returning by stress of
contrary winds, or on account of accident, into ports in the district of the Isle of Wight,
, and Falmouth, shall be subject to pay half the common pilotage in such ports.— § 8.

majority of the pilots licensed by the Trinity-house corporation in any port or place, or any
r in the same, be dissatisfied with the rates, they may appeal to the privy council, who may
on the matter as they think fit. — § 9.

erson applying for a licence to act as a pilot, shall, before any such licence be granted to him,
bond in a penal sum, at the discretion of the Trinity-house corporation, or of the Lord Warden
nque Ports, to an amount not exceeding 100*l.*, for better securing his due obedience to the by-
s, regulations, &c. to be made by competent authority. — § 27.

s may be annulled, suspended, or adjudged forfeited, at the pleasure of the foresaid corporation
Warden; but pilots, whose licences are so annulled, suspended, &c., may appeal to the privy
ho are authorised to make such adjudication in the premises as they may think fit. — §§ 29, 30.

sing of Pilot Boats. — The Trinity corporation and the fellowship of the Cinque Port pilots are
d to license pilot vessels of such size and description as may appear to them to be proper for
lots constantly in attendance in such vessels at sea; and the licensed pilots are authorised to

form themselves into companies, with consent of the corporations aforesaid, for providing and maintai
such pilot vessels, such companies and vessels being at all times subject to such rules and regulatio
shall from time to time be sanctioned by the said corporate bodies. — § 31.

Pilot boats or vessels are to be distinguished by being at all times and on every station fitted with b
sides, and having the upper streak next the gunwale painted white; they are, while afloat, to carry a
of large dimensions proportioned to the size of the vessel, at the mast head, or on a sprit or staff in s
conspicuous situation, which flag shall be half red and half white, in horizontal stripes, the white u
most. The name of the pilot on board is to be painted in large white letters (3 inches long)
black ground on the stern, and on each bow the number of the licence of such pilot; and the conceal
of such name or number, or the evasion of any of the before mentioned provisions, incurs a penalty of
to be paid by the senior pilot on board, who is answerable for their observance. Any pilot carried c
a boat other than a pilot boat, is to hoist a flag as previously ordered, on pain of forfeiting 20l. unles
show reasonable cause for having omitted it. — § 32.

The owners or master of any boat or vessel carrying a pilot's flag, without having a licensed pilo
board, shall for every such offence forfeit 100l. — § 33.

The Trinity-house corporation, the court of *Loadmanage* of the Cinque Ports, and all other corpora
and persons authorised to manage or direct pilots in any part of England, shall, on the 1st of Januar
each year, or within the month next following, transmit to the officer of the sixpenny duty in the po
London, a list of all the vessels of every description employed by them or by those under them, for
purposes of pilotage, with the number of men and boys belonging to or serving in such vessels. — §

4 *Duties of Pilots.* — In order to secure the due performance of his important duties by the pilot,
enacted, that every pilot, duly licensed, who shall, without sufficient cause, refuse or decline going o
any vessel wanting a pilot, upon signal being made by the same, or upon being required to do so by
master of such ship, or by any person interested therein as principal or agent, or by any officer of
corporation to which such pilot shall belong, or by any principal officer of the customs; or who shal
any frivolous pretext, quit any ship or vessel, or decline piloting thereof, after he has been engaged to
the same, or after going alongside thereof, without leave of the master; shall, for every such offe
forfeit not more than 100l. and not less than 10l. — § 72.

Any licensed pilot employing or making use of, or compelling or requiring any person having the ch
of any ship or vessel to employ or make use of, any boat, anchor, cable, &c. beyond what is act
necessary, shall forfeit and pay for every such offence not more than 50l. and not less than 10l., and
also be deprived of his licence, or suspended, at the discretion of those by whom he was licensed. —

If any licensed pilot shall lend his licence to an unlicensed person, to assist him in acting or claimi
act as pilot, and if such unlicensed person shall by drunkenness render himself incapable of condu
any ship or vessel, or negligently or wilfully lead, decoy, or betray any ship into danger, or shall unn
sarily or improperly cut any cable or cables belonging to any vessel; or if any such person shall, by w
misrepresentation of any circumstances upon which the safety of the vessel shall appear natural
depend, obtain or endeavour to obtain the conduct of such vessel, then, and in every such case, the pe
so offending, or who shall aid in, procure, abet, or connive at the committing any such offence or offe
shall, *besides being liable to damages at the suit of the party grieved*, forfeit and pay a sum of not
than 100l. and not less than 20l.; and if the person offending be a pilot, he shall be liable to be depriv
his licence, at the discretion of those by whom he was appointed. — § 74.

Pilots keeping public houses, or selling wine, spirituous liquors, tobacco, or tea (unless authorise
the competent authorities), or being concerned in any fraud or offence against the revenue laws,
relation to any branch of their duty, shall, over and above all mulcts, penalties, &c. for such offe
be adjudged to forfeit their licence, or be suspended, at the discretion of those by whom the
licensed. — § 68.

A pilot, when taken on board, shall enter his name in the log book of every ship entering the po
London requiring to be piloted under this act, and if any pilot or other person insert a false name,
to forfeit 20l.; and the name or names of the pilot or pilots so entered in the log book and employ
piloting the vessel, are to be inserted in the *entry* or *report* of such vessel inwards; and this insert
to be made (without fee or reward) by the proper officer of the customs, who shall report the same
to the Trinity-house, and monthly to the Lord Warden of the Cinque Ports. The principal searc
officer of the customs at Gravesend is to demand and take the name or names of the pilot or pilots
vessels clearing outwards, and shall transmit monthly lists thereof to the Trinity-house, on pa
forfeiting a sum not more than 10l., nor less than 5l., to be paid by each and every of the persons for
who shall neglect to comply with any of the foresaid regulations. — § 43.

Pilots quitting any vessel in the Thames or Medway before she has arrived at the place to whic
was bound, without the consent of the captain or other person in command, and unless some othe
qualified person shall with such consent come on board and take charge of the ship, shall forfeit for
offence all pay or reward they might be entitled to, and shall also be subject to such other pena
punishment as may legally affect them in consequence of any by-law, &c. — § 42.

Pilots neglecting or refusing to obey the orders of the different dock masters within their resp
jurisdictions incur a penalty of not more than 50l. and not less than 20l. for each offence, and may b
missed or suspended. — § 75.

Licensed pilots may supersede unlicensed ones. And if any unlicensed person shall act after
licensed pilot has offered to come on board and take charge of the ship, she being at the time with
limits for which he is qualified, such unlicensed person shall forfeit not more than 5l. and not les
20l. — § 70.

But unlicensed persons may act so long as no licensed pilot offers to take charge of the sh
makes a signal for that purpose, or where and so long as the ship shall be in distress. — § 71.

Licensed pilots who have executed the bond before mentioned shall not be liable to any acti
damages on account of neglect or want of skill, at the suit of the part grieved, in any greater sun
the amount which shall have been specified by way of penalty in such bond, and the pilotage paya
him in respect of the voyage during which the neglect or want of skill are alleged to have been exh
— § 57.

5. *Fees of Pilotage.* — The charge on account of pilotage is regulated in various places by us
statute, and generally increases in proportion to the depth of water which the vessel draws. The T
house corporation and the Lord Warden of the Cinque Ports have authority, as before mention
fix the rates on account of pilotage to be charged by all pilots licensed by them.—(Subjoined to this
are tables of the present rates.)

Any pilot carried to sea beyond the limits of his district without his free consent, except in ca
absolute necessity, shall, over and above his pilotage, receive 10s. 6d. a day, to be computed from a
clusive of the day next after the day on which the vessel shall pass the limit to which the pilo
engaged to conduct her, and until he shall be returned to the port or place where he was taken on
or be discharged for a sufficient time to enable him to return there. — § 38.

Pilots are to qualify themselves for conducting vessels in and out of Ramsgate harbour, and th
bours of Dover, Sandwich, and Margate, and shall be entitled to and receive for such pilotage at th
of 5s. for every foot of the draught of water of every vessel so piloted. — §§ 39, 40.

Ships bound to the Thames, repairing to Standgate Creek, or other place appointed for the perfor
of *quarantine*, are to pay the full charges of pilotage to such place, and a further sum of 8s. a day
days the pilot shall be obliged to remain on quarantine.

Any boat or vessel running before a ship or vessel, not having a licensed pilot on board, when su

cannot be boarded for the purpose of directing her course, the pilot on board such boat or vessel, pilot be on board, the person having the command thereof, and who shall run before such he request or by direction of the master, shall be entitled to full pilotage for the distance 34.

sums which shall become due to any licensed pilot for the pilotage of foreign ships or vessels o or from the port of *London* may be recovered from the owners or masters of such ships or r from the consignees or agents thereof, who shall have paid, or made themselves liable to pay, charge for the ship or vessel in the port of her arrival or delivery as to pilotage inwards, and rt from whence she shall clear out or sail as to pilotage outwards; and may be levied in like according to the amount, as any penalty may be recovered and levied by virtue of the act, demand eing made in writing at least *fourteen* days before such levy. And the master or other person e charge of ships or vessels, *not having British registers*, which shall enter into or sail from the ndon, and which are by law required to be piloted by persons licensed by the corporation of the ouse, or the consignees or agents thereof, are to pay at the Trinity-house, in *London*, to pointed by the corporation of the Trinity-house, the full pilotage inwards and outwards; viz. age outwards, the amount for the distance which the ship is by law required to be piloted; as e inwards, where a pilot shall have been on board, the amount for the distance piloted by him, if an that which she shall be required to be piloted; if less, or if no pilot shall have been on board, t for the distance which she was by law required to be piloted: the pilotage inwards may be . upon the master or other person in charge, consignee, or agent, in the same manner as in the ips *having British registers*, if such pilotage inwards be not paid within *fourteen* days from the ship's reporting inwards. — §§ 44. 46.

otage outward upon foreign vessels is to be calculated according to the scale or amount of on which such ships or vessels are rated in the port of *London* for payment of light and other according to the draught of water thereof, as the Trinity-house may think most proper.

 to prevent controversies with respect to the draught of water of ships not having British the Trinity-house is empowered to appoint an officer to measure the draught of water of ships ct to which there is any controversy, such officer receiving 1*l*. 1*s*. for his trouble if the ship be entrance to the London docks, and 10*s*. 6*d*. if above such entrance, from the party against whom cide. If arriving inwards, application for such officer must be made within 12 hours after the me to her moorings, and before she begin to unlade, and before quitting her moorings if clear- rds. — § 50.

nity-house are empowered to take measures for the relief of foreign vessels coming to the port with fish, corn, and other provisions on board, either from the whole or a part of the charges . of pilotage that would fall upon them under this act. — § 51.

gn vessel shall be cleared outwards until a certificate signed by the person appointed for that the Trinity-house that the pilotage has been paid, has been produced; the corporation pay the yed, on proof that he has duly performed his service, the pilotage, after deducting the sixpenny 47.

signees or agents of any ship or vessel are authorised a..d empowered to retain in their hands y, out of any monies which they may have received or shall thereafter receive for or on account ip or vessel, or the owner or owners thereof, so much as shall be sufficient to pay and discharge ge and any expenses attending the same. — § 45.

nsibility, &c. of Masters. — Ships coming from the westward, bound to any place in the Thames , not having a duly qualified Cinque Port pilot on board, shall, on arriving at *Dungeness*, and ave passed the south buoy of the *Brake*, display and keep flying the usual signal for a pilot to ard; and the master shall heave to and shorten sail, so as to facilitate the entry of the pilot. displaying such signal, &c. shall forfeit and pay double the amount of the sum that the charge would have amounted to. And it is further provided, that all masters of vessels acting them- lots, or employing any unlicensed person as such, or any licensed person out of the limit of his n, after any licensed and qualified pilot shall have offered to come on board, or made a signal rpose, shall forfeit double the sum that would have been legally demandable as pilotage, and an enalty of 5*l*. for every 50 tons burthen of the ship, if the Trinity-house or Lord Warden of the ts, as the case may be, shall think it proper to certify the same.

master of any of the following vessels may pilot the same, *so long as he is not assisted by any pilot or other person than the ordinary crew*: viz. the master of any collier, or of any ship or ng to *Norway*, or to the *Cattegat* or *Baltic*, or round the *North Cape*, or into the *White Sea*, on d or outward voyages, or of any constant trader inwards, from the ports between *Boulogne* and the *Baltic* (all such ships or vessels having *British* registers, and coming up by the nnel, but not otherwise), or of any *Irish* trader using the navigation of the rivers *Thames y*, or of any ship or vessel employed in the regular coasting trade of the kingdom, or of any sel wholly laden with stone from *Guernsey, Jersey, Alderney, Sark*, or *Man*, and being the thereof, or of any ship or vessel, not exceeding the burthen of 60 tons, and *having a British* r not exceeding the burthen of 60 tons, and *not having a British register*, if authorised so to do of the privy council,) or of any other ship or vessel whatsoever, whilst the same is within the e port or place to which she belongs, the same not being a port or place in relation to which rovision hath heretofore been made by any act or acts of parliament, or by any charter or the appointment of pilots. — §§ 59, 60.

er or mate of any vessel, being the owner or part owner thereof, and residing at Dover, Deal, of Thanet, shall not be liable to any penalty for conducting or piloting his own ship or vessel the rivers Thames or Medway, or into or out of any place within the jurisdiction of the Cinque 52.

hall not extend, or be construed to extend, to subject the master or owner of any ship or vessel e penalties of this act, for employing any person or persons whomsoever, as a pilot or pilots, he assistance of such ship or vessel whilst the same shall be in distress, or in consequence under any circumstances which shall have rendered it necessary for such owner or master to f of the best assistance which at the time could be procured. — § 61.

or master of any ship or vessel shall be answerable for any loss or damage which shall happen on or persons whatsoever, from or by reason or means of no licensed pilot, or of no duly ot, being on board thereof, unless it shall be proved that the want of such licensed or of such ed pilot respectively shall have arisen from any refusal to take such licensed or qualified rd, or from the wilful neglect of the master of such ship or vessel in not heaving to, or using le means, consistently with her safety, for the purpose of taking on board thereof any pilot e ready and offer to take charge of the same. — § 53.

n this act shall extend, or be construed to extend, to make the owner of any ship or vessel y such case, for any loss or damage beyond the value of such ship or vessel, and her es, and the freight due, or to grow due, for and during the voyage wherein such loss or happen or arise. — § 54.

or master of any ship or vessel shall be answerable for any loss or damage which shall happen n or persons whomsoever, from or by reason or means of any neglect, default, incompetency, y of any licensed pilot acting in the charge of any such ship or vessel, under or in pursuance e provisions of this act, where and so long as such pilot shall be duly qualified to have the

charge of such ship or vessel, or where and so long as no duly qualified pilot shall have offered charge thereof. — § 55.

Nothing in this act shall be construed to extend to deprive any person or persons of any remedies upon any contract of insurance, or of any other remedy whatsoever, which he or the have had if this act had not been passed, by reason or on account of the neglect, default, incomp or incapacity of any pilot duly acting in the charge of any ship or vessel, under or in pursuance o the provisions of this act, or by reason or on account of no pilot, or of no duly qualified pilot, b board of any such ship or vessel, unless it shall be proved that the want of a pilot arises from a re the part of the master to take such pilot on board, or to heave to for him. — § 56.

All masters or other persons having the command of any ship, who shall report, or be privy to a reporting, a false account of the draught of water of such ship, shall, besides the full pilotage double the amount thereof; and any master or other person having any interest, share, or pro any vessel, who shall fraudulently alter any marks on the stem or stern post thereof, diminis draught of water, or shall be privy or consent thereto, shall for every such offence forfeit and sum of 500*l*.

7. *Recovery of Penalties.* — Penalties incurred under this act, not exceeding 20*l.*, are to be re before a justice by prosecution within *six* months; and penalties *above* 20*l.* by action of debt in the courts of record at *Westminster*, to be commenced within *twelve* months; but if it shall be n appear, as soon after as the circumstances of the case will admit, that the commencement of th cution or action has been delayed by reason of the absence of any party or parties, whether offen complaining, or of any necessary witness, then upon such circumstances being stated by affidav before any judge of any of his Majesty's courts of record at *Westminster*, any such judge ma or authorise the commencement of the prosecution or action within such further time as he sha fit to limit.

It is, however, provided, that nothing therein contained shall affect or impair the jurisdictio Court of Loadmanage, or High Court of Admiralty, nor the right of the city of London, nor (in any separate jurisdictions established under any act of parliament or charter. — §§ 76, 77. 87, 88,

---

By-Laws, Regulations, and Ordinances as to Pilots, framed by the Trinity Corporation sanctioned by Lord Tenterden, 19th April, 1826.

I. Annuls the previous regulations.

II. It is ordained, that every pilot who shall be ordered to proceed on his Majesty's service, by a signed by the deputy master or secretary of the said corporation, or by the officer for the time b the said corporation at Yarmouth, or elsewhere, duly authorised to act in matters of pilotage, or w be so ordered, in writing or otherwise, by any officer in his Majesty's service, shall immediately thereon; and every pilot who shall fail so to do, or shall evade the receipt of any such order, or w quit or decline such service, shall for the first offence forfeit 5*l.*, and for the second and every sub offence 10*l.* each.

III. It is ordained, that every pilot engaged in the charge of any ship employed by governmer transport service, shall observe particularly if any unnecessary delay takes place on the part of the in proceeding towards his destination; and if any delay does take place, such pilot shall, on his report the same to the secretary of the said corporation, and upon going on board, such pilot sh notice to the master that he has orders so to do.

IV. It is ordained, that no pilot having the charge of a merchant ship shall stop the same along moorings of his Majesty's ships at Deptford, or elsewhere, or between the Round Tree and Bathin Gravesend (except in either of such cases there be an extreme necessity for so doing, or leave be for that purpose from the proper officer or officers in that behalf), and all pilots licensed by corporation are at all times to be particularly careful to steer clear of the king's ships in passing

V. It is ordained, that every pilot, when called upon or required to pilot any ship or vessel, shall engagements to any other ship, forthwith make known such engagement, and specify the pa thereof truly and faithfully to the person calling for or requiring such pilot's service; and in cas concealment, misrepresentation, or falsehood, in respect of such alleged previous engagement, offending shall forfeit 10*l.*

VI. It is ordained, that every pilot who shall have taken charge of any ship from the river T the Downs, or elsewhere, shall, without any additional compensation in that behalf, wait on boar space of three complete days while such ship may be detained at Gravesend, or elsewhere, for seamen, or by any other casualty; nor shall he at the end of three complete days be at liberty to q ship, or receive any additional compensation, if she shall be further detained by winds, weather, and should the ship be detained beyond three complete days on any other account except winds, or tides, the pilot having the charge thereof shall nevertheless still (if required so to do) rema charge of her, provided a compensation of 6*s.* per day be offered to him in that behalf by the r owner.

VII. It is ordained, that every pilot shall in all cases demean himself civilly and respectfully all persons who may require his service, and towards all officers in his Majesty's navy, and shall a strict temperance and sobriety in the exercise of his office, and shall use his utmost care and for the safe conduct of every ship which he shall be intrusted with the charge of, and to pre doing damage to others.

VIII. It is ordained, that every pilot who shall undertake the charge of any ship downwar before his departure, leave, or cause to be left, notice thereof, in writing, at the proper office at the house in London, with one of the clerks there attending, and shall be considered as disengaged shall have done so; and upon such pilot's return, he shall immediately, in his own person, atte said office, and make and sign such entry, in a book there kept for that purpose, as the said co shall from time to time direct or require.

IX. It is ordained, that every pilot licensed by the said corporation shall, from time to time, times, in obedience to the order or summons of the said corporation, under the hand of the thereof for the time being, duly delivered or offered to such pilot, or left a reasonable time at or last known place of residence of such pilot, attend the said corporation, at their courts, by-l committees, or their secretary for the time being, at the Trinity-house in London; and that e licensed by the said corporation, upon a certificate of qualification from sub-commissioners of shall, in like manner, attend the sub-commissioners of the port or place for which such pilot s licensed, in obedience to the order or summons of the said sub-commissioners, under their han hands of the major part of them, duly delivered, offered, or left as aforesaid, to answer to an brought against such pilots respectively, or for the performance of any public service, or for purpose whatsoever; and in default of such attendance, every pilot so offending shall forfeit, fo offence, 40*s.*, and for the second and every subsequent offence 5*l.* each.

X. It is ordered, and hereby directed, that every pilot licensed or to be licensed by the said co upon their receiving a certificate of examination by any sub-commissioners of pilotage, shall examination, and for granting the licence thereon, pay the sum of 2 guineas to the said sub-comr of pilotage by whom he shall be examined, or to one of them; and shall also, for the renewing o ing such licence from time to time, pay to the sub-commissioners of pilotage for the time being the port or place specified in such licence, or to one of them, the annual sums following; say,) every pilot so licensed or to be licensed as aforesaid, for the ports of Plymouth, Porto

respectively, the annual sum of 2 guineas; and every pilot licensed or to be licensed as afore-
 or any other port or place, the annual sum of 1 guinea, unless the pilots at or for such port or place
e divided into two classes; and, in that case the pilots of the first class are to pay the annual sum
uineas each, and pilots not of the first class the annual sum of 1 guinea each.

It is ordained, that no pilot shall add to or in any way alter his licence, or make or alter any
ment thereon, nor shall he be privy to any such licence or endorsement being altered.

It is ordained, that every pilot who shall observe any alteration in any of the sands or channels,
any of the buoys or beacons of the said corporation are driven away, broken down, or out of
shall forthwith deliver or send a correct statement thereof, in writing, to the secretary of the said
ation for the time being.

. It is ordained, that every pilot shall, whenever he comes to an anchor, carefully observe the
of the tide, and the force of the stream; and if it shall happen, that he comes near to a sand or
bject or cause of danger, and there be any other ships or ship in company likely to fall in there-
uch pilot shall immediately give notice thereof to the captain or principal officer of the ship under
, that he may make a signal to such other ship or ships for avoiding the same.

It is ordained, that no pilot shall, on any pretence, aid or assist, either in his own person or with
or servants, or by any other means whatever, the landing, removing, or secreting any seamen
y merchant ship or vessel, to avoid serving in his Majesty's navy, or escape the impress for the

It is ordained, that every pilot shall from time to time conform himself strictly to all directions
shall be given to him by any of the harbour masters authorised by act of parliament, under the
tion of the city of London, touching the mooring, unmooring, placing, or removing of any ship
l under his charge, as long as such ship or vessel shall be lying and situate within the limits of the
ty of such harbour master.

It is ordained, that each and every pilot belonging to a licensed pilot vessel shall be at liberty to
n one apprentice and no more.

It is ordained, that for any work done on the rivers Thames or Medway by men in boats, being
n the work for the whole tide, the pay shall be, for half a tide's work, 4s. to each man, and so in
on for any time less than a whole tide, the pay for which is settled by the said act of the 6th year
eign of his present Majesty at 8s.

1. It is ordained, that in all cases where pecuniary penalties and forfeitures are annexed to the
of the foregoing by-laws, rules, orders, regulations, and ordinances, the said corporation of
house may mitigate and reduce the same to one fourth part at their discretion.

It is ordained, that every pilot who shall offend against any or either of the foregoing by-laws,
regulations, and ordinances, shall, for every such offence (whether the same shall subject him to
uniary penalty or not, and in addition to such penalty if any), be liable to have his licence an-
nd forfeited, or suspended, at the discretion of the said corporation.

— Besides conforming themselves diligently so the above by-laws, rules, orders, regulations, and
es, the pilots licensed by the corporation of Trinity-house are, of course, in all things to observe
the same enactments and provisions relating to such pilots contained in the said act of parliament
d passed in the 6th year of the reign of his Majesty King George the Fourth, a copy of which
een delivered to each of the said pilots.

he following tables of the charges on account of pilotage, &c., are the most complete that have
been published. They have all been derived from official sources, so that their accuracy may
ded upon.

CHARGES ON ACCOUNT OF PILOTAGE.

Table of the Rates of Pilotage to be demanded and received by Pilots licensed by the Corporation of Trinity-house of Deptford Strond, for piloting Vessels.

From	To	7 Feet and under.	8 Feet.	9 Feet.	10 Feet.	11 Feet.	12 Feet.	13 Feet.	14 Feet.	15 Feet.	16 Feet.	17 Feet.	18 Feet.	19 Feet.	20 Feet.	21 Feet.	22 Feet.	23 Feet and upwards.
The Sea, Orfordness, the Downs, Hoseley Bay, and vice versâ.	Nore or Warps																	
	Gravesend, Chatham, Standgate Creek, or Blackstakes																	
	Long Reach																	
	Woolwich or Blackwall																	
	Moorings or London Docks																	
The Nore or Warps, and vice versâ.	Grave-end, Standgate Creek, or Blackstakes																	
	Long Reach or Chatham																	
	Woolwich or Blackwall																	
	Moorings or London Docks																	
Gravesend Reach, and vice versâ.	Long Reach																	
	Woolwich or Blackwall																	
	Moorings or London Docks																	
	Sheerness, Standgate Creek, or Blackstakes																	
	Chatham																	
Long Reach, and vice versâ.	Woolwich or Blackwall																	
	Moorings or London Docks																	
	Sheerness, Standgate Creek, or Blackstakes																	
	Chatham																	
Woolwich, or Blackwall, and vice versâ.	Moorings or London Docks																	
	Sheerness, Standgate Creek, or Blackstakes																	
	Chatham																	

Ships not having British registers are to pay one fourth more than ships having British registers, except when such first-mentioned ships shall be chiefly laden with corn or other provisions, or shall, by any order of his Majesty's most honourable privy council, be privileged to enter the ports of this kingdom, upon paying the same duties of tonnage and pilotage as are paid by British vessels: but in entering or leaving the port of London, &c. such rates of pilotage only as are payable by ships having British registers. — For half a foot exceeding the above draughts of water, the medium price between the two limits. — For intermediate distances a proportionate rate. — For removing a ship or vessel from moorings into a dry or wet dock, for a ship under 300 tons, 15s.; 300 to 600 tons, 1l.; above 600 to 1,000 tons, 1l. 11s. 6d.; above 1,000 tons, 2l. 2s. — In the river Thames, above Gravesend, for a boat of a class carrying an anchor of above a level, ditto, above 1l/10, ditto, with a whole distancing from Gravesend to London; and in proportion for any part of that distance. — And for each man's service in those boats, 8s. per tide.

Table of the Rates of Pilotage to be demanded and received by Pilots licensed by the Lord Warden of the Cinque Ports and Constable of Dover Castle, or his Lieutenant for the time being, for piloting Ships and Vessels within the Limits in the said Table mentioned.

From	To	Under 7 Feet.	From 7 Feet to 10 Feet.	11 Feet.	12 Feet.	13 Feet.	14 Feet.	15 Feet.	16 Feet.	17 Feet.	18 Feet.	19 Feet.	20 Feet.	21 Feet.	22 Feet.	23 Feet and upwards.
The Downs	Nore, Sheerness, Standgate Creek, Gravesend															
	Long Reach															
	Blackwall or London															
	Gravesend															
Standgate Creek																

g a Pilot on Board, and age of Ships and Vessels nchorage in the Downs.*	60 Tons, and under 150.	150 Tons, and under 250.	250 Tons, and under 400.	400 Tons, and under 600.	600 Tons, and upwards.
	L. s. d.	L. s. d.	L. s. d.	L. s. d.	L. s. d.
Dungeness to off Folke-he Church bearing N. y compass	2 0 0	3 0 0	3 10 0	4 0 0	5 5 0
Folkestone to the South , the Lights in one the South Foreland to ns	1 10 0	2 0 0	2 10 0	3 0 0	4 4 0
	1 5 0	1 5 0	1 10 0	2 0 0	3 3 0

e Thames avesend	For a boat of a class carrying an anchor of above 4 cwt. with a corresponding tow-line	L. s. d. 2 2 0	Per trip for the whole distance from Gravesend to London ; and in proportion for any part of that distance.
	Do. do. 2 cwt.	1 1 0	
	Do. do. under 2 cwt.	0 15 0	
	And for each man's service in these boats, 8s. per tide.		

HARGED FOR THE PILOTAGE OF VESSELS, WITH AN ACCOUNT OF OTHER CHARGES AFFECTING THEM IN SOME OF THE UNDERMENTIONED PORTS.

s District, viz. — From Bangor to a line drawn Ormes Head to Point Linas; and to and from, out of, all ports and places within those limits. o master of a vessel is compelled to take a pilot istrict, unless coming into or going out of port ; take a pilot, it must be one of the district pilots,

ilotage, for piloting Ships within the Beaumaris District.

Innwards.

			L. s. d.
tside d } into the Bay		Under 100 tons	0 15 0
		100 to 200	1 1 0
		200 to 300	1 11 6
		300 and upwards	2 2 0
side d } into the Bay		Under 100 tons	0 10 6
		100 to 200	0 15 0
		200 to 300	1 1 0
		300 and upwards	1 11 6

Outwards.

	L. s. d.
ons	0 10 6
	0 15 0
	1 1 0
ards	1 14 6

aving British registers are to pay one fourth more t in the above table.

	L. s. d.
ilot be landed at Great Ormes Head— }	2 2 0
of the limits of his licence, to Chester } ol	
lot should happen to have charge of the } her of the said places	5 6 0

7s. 6d. per day is to be allowed to the pilot for h pilot may be detained on board in consequence vessel performing quarantine, or detained under rictions or circumstances such ship may be liable

	Foreign Rate.	British Rate.
	L. s. d.	L. s. d.
ies	0 0 3 per ton	0 0 2 per ton
never to exceed	3 0 0 per ves.	2 0 0 per ves.
ivered at the		
	0 2 8 per ton	0 2 0 per ton
	0 4 0 —	0 3 0 —
ed at Garmoyle	0 3 4 —	0 2 6 —
	0 4 6 —	0 3 6 —
m Whitehouse Garmoyle, and	0 14 0 per ves.	0 10 6 per ves.
10 —	1 0 0 —	0 15 0 —
12 —	1 8 0 —	1 1 0 —
14 —	2 16 0 —	2 2 0 —
oyle to the Quay, ersad - 4 feet	0 6 7 —	0 5 0 —
6 —	0 10 8 —	0 8 0 —
7 —	0 13 4 —	0 10 0 —
8 —	0 16 0 —	0 12 0 —
9 —	1 1 0 —	0 15 9 —
10 —	1 10 0 —	1 2 6 —
12 —	2 2 0 —	1 11 6 —
14 —	4 0 0 —	3 3 0 —
tehouse Road y, and vice versâ		
9 feet	1 15 0	1 7 6
10 —	2 10 0	1 17 6
12 —	3 10 0	2 12 6
14 —	7 0 0	5 5 0
Vessels trading Berwick and f the coast be-nkirk and the pe	0 2 0 per ton	0 1 0 per ton
altic, and be-nkirk and the	0 2 4 —	0 1 2 —
Gibraltar hite or Medi- Seas, West merica, Green-any other fo-e not before		
l	0 3 0 —	0 1 6 —
o the Port for Ballast	0 4 0 —	0 2 0 —
Laden	0 6 0 —	0 3 0 —
rom 1st April		
ober —	0 1 8 per foot	0 1 3 per foot
to 1st April	0 2 0 —	0 1 6 —

BRIGHTON.,–Pilotage for the Beaches at Brighthelmstone, Hastings, or Bexhill.

8 Feet and under.	8 to 10 Feet.	Above 10 Feet.
1s. 3d. per Foot.	1s. 9d. per Foot.	2s. per Foot.

The above rates for the harbours and beaches are due both inwards and inwards ; but no charge whatever is to be made for the use of pilot boats.

Ships going into the harbours of Rye and Shoreham, and unloading near the harbour's mouth, are subject to half pilotage only ; but if such ships are afterwards removed by pilots to any dock or wharf near the town, where such ships may be for the purpose of taking in a cargo, in that case the full pilotage is due.

Ships taken charge of in distress are to pay according to circumstances, to be settled by the sub-commissioners.

Ships not having British registers are to pay one fourth more of the rates of pilotage for the harbours and beaches, than stated in the above tables.

BRISTOL.

	Foreign Rate.	British Rate.
	Per Ves.	Per Ves.
	L. s. d.	L. s. d.
Pilotage from Lundy Island or the west-ward thereof to Kingroad, under 100 tons	3 18 9	3 3 0
100 and under 200 —	5 5 0	4 4 0
200 — 300 —	6 11 3	5 5 0
300 and upwards	7 17 6	6 6 0
From Coombe to Kingroad, under 100 tons	2 12 6	2 2 0
100 and under 200 —	3 10 0	2 16 0
200 — 300 —	4 7 6	3 10 0
300 and upwards	5 5 0	4 4 0
From Minehead to Kingroad, under 100 tons	1 6 3	1 1 0
100 and under 200 —	1 15 0	1 8 0
200 — 300 —	2 3 9	1 15 0
300 and upwards	2 12 6	2 2 0
From the Holms to Kingroad, under 100 tons	0 13 1½	0 10 6
100 and under 200 —	0 17 6	0 14 0
200 — 300 —	1 1 10½	0 17 6
300 and upwards	1 6 3	1 1 0
From Portishead, Kingroad, Hung-road, or Broad Pill, to Cumberland or Bathurst Basin, or vice versâ, under 40 tons	0 5 0	0 4 0
40 and under 60	0 6 3	0 5 0
60 — 80	0 9 4½	0 7 6
80 — 100	0 12 6	0 10 0
100 — 200	0 18 9	0 15 0
200 — 300 —	1 5 0	1 0 0
300 and upwards	1 11 3	1 5 0
From Portishead, Kingroad, Hung-road, or Broad Pill, to either of them, under 100 tons	0 12 6	0 10 0
100 and under 200 —	0 18 9	0 15 0
200 — 300 —	1 5 0	1 0 0
300 and upwards	1 11 3	1 5 0

DARTMOUTH District. — From Bob's Nose to the Start, and vice versâ ; and to and from, and in and out of, all ports and places within those limits.

N. B.— No master of a vessel is compelled to take a pilot within this district, unless going into or coming out of port, within a line drawn from the Mewstone to the Blackstone , but if he do take a pilot between Bob's Nose and the Start, it must be one of the district pilots, if one offer.

Rates of Pilotage, for piloting Ships within the Dartmouth District. — All British ships, if boarded without the run of the Mewstone East, or the Blackstone West, are to pay as follows ; viz.—

	Per Foot.
	s. d.
Drawing 10 feet of water and under	2 6
10 to 12 feet	3 0
12 to 14 feet	3 6
14 to 16 feet	4 0
16 feet and upwards	5 0

All British ships, if boarded within that line, are to pay one fourth part less.

All British ships, boarded within the Castle, are to pay only half pilotage : subject to the consideration of the weather, which is to be settled by the sub-commissioners.

In carrying ships out of the harbour, the pilotage is to be in all cases one third less than the inward pilotage.

pilot is put on board by a boat from the shore, one seventh to the pilot, and the remaining six sevenths to the boat

All ships not having British registers are to pay one fourth more than the rates above stated.

Masters of ships taking a pilot at sea, viz. two leagues or more from the harbour's mouth, are to pay according to circumstances attending the hazard run, assistance required, &c., which is to be regulated, in case of dispute, by the sub-commissioners. The pilot is to provide one proper tow-boat, with at least four men it; and if further assistance of another boat or boats and men be required, the master or owners of the ship to pay the additional charge ;—and, in case of dispute, to be settled by the sub-commissioners, and the assistants rewarded according to the risk, time, and trouble.

DUBLIN.

	Foreign Rate.			British Rate.		
	L.	s.	d.	L.	s.	d.
Ballast Dues. Taken on board within the Harbour	0	2	6 per ton	0	1	8 per ton
thrown out	0	0	10 —	0	0	8 —
Tonnage Dues -	0	1	6 —	0	0	9 —
Inwards.						
Pilotage over the Bar from without the Banks	0	6	0 per foot	0	3	0 per foot
within	0	4	0 —	0	2	0 —
within the Heads	0	3	0 —	0	1	6 —
From Poolbeg to the Quays	0	1	6 —	0	1	0 —
Outwards.						
From the Quays to Poolbeg Laden	0	1	6 —	0	1	0 —
From Poolbeg over the Bar Laden	0	1	6 —	0	1	0 —

DUNDEE.

	Foreign Rate.			British Rate.		
	L.	s.	d.	L.	s.	d.
Harbour Dues. Vessels from India or China -	0	5	0 per ton	0	2	6 per ton
West Indies, Azores, Madeira, Teneriffe, Cape de Verd Isles, Greenland, and Davis Straits	0	1	4 —	0	0	8 —
America, Mediterranean, or any part north of Drontheim	0	1	0 —	0	0	6 —
Any part between Dunkirk and Gibraltar (including Dunkirk) and from any part in the Baltic	0	0	8 —	0	0	4 —

N. B.— British vessels navigated by non-freemen pay one half more.

EXETER District, viz. — From Lyme to Bob's Nose, and *vice versâ*; and to and from, and into and out of, all ports and places within those limits.

N. B.— No master of a ship is compelled to take a pilot within this district, until he comes off the ports of Exmouth and Teignmouth; but if he do take a pilot between Lyme and Bob's Nose, it must be one of the district pilots, if one offer.

Rates of Pilotage for Vessels in and over Exmouth Bar, to the Moorings in the Bight at Exmouth, and out again over the Bar.

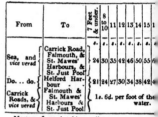

Coasters.
If above per register
60 tons	80 tons	3 6
80 —	90 —	4 0
90 —	100 —	4 6
100 —	125 —	5 6
125 —	150 —	6 0
150 —	175 —	7 0
175 —	200 —	7 6
200 —	250 —	9 6
250 —	300 —	11 6
300 —	400 —	12 6
and not exceeding — Per foot, draught of water.

And if carried up to Topsham Quay and back, 1 guinea extra.

Ships from Foreign Parts.
If above per register or measurement
60 tons	80 tons	6 6
80 —	100 —	7 6
100 —	150 —	9 6
150 —	200 —	10 6
200 —	250 —	12 6
250 —	300 —	13 6
300 —	350 —	15 6
and not exceeding — Per foot, draught of water.

And if carried up to Topsham Quay and back, 1 guinea extra.

For Vessels in and out, over Teignmouth Bar.

Ships from Foreign Parts.
If above per register:
60 tons	100 tons	3 0
100 —	150 —	3 6
150 —	200 —	4 0
200 —	250 —	4 6
250 —	300 —	5 0
300 —	400 —	6 6
and not exceeding — Per foot, draught of water.

Coasters.
If above per register or measurement
60 tons	80 tons	3 0
80 —	100 —	3 6
100 —	150 —	4 0
150 —	200 —	4 6
200 —	250 —	5 0
250 —	300 —	6 0
300 —	400 —	7 0
and not exceeding — Per foot, draught of water.

Ships not having British registers to pay one fourth more than is stated in the preceding table.

Pilots to provide a boat and crew to assist over the bar to a mooring berth ; for which they shall be paid, over and above the pilotage, 2s. 6d. for each man or oar employed for that purpose.

Masters of ships taking a pilot off the Bill of Portland, or the Start (which is optional to them), are to pay, beyond the pilotage, from Bob's Nose, or Lyme, as follows, viz. :— Colliers and coasters, 2 guineas ; ships from foreign ports, 3 guineas ; and proportionately for intermediate distances.

FALMOUTH District, viz. — From the Dodman to and *vice versâ*; and to and from, and into and ports and places within those limits.

N. B.— No master of a vessel is compelled to t within this district, unless going into or coming port within a line drawn from the Manacles to the but if he does take a pilot between the Dodma Lizard, it must be one of the district pilots, if one

Table of the Rates of Pilotage, for piloting Ships Falmouth District.

From	To	7 Feet & under.	8 to 10	11	12	13	14	15	1
		s.	s.	s.	s.	s.	s.	s.	
Sea, and *vice versâ*	Carrick Road, Falmouth, & St. Mawes' Harbours, & St. Just Pool	24	30	35	42	46	50	55	6
Do. .. do.	Helford Harbour	21	24	27	30	34	38	42	
Carrick Roads, & *vice versâ*	Falmouth & St. Mawes' Harbours & St. Just Pool	1s. 6d. per foot of the water.							

Masters of vessels taking a pilot at sea, are to pay

For putting a pilot on board without a line drawn from the Manacles to the Dodman

Ditto, from the entrance of Helford Harbour to the Gull Rock

Ditto, a mile without the Shag Rock or Pendennis Point

Ditto, of the Lizard, or in the parallel of the Lizard, or meeting a vessel there, and running before her, not being able to put a pilot on board, provided the master of the vessel consents to receive a pilot at that distance

Ships not having British registers to pay one of the rates of pilotage than stated in the above tal

N.B.— No allowance for a pilot going on board a harbour to take charge, except in extremely bad when ships are on shore or making signals of distres cases a reasonable compensation is to be made.

Fowey District, viz.—From Looe, inclusive, to th and *vice versâ*; and to and from, and into and ports and places within those limits.

N. B.— No master of a vessel is compelled to within this district till he comes off the port o within a line drawn from Looe to the Gribben H port of Fowey; or from the Gribben Head to Bla Polkerris Bay; or from the Gribben Head to t for Mevagissey; but if he do take a pilot betwee the Dodman, it must be one of the district pi offer.

Rates of Pilotage, for piloting Ships within the trict. — All British ships of 14 feet water, and boarded without the land, off Looe or the Dods must be known by the western land, called the open off the Dodman, shall pay 5s. per foot pilot ried into the harbour of Fowey, Mevagissey Pi town Basin, or Looe.

British ships under 14 feet water, boarded as a to pay 4s. per foot for the like service.

British ships above 14 feet, within that line, to per foot ; and ships under 14 feet, boarded as ab per foot, for the like service.

All ships not having a British register to pay more than the rates above stated.

All the above rates to be paid in proportion fo foot of water, but no allowance to be made for of water above, or under, half a foot.

In carrying ships to sea from the said harbour, to be in all cases one third less than the inward mentioned in the third article.

All ships which may anchor on their arrival e vagissey Bay, or the Sands off Fowey, to pay onl the before-mentioned rates of pilotage.

All pilots employed to carry ships from any on bours to another, to be paid the same pilotage ships had been boarded within the headlands c sea.

Masters of ships taking a pilot at sea (which with them) —

3 Leagues without a line drawn from the Looe the Dodman, are to pay
6 Leagues ditto - -
10 Leagues ditto - - -
and proportionately for intermediate distance

GALWAY.

	Foreign Rate.			Br	
	L.	s.	d.	L.	s.
Pilotage from Sea to the Roads, and *vice versâ*					
20 to 60 tons	0	10	0 per ves.	0	5
60 — 100	0	14	0 —	0	7
100 — 150	1	0	0 —	0	10
150 — 200	1	8	0 —	0	14
200 and upwards	1	14	8 —	0	17
From the Roads to the Dock, and *vice versâ*					
20 to 60 tons	0	15	0 —	0	7
60 — 100	1	1	0 —	0	10
100 — 150	1	10	0 —	0	15
150 — 200	2	2	0 —	1	1
200 and upwards	2	12	0 —	1	

OCK.

	Foreign Rate.	British Rate.
r Dues. - Oversea	0 1 4 per ton	0 0 8 per ton
Coastwise	0 0 8 —	0 0 4 —
age - -	0 0 1 —	0 0 0½ —
-	0 0 2¼ —	0 0 1¼ —

. — *Rates of Pilotage, for piloting Ships into and out of Harwich Harbour.*

rom	To	Under 10 Feet.	10 to 13 Feet.	13 Feet and upwards.
Orford - {	HarwichHarbour }	2 2 0	3 3 0	4 4 0
Rolling nds {	HarwichHarbour }	1 1 0	1 11 6	2 2 0
chHar- {	Sea or Orfordness }	1 11 6	2 2 0	3 3 0
	The Rolling Grounds }	Two thirds of the above.		

ot having British registers are to pay one fourth
.e rates of pilotage than stated in the above table, to
the Custom-house, Harwich.

AD *District, viz.*— To and from the anchorages at
nes Head, along the coast of the Isle of Anglesea and
.far as Bardsey Island, and to and from, and into and
ports and places within those limits (except the bar
ur of Caernarvon, and the Swellies).

No master of a vessel is compelled to take a pilot
.s district, till he comes to the North Stack, bound to
Harbour; but if he do take a pilot between Great
ad and Bardsey Island, it must be one of the district
ne offer.

Pilotage, for piloting Ships into and out of the Harbour of Holyhead.

Vessels per register to pay, for

200 and less than 300 Tons.	120 and less than 200 Tons.	80 and less than 120 Tons.	60 and less than 80 Tons.	Under 60 Tons.
2 2 0	1 11 6	1 1 0	0 15 0	0 10 6

ot having British registers are to pay one fourth
stated in the above table.

and vessels, under any circumstances of distress,
such pilot a further sum of money, to be calculated
o the extent and circumstances of such distress,
vice afforded.

l vessels which shall be boarded by pilots, at
three leagues or farther to the southward and
f Holyhead (where it is optional to masters of ves-
pilots), are to pay the several rates following, viz.

a Liverpool pilot on board, off Point d landing the Holyhead pilot there }	3 3 0
the pilot at the Great Ormes Head }	4 4 0
taken beyond the limits of his licence r Water or to Liverpool }	5 5 0

sum of 7s. 6d. per day for every day such pilot may
on board in consequence of the ship or vessel per-
arantine, or detained under any other restrictions
may be liable to.

arding ships and vessels at a less distance than 3
n the Head, as above, are to receive 10s. 6d. less for
n the above rates.

ticularly requested that commanders of ships, on
their pilots off Port Linas, or the Ormes Head,
ertain that such pilots will be taken on shore with-
elayed on board such vessels or boats as may receive
pilot will be entitled to 7s. 6d. per day for every day
m the ship or vessel he may have piloted, unless it is
ed that such delay had unavoidably happened from
e of the wind and weather.

Town Dues for Alien Vessels.

	L. s. d.
e, under 100 tons -	0 1 6
100 and not 200 tons -	0 2 0
200 and upwards -	0 3 0
nder 100 tons -	0 13 6
if loads out more -	0 3 6
100 and not 200 tons -	0 17 0
if loads out more -	0 5 0
200 and upwards -	1 0 0
if loads out more -	0 7 0
per each 1l. sterling of the freight	
	0 0 2
ngst the officers, per ship -	0 3 0
r each ton taken on board Outwards	0 0 2

HULL — *continued.*

	Foreign Rate.	British Rate.
Sea Pilotage. From the Humber to Lyme or Boston Deeps	0 12 0 per foot	0 8 0 per foot
Trinity House Dues.		
Buoyage - under 20 tons	0 11 0 per ves.	0 2 0 per ves.
30 —	0 11 0	0 2 6 —
40 —	0 11 0	0 3 0 —
50 —	0 11 0	0 3 6 —
60 —	0 11 0	0 4 0 —
65 —	0 11 0	0 4 0 —
70 —	0 11 0	0 4 6 —
80 —	0 11 0	0 5 0 —
90 —	0 11 0	0 5 6 —
100 —	0 11 0	0 6 0 —
110 —	0 14 0	0 6 6 —
120 —	0 14 0	0 7 0 —
130 —	0 14 0	0 7 6 —
135 —	0 14 0	0 7 6 —
140 —	0 17 0	0 8 0 —
150 —	0 17 0	0 8 6 —
160 —	0 17 0	0 9 0 —
170 —	0 17 0	0 9 6 —
180 —	1 0 0	0 10 0 —
For every additional 10 —	1 0 0	0 0 6 —
Fine on importing a cargo	1 0 0 per ves.	Nil.
Do. exporting	6 13 4 —	
Harbour Master's Dues	0 2 8 —	

Town Dues for British Vessels.

	Anchorage.	Jettage. Inwards.	Jettage. Outwards.
	L. s. d.	L. s. d.	L. s. d.
Under 40 tons -	0 1 0	0 1 6	0 1 0
40 and not 45 tons -	0 1 0	0 2 0	0 1 0
45 — 50 —	0 1 6	0 2 0	0 1 6
50 — 100 —	0 1 6	0 2 6	0 2 6
100 — 150 —	0 2 0	0 3 6	0 3 6
150 — 200 —	0 2 0	0 4 0	0 4 0
200 — 250 —	0 2 6	0 5 0	0 5 0
250 — 300 —	0 2 6	0 6 0	0 6 0
300 and upwards	0 2 6	0 7 0	0 6 6
	Exempt if belonging to Freemen.	Not due unless with goods landed at, or taken in at Hull, or within the Harbour.	

	Foreign Rate.	British Rate.
	L. s. d.	L. s. d.
Inwards.		
River Pilotage. From the Northness of Dimlington seen open, or clear of the Land to the southward thereof -	0 7 0 per foot	0 5 0 per foot
From the same, for vessels coming from the southward -	0 7 0 —	0 5 0 —
From the same, for vessels coming from the northward and eastward	0 7 0 —	0 5 0 —
From the Floating Light until Spurn Lights at north-east -	0 5 3 —	0 3 6 —
From Spurn Lights at north-east, to the Buoy of the Burcome or Grimsby -	0 3 6 —	0 2 6 —
Outwards.		
With Goods -	0 6 0	0 4 0 —
Ballast -	0 4 0	0 2 8 —
Goods from Grimsby	0 3 0	0 2 0 —
Ballast -	0 2 0	0 1 4 —
Pilots attending on vessels	0 10 6 per day	0 7 0 per day
Dock Dues. Vessels coming to, or going between, Hull and the West Indies, North or South America, Africa, Greenland, or any place east of the North Cape of Norway, within the Straits of Gibraltar, and south of Cape St. Vincent -	0 3 6 per ton	0 1 9 per ton
Between Hull, and all places above the Sound, and westward of Ushant in Europe, without the Straits of Gibraltar -	0 2 6 —	0 1 3 —
Between Hull, and any Port in Sweden, Denmark, or Norway, below Elsineur, Germany, Holland, Flanders, or France, to the eastward of Ushant -	0 1 8 —	0 0 10 —

IPSWICH.

	Foreign Rate.	British Rate.
	L. s. d.	*L. s. d.*
Water Bailiff's Dues	0 3 4 per ves.	0 1 8 per ves.
River Dues, under 40 tons	0 0 2 per ton	0 0 1 per ton
40 to 50 —	0 0 3 —	0 0 2 —
50 — 60 —	0 0 4 —	0 0 3 —
60 — 70 —	0 0 6 —	0 0 4 —
70 — 80 —	0 0 8 —	0 0 5 —
80 — 90 —	0 1 0 —	0 0 6½ —
90 — 100 —	0 1 4 —	0 0 8 —
100 — 180 —	0 1 8 —	0 0 10 —
180 and upwards	0 1 8 —	
If delivering or taking in a cargo, at or below Downham Reach	- - -	0 0 5 per ton
Pilotage from Downham Reach to Levington Creek, and *vice versâ*	0 1 6 per foot	0 0 9 per foot
From Levington Creek to Harwich Harbour, and *vice versâ*	0 1 0 —	0 0 6 —
From Downham Reach to Harwich Harbour, and *vice versâ*	0 2 6 —	0 1 3 —
From Ipswich Quay to Downham Reach, and *vice versâ.*—Vessels with one mast	0 2 6 —	0 1 3 —
With two or more	0 3 0 —	0 1 6 —

LIVERPOOL.

	Foreign Rate.	British Rate.
Innards.	*L. s. d.*	*L. s. d.*
Pilotage. From the length of the West End of the Great Ormshead bearing S. by W., or before Penman Bachan be shut in with the Great Ormshead	0 12 0 per foot	0 9 0 per foot
From the eastward of the Great Ormshead, as above	0 11 0 —	0 8 0 —
From the only House now on Great Hilbree Island bearing S.S.W. by the compass, or shall be piloted from the Road of Hoylake only, or from the Buoy of the Fairway in Formby Channel	0 5 6 —	0 4 0 —
Outwards.		
Whether through the Rock or Formby Channel	0 8 0 —	0 5 0 —
Into Beaumaris, the same as to Liverpool, and half as much mo'.		

LONDONDERRY.

	Foreign Rate.	British Rate.
	L. s. d.	*L. s. d.*
Quay Dues (except French) Oversea	0 0 6 per ton	0 0 3 per ton
Coasting		0 0 2 —
Harbour Dues - Oversea	0 0 6 -	0 0 3 —
Coasting		0 0 2 —
Innards.		
Pilotage. 7 feet and under	0 3 0 per foot	0 14 0 per ves.
Above 7 ft. and under 8 ft.	0 3 4 —	0 2 0 per foot
8 — 9 —	0 3 6 —	0 2 2 —
9 — 10 —	0 3 8 —	0 2 4 —
10 — 11 —	0 4 0 —	0 2 8 —
11 — 12 —	0 4 4 —	0 3 0 —
12 — 13 —	0 4 8 —	0 3 4 —
13 — 14 —	0 5 0 —	0 3 8 —
14 — 15 —	0 5 4 —	0 4 0 —
15 and upwards	0 5 8 —	0 4 4 —
Outwards.		
7 feet and under	0 17 6 per ves.	0 10 6 per ves.
Above 7 ft. and under 8 ft.	0 2 6 per foot	0 1 6 per foot
8 — 9 —	0 2 9 —	0 1 9 —
9 — 10 —	0 3 0 —	0 2 0 —
10 — 11 —	0 3 3 —	0 2 3 —
11 — 12 —	0 3 6 —	0 2 6 —
12 — 13 —	0 3 9 —	0 2 9 —
13 — 14 —	0 4 0 —	0 3 0 —
14 — 15 —	0 4 4 —	0 3 3 —
15 and upwards	0 4 4 —	0 3 6 —

N.B.—All British ships from foreign parts to pay 4d. per foot extra; or if bound to foreign ports, having on board half a cargo, or with passengers, to pay 4d. per foot extra, in addition to the above charges.

LYNN.

	Foreign Rate.	British
	L. s. d.	*L. s. d.*
Town Dues. Beaconage	0 0 1½ per ton	0 0 1 —
Stakage	0 0 0½ —	0 0 0½ —
and one-fifth of the Beaconage, if at the Boat		
Ballast	0 0 8 pr 3 tns.	0 0 4 —
Mooring Dues	0 0 1½ per ton goods	0 0 0½ —
which may be increased to	0 0 2 —	0 0 1 —
Pilotage, 10 feet and under	0 3 0 per foot	0 1 6 —
10½ to 12	0 3 6 —	0 1 9 —
12½ to 14½	0 4 0 —	0 2 0 —
14½ and upwards	0 5 0 —	0 2 6 —

MILFORD *District, viz.*—From Caldy Island, along the to St. David's Head, and from thence to Cardigan Island *vice versâ*; and to and from, and into and out of, all places within those limits.

N. B.—No master of a vessel is compelled to take within this district, unless going into or coming out within a line drawn from Lenny Point to Skokam but if he do take a pilot between Caldy Island and C Island, it must be one of the district pilots, if one offe

Rates of Pilotage, for piloting Ships into the Harbour of and up and down the said Harbour.

From	To	Rate Fo Under 14 Ft.
		L. s. d.
A line drawn from St. Anne's Point to Sheep's Island	Any part of the Harbour below a line drawn from Newton Nose Point to St. Martin's Haven	0 2 6
A line drawn from St. Anne's Point to Sheep's Island, or from Hubberstone Road	Any place above a line drawn from Newton Nose Point to Martin's Haven, in addition	0 2 0

Additional Rates for Ships boarded without the Entra Harbour.

From a line drawn from Lenny Point to Skokam Island, in addition, per foot	
If to the southward of St. Gowen's Head, ditto	
Or from Caldy Island eastward, or from the westward of the Grassholm, or three leagues without Lenny Point, in addition to the harbour pilotage	
Six leagues ditto	
Ten leagues ditto	

One fourth part is to be added to the harbour rates not having British registers.

Rates for Services and Assistance performed in the H

For a boat carrying an anchor of above 6 cwt. with sponding hawser —

		L. s. d.	
If in Hubberstone Roads		2 2 0	
Each man in the boat, each tide		0 5 0	
If below Hubberstone Road, a line drawn from the E. point of Gilliswick, to the E. point of Angle Bay and above the Stack Rock		2 12 6	Not exceed the discret sub-comm
Each man in the boat, each tide		5 0	
If in Dale Road, and the anchor is brought from Milford		4 4 0	
Or if carried off from Dale		2 12 6	
Each man in the boat, each tide		0 5 0	

For a boat carrying an anchor of 3 cwt. and not ing 6 cwt., with a corresponding hawser, the boat to have three fourths of the sums above specified.

For a boat with an anchor of 2 cwt. and not exc cwt. with a corresponding hawser, the boat and me one half of the said sums above specified.

For unmooring a ship drawing 14 feet water, and bringing her alongside the quay, or into Hubberstone Pill —

From the situation, first or second, before mention

		L. s. d.	
For the pilot		1 1 0	
If with a boat, an additional sum of		0 10 6	Not excee the discre sub-comm
Each person employed		0 5 0	
From the third station specified—			
For the pilot		1 11 6	
If with a boat, an additional sum of		0 10 6	Not excee the discre sub-comm
Each person employed		0 5 0	

And for taking a ship of 14 feet draught of water wards, from the quays, or Hubberstone Pill, to m any of the situations before mentioned, the like s specified.

Ships under 14 feet draught of water, to or from ations before mentioned, three fourths of the su pilot; the boats and men as above specified.

For new mooring a ship drawing 14 feet water, i the situations before described —

		L. s. d.	
For the pilot		0 10 6	
If with a boat, an additional sum of		0 10 6	
Each person employed		0 5 0	Not excee

.g.

	Foreign Rate.	British Rate.
	L. s. d.	L. s. d.
nto or out of th- or into, or out of the Creeks or ers thereof, from 1st April	0 1 9 per foot	0 1 3 per foot
1st Oct.	0 2 0 —	0 1 0 —
wn the Tyne be- North and South s, and any part of iver above Bil	0 2 0 —	0 1 6 —
wn the River be- l Point	0 1 6 —	0 1 0 —
	N. B. — 5s. per vessel extra, if with Lee- Boards.	
and Beaconage. loaded 50 ton der	0 1 6 per ves.	0 0 4 per ves.
51 to 100	0 1 6 —	0 0 9 —
101 — 200	0 1 6 —	0 0 11 —
201 — 300	0 1 6 —	0 1 1 —
301 and above	0 1 6 —	0 1 3 —
s. On Coals and ones exported	0 1 4per chal.	0 0 2per chal.
ues Laden	0 6 10 per ves.	0 4 6 per ves.
Ballast	5 5 10 —	0 4 2 —
icular kind of du.	0 8 4 —	0 7 0 —
Ballast or Good	4 4 10 —	0 3 2 —
Dues. Grind		
	0 0 8per chal.	0 0 4per chal.
	0 1 0 per ves.	Nil.

n District, viz. — From Dungeness to the Owers, *d*; and to and from, and into and out of all ces within those limits.

o master of a vessel is compelled to take a pilot district, until he comes to the entrance of Rye, r Newhaven, and is bound to one of those ports; s take a pilot between Dungeness and the Owers, licensed pilot, if offers.

ilotage for piloting Ships within the Newhaven Dis- pilotage from Dungeness to the west end of the feet draught and under, 2l. 16s. 6d.; 7 to 10 feet, 4 feet, 4l. 13s.; 12 feet, 5l. 1s. 6d.; 13 feet, 5l. feet, 5l. 18s.; 15 feet, 6l. 6s.; 16 feet, 6l. 13s.; .; 18 feet, 8l. 5s.; 19 feet, 9l. 15s.; 20 feet, 11l. 12l. 15s.; above 21 feet, 13l. 10s.

ilotage. — Newhaven. — 8 feet draught and under, 5d.; 8 to 10 feet, 1s. 9d.; above 10 feet, 3s. er. — 8 feet draught and under, per foot, 2s. 6d.; s.; above 10 feet, 4s. r. — 8 feet draught and under, per foot, 2s. 6d.; 8 to above 10 feet, 4s.

ANNEL, &c. upwards, from Orfordness to London. ots within this district, some are licensed from light-vessel to Orfordness, and thence to the ers are farther distant from Smith's Knoll to But the taking of pilots along the coast, to the Orfordness, is optional to masters of vessels; pilot be employed, he must be licensed as above,

ranted for the northward of Orfordness do not pilotage into or out of Yarmouth Roads or Har- as may be requisite in the passage to the Downs

District, viz. — From the Lizard to Cape Corn- *versed*; and to and from, and into and out of, all ces within those limits.

master of a vessel is compelled to take a pilot strict, until he comes within a line drawn from Isle to Trewavas Head, for Mount's Bay and ut if he does take a pilot between the Lizard and rnwall, it must be one of the district pilots, if

ates of Pilotage, for piloting Ships within the Penzance District.

To	7 feet & under.	8 to 10	11	12	13	14	15	16	17	18	19	20
	s.	s.	s.	s.	s.	s.	s.	s.	s.	s.	s.	s.
er of the adsteads Piers in nt's Bay er of the rentPiers Mount's	10	16	24	30	35	40	45	50	55	60	67	77
	1s. 6d. per foot of the draught of water.											

having British registers are to pay one fourth ed in the above table. essels boarded by pilots at a distance southward

	L. s. d.
pilot on board without a line drawn rd to Tol Pedan	2 2 0
a line drawn from the Lizard to Tol without a line drawn from Carn Dew on Point	1 1 0
a line drawn from Carn Dew to Point, and within a line drawn from Isle to Trewavas Head	0 10 0
hose limits to be charged inwards	0 5 0

Rates of Pilotage, for piloting Vessels within the Scilly District, in and out.

Vessels from foreign ports —		L. s. d.
60 tons		2 2 0
100		2 12 6
200		4 4 0
300		5 15 6
400		6 6 0
Coasting vessel of 60 tons		1 1 0
60 to 75		1 11 6
75 to 100		2 2 0
100 to 200		2 12 6
200 tons		3 3 3

And in proportion for greater tonnage. Ships not having British registers are to pay one fourth more than is above stated.

PLYMOUTH District, viz. — To the westward as far as Looe and eastward as far as the Start; and to and from, and into and out of, all ports and places within those limits.

N. B. — No master of a vessel is compelled to take a pilot within this district, unless going into or coming out of the port, within a line drawn from Rame Head to the Mewstone; but if he do take a pilot between the Start and Looe, it must be one of the district pilots, if one offer.

Rates of Pilotage, for piloting Ships within the Plymouth District. — 1. All British ships of 14 feet water and upwards, except East Indiamen, if boarded without the land off Penlee Point or the Mewstone, which must be known by the western land being open off Rame Head, shall pay 5s. per foot pilot- age, if carried into the harbour of Hamoaze, Catwater, or Sutton Pool.

2. British ships under 14 feet water, down to 8 feet, boarded as above stated, are to pay 4s. per foot for the like service.

3. Ships above 14 feet, within that line, are to pay only 4s. per foot; and ships under 14 feet, boarded as above, only 3s. per foot, for the like service.

4. All ships under 8 feet water, are to pay as above stated, as if the vessel was of that draught.

5. All the above rates are to be paid in proportion for every half foot of water, but no allowance is to be made for any draught of water less than half a foot.

6. In carrying ships to sea from the said harbours, the pi- lotage is to be, in all cases, the same as the inward pilotage.

7. All ships which may anchor on their arrival, either in Cawsand Bay or Plymouth Sound, are to pay only one half of the before-mentioned rates of pilotage.

8. All pilots employed to carry ships from any one of the harbours to another, are to be paid the same pilotage as if the said ship had been boarded within the headlands coming from sea.

9. Should any ship above 17 feet water be boarded while the western land is open off Rame Head by one of the second class pilots, and he runs the ship as far in as either of the buoys on the Panther or Shovel, and is there superseded by one of the first class, he shall be entitled to one third of the pilotage.

10. Masters of ships taking a pilot at sea —

	L. s. d.
5 Leagues without a line drawn from Rame Head to the Mewstone, are to pay	3 3 0
6 Leagues ditto	4 4 0
10 Leagues ditto	6 6 0

and proportionably for intermediate distances.

11. Ships not having British registers are to pay one fourth more than is stated in the above table.

12. If a master choose to retain or employ a pilot whilst at anchor, the rate for the lay-days is to be 7s. 6d. a day, not including the day coming in or going out.

	Spanish Vessels.	British Rate.	Foreign Rate.
	Per Ves. L. s. d.	Per Ton. L. s. d.	Per Ton. L. s. d.
Sutton Pool Dues Citadel Dues. Vessels lying at Catwater, Sutton Pool, or 24 hours in the Sound, from or		0 0 4	0 0 2
to any port in England or Wales	0 6 8	Per Ves. 0 2 0	Per Ves. 0 0 6
As above, if to or from Ireland, or any of the British Islands or Plantations	0 6 8	0 2 0	0 1 0
Lying in Hamoaze, if from or to any part of England, Scot- land, or Wales	0 10 0	0 3 0	0 1 0
As above, if from or to Ireland, or any of the British Islands or Plantations	0 10 0	0 3 0	0 1 6

POOLE District, viz. — From Christ Church, inclusive, to St. Alban's Head, and vice versâ; and to and from, and into and out of, all ports and places within those limits.

N. B. No master of a vessel is compelled to take a pilot within this district until he comes to the entrance of Poole, Studland Bay, or Christ Church, bound to one of those places; but if he do take a pilot between Christ Church and St. Alban's Head, it must be one of the district pilots, if one offer.

Rates of Pilotage for piloting Ships within the Poole District. — For the pilotage of any vessel from Studland Bay to Poole Quay, 3s. per foot.

For the pilotage of any vessel from Studland Bay to Brown- sea, two thirds of the above.

For the pilotage of any vessel from St. Alban's or Christ Church Head, to Poole Quay, 4s. per foot, and in proportion from those Heads to Brownsea, &c.

For the pilotage of any vessel from any place between either of those Heads and Studland Bay, to Poole Quay, 3s. 6d. per foot; and in proportion from the same place to Brownsea, &c.

For the pilotage of any vessel outwards, the same as for a vessel inwards.

Ships not having British registers are to pay one fourth more of the rates of pilotage than above stated.

The pilot having charge of any ship or vessel, either inwards or outwards, and being required by the master or owner to remain on board any such ship or vessel, shall be paid 4s. per day in addition to the limited pilotage for every day after the first.

The pilot of any vessel shall, if required by the owner or master only, provide a boat, with four men to attend her, from Stakes to the quay, or from the quay to Stakes, to tow her in or out, or to carry ropes on shore or to the buoys, as may be necessary; for which service there shall be paid the sum of 10s.

The pilots shall at all times, when required by the master or owner, lend their assistance to work any vessel to or from the quay, into or out of the harbour, for which service they shall be paid as follows, viz.:—For working a vessel to or from the bay, 5s. per man; to or from Brownsea, 3s. ditto; and to or from Stakes, 2s. ditto; and the same for the boat they attend in; and 4s. per day each man, if detained on board after the first day.

Coasting vessels to pay two thirds of the above rates.

PORT-GLASGOW.

	Foreign Rate.	British Rate.
	L. s. d.	L. s. d.
Harbour Dues. If a foreign voyage	0 1 0 per ton	0 0 6 per ton
Above 30 tons coasting	0 0 6 —	0 0 3 —
Pilotage. From any place betwixt Light and the Clough Light, or from the Anchorage at Fairlee Roads, Rothsay Bay, or Quarantine Station Holy Loch, to Greenock Roads, mooring and berthing, or vice versā	0 0 2½ —	0 0 1½ —
From any place inside the Clough Light, or from the Anchorage at Gourock Roads, or the Tail of the Bank	0 0 1½ —	0 0 1 —
Vessels inward bound, not boarded until nearer Gourock than the Bay of Quirk	0 0 0¾ —	0 0 0½ —
From Greenock to Port Glasgow, which rate is to be added to above, for vessels from any of these stations for that port	0 0 1½ —	0 0 1 —

PORTSMOUTH and Cowes District, viz.—From the Owers, within and without the Isle of Wight, to Peverell, and vice versā; and to and from, and into and out of, all ports and places within those limits.

The pilots of this district have authority to supersede such of the London or Cinque Port pilots as are licensed by the corporation of Trinity-house, for the charge of vessels to the Isle of Wight, when they arrive near the channels leading into the ports and harbours within the Isle of Wight; but no master of a vessel is compelled to take a Portsmouth or Cowes pilot, till within five miles of Bembridge Ledge, or three miles of Dunnose, St. Catherine's, or the Needles, (or till at St. Helen's, if he is piloted thereto by a duly licensed London or Cinque Port pilot,) but if he do take on board a pilot between the Owers and Peverell, it must be one of the district.

Rates of Pilotage for piloting Ships within the Portsmouth and Cowes District.—From five miles without Bembridge Ledge, or three miles without Dunnose or St. Catherine's, or three miles from the Needles' Point, coming in at that passage.

To Spithead, Motherbank, Stoke's Bay or Cowes Road.

                                          Per foot.
For ships of every draught, as far as 17 feet, inclusive   5s. 0d.
From 17 feet to 20 feet draught, inclusive - - 6s. 0d.
Above 20 feet draught - - - - - 7s. 0d.

But if the ship be boarded within two miles of the buoys off Bembridge, the rate to be 1s. per foot less than the above for each foot the ship draws. And the same rates as the above for pilotage outwards.

Ships anchoring and remaining at St. Helen's, either inward or outward bound, to pay half the rate of pilotage.

Pilots taken on board by the captain without the above limits, to receive the following pay; viz.

                                        L. s. d.
If at 3 leagues from the Wight - - 3 3 0
   6 ditto   ditto - - 4 4 0
  10 ditto   ditto - - 6 6 0

and proportionally for any intermediate distances.

Ships coming into Cowes harbour to pay 1s. 6d. per foot, and the same on going out, as harbour pilotage.

Pilots of ships drawing 17 feet water and under, are to have 2s. per foot addition to the pilotage from sea, from any place within the Isle of Wight to Portsmouth harbour, or to Southampton, or to Buckler's Hard, or to Langstone harbour and Lymington; and for all vessels drawing above 17 feet water, 3s. per foot.

Ships coming from the Downs with a London or Cinque Port pilot, to the Isle of Wight, and he continuing the charge into any of the places within the said island, no duly licensed pilot offering, is to be allowed half pilotage from St. Helen's to the anchorage, but not otherwise.

Ships not having British registers are to pay one fourth more of the rates of pilotage than stated in the above table.

If a master choose to retain or employ a pilot whilst at anchor, the rate for the lay-days is to be 7s. 6d. per day, not including the day coming in or going out.

SLIGO.

	Foreign Rate.	British
	L. s. d.	L. s. d.
Harbour Dues -	0 0 9 per ton	0 0 6
	From April 1. to Sept. 30.	From Oct. 1. to Mar. 31.	From April 1. to Sept. 30
	s. d.	s. d.	s. d.
Inward. Pilotage from the Wheaten Rock to the Oyster Island	2 0	2 6	1 6
Roghley Point to do.	1 6	2 0	1 2
Outside the Bar to do.	1 1	1 3	0 10
Sligo side the Bar to do.	0 5	0 7	0 4
The Island to the Quay	1 6	1 6	1 0
Do. to the Pool -	0 9	0 9	0 6
Outward. From any place to the Sea -	3 0	3 6	2 0
	per foot draught of w

STOCKTON.

	Foreign Rate.	Brit
	L. s. d.	L. s.
Tees Navigation Dues. Vessels trading to or from the River Tees from or to any foreign port (except laden with Norway timber only)	0 1 6 per ton	0 0
If laden with Norway Timber only	0 1 0 —	0 0
Town Dues -	0 5 0 per ves.	0 2
Pilotage from Sea to the Eighth Buoy	0 1 9 per foot	0 1
From Sea to Cargo Fleet	0 3 0 —	0 2
From Cargo Fleet to Middleburg	0 1 0 —	0 0
From Cargo Fleet to Newport or Portrack	0 2 6 —	0 1
From Cargo Fleet to Stockton	0 3 0 —	0 2
N. B.— 5s. per Vessel extra if with Lee-Boards.		

WATERFORD.

Pilotage. Taking Pilots at the following distances.	12 Feet and tween 25th 29th Septem			
	Above Creden Head, and no further than Passage.	To Cheek Point or Glasshouse		
Westward.	*Eastward.*	Brit.	For.	Brit
		s. d.	s. d.	s. d.
Grt. Newtown Head	Saltees -	1 8	3 0	2 7
Foilskirt -	Bag & Bun Hd.	1 4	2 7	2 3
Below Duncannon and nearer than Foilskirt or Bag and Bun		1 0	2	1 2 0
		Between 29 and 25th Ma		
Grt. Newtown Head	Saltees -	2 1	3 . 6	3 0
Foilskirt -	Bag & Bun Hd.	1 8	3 9	2 7
Below Duncannon and nearer than Foilskirt or Bag and Bun		1 4	2 7	2 3
		More than 6 12 Feet, betw and 29th Se		
Grt. Newtown Head	Saltees -	1 2½	7	1 11
Foilskirt -	Bag & Bun Hd.	1 0	2	1 1 9
Below Duncannon and nearer than Foilskirt or Bag and Bun		0 9	1	8 1 5
		Between 29 and 25th M		
Grt. Newtown Head	Saltees -	1 8	3 0	2
Foilskirt -	Bag & Bun Hd.	1 6	2 7	2
Below Duncannon and nearer than Foilskirt or Bag and Bun		1 2	2	1 10
Pilotage outwards, the same as Foilskirt, or Bag				

RFORD — continued.

	Foreign Rate.	British Rate.
	L. s. d.	L. s. d.
re Dues. Vessels arriving at the 'Custom-e, (vessels, two ds of whose Cargo l be Coals, or *from* Port of Ireland, ex-ed)	0 0 5 per ton	0 0 2½ per ton
s two thirds of whose o shall be Coals	0 0 3 —	0 0 1½ —
s arriving from any in Ireland - -	0 0 2 —	0 0 1 —

		If above the River or Pill of Kilma-cow, and below the Cove.	If between the River or Pill of Kilmacow, and the Cove.	
			If by Lighters.	If at Bal-last Quay.
		Per Ton. L. s. d.	Per Ton. L. s. d.	Per Ton. L. s. d.
Dues.	Taken on rd British	0 3 3	0 1 10	0 1 4
	Foreign	0 4 6	0 2 8	0 2 2
wn out British	0 1 15	0 0 11	0 0 9
	Foreign	0 2 9	0 1 7	0 1 5

UTH *District.* — From St. Alban's Head to Lyme, and ; and to and from, and into and out of, all ports and hin those limits.
o master of a vessel is compelled to take a pilot a district, until he comes within a line drawn from Cove to the Shambles, or within the Race, into the ortland and Weymouth, and off those of Bridport ; but if he do take a pilot between St. Alban's Lyme, it must be one of the district pilots, if one

lotage for piloting Ships within the Weymouth District.

rom	To	Under 8 Feet.	From 8 Feet to 10 Feet.	Above 10 Feet.
		Per Foot. s.	Per Foot. s. d.	Per Foot. s.
awn from th to the art of the Shambles ath or d Roads	Weymouth or Portland Roads or Bay	2	2 6	3
	Weymouth Harbour	2	2 6	3
- -	Bridport Har-bour	2	2 6	3
- -	Lyme Harbour	2	2 6	3

e same rates of pilotage to be paid outwards.

Ships not having British registers to pay one fourth more than is stated in the above table.

The pilot of any vessel shall, if required by the owner or master only, provide a boat, with four men to attend her, from the roads to the quay, or from the quay to the roads, to tow her in or out, or carry ropes on shore or to the posts, &c. as may be necessary, for which service each man is to be paid 4s. per tide ; the owner of the boat to be paid the same as a man.

Masters of ships taking a pilot at sea (which is optional to them) to pay as follows, viz. : —

		L. s. d.
From St. Alban's Head or Bill of Portland, to off Bridport or Lyme		2 2 0
If 3 leagues from the limits of Weymouth, Bridport, or Lyme		3 3 0
If 6 ditto ditto		4 4 0
If 10 ditto ditto		6 6 0

YARMOUTH. — *Rates of Pilotage for piloting Ships within the Yarmouth District.* — For ships above 14 feet draught of water,

From	To	Amt.
		L. s. d
The Dudgeon Light, its parallel of latitude, or the Northward there-of, and *vice versa*	Orfordness	10 10
	Yarmouth Roads, within or without the Sands	7 7
	Downs	7 7
Yarmouth, and *vice versa*	Orfordness	5 5
	Downs	16 16
Yarmouth Roads	Sea, through the Cockle Gat, St. Nicholas Gat, or over the Stanford	3 3
Sea	Yarmouth Roads, through any of the Channels	5 5
	Orfordness	5 5
Smith's Knoll, and *vice versa*	The Entrance of the Gat-ways leading into Yar-mouth Roads	3 3
Orfordness	The Entrance of the Gat-ways leading into Yar-mouth Roads	3 3

For ships of 14 feet draught of water, and under, two thirds of the above rate.

Into and out of the Harbour of Yarmouth or Southwold. — For all laden ships ;

			L. s. d.
Of above 50 and not exceeding 60 tons			1 1 0
60	—	70	1 4 0
70	—	80	1 6 0
80	—	90	1 8 0
90	—	100	1 10 0
100	—	110	1 15 0
110	—	120	1 16 0
120	—	130	2 0 0
130	—	140	2 4 0
140	—	150	2 8 0
150	—	175	2 15 0
175	—	200	3 0 0

The pilotage for ships in ballast is to be one third part of the pilotage of laden ships ; and ships returning into port by distress of weather, contrary winds, or on account of accident, are to pay two thirds of their common pilotage. Ships not having British registers are to pay one fourth more than the sums stated in the preceding table.

ENTO, ALLSPICE, OR JAMAICA PEPPER (Fr. *Poivre de Jamaïque ; elkenpfeffer ;* It. *Pimenti*), the fruit of the *myrtus pimenta*, a beautiful tree grows in great plenty on the hills on the north side of Jamaica. The berries erical, and, when ripe, of a black or dark purple colour. But as the pulp is state moist and glutinous, the berries are plucked when green ; and being d in the sun to dry, they lose their green colour, and become of a reddish They are packed in bags and hogsheads for the European market. The agrant and smaller they are, the better are they accounted. They have matic, agreeable odour, resembling that of a mixture of cinnamon, cloves, megs, with the warm, pungent taste of the cloves. Pimento is used in me-but its principal use is in the seasoning of soups and other dishes.

eturns," says Mr. Bryan Edwards, " from a pimento walk in a favourable season are prodi-single tree has been known to yield 150 lbs. of the raw fruit, or 100 lbs. of the dried spice ; there monly a loss in weight of one third in curing ; but this, like many other of the minor pro-is exceedingly uncertain, and perhaps a very plenteous crop occurs but once in five years. The he British market, as may be supposed, fluctuates accordingly ; but I believe its average for s past may be set down at 7d. per lb., exclusive of the duty (3d.)."—(Vol. ii. p. 372. ed. 1819.) t (November, 1831) the price of pimento in bond, in the London market, varies from 4d. to 0.

period when Mr. Edwards's work was published, the annual imports of pimento from Jamaica to about 672,000 lbs. and were decreasing every year (*loc. cit.*).—But there has since then been a increase. In 1829, the imports amounted to 3,599,268 lbs., of which 3,585,694 lbs. were from the est Indies, being almost entirely from Jamaica.—(*Parl. Paper,* No. 153. Sess. 1831.) About s. of pimento are annually entered for home consumption. The duty is 5d. per lb., being more er cent. upon the price of the article. It produces about 7,250l. The best policy would be to ltogether.

CHBECK (Ger. *Tombach ;* Du. *Tombak ;* Fr. *Tambac, Similor ;* It. *Tom-* Sp. *Tambac, Tumbaga*), a name given to one of the many imitations of By melting zinc in various proportions with copper or brass, some alloys

result, the colours of which approach more or less to that of gold. This c
position is frequently employed as a substitute for gold, in the formation of wa
cases, and various other articles of a like description. Pinchbeck is someti
called *Tambac*, and sometimes *Similor*, and *Petit-or*.

PINE, or FIR, a species of forest tree, next, if not superior, to the oak
point of utility and value. There are above 20 species of pines. They do
bear flat leaves, but a species of spines, which, however, are real leaves. T
are mostly, though not all, evergreens; but the appearance of the tree, as wel
the quality of the timber, varies with the species, and also with the situatio
which it grows. Generally speaking, the timber is hardest and best in expo
cold situations, and where its growth is slow. We shall only notice those spe
the timber of which is most in use in this country.

1. Scotch Pine (*Pinus Sylvestris*), is a native of the Scotch mountains, and of a
northern parts of Europe; being common in Russia, Denmark, Sweden, Norway,
Lapland. It is straight, abruptly branched, rising in favourable situations to the he
of 80 or 90 feet, and being from 3 to 4 feet in diameter. It is at perfection when 7
80 years old. The colour of the wood differs considerably; it is generally of a red
yellow, or a honey yellow, of various degrees of brightness. It has no larger transv
septa, and it has a strong resinous odour and taste. In the best timber the annual r
are thin, not exceeding $\frac{1}{70}$th of an inch in thickness; the dark parts of the rings of a br
reddish colour; the wood hard and dry to the feel, neither leaving a woolly surface
the saw, nor filling its teeth with resin. The best Norway is the finest of this kind,
the best Riga and Memel are not much inferior. The inferior sorts have thick an
rings; in some, the dark parts of the rings are of a honey yellow, the wood heavy,
filled with a soft resinous matter, feels clammy, and chokes the saw. Timber of
kind is not durable, nor fit for bearing strains. In some inferior species, the wo
spongy, contains less resinous matter, and presents a woolly surface after the
Swedish timber is often of this kind.

Scotch fir is the most durable of the pine species. It was the opinion of the celeb
Mr. Brindley, "that red Riga deal, or pine wood, would endure as long as oak i
situations." Its lightness and stiffness render it superior to any other material for be
girders, joists, rafters, &c. It is much used in joiners' work, as it is more easily wro
stands better, is much cheaper, and is nearly, if not quite, as durable as oak.

Scotch fir is exported from Norway and Sweden, under the name of *redwood*. No
exports no trees above 18 inches' diameter, consequently there is much sap wood;
the heart wood is both stronger and more durable than that of larger trees from
situations. Riga exports a considerable quantity under the name of masts and s
pieces from 18 to 25 inches' diameter are called *masts*, and are usually 70 or 80 fe
length: those of less than 18 inches' diameter are called *spars*. — (See Riga.) Y
deals and planks are imported from various ports of Norway, Sweden, Prussia, R
&c. Tar, pitch, and turpentine, are obtained from the Scotch fir. — (See these ti
When the tree has attained to a proper age, it is not injured by the extraction of
products.

2. Spruce Pine. — Of this there are three species: the Norway spruce, or *Pinus*
white spruce, or *Pinus alba*; and black spruce, or *Pinus nigra*. These are noble
rising in straight stems from 150 to 200 feet in height. They yield the timber knov
the name of *white fir*, or *deal*, from its always being imported in deals or planks.

Deals imported from Christiania are in the highest estimation. — (See Christia
The trees are usually cut into three lengths, generally of about 12 feet each; ar
afterwards cut into deals by saw-mills, each length yielding 3 deals. The Norway s
thrives very well in Britain, and produces timber little inferior to the foreign; it is
what softer, and the knots are extremely hard.

The white spruce, or *Pinus alba*, is brought from British North America. The
is not so resinous as the Norway spruce: it is tougher, lighter, and more liable to
in drying.

The black spruce, or *Pinus nigra*, is also an American tree; but it is not muc
ported into this country. The black and white spruce derive their names from the
of the bark; the wood of both being of the same colour.

The colour of spruce fir, or white deal, is yellowish or brownish white; the har
of the annual ring a darker shade of the same colour; often has a silky lustre, esp
in the American and British grown kinds. Each annual ring consists of two par
one hard, the other softer. The knots are generally very hard; the clear and st
grained kinds are often tough, but not very difficult to work, and stand extreme
when properly seasoned. White deal, as imported, shrinks about $\frac{1}{70}$th part in bec
quite dry.

EYMOUTH PINE, or WHITE PINE (*Pinus strobus*), is a native of North America, nported in large logs, often more than 2 feet square and 30 feet in length. It f the largest and most useful of the American trees, and makes excellent masts; not durable, nor fit for large timbers, being very subject to dry rot. It has ar odour.

VER FIR (*Pinus picea*), is a native of the mountains of Siberia, Germany, and land, and is common in British plantations. It is a large tree, and yields the rgh turpentine. The wood is of good quality, and much used on the Continent carpentry and ship-building. The harder fibres are of a yellow colour, com-d resinous; the softer nearly white. Like the other kinds of fir, it is light and d does not bend much under a considerable load; consequently, floors constructed nain permanently level. It is subject to the worm. It has been said to last n the air than in the water; and, therefore, to be fitter for the upper parts of than for piles and piers.

RCH (*Pinus Larix*). There are three species of this valuable tree; one European, American. The variety from the Italian Alps is the most esteemed, and has en extensively introduced into plantations in Great Britain. It is a straight and e of rapid growth. A tree 79 years of age was cut down at Blair Athol, in 1817, ontained 252 cubic feet of timber; and one of 80 years of age, at Dunkeld, d 300 cubic feet. The mean size of the trunk of the larch may be taken at 45 ngth, and 33 inches' diameter. The wood of the European larch is generally ey yellow colour, the hard part of the annual rings of a redder cast; sometimes vnish white. In common with the other species of pine, each annual ring con-a hard and a soft part. It generally has a silky lustre; its colour is browner of the Scotch pine, and it is much tougher. It is more difficult to work than Memel timber; but the surface is better when once it is obtained. It bears bolts and nails better than any other species of resinous wood. When per-y, it stands well; but it warps much in seasoning.

a all situations extremely durable. It is useful for every purpose of building, external or internal; it makes excellent ship timber, masts, boats, posts, rails, ture. It is peculiarly adapted for flooring boards, in situations where there is ar, and for staircases: in the latter, its fine colour, when rubbed with oil, is much e to that of the black oaken staircases to be seen in some old mansions. It is ited for doors, shutters, and the like; and, from the beautiful colour of its wood nished, painting is not necessary. — (We have abstracted these particulars from gold's excellent work, *The Principles of Carpentry*, pp. 209—217.)

-APPLE, OR ANANAS, though a tropical fruit, is now extensively d in hothouses in this country, and is well known to every one. When sort and healthy, it is the most luscious, and, perhaps, the best fruit that atry produces; and when carefully cultivated, is equal in point of quality produced in the West Indies. A pine-apple, raised at Stackpool Court, eshire, and served up at the coronation dinner of George IV., weighed oz. — (*Vegetable Substances*, p. 379. *Lib. Entert. Knowledge*.)

, a measure used chiefly in the measuring of liquids. The word is High nd signifies a little measure of wine. The English pint used to be of two e one for wine, the other for beer and ale. Two pints make a quart; 2 pottle; 2 pottles a gallon, &c. The pint, imperial liquid measure, 34·659 cubic inches.

, a wine measure, usually containing from 110 to 140 gallons. Two pipes, llons, make a tun. The pipe of port contains 138 gallons, of sherry 130, a and Bucellas 140, of Madeira 110, and of Vidonia 120. The pipe of s to be observed, is seldom accurately 138 gallons, and it is not unusual what the vessel actually contains.

-CLAY, a species of clay abounding in Devonshire and other parts of employed in the manufacture of various sorts of earthenware, and in

CY, consists in committing those acts of robbery and violence upon the , if committed upon land, would amount to felony.

hold no commission or delegated authority from any sovereign or state, em-them to attack others. They can, therefore, be only regarded in the light of assassins. They are, as Cicero has truly stated, the common enemies of all s *hostes omnium*); and the law of nations gives to every one the right to pursue ninate them, without any previous declaration of war; but it is not allowed to without trial, except in battle. Those who surrender, or are taken prisoners, ought before the proper magistrates, and dealt with according to law.

By the ancient common law of England, piracy, if committed by a *subject*, wa to be a species of treason, being contrary to his natural allegiance; and, by an al. be felony only: but since the statute of treasons (25 Edw. 3. c. 2.), it is held to b felony in a subject. Formerly this offence was only cognisable by the Admiralty (which proceed by the rules of the civil law; but it being inconsistent with the li of the nation that any man's life should be taken away unless by the judgment peers, the statute 28 Hen. 8. c. 15. established a new jurisdiction for this purpose, proceeds according to the course of the common law.

It was formerly a question whether the Algerines, and other African states, sho considered pirates; but, however exceptionable their conduct may have been on occasions, and however hostile their policy may be to the interests of humanity, s they have been subjected to what may be called regular governments, and hav admitted to enter into treaties with other powers, they are no longer to be trea pirates.

Pirates having no right to make conquests, or to seize upon what belongs to capture by them does not divest the owner of his property. At a very early per our history, a law was made for the restitution of property taken by pirates, if within the realm, whether belonging to strangers or Englishmen: but any fo suing upon this statute must prove that, at the time of the capture, his own sov and the sovereign of the captor were in mutual amity; for it is held that piracy be committed by the subjects of states at war with each other.

Piracy was almost universally practised in the heroic ages. Instead of being est infamous, it was supposed to be honourable. (*Latrocinium maris gloriæ habeba* Justin. lib. xliii. c. 3.) Menelaus, in the Odyssey, does not hesitate to inform his who admired his riches, that they were the fruit of his piratical expeditions—(Lib. iv. v and such, indeed, was the way in which most of the Greek princes amassed great v — (*Goguet, Origin of Laws*, vol. i. p. 383. Eng. trans.)

The prevalence of this piratical spirit in these early ages may, perhaps, be exp by the infinite number of small independent states into which the country was d and the violent animosity constantly subsisting amongst them. In this way fe and predatory habits were universally diffused and kept alive; and it is not to b posed that those who were at all times liable to be attacked by hosts of enemies, very accurately examine the grounds upon which they attacked others. Acc however, as a more improved system of government grew up in Greece, and a few as Athens, Corinth, &c. had attained to distinction by their naval power, pira made a capital offence: but though repressed, it was never entirely put down. was at all times the great stronghold of the pirates of antiquity: and of consequ the decline of the maritime forces of Athens, Rhodes, &c., which had kept them in they increased so much in numbers and audacity as to insult the majesty of Ror self; so that it became necessary to send Pompey against them, with a large fl army, and more extensive powers than had been ever previously conferred on any general.

During the anarchy of the middle ages, when every baron considered himself of independent prince, entitled to make war on others, piracy was universally pr The famous Hanseatic League was formed chiefly for the purpose of protecting th of the confederated cities from the attacks of the pirates by which the Baltic w infested. The nuisance was not finally abated in Europe till the feudal system h subverted, and the ascendancy of the law every where secured. In more moder some of the smaller West India islands have been the great resort of pirates: however, they have been driven from most of their haunts in that quarter. T still not unfrequently met with in the Indian seas east of Sumatra.

Besides those acts of robbery and depredation upon the high seas which, at common law, c piracy, some other offences have been included under that term. Thus, by the stat. 11 & 12 Wi if any natural-born subject commits any act of hostility upon the high seas against others of his subjects, under colour of a commission from any foreign power, this, though it would only be war in an alien, shall be construed piracy in a subject. And further, any commander or other person betraying his trust, and running away with any ship, boat, ordnance, ammunition, or *yielding them up voluntarily to a pirate*, or conspiring to do these acts; or any person assaulting mander of a vessel, to hinder him from fighting in defence of his ship, or confining him, or c endeavouring to cause a revolt on board; shall for each of these offences be adjudged a pirate, robber, and shall suffer death, whether he be principal, or merely accessory by setting forth suc or abetting them before the fact, or receiving them, or concealing them or their goods after it stat. 4 Geo. 1. c. 2. expressly excludes the principals from the benefit of clergy. By the stat. 8 Ge the trading with known pirates, or furnishing them with stores or ammunition, or fitting out a for that purpose, or in any wise consulting, combining, confederating, or corresponding with the forcibly boarding any merchant vessel, though without seizing or carrying her off, and dest throwing any of the goods overboard, shall be deemed piracy; and such accessories to pira described by the statute of King William are declared to be principal pirates, and all pirates by virtue of this act are made felons without benefit of clergy. To encourage the defence of vessels against pirates, the commanders and seamen wounded, and the widows of such seamen a in any engagement with pirates, are entitled to a bounty, to be divided among them, not exc *one fiftieth* part of the value of the cargo saved; and the wounded seamen are entitled to the

ich Hospital.— (11 & 12 *Will.* 3. c. 7. ; 8 *Geo.* 1. c. 24.) The first of these statutes also enacts, that mariner or inferior officer of any English ship decline or refuse to fight when commanded by the or shall utter any words to discourage the other mariners from defending the same, he shall lose wages due to him, together with such goods as he hath in the ship, and be imprisoned and kept to our for six months.

Geo. 4. c. 49. enacts that a bounty shall be paid to the officers and crews of such of his Majesty's war as may be engaged in the actual taking, sinking, burning, or otherwise destroying any vessel manned by pirates, of 20*l.* for each pirate taken or killed during the attack, and 5*l.* for every an of the crew not taken or killed, who shall have been alive on board the said piratical vessel at ck thereof.

me statute (§ 3.) enacts that vessels and other property taken from pirates, proved to have be- to any of his Majesty's subjects, are to be delivered up to them, on their paying a sum of money, as equal to one eighth part of the true value of the same.

STACHIA, OR PISTACHIO NUTS (Ger. *Pistaschen;* Du. *Pistasjes;* Fr. hes; It. *Pistacchi, Fastucchi;* Sp. *Alfocigos;* Lat. *Pistaciæ*), the fruit of stachia vera, a kind of turpentine tree. It grows naturally in Arabia, Persia, yria ; also in Sicily, whence the nuts are annually brought to us. They are ; and pointed, about the the size and shape of a filbert, including a kernel le greenish colour, covered with a yellowish or reddish skin. They have a nt, sweetish, unctuous taste, resembling that of sweet almonds ; their prin- difference from which consists in their having a greater degree of sweetness, panied with a light grateful flavour, and in being more oily. Pistachias im- from the East are superior to those raised in Europe.—(*Lewis's Mat. Med.*)

CH (Ger. *Pech;* Fr. *Poix, Brai;* It. *Pece;* Sp. *Pez;* Rus. *Smola gustaja*), siduum which remains on inspissating tar, or boiling it down to dryness. It nsively used in ship-building, and for other purposes. Large quantities are actured in Great Britain. The duty on pitch, which is 10*d.* a cwt., pro- in 1829, 448*l.*, so that 10,752 cwt. must have been entered for home con- on.

lowance is to be made for tare on pitch of 93 lbs. each on Archangel casks, 36 lbs. each on do., and 56 lbs. each on American do.

NE, a forest tree, of which there are two species ; the Oriental plane (*Pla- Orientalis*), and the Occidental plane (*Platanus Occidentalis*).

Oriental plane is a native of the Levant, and other Eastern countries, and is con- one of the finest of trees. It grows to about 60 feet in height, and has been to exceed 8 feet in diameter. Its wood is much like beech, but more figured, used for furniture and such like articles. The Occidental plane is a native of America, and is one of the largest of the American trees, being sometimes more feet in diameter. The wood of the Occidental plane is harder than that of the l. It is very durable in water.

tree known by the name of plane in England is the sycamore, or great maple seudo-platanus). It is a large tree, grows quickly, and stands the sea spray better st trees. The timber is very close and compact, easily wrought, and not liable o splinter or warp. It is generally of a brownish white, or yellowish white and sometimes it is very beautifully curled and mottled. In this state it takes olish, and bears varnishing well. It is chiefly used in the manufacture of saddle ooden dishes, and a variety of articles both of furniture and machinery. When y, and protected from worms, it is pretty durable ; but it is quite as liable as beech tacked by them. — (*Tredgold*, p. 196.)

NKS (Ger. and Du. *Planken;* Da. *Planker;* Sw. *Plankor;* Fr. *Planches,* es; Rus. *Tolstüle olosku*), thick strong boards, cut from various kinds of especially oak and pine. Planks are usually of the thickness of from to 4. They are imported in large quantities from the northern parts of , particularly from the ports of Christiania, Dantzic, Archangel, Peters- Narva, Revel, Riga, and Memel, as well as from several parts of North a.

TE, the denomination usually given to gold and silver wrought into of household furniture.

ler partly to prevent fraud, and partly for the purpose of collecting a revenue, ufacture of plate is placed under certain regulations. Those who carry it obliged to take out a licence, renewable annually on the 31st of July. e, p. 707.) Assay offices are established in different places ; and any one selling le previously to its having been assayed and marked, forfeits 50*l.* — (24 *Geo.*) No plate is passed at the assay offices, unless it be of the fineness of the old , or 11 oz. and 2 dwts., or of the new standard of 11 oz. and 10 dwts. Gold th the exception of gold watch-cases, is to pay a duty of 17*s.* an oz., and silver uty of 1*s.* 6*d.* ; but watch-cases, chains, tippings, mountings, collars, bottle

tickets, teaspoons, &c. are exempted. The 52 Geo. ?. c. 143. made the counterfei
or the transference from one piece of plate to another, of the marks, stamps, &c.
pressed on plate by the assayers, felony without the benefit of clergy. But the off
is now punishable by transportation or imprisonment only. — (1 *Will.* 4. c. 66.)

In his able speech on the state of the country, 18th of March, 1830, Mr. Huskisson said, " The ra
duty upon silver wrought plate in 1804 was 1s. 3d., upon gold 16s. an ounce; it was afterwards rais
1s. 6d. upon silver, and 17s. on gold. But what has been the increase in the nett produce of the dut
has risen from less than 5,000l. in 1804, to 105,000l. in 1828 ; a rise of more than twenty fold, notwithstar
the greatly diminished supply from the mines, and the consequent increasing value of the precious m
It may be further remarked, that this augmentation shows how large a portion of gold and silver is a
ally diverted from the purposes of coin to those of ornament and luxury."
Mr. Huskisson does not refer to any document in support of this statement, and we do not kno
what authority it is founded. We are, however, pretty confident that it involves a most material e
It appears from the official account, published by Mr. Jacob (*Precious Metals*, vol. ii. Appendix 13
the number of ounces of gold and silver plate " for which *duty was paid* in each year, from 1799 to 1
that in 1804, duty was paid upon 5,445 ounces of gold plate, and upon 1,048,869 ounces of silver ditto; w
in 1828, duty was paid upon 7,266 ounces of gold plate, and upon 1,207,887 ounces of silver ditto
1830, duty was paid on 6,441 ounces of gold, and upon 1,271,322 ounces of silver plate. It is clear, t
fore, that the increase in the consumption of plate has been nothing like what Mr. Huskisson suppe
indeed, it has not been nearly so considerable as might have been expected ; a circumstance whi
perhaps, to be explained by the facility with which the regulations are evaded. The increase amo
comparing 1804 with 1830, to 28 per cent. upon gold plate, and to 21 per cent. upon silver ditto.
obvious too, that the duty on plate, in 1804, must, if fairly collected, have amounted to more than *thi*
times the sum stated by Mr. Huskisson ; while, unless arrears of duty were paid up in 1828, he has
siderably over-rated the revenue of that year. Last year the duty produced 82,000l.

PLATINA, a metal which, in respect of scarcity, beauty, ductility, and i
structibility, is hardly inferior to gold, was unknown in Europe till about
middle of last century, when it began to be imported in small quantities f
South America. It has since been discovered in Estremadura in Spain.

Platina is of a white colour, like silver, but not so bright, and has no taste or sr
Its hardness is intermediate between copper and iron. Its specific gravity is about £
that of gold being 19·3 ; so that it is the heaviest body with which we are acquair
It is exceedingly ductile and malleable ; it may be hammered out into very thin pl
and drawn into wires not exceeding $\frac{1}{1945}$ inch in diameter. In these properties it is
bably inferior to gold, but it seems to surpass all the other metals. Its tenacity is s
that a wire of platina 0 078 inch in diameter is capable of supporting a weigl
274·31 lbs. avoirdupois without breaking. It is one of the most infusible of all me
but pieces of it may be welded together without difficulty when heated to whiteness.
not in the smallest degree altered by the action of air or water. — (*Thomson's Chemis*

PLATTING, slips of bast, cane, straw, &c. woven or plaited for making
hats, &c. The best straw platting is imported from Leghorn. Its superiority is
to depend on the peculiar quality of the straw employed in its manufacture, w
is nowhere obtained in such perfection, for this purpose, as in the vicini
Florence. In order to blanch the straw, it is suspended in the smoke of sul
previously to being wrought; and the platting is afterwards subjected to the
process. Fine plait is wrought with wet straw. All the details of the man
ture are understood better in Tuscany than anywhere else. — (See HATS.)

PLUMS, the fruit of the *Prunus domestica*, are too well known to require
description. They were introduced into England in the fifteenth century,
are cultivated in all parts of the country. There are said to be nearly 300 vari
of plums.

PLUMBAGO. See BLACK LEAD.

POMEGRANATE, POMEGRANATES (Ger. *Granatäpfel:* Fr. *Grenades
Granati, Melagrani;* Sp. *Granadas*), the fruit of the pomegranate tree. This
is a native of the south of Europe, Asia, and Barbary ; but in the West In
where it was introduced from Europe, it succeeds better than in its native
mates. The fruit is a pulpy, many-seeded berry, the size of an orange, co
with a thick coriaceous rind. The red succulent pulp is pleasantly acid
sembling that of the orange. — (*Thomson's Dispensatory.*)

POPLAR (Ger. *Pappel, Pappelhaum;* Du. *Popelier;* Fr. *Peuplier;* It. *Pio
Sp. Alamo;* Lat. *Populus*). Of the poplar (*Populus* of botanists), there are a
15 species described ; of these, 5 are common in England ; viz. the comm
white, the *black*, the *aspen* or trembling poplar, the *abele* or great white po
and the Lombardy poplar. In most favourable situations, the white poplar g
with great rapidity, sometimes sending forth shoots 16 feet long in a single se
The wood is soft, and not very durable, unless kept dry; but it is light, no
either to swell or shrink, and easily wrought. The Lombardy poplar grows ra
and shoots in a complete spire to a great height ; its timber does not diffe
terially from that of the white poplar. It is very light ; and is, therefore,

for the manufacture of packing-cases.' None of the species is fit for
mbers. — (*Tredgold's Principles of Carpentry; Veget. Sub., Lib. of Entert.*
dge.)

CELAIN, or CHINA WARE, a very fine species of earthenware.

irst specimens of porcelain were brought to Europe from China and Japan,
e manufacture has attained to great perfection, and has been carried on from a
ote era. It is of a very fine texture, white, semi-transparent, and sometimes
lly coloured and gilt; is infusible, and not subject to break by the sudden appli-
f heat or cold. The Chinese term for porcelain is *tse-ki*. But the Portuguese,
it was first brought in considerable quantities into Europe, bestowed on it the
porcelain, from *porcella*, a cup. The beauty of the fabric soon brought it into
uest, notwithstanding its high price, as an ornament for the houses and tables of
and the great. The emulation of European artists was in consequence excited.
le information was, however, obtained as to the mode of manufacturing porce-
he early part of last century, when the process was developed in a letter from
Jesuit in China, who had found means to make himself pretty well acquainted
subject. The knowledge that had thus transpired, and the investigations of
r and other chemists, prepared the way for the establishment of the manufacture
e. It was first commenced at Dresden, which has been famous ever since for
ty of its productions; but the finest and most magnificent specimens of Eu-
hina have been produced at Sèvres in France, in the factory carried on at the
of the French government.

Porcelain Manufacture.—This, though unable to boast of such fine specimens
workmanship as have been produced at Sèvres and Dresden, is of much greater
importance. Instead of exclusively applying themselves to the manufacture
s fitted only for the consumption of the rich, the artists of England have
hemselves in preference to produce China-ware suitable for the middle classes;
succeeded in producing articles at once excellent in quality, elegant in form,
o. We are principally indebted for the improvements made in this important
ure to the genius and enterprise of the late Mr. Josiah Wedgwood. This ex-
ry man owed none of his success to fortuitous circumstances. Devoting his
atient investigation, and sparing neither pains nor expense in accomplishing his
gathered round him artists of talent from different countries, and drew upon the
science for aid in pursuing the objects of his praiseworthy ambition. The
signal prosperity that attended his efforts served only as an incentive to urge
ard to new exertions, and as means for calling forth and encouraging talent in
a manner calculated to promote the welfare of his country. Previously to his
otteries of Staffordshire produced only inferior fabrics, flimsy as to their mate-
void of taste in their forms and ornaments; the best among them being only
imitations of the grotesque and unmeaning scenes and figures portrayed on
lain of China. But such have been the effects resulting from the exertions
ple of this one individual, that the wares of that district are now not only
to general use in this country, to the exclusion of all foreign goods, which
largely imported; but English pottery has since been sought for and celebrated
t the civilised world, and adopted even in places where the art was previously
An intelligent foreigner, M. Faujas de St. Fond, writing on this subject,
s excellent workmanship, its solidity, the advantage which it possesses of sus-
e action of fire, its fine glaze impenetrable to acids, the beauty and conve-
its form, and the cheapness of its price, have given rise to a commerce so
so universal, that, in travelling from Paris to Petersburgh, from Amsterdam
thest part of Sweden, and from Dunkirk to the extremity of the south of
ne is served at every inn upon English ware. Spain, Portugal, and Italy are
vith it; and vessels are loaded with it for both the Indies and the continent of
'—(See the quotation in the Account of the Porcelain Manufacture, p. 16. in
ner's Cyclopædia; for the statistical details with respect to the manufacture,
icle Earthenware, in this work.)

itish porcelain manufacture is principally carried on at the potteries in Stafford-
at Worcester, Derby, Colebrook Dale, and other places.

ne Cups.—It was long a prevalent opinion among modern critics, that the *vasa*
so famous in Roman history, were formed of porcelain. Pompey was the first
ght them to Rome from the East about 64 years before the Christian era. They
as drinking cups, and fetched enormous prices; Nero having given, according
mon method of interpreting, 58,000*l.* for a single cup! The extravagance of
ser may, in this instance, be supposed to have increased the price; so that the
estimation in which these cups were held may be more accurately inferred from

the fact, that, of all the rich spoils of Alexandria, Augustus was content to select c his share. — (*Sueton.* lib. ii. c. 71.) Pliny (lib. xxxvii. c. 2.) says they were m Persia, particularly in Karamania. But those who contend they were China chiefly found on the following line of Propertius : —

> Murrheaque in Parthis pocula COCTA FOCIS.—(Lib. iv. Eleg. 5. lin. 26.)

In despite, however, of this apparently decisive authority, M. le Bland and M cher have, in two very learned dissertations (*Mémoires de Littérat.* tom. xliii.), whi Robertson has declared are quite satisfactory, endeavoured to prove that the *vasa rhina* were formed of transparent stone, dug out of the earth in some Eastern pro and that they were imitated in vessels of coloured glass.—(*Robertson's Disquisition on* note 39.) Dr. Vincent (*Commerce and Navigation of the Ancients*, vol. ii. p. 723 clines to the opposite opinion; but the weight of authority is evidently c other side. At all events, it is plain that if the murrhine cups were really porcel had been exceedingly scarce at Rome, as their price would otherwise have been cor tively moderate. But it is most probable that the ancients were wholly unacqu with this article; which, indeed, was but little known in Europe till after the dis of the route to India by the Cape of Good Hope.—(For some further details question, see *Kippingü Antiq. Rom.* lib. iv. c. 3.)

PORK, the flesh of the hog. Salted and pickled pork forms a conside article of export from Ireland to the West Indies and other places.

Pork and Bacon exported from Ireland in the under-mentioned Years.

Years.	Pork.		Bacon.		Years.	Pork.		Bacon.	
	Quantity.	Official Value.	Quantity.	Official Value.		Quantity.	Official Value.	Quantity.	Of V.
	Cwt.	*£*	*Cwt.*	*£*		*Cwt.*	*£*	*Cwt.*	
1815	154,719	214,226	236,349	327,252	1821	141,211	195,559	366,209	50
1816	103,585	143,425	227,668	315,205	1822	115,936	160,527	241,865	33
1817	133,095	184,285	191,025	264,496	1823	120,046	166,218	343,675	47
1818	118,345	163,862	214,956	297,631	1824	106,543	147,521	313,788	43
1819	120,334	166,616	224,131	310,340	1825	108,141	149,734	362,278	50
1820	142,431	197,212	262,736	363,797					

Most part of the bacon is exported to England — (see BACON), and also a good deal of the por account cannot be brought further down than 1825, the trade between Great Britain and Irelanc since then been placed on the footing of a coasting trade.

PORT. See WINE.

PORT-AU-PRINCE, the capital of Hayti, or St. Domingo, in lat. l N., lon. 73° 10' W. Population variously estimated, probably about 8,00 is situated on the west coast of the island, at the bottom of a large and dee It was founded in 1749; since which, with few intervals, it has been the of French St. Domingo, as it is now of the entire island. It is partially for the harbour being protected by a battery on a small island at a little distanc the shore. The country around is low and marshy; and the heat in the s months being excessive, the climate is then exceedingly unhealthy. The bu are principally of wood, and seldom exceed two stories in height.

Haytı is, next to Cuba, the largest of the West India islands. It was discove Columbus, on the 5th of December, 1492. Its greatest length is estimated at abc leagues, and its greatest breadth at about 40. Its superficies is estimated at abou square leagues. Three principal chains of mountains (from which emanate mountain arms) run from the central group of Cibao. The whole of these are de as fertile and susceptible of cultivation, even to their summits; affording great of climate, which, contrary to what is the fact in the plains, is remarkably healthy soil of the plains is, in general, a very rich vegetable mould, exceedingly fertile, a watered. There are several large rivers, and an immense number of smaller s some tributary and others independent. The ports are numerous and good. 1 bour of Cape St. Nicholas, the fortifications of which are now in ruins, is one finest in the West Indies; being inferior only to the Havannah. Timber of th description is most abundant; and mines of gold, silver, copper, tin, iron, and r besides other natural productions, are said not to be wanting. The French are, th fully justified in designating this magnificent island, *La Reine des Antilles.* T cipal towns besides Port-au-Prince, are Cap Haytien, formerly Cap François, north coast, St. Domingo on the south, Les Cayes, and Jacmel.

Previously to the revolt of the blacks, Hayti was divided in unequal portions the French and Spaniards; the former possessing the west, and the latter the cas larger portion of the island. The revolution began in 1789; and terminat the most dreadful massacres, and the destruction of a vast deal of property, in

on of slavery, and the establishment of an independent black republic. The
sh part of the island and the French were finally consolidated in 1822.

ulation. — In 1789, the French part of Hayti was by far the most valuable and
hing colony in the West Indies. The population was estimated at 524,000; of
31,000 were whites, 27,500 people of colour, and 465,500 slaves. The Spanish
f the island was much less densely peopled; the number in 1785 being estimated
,640; of which 122,640 were free people of all colours, mostly mulattoes, and the
aves. The population of the entire island in 1827 was estimated by M. Hum-
at 820,000, of whom 30,000 were whites.

orts. — There has been an extraordinary decline in the quantity and value of the
s exported from Hayti since 1789. Sugar, for example, has fallen off from
0,000 lbs. to almost nothing; coffee from about 77,000,000 lbs. to little more
32,000,000 lbs.; cotton from 7,000,000 lbs. to 620,000 lbs.; indigo from
0 lbs. to nothing, &c.! Mahogany is almost the only article, the exports of
have rapidly increased of late years. The following table illustrates what has now
tated.

ral Table of Exports from Hayti, during the Years 1789, 1801, and from 1818 to 1826, both inclusive.

	Muscovado Sugar.	Coffee.	Cotton.	Cacao.	Indigo.	Molasses.	Dye Woods.	Tobacco.	Castor Oil.	Mahogany.	Cigars.
	Lbs.	*Lbs.*	*Lbs.*	*Lbs.*	*Lbs.*	*Lbs.*	*Lbs.*	*Lbs.*	*Gal.*	*Feet.*	
31	93,573,300	76,835,219	7,004,274	- -	758,628	25,749	- -	- -	-	- -	
40	18,518,572	43,420,270	2,480,340	648,518	804	99,419	6,768,634	- -	- -	5,217	
98	5,443,567	26,065,200	474,118	434,368	- -	-	6,819,300	19,140	121	129,962	
57	3,790,143	29,240,919	216,103	370,439	- -	-	3,094,409	39,698	711	141,577	
87	2,514,502	35,137,759	346,839	556,424	- -	-	1,919,748	97,600	157	129,509	
	600,934	29,925,951	820,563	264,792	-	-	3,728,186	76,400	-	55,005	
	200,454	24,235,372	592,368	464,154	-	211,927	8,295,080	588,957	-	2,622,277	279,000
	14,920	33,802,837	332,256	335,540	-	-	6,607,308	387,014	-	2,369,047	393,800
	5,106	44,269,084	1,028,045	461,694	1,240	-	3,858,151	718,679	-	2,181,747	175,000
	2,020	36,034,300	815,697	339,937	-	-	3,948,190	503,425	-	2,986,469	
	32,864	32,189,784	620,972	457,592	-	-	5,307,745	340,588	-	2,136,984	179,500

Gum Guaiacum, in 1822, 7,338 lbs. — 1823, 13,056 lbs. — 1824, 68,692 lbs.

exports of coffee have, we believe, been a good deal increased within the last 4 or

destruction caused by the deplorable excesses which accompanied the revolution
s a part of this extraordinary falling off: but the greater part is to be accounted
the change in the condition of the inhabitants. It could not reasonably be ex-
that the blacks were to make the same efforts in a state of independence they
when goaded on by the lash to exertions almost beyond their powers. It may,
r, be fairly anticipated that they will become more industrious, according as the
ion becomes denser, and as they become more civilised, and acquire a taste for
ences and luxuries. Hitherto industry in Hayti cannot be said to be free. The
ions laid down in the *Code Rural* direct the mode in which property is to be cul-
; and hinder the inhabitants from leaving the country without permission. The
ents against vagrancy are very severe. One of the greatest obstacles to industry
o be the enormous weight of the taxes imposed to defray the French indemnity.
re greatly beyond the means of the Haytians; so that the stipulated payments are
r, and will have to be abandoned.

des the articles specified in the above table, hides, tortoiseshell, wax, ginger, and
s' horns are exported in considerable quantities. Hides are principally exported
e eastern, or, what was, the Spanish part of the island. They constitute a valuable

f Tonnage and Value of Imports into Hayti, during the Year 1825, and the Three First Quarters of 1826.

5.	Vessels.	Tonnage.	Value of Cargoes in Dollars.	1826.	Vessels.	Tonnage.	Remarks.
an -	374	39,199	1,958,921	American	250	25,559	No Returns
- -	78	11,952	1,457,281	British -	37	6,376	to be ob-
an -	16	1,195	46,197	Colombian -	11	740	tained of the
- -	2	133	4,687	Danish - -	8	412	value of the
- -	65	11,136	763,404	French -	66	12,025	Imports for
- -	17	3,185	429,754	German -	4	747	1826.
				Dutch - -	11	645	
				Haitian -	5	319	
				Portuguese -	1	92	
				Russian -	1	181	
				Spanish - -	1	5	
Total	552	66,800	4,660,174	Total	395	47,101	

Imports. — The principal articles of import are provisions, such as flour, rice, and cargo beef, fish, &c. and timber, from the United States; cotton goods of all sorts, and Scotch linens, earthenware, cutlery, ammunition, &c. from England; wines, sa liqueurs, jewellery, toys, haberdashery, &c. from France; and linens, canvass, gin, from Holland and Germany. Nearly half the trade of the island is in the hands of Americans.

Regulations as to Trade. — It is enacted, that all persons exercising any trade or profession, exce that of cultivating the soil, must be provided with a patent or licence to carry on such trade or profes that all strangers admitted as merchants to the republic must, in the first place, procure the permi of the president to take out a patent, which, when obtained, only authorises them; under heavy pen to carry on a wholesale business, not with each other, but with the Haytians, in the open ports, v are Port-au-Prince, Gonaives, Cape Haytien, Port-à-Plate, Santo Domingo, Jacmel, Cayes, and Jer The minimum quantities of goods that may be sold are fixed by the same law. The Haytian cons may be also a retailer, on taking out a corresponding patent.

A charge of 2,000 dollars is made for each patent to a foreigner trading at Port-au-Prince; 1,8C Cayes, Cape Haytien, and Jacmel; and 1,600 for each of the remaining ports.

By an arrêté of the late President Petion, the duties on British goods were reduced to 7 per while those on all other merchandise were 10 per cent. The exception in favour of Great Britain confirmed by law, of April 3d, 1819, when the duties on all other foreign goods were raised to 12 per and those imported in native vessels fixed at 9 per cent.

By the last general law of the customs, the duty on all foreign merchandise imported in foreign v is fixed at 18 per cent. on an established tariff; and by a subsequent enactment, that leviable on the goods in Haytian bottoms, on Haytian account, is reduced to less than that paid by the most fav nation.

But the general law is partially abrogated by the acceptance, on July 11. 1825, of the king of Fra ordinance of the 17th of the preceding April, in which it is stipulated that French ships and good only half duties.

The following articles are duty free in all bottoms: — Shot of all sizes, grenades, howitzers, bomb-s and other projectiles of artillery; iron and bronze cannon, mortars, muskets and bayonets, carbine tols, and cavalry sabres, briquets, or short swords for infantry; machines, and instruments for simpl and facilitating the cultivation of the soil, and the preparation of its products; horses and cattle, m asses; gold and silver coin; classical and elementary works, sewed in boards, or bound in parchmen the instruction of youth.

The following is a list of articles absolutely prohibited, without reference to their place of grow Mahogany, logwood, lignumvitæ, fustic, coffee, cotton wool, cacao, raw and clayed sugar, rum, syrup, molasses, canes, whips, and umbrellas, containing swords, stilettoes, or other arms; books other works, opposed to good morals.

Produce or merchandise exported in Haytian vessels, on Haytian account, pays one tenth less e duties than the most favoured nation.

Besides the export, there is also a territorial duty levied equally on the produce of the soil, whethe ported in national or foreign ships.

The export of the following articles is strictly prohibited : — Gold and silver coin, side and fire-munitions, and other articles of war, old or new iron and copper; horses, brood mares, mules, asse wood for ship building.

The coasting trade is entirely confined to Haytian citizens.

There are also levied wharf and tonnage dues, port charges, and water money.

Haytian vessels, as they pay for a licence, are not subject to the tonnage duty.

The warehousing system has been partially adopted. By a law of April 25th, 1826, it is enacte *depôt* warehouses shall be established at Port-au-Prince, Cayes, Cape Haytien, Santo Domingo Jacmel, under certain regulations to the following effect : — Vessels coming from foreign parts must de on entry what goods are destined for sale in the country, and what are to be warehoused. No goo allowed to remain on board.

Certain colonial products, the import of which is prohibited, such as coffee, sugar, &c., cannot be er to be warehoused.

Goods warehoused may remain in store one year, paying a rent of 1 per cent.; but they may be with at any anterior period, on payment of the dues, which, besides the rent, are for weighing and whan

The commerce of Port-au-Prince is carried on by various classes of persons. The imports from E and America are principally consigned to European and North American commission houses, be few Haytian establishments. The capital is one of the ports to which foreign merchants are confin the law of patents; but they are, or at least were during the time of my residence, restricted by penalties to wholesale business. Of course they cannot deal with the consumers, but with the nati tailers, who are chiefly women, styled "marchandes;" these employ hucksters, also women, who tr the country, attend the markets, and give an account of their transactions to their employers, either evening, once a week, or once a month, according to their character for integrity.

As the payments of the importer are generally in money, and there is only one important article port—coffee—the purchases for returns can only be made after the crops have been gathered; and the effected by brokers, who often bargain with a class of natives called coffee speculators, from their d for the chance of the market with the cultivators, and either sell to the best advantage, or fulfil con previously entered into.

Among the respectable *marchandes* there is said to be much good faith; but with the great body customers, I believe, the merchants are obliged to use the utmost circumspection.

All the ordinary tradesmen, such as tailors, shoemakers, and even a water-proof hat manufactur to be found at Port-au-Prince. And I confess I was struck with the respectable appearance of s booksellers' shops, having looked in vain for such things both in Barbadoes and Antigua. The boc generally elementary, French publications, and romances. The works of Voltaire, Rousseau, and of the same class, abound.

There are also two printing presses; one at which the government Gazette *Le Télégraphe* is p and the other from which the *Feuille de Commerce* issues. The former rarely contains more th documents issued by the government; the latter occasionally some spirited papers, and is conduc M. Courtois, who was for a short time director of the post-office.

The apothecaries' shops are numerous, as they ought to be in such a horrible climate, and are we plied with all the contents of the French Pharmacopœia. There are also some tanneries, in which tl of the mangrove is used as the tanning material. As far as I could ascertain, the great bulk of the people were either of that class of Europeans called in the French time "*petits blancs,*" or pe colour. The labourers in town and country are generally black.

Monies, Weights, and Measures. — In the French part of the island, accounts were formerly livres and sols; but they are now kept, as in the United States, in dollars and cents. Dollars are va 4s. 6d. sterling, with halves and quarters in proportion. Weights and measures same as those of previously to the Revolution. — (See WEIGHTS AND MEASURES.)

We are indebted for these details with respect to Hayti principally to the valuable N *Hayti,* by Charles Mackenzie, *Esq.,* late Consul General in that island.

.TERS AND PORTERAGE. Porters are persons employed to carry
es or parcels, &c.

.ion, they are divided into different classes. It is enacted by 39 Geo. 3. c. 58., that the following
.l be the maximum charge upon all parcels not exceeding 56 lbs. weight, in London, West-
Southwark, and the suburbs; viz. —

	s. d.		s. d.
.istance not exceeding one quarter		Not exceeding one mile - -	0 6
e . . . -	0 3	Not exceeding one mile and a half -	0 8
.ding half a mile - -	0 4	Not exceeding two miles - -	0 10

like manner the additional sum of 3d. for every further distance not exceeding ¼ a mile.
to be made out at the inns, and given to the porters, who are to deliver them with the parcels;
.nkeeper not making out such tickets to forfeit not exceeding 40s., nor less than 5s.; porters
ring, or defacing the same, to forfeit 40s., and if they make any overcharge they are to for-
Parcels brought by coaches to be delivered *within six hours*, under a penalty not exceeding 20s.,
.an 10s. Parcels brought by wagons to be delivered *within twenty-four hours*, under a like
Parcels directed to be left till called for, to be delivered to those to whom the same may be di-
.· payment of the carriage, and 2d. for warehouse room, under like penalty. If parcels be not
.ll the expiration of a week, 1d. more for warehouse rent may be charged. Parcels not directed,
.ill called for, to be delivered on demand, under the above penalty. *Misbehaviour* of porters
.nished by a fine not exceeding 20s., nor less than 5s. The porters of London have the exclusive
.f taking up and carrying goods within the city, and the employment of any one else may be pu-
.fine.

.s (TACKLE-HOUSE), are regulated by the city of London. They have the privilege of perform-
.our of unshipping, landing, carrying, and housing the goods of the South Sea Company, the
.. Company, and all other goods, except from the East country, the produce of the British
.s and Ireland, and goods coastwise. They give bond for 500l. to make restitution in case of loss
., and are limited to rates fixed by the corporation.

.(TICKET), are persons appointed by the city of London, and have granted to them the exclusive
.f unshipping, loading, and housing pitch, tar, soap, ashes, wainscot, fir, poles, masts, deals, oars,
les, flax, and hemp, brought to London from the East country; also iron, cordage, and timber,
.ds of the produce of Ireland and the British plantations, and all goods coastwise, except lead.
.reemen of the city, give security in 100l. for fidelity, and have their names and numbers en-
a metal badge. They are under the tackle porters; who may, in performing the business of
.mploy other labourers, if ticket porters be not at hand. — (*Montefiore's Dictionary*.)
.son may bring goods into the city of London; but he is liable to a fine if he either take up, or
. within the city. It is astonishing that such absurd regulations should be still kept up: why
. the merchants of London, as well as those of Manchester, be allowed to employ any one they
.the conveyance of goods? Does any one doubt that competition would, in this, as in every
. be productive of the greatest advantage? The regulations in question merely tend to keep
.ve privileges, injurious to the public interests, and disadvantageous even to those in whose
.. are enacted.

T LOUIS, or NORTHWEST PORT, the capital of the Mauritius, in lat.
.., lon. 57° 32′ E. It is situated at the bottom of a triangular bay, the en-
. which is rather difficult. Every vessel approaching the harbour must
. flag and fire two guns; if in the night, a light must be shown; when a pilot
. board and steers the ship to the entrance of the port. It is a very con-
.ort for careening and repairing; but provisions of all sorts are dear. In
. cane months the anchorage in Port Louis is not good; and it can then
.ommodate a very few vessels. The houses are low, and are principally
.vood. The town and harbour are pretty strongly fortified. Almost all
.n trade of the island is carried on here.

.Iauritius was so called by the Dutch in honour of Prince Maurice; but
.st settled by the French in 1720; and is indebted for most part of its
.y to the skilful management of its governor, the famous M. de la Bour-
. It was taken by the English in 1810; and was definitively ceded to us

and Imports, &c. — Mauritius is not very fertile, a considerable part of the
.eing occupied by mountains. Its shape is circular, being about 150 miles
.ference. The climate is healthy, but is very subject to hurricanes. The
. product of the island is sugar, which is now cultivated to the almost total
. every thing else; but it also produces excellent coffee, indigo, and cotton.
.kwood or ebony of the Mauritius is very abundant, and of a superior quality.
.: corn or grain of any kind is raised in the island; most articles of provision
.orted. Previously to 1825, the sugar and other articles brought to Great
.om the Mauritius were charged with the same duties as the like articles from
.at in the above-mentioned year this distinction was done away, and it was en-
.Geo. 4. c. 111. § 44.), that all goods of the growth, produce, or manufacture of
.tius, should, upon importation into any port of the United Kingdom, be sub-
.. same duties and regulations as the like goods being of the growth, produce,
.cture of the British colonies in the West Indies; and that the trade with the
. should be placed as nearly as possible on the same footing as that of the West
.ids.

.. great boon to the Mauritius, and the exports of sugar from it have since rapidly increased.
.. Mr. Milburn (*Oriental Commerce*, vol. ii. p. 568.), they amounted, in 1812, to about 5,000,000 lbs.
. amounted to about 8,000,000 lbs.; and in 1824, to 23,334,553 lbs. During the 3 years ending
..e exports were as under: —

1826   -   42,489,416 lbs. | 1828   48,638,780 lbs.
1827   -   40,616,254 lbs. | (*Parl. Paper*, No. 354. Sess. 18.

Last year (1830) the quantity of sugar imported from the Mauritius into Great Britain amou
485,326 cwt. or 54,356,512 lbs.

The cultivation of sugar being found more profitable than that of coffee, the exports of the
though of excellent quality, have declined so far, that last year we only obtained from the Ma
29,506 lbs. The exports of cotton are also inconsiderable. The exports of ebony in 1826 amou
2,002,783 lbs., of the estimated value of 9,017*l*. The value of the tortoiseshell exported in the sar
was also estimated at about 9,000*l*. Considerable quantities of Indian piece goods are exporte
principal imports consist of provisions, particularly grain and flour; the supply required
use of the island being almost entirely derived from the Cape of Good Hope, Madagascar, India
bon, &c. Earthenware, machinery, furniture, hardware, piece goods, wine, &c. are also largely in
The total estimated value of the imports in 1826 amounted to 657,107*l*.; the estimated value of
ports for the same year being 572,553*l*. In 1826, 330 ships cleared outwards, of the burthen of 63,19
of which 47 ships, of the burthen of 15,297 tons, were British.

In 1826, the population of the Mauritius amounted to 94,624 souls; of which 8,111 were whites
sive of the king's troops), 15,444 free blacks, 69,076 slaves, 1,736 troops, and 257 resident stranger
population of the Seychelles — small islands dependent on the Mauritius — amounted at the same
7,665, of whom 6,525 were slaves.

Monies, Weights, and Measures. — According to the regulations of government, the franc is
equal to 10*d*., and the Spanish dollar to 4*s*. 4*d*. The government accounts are kept in sterling ▪
but merchants, shopkeepers, &c. keep their accounts in dollars and cents, and dollars, livres, and

The measures and weights are those of France previously to the Revolution. —100 lbs. French ═
English; the French foot is to the English foot as 100 to 93·89, but in practice they are supposed
16 to 15. The velte = 1 gallon 7¼ pint English; but in commercial transactions it is always taker
gallons.

Duties, &c. — A duty of 6 per cent. *ad valorem* is laid on all goods imported for consumption in
vessels from all quarters of the world. The duties on the goods imported in foreign ships are,
most part, also 6 per cent. A duty of 25 cents or 1*s*. 1*d*. per cwt. is laid on all sugar exported on
bottoms, to all places except Bourbon; and an additional duty of 8 per cent. *ad valorem* is laid
goods exported on foreign bottoms. The charges for pilotage, wharfage, &c. are fixed by gover
and may be learned at the Custom-house. For the most part they are very moderate.

Finance. — In a financial point of view, the Mauritius does not seem to be a very valuable acqu
During the 15 years ending with 1825, the expenditure of government in the island exceeded the ▪
by no less than 1,026,208*l*.! According to the estimate of the commissioners of inquiry, the probable
revenue of the Mauritius may be estimated at 184,253*l*. a year; but the commissioners state that
penditure in the island in 1828 amounted to 166,509*l*., and the expenditure in Great Britain on ac
the island to 77,857*l*.; making together 244,366*l*.— (*Parl. Paper*, No. 194. Sess. 1831.) We believ
ever, that by enforcing a system of unsparing retrenchment in the island, this unfavourable balanc
be considerably diminished: at present, both the number of functionaries and their salaries see
quite excessive. — (This article has been almost entirely compiled from official documents.)

PORTS. See HARBOURS.

POSTAGE AND POST-OFFICE. Postage is the duty or charge in
on letters or parcels conveyed by post; the Post-office being the establishme
which such letters or parcels are conveyed.

1. *Establishment of Post-offices.* — Regular posts or couriers were instituted at
early period, for the safe, regular, and speedy transmission of public intelligence.
dotus informs us— (Lib. viii. c. 98.), that in Persia, men and horses, in the ser
the monarch, were kept at certain stations along the public roads; and that the desp
being given to the first courier, were by him carried to the second, and so on, v
expedition that neither snow, nor rain, nor heat, nor darkness, could check. A
institution, under the name of *cursus publicus*, was established at Rome by Au
and was extended and improved by his successors. Horses and carriages were
readiness at the different stations along the public roads, not only for the transi
of despatches, but also for the conveyance of official personages, or others who ▪
tained an order from authority allowing them to travel post. By this means ᶢ
ment was speedily apprised of whatever took place in the remotest corners
empire; and instructions or functionaries could be sent to, or recalled from, th
distant provinces, with a celerity that would even now appear considerable. — (
Histoire des Grands Chemins, liv. iv. c. 4. *Bouchaud sur la Police des R*
pp. 136—151.)

Posts appear to have been established, for the first time, in modern Europe, i
by Louis XI. They were originally intended to serve merely, as the ancient pc
the conveyance of public despatches, and of persons travelling by authority of ᵍ
ment. Subsequently, however, private individuals were allowed to avail thems
this institution; and governments, by imposing higher duties or rates of postage
letters and parcels sent through the post-office than are sufficient to defray the ▪
of the establishment, have rendered it productive of a considerable revenue. No
the rates of postage are confined within due limits, or not carried so high as to fc
serious obstacle to correspondence, is there, perhaps, a more unobjectionable tax.

English Post-office. — The post-office was not established in England till tl
century. Postmasters, indeed, existed in more ancient times; but their busin
confined to the furnishing of post-horses to persons who were desirous of travell
peditiously, and to the despatching of extraordinary packets upon special occasic
1635, Charles I. erected a letter-office for England and Scotland; but this e
only to a few of the principal roads, the times of carriage were uncertain, and t
masters on each road were required to furnish horses for the conveyance of the l

te of 2¼d. a mile.   This establishment did not succeed; and at the breaking out
civil war, great difficulty was experienced in the forwarding of letters.   At
a post-office, or establishment for the *weekly* conveyance of letters to all parts
kingdom, was instituted in 1649, by Mr. Edmund Prideaux, attorney-general for
mmonwealth; the immediate consequence of which was a saving to the public of
. a year on account of postmasters.   In 1657, the post-office was established
on its present footing, and the rates of postage that were then fixed were con-
till the reign of Queen Anne. — (*Black. Com.* book i. c. 8.)

m the establishment of the post-office by Cromwell, down to 1784, mails were con-
either on horseback, or in carts made for the purpose; and instead of being the
xpeditious and safest conveyance, the post had become, at the latter period, one
slowest and most easily robbed of any in the country.   In 1784, it was usual for
igences between London and Bath to accomplish the journey in *seventeen* hours,
the post took *forty* hours; and on other roads their rate of travelling was about
same proportion.   The natural consequence of such a difference in point of de-
was, that a very great number of letters was sent by those conveyances; the law
very easily evaded, by giving them the form of small parcels.

ler these circumstances, it occurred to Mr. John Palmer, of Bath, comptroller
l of the post-office, that a very great improvement might be made in the convey-
f letters, in respect of economy, as well as of speed and safety, by contracting with
prietors of the coaches for the carriage of the mail; the latter being bound to
n the journey in a specified time, and to take a guard with the mail for its pro-
. Mr. Palmer's plan encountered much opposition, but was at length carried
fect.   The consequences have proved most beneficial: the use of mail-coaches
ended to every part of the empire; and while the mail is conveyed in less than
e time that was required under the old system, the coaches by which it is con•eyed
by their regularity and speed, a most desirable mode of travelling.   Mr. Palmer
e author of several other improvements in the economy of the post-office; nor is
ny other individual to whose exertions this department owes so much. — (*Mac-
's History of Com. Anno* 1784.)

oes not really seem, though the contrary has been sometimes contended, that the
fice could be so well conducted by any one else as by government: the latter
an enforce perfect regularity in all its subordinate departments; can carry it to
allest villages, and even beyond the frontier; and can combine all its separate
ato one uniform system, on which the public may confidently rely both for security
spatch.   The number of letters and newspapers conveyed by the British post-office
immense.   The letters only, despatched from London, may, we believe, be esti-
at an average, at about 40,000 a day! — (See *App. to* 18*th Report of Revenue*
ssioners, p. 299.)

relating to the Post-office. — The postmaster general does not come under the denomination of a
or he enters into no contract, and has no hire; the postage of letters being an article of revenue,
a mere reward for the conveyance.   He is, therefore, not liable to constructive negligence.
ne safety of letters by the post is provided for by numerous statutes; and for inferior offences,
not amount to absolute crimes, by the regulations of the general post-office, all inferior officers
shed by dismission, on complaint to the postmaster general, or his deputies.
arly statutes for the protection of letters, before mail-coaches were invented, still apply to those
which such coaches are not established.   The first necessary to be noticed is 5 Geo. 3. c. 25.,
acts, that if post-boys conveying the mail-bag shall quit the mail, or suffer any other person to
he horse or carriage, or shall loiter on the road, or not, if possible, convey the mail at the rate of
an hour, they shall, on conviction before one justice, on oath of one witness, be sent to the house of
n for not exceeding one month, nor less than 14 days.   For unlawfully collecting letters to con-
, being convicted in like manner, shall forfeit for every such letter 10s. to informer, and be com-
or two months, mitigable to one.   And any persons *intrusted to take in letters and receive the*
embezzling, or employing to their own use, the same; or burning or destroying said letters; or
g the rates of postage, and not accounting for the money; shall be guilty of felony.
Geo. 3. c. 5. extends the punishment to *all persons whatever employed in the business of the post-*
ilty of the like offences, and for stealing out of any letter, any bill, note, or other security for
nd makes the offence felony without benefit of clergy.   This statute did not extend to embez-
ney itself, or to *parts* of securities.
Geo. 3. c. 81. extends the punishment of felony without benefit of clergy to all *such* persons,
parts of notes, bills, and other securities, out of letters, as also to all persons buying or receiving
; and the accessaries may be tried whether the principals be apprehended or not, and the offence
ried either where the offence was committed or the offender apprehended.
y the same statute, if any person shall wilfully secrete, or detain, or refuse to deliver to any
the post-office authorised to demand the same, any letter or bag of letters intended to be con-
the mail, which he shall have found or picked up, or which shall by accident or mistake have
with any other person, he shall be guilty of a misdemeanor, and punished by fine and impri-

Geo. 3. c. 143., if any deputy, clerk, agent, letter-carrier, post-boy or rider, or any other officer
by or under the post-office, on receiving, stamping, sorting, changing, carrying, conveying, or
g letters or packets, in any way relating to the post-office, shall secrete, embezzle, or destroy any
cket, or bag or mail of letters, which shall have come into his hands in consequence of such
ent, containing the whole, or any part of any bank note, bank post bill, bill of exchange, ex-
ill, South Sea or East India bond, dividend warrant of the same, or any other company, society,
ation; navy, or victualling, or transport bill: ordnance debenture, seaman's ticket, state lottery
debenture, bank receipt for payment on any loan, note of assignment of stock in the funds,
attorney for receiving dividends or selling stock in the funds, or belonging to any company;

American provincial bill of credit, goldsmiths' or bankers' letter of credit, or note relating to the payr
of money, or other bond, warrant, draft, bill, or promissory note whatever, for payment of money
shall steal and take out of any letter, with which he shall have been so intrusted, or which shall l
come to his hand, the whole or any part of any such bank note, bank post bill, &c.; shall be guil
felony without benefit of clergy.

Any person stealing or taking away from any carriage, or from the possession of any person
ployed to convey letters sent by the post, or from any receiving-house for the post-office, or from
bag or mail sent or to be sent by the same, any letter, packet, bag, or mail, shall suffer death wit
benefit of clergy.

And all persons who shall counsel, command, hire, persuade, promise, aid, or abet such persons, or a
with a fraudulent intention buy or receive any such securities, instruments, &c., shall suffer in like r
ner: accessaries may be tried before apprehension or trial of principals. Trials may be in the co
where offenders are apprehended.

Exemptions from Postage, Franking, &c. — The statutes for regulating the rates of postage, and
exemptions from postage, from the 9th of Anne to the 53d of Geo. 3., are too numerous to be inse
but the principal regulations of them are the following : —

The king, the persons filling the principal offices of government, the public Boards, and the post-o
may send and receive letters duty free.

Also all members of either house of parliament during the sitting of the same, or within 40 days be
or after, any summons or prorogation, not exceeding one ounce in weight, on condition that the na
of the member, and the post town from which sent, the day of the month at full length, and the y
shall be indorsed thereon; also that the member directing it shall be at, or within 20 miles, of the
town, on the day, or day before, the letter is put into the post-office; and also on condition that no m
ber send more than ten, or receive more than fifteen, letters in one day.

Printed votes of parliament, and newspapers in covers open at the sides, &c. are exempted from post
But the postmasters may search to see if any thing else be contained in the cover; and if there be
such found, it shall be charged treble postage.

Persons altering the superscription of franked letters, or counterfeiting the handwriting of membe
them to avoid postage, guilty of felony, and to be transported for seven years.

But nevertheless, members who from infirmity are unable to write, may authorise and depute and
to frank for them, sending notice thereof under hand and seal, attested by a witness, to the postma
general.

Bills of exchange, invoices, merchants' accounts, &c. written on the same piece of paper with a le
or several letters written to several persons on one piece of paper, to pay as *one* letter. — (7 & 8 Ge
c. 21.)

So writs or other legal proceedings.

Patterns and samples of goods in covers open at the sides, without any writing inside, to be charge
single letters. But, by 52 Geo. 3., if not open at the sides, and weighing only 1 oz, an additional ra
2d.; but if less than 1 oz. and open at the side only, the additional rate of 1d.

Foreign letters suspected to contain prohibited goods may be opened in the presence of a justic
magistrate, of the place, or district, on oath of person suspecting. If contraband goods found, to b
stroyed, and the letter sent to the commissioners of customs; if none found, the letter to be forwa
with an attestation of the circumstances by the justice, or magistrate.

By 9 Anne, c. 10., no person except the postmaster, and persons authorised by him, shall carry or
vey any letters on pain of 5l. for every offence, and a penalty of 100l. per week besides, to be recover
any court of record. And by 5 Geo. 4. c. 20., no person shall send or tender, or deliver to be sent, o
wise than by the authority of the postmaster or his deputies, or to the nearest or most convenient
town to be forwarded by the post, any letter or packet, on pain of 5l. for each letter so sent, to be recov
in any court of record at Westminster.

Except letters *concerning goods* to be delivered *with such goods*, sent by a common carrier; lette
merchants, owners of ships or merchant vessels with cargoes to be delivered; such letters being ca
without hire or reward; any commission or return thereof; process or return thereof out of any c
or any letter sent by any private friend in their way of journey; or by any messenger sent on pu
concerning private affairs.

Postmasters may make private agreements with persons living in places (not being post towns), fo
receiving and sending to them respectively, letters to and from the post town; but for the delive
letters within the limits of the post town, he is entitled to no remuneration.

RATES OF POSTAGE. — Letters containing one enclosure are chargeable with two single rates. L
containing more than one enclosure, and not weighing one ounce, are chargeable with three single
Letters weighing one ounce, whatever the contents may be, are chargeable with four single rates;
for every quarter of an ounce above that weight, an additional single rate is chargeable.

Letters to soldiers and sailors, if single, and in conformity to the act of parliament, are chargeable
one penny only.

GREAT BRITAIN.

											Postage Single I in Per
From any post-office in England or Wales to any place not exceeding 15 miles from such office											4
For any distance above 15 miles, and not exceeding 20 miles			.	.	.	.	.	.	.	.	5
—	20	—	30	—	.	.	.	.	.	.	6
—	30	—	50	—	.	.	.	.	.	.	7
—	50	—	80	—	.	.	.	.	.	.	8
—	80	—	120	—	.	.	.	.	.	.	9
—	120	—	170	—	.	.	.	.	.	.	10
—	170	—	230	—	.	.	.	.	.	.	11
—	230	—	300	—	.	.	.	.	.	.	12

And so in proportion; the postage increasing progressively one penny for a single letter for eve
excess of distance of 100 miles.

IRELAND.

											Postag Single i in Per
From any post-office in Ireland to any place within the same, not exceeding 7 Irish miles from such office			.	.	.	.	.	.	.	.	2
Exceeding 7 and not exceeding 15 Irish miles			.	.	.	.	.	.	.	.	3
—	15	—	25	—	.	.	.	.	.	.	4
—	25	—	35	—	.	.	.	.	.	.	6
—	35	—	45	—	.	.	.	.	.	.	7
—	45	—	55	—	.	.	.	.	.	.	8
—	55	—	65	—	.	.	.	.	.	.	9
—	65	—	95	—	.	.	.	.	.	.	10
—	95	—	120	—	.	.	.	.	.	.	11
—	120	—	150	—	.	.	.	.	.	.	12
—	150	—	200	—	.	.	.	.	.	.	13
—	200	—	250	—	.	.	.	.	.	.	14
—	250	—	300	—	.	.	.	.	.	.	15

very 100 miles, Irish measure, above 300 miles, a further sum of 1d.   Double and treble letters
according to the same scale of advance as in England.

GREAT BRITAIN AND IRELAND.

Postage to be taken in the Currency of the United Kingdom for the Port and Conveyance of
and Packets by the Post from any Place in Great Britain to any Place in Ireland, or from
ce in Ireland to any Place in Great Britain.

Distance.	Single Letter.	Double Letter.	Treble Letter, or other under an Ounce Weight.	For every Ounce Weight, and for every Packet not exceeding an Ounce in Weight.
	s. d.	s. d.	s. d.	s. d.
distance of such places shall not exceed 15 miles, h measure - - - - - - -	0 4	0 8	1 0	1 4
ing 15, and not exceeding 20 such miles - - -	0 5	0 10	1 3	1 8
20 — — 30 — - - -	0 6	1 0	1 6	2 0
30 — — 50 — - - -	0 7	1 2	1 9	2 4
50 — — 80 — - - -	0 8	1 4	2 0	2 8
80 — — 120 — - - -	0 9	1 6	2 3	3 0
120 — — 170 — - - -	0 10	1 8	2 6	3 4
170 — — 230 — - - -	0 11	1 10	2 9	3 8
230 — — 300 — - - -	1 0	2 0	3 0	4 0
300 — — 400 — - - -	1 1	2 2	3 3	4 4
400 — — 500 — - - -	1 2	2 4	3 6	4 8
500 — — 600 — - - -	1 3	2 6	3 9	5 0
600 — — 700 — - - -	1 4	2 8	4 0	5 4
700 - - - - - - -	1 5	2 10	4 3	5 8
and packets conveyed by packet boats between the of Portpatrick and Donaghadee, a packet postage and above all other rates - - - -	0 4	0 8	1 0	1 4
and packets conveyed by packet boats from or to ead or Milford Haven, to or from any port in Ire- a packet postage over and above all other rates -	0 2	0 4	0 6	0 8
and packets conveyed by packet boats to or from bool, from or to Dublin, or any other port in Ireland, et postage over and above all other rates - - vided that no letter sent by way of Liverpool shall chargeable with a higher rate of postage than if it ere sent by way of Holyhead.	0 8	1 4	2 0	2 8
and packets to and from any part of Great Britain land, by way of Dublin and Holyhead, in addition other rates (Menai Bridge) - - - -	0 1	0 2	0 3	0 4
and packets to and from any part of Great Britain and, by way of Conway and Chester, in addition to er rates (Conway Bridge) - - - -	0 1	0 2	0 3	0 4
so in proportion in all the aforesaid cases for any her letter or packet of greater weight than an ounce.				

FOREIGN PARTS. — Postage of a Single Letter to and from London.

	s. d.		s. d.		s. d.
- - -	1 2	Spain - - -	2 2	Brazils - -	3 6
		Holland & the Netherlands	1 4	Buenos Ayres - -)	
s and Turkey,}	1 11	America - - -	2 2	Chili - - -}	3 6
e - -)		West India Islands -	2 2	Peru - - -)	
- - -)		St. Domingo - -	2 2	Colombia - -)	
- -		Gibraltar - - -	2 10	La Guayra - -)	
- -		Malta & the Mediterranean	3 2	Honduras - -}	3 0
- - -}	1 8	Madeira - -)		Mexico - -)	
- - -)		The Azores - -}	2 7	Tampico - -)	
- - -)		The Canaries - -)		Cuba - - -	3 0
- - -)		Portugal - -	2 6		

to any of the above places and parts (except the West India colonies and British America) can
ded unless the postage be first paid.

Mails made up in London as follows.

onday, Tuesday, Thursday, and Friday.   Letters received on Tuesday and Friday till 11 P. M.,
onday and Thursday till 7 P. M.
nd NETHERLANDS, GERMANY, and the NORTH OF EUROPE, every Tuesday and Friday.   Letters
ill 11 P. M.
ery Friday.   Letters received till 11 P. M.
first Wednesday, monthly.
EEWARD ISLANDS and DEMERARA, first and third Wednesday, monthly.
st and third Tuesday in each month.
irst Tuesday in each month.
every Tuesday.
, MALTA, and MEDITERRANEAN, first Tuesday in each month.
RES, third Tuesday in each month.
first Wednesday, monthly.
first Wednesday, monthly.
, first Wednesday, monthly.   MEXICO, CUBA, and ST. DOMINGO, third Wednesday, monthly.

er Office. — The postage for letters forwarded through this office, to the Cape of Good Hope,
Wales, Isle of France, Bombay, Ceylon, Madras, Bengal, Singapore, and Prince of Wales's
e full inland rate of postage, to the port where the ship may be, and 2d. sea-postage in addition,
tter not exceeding three ounces, and 1s. per ounce for every ounce above.
om the country for the above places, are charged with the full inland postage to London, and
age in addition, for every letter not exceeding three ounces; and 1s. per ounce for every ounce

Newspapers and price currents that have paid the stamp duty, are forwarded to India, if made u at the ends, for one penny on each packet, not exceeding one ounce, and for each packet exceed ounce, one penny per ounce.

But letters, newspapers, and price currents to the coast of Africa, St. Helena, Batavia, and all where there are no packets, one half of the highest rate of packet postage is charged.

All letters from abroad, except the Cape of Good Hope, Isle of France, New South Wales, B Ceylon, Madras, Bengal, Singapore, and Prince of Wales's Island, are liable to a sea-postage of 8*d.* and 1*s.* 4*d.* double, and so on over and above all inland rates whatever; but those from the Cape o Hope, Isle of France, Bombay, Ceylon, Madras, Bengal, Singapore, and Prince of Wales's Isla liable to the full inland rates, and a sea-postage of 4*d.* for every letter not exceeding the weight o ounces, and 1*s.* per ounce for every ounce exceeding that weight.

Newspapers printed within his Majesty's colonies, and brought into the United Kingdom by a other than a packet, if left open at the ends, and containing no other enclosure or corresponden charged 3*d.* each paper.

*** All letters forwarded through this office, must be paid for at the time they are put into the o

Seamen's and soldiers' single letters are forwarded through this office to the East Indies and New Wales, on payment of 1*d.* at the time of putting in; and letters from the East Indies are chargeab 1*d.*, or 3*d.* if the penny is not paid when the letter is put into the office; and to places abroad, to there are no regular packets, on the payment of 3*d.*, and those received from such places are charg

Seamen and Soldiers, within any part of his Majesty's dominions, to and from which th regular mails, can send and receive single letters on their own private concerns only, while they a ployed on his Majesty's service, for 1*d.*

Letters coming from a Seaman, or from a Serjeant, Corporal, Trumpeter, Fifer, or Private Sol. The penny must be paid at the time it is put into the post-office. The name of the soldier or sai class or description, and the name of the ship or regiment, corps or detachment, to which he b must be specified. And the officer having the command, must sign his name, and specify the n the ship or regiment, corps or detachment, he commands.

Letters going to Seamen or Soldiers.—The penny must be paid at the time it is put into th office.

Newspapers for his Majesty's Colonies, and Places beyond Seas.—Every such newspa other printed paper *liable to the stamp* duty, *and for the conveyance of which any duty of po chargeable,* to be put into the post-office of the town or place in Great Britain or Ireland, on a within *seven* days next after the day on which the same shall be published, the day of publicatio ascertained by the date of such paper; and in case any such paper be put into any post-office, a *expiration of such seven days,* such paper to be charged as a *single* letter.

Printed votes and proceedings in parliament from Great Britain and Ireland to any of his M colonies, are to be charged with a rate of *one penny half-penny per ounce,* and so on in proportion, of any sum payable under any former act, *to be paid on putting the said votes and proceedings i post-office.*

N. B.—If such printed vote, proceeding, newspaper, pamphlet, magazine, &c., be not sent *without or in a cover open at the sides,* or if *any writing be thereon,* other than the superscription, or *an paper or thing* be enclosed therein, the packet will be liable to the full rates of postage, as a letter.

Bank Notes and Drafts.—Persons wishing to send bank notes or drafts by post, are advised to c notes or drafts in halves, and send them at two different times, waiting till the receipt of one acknowledged before the other is sent.

Money, Rings, or Lockets, &c.—When money, rings, or lockets, &c. are sent by the post from I particular care should be taken to deliver the same to the clerk at the window at the general post and when any such letter is to be sent from the country, it should be delivered into the hands of t master: but it is to be observed, that this office does not engage to insure the party from loss.

Twopenny Post-office.—Besides the general post-office, or that intended for th veyance of letters from one part of the kingdom to another, letters are received metropolis and other large towns for delivery in the same. In London these are charged 2*d.*, but in other towns they are only charged 1*d.* The limits of th penny post extend generally 7 or 8 miles round the metropolis; there are daily s deliveries, and the establishment is extremely convenient. The twopenny post-o dependent upon, though in some measure distinct from, the general post-office principal offices are at the general post-office, and Gerrard-street, Soho. There are number of receiving-houses scattered up and down the town and the adjacent cou

The gross receipt and nett revenue derived from the twopenny post in the met in the under-mentioned years, has been as follows:—

Years.	Gross Receipt.			Nett Revenue.			Rate per Cent. of Charge of Collection.		
	£	s.	d.	£	s.	d.	£	s.	d.
1826	118,743	15	3	78,942	12	0	33	10	4¼
1827	115,800	8	11¼	75,866	17	7¼	34	9	8¼
1828	117,205	8	2¼	77,317	7	9¼	34	0	7¾

The gross number of letters collected in the two separate grand divisions, wit same period of six days, gives the following result:—

G. Post-office division - - - 73,427 letters.
Gerrard-street division - - - 69,157 —

The number of letters delivered in the respective divisions in the same period follows:—

G. Post-office division - - - - 68,693 letters.
Gerrard-street division - - - - 80,578 —

The reciprocal transfers between the two divisions of the letters collected by destined for delivery within the limits of the other, are as follow:—

From G. Post-office to Gerrard-street - - 40,896 letters.
From Gerrard street to the G. Post-office - - 25,906 —

(21*st Report of Revenue Commission*

ATIONS AS TO THE TWOPENNY POST-OFFICE. — There principal offices — at the general post-office, and the Gerrard-street, Soho; the hours of receipt and de-d all the regulations of which, are the same at the e other. There are, besides, numerous receiving r letters in and around London:—

are six collections and deliveries of letters in town d three deliveries at, and two departures from, most the country districts of this office. General post e despatched to the country letter-carriers the same of their arrival in London.

ne by which letters should be put into the receiving r either of the two principal offices, for each delivery r, and that by which they are despatched for delivery, lows:—

tters going from one Part of the Town to another.

to the re- houses by	Or either of the two principal offices by	They are sent out for delivery at
ng	9 morning	10 morning
	11 —	12 —
	1 afternoon	2 afternoon
on	3 —	4 —
	6 —	7 —
	9 —	8 next morning.

ch delivery should be completed generally in about and a half after the despatch from the principal according to distance and number of letters, &c. At e out parts of the town, however, five deliveries and s only can be given, on account of their distance from ipal offices; and for the same reason, the deliveries and the collections earlier than in the interior.

t parts served but five times a day, and to which the delivery at night does not extend, are (alphabeti-ollows:—)

sey, beyond the Spa	Mill Bank, Westminster, to Thames Bank Place
Green and Road	New Kent Road
Road	New Grove, Mile End
n	Pimlico, beyond Vauxhall Bridge
l Road to the Bridge , beyond Church-St.	Rotherhithe, beyond the Church
se,beyond theBridge	Tothill Fields, Vauxhall
, beyond the 1 mile	Bridge Road, Pimlico Sloane Street.

Mile End and other out parts letters are collected a an hour earlier than the above periods. And for the , or last delivery of the day, at these parts, let-be put in at the interior receiving houses by 2 o clock, ncipal offices by 3.

From London to the Country.

o the re- houses by	Or either of the two principal offices by	They are despatched from the latter at
g	9 morning	10 morning
on	3 afternoon	4 afternoon
	6 —	7 —

es having but two deliveries a day, letters are sent off ve hours of 10 in the morning, and 4 or 7 in the Such as go off at 10 are delivered at noon; those livered the same evening; and such as go off at 7 livery early next morning. To places having only n, they go off at 10, and are delivered the same n.

veries in the country should be completed, generally, e hours of 11 and 1; between 6 and 8 in the even-oy, or about, 9 in the morning.

Country to London. — If put into the post in time rning despatch, they arrive in town between 10 and and are sent out at 12 from the principal offices, for delivery in all parts of London. If put in for the afternoon despatch, they arrive between the hours of 5 and 6, and are sent out at 7 for delivery the same evening.

From one Part of the Country to another. — If going from one part of a ride or district to another part of the same ride or district, and put in for the morning despatch, they are deli-vered, through the means of a by post arrangement, the same day at noon. If put in for the afternoon despatch, they are delivered the same evening, where an evening delivery is given. If going to parts not belonging to the same ride, they come to London: such letters put into the post for the morn-ing despatch, are delivered in the country the same evening, where an evening delivery is given; if for the afternoon de-spatch, the next morning, where a morning delivery is given; or otherwise at noon.

Stamps. — The date stamp on letters, or, if there be more than one, that having the latest hour, shows the day and time of day they were despatched for delivery; that on returned letters excepting, which shows the time they were returned to the office as dead letters. The oval stamp is used at the chief office; the indented stamp at the Westminster; and the cir-cular at the country offices. Persons having occasion to com-plain of the delay of their letters, are requested to transmit to the comptroller the covers, with a statement of the time of delivery, as the date and stamp will assist materially in tracing their course.

Postage.—The postage of each letter or packet, passing from one part of the town to another, both being within the limits of the *general post-office delivery*, is 2d. To or from the country, or from one part of the country to another, 3d. The postage of this office on each letter or packet, passing to or from the general or foreign office, is 2d. in addition to the general or foreign rates. To prevent mistakes, it is recom-mended to persons paying the postage of letters at putting in, to see them stamped with the paid stamp before they leave the office.

Soldiers and Sailors. — Single letters *from* or *to* soldiers and sailors, under certain restrictions, pass throughout both this and the general post, or either, for 1d. only, if paid at putting in.

Newspapers. — Newspapers pass *from* London *to* the country, in covers open at the ends, for 1d. each: but from one part of London to another, or from the country to London, or one part of the country to another, the postage is the same as for letters.

Letters of Value. — This office is not liable to make good the loss of property contained in letters. But for the greater security of such property, it is recommended that notice of it be given to the office-keepers at putting into the post. This, however, with the exception of bank or other notes, or drafts payable to bearer, which should be cut in halves, and sent at twice, the first half to be acknowledged before the other is sent.

Weight. — No letters or packets exceeding the weight of four ounces can be sent by this post, except such as have first passed by, or are intended to pass by, the general or foreign mails.

Letters for this Post not to be put into the General Post. — Let-ters for the twopenny post are sometimes put into the general post, by which they are unavoidably delayed. It is therefore recommended that they be put into the twopenny post-offices or receiving houses, that they may be regularly for-warded by their proper conveyance.

Letters not to be delivered back. — And to prevent the possi-bility of letters being surreptitiously obtained from the offices where put in, office-keepers are strictly forbid returning, to any persons whatsoever, letters that may be applied for, under whatever circumstances the recovery may be urged. This is moreover forbid by the established principle, that the instant a letter is committed to the post, it is no longer the property of the sender.

office Revenue. — The progress of the post-office revenue of Great Britain has ry remarkable. Most part of its increased amount is, no doubt, to be ascribed to atly increased population of the country, and the growing intercourse among all of the community; but a good deal must also be ascribed to the efforts made in y part of the reign of George III. to suppress the abuses that had grown out of ilege of franking, and still more to the additions that have repeatedly been made ates. We believe, however, that these have been completely overdone; and, con- the vast importance of a cheap and safe conveyance of letters to commerce, it mediately be seen that this is a subject deserving of grave consideration. In fact, the post-office revenue has *been about stationary since* 1814; though, from ease of population and commerce in the intervening period, it is pretty obvious d the rates of postage not been so high as to force recourse to other channels, the must have been decidedly greater now than at the end of the war. Were the oderate, the greater despatch and security of the post-office conveyance would any considerable number of letters from being sent through other channels. But, stimation of very many persons, the present duties more than countervail these ges: and the number of coaches that now pass between all parts of the country, facility with which the law may be evaded, by transmitting letters in parcels d by them, renders the imposition of oppressive rates of postage quite as injurious evenue as to individuals.

ross produce of the post-office revenue of Great Britain, in the under-mentioned as been as follows:—

Years.	Duty.	Years.	Duty.	Years.	Duty.	Years.	Duty.
	£		£		£		£
1722	201,804	1795	745,238	1814	2,005,987	1828	2,048,042
1755	210,663	1800	1,083,950	1820	1,993,885	1829	2,024,418
1775	345,321	1810	1,675,076	1825	2,160,390	1830	2,053,720

The expenses of collection amount, at an average, to from 24 to 30 per cent. on gross receipt. In 1830, they were 594,349*l.*, being at the rate of very near 29 per c. After all deductions on account of collection, over-payments, drawbacks, &c., the t. nett payments into the exchequer on account of the post-office revenue of Great Bri. amount to about 1,350,000*l.* a year.

The British post-office is admitted on all hands to be managed with great intellige. But there are several departments in which it is believed that a very considerable sav. of expense might be effected. The packet service costs 106,000*l.* a year. The mile to mail coaches, and the payments to guards, tolls, &c. amount to about 84,000*l.* conveyance of mails in Canada, Nova Scotia, and Jamaica, is an item of above 12,50.

There may, in all, be about 3,000 persons employed in the carriage and distribu. of letters in Great Britain only; besides about 180 coaches, and from 4,000 to 5, horses.

Irish Post-office. — The most gross and scandalous abuses have long been p. valent in every department of the Irish post-office. The commissioners of reve. inquiry exerted themselves to abate the nuisance; but, as it would appear from evidence of the Duke of Richmond, before the committee of the House of Comm. on public salaries, without much effect. His Grace is, however, labouring with laud. activity and zeal to introduce something like honesty, order, and responsibility into department. The gross revenue of the Irish post-office amounted last year to 247,71 the expenses of collection were 99,905*l.*, and the nett payments into the exche. 108,000*l.*

UNITED STATES. — We subjoin an account of the number of post-offices, the extent of post roads the rates of postage, in the United States.

POST-OFFICES AND POSTAGE.

Post-offices in 1790	75;	Extent of post roads in miles	1,875
—	1800 903;	—	20,817
—	1810 2,300;	—	36,406
—	1820 4,500;	—	72,492
—	1829 8,004;	—	115,000

RATES OF POSTAGE.

For Single Letters, composed of One Piece of Paper.
Any distance, not exceeding   30 miles,   6 cents.
Over 30, and not exceeding   80   —   10   —
—   80   —   150   —   12½   —
—   150   —   400   —   18½   —
—   400 miles   ·   —   25   —

Double letters, or those composed of two pieces of paper, are charged with double the above rates.
Triple letters, or those composed of three pieces of paper, are charged with triple the above rates.
Quadruple letters, or those composed of four pieces of paper, are charged with quadruple the above rates.
All letters weighing one ounce, avoirdupois, or more, are charged at the rate of single postage for each quarter of an ounce, or quadruple postage for each ounce, according to their weight; and no letter can be charged with more than quadruple postage, unless its weight exceeds one ounce avoirdupois.

The postage on ship letters, if delivered at the office the vessel arrives, is 6 cents; if conveyed by post, 2 c. addition to the ordinary postage.
Newspaper Postage. — For each newspaper, not carri. of the state in which it is published, or if carried out state, but not carried over 100 miles, 1 cent.
Over 100 miles, and out of the state in which it is lished, 1½ cent.
Magazines and Pamphlets. — If published periodical! tance not exceeding 100 miles, 1½ cent per sheet.
—   over 100   —   2½   —
If *not* pub. period. dist. not exceed. 100 miles, 4 cts. pe.
over 100   —   6
Small pamphlets, containing not more than a half ro.al, are charged with half the above rates. Eight quarto are rated as *one sheet*, and all other sizes in th. proportion.
The number of sheets in a pamphlet sent by mail m. printed or written on the outer pages. When th. ber of sheets is not truly stated, double postage is charg.
Every thing not coming under the denomination of papers or pamphlets, is charged with letter postage.

POST ENTRY.

When goods are weighed or measured, and the merc. has got an account thereof at the Custom-house, and finds his entry, already m. too small, he must make a *post* or additional *entry* for the surplusage, in the s. manner as the first was done. As a merchant is always in time, prior to the c. ing of the vessel, to make his post, he should take care not to over enter, to a. as well the advance, as the trouble of getting back the overplus. However, if. be the case, and an over entry has been made, and more paid or bonded for. toms than the goods really landed amount to, the land-waiter and surveyor. signify the same, upon oath made, and subscribed by the person so over ent. that neither he nor any other person, to his knowledge, had any of the said g. over entered on board the said ship, or any where landed the same without pay. of custom; which oath must be attested by the collector or comptroller, or. deputies, who then compute the duties, and set down on the back of the ce. cate, first in words at length, and then in figures, the several sums to be pai.

POSTING, travelling along the public road with hired horses, and wit. without hired carriages. Duties are charged upon the horses and carriag. hired. — (For the duties on the latter, see *antè,* p. 263.) The duties on post h. are regulated by the 4 Geo. 4. c. 62.

Duties. — Every postmaster to pay 5*s.* annually for a licence. For every horse, mare, o. ing, let for hire, by the mile, 1½*d.* for every mile; if let to go no greater distance than 8 miles, 1-5th. the sum charged for such letting, or 1*s.* 9*d.*, ; if let to go no greater distance than 8 miles, and not t. back any person nor deviate from the usual line of road, 1*s.*; if let for any time less than 28 suc. days, or in any other manner than by the mile, or to go no greater distance than 8 miles, in either cas.

e sum charged on every such letting; or the sum of 2s. 6d. for each day not exceeding 3 days; ւm of 1s. 9d. for each day exceeding 3, and not exceeding 13 days; and the sum of 1s. 3d. for each ·ding 13, and less than 28 days. If let for 28 successive days, or for longer period, and returned ·riod of time than *twenty-eight* successive days, and not exchanged for another horse, mare, or ․n continuation of the same hiring, 1-5th part of the sum agreed to be received for such letting, or ‹f 2s. 6d. for each day not exceeding 3 days; and the sum of 1s. 9d. for each day exceeding 3, ‹ceeding 13 days; and the sum of 1s. 3d. for each day exceeding 13, and less than 28 days, during ·very such horse, &c. shall have been under the direction of the person hiring the same.

․ies imposed by the act do not extend to horses used in stage or hackney coaches duly licensed; ·‹ mourning coach or hearse, where the same is hired to go no greater distance than 10 miles from ․ır; nor to any cart or carriage kept for the conveyance of fish.

letting any horse, mare, or gelding, *for hire*, without licence from the commissioners of stamps, ·t to a penalty of 10l. No postmaster to keep more than one house by virtue of one licence, un- ․ilty of 10l.; and the words *licensed to let horses* for hire to be painted in legible characters on the ‹heir houses, under a penalty of 5l. Postmasters are to give security by bond, renewable at the ·‹ of three years. The commissioners or collector of stamps to furnish *blank tickets* and *certifi-* ·stmasters, and *exchange* and *check tickets* to the toll-gate keepers: the former containing the ·abode of the postmaster, the number of horses, whether let for a day or longer period; the ‹ name of the toll-keeper, the place where he lives, and the places the horses hired are going to. ·ses are returned within the period for which they were hired, check tickets are to be delivered ‹collector; penalty 20l. Improperly using a check ticket, subjects to a penalty of 50l. Travellers ·ver up their tickets at the *first* toll-gate, and to *ask for* and receive the necessary exchange and ·ets in return.

nf Duties to Farm.—The commissioners of stamps, by authority of the Lords of the Treasury, are ‹ to let the post-horse duties to farm for any period not longer than 3 years, either in whole, or ·‹o divisions or districts. The biddings are conducted under regulations issued by the commis- ·t least a month's notice being given of the time and place of letting the duties. The highest bidder ·erred, must forthwith execute a contract, and give bond with *three* or more securities for pay- ·‹e yearly rent contracted for at the head office of stamps in equal portions by *eight* several annual ‹ The commissioners have also the power to appoint a time for making a deposit, and the ·ereof; and in case any bidder fail of making such deposit, or of executing a proper contract ‹ security, the duties to be again put up. Duties not to be farmed by persons licensed to let post-

nt of the Produce of the Duties on Posting, in each of the Five Years ending 1st January 1830.—(*Parl. Paper*, No. 689. Sess. 1830.)

	£	s.	d.		£	s.	d.
‹ling 1st January 1826 -	232,651	2	4	Year ending 1st January 1829 -	238,858	0	4
1827 -	239,375	19	5	1830 -	235,318	17	8
1828 -	225,864	5	0				

⸝SH (Da. *Potaske*; Fr. *Potasse*; Ger. *Pottasche*; It. *Potassa*; Pol. *Potasz*; *tasch*). If vegetables be burned, the ashes lixiviated, and the solution ‹ dryness in iron vessels, the mass left behind is the *potash* of commerce ‹pure carbonate of potass of chemists. It is intensely alkaline, solid, and ‹ brown by the admixture of a small portion of vegetable inflammable ‹which generally becomes moist. When potash is calcined in a rever- furnace, the colouring matter is destroyed, it assumes a spongy texture, ·hitish pearly lustre; whence it is denominated *pearl-ash*. The latter ‹ contains from 60 to 83 or 84 per cent. of pure carbonate of potass. — ‹, p. 20.)

‹hes of those vegetables only which grow at a distance from the sea, are em- ‹the manufacture of potash. Herbaceous plants yield the largest portion, and ‹ore than trees. It is principally manufactured in America, Russia, and ‹he vast forests of which furnish an inexhaustible supply of ashes.

‹is of great importance in the arts, being largely employed in the manufacture ‹ass and soft soap, the rectification of spirits, bleaching, making alum, scouring Of 162,256 cwt. of pot and pearl ash imported in 1829, 145,730 cwt. were ‹rom the British possessions in North America, the remainder being almost en- ‹ished by Russia. The ashes of the United States are the purest, and bring ‹st price.

‹ices of pot and pearl ash in the London market, in October, 1831, were as ‹.

	£	s.	d.	£	s.	d.			£	s.	d.	£	s.	d.	
‹, 1st -	1	11	6 to	1	12	0	per cwt.	United States Pearl, *bd.*	1	16	0 to	0	0	0	per cwt.
⸝rl, 1st -	1	15	6 —	1	16	0	—	Russia, *bd.* -	1	3	6 —	0	0	0	—
⸝es Pot, *bd.* -	1	15	6 —	0	0	0	—								

‹m Canada are duty free; those from Russia and the United States pay a duty of 6s. a cwt. ‹e duty on ashes produced 4,930l. 14s.; showing that 16,466 cwt. from Russia and the United ‹been entered for home consumption.

⸝TOES (Ger. *Kartoffeln*; Du. *Aardappelen*; Fr. *Pommes de terre*; It. *Pomi di terra*; Sp. *Patatas manchegas*; Rus. *Jabloki semlenüe*), the roots *lanum tuberosum*, of innumerable varieties, and too well known to require ·iption.

‹rical Notice. — The potato, which is at present to be met with every where in ‹nd forms the principal part of the food of a large proportion of its inhabitants, ‹ly unknown in this quarter of the world till the latter part of the 16th cen-

tury. It is a native of America, but whether of both divisions of that contin
doubtful. — (*Humboldt, Nouvelle Espagne*, liv. iv. c. 9.) Some authors affirm t
was first introduced in Europe by Sir John Hawkins, in 1545; others, that
introduced by Sir Francis Drake, in 1573; and others, again, that it was for th
time brought to England from Virginia, by Sir Walter Raleigh, in 1586. B
discrepancy seems to have arisen from confounding the common, or Virginian
(the *solnnum tuberosum* of Linnæus), with the sweet potato (*convolvulus battatas*).
latter was introduced into Europe long before the former, and it seems most pr
that it was the species brought from New Granada by Hawkins. Sweet pc
require a warm climate, and do not succeed in this country; they were, howeve
ported in considerable quantities, during the 16th century, from Spain and the Ca
and were supposed to have some rather peculiar properties. The kissing com
Falstaff, and such like confections, were principally made of battatas and eringo
On the whole, we are inclined to think that we are really indebted for the potato (
as for tobacco) to Sir Walter Raleigh, or the colonists he had planted in Vi
Gerarde, an old English botanist, mentions, in his *Herbal*, published in 1597, that
planted the potato in his garden at London about 1590; and that it succeeded th
well as in its native soil, Virginia, whence he had received it. Potatoes were
cultivated by a very few, and were looked upon as a great delicacy. In a man
account of the household expenses of Queen Anne, wife of James I., who died in
and which is supposed to have been written in 1613, the purchase of a very
quantity of potatoes is mentioned at the price of 2s. a pound. The Royal Soc
1663, recommended the extension of their cultivation as a means of preventing fa
Previously, however, to 1684, they were raised only in the gardens of the nobili
gentry; but in that year they were planted, for the first time, in the open fields i
cashire, a county in which they have long been very extensively cultivated.

Potatoes, it is commonly thought, were not introduced into Ireland till 1610,
a small quantity was sent by Sir Walter Raleigh to be planted in a garden
estate in the vicinity of Youghall. Their cultivation extended far more rapidl
in England; and have long furnished from three fifths to four fifths of the entir
of the people of Ireland!

Potatoes were not raised in Scotland, except in gardens, till 1728, when the
planted in the open fields by a person of the name of Prentice, a day labourer
syth, who died at Edinburgh in 1792.

The extension of the potato cultivation has been particularly rapid during the
years. The quantity that is now raised in Scotland is supposed to be from 1
times as great as the quantity raised in it at the end of the American war; and
the increase in England has not been so great as in Scotland, it has been far
than during any previous period of equal duration. The increase on the Contin
been similar. Potatoes are now very largely cultivated in France, Italy, and Ger
and, with the exception of the Irish, the Swiss have become their greatest cons
They were introduced into India from the Cape of Good Hope about 30 year
and are cultivated with great success in the Bengal provinces. So rapid an
sion of the taste for, and the cultivation of, an exotic, has no parallel in the his
industry; it has had, and will continue to have, the most powerful influence
condition of mankind. — (For further details with respect to the history of the pot
Sir F. M. Eden on the State of the Poor, vol. i. p. 508.; Humboldt, Essai
Nouvelle Espagne, tome iii. pp. 460. 465. 2d ed.; Sir Joseph Banks on the In
tion of the Potato; Phillips's History of Cultivated Vegetables, vol. ii. art. *Pota*

2. *Influence of the Cultivation of the Potato on the Number and Condition of the*
— There is a considerable discrepancy in the statements of the best authors as
number of individuals that might be supported on an acre of land planted with p
as compared with those that might be supported on an acre sown with wheat
stating the proportion as high as *six* to *one*, and others at only *two* to *one*. Acc
to Mr. Arthur Young, one pound of wheat is about equal in nutritive power
pounds of potatoes. But Mr. Newenham, who has carefully investigated this
states that "three pounds of good mealy potatoes are, undoubtedly, more than equ
to a pound of bread,"—(*Newenham on the Population of Ireland*, p. 340.); and his e
is rather above Mr. Wakefield's. Supposing, however, that one pound weight o
is fully equal to *four* pounds of potatoes, still the difference in favour of the s
quantity of food derived from a given quantity of land planted with the l
very great. According to Mr. Young, the average produce of potatoes in
may be taken at 82 barrels the Irish acre; which, at 20 stones the barrel, is
22,960 lbs.; and this, being divided by *four*, to bring it to the same standard,
of nutritive power, as wheat, gives 5,740 lbs. Mr. Young further estimates the
produce of wheat, by the Irish acre, at four quarters; which, supposing the qu

480 lbs. gives in all 1,920 lbs., or about one third part of the solid nourishment
ed by an acre of potatoes. — (*Tour in Ireland*, Appen. pp. 12. 24. &c. 4to ed.)
stimate must, however, be somewhat modified when applied to Great Britain ;
ll of which, while it is better adapted to the growth of wheat, is generally supposed
be quite so suitable for the potato as that of Ireland. But it notwithstanding
of demonstration, that even here " *an acre of potatoes will feed double the number*
viduals that can be fed from an acre of wheat." — (*General Report of Scotland*, vol. i.
)

clear, therefore, on the most moderate estimate, that the population of a potato-
g country may become, *other things being about equal*, from two to three times as
as it could have been, had the inhabitants fed wholly on corn. But it is exceedingly
ul whether an increase of population, brought about by a substitution of the po-
r wheat, be desirable. Its use as a subordinate or subsidiary species of food is
ed with the best effects — producing both an increase of comfort and security ; but
are certain circumstances inseparable from it, which would seem to oppose the
ormidable obstacles to its advantageous use as a *prime* article of subsistence.
scussion of this subject can hardly be said properly to belong to a work of this
ut its importance may, perhaps, excuse us for making a few observations with
to it.

admitted on all hands, that the rate of wages is principally determined by the
of food made use of in a country. Now, as potatoes form that species which is
ed at the very least expense, it may be fairly presumed, on general grounds, thta
vill be reduced to a minimum wherever the labouring classes are mainly dependent
toes ; and the example of Ireland shows that this conclusion is as consistent with
with principle. It is clear, however, that when the crop of potatoes happens to be
t in a country thus situated, the condition of its inhabitants must be in the last
unfortunate. During a period of scarcity, men cannot go from a low to a high
if they would elude its pressure, they must leave the dearer and resort to
species of food. But to those who subsist on potatoes this is not possible ; they
ready reached the lowest point in the descending scale. Their wages being de-
d by the price of the least expensive sort of food, they cannot, when it fails, buy
ich is dearer ; so that it is hardly possible for them to avoid falling a sacrifice to
e want. The history of Ireland abounds, unfortunately, in examples of this sort.
g is more common than to see the price of potatoes in Dublin, Limerick, &c.
ause of a scarcity, to five or six times their ordinary price, and the people to be in-
n the extreme of suffering ; and yet it rarely happens, upon such occasions, that
e of corn is materially affected, or that any less quantity than usual is exported to
d.

ay be said, perhaps, that had potatoes not been introduced, wheat, or barley,
would have been the lowest species of food ; and that whenever they happened
he population would have been as destitute as if they had been subsisting on
. It must, however, be observed, that the proportion which the price of
r any species of grain, bears to the price of butcher's meat, tea, beer, &c. is
decidedly greater than the proportion which the price of potatoes bears to
ticles : and it therefore follows, that a people, who have adopted wheat, or
ies of corn, for the principal part of their food, are much better able to make
al purchases of butcher's meat, &c. ; and will consequently be more likely to
eir habits elevated, so as to consider the consumption of a certain quantity of
food, &c. as indispensable to existence. And hence it appears reasonable to
, that a people who chiefly subsist on corn, would, in most cases, subsist par-
butcher's meat, and would enjoy a greater or less quantity of other articles ;
t would be possible for them, in a period of scarcity, to make such retrench-
would enable them to elude the severity of its pressure.

hough the population in corn-feeding countries were dependent on the cheapest
of grain, not for a part only, but for the whole of their food, their situation
otwithstanding, be less hazardous than that of a population subsisting wholly
oes.

e *first* place, owing to the impossibility, as to all practical purposes at least, of
g potatoes, the surplus produce of a luxuriant crop cannot be stored up or
as a stock to meet any subsequent scarcity. The whole crop must necessarily
usted in a single year ; so that when the inhabitants have the misfortune to be
n by a scarcity, its pressure cannot be alleviated, as is almost uniformly the
orn-feeding countries, by bringing the reserves of former harvests to market.
ear is thus left to provide subsistence for itself. When, on the one hand, the
uxuriant, the surplus is of comparatively little use, and is wasted unprofitably ;
n, on the other hand, it is deficient, famine and disease necessarily prevail.

In the *second* place, the general opinion seems to be, that the variations in the q
tities of produce obtained from land planted with potatoes, are greater than the
ations in the quantities of produce obtained from land on which wheat, or any
species of grain, is raised.

And *lastly*, owing to the great bulk and weight of potatoes, and the difficulty of
serving them on shipboard, the expense of conveying them from one country to an
is so very great, that a scarcity can never be materially relieved by importing them
abroad. In consequence, those who chiefly depend on potatoes are practically excl
from participating in the benevolent provision made by nature for equalising the
ations in the harvests of particular countries by means of commerce, and are th
almost wholly on their own resources.

We should, therefore, be warranted in concluding, even though we were not posse
of any direct evidence on the subject, from the circumstance of the potato being a
that cannot be kept on hand, from its natural fickleness, and from the incapaci
importing it when deficient, or of exporting it when in excess, that the oscillations
price must be greater than in the price of wheat; and such, in point of fact, is the
The oscillation in wheat is thought great when its price is doubled; but in a scarce
the potato is not unfrequently *six* times as dear as in a plentiful one! — (*Minu*
Evidence taken before the Agricultural Committee of 1821, p. 212.) And the comp
tively frequent recurrence of scarcities in Ireland, and the destitution and mise
which they involve the population, afford but too convincing proofs of the accura
what has now been stated.

It is, therefore, of the utmost consequence to the well-being of every people, a
their protection in years of scarcity, that they should not subsist principally o
potato. In this country the pressure of a scarcity is evaded by resorting to in
species of food, such as potatoes, and a lower standard of comfort; but if our p
were habitually fed on the potato, this would be impracticable. The chances of fa
would thus be vastly increased; while, owing to the low value of the potato as comp
with most other things, the labourers would have less chance of preserving or acqu
a taste for animal food, or other necessaries and luxuries; and, consequently, of ch
ing, at any future period, their actual condition for a better.

It is not easy to form any very accurate estimate of the profit and loss attendin
cultivation of potatoes to the farmer, as compared with other crops. This is a point
which the statements of those best qualified to give an opinion differ very consider
Mr. Loudon says, "they require a great deal of manure from the farmer;
generally speaking, little is returned by them; they are a bulky, unhandy article,
blesome in the lifting and carrying processes, and interfering with the seed seas
wheat — the most important one to the farmer. After all, from particular circumst
they cannot be vended unless when raised in the vicinity of large towns; hence
are in most respects an unprofitable article to the agriculturist. To him, the re
terion is the profit which potatoes will return in feeding beasts; and here we appr
the result will be altogether in favour of turnips and *rutabaga* as the most pro
articles for that purpose."

It seems difficult to reconcile this statement with the rapid progress of the
cultivation: but those who assent to what has been previously advanced with r
to the mischievous consequences that arise from the mass of the population bec
dependent on the potato as a principle article of food, will not regret though it s
turn out to be accurate.

3. *Price and Value of Potatoes.* — Where potatoes form, as in England, only
sidiary species of food, the fluctuations in their price are confined within compar
narrow limits. But even in this case they are very considerable, as is evinced
following statement of their price at the ship's side in the Thames from 1824 to 18

Prices of Potatoes, 1824 to 1829. By Messrs. Hooper and Moxon, Hays Lane, Tooley Stree

			s.				s.
December, 1824	-	Red -	90 per ton.	January, 1827	-	White	55
January, 1825	- -	Red	100 —	May	- -	White	80
February	-	Kidney	120 —	January	-	Kidney	100
April	-	Kidney -	160 —	October	-	Kidney	60
April	-	Red -	95 —	November	-	Kidney	80
January	-	White	100 —	December	-	Kidney	100
March	-	White -	80 —	March, 1828	-	White	40
November	-	White -	80 —	April	-	White	40
January, 1826	-	Kidney	120 —	March	-	Red	60
April	-	Kidney -	140 —	March	-	Kidney	60
March	-	White -	85 —	November	-	Kidney	100
November	-	White -	70 —	June	-	Red	45
April	-	Red -	110 —	December	-	Red	80
May	-	Red -	105 —	January, 1829	-	Red	70
May	-	Red -	120 —	February	-	White	70
May	-	Red -	140 —	March	- -	Kidney	100
November	-	Red	85 —	March	-	Red -	70 to 55
December	-	Red -	100 —	April	-	Red -	65 to 50

Colquhoun estimated the entire value of the potatoes annually consumed in Britain and Ireland at the end of the late war at *sixteen millions* sterling. But it less to say that there are no materials by which to form an estimate of this sort pretensions to accuracy. The one in question has been suspected, like most put forth by the same learned person, of exaggeration. And we incline to think that he estimated the value of the yearly produce of potatoes in the empire at *twelve* he would have been nearer the mark. But on a point of this sort it is not to speak with any thing like confidence.

ND, a certain weight used as a standard to determine the gravity and of bodies. See WEIGHTS AND MEASURES.

ND, a money of account = 20*s*.

DER, GUN. See GUNPOWDER.

CIOUS METALS, a designation frequently applied to gold and silver. c given, under the articles GOLD, and SILVER, a short account of each and we now propose laying before the reader a few details with respect to pply and consumption.

ter fully into this interesting and difficult subject would require a long rather a large volume. Mr. Jacob has recently published an "Histori- iry into the Introduction and Consumption of the Precious Metals," in e takes up the subject at the earliest period, and continues it to the pre- . This work, though neither so complete nor satisfactory as might have pected, contains a good deal of valuable information, and deserves the of all who take an interest in such inquiries. We confess, however, ral of the learned author's statements and conclusions seem to us to be le wide of the mark. We shall notice one or two of them in the course rticle.

ply of the Precious Metals. — Since the discovery of America, the far greater ae supplies of gold and silver have been derived from that continent. Pre- o the publication of Humboldt's great work, *Essai Politique sur la Nouvelle* several estimates, some of them framed by individuals of great intelligence, irculation, of the quantities of gold and silver imported from America. They, differed widely from each other, and were all framed from comparatively urces of information.* But these have been wholly superseded by the more and laborious investigations of M. Humboldt. This illustrious traveller, ing acquainted with all that had been written on the subject, and having ready official sources of information unknown to the writers already alluded to, was d in the theory and practice of mining, and critically examined several of the brated mines. He was, therefore, incomparably better qualified for forming nclusions as to the past and present productiveness of the mines, than any of had hitherto speculated on the subject. His statements have, indeed, been f exaggeration; and we incline to think that there are grounds for believing harge is, in some measure, well founded, particularly as respects the accounts fits made by mining, and of the extent to which the supplies of the precious y be increased. But this criticism applies, if at all, in a very inferior degree, unts M. Humboldt has given of the total produce of the mines, and the ex- urope. And making every allowance for the imperfection inseparable from tigations, it is still true that the statements in question, and the inquiries on y are founded, are among the most valuable contributions that have ever been atistical science.

ng to M. Humboldt, the supplies of the precious metals derived from Ame- een as follows: —

	Dollars a Year at an Average.				Dollars a Year at an Average.
to 1500	250,000	From 1600 to 1700	-	-	16,000,000
—1545	3,000,000	— 1700 — 1750	-	-	22,500,000
—1600	11,000,000	— 1750 — 1803	-	-	35,300,000

(*Essai sur la Nouvelle Espagne,* tome iii. p. 428. 2d ed.)

It has brought these estimates together as follows : —

	Epochs.	Dollars.	Authors.	Epochs.	Dollars.
-	1492—1724	3,536,000,000	Gerboux	1724—1800	1,600,000,000
-	1492—1628	1,500,000,000	The Author of the		
-	1492—1595	2,000,000,000	Recherches sur le	1492—1775	5,072,000,000
-	1519—1617	1,536,000,000	Commerce, Amst.		
-	1492—1780	5,154,000,000	1779.		
-	1492—1775	8,800,000,000			
-	1763—1777	301,000,000			

(*Essai sur la Nouvelle Espagne,* tome iii. p. 412.)

The following is M. Humboldt's estimate of the annual produce of the mines New World, at the beginning of the present century : —

Annual Produce of the Mines of America at the Commencement of the Nineteenth Centu

Political Divisions.	Gold.		Silver.		Value of and Sil Doll
	Marcs of Castile.	Kilogs.	Marcs of Castile.	Kilogs.	
Vice-Royalty of New Spain -	7,000	1,609	2,338,220	537,512	23,000
Vice-Royalty of Peru -	3,400	782	611,090	140,478	6,240
Captain-Generalship of Chili -	12,212	2,807	29,700	6,827	2,050
Vice-Royalty of Buenos Ayres	2,200	506	481,830	110,764	4,850
Vice Royalty of New Granada	20,505	4,714	-	-	2,990
Brazil - -	29,900	6,873	-	-	4,360
Total - - - -	75,217	17,291	3,460,840	795,581	43,500

Taking the dollar at 4s. 3d. this would give 9,243,750l. as the total annual p of the American mines. M. Humboldt further estimated the annual produce European mines of Hungary, Saxony, &c., and those of northern Asia at the period, at about a million more.

The *quantity* of gold produced in America at the beginning of the century, the quantity of silver as 1 to 46 ; in Europe the proportions were as 1 to 40. *value* of equal quantities of gold and silver were then in the proportion of 15 to 1. Latterly the quantity of gold produced has increased as compared w quantity of silver.

From 1800 to 1810, the produce of the American mines was considerably inc but in the last mentioned year, the contest began, which terminated in the diss of the connection between Spain and the South American colonies. The conv and insecurity arising out of this struggle, the proscription of the old Spanish fa to whom the mines principally belonged, who repaired with the wrecks of the tunes, some to Cuba, some to Spain, and some to Bordeaux and the so France, have caused the abandonment of several of the mines, and an extrao falling off in the amount of their produce. There are no means of accurately e ing the precise extent of this decline; but according to Mr. Jacob, who has co and compared all the existing information on the subject, the total produce American mines, inclusive of Brazil, during the 20 years ending with 1829, estimated at 80,736,768l. or at 4,036,838l. a year; less considerably than the their produce at the beginning of the century ! — (*Jacob*, vol. ii. p. 267.)

The European mines have declined within the last 20 years ; but there is a n increase in the produce of the Russian mines. According to M. Humboldt, it a at present to about 1,250,000l. a year.

On the whole, therefore, the present annual average produce of the Ameri European mines, including those of Russia, may be estimated at between 5,50 and 6,000,000l., being thrown from 4,500,000l. to 4,000,000l. less than the annual pro the beginning of the century.

2. *Consumption of the Precious Metals.* — Gold and silver are supplied either as coin, or are made use of in the arts. There are no means whatever by which cover the proportion in which they are applied, at any given period, to these pu and the proportion is perpetually varying with the varying circumstances country ; as, for example, with the greater or less abundance of paper money, degree in which the use of coins is saved by the various devices resorted to by n banking and otherwise for economising currency, the greater or less wealth inhabitants, the fashion as to plate, the feeling of security at the moment thousand other circumstances, — all of which are liable to great and sometimes changes.

According to Mr. Jacob, the value of the precious metals annually applied mental and luxurious purposes in Europe, may be estimated as follows : —

Great Britain	-	-	-	-	£ 2,457,
France	-	-	-	-	1,200,
Switzerland	-	-	-	-	350,
Remainder of Europe		-	-	-	1,605,
	Total	-	-	-	£ 5,612,

And adding to this the sums directly applied to the same purposes in Am whole will be about 5,900,000l.

The data upon which this estimate has been founded, are in the last degree v unsatisfactory. It can hardly, indeed, be looked upon as any thing better tha guess ; and as such, we do not think that it is a very happy one. M. Chabro

ches are far more worthy of confidence than those of M. Chaptal, to which Mr.
refers) estimates the consumption of gold and silver in the arts at Paris at
,000 francs a year — (*Recherches Statistiques sur la Ville de Paris*, 1823. Tab.
.); which corresponds with the elaborate estimate of M. Benoiston de Château-
- (*Recherches sur les Consommations de Paris en* 1817, 2de partie, p. 78.). Both
authorities agree that the consumption of the precious metals in the arts at Paris
le that of the rest of France; so that we have 21,828,000 francs, or 866,190*l.* for
sumption of the whole kingdom, which is 333,810*l.* a year under Mr. Jacob's
e.

have been assured, by those who have good means of forming a correct opinion
uch a point, that the quantity assigned by Mr. Jacob for the consumption of
Britain is over-rated in about the same proportion as the consumption of France,
ut a fourth part. There has, no doubt, been a considerable increase of late years
consumption of plate and gilt articles; but it would require far better evidence
y hitherto laid before the public, to warrant the conclusion that so large a sum as
000*l.* is appropriated to such purposes.

consumption of Switzerland, as set down by Mr. Jacob, is probably not far from
e. But the sum assigned for the aggregate consumption of the rest of Europe
to be quite as much exaggerated as that allowed for France and England.
ording to this view of the matter, the consumption will be —

reat Britain	-	-	-	-	-	-	£ 1,842,916
ance	-	-	-	-	-	-	866,190
witzerland	-	-	-	-	-	-	350,000
est of Europe	-	-	-	-	-	-	1,204,118
Total		-		-		-	£ 4,263,224

s must be added 300,000*l.* for the consumption of America; making the entire
ption 4,563,224*l.*

ably this valuation is still too high. According to M. Humboldt (*Nouvelle
e*, 2d edit. tome iii. p. 464.), the total consumption of the precious metals in
, for other purposes than those of coin, amounts to only 87,182,800 francs;
at the exchange of 25·20, to 3,459,714*l.* : and adding to this, 300,000*l.* for the
ption of America, the grand total will be, in round numbers, 3,760,000*l.* ; being
l. under our estimate, and no less than 2,140,000*l.* under that of Mr. Jacob !
a portion of the gold and silver annually made use of in the arts is derived from
on of old plate, the burning of lace, picture frames, &c. Here, however, we
lament the impossibility of ascertaining the proportion the supply from this
bears to the total quantity wrought up. Mr. Jacob estimates it at only $\frac{1}{40}$th
$2\frac{1}{2}$ per cent. ; but so small a sum seems to be quite out of the question. Most
the precious metals employed in plating, gilding, &c., is certainly destroyed ; but
ntity of metal so made use of is admitted by every one to be decidedly less than
ntity used in the manufacture of plate, watch-cases, and other articles of that
ion. And these, when they either become unfashionable, or are broken or in-
re, for the most part, sent to the melting pot. According to the statement of
quoted and sanctioned by Humboldt, a *half* of the gold and silver used in
by goldsmiths and others in the arts, is supposed to be obtained from the fusion
late, &c. — (*Nouvelle Espagne*, tome iii. p. 467.)
notwithstanding the high authority by which this estimate is supported, we
that it is nearly as much above the mark as Mr. Jacob's is certainly below it.
ng, therefore, that, at a medium, 20 per cent. or $\frac{1}{5}$th part of the precious
nnually made use of in the arts is obtained from the fusion of old plate, we
ve, by deducting this proportion from the 4,563,000*l.* applied to the arts in
and America, 3,650,000*l.* as the total annual appropriation of the new gold and
g from the mines to such purposes, leaving about 2,000,000*l.* a year to be
tured into coin.

ot much more easy to determine the consumption of the precious metals when
tured into coin, than when in plate. Mr. Jacob has entered into some curious
vol. ii. c. 28.) to determine the abrasion or loss of coins from wear, which he
s at $\frac{1}{500}$th part a year for gold, and $\frac{1}{200}$th part for silver coins. This, however,
give the total wear and tear of the coins. To determine the latter, the quan-
t by fire, shipwrecks, and other accidents, must be taken into account. The
these sources can only be guessed at; but adding it to the loss by abrasion,
we shall not be far wrong in estimating the whole at 1 per cent.
ngular that, in estimating the consumption of gold and silver, Mr. Jacob should
made the slightest allusion to the practice which has uniformly prevailed in all

countries harassed by intestine commotions, or exposed to foreign invasion, of bu▮ treasure in the earth. Of the hoards so deposited, a very considerable proportion ▮ been altogether lost; and there can be no doubt that this has been one of the prin▮ means by which the stock of the precious metals has been kept down to its pr▮ level. Every one is aware that, during the middle ages, *treasure trove*, or money ▮ from the ground by chance finders, belonged to the crown, and formed no incons▮ able part of the royal revenue of this and other countries. The practice has al▮ prevailed to a very great extent in the East. — (*Bernier, Voyage de Mogol*, Amst. ▮ tome i. p. 209.; *Scrafton on the Government of Hindostan*, p. 16. &c.) But it i▮ confined to that quarter. Wherever property is insecure, it is invariably resorte▮ Mr. Wakefield tells us that it is common in Ireland. — (*Account of Ireland*, ▮ p. 593.) It has always prevailed to a considerable extent in Russia and France; ▮ in the latter, during the revolutionary anarchy, immense sums were buried, of whic▮ abundantly certain a large proportion will never be resuscitated. The wars and ▮ vulsions by which Europe was desolated for more than 20 years extended the pra▮ to all parts of the Continent; withdrawing in this way from circulation a very ▮ siderable part of the increased produce of the mines. — (*Storch, Economie Poli*▮ tome i. p. 221. Paris, 1823.)

3. *Exportation of the Precious Metals to the East.* — It must be well known to al▮ traders, that from the remotest era down to a comparatively late period, bullion has al▮ formed one of the principal and most advantageous articles of export to the ▮ Humboldt estimated that, of the entire produce of the American mines at the begi▮ of this century, amounting, as already seen, to 43,500,000 dollars, no less than 25,50▮ were sent to Asia, — 17,500,000 by the Cape of Good Hope, 4,000,000 by the L▮ and 4,000,000 through the Russian frontier. — (*Nouvelle Espagne*, tome iii. p. ▮ Latterly, however, this immense drain has almost entirely ceased. The expor▮ opium from India to China, and the vastly increased exportation of British cotton▮ other goods to the East Indies and China, since the opening of the trade in 1814▮ only suffice to pay for our own, but also for the imports of other nations from ▮ countries, without, in ordinary seasons, requiring the exportation of a single oun▮ bullion. It would seem, too, that the efflux of bullion to China from Russia had ce▮ and that the current had even begun to set in the opposite direction. — (*Jacob*, v▮ p. 320.) And if there be any sums still exported by way of the Levant, whi▮ doubtful, they are certainly quite inconsiderable.

4. *Influence of the diminished Productiveness of the Mines on Prices.* — It has ▮ customary in this country to ascribe almost the whole fall that has taken place i ▮ price of most commodities since the peace, to the diminished supply of bullion fro▮ mines. But we doubt whether this circumstance has not been fully counterbal▮ by others, and whether it has had any influence in the way now mentioned. ▮ cessation of the drain to the East, even admitting that M. Humboldt has som▮ over-rated its amount, must of itself have gone far to counteract the decreased ▮ ductiveness of the mines. In addition to this, the greater security and tranq▮ enjoyed on the Continent since the peace, must not only have checked that bu▮ of money, formerly so prevalent, but must have caused the bringing to light of a ▮ many of the subterranean hoards. The institution of savings banks, now so co▮ every where, has also, no doubt, tended to prevent hoarding, and to bring a good ▮ of coin into circulation, that would otherwise have been locked up. These ci▮ stances, coupled with others that might be mentioned, such as the cessation ▮ demand for military chests, &c., afford the best grounds for doubting wheth▮ quantity of the precious metals annually applicable to the purposes of circulation ▮ as great at present, as in 1809 or 1810. It is contended, indeed, that the fall whi▮ taken place in the price of *all* commodities during the last dozen years, proves th▮ value of money must have sustained a corresponding advance. But though the f▮ been pretty general, it has not been universal; and we venture to affirm that there ▮ without any exception whatever, a single commodity that has fallen in price since ▮ the fall of which may not be satisfactorily accounted for without reference to the su▮ gold and silver. — (See *ante*, p 72.) Multiplied proofs of what is now stated, ▮ found in various articles throughout this work. And we have little doubt that thos▮ investigate the matter with any degree of care will agree with us in thinking, tha▮ the influence of the decreased productiveness of the mines on prices estimated a▮ .5 to 10 per cent, it would be very decidedly beyond the mark. We believe its in▮ has been hardly perceptible.

5. *Probable future Supply of Gold and Silver.* — Nothing but conjectural stat▮ can be made as to the probable future supply of the precious metals. On the ▮ however, we should think that a considerable increase may be fairly anticipated.▮ anarchy in which the new South American states have hitherto been involved, wi▮

se ; and, with the increase of population and capital, renewed attention will
s be paid to the mines. It is reasonable also, we think, to anticipate that the
from the Russian mines will continue to increase.

MIUM. See INSURANCE.

CES. By the price of a commodity is meant its value estimated in money,
y the quantity of money for which it will exchange. The price of a com-
rises when it fetches more, and falls when it fetches less money.

ce of freely produced Commodities. — The exchangeable value of commodities—that
ower of exchanging for or buying other commodities — depends, at any given
artly on the comparative facility of their production, and partly on the relation of
y and demand. If any two or more commodities respectively required the same
capital and labour to bring them to market, and if the supply of each were adjusted
ccording to the effectual demand — that is, were they all in sufficient abundance,
ore, to supply the wants of those able and willing to pay the outlay upon them,
ordinary rate of profit at the time — they would each fetch the same price, or
for the same quantity of any other commodity. But if any single commodity
ppen to require less or more capital and labour for its production, while the quan-
red to produce the others continued stationary, its value, as compared with them,
the first case, fall, and in the second, rise ; and, supposing the cost of its pro-
ot to vary, its value might be increased by a falling off in the supply, or by
se of demand, and conversely.

is of importance to bear in mind, that all variations of price arising from any
tion in the supply and demand of such commodities as may be *freely produced
ite quantities*, are *temporary* only ; while those that are occasioned by changes
ost of their production are *permanent*, at least as much so as the cause in
ey originate. A general mourning occasions a transient rise in the price of
th : but supposing that the fashion of wearing black were to continue, its price
t permanently vary ; for those who previously manufactured blue and brown
., would henceforth manufacture only black cloth ; and the supply being in this
ased to the same extent as the demand, the price would settle at its old level.
e importance of distinguishing between a variation of price originating in a
f fashion, or other accidental circumstance — such, for example, as a deficient
and a variation occasioned by some change in the cost of production. In the
se, prices will, at no distant period, revert to their old level ; in the latter, the
will be lasting.

the *price* of a freely produced commodity rises or falls, such variation may evi-
occasioned either by something affecting the commodity, or by something affect-
lue of money. But when, instead of being confined to one, the generality of
ies rise or fall, the fair presumption is that the change is not in them, but in the
h which they are compared. This conclusion will not, however, apply in all cases ;
ieve that most part of that fall in the price of commodities, which has taken place
peace, and which has been so generally ascribed to a rise in the value of money
by a decline in the productiveness of the mines, has been caused by the in-
oductiveness of industry arising from the abolition of oppressive restraints on
, the opening of new and more abundant sources of supply, and the discovery
ventions, and improved methods of production. — (See PRECIOUS METALS.)

e of Monopolised Commodities. — Exclusive, however, of the commodities now
, there is a considerable class, whose producers or holders enjoy either an *absolute
l* monopoly of the supply. When such is the case, prices depend entirely or
y on the proportion between the supply and demand, and are not liable to be
, or only in a secondary degree, by changes in the cost of production. An-
es and gems ; the pictures of the great masters ; wines of a peculiar flavour,
in small quantities, in particular situations ; and a few other articles, exist
t may be called absolute monopolies : their supply cannot be increased, and
e must, therefore, depend entirely on the competition of those who may
y them, without being in the slightest degree influenced by the cost of their

lies are sometimes established by law ; as when the power to supply the
th a particular article is made over to one individual or society of individuals,
ny limitation of the price at which it may be sold ; which, of course, enables
essed of the monopoly to exact the highest price for it that the competition of
will afford, though such price may exceed the cost of production in any con-
gree. Monopolies of this sort used to be common in England, particularly
n of Elizabeth ; but they were finally abolished by the famous act of the
c. 3. — an act which, by establishing the freedom of competition in all

businesses carried on at home, has been productive of the greatest advantage. Monopoly.)

The corn laws establish a partial monopoly of the supply of Great Britain wi in favour of the agriculturists; but as competition is carried to as great an ex agriculture as in any other business, this monopoly does not enable them to o higher price for their produce than is sufficient to pay the expenses of its produ though, owing to the peculiar circumstances under which this country is place price is higher than the price in the surrounding countries. Hence it results monopoly is injurious to the public, without being of any advantage to those e in the business of agriculture. Neither, indeed, can it be truly said to be advant to the landlords. — (See *antè*, p. 390.)

The rights conveyed by patents sometimes establish a valuable monopoly ; f enable the inventors of improved methods of production to maintain, during tinuance of the patent, the price of the article at a level which may be much than is required to afford them the ordinary rate of profit. This advantage, howe stimulating invention, and exciting to new discoveries, of which it is the natu appropriate reward, instead of being injurious, is beneficial to the public. Patents.)

There are also partial monopolies, depending upon situation, connection, f &c. These, and other inappreciable circumstances, sometimes occasion a diffe 30 per cent., or more, in the price of the same article in shops not very dista each other.

Generally speaking, the supply of monopolised commodities is less liable to va those that are freely produced; and their prices are commonly more steady. B are various exceptions to this rule, and of these the corn monopoly is one. The variations in the harvests of particular countries, and their average equality thro the world, exposes a nation which shuts foreign corn out of its ports to des vicissitudes of price, from which it would enjoy a nearly total exemption were t open. — (See *antè*, p. 386.) Sometimes the expiration of a monopoly — a pat example — has occasioned a sudden and extraordinary increase of supply, and quent fall of price ; entailing, of course, a serious loss on the holders of large st goods produced under the monopoly.

3. *New Sources of Supply.* — The effects on prices produced by the opening markets, or new sources of supply, are familiar to every one. The fall that ha place in the price of pepper, and of all sorts of commodities, with *the exception* brought from the East, since the opening of the trade in 1814, is a conspicuo of what is now stated.

4. *Influence of War on Prices.* — The effect of war in obstructing the ordinary of commercial intercourse, and occasioning extreme fluctuations in the supply a of commodities, is well known. In this respect, however, the latter part of the is perhaps entitled to a pre-eminence. We had then to deal with an enemy w extended his sway over most part of the Continent; and who endeavoured, b means in his power, to shut us out of the continental markets. Mr. Tooke ha in his elaborate and valuable work on High and Low Prices, a variety of detail strikingly illustrate the effect that the regulations then adopted by the belligeren had on prices. " Among the means," says Mr. Tooke, " devised by the ingen enterprise of adventurers to elude or overcome the obstacles presented by the de the enemy, one in particular, which was resorted to on an extensive scale, mention, as illustrating in a striking manner the degree in which those obstac calculated to increase the cost to the consumer. Several vessels laden with sugar tobacco, cotton, twist, and other valuable commodities, were despatched from l very high rates of freight and insurance to Salonica, where the goods were land thence conveyed on mules and horses through Servia and Hungary to Vienna purpose of being distributed over Germany, and possibly into France. Thus i happen that the inhabitants of that part of the Continent most contiguous country could not receive their supplies from hence, without an expense of co equivalent to what it would be, if they were removed to the distance of a sea twice round the globe, but not subject to fiscal and political regulations." An sequence of these, and other causes of the same sort, Mr. Tooke mentions that of sugar in France, and other parts of the Continent, during the latter yea war, was as high as 5s. and 6s. a pound ; that coffee rose to 7s. ; indigo to so on.

But the sums charged for freight and insurance were the most extra Mr. Tooke states, that he has known instances in which the licence, freight, charges on account of a vessel of about 100 tons burthen, making a voyage fr to London and back, have amounted to the almost incredible sum of 50,000*l.*

ich the whole cost and outfit did not amount to 4,000l., earned, during the latter
of the war, a gross freight of 80,000l. on a voyage from Bordeaux to London
ick! The freight of indigo from London to the Continent does not at present
1d. a pound; whereas it amounted, at the period referred to, to about 4s. 6d.
igh and Low Prices, 2d ed. p. 212.)

Influence of Taxes on Prices. — It is unnecessary to dilate on a topic so familiar to
one. When a tax is laid on a commodity, its price necessarily rises in a cording proportion; for otherwise the producers would not obtain the ordinary rate
fit, and would, of course, withdraw from the business. The rise in the price of
of the articles in the annexed table, is principally to be ascribed to the increase of
n.

se statements will probably suffice to give our readers a general idea of the prin-
which determine the value of commodities. To go deeper into the subject would
us in discussions that belong to political economy, and are among the most
te in that science. The influence of speculation on prices must not, however,
sed over in a work of this sort.

Influence of Speculation on Prices. — It very rarely happens that either the actual supply
species of produce in extensive demand, or the intensity of that demand, can be ex-
easured. Every transaction in which an individual buys produce in order to sell it
is, in fact, a speculation. The buyer anticipates that the demand for the article he
chased will be such, at some future period, either more or less distant, that he will be
dispose of it with a profit; and the success of the speculation depends, it is evident,
skill with which he has estimated the circumstances that must determine the future
f the commodity. It follows, therefore, that in all highly commercial countries,
merchants are possessed of large capitals, and where they are left to be guided in
of them by their own discretion and foresight, the prices of commodities will
tly be very much influenced, not merely by the actual occurrence of changes in
ustomed relation of the supply and demand, but by the anticipation of such
s. It is the business of the merchant to acquaint himself with every circumstance
g the particular description of commodities in which he deals. He endeavours
in, by means of an extensive correspondence, the earliest and most authentic
ation with respect to every thing that may affect their supply or demand, or the
their production: and if he learned that the supply of an article had failed, or
ving to changes of fashion, or to the opening of new channels of commerce, the
for it had been increased, he would most likely be disposed to become a buyer,
ipation of profiting by the rise of price, which, under the circumstances of the
uld hardly fail of taking place; or, if he were a holder of the article, he would
o part with it, unless for a higher price than he would previously have accepted.
ntelligence received by the merchant had been of a contrary description — if, for
e, he had learned that the article was now produced with greater facility, or that
as a falling off in the demand for it, caused by a change of fashion, or by the
up of some of the markets to which it had previously been admitted — he
ave acted differently: in this case he would have anticipated a fall of prices,
ld either have declined purchasing the article, except at a reduced rate, or have
ured to get rid of it, supposing him to be a holder, by offering it a lower price.
equence of these operations, the prices of commodities, in different places and
are brought comparatively near to equality. All abrupt transitions, from
to abundance, and from abundance to scarcity, are avoided; an excess in one
made to balance a deficiency in another, and the supply is distributed with a
f steadiness and regularity that could hardly have been deemed attainable.

obvious, from what has now been stated, that those who indiscriminately con-
ll sorts of speculative engagements, have never reflected on the circumstances
to the prosecution of every undertaking. In truth and reality, they are all
ions. Their undertakers must look forward to periods more or less distant, and
cess depends entirely on the sagacity with which they have estimated the proba-
certain events occurring, and the influence which they have ascribed to them.
ion is, therefore, really only another name for foresight; and though fortunes
netimes been made by a lucky hit, the character of a successful speculator is,
st majority of instances, due to him only who has skilfully devised the means
ing the end he had in view, and who has outstripped his competitors in the
t with which he has looked into futurity, and appreciated the operation of causes
g distant effects. Even in those businesses, such as agriculture and manufac-
at are apparently the most secure, there is, and must be, a great deal of specu-
Those engaged in the former have to encounter the variations of seasons, while
gaged in the latter have to encounter the variations of fashion; and each is, be-
ble to be affected by legislative enactments, by new discoveries in the arts, and

by an endless variety of circumstances which it is always very difficult, and some
quite impossible, to foresee. On the whole, indeed, the gains of the undertakers a
adjusted that those who carry them on obtain, at an average, the common and ord
rate of profit. But the inequality in the gains of individuals is most commonly
great: and while the superior tact, industry, or good fortune of some enable the
realise large fortunes; the want of discernment, the less vigilant attention, or the
fortune of others, frequently reduces them from the situation of capitalists to th
labourers.

The risk to which merchants are exposed, when they either sell off any commod
a reduced price in anticipation of a fall, or buy at an advanced price in anticipati
a future rise, is a consequence principally of the extreme difficulty of ascertainin
true state of the fact with respect to the grounds on which an abundant or a defi
supply, or an increasing or decreasing demand, may be expected. Rules can here be
service; every thing depends upon the talent, tact, and knowledge of the party.
questions to be solved are all practical ones, varying in every case from each other
skill of the merchant being evinced by the mode in which he conducts his business u
such circumstances, or by his sagacity in discovering coming events, and appreci
their character and the extent of their influence. Priority, but, above all, accura
intelligence, is, in such cases, of the utmost consequence. Without well authenti
data to go upon, every step taken may only lead to error. The instances, indee
which speculations, apparently contrived with the greatest judgment, have ende
bankruptcy and ruin, from a deficiency in this essential requisite, are so very num
that every one must be acquainted with them. Hence the importance of selecting
and cautious correspondents; and hence also the necessity of maturely weighing
reports, and of endeavouring, by the aid of information, gleaned from every auth
accessible source, to ascertain how far they may be depended upon.

The great cotton speculation of 1825 took its rise partly and chiefly from a sup
deficiency in the supply of cotton, partly from an idea that there was a greatly incr
demand for raw cotton in this country and the Continent, and partly from a belief
the stocks on hand were unusually low. Now it is obvious, that the success of
who embarked in this speculation depended entirely on two circumstances; viz.
that they were right in the fundamental supposition on which the whole specu
rested, that the supply of cotton was no longer commensurate with the demand ;
second, that their competition did raise the price so high as to diminish the consum
by the manufacturers in too great a degree to enable them to take off the quantity
actually brought to market. If the merchants had been well founded in their s
sitions, and if their competition had not raised the price of cotton too high, the s
lation would certainly have been successful. But, instead of being well founde
hypothesis on which the whole thing rested was perfectly visionary. There was n
ficiency in the supply of cotton, but, on the contrary, a great superabundance
though there had been such a deficiency, the excess to which the price was carried
have checked consumption so much as to occasion a serious decline. The falling
the imports of cotton from America, in 1824, seems to have been the source of the
sion. It was supposed that this falling off was not accidental, but that it was a c
quence of the price of cotton having been for a series of years so low as to be i
quate to defray the expenses of its cultivation. The result showed that this calcu
was most erroneous. And besides, in entering on the speculation, no attention wa
to Egypt and Italy, — countries from which only about 1,400,000 lbs. of cotton
obtained in 1824, but from which no less than 23,800,000 lbs. were obtained in
This unlooked-for importation was of itself almost enough to overturn the combin
of the speculators; and, coupled with the increased importation from America and
countries, actually occasioned a heavy glut of the market.

When a few leading merchants purchase in anticipation of an advance, or s
anticipation of a fall, the speculation is often pushed beyond all reasonable lim
the operations of those who are influenced by imitation only, and who have neve
haps, reflected for a moment on the grounds on which a variation of price is antici
In speculation, as in most other things, one individual derives confidence from an
Such a one purchases or sells, not because he has any really accurate informatio
the state of the demand and supply, but because some one else has done so before
The original impulse is thus rapidly extended; and even those who are satisfied
speculation, in anticipation of a rise of prices, is unsafe, and that there will be a
not unfrequently adventure, in the expectation that they will be able to withdraw
the recoil has begun.

It may, we believe, speaking generally, be laid down as a sound practical r
avoid having any thing to do with a speculation in which many have already en
The competition of the speculators seldom fails speedily to render an adventu

ave been originally safe, extremely hazardous. If a commodity happen to be at
ually reduced price in any particular market, it will rise the moment that
buyers appear in the field; and supposing, on the other hand, that it is fetch-
nusually high price, it will fall, perhaps far below the cost of production, as
supplies begin to be poured in by different merchants. Whatever, therefore,
the success of those who originate a speculation, those who enter into it at
nced period are almost sure to lose. To have been preceded by others ought
uch matters, to inspire confidence; on the contrary, it ought, unless there be
g special in the case, to induce every considerate person to decline interfering

naintenance of the freedom of intercourse between different countries, and the
neral diffusion of sound instruction, seem to be the only means by which those
lations, that are often productive of great national as well as private loss, can
obviated or mitigated. The effects consequent to such improvident specula-
ng always far more injurious to the parties engaged in them than to any other
presumption is that they will diminish both in frequency and force, according
ue principles of commerce come to be better understood. But whatever
ience may occasionally flow from them, it is abundantly plain, that instead of
sened, it would be very much increased, were any restraints imposed on the
of adventure. When the attention of many individuals is directed to the same
peculation; when they prosecute it as a business, and are responsible in their
ate fortunes for any errors they may commit; they acquire a knowledge of the
ircumstances influencing prices, and give by their combinations a steadiness to
ich it is easy to see could not be attained by any other means. It is material,
ar in mind, as was previously stated, that many, perhaps it might be said *most*,
who press so eagerly into the market, when any new channel of commerce is
r when any considerable rise of price is anticipated, are not merchants, but
ngaged in other businesses, or living, perhaps, on fixed incomes, who speculate
pe of suddenly increasing their fortune. This tendency to gambling seldom
reak out upon such occasions: but, fortunately, these are only of comparatively
rrence; and in the ordinary course of affairs, mercantile speculations are left
ducted by those who are familiar with business, and who, in exerting them-
equalise the variations of price, caused by variations of climate and of seasons,
istribute the supply of produce proportionally to the effective demand, and
much providence that it may not at any time be wholly exhausted, perform
that are in the highest degree important and beneficial. They are, it is true,
only by a desire to advance their own interests; but the results of their
s are not less advantageous than those of the agriculturist who gives greater
the soil, or of the mechanist who invents new and more powerful machines.
es of Prices. — It is superfluous, perhaps, to observe that the precious metals are
ll the variations of value already alluded to. Not only, therefore, are prices,
eady remarked, affected by variations in the cost and supply of commodities,
re also affected by changes in the cost and supply of gold and silver, whether
m the exhaustion of old, or the discovery of new mines, improvements in
mining, changes of fashion, &c. Hence it is, that tables of the prices of
ies, extending for a considerable period, communicate far less solid inform-
is generally supposed, and, unless the necessary allowances be made, may
most unfounded conclusions. The real value of any commodity depends
ntity of labour required for its production; but supposing that we were to
inferring this real value, or the ultimate sacrifice required to obtain the
, from its price, it might happen, (had the quantity of labour required for its
declined, but in a less degree than the quantity required to produce gold
, that its value would appear to rise when it had really been diminished.
wever, the rate of wages, as well as the price of commodities, is given upon
data, a table of prices is valuable, inasmuch as it shows the extent of the
over the necessaries and conveniences of life enjoyed by the bulk of the com-
ring the period through which it extends. The subjoined table of the prices
commodities, and of the wages paid to different descriptions of tradesmen, at
Hospital, for the last 100 years, is the most complete table of the sort that
ublished; and is one of the few that are founded upon data, the accuracy of
not be questioned. Unfortunately it applies only to a small part of the
But many important conclusions may, notwithstanding, be deduced from it.
r will find, under the more important articles described in this work, pretty
unts of their prices. Sometimes, as in the case of corn, these accounts go
ery distant period.

An Account of the Contract Prices of the following Articles of Provision, &c. at the Roy

Year.	Flesh, per Cwt.	Bread, per Lb.	Flour, per Sack.	Butter, per Lb.	Cheese, per Lb.	Peas, per Bushel.	Oatmeal, per Bushel.	Salt, per Bushel.	Malt, per Quarter.	Hops, per Cwt.
	£ s. d.	Average.	£ s. d.	s. d.	s. d.	s. d.	£ s. d.	s. d.	£ s. d.	£ s. d.
1729	1 5 8	1d. for 10 6/16 oz.	- -	0 4¼	0 3⅛	4 0	0 4 6	5 0	1 9 0	2 5 0
1730	1 5 8	1d. for 14¼ oz.	- -	0 5	0 3¼	4 0	0 4 6	5 0	1 0 6	2 5 10
1735	0 16 11	1d. for 12¾ oz.	- -	0 3⅝	0 2¼	3 6	0 4 0	4 0	1 0 3	3 9 6¾
1740	1 8 0	1d. for 9 13/16 oz.	- -	0 5	0 3¼	3 6	0 4 0	4 0	1 7 3½	2 10 7¾
1745	1 2 2	1d. for 15 9/16 oz.	- -	0 3⅝	0 2¼	3 6	0 4 0	4 0	1 3 1	3 11 1
1750	1 6 6	1d. for 13¼ oz.	- -	0 5⅛	0 3¼	3 6	0 4 0	4 0	1 4 0	5 4 0
1755	1 7 9½	1d. for 14 6/16 oz.	- -	0 5½	0 3½	3 6	0 4 0	4 0	1 2 0	2 15 0
1760	1 11 6	1d. for 13¼ oz.	- -	0 5½	0 3⅛	3 6	0 4 0	4 0	1 4 9	4 13 4
1765	1 7 3	id. for 9½ oz.	- -	0 5½	0 3¼	3 6	0 4 0	4 0	1 10 8	7 3 6
1770	1 8 6	1d. for 11 3/16 oz.	- -	0 6½	0 3¾	4 3	0 4 9	4 8	1 8 3	5 16 4
1775	1 13 5	1d. for 9 5/16 oz.	- -	0 6¾	0 3¼	7 6	0 5 3	4 8	1 17 3	4 16 6
1780	1 12 6	1d. for 11 6/16 oz.	- -	0 6⅛	0 3⅜	7 6	0 5 3	4 8	1 11 1	2 14 8
1785	1 17 6½	1d. for 10¼ oz.	- -	0 6¾	0 3¾	7 6	0 5 3	4 8	2 0 3	5 6 4
1790	1 16 10	- -	2 3 4	0 6½	0 4	7 6	0 5 3	4 8	1 15 6	6 13 9
1795	2 2 10	- -	3 5 8	0 8¼	0 5¼	9 6	0 6 4¾	6 1¼	2 8 3	7 7 10
1800	3 4 4	- -	4 16 0	0 11⅓	0 6¼	13 5	0 14 0	14 0	4 4 0	16 15 9
1805	3 0 4	- -	4 2 3	0 11¾	0 7¼	7 9	0 12 0	16 10½	4 5 7	6 11 6
1806	3 1 0	- -	3 9 6½	0 11½	0 7⅛	8 4½	0 10 3	19 9	3 16 0	6 7 9
1807	3 3 0	- -	3 3 8¾	1 0⅛	0 7½	14 4¼	0 9 4¾	19 9	3 13 1½	5 19 0
1808	3 3 0	- -	3 9 10½	1 0¼	0 7⅞	19 2¾	0 10 10	19 9	3 16 1½	4 12 6
1809	3 6 6	- -	4 5 1½	1 1	0 8	14 10¾	0 11 9	19 9	4 4 5¼	7 6 8
1810	3 12 0	- -	4 8 4	1 1⅜	0 8⅛	9 5	0 11 7	19 9	4 4 5	7 6 8
1811	3 14 0	- -	4 11 0	1 2½	0 8¼	8 9	0 11 6	19 9	3 13 6	7 13 6
1812	3 18 0	- -	5 7 5	1 3½	0 8½	12 8½	0 13 3	19 9	4 18 6	9 17 0
1813	4 5 0	- -	4 13 0	1 3	0 8¾	13 8¼	0 13 3	19 9	4 16 6	11 11 8
1814	3 14 6	- -	3 10 6	1 2	0 8¾	9 4	0 10 4	19 9	3 17 8	9 10 0
1815	3 8 0	- -	2 4 9	1 2	0 8	6 7¼	0 10 3	19 9	3 9 7¼	9 13 7
1816	2 11 4	- -	3 4 1	0 9½	0 6½	7 0½	0 9 2	19 9	3 9 4½	14 0 0
1817	2 11 4	- -	4 6 4	0 8¾	0 5½	8 6¾	0 13 9	19 9	4 6 10½	22 4 0
		d.								Pockets
1818	2 17 1	Per lb. 2 6/12	3 8 5½	0 11	0 6	9 3¾	0 13 5½	19 9	4 1 8½	8 8 0
1819	3 4 3	— 1¾ 11/12	2 17 5	0 11	0 8	7 8	0 12 9	19 9	3 12 11¾	4 12 0
1820	3 10 4½	— 1¾ 5/12	2 15 1	0 9½	0 7	7 5¾	0 13 4¼	19 9	3 8 8¼	4 0 0
1821	2 18 10	— 1½ 1/12	2 5 3¼	0 8¾	0 6	5 9	0 8 8¼	19 4½	3 1 11	3 12 0
1822	1 19 5½	— 1¼ 8/12	1 17 5¾	0 7½	0 5	5 0½	0 8 6	18 0	2 12 8½	3 10 0
1823	2 2 7¼	— 1⅛	2 2 5	0 7¼	0 4	5 6	8s. 3d. ⅌ bush. 15s. 6d. ⅌ cwt.	4 10	2 19 11	9 19 0
1824	2 2 8¼	— 1½ 5/12	2 6 2	0 8¼	0 4½	5 11	17s. ⅌ cwt.	4 9	3 2 1	7 5 0
1825	2 19 6½	— 1¾ 5/12	2 13 4	0 10½	0 5¼	split peas 11s	0 17 6	2 10	3 11 10¼	23 0 0
1826	2 17 8	— 1½ 3/12	2 5 2¾	0 9½	0 6⅓	11 0	0 19 0	1 10¼	3 5 1	15 5 0
1827	2 15 4½	— 1⅓ 3/12	2 3 6	0 8¼	0 5¼	10 6	1 5 0	1 8	3 4 10	4 10 0
1828	2 10 7¼	— 1½ 288/360	2 6 0¾	0 8½	0 5¼	9 6	0 18 6	1 10	3 1 7	- -
1829	2 6 3¼	— 2 18/360								
1830	2 3 6	— 2 48/360								

It may be right to observe, that in the infancy of the Institution, the clothes and b
the blue cloth now used for the Pension

, for the Years under-mentioned.—(*From the Parl. Papers*, Nos. 54. 72. and 87. Sess. 1830.)

…s,	Bricklayers, per Day.	Masons, per Day.	Plumbers, per Day.	Candles, per Doz. lb.	Shoes, per Pair.	Coals, per Chaldron.	Mops, each.	Stockings, per Pair.	Hats, each.	Complete Suits of Bedding.	Suits of Clothes.	Coats, each.
d.	s. d.	s. d.	s. d.	s. d.	s. d.	£ s. d.	£ s. d.	s. d.	s. d.	£ s. d.	£ s. d.	£ s. d.
	- -	- -	- -	6 5	4 0	1 8 5	0 0 10½	1 9	2 8	3 5 0	2 12 0	
6 6	2 6	2 6	3 0	6 4	4 0	1 4 6	per dozen. 0 10 0	1 6	2 8	2 13 0	2 12 0	
6 8	2 6	2 6	3 0	4 2	4 0	1 5 0	0 10 6	1 6	2 3	Blankets, each. 0 4 0	2 2 6	
6 8	2 6	2 8	3 0	5 6	3 10	1 9 0	0 10 0	1 6	2 0	0 4 6	2 3 6	
6 8	2 6	2 8	2 6	6 0	3 6	1 10 0	0 11 0	1 6	2 0	0 4 6	- -	1 2 4
6 8	2 6	2 8	2 6	6 2	3 9	1 7 7½	0 10 9	1 6	2 0	0 4 6	- -	1 1 5
6 8	2 6	2 8	2 6	6 10	4 0	1 8 7¾	0 11 0	1 8	2 0	0 4 4½	-	1 1 6
6 8	2 6	2 8	2 6	6 6	4 0	1 12 8	0 12 0	1 8	2 0	0 4 4½	- -	1 1 0
6 8	2 4	2 8	3 0	6 2	4 0	1 12 4½	0 11 3	1 8	2 6	0 4 6	- -	1 1 6
6 8	2 4	2 8	3 0	6 10¾	4 0	1 9 1½	0 11 0	1 6	2 6	0 4 6	- -	1 0 5
6 8	2 4	2 10	3 0	6 3	3 10	1 10 11¼	0 10 6	1 4	2 2	0 5 4½	- -	0 19 11
6 8	2 4	2 10	3 0	6 9½	3 11½	1 17 3¾	0 12 0	1 6	2 2	0 5 4½	- -	0 19 5
6 8	2 4	2 10	3 3	6 6	3 6	1 14 2½	0 11 0	1 6	2 4	0 5 4½	- -	1 0 3
6 0	2 4	2 10	3 3	7 9	3 11½	1 14 4¼	0 14 0	1 6	2 6	0 5 4½	- -	1 0 8
6 0	3 0	2 10	3 3	9 2	4 0	1 19 9	0 15 0	1 6	2 3	0 6 6	- -	1 0 2
0 2	3 0	2 10	3 3	10 4	5 8	2 11 7	0 15 0	1 6	2 3	0 6 6	- -	1 0 0
5	4 10	5 0	4 6	10 7	5 9	2 11 8¾	0 17 0	2 2	3 0	0 8 9	- -	1 1 10
6	4 8	5 0	4 6	10 3	5 9	2 13 4	0 17 0	2 2	3 0	0 8 9	- -	1 1 10
0	4 8	5 0	4 6	9 10	5 0	2 14 0	0 17 0	2 2	3 0	0 8 9	- -	1 1 6
0	5 0	5 0	4 6	13 2½	5 0	2 15 9¾	0 17 0	2 2	3 0	0 8 9	-	1 1 4
4	5 1	5 1	5 3	14 5½	5 6	3 0 9¾	0 17 0	2 2	3 0	0 8 9	- -	1 1 4
	5 2	5 3	5 9	12 0	5 6	3 0 8	0 17 0	2 2	3 0	0 8 9	- -	1 1 4
5	5 5	5 9	5 9	10 9¾	4 11	3 1 6	0 17 0	2 2	3 0	0 8 9	- -	1 2 2
	5 5	5 9	5 9	12 6	4 11	2 16 1	0 17 0	2 6	3 0	0 8 9	- -	1 2 2
	5 5	5 9	5 9	14 2	4 8	2 16 7¼	0 18 0	2 6	3 0	0 8 9	- -	1 2 2
	5 5	5 9	5 9	14 6	4 8	3 2 2¼	1 10 0	3 3	3 0	0 11 6	- -	1 4 6
	5 1	5 9	5 9	11 7	4 7	2 15 6¾	1 10 0	3 3	3 0	0 11 3	- -	1 4 9
	5 1	5 3	5 5	9 3	4 7	2 9 6½	1 10 0	2 9	3 0	0 9 4½	- -	1 4 9
	5 1	5 3	5 9	9 10	3 10	2 6 7	1 10 0	2 9	3 0	0 9 4½	- -	1 0 7
	5 1	5 3	5 9	11 5½	3 10	2 8 6	Each. 0 2 6	2 10	3 0	Suits. 2 19 10½	2 1 0½	1 1 7
	5 1	5 3	5 9	8 6¼	4 2¾	2 6 8	0 2 6	2 11	3 0	2 19 10½	2 1 7¼	1 1 10½
	5 1	5 3	5 9	8 2¾	4 4½	2 5 9	0 1 10½	2 9½	3 0	2 19 10½	2 3 3¼	1 2 7
	5 1	5 3	5 9	7 1¼	4 3	2 6 6	0 1 4¾	2 8	3 0	2 19 10½	2 1 9	1 1 11
	5 0	5 1½	5 7½	6 1½	4 2½	2 4 6¼	0 1 3½	2 5	3 0	2 19 10½	2 0 2¾	1 1 3
	4 10	5 0	5 6	5 6	4 7¾	2 6 7	0 1 2	2 2	3 0	2 19 10½	1 19 11¼	1 1 1½
	4 10	5 0	5 6	5 6	4 9½	2 3 8	0 1 1¼	2 1¾	3 0	2 19 10½	1 19 11¼	1 1 2
	4 10	5 0	5 6	6 0	4 6	2 3 2	0 1 2¼	2 1½	3 0	2 19 10½	2 0 8½	1 1 8
	4 10	5 6	5 6	5 9½	4 5	2 0 4	0 1 1¼	2 0¼	3 0	2 19 10½	2 1 6¼	1 2 2
	4 10	5 6	5 9	5 10	4 3½	2 1 5¼	0 1 1¾	1 10¼	3 0	2 8 3	1 19 10¾	1 1 4
	4 10	5 6	5 9	5 10¼	4 3	2 0 8¼	0 1 2	1 9½	3 0	2 5 9	1 18 1	1 0 7

r in suits; and it is so stated in the account. It is also necessary to remark, that
ery inferior to the ancient pattern.

Those desirous of detailed information as to the prices of commodities in C
Britain, in remoter ages, may consult the elaborate tables in the 3d volume of S
M. Eden's work on the Poor; and the 4th volume of Macpherson's Annals of C
merce. Arbuthnot's Tables of Ancient Coins, Weights, Measures, Prices, &c. are
known; but the statements are not much to be depended upon. The *Traité de Métr*
of M. Paucton, 4to. Paris, 1780, is the best work on this curious and difficult subje

PRICE-CURRENT, a list or enumeration of various articles of merchan
with their prices, the duties payable thereon, and the drawbacks allowed
particular sorts of goods. Lists of this description are published periodic
generally once or twice a week, in most of the great commercial cities and to
of Europe.

PRIMAGE, is a certain allowance paid by the shipper or consignee of go
to the mariners and master of a vessel, for loading the same. In some places
1*d.* in the pound; in others 6*d.* for every pack or bale; or otherwise, accor
to the custom of the place.

PRINTS, impressions on paper, or some other substance, of engraving
copper, steel, wood, stone, &c., representing some particular subject or com
tion.

Prints, like paintings, embrace every variety of subject; and differ very w
in the manner in which they are engraved. Their price varies according t
style of the engraving, the fineness of its execution, the goodness of the
pression, its rarity, &c. The art seems to have taken its rise in the fifte
century. But as a dissertation on one of the most beautiful of the fine arts w
be singularly out of place in a work of this sort, we have introduced it fo
purpose merely of stating the law with respect to the copyright of prints.

This is laid down in the acts 8 Geo. 2. c. 13., 7 Geo 3. c. 38., and 17 Geo. 3. c. 57. By these ac
copyright of all sorts of prints, including maps and charts, is secured to the engraver, or auth
twenty-eight years. The last mentioned act declares that every individual who shall within the
years engrave, etch, or work, or in any other manner copy in the whole or in part, by varying, add
or diminishing from the main design; or shall print, reprint, or import for sale, or shall publish,
otherwise dispose of any copy of any print whatever, which has been or shall be engraved, etched,
or designed in Great Britain, without the express consent of the proprietor thereof first obtained i
ing, signed by him with his own hand in the presence of, and attested by, two or more credible witn
then every such proprietor may, by a special action upon the case to be brought against the person
fending, recover such damages as a jury, on the trial of such action, or on the execution of a writ
quiry thereon, shall give or assess, together with double costs of suit.

In questions as to the piracy of prints, the courts proceed upon the same principles that are follo
those with respect to the piracy of books. — (See Books; see also Mr. Godson's excellent work on th
of Patents and Copyright, pp. 287—301.)

PRISAGE, or BUTLERAGE, was a right of taking 2 tons of wine
every ship importing into England 20 tons or more; which was chang
Edward I. into a duty of 2*s.* for every ton imported by merchant strangers
called butlerage, because paid to the king's butler. The term is now fallen
disuse. — (*Blackstone.*)

PRIVATEERS, ships of war fitted out by private individuals, to a
and plunder the public enemy. But before commencing their operations,
indispensable that that they obtain *letters of marque and reprisal* from the go
ment whose subjects they are, authorising them to commit hostilities, and
they conform strictly to the rules laid down for the regulation of their co
All private individuals attacking others at sea, unless empowered by lett
marque, are to be considered pirates; and may be treated as such, either by
they attack, or by their own government.

1. *Policy of Privateering.* — The policy of this system is very questionable. It
to be a remnant of that species of private war exercised by all individuals in early
but which gradually disappears as society advances. In wars carried on by lan
property of the peaceable inhabitants who take no part in the operations of the
is uniformly protected; and it is difficult to discover any solid grounds why the
rule should not be followed at sea. Privateers rarely attack ships of war.
object is merely to plunder and destroy merchantmen. They cause an infinite d
mischief to individuals, and aggravate all the miseries of war, without havi
slightest influence on the result of the contest. Experience has also shown that it
possible, whatever precautions may be adopted, to prevent the greatest abuses from
perpetrated by privateers. The wish to amass plunder is the only principle by
they are actuated; and such being the case, it would be idle to suppose that they
be very scrupulous about abstaining from excesses. A system of this sort, if it
useful, can be so only to nations who have little trade, and who may expect to
themselves during war by fitting out privateers to plunder the merchant ships

In all other cases it seems to be productive only of mischief; though it is, e, most injurious to those states that have the greatest mercantile navy. Instead, , of encouraging the practice of privateering, we think that a due regard to the d interests of humanity would suggest to the great powers the expediency of g it altogether. A few efforts have, indeed, been already made towards this object. Thus, it was stipulated in the treaty between Sweden and the United s, in 1675, that neither party should, in any future war, grant letters of marque the other. In 1767, Russia abstained from licensing privateers. And in the tween the United States and Prussia, in 1785, a stipulation was inserted as to s, similar to that in the treaty between Sweden and the United Provinces in But nothing short of a convention and agreement to that effect amongst the wers will be able to effect this desirable object. — (*Essai concernant les Arma-r Martens,* 1794.)

intment of Privateers. — The captain of a privateer is nominated by the owners, who may dis-t pleasure. The commission or letters of marque given to the owners, authorises them to attack he ships of the power or powers specified therein; but they are not to look upon them as their r to appropriate them, or any part of them, to their own use, *till they have been legally con-* Besides the stimulus afforded by the hope of booty, government has been in the habit of allow-5*l.* for every man on board such enemy's ships of war or privateers as they may capture.— c. 66.) A privateer cruising under letters of marque against one state may, on obtaining information of hostilities being commenced by her government against another, capture its ships dvantage to herself. The king has in all cases the right to release any prize previously to its ion; this being an implied exception in the grant of prizes by the crown. — (*Chitty on Com-w,* vol. i. c. 8.)

privateering adventures, the crew are engaged on the terms of no prize no pay; and, in such produce of whatsoever prizes may be taken goes half to the ship (for the owners), and half to ivided among them according to the articles of agreement; but when the men sail for wages, es belong entirely to the owners, except a small share, which is commonly stipulated to be given r over and above their wages in order to stimulate their enterprise. Both ways of arming are y the articles entered into between the owners and crews.

rs are forbidden from doing any thing contrary to the law of nations, as to assault an enemy in aven under the protection of any prince or republic, be he friend, ally, or neutral; for the peace ce must be preserved inviolable. — (*Molly, De Jure Maritimo,* book i. c. 3.)

tters of marque are granted, it is usual, in most countries, to exact security that the regulations t to the conduct of privateers will be observed. In Great Britain, a bond for 1,500*l.* must be sponsible persons, not concerned in the ship, for all ships carrying less than 150 men, and very ship carrying more, that they will give full satisfaction for any damage or injury they it at sea, contrary to the regulations under which they are to act, and to their duty as

eers wilfully commit any spoil, depredation, or other injury, on friendly or neutral ships, hips or goods of their fellow subjects, they are to be punished, according to the crime, either or otherwise; and the vessels are subject to forfeiture.

a ship taken be lawful prize, or not, shall be tried in the admiralty; and no ship or cargo, a ship or part of a cargo, is to be sold, or disposed of in any way, till after judgment has been

ips with letters of marque accidentally meet with a prize at sea, though only one attack and t the other, being in sight, shall have an equal share of the prize, though he afforded no n the capture; because his presence may be presumed to have struck terror into the enemy, and ield; which perhaps he would not have done, had his conqueror been single: so that all ships ight, though they cannot come up to assist in the engagement, are entitled to the *common* ribution of the spoil. — (*Beawes, Lex Mercatoria,* art. *Privateers.*)

o whom letters of marque are granted should, instead of taking the ship and goods appertain-nation against which the said letters are awarded, *wilfully* take or spoil the goods of another nity with us, this would amount to *piracy;* and the persons so offending would, for such fault, vessel, and the penalties in which their securities are, according to custom, bound on taking tters. But such penalties would not follow, unless the capture were made in a piratical or if the circumstances incident to the captured vessel were such as to afford a strong pre-at she really belonged to the country against which the letters were granted, the captors be liable to punishment, though they might be to damages. " It being impossible," says tways to determine an affair of this sort at sea, it is allowable to bring a dubious capture into er to more nice and just scrutiny and inspection; otherwise the goods of an enemy would . However, to guard against unlawful seizures, the government have wisely directed suffi-n to be given (as before-mentioned) for the due observance of the letters according to law, permit their issuing; and when there is a breach committed, the penalties are inflicted." — toria, art. *Privateers.*)

tions for the Government of Privateers, &c. — The following instructions to privateers were r an order in council, at the commencement of the last war with France, 16th May, 1803 : —

inst what, and where, Letters of Marque may act shall be lawful for the commanders of ships etters of marque and reprisals for private men-pon by force of arms, and subdue and take the ips and vessels, goods, wares, and merchandises, e French republic, or to any person being sub-nch republic, or inhabitants within any of the e French republic; but so that no hostility be r prize attacked, seized, or taken within the nces or states in amity with us, or in their rivers n the shot of their cannon, unless by permission or states, or their commanders or governors in aces.

ures to be brought into Port. — The commanders l vessels so authorised as aforesaid, shall bring s, and goods, which they shall seize and take, f England, or some other port of our dominions, convenient for them, in order to have the same d by our high court of admiralty of England, or ge of any other admiralty court, lawfully au-n our dominions.

duct of the Captors after the Capture is brought ter such ships, vessels, and goods shall be taken o any port, the taker, or one of his chief officers,

or some other person present at the capture, shall be obliged to bring or send, as soon as possibly may be, three or four of the principal of the company (whereof the master, supercargo, mate, or boatswain, to be always two) of every ship or vessel so brought into port, before the judge of our high court of ad-miralty of England, or his surrogate, or before the judge of such other admiralty court within our dominions, lawfully authorised as aforesaid, or such as shall be lawfully commis-sioned in that behalf, to be sworn and examined upon such interrogatories as shall tend to the discovery of the truth, con-cerning the interest or property of such ship or ships, vessel or vessels, and of the goods, merchandises, and other effects found therein; and the taker shall be further obliged, at the time he produceth the company to be examined, and before any moni-tion shall be issued, to bring in and deliver into the hands of the judge of the high court of admiralty of England, his surrogate, or the judge of such other admiralty court within our do-minions, lawfully authorised, or others commissioned as afore-said, all such papers, passes, sea-briefs, charterparties, bills of lading, cockets, letters, and other documents and writings, as shall be delivered up or found on board any ship; the taker, or one of his chief officers, or some other person who shall be pre-sent at the capture, and saw the said papers and writings delivered up, or otherwise found on board at the time of the

capture, making oath that the said papers and writings are brought and delivered in as they were received and taken, without any fraud, addition, subduction, or embezzlement whatever, or otherwise to account for the same upon oath, to the satisfaction of the court.

Art. IV. *Not to break Bulk before Judgment.* — The ships, vessels, goods, wares, merchandises, and effects, taken by virtue of letters of marque and reprisals as aforesaid, shall be kept and preserved, and no part of them shall be sold, spoiled, wasted, or diminished, and the bulk thereof shall not be broken, before judgment be given in the high court of admiralty of *England*, or some other court of admiralty, lawfully authorised in that behalf, that the ships, goods, or merchandises are lawful prize.

Art. V. *Privateers to assist Ships in Distress.* — If any ship or vessel belonging to us, or our subjects, shall be found in distress by being in fight set upon or taken by the enemy, or by reason of any other accident, the commanders, officers, and company, of such merchant ships or vessels as shall have letters of marque and reprisals as aforesaid, shall use their best endeavours to give aid and succour to all such ship and ships, and shall, to the utmost of their power, labour to free the same from the enemy, or any other distress.

Art. VI. *Application to the Admiralty for Letters of Marque.* — The commanders or owners of such ships and vessels, before the taking out letters of marque and reprisals, shall make application in writing, subscribed with their hands, to our high admiral of *Great Britain*, or our commissioners for executing that office for the time being, or the lieutenant or judge of the said high court of admiralty, or his surrogate, and shall therein set forth a particular, true, and exact description of the ship or vessel for which letter of marque and reprisal is requested, specifying the burthen of such ship or vessel, and the number and nature of the guns, and what other warlike furniture and ammunition are on board the same, to what place the ship belongs, and the name or names of the principal owner or owners of such ship or vessel, and the number of men intended to be put on board the same, and for what time they are victualled; also the names of the commanders and officers.

Art. VII. *Correspondence with the Admiralty.* — The commanders of ships and vessels having letters of marque and reprisals as aforesaid, shall hold and keep, and are hereby enjoined to hold and keep, a correspondence, by all conveniences, and upon all occasions, with our high admiral of *Great Britain*, or our commissioners for executing that office for the time being, or their secretary, so as from time to time to render or give him or them, not only an account or intelligence of their captures and proceedings by virtue of such commission, but also of whatever else shall seem unto them, or be discovered and declared to them, or found out by them, or by examination of, or conference with, any marines or passengers of or in the ships or vessels taken, or by any other ways or means whatsoever, touching or concerning the designs of the enemy, or any of their fleets, ships, vessels, or parties, and of the stations, sea-ports, and places, and of their intents therein; and what ships or vessels of the enemy bound out or home, or where cruising, as they shall hear of; and of what else material in these cases may arrive at their knowledge; to the end such course may be thereon taken, and such orders given, as may be requisite.

Art. VIII. *What Colours a Privateer is to wear.* — No commander of any ship or vessel, having a letter of marque and reprisals as aforesaid, shall presume, as they will answer it at their peril, to wear any flack, pendant, or other ensign or colours usually borne by our ships; but, besides the colours usually borne by merchants' ships, they shall wear a red jack, with the union jack described in the canton, at the upper corner thereof, near the staff.

Art. IX. *Not to ransom any Capture.* — No commander of any ship or vessel, having a letter of marque and reprisal as aforesaid, shall ransom, or agree to ransom, or quit or set at liberty, any ship or vessel, or their cargoes, which shall be seized and taken.

Art. X. *To deliver their Prisoners to the proper Commissioners.* — All captains or commanding officers of ships having letters of marque and reprisals, shall send an account of, and deliver over, what prisoners shall be taken on board any prizes, to the commissioners appointed or to be appointed for the exchange of prisoners of war, or the persons appointed in the sea-port towns to take charge of prisoners; and such prisoners shall be subject only to the orders, regulations, and directions of the said commissioners; and no commander or other officer of any ship, having a letter of marque or reprisal as aforesaid, shall presume, upon any pretence whatsoever, to ransom any prisoner.

Art. XI. *Commission forfeited for acting contrary* &c., case the commander of any ship, having a letter of m reprisal as aforesaid, shall act contrary to these instr any such further instructions; of which he shall notice, he shall forfeit his commission to all in purposes, and shall, together with his bail, be against according to law, and be condemned in damages.

Art. XII. *Copies of Journals.* — All commands and vessels, having letters of marque and reprisals every opportunity, send exact copies of their jou secretary of the admiralty, and proceed to the com of the prizes as soon as may be, and without delay.

Art. XIII. *To observe all Orders.* — Commander and vessels, having letters of marque and reprisals, due notice being given to them, observe all such oth tions and orders as we shall think fit to direct fre time, for the better carrying on this service.

Art. XIV. *Violating these Instructions.* — All pe shall violate these, or any other of our instruction severely punished, and also required to make full re persons injured contrary to our instructions, for a they shall sustain by any capture, embezzlement, or otherwise.

Art. XV. *Bail to be given.* — Before any letter of reprisal for the purposes aforesaid shall issue unde shall be given with sureties, before the lieutenant an our high court of admiralty of *England*, or his su the sum of 3000l. sterling, if the ship carries above and if a less number, in the sum of 1,500l. sterling; shall be to the effect and in the form following:—

Which day, time and place, personally appeared _____ and submitting themselves to the jurisdiction of the hi admiralty of *England*, obliged themselves, their he tors, and administrators, unto our Sovereign Lord t' the sum of _____ poun money of *Great Britain*, to this effect; that is to whereas _____ is duly au letters of marque and reprisals, with the ship called _____ of the burthen of abou _____ tons, whereof he the said _____ master, by force of arms to attack, surprise, seize, a ships and vessels, goods, wares, and merchandises, effects, belonging to the French Republic, or to being subjects of the French Republic, or inhabi any of the territories of the French Republic; exc within the harbours or roads within shot of the princes and states in amity with his Majesty. And the said _____ copy of certain instructions, approved of and pa Majesty in council, as by the tenour of the sai marque and reprisals, and instructions thereto rela at large appeareth: if therefore nothing be done _____ or any of _____ marines, or company, contrary to the true meaning instructions, and of all other instructions which ma in like manner hereafter, and we shall, reof due notice sh him; but that such letters of marque and reprisal and the said instructions, shall in all particulars t duly observed and performed, as far as they shall th master, and company, any way concern; and if th full satisfaction for any damage or injury which sh by them or any of them to any of his Majesty's sub foreign states in amity with his Majesty, and als and truly pay, or cause to be paid, to his Majesty, tomers or officers appointed to receive the same jesty, the usual customs due to his Majesty, of and and goods so as aforesaid taken and adjudged as moreover if the said _____ shall not take any ship or vessel, or any goods or m belonging to the enemy, or otherwise liable to c through consent or clandestinely, or by collusion colour, or pretence of his said letters of marque a that then this bail shall be void and of none effect; they shall so do, they do all hereby severally cons ecution issue forth against them, their heirs, exe administrators, goods and chattels, wheresoever th be found, to the value of the sum of _____ pounds before mentioned; and in testimony o thereof they have hereunto subscribed their names

By his Majesty's command, (Signed) P

PROMISSORY NOTE. See BANKS, BANKING.

PROTECTION, in mercantile navigation, a privilege granted to cer scriptions of seamen, by which they are protected from impressment. IMPRESSMENT.)

PRUNES AND PRUNELLOES, dried plums, of which there ar varieties. The finest are imported from France, in the south of which this very abundant. The best prunes are packed in hampers or baskets made osiers, weighing from 6 to 10 lbs. each; the second quality in quarters, third in puncheons. In 1829, there were 6,283 cwt. of prunes imported the whole of which were retained for home consumption. The duty is 1 a cwt., being more than 50 per cent. upon the price of the inferior qualities cannot be a doubt that it would be more productive were it reduced to 10

PRUSSIAN BLUE, OR PRUSSIATE OF IRON (Ger. *Berlinerb Bleu de Prusse*; It. *Azurro Prussiano*; Sp. *Azul de Prussia*; Rus. *Lazo skaja*), a beautiful deep blue powder, accidentally discovered at Berlin in 1 is of considerable importance in the arts, being extensively used by paint

actured in this country. Many attempts have been made to render Prussian
available for the dyeing of broad cloths, but without much success. The dif-
· is to diffuse the colour equally over the surface; for, from its extraordinary
ty and lustre, the slightest inequalities strike and offend the eye. Prussian
esists the air and sun extremely well; but it cannot be used in the dyeing of
is, or any sort of stuff that is to be washed with soap, as the alkali contained
soap readily dissolves and separates the colouring matter. — (*Bancroft on*
's, vol. ii. pp. 60—94.)

BLICANS, are persons authorised by licence to retail beer, spirits, or
Under the term publicans are comprised innkeepers, hotel keepers,
ise keepers, keepers of wine vaults, &c. An inn differs from an alehouse
i, — that the former is a place intended for the lodging as well as the enter-
ent of guests, whereas the latter is intended for their entertainment only.
wever, ale or beer be commonly sold in an inn, as is almost invariably the
t is also an alehouse; and if travellers be furnished with beds, lodged, and
ained in an alehouse, it also is an inn. It is not material to the character
innkeeper that he should have any sign over his door; it is sufficient that
kes it his business to entertain passengers and travellers, providing them
·dgings and other accommodations.

Licensing of Publicans. — The provisions with respect to the licensing of public
are embodied in the 9 Geo. 4. c. 61., of which we subjoin an abstract.

al Meetings. — There shall be annually holden in county divisions, cities, and towns, a special
of justices, to be called the "*General Annual Licensing Meeting*," for the purpose of granting
to persons keeping or about to keep inns, alehouses, &c.; such meetings to be held, in Middlesex
ey, within the first 10 days of the month of March; and in every other place, between the 20th
st and the 14th of September both inclusive.

of General Meeting. — Within every division, 21 days before the annual licensing meeting, a
sion of justices to be held, a majority of whom shall fix the day and hour for holding the general
eeting; and shall direct a precept to the high constable, requiring him, within 5 days after the
hereof, to order the petty constables to affix on the door of the church, chapel, or other public
notice of such annual meeting, and give or leave at the dwelling-house of each justice acting for
ion, and of each person keeping an inn, or who shall have given notice of his intention to apply
nce to keep an inn, a copy of such notice. — § 2.

inual meeting may be adjourned, but the adjourned meeting is not to be held on any of the 5
nediately following the adjournment; and every adjournment to be held in the month of March
esex and Surrey, and in August and September in every other county. — § 3.

s for Transfer of Licences. — At the annual meeting, justices to appoint not less than four nor
n eight special sessions, to be held as near as possible at equidistant periods, for the purpose of
ing licences. — § 4.

of holding any adjourned meetings, or of any special session for the transfer of licences, to be
the same manner and to the same parties as mentioned above. — § 5.

s disqualified. — No justice who is a common brewer, distiller, maker of malt for sale, or retailer
r any exciseable liquor, shall act or be present at any annual licensing meeting, or adjournment,
session for transferring licences, or take part in the adjudication upon any application for a
r upon an appeal; nor in the case of licensing any house of which he is owner, or agent of the
of any house belonging to any common brewer, maker of malt, &c. to whom he shall be, either
or marriage, the father, son, or brother, or with whom he shall be partner in *any other trade ;*
these cases knowingly or wilfully to act, subjects to a penalty of 100*l.* But disqualification does
where a justice, having no *beneficial interest* in a house licensed or about to be licensed, holds
egal estate therein as trustee, or for a charitable or public use. — § 6.

in any liberty, city, or town, two qualified justices do not attend, the county justices may act. —

wer given to county justices not to extend to the Cinque Ports. — § 8.

ns respecting licences to be determined, and licences to be signed, by a majority of the justices
— § 9.

ation for a Licence. — Persons intending to apply for a licence to a house *not before licensed*, to
tice on the door of such house, and on the door of the church or chapel of the parish, and where
l be no church or chapel, on some other conspicuous place within the parish, on *three several*
between the 1st of January and the last day of February in the counties of Middlesex and
nd elsewhere between the 1st of June and the last day of July, at some time between the hours
he forenoon and 4 in the afternoon, and shall serve a copy of such notice upon one of the over-
e poor, and upon one of the constables or peace-officers of the parish, within the month of Fe-
the counties of Middlesex and Surrey, and elsewhere within the month of July, prior to the
eeting; such notice to be in a legible hand, or printed, and signed by the applicant. The appli-
st state the Christian and surname of the party, with the place of his residence, and his trade or
ring the six months previous to the serving of the notice. — § 10.

o *transfer Licence.* — Persons desirous of transferring a licence, and intending to apply to the
ial sessions, must, 5 days previously, serve a notice upon one of the overseers and one of the
s of the parish. Persons hindered, by sickness or other reasonable cause, from attending any
meeting, and proof thereof adduced *on oath*, may authorise another person to attend for them.

s to be in force, in Middlesex and Surrey, from the 5th of April; elsewhere from the 10th of
for one whole year. — § 13.

m for Death or other Contingency. — If any person licensed shall die, or become incapable, or a
or insolvent, or if he, or his heirs, executors, or assigns, shall remove, or neglect to apply for a
ion of his licence, the justices at special session may grant a licence to the heirs, executors, or
such party, or to any new tenant; or if any man's house should be, or be about to be, pulled
a public purpose, or rendered, by fire, tempest, or other unforeseen calamity, unfit for the
of an inn, licence may be granted to the occupier, if he intend to open another house as an
transferred licences shall continue only in force to the end of the year; and in case of removal
house, notice must be given on some Sunday, within 6 weeks before the special session, in the
d form before described. — § 14.

Fees for Licences. — The clerk of the justices may lawfully receive from every person to whom a li is granted, for trouble and *all expenses*, the following sums : —

	s.	d.
For constable or officer serving notices	1	0
For clerk of justices for licence	5	0
For precept to the high constable, and notices to be delivered by the petty constable	1	6

Clerks demanding or receiving more than these fees to forfeit 5*l.* — § 15.

No sheriff's officer, or officer executing the process of any court of justice, qualified to hold or us licence under this act. — § 16.

Excise Licences. — No licence for the sale of any exciseable liquors, to be consumed on the pre shall be granted by the excise to any person, unless such person be previously licensed under this act . -

Penalties. — Any person *without a licence* selling or exchanging, or for valuable consideration dis of any exciseable liquor by retail, to be consumed in his premises ; or *with a licence*, and so selling i mises other than those specified in his licence ; shall for every offence, on conviction before one ji forfeit not exceeding 20*l.* nor less than 5*l.* with costs ; but the penalty not to attach in case of de insolvency, and sale by the heir or assigns, prior to the next special sessions. — § 18.

Every licensed person shall, if required, sell all liquors by retail (except in quantities less than a pint) by the gallon, quart, pint, or half-pint, sized according to the standard ; in default thereof to the illegal measure, and pay not exceeding 40*s.* with costs, to be recovered within 30 days before or tice. — § 19.

In cases of riot, or probability of riot, houses licensed in the neighbourhood may be closed by the of two justices. — § 20.

Any person convicted of a *first offence*, before two justices, against the tenour of his licence, to forf exceeding 5*l.* with costs ; guilty of a *second offence* within 3 years of the first, to forfeit not exceedi with costs ; and guilty of a *third offence* within 3 years, to forfeit not exceeding 50*l.* with costs : or th in the last instance may be adjourned to the petty sessions, or the annual meeting, or the general q sessions ; and if the offender is found guilty by a *jury*, he may be fined 100*l.*, or adjudged to forf licence, or both, and rendered incapable of selling any exciseable liquor in any inn kept by him for 3 — § 21.

Proceedings at the session in certain cases, may be directed by the justices to be carried on by th stable, and the expenses defrayed out of the county rates. — § 22.

Witnesses refusing to attend without lawful excuse, may be fined not more than 10*l.* — § 23.

Penalties against justices may be sued for in any court in Westminster ; a moiety to the king, moiety to the party suing. — § 24.

Penalties adjudged by justices may be recovered by distress, or the party imprisoned 1, 3, or 6 ca months. — § 25.

The next sections relate to the mode of prosecuting actions.

The last section of the act bears that the word "*inn*" shall include any inn, alehouse, or victu house, in which is sold by retail any exciseable liquor, to be drunk or consumed on the premises ; a words exciseable liquor are to include all such fermented or spirituous liquors as may now or herea charged with any customs or excise duty. — § 37.

The act does not affect the two Universities, nor the privileges of the Vintners' Company, excep freemen who have obtained their freedom by redemption ; and it does not alter the time of gr licences in the city of London.

Innkeepers are bound, by the tenour of their licence, to keep order in their houses, to prevent dru ness and disorderly conduct, and gambling. If they fail in these respects, they forfeit their licenc subject themselves to the penalties mentioned before. Allowing seditious or immoral books to be r an inn, also forfeits the licence, and subjects to penalties. — (39 Geo. 3. c. 79. § 31.)

2. *Duties of Innkeepers.* — Innkeepers are bound by law to receive com their inns, and they are also bound *to protect their property when there.* They ha option to reject or refuse a guest, unless their house be already full, or they are a assign some other reasonable and sufficient cause. Neither can they impose unre able terms on such as frequent their houses : if they do, they may be fined, and inns indicted and suppressed. An innkeeper who has stables attached to his pre may be compelled to receive a horse, although the owner does not reside in his h but he cannot, under such circumstances, be compelled to receive a trunk or other thing. By the annual mutiny act, constables, or, in their default, justices of the p may quarter soldiers in inns, livery-stables, alehouses, &c., under the condition regulations set forth in the statute.

3. *Responsibility of Innkeepers.* — An innkeeper is bound to keep safely whatever t his guests deposit in his inn, or in his custody as innkeeper ; and he is civilly liab all losses, except those arising from *irresistible force*, or what is usually termed the a God and the king's enemies. " It has long been holden," says Sir William Jones, an innkeeper is bound to restitution, if the trunks or parcels of his guests, comr to him either personally or through one of his agents, be damaged in his inn, or out of it by any person whatever (except the servant or companion of the guest) shall he discharge himself of this responsibility by a refusal to take any care of the g because there are suspected persons in the house, for whose conduct he cannot be ar able : it is otherwise, indeed, if he refuse admission to a traveller because he rea no room for him, and the traveller, nevertheless, insist upon entering, and pla baggage in a chamber without the keeper's consent. Add to this, that if he fail t vide honest servants and honest inmates, according to the confidence reposed in b the public, his negligence in that respect is highly culpable, and he ought to a civilly for their acts, even if they should rob the guests that sleep in their cha Rigorous as this law may seem, and hard as it may actually be in one or two par instances, it is founded on the great principle of public utility, to which all privat siderations ought to yield ; for travellers, who must be numerous in a rich and mercial country, are obliged to rely almost implicitly on the good faith of innk whose education and morals are usually none of the best, and who might have fr

ities of associating with ruffians or pilferers, while the injured guest could never
gal proof of such combinations, or even of their negligence, if no actual fraud
n committed by them. Hence the prætor declared, according to Pomponius,
e of securing the public from the dishonesty of such men; and by his edict gave
against them, if the goods of travellers or passengers were lost or hurt by any
xcept by inevitable accident (*danno fatali*): and Ulpian intimates, that even
rity could not restrain them from knavish practices or suspicious neglect." —
n *the Law of Bailments*, 2d ed. pp. 95, 96.)

if an innkeeper bid the guest take the key of his chamber and lock the
ling him that he cannot undertake the charge of the goods, still, if they be
is held to be responsible. In all such cases it is not competent to the innkeeper
that he took *ordinary* care, or that the *force* which occasioned the loss was truly
e. A guest is not bound to deliver his goods in special custody to the inn-
or, indeed, to acquaint him that he has any. If he have property with him, or
person, the innkeeper must be responsible for it without communication. But
eeper may require that the property of his guest be delivered into his hands, in
t it may be put into a secure place; and if the guest refuse, the innkeeper is not
its safety. The guest exonerates the innkeeper from liability, when he takes
self the exclusive custody of the goods, so as to deprive the innkeeper of having
over them: thus, if a guest demand and have exclusive possession of a room,
urpose of a shop or warehouse, he exonerates the landlord from any loss he may
the property which he keeps in that apartment; but it is otherwise if he have
clusive possession of the room. The innkeeper cannot oblige the guest to take
his own goods; for this, in effect, would be a refusal to admit them into the
nd it is no excuse for an innkeeper to say that he delivered the key of the
whence the property was stolen to the guest, who left the door open. A case
t occurred very recently, at Brighton.—A lady having left the door of her bed-
which she had the key, open for a few minutes, 50*l.* were abstracted from her
The innkeeper contended that the plaintiff, by selecting particular apartments,
g the key, had exonerated him from his liability. The jury found for the
and upon a motion for a new trial, Lord Tenterden said — " By the common
s country, and also by the civil law, the principle of the liability of innkeepers
led on two reasons: first, to compel the landlord to take care that no improper
was admitted into his house; and, secondly, to prevent collusion. — The prin-
stated in the civil law was this — ' *Ne, quisquam putet graviter hoc in eos consti-
nam est in ipsorum arbitrio nequem recipient; et nisi hoc esset statutum, materia
m furibus, adversus eos quos recipiunt, coeundi: cum ne nunc quidem abstinent
fraudibus.'* It was true, that in the present state of society, it was very diffi-
event the intrusion of improper company into inns. But still the principle
as he had stated it to be, and it would be dangerous to relax it; and he did not
the taking rooms in this way was sufficient to discharge the landlord. Then,
bjection that the cases did not extend to money, it was clear that money was
ithin the principle as goods, and that no substantial distinction could be made.
erefore of opinion that the verdict was right." — Rule refused.

ord may exempt himself from liability, if he can show that the loss was
by the misconduct of the guest; as, if his goods are stolen by his own servant
ion.

een decided that a man is a guest at an inn, if he leave his horse at it, though
t gone into it himself. If a man come to an inn, and make a contract for
r a set time, and do not eat or drink there, he is no guest, but a lodger, and,
ot under the innkeeper's protection; but if he eat and drink, or pay for his
it is otherwise. Any innkeeper or alehouse keeper, knowingly receiving and
g any person convicted of an offence against the revenue laws for which he has
ison, or for which he has fled, shall forfeit 100*l.*, and have no licence for the

of an Innkeeper against his Guest.— An innkeeper may, without any agreement to that
the person of a guest who has eat in his house, until payment; and he may do the same by
his stable.
per is not entitled to recover for any items for spirits supplied to his guests, unless of the
and upwards, and contracted for at one time. — (25 Geo. 2. c. 40.)
stom of London and Exeter, if a man commit a horse to an hostler, and the expense of his
equivalent to his price, the hostler may appropriate the horse to himself upon the appraise-
of his neighbours, or may have him sold. But innkeepers in other parts of the country have
sell horses detained by them.
mmitted to an innkeeper cannot be detained as a security for the board of his master.
ted by stat. 11 & 12 Wm. 3. c. 15., that innkeepers, alehouse keepers, &c., refusing to specify
nt the number of pints or quarts for which demand is made, or selling in unmarked
all have no power to detain any goods or other things belonging to the person from whom
le, but shall be left to their action for recovery of the same.

PUMICE-STONE, (Ger. *Bimstein;* Fr. *Pierre pouce;* It. *Pietra p* Sp. *Piedra pomez;* Lat. *Pumex*), a light, spongy, vitreous stone, found use the neighbourhood of volcanoes. It is used for polishing metals and marb smoothing the surface of wood and pasteboard. It is said to form a good for pottery. The lighter pumice-stones swim on water, their specific grav exceeding ·914. The island of Lipari, in the Mediterranean, is chiefly forr pumice-stone, and may be said to be the magazine whence all Europe is su with this useful article. There are several species of pumice-stones; but only that are light and spongy are exported. The price varies in the L market from 8*l.* to 10*l.* a ton.

Q.

QUARANTINE, a regulation by which all communication with indiv ships, or goods, arriving from places infected with the plague, or other con disease, or supposed to be peculiarly liable to such infection, is interdicte certain definite period. The term is derived from the Italian *quaranta,* fo being generally supposed, that if no infectious disease break out within 4 or 6 weeks, no danger need be apprehended from the free admission of dividuals under quarantine. During this period, too, all the goods, cloth that might be supposed capable of retaining the infection, are subjected to cess of purification. This last operation, which is a most important part quarantine system, is performed either on board ship, or in establishments minated *lazarettos.* — (See *post.*)

Policy of Quarantine. — The regulations as to quarantine are entirely precaut they have their origin in the belief that various diseases, but especially the plag contagious; and supposing such to be the case, the propriety of subjecting those from an infected or suspected place to a probation is obvious. Indeed no gove could, until the belief in question be proved to be ill-founded, abstain from er precautionary measures, without rendering itself liable to the charge of having c neglected one of its most important duties, — that of providing, by every mea power, for the safety of its subjects. Latterly, however, it has been contended plague is never imported; that it is always indigenous; originating in some state of the atmosphere, or in something peculiar in the condition of the peop that, consequently, quarantine regulations merely impose a heavy burden on co without being of any real utility. But though there does not seem to be any re doubting that infectious diseases have originated in the way described, the fact t have, in innumerable instances, been carried from one place to another, seems to blished beyond all question. Even if the evidence as to the importation of in diseases were less decisive than it is, or the opinions of medical men more di would not warrant the repeal of the restraints on the intercourse with suspecte This is not a matter in which innovations should be rashly introduced; wherev is doubt, it is proper to incline to the side of security. In some cases, perhaps, tine regulations have been carried to a needless extent; but they have more fre we believe, been improperly relaxed.

Institution of Quarantine. — The notion that the plague was imported from into Europe, seems to have prevailed in all ages. But it would appear that th tians were the first who endeavoured to guard against its introduction from ab obliging ships and individuals from suspected places to perform quarantine. gulations upon this subject were, it is most probable, issued for the first time — (*Beckmann, Hist. of Invent.* vol. ii. art. *Quarantine.*) They have since b dually adopted in every other country. Their introduction into England was c tively late. Various preventive regulations had been previously enacted; but qu was not systematically enforced till after the alarm occasioned by the dreadful p Marseilles in 1720. The regulations then adopted were made conformabl suggestions of the celebrated Dr. Mead, in his famous " Discourse concern tilential Contagion."

Lazarettos or Pest-houses, are establishments constructed to facilitate the per of quarantine, and particularly the purification of goods. They have usual in which ships from a suspected place may anchor; and when perfect, are with lodgings for the crews and passengers, where the sick may be separated healthy; and with warehouses where the goods may be deposited; all interce

the lazaretto and the surrounding country being, of course, interdicted, except mission of the authorities. The lazarettos at Leghorn, Genoa, and Marseilles, ae most complete of any in Europe. The facilities they afford to navigation ry great; for, as ships from suspected places may discharge their cargoes in :aretto, they are not detained longer than they would be were there no quarantine tions. The goods deposited in the lazaretto, being inspected by the proper officers, urified, are then admitted into the market.

npared with these, the quarantine establishments in this country are exceedingly ve. There is not, even in the Thames, a lazaretto where a ship from a suspected may discharge her cargo and refit: so that she is detained frequently at an enor-expense, during the whole period of quarantine; while, if she have perishable on board, they may be very materially injured. It is singular that nothing should o have been done to obviate such grievances. The complaints as to the oppres-s of quarantine regulations are almost wholly occasioned by the want of proper es for its performance. Were these afforded, the burdens it imposes would dered comparatively light; and we do not know that many more important ser-ould be rendered to the commerce of the country, than by constructing a proper tine establishment on the Thames.

of Health. — The period of quarantine varies, as respects ships coming from the lace, according to the nature of their bills of health. These are documents, ificates, signed by the consul or other competent authority in the place which the s left, describing its state of health at the time of her clearing out. A *clean* bill s that, at the time of her sailing, no infectious disorder was known to exist. A ed, or, as it is more commonly called, a *touched* bill, imports that rumours were f an infectious disorder, but that it had not actually appeared. A *foul* bill, or the of *clean bills*, imports that the place was infected when the vessel sailed. — (See)F HEALTH.) The duration of the quarantine is regulated by the nature of these ents. They seem to have been first issued in the Mediterranean ports in 1665; obviously of great importance.

antine Regulations. — The existing quarantine regulations are embodied in the act 4. c. 78., and the different orders in council issued under its authority. These specify what vessels are liable to perform quarantine; the places at which it be performed; and the various formalities and regulations to be complied The publication in the Gazette of any order in council with respect to qua-is deemed sufficient notice to all concerned; and no excuse of ignorance is d for any infringement of the regulations. To obviate, as far as possible, any ion for such plea, it is ordered that vessels clearing out for any port or place with to which there shall be at the time any order in council subjecting vessels from it antine, are *to be furnished* with an abstract of the quarantine regulations; and *urnish themselves* with quarantine signal flags and lanterns, and with materials truments for fumigating and immersing goods. The following are the clauses ct as to signals: —

commander, master, or other person having the charge of any vessel liable to quarantine, shall, es, when such vessel shall meet with any other vessel at sea, or shall be within two leagues of the he United Kingdom, or the islands of Guernsey, Jersey, Alderney, Sark, or Man, hoist a signal that his vessel is liable to quarantine; which signal shall in the day time, if the vessel shall ean bill of health, be a large yellow flag, of six breadths of bunting, at the main top-mast-head; h vessel shall not have a clean bill of health, then a like yellow flag, with a circular mark or rely black, in the middle thereof, whose diameter shall be equal to two breadths of bunting; and ght time, the signal shall in both cases be a large signal lantern with a light therein (such as is oard his Majesty's ships of war), at the same mast head: and such commander, master, or other all keep such signals hoisted during such time as the said vessel shall continue within sight of r vessel, or within two leagues of the said coast or islands, and while so in sight, or within such until such vessel so liable to quarantine shall have arrived at the port where it is to perform e, and until it shall have been legally discharged from the performance thereof; on failure such commander, master, or other person, shall forfeit 100*l.*—§ 8.

ommander, master, or other person having the charge of any vessel on board whereof the plague fectious disease highly dangerous to the health of his Majesty's subjects shall actually be, shall es when such vessel shall meet with any other vessel at sea, or shall be within two leagues of the e United Kingdom, or the islands of Guernsey, Jersey, Alderney, Sark, or Man, hoist a signal that a vessel has the plague or other infectious disease; which signal shall be in the day time a low and black, borne quarterly, of eight breadths of bunting, at the main top-mast-head; and ht time, the signal shall be two large signal lanterns, commonly used on board ships of war, one ther, at the same mast head: and such commander, master, or other person, shall keep such sted during such time as the said vessel shall continue within sight of such other vessel, or within es of the coasts or islands aforesaid, while so in sight, or within such distance, until such vessel arrived at the port where it is to perform quarantine, and until it shall have been legally dis-rom the performance thereof; on failure thereof, such commander, master, or other person, it 100*l.* — § 9.

ommander, master, or other person, knowing that the same is not liable to the performance of e, shall hoist such signal, by day or night, such commander or other person shall forfeit 50*l.*

stead of printing the act, and the various orders in council that have grown out ill be sufficient to lay the following abstract of them before the reader. This

abstract has been prepared by the Custom-house; and contains a distinct summa:
the various rules and regulations to be complied with.

ABSTRACT OF QUARANTINE REGULATIONS.

It is in the first place to be observed, that all persons are presumed to know, and are bound to notice, not only of the quarantine regulations established by act of parliament (as they are of any public act), but likewise of every order in council made for the performance of quarantine, and pub: in the London Gazette; and as it is easily in their power to inform themselves of such regulation: particular care is taken by this and other means to promulgate such of them as apply to their resp: situations, *previously to their being actually put under quarantine*, when they will receive directio: their guidance from the quarantine officers, no plea of ignorance will be admitted as an excuse fc neglect, breach, or violation thereof; but for the sake of example, and for the security of the health, the pains, penalties, and punishments of the law will be enforced with the utmost severity.

Duty of Commanders and Masters of Vessels.

Upon arrival off the coasts of the United Kingdom, or the islands of Guernsey, Jersey, Alderney, or Man,

To deliver to the pilot who shall go on board, a written paper, containing a true account of the na: the place at which his ship loaded, and of all the places at which he touched on the hom: voyage. Neglecting or refusing to deliver such papers, or making any false representation or omission therein, subjects him to a penalty of 500*l*.

Upon entering or attempting to enter any port, and being spoke by any quarantine officers,

To give a true answer in writing or otherwise, and upon oath or not upon oath (according as he sh: required), to the preliminary questions put to him by such quarantine officer, for the purp: ascertaining whether his vessel is or is not liable to quarantine. Neglecting or refusing to bri: vessel to as soon as it can be done with safety, in obedience to the requisition of the quarantine c: subjects him to the penalty of 200*l*.

Refusing to answer such questions, or giving any false answer thereto (if not upon oath), subject: to the penalty of 200*l*.

If upon oath, to the punishment for wilful and corrupt perjury.

If any infectious disease shall appear on board, the master is to repair to such place as his M: shall direct, and make known his case to the officer of customs, and he is to remain at that place: directions are given by the Lords of the Privy Council. He is not to permit any of the crew or passe: on board to go on shore, and he, his crew, and passengers, are to obey such directions as are receive: the Lords of the Privy Council.

Not acting in conformity to the regulations herein directed, or acting in disobedience to such dire: as shall be received from the privy council, he incurs the penalty of 100*l*.

Upon meeting with any other vessel at sea, or when he shall be within two leagues of the coast United Kingdom or the islands aforesaid, to hoist the proper quarantine signals as herein-after state: to keep the same hoisted whilst in sight of such vessel, or within such distance from the coast, an: discharged from quarantine; any neglect or omission thereof incurs the penalty of 100*l*.

If informed by the pilot that his vessel has become liable to quarantine, by reason of any procla: made subsequent to his departure, to hoist and keep hoisted a like signal, under the same pen: 100*l*.

To give to the pilot coming on board a written paper containing a true account of the different a: composing his cargo. Neglecting or refusing to do so, or making a false representation or wilful om: subjects him to a penalty of 50*l*.

Masters of vessels liable to quarantine, and other persons on board them or having communicatio: them, are to repair to the appointed quarantine stations, and may be compelled to do so by force.

The master of any vessel having disease on board, on meeting with any other vessel at sea, or two leagues of the coast of the United Kingdom, or the islands of Guernsey, Jersey, Alderney, S: Man, is to hoist a signal to denote that his vessel has such disease on board, and is to keep such hoisted during such time as he shall continue within sight of such vessel, or within two leagues coast or islands aforesaid, while so in sight or within such distance, until the vessel shall arrive port where she is to perform quarantine, and until she shall be legally discharged from the perfor: thereof. Failing herein, the master incurs the penalty of 100*l*.

If he shall refuse or omit to disclose the circumstances of such infection prevailing either at an: at which he has been, or on board his vessel, in his answers to the preliminary questions put : by the quarantine officer, or if he shall wilfully omit to hoist, and to keep hoisted, the proper q: tine signal to denote that his ship is liable to quarantine, he incurs the penalty of 300*l*.

Upon attempting to enter any port, which is not the port at which he ought to perform quaranti: may be compelled to desist therefrom, in order that he may proceed to the proper quarantine po: guns being fired upon the ship, or any other kind of force being used that may be necessary attainment of that object.

Quitting or knowingly suffering any seamen or passenger to quit his ship by going on shore, or b: on board any other vessel or boat, before discharged from quarantine, or,

Not repairing to the proper quarantine station within a convenient time after due notice given, a penalty of 100*l*.

To repair in all cases to the proper quarantine port, as herein-after stated in the Appendix, accor: he shall or shall not be furnished with a clean bill of health, and according to the port or place to he shall be bound, as herein stated.

But if through ignorance, or by stress of weather, damage, loss, or accidents of the seas, he sha: passed the proper quarantine port, he may (having a clean bill of health on board, and upon: satisfactory proof thereof upon oath, and by the oath of the pilot, if any on board, and that th: was not wilfully or intentionally done or occasioned), be permitted to proceed to some other: tine port, in the discretion of the quarantine officer, keeping the proper quarantine signal during the whole time.

Upon his arrival at the proper quarantine port, to give true answers upon oath to all the qua: questions, and to make oath to the truth of his log-book, and the times at which the entries were made: failing herein, he incurs the penalty of wilful and corrupt perjury.

He is also to repair to the particular station which shall be appointed by the quarantine officer said ship or vessel.

To deliver up to the quarantine officer his bill of health, manifest, log-book, and journal. Wilfully refusing or neglecting so to do, subjects him to a penalty of 100*l*.

If not bound to any port of the United Kingdom, or the islands aforesaid, and attempting to er: port thereof (except to wait for orders, or in consequence of stress of weather or accidents of th: he shall give satisfactory proof thereof to the quarantine officer, and give true answers upon oat: preliminary questions, and strictly conform to all such directions as he shall receive from the qua: officer, touching his continuance at such port, or departure from thence, or repairing to any othe: also with respect to all other quarantine regulations; in default of which, he may be comp: proceed to sea by any means or by any kind of force that shall be necessary for that purpose.

performed quarantine in any foreign lazaret, the vessel is to be put under quarantine at some
rts herein-after appointed, until the master shall produce to the quarantine officer the proper
s in proof thereof, upon production whereof the said vessel shall not be obliged to perform
e, but shall remain at such station until released by order in council.

ping, or moving in order to unship, any goods from on board any vessel liable to quarantine,
a penalty of 500l.

tinely conveying, or secreting or concealing for the purpose of conveying, any letter, goods, or
cles, from any vessel actually performing quarantine, subjects to a penalty of 100l.

Every commander or master of any vessel clearing out or about to sail for any port or place in the
nean, or in the West Barbary on the Atlantic Ocean, or for any port or place respecting which
t at the time be any order of his Majesty in council in force, subjecting vessels coming from
quarantine, is to receive from the principal officer of the customs at such port or place, this
stract of the Quarantine Regulations, which such commander or master is to cause to be affixed
onvenient and conspicuous part of his said vessel, and to remain so affixed until his return with
ssel to some port or place in the United Kingdom or the islands aforesaid.

ry such commander and master is likewise to provide and take on board one at least of each of
quarantine signal flags and lanterns, and likewise materials and instruments for fumigation
rsion, and to keep the same on board, to be used upon his return to the United Kingdom or the
resaid.

Duty of Pilots.

e strictly to observe the following directions :—

ve an account in writing from every commander or master of any vessel coming from foreign
he places at which his vessel loaded, and at which he touched on his said homeward voyage.
notice to such commander or master of any proclamation, or order in council, made after the
of such vessel from the United Kingdom or the islands aforesaid, and then in force, by which
ning from any place mentioned in such account shall be liable to quarantine. Neglecting or
give such notice subjects them to a penalty of 100l.

a like notice of any proclamation then in force, by which vessels having on board any of the
ntioned in the master's account shall be liable to quarantine. Neglecting or omitting to give
subjects them to a penalty of 100l.

in on board in the same manner as any of the officers, crew, or passengers, and not to quit the
before or after the arrival, either by going on shore, or by going on board any other vessel or
ntent to go on shore, until she is regularly discharged from quarantine, and they may be com-
ny persons whatsoever, and by any kind of necessary force, to return on board the same. If
herein they incur a penalty of 300l. and six months' imprisonment.

ring any such vessel into any port or place other than the port or place appointed for the
f vessels so liable to quarantine, as stated in the Appendix, unless compelled by stress of wea-
se winds, or accidents of the seas, of which the pilot, as well as the commander or master of
is to give satisfactory proof upon oath. If they offend herein they incur a penalty of 200l.
the ship to, as soon as it can be done with safety, in obedience to the requisition of the quaran-
Failing herein subjects them to a penalty of 100l.

Duty of other Persons.

y infectious disease actually appears on board any vessel, all persons on board are to obey the
the privy council, under a penalty of 100l.

it such vessel, either by going on shore or by going on board any other vessel or boat with
on shore, until regularly discharged from quarantine ; and if they quit the ship they may be
y any persons whatsoever, and by any kind of necessary force, to return on board the same ;
liable to a penalty of 300l. and six months' imprisonment.

liable to quarantine, or actually performing quarantine, or having had any intercourse or
tion with any such persons so liable to or under quarantine, all persons are to obey all such
hey shall receive from the quarantine officer, and to repair to the lazaret, vessel, or place
or the performance of quarantine. Wilfully refusing or neglecting to repair forthwith, when
to do by such officers, or escaping from or out of such lazaret, vessel, or place, may be com-
pair or return thereto by any kind of necessary force, and are subject to a penalty of 200l.

or unshipping, or moving in order to the landing or unshipping, of any goods, packets, packages,
aring apparel, books, letters, or any other articles whatever, from vessels liable to quarantine,
a penalty of 500l.

nely conveying, or secreting or concealing for the purpose of conveying, any goods, letters, or
s as aforesaid, from any vessel actually performing quarantine, or from the lazaret or other
such goods or other articles shall be performing quarantine, are liable to a penalty of 100l.

uitted or come on shore from any vessel liable to or under quarantine, or having escaped from
or other place appointed in that behalf, may be seized and apprehended by any constable or
officer, or by any other person whatever, and carried before a justice of the peace, who may
arrant for conveying such person to the vessel, lazaret, or other place from which he shall have
for confining him in any place of safe custody (not being a public gaol) until directions can be
m the privy council.

y and wilfully forging or counterfeiting, interlining, erasing, or altering, or procuring to be
any certificate directed by any order in council touching quarantine, or publishing the same
ttering any such certificate with intent to obtain the effect of a true certificate, knowing its
e false, are guilty of felony.

What Vessels are liable to Quarantine.

(as well ships of war as all others) with or without clean bills of health, coming—
having touched at any place in the Mediterranean, or the West Barbary on the Atlantic

other place from which his Majesty shall from time to time adjudge it probable (and shall so
by proclamation or order in council) that the plague, or any other infectious disease or
r highly dangerous to the health of his Majesty's subjects, may be brought.
ey are considered as liable to quarantine from the time of their leaving any of the said

having communication with any of the before-mentioned ships or vessels, or receiving—
whatever from or out of such vessel, whether such person shall have come from any of the
es, or shall have gone on board of such vessel, either in the course of her voyage, or upon
al off the coast of the United Kingdom, &c.— Or,
wares, or merchandise, packets, packages, baggage, wearing apparel, goods, letters, or any
cles whatever, from or out of such ship or vessel.
ey are liable to quarantine from the time of their receiving any such persons or goods.

coming from any port or place in Europe without the Streights of Gibraltar, or on the
America, and having on board—
articles enumerated (a list of which articles see in the Appendix) ;
oducing a declaration upon oath, made by the owner, proprietor, shipper, or consignee, stating

either that such articles are not the growth, produce, or manufacture of Turkey, or of a
in Africa within the Streights of Gibraltar, or in the West Barbary on the Atlantic Ocean, o
of what place they are the growth, produce, or manufacture.

All vessels and boats receiving —
Any of the said goods, wares, and merchandise, or other articles enumerated.

Signals.

For vessels with the plague or other highly infectious disease actually on board —
In the daytime — A flag of yellow and black, borne quarterly, of eight breadths of bunting
main top-mast-head.
In the night time — Two large signal lanterns, with a light therein, such are commonly used
his Majesty's ships of war, one over the other, at the same mast-head.

For vessels with clean bills of health —
In the daytime — A large yellow flag, of six breadths of bunting, at the main top-mast-head.
In the night time — A large signal lantern, with a light therein, such as is commonly used o
his Majesty's ships of war, at the same mast-head.

For vessels without clean bills of health —
In the daytime — A large yellow flag, with a circular mark or ball, entirely black in the middle
whose diameter shall be equal to two breadths of bunting, at the main top-mast-head.
In the night-time — Same as for vessels with clean bills of health.

Note. — Every commander or master of a vessel about to sail for the Mediterranean, or for a
respecting which an order in council shall be in force, subjecting vessels coming from thence to
tine, to be provided with the quarantine signals above mentioned, and to keep the same on boa
used on his return to the United Kingdom.

Any commander or master hoisting either of the said quarantine signals, by day or night,
that his vessel is not liable to quarantine, incurs the penalty of 50l.

APPENDIX. — A List of Articles enumerated considered as most liable to Infection.

Apparel of all kinds	Goats' hair	Platting or bast, chip, cane,
Artificial flowers	Gold or silver on thread, cotton, hair,	horse hair
Bast, or any articles made thereof	wool, or silk, or any other substance	Quills
Beads, bracelets, or necklaces in strings	herein-before mentioned	Rags
Beds and bed ticks	Grogram	Sail and sail cloths
Books	Hats, caps, or bonnets of straw, chip,	Silk, viz. — crapes and tiffa
Brooms of all sorts	cane, or any other material	and knubs, raw silk, throw
Brushes of all sorts	Hemp	ganzine silk, waste silk, wro
Burdets	Hoods	Skins, hides, and furs, and par
Camlets	Horn and horn tips	of skins, hides, and furs, w
Canvass	Hair of all sorts	dressed, or in part or who
Carmenia wool	Leather	tawed, or dressed
Carpets	Linen	Sponges
Cordage not tarred	Lute strings, bathings, or harp strings	Straw, or any article made
Cotton wool	Maps	with straw
Cotton yarn	Mattresses	Stockings of all sorts
Cotton thread	Mats and matting	Thread, tow, vellum, whisks,
All articles wholly made of or mixed	Mohair yarn	ther raw or any wise wrou
with cotton, silk, wool, thread, or yarn	Nets, new or old	Yarn of all sorts
Down	Paper	And all other goods whatsoe
Feathers	Packthread	shall have arrived in or wit
Flax	Parchment	consisting wholly or in pa
Furriers' waste	Pelts	the said articles.

QUARANTINE PORTS. — For Vessels liable to Quarantine not coming from any Place actually i
nor having any Infection actually on Board.

Without clean Bills of Health.

All vessels, ships of war, &c. as herein-after specified, to
perform quarantine at Standgate Creek or Milford Haven.
Ships of war, transports, or other ships in the actual service
of government, under the command of a commissioned officer
in the service of his Majesty's navy, whithersoever bound; to
perform quarantine at the Motherbank near Portsmouth, at a
place marked out with yellow buoys.

With clean Bills of Health.

All ships and vessels bound to the following places, to perform quarantine at Standgate Creek : —
London, Rochester, Faversham, or any creeks or places belonging to or within any or either of the above ports.

All ships and vessels bound to the following places, to per-
from quarantine at Whitebooth Road, between Hull and
Grimsby : —

Leigh	Wisbeach
Maldon	Boston
Colchester	Grimsby
Harwich	Hull
Ipswich	Bridlington
Woodbridge	Scarborough
Aldborough	Whitby
Southwo'd	Stockton
Yarmouth	Sunderland
Blackney and Clay	Newcastle
Wells	Berwick
Lynn	

And any creeks or places belonging to or within any or either
of the above ports.

All ships and vessels bound to the following places, to perform quarantine at Banbury Pool, near Liverpool, or Milford
Haven : —

Carlisle	Liverpool
Whitehaven	Chester
Lancaster	Beaumaris
Preston	Isle of Man

And any creeks or places belonging to or within any or either
of the above ports.

All ships and vessels bound to the following places, to perform quarantine at the Motherbank near Portsmouth.

Sandwich	Arundel
Deal	Chichester
Dover	Portsmouth
Rye	Southampton
Newhaven	Cowes
Shoreham	

And any creeks or places belonging to or within any or either
of the above ports.

All ships and vessels bound to the following pla
form quarantine at St. Just's Pool, within the m
harbour of Falmouth : —

Poole	Fowey
Weymouth	Falmouth
Lyme	Gweek
Exeter	Penryn
Dartmouth	Truro
Plymouth	Penzance
Looe	Scilly

And any creeks or places belonging to or within a
of the above ports.

All ships and vessels bound to the following pla
form quarantine at King Road and Portshute Pill :

Bridgewater	Chepstow
Minehead	Cardiff
Bristol	Swansea
Gloucester	

And any creeks or places belonging to or within s
of the above ports.

All ships and vessels bound to the following pl
form quarantine at Milford Haven : —

St. Ives	Llanelly
Padstow	Pembroke
Bideford	Milford
Barnstaple	Cardigan
Ilfracombe	Aberystwith

Or any creek or places belonging to or within
of the above ports.

All ships and vessels bound to the following p
form quarantine at the Motherbank, near Portm
Just's Pool, within the mouth of the harbour of F

Jersey	Sark
Guernsey	Alderney

Or either of them, or any part of them, or eithe

All ships and vessels bound to the following p
form quarantine at Inverkeithing Bay : —

The eastern coasts of Scot-	Anstruther
land, comprehending the	Prestonpans
ports of Leith	Dundee
Borrowstouness	Perth
Alloa	Montrose
Dunbar	Aberdeen
Kirkaldy	

Or any member, creek, or other place belonging
any or either of the above ports.

All ships and vessels bound to the following p
form quarantine at Holy Loch, in the Frith of Cly

...tern coast of Scot- comprehending the " Glasgow ...eenock ...ine ...mpbell Town ...n	Rothsay Fort William Ayr Port Patrick Stranraer Wigtown

...ember, creek, or other place belonging to or within any or either of the above ports.

...ps and vessels bound to the following places, to per-...rantine at *Innerkeithing Bay* : —

...hern ports of Scot- ...omprehending the ' Inverness ...land	Orkney Caithness Stornaway

...nember, creek, or other place belonging to or within ...ther of the above ports.

...ps and vessels bound to the following places, to per-...rantine at *Holy Loch*, in the *Frith of Clyde* : —

The south-west ports of Scotland, comprehending the ports of Dumfries and Kircudbright, or any member, creek, or other place belonging to or within any or either of the above ports.

Bound to any port of Ireland, between Missen Head and Tuskard, to perform quarantine at *Bay of Baltimore*.

Bound between Tuskard and Rathlin, to perform quarantine at *Lough Larn* and the *Bay of Carlingford*, near *Killoween Point*, opposite to the town of *Carlingford*.

Bound to Rathlin and Tory Island, to perform quarantine at *Ballymostoker Bay* or *Red Castle Road*, near *Londonderry*.

Bound to Tory Island and Blacksod Bay, to perform quarantine at the harbour of *Killy Begs*.

Bound to Loop Head and Missen Head, to perform quarantine at *Scattery Bay*, in the river of *Limerick*.

Bound to any place on the coasts of the United Kingdom, not within any of the ports or limits herein-before mentioned or described, to perform quarantine at such places herein-before appointed for performance of quarantine, as shall be nearest to the port or place to which such vessels respectively shall be so bound.

Preliminary Questions.

...t is the name of the vessel, and the name of the commander or master?
...you the commander or master? Where does she belong?
...a whence do you come?
...hat place are you bound?
...hat ports have you touched since you left the port of your lading on your homeward voyage?
...t vessels have you had intercourse or communication with on your passage, and from whence did ...y come?
...he plague or any other infectious disease or distemper prevail in any degree at the place from ...nce you sailed on your homeward voyage, or at any of the places at which you have touched? ...t any, say at which and when. Are any persons on board your ship suffering under any infec-...s disease? or have any persons died or been ill of a disease of that nature on the homeward ...age? and if any, what number? And if any have died or been ill of such disease, were their ...ling and clothes destroyed?
...e vessel shall have sailed from any port in Europe without the Streights, or on the continent of America.]
...you on board any goods enumerated in this list?
[Handing up a list of articles enumerated.]
...have, specify the same, and whether they are of the growth, produce, or manufacture of Turkey, ...y place in Africa within the Streights of Gibraltar, or in the West Barbary on the Atlantic ...r of what other place? Have you any declaration to prove of what place they are the growth, or manufacture?
...e vessel comes from the Mediterranean, or from any other place respecting which there is any order in council in force concerning quarantine.]
...e you any, and what bill of health?
...t number of officers, mariners, and passengers have you on board?
...in cases of vessels coming from or having touched at any port or place on the continent of ...erica, or the islands adjacent thereto, or coming from or having touched at any ports in the West ...es, the following questions are to be put, in addition to the aforesaid questions :]
...e course of your voyage have any persons on board suffered from sickness of any kind? What ...the nature of such sickness? and when did it prevail? How many persons were affected by it? ...have any of them died in the course of the voyage?
...long after sailing from your port of lading, or having touched at any port on the continent of ...rica or the islands adjacent thereto, or any of the ports in the West Indies, was the first appear-...of disease observed?
...had the persons attacked been employed before they came on board?
...they been employed in loading or unloading the vessel before she left the port?
...the place which they inhabited before they sailed, the reputation of being healthy; or was it ...ct particularly to the fever incident to the country?
...the fever been frequent in the place before the vessel sailed?
...he persons who were ill on board your vessel fall sick nearly about the same time, or within a ...ays of each other? Or, did the disorder spread successively from one to another, and increase ...derably? Or, did it abate gradually, and cease to multiply as the distance from the ports you ...from or touched at as aforesaid increased?
...s was the greatest number of persons ill at the most sickly period of your voyage?
...was the whole number of persons on board your vessel when you sailed?
...is the whole number of persons now ill on board your vessel?
...ou state what were the symptoms of illness with which your crew was first attacked; and what ...he daily succession and change in them till their death?
...her any and what medicines have been used? and what methods have been adopted to prevent ...reading among the crew?
...her attention has been paid to cleanliness and ventilation on board your vessel?
...did you sail from the port or place from whence you took on board your outward cargo? and ...at place did you touch before you arrived at the port or place where you took in your present ?
...ou carry any bill of health with you to the port or place where you took in the cargo you have ...n board? From what place? Were the said bills of health clean, unclean, or suspected?

Quarantine Questions.

...s the name of the vessel, and the name of her commander or master?
...u the commander or master?
...t port or place does she belong?
...lid you sail from the port or place from whence you took on board your outward cargo? and at ...places did you touch before you arrived at the port or place where you took in your present ?
...a carry any bill or bills of health with you to the port or place where you took in the cargo you ...iow on board? From what places? Were the said bills of health clean, unclean, or suspected? ...hat port or place does she now come? When did you sail from such port or place? and at what ...or places have you touched in the course of the voyage?
...ou any bill or bills of health on board? From what place or places? Are the same clean, ...n, or suspected? Produce them.
...vessel shall have sailed from any port or place in Europe without the Streights, or on the con-tinent of America.]
...t articles does your cargo consist? Have you on board any goods enumerated in this list.
[Handing up a list of articles enumerated.]
...ve, specify the same, and whether they are of the growth, produce, or manufacture of Turkey,

or of any place in Africa, within the Streights of Gibraltar, or in the West Barbary on the At
Ocean, or of what other place: Have you any declaration to prove of what place they are the gr
produce, or manufacture?

9. At what place or places was the cargo or any part thereof taken on board? On what day di
arrive at the place or places where you took in the whole, or any and what part of the cargo?
on what day did you sail from such place or places? and what part of your cargo was taken in af
place, and when?

10. Did the plague or any other infectious disease or distemper prevail in any degree at the places
whence you sailed, or at any of the places at which your cargo was taken on board, or at whic
touched? If at any, say at which and when.

11. Did you hear of any report, or are you aware of any suspicion having existed, at the time of
sailing, that the plague or any other infectious disease prevailed at the place from whence you s
or at any other place in the Mediterranean (or in America or the West Indies, as the case may
12. What number of officers, mariners, passengers, or other persons have you on board? Descri
number of each.

13. At what port did you take on board your passengers?

14 Were they residents at that place, or had they been embarked as passengers on board any other
from any other places? and from what places and at what time?

15. Do the said officers, mariners, passengers, and other persons, consist of the same individuals a
on board at the port from which you sailed upon your homeward voyage? If any other person
been taken on board, or if any of your officers, crew, or passengers, have quitted your vessel sin
sailed from such port, or before your arrival at this place, or if any other alterations in that r
have taken place, specify the same, the causes and the time or times of such alterations.

16. What number of persons (if any) have died on board during the voyage outwards and homewa
at any port at which vou have touched? When, and in what part of the voyage did such per
persons die? Of what disease or distemper?

17. Have any of your officers, mariners, or other persons of your crew, who sailed with you on you
ward voyage, died or left the vessel?

18. In the course of your voyage outwards or homewards, or at any port at which you have touche
any persons on board suffered from sickness of any kind? What was the nature of such sic
When did it prevail? How many persons were affected by it? Are there any convalesce
board? Or, are all persons on board at present in good health?

19. Were any of those who died, or who have been sick in the course of the voyage, or any port at
you have touched, affected, or suspected to have been affected, by any infectious disease or diste
Were the bedding and clothes of such deceased and sick persons destroyed? If so, when and ir
manner were any of the persons immediately employed about the sick afterwards taken ill?
of what disease? and in how many days after having been so employed?

20. At what precise time did such deaths happen? In how many days after being indisposed, did th
die? What were the most obvious appearances of the disease?

21. Have you spoken to or otherwise had any communication with any vessels at sea, during the vo
What where the names of such vessels? and to what country, port, or place did they belong?
what ports or places were they coming, or at what ports or places had they touched on their vo
and to what country, ports, or places were they bound? What was the nature of the communi
held? What do you know respecting the state of health on board such vessels?

22. Have there been any letters, parcels, or other articles delivered out of or received into your
from any vessel or boat met with on the voyage, or before or since your arrival at this place?
what were such letters, parcels, or articles? And where were the same delivered or received
into or out of what vessel or boat?

23. Have you any packages or parcels which you have taken charge of? If so, what are their con
and when and where did you take them on board?

24. What pilots or other persons from the shores of the United Kingdom, or from the islands of
Guernsey, Jersey, Alderney, Sark, or Man, have been or are now on board your vessel, or ha
any communication whatever with the ship's company, or any of the passengers, during the ·
homewards, or before or since your arrival at this place? If any such pilots or other person
come on board, and have afterwards quitted your vessel, specify the names of such persons, a
time, manner, and circumstances of their so quitting your vessel.

25. Did you leave any British vessels at any of the ports you sailed from? If you did, mentio
names and the names of their commanders.

26. Were such vessels loading? were they near their departure? and whither were they bound.

27. Did you meet with any British vessels at any of the places you touched at? If you did, say
where, and what were the names and destinations of such vessels; and to what ports or pla
they belong?

28. Do you know whether any foreign vessels loading at the port from which you sailed, were
beyond the Streights of Gibraltar? And if so, what were they? and whither were they boun

29. Do you know whether any person whatever employed in loading your vessel, or in bringir
articles into it, or having any communication on board thereof, was taken ill during such empl
or communication? or whether, by the absence of such person or persons in the course of su
ployment, any suspicion was entertained of their having been ill? If so, of what disease?

30. Do you know whether or not your cargo, or any part thereof, had been long in warehouse be
being taken on board? If you do, say how long. Have you any knowledge of its being pac
handled on shore, or conveyed from shore, or stowed on board, by persons affected with the pla
any other infectious disease or distemper?

QUASSIA (Ger. *Quassienholz;* Fr. *Bois de quassie;* Sp. *Leno de quassi*
beautiful tall tree growing in North and South America, and the West Indi
which there are several varieties. The wood is of a pale yellow colour, a
odorous; it, as well as the fruit, and bark of the tree, has a place in the m
medica. Its taste is intensely bitter. It is said to have been sometimes us
the brewers in the preparation of beer, instead of hops; but the use of it fo
purpose is prohibited under severe penalties. — (See ALE AND BEER.)
price of quassia in bond varies from 1*l*. 4*s*. to 1*l*. 6*s*. a cwt. The duty is 8*l*. 17.
it is of course intended to be prohibitory; and it is one of the few impos·
such a purpose, against which no good objection can be urged.

QUEBEC, the capital of Canada, and of the British possessions in
America, on the north-west bank of the river St. Lawrence, about 340 mile
its mouth, in lat. 46° 50′ N., lon. 71° 16¼′ W. Population about 30,000.

ec is situated on a ridge, or promontory, formed by the St. Lawrence on the
d west, and the river St. Charles on the east. The extremity of this headland
Cape Diamond. It is about 345 feet above the level of the water, and on it
el is built. The town extends from the citadel, principally in a north-east di-
down to the water; and is, from the difference of elevation, divided into the
d lower towns. The fortifications, which are very strong, extend across the
a; the circuit within them being about 2¾ miles. From their situation, many of
ts are uneven; they are also, for the most part, narrow; but they are either well
Macadamised. The greater number of the houses are built of stone, with
oofs. Some of the public buildings are elegant, and well adapted for their pur-
The harbour, or basin, lies between the town, and the island of Orleans. It is
commodious: the water is about 28 fathoms deep, with a tide rising from 17
t; and at springs from 23 to 25 ditto. Quebec was founded by the French in
n 1629, it was taken by the English; but was restored in 1632. It was again
the English under General Wolfe, who fell in the engagement, in 1759; and
y ceded to us by the treaty of Paris in 1763.

apid increase of population in Upper Canada has occasioned a proportional
of intercourse between Quebec, Montreal, &c. The first steam boat that plied
t. Lawrence was launched in 1812. In 1829, 10 steam boats, 1 of them of
burthen, were engaged in the trade between Quebec and Montreal; and in the
ear a steam ship of from 700 to 800 tons burthen was launched at Quebec, to
en that city and Halifax in Nova Scotia. Thus will be formed a line of steam
cation from the Atlantic to Amherstburgh, one of the remote settlements of
nada,—a distance of more than 1,500 miles; which we may soon expect to see
to the head of Lake Huron, and eventually to the western extremity of Lake
about 700 miles beyond Amherstburgh; giving to Quebec a command of
avigation inferior only to that of New Orleans. The navigation at Quebec
he end of November or beginning of December, and opens in April. Below
he river is seldom frozen over; but the masses of floating ice, kept in constant
by the flux and reflux of the tide, render navigation impracticable. The waters
Lawrence are very pure; and in point of depth and magnitude it is one of the
vers in the world. — (*Bouchette's British Dominions in America,* vol. i. p. 272.
elaborate and valuable work.) Quebec is a free warehousing port.

ve already given (see *antè,* p. 327.) an account of the aggregate value and
f the trade and navigation of Canada, and our other possessions in North
for three different periods; viz. 1806, 1825, and 1829. The acts 6 Geo. 4.
d 1 Wm. 4. c. 24., regulating the colonial trade, and the duties upon the
rticles imported into Canada and the other colonies, are given *antè,* pp. 328—
nce the following statements refer only to the trade, charges, &c. peculiar to
d the St. Lawrence.

ere arrived at Quebec,

	Ships with Cargoes.	Ships in Ballast.	Tonnage of both.	Men.
at Britain - - - -	219	320	163,439	7,134
nd - - - -	54	111	44,426	1,999
ey - - - -	1	- -	88	5
raltar - - - -	1	- -	105	8
ce - - - -	- -	2	471	18
herlands - - -	- -	4	1,358	61
n - - - -	2	- -	572	25
ugal - - -	8	- -	1,290	61
y - - - -	2	- -	231	18
den - - - -	1	- -	316	16
eriffe - - -	1	- -	104	8
sh North American Colonies -	72	32	12,898	606
sh West Indies - - -	57	4	8,996	495
ed States - - -	5	4	2,271	113
Totals - - -	423	477	236,565	10,567

e same year there entered at Gaspé,

Vessels. Tons. Men.
34 - - - 4,616 - - - 257

arlisle, to 10th October, 1829,
33 - - - 13,701 - - - 352

e same year there cleared out

	Vessels.	Tons.	Men.
é - - - - - -	33	4,587	253
Carlisle, to 10th October - - - - -	31	5,925	303

During the same year there cleared out from Quebec,

	Vessels.	Tons.	N
or Great Britain - - - - -	537	162,883	7
Ireland - - - - -	34	63,053	2
Portugal - - - - -	1	209	
Fayal - - - - -	1	105	
Cape of Good Hope - - -	1	170	
British North American Colonies	96	7,132	
British West Indies - - -	58	8,043	
United States - - - - -	5	769	

There has been, during the last two years, a very extraordinary increase in the number of e from this country to Canada. According to the accounts published by the Committee of Quebec, the following emigrants arrived in that city, viz. in 1827, 16,862; 1828, 13,694; 1829, 1830, 24,391; 1831, 49,082. The account for 1831 is made up to the 25th of November only. Mo emigrants were destined for Upper Canada. We have given, (*ante*, p. 321.) some details as to mode of proceeding from Quebec to Upper Canada.

Rates of Pilotage for the River St. Lawrence.

From Bic to Quebec (153 miles distance)— *Per Foot.*

	L.	s.	d.
From the 2d to the 30th April, inclusive -	1	0	0
From the 1st May to the 10th Nov., inclusive -	0	18	0
From the 11th to the 18th November, inclusive	1	3	0
From the 19th Nov. to the 1st March, inclusive	1	8	0

From Quebec to Bic—

From the 2d to the 30th April, inclusive -	0	18	0
From the 1st May to the 10th November, inclusive	0	15	9
From the 11th to the 18th November, inclusive	1	0	9
From the 19th Nov. to the 1st March, inclusive	1	5	9

Rates of pilot water and poundage on pilot money are payable at the Naval Office, by masters and commanders of vessels, viz.—

For every foot of water for which masters or commanders of vessels are bound to pay their pilots, from Bic to Quebec, and from Quebec to Bic, 2*s.* 6*d.* currency per foot.

For vessels going to Three Rivers or Montreal,

Of 100 to 150 tons inclusive - -	*L.* 2	currency
Of 151 to 200 tons inclusive - -	3	—
Of 201 to 250 tons inclusive - -	4	—
Of 251 tons and upwards - -	5	—

On settling with pilots, masters or commanders of vessels, or the consignees of such vessels, are to deduct 1*s.* in the pound for the amount of the sums to be paid for pilotage; which will be exacted by the naval officer at clearing out; the same being funded by law, under the direction of the Trinity-house, for the relief of decayed pilots, their widows, and children.

Regulations for the Payment of Pilotage above Bic to Quebec.

At or above the anchorage of the Brandy Pots, 2-3ds of the present rate for a full pilotage.

Above the Point of St. Roc, 1-3d do.

Above the Point aux Pins, on the Isle aux Grues, and below Patrick's Hole, 1-4th do.

At and above Patrick's Hole - - - -

For shifting a vessel from one wharf to another, between Bréhaut's wharf and Point à Carcis; or from or to the stream, from or to any of the above wharfs - - -

For shifting a vessel from the stream, or from either of the above wharfs to St. Patrick's Hole, or to the basin of Montmorency, or to the ballast ground, the basin of the Chaudière, Wolfe's Cove, and as far as the river Cap Rouge - - -

Rates above the Harbour of Quebec.

From Quebec to Port Neuf, 4*l.* currency	For vessels of registered measurement not exceeding 200 tons	—	To Que Port N currenc
—	5*l.*	If above 200 and not exceeding 250 tons	—	
To Three Rivers, on above Port Neuf, 6*l.* currency	For vessels not exceeding 200 tons	—	FromTh and a Neuf,
—	7*l.*	If above 200 and not exceeding 250 tons	—	
To Montreal, and above Three Rivers, 11*l.* currency	For vessels not exceeding 200 tons	—	From and al Rivers curren
—	13*l.*	If above 200 and not exceeding 250 tons	—	
—	16*l.*	If above 250 tons	—	

Pilots are at liberty to leave vessels 48 hours arrive at the place of their destination.

Imports and Exports.

We extract from the papers laid before the Financ mittee, the following detailed statement of the *quantities* of the different articles in into and exported from Quebec and the other ports of Lower Canada, in 1826. comprise the entire imports and exports of Upper as well as Lower Canada.

IMPORTS IN THE YEAR 1826.

At QUEBEC.

714 Vessels. 179,949 Tons.
8,263 Men.

16,269 Gallons Madeira Wine, in 123 pipes, 50 hogsheads, 23 quarter casks, and 44 casks, cases.
41,058 Gallons Port Wine, in 257 pipes, 78 hogsheads, 54 qr. casks, and 143 casks, cases.
31,642 Gallons Teneriffe Wine, in 231 pipes, 140 hogsheads, 296 qr. casks, and 4 casks, cases.
116,270 Gallons Spanish Wine, in 17 butts, 749 pipes, 354 hogsheads, and 289 casks, cases.
65,389 Gallons Sicilian Wine, in 467 pipes, 196 hogsheads, and 9 quarter casks.
8,580 Gallons Italian Wine, in 61 pipes, 10 hhds. and 1 cask.
8,476 Gallons French Wine, in 30 pipes, 52 hogsheads, and 221 casks, cases.
241 Gallons Whiskey, in 3 puncheons and 2 kegs.
37,356 Gallons Brandy, in 251 pipes, 123 hogsheads, and 1 cask.
25,330 Gallons Gin, in 192 pipes and 7 hogsheads.
350,885 Gallons Jamaica Rum, in 3,230 puncheons, 128 hogsheads, and 2 casks.
79,349 Gallons Leeward Island Rum, in 7,207 puncheons, 528 hogsheads, and 123 casks.
870 Gallons Shrub, in 7 puncheons, 2 hogsheads, and 4 casks.
213 Gallons Cordials, in 12 hampers and 43 casks, cases.
100,975 Lbs. Molasses, in 1,088 casks.
229,542 Lbs. Refined Sugar, in 276 casks.
2,371,508 Lbs. Muscovado Sugar, in 3,636 casks and 697 bags.

QUEBEC—*continued.*

75,636 Lbs. Coffee in 192 casks, and 33 bags.
77,601 Lbs. Leaf Tobacco, in 71 casks.
11,219 Lbs. Manufactured Tobacco, in 66 kegs, 58 boxes, 44 half boxes, and 299 qr. boxes.
19,952 Packs Playing Cards.
209,783 Minots Salt.
32,074 Lbs. Hyson Tea, in 484 chests and 19 packages (from London).
1,042,318 Lbs. other Teas, in 13,310 chests, 3,583 boxes, and 58 packages (from London).

N. B.—Three per cent. has been deducted from all the above Articles, except the Playing Cards.

		L.	*s.*	*d.*
Value of Merchandise paying 2½ per cent. -		715,856	9	8
Value of Free Goods -		15,086	3	3
		*l.*730,922	12	11

TEAS *from* CHINA.

Chests & Boxes.

Teas imported in 1825 -	15,480	
Of which there appears to have been sold, as the Duty thereon has been paid -	12,651	
Remaining -		2,829
Teas imported in 1826 -	17,777	
Of which have been sold	144	
Remaining -		17,255
Total remaining in the Agent's Warehouse -		20,062
Of the quantity sold, there have been exported -		1,014
Nett Sales for Home Consumption in 1825, 1826, and 1827 -	11,781	

N. B.—A Sale will take place in May.

At NEW CARLIS

From 10th *October*, 1825 *October*, 1826.

29 Vessels. 5,307 Tons.

138 Gallons Wine.
878 ditto Brandy.
3,122 ditto Rum.
3,099 ditto Molasses.
2,138 Lbs. Refined Sugar.
7,814 Lbs. Muscovado ditto.
157 Lbs. Coffee.
54 Lbs. Leaf Tobacco.
472 Lbs. Manufactured di
39 Lbs. Tea.

N. B.—Three per cent. h ducted from the above Article

37,280 Bushels Salt, due

Value of Merchandise pay cent.	8,994*l.* 5*s.*

At GASPE'.

From 10th *October*, 1825, t 1826.

9 Vessels. 837 Tons.

107 Gallons Brandy.
868 ditto Rum.
630 ditto Molasses.
1,338 Lbs. Muscovado Suga
54 Lbs. Manufactured T

N. B.—Three per cent. h ducted from the above Artic

256 Tons Salt, duty
6,000 Bushels di

Value of Merchandise pay cent.	2,520*l.* 14*s.*

EXPORTS IN THE YEAR 1826.

m QUEBEC.

els. 198,818 Tons.
Men. 59 of which
is year, 17,823 Tons.

Masts and Bow-
  sprits.
Spars.
Tons Oak Timber.
Feet   ditto.
Tons Pine Timber.
Feet   ditto.
Tons Ash Timber.
Feet   ditto.
Tons Elm Timber.
Feet   ditto.
Tons Maple, &c.
Feet   ditto.
Pieces of Standard
  Staves and Head-
  ings.
Ps. Pipe and Pun-
  cheon Staves and
  Heading.
's. Stave Ends.
's. Deals, 3-inch.
's. Boards and
  Planks.
's. Deal Ends.
's. Battens.
's. Batten Ends.
ars.
andspikes.
ords Lathwood.
Ton Timber Ends.
ords Oak Billets.
ieces   ditto.
s. Wood Hoops.
uncheon Stave
  Packs.
ogsheads ditto.
arrels   ditto.
r. Casks ditto.
eces Treenails.
nees.
nchor Stocks.
ocks.
ingles.
wt. 1 qr. 24 lbs.
Pearl Ashes, in
  18,371 barrels.
wt. 3 qrs. 19 lbs.
Pot Ashes, in
  21,218 barrels.
ishels Wheat.
tto Barley.
tto Oats.
tto Peas.
tto Ind. Corn.
tto Malt.
tto Flaxseed.
tto Rye.
rrels Flour.
lf Barrels ditto.
gs   ditto.
t. Biscuit.
s. Crackers, in
  11 Barrels and 18
  Kegs.
shels Potatoes.
to Carrots and
  Turnips.
shels Onions.

QUEBEC —continued.

9,228 Barrels Pork.
537 Half Barrels ditto.
5,173 Barrels Beef.
1,364 Half Barrels ditto.
14,749 Lbs. Rounds, &c. in
  12 half barrels and
  211 kitts.
6,066 Barrels Hams, in 9 puncheons and 10 bar-
  rels ; 21 loose.
6,717 Lbs. Tongues, in 7
  barrels and 261 kegs
636 Lbs. Dried Beef.
1,250 Lbs. Fresh Beef.
1,680 Lbs. Sausages, in 7
  jars and 55 kegs.
1,450 Lbs. Tripe, in 29 kegs.
500 Lbs. Mutton, in 5 half
  barrels.
249 Lbs. Bacon.
23,817 Lbs. Lard, in 699 kegs.
98,046 Lbs. Butter, in 1,933
  kegs.
1,163 Lbs. Cheese, in 5 hampers and 5 cases.
18,020 Cwt. Cod-fish, in 2,281
  casks,254 boxes, and
  25 bundles.
242 Tierces Salmon.
659 Barrels ditto.
18 Kitts ditto.
550 Barrels Mackerel.
89 Ditto Shad.
39 Kitts Trout.
573 Barrels Herrings.
120 Boxes ditto.
25 Lbs. Cod Sounds, in 1
  cask.
21,849 Gallons Oil, in 438
  casks.
88 Kegs ditto.
270 Jars ditto.
205 Cwt. Oil Cake, in 31
  punch. and loose.
31,674 Lbs. Soap, in 557 bxs.
15,018 Lbs. Candles, in 376
  boxes.
12,079 Gals. Ale, in 230 casks.
2 Boxes Essence Spruce.
9 Casks ditto.
264 Gals. Cider, in 1 casks.
12 Doz. ditto, in 12 cases.
35 Gals. Peppermint, in
  1 barrel.
10 Casks Canada Balsam.
2 Kegs ditto.
929 Barrels Apples.
1 ditto Berries.
6 Punch. Cranberries.
5 Barrels ditto.
5 Kegs ditto.
49 Packages Trees and
  Plants.
277 Lbs. Honey, in 3 kegs.
3 Casks Bees' Wax.
1 Bag Wool.
1 Case Bones.
15 Hogsheads Horns.
2 Casks ditto.
1 Basket ditto.
987 Pairs Moccasins.
1,452 Lbs. Leather, in 13
  bales.
9 Cases ditto.

QUEBEC —continued.

174 Hides.
1 Hhd. Leaf Tobacco.
7,733 Lbs. Plug ditto, in 49
  kegs.
1,358 Lbs. Cut ditto, in 11
  boxes and 2 barrels.
7 Barrels Segars.
1,482 Lbs. Snuff, in 27 kegs,
  90 blad. and 1 box.
4 Bark Canoes.
20 Wooden Clocks.
12 Packages Indian Cu-
  riosities.
5 Boxes Bark-work.
5 Horses.
3 Barrels Nuts.
4 Kegs ditto.
9 Boxes Maple Sugar
105 Stoves.
150 Pairs of Iron Hooks.

FURS and PELTRIES.

39,619 Marten Skins.
600 Hare ditto.
7,510 Beaver ditto.
940 Fisher ditto.
6,433 Raccoon ditto.
3,782 Bear and Cub ditto.
1,698 Otter ditto.
15,028 Musk Rat ditto.
4,218 Minx ditto.
362 Lynx ditto.
3,292 Fox ditto.
187 Cat ditto.
5,459 Deer ditto.
4 Wolf ditto.
17 Wolverine ditto.
14 Buffalo Robes.
2 Lbs. Bear Coating.
383 Lbs. Castorum, in 2
  casks and 1 case.

**IMPORTED GOODS EX-
PORTED.**

677 Gals. Wine, in 5 hhds.
  and 13 qr. casks.
6 Cases Bottled Wine.
859 Gals. Rum, in 6 pun-
  cheons and 6 casks.
242 Gallons Molasses, in
  3 casks.
1,904 Lbs. Muscovado Su-
  gar, in 2 hogsheads
  and 4 barrels.
28 Lbs. Coffee, in 1 box.
32,432 Lbs. Tea, in 535 chests
  and boxes, 18 pack.
  and 1 qr. chest.
6 Boxes Chocolate.
28 Casks Raisins.
289 Boxes ditto.
123 Ditto Prunes.
9 Ditto Figs.
4 Bags Almonds.
1 Barrel Candy.
1 Box Pepper.
3 Barrels ditto.
2 Tierces Rice.
2 Puncheons Lime Juice
2 Tons Logwood.
1 Puncheon Paint.
253 Kegs ditto.

QUEBEC —continued.

846 Bars Iron.
5 Bundles ditto.
39 Tons ditto.
3 Cases Sheet Iron.
146 Bundles Iron Hoops.
3 Grates.
2 Iron Pots.
160 Sheets Copper.
2 Boxes Axes.
1 Cwt. Steel.
34 Gross Bottles.
1 Cable.
12 Coils Cordage.
1 Bale Cotton Wool.
10 Bales Canvass.
10 Bolts ditto.
20,000 Bricks.
20 Tons Coals.
2 Barrels Pitch.
3 Ditto Tar.
8 Ditto Spirits Tur-
  pentine.
10 Boxes Glass.
5 Punch. Broken Glass.
1 Hogshead ditto.
1 Case Castor Oil.
600 Minots Salt.
4 Cwt. Shot.
295 Barrels Gunpowder.
56 Kegs ditto.
158 Pack. Merchandise.

From GASPÉ.

13 Vessels. 1,701 Tons.
  81 Men.

14,356 Cwt. Cod-fish.
3 Barrels Eels.
10 Ditto Salmon.
3 Ditto Oil.
20 Pieces Oak Timber.
155 Ditto Pine ditto.
61 Ditto Elm, Ash, &c.
11 Spars.
4,008 Pieces Staves.
7,971 Ditto Deals.
273 Ditto Deal Ends.
8 Cords Lathwood.

*From NEW CAR-
LISLE.*

30 Vessels. 4,787 Tons.
  261 Men.

19,661 Cwt. Cod-fish.
4 Barrels Salmon.
9 Ditto Shad.
204 Ditto Herrings.
2 Ditto Oil.
12 Ditto Pork.
36 Ditto Flour.
3,599 Tons Pine Timber.
89 Tons Birch, &c.
125 Spars.
318 Pieces Planks.
2,484 Feet Boards.
40 Oars.
5,530 Treenails.
2,500 Minots Salt.

Monies. — Table of Coins in Circulation.

Portuguese, American, h. and French Coins.	Weight.	Halifax Currency.	OldCurrency.	English, Portuguese, American, Spanish, and French Coins.	Weight.	Halifax Currency.	OldCurrency.
Gold.	Dwt.gr.	L. s. d.	Liv.sols.	*Silver.*	Dwt.gr.	L. s. d.	Liv.sols.
-	5 6	1 3 4	28 0	A Crown -	—	0 5 6	6 12
-	5 3	1 2 3	26 14	English Shilling -	—	0 1 1	1 6
ea -	2 15	0 11 8	14 0	Spanish and American Dollar -	—	0 5 0	6 0
Guinea -	1 18	0 7 9¼	9 6¾	Pistareen - -	—	0 1 0	1 4
-	18 0	4 0 0	96 0	French Crown, coined before			
-	9 0	2 0 0	48 0	1793 -	—	0 5 6	6 12
-	6 18	1 10 0	36 0	French Piece, of 4 Liv. 10 Sols.			
-	11 6	2 10 0	60 0	Tournois -	—	0 4 2	5 0
-	5 15	1 5 0	30 0	French Piece of 6 Francs, since			
n -	17 0	3 11 6	89 8	1792 -	—	0 5 6	
-	8 12	1 17 3	41 14	French Piece of 5 Francs, do. -	—	0 1 8	
, coined before 1793 -	5 4	1 2 8	27 4				
do. -	4 4	0 18 3	21 18				
Francs, coined since							
-	8 6	1 16 2					
ty Francs, do. -	4 3	0 18 1					

Deducting one tenth from the currency value of these coins will give their sterling value.

rency. — There is no established government bank
nce ; but there are private chartered banks, which
owing sums of paper currency in circulation, viz.

	L.	s.	d.
bec Bank -	28,395	0	0
treal Bank -	88,543	5	0
ada Bank -	8,432 10	0	
	L.125,368	15	0

o notes or other paper money are issued on the
province.
pt in Halifax currency.

Weights same as in England.
Measures. — Standard wine gallon, liquid measure of the
province. The Canada minot for all grain, &c., except where
specially agreed upon to the contrary ; and this measure is
about one eighth larger than the Winchester bushel. The
English Winchester bushel, when specially agreed for. The
Paris foot, for all measures of lands granted previous to the
conquest ; and all measures of length, where an agreement is
made to the contrary. The English foot, for measure of lands
granted since the conquest, and wherever specially agreed
upon. The standard English yard for measuring all cloths
or stuffs, sold by the yard or measure of length. The English
ell, when specially agreed upon.

MONTREAL, the second town of Canada, is situated on the south side of an island of the same nam the St. Lawrence, about 180 miles above Quebec, in lat. 45° 31′ N., lon. 73° 35′ W. Population 30,000. harbour is not large, but it is safe and commodious; the facilities for navigation afforded by the noble on which it is situated being such, that vessels of 600 tons burthen may ascend thus far without diffi The North American fur trade principally centres in Montreal ; which also enjoys the principal sh the commerce between Canada and the United States. It is increasing faster than Quebec, or tha city in British America. Imports and exports included in those of Quebec.

QUERCITRON BARK, the bark of a species of oak growing in many p of North America. It is used in dyeing yellow colours. — (See BARK.)

QUILLS (Fr. *Plumes à écrire*; Ger. *Posen, Federkiele*; It. *Penne da scri* Rus. *Stivoli*; Sp. *Canones para escribir*), the hard and strong feathers of the w of geese, ostriches, swans, turkeys, crows, &c. They are classified accordir the order in which they are fixed in the wing; the second and third quills t the best. Crow quills are chiefly used for drawing.

The goodness of quills is judged partly by the size of the barrels, but more b weight ; hence the denomination of quills of 14, 15, &c. loths ; viz. the 1,000, consi of 1,200 quills, weighing 14, 15, &c. loths. Particular attention should be take purchasing quills, that they be not *left-handed*, that is, out of the left wing. The on goose quills produced, in 1829, 4,842*l.* 16*s.* ; which, as the duty is at the ra 2*s.* 6*d.* the 1,000, shows that the number of quills imported for home consumption year must have amounted to 38,742,000. Quills are principally imported from Netherlands and Germany ; but those from Van Diemen's Land are said to be the fi The price of quills in London, in October, 1831, duty paid, was as under : —

				£	s.	d.	£	s.	d.							£	s.	d.	£
Quills, Swan, 100	-	-	-	0	2	0 to 0	10	6		Quills, Goose, 13 loth per *mille*				0	9	0 to 0
Goose, 17 loth per *mille*	3	4	0 — 3	6	0			12	-	-	-	0	7	0 — 0
16	-	-	2	0	0 — 2	2	0			11	-	-	-	0	5	6 — 0
15	-	-	1	4	0 — 1	6	0		Pinions	-	-	-	-	0	5	6 — 0
14	-	-	0	15	0 — 0	17	0									

R.

RAGS (Du. *Lompen, Vodden*; Fr. *Chiffes, Chiffons, Drapeaux, Drilles*; *Lumpen*; It. *Strasci, Strazze*; Rus. *Trepje*; Sp. *Tropos, Harapos*), shred fragments of (generally decayed) linen, woollen, or cotton cloth. Though monly held in little estimation, rags are of great importance in the arts, being for various purposes, but especially in the manufacture of paper, most of w is entirely prepared from them. As the mode in which British rags are colle must be well known to every one, the following statements apply only to the t in foreign rags.

Woollen Rags. — Woollen and linen rags are imported in considerable quantities the continent of Europe, and from Sicily. The woollen rags are chiefly used for nure, especially in the culture of hops ; but rags of loose texture, and not too v worn or decayed, are unravelled and mixed up with fresh wool in the making of yar practice more favourable to the cheapness than to the strength and durability of the f into which this old wool is introduced. Woollen rags are also used for making or stuffing for beds, &c. : this process is performed chiefly by the aid of the same ki engines that prepare pulp for paper ; these wash the rags thoroughly, at the same tim they grind and tear them out into separate threads and fibres. The chief importat woollen rags is from Hamburgh and Bremen ; and there are some got from Ro but the quantity is trifling. The total average importation varies from 300 to 500 and the price ranges from 4*l.* to 5*l.* per ton, duty (7*s.* 6*d.*) and freight paid, on as are used for manure ; and from 13*l.* to 15*l.* for coloured woollens of loose texture 18*l.* to 20*l.* for white of the same description.

Linen Rags are principally imported from Rostock, Bremen, Hamburgh, Leg Ancona, Messina, Palermo, and Trieste. Their export from Holland, Belgium, F Spain, and Portugal, is strictly prohibited. The imports usually amount to 10,000 tons ; worth, at an average, from 21*l.* to 22*l.* per ton, duty (5*s.*) and freig cluded. Exclusive of the very large quantity collected at home, the whole rag ported were, until very recently, employed in the manufacture of paper ; bu Americans, who have for some years been large importers from the Mediterranea Hamburgh, have lately come into the London market, and purchased several ca a circumstance sufficiently indicative of the languid state of the paper manufact this country, occasioned by the oppressive amount of the duties with which it is dened, and of the duty on advertisements. — (See PAPER.)

nported rags are coarser and inferior in appearance to the English; but, being
xclusively linen, they are stronger, and bear a price disproportioned to the ap-
ifference in quality : this disproportion has been materially augmented since the
tion of the process of boiling the rags in ley, and afterwards bleaching them
orine, has rendered foreign rags fit for making fine paper, and, indeed, in some
preferable for that purpose, by their affording greater strength of texture com-
th equal whiteness of colour.

is considerable variety in the appearance of rags from different ports; but, in
those from the north of Europe are darker and stronger than those from the
anean ports. The latter are chiefly the remains of outer garments, and have
whitened by exposure to the sun and air; but since the improvements in bleach-
does not much enhance their value in the British market. The rags shipped
este are chiefly collected in Hungary. It is only within these few years that
brought rags from this port, which now furnishes us with considerable sup-
ost part of the rags collected in the Tuscan states, to the extent of 10,000 or
ags a year, goes to America.

are, at an average, about — Hamburgh and Bremen, linen 22s. per ton, woollen 26s.;
s. ; Ancona and Leghorn, 45s. to 50s.; Trieste and Sicily, 55s. to 60s. Linen rags are almost,
and assorted previously to their shipment from the foreign port. Their distinguishing marks
per cwt. in the London market, January, 1832, were as follow; viz.

	Rostock.	Hamburgh.	Bremen.	Trieste.
S P F F	38s.	33s.	32s.	31s. to 36s.
S P F	32s.	27s. 6d.	26s.	27s. to 30s.
F F	28s.	23s.	22s.	22s. to 25s. 6d.
F X or F M	17s.	14s. 6d.	13s.	17s.
F B	16s.	13s. 6d.	12s.	

-ROAD, TRAM or WAGON ROAD, a species of road having tracks
formed of iron, stone, or other solid material, on which the wheels of
ages passing along it run. The object in constructing such roads is, by
ng the friction, to make a less amount of power adequate either to impel
e with a greater velocity, or to urge forward a greater load.

ction of Rail-roads. — The friction on a perfectly level rail-road, properly con-
is estimated to amount to from $\frac{1}{10}$th to $\frac{1}{4}$th only of the friction on an ordinary
; so that, supposing the same force to be applied in both cases, it would move a
m 10 to 7 times as great on the former as on the latter. But if there be a very
ascent, such as 1 foot in 50, which in an ordinary road would hardly be perceived,
crease of power on the rail-road is required to overcome the resistance that is
ioned. The reason is, that the ordinary load on a *level* rail-road is about *seven*
reat as on a common turnpike road; so that when the force of gravity is brought
tion by an ascending plane, its opposing power, being *proportioned to the load,*
mes as great as on a common road. Hence the vast importance of having
either level, or as nearly so as possible.

o of great importance that rail-roads should be straight, or, at least, free from
t curves. Carriages being kept on the road by *flanges* on the wheels, it is ob-
t where the curves are quick, the friction on the sides of the rails, and con-
tardation, must be very great. In the Manchester and Liverpool rail-road,
form segments of a circle which, if extended, would embrace a circumference
s.

-roads, the kind now generally used, are of two descriptions. The *flat rail* or
consists of cast-iron plates about 3 feet long, 4 inches broad, and $\frac{1}{2}$ inch or
k, with a flaunch, or turned up edge, on the inside, to guide the wheels of the
The plates rest at each end on stone *sleepers* of 3 or 4 cwt. sunk into the
they are joined to each other so as to form a continuous horizontal pathway.
of course, double; and the distance between the opposite rails is from 3 to
cording to the breadth of the carriage or wagon to be employed. The *edge*
is found to be superior to the tram rail, is made either of wrought or cast
e latter be used, the rails are about 3 feet long, 3 or 4 inches broad, and
2 inches thick, being joined at the ends by cast metal sockets attached to the
The upper edge of the rail is generally made with a convex surface, to which
of the carriage is attached by a groove made somewhat wider. When wrought
, which is in many respects preferable, the bars are made of a smaller size, of
ape, and from 12 to 18 feet long; but they are supported by sleepers, at the
every 3 feet. In the Liverpool rail-road the bars are 15 feet long, and
s. per lineal yard. The wagons in common use run upon 4 wheels of from
in diameter. Rail-roads are either made double, one for going and one for
or they are made with *sidings* where the carriages may pass each other. —(See

the able and original Essays on Rail-roads by Charles Maclaren, Esq., in the Sc
for 1824, Nos. 511, 512. and 514. See also Mr. Booth's pamphlet on the Liv
and Manchester Rail-road.)

Speed of Carriages on Rail-roads, &c. — The effect of rail-roads in diminishing
is familiar to every one; and they have long been used in various places of this an
countries, particularly in the vicinity of mines, for facilitating the transport of
loads. But it is only since the application of locomotive engines as a moving
that they have begun to attract the public attention, and to be regarded as of the
national importance. These engines were first brought into use on the Darlingt
Stockton rail-road, opened on the 27th of December, 1825. But the rail-ro
tween Liverpool and Manchester is by far the greatest undertaking of this sort th
hitherto been completed. This splendid work, which is executed in the most ap
manner, cost between 800,000l. and 900,000l.; and as far as speed is concern
completely verified, and, indeed, far surpassed, the most sanguine anticipations.
road has the advantage of being nearly level; for, with the exception of a short s,
Rainhill, where it is inclined at the rate of 1 foot in 96, there is no greater incl
than in the ratio of 1 foot in 880. The length of the rail-road is 31 miles; an
usual to perform this journey in handsome carriages attached to the locomotive er
in an hour and a half, and sometimes less! So wonderful a result has gone far to
space and time out of the calculations of the traveller : it has brought, in so far, a
as respects the facility of passing from the one to the other, Liverpool as near to
chester as the western part of London is to the eastern part!

The extraordinary speed of carriages on rail-roads depends on the fact, that the
which on a perfectly level rail-road is the only resistance to be overcome, is *the s*
all velocities; so that, abstracting from the resistance of the air, which is so tri
not to require to be taken into account, we have merely, in order to double or tre
velocity, to double or treble the power. But in vessels at sea, or in canals, whic
to make their way through a comparatively dense medium, the resistance to be ov
increases as the *square of the velocity;* so that to double the speed, the power m
multiplied by 4, and to treble it, it must be multiplied by 9, and so on.

Comparative Advantages of Rail-roads and Canals. — Astonishing, however,
the results of the performances on the Manchester and Liverpool rail-road, we
much whether there be many more situations in the kingdom where it would be p
to establish one. That carriages with passengers may be safely impelled along
fectly level rail-road at a speed of 20 or 30 miles an hour, is a fact that is now
experimentally; but before deciding as to the expediency of opening such a n
communication between any two places, it is necessary to look carefully into
pense attending the formation of a rail-road with a suitable establishment of ca
at the expense of keeping it and them in repair, and at the probable returns. T
lay, judging from what has taken place between Liverpool and Manchester,
enormous; the wear and tear of the engines, which is great under all circumstal
increased in an extraordinary degree with every considerable increase of speed.
not, therefore, consider the success that has hitherto attended the Liverpool an
chester rail-road as at all warranting the construction of similar roads in mos
places. The great size of these two towns, and still more their intimate con
— Liverpool being, in fact, the port of Manchester and of the entire cotton dist
occasions a very great intercourse between them : the number of passengers
quantity of goods that are always in the course of being conveyed from the on
other, is far greater than between any two equally distant places in the empir
rail-road had not succeeded in such a situation, it would have been madness to
the formation of one, at least as a mercantile speculation, any where else.

No general estimate can be formed of the comparative cost of canals and rai
as it must, in every given instance, depend on special circumstances. It is, h
certain, that the cost of rail-roads, and particularly of keeping up the locomotive
is far greater than it was supposed it would be a short time since. It is reasona
deed, inasmuch as these engines are only in their infancy, to suppose that they
gradually improved, and that ultimately their expense will be materially reduc
at present it is a heavy drawback from the other advantages of rail-roads.

In as far as respects the conveyance of heavy goods, we believe that, even
Manchester and Liverpool, canals are generally preferred. It is not very mate
ther a ton of lime, or coal, or of manure, be moved with a velocity of 3 or 10
hour; at least, the advantage of superior speed would, in such a case, be e
overbalanced by a small additional charge.

The wonderful performances of the engines between Liverpool and Mancheste
in the first instance, every one with astonishment, and led to the most extravag
culations. It was supposed that the whole country would be forthwith inters

ads ; that locomotive engines would be as common as stage coaches ; and that
ly way in which the canal proprietors could escape ruin, would be by converting
into rail-roads ! Soberer and sounder views are now entertained. The price of
stock has recovered from the depression which it suffered in 1826. And it seems
generally admitted, that rail-roads between distant places, at least where a canal
lready been constructed, must depend for returns chiefly on the conveyance of
gers and light goods; and that it would not be prudent to undertake their con-
on, except between places that have a very extensive intercourse together.

m Carriages on common Roads. — The late committee of the House of Com-
have collected a good deal of evidence as to the probability of advantageously
locomotive engines, or steam carriages, on common roads. Most of the witnesses
o be very sanguine in their expectations ; nor, after what has been effected, can
anticipations be deemed unreasonable. Mr. Farey, a very eminent practical en-
, declares that " what has been done proves to his satisfaction the practicability of
ing stage coaches by steam on good common roads, in tolerably level parts of the
y, without horses, at a speed of 8 or 10 miles an hour." Mr. Farey further states,
e believes " that steam coaches will, very soon after their first establishment, be *run
third of the cost of the present stage coaches.*" We suspect that the latter part of
atement is a good deal more problematical than the first ; but since there is nothing
than conjecture on which to found an opinion, it would be useless to indulge in
speculations.

ISINS (Fr. *Raisins secs, ou passés;* Ger. *Rosinen;* It. *Uve passe;* Por
; Rus. *Issum;* Sp. *Pasas*), the dried fruit of the vine. They are pro-
from various species of vines ; deriving their names partly from the place
they grow, as Smyrnas, Valencias, &c.; and partly from the species of
of which they are made, as muscatels, blooms, sultanas, &c. Their quality
s, however, to depend more on the method of their cure than on any thing
The finest raisins are cured in two methods ; — either by cutting the stalk of
nches half through, when the grapes are nearly ripe, and leaving them sus-
d on the vine till the watery part be evaporated, and the sun dries and
s them ; or by gathering the grapes when they are fully ripe, and dipping
n a ley made of the ashes of the burnt tendrils ; after which they are exposed
sun to dry. Those cured in the first way are most esteemed, and are de-
ated raisins of the sun. The inferior sorts are very often dried in ovens.—
son's Dispensatory.)

s are imported in casks, barrels, boxes, and jars. The finest come in jars and quarter boxes
; about 25 lbs. Some of the inferior sorts are brought to us in mats.
,750 cwt. of raisins imported in 1829, 81,370 came from Turkey, 58,660 from Turkey, and 5,273 from
Malaga raisins are in the highest estimation. The muscatels from Malaga fetch nearly twice the
any other description of raisins. The Smyrna black is the cheapest variety, and may average
to 35s. a cwt., duty included ; muscatels vary from 80s. to 130s., duty included. But the price de-
uch on the season, and the period of the year.
ty on raisins varies, according to the species, from 21s. to 42s. 6d. a cwt. ; that is, it varies from
per cent. on the cheapest sorts, to from 50 to 35 per cent. on the dearest ! It is impossible too severely
mn such exorbitant duties. Raisins are, at present, a luxury that can be enjoyed only by the
were the duty reduced, as it ought to be, to 5s. a cwt. on the cheapest sorts, and 10s. or 12s. on
est, we are well assured that they would be very largely consumed by the middle classes ; and
would not unfrequently be used even by the lower. Nothing but the magnitude of the duties
them from becoming of very considerable importance as an article of food. And it is really
nstrous, that the public should be debarred from the use of a desirable article, on the stale and
etence of its being necessary, in order to keep up the revenue, that it should be loaded with an
e duty. We admit the importance of keeping up the revenue ; but so far from exorbitant duties
ich an effect, they contribute more than any thing else to its reduction. They either limit tho
tion of the articles on which they are laid to the very richest classes, or they cause them to bo
nely supplied ; reducing the revenue as well as the consumption far below the level to which it
ain were the duties moderate. But it is needless to reason speculatively on such a point. Have
een the revenue derived from spirits increased, by reducing the duty from 5s. 6d. a gallon to
nd the revenue derived from coffee trebled, by reducing the duty from 1s. 7d. per lb. to 6d. ?
either of these articles was more grossly overtaxed than raisins, have we not every reason to ex-
a like effect would be produced by an adequate reduction of the duties by which they are
?
ve of raisins, a considerable quantity of undried grapes is annually imported from Spain and
in jars, packed in sawdust. The duty on these grapes, which is 20 per cent. *ad valorem*, produced,
,641*l*.
, the produce of Europe, may not be imported for home consumption, except in British ships,
s of the country of which they are the produce, or from which they are imported. — (6 *Geo.* 4.
)
ement of duty is made on account of any damage received by raisins. — (6 *Geo.* 4. c. 107. § 30.)
imported in foreign ships, deemed *alien* goods, and pay town and port dues accordingly.—
c. 111. § 26.)

E, a biennial plant of the turnip kind (*Brassica Napus*, Lin.), but with a
usiform root scarcely fit to be eaten. It is indigenous, flowers in May, and
ts seeds in July. It is cultivated in many parts of England, particularly in

Lincoln and Cambridge; partly on account of its seed, which is crushed for
and partly for its leaves as food for sheep. The culture of rape for seed has b
much objected to by some, on account of its supposed great exhaustion of the la
but Mr. Loudon says that, where the soil and preparation are suitable; the after-
ture properly attended to; and the straw and offal, instead of being burnt, as is
common practice, converted to the purposes of feeding and littering cattle; it n
in many instances, be the most proper and advantageous crop that can be
ployed by the farmer. The produce, when the plant succeeds well, and the sea
is favourable for securing the seed, amounts to from 40 to 50 bushels an a
The seed is sold by the last of 10 quarters; and is crushed in m:lls constru
for that purpose. — (*Loudon's Ency. of Agriculture.*)

In addition to the rape seed raised at home, we import considerable quanti
principally from Denmark. In 1829, our imports amounted to 378,304 bushels
which 266,596 were from Denmark, 83,522 from Germany, 12,489 from Fra
7,544 from the Netherlands, 6,931 from the East Indies, and 1,222 from Pru
The price of English rape seed is at present (November, 1831) from 26*l.* to 27*l.*
last; the duty on foreign rape seed is 10*s.* a last.

Rape seed, the produce of Europe, may not be imported for home consumption, except in British s
or in ships of the country of which it is the produce, or from which it is imported. — (6 *Geo.* 4. c.
7 & 8 *Geo.* 4. c. 56.)

RAPE CAKE, is the adhering masses of the husks of rape seed, after the oil has been expressed. The
reduced to powder by a malt mill or other machine; and are used either as a top dressing for cro
different kinds, or are drilled along with turnip seed. Rape cakes are at present (November, 1831) v
from 5*l.* to 6*l.* a ton; and rape oil from 1*l.* 15*s.* to 1*l.* 17*s.* a cwt. Last year we imported about 330,000
of rape and other oil cake. It is charged with a duty of 2*d.* a cwt., last year's produce of v
amounted to 2,731*l.*

RATTANS, OR CANES, the long slender shoots of a prickly bush (*Cala*
Rotang, Lin.), one of the most useful plants of the Malay peninsula, and
Eastern islands. They are exported to Bengal, to Europe, and above a
China, where they are consumed in immense quantities. For cane work
should be chosen long, of a bright pale yellow colour, well glazed, and of a s
size, not brittle or subject to break. They are purchased by the bundle, w
ought to contain 100 rattans, having their ends bent together, and tied ir
middle. In China they are sold by the picul, which contains from 9 to 12 bun
Such as are black or dark coloured, snap short, or from which the glazing flie
on their being bent, should be rejected. When stowed as dunnage, the
generally allowed to pass free of freight. The imports into this country are
considerable.   In 1827, the number imported was 3,158,641; and in 1
6,891,321. — (*Milburn's Orient. Com.,* &c.)

"The rattan," says Mr. Crawfurd, "is the spontaneous product of all the forests of the Archipe
but exists in great perfection in those of the islands of Borneo, Sumatra, and of the Malayan peni
The finest are produced in the country of the *Bataks* of Sumatra. The wood-cutter, who is incli
deal in this article, proceeds into the forest without any other instrument than his *parang* or cleave
cuts as much as he is able to carry away. The mode of performing the operation is this;—He m
notch in the tree at the root of which the rattan is growing, and cutting the latter, strips off a sma
tion of the outer bark, and inserts the part that is peeled into the notch. The rattan now being
through as long as it continues of an equal size, is by this operation neatly and readily freed fr
epidermis. When the wood-cutter has obtained by this means from 300 to 400 rattans,—being as m
an individual can conveniently carry in their moist and undried state,—he sits down, and ties them
bundles of 100, each rattan being doubled before being thus tied up. After drying, they are fit f
market without further preparation. From this account of the small labour expended in bringing
to market, they can be sold at a very cheap rate. The Chinese junks obtain them in Borneo at tl
rate of 5 Spanish dollars per hundred bundles, or 5 cents for each 100 rattans, or 27 for a penny. The r
always vend them by tale; but the resident European merchants, and the Chinese, by weight, count
piculs. According to their quantity, and the relative state of supply and demand, the European
chants dispose of them at from 1½ to 2½ dollars the picul. In China, the price is usually about 3½ e
per picul, or 75 per cent. above the average prime cost. In Bengal they are sold by tale, each t
of about 100 rattans bringing about 20½*d.*"— (*Indian Archipelago,* vol. iii. p. 423.)

REAL, in the Spanish monetary system, is of two sorts; viz., a re
plate, and a *real vellon.* The former is a silver coin, varying in value
about 6½*d.* to 5*d.* — (See COINS.) A real vellon is a money of account, v
about 2½*d.*

REAM, a quantity of paper. The ream of writing paper consists of 20 q
each of 24 sheets; but the ream of printing paper, or, as it is sometimes c
the *printer's ream,* extends to 21½ quires, or 516 sheets. Two reams of
make a *bundle.*

RECEIPT, is an acknowledgment in writing of having received a su
money, or other valuable consideration. It is a voucher either of an oblig
or debt discharged, or of one incurred.

eo. 3. c. 55. enacts, that every note, memorandum, whatever, given to any person on the payment of nowledging such payment, on whatever account it ether signed or not, shall be considered a receipt, a stamp duty.

y person who shall write, or cause to be written, any 1oney on unstamped paper, (except in certain ex- hereafter enumerated,) or on a lower stamp than ne, shall forfeit 10l. if for a sum under 100l.; if

ceipts for less than actually paid, writing off sums, idulent contrivances, penalty 50l.; but receipts may if brought *within fourteen days after date*, on pay- nalty of 5l. over and above the duty; and if brought alendar month, on payment of a penalty of 10l.

n refusing to give a receipt upon demand, or to pay of the stamp, is liable to a penalty of 10l.

cale of Stamp Duties per 55 Geo. 3. c. 184.

		L. s. d.
scharge, given for or upon the payment of		
iounting to 2l. and under 5l.		0 0 2
i under 10l.		0 0 3
— 20l.		0 0 6
— 50l.		0 1 0
— 100l.		0 1 6
— 200l.		0 2 6
— 300l.		0 4 0
— 500l.		0 5 0
— 1,000l.		0 7 6
ipwards		0 10 0
any sum shall be therein expressed to be a full of all demands		0 10 0

e, memorandum, or writing whatsoever, given to any person for or upon the payment of money, whereby any sum of money, debt, or demand, or any part of any debt or demand, therein specified, and amounting to 2l. or upwards, shall be expressed to have been paid, settled, balanced, or otherwise dis- charged or satisfied, or which shall import or signify any such acknowledgment, and whether the same shall or shall not be signed with the name of any person, shall be deemed to be a receipt for a sum of money of equal amount with the sum so expressed to have been paid, settled, balanced, or otherwise discharged or satisfied, and shall be charged with a duty ac- cordingly.

Exemptions. — Receipts exempted from stamp duty by any act relating to the assessed taxes. Receipts given by the Treasurer of the Navy. Receipts on account of the pay of the army or ordnance. Receipts by any officer, seaman, marine, or soldier, or their representatives. Receipts for the consideration money for the purchase of any parliamentary stocks or funds, and for any dividend paid on any share of the said stocks or funds. Re- ceipts on exchequer bills. Receipts given for money deposited in the Bank of England, or in the hands of any banker, to be accounted for on demand; provided the same be not expressed to be received of, or by the hands of, any other than the person to whom the same is to be accounted for. Receipts written upon promissory notes, bills of exchange, drafts, or orders for the payment of money. Receipts given upon bills or notes of the Bank of England. Letters by the general post acknowledging the safe arrival of any bills of exchange, promissory notes, or other securities. Receipts indorsed upon any bond, mortgage, or other security, or any conveyance whatever. Releases or discharges for money by deeds duly stamped. Receipts or dis- charges for drawbacks or bounties. Receipts or discharges for the return of duties of customs. Receipts indorsed upon navy bills. Receipts upon victualling and transport bills. Receipts given solely for the duty on insurances against fire.

In 1830, the nett produce of the receipt duty was as follows : —Great Britain, 205,640l. 16s. 9¼d.; Ireland, 18,019l. 9s. 5¼d.

ISTRY, in commercial navigation, the registration or enrolment of ships ustom-house, so as to entitle them to be classed among, and to enjoy the s of, British built ships.

gistry of ships appears to have been first introduced into this country by the on Act (12 Cha. 2. c. 18. anno 1660). Several provisions were made with o it by the 7 & 8 Will. 3. c. 22.; and the whole was reduced into a system Geo. 3. c. 19.

be laid down in general, that a vessel, in order to be admitted to registry, and ntly to enjoy the privileges and advantages that exclusively belong to a British t be the property of his Majesty's subjects in the United Kingdom or some of dencies; and that it must have been built in the said United Kingdom, &c., prize vessel legally condemned, or a vessel legally condemned for a breach of laws.

eat, and, perhaps, the only original object of the registration of ships, was to the exclusion of foreign ships from those departments in which they were pro- om engaging by the navigation laws, by affording a ready means of distinguish- as were really British. It has also been considered advantageous to indivi- preventing the fraudulent assignment of property in ships; but Lord Ten- s observed, in reference to this supposed advantage, that "the instances in and honest transactions are rendered unavailable through a negligent want of e with the forms directed by these and other statutes requiring a public register ances, make the expediency of all such regulations, considered with reference benefit only, a matter of question and controversy." — (*Law of Shipping,* .)

sting regulations as to the registry of ships, are embodied in the act 6 Geo. 4. which, on account of its importance, is subjoined nearly entire.

ACT 6 GEO. 4. c. 110. FOR REGISTERING OF BRITISH VESSELS.

ement of Act. — From 5th of January, 1826, except where any other commencement is herein- ularly directed.

to enjoy Privileges until registered. — No vessel shall be entitled to any of the privileges or of a British registered ship, until the persons claiming property therein have caused the same ered, in manner herein-after mentioned, and have obtained a certificate of such registry from authorised to make such registry, and grant such certificate, as herein-after directed; the form rtificate shall be as follows, viz.: —

ertify, that in pursuance of an act passed in the 1e reign of King George the Fourth, intituled, *insert the title of this act,* the names, occupation, *of the subscribing owners*], having taken and oath required by this act, and having sworn y] together with [*names, occupations, and resi- subscribing owners*] [is or are] sole owner or proportions specified on the back hereof, of the called the [*ship's name*] of [*place to which the ,* which is of the burthen of [*number of tons*], naster's name*] is master, and that the said ship *when and where built, or condemned as prize,* dder's certificate, judge's certificate, or certificate then delivered up to be cancelled*], and [*name of surveying officer*] having certified to us that vessel has [*number*] decks and [*number*] masts, from the fore part of the main stem to the after part of the stern post aloft is [*number of feet and inches*], her breadth at the broadest part [*stating whether that be above or below the main wales*] is [*number of feet and inches*], her [*height between decks, if more than one deck, or depth in the hold, if only one deck*] is [*number of feet and inches*], that she is [*how rigged*] rigged with a [*standing or running*] bowsprit, is [*description of stern*] sterned [*carvel or clinker*] built, has [*whe- ther any or no*] gallery, and [*kind of head, if any*] head; and the said subscribing owners have consented and agreed to the above description, and having caused sufficient security to be given, as is required by the said act, the said ship or vessel called the [*name*] has been duly registered at the port [*name of port*]. Certified under our hands at the Custom-house, in the said port of [*name of port*], this [*date*] day of [*name of month*], in the year [*words at length*].

[*Signed*]   Collector.
[*Signed*]   Comptroller."

And on the back of such certificate of registry there shall be an account of the parts or shares each of the owners mentioned in such certificate, in the form following. — § 2.

" Names of the several owners within mentioned.	Number of sixty-fourth shares held by each owner.
[Name]	*Thirty-two.*
[Name]	*Sixteen.*
[Name]	*Eight.*
[Name]	*Eight.*

[Signed]	Collector.
[Signed]	Comptroller."

Persons authorised to make Registry and grant Certificates. — The persons authorised to ma registry and grant such certificates shall be the collector and comptroller of customs in any par United Kingdom, and in the Isle of Man, in respect of ships or vessels to be there registered ; principal officers of customs in the island of Guernsey, or Jersey, together with the governor, lieu governor, or commander-in-chief of those islands, in respect of ships or vessels to be there reg and the collector and comptroller of customs of any port in the colonies, plantations, islands, ar tories in Asia, Africa, and America, together with the governor, lieutenant-governor, or comma chief of such territories, in respect of ships or vessels to be there registered ; and the collector of c any port in the territories under the government of the East India Company, and within the limi charter of the said Company, payable to the said Company, or any other person of the rank c merchant, or of six years' standing in the said service, being appointed to act in the execution of by any of the governments of the said Company in India, in any ports in which there shall be no c and comptroller of customs, in respect of ships or vessels to be there registered (see *infrà* *) ; governor, lieutenant-governor, or commander-in-chief of Malta, Gibraltar, Heligoland, and Cape Hope, in respect of ships or vessels to be there registered : Provided always, that no ship or ves be registered at Malta, Gibraltar, or Heligoland, except such as are wholly of the built of thos and such ships or vessels shall not be registered elsewhere (see *infrà*†) ; and such ships or v registered shall not be entitled to the privileges of British ships in any trade between the said Kingdom and any of the colonies, plantations, islands, or territories in America : Provided a wherever by this act it is directed that any act shall be done by, to, or with any collector and con of customs, the same may be done by, to, or with the principal officers of customs in the islands of sey or Jersey, together with the governor, lieutenant-governor, or commander-in-chief of those and also by, to, or with such collector or other person in India in the service of the East India Cc and also by, to, or with the governor, lieutenant-governor, or commander-in-chief of Malta, G Heligoland, or Cape of Good Hope : Provided also, that wherever in and by this act it is direc any thing shall be done by, to, or with the commissioners of customs, the same shall or may or performed by, to, or with the commissioners in England, Ireland, or Scotland, and also by, to, the governor, lieutenant governor, or commander-in-chief of any place where any ship or vesse registered under this act, so far as such thing can be applicable to the registering of any ship or such place. — § 3.

Ships exercising Privileges before Registry to be forfeited. — In case any ship or vessel, not du tered, and not having obtained a certificate of registry, shall exercise any of the privileges of a ship, the same shall be subject to forfeiture, and also all the guns, furniture, ammunition, tac apparel, and shall be seized by any officer of customs : Provided always, that nothing in this extend to affect the privileges of any ship or vessel registered prior to the 31st of December, 18 virtue of any act in force at the time of the commencement of this act, until such time as such vessels shall be required by this act to be registered *de novo.* — § 4.

What Ships are entitled to be registered. — No ship or vessel shall be registered, or, having be tered, shall be deemed to be duly registered by virtue of this act, except such as are wholly of the the said United Kingdom, or of the Isle of Man, or cf the islands of Guernsey or Jersey, or of sor colonies, plantations, islands, or territories in Asia, Africa, or America ; or of Malta, Gibraltar, goland, which belonged to his Majesty at the time of the building of such ships or vessels ; or st or vessels as shall have been condemned in any court of admiralty as prize of war, or such ships as shall have been condemned in any competent court as aforesaid, for the breach of the laws fo vention of the slave trade, and which shall wholly belong and continue wholly to belong to subj entitled to be owners of ships or vessels registered by this act. — § 5.

Foreign Repairs not to exceed 20s. per Ton. — No ship or vessel shall continue to enjoy the priv a British ship after the same shall have been repaired in a foreign country, if such repairs sha 20s. for every ton of the burthen, unless such repair shall have been necessary by reason of extra damage sustained during her absence from his Majesty's dominions, to enable her to perform th in which she shall have been engaged, and to return to some port of the said dominions ; and v any ship or vessel which has been so repaired in a foreign country shall arrive at any port as registered ship or vessel, the master shall, upon the first entry thereof, report upon oath to the and comptroller of customs that such ship has been so repaired, under penalty of 20s. for every t burthen, according to the admeasurement thereof ; and if it shall be proved to the satisfacti commissioners of customs, that such ship was seaworthy at the time when she last departed, an greater quantity of such repairs have been done to the said vessel than was necessary, it shall f for the said commissioners, upon full consideration of all the circumstances, to direct the colle comptroller to certify on the certificate of the registry, that it has been proved to the satisfacti commissioners of customs, that the privileges of the said ship have not been forfeited, notwithsta repairs done in a foreign country. — § 6.

On Combination of Workmen. — And as it has recently happened that the owners of British sh been unable to effect the necessary repairs to their vessels in British ports, by reason of combi workmen ; it is enacted, that for two years from and after the passing of this act, when and as c shall appear expedient to the Lords of his Majesty's Privy Council, it shall be lawful for them to is order in behalf of the master or owners of any such ship, permitting the same to proceed to son port, to be named in such order, and there to be repaired to such extent as shall be necessa voyage in which such ship is engaged. — § 7.

Power to Privy Council to permit Vessels to proceed on their Voyage with a less Number of B *men than required.* — And as by the law of navigation British ships cannot proceed to sea unle navigated by a crew, of which three fourths at least are British seamen ; it is enacted, that for from and after the passing of this act, when and as often as it shall appear expedient to the Lo Privy Council, it shall be lawful for them to issue their order in behalf of the master or owners of

---

The 10 Geo. 4. c. 43. authorises any person appointed to act as collector of duties in any British possession within the limits of the East India Company's charter, not under the Company's government, and where a Custom-house is not established, together with the governor, lieutenant-governor, or commander-in-chief of any such possession, to register British vessels, and grant certificates thereof, under the regulations of the above act. — s. 12.

So much of the act 6 Geo. 4. c. 110. as requires the governor, lieutenant-governor, or commander-in-chief in the colonies, &c. in Asia, Africa, and America, where collectors and comptrollers of customs have been appointed by the Treasury, and

are under the management of the commissioners of be a party to the registry of British vessels, and t certificates thereof, is repealed. — s. 13.
† The act 7 & 8 Geo. 4. c. 56. repeals so much 6 Geo. 4. c. 110. as prohibits the registering, at M raltar, of any vessels, except such as are of the b places : but it declares that no ship or vessel r Malta or Gibraltar shall afterwards be registered and that they shall not be entitled to the privile tages of British ships in the trade between the U dom and the British possessions in America. — s.

ermitting such ship to proceed upon her voyage with a less number of British seamen than is
l by the law of navigation; and every ship which shall be navigated with the number of British
required in such order, shall be deemed to be duly navigated. — § 8.

declared unseaworthy. — If any ship or vessel registered, shall be deemed or declared to be
d or unseaworthy, and incapable of being recovered or repaired, and shall for such reasons be sold
r of any competent court for the benefit of the owners, the same shall be deemed to be a ship lost
en up, and shall never again be entitled to the privileges of a British built ship for any purposes of
r navigation. — § 9.

h Ships captured. — No British ship or vessel captured by and become prize to an enemy, or sold
gners, shall again be entitled to the privileges of a British ship; but nothing contained in this act
tend to prevent the registering of any ship which shall be condemned in any court of admiralty as
war, or in any competent court, for breach of laws made for the prevention of the slave trade. —

shall be registered at the Port to which they belong. — No such registry shall hereafter be made, or
te thereof granted, by any persons herein-before authorised, in any other port than the port to
uch ships shall properly belong, except as to ships condemned as prizes in Guernsey, Jersey, or
hich ships shall be registered in manner herein-after directed; but every registry and certificate
in any port to which such ship does not properly belong, shall be utterly void, unless the officers
d shall be specially authorised to make such registry and grant such certificate in any other port,
rder in writing under the hands of the commissioners of customs, if they shall see fit; and at every
ere registry shall be made in pursuance of this act, a book shall be kept by the collector and comp-
n which all the particulars contained in the form of the certificate of the registry herein-before
to be used, shall be duly entered; and every registry shall be numbered in progression, beginning
gressive numeration at the commencement of each year; and such collector and comptroller shall
h, or within one month at the farthest, transmit to the commissioners of customs a true and exact
gether with the number of every certificate so granted. — § 11.

to which Vessels shall be deemed to belong. — Every ship or vessel shall be deemed to belong to
rt at or near to which some or one of the owners, who shall take and subscribe the oath required
ct before registry be made, shall reside; and whenever such owners shall have transferred all
res, the same shall be registered *de novo* before such ship shall sail from the port to which she shall
ong, or from any other port in the same part of the United Kingdom, or the same colony, plant-
and, or territory: Provided that if the owners cannot in sufficient time comply with this act, so
stry may be made before it shall be necessary for such ship to sail upon another voyage, it shall
l for the collector and comptroller of the port to certify upon the back of the existing certificate
ry, that the same is to remain in force for the voyage upon which the said ship is about to sail;
ny ship shall be built in any of the colonies, plantations, islands, or territories in Asia, Africa, or
, to his Majesty belonging, for owners residing in the United Kingdom, it shall be lawful for such
roceed to any part of the United Kingdom, whether by a direct or circuitous voyage, and there
t a cargo before registry shall have been made; provided the master of such vessel, or the agent for
er or owners, shall have produced to the collector and comptroller of the port at or near to which
was built, or from which she shall be cleared for her voyage, the certificate of the builder, and
e made oath before such collector and comptroller, of the names and descriptions of the principal
and that she is the identical ship mentioned in such certificate of the builder, and that no
, to the best of his knowledge, has any interest therein; whereupon the collector and comp-
all cause such ship to be surveyed and measured, and shall give the master a certificate under
ds and seals, purporting to be under the authority of this act, and stating when and where, and
, such ship was built, the description, tonnage, and other particulars required on registry, and
ge for which such ship is cleared; and such certificate shall, for such voyage, have all the force
ficate of registry; and such collector and comptroller shall transmit a copy of such certificate to
issioners of customs. — § 12.

s residing in foreign Countries may not be Owners. — No person who has taken the oath of alle-
r any foreign state, except under the terms of some capitulation, unless he shall afterwards
denizen or naturalised subject; nor any person usually residing in any country not under the
of his Majesty, unless he be a member of some British factory, or agent for or partner in any
rying on trade in Great Britain or Ireland, shall be entitled to be the owner, in whole or in part,
r indirectly, of any ship required to be registered by this act. — § 13.

be taken by subscribing Owners previous to Registry. — No registry shall be made, or certificate
ntil the following oath be taken and subscribed before the persons herein-before authorised to
h registry, by the owner of such ship, if such ship belongs to one person only; or in case there
wo joint owners, then by both of such joint owners, if both shall be resident within twenty miles
t, or by one of such owners, if one or both shall be resident at a greater distance from such port;
umber of such owners shall exceed two, then by the greater part of the number, if the greater
hall be resident within twenty miles of such port, not in any case exceeding three of such
nless a greater number shall be desirous to join in taking and subscribing the oath; or by one
wners, if all, or all except one, shall be resident at a greater distance: —

of [*place of residence and occupation*] do make
the ship or vessel [*name*] of [*port or place*] whereof
me] is at present master, being [*kind of built, bur-
ra, as described in the certificate of the surveying
[*when and where built, or if prize or forfeited, cap-
demnation as such*], and that I the said *A. B.* [*and
ers' names and occupations, if any, and where they
reside, videlicet, town, place, or parish, and county,
of and resident in any factory in foreign parts, or
ign town or city, being an agent for or partner in
copartnership actually carrying on trade in Great
reland, the name of such factory, foreign town, or
names of such house or copartnership*] am [*or are*]
or owners] of the said vessel, and that no other
ersons whatever hath or have any right, title, in-
, or property therein or thereto; and that I the said
he said other owners, if any*] am [*or are*] truly and

bona fide a subject [*or subjects*] of Great Britain; and that I
the said *A. B.* have not [*nor have any of the other owners, to
the best of my knowledge and belief*] taken the oath of allegiance
to any foreign state whatever [*except under the terms of some
capitulation, describing the particulars thereof*], or that since
my taking [*or his or their taking*] the oath of allegiance to
[*naming the foreign states respectively to which he or any of the
said owners shall have taken the same*] I have [*or he or they
hath or have*] become a denizen [*or denizens, or naturalised
subject or subjects, as the case may be*] of the United Kingdom
of Great Britain and Ireland, by his Majesty's letters patent,
or by an act of parliament [*naming the times when such letters
of denization have been granted respectively, or the years in which
such act or acts for naturalisation have passed respectively*], and
that no foreigner, directly or indirectly, hath any share or part
interest in the said ship or vessel."

that if it shall become necessary to register any ship belonging to any corporate body, the
oath, in lieu of the above oath, shall be taken and subscribed by the secretary or other proper
§ 14.

ecretary or officer of [*name of company or corpora-
ce oath, that the ship or vessel [*name*] of [*port]
aster's name*] is at present master, being [*kind of
, et cætera, as described in the certificate of the sur-

veying officer*] was [*when and where built, or if prize or forfeited, capture or condemnation as such*] and that the same
doth wholly and truly belong to [*name of company or corporation*]."

s to Oath in case the required Number of Owners do not attend. — In case the required number
wners shall not personally attend, then such owner or owners as shall personally attend, and
subscribe the oath, shall further make oath, that the part owner or part cwners of such ship
at is or are not resident within twenty miles of such port, and hath or have not, to the best of
ir knowledge, wilfully absented himself or themselves in order to avoid taking the oath, or is
ented by illness from attending. — § 15.

3 M 4

Vessels to be surveyed previous to Registry. — Previous to the registering, or granting of any certi of registry, some person or persons, appointed by the commissioners of customs, (taking to his or assistance, if he or they judge it necessary, one or more person or persons skilled in the building admeasurement of ships,) shall go on board, and shall strictly examine and admeasure every such sl to every particular contained in the form of the certificate before directed, in the presence of the m or any other person appointed on the part of the owners, or in his absence by the said master; and deliver a true account in writing of all such particulars as are specified in the form of the certificate recited, to the collector and comptroller authorised to make such registry and grant such certificate the said master or other person is to sign his name also to the certificate of such surviving officer, pro such master or person shall agree to the particulars set forth therein. — § 16.

Sections 17, 18, 19, and 20. relate to the mode of ascertaining the tonnage. — (See TONNAGE.)

Bond to be given at the Time of Registry. — At the time of obtaining the certificate of registry, suff security shall be given to his Majesty, by the master and such of the owners as shall perse attend, as before required, to be approved of and taken by the persons authorised to make registry, penalties following; that is to say, if such ship shall be a decked vessel, or be above the burthen of I and not exceeding 50 tons, in the penalty of 100*l.*; if exceeding the burthen of 50 tons and not exce 100 tons, in the penalty of 300*l.*; if exceeding the burthen of 100 tons and not exceeding 200 tons, penalty of 500*l.*; if exceeding the burthen of 200 tons and not exceeding 300 tons, in the penalty of and if exceeding the burthen of 300 tons, in the penalty of 1,000*l.*; and the condition of every such shall be, that such certificate shall not be sold, lent, or otherwise disposed of, to any person or pe whatever, and that the same shall be solely made use of for the service of the ship for which it is gra and that in case such ship shall be lost, or taken by the enemy, burnt or broken up, or otherwise prev from returning to the port, or shall on any account have lost and forfeited the privileges of a British or shall have been seized and legally condemned for illicit trading, or shall have been taken in exec for debt and sold by due process of law, or shall have been sold to the crown, or shall under any cir stances have been registered *de novo*, the certificate, if preserved, shall be delivered up within one r after the arrival of the master in any port, to the collector and comptroller of some port in Great Br or of the Isle of Man, or of the British plantations, or to the governor, lieutenant-governor, or comma in-chief of the islands of Guernsey or Jersey; and if any foreigner, or any person for his use, shal chase or otherwise become entitled to any interest in such ship, and the same shall be within the of any port of Great Britain, Guernsey, Jersey, Man, or the British colonies or territories, then th tificate of registry shall, within seven days after such purchase or transfer, be delivered up to the pe authorised to make registry at such port; and if such ship shall be in any foreign port when such chase or transfer shall take place, then the same shall be delivered up to the British consul, or British officer at or nearest to such foreign port, or if such ship shall be at sea when such purcha transfer shall take place, then the same shall be delivered up to the British consul or chief British at the foreign port at which the master shall first arrive after such purchase or transfer at sea, diately after his arrival at such foreign port; but if such master shall not arrive at a foreign por shall arrive at some port of Great Britain, Guernsey, Jersey, Man, or his Majesty's said colonies ritories, then the same shall be delivered up in manner aforesaid, within fourteen days after the arr such ship in any port of Great Britain, Guernsey, Jersey, Man, or any of his Majesty's said colon territories: Provided always, that if it shall happen that at the time of registry of any ship, the sam be at any other port than that to which she belongs, so that the master cannot attend at the port gistry to join with the owners in such bond, it shall be lawful for him to give a separate bond, to tl effect, at the port where such ship may then be, and the collector and comptroller shall transmit bond to the collector and comptroller of the port where such ship is to be registered; and such and the bond also given by the owners, shall together be of the same effect against the master or o or either of them, as if they had bound themselves jointly and severally in one bond. — § 21.

When Master is changed, new Master to give similar Bond. — When and so often as the master ship registered shall be changed, the master or owner shall deliver to the persons authorised to registry at the port where such change shall take place, the certificate of registry, who shall ther endorse and subscribe a memorandum of such change, and shall forthwith give notice to the off the port where such ship was last registered, who shall make a memorandum of the same in the b registers, and shall forthwith give notice thereof to the commissioners of customs: Provided, that the name of such new master shall be endorsed on the certificate of registry, he shall give a bond, like penalties and under the same conditions as are contained in the bond required to be given at th of registry. — § 22.

Certificate of Registry to be given up, as directed by the Bond. — If any person shall have posses and wilfully detain any certificate of registry, which ought to be delivered up to be cancelled, such is enjoined to deliver up such certificate of registry, in manner directed by the conditions of such under the penalties therein provided. — § 23.

Name of Vessels registered, never afterwards to be changed. — It shall not be lawful for any ow give any name to such ship, other than that by which she was first registered; and the owners before such ship (after registry) shall begin to take in any cargo, paint in white or yellow lett a length not less than four inches, upon a black ground, upon some conspicuous part of the the name by which such ship shall have been registered, and the port to which she belong legible manner, and shall so keep the same; and if such owners or master shall permit such s begin to take in any cargo before the name has been so painted, or shall wilfully alter, erase, obli or in anywise hide or conceal (unless in the case of square-rigged vessels in time of war,) or s any written or printed paper, or other document, describe such ship by any name other than that by she was first registered, or shall verbally describe, or cause or permit such ship to be described, other name, to any officer of revenue in the execution of his duty, then such owners, or maste forfeit 100*l.* — § 24.

Builder's Certificate of Particulars of Ship. — All persons who shall apply for a certificate of r are to produce, to the person authorised to grant such certificate, a true account, under the hand builder, of the proper denomination, and of the time when and the place where such ship wa and also an exact account of the tonnage, together with the name of the first purchaser, (wh count such builder is to give under his hand, on the same being demanded by such persons so a for a certificate,) and shall also make oath before the persons authorised to grant such certificate, th ship is the same with that which is so described by the builder. — § 25.

Certificate of Registry lost or mislaid. — If the certificate of registry of any ship shall be lost or r so that the same cannot be found or obtained, and proof thereof shall be made, to the satisfac the commissioners of customs, such commissioners shall permit such ship to be registered de and a certificate thereof to be granted: Provided, that if such ship be absent and far distant fr port to which she belongs, or by reason of the absence of the owners, or of any other imped registry of the same cannot then be made in sufficient time, such commissioners shall grant a for the present use of such ship, which licence shall, for the time and to the extent specified and no longer, be of the same force as a certificate of registry under this act: Provided alway before such registry *de novo* be made, the owners and master shall give bond to the commission such sum as to them shall seem fit, with a condition that if the certificate of registry shall afte be found, the same shall forthwith be delivered to the officers of customs to be cancelled, and illegal use has been or shall be made thereof with their privity; and further, that before an licence shall be granted, the master shall also make oath that the same has been registered as a

ing the port and time when such registry was made, and all the particulars contained in the
thereof, to the best of his knowledge, and shall also give such bond, and with the same
as before mentioned : also, before any such licence shall be granted, such ship shall be surveyed
nner as if a registry *de novo* were about to be made, and the certificate of such survey shall be
by the collector and comptroller of the port to which such ship shall belong ; and in virtue
shall be lawful for the commissioners to permit such ship to be registered after her departure,
the owners shall personally attend to take and subscribe the oath required before registry,
also comply with all other requisites of this act, except so far as relates to the bond to be
he master ; which certificate of registry the commissioners shall transmit to the collector and
r of any other port, to be by them given to the master upon his giving such bond, and deliver-
licence granted for the then present use of such ship. — § 26.

detaining Certificate of Registry to forfeit 100*l.* — In case the master or any other person, who
received or obtained by any means, or for any purpose whatever, the certificate of registry,
part owner or not,) shall wilfully detain and refuse to deliver up the same to the proper officers
, for the purposes of such ship, it shall be lawful for any owners to make complaint on oath
master of the ship, or other person, of such detainer and refusal, to any *justice of the peace*
place in Great Britain or Ireland, or to any member of the supreme court of justice, or any
he peace in the islands of Jersey, Guernsey, or Man, or in any colony, plantation, island, or
his Majesty belonging, in Asia, Africa, or America, or Malta, Gibraltar, or Heligoland, where
er and refusal shall be ; and on such complaint the said justice or magistrate shall, by warrant
hand and seal, cause such master or person to be brought before him to be examined, and if it
r to the said justice or magistrate, on examination, that the said certificate of registry is not
laid, but is wilfully detained by the said master or other person, such master or other person
ereof convicted, and shall forfeit 100*l.*, and on failure of payment he shall be committed to the
ol, there to remain for such time as the said justice or magistrate shall deem proper, not being
ree months nor more than twelve months ; and the said justice or magistrate shall certify the
etainer, refusal, and conviction, to the persons who granted such certificate of registry, who
e terms and conditions of law being complied with, make registry of such ship *de novo*, and
tificate thereof, notifying on the back of such certificate the ground upon which the ship was
d *de novo ;* and if such master or other person shall have absconded, so that the said warrant
executed upon him, and proof thereof shall be made to the satisfaction of the commissioners of
shall be lawful for the said commissioners to permit such ship to be registered *de novo*, or
n their discretion to grant a licence for the present use of such ship, in like manner as in the
in the certificate of registry is lost or mislaid. — § 27.*

red in certain Manner to be registered de novo. — If any ship after registered, shall in any
atever be altered, so as not to correspond with all the particulars contained in the certificate of
ch ship shall be registered *de novo*, as soon as she returns to the port to which she belongs, or
r port of the United Kingdom, or in the same colony, plantation, island, or territory, on failure
h ship shall be deemed to be a ship not duly registered. — § 28.

ndemned as Prize, or for Breach of Laws against the Slave Trade. — The owners of all such
ll be taken by any of his Majesty's ships of war, or by any private or other ship, and condemned
any court of admiralty, or of such ships as shall be condemned for breach of the laws for the
of the slave trade, shall, upon registering such ship, before they shall obtain such certificate,
he collector and comptroller a certificate of the condemnation, under the hand and seal of the
also a true account in writing of all the particulars contained in the certificate herein-before set
made and subscribed by one or more skilful person or persons, to be appointed by the court to
ship, and shall also make oath before the collector and comptroller, that such ship is the same
entioned in the certificate of the judge. — § 29.

sels not to be registered at Guernsey, Jersey, or Man. — Provided always, that no ship con-
prize or forfeiture, shall be registered in Guernsey, Jersey, or the Isle of Man, although
o subjects in those islands, but the same shall be registered either at Southampton, Wey-
ster, Plymouth, Falmouth, Liverpool, or Whitehaven, by the collector and comptroller at
— § 30.

of Interest to be made by Bill of Sale. — When and so often as the property in any ship, or
ereof, belonging to subjects, shall after registry be sold to any other subjects, the same shall be
by bill of sale, or other instrument in writing, containing a recital of the certificate of registry,
ipal contents thereof, otherwise such transfer shall not be valid for any purpose whatever,
or in equity : Provided always, that no bill of sale shall be deemed void by reason of any
h recital, or by the recital of any former certificate of registry instead of existing certificate,
identity of the ship be effectually proved thereby. — § 31.

n Ships to be divided into Sixty four Parts or Shares. — The property in every ship of which
ore than one owner, shall be considered to be divided into sixty-four parts or shares, and the
eld by each owner shall be described in the registry as being a certain number of sixty-fourth
es ; and no person shall be entitled to be registered as an owner in respect of any proportion
not be an integral sixty-fourth part of the same ; and upon the first registry, the owners
ke and subscribe the oath required by this act, before registry be made, shall also declare
e number of such parts then held by each owner, and the same shall be so registered accord-
ided always, that if it shall at any time happen that the property of any owner cannot be
division, into any number of integral sixty-fourth parts, it shall be lawful for the owner of
al parts, to transfer the same one to another, or jointly, to any new owner, by memorandum
ills of sale, or by fresh bill of sale, without such transfer being liable to stamp duty : Also,
such owners to such fractional parts shall not be affected by reason of the same not having
red : Also, it shall be lawful for any number of such owners, described in such registry,
rs, to hold any ship, or any shares of any ship, in the name of such copartnership, as joint
out distinguishing the proportionate interest of each, and such ship, or the share or shares
eld in copartnership, shall be deemed to be partnership property, and shall be governed by
es as relate to all other partnership property in any other goods. — § 32.

ty-two Persons to be Owners of any Ship at one Time. — No greater number than thirty-two
be entitled to be legal owners at one time of any ship, as tenants in common, or to be regis-
h : Provided always, that nothing herein shall affect the equitable title of minors, heirs,

---

& 8 Geo. 4. c. 56. enacts, if any person shall
the certificate of registry of any ship or vessel,
eliver up the same to the proper officer of cus-
urposes of such ship or vessel, as occasion shall
erson may be proceeded against in a manner
last mentioned act; and doubts having arisen
roceedings may be had, unless the certificate of
ve been first demanded of such person by the
f the customs; and it is expedient to remove
is therefore enacted, that it shall be lawful for
her person having jurisdiction, and he is hereby
ive proof on oath from the person making com-
such detainer and refusal, that such occasion
ough the certificates shall not have been de-
fficer of the customs ; and the endorsing of any

transfer of property, or of the name of any new master upon
the certificate of registry, by the officers of customs, shall be
deemed to be purposes for which there is occasion to deliver
the certificate of registry to the officers of customs; and if
any person who is not in actual possession of a ship, shall
detain the certificate of registry from some person who is in actual possession of such ship as ostensible master thereof, or who
has the actual charge or command of such ship or vessel as ostensible master thereof, then occasion shall be deemed to have
arisen for delivering of such certificate to the officers of the
customs at the port where such ship shall then be, in order
that such certificate may be given to some person who is in actual possession of such ship or vessel, as such ostensible owner
or master. — s. 20.

legatees, creditors, or others, exceeding that number, holding from any of the persons within number : Also, if it shall be proved to the satisfaction of the commissioners of customs, that any of persons have associated themselves as a joint stock company, for the purpose of owning any number of ships, as joint property, and such company have elected or appointed any number, not l three of the members, to be trustees of the property, it shall be lawful for such trustees, or three with the permission of such commissioners, to take the oath required before registry be made, that instead of stating therein the names and descriptions of the other owners, they shall state t and description of the company. — § 33.

Shares to be registered on Registry de novo under this Act. — Whenever any ship (registered be said 31st of December, 1823, and not registered *de novo* since that day, and before the commence this act) shall be registered *de novo*, the number of shares held by each owner shall be registered practicable; and to that intent the owners, who shall take the oath required before registry, shall the bills of sale of themselves and of the other owners, in order that the number of shares held may be ascertained and registered; and if the registry then in force shall be the first registry, shares of any of the owners shall remain the same, and the owner or owners, or any one of them, w attend to take the oath required before registry, shall be the same who took such oath before s registry was made, such original owner or owners, instead of producing the bill of sale, shall decla oath, to the best of their knowledge and belief, the number of such shares held by them, or by a original owners whose property shall have remained unchanged : Provided always, that if at the such registry *de novo* such owners shall make oath that they are unable to produce the bill or bills or to give any certain account or proof of the shares of the other previous owners, it shall be la the collector and comptroller to register such ship without requiring the shares of such owners t clared and specified. — § 34.

Shares must be registered within a certain Time. — After the commencement of this act, or a first arrival and entry of any ship after such commencement, at the port to which she belongs, c other port, no certificate of registry shall be in force, except such as shall be granted under th which shall have been granted under 4 Geo. 4. c. 41., intituled " An Act for the registering of \ and in which the shares held by each owner shall be set forth, unless it shall be certified thereo collectors and comptroller of the port to which such ship belongs, that further time has been gra the commissioners of customs for ascertaining and registering the numbers of such shares as can be ascertained. — § 35.

No Stamp Duty on first Registry. — Upon the first registry, in compliance with this act, of before registered, no stamp duty shall be charged upon the bond required to be given ; and if th cate of such former registry, then delivered up to be cancelled, shall have a Mediterranean pass thereto, no stamp duty shall be charged on account of the new Mediterranean pass in lieu of the livered up. — § 36.

Bills of Sale not effectual until produced to Officers of Customs, and entered in the Book of Reg No bill of sale or other instrument in writing shall be valid to pass the property in any ship, c share thereof, or for any other purpose, until such bill of sale or instrument shall have been p to the collector and comptroller of the port at which such ship is registered, or to the colle comptroller of any other port at which she is about to be registered *de novo*, nor until such colle comptroller shall have entered in the book of registry the name, residence, and description of th or mortgagor, or of each vendor or mortgagor, if more than one, the number of shares transfe name, residence, and description of the purchaser or mortgagee, or of each purchaser or mort more than one, and the date of the bill of sale or instrument, and of the production of it ; and ship is not about to be registered *de novo*, the collector and comptroller of the port where suc registered shall endorse the aforesaid particulars on the certificate of registry, when produced purpose, in manner following : —

" Custom House [*port and date: name, residence, and description of vendor or mortgagor*] has transferred by [*bill of s instrument*] dated [*date; number of shares*] to [*name, residence, and description of purchaser or mortgages.*]
> A. B. Collector.
> C. D. Comptrol.

And forthwith to give notice thereof to the commissioners of customs; and in case the colle comptroller shall be desired so to do, and the bill of sale or instrument shall be produced for that then the collector and comptroller are to certify, by endorsement upon the bill of sale, that the pa have been so entered in the book of registry, and endorsed upon the certificate of registry. — § 3

Entry of Bill of Sale to be valid. — When the particulars of any bill of sale shall have been so e the book of registry, the said bill of sale shall be valid and effectual to pass the property, as a persons whatsoever, and to all intents and purposes, except as against subsequent purchasers a gagees, who shall first procure the endorsement to be made upon the certificate of registry in herein-after mentioned. — § 38.

When a Bill of Sale has been entered for any Shares, Thirty Days shall be allowed for endo Certificate of Registry, before any other Bill of Sale for the same shall be entered. — After the pa of any bill of sale shall have been so entered in the book of registry, the collector and comptro not enter in the book of registry the particulars of any other bill of sale, purporting to be a transf same vendor or mortgagor of the same ship or shares, to any other person or persons, unless th shall elapse from the day on which the particulars of the former bill of sale were entered in th registry ; or in case the ship was absent from the port to which she belonged at the time when culars of such former bill of sale were entered, then unless thirty days shall have elapsed from th which the ship arrived at the port to which the same belonged ; and in case the particulars a more such bills of sale shall at any time have been entered in the book of registry, the colle comptroller shall not enter in the book of registry the particulars of any other bill of sale, unl days shall in like manner have elapsed from the day on which the particulars of the last of suc sale were entered in the books of registry, or from the day on which the ship arrived at the port she belonged, in case of her absence as aforesaid ; and in every case where there shall at any tim to be two or more transfers, by the same owners, of the same property in any ship entered, the and comptroller are to endorse upon the certificate of registry the particulars of that bill of s which the persons claim property, and shall produce the certificate of registry for that purpo thirty days after the entry of his said bill of sale, or within thirty days next after the return of t the port, in case of absence at the time of such registry ; and in case no person shall produce t cate of registry within either of the said spaces of thirty days, then it shall be lawful for the coll comptroller to endorse upon the certificate of registry the particulars of the bill of sale to such shall first produce the certificate of registry ; it being the true meaning of this act that the sev chasers and mortgagees, when more than one appear to claim the same property, shall have pr over the other, not according to the times when the particulars of the bill of sale were enter book of registry, but according to the time when the endorsement is made upon the certificate of Provided always, that if the certificate of registry be lost or mislaid, or shall be detained by a so that the endorsement cannot in due time be made thereon, and proof thereof shall be made b chaser or mortgagee, or his agent, to the satisfaction of the commissioners of customs, it shall for the commissioners to grant further time for the recovery of the certificate of registry, or for try *de novo* of the said ship, and thereupon the collector and comptroller shall make a memo the book of registers of the further time granted, and during such time no other bill of sale shall or the transfer of the same ship or the same shares. — § 39.

f Sale may be produced after Entry at other Ports than those to which Vessels belong, and Trans-
rsed on Certificate of Registry. — If the certificate of registry of such ship shall be produced to the
r and comptroller of any port where she may then be, after such bill of sale shall have been
d at the port to which she belongs, together with such bill of sale, containing a notification of such
signed by the collector and comptroller of such port, it shall be lawful for the collector and comp-
f such other port to endorse on such certificate (being required so to do) the transfer mentioned
bill of sale ; and such collector and comptroller shall give notice thereof to the collector and comp-
f the port to which such ship belongs, who shall record the same in like manner as if they had
ich endorsement themselves, but inserting the name of the port at which such endorsement was
Provided always, that the collector and comptroller of such other port shall first give notice to the
r and comptroller of the port to which such ship belongs, of such requisition to endorse the certifi-
registry, and the collector and comptroller of the port to which such ship belongs shall thereupon
ormation to the collector and comptroller of such other port, whether any and what other bill or
have been recorded in the book of the registry of such ship ; and the collector and comptroller
other port, having such information, shall proceed in manner directed by this act in all respects
ndorsing of the certificate of registry, as they would do if such port were the port to which such
elonged. — § 40.

n Registry de novo, Bill of Sale not recorded. — If it shall become necessary to register any ship
and any shares shall have been sold since she was last registered, and the transfer shall not have
orded and endorsed, the bill of sale shall be produced to the collector and comptroller, who are to
zistry, or otherwise such sale shall not be noticed in such registry *de novo*, except as herein-after
: Provided always, that upon the future production of such bill of sale, and of the existing cer-
f registry, such transfer may be recorded and endorsed as well after registry *de novo* as before.—

Change of Property, Registry de novo may be granted if desired. — If upon any change of property
ip, the owners shall desire to have the same registered *de novo*, although not required by this act,
wners shall attend at the Custom-house at the port to which such ship belongs for that purpose,
e lawful for the collector and comptroller at such port to make registry *de novo* of such ship, and
a certificate thereof, the several requisites herein mentioned being first complied with. — § 42.

of Oaths, and Extracts from Books of Registry. — The collector and comptroller of customs at any
the persons acting for them, shall, upon every request by any person whomsoever, produce and
for inspection and examination any oath or affidavit sworn by any such owners, and also any
or entry in any book of registry, and shall, upon request by any person whomsoever, permit him
copy or an extract thereof ; and the copies shall, upon being proved to be true copies, be received
ce upon every trial at law, without the production of the originals, and without the testimony or
ce of any collector or comptroller, as fully as such originals, if produced by any collector or comp-
r other person acting for them, could be admitted in evidence. — § 43.

or Shares sold in the Absence of Owners without formal Powers. — If the ship or the shares of
er (out of the kingdom) shall be sold in his absence by his known agent or correspondent, and
nt or correspondent who shall have executed a bill of sale to the purchaser shall not have received
ower to execute, it shall be lawful for the commissioners of customs, upon application, and proof
r dealings of the parties, to permit such transfer to be registered, if registry *de novo* be necessary
orded and endorsed, as the case may be, as if such legal power had been produced ; and if any
e cannot be produced, or if, by reason of distance of time, or the absence or death of parties con-
t cannot be proved that a bill of sale for any shares had been executed, and registry *de novo* shall
ome necessary, it shall be lawful for the commissioners of customs, upon proof of the fair dealings
arties, to permit such ship to be registered *de novo*, in like manner as if a bill of sale for the
f such shares had been produced : Provided always, that in any of the cases mentioned, good
shall be given to produce a legal power or bill of sale within a reasonable time, or to abide the
aims of the absent owner ; and at the future request of the party whose property has been so
ed without the production of a bill of sale, such bond shall be available for the protection of his
n addition to any powers which he may have in law or equity against the ship, or against the
ncerned, until he shall have received full indemnity for any loss sustained. — § 44.

r by way of Mortgage. — When any transfer of any ship, or of any shares, shall be made only as
for the payment of a debt, either by way of mortgage, or of assignment to trustees for the pur-
lling the same, then the collector and comptroller of the port where the ship is registered shall,
try in the book of registry, and also in the endorsement on the certificate of registry, state that
sfer was made only as a security for the payment of a debt, or by way of mortgage ; and the
whom such transfer shall be made, or any other person claiming under him as a mortgagee, or a
ly, shall not by reason thereof be deemed to be the owner ; nor shall the person making such
e deemed to have ceased to be an owner of such ship, any more than if no such transfer had been
cept so far as may be necessary for the purpose of rendering the ship or shares transferred avail-
le for the payment of the debt. — § 45.

rs of Ships for Security of Debts being registered, Rights of Mortgagee not affected by any Act
uptcy of Mortgagor, &c. — When any transfer of any ship, or of any shares thereof, shall have
e as a security for the payment of any debt, either by way of mortgage or of assignment as afore-
such transfer shall have been duly registered according to this act, the right or interest of the
e or other assignee shall not be in any manner affected by any act of bankruptcy committed after
when such mortgage or assignment shall have been so registered, notwithstanding such mort-
ssignor, at the time, shall have in his possession, order, and disposition, and shall be the reputed
the said ship, or the shares thereof, by him mortgaged or assigned ; but such mortgage or
t shall take place of and be preferred to any right, claim, or interest which may belong to the
of such bankrupt. — § 46.

sioners in Scotland, &c. — The commissioners of customs in Scotland and Ireland shall transmit, at
every month, to the commissioners of customs in England, true copies of all such certificates
granted by them, or by any officers within the limits of their commission, in pursuance of this
.

rs of Colonies may cause Proceedings in Suits to be stayed. — It shall be lawful for any governor,
-governor, or commander-in-chief of any colonies, plantations, or territories, if any suit or pro-
any nature shall have been commenced, in any court whatever in any of the said territories,
he force of any register granted to any ship, upon representation made, to cause all proceedings
be stayed, if he see just cause, until his Majesty's pleasure shall be known ; and such governor,
-governor, or commander-in-chief, is to transmit to one of the secretaries of state, to be laid
Majesty in council, an authenticated copy of the proceedings, together with his reasons for
e same to be stayed (properly verified). — § 48.

making false Oath, &c. — If any person shall falsely make oath to any of the matters before re-
be verified, such person shall suffer the like pains and penalties as are incurred by persons
g wilful and corrupt perjury ; and if any person shall counterfeit, erase, alter, or falsify any
or other instrument in writing, required to be obtained, granted, or produced, by this act, or
or wilfully make use of any certificate or other instrument so counterfeited, &c., or wilfully
certificate or other instrument in writing, knowing it to be false, such person shall, for every
ce, forfeit 500*l.* — § 49.

REPORT, in commercial navigation, a paper delivered by the masters o
ships arriving from parts beyond seas to the Custom-house, and attested u
oath, containing an account of the cargo on board, &c. — (See *antè*, p. 603.)

REPRISALS. Where the people of one nation have unlawfully seized
detained property belonging to another state, the subjects of the latter are au
rised, by the law of nations, to indemnify themselves, by seizing the propert
the subjects of the state aggressing. This is termed making reprisals; and o
missions to this effect are issued from the Admiralty. — (See PRIVATEERS.)

RESPONDENTIA. See BOTTOMRY and RESPONDENTIA.

RHUBARB (Du. *Rhubarber;* Fr. *Rhubarbe, Rubarbe;* It. *Rabarbaro,*
barbaro; Sp. *Ruibarbo;* Rus. *Rewen;* Arab. *Rawend;* Chin. *Ta-hwang*),
root of a plant, a native of China and Tartary. Three varieties of rhubar
known in the shops; viz., Russian, Turkey, and East Indian or Chinese rhul
The two first resemble each other in every respect. They are, in fact, the s
article, being both derived from Tartary. The portion destined for the Pe
burgh market, being selected and sorted at Kiachta, acquires the name of Rus
rhubarb; while the portion that is sent from Tartary to Smyrna and other pl
in Turkey, is called Turkey rhubarb. The best pieces only are sent to Pe
burgh; and according to the contract with the government, on whose accou
is bought, all that is rejected must be burnt; and that which is approved ur
goes a second cleaning before being finally packed up for Petersburgh. The
pieces of Russian and Turkey rhubarb are roundish, and perforated with a l
hole, of a reddish or yellow colour on the outside, and when cut or broker
hibit a mottled texture, and alternate streaks of red and grey. Its odo
peculiar; and its taste nauseous, bitter, and astringent. It should not be po
but rather compact and heavy. East Indian or Chinese rhubarb is in oblong
pieces, seldom perforated; has a stronger odour, and is more nauseous to
taste, than the other; it is heavier, more compact, breaks smoother, and affor
powder of a redder shade. — (*Thomson's Dispensatory; Ainslie's Mat. Indica,*

The total quantity of rhubarb imported in 1829 amounted to 146,881 lbs.; of which 10,659 lbs. came
Russia, 127,443 from the East Indies, and 8,074 lbs. from the Cape of Good Hope. Of the quanti
ported, 33,673 lbs. were retained for home consumption. The price of rhubarb in bond varies from 5
lb. for the inferior East Indian, to 9s. for the best Russian.

RICE (Fr. *Riz;* It. *Riso;* Arab. *Aruz;* Hind. *Chawl*), a very valuable sp
of grain (*Oryza sativa,* Lin.).

It is largely cultivated in India, China, and most Eastern countries; in the
Indies; in many parts of America; and in some of the southern countries of Eu
When rough, or in its native state in the husk, it is called *paddy.* It is more extens
consumed than wheat, or any other species of grain, and forms the chief part of the
of all Eastern nations between the tropics; it is light and wholesome, but is said to
tain less of the nutritive principle than wheat. There are an immense number of dif
sorts of rice. The rice exported from Bengal is chiefly of the species denominated
rice; it is of a coarse reddish cast, but peculiarly sweet and large grained; it doe
readily separate from the husk, but is preferred by the natives to all the others. I
rice is more esteemed in Europe, and is of a very superior quality; it is small gra
rather long and wiry, and is remarkably white. No hill rice, or rice raised on gr
not flooded, is exported from Bengal; but it is common in the Eastern islands.

A few years ago England was principally supplied with cleaned rice from Carolina, produced
marshy banks of the rivers of that state. Latterly, however, the imports of Carolina rice have been
reduced. A very improved method of separating the husk, which throws out the grain clean a
broken, has recently been practised in this country; and as the grain, when in the husk, is found
serve its flavour and sweetness better during a long voyage than when shelled, it is now prin
imported rough from Bengal and the United States. No doubt, however, the heavy duty on An
cleaned rice must have contributed powerfully to increase the imports of the rough grain.
The consumption of rice is rapidly extending; the deliveries for home use having amounted,
and 1830, to above 100,000 bags a year, whereas a few years ago they did not exceed 20,000 or 25,0
a year. The principal part of this great increase is certainly to be attributed to the reduction in th
on Indian rice, from 5s. to 1s. a cwt.; but it may also in some degree have been owing to the co
tively high price of corn during the last two years. It has now, however, been very generally intr
among the middle, and to a certain extent also among the lower, classes; and there can be little
that its consumption will continue to increase according as the various excellent qualities of this
and highly useful grain come to be known. It is likely, therefore, that it will in future form an a
importance in the trade with India. — (*Milburn's Orient. Com.; Ainslie's Mat. Indica; Cook's*
Great Britain in 1830, &c.)

The price of rice in the London market, 23d of June, 1831, was as under: —

				L. s. d.	L. s. d.	
American	Carolina, new - duty paid, per cwt.			1 11 0 to 1 13 0		Duty on paddy, the produce of and impor
	old	—				British possessions, 1d. per quarter.
	Bengal, yellow - in bond		-	0 11 6 — 0 12 6		From America and other foreign places, 2
	white	—	-	0 13 0 — 6 14 6		bushel.
East India	cargo	— -	-	0 10 0 — 0 10 6		Duty on American, and other foreign
	Patna	— -	-	0 16 0 — 0 18 0		growth, 15s. per cwt. — Bengal, and ot
	Java and Madagascar	-	-	0 9 0 — 0 10 0		1s. per cwt.

y foreign rice or paddy, cleaned in the United Kingdom, which has paid the duty on import-
g exported, a drawback shall be allowed on every cwt. thereof, equal in amount to the duty paid
bushels of the rough rice from which the same shall have been cleaned.—(6 *Geo.* 4. c. 111. § 6.)
awback shall be paid and allowed only upon such clean rice as shall be deposited for the purpose
ation within a calendar month from the day on which the duty thereon has been paid, in some
(in which rice may be warehoused on importation without payment of duty), and shall there
ured until duly shipped to be exported from such warehouse ; provided that the exporter of
hall make oath before the collector or comptroller that the rice so warehoused for exportation
d from the rough rice or paddy upon which the duties had been so paid. — § 7.

A, a city of European Russia, and the capital of Livonia, situated on the
bout 9 miles from the sea, in lat. 56° 5′ N., lon. 24° 7¾′ E. Population
,000. Owing to its advantageous situation near the mouth of a great
e river, the trade of Riga is very extensive ; being, of the Russian towns on
ic, in this respect second only to Petersburgh. The trade is chiefly car-
oy foreign merchants, particularly by the English. The principal exports
, hemp and flax, linseed, iron, timber, masts, leather, tallow, &c.; the im-
e, salt, cloth and cotton stuffs, silks, wine, sugar, coffee, and groceries of
indigo, dye-woods, salted herrings, &c.

ast trade is very extensive. The burghers of Riga send persons who are called
kers into the provinces to mark the trees, which are purchased standing. They
stly in the districts which border on the Dnieper, are sent up that river to a
place, transported 30 versts to the Duna, are there formed into rafts of from 50
ices, and descend the stream to Riga. The tree which produces the largest masts
tch fir. Those pieces which are from 18 to 25 inches in diameter are called
nder those dimensions, spars, or, in England, Norway masts, because Norway
o trees more than 18 inches in diameter. Great skill is required in distinguish-
masts that are sound, from those which are in the least internally decayed.
usually from 70 to 80 feet in length.

is brought from the Ukraine and Poland, and requires 2 years in its passage
The barks in which it is conveyed are from 250 to 300 tons burthen, are
ith mats sloping like a pent-house roof, and have a false bottom. They ascend
er and the Duna ; but on account of numerous shoals, can only pass the Duna
ing, or about 3 weeks after the snow begins to melt ; and if they miss that time,
ed till autumn. The hemp exported from Riga is considered the best in Europe,
erally about 30 per cent. dearer than that exported from Petersburgh. Riga
hiefly used for the shrouds and stays of men-of-war. — (*Coxe's Travels in the
Europe,* 5th ed. vol. ii. p. 241.)

st kind of flax shipped from Riga is grown in White Russia, and is called
akitzer ; its colour is very white, and the threads long, fine, and loose, but it
imes black spots : the next quality, coming from the province of Trockic in Li-
called Lithuanian rakitzer, and is very little inferior to Druana, but its colour
orown ; of this kind the best sort is Thiesenhausen : the best kind of Courland
ed from Riga is Marienburg ; that grown in Livonia is of inferior quality.
two kinds of linseed : that of the last crop, which is used for sowing ; and that
years, for crushing. To prevent deception, the year of its growth is stamped
rel by sworn inspectors (*brackers*). Some hemp-seed is occasionally shipped,
Holland. Riga wheat is very inferior to that of Dantzic. Two descriptions
d — one the growth of Russia, the other of Courland : the last is much the best,
er bodied, and of a brighter colour, than the Russian ; still, however, it makes
rent flour. Oats are of a good quality, and are largely exported ; peas are also
y exported.

ing masts, the rest of the cargo generally consists of deals and wainscot logs ;
are much exported to England, and are very superior. Tallow is not so cheap
Petersburgh.

For the monies of Riga, see PETERSBURGH. The current rixdollar of Riga = 37½d. sterling ;
rling = 6 rixdollars 36 groschen currency ; the Riga dollar being divided into 90 groschen.
nd *Measures.* — The commercial pound is divided into 2 marcs, or 32 loths ; and also into
ers, &c. It contains 6,452 English grains. Hence 100 lbs. of Riga = 92·17 lbs. avoirdupois =
86·32 lbs. of Hamburgh = 84·64 lbs. of Amsterdam. The lispound = 20 lbs. ; the shippound =

the measure for grain : 48 loofs = 1 last of wheat, barley, or linseed ; 45 loofs = 1 last of rye ;
= 1 last of oats, malt, and beans. According to Dr. Kelly, the loof = 1·9375 Winchester
consequently, the last of wheat = 11·625 quarters. Nelkenbrecher does not value the loof
as Dr. Kelly.
the measure for liquids, is divided into 6 ahms, 24 ankers, 120 quarts, or 720 stoofs. The
English wine gallons.
Riga = 10·79 English inches. The ell = 2 feet ; the clafter = 6 feet.
burgh Gazette of the 15–27th of January, 1829, gives the following details with respect to the
Riga in 1827 and 1828.

	1827.		1828.
els entered	1,396		1,162
despatched	1,378		1,180
e of commodities imported	16,410,875 roubles		15,599,556 roubles.
ditto exported	40,668,678 —		38,826,85 —

RIO DE JANEIRO, the capital of Brazil, situated in lat. 22° 56′ S., lo
44′ W.　Population about 110,000.　The harbour of Rio is one of the fi
the world, both as respects capaciousness and security for all sorts of vessel
coming from the N. E. it is usual to make Cape Frio, in lat. 23° 1′ S., lon. 41° ‡
about 18 leagues due E. of Rio.　The entrance into the harbour is know
remarkable hill in the form of a sugarloaf, at the west point of the bay.
east point, or starboard side of the entrance into the harbour, is the fort of
Cruz.　The entrance is not very wide; but the sea breeze, which blows eve
from 10 or 12 o'clock till sunset, enables ships to go in before the wind;
grows wider as the town is approached, so that abreast of it there is roc
the largest fleet.　The trade of Rio is extensive, and has increased rapidly
years.　The principal articles of export are sugar, coffee, cotton, rum, hides,
indigo, coarse cotton cloths, gold, diamonds, precious stones, tobacco, cabin
dye woods, rice, &c.　The imports consist principally of flour, dried fish, wo
cottons, hardware, soap and candles, wines, oils, &c.　Until last year, slaves
one of the principal articles of import into Rio and other Brazilian por
many as 45,000 having been imported in one year, of which Rio receiv
greater proportion.　But according to the conventions entered into wit
country, this infamous traffic ceased in February, 1830.

The increase in the exports of sugar and coffee from Brazil during the
years has been quite unprecedented.　In 1822, the total export of sugar fr
empire was only 40,000 tons, whereas in 1830 it amounted to 70,000 tons; of
about 15,000 tons were exported from Rio, 44,000 from Bahia, and 11,00
Pernambuco.　In 1821, the quantity of coffee exported from Rio did not ‡
7,500 tons; but in 1830 it amounted to nearly four times that quantity,
28,000 tons!　The exports of cotton have also increased, but not so rapidly
exports of cotton from Brazil to England in 1828, were 29,143,279 lbs.,
between a seventh and an eighth of the total quantity that imported that ye

A considerable part of the extraordinarily rapid increase of the sugar and
cultivation in Brazil must be ascribed to the facility with which slaves h
cently been imported; and it is possible that the cessation of their impor
supposing the convention to that effect to be executed, may check, for a
the extension of cultivation in Brazil.

The exports of British goods to Brazil amount to about 5,000,000*l.* a
greatly exceeding the value of the articles we import in return.　The bala
for the most part, paid by bills on the Continent, particularly on Hamburg
sterdam, and Antwerp, the great European markets for Brazilian produce.

Account of the Trade of Great Britain with Brazil, for the Five Years ending with 1830, acc
the Official Returns and Values.

| Years. | Exports. | | Totals. | Imports fr |
	British and Irish Manufactures.	Foreign & Colonial Produce.		Brazil.
	£	*£*	*£*	*£*
1826	4,116,130	80,743	4,196,873	1,818,28
1827	2,556,140	37,591	2,593,731	767,91
1828	3,757,014	65,473	3,822,487	1,382,81
1829	6,055,902	99,819	6,155,721	1,488,27
1830	4,566,010	76,314	4,642,324	1,469,01
			21,411,136	6,926,30

The number of ships which arrived at Rio, in 1826, were —

From Great Britain	-	-	62	From North of Europe	-	-	37
France	-	-	19	Cape of Good Hope, and {			12 Briti
Spain	-	-	{ 4 Spanish. 15 Foreign.	Cape Verd Islands	- {		3 Fren
Portugal	-	-	{ 51 Portuguese 10 British.	Slave Settlements	- {		53 Port Bra
Holland	-	-	{ 14 Dutch. 5 Foreign.	South America	-	-	81
Hanse Towns	-	-	15	Total	-		440
United States	-	-	{ 53 American. 6 Foreign.				

In 1828, 212 British ships, of the bu
44,000 tons, entered Rio Janeiro.

The outward freights from the continent of Europe to Brazil may be stated at 2*l.* per ton; th
ward freights at 3*l.* 10*s.* per ton.　Woollens, linens, and iron manufactures, are from 12½ to 15
cheaper in Brazil than in the British West India colonies.　Very little sugar is shipped on acco
planters.　It is all purchased by European merchants. — (*Parl. Paper*, No. 120. Sess. 1831.)
Coffee pays on exportation a duty of 80 rees per arroba of consulado, and 8 or 9 per cent
Sugar pays 160 rees per chest, and 40 rees per feixo.　Hides pay 20 rees when dried, and 10
raw.　Tobacco pays 40 rees per *rollo* and 2 per cent.　Most other articles of export pay 2 per cen

s, Weights, and Measures, are the same at Rio as at Lisbon ; which see.

orrow the following details as to the trade of Brazil from Mr. Caldcleugh's Travels in South
a : — " The colonial system, which was strictly preserved until the arrival of the court, kept the
in a state of ignorance of many of those beautiful articles of English manufacture, now so
· purchased by all. The Brazil trade may be considered as entirely in the hands of the British,
exclusive monopoly existed in their favour. By the commercial treaty of 1810 — a treaty abused
des, and consequently supposed to be very equitable — British goods are admitted at a duty of 15
ad valorem, while those of other nations pay 24. But I am assured that even if this difference did not
ven if our manufactures paid a more considerable duty than any other, they would still command
·ket. They could always be furnished at a cheaper rate, which, in a new country with a slave
on, is, after all, the main object. Brazil takes from us every thing it requires, excepting wine
rtugal ; and the importance of this trade to England may be well conceived, when it is mentioned,
er the East and West Indies and the United States, it forms the greatest mart for our fabrics, and
: is most rapidly increasing.
820, the exports of British manufacture amounted to 1,860,000*l.* in 1821, to 2,230,000*l.* The im-
1820 were 950,000*l.* ; in 1821, 1,300,000*l.* ; showing a great and progressive increase.
he amount of exports, about *three fifths* are sent to the capital, owing to the greater consumption,
n its being in communication with the mines, the most inhabited districts of the interior.
returns for this large sum are made in diamonds and precious stones, gold, coffee, cotton, sugar,
brought from a considerable distance inland, some drugs, and dye-woods. The larger portion of
is made from the northern parts — Bahia, Pernambuco, and Maranham — as produce is in them,
ariety of circumstances, much cheaper than at Rio de Janeiro. In sugar alone, the difference is
per cent. in favour of the northern markets.
other nations trading to Brazil exhibit a poor figure after Great Britain. By far the most active
—the United States — exported to Brazil only to the amount of 320,000*l.*, chiefly in flour, fish, and
ticles. It is impossible to say what may happen, but at present it does not appear that England
h to fear in this quarter. The immense command of capital which our merchants possess strikes
ners with astonishment, and forces them to abandon all idea of competition. The trade carried
e rest of the world amounts, in the aggregate, to little : that of France being chiefly confined to
of dress and fashion ; and of Sweden, to a few ship-loads of iron annually.
trade expressly confined to Brazilian vessels is the coasting and African. This latter traffic, it is
wn, is now restricted, by treaty, to that part of Africa south of the line, which comprehends, in
ost the whole of the Portuguese possessions. The importation of negroes varies in amount ; but
ears it cannot be estimated, on an average, at less than 21,000 into Rio de Janeiro only. It affords
a return of gain to be easily abandoned ; more especially when, strange to say, patriotic feelings
dered, in this instance, to go hand in hand with profit ; and when it is imagined, that the moment
is prohibited, the prosperity of the country must decay. When it is considered that this num-
nually received into the capital, and that there are three other ports trading to the same extent,
scarcely two thirds of the negroes taken from the coast live to be landed, the number of negroes
way by this outlet only in the course of the year appears prodigious.
y years since, a considerable capital was employed in the whale fishery. The black whale was
y common near the mouth of the harbour, but an increasing traffic has driven this animal to
ward, and the only establishments at present are in the province of St. Catharine's. It forms
of the royal monopolies ; and, in 1820, was farmed by some Frenchmen.
other trade carried on in Brazilian bottoms is very much confined to that with the mother
its dependencies, as Madeira, and its possessions in Africa and the East. The traffic with China
ntinued, but no longer in that way which made Portugal at one time the envy of all maritime

internal trade is very much confined to the products of the district of the mines ; and is carried
ans of large troops of mules, some of which, from the western provinces of Gozaz and Matto
re four months on the journey. It is not easy to learn with accuracy the produce of the diamond
s they are worked by government, and strictly monopolised : much smuggling consequently pre-
some years, the quantity recovered by government has amounted to as much as 4,000 octavas
ats ; but these are years of rare occurrence : taking the average, however, of some years, the
of octavas would come to near 1,200. In this quantity there would be, of course, many of large
ng immensely to their value. It is calculated that about the same quantity is smuggled ; and
strong reasons to suppose, that if no difficulties were thrown in the way, owing to the facility
h they are obtained, the produce of Brazil diamonds, in every way as fine as the Oriental, would
siderable effect on the demand.
respect to the quantity of gold which comes from the mines, it is immersed in a certain degree
ty. The one fifth due to government is the principal cause that I could never ascertain, in
which I visited, its exact produce. I shall have another opportunity of saying more on this
explaining why the produce of gold mines is on the decrease, which I certainly conceive to be
Knowing the amount of the workings at the commencement of the century, and from information
d in Rio de Janeiro, and in the mines, and making allowance for that exaggeration so common
and all new countries, I consider the annual value of gold certainly does not exceed 900,000*l.*, in-
e contraband.
ver is produced in Brazil. As there is lead, it would be too much to affirm that none exists ;
bly the quantity would be trifling. The silver coin is mostly Spanish dollars, restamped into
c pieces, by which a considerable profit is obtained on each.
uantity of precious stones shipped is now very considerable. In most cases they are sent to a
ket ; being, in fact, more valuable in Brazil than in London or Paris. Aqua marines—(see BERYL)
· large size have been found. In January, 1811, one was found in the Riberao das Americanas,
iamond district, which weighed 15 lbs. ; and in the same place, in the October following, one
ered weighing 4 lbs. Topazes of fine quality, but seldom large, amethysts, and chrysolites, are
s of exportation ; and at times some fine specimens of these gems are to be met with in the
shops.
tly speaking, there are no trading companies in Rio de Janeiro : there is a society for effecting
ssurances, but no other.
ank of Brazil has had very extensive concessions made in its favour, and ought to be in a
state. It has the power of issuing notes ; and all disputed monies and property of the deceased
(*mortes e auzentes*) must be placed in its hands, and 2 per cent. per annum charged for the care
e. This, in addition to the interest which might be obtained for the deposit, would alone, in an
cantile country, form no inconsiderable revenue. Specie is prohibited from being carried
merchants who wish to deposit cash in one of the northern ports, where the largest purchases
are therefore forced to take hand bills, and pay a premium for them, varying from 3 to 5 per

enormous capitals have been amassed ; but generally the speculations of the native merchants
ted on a very limited scale.
gal rate of interest is 6 per cent. ; but money can seldom be obtained under 12."—(*Cald-
avels in South America,* vol. i. pp. 53—59.)

ROADS, pathways formed through the country with more or less art
care, for facilitating the transit of individuals, carriages, &c. between diffe
places. They are of every variety of form — from rude, narrow, rugged, and
formed paths, carried over mountains, interrupted by every petty rivulet,
almost impracticable to any but foot passengers, to smooth, broad, and l
ways, formed of solid materials, winding round or cut through mountains,
carried over swamps and rivers at an immense expense, and admitting of
easy passage of carriages and of all sorts of goods.

The laying out of improved roads, and their construction, forms an important pa
what is denominated the science of civil engineering. But as it would be quite for
to our purpose to enter into any details as to the formation of roads, we shall satisfy
selves with laying before the reader the following statements as to their importance
commercial point of view.

Importance and Utility of improved Roads. — Next to the introduction of money,
weights and measures, the formation of good roads and bridges gives the greatest
lity to commerce, and contributes more powerfully, perhaps, than any thing else to
progress of improvement. They have been denominated national veins and arte
and the latter are not more indispensable to the existence of individuals, than imp
communications are to a healthy state of the public economy. It were vain to attem
point out in detail the various advantages derived from the easy means of communic
that exist in Great Britain. There is not a single district that is not indebted to or
for a large part of its supplies, even of some of the bulkiest commodities. Beside
coal, metals, minerals, timber, corn, &c. conveyed from one part of the empi
another by sea, immense quantities are conveyed from place to place in the interio
roads and canals; and every improvement effected in the means of conveyance has
viously the same effect upon the cost of commodities that have to be conveyed, a
improvement in the methods by which they are raised or manufactured.

Wherever the means of internal communication are deficient in a country, the i
bitants must unavoidably disperse themselves over the surface. Cities were origi
founded by individuals congregating more, perhaps, for the purpose of national de
and protection, than for any other cause. But in countries where good governme
established, and property is secure, men resort to cities only from a sense of the ac
tages they afford. The scale on which business is here conducted presents facilitie
cannot be elsewhere afforded for making a fortune; and the extent to which the
division of employments is carried opens a field for the exercise of all sorts of ta
at the same time that it improves and perfects all sorts of arts, whether subservie
industrious or scientific pursuits, or to those of pleasure and dissipation. It is
that attracts the aspiring, the industrious, the gay, and the profligate, to cities, —
fills them with the best and the worst part of the species. The competition that
place in a great town, — the excitement that is constantly kept up, the collision
many minds brought into immediate contact, and all endeavouring to outstrip each
in their respective departments, — developes all the resources of the human mind
renders a great city a perpetually radiating focus of intelligence and invention.
are, however, considerable clogs upon the continued increase of cities. The food
fuel made use of by the inhabitants, and the raw products on which their industry
be exerted, must all be brought from the country; and according as the size of th
increases, the distances from which its supplies must be brought become so muc
greater, that ultimately the cost of their conveyance may be so great as to balan
more the peculiar advantages resulting from a residence in town. Hence the im
bility of a large, or even a considerable city existing any where without possessing
siderable means of communication either with the surrounding country, or with
countries; and hence, too, the explanation of the apparently singular fact, of alm
large cities having been founded on or near the sea, or a navigable river. Had L
been an inland town, fifty miles from the shore, it is abundantly certain that she
not have attained to one third her present size; but the facilities afforded by her a
able situation on the Thames, for the importation of all sorts of produce from al
as well as from other parts of England, will enable her, should her commerce co
to prosper, to add to her colossal magnitude for centuries to come.

But all towns cannot be founded on the sea coast or the banks of navigable r
and the growth of those in inland situations must, in all cases, depend on their
of communication with the surrounding country. Without our improved roa
great inland manufacturing towns with which England is studded, such as Manc
Leeds, Birmingham, Sheffield, Bolton, Preston, &c., could not exist. They enab
inhabitants to obtain the rude products of the soil and the mines almost as cheap as i
lived in country villages. There is thus nothing, or next to nothing, to detract fr
advantages which the inventive and enterprising artisan may expect to realise fr

o these great hives of industry. And, owing to the gigantic scale on which all
industry are conducted in them, the scope afforded for the employment of the
werful machines, and the appropriation of particular sets of workmen to every
process, however minute, manufacturing industry is carried to a degree of per-
hat almost exceeds belief.

nfluence that the growth of a large town has upon agriculture is great and
" In the neighbourhood," says Dr. Paley, " of trading towns, and in those dis-
ich carry on a communication with the markets of trading towns, the husband-
busy and skilful, the peasant laborious ; the land is managed to the best advan-
d double the quantity of corn or herbage (articles which are ultimately converted
an provision) raised from it, of what the same soil yields in remoter and more
d parts of the country. Wherever a thriving manufactory finds means to esta-
lf, a new vegetation springs up around it. I believe it is true, that agriculture
ives at any considerable, much less at its highest, degree of perfection, when it
nnected with trade ; that is, when the demand for the produce is not increased
nsumption of trading cities." — (*Moral Philosophy*, book vi. c. 11.)

e fact of their being mainly conducive to the growth of cities, is not the only
e which improved roads confer upon agriculture. Without their aid it would
sible to carry to distant places sufficient supplies of such bulky and heavy arti-
ne, marl, shells, and other manures necessary to give luxuriance to the crops
ils, and to render those that are poor productive. Not only, too, would infe-
s lessen the market for farm produce, and consequently the quantity raised, but
roportional number of horses or other cattle would be required to convey the
d produce to market. It is plain, therefore, that good roads are both directly
ctly a prime source of agricultural improvement ; — directly, by increasing the
nd reducing the cost of manure, and by increasing the quantity and reducing
of conveying farm produce to market ; and indirectly, by providing for the
d indefinite extension of cities and towns, that is, of the markets for agricul-
uce.

ed speed of conveyance is one of the principal advantages that have resulted
ormation of good roads, the invention of steam packets, &c. Suppose that it
days to travel by an uneven ill-made road between any two places ; and that,
ing the road, the journey may be accomplished in one day : the effect is the
the distance were reduced a half ; and there is not only a great saving of time
rs, but also a great saving of cost from the more speedy conveyance of commo-
his latter is a point of much more importance than is commonly supposed.
ossible to form any correct estimate of the value of the products that are con-
the act of being carried from place to place in Great Britain and Ireland. It
however, that it is very great ; and every additional facility of conveyance, by
uch products more rapidly to their destination, and enabling them to be sooner
the purposes for which they are intended, renders large quantities of capital
or industrious purposes, that would otherwise be locked up.

defraying Cost of Roads. — Roads of one sort or other must, of course, exist
untry emerged from barbarism, — but in England, the statute of the 28th of
d Mary, which is still in force, is the first legislative enactment in which a re-
ision was made for the repair of the roads. The preamble to this statute de-
t the roads were tedious and noisome to travel on, and dangerous to passengers
ges ; and, therefore, it enacts, that in every parish two surveyors of the high-
be annually chosen, and the inhabitants of all parishes obliged, according to
ctive ability, to provide labourers, carriages, tools, &c. for *four* days each
rk upon the roads, under the direction of the surveyors. This system, though
spects exceedingly defective, was at the time justly considered a great improve-
answered pretty well till the reign of Charles II., when, owing to the increase
s, particularly about London, it became necessary to adopt more efficient
or the formation and repair of roads ; and the plan of imposing tolls upon
made use of them began then to be adopted. But this system was not
full effect, and placed upon a solid footing, till about 1767, when it was ex-
he great roads to all parts of the country ; the contributions of labour under
Philip and Mary being then appropriated entirely to the cross or country
money payment is also very frequently made instead of a contribution in

e plan for extending turnpike roads from the metropolis to distant parts of
was in agitation, the counties in the neighbourhood of London petitioned
against it, alleging that the remoter counties would be able, from the com-
eapness of labour in them, to sell their produce in London at a lower rate
ould do ; and that their rents would be reduced, and cultivation ruined, by the

measure! Luckily this interested opposition proved ineffectual; and instead of
injurious to the counties adjoining the metropolis, the improvement of the roa
been quite as beneficial to them as to those at a distance, inasmuch as, by providi
the indefinite extension of the city, it has rendered it a far better market for their
liar productions, than it would have been, had its growth been checked, which mus
been the case long ago, had the improvements in question not been made.

The plan of making and repairing roads by contributions of labour is not pecu
England, but was at one period general all over Europe. By an act of the Scot
liament, passed in 1669, all persons engaged in husbandry were obliged to lab
days each year, before or after harvest, upon the public roads; the farmers and la
being, at the same time, obliged to furnish horses, carts, &c. according to the ex
land occupied by them. The inconveniences of such a system are many and ol
Those who get no pay for their work, and who perform it against their will, wast
time and industry; and there is, besides, a great loss incurred by the interruption
regular pursuits of the labourer. A sense of these disadvantages led, in the ear
of the reign of George III., to a commutation of the labour contribution for a mo
on land, rated according to its valuation in the cess books. This measure has be
ductive of the best effects. Previously to its taking place, the roads, even in th
cultivated districts of Scotland, were in the worst possible state; now, howeve
are about the very best in Europe.

A similar system has been followed on the Continent. When Turgot entered
administration, he sent a circular letter to the road surveyors and engineers of
ferent provinces of France, desiring them to transmit estimates, framed on th
liberal scale, of the sums of money for which the usual repairs might be made
old roads, and the ordinary extent of new ones constructed. The average of t
mates showed that a money contribution of about 10,000,000 livres a year would
for these objects: whereas Turgot showed, that the execution of these repairs a
structions, by contributions of forced labour, or *corvées*, cost not less than 40,0
livres! — (Art. *Taxation, Supp. to Ency. Brit.*)

There is still, however, a great deal of labour performed on the cross and
roads of England, under the system established by the act of Philip and Mar
continuance is most probably to be ascribed to the want of any ready means
commutation.

It is the duty of government to furnish assistance towards the formation of ro
bridges in parts of the country where they are necessary, and where the funds r
for their formation cannot otherwise be obtained. But it is in such cases ex
desirable, in order to prevent government from being deceived by interested rep
ations, that those more immediately concerned in the undertaking should be b
contribute a considerable portion of its expense. This has been done in the cas
Highland roads. Down to a very recent period, large tracts in the Highlan
quite inaccessible, and were, consequently, in a great measure shut out from
provement; while the rugged nature of the country and the poverty of the inh
rendered any attempt to construct improved roads an undertaking beyond their
Under these circumstances, government came forward, and engaged to advance
expense of making roads and bridges in certain districts, on condition that the la
and others interested should advance the other half, and that the work should
cuted under the direction of parliamentary commissioners and engineers. This
ment has been highly beneficial. Through its means about 600 miles of excelle
have been constructed; and in consequence of the easy means of communicat
afford, a spirit of improvement has been excited even in the wildest and least fre
districts.

Dr. Smith seems to have inclined to the opinion, that the roads of a countr
be better attended to, and more economically managed, were they placed ur
control of government, than when they are left to be planned and superintended
vate individuals. But this opinion does not seem to rest on any good foundat
is, perhaps, true that a few of the great roads between the principal towns of
might be better laid out by government surveyors, than by surveyors appointe
gentlemen of the different counties through which they pass. But these gre
bear but a very small proportion to the total extent of cross and other roads wi
every county either is, or ought to be, intersected; and, besides, it is abundantl
that when the formation of the great roads is left, as in Great Britain, to th
those who, either by themselves or their tenants, have to defray the greater pa
expense of their construction and repair, they will be managed, if not with grea
at least with far more economy than if they were intrusted to the agents of gove
M. Dupin has set this matter in the clearest point of view, in the remarks he
on the administration of the roads in France and England. In the former

y under the control of government; and the consequence is, that while there is
ess expenditure upon a few great roads, the cross roads are almost entirely ne-
l, and the facilities of internal intercourse are incomparably inferior to ours.

gth of Roads. — It appears from a paper printed by order of the House of Com-
in 1818, that the length of the different paved streets and turnpike roads in
nd and Wales, at that period, amounted to about 20,000 miles, and the length of
er highways to about 95,000 miles. The value of the labour performed in kind
he roads is estimated, in the same paper, at 515,000*l.* a year; the commutation
, paid for contributions of labour, is estimated at 271,000*l.*; and the average
e of the tolls is estimated at 570,000*l.*; making the total yearly expenditure upon
roads of England and Wales, in 1818, 1,356,000*l.* At this moment it may be
ted at 1,600,000*l.*

.. — In fixing the rate of tolls, great care should be taken to keep them as low as
e. When they are either too much multiplied, or too high, they have a very per-
influence. They then operate as a most oppressive and unequal tax on com-
and obstruct that intercourse they are intended to promote. The same remark is
ble to all sorts of dock and harbour dues, light-house dues, &c. When confined
due bounds, they cannot justly be objected to; for nothing can be fairer than
ose who benefit by such increased facilities and security in the prosecution of
usinesses should pay for them. But whenever they exceed the proper limits, they
the navigator to resort to ports where the charges are lower, and to direct his
through more insecure but less costly channels.

ovement of Roads. — It is not easy for those accustomed to travel along the
and level roads by which every part of this country is now intersected, to form
urate idea of the difficulties the traveller had to encounter a century ago. Roads
en hardly formed; and, in summer, not unfrequently consisted of the bottoms of
. Down to the middle of last century, most of the goods conveyed from place
in Scotland, at least where the distances were not very great, were carried, not
s or wagons, but on horseback. Oatmeal, coals, turf, and even straw and hay,
nveyed in this way! At this period, and for long previous, there was a set of
orse traffickers (cadgers) that regularly plied between different places, supplying
abitants with such articles as were then most in demand, as salt, fish, poultry,
rthenware, &c.: these were usually conveyed in sacks or baskets, suspended one
side the horse. But in carrying goods between distant places, it was necessary
oy a cart, as all that a horse could carry on his back was not sufficient to defray
of a long journey. The time that the *carriers* (for such was the name given to
at used carts) usually required to perform their journeys, seems now almost in-
. The common carrier from Selkirk to Edinburgh, *thirty-eight* miles distant,
a *fortnight* for his journey between the two places, going and returning! The
ginally was among the most perilous in the whole country; a considerable ex-
t lay in the bottom of that district called Gala-water, from the name of the
l stream, the channel of the water being, when not flooded, the track chosen as
level, and easiest to travel in.

between the largest cities, the means of travelling were but little superior. In
agreement was made to run a coach between Edinburgh and Glasgow, a dis-
44 miles, which was to be drawn by *six* horses, and to perform the journey from
to Edinburgh and back again in *six* days. Even so late as the middle of last
it took a day and a half for the stage-coach to travel from Edinburgh to Glas-
ourney which is now accomplished in 4½ or 5 hours.

e as 1763, there was but one stage-coach from Edinburgh to London, and it
only once a month, taking from 12 to 14 days to perform the journey! At
notwithstanding the immense intercourse between the two cities by means of
ckets, smacks, &c., 6 or 7 coaches set out each day from the one for the other,
ng the journey in from 45 to 48 hours. — (*Robertson's Rural Recol.* pp. 39—44.)
ffects of this extraordinary improvement in the means of travelling have been
g on the manners as on the industry of all classes. The remark of Dr. Smith,
an is the least transportable species of luggage," is no longer true as applied
Britain. During spring, the metropolis is crowded with visiters of all ranks
rs from the remotest provinces; and during summer and autumn vast numbers
izens are spread over the country. Hence it is, that manners as well as prices
ed nearly to the same standard. A respectable family in Penzance or Inver-
very much in the same way as a respectable family in London. Peculiarities
ts have disappeared; every thing is, as it were, brought to a level; the fashions
ons of the metropolis are immediately diffused over every part of the country,
se that originate in the latter powerfully influence the former.

etails are borrowed from the treatise on *Commerce*, published by the Society for the Diffusion
nowledge, contributed by the author of this work.}

ROPE consists of hemp, hair, &c. spun into a thick yarn, of which several st
are twisted together by means of a wheel. When made very small it is c
a cord; and when very thick, a cable. All the different kinds of this manufac
from a fishing-line, or whip-cord, to the cable of a first-rate ship of war, g
the general name of cordage. — (See CABLE.)

ROSEWOOD (Ger. *Rosenholz ;* Fr. *Bois du rose, de Rhode ;* It. *Legno r*
Sp. *Leno de rosa ;* Port. *Páo de rosado*), is produced in Brazil, the Canary isla
and other places. It is in the highest esteem as a fancy wood. The width of
log imported into this country averages about 22 inches, so that it must be
produce of a large tree. Rosewood has a slightly bitterish, somewhat pun
balsamic taste, and a fragrant smell, whence its name. It should be chosen so
heavy, of the deepest colour, in the largest pieces that can be procured, and o
most irregular knotty grain. The small, light coloured, and large shivered p
should be rejected. The more distinct the darker parts are from the purple
which forms the ground, the more is the wood esteemed. It is usually cut
veneers of 9 to an inch. — (*Milburn's Orient. Com.*, &c.)

Rosewood is one of the dearest as well as most beautiful of the fancy woods. Its price in bond
from about 120*l.* to 125*l.* per ton. The duty, which is 10*l.* per ton, produced, in 1830, 10,491*l.* 19*s.*, sh
that 1,049 tons had been entered for home consumption.

ROSIN. " This substance is obtained from different species of fir ; as the
abies, sylvestris, larix, balsamea. It is well known that a resinous juice exudes
the *pinus sylvestris*, or common Scotch fir, which hardens into tears. The
exudation appears in the *pinus abies*, or spruce fir. These tears constitute
substance called *thus*, or frankincense. When a portion of the bark is stripp
these trees, a liquid juice flows out, which gradually hardens. The juice ha
tained different names, according to the plant from which it comes. The
sylvestris yields common turpentine ; the *larix*, Venice turpentine — (see
PENTINE) ; the *balsamea*, balsam of Canada — (see BALSAM), &c. All these j
which are commonly distinguished by the name of turpentine, are consider
composed of two ingredients ; namely, oil of turpentine and rosin. When the
pentine is distilled, the oil comes over, and the rosin remains behind. Whe
distillation is continued to dryness, the residuum is known by the name of
mon rosin, or *colophonium ;* but when water is mixed with it while yet fluid,
incorporated by violent agitation, the mass is called *yellow rosin.* During w
the wounds made in the fir trees become incrusted with a white brittle subst
called *barras* or *galipot*, consisting of rosin united to a small portion of oil.
yellow rosin, made by melting and agitating this substance in water, is pref
for most purposes, because it is more ductile, owing, probably, to its still con
ing some oil. The uses of rosin are numerous and well known." — (*Thon*
Chemistry.)

ROTTERDAM, on the north bank of the Maese, in lat. 51° 55¼' N.
4° 29¼' E. Population about 60,000. Rotterdam is the second commercial
Holland. It is more advantageously situated than Amsterdam ; it is near th
and the canals which intersect it are so deep as to admit of the largest v
coming up to the quays and warehouses of the merchants. Its commerce, c
the last 15 years, has increased more rapidly than that of any town in
land. The exports and imports are similar to those of Amsterdam. The
Zealand wheat shipped here is of a peculiarly fine quality ; and it is the
market for madder and geneva. Our imports of madder from the Nether
in 1829, amounted to about 41,000 cwt., most of which came from Rotterd
(See MADDER.) Geneva is sold by the aam ; but, for the convenien
smuggling to England, it is divided into ankers and half ankers. The legi
imports of geneva from the Netherlands, in 1828, amounted to 335,424 gallo

Monies, Weights, and Measures. — See the article AMSTERDAM, for an account of the current
weights, and measures of Holland.
Two different commercial pounds were formerly used at Rotterdam : one was the Amsterdam
100 lbs. of which = 108·93 lbs. avoirdupois ; the other, used by retailers, was 5 per cent. lighter, —
of it being = 103·48 lbs. avoirdupois.
The Rotterdam last of corn = 10·642 Winchester bushels.
The aam = 40 English wine gallons very nearly.
A hogshead of flax seed contains from 7¾ to 8 Winchester bushels. Rock salt is sold per great
of 404 maaten, containing from 21 to 22 tons. Coals per hoed, equal to half a chaldron of Newcas
The liquid measures were divided in the same manner as at Amsterdam, but were larger ; thus, 1
of Rotterdam were = 67¾ English wine gallons. Brandies were sold per 30 viertels ; whale oil per
vegetable oils per 340 stoops.
The ell is the same as at Amsterdam. 100 feet of Rotterdam = 109¼ feet of Amsterdam, or 10
feet.

Tares and Allowances.

	Tares.	Drafts.	Allowances.
e, Surinam - ⎫ St. Domingo - ⎬	6 per cent.	1 per cent.	1 per cent.
Bourbon -	10 lbs. per bale	1 —	—
Mocha -	24 lbs. per bale	1 —	1 —
Java -	14 lbs. per bale of 270 lbs.	1 —	3 —
r, Jamaica -	18 per cent.		
Surinam -	20 per cent. ⎫	1 —	1 —
East India, in bags -	10 per cent. ⎬		
Havre chests, below			
454 lbs. -	80 lbs. per chest	1 —	1 —
above	13 per cent.		
Martinique - ⎫ St. Domingo - ⎬	18 per cent. ⎫⎬	1 —	1 —
n -	6 per cent.	1 —	1 —
s, Buenos Ayres -	2 lbs. per hide	2 —	1 —
cco, Virginia -	3 per cent.	2 —	3 —
ood -	3 per cent.	1 —	1 —
nto -	real tare	1 —	1 —
o -	3 per cent.	-	2 —
r -	5 lbs. per bale	1 —	2 —
e oil -	1 per cent.	-	1 —
ers -	real tare		1 —

umber of ships entering the Maese and the Goré, chiefly destined for Rotterdam, in the 5 years
vith 1828, was as follows : —

irs.	Ships.	Years.	Ships.
24 -	1,373	1827 -	1,731
25 -	1,396	1828 -	2,085
26 -	1,587		

BY, a precious stone, very highly esteemed ; but under this name a variety
erals have not unfrequently been sold, which differ essentially in their
ers.

Oriental Ruby is, in fact, a red variety of the sapphire. When perfect, its colour is
eal red, presenting a richness of hue the most exquisite and unrivalled : it is,
r, in general, more or less pale, and often mixed with blue ; hence it occurs rose
ch blossom red, and lilac blue, passing into the amethyst. It is harder than any
ineral, except the diamond. Easily frangible. Specific gravity from 3·916 to
Infusible before the blowpipe. Oriental rubies of 10 carats are extremely
valuable. One of 22 grains was sold for 160*l.* Rubies in lots, Indian cut, of
zes, and of different qualities, are at all times to be had, and sell at from 15*s.* to
arat ; but a perfect stone of a carat, or 6 grains, may be deemed rare, and falls
rt of the value of the diamond : nay, in some cases, rubies of 2, 3, or 4 carats, if
, are much scarcer, and even more valuable, than diamonds of equal weight.
est ruby in England, or, perhaps, in Europe, is in the collection of the late
pe, author of "Anastasius."

are two other species of ruby, the *Spinelle* and *Balais.* When perfect, the Spi-
gem of great value and scarcity. Its colour is a fine full carmine or rose red,
ver presents that rich mellow tinge that attends the Oriental ruby. It is also
to the latter in hardness and specific gravity. Stones of 3 carats and upwards
rare and valuable.

Balais Ruby is a pale variety of the Spinelle. It varies in colour from light
llowish red. Though not so rare as the Spinelle, it is by no means common.
ch admired for its agreeable tinge of colour ; and, when pure and perfect, fetches
gh price ; though considerably less than the other varieties.
s are found in Pegu and the island of Ceylon. — (*Mawe on Diamonds,* 2d ed.
101. ; *Thomson's Chemistry.*)

, a well known and highly esteemed spirituous liquor, imported from the
idies, of which it forms one of the staple products. It is obtained, by
f fermentation and distillation, from molasses, the refuse of the cane juice,
tions of the cane, after the sugar has been extracted. The flavour and
culiar to rum are derived from the essential oils carried over in distillation.
ie distillation has been carelessly performed, the spirit contains so large
ty of the grosser and less volatile part of the oil as to be unfit for use till
tained a considerable age. When it is well rectified, it mellows much
Rum of a brownish transparent colour, smooth oily taste, strong body
istence, good age, and well kept, is the best. That of a clear, limpid
ind hot pungent taste, is either too new, or mixed with other spirits.
rum is the first in point of quality ; the Leeward Island rum, as it is
eing always inferior to it, both in flavour, strength, and value. The price
tter is usually 20 per cent. below that of the former. We import all our

rum in puncheons, containing from 84 to 90 gallons each. It is custom some of the West India islands, to put sliced pine-apples in puncheons o this gives the spirit the flavour of the fruit, and hence the designation, *apple rum.* The best state in which rum can be imported, or preserved, of rectified spirit, as it may thus be conveyed in half its usual bulk, being wards reduced to the proper degree of strength by means of spring water.

Rum is usually very much adulterated by the retail dealers in England, times with corn spirit; but if done with molasses spirit, the tastes of both nearly allied, that the cheat is not easily discovered.

Consumption of, and Duties upon, Rum, &c.—The following tables show the q of rum consumed in Great Britain and Ireland since 1800, the rates of duty c upon it, and the produce of the duties; the quantities derived from our different c last year, and the countries to which the excess of imports has been again export

I. Account, stated in *Imperial Proof Gallons*, of the Rum annually entered for Home Consumpti United Kingdom, from 1800 to 1829; distinguishing England, Ireland, and Scotland; the Duty payable respectively thereon; the Produce of the Duties; and the Price of Rum since 1814.

Years.	Quantities Entered for Home Consumption.				Rates of Duty payable (Customs and Excise.)				Nett Produce of the Duties in Great Britain.			Neu Produce of Duties in Ireland.			Pri Jamai in
	England.	Scotland.	Ireland.	United Kingdom.	In England and Scotland.		In Ireland.								
	Gallons.	*Gallons.*	*Gallons.*	*Gallons.*	*Per Gal.* *s.*	*d.*	*Per Gal.* *s.*	*d.*	*L.*	*s.*	*d.*	*L.*	*s.*	*d.*	*Per*
1800	1,945,266	239,913	864,411	3,049,590	9	0¼	6	8¾	920,827	6	4	263,355	0	0	
1801	1,687,839	349,237	1,057,316	3,094,392	8	10¼	-	-	955,177	1	5	347,455	7	9	
1802	2,204,897	468,163	637,005	3,310,065	9	0¾	6	11¼	1,222,989	11	2	206,861	2	10	
1803	2,573,602	379,043	259,966	3,212,611	13	4¾	8	6¾	1,368,870	13	4	88,140	7	8	
1804	1,508,899	124,548	180,289	1,813,736	13	5¾	9	2¾	1,054,625	1	6	69,292	8	3	
1805	1,696,384	153,635	123,049	1,973,068	13	5¼	-	-	1,223,770	0	9	56,401	2	4	
1806	1,857,321	188,811	160,148	2,206,280	13	6½	-		1,373,986	5	0	72,615	16	0	
1807	1,999,783	226,296	210,822	2,436,901	-	-	-	-	1,496,814	1	8	69,776	13	3	
1808	2,174,751	239,263	343,333	2,757,347	-	-	10	3½	1,637,475	16	2	161,789	3	9	
1809	2,260,625	289,325	1,063,661	3,613,611	13	7¾	-	-	1,738,074	5	8	546,747	1	7	
1810	2,703,718	330,560	336,658	3,370,936	-	-	-	-	2,059,170	0	7	172,424	11	8	
1811	2,711,945	300,306	150,290	3,162,541					2,055,161	4	0	77,378	3	11	
1812	3,205,465	286,569	285,155	3,775,169	-	-	-	-	2,366,338	12	10	149,817	9	1	
1813	3,044,680	241,686	463,008	3,749,374	13	10½	12	10¼	2,278,636	10	0	251,639	9	2	
1814	3,332,188	280,493	91,154	3,703,835	-	-	12	8¾	2,513,578	2	7	58,060	6	6	4*s.* 6*d.*
1815	3,019,201	281,748	64,833	3,365,785	-	-		-	2,240,472	17	10	41,295	5	10	3*s.* 2*d.*
1816	2,221,533	185,874	21,543	2,428,950	-	-	-		1,636,386	13	10	12,171	5	0	3*s.* 7*d.*
1817	2,179,213	198,412	30,686	2,408,311		-	-		1,619,425	16	5	19,423	6	2	3*s.* 9*d.*
1818	2,406,266	203,951	21,366	2,631,583	-	-	-		1,775,714	12	2	13,587	15	4	3*s.* 5*d.*
1819	2,390,193	148,955	25,735	2,564,883	13	11½	-	-	1,730,446	14	9	16,289	14	6	2*s.* 6*d.*
1820	2,325,733	142,997	20,390	2,489,120	-	-	-	-	1,684,425	7	8	12,981	5	2	2*s.* 8*d.*
1821	2,166,441	138,189	19,685	2,324,315	-	-		-	1,576,377	1	4	12,538	6	0	1*s.* 6*d.*
1822	2,100,925	130,879	15,035	2,246,859	-		-	-	1,516,645	11	6	9,557	6	8	1*s.* 8*d.*
1823	2,222,923	108,562	18,175	2,349,660	-	-	13	11½	1,590,666	18	6	11,534	6	5	1*s.* 8*d.*
1824	2,407,207	134,986	9,453	2,551,646	12	7½	12	7½	1,600,827	6	6	6,097	7	1	1*s.* 7*d.*
1825	1,980,807	104,752	10,128	2,095,687	-	-	-	-	1,278,313	19	1	6,313	19	4	2*s.* 6*d.*
1826	3,982,053	295,505	27,758	4,305,316	8	6	8	6	1,817,108	2	3	11,770	6	6	3*s.* 0*d.*
1827	3,080,152	185,214	23,240	3,288,606	-	-	-	-	1,386,726	1	1	9,850	7	10	3*s.* 4*d.*
1828	3,064,856	188,089	24,708	3,277,653	-	-			1,382,624	19	5	10,528	17	9	3*s.* 3*d.*
1829	3,202,143	152,461	21,262	3,375,866	-	-	-	-	1,425,746	18	8	9,035	14	5	2*s.* 3*d.*

This account has been prepared partly from published and partly from unpublished *official* d The column of prices has been taken from *Mr. Cook's* tract on the *Commerce of Great Britain*

II. Account of Rum entered for Home Consumption in the United Kingdom in 1830, and o ceived thereon.

Quantity - -	3,658,958 proof gallons.	Duty received - -	£1,599,9
Price in bond -	2*s.* 1*d.* to 3*s.* 3*d.*		

III. Account of the Quantity of Rum imported into the United Kingdom, distinguishing t Colonies and Countries from which the same was imported, in the Year ended 5th January

British Colonies and Plantations in America; viz.	*Proof Gallons.*	British Colonies and Plantations in America; viz. (*continued.*) -	*Pro*
Antigua - - - -	155,514	Berbice - - - -	
Barbadoes - - - -	2,357	Honduras - - -	
Dominica - - - -	36,321	British N. American Colonies	
Grenada - - - -	298,933		
Jamaica - - - -	3,213,503	Foreign Colonies in the West Indies, viz.	
Montserrat - - -	49,075		
Nevis - - - -	51,243	Cuba - - - -	
St. Christopher - - -	219,706	Porto Rico - - -	
St. Lucia - - - -	12,817	St. Thomas - - -	
St. Vincent - - - -	173,262	United States of America - -	
Tobago - - - -	428,810	Philippine Islands - -	
Trinidad - - - -	12,941	Other Countries - -	
Bermudas	2,987		
Demerara - - -	1,859,710	Total - -	6

count of the Quantity of Rum exported from the United Kingdom, distinguishing the Countries to which the same was exported, in the Year ended 5th January, 1831.

	Proof Gallons.		Proof Gallons.
a - - - -	66,698	Brought up - -	1,048,615
en - - -	12,341	East Indies and China -	8,480
ay - - -	4,527	New South Wales, Swan River, and Van Diemen's Land	133,304
ark - - -	19,342		
ta - - -	214,105	Cape of Good Hope - -	3,948
any - - -	413,479	Other Parts of Africa - -	158,418
Netherlands -	92,256	British North American Colonies -	167,198
e - - -	730	British West Indies -	24,147
gal, Azores, and Madeira -	861	Foreign West Indies -	3,589
and Canaries - -	3,024	United States of America -	7,835
ltar - - -	19,481	Mexico - - -	211
- - - -	86,463	Colombia - -	196
- - - -	12,854	Brazil - -	1,656
n Islands - -	12,654	States of the Rio de la Plata -	2,898
y - - -	7,785	Chili - - -	2,497
sey, Jersey, Alderney, and	82,015	Peru - - -	8,562
		The Whale Fisheries -	7,027
	1,048,615	Total -	1,578,581

ugh rum has not been so much over-taxed as brandy, geneva, and wine, still it pretty clear that even in its case taxation has been carried far beyond its proper During the 3 years ending with 1802, when the duty of Great Britain was s. a gallon. and in Ireland 6s. 8¾d., the consumption in the United Kingdom ed to 3,150,000 gallons a year; while, notwithstanding the great increase of ion, during the 3 years ending with 1823, when the duty in Great Britain was ¾d. a gallon, and in Ireland 12s. 8¾d., the annual consumption amounted to 307,000 gallons! The reduction of the duty in 1826 to 8s. 6d. has increased the ption from about 2,500,000 to above 3,600,000 gallons a year; and the demand greater than before the reduction. The great demand for rum from 1811 to as occasioned chiefly by the high price and inferior quality of the British spirits re then manufactured.

decrease in the consumption of rum in Ireland is most striking. Unfortunately, ·, this is not the only instance the sister kingdom affords of the destructive effects ssive taxes. The excessive additions made to the duties on brandy, wine, sugar, e 1805, have had similar effects; the quantity of these articles consumed in Ire- ng *incomparably less now than it was 30 years ago !*—(See BRANDY, SUGAR, &c.) ant taxes have gone far to deprive the Irish of every comfort; and, consequently, from them some of the most powerful incentives to industry and good conduct. erty of the people has set at nought the calculations of our finance ministers; *crease of taxation in Ireland having produced a diminution of revenue and an of crime !* Surely it is high time to abandon so odious a system; particularly e experience of the beneficial effects that have resulted from the diminution of t duties. As a means of raising revenue the taxation of Ireland is utterly ve; but the wit of man never contrived any thing better fitted to produce m and disaffection.

he produce of the British possessions in America, is not liable to the duty charged on sweetened less the actual strength exceed the strength denoted by Sykes's hydrometer by more than 10 er cent.; and in lieu of such duty there shall be charged upon every degree per cent. more than and not more than 10 degrees, by which the actual strength shall exceed the strength denoted hydrometer, a duty of 9s. 6d.: Provided, that if the importer cannot make a perfect entry thereof nt of duty on the actual strength, he may demand in writing, upon the entry, that trial be made tual strength (he paying the expenses of such trial), instead of entering such rum for the pay- uty upon any stated number of such excessive degrees of strength: Provided, also that all trials strength of such rum shall be made by some skilful person appointed by the commissioners of or such purpose. — (7 Geo. 4. c. 48. § 31.)

he produce of the British plantations, must be imported in casks containing not less than 20 · in cases containing not less than 3 dozen reputed quart bottles, under penalty of forfeiture. — c. 107.)

bonded warehouses may be drawn off into casks containing not less than 20 gallons each, as hips, and may be delivered into the charge of the searcher, to be shipped as stores for any ship, ntry or payment of duty, the same being duly borne upon the victualling bill of such ships y. — (6 Geo. 4. c. 112.)

bonded warehouses may also be drawn off into reputed quart or reputed pint bottles, and cases containing not less than 3 dozen such quarts, or 6 dozen such pint bottles each, for the being exported from the warehouse. — (6 Geo. 4. c. 112.)

cations referring to a former order allowing the admixture of rums of different strengths for n, and praying that the rum remaining in the vats after the operation of racking might be or home consumption, the Board were of opinion that the request might be complied with, to of an ullage of 20 gallons, the legal quantity allowed to be exported, and that the duty should cording to the strength, at the time of delivery of the said rum. — (Min. Com. Cus. 27th Sept.

ny rum shall be entered as being the produce of any British possession in America, or of the the master of the ship importing the same must deliver a certificate of origin to the collector ller, and make oath that the goods are the produce of such place. — (6 Geo. 4. c. 107 § 35.; see 5.)

RUSSIA COMPANY, a regulated company for conducting the trade Russia. It was first incorporated by charter of Philip and Mary, sanctioned act of parliament in 1566. The statute 10 & 11 Will. 3. c. 6., enacts, every British subject desiring admission into the Russia Company shall be mitted on paying 5*l.*; and every individual admitted into the Company cond his business entirely as a private adventurer, or as he would do were the Com abolished.

Table of Duties payable to the Russia Company.

		s.	d.
Aniseed	the cwt.	0	3
Ashes, pearl and pot	the ton	0	9
Books, bound	the cwt.	0	3
unbound	the cwt.	0	2
Bristles	the dozen lbs.	0	0¼
Castoreum	the lb.	0	1
Caviare	the cwt.	0	2
Cordage	the cwt.	0	2
Down	the 100 lbs.	0	4
Feathers, bed	the cwt.	0	4
Flax	the ton	0	9
Hair, cow or ox	the cwt.	0	2
Hemp	the ton	0	7
Hides, of cows or horses, undressed	each	0	0½
red or Muscovy	each	0	1
Iron	the ton	0	5
Isinglass	the cwt.	0	4
Linen, drillings	the 120 ells	0	1½
narrow or diaper	the 120 ells	0	2
22½ to 31½	the 120 ells	0	3
31½ to 45	the 120 ells	0	4
45	and upwards	0	6
sail cloth	the 120 ells	0	3
Linseed	the quarter	0	2
Mats	the hundred	0	2
Oats	the quarter	0	1
Pitch	the last	0	2
Rhubarb	the lb.	0	1½
Rosin	the cwt.	0	1½
Saltpetre	the cwt.	0	1½
Seeds, garden	the 100 lb.	0	3
Skins and Furs, viz.			
armins or ermines	the zimmer of 40 skins	0	2
bear	each	0	2
Calabar	the zimmer	0	2
calf	the hundred	0	3

Skins and Furs; viz.	
fox	the hundred
hare	the 100 dozen
sables	the zimmer
swan	each
wolf	each
Tallow	the ton
Tongues	the hundred
Tow	the ton
Wax, bees'	the cwt.
Wheat	the quarter
Wood, viz.	
balks, above 5 inches sq.	the 120
under do.	the 120
barrel boards	the 120
battens	the 120
capravens	the 120
clap boards	the 120
deals, under 20 feet long	the 120
above do.	the 120
fire wood	the fathom
fir timber	the load
handspikes	the 120
lathwood	the fathom
masts, great	each
all others	each
oak boards	the 120
plank	the load
timber	the load
oars	the 120
paling boards	the 120
spars	the 120
staves	the 120
tar	the last
wainscot logs	the load

All goods not enumerated, pay one eighth per cent. *ad* on the declaration of the importer.

RUSSIA LEATHER (Fr. *Cuir de Russie;* Ger. *Juften;* It. *Cuojo di Ru* Pol. *Jachta;* Rus. *Juft*, *Youft;* Sp. *Moscovia*), the tanned hides of oxen other kine, denominated by the Russians *youfts*, or *juffs*,—a designation said derived from their being generally manufactured in pairs. The business of ta is carried on in most towns of the empire, but principally at Moscow and P burgh. Russia leather is soft, has a strongly prominent grain, a great deal of l and a powerful and peculiar odour. It is principally either red or black; the fo is the best, and is largely used in this and other countries in bookbindin which purpose it is superior to every other material. The black is, howev very extensive demand in Russia, large quantities being made up into and shoes. The process followed by the Russians in the preparation o valuable commodity has been frequently described; but notwithstanding circumstance, and the fact that foreigners have repeatedly engaged in the bu in Russia, with the intention of making themselves masters of its details undertaking it at home, the efforts made to introduce the manufacture into countries have hitherto entirely failed. One of the best tests of genuine R leather is its throwing out a strong odour of burnt hide upon being rub little. —(*Ricard, Traité Général du Commerce*, tome i. p. 275. ed. 1781.)

We borrow from Mr. Borrisow's work on the Commerce of Petersburgh the following details w spect to this article: — "Russia leather forms one of the principal export commodities of Peter But since the ports of the Black Sea have been opened, the exports of leather from this port ha siderably decreased; Italy, the principal consumer, supplying its wants from Odessa and Taganro easily, cheaply, and expeditiously, than from Petersburgh. The chief exportation from the lat Prussia, Germany, and England. Frankfort on the Maine and Leipzic are of great importanc spects the trade in Russia leather, on account of the fairs held in them.

Juffs are never bought on contract, but always on the spot at cash prices. It nevertheless often h that agents, in order to secure a lot of juffs, pay a certain sum in advance, and settle for the am the first market prices; no prices being fixed in the months of January, February, March, an times even April.

Juffs are assorted or *bracked* when received, according to their different qualities, into *Gave*, *Malja*, and *Domashna*. The three first sorts are again divided into *heavy* and *light Gave*, *heavy* a *Rosval*, &c. Domashna is the worst, and consequently the cheapest sort. It often happens that j bought unassorted, and then the prices are regulated according as the quantity of Domashna cont the lot is greater or less. Persons well acquainted with the nature of Russia leather prefer purch in this state.

Juffs are sold by the pood, which consists, as it is commonly expressed, of 4, 4¼, 4½, 5, 5½, and 5 By this is understood, that so many hides make a pood, calculated upon the whole lot; and it observed that the lightest juffs are esteemed the best in quality. Heavy juffs, or those of 4 and 4 are shipped for Italy: the Germans, on the contrary, prefer the lighter sort.

Juffs are packed in rolls, each containing 10 hides; and from 10 to 15 of these rolls are packed t in a bundle, which is well secured by thick matting. There are red, white, and black juffs; but

in demand. Their goodness is determined by their being of a high red colour, of equal size,
ked with small hides : they must also be free from holes, well stretched, and equally thin. In a
hed lot, no thick head or feet parts should be found. If spots resembling flowers are seen on
des, it is an additional sign of their good quality ; and they are then called *bloomed juffs*. The
uld be clean, soft, and white, and, when taken in the hand, should feel elastic. The best con-
of Russia leather can nearly determine the quality by the smell alone.
ttention must be paid, in shipping juffs, to secure them from being wetted, as damp air alone
t to injure them.
of juffs make a last ; 88 poods nett weight, when shipped for Italy, make a last ; and 44 poods a
gland.

(Ger. *Rogken, Rocken* ; Du. *Rog, Rogge* ; Fr. *Seigle* ; It. *Segale, Segala* ;
eno ; Rus. *Rosch, Sel, Jar* ; Lat. *Secale*), according to some, is a native
; but it is very doubtful if it be found wild in any country. It has been
d from time immemorial, and is considered as coming nearer in its pro-
o wheat than any other grain. It is more common than wheat in many
the Continent ; being a more certain crop, and requiring less cul-
manure. It is the bread corn of Germany and Russia. In Britain it is
little grown ; being no longer a bread corn ; and, therefore, of less value
rmer than barley, oats, or peas. — (*Loudon's Ency. of Agriculture.*)
e regulations as to the importation and exportation of rye, see CORN
ID CORN TRADE.

S.

E (Ger. *Zobel* ; Fr. *Zibelline* ; It. *Zibellino* ; Rus. *Sohol*), an animal of the
ibe, found in the northern parts of Asiatic Russia and America, hunted
ke of its fur. Its colour is generally of a deep glossy brown, and some-
a fine glossy black, which is most esteemed. Sable skins have some-
ough very rarely, been found yellow, and white. The finer sorts of the
bles are very scarce and dear.—(See FUR TRADE.)
LES (Fr. *Selles* ; Ger. *Sattel* ; It. *Selle* ; Rus. *Sädla* ; Sp. *Selles*), seats
o the horse's back, for the convenience of the rider. Those made in
are reckoned the best. Sherborne and Lynn are particularly remarkable
nanufacture. The hogskins, which, when tanned, are used for the seat
dle, are mostly imported from Russia.
LOWER, OR BASTARD SAFFRON (Ger. *Safflor* ; Du. *Saffloer,*
affran ; Fr. *Cartame, Saffran batard* ; It. *Zaffrone* ; Sp. *Alazor, Azafran*
Rus. *Polerroi, Prostoi schafran*), the flower of an annual plant (*Carthamus*
Lin.) growing in India, Egypt, America, and some of the warmer parts
e. It is not easily distinguished from saffron by the eye, but it has
f its smell or taste.

rs, which are sometimes sold under the name of *saffranon*, are the only parts employed in
ey yield two sorts of colouring matter : one soluble in water, and producing a yellow of but
; the other is *resinous*, and best dissolved by the fixed alkalies : it is this last which alone
ower valuable in dyeing ; as it affords a red colour exceeding in delicacy and beauty, as it does
any which can be obtained even from cochineal, though much inferior to the latter in dura-
olour of safflower will not bear the action of soap, nor even that of the sun and air for a long
eing very costly, it is principally employed for imitating upon silk the fine scarlet (*ponçeau* of
and rose colours dyed with cochineal upon woollen cloth.
ose colour of safflower, extracted by crystallised soda, precipitated by citric acid, then slowly
ground with the purest talc, produces the beautiful *rouge* known by the name of *rouge*

hould be chosen in flakes of a bright pink colour, and of a smell somewhat resembling tobacco.
s in powder, dark coloured, or oily, ought to be rejected. —(*Hasselquist's Voyages*, Eng. ed.
croft's Permanent Colours*, vol. i. pp. 286—289. ; *Milburn's Orient. Com.*)
wt. of safflower imported in 1829, 2,689 came from the East Indies, 1,778 from the United
155 from Egypt. The price of safflower in bond varies from 5l. to 10l. a ton. The duty is

RON (Ger. *Saffran* ; Du. *Safran* ; It. *Zafferano* ; Sp. *Saffron* ; Fr. *Azafran* ;
fran*), a sort of cake prepared from the stigmas, with a proportion of the
perennial bulbous plant (*Crocus sativus*, Lin.) cultivated to a small extent
dgeshire. It is also imported from Sicily, France, and Spain ; but the
s being fresher, more genuine, and better cured, is always preferred.
d, saffron has a sweetish, penetrating, diffusive odour ; a warm, pungent,
aste ; and a rich, deep, orange red colour. It should be chosen fresh, in
h, compact cakes, moderately moist, and possessing in an obvious de-
e above mentioned qualities. The not staining the fingers, the making
and a whitish yellow or a blackish colour, indicate that it is bad, or

too old. Saffron is used in medicine, and in the arts; but in this country th
sumption seems to be diminishing. It is employed to colour butter and (
and also by painters and dyers. —(*Thomson's Dispensatory; Loudon's E*
Agriculture.)

SAGAPENUM (Arab. *Sugbenuj*), a concrete gum resin, the produce
unknown Persian plant. It is imported from Alexandria, Smyrna, &c.
an odour of garlic; and a hot, acrid, bitterish taste. It is in agglutinated
or masses, of an olive or brownish yellow colour, slightly translucent, and
ing with a horny fracture. It softens and is tenacious between the fingers.
at a low heat, and burns with a crackling noise and white flame, giving out
dance of smoke, and leaving behind a light spongy charcoal. It is used
medicine. — (*Thomson's Dispensatory.*)

SAGO (Malay, *Sagu*; Jav. *Sagu*), a species of meal, the produce of
(*Metroxylon Sagu*) indigenous to and abundant in the Eastern islands, wl
supplies the principal part of the farinaceous food of the inhabitants.

The tree, when at maturity, is about 30 feet high, and from 18 to 22 inches
ameter. Before the formation of the fruit, the stem consists of an external wal
2 inches thick, the whole interior being filled up with a sort of spongy medullary
When the tree attains to maturity, and the fruit is formed, the stem is quite
Being cut down at the proper period, the medullary part is extracted from the
and reduced to a powder like sawdust. The filaments are next separated by w;
The meal is then laid to dry; and being made into cakes and baked, is eaten
islanders. For exportation, the finest sago meal is mixed with water, and the paste
into small grains of the size and form of coriander seeds. This is the species pri
brought to England, for which market it should be chosen of a reddish hue, and
dissolving in hot water into a fine jelly. Within these few years, however, a
has been invented by the Chinese for refining sago, so as to give it a fine pearly
and the sago so cured is in the highest estimation in all the European markets.
light, wholesome, nutritious food.

During the 3 years ending with 1828, the imports of sago amounted to about 8,000 cwt. a ye
duty on the sago entered for home consumption produced, in 1830, 1,623*l*. 13*s*.; but as the duty is c
amounts, we are thence unable to determine the quantity that paid duty. Probably, however, it
2,000 cwt. The price of common sago in bond varies from 14*s*. to 1*l*.; while pearl sago fetches
to 1*l*. 15*s*. a cwt.; but the price is liable to great fluctuation. It is largely exported from the India
to China and Bengal. The best is said to be produced at Siak, on the north coast of Sumatra. —
Mat. Indica; Crawfurd's East. Archip. vol. i. pp. 383—393., vol. iii. p. 348.; *Bell's Review of
merce of Bengal*, &c.)

SAIL, a coarse linen or canvass sheet attached to the masts and y
ships, the blades of windmills, &c., to intercept the wind and occasio
movement.

Foreign sails, when imported by, and fit and necessary for, and *in the actual use* of any Bri
are exempted from duty; but when otherwise disposed of, they pay a duty of 20 per cent. *ad*
— (9 *Geo.* 4. c. 76. § 12.)

Sails and cordage of British manufacture, exported from Great Britain to the colonies, and a
imported into the United Kingdom, are in all cases, other than those in which they are imported
store, to be deemed foreign; and such sails and cordage, although not liable to duty so l
vessel continues to belong to the colony, become subject to the duties in question as soon as
becomes the property of persons residing in this country. — (*Treasury Order*, 29 Jan. 1828.)

SALEP, a species of powder prepared from the dried roots of a plant
orchis kind (*Orchis Mascula*, Lin.). That which is imported from Indi
white oval pieces, hard, clear, and pellucid, without smell, and tasti
tragacanth. As an article of diet, it is said to be light, bland, and nu
The plant thrives in England, but it is not cultivated to any extent; a
little is imported. — (*Ainslie's Mat. Indica; Milburn's Orient. Com.*)

SALMON (Ger. *Lachs, Salm*; Fr. *Saumon*; It. *Sermone, Salamone*;
mon; Rus. *Lemga*). This capital fish is too well known to require any
tion. It is found only in northern seas, being unknown in the Medite
and other warm regions. In this country it is an article of much value
portance.

"Salmon fisheries," Marshall observes, "are copious and constant sources of human food;
next to agriculture. They have, indeed, one advantage over every other internal produce,—
crease does not lessen other articles of human subsistence. The salmon does not prey on the
the soil, nor does it owe its size and nutritive qualities to the destruction of its compatriot
leaves its native river at an early state of growth; and going, even naturalists know not whe
of ample size, and rich in human nourishment; exposing itself in the narrowest streams, a
intended it as a special boon to man. In every stage of savageness and civilisation, the sa
have been considered as a valuable benefaction to this country."

Being rarely caught, except in estuaries or rivers, the salmon may be considered in a grea
private property. The London market, where the consumption is immense, is principally sur
the Scotch rivers. The Tweed fishery is the first in point of magnitude of any in the kin
take is sometimes quite astonishing, several hundreds having been frequently taken by a sing

Salmon are despatched in fast sailing vessels from the Spey, the Tay, the Tweed, and other rivers, for London, packed in ice, by which means they are preserved quite fresh. When the ~~s~~ at its height, and the catch greater than can be taken off fresh, it is salted, pickled, or dried for consumption at home, and for foreign markets. Formerly such part of the Scotch salmon as was ~~con~~sumed at home, was pickled and kitted after being boiled, and was in this state sent up to London ~~th~~e name of Newcastle salmon; but the present method of disposing of the fish has so raised its ~~price~~s to have nearly deprived all but the richer inhabitants in the environs of the fishery of the use of

Within the memory of many now living, salted salmon formed a material article of household ~~diet~~ in all the farm-houses in the vale of the Tweed; insomuch, that in-door servants used to sti~~pulate~~ that they should not be obliged to take more than two weekly meals of salmon. Its ordinary price ~~was~~ 2s. a stone of 19 lbs.; but it is now never below 12s., often 36s., and sometimes 42s. a stone! ~~The ris~~e in the price of the fish has produced a corresponding rise in the value of the salmon fisheries, which yield very large rents. The total value of the salmon caught in the Scotch rivers has ~~been es~~timated at 150,000l. a year. There are considerable fisheries in some of the Irish and English ~~rivers,~~ but inferior to those of Scotland. — (*Loudon's Ency. of Agriculture; General Report of Scotland,* ~~p~~. 327.)

~~C~~ase of the Supply of Salmon, Poaching, &c. — The decrease of salmon in the English and Scotch ~~rivers, p~~articularly of late years, is a fact as to which there can be no manner of doubt. Much unsatis~~factory~~ discussion has taken place as to its causes, which are, probably, of a very diversified character. ~~Some~~ deal has been ascribed to the increase of water machinery on the banks of the different rivers; ~~but we~~ hardly think that this could have much influence, except, perhaps, in the case of the smaller ~~r~~ivers. *Weirs,* or salmon traps, have also been much objected to; though, as we have been assured, ~~with~~ less reason. On the whole, we are inclined to think that the falling off in the supply of this fish is principally to be ascribed to the temptation to over-fish the rivers, caused by the extraor~~dinary ri~~se in the price of salmon; to the prevalence of poaching; and, more than all, to the too limited of the *close time*. In 1828, after a great deal of discussion and inquiry, an act was passed ~~(9 Geo.~~ c. 39.), which has done a good deal to remedy these defects — in so far, at least, as respects the ~~fi~~sheries. The rivers are to be shut from the 14th of September to the 1st of February; and ~~any pe~~rson catching or attempting to catch fish during that period is to forfeit not less than 1l. and not ~~more tha~~n 10l. for every offence, besides the fish, if he have caught any, and such boats, nets, or other ~~impleme~~nts, as he may have made use of. Pecuniary penalties are also inflicted upon poachers and ~~othe~~rs; and provision is made for the watching of the rivers. We understand that this act has had ~~a go~~od effect; though it is believed that it would be better were the *close time* extended from the ~~Se~~ptember to the middle of February.

~~It is e~~nacted by stat. 1 Geo 1. st. 2. c. 18., that no salmon shall be sent to any fishmonger or fish-seller ~~in Lon~~don, of less than 6 lbs. weight, under a penalty of 5l. The 58 Geo. 3. c. 43. authorises the justices ~~in thei~~r sessions to appoint conservators of rivers, and to fix the beginning and termination of the *close* ~~time; t~~he penalty upon poaching and taking fish in *close time* is by the same act fixed at not more than ~~5l.;~~ ~~n~~ot less than 5l., with forfeiture of fish, boats, nets, &c.

~~SAL~~T (Ger. *Salz;* Du. *Zout;* Fr. *Sel;* It. *Sale;* Sp. *Sal;* Rus. *Sol;* Lat. *Sal;* ~~Arab.~~ *Melh;* Chin. *Yen;* Hind. *Nimmuck*), the *chloride of sodium* of modern ~~chemis~~ts, has been known and in common use as a seasoner and preserver of ~~food fr~~om the earliest ages. Immense masses of it are found in this and many ~~other c~~ountries, which require only to be dug out and reduced to powder. In ~~this sta~~te it is called rock-salt. The water of the ocean also contains a great ~~deal of~~ salt; to which, indeed, it owes its taste, and the power which it pos~~sesses o~~f resisting freezing till cooled down to 28·5°. When this water is suffi~~ciently~~ evaporated, the salt precipitates in crystals. This is the common process ~~by whic~~h it is obtained in many countries. There are various processes by which ~~it may b~~e obtained quite pure. Common salt usually crystallizes in cubes. Its ~~taste is~~ universally known, and is what is strictly denominated *salt*. Its specific ~~gravity~~ is 2·125. It is soluble in 2·82 times its weight of cold water, and in 2·76 ~~it~~s weight of boiling water. — (*Thomson's Chemistry.*)

~~Salt ha~~s its vast utility in seasoning food, and preserving meat both for domestic con~~sumptio~~n and during the longest voyages, and in furnishing muriatic acid and soda, ~~It is use~~d as a glaze for coarse pottery, by being thrown into the oven where it is baked; ~~it impro~~ves the whiteness and clearness of glass: it gives hardness to soap; in melting ~~metals i~~t preserves their surface from calcination, by defending them from the air, and ~~is empl~~oyed with advantage in some assays; it is used as a mordant, and for improving ~~some c~~olours, and enters more or less into many other processes of the arts. Many ~~contradi~~ctory statements have been made as to the use of salt as a manure. Probably ~~it may b~~e advantageous in some situations, and not in others.

~~Mi~~nes, Springs, &c. — The principal salt mines are at Wielitska in Poland, Catalonia in Spain, ~~thos~~e in Calabria, Loowur in Hungary, in many places in Asia and Africa, and in Cheshire in this ~~country.~~ The mines at Wielitska are upon a very large scale; but the statements that have frequently ~~been publi~~shed of their containing villages, inhabited by colonies of miners who never saw the light, are ~~quite~~ without foundation. These mines have been wrought for more than 600 years. — (*Coxe's ~~Travels in~~ the North of Europe,* vol. i. p. 149. 8vo ed.)

~~The~~ mines in the neighbourhood of Northwich in Cheshire are very extensive. They have been ~~worked si~~nce 1670; and the quantity of salt obtained from them is greater, probably, than is obtained ~~from any o~~ther salt mines in the world. In its solid form, when dug from the mine, Cheshire salt is not ~~sufficientl~~y pure for use. To purify it, it is dissolved in sea water, from which it is afterwards separated ~~by evapora~~tion and crystallisation. The greater part of this salt is exported.

~~Salt spri~~ngs are met with in several countries. Those in Cheshire and Worcestershire furnish a large ~~part~~ of the salt made use of in Great Britain. The brine, being pumped up from very deep wells, is ~~boiled~~ in wrought iron pans from 20 to 30 feet square and 10 or 12 inches deep, placed over a

~~Much of~~ the salt used in Scotland previously to the repeal of the duty, was obtained by the evaporation ~~of sea wate~~r nearly in the way now mentioned; but several of the Scotch salt works have since been relin·

In warm countries, salt is obtained by the evaporation of sea water by the heat of the sun; an crystals of salt made in this way are more perfect and purer, from the greater slowness of the pr French salt is manufactured in this mode, and it has always been in considerable demand in th other countries; but the principal imports of foreign salt into Great Britain at present are from Por

Account of the Foreign Salt imported into Great Britain and Ireland in the Years 1829 and 183

Countries from which imported.	Quantities of Foreign Salt imported into Great Britain and Ireland.	
	1829.	1830.
	Bushels.	*Bushels.*
France - - - - - -	81,128	25,760
Portugal - - - - -	284,225	331,244
Spain - - - - -	18,205	6,205
Naples and Sicily - - -	11,630	9,910
Ionian Islands - - -	4,000	
East India Company's Territories -		8
Total - -	399,188	373,127

Consumption of Salt. — The consumption of salt in this country is immense. Necker estimate consumption in those provinces of France which had purchased an exemption from the *gabelle* *francs redimées*) at about 19½ lbs. (Eng.) for each individual. — (*Administration des Finances*, to p. 12.) From all that we have been able to learn on the subject, we believe that the consumption people of this country may be estimated a little higher, or at 22 lbs.; the difference in our food and as compared with the French, fully accounting for this increased allowance. On this supposition taking the population at 16,000,000, the entire consumption will amount to 352,000,000 lbs., or 144,20 Exclusive of this immense home consumption, we annually export about 10,000,000 bushels, wh 56 lbs. a bushel, are equivalent to 250,000 tons. The Americans are the largest consumers of Britis the exports to the United States in 1829 having amounted to 3,515,924 bushels. During the same y exported to the Netherlands, 1,583,517 bushels; to the British North American colonies, 1,472,0 to Russia, 1,388,490 do.; to Prussia, 949,834 do., &c. The cheapness of this important necessary of life is not less remarkable than its diffusion. Its cost may be estimated, at a medium, at from 14s. to 16s. a ton.

Duties on Salt. — In ancient Rome salt was subjected to a duty (*vectigal salinarum*, see *Burma* *sertatio de Vectigalibus Pop. Rom.* c. 6.); and it has been heavily taxed in most modern states *gabelle*, or code of salt laws, formerly established in France, was most oppressive. From 4,000 t persons are calculated to have been sent annually to prison and the galleys for offences connecte these laws, the severity of which had no inconsiderable share in bringing about the Revolut (*Young's Travels in France*, vol. i. p. 598.) In this country, duties upon salt were imposed in the re William III. In 1798, they amounted to 5s. a bushel; but were subsequently increased to 15s. a or about *forty times* the cost of the salt! So exorbitant a duty was productive of the worst effect occasioned, by its magnitude, and the regulations for allowing salt, duty free, to the fisheries, a va of smuggling. The opinion of the public and of the House of Commons having been strongly pron against the tax, it was finally repealed in 1823.

That the repeal of so exorbitant a duty has been productive of great advantage, no one can doub seeing that a large revenue must be raised, we question whether government acted wisely in totally quishing the tax. Had the duty been reduced to 2s. or 2s. 6d. a bushel, and no duty-free salt allo the fisheries, but a drawback given on the fish exported, a revenue of a million a year might ha derived from this source with but little injury. It was not the nature of the salt tax, but the extent to which it had been carried, that rendered it justly odious. When at the highest, it pr about 1,500,000l. a year.

SALTPETRE or NITRATE OF POTASH (Ger. *Salpeter;* Fr. *Salpetre;* It. *Nitro, Salnitro;* Sp. *Nitro, Salitre;* Rus. *Senitra;* Lat. *Nitrum; Ubkir*), a salt well known in commerce, and of very great importance. I be regarded both as a natural and an artificial production; being found surface of the soil in many parts of India, Egypt, Italy, &c., while in thes other places it is obtained by an artificial process, or by lixiviating earth th been formed into *nitre* beds. The saltpetre consumed in England is br from Bengal in an impure state, but crystallised, in bags, each containing 1 Saltpetre forms the principal ingredient in the manufacture of gunpowder is also used in various arts. It is possessed of considerable antiseptic p That which is of the best quality and well refined, is in long transparent cry its taste is sharp, bitterish, and cooling; it flames much when thrown burning coals; it is very brittle; its specific gravity is 1·933. It is not a by exposure to the air.

Beckmann contends, in a long and elaborate dissertation (*Hist. of Invent.* vol. iv. pp. 525—5 ed.) that the ancients were unacquainted with saltpetre, and that their *nitrum* was really an alkal But, as saltpetre is produced naturally in considerable quantities in Egypt, it is difficult to supp they could be entirely ignorant of it; though it would appear that they had confounded it wi things. It has been known in the East from a very early period. Beckmann concurs in opini those who believe that gunpowder was invented in India, and brought by the Saracens from A the Europeans; who improved its manufacture, and made it available for warlike purposes. — p. 571.)

The consumption of saltpetre during periods of war is very great. Its price is consequently extreme fluctuation. In remarking on the varieties in the price of saltpetre, Mr. Tooke observ reached its greatest height in 1795, viz. 170s. a cwt.; in 1796, it fell at one time to 45s., and rose agai It seems to have been affected considerably by the scale of hostilities on the Continent. But in cons of the discoveries in chemistry, by which the French were enabled to dispense with a foreign and by the increased importation from India to this country, by which we were enabled to supply of the Continent at a reduced cost; the price declined permanently after 1798–9, when it had 145s.; and never after was so high as 100s., except during the short interval of speculation in during the peace of 1814, and again upon the breaking out of the war terminated by the battle terloo." The price of saltpetre in the London market varies at this moment (October, 1831) f

wt. The total quantity imported in 1829 amounted to 176,489 cwt., of which 155,095 were
t home. The duty of 6d. a cwt. produced, in 1830, 3,690l. 18s., showing that 147,636 cwt had
·ed for home consumption.

ONICA, a large city and sea-port of European Turkey, at the north-east
ty of the gulf of the same name, in lat. 40° 41′ N., lon. 23° 8′ E. Popula-
imated at 70,000. During that period of the late war when the anti-
cial system of Napoleon was at its height, Salonica became a great *depôt*
·sh goods; whence they were conveyed to Germany, Russia, and other
Europe. At all times, however, Salonica has a considerable trade.
·orts principally consist of wheat, barley, and Indian corn, cotton, wool,
, and timber. The average exportation of cotton is about 110,000 bales;
·co about 30,000 bales; each bale containing about 275 lbs. The ex-
wool is said to amount to about 1,000,000 lbs. The imports are
offee, dye-woods, indigo, muslins, printed calicoes, iron, lead, tin, watches,

, *Weights, and Measures.* — Accounts are kept in piastres of 40 paras, or 120
The coins are those of Constantinople; which see.
·eights and measures are the same as those of Smyrna, except that the kisloz,
· corn measure of Salonica = 3·78 kisloz of Smyrna.

·AGE, as the term is now understood, is an allowance or compensation
those by whose exertions ships or goods have been saved from the
of the seas, fire, pirates, or enemies.
·opriety and justice of making such an allowance must be obvious to every one.
owed by the laws of Rhodes, Oleron, and Wisby; and in this respect they have
·wed by all modern maritime states. At common law, the party who has saved
of another from loss or any imminent peril has a *lien* upon them, and may
·m in his possession till payment of a reasonable salvage.
·age *upon Losses by Perils of the Sea.* — If the salvage be performed at sea, or
·gh or low water mark, the court of admiralty has jurisdiction over the subject,
·x the sum to be paid and adjust the proportions, and take care of the property
·he suit; or, if a sale be necessary, direct it to be made; and divide the
·between the salvors and the proprietors according to equity and reason. And
the rate of salvage, the court usually has regard not only to the labour and
·red by the salvors, but also to the situation in which they may happen to stand
of the property saved, to the promptitude and alacrity manifested by them,
value of the ship and cargo, as well as the degree of danger from which they
·ued. Sometimes the court has allowed as large a proportion as *a half* of
·ty saved as salvage; and in others, not more than *a tenth.*
·w of a ship are not entitled to salvage, or any unusual remuneration for the
·ary efforts they may have made in saving her; it being their duty as well as
contribute their utmost upon such occasions, the whole of their possible ser-
pledged to the master and owners. Neither are passengers entitled to claim
·for the *ordinary assistance* they may have been able to afford to a vessel in dis-
·t a passenger is not bound to remain on board a ship in the hour of danger,
·e can leave her; and if he perform any *extraordinary services,* he is entitled to
·nal recompence.
·ase of valuable property, and of numerous proprietors and salvors, the juris-
·l proceedings of the court of admiralty are well adapted to further the
·f justice. But as the delay and expense necessarily incident to the proceed-
·ourt sitting at a distance from the subject will often be very burdensome
·arties, in cases where the property saved is not, perhaps, very considerable, the
·has endeavoured to introduce a more expeditious and less expensive method
·ing.

·ict for this purpose is the 12 Ann. stat. 2. c. 18. It appears from the preamble, that the
·ctices, once so common, of plundering ships driven on shore, and seizing whatever could be
·s lawful property—(see WRECK)—had not been wholly abandoned; or that if the property was
·e owners, the demand for salvage was so exorbitant, that the inevitable ruin of the trader
·ediate consequence. To remedy those mischiefs in future, it was enacted, "that if a ship
·r of being stranded, or being run ashore, the sheriffs, justices, mayors, constables, or officers
·ns, nearest the place of danger, should, upon application made to them, summon and call
·any men as should be thought necessary to the assistance, and for the preservation, of such
·s, and her cargo; and that if any ship, man-of-war, or merchantman, should be riding at
·he place of danger, the constables and officers of the customs might demand of the superior
·h ship, the assistance of her boats, and such hands as could be spared; and that, if the supe-
·ould refuse to grant such assistance, he should forfeit 100l."
·ws the section respecting salvage. It enacts, "that all persons employed in preserving ships
distress, or their cargoes, shall, within 30 days after the service is performed, be paid a
·ward for the same, by the commander, master, or other superior officer, mariners, or owners,
·vessel so in distress, or by any merchant whose vessel or goods shall be so saved; and, in

default thereof, the said ship or vessel so saved shall remain in the custody of the officers of
until all charges are paid, and until the officers of the customs, and the master or other officer
ship or vessel, and all others employed in the preservation of the ship, shall be *reasonably grat*
their assistance and trouble, or good security given for that purpose : and if any disagreement sh
place between the persons whose ships or goods have been saved, and the officer of the customs, t
the monies deserved by any of the persons so employed, it shall be lawful for the commander of t
or vessel so saved, or the owner of the goods, or the merchant interested therein, and also for th
of the customs, or his deputy, to nominate three of the neighbouring justices of the peace, w
thereupon adjust the *quantum* of the monies or gratuity to be paid to the several persons acting
employed in the salvage of the said ship, vessel, or goods ; and such adjustment shall be binding t
parties, and shall be recoverable in an action at law ; and in case it shall so happen, that no pers
appear to make his claim to all or any of the goods that may be saved, that then the chief office
customs of the nearest port to the place where the said ship or vessel was so in distress shall
three of the nearest justices of the peace, who shall put him or some other responsible person in po
of the said goods, such justices taking an account in writing of the said goods, to be signed by
officer of the customs ; and if the said goods shall not be legally claimed, within the space of 12
next ensuing, by the rightful owner thereof, then public sale shall be made thereof ; and, if pe
goods, forthwith to be sold, and, after all charges deducted, the residue of the monies arising tro
sale, with a fair and just account of the whole, shall be transmitted to her Majesty's exchequer,
remain for the benefit of the rightful owner, when appearing ; who, upon affidavit, or other proc
of his or their right or property thereto, to the satisfaction of one of the barons of the coif of the
quer, shall, upon his order, receive the same out of the exchequer."

By a subsequent statute, 26 Geo. 2. c. 19. it is enacted, " that in case any person or perse
employed by the master, mariners, or owners, or other person lawfully authorised, in the salvage
vessel, or the cargo or provision thereof, shall, in the absence of the person so employed and aut
save any such vessel, goods, or effects, and cause the same to be carried, for the benefit of the ov
proprietors, into port, or to any near adjoining Custom-house, or other place of safe custody, imm
giving notice thereof to some justice of the peace, magistrate, or Custom-house or excise officer,
discover to such magistrate or officer, where any such goods or effects are wrongfully bought,
concealed, then such person or persons shall be entitled to a *reasonable reward* for such servic
paid by the masters or owners of such vessels or goods, and to be adjusted, in case of disag
about the *quantum*, in like manner as the salvage is to be adjusted and paid by 12th Anne,
as follows : —

" And be it further enacted, that, for the better ascertaining the salvage to be paid in pursuane
present act and the act before-mentioned, and for the more effectually putting the said acts inte
tion, the justice of the peace, mayor, bailiff, collector of the customs, or chief constable, who
nearest to the place where any ship, goods, or effects shall be stranded or cast away, shall fe
give public notice for a meeting to be held as soon as possible, of the sheriff or his deputy,
tices of the peace, mayors, or other chief magistrates of towns corporate, coroners, or comm
of the land tax, or any five or more of them, who are hereby empowered and required to give a
execution of this and the said former act, and to employ proper persons for the saving ships in
and such ships, vessels, and effects, as shall be stranded or cast away ; and also to examine perse
oath, touching the same, or the salvage thereof, and to adjust the *quantum* of such salvage, ar
bute the same among the persons concerned in such salvage, in case of disagreement among th
or the said persons ; and that every such magistrate, &c. attending and acting at such meeti
be paid 4s. a day for his expenses in such attendance, out of the goods and effects saved by t
or direction.'

" Provided always, that if the charges and rewards for salvage directed to be paid by the
statute, and by this act, shall not be fully paid, or sufficient security given for the same, within
next after the said services performed, then it shall be lawful for the officer of the customs, conc
such salvage, to borrow or raise so much money as shall be sufficient to satisfy and pay such cha
rewards, or any part thereof, then remaining unpaid, or not secured as aforesaid, by or upon one
bill or bills of sale, under his hand and seal, of the ship or vessel, or cargo saved, or such part th
shall be sufficient, redeemable upon payment of the principal sum borrowed, and interest upon
at the rate of 4l. per cent. per annum."

An act of the 53 Geo. 3. c. 87., continued and extended by the 1 & 2 Geo. 4. c. 76., conta
regulations supplying defects in former statutes. They enact, that goods of a perishable natu
much damaged that they cannot be kept, may, at the request of any person interested or concern
same, or in saving thereof, be sold with the consent of a justice, the money being deposited in t
of the lord of the manor, and an account of the sale transmitted to the deputy vice admiral. T
authorise the passage of horses, carts, carriages, &c. to the part of the sea coast where a vesse
wrecked, over the adjoining lands, if there be no road leading as conveniently thereto, under
of 100l., the damages to be settled by two justices in the event of the parties not agreeing.
Geo. 4. §§ 27. 29, 30.)

It is ordered by the same statute, that no lord of the manor, or other person claiming to be e
wreck or goods, shall appropriate or dispose of the same until he shall have caused to be
writing to the deputy vice admiral of that part of the coast, or to his agents if they reside v
miles, if not, then to the corporation of the Trinity-house, a report containing an accurate and p
description of the wreck or goods found, and of the place where and time when found, and of a
thereon, and of such other particulars as may better enable the owner to recover them, and al
place where they are deposited, and may be found and examined by any person claiming any
them, nor until the expiration of one whole year and a day after the expiration of such notice
puty vice admiral, or his agent, is, within 48 hours of receiving such report, to transmit a copy
the secretary of the corporation of the Trinity-house, upon pain of forfeiting, for every neglect
mit such account, 50l. to any person who shall sue for the same, and the secretary is to cause such
to be placed in some conspicuous situation for the inspection of all persons claiming to inspect
mine it. — (1 & 2 *Geo.* 4. c. 75. § 26.)

It is further ordered by the same statute, that pilots and others taking possession of anchors,
other wrecked or left materials upon the coast, or within any harbour, river, or bay, shall se
thereof, within *twenty-four* hours, to the nearest deputy vice admiral, or his agent, delivering th
at such place as may be appointed, under pain of being deemed receivers of stolen goods. Th
vice admiral, or his agent, may also seize *such articles as have not been reported to him*, and is
to keep and report them to the Trinity-house as aforesaid ; and if he seize them without pr
formation, he is to have one third of the value ; if he seize in pursuance of information, the thi
divided between him and the informer. If the articles are not claimed within a year and a day
to be sold, and the money applied as directed by the act of Queen Anne (12 Anne, stat. 2. c. 18.
quoted), the deputy vice admiral, or his agent, and the person who may have given informatior
such cases entitled to the salvage allowed upon unclaimed property. And it is further enact
any dispute shall arise between the salvors of any goods found, lodged, and reported as aforesai
owners thereof, as to the salvage to be paid in respect of the same, it is to be determined by th
of three justices ; or if they differ, by their nominee, who is to be a person conversant with
affairs. Masters and others bound to foreign parts, finding or taking on board anchors, g

g them to be found, are to enter the same in the log book, with the place and time of finding, transmit a copy of such entry, by the first possible opportunity, to the Trinity-house, and to up the articles on their return home, which, if not claimed, are to be sold within a year and cording to the aforementioned statute of Anne. Masters selling such articles incur a penalty ess than 30*l.* and not more than 100*l.*

, boatmen, or other persons, conveying anchors and cables to foreign countries, and disposing there, are to be adjudged guilty of felony, and may be transported for seven years.

ame statute authorises three justices, or their nominee, to decide upon all claims made by , pilots, and other persons, for services of any description (except pilotage) rendered by them hip or vessel, whether in distress or not.

s dissatisfied with the award of the justices or their nominee may appeal to the court of admi- ut the justices are in such cases to deliver the goods to the proprietors, or their agent, on their ood security for double their value. This act does not extend to Scotland.

of the previously mentioned acts have any force within the *Cinque Ports ;* but the Lord Warden ed by stat. 1 & 2 Geo. 4. c. 76. to appoint three or more substantial persons in each of these towns, authorised to decide upon all claims for services of any sort or description rendered to any vessel, ving or preserving, within the jurisdiction, any goods or merchandise wrecked, stranded, or cast : for bringing anchors or cables ashore, &c. No commissioner can act for any other place than which, or within a mile of which, he is resident. Either party may, within eight days of the leclare his intention of bringing the matter before some competent court of admiralty ; selecting, ay judge best, the admiralty of England or that of the Cinque Ports. The provisions in this sta. e been justly eulogised by Lord Tenterden, for the cheap and easy means they afford for settling estions.

npossible, as Mr. Justice Park has observed (*Law of Insurance*, c. 8.), to suppose two instances of ipwreck, or other peril of the sea, so similar to each other, that the trouble, danger, and expense lvors should be exactly equal ; and it would, consequently, be contrary to the first principles of award the same sum for all possible cases of salvage. There was, therefore, no other resource point competent persons to decide as to the allowance due in any case of salvage that might arise, ng the various circumstances with respect to it into account.

age upon Recapture. — It was the practice of our courts, previously to any regulations on the o order restitution of ships or goods, if retaken before condemnation, to be made to the original on payment of a *reasonable salvage* to the recaptors ; but by stat. 43 Geo. 3. c. 160. it has been , that " if any ship or vessel taken as prize, or any goods therein, shall appear, in the court of , to have belonged to any of his Majesty's subjects, which were before taken by any of his enemies, and at any time afterwards retaken by any of his Majesty's ships, or any privateer, or or vessel under his Majesty's protection, such ships, vessels, and goods shall, in all cases (save er excepted), be adjudged to be restored, and shall be accordingly restored, to such former owner , he or they paying for salvage, if retaken by any of *his Majesty's ships, one eighth* part of the e thereof, to the flag officers, captains, &c., to be divided as the same act directs ; and if retaken *rivateer*, or other ship or vessel, *one sixth* part of the true value of such ships and goods, to be ie owners, officers, and seamen of such privateer or other vessel, without any deduction ; and if)y the joint operation of one or more of his Majesty's ships, and one or more private ships of war, e of the court of admiralty, or other court having cognizance thereof, shall order such salvage, ch proportions, to be paid to the captors by the owners, as he shall, under the circumstances of deem fit and reasonable ; but if such recaptured ship or vessel shall appear to have been set he enemy as a ship or vessel of war, the said ship or vessel shall not be restored to the former ut shall in all cases, whether retaken by any of his Majesty's ships or any privateer, be adjudged ize for the benefit of the captors."

t is decidedly more favourable to the merchants than the old law, which adjudged that all ships d after sentence of condemnation should be the property of the captors.

case of neutral ships captured by an enemy, and retaken by British men-of-war or privateers, s of admiralty have a discretionary power of allowing such salvage, and in such proportions, as, e circumstances of each particular case, may appear just ; but there is no positive law or binding n to which parties may appeal, for ascertaining the rate of such salvage. " The maritime law of " says Lord Stowell, " having adopted a most liberal rule of restitution on salvage, with respect aptured property of its own subjects, gives the benefit of that rule to its allies, till it appears that owards British property on a less liberal principle ; *in such a case it adopts their rule*, and treats ording to their own measure of justice."—(1 *Rob. Adm. Rep.* 54.)

is one of those charges which are usually provided against by insurance. When, however, the very high, and the object of the voyage in so far defeated, the insured is, by the laws of this her maritime nations, allowed to abandon, and to call upon the insurer as for a total loss.—(See MENT.)

her information with respect to salvage, see Abbott on the Law of Shipping, part iii. c. 10. ; Park nce, c. 8. ; and Marshall on Insurance, book i. c. 12. § 8.

PLE, a small quantity of a commodity exhibited at public or private a specimen. Sugars, wool, spirits, wine, coffee, and, indeed, most species handise, are sold by sample. If an article be not, at an average, equal sample by which it is sold, the buyer may cancel the contract, and re- article to the seller.

ined is a list of most articles that may be warehoused, and of the quan- at may be taken out as samples. — (*Customs Min.* Oct. 11. 1825.)

Barilla	5 lbs. per pile 5 tons.	Cream of Tartar	1 lb. per package.	exceeding 1¼
	2 oz. per package.	Currants -	½ lb. do.	lb. to be
	½ lb. do.	Essence of Ber-		charged with
ot	½ lb. do.	gamot or Le-		duty on de-
aptivi	2 oz. do.	mon -	1 oz. do.	livery of the
alt's	½ lb. do.	Euphorbium	1 oz. do.	package.
neral		Feathers, Bed	½ lb. per lot 6 bags.	Isinglass -	½ lb. per package.
esuit's	½ lb. do.	Galls -	1 lb. do.	Juice of Lemons	½ pint do.
		Gentian -	½ lb. do.	Lac Dye -	1 oz. do.
	2 lb. per pile.	Ginger -	8 oz. do.	Lead, Black	1 lb. do.
	1 lb. per package.	Granilla, *see Co-*		Lemon Peel	½ lb. each entry.
	½ lb. do.	*chineal.*		Liquorice Juice	½ lb. per package.
s	2 oz. do.	Gum Arabic -	1 lb. per package.	Root -	¼ lb. do.
	1 lb. do.	Senegal -	½ lb. do.	Madder, manu-	
	2 oz. do.	Tragacanth	2 oz. do.	factured -	½ lb. do.
Dust	2 oz. do.	Other Gum -	4 oz. do.	Root -	½ lb. do.
Oil	½ pint each cask.	Honey -	½ oz. do.	Oil of Almonds	1 oz. do.
	2 oz. per bag.	Jalap -	1 oz. do.	Aniseed	1 oz. do.
la	2 oz. per package.	Indigo -	¼ lb. do.	Juniper -	1 oz. do.
dicus	1 oz. do.	Any further		Olive	½ pint per cask.
	4 oz. do.	quantity (not		Palm	½ pint do.

Oil of Rosemary 1 oz. per package.	Salep - 1 oz. per package.	Sugar, British } 1½ lb. per hogshea
Spike - 1 oz. do.	Sarsaparilla - 1 oz.	1½ lb. per tierce.
Thyme - 1 oz. do.	Saltpetre - 56 lbs. each mark.	Plantation } 1½ lb. per chest.
Orange Peel - ½ lb. do.	Seed, Aniseed - 1 oz. per package.	12 oz. per barrel.
Orchelia - 2 oz. do.	Clover - 2 oz. do.	¼ lb. molasses p
Orrice Root - ½ lb. do.	Carraway 2 oz. do.	hhd. or cask.
Oil of Bay - 1 oz. do.	Lac - 1 oz. do.	Tallow - 4 lb. per lot 10 pa
Pepper - 1 oz. per bag.	Mustard 1 oz. do.	Tapioca - 1 oz. per package
Pimento - 2 oz. do.	Senna - 1 oz. per package.	Turmeric - 2 lb. per pile.
Radix Contra.	Shumac - 1 lb. per lot 10 bags.	Valonea - 3 lb. per lot.
yerva - 1 oz. per package.	Silk, Raw - 2 oz. per package.	Wax, Bees' - ½ lb. per package
Galanga - 2 lb. per pile.	Thrown - 1 oz. do.	Wine - ½ pint.
Ipecacu-	Waste - 2 oz. do.	Wool, Cotton 4 oz. per package
anhæ - 1 oz. per package.	Smalts - 1 oz. do.	Sheep or
Senekæ - 1 oz. do.	Spirits - ½ pint.	Lambs' 1 lb. do.
Raisins - ½ lb. each mark.		Spanish 1 lb.; do.
Rhubarb - 1 oz. per package.	Sugar, Foreign { 2 oz. per bag.	Yarn, Mohair - ½ lb. do.
Rice - ½ lb. do.	8 oz. per box not exceeding 5 cwt.	Cotton ½ lb. do.
Saffron - ½ oz. do.	16 oz. per box or chest	Mother of Pearl 7 lb. per lot of 1
Sago - 2 lb. per pile.	exceeding 5 cwt.	Shells } packages.
		Vermicelli - 1 oz. per package

SANDAL WOOD, the wood of a tree (*Santalum album*, Lin.) having s
what of the appearance of a large myrtle. The wood is extensively employe
a perfume in the funeral ceremonies of the Hindoos. The deeper the colour,
the nearer the root, the higher is the perfume. Malabar produces sandal w
of the finest quality. It is an article of export to Bengal and China; b
seldom brought to Europe, except by individuals for their own use, or as
sents for their friends.—(*Milburn's Orient. Com.; Bell's Review of Con
Bengal.*)

SANDARACH, a resinous substance commonly met with in loose grar
a little larger than a pea, of a whitish yellow colour, brittle, inflammabl
a resinous smell, and acrid aromatic taste. It exudes, it is said, in warm clim
from cracks and incisions in the common juniper bush. It is used as a var
dissolved in spirits of wine.—(*Ainslie's Mat. Indica.*)

SAPAN WOOD, is obtained from a species of the same tree that yield
Brazil wood (*Cæsalpinia Sapan*, Lin.). It is a middle-sized tree indigeno
Siam, Pegu, the coast of Coromandel, the Eastern islands, &c. It has beer
ployed for dyeing in the greater part of Asia for many centuries. It found its
into Europe some time before the discovery of America; but very little is
imported. Its colouring matter differs but little from that of Brazil wood
the best sapan wood does not yield more than half the quantity that may b
tained from an equal weight of Brazil wood, and the colour is not quite so b
—(*Bancroft on Colours*, vol. ii. p. 329.) Its price in the London market varies
8l. to 14l. a ton.

SAPPHIRE (Ger. *Sapphir*; Du. *Saffiersteen*; Fr. *Saphir*; It. *Zaffiro*
Safiro, Safir; Rus. *Jachant*; Lat. *Sapphirus*). A precious stone in very
estimation. Colours blue and red; also gray, white, green, and yellow
occurs in blunt-edged pieces, in roundish pebbles, and crystallised. Varies
transparent to translucent. Refracts double. After diamond, it is the ha
substance in nature. The blue variety, or sapphire, is harder than the rul
red variety. Brittle. Specific gravity 4 to 4·2.

It is found at Potsedlitz and Trealitz in Bohemia, and Hohenstein in Saxony; Expailly in F
and particularly beautiful in the Capelan mountains, in Pegu. Next to diamond, it is the most v
of the gems. The white and pale blue varieties, by exposure to heat, become snow white, and wh
exhibit so high a degree of lustre, that they are used in place of diamond. The most highly
varieties are the crimson and carmine red; these are the Oriental *ruby* of the jeweller; the
sapphire; and last, the yellow or Oriental *topaz*. The *asterias*, or star-stone, is a very beautiful
in which the colour is generally of a reddish violet, and the form a rhomboid, with truncated
which exhibit an opalescent lustre. A sapphire of 10 carats' weight is considered to be worth 50 g
—(*Jameson's Mineralogy.*)

SARCOCOLLA, a subviscid, sweetish, and somewhat nauseous gum res
is brought from Arabia and Persia in small grains of a pale yellow colou
whitest, as being the freshest, is preferred. It is but seldom imported. —
burn's Orient. Com.)

SARDINES, OR **SARDINIAS** (Ger. *Sardellen*; Fr. *Sardines*; It. *Sa*
Sp. *Sardinas*), a species of fish of the herring tribe, but smaller. The
taken in considerable quantities on our coasts, and are exceedingly ple
on the coasts of Algarve in Portugal, Andalusia and Granada in Spain
along the shores of Italy. The small sardines, caught on the coast o
vence, in France, are esteemed the best. From 1,000 to 1,200 fishing s
are engaged in catching these fish on the coast of Britany, from June
middle of October. The French frequently cure them in red brine; and
thus prepared, designate them *anchoisées*, or *anchovied sardines*. The
packed in vessels previously employed for holding wine, and exported

When perfectly fresh, sardines are accounted excellent fish; but if kept time, they entirely lose their flavour, and become quite insipid.

DONYX, a precious stone, a variety of chalcedony.

ients selected this substance to engrave upon, no doubt from its possessing two peculiar and qualities, viz. hardness and tenacity, by which it is capable of receiving the finest touch or the tool without chipping, and showing the art of the engraver to the highest perfection. — *Diamonds*, 2d ed. p. 121.)

SAPARILLA (Ger. *Sarsaparille*; Fr. *Salsepareille*; It. *Salsapariglia*; zaparilla), the root of the *Smilax Sarsaparilla*, a plant growing in South , and the West Indies. It is imported in bales. It is known in the market by the names of Lisbon, Honduras, and Vera Cruz, but it is also from Jamaica. The Lisbon root, which is the produce of Brazil, ·ddish or dark brown cuticle, is internally farinaceous, and more free ·re than the other kinds: the Honduras has a dirty brown, and some-hitish cuticle; is more fibrous, and has more ligneous matter than the ·nd Vera Cruz. It is in long, slender twigs, covered with a wrinkled ·uticle, and has a small woody heart. The Jamaica differs from the ·n having a deep red cuticle of a close texture; and the red colour par-·fused through the ligneous part. The root is inodorous, and has a muci-, very slightly bitter taste: the bark is the only useful part of the plant; ·ous part being tasteless, inert, woody fibre. — (*Thomson's Dispensatory.*) ·ntity imported in 1828 amounted to 169,518 lbs., of which 85,520 lbs. ·ained for home consumption. The duty, which varies, according as it ·t from a foreign country or a British possession, from 1*s.* 3*d.* to 1*s.* ·roduced, in 1829, 6,133*l.* 2*s.* 10*d.*

AFRAS (Ger. and Fr. *Sassafras*; It. *Sassafrasso*; Sp. *Sasafras*), a ·f laurel (*Laurus Sassafras*, Lin.), a native of the southern parts of North and Cochin-China. Sassafras wood, root, and bark, have a fragrant ·d a sweetish aromatic taste. The wood is of a brownish white colour; ·ark ferruginous within, spongy, and divisible into layers. Their sensible and virtues depend on an essential oil, which may be obtained separate ·ing the chips or the bark with water. It is very fragrant, hot, and pene-· the taste, of a pale yellow colour, and heavier than water. It is used ·1e *materia medica.* Very little is imported. — (*Thomson's Dispensatory.*)

·DERS (RED) (Arab. *Sundal-ahmer*; Hind. *Ruckut-chundum*), the · lofty tree (*Pterocarpus Santalinus*) indigenous to various parts of India, ·imor, &c. The wood is brought to Europe in billets, which are very ·l sink in water. It is extremely hard, of a fine grain, and a bright garnet ·r, which brightens on exposure to the air. It is employed to dye lasting ·rown colours on wool. It yields its colouring matter to ether and ·ut not to water. The quantity imported is but inconsiderable. The ·ond varies at this moment (October, 1831) from 15*l.* to 16*l.* a ton. — ·'s *Dispensatory*; *Bancroft on Colours*, vol. ii. p. 236.)

MONY (Ger. *Skammonien*; Fr. *Scammonée*; It. *Scammonea*; Sp. *Esca-*gum resin, the produce of a species of convolvulus, or creeper plant, ·ws abundantly in Syria. When an incision is made into the roots, they ·lky juice, which being kept grows hard, and is the scammony of the ·t is imported from Aleppo in what are called drums, weighing from 75 ·. each; and from Smyrna in cakes like wax, packed in chests. The ·light and friable, and is considered the best; that from Smyrna is more ·nd ponderous, less friable, and fuller of impurities. It has a peculiar ·ur, not unlike that of old cheese; and a bitterish, slightly acrid taste. ·ir is blackish or bluish gray, changing to dirty white, or lathering when ·e is rubbed with a wet finger. Its specific gravity is 1·235. It is very ·)e adulterated; and when of a dark colour, heavy, and splintery, it ·)e rejected. It is used only in medicine — (*Thomson's Dispensatory.*) ·on scammony, which is as high as 6*s.* 4*d.* per lb., produced, in 1829, ·8*d.*, showing that 5,890 lbs. had been entered for home consumption.

·PTURES, figures cut in stone, metal, or other solid substance, repre-·describing some real or imaginary object. The art of the sculptor, or ·vas carried to the highest pitch of excellence in ancient Greece. For-·everal of the works of the Grecian sculptors have been preserved; ·at once to stimulate and direct the genius of modern artists.

3 O

Models, are casts or representations of sculptures.

The act 54 Geo. 3. c. 56. vests the property of sculptures, models, copies, and casts, in the propr 14 years; provided he cause his name, with the date, to be put on them before they are publishe the same term in addition, if he should be living at the end of the first period. In actions fo double costs to be given. The act 6 Geo. 4. c. 107. prohibits the importation, on pain of forfeitur sculptures, models, casts, &c. first made in the United Kingdom.

SEAL (Lat. *Sigillum*), a stone, piece of metal, or other solid substan nerally round or elliptical, on which is engraved the arms, crest, name, &c. of some state, prince, public body, or private individual. It is emplo a stamp to make an impression on sealing wax, thereby authenticating publ deeds, &c., or to close letters or packets. Seals were very early invent much learning has been employed in tracing their history, and explaini figures upon them. — (See particularly the work of Hopkinck, *De Sig Prisco et Novo Jure*, 4to, 1642.) They are now very generally used.

The best are usually formed of precious stones, on which the crest or the initials of the perso are engraved, set in gold. But immense numbers are formed of stained glass, and set in gil They are manufactured at London, Birmingham, &c., and are extensively exported.

SEALING-WAX (Ger. *Siegellack;* Fr. *Cire d'Espagne, Cire à cachet Cera Lacca, Cera di Spagna;* Sp. *Lacre;* Rus. *Surgutsch*), the wax us sealing letters, legal instruments, &c. It is a composition of gum lac, mel incorporated with resin, and afterwards coloured with some pigment, as ver verditer, ivory-black, &c.

SEAMEN, the individuals engaged in navigating ships, barges, &c. up high seas. Those employed for this purpose upon rivers, lakes, or can denominated watermen.

A *British Seaman* must be a natural born subject of his Majesty; or be nat by act of parliament; or made a denizen by letters of denization; or have be British subject by the conquest or cession of some newly acquired territory; ot a foreigner) have served on board his Majesty's ships of war, in time of war, space of 3 years. — (6 *Geo*. 4. c. 109. § 16.) But his Majesty may, by procl during war, declare that foreigners who have served *two* years in the royal navy, such war, shall be deemed British seamen. — (§ 17.)

Various regulations have been enacted with respect to the hiring of seame conduct while on board, and the payment of their wages. These regulations c different countries; but in all they have been intended to obviate any dispu might otherwise arise between the master and seamen as to the terms of the c between them, to secure due obedience to the master's orders, and to interest the in the completion of the voyage, by making their earnings depend on its su termination.

1. *Hiring of Seamen.* — To prevent the mischiefs that frequently arose f want of proper proof of the precise terms upon which seamen engaged to perfor service in merchant ships, it is enacted by statute (2 Geo. 2. c. 36.), "that it s be lawful for any master or commander of any ship or vessel, bound to parts the seas, to carry any seaman or mariner, except his apprentice or apprentice from any port or place where he or they were entered or shipped, to proceed voyage to parts beyond the seas, without first coming to an agreement or contr such seamen or mariners for their wages; which agreement or agreements made in writing, declaring what wages each seaman or mariner is to have resp during the whole voyage, or for so long time as he or they shall ship themsel and also to express in the said agreement or contract the voyage for which such or mariner was shipped to perform the same;" under a penalty of 5l. for each carried to sea without such agreement, to be forfeited by the master to th Greenwich Hospital. This agreement is to be signed by each mariner withi after he shall have entered himself on board the ship; and is, when signed, cc and binding upon all parties. By a subsequent statute, these provisions ha extended to vessels of the burthen of 100 tons and upwards, employed in the *trade*. — (31 *Geo*. 3. c. 39.)

The following is the form of the articles of agreement required by statute (3? c. 73.) to be entered into between the masters and mariners of ships engage West India trade. It is substantially the same with that which previously still continues to be, in common use for all ships employed in foreign trade.

Ship

IT is hereby agreed between the master, seamen, and mariners of the ship　　　 now the port of　　　　and　　　　the master or commander of the said ship, That, in con of the monthly or other wages against each respective seaman or mariner's name hereunt severally shall and will perform the above-mentioned voyage: and the said master doth he with and hire the seamen and mariners for the said voyage at such monthly wages, to be pai to the laws of Great Britain; and they, the said seamen and mariners, do hereby promise

ves to do their duty, and obey the lawful commands of their officers on board the said ship or
ereunto belonging, as become good and faithful seamen and mariners, and at all places where the
p shall put in or anchor during the said ship's voyage, to do their best endeavours for the pre-
n of the said ship and cargo, and not to neglect or refuse doing their duty by day or night; nor
out of the said ship on board any other vessel, or be on shore under any pretence whatsoever,
voyage is ended, and the ship discharged of her cargo, without leave first obtained of the master,
or commanding officer on board; and, in default thereof, they freely agree to be liable to the
s mentioned in the act of parliament, made in the second year of the reign of King George the
intituled "An Act for the better Regulation and Government of Seamen in the Merchants' Ser-
and the act made in the thirty-seventh year of the reign of King George the Third, intituled
ct for preventing the Desertion of Seamen from British Merchant Ships trading to his Majesty's
s and Plantations in the West Indies." And it is further agreed by the parties to these presents,
nty-four hours' absence without leave shall be deemed a total desertion, and render such seamen
iners liable to the forfeitures and penalties contained in the acts above recited; that each and
wful command which the said master shall think necessary to issue for the effectual government
aid vessel, suppressing immorality and vice of all kinds, be strictly complied with under the
of the person or persons disobeying, forfeiting his or their whole wages or hire, together with
ing belonging to him or them on board the said vessel; and it is further agreed, that no
seaman, or person belonging to the said ship, shall demand or be entitled to his wages, or any
reof, until the arrival of the said ship at the above-mentioned port of discharge, and her cargo
, nor less than twenty days, in case the seaman is not employed in the delivery; and it is hereby
greed between the master and officers of the said ship, that whatever apparel, furniture, and
ach of them may receive into their charge, belonging to the said ship, shall be accounted for on
rn; and in case any thing shall be lost or damaged through their carelessness or insufficiency, it
made good by such officer or seaman, by whose means it may happen, to the master and owner
id ship: and whereas it is customary for the officers and seamen, on the ship's return home in
, and during the time their cargoes are delivering, to go on shore each night to sleep, greatly
ejudice of such ship and freighters; be it further agreed by the said parties, that neither officer
an shall, on any pretence whatsoever, be entitled to such indulgence, but shall do their duty by
scharge of the cargo, and keep such watch by night as the master or commander of the said ship
k necessary, in order for the preservation of the above: and whereas it often happens that part
rgo is embezzled after being delivered into lighters; and, as such losses are made good by the
f the ships, be it therefore agreed, by these presents, that whatever officer or seaman the master
k proper to appoint, shall take charge of the cargo in the lighters, and go with the same to the
ay, and there deliver his charge to the ship's husband, or his representative, or see the same
ighed at the king's beam; and, in consequence of their true fidelity, such seamen shall be en-
2s. 6d. each lighter, exclusive of their monthly pay; and should it so happen that lighters are
any considerable time at the quay before they can be unloaded, such officer and seaman so
d shall in that case be entitled to 2s. 6d for ever twenty-four hours, exclusive of their monthly
t each seaman and mariner, who shall well and truly perform the above-mentioned voyage,
, always, that there be no plunderage, embezzlement, or other unlawful acts, committed on the
argo or stores,) shall be entitled to their wages or hire that may become due to him, pursuant to
ement; that, for the due performance of each and every the above-mentioned articles and agree-
d acknowledgment of their being voluntary and without compulsion, or any other clandestine
ing used, the said parties have hereunto subscribed their names, the day and month set opposite
espective names.

ime	Men's Names.	Quality.	Witnesses to each Man's signing.	Pay in the River.		Wages per Month, or for the Voyage.	Whole Wages.
				Whole.	Half.		

tatutes do not render a verbal agreement for wages absolutely void; but impose
y on the master if a written agreement be not made. When a written agree-
made, it becomes the only evidence of the contract between the parties; and a
cannot recover any thing agreed to be given in reward for his services, which is
ified in the articles.

man who has engaged to serve on board a ship, is bound to exert himself to
st in the service of the ship; and, therefore, a promise made by the master of
distress, to pay an extra sum to a seaman, as an inducement to extraordinary
on his part, is held to be essentially void.

duct of Seamen. — It is essential to the business of navigation that the most
nd ready obedience should be paid to the lawful commands of the master.
effect it is covenanted in the articles of agreement previously quoted, that
d every lawful command which the said master shall think necessary to issue
fectual government of the said vessel, suppressing immorality and vice of all
strictly complied with, under the penalty of the person or persons disobeying
; his or their whole wages or hire, together with every thing belonging to him
on board the said vessel."

e of disobedience or disorderly conduct on the part of the seamen, the master
ect them in a reasonable manner. Such an authority is absolutely necessary
fety of the ship and of those on board; but it behoves the master to act in such
h great deliberation, and not to pervert the powers with which he is intrusted
ood of the whole to cruel or vindictive purposes. Masters abusing their au-
ust answer at law for the consequences. In the case of actual or open mutiny
ew, or any part of them, the resistance of the master becomes an act of self
nd is to be considered in all its consequences in that point of view. The
s of Oleron and Wisby declare that a mariner who strikes the master shall

either pay a fine or lose his right hand ; a singular as well as cruel alternative, unk*
in modern jurisprudence.

But although the master may by force restrain the commission of great cri
he has no judicial authority over the criminal, but is bound to secure his person
bring him before a proper tribunal. And all justices of the peace are empower
receive informations touching any murder, piracy, felony, or robbery upon the sea,
to commit the offenders for trial. — (43 *Geo.* 3. c. 160.)

The *desertion* or absence without leave of seamen from a ship, while on a voya
foreign parts, being attended with many bad consequences, has been provided ag
in all maritime laws. It was enacted in this country, in the reign of William
(11 & 12 Will. 3. c. 7.),

" That all such seamen, officers, or sailors, who shall desert the ships or vessels wherein they are
to serve for that voyage, shall for such offence forfeit all such wages as shall be then due to h
them." By subsequent statutes (2 Geo. 2. c. 36., and 31 Geo. 3. c. 39.), it is enacted, that if, after h
entered into the agreement previously referred to, a mariner deserts or refuses to proceed on the v
he forfeits to the owners all the wages then due to him, and a justice of the peace may, on compla
the master, owner, or person having charge of the ship, issue a warrant to apprehend him ; and in c
his refusal to proceed on the voyage, or of his not assigning a sufficient reason for such refusa
commit him to hard labour in the house of correction for not more than *thirty* nor less than *for*
days. A mariner *absenting* himself from the ship without leave of the master or other chief c
having charge of the ship, forfeits *two* days' pay for every such day's absence, to the use of Gree
Hospital. And in the case of foreign voyages, if upon the ship's arrival at her port of delivery
he leaves her without a *written discharge* from the master or other person having charge of the sl
if in the coasting trade he quits the ship before the *voyage is completed and* THE CARGO DELIVER
before the expiration of the term for which he engaged, or before he has obtained a discharge in w
he forfeits one month's pay to the said hospital. But these provisions do not debar seamen from en
on board any of his Majesty's ships."

In order still further to discountenance desertion, a penalty of 100*l.* is impose
Geo. 3. c. 73.) on every master or commander of any British merchant ship
engages any seaman, or other person to serve on board such ship, in the event of
master or commander being aware, at the time, that such seaman or person had des
from any other ship or vessel.

For an account of the penalties imposed on the master for leaving seamen in fo
countries, or refusing to bring them back, see MASTER.

Neglect of duty, disobedience of orders, habitual drunkenness, or any cause v
will justify a master in discharging a seaman during the voyage, will also depriv
seaman of his wages.

If the cargo be embezzled or injured by the fraud or negligence of the seame
that the merchant has a right to claim satisfaction from the master and owners, they
by the custom of merchants, deduct the value thereof from the wages of the seam
whose misconduct the injury has taken place. And the last proviso introduced int
usual agreement signed by the seamen, is calculated to enforce this rule in the c
embezzlement either of the cargo, or of the ship's stores. This proviso, however
be construed individually, as affecting only the particular persons guilty of the emb
ment, and not the whole crew. Nor is any innocent person liable to contribute a
tion of his wages to make good the loss occasioned by the misconduct of others.

The offences of running away with the ship, or voluntarily yielding her up
enemy, or making a revolt, are punishable by death. The statute 11 & 12 Will. 3
enacts,

" That if any commander or master of any ship, or any seaman or mariner, shall in any place
the admiral hath jurisdiction, betray his trust and turn pirate, enemy, or rebel, and piratica
feloniously run away with his or their ship or ships, or any barge, boat, ordnance, ammunition, go
merchandises, or yield them up voluntarily to any pirate, or shall bring any seducing messages fr
pirate, enemy, or rebel, or consult, combine, or confederate with, or attempt or endeavour to corr
commander, master, officer, or mariner, to yield up or run away with any ship, goods, or mercha
or turn pirate, or go over to pirates ; or if any person shall lay violent hands on his commander, w
to hinder him from fighting in defence of his ship and goods committed to his trust, or that shall
his master, or make or endeavour to make a revolt in the ship ; shall be adjudged, deemed, and t
be a *pirate, felon,* and *robber,* and being convicted thereof according to the directions of this ac
have and suffer pain of *death,* loss of lands, goods, and chattels, as *pirates, felons,* and *robbers* u
seas ought to have and suffer."

The wilful destruction or loss of the ship is, in all countries, punishable by
But doubts having been entertained whether the destruction of a ship that had be
sured came within the scope of the previously existing statutes, they were repea
the 43 Geo. 3. c. 113., and the following provision substituted in their stead : —

" That if any person or persons shall, from and after the *sixteenth* day of *July,* 1803, wilfully cas
burn, or otherwise destroy, any ship or vessel, or in any wise counsel, direct, or procure the sam
done, and the same be accordingly done, with intent or design thereby wilfully and maliciously to p
any owner or owners of such ship or vessel, or any owner or owners of any goods laden on board th
or any person or persons, body politic or corporate, that hath or have underwritten or shall und
any policy or policies of insurance upon such ship or vessel, or on the freight thereof, or upon an
laden on board the same, the person or persons offending therein, being thereof lawfully convicte
be deemed and adjudged a principal felon or felons, and shall suffer death as in cases of felony,
benefit of clergy."

3. *Payment of Seamen's Wages, &c.*—In order to stimulate the zeal and atten
seamen, it has been the policy of all maritime states to make the payment of their

n the successful termination of the voyage. "*Freight is the mother of wages ; the the ship the mother of freight.*" When, therefore, by any disaster happening in se of the voyage, such as the loss or capture of the ship, the owners lose their he seamen also lose their wages.

ip destined on a voyage out and home has delivered her outward bound cargo, hes in the homeward voyage, the freight for the outward voyage is due; so in case the seamen are entitled to receive their wages for the time employed in the voyage and the unloading of the cargo, unless by the terms of their contract ard and homeward voyages are consolidated into one. If a ship sail to several ages are payable to the time of the delivery of the last cargo. Upon the same , where money had been advanced to the owners in part of the freight out- d the ship perished before her arrival at the port of delivery, it was held that the vere entitled to wages in proportion to the money advanced.

er seamen have been hired, the owners of a ship do not think proper to send her tended voyage, the seamen are to be paid for the time during which they may employed on board the ship; and in the event of their sustaining any special y breaking off the contract, it is but reasonable that they should be indemnified. case of shipwreck, it is the duty of the seamen to exert themselves to the ut- ave as much as possible of the vessel and cargo. If the cargo be saved, and a n of the freight paid by the merchant in respect thereof, it seems, upon principle, eamen are also entitled to a proportion of their wages. And for their labour the cargo, or the remains of the ship, they, as well as other persons, may be en- a recompence by way of *salvage*. The laws of Oleron rule, that if, in case of , " the seamen preserve a part of the ship and lading, the master shall allow asonable consideration to carry them home to their own country; and in case enough to enable the master to do this, he may lawfully pledge to some honest ich part thereof as may be sufficient for the occasion."

laws of Wisby, " the mariners are bound to save and preserve the merchan- e utmost of their power, and whilst they do so (*ce-faisant*, according to the anslation), ought to be paid their wages, otherwise not." By the Hanseatic , if a ship happens to be cast away, the mariners are obliged to save as much as es, and the master ought to requite them for their pains to their content, and em at his own charge to their dwelling places; but if the mariners refuse to master, in such case they shall have neither reward nor wages paid them." uite clear, from the language of these ancient ordinances, whether the payment be made to seamen on those melancholy occasions, is to be a reward only bour in the salvage, or a recompence for their former services in the ship, for ording to general principles, they are entitled to no payment, if no freight is But Cleirac, in his Commentary on the Laws of Oleron, says, that by an of Philip II. of Spain, made in the year 1563, it is ordained, that the seamen as much as they can from shipwreck; and, in that case, the master is bound m their wages, and to give them a further reward for their labour out of the nd the Hanseatic ordinance of the year 1614 expressly directs, that if so e ship be saved as equals the value of the wages of the seamen, they shall be whole wages. In like manner, the ordinance of Rotterdam and the *French* also expressly direct the payment of wages out of the relics and materials of - (*Abbott on the Law of Shipping*, part iv. c. 2.)

not been able," says Lord Tenterden, " to find any decision of an English e point, and the legislature has made no provision relating to it. As an t to the mariners to exert themselves in the hour of danger, it may not be ld out to them the prospect of obtaining their wages, if they save so much of shall be sufficient to pay them; but their claim upon the ship seems not to case, wherein, according to the principles of the law upon which their claim , no wages are payable to them." — (Part iv. c. 2.)

s of Oleron, Wisby, and the Hanse towns, direct, that if a seaman die during , wages shall be paid to his heirs : but it is not clear whether the sum thus be paid is to be understood as meaning a payment proportioned to the time ice, or the whole sum that he would have earned had he lived till the con- he voyage. This question has not been judicially decided in England; but 37 Geo. 3. c. 73. it is ordered, that the wages due to any seaman, who has ard any ship trading to the West Indies, shall be paid, within three months of of such ship in Great Britain, to the receiver of the sixpenny duty for Green- ital, for the use of the seaman's executor or administrator. All masters or refusing to pay the same incur a penalty of 50*l.*, and pay double wages ence.

n impressed from a merchant ship into the royal service, is entitled to receive

the proportion of his wages due to him at the time of impressment, provid
merchant ship *arrive in safety* at the port of her discharge.

Policy requires that the wages of seamen should not be paid to them in foreig
tries, as well to prevent desertion, as to preserve, for the benefit of their famili
might otherwise be spent in riot and debauchery.   Conformably to this principl
been enacted,

" That no master or owner of any merchant ship or vessel shall pay or advance, or cause to b
advanced, to any seaman or mariner, during the time he shall be in parts beyond the seas, any r
effects upon account of wages, exceeding *one moiety* of the wages which shall be due at the time
payment, until such ship or vessel shall return to *Great Britain* or *Ireland*, or the plantations, or
other of his Majesty's dominions, whereto they belong, and from whence they were first fitted
if any such master or owner of such merchant ship or vessel shall pay or advance, or cause to b
advanced, any wages to any seaman or mariner above the said moiety, such master or owner sha
and pay *double* the money he shall so pay or advance, to be recovered in the high court of adm
any person who shall first discover and inform of the same."—(8 *Geo.* 1. c. 24.)

The time when wages should be paid has also been made the subject of parliar
enactments.   Thus, as to ships engaged in *foreign voyages*, it is ordered, that u
arrival of any ship in *Great Britain* from parts beyond the seas, the master or com
shall be obliged to pay the seamen thereto belonging their wages, if demanded, i
days after the ship's entry at the Custom-house, except in cases where a covenar
be entered into to the contrary ; or at the time the seamen shall be discharged
shall first happen, if demanded ; deducting the penalties and forfeitures imposec
act, " under the penalty of paying to each seaman or mariner that shall be
contrary to the intent and meaning of this act, *twenty shillings* over and above th
that shall be due to each person, to be recovered by the same means and method
wages may be recovered ; and such payment of wages aforesaid shall be good ar
in law, notwithstanding any action, bill of sale, attachment, or incumbrance whats
— (2 *Geo.* 2. c. 36.)

And as to ships employed in the *coasting trade* in the manner before mention
enacted, that the master, commander, or person having charge of the ship, s
obliged to pay the seamen their wages, if demanded, within *five days* after the sl
be entered at the Custom-house, or the cargo be delivered, or at the time the
shall be discharged, which shall first happen, unless an agreement shall have bee
to the contrary ; in which case the wages shall be paid according to such agr
deducting in every case the penalties imposed by this act, under the like fe
of *twenty shillings*, to be recovered in the same manner as with regard to ships
from abroad ; and such payment shall be good in law, " notwithstanding any
bill of sale, attachment, or incumbrance whatsoever." — (31 *Geo.* 3. c. 39.)

Seamen have a threefold remedy for the recovery of wages ; viz. against the s
owner, and the master ; and they may proceed either in the admiralty or the c
common law : in the former case all may join, and payment may be obtained or
value of the ship.   The contract remains in the custody of the master or ow
they are bound to produce it when required, and it is conclusive evidence of the
between the parties.

By the act 59 Geo. 3. c. 58., justices of the peace are authorised summaril
cide upon the complaint of any seaman as to the nonpayment of wages not e>
20*l.* ; and if they find the claim well founded, may, in the event of its not be
within two days, issue their warrant for the levy of the same by distress :
dissatisfied may appeal to the admiralty.

4. *Payment to Greenwich Hospital.* — During the reign of George II. an estab
attached to Greenwich Hospital was erected (20 Geo. 2. c. 38.) "*for the re
support of maimed and disabled seamen, and the widows and children of such as
killed, slain, or drowned, in the merchant service.*   To provide a fund for this c
institution, every person serving in any merchant ship, or other private ship c
belonging to any of his Majesty's subjects in *England*, (except apprentices u
age of 18, persons employed in boats upon the coasts in taking fish w
brought fresh on shore, or in boats within rivers, or upon boats on the coast, ar
(except persons employed in the service of the *East India Company*, and
not entitled to the benefit of this institution, being provided for by a fund establ
the Company), pays *sixpence per month*, which is deducted out of his wages by th
and by him paid over to the persons appointed under the authority of the a
port to which the ship belongs, before she shall be allowed to clear inwards.
management and distribution of this fund, a corporation was created, compose
of eminent merchants, with power to purchase land and erect an hospital
provide for seamen rendered incapable of service by sickness, wounds, or other a
misfortunes, and decrepit and worn out by age, either by receiving them
hospital, or by pensions ; and also to relieve the widows and children of seam
or drowned in the merchant service, provided the children are not of the age of

f that age and upwards, are incapable of getting a livelihood by reason of lameness, ess, or other infirmity, and are proper objects of charity; and to make reasonable nces to those who shall lose an eye or limb, or be otherwise hurt or maimed, in g, defending, or working their ships, or doing any other duty in their service, in tion to their hurt; so far forth as the income and revenues of the charity will for these purposes. But no person is to be provided for as a worn-out seaman, s not been employed in the merchant service *five* years, and paid the contribution. providing for this class, a preference is given to such as have served longest and uted most.

rder to ascertain the times of service and payment of the contribution, the master eep a *muster-roll* of the persons employed in the ship, and before its departure a duplicate to the collector of these duties at the port; and, during the voyage, e time and place of discharge, quitting, and desertion, and of receiving other on board, and of any hurt, damage, death, or drowning; of which he must also a duplicate at his return, under the penalty of 20*l.*, to the truth whereof he may ined upon oath by the collector. And in case any person employed on board o or vessel shall, in doing his duty on shore or on board, break an arm or leg, or wise hurt or maimed, he is to be properly relieved until sufficiently recovered to to the place to which the ship belongs.

notwithstanding the *principle* of this charity is excellent, it has been alleged, and rehend on pretty good grounds, that the conditions under which merchant are admitted to participate in its benefits are too onerous, that they have not from it an advantage equivalent to the sacrifice it imposes on them, and that the s of collection have been quite enormous.

last part of this statement is, indeed, completely borne out by the first of the d documents, which shows that the expense of collection is, in future, to be to a *half* of what it has hitherto been; and we have been well assured that the n may be safely carried a good deal further.

second of the subjoined accounts shows that there is not at present a single in Greenwich Hospital, except such as have served in the navy; a circumstance onsidering the number of men in the merchant service, the large sum (26,000*l.*) y paid by them to the hospital, and the period that has elapsed since the ter- n of the war, strikes us as not a little extraordinary. The subject is one that o require a thorough investigation. Merchant seamen ought to participate, with those in his Majesty's service, in the benefits of an institution to which they te so largely.

count of the Money deducted out of the Wages of Seamen employed in the Merchant Service of ntry, for the Years 1828 and 1829; showing the Gross Amount collected, the Nett Money paid nwich Hospital, and the Amount and Rate per Cent. paid for collecting the same in each Year, what Purposes employed.

	1828.	1829.
	£ s. d.	£ s. d.
nount of the collection - - - - -	23,683 1 1	26,137 2 3½
aid to Greenwich Hospital - - -	18,845 19 8	21,412 17 5¼
pense of collection - - - - -	4,837 1 5	4,724 4 10¼
Detail of the Total Expense of Collection:		
eputy receivers of Great Britain and Ireland, America, Guern- rsey, and Newfoundland, 12½ per cent. for collecting, except the Liverpool, which is 7½ per cent. - - - -	2,081 3 6	2,343 4 1
receivers general for Scotland and Ireland, a salary of 50*l.* per each - - - - -	100 0 0	100 0 0
n clerk at the Custom-house, 10 per cent. on the amount ed in America - - - - -	78 4 5	77 2 10
f the chief receiver at Newfoundland, 7½ per cent. on the on - - - - - -	- -	81 8 1½
o the receiver general and comptroller at the port of London, lerks, clerk at the customs, messenger, and housekeeper -	1,635 0 0	1,655 0 0
- - - - - - -	437 11 8	
uation allowances - - - - -	36 5 0	36 5 0
stationery, taxes, and housekeeper's disbursements -	468 16 10	431 4 10
£	4,837 1 5	4,724 4 10¼

ies paid to Greenwich Hospital are applied to the general purposes of the institution.

P. C. LE GEYT, Clerk of the Cheque.

l expense of collecting amounted in the year 1828 to 20½ per cent., and in 1826 to 18 per cent. s receipts; but arrangements are now ordered to be carried into effect, by which the whole ll be reduced to about 10 per cent.

W. H. HOOPER, Secretary.

Hospital, Greenwich, 10th May, 1830.

II. Account of Merchant Seamen now in the Royal Hospital for Seamen at Greenwich, with the parative Amount of Service in the Navy and in the Merchants' Employ.

Number of Men who have never served in the Navy.	Number of Men who have served in the Navy and in the Merchants' Service.	Total Number of Years served by them in the King's Service.	Total Number of Years served by them in the Merchants' Service.	Average Number of Years served by each Man in the Navy.	Average N of Yea served each Man Merchants'
Nil.	1,121	18,195	14,485	16¼	13

The Establishment of Greenwich Hospital is - - - -	2,7
Of these are —	
Seamen who have served in merchant ships - - - - - -	1,
Seamen who have served in King's ships only - - - - -	1,
Royal Marines - - - - - - - - -	4
Lunatics - - - - - - - - - -	
Absent - - - - - - - - - -	
Vacancies - - - - - - - - -	
	2,7

III. Account of Children of Merchant Seamen in the School of Greenwich Hospital.

Number of Children of Merchant Seamen whose Fathers have never served in the Navy.	Number of Children of Merchant Seamen whose Fathers have also served in the Navy.	Remarks.
89	23	The original Greenwich Hospital School, to which the chi of merchant seamen are eligible, consisted of 200 children, unt a regulation of 1829, it was increased to 300.

Royal Hospital, Greenwich, April 9th, 1831.   R. G. KEATS, Govern

For further details with respect to this important subject, see Abbott's (now Tenterden's) valuable work on the Law of Shipping.

SEAWORTHY, a term applied to a ship, indicating that she is in every re fit for her voyage.

It is provided in all charterparties, that the vessel chartered shall be " tight, sta and strong, well apparelled, furnished with an adequate number of men and mar tackle, provisions, &c." If the ship be insufficient in any of these particulars owners, though ignorant of the circumstance, will be liable for whatever damage in consequence, be done to the goods of the merchant; and if an insurance has effected upon her, it will be void.

But whether the condition of seaworthiness be expressed in the charterparty or is always implied. " In every contract," said Lord Ellenborough, " between a holding himself forth as the owner of a lighter or vessel ready to carry goods fo and the person putting goods on board, or employing his vessel or lighter fo purpose, it is a term of the contract on the part of the lighterman or carrier *imp law*, that his vessel is tight, and fit for the purpose for which he offers and holds i to the public : it is the immediate foundation and substratum of the contract that it *the law presumes a promise to that effect on the part of the carrier, without any actual* and every reason of sound policy and public convenience requires that that it be so."

Not only must the ship and furniture be sufficient for the voyage, but she mus be furnished with a sufficient number of persons of competent skill and ability to gate her. And for sailing down rivers, out of harbours, or through roads, &c., either by usage or the laws of the country a pilot is required, a pilot must be tal board. But no owner or master of a ship shall be answerable for any loss or d by reason of no pilot being on board, unless it shall be proved that the want of shall have arisen from any refusal to take a pilot on board; or from the neglige the master in not heaving to, for the purpose of taking on board any pilot who sh ready and offer to take charge of the ship. — (48 *Geo.* 3. c. 164.)

A ship is not seaworthy unless she be provided with all the documents or pape cessary for the manifestation of the ship and cargo. Neither is she seaworthy, if, war, she be not supplied with the sails required to facilitate her escape from an ene

It is only necessary to guarantee the owners from loss, that the ship should b worthy at the time of her departure. She may cease to be so in a few hours, a they may not be liable. The question to be decided in such cases always is, w the ship's disability arose from any defect existing in her *before* her departure, or cause which occasioned it *afterwards*. But if a ship, within a day or two of parture, become leaky or founder at sea, or be obliged to put back, without any vis

cause to produce such an effect — such as the starting of a plank or other ac-
which the best ships are liable, and which no human prudence can prevent —
presumption is that she was not seaworthy when she sailed; and it will be in-
on the owners to show that she was seaworthy at that time.' They are liable for
occasioned by every injury arising from any *original defect* in the ship, or from
age: but they are not liable for any injury arising from the act of God, the
emies, or the perils of the sea.

urther to be observed, that how perfect soever a ship may be, yet if, from the
of her construction, or any other cause, she be incapable of performing the pro-
yage, with the proposed cargo on board, she is not seaworthy. *She must be, in
ts, fit for the trade in which she is meant to be employed.* And it is a wholesome
the owners should be held to a pretty strict proof of this.

been already observed, that any defect in point of seaworthiness invalidates an
upon a ship. There is not only an express but an implied warranty in every
at the ship shall be " tight, staunch, and strong, &c.;" and the reason of this is
The insurer undertakes to indemnify the insured against the *extraordinary and
perils of the sea;* and it would be absurd to suppose that any man would insure
ose perils, but in the confidence that the ship is in a condition to encounter the
perils to which every ship must be exposed in the usual course of the proposed

old law of France it was directed, that every merchant ship, before her de-
om the place of her outfit, should be surveyed by certain sea-officers appointed
urpose, and reported to be seaworthy, " *en bon état de navigation;*" and that
o her return, before she took her homeward cargo on board, she should be
veyed. Valin has shown — (Tit. *Fret,* art. 12.), that very little confidence
placed in these surveys, which, he tells us, were only made upon the external
the ship was not unsheathed; and, therefore, her internal and hidden defects
be disclosed. This practice seems now to be abandoned by the French; at
e is no allusion to it in the *Code de Commerce.* It is, one should think, much
eave the question as to the seaworthiness of the ship to be ascertained, as in
after a loss has happened, by an investigation of the true cause of such loss,
rmit so important a question to be decided upon the report of officers without
e to inquire carefully into her actual condition. A ship may, to all ap-
be perfectly capable of performing a voyage; and it is only after a loss has
that her latent defects can be discovered, and her true state at the time of her
rendered manifest. Indeed, the survey made by the French was not deemed
ve proof that the ship was, at her departure, really seaworthy: it merely raised
ion that such was the case; but it was still open to the freighter or the insurer
e contrary.

ther information upon this point, the reader is referred to the able and ex-
ks of Chief Justice Abbott (Lord Tenterden) on the Law of Shipping (part iii.
of Mr. Serjeant Marshall on Insurance (book i. c. 5. § 1.).

S, in commerce, the grains of several species of gramina. Those of
rtance are clover seed, flax or linseed, hemp seed, mustard seed, rape
, &c.; for which, see the respective articles.

RS, OR CIGARS. See TOBACCO.

A. See CASSIA SENNA.

REEN (Ger. *Schagrin;* Fr. *Chagrin;* Rus. *Schagrim, Schagren*), a kind
leather, used for various purposes in the arts. It is extensively ma-
d at Astrachan in Russia. — (See *Tooke's Russia,* vol. iii. p. 403.)

MY, OR CHAMOIS LEATHER (Ger. *Sämischleder;* Fr. *Chamois;*
io; Rus. *Samschaniii, Koshi*), a kind of leather dressed in oil, or tanned,
esteemed for its softness, pliancy, and capability of bearing soap with-
The real shammy is prepared of the skin of the chamois goat. But
pared from the skins of the common goat, kid, and sheep, is frequently
in its stead.

KS' FINS form a regular article of trade to China; and are collected
urpose in every country from the eastern shore of Africa to New
In the Canton Price Currents they are as regularly quoted as tea
and the price of late years has been, according to quality, from 15 to
per picul, equal to from 50s. to 60s. per cwt.

LS (Ger. *Schalen;* Fr. *Chals, Chales;* It. *Shavali;* Sp. *Schavalos*), ar-
ne wool, silk, or wool and silk, manufactured after the fashion of a
kerchief, used in female dress. The finest shawls are imported from
Indies, where they are highly esteemed, and cost from 50 to 300

guineas. But the British shawls manufactured at Norwich, Paisley, and p
larly Edinburgh, have recently been very much improved ; and are ver
inferior, in point of quality, to the finest specimens brought from the East
they are much cheaper. The shawl manufacture is of very considerable
and importance.

SHEEP (Ger. *Schafe ;* Fr. *Brebis, Bétes à laine, Moutons ;* It. *Pecor*
Pecora, Ovejas ; Rus. *Owzü ;* Lat. *Oves*). These well known and most
animals are, in more than one respect, of great importance to the trading
the community, as well as to society in general. Their wool, skins, an
and even their entrails, constitute articles of extensive traffic. The impo
of sheep from a foreign country is prohibited under pain of forfeiture.—(6
c. 107. § 52.) (See CATTLE, and WOOL.)

SHERRY. See WINE.

SHIPS. Nautical men apply the term ship to distinguish a vessel havin
masts, each consisting of a lower mast, a top-mast, and top-gallant-mas
their appropriate rigging. In familiar language, it is usually employed to
guish any large vessel, however rigged : but it is also frequently used as a
designation for all vessels navigated with sails; and it is in this sense that v
employ it.

Merchant Ships. — It is hardly possible to divide merchant ships into
at least with any degree of precision. Their size, shape, the mode of th
ging, &c. depend not merely on the particular trade for which they are de
but on the varying tastes and fancies of their owners. The ships employed
China trade, by the East India Company, are the largest merchantmen be
to this country; the private traders to the East and West Indies rank next
follow the whale ships, those engaged in the trade to the Baltic and Cana
Mediterranean, and a host of others of every variety of burthen and shape

The reader will find, in the articles NAVIGATION LAWS, and REGISTRY,
count of the peculiar privileges enjoyed by British ships, of the conditio
formalities necessary to be observed in order to acquire and preserve th
vileges, of the mode of transferring property in ships, &c. And in the
CHARTERPARTY, FREIGHT, MASTER, OWNERS, SEAMEN, &c., the law v
spect to ships and ship-owners, in their capacity of carriers or public servan
the reciprocal duties and obligations of the masters and crews, is pretty fu
pounded. In this place, therefore, we shall content ourselves with laying
the reader some official statements exhibiting the progress and present ma.
of the mercantile navy of Great Britain.

Increase of Shipping in England. — It would be to no purpose, even if ou
permitted, to enter into any details with respect to the shipping of Engla
viously to the Revolution. Those who wish to examine the subject, v
most of the scattered notices of contemporary writers collected by Anderso
" Chronological History of Commerce." The mercantile navy of Engla
became considerable in the reign of Elizabeth ; and gradually increased un
successors, James I. and Charles I. At the Restoration, the British s
cleared outwards amounted to 95,266 tons; but such was the increase
gation during the reigns of Charles II. and James II., that, at the Rev
the British ships cleared outwards amounted to 190,533 tons. The wa
nated by the treaty of Ryswick, in 1697, checked this progress. But co
and navigation have steadily advanced, with the exception of two short
during the war of 1739, and the American war, from the beginning of last
down to the present day.

The first really authentic account of the magnitude of the commercial
England was obtained in 1701–2, from returns to circular letters of th
missioners of customs, issued in January of that year. From these it
that there belonged, at the period in question, to *all* the ports of Engl
Wales, 3,281 vessels, measuring (or rather estimated to measure) 261,2
and carrying 27,196 men and 5,660 guns. Of these there belonged to

	Vessels.	Tons.	Men.		Vessels.	Tons.
London	560	84,882	10,065	Hull	115	7,564
Bristol	165	17,338	2,359	Whitby	110	8,292
Yarmouth	143	9,914	668	Liverpool	102	8,619
Exeter	121	7,107	978	Scarborough	100	6,860

e of the other ports had 100 vessels; and there is some mistake in the reas to the tonnage assigned to Newcastle and Ipswich. Of the Hull vessels,
re at the time laid up, which accounts for the small number of men in that
— (*Macpherson's Annals of Commerce, Anno* 1701.)

following table of the British and foreign shipping *cleared outwards* from
to 1811, both inclusive, is taken from the last edition of *Mr. Chalmers's*
rative Estimate. It gives a very complete view of the progress of the navi-
of the country; and from the attention paid by the author to such subjects,
e facilities which his situation in the Board of Trade gave him for acquiring
tic information, its accuracy may be depended upon.

I. Table of Ships cleared Outwards from 1663 to 1811.

Years.	Tons. English.	Tons. Foreign.	Total.	Years.	Tons. British.	Tons. Foreign.	Total.
1663 } 1669 }	95,266	47,634	142,900	1773	874,421	57,994	932,415
				1774	901,016	68,402	969,418
1688	190,533	95,267	285,800	1775	882,579	68,034	950,613
1697	144,264	100,524	244,788	1776	872,108	74,323	946,431
1700 } 1701 } 1702 }	273,693	43,635	317,328	1777	827,067	102,638	929,705
				1778	732,558	93,778	826,336
				1779	642,981	149,040	791,021
1709	243,693	45,625	289,318	1780	731,286	154,111	885,397
1712	326,620	29,115	355,735	1781	608,219	170,775	778,994
1713 } 1714 } 1715 }	421,431	26,573	448,004	1782	615,150	225,456	840,606
				1783	865,967	170,938	1,037,905
				1784	932,219	118,268	1,050,487
1726 } 1727 } 1728 }	432,832	23,651	456,483	1785	1,074,862	107,484	1,182,346
				1786	1,115,024	121,197	1,236,221
				1787	1,279,033	138,220	1,417,253
1736 } 1737 } 1738 }	476,941	26,627	503,568	1788	1,411,689	128,997	1,540,686
				1789	1,515,021	103,722	1,618,743
1739 } 1740 } 1741 }	384,191	87,260	471,451	1790	1,424,912	148,919	1,573,831
				1791	1,511,246	184,729	1,695,975
				1792	1,561,158	175,405	1,736,563
1749 } 1750 } 1751 }	609,798	51,386	661,184	1793	1,240,202	187,032	1,427,234
				1794	1,382,166	218,077	1,600,243
				1795	1,145,450	382,567	1,528,017
1755 } 1756 } 1757 }	British. 496,254	76,456	572,710	1796	1,254,624	478,356	1,732,980
				1797	1,103,781	396,271	1,500,052
				1798	1,319,151	365,719	1,684,870
1760	540,241	107,237	647,478	1799	1,302,551	414,774	1,717,325
1761	582,020	122,735	704,755	1800	1,445,271	685,051	2,130,322
1762	543,444	124,926	668,370	1801	1,345,621	804,880	2,150,501
1763	631,724	91,593	723,317	1802	1,626,966	461,723	2,088,689
1764	662,434	79,800	742,234	1803	1,453,066	574,542	2,027,608
1765	726,402	72,215	798,617	1804	1,463,286	587,849	2,051,135
1766	758,081	66,153	824,234	1805	1,495,209	605,821	2,101,030
1767	725,835	68,006	793,841	1806	1,486,302	568,170	2,054,472
1768	761,786	77,984	839,770	1807	1,424,103	631,910	2,056,013
1769	805,305	68,420	873,725	1808	1,372,810	282,145	1,654,955
1770	806,495	63,176	869,671	1809	1,531,152	699,750	2,230,902
1771	877,004	66,898	943,902	1810	1,624,274	1,138,527	2,762,801
1772	923,456	72,931	996,387	1811	1,507,353	696,232	2,203,585

unt of the Total Number of Vessels engaged in the *Foreign* Trade of the United Kingdom,
Amount of their Tonnage, and the Number of Men and Boys employed in navigating the
at entered Inwards from all Parts of the World, in the several Years from 1814 to 1830, both
; distinguishing British from Foreign.

Years.	British and Irish Vessels.			Foreign Vessels.		
	Vessels.	Tons.	Men.	Vessels.	Tons.	Men.
1814	8,975	1,209,248	83,793	5,286	599,287	37,875
1815	8,880	1,372,108	86,390	5,411	764,562	44,000
1816	9,744	1,415,723	90,119	3,116	379,465	25,345
1817	11,255	1,625,121	97,273	3,396	445,011	27,047
1818	13,006	1,886,394	111,880	6,230	762,457	43,936
1819	11,974	1,809,128	107,556	4,215	542,684	32,632
1820	11,285	1,668,060	100,325	3,472	447,611	27,633
1821	10,805	1,599,423	97,485	3,261	296,107	26,043
1822	11,087	1,663,627	98,980	3,389	469,151	28,421
1823	11,271	1,740,859	112,244	4,069	582,996	33,828
1824	11,731	1,797,089	108,686	5,655	759,672	42,126
1825	13,503	2,143,317	123,028	6,981	959,312	52,722
1826	12,473	1,950,630	113,093	5,729	694,116	39,838
1827	13,133	2,086,898	118,686	4,955	751,864	43,536
1828	13,436	2,094,357	119,141	4,955	634,620	36,753
1829	13,659	2,184,535	122,185	5,218	710,303	39,342
1830	13,548	2,180,042	122,103	5,359	758,828	41,670

III. Number of Ships and Vessels belonging to the different Ports or Places of the British Emp[ire] 1829, stated in succession, agreeably to the Amount of Tonnage belonging to each.

ENGLAND.	Ships.	Tons.		Ships.	Tons.		Ships.
London	2,663	572,835	Ramsgate	70	4,397	Port Glasgow	46
Newcastle	987	202,379	Ilfracombe	64	4,095	Banff	133
Liverpool	805	161,780	Wells	66	3,962	Lerwick	94
Sunderland	624	107,628	Newport	50	3,824	Kirkwall	68
Whitehaven	496	72,967	Rye	68	3,704	Stornoway	74
Hull	579	72,248	Goole	50	3,625	Campbeltown	68
Bristol	316	49,535	Padstow	68	3,587	Thurso	39
Yarmouth	585	44,134	Blackney and Clay	50	3,380	Stranraer	42
Whitby	258	41,576	Lyne	39	3,335		
Scarborough	169	28,070	Llanelly	69	3,264		3,228
Plymouth	302	24,838	Bridgewater	46	2,921		
Dartmouth	349	24,114	Carlisle	40	2,886		
Beaumaris	389	22,076	Chichester	62	2,805	IRELAND.	
Poole	168	17,860	Cardiff	38	2,742	Belfast	247
Exeter	196	17,166	Arundel	25	2,711	Dublin	289
Lynn	118	14,659	Aldborough	49	2,698	Cork	256
Cardigan	281	14,643	Woodbridge	38	2,659	Newry	161
Gloucester	247	13,026	Southwold	37	2,638	Waterford	26
Rochester	255	10,816	Wisbech	43	2,487	Wexford	135
Bideford	116	10,182	Shoreham	42	2,272	Londonderry	32
Lancaster	107	9,410	Barnstaple	40	2,087	Baltimore	86
Ipswich	138	8,532	Truro	25	1,727	Drogheda	30
Portsmouth	184	8,485	Grimsby	39	1,390	Limerick	39
Southampton	178	8,120	Newhaven	21	1,205	Sligo	20
Milford	116	8,104	Minehead	20	957	Galway	19
Boston	152	8,059	Scilly	22	792	Coleraine	10
Swansea	122	7,772	Deal	19	557	Dundalk	6
Faversham	217	7,592	Gweek	8	557	Westport	7
Maldon	190	7,373					
Stockton	74	7,296	Total	13,977	1,758,065		1,413
Weymouth	85	7,175					
Colchester	235	6,745	SCOTLAND.			Isle of Jersey	200
Falmouth	78	6,614	Aberdeen	350	46,201	Guernsey	75
Aberystwith	120	6,423	Glasgow	235	41,121	Man	217
Bridlington	40	6,290	Greenock	371	36,241		
Cowes	151	6,015	Dundee	299	31,986	Total of the United Kingdom and British Islands }	19,110
Chepstow	72	5,805	Leith	263	26,362		
St. Ives	87	5,570	Grangemouth	204	24,327	Plantations	4,343
Dover	120	5,525	Montrose	173	16,179		
Harwich	96	5,513	Kirkaldy	192	14,802	Grand Total	23,453
Fowey	81	5,470	Irvine	135	13,379		
Penzance	92	4,981	Dumfries	183	12,192		
Chester	74	4,816	Bowness	123	9,108		
Berwick	57	4,784	Inverness	136	7,338		

Number of men belonging to ships of United Kingdom and British Islands   - - - 1
Number of men belonging to ships of Plantations   - - - - -

Total of men belonging, in 1829, to the mercantile navy of the United Kingdom and Plantations 1

Mercantile Navy in 1830.

	Vessels.	Tons.	Men.
Great Britain and Plantations	23,721	2,531,819	154,812

IV. Shipping entered Inwards in Great Britain from *all* Parts of the World.

Years ending Jan. 5th.	British and Irish Vessels.			Foreign Vessels.			Total.		
	Vessels.	Tons.	Men.	Vessels.	Tons.	Men.	Vessels.	Tons.	Men.
1829	23,356	3,005,819	181,723	4,771	604,097	34,958	28,127	3,609,916	216,6..
1830	23,536	3,096,759	186,719	5,028	682,048	37,689	28,564	3,778,807	224,..
1831	23,086	3,088,498	188,538	5,212	736,297	40,262	28,298	3,824,795	228,8..

V. Shipping entered Inwards in Ireland from *all* Parts of the World.

Years ending Jan. 5th.	British and Irish Vessels.			Foreign Vessels.			Total.		
	Vessels.	Tons.	Men.	Vessels.	Tons.	Men.	Vessels.	Tons.	Men.
1829	13,107	1,278,050	75,848	184	30,523	1,775	13,291	1,308,573	77,6..
1830	14,781	1,442,722	86,045	190	28,255	1,703	14,971	1,470,977	87,7..
1831	14,160	1,385,452	85,544	147	22,531	1,408	14,307	1,407,983	86,9..

SHIPS.

The year headings for the upper table are cut off at the top edge of the page; the five year-groups (each with British and Foreign — Ships and Tons) are shown below without legible year labels.

	British Ships	British Tons	Foreign Ships	Foreign Tons	British Ships	British Tons	Foreign Ships	Foreign Tons	British Ships	British Tons	Foreign Ships	Foreign Tons	British Ships	British Tons	Foreign Ships	Foreign Tons	British Ships	British Tons	Foreign Ships	Foreign Tons
Europe, Northern*	3,138	439,090	1,229	178,572	3,498	518,432	1,653	259,657	3,298	481,825	2,252	350,196	3,400	504,710	3,884	535,604	5,016	775,487	4,943	675,898
Southern †	2,982	267,528	1,580	76,701	2,899	255,137	1,335	60,340	2,837	269,500	1,299	65,372	2,854	265,647	1,298	68,473	2,994	297,200	1,407	81,404
Asia	119	77,946	—	—	103	68,160	—	—	123	81,855	—	198	150	86,758	—	330	132	77,311	—	—
Africa	92	19,447	—	—	75	12,394	—	—	97	18,066	—	102	106	21,916	—	—	139	34,621	—	—
America, British Northern Colonies	1,403	537,446	—	—	1,416	356,448	—	—	1,579	401,669	—	—	1,683	427,832	—	—	1,858	489,844	—	—
British West Indies	884	245,321	—	—	839	232,426	—	—	861	233,790	—	—	899	244,971	—	—	872	232,357	—	—
Foreign West Indies	79	15,204	1	57	62	11,825	—	—	64	12,592	1	290	52	9,566	—	—	75	12,901	8	1,848
United States	103	98,411	450	140,776	138	37,385	500	156,054	237	63,606	509	165,699	157	44,994	460	153,475	133	38,943	599	196,863
Foreign Continental Colonies	204	37,154	—	—	213	38,903	—	—	223	40,574	3	682	251	46,787	1	200	314	57,553	7	1,576
The Fisheries, viz. the Whale	197	60,257	—	—	157	43,204	—	—	170	51,796	—	—	148	45,925	—	—	138	42,736	—	—
the Pearl	—	—	—	—	—	—	—	—	—	—	—	—	—	—	—	—	—	—	—	—
Isles of Guernsey, Jersey, and Man	1,609	79,170	1	150	1,757	84,863	1	100	1,852	85,936	5	367	2,053	98,214	5	492	1,845	85,645	4	543
Total	10,810	1,599,274	3,261	396,256	11,087	1,664,186	3,389	469,151	11,271	1,740,859	4,069	582,996	11,733	1,797,390	5,653	759,441	13,516	2,144,598	6,968	958,132

	1826				1827				1828				1829			
	British		Foreign		British		Foreign		British		Foreign		British		Foreign	
	Ships	Tons	Ships	Tons	Ships	Tons	Ships	Tons	Ships	Tons	Ships	Tons	Ships	Tons	Ships	Tons
Europe, Northern*	4,102	604,838	3,930	468,446	4,992	770,738	3,733	449,211	4,728	691,273	3,291	410,215	4,857	744,563	3,510	465,138
Southern †	2,858	273,790	1,338	71,597	3,160	318,712	1,659	83,175	3,040	311,144	1,267	82,356	3,001	311,489	1,294	78,256
Asia	196	101,683	—	—	191	103,436	1	300	200	101,467	—	—	223	111,359	—	—
Africa	133	33,192	—	—	136	35,464	—	—	151	38,181	—	—	191	50,378	—	—
America, British Northern Colonies	1,770	472,588	7	1,362	1,357	359,793	5	1,250	1,526	400,841	3	683	1,611	431,901	1	89
British West Indies	891	243,448	448	151,765	872	243,721	646	217,535	1,013	272,800	872	138,174	958	263,338	450	162,327
Foreign West Indies	52	9,649	3	675	51	10,338	—	293	45	8,899	5	976	57	10,530	5	910
United States	158	47,711	—	—	238	73,304	—	—	256	80,158	—	—	192	61,343	—	—
Foreign Continental Colonies	157	27,947	—	—	203	40,531	—	—	251	51,784	—	—	271	55,925	—	—
The Fisheries, viz. the Whale	125	39,394	—	—	118	37,741	—	—	106	34,029	—	—	113	35,982	—	—
the Pearl	—	—	—	—	1	261	—	—	—	—	—	—	1	259	—	—
Greenland (a Cargo of Ice)	—	—	—	—	—	—	1	100	1	100	—	—	—	—	—	—
Isles of Guernsey, Jersey, and Man	2,031	96,460	3	271	1,814	99,959	—	—	2,119	103,681	17	2,216	2,184	108,068	10	1,393
Total	12,473	1,950,630	5,729	694,116	13,133	2,086,898	6,046	751,864	13,436	2,094,357	4,955	634,620	13,659	2,184,535	5,918	710,303

* Europe, Northern, viz. Russia, Sweden, Norway, Denmark, Prussia, Germany, Netherlands.
† Europe, Southern, viz. France, Portugal, Spain, Gibraltar, Italy, Malta, Ionian Islands, Turkey, and the Levant.

VII. General Statement of the Shipping employed in the Trade of the United Kingdom, in the Year hibiting the Number and Tonnage of Vessels entered Inwards and cleared Outwards (includi repeated Voyages), with the Number of their Crews; separating British from Foreign Ships, tinguishing the Trade with each Country. — (*Parl. Paper*, No. 350. Sess. 1831.)

| Countries, &c. | Inwards | | | | | | Outwards | | | |
| | British. | | | Foreign. | | | British. | | | F |
	Ships.	Tons.	Men.	Ships.	Tons.	Men.	Ships.	Tons.	Men.	Ships.
Russia	1,661	321,426	14,698	90	26,905	1,280	1,231	240,638	11,253	88
Sweden	82	32,116	583	127	23,158	1,175	55	8,020	412	67
Norway	66	6,459	395	556	84,585	4,570	53	5,148	326	582
Denmark	111	12,210	608	655	51,490	3,175	540	85,981	4,135	926
Prussia	666	102,758	4,920	720	139,646	6,132	341	50,931	2,559	380
Germany	986	150,997	7,516	616	54,869	3,018	876	133,847	6,724	612
United Netherlands	1,156	120,301	7,030	863	92,811	5,096	887	87,559	5,301	783
France	1,367	110,766	10,029	933	47,940	6,369	1,330	111,779	9,968	642
Portugal, Proper	395	43,336	2,542	78	8,394	705	339	36,930	2,313	99
the Azores	161	12,906	836	2	185	18	105	8,332	571	4
Madeira	8	1,339	73	-	-	-	7	1,327	90	1
Spain and the Balearic Islands	428	46,508	2,645	61	5,639	450	353	37,412	2,230	58
Canaries	42	4,793	258	-	-	-	46	5,590	324	2
Gibraltar	30	4,196	239	-	-	-	83	10,677	606	8
Italy and the Italian Islands	353	51,512	2,848	13	2,253	157	418	58,307	3,547	14
Malta	17	2,162	118	1	225	10	38	9,306	512	1
Ionian Islands	32	4,304	240	-	-	-	38	5,513	292	
Turkey and Continental Greece	95	13,610	780	-	-	-	95	13,424	783	
Morea and Greek Islands	7	1,055	55	-	-	-	11	1,607	98	
Egypt (Ports on the Mediterranean)	14	3,855	188	-	-	-	22	4,281	236	1
Tripoli, Barbary and Morocco	11	1,127	65	-	-	-	3	331	19	
Coast of Africa, from Morocco to the Cape of Good Hope	126	34,763	1,852	-	-	-	137	38,661	2,192	
Cape of Good Hope	23	4,276	230	-	-	-	38	7,737	463	1
Cape Verd Islands	-	-	-	-	-	-	2	307	19	
Saint Helena and Ascension	1	142	13	-	-	-	3	615	33	2
Isle of Bourbon	-	-	-	-	-	-	-	-	-	
Mauritius	55	17,189	893	-	-	-	33	8,036	481	
East India Co.'s Territories and Ceylon	148	65,498	4,525	-	-	-	141	59,605	4,043	2
China	22	27,782	2,700	-	-	-	16	21,033	2,169	2
Sumatra and Java	3	1,189	59	1	370	20	2	577	53	1
Philippine Islands	6	2,486	121	-	-	-	1	237	16	2
Other Islands of the Indian Seas	-	-	-	-	-	-	1	569	31	
New S. Wales and Van Diemen's Land	26	8,668	502	-	-	-	65	22,587	1,633	
Swan River	-	-	-	-	-	-	2	764	42	
New Guinea	-	-	-	-	-	-	1	405	30	
New Zealand and South Sea Islands	2	431	26	-	-	-	7	728	71	
British North American Colonies	1,709	452,397	21,358	-	-	-	1,714	450,987	22,015	
British West Indies	911	253,872	13,782	-	-	-	868	240,664	13,647	
Hayti	21	3,712	189	-	-	-	46	7,642	472	
Cuba and other Foreign West Indies	25	4,637	238	12	3,111	139	67	12,584	741	16
United States of America	197	65,130	2,948	609	214,166	9,189	281	91,551	4,344	611
Mexico	35	6,236	351	-	-	-	51	8,574	503	2
Colombia	17	3,268	186	-	-	-	16	3,108	178	
Brazil	168	38,322	1,968	1	270	9	254	57,682	5,044	
States of the Rio de la Plata	51	9,784	531	1	320	21	36	6,294	373	3
Chili	7	1,242	78	-	-	-	14	2,510	152	
Peru	11	2,085	116	-	-	-	10	1,899	118	
The Whale Fisheries	97	31,897	3,835	-	-	-	123	40,166	5,044	
The Isles of Guernsey, Jersey, Alderney and Man	2,199	117,298	8,949	20	2,561	141	1,897	95,547	7,829	250
Foreign Parts, not otherwise described	-	-	-	-	-	-	34	4,338	202	
Total, all Parts of the World	13,548	2,180,012	122,105	5,359	758,828	41,670	12,747	2,102,147	122,025	5,158

VIII. Steam-boats belonging to Great Britain in 1829, and to Ireland in 1828.

	Vessels.	Tons.
England	241	20,611
Scotland	75	5,953
Ireland	26	4,791

SHIPS' PAPERS, the papers or documents required for the manif of the property of the ship and cargo, &c. They are of two sorts; viz. 1 required by the law of a particular country — as the certificate of registry, charterparty, bills of lading, bill of health, &c.—(see these titles)—require law of England to be on board British ships; and 2dly, those required by of nations to be on board neutral ships, to vindicate their title to that ch Mr. Serjeant Marshall, following M. Hubner (*De la Saisie des Bâtimens* tome i. pp. 241—252.) has given the following description of the latter documents: —

1. *The Passport, Sea Brief, or Sea Letter.*—This is a permission from the neu to the captain or master of the ship, to proceed on the voyage proposed, and usu tains his name and residence; the name, property, description, tonnage, and de of the ship; the nature and quantity of the cargo, the place from whence it co its destination; with such other matters as the practice of the place requires. cument is indispensably necessary for the safety of every neutral ship. Hubi that it is the only paper rigorously insisted on by the Barbary corsairs; by the p of which alone their friends are protected from insult.

2. *The Proofs of Property.*—These ought to show that the ship really belor subjects of a neutral state. If she appear to either belligerent to have been bu enemy's country, proof is generally required that she was purchased by the ne fore, or captured and legally condemned and sold to the neutral after, the decl

nd in the latter case the *bill of sale*, properly authenticated, ought to be produced. ibner admits that these proofs are so essential to every neutral vessel, for the pre- of frauds, that such as sail without them have no reason to complain if they be pted in their voyages, and their neutrality disputed.

he Muster Roll.—This, which the French call *rôle d'équipage*, contains the names, uality, place of residence, and, above all, *the place of birth*, of every person of the ompany. This document is of great use in ascertaining a ship's neutrality. It aturally excite a strong suspicion, if the majority of the crew be found to consist igners; still more, if they be natives of the enemy's country. — (See SEAMEN.)

he Charterparty.—Where the ship is chartered, this instrument serves to authen- nany of the facts on which the truth of her neutrality must rest, and should there- always found on board chartered ships.

he Bills of Lading.—By these the captain acknowledges the receipt of the goods d therein, and promises to deliver them to the consignee or his order. Of these re usually several duplicates; one of which is kept by the captain, one by the of the goods, and one transmitted to the consignee. This instrument, being only lence of a private transaction between the owner of the goods and the captain, does y with it the same degree of authenticity as the charterparty.

he Invoices.—These contain the particulars and prices of each parcel of goods, e amount of the freight, duties, and other charges thereon, which are usually trans- from the shippers to their factors or consignees. These invoices prove by whom ds were shipped, and to whom consigned. They carry with them, however, but thenticity; being easily fabricated where fraud is intended.

he Log Book, or Ship's Journal.—This contains a minute account of the ship's with a short history of every occurrence during the voyage. If this be faithfully will throw great light on the question of neutrality; if it be in any respect fa- , the fraud may in general be easily detected.

ie Bill of Health.—This is a certificate, properly authenticated, that the ship comes place where no contagious distemper prevails; and that none of the crew, at the her departure, were infected with any such disorder. It is generally found on board ming from the Levant, or from the coast of Barbary, where the plague so fre- prevails.

p using false or simulated papers is liable to confiscation.—(*Marshall on Insur- ok* i. c. 9. § 6.)

ES (Du. *Schoenen*; Fr. *Souliers*; Ger. *Schuhe*; It. *Scarpe*; Rus. *Basch- Sp. Zapatos*), articles of clothing that are univerally worn, and require no ion.

hoe manufacture is of great value and importance. The finest sort of shoes is London; but the manufacture is carried on upon the largest scale in Northamp- and Staffordshire. The London warehouses derive considerable supplies from h, Congleton, and Sandbach, in Cheshire. During the late war, the contractor generally furnished about 600,000 pairs annually. For an estimate of the the shoes annually manufactured in Britain, see LEATHER.

MAC OR SUMACH (Ger. *Schmack, Sumach*; Fr. *Sumac, Roure*, It. *Sommaco*; Sp. *Zumaque*; Rus. *Sumak*). Common shumac (*Rhus* is a shrub that grows naturally in Syria, Palestine, Spain, and Portugal. ich is cultivated in Italy, and is improperly called *young fustic*, is the *Rhus* It is cultivated with great care: its shoots are cut down every year quite ot; and, after being dried, they are chipped or reduced to powder by a thus prepared for the purposes of dyeing and tanning. The shumac cul- n the neighbourhood of Montpellier is called *rédoul* or *roudou*. Shumac considered of good quality, when its odour is strong, colour of a lively ell ground, and free from stalks. Italian shumac is used in dyeing a yellow, approaching to the orange, upon wool or cloth; but the colour e. Common shumac is useful for drab and dove colours in calico print- is also capable of dyeing black. — (*Bancroft on Colours*, vol. ii. p. 100.)

ntity imported in 1828, amounted to 95,935 cwt., none of which was re-exported. The duty, unts at present to 1s. per cwt., produced, in 1830, 5,276l. 8s.; so that the quantity entered onsumption that year must have been 105,528 cwt. The imports are almost entirely from

RA LEONE, an English settlement, near the mouth of the river of the ne, on the south-west coast of Africa, in lat. 8° 30′ N., lon. 13° 15′ W.

of the Colony. — This colony was founded partly as a commercial establish- t more from motives of humanity. It was intended to consist principally of s, who, being instructed in the Christian religion, and in the arts of Europe,

should become, as it were, a focus whence civilisation might be diffused among the
rounding tribes. About 1,200 free negroes, who, having joined the royal standa
the American war, were obliged, at the termination of that contest, to take refu
Nova Scotia, were conveyed thither in 1792: to these were afterwards added the
roons from Jamaica; and, since the legal abolition of the slave trade, the negroes t
in the captured vessels, and liberated by the mixed commission courts, have been ca
to the colony. The total number of liberated Africans under the superintendenc
the colonial authorities, on the 21st of December, 1829, was 21,205.

Success of the Efforts to civilise the Blacks. — Great efforts have been made to intro
order and industrious habits amongst these persons. We are sorry, however,
obliged to add, that these efforts, though prosecuted at an enormous expense of 'b
and treasure, have been signally unsuccessful. There is, no doubt, much discrep
in the accounts as to the progress made by the blacks. It is, however, sufficiently c
that it has been very inconsiderable, and we do not think that any other r
could be rationally anticipated. Their laziness has been loudly complained of,
without reason. Men are not industrious without a motive; and most of those mo
that stimulate all classes in colder climates to engage in laborious employments
unknown to the indolent inhabitants of this burning region, where clothing is of
importance, where sufficient supplies of food may be obtained with little exer
and where more than half the necessaries and conveniences of Europeans wou
positive incumbrances. And had it been otherwise, what progress could a color
expected to make, into which there are annually imported thousands of liberated neg
most of whom are barbarians in the lowest stage of civilisation?

Influence of the Colony upon the illicit Slave Trade. — As a means of checking
prevalence of the illicit slave trade, the establishment of a colony at Sierra Leone
been worse than useless. That trade is principally carried on with the countries r
the bight of Biafra and the bight of Benin, many hundred miles distant from S
Leone; and the mortality in the captured ships during their voyage to the latt
often very great. In fact, there is but one way of putting down this nefarious tra
and that is by the great powers declaring it to be *piracy*, and treating those engag
it, wherever and by whomsoever they may be found, as sea-robbers or pirates. S
declaration would be quite conformable to the spirit of the declaration put forth b
congress of Vienna in 1824. — (See SLAVE TRADE.) And were it subscribe
England, France, the United States, Russia, &c., the Spaniards and Portuguese v
be compelled to relinquish the trade; but unless something of this sort be don
are afraid there are but slender grounds for thinking that humanity will speedi
relieved from the guilt and suffering inseparable from the traffic.

Climate of Sierra Leone. — The soil in the vicinity of Sierra Leone seems to be
indifferent fertility, and the climate is about the most destructive that can be imag
The mortality among the Africans sent to it seems unusually great; and amongs
whites it is quite excessive. Much as we desire the improvement of the black
protest against its being attempted by sending our countrymen to certain destr
in this most pestiferous of all pestiferous places. It would seem, too, that it is
unnecessary, and that instructed blacks may be advantageously employed to fi
official situations in the colony. But, if otherwise, it ought to be unconditi
abandoned.

Expenses incurred on Account of Sierra Leone. — The pecuniary expense occas
by this colony, and our unsuccessful efforts to suppress the foreign slave trade, hav
altogether enormous. Mr. Keith Douglas is reported to have stated, in his place
House of Commons, in July last (1831), that "Down to the year 1824, th
expenses of Sierra Leone amounted to 2,268,000*l.*; and that the same expense
amounted, from 1824 to 1830, to 1,082.000*l.* The naval expenses, from 1807 to
had been 1,630,000*l.* The payments to Spain and Portugal, to induce them to
quish the slave trade, amounted to 1,230,000*l.* The expenses on account of ca
slaves were 533,092*l.* The expenses incurred on account of the mixed comm
courts were 198,000*l.* Altogether this establishment had cost the country
8,000,000*l.*!"

The prodigality of this expenditure is unmatched, except by its uselessness.
doubtful whether it has prevented a single African from being dragged into s'
or conferred the smallest real advantage on Africa. The kings of Spain and Po
have certainly turned their spurious humanity to pretty good account. We hop
is now, at least, an end of all attempts to bribe such monarchs to respect the ri
humanity, or the treaties into which they have entered.

Commerce of Sierra Leone, and the West Coast of Africa. — Commercially cons
Sierra Leone appears to quite as little advantage as in other points of view.
port from it teak wood, camwood, ivory, palm oil, hides, gums, and a few other a
but their value is inconsiderable, amounting to not more than from 40,000*l.* to 6

The great article of import from the coast of Africa is palm oil, and of this [i]n *fifty times* as much is imported from the coast to the south of the Rio Volta, [h]undred miles from Sierra Leone, as from the latter. We doubt, indeed, [t]he commerce with the western coast of Africa will ever be of much import-['t]he condition of the natives would require to be very much changed before they [beco]me considerable consumers of European manufactures. It is singular, that [w]e persons in this country should be so much bent on prosecuting, without [?] expense, a trade with barbarous uncivilised hordes, while they contribute to [?]ct or oppression of the incomparably more extensive and beneficial intercourse [we] carry on with the opulent and civilised nations in our immediate vicinity. [?]lisation of the duties on Canada and Baltic timber, and the abolition of the [?]restraints on the trade with France, would do ten times more to extend our [trad]e, than the discovery of fifty navigable rivers, and the possession of as many [t]he African coast. If, however, an establishment be really required for the [zeal]ous prosecution of the trade to Western Africa, it is abundantly obvious that [it should] be placed much further to the south than Sierra Leone. The island of Fer-[nando Po] has been suggested for this purpose; but after the dear-bought experience [a]lready had, it is to be hoped that nothing will be done with respect to it without [co]nsideration.

into the United Kingdom in 1829, from the Western Coast of Africa, distinguishing their Quantities and Values.

	Quantities imported.				Official Value of Imports.				
	Sierra Leone, the River Gambia, and the Coast between the Gambia and the Mesurada.	Windward Coast, from the River Mesurada to Cape Apollonia.	Cape Coast Castle and the Gold Coast, from Cape Apollonia to the Rio Volta.	Coast Southward of the Rio Volta, with the Island of Fernando Po.	Sierra Leone, the River Gambia, and the Coast between the Gambia and the Mesurada.	Windward Coast, from the River Mesurada to Cape Apollonia.	Cape Coast Castle and the Gold Coast, from Cape Apollonia to the Rio Volta.	Coast Southward of the Rio Volta, with the Island of Fernando Po.	Total.
					L. s. d.	L. s. d.	L. s. d.	L. s. d.	L. s. d.
lbs.	1,327	-	-	6,766	82 18 9	-	-	422 17 6	505 16 3
qr. lb	103 4 1 3	-	-	246 15 2 13		-	-	9,871 4 8	9,871 4 8
qr. lb.	-	-	-	15 18 0 19	825 14 3	-	-	127 5 4	952 19 7
qr. lb.	-	-	-	12 4 2 20	-	-	-	201 17 2	201 17 2
qr. lb.	-	-	-	3 1 3 15	-	-	-	125 15 4	125 15 4
qr. lb.	518 2 24	-	636 3 6	1,258 2 22	1,912 5 9	-	3,820 16 5	7,432 3 7	13,165 5 9
lbs.	9,007	-	5,302	-	131 7 1	-	77 6 5	-	208 13 6
lbs.	12,576	-	566	423	524 0 0	-	23 11 8	17 12 6	565 4 2
qr. lb.	2,587 1 6	-	-	-	5,498 0 4	-	-	-	5,498 0 4
qr. lb.	3,696 2 25	-	-	-	11,101 12 9	-	-	-	11,101 12 9
qr. lb.	2,963 1 15	400 0 0	7,001 2 18	169,556 3 7	2,963 7 9	400 0 0	7,001 13 2	169,556 16 3	179,921 17 2
qr. lb.	827 1 21	0 3 6	-	-	2,606 8 6	2 10 7	-	-	2,608 19 1
&feet	16,015 26	-	-	-	10,207 15 9	-	-	-	10,207 15 9
qr. lb.	4,510 1 19	-	-	64 2 0	21,486 11 11	-	-	306 7 6	21,792 19 5
value	-	-	-	-	767 12 7	1 5 0	464 4 4	611 3 5	1,847 5 4
					58,107 15 5	403 15 7	11,387 12 0	189,674 3 3	258,573 6 3

British Produce and Manufactures from the United Kingdom in 1829, to the Western Coast of Africa, distinguishing their Quantities and Values.

	Quantities exported.				Official Value of Exports.				
	Sierra Leone, the River Gambia, and the Coast between the Gambia and the Mesurada.	Windward Coast, from the River Mesurada to Cape Apollonia.	Cape Coast Castle and the Gold Coast, from Cape Apollonia to the Rio Volta.	Coast Southward of the Rio Volta, with the Island of Fernando Po.	Sierra Leone, the River Gambia, and the Coast between the Gambia and the Mesurada.	Windward Coast, from the River Mesurada to Cape Apollonia.	Cape Coast Castle and the Gold Coast, from Cape Apollonia to the Rio Volta.	Coast Southward of the Rio Volta, with the Island of Fernando Po.	Total.
					L. s. d.	L. s. d.	L. s. d.	L. s. d.	L. s. d.
r. lb	328 2 0	10 0 0	77 2 0	242 0 7	7,172 14 0	10 0 0	670 2 6	1,335 15 0	9,186 11 6
yds.	558,187	119,484	551,908	681,561	1,637 9 0	45 0 0	40,049 6 9	1,162 10 3	141,581 1 2
wares	-	-	-	-	218 15 0	-	-	-	218 15 0
No.	-	-	-	-	878 11 4	1315 10 0	139 7 1	931 0 1	1,962 14 4
No.	21,151	2,960	14,585	37,955	15,783 5 0	2,220 0 0	10,958 15 0	28,466 5 0	57,408 5 0
lbs.	357,604	25,000	250,800	1,549,350	10,802 12 5	755 4 2	6,960 0 0	46,803 5 7	65,321 2 2
r. lb.	420 0 0	2 0 0	45 2 0	1,194 2 20	1,157 1 3	5 10 0	119 12 6	3,285 7 3	4,567 11 0
qr. lb.	527 18 0 17	20 0 0 0	151 8 2 6	1,157 12 0 0	8,647 16 6	210 0 0	2,220 3 1	11,684 15 0	22,762 14 7
r. lb.	8 3 2 0	4 7 0 0	35 3 0 0	4 6 2 0	85 16 9	47 13 6	369 1 6	45 8 3	548 0 0
ught	-	-	-	-	772 19 10	-	171 3 9	-	947 3 7
ards	36,502	-	3,818	1,853	1,736 17 0	-	178 0 0	79 10 0	1,994 7 0
shels	38,440	-	-	141,700	1,279 16 8	-	-	4,723 6 8	6,003 3 4
r. lb.	500 3 21	-	20 2 26	270 0 16	1,795 18 5	-	69 4 6	810 8 7	2,675 9 6
	-	-	-	-	958 9 0	-	44 10 0	-	1,002 19 0
r. lb.	199 1 2	-	14 3 22	261 3 3	590 11 3	-	41 2 0	478 1 0	1,110 7 6
No.	16,193	-	400	12,162	4,048 5 0	-	100 0 0	3,040 10 0	7,188 15 0
acks	170	200	1,285	10,747	113 6 8	50 0 0	756 13 4	7,164 13 4	8,084 13 4
ieces	196	3	228	40	934 3 4	13 10 0	435 0 0	180 0 0	1,552 13 4
ards	800	-	80	650	55 10 0	-	5 0 0	48 15 0	107 5 0
	-	-	-	-	161 19 0	3 0 0	66 6 9	1,323 10 0	1,554 15 9
	-	-	-	-	7,560 19 2	133 4 5	2,095 2 10	1,588 7 6	11,377 13 11
					107,882 13 5	12,468 3 11	65,791 18 7	164,218 11 4	350,361 7 5

Exclusive of the above, we exported, in 1829, to the western coast of Africa, 16
worth of foreign and colonial merchandise : of this amount, 43,550l. worth
the coast south of the Rio Volta.

For further details with respect to Sierra Leone, and the trade of Western
see the Report of the Select Committee of the House of Commons, No. 661. Sess

SILK (Lat. *Sericum*, from *Seres*, the supposed ancient name of the Ch
a fine glossy thread or filament spun by various species of caterpill
larvæ, of the *phalæna* genus. Of these; the *Phalæna Atlas* produces the g
quantity; but the *Phalæna Bombyx* is that commonly employed for this p
in Europe. The silkworm, in its caterpillar state, which may be conside
the first stage of its existence, after acquiring its full growth (about 3 in
length), proceeds to enclose itself in an oval shaped ball, or cocoon, w
formed by an exceedingly slender filament of fine yellow silk, from 10
yards in length, emitted from the stomach of the insect preparatory to
suming the shape of the chrysalis or moth. In this latter stage, after emanc
itself from its silken prison, it seeks its mate, which has undergone a similar
formation; and in 2 or 3 days afterwards, the female having deposited h
(from 300 to 500 in number), both insects terminate their existence. Acc
to Reaumur, the *phalæna* is not the only insect that affords this material, — s
species of the *aranea* or spider enclose their eggs in very fine silk.

Raw Silk is produced by the operation of winding off, at the same time, s
of the balls or cocoons (which are immersed in hot water, to soften the
gum on the filament) on a common reel, thereby forming one smooth even
When the skein is dry, it is taken from the reel and made up into hank
before it is fit for weaving, and in order to enable it to undergo the pro
dyeing, without furring up or separating the fibres, it is converted into
three forms; viz. *singles*, *tram*, or *organzine*.

Singles (a collective noun) is formed of *one* of the reeled threads being t
in order to give it strength and firmness.

Tram is formed of two or more threads twisted together. In this sta
commonly used in weaving, as the *shoot* or *weft*.

Thrown Silk is formed of two, three, or more singles, according to t
stance required, being twisted together in a *contrary* direction to that in
the singles of which it is composed are twisted. This process is termed
zining; and the silk so twisted, *organzine*. The art of throwing was origina
fined to Italy, where it was kept a secret for a long period. Stow says
known in this country since the 5th of Queen Elizabeth, " when it was
from the strangers;" and in that year (1562), the silk throwsters of the me
were united into a fellowship. They were incorporated in the year 16
the art continued to be very imperfect in England until 1719. — (See po

1. *Historical Sketch of the Manufacture.* — The art of rearing silkworms, of unr
the threads spun by them, and manufacturing the latter into articles of dress ar
ment, seems to have been first practised by the Chinese. Virgil is the earlie
Roman writers who has been supposed to allude to the production of silk in Ch
the terms he employs show how little was then known at Rome as to the real r
the article.

Velleraque ut foliis depectant tenuia Seres. — (*Georg.* book ii. lin. 121.

But it may be doubted whether Virgil do not, in this line, refer to cotton rat
silk. Pliny, however, has distinctly described the formation of silk by the *bombyx*.
Nat. lib. xi. c. 17.) It is uncertain when it first began to be introduced at Rom
was most probably in the age of Pompey and Julius Cæsar; the latter of whom dis
profusion of silks in some of the magnificent theatrical spectacles with which he s
once to conciliate and amuse the people. Owing principally, no doubt, to the g
tance of China from Rome, and to the difficulties in the way of the intercourse
country, which was carried on by land in caravans whose route lay through the
empire, and partly, perhaps, to the high price of silk in China, its cost, when
at Rome, was very great; so much so, that a given weight of silk was someti
for an equal weight of gold! At first it was only used by a few ladies eminent
rank and opulence. In the beginning of the reign of Tiberius, a law was p
vestis serica viros fœdaret — that no man should disgrace himself by wearing
garment. — (*Tacit. Annal.* lib. ii. c. 33.) But the profligate Heliogabalus
this law, and was the first of the Roman emperors who wore a dress compose
of silk (*holosericum*). The example once set, the custom of wearing silk soo

among the wealthy citizens of Rome, and throughout the provinces. According
demand for the article increased, efforts were made to import larger quantities;
price seems to have progressively declined from the reign of Aurelian. That
st have been the case, is obvious from the statement of Ammianus Marcellinus,
k was, in his time (anno 370), very generally worn, even by the lowest classes.
n ad usum antehac nobilium, nunc etiam infimorum sine ulla discretione proficiens.
. 18. c. 6.)

a continued to draw considerable sums from the Roman empire in return for
w become indispensable to the Western world, till the sixth century. About the
0, two Persian monks, who had resided long in China, and made themselves ac-
d with the mode of rearing the silkworm, encouraged by the gifts and promises
nian, succeeded in carrying the eggs of the insect to Constantinople. Under
rection they were hatched and fed; they lived and laboured in a foreign climate;
ent number of butterflies was saved to propagate the race, and mulberry trees
anted to afford nourishment to the rising generations. A new and important
of industry was thus established in Europe. Experience and reflection gradually
d the errors of a new attempt; and the Sogdoite ambassadors acknowledged, in
ceeding reign, that the Romans were not inferior to the natives of China, in the
on of the insects, and the manufacture of silk. — (*Gibbon, Decline and Fall*,
p. 99.)

ce, particularly the Peloponnesus, was early distinguished by the rearing of silk-
and by the skill and success with which the inhabitants of Thebes, Corinth, and
carried on the manufacture. Until the twelfth century, Greece continued to be
European country in which these arts were practised: but the forces of Roger
Sicily, having, in 1147, sacked Corinth, Athens, and Thebes, carried off large
s of the inhabitants to Palermo; who introduced the culture of the worm, and
ufacture of silk, into Sicily. From this island the arts spread into Italy; and
Milan, Florence, Lucca, &c. were soon after distinguished for their success in
silkworms, and for the extent and beauty of their manufactures of silk —(*Gibbon*,
. 110.; *Biographie Universelle*, art. *Roger II.*)

ilk manufacture was introduced into France in 1480; Louis XI. having invited
n from Italy, who established themselves at Tours. The manufacture was not
t Lyons till about 1520; when Francis I., having got possession of Milan, pre-
1 some artisans of the latter city to establish themselves, under his protection, in
er. Nearly at the same period the rearing of silkworms began to be success-
osecuted in Provence, and other provinces of the south of France. Henry IV.
d such of the early manufacturers as had supported and pursued the trade for
with patents of nobility.

anufacture of England. — The manufacture seems to have been introduced into
d in the fifteenth century. Silk had, however, been used by persons of distinc-
centuries previously. The manufacture does not appear to have made much
till the age of Elizabeth; the tranquillity of whose long reign, and the influx of
s occasioned by the disturbances in the Low Countries, gave a powerful stimulus
anufactures of England. The silk throwsters of the metropolis were united,
y observed, in a fellowship, in 1562; and were incorporated in 1629. Though
by the civil wars, the manufacture continued gradually to advance; and so
ng had it become, that it is stated in the preamble to a statute passed in 1666
Cha. 2. c. 15.), that there were at that time, no fewer than 40,000 individuals
in the trade! And it is of importance to observe, that though the importation
h and other foregn silks was occasionally prohibited, during the reigns of James
harles I., the Protectorate, and the reign of Charles II., the prohibition was
y enforced; and, generally speaking, their importation was quite free.

siderable stimulus, though not nearly so great as has been commonly supposed,
1 to the English silk manufacture by the revocation of the edict of Nantes, in
Louis XIV. drove, by that disgraceful measure, several hundreds of thousands
st industrious subjects to seek an asylum in foreign countries; of whom it is
about 50,000 came to England. Such of these refugees as had been engaged
k manufacture, established themselves in Spitalfields, where they introduced
ew branches of the art. When the refugees fled to England, foreign silks were
mitted; and it appears from the Custom-house returns, that from 600,000*l.* to
worth were annually imported in the period from 1685 to 1692, being the
od during which the British silk manufacture made the most rapid advances.
manufacture was not long permitted to continue on this footing. In 1692, the
who seem to have been quite as conversant with the arts of monopoly as with
er of spinning or weaving, obtained a patent, giving them an exclusive right
icture lustrings and *à-la-modes*, — the silks then in greatest demand. This,
was not enough to satisfy them; for, in 1697, parliament passed an act, in

3 P 2

compliance with their solicitations, prohibiting the importation of all French and European silk goods; and, in 1701, the prohibition was extended to the silk goo India and China.

These facts show the utter fallacy of the opinion, so generally entertained, that w the introduction and establishment of the silk manufacture to the prohibitive sy So far from this being the case, it is proved, by statements in numerous acts of p ment, and other authentic documents, that the silk manufacture had overcome a difficulties incident to its first establishment, had been firmly rooted, and had beco great value and importance, long before it was subjected to the trammels of mono that is, before the manufacturers were taught to trust more to fiscal regulations, an exertions of Custom-house officers, than to their skill and ingenuity, for the sale of goods.

The year 1719 is an important epoch in the history of the British silk manufac a patent being then granted to Mr. (afterwards Sir Thomas) Lombe and his brothe the exclusive property of the famous silk mill erected by them at Derby, for thro silk, from models they had clandestinely obtained in Italy. At the expiration o patent, parliament refused the prayer of a petition of Sir Thomas Lombe for its rene but granted him 14,000l. in consideration of the services he had rendered the count erecting a machine which, it was supposed, would very soon enable us to dispense w with the supplies of thrown silk we had previously been in the habit of importing Italy: but instead of being of any advantage, it is most certainly true that the esta ment of throwing mills in England has proved one of the most formidable obs to the extension of the manufacture amongst us. These mills could not have constructed unless oppressive duties had been laid on thrown or organzine silk; ar circumstance of their having been erected, and a large amount of capital vested in was successfully urged, for more than a century, as a conclusive reason for conti the high duties!

From this period down to 1824, the history of the silk manufacture presents little than complaints, on the part of the manufacturers, of the importation of foreign impotent efforts on the part of parliament to exclude them; and combinations and ou on the part of the workmen. Of the multitude of acts that have been passed in refe to this manufacture, from 1697 to the era of Mr. Huskisson, we believe it wou exceedingly difficult to point out one that is bottomed on any thing like a sound ciple, or that was productive of any but mischievous consequences. The French w estimate the average exportation of silks from France to England, during the period 1688 to 1741, at about 12,500,000 francs, or 500,000l. a year! In 1763, attempts made to check the prevalence of smuggling; and the silk mercers of the metropo show their anxiety to forward the scheme, are said to have recalled their orders for f goods! It would seem, however, either that their patriotic ardour had very soon c or that they had been supplanted by others not quite so scrupulous; for it appears a report of a committee of the privy council, appointed, in 1766, to inquire in subject, that smuggling was then carried on to a greater extent than ever, and that looms were out of employment. The same committee reported, that though the were decidedly superior to us in some branches of the trade, we were quite equa even superior, to them in others; but instead of proposing, consistently with their to admit French silks on a reasonable duty,—a measure which would have prove advantageous to those branches of the manufacture in which we were superior, or equal, to the French, without doing any material injury to the others, which were a in the most depressed condition,—they recommended the continuance of the old sy substituting absolute prohibitions in the place of the prohibitory duties that for existed! Whatever immediate advantages the manufacturers might have reape this measure, the ultimate tendency of which could not fail of being most injuriou effectually countervailed by the turbulent proceedings of the workmen, who succ in 1773, in obtaining from the legislature an act which, by itself, was quite suffic have destroyed even a prosperous trade. This, which has been commonly cal Spitalfields act, entitled the weavers of Middlesex to demand a fixed price fo labour, which should be settled by the magistrates; and while both masters an were restricted from giving or receiving more or less than the fixed price, the ma turers were liable in heavy penalties if they employed weavers out of the district monopoly which the manufacturers had hitherto enjoyed, though incomplete, h sufficient influence to render inventions and discoveries of comparatively rare occ in the silk trade; but the Spitalfields act extinguished every germ of improv Parliament, in its wisdom, having seen fit to enact that a manufacturer should be to pay as much for work done by the best machinery as if it were done by h would have been folly to have thought of attempting any thing new! It is no ever, to be denied that Macclesfield, Manchester, Norwich, Paisley, &c. are obligations to this act. Had it extended to the whole kingdom, it would have

d the manufacture; but being confined to Middlesex, it gradually drove the
uable branches from Spitalfields to places where the rate of wages was deter-
y the competition of the parties, on the principle of mutual interest and com-
advantage. After having done incalculable mischief, the act was repealed in
Had it continued down to the present day, it would not have left employment
etropolis for a single silk weaver.

the effects of this act did not immediately manifest themselves, it was at first
gly popular. About 1785, however, the substitution of cottons in the place of
e a severe check to the manufacture, and the weavers then began to discover the
re of the Spitalfields act. Being interdicted from working at reduced wages,
: totally thrown out of employment; so that, in 1793, upwards of 4,000 Spital-
ms were quite idle. In 1798, the trade began to revive; and continued to
owly till 1815 and 1816, when the Spitalfields weavers were again involved in
far more extensive and severe than at any former period.

cars from this brief sketch of the progress of the English silk trade, that
year 1695, down to our own times, it has been exposed to the most ap-
cissitudes. The reason is obvious. The monopoly enjoyed by the manufac-
id the Spitalfields act, effectually put a stop to all improvement; so that the
ure continued stationary in England, while on the Continent it was rapidly
. Whenever, therefore, the markets were, either from the miscalculation of
facturers or a change of fashion, overloaded with silks, there were no means of
of the surplus profitably abroad, and the distress became extreme. Notwith-
he unparalleled advances we had made in other departments of manufacturing
it was affirmed, in 1826, by the member for Coventry (Mr. Ellice), in his place
use of Commons, " that there were in that city 9,700 looms; 7,500 of which
e hands of operative weavers, who applied their manual labour, as well as their
, to the manufacture of ribands. These looms were, for the most part, of the
ble construction; and it would scarcely be believed that the improved loom in
uld, in a given time, produce five times as much riband as the common loom
d with the same manual labour! He could also state that there existed an
manufacture in Germany, by which one man could make forty-eight times as
t as could be made in an equal time by an English machine. What chance was
the English manufacturer could maintain such a competition?"

these statements may be somewhat exaggerated; but there can be no doubt
are substantially well founded. Surely, however, no one believes that the
of the machinery used by the English manufacturers is to be ascribed to any
ot that the protection they enjoyed had made them indifferent to improvements.
lieves that the French or Germans are superior to the English in the construc-
chines; on the contrary, their inferiority is admitted by themselves, and by
else. That that spirit of invention, which has effected such astonishing
he cotton manufacture, should have been wholly unknown in that of silk, is
be ascribed to the fact of the former never having been the object of legislative
The cotton manufacturers were not bribed into the adoption of a routine
ey could not rest satisfied with mediocrity; but being compelled to put forth
wers, to avail themselves of every resource of science and of art, they have,
ears, raised the British cotton manufacture from a subordinate and trifling,
first place amongst the manufactures, not of this country only, but of the

in 1826, of the Monopoly System. — At length, however, the impolicy of the
which the silk manufacture had been so long depressed, became obvious to
igent individual. The principal manufacturers in and about London sub-
1824, a petition to the House of Commons, in which they stated that " this
manufacture, though recently considerably extended, is still depressed below
level, by laws which prevent it from attaining that degree of prosperity which,
favourable circumstances, it would acquire." Fortified by this authority,
rience of 130 years, during which the prohibitive system had been allowed
the energies of the manufacturers, and by the sanction of parliamentary com-
r. Huskisson moved, on the 8th of March, 1824, that the prohibition of
s should cease on the 5th of July, 1826, and that they should then be
r importation on payment of a duty of 30 per cent. ad valorem. On this
r. H. observed — " The monopoly had produced, what monopoly was always
duce, an indifference with regard to improvement. That useful zeal, which
o industry, which fosters ingenuity, and which in manufactures occasions
fforts to produce the article in the most economical form, had been compara-
guished. To the prohibitive system it was to be ascribed, that in silk only, in the
of manufactures, we were left behind our neighbours! We have here a proof
ling and benumbing effect which is sure to be produced when no genius is

called into action, and when we are rendered indifferent to exertion by the indo
curity derived from restrictive regulations. I have not the slightest doubt, that
same system had been continued with respect to the cotton manufacture, it wou
been at this moment as subordinate in amount to the woollen as it is junior in it
duction into the country." — (*Speeches*, vol. ii. p. 249.)

We have already alluded to the enormous duties imposed, in 1719, when Sir '
Lombe erected his throwing mill at Derby, on foreign organzined silk. These,
subsequently reduced, amounted, in 1824, to no less than 14s. 7½d. per lb. ! Th
also, at the same time, a duty of 4s. per lb. on raw silk imported from Bengal,
5s. 7½d. per lb. on that imported from other places. Even had the manufactu
otherwise in a flourishing condition, such exorbitant duties on the raw materi
enough to have destroyed it. Mr. Huskisson, therefore, proposed, by way of pr
the manufacturers for the approaching change of system, that the duty on foreign
silk should be immediately reduced to 7s. 6d. (it was further reduced to 5s. in
and the duty on raw silk to 3d. per lb. These proposals were all agreed to; a
siderable reductions were at the same time effected in the duties charged on mos
dye stuffs used in the manufacture.

It is to be regretted that Mr. Huskisson did not propose that the reduction
duties on raw and thrown silk, and the legalised importation of foreign silks, sh
simultaneous and immediate. During the interval that was allowed our manuf
to make preparations for the change, the French had been accumulating a large
goods to pour into our markets. To quiet the alarm occasioned by this circums
singular device was fallen upon.—The French had long been accustomed to man
their goods of a certain length; and, in the view of rendering their accumulate
unfit for our markets, a law was passed in 1826, prohibiting the importation of a
except such as were of entirely different lengths from those commonly manufac
the French! No one can regret that this wretched trick, for it deserves no bett
entirely failed of its object. The French manufacturers immediately commenc
redoubled zeal, the preparation of goods of the legitimate length; and the others
become unsaleable at any thing like fair prices, were purchased up by the sm
and imported, almost entirely, into this country.

But no permanent injury arose from this circumstance; and, on the whole, th
of the opening of the trade has been such as to justify all the anticipations w
advocates of the measure had formed of its success.

Effects of the Change of 1826. — We do not exaggerate, we only state the plai
of fact, when we affirm that the silk manufacture has made a more rapid progres
the last 5 years, or since the abolition of the prohibitive system in 1826, tha
during the preceding century. So unprecedented has been its advance, th
once existing disparity in quality between goods of French and English make h
some very unimportant exceptions, not merely disappeared, but actually ranged
the side of the British artisan."

Most of the machines and processes known on the Continent have been int
amongst us, and many of them have been materially improved. Nor, after v
taken place, can the least doubt remain in the mind of any one, that had the same
been given to the silk manufacture 50 years ago that was given to it in 1826, i
now have ranked among the most important and valuable businesses in the k
and would have had nothing whatever to fear from the admission of forei
free of duty. It is the opinion of the most intelligent persons in the trade,
existing duty of 30 per cent. on foreign silks ought to be immediately re
20 per cent.; and that it should be further reduced 1 per cent. per annum f
brought to 12 or 15 per cent., at which it might be allowed to continue statio
as a protecting duty, but as a duty imposed for the sake of revenue. A measur
sort, by increasing *fair* competition, would continue the impulse already giv
manufacture, and excite to new efforts of invention. Under such a system, we
assured that, in a very few years, perhaps not more than 5 or 6, our superic
France in some important departments of the silk manufacture would be l
decided than in that of cotton.

" I maintain," said Mr. Poulett Thomson, in his excellent speech on the sta
silk trade (14th of April, 1829), — a speech equally distinguished for soundnes
ciple and beauty of illustration, — " I maintain, without fear of contradiction, tha
essence of commercial and manufacturing industry is freedom from legislati
ference and legislative protection. Attempt to assist its course by legislative en
by fostering care, you arrest its progress, you destroy its vigour. Unbind the
in which your unwise tenderness has confined it — permit it to take unrestraine
course — expose it to the wholesome breezes of competition, — you give it new
restore its former vigour. Industry has been well likened to the hardy Alpi
self sown on the mountain side, exposed to the inclemency of the season, i

h in its struggles for existence — it shoots forth in vigour and in beauty. Trans-
I to the rich soil of the parterre, tended by the fostering hand of the gardener,
in the artificial atmosphere of the forcing-glass, it grows sickly and enervated,
ots are vigourless, its flowers inodorous. In one single word lies the soul of
y — competition. The answer of the statesman and the economist to his sovereign
ng what he could do to assist the industry of his kingdom was, ' Let it take its
ay.' Such is my prayer. Relieve us from the chains in which your indiscreet
less has shackled us; remove your oppressive protection; give us the fair field
; and we demand no more. The talent, the genius, the enterprise, the capital,
ustry of this great people will do the rest; and England will not only retain, but
I take a yet more forward place in the race of competition for wealth and improve-
hich, by the nature of things, she is destined to run amongst the nations of the
Place us in that condition, not by any violent change, but by slow and easy
on. Here we shall find security for our enterprise, and reward for our labours.

> ' Hic patet ingeniis campûs; certusque merenti
> Stat favor; ornatur propriis industria donis.' "

is not, however, to be supposed, that all departments of the silk manufacture
be equally benefited by the change of system that has taken place — *Non omnia*
s. The probability is, that the trade will in future be divided between the
and French. In point of substantial excellence, the plain silk goods manu-
I in England are superior to those of France; and the difference in favour of
r in point of *finish* is every day becoming less perceptible; while in all mixed
ctures, of silk and wool, silk and cotton, silk and linen, &c., our ascendancy is
d by the French themselves. On the other hand, the ribands, figured gauzes,
it fancy goods, manufactured in France, are superior to those of this country.
this department we have made a very great progress; and fancy goods are now
d at Spitalfields, Coventry, and other places, contrasting most advantageously,
of taste and beauty, with those produced previously to the introduction of the
tem. Still, however, we are not sanguine in our expectations of our country-
ng able to maintain a successful competition with our neighbours in the manu-
of this class of articles. The greater attention paid to the art of designing in
the consequent better taste of the artists, and the superior brightness and lustre
colours, give them advantages with which it will be very difficult to contend.
upposing that the trade is partitioned between the two countries in the way now
: is easy to see that the best share will belong to us, and that that share will be
rably more valuable than the whole manufacture formerly was. The proofs of
racy of this statement are at hand. Notwithstanding the distress of the riband
of Coventry and a few other places, the manufacture, taken as a whole, is
ncreasing. The greatest importation of raw and thrown silk that took place in
year previously to the repeal of the prohibitory system, was in 1823, when
6 lbs. were imported. But last year, in despite of all the sinister predictions
e been indulged in with respect to the ruin of the manufacture, the imports of
thrown silk amounted to 4,693,517 lbs., being nearly *twice the quantity imported*
monopoly was in its vigour!
ncrease in the exports of wrought silks affords, if possible, a still more decisive
the extraordinary improvement and extension of the manufacture. Instead of
ny thing to fear from the competition of the French at home, we are actually
ing them in the heavier and more important species of goods, in every foreign
qually accessible to both parties. The exports of silks from France have been
;, while those from England have been increasing beyond all precedent. The
alue of our exports of silk goods, in 1823, amounted to 140,320*l.*, whereas in
mounted to 437,880*l.*, being *an advance of more than three hundred per cent.!*
, therefore, are the statements as to the ruin of the silk manufacture proved to
7 without even the shadow of a foundation, but the expectations of those who
I that the repeal of the restrictive system would be the commencement of a
of invention and improvement, have been realised to the utmost extent.
has now been stated renders it obvious, that though the manufacturers of fancy
y be obliged to change their employment, a new, and at the same time a more
and fruitful, field is opened for their exertions. We lament the hardships in-
the transition even from one department of the same business to another, but
ring thence arising will speedily disappear; and when the change has been
the manufacturers will enter with fresh vigour on a new career of prosperity.
be regretted, that it is not possible either to abandon a routine system, or to
new and improved methods of production, without injury to individuals.
use such is the fact — because the bridge cannot be built without displacing
, nor the plough introduced without superseding the spade, nor wine brought

from abroad without diminishing the demand for ale and beer — is that any reaso
proscribing inventions, and denying ourselves gratifications within our reach?
maintain the affirmative, would be evidently absurd, — it would be equivalent to m
taining that the interests of society are best promoted by perpetuating poverty, ignor
and barbarism! The injury occasioned by the adoption of an improved meth
production, or the opening of new markets whence cheaper supplies of any article
be obtained, is temporary only, and affects but a very small portion of the commu
while the advantage is permanent, and benefits every individual, even those wh
may, in the first instance, have forced to resort to other businesses.

Those unacquainted with the history of the silk trade, who may have looked int
pamphlets and speeches of those opposed to the late alterations, will probably b
posed to think that, though more limited in point of numbers, the condition o
workmen engaged in the trade was better previously to 1825 than it has been s
But those who have looked, however cursorily, into the history of the trade, must b
that such is not the fact; and that, speaking generally, the situation of those engag
it has been materially improved since 1825. We have already adverted to the sta
the trade in 1793 and 1816. At the last mentioned period, 7 years before any relax
of the monopoly had been so much as thought of, the distress in the silk trad
infinitely more severe than it has ever been since the introduction of the new sy
In proof of this, we may mention that, at a public meeting held for the relie
the Spitalfields weavers, at the Mansion House, on the 26th of November, 1816
secretary stated, that *two thirds* of them were without employment, and withou
means of support; "that some had deserted their houses in despair, unable to e
the sight of their starving families; and many pined under languishing diseases bro
on by the want of food and clothing." And Mr. Fowell Buxton, M.P., stated, a
same meeting, that the distress among the silk manufacturers was so intense, tha
partook of the nature of a pestilence, which spreads its contagion around, and deva
an entire district." Such was the state of the workmen under that monopoly s
that has been the worthless theme of so much recent eulogy. But such, we are
to say, is not their state at present. The trade, being now mostly diverted into
branches in which we have a superiority, is comparatively secure against revuls
and it would be an absurdity to imagine, that measures that have about double
manufacture, should have reduced the rate of wages, or been otherwise than a
tageous to the workmen.

We have already noticed the smuggling of foreign silks carried on in the earl
and towards the middle of last century. The evil was not afterwards abated.
vigilance of the Custom-house officer was no match for the ingenuity of the smug
and at the very moment when the most strenuous efforts were made to exclude the
silks of France and Hindostan were openly displayed in the drawing-rooms of St. Ja
and in the House of Commons, in mockery of the impotent legislation which sou
exclude them. We doubt, indeed, whether the substitution of the *ad valorem* d
30 per cent., in place of the old system of prohibition, has been productive of any
rially increased importation of foreign silks. "I have lately," said Mr. Huskiss
his famous speech in vindication of his policy as to the silk trade, "taken some p
ascertain the quantity of smuggled silks that has been seized inland throughout the
dom during the last 10 years; and I find that the whole does not exceed 5,000*l.*
I have endeavoured, on the other hand, to get an account of the quantity of silk
actually smuggled into this country. Any estimate of this quantity must be very v
but I have been given to understand that the value of such goods as are regularly e
at the Custom-houses of France, for exportation to this country, is from 100,0
150,000*l.* a year; and this, of course, is exclusive of the *far greater supply* wh
poured in throughout all the channels of smuggling, without being subjected to any
In fact, to such an extent is this illicit trade carried, that there is scarcely a haberd
shop in the smallest village of the United Kingdom, in which prohibited silks a
sold; and that in the face of day, and to a very considerable extent.

"The honourable member for Coventry (Mr. Ellice) has mentioned the silk
from India as those against which any thing but prohibition would prove an una
protection. Now, in my opinion, it is scarcely possible to conceive a stronger ca
those very silks furnish against the honourable member's own argument. I belie
universally known that a large quantity of Bandana handkerchiefs are sold every y
exportation, by the East India Company. But does any gentleman suppose tha
Bandanas are sent to the Continent for the purpose of remaining there? No such
They are sold at the Company's sales, to the number of about 800,000 or 1,00
year, at about 4*s.* each; they are immediately shipped off for Hamburgh, Antwer
terdam, Ostend, or Guernsey, and from thence they nearly all illicitly find the
back to this country.

"Mark, then, the effect of this beautiful system. — These Bandanas, which h

een sold for exportation at 4s., are finally distributed in retail to the people of
at about 8s. each; and the result of this prohibition is to levy upon the con-
ax, and to give those who live by evading your law, a bounty of 4s. upon each
hief sold in this country!" — (*Speeches*, vol. ii. p. 510.)

, one of the principal objections to the present duty of 30 per cent. on foreign
hat it is high enough to enable a considerable smuggling trade to be still carried
acility for smuggling being increased by means of the legalised importation. A
2 or 15 per cent. would not, however, be so high as to balance the risks run in
g; and would, therefore, really afford the manufacturer a more efficient protec-
he derives from the existing duty, at the same that it would place all classes of
1 the same footing; whereas the advantage is at present on *the side of those who
fraudulent schemes.*

ms as to the Importation of Silks. — Silk manufactures are not to be imported in any vessel
ns burthen, except by license from the commissioners of the customs, to vessels belonging to
import such manufactures direct from Calais, though such vessels may not exceed 60 tons
Silk goods, the manufacture of Europe, not to be imported except into the port of London or
Dublin direct from Bordeaux, or the port of Dover direct from Calais. — (10 *Geo.* 4. c. 22.

try of silk goods which are subject to duty according to the weight or to the value thereof, at
of the officers of the customs, the weight and the value of such goods shall be both stated; and
shall be affirmed in like manner as the value of any goods charged to pay duty according to
ereof, as affirmed under the provisions of the act 6 *Geo.* 4. c. 107. § 19. — (*Ante*, p. 605.) And
lawful for the officers of the customs to detain any such goods, and to take the same for the
rown, in like manner and upon the same terms as such officers may, under the provisions of
t, detain and take any goods entered for payment of duty according to the value thereof as
. § 4.

e shoot or the warp only is of silk, the article is to be considered as composed of *not more* than
rt of silk, and subject to the *ad valorem* duty of 30 per cent.; but if the shoot or the warp be
silk, and a portion of the other be of silk also, the article is to be considered to be composed of
ne half part of silk, and subject to the rated duties at per lb., or to the *ad valorem* duties, at
f the officers. — (*Min. Com. Cus.* 14th of August, 1829.)

ks shall not be imported except in packages, each of which shall contain at least 100 lbs. of
lk;

g crape, gauze, lace, net, or tulle, fancy net or tricot, millinery, or dresses), in packages each
ich shall be of the capacity of 9 cubic feet at least, and shall contain only such silks;
road silks or ribands (except handkerchiefs, shawls, scarfs, net, or tulle, fancy net or tricot,
xcept silks the produce of, and imported from, places within the limits of the East India Com-
charter), shall not be imported for home use unless in pieces or half pieces, of the respective
s herein after mentioned; (that is to say),

lks, in pieces not less than 60 yards in length, nor more than 66 yards in length;
being velvets, or silks, mixed with other materials), in half pieces not less than 29 yards in
igth, nor more than 32 yards in length:
, in pieces not less than 35 yards in length, nor more than 37 yards in length; or in half
not less than 17 yards in length, nor more than 19 yards in length:
pieces and half pieces shall be separate and entire, and each of uniform quality throughout;
of broad silks, shall be finished in the loom with ferrels or marks at each end wove in.
ks in pieces, wound or rolled, whether on blocks or rollers, or not, shall not be imported for

lks the produce of, and imported from, places within the limits of the East India Company's
.

ing articles, although mostly composed of silk, shall not be subject to the regulations or
:ontained in this table, viz.: — Artificial flowers, and other similar imitations; umbrellas,
, screens, and other articles not for dress or furniture; articles of materials other than silk,
h silk, or to which silk is only applied by needlework or embroidery; stuffs, of the materials
shall not amount to one tenth part.

' Silks. — Nothing in this act shall extend to prohibit the entering, for home use, of any
s which shall have been warehoused before the 15th of March, 1826; nor to prevent any
ning into the United Kingdom from bringing with him or her, into any port, any wrought
es which may be legally imported for home use, and any articles of silk made up, whether
although not in packages of the weight or size herein-before required, provided such pieces
:cles be *bonâ fide* for his or her own use, and not for sale, and the quantity in the whole be
n 10 lbs.; provided that the duty on such articles, whether worn or not, be paid, and be in
rtained according to the value thereof. — (7 *Geo.* 4. c. 53. §§ 2, 3.)

ties on silks, see TARIFF.

of Foreign Raw, Waste, and Thrown Silk entered for Home Consumption in the United
n 1830; distinguishing the Species of Silk, and the Quantities brought from each Country.

	From the Netherlands.	France.	Spain and Gibraltar.	Italy.	Turkey.	The East Indies, China, St. Helena, and Cape of Good Hope.	The United States of America.	Other Parts.	Total Quantity imported.	Amount of Duty received.		
	Lbs.	*Lbs.*	*Lbs.*	*Lbs.*	*Lbs.*	*Lbs.*	*Lbs.*	*Lbs.*	*Lbs.*	£	s.	d.
and	71,142	852,788	2,585	269,939	491,752	2,047,725	35,060	980	3,771,969	15,776	2	6
ed;	12,481	255,574	1,368	210,793	91	1,176	-	3,530	485,013	216	17	3
ape	38,576	354,065	- -	5,993	- -	- -	- -	-	398,634	69,769	10	10
	3,838	33,695	- -	- -	- -	- -	-	37	37,570	3,698	18	0
		137	- -	188	- -	3	- -	3	331	82	11	10
	126,037	1,496,259	3,953	486,913	491,843	2,048,902	35,060	4,550	4,693,517	89,544	0	5

II. Manufactured Silks, of the East Indies, entered for Home Consumption in 1830.

Species of Goods.		Quantity.	Am of rec
			£
Bandanas and other Silk Handkerchiefs in pieces - -	*pieces*	77,953	14,98
Silks and Crapes in pieces - - - -	*pieces*	2,978	} 4,81
Crape Shawls, Scarfs, and Handkerchiefs - -	*number*	17,620	}
Manufactures of Silk, or of Silk and any other Material, not } particularly enumerated, and Manufactures of Silk made up }	*value*	£ 4,790 11 3	1,54
Total Amount of Duty received on Manufactured Silks of the East } Indies - - - - - - - }		£	21,14

III. Foreign Manufactured Silks, not of the East Indies, entered for Home Consumption in 183 guishing the Species of Goods, and the Quantities brought from each Country.

Species of Goods (Stated agreeably to their designations in the Schedule of the Act 10 Geo. 4. c. 23., which regulates the Entry at the Custom-house).	Countries and Quantities.					Amo Duty »
	From the Hanseatic Towns.	The Netherlands.	France.	Other Parts.	Total.	
	Lbs. oz.	Lbs. oz.	Lbs. oz.	Lbs. oz.	Lbs. oz.	£
Silk or Satin, plain -	15 14	36 5	35,908 2½	23 8	35,983 13½	19,8
figured or brocaded	29 7	1 11	15,363 10	38 13	15,433 9	11,5
Gauze, plain . - -	-	0 4	2,314 0	- -	2,314 4	1,9
striped, figured or brocaded -	20 1	0 4	27,906 6	0 4	27,926 15	38,4
Crape, plain - -	- -	1 15	25,203 13	5 6	25,211 2	20,1
figured -	4 0	0 6	3,657 15	6 13	3,669 2	3,5
Velvet, plain - -	13 0	9,510 3	3,648 5	303 8	13,475 0	14,8
figured -	- -	38 7	1,330 14	3 1	1,372 6	1,8
Ribands embossed or figured with Velvet -	..	516 6	12 13	- -	529 3	4
Fancy Silk Net or Tricot	- -	- -	42 11	- -	42 11	
Silk mixed with Metal; viz.						
Silk or Satin, plain	- -	- -	126 13	- -	126 13	}
figured -	- -	- -	99 0	- -	99 0	}
Gauze, plain -	- -	- -	53 15	0 4	54 3	}
striped, figured or brocaded -	- -	- -	103 2	- -	103 2	}
Crape, plain -	- -	- -	2 0	- -	2 0	
figured -	- -	- -	3 11	- -	3 11	
Velvet, plain -	- -	- -	23 10	- -	23 10	
Total entered by Weight	82 6	10,105 13	115,800 12½	381 9	126,370 8½	
Plain Silk Lace or Net, called Tulle, *sq. yrds.*	1	-	114,380½	-	114,381¼	7,«
Millinery ; viz.						
Turbans or Caps, *No.*	2		363	3	368	}
Hats or Bonnets -	1	2	531	1	535	}
Dresses -	1	8	285	4	298	}
At Value - *value*	£ s. d. 27 15 0	£ s. d. 14 0 0	£ s. d. 61 4 0	£ s. d 51 5 0	£ s. d. 154 4 0	
Manufactures of Silk, or of Silk and any other Material, not particularly enumerated, and Manufactures of Silk made up -	1,354 7 6	5,287 3 6	37,578 8 10	703 16 0	44,923 15 10	13,
Total Amount of Duty received on Manufactured Silks not of the East Indies -						£135

IV. Account of the Quantities and declared Value of the British Manufactured Silks exception of British Thrown Silk), exported from the United Kingdom during 1830; disti the Sorts of Goods, the Countries to which they were sent, and the Quantities sent to each.

Countries to which exported.	Quantities of Silks exported.						Declared Value of Britis Silks expor	
	Manufactures of Silk only.				Silks mixed with other Materials.		Manufactures of Silk only.	Silks mix with oth Materia
	Entered by Weight.	the Yard.	At Value.	Stockings.	Entered by Weight.	Stock- ings.		
	Lbs. oz.	Yards.	L. s. d.	Doz. prs.	Lbs. oz.	Doz.prs.	L. s. d.	L.
Russia -	44 0			120 0	175 0		301 0 0	208
Sweden -					20 0			15
Norway -	142 0				273 0		198 10 0	263 1
Denmark -	30 0						61 0 0	
Germany -	3,620 12	2,342			78 0		6,683 10 0	8,643 1
The Netherlands -	3,324 3	993	86 0 0	14 0	18,310 7		6,807 15 0	3,410 1
France -	25,674 12		10 0 0		9,414 0		33,939 10 0	536 1
Portugal, Azores, & Madeira	257 1	120			639 0		852 0 0	3,852 1
Spain and the Canaries -	8,882 12	220		742 0	5,437 4		3,852 0 0	
Gibraltar -	1,309 10				16,267 11	90 0	15,397 0 0	15,293 »
Italy -	6,246 10	2,042		4 0	5,373 0		2,734 0 0	2,253 «
Malta -	113 0				2,300 0		10,429 0 0	1,629
Ionian Islands -	43 0			5 0	156 0		206 0 0	103 »
Turkey -	100 8	700		1 0	76 0		107 0 0	42
East Indies and China -	1,273 10			434 8	1,460 0		276 0 0	1,056
					4,700 14		4,069 10 0	3,202

	Quantities of Silks exported.						Declared Value of British Manufactured Silks exported.		
to which ...ted.	Manufactures of Silk only.				Silks mixed with o...her Materials.		Manufactures of Silk only.	Silks mixed with other Materials.	Total.
	Entered by Weight.	the Yard.	At Value.	Stockings.	Entered by We..ght.	Stock-ings.			
	Lbs. oz.	Yards.	L. s. d.	Doz. prs.	Lbs. oz.	Doz. prs.	L. s. d.	L. s. d.	L. s. d.
...les and Van	3,340 7	-	-	50 0	1,244 4	-	7,676 17 0	900 10 0	8,577 7 0
...d	2,475 12	-	-	97 0	1,868 13	-	5,624 0 0	1,124 0 0	6,748 0 0
...ope -	706 0	-	-	90 0	3,153 0	-	1,278 0 0	1,816 12 0	3,094 12 0
...Africa American	29,497 9	-	140 0 0	201 0	16,652 13	-	62,302 7 8	9,310 17 6	71,613 5 2
...ndies	7,421 12	-	-	338 6	20,085 13	21 0	17,218 6 0	11,510 5 6	28,728 11 6
...ndies	1,671 2	-	-	1,706 0	10,625 12	-	6,097 15 6	6,288 0 2	12,385 15 8
...America	5,129 14	2,000	490 0 0	3,335 0	142,811 6	-	120,035 0 0	75,791 18 6	195,826 18 6
...	1,498 8	700	255 0 0	4,592 0	3,746 0	-	14,396 10 0	2,575 0 0	16,971 10 0
...	31 0	-	-	-	2,512 0	-	65 0 0	1,805 4 0	1,870 4 0
...de la Plata	1,756 0	8,416	82 0 0	1,730 0	9,051 0	-	8,687 0 0	5,061 0 0	13,748 0 0
...	2,366 0	-	-	1,450 0	4,604 0	-	7,479 0 0	2,886 0 0	10,365 0 0
...	597 0	-	-	605 0	3,829 0	-	2,834 0 0	1,960 0 0	4,794 0 0
...	109 0	575	-	2,329 0	3,405 0	-	6,991 0 0	1,889 0 0	8,880 0 0
...y, Alderney,	5,532 13	-	-	6 0	3,295 1	-	7,700 16 0	1,783 0 0	9,483 16 0
- -	182,994 11	18,108	1,063 0 0	17,928 8	289,346 2	111 0	350,447 7 2	165,219 15 8	515,667 2 10

...nt of the Amount of Drawback paid on the Exportation of British Silk Manufactured Goods ... Year ended 5th January, 1831; distinguishing the Amount upon Stuffs or Ribands of Silk only, ...uffs or Ribands of Silk and Cotton mixed, and upon Stuffs or Ribands of Silk and Worsted mixed.

Articles.	Amount of Drawback paid in the United Kingdom on British Silk Manufactured Goods exported. Year ended 5th January, 1831.
	£ s. d.
...r Ribands of Silk only - - - -	24,973 4 0¼
...r Ribands of Silk and Cotton mixed - - -	9,296 10 11¼
...r Ribands of Silk and Worsted mixed - - -	2,420 13 6¼
Total - - - -	£ 36,690 8 7

...nt of the Total Quantities of Raw and Waste Silk entered for Home Consumption, in Great ... and Ireland, in each Year from 1814 to 1828, both inclusive; distinguishing the Quantity of ...m Waste, including Knubs and Husks; specifying also, the Annual Quantity of Raw and ...eparately, at an Average of three Periods of Five Years each, viz. in the Five Years from 1814 ...from 1819 to 1823, and from 1824 to 1828; with the Rate of Duty paid separately on Raw, and ...cluding Knubs and Husks.

Quantities of Raw and Waste Silk entered for Home Consumption in the United Kingdom.			Rates of Duty per lb.				
Raw Silk.	Waste Silk, including Knubs and Husks.	Total of Raw and Waste Silk.	Raw Silk.			Waste Silk.	
			Of Bengal.	Of China.	Of other Sorts.	Of India and China.	Of other Sorts.
Lbs.	Lbs.	Lbs.					
1,504,235	29,234	1,533,469	3s. 9d.	5s. 7½d.	5s. 6d.	3s. 9d.	3s. 4d.
1,069,596	27,971	1,097,567					
873,414	4,162	877,576					
1,343,051	49,055	1,392,106					
1,444,881	86,940	1,531,821					
...verage above ...ears	1,247,035	39,473	1,286,508				
1,446,097	71,331	1,517,428	4s.	5s. 6d.	5s. 6d.	3s. 9d.	4s.
1,622,799	94,883	1,717,682					
1,864,513	105,047	1,969,560					
1,993,764	64,921	2,058,685					
2,051,895	52,362	2,104,257					
...verage above ...ars	1,795,813	77,709	1,873,522				
3,414,520	133,257	3,547,777	On Raw and Waste Silk of all Sorts: 3d.				
2,848,506	195,910	3,044,416					
During these years raw and waste silk were not distinguished from each other in the entries at the Custom House.		1,964,188	1d.				
		3,759,138					
		4,162,550					
...verage above ...ars	- -	- -	3,295,614				

VII. Account of the Quantity of Raw and Waste Silk entered for Home Consumption, in Great B
and Ireland, during the Year 1829; distinguishing Raw from Waste, including Knubs and Hus

| | Quantities entered for Home Consumption in the United Kingdo | | |
	Raw Silk.	Waste Silk, including Knubs and Husks.	Total of Raw an Waste Silk.
	Lbs.	Lbs.	Lbs.
From 5th January to 5th July, 1829	During this period raw and waste silk were not distinguished from each other in the entries at the Custom-house		1,102,833
From 5th July, 1829, to 5th January, 1830	1,460,950	156,179	1,617,129
Year ended 5th January, 1830	-	-	2,719,962

SILVER (Ger. *Silber ;* Du. *Zilver ;* Da. *Sölv ;* Sw. *Silfver ;* Fr. *Argent
Argento ;* Sp. *Plata ;* Port. *Prata ;* Rus. *Serebro ;* Pol. *Srebro ;* Lat. *Argen
Gr.* ἄργυρος ; Arab. *Fazzeh*), a metal of a fine white colour, without either
or smell; being in point of brilliancy inferior to none of the metallic bodi
we except polished steel. It is softer than copper, but harder than gold.
melted, its specific gravity is 10·474; when hammered, 10·51. In mallea
it is inferior to none of the metals, if we except gold. It may be beaten out
leaves only $\frac{1}{100000}$ inch thick. Its ductility is equally remarkable: it m
drawn out into wire much finer than a human hair; so fine, indeed, that a
grain of silver may be extended about 400 feet in length. It tenacity is
that a wire of silver 0·078 inch in diameter is capable of supporting a wei
187·13 lbs. avoirdupois without breaking. Silver is easily alloyed with copp
fusion. The compound is harder and more sonorous than silver, and retai
white colour even when the proportion of copper exceeds a half. The har
is a maximum when the copper amounts to *one fifth* of the silver. The sta
or sterling silver of Britain, of which coin is made, is a compound of 12$\frac{1}{3}$
silver and 1 copper. Its specific gravity is 10·2. The specific gravity of
standard silver, composed of 137 parts silver and 7 copper, is 10·175.
French silver coin during the old government was not nearly so fine, being
posed of 261 parts silver and 27 of copper, or 9$\frac{2}{3}$ parts of silver to 1 p
copper. The Austrian silver coin contains $\frac{13}{288}$ of copper. The silver co
the ancients was nearly pure, and appears not to have been mixed with all
(*Thomson's Chemistry.*)

The most productive silver mines are in America, particularly in Mexic
Peru. There are also silver mines in Hungary, Saxony, and other pa
Europe, and in Asiatic Russia.

Besides being used as coin, or money, silver is extensively employed in the
The value of the silver plate annually manufactured is very considerable. —
PLATE.) Large quantities are also used in plating. (See PRECIOUS META

Account of the Quantity of the several Denominations of Silver Monies coined since the Com
ment of the New Silver Coinage in 1816, to the 31st of December, 1829.

Crowns.	Half Crowns.	Shillings.	Sixpences.	Maundy.	Total.
£ s. d.	£ s. d.	£ s. d.	£ s. d.	£ s. d.	£ s
462,476 7 1	3,500,936 7 0	4,183,146 0 0	1,000,692 0 0	1,735 16 0	9,148,986 1

SINGAPORE, an island and recent British settlement at the easte
tremity of the Straits of Malacca. The town is in lat. 1° 17′ 22″ N., lo
51′ 45″ E.

The island is of an elliptical form, about 27 miles in its greatest length, and 1
greatest breadth, containing an estimated area of 270 square miles. The whole
settlement, however, embraces a circumference of about 100 miles ; in which is i
about 50 desert islets, and the seas and straits within 10 miles of the coast of the
pal island. Singapore is separated from the main land by a strait of the same n
small breadth throughout, and scarcely, indeed, a quarter of a mile wide in its na
part. In the early period of European navigation, this channel was the thoro
between India and China. Fronting the island, on its southern side, and at the
of about 9 miles, is an extensive chain of islands, all desert, or at least inhabited
a few wild races, of which nothing is known but their mere existence. The inte
channel is now the grand route of the commerce between the eastern and weste
tions of maritime Asia; the safest and most convenient track, being so near to Si
that ships in passing and repassing approach close to the roads. The town is

...le of the island, and is situated on a river, or rather salt creek, navigable by
...or about three quarters of a mile from the sea. Ships lie in the roads, or open
...at the distance of from a mile to two miles from town, according to their
...of water. The assistance of a number of convenient lighters, which are always
...ess, enables ships to load and unload, with scarcely any interruption, through-
...ear. The river or creek is accessible to the lighters, and the goods are taken
...ischarged at convenient quays, at the doors of the principal warehouses. —
...rt of the *Island of Singapore* in the *Mercator's Chart* in this work.)
...imate of Singapore is hot but healthy. Fahrenheit's thermometer ranges from
...°. In a place only about 80 miles from the equator there is, of course,
... variety in the seasons. There is neither summer nor winter; and even the
... rains are short, and not very well marked — moderate showers of rain falling
...150 days each year. The settlement of Singapore was formed in February
...its sovereignty and property, in their present extent, confirmed to the British
...nt in 1825, by a convention with the king of the Netherlands, and a treaty
...Malay princes of Johore, to whom it belonged. When taken possession of
...glish, it had been inhabited for about 8 years by a colony of Malays, half
... and half pirates. When the first census of the population was taken, in
...824, it was found to amount to 10,683. In 1828, it had increased to 15,834;
...ses, exclusive of troops, camp followers, Indian convicts, and a floating popu-
...about 3,000. The following statement of the census of 1827 will show the
...lasses of inhabitants, and their proportions to each other: —

	Males.	Females.	Total.		Males.	Females.	Total.
...istians	69	18	87	Siamese - - -	5	2	7
...	128	60	188	Bugis - - -	666	576	1,242
...	16	3	19	Malays - -	2,501	2,289	4,790
...	18	- -	18	Javanese - -	174	93	267
...Coromandel } ...abar - - }	772	5	777	Chinese - -	5,747	341	6,088
				African Negroes	2	3	5
Bengal and } ...rts of Hin- }	209	35	244	Total -	10,307	3,425	13,732

...of January, 1830, the population amounted to 16,634; of whom 12,213 were males, and 4,421

...cipal merchants and agents are Englishmen, of whom also there are a few shopkeepers,
...&c. There are also some respectable Chinese merchants; and the bulk of the shopkeepers,
...st valuable part of the labouring population, consist of Chinese. About 5,000 adult males
...lly from China by the junks; about 1,000 of whom remain at Singapore, the rest dispersing
...mong the neighbouring Dutch, English, and Malay settlements. The boatmen are chiefly
...e Coromandel coast; and the Malays employ themselves as fishermen, in cutting timber, and
...the settlement with the rude produce of the neighbourhood. There are two good daily mar-
...all hours, and well supplied with vegetables, fruits, grain, fish, pork, and green turtle; the
...eapest animal food that can be procured. At Singapore there are no export or import duties
...anchorage, harbour, lighthouse dues, or any fees; but a register is kept of all exports and
...orts must be made to the master attendant by the masters of vessels, and invoices delivered
...intendent of imports and exports.

Weights, Language, &c. — The currency and weights are simple and convenient. Merchants'
...kept in Spanish dollars, divided into 100 parts, represented either by Dutch doits, or by
...er coins of the same value. The weights in use (and almost every thing is sold by weight,
...are the Chinese picul of 100 catties or 133¼ lbs. avoirdupois. Rice (the produce of Siam and
...ago) and salt are sold by the coyan of 40 piculs. Gold dust is sold by a Malay weight called
...which weighs 2 Spanish dollars, or 832 grains Troy. Bengal rice, wheat, and pulses of the
..., are sold by the bag, containing 2 Bengal maunds, or 164½ lbs. avoirdupois. Piece goods, &c. are
...rge or score. English weights and measures are frequently used in reference to European com-
...e mode of transacting business among the European merchants is simple and efficient. Instead
...eir affairs to native agents, as in other parts of India, they transact them in person, with the
...sistance of a Chinese creole as an interpreter and broker. The European merchants transact
...heir own account; but a great deal of their employment consists in acting as agents for houses
...iverpool, Glasgow, Amsterdam, Antwerp, Calcutta, Bombay, Madras, Canton, and Batavia.
...agents for various insurance offices at Calcutta and elsewhere, and policies of insurance to any
...e effected without difficulty. The language of commercial intercourse, where any of the
... East are concerned, is universally Malay, — a simple and easy dialect, of which all the resi-
...ts have a sufficient acquaintance for the transacting of ordinary business. A newspaper, the
...ronicle, is published once a week, and contains a price current, an account of arrivals and
... shipping, and an official detail of all the exports and imports of the preceding week. The
...n of justice is entirely English, there being a recorder's court for the settlement, in common
...neighbouring ones of Penang and Malacca. The following are the rates of commission and
...nt charged at Singapore, except in cases of special agreement: —

Commission.

...or purchases, except the following, 5 per cent.
...es of goods or produce for returns, 2½ per

...purchases of opium, 3 per cent.
...purchase of ships, vessels, houses, or lands,
...t.
...chase, or shipment of bullion, 1 per cent.
...rchase of diamonds, jewels, &c., 2 per cent.
...n treasure, bullion, or bills, 1 per cent.
...consigned and withdrawn, half commission.
...chase, or negotiating of bills not serving for
...of goods or produce, 1 per cent.
...sold by auction by the agents themselves, in
... the above, 2½ per cent.
...ere, or guaranteeing sales when specially re-
...per cent.
...per cent. per mille.

13. On all advances of money for the purpose of trade, whether
the goods are consigned to the agent or not, and where
a commission of 5 per cent. is not charged, 2½ per cent.
14. On ordering goods, or superintending the fulfilment of
contracts whence no other commission is derived,
2½ per cent.
15. On guaranteeing bills, bonds, or other engagements, and
on becoming security for administrations of estates, or
to government or individuals for contracts, agreements, &c., 2½ per cent.
16. On acting for the estates of persons deceased as executors
or administrators, 5 per cent.
17. On the management of estates for others, on the amount
received, 2½ per cent.
18. On procuring freight, or advertising as the agent of owner
or commanders, on the amount of freight, whether the
same passes through the hands of the agent or not,
5 per cent.

19. On chartering ships for other parties, 2½ per cent.
20. On making insurance, or writing orders for do., ½ per cent.
21. On settling insurance losses, total or partial, and on procuring return of premium, 1 per cent.
22. On debts, when a process at law or arbitration is necessary, 2½ per cent.
    And if received by such means, 5 per cent.
23. On bills of exchange noted or protested, ½ per cent.
24. On collecting house rent, 5 per cent.
25. On ships' disbursements, 2½ per cent.
26. On negotiating loans on respondentia, 2 per cent.
27. On letters of credit granted for mercantile purposes, 2½ per cent.
28. On purchasing or selling government securities, or on exchanging or transferring the same, ½ do.
29. On delivering up do., ½ per cent.
30. On all advances not punctually liquidated, the agent to have the option of charging a second commission, as upon a fresh advance, provided the charge be only made once in the same year.
31. On trans-shipping all goods or produce except the following, 1 per cent.
32. On trans-shipping whole chests of cassia, cassia-buds,

aniseed, camphor, nankeens, and gunny package, 1 dollar.
33. At the option of the agent, on the amount credited within the year, including interest excepting only such items, on which at least 2½ has been charged, 1 per cent.
    This charge not to apply to paying over a balan an account made up to a particular period, unless w balance is withdrawn without reasonable notice.

Warehouse Rent per Month.

Chests of opium or silk, bales of woollens, pipes o brandy, leaguers of arrack, &c., 1 dollar.
Bales of Indian piece goods, cotton, and g 50 cents.
Cases of European piece goods, trusses of woo 25 cents.
Hogsheads of liquor, half chests of wine, &c., 40 ce
Pepper, rice, coffee, sugar, saltpetre, &c., 10 per ce
Iron, tin, tinnague, spelter, copper, lead, &c., 5 p
All other goods not mentioned, to pay accordi measurement, at the rate of, per ton of 50 1 dollar.

Commodities and Prices. — Singapore is chiefly an *entrepôt*, having, with the exception of p manufactured on the spot from the raw material imported from the north coast of Sumatra, im of agriculture, and some others fabricated by the Chinese from European iron, and gambier or grown and manufactured on the island, few commodities of its own for exportation. The followi price current of the 24th of March, 1831, will convey the best idea of the miscellaneous articles the commerce of the port consists : —

Eastern Articles.		Dollars.		Eastern Articles.		D
		From	To			From
Bees' wax	per picul	35	40	Sugar candy	per picul	12
Biche de mer (tripang) first sort	per picul	45	50	Tin, Banca		15
inferior		20	25	Straits		14
Isle of France		10	25	Tobacco, Java	40 baskets	200
Benjamin		10	15	China	per picul	19
Betel nut				Tortoise shell		1,000
Birds' nests, white	per catty	40		Turmeric		2
black	per picul	25	125			
Camphor, Baras	per catty	12	50	*Western Articles.*		
China	per picul	27	29			
Canvass, Bengal	per bolt	5	6	Ale, Hodgson	per hogshead	40
Cassia lignea	per picul	10	12	Anchors and grapnells	per picul	1
Coffee, Java		8	8½	Bottles, English	per 100	4
Malay		6½	7	Books, &c.		
Copper, Japan		30	33	Canvass	per bolt	10
Peruvian		27	28	Copper nails and sheathing	per picul	40
Cordage, coir		4	5	Cordage		1
Dammer, raw		¾	1	Cotton		1
Dholi	per bag	2½	3	Cotton twist, No. 16. to 36.		50
Dragons' blood, first sort	per picul	—		No. 38. to 70.		80
inferior		5	30	No. 40. to 80.		85
of other parts		3	3½	Earthenware		
Ebony, Isle of France		1	2	Flints		
Elephants' teeth, first sort		15	190	Glass ware		
second sort		90	100	Gunpowder, cannister	per 100 lbs.	30
third sort		170	75	Hardware, assorted		
Gambier, Rhio and Singapore		1¼	1¾	Iron, Swedish	per picul	
Siak		6	6½	English		
Gamboge		50	75	nails		
Ghee, cow		25	30	Lead, pig		
buffalo		16	18	sheet		
Grain, rice, white	per coyan	55	60	Oilman's stores		
cargo, first sort		50	55	Patent shot	per bag	
cargo, inferior		38	40	Paints, black		
Bengal	per bag	1¼	1¾	green		
wheat		2	2½	white lead		
Gram		2½	3	Provisions, beef	per tierce	3
Gold dust, of Pahang and Siae	per bungkal	30	31	pork	per barrel	2
of other parts		25	29	biscuit	per picul	
Gunnies	per 100	8	11	flour		
Mother of pearl shells	per picul	19	20	Piece goods, Madapolams, 25 yds. by 32 in., per piece		
Nankeens, long junk	per 100	45	55	imitation Irish, 25 yds. by 32 in., per piece		
short	per corge	—		long cloths, 38 to 40 yds. by 34 to 36 in., per piece		
Oil, cocoa nut	per picul	4	4½	38 to 40 yds. by 38 to 40 in.,		
Opium, Patna	per chest		1,000	— by 44 in.		
Benares			1,000	— by 50 in.		
Malwa				— by 55 in.		
Pepper, black	per picul	5	5½	— by 60 in.		
white		7½	8	prints, 7-8, light grounds, single colours, per piece		
long		6½	7	9-8		
Piece goods, Bengal, sunnahs	per corge	36	40	7-8, dark		
Mahmoodies		30	32	9-8		
Gurrahs		22	26	7-8 and 9-8, two colours		
Baftahs		22	24	9-8, Turkey red ground, 2¼ yds.,		
chintz of 12 cubits		15	17½	cambric, 12 yds. by 40 in.		
chintz of 10 cubits		10	14	12 yds. by 42 in.		
Madras, moorees, white		12	25	— by 45		
blue		30	35	Jacconet, 20 yds. by 44 to 46 in.,		
salempires, blue		30	40	handkerchiefs, imitation Batteck, double, per corge		
brown		28	32	Pulicat		
handkerchiefs		30	100	Rosin	per barrel	
kolamhories		20	45	Spelter	per picul	
kambayas		12	13	Steel, Swedish		
bugis sarungs		18	40	English		
Bali cloths		5	7	Tar, Stockholm	per barrel	
Batick handkerchiefs		14	24	Woollens, long ells	per piece	
Rattans	per picul	1½	2	camblets		
Sago, pearl, in cases		2½	2½	ladies' cloth	per yard	
Salt, Siam	per coyan	22	24	Wines and spirits. Sherry	per dozen	
Saltpetre	per picul	7	8	Madeira		
Sapan wood, Manilla		—	2	port		
Siam		2	2½	claret, French		
Silk, raw, China, junk	72 cts.	200	250	English		
Canton, No. 2.	100 cts.	300	325	brandy	per gallon	
No. 3.	95 cts.	285	290	rum		
Spices, nutmegs	per picul			gin		
cloves		20	30			
mace		40	49			
Spirits, arrack	per gallon	30	40 ct.			
Stick lac	per picul	13	15			
Sugars, Manilla	per 1,000	6	7			
Sugar, Java	per picul	5½	7			
Siam, first sort		6½	7			
Manilla		5½	6			

ollowing **statement** of the imports and exports of Singapore, for the year 1827-28, shows the the trade, and the countries with which it is conducted : —

Names of Places.	Imports.	Exports.	Names of Places.	Imports.	Exports.
	£	£		£	£
ta - - -	231,646	163,134	Mauritius, &c. - -	15,595	11,912
s - - -	41,469	113,809	Ceylon - - -	1,935	
y - - -	37,688	18,401	Siam - - -	27,581	45,715
d - - -	192,012	278,951	Cochin China - -	10,844	8,557
n Europe - -	54,167	27,223	Acheen - - -	289	
	179,267	151,989	Other native Ports -	351,472	351,743
of Wales Island -	88,301	64,612			
a - - -	27,862	48,055	Total -	£1,488,599	1,387,201
	228,463	102,637			

—The difference between the exports and imports is chiefly owing to bills of exchange principally wn by the government on Bengal for Spanish dollars, paid in by the merchants, and which are oned in the exports.
ports at present are understood to exceed considerably 3,000,000*l.* per annum; a new article for d Chinese consumption, cotton twist, having been largely introduced within the last few years.
wing are the quantities of some of the staple articles exported in the same year, 1827-28 : —

nests - - -	cwt.	224	Rice, Malay and Siam -	cwt.	86,820
in, Siam - - -	cwt.	700	Salt, Siam - -	cwt.	54,683
or, Malay . -	cwt.	10	Camphor, China -	cwt.	1,476
Java and Sumatra -	cwt.	37,358	Tea - - -	chests	2,640
st, Borneo, &c. -	oz.	11,000	Silk, raw, China -	bales	855
Sumatra - -	cwt.	44,672	Opium, Indian -	lbs.	94,169
ngapore - - -	cwt.	10,944	Gunnies, Bengal - -	number	146,557
nca, and Malay penins,	cwt.	16,044	Iron, bar, British -	cwt.	9,555
Siam - - -	cwt.	17,349	Cottons, British -	pieces	178,791

urnal of an Embassy to Siam and Cochin China, by *John Crawfurd, Esq.* chap. xix. ; *Return of lation of British India in Report of the Select Committee of the Commons*, 1831 ; *Report of the mmittee of the Commons, for* 1830.)

NS. The term is applied in commercial language to the skins of those , as calves, deer, goats, lambs, &c., which, when prepared, are used in the works of bookbinding, the manufacture of gloves, parchment, &c. ; while n hides is applied to the skins of the ox, horse, &c., which, when tanned, d in the manufacture of shoes, harness, and other heavy and strong articles. nd kid skins are principally used in the glove manufacture : 120 skins being d to produce, at an average, 18 dozen pairs of gloves.

of the Skins imported in 1829, specifying the Countries whence they came, and the Numbers brought from each.

es from which imported.	Skins.						
	Calf and Untanned.	Deer, Undressed	Goat, Undressed	Kid, Undressed	Kid, Dressed.	Lamb, Undressed	Seal, Undressed
	Cwt. qrs. lbs.	Number	Number	Number	Number	Number	Number
- - -	21,121 1 19	- -	5,186				
		15	34				
s - - -	27 1 0	42	15 599	2,978	22		
- - -	636 3 14	- -	- -	- -	- -	10,900	400
- - -	5,671 1 10	- -	7,496				
ands - -	7,919 2 22	- 75	3,323	140	15,668	62,015	887
- - -	7,159 1 27	- -	7,840	- -	10,160	624	264
			36,578	4,463	564,571	76,757	
e Balearic Islands -	- -	- -	7,515	16,034	- -	239,964	
e Italian Islands -	0 2 0	- -	31	82,149	673	1,497,669	
Continental Greece (exclu- } Morea) }	-	- -	387	302	- -	262	
ary, and Morocco -	10 1 27	- -	104,446				
ast of Africa - -	828 0 27	345	- -	- -	- -	- -	2
d Hope - -	67 3 7	15	87,058	- -	- -	- -	4,654
			2				
- - -	- -	- -	1,247	253	- -	- -	43
ompany's Territories and }	180 0 0	675	29,476	- -	- -	- -	1,659
Wales and Van Diemen's }	0 0 22	- -	- -	- -	- -	- -	9,956
ern Colonies - -	24 1 6	1,778	368	- -	- -	- -	227,700
Indies - -	- -	67					
of America - -	- -	120,238	- -	- -	- -	- -	15,125
entral and Southern Ame- rica, viz.—		26					
							300
Rio de la Plata - -	107 0 25	- -	- -	- -	- -	- -	909
isheries - -	-	- -	- -	- -	- -	- -	18,813
		- -	- -	- -	- -	- -	8,829
rnsey, Jersey, Alderney, }	9 2 20	- -	- -	- -	- -	296	
antity imported - -	43,764 2 2	123,276	306,579	106,319	591,094	1,888,487	289,541
ained for Home Consump- ting the Quantity exported y to the Payment of Duty }	43,046 2 4	36,314	182,062	107,513	591,091	1,887,891	262,446

SLATE (Ger. *Schiefer;* Fr. *Ardoise;* It. *Lavagna, Lastra;* Sp. *Pizarr* fossil or compact stone that may be split into plates. There are several vari of this mineral, chiefly distinguished by their colour, which is in general gra termixed with blue, green, or black streaks, though sometimes purplish, yello brown, bluish black, and occasionally streaked with a darker hue than the gr itself. There are very valuable slate quarries in many parts of Scotland; at Cardigan and other places in Wales. The principal use of slates is in covering of houses, for which purpose they are infinitely superior to either or thatch.

Slates carried by land have never been subjected to any duty; but those ried coastwise were, until last year, charged with duties, varying accordi their size and species. The injustice of this distinction, and the impolicy o ing any duty on an article of this sort, are obvious. The revenue it produce quite inconsiderable, not exceeding 35,000*l.* a year. It was **repealed** at the time as the duty on coal carried coastwise.

SLAVES AND SLAVE TRADE. A slave, in the ordinary sense of term, is an individual at the absolute disposal of another, who has a rig employ and treat him as he pleases. But the state of slavery is susceptib innumerable modifications; and it has been usual, in most countries where i been long established, to limit in various ways the power of the master the slave. The *slave trade* is, of course, the business of those who deal in sl

Origin of Slavery. — A great deal of learning has been employed in tracing th tory of slavery, though the subject is still far from being exhausted. It seems probable that it originally grew out of a state of war. In rude uncivilised com ties, where the passion of revenge acquires a strength unknown in more advanced of society, captives taken in war are adjudged to belong to the victors, who may put them to the sword, or reduce them to a state of servitude. In antiquity the of war and slavery were inseparable. Probably, in very remote ages, prisoners most commonly put to death; but the selfish gradually predominated over the passionate feelings, and for many ages it was usual to reduce them to the condit slaves; being either sold by their captors to others, or employed by them as they think fit. "*Jure gentium,*" says Justinian, "*servi nostri sunt, qui ab hostibus capiunt* (*Instit.* lib. i. 5.)

The practice of reducing men to a state of slavery having once begun, was ext in various ways. The progeny of slaves, or of women in a state of slavery, slaves; men born free might sell themselves as slaves; and parents had author Judea and Rome, to dispose of their children for the same purpose. — (*Michaelis Laws of Moses,* vol. ii. p. 163. Eng. ed.) It was the law of Rome, and of most ancient states, that the persons of debtors who had contracted obligations which could not discharge, should become the property of their creditors.

Treatment of Slaves. — The treatment of slaves in antiquity, as in more modern differed very widely in different countries and periods, and among different cla slaves in the same country and at the same time. A great deal also depended character of particular masters. Slaves bred up in the house or family of the n were uniformly treated with greater indulgence than others, and became entitl custom, to several important privileges. At Athens, slaves appear to have been treated than in any other ancient state; and Demosthenes mentions, in his s Philippic, that "a slave was better off at Athens than a free citizen in many countries." In republican Rome, the masters had the power of life and death ove slaves, who were often treated with the most detestable barbarity. It was not a common practice to expose old, useless, or sick slaves to starve in an island Tiber! We may, as Mr. Hume has justly remarked, "imagine what others practise, when it was the professed maxim of the elder Cato, to sell his superan slaves at any price, rather than maintain what he esteemed a useless burden." — tarch, in *Vitâ Catonis.*) *Ergastula,* or dungeons, where slaves were confine chained at night, and where they were sometimes made to work in the day common all over Italy. Columella advises that they be always built under gro (lib. i. c. 6.); and remains of them are still seen in the lower stories of ancient bu in Italy and Sicily. Hundreds of slaves were sometimes put to death for the cr one only; and they were exposed, when they committed any petty fault, to violence of the most capricious and unrestrained despotism.

It was not uncommon in the barbarous ages to immolate captives on the tomb chiefs as had fallen in battle; and magnificent games were celebrated on thes sions.* The gladiatorial exhibitions, so common at Rome after the Punic war

---

* Achilles sacrificed 12 Trojan captives on the tomb of Patroclus. — (*Iliad,* lib. 23.)

,rown out of this practice. These were contests between slaves, denominated
s, trained to fight in public for the amusement of a ferocious populace, who
greatest delight in their sanguinary combats. Thousands of unfortunate
were annually sacrificed in this inhuman sport. After his triumph over the
Trajan exhibited spectacles, in which no fewer than 11,000 wild beasts of
kinds were killed, and 10,000 gladiators fought! — (*Adam's Roman Antiqui-*
7.)

uelties inflicted on the slaves occasioned frequent revolts, attended by the most
excesses. Spartacus a Thracian captive, destined for the profession of a
headed a rebellion of gladiators and slaves, which continued for three years,
ired all the force of the republic to suppress. When finally defeated by
about 6,000 of his followers were nailed to the cross, in double rows, that ex-
most from Capua to Rome. — (*Ferguson, Rom. Republic,* c. 16.) No one
d with the manners of the Romans can be surprised at the atrocities of so
the emperors. The worst of them treated the citizens better than the latter
ae slaves. Humanity could not be looked for in the rulers of a state in
man life was held in contempt, and human suffering made the subject of
oort.

:equence partly of their ill usage, and partly of its being accounted cheaper
an to breed slaves, vast numbers were annually imported into Italy. Thrace
ountries round the Black Sea furnished large supplies of the best slaves; and
were obtained from Egypt, Syria, Cappadocia, and other places. Delus in
s the greatest slave market of antiquity; as many as 10,000 slaves have been
in a single day. — (*Strabo,* lib. 14.)

its brutalising influence on the manners of the people, the institution of
as in other respects productive of the worst effects. The best Roman writers
aony to the negligence, waste, and bad conduct of slaves. — (*Columella,* lib. i.
n. *Hist. Nat.* lib. 17. § 3.) The inferiority of the ancients in most of the
s is principally to be ascribed to the prevalence of slavery, which not only
ed all emulation and invention on the part of most of those engaged in in-
employments, but made the employments be considered in some measure
l. In the ancient world agriculture and arms were the only occupations that
ned worthy of a freeman. The mechanical arts were carried on either wholly
or by the very dregs of the people; and remained for ages in the same state.

ablishment of Christianity contributed more, perhaps, than any thing else, first
e, and finally to suppress the abomination of slavery. But within no very
d after its abolition had been completely effected in every part of Europe, its
gan to be inflicted on America.

Slave Trade. — This infamous traffic was commenced by the Portuguese,
The trade, however, was but of trifling extent till the commencement of the
entury. In consequence, however, of the rapid destruction of the Indians
n the mines of St. Domingo or Hayti, Charles V. authorised, in 1517, the
n into the island of African slaves from the establishments of the Portuguese
t of Guinea. The concurrence of the emperor was obtained by the inter-
the celebrated Las Casas, bishop of Chiapa, who, contradictorily enough,
protect the Indians by enslaving the Africans. The latter were certainly
ous and capable of bearing fatigue than the former. But this circumstance
eal justification of the measure, which, at best, was nothing more than the
a of one species of crime and misery in the place of another. — (*Robertson's*
ica, book iii.)

ortation of negroes into the West Indies and America having once begun,
ncreased, until the extent and importance of the traffic rivalled its cruelty and
John Hawkins was the first Englishman who engaged in it: and such was
with which our countrymen followed his example, that they exported from
e than 300,000 slaves between the years 1680 and 1700; and between 1700
610,000 Africans were imported into Jamaica only; to which adding the
o the other islands and the continental colonies, and those who died on their
e number carried from Africa will appear immense. — (*Bryan Edwards,*
Indies, vol. ii. p. 64.) The importations by other nations, particularly the
Portuguese, were also very great.

easy to say whether this traffic has been more injurious to Africa or America.
er it has perpetuated and multiplied every sort of enormity and abuse. The
s have been tempted to make war on each other, that they might obtain cap-
to the European traders; and when these could not be found, have seized
ir own subjects. Many, too, have been kidnapped by the crews of the slave
is there any sort of crime known among pirates and banditti, which, for more

than three centuries, the civilised inhabitants of Europe have not perpetrated up
unoffending natives of Central Africa. In the West Indies, and those parts of A
into which slaves have been largely imported, its effect has been equally disastro
has led to the most violent antipathy between the whites and the blacks; and b
fruitful source of crimes, convulsions, and disorders, of which it is difficult to
termination. — (There are some good remarks on slavery as it exists in Ameri
on the multiplied evils of which it is productive, in a volume entitled "Excu
an English Gentleman through the United States and Canada," published in 18

It would be to no purpose to enter into any examination of the sophisms by
it was formerly attempted to justify the slave trade. We shall not undertake
nounce any opinion upon the question as to the inferiority of the blacks; th
does not appear to us that the statements of Mr. Jefferson on this subject, in his
on Virginia," and similar statements made by others, have received any su
answer. But supposing the inferiority of the negroes were established bey
question, that would be no justification of the infamous cruelties inflicted upo
Did any one ever think of vindicating a robber, because he happened to be stro
cleverer than his victim?

Abolition of the Slave Trade. — Notwithstanding the sanction it had receive
parliament, and the supineness of the public, the slave trade was frequently der
by distinguished individuals in this and other countries, as essentially cruel a
just. Of these, Montesquieu is, perhaps, the most conspicuous. He succ
exposed the futility of the different pleas put forth by the advocates of slavery.
prit des Loix, liv. 15.); and the extensive circulation of his great work, and
ference paid to the doctrines advanced in it, contributed powerfully to awa
public to a just sense of the iniquity of the traffic. The Quakers early distin
themselves by their hostility to the trade; of which they always were the co
and uncompromising enemies.

The first motion on the subject in parliament was made in 1776; but without
The subject was not taken up systematically till 1787, when a committee was
of which Mr. Granville Sharp and Mr. Clarkson, whose names are imperishab
ciated with the history of the abolition of the slave trade, were members. Tl
mittee collected evidence in proof of the enormities produced by the trade, proc
circulation throughout the country, and succeeded in making a very great impres
the public mind. After a number of witnesses on both sides had been examine
the privy council, Mr. Wilberforce, on the 12th of May, 1789, moved a series of
tions condemnatory of the traffic. They were supported by Mr. Burke in one of
speeches; and by Mr. Pitt and Mr. Fox. But notwithstanding the resolutio
carried, nothing was done to give them effect. The friends of the trade having
leave to produce evidence at the bar of the house, contrived to interpose s
delays that the session passed off without any thing being done. In the fo
sessions the great struggle was continued with various success, but without any
result. At length the triumph of humanity and justice was finally consumm
1807; a bill for the total and immediate abolition of the slave trade, having been
in both houses by immense majorities, received the royal assent on the 25th of
being the last act of the administration of Mr. Fox and Lord Grenville.
ended," says Mr. Clarkson, "one of the most glorious contests, after a continu
20 years, of any ever carried on in any age or country: a contest, not of
violence, but of reason; a contest between those who felt deeply for the happi
the honour of their fellow creatures, and those who, through vicious custom,
impulse of avarice, had trampled under foot the sacred rights of their nature,
even attempted to efface all title of the divine image from their minds."

America abolished the slave trade at the same time as England.

But notwithstanding what had been done, further measures were soon disc
be necessary. The Spaniards and the Portuguese continued to carry on the tr
greater extent than ever; and British subjects did not hesitate, under cover
flags, to become partners in their adventures. An effectual stop was put to this
in 1811, by the enactment of a law introduced by Mr. (now Lord) Brough
made trading in slaves punishable by transportation for 14 years, or by confin
hard labour for a term not more than 5 nor less than 3 years.

The British laws relative to the slave trade were consolidated by the act 5
c. 113., of which we subjoin the more important clauses.

Dealing in Slaves in the High Seas, &c. to be deemed Piracy. — And if any subject or subj
Majesty, or any person or persons residing or being within any of the dominions, forts, settle
tories, or territories, now or hereafter belonging to his Majesty, or being in his Majesty's oc
possession, or under the government of the United Company of Merchants of England trading
Indies, shall, except in such cases as are by this act permitted, after the 1st day of January,
the high seas, or in any haven, river, creek, or place, where the admiral has jurisdiction, kno
wilfully carry away, convey, or remove, or aid or assist in carrying away, conveying, or rem

r persons as a slave or slaves, or for the purpose of his, her, or their being imported or brought as
r slaves into any island, colony, country, territory, or place whatsoever, or for the purpose of his,
heir being sold, transferred, used, or dealt with as a slave or slaves; or shall after the said 1st
anuary, 1825, except in such cases as are by this act permitted, upon the high seas, or within the
ion aforesaid, knowingly and wilfully ship, embark, receive, detain, or confine, or assist in ship-
nbarking, receiving, detaining, or confining, on board any ship, vessel, or boat, any person or
for the purpose of his, her, or their being carried away, conveyed, or removed as a slave or slaves,
ie purpose of his, her, or their being imported, or brought as a slave or slaves into any island,
country, territory, or place whatsoever, or for the purpose of his, her, or their being sold, trans-
ssed, or dealt with as a slave or slaves; then and in every such case, the *persons so offending shall*
ed and adjudged guilty of piracy, felony, and robbery, and being convicted thereof shall suffer
thout benefit of clergy,—and loss of lands, goods, and chattels, as pirates, felons, and robbers
e seas ought to suffer.—§ 9.

s dealing in Slaves, or exporting or importing Slaves, &c. guilty of Felony.—And (except in such
ases as are by this act permitted) if any persons shall deal or trade in, purchase, sell, barter, or
or contract for the dealing or trading in, purchase, sale, barter, or transfer of slaves, or persons
to be dealt with as slaves; or shall, otherwise than as aforesaid, carry away or remove, or con-
the carrying away or removing of slaves or other persons, as or in order to their being dealt with
; or shall import or bring, or contract for the importing or bringing into any place whatsoever,
other persons, as or in order to their being dealt with as slaves; or shall, otherwise than as afore-
, tranship, embark, receive, detain, or confine on board, or contract for the shipping, tranship-
barking, receiving, detaining, or confining on board of any ship, vessel, or boat, slaves or other
for their being carried away or removed, as or in order to their being dealt with
; or shall ship, tranship, embark, receive, detain, or confine on board, or contract for the ship-
nshipping, embarking, receiving, detaining, or confining on board of any ship, vessel, or boat,
other persons, for the purpose of their being imported or brought into any place whatsoever, as
der to their being dealt with as slaves; or shall fit out, man, navigate, equip, despatch, use,
et or take to freight or on hire, or contract for the fitting out, manning, navigating, equipping,
ing, using, employing, letting, or taking to freight or on hire, any ship, vessel, or boat, in order
plish any of the objects, or the contracts in relation to the objects, which objects and contracts
einbefore been declared unlawful; or shall knowingly and wilfully lend or advance, or become
or the loan or advance, or contract for the lending or advancing, or becoming security for the
vance of money, goods, or effects, employed or to be employed in accomplishing any of the
r the contracts in relation to the objects, which objects and contracts have hereinbefore been
unlawful; or shall knowingly and wilfully become guarantee or security, or contract for the
guarantee or security, for agents employed or to be employed in accomplishing any of the
r the contracts in relation to the objects, which objects and contracts have hereinbefore been
unlawful, or in any other manner to engage, or contract to engage, directly or indirectly therein,
er, agent, or otherwise; or shall knowingly and wilfully ship, tranship, lade, or receive or put
or contract for the shipping, transhipping, lading, receiving, or putting on board of any ship,
boat, money, goods or effects, to be employed in accomplishing any of the objects, or the con-
elation to the objects, which objects and contracts have hereinbefore been declared unlawful; or
the charge or command, or navigate, or enter and embark on board, or contract for the taking
e or command, or for the navigating or entering and embarking on board of any ship, vessel, or
aptain, master, mate, surgeon, or supercargo, knowing that such ship, vessel, or boat is actually
, or is in the same voyage, or upon the same occasion, in respect of which they shall so take the
command, or navigate or enter and embark, or contract so to do as aforesaid, intended to be
in accomplishing any of the objects, or the contracts in relation to the objects, which objects
acts have hereinbefore been declared unlawful; or shall knowingly and wilfully insure, or con-
he insuring of any slaves, or any property or other subject matter engaged or employed in
hing any of the objects, or the contracts in relation to the objects, which objects and contracts
einbefore been declared unlawful; or shall wilfully and fraudulently forge or counterfeit any
, certificate of valuation, sentence, or decree of condemnation or restitution, copy of sentence
of condemnation or restitution, or any receipt (such receipts being required by this act) or any
ich certificate, certificate of valuation, sentence or decree of condemnation or restitution,
ntence or decree of condemnation or restitution, or receipt as aforesaid; or shall knowingly
ly utter or publish the same, knowing it to be forged or counterfeited, with intent to defraud
v, or any other person or persons whatsoever, or any body politic or corporate; then, and in
r case the persons so offending, and their procurers, counsellors, aiders, and abettors, *shall be*
shall be transported for a term not exceeding 14 years, or shall be confined and kept to hard
a term not exceeding 5, nor less than 3 years, at the discretion of the court before whom such
hall be tried.— § 10.

&c. serving on Board such Ships guilty of Misdemeanor. — And (except in such special cases,
special purposes as are by this act permitted) if any persons shall enter and embark on board,
for the entering and embarking on board of any ship, vessel, or boat, as petty officer, seaman,
servant, or in any other capacity not hereinbefore specifically mentioned, knowing that such
l, or boat is actually employed, or is in the same voyage, or upon the same occasion, in respect
hey shall so enter and embark on board, or contract so to do as aforesaid, intended to be em-
accomplishing any of the objects, or the contracts in relation to the objects, which objects and
ave hereinbefore been declared unlawful; then, and in every such case, the persons so offend-
eir procurers, counsellors, aiders, and abettors, shall be guilty of a misdemeanor only, and
nished by imprisonment for a term not exceeding 2 years. — § 11.

herein shall prevent Persons from purchasing Slaves in any Islands, &c. belonging to his Ma-
ided such Slaves shall be employed in the same Island, &c. — Provided always, that nothing in
all prevent or be construed to prevent any persons from dealing or trading in, purchasing,
tering, or transferring, or from the contracting for the dealing or trading in, purchase, sale,
ransfer of any slave or slaves lawfully being within any island, colony, dominion, fort, settle-
ry, or territory belonging to or in the possession of his Majesty, in case such dealing or trading,
ale, barter, transfer, or contract shall be made and entered into with the true intent and pur-
ploying or working such slave or slaves within such and the same island, colony, dominion,
nent, factory, or territory in which they, he, or she may lawfully be at the time of the making
into any such dealing or trading, purchase, sale, barter, transfer, or contract. — § 13.

es may be removed Coastwise, or by Land, to any other Part of the same Island, &c. Where
wo or more Islands comprised in the same Colonial Government, Proprietors of Slaves may
m to any Island within the Government, the Governor granting Licence for that Purpose. —
lways, that nothing in this act shall prevent any person from carrying away or removing by
stwise, or from contracting for the carrying away or removing by land or coastwise, of any
ully being in any part of any island, colony, dominion, fort, settlement, factory, or territory
o or in the possession of his Majesty, to any other part of the same island, colony, dominion,
nent, factory, or territory: Provided always, that where two or more islands are comprised in
lonial government, nothing in this act shall prevent any proprietor of slaves, lawfully being
of such islands, from carrying away or removing such slaves to any other island, within the
ment, for the purpose of cultivating any estate or plantation belonging to such proprietor him.

self, provided that such special purpose for the removal shall previously be made to appear to the sation of the governor or lieutenant-governor, or other person having the chief civil command within government, who thereupon shall grant a licence for such removal, specifying therein the special thereof; but before any slave or slaves shall, by virtue of any such licence, be so removed or emb on board of any ship or vessel, such clearances or permits, and such certificates, shall be obtained herein-after mentioned and directed in regard to domestic slaves attending on their owner or ma his family by sea. — § 14.

His Majesty in Council may authorise, until July 31. 1827, the Removal of Slaves from any Island in the West Indies to another British Island there, in case it shall appear that such Rem essential for the Welfare of the Slaves : and such Stipulations and Conditions shall be established Benefit of such Slaves as his Majesty in Council shall think fit. — Provided also, that it shall be law his Majesty, by any order or orders, with the advice of his privy council, to authorise, until the July, 1827, and to the end of the next ensuing session of parliament, and no longer, the removal slaves from any island in the West Indies belonging to his Majesty, to any other island in the West belonging to his Majesty, in case it shall be made appear to his Majesty and his council, that such re is essential to the welfare of the slaves proposed to be removed : also, it shall be lawful for his M by any such order or orders, to make such stipulations, conditions, and regulations for the benefit o slaves, in the island to which they may be removed, as to his Majesty, with the advice of his counc seem meet, and to take security in double the value of the slaves so to be removed (such value estimated according to the price of slaves in the island) by bond or recognisance to be entered i the person on the application of whom such licence may be granted, with two sufficient sureties, f due observance of all such stipulations, conditions, and regulations ; and all orders in council so shall be laid before both houses of parliament within sixteen weeks next after the commencement o session. — § 15.

Convict Slaves may be transported from a British Island to a Foreign Settlement. — Nothing in t shall prevent the transportation to any foreign colony or place, of any slaves that shall have bee victed in any court of record, in any present or future British island or colony, of any crime to whi punishment of transportation shall be annexed by the law of such island or colony ; but in ever case a copy of the judgment or sentence, certified by the court, shall be put on board in the ship or in which any such convict shall be transported. — § 16.

Domestic Slaves may accompany their Masters, under certain Regulations. — Nothing in this ac prevent any slave, who shall be really the domestic servant of any person, from attending his ow master, or any part of his family, by sea, to any place whatever ; nevertheless, under the following lations; that is to say, first, the name and occupation of every such domestic slave shall be inse or endorsed upon the clearance or permit to depart, by or in the presence of the collector, comptrol chief officer of customs from which such ship or vessel shall clear outwards, who shall, witho certify, under his hand, that the slaves so embarked or carried were reported to him as domestic ser secondly, the master or owner of any such domestic slaves shall obtain from the registry of the c an extract, certified by the registrar thereof, showing that such domestic slaves have been duly e in the slave registry of the said colony, by their names and descriptions therein specified, which e and certificate shall always be on board the ship or vessel in which any such domestic slaves are ca and upon such slaves being brought into or landed in any British colony, the extract and certifi their registration in the colony from which they may have come, shall be forthwith produced collector or principal officer of customs, and a copy thereof shall be by him delivered to the regi slaves in the colony into which they may be brought ; and if the domestic slaves shall be again re from the colony into which they may have been so brought, previous to the next period for n returns of slaves therein, the collector shall, previous to the embarkation of such domestic slaves, to the party requiring it the original extract and certificate of registration delivered into his offic kept on board the ship or vessel in which such domestic slaves may be carried ; and if the regu herein contained be not complied with, the owners of the said slaves shall forfeit 100*l.* for every and the master or other person having the charge of such ship or vessel shall in every such case 100*l.* for every domestic slave so unlawfully taken on board. — § 17.

Slaves may be employed in Navigation, under certain Regulations. — Nothing in this act shall p any slaves from being employed in navigation, in numbers not exceeding in any one vessel or boa usually employed in navigating such vessels or boats ; nevertheless where they shall be design employed in navigating from any British island, colony, plantation, or territory, the regulatio scribed for the transit of domestic slaves as aforesaid shall be duly observed. — § 18.

As also in Fishing, or other their ordinary Occupations. — Nothing in this act shall prevent any from being employed in fishing, or any other his ordinary business upon the seas ; nevertheless they shall be so employed in the course of a navigation designedly undertaken from any British colony, plantation, or territory, the regulations prescribed for the transit of domestic slaves as ar shall be duly observed. — § 19.

Slaves may be employed in the Military and Naval Services. — Nothing in this act shall prev slaves from being put on board any ship or vessel by the order of his Majesty's commander-i either by sea or land, in any island, colony, plantation, or territory belonging to or under th nion of his Majesty, in order to be employed in his Majesty's military or naval service, and fro by such order so employed, however or wheresoever the said service may require. — § 20.

Slaves in Vessels in Distress may be assisted. — Nothing in this act shall prevent the transhipp assisting at sea any slave or slaves which shall be in any ship or vessel in distress. — § 21.

Foreign Slave Trade. — At the Congress of Vienna, in 1814, the plenipotentia the great powers agreed to a declaration that the slave trade was "repugnant principles of humanity and of universal morality ; and that it was the earnest de their sovereigns to put an end to a scourge which has so long desolated Africa, deg Europe, and afflicted humanity."

But notwithstanding this memorable declaration, the immediate abolition of th was not agreed to. France was allowed to continue it for *five* years. It is b abundantly certain that, though the trade nominally ceased in 1819, it has sinc clandestinely carried on to a great extent in French ships, if not with the conni at least without much opposition, on the part of the late government of France. is now, however, reason to hope that it will be effectually suppressed ; for accor a recent arrangement (Nov. 30. 1831) made with his Majesty Louis-Philippe, th of search is reciprocally conceded, within certain limits, by the French and E so that French ships suspected of being engaged in the trade may be stopped by cruisers.

Considering the efforts Great Britain made in behalf of Spain and Portugal, a influence she might have been supposed to have acquired with the restored mona

ntries, it may well excite astonishment that our negotiators (whether from the
lity of those with whom they had to deal, or from want of address and firmness
arts, we leave it to others to decide,) were unable to prevail on these powers
ice the trade till after the lapse of a considerable period. They succeeded, in-
nducing them to exempt that portion of the African coast north of the Equator
r piratical attacks; and for this concession, and damages alleged to have been
by their slave ships from our cruisers, Great Britain has paid them no less than
l. ! —(See SIERRA LEONE.)

anish slave trade was to have finally ceased, according to the stipulations in
between Spain and this country of the 5th of July and 28th of August, 1814,
But within these two years, and, perhaps, at this very moment, slave ships
publicly fitted out from Cuba, and immense numbers of slaves have been
into that island, with the open connivance of the authorities. A mixed com-
ourt, consisting of British and Spanish commissioners, has been established
nah, for the condemnation of vessels proved to have been engaged in the slave
ut we are officially informed by Mr. Macleay, one of the commissioners, that
establishment of the court no seizure of a slave vessel has ever taken place, but
erference and denunciation of the British commissioners; and even then *such*
s only been made to be instantly followed by a perfect acquittal in the Spanish
" — (*Parl. Paper*, No. 120. Sess. 1831, p. 53.)

were freely imported in immense numbers into Brazil, till February, 1830,
trade was to cease, conformably to the convention entered into with this
n the 23d June, 1826.— (See RIO DE JANEIRO.) But whether the clan-
d illegal, as well as the open and legitimate importation of slaves, be at end,
an we can undertake to say.

whole, we are afraid that nothing short of a declaration by the great powers,
e slave trade piracy, will be sufficient entirely to rid humanity of its guilt and

T, OR SMALTZ (Ger. *Smalte;* Du. *Smalt;* Fr. *Smalte;* It. *Smalto az-
altino;* Sp. *Esmalte, Azul azur;* Rus. *Lasor*), an oxide of cobalt, melted
eous earth and potash. It is a sort of glass, of a beautiful deep blue
nd being ground very fine, is known by the name of powder blue. The
smaltz is not affected by fire; and it is consequently in great demand in
ng of earthenware. It is also employed in the colouring of paper, and for
poses in the arts. Beckmann has proved that the process used in the
n of smaltz was invented about the end of the fifteenth or the begin-
e sixteenth century; and that the blue glass of the ancients owes its
t to the presence of cobalt or of smaltz, but to that of iron. — (*Hist. of
, vol. ii. art. Cobalt.*) Smaltz is principally manufactured in Germany
ay. Of 496,160 lbs. imported into Great Britain in 1828, 281,231 lbs.
t from Germany, 59,440 from the Netherlands, and 155,487 from Nor-

GLING, the offence of defrauding the revenue by the introduction of
to consumption, without paying the duties chargeable upon them. It
mmitted indifferently either upon the excise or customs' revenue.

nd Prevention of Smuggling. — This crime, which occupies so prominent a
criminal legislation of all modern states, is wholly the result of vicious com-
d financial legislation. It is the fruit either of prohibitions of importation,
ssively high duties. It does not originate in any depravity inherent in man;
folly and ignorance of legislators. A prohibition against importing a com-
s not take away the taste for it; and the imposition of a high duty on any
sions a universal desire to escape or evade its payment. Hence, the rise
tion of the smuggler. The risk of being detected in the clandestine intro-
commodities under any system of fiscal regulations may always be valued at
erage rate; and wherever the duties exceed this rate, smuggling immediately
Now, there are plainly but two ways of checking this practice, — either
ion to smuggle must be diminished by lowering the duties, or the difficulties
of smuggling must be increased. The first is obviously the more natural
t method of effecting the object in view; but the second has been most ge-
rted to, even in cases when the duties were quite excessive. Governments
mly almost consulted the persons employed in the collection of the revenue
t to the best mode of rendering taxes effectual; though it is clear that the
rejudices, and peculiar habits of such persons utterly disqualify them from
sound opinion on such a subject. They cannot recommend a reduction of

duties as a means of repressing smuggling and increasing revenue, without a
ledging their own incapacity to detect and defeat illicit practices: and the re
been, that, instead of ascribing the prevalence of smuggling to its true causes,
cers of customs and excise have almost universally ascribed it to some defect in th
or in the mode of administering them, and have proposed repressing it by new
tions, and by increasing the number and severity of the penalties affecting the sm
As might have been expected, these attempts have, in the great majority o
proved signally unsuccessful. And it has been invariably found, that no vigil
the part of the revenue officers, and no severity of punishment, can prevent the
gling of such commodities as are either prohibited or loaded with oppressive
The smuggler is generally a popular character; and whatever the law may dec
the subject, it is quite ludicrous to expect that the bulk of society will ever be I
to think that those who furnish them with cheap brandy, geneva, tobacco, &c. are
of any very heinous offence.

"To pretend," says Dr. Smith, "to have any scruple about buying smuggled
though a manifest encouragement to the violation of the revenue laws, and to th
jury which almost always attends it, would, in most countries, be regarded as one c
pedantic pieces of hypocrisy, which instead of gaining credit with anybody, seems
expose the person who affects to practise them to the suspicion of being a greater
than most of his neighbours. By this indulgence of the public, the smuggler i
encouraged to continue a trade, which he is thus taught to consider as, in some m
innocent; and when the severity of the revenue laws is ready to fall upon hin
frequently disposed to defend with violence what he has been accustomed to re
his just property; and from being at first rather imprudent than criminal, he,
too often becomes one of the most determined violators of the laws of soci
(*Wealth of Nations*, vol. iii. p. 491.)

To create by means of high duties an overwhelming temptation to indulge in
and then to punish men for indulging in it, is a proceeding completely subve
every principle of justice. It revolts the natural feelings of the people; and
them to feel an interest in the worst characters — for such smugglers generally a
espouse their cause, and avenge their wrongs. A punishment which is not propo
to the offence, and which does not carry the sanction of public opinion along with
never be productive of any good effect. The true way to put down smuggli
render it unprofitable; to diminish the temptation to engage in it; and this is
be done by surrounding the coasts with cordons of troops, by the multiplic
oaths and penalties, and making the country the theatre of ferocious and bloody
in the field, and of perjury and chicanery in the courts of law, but by repeali
hibitions, and reducing duties, so that their collection may be enforced with a m
degree of vigilance; and that the forfeiture of the article may be a sufficient
upon the smuggler. It is in this, and in this only, that we must seek for an e
check to illicit trafficking. Whenever the profits of the fair trader become near
to those of the smuggler, the latter is forced to abandon his hazardous professio
so long as prohibitions or oppressively high duties are kept up, or, which is, in
same thing, so long as *high bounties* are held out to encourage the adventurous, th
and the profligate, to enter on this career, we may be assured that armies o
and custom-house officers, backed by the utmost severity of the revenue laws,
insufficient to hinder them.

The penalties imposed on illicit dealing in commodities subject to duties
have been specified in the articles on such commodities. The following fo
statute, with its multiplied provisions and penalties, refers entirely to custom
The importance of the subject has induced us to give it entire; mentioning th
in which it has been modified by subsequent statutes.

ACT 6 GEO. IV. c. 108, "FOR THE PREVENTION OF SMUGGLING."

Commencement of the act, to take effect from 5th of January, 1826. — § 1.
*Any Vessel belonging wholly or in part to his Majesty's Subjects, found within certain Distar
Coast of the United Kingdom with prohibited Goods on board, and not proceeding on her Voyage, f*
If any vessel or boat belonging in the whole or in part to his Majesty's subjects, or whereof
the persons on board or discovered to have been on board the said vessel or boat shall be subj
Majesty, shall be found within *four* * leagues of the coast of that part of the United Kingdo
between the North Foreland on the coast of Kent and Beachy Head on the coast of Sussex,
eight leagues of the coast of any other part of the said United Kingdom, or shall be discover
been within the said distances, not proceeding on her voyage, wind and weather permitting,
board or in any manner attached or affixed thereto, or having had on board or in any manne
or affixed thereto, or conveying or having conveyed in any manner, any goods whatsoever lia
feiture by this or any other act relating to the revenue of customs upon being imported into
Kingdom, then not only all such goods, together with their packages, and all goods containe
but also the vessel or boat, together with all her guns, furniture, ammunition, tackle, and appa
forfeited: Provided always, that such distance of eight leagues shall be measured in any directic

---

* Under the former acts the distance was fixed at *eight* leagues.

hward and eastward of Beachy Head; and the provisions of this act shall extend to such distance leagues in every direction from Beachy Head, although any part of such limits may exceed the of four leagues from any part of the coast of Great Britain to the eastward of Beachy Head. —

essel or Boat (not square rigged) found in the British or Irish Channels, or within 100 Leagues of ', with Spirits or Tobacco in certain Packages, or with other Goods. — If any vessel or boat, not being gged, belonging in the whole or in part to his Majesty's subjects, shall be found in any part of sh or Irish channels, or elsewhere on the high seas, within 100 leagues of any part of the coasts of ed Kingdom, or shall be discovered to have been within the said limits, having on board, or having oard, any brandy or other spirits in any cask or package of less size than forty gallons, (excepting the use of the seamen, not exceeding two gallons for each,) or any tea exceeding six pounds r any tobacco or snuff in any cask or package containing less than 450 pounds weight, or packed y within such cask or package, (except loose tobacco for the use of the seamen, not exceeding five or each,) or any cordage or other article adapted for slinging small casks, or any casks or other apable of containing liquids, of less size than forty gallons, of the sort used or fit for smuggling , or any materials for the forming such casks or vessels, or any siphon, tube, hose, or implements er, for the broaching or drawing any fluid, or any articles or implements or materials adapted for king tobacco or snuff, (unless the said cordage or articles are really necessary for the use of the are a part of the cargo, and included in the regular official documents of the said vessel,) then spirits, tea, tobacco, or snuff, together with the casks or packages, and the cordage or other and also the vessel or boat, with all her guns, furniture, ammunition, tackle, and apparel, shall ed. — § 3. *

reign Vessel (not square rigged) in which there shall be one or more Subjects of his Majesty. — If *gn vessel or boat* (not being square rigged) in which there shall be one or more subjects of his shall be found within four leagues of the North Foreland on the coast of Kent and Beachy Head ast of Sussex, or within eight leagues of any other part of the coast, not proceeding on her voyage, weather permitting, having on board or in any manner attached or affixed thereto, or conveying, conveyed in any manner, any brandy or other spirits, in any cask or package of less size than ons, (except only for the use of the seamen, not exceeding two gallons for each,) or any tea : six pounds, or any tobacco or snuff in any cask or package containing less than 450 pounds r packed separately within such cask or package, (except loose tobacco for the use of the sea- exceeding five pounds for each,) then such vessel or boat, with all her guns, furniture, ammuni- le, and apparel, shall be forfeited. — § 4. †

reign Vessel found at Anchor, or hovering within One League of the Coast. — If any foreign vessel er shall be found within one league of the coast, not proceeding on her voyage, having on board ed thereto, or having had on board, or conveying or having conveyed, within such distance, any le to forfeiture upon being imported into the United Kingdom, in such case the said vessel, with her guns, furniture, ammunition, tackle, and apparel, and all such goods, shall be for- § 5. ‡

throwing overboard Goods during Chase. — When any vessel or boat belonging in the whole or his Majesty's subjects, shall be found within four or eight leagues of the coast, or shall be found tish or Irish channels, or elsewhere within 100 leagues of the coast, and chase shall be given or de by any vessel in his Majesty's service, or in the service of the revenue, hoisting the proper s herein-after mentioned, in order to bring such vessel or boat to, if any person on board shall, e chase, or before such vessel or boat shall bring to, throw overboard the cargo, or any part, rough unavoidable necessity, or for the preservation of such vessel or boat, having a legal cargo or shall stave or destroy any part of the cargo to prevent seizure thereof, the said vessel or all her guns, furniture, ammunition, tackle, and apparel, shall be forfeited. — § 6.

(not square rigged) coming from Brest, or Places between Brest and Cape Finisterre, having on rits. — If any vessel (not being square rigged, nor a galliot of not less than 50 tons burthen) or oming from Brest on the coast of France, or from any place between Brest and Cape Finisterre st of Spain, including all islands, or coming from any place between the Helder Point on the olland and North Bergen on the coast of Norway, or from any place as far up the Cattegat as

s or Boats arriving in Port with Spirits or Tobacco in small Packages forfeited, and Persons Board knowing thereof, to forfeit 100l. — If any vessel or boat whatever shall arrive, or shall be iscovered to have been within any port, harbour, river, or creek, of the United Kingdom, not en therein by stress of weather, or other unavoidable accident, having on board, or in any man- ed or affixed thereto, or having had on board, or in any manner attached or affixed thereto, or or having conveyed in any manner within any such port, harbour, river, or creek, any brandy spirits, except rum, in any cask or package of less size or content than 40 gallons, except only of the seamen then belonging to and on board such vessel or boat, not exceeding 2 gallons for an ; or any tobacco or snuff in any cask or package, in which such tobacco or snuff could not mported into the United Kingdom in such vessel (except loose tobacco for the use of the seamen, ing 5 lbs. weight for each seaman,) every such vessel or boat, together with such spirits or tobacco rfeited; and every such person found, or discovered to have been on board such vessel or boat e of her becoming so liable to forfeiture, and knowing such spirits or tobacco to be or to have ard or attached to such vessel or boat, shall forfeit the sum of 100l., and shall be liable to deten- rosecution, and to be dealt with in the manner directed by the said act for the prevention of , in cases of persons found or discovered to have been on board of vessels liable to forfeiture act : Provided always that if it shall be made appear by proof on oath to the satisfaction of the ners of his Majesty's customs, that the said spirits or tobacco were on board without the know- ivity of the owner or master of such vessel or boat, and without any wilful neglect or want of care on their or either of their behalfs, then, and in such case, the vessel or boat shall not be rfeiture, although the persons concerned in placing the said spirits or tobacco on board, or ereof, shall be liable to detention and prosecution as aforesaid. — (7 Geo. 4. c. 48. § 16.)

as by the act 6 Geo. 4. c. 108., for the prevention of smuggling, foreign vessels laden with spirits less content than 40 gallons, or with certain other modes in which there shall be a certain pro- British subjects, are liable to seizure, if found within certain distances of the coast ; and it frequently happens that during chase, and previously to such vessels being taken possession of, sons who are believed to be British subjects, but of which there is no legal proof, quit such ving only foreigners on board, by which the law is evaded, and the vessels and cargoes escape n, although the cargoes may be evidently intended to be smuggled into the United Kingdom : It that in all such cases where any person shall escape from any such vessel or boat before pos- ken of it, every such person so escaping shall be deemed to be a subject of his Majesty within g of the said last mentioned act, unless it shall be proved to the contrary. — (7 & 8 Geo. 4.

hereas by the said act (6 Geo. 4. c. 108.) for the prevention of smuggling, it is enacted, that if vessel shall in certain cases therein described be found within 1 league of the coast of the gdom, such vessel shall be forfeited ; be it therefore enacted, that the like forfeiture shall, in s, attach equally to any foreign boat as fully and effectually, as if in the said act such forfeiture ade to attach to any foreign vessel or boat. — (7 & 8 Geo. 4. c. 56. § 15.)

Gottenburg, including all the islands, shall arrive in any of the ports of the United Kingdom, or sh
found at anchor or hovering within the limits of any of the ports, and not proceeding on her vo
having on board, for the use of the seamen, any spirits exceeding one half gallon for each, or havi
board any tea exceeding four pounds in the whole, or having on board any tobacco, (excepting
tobacco, not exceeding two pounds for each seaman,) then not only all such goods, but also the ves
boat, with all her materials, shall be forfeited. — § 7.

*Vessels (not square rigged) coming from Places between Brest and the Helder, having on board S,
&c.* — If any vessel (not being square rigged, nor a galliot of not less than 50 tons burthen) or an
coming from any place between Brest on the coast of France and the Helder Point on the coast of
land, including the Texel Isle, and all places on the Zuyder Zee, and all islands on the coasts of F
the Netherlands, and Holland, between Brest and the Texel, shall arrive in any of the ports of the U
Kingdom, or shall be found at anchor or hovering within the limits of any of the ports, and not pro
ing on her voyage, having on board, for the use of the seamen, any spirits exceeding one half gall
each, or having on board any tea exceeding two pounds, or having on board any tobacco, except
tobacco, not exceeding one pound for each seaman, then not only all such goods, but also the ves
boat, with all her materials, shall be forfeited. — § 8.

Vessels found or discovered within certain Distances of Guernsey, &c. — If any vessel or boat, wh
British or foreign, shall be found or discovered to have been within one league of the islands of Gue
Jersey, Alderney, Sark, or Man, not proceeding on her voyage, or within any bay, harbour, riv
creek of any one of the said islands, having on board, or in any manner conveying or having con
within the said distances or places, any goods which, by this or any other act relating to the custom
liable to forfeiture upon being imported into, exported from, or carried coastwise into the said is
the said vessel or boat, with all her guns, furniture, ammunition, tackle, and apparel, and all such
with their packages, and any other goods contained therein, shall be forfeited. — § 9.

*Vessels sailing from Guernsey, Jersey, Alderney, Sark, or Man, with a greater Number of Me
allowed.* — If any vessel or boat, belonging wholly or in part to his Majesty's subjects, shall sail
Guernsey, Jersey, Alderney, Sark, or Man, navigated by a greater number of persons than is allow
this act (as herein-after mentioned) in a vessel or boat of like size ; or if any vessel or boat shall sai
any of the said islands, having on board, or which shall take or have taken on board during the ve
any small cordage adapted for slinging small casks, or any more ankers, half ankers, or other small
or any tin or other cases, or bladders of less content than 40 gallons, and capable of containing flu
the sort used for smuggling spirits, than shall be necessary for the use of such vessel, or any materi
making any such small casks, cases, boxes, or bladders, or any siphon, tube, hose, or impleme
drawing off any fluid, more than is necessary for the ordinary purposes of the voyage, or any a
implements, or materials adapted for repacking tobacco or snuff on board, during the voyage, suc
vessel, or boat, with her guns, furniture, ammunition, tackle, and apparel, shall be forfeited, to
with all such articles. — § 10.

Vessels sailing from thence without a Clearance, forfeited. — No vessel or boat belonging wholl
part to his Majesty's subjects shall sail from Guernsey, Jersey, Alderney, Sark, or Man, without a
ance, whether in ballast or having a cargo, and if with a cargo the master shall give bond, in doub
value of the vessel or boat and of the cargo, for duly landing the same at the port for which the
clears ; and every such vessel or boat not having such clearance, or having a clearance for a carg
be found light, or with any part of the cargo discharged before delivery at the port specified in the
ance, (unless through necessity or for preservation of the vessel or boat, to be proved to the satis
of the commissioners of customs,) shall be forfeited. — § 11.

Vessels departing from Guernsey, &c. breaking Bulk. — If, after the departure from Guernsey,
Alderney, or Sark, of any vessel or boat belonging wholly or in part to his Majesty's subjects, hav
board any spirits, tobacco, snuff, tea, or wine, bulk be broken, or any of the cargo unladen, or any
ation be made in the form, size, description, or number of the packages, or in the quantity, qua
mode of package, at any time in the prosecution of the voyage towards the United Kingdom, or an
place for which the vessel or boat shall have cleared out, such vessel or boat, with her tackle and
ture, shall be forfeited ; but no forfeiture shall be incurred for breaking bulk or unlading the
through unavoidable necessity and distress, nor for any alteration in the cargo, if occasioned by ne
or accident, or made for the preservation of the vessel or boat, to be proved to the satisfaction of th
missioners of customs. — § 12.

Vessels found within the Limits of a Port with a Cargo, and afterwards found light. — If any v
boat whatever shall be found within the limits of any port with a cargo on board, and such vess
afterwards be found light or in ballast, and the master is unable to give a due account, such vessel
with the guns, furniture, ammunition, tackle, and apparel, shall be forfeited. — § 13.

Vessels not bringing to during Chase may be fired at. — In case any vessel or boat, liable to sei
examination, shall not bring to on being required, on being chased by any vessel in his Majesty'
having the proper ensign hoisted, or by any vessel employed for the prevention of smuggling un
admiralty or the commissioners of customs, having a pendant and ensign hoisted, of such descrip
his Majesty, by order in council, or by proclamation under the great seal, shall have ordered, it s
lawful for the captain, master, or other person having the command of such vessel (first causing a
be fired as a signal) to fire at or into such vessel or boat ; and such captain, master, or other perso
be indemnified from any indictment, penalty, or action for damages for so doing ; and in case any
shall be wounded, maimed, or killed by such firing, and the said captain, master, or other person,
sued, molested, or prosecuted, or shall be brought before any justices of the peace for such firing,
ing, maiming, or killing, all such justices are authorised to admit every such captain, master, or
to bail. — § 14.

Persons not to hoist Flags in Imitation of those used in the Navy. — If any person shall wear, ca
hoist in or on board any ship, vessel, or boat belonging to any of his Majesty's subjects, whether me
or otherwise, without particular warrant from his Majesty, or the commissioners for executing th
of high admiral, the union jack, or any pendant, ensign, or colours usually worn by his Majesty's s
any flag, jack, pendant, ensign, or colours, resembling those of his Majesty, or used on board his M
ships, or any other ensign or colours than the ensign or colours by any proclamation prescribe
worn ; in every such case the master, or the owner or owners being on board, and every other p
offending, shall forfeit 50l., which shall be recovered, with costs, either in the High Court of Ad
or in the courts of King's Bench or Exchequer at Westminster or Dublin, or in the courts of
or Exchequer in Scotland, or before any two justices of the peace ; and it shall be lawful for any c
the navy, customs, or excise, to enter on board any such ship, vessel, or boat, and to seize any s
hibited flag, jack, pendant, ensign, or colours, and the same shall thereupon become forfeite
Majesty's use. — § 15.

All vessels and boats made use of in the removal, carriage, or conveyance of any goods liab
feiture under this or any other act relating to the customs, shall be forfeited. — § 16.

Boats belonging to Vessels. — The owner of every vessel belonging in whole or in part to an
Majesty's subjects shall paint upon the outside of the stern of every boat belonging to such ve
name of such vessel, and the port to which she belongs, and the master's name withinside the
in white or yellow Roman letters, not less than two inches in length, on a black ground, on pa
forfeiture of such boat. — § 17.

Boats not belonging to Vessels. — The owner of every boat not belonging to any vessel, shall pa
the stern in white or yellow Roman letters of two inches in length, on a black ground, the nar
owner of the boat, and the port to which she belongs, on pain of the forfeiture of such boat. — §

ving double Sides or Bottoms. — All vessels and boats, belonging in the whole or in part to his *ubjects*, having false bulkheads, false bows, double sides or bottoms, or any secret or disguised *soever* in the construction of the said vessel or boat, for the purpose of concealing goods, or *hole*, pipe, or other device in or about the vessel or boat, adapted for the purpose of running *be* forfeited, with all the guns, furniture, ammunition, tackle, and apparel belonging to such *at*; and all goods liable to the payment of duties, or prohibited to be imported, found concealed *r* in or underneath the ballast, or in any other place on board, shall be forfeited. — § 19.

LICENCES.

&c. forfeited, unless licensed. — All vessels belonging in the whole or in part to his Majesty's *nless* square rigged), and all vessels whatsoever belonging as aforesaid, the length of which *eater* than in the proportion of three feet to one foot in breadth; and all vessels belonging as *rmed* for resistance (otherwise than is herein-after provided); and all boats whatsoever belong- *said*, which shall be found within any of the limits or distances aforesaid; shall be forfeited, *wners* thereof shall have obtained a licence for navigating the same from the commissioners as herein-after directed. — § 20.

be navigated by a certain Number of Men. — No vessel or boat so belonging (not being a *at* the time fitted and rigged as such) shall be navigated by a greater number of men (officers *cluded*) than in the following proportions; that is to say,

30 tons or under, and above 5 tons, 4 men.
60 tons or under, and above 30 tons, 5 men.
80 tons or under, and above 60 tons, 6 men.
100 tons or under, and above 80 tons, 7 men.

that tonnage, one man for every 15 tons of such additional tonnage.

gger, in the following proportions; that is to say, if of

30 tons or under, 8 men.
50 tons or under, and above 30 tons, 9 men.
60 tons or under, and above 50 tons, 10 men.
80 tons or under, and above 60 tons, 11 men.
100 tons or under, and above 80 tons, 12 men.

e 100 tons, 1 man for every 10 tons of such additional tonnage.

vessel, boat, or lugger, navigated with a greater number of men than in the proportions *tioned*, be found within any of the distances aforesaid, the same shall be forfeited, unless such *or* lugger, shall be especially licensed for that purpose by the commissioners of customs. —

ot required for certain Vessels. — Nothing in this act shall extend to forfeit any square rigged *e* burthen of 200 tons or upwards by admeasurement, for being armed for resistance, having *o* carriage guns of the caliber not exceeding four pounds, and small arms not exceeding two *every* ten men; or any vessel, boat, or lugger belonging to the royal family, or being in the *e* navy, victualling, ordnance, customs, excise, or post-office; nor any whale boat, or boat *ved* in the fisheries, or any boat belonging to any square rigged vessel in the merchants' ser- *ty* life boat or tow boat used in towing vessels belonging to licensed pilots; nor to any boat *n* rivers or inland navigation, on account of such ship, vessel, boat, or lugger not being li- *22.*

contain certain Particulars. — Every licence granted by the commissioners of customs for *quiring* licence, shall contain the proper description of such vessel, the names of the owners, *ode*, and the manner and the limits in which the same is to be employed; and, if armed, the *l* description of arms, and the quantity of ammunition, together with any other particulars *mmissioners* may require. — § 23.

ence granted to a Ship, Owners to give Security by Bond in certain Conditions. — Before such *be* delivered, or have effect, the owners shall give security by bond of two or more sufficient *g* housekeepers), in treble the value of such vessel (not exceeding in any case 3,000*l.* for a *l* vessel) with condition, that the vessel shall not be employed in the importation, landing, or *any* prohibited or uncustomable goods, contrary to this act, or any other act relating to the *cise*, nor in the exportation of any goods which are or may be prohibited to be exported, *landing* of any goods contrary to law; nor shall receive on board, or be found at sea or in *y* goods subject to forfeiture; nor shall do any act contrary to this act, or any act hereafter *elating* to the customs or excise, or for the protection of trade and commerce; nor shall be *erwise* than mentioned in the licence, and within the limits therein mentioned; and in case *ing* up, or disposal of the vessel, then the licence shall be delivered within six months from *uch* loss, breaking up, or disposal, to the collector or principal officer at the port to which such *elong.* — § 24.

nd to be given at the Port to which the Vessel belongs. — Such bond shall be given at the port *n* vessel shall belong, and at no other, without the consent of the commissioners of customs; *ns* who are to become such security shall be persons, whether owners or not, approved by *and* comptroller of the port, and residing at or near such port; and the collector and *hall* certify upon such licence, before they issue the same, that the security has been given. —

Boat to contain certain Particulars. — Every licence granted for any boat requiring licence *the* description of the boat, with the names of the owners, and their abode, and the manner *which* such boat is to be used, together with any other particulars which the commissioners *and* the owners of the said boat shall give their own security by bond, in treble the value *the* like condition as is herein-before required on licences granted for vessels; and such bond *able* to the same stamp duty. — § 26.

ers may refuse Licence, or revoke Licence when granted. — It shall be lawful for the com- *restrict* the granting of a licence for any vessel or boat, in any way that they may deem *the* security of the revenue; and in case the commissioners shall have granted a licence for *d* shall deem it necessary to require fresh security, they are empowered so to do, by an order *der* their hands; and a copy of such order shall be left either with the owners of such vessel, *erson* in whose custody the same shall then be; and after the delivery of such order, the *d* shall be null and void, and the owners are to deliver up the said licence to the collector at *hich* such vessel or boat shall belong, within three months from the day when such order *ered*; and in default, the owners shall forfeit 100*l.*; and if any vessel or boat requiring such *e* found without such licence, or shall be found to have been used in any trade, or in any *nan* such as shall be specified in such licence, in such case the said vessel or boat, with all *aiture*, ammunition, tackle, and apparel, and all the goods laden on board, shall be forfeited.

be taken to the Collector at the Port to be registered. — The owner of every vessel or boat *, before* such vessel or boat first proceeds to sea, or departs out of any port, bring such licence *r* or proper officer, and the said collector or officer is to register the same; and in default of *nging* the same, the said licence shall be void; and the master is to produce such licence to

any officer of the army, navy, or marines, duly authorised and on full pay, or officer of customs o who shall board such vessel or boat within the limits aforesaid, and shall demand a sight of the sa in case of a refusal to produce the same, or the same shall not be on board, or if the licence p shall be without an endorsement thereon that the proper security hath been given, in such case t or boat shall be forfeited, with her guns, furniture, ammunition, tackle, and apparel. — § 28.

Vessels in course of Removal to obtain Certificate. — It shall be lawful for the commissioners, to their satisfaction that the master or owner is desirous of removing such vessel or boat to the which she belongs, for the purpose of obtaining a licence and giving security, to grant a certificate master or owner of such proof having been made; and in such case, so long as such vessel or b be in her voyage to the port to which the vessel or boat belongs, such vessel or boat shall not be forfeiture on account of not being licensed. — § 29.

Counterfeiting Licences. — If any person shall counterfeit, erase, alter, or falsify any licence, knowingly make use of any licence so counterfeited, erased, altered, or falsified, such person sha 500*l.* — § 30.

Licensed Vessel being lost, broken up, &c. — Whenever any licensed vessel or boat shall be lost up, captured, burnt, seized, and condemned, sold, or otherwise disposed of, the licence shall be d up to the collector at the port to which such vessel or boat belongs, within six calendar month case of the licence being lost or taken by the enemy, proof thereof on oath shall be made within period before the collector; and in default, the owner and the master shall forfeit 100*l.* — § 31.

Goods.

Uncustomed or prohibited Goods unshipped or removed illegally, &c. forfeited. — If any goods the payment of duties shall be unshipped from any vessel or boat (customs and other duties not b paid or secured), or if any prohibited goods shall be imported; or if any goods whatsoever, wh have been imported, warehoused, or otherwise secured, either for home consumption or exportat be clandestinely or illegally removed out of any warehouse or place of security; in such case all s shall be forfeited, together with all horses and other animals, and all carriages and other things, of in the removal of such goods. — § 32.

Prohibited Goods shipped or brought to the Quay. — If any goods prohibited to be exported sha on board any vessel or boat, with intent to be shipped for exportation, or shall be brought to a wharf, or other place, in order to be put on board any vessel or boat for the purpose of being exp if any goods prohibited to be exported shall be found in any package, produced to the officers of as containing goods not prohibited; in such case not only all such prohibited goods, but also goods packed therewith, shall be forfeited. — § 33.

Goods liable to Forfeiture may be seized. — All vessels and boats, and all goods whatsoever liab feiture under this or any other act, may be seized in any place, either upon land or water, by ar of his Majesty's army, navy, or marines, duly authorised and on full pay, or officers of customs c or any person having authority to seize from the commissioners of customs or excise; and all boats, and goods, so seized, shall be delivered into the care of the proper officer. — § 34.

Making collusive Seizures. — If any officer of the customs, or any officer of the army, navy, or and any other person employed by the commissioners of the customs, shall make any collusive se deliver up, or make any agreement to deliver up, or not to seize, any vessel or boat, or any go to forfeiture, or shall take any bribe, gratuity, recompence, or reward, for the neglect or non-per of his duty, every such officer or other person shall forfeit 500*l.*, and be rendered incapable of se Majesty in any office, either civil or military; and if any person shall give, or offer, or promise any bribe, recompence, or reward, or make any collusive agreement with any such officer, to ind in any way to neglect his duty, or to do, conceal, or connive at, any act whereby any of the pro any act of parliament may be evaded, every such person shall, whether the offer be accepted or p or not, forfeit 500*l.* — § 35.

Search for prohibited and uncustomed Goods. — It shall be lawful for any officer of the army, marines, authorised and on full pay, or for any officer of customs, producing his warrant or depu required), to go on board any vessel within the limits of any of the ports of this kingdom, and to and to search the cabin, and all other parts, for prohibited and uncustomed goods, and to remain during the whole time that such vessel shall continue within the limits of such port; and also any person or persons, either on board or who shall have landed from any vessel; provided su shall have good reason to suppose that such person hath any uncustomed or prohibited goods about his person; and if any person shall obstruct, oppose, or molest any such officer in going o ing on board, or in entering or searching such vessel or person, such person shall forfeit 100*l.* —

Officers, before searching People, to take them before a Justice, Collector, or Comptroller of Cu Before any person shall be searched by any such officer, it shall be lawful for such person to req officer to take him before any justice of the peace, or before the collector, comptroller, or othe officer of customs, who shall determine whether there is reasonable ground to suppose that su has any uncustomed or prohibited goods about his person; and if it shall appear to such justice, comptroller, or other officer of customs, that there is reasonable ground, then such justice, comptroller, or other officer of customs, shall direct such person to be searched in such manner a think fit; but if it shall appear that there is not reasonable ground, then such justice, collect troller, or other officer of customs, shall forthwith discharge such person, who shall not in sue liable to be searched; and every such officer is authorised to take such person, upon demand, l such justice, collector, comptroller, or other officer of customs, detaining him in the mean time : that no person, being a female, shall be searched by any other person than a female duly authori commissioners of customs. — § 37.

Officer not taking suspected Persons before a Magistrate. — If any such officer shall not person with reasonable despatch before such justice, collector, comptroller, or other officer o when required, or shall require any person to be searched by him, not having reasonable suppose that such person has any uncustomed or prohibited goods about his person, such o forfeit 10*l.* — § 38.

Passengers having Goods in Possession. — If any passenger or other person on board any boat shall, upon being questioned by any officer of customs, whether he has any foreign g his person, or in his possession, deny the same, and any such goods shall, after such denial vered upon his person, or in his possession, such goods shall be forfeited, and such person s treble the value. — § 39.

Officers with Writs of Assistance may enter Houses to search. — It shall be lawful for an customs, or persons acting under the direction of the commissioners, authorised by writ of under the seal of the court of Exchequer, to take a constable, headborough, or other pu inhabiting near the place, and in the daytime, to enter into any house, shop, cellar, wareho or other place, and, in case of resistance, to break open doors, chests, trunks, and other pack to seize any uncustomed or prohibited goods, and to put the same in the Custom-house wa the port next to the place from whence such goods shall be so taken : Provided always, t purposes of this act, any such constable, headborough, or other public officer duly swo may act as well without the limits of any parish or place for which he shall be sworn, as limits. — § 40.

All writs of assistance so issued from the court of Exchequer shall continue in force durin of the reign in which such writs shall have been granted, and for six months from the co such reign. — § 41.

Officers seizing Goods to carry them to the Custom-house Warehouse. — If any goods liable
ture under this or any other act relating to the revenue of customs, shall be stopped by any
fficer, or other person acting by virtue of any act of parliament, or otherwise duly authorised,
ods shall be carried to the Custom-house warehouse next to the place where the goods were
and delivered to the proper officer, within 48 hours after the said goods were stopped. — § 42.

stopped by Police Officers may be retained until Trial. — If any such goods shall be stopped by
lice officer, on suspicion that the same have been feloniously stolen, it shall be lawful for the
o carry the same to the police office to which the offender is taken, there to remain until the
he offender ; and in such case the officer is to give notice in writing to the commissioners of
of his having so detained the said goods, with the particulars of the same; and immediately after
, all such goods are to be deposited in the Custom-house warehouse, to be proceeded against
g to law ; and in case any police officer shall neglect to convey the same to such warehouse, or
he notice of having stopped the same, such officer shall forfeit 20*l.* — § 43.

issioners of Treasury or Commissioners of Customs may restore Seizures. — It shall be lawful for
missioners of the treasury, or the commissioners of customs, by any order under their hands, to
ny vessel, boat, goods, or commodities whatever, seized as aforesaid, to be delivered to the pro-
whether condemnation shall have taken place or not, upon such terms as they may deem ex-
and which shall be mentioned in the said order ; and it shall be also lawful for the said commis-
f the treasury, and the said commissioners of customs, to mitigate any penalty, or any part of
alty, incurred under any laws relating to customs, or to trade and navigation : Provided, that no
nall be entitled to the benefit of any order for delivery or mitigation, unless the terms expressed
id order are fully complied with. — § 44.

PENALTIES.

y on Persons unshipping or harbouring prohibited or uncustomed Goods, treble their Value, or
*every person not arrested and detained as herein-after mentioned, who shall, either in the United
a or the Isle of Man, assist in the unshipping of any goods prohibited, or the duties for which
t been paid or secured, or who shall knowingly harbour, keep, or conceal, or shall knowingly
r suffer to be harboured, kept, or concealed, any goods which have been illegally unshipped
payment of duties, or which have been illegally removed without payment of the same, from any
se or place of security, or shall knowingly harbour, keep, or conceal, or permit or suffer to be
d, kept, or concealed, any goods prohibited to be imported, or to be used or consumed ; and
son, either in the United Kingdom or the Isle of Man, to whose possession any such uncustomed
ited goods shall knowingly come ; shall forfeit either treble value, or 100*l.*, at the election of the
oners of customs. — § 45.

y on Persons unshipping Drawback or Bounty Goods. — If any goods, upon which there is a
or bounty, shall be shipped to be exported, and shall afterwards be unshipped with intention
nded (unless in case of distress), in such case the said goods shall be forfeited, and the master
r person concerned in the unshipping, and the person to whose hands the same shall knowingly
who shall knowingly harbour, keep, or conceal, or suffer to be harboured, kept, or concealed,
s, shall for every such offence forfeit treble value, or 100*l.*, at the election of the commissioners
ns. — § 46.

s insuring the Delivery of smuggled Goods. — Every person who, by way of insurance or other-
il undertake to deliver any goods to be imported at any port, without paying the duties due on
on, or any prohibited goods, or in pursuance of such insurance, or otherwise, shall deliver any
ed or prohibited goods; every such person, and every aider or abettor thereof, shall forfeit 500*l.*
above any other penalty to which by law he may be liable ; and every person who shall agree
y money for the insurance or conveyance of such goods, or shall receive such goods into his
, or suffer the same to be so received, shall also forfeit 500*l.* over and above any penalty to
law he may be liable on account of such goods. — § 47.

Goods for Sale under Pretence of being run or prohibited — If any person shall offer for sale
, under pretence that the same are prohibited, or have been unshipped and run on shore without
f duties, in such case all such goods, (although not liable to duties, or prohibited,) shall be for-
t the person offering the same for sale shall forfeit treble value, or 100*l.*, at the election of the
ners of customs. — § 48.

found on board Vessels liable to Forfeiture, or carrying smuggled Goods. — Every person, *being*
who shall be found or discovered to have been on board any vessel or boat liable to forfeiture,
found within four or eight leagues of the coast, or for being found or discovered to have been
y of the distances in this act mentioned, having on board, or in any manner attached thereto,
had on board, or in any manner attached thereto, or conveying, or having conveyed in any
uch goods as subject such vessel or boat to forfeiture, or who shall be found or discovered to
on board any vessel or boat, from which any part of the cargo shall have been thrown over-
ing chase, or staved or destroyed, shall forfeit 100*l.* ; and every person, *not being a subject,*
be found or discovered to have been on board any vessel or boat, liable to forfeiture for any of
f aforesaid, within one league of the coast of the United Kingdom, or of the Isle of Man, or
y bay, harbour, river, or creek of the said island, shall forfeit 100*l.* ; and it shall be lawful for
of the army, navy, or marines, duly authorised and on full pay, or any officer of customs or
other person acting in their aid, or duly employed for the prevention of smuggling, to stop,
d detain every such person, and to carry such person before two justices of the peace in the
ngdom, or a governor, deputy governor, or deemster in the Isle of Man, to be dealt with as
er directed : Provided always, that any such person proving, to the satisfaction of such justices,
deputy governor, or deemster, that he was only a passenger in such vessel or boat, and had no
natever either in the vessel or boat, or in the cargo on board the same, shall be forthwith dis-
r such justices. — § 49.

unshipping Spirits or Tobacco. — Every person who shall unship, or be aiding in the unshipping
rits or tobacco, liable to forfeiture, either in the United Kingdom or the Isle of Man, or who
r, convey, or conceal, or be aiding or concerned in the carrying, conveying, or concealing of
spirits or tobacco, shall forfeit 100*l.* ; and every such person may be detained by any officer
esty's army, navy, or marines, or any officer of customs or excise, or other person acting
or duly employed for the prevention of smuggling, and taken before two justices of the
a governor, deputy governor, or deemster of the Isle of Man, to be dealt with as herein-
ted. — § 50.

arrested, and making Escape. — If any person liable to be arrested, shall not be detained at
f committing the offence, or after detention shall make his escape, it shall be lawful for
of the army, navy, or marines, or any officer of customs or excise, or any other person acting
d, to arrest and detain such person at any time afterwards, and to carry him before two justices
e, to be dealt with as if detained at the time of committing the offence. — § 51.

on Persons making Signals to Smugglers. — No person shall, after sunset and before sunrise
e 21st of September and the 1st of April, or after 8 in the evening and before 6 in the
; any other time of the year, make, aid, or assist in making, or be present for the purpose
r assisting in the making of any light, fire, flash, or blaze, or any signal by smoke, or by any
works, flags, firing of any gun or other fire-arms, or any other contrivance or device, or any
al in or on board or from any vessel or boat, or on or from any part of the coast or shore, or

within six miles of any part of such coasts or shores, for the purpose of making or giving any sig
any person on board any smuggling vessel or boat, whether any person so on board be or be not v
distance to see or hear any such light, fire, flash, blaze, or signal; and if any person, contrary t
act, make or cause to be made, or aid or assist in making, any such light, fire, flash, blaze, or signal
person shall be guilty of a misdemeanor; and it shall be lawful for any person to arrest the perso
to carry such person so offending before any two justices of peace residing near the place, who, i
see cause, shall commit the offender to the next county gaol, there to remain until the next co
oyer or terminer, great session or gaol delivery, or until such person shall be delivered by due c
of law; and it shall not be necessary to prove, on any indictment or information, that any vessel o
was actually on the coast; and the offender being convicted, shall, by order of the court,
forfeit and pay the penalty of 100l., or, at the discretion of such court, be sentenced or committ
the common gaol or house of correction, there to be kept to hard labour for not exceeding one
— § 52.

Proof of not making Signal to lie on the Defendant. — In case any person be charged with or in
for having made or caused to be made, or been aiding in making, or been present for the purp
making or aiding in making any such fire, light, flash, blaze, or other signal, the proof that such
was not made with such intent, and for such purpose, shall be upon the defendant against whom
charge is made, or such indictment is found. — § 53.

Any Person may put out Lights for Signals. — It shall be lawful for any person to put out and
guish or prevent any such light, fire, flash, or blaze, or any smoke, signal, rocket, firework, noise, or
device or contrivance, and to enter into and upon any lands for that purpose, without being liable
indictment, suit, or action. — § 54.

Persons resisting Officers, or destroying Goods, to prevent Seizure. — If any person shall hinder, o
molest, or obstruct any officer of the army, navy, or marines, or any officer of customs or excise,
execution of his duty, or in the due seizing of any goods liable to forfeiture, or any person acting
aid, or duly employed for the prevention of smuggling, or shall rescue or cause to be rescued any
which have been seized, or shall attempt to do so, or shall, before or at or after any seizure, stave,
or otherwise destroy any goods, to prevent the seizure thereof, or the securing the same, the p
offending shall forfeit for every such offence 200l. — § 55.

FELONIES.

*Three or more Persons armed with Fire-arms, assembled to assist in the illegal Exportation or Le
of prohibited or uncustomed Goods.* — If any persons to the number of three or more, armed with fir
or other offensive weapons, shall, within the United Kingdom, or within the limits of any port, ha
or creek thereof, be assembled in order to be aiding and assisting in the illegal exportation of any
prohibited to be exported, or in the carrying of such goods in order to such exportation, or in the
landing, running, or carrying away of prohibited or uncustomed goods, or goods liable to pay any
which have not been paid or secured, or in the illegal carrying of any goods from any warehouse o
place, as shall have been deposited therein, for the security of the home consumption duties there
for preventing the use or consumption thereof in the United Kingdom, or in the illegal relanding
goods which shall have been exported upon debenture or certificate, or in rescuing or taking aw
such goods as aforesaid, after seizure, from the officer of customs authorised to seize the same,
person employed by them or assisting them, or from the place where the same shall have been loc
them, or in rescuing any person who shall have been apprehended for any of the offences made fel
in the preventing the apprehension of any person who shall have been guilty of such offence; or
any persons to the number of three or more, so armed as aforesaid, shall, within this kingdom, or
the limits of any port, harbour, or creek thereof, be so aiding; every person so offending, and eve
son assisting therein, shall be guilty of *felony*, and suffer death as a felon, *without benefit of*
— § 56.

Persons shooting at any Boat belonging to the Navy or Customs. — If any person shall maliciously s
or upon any vessel or boat belonging to his Majesty's navy, or in the service of the revenue in any
the British or Irish channels, or elsewhere on the high seas, within 100 leagues of any part of the c
the United Kingdom, or shall maliciously shoot at, maim, or dangerously wound, any officer of th
navy, or marines, or any officer of customs or excise, or any person acting in his aid, or employed
prevention of smuggling, in the due execution of his office, every person so offending, and every
aiding, shall be guilty of *felony*, and suffer death as a felon, *without benefit of clergy.* — § 57.

*Any Person in Company with Four others passing with Goods liable to Forfeiture, armed or disgu
If any person, being in company with more than four other persons, be found with any goods liable
feiture, or in company with one other person, within five miles of any navigable river, carrying o
arms or weapons, or disguised in any way, every such person shall be guilty of *felony*, and, on con
be *transported as a felon* for seven years; and if such offender shall return before the expiration of th
years, he shall suffer as a felon, and have execution awarded against him as a person attainted of
without benefit of clergy. — § 58.

Persons assaulting Officer by Force or Violence may be transported, &c. — If any person shall by
violence assault, resist, oppose, molest, hinder, or obstruct any officer of the army, navy, or mari
any officer of customs or excise, or other person acting in their aid, or duly employed for the pre
of smuggling, in the due execution of their office or duty, such person shall be adjudged a felon, a
be transported for seven years, or sentenced to be imprisoned in any house of correction or c
gaol, and kept to hard labour for not exceeding three years, at the discretion of the court. — § 59.

OFFICERS.

*Commanding Officers of Vessels in the Service may haul their Vessels on Shore, without being liable
Action for so doing.* — It shall be lawful for the commanding officer of any vessel or boat employed
prevention of smuggling, to haul any such vessel or boat upon any part of the coasts of the United
dom, or the shores, banks, or beaches of any river, creek, or inlet of the same, (not being a ga
pleasure ground, or place ordinarily used for any bathing machine,) which shall be deemed m
venient for that purpose, and to moor any such vessel or boat below high water mark, and over wh
tide flows on ordinary occasions, and to continue such vessel or boat so moored, for such time as
officer shall deem necessary; and such officer, or persons acting under his direction, shall not be
any indictment, action, or suit for so doing. — § 60.

Persons wounded in the Service of the Customs. — In all cases where any officer or seaman emp
the service of the customs or excise shall be killed, maimed, wounded, or in any way injured in
execution of his office, or if any person acting in his aid shall be so killed, maimed, wounded, o
way injured while so aiding, it shall be lawful for the commissioners of customs and excise to ma
provisions for the officer or person so injured, or for the widows and families of such as shall be k
they shall be authorised to do by warrant from the commissioners of the treasury. — § 61.

SEIZURES.

Condemned Vessels and Goods, how to be disposed of. — All vessels and boats, and all goods wha
which shall have been seized and condemned, shall be disposed of as soon as conveniently may
condemnation, in the following manner; (that is to say,) all goods of a description admissible
shall be sold by public auction, at a price not less than the duty upon importation; and in case su
will not fetch the duty, shall be put up to sale for exportation, and in case they do not sell for exp

ods shall be destroyed; and all prohibited goods shall be put up for sale for exportation to the
, and in case they do not sell, then shall be destroyed; all vessels or boats calculated for the
ercantile trade of this kingdom shall be put up for sale to the best bidder; and all vessels or
lated for smuggling shall be broken up and destroyed, and the materials shall be put up to sale
bidder: Provided always, that if the commissioners of customs shall deem any of the vessels or
ssary for the public service, it shall be lawful for them to cause the same to be used for the said
§ 62.

REWARDS.

to Officers for detaining Smugglers. — It shall be lawful for the commissioners of customs to
ny officer or person detaining any person liable to detention, to be paid upon conviction, any re-
may think fit, not exceeding 20l. for each person. — § 63.
where pecuniary Penalties are recovered. — It shall be lawful for the commissioners of customs
following reward to any officers, or persons aforesaid, by whose means any pecuniary penalty
ion is recovered; (that is to say,) one third of the penalty or sum recovered. — § 64.
for Seizures. — There shall be paid for any seizure made by any officer of the army, navy, or
any officer of customs or excise, or other person deputed or employed by the commissioners of
excise, the following rewards: —

In the case of seizures of spirits and tobacco:
arties are detained and carried before two justices of the peace, the whole:
ore, not being the whole, are detained and convicted, seven eighths:
g a seafaring man and convicted, three fourths:
ained with the vessel or means of conveyance, three fourths:
n is detained and convicted, not a seafaring man, five eighths:
carriage with its lading is seized, without any person being detained, one third:
ad sunk and concealed, and the smuggler afterwards convicted in consequence thereof, and by
ons of the individuals so finding them, one half:
nd and no person subsequently convicted, one eighth:
ed and parties subsequently convicted in consequence of such seizure, and by the exertion of
s, one half:
zed only, one eighth, or such other part as the commissioners of the customs shall think pro-
xceeding one fourth.

In the case of seizures of goods prohibited to be imported:
r importation, or other means of conveyance, seized, or any person prosecuted to conviction on
the same, two thirds:
, one half.

In the case of seizures of goods not before enumerated:
other means of conveyance, seized, or any person prosecuted to conviction on account of the
half.
, one fourth.

In the case of goods destroyed:
other means of conveyance, seized, or any person prosecuted to conviction on account of the
iety of the appraised value or amount of duty:
, one fourth of appraised value or amount of duty.

In the case of seizures of vessels and boats:
iety of the produce:
the public service or broken up, a moiety of appraised value.

In the case of seizures of cattle and carriages:
three fourths of the produce of the sale. — § 65.

lways, that the aforesaid rewards shall be paid, subject to a deduction of ten per cent on ac-
charges and other expenses. — § 66.
is and Seizures to be regulated by Orders in Council. — Every such reward, or part of any such
the value thereof, as shall be payable to any officers, non-commissioned officers, petty officers,
rivates of his Majesty's army, navy, or marines, or acting under the orders of the admiralty,
ibuted in such proportions, and according to such rules, as his Majesty shall by order in coun-
clamation, be pleased to direct. — § 67.
ners may distribute Officers' Shares of Seizures so as to reward Persons not present. — It shall
the commissioners of customs or excise, in case of any seizure of vessels, boats, or goods, or
sion of any parties, to direct the distribution of the seizor's share of such vessels, boats, or
ny penalties or rewards, so as to enable any officers, or persons acting under the authority of
missioners, or through whose information or means such seizure shall have been made, or
ered, or party apprehended, *who shall not have been actually present at the making of the*
icipate in such proportions as the said commissioners shall deem expedient. — § 68.
cers act negligently or collusively. — Upon proof being made to the satisfaction of the com-
customs or excise, that any officer, or person as aforesaid, shall have acted collusively or
the making of any seizure, it shall be lawful for the commissioners to direct that the whole,
the proportion of such seizure, be applied to the use of his Majesty. — § 69.
ting on the Sea, not to be taken up but by Officers. — And as it hath frequently happened that
been imported, and that the persons importing have alleged that the same had been found
or sunk in the sea; and great frauds have been practised with regard to such spirits, by the
porting the same, it is enacted, that no person or persons, being a subject or subjects, other
of the navy, customs, or excise, or some person authorised in that behalf, shall intermeddle
up any spirits, being in casks of less content than forty gallons, which may be found floating
in the sea; and if any spirits shall be taken up, and shall be found on board any vessel or
he limits of any port in the United Kingdom or Isle of Man, or within the distances in this
d, the vessel or boat, together with such spirits, shall be forfeited, and the persons in whose
same shall be found shall forfeit treble value, or 50l., at the election of the commissioners
§ 70.
Persons giving Information of Goods floating or sunk. — Provided always, that if any person
any spirits, being in casks of less content than forty gallons, which may be found floating
in the sea, and shall give information to any officer of customs or other person authorised to
so that seizure shall be made, the person giving such information shall be entitled to receive
as the commissioners of customs may direct. — § 71.
o poor Persons confined for Offences against Laws of Customs and Excise. — For the necessary
f any poor person confined in the United Kingdom, or in the Isle of Man, under any ex-
ner process for the recovery of any duties or penalties, either upon bond or otherwise, under
her act relating to the revenue of customs or excise, sued for under any order of the com-
customs or excise, it shall be lawful for the commissioners of customs or excise, to cause an
t exceeding 7½d., and not less than 4½d. per day, to be made to any such poor person, out of
ising from the duties of customs or excise, as the case may require. — § 72.

JURISDICTION.

Penalties and Forfeitures, how to be sued for.—All penalties and forfeitures incurred or impose
and may be sued for, prosecuted, and recovered by action of debt, bill, plaint, or information in an
of record at Westminster, or in the courts of Exchequer in Scotland or in Dublin, or in the royal c
the islands of Guernsey, Jersey, Alderney, Sark, or Man, in the name of his Majesty's attorney gen
in the name of some officer of customs, or by information before any two justices of the peace in the
Kingdom, or before any governor, deputy governor, or deemster in the Isle of Man : Provided alwa
all the powers vested in any justices by virtue of this act shall be vested in the commissioners or a
commissioners of customs in Ireland, or any two of them, and the sub-commissioners lawfully appo
Ireland to hear and determine complaints, so far as regards any offences committed in Ireland. —

Offences on the High Seas deemed to have been committed at the Place into which the Offender is
In case any offence shall be committed upon the high seas, or any penalty or forfeiture shall be i
upon the high seas, such offence shall, for the purpose of prosecution, be deemed to have been commit
such penalties and forfeitures to have been incurred, at the place on land, into which the person con
such offence or incurring such penalty or forfeiture shall be taken ; and in case such place on la
tuated within any city, borough, liberty, division, franchise, or town corporate, as well any justic
peace for such city, borough, liberty, division, franchise, or town corporate, as any justice of the pea
county, shall have jurisdiction to hear and determine all cases of offences so committed upon
seas : Provided always, that all offences committed in any city, borough, liberty, division, franc
town corporate, shall be deemed to have been committed in the county within which such city, b
liberty, division, franchise, or town corporate is situated, and as well any justices of the said city, b
liberty, division, franchise, or town corporate, as any justices of any county in which such city, b
liberty, division, franchise, or town corporate is situated, shall have jurisdiction to hear and deterr
same. — § 74.

Justices to summon Party accused, and in Default of Appearance to proceed to the Hearing and
tion.—In cases where any information shall be exhibited before two or more justices, or governor
governor, or deemster of the Isle of Man, for the recovery of any penalty (except as herein-after pr
it shall be lawful for the said justices, or governor, deputy governor, or deemster, to summon t
accused, and upon his appearance or default, to proceed to the examination of the matter, and u
proof thereof, either upon the voluntary confession of such party, or upon the oath of one or mo
ble witness or witnesses, to convict the offender in the said penalty ; and in case of the nonpayment
the justices, or governor, deputy governor, or deemster, is to cause the same, by warrant of dist
sale, to be levied upon the goods of the offender ; (or, in case it shall appear that such offender
sufficient goods whereon to levy the said penalty, it shall be lawful for such justices, or governor
governor, or deemster,) to commit such offender to any of his Majesty's gaols in the county wher
fence shall have arisen, or wherein the offender shall have been found, there to remain until the
shall be paid : Provided always, that when any person shall have been committed by any justice
vernor, deputy governor, or deemster, to any prison for nonpayment of such penalty, or in defau
tress, it shall be lawful for the gaoler to discharge such person at the end of six calendar mon*
the date of such warrant by which the said person is committed to his custody, and he shall b
discharged from the payment of such penalty. — § 75.

Justices empowered to mitigate in certain Cases.—Where any party shall be convicted before
justices, or governor, or deputy governor, or deemster, in any penalty (except as herein-after p
it shall be lawful, in cases where, upon consideration of the circumstances, he or they shall deem
dient so to do, to mitigate the payment of the said penalty, so as the sum be not less than one four
amount of the penalty. — § 76.

Suits to be commenced within Three Years.—All suits, indictments, or informations, in any of t
of record, shall be brought, sued, or exhibited, within three years next after the date of the off
shall be exhibited before any two or more justices of the peace, or governor, or deputy gove
deemster in the Isle of Man, within six months next after the date of the offence committed. —

Indictments and Informations may be inquired into in any County.—Any indictment or inf
found or prosecuted for any offence, shall and may be inquired of, tried, and determined in any c
England ; and such indictment or information which shall be found or prosecuted in Scotland,
inquired of, tried, and determined in any county in Scotland ; and any such indictment or inf
found or commenced in Ireland, may be inquired of, tried, and determined in any county in Ir
if the offence had been committed in the said county. — § 78.

Mode of Proceeding before Justices for Condemnation of seized Goods.—In all cases of inform
hibited before any two justices of the peace, or any governor, deputy governor, or deemster as a
for the forfeiture of any goods seized, and where the party to whom such goods belonged, or fro
they were seized, is known, it shall be lawful for the said justices, or governor, deputy gove
deemster, to summon the said party, and upon his appearance or default to proceed to the exa
of the matter of fact, and on due proof that the goods are liable to forfeiture to condemn the sa
and in case the party from whom the said goods have been seized is not known, it shall be lawf
said justices, or governor, deputy governor, or deemster, to cause public notice to be stuck up in
Exchange if the seizure is made in London, at the market cross if in Edinburgh, and at the F
change if in Dublin ; and if the seizure is made at any other place, then a notice shall be public
the public crier at the next market-place, stating that the goods have been so seized, and that th
will take place on a certain day, not being less than eight days from the date of the said notic
default of any person's attendance in consequence of the said notice, the said justices, or gove
puty governor, or deemster, are to proceed to the hearing and condemnation of the said goods
said. — § 79.

Persons detained for certain Offences, to pay 100l., or if Seafaring Men, to be sent into the Nave
—It shall be lawful for any two justices of the peace, or governor, deputy governor, or de
aforesaid, before whom any person liable to be arrested, and who shall have been arrested, for be
or discovered to have been on board any vessel or boat liable to forfeiture, or for unshipping,
conveying, or concealing, or aiding or being concerned in unshipping, carrying, conveying, or c
any spirits or tobacco liable to forfeiture, shall be carried, on the confession of such person, o
upon the oaths of one or more credible witness or witnesses, to convict such person of any such
and every such person so convicted shall, immediately upon conviction, pay into the hand
justices, or governor, deputy governor, or deemster, the penalty of 100l., without any mitigat
ever ; or in default thereof the said justices, or governor, deputy governor, or deemster, shall, by
commit such person to any gaol or prison until such penalty shall be paid : Provided, that if t
convicted shall be a seaman or seafaring man, and fit to serve his Majesty in his naval service,
not prove that he is not a subject of his Majesty, it shall be lawful for such justices, or governo
governor, or deemster, in lieu of such penalty, by warrant to order any officer of the army, na
rines, or officer of customs or excise, to carry such person on board of any of his Majesty's ship
to his serving his Majesty in his naval service for five years ; and if such person shall within t
escape or desert, he shall be liable at any time afterwards to be again arrested and detained by
of customs, or any other person, and delivered over to complete his service of five years : Prov
if it shall be made to appear to any such justices, or governor, deputy governor, or deemster, that
venient arrangement cannot be made at the time of conviction, for immediately carrying su
or seafaring man on board any of his Majesty's ships, it shall be lawful for any such justices, or

overnor, or deemster, to commit such seaman or seafaring man to any gaol, there to remain for
od not exceeding one month, in order that time may be given to make arrangements for convey-
seaman or seafaring man on board as aforesaid : Provided also, that the commissioners of the
shall have full power to remit or mitigate any such penalty, punishment, or service, whether the
hall be seafaring men or otherwise. — § 80.

as convicted and sent on board his Majesty's Ships found unfit.—If any person so convicted as a
and carried on board any of his Majesty's ships of war, shall, on examination by any surgeon,
ne week, be deemed to be unfit, and shall be refused to be received, such person shall, as soon as
nt, be conveyed before any two justices, or any governor, deputy governor, or deemster as afore-
d upon proof that he has been refused to be received on board one of his Majesty's ships, such
governor, deputy governor, or deemster, shall call upon the said person to pay the penalty of
hout hearing any evidence other than such proof; and in default of immediate payment into the
the said justices, governor, deputy governor, or deemster, shall commit the said person to any
re to remain until such penalty shall be paid : Provided, that no person so convicted, and ordered
on board any of his Majesty's ships, shall be sent away from the United Kingdom on board of
in a less time than one month from the date of conviction. — § 81.

ations, &c. to be in the Form given in the Schedule. — All informations before justices of the
vernors, deputy governors, or deemsters, and all convictions and warrants, shall be drawn in the
o the effect in the schedules to this act annexed.—§ 82.

s arrested for certain Offences may be detained by Order of Justices.—Where any person shall have
sted and detained by any officer of the army, navy, or marines, on full pay, or any officer of cus-
xcise, or any person acting in their aid, or duly employed for the prevention of smuggling, and
been taken before any two justices, if it shall appear to such justices that there is reasonable
etain such person, such justices may order such person to be detained a reasonable time, as well
after any information exhibited ; and at the expiration of such time, such justices may proceed
hear and determine the matter. — § 83. (N. B. The act 9 Geo. 4. c. 76., authorises *one* justice to
fore and after hearing the case.)

may issue against Persons sued under this Act.—Whenever any penalty shall be sued for by in-
in any of the courts of record at Westminster, or in the courts of Exchequer in Scotland or in
capias shall issue as the first process, specifying the amount of the penalty ; and such person
bliged to give sufficient bail by natural-born subjects or denizens, to appear at the day of the reach writ; and shall likewise, at the time of such appearing, give bail as aforesaid, to pay all the
s incurred, in case he shall be convicted thereof, or to yield his body to prison. — § 84.

s arrested on Capias, and not pleading.—If any person shall be arrested upon such capias, and
rison for want of bail, a copy of the information shall be served upon him in gaol, or delivered
ler, keeper, or turnkey ; and if such person shall neglect or refuse to appear or plead for the
ne term, judgment shall be entered by default ; and in case judgment shall be obtained by de-
dict, or otherwise, and such person shall not pay the sum recovered, execution shall be there-
ed, not only against the body of the person so in prison, but against all the real and personal
such person, for such sum so recovered. — § 85.

not worth 5l. may defend Suits in Formâ Pauperis.—In case any person arrested and imprisoned
as aforesaid, shall make affidavit before the judge, or any person commissioned to take affidavits,
not worth, over and above his wearing apparel, the sum of 5l., and such person shall thereupon
defend himself *in formâ pauperis,* then the judge or judges shall, according to their discretion,
person to defend himself, in the same manner and with the same privileges as the judges are
ected to admit poor subjects to commence actions ; and for that end it shall be lawful for the
assign counsel, and to appoint an attorney and clerk of court to advise and carry on any legal
at such person can make against such action or information, and which counsel, attorney, and
to give their advice and assistance to such person, and to do their duties without fee or reward.

to grant Warrant on Writ of Capias endorsed by one of the Solicitors for the Customs. — Where
f capias shall issue, directed to any sheriff, mayor, bailiff, or other person, every such sheriff,
bailiff, and other person, and their under sheriffs, deputies, and other persons acting for them,
the application of one of the solicitors for the customs (such request to be in writing, and
apon the back of the said process, and signed by such solicitor with his name and addition
for the customs), grant a special warrant to such person or persons as shall be named to
ach solicitor, for the apprehending such offender ; or in default thereof, every such sheriff,
diff, under sheriff, and other person, shall be subject to such process of contempt, fines,
nts, penalties, and forfeitures, as they are now liable to in case of refusing or neglecting to
e like process where the defendant might have been taken thereupon in the usual method
ng. — § 87.

demnified from Escapes. — Every such sheriff, mayor, bailiff, under sheriff, and other persons
t special warrant, shall be indemnified against his Majesty, and against all other persons,
scapes of any person who shall be taken by virtue of such warrant, from the time of taking
der till he shall be committed to gaol, or tendered to the gaol-keeper, (who is to receive every
n, and give a receipt for his body,) and from all actions, prosecutions, process of contempt, and
edings for such escape. — § 88.

r seized Goods to be entered in the Name of the real Owner. — No claim shall be permitted to be
any vessel, boat, or goods seized for any cause of forfeiture, and returned into the courts of
, unless such claim is entered in the real name of the owner or proprietor, describing the
nd business of such person ; and if such person shall reside at London, Edinburgh, or Dublin,
he liberties thereof, oath shall be made by him before one of the barons of the court of Ex-
at the vessel, boat, or goods so claimed was or were really the property of him at the time of
t if such person shall not be resident in London, Edinburgh, or Dublin, or the liberties
en oath shall be made in like manner by the agent or attorney, or solicitor, by whom such
be entered, that he has full power from such owner or proprietor to enter such claim, and that
of his knowledge and belief such vessel, boat, or goods, were at the time of the seizure *bond*
al property of the person in whose name such claim is entered, which oath shall be endorsed
d on the back of the indenture of appraisement, and on failure thereof the vessel, boat, or
be absolutely condemned, and judgment shall be entered thereon by default, in the same
if no claim had been entered thereto ; and every person who shall be convicted of taking a
shall be guilty of perjury, and liable to the pains for wilful and corrupt perjury. — § 89.

Delivery for seized Goods. — No writ of delivery shall be granted out of the court of Exche-
person making claim as aforesaid, unless a delay of proceeding to trial and condemnation for
f three terms shall have taken place, and in that case not until good security be given in
appraised value of such vessel, boat, or goods, to return the same, or to pay the full amount of
ty upon condemnation. — § 90.

ry of Claim, Security to be given. — Upon the entry of any claim, the persons who shall enter
s the owners (in case such claimant shall reside in the United Kingdom) shall be bound with
nt sureties in 100l., to pay the costs occasioned by such claim ; and if such owner or pro-
l not reside in the United Kingdom, then the attorney or solicitor shall in like manner be
two sufficient securities, in the like penalty, to pay the costs occasioned by such claim. —

If Suit brought on any Seizure, and the Judge certify that there was probable Cause, Claimant sho
have Costs. — In case any suit shall be commenced or brought to trial on account of any seizure, w[…]
a verdict shall be found for the claimant, and it shall appear to the court before whom the same
have been tried, that there was a *probable cause of seizure*, such court shall certify on the record
there was such probable cause, and in such case the claimant shall not be entitled to any costs w[…]
ever, nor shall the person who made such seizure be liable to any action, indictment, or other suit o[…]
secution ; and in case any action, indictment, or other suit or prosecution shall be commence[…]
brought to trial against any person, on account of any such seizure, wherein a verdict shall be
against the defendant, if the court shall have certified on the said record that there was a pr[…]
cause for such seizure, then the plaintiff, besides the things seized, or the value thereof, shall […]
entitled to above 2*d.* damages, nor to any costs of suit, nor shall the defendant in such prosecution be[…]
above 1*s.* — § 92.

No Process to be sued out against any Officer until One Calendar Month next after Notice. — N[…]
shall be sued out against, nor a copy of any process served upon, any officer of the army, navy, ma[…]
customs, or excise, or against any person acting under the direction of the commissioners of custom
any thing done in the execution of his office, until one calendar month next after notice in w[…]
shall have been delivered to him, or left at his usual place of abode, by the attorney for the part[…]
intends to sue out such writ or process, in which notice shall be explicitly contained the cause of a[…]
the name and abode of the person who is to bring such action, and the name and abode of the atto[…]
and a fee of 20*s.* shall be paid for the preparing or serving of every such notice. — § 93.

No Evidence to be adduced but what is contained in the Notice. — No plaintiff, in any case w[…]
action shall be grounded on any act done by the defendant, shall be permitted to produce any evi[…]
of the cause of such action, except such as shall be contained in the notice, or shall receive any v[…]
against such officer, unless he shall prove on the trial that such notice was given ; and in default o[…]
proof the defendant shall receive a verdict and costs. — § 94.

Officer may tender Amends. — It shall be lawful for any such officer or person to whom such notic[…]
have been given, at any time within one calendar month after such notice, to tender amends to the
complaining, or to his agent or attorney, and in case the same is not accepted to plead such tender
with the plea of not guilty, and other plea with leave of the court ; and if, upon issue joined, th[…]
shall find the amends so tendered to have been sufficient, then they shall give a verdict for the defen[…]
and in such case, or in case the plaintiff shall become nonsuited or discontinue, or in case judgmen[…]
be given for such defendant upon demurrer, then such defendant shall be entitled to the like cos[…]
he had pleaded the general issue only ; but if, upon issue joined, the jury shall find that no amend[…]
tendered, or that the same were not sufficient, or shall find against the defendant in such othe[…]
then they shall give a verdict for the plaintiff, and such damages as they shall think proper, togethe[…]
costs of suit. — § 95.

Officer neglecting to tender Amends may pay Money into Court. — In case such officer or perso[…]
neglect to tender amends, or shall have tendered insufficient amends before action brought, it sh[…]
lawful for him, by leave of the court, at any time before issue joined, to pay into court such sum[…]
shall see fit, whereupon such proceedings shall be had as in other actions where the defendant is a[…]
to pay money into court. — § 96.

Action to be commenced within Six Months. — If any action shall be brought, such action shall be b[…]
within six months next after the cause of action shall have arisen, and not afterwards, and shall […]
and tried in the county where the facts were committed, and not in any other county, and the def[…]
may plead the general issue, and give the special matter in evidence ; and if the plaintiff shall b[…]
nonsuited, or discontinue, or if, upon a verdict or demurrer, judgment shall be given against the pl[…]
the defendant shall receive treble costs. — § 97.

Judges of the Court of King's Bench may issue Warrant for the Apprehension of Offenders. — […]
ever any person shall be charged with any offence against this or any act relating to the customs,
which he may be prosecuted by indictment or information in the court of King's Bench, and the[…]
shall be made appear to any judge of the same court, by affidavit, or by certificate of an informa[…]
indictment being filed, it shall be lawful for such judge to issue his warrant under his hand and se[…]
thereby to cause such person to be apprehended and brought before him, or some other judge[…]
same court, or before one of his Majesty's justices of the peace, in order to his being bound to th[…]
with two sufficient sureties, in such sum as in the said warrant shall be expressed, with conditio[…]
pear in the said court at the time mentioned in such warrant, and to answer to all indictments or i[…]
ations ; and in case any such person shall neglect or refuse to become bound, it shall be lawful fo[…]
judge or justice to commit such person to the common gaol of the county, or place where the offen[…]
have been committed, or where he shall have been apprehended, there to remain until he become[…]
as aforesaid, or shall be discharged by order of the court in term time, or of one of the judges in va[…]
and the recognizance to be thereupon taken shall be returned and filed in the said court, and sha[…]
tinue in force until such person shall have been acquitted, or in case of conviction, shall have r[…]
judgment, unless sooner ordered by the court to be discharged ; and where any person, either by[…]
of such warrant of commitment aforesaid, or by virtue of any writ of capias ad respondendum[…]
out of the said court, is now detained, or shall hereafter be committed to and detained in any […]
want of bail, it shall be lawful for the prosecutor of such indictment or information to cause[…]
thereof to be delivered to such person, or to the gaoler, keeper, or turnkey, with a notice there[…]
dorsed, that unless such person shall, within eight days from the time of such delivery, cause an[…]
ance, and also a plea or demurrer to be entered, an appearance and the plea of not guilty will be[…]
thereto in the name of such person ; and in case he shall thereupon, for the space of eight days,
to cause an appearance, and also a plea or demurrer, to be entered, it shall be lawful for the pros[…]
upon affidavit being made and filed in the court of the delivery of a copy of such indictment or
ation, with such notice endorsed thereon as aforesaid, to such person, or to such gaoler, keeper, […]
key, which affidavit may be made before any judge or commissioner of the said court, to c[…]
appearance and the plea of not guilty to be entered in the said court ; and such proceedings
had thereupon as if the defendant in such indictment or information appeared and pleaded no[…]
according to the usual course ; and if, upon trial, any defendant shall be acquitted, it shall be la[…]
the judge before whom such trial shall be had, to order that such defendant shall be forthwith dis[…]
out of custody, and such defendant shall be discharged accordingly. — § 98.

Sheriff to assign Bail Bond at the Request of the Prosecutor. — If any person shall be arrested b[…]
of capias, issuing out of any court of record at Westminster, or out of any of the superior c[…]
record of either of the counties palatine, or out of any of the courts of great session in Wale[…]
suit of the king, and the sheriff shall take bail, the sheriff, at the request and costs of the pro[…]
shall assign to the king the bail bond, by endorsing the same and attesting it under his hand an[…]
the presence of two witnesses, which may be done without any stamp, provided the assignment
stamped before suit commenced ; and if such bail bond be forfeited, such process shall thereupon[…]
on bonds originally made to the king ; and the court in which such bail bond is put in suit may[…]
of court, give such relief to the defendant as is agreeable to justice. — § 99.

Suits to be commenced in the Name of Attorney-General, or an Officer of the Customs. — No in[…]
shall be preferred, or suit commenced for the recovery of any penalty, (except in the cases o[…]
detained and carried before two justices,) unless such suit shall be commenced in the name of […]
jesty's attorney-general, or unless such indictment shall be preferred under the direction of the[…]

customs or excise, or unless such suit shall be commenced in the name of some officer of
excise, under the direction of the said commissioners. — § 100.

rney-General may enter a noli prosequi. — If any prosecution whatever shall be commenced
:overy of any fine, penalty, or forfeiture under this or any other act relating to the customs
, it shall be lawful for his Majesty's attorney-general, if he is satisfied that such fine, pe-
orfeiture, was incurred without any intention of fraud, or that it is inexpedient to proceed
prosecution, to stop all further proceedings, by entering a noli prosequi, as well with respect
e to which any officer may be entitled, as to the king's share. — § 101.

bandi to lie on the Claimer. — If any goods shall be seized for nonpayment of duties or any
e of forfeiture, and any dispute shall arise whether the customs, excise, or inland duties
paid, or the same have been lawfully imported, or concerning the place from whence such
brought, in such case the proof thereof shall lie on the owner or claimer, and not on the
102.

x who is a Collector to take Cognisance of Convictions. — § 103.

of certain Matters to be sufficient until the contrary is proved. — In case of any information
ngs, the averment that the commissioners of customs and excise have directed or elected such
or proceedings to be instituted, or that any vessel is foreign or British, or that any person
not a subject of his Majesty, or that any person detained is or is not a seaman, or fit and able
Majesty in his naval service, or that any person is an officer of the customs, shall be sufficient
of as to such facts, unless the defendant in such case shall prove to the contrary. — § 104.

Evidence may be given that a Party is an Officer. — If upon any trial a question shall arise
y person is an officer of the army, navy, or marines, or officer of customs or excise, evidence
g acted as such shall be deemed sufficient, and such person shall not be required to produce
ion or deputation unless sufficient proof shall be given to the contrary; and every such officer
son acting in his aid or assistance shall be deemed a competent witness upon the trial of any
mation on account of any seizure or penalty as aforesaid, notwithstanding such officer or other
be entitled to the whole or any part of such seizure or penalty. — § 105.

this act not to extend to officers of the army, navy, or marines, unless on full pay, and duly
: the prevention of smuggling.

:NA, a large city and sea-port of Asiatic Turkey, on the western side of
or, lat. 38° 29′ N., lon. 27° 4¼′ E. Population probably about 120,000;
60,000 may be Turks, 40,000 Greeks, and the remainder Armenians,
ews, &c. Smyrna is situated at the bottom of a pretty deep gulf;
ace has the island of Mytilene on the north, and Cape Caraburun on
. The best way to go in is to keep about mid channel, rather inclining
uth, and to wait for the sea breeze, which blows from morning till
The bay is capacious, the anchorage excellent, and the water so deep
ships come close to the wharfs. Smyrna is a place of great antiquity
lence of its port, and its admirable situation, have made it be several
ilt, after being destroyed by earthquakes. It is admirably situated; and
ching it from the sea, it has the appearance of an amphitheatre: the
: the back of the town, which it commands, on the top of the hill; but
tate of decay, and could oppose no resistance to an invading force.
or of the city does not correspond to its external appearance; the
ng, for the most part, narrow, dirty, and ill paved. Owing to the want
ess, and of all sorts of precautions on the part of the Turks, Smyrna is
visited by the plague. So late as 1814, from 50,000 to 60,000 of the
s are said to have been cut off by this dreadful scourge. The trade of
more extensive than that of any other in the Turkish empire. The
rom Persia are chiefly composed of Armenians. They arrive and de-
:ed periods, which are nearly identical with those of the arrival and
of most of the foreign ships frequenting the port. Bargains are prin-
:cted by Jew brokers, many of whom have amassed considerable fortunes.
pal articles of import consist of grain, furs, iron, butter, &c. from Odessa
rog; and of cotton stuffs and twist, silk and woollen goods, coffee, sugar,
and dye-woods, iron, tin and tin-plates, rum, brandy, paper, cheese, glass,
rom Great Britain, France, Italy, the United States, &c. The exports
acipally of raw silk and cotton, fruits —particularly raisins; opium, rhu-
. variety of drugs and gums; olive oil, madder roots, Turkey carpets, va-
ige, galls, wax, copper, hare skins, goats' wool, safflower, &c. — (For
ails, see *Tournefort, Voyage du Levant,* tome ii. pp. 495—507, 4to edit.;
ll's Travels in Turkey, vol. i. letters 5, 6, 7, 8, and 9.)

ights, and Measures, same as at Constantinople; which see. Accounts are kept in piastres,
medini. The value of the piastre fluctuates according to the exchange. It has been very
d; and is at present worth about 4d. The oke is the principal weight used. It is equiva-
43 oz. 5 dr. avoirdupois; 45 okes = 1 kintal = 100 rottolos = 127·48 lbs. avoirdupois. The
tantinople is only 44 okes. A teffee of silk = 4½ lbs. avoirdupois. A chequee of opium =
uee of goats' wool = 5⅘ lbs. do. Corn is measured by the killow = 1·456 Winch. bushel.
ig measure = 27 Eng. inches. — (*Kelly's Cambist,* &c.)

:E OF SMYRNA. — The following details with respect to the commerce of
th Western Europe, are copied from a letter addressed by an intel-
'ish merchant, established in Smyrna, to his correspondent in London,

to whom we are indebted for it. Nothing so complete or satisfactory has ev
published as to the trade of this great emporium.

Charges on Selling and Buying. — As we conceive that a correct list of selling and buying ch
essential piece of information for those interested in the commerce of the Levant, we annex
including every item of expense, namely:

ON SELLING.		ON BUYING.
	Per Cent.	
Freight (according to the rate agreed upon in England) say - - - - 2		Custom duty (according to the quality of article) - - - -
Custom duty (on general goods) - - 3		Porterage (included in the cost of packa which vary according to the quality of goods packed).
Porterage from 1 to 2 piastres per package (according to size).		
Shroffage - - - - 0½		House and street brokerage - -
House and street brokerage - - 2		Commission (except on figs, which is 6 cent.)
Commission for effecting sale - - 3		Warehouse rent - - -
Ditto, if proceeds are remitted by bill or specie 1½		
Del credere ditto (when required to be charged) 2		
Warehouse rent - - - - 0½		

With regard to the cost of packages, those for silk are about 2½ piastres each; for galls, 18
mastic, tragacanth, &c., 20 do.; scammony, 18 do.; opium, 30 to 36 do.; raisins, 12 to 14 do.;
30 paras; cotton wool, from 12 to 20 piastres, &c.

We learn from ———— that your firm deals largely in skins and furs, but he does no
quality of either; the latter article is, however, of a very limited and ordinary nature wi
chiefly consists of hare skins, which are abundant and shipped in considerable quantities fo
man and French markets. They are most plentiful during the winter season, when the
cheaper and keep better than in the hot months of the year. Sheep, goat, lamb, and kic
plentiful, and are often in request for America; particularly the two latter when in seasor
for lamb skins from the middle of March to the beginning of June, and for goat skins from
until April. We have no want of ox and cow hides both dried and salted, the leather of w
to be more pliable than those of Europe. They are now and then sent to Marseilles in sma
but as it would be difficult to convey, by a written description, the exact quality of those skins,
making up a little bale of such kinds as may for the moment be met with, and to forward it b
vessel to London, when it shall be submitted to your inspection with an invoice, and remain, i
proper, at your disposal.

We now proceed to make you acquainted with the manner in which our sales, purchases, a
are effected, together with the nature of sales made on credit or for cash, &c.

Sales are effected in this country between our house's brokers, and what is termed a st
door broker; the former receiving their instructions from us, and the latter acting on behalf of
When the terms are mutually agreed upon, the real buyer and seller personally meet; and a bo
gatory note stating the terms and amount of the transaction is drawn out and signed by the
when not much approved of, one or more signatures are required to the bond, who indiv
collectively become responsible for the fulfilment of it.

Purchases are similarly made, except that the purchaser or agent himself, in the first in
his brokers, inspect the goods he is about to treat for; cash down is generally expected;
but seldom that a short credit of one or two couriers is obtained: it not unfrequently happen
a quarter or even a half of the purchase amount is advanced to the seller, when an insuffic
tity of the article wanted by the buyer is in the place, and which must then be procured fro
rior or place of growth. The money advanced (which is to be returned if the quality does
sent by a confidential person on the part of the purchaser, accompanied either by the seller in
by some one representing him.

Barters are generally attended with delay, impediments, and sacrifices to the European
exchanges his constituents' goods for native produce, and are never completed without h
large portion in cash, which is mostly a half, sometimes even three quarters, but never
third of the full amount; besides always paying a higher price for the produce than if it w
for ready money. On the other hand, so far as the agent's transaction goes in goods, the pri
he also advances, it is equal to an advantageous cash sale, deducting a discount; but still he
have just stated, on that part of the operation which subjects him to the necessity of g
money for such part of the produce as remains above the counter-value given in goods,
rate than it is worth in the open market. Thus the advantage is all in favour of this c
against the agent. Indeed, barters are seldom undertaken unless when a profitable result is
when European goods are difficult to be placed upon saving conditions, either from the want
or a glutted market, or when (which is mostly the case) the holder of such goods has orde
owners of them to remit them in produce, and thus realise their property, if not upon profi
at least without the risk arising from bad debts; sometimes, also, outstanding bonds are ta
payment, to the extent occasionally of one third; another third is taken in goods at an adva
5 to 10 or 12 per cent. above current prices; and the remaining third in cash, against prod
5 to 10 per cent. more than it fetches in the bazaars. However, it is by barter alone that
sive transaction ever takes place, or that it can be either readily or safely effected.

Sales on Credit. — The terms of credit vary considerably, and depend entirely upon the qu
goods which the agent sells: for current or demanded merchandise, two couriers (or tw
15 days), and two and three 31 days, are the present terms; which are extended to four, five
days for articles not much in request. Couriers mean post days; of which we have two in e
at each courier, and 31 days, a proportionate payment becomes payable; for instance, on
six 31 days, one sixth falls due at the expiration of the first month; and if paid, is noted
on the bond, and so on until the remaining five periods are expired: it must, however,
that payments are by no means punctually made, except by a few of our more wealthy ba
although for the first three or four periods of a long credit some regularity is observed;
time begins to shorten, payments are proportionally retarded, so that two 31 days on a bo
for six months, may be considered as a fair average of time in addition to the limited term.

Sales for Cash. — These very seldom occur, indeed, and then only when money is abundan
cle sold scarce and in great demand; in fact, not one sale in a hundred is made on these ter
about the same ratio is a discount taken off from a bazaar bond at even an exorbitant ra
short the period may be that it has to run: occasionally a sale is, however, effected for on
and the other half short credit, for some very current goods.

Character of Dealers. — Before entering upon the articles of commerce, we are desirou
you acquainted with the character and customs of our bazaar dealers. The Greek dealers a
petty shopkeepers, very cunning, and very bad payers. The Jews have similar defects, but a
ported by their brethren, who generally become guarantee for each other. The Armenian
the largest traffickers both for buying and selling; and though hard bargainers, are most
and honourable as well as honest. The Turks are, however, as far superior to the foregoin

ualities, as they are inferior to them in means and commercial abilities; yet they sometimes
gely, and their bond is as punctually discharged, in general, as the day comes when it falls due.
vs in this country mostly favour the debtor at the expense of the creditor; and so far they
ge dishonesty. The number of insolvent, native dealers, was at one time excessive; but of late
ns of each individual buyer have been so carefully investigated, that at present we are not aware
ere is one bazaar dealer who is not able to meet the demands of those from whom he has pur-
The European consuls, who enjoy much consideration by the Turks, protect the interests of
untrymen in disputed points; and, in general, questions of a commercial nature are submitted
decision of a Turkish tribunal, where very little pleading, but a good deal of plain straight-
justice, goes forward; except that, *perhaps*, the European is, if any thing, rather less favoured
native.
ow proceed to offer some observations on the leading articles of our imports and exports for
ernment, the correctness of which may be relied upon.

IMPORTS.

—This is by far the most current article received here, and is sent from England, France,
Trieste, Marseilles, Leghorn, Genoa, and America; but first and principally, of late years,
latter country; the vessels of which are frequently laden with coffee, and always partly so:
in point of quantity comes from England; but is shipped mostly in small parcels at a time, of
to 600 sacks, although occasionally that amount is doubled. France follows, but on a less ex-
cale; and Austria, Holland, and the small ports in the south of Europe, do not together export
in what is received from England alone. We have four different qualities of coffee in our mar-
mely, Mocha, St. Domingo, Havannah, and Brazil: the first is sent from Alexandria, and by
in vessels, and but seldom from Europe; the consumption is however limited, and does not ex-
00 okes annually. At Constantinople, about three times that quantity is sold yearly. We never
r to have known such heavy importations of West India coffee as within these last 6 months,
n November, 1827); the consequence of which has been such an excess beyond the wants of the
at not only buyers are fully supplied for some time to come, but also the heavy stock in first
n only be diminished either by forced or ruinous sales, or must wait for 2 or 3 months, until the
gain comes round; which is however certain to take place, as coffee forms one of the necessaries
this country: in short, an Asiatic cannot do without his coffee; and it is well known that in
lone not less than perhaps 4'00,000 cups of it are daily drunk, which, computed at the cost
paras each, amount to 20,000 piastres! The St. Domingo and Havannah coffee are preferred
azil, although, when the latter is of a fair round quality, there is not more than 5 per cent.
in price. the small green West India berry certainly commands a ready sale; but, for the
, not more than 6 or 8 per cent. can be obtained above the middling and sound quality. Coffee
t the very few articles which occasionally meet with a partial and entire cash sale and short
nd is, moreover, from the means and character of the dealers in it, the least liable to risk from
y. It is also the easiest through which an advantageous barter can be effected, as a much
antity of coffee will be taken in exchange for produce than almost any other item of European
ise. Annual consumption, about 3,000,000 okes.
s the next in consequence. This article is supplied from the same sources as coffee, and is
in its disposal with similar results. We receive the following qualities:—white crushed,
avannah, brown do., white East India, refined in small loaves of 4 lbs. and in large of 8 lbs.
two latter are mostly shipped from America and England. The brown and ordinary sorts
o current. Annual consumption, 10,000 okes.
ollows the two preceding articles, not so much in extent as meeting a ready sale always, and
quently a profitable one: it is attended likewise with all the advantages and facilities attached
nd sugar, and is furnished by Europe and America, but principally by England. The quali-
ceive consist of East India purple and copper, ditto common, and Guatemala. The first of the
e kind best adapted for our markets, and is placed sooner and better than the other two; but
ase with coffee, the *very fine* will not pay cost price, and ought therefore never to be sent.
s suited for our buyers ought to be good sized, with about an equal proportion of purple
r in each piece. The few chests on sale are all ordinary, and consequently dull; and the
al of 15 or 20 chests (and not more ought ever to be shipped at one time) of fair East India
with a ready and favourable sale at 20 piastres per oke. Annual consumption, 80 chests.
ctures.—This is, in point of amount, the most extensive branch of trade carried on in
We have, as you will perceive from our Price Current, a numerous assortment of British and
cotton goods and English shalloons. The white or unprinted cotton goods are most in demand
e warm weather, and the coloured or printed stuffs during winter, although a considerable
f all sorts is regularly and largely sold throughout the whole year. The East Indian manure supplied by America and England exclusively; the latter country also sends fair imita-
e East India loom, in long cloths, seersuckers, &c. The native consumers are exceedingly
in their choice of designs and colours, which ought very frequently to be altered, in order to
capricious taste. Manufactured goods are always sold at long credits, but large barters are
ted through them. A person desirous of entering into this item of our commerce is almost
imately to reap an advantage; but he must have patience, a large capital, and must not be dis-
at the first or second result of his enterprise, should it disappoint his hopes of profit. He
enter into the thing with spirit, and keep his agent always supplied with the goods he may
d; and he is to remember that many months must elapse before he can expect a return by bills
ge, but sooner if he order a barter. The capital employed must also at least be to the
20,000l. to do any good; and further, this sum ought to be disbursed by him without any
embarrassment or inconvenience. For a person willing to undertake such a step, he would
be regularly furnished with patterns, and advices of the manner in which they ought to be
varied; and we again repeat, that with *competent means*, a real desire to follow the branch
and full information hence of what is required, a most extensive and finally lucrative busi-
be done; and we recommend the matter strongly to your best consideration. Annual con-
f all kinds (British), about 367,000 pieces.
wist forms no inconsiderable article in our trade, and is supplied exclusively from England.
has, however, superseded, in some degree, the demand which formerly existed for water twist,
equently more in request. Water twist is nevertheless saleable, and both qualities ought to
r high numbers. This article is often given in barter, but mostly sold at rather long credits,
ever for cash. Annual consumption of water twist, 10,000 okes; ditto of mule ditto,

ars, English, was formerly largely consumed; but from the buyers being plentifully sup-
at present but little demanded, even at the losing price of the day. Barters are very
effected through irons of all descriptions, and command a short credit, and sometimes a cash
ual consumption, 16 to 18,000 kintals.
es are generally employed for building purposes, and store doors.
are always saleable.
ns are most saleable in August, September, and October, for fruit and other export barrels.
ssia and Swedish Bars.— These kinds are sent in rather large parcels, particularly the
fetch a higher price than the English, owing to their malleable qualities, which render

labour easier, and by that advantage command a preference; though the high price, beyond the E▮ make, puts the two qualities upon a level, and commands a larger consumption of the latter. A▮ consumption, 3,500 kintals.

Tin in Bars is a good, steady, saleable article; is often given on fair terms in barter, always di▮ of on short credit, and now and then placed for cash. It comes from England exclusively. A▮ consumption, 800 to 1,000 barrels of 4 cwt. each.

Tin in Plates is attended with the foregoing advantages, and is also supplied by England Annual consumption, 1,200 double boxes.

Lead in Sheets, Pigs, and Shot. — These three items have lately, particularly shot, been sent Germany, and prove dangerous competitors with the English; in consequence of which the thing i▮ done, and we have more in market than meets the demand at losing prices.

Lead, Red and White. — These two articles have lately been much in request for the format▮ paint. Some large parcels of red have lately arrived, and sell well and currently, but we are altog▮ without white. The consumption of all sorts of lead has, however, considerably decreased of late and no longer forms an item of any great consequence in our trade.

Rum and Brandy. — Leeward Island and Jamaica, are furnished by America and England; the f▮ particularly in the lower qualities, of which we have a full market at low prices. The better kin▮ brandy are supplied from England, but do not obtain a proportionate advance compared with the mon sorts. Brandy is but of limited demand, and two or three puncheons are sufficient at a tim▮ ought, as well as rum, to be deeply coloured. Annual consumption of rum, 300 puncheons.

Spices are all saleable in small parcels at a time, particularly pepper and pimento; the latter of v▮ in small sound berries, is demanded at good prices. Nutmegs are very abundant, and offering ve▮ without finding purchasers. France, America, and England supply us with spices, but France m▮ in cloves than in other kinds; and it may be remarked that the qualities received from Englan▮ preferred. Credit on selling is generally short.

Cochineal is a fair article now and then in small qualities; and, when in demand, at times f▮ good prices, occasionally a cash sale, and always one of the shortest credits. Annual consum▮ 4,500 okes.

In concluding our observations on imports, we could wish to impress the conviction, that a poor purpose cannot be answered in speculating *to* this country; for, should his circumstances req▮ speedy remittance in bills, he must submit to a heavy sacrifice, in order to meet his wants, by selli▮ property for whatever it may fetch in cash; and such a measure cannot but be attended with very loss. On the contrary, when an opulent person finds that his property cannot be realised at ▮ prices, he can afford to wait until a more favourable moment presents itself; and such a moment, than 12 months, is almost certain to arrive, when he retires his money with an advantage more thar to any interest he could obtain for it in Europe.

That the rate of exchange has regularly advanced, and will continue to advance, is the natural of the continual deterioration of the Turkish specie. We remember when the piece of money, d▮ nated ' Mahmoudia,' passed at about its value, or nearly so, of 10 piastres: it rose to 25 soon after▮ and the few which remain are at present worth 38 each. At the period we allude to (1812), the ex▮ on London was at 25 piastres the pound sterling; and until lately (owing to the great stagnat▮ trade, and to political events, which has lowered it), the rate has been up to 60! It cannot, ho▮ increase beyond that rate more than 5 per cent., as it then will nearly be on a par with the value gold and silver current coin of the realm, when it will be better to remit in specie than by a 63 piastres for 61 days' sight. The rates of exchange fluctuate considerably, and a difference of per cent. often occurs between one post day and another, and are attributable to the quantity or s▮ of paper in market: it is for this reason that the rate always decreases during the fruit season, takes place at the latter end of August, and continues until the middle of October; when it rises a meet the limited wants of drawers, and the larger demands of those remitters who did not ship fru▮ invest the funds of their employers in that article. These observations lead us to submit the ques the advantage which a person in Europe has in receiving *from* this country, instead of sendin▮ Late extensive barters have proved to us, and which we have endeavoured to show to you, the u▮ able terms upon which they are conducted, were it only in paying, and that in cash too, for at le third of the amount, at a higher rate than was current; now this higher rate is, in itself, suppos▮ produce taken in barter to meet with a saving sale in Europe, of no small consideration; — then y▮ the advantage of drawing at a high exchange in making a purchase; and again you have the ch▮ selecting the good part of the produce, and of rejecting the inferior, — a choice which is not all▮ taking it in barter; lastly, the principal advantage in buying over bartering is, that you can ava▮ self of a depression in the produce market, and effect your purchase upon easy terms, whereas ▮ barter is proposed, it has the immediate effect of producing a general rise in the whole market, a▮ of engendering the most absurd pretensions on the part of produce holders, who are too conversa▮ commerce, not to see that either the European house, wishing to barter, is in want of procuring for his principal, or else that the articles of produce wanted are in great demand in Europe — ▮ which, the European agent would never submit to take produce at so much higher a price than h▮ procure it for with cash! The only time in which the person sending *to* this country can calcula▮ a profitable return, is during the fruit season; and for that reason he ought to forward his shipme▮ Europe so as to meet the demand, and to be cashed by the beginning of August. A vessel from ▮ hence is in general from 40 to 50 days in performing her voyage, sometimes much less, and but longer: goods ought, if possible, always to be shipped in a fast and first classed ship.

We now continue our remarks on the articles of our trade, and the following are some of th▮ hence, and deserving of serious attention.

EXPORTS.

Silk. — This is the richest raw article in our export trade with Europe in general, but almos▮ sively with England, which consumes nearly our entire produce. There are three different q▮ viz. fine, middling, and coarse. Bales, adapted for the English market, are composed of the th▮ lities, but the lesser quantity is of the coarse kind; at one time, all coarse was in request in Lon▮ at present an assortment of the three qualities is preferred. When an order is given, it oug▮ accompanied by a description of the quality required; and it is necessary to state that, for *all* of t▮ without being mixed, a higher price is demanded. A bale contains 40 teffees; and, before being is carefully examined and approved of by competent native judges. Silk is produced at Brussa▮ city about 200 miles distant from Smyrna, whence it is forwarded by caravans to the different ▮ consumption, which are Constantinople and this town. Until very lately, almost the entire cro▮ came for sale to Smyrna, but at present the most considerable part is sent to Constantinople, w▮ price is higher; we have therefore here an advantage, not only in price, but also in our manner▮ ing, which fetches 5 or 6 per cent. more in England than if packed in the capital. Silk is mostly ▮ money article, though it sometimes may be had in small quantities at a short credit; or half ▮ half one or two couriers: it is also now and then given in barter. Annual average produce, 2,5▮ or about 480,000 lbs.

Opium, in point of value, and as an article of speculation, hardly gives way to silk; but as it i▮ shipped by Americans, and sent in smaller quantities to Holland and the south of Europe, it is s▮ much competition and variation of price, although we have invariably observed that the open▮ of the new crop is always the lowest, which, however, is in some measure counterbalanced by the

which occurs by keeping. This is also a cash article, and indeed subject to the same conditions
ing or bartering for silk ; it nevertheless has one inferiority, which the silk is not liable to—
difference in the quality of the crops : last year, for instance, opium was of a very bad kind, and
table in England ; this year, though small, it is fine. On the Continent and in America, the
is preferred to the larger sized. We observe that, in England, the prices of opium fluctuate
ly ; but we are not aware that, by holding it, any loss has ever happened,—another reason why
man only should embark in the Turkey trade. It would be impossible, or at least difficult,
ed with much expense, to obtain a monopoly of the opium crop, as it is produced through some
of individuals, each one (and they are all poor) adding his produce ; and when collected in
uantities, it is brought to market by the natives, having each of them one or two baskets for
t might be done is this : — Send a person to the place of growth with ready money to purchase
ut limited quantity, and which he can do easily, if not hurried, to the extent of 50, or even a
s, and upon terms of advantage, from the simple fact that the collectors of it prefer to receive a
ng price on the spot of growth, rather than perform a long and expensive journey, with the
ot finding purchasers immediately. Opium is produced at sundry places in the interior, of
30 days' distance hence ; but that grown at Caissar, about 600 miles from Smyrna, is the
med, from its cleanness and good quality ; it comes to market in June, and finishes about
or January. Annual average produce, 3,000 baskets, or about 400,000 lbs.

d Gums form one of our principal branches of commerce, and is almost entirely in the hands
s. At present gum Arabic and mastic are exceedingly scarce ; and it is only when that
or the demand for exportation is very brisk, that much variation exists in the price of drugs.
d occasionally America, consume a considerable portion of gums, but the largest quantity goes
sh markets. Barters are often effected through this medium ; but it is not attended with
ntage, as they are conducted by a race who never lose in any transaction they undertake. It
e to ascertain the quantities of drugs received in Smyrna, and equally so to know the quantity
as they are dispersed all over the city, and consumed so irregularly in Europe, as bids defiance
ar calculation.

ave been, and still are, an article of considerable moment, particularly for the English mar-
e found about the islands in the Grecian Archipelago, brought here, and cleaned for export-
y vary in price from 6 to 90 piastres per oke, according to fineness and quality : the better sort
rs for speculation, and which it would appear, from the considerable quantity sent to London,
od account. The produce depends so entirely on chance, that no correct estimate of the
tity can be formed ; however, we are seldom in want of a moderate supply.

shipped in considerable quantities for the English, German, and French markets ; the two
ever, being the largest consumers : for England, the blue galls are those principally sent ;
market there for their sale being dull and low, prices with us, moderate as they are
o last year, will still further decline, should a demand not spring up, of which there is no
Annual produce of all sorts, 5,500 kintals.

ool, of which we have several qualities, is chiefly exported to Trieste and Marseilles. The
present for all kinds of this produce is extremely limited, and we expect that prices will go
as before long, when perhaps something good might be done in Soubougea's to England,
rally receives only that quality. Barters are made to a large extent in cottons. Annual
luce of all sorts, 60,000 kintals.

nploys more British shipping for full cargoes of only one article, than any other species of
ve except perhaps fruit : it is also sent to Dublin and to the German markets in considerable
Almost any supply can be obtained, and it is shipped generally near the places of growth,
umerous, although there is never any want of it in the Smyrna market. It is much resorted
s of making barters, which perhaps are as easily effected, upon pretty fair terms, as with any
of produce. The annual produce is sufficient to meet the wants of all Europe. It can be had
t and at all periods.

This is an article which occupies the attention of all Smyrna, more or less, and produces
ason great interest and activity. Figs come to market early in September, and raisins are
pping early in October : the former are procurable only at Smyrna, where the latter in all
s may be procured ; but the shipments are generally made at Cesmé, Vouria, Carabourna,
from which ports the name of the raisin takes its origin. Large sums are frequently gained
ulations ; and when the demand in England is brisk, and the prices and quality fair with us,
n happens indeed that any loss is sustained : it is, however, attended with risk ; must be
and ought only to go in a very fast, sound vessel, as much depends upon a first, or at least
val, which obtains in general a higher price than the later arrivals. The quantity produced
ertain.

maining articles of exports hence, we refer you to our Price Current. Carpets are produced
of about 80,000 to 100,000 pikes a year. Oil (olive) to the amount of 10 to 15 middling sized
s the islands of Mytilene, Candia, &c., is generally shipped for America and France, seldom
the season commences in September, but the crops of olives fluctuate exceedingly in point
hence arise dear and cheap years : last year was a high one, and it is expected to be lower this.
nd new, may be computed at 30,000 okes, which are generally brought up as soon as offered,
Hare skins are computed at from 350,000 to 400,000 annually. Madder roots at 12,000 kintals.
2,000 to 15,000 chequees. Goats' wool of all kinds may be calculated per year at 45,000 to
es ; sheep's wool at 23,000 kintals. Wax (yellow), 1,600 kintals.
ow finished our general remarks on the exports and imports of the place ; and in concluding
to state that upon an average of all of them, (with the exception of fruit from, and of iron
the selling charges may (excluding del credere commission) be calculated at about 12 per
purchasing at about 8 per cent.

(Ger. *Schnupftaback;* Fr. *Tabac en poudre;* It. *Tabacco da naso;* Sp.
polvo; Rus. *Nosowoi tabak*), a powder in very general use as an er-
bacco is the usual basis of snuff; but small quantities of other articles
ntly added to it, to vary its pungency, flavour, scent, &c. Though sub-
he same, the kinds and names of snuff are infinite, and are perpetually
There are, however, three principal sorts : the first, granulated ; the
impalpable powder ; and the third, the bran, or coarse part remaining
the second sort. Unless taken in excess, no bad consequences result
e.

obacco and snuff are obliged to take out a licence renewable annually which costs 5s. They
ed to enter their premises, and have their names written in large legible characters over
on some conspicuous part of their house, under a penalty of 50l. The dyeing of snuff with
or any other colouring matter except water tinged with colour, is prohibited under a
l. ; and its intermixture with fustic, yellow ebony, touchwood, sand, dirt, leaves, &c.

is prohibited under a penalty of 100*l.* and the forfeiture of the article. — (1 & 2 *Geo.* 4. c.
snuff be found to contain 4 per cent. of any substance, not being tobacco, and other than wa
or water tinged with colour, or flavoured only, such snuff shall be deemed adulterated, and sha
feited, and the parties subjected to a penalty of 100*l.* over and above all other penalties and forfe
(*Ib.*) No quantity of snuff weighing above 2 lbs. shall be removed by land or water without a p
(29 *Geo.* 3. c. 68.) See Tobacco.

SNUFF-BOXES, are made of every variety of pattern, and of an
variety of materials. We only mention them here for the purpose of giv
following details, not to be met with in any other publication, with respect
manufacture of Laurencekirk or Cumnock boxes. These are made of
admirably jointed, painted, and varnished.

These beautiful boxes were first manufactured at the village of Laurencekirk, in Kincardineshi
forty years since. The original inventor was a cripple hardly possessed of the power of locomo
place of curtains, his bed (rather a curious workshop) was surrounded with benches and ro
for tools, in the contrivance and use of which he discovered the utmost ingenuity. The invento
of taking out a patent, confided his secret to a joiner in the same village, who in a few years a
considerable property; while the other died, as he had lived, in the greatest poverty. The great
of the manufacture lies in the formation of the hinge, which in a genuine box is so delicately
hardly to be visible. Peculiar, or, as they are called, secret tools are required in its formation; ar
they must have been improved by time and experience, the mystery attached to their preparati
so studiously kept up, that the workmen employed in one shop are rigorously debarred from ha
communication with those employed in another.

About the beginning of this century, an ingenious individual belonging to the village of Cur
Ayrshire, of the name of Crawford, having seen one of the Laurencekirk snuff-boxes, succee
various attempts, by the assistance of a watchmaker of the same village, who made the tools, i
ing a similar box; and by his success, not only laid the foundation of his own fortune, but greatl
his native parish and province. For a while, the Laurencekirk boxes were most in dem
Mr. Crawford and his neighbours in Cumnock not only copied the art, but so improved and pe
that in a very few years, for every box made in the north there were, probably, twenty made in
In 1826, the Cumnock trade was divided amongst eight master manufacturers, who employed co
more than 100 persons. The demand at that time equalled the supply, and it was calculated that
yielded from 7,000*l.* to 8,000*l.* annually, — a large product for a manufacture seemingly so ins
and consisting almost exclusively of the wages of labour. Plane is the wood in common use, ar
of the wood in an ordinary sized box does not exceed 1*d.*; the paints and varnish are rated at
though something is lost by selecting timber of the finest colour, the whole expense of the ra
falls considerably short of ½ per cent. on the return it yields!

Snuff-box, like pin making, admits of subdivision of labour; and in all workshops of any
classes of persons are employed — painters, polishers, and joiners. At the period alluded to,
trious joiner earned from 30*s.* to 40*s.* weekly, a painter from 45*s.* to 3*l.*, and a polisher conside
than either. When Mr. Crawford first commenced business he obtained almost any price h
ask; and many instances occurred, in which ordinary sized snuff-boxes sold at 2*l.* 12*s.* 6*d.*, and la
boxes at 25*l.* But as the trade increased, it became necessary to employ apprentices, who fi
journeymen and then masters; and such have been the effects of improvement and compe
articles such as are specified above may now be obtained at the respective prices of *six* and
shillings. While the joiner's part of the art has remained pretty stationary, that of the painte
gradually improving. By means of the *Pentagraph*, which is much employed, the largest eng
reduced to the size most convenient for the workman, without injuring the prints in the slighte
and hence a snuff-box manufacturer, like a Dunfermline weaver, can work to order by exhibitio
his employer's coat of arms, or, in short, any object he may fancy within the range of the pi
Some of the painters display considerable talent, and as often as they choose to put forth thei
produce box-lids, which are really worthy of being preserved as pictures. At first, nearly the
jects chosen as ornaments, were taken from Burns's poems; and there can be no doubt, that the
Saturday Night," "Tam O'Shanter," "Willie brewed a peck o' maut," &c. &c., have penetra
form into every quarter of the habitable globe. Now, however, the artists of Cumnock ta
range; the studios of Wilkie, and other artists, have been laid under contribution; landscapes a
met with as figures; and there is scarcely a celebrated scene in the country that is not pictured
or less perfectly on the lid of a Cumnock snuff-box. A few years ago, the art in question
affected by the long-continued depression of the weaving business; so much so, that many left
other employment. And some of those who emigrated, having made a good deal of money
being cooped up in a work shop, are now thriving proprietors in Upper Canada. But after a br
the trade rallied; and though prices are low, it is now more flourishing than ever. In Cumnock,
of hands has increased considerably, and in Mauchline there is one workshop so extensive
almost be compared to a cotton mill or factory. In other quarters the trade is extending, such
burgh near Greenock, Catrine, Maxwelltown, Dumfries, &c. The principal markets for the s
are London, Liverpool, Glasgow, and Edinburgh. At one time large lots of boxes were export
America, and probably are so at present. Cumnock, in a word, in regard to its staple manufa
that palmy state so well described by a modern writer: — "The condition most favourable to
is that of a laborious frugal people ministering to the demands of opulent neighbours; becaus
ation, while it leaves them every advantage of luxury, exempts them from the evils which acc
admission into a country. Of the different kinds of luxury, those are the most innocent wh
employment to the greatest number of artists and manufacturers; or those in which the p
work bears the greatest proportion to that of the raw material." Some very wretched imitatio
nock boxes have been produced in different parts of England; but they can deceive no one wh
a genuine box. The hinge, as well as the finishing, is clumsy in the extreme.

*** We are indebted for this curious and instructive article to our esteemed friend, John N
Esq., Editor of the Dumfries Courier, one of the best provincial papers published in the emp

SOAP (Ger. *Seife*; Fr. *Savon*; It. *Sapone*; Sp. *Jabon*; Rus. *Mi*
Sapo). The soap met with in commerce is generally divided into two s
and *soft:* the former is made of soda and tallow or oil, and the latter o
and similar oily matters. Soap made of tallow and soda has a whitis
and is, therefore, sometimes denominated *white* soap: but it is usual
makers, in order to lower the price of the article, to mix a considerabl
of rosin with the tallow; this mixture forms the common *yellow* soa
country. Soap made of tallow, &c. and potash does not assume a so

sistence is never greater than that of hog's lard. Tho properties of soft
s a detergent do not differ materially from those of hard soap, but it is not
so convenient for use. The alkali employed by the ancient Gauls and
ns in the formation of soap was potash; hence we see why it was
ed by the Romans as an unguent. The oil employed for making soft
this country is whale oil. A little tallow is also added, which, by a pecu-
nagement, is dispersed through the soap in fine white spots. The soap
in countries which produce olive oil, as the south of France, Italy, and
is preferable to the soap of this country, which is usually manufactured
ease, tallow, &c. — (*Thomson's Chemistry.*)

e of soap as a detergent is well known: it may, in fact, be considered as a necessary of life
mption in most civilised countries is immense. Pliny informs us, that soap was first discovered
uls; that it was composed of tallow and ashes; and that the German soap was reckoned the
Lib. xviii. c. 51.)

tions as to the Manufacture. — Soap is charged with a duty of excise, and its manufacture is
ntly regulated by several provisions intended for the protection of the revenue. No person is
to make soap within the limits of the head office of excise in London, unless he occupy a tene-
10*l.* a year, and is assessed to and pays the parish rates; nor elsewhere, unless he is assessed and
urch and poor; and every soap-maker is required to take out a licence to be renewed annually,
he is to pay 4*l.*; but persons in partnership require only one licence for one house. They are
red to provide sufficient wooden covers for all coppers and other utensils wherein they boil hard
ich covers are to be locked and sealed down by the officer whenever any soap is left in the
d the furnace door, cover, and the ash-hole door is also to be locked and sealed at all times
hen the same is at work. Regulations are also made for preventing the use of any private con-
or pipes, empowering officers to break up the ground to search for the same, and cut them up
if not the officers must make compensation for the injury done. On cleansing or taking
f the coppers, the makers are required to give notice; and certain spaces of time are limited
eting the cleansing and taking out of the soap, according to the kind of soap, and the number
into which the same is put. Coppers and other utensils must be cleansed once in every month.
es used in making hard soap, for cleansing and putting the same into when taken out of the
hen boiled and prepared, must be either square or oblong, and the bottom, sides, and end
ames are to be 2 inches thick and not more than 45 inches long, and 15 inches broad, the same
ked and numbered at the expense of the soap-maker. The making of yellow or mottled soap
ed by 59 Geo. 3. c. 90., by which every maker is required, as soon as the same is cleansed or
of the vessel in which it has been made, to add and put into the copper or vessel all the fob and
s taken out of the same, and also grease, in the proportion of at least 100 cwt. of grease for
of yellow or mottled soap which the copper or vessel shall be by the officer computed to boil or
immediately re-melt such grease in the presence of the officer of excise. No fees fit for the
soap may be manufactured for sale; nor may any barilla be ground or pounded for sale; nor
nd or pounded be sold exceeding the weight of 28 lbs. of such barilla at one time. In the re-
soap exceeding the quantity of 28 lbs., the word "soap" must be painted or marked in large
at least 2 inches long on every chest, basket, box, cask, or package containing the same; and
word must be painted or marked in letters of at least 3 inches in length on every waggon,
her carriage carrying more than 28 lbs in some conspicuous and open part of the same, unless
I by a person being a known and public or common carrier of goods and merchandise from one
ther; officers may inspect the soap and the accompanying certificate. Soap-makers are also to
s, and enter therein all quantities of soap sold exceeding 28lbs. Every barrel of soap must
6 lbs. avoirdupois; every half barrel 128 lbs.; every firkin 64 lbs., and every half firkin 32 lbs.;
weight and tare of the cask. Soap-makers must keep scales and weights, and assist the excise
the use of them, and must weigh their materials for making soap before the officer, on penalty
Chitty's Com. Law, v. ii. pp. 418—420.)

of Soap and Candles. — We annually export from 10,000,000 to 12,000,000 lbs. of soap and
orth from 250,000*l.* to 300,000*l.* Nearly two thirds are exported to the British West Indian and
colonies. A very large quantity is also exported to Brazil.

veness of the Duty. — The direct duty charged on hard soap, which is by far the most extensively
per lb., or 28*s.* per cwt., while the price of soap rarely exceeds 6*d.* per lb or 56*s.* per cwt., so that
luty is fully 100 per cent.! But besides this enormous duty, the substances of which soap is made,
barilla, and turpentine, or rosin, are respectively charged with duties of 3*s.* 4*d.*, 2*s.*, and 4*s.* 4*d.* a
aking these indirect taxes into account, it may be truly stated that soap is taxed from 120 to 130
l valorem! The imposition of so exorbitant a duty on an article that is indispensable to the pro-
many branches of manufacture, and to the comfort and cleanliness of all orders of persons, is in
ree inexpedient. There are good reasons, too, for thinking that in consequence of the encourage-
this excessive duty gives to smuggling and fraud, the revenue derived from it is decidedly less
ld yield were it reduced to half its present amount. During the last five years, the consumption
d soap has been nearly stationary; though there can be no doubt, from the increase of manu-
d population during that period, that it would have been very considerably extended, but for
e of smuggling. This baneful practice is facilitated by the total exemption which Ireland
this duty; for it not unfrequently happens that the soap made in this country, and sent to
ler a drawback, is again clandestinely introduced into Great Britain. It is, perhaps, needless
nothing but the effectual reduction of the duty can put a stop to the smuggling and fraud that
enerally practised. So long as the profit to be made by breaking the law is so high as 120 or
t., so long will it be broken, in despite of the multiplication of penalties and the utmost acti-
gilance of the officers. But were the duty lowered to *half its present amount*, the profit to be
m smuggling would not be enough to make it be carried on to any considerable extent. And
irly concluded, that the great increase of consumption that would infallibly take place in con-
the fall that this reduction of the duty would occasion in the price of so necessary an article,
o distant period, go far to render the lower duty as productive as the higher one is at this
o that the immense advantages that would result from the proposed diminution of the duties,
ng smuggling and fraud, in facilitating manufacturing industry, and in promoting habits of
amongst the population, would be obtained without any loss, and most probably, indeed, with
ole increase of revenue.

e repeal of the soap duty would be a popular measure; but, seeing that a large amount of
st be raised, and that those taxes only are productive which affect all classes of the commu-
uld not be disposed to recommend such a measure. It is not the tax itself, but the oppressive
which it has been carried, that is objectionable. Provided it were adequately reduced, and
n of the duty simplified as much as possible, we do not think it could justly be found fault

I. Account of the Quantity of *Hard* and *Soft Soap* charged with Excise Duty in Great Britain, i
of the Ten Years ending 5th January, 1831 ; the Rates of Duty ; and the *Gross* and *Nett* Proc
the Duties. — (Compiled from different *Parliamentary Papers*.)

Years.	Pounds' Weight of Soap.		Rates of Duty.		Gross Produce of the Duties.	Nett Produce of th Duties.
	Hard.	Soft.	Hard, per lb.	Soft, per lb.		
			d.	d.	£. s. d.	£. s. d
1822	89,168,934	7,583,938	3	1¾		
1823	92,901,382	8,073,803	—	—		
1824	97,071,456	8,226,922	—	—		
1825	100,261,353	9,297,485	—	—		
1826	102,623,165	8,910,504	—	—	1,347,761 19 10	1,179,612 2 4
1827	96,859,694	7,278,446	—	—	1,263,818 3 8	1,147,060 7 10
1828	104,372,807	9,646,477	—	—	1,374,998 19 7	1,199,409 18 0
1829	108,110,198	10,024,665	—	—	1,425,516 11 9	1,210,754 11 3
1830	103,041,961	9,068,918	—	—	1,354,152 0 9	1,151,909 15 9
1831	117,324,320	10,809,519	—	—	1,513,149 19 9¼	1,249,684 13 10

II. Account of all Soap exported to Ireland and Foreign Countries, on which a Drawback was a
during the Seven Years ending with 5th January, 1831. — (*Parl. Paper*, No. 23. Sess. 1831.)

Years.	Ireland.			Foreign Countries.		
	Pounds' Weight of Soap exported.		Drawback allowed thereon.	Pounds' Weight of Soap exported.		Drawback allow thereon.
	Hard.	Soft.		Hard.	Soft.	
			£. s. d.			£. s. d.
1824	116,401	72,814	1,985 18 11½	4,993,694	3,729	62,448 7 3
1825	146,855	83,041	2,441 3 10½	5,764,070	3,526	72,076 11 8
1826	210,912	88,890	3,284 11 1¼	4,073,973	2,773	50,944 17 7
1827	301,642	89,280	4,421 10 6	7,445,467	6,491	93,115 13 4
1828	947,326	90,875	12,504 4 1½	7,936,569	12,734	99,299 19 3
1829	2,751,558	140,673	35,420 4 3¾	6,884,061	4,467	86,083 6 8
1830	6,559,461	120,992	82,375 9 11	8,098,205	10,324	101,302 16 10

SODA.   See ALKALI.

SOUTH SEA DUTIES. The act of the 9 Ann. c. 21., establishing the S
Sea Company, conveyed to them the exclusive privilege of trading to the I
Ocean, and along the east coast of America from the Orinoco to Cape Hor

This privilege was taken away by the 47 Geo. 3. c. 23. ; and in order to raise a guarantee fund
indemnification of the Company, a duty of 2 per cent. *ad valorem* was imposed by the 55 Geo. 3.
all goods (with the exception of those from Brazil and Dutch Surinam* ; and with the excep
blubber, oil, &c. of whales, or fish caught by the crews of British or Irish ships), imported from
the aforesaid limits. A duty of 1s. 6d. per ton was also imposed on all vessels (except in ballast
porting the produce of the fishery of British subjects) entering inwards or clearing outwards fro
places within the said limits. The duties are to cease when the guarantee fund is completed.

SOY, a species of sauce prepared in China and Japan, and eaten with fis
other articles. It should be chosen of a good flavour, not too salt nor too
of a good thick consistence, a brown colour, and clear ; when shaken in a g
should leave a coat on the surface of a bright yellowish brown colour ; if it c
it is of an inferior kind, and should be rejected. Japan soy is deemed supe
the Chinese. It is worth, in bond, from 6s. to 7s. a gallon. It is believed
extensively counterfeited. — (*Milburn's Orient. Com.*)

SPELTER, a name sometimes given to ZINC ; which see.

SPERMACETI (Ger. *Wallrath* ; Fr. *Blanc de Baleine, Sperme de B*
It. *Spermaceti* ; Sp. *Esperma de Ballena* ; Rus. *Spermazet*), a product ob
from the brain of the *physeter macrocephalus*, a species of whale inhabiti
Southern Ocean. The brain being dug out from the cavity of the head, th
separated from it by dripping. The residue is crude spermaceti, of wh
ordinary sized whale will yield 12 barrels. After being brought to Englan
purified. It then concretes into a white, crystallised, brittle, semi-trans
unctuous substance, nearly inodorous and insipid. On being cut into
pieces it assumes a flaky aspect. It is very heavy ; its specific gravity being
It is used in the manufacture of candles, in medicine, &c.

SPICES (Ger. *Spezereyen* ; Du. *Specceryen* ; Fr. *Epiceries, Epices* ; It
Spezierie ; Sp. *Especias, Especerias* ; Port. *Especiaria* ; Rus. *Pränüe k*
Under this denomination are included all those vegetable productions wh
fragrant to the smell and pungent to the palate ; such as cloves, ginger, n
allspice, &c. These will be found under their proper heads.

* The provinces of the Rio de la Plata have since been ad led... (*Treas. Order*, 12th of Marc

IT OF WINE. See Alcohol.

ITS. All inflammable liquors obtained by distillation, as brandy, rum, whisky, gin, &c., are comprised under this designation. The term *British* applied indiscriminately to the various sorts of spirits manufactured in ritain and Ireland. Of these, gin and whisky are by far the most im-

anufacture of spirits is placed under the *surveillance* of the excise, and a e revenue is obtained from it. The act 6 Geo. 4. c. 80. lays down the ns to be followed by the distillers in the manufacture, and by the officers ng the duties. This act is of great length, having no fewer than 151 it is, besides, exceedingly complicated, and the penalties in it amount to ousand pounds. It would, therefore, be to no purpose to attempt giving ract of it in this place. Every one carrying on the business of distillation e the act in his possession, and must be practically acquainted with its n.

it Duties; Consumption of British Spirits in Great Britain and Ireland.—There aps, no better subjects for taxation than spirituous and fermented liquors. essentially luxuries; and while moderate duties on them are, in consequence eing very generally used, exceedingly productive, the increase of price which sion has a tendency to lessen their consumption by the poor, to whom, when xcess, they are exceedingly pernicious. Few governments, however, have been ith imposing moderate duties on spirits; but partly in the view of increasing ne, and partly in the view of placing them beyond the reach of the lower ve almost invariably loaded them with such oppressively high duties as have efeated both objects. The imposition of such duties does not take away the r spirits; and as no vigilance of the officers or severity of the laws has been cient to secure a monopoly of the market to the legal distillers, the real effect h duties has been to throw the supply of a large proportion of the demand nds of the illicit distiller, and to superadd the atrocities of the smuggler to ss and dissipation of the drunkard.

the latter part of the reign of George I., and the earlier part of that of I., gin drinking was exceedingly prevalent; and the cheapness of ardent. the multiplication of public houses, were denounced from the pulpit, and in ments of grand juries, as pregnant with the most destructive consequences to and morals of the community. At length, ministers determined to make a ffort to put a stop to the further use of spirituous liquors, except as a cordial e. For this purpose, an act was passed in 1736, the history and effects of erve to be studied by all who are clamorous for an increase of the duties on ts preamble is to this effect:—"Whereas the drinking of spirituous liquors, vater, is become very common, especially among people of lower and inferior onstant and excessive use of which tends greatly to the destruction of their dering them unfit for useful labour and business, debauching their morals, g them to perpetrate all vices; and the ill consequences of the excessive use quors are not confined to the present generation, but extend to future ages, the destruction and ruin of this kingdom." The enactments were such as xpected to follow a preamble of this sort. They were not intended to repress gin drinking, but to root it out altogether. To accomplish this, a duty of *lings* a gallon was laid on spirits, exclusive of a heavy licence duty on Extraordinary encouragements were at the same time held out to informers, of 100*l.* was ordered to be rigorously exacted from those who, were it even advertency, should vend the smallest quantity of spirits which had not paid ty. Here was an act which might, one should think, have satisfied the emy of gin. But instead of the anticipated effects, it produced those directly The respectable dealers withdrew from a trade proscribed by the legislature; spirit business fell almost entirely into the hands of the lowest and most pro- acters, who, as they had nothing to lose, were not deterred by penalties from rough all its provisions. The populace having in this, as in all similar sed the cause of the smugglers and unlicensed dealers, the officers of the re openly assaulted in the streets of London and other great towns; in- e hunted down like wild beasts; and drunkenness, disorders, and crimes, ith a frightful rapidity. "Within two years of the passing of the act," , "it had become *odious and contemptible*, and policy as well as humanity ommissioners of excise to mitigate its penalties."—(*Continuation of Rapin*, 358. ed. 1759.) The same historian mentions (vol. viii. p. 390.), that during s in question, no fewer than 12,000 persons were convicted of offences con-

nected with the sale of spirits. But no exertion on the part of the revenue offic
magistrates could stem the torrent of smuggling. According to a statement m
the Earl of Cholmondely in the House of Lords — (*Timberland's Debates in the I
Lords*, vol. viii. p. 388.), — it appears, that at the very moment when the sale of
was declared to be illegal, and every possible exertion made to suppress it, upw
SEVEN MILLIONS of gallons were annually consumed in London, and other parts
diately adjacent! Under such circumstances, government had but one course to
— to give up the unequal struggle. In 1742, the high prohibitory duties were
ing repealed, and such moderate duties imposed, as were calculated to incre
revenue, by increasing the consumption of legally distilled spirits. The bill
purpose was vehemently opposed in the House of Lords by most of the bishe
many other peers, who exhausted all their rhetoric in depicting the mischievous
quences that would result from a toleration of the practice of gin-drinking. . T
declamations it was unanswerably replied, that whatever the evils of the practic
be, it was impossible to repress them by prohibitory enactments; and that the a
to do so had been productive of far more mischief than had ever resulted, or c
expected to result, from the greatest abuse of spirits. The consequences of the
were highly beneficial. An instant stop was put to smuggling; and if
of drunkenness was not materially diminished, it has never been stated that
increased.

But it is unnecessary to go back to the reign of George II. for proofs of
potency of high duties to take away the taste for such an article, or to lessen
sumption. The occurrences that took place in the late reign, though they
seem to be already forgotten, are equally decisive as to this question.

Duties in Ireland. — Perhaps no country has suffered more from the excessive I
which duties on spirits have been carried than Ireland. If heavy taxes, enfc
severe fiscal regulations, could make a people sober and industrious, the Iris
be the most so of any on the face of the earth. In order to make the posse
property join heartily in suppressing illicit distillation, the novel expedient was
sorted to, of imposing a heavy fine on every parish, town land, manor land, or lor
which an unlicensed still was found; while the unfortunate wretches found
it were subjected to *transportation for seven years.* But instead of putting dov
distillation, these unheard of severities rendered it universal, and filled the cour
bloodshed, and even rebellion. It is stated by the Rev. Mr. Chichester, in his
pamphlet on the Irish Distillery Laws, published in 1818, that "the Irish systen
to have been formed in order to perpetuate smuggling and anarchy. It has cul
the evils of savage and civilised life, and rejected all the advantages which they
The calamities of civilised warfare are, in general, inferior to those produce
Irish distillery laws; and I doubt whether any nation of modern Europe, whi
in a state of actual revolution, can furnish instances of legal cruelty commen
those which I have represented " — (pp. 92—107.).

These statements are borne out to the fullest extent by the official details in
ports of the Revenue Commissioners. In 1811, say the commissioners — (*Fift*
p. 19.), — when the duty on spirits was 2s. 6d. a gallon, duty was paid in I
6,500,361 gallons (Irish measure); whereas, in 1822, when the duty was 5s.
2,950,647 gallons were brought to the charge. The commissioners estimate,
annual consumption of spirits in Ireland was at this very period not less
MILLIONS of gallons; and, as scarcely *three* millions paid duty, it followed,
millions were illegally supplied; and " taking *one* million of gallons as the
fraudulently furnished for consumption by the licensed distillers, the produ
unlicensed stills may be estimated at *six millions of gallons.*" — (*Ib.* p. 8.) I
material to keep in mind, that this vast amount of smuggling was carried
teeth of the above barbarous statutes, and in despite of the utmost exe
the police and military to prevent it; the only result being the exasperati
populace, and the perpetration of revolting atrocities both by them and
tary. " In Ireland," say the commissioners, " it will appear, from the
annexed to this Report, that parts of the country have been absolutely disorga
placed in opposition not only to the civil authority, but to the military for
government. The profits to be obtained from the evasion of the law have bee
to encourage numerous individuals to persevere in these desperate pursuits
standing the risk of property and life with which they have been attended."

To put an end to such evils, the commissioners recommended that the duty
should be reduced from 5s. 6d. to 2s. the wine gallon (2s. 10d. the imperi
and government wisely consented to act upon this recommendation. In 1823,
were accordingly reduced; and the following official account will show wha
the result of this measure : —

ount of the Quantities of Spirits made in Ireland, which have paid the Duties of Excise for Home
mption; stating the Rate of Duty paid ; and also the Nett Amount of Revenue received in each
since the Year 1820.— *Parl. Paper*, No. 340. Sess. 1829., and No. 61. Sess. 1831.)

ears:	Number of Gallons.	Rate per Gallon.	Nett Amount of Revenue.
	Imp. Measure.		£ s. d.
821	2,649,179	5s. 6d. per Irish gallon.	912,288 7 5
822	2,328,387	Ditto.	797,518 13 3
823	3,348,505	Ditto ; from 10th Oct. 1823, 2s. per English wine gallon.	634,460 7 2
824	6,690,315	Ditto.	771,690 16 0
825	9,262,744	Ditto.	1,084,191 6 5
826	6,837,408	2s. 10d. per Imperial gallon.	964,509 10 8
827	8,260,919	Ditto.	1,122,096 14 10
828	9,937,903	Ditto.	1,395,721 12 11
829	9,212,223	Ditto.	1,305,064 18 6
830	9,004,539	3s and 3s. 4d. per ditto.	1,412,917 7 2

ay appear, on a superficial view of this table, as if the consumption of spirits in
had been trebled since 1823 ; but, in point of fact, it has not been in any degree
d. The reduction of the duties has substituted legal for illicit distillation, and
e country from the perjuries and other atrocities that grew out of the previous
but it would be wholly erroneous to say that it has increased drunkenness. We
eady seen that the commissioners, who had the best means of obtaining accurate
tion, estimated the consumption of spirits in Ireland, in 1823, at TEN millions
ns ; and it is less at this moment. The measure has, therefore, been in every
view most successful ; and we trust that no senseless clamour, and no pecuniary
, will ever tempt ministers to add farther to the duties on spirits. Such a mea-
uld not bring a shilling into the public treasury, nor cause any diminution of
; it would merely add smuggling to the other disorders with which Ireland is

s *in Scotland*. — The experience of Scotland is hardly less decisive as to this ques-
he exorbitancy of the duties produced nearly the same effects there as in Ireland.
n Hay Forbes, formerly sheriff-depute of Perthshire, now one of the Lords of
stated in evidence before the commissioners, that, according to the best informa-
ould obtain, the quantity of illegally distilled spirits annually produced in the
ds could not amount to less than TWO *millions of gallons*. In corroboration of this
, that in 1821, only 298,138 gallons were brought to the charge in the High-
nd of these, 254,600 gallons were permitted to the Lowlands, leaving only
allons for the consumption of the whole country ; — a supply which, we are
red, would hardly be sufficient for the demand of two moderately populous
In a letter of Captain Munro of Teaninich to the commissioners, it is stated
t Tain, where there are upwards of twenty licensed public houses, *not one gallon
permitted from the legal distilleries for upwards of twelve months*," though a small
of smuggled whisky had been purchased at the excise sales, to give a colour of
o the trade. The same gentleman thus expresses himself in another part of his
" The moral effects of this baneful trade of smuggling on the lower classes is
spicuous, and increasing in an alarming degree, as evidenced by the multiplicity
, and by a degree of insubordination formerly little known in this part of the
In several districts, such as Strathconon, Strathcarron, &c., the excise officers
often deforced, and dare not attempt to do their duty ; and smuggled whisky is
ried to market by smugglers escorted by *armed* men, in defiance of the laws.
the Irish system is making progress in the Highlands of Scotland."
est the progress of demoralisation, government, pursuant to the judicious advice
mmissioners, reduced the duties on Scotch to the same level as those on Irish
and the consequences have been equally salutary. Smuggling is now almost
; the revenue has been greatly increased ; and though drinking is, perhaps,
t more prevalent in Edinburgh and some of the other large towns, it has
very much throughout the Highlands. We believe, indeed, we are warranted
ng, that the total consumption of spirits in Scotland at this moment is decidedly
in 1823. The subjoined official statement shows the effect of the measure
nsumption of legally distilled spirits, and on the revenue : —

An Account of the Quantities of Spirits made in Scotland, which have paid the Duties of Excise for Consumption; stating the Rate of Duty paid; and also the Nett Amount of Revenue received in Year, since the Year 1820.—(*Parl. Paper*, No. 340. Sess. 1829., and No. 61. Sess. 1831.)

Years.	Number of Gallons.	Rate per Gallon.	Nett Amount of Revenue.
	Imp. Measure.		£. s. d.
1821	2,229,435	5s. 6d. per English wine gallon.	727,650 19 7
1822	2,079,556	Ditto.	691,136 6 6
1823	2,232,728	Ditto ; { from 10th Oct. 1823, 2s. per English } wine gallon.	536,654 17 8
1824	4,350,301	Ditto.	520,624 18 4
1825	5,981,550	Ditto.	682,848 11 1
1826	3,988,788	2s. 10d. per Imperial gallon.	563,263 4 0
1827	4,752,199	Ditto.	672,441 6 6
1828	5,716,180	Ditto.	809,559 6 7
1829	5,777,280	Ditto.	818,448 0 0
1830	6,007,539	3s. and 3s. 4d. per ditto.	939,534 1 10

Duties in England.—Previously to the reduction of the duty on Irish and Scotch s the duty on English spirits had been as high as 10s. 6d. a gallon. This high dut, the restrictions under which the trade was placed, were productive of the worst c They went far to enable the distillers to fix the price of spirits, " and consequently, quote the words of the commissioners) " to raise it much beyond that which was cient to repay, with a profit, the cost of the manufacture, and the duty advanced crown." And, in proof of this, the commissioners mention, that in November, " when corn spirits might be purchased in Scotland for about 2s. 3d. a gallo: spirits could not be purchased in England for less than 4s. 6d. ready money, and 4 credit, omitting, in both cases, the duty." In consequence of this state of thin, adulteration of spirits was carried on to a great extent in England; and the profits made by the smuggler occasioned clandestine importation in considerable tities from Scotland and Ireland. To obviate these inconveniences, and, at the time, to neutralise the powerful additional stimulus that the reduction of the du Scotland and Ireland would have given to smuggling, had the duties in Englan continued at their former amount, the latter were reduced, in 1825, to 7s. a gallon lities being at the same time given to the importation of spirits from the other p. the empire. It is of the effects of this measure that so many complaints are though nothing can well be imagined more completely destitute of foundation. commissioners estimate the consumption of British spirits in England and W 1823, at 5,000,000 gallons — (*Sup. to Fifth Report*, p. 8.); and it appears from th joined account, that it amounted, for the year ending 5th January, 1831, to 7,7 gallons; producing 2,857,147l. 19s. of revenue: so that, making allowance f increase of population, and the check given to adulteration and smuggling, the i must appear very trifling indeed; and we are warranted in affirming, that the red of the duties has been as eminently successful in England as in either Scotl Ireland.

Account of the Quantities of British, Colonial, and Foreign Spirits, which paid the Home Cons Duty for England ,Scotland, and Ireland, from the Year 1821 to 1830 inclusive. — (*Parl. Paper*, Sess. 1831.)

Years.	England.			Scotland.			Ireland.		
	Foreign.	Colonial.	British.	Foreign.	Colonial.	British.	Foreign.	Colonial.	B:
	Imp. Gal.	*Imp. Gal.*	*Imp. Gal.*	*Imp. Gal.*	*Imp. Gal.*	*Imp. Gal.*	*Imp. Gal.*	*Imp. Gal.*	*Im*
1821	969,474	2,166,441	3,820,015	34,601	138,189	2,229,435	9,325	19,685	2,6
1822	1,054,540	2,100,925	4,346,348	35,739	130,879	2,079,556	10,225	15,035	2,3
1823	1,131,099	2,222,923	3,521,586	34,297	108,562	2,232,728	25,282	18,175	3,3
1824	1,268,609	2,407,207	4,067,233	47,710	134,986	4,350,301	1,352	9,453	6,6
1825	1,348,482	1,980,807	3,443,554	56,554	104,752	5,981,549	4,550	10,128	9,2
1826	1,498,230	3,982,053	7,407,205	42,092	295,505	3,988,789	9,452	27,758	6,8
1827	1,321,221	3,080,152	6,671,562	42,756	185,214	4,752,200	9,179	23,240	8,5
1828	1,325,197	3,064,856	7,759,687	45,749	188,089	5,716,180	9,779	24,708	9,5
1829	1,293,523	3,202,143	7,700,766	43,228	152,461	5,777,280	10,374	21,262	9,2
1830	1,267,397	3,503,141	7,732,101	38,967	137,806	6,007,631	10,406	18,011	9,0

The entire revenue from spirits in the United Kingdom, in 1830, amounted t

	£	s.	d.
British Spirits - -	5,209,559	0	0
Colonial and Foreign Spirits -	3,079,339	0	0
Total -	8,288,898	0	0

Owing to that absurd consolidation of the trade and revenue accounts of the Kingdom, previously alluded to (see *antè*, p. 431.), we are unable to give the

of duties collected in 1830, on the foreign spirits consumed in England,
and Ireland.

Spirits. — No spirits made in England, Scotland, or Ireland, shall be conveyed from England
or Ireland, or from Scotland or Ireland to England, otherwise than in casks containing *eighty*
the least, and in vessels of not less than *fifty* tons burthen.

ons whatsoever, not being licensed distillers, rectifiers, or compounders, having more than *eighty*
spirits in their possession, shall be deemed dealers in spirits, and subject to the survey of
of excise, and to all the regulations, penalties, &c. to which such persons are liable. — (6 Geo. 4.
.)

n British spirits are prohibited selling or having in their possession any plain British spirits,
its of wine, of any strength exceeding the strength of 25 per cent. above hydrometer, or of
h below 17 per cent. under hydrometer proof; or any compounded spirits, except shrub, of
strength than 17 per cent. under hydrometer, under pain of forfeiting all such spirits, with the
— § 124.

n foreign and British spirits are to keep them separate, in cellars, vaults, or other places
tered for that purpose, under a heavy penalty; and any person mixing, selling, or sending out
spirits mixed with foreign or colonial spirits, shall forfeit 100*l*. for every such offence. —

er of spirits, or any other person licensed or unlicensed, shall sell or send out from his stock or
y quantity of spirits exceeding one gallon, unless the same be accompanied by a true and law-
under pain of forfeiting 200*l*.; and any rectifier, compounder, or dealer in spirits, receiving the
heir stock, or allowing any one else to receive it, and any carrier, boatman, or other person,
carrying the same, shall forfeit the sum of 200*l*., with the boat, horse, cart, &c. used in the
§ 116.

e to be granted for retailing spirits within gáols, houses of correction, or workhouses for parish
re spirits to be used there, except medicinally prescribed by a regular physician, surgeon, or
Penalty for a first offence of this sort committed by goalers, &c., 100*l*.; a second offence to
forfeiture of their office. — § 134.

awking spirits to forfeit them and 100*l*.; and if the penalty be not immediately paid, they are
itted to the house of correction for 3 months, or until paid. — (§ 138.) Any person is
o detain a hawker of spirits, and give notice to a peace officer, who is to carry the offender
tice. — § 140.

er of excise, or other person employed in the excise, taking any sum of money or other
, or entering into any collusive agreement with, any person, to act contrary to his duty, to for-
d be incapacitated; and any person offering such reward or proposing such agreement, to
— § 145.

gulations as to the importation, &c., of foreign spirits, see BRANDY, GENEVA, and RUM.

GE (Ger. *Schwamm*; Fr. *Eponge*; It. *Spugna*; Sp. *Esponja*), a soft,
y porous, and compressible substance, readily imbibing water, and as
ing it out again. It is found adhering to rocks, particularly in the Me-
n sea, about the islands of the Archipelago. It was formerly supposed
egetable production, but is now classed among the zoöphytes; and
it yields the same principles as animal substances in general. The in-
in several of the Greek islands have been trained from their infancy to
onges. They adhere firmly to the bottom; and are not detached with-
l deal of trouble. The extraordinary clearness of the water facilitates the
s of the divers. Smyrna is the great market for sponge. The price
n 6 to 16 piastres per oke for ordinary and dirty, and from 80 to 100
er oke for fine and picked specimens. Sponge is also fished in the Red
Jre's Dictionary, and private communications.)

sed in surgery, and for a variety of purposes in the arts. The duty on it, in 1829, produced
The duty is 2*s*. on all that is imported from foreign countries, and 6*d*. on that imported from
session. The far greater portion is brought from the former. No deduction is to be made
y on account of sand or dirt, unless it shall exceed 7 per cent., and then only for the excess
ent.

L (Ger. *Meerzwiebel*; Fr. *Scille, Oignon marin*; It. *Scilla, Cipolla marina*;
albarrana), or, as it is sometimes denominated, the sea onion, is a
a large bulbous root, which is the only part that is used. It grows
usly on sandy shores in Spain, and the Levant; whence we are an-
plied with the roots. They should be chosen large, plump, fresh, and
ammy juice: some are of a reddish colour, and others white; but no
is observed in the qualities of the two sorts. The root is very nauseous,
itter, and acrimonious; much handled, it ulcerates the skin. The bulbs
t to England, preserved fresh in sand. The acrimony of the roots, on
r virtue depends, is partially destroyed by drying and long keeping, and
ely destroyed by exposure to heat above 212°. Squill is one of the
rful and useful remedies in the materia medica. — (*Lewis's Mat. Med.*;
Dispensatory.)

, a small city of Hanover, on the Schwinge, 22 miles W. by N. of
It has very little trade; and would be quite unworthy of notice in a
s sort, except for the circumstance that a duty is paid here by all ships
e Elbe. This duty is generally about ½ per cent. *ad valorem*, but is a
heavier on some articles, and lighter on others. English ships may
ustom-house at Brunshausen, near Stade, without coming to an an-

chor. The following are the regulations they must observe, as laid do[wn in a]
proclamation of George II., dated the 1st of December, 1736 : —

1. That all English vessels be exempted from coming to an anchor before the river Schwinge, and allowed to sail directly up to Hamburgh.

2. Such English vessels shall be obliged, at their approach, within about a quarter of a league thereof, to hoist their colours, to lower their sails, and only to drive, till the legitimation is made at the king's frigate lying there.

3. The master of the ship, or a proper person fully provided with the necessary documents, is to go on board the frigate, and afterwards to the Custom-houses at Brunshausen and Stade ; and there to produce an exact manifest, and the original bills of lading, cockets, &c.

4. The documents being produced, the account shall be stated, and all duties must be paid at Brunshausen, Stade, or Hamburgh.

5. The clearance shall be given at Brunshausen to the person sent thither by the master of the vessel ; by whom it must be delivered to the king's commissary in Hamburgh, together with the documents of the cargo, and a specification of the parcels, bales, casks, &c. which were received on board at the port of lading, whether designed for Hamburgh or other places.

6. Bulk must not be broken till all this has been performed, except the king's commissary in Hamburgh permits, in urgent cases, the unloading.

7. The vessels being thus allowed to pass the frigate without being searched, in case of suspecting any fraud, the masters shall be obliged to sign a proper oath ; and the merchants in

Hamburgh, who receive effects by those vessels, sha[ll make]
exact report thereof, and give a certificate in lieu [of it]
— That they neither have received nor expected [more]
than have been specified : — which must be deli[vered to the]
Majesty's commissary in Hamburgh, to enable him [to make]
the report made by the master.

8. No master is to depart from Hamburgh before h[e gets]
a certificate from his Majesty's commissary, provi[ng that he]
has been duly performed ; which is to be sent to [the]
frigate, near Brunshausen.

9. The signals mentioned in the second article [are]
to be made when the ship repasses Stade.

10. The taking cognizance of, and punishing mis[demeanors,]
frauds, and mismanagements, as well as the negle[ct of the]
preceding articles, remains in the court of the Kin[g]
at Stade : so that both merchants and masters of [ships]
may be called to an account, shall, when summon[ed appear]
before the said court, and submit to its decisions [and]
have the liberty of appeal to the superior courts fo[r redress]
and relief.

11. As to all other points not expressly menti[oned in the]
foregoing articles, they shall be observed at the Ki[ng's Custom-]
houses at Brunshausen, Stade, and Hamburgh, a[ccording to]
the regulations and customs heretofore practised.

12. This gracious concession is hereby granted [during his]
lene placito ; the king reserving to himself and his s[uccessors in]
his German dominions the right of revoking it, [and of making]
any alterations or new orders, whenever they shall [see fit.]

STARCH (Ger. *Amidan;* Fr. *Amidon;* It. *Amido, Amito;* Sp. *Amidon, A[midon;*
Rus. *Kruchmal*), a substance obtained from vegetables. It has a fine white [colour,]
and is usually concreted in longish masses ; it has scarcely any smell, a[nd but]
little taste. When kept dry, it continues for a long time uninjured, tho[ugh ex-]
posed to the air. It is insoluble in cold water ; but combines with boiling [water,]
forming with it a kind of jelly. It exists chiefly in the white and brittle [parts of]
vegetables, particularly in tuberose roots, and the seeds of the gramineous [plants.]
It may be extracted by pounding these parts, and agitating them in cold [water ;]
when the *parenchyma,* or fibrous parts, will first subside ; and these being re[moved,]
a fine white powder, diffused through the water, will gradually subside, [which is]
the starch. Or the pounded or grated substance, as the roots of potatoes, [wheat,]
or horse chestnuts, for instance, may be put into a hair sieve, and the[n being]
washed through with cold water, leaving the grosser matters behind. Fari[naceous]
seeds may be ground and treated in a similar manner. Oily seeds require [that]
the oil expressed from them before the farina is extracted. Potato starch [swells a]
good deal further than wheat starch—a less quantity of it sufficing to form [a jelly]
of equal thickness, with water. It has a very perceptible crystallised app[earance,]
and is apparently heavier than common starch. — (*Thomson's Chemistry [and]
Dictionary.*)

Starch is charged with a duty of 3½d. per lb. ; and its manufacture is, consequently placed [under the]
control of the excise. Every maker of starch for sale must take out an annual licence, whi[ch &c. ...]
Notice must be given to the excise of the erection, and of all changes in the construction, of w[orking]
implements, &c. used in the manufacture of starch, under a penalty of 200l. All starch, befo[re being put]
into any stove or place to dry, must be papered and sealed or stamped by the officer, under a [penalty of]
100l. Any person forging or counterfeiting such stamp or seal is guilty of felony, but with the [benefit of]
clergy. Any person knowingly selling any starch with a forged or counterfeit stamp, &c., fo[rfeits &c.]
No quantity of starch exceeding 28 lbs. to be removed from one place to another, unless the w[hole shall]
be marked on the package in legible letters three inches long, under forfeiture of the package, [and of the]
cattle and carts conveying the same. Any dealer in starch receiving any quantity exceeding [28 lbs. not]
marked as above, shall forfeit 200l. Starch-makers are to make weekly entries of the starch [made by]
them, under a penalty of 50l. ; and are to make payment of the duties within a week of s[ending it out.]
Cockets granted for shipping starch to be carried coastwise are to express the quality, quanti[ty, and]
the mark of the package, by whom made and sold, and to whom consigned ; and if shipped wi[thout a]
cocket, it may be seized. No starch is to be imported, unless in packages containing at le[ast &c.,]
stowed openly in the hold, on pain of forfeiture and of incurring a penalty of 50l. No starch [to be ex-]
ported, unless the package as originally sealed or stamped by the officer be entire, and unless [it have the]
mark the word *exportation* upon it. The duties must have been paid on all starch exported ; [and the ex-]
porter is entitled to an excise drawback of 3½d. per lb. — (*Burn's Justice of the Peace,* Marri[ott on]
Starch.*)

Account of the Quantity of Starch that paid Duty in England and Scotland during the T[hree Years]
ending with 1829.

Years.	England.	Scotland.
	lbs.	*lbs.*
1827	6,756,936	601,033
1828	6,998,245	767,654
1829	5,554,874	812,333

STEEL (Fr. *Acier;* Ger. *Stahl;* It. *Acciajo;* Lat. *Chalybs;* Rus. [*Stal;*
Acero;* Sw. *Stål*), is iron combined with a small portion of carbon ; an[d it is]
for that reason, called carburetted iron. The proportion of carbon has [been]
ascertained with much precision. It is supposed to amount, at an average [to 1/100th]
part. Steel is so hard as to be unmalleable while cold ; or at least it acq[uires]

ty by being immersed, while ignited, in a cold liquid; for this immersion, it has no effect upon iron, adds greatly to the hardness of steel. It is resists the file, cuts glass, affords sparks with flint, and retains the mag- irtue for any length of time. It loses this hardness by being ignited, and very slowly. It is malleable when red hot, but scarcely so when raised to e heat. It may be hammered out into much thinner plates than iron. It e sonorous; and its specific gravity, when hammered, is greater than that of varying from 7·78 to 7·84. Steel is usually divided into three sorts, accord- the method in which it is prepared; as *natural steel*, *steel of cementation*, and *el*. The latter is the most valuable of all, as its texture is the most com- nd it admits of the finest polish. It is used for razors, surgeons' instru- and similar purposes. Steel is chiefly employed in the manufacture of , knives, and cutting instruments of all sorts used in the arts; for which it liarly adapted by its hardness, and the fineness of the edge which may be o it. — (*Thomson's Chemistry*; see IRON.)

OCKHOLM, the capital of Sweden, situated at the junction of the lake , with an inlet of the Baltic, in lat. 59° 20⅓′ N., lon. 18° 3½′ E. A well ndsome city; population about 100,000. The entrance to the harbour is dangerous; but the harbour itself is excellent, the largest vessels lying the quays. Stockholm possesses half the foreign trade of Sweden; but onfined within comparatively narrow limits, in consequence of the impo- orts of the government to promote industry by excluding foreign pro- Iron, steel, and copper, particularly the first, form the great articles of Swedish iron is of very superior quality, and is extensively used in Britain; the imports of it, in 1829, having amounted to about 9,000 tons, e of 400 tons of steel. In addition to the above leading articles, Stock- ports pitch, tar, and timber; but the latter is inferior to that from the n ports of the Baltic. The imports principally consist of corn, colonial s, fruit, salt, a small quantity of British manufactured goods, and a very antity of wine.

y. — Accounts are kept here and at Gottenburgh, and generally throughout in rixdollars, or crowns, of 48 schellings, each of 12 pfennings. Since 1777, in circulation have been gold ducats = 94 schellings, and silver rixdollars s, and ⅔, ⅓, ⅙, $\frac{1}{12}$, and $\frac{1}{24}$ rixdollars. The Swedish ducat is worth 9*s.* 2½*d.* in English gold coin; but in Sweden it passes only for 94 schellings, and worth only 9*s.* 1*d.* in English silver coin. The Swedish rixdollar = 4*s.* 7½*d.* so that 1*l.* = 207 schellings. The paper currency of Sweden is very ex- circulated, and is often at a heavy discount.

s and Measures. — The victuali or commercial weights are pounds, lispounds, ounds; 20 pounds being equal to 1 lispound, and 20 lispounds = 1 shippound; Swedish commercial weight = 93¾ lbs. avoirdupois = 42½ kilog. = 87¾ lbs. urgh.

on weights are ⅘ths of the victuali or commercial weights; 20 marks = 1 mark 20 mark pounds = 1 shippound; and 7½ shippounds = 1 ton English. 00 lbs. Swedish iron weight = 75 lbs. avoirdupois, and 100 lbs. avoirdupois bs. Swedish iron weight.

neasure: —

els -	=	1	Spann.
n - -	=	1	Ton.
-	=	4⅛	Winch. bush.
of rye from Riga	=	18	tons.
Ditto Liebau	=	19½	—
Ditto Stettin	=	22⅓	—
Ditto Stralsund	=	24	—

co, grain measure, equals 3¼ Winchester he turma of 32 kapper contains 4⅛ Win- hels.

In liquid measure: —

2 Stoof	=	1	Kanne.
15 Kannes	=	1	Anker.
2 Ankers	=	1	Eimer.
2 Eimers	=	1	Ahm.
1½ Ahm	=	1	Oxhoft.
2 Oxhoft	=	1	Pipe.

The pipe = 124¼ English wine gallons; and, consequently, the ahm = 41 $\frac{5}{12}$ ditto, and 100 kannes = 69$\frac{}{3}$ ditto.

ish foot = 11·684 English inches; the ell = 2 feet; the fathom = 3 ells; the rod = 8 ells.

ting by lasts: —

tch, ashes, &c. = 12 barrels.
ar, oil, &c. = 13 ditto.
1 Last of hemp, flax, tallow, &c. = 6 shippounds.
1 Ton of Liverpool common salt = 7 tons Swed.

wing is the account given by the Royal Directory of the Mines of the exports of iron from the 4 years ending with 1824: —

	Iron in bars.	Iron in pigs, &c.
1821	314,945 shippounds.	26,045 shippounds.
1822	346,754 —	27,760 —
1823	402,001 —	27,711 —
1824	345,377 —	28,515 —

(*Bulletin des Sciences Géographiques*, xv. p. 280.)

The College of Commerce of Sweden have published the following details with respect to the [...] and navigation of the kingdom in 1829 : —

In 1829, the number of vessels belonging to the different towns of the kingdom was 1,178, of th[...] then of 61,000 67-100ths tons ; of this number, only 389 were occupied in the interior navigation. S[...] landed proprietors possess vessels of various sizes for interior commerce, the number of which wa[...] mated at 486, carrying 9,000 tons.   The most part of those navigate the great lakes and canals, an[...] blish communication between the different provinces : they are principally employed in transporti[...] produce of the mines, and wood to the various sea ports, or in carrying merchandise and wheat fro[...] province to the other.

101 vessels, of the burthen of 45,231 9-12ths tons, manned by 4,797 sailors, were engaged in f[...] commerce.

Comparative Table of the Commerce direct from Sweden with Foreign Countries, in 1829.

| | Commerce | | | | | | Navigation | | | | |
| | Value of the Merchandise imported from Foreign Countries. | | | Value of the Merchandise exported from Sweden. | | | Tonnage of the Ships arrived at Sweden. | | | Tonnage of t[...] sailed from [...] | |
	By Swedish Ships.	By Foreign Ships.	Total.	By Swedish Ships.	By Foreign Ships.	Total.	Swedish Ships.	Foreign Ships.	Total.	Swedish Ships.	Foreign Ships.
			Rixdollars banco.*			Rixdollars banco.					
Norway - -	687,782	865,220	1,551,002	161,228	276,344	437,572	4,728	22,557	27,285	11,175	23,5[...]
Finland - -	12,544	1,481,200	1,493,744	27,367	621,805	642,172	1,386	33,139	34,597	1,360	43,3[...]
Russia - -	1,086,369	-	1,086,369	200,098	1,362	201,460	3,997	99	4,096	8,287	-
Prussia - -	7,450	31,864	39,314	275,183	48,852	324,035	2,074	436	2,510	4,225	4
Mecklenburgh -	149,290	281	149,574	390,441	10,086	400,527	4,096	651	4,747	4,546	6
Denmark, Copenhagen excepted -	51,606	156,274	207,880	640,545	99,111	739,656	17,099	1,137	18,236	20,834	1,0[...]
Netherlands, Rotterdam excepted -	19,790	24,617	44,307	537,336	244,012	781,348	2,641	513	3,154	6,259	5[...]
England - -	1,327,660	400,605	1,788,265	2,931,699	1,296,567	4,228,266	4,799	9,937	14,736	9,455	9,9[...]
France, Havre excepted -	311,537	16,910	328,447	800,789	193,317	994,106	2,557	98	2,655	14,294	
Spain - -	130,851	-	130,854	199,277	2,782	202,059	4,360	-	4,360	13,827	
Portugal - -	243,448	-	243,448	610,102	-	610,102	5,129	-	5,129	9,843	
Gibraltar - -	-	-	-	60,521	-	60,521	-	-	-	5,327	
Sardinia - -	-	-	-	51,079	-	51,079	227	-	227	1,342	
The Two Sicilies	15,146	-	15,146	25,773	-	25,773	1,736	-	1,736	3,494	
United States -	175,000	450,000	625,000	160,000	2,540,000	2,700,000	609	7,791	8,400	1,666	8,2[...]
Brazil - -	495,900	-	495,900	477,920	-	477,920	1,550	-	1,550	5,386	-
			8,199,244			12,883,396					

★ A rixdollar banco is worth, according to the exchange of 1829, about 20d.

STOCKINGS, as every one knows, are coverings for the legs. They [...] formed of only one thread entwined, so that it forms a species of tissue, extre[...] elastic, and readily adapting itself to the figure of the part it is employed to c[...] This tissue cannot be called cloth, for it has neither warp nor woof, but i[...] proaches closely to it. For the purposes to which it is applied, it is, how[...] very superior.

1. *Historical Sketch of the Stocking Manufacture.*—It is well known that the Ro[...] and other ancient nations had no particular clothing for the legs. During the middle [...] however, hose or *leggins*, made of cloth, began to be used ; and at a later perio[...] art of knitting stockings was discovered.   Unluckily, nothing certain is known as [...] individual by whom, the place where, or the time when, this important inventio[...] made.   Howell, in his History of the World (vol. iii. p. 222.), says, that Henry [...] wore none but cloth hose, except there came from Spain by great chance a pair [...] stockings ; that Sir Thomas Gresham, the famous merchant, presented Edwar[...] with a pair of long silk stockings from Spain, and that the present was much [...] notice of ; and he adds, that Queen Elizabeth was presented, in the third year [...] reign, with a pair of black knit silk stockings, and that from that time she ceased t[...] cloth hose. It would appear from this circumstantial account, that the art of k[...] stockings, or at least that the first specimens of knit stockings, had been introduce[...] England from Spain about the middle of the sixteenth century ; and such se[...] have been the general opinion, till an allusion to the practice of knitting, in t[...] tended poems of Rowley, forged by Chatterton, caused the subject to be more [...] investigated.   The result of this investigation showed clearly that the prac[...] knitting was well known in England, and had been referred to in acts of parlian[...] good many years previously to the period mentioned by Howell. But it had ther[...] probably, been applied only to the manufacture of woollen stockings ; and the [...] use of cloth hose shows that even these had not been numerous.   There is no ev[...] to show whether the art is native to England, or has been imported.—(See Beck[...] *Inventions*, vol. iv. art. *Knitting Netts and Stockings*.)

It is singular that the stocking frame, which, even in its rudest form, is a ver[...] plex and ingenious machine, that could not be discovered accidentally, but mu[...] been the result of deep combination and profound sagacity, should have been dis[...] so early as 1589, before, in fact, the business of knitting was generally introduce[...] inventor of this admirable machine was Mr. William Lee, of Woodborough, in N[...]

. He attempted to set up an establishment at Calverton, near Nottingham, for
.facture of stockings, but met with no success. In this situation he applied to
. for assistance ; but instead of meeting with that remuneration to which his
.d inventions so well entitled him, he was discouraged and discountenanced !
.not, therefore, excite surprise that Lee accepted the invitation of Henry IV.
., who, having heard of the invention, promised him a magnificent reward if he
.rry it to France. Henry kept his word, and Lee introduced the stocking
.Rouen with distinguished success ; but after the assassination of the king, the
.got into difficulties, and Lee died in poverty at Paris. A knowledge of the
.was brought back from France to England by some of the workmen who had
.l with Lee, and who established themselves in Nottinghamshire, which still
.the principal seat of the manufacture.—(See *Beckmann's Inventions*, vol. iv.
.-324. ; and *Letters on the Utility and Policy of Machines*, Lond. 1780.)
.g the first century after the invention of the stocking frame, few improvements
.e upon it, and two men were usually employed to work one frame. But in
.e of last century the machine was very greatly improved. The late ingenious
.diah Strutt, of Derby, was the first individual who succeeded in adapting it to
.facture of *ribbed* stockings.
.*e of the Manufacture.* — Estimating the population of Great Britain at
.0, and the average annual expenditure of each individual upon stockings and
.s at 5s., the total value of the manufacture will be 4,000,000l. Of this sum,
.of the silk and cotton stockings and gloves may amount to 2,500,000l.

.AX. See BALSAM.

.ES, MILITARY AND NAVAL, include arms, ammunition, &c. It is
.that no arms, ammunition, or utensils of war, be imported by way of mer-
.except by licence, for furnishing his Majesty's public stores only. —
.. e. 107.)

.ES, in commercial navigation, the supplies of different articles pro-
.the subsistence and accommodation of the ship's crew and passengers.

.own, in general, that the surplus stores of every ship arriving from parts beyond seas are to
.the same duties and regulations as those which affect similar commodities, when imported
.ise ; but if it shall appear to the collector and comptroller that the quantity of such stores is
., nor unsuitable, under all the circumstances of the voyage, they may be entered for the
.f the master, purser, or owner of such ship, on payment of the proper duties, or be ware-
.he future use of such ship, although the same could not be legally imported by way of
. — (6 Geo. 4. c. 107. § 33.)

.NDING, in navigation, the running of a ship on shore or on the

.invariable practice to subjoin the following *memorandum* to policies of insur-
.ated by private individuals in this country :—" N. B.— Corn, fish, salt, fruit,
.seed, are warranted free from average, unless general, *or the ship be stranded ;*
.acco, hemp, flax, hides, and skins, are warranted free from average under 5l.
. and all other goods, also the ship and freight, are warranted free of average
.er cent., unless general, *or the ship be stranded.*"
.erefore, of the greatest importance accurately to define what shall be deemed
.. But this is no easy matter ; and much diversity of opinion has been en-
.ith respect to it. It would, however, appear that merely striking against a
.or shore, is not a stranding ; and that to constitute it, the ship must be upon the
.or some time (how long ?).—Mr. Justice Park has the following observations
.ject :—" It is not every touching or striking upon a fixed body in the sea or
.ill constitute a stranding. Thus Lord Ellenborough held, that in order to
.stranding, the ship must be *stationary ;* for that merely striking on a rock,
.*ing there a short time* (as in the case then at the bar, about a minute and a half),
.ssing on, though the vessel may have received some injury, is not a stranding.
.borough's language is important.—*Ex vi termini* stranding means lying on the
.mething analogous to that. To use a vulgar phrase, which has been applied
.ect, if it be *touch and go* with the ship, there is no stranding. It cannot be
.t the ship lie for a few moments on her beam ends. Every striking must
.produce a retardation of the ship's motion. If by the force of the elements
.ground, and becomes stationary, it is immaterial whether this be on piles, on
.bank of a river, or on rocks on the sea shore : but a mere *striking* will not do,
.t may happen. I cannot look to the consequences, without considering the
.s. There has been a curiosity in the cases about stranding not creditable to
.a little common sense may dispose of them more satisfactorily."
.e clearest and most satisfactory statement we have met with on this subject ;
.er, it is very vague. Lord Ellenborough and Mr. Justice Park hold, that
. a stranding. the ship must be *stationary ;* but they also hold, that if she

merely remain upon a rock, &c. for a *short time*, she is not to be considered as havi
stationary. Hence every thing turns upon what shall be considered as a sho
And we cannot help thinking that it would be better, in order to put to rest al
upon the subject, to decide either that every striking against a rock, the shore,
which damage is done to the ship, should be considered a stranding; or that no
against a rock, &c. should be considered as such, provided the ship be got off
specified time. Perhaps a *tide* would be the most proper period that could be fix
The Insurance Companies exclude the words, " or the ship be stranded," from
morandum.—(See Insurance, Marine.)

SUCCORY, or CHICCORY, the wild endive, or *Cichorium Intybus*
næus.

This plant is found growing wild on calcareous soils in England, and
countries of Europe, In its natural state the stem rises from 1 to 3 feet high, b
cultivated it shoots to the height of 5 or 6 feet. The root runs deep into the
and is white, fleshy, and yields a milky juice. It is cultivated to some extent
country as an herbage plant, its excellence in this respect having been strongly
upon by the late Arthur Young. But in Germany, and in some parts of the
lands and France, it is extensively cultivated for the sake of its root, which is u
substitute for coffee; and it is this circumstance only that has induced us to me
When prepared on a large scale, the roots are partially dried, and sold to the
facturers of the article, who wash them, cut them in pieces, kiln-dry them, an
them between fluted rollers into a powder, which is packed up in papers co
from 2 oz. to 3 or 4 lbs. The powder has a striking resemblance to dark groun
and a strong odour of liquorice. It has been extensively used in Prussia, Br
and other parts of Germany, for several years; but as it wants the essential oil
rich aromatic flavour of coffee, it has little in common with the latter except its
and has nothing to recommend it except its cheapness. It is only lately that
powder began to be used in England; but since the rise in the price of coffee, v
quantities have been imported from Hamburgh, Antwerp, &c. We believe, to
small quantity has been produced in the isle of Thanet. — (*Loudon's Ency.
culture; Rees's Cyclopædia*, and private information.)

Succory, being an unenumerated article, is charged with a duty of 20 per cent. *ad valorem.*
average price of British plantation coffee may be taken at this moment (10th of January, 1832)
cwt. in bond; and the duty, being 56s. per cwt., is equivalent to an *ad valorem* duty of about 60
so that *coffee is taxed three times as much as succory*. Had coffee been always sold ungroun
tinction in the duties would have been less objectionable; but as the lower classes, who are nov
consumers of coffee, have no facilities for roasting and grinding it at home, they uniformly bu
shape of powder. It is plain, therefore, that the discriminating duty in favour of succory mu
premium upon, and an incitement to, the adulteration of coffee. Instead, therefore, of its being
it is for the interest of the lower classes that the duties should remain on their present footi
their interest that they should be equalised. We have already shown that the duty on coffee c
reduced to 3d. per lb., or to about 30 per cent. *ad valorem*, and the duty on succory ought to b
the same level. The imposition of different duties upon *convertible articles* is quite subversiv
sound principle; and, whether it be so intended or not, is calculated only to promote adulte
fraud.

SUGAR (Fr. *Sucre*; Ger. *Zucker*; It. *Zucchero*; Russ. *Sachar*; Sp.
Arab. *Sukhir*; Malay *Soola*; Sans. *Sarkarā*), a sweet granulated substa
well known to require any particular description. It is every where in e
use; and in this country ranks rather among the indispensable necessarie
than among luxuries. In point of commercial importance, it is secon
articles. It is chiefly prepared from the expressed juice of the *arundo sac*
or sugar cane; but it is also procured from an immense variety of othe
as maple, beet, birch, parsnep, &c.

I. *Species of Sugar.* — The sugar met with in commerce is usually of four
brown or muscovado sugar, clayed sugar, refined or loaf sugar, and sugar candy.
ference between one sort of sugar and another depends altogether on the differe
in which they are prepared.

1. *Brown or Muscovado Sugar.* — The plants or canes being crushed in a
juice, having passed through a strainer, is collected in the clarifier, where it
posed to the action of a gentle fire after being " tempered " (mixed with alkal
purpose of facilitating the separation of the liquor from its impurities. It is
veyed into the large evaporating copper, and successively into two others, each
size; the superintending boiler freeing it, during the process, from the scum an
matters which rise to the surface. The syrup then reaches the last copper ves
the "striking tache," where it is boiled till sufficiently concentrated to be
granulating in the cooler, whence it is transferred with the least possible del
vent charring. Here it soon ceases to be a liquid; and when fully crystalli
into hogsheads (called " potting "), placed on their ends in the curing-house, w

es in their bottoms, through which the molasses drain into a cistern below. In
te they remain till properly cured, when the casks are filled up, and prepared for
nt.

layed Sugar is prepared by taking the juice, as in the case of muscovado sugar,
oiled to a proper consistency, and pouring it into conical pots with the apex
ards. Those pots have a hole at the lower extremity, through which the mo-
r syrup is allowed to drain. After this drain has continued for some time, a
a of moistened clay is spread over the surface of the pots; the moisture of which
ting through the mass, is found to contribute powerfully to its purification.

efined Sugar is prepared from muscovado or clayed sugar, by redissolving the
n water, and after boiling it with some purifying substances, pouring it, as before,
nical pots, which are again covered with moistened clay. A repetition of this
produces *double refined* sugar.

ugar Candy. — Solutions of brown or clayed sugar, boiled till they become
and then removed into a hot room, form, upon sticks or strings put into the
for that purpose, into crystals, or candy.

Historical Notice of Sugar. — The history of sugar is involved in a good deal of
y. It was very imperfectly known by the Greeks and Romans. Theophrastus,
ed about 320 years before the Christian era, the first writer whose works have
own to us by whom it is mentioned, calls it a sort of " honey extracted from
reeds." Strabo states, on the authority of Nearchus, Alexander's admiral, that
in India yield honey without bees." And Seneca, who was put to death in the
ar of the Christian era, alludes (Epist. 84.) to the sugar cane, in a manner which
nat he knew next to nothing of sugar, and absolutely nothing of the manner in
is prepared and obtained from the cane.

e ancients, Dioscorides and Pliny have given the most precise description of
The former says it is " a sort of concreted honey, found upon canes, in India
bia Felix; it is in consistence like salt, and is, like it, brittle between the teeth."
ny describes it as " honey collected from canes, like a gum, white and brittle
the teeth; the largest is of the size of a hazel nut: it is used in medicine only."
aron et Arabia fert, sed laudatius India; est autem mel in arundinibus collectum,
m modo candidum, dentibus fragile, amplissimum nucis avellanæ magnitudine, ad
tantum usum. — Lib. xii. c. 8.)

vident, from these statements, that the knowledge of the Greeks and Romans
pect to the mode of obtaining sugar was singularly imperfect. They appear
thought that it was found adhering to the cane, or that it issued from it in
of juice, and then concreted like gum. Indeed, Lucan expressly alludes to
near the Ganges —

Quique bibunt tenerâ dulces ab arundine succos. — (Lib. iii. l. 237.)

nese statements are evidently without foundation. Sugar cannot be obtained
cane without the aid of art. It is never found native. Instead of flow-
. the plant, it must be forcibly expressed, and then subjected to a variety of
.

oseley conjectures, apparently with much probability, that the sugar described
and Dioscorides, as being made use of at Rome, was sugar candy obtained
na. This, indeed, is the only sort of sugar to which their description will at
And it would seem that the mode of preparing sugar candy has been under-
practised in China from a very remote antiquity; and that large quantities of
een in all ages exported to India, whence, it is most probable, small quantities
eir way to Rome. — (*Treatise on Sugar*, 2d edit. pp. 66—71. This, as well
loseley's Treatise on Coffee, is a very learned and able work.)

e seems to be indebted to the Saracens not only for the first considerable sup-
ugar, but for the earliest example of its manufacture. Having, in the course
th century, conquered Rhodes, Cyprus, Sicily, and Crete, the Saracens intro-
o them the sugar cane, with the cultivation and preparation of which they
iliar. It is mentioned by the Venetian historians, that their countrymen im-
a the twelfth century, sugar from Sicily at a cheaper rate than they could import
gypt. — (*Essai de l'Histoire du Commerce de Venise*, p. 100.) The crusades
spread a taste for sugar throughout the Western world; but there can be no
t it was cultivated, as now stated, in modern Europe, antecedently to the era
usades; and that it was also previously imported by the Venetians, Amal-
ud others, who carried on a commercial intercourse, from a very remote epoch,
andria and other cities in the Levant. It was certainly imported into Venice
.(See the *Essai, &c.* p. 70.)

of refining sugar, and making what is called loaf-sugar, is a modern Eu-
vention, the discovery of a Venetian about the end of the fifteenth or the
of the sixteenth century. — (*Moseley*, p. 66.)

The Saracens introduced the cultivation of the sugar cane into Spain soon after obtained a footing in that country. The first plantations were at Valencia; but were afterwards extended to Granada and Murcia. Mr. Thomas Willoughby, travelled over great part of Spain in 1664, has given an interesting account of the st the Spanish sugar plantations, and of the mode of manufacturing the sugar.

Plants of the sugar cane were carried by the Spaniards and Portuguese to the C islands and Madeira, in the early part of the fifteenth century; and it has been ass by many, that these islands furnished the first plants of the sugar cane that ever in America.

But though it is sufficiently established, that the Spaniards early conveyed pla the sugar cane to the New World, there can be no doubt, notwithstanding Hum seems to incline to the opposite opinion, — (*Essai Politique sur la Nouvelle Es*; liv. iv. c. 10.),—that this was a work of supererogation, and that the cane was indig both to the American continent and islands. It was not for the plant itself, flourished spontaneously in many parts when it was discovered by Columbus, b the secret of making sugar from it, that the New World is indebted to the Spaniar Portuguese; and these to the nations of the East. — (See *Lafitau, Mœurs des Sau* tome ii. p. 150.; *Edwards's West Indies*, vol. ii. p. 238.)

Barbadoes is the oldest settlement of the English in the West Indies. The possession of it in 1627; and so early as 1646 began to export sugar. In 167 trade of Barbadoes is said to have attained its maximum, being then capable of emp 400 sail of vessels, averaging 150 tons burthen.

Jamaica was discovered by Columbus, in his second voyage, and was first occup the Spaniards. It was wrested from them by an expedition sent against it by Cro in 1656; and has since continued in our possession, forming by far the most valu our West Indian colonies. At the time when it was conquered, there were onl small sugar plantations upon it. But, in consequence of the influx of English from Barbadoes and the mother country, fresh plantations were speedily forme continued rapidly to increase.

The sugar cane is said to have been first cultivated in St. Domingo, or Hayti, in It succeeded better there than in any other of the West Indian islands. Peter I in a work published in 1590, states that in 1518 there were twenty-eight sugar-w St. Domingo established by the Spaniards. "It is marvellous." says he, "to c how all things increase and prosper in the island. There are now twenty-eigh presses, wherewith great plenty of sugar is made. The canes or reeds where sugar groweth are bigger and higher than in any other place; and are as big as wrist, and higher than the stature of a man by the half. This is more wonderf whereas in Valencia, in Spain, where a great quantity of sugar is made yearly, v ever they apply themselves to the great increase thereof, yet doth every root brin not past five or fix, or, at the most, seven of these reeds; whereas in St. Domir root beareth twenty, and oftentimes thirty."— (Eng. Trans. p. 172.)

Sugar from St. Domingo formed, for a very long period, the principal par European supplies. Previously to its devastation in 1790, no fewer than 65,000 sugar were exported from the French portion of the island.

III. *Sources whence the Supply of Sugar is derived.* — The West Indies, Brazil, Surinam, the E including the islands of Java, Mauritius, and Bourbon, are the principal sources whence the required for the European and American markets are derived. The average quantities expo these countries during the three years ending with 1830 were nearly as follows: —

	Tons.
British West Indies, including Demerara and Berbice	193,000
Mauritius	25,000
Bengal, Isle de Bourbon, Java, &c.	30,000
Cuba and Porto Rico	95,000
French, Dutch, and Danish West Indies	95,000
Brasil	70,000
	508,00

The consumption of sugar is rapidly extending on the Continent; the imports into which fror may amount to about 280,000 tons, including what is sent from Great Britain. The United State from 70,000 to 75,000 tons; but of these from 30,000 to 40,000 tons are produced in Louisiana. Abc tons are retained for home consumption in Great Britain, exclusive of about 9,000 tons of coarse bastards, made in this country from molasses. The quantity retained for home consumption in Ir not exceed 14,000 tons; she, however, derives a portion of her supply at second hand from Liver tol, and Glasgow; but there are no means of estimating what this may amount to. We hav stated at 5,000 tons.

IV. *Progressive Consumption of Sugar in Great Britain.*—We are not aware that there are any accounts with respect to the precise period when sugar first began to be used in England. It was imported in small quantities by the Venetians and Genoese in the fourteenth and fifteenth ce but honey was then, and long after, the principal ingredient employed in sweetening liquors a Even in the early part of the seventeenth century, the quantity of sugar imported was very incor and it was made use of only in the houses of the rich and great. It was not till the latter part o tury, when coffee and tea began to be introduced, that sugar came into general demand. In quantity consumed was about 10,000 tons, or 22,000,000 lbs.; at this moment the consumption ha (bastards included) to above 180,000 tons, or more than 400,000,000 lbs.; so that sugar forms no of the principal articles of importation and sources of revenue, but an important necessary of li

* In Marin's *Storia del Commercio de' Veneziani* (vol. v. p. 306.) there is an account of a shipm at Venice for England in 1319, of 100,000 lbs. of sugar, and 10,000 lbs. of sugar candy. The su to have been brought from the Levant.

wever, as the increase in the use of sugar has certainly been, it may, we think, be easily the demand for it is still very far below its natural limit; and that, were the existing duties le reduced, and the trade placed on a proper footing, its consumption, and the revenue derived ld be greatly increased.

e first half of last century, the consumption of sugar increased five-fold. It amounted, as d —

10,000 tons - or 22,000,000 lbs.	In 1754 to 53,270 tons - or 119,320,000 lbs.
14,000 — - 31,360,000 —	1770 — 1775, 72,500 (average) 162,500,000 —
42,000 — - 94,080,000 —	1786 — 1790, 81,000 - 181,500,000 —

n of Queen Anne the duty on sugar amounted to 3s. 5d. per cwt. Small additions were made eign of George II.; but in 1780 it was only 6s. 8d. In 1781, a considerable addition was made us duty; and in 1787 it was as high as 12s. 4d. In 1791, it was raised to 15s.; and while its d increasing consumption pointed it out as an article well fitted to augment the public revenue, on the public finances, caused by the French war, occasioned its being loaded with duties, h they yield a large return, would, there is good reason to think, have been more productive n lower. In 1797, the duty was raised to 17s. 6d.; two years after, it was raised to 20s.; and, augmentations in 1803, 1804, and 1806, it was raised to 30s.; but in the last mentioned year d, that, in the event of the market price of sugar in bond, or exclusive of the duty, being, for hs previous to the 5th of January, the 5th of May, or the 5th of September, below 49s. a cwt., the Treasury might remit 1s. a cwt. of the duty; that if the prices were below 48s. they might remit ow 47s. they might remit 3s., which was the greatest reduction that could be made. In 1826, declared to be constant at 27s., without regard to price; but last year it was reduced to 24s. a sugar, and to 32s. on East India sugar.

n foreign sugars is a prohibitory one of 63s. a cwt. Sugar from the Mauritius is, however, rovision, allowed to be imported at the same duty as West India sugar.

the Quantity of Sugar retained for Home Consumption in Great Britain, the Nett Revenue m it, and the Rates of Duty with which it was charged; and the Price, exclusive of the ch Year from 1789 to 1829, both inclusive.

Quantities re-ined for Home Consumption.	Nett Revenue.	Rates of Duty.			Price of Jamaica Brown or Muscovado Sugar in Bond. Per Gazette Average.
		British Plantation Sugar.	East India Sugar.		
Cwt.	£ s. d.	Per Cwt. £ s. d.	Per Cwt. £ s. d.	Per Cent. ad valorem. £ s. d.	Per Cwt. £ s. d.
1,547,109	862,632 11 11	0 12 4	-	37 16 3	
1,536,232	908,954 17 4				
1,403,211	1,074,903 16 5	0 15 0	0 2 8	37 16 3	
1,361,592	1,012,538 12 1				
1,677,097	1,316,502 14 3				
1,489,392	1,031,492 4 2				
1,336,230	949,961 16 1				
1,554,062	1,225,213 7 5				
1,273,722	1,299,744 0 7	0 17 6	0 5 2	37 16 3	
1,476,552	1,794,990 15 9	0 19 0	0 5 2	40 16 3	
2,772,438	2,321,935 16 5	1 0 0	0 2 6	42 16 3	
1,506,921	1,835,112 11 1				
2,773,795	2,782,232 18 1	- -	0 3 2	42 16 3	
2,250,311	2,210,801 6 11				
1,492,565	1,551,457 17 11	1 4 0	1 6 4¾	1 4 0	
2,144,369	2,458,124 18 3	1 6 6	1 9 1¾	1 6 6	
2,076,103	2,439,795 1 10	1 7 0	1 9 8¾	1 7 0	
2,801,747	3,097,590 3 6				
2,277,665	3,150,753 6 3				
2,842,813	4,177,916 3 4	- -	1 10 0	1 0 0	
2,504,507	3,273,995 2 8				
3,489,312	3,117,330 12 9	1 9 0 1 8 0	1 12 0 1 11 0	1 0 0 1 0 0	
3,226,757	3,339,218 4 3	1 7 0	1 10 0	1 0 0	
2,604,019	3,939,939 17 2				
2,209,063	3,447,560 4 5	1 10 0	1 13 0	1 0 0	
			Per Cwt.		
,997,999	3,276,513 6 5	- -	£1 10 1 11 1 19		
,888,965	2,957,403 2 4	- -	1 10 1 17		3 2 8
,228,156	3,166,851 18 0	1 7 0	1 19 2 0 1 17		2 8 1½
,960,794	3,967,154 5 0	- -	1 17		2 9 7½
,457,707	2,331,472 3 5	1 10 0	2 0		2 11 1
,474,738	3,507,844 11 0	1 8 0 1 7 0	1 18 1 17		2 1 5¼
,581,256	3,477,770 11 4	1 7 0	1 17		1 16 3¾
,676,274	3,660,567 6 7	- -	-	-	1 14 4¾
,618,490	3,579,412 12 1	- -	-	-	1 11 2¾
,842,676	4,022,782 4 1	- -	-	-	1 13 2¾
,957,261	4,223,240 18 5	- -	-	-	1 11 0¾
,655,959	3,766,654 0 1	- -	Duty on Mauritius Sugar reduced to 27s.		1 18 11¾
,255,075	4,518,690 15 9	- -			1 11 8¾
,021,191	4,218,623 6 7	- -	-	-	no average.
,285,843	4,576,287 13 4	- -	-	-	1 11 8¾
,495,709	4,452,793 18 11	- -	-	-	1 7 10

m the distilleries included in these years.

to 1820, the importation of East India sugar was comparatively trifling, and does not at nount to above 190,000 cwt. The imports from the Mauritius have increased rapidly five years, more especially since 1826, when the duty on sugar from that island was re- ne level as that on sugar from the West Indies. They now exceed 450,000 cwt.

II. An Account of the Quantities of Unrefined Sugar retained for Home Consumption in the Unit[ed King]dom, during each of the Years ending 5th January, 1815 to 1831 (both inclusive); distingui[shing the] Quantities of British Plantation, of Mauritius, of East India, and of Foreign Plantation, en[tered for] Home Consumption, or for being refined for Exportation; the Nett Amount of Duty an[d Re]ceived on the whole, after deducting the Drawback on British Refined Sugar exported, an[d Pay]ments for Over-entries.

Years.	Quantities of Unrefined Sugar charged with Duty, either for the Actual Consumption of the United Kingdom, or the Purpose of Exportation in a Refined State.							Quantities of Sugar retained for Home Consumption in the United Kingdom, after deducting the Amount exported in a Refined State subsequently to the Payment of Duty.	Ne[tt Amount] of the [Duty on] Su[gar] Un[ited King]dom [paid] du[ring] Dr[awback] Brit[ish Refined] Suga[r] an[d Pay]men[ts]
	Of the British Plantation.	Of Mauritius.	Of the East Indies.		Of the Foreign Plantations, including Sugar of Martinique and Guadaloupe, admitted under Act 53 Geo. 3. c. 62.		Total of all Sorts.		
			For Home Consumption.	For Refining.	For Home Consumption.	For Refining.			
	Cwt.	Cwt.	Cwt.	Cwt.	Cwt.	Cwt.	Cwt.	Cwt.	
1814	3,054,736		14,116	- -	205,297	- -	3,274,149	2,324,051	
1815	3,144,868		43,041	- -	37,228	- -	3,225,137	2,211,299	
1816	3,413,236		33,979	- -	49,493	- -	3,496,708	2,529,931	
1817	4,414,679	Consider-	27,332	- -	4,575	- -	4,446,586	3,298,941	
1818	2,872,070	ed as	25,056	- -	418	- -	2,897,544	1,726,896	
1819	3,571,054	East India	100,047	- -	244	- -	3,671,345	2,820,900	
1820	3,911,512	Sugar	84,795	- -	280	- -	3,996,587	2,901,864	
1821	3,962,300	in these	120,203	- -	268	- -	4,082,771	3,056,882	
1822	3,410,987	years.	137,093	- -	286	- -	3,548,366	2,989,057	
1823	3,802,931		102,901	- -	183	- -	3,906,015	3,228,991	
1824	3,854,789		152,673	- -	50	- -	4,007,512	3,367,424	
1825	3,443,734	{78,671 from 5 July 1825.}	107,200	- -	25	- -	3,629,630	3,079,848	
1826	3,905,538	111,285	143,312	- -	26	- -	4,160,161	3,573,990	
1827	3,747,232	170,257	69,945	29,406	186	19,304	4,036,330	3,340,927	
1828	4,037,450	241,794	97,245	38	11	1,505	4,378,043	3,601,419	
1829	3,980,453	240,318	118,400	2,873	11	6,200	4,348,255	3,539,821	
1830	4,145,733	435,010	131,979	3,922	25	38,261	4,754,930	3,722,044	

III. Account of the Quantity of Sugar imported into the United Kingdom, from the several [British Colonies] and Plantations, from the British Possessions in the East Indies and from Foreign Countr[ies in the Year] ended 5th January 1831; distinguishing the several Sorts of Sugar, and the Colonies and [Countries from] which the same was imported.

	Unrefined Sugar imported into the United Kingdom, in th[e Year ended] 5th January 1831.			
	Of the British Plantations.	Of Mauritius.	Of the East Indies.	Of the Foreign Plantations.
	Cwt. qrs. lbs.	Cwt. qrs. lbs.	Cwt. qrs. lbs.	Cwt. qrs. lbs.
British Colonies and Plantations in America, viz.				
Antigua	158,611 1 16	- -	- -	- -
Barbadoes	336,881 0 11	- -	- -	- -
Dominica	60,063 0 20	- -	- -	- -
Granada	213,160 1 13	- -	- -	- -
Jamaica	1,379,347 3 2	- -	- -	0 0 8
Montserrat	20,646 0 17	- -	- -	- -
Nevis	54,236 1 21	- -	- -	- -
St. Christopher	133,452 0 22	- -	- -	- -
St. Lucia	86,971 0 10	- -	- -	- -
St. Vincent	261,551 2 9	- -	- -	0 0 3
Tobago	93,471 2 4	- -	- -	- -
Tortola	17,099 3 7	- -	- -	- -
Trinidad	204,987 0 10	- -	- -	- -
Bermudas	894 2 13	- -	- -	- -
Demerara	780,286 2 12	- -	- -	- -
Berbice	110,967 2 21	- -	- -	- -
British North American Colonies	640 1 8	- -	- -	- -
Mauritius	- -	485,326 0 15	- -	- -
British Possessions in the East Indies, viz.				
East India Company's Territories, exclusive of Singapore.	- -	- -	213,494 0 23	- -
Singapore	- -	- -	38,535 0 4	- -
Java	- -	- -	5,950 3 11	- -
Philippine Islands	- -	- -	35,780 3 0	- -
China	- -	- -	8 1 4	- -
New South Wales	0 0 18	- -	- -	- -
Foreign Colonies in the West Indies:				
Cuba	- -	- -	- -	118,338 0 [..]
Porto Rico	- -	- -	- -	6,921 3 [..]
St. Thomas	- -	- -	- -	1 3 [..]
Surinam	- -	- -	- -	645 2 [..]
United States of America	- -	- -	- -	1,521 2 [..]
Colombia	- -	- -	- -	197 1 [..]
Brazil	- -	- -	- -	94,549 3 [..]
Peru	- -	- -	- -	1 1 [..]
Europe	- -	383 3 8	- -	1,079 0 [..]
Total	3,913,269 0 10	485,709 3 23	293,769 0 14	223,256 3 [..]

...ount of the Amount of Duties received on Sugar in the United Kingdom, in the Year ended ...nuary 1831, distinguishing each Sort of Sugar; also, of the Amount of Drawbacks and Boun...owed upon the Exportation thereof, and the Nett Produce of the Duties on Sugar, in the United ...om, in such Year.

	Gross Receipt of Duties on Sugar.				
	Of the British Plantations.	Of Mauritius.	Of the East Indies.	Of the Foreign Plantations, and Refined Sugar.	Total.
	£ s. d.	£ s. d.	£ s. d.	£ s. d.	£ s. d.
...ded 5th Ja-⎱ ...y 1831 ⎰	5,226,965 17 1	558,207 4 11	230,184 12 2	47,964 2 4	6,063,321 16 6

	Payments out of the Gross Receipt of Duties on Sugar.			Nett Produce of the Duties on Sugar in the United Kingdom.
	Bounties paid on British Refined Sugar exported.	Repayments on Over-Entries, Damages, &c.	Total.	
	£ s. d.	£ s. d.	£ s. d.	£ s. d.
...ded 5th Ja-⎱ ...1831 ⎰	1,286,753 4 10	9,226 11 1	1,295,979 15 11	4,767,342 0 7

...nt of the Quantity of Raw and Refined Sugar exported from the United Kingdom, in the Year ...th January 1831; reducing the Quantity of Refined into its Proportion of Raw; distinguishing ...ral Sorts of Sugar, and the Countries to which the same was exported.

	Raw Sugar.					Refined Sugar.		Total (stated in Cwts.) of Raw Sugar.
...s to which exported.	Of the British Plantations.	Of Mauritius.	Of the East Indies.	Of the Foreign Plantations.	Total of Raw Sugar.	Actual Weight exported.	The same stated as Raw Sugar, in the Proportion of 34 Cwt. of Raw to 20 Cwt. of Refined.	
	Cwt. qrs.	Cwt. qrs.	Cwt. qrs.	Cwt. qrs.	Cwt. qrs.	Cwt. qrs.	Cwt. qrs.	Cwt. qrs.
. . .	0	9 2	4,343 0	44,280 2	48,640 2	4,558 2	7,749 3	56,390 1
. . .	.	746 1	6,473 1	12,166 1	19,386 1	3,359 3	5,711 2	25,097 3
. . .	.	816 2	565 3	453 0	1,835 1	1,227 3	2,087 0	3,922 2
. . .	4 1	837 2	1 3	456 1	1,300 0	1,506 0	2,360 1	3,860 1
. . .	1,527 2	4,962 2	9,595 3	13,039 3	29,126 0	40,024 3	68,042 0	97,168 1
...s	489 3	20,340 0	9,014 1	16,033 2	45,877 3	251,336 1	427,271 3	473,149 3
. . .	4 2	6,070 3	23,211 3	42,936 1	72,223 3	1,157 0	1,967 0	74,191 0
...s, and Madeira	29 0	80 0	1,855 3	406 2	2,371 0	.	62 3	2,434 3
...ries	10 1	0 3	.	308 1	319 2	.	.	319 2
. . .	.	851 0	495 1	844 0	4,087 2	5,714 2	9,714 3	13,802 0
. . .	3 3	2,748 0	369 2	3,165 1	4,390 0	5,154 0	8,761 3	13,152 2
. . .	1,942 1	7,828 3	16,187 2	25,366 1	51,364 3	214,020 3	363,835 1	415,200 1
. . .	236 3	346 3	3,162 0	3,018 2	6,764 2	17,944 1	30,505 2	37,270 1
. . .	1 3	320 1	816 0	75 0	1,213 1	10,720 2	18,224 3	19,438 1
. . .	38 2	201 0	4,801 3	594 0	5,638 3	27,282 0	46,379 1	52,018 0
...y, Alderney, and Man	5,715 1	259 0	.	1,800 1	7,774 3	3,087 1	5,248 2	13,023 2
	10,052 3	46,420 0	80,897 2	164,946 0	302,316 2	587,131 3	998,124 0	1,300,440 2
...China	140 0	599 3	122 1	308 2	1,171 2	844 2	1,435 2	2,607 1
...es, Swan River, and⎱ ...Land ⎰	30 3	227 0	45 0	14 0	317 0	491 2	835 3	1,153 0
...pe	7 3	32 0	7 0	26 3	73 3	335 3	571 0	645 0
...frica	133 0	140 2	433 2	178 0	885 1	914 1	1,554 1	2,439 2
...merican Colonies	2,742 1	713 0	731 0	487 3	4,677 1	10,677 3	18,152 1	22,829 3
...lies	31 0	171 0	432 3	41 3	682 3	4,096 2	6,964 0	7,646 3
...dies	29 1	34 1	182 0	167 0	412 3	263 3	448 1	861 1
...America	43 2	.	522 1	64 3	630 3	2,521 3	4,287 1	4,918 0
. . .	27 0	4 1	9 2	18 0	59 0	2 0	3 3	62 3
. . .	11 1	.	3 2	5 3	20 3	9 3	16 3	37 3
...de la Plata .	42 3	26 3	7 2	38 3	116 0	9 0	15 1	131 1
. . .	29 3	1 0	.	9 1	40 1	148 2	252 3	293 0
. . .	18 0	5 3	13 0	1 0	38 1	130 0	221 1	259 3
. . .	11 0	3 0	1 3	1 1	17 2	1 3	3 0	20 3
Total . .	13,355 0	48,383 0	83,413 1	166,310 1	311,461 2	607,580 1	1,032,886 1	1,344,348 0

...e of the Duties. — The price of sugar, exclusive of the duty, may be taken, at an average of ...years, at from 22s. to 35s. But to lay a tax of 24s. on a necessary of life costing only 22s. or 35s. ...per cwt. freight and charges, is obviously a most oppressive proceeding. Indeed, there does ...e much room for doubting that the consumption, and consequently also the revenue, would be ...increased by reducing the duty to 16s. or 18s. This may be pretty confidently inferred from ...of consumption that has invariably followed every fall in the price of sugar. During the ...ending with 1808, when the price of brown or muscovado sugar, inclusive of the duty, was ...wt., there were, at an average, 2,640,741 cwt. retained for home consumption. During the ...nding with 1816, the price was about 93s., and the average quantity retained for home con-...d off to 2,038,373 cwt. But during the three years ending with 1829, the price having ...ut 57s., the average quantity retained for home consumption rose to 3,267,581 cwt.; being ...f more than fifty per cent. upon the quantity consumed during the previous period ! ...oserved that the duty was either the same, or very nearly the same, in those three periods; ...en imposed on an ad valorem principle, or made to vary directly as the price, the reduction ...entioned period would have been proportionally greater, and there would, consequently, have ...reater increase of consumption. ...ion of 3s. a cwt. from the duty in 1830 was too trifling to have much effect; and it is difficult ...portion of the increased consumption that has taken place is to be ascribed to it, and ...r things. But if, instead of reducing the duty from 27s. to 24s., it had been reduced from 27s. ...., the reduction would have had a powerful influence; and would certainly have occasioned ...se in the consumption of the lower priced sugars, particularly in Ireland. ...ty of sugar consumed in Great Britain is, at present, allowing for the quantity sent to Ireland, ...ouble what it was in 1790. But had the duty continued at 12s. 4d., its amount in 1790, there ...ink, be much doubt that the consumption would have been quadrupled. During the interven-...e population has been little less than doubled; and the proportion which the middle classes ...e whole population has been decidedly augmented. The consumption of coffee — an article ...ation of which a great deal of sugar is used in this country, by all who can afford it — is more ...wo times as great now as in 1790; that is, it has increased from under 1,000,000 lbs. to above ...! The consumption of tea has about doubled; and there has been a vast increase in the

use of home made wines, preserved and baked fruits, &c. Instead, therefore of having done lit
than increase proportionally to the increase of the population, it may be fairly presumed that
sumption of sugar would, had there not been some powerful counteracting cause in operation,
creased in a far greater degree. Instead of amounting to little more than 3,000,000 cwt. it ought
amounted to 5,000,000 cwt.

Taking the aggregate consumption of Great Britain at 3,300,000 cwt., and the population at 16
the average consumption of each individual will be about 23 lbs. This, though a far greater avera
that of France, or any of the continental states, is small compared with what it might be were su
plied under a more liberal system. In workhouses, the customary annual allowance for each in
is, we believe, 34 lbs.; and in private families, the smallest separate allowance for domestic
a week, or 59 lbs. a year. These facts strongly corroborate what we have already stated as to th
to which the consumption of sugar may be increased; and others may be referred to, that are, if
still more conclusive. Mr. Huskisson stated, in his place in the House of Commons, on Mr
motion for a reduction of the sugar duties, 25th May, 1829, that "in consequence of the present e
duty on sugar, the poor working man with a large family, to whom pence were a serious consi
was denied the use of that commodity; and he believed *he did not go too far when he stated,*
THIRDS *of the poorer consumers of coffee drank that beverage without sugar.* If, then, the price
were reduced, it would become an article of his consumption, like many other articles — woo
example, which are now used from their cheapness — which he was formerly unable to purc
(*Speeches*, vol. iii. p. 455.) There are no grounds for thinking that this statement is in any degr
gerated; and it strikingly shows the very great extent to which the consumption of sugar mig
creased, were it brought fully under the command of the labouring classes.

It is in Ireland, however, that we should anticipate the greatest and most salutary effects f
duction of the duties on sugar. The direct importations into Ireland do not exceed 14,000 tons;
add to these 6,000 tons for the second hand importations from Great Britain, which, we believe
as much, or more than they amount to, the entire consumption of that country will be 20,00
44,800,000 lbs., which, taking the population of Ireland at 8,000,000, gives about 5½ lbs. to each in
or between one fourth and one fifth part of the average consumption of each individual in Grea
So singular a result must, we believe, be ascribed, in a considerable degree, to the comparative p
the Irish; but there can be no doubt that it is partly, if not principally, owing to over-taxati
direct imports of sugar into Ireland were twice as great 30 years ago as they are at this mom
there is no reason for thinking that the increase in the second hand imports has been equivale
increase in the population. Hence, in order to diffuse a taste for so necessary an article as sug
the population of Ireland, it would be very desirable, if possible, to reduce the duties even as l
a cwt.; and we are well convinced that such reduction, though it might occasion an immediate lo
in the end, be productive of a great increase of revenue, besides being attended with other and
beneficial consequences. The "one thing needful" in Ireland is to inspire the population w
for the conveniences and enjoyments of civilised life; but how is it possible to do this while t
veniences are burdened with oppressive duties, that form an insuperable obstacle to their bein
any but the richest classes? Hence, the first step towards supplying what is confessedly the g
deratum in the case of Ireland, is to reduce the duties on articles of convenience and luxury, so
may become attainable by the mass of the people. If this be done, we may rest assured that
inherent in all individuals of improving their condition, will impel them to exert themselves
them. A taste for the articles in question will be gradually diffused amongst all ranks, and, ult
will be thought discreditable to be without them.— (*Parl. Paper*, No. 97. Sess. 1831.)

We have already seen that the imports of sugar from the British West Indies and the Mau
be estimated at 220,000 tons, and the consumption of Great Britain and Ireland at 189,000-ton
the latter, about 6,000 tons is Bengal sugar,—making the nett consumption of West India and
sugar 183,000 tons, leaving 37,000 tons of the latter for exportation, exclusive of the surplus
sugar. But were the duty on British sugar reduced to 16s. or 18s. a cwt., without any reductio
the same time made of the prohibitory duty on foreign sugar, the consequence would be, that t
the former would speedily rise, because of the increased demand, either to the present, or, whi
probable, to a higher level; so that the planters would reap the principal benefit from the
Hence the propriety of reducing the duty on foreign sugars, so that they might find their wa
markets, in the event of prices here being materially advanced. According to the resolution
sugar duties, submitted to the House of Commons in 1829 by Mr. Grant, the duties on British
and Mauritius sugar were fixed at 20s., those on East India sugar at 25s., and those on foreig
28s. a cwt. But, for the reasons already stated, these duties ought to be at least 4s. lower; th
ought to be respectively 16s., 21s., and 24s. At all events, however, it is abundantly clear, tha
ever degree the duty on British plantation sugar may be reduced, we must, in order to secu
advantage of the measure, reduce the duties on foreign sugar; so that, while our planters may
a preference proportioned to the greater burdens laid on them, it may be kept within due lim
interests of the public be adequately protected.

The duty on East India sugar ought to be reduced to the same level as that on West India
is difficult to imagine that there can be any good reason why all the productions of the diffe
dencies of the empire should not be allowed to come into the home market on paying the
The admission of Mauritius sugar at a duty of 27s. is, indeed, a full concession of the principle
is not a single argument that could be alleged in favour of admitting Mauritius sugar at the sa
West India sugar, that will not equally apply to Bengal sugar. However, we do not think tha
is of so much practical importance as is generally supposed. East India sugar has not, as yet
way in the continental markets, most of which are open to it on the same terms as to other s
unless its quality be materially improved, or its price considerably reduced, there is but little
its being able to come into competition with the sugars of Jamaica, Brazil, and Cuba.

Inquiry had become necessary as to the real operation of the present plan of granting
on the exportation of refined sugar. Previously to 1826, the drawback allowed was 46s.
single refined sugar, and since then it has been 41s. 6d.; but even at its present reduced rate,
be considerably more than the fair equivalent of the duty paid on the raw; and the fact, t
nothing save refined sugar is exported, would seem to prove that this is the case. It is the
making up returns to parliament, to reduce the refined sugar exported into raw sugar, by
cwt. of the latter to 20 of the former. But the export of sugar is thus made to appear gre
really is; for, though 34 cwt. of raw may be required to produce 20 cwt. of refined sugar, the
molasses and bastards that remain (about 13 cwt.), are consumed at home. It is therefore h
able that this matter should be inquired into, and carefully adjusted; and we are glad to h
that government have recently taken a sugar house in London, which they are now (Jan
working, in order to ascertain the exact quantity of refined sugar which each description
yield; and, consequently, to determine whether there be any latent bounty in the drawbac
sugar. The idea of giving a bounty on the exportation of sugar is out of the question.

The liberty recently granted to the British sugar refiners, to refine foreign sugars in this c
been much objected to by the West Indians; but, as it would appear, without any good reaso
gulations must have been very defective, if any part of such foreign sugar was admitted int
sumption: while, in consequence of the repeal of the prohibition, we have made Great Britain
for the sugar trade; and acquired a new and valuable business, which is better understood he
where else; and for the successful prosecution of which, the cheapness of our fuel, the magn
capital, and our other facilities, give us immense advantages.

s as to Importation, &c. of Sugar. — No allowance is to be made for damage or increase of
ater, on sugar, without special permission.

ritish plantation sugar — Under 8 cwt.						14 per cent.
8 cwt. and under 12 —						1 cwt. each cask.
12 — 15 —						1 cwt. 1 qr. 12 lbs. each cask.
15 — 17 —						1 2 0 —
17 and upwards						1 3 0 —

orted in foreign ships to be deemed *alien* goods, and to pay town and port dues accordingly.
c. 181. § 26.)

s of Growth are required before any sugar can be entered as the produce of a British pos-
merica, or of the Mauritius; and before it can be entered as the produce of any British posses-
the limits of the East India Company's charter. — (See the clauses in the act 6 Geo. 4. c. 107.,
).

Drawback on Sugar exported. — For this, see TARIFF. The exporter is obliged to give a bond
e value of the goods, with one sufficient surety, that the same shall be duly exported, and
relanded in the United Kingdom or any of its dependent islands. — (6 Geo. 4. c. 113. § 3.)

r is to be crashed. — If any sugar in lumps or loaves is to be pounded, crashed, or broken,
me be exported for the bounty payable thereon, such lumps or loaves shall, after due entry
odged in some warehouse provided by the exporter, and approved by the commissioners of
such purpose, to be then first examined by the officers of customs while in such lumps or
for immediate shipment; and afterwards to be there pounded, crashed, or broken, and
xportation, in the presence of such officers, and at the expense of the exporter; and such
e kept in such warehouse, and be removed thence for shipment, and be shipped under the
he charge of the searchers, in order that the shipment and exportation thereof may be duly
hem upon the debenture, according to the quality ascertained by them while in such lumps
§ 5.

rts of crashed Sugar to be kept separate. — *Sugar of inferior Quality.* — The different
sugar shall be kept apart from each other, in such a manner, and in such distinct rooms or
uch warehouse, as shall be directed and appointed by the commissioners of customs; and if
ich sugar be found in any part of such warehouse appointed for the keeping of sugar, of a
in quality thereto, the same shall be forfeited; and if any sort of such sugar be brought to
ise to be pounded, crashed, or broken, which shall be of a quality inferior to the sort of
ed in the entry for the same, such sugar shall be forfeited. — § 6.

amples. — There shall be provided by and at the expense of the committee of sugar refiners
id in like manner by and at the expense of the committee of merchants in Dublin, as many
ile refined sugar, prepared in manner herein-after directed, as the commissioners of customs
ecessary; which loaves, when approved of by the said commissioners, shall be deemed to be
ples; one of which loaves shall be lodged with the said committees respectively, and one
ch persons as the said commissioners shall direct, for the purpose of comparing therewith
I sugar, or sugar equal in quality to double refined sugar, entered for exportation for the
fresh standard samples shall in like manner be again furnished by such committees respect-
ike manner lodged, whenever it may be deemed expedient by the said commissioners: Pro-
that no loaf of sugar shall be deemed to be a proper sample loaf of double refined sugar, as
be of greater weight than 14 lbs., nor unless it be a loaf complete and whole, nor unless the
ve been made, by a distinct second process of refinement, from a quantity of single refined
art of which had first been perfectly clarified and duly refined, and had been made into
is which were of a uniform whiteness throughout, and had been thoroughly dried in the
o. 4. c. 76. § 18.)

in Quality to Double Refined Sugar. — In respect of refined sugar which is equal in quality
ied sugar, the like bounty shall be paid as is granted by the said act in respect of double
Provided always, that no sugar shall be entitled to bounty as double refined sugar, or as
i quality to double refined sugar, unless it be in loaves complete and whole, not weighing
bs. each loaf, nor unless it corresponds with, or be equal in quality to, the sample loaves
19.

ual to Standard. — In case any sugar be entered, in order to obtain the bounty on double
or sugar equal in quality to double refined sugar, which shall, on examination by the proper
id to be of a quality not equal to such standard sample, all sugar so entered shall be for-
y be seized. — § 20.

her of British Plantations or not. — The several bounties on refined sugar granted by the
ie granted equally in respect of all refined sugar, without regard to whether the same be
the produce of the British plantations or of the East Indies, or of sugar the produce *of any*
§ 21.

lations as to the taking out of sugar from warehouses to be refined, see WAREHOUSING.

oT SUGAR. — The manufacture of sugar from beet root is carried on to a very
extent in several parts of the Continent, particularly in France, where
roduce of the sugar from this source may at present be estimated at about
This branch of industry began during the exclusion of colonial products
in the reign of Napoleon. It received a severe check at the return of
e admission of West India sugars at a reasonable duty; and would, it is
ie, have been entirely extinguished, but for the oppressive additions made to
colonial sugars in 1820 and 1822. It is supposed by some, that at no dis-
he manufacture of sugar from beet root will be so much improved, that it
to stand a competition with colonial sugar at the same duty; but we have
this supposition will ever be realised. It is of importance, however, to bear
t were the culture of beet root sugar to be extensively carried on at home,
quite impossible to collect a duty upon it; so that the large amount of re-
ay be advantageously derived from a moderate duty on imported sugar,
iost entirely lost. — (For an account of the beet root cultivation in France,
e on the *French Commercial System,* in the Edinburgh Review, No. 99.)
stand that a few small parcels of beet root sugar have recently been pro-
country; and with the present enormous duty on colonial sugar, we are
the manufacture may not succeed. But as the preservation of the revenue
of infinitely more importance than the introduction of this spurious busi-
idations of which must entirely rest on the miserable machinery of Custom-

house regulations, sound policy would seem to dictate that the precedent establi
the case of tobacco should be followed in this instance, and that the beet ro
manufacture should be abolished. Inasmuch, too, as it is better to check an ev
outset, than to grapple with it afterwards, we trust that no time may be lost i
vigorous measures, should there be any appearance of the business extending.

MAPLE SUGAR. — A species of maple (*Acer Saccharinum*, Lin.) yields a cons
quantity of sugar. It grows plentifully in the United States and in Canada; and
districts furnishes the inhabitants with most of the sugar they make use of. Th
ferior both in grain and strength to that which is produced from the cane, map
granulates better than that of the beet root, or any other vegetable, the cane exce
is produced from the sap, which is obtained by perforating the tree in the sprin
depth of about 2 inches, and setting a vessel for its reception. The quantity
varies with the tree and the season. From 2 to 3 gallons may be about the daily
yield of a single tree; but some trees have yielded more than 20 gallons in a
others not more than a pint. The process of boiling the juice does not differ m
from what is followed with the cane juice in the West Indies. It is necessa
should be boiled as soon after it is drawn from the tree as possible. If it be al
stand above 24 hours, it is apt to undergo the vinous and acetous fermentation,
its saccharine quality is destroyed. — (*Bouchette's British America*, vol. i. p. 371
Trees and Fruits, Library of Entertaining Knowledge.)

Prices of Sugar in the London Market, January, 1832.

British Plantation.	Prices, Duty paid.					Exclusive of Duty 32s. per Cwt.		Exclusive
Present Duty, 24s. per Cwt.	Brown.	Middling.	Good.	Fine.	East India. (InBond.)	Benares.	Bengal.	Java.	M
Jamaica per Cwt. St. Kitt's, Antigua and Demerara,	46s. to 47s.	48s. to 52s.	51s. to 56s.	58s.		16s. to 17s.	15s. to 16s.	—	16
St. Vincent's & Montserrat	45s.6d.—46s.6d.	47s. 6d. to 51s.	52s.—54s.	55s.—57s.	per Cwt. Low Brown	18s.—20s.	17s.—19s.	18s. to 19s.	18
Grenada, Tobago and Trinidad, St. Lucia, Berbice, &c.	45s.—46s.	47s.—50s.	51s.—52s.	53s.—54s.	row n Yellow	21s.—23s.	20s.—21s.	20s.—22s.	21
Barbadoes	47s.—48s.	49s.—51s.	55s.—58s.	59s.—60s.	White	24s.—26s.	23s.—25s.	23s.—24s.	25
						Brown.		Yellow.	
Foreign. In Bond.	Brown.	Yellow.	White.	Fine White.	Mauritius Duty 24s. per Cwt. paid.	44s. to 45s.		47s. to 52s.	
Duty 63s. if taken for home use.									
Havannah per Cwt. Brazil	20s. to 21s. 15s.—17s.	22s. to 25s. 18s.—20s.	30s. to 32s. 23s.—31s.	33s. to 34s. —					

ACCOUNTS OF SALES OF SUGAR. — Subjoined are accounts of actual sales of sugar from J
Berbice. These accounts are interesting, inasmuch as they exhibit the various charges a
necessary article, from the time it is shipped in the colonies till it finds its way into the h
grocer. It will be observed, that *the duties are very much greater than the sums received by th*

1. ACCOUNT SALES of 10 Hogsheads and 5 Tierces Sugar, per Rambler, Capt. Smith, from
account of Messrs. James Morrison and Co.

1831. July.	15	By William Gadsden for 1-10 — 10 Hogsheads Ditto 11-15 — 5 Tierces			} Sugar, viz.—		L. s.

```
          IM         Cwt.  qr.  lb.              Cwt.  qr.  lb.
           C      1.  15   0   4          11.   9   3  13
                  2.  15   2   0          12.   9   2   6
                  3.  15   3   2          13.  10   0  11
                  4.  15   2   6          14.   9   0  27
                  5.  16   2   6          15.  10   1  14
                  6.  15   2   9                 ———————
                  7.  15   3   2                 49   0  15
                  8.  15   3  23                  5   0   0  Tare
                  9.  14   2  13                 ———————
                 10.  15   2   9                 44   0  15   Nett, at 47s.    .   103 14
                      —————————
                     156   0   0
                      14   1  23  Tare
                      —————————                                  .    47s.            332 1
                     141   2   5   Nett
```

CHARGES.

To Insurance on 290l., valuing each hogshead at 15l., and each tierce at 10l. at 60s. per cent. and policy and commission	} 10 18 9	
Less return for short interest, 90l. at 57s. per cent.	2 11 4	8 7
Duty on 186 cwt. 2 qrs. 9 lbs.* at 24s. per cwt. with fees of entry		224 8
Freight on ditto · 5s. per cwt. with primage, pierage, and trade ·	} 47 10 2	
Dock rate on ditto at 8d. per cwt.	6 4 0	53 14
Interest on duty 73 days	2 4 10	
Ditto on freight and dock rate	0 7 0	2 11
Extra warehouse rent on 10½ tons for 3 weeks, at 5d. per ton per week, 12s.10d.		0 17
Receipt stamp, 5s.		
Brokerage ½ per cent.		2 3
Commission 2½ per cent.		10 18
	Nett proceeds ·	
	London errors excepted.	

* Duties, freight, and charges of all sorts, are paid upon the *landing weight*, or the weight as ascertained
officers at the docks when the sugar is imported. When sugar is sold to the grocers it is weighed; and owin
through the casks this latter weight is invariably less than the former. This accounts for the discrepancy in
lowing account between the weights on which duties, freights, &c. are paid, and those accounted for to the grov

 NT SALES of A C. 30 Hhds. and 30 Tierces of Sugar, per Hero, from Berbice, on Account of Messrs. Brown, Stokes, and Co.

Jones for 30 Tierces. Payment 2 and 2 months.

Gross. Cwt.qrs.lbs.	Tare. Cwt.qrs.lbs.	No.	Gross. Cwt.qrs.lbs.	Tare. Cwt.qrs.lbs.	No.	Gross. Cwt.qrs.lbs.	Tare. Cwt.qrs.lbs.		L. s. d.	L. s. d.
8 0 4	1 0 7	11	8 0 12	1 0 7	21	7 3 15	0 3 20			
7 2 22	0 3 24	2	8 3 2	1 0 7	2	7 3 16	0 3 27			
7 3 21	1 0 0	3	7 1 6	0 3 9	3	7 3 2	0 3 25			
7 1 1	0 3 18	4	7 2 10	0 3 23	4	7 2 4	0 3 22			
7 0 17	0 3 17	5	8 3 20	1 0 7	5	8 0 22	1 0 7			
7 2 25	0 3 25	6	7 3 26	1 0 0	6	7 0 27	0 3 17			
6 2 22	0 3 10	7	8 2 14	1 0 7	7	7 0 23	0 3 16			
8 3 26	1 0 14	8	8 2 6	1 0 7	8	7 2 9	0 3 22			
7 3 18	0 3 27	9	7 3 17	0 3 20	9	7 2 10	0 3 22			
7 1 17	0 3 21	20	7 0 2	0 3 25	30	7 1 12	0 3 18			
76 3 5	9 2 23		80 3 3	10 0 14		75 2 26	9 2 0			

	Gross. Cwt. qrs. lbs.	Tare. Cwt. qrs. lbs.			
	76 3 5	9 2 23			
	80 3 3	10 0 14			
	75 2 26	9 0 2			
	233 1 6	29 1 9			
Deduct	29 1 9				
	203 3 25	Nett, at - - 2 11 0		520 2 7	
dutv on 205 cwt. 0 qrs. 21 lbs. nett landing weight, at 1l. 4s.		- 246 4 6			
Four months interest		- 4 2 0			
				250 6 6	269 16 1

d Co. for 30 Hhds. Payment as above.

Gross. Cwt.qrs.lbs.	Tare. Cwt.qrs.lbs.	No.	Gross. Cwt.qrs.lbs.	Tare. Cwt.qrs.lbs.	No.	Gross. Cwt.qrs.lbs.	Tare. Cwt.qrs.lbs.
16 1 22	1 2 0	41	15 3 21	1 2 0	51	15 3 27	1 2 0
16 2 20	1 2 0	2	15 1 8	1 2 0	2	15 2 16	1 2 0
16 2 6	1 2 0	3	15 2 24	1 2 0	3	15 3 24	1 2 0
15 3 17	1 2 0	4	15 2 27	1 2 0	4	16 1 15	1 2 0
14 1 88	1 1 12	5	15 0 25	1 2 0	5	15 1 8	1 2 0
14 3 26	1 2 0	6	15 2 22	1 2 0	6	15 3 16	1 2 0
15 1 7	1 2 0	7	15 2 24	1 2 0	7	16 0 2	1 2 0
15 3 3	1 2 0	8	16 2 18	1 2 0	8	16 0 20	1 2 0
15 3 25	1 2 0	9	15 2 3	1 2 0	9	16 3 16	1 3 0
15 2 15	1 2 0	50	14 2 11	1 1 12	60	15 1 22	1 2 0
57 2 9	14 3 12		156 0 15	14 3 12		159 2 26	15 1 0

	Gross. Cwt. qrs. lbs.	Tare. Cwt. qrs. lbs.			
	157 2 9	14 3 12			
	156 0 15	14 3 12			
	159 2 26	15 1 0			
	473 1 22	44 3 24			
Deduct	44 3 24				
	428 1 26	Nett, at 2l. 3s. 6d. - -			931 18 11
					1201 15 0

CHARGES.

			L. s. d.
n, and trade dues, and bond	-	4 13 3	
30 hhds. weighing 434 cwt. 1 qr. 22 lbs.* nett, at 1l. 4s.		521 6 8	
a 639 cwt 2 qrs. 15 lbs.* nett, at 4s.	- 127 18 6		
Primage	- 1 5 0	129 3 6	
porterage, and cooperage	-	8 15 0	
ing, and removing scales	-	2 8 6	
and paper	-	1 0 0	
se rent, at 3d. per hhd. and 2d. per tierce per week	-	16 18 11	
against fire, at 5s. per cent.	-	1 15 0	
interest on dues L. 4 13 3		- 0 3 6	
do. duty 521 6 8		- 8 16 11	
do. freight 129 3 6		- 2 17 11	
imission on 655 3 5	-	- 1 12 9	
e on 1,452l. 1s. 6d. at ½ per cent.		-	13 11 1
on on do. at 2½ per cent.		-	14 10 5
			36 6 0
Nett proceeds	-		7 50 8 4
			451 6 8

ctober. 1831.   Errors and debts excepted.   FRIEND and CO.

* See note, previous page.

HUR, or BRIMSTONE (Fr. Soufre; Ger. Schwefel; It. Zolfo, Solfo; e; Arab. Kibreet), is a crystallised, hard, brittle substance, commonly ish yellow colour, without any smell, and of a weak though perceptible specific gravity is from 1·9 to 2·1. It burns with a pale blue flame, and eat quantity of pungent suffocating vapours. In some parts of Italy it is dug up in a state of comparative purity. That which is manufac- his country is obtained by the roasting of pyrites. It is denominated oll sulphur, from its being cast in cylindrical moulds, and contains 7 per rpiment. The Italian roll sulphur does not contain more than 3 per simple earth; and is, therefore, in higher estimation than the English. sulphur is purified, it receives the name of sublimed sulphur, and is in f a bright yellow powder. — (Thomson's Chemistry, &c.)

is of great importance in the arts. It is used extensively in the manu-

facture of gunpowder, and in the formation of sulphuric acid or oil of vitriol also used extensively in medicine, and for other purposes. In 1829, 302,03 of rough or roll sulphur were imported into Great Britain, of which no less 285,108 cwt. were brought from Italy, or rather Sicily. The duty (6d. a cw rough or roll sulphur, produced, in 1830, 6,628l. 16s., showing that 265,15 had been entered for home consumption.

SYDNEY, the capital of New South Wales, and of the British settle in New Holland, or Australia, in lat. 33° 15′ S., lon. 151° 15′ E. Popu about 11,000. Sydney is situated on a cove on the south side of Port Ja about 7 miles from its mouth. The water is of sufficient depth to allo largest ships to come close to the shore. The inlet or harbour, denom Port Jackson, is one of the finest natural basins in the world. It str about 15 miles into the country, and has numerous creeks and bays; t chorage is every where excellent, and ships are protected from every There is a light-house at the entrance. Owing to a want of attention a the streets of Sydney were laid out, and the houses built, according to the of individuals, without any fixed or regular plan. But latterly this def been to a considerable degree remedied in the old streets; and the new o systematically laid out. The town covers a great extent of land; almost house having a considerable piece of ground attached to it. There are d banks at Sydney; some of which are joint stock associations, and others copartneries. There is also a Savings' Bank. Schools for the instruc poor children have been established; and there are numerous seminarie of them said to be very well conducted, for the education of the midd upper classes. There are several periodical publications.

Population, &c. — The British settlements in New South Wales were origin tended to serve as penal establishments to which convicts might be transport employed in public and private works; and are still used for this purpose first vessel with convicts arrived at Botany Bay in January, 1788; but it been found to be quite unsuitable as a site for a colony, the establishme removed to Port Jackson. The progress of the colony has been much mo than might have been anticipated, considering the character and habits convicts annually landed upon its shores, and the difficulties which th distance from England interpose in the way of an emigration of voluntary Owing to the circumstance of the great majority of the convicts and other er being males, a great disproportion has always existed between the sexes in the which has materially retarded its progress, and been, in other respects, pr of very pernicious results. Government, however, has recently come to the det tion to pay a sum of 8l. each, on their arrival in the colony, to every well unmarried young woman, between the ages of 18 and 30, not exceeding 1,20 who may emigrate either to New South Wales or Van Diemen's Land. In 1 date of the last census, the entire population of the colony, exclusive of ab was 36,598, distributed as follows: —

Free Emigrants	-	-	-	Males	-	2,846	4,673
				Females	-	1,827	
Born in the Colony	-	-	Males	-	4,473	8,727	13,400
				Females	-	4,254	
Convicts become free by servitude	-	Males	-	5,302	6,644	
				Females	-	1,342	
Convicts pardoned	-	-	Males	-	835	886	7,530
				Females	-	51	
Convicts	-	-	-	Males	-	14,155	
				Females	-	1,513	-	15,668
						Total -	36,598

Produce, Exports, Imports, &c. — The climate of such parts of New Sou as have been explored by the English is mild and salubrious. Wheat and al European grain succeed remarkably well, and are extensively cultivated; bu still continues to be indebted for a portion of her supplies of corn to other c particularly to Van Diemen's Land. Wool is by far the most important article o and from the great and growing attention paid to the improvement of the breed their rapid multiplication, and the extraordinary increase in the quantity o ported, there seems little doubt but that, at no distant period, New South Wal one of the principal wool-growing countries in the world. In 1822, the e wool amounted to only 152,880 lbs.; in 1825, they had increased to 411,60 1828, they were 834,343 lbs.; and now, we believe, they exceed 1,100,000 lbs

owing statements show the progress of cultivation in the colony, from 1819

The Stock was

In 1819				In 1828.			
Horses	-	-	3,572	Horses	-	-	12,479
Horned Cattle	-	-	42,789	Horned Cattle	-	-	262,868
Sheep	-	-	75,369	Sheep	-	-	536,391

The Number of Acres held was

In 1819	-	-	337,114	In 1828	-	-	2,906,346
Of which were cultivated	47,973			Of which were cleared	-		231,573
				And cultivated	-	-	71,523

e value of the imports from all places into Sydney in 1828 was 570,000l.
st principally of cotton, woollen, and linen goods, hardware, iron, sugar, tea,
e, gunpowder, &c. The exports do not as yet amount to half the value of
; but the discrepancy is every day diminishing. The official values of the
en Great Britain and New South Wales, in 1829, were, exports from the
he latter, 250,620l.; imports, 92,528l. During the same year, 30 ships, of
burthen, entered inwards from New South Wales, Van Diemen's Land, and
r; and 81 ships, of 28,719 tons burthen, cleared outwards for the same.
ere belonged to Sydney 34 vessels, of the burthen of 4,129 tons. The whale
neries have been carried on from Sydney with great vigour and success.

nd Expenditure. — The revenue of the colony in 1828, exclusive of parlia-
ants, was 122,722l. 14s. 3d. The total public expenditure on account of the
ng the same year amounted to 401,283l. 16s. 6d., including 79,007l. 18s. 8d.,
xpense of conveying convicts and troops to the colony. In fact, were it not
y expenses necessarily incurred on account of the conveyance and superin-
convicts, the revenue of the colony would be adequate to meet the out-

ights, and Measures. — Accounts are kept in sterling money.; but Spanish dollars are
. They pass current at 5s. each. The weights and measures are the same as those of

cy, Commission, and Warehouse Rent, agreed to at a Meeting of the New South Wales
Chamber of Commerce, 1828.

Commission.

es or purchases of ships and other
iouses, or lands, where no advance on
been made, 2½ per cent.
her sales, purchases, or shipments,
.
onsigned and afterwards withdrawn,
o public auction, if no advance on
been made, 2½ per cent.
orders for the provision of goods,
t.
teeing sales, bills, bonds, or other en-
s, 2½ per cent.
nagement of estates for others, 5 per
ng freight or charter, and on freight
5 per cent.
ces effected, ½ per cent.
losses, partial or general, 1 per cent.
g remittances, or purchasing, selling,
ting bills of exchange, 1 per cent.
overy of money, 2½ per cent. If by
iltration, 5 per cent.

10. On collecting house rent, 5 per cent.
11. On attending the delivery of contract goods, 2 per cent.
12. On becoming security for contracts, 5 per cent.
13. On ships' disbursements, 5 per cent.
14. On obtaining money on respondentia, 2 per cent.
15. On letters of credit granted, 2½ per cent.
16. On purchasing, selling, receiving from any of the public offices, lodging in ditto, delivering up or exchanging government paper or other public securities, ½ per cent.
17. On all items on the debit or credit side of an account, on which a commission of 5 per cent. has not been previously charged in the same account, including government paper, 1 per cent.
18. On entering and clearing ships at the Custom-house, each, 1 guinea.
19. On the dishonour of foreign bills, exclusive of protest and other law expenses, a re-exchange of, 25 per cent.

Warehouse Rent.

ment goods, 1s. per ton of 40 cubic
.
3d. per tun of 252 gallons (old mea-
k.
salt, and similar articles, 6d. per ton

On grain, 4d. per bushel for first month, and one half ditto per bushel per week afterwards.
On iron, lead, &c. 4d. per ton per week.

Duties levied at Sydney under Acts of Parliament.

t l.	Articles upon which levied.	Present Duties levied.	Acts of Parliament under which levied.	Articles upon which levied.	Present Duties levied.
	Spirits made or dis-tilled from grain the produce of the colony or its depen-cies - -	2s. 6d. per gallon.		jesty's plantations in the West Indies, imported directly from the United Kingdom -	6s. 6d. per gallon.
			3 Geo. 4. c. 96.	All other spirits -	8s. 6d. per do.
	Ditto ditto ditto, from sugar and molasses - -	8s. 6d. per do.	1d. - -	Tobacco imported unmanufactured -	1s. 6d. per pound.
	Spirits, the produce and manufacture of the United King-dom, or his Ma-		1d. - -	Ditto ditto manufac-tured, and snuff -	2s. 0d. per do.
			1d. - -	Foreign goods im-ported - -	5 per cent. ad val.

Duties, Rates, Tolls, &c. levied at Sydney under Acts of the Colonial Legislature.

DUES PAYABLE AT CUSTOM-HOUSE.
Dues on Entry and Clearance of Vessels.

	Entry.	Clearance.
	s. d.	*s. d.*
Vessels not colonial, in government service -	15 5	5
Ditto ditto, not in ditto -	30 5	5
Colonial vessels - -	5 5	5

Dues on Registering of Vessels.

	L. s. d.
For all vessels not exceeding 40 tons - - - -	2 0 0
Exceeding 40 tons, per ton -	0 1 0

Permits to remove spirits and wines, 6d. each permit.

Wharfage Dues.
Packages, 9d. each.
Iron, 9s. per ton.
Salt, 4s. per do.
Wheat and other grain, 1d. per bushel.

Light-house Dues.
Every ship or vessel arriving within Port Jackson, 2d. per ton register.

Dues received by the Harbour Master.
Mooring chains or buoys, 1l. 1s. per week.
Use of the government heaving down place, 18s. per day.

Postage of Single Letters from Sydney.

	d.
To Parramatta - - -	4
Emu Plains (Penrith) - -	8
Windsor - - -	8
Liverpool - - -	6
Cambell Town - - -	8
Newcastle - - -	4
Port Macquarrie - - -	4
Bathurst - - -	12

And at corresponding rates from other places.
Double and treble letters to be charged proportionally to the aforesaid rates. Letters the weight of an ounce to be charged four times the rate of postage of a single letter.

Newspapers printed in New S[outh] or Van Diemen's Land, 1d.

Letters from and to New S[outh] and Van Diemen's Land to postage of 3d., and all other a sea postage of 4d. for letter, and a sea postage all other letters.

Parcels of Newspapers, pri Current, or other periodical exported or imported, to b sea postage at the rate of 1 4 ounces of their weight.

Auction Duty.
For each and every 100l. a the sale by auction of any e or effects whatsoever, 1l. 1

Licences.

Auctioneers, annually - -
Beer and spirits, to retail, d[o]
Distilling, do. - -
Hawkers do. - -
Carts - - - -

Emigration to New South Wales, Rate of Wages, &c. — Were it not for th[e] expenses attending emigration to so distant a country as New South Wales, vantages it holds out to the industrious emigrant are very considerable. Lab[our] great demand, the rate of wages high, provisions cheap, and the climate mild unsuitable to European constitutions. The commissioners for facilitating er[?] (that is, for contracting with individuals or parishes willing to defray the of removing voluntary emigrants to the colonies), have issued the following

INFORMATION WITH RESPECT TO THE AUSTRALIAN COLONIES.

Price of Passage. — The commissioners for emigration have reason to expect, from the r[e] inquiries which they have made on this subject, that passages can be provided for people of t[he] classes, including their maintenance during the voyage, at a charge not exceeding 16l. for ad[ults] for children. More exact particulars, and the precise charge for which passages can be provi[ded] stated at the time of entering into the agreements with such persons as may apply to the com[missioners] for that purpose.

Probability of Employment, and Rates of Wages. — The commissioners have examined a c[ertain] number of letters upon these subjects from respectable inhabitants of New South Wale[s and Van] Diemen's Land; and they find that all concur in representing the existence of a great [demand for] labour. These representations are further confirmed by official reports received from those the secretary of state.

The following general statements, collected from a variety of sources, will afford a view of rates of wages in the Australian colonies : —

Twenty-five or thirty pounds a year, besides board and lodging, seem to be the wages which are to common labourers : artisans of very ordinary qualifications are reported to find no difficult[y] ing 50l. a year, besides board and lodging. The following advertisement, which appeared in Gazette of the 12th of August, 1830, contains a list of several descriptions of workmen wante[d] as well as an account of the high wages which some of them might obtain : —

Wanted, in Sydney, New South Wales, the following Tradesmen and Mechanics.

Bread and Biscuit Bakers.
Butchers.
*Boat Builders.
*Brick Makers.
*Ditto Layers.
Bellows Makers.
*Blacksmiths.
Bell Hangers.
Brass Founders.
Brewers.
Boatmen.
*Collar Makers.
Confectioners.
Chair Makers.
*Curriers.
*Carpenters.
*Caulkers.
*Coopers.
Cart Makers.
Coach Makers.
Compositors.
Candle Makers.
Cabinet Makers.
Cheese Makers.
Coach Spring Makers.
Cooks.
Colliers.
*Coppersmiths.
Cutlers.
Dyers.

Dairywomen.
Distillers.
*Engineers.
Farriers.
Flax Dressers.
Fencers.
Fellmongers.
Gardeners.
Glaziers.
Glass Blowers.
Glue Makers.
Gilders.
Gunsmiths.
Hairdressers.
Hat Makers.
—— Finishers.
*Harness Makers.
Horse Breakers.
Hoop Benders.
*Joiners.
Japanners.
Ironmongers.
Iron Founders.
Leather Dressers.
Lime Burners.
Locksmiths.
Millers.
Mealmen.
*Millwrights.

Milliners.
Maltsters.
Mustard Makers.
Milkmen.
Nurserymen.
Nailers.
Painters.
Parchment Makers.
Pump Makers.
Plough Makers.
Potters.
Paper Makers.
*Plasterers.
Ploughmen.
Provision Curers.
Plumbers.
Printers and Pressmen.
Quarrymen.
Quill Preparers.
Rope Makers.
Reapers.
Saddlers.
Shoemakers.
*Sawyers.
Shipwrights.
*Stone Masons.
*Stone Cutters.
*Stone Setters.
Stone Quarrymen.

Sail Makers.
*Slaters and Sl[aters]
Shepherds.
Sheepshearers.
Soap Makers.
Sign Painters.
Sailors.
Sail Cloth Mak[ers]
Sieve Makers.
Starch Makers
Straw Platters
Straw Hat Ma[kers]
Turners.
*Tanners.
Tailors.
Tin Plate Wo[rkers]
Tobacco Pipe
Tobacco Grow[ers]
Tallow Melte[rs]
Vine D[r]essers
Upholsterers.
Wheelwrights
Wagon Make[rs]
Wool Sorters.
Whalers.
Weavers of
   Coarse Woo[llens]
Wire Drawers
Wood Splitte[rs]

Those marked thus (*) are particularly wanted, and earn 10s. a day and upwards, *all the year round.* and millwrights earn 20s. a day.

All articles of provision are very cheap : beef and mutton, 2d. per lb. by the joint, and 1d. per lb. by the case. Tea (green), 1s. 6d. ; sugar, 3d. Indian corn, 1s. 6d. per bushel, &c. &c.

The agent for New South Wales and Van Diemen's Land, in a letter addressed to the cha[irman] emigration committee in the year 1827, since which period the price of labour is underst[ood to have] risen, stated the rates of wages as follows : —

	Per Day.	
Common labourers - - -	3s.	And to mechanics of peculiar quali
Common mechanics - - -	7s.	tions, or agricultural labourers, ca[pable]
2d rate ditto - -	8s. to 12s.	of managing a farm in the capacit[y of]
3d rate ditto - -	12s. to 15s.	bailiffs - - - -

Prices at Sydney. — The commissioners have collected from newspapers published in New [Wa]les, the following accounts of the market prices at Sydney on the 1st day of each month during [1]830 :—

	Jan.			Feb.			March.			April.			May.			June.			July.			August.			Sept.			October.			Nov.			Dec.		
	L.	s.	d.	L.	s.	d.	L.	s.	d.	L.	s.	d.	L.	s.	d.	L.	s.	d.	L.	s.	d.	L.	s.	d.	L.	s.	d.	L.	s.	d.	L.	s.	d.	L.	s.	d.
per bush.	0	6	6	0	8	3	0	6	9	0	8	0	0	9	6	0	7	6	0	7	0	0	6	0	0	6	0	0	5	3	0	4	9	0	5	3
do.	0	5	0	0	3	0	0	3	6	0	4	6	0	3	9	0	4	3	0	3	9	0	1	9	0	1	9	0	1	8	0	1	10	0	2	0
do.	-	-	-	0	3	0	0	3	6	0	3	6	0	3	6	0	3	6	0	3	6	0	3	6	0	3	0	0	3	0	0	3	6	0	3	6
do.	0	5	0	0	3	6	0	3	6	0	3	6	0	3	6	0	3	6	0	3	6	0	3	6	0	3	0	0	3	0	0	2	9	0	3	6
per cwt.	0	8	6	0	4	0	0	5	0	0	5	6	0	10	0	0	7	0	0	7	0	0	6	6	0	10	0	0	13	0	0	11	0	0	9	0
per lb.	0	1	9	0	1	3	0	1	0	0	1	0	0	1	0	0	0	9	0	0	9	0	1	0	0	1	6	0	1	9	0	1	2	0	0	9
do.	-	-	-	-	-	-	-	-	-	-	-	-	-	-	-	-	-	-	-	-	-	-	-	-	0	0	11	0	0	11	-	-	-	0	0	7
do.	-	-	-	-	-	-	-	-	-	-	-	-	-	-	-	-	-	-	-	-	-	-	-	-	0	0	11	0	0	10	0	0	10	0	0	9
per dozen.	0	1	9	0	0	9	0	0	9	0	0	9	0	0	10	0	1	1	0	1	0	0	0	11	0	1	0	0	1	0	0	0	11	0	0	9
do.	0	7	0	0	6	0	0	5	0	0	4	0	0	5	0	0	3	6	0	2	0	0	2	3	0	5	0	0	5	6	0	6	0	0	5	0
do.	0	5	0	0	4	0	0	3	9	0	3	6	0	3	6	0	2	0	0	2	0	0	2	0	0	3	0	0	3	0	0	3	6	0	3	3
per pair.	0	16	0	0	11	3	0	10	0	0	9	0	0	10	0	0	10	0	0	10	0	0	10	6	0	10	6	0	10	6	0	12	0	0	10	0
do.	1	0	0	0	16	0	0	12	0	0	12	0	0	12	6	0	10	0	0	10	0	0	9	6	0	12	6	0	14	0	0	13	0	0	12	0
per ton. { per load. {	2	10	0																																	
per ton. {	6	10	0	0	6	0	0	6	0	0	6	0	0	6	0	5	10	0	5	10	0	5	8	0	5	17	6	6	6	0	6	8	0			
per load.	1	0	0	0	17	0	1	0	0	1	0	0	1	0	0	1	3	0	1	3	0	0	12	6	0	12	6	0	13	0	0	12	6	0	13	6
4lb. loaf {	10d. to 11d.			8d. to 9d.			7d. to 8d.			10d. to 11d.			8d. to 9d.			8d. to 9d.			8d. to 9d.			8d. to 9d.			7d. to 8d.			7d. to 8d.			} 8d.		
tone.																																				
·	:			0	1	3	0	1	3	0	1	3	0	1	3	0	1	3	0	1	3	0	1	2	0	1	9	0	2	0	0	1	6	0	2	4
·	:			0	1	5	0	1	5	0	1	5	0	1	5	0	1	5	0	1	5	0	1	4	0	2	4	0	3	0	0	2	6	0	3	4
·	:			0	2	6	0	2	8	0	2	8	0	2	8	0	2	8	0	2	8	0	2	8	0	5	3	0	5	3	0	5	9	0	4	6
·	:			0	3	1	0	2	6	0	2	6	0	2	6	0	2	6	0	2	6	0	2	4	0	4	4	0	4	6	0	5	9	0	4	6
0 lbs.	1	2	0	1	6	0	0	17	6	0	17	6	1	7	0	0	6	0	1	0	0	0	18	0	0	17	0	0	15	0	0	13	0	0	13	0
·	0	19	0	1	2	0	0	15	0	0	15	0	1	2	0	0	18	0	1	0	16	8	0	15	0	0	14	0	0	13	0	0	11	0			

necessary that emigration to the Australian colonies should be confined to any particular [...] d the commissioners for emigration will therefore be ready immediately to afford their assist-[rsons] desirous of going to New South Wales and Van Diemen's Land. In consequence, [o]f the state of the population in the Australian colonies, the commissioners do not propose to [...] the conveyance of any but married men and their families, or of females belonging to the [...] lasses.

[com]missioners for emigration take this opportunity of announcing, that they are not prepared to [...] the conveyance of emigrants to the settlement on the Swan River.

[We sub]join, in illustration of the same subject, the following extract from the Sydney [... of] the 22d of May, 1830, which is not, we believe, more striking than true : —

[Here], then, is a country prepared to our very hands for all the purposes of civilised [... wh]ile England is groaning under a population for which she cannot provide [... her]e is an unmeasured extent of rich soil, that has lain fallow for ages, and to [... the] starving thousands of the North are beckoned to repair. The great want of [...]is employment; the great want of New South Wales is labour. England has [... mou]ths than food; New South Wales has more food than mouths. England [...]the gainer by lopping off one of her superfluous millions; New South Wales [...]the gainer by their being planted upon her ample plains. In England, the [...]rs are perishing for lack of bread; in New South Wales, they are, like Je-[...]waxing fat and kicking" amid superabundance. In England, the master is [...]to find work for his men; in New South Wales, he is distracted to find men [...]k. In England, the capitalist is glad to make his 3 per cent.; in New South [...]looks for 20. In England, capital is a mere drug,—the lender can scarcely [...]rower, the borrower can scarcely repay the lender; in New South Wales, [...]he one thing needful,—it would bring a goodly interest to the lender, and [...]e the fortune of the borrower.

[...]et the capitalist wend his way hither, and his 1 talent will soon gain 10; and

Let the labouring pauper come hither; and, if he can do nothing but dig, [...]on be welcome to 23s. a week, and shall feast on fat beef and mutton at 1d. [...]ound! Let the workhouses and jails disgorge their squalid inmates on our [...]the heart-broken pauper and the abandoned profligate shall be converted [...], industrious, and jolly-faced yeomen."

[...]to provide a fund for defraying the expenses of emigration to Australia, [...]t has resolved to impose a tax of 1l. each, upon the convicts assigned to [... i]viduals. Doubts, however, may be entertained as to the policy of any such [...]ty upon labour is certainly a novel expedient for increasing the prosperity [...]; though, perhaps, under the peculiar circumstances of the case, it may be

[...]*of Land in Australia.* — We have previously given (*ante*, p. 389.) a copy of [...]n which lands are henceforth to be granted to emigrants to New South [...]Van Diemen's Land. We have little to add, in this place, to the remarks [...]de — (see *loc. cit.*) — on this subject. The colonial secretary's letters to the [...]erely tell him that in future all land is to be sold by auction; that the mini-[...]pset price is to be 5s. an acre; and that he has a *discretionary power* of [...]her minimum price on superior lots, and of declining to sell them till this [...]ained. We have little fault to find with the *principle* of this plan, if any [...]y vague deserve that name; but we have very little doubt that in its prac-

tical operation it will generate every species of abuse. The local government, h
the power of limiting the quantity of land to be put up to auction, has it complet
its power to fix its price; for it may either increase the quantity of land so that it
fetch no more than the upset price, or it may limit it so that it shall fetch any gr
sum. Such auctions must in reality be a mere farce; it is not possible that the
be conducted on a fair principle. The price must, in every instance, really deper
the pleasure of the sellers, and not on the competition of the buyers. Supposir
local authorities to be uniformly actuated by the sincerest desire to deal fairly by
one, by what test are they to discover the probable number of offerers at dif
periods, the amount of their funds, and the intensity of their desire to purchase?
yet, without knowing all these things, they cannot decide upon the quantity of land
put up, so as to have any thing like a fair sale. And supposing them to be influenc
the partialities and weaknesses incident to humanity, how easy, when they wish to o
will it be for them to increase the number of lots put up, and conversely! To ob
in some degree at least, the chance of such abuses, the better way would be to
large tract of country divided into lots, and to fix prices on these according
estimate formed of their various advantages, assigning them in absolute property
first applicant ready to pay down the price, and to conform to the regulations as
cupancy, &c. It is to no purpose to contend that the plan of selling land by auc
adopted in America. What is there in common between the political conditi
Australia and the United States? Jobbing, that would be instantly detected an
down in the latter, may attain to the rankest luxuriance in the former. The infl
of a government and a public on the spot is altogether different from that of a g
ment and a public many thousand miles distant. At all events, Lord Goderich
not confine himself to the holiday task of setting a *minimum* price upon land
real desideratum is the establishment of some certain, fixed, and *fair* principles for
its *maximum* price; and few are better are better able than his Lordship to devis
principles.

In compiling this article we have chiefly made use of *Parliamentary Paper
Report of Mr. Bigge, on the Agriculture and Trade of New South Wales,* N
Sess. 1823 ; *Report of Commissioners of Inquiry,* No. 328. Sess. 1831 ; *Pape
before the Finance Committee,* &c.

T.

TACAMAHAC, a resin obtained from the *fagara octandra;* and likewis
supposed, from the *populus balsamifera.* It is imported from America i
oblong masses, wrapt in flag leaves. It is of a light brown colour, very
and easily melted when heated. When pure, it has an aromatic smell be
that of lavender and musk; and dissolves completely in alcohol; water ha
action upon it. — (*Thomson's Chemistry.*)

TALC, a species of fossil nearly allied to mica. It is soft, smooth, gre
the feel, and may be split into fine plates or leaves, which are flexible, b
elastic. It has a greenish, whitish, or silver-like lustre. The leaves are
parent, and are used in many parts of India and China, as they were used in a
Rome — (*Plin. Hist. Nat.* lib. xxxvi. c. 22.) — in windows instead of
In Bengal, a seer of talc costs about 2 rupees, and will sometimes yield a
panes 12 inches by 9, or 10 by 10, according to the form of the mass, tran
enough to allow ordinary subjects to be seen at 20 or 30 yards' distance. It
be chosen of a pure pearl colour; but it has, in general, either a yellowish
blue tinge. Its beautiful translucent flakes are frequently used by the I
for ornamenting the baubles employed in their ceremonies. Talc is empl
the composition of *rouge végétal.* The Romans prepared with it a beautifi
by combining it with the colouring fluid of particular kinds of testaceous a
Talc is met with in Aberdeenshire, Perthshire, and Banffshire in Scotland ;
various parts of the Continent, where rocks of serpentine and porphyry occu
talc brought from the Tyrolese mountains is called in commerce Veneti
Several varieties are found in India and Ceylon. — (*Thomson's Chemistry;
Cyclopædia; Milburn's Orient. Com.; Ainslie's Mat. Indica.*)

TALLOW (Fr. *Suif;* Ger. *Talg;* It. *Sevo, Sego;* Rus. *Salo, t
Sp. *Sebo*), animal fat melted and separated from the fibrous matter mi
it. Its quality depends partly on the animal from which it has been pr

e, perhaps, on the care taken in its purification. It is firm, brittle, and
culiar heavy odour. When pure, it is white, tasteless, and nearly in-
ut the tallow of commerce has usually a yellowish tinge; and is divided,
g to the degree of its purity and consistence, into candle and soap

is an article of great importance. It is manufactured into candles and soap;
:ensively used in the dressing of leather, and in various processes of the arts.
ur extensive supplies of native tallow, we annually import a very large quan-
ipally from Russia. The exports of tallow from Petersburgh amount, at
;e, to between 3,000,000 and 4,000,000 poods, of which the largest portion
brought to England; the remainder being exported to Prussia, France, the
owns, Turkey, &c.
·row from the work of Mr. Borrisow, on the Commerce of Petersburgh, the
details with respect to the tallow trade of that city: —

divided into different sorts; namely, white and yellow *candle tallow*, and common and Sibe-
llow; although it is allowed that the same sort often differs in quality.
brought to Petersburgh from the interior; and the best soap tallow from Siberia, by various
e lake Ladoga; and thence, by the canal of Schlusselburg, to the Neva.
·re, or warehouse, is appropriated for the reception of tallow, where, on its arrival, it is
assorted (*bracked*). The casks are then marked with three circular stamps, which state
of the tallow, the period of selecting, and the name of the selector (*bracker*).
in which white tallow is brought have a singular appearance; their form being conical, and
·ter at one end about 2¼ feet, and at the other only 1¼ foot: the casks of yellow tallow are
·on shape. There are also others, denominated half casks.
·te the tare, the tallow is removed from a certain number of casks, which are weighed,
·age tare is thence deduced for the whole lot. A cask weighs 8½, 9, 10, or 11 per cent.,
·age is generally about 10 per cent., of the entire weight of tallow and cask.
·idle tallow, when good, should be clean, dry, hard when broken, and of a fine yellow colour
The white candle tallow, when good, is white, brittle, hard, dry, and clean. The best
· is brought from Woronesch. As for soap tallow, the more greasy and yellow it is, the
uality. That from Siberia is the purest, and commonly fetches a higher price than the

the oil and tallow warehouses were the same; and this occasioned great difficulties in
·cause all vessels or lighters taking in tallow or oil were obliged to haul down to the
· wait in rotation for their cargoes. The consequence was, that when much business was
·el was often detained for several weeks at the *ambare* before she could get her cargo on
· the tallow and oil warehouses are separated, and every article has its own place. When
·of tallow is made, the agent is furnished by the selector (*bracker*) with a sample from each

in order to obtain more freight, usually load some casks of tallow upon deck; but it is
· interest of the owner to avoid this if possible, because the tallow loses, through the heat
·onsiderably both in weight and quality.
·ed and twenty poods of tallow gross weight, make a Petersburgh last, and 63 poods an

·8 cwt. of tallow imported in 1829, 1,164,180 came from Russia, 6,143 from the United
·from Turkey, 1,992 from France, and 1,626 from Sweden.
·n an official account of the export of tallow from Russia in 1831.

Exports of Tallow from Russia in 1831.

From		Poods.	To			Poods.
h	-	3,579,224	Great Britain	-	-	3,223,434
	-	89,258	France	-	-	141,829
	-	126,006	Holland	-	-	55,443
	-	244,818	Prussia	-	-	307,073
	-	1,092	Denmark	-	-	8,304
,	-	19,035	Sweden	-	-	39,507
	-	2,543	Hanse Towns	-	-	123,058
.ces	-	29,658	Spain and Portugal	-	-	612
			Austria	-	-	19,501
Total	-	4,091,544	Turkey	-	-	113,487
			Elsinore	-	-	23,642
			Other Places	-	-	32,952
			Per Asiatic Frontier	-	-	107
			Kiachta	-	-	2,453
receive, at the Sound, orders for their			To Georgia	-	-	142
.ination, and the cargoes are princi-						
.t Britain.			Total	-	4,091,544

·f tallow fluctuated very much during the war. This was occasioned, principally, by the
· were at different periods thrown in the way of supplies from Russia. The price of
· affected by the state of the seasons. Some very extensive speculations have at various
·attempted in tallow; but seldom, it is believed, with much advantage to the parties.

·ng is a statement of the prices per cwt. of foreign and British tallow in the London
· 10th of January, 1832: —

	s. d.		Market Letter.		Committee.	
				s. d.	s. d.	s. d.
·, &c. duty (3s. 2d.)	42 9 to 43 0		Town Tallow, cwt. -	53 6 to 0 0	51 6	
·rt. -	42 3 — 42 6		Russian Candle -	44 0 — 0 0	45 0	
	40 0 — 0 0		Melted Stuff -	36 0 — 0 0	36 0	
	40 6 — 0 0		Rough ditto -	22 0 — 0 0	22 0	
	40 6 — 41 0		Whitechapel Mar- ⎱	2 11 — 0 0	0 0	
	41 6 — 41 9		ket, stone - ⎰			
	42 6 — 0 0		St. James's ditto	3 0 — 0 0	0 0	
·ica -	0 0 — 0 0		Average -	2 11½ — 0 0	2 10½	

TAMARINDS (Ger. *Tamarinden;* Fr. *Tamarins;* It. and Sp. *Tam*
Arab. *Umblic;* Hind. *Tintiri*), the fruit of the *Tamarindus Indica*, a tree whic
in the East and West Indies, in Arabia, and Egypt. In the West Ind
pods or fruit, being gathered when ripe, and freed from the shelly fragme
placed in layers in a cask, and boiling syrup poured over them, till the
filled; the syrup pervades every part quite down to the bottom, and wh
the cask is headed for sale. The East India tamarinds are darker colou
drier, and are said to be preserved without sugar. When good, tamari
free from any degree of mustiness; the seeds are hard, flat, and clean; the
tough and entire; and a clean knife thrust into them does not receive any
of copper. They should be preserved in closely covered jars. — (*Thomso*
pensatory.) The duty on tamarinds produced, in 1829, 1,433*l.* 14*s.* 5*d.*

TAPIOCA, a species of starch or powder prepared from the roots
Jatropha manihat, an American plant. The roots are peeled, and subj
pressure in a kind of bag made of rushes. The juice which is forced
deadly poison, and is employed by the Indians to poison their arrows; b
posits gradually a white starch, which, when properly washed, is innocent
remains in the bag consists chiefly of the same starch. It is dried in smo
afterwards passed through a kind of sieve. Of this substance the cassa
is made. — (*Thomson's Chemistry.*)

TAR (Fr. *Goudron;* Ger. *Theer;* It. *Catrame;* Pol. *Smola gesta;* Rus
Smola shitkaja; Sw. *Tjära*), a thick, black, unctuous substance, chiefly c
from the pine, and other turpentine trees, by burning them in a close sm
heat.

The tar of the north of Europe is very superior to that of the United Stat
an article of great commercial importance. The process followed in making it
described as follows by Dr. Clarke: — " The inlets of the gulf (Bothnia) ever
appeared of the grandest character; surrounded by noble forests, whose t
flourishing luxuriantly, covered the soil quite down to the water's edge. From
southern parts of Westro-Bothnia, to the northern extremity of the gulf, the in
are occupied in the manufacture of tar; proofs of which are visible in the who
of the coast. The process by which the tar is obtained is very simple: and as
witnessed it, we shall now describe it, from a tar-work we halted to inspect
spot. The situation most favourable to the process is in a forest near to a marsh
because the roots of the fir, from which tar is principally extracted, are always n
ductive in such places. A conical cavity is then made in the ground (generally ir
of a bank or sloping hill); and the roots of the fir, together with logs and bille
same, being neatly trussed in a stack of the same conical shape, are let into th
The whole is then covered with turf, to prevent the volatile parts from being d
which, by means of a heavy wooden mallet, and a wooden stamper worked s
by two men, is beaten down and rendered as firm as possible above the woo
stack of billets is then kindled, and a slow combustion of the fir takes place
flame, as in making charcoal. During this combustion the tar exudes; and a
pan being at the bottom of the funnel, with a spout which projects through t
the bank, barrels are placed beneath this spout to collect the fluid as it comes a
fast as the barrels are filled, they are bunged and ready for immediate exportatio
this description it will be evident that the mode of obtaining tar is by a kind o
tion *per descensum;* the turpentine, melted by fire, mixing with the sap and
the fir, while the wood itself, becoming charred, is converted into charcoal.
curious part of the story is, that this simple method of extracting tar is pre
which is described by Theophrastus and Dioscorides; and there is not the
difference between a tar-work in the forests of Westro-Bothnia, and those c
Greece. The Greeks made stacks of pine; and having covered them with
were suffered to burn in the same smothered manner; while the tar, melting,
bottom of the stack, and ran out by a small channel cut for the purpose."

Of 12,212 lasts of tar imported in 1828, 9,064 were brought from Russia, and 2,539 from
States. The last contains 12 barrels, and each barrel 31½ gallons.
Tar produced or manufactured in Europe is not to be imported for home consumptio
British ships, or in ships of the country of which it is the produce, or from which it is impo
penalty of forfeiting the same, and 100*l.* by the master of the ship. — (6 *Geo.* 4. c. 109.)

TARE, an abatement or deduction made from the weight of a parcel
on account of the weight of the chest, cask, bag, &c. in which they are c
Tare is distinguished into *real tare, customary tare*, and *average tare.* T
the actual weight of the package; the second, its supposed weight acc
the practice among merchants; and the third is the medium tare, dede

ng a few packages, and taking it as the standard for the whole. In Amster-
nd some other commercial cities, tares are generally fixed by custom; but
country, the prevailing practice, as to all goods that can be unpacked with-
ury, both at the Custom-house and among merchants, is to ascertain the
re. Sometimes, however, the buyer and seller make a particular agree-
bout it. We have, for the most part, specified the different tares allowed
articular commodities, in the descriptions given of them in this work.
he tares at Amsterdam, Bordeaux, &c., see these articles; see also
ANCES.)

RE, VETCH, OR FITCH, a plant (*Vicia sativa*, Lin.) that has been cul-
in this country from time immemorial; principally for its stem and leaves,
are used in the feeding of sheep, horses, and cattle; but partly, also, for its
Horses thrive better upon tares than upon clover and rye grass; and
at are fed upon them give most milk. The seed is principally used in
ling of pigeons and other poultry. In 1829, we imported 87,101 bushels
s, principally from Denmark and Prussia.

IFF, a table, alphabetically arranged, specifying the various duties, draw-
ounties, &c. charged and allowed on the importation and exportation of
of foreign and domestic produce.

nded at one time to have given the tariffs of some of the principal foreign states, and had some
ranslated for that purpose; but as the duties and regulations in them are perpetually changing,
d very soon have become obsolete, and would have tended more to mislead than to instruct.
lars issued by foreign houses usually specify the duties on importation and exportation. The
e United States, having excited a more than ordinary degree of attention and discussion in this
s given under the article NEW YORK. Subjoined is the British tariff, as it stood on the 1st of
st.

TARIFF (BRITISH). — 1st of January, 1832.

DUTIES INWARDS

three fourths of the following Duties were established by the 6 Geo. 4. c. 111. The principal
ations have been made by the 7 Geo. 4. c. 48., the 9 Geo. 4. c. 76., and the 10 Geo. 4. c. 43.

	Duty.	Draw-back.		Duty.	Draw-back.
A.	*L. s. d.*	*L. s. d.*	Antimony, crude, per cwt.	0 15 0	*L. s. d.*
e Vinegar.	0 2 0	0 1 4	regulus of antimony, per cwt.	2 0 0	
d.			Apples, per bushel	0 4 0	
	0 0 10	0 0 6	dried, per bushel	0 7 0	
o.	0 0 8	0 0 5	Aquafortis, per cwt.	0 14 3	
	1 18 0		Arangoes, for every 100*l.* of the value	20 0 0	
ns, viz.			Argol, per cwt.	0 2 0	
100*l.* value	20 0 0		the produce of, and imported from, any		
ry 100*l.* value	10 0 0		British possession, per cwt.	0 1 0	
barilla, viz.			Aristolochia, per lb.	0 0 10	0 0 6
ontaining soda or mineral			Arrow root or powder, per lb.	0 0 2	
eof mineral alkali is the			the produce of any British possession,		
le part (such alkali not be-			per lb.	0 0 1	
se particularly charged with			Arsenic, white, per cwt.	0 14 3	
			of any other sort, per cwt.	0 18 8	
ntaining a greater propor-			Asafœtida, per lb.	0 0 10	0 0 6
uch alkali than 20 per cent.	0 11 4	0 5 8	Asarum root, per lb.	0 0 8	0 0 5
			Ashes, pearl and pot, per cwt.	0 6 0	
ng more than 20 per cent.,			the produce of any British possession, and		
exceeding 25 per cent. of			imported direct from thence	Free.	
ali, per cwt.	0 15 0	0 7 6	soap and wood, per cwt.	0 1 8	
ng more than 25 per cent.,			weed	0 1 8	
exceeding 30 per cent. of			not otherwise described, for every 100*l.* of		
ali, per cwt.	0 18 4	0 9 2	the value	20 0 0	
ng more than 30 per cent.,			Asphaltum, per lb.	0 0 10	0 0 6
exceeding 40 per cent. of			the produce of, and imported from, any		
ali, per cwt.	1 3 4	0 11 8	British possession, per lb.	0 0 5	
ng more than 40 per cent.	1 10 0	0 15 0	Asses, each	0 10 0	
lkali, per cwt.	0 0 10	0 0 6	**B.**		
n of, per oz.	0 1 8		Balau-tia, per cwt.	1 8 0	
very 100*l.* value	60 0 0		Balaustia, per lb.	0 0 10	
r cwt.	1 11 8	1 8 0	Balsam, Canada, per lb.	0 1 3	0 0 10
duce of any British pos-			copaiba or caprivi, per lb.	0 2 0	0 1 4
wt.	0 15 10	0 14 0	Riga, per lb.	0 1 0	
t.	4 15 0	4 4 0	and further, as foreign spirits, for		
e of any British possession,			every gallon	1 10 0	
	2 7 6	2 2 0	balm of Gilead, balsam of Peru, of		
, per cwt.	2 7 6	2 2 0	Tolu, and all balsams not otherwise		
arbadoes aloes, per lb.	0 1 3	0 0 10	described, per lb.	0 1 6	
o.	0 2 6	0 1 8	Bandstring twist, the dozen knots, each 32		
e of the Cape of Good			yards	0 5 0	
d imported direct from			Barilla, per ton	2 0 0	
er lb.	0 0 3		Barilla and alkali from places within the limits		
, per lb.	0 0 9	0 0 6	of the charter of the East India Com-		
	0 17 6		pany, per ton	2 0 0	
	0 11 8		(The barilla duties were reduced by act		
	0 1 8	0 1 1	1 and 2 Will. 4. c. 16.)		
o.			Bark, viz.		
of amber, not otherwise			Angustura bark, per lb.	0 2 0	0 1 4
lb.	0 12 0		clove bark, per lb.	0 0 10	0 0 6
duce of British fishing,			eleutheria, or cascarilla bark, per lb.	0 0 1	
	0 2 0		guaiacum bark, per lb.	1 8 0	
reign fishing, per oz.	0 5 0		oak bark, per cwt.	0 0 5	
b.	0 3 1		black oak, or quercitron bark, per cwt.	0 1 0	
	0 0 2		otherwise imported, for every 100*l.* of		
	0 0 3		the value	20 0 0	
g, per lb.	0 0 2		Peruvian or Jesuits' bark, per lb.	0 0 1	
er sort, not otherwise			red mangrove bark, per cwt.	0 0 8	
b.	0 1 0				

3 T 2

	Duty.	Draw-back.
	L. s. d.	L. s. d.
Bark—*continued.*		
sassafras bark, per lb.	0 0 8	0 0 5
simarouba bark, per lb.	0 1 0	0 0 8
Winter's bark, per lb.	0 0 8	0 0 5
the produce of any British possession, per lb.	0 0 4	0 0 3
bark not otherwise described, being for the use of dyers or of tanners, and no other use, for every 100*l.* of the value	20 0 0	
the produce of and imported from any British possession, for every 100*l.* of the value	10 0 0	
bark not particularly described, nor otherwise charged with duty, whether pulverised or not, per lb.	0 2 0	
Bar wood, per ton	0 7 0	
Basket rods, the bundle not exceeding 3 feet in circumference at the band	0 3 2	
Baskets, for every 100*l.* of the value	20 0 0	
Bast ropes, per cwt.	0 10 0	
Bdellium, per lb.	0 1 8	0 1 1
Beads, viz.		
amber beads, per lb.	0 12 0	
beads, arango, for every 100*l.* of the value	20 0 0	
coral beads, per lb.	0 15 10	
crystal beads, per 1,000	1 8 6	
jet beads, per lb.	0 3 2	
not otherwise described, for every 100*l.* of the value	30 0 0	
Beans, kidney or French beans, per bushel	0 0 10	
Beef, salted, not being corned, per cwt.	0 12 0	
Beef wood, unmanufactured, imported from New South Wales, per ton	0 5 0	
Beer, viz.		
mum, per barrel of 32 gallons	3 1 1	
spruce beer, do.	3 6 0	
or ale of all other sorts, do.	2 13 0	
Benjamin, or benzoin, per lb.	0 2 0	0 1 4
Berries, viz.		
bay, per cwt.	0 11 1	
juniper, per cwt.	0 11 1	
yellow, for dyers' use, per cwt.	0 14 0	
for dyers' use, not otherwise described, per cwt.	0 12 0	
not for dyers' use, nor otherwise described, for every 100*l.* of the value	30 0 0	
Bezoar stones, per oz.	0 2 6	
Birds, viz. singing-birds, per dozen	0 8 0	
Bitumen Judaicum, per lb.	0 0 10	0 0 6
Blacking, per cwt.	3 12 0	
Bladders, per dozen	0 0 6	
Bole Armenic or Armenian bole, per cwt.	0 8 0	0 5 4
Bones of cattle and other animals, and of fish, except whale fins, for every 100*l.* of the value	1 0 0	
Books, viz.		
being of editions printed prior to the year 1801, bound or unbound, per cwt.	1 0 0	
being of editions printed in or since the year 1801, bound or unbound, per cwt.	5 0 0	
Boots, shoes, and calashes, viz.		
women's boots and calashes, per dozen pair	1 10 0	
if lined or trimmed with fur or other trimming, per dozen pair	1 16 0	
women's shoes with cork, or double soles, quilted shoes and clogs, per dozen pair	1 6 0	
if trimmed, or lined with fur, or any other trimming, per dozen pair	1 9 0	
women's shoes of silk, satin, jean, or other stuffs, kid, morocco, or other leather, per dozen pair	0 18 0	
if trimmed, or lined with fur, or other trimming, per dozen pair	1 4 0	
men's boots, per dozen pair	2 14 0	
men's shoes, per dozen pair	1 4 0	
children's boots, shoes, and calashes, not exceeding 7 in. in length, to be charged with two thirds of the above duties.		
(Duties on boots and shoes imposed by 10 Geo. 4. c. 48.)		
Boracic acid, per lb.	0 0 4	
Borax or tincal, viz.		
refined, per lb.	0 0 6	
unrefined, per lb.	0 0 3	
Rotargo, per lb.	0 1 0	
Bottles, viz.		
of earth or stone, empty, per dozen	0 3 2	
and further, full or empty, for every cwt.	0 5 0	
of glass covered with wicker, per dozen quarts content	1 2 0	
and further, for every cwt.	4 0 0	
of green or common glass, not of less content than one pint, and being phials, viz.		
full, if containing wine or spirits, per dozen quarts content	0 4 0	
empty, per dozen quarts content	0 2 0	
full, but not containing wine or spirits, computing all bottles of not greater content than half a pint as of the content of half a pint; and all bottles of greater content than half a pint, and not of greater content than a pint, or a reputed pint, as of the content of a pint, or of a reputed pint : viz.		
imported from any foreign place, per dozen quarts content	0 2 0	
imported from any British possession, and although containing wine or spirits, per dozen quarts content	0 1 0	

	Duty	
	L. s.	
Bottles—*continued.*		
of glass, not otherwise enumerated or described, for every 100*l.* of the value	25 0	
and further, for every cwt.	4 0	
Note. — Flasks in which wine or oil is imported are not subject to duty.		
Boxes of all sorts, for every 100*l.* of the value	20 0	
Box wood, per ton	5 0	
the produce of, and imported from, any British possession, per ton	1 0	
Brass, viz.		
manufactures of, not otherwise enumerated or described, for every 100*l.* of the value	30 0	
powder of, for japanning, per lb.	0 2	
Brazil wood, not otherwise described, per ton	5 0	
Braziletto, or Jamaica wood, imported from a British possession, per ton	0 3	
not so imported, per ton	0 4	
Bricks or clinkers, per 1,000	1 2	
Brimstone, rough, per cwt.	0 0	
refined, per cwt.	0 6	
in flour, per cwt.	0 9	
Bristles, viz.		
rough, and in the tufts, and not in any way sorted, per lb.	0 0	
in any way sorted, or arranged in colours, and not entirely rough, and in the tufts, per lb.	0 0	
Brocade of gold or silver, for every 100*l.* of the value	30 0	
Bronze, all works of art made of bronze, per cwt.	1 0	
powder, for every 100*l.* of the value	25 0	
Buck wheat. See Corn.		
Bugles, of all sorts, per lb.	0 2	
Bullion and foreign coin, of gold or silver, and ore of gold or silver, or of which the major part in value is gold or silver	Free	
Bulrushes, per load of 63 bundles	0 12	
Burrachas, or caoutchouc, per lb.	0 5	
Burrs for millstones, per 100	3 16	
Butter, per cwt.	1 0	
Buttons, for every 100*l.* of the value	20 0	
C.		
Cables, tarred or untarred, per cwt.	0 10	
not of iron, in use of any British ship, being fit and necessary for such ship, and in the actual use of the same, and not otherwise disposed of	Free	
if otherwise disposed of, for every 100*l.* of the value	20 0	
Calamus aromaticus, per lb.	0 0	
Calves velves, per cwt.	0 11	
Camomile flowers, per lb.	0 0	
unrefined, per lb.	0 0	
Camphor, refined, per lb.	0 0	
Camwood, per ton	0 15	
Cancrorum oculi, per lb.	0 2	
Candles, spermaceti, per lb.	0 2	
tallow, per lb.	3	
wax, per lb.	4	
Candlewick, per cwt.	4 8	
Canella alba, per lb.	0	
Canes, bamboo, per 1,000	1 14	
rattans, not ground, per 1,000	1 1	
reed canes, per 1,000	1 6	
walking-canes or sticks, mounted, painted, or otherwise ornamented, for every 100*l.* value	30 0	
whangees, jumbo, ground rattans, dragon's blood, and other walking-canes or sticks, per 1,000	4	
Cantharides, per lb.	0	
Caoutchouc, or elastic gum, per lb.	0	
Capers, per lb.	0	
Capita papaverum, per 1,000	0	
Cardamoms, per lb.	0	
Cards, viz.		
playing-cards, per dozen packs	4	
Carmine, per oz.	0	
Carriages of all sorts, for every 100*l.* value	30 0	
Casks, empty, for every 100*l.* value	50	
Cassia, viz.		
buds, per lb.	0	
fistula, per lb.	0	
lignea, per lb.	0	
imported from any British possession, per lb.	0	
Castor, per lb.	0	
Casts of busts, statues, or figures, per cwt.	0	
Catechu, or terra Japonica, per cwt.	0	
Catlings, harpstrings, or lutestrings, per gross, containing 12 dozen knots	0	
Caviare, per cwt.	0	
Cedar wood, per ton	2	
the produce of, and imported from, any British possession, per ton	0	
Chalk, prepared or otherwise manufactured, and not otherwise described, for every 100*l.* value	10	
unmanufactured, and not otherwise described, for every 100*l.* value	20	
Charts or maps, plain or coloured, each chart or map, or part thereof	0	
Cheese, per cwt.	0	
Cherries, per cwt.	0	
dried, per lb.	0	
China root, per lb.	0	
China or porcelain ware, viz.		
plain, for every 100*l.* value	15	

	Duty.			Drawback.		
	L.	s.	d.	L.	s.	d.
in ware—*continued.*						
ornamented, for every 100*l.*	30	0	0			
coa paste, the produce of, rom, any British possession,	0	1	9			
f any other place, or if other- ed, per lb.	0	4	4			
	21	10	0			
	2	0	0			
, per lb.	0	0	3	0	0	2
	0	1	0			
f, and imported from, any ession, per lb.	0	0	6			
r lb.	0	1	6			
with salt, for every 100*l.*	20	0	0			
	0	4	9			
per 1,000	1	2	6			
00*l.* value	25	0	0			
	0	3	0	0	2	7
f, and imported from, any ssion, within or without the he East India Company's lb.	0	2	0	0	1	9
	2	0	0			
	0	0	3			
	0	0	6			
	0	0	2			
ny British possession, per lb.	0	0	2			
	0	0	1			
	0	1	3			
f any British possession in r lb.	0	0	6			
any British possession within the East India Company's lb.	0	0	9			
any other place within the East India Company's char-	0	1	0			
or cocoa shells, per lb.	0	0	2			
er lb.	0	2	6			
roduce of any British posses-	0	3	0			
ce of any British possession lb.	0	0	6			
any British possession within the East India Company's lb.	0	0	9			
any other place within the East India Company's char-	0	1	0			
, and imported from, Sierra .	0	0	9			
	0	5	0			
nly to be made into mats,	0	5	0			
locynth, per lb.	0	1	8	0	1	1
lb.	0	2	0	0	1	4
	0	2	6			
	0	12	0			
e remanufactured, per cwt.	0	15	0			
opper coins, per cwt.	1	10	0			
.						
r pigs, rose copper, and all er, per cwt.	1	7	0			
t, viz.						
or ingots, hammered or r cwt.	1	15	0			
rwise enumerated or de- cwt.	2	10	0			
of copper, not otherwise or described, and copper ed, for every 100*l.* value	30	0	0			
y British possession within the East India Company's						
	0	1	0			
e remanufactured, per cwt.	0	9	2			
pper coin, per cwt.	0	15	0			
r pigs, rose copper, and all er, per cwt.	0	9	2			
t, viz.						
or ingots, hammered or r cwt.	1	11	3			
of copper, not otherwise or described, and copper ed, for every 100*l.* value	30	0	0			
cwt.	0	5	0			
	0	3	0			
	0	12	0			
	0	15	10			
er lb.	0	1	0			
, per lb.	0	12	0			
per lb.	0	5	6			
g or taking, per lb.	0	0	6			
ntarred, per cwt.	0	10	9			
ritish ship, and being fit for such ship	Free.					
posed of, for every 100*l.*	20	0	0			
	0	8	0			
per lb.	0	7	0			
a foreign country, viz.						
under 34*s.* per quarter	0	12	4			
ect of every integral shil- such price shall be above y shall be decreased by ch price shall be 41*s.*						
1*s.* per quarter	0	1	0			

	Duty.			Drawback.		
	L.	s.	d.	L.	s.	d.
Corn—*continued.*						
under 33*s.* and not under 32*s.* per quarter	0	13	10			
And in respect of each integral shilling, or any part of each integral shilling, by which such price shall be under 32*s.*, such duty shall be increased by 1*s.* 6*d.*						
Oats, 25*s.* and under 26*s.* per quarter	0	9	3			
And in respect of every integral shilling by which such price shall be above 25*s.*, such duty shall be decreased by 1*s.* 6*d.* until such price shall be 31*s.*						
at or above 31*s.* per quarter	0	1	0			
under 25*s.* and not under 24*s.* per quarter	0	10	9			
And in respect of each integral shilling, or any part of each integral shilling, by which such price shall be under 24*s.*, such duty shall be increased by 1*s.* 6*d.*						
Wheat, viz. whenever such price shall be						
62*s.* and under 63*s.* per quarter	1	4	8			
63*s.* — 64*s.* —	1	3	8			
64*s.* — 65*s.* —	1	2	8			
65*s.* — 66*s.* —	1	1	8			
66*s.* — 67*s.* —	1	0	8			
67*s.* — 68*s.* —	0	18	8			
68*s.* — 69*s.* —	0	16	8			
69*s.* — 70*s.* —	0	13	8			
70*s.* — 71*s.* —	0	10	8			
71*s.* — 72*s.* —	0	6	8			
72*s.* — 73*s.* —	0	2	8			
at or above 73*s.* per quarter	0	1	0			
under 62*s.* and not under 61*s.* per quarter	1	5	8			
And in respect of each integral shilling, or any part of each integral shilling, by which such price shall be under 61*s.*, such duty shall be increased by 1*s.*						
Oatmeal, for every quantity of 181½ lbs., a duty equal in amount to the duty payable on a quarter of oats.						
Maize or Indian Corn, Buck Wheat, Beer or Bigg, for every quarter, a duty equal in amount to the duty payable on a quarter of barley.						
Rye, Peas, and Beans, 36*s.* and under 37*s.* per quarter	0	15	6			
And in respect of every integral shilling by which such price shall be above 36*s.*, such duty shall be decreased by 1*s.* 6*d.* until such price shall be 46*s.*						
at or above 46*s.* per quarter	0	1	0			
under 36*s.* and not under 35*s.* per quarter	0	16	9			
And in respect of each integral shilling, or any part of each integral shilling, by which such price shall be under 35*s.*, such duty shall be increased 1*s.* 6*d.*						
Wheat meal and Flour, for every barrel, being 196 lbs., a duty equal in amount to the duty payable on 38½ gallons of wheat.						
produce of, and imported from, any British possessions in North America, or elsewhere out of Europe, viz.						
Barley, per quarter, until the price of British barley be 34*s.* per quarter	0	2	6			
at or above 34*s.* per quarter	0	0	6			
Oats, per quarter, until the price of British oats be 25*s.* per quarter	0	2	0			
at or above 25*s.* per quarter	0	0	6			
Wheat, per quarter, until the price of British wheat be 67*s.* per quarter	0	5	0			
at or above 67*s.* per quarter	0	0	6			
Maize or Indian Corn, Buck Wheat, Beer or Bigg, for every quarter a duty equal in amount to the duty payable on a quarter of barley.						
Oatmeal, for every quantity of 181½ lbs., a duty equal in amount to the duty payable on a quarter of oats.						
Rye, Peas, or Beans, per quarter, until the price of British rye, peas, or beans shall be 41*s.*	0	3	0			
at or above 41*s.* per quarter	0	0	6			
Wheat meal and Flour, for every barrel, being 196 lbs., a duty equal in amount to the duty payable on 38½ gallons of wheat.						
N. B. — The corn duties are regulated by 9 Geo. 4. c. 60.—(See *antè*, pp. 393, 394.)						
Cornu cervi calcinatum, per lb.	0	0	8			
Costus, per lb.	0	1	0	0	0	8
Cotton, manufactures of, for every 100*l.* value	10	0	0			
articles of manufactures of cotton, wholly or in part made up, not otherwise charged with duty, for every 100*l.* value	20	0	0			
Ceiba tree cotton or silk cotton, imported from any British possession, per cwt.	0	0	1			
wool, or waste of cotton wool. See Wool.						
Couhage or cowitch, per lb.	0	1	3	0	0	10
Cowries, for every 100*l.* value	20	0	0			
Cranberries, per gallon	0	0	6			
Crayons, for every 100*l.* value	40	0	0			
Cream of tartar, per cwt.	0	4	8			
Crystal, rough, for every 100*l.* value	20	0	0			
cut, or in any way manufactured, for every 100*l.* value	30	0	0			
beads, per 1,000	1	8	6			
Cubebs, per lb.	0	2	0			
Cucumbers, viz.						
pickled, including the vinegar, per gallon	0	3	0			

	Duty.	Drawback.
	L. s. d.	L. s. d.
Cucumbers—*continued.*		
preserved in salt and water, for every 100l. value	20 0 0	
Culm, per ton	2 0 0	
Currants, per cwt.	2 4 4	2 0 0
Cuttle shells, per 1,000	0 12 6	
D.		
Dates, per cwt.	4 10 3	4 0 0
Derelict. Foreign liquors, derelict, jetsam, flotsam, lagan, or wreck, brought or coming into Great Britain or Ireland, are subject to the same duties, and entitled to the same drawbacks, as liquors of the like kind regularly imported.		
Diamonds	Free.	
Dice, per pair	1 6 2	
Dittany, per lb.	0 1 0	
Down, per lb.	0 1 3	0 0 8
Drugs, not particularly enumerated nor otherwise charged with duty, for every 100l. value	20 0 0	
E.		
Earthenware, not otherwise enumerated, for every 100l. value	15 0 0	
Ebony, per ton	10 0 0	
the produce of, and imported from, any British possession, per ton	0 15 0	
green ebony, the produce of, and imported from, any British possession, per ton	0 3 0	
Eggs, per 120	0 0 10	
Embroidery and needlework, for every 100l. value	30 0 0	
Enamel, per lb.	0 7 2	
Essence, viz.		
of bergamot or of lemon, per lb.	0 4 6	
of spruce, for every 100l. value	20 0 0	
not otherwise enumerated or described, per lb.	0 4 6	
Euphorbium, per lb.	0 0 8	0 0 5
Extract or preparation of cardamoms, coculus Indicus, grains, viz.		
Guinea grains of Paradise, liquorice, nux vomica, for every 100l. value	75 0 0	
oak bark, solid vegetable extract from oak bark, or other vegetable substances, to be used for purposes of tanning leather, and for no other purpose whatever, per cwt.	0 3 0	
the produce of New South Wales and its dependencies, and imported direct from thence, until the 1st of January, 1833	Free.	
opium, pepper, viz. Guinea pepper, extract of, for every 100l. value	25 0 0	
Peruvian or Jesuits' bark, per lb.	0 5 0	
quassia, for every 100l. value	50 0 0	
radix rhataniae, per lb.	0 5 0	
vitriol, for every 100l. value	25 0 0	
extract or preparation of any article, not being particularly enumerated, nor otherwise charged with duty, for every 100l. value	20 0 0	
F.		
Feathers, viz.		
for beds, in beds or not, per cwt.	2 4 0	
ostrich, dressed, per lb.	1 10 0	
undressed, per lb.	0 10 0	
not otherwise enumerated or described, viz.		
dressed, for every 100l. value	20 0 0	
undressed, for every 100l. value	10 0 0	
Figs, per cwt.	1 1 6	0 19 0
Fish, viz.		
eels, per ship's lading	13 1 3	
lobsters	Free.	
oysters, per bushel	0 1 6	
stock fish, per 120	0 5 0	
sturgeon, per keg, not containing more than 5 gallons	0 9 0	
turbots	Free.	
fresh fish, of British taking, and imported in British ships or vessels	Free.	
cured fish, of British taking and curing	Free.	
Flax, and tow or codilla of hemp or flax, whether dressed or undressed, per cwt.	0 0 1	
the growth or produce of New South Wales or its dependencies, or of Norfolk Island, or Van Diemen's Land, or of New Zealand, imported direct from those places respectively, until the 1st of Jan. 1833	Free.	
Flocks, per cwt.	0 19 0	
Flower roots, for every 100l. value	20 0 0	
Flowers, artificial, not made of silk, for every 100l. value	25 0 0	
Fossils, not otherwise enumerated, for every 100l. value	20 0 0	
Frames for pictures, prints, or drawings, for every 100l. value	20 0 0	
Furriers' waste, for every 100l. value	10 0 0	
Fustic, per ton	0 4 6	
imported from any British possession, per ton	0 3 0	
G.		
Galangal, per lb.	0 0 6	0 0 4
Galbanum, per lb.	0 1 4	0 0 10
Galls, per cwt.	0 5 0	
Gamboge, per lb.	0 1 8	0 1 1
Garnets, viz.		
cut, per lb.	1 10 0	
rough, per lb.	0 10 0	
Gauze of thread, for every 100l. value	30 0 0	

	Duty.
	L.
Gentian, per lb.	0
Ginger, per cwt.	2
preserved, per lb.	0
the produce of any British possession, per cwt.	0
preserved, per lb.	0
Ginseng, per lb.	0
Glass, viz.	
crown glass, or any kind of window glass (not being plate glass or German sheet glass), per cwt.	8
German sheet glass, per cwt.	10
plate glass, superficial measure, viz.	
not containing more than 9 square feet, per square foot	0
containing more than 9 square feet, and not more than 14 square feet, per square foot	0
containing more than 14 square feet, and not more than 36 square feet, per square foot	0
containing more than 36 square feet, per square foot	0
glass manufactures not otherwise enumerated or described, and old broken glass, fit only to be remanufactured, for every 100l. value	20
and further, for every cwt.	4
Glovers' clippings, fit only to make glue, per cwt.	0
Gloves, of leather, viz.	
habit gloves, per dozen pair	0
men's gloves, per dozen pair	0
women's gloves or mitts, per dozen pair	0
Glue, per cwt.	0
Grains, viz.	
Guinea grains, per lb.	0
of Paradise, per lb.	0
Granilla, per lb.	0
the produce of any British possession, per lb.	0
Grapes, for every 100l. value	20
Grease, per cwt.	0
Greaves for dogs, per cwt.	0
Gum, viz.	
ammoniac, per lb.	0
animi, rough, and in no way cleaned, per lb.	0
scraped, or in any way cleaned, per lb.	0
Arabic, per cwt.	0
cashew, per cwt.	0
copal, rough, and in no way cleaned, per lb.	0
scraped, or in any way cleaned, per lb.	0
elemi, per lb.	0
guaiacum, per lb.	0
imported from any British possession, per lb.	0
kino, or gum rubrum astringens, per lb.	0
lac, viz.	
cake lac, lac lake } for every 100l. value	10
lac dye	
seed lac } for every 100l. value	5
stick lac	
shell lac, for every 100l. value	20
opoponax, per lb.	
sagapenum, per lb.	
sandarack, or juniper, per cwt.	
sarcocolla, per lb.	
Senegal, per cwt.	
imported from any British possession, per cwt.	
tacamahaca, per lb.	
tragacanth, per lb.	
not particularly enumerated or otherwise charged with duty, for every 100l. value	
Gunpowder, per cwt.	
Gypsum, per ton	
the produce of, and imported from, any British possession, per ton	
H.	
Hair, viz.	
camels' hair or wool, per lb.	
the produce of, and imported from, any British possession	
cow, ox, bull, or elk hair, per cwt.	
goat's hair, per lb.	
horse hair, per cwt.	
human hair, per lb.	
not otherwise enumerated, for every 100l. value	
manufactures of hair or goats' wool, or of hair or goats' wool and any other material, not particularly enumerated or otherwise charged, for every 100l. value	
articles of manufactures of hair or goats' wool, or of hair or goats' wool and any other material, wholly or in part made up, not otherwise charged with duty, for every 100l. value	
Hams, per cwt.	
Harpstrings, per gross, containing 12 dozen knots	
Hats, viz.	
bast, chip, cane, or horse hair hats or bonnets, each hat or bonnet not exceeding 22 inches in diameter, per dozen	
each hat or bonnet exceeding 22 inches in diameter, per dozen	
straw hats or bonnets, each hat or bonnet not exceeding 22 inches in diameter, per dozen	

	Duty. L. s. d.	Draw-back. L. s. d.
ᵻ.		
t or bonnet exceeding 22 inches meter, per dozen	6 16 0	
mixed with, felt, hair, wool, or er hat	0 10 6	
ontaining 36 trusses, each truss	1 4 0	
ies, per cwt.	0 9 2	
b.	0 0 6	0 0 4
cwt.	4 15 0	
dressed, or any other vegetable of the nature and quality of hemp, and applicable to the poses, per cwt.	0 4 8	
duce of, and imported from, ritish possession	Free.	
duce of, and imported from, Zealand, until 1st of Jan. 1833	Free.	
, gelding, buffalo, bull, cow, or n the hair, not tanned, tawed, r in any way dressed; viz.		
cwt.	0 4 8	
cwt.	0 2 4	
uce of, and imported from, the coast of Africa, each hide not ding 14 lbs. weight, per cwt.	0 2 4	
uce of, and imported from, any n possession, viz.		
per cwt.	0 2 4	
per cwt.	0 1 2	
and not otherwise dressed,	0 0 6	
uce of, and imported from, any n possession, per lb.	0 0 3	
immed, per lb.	0 0 9	
uce of, and imported from, any n possession, per lb.	0 0 4	
f hides, tawed, curried, or in essed, per lb.	0 0 9	
uce of, and imported from, any n possession, per lb.	0 0 4½	
immed, per lb.	0 1 2	
uce of, and imported from, any , possession, per lb.	0 0 7	
	0 1 8	
Russia, tanned, coloured, otherwise dressed, per hide	0 5 0	
anned, coloured, shaved, or ise dressed, per lb.	0 2 6	
f hides, raw or undressed, cularly enumerated or de- or otherwise charged with rted from any British posses- erica, for every 100*l*. value	5 17 6	
hides, raw or undressed, cularly enumerated or de- or otherwise charged with very 100*l*. value	20 0 0	
hides, tanned, tawed, cur- any way dressed, not par- numerated or described, nor harged with duty, for every	40 0 0	
	1 3 0	
ice of any British possession,	0 5 0	
of any other place, per cwt.	0 15 0	
r every 100*l*. value	20 0 0	
wt.	1 3 9	
ding 6 feet in length, per 1,000	0 5 0	
6 feet, and not exceeding length, per 1,000	0 7 6	
9 feet, and not exceeding in length, per 1,000	0 10 0	
12 feet, and not exceeding n length, per 1,000	0 12 6	
15 feet in length, per 1,000	0 15 0	
	8 11 0	
, and pieces of horns, not ed with duty, per cwt.	0 2 4	
geldings	1 0 0	
I. and J.		
	0 2 0	0 1 4
or every 100*l*. value	20 0 0	
	0 2 0	
rubies, and all other precious iamonds), viz.		
00*l*. value	20 0 0	
ry 100*l*. value	10 0 0	
	0 0 4	
f, and imported from, any ssion, per lb.	0 0 3	
er cwt.	1 1 0	
er lb.	0 0 10	
b.	0 5 2	
, per cwt.	1 8 6	
unwrought, the produce of ession, and imported from on	0 2 6	
f any other country, per	1 10 0	
ed into rods, and iron drawn d less than ¾ of an inch wt.	0 5 0	
100*l*. value	10 0 0	
d old cast iron, per ton	0 12 0	
	0 5 0	

	Duty. L. s. d.	Draw-back. L. s. d.
Iron—*continued.*		
pig, per ton	0 10 0	
the produce of, and imported from, any British possession, per ton	0 1 3	
wrought, not otherwise enumerated, for every 100*l*. value	20 0 0	
Isinglass, per cwt.	2 7 6	
the produce of, and imported from, any British possession, per cwt.	0 15 10	
Juice of lemons, limes, or oranges, viz.		
raw, per gallon, for every degree of specific gravity or strength	0 0 0¼	
concentrated, per gallon, for every degree of specific gravity or strength	0 0 0½	
the produce of, and imported from, any British possession, whether concentrated or raw, the gallon, for every degree of specific gravity or strength	0 0 0¼	
K.		
Kelp. See Alkali.		
L.		
Lac. See Gum.		
Lace, viz.		
silk lace. See Silk.		
thread lace, for every 100*l*. value	30 0 0	
Lackered ware, for every 100*l*. value	30 0 0	
Lamp black, per cwt.	3 6 6	
Lapis, viz.		
calaminaris, per cwt.	0 1 0	
lazuli, per lb.	0 3 2	
tutiæ, per lb.	0 0 8	
Lard, per cwt.	0 8 0	
Latten, viz.		
black, per cwt.	0 8 0	
shaven, per cwt.	0 12 0	
Lavender flowers, per lb.	0 0 10	
Lead, viz.		
black, per cwt.	0 4 0	
chromate of lead, per lb.	0 2 0	
ore, per ton	1 5 0	
pig, per ton	2 0 0	
red, per cwt.	0 6 0	
white, per cwt.	0 7 0	
Leather, any article made of leather, pieces of leather, or any manufacture whereof leather is the most valuable part, not otherwise enumerated or described, for every 100*l*. value	30 0 0	
Leaves of gold, per 100 leaves	0 3 0	
of roses, per lb.	0 0 10	
Lemons, peel of, per lb.	0 0 5	
preserved in salt and water, for every 100*l*. value	20 0 0	
Lentils, the bushel	0 0 10	
Lignum, viz.		
quassia, per cwt.	8 17 6	One eighth part of the under-mentioned sums, being part of the duties on linens, ceased on 6th Jan. 1827, and every subsequent 6th Jan. till 1831.
rhodium, per cwt.	1 0 0	
vitæ, the produce of, and imported from, any British possession, per ton	0 10 0	
of any other place, or if otherwise imported, the ton	2 0 0	
LINEN, or linen and cotton, viz.		
cambrics, and lawns, commonly called French lawns, the piece not exceeding 8 yards in length, and not exceeding 7-8ths of a yard in breadth, and so in proportion for any greater or less quantity,		
plain	0 6 0	
bordered handkerchiefs	0 5 0	
lawns of any other sort, not French, viz.		
not containing more than 60 threads to the inch of warp, per square yard	0 0 9	
containing more than 60 threads do.	0 1 0	
damask and damask diaper, per square yd.	0 3 0	0 1 0
from 5 Jan. 1834, per square yd.	0 2 0	
drillings, ticks, and twilled linens, sq. yd.	0 0 11	0 0 3
from 5 Jan. 1834, per square yd.	0 0 8	
sail cloth, per square yard	0 0 7½	
plain linens, and diapers, not otherwise enumerated or described, whether chequered or striped, with dyed yarn or not, viz. not containing more than 20 threads to the inch of warp, per square yd.	0 0 3	0 0 0¾
from 5 Jan. 1834, per square yd.	0 0 2¼	
exceeding 20 and not more than 24 threads, do.	0 0 3½	0 0 0½
from 5 Jan. 1834, do.	0 0 3	
— 24 — 30 threads do.	0 0 5	0 0 1
from 5 Jan. 1834, do.	0 0 4	
— 30 — 40 threads do.	0 0 6	0 0 1½
from 5 Jan. 1834, do.	0 0 4½	
— 40 — 60 threads do.	0 1 0	0 0 4
from 5 Jan. 1834, do.	0 0 8	
— 60 — 80 threads do.	0 1 2	0 0 4
from 5 Jan. 1834, do.	0 0 10	
— 80 — 100 threads do.	0 1 4	0 0 4
from 5 Jan. 1834, do.	0 1 0	
containing more than 100 threads do.	0 2 0	0 0 6
from 5 Jan. 1834, do.	0 1 6	
Or, instead of the duties herein before imposed, upon linen of all sorts, at the option of the importer, for every 100*l*. value	40 0 0	
Note. — No increased rate of duty to be charged on any linen or lawns for any additional number of threads not exceeding two threads, for such as are not of 30 threads to the inch, nor for any additional number of threads not exceeding five threads,		

	Duty.		
	L.	s.	d.
LINEN—continued.			
for such as are of 30 threads and upwards to the inch.			
printed linen, in addition to the rated duties thereon, for every square yard	0	0	3½
sails, for every 100l. value	30	0	0
in use of any British ship, and being fit and necessary for such ship	Free.		
if otherwise disposed of, for every 100l. value	2	0	0
manufactures of linen, or of linen mixed with cotton or with wool, not particularly enumerated, or otherwise charged with duty, for every 100l. of the value	25	0	0
and further, if printed, for every square yard	0	0	3½
articles of manufactures of linen, or of linen mixed with cotton or with wool, wholly or in part made up, not otherwise charged with duty, for every 100l. value	40	0	0
Linseed cakes, per cwt.	0	0	2
Liquorice juice, or succus liquoritiæ, per cwt.	3	15	0
powder, per cwt.	5	10	0
root, the cwt.	3	3	4
Liquors. Foreign liquors, derelict. See Derelict.			
Litharge of gold or silver, per cwt.	0	2	0
Litmus, per cwt.	0	4	0
Logwood, per ton	0	4	6
imported from any British possession, per ton	0	5	0
Lupines, per cwt.	0	5	0

M.

	Duty.			Draw-back.		
	L.	s.	d.	L.	s.	d.
Macaroni, per lb.	0	0	8			
Mace, per lb.	0	4	6	0	4	0
the produce of, and imported from, any British possession, per lb.	0	3	6	0	3	2
Madder, per cwt.	0	6	0			
root, per cwt.	0	1	6			
Magna grecia ware, for every 100l. value	50	0	0			
Mahogany, per ton	7	10	0			
of the growth of Bermuda, or any of the Bahama islands, and imported direct from thence respectively, and mahogany imported direct from the bay of Honduras, in a British ship, cleared out from the port of Belize, per ton	2	10	0			
imported from Jamaica, per ton	4	0	0			
Mangoes, per gallon	0	6	0			
Manna, per lb.	0	1	3	0	0	10
Manuscripts, per lb.	0	0	2			
Maps or charts, plain or coloured, each map or chart, or part thereof	0	0	6			
Marmalade, per lb.	0	1	3			
the produce of, and imported from, any British possession, per lb.	0	0	3			
Mastic, per lb.	0	1	4	0	0	10
Mats, and matting, imported from any British possession, for every 100l. value	5	0	0			
of Russia, the 100	1	3	9			
not otherwise enumerated or described, for every 100l. value	20	0	0			
Matting, for every 100l. value	20	0	0			
Mattresses, for every 100l. value	20	0	0			
Mead or metheglin, per gallon	0	6	7			
Medals, viz.						
of gold or silver	Free.					
of any other sort, for every 100l. value	5	0	0			
Medlars, per bushel	0	5	0			
Molasses, per cwt.	1	3	9			
the produce of, and imported from, any British possession, per cwt.	0	9	0			
Mercury, prepared, for every 100l. of the value	30	0	0			
Metal, viz.						
bell metal, per cwt.	1	0	0			
leaf metal (except leaf gold) the packet containing 250 leaves	0	0	3			
Mill boards, per cwt.	3	8	2			
Minerals, not otherwise enumerated or described, for every 100l. value	20	0	0			
Models of cork or wood, for every 100l. value	5	0	0			
Morels, per lb.	0	2	9			
Moss, viz.						
lichen Islandicus or liverwort, per lb.	0	0	8			
rock, for dyers' use, the ton	0	15	0			
not otherwise enumerated, for every 100l. value	20	0	0			
Mother of pearl shells, for every 100l. value	5	0	0			
Mules, each	0	10	0			
Musical instruments, for every 100l. value	20	0	0			
Musk, per oz.	0	5	0	0	5	4
Myrrh, per lb.	0	1	8	0	1	1

N.

Nardus Celtica, per cwt.	1	0	0	0	13	4
Needlework, for every 100l. value	30	0	0			
Nets, viz.						
old fishing nets, fit only to make paper and pasteboard, per ton	0	5	0			
Nicaragua wood, per ton	0	15	0			
Nitre, viz.						
cubic nitre, per cwt.	0	0	6			
Nutmegs, per lb.	0	3	6	0	3	2
the produce of, and imported from, any British possession, per lb.	0	2	6	0	2	3
Nuts, viz.						
cashew nuts, per lb.	0	2	0	0	1	4
the produce of, and imported from, British possessions, per lb.	0	0	1			
kernel, per lb.	0	0	2			
castor nuts, per lb.	0	0	2			

	Duty.	
	L.	s.
Nuts—continued.		
nuts or seeds, the produce of any British possession, per cwt.	0	0
coker or cocoa nuts, the produce of any British possession, per 120 nuts	0	5
chestnuts, per bushel	0	2
pistachio nuts, per lb.	0	0
small nuts, per bushel	0	2
walnuts, per bushel	0	2
not otherwise enumerated, for every 100l. value	20	0
Nux vomica, per lb.	0	0

O.

Oakum, per cwt.	0	4
Ochre or oaker, per cwt.	0	6
Oil seed cakes of all sorts, per cwt.	0	0
Oil of almonds, per lb.	0	5
amber or succinum, per lb.	0	4
aniseed, per lb.	0	4
bay, per lb.	0	4
cajeputa, per oz.	0	0
carawa, per lb.	0	4
cassia, per oz.	0	4
castor, per lb.	0	1
the produce of, and imported from, any British possession, per lb.	0	0
chemical, not otherwise enumerated, per lb.	0	4
cinnamon, per oz.	0	1
cloves, per oz.	0	2
cocoa nut, per cwt.	0	2
fennel, per lb.	0	4
hemp seed, per tun	39	18
jessamine, per lb.	0	2
juniper, per lb.	0	4
lavender, per lb.	0	4
linseed, per tun	39	18
mace, per lb.	0	2
marjoram, per lb.	0	4
nutmegs, per lb.	0	2
olives, per tun	8	8
imported in a ship belonging to any of the subjects of the king of the Two Sicilies, and not warehoused before 1st of August, 1828, in addition to the duties imposed by any other act (9 Geo. 4. c. 76.), the tun		1
imported in a ship belonging to any of the subjects of the king of the Two Sicilies, in addition to the duties imposed by any other act or acts (10 Geo. 4. c. 43.), the tun		1
orange flower or neroli, per oz.	0	
palm, per cwt.	0	2
perfumed, not otherwise enumerated, per lb.	0	4
pine, per lb.	0	
rape seed, the tun	39	18
rhodium, per oz.	0	
rock, per lb.	0	
rosemary, per lb.	0	
rosewood, per oz.	0	
sandal wood, per oz.	0	
sassafras, per lb.	0	
seed, not enumerated, the tun	39	18
spike, per lb.	0	
thyme, per lb.	0	
train oil, blubber, spermaceti oil, and head matter, viz.		
the produce of fish, or creatures living in the sea, taken and caught by the crews of British ships, and imported direct from the fishery, or from any British possession, in a British ship, the tun	0	
the produce of fish, or creatures living in the sea, of foreign fishing, the tun	26	0
turpentine, per lb.	0	
vitriol, per lb.	0	
walnut, per lb.	0	
hemp seed, linseed, and rape seed, and seed oil, not particularly charged with duty, imported from any British possession, the tun	1	
not enumerated, nor otherwise charged with duty, for every 100l. value	50	
Olibanum, per cwt.	2	
Olives, per gallon	0	
Olive wood, viz.		
the produce of, and imported from, any British possession, the ton	0	
of any other place, or if otherwise imported, the ton	8	
Onions, the bushel	0	
Opium, per lb.	0	
Orange flower water, per gallon	0	
Oranges and lemons, viz.		
the chest or box, not exceeding 5,000 cubic inches	0	
the chest or box, exceeding 5,000 cubic inches, and not exceeding 7,500	0	
the chest or box, of 7,500 cubic inches, and not exceeding 14,000	0	
for every 1,000 cubic inches exceeding the above rate of 14,000 cubic inches, and so in proportion for any greater or less excise	0	
loose, per 1,000	0	
or, and at the option of the importer, for every 100l. value	75	

	Duty.	Draw-back.
	L. s. d.	L. s. d.
ns—*continued*.		
or archelia, per cwt.	0 0 6	
e enumerated, for every 100*l*.	0 3 0	
t.	20 0 0	
per cwt.	1 8 6	
	1 8 6	
il of roses, per oz.	0 0 6	
	0 2 0	
P.		
not otherwise enumerated, value	10 0 0	
for every 100*l*. value	30 0 0	
or every cwt. of glass	4 0 0	
nade of old rope or cordage t separating or extracting tar therefrom, and without e of other materials there-	0 0 3	
d, or stained paper, or paper flock paper, per square yd. paper of any other sort, not enumerated or described, with duty, per lb.	0 1 0	
zen sheets	0 0 9	
wt.	0 10 0	
	3 8 2	
wt.	0 17 6	
00*l*. value	5 0 0	
	0 7 6	
el	0 10 0	
	0 0 6	
00*l*. value	30 0 0	
ry 100*l*. value	20 0 0	
l. value	30 0 0	
, the produce of, and im- British possession, per lb.	0 1 0	
n any British possession imits of the East India harter, per lb.	0 1 0	
any place within the limits dia Company's charter, and h possession, per lb.	0 1 2	
lace, or if otherwise im-	0 1 6	
res of, not otherwise enu- y 100*l*. value	22 13 8	
not otherwise enumerated, gar, per gallon	20 0 0	
	0 6 0	
	0 1 0	
, per square foot et square or upwards, each	0 1 0	
	10 0 0	
any British possession,	0 0 5	
ny other place, per lb.	0 1 5	
	0 0 10	0 0 6
	0 0 10	
, per cwt.	0 0 9	
rces alive	0 14 4	
cwt.	Free.	
	0 1 0	
y to be remanufactured.		
roy	3 16 9	
oz. Troy	0 6 4	
oz. Troy	0 6 0	
z. Troy	0 4 6	
ATR, viz. manufactured in Great hich shall or ought to be arked in Great Britain, viz. the 5th of July, 1797,		0 16 0
he 31st of August, 1815,		0 17 0
owed on gold watch cases, any articles of gold not weight of two ounces.) , manufactured in Great hich shall or ought to be rked in Great Britain, viz. he 5th of July, 1797, per		0 1 0
e 10th of October, 1804,		0 1 5
e 31st of August, 1815,		0 1 6
llowed on silver watch ecklaces, beads, lockets, irt buckles or brooches, s, and spouts to China, nware teapots, whatever		
, or mounts, not weigh- silver each, and not being for castors, cruets, or ning to any sort of stands s of silver, not weighing each ; but this exemp- ade necks, collars, and ruets, or glasses, apper- rt of stands or frames. ffixed to or set on any solid silver buttons and having a bezelled edge		

	Duty.	Draw-back.
	L. s. d.	L. s. d.
Plate—*continued*.		
soldered on ; wrought seals, blank seals, bottle tickets, shoe clasps, patch boxes, salt spoons, salt ladles, tea spoons, tea strainers, caddy ladles, buckles, and pieces to garnish cabinets, or knife cases, tea chests, bridles, stands or frames.)		
Platina, per oz.	0 1 0	
ore of, for every 100*l*. value	5 0 0	
Platting or other manufactures to be used in making hats or bonnets, viz.		
of bast, chip, cane, or horse hair, per lb.	1 0 0	
of straw, per lb.	0 17 0	
Plums, dried, per cwt.	1 7 6	
Polishing rushes, for every 100*l*. value	20 0 0	
Pomatum, for every 100*l*. value	30 0 0	
Pomegranates, per 1,000	1 10 0	
peel of, per cwt.	0 15 0	
Pork, salted (not hams or bacon), per cwt.	0 12 0	
Potatoes, per cwt.	0 2 0	
Pots, viz.		
melting pots for goldsmiths, per 100	0 3 2	
of stone, for every 100*l*. value	30 0 0	
Powder, viz.		
hair powder, per cwt.	9 15 0	
perfumed, or perfumed dust, per cwt.	13 13 0	
not otherwise enumerated, that will serve for the same uses as starch, per cwt.	9 10 0	
Prints and drawings, viz.		
plain, each	0 0 1	
coloured, each	0 0 2	
Prunelloes, per cwt.	1 7 6	
Prunes, per cwt.	1 7 6	
Q.		
Quassia, per cwt.	8 17 6	
Quicksilver, per lb.	0 0 6	0 0 3
Quills, viz.		
goose quills, per 1,000	0 2 6	
swan quills, per 1,000	0 12 0	
Quinces, per 100	0 4 0	
Quinine, sulphate of, per oz.	0 0 1	
R.		
Radix, viz.		
contrayervæ, per lb.	0 1 8	0 1 1
enulæ campanæ, per cwt.	0 13 6	0 9 0
eringii, per lb.	0 0 6	0 0 4
ipecacuanhæ, per lb.	0 4 0	0 2 8
rhataniæ, per lb.	0 2 0	0 1 4
sen kæ, per lb.	0 1 9	0 1 2
serpentariæ, or snakeroot, per lb.	0 1 9	0 1 2
Rags, viz.		
old rags, old ropes, or junk, or old fishing nets, fit only for making paper or paste-board, per ton	0 5 0	
woollen rags, fit only for manure, per ton	0 7 6	
Raisins, viz.		
of the sun, per cwt.	2 2 6	1 18 0
not being raisins of the sun, and not being the produce of any British possession, the cwt.	1 0 0	
of all other sorts, the produce of any British possession, per cwt.	0 10 0	0 9 0
Rape cakes, per cwt.	0 0 2	
of grapes, per tun	13 6 0	
Red wood, or Guinea wood, per ton	0 15 0	
Rennet, per gallon	0 0 6	
Resina jalapæ, per lb.	0 6 9	0 4 6
Rhinehurst, per cwt.	0 14 3	0 9 6
Rhubarb, per lb.	0 2 8	
the produce of any British possession, per lb.	0 2 6	
Rice, viz.		
not being rough and in the husk, per cwt.	0 15 0	
rough and in the husk, or paddy, per bushel	0 2 6	
the produce of any British possession, not being rough and in the husk, per cwt.	0 1 0	
rough and in the husk, or paddy, per quarter	0 0 1	
Rosewood, per cwt.	0 10 0	
Rosin, or colophonia, per cwt.	0 4 9	
the produce of any British possession, per cwt.	0 3 2	
S.		
Saccharum saturni, per lb.	0 0 10	0 0 6
Safflower, per cwt.	0 2 6	
Saffron, per lb.	0 1 0	
Sago, viz.		
pearl, per cwt.	0 15 0	
common, per cwt.	0 5 0	
powder, per cwt.	0 15 0	
imported from any British possession, viz.		
pearl, per cwt.	0 10 0	
common, per cwt.	0 1 0	
powder, per cwt.	0 10 0	
Sal, viz.		
ammoniac, per lb.	0 0 3	
gem, per cwt.	0 8 0	
limonum, per lb.	0 4 9	
prunelle, per lb.	0 0 6	
succini, per lb.	0 3 2	
Salep, or salop, per lb.	0 1 3	0 0 10
Salt	Free.	
Saltpetre, per cwt.	0 0 6	
Sanguis draconis, per lb.	0 1 8	0 1 1
Santa Maria wood, for every 100*l*. value	20 0 0	
Sapan wood, per ton	0 15 0	

	Duty. L. s. d.	Drawback. L. s. d.
Sarsaparilla, per lb.	0 1 3	0 0 10
the produce of any British possession per lb.	0 1 0	0 0 10
Sassafras, per cwt.	0 6 4	
Saunders, viz.		
red, per ton	0 12 0	
white or yellow, per lb.	0 0 10	
Sausages, or puddings, per lb.	0 1 3	
Scaleboards, per cwt.	3 8 2	
Scammony, per lb.	0 6 4	0 4 2
Seeds, viz.		
acorns, per bushel	0 1 0	
ammi, or ammios seed, per lb.	0 0 6	
aniseed, per cwt.	3 0 0	
burnet, per cwt.	1 0 0	
canary seed, per cwt.	3 0 0	
caraway, per cwt.	1 10 0	
carrot seed, per lb.	0 0 9	
carthamus, per lb.	0 0 6	
castor, per lb.	0 0 1	
nuts, or seeds imported from any British possessions, per cwt.	0 0 6	
clover, per cwt.	1 0 0	
cole, per last	0 10 0	
coriander, per cwt.	0 15 0	
cummin, per cwt.	1 0 0	
fennel, per lb.	0 0 9	
fenugreek, per cwt.	0 9 6	
flax, per quarter	0 1 0	
forest, per lb.	0 0 6	
garden, not particularly enumerated, nor otherwise charged with duty, per lb.	0 0 6	
grass of all sorts, per cwt.	1 0 0	
hemp, per quarter	2 0 0	
the produce of, and imported from, any British possession, per quarter	0 1 0	
leek, per lb.	0 1 6	
linseed, per quarter	0 1 0	
lucerne, per cwt.	1 0 0	
maw, per cwt.	3 0 0	
millet, per cwt.	0 11 6	
mustard, per bushel	0 8 0	
onion, per lb.	0 1 6	
parsley, per lb.	0 0 1	
peas, when prohibited to be imported as corn, per bushel	0 7 6	
piony, or peony, per lb.	0 0 6	
quince, per lb.	0 3 0	
rape, per last	0 10 0	
sabadilla or cevadilla, per lb.	0 1 0	
shrub, or tree, not otherwise enumerated, per lb.	0 0 6	
trefoil, per cwt.	1 0 0	
worm, per lb.	0 1 6	0 1 0
all seeds not enumerated, nor otherwise charged with duty, commonly made use of for extracting oil therefrom, per last	0 10 0	
all other seed not enumerated, nor otherwise charged with duty, for every 100*l.* value	30 0 0	
Segars, per lb.	0 9 0	
Senna, per lb.	0 1 3	0 0 10
Ships to be broken up, with their tackle, apparel, and furniture (except sails), viz.		
foreign ships or vessels, for every 100*l.* of the value	50 0 0	
British ships or vessels entitled to be registered as such, not having been built in the United Kingdom, for every 100*l.* of the value	15 0 0	
Shumac, per cwt.	0 1 0	
Silk, viz.		
knubs or husks of silk, and waste silk, per cwt.	0 1 0	
raw silk, per lb.	0 0 1	
thrown silk, not dyed, viz.		
singles, per lb.	0 1 6	
tram, per lb.	0 2 6	
organzine and crape silk	0 3 6	
thrown silk, dyed, viz.		
singles or tram, per lb.	0 3 0	
organzine or crape silk, per lb.	0 5 2	
manufactures of silk, or of silk mixed with any other material, the produce of Europe, viz.		
silk or satin, plain per lb.	0 11 0	
or, and at the option of the officer of the customs, for every 100*l.* of the value	25 0 0	
silk or satin, figured or brocaded, per lb.	0 15 0	
or, and at the option, &c. for every 100*l.* value	30 0 0	
gauze, plain, per lb.	0 17 0	
or, and at the option, &c. for every 100*l.* value	30 0 0	
gauze, striped, figured, or brocaded, per lb.	1 7 6	
or, and at the option, &c. for every 100*l.* value	30 0 0	
crape, plain, per lb.	0 16 0	
or, and at the option, &c. for every 100*l.* value	30 0 0	
crape, figured, per lb.	0 18 0	
or, and at the option, &c. for every 100*l.* value	30 0 0	
velvet, plain, per lb.	1 2 0	
or, and at the option, &c. for every 100*l.* value	30 0 0	
velvet, figured, per lb.	1 7 6	
or, and at the option, &c. for every 100*l.* value	30 0 0	
ribands, embossed or figured with velvet, per lb.	0 17 0	

	Duty (L.)
Silk – *continued.*	
or, and at the option, &c. for every 100*l.* value	30
and further, if mixed with gold, silver, or other metal, in addition to the above rates, when the duty is not charged according to the value, per lb.	0
fancy silk net or tricot, per lb.	1
plain silk lace or net, called tulle, per square yard	0
manufactures of silk, or of silk mixed with any other material, the produce of, and imported from, British possessions within the limits of the East India Company's charter, for every 100*l.* value	20
millinery of silk, or of which the greater part of the materials is of silk, viz.	
turbans or caps, each	0
hats or bonnets, each	1
dresses, each	2
or, and at the option of the officers of the customs, for every 100*l.* of the value	40
manufactures of silk, or of silk and any other material, not particularly enumerated or otherwise charged with duty, for every 100*l.* value	30
articles of manufacture of silk, or of silk and any other material, wholly or in part made up, not particularly enumerated or otherwise charged with duty, for every 100*l.* of the value	30
Silkworm gut, for every 100*l.* value	20
Drawback on the Exportation of Silk Goods manufactured in the United Kingdom.	
For every lb. of stuffs or ribands of silk, composed of silk only, and being of the value of 14s. at least	
for every lb. of stuffs or ribands of silk and cotton mixed, whereof one half at least shall be silk, and being of the value of 4s. 8d. at least	
for every lb. of stuffs or ribands of silk and worsted mixed, whereof one half at least shall be silk, and being of the value of 2s. 4d. at least	
Skates for sliding, for every 100*l.* value	20
Skins, furs, pelts, and tails, viz.	
badger, undressed, per skin	0
bear, undressed, per skin	0
undressed, imported from any British possession in America, per skin	0
beaver, undressed, per skin	0
undressed, imported from any British possession in America, per skin	0
calf and kip, in the hair, not tanned, tawed, curried, or in any way dressed,	
dry, per cwt.	0
wet, per cwt.	0
produce of, and imported from, any British possession, viz.	
dry, per cwt.	0
wet, per cwt.	0
produce of, and imported from, the West Coast of Africa, each skin not exceeding 7 lbs. weight, per cwt.	
tanned, and not otherwise dressed, per lb.	
produce of, and imported from, any British possession, per lb.	
cut or trimmed, per lb.	
produce of, and imported from, any British possession, per lb.	
tawed, curried, or in any way dressed, per lb.	
produce of, and imported from, any British possession, per lb.	
cut, or trimmed, per lb.	
produce of, and imported from, any British possession, per lb.	
cat, undressed, per skin	
undressed, imported from any British possession in America, per skin	
coney, undressed, per 100 skins	
deer, undressed, per skin	
undressed, produce of, and imported from, any British possession in America, per 100 skins	
Indian, half dressed, per skin	
undressed or shaved, per skin	
dog, in the hair, not tanned, tawed, or in any way dressed, per dozen skins	
dogfish, undressed, per dozen skins	
undressed, of British taking, and imported direct from Newfoundland, per dozen skins	
elk, in the hair, not tanned, tawed, curried, or in any way dressed, per skin	
ermine, undressed, per skin	
fisher, undressed, per skin	
undressed, imported from any British possession in America, per skin	
fitch, undressed, per dozen skins	
fox, undressed, per skin	
undressed, imported from any British possession in America, per skin	
tails, undressed, for every 100*l.* value	
goat, viz.	
raw or undressed, per dozen skins	
tanned, per dozen skins	
hare, undressed, per 100 skins	

	Duty.	Draw-back.
	L. s. d.	L. s. d.
tails—*continued.*		
, undressed, per skin -	0 0 6	
the hair, per 100 skins -	0 0 4	
, per 100 skins	0 10 0	
kins, foreign, raw and un-		
r every 100*l.* value -	20 0 0	
l undressed, imported from any		
sh possession, for every 100*l.*		
	5 0 0	
hair, undressed, per 100 skins -	0 0 4	
, per 100 skins	0 10 0	
d or coloured, per 100 skins -	0 15 0	
essed, in the wool, per 100		
	0 0 4	
or tawed, per 100 skins -	0 10 0	
or tawed, and dyed or coloured,		
00 skins	0 15 0	
in oil, per 100 skins -	4 0 0	
ressed, per skin -	0 9 6	0 9 0
ssed, per skin	0 6 0	
ressed, per skin -	0 0 6	
ed, imported from any British		
sion, per skin	0 0 3	
dressed, per 100 tails -	0 16 3	0 15 6
essed, per skin -	0 0 4	
d, imported from any British		
sion in America, per skin -	0 0 2	
per skin	0 2 0	
essed, per dozen skins -	0 0 6	0 0 5
undressed, per 100 skins -	0 1 0	
essed, per 100 skins	0 12 6	
ssed, per skin	0 1 6	
ed, imported from any British		
sion in America, per skin -	0 1 0	
essed, per skin	0 7 6	
ressed, per skin -	0 9 6	
rs, undressed, per dozen pelts -	0 3 0	
per dozen pelts	0 6 0	
ther sorts, undressed, per 100		
	0 17 0	
essed, per skin	0 0 2	
d, imported from any British		
sion in America, per skin -	0 0 1	
ssed, per skin	0 8 4	0 7 6
tips of sable, undressed, per		
	0 1 3	0 1 1
air, not tanned, tawed, or any		
d, per skin	0 0 3	
taking, and imported direct-		
Newfoundland, per skin -	0 0 1	
any foreign fishery by persons		
ng British subjects, per skin -	0 1 0	
ssed, in the wool, per dozen		
	0 1 0	
r tawed, per 100 skins -	2 0 0	
in oil, per 100 skins -	4 0 0	
calabar, undressed, per 100		
	0 11 6	
r 100 skins	0 17 6	0 10 4
ressed, for every 100*l.* value	20 0 0	
sed, per skin	0 1 0	
sed, per skin	0 9 6	0 8 6
essed, per 100 skins	0 4 9	0 4 9
ed, per skin	0 2 0	
d, imported from any British		
on in America, per skin -	0 1 0	
r skin	0 17 6	
ndressed, per skin	0 1 0	
d, imported from any British		
on in America, per skin -	0 0 6	
, or pieces of skins and furs,		
r described, nor otherwise		
h duty, for every 100*l.* value	20 0 0	
s, or pieces of skins and furs,		
red, curried, or in any way		
particularly enumerated or		
nor otherwise charged with		
ery 100*l.* value	75 0 0	
	0 0 6	
	0 6 0	
	4 10 0	
	3 11 3	
f any British possession in		
dies, viz.		
cwt.	1 8 0	
wt.	1 3 0	
ton	0 3 2	
100*l.* value	30 0 0	
h minerals, fossils, or ores,		
particularly enumerated or		
herwise charged with duty,		
not exceeding in weight	Free.	
weight 14 lbs. each, for		
alue	5 0 0	
natural history, not other-		
ated or described	Free.	
f, and imported from, any		
sion, per ton	0 16 3	
place, or if otherwise im-		
on	8 14 2	
	0 10 0	
er lb.	0 1 6	
us Indica, per lb.	0 2 9	0 1 10
aters of all sorts, viz.		
n of such spirits or strong		
y strength not exceeding		
of proof by Sykes's hydro-		
so in proportion for any		
gth than the strength of		

Spirits, or strong waters—*continued.*	Duty.	Draw-back.
	L. s. d.	L. s. d.
proof, and for any greater or less quan-		
tity than a gallon, viz.		
not being spirits or strong waters, the		
produce of any British possession in		
America, or any British possession		
within the limits of the East India		
company's charter, and not being sweet-		
ened spirits or spirits mixed with any		
article, so that the degree of strength		
thereof cannot be exactly ascertained by		
such hydrometer	1 2 6	
or strong waters, the produce of any		
British possession in America, not		
being sweetened spirits or spirits so		
mixed as aforesaid	0 9 0	
or strong waters, the produce of any		
British possession within the limits		
of the East India Company's charter,		
not being sweetened spirits or spirits so		
mixed as aforesaid	0 15 6	
cordials, or strong waters respectively,		
(not being the produce of any Bri-		
tish possession in America,) sweet-		
ened or mixed with any article, so that		
the degree of strength thereof cannot be		
exactly ascertained by such hydrometer	1 10 6	
cordials, or strong waters respectively,		
being the produce of any British		
possession in America, sweetened or		
mixed with any article, so that the de-		
gree of strength thereof cannot be exactly		
ascertained by such hydrometer	1 0 6	
Sponge, per lb.	0 2 0	0 1 4
the produce of any British possession,		
per lb.	0 0 6	
Squills, dried, per cwt.	1 0 0	
not dried, per cwt.	0 5 0	
Starch, per cwt.	9 10 0	
Stavesacre, per cwt.	1 8 0	0 18 8
Steel, or any manufactures of steel, not other-		
wise enumerated, for every 100*l.* value	20 0 0	
Stone, viz.		
burrs for mill stones, per 100	3 16 0	
dog stones, not exceeding 4 feet in diame-		
ter, above 6 and under 12 inches in		
thickness, per pair	6 3 6	
emery stones, per cwt.	0 2 0	
filtering stones, for every 100*l.* value	50 0 0	
flint stones for potters, per ton	0 2 6	
grave stones of marble, polished, each not		
containing more than 2 feet square, per		
foot square, superficial measure	0 2 6	
unpolished, per foot square, superficial		
measure	0 0 10	
not of marble, polished or unpolished,		
per foot square, superficial measure	20 0 0	
limestone, for every 100*l.* value	0 1 0	
marble blocks, per solid foot		
marble, in any way manufactured, (except		
grave stones and paving stones, each not		
containing more than 2 feet square,)		
per cwt.	0 3 0	
marble paving stones, polished, each not		
containing more than 2 feet square, per		
foot square, superficial measure	0 0 10	
rough, per foot square, superficial		
measure	0 0 6	
mill stones above 4 feet in diameter, if 12		
inches in thickness or upwards, per pair	11 8 0	
paving stones, not of marble, per 100 feet		
square, superficial measure	0 12 0	
pebble stones, per ton	0 13 6	
polishing stones, for every 100*l.* value	20 0 0	
pumice stones, per ton	1 13 4	
quern stones, under 3 feet in diameter,		
and not exceeding 6 inches in thickness,		
per pair	0 8 9	
3 feet in diameter, and not above 1		
feet in diameter, and not exceeding		
6 inches in thickness, per pair	0 17 6	
rag stones, for every 100*l.* of the value	20 0 0	
slates, the produce of any foreign country,		
not otherwise enumerated or described,		
for every 100*l.* value	66 10 0	
slates in frames, per dozen	0 3 0	
slick stones, per 100	0 8 0	
sculptured, or Mosaic work, per cwt.	0 2 6	
to be used for the purpose of lithography,		
per cwt.	0 5 0	
whetstones, per 100	0 8 9	
stones not enumerated, nor otherwise		
charged with duty, for every 100*l.*		
value	66 10 0	
Note. — If any statue, group of figures,		
or other stone or marble ornament,		
carved out of the same block, shall		
exceed one ton weight, the duty to		
be charged thereon shall be estimated		
at the rate payable for one ton		
weight, and no more.		
Storax or styrax, viz.		
calamita, per lb.	0 2 0	0 1 4
liquida, per lb.	0 3 4	0 2 2
in the tear or gum, per lb.	0 8 4	0 5 5
Succades, viz.		
the produce of any British possession in		
America, per lb.	0 0 3	
the produce of any British possession		
within the limits of the East India		
company's charter, per lb.	0 0 6	
the produce of any other place, per lb.	0 3 2	
Succinum, per lb.	0 1 8	0 1 1

	Duty.	Draw-back.
	L. s. d.	*L. s. d.*
Sugar, brown or muscovado, or clayed, not being refined, viz.		
the growth, produce, or manufacture of any British possession within the limits of the East India company's charter, per cwt.	1 12 0	
the growth, produce, or manufacture of any British possession in America, or the Mauritius, per cwt.	1 4 0	
of any other place, per cwt.	3 5 0	
refined, per cwt.	8 8 0	
Sugar candy, viz.		
brown, per cwt.	5 12 0	
white, per cwt.	8 8 0	
(N. B.—By the 1 W. 4. c. 50. *eight tenth parts of the following bounties or drawbacks on sugar are continued so long as the duties imposed by that act.*)		
Sugar, viz. refined, made in the United Kingdom from sugar, viz. bastards, or refined loaf sugar, broken in pieces, or being ground or powdered sugar, or such sugar, pounded, crashed, or broken, exported in a British ship, per cwt.		1 10 0
in a ship, not British, per cwt.		1 9 0
other refined sugar, in loaf, complete, and whole, or lumps, duly refined, having been perfectly clarified and thoroughly dried in the stove, and being of uniform whiteness throughout, or such sugar pounded, crashed, or broken, and sugar candy, exported in a British ship, for every cwt.		2 6 0
in a ship not British, per cwt.		2 4 6
double refined sugar, additional bounty for every cwt.		0 8 0
Sulphur impressions, for every 100*l.* value	5 0 0	
Sweet wood, viz.		
the produce of, and imported from, any British possession, per ton	0 16 3	
of any other place, or if otherwise imported, per ton	10 13 0	
T.		
Tails, viz.		
buffalo, bull, cow, or ox tails, per 100	0 6 0	
Talc, per lb.	0 8 0	
Tallow, per cwt.	0 3 2	
imported from any British possession, per cwt.	0 1 0	
Tamarinds, per lb.	0 0 8	
the produce of any British possession within the limits of the East India company's charter, per lb.	0 0 6	
the produce of any British possession in America, or on the west coast of Africa, per lb.	0 0 2	
Tapioca, or tapioca powder, per cwt.	0 10 0	
Tar, viz.		
the last containing 12 barrels, each barrel not exceeding 31½ gallons	0 15 0	
the produce of any British possession, the last containing 12 barrels, each barrel not exceeding 31½ gallons	0 12 6	
Barbadoes, per cwt.	0 2 6	
Tares, per quarter	0 10 0	
Tarras, per bushel	0 1 3	
Tea, subject only to an excise duty.		
Teasles, per 1,000	0 1 0	
Teeth, viz.		
elephants' teeth, per cwt.	1 0 0	
sea cow, sea horse, or sea morse teeth, per cwt.	3 4 0	
Telescopes, for every 100*l.* value	30 0 0	
Terra, viz.		
Japonica or catechu, per cwt.	0 3 0	
Sienna, per cwt.	1 11 8	
umbra, per cwt.	0 12 0	
verde, per cwt.	0 16 0	
Thread, viz.		
Bruges thread, per dozen lbs.	0 15 0	
Outnal thread, per dozen lbs.	0 15 0	
pack thread, per cwt.	0 15 0	
Sister's thread, per cwt.	0 4 0	
whited brown thread, per dozen lbs.	0 18 0	
not otherwise enumerated, for every 100*l.* value	25 0 0	
Tiles of all sorts, for every 100*l.* value	50 0 0	
Dutch, for every 100*l.* value	15 0 0	
Tin, per cwt.	2 10 0	
manufactures of, not otherwise enumerated, for every 100*l.* value	20 0 0	
Tinfoil, for every 100*l.* value	25 0 0	
Tobacco, viz.		
unmanufactured, per lb.	0 3 0	
the produce of, and imported from, any British possession in America, manufactured, per lb.	0 2 9	
manufactured, or segars, per lb.	0 9 0	
manufactured in the United Kingdom, at or within two miles of any port into which tobacco may be imported, made into shag, roll, or carrot tobacco, per lb.		0 2 7½
Tobacco pipes, for every 100*l.* value	30 0 0	
Tongues, per dozen	0 3 0	
Tooth powder, for every 100*l.* value	30 0 0	
Tornsal or turnsole, per cwt.	0 5 0	
Tortoise shell, unmanufactured, per lb.	0 2 0	
the produce of any British possession, per lb.	0 0 6	
Touchstones, for every 100*l.* value	20 0 0	
Toys, for every 100*l.* value	20 0 0	
Treacle of Venice, per lb.	0 3 6	

	Duty
	L. s.
Truffles, per lb.	0 2
Turbith, per lb.	0 2
Turmeric, per cwt.	0 10
the produce of any British possession, per cwt.	0 2
Turnery, not otherwise enumerated, for every 100*l.* value	30 0
Turpentine, viz.	
not being of greater value than 12*s.* per cwt. thereof, per cwt.	0 4
being of greater value than 12*s.* and not of greater value than 15*s.* per cwt. thereof, per cwt.	0 5
of Venice, Scio, or Cyprus, per lb.	0 0
Twine, per cwt.	1 11
V.	
Valonia, per cwt.	0 1
Vanelloes, per lb.	0 16
Varnish, not otherwise enumerated, for every 100*l.* value	30 0
Vases, viz.	
ancient, not of stone or marble, for every 100*l.* value	5 0
Vellum, per skin	0 2
Verdigrise of all sorts, per lb.	0 7
Verjuice, per tun	73 12
Vermicelli, per lb.	0 0
Vermilion, per lb.	0 1
Vinegar, or acetous acid, per tun	18 18
W.	
Wafers, per lb.	0 1
Washing balls, per lb.	0 1
Watches of gold, silver, or other metal, for every 100*l.* value	25 0
Watch-glasses, for every 100*l.* value	20 0
and further for every cwt.	4 0
Water, viz.	
Cologne water, the flask, 30 of such flasks containing not more than one gallon	0 1
mineral or natural water, per dozen bottles or flasks, each bottle or flask not exceeding 3 pints	0 4
Wax, viz.	
bees', unbleached, per cwt.	1 10
in any degree bleached, per cwt.	3 0
imported from any British possession in Asia, Africa, or America, viz.	
unbleached, per cwt.	0 10
in any degree bleached, per cwt.	2 10
myrtle wax, per lb.	0
sealing wax, for every 100*l.* value	30 0
Weld, per cwt.	0
Whale-fins, viz.	
taken and caught by the crew of a British ship, and imported direct from the fishery, or from any British possession, in a British ship, per ton	1 0
of foreign fishing, per ton	95 0
Whipcord, per cwt.	0
Wine, viz.	
the produce of his Majesty's settlement of the Cape of Good Hope, or the territories or dependencies thereof, imported directly from thence, per gallon	0
all wine, except Cape, per gallon	0
Wire, viz.	
brass or copper, not otherwise enumerated, per cwt.	2 1
gilt or plated, for every 100*l.* value	25
iron, not otherwise enumerated or described, per cwt.	1
latten, for every 100*l.* value	25
silver, for every 100*l.* value	25
steel, per lb.	0
Woad, per cwt.	0
Wood, viz.	
anchor stocks, per piece	0
of the growth and production of any British possession in America, and imported directly from thence, per piece	0
balks, under 5 inches square, and under 24 feet in length, per 120	18
under 5 inches square, and 24 feet in length or upwards, per 120	27
5 inches square or upwards are subject and liable to the duties payable on fir timber.	
of the growth and produce of any British possession in America, and imported directly from thence, viz.	
under 5 inches square, and under 24 feet in length, per 120	3
under 5 inches square, and 24 feet in length or upwards, per 120	4
5 inches square or upwards are subject and liable to the duties payable on fir timber.	
battens, imported into Great Britain, viz.	
6 feet in length, and not exceeding 16 feet in length, not above 7 inches in width, and not above 2¾ inches in thickness, per 120	10
exceeding 16 feet in length, and not exceeding 21 feet in length, not above 7 inches in width, and not exceeding 2½ inches in thickness, per 120	11
exceeding 21 feet in length, not above	

	Duty. L. s. d.	Draw-back. L. s. d.
in width, or if exceeding 2¾ thickness, per 120	20 0 0	
45 feet in length, or ex- 2¾ inches in thickness, (not mber 8 inches square,) the taining 50 cubic feet	2 10 0	
r, per 120	6 0 0	
owth and produce of any possession in America, and directly from thence into itain, viz.		
ngth, and not exceeding 16 ngth, not above 7 inches in nd not exceeding 2¾ inches ess, per 120	1 0 0	
16 feet in length, and not 21 feet in length, and not inches in width, and not 2¾ inches in thickness,	1 3 0	
21 feet in length, not above in width, or if exceeding in thickness, per 120	2 0 0	
to Ireland, viz.		
ngth, and not exceeding 12 gth, not above 7 inches in d not exceeding 3½ inches ess, per 120	8 6 3	
12 feet in length, and not 14 feet in length, not nches in width, and not 3½ inches in thickness,	9 14 0	
4 feet in length, and not 16 feet in length, not nches in width, and not 3½ inches in thickness,	11 1 8	
6 feet in length, and not 18 feet in length, not nches in width, and not 3½ inches in thickness,	12 9 4	
8 feet in length, and not 20 feet in length, not ches in width, and exceed- hes in thickness, per 120	13 17 2	
) feet in length, not above width, and not exceeding in thickness, per 120	34 6 1	
ported into Great Britain,		
in length, not above 7 width, and not exceeding n thickness, per 120	3 0 0	
t in length, not above 7 width, and exceeding 2¾ hickness, per 120	6 0 0	
th and produce of any session in America, and directly from thence into ain, viz.		
in length, not above 7 width, and not exceeding n thickness, per 120	0 7 6	
in length, not above 7 width, and exceeding 2¾ hickness, per 120	0 15 0	
to Ireland, viz.		
in length, not above 7 width, and not exceeding n thickness, per 120	4 14 5	
in length, if exceeding n thickness, per 120	9 3 1	
en ends of all sorts, of d produce of any British America, and imported hence, per 120	0 8 3	
ches in thickness, or up- , containing 50 cubic feet	2 8 9	
of the growth and pro- ny British possession in nd imported directly from 120	0 8 4	
z.		
es square, and under 24 h, per 120	4 10 8	
re, and under 8 inches 24 feet in length, or up- 120	12 3 6	
nder 8 inches square, of and produce of any Bri- on in America, and im- tly from thence, per 120	0 16 3	
viz.		
s in thickness, and under ngth, per 120	4 9 6	
s in thickness, and if 15 h, or upwards, per 120	8 19 0	
5 feet 3 inches in length, inches square, per 120	6 2 0	
and produce of any Bri- on in America, and im- tly from thence, per 120	0 12 4	
white boards for shoe-		
in length, and under 6 ckness, per 120	6 16 6	
th, or 6 inches in thick- rds, per 120	13 13 0	

	Duty. L. s. d.	Draw-back. L. s. d.
Wood—*continued.*		
oak boards, viz.		
under 2 inches in thickness, and under 15 feet in length, per 120	18 1 0	
under 2 inches in thickness, and if 15 feet in length, or upwards, per 120	36 2 0	
outside slabs, or paling boards, hewed on one side, not exceeding 7 feet in length, and not above 1½ inch in thickness, per 120	2 0 0	
or paling boards, hewed on one side, exceeding 7 feet in length, and not exceeding 12 feet in length, and not above 1½ inch in thickness, per 120	4 0 0	
or paling boards, hewed on one side, exceeding 12 feet in length, or exceeding 1½ inch in thickness, are subject and liable to the duties payable on deals.		
or paling boards, hewed on one side, of the growth and produce of any British possession in America, and imported directly from thence, viz.		
not exceeding 7 feet in length, and not above 1½ inch in thickness, per 120	0 5 0	
exceeding 7 feet in length, and not exceeding 12 feet in length, and not above 1½ inch in thickness, per 120	0 10 0	
exceeding 12 feet in length, or exceeding 1½ inch in thickness, are subject and liable to the duties payable on deals.		
pipe boards, viz.		
above 5 feet 3 inches in length, and not exceeding 8 feet in length, and under 8 inches square, per 120	9 3 0	
exceeding 8 feet in length, and under 8 inches square, per 120	18 6 0	
of all sorts, exceeding 5 feet 3 inches in length, and under 8 inches square, of the growth and produce of any British possession in America, and imported directly from thence, per 120	0 19 6	
wainscot boards, viz.		
the foot, containing 12 feet in length, and 1 inch in thickness, and so in proportion for any greater or lesser length or thickness	0 4 0	
boards of all sorts, not otherwise enumerated or described, of the growth and produce of any British possession in America, and imported directly from thence, per 120	0 8 4	
bowsprits. See masts.		
deals, to be used in mines, viz.		
above 7 inches in width, being 8 feet in length, and not above 10 feet in length, and not exceeding 1½ inch in thickness, per 120	8 2 6	
imported into Great Britain, viz.		
above 7 inches in width, being 6 feet in length, and not above 16 feet in length, and not exceeding 3½ inches in thickness, per 120	19 0 0	
above 7 inches in width, above 16 feet in length, and not above 21 feet in length, and not exceeding 3½ inches in thickness, per 120	22 0 0	
above 7 inches in width, above 21 feet in length, and not above 45 feet in length, and not above 3½ inches in thickness, per 120	44 0 0	
above 45 feet in length, or above 3½ inches in thickness, (not being timber 8 inches square or upwards,) the load, containing 50 cubic feet	2 10 0	
and further, per 120	6 0 0	
of the growth and produce of any British possession in America, and imported directly from thence into Great Britain, viz.		
above 7 inches in width, being 6 feet in length, and not above 16 feet in length, and not exceeding 3½ inches in thickness, per 120	2 0 0	
above 7 inches in width, above 16 feet in length, and not above 21 feet in length, and not exceeding 3½ inches in thickness, per 120	2 10 0	
above 7 inches in width, being 6 feet in length, and not above 21 feet in length, and exceeding 3½ inches in thickness, per 120	4 0 0	
above 7 inches in width, exceeding 21 feet in length, and not exceeding 4 inches in thickness, per 120	5 0 0	
above 7 inches in width, exceeding 21 feet in length, and exceeding 4 inches in thickness, (not being timber 8 inches square, or upwards,) per 120	10 0 0	
imported into Ireland, viz.		
above 7 inches in width, and not exceeding 12 inches in width, and not exceeding 3½ inches in thickness, viz.		
8 feet in length, and not exceeding 12 feet in length, per 120	12 9 5	
exceeding 12 feet in length, and not exceeding 14 feet in length, per 120	14 11 0	
exceeding 14 feet in length, and not exceeding 16 feet in length, per 120	16 12 6	
exceeding 16 feet in length, and not exceeding 18 feet in length, per 120	18 14 1	

Wood—continued.

Description	Duty	Draw-back
	L. s. d.	L. s. d.
exceeding 18 feet in length, and not exceeding 20 feet in length, per 120	20 15 7	
above 7 inches in width, and not exceeding 12 inches in width, and exceeding 3½ inches in thickness, viz.		
8 feet in length, and not exceeding 20 feet in length, per 120	31 11 3	
above 7 inches in width, and not exceeding 12 inches in width, and not exceeding 4 inches in thickness, and exceeding 20 feet in length, per 120	51 9 2	
imported into Ireland, viz.		
above 7 inches in width, and not exceeding 12 inches in width, and exceeding 4 inches in thickness, and exceeding 20 feet in length, per 120	100 6 1	
deal ends imported into Great Britain, viz.		
above 7 inches in width, being under 6 feet in length, and not exceeding 3½ inches in thickness, per 120	6 0 0	
above 7 inches in width, being under 6 feet in length, and exceeding 3½ inches in thickness, per 120	12 0 0	
of the growth and produce of any British possession in America, and imported directly from thence into Great Britain, viz.		
above 7 inches in width, being under 6 feet in length, and not exceeding 3½ inches in thickness, per 120	0 15 0	
above 7 inches in width, being under 6 feet in length, and exceeding 3½ inches in thickness, per 120	1 10 0	
imported into Ireland, viz.		
above 7 inches in width, and not exceeding 12 inches in width, and under 8 feet in length, viz.		
not exceeding 3½ inches in thickness, per 120	7 1 8	
exceeding 3½ inches in thickness, per 120	13 14 8	
deals and deal ends, viz.		
of all sorts, of the growth and produce of any British possession in America, and imported directly from thence into Ireland, per 120	0 8 3	

and further, on all deals and deal ends imported into Ireland of the aforesaid lengths and thicknesses, but of the following widths, the additional duties following, viz.

if exceeding 12 inches in width, and not exceeding 15 inches in width, 25 per cent., or one fourth of the aforesaid rates.

if exceeding 15 inches in width, and not exceeding 18 inches in width, 50 per cent., or one half of the aforesaid rates.

if exceeding 18 inches in width, and not exceeding 21 inches in width, 75 per cent., or three fourths of the aforesaid rates.

if exceeding 21 inches in width, 100 per cent., or an additional duty, equal to the aforesaid rates respectively.

Description	Duty	Draw-back
firewood, not fit or proper to be used other than as such, viz.		
per fathom, 6 feet wide and 6 feet high	0 19 0	
of the growth and produce of any British possession in America, and imported directly from thence, per fathom, 6 feet wide and 6 feet high	0 0 10	
fir quarters, viz.		
under 5 inches square, and under 24 feet in length, per 120	18 2 7	
under 5 inches square, and 24 feet in length, or upwards, per 120	27 0 0	
5 inches square, or upwards, are subject and liable to the duties payable on fir timber.		
of the growth and produce of any British possession in America, and imported directly from thence, viz.		
under 5 inches square, and under 24 feet in length, per 120	3 5 0	
under 5 inches square, and 24 feet in length, or upwards, per 120	4 17 6	
5 inches square, or upwards, are subject and liable to the duties payable on fir timber.		
fir timber. See timber.		
handspikes, viz.		
under 7 feet in length, per 120	2 0 0	
7 feet in length, or upwards, per 120	4 0 0	
of the growth and produce of any British possession in America, and imported directly from thence, viz.		
under 7 feet in length, per 120	0 2 6	
7 feet in length or upwards, per 120	0 5 0	
knees of oak, viz.		
under 5 inches square, per 120	0 10 0	
5 inches square, and under 8 inches square, per 120	1 0 0	
8 inches square, or upwards, per load, containing 50 cubic feet	1 6 0	
of the growth of any British possession in America, and imported directly from thence, viz.		
under 5 inches square, per 120	0 2 0	
5 inches square, and under 8 inches square, per 120	0 15 0	

Wood—continued.

Description	Duty
8 inches square, or upwards, per load, containing 50 cubic feet	0
lathwood, viz.	
in pieces under 5 feet in length, per fathom, 6 feet wide and 6 feet high	4
in pieces 5 feet in length, and under 8 feet in length, per fathom, 6 feet wide and 6 feet high	6
8 feet in length, and under 12 feet in length, per fathom, 6 feet wide and 6 feet high	10
12 feet long, or upwards, per fathom, 6 feet wide and 6 feet high	13
of the growth of any British possession in America, and imported directly from thence, viz.	
in pieces under 5 feet in length, per fathom, 6 feet wide and 6 feet high	0
in pieces 5 feet in length, or upwards, per fathom, 6 feet wide and 6 feet high	1
masts, yards, or bowsprits, viz.	
6 inches in diameter, and under 8 inches, each	0
8 inches in diameter, and under 12 inches, each	1
12 inches in diameter, or upwards, per load, containing 50 cubic feet	2
of the growth of any British possessions in America, and imported directly from thence, viz.	
6 inches in diameter, and under 8 inches, each	0
8 inches in diameter, and under 12 inches, each	0
12 inches in diameter, or upwards, per load, containing 50 cubic feet	0
oak plank, viz.	
2 inches in thickness, or upwards, per load, containing 50 cubic feet	4
of the growth of any British possession in America, and imported directly from thence, viz.	
2 inches in thickness, or upwards, per load, containing 50 cubic feet	0
oak timber. See timber.	
oars, per 120	14
of the growth of any British possession in America, and imported from thence, per 120	0
spars, viz.	
under 22 feet in length, and under 4 inches in diameter, exclusive of the bark, per 120	2
22 feet in length or upwards, and under 4 inches in diameter, exclusive of the bark, per 120	4
4 inches in diameter, and under 6 inches in diameter, exclusive of the bark, per 120	9
of the growth of any British possession in America, and imported directly from thence, viz.	
under 22 feet in length, and under 4 inches in diameter, exclusive of the bark, per 120	0
22 feet in length or upwards, and under 4 inches in diameter, exclusive of the bark, per 120	0
4 inches in diameter, and under 6 inches in diameter, exclusive of the bark, per 120	1
spokes for wheels, viz.	
not exceeding 2 feet in length, per 1,000	3
exceeding 2 feet in length, per 1,000	6
of all sorts, of the growth of any British possession in America, and imported directly from thence, per 1,000	0

staves, viz.

not exceeding 36 inches in length, not above 3 inches in thickness, and not exceeding 7 inches in breadth, per 120

above 36 inches in length, not exceeding 50 inches in length, not above 3 inches in thickness, and not exceeding 7 inches in breadth, per 120

above 50 inches in length, not exceeding 60 inches in length, and not above 3 inches in thickness, and not exceeding 7 inches in breadth, per 120

above 60 inches in length, and not exceeding 72 inches in length, not above 3 inches in thickness, and not exceeding 7 inches in breadth, per 120

above 72 inches in length, not above 3 inches in thickness, and not exceeding 7 inches in breadth, per 120

above 3 inches in thickness, or above 7 inches in breadth, and not exceeding 63 inches in length, shall be deemed clap boards, and be charged with duty accordingly.

above 3 inches in thickness, or above 7 inches in breadth, and exceeding 63 inches in length, shall be deemed pipe boards, and be charged with duty accordingly.

imported from any foreign country in

	Duty.	Draw-back.
	L. s. d.	L. s. d.
d. ica, or from the Ionian Islands, charged with the same duty as e staves are charged with when ted from other foreign coun-		
rowth of any British possession nerica, and imported directly hence, viz.		
eding 36 inches in length, not 3½ inches in thickness, and ng 7 inches in breadth, per 120	0 2 0	
inches in length, and not ing 50 inches in length, and 3½ inches in thickness, and ceeding 7 inches in breadth,)	0 4 0	
inches in length, and not ex g 60 inches in length, not 3½ inches in thickness, and ceeding 7 inches in breadth,)	0 6 0	
inches in length, and not ing 72 inches in length, not 3½ inches in thickness, and ceeding 7 inches in breadth,)	0 8 0	
inches in length, not above es in thickness, and not ex 7 inches in breadth, per 120 eding 1½ inch in thickness, e charged with one third part duty herein proposed on such	0 10 0	
inches in thickness, or above s in breadth, and not exceed- s inches in length, shall be clap boards, and be charged ity accordingly.		
inches in thickness, or above s in breadth, and exceeding es in length, shall be deemed ards, and be charged with cordingly.		
er load, containing 50 cubic	1 10 0	
wth of any British possession ica, per load, containing 50 et	0 10 0	
inches square or upwards, per ning 50 cubic feet	2 15 0	
wth of any British possession rica, and imported directly nce, 8 inches square or up- er load, containing 50 cubic	0 10 0	
inches square or upwards, ntaining 50 cubic feet	2 15 0	
owth of any British posses- America, imported directly nce, 8 inches square or up- er load, containing 50 cubic	0 10 0	
sorts, not particularly enu- described, nor otherwise n duty, being 8 inches square per load, containing 50	1 8 0	
ularly enumerated or de- nor otherwise charged with eing of the growth of any possession in America, and directly from thence, being square or upwards, per load, ng 50 cubic feet	0 5 0	
ches square, and under 24 ngth, per 120	18 2 7	
ches square, and 24 feet in upwards, per 120	27 0 0	
quare or upwards, are sub- liable to the duties payable aber.		
th of any British possession ca, and imported directly nce, viz.		
ches square, and under 24 ngth, per 120	3 5 0	
hes square, and 24 feet in upwards, per 120	4 17 6	
uare or upwards are sub- lable to the duties payable ber. iz.		
uare or upwards, per load, 50 cubic feet	2 15 0	
th of any British possession ca, and imported directly ce, per load, containing 50	0 12 0	
ured, of the growth of any ossession in America, not y enumerated or de-		

	Duty.	Draw-back.
	L. s. d.	L. s. d.
Wood—continued. scribed, nor otherwise charged with duty, for every 100l. value	5 0 0	
unmanufactured, not particularly enumerated or described, and on which the duties due on the importation are payable according to the value thereof, being of the growth of the British limits within the province of Yucatan in the bay of Honduras, and imported directly from the said bay, for every 100l. value	5 0 0	
unmanufactured, not particularly enumerated or described, nor otherwise charged with duty, for every 100l. value	20 0 0	
teak wood, or other wood fit for ship-building, 8 inches square or upwards, the growth of any British possession within the limits of the East India Company's charter, per load, containing 50 cubic ft.	Free.	
Wool, viz.		
beaver wool per lb.	0 1 7	
cut and combed, per lb.	0 4 9	
bison or buffalo wool, the produce of, and imported directly from, any British possession, per lb.	0 0 4	
of any other place, or otherwise imported, per lb.	0 0 6	
Carmenia wool, per lb.	0 0 1	
coney wool, per lb.	0 0 3	
cotton wool, or waste of cotton wool, viz.		
the produce of, and imported direct from, any British possession, per cwt.	0 0 4	
the produce of any other country or place, per cwt.	0 5 10	
goats' wool or hair, per lb.	0 0 1	
the produce of, and imported from, any British possession	Free.	
hares' wool, per lb.	0 0 2	
ostrich wool, per lb.	0 0 6	
Polonia wool, per lb.	0 0 6	
red wool, per lb.	0 0 6	
sheep or lambs' wool, viz.		
the produce of, and imported from, any British possession	Free.	
the produce of, or imported from, any other place, viz.		
not being of the value of 1s. per lb. thereof	0 0 0½	
being of the value of 1s. per lb. or upwards, per lb.	0 0 1	
Woollens, viz.		
manufactures of wool (not being goats' wool), or of wool mixed with cotton, not particularly enumerated or described, nor otherwise charged with duty, for every 100l. value	15 0 0	
articles of manufactures of wool (not being goats' wool), or of wool mixed with cotton, wholly or in part made up, not otherwise charged with duty, for every 100l. value	20 0 0	
Y.		
Yarn, viz.		
cable yarn, per cwt.	0 10 9	
camel or mohair yarn, per lb.	0 0 1	
grogram yarn, per lb.	0 0 6	
raw linen yarn, per cwt.	0 1 0	
worsted yarn, of all sorts, per lb.	0 0 6	
Z.		
Zaffre, per lb.	0 0 1	
Zebra wood, per ton	2 0 0	
Zedoaria, per lb.	0 1 3	0 0 10
Goods, wares, and merchandise, being either in part or wholly manufactured, and not being enumerated or described, nor otherwise charged with duty, and not prohibited to be imported into or used in Great Britain or Ireland, for every 100l. value	20 0 0	
Goods, wares, and merchandise, not being either in part or wholly manufactured, and not being enumerated or described, nor otherwise charged with duty, and not prohibited to be imported into or used in Great Britain or Ireland, for every 100l. value	10 0 0	
Note.—All goods, the produce or manufacture of the island of Mauritius, are subject to the same duties as are imposed in this table on the like goods the produce or manufacture of the British possessions in the West Indies.		
All goods, the produce or manufacture of the Cape of Good Hope, or the territories or dependencies thereof, are subject to the same duties as are imposed in this table on the like goods the produce or manufacture of the British possessions within the limits of the East India Company's charter, except when any other duty is expressly imposed thereon.		

DUTIES COASTWISE.

e of the repeal of the duty on sea-borne coal, and the duty on slates carried coastwise, o public duties under this head.

See MAN, ISLE OF.

ESSIONS ABROAD. See *antè*, pp. 328—336.

DUTIES OUTWARDS.

	L.	s.	d.
Coals, not being small coals, exported to any place not a British possession, viz.			
in a British ship, per ton	0	3	4
in a foreign ship, per ton	0	6	8
Small coals, culm, and cinders, exported to any place not a British possession, viz.			
in a British ship, per ton	0	2	0
in a foreign ship, per ton	0	4	0
Skins, viz.			
coney skins, per 100	0	1	0
hare skins, per 100	0	1	0
Wool, viz.			
of sheep or lambs, and of hares and conies, per cwt.	0	1	0
Woollen manufactures, viz.			
woolfels, mortlings, shortlings, yarn, worsted, wool-flacks, crewels, coverlids, waddings, or other manufactures or pretended manufactures, slightly wrought up or put together, so as the same may be reduced to and made use of as wool again, mattresses or beds stuffed with combed wool, or wool fit for combing or carding, per cwt.	0	1	0
The following duty is also payable on goods of the growth, produce, or manufacture of the United Kingdom, exported from thence, except upon such as are subject to any other export duty, viz.			
Goods, wares, and merchandise, of the growth, produce, or manufacture of the United Kingdom (except as herein-after mentioned), exported to any port or place whatever, for every 100l. of the true value thereof	0	10	0

EXCEPT

Bullion; corn, grain, meal, malt, flour, biscuit, bran, grits, pearl barley and Scotch barley; cotton yarn, or other cotton manufactures; fish; linen, or linen with cotton mixed; molasses; military clothing, accoutrements, or appointments, exported under the authority of the commissioners of his Majesty's treasury, and sent to any of his Majesty's forces serving abroad; military stores exported to India by the East India Company; salt; sugar, refined, of all sorts, and sugar candy.

Goods, wares, and merchandise, exported to the Isle of Man by virtue and under the authority of any licence which the commissioners of his Majesty's customs are or may be authorised and empowered to grant.

Any sort of craft, food, victuals, clothing, or implements or materials necessary for the British fisheries established in the island of Newfoundland, or in any of his Majesty's colonies, islands, or plantations in North America, on due entry thereof, and exported direct to the said colonies, islands, or plantations.

Wool.

Woollen goods, or woollen and cotton mixed, exported to any port or place within the limits of the East India Company's charter.

EXCISE DRAWBACKS.

	L.	s.	d.
Beer, brewed by any entered brewer for sale in the United Kingdom, and duly exported from any part of the same to foreign parts, as merchandise, per barrel of 36 gallons imperial measure	0	5	0
Bottles, of stone, not exceeding 2 quarts in measure, and not being blacking bottles, per cwt.	0	5	0
of glass. See Glass.			
Bricks, viz.			
not exceeding 10 inches long, 3 inches thick, and 5 inches wide, per 1,000	0	5	10
exceeding the above dimensions, per 1,000	0	10	0
smoothed or polished on one or more sides, not exceeding 10 inches long by 5 inches wide, per 1,000	0	12	10
Glass, viz.			
plate glass, made in any part of the United Kingdom, exported to foreign parts, ground or polished, in rectangular plates at least 6 inches long and 4 inches broad, and 1-8th of an inch thick throughout, free from stains, and of good and fair quality, per square foot superficial measure	0	2	9
unground and unpolished, made in the United Kingdom, and exported from any part thereof to foreign parts, or to the islands of Jersey, Guernsey, Alderney, or Sark, in rectangular plates 6 inches long and 4 inches broad at the least, and not less than 2-8ths or more than 5 8ths of an inch thick, and of good and fair quality, per cwt.	3	0	0
window glass, not being spread glass, flashed or otherwise, and commonly called crown glass or German sheet glass, made in the United Kingdom, and exported from any part thereof to foreign parts, or to the islands of Jersey, Guernsey, Alderney, or Sark, in whole, half, or quarter tables, per cwt., and proportionally for greater or less quantities	3	13	6
panes of ditto, made in the United Kingdom, and exported from any part thereof to foreign parts, being in rectangular figures, not less than 6 inches long by 4 inches broad, and not containing any part of the bullion or thick centre part of the table from which such panes are cut, per cwt.	4	18	0

	L.	s.	d.
Glass — continued.			
spread window glass, or broad glass, made in the United Kingdom, and exported to foreign parts or to the islands of Jersey, Guernsey, Alderney or Sark, per cwt.			
common bottles (not being phials), vessels made use of in chemical laboratories, garden glasses, and all other vessels or utensils of common bottle metal, made in the United Kingdom, and exported to foreign parts, or to the islands of Jersey Guernsey, Alderney, or Sark, per cwt.			
flint glass wares, vessels, or utensils (in which phial glass is included), made in the United Kingdom and exported to foreign parts, per cwt.			
(See art. GLASS.)			
Hops, British, fit for use, per lb.			
Paper, first class, per lb.			
second class, per lb.			
mill-board, scale-board, sheathing-paper, button board, and button-paper, per cwt.			
books in complete sets, or, if periodical publications, in perfect parts or numbers, and blank plain, and ruled account books, bound or unbound, made of paper of the first class, per lb.			
pasteboard, of paper of first class, per cwt.			
of paper of second class, per cwt.			
printed, painted, or stained, per square yard			
Soap, viz.			
hard cake or ball, per lb.			
soft, per lb.			
Starch, and hair powder, per lb.			
Tiles, viz.			
pan or ridge tiles, per 1,000			
paving, not exceeding 10 inches square, per 100			
exceeding 10 inches square, per 100			
plain, per 1,000			
not otherwise enumerated, per 1,000			
Tobacco, manufactured in the United Kingdom, at or within two miles of any port into which tobacco may be imported, made into shag, roll, cut, or carrot tobacco, per lb.			

TARTAR. See ARGAL.

TEA (in one dialect of Chin. *Cha;* in another *Te;* Du. *Te;* Fr. *Thé;* Rus. *Tchai;* Hind. *Cha;* Malay, *Teh*), the leaves of the tea tree or shrub *viridis*, Lin.).

I. DESCRIPTION OF THE TEA PLANT. — TEA TRADE OF CHINA.
II. RISE AND PROGRESS OF THE BRITISH TEA TRADE.
III. INFLUENCE OF THE EAST INDIA COMPANY'S MONOPOLY ON THE AND QUALITY OF TEA.
IV. CONDITIONS UNDER WHICH THE EAST INDIA COMPANY HOLDS IT NOPOLY.
V. INFLUENCE OF THE MONOPOLY ON THE DUTIES ON TEA. — P MADE BY THE COMPANY, &c.

I. DESCRIPTION OF THE TEA PLANT. — TEA TRADE OF CHINA.

Description of the Plant. — *Places where it is cultivated.* — The tea tree or grows to the height of from 3 to 6 feet, and has a general resemblance to the my

is seen in congenial situations in the southern countries of Europe. It is a
ous plant, of the natural order *Columniferæ*, and has a white blossom, with
yle and anthers, not unlike those of a small dog rose. The stem is bushy, with
s branches, and very leafy. The leaves are alternate, on short, thick, channeled
, evergreen, of a longish elliptic form, with a blunt, notched point, and ser-
ept at the base. These leaves are the valuable part of the plant. The *Camel-*
cularly the *Camellia Sasanqua* of the same natural family as the tea tree, and very
sembling it, are the only plants liable to be confounded with it by a careful
The leaves of the particular camellia just named are, indeed, often used in
s of China, as a substitute for those of the tea tree.
fects of tea on the human frame are those of a very mild narcotic, and, like
nany other narcotics taken in small quantities, — even of opium itself, — they
rating. The green varieties of the plant possess this quality in a much higher
an the black ; and a strong infusion of the former will, in most constitutions,
onsiderable excitement and wakefulness. Of all narcotics, however, tea is the
icious ; if, indeed, it be so at all in any degree, which we very much doubt.
a shrub may be described as a very hardy evergreen, growing readily in the
from the equator to the 45th degree of latitude. For the last 60 years, it has
d in this country, without difficulty, in greenhouses ; and thriving plants of it
seen in the gardens of Java, Singapore, Malacca, and Penang ; all within 6
the equator. The climate most congenial to it, however, seems to be that
ue 25th and 33d degrees of latitude, judging from the success of its cultivation
For the general purposes of commerce, the growth of good tea is confined
and is there restricted to five provinces, or rather parts of provinces, viz.
d Canton, but more particularly the first, for black tea ; and Kiang-nan,
and Che-kiang, but chiefly the first of these, for green. The tea districts all
n the latitudes just mentioned, and the 115th and 122nd degrees of East longi-
wever, almost every province of China produces more or less tea, but generally
rior quality, and for local consumption only ; or when of a superior quality,
of the fine wines of France, losing its flavour when exported. The plant is
sively cultivated in Japan, Tonquin, and Cochin-China ; and in some of the
us parts of Ava ; the people of which country use it largely as a kind of *pickle*
a *oil !*
ally considered, the tea tree is a single species ; the green and black, with all
ies of each, being mere varieties, like the varieties of the grape, produced by
of climate, soil, locality, age of the crop when taken, and modes of preparation
ket. Considered as an object of agricultural produce, the tea plant bears a
blance to the vine. In the husbandry of China, it may be said to take the
e which the vine occupies in the southern countries of Europe. Like the
growth is chiefly confined to hilly tracts, not suited to the growth of corn.
capable of producing the finest kinds are within given districts, limited, and
kill and care, both in husbandry and preparation, are quite as necessary to the
of good tea, as to that of good wine.
t wine is produced only in particular latitudes, as is the best tea ; although,
e latter is not restricted to an equal degree. Only the most civilised nations
have as yet succeeded in producing good wines ; which is also the case in
ith tea ; for the agricultural and manufacturing skill and industry of the
e there unquestionably pre-eminent. These circumstances deserve to be
, in estimating the difficulties which must be encountered in any attempt to
he tea plant in colonial or other possessions. These difficulties are obviously
and, perhaps, all but insuperable. Most of the attempts hitherto made to
foreign countries were not, indeed, of a sort from which much was to be
Within the last few years, however, considerable efforts have been made by
government of Java, to produce tea on the hills of that island ; and having
ce of Chinese cultivators from Fokien, who form a considerable part of the
o Java, a degree of success has attended them, beyond what might have been
so warm a climate. The Brazilians have made similar efforts ; having also,
sistance of Chinese labourers, attempted to propagate the tea shrub near Rio
and a small quantity of tolerably good tea has been produced. But owing
price of labour in America, and the quantity required in the cultivation and
n of tea, there is no probability, even were the soil suitable to the plant, that
an be profitably carried on in that country.
probably be successfully attempted in Hindostan, where labour is compara-
, and where the hilly and table lands bear a close resemblance to those of the
of China ; but we are not sanguine in our expectations as to the result.
  Tea. — Manner in which they are manufactured. — The *black* teas usually

exported by Europeans from Canton are as follows, beginning with the lowest q
—Bohea, Congou, Souchong, and Pekoe.   The *green* teas are Twankay, Hys
young Hyson, Hyson, Imperial, and Gunpowder.   All the black teas exported (
exception of a part of the bohea, grown in Woping, a district of Canton) are g
Fokien, a hilly, maritime, populous, and industrious province, bordering to th
east on Canton.   Owing to the peculiar nature of the Chinese laws as to inh
and probably, also, in some degree to the despotic genius of the government,
property is much subdivided throughout the empire; so that tea is generally g
gardens or plantations of no great extent.   The plant comes to maturity and
crop in from 2 to 3 years.   The leaves are picked by the cultivator's family, an
diately conveyed to market; where a class of persons, who make it their p
business, purchase and collect them in quantities, and manufacture them in pa
is, expose them to be dried under a shed.   A second class of persons, commonl
in the Canton market as "the tea merchants," repair to the districts where th
produced, and purchase it in its half prepared state from the first class, and com
manufacture by garbling the different qualities; in which operation, women and
are chiefly employed.   A final drying is then given, and the tea packed in ch
divided, according to quality, into parcels of from 100 to 600 chests each.
parcels are stamped with the name of the district, grower, or manufacturer, e
is practised with the wines of Bordeaux and Burgundy, the indigo of Bengal, a
other commodities; and, from this circumstance, get the name of *chops;* the
term for a seal or signet.   Some of the leaf buds of the finest black tea p
picked early in the spring, before they expand.   These constitute pekoe, or b
of the highest quality; sometimes called "white-blossom" tea, from there bein
mixed with it, to give it a higher perfume, a few blossoms of a species of ol
fragrans), a native of China.   A second crop is taken from the same plants in
ginning of May, a third about the middle of June, and a fourth in August; wh
consisting of large and old leaves, is of very inferior flavour and value.   The
the leaf, the more high flavoured, and consequently the more valuable, is the te
some of the congous and souchongs are occasionally mixed a little pekoe, to
their flavour; and hence the distinction, among the London tea dealers, of these
tea, into the ordinary kinds and those of "Pekoe flavour."   Bohea, or the low
tea, is partly composed of the lower grades; that is, of the fourth crop of th
Fokien, left unsold in the market of Canton after the season of exportation has
and partly of the teas of the district of Woping in Canton.   The green teas a
and selected in the same manner as the black, to which the description now gi
particularly refers; and the different qualities arise from the same causes.
powder here stands in the place of the pekoe; being composed of the unopened
the spring crop.   Imperial, hyson, and young hyson, consist of the second a
crops.   The light and inferior leaves, separated from the hyson by a winnowing
constitute hyson-skin,—an article in considerable demand amongst the America
process of drying the green teas differs from that of the black; the first being
iron pots or vases over a fire, the operator continually stirring the leaves with l
hand.   The operation is one of considerable nicety, particularly with the finer
is performed by persons who make it their exclusive business.

Tea Trade in China. — The tea merchants commonly receive advances from
merchants and other capitalists of Canton; but, with this exception, are altog
dependent of them; nor have the latter any exclusive privilege or claim of pre
They are very numerous; those connected with the green tea districts alone be
400 in number.   The black tea merchants are less numerous, but more wealth
greater part of the tea is brought to Canton by land carriage or inland naviga
chiefly by the first: it is conveyed by porters; the roads of China, in the sout
vinces, not generally admitting of wheel carriages, and beasts of burden being
A small quantity of black tea is brought by sea, but probably smuggled;
cheaper mode of transportation is discouraged by government, which it depri
transit duties levied on inland carriage.   The length of land carriage from
cipal districts where the green teas are grown, to Canton, is probably not less
miles; nor that of the black tea, over a more mountainous country, less than
The tea merchants begin to arrive in Canton about the middle of October, and
season continues until the beginning of March; being briskest in November, I
and January.   Tea, for the most part, can only be bought from the Hong o
merchants; but some of these, the least prosperous in their circumstances, are
by wealthy *outside* merchants, as they are called; and thus the trade is co
extended.   The prices in the Canton market vary from year to year with the
stock on hand, and the external demand, as in any other article, and in any oth
After the season is over, or when the westerly monsoon sets in, in the month

pedes the regular intercourse of foreigners with China, there is a fall in the price
not only arising from this circumstance, but from a certain depreciation in quality,
e age of the tea; which, like most other vegetable productions, is injured by
, particularly in a hot and damp climate. The relative prices and values of the
t teas, and their values at different seasons, will be seen from the following com-
 statement, taken from Canton Price Currents, reckoned in *tales* per picul, the
and weight by which tea is always sold in China * : —

Teas.	In Season 1828. December 13.	Out of Season 1829. May 2.	Teas.	In Season 1828. December 13.	Out of Season 1829. May 2.
hea - -	14 to 15	14 to 15	Hyson -	44 to 54	36 to 45
ngou - -	24 — 28	18 — 20	Hyson-skin -	24 — 28	10 — 20
mpoi - -	24 — 28	18 — 20	Hyson, young -	34 — 0	16 — 20
chong - -	20 — 36	17 — 24	Gunpowder -	50 — 54	45 — 50
koe -	50 — 60	50 — 60	Twankay -	24 — 28	18 — 22
koi -	20 — 24	15 — 20			

ll be seen from this statement that the only two teas of which the prices are the
 both seasons, are bohea and pekoe — both articles of domestic consumption, and
 in extensive demand for the Russian market of Kiachta; and that the variation
st in the green teas, which are exclusively grown for the European and American
er.

gn *Trade in Tea.* — There seems to be little mystery in the selection and pur-
 teas; for the business is both safely and effectively accomplished, not only by
rcargoes of the American ships, but frequently by the masters; and it is ascer-
om the sales at the East India House, that there is no difference between the
 of the teas purchased by the commanders and officers of the Company's ships,
any assistance from the officers of the factory, and those purchased for the Com-
the latter. An unusual degree of good faith, indeed, appears to be observed,
art of the Chinese merchants, with respect to this commodity; for it was proved
e select committee of the House of Commons, in 1830, that it is the regular
of the Hong merchants to receive back, and return good tea for, any chest
l upon which any fraud may have been practised, which sometimes happens
nveyance of the teas from Canton on board ship. Such restitution has occa-
been made even at the distance of 1 or 2 years. The Company seem to
advantage over other purchasers in the Canton market, except that which the
urchaser has in every market, viz. a selection of the teas, on the payment of the
ces as others; and this advantage they enjoy only as respects the black teas;
Americans are the largest purchasers of green teas.

II. Rise and Progress of the British Tea Trade.

te rise and present magnitude of the British tea trade are among the most
nary phenomena in the history of commerce. Tea was wholly unknown to
ks and Romans, and even to our ancestors previously to the end of the
the beginning of the 17th century. It seems to have been originally im-
small quantities by the Dutch; but was hardly known in this country
1650. In 1660, however, it began to be used in coffee houses; for, in
assed that year, a duty of 8*d.* is laid on every gallon of " coffee, chocolate,
nd tea," made and sold. But it is abundantly evident that it was then only
g to be introduced. The following entry appears in the Diary of Mr. Pepys,
to the admiralty:—" September 25. 1661. I sent for a cup of tea (a China
' which I had never drunk before." In 1664, the East India Company bought
z. of tea as a present for his Majesty. In 1667, they issued the first order
tea, directed to their agent at Bantam, to the effect that he should send home
f the best tea he could get! — (See the references in *Milburn's Orient. Com.*
530.; *Macpherson's Hist. of Com. with India*, pp. 130—132.) Since then
mption seems to have gone on regularly though slowly increasing. In 1689,
charging a duty on the decoction made from the leaves, an excise duty of 5*s.* per
id on the tea itself. The importation of tea from 1710 downwards is exhibited
le annexed to this section.

at increase that took place in the consumption of tea in 1784 and 1785, over
ption in the preceding years, is to be ascribed to the reduction that was then
the duties. In the *nine* years preceding 1780, above 180,000,000 lbs. of tea
exported from China to Europe, in ships belonging to the Continent, and about
0 lbs. in ships belonging to England. But from the best information attain-
pears that the real consumption was almost exactly the reverse of the quanti-

* The value of the tale is about 6*s*., and the picul weighs 133⅓ lbs. avoirdupois.

ties imported; and that while the consumption of the British dominions amount above 13,000,000 lbs., the consumption of the Continent did not exceed 5,500,00 If this statement be nearly correct; it follows that an annual supply of above 8,000,00 was clandestinely imported. It was well known, indeed, that smuggling was carri to an enormous extent; and after every other means of checking it had been tried purpose, Mr. Pitt proposed, in 1784, to reduce the duties from 119 to 12½ per cent. measure was signally successful. Smuggling and the practice of adulteration we immediately put an end to, and the legal imports of tea were about trebled. In 1795 ever, the duty was raised to 25 per cent.; and after successive augmentations in 1790, 1803, and 1803, it was raised, in 1806, to 96 per cent. *ad valorem*, at which i tinued till 1819, when it was raised to 100 per cent. on all teas that brought abo per lb. at the Company's sales.

In consequence partly of this increase of duty, but far more of the conduct p by the East India Company in relation to the trade, the consumption of tea, as con with the population, has been *steadily declining since* 1800! That such is the case vious from the following statement:—

Years.	Population.	Total.	Consumption per Head.
		Lbs.	*Lbs. oz.*
1801	10,942,646	20,257,753	1 13·6
1811	12,609,864	20,702,809	1 10·2
1821	14,391,631	22,892,913	1 9·4
1831	16,537,398	26,043,223 *	1 9·2

It appears from this table, not only that the decline has been constant, but amounts, comparing the individual consumption of 1801 with the individual con tion of 1831, to full 17 per cent.! The subjoined statements show how this decl been occasioned.

A Return of the Quantities and Prices of the several Sorts of Tea sold by the East India Com each Year during the present Charter (1st May to 1st May).

Years.	Bohea		Congou		Campoi		Souchong		Pekoe	
	Quantity.	Average Sale Price per Pound.	Quantity.	Average Sale Price per Pound.	Quantity.	Average Sale Price per Pound.	Quantity.	Average Sale Price per Pound.	Quantity.	Average Sale Price per Pound.
	Lbs.	s. d.	*Lbs.*	s. d.	*Lbs.*	s. d.	*Lbs.*	s. d.	*Lbs.*	s.
1814-15	397,909	2 10·20	21,283,519	3 2·55	1,002,000	3 4·67	1,520,035	3 7·51	22,625	6 1
1815-16	839,198	2 1·57	17,908,827	2 11·02	823,507	3 4·94	982,816	3 6·55	30,700	5
1816-17	1,597,276	2 5·56	14,895,681	2 10·39	925,550	3 1·73	1,862,135	3 0·47	98,562	4
1817-18	1,972,736	2 5·73	15,736,003	2 11·82	866,304	3 3·12	2,018,058	3 2·88	76,302	4
1818-19	1,441,636	2 4·78	18,441,066	2 11·22	533,821	3 4·49	1,183,051	3 5·11	69,760	4
1819-20	1,497,592	1 9·25	17,664,433	2 7·94	479,081	3 4·64	1,168,605	3 2·01	27,802	4
1820-21	2,522,927	2 1·88	15,939,795	2 7·31	319,775	3 6·04	1,285,496	3 2·96	133,964	4
1821-22	3,583,486	2 5·28	17,249,982	2 8·59	121,293	3 7·00	1,397,931	3 1·25	92,957	3
1822-23	1,873,881	2 5·43	18,822,848	2 7·82	323,063	3 6·30	1,391,668	2 10·62	44,757	4
1823-24	1,853,394	2 4·92	19,006,594	2 8·06	242,562	3 6·56	1,322,326	2 11·82	46,005	5
1824-25	2,093,276	2 4·59	20,598,958	2 7·90	227,722	3 0·88	473,476	3 4·74	86,051	4
1825-26	2,713,011	2 0·50	21,034,635	2 6·75	207,971	3 1·77	547,128	3 1·28	148,038	4
1826-27	2,588,124	1 7·02	20,472,625	2 4·73	166,701	2 9·04	475,796	3 2·17	165,842	3
1827-28	3,759,199	1 7·44	19,389,592	2 3·95	297,346	2 9·81	448,163	3 0·53	280,308	3
1828-29	3,778,012	1 6·65	20,142,073	2 3·88	284,187	2 9·14	601,739	2 10·38	131,281	3

Years.	Twankay.		Hyson-skin.		Young Hyson.		Hyson.		Gunpowder.	
	Quantity.	Average Sale Price per Pound.	Quantity.	Average Sale Price per Pound.	Quantity.	Average Sale Price per Pound.	Quantity.	Average Sale Price per Pound.	Quantity.	Average Sale Price per Pound.
	Lbs.	s. d.	*Lbs.*	s. d.	*Lbs.*	s. d.	*Lbs.*	s. d.	*Lbs.*	s.
1814-15	3,646,048	3 6·11	795,907	3 9·57	-	-	1,008,948	5 9·15	9,189	7
1815-16	3,784,868	3 3·06	708,480	3 5·26	-	-	1,059,225	5 5·75		
1816-17	3,239,210	2 11·92	554,270	3 0·76	-	-	882,820	4 11·61	15,425	5
1817-18	3,763,123	3 0·09	451,904	3 1·97	-	-	992,439	4 10·34		
1818-19	4,730,297	2 11·87	193,852	3 2·78	-	-	909,637	4 11·83		
1819-20	4,288,345	2 10·83	161,919	3 4·38	-	-	700,319	5 3·66		
1820-21	4,900,764	3 0·33	343,095	3 0·84	-	-	782,482	5 6·04		
1821-22	4,401,778	3 1·48	225,636	3 1·89	-	-	1,044,256	4 8·53		
1822-23	4,165,896	3 4·77	205,658	3 3·99	-	-	816,872	4 3·24		
1823-24	3,987,206	3 5·71	259,209	3 4·72	-	-	980,753	4 3·23		
1824-25	3,754,120	3 5·17	324,987	3 3·29	9,055	4 3·68	985,566	4 2·71		
1825-26	3,768,406	3 4·88	229,961	3 4·57	-	-	932,099	4 5·38		
1826-27	4,424,262	3 1·94	298,960	3 2·26	51,421	4 0·75	801,724	4 8·72		
1827-28	4,537,672	2 7·04	242,313	2 7·19	-	-	1,013,771	4 5·58		
1828-29	4,101,845	2 5·72	213,993	2 3·84	-	-	1,014,923	4 1·75	645	6

East India House, 21st September, 1829. (Errors excepted.) THO. G. LLOYD, A

* This is what the consumption amounted to in 1827; for it is not now possible to distingu the quantities consumed in Great Britain and Ireland. Owing, however, to the degree in w has recently gained upon tea in England, we believe that in estimating the present consum part of the empire at 26,043,233 lbs., we are above rather than under the mark.

f the Quantity of Tea remaining for Home Consumption in Great Britain from 1711 to 1786, ned by deducting the Quantity exported, from the Quantity sold at the Company's Sales.

Lbs.		Lbs.		Lbs.		Lbs.
141,995	1741	1,031,540	1771	5,566,793	1784	8,608,473
149,929	1751	2,114,922	1781	3,578,499	1785	13,165,715
816,773	1761	2,619,277	1783	3,087,616	1786	13,985,506

duties amounted, at an average of a few years preceding 1784, to about 700,000l. a year.

the Quantity of Tea retained for Home Consumption in Great Britain from 1789 to 1828, e Quantity that paid Duty for Home Consumption in Ireland from 1789 to 1827; specifying Produce of the Duties in each Country, and the Rates of Duty.

Great Britain.		Ireland.				
Nett Amount of Duty. L. s. d.	Rates of Duty.	Quantity charged with Duty for Home Consumption. Lbs.	Nett Amount of Duty. (British Currency.) L. s. d.	Rates of Duty. Black:	Green:	
562,038 14 5	12l. 10s per cent.	1,970,898	38,038 14 S	4d. per lb.	6d. per lb.	Irish Currency.
547,230 4 8	—	1,736,796	33,132 12 2	ditto	ditto	
607,430 8 4	—	1,994,787	43,295 12 4	4½d. per lb.	6½d. per lb.	
616,775 6 9	—	1,844,598	35,110 0 8	ditto	ditto	
609,846 5 6	—	2,148,755	39,274 9 6	ditto	ditto	
628,081 6 5	—	2,041,290	43,892 6 2	ditto	ditto	
695,108 5 9	20l. per cent.	2,970,701	64,093 16 10	ditto	ditto	
877,042 13 0	—	2,326,306	48,633 14 9	ditto	ditto	
1,028,060 9 7	At or above 2s. 6d. per lb. 30l. per ct Under 2s. 6d. per lb. 20l. per ditto.	2,402,25[illegible]	60,817 6 5	ditto	ditto	
1,111,898 9 1	At or above 2s. 6d. per lb. 35l. per ct. Under 2s. 6d. per lb. 20l. per ditto.	2,953,24[illegible]	108,016 5 5	ditto	ditto	
1,176,861 9 9	—	2,873,71[illegible]	101,727 11 6	5½d. per lb.	7d. per lb.	
1,152,262 0 0	At or above 2s. 6d. per lb. 40l. per ct. Under 2s. 6d. per lb. 20l. per ditto.	2,926,16[illegible]	69,824 17 [illegible]	ditto	ditto	
				All Sorts: Sold at or above 2s. 6d. per lb.	Sold under 2s. 6d per lb.	
,287,808 2 6	At or above 2s. 6d. per lb. 50l. per ct Under 2s. 6d. per lb. 20l. per ditto.	3,499,801	135,852 3 4	35l. per ct ad val.	20l. per ct. ad val.	
,450,252 7 9	—	3,576,775	182,214 17 7	38l. 10s. per do.	23l. 10s. per do.	
,757,257 18 4	At or above 2s. 6d. per lb. 95l. per ct. Under 2s. 6d. per lb. 65l. per ditto.	3,239,937	172,355 15 6	ditto	ditto	
,348,004 4 6	—	3,337,125	251,734 8 9	34l. 14s. per do.	51l. 14s. per do.	
,925,298 17 9	At or above 2s. 6d. per lb. 95l. 2s. 6d. per ditto. Under 2s. 6d. per lb. 65l. 2s. 6d. per do	3,267,71[illegible]	[illegible]11,225 1 4	ditto	ditto	British Currency.
,098,428 19 2	On all Teas 96l. per ditto.	2,611,45[illegible]	[illegible]48,242 7 2	84l. 14s. per do.	71l. 14s. per do.	
043,224 11 3	—	3,555,129	476,949 4 3	ditto	ditto	
370,610 0 10	—	3,706,771	[illegible]34,685 1 7	ditto	ditto	
130,616 14 9	—	3,391,66[illegible]	4[illegible]2,088 12 3	ditto	ditto	
				On all Teas:		
212,430 1 1	—	2,922,565	435,307 10 2	93l. per cent. ad valorem.		
240,294 0 9	—	3,517,384	702,816 16 11	ditto		
258,798 2 9	—	3,758,49[illegible]	[illegible]67,186 11 0	ditto		
Customs record destroyed.	—	23,522,94	[illegible]21,299 12 3	ditto		
428,236 8 4	—	3,387,012	529,818 7 11	96l. per cent. ad valorem, and henceforth the same as in Great Britain.		
526,590 18 3	—	3,462,776	531,590 15 2			
[illegible]56,719 0 5	—	2,990,580	405,777 16 3			
[illegible]03,650 18 7	—	3,141,035	427,713 7 3			
362,588 10 1	—	3,560,431	510,105 6 6			
256,433 12 10	At or under 2s. per lb. 96l. per ditto. Above 2s. per lb. 100l. per ditto.	3,238,498	433,571 11 6			
128,410 17 0	—	3,150,344	398,742 5 4			
275,642 17 6	—	3,493,960	462,819 16 [illegible]			
434,292 19 10	—	3,816,966	511,299 5 2			
407,983 1 8	—	3,367,710	410,139 4 11			
420,205 11 11	—	3,387,510	415,271 15 11			
[illegible]27,944 4 11	—	3,889,658	503,074 13 4			
[illegible]91,813 19 5	—	3,807,785	446,229 5 1			
[illegible]63,206 19 3	—	3,887,955	442,382 14 10			
77,179 8 0	—					

nt includes all tea shipped to Ireland for consumption in that country subsequently to the passing of the act 9 Geo. 4. c. 44.

We regret that the Parliamentary Papers do not enable us to continue the pr account down to the present time. We, however, subjoin the following offici ments. (The years in the Company accounts are from the 1st May to 1st May

An Account of the Quantity and Sale Amount of Teas sold by the East India Company in t 1828-29 and 1829-30.

	Sales in England.		Sales in North American Colonies.		Total.	
	Quantity.	Sale Amount.	Quantity.	Sale Amount.	Quantity.	Sale A
	Lbs.	£	Lbs.	£	Lbs.	
1828—29	28,230,383	3,286,272	1,012,216	107,905	29,242,599	3,3
1829—30	27,411,196	3,024,138	1,047,134	115,915	28,458,330	3,1

Nett Produce of the Duties on Tea in the United Kingdom in the Years ending 5th January 1831.

	1829.	1830.
Tea Duties - - - - -	£3,321,722	3,387,097

III. Influence of the East India Company's Monopoly on the Pri Quality of Tea.

Influence of the Monopoly on Prices.—Every one is aware that hitherto the Ea Company have enjoyed a monopoly of the trade in tea. Very large quantities h deed, been smuggled at different periods into the country; but no British subj authorised by the East India Company, has ever been allowed openly to imp Being thus the *only sellers*, they have plainly had it in their power, by limiting th tities of tea brought to market, to raise its price above its natural elevation, and t an excessive profit at the expense of the public. No doubt they might have availing themselves of this power; but no such degree of forbearance could be ra expected, from the Company or any other body of men. All individuals an ciations naturally exert themselves to obtain the highest possible price for v they have to sell. And it is found that those who are protected from the compe others, or who have obtained a monopoly of any market, invariably raise the price commodities to a very high pitch. In supposing that the East India Company ha this, we do not suppose that they are better or worse than others: we merely supp they have acted as all associations have done when placed under nearly similar stances; or that they have availed themselves of their privileges to promote t culiar interests. So reasonable an inference is not to be defeated, except by di unimpeachable evidence.

But it is unnecessary to argue speculatively on a point of this sort. The deciding accurately with respect to it are in every one's hands. The Americans &c. import teas from China under a system of fair competition; and as no one that there can be any reason other than the existence of the monopoly, why tea s higher priced in London than in Hamburgh or New-York, we have, in order to the precise use made by the Company of their monopoly, merely to compare of tea as sold at their sales, with its price, duty free, in the cities referred to.

Instead, however, of resorting to Price Currents to learn the price of tea abroa furnished officially with its price in 1829. In the course of that year, governm orders to our consuls in foreign parts, directing them to purchase large sample specifying their cost price, the duty upon them, &c. These teas, when brought to were classified by the most skilful tea brokers, who, without knowing what had for them, fixed the prices which, in their estimation, they would bring at the C sales. Their cost price abroad was at the same time converted into sterling mone Kelly, the author of the Cambist. The table on next page contains the resul investigations, and the price of tea at the Company's quarterly sales in 1828–2

The extraordinary excess of the Company's prices over those of Hamburgh, R &c. is obvious at a glance. But taking the prices at Hamburgh as a standar crepancy may be set in a still clearer point of view as follows:—

Comparative Account of the Prices of Tea at London and Hamburgh.

Species of Tea.	Company's selling Price per Pound in 1828-29.		Prices at Hamburgh, per Pound, in 1828-29.		Excess of Company's Prices over those of Hamburgh.		Excess of Prices over Cor
	s.	d.	s.	d.	s.	d.	s.
Bohea - -	1	6½	0	8¼	0	10	
Congou -	2	4	1	2¾	1	1¼	
Campoi - -	2	9	1	2	1	7	
Souchong -	2	10¼	1	1¾	1	8½	
Pekoe - -	3	9¼	4	6¾	-	-	0
Twankay -	2	5¾	1	2¼	1	3½	
Hyson-skin -	2	4	0	11¼	1	4¾	
Hyson - -	4	1¾	2	8	1	5¾	
Gunpowder -	6	6½	3	5½	3	1	

owing the Cost Prices of Tea at Hamburgh, Rotterdam, and New-York, the Value affixed to the
es by the London Brokers, and the Price of Tea at the Company's Quarterly Sales in 1828-9.

Teas.	Samples.						Prices at the Company's Quarterly Sales in 1828-29.
	Hamburgh.		Rotterdam.		New York.		
	Cost Price abroad.	Value affixed by the London Brokers.	Cost Price abroad.	Value affixed by the London Brokers.	Cost Price abroad.	Value affixed by the London Brokers.	
	d. per lb.	d. per lb.	d. per lb.	d. per lb.	d. per lb.	d. per lb.	d. per lb.
	7·3850	16·	9·6375	17·5	-	-	} 18·65
	9·7025	16·5	11·3900	17·	-	-	
	12·6050	25·5	19·2775	25·5	-	-	
	16·8250	30·	21·9050	25·5	-	-	} 27·28
			26·2875	26·5			
	12·6050	25·	17·5250	28·	-	-	} 33·14
	15·7700	24·5	20·1525	25·	-	-	
ng	12·1350	24·5	19·2750	24·5	31·5675	26·	} 34·38
ng	20·2125	27·	31·5250	27·	24·3725	24·	
	-	-	-	-	16·5600	24·	None.
					32·6025	24·	None.
	36·9250	46·	78·8625	63·	-	-	
	55·9150	48·	84·1200	62·	-	-	} 45·23
	71·7400	66·					
y	10·5500	32·	17·5250	25·5	-	-	} 29·72
	15·8250	35·	19·2775	26·	-	-	
			19·2775	36·	-	-	None.
			20·1525	26·			None.
kin	7·3850	24·5	15·7600	25·	19·6625	32·	} 27·84
	11·6050	26·5	19·2775	25·5	12·9375	25·	
	27·7400	46·	33·2975	43·	23·8050	52·	
	31·6500	50·	37·6775	44·	27·4275	45·	} 49·75
	37·2300	60·	42·0600	46·	24·3925	43·	
Hyson	12·6500	36·	26·2875	43·	31·0500	45·	None.
	22·1500	47·	33·2975	45·	23·0375	43·	None.
	35·1200	58·	43·8125	54·			None.
			50·8225	62·			None.
			61·3375	66·			None.
der	39·0350	63·	52·5750	57·	40·3650	62·	} 78·51
	44·3100	68·	59·5850	64·	33·1200	60·	
			66·5950	72·			

it is obvious that to learn the total sacrifice occasioned by the monopoly, we have
ultiply the quantities of the different teas (with the exception of pekoe) disposed
Company's sales, by the excess of their prices over those of Hamburgh (see
page), and to deduct from this sum the quantity of pekoe, multiplied by the ex-
e Hamburgh price over that of the Company. — The account stands as follows : —

Species of Tea.	Quantities of Tea sold by the Company in 1828-29.	Excess of Company's Price per Pound, over Price at Hamburgh.	Excess of Price received by the Company.
	Lbs.	s. d.	£
Bohea	3,778,012	0 10	157,417
Congou	20,142,073	1 1¼	1,132,992
Campoi	284,187	1 7	22,493
Souchong	601,739	1 8¼	51,398
Twankay	4,101,845	1 3¼	260,638
Hyson-skin	213,933	1 4¾	14,930
Hyson	1,014,923	1 5¾	75,062
Gunpowder	645	3 1	99
			1,715,034
Deduct Pekoe, 131,281 lbs. at 9½d.	- -		5,197
Total Excess of Price received by the Company over and above the Price of similar Teas at Hamburgh - }			£1,709,837

g a similar computation for 1830, the total excess of price charged by the
on the 30,612,484 lbs. of tea sold by them that year over the Hamburgh price,
o amount to 1,889,975l. From the commencement of the present charter in
he end of 1830, the total quantity of tea sold at the Company's sales has been
51 lbs. ; so that, supposing the excess of price charged by the Company to
throughout the same as in 1830, the total surplus price received by them will
28,815,820l. ! Nearly the whole of this immense sum has been paid by the
d Irish consumer ; for the exportations to the colonies and foreign parts have
aratively inconsiderable.
ce of the Monopoly on the Qualities of Tea. *Comparison between the Teas of Great*
d those of the Continent. — It must, however, be admitted, that the mere com-
the prices of tea at Hamburgh and London does not afford a fair test of the
of the Company's monopoly, except on the supposition that the qualities of
ld in both places are about the same. The Company's advocates have, how-

ever, been in the habit of contending that the teas with which the British markets supplied are decidedly superior, in point of quality, to the teas met with on the C tinent and in the United States; and this, it was said, was merely the natural r of the Company's mode of managing the trade at Canton, where, it was alleged Company's agents had the choice of all the teas brought to market. But these s ments have been proved to be destitute of any good foundation. The samples o purchased abroad by the consuls in 1829, were taken without any discrimination the ordinary sorts met with in the foreign markets; and yet the prices which the bro to whose inspection they were submitted, supposed they would bring in the Lo market, are, in most cases, as high, and in some higher, than the sale prices of t London. The result of this comparison, in as far as Hamburgh is concerned, follows: —

Species of Tea.	Prices per Pound at the Company's Sales in 1828-29.		Prices of Samples bought at Hamb as fixed by the Brokers.	
	s.	d.	s.	d.
Bohea	1	6½	1	4¼
Congou	2	4	2	3¾
Campoi	2	9	2	0¾
Souchong	2	10¼	2	1¾
Pekoe	3	9¼	6	8
Twankay	2	5½	2	8
Hyson-skin	2	4	2	2¼
Hyson	4	1¾	4	3
Gunpowder	6	6½	5	6

It appears, therefore, from the award of the most competent persons that co selected for the purpose, that the common teas, such as bohea, and congou, s Hamburgh, are about as good as those sold at the Company's sales; and that m the finer teas, such as pekoe, twankay, hyson, &c., are decidedly better. He follows, that the consumers get no indemnification in the superiority of the arti the higher price they are compelled to pay for it. If the monopoly is to be vindi other grounds than this must be resorted to.

Prices of Bohea and Congou at Company's Sales. — Species of Tea brought to M — Bohea is the cheapest of all sorts of tea brought from China; and is, quently, most generally consumed by the lowest classes. From 1793 to 18 price, at the Company's sales, amounted to about 1*s*. 6*d*. per lb. In 1812, i raised from 1*s*. 7*d*. to 2*s*. 3*d*., and continued at about that rate till 1825-26, when reduced to 2*s*., and has since fluctuated between 1*s*. 6*d*. and 1*s*. 7*d*. This fall h the effect of increasing the consumption of bohea from about 2,000,000 lbs. in 18 to 3,788,012 lbs. in 1828-29, — a striking proof of the powerful influence of a red of price in augmenting consumption! But were it not for the monopoly, the p bohea might be farther reduced from 1*s*. 6*d*. or 1*s*. 7*d*. to 8½*d*. or 9*d*.; for such difference between the price charged for it by the Company and its price at Ham New-York, &c.! Were it reduced to this extent, it may be fairly presumed t consumption of bohea would amount to 7,000,000 or 8,000,000 lbs. The v crease that has taken place in the consumption of coffee since 1807, shows th digious influence of low prices in extending the demand for such articles. however, is troublesome to make; and is neither so suitable for, nor so well lik the poorer classes as tea. Its increased consumption is, in fact, quite as much to the system followed in the tea trade, as to the reduction of the duty affecting i

Congou is the next cheapest tea disposed of by the Company. It was sold b at 2*s*. 11*d*. per lb. in 1815-16, and they have since permitted it to fall to 2*s*. 4*d*., — an inconsiderable decline, compared with that which has taken place the same period in the price of pepper — (see *antè*, p. 826.), and other Eastern imported by free traders. Congou is used by the middle classes, and forms abo *thirds* of all the tea consumed in the empire. Notwithstanding the reduction price, it is still sold, like bohea, at an advance of about 100 per cent. over its p Hamburgh. The rate of advance on the finer species of tea is not so great, so t weight of the monopoly falls principally on the lower and middle classes. It s however, be observed, that the exorbitant price of tea in this country has driven the very wealthiest class to the secondary qualities; and it is to this that it is owin notwithstanding England is the richest country in the world, and the taste fo more generally diffused amongst us than amongst any other people, we consum little of the superior qualities! Indeed, some of the finest are not to be m in our markets; and while about a dozen kinds of tea are regularly quoted in burgh, Amsterdam, and New-York Price Currents, there are never more than sev sometimes only six, species to be met with here. Imperial, — a very fine gre regularly imported into America and all parts of the Continent, — is unknown English market. Singlo, once imported by the Company, has disappeared fo

Pekoe and gunpowder, the finest qualities of black and green, are little
the English market; and, in fact, are only imported in small quantities by
rs of the Company's ships. Thus, like all other monopolies, that of the
tea has not only the effect of adding enormously to its price, but of substi-
erior in the room of better qualities. Were their prices the same, can there
bt that superior teas would be in as great demand here as in the United

Conditions under which the East India Company holds its Monopoly.

ns, &c. — The legislature seems to have been early aware that the Company
their power, under the monopoly, to exact an exorbitant price for tea; and
ough (as we have seen) entirely unavailing, efforts have been made at different
eep prices at their fair level. In 1745, for example, a very great deduction
from the amount of the tea duties; and by a statute passed in that year
2. c. 26.), it was enacted, in order to prevent the Company from depriving the
the benefit of this reduction, that in case the tea imported by the East India
shall not always be sufficient to answer the consumption thereof in Great
d to *keep the price of tea in this country upon an* EQUALITY WITH THE PRICE
N THE NEIGHBOURING CONTINENT OF EUROPE, it shall be lawful for the said
and their successors, to import into Great Britain such quantities of tea as
think necessary from any part of Europe: and by another section of the same
s enacted, that if the East India Company shall, at any time, neglect to keep
market supplied with a *sufficient quantity of tea at reasonable prices*, it shall
for the Lords of the Treasury to *grant licences to any other person or persons,*
ic or corporate, to import tea into Great Britain from any part of Europe.
s statute been enforced, it would certainly have restrained the demands of the
within reasonable limits; but it was very soon forgotten, and the Company
as before, to sell their teas at an enormous advance as compared with their
Iamburgh and Amsterdam.

ne well-founded jealousy, which dictated the act of 1745, was again dis-
he proceedings at the reduction of the duties in 1784. It was then enacted (24
38.), that the East India Company shall make four sales of tea every year,
conveniently may be at equal distances of time from each other, and shall put
sales such quantities of tea as shall be judged sufficient to supply the demand;
sale, the tea to be put up shall be sold without reserve to the highest bidder,
n advance of 1d. per lb. be bid upon the price at which the same is put
nother clause it is enacted, that it shall not be lawful for the East India Com-
out up their teas for sale at any price which shall, upon the whole of the teas
t any sale, exceed the prime cost thereof, with the freight and charges of im-
together with lawful interest from the time of arrival of such teas in Great
d the common premium of insurance as a compensation for the sea risk in-
eon." The Company are further ordered to keep a stock, equal to at least one
amption, according to the sales of the preceding year, always before-hand.
re bound to lay before the Lords of the Treasury, copies of the accounts and
oon which their orders for importation, prices for sale, and quantities put up
l be grounded.

ct of these conditions is obvious. They were intended to secure a plentiful
ea to the public, and to prevent its being sold at an oppressive increase of price.
oly and low prices are altogether incompatible. The conditions now referred
n, as to all practical purposes at least, quite inoperative.

first place, the Company have made various additions to the prime cost, and
y to the putting up price of their tea, which they ought not to have made,
he Lords of the Treasury, had they been so disposed, could hardly disallow.
lways, for example, charged the cost of the factory at Canton to the price of
establishment consists of about 20 persons, and costs at an average about
year! We have not, we confess, been able to discover the shadow of a rea-
ing up so very expensive an establishment. The whole American business
transacted by the captains of the ships; and every one knows that they have
r disturbances with the natives than the English. Perhaps, however, a con-
assessor, an interpreter, and one or two other officers, might be advantage-
n the public service at Canton; but instead of costing 100,000l. such func-
uld be exceedingly well paid if they received 5,000l., or, at most, 8,000l.
second place, it is established in the evidence taken before the select committee
at the Company's practice for many years has been to throw the whole losses
their outward investment upon tea, by estimating the value of the tale, or
ney in which the accounts are kept, at the price which it cost for the purpose

of being invested in tea. This was a complete evasion of the provisions of the s
but it was one which it was very difficult, if not impossible, to defeat.

3. In the third place, the obligation imposed on the Company, of keeping
supply of tea in their warehouses, has contributed both to raise its price, and de
its quality.   From a return made to an order of the select committee of the H
Commons in 1830 (*First Report*, App. p. 23.), it appears that the shortest time
sold by the Company had been in store was 14 months ; and that, at an average
teas sold during the three years ending with 1829 had been 17 months in store
according to the evidence of the most respectable American witnesses, the bla
coarser kinds of tea are depreciated at least 5 per cent. by being kept a twelve
and are, indeed, hardly saleable after the arrival of fresh teas from China.   .
therefore, warehouse rent, interest of capital, and insurance for 17 months, to
terioration in point of quality, we may estimate the loss to the public, by this wea
but most injudicious interference of the legislature, at 15 per cent. upon the pri
the teas sold.

4. In the fourth place, it is obvious, even supposing the prime cost of the Co
teas were not improperly enhanced, that the regulation obliging them to be so
advance of 1*d*. per lb. if offered, on the putting up price, could not be otherw
nugatory.   Were the trade open, private merchants would endeavour to under
other ; so that the price of tea, like that of sugar or coffee, would be reduced to
lowest point that would yield the sellers the customary rate of profit.   But th
pany is in an entirely different situation.   Being the *only sellers*, they invariabl
stock the market.   Instead of bringing forward such quantities of tea as might
its sale at a small advance upon the upset price, they adjust the supply so that t
is raised to a much higher elevation.   Now, it will be observed, that all that thi
of management puts into the Company's coffers consists of *extra profit ;* for the
up price embraces every item that can fairly enter into the cost of the tea, includ
interest on capital and insurance, and including also, as we have seen, several it
have but little to do with it.   To show the extent to which this source of profit
vated, we may mention, that at the June sale in 1830, the Company put up c
1*s*. 8*d*. and 2*s*. 1*d*. per lb. ; the lowest sort, or that put up at 1*s*. 8*d*., being so
at 2*s*. 1½*d*., being an advance of *twenty-two and a half* per cent., and partly at
being an advance of FORTY-FIVE per cent. ; while the highest sort, or that p
2*s*. 1*d*., was sold partly at 2*s*. 2*d*., being an advance of *four* per cent., and partly a
being an advance of no less than SEVENTY-TWO per cent. above the upset price
above a price calculated to yield *ordinary profits*.   Mr. Mills, an intelligent ar
sive wholesale tea merchant, in a paper laid before the Lords' committee, shows
advance on the teas sold at the Company's June sale in 1830, above the putting
amounted to 122,177*l*. 18*s*. 1*d*. ; and as there are four such sales in the year,
advance may be estimated at about 500,000*l*.! And it is admitted, that this
considerably less than it was three or four years since.

These statements show generally how the Company have defeated the provisi
act of 1784, and, indeed, turned them to its own advantage.   But, as already
it is nugatory to attempt to combine monopoly with low prices and good
They never have existed, and it is not possible they ever should exist, togethe
nopoly is the parent of dearness and scarcity ; freedom, of cheapness and plent

V. INFLUENCE OF THE MONOPOLY ON THE DUTIES ON TEA. — PROFITS MAD
COMPANY, &c.

Duties on Tea. — The duty on tea, as already observed, is an *ad valore*
100 per cent. on all teas sold at above 2*s*. per lb., and of 96 per cent. o
are sold at 2*s*. and under.   This is certainly a high duty; but seeing tha
revenue must be raised, we do not know, were tea supplied under a free syste
could be fairly objected to.   Under the present system, however, the duty beco
exorbitant ; for being rated according to its sale price, when that is doubl
Company, the duty also is doubled, or amounts to 200 per cent. upon the rea
the article !   Thus, the ordinary price of congou at Hamburgh is about 1*s*. 2½c
and if the Company sold congou at the same rate, the duty would be 1*s*. 2
would cost the dealer 2*s*. 4½*d*. : but instead of this, the Company sell congou
or 2*s*. 4*d*., and the duty being as much, the cost to the dealer is 4*s*. 6*d*. c
so that the duty, though only 100 per cent. on the Company's price, is real
cent. on its price in an open market !   The mischief of the monopoly is thus a
almost beyond endurance ; for, besides doubling the cost price of the article,
the duty laid upon it !

The subjoined table, to which we invite the reader's attention, shows th
operation of this system.   In the first place, we have taken the cost price

rgh as purchased by the consul in that city (col. 3.), and adding to these
he English duties (col. 4.), the results (col. 5.) are the prices at which, under the
uties, the consumers might purchase teas in an open market. We have next
he prices affixed to the Hamburgh teas by the London brokers (col. 6.), and ad-
them, as before, the English duties (col. 7.), we have the prices (col. 8.) which
as would cost under the monopoly system. And deducting from the latter the
ce of tea at Hamburgh, we have (col. 9.) the addition caused by the monopoly,
actual duty, to the price of tea per pound, and the amount per cent. of such
.

	2.	3.	4. English Duty on Cost Price at Hamburgh.		5. Amount of Hamburgh Price, and English Duty.	6. London Value affixed to Hamburgh Teas by the Brokers.	7. Duty.		8. Amount of London Price and Duty.	9. Real Duty to the Consumer on the Cost Price of Tea.	
s.	Qualities.	Hamburgh Cost Price.	Per Cent. 96.	100.			Per Cent. 96.	100.		Per Lb.	Per Cent.
		d.	d.	d.	d.	d.	d.	d.	d.	d.	
-	Lowest	7·38	7·08	- -	14·46	16·	15·36	- -	31·36	23·98	325
-	Lowest	12·60	12·09	- -	24·69	25·5	- -	25·5	51·	38·40	305
g -	Best	20·21	19·40	- -	39·61	27·	-	r	27·	54·	33·79	167
-	Best	37·23	- -	37·23	74·46	60·	-	-	60·	120·	82·77	222
der -	Best	66·59	- -	66·59	133·18	72·	-	-	72·	144·	77·41	116
-	Best	71·74	- -	71·74	143·48	66·	-	-	66·	132·	60·26	84

ears from this statement, on the accuracy of which our readers may rely, that
of an *ad valorem* duty of 96 per cent., the teas consumed by the lower and
lasses pay, in monopoly price and duty together, a tax of above 300 per cent.
cost in the market of Hamburgh! Here is the real and sufficient cause of the
g consumption of tea. It never was attempted, in any other country, to levy a
·5 per cent. on the beverage of the poor, or rather, we should say, on one of the
t necessaries consumed by them. Instead of wondering at the decrease of
tion that has taken place, the only thing to excite the surprise of any reasonable
that this decrease has not been incomparably greater. Besides its other in-
ffects, the exorbitant price of tea has led to its extensive adulteration, and to a
l of smuggling in the finer qualities. It also has driven the poor to less sa-
stimulants, and is the principal cause of that prevalence of gin drinking which
ch lamented. We venture to affirm that the abolition of the Company's mo-
ould do ten times more to promote sobriety and good order among the poor,
formation of a thousand temperance societies, and the preaching of as many

a duties have recently declined to less than 3,400,000*l.*; at an average, however,
t 14 years, they have amounted to about 3,800,000*l.* a year. But had tea been
under a free system, and government imposed a duty on it equal to the present
the increased price caused by the monopoly, it would have produced a revenue
5,400,000*l.*; the balance, or 1,600,000*l.* a year, being the sum which the mo-
sts this country, exclusive of what it has cost the colonies, and of its influence
the duty, and in depressing the trade with China and the East.
, perhaps, be imagined that, were the trade thrown open, the price of tea would
ch reduced that government, instead of receiving 3,800,000*l.* or 3,400,000*l.*
revenue, would hardly receive half that sum. But this would be to suppose
consumption should remain stationary: whereas it is abundantly certain
uld be far more than doubled; and that while the consumer would get better
than half the present price, the revenue derived from it would be increased.
made by the East India Company on the Tea Trade. — Vast as the sacrifice
the Company's monopoly occasions to the people of Britain, it is doubtful
t yields any profit to the Company. Every one, indeed, must be satisfied
Company cannot possibly make the same profit by the privileges conceded
that would be made by private individuals enjoying similar advantages.
rit of monopolists," to borrow the just and expressive language of Gibbon,
w, lazy, and oppressive. Their work is more costly and less productive than
dependent artists; and the new improvements so eagerly grasped by the com-
f freedom, are admitted with slow and sullen reluctance, in those proud cor-
above the fear of a rival, and below the confession of an error." Even
e directors of a great association like the East India Company were disposed
its commerce, and to manage it according to the most approved principles,
holly without the means of giving effect to their wishes. They must operate
rvants; and is it to be imagined that the *employés* of such a body will ever

display that watchful attention to the Company's interests, or conduct the busines
trusted to their care with the unsparing economy practised by private merchants tra
on their own account, superintending their own concerns, and responsible in their
private fortunes for every error they may commit? The affairs of the Company,
withstanding the efforts of the directers to introduce activity and economy, have al
been managed, and must necessarily continue to be managed, according to a syste
routine. Their captains and mercantile agents are, we doubt not, " all honou
men ;" but it were an insult to common sense to suppose that they may be compare
a moment with individuals trading on their own account, in the great requisites of
conduct, and skill.

We have already (*antè*, p. 507.) noticed the controversy now going on as to wh
the Company has gained or lost by their trade. This, however, is not a matte
which it is necessary for us to enter ; but we entertain very little doubt that the op
of those who contend that the Company have been heavy losers by their comm
transactions, will turn out to be well founded. Taking, however, the Company
counts as they stand, they say they have realised a profit on the trade with (
during the three years ending with 1827–8, of 2,542,569*l.*, being at the rate of 847
a year. — (*Appen. to Second Report of Select Committee of* 1830, p. 95.) But we
already seen that the excess of price received by the Company during the same
years, over the price of similar teas sold at Hamburgh, amounted to at least 1,700
a year; so that, according to the Company's own showing, their monopoly occasie
absolute loss of 852,477*l.*, exclusive of its mischievous influence in doubling the
and in confining our trade with China to less than a third of what it would amo
under a system that gave free scope to the energies of individual enterprise.

But supposing that the Company gains every farthing that the public loses
monopoly, will any one pretend that *that* is any reason for its continuance? We
undervalue the East India Company ; we believe that the " ladies and gentlem
which it consists, are very worthy persons; but their deserts are not such that the
should be taxed directly and indirectly 3,000,000*l.* a year for their advantage.
idea of maintaining a monopoly which more than doubles the cost of an importa
cessary of life, because it may be advantageous to 2,500 out of 25,000,000 of p
is something too absurd to deserve any remark.

Capacity of China to furnish additional Supplies of Tea. — It has been som
contended, that were the tea trade thrown open, the increased demand of this e
could not be supplied, and that the abolition of the monopoly would not really
the British consumer, but the Chinese government. Our readers will hardly
that we should enter at any length into the refutation of so absurd a notion.
commencement of last century, the entire annual consumption of tea in this e
the Continent, and America, did not certainly amount to 500,000 lbs. ; whereas t
sumption of Great Britain, the Continent, and United States, amounts at pre
about 50,000,000 lbs. ; and yet every one acquainted with the history of the
aware, that though the consumption has increased *a hundred fold*, the prices in
markets have been regularly declining, and even at the Company's sales the
good deal less now than they were 50 or 60 years since. We may, therefore, re
easy upon this point. The production of tea is rapidly extending in China ; and
extent of that empire, its capacities for raising unlimited quantities of tea, and th
to which it is there used, negative the idea that any possible increase of the cons
of this country could have any perceptible or permanent influence on its cost pri

Sales of Tea at the East India House. — The biddings for lots are always made by professional
and from the disorder and noise which prevail in the sale room, and the rapidity of the bie
stranger could attempt it. One of the junior directors sits in the auction room as umpire. Th
be put up for sale are previously examined by the brokers, who mark each box with a convent
expressive of its quality. The Company make no allowance on account of any damage, rub
packing, or inequality of goodness, found, or pretended to be found, in any box or lot of tea
supposed that the brokers have, by means of their previous examination, made themselves a
with the state of every lot.

For the tares and allowances at the Company's sales, see *antè*, p. 499.

Purchasers at the Company's sales pay the duty to the Company at the same time that the
price of the tea ; and the Company pays it over to the excise, in the same way as distillers, soap b
It was shown in the evidence before the Commons' committee of 1830, that, exclusive of custom
above 80 excise officers are employed at the East India docks and Company's warehouses in att
the tea duties.

Retail Dealers in Tea. — Retailers of tea are obliged to take out a licence, wh
11*s.* a year. Being classed with coffee and pepper retailers, their exact numbe
be specified. We believe, however, that they are little, if at all, under 80,000
—(See LICENCES.)

Consumption of Tea on the Continent and in the United States. — Of the co
states, Russia and Holland are the only ones in which the consumption of tea
derable. In 1830, the imports of tea into Russia amounted to 154,554 f

s. The imports consist almost entirely of black tea. The consumption
olland amounts to about 2,700,000 lbs. a year; the duty on which varies
o 4½d. per lb. The consumption of France is not supposed to exceed
The importations into Hamburgh vary between 1,500,000 and 2,000,000
ater part of which is forwarded to the interior of Germany. The imports
and Trieste do not exceed 7 cwt. a year.
umption of the United States fluctuates from 6,000,000 to 8,000,000 lbs.
e American duties are specific, varying from about 6¼d. per lb. on bohea,
er ditto on congou, to 2s. 1d. on gunpowder. The tea duties form one
st items of American revenue, having in some years produced 650,000l.
tude has, however, been justly complained of; and it is probably owing to
ance that, while the consumption of tea continues pretty stationary in the
s, that of coffee is increasing with far greater rapidity than even in England.
y of the treasury of the United States, in his Report for 1827, observes —
f tea has become so general throughout the United States, as to rank
ecessary of life. When to this we add that there is no rival production
ne fostered by lessening the amount of its importation, the duty upon
be regarded as too high. Upon some of the varieties of the article it
exceeds 100 per cent., and is believed to be generally above the level
policy points out. A moderate reduction of the duty would lead to an
sumption of the article, to an extent that, in all probability, would, in the
enefit than injure the revenue. Its tendency would be to enlarge our trade
o China; a trade of progressive value, as our cottons and other articles of
tion (aside from specie) are more and more entering into it. It would
the trade in teas to centre in our ports; the present rate of duty driving
not unfrequently, to seek their markets in Europe, not in the form of
, but in the direct voyage from China. It would also serve to diminish
e United States losing any portion of a trade so valuable, through the
gulations of other nations." There is reason to think that these excellent
ll now be attended to. The consumption of bohea in the United States
siderable; nor does the total consumption of congou, souchong, and
as, amount to a third part of the consumption of green teas.

OOD, or **INDIAN OAK,** the produce of the *Tectona grandis,* a
ree, a native of the mountainous parts of the Malabar and Coro-
s, the Burman empire, Pegu, Java (where it is produced in great
Sumatra, the western coast of Africa, &c. The wood of the teak
the most useful timber in India; it is light, easily worked, and,
s, is strong and durable; it is easily seasoned, and shrinks very
ther of an oily nature, and, therefore, does not injure iron. Mr.
s, that in comparing teak and oak together, the useful qualities of
ll be found to preponderate. " It is equally strong, and somewhat
t. Its durability is more uniform and decided; and to ensure that
demands less care and preparation; for it may be put in use almost
forest, without danger of dry or wet rot. It is fit to endure all cli-
rnations of climate." Malabar teak is deemed superior to every other,
vely used for ship-building at Bombay. Teak ships of 40 years' old
re not uncommon in the Indian seas. Some men-of-war have been
nd have answered exceedingly well, except that they are said to
y sailers; but as teak timber is light, this has been, probably, owing
in their form. In 1829, 16,015 loads of teak wood were imported
tain from the western coast of Africa.—(See *Tredgold's Principles of*
06.; *Crawfurd's East. Archip.* vol. i. p. 451.; *Rees's Cyclopædia,* &c.

or **FULLERS' THISTLE** (Ger. *Weberdistel, Kratzdistel;*
carder; It. *Cardo da cardare;* Sp. *Cardeucha, Cardo peinador*).
ich is cultivated in the north and west of England, is an article
importance to clothiers, who employ the crooked awns of the
ng the nap on woollen cloths; for this purpose they are fixed
phery of a large broad wheel, against which the cloth is held while
s turned. In choosing teasels, the preference should be given to
largest bur, and most pointed, which are generally called *male*
re mostly used in preparing and dressing stockings and coverlets;
nd, commonly called the fullers' or drapers', and sometimes the
re used in the preparation of the finer stuffs, as cloths, rateens, &c.

THREAD (Ger. *Zwirn;* Du. *Garen;* Fr. *Fil;* It. *Refe;* Sp. *Hilo,* Rus. *Nitki*), a small line made up of a number of fine fibres of any veget animal substance, such as flax, cotton, or silk; whence its names of cotton, or silk, thread.

TILES (Ger. *Dachziegel;* Fr. *Tuiles;* It. *Tegole, Embrici;* Sp. *Tejas Tscherepiza*), a sort of thin bricks, dried in kilns, and used in covering and different kinds of buildings. The best brick earth only should be made in — (See Bricks and Tiles.)

TIMBER (Ger. *Bauholz, Zimmer;* Du. *Timmerhout;* Fr. *Bois de ch Bois à bâtir;* It. *Legname da fabbricare;* Sp. *Madera de construccion Ströewoi Gess;* Pol. *Cembrowina*), the term used to express every lar squared, or capable of being squared, and fit for being employed in house building. In the language of the customs, when a tree is sawn into thin not above 7 inches broad, it is called batten; when above that breadth, s pieces are called deal. Wood is the general term, comprehending under ber, dye-woods, fire-wood, &c.

Timber is generally sold by the load.

The following are the contents of the loads of different species of timber-h unhewn: —

A load of timber unhewn	40 cubic feet.	A load of 2½ inch plank	240 s
squared timber	50 —	3 inch plank	200
1 inch plank	600 square feet.	3½ inch plank	170
1½ inch plank	400 —	4 inch plank	150
2 inch plank	300 —		

36⅓	Russian stand. deals	12 ft. long,	1½	inch. thick,	11	inch. broad	make	1 loa
58$\frac{12}{33}$	Christiania ditto	11 —	1¼	—	9	—		1
53⅓	Dram ditto	10 —	1½	—	9	—		1
3	Riga logs	-	-	-	-	-		1

The following were the prices of the principal species of timber in the markets, March 1832, duty paid. — (For the duties, see Tariff.)

		L.	s.	d.		L.	s.	d.
Teak, African	per load	7	0	0	to	8	0	0
Oak, European	—	7	10	0	—	0	0	0
Quebec	—	5	10	0	—	6	0	0
Fir, Riga	—	5	10	0	—	0	0	0
Dantzic	—	5	0	0	—	5	7	6
Memel	—	5	0	0	—	5	7	6
Swedish	—	4	7	6	—	0	0	0
Norway Balks	per 120	36	0	0	—	0	0	0
Pine, Quebec red	per load	4	0	0	—	4	5	0
yellow	—	3	12	6	—	3	15	0
New Brunswick	—	3	10	0	—	0	0	0
red	—	3	12	6	—	3	15	0
Miramichi yellow	—	3	15	0	—	4	0	0
Birch	—	3	0	0	—	4	0	0
Wainscot Logs, 14 feet	each	4	0	0	—	4	10	0
Rose Wood	per ton	12	0	0	—	30	0	0
Masts, Quebec red, 14 to 18 inches		8	0	0	—	9	0	0
yellow	per load	7	0	0	—	8	0	0
Riga	—	0	0	0	—	0	8	0
Norway and Swedish	—	5	0	0	—	5	10	0
Plank, Dantzic Oak	—	9	0	0	—	10	10	0
Memel	—	0	0	0	—	0	0	0

		L.	s.	d
Deals, Gefle, 14 feet 3 inches,	per 120	40	0	
Stockholm —	—	36	0	
Gottenburg, 12 ft. 3 in. 9	—	26	0	
Christiania, 1st and 2d	—	32	0	
Frederickshal —	—	29	0	
Onega, Archangel	—	17	0	
Petersburgh, Narva, or Memel,	per standard hundred	16	10	
Dantzic	—	17	0	
Deal Ends, &c. 2-3ds the price of deals				
If white wood, from 2*l.* to 3*l.* less				
Quebec red Pines, per stand. hun.		15	0	
yellow	—	11	10	
white Spruce	per 120	18	0	
Dantzic Deck	each	19	0	
Spars	—	0	0	
Lathwood, Memel, &c.	per fathom	8	10	
British America		4	10	
Staves, Baltic	per 1,200	130	0	
Hhd. 2-3ds, barrel half, longhdng. 1-3rd.				
Quebec pipe	per 1,200 pieces	47	10	
Hdh. 2-3rd and barrel half the price of pip				

TIMBER TRADE. Having, in separate articles, described those s timber most in demand in this country, we mean to confine ourselves in th to a few remarks on the policy of the regulations under which the trade is conducted.

1. *Importance of a cheap Supply of Timber.* — It is surely unnecessary to any lengthened statements on this head. If there be one article more tha with which it is of primary importance that a great commercial nation like should be abundantly supplied on the lowest possible terms, that article is timbe to the deficiency of our home supplies, most of the timber, with the exceptio required for building ships and houses, and most part, also, of that emplo construction of machinery, is imported from abroad. Any individual acquai the purposes to which timber is applied, but ignorant of our peculiar policy wi to it, would never, certainly, imagine that such an article could be made the oppressive duties, and of still more oppressive preferences. Timber is not to be in the same light as most other commodities. It is against all principle duties on materials intended to be subsequently manufactured; but timber material of the most important of all manufactures — that of the instruments tion! Suppose it were proposed to lay a heavy tax on ships, wagons, looms shops when completed, would not such a monstrous proposal be universally scou yet this is what is really done. The finished articles are not, indeed, direc but the principal material of which they are made, and without which they be constructed, is burdened with an exorbitant duty! To dwell on the ab

tax would be worse than useless. Of all things essential to the prosperity of
cturing industry, improved and cheap machinery is the most indispensable.
dividuals amongst us are ready enough to ridicule the contradictory conduct of
nch government, who, at the very moment that they are endeavouring to bolster
anufacturing interest, lay enormous duties on foreign iron, and thus double or
he price of some of the most important manufacturing implements. Timber is,
r, of quite as much importance in this respect as iron ; and our conduct in bur-
it with exorbitant duties partakes as largely of the *felo de se* character as that of
ghbours ! Indeed, as will be immediately seen, it is decidedly less defensible.
lausible though inconclusive reasonings might be urged in defence of duties on
d timber, were they imposed for the sake of revenue : but even this poor
for financial ignorance and rapacity cannot be set up in defence of the iron
of France or the timber duties of England. The former, however, are the
jectionable ; they were imposed, and are still kept up, to encourage the produc-
iron in France : whereas the duties on timber in England have been imposed
sake, principally, of promoting the lumber trade of Canada, and of forcing
loyment of a few thousand additional tons of shipping ! We do not sacrifice the
r the sake of the golden eggs, but for the sake of the offal she has picked up.
gin and Operation of the discriminating Duty in favour of American Timber. —
ctice of encouraging the importation of the timber of Canada and our other
ns in North America, in preference to that of foreign countries, is but of recent
It took its rise during the administration of Mr. Vansittart, and bears in
art the impress of his favourite policy. The events that took place in 1808
eriously affected our previous relations with the Baltic powers, a deficiency in
stomed supply of timber began to be apprehended ; and the ship owners and
merchants naturally enough availed themselves of this circumstance, to excite
of the ministry, and to induce them to change the fair and liberal system on
e trade in timber had been conducted down to that time, by granting extraor-
ncouragement to its importation from Canada. Even as a temporary expedient,
e to a peculiar emergency, the policy of giving any such encouragement is
y doubtful. Supposing timber not to have been any longer obtainable from
n of Europe, its price would have risen, and it would, of course, have been
from Canada, the United States, or wherever it could be had, without any
nce on the part of government. But, in 1809, a large addition was made to
s previously charged on timber from the north of Europe, at the same time
e previously charged on timber from Canada and our other possessions in
were almost entirely repealed ; and in the very next year (1810 , the duties
osed on Baltic timber were *doubled !* Nor did the increase of duties on such
op even here. In 1813, after Napoleon's disastrous campaign in Russia, and
free navigation of the Baltic had been restored, 25 per cent. was added to the
European timber ! The increase of the revenue was pleaded as a pretext for
ure ; but we believe it was really intended to augment the preference in favour
a timber ; for how could it be supposed that an increase of the duties on an
ported from a particular quarter of the world, that was already taxed up to
highest point, could add any thing considerable to the revenue, when a con-
rticle might be imported from another quarter duty free ? The various duties
uropean timber amounted, when consolidated by the act 59 Geo. 3. c. 52.,
per load.
ting for the moment that the peculiar and unprecedented aspect of things
and 1809 warranted the giving of some preference to the importation of
om Canada, such preference should plainly have ceased in 1813. So long
mmunication with the bridge is interrupted, we may be forced to use a boat
he river ; but when the communication is again opened, and when there is not
est chance of its future interruption, it would be a singular absurdity to
resume the use of the bridge, and to continue the costly and inconvenient
f being ferried over ! This, however, is exactly what we have done in the
e Canada trade. Because a fortuitous combination of circumstances obliged
ne occasion to import inferior timber at a comparatively high price, we resolve
e the practice in all time to come ! The history of commerce affords no
splay of gratuitous folly.
surdity of this conduct will appear still more striking, if we reflect for a moment
uliar situation of the countries in the north of Europe. The nations round
have made little progress in manufacturing industry. They abound in
aw products ; but they are wholly destitute as well of the finer species of manu-
ommodities, as of colonies. Nor have they any real inducement to attempt
themselves directly with the former, or to establish the latter. Their iron and

copper mines, their vast forests, and their immense tracts of fertile and hitherto
cupied land, afford far more ready and advantageous investments for their def
capital, than could be found in manufactures or foreign trade. Russia and Prussia
indeed, been tempted, by our corn and timber laws, to exclude some species of n
factured goods; but it is not possible that they should succeed in materially lim
our exports to them, provided we do not second their efforts by refusing to admit
products.

Of all the countries in the world, there is obviously none which has so many fac
for carrying on an advantageous trade with the North as Great Britain. We h
surplus of all those products of which Russia, Prussia, Sweden, Denmark, and
way stand most in need; and, on the other hand, they have a surplus of many of
of which we are comparatively destitute. The immense traffic we carry on wi
Baltic does not, therefore, depend in any considerable degree on artificial or accic
circumstances. It does not rest on the wretched foundation of Custom-house regul
or discriminating duties, but on the gratification of mutual wants and desires.
been justly remarked by the Marquis Garnier, the excellent translator of the " W
of Nations," that no inconsiderable portion of the increased power and wea
England may be traced to the growing opulence of Russia. But the Russian e
is yet only in the infancy of civilisation; she must continue for a very long per
advance in the career of improvement, and it will be our own fault if we do not
still greater advantages from her progress.

Such is the nature of that commerce against which the discriminating duti
timber from the north of Europe aimed a severe blow! In 1809, when this s
began, 428,000 tons of British shipping entered inwards from the Baltic. In
the year after the 25 per cent. of additional duty had been imposed on Baltic ti
and when all the ports of that sea were open to our ships, only 242,000 tons of
shipping entered inwards,—being little more than the half of what it amounted to
the system began. In 1816, the British shipping entered inwards from the
amounted to 181,000 tons. It was materially augmented in 1818 and 1819, i
sequence of the failure of the crops in this country in 1817 and 1818; but even i
the entries inwards were 55,000 tons under what they had been 10 years before!

By diminishing our imports from the northern nations, the high discriminatinε
on timber necessarily diminished our exports to them in the same proportion.

The following extract from the evidence of Mr. Edward Patzcker, a merch
Memel, given before the committee of the House of Commons, on the foreig
of the country in 1821, shows the effect that the increased duties on timber had
commerce with Prussia: —

" Has there been a great alteration in the timber trade between Memel and this country of late
— " Since the war, a great alteration; before the war we used to have 950 to 1,000 English ship
year, and since the war we have had from 200 to 300 only."
" When you talk of 900 ships, do you mean 900 ships trading between Great Britain and Men
" Yes."
" Do you mean that number of cargoes were loaded in the year for England?" — " Yes."
" How many cargoes were loaded for Great Britain during the last year (1820) ?" —" About 2
cargoes; there have not been more."
" To what cause do you attribute that diminution in the trade ?" — " *To the high duties in E
for formerly the duties were only 16s. and some pence; now they are 3l. 5s. in a British, and 3l.
foreign ship."
" Has that diminished trade in timber produced a great alteration in the circumstances of th
of Prussia ?" — " Yes: for it is the only trade which we can carry on; wheat and all the re
articles cannot be brought here; *timber* is the only one that can be brought, and the trade fror
has very much ceased in consequence of the diminished demand for it; the people cannot sell the
and we cannot take such quantities of timber as we used to do; and, therefore, they cannot take
goods from us."
" If such an alteration was to take place in the duties on timber in this country, as to give the
a larger share of the trade than they at present enjoy, do you think that would produce increased
feelings on the part of the people of your country to the people of this country ?" — " It woul
would certainly take far more goods from hence, as they could get better rid of them. The P
would take more of them." — (*Report*, 9th March, 1821, p. 107.)

The effect that the increased duties had on the trade with Norway and
aggravated as they in some degree were by an absurd method of charging the
deals, was still more striking and extraordinary. These countries had few p
except timber and iron, to exchange for our commodities; and as neither of the
be advantageously imported into England under the new system, the trade wi
almost entirely ceased; and they were reluctantly compelled to resort to the ma
France and Holland for the articles they had formerly imported from us. In
this, we may mention, that the exports to Sweden, which had amounted in
511,818l., declined in 1819 to 46,656l.; and the exports to Norway, which had
amounted to 199,902l., amounted in 1819 to only 64,741l.* — (*Lords' Repo
Foreign Trade of the Country*, 3d July, 1820, p. 34.)

* Even at present the official value of the total exports, including colonial produce, from
Kingdom to Sweden, does not exceed 160,000l. a year. Our exports of all sorts to Norway amour

aordinary falling off in so very important a branch of our commerce having
shed beyond all question by the evidence taken before the committees now
an approach to a better system was made in 1821, when the duty on
the north of Europe was reduced from 3l. 5s. to 2l. 15s. per load, at the
hat a duty of 10s. per load was laid on timber from British America. This,
as a comparatively inefficient measure. It was stated, to be sure, at the
he 2l. 5s. per load of excess of duty that was thus continued on Baltic
that laid on timber imported from Canada, was not more than enough to
higher prime cost, the greater freight, and other charges consequent upon
tion of the latter; and that it would, therefore, be in future indifferent to
whether he imported timber from Memel or Miramichi! In point of fact,
discriminating duty continued in favour of Canada timber has been far too
of this equalisation being effected. So much so is this the case, that there
stances of ships loading with timber in the north of Europe, carrying that
anada, and then bringing it to England as Canada timber; the difference of
been about sufficient to indemnify the enormous expense of this round-
! We do not mean to say that this has been a common practice; but what
nk of a commercial regulation that admits of such an adventure being under-
ay prospect of success? Admitting, however, that the duty had been adjusted
had the anticipated effect, could any thing be more preposterous and absurd
se it on such a principle? There are mines of coal in New Holland; but
we think, were an attempt made to impose such duties on coals from New-
uld render it indifferent to a London merchant whether he imported a cargo
the Tyne or Botany Bay? Now, the case of the timber duties is, in point of
cisely the same. We may obtain timber from countries so near at hand
ps may make three, four, five, and even six voyages a year to them * ;
e to admit it unless loaded with a duty that has the effect to raise its price
h that which is brought from the other side of the Atlantic — a voyage
ps cannot, at most, perform above twice a year!

ing official account shows the extent to which the system of preference has
—

st of the Rates of Duty payable in Great Britain on the Principal Articles of Wood.

mber.	Of Foreign Countries.			Of the British Plantations in America.			Timber.	Of Foreign Countries.			Of the British Plantations in America.		
	L.	s.	d.	L.	s.	d.		L.	s.	d.	L.	s.	d.
ot exceeding 16 feet exceeding 2¾ inches - per 120	10	0	0	1	0	0	Lathwood, in pieces under 5 feet long, per fathom	4	5	0	0	15	0
eeding 21 feet long, ding 2½ inches thick,							5, and under 8 feet long —	6	16	0	} 1	5	0
per 120	11	10	0	1	5	0	8, and under 12 feet long —	10	4	0			
et long, or if exceed-							12 feet long and upwards —	13	12	0			
thick per 120	20	0	6	2	0	0	Masts, 6, and under 8 inches in diameter - each	0	8	0	0	1	6
ding 1½ inch thick,							8, and under 12 inches in diameter, each	1	2	0	0	4	0
per 120	8	2	6				12 inches in diameter or upwards, per load	2	15	0	0	10	0
16 feet long, and not nches thick, per 120	19	0	0	2	0	0	Oak Plank, 2 inches thick or upwards —	4	0	0	0	15	0
eeding 21 feet long, ding 3½ inches thick,							Spars, under 4 inches in diameter, and under 22 feet long - per 120	2	8	0	0	9	0
per 120	22	0	0	2	10	0	and 22 feet long or upwards, per 120	4	5	0	0	16	0
ve 45 feet long, and 3½ inches thick,							4 and under 6 inches in diameter —	9	0	0	1	15	0
per 120	44	0	0				Staves, not exceeding 36 inches long	1	3	0	0	2	0
et long, or above 3½ not being timber 8							above 36, and not exceeding 50 inches long - - per 120	2	6	0	0	4	0
or upwards) the load							above 50, and not exceeding 60 inches long - - per 120	3	0	0	0	6	0
cubic	2	10	0				above 60, and not exceeding 72 inches long - - per 120	4	4	0	0	8	0
120	6	0	0				above 72 inches long —	4	16	0	0	10	0
lass of deals brought onies of the same the two previous e preference on those corresponds to its ther articles. — (See							N.B.—Staves of the United States of America, of Florida, of the Ionian Islands, or of the British colonies, and not exceeding 1½ inch in thickness, are chargeable with one third part only of the above rates.						
							Fir, 8 inches square or upwards, per load	2	15	0	0	10	0
feet long, and not nches thick, per 120	6	0	0	0	15	0	Oak do. - -	2	15	0	0	10	0
ding 3½ inches thick,							Unenumerated do. -	1	8	0	0	5	0
per 120	12	0	0	1	10	0	Wainscot Logs, 8 inches square or upwards - per load	3	15	0	0	12	0

while our imports hardly amount to 70,000l. In fact, were it not that Norway finds means
rafts on Holland, into which her produce is admitted, she could import almost nothing
The injury done to our commerce with these two nations, by our heavy discriminating
cipal equivalent they have to give in exchange for commodities brought from abroad, was
riking point of view by Lord Althorp, in the debate on the timber duties, 18th March, 1831.
the evidence of Mr. J. D. Powles, an extensive ship and insurance broker, ships can
from Norway, three or four from Prussia, and two from Russia, in a season. — (Com.
39.)

So long as the foreigner can lay his finger on such a table as this, it will not
to convince him that our commercial system has lost so much of its exclusive c
as it really has done during the last few years. Having set such an exampl
Russians and Prussians, need we wonder at their having attempted to shut se
our peculiar productions out of their markets? Could we expect that they were t
our precepts rather than our practice?

8. *Comparative Quality of Baltic and Canada Timber.* — Had the timber of Cana
decidedly superior to that of the north of Europe, something might have bee
to say in favour of the discriminating duty: for it might have been contend
some show of reason, that it was of the utmost consequence, considering the app
of timber to ship and house building, and other important purposes, to prevent
portation of an inferior species, even though it might be cheaper. But the sy
have adopted is of a totally different character. We have not attempted to shu
article which, though cheap, is inferior; but have committed the twofold absu
shutting out one that is at once *cheap and superior!*

The committee of the House of Lords observe, in their First Report on the
Trade of the Country, that " the North American timber is more soft, less dura
every description of it more liable, though in different degrees, to the dry i
timber of the north of Europe. The red pine, however, which bears a small
tion to the other descriptions of timber, and the greater part of which, though i
from Canada, *is the produce of the United States,* is distinguished from the white
its greater durability. On the whole, it is stated by one of the commissioner
Majesty's navy, most distinguished for practical knowledge, experience, and s
the timber of Canada, both oak and fir, *does not possess, for the purpose of ship-
more than half the durability of wood of the same description, the produce of the
Europe.* The result of its application to other purposes of building is desc
timber merchants and carpenters to be nearly similar. — (p. 4.)

We subjoin the following extracts from the evidence of Sir Robert Sepp
commissioner alluded to by the committee, whose great intelligence and ex
render his opinion of the highest authority: —

" Can you state to the committee the result of any observations that you or others in his
service have made, on the durability of timber, the produce of the North American colonies,
imported from the north of Europe, applied to the same purposes?" — " About the year 1796,
a certain number of frigates built of the fir of the Baltic, and *their average durability was ar*
years. About the year 1812, there were a considerable number of frigates built also, of fir of t
of North America, and their *average durability was not* HALF *that time.*"

" You have stated that Canada timber is peculiarly subject to the dry rot, and the dry rot is
have prevailed lately to a great degree in the navy; has that prevailed principally since the a
of Canada timber to the uses of the navy?" — " I believe *the navy has suffered very consider*
the introduction of Canada timber, or timber of the growth of North America; and in consequ
experience, we have *entirely discontinued the use of it,* except for deals and masts." — (p. 56.)

Mr. Copland, an extensive builder and timber merchant, being asked by
mittee what was his opinion with respect to the comparative qualities of Ame
Baltic timber, answered, — " The timber of the Baltic in general, speaking of
Russian, Prussian, and Swedish timber, is of very superior quality to that
from America; the bulk of the latter *is very inferior in quality, much softer in its n*
so durable, and very liable to dry rot; indeed, it is not allowed by any professi
under government to be used, nor is it ever used in the *best* buildings in Lond
only speculators that are induced to use it, from the price of it being much
consequence of its exemption from duty) than the Baltic timber; if you w
two planks of American timber upon each other, in the course of a twelvem
would have the dry rot, almost invariably, to a certain extent." — (p. 56.) A
passages to the same effect might be produced, from the evidence of perso
greatest experience in building.

Now, we would beg leave to ask, whether any thing can be more absolu
strous, than to force, by means of a system of discriminating duties, a very
portion of the public to use that very timber in the construction of their ships a
which government will not use for either of these purposes, and which the m
rienced engineers and builders pronounce to be utterly unfit for them? Thi
impose duties on a fair and equal principle for the sake of revenue, but for t
securing a preference to a worthless article: it is not imposing them in t
which they may be least, but in that in which they are certain to be *most i*
those who have to pay them.

It appears from the official account subjoined to this article, that, at an avei
years 1828 and 1829, the revenue would have gained considerably more than 1
a year, had the same duty been laid on Canada timber that is laid on timbe
north of Europe; and this, therefore, may be considered as the amount of the
sacrifice we consent to make, in order that our ships and houses may be i
with dry rot!

pologies for the discriminating Duty. — If any thing ought, more than another, to
egislators pause before enacting a restrictive regulation, it is the difficulty of
g from it. After it has been enforced for a while, a variety of interests usually
p under its protection, which may be materially injured by its repeal. *All,*
r, that the persons so interested can justly claim, is, that sufficient time, and every
e facility, should be afforded them to prepare for a change of system. Because
erests of a comparatively small portion of the community may be injuriously
l by the abolition of a regulation ascertained to be in the last degree inimical to
lic, is it, therefore, to be contended that we ought, at all hazards, to continue
ce the regulation we have so unwisely enacted? To maintain the affirmative,
be to give perpetuity to the worst errors and absurdities; and would be an
l bar to every sort of improvement. No change, even from a bad to a good
ought to be rashly set about; but when once the expediency of an alteration
a clearly established, it ought to be resolutely carried into effect.
objected to the abolition of the discriminating duties on timber, that it would be
s to Canada and the shipping interest. We believe, however, that the injury
not be nearly so great as has been represented; that it would, in fact, be quite
lerable. So far from the *lumber trade*—or the trade of felling wood, squaring it,
ting it down the rivers to the shipping ports—being advantageous to a colony, it
ctly and completely the reverse. The habits which it generates are quite sub-
of that sober, steady spirit of industry, so essential to a settler in a rude country;
a degree, indeed, is this the case, that lumberers have been described as the pests
ony, "made and kept vicious by the very trade by which they live."— But
ng altogether from the circumstances now alluded to, Mr. Poulett Thomson
in his unanswerable speech on the timber question (March 18. 1831), that the
s of the lumber trade would materially benefit the real interests of the colonies.
dicrous, indeed, seeing that not one tree in a hundred is fit for the purpose of
uared for timber, to suppose that the discontinuance of the trade could be any
oss. But the fact is, that when trees are cut down by lumberers for export as
nstead of being burnt down, so great a growth of brushwood takes place, that
y costs more to clear the ground where the lumberers have been, than where
e not been. Mr. Richards, who was sent out by government to report on
ence of the lumber trade, represents it as most unfavourable; and observes,
hen time or chance shall induce or compel the inhabitants to desist from this
ent, agriculture will begin to raise its head." The statements of Captain
a, in his "Letters from Nova Scotia," are exactly similar. He considers the
n of the timber market, although a severe loss to many individuals, a "decided
he colony," from the check it has given to the "lumbering mania."—(p. 53.)
atements that have been made as to the amount of capital expended on saw
l other fixed works for carrying on the lumber trade, have been singularly ex-
l. Mr. Thomson, who had the best means of acquiring accurate information on
, made the following statement with respect to it in his speech already referred
from the means I have had of calculating the amount of capital embarked in
r mills, I believe it is about 300,000*l*. : I am sure I may say that if 500,000*l*.
en as the amount, it would be a great deal above rather than under the real
ut after all, this description of property is not to be sacrificed by the arrange-
oposed, even if they were carried to the fullest extent. I am ready at once to
at the consequence of the proposed alteration may be, that it will diminish the
f timber from Canada to England, and affect the productiveness of the capital
the mills to which I have referred; but the committee ought not to lose sight
t, that though in this one branch of industry there will be a great falling off,
me amount of labour might be applied to much greater advantage on land in
ies; and the mills, which will be rendered useless for their original purposes,
nverted into useful auxiliaries to the agricultural and other pursuits of the
so that the enormous losses that have been placed in so frightful a point of
, as I have shown, be absolutely next to nothing."
therefore, as the interests of the colonies are concerned, it is plain they would
lose, but gain, by a repeal of the discriminating duties on foreign timber. They
l continue to possess a respectable share of the trade; for their timber,
afit for more important purposes, is well suited, by its softness and freedom
s, for the finishing of rooms and cabins, the manufacture of boxes, &c.; and in
ade, it is believed, that they would be able to maintain a successful competition
. It might also be expedient to assist in turning the industry of the colonies
rofitable channel of agriculture, by giving their corn and flour a still more
reference than they now enjoy in our markets. In our opinion, it would be
y to admit them, at all times, duty free.
p owners would undoubtedly have more cause to complain of injury from the

equalisation of the duties; but even as respects them, it would not be nearly so grea
commonly supposed. The statement usually put forward by those who represent the
trade to North America as of vital importance to the shipping interest, is, that it em
1,800 ships, of 470,000 tons, navigated by 20,000 sailors. But Mr. Poulett The
showed, in his previously quoted speech, that this statement is utterly erroneous. T
tries inwards of British ships from our possessions in North America correspond w
sums now stated; but, at an average, every ship employed in the trade makes $1\frac{3}{4}$ v
a year; so that, in point of fact, only 1,028 ships, of 270,000 tons and 11,427 men a
ployed in the trade.[*] From this latter number must, however, be struck off ships em
in other branches of trade; for no one pretends that the only trade we carry on wit
tish North America is the importation of timber. We believe that the number to
struck off may be safely estimated at 200 ships, of 54,000 tons and 2,200 men, l
about 800 ships, of 216,000 tons and 9,200 men, to be affected by the change.
much, however, as about a third part of the timber now brought from Canada woul
probably continue to be brought for the purposes already referred to, were the
equalised, only 534 ships, of 144,000 tons and 6,134 men, would be forced to c
their employments. Now of these, a half, at least, would be immediately emplo
bringing from the Baltic the same quantity of timber that is brought from Americ
as the price of timber would be materially lowered by the reduction of the du
demand for it would no doubt materially increase; so that it is abundantly plai
very few, if any, ships would be thrown out of employment by the abolition of t
criminating duties. It is material, too, to observe that whatever temporary inconve
the shipping interest might sustain from the change, its future consequences wo
singularly advantageous to it. The high price of timber employed in the building c
is at present the heaviest drawback on the British ship owners; but the equalisa
the duties would materially reduce this price; and we have the authority of th
practical judges for affirming, that were the duty (as it ought to be) entirely re
ships might be built decidedly cheaper in England than in any part of the world

It would be desirable, however, to secure the interests of so important a class
of the ship owners from any chance even of temporary loss or inconvenience f
equalisation of the duties. And it is fortunate that this object may be at
not only without any loss, but with certain benefit to the public. The expedie
encouraging emigration to the colonies, as a means of relieving parts of Englan
Ireland from that mass of paupers by which they are burdened, is no longer ques
and we incline to think that no more effectual means of promoting emigration c
devised, than the giving a bounty to the owners of ships landing emigrants in Cana
Cape of Good Hope, or New South Wales. We have already seen that the
of emigrants to Canada last year amounted to about 50,000 (ante, p. 894.); and
ing that a bounty of 30s. or 40s. a head were in future to be paid on the ar
emigrants at Quebec, it would more than indemnify the ship owners for any i
nience resulting from a new arrangement of the timber duties; at the same ti
the stimulus it would give to emigration would be of the utmost importance t
Britain and to the colonies.

5. *Alteration proposed in the Timber Duties in* 1831. — To suppose that the
trade should be allowed to continue on its present footing seems to be quite ou
question. We have already seen that the discriminating duties impose a pecun
crifice of 1,500,000l. a year on the British public, besides forcing the use of a
ratively worthless article where none but the very best ought to be employed.
also seen that this sacrifice produces no real benefit to the colonies; and that the
it does produce to the ship owners is but trifling, and may be more than made up
without loss to the public. Lord Althorp and the present government seem
been early satisfied of the necessity of attempting to introduce a less objectiona
tem; and on the 18th of March, 1831, his Lordship moved that the duties o
timber should be reduced 6s. a load on the 1st of January, 1832; 6s. more on
of January, 1833; and 3s. on the 1st of January, 1834; making the total r
15s. a load, and leaving a protection in favour of Canada timber of 30s. a loa
only real objection to this scheme is, that it does not go far enough. " It scot
snake, without killing it." There is not the shadow of a ground on which t
the granting of a bounty (for such is the real operation of the duty) to force th
an inferior and more costly article; and even if a reasonable bounty could
tified, one of 30s. a load is quite excessive. But, singular as it may seem, this
moderate as it certainly was, encountered the most furious opposition. Some
who had previously expressed their concurrence in the expediency of some me
the sort, thought proper to vote against it; and, upon a division, it was lost b

---

[*] It is singular that Mr. Bouchette should have fallen into the common but palpable error on
— (See the Preface to his valuable work on British America.)

46.* It is impossible, however, notwithstanding this division, that a system, ...ctive of the public interests should be allowed to continue ; and we trust that ...will not be deterred, by the ill success of this attempt, from bringing forward, ...tant period, a new and more comprehensive measure. It were much to be ...at the duties could be wholly dispensed with. Timber is about the very worst ...r taxation ; but, at all events, an end must be put to the discriminating duties. ...o be endured, that so essential an article — that *the prime necessary of manu-* ...*industry* — should be loaded with exorbitant duties, imposed not for the sake of ...ut for the sake of those who either reap no advantage from them, or none that ...

of the Quantities of the different Species of Timber imported into the United Kingdom in ...cifying the Countries whence they were brought, and the Quantities brought from each.

...m-	Battens and Batten Ends.	Deals and Deal Ends.	Lath-wood.	Masts, Yards and Bowsprits under 12 Inches in Diameter.	Masts, Yards and Bowsprits 12 Inches in Diameter, and upwards.	Oak Plank 2 Inches thick, or upwards.	Staves.	Teak.	Timber, Fir, Oak, and unenumerated, 8 Inches square, or upwards.	Wainscot Logs 8 Inches square, or upwards.
	Gt.Hds.qrs.No	Gt.Hds.qrs.No	Fathoms	Number.	Loads.Feet	Loads.Feet	Gt.Hds.qrs.No	Loads.Feet	Loads. Feet.	Loads.Feet
	2,811 1 3	11,887 1 22	2,691	2,264	653 1	25 18	18 1 1	-	4,923 24	2,116 18
	1,135 2 16	3,265 0 17	15	2,113	11 17				1,255 33	
	6,360 2 2	9,809 1 1	31	3,582		4 12			17,261 42	
	3 0 12	8 2 5	5	18	203 6	1,281 25	17,710 2 11		133 10	75 32
	257 2 6	5,359 3 1	2,587	369	70 31	111 25	1,056 1 24	23 33	127,555 20	2,031 17
	0 1 18	1 1 3		5	0 38	1 0			1,841 4	
		1 0 19		2	19 30				215 49	
	0 1 5	3 1 28		7				16,015 20	59 78	
									0 44	
...er }		0 3 22		1				421 5	20 30	
...e }								463 31		
...an }									1,759 1	
...ea }									429 15	
	577 2 20	18,256 0 2	5,057	5,039	3,592 0	2 7	72,634 1 19		395,172 11	
		2 2 28		30	1 0		108 0 29		58 46	
		11 0 6		15	270 21	8 1	4,125 0 20		0 9	
		1 0 11		30	1 4				291 5	
									12	
	11,149 1 22	51,587 3 15	10,586	13,475	4,803 1	1,133 36	95,953 1 1	16,924 0	549,289 36	4,221 17

of the Customs Duties on the different Sorts of Timber imported into the United Kingdom in 1830, specifying the Amount of the Duties on each.

...uties Inwards.	Gross Receipt.			Payments out of the Gross Receipt.						Nett Produce.		
				Drawbacks, and Bounties of the Nature of Drawbacks.			Repayments on over Entries, Damaged Goods, &c.					
	£	s.	d.	£	s.	d.	£	s.	d.	£	s.	d.
...ers, under 5 inches square	1,208	1	11		-		11	0	7	1,197	1	4
...Batten Ends	111,305	10	4	5	16	8	481	4	9	110,818	8	11
...al Ends	568,615	5	10	55	14	6	8,063	13	5	560,531	17	11
...	3,930	15	3		-		30	15	1	3,900	0	2
...	3,083	7	3		-		5	8	2	3,077	19	1
...	1,160	18	11		-		4	4	6	1,156	14	5
...ars	30,912	14	6		-		307	10	9	30,605	3	9
...	12,051	9	11		-		57	17	7	11,993	12	4
...	6,219	1	4		-		6	7	0	6,212	14	4
...	808	9	4		-		3	9	10	804	19	6
...	47,181	14	0		-		509	2	10	46,672	11	2
...	11,104	0	11		-		22	13	4	11,081	7	7
...8 ins. square or upwards	542,227	1	8	33,878	12	1	15,294	12	8	493,053	16	11
...o	23,821	16	2		-		85	7	3	23,736	8	11
...Sorts, ditto	6,305	5	4		-		187	5	9	6,117	19	7
...s	8,309	9	8		-		36	15	8	8,272	14	0
							Total - £			1,319,233	9	11

of the Amount of Duties paid in the United Kingdom on Timber and other Articles of ...rted from the British Provinces of North America, in each of the Years ending 5th January, ...nuary 1829, and 5th January 1830; and of the Amount of Duties which would have been ... Timber and other Articles of Wood, if they had been charged with the Rates of Duty pay-...lar Articles imported from the Baltic.

	Amount of Duty paid in the United Kingdom on Timber, Deals, and other Articles of Wood, imported from the British Provinces in North America.			Amount of Duty which would have been paid upon such Timber, Deals, and other Articles of Wood, if they had been imported from the Baltic.		
	£	s.	d.	£	s.	d.
...ing 5th January, 1828 -	213,749	15	4	1,251,922	13	4
— 1829 -	224,108	12	9	1,494,867	4	1
— 1830 -	233,799	17	0	1,580,795	9	4

* Thomson's speech in vindication of this measure deserves the attention of the reader. ...th, and successfully answered every objection to it. The ascendancy which those familia ...ciple and practice have over those acquainted with detail merely, was never more strik-...han in this speech.

TIN (Ger. *Blech, Weissblech;* Fr. *Fer blanc;* It. *Latta, Banda stagna*
Hoja de lata; Rus. *Blächa, Shest;* Arab. *Resas;* Sans. *Trapu* and *Ra*
metal which has a fine white colour like silver; and when fresh, its brill
very great. It has a slightly disagreeable taste, and emits a peculiar sme
rubbed. Its hardness is between that of gold and lead. Its specific gr
7·29. It is very malleable; *tinfoil,* or tin leaf, is about $\frac{1}{1000}$th part of ⸱
thick; and it might be beat out into leaves as thin again, if such were requ
the purposes o art. In ductility and tenacity it is very inferior. A t
0·078 inch in diameter is capable of supporting a weight of 34·7 pounds on
out breaking. Tin is very flexible, and produces a crackling noise when
It may be readily alloyed with copper, zinc, &c., forming very valuabl
pounds. — (*Thomson's Chemistry.*)

The ores of this metal are found in comparatively few places; the principal, and perhaps the ⸱
are Cornwall, Galicia, Erzgebirge, in Saxony, Bohemia, the Malay countries, China, and
Asia. They are peculiar to primitive rocks, generally in granite, either in veins or beds, and
associated with copper and iron pyrites.
Tin is much used as a covering to several other metals: iron is tinned to prevent its rapid
when exposed to air and moisture, and the same process is applied to copper to avoid the injuri
to which those who are in the habit of employing cooking utensils made of this metal are alw
The solutions of tin in the nitric, muriatic, nitro-sulphuric, and tartaric acids, are much used
as giving a degree of permanency and brilliance to several colours, to be attained by the use o
mordants with which we are at present acquainted: tin forms the basis of pewter, in the com
which it is alloyed with lead; when rolled into thin sheets it is called tin foil, and is applied
addition of mercury, to cover the surface of glass, thus forming looking-glasses, mirrors, &
combination with sulphur it constitutes what is called mosaic gold.—(*Joyce's Chem. Min.*)

Historical Notice of the British Tin Trade. — The tin mines of Cornwall h
worked from a very remote era. The voyages of the Phœnicians to the Cas
or tin islands, are mentioned by Herodotus (lib. iii. c. 115.), Diodorus Siculus
p. 301. ed. 1604), and Strabo (*Geog.* lib. iii.). Some difference of opinion
deed, been entertained as to the particular islands to which the Phœnicians
the term Cassiterides; but Borlase (Account of the Scilly Islands, p. 72.),
(*Herodote,* tome iii. p. 384. ed. 1802), and the ablest critics, agree that they
Scilly islands, and the western extremity of Cornwall. After the destru
Carthage, the British tin trade, which was always reckoned of peculiar importa
carried on by the merchants of Marseilles, and subsequently by the Romans.
Britain, Spain furnished the ancients with considerable quantities of tin. We
very precise information as to the purposes to which they applied this metal. It
supposed that the Phœnicians, so famous for their purple dyes, were acquai
the use of the solution of tin in nitro-muriatic acid in fixing that colour. T
the ancient mirrors, or *specula,* were also made of a mixture of copper and tin
was used in the coating of copper vessels. — (*Watson's Chemical Essays,* vol. iv
In modern times, the tin mines of Cornwall and Devon have been wrought wit
degrees of energy and success. Queen Elizabeth brought over some Germa
by whom some of the processes were improved. During the civil wars, the m
much neglected. At the commencement of last century, however, the b⸱
mining was carried on with renewed vigour; and from 1720 to 1740, the an
duce was about 2,100 tons. The produce went on gradually increasing, till it a
in the 10 years from 1790 to 1800, to 3,254 tons a year. During the nex
the produce fell off; but the following account shows that it has again incre
siderably: —

I. Tin coined in Cornwall and Devon, from 1822 to 1829 inclusive. — (*Mining Review,*

Years.	Blocks.	Tons.	Years.	Blocks.	Tons.
1822	18,732	= 3,137	1826	26,299	= 4,406
1823	24,077	= 4,031	1827	31,744	= 5,316
1824	28,602	= 4,819	1828	28,179	= 4,696
1825	24,902	= 4,170	1829	26,344	= 4,290

II. Tin imported into the United Kingdom in the Year ending 5th of January, 1831; d
from what Countries imported.

Countries.	Cwt. qrs. lbs.	Countries.	Cwt
The Netherlands	358 3 2	Java	9
East IndiaCompany'sTerritories, exclusive of Singapore	4,110 3 11	China	6
Singapore	10,217 0 25	Total	15,5

exported from the United Kingdom in the Year ending 5th of January, 1831; distinguishing to what Countries exported.

Countries.	British Tin. Cwt.	qrs.	lbs.	Foreign Tin. Cwt.	qrs.	lbs.	Countries.	British Tin. Cwt.	qrs.	lbs.	Foreign Tin. Cwt.	qrs.	lbs.
- -	5,149	1	26	2,471	2	6	Turkey - -	3,659	0	0			
- -	508	3	20				Morea and Greek Islands	92	0	0			
- -	64	2	17				Asia - -	0	2	0			
k - -	185	2	26	7	0	26	Africa - -	28	0	7			
- -	1,115	3	26	14	1	0	British North American Colonies -	62	0	0			
y - -	620	3	23	184	2	15							
therlands -	1,242	1	19	1,325	0	0	British West Indies -	299	2	21			
- -	7,396	3	11				Foreign West Indies -	18	0	0			
, Azores, and ira - -	380	0	0				United States of America	2,231	1	13	4,879	3	22
							Brazil - -	208	2	0			
nd the Canaries	720	0	0				Guernsey, Jersey, Alderney, and Man -	52	3	0			
r -	22	2	0										
-	6,205	3	23	1,543	1	20							
- -	160	0	0				Total - -	30,425	1	8	10,426	0	5

IV. Prices of British Tin and Tin Plates. — March 1832.

	lbs.	£	s.	d.		£	s.	d.
ocks on board, per cwt.		3	12	6	to	0	0	0
ts - -	-	3	13	0	—	0	0	0
rs - -		3	14	6	—	0	0	0
u blocks -	-	4	13	0	—	0	0	0
broke - -		5	3	0	—	0	0	0
tes, per box of 225 sheets.								
. C - 13¾ by 10 in.	112	1	12	0	—	0	0	0
. X - -	140	1	18	0	—	0	0	0
. XX - - -	161	2	4	0	—	0	0	0
. XXX - - -	182	2	10	0	—	0	0	0
. XXXX - -	203	2	16	0	—	0	0	0
I. C 13¼ by 9¾ in.	105	0	0	0	—	1	10	0
I. X - -	133	0	0	0	—	1	16	0
II. C - 12¾ 9¼	98	0	0	0	—	1	8	0
II. X - - -	126	0	0	0	—	1	14	0

	Lbs.	£	s.	d.
Small Dble. SDC 15 by 11 in. 200 sheets	167	2	14	0
Small Dble. SDX	188	3	0	0
Small Dble. SDXX - -	209	3	6	0
SDXXX - -	230	3	12	0
SDXXXX - -	251	3	18	0
Double C 16¾ by 12¼ in.	98	1	8	0
Ditto X 100 sheets -	126	1	14	0
Ditto XX - -	147	2	0	0
Ditto XXX -	168	2	6	0
Ditto XXXX - -	189	2	12	0
Taggers, 14 in. by 10 in. 450 s.	.	4	3	0
Ditto 14½ in. by 10½ in. -	-	4	9	0
Wasters of No. 1. C. No. 1. X. and No. 1. XX. 3*s.* per box less than perfect plates; all other sorts of wasters 6*s.* per box less; odd sizes 6½*d.* per lb.; duty and shipping charges 6*d.* per box.				

IENTAL, (Malay, *Tima*; Hind *Kalai*; Siamese, *Dibuk*; Burmese, *Kye-p'hyu*, white copper), rcial language usually called Banca tin. It is found in several provinces of China; but extensive and, probably, richest tin district in the world, exists in the Malay countries. rehends the whole of the peninsula, from the extreme cape to the latitude of 14° on its de, and to 11° on its eastern, and comprehends several of the small islands lying in the een the peninsula and Java, as far as the latitude of 3° south; so that the whole of this t has an extreme length of near 1,200 miles. By far the greater number of the mines se limits are as yet unwrought and unexplored. It was only in the beginning of last century nines of Banca, the most productive at present worked, were accidentally discovered. The of the Malay countries is the produce of alluvial ores, or what is called, in Cornwall, vork;" and from the abundance in which the mineral has been found by the mere washing of attempt has hitherto been made at regular mining, or obtaining the ore from its rocky matrix. consequently, is grain tin, or tin in a very pure state; that being the species which alluvial ore produces. The mines, or rather excavations, are perpendicular pits of from 15 to 25 feet deep; he soil and a superstratum of common clay are removed, the bed containing the ore, consisting nd granitic gravel, is reached. The sand and gravel are separated from the ore by passing a vater through the whole materials. The ore so obtained is preserved in heaps, and smelted with charcoal in a blast furnace. The mine or pit is kept clear of water by the Chinese cattle are used in any part of the process; human labour being had recourse to throughout f its stages. The most imperfect part of the process is the smelting. The stream ores of which are generally poor, afford from 65 to 75 per cent. of grain tin; whereas, owing to the n of the process, from those of Banca not more than 55 or 60 are usually obtained. The dif. he produce suggested, a few years ago the practicability of sending the ore to England for the being smelted; and the experiment was tried; but our customs regulations not allowing the be bonded and re-exported without duty, rendered the scheme abortive.

y trifling exceptions, the whole tin of the Malay islands is mined and smelted by Chinese id before their skill and enterprise were applied to its production, the metal seems to have been the inhabitants of the countries which produced it, by processes hardly more skilful than hich the precious metals were procured by the native inhabitants of America, prior to the n of European skill and machinery. The following estimate has been given of the annual the principal states and places producing tin:—

	Piculs.	West coast of the Malay peninsula and islands—	Piculs.
t of the Malay peninsula—			
Ceylon - -	5,000	Sungora and Patani - -	3,000
a - - - - -	2,000	Tringanu - - -	7,000
- - -	3,000	Pahang - - - -	3,000
gore - -	3,000	Singkep - - -	5,000
cca - - -	4,000	Banca - - -	35,000
Total - - Piculs	17,000	Total - - Piculs	53,000

e considered only as a rough estimate; but we believe it is not far wide of the truth. At an he two years 1826-27 and 1827-28, the exports of Singapore amounted to 16,342 piculs, or about he most considerable port of exportation is Batavia; from which there is sent annually, either hrough orders from the Dutch government or the authorities at Banca, 2,000 tons. From Prince and there is also a considerable quantity exported; and a smaller one direct to China in junks, of the native ports on the eastern shore of the Malay peninsula. The great marts for the contin are China, Hindostan, and the continent of Europe. The quality of the different descrip. ay tin, although there may be some inconsiderable difference in the quality of the original

ores, seems to be derived chiefly from the greater or less skill with which the process of smelting
ducted; and this, again, necessarily depends upon the extent of capital, and goodness of the mac
employed. The mining operations of Banca have long been conducted upon a larger scale, and wit
skill, than in any other of the Malay countries; and consequently, the metal produced in this is
superior by from 10 to 12 per cent. : in the market of Canton it is called "old tin," in contradist
to " new tin," the produce of the other Malay countries. Next, in point of quality, to the proc
Banca, are those of Tringanu and Singkep, which are not more than 5 per cent. inferior to it. Th
the state of Pera, a considerable part of which is produced by the natives themselves, without c
assistance, is the worst, and usually about 15 per cent. below that of Banca. The native tin of Chi
per cent. inferior to that of Banca, and is probably block tin, like the greater part of that of Cornwa
like it, the produce of regular mining operations, and not alluvial. The produce of the Chinese n
said of late years to have greatly decreased; probably owing to the great increase which has recentl
place in the produce of the Malay countries, and the cheapness and abundance with which it finds its
China. It should be added, that of late years, and chiefly owing to the very low price and abund
German spelter (zinc) in the Indian market, this commodity has occasionally been fraudulently
with tin. The Chinese brokers of Canton, however, are sufficiently expert to detect the adulteratic
it is believed that this discreditable practice has lately ceased.

The price of tin, taking the market of Singapore as the standard, has fluctuated of late years fro
20 Spanish dollars per picul; equal, at the exchange of 4s. per dollar, to 47s. and 67s. per cwt.
average of these prices the annual value of the whole Malay tin will be about 240,000l. per an
(*Crawfurd's History of the Indian Archipelago*; *Dr. Horsfield's MS. Statistical View of the Is.
Banca*; *Singapore Chronicle*; *Canton Register, &c.*)

TOBACCO (Da. *Tobak;* Du. *Tabak;* Fr. *Tabac;* Ger. *Taback;* It. *Tab*
Pol. *Tobaka;* Rus. *Tabak;* Sp. *Tabaco;* Arab. *Bujjerbhang;* Hind. *Tym*
Malay, *Tambracoo*), the dried leaves of the *Nicotiana Tabacum*, a plant indig
to America, but which succeeds very well, and is extensively cultivated, in
parts of the Old World. The recent leaves possess very little odour or '
but, when dried, their odour is strong, narcotic, and somewhat fetid; their
bitter and extremely acrid. When well cured, they are of a yellowish
colour. When distilled, they yield an essential oil, on which their
depends, and which is said to be a virulent poison. The leaves are us
various ways; being chewed, smoked, and ground and manufactured into
It is in the last mentioned form that tobacco is principally used in Grea
tain; and, though the contrary has been often asserted, its use does not se
have been productive of any peceptible bad consequence.

1. *Historical Sketch of Tobacco.* — The taste for tobacco, though apparently a
stering only to a frivolous gratification, has given birth to a most extensive com
and been a powerful spur to industry. Being a native of the New Wor
introduction into Europe dates only from the early part of the 16th century. S
the plant were sent, in 1560, from Portugal, to Catherine de' Medici, by Jean Nic
French ambassador in that country, from whom it has received its botanical name
notion, at one time so general, that the specific appellation tobacco was derive
its having been imported from Tobago, is now universally admitted to be v
foundation. Humboldt has shown, that tobacco was the term used in the H
language to designate the pipe, or instrument made use of by the natives in sr
the herb; and the term, having been transferred by the Spaniards from the pipe
herb itself, has been adopted by the other nations of the ancient world. — (*Es
litique sur la Nouvelle Espagne*, vol. iii. p. 50. 2d edit.) Tobacco is believed t
been first introduced into England by the settlers who returned, in 1586, from the
which it had been attempted to found in Virginia, under the auspices of Sir
Raleigh, in the preceding year. Harriott, who accompanied this expedition, gi
his description of Virginia, an account of the tobacco plant, and of the manner ir
it was used by the natives; adding, that the English, during the time they were
ginia, and since their return home, were accustomed to smoke it after the fashion
Indians, " and found many rare and wonderful experiments of the virtue there
(*Hakluyt*, vol. i. p. 75.)

Raleigh, and other young men of fashion, having adopted the practice of sr
it spread amongst the English; as it had previously spread amongst the Sp
Portuguese, French, and other continental nations. But it made its greatest
in this country after the foundation of the colony at James Town in Vir,
1607. The soil of the colony being found particularly well fitted for the cu
tobacco, considerable quantities were raised and sent home; and the numero
viduals interested in the colony contributed to introduce that taste for it wł
diffused amongst all classes with astonishing rapidity.

James I. attempted, by repeated proclamations and publications, some of them
in very strong terms, to restrain the use of tobacco. But his efforts had v
effect; and the settlers in Virginia continued to experience a more rapidly in
and better demand for tobacco than for any other product of the colony.

During the earlier part of the reign of Charles I., the trade in tobacco wa
polised by the crown. This monopoly was not, however, of long continuar
totally ceased at the breaking out of the civil war.

o plants had been early introduced into England, and were found to answer
ly well. Their cultivation was, indeed, prohibited by James, and afterwards
:s, but apparently without effect. At length, however, the growing con-
of tobacco having excited the attention of the government financiers, it was
by imposing a duty on its importation a considerable revenue might be raised ;
were it allowed to be freely cultivated at home, it would be very difficult to
luty upon it. In 1643, the Lords and Commons imposed a moderate duty,
ke of revenue, on plantation tobacco ; but instead of directly prohibiting the
tive tobacco, they burdened it with such a duty as, it was supposed, would
ts culture to be abandoned. The facility, however, with which the duty was
oon satisfied the republican leaders that more vigorous measures were required
cultivation, and consequently to render its importation a source of revenue.
1652, an act was passed, prohibiting the growth of tobacco in England, and
; commissioners to see its provisions carried into effect. This act was con-
the Restoration, by the act Charles 2. c. 34., which ordered that all tobacco
s should be destroyed. These measures were believed, at the time, to have
:ipally brought about by the solicitations of the planters ; but their real inten-
ot so much to conciliate or benefit the latter, as to facilitate the collection of
from tobacco ; and, considered in this point of view, their policy seems quite
nable.

t did not, however, extend to Ireland ; and of late years the cultivation of
ide considerable progress in that country. Had this been allowed to continue,
be no question that in a few years the revenue from tobacco, amounting to
0,000l. a year, would have been materially diminished ; for it would be quite
o suppose that any plan could have been devised for collecting a duty even of
nt. upon tobacco — (see *post*) — supposing it to have been generally cultivated

We therefore cordially approve of the late act prohibiting its growth in that
id we trust its provisions will be rigorously enforced. Any advantage Ireland
gained by its cultivation would have been but a poor compensation for the
revenue it must have occasioned.

countries, as England, tobacco is principally used in the form of snuff; in
principally chewed ; but in one form or other it is every where made use of.
1624, Pope Urban VIII. issued a bull excommunicating those who smoked
s ! The practice of smoking was at one time exceedingly prevalent in this
ut during the reign of George III. it was well nigh superseded, at least
e higher and middle classes, by the practice of snuff taking. Latterly, how-
ng has been in some measure revived, though it is still very far from being
ely practised as formerly.

e the following statement as to the universality of the use of tobacco from a
able paper on its " Introduction and Use," in the 22d volume (p. 142.) of the
rnal : — " In Spain, France, and Germany, in Holland, Sweden, Denmark,
, the practice of smoking tobacco prevails amongst the rich and poor, the
I the gay. In the United States of America, smoking is often carried to an
is not uncommon for boys to have a pipe or cigar in the mouth during the
t of the day. The death of a child is not unfrequently recorded in American
, with the following remark subjoined : — ' supposed to be occasioned by ex-
king.' If we pass to the East, we shall find the practice almost universal.
the pipe is perpetually in the mouth ; and the most solemn conferences are
ncluded with a friendly pipe, employed like the *calumet of peace* amongst the
n the East Indies, not merely all classes, but both sexes, inhale the fragrant
only distinction among them consisting in the shape of the instrument em-
the species of the herb smoked. In China, the habit equally prevails ; and
aveller in that country (Barrow) states, that every Chinese female, from the
9 years, wears, as an appendage to her dress, a small silken purse or pocket
cco, and a pipe, with the use of which many of them are not unacquainted
r age. This prevalence of the practice, at an early period, amongst the
appealed to by M. Pallas as an evidence that ' in Asia, and especially in
se of tobacco for smoking is more ancient than the discovery of the New
e adds — ' Among the Chinese, and amongst the Mongol tribes who had
ercourse with them, the custom of smoking is so general, so frequent, and
so indispensable a luxury ; the tobacco purse affixed to their belt so necessary
dress ; the form of the pipes, from which the Dutch seem to have taken the
eirs, so original ; and, lastly, the preparation of the yellow leaves, which are
ed to pieces and then put into the pipe, so peculiar ; that they could not pos-
all this from America by way of Europe ; especially as India, where the
moking is not so general, intervenes between Persia and China.'

This, however, is a very doubtful proposition. It seems sufficiently establis
the tobacco plant was first brought from Brazil to India, about the year 1617.;
most probable that it was thence carried to Siam, China, and other Eastern co
The names given to it in all the languages of the East, are obviously of Euro
rather American, origin; a fact which seems completely to negative the ide
being indigenous to the East.

Sources of Supply. — *Importation into Great Britain.* — Tobacco is now ver
sively cultivated in France and other European countries, in the Levant, and ir
but the tobacco of the United States is still very generally admitted to be d
superior to most others. It is much higher flavoured than the tobacco of Eu
superiority attributable in some degree, perhaps, to a different mode of treatm
far more, it is believed, to differences of soil and climate.

Previously to the American war, our supplies of tobacco were almost entirely
from Virginia and Maryland; and they are still principally imported from thes
so much so, that of 22,399,335 lbs. of unmanufactured tobacco imported i
21,751,602 lbs. came from the United States. Mr. Jefferson, in his " Notes
ginia," has given a very unfavourable view of the effects of the tobacco cult
was, indeed, well known to be a crop that speedily exhausted all but the v
lands; and in addition to this, Mr. J. says that " it is a culture productive of
wretchedness. Those employed in it are in a continued state of exertion be
powers of nature to support. Little food of any kind is raised by them; so
men and animals on these farms are badly fed, and the earth is rapidly impove
— (English ed. p. 278.)

Tobacco is extensively cultivated in Mexico, but only for home consumpt
might probably, however, were it not for the restrictions under which it is
form a considerable article of export from that country. Under the Spanish
ment, the tobacco monopoly was one of the principal sources of revenue; yieldi
4,000,000 to 4,500,000 dollars, exclusive of the expenses of administration, an
to about 800,000 dollars. No tobacco was allowed to be cultivated, except
specified places. Commissioners, or *guardas de tabaco*, were appointed, whos
was to take care that all tobacco plantations without the privieged districts s
destroyed. The government fixed the price at which the cultivators of toba
obliged to sell it to its agents. The sale of the manufactured tobacco was far
and *cigars* were not allowed to be sold except at the royal *estancos*. No one was
to use cigars of his own manufacture. This most oppressive monopoly was es
in 1764. It has been continued, from the difficulty of supplying the revenue
produces, by the present government. — (*Humboldt, Nouvelle Espagne,* vol. ii
Poinsett's Notes on Mexico, note 116. Lond. ed.)

Cuba is celebrated for its tobacco, particularly its cigars. These consist of
formed into small rolls, for the purpose of smoking. Formerly their importa
this country was prohibited; but they may now be imported on paying the e
duty of 9s. per lb. Havannah cigars are usually reckoned the best. Previousl
the cultivation and sale of tobacco was subjected to the same sort of monopol
as in Mexico; but at the period referred to, the trade was thrown open. Its p
has not, however, been extended so rapidly as might have been expected; the
sugar and coffee is reckoned more profitable. Recently, the exportation of ci
Cuba is said to have amounted to 200,000 boxes a year, worth 2,000,000 dol
Humboldt suspects this estimate of exaggeration. — (*Essai Politique sur l'Isle*
vol. i. p. 256.) The tobacco used in Cuba by the lower classes is chiefly impo
the United States.

Consumption of Duty-paid Tobacco in the United Kingdom. — It appears fro
lowing official account, that the consumption of duty-paid tobacco in Great B
increased from about 8,000,000 lbs., in 1789, to 14,500,000, in 1828; the du
fluctuated during the same period from 1s. 3d. to 4s. and 3s. per lb. There
ever, sufficient grounds for thinking that the consumption would have been a
fourth part greater, had the duty been less. But whatever difference of opi
exist as to the influence of the duty in Great Britain, there can be none as
fluence in Ireland. The subjoined table shows that during the 5 years en
1798, when the duty was 8d. a pound, the annual average consumption of
tobacco was 7,337,217 lbs. Since 1798 the population of Ireland has been full
and yet, during the 5 years ending with 1828, when the duty was 3s. per lb.,
average consumption amounted to only 3,972,703 lbs. ; which, making allowa
increase of population, shows that the consumption has sunk to about a *four*
what it amounted to at the former period! This statement warrants the concl
were the duty on tobacco in Ireland reduced to 1s. per lb., the consumption
so much increased, that the revenue would gain and not lose by the reductio

uggling. — The price of tobacco in bond varies from 2½*d.* to 6*d.* per lb.; so that luty of 3*s.* amounts to 1,440 per cent. on the inferior, and to 600 per cent. on the rior qualities. Now, though the use of tobacco be a frivolous, it is, at the same time, nocent gratification; and we do not really see any reason whatever for loading it such oppressive duties, even supposing it were possible to collect them. The more ants and desires of men are multiplied, the more inventive and industrious they me; and so far from preventing luxurious indulgences, a wise government should itself to increase their number, and to diffuse a taste for them as widely as possible. supposing it to be otherwise, still the magnitude of the tobacco duty is altogether ensible: it is neither calculated to produce the largest amount of revenue, nor to ate the taste for the article. Its exorbitancy is advantageous to the smuggler, and m only. With the exception of brandy and geneva, tobacco is the principal clandestinely imported. If, as one might be half inclined to suspect, the duty intended to give life and activity to the nefarious practices of the illicit traders, it mpletely answered its object; but in every other point of view, its failure has been and complete. "According," said Mr. Poulett Thomson, in his admirable speech taxation of the empire, on the 26th of March, 1830, "according to all accounts efore the house on this subject, smuggling in this article in England, Ireland, and nd, is carried on to the greatest possible extent. I have heard it stated, and I he fact upon the best authority, that numbers of vessels are constantly leaving the of Flushing, Ostend, &c., carrying contraband tobacco to this country. It is a fact was established in evidence before a committee of this house, that *seventy* cargoes acco, containing 3,644,000 lbs., were smuggled in one year, on the coast of Ireland, e port of Waterford to the Giant's Causeway alone! In Scotland, smuggling in icle is also carried on to a great extent. There is no doubt," added the Right Hole gentleman, "that the only mode of meeting this system of smuggling con- *fairly reducing the duty upon the article.* I believe, that were the duty upon it d to 1*s.* or 1*s.* 6*d.* per lb., the public would be greatly served, and smuggling put

question, indeed, whether, allowing for the clandestine importation, the consump- relatively less at this moment in Ireland, than at any former period. Under the system, government collects an exorbitant duty upon about a *fourth part* of the consumed in Ireland, the other *three fourths* being supplied by the smuggler; y being at once an incentive to his energies, and a premium to indemnify him risks! A *fourth part* of the demand of Great Britain is, probably, supplied in e way.

of the Number of Pounds' Weight of Leaf Tobacco, Manufactured Cigars and Snuff, that paid the United Kingdom, for the Year ending 5th of January, 1831; with the Rates of Duty, and mount of the same.

	Quantities entered for Home Consumption in the United Kingdom.				Amount of Duty received thereon.			
	Leaf Tobacco.	Manufactured Tobacco and Cigars.	Snuff.	Total.	Leaf Tobacco.	Manufactured Tobacco and Cigars.	Snuff.	Total.
	Lbs.	*Lbs.*	*Lbs.*	*Lbs.*	*L. s. d.*	*L. s. d.*	*L. s. d.*	*L. s. d.*
ded 831	19,301,332	104,898	172	19,406,402	2,890,787 11 3	47,211 2 0	51 14 7	2,938,050 10 10

4,148 lbs. of unmanufactured tobacco imported in 1828, 24,823,522 lbs. were from the United uring the same year 49,130 lbs. of manufactured tobacco were imported, of which 32,127 lbs. Cuba.

Prices of Tobacco, in Bond, in the London Market, January, 1832.

per lb.	s. d.	s. d.
d Scrubs	0 3½	to 0 5½
and leafy	0 4½	— 0 5
y and yellow	0 5	— 1 2
ellow	1 0	— 1 6
Fine Irish and Spinners	0 4	— 0 6
ng	0 3½	— 0 4½
	0 3½	— 0 4
ry and dry	0 2½	— 0 3
ack	0 4½	— 0 5
ng	0 3½	— 0 3¾
tto	0 2¾	— 0 3

Tobacco per lb.	s. d.	s. d.
Virginia, ordinary	0 2½	— 0 3
Stript fine	0 4½	— 0 6
Ordinary and middling	0 2¾	— 0 4
Kentucky, fine and leafy	0 3¼	— 0 4
Good midling	0 2¾	— 0 3
Ordinary and old	0 2½	— 0 2¾
Stript	0 3½	— 0 5½
Havannah	2 0	— 4 0
Cuba	1 3	— 1 6
East India	0 0	— 0 0
Cigars	5 0	— 13 0

Rates of Duty charged in the Year ended 5th of January, 1831.

	s. d.
tured Tobacco, the produce of and imported from any British Possession in	2 9 per lb.
tured Tobacco, otherwise imported	3 0 —
ed Tobacco and Cigars	9 0 —
	6 0 —

Account of the Quantities of Tobacco retained for Home Consumption; the Rates of Duty thereon; the Total Nett Produce of the Duties, in Great Britain and Ireland, from 1789 to 1828, both inclus — (*Parl. Paper*, No. 340. Sess. 1829.)

			Great Britain.			Ireland.	
Years.	Quantities retained for Home Consumption.	Nett Revenue of Customs and Excise.	Total Rates of Duty per lb. on unmanufactured Tobacco.		Quantities entered for Home Consumption.	Nett Revenue of Customs and Excise.	Total Rate of per lb. on unma...tured Tobac...
			American.	Of the Dominions of Spain and Portugal.			
	Lbs.	*£ s. d.*			*Lbs.*	*£ s. d.*	
1789	8,152,185	408,037 4 1	1s. 3d.	3s.	2,765,441	128,704 8 4	1s. Irish cur
1790	8,960,224	512,383 7 1	1s. 3d.	3s. 6d.	2,900,437	133,195 18 10	
1791	9,340,875	585,966 9 1	-	-	2,549,043	117,420 0 2	
1792	8,979,221	582,096 7 7	-	-	1,767,581	80,693 4 5	
1793	8,617,967	547,217 14 4	-	-	5,568,857	125,844 17 1	6d. ditto
1794	9,723,536	606,262 12 10	-	-	9,426,211	193,158 10 7	
1795	10,972,368	659,989 3 4	-	-	7,874,409	215,719 9 0	8d. ditto
1796	10,047,843	755,451 15 1	1s. 7d.	4s. 6d.	6,045,790	186,759 19 0	
1797	9,822,439	813,027 16 2	1s. 7d. 6-20ths.	4s. 6d. 13-20ths.	8,445,555	267,721 16 4	
1798	10,286,741	867,302 14 0	1s. 7d. 12-20ths.	4s. 7d. 4-20ths.	4,894,121	215,317 12 7	1s. ditto
1799	10,993,113	799,369 14 2	-	-	5,876,172	288,028 4 9	1s. 7-10ths d
1800	11,796,415	987,110 8 8	-	-	6,737,275	327,916 9 0	
1801	10,514,998	923,855 3 5	1s. 7d. 6-20ths.	4s. 6d. 18-20ths.	6,389,754	285,482 6 4	
1802	12,121,278	928,678 9 1	1s. 7d. 33-50ths.	4s. 7d. 13-50ths.	6,327,542	309,738 9 2	{1s. 7-10ths and 3s. per
1803	12,589,570	1,028,563 16 1	1s. 7¾d.	4s. 8¼d.	5,278,511	265,944 3 4	
1804	12,254,494	1,060,319 18 0	1s 8½d.	4s. 10¼d.	5,783,487	314,007 5 8	1s.5d.Brit.cu
1805	12,656,471	1,088,821 4 5	1s. 8d. 13-20ths.	4s. 10d. 19 20ths.	4,158,794	302,316 8 1	
1806	12,435,035	1,185,830 14 1	2s. 2d. 13-20ths.	5s. 4d. 19-20ths.	5,082,186	359,867 6 4	
1807	12,432,994	1,336,542 17 9	-	-	4,531,049	315,417 4 3	1s. 5d. ditt
1808	12,876,119	1,448,296 3 7	-	-	5,847,416	403,973 3 8	
1809	13,054,870	1,325,154 5 7	2s. 2d. 13-20ths.	4s. 1d. 13-20ths.	6,497,662	451,278 19 11	
1810	14,108,193	1,599,376 18 9	-	-	6,221,646	444,198 5 0	
1811	14,923,243	1,701,848 8 2	-	-	6,453,024	552,082 9 9	2s. 2d. 13-20t
1812	15,043,533	1,679,912 2 2	2s. 4d. 13-20ths.	4s. 5d. 18-20ths.	5,896,702	697,897 9 11	
1813	13,648,245	{Customs Records destroyed}	2s.8d. 3-16ths.	4s.11d. 11-16ths.	5,944,817 / 4,869,304	746,006 5 2 / 653,708 12 11	2s. 8d. 3-16t
1814	10,503,917	1,581,684 12 9	-	-	4,748,205	740,279 13 1	3s. 2d. dit
1815	13,207,192	1,764,487 7 10	3s. 2d.	5s. 5¼d.	4,732,085	750,510 7 9	
1816	12,815,808	2,035,109 2 8	-	-	4,778,469	757,316 8 3	
1817	13,593,089	2,158,500 3 11	-	-	4,194,041	664,183 9 1	
1818	13,688,437	2,173,866 19 2	-	-	3,466,852	614,989 5 7	4s. di
1819	12,911,285	2,235,045 2 10	4s.	6s.	2,582,498	516,446 6 6	
1820	13,016,562	2,610,972 7 9	-	-	2,614,954	522,168 6 9	
1821	12,983,198	2,600,415 7 8	-	-	3,309,072	664,016 7 4	
1822	12,970,566	2,599,155 15 1	-	-	3,546,126	730,507 12 8	
1823	13,418,554	2,695,009 15 0	-	-	3,749,732	750,589 5 4	
1824	13,083,094	2,627,955 12 6	-	-	4,160,049	728,288 13 11	3s. di
1825	14,510,555	2,530,617 6 3	3s.	5s.	3,898,647	580,893 11 0	
1826	13,784,370	2,077,875 14 7	3s.	3s.	4,041,172	603,037 18 9	
1827	14,704,655	2,223,340 18 4	-	-	4,013,915	595,683 4 3	
1828	14,540,368	2,198,142 18 2	-	-			

Regulations as to Importation. — Tobacco is not to be imported in a vessel of less than 120 tons b... nor unless in hogsheads, casks, chests, or cases, containing at least 100 lbs. nett weight, if from t... Indies; or 450 lbs. weight, if from any other place; or 100 lbs. weight, if cigars; except tobac... Turkey, which may be packed in separate bags or packages, provided the outward package be a ho... cask, chest, or case, containing 450 lbs. nett at least; and except Guatemala and Colombian ... which may be imported in packages of not less than 90 lbs. Tobacco is not allowed to be imported... into the following ports, viz. London, Liverpool, Bristol, Lancaster, Cowes, Falmouth, Whitehaven... Port Glasgow, Greenock, Leith, Newcastle, Plymouth, Belfast, Cork, Drogheda, Dublin, ... Limerick, Londonderry, Newry, Sligo, Waterford, and Wexford. A rent of *four* shillings is charg... every hogshead, cask, chest, or case of tobacco, warehoused in every warehouse approved by the ... 2s. being paid immediately upon depositing the tobacco in the warehouse, and 2s. more before the ... is taken out for home consumption, or exportation: it may remain for *five* years in the warehou... out any additional charge for rent. No abatement is made from the tobacco duties on account of ... but the merchant may, if he choose, abandon the tobacco, which is to be destroyed. The allo... duty-free tobacco for each sailor on board his Majesty's navy, and for each soldier on foreign s... fixed at 2 lbs. per lunar month. Tobacco that has been exported cannot be re-imported, witho... subject to the same duty as if it were imported for the first time. Tobacco cannot be entere... portation in any vessel of less than 70 tons burthen. — (See 6 *Geo.* 4. c. 107., 9 *Geo.* 4. c. 76., 4... c. 100., &c.)

TON, an English weight containing 20 cwt.

TONNAGE, in commercial navigation, the number of tons burthen that... will carry. It is enacted by the 6 *Geo.* 4. c. 110. that the tonnage of... ships shall be ascertained as follows: —

When the Ship is dry. — The length shall be taken on a straight line along the rabbet of the keel... back of the main sternpost to a perpendicular line from the fore part of the main stem under the... from which subtracting three fifths of the breadth, the remainder shall be esteemed the just len... keel, to find the tonnage; and the breadth shall be taken from the outside of the outside pl... broadest part of the ship, whether that shall be above or below the main wales, exclusive of all... doubling planks that may be wrought upon the sides of the ship; then multiplying the length o... by the breadth so taken, and that product by half the breadth, and dividing the whole by 94, th... shall be deemed the true contents of the tonnage. — § 17.

When Ship is afloat. — In cases where it may be necessary to ascertain the tonnage of any... afloat, according to the foregoing rule, the following method shall be observed; that is to s... plumb line over the stern of the ship, and measure the distance between such line and the a...

post at the load water-mark; then measure from the top of the plumb line, in a parallel direction
water, to a perpendicular point immediately over the load water-mark at the fore part of the
m, subtracting from such measurement the above distance; the remainder will be the ship's ex-
roin which is to be deducted 3 inches for every foot of the load draught of water for the rake abaft,
e fifths of the ship's breadth for the rake forward, the remainder shall be esteemed the just length
el to find the tonnage: and the breadth shall be taken from outside to outside of the plank in the
part of the ship, whether that shall be above or below the main wales, exclusive of all manner of
g or doubling that may be wrought on the side of the ship; then multiplying the length of the
tonnage by the breadth so taken, and that product by half the breadth, and dividing by 94, the
shall be deemed the true contents of the tonnage. — § 18.

Room in Steam Vessels to be deducted. — Provided always, that in each of the several rules be-
cribed, when used for the purpose of ascertaining the tonnage of any ship propelled by steam, of
the engine room shall be deducted from the whole length of such ship, and the remainder shall,
purpose, be deemed the whole length. — § 19.

e, when so ascertained, to be ever after deemed the Tonnage. —Whenever the tonnage shall have
ertained according to the rules prescribed (except ships which have been admeasured afloat),
unt of tonnage shall ever after be deemed the tonnage of such ship, and shall be repeated in
sequent registry, unless any alteration shall be made in the form and burthen, or it shall be dis-
hat the tonnage has been erroneously computed. — § 20.

nage of goods and stores is taken sometimes by weight and sometimes by measurement; that
eing allowed to the vessel which yields the most tonnage. In tonnage by weight, 20 cwt. make
tonnage by measurement, 40 cubic feet are equal to a ton. All carriages, or other stores
by the tonnage, are taken to pieces and packed so as to occupy the least room. Ordnance,
rass or iron, is taken in tonnage at its actual weight; as are musket-cartridges in barrels or
munition in boxes, &c.

the article SHIPS went to press, the subjoined table has been printed.

ve Statement of the British and Foreign Tonnage which have entered the several Ports of
ritain from Foreign Countries, during the Five Years ending with 5th January, 1832.—(*Parl.*
No. 235. Sess. 1832.)

s.	1827.		1828.		1829.		1830.		1831.	
	British Tonnage.	Foreign Tonnage	British Tonnage.	Foreign Tonnage	British Tonnage.	Foreign Tonnage	British Tonnage.	Foreign Tonnage	British Tonnage.	Foreign Tonnage
	359,314	29,267	261,137	24,281	338,514	25,038	311,989	26,905	338,610	33,711
	11,380	20,872	14,797	23,836	16,028	24,214	11,782	23,158	11,017	37,276
	6,289	84,253	6,431	74,148	5,482	76,691	2,593	76,904	2,649	106,247
	10,825	52,456	17,210	49,207	24,424	53,390	11,926	51,420	6,552	62,190
	147,489	106,722	122,288	96,100	116,630	124,368	95,190	136,739	78,783	136,224
	94,296	57,933	113,219	45,765	100,340	49,830	150,171	54,869	109,651	58,194
	118,336	76,813	127,582	78,106	116,486	93,995	119,555	92,158	186,634	80,851
	100,704	66,903	100,459	63,184	102,929	59,279	107,728	47,940	95,766	71,608
	67,502	2,704	65,318	2,574	54,111	1,430	53,790	1,321	59,909	2,549
	45,726	6,064	49,657	7,741	58,919	5,981	45,018	5,514	71,707	8,800
	5,354	-	2,341	-	882	-	1,510	-	420	
	53,154	1,449	41,487	2,590	47,690	4,734	45,562	2,253	69,163	19,416
	2,500	-	784	-	2,034	-	2,162	225	4,509	
	7,721	-	7,385	120	5,326	-	4,304	-	8,482	
ant	15,607	-	13,105	-	9,469	-	13,031	-	18,022	
Guern										
Man	91,580	100	101,365	2,216	105,689	1,393	116,017	2,561	104,864	907
	103,436	300	101,467	-	111,359	-	106,054	370	106,828	
	40,453	-	46,191	-	56,822	-	60,984	-	70,257	235
eries	37,741	-	33,887	-	35,982	-	31,897	-	37,454	
to	261	-	-	-	259	-				
Colonies	298,941	-	332,372	-	347,800	-	372,425	-	402,681	
ies	232,289	-	258,727	-	250,578	-	239,663	-	233,140	
dies	71,160	208,445	79,102	132,570	60,607	158,605	63,946	210,259	90,472	225,093
	10,338	1,250	8,899	683	10,530	2,190	8,132	3,111	11,847	2,386
ntal Co-	40,307	293	50,238	976	54,973	910	60,662	590	67,029	1,633
	104	-	-	-						
of Ice)	-	-	100	-						
al	1,972,780	715,834	1,955,548	604,097	2,033,854	682,048	2,036,091	736,997	2,236,446	847,320

S AND MACHINES. Under this designation are comprised all sorts
ents employed to assist in the performance of any undertaking, from
and simplest to the most improved and complex. But we only mention
for the purpose of making one or two remarks on the restrictions to
trade in them is subjected.

ion and Exportation of Tools and Machines. — Tools and machines being in-
f production, it is obviously of the utmost importance that they should be as
ved as possible, and hence the expediency of allowing their free importation.
sion, or the exclusion of the articles of which they are made, would obviously
anch of industry carried on in a nation less advanced than others in their
e, under the most serious disadvantages. And supposing the implements it
be superior to those of other countries when the exclusion took place, the
oreign competition, and of the emulation which it inspires, would most pro-
very short time, occasion the loss of this superiority. The injury arising
ohibition of most other articles is comparatively limited, affecting only the
d consumers of those that are prohibited. But a prohibition of machines

strikes at the root of every species of industry : it is not injurious to one, or a branches, but to all.

The question whether the exportation of machinery ought to be free, is not so of solution. It is the duty of a nation to avail itself of every fair mean its own aggrandisement; and supposing the machinery belonging to any pa lar people were decidedly superior to that employed by their neighbours, and that had it in their power to preserve this advantage, their generosity would certainly run their sense, were they to communicate their improved machinery to others. do not, however, believe that it is possible, whatever measures may be adopted i view, for one country to monopolise, for any considerable period, any materia provement in machinery or the arts; and on this ground we think that the ex restraints on the exportation of machinery had better be abolished. Drawing models of all sorts of machines used in Manchester, Glasgow, and Birmin are to be found in most parts of the Continent; and at Rouen, Paris, &c., nu of the best English workmen are employed in the manufacture of prohibited chines. Now, it does certainly appear not a little preposterous to prevent the e ation of a machine, at the same time that we allow (it could not, indeed, be preve the free egress of the workmen by whom it is made ! The effect of this absurd is, not to secure a monopoly of improved machines for the manufacturers of En but to occasion the emigration of English artisans to the Continent, and the est ment there of machine manufactories under their superintendence. The prejudi must arise from this state of things to the interests of England, is too obvious to being pointed out. It is plain, therefore, that the exportation of all sorts of mach on payment of a moderate duty, ought to be allowed. A policy of this sort afford a much more efficient protection to our manufacturers than they enjoy at p at the same time that it would tend to keep our artisans at home, and make E the grand seat of the tool as well as of the cotton manufacture.

For an account of the restrictions on the exportation of machinery from Great see *ante*, p. 613.

Account of the Value of the Machinery exported from Great Britain, during the Six Year with 1829. — (*Parl. Paper*, No. 373. Sess. 1830.)

Years.	Steam Engines and Parts of Steam Engines.	Mill Work of all Sorts allowed by Law to be exported.	Machinery of all other Kinds allowed by Law to be exported.	Machinery exported under Licence from the Treasury or Privy Council.	Total.
	£	£	£	£	£
1824	28,123	22,996	33,575	44,958	129,652
1825	78,027	25,654	104,263	4,472	212,416
1826	128,826	25,724	66,247	13,158	233,955
1827	111,930	24,558	60,507	17,154	214,129
1828	123,969	65,372	56,413	19,614	265,368
1829	133,573	47,543	52,019	23,404	256,539

TOPAZ (Ger. *Topas*; Fr. *Topase*; It. *Topazio*; Sp. *Topacio*; Rus. *Topa* name topaz has been restricted by M. Haüy to the stones called by mine Occidental ruby, topaz, and sapphire; which, agreeing in their crystallisat most of their properties, were arranged under one species by M. Romé d The word topaz, derived from an island in the Red Sea, where the ancie to find topazes, was applied by them to a mineral very different from our variety of our topaz they denominated chrysolite. Colour, wine yellow. pale wine yellow it passes into yellowish white, greenish white, mounta sky blue : from deep wine yellow into flesh red and crimson red. Specifi from 3·464 to 3·641. — (*Thomson's Chemistry*.)

TORTOISE-SHELL (Fr. *Ecaille de Tortue*; It. *Scaglia de Tartaru Schilpad*; Malay, *Sisik kurakura*), the brown and yellow scales of the *imbricata*, or tortoise, a native of the tropical seas. It is extensively us manufacture of combs, snuffboxes, &c., and in inlaying and other or work.

The best tortoise-shell is that of the Indian Archipelago, and the finest of tl is obtained on the shores of the Spice Islands and New Guinea. When the f Indian tortoise-shell is worth, in the London market, 46s., the finest East India 60s per lb. Under the latter name, however, a great deal of inferior sh ported, brought from various parts of the East Indies. The goodness o shell depends mainly on the thickness and size of the scales, and in a smaller the clearness and brilliancy of the colours. Before the opening of the Bri course with India, the greater part of the tortoise-shell, which eventually fou to Europe, was first carried to Canton, which then formed the principal ma

dity. It is still an article of considerable export from that city; but at present Sin-
is the chief mart. There were exported from it, in 1825, about 21,500 lbs. weight,
ed at the time to be worth about 150,000 Spanish dollars. The quantity has since
rably increased, and the price has risen from 750 and 900 to from 1,000 to 1,600
per picul, according to quality. — (*Crawfurd's Indian Archipelago ; Singapore*
le ; Canton Register.)

ty, which is 2s. per lb. on the shells imported from foreign countries, and 1s. per lb. on those im-
om a British possession, produced, in 1829, 732l, 4s. 11d.

'S (Ger. *Spielzeug, Speilsachen ;* Du. *Speelgöed ;* Fr. *Jouets, Bimbelots ;*
stulli ; Sp. *Dijes, Juguetes de ninnos ;* Rus. *Igrushki*), include every trifling
made expressly for the amusement of children. How frivolous soever these
may appear in the estimation of the merely casual observer, their manu-
employs hundreds of hands, and gives bread to many families in London
vicinity; at the same time that the demand for them occasions a consider-
.de to Holland. From the latter country we procure most sorts of toys
e reasonable terms than we can afford to produce them. But of late
.ey have been made in greater abundance in England than formerly. The
toys, which is an *ad valorem* one of 20 per cent., produced, in 1829,
16s. showing that the value of the toys imported must have amounted to

GACANTH, a species of gum, the produce of the *Astragalus Tragacantha*,
' shrub growing in Persia, Crete, and the islands of the Levant. It exudes
e end of June from the stem and larger branches, and soon dries in the sun.
.dorous ; impressing a very slightly bitter taste as it softens in the mouth.
whitish colour ; is semi-transparent; and in very thin, wrinkled, vermiform
it is brittle, but not easily pulverised, except in frosty weather, or in a
mortar. It should be chosen in long twisted pieces, white, very clear,
e from all other colours; the brown, and particularly the black pieces,
.e wholly rejected.—(*Thomson's Chemistry ; Dr. A. T. Thomson's Dispensa-
Tilburn's Orient. Com.*)

.ry, 1832, tragacanth sold in the London market at from 14l. 10s. to 20l. per cwt., duty (5l. 12s.)

.ATIES (COMMERCIAL). By a commercial treaty is meant a treaty
two independent nations for facilitating, and most commonly, also, re-
the commerce carried on between them.

Objects, and Policy of modern Commercial Treaties.—During the middle ages,
.n, indeed, to a comparatively recent period, foreigners resident in a country,
.or commercial or other purposes, were, for the most part, subject to very harsh
.'. At one time it was usual in England to make aliens liable for the debts and
each other ; and the practice, formerly so common, of laying heavier duties on
imported and exported by aliens, than by British subjects, is not even yet, we
say, altogether abandoned. In France, and some other countries, during the
15th centuries, a stranger was incapable of bequeathing property by will ; and
.e of his personal as well as real estate fell, at his death, to the king or the lord
.rony. This barbarous law was known by the name of *Droit d'Aubaine,* and
.ompletely abolished in France till a very late period.—(*Robertson's Charles V.*
.e 29.) Previously to last century, the laws with respect to shipwreck, though
.more humane than they had been at a more remote period, were calculated
promote the interests of the sovereign of the country, or the feudal lords on
.ritories shipwrecked vessels might be thrown, than those of the unfortunate
survivors.— (See WRECK.*) The most serious obstacles were then, also, op-
the prevalent insecurity, and the arbitrary nature of the tolls which the lords
.e habit of exacting, to the transit of commodities through the territories of
.o those of another.

.such circumstances, it became of much importance for commercial states to
to obtain, by means of treaties, that protection and security for the persons
.rties of their subjects, when abroad, against unjust treatment and vexatious
which they could not have obtained from the laws of the countries in which
.t happen to reside. Thus, it was stipulated by Edward II., in 1325, that

.ctice of confiscating shipwrecked property continued in France till 1681, when it was abolished
.f Louis XIV. It was at one time common in Germany, to use the words of M. Bouchaud,
.édicateurs de prier Dieu en chaire, *qu'il se fasse bien des naufrages sur leurs côtes!* "— (*Thé-*
.tés de Commerce, p. 118.) And the fact that the celebrated jurist Thomasius wrote a dis-
.defence of such prayers, affords, if possible, a still more striking proof of the spirit of the

the merchants and mariners of Venice should have power to come to England
years, with liberty to sell their merchandise and to return home in safety, " *u
having either their persons or goods stopped on account of other people's crimes or a
— (Anderson, Anno 1325.) The commercial treaties negotiated during the 15th,
and 17th centuries, are full of similar conditions; and there can be no doubt that b
viding for the security of merchants and seamen when abroad, and suspending
respect to them, the barbarous laws and practices then in force, they contributed
rially to accelerate the progress of commerce and civilisation.

Commercial treaties were also negotiated at a very early period for the regulati
neutral commerce during war; and for defining the articles that should be d
contraband, or which it should not be lawful for neutral ships to convey or ca
either belligerent. These are obviously points that can only be decided by express
lations. *

Instead, however, of confining commercial treaties to their legitimate and prope
poses — the security of merchants and navigators, and the facility of commercial tr
tions — they very soon began to be employed as engines for promoting the comme
one country at the expense of another. For more than two centuries, those er
in framing commercial treaties have principally applied themselves to secure,
by force or address, some exclusive advantage in favour of the ships and prodt
their particular countries. Hence these compacts are full of regulations as
duties to be charged on certain articles, and the privileges to be enjoyed by e
ships, according as they were either produced by or belonged to particular countri
was in the adjustment of these duties and regulations that the skill of the negotiat
chiefly put to the test. It was expected that he should be thoroughly acquainte
the state of every branch of industry, both in his own country, and in the countr
which he was negotiating; and he was to endeavour so to adjust the tariff of dutie
those branches in which his own country was deficient might be benefited, and
in which the other was superior might be depressed! The idea of conducting a
tiation of this sort on a fair principle of reciprocity is of very late origin; to suce
circumventing, in over-reaching, or in extorting from fear or ignorance some opp
but at the same time worthless, privilege, were long esteemed the only proofs of s
talent in negotiators.

In an able tract, attributed to Mr. Eden, afterwards Lord Auckland, published
(Historical and Political Remarks on the Tariff of the French Treaty), there is the fo
outline of the qualifications necessary to the negotiator of a commercial treaty. —
side a general knowledge of the trade and reciprocal interests of the contracti
ties, he ought to be precisely acquainted with their several kinds of industry and
to discover their wants, to calculate their resources, and to weigh with nicety the
their finances, and the proportionate interest of their money: nay, further, he sh
able to ascertain the comparative population and strength of each country, togeth
the price and quality both of first materials, and also of the labour bestowed upon
for this purpose he should inquire into the operations of every class of mercha
manufacturers concerned in the trade; should consult their expectations on eac
several branches; and collect their hopes and fears on the effect of such a com
revolution, on the competition of rival nations. A good treaty of commerce
pendent of the art of negotiation, is pronounced, by one who well knew the ext
difficulty of the subject, to be a ' masterpiece of skill.' "—(p. 10.)

Had Mr. Eden concluded by stating that no individual, or number of indi
ever possessed, or ever would possess, the various qualifications which in his es
were required in negotiating a " good commercial treaty," he would only have a
what is most certainly true. We believe, however, that he had formed a tota
estimate, not only of the qualifications of a negotiator, but of the objects he o
have in view. It was the opinion of the Abbé Mably (Droit Publique de l'
tome ii. p. 561.) — an opinion in which we are disposed, with very little modific
concur, — that when a few general rules are agreed upon for the effectual security
and navigation, including the importation and exportation of all commodities
hibited by law; the speedy adjustment of disputes; the regulations of pilotage,
and light-house duties; the protection of the property and effects of merchant
event of a rupture, &c.; all is done that ought to be attempted in a commercia
It may, indeed, be properly stipulated that the goods of the contracting powers
admitted into each other's ports on the same terms as " those of the most
nations,"—that is, that no higher duties shall be charged upon them than on
others. But here stipulations ought to cease. It is an abuse and a perversion
mercial treaties, to make them instruments for regulating duties or prescribing
house regulations.

* There is a good collection of treaties as to this point, in the Appendix to the excellent wor
predi, Del Commercio de' Popoli Neutrali. — (See CONTRABAND.)

nit, indeed, that occasions may occur in which it may be expedient to stipu-
reduction of duties or an abolition of prohibitions on the one side, in return
r concessions on the other. But all arrangements of this sort ought to be deter-
a convention limited to that particular object; and a fixed and not very distant
ld be agreed upon, when the obligation in the convention should expire, and
ies be at liberty to continue or abandon the regulations agreed upon. Ge-
eaking, all treaties which determine what the duties on importation or ex-
shall be, or which stipulate for preferences, are radically objectionable. Nations
regulate their tariffs in whatever mode they may judge best fitted to promote
interests, without being shackled by engagements with others.* If foreign
e all treated alike, none of them has just grounds of complaint; and it
be for the interest of any people to show preferences to one over another.
r example, by whom we may be most advantageously supplied with foreign
equire no preferences; and if we exclude them, or give a preference to others,
estably injure ourselves: and yet 19 out of 20 of the regulations as to duties
cial treaties have been founded on this preposterous principle. They have
oyed to divert trade into channels, where it would not naturally flow; that is,
t less secure and less profitable than it would otherwise have been.
deal of stress has usually been laid upon the advantages supposed to be derived
privileges sometimes conceded in commercial treaties. But we believe that
inquire into the subject will find that such concessions have, in every case,
nly injurious to the party making them, but also to the party in whose favour
been made. The famous commercial treaty with Portugal, negotiated by
uen in 1703, was almost universally regarded, for a very long period, as ad-
lculated to promote the interests of this country; but it is now generally
y every one who has reflected upon such subjects, that few transactions have
e by which these interests have been more deeply injured. It stipulated
admission of British woollens into Portugal, from which they happened, at
o be excluded; but in return for this concession — a concession far more ad-
to the Portuguese than to us — we bound ourselves "for ever hereafter" to
s of the growth of Portugal into Great Britain at two thirds of the duty pay-
wines of France! Thus, in order to open an access for our woollens to the
rket of Portugal, we consented, in all time to come, to drink inferior wine,
comparatively high price! — (See WINE.) This, however, was not all: by
ne of the principal equivalents the French had to offer for our commodities,
ily lessened their ability to deal with us; at the same time that we provoked
opt retaliatory measures against our trade. It is owing more to the sti-
the Methuen treaty than to any thing else, that the trade between England
— a trade that would naturally be of vast extent and importance — is con-
the narrowest limits; and is hardly, indeed, of as much consequence as the
Sweden and Norway. — (See antè, p. 588.)
ionary to imagine that any nation will ever continue to grant to another
ve advantage in her markets, unless she obtain what she reckons an equivalent
in the markets of the other. And if a commercial treaty stipulating for
e privilege be really and bonâ fide observed by the country granting the
e may be sure that the concessions made by the country in whose favour it is
sufficient fully to countervail it. Those who grasp at exclusive privileges in
his sort, or who attempt to extort valuable concessions from the weakness or
their neighbours, are uniformly defeated in their object. All really beneficial transactions are bottomed on a fair principle of reciprocity; and that
lways flourish most, and have the foundations of her prosperity best secured,
versal merchant, and deals with all the world on the same fair and liberal

ess of these principles, we are glad to observe, is now beginning to be very
mitted. Stipulations as to duties and Custom-house regulations are dis-
rom commercial treaties; and it is to be hoped that at no distant period
f them may have vanished.

on the principles, style, and history of commercial treaties is a desideratum. The best we
Mascovius *De Fœderibus Commerciorum*, 4to. Leipsic, 1735; and Bouchaud, *Théorie des
nmerce*, 12mo. Paris, 1777. But these are principally works of erudition, and were written
nd principles of commercial policy had been unfolded. There is no good collection of trea-
lish language; but Mr. Hertslet's work is valuable, as containing the recent treaties in an
We understand that a work containing new treaties and state papers is annually compiled
Office, and that a few copies of it are circulated; but we are ignorant of the peculiar
ontents, and of the principle on which it is distributed, not having been able to obtain a
nay be some reason for this mystery; but it is not affected by the American, French, or
nments, who do themselves honour by the liberality with which they distribute all papers
expense.

---

ple is laid down as fundamental by a very high authority, Sir Henry Parnell, in his tract
rs des Rélations Commerciales entre la France et l'Angleterre.

We subjoin copies of some of the commercial treaties and conventions existin moment between Great Britain and other powers.

AUSTRIA.

Convention of Commerce and Navigation between His Britannic Majesty and the Emperor o signed at London, December 21. 1829.

Article 1. From the 1st day of February, 1830, Austrian vessels entering or departing from th the United Kingdom of Great Britain and Ireland, and British vessels entering or departing from of his Imperial and Royal Apostolic Majesty's dominions, shall not be subject to any other duties or charges whatever than are or shall be levied on national vessels entering or departing ports respectively.

2. All articles of the growth, produce, or manufacture of any of the dominions of either of contracting parties, which are or shall be permitted to be imported into or exported from the po United Kingdom and of Austria, respectively, in vessels of the one country, shall, in like m permitted to be imported into and exported from those ports in vessels of the other.

3. All articles not of the growth, produce, or manufacture of the dominions of his Britannic which can legally be imported from the United Kingdom of Great Britain and Ireland into th Austria, in British ships, shall be subject only to the same duties as are payable upon the like imported in Austrian ships: and the same reciprocity shall be observed in the ports of t. Kingdom, in respect to all articles not the growth, produce, or manufacture of the dominic Imperial and Royal Apostolic Majesty, which can legally be imported into the ports of t' Kingdom in Austrian ships.

4. All goods which can legally be imported into the ports of either country shall be admit same rate of duty, whether imported in vessels of the other country or in national vessels; and which can be legally exported from the ports of either country shall be entitled to the same drawbacks, and allowances, whether exported in vessels of the other country or in national vess

5. No priority or preference shall be given, directly or indirectly, by the government of eithe or by any company, corporation, or agent acting in its behalf, or under its authority, in the p any article the growth, produce, or manufacture of either country, imported into the other, c of or in reference to the national character of the vessel in which such article may be imported the true intent and meaning of the high contracting parties, that no distinction or difference shall be made in this respect.

6. In respect to the commerce to be carried on in Austrian vessels with the British dominic East Indies, or now held by the East India Company in virtue of their charter, his Britann consents to grant the same facilities and privileges, in all respects, to the subjects of his Im Royal Apostolic Majesty, as are or may be enjoyed under any treaty or act of parliament by th or citizens of the most favoured nation; subject to the laws and regulations which are, c applicable to the ships and subjects of any other foreign country enjoying the like facilities and of trading with the said dominions.

7. All the possessions of his Britannic Majesty in Europe, except the British possessions in terranean Sea, shall, for all the purposes of this convention, be considered as forming part of Kingdom of Great Britain and Ireland.

8. That clause of article 7. of the convention concluded at Paris on the 5th of November, 18 the courts of Great Britain, Austria, Prussia, and Russia, which relates to the commerce be dominions of his Imperial and Royal Apostolic Majesty and the United States of the Ionian hereby confirmed.

9. The present convention shall be in force until the 18th day of March, 1836; and furthe end of twelve months after either of the high contracting parties shall have given notice to t its intention to terminate the same; each of the high contracting parties reserving to itself t giving such notice to the other, on or at any time after the said 18th day of March, 1836 hereby agreed between them, that, at the expiration of twelve months after such notice shal received by either party from the other, this convention, and all the provisions thereof, shall cease and determine.

10. The present convention shall be ratified, and the ratifications shall be exchanged at Lon one month from the date hereof, or sooner if possible.

In witness whereof the respective plenipotentiaries have signed the same, and have affixed seals of their arms.

Done at London, the 21st day of December,   ABERDEEN.
in the year of our Lord 1829.   W. F. VESEY FITZG
     ESTERHAZY.

Austrian ships may import from the dominions of his Majesty the Emperor of Austria int British possessions abroad, goods the produce of such dominions, and export goods from s possessions abroad, to be carried to any foreign country whatever. — (*Order in Council, April*

DENMARK.

Convention of Commerce between Great Britain and Denmark, signed at London, the 16th J

Article 1. From and after the 1st day of July next, Danish vessels entering or departi ports of the United Kingdom of Great Britain and Ireland, and British vessels entering or de the ports of his Danish Majesty's dominions, shall not be subject to any other or higher dutie whatever, than are or shall be levied on national vessels entering or departing from respectively.

2. All articles of the growth, produce, or manufacture of any of the dominions of either contracting parties, which are or shall be permitted to be imported into or exported from the United Kingdom and of Denmark respectively, in vessels of the one country, shall, in l: be imported into and exported from those ports in vessels of the other.

3. All articles not of the growth, produce, or manufacture of the dominions of his Britan which can legally be imported from the United Kingdom of Great Britain and Ireland into t dominions of the King of Denmark, in British ships, shall be subject only to the same dutie able upon the like articles if imported in Danish ships; and the same reciprocity shall be o regard to Danish vessels in the ports of the said United Kingdom of Great Britain and Irelan to all articles not the growth, produce, or manufacture of the dominions of his Danish Majes legally be imported into the ports of the United Kingdom in Danish ships.

4. All goods which can legally be imported into the ports of either country, shall be ad same rate of duty, whether imported in vessels of the other country, or in national vessels; which can be legally exported from the ports of either country, shall be entitled to the sa drawbacks, and allowances, whether exported in vessels of the other country, or in national

5. No priority or preference shall be given, directly or indirectly, or by the governm country, or by any company, corporation, or agent, acting on its behalf, or under its auth purchase of any article the growth, produce, or manufacture of either country imported i on account of or in reference to the character of the vessel in which such article was impor

intent and meaning of the high contracting parties that no distinction or difference whatever
made in this respect.

high contracting parties having mutually determined not to include, in the present convention,
ective colonies, in which are comprehended, on the part of Denmark, Greenland, Iceland, and
ds of Ferroe; it is expressly agreed that the intercourse which may at present legally be carried
subjects or ships of either of the said high contracting parties with the colonies of the other,
ain upon the same footing as if this convention had never been concluded.

present convention shall be in force for the term of ten years from the date hereof; and further,
end of twelve months after either of the high contracting parties shall have given notice to the
ts intention to terminate the same; each of the high contracting parties reserving to itself the
giving such notice to the other, at the end of the said term of ten years; and it is hereby agreed
them, that, at the expiration of twelve months after such notice shall have been received by
ty from the other, this convention, and all the provisions thereof, shall altogether cease and
c.

present convention shall be ratified, and the ratifications shall be exchanged at London, within.
h from the date hereof, or sooner if possible.

ess whereof, the respective plenipotentiaries have signed the same, and have affixed thereto the
eir arms.

at London, the 16th of June, 1824.

GEORGE CANNING.
W. HUSKISSON.
C. E. MOLTKE.

Separate Article.

h contracting parties reserve to themselves to enter upon additional stipulations for the purpose
ting and extending, even beyond what is comprehended in the convention of this date, the
al regulations of their respective subjects and dominions, upon the principles either of reciprocal
ent advantages, as the case may be. And in the event of any articles or article being con-
tween the said high contracting parties, for giving effect to such stipulations, it is hereby agreed,
rticle or articles which may hereafter be so concluded shall be considered as forming part of the
convention.

Additional Article.

ritannic and Danish Majesties mutually agree, that no higher or other duties shall be levied in
heir dominions (their respective colonies being excepted from the convention of this date), upon
al property of their respective subjects, on the removal of same from the dominions of their
ties reciprocally, either upon the inheritance of such property, or otherwise, than are or shall
in each state, upon the like property, when removed by a subject of such state, respectively.

FRANCE.

*of Commerce between His Britannic Majesty and the Most Christian King, together with two
additional Articles thereunto annexed, signed at London, January 26. 1826.*

. French vessels coming from or departing for the ports of France, or, if in ballast, coming
parting for any place, shall not be subject, in the ports of the United Kingdom, either on
to or departing from the same, to any higher duties of tonnage, harbour, light-house, pilotage,
or other similar or corresponding duties, of whatever nature, or under whatever denomination,
to which British vessels, in respect of the same voyages, are or may be subject, on entering
arting from such ports; and, reciprocally, from and after the same period, British vessels
m or departing for the ports of the United Kingdom, or, if in ballast, coming from or departing
ce, shall not be subject, in the ports of France, either on entering into or departing from the
y higher duties of tonnage, harbour, light-house, pilotage, quarantine, or other similar or cor-
duties, of whatever nature, or under whatever denomination, than those to which French
respect of the same voyages, are or may be subject, on entering into or departing from such
ther such duties are collected separately, or are consolidated in one and the same duty;—his
tian Majesty reserving to himself to regulate the amount of such duty or duties in France,
o the rate at which they are or may be established in the United Kingdom: at the same time,
of diminishing the burthens imposed upon the navigation of the two countries, his Most
Majesty will always be disposed to reduce the amount of the said burthens in France, in
to any reduction which may hereafter be made of those now levied in the ports of the United

which can or may be legally imported into the ports of the United Kingdom, from the ports of
o imported in French vessels, shall be subject to no higher duties than if imported in British
, reciprocally, goods which can or may be legally imported into the ports of France, from the
United Kingdom, if so imported in British vessels, shall be subject to no higher duties than if
French vessels. The produce of Asia, Africa, and America, not being allowed to be imported
id countries, nor from any other, in French vessels, nor from France in French, British, or
essels, into the ports of the United Kingdom, for home consumption, but only for warehousing
ortation, his Most Christian Majesty reserves to himself to direct that, in like manner, the
Asia, Africa, and America, shall not be imported from the said countries, nor from any other,
essels, nor from the United Kingdom in British, French, or any other vessels, into the ports
or the consumption of that kingdom, but only for warehousing and re-exportation.
rd to the productions of the countries of Europe, it is understood between the high contracting
such productions shall not be imported, in British ships, into France, for the consumption of
m, unless such ships shall have been laden therewith in some port of the United Kingdom;
Britannic Majesty may adopt, if he shall think fit, some corresponding restrictive measure,
to the productions of the countries of Europe, imported into the ports of the United Kingdom
essels: the high contracting parties reserving, however, to themselves the power of making,
consent, such relaxations in the strict execution of the present article, as they may think
respective interests of the two countries, upon the principle of mutual concessions, affording
other reciprocal or equivalent advantages.
ds which can or may be legally exported from the ports of either of the two countries, shall,
ort, pay the same duties of exportation, whether the exportation of such goods be made in
French vessels, provided the said vessels proceed, respectively, direct from the ports of the
to those of the other. And all the said goods so exported in British or French vessels, shall
ly entitled to the same bounties, drawbacks, and other allowances of the same nature, which
by the regulations of each country, respectively.
utually agreed between the high contracting parties, that in the intercourse of navigation
ir two countries, the vessels of any third power shall, in no case, obtain more favourable
an those stipulated, in the present convention, in favour of British and French vessels.
hing-boats of either of the two countries, which may be forced by stress of weather to seek
ports, or on the coast of the other country, shall not be subject to any duties or port charges
ption whatsoever; provided the said boats, when so driven in by stress of weather, shall not

discharge or receive on board any cargo, or portion of cargo, in the ports, or on the parts of th
where they shall have sought shelter.

6. It is agreed that the provisions of the present convention between the high contracting
shall be reciprocally extended and in force, in all the possessions subject to their respective domir
Europe.

7. The present convention shall be in force for the term of ten years, from the 5th of April
present year ; and further, until the end of twelve months after either of the high contracting parti
have given notice to the other of its intention to terminate its operation ; each of the high cont
parties reserving to itself the right of giving such notice to the other, at the end of the said term
years : and it is agreed between them, that, at the end of the twelve months' extension agreed to
sides, this convention, and all the stipulations thereof, shall altogether cease and determine.

8. the present convention shall be ratified, and the ratifications shall be exchanged in London,
the space of one month, or sooner if possible.

In witness whereof the respective plenipotentiaries have signed the same, and have affixed ther
seals of their arms.

Done at London, the 26th day of January, in the year of our Lord 1826.

     GEORGE CANNING.   LE PRINCE DE POLIGN
     WILLIAM HUSKISSON.

Additional Articles.

Article 1. French vessels shall be allowed to sail from any port whatever of the countries un:
dominion of his Most Christian Majesty, to all the colonies of the United Kingdom (except those pe
by the East India Company), and to import into the said colonies all kinds of merchandise (being
tions the growth or manufacture of France, or of any country under the dominion of France), w
exception of such as are prohibited to be imported into the said colonies, or are permitted to be i
only from countries under the British dominion ; and the said French vessels, as well as the merc
imported in the same, shall not be subject, in the colonies of the United Kingdom, to other or
duties than those to which British vessels may be subject, on importing the same merchandise fr
foreign country, or which are imposed upon the merchandise itself.

The same facilities shall be granted, reciprocally, in the colonies of France, with regard to the
ation, in British vessels, of all kinds of merchandise, (being productions the growth and manufa
the United Kingdom, or of any country under the British dominion,) with the exception of suc
prohibited to be imported into the said colonies, or are permitted to be imported only from c
under the dominion of France. And whereas all goods, the produce of any foreign country, may
imported into the colonies of the United Kingdom, in the ships of that country, with the except
limited list of specified articles, which can only be imported into the said colonies in British s
Majesty the King of the United Kingdom reserves to himself the power of adding to the sai
excepted articles any other, the produce of the French dominions, the addition whereof may a
his Majesty to be necessary for placing the commerce and navigation to be permitted to the sub
each of the high contracting parties with the colonies of the other, upon a footing of fair reciproc

2. French vessels shall be allowed to export from all the colonies of the United Kingdom (exce
possessed by the East India Company), all kinds of merchandise, which are not prohibited to be e
from such colonies in vessels other than those of Great Britain ; and the said vessels, as well as
chandise exported in the same, shall not be subject to other or higher duties than those to which
vessels may be subject, on exporting the said merchandise, or which are imposed upon the mer
itself; and they shall be entitled to the same bounties, drawbacks, and other allowances of th
nature, to which British vessels would be entitled, on such exportation.

The same facilities and privileges shall be granted, reciprocally, in all the colonies of France,
exportation, in British vessels, of all kinds of merchandise, which are not prohibited to be export
such colonies in vessels other than those of France.

These two additional articles shall have the same force and validity as if they were inserted,
word, in the convention signed this day. They shall be ratified, and the ratifications shall be ex
at the same time.

In witness whereof the respective plenipotentiaries have signed the same, and have affixed the
seals of their arms.

Done at London, Jan. 26. 1826.

     GEORGE CANNING.   LE PRINCE DE POLIG
     WILLIAM HUSKISSON.

A Treasury letter, dated 28th March, 1826, directs that French vessels, and their cargoe
imported or exported on board the same, according to the terms of the convention in the precedi
are, from 5th April, 1826, to be charged with such and the like duties only, of whatever kind they
that are charged on British vessels, and similar cargoes laden on board thereof ; and in like ma
same bounties, drawbacks, and allowances are to be paid on articles exported in French vessels,
paid, granted, or allowed on similar articles exported in British vessels. And the necessary ins
are to be transmitted to the officers in the colonies for carrying into effect the stipulations c
in the two additional articles of the said convention, respecting French vessels and their cargoes,
1st October, 1826.

HANSE TOWNS.

Convention of Commerce between His Britannic Majesty and the Free Hanseatic Republics of
Bremen, and Hamburgh, signed at London, Sept. 29. 1825.

Article 1. From and after the date hereof, British vessels entering or departing from the po
free Hanseatic republics of Lubeck, Bremen, or Hamburgh ; and Lubeck, Bremen, or H
vessels entering or departing from the ports of the United Kingdom of Great Britain and Irela
not be subject to any other or higher ship duties or charges than are or shall be levied on nation
entering or departing from such ports respectively.

2. All goods, whether the production of the territories of the free Hanseatic republics of
Bremen, or Hamburgh, or of any other country, which may be legally imported from any of th
the said republics into the United Kingdom of Great Britain and Ireland in British vessels, sha
manner, be permitted to be imported in Lubeck, Bremen, or Hamburgh vessels ; and all goods
the production of any of the dominions of his Britannic Majesty, or of any other country, whi
legally exported from the ports of the United Kingdom in British vessels, shall, in like manne
mitted to be exported from the said ports, in Lubeck, Bremen, or Hamburgh vessels. And
which may be legally imported into or exported from the ports of Lubeck, Bremen, or Han
national vessels, shall, in like manner, be permitted to be imported into or exported from th
Lubeck, Bremen, or Hamburgh, in British vessels.

3. All goods which can be legally imported into the ports of the United Kingdom directly
ports of Lubeck, Bremen, or Hamburgh, or either of them, shall be admitted at the same rat
whether imported in British vessels, or in vessels belonging to either of the said republics ; an
which can be legally exported from the United Kingdom, shall be entitled to the same boun
backs, and allowances, whether exported in British or Hanseatic vessels. And the like recipr

, in the ports of the said republics, in respect to all goods which can be legally imported into
from any or either of the said ports in vessels belonging to the United Kingdom.

ority or preference shall be given, directly or indirectly, by any or either of the contracting
by any company, corporation, or agent, acting on their behalf or under their authority, in the
any article, the growth, produce, or manufacture of their states respectively, imported into
n account of or in reference to the character of the vessel in which such article was imported ;
e true intent and meaning of the high contracting parties that no distinction or difference
all be made in this respect.

sideration of the limited extent of the territories belonging to the republics of Lubeck, Bremen,
rgh, and the intimate connection of trade and navigation subsisting between these republics,
stipulated and agreed, that any vessel which shall have been built in any or either of the ports
republics, and which shall be owned exclusively by a citizen or citizens of any or either of
f which the master shall also be a citizen of either of them, and provided three fourths of the
e subjects or citizens of any or either of the said republics, or of any or either of the states
n the Germanic Confederation, such vessel, so built, owned, and navigated, shall, for all the
this convention, be taken to be and be considered as a vessel belonging to Lubeck, Bremen,
h.

ssel, together with her cargo, belonging to either of the three free Hanseatic republics of
men, or Hamburgh, and coming from either of the said ports to the United Kingdom, shall,
urposes of this convention, be deemed to come from the country to which such vessel belongs ;
ish vessel and her cargo trading to the ports of Lubeck, Bremen, or Hamburgh, directly or in
hall, for the like purposes, be on the footing of a Hanseatic vessel and her cargo making the

rther mutually agreed, that no higher or other duties shall be levied, in any or either of the
e high contracting parties, upon any personal property of the subjects and citizens of each
on the removal of the same from the dominions or territory of such states, (either upon
of such property, or otherwise,) than are or shall be payable, in each state, upon the like
en removed by a subject or citizen of such state respectively.

h contracting parties reserve to themselves to enter upon additional stipulations for the pur-
tating and extending, even beyond what is comprehended in the convention of this date, the
relations of their respective subjects and dominions, citizens and territories, upon the principle
iprocal or equivalent advantages, as the case may be; and, in the event of any article or
concluded between the said high contracting parties, for giving effect to such stipulations, it
reed that the article or articles which may hereafter be so concluded shall be considered
art of the present convention.

sent convention shall be in force for the term of ten years from the date hereof; and further,
of twelve months after the King of the United Kingdom of Great Britain and Ireland, on
or the governments of the free Hanseatic republics of Lubeck, Bremen, or Hamburgh, or
m, on the other part, shall have given notice of their intention to terminate the same; each
gh contracting parties reserving to itself the right of giving such notice to the other, at the
d term of ten years: and it is hereby agreed between them, that, at the expiration of twelve
such notice shall have been received by either of the parties from the other, this convention,
ovisions thereof, shall altogether cease and determine, as far as regards the states giving and
h notice; it being always understood and agreed, that, if one or more of the Hanseatic
esaid shall, at the expiration of ten years from the date hereof, give or receive notice of the
aination of this convention, such convention shall, nevertheless, remain in full force and
ar as regards the remaining Hanseatic republics or republic which may not have given or
notice.

sent convention shall be ratified, and the ratification shall be exchanged at London within
om the date hereof, or sooner if possible.

whereof the respective plenipotentiaries have signed the same, and have affixed thereto the
arms.

London, Sept. 29. 1825.

GEORGE CANNING.
W. HUSKISSON.
JAMES COLQUHOUN.

MEXICO.

*ity, Commerce, and Navigation, between Great Britain and Mexico, signed at London,
December 26. 1826.*

here shall be perpetual amity between the dominions and subjects of his Majesty the King
Kingdom of Great Britain and Ireland, and the United States of Mexico, and their citizens.
all be, between all the territories of his Britannic Majesty in Europe and the territories of
iprocal freedom of commerce. The inhabitants of the two countries, respectively, shall
eely and securely to come, with their ships and cargoes, to all places and rivers in the
resaid, saving only such particular ports to which other foreigners shall not be permitted to
r into the same, and to remain and reside in any part of the said territories respectively ;
d occupy houses and warehouses for the purposes of their commerce : and, generally, the
traders of each nation, respectively, shall enjoy the most complete protection and security
erce.

ner, the respective ships of war, and post-office packets of the two countries, shall have
nd securely to come to all harbours, rivers, and places, saving only such particular ports (if
other foreign ships of war and packets shall not be permitted to come, to enter into the
or, and to remain there and refit ; subject always to the laws and statutes of the two
ectively.

of entering the places, ports, and rivers, mentioned in this article, the privilege of carrying
g trade is not understood, in which national vessels only are permitted to engage.
sty the King of the United Kingdom of Great Britain and Ireland engages further, that the
Mexico shall have the like liberty of commerce and navigation stipulated for in the pre-
in all his dominions situated out of Europe, to the full extent in which the same is permitted
hall be permitted hereafter, to any other nation.

or other duties shall be imposed on the importation into the dominions of his Britannic
y article of the growth, produce, or manufacture of Mexico, and no higher or other duties
ed on the importation into the territories of Mexico, of any articles of the growth, produce,
e of his Britannic Majesty's dominions, than are or shall be payable on the like articles,
th, produce, or manufacture of any other foreign country ; nor shall any other or higher
ges be imposed in the territories or dominions of either of the contracting parties, on the
any articles to the territories of the other, than such as are or may be payable on the
the like articles to any other foreign country ; nor shall any prohibition be imposed upon
of any articles the growth, produce, or manufacture of his Britannic Majesty's dominions,
erritories of Mexico, to or from the said dominions of his Britannic Majesty, or to or from
ries of Mexico, which shall not equally extend to all other nations.

5. No higher or other duties or charges on account of tonnage, light or harbour dues, pilotag in case of damage or shipwreck, or any other local charges, shall be imposed, in any of th Mexico, on British vessels, than those payable in the same ports by Mexican vessels*; nor, in of his Britannic Majesty's territories, on Mexican vessels, than shall be payable, in the sa on British vessels.

6. The same duties shall be paid on the importation into the territories of Mexico, of any growth, produce, or manufacture of his Britannic Majesty's dominions, whether such importa be in Mexican* or in British vessels; and the same duties shall be paid on the importatio dominions of his Britannic Majesty, of any article the growth, produce, or manufacture o whether such importation shall be in British or in Mexican vessels. The same duties shall be the same bounties and drawbacks allowed, on the exportation to Mexico of any articles of th produce, or manufacture of his Britannic Majesty's dominions, whether such exportation s Mexican or in British vessels; and the same duties shall be paid, and the same bounties and allowed, on the exportation of any articles the growth, produce, or manufacture of Mexico, to hi Majesty's dominions, whether such exportation shall be in British or in Mexican vessels.

7. In order to avoid any misunderstanding with respect to the regulations which may re constitute a British or Mexican * vessel, it is hereby agreed that all vessels built in the domini Britannic Majesty, or vessels which shall have been captured from an enemy by his Britannic ships of war, or by subjects of his said Majesty furnished with letters of marque by the Lords Com of the Admiralty, and regularly condemned in one of his said Majesty's prize courts as a lawf which shall have been condemned in any competent court for the breach of the laws made f vention of the slave trade, and owned, navigated, and registered according to the laws of Gre shall be considered as British vessels; and that all vessels built in the territories of Mexico, c from the enemy by the ships of Mexico, and condemned under similar circumstances, and w be owned by any citizen or citizens thereof, and whereof the master and three fourths of the m citizens of Mexico, excepting where the laws provide for any extreme cases, shall be con Mexican vessels.

And it is further agreed, that every vessel, qualified to trade as above described, under the of this treaty, shall be furnished with a register, passport, or sea letter, under the signature of person authorised to grant the same, according to the laws of the respective countries (the form shall be communicated), certifying the name, occupation, and residence of the owner or own dominions of his Britannic Majesty, or in the territories of Mexico, as the case may be; and they, is, or are, the sole owner or owners, in the proportion to be specified; together with burthen, and description of the vessel as to built and measurement, and the several particulars c the national character of the vessel, as the case may be.

8. All merchants, commanders of ships, and others, the subjects of his Britannic Majesty, full liberty, in all the territories of Mexico, to manage their own affairs themselves, or to comm the management of whomsoever they please, as broker, factor, agent, or interpreter; nor sh obliged to employ any other persons for those purposes than those employed by Mexicans, nor t any other salary or remuneration than such as is paid, in like cases, by Mexican citizens; ar freedom shall be allowed, in all cases, to the buyer and seller, to bargain and fix the price of imported into or exported from Mexico, as they shall see good, observing the laws and customs of the country. The same privileges shall be enjoyed in the dominions of his Britann by the citizens of Mexico, under the same conditions.

The citizens and subjects of the contracting parties, in the territories of each other, shall enjoy full and perfect protection for their persons and property, and shall have free and ope the courts of justice in the said countries, respectively, for the prosecution and defence of their and they shall be at liberty to employ, in all causes, the advocates, attorneys, or agents o description, whom they may think proper; and they shall enjoy, in this respect, the same privileges therein as native citizens.

9. In whatever relates to the succession to personal estates, by will or otherwise, and the personal property of every sort and denomination, by sale, donation, exchange, or testament other manner whatsoever, as also the administration of justice, the subjects and citizens of th tracting parties shall enjoy, in their respective dominions and territories, the same privilege and rights, as native subjects; and shall not be charged, in any of these respects, with any hig or duties, than those which are paid, or may be paid, by the native subjects or citizens of th whose dominions or territories they may be resident.

10. In all that relates to the police of the ports, the lading and unlading of ships, th merchandise, goods, and effects, the subjects of his Britannic Majesty, and the citizens respectively, shall be subject to the local laws and regulations of the dominions and territori they may reside. They shall be exempted from all compulsory military service, whether by No forced loans shall be levied upon them; nor shall their property be subject to any oth requisitions, or taxes, than such as are paid by the native subjects or citizens of the contractir their respective dominions.

11. It shall be free for each of the two contracting parties to appoint consuls for the protecti to reside in the dominions and territories of the other party; but, before any consul shall act shall, in the usual form, be approved and admitted by the government to which he is sent; a the contracting parties may except from the residence of consuls such particular places as eit may judge fit to be excepted. The Mexican diplomatic agents and consuls shall enjoy, in th of his Britannic Majesty, whatever privileges, exceptions, and immunities are or shall be gran of the same rank belonging to the most favoured nation; and, in like manner, the diplomati consuls of his Britannic Majesty in the Mexican territories shall enjoy, according to the s procity, whatever privileges, exceptions, and immunities are or may be granted to the Mexica agents and consuls in the dominions of his Britannic Majesty.

12. For the better security of commerce between the subjects of his Britannic Majesty and of the Mexican States, it is agreed that if, at any time, any interruption of friendly interco rupture, should unfortunately take place between the two contracting parties, the mercha upon the coasts shall be allowed six months, and those of the interior a whole year, to w accounts, and dispose of their property; and a safe conduct shall be given to them to embark which they shall themselves select. All those who are established in the respective dominio tories of the two contracting parties, in the exercise of any trade or special employment, s privilege of remaining and continuing such trade and employment therein, without any mar ruption, in full enjoyment of their liberty and property, as long as they behave peaceably, ar offence against the laws: and their goods and effects, of whatever description they may be liable to seizure or sequestration, or to any other charges or demands than those which upon the like effects or property belonging to the native subjects or citizens of the respectiv or territories in which such subjects or citizens may reside. In the same case, debts, betweer public funds, and the shares of companies, shall never be confiscated, sequestered, or detaine

13. The subjects of his Britannic Majesty, residing in the Mexican territories, shall en houses, persons, and properties, the protection of the government; and, continuing in posses they now enjoy, they shall not be disturbed, molested, or annoyed, in any manner, on acc

---

* See additional articles at the end of this treaty.

provided they respect that of the nation in which they reside, as well as the constitution, laws,
ms of the country. They shall continue to enjoy, to the full, the privilege already granted to
urying, in the places already assigned for that purpose, such subjects of his Britannic Majesty
e within the Mexican territories; nor shall the funerals and sepulchres of the dead be disturbed
ay, or upon any account. The citizens of Mexico shall enjoy, in all the dominions of his
Majesty, the same protection, and shall be allowed the free exercise of their religion, in
private, either within their own houses, or in the chapels and places of worship set apart for
ose.

subjects of his Britannic Majesty shall, on no account or pretext whatsoever, be disturbed or
in the peaceable possession and enjoyment of whatever rights, privileges, and immunities they
ny time enjoyed within the limits described and laid down in a convention signed between his
sty and the King of Spain, on the 14th of July, 1786; whether such rights, privileges, and
es shall be derived from the stipulations of the said convention, or from any other concession
ty, at any time, have been made by the King of Spain, or his predecessors, to British subjects
ers residing and following their lawful occupations within the limits aforesaid: the two
g parties reserving, however, for some more fitting opportunity, the further arrangements on
e.

government of Mexico engages to co-operate with his Britannic Majesty for the total abolition
ve trade, and to prohibit all persons inhabiting within the territories of Mexico, in the most
manner, from taking any share in such trade.

two contracting parties reserve to themselves the right of treating and agreeing hereafter,
e to time, upon such other articles as may appear to them to contribute still further to the
ent of their mutual intercourse, and the advancement of the general interests of their respective
nd citizens; and such articles as may be so agreed upon, shall, when duly ratified, be regarded
g a part of the present treaty, and shall have the same force as those now contained in it.

present treaty shall be ratified, and the ratifications shall be exchanged at London, within the
x months, or sooner if possible.

ss whereof the respective plenipotentiaries have signed the same, and have affixed thereto their
seals.

at London, the 26th day of December, in the year of our Lord 1826.

WILLIAM HUSKISSON   SEBASTIAN CAMACHO.
JAMES J. MORIER.

Additional Articles.

reas in the present state of Mexican shipping, it would not be possible for Mexico to receive the
tage of the reciprocity established by the articles 5, 6, 7. of the treaty signed this day, if that
e 7th article which stipulates that, in order to be considered as a Mexican ship, a ship shall
ave been *built* in Mexico, should be strictly and literally observed, and immediately brought
tion; it is agreed that, for the space of ten years, to be reckoned from the date of the exchange
ications of this treaty, any ships, *wheresoever built*, being *bonâ fide* the property of and wholly
one or more citizens of Mexico, and whereof the master and three fourths of the mariners, at
lso natural-born citizens of Mexico, or persons domiciliated in Mexico, by act of the govern-
wful subjects of Mexico, to be certified according to the laws of that country, shall be consi-
exican ships: his Majesty the King of the United Kingdom of Great Britain and Ireland
o himself the right, at the end of the said term of ten years, to claim the principle of reciprocal
stipulated for in the article 7. above referred to, if the interests of British navigation shall be
e prejudiced by the present exception to that reciprocity, in favour of Mexican shipping.

urther agreed that, for the like term of ten years, the stipulations contained in articles 5. and 6.
ent treaty being suspended; and in lieu thereof, it is hereby agreed that, until the expiration
term of ten years, British ships entering into the ports of Mexico, from the United Kingdom
ritain and Ireland, or any other of his Britannic Majesty's dominions, and all articles the
oduce, or manufacture of the United Kingdom, or of any of the said dominions, imported in
shall pay no other or higher duties than are or may hereafter be payable, in the said ports, by
and the like goods, the growth, produce, or manufacture of the most favoured nation; and,
y, it is agreed, that Mexican ships entering into the ports of the United Kingdom of Great
d Ireland, or any other of his Britannic Majesty's dominions, from any port of the states of
d all articles the growth, produce, or manufacture of the said states, imported in such ships,
o other or higher duties than are or may hereafter be payable, in the said ports, by the ships,
e goods, the growth, produce, or manufacture of the most favoured nation; and that no higher
be paid, or bounties or drawbacks allowed, on the exportation of any article, the growth, pro-
anufacture of the dominions of either country, in the ships of the other, than upon the
s of the like articles in the ships of any other foreign country.

nderstood that, at the end of the said term of ten years, the stipulations of the said 5th and
shall, from thenceforward, be in full force between the two countries.

ent additional articles shall have the same force and validity as if they were inserted, word for
e treaty signed this day. They shall be ratified, and the ratifications shall be exchanged at the

s whereof the respective plenipotentiaries have signed the same, and have affixed thereto their
eals.

t London, the 26th day of December, in the year of our Lord 1826.

WILLIAM HUSKISSON.   SEBASTIAN CAMACHO.
JAMES J. MORIER.

in council, dated September 3. 1827, orders, that vessels of the United States of Mexico,
e ports of the United Kingdom of Great Britain and Ireland in ballast, or laden direct from
orts of Mexico, or departing from the ports of the said United Kingdom, together with the
oard the same, such cargoes consisting of articles which may be legally imported or exported,
subject to any other or higher duties or charges whatever than are or shall be levied on
els entering or departing from such ports, or on similar articles when imported into, or
m, such ports in British vessels; and also such articles, when exported from the said ports in
e United States of Mexico respectively, shall be entitled to the same bounties, drawbacks, and
hat are granted on similar articles when exported in British vessels.

— Treaties similar to the above have been negotiated with Columbia, Buenos Ayres, &c.

NETHERLANDS.

ween *His Britannic Majesty and the King of the Netherlands, respecting Territories and
Commerce in the East Indies, signed at London, March* 17. 1824.

The high contracting parties engage to admit the subjects of each other to trade with their
ossessions in the Eastern Archipelago, and on the continent of India, and in Ceylon, upon the
e most favoured nation; their respective subjects conforming themselves to the local regu-
ch settlement.

jects and vessels of one nation shall not pay, upon importation or exportation, at the ports of

the other in the Eastern seas, any duty at a rate beyond the double of that at which the subjec vessels of the nation to which the port belongs, are charged.

The duties paid on exports or imports at a British port, on the continent of India, or in Ceyl Dutch bottoms, shall be arranged so as, in no case, to be charged at more than double the amount duties paid by British subjects, and on British bottoms.

In regard to any article upon which no duty is imposed, when imported or exported by the subje on the vessels, of the nation to which the port belongs, the duty charged upon the subjects or ve the other shall, in no case, exceed six per cent.

3. The high contracting parties engage, that no treaty hereafter made by either, with any native in the Eastern seas, shall contain any article tending, either expressly, or by the imposition of u duties, to exclude the trade of the other party from the ports of such native power: and that if, treaty now existing on either part, any article to that effect has been admitted, such article shall b gated upon the conclusion of the present treaty.

It is understood that, before the conclusion of the present treaty, communication has been m each of the contracting parties to the other, of all treaties or engagements subsisting between them, respectively, and any native power in the Eastern seas; and that the like communication made of all such treaties concluded by them, respectively, hereafter.

4. Their Britannic and Netherland Majesties engage to give strict orders, as well to their ci military authorities, as to their ships of war, to respect the freedom of trade, established by articl and 3.; and, in no case, to impede a free communication of the natives in the Eastern Archipelag the ports of the two governments, respectively, or of the subjects of the two governments with th belonging to native powers.

5. Their Britannic and Netherland Majesties, in like manner, engage to concur effectually in rep piracy in those seas: they will not grant either asylum or protection to vessels engaged in pira they will, in no case, permit the ships or merchandise captured by such vessels, to be introduced sited, or sold, in any of their possessions.

6. It is agreed that orders shall be given by the two governments to their officers and agents East, not to form any new settlement on any of the islands in the Eastern seas, without previous au from their respective governments in Europe.

7. The Molucca islands, and especially Amboyna, Banda, Ternate, and their immediate depend are excepted from the operation of the 1st, 2d, 3d, and 4th articles, until the Netherland gove shall think fit to abandon the monopoly of spices; but if the said government shall, at any time p to such abandonment of the monopoly, allow the subjects of any power, other than an Asiatic power, to carry on any commercial intercourse with the said islands, the subjects of his Britannic shall be admitted to such intercourse, upon a footing precisely similar.

8. His Netherland Majesty cedes to his Britannic Majesty all his establishment on the cont India; and renounces all privileges and exemptions enjoyed or claimed in virtue of those establis

9. The factory of Fort Marlborough, and all the English possessions on the island of Sumatra, are ceded to his Netherland Majesty: and his Britannic Majesty further engages that no British set shall be formed on that island, nor any treaty concluded by British authority, with any native chief, or state therein.

10. The town and fort of Malacca, and its dependencies, are hereby ceded to his Britannic M and his Netherland Majesty engages, for himself and his subjects, never to form any establishmen part of the peninsula of Malacca, or to conclude any treaty with any native prince, chief, or state

13. All the colonies, possessions, and establishments which are ceded by the preceding articles, delivered up to the officers of the respective sovereigns on the 1st March, 1825. The fortificatic remain in the state in which they shall be at the period of the notification of this treaty in India; claim shall be made, on either side, for ordnance, or stores of any description, either left or rem the ceding power, nor for any arrears of revenue, or any charge of administration whatever.

16. It is agreed that all accounts and reclamations, arising out of the restoration of Java, ar possessions, to the officers of his Netherland Majesty in the East Indies, — as well those which subject of a convention made at Java on the 24th of June, 1817, between the commissioners of nations, as all others, — shall be finally and completely closed and satisfied, on the payment of th 100,000l., sterling money, to be made in London on the part of the Netherlands, before the expi the year 1825.

17. The present treaty shall be ratified, and the ratifications exchanged at London within three from the date hereof, or sooner if possible.

In witness whereof the respective plenipotentiaries have signed the same, and affixed there seal of their arms.

Done at London, the 17th day of March, in the year of our Lord 1824.

GEORGE CANNING. CHARLES WATKINS WILLIAMS WYNN. H. FAGEL. A. R. F

PORTUGAL.

Treaty of Commerce between Great Britain and Portugal, signed at Lisbon, December 27.

Article 1. His Sacred Royal Majesty of Portugal promises, both in his own name and th successors, to admit, for ever hereafter, into Portugal, the woollen cloths, and the rest of th manufactures of the Britons, as was accustomed till they were prohibited by the laws; neverthel this condition;

2. That is to say, that her Sacred Royal Majesty of Great Britain shall, in her own name an her successors, be obliged for ever hereafter, to admit the wines of the growth of Portugal into so that at no time, whether there shall be peace or war between the kingdoms of Br France, any thing more shall be demanded for these wines, by the name of custom or duty, or soever other title, directly or indirectly, whether they shall be imported into Great Britain in hogsheads, or other casks, than what shall be demanded from the like quantity or measure c wine, deducting or abating a third part of the custom or duty: but if at any time this ded abatement of customs, which is to be made as aforesaid, shall in any manner be attempted a diced, it shall be just and lawful for his Sacred Royal Majesty of Portugal again to prohibit th cloths, and the rest of the British woollen manufactures.

3. The most excellent Lords of the plenipotentiaries promise, and take upon themselves, above named masters shall ratify this treaty, and that within the space of two months the ra shall be exchanged.

Given at Lisbon, the 27th of December, 1703.

JOHN METHUEN. MARCHIS ALEGRET

Treaty of Commerce and Navigation between Great Britain and Portugal, signed at Rio de Ja 19th February, 1810.

1. Peace established.

2. There shall be reciprocal liberty of commerce and navigation between the respective subj two high contracting parties, in all the territories and dominions of either. They may tra sojourn, or establish themselves, in all the ports, cities, towns, countries, provinces, or places w

each of the two high contracting parties, except in those from which all foreigners whatso-
enerally and positively excluded, the names of which places may be hereafter specified in a
icle of this treaty. Provided, however, that it be thoroughly understood that any place be-
either of the two high contracting parties, which may hereafter be opened to the commerce
cts of any other country, shall thereby be considered as equally opened, and upon correspond-
to the subjects of the other high contracting party, in the same manner as if it had been ex-
ilated by the present treaty. And his Britannic Majesty, and his Royal Highness the Prince
'ortugal, do hereby bind themselves not to grant any favour, privilege, or immunity in matters
e and navigation, to the subjects of any other state, which shall not be also at the same time
extended to the subjects of the high contracting parties, gratuitously, if the concession in
at other state should have been gratuitous, and on giving, *quam proxime*, the same compen-
uivalent, in case the concession should have been conditional.

bjects of the two sovereigns respectively shall not pay in the ports, harbours, roads, cities,
laces whatsoever, belonging to either of them, any greater duties, taxes, or imposts (under
names they may be designated or included), than those that are paid by the subjects of the
ed nation; and the subjects of each of the high contracting parties shall enjoy, within the
f the other, the same rights, privileges, or exemptions, in matters of commerce and naviga-
e granted, or may hereafter be granted, to the subjects of the most favoured nation.

itannic Majesty, and his Royal Highness the Prince Regent of Portugal, do agree, that there
rrfect reciprocity on the subject of the duties and imposts to be paid by the vessels of the high
parties, within the several ports and anchoring places belonging to each of them; to wit, that
or the subjects of his Britannic Majesty shall not pay any higher duties or imposts (under
name they be designated or implied), within the dominions of his Royal Highness the Prince
ortugal, than the vessels belonging to the subjects of his Royal Highness the Prince Regent
shall be bound to pay within the dominions of his Britannic Majesty, and *vice versâ*. And
nt shall particularly extend to the payment of the duties known by the name of *Port Charges*,
d *Anchorage Duties*, which shall not, in any case, or under any pretext, be greater for British
in the dominions of Portugal, than for Portuguese vessels within the dominions of his
ajesty, and *vice versâ*.

high contracting parties do also agree, that the same rates of bounties and drawbacks shall
d in their respective ports upon the exportation of goods, whether those goods be exported
Portuguese vessels; that is, that British vessels shall enjoy the same favour in this respect,
ominions of Portugal, that may be shown to Portuguese vessels within the dominions of his
ajesty, and *vice versâ*. The two high contracting parties do also agree, that goods coming
from the ports of either of them, shall pay the same duties, whether imported in British or
essels; or otherwise, that an increase of duties may be imposed upon goods coming into the
lominions of Portugal from those of his Britannic Majesty in British ships, equivalent, and
oortion to any increase of duties that may hereafter be imposed upon goods coming into the
iritannic Majesty from those of his Royal Highness the Prince Regent of Portugal, imported
e ships. And in order that this matter may be settled with due exactness, and that nothing
undetermined concerning it, it is agreed, that tables shall be drawn by each government,
specifying the difference of duties to be paid on goods so imported; and the tables (which
applicable to all the ports within the respective dominions of each of the contracting parties)
lged to form part of this present treaty.

avoid any differences or misunderstandings with respect to the regulations which may re-
istitute a British or Portuguese vessel, the high contracting parties agree in declaring, that
ilt in the dominions of his Britannic Majesty, and owned, navigated, and registered accord-
vs of Great Britain, shall be considered as British vessels; and that all vessels built in the
onging to Portugal, or ships taken by any of the vessels of war belonging to the Portuguese
or any of the inhabitants of the dominions of Portugal, having commissions or letters of
eprisal from the government of Portugal, and condemned as lawful prize in any court of
he Portuguese government, and owned by the subjects of his Royal Highness the Prince
rtugal, and whereof the master and three fourths of the mariners, at least, are subjects of
ghness the Prince Regent of Portugal, shall be considered as Portuguese vessels.

ual commerce and navigation of the subjects of Great Britain and Portugal, respectively,
nd seas of Asia, are expressly permitted to the same degree as they have heretofore been
e two crowns: and the commerce and navigation thus permitted, shall be placed on the
commerce and navigation of the most favoured nation trading in the ports and seas of Asia,
that neither of the high contracting parties shall grant any favour or privilege in matters
and navigation to the subjects of any other state trading within the ports and seas of Asia,
ot be also granted, *quam proxime* on the same terms, to the subjects of the other contracting
ritannic Majesty engages not to make any regulation which may be prejudicial or incon-
commerce and navigation of the subjects of his Royal Highness the Prince Regent of
in the ports and seas of Asia, to the extent which is or may hereafter be permitted to the
nation. And his Royal Highness the Prince Regent of Portugal does also engage not to
ilations which may be prejudicial or inconvenient to the commerce and navigation of the
Britannic Majesty within the ports, seas, and dominions opened to them by virtue of the

shall be established for the purpose of furthering the public service of the two courts, and
commercial intercourse of their respective subjects. A convention shall be concluded
he basis of that which was signed at Rio de Janeiro, on the 14th day of September, 1808, in
the terms upon which the packets are to be established, which convention shall be ratified
me with the present treaty.

ds and articles whatsoever, of the produce, manufacture, industry, or invention of the do-
ubjects of his Britannic Majesty, shall be admitted into all the ports and dominions of his
ss the Prince Regent of Portugal, as well in Europe as in America, Africa, and Asia,
gned to British or Portuguese subjects, on paying, generally and solely, duties to the amount
according to the value which shall be set upon them by a tariff or table of valuations,
Portuguese language *pauta*, the principal basis of which shall be the sworn invoice cost of
oods, merchandises, and articles, taking also into consideration (as far as may be just or
e current prices thereof in the country into which they are imported. This tariff or valua-
etermined and settled by an equal number of British and Portuguese merchants of known
onour, with the assistance on the part of the British merchants, of his Britannic Majesty's
, or consul, and on the part of the Portuguese merchants with the assistance of the super-
dministrator general of the customs, or of their respective deputies. And the aforesaid
made and promulgated in each of the ports belonging to his Royal Highness the Prince
ugal, in which there are or may be Custom-houses. And it shall be revised and altered if
n time to time, either in the whole, or in part, whenever the subjects of his Britannic
nt within the dominions of his Royal Highness the Prince Regent of Portugal, shall make
that effect through the medium of his Britannic Majesty's consul general, or consul, or
rading and commercial subjects of Portugal shall make the same requisition on their own

n goods should hereafter arrive in the ports of the Portuguese dominions without having

been specifically valued and rated in the new tariff or *pauta*, they shall be admitted on paying
duties of 15 per cent. *ad valorem*, according to the invoices of the goods, which shall be duly
and sworn to by the parties importing the same. And in case that any suspicion of fraud, or un
tices, should arise, the invoices shall be examined, and the real value of the goods ascertained b
ence to an equal number of British and Portuguese merchants of known integrity and honou
case of a difference of opinion amongst them, followed by an equality of votes upon the subject,
then nominate another merchant likewise of known integrity and honour, to whom the matte
ultimately referred, and whose decision thereon shall be final, and without appeal. And in ca
voice should appear to have been fair and correct, the goods specified in it shall be admitted,
the duties above mentioned of 15 per cent. ; and the expenses, if any, of the examination of th
shall be defrayed by the party who called its fairness and correctness into question. But if th
should be found to be fraudulent and unfair, then the goods and merchandises shall be bought
officers of the customs on the account of the Portuguese government, according to the value sp
the invoice, with an addition of 10 per cent. to the sum so paid for them by the officers of the
the Portuguese government engaging for the payment of the goods so valued and purchase
officers of the customs within the space of 15 days ; and the expenses, if any, of the examinat
fraudulent invoice shall be paid by the party who presented it as just and fair.

17. Articles of military and naval stores brought into the ports of his Royal Highness the Prin
of Portugal, which the Portuguese government may be desirous of taking for its own use, sha
for without delay at the prices appointed by the proprietors, who shall not be compelled to
articles on any other terms.

If the Portuguese government shall take into its own care and custody any cargo, or part o
with a view to purchase, or otherwise, the Portuguese government shall be responsible for ar
or injury that the same may receive while in the care and custody of the officers of the P
government.

18. His Royal Highness the Prince Regent of Portugal is pleased to grant to the subject
Britain the privilege of being *assignantes* for the duties to be paid in the Custom-houses of
Highness's dominions, on the same terms, and on giving the same security, as are required
subjects of Portugal.

On the other hand, the subjects of the crown of Portugal shall receive, as far as it may be ju
the same favour in the Custom-houses of Great Britain as is shown to the natural subjects of his
Majesty.

19. His Britannic Majesty does promise and engage, that all goods and articles whatsoever,
duce, manufacture, industry, or invention of the dominions or subjects of the Prince Regent of
shall be admitted into the ports and dominions of his Britannic Majesty, on paying generally an
same duties that are paid upon similar articles by the subjects of the most favoured nation.

If any reduction of duties should take place exclusively in favour of British goods importe
dominions of Portugal, an equivalent reduction shall take place on Portuguese goods and me
imported into his Britannic Majesty's dominions, and *vice versâ* ; the articles upon which su
lent reduction is to take place being settled by previous concert and agreement between th
contracting parties.

It is understood, that any such reduction so granted by either party to the other, shall not
afterwards (except upon the same terms and for the same compensation) in favour of any oth
nation whatsoever. And this declaration is to be considered as reciprocal on the part of th
contracting parties.

20. But as there are some articles of the growth and production of Brazil, which are excl
the markets and home consumption of the British dominions, such as sugar, coffee, and oth
similar to the produce of the British colonies ; his Britannic Majesty, willing to favour and
much as possible) the commerce of the subjects of his Royal Highness the Prince Regent o
consents and permits that the said articles, as well as all others the growth and produce of Bra
other parts of the Portuguese dominions, may be received and warehoused in all the ports of his
which shall be by law appointed to be warehousing ports for those articles, for the purpose of
ation, under due regulation, exempted from the greater duties with which they would be ch
they destined for consumption within the British dominions, and liable only to the reduced
expenses on warehousing and re-exportation.

21. In like manner, notwithstanding the general privilege of admission thus granted i
article of the present treaty by the Prince Regent of Portugal, in favour of all goods the pr
manufacture of the British dominions, his Royal Highness reserves to himself the right o
heavy, and even prohibitory duties on all articles known by the name of *British East Indian
West Indian Produce*, such as sugar and coffee, which cannot be admitted for consumption in
guese dominions, by reason of the same principle of colonial policy which prevents the free adr
the British dominions of corresponding articles of Brazilian produce.

But his Royal Highness the Prince Regent of Portugal consents that all the ports of his
where there are or may be Custom-houses, shall be free ports for the reception and admission o
whatsoever, the produce and manufacture of the British dominions, not destined for the cons
the place at which they may be received or admitted, but for re-exportation, either for other
dominions of Portugal, or for those of other states. And the articles thus received and admit
to due regulations) shall be exempted from the duties with which they would be charged, if
the consumption of the place at which they may be landed or warehoused, and liable only
expenses that may be paid by articles of Brazilian produce received and warehoused for re
in the ports of his Britannic Majesty's dominions.

22. His Royal Highness the Prince Regent of Portugal is pleased to declare the port of St. C
be a *Free Port*, according to the terms mentioned in the preceding article of the present treat

23. His Royal Highness the Prince Regent of Portugal is pleased to render Goa a *Free I
permit the free toleration of all religious sects whatever in that city and in its dependencies.

24. All trade with the Portuguese possessions situated upon the eastern coast of the contine
(in articles not included in the exclusive contracts possessed by the crown of Portugal) whic
been formerly allowed to the subjects of Great Britain, is confirmed and secured to them r
ever, in the same manner as the trade which has hitherto been permitted to Portuguese su
ports and seas of Asia is confirmed and secured to them by virtue of the 6th article of the pre

25. His Britannic Majesty consents to wave the right of creating factories or incorporat
British merchants, within the dominions of Portugal : provided, however, that this shall not
subjects of his Britannic Majesty, residing within the dominions of Portugal, of the full en
individuals engaged in commerce, of any of those rights and privileges which they did or m
as members of incorporated commercial bodies ; and also that the commerce and trade ca
British subjects shall not be restricted, or otherwise affected, by any commercial compan
possessing exclusive privileges and favours within the dominions of Portugal. And his Roy
the Prince Regent of Portugal does also engage, that he will not permit that any other nat
shall possess factories or incorporated bodies of merchants within his dominions, so long as Bri
shall not be established therein.

26. The two high contracting parties agree, that they will forthwith proceed to the revisior
former treaties subsisting between the two crowns, for the purpose of ascertaining what stip
tained in them are, in the present state of affairs, proper to be continued or renewed.

reed, that the stipulations contained in former treaties concerning the admission of the wines of on the one hand, and the woollen cloths of Great Britain on the other, shall at present remain . In the same manner it is agreed, that the privileges and immunities granted by either con-party to the subjects of the other, whether by treaty, decree, or *alvara*, shall remain unaltered, e power granted by former treaties, of carrying in the ships of either country, goods of any de-whatever, the property of the enemies of the other country, which power is now mutually and renounced and abrogated.

 reciprocal liberty of commerce and navigation, declared by the present treaty, shall be con- extend to all goods whatsoever, except those articles the property of the enemies of either contraband of war.

der the name of contraband or prohibited articles shall be comprehended not only arms, cannon, ses, mortars, petards, bombs, grenades, saucisses, carcasses, carriages for cannon, musket rests, s, gunpowder, match, saltpetre, ball, pikes, swords, head pieces, helmets, cuirasses, halberts, holsters, belts, horses, and their harness, but generally all other articles that may have been as contraband in any former treaties concluded by Great Britain or by Portugal with other But goods which have not been wrought into the form of warlike instruments, or which cannot uch, shall not be reputed contraband, much less such as have been already wrought and made her purposes, all which shall be deemed not contraband, and may be freely carried by the sub-th sovereigns, even to places belonging to an enemy, excepting only such places as are besieged, , or invested by sea or land.

ase any vessels of war, or merchantment, should be shipwrecked on the coasts of either of the racting parties, all such parts of the vessels, or of the furniture or appurtenances thereof, as also s shall be saved, or the produce thereof, shall be faithfully restored upon the same being claimed prietors or their factors duly authorised, paying only the expenses incurred in the preservation cording to the rate of salvage settled on both sides (saving at the same time the rights and f each nation, the abolition or modification of which shall, however, be treated upon in the re they shall be contrary to the stipulations of the present article); and the high contracting l mutually interpose their authority, that such of their subjects as shall take advantage of any rtune may be severely punished.

further agreed, that both his Britannic Majesty and his Royal Highness the Prince Regent of shall not only refuse to receive any pirates or sea-rovers whatsoever into any of their havens, es, or towns, or permit any of their subjects, citizens, or inhabitants, on either part, to receive them in their ports, to harbour them in their houses, or to assist them in any manner whatso-further, that they shall cause all such pirates and sea-rovers, and all persons who shall receive, assist them, to be brought to condign punishment for a terror and example to others. And hips, with the goods or merchandises taken by them, and brought into the ports belonging to the high contracting parties, shall be seized, as far as they can be discovered, and shall be re-he owners, or the factors duly authorised or deputed by them in writing, proper evidence being to prove the property, even in case such effects should have passed into other hands by sale, certained that the buyers knew or might have known that they had been piratically taken.

any time there should arise any disagreement, breach of friendship, or rupture between the the high contracting parties, which God forbid, (which rupture shall not be deemed to exist ecalling or sending home of their respective ambassadors and ministers,) the subjects of each parties, residing in the dominions of the other, shall have the privilege of remaining and con-eir trade therein, without any manner of interruption, so long as they behave peaceably, and offence against the laws and ordinances; and in case their conduct should render them sus-l the respective governments should be obliged to order them to remove, the term of twelve all be allowed them for that purpose, in order that they may retire with their effects and pro-ther intrusted to individuals, or to the state.

ame time it is to be understood that this favour is not to be extended to those who shall act in r contrary to the established laws.

present treaty shall be unlimited in point of duration, that the obligations and conditions ex-mplied in it shall be perpetual and immutable; and they shall not be changed or affected in r in case his Royal Highness the Prince Regent of Portugal should again establish the seat of uese monarchy within the European dominions of that crown.

he two high contracting parties do reserve to themselves the right of jointly examining and e several articles of this treaty at the end of fifteen years, counted in the first instance from the exchange of the ratifications thereof *, and of then proposing, discussing, and making such ts or additions, as the real interests of their respective subjects may seem to require. It being that any stipulation which at the period of revision of the treaty shall be objected to by either contracting parties, shall be considered as suspended in its operation until the discussion con-t stipulation shall be terminated, due notice being previously given to the other contracting intended suspension of such stipulation, for the purpose of avoiding mutual inconvenience.

everal stipulations and conditions of the present treaty shall begin to have effect from the Britannic Majesty's ratification thereof; and the mutual exchange of ratifications shall take city of London, within the space of four months, or sooner if possible, to be computed from he signature of the present treaty.

 the city of Rio de Janeiro, on the 19th day of February, in the year of our Lord 1810.

STRANGFORD.   CONDE DE LINHARES.

---

between the British and Portuguese Commissioners, on four Points connected with the Execution of the Treaty of 1810. Signed at London, 18th December, 1812.

icial certificate of registry, signed by the proper officer of the British customs, shall be deemed identify a British built ship; and on the production of such certificate she shall be admitted ny of the ports within the dominions of Portugal.

he importation of any goods from the United Kingdom, into any of the ports in the dominions all such goods shall be accompanied by the original cockets, signed and sealed by the proper he British customs at the port of shipping, and the cockets belonging to each ship shall be rogressively, the total number stated on the first and last cocket, by the proper officers of the final clearance of each vessel at the British port: and it is further agreed, that prior to arance by the searchers at the shipping port, the cockets for each ship must be collected together, to which shall be annexed a paper, with the number of the cockets, sealed with eal, and signed by the searchers; the cockets, so collected, shall be produced, together with sworn to by the captain, to the Portuguese consul, who shall certify the same on the mani-kets, thus secured together, and the manifest, so authenticated, to be returned to the searcher, he final clearance of the ship.

ced to place the Portuguese merchant on the same footing with the British, both with regard of scavage and package payable to the corporation of London, and the duties payable on he corporation of the Trinity-house in London. To effect this, and at the same time to pre-artered rights of the corporation of London, and of the Trinity-house, it will be necessary

* These ratifications were exchanged in London, on the 19th of June, 1810.

that those duties should, in the first instance, be paid as at present, and in all cases where it shall
that the Portuguese merchant shall have paid more than the British, the difference to be returne
out expense, in such manner as the British government shall direct.

4. The importer shall, on making the entry at the Portuguese Custom-house, sign a declaration
value of his goods, to such amount as he shall deem proper; and in case the Portuguese exa
officers should be of opinion that such valuation is insufficient, they shall be at liberty to take the
on paying the importer the amount, according to his declaration, with the addition of 10 per ce
also returning the duty paid.

The amount to be paid on the goods being delivered to the Portuguese officer, which must be
fifteen days from the first detention of the goods.

London, 18th December, 1812.

R. Frewin.　　　　　　　　　　　　A. T. Sm. Pa
Wm. Burn.　　　　　　　　　　　　A. I. Da Cos

PRUSSIA.

Convention of Commerce between His Britannic Majesty and the King of Prussia, signed at
April 2. 1824.

Article 1. From and after the 1st day of May next, Prussian vessels entering or departing f
ports of the United Kingdom of Great Britain and Ireland, and British vessels entering or departi
the ports of his Prussian Majesty's dominions, shall not be subject to any other or higher d
charges whatever, than are or shall be levied on national vessels entering or departing from su
respectively.

2. All articles of the growth, produce, or manufacture of any of the dominions of either of t
contracting parties, which are or shall be permitted to be imported into or exported from the por
United Kingdom and of Prussia, respectively, in vessels of the one country, shall, in like manner,
mitted to be imported into and exported from those ports in vessels of the other.

3. All articles not of the growth, produce, or manufacture of the dominions of his Britannic I
which can legally be imported from the United Kingdom of Great Britain and Ireland into the
Prussia, in British ships, shall be subject only to the same duties as are payable upon the like ar
imported in Prussian ships; and the same reciprocity shall be observed in the ports of the Unite
dom, in respect to all articles not the growth, produce, or manufacture of the dominions of his I
Majesty, which can legally be imported into the ports of the United Kingdom in Prussian ships.

4. All goods, which can legally be imported into the ports of either country, shall be admitte
same rate of duty, whether imported in vessels of the other country, or in national vessels; and a
which can be legally exported from the ports of either country, shall be entitled to the same b
drawbacks, and allowances, whether exported in vessels of the other country, or in national vesse

5. No priority or preference shall be given, directly or indirectly, by the government of either
or by any company, corporation, or agent, acting on its behalf, or under its authority, in the pur
any article, the growth, produce, or manufacture of either country, imported into the other, on
of, or in reference to, the character of the vessel in which such article was imported; it being
intent and meaning of the high contracting parties, that no distinction or difference whatever
made in this respect.

6. The present convention shall be in force for the term of ten years from the date hereof; and
until the end of twelve months after either of the high contracting parties shall have given noti
other of its intention to terminate the same; each of the high contracting parties reserving to
right of giving such notice to the other, at the end of the said term of ten years: and it is hereb
between them, that at the expiration of twelve months after such notice shall have been rec
either party from the oher, this convention, and all the provisions thereof, shall altogether ce
determine.

7. The present convention shall be ratified, and the ratifications shall be exchanged at Londo
one month from the date hereof, or sooner if possible.

In witness whereof the respective plenipotentiaries have signed the same, and have affixed the
seals of their arms.

Done at London, the second day of April, in the year of our Lord one thousand eight hun
twenty-four.　　　　　　　　　　　　GEORGE CANNING.　W. HUSKISSON.　WE

An order in council, dated May 25. 1824, directs that from May 1. 1824, Prussian vessels ent
departing from the ports of the United Kingdom of Great Britain and Ireland, shall not be subje
other or higher duties or charges whatever than are or shall be levied on British vessels enteri
parting from such ports; that all articles of the growth, produce, or manufacture of any of the d
of his Prussian Majesty, which are or shall be permitted to be imported into or exported from
of the United Kingdom of Great Britain and Ireland in British vessels, shall, in like manner, be
to be imported into and exported from the said ports in Prussian vessels; that all articles
growth, produce, or manufacture of the dominions of his Prussian Majesty, which can legally be
from Prussia into the ports of the United Kingdom in Prussian vessels, shall be subject only to
duties as are payable upon the like article if imported in British ships; that all goods, which ca
be imported into the ports of the United Kingdom, shall be admitted at the same rate of duty,
ported in Prussian vessels, that is charged on similar articles imported in British vessels; and
goods which can be legally exported from the ports of the United Kingdom, shall be entitled to
bounties, drawbacks, and allowances, when exported in Prussian vessels, that are granted, paid, c
on similar articles when exported in British vessels.

A Treasury letter, dated October 13. 18 24, directs, that with respect to pilotage and all oth
charged on vessels belonging to Prussia, Sweden, and Norway, Denmark, Hanover, and H
which have entered, or which may enter, the ports of the United Kingdom, either from stress o
or from any other causes, it was the intention of the Lords of the Committee of Privy Council
that such dues should not be higher than are charged upon British vessels, and that it is only t
of goods imported into this kingdom, and not brought direct from the country to which the vesse
that the equality of duty does not apply.

An order in council, dated May 3. 1823, states, that his Majesty is pleased to declare, that th
and belonging to the dominions of his Majesty the King of Prussia are entitled to the privilege
by the law of navigation, and may import from the dominions of his Majesty the King o
into any of the British possessions abroad, goods the produce of such dominions, and may ex
from such British possessions abroad, to be carried to any foreign country whatever.

RUSSIA.

Convention between His Britannic Majesty and the Emperor of Russia, signed at Peter
February, 1825.

Article 1. It is agreed that the respective subjects of the high contracting parties shall not b
or molested, in any part of the ocean commonly called the Pacific Ocean, either in navigating

herein, or in landing at such parts of the coast as shall not have been already occupied, in
de with the natives, under the restrictions and conditions specified in the following articles.
er to prevent the right of navigating and fishing, exercised upon the ocean by the subjects of
ntracting parties, from becoming the pretext for an illicit commerce, it is agreed that the sub-
Britannic Majesty shall not land at any place where there may be a Russian establishment,
permission of the governor or commandant: and, on the other hand, that Russian subjects
id, without permission, at any British establishment on the north-west coast.

ne of demarcation between the possessions of the high contracting parties, upon the coast of
it, and the islands of America to the north-west, shall be drawn in the manner following:—
ing from the southernmost point of the island called Prince of Wales Island, which point lies
iel of 54 degrees 40 minutes north latitude, and between the 131st and the 133d degree of west
ieridian of Greenwich), the said line shall ascend to the north along the channel, as far as the
continent where it strikes the 56th degree of north latitude; from this last mentioned point,
demarcation shall follow the summit of the mountains situated parallel to the coast, as far as
intersection of the 141st degree of west longitude (of the same meridian); and, finally, from
nt of intersection, the said meridian line of the 141st degree, in its prolongation as far as the
un, shall form the limit between the Russian and British possessions on the continent of
the north-west.

eference to the line of demarcation laid down in the preceding article it is understood;
the island called Prince of Wales Island shall belong wholly to Russia.
wherever the summit of the mountains which extend in a direction parallel to the coast, from
ree of north latitude to the point of intersection of the 141st degree of west longitude, shall
it the distance of more than 10 marine leagues from the ocean, the limit between the British
and the line of coast which is to belong to Russia, as above mentioned, shall be formed by a
to the windings of the coast, and which shall never exceed the distance of 10 marine leagues

reover agreed, that no establishment shall be formed by either of the two parties within the
ed by the two preceding articles to the possessions of the other: consequently, British sub-
ot form any establishment either upon the coast, or upon the border of the continent com-
i the limits of the Russian possessions, as designated in the two preceding articles; and, in
, no establishment shall be formed by Russian subjects beyond the said limits.
derstood, that the subjects of his Britannic Majesty, from whatever quarter they may arrive,
n the ocean, or from the interior of the continent, shall for ever enjoy the right of navigating
'ithout any hindrance whatever, all the rivers and streams which, in their course towards the
n, may cross the line of demarcation upon the line of coast described in article 3. of the pre-
ion.

understood that, for the space of ten years from the signature of the present convention, the
e two powers, or those belonging to their respective subjects, shall mutually be at liberty to
hout any hindrance whatever, all the inland seas, the gulfs, havens, and creeks on the coast
article 3, for the purposes of fishing and of trading with the natives.
t of Sitka, or Novo Archangelsk, shall be open to the commerce and vessels of British sub-
space of ten years from the date of the exchange of the ratifications of the present conven-
event of an extension of this term of ten years being granted to any other power, the like
ill be granted also to Great Britain.
ve-mentioned liberty of commerce shall not apply to the trade in spirituous liquors, in fire-
r arms, gunpowder, or other warlike stores; the high contracting parties reciprocally
to permit the above-mentioned articles to be sold or delivered, in any manner whatever, to
' the country.
ritish or Russian vessel navigating the Pacific Ocean, which may be compelled, by storms or
o take shelter in the ports of the parties, shall be at liberty to refit therein, to provide itself
ssary stores, and to put to sea again, without paying any other than port and light-house
hall be the same as those paid by national vessels. In case, however, the master of such
be under the necessity of disposing of a part of his merchandise in order to defray his
shall conform himself to the regulations and tariffs of the place where he may have

of complaint of an infraction of the articles of the present convention, the civil and military
the high contracting parties, without previously acting or taking any forcible measure,
exact and circumstantial report of the matter to their respective courts, who engage to
e, in a friendly manner, and according to the principles of justice.
sent convention shall be ratified, and the ratifications shall be exchanged at London within
x weeks, or sooner if possible,
hereof the respective plenipotentiaries have signed the same, and have affixed thereto the
arms.
t. Petersburgh, the 28th [16.] February, 1825.

> STRATFORD CANNING.
> THE COUNT DE NESSELRODE.
> PIERRE DE POLETICA.

THE TWO SICILIES.

*mmerce and Navigation between His Britannic Majesty and the King of the Two Sicilies,
signed at London, September 26. 1816.*

his Britannic Majesty consents that all the privileges and exemptions which his subjects,
e and shipping, have enjoyed, and do enjoy, in the dominions, ports, and domains of his
ty, in virtue of the treaty of peace and commerce concluded at Madrid on the 10th of May
667, between Great Britain and Spain; of the treaties of commerce between the same
d at Utrecht, the 9th of December, 1713, and at Madrid, the 13th of December, 1715;
vention concluded at Utrecht, the 8th March, 1712-1713, between Great Britain and the
ily, shall be *abolished;* and it is agreed upon in consequence, between their said Britannic
Majesties, their heirs and successors, that the said privileges and exemptions, whether of
ags and shipping, are and shall continue for ever abolished.
in Majesty engages not to continue, nor hereafter to grant to the subjects of any other
r, the privileges and exemptions abolished by the present convention.
in Majesty promises that the subjects of his Britannic Majesty shall not be subjected within
o a more rigorous system of examination and search by the officers of customs, than that
ibjects of his said Sicilian Majesty are liable.
ty the King of the Two Sicilies promises that British commerce in general, and the British
irry it on, shall be treated throughout his dominions upon the same footing as the most
is, not only with respect to the persons and property of the said British subjects, but also
every species of article in which they may traffic, and the taxes or other charges payable
cles, or on the shipping in which the importation shall be made.
ect to the personal privileges to be enjoyed by the subjects of his Britannic Majesty in the
Two Sicilies, his Sicilian Majesty promises that they shall have a free and undoubted right

to travel, and to reside in the territories and dominions of his said Majesty, subject to the sa[m] tions of police which are practised towards the most favoured nations. They shall be entitled dwellings and warehouses, and to dispose of their personal property of every kind and descr sale, gift, exchange, or will, and in any other way whatever, without the smallest loss or hindra given them on that head. They shall not be obliged to pay, under any pretence whatever, oth[e] rates than those, which are paid, or that hereafter may be paid, by the most favoured nat[i] dominions of his said Sicilian Majesty. They shall be exempt from all military service, wheth or sea; their dwellings, warehouses, and every thing belonging or appertaining thereto for obje[c] merce or residence, shall be respected. They shall not be subjected to any vexatious search or v arbitrary examination or inspection of their books, papers, or accounts, shall be made under th of the supreme authority of the state, but these shall alone be executed by the legal sentence o[f] petent tribunals. His Sicilian Majesty engages on all these occasions to guarantee to the subje Britannic Majesty who shall reside in his states and dominions, the preservation of their pr[e] personal security, in the same manner as those are guaranteed to his subjects, and to all foreigne ing to the most favoured and most highly privileged nations.

6. According to the tenor of the articles 1. and 2. of this treaty, his Sicilian Majesty enga[ges] declare null and void the privileges and exemptions which actually exist in favour of British within his dominions, till the same day, and except by the same act, by which the privileges a tions, whatsoever they are, of all other nations, shall be declared null and void within the sam[e]

7. His Sicilian Majesty promises, from the date when the general abolition of the privileges to the articles 1, 2. and 6. shall take place, to make a reduction of 10 per cent. upon the amo duties, payable according to the tariff in force the 1st of January, 1816, upon the total of the m[e] or production of the United Kingdom of Great Britain and Ireland, her colonies, possessions, a dencies, imported into the states of his said Sicilian Majesty, according to the tenor of articl present convention; it being understood that nothing in this article shall be construed to p King of the Two Sicilies from granting, if he shall think proper, the same reduction of dut foreign nations.

8. The subjects of the Ionian Islands shall, in consequence of their being actually under the protection of his Britannic Majesty, enjoy all the advantages which are granted to the comme the subjects of Great Britain by the present treaty; it being well understood that, to prevent and to prove its identity, every Ionian vessel shall be furnished with a patent, signed by the Commissioner or his representative.

9. The present convention shall be ratified, and the ratifications thereof exchanged in Lon the space of six months, or sooner if possible.

In witness whereof, the respective plenipotentiaries have signed it, and thereunto affixed their arms.

Done at London, the 26th of September, 1816.

CASTLEREAGH.   CASTEL[C]

Separate and Additional Article.

In order to avoid all doubt respecting the reduction upon the duties in favour of British which his Sicilian Majesty has promised in the 7th article of the convention, signed this day b Britannic Majesty and his Sicilian Majesty, it is declared, by this present separate and additio[n] that by the concession of 10 per cent. of diminution, it is understood that in case the amount should be 20 per cent. upon the value of the merchandise, the effect of the reduction of 10 per reduce the duty from 20 to 18; and so for other cases in proportion. And that for the article[s] not taxed *ad valorem* in the tariff, the reduction of the duty shall be proportionate; that deduction of a tenth part upon the amount of the sum payable shall be granted.

The present separate and additional article shall have the same force and validity as if i[t] inserted word for word in the convention of this day — it shall be ratified, and the ratificat shall be exchanged at the same time.

In witness whereof, the respective plenipotentiaries have signed it, and have thereunto affi[x] of their arms.

Done at London, the 26th of September, 1816.

CASTLEREAGH.   CASTEL[C]

TURKEY.

Capitulations and Articles of Peace between Great Britain and the Ottoman Empire, as a augmented, and altered, at different Periods, and finally confirmed by the Treaty of Peace the Dardanelles, in 1809.

SULTAN MEHEMED,

MAY HE LIVE FOR EVER.

"*Let every thing be observed in conformity to these capitulations, and contrary thereto le done.*"

1. The English nation and merchants, and all other merchants sailing under the Engli[sh] their vessels, and merchandise of all descriptions, may pass safely by sea, and go and co[m] dominions, without any the least prejudice or molestation being given to their persons, effects, by any person whatsoever, but they shall be left in the undisturbed enjoyment of the and be at liberty to attend to their affairs.

2. If any of the English coming into our dominions by land be molested or detained, such be instantly released, without any further obstruction being given to them.

3. English vessels entering the ports and harbours of our dominions shall and may at all and securely abide and remain therein, and at their free will and pleasure depart therefrom, opposition or hindrance from any one.

4. If it shall happen that any of their ships suffer by stress of weather, and not be provide[d] sary stores and requisites, they shall be assisted by all who happen to be present, whether the Imperial ships, or others, both by sea and land.

5. Being come into the ports and harbours of our dominions, they shall and may be at li chase at their pleasure, with their own money, provisions and all other necessary articles, a[nd] themselves with water, without interruption or hindrance from any one.

6. If any of their ships be wrecked upon any of the coasts of our dominions, all beys, cad[is] commandants, and others our servants, who may be near or present, shall give them all hel[p] and assistance, and restore to them whatsoever goods and effects may be driven ashore; and of any plunder being committed, they shall make diligent search and inquiry to find out which, when recovered, shall be wholly restored by them.

7. The merchants, interpreters, bankers, and others, of the said nation, shall and may, bo[th] land, come into our dominions, and there trade with the most perfect security; and in com[merce] neither they nor their attendants shall receive any the least obstruction, molestation, or in their persons or property, from the beys, cadis, sea-captains, soldiers, and others our slav[es]

17. Our ships and galleys, and all other vessels, which may fall in with any English ship[s]

nions, shall not give them any molestation, nor detain them by demanding any thing, but shall
d and mutual friendship the one to the other, without occasioning them any prejudice.

he corsairs or galliots of the Levant be found to have taken any English vessels, or robbed or
I them of their goods and effects, also if any one shall have forcibly taken any thing from the
all possible diligence and exertion shall be used and employed for the discovery of the property,
ting condign punishment on those who may have committed such depredations; and their ships,
I effects, shall be restored to them without delay or intrigue.

ties shall not be demanded or taken, of the English, or the merchants sailing under the flag of
on, on any piastres and sequins they may import into our sacred dominions, or on those they
port to any other place.

glish merchants, and all others sailing under their flag, may, freely and unrestrictedly, trade
ase all sorts of merchandise (prohibited commodities alone excepted), and convey them, either
r sea, or by way of the river Tanais, to the countries of Muscovy or Russia, and bring back
her merchandise into our sacred dominions, for the purposes of traffic, and also transport
Persia and other conquered countries.

uld the ships bound for Constantinople be forced by contrary winds to put into Caffa, or any other
hose parts, and not be disposed to buy or sell any thing, no one shall presume forcibly to take
ke any part of their merchandise, or give to the ships or crews any molestation, or obstruct the
at are bound to those ports.

their ships arriving at any port, and landing their goods, they may, after having paid their
ely and securely depart, without experiencing any molestation.

lish ships bound to Constantinople, Alexandria, Tripoli of Syria, Scanderoon, or other ports of
dominions, shall in future be bound to pay duties, according to custom, on such goods only as
, of their own free will, land with a view to sale; and for such merchandise as they shall not
no duty shall be demanded, neither shall the least molestation or hindrance be given to them.

lish and other merchants navigating under their flag, who trade to Aleppo, shall pay such
he silks, brought and laden by them on board their ships, as are paid by the French and Vene-
not one asper more.

Imperial fleet, galleys, and other vessels, departing from our sacred dominions, and falling in
sh ships at sea, shall in no wise molest or detain them, nor take from them any thing whatso-
glish ships shall no longer be liable to any further search, or exaction at sea, under colour of
examination.

lish ships coming to the ports of Constantinople, Alexandria, Smyrna, Cyprus, and other ports
ed dominions, shall pay 300 aspers for anchorage duty, without an asper more being demanded

olestation shall be given to any of the aforesaid nation buying camlets, mohairs, or grogram
ngora and Beghbazar, and, desirous of exporting the same from thence, after having paid the
er cent., by any demand of customs for the exportation thereof, neither shall one asper more
ed of them.

it being represented to us that English merchants have been accustomed hitherto to pay no
scale duty, either on the silks bought by them at Brussa and Constantinople, or on those which
Persia and Georgia, and are purchased by them at Smyrna from the Armenians; if such
stom really exists, and the same be not prejudicial to the empire, such duty shall not be paid

. These capitulations may be found entire in *Hertslet's Treaties*, and in *Chitty's Common Law*,
90-311. Appen.)

ween *Great Britain and the Sublime Porte. Concluded at the Dardanelles, the 5th of
January*, 1809.

the moment of signing the present treaty, every act of hostility between England and Turkey

arn for the indulgence and good treatment afforded by the Sublime Porte to English merchants,
t to their goods and property, as well as in all matters tending to facilitate their commerce,
all reciprocally extend every indulgence and friendly treatment to the flag, subjects, and mer-
he Sublime Porte, which may hereafter frequent the dominions of his Britannic Majesty for
s of commerce.

st Custom-house tariff established at Constantinople, at the ancient rate of 3 per cent., and
the article relating to the interior commerce, shall continue to be observed, as they are at
ulated, and to which England promises to conform.

sh patents of protection shall not be granted to dependants, or merchants who are subjects of
Porte, nor shall any passport be delivered to such persons, on the part of ambassadors or
hout permission previously obtained from the Sublime Porte.

ear the Castles of the Dardanelles, the 5th of January, 1809, which corresponds with the year of
legira 1223, the 19th day of the Moon Zilkaade.

SEYD MEHEMMED EMIN VAHID EFFENDI.
ROBERT ADAIR.

UNITED STATES.

of *Commerce between Great Britain and the United States of America, signed at London, the
3d July*, 1815.

There shall be between all the territories of his Britannic Majesty in Europe, and the terri-
e United States, a reciprocal liberty of commerce. The inhabitants of the two countries
shall have liberty freely and securely to come with their ships and cargoes to all such places,
vers in the territories aforesaid, to which other foreigners are permitted to come, to enter
e, and to remain and reside in any part of the said territories respectively; and also to hire
houses and warehouses for the purpose of their commerce; and generally the merchants and
ach nation respectively shall enjoy the most complete protection and security, for their com-
subject always to the laws and statutes of the two countries respectively.

her or other duties shall be imposed on the importation into the territories of his Britannic
lurope, of any articles, the growth, produce, or manufacture of the United States, and no
ther duties shall be imposed on the importation into the United States, of any articles, the
luce, or manufacture of his Britannic Majesty's territories in Europe, than are or shall be
he like articles, being the growth, produce, or manufacture of any other foreign country; nor
her or other duties or charges be imposed in either of the two countries on the exportation
es to his Britannic Majesty's territories in Europe, or to the United States respectively, than
ayable on the exportation of the like articles to any other foreign country; nor shall any pro-
mposed upon the exportation or importation of any articles, the growth, produce, or manu-
he United States, or of his Britannic Majesty's territories in Europe, to or from the said
f his Britannic Majesty in Europe, or to or from the said United States, which shall not
nd to all other nations.

or other duties or charges shall be imposed in any of the ports of the United States on British
those payable in the same ports by vessels of the United States; nor in the ports of any of

his Britannic Majesty's territories in Europe on the vessels of the United States, than shall be pay
the same ports on British vessels.

The same duties shall be paid on the importation into the United States of any articles, the p
produce, or manufacture of his Britannic Majesty's territories in Europe, whether such importatio
be in the vessels of the United States, or in British vessels; and the same duties shall be paid
importation into the ports of any of his Britannic Majesty's territories in Europe, of any artic
growth, produce, or manufacture of the United States, whether such importation shall be in
vessels, or in vessels of the United States.

The same duties shall be paid, and the same bounties allowed, on the exportation of any artic
growth, produce, or manufacture of his Britannic Majesty's territories in Europe, to the United
whether such exportation shall be in vessels of the United States, or in British vessels; and th
duties shall be paid, and the same bounties allowed, on the exportation of any articles, the grow
duce, or manufacture of the United States, to his Britannic Majesty's territories in Europe, wheth
exportation shall be in British vessels, or in vessels of the United States.

It is further agreed, that in all cases where drawbacks are or may be allowed, upon the re-expo
of any goods, the growth, produce, or manufacture of either country respectively, the amount
said drawbacks shall be the same, whether the said goods shall have been originally imported in a
or American vessel; but when such re-exportation shall take place from the United States in a
vessel, or from the territories of his Britannic Majesty in Europe in an American vessel, to ar
foreign nation, the two contracting parties reserve to themselves, respectively, the right of regul
diminishing, in such case, the amount of the said drawback.

The intercourse between the United States and his Britannic Majesty's possessions in the West
and on the continent of North America, shall not be affected by any of the provisions of this
but each party shall remain in the complete possession of its rights, with respect to such an inte

3. His Britannic Majesty agrees that the vessels of the United States of America shall be ad
and hospitably received, at the principal settlements of the British dominions in the East Ind
Calcutta, *Madras*, *Bombay*, and *Prince of Wales's Island*, and that the citizens of the said Unite
may freely carry on trade between the said principal settlements and the said United States, in all
of which the importation and exportation respectively, to and from the said territories, shall
entirely prohibited; provided only, that it shall not be lawful for them in any time of war, betw
British government and any state or power whatever, to export from the said territories, with
special permission of the British government, any military stores, or naval stores, or rice. The
of the United States shall pay for their vessels, when admitted, no higher or other duty or cha
shall be payable on the vessels of the most favoured European nations, and they shall pay no h
other duties or charges on the importation or exportation of the cargoes of the said vessels, than
payable on the same articles when imported or exported in the vessels of the most favoured E
nations.

But it is expressly agreed, that the vessels of the United States shall not carry any articles f
said principal settlements to any port or place, except to some port or place in the United
America, where the same shall be unladen.

It is also understood, that the permission granted by this article is not to extend to allow the v
the United States to carry on any part of the coasting trade of the said British territories; but th
of the United States having, in the first instance, proceeded to one of the said principal settle
the British dominions in the East Indies, and then going with their original cargoes, or any part
from one of the said principal settlements to another, shall not be considered as carrying on the
trade. The vessels of the United States may also touch for refreshments, but not for commerc
course of their voyage to or from the British territories in India, or to or from the dominion
Emperor of China, at the Cape of Good Hope, the island of St. Helena, or such other places as
in the possession of Great Britain, in the African or Indian seas; it being well understood, that
that regards this article, the citizens of the United States shall be subject in all respects to the
regulations of the British government from time to time established.

4. It shall be free for each of the two contracting parties respectively to appoint consuls, for the p
of trade, to reside in the dominions and territories of the other party; but before any consul sh
such, he shall in the usual form be approved and admitted by the government to which he is se
it is hereby declared, that in case of illegal and improper conduct towards the laws or governme
country to which he is sent, such consul may either be punished according to law, if the laws w
the case, or be sent back, the offended government assigning to the other the reasons for the san

It is hereby declared, that either of the contracting parties may except from the residence o
such particular places as such party shall judge fit to be so excepted.

5. This convention, when the same shall have been duly ratified by his Britannic Majesty ar
President of the United States, by and with the advice and consent of their Senate, and the r
ratifications mutually exchanged, shall be binding and obligatory on his Majesty and on the sai
States for four years from the date of its signature; and the ratifications shall be exchanged in si
from this time, or sooner if possible.

Done at London, the 3d July, 1815.

FRED. J. ROBINSON.
HENRY GOULBURN.
WILLIAM ADAMS.

JOHN Q. AD.
H. CLAY.
ALBERT GAL.

This convention was subsequently prolonged by conventions for that purpose in 1818 and 1827

TRIESTE, a large city and sea-port of the Austrian dominions, the ca
a district of Illyria, situated near the north-east extremity of the Gulf of
in lat. 40° 43' N., lon. 12° 58½' E. Population, 70,000.—(*Edin. Gazet.*)
has no command of internal navigation; but being the only, or at least th
convenient, sea-port, not of the Illyrian provinces only, but of the whole s
Germany, and great part of Hungary, it enjoys a very extensive comme
has a large and convenient harbour. Among the exports is quicksilver, c
partly from mines in the neighbourhood of the town, partly from those
and partly from the mines of Hungary. Linen, tobacco, and woollens,
from different parts of Germany; Dalmatian red wine, Tokay and othe
garian wines, printed cottons from Switzerland, rags from Hungary, and
articles brought from Smyrna and other places of the Levant, enter into
of exports. The imports consist of cotton wool (of which nearly 20,000
were imported in 1831), coffee, sugar, spices, fish, iron, indigo, dye-wood

Accounts are kept at Trieste in florins of 60 creutzers; also in lire of 20 soldi. The par of 10 florins = 1*l.* sterling. The florin Austrian currency is worth 5 5-17ths of a lire Trieste cur-

nd Measures. — Those chiefly in use at Trieste are those of Vienna and Venice. The com-nd contains 4 quarters, 16 ounces, or 32 loths: it is = 8,639 English grains. Thus, 100 lbs. at 23·6 lbs. avoirdupois; or 90½ lbs. of Trieste = 112 lbs. avoirdupois.

ipal dry measure is the stajo or staro = 2·34 Winch. bushels. The Vienna metzen, which is used, = 1·723 Winch. bushel. The polonick = 0·861 Winch. bushel.

ipal liquid measure is the orna or eimer = 40 boccali = 15 English wine gallons very nearly. = 173½ English wine gallons.

of oil contains 5¼ caffisi, and weighs about 107 commercial pounds. It is = 17 English wine

oollen measure = 26·6 English inches. The ell for silk = 25·2 English inches.

ges at Trieste are very moderate: they do not exceed 5 per cent. on sales; commission, gua-bts, brokerage, and every other charge of landing, warehousing, &c. included. There is no se duty to pay. Trieste being a free port—that is, a port where goods may be warehoused free e shipping expenses, besides 2 per cent. commission, are trifling.

Customary Tares.

nnah, in boxes	- 50 lbs. per box.	Pepper, in bales	-	- 4 lbs. per bale.
n long chests -	- 270 lbs. per chest.	in bags -		⎫
astard ditto -	- 243 lbs. —	Coffee, in ditto -		⎬ 1 to 2 lbs. per bag.
nort ditto -	- 216 lbs. —	Cocoa, &c. in ditto		⎭
ags -	- 3 lbs. per cent.	Cotton, Brazil	-	2 lbs. per cent.
, in casks	- 12 lbs. —	American and Levant	-	4 lbs. —
dia, white	- 12 lbs. —	On other articles the weight of the package is
covado	- 14 lbs. —	usually taken.
lia, in mats	- 5 lbs. —	No extra tare is customary.

Statement of the Quantities of some of the Principal Articles imported into Trieste, and of the Warehouses for Consumption in the Interior and elsewhere, during the Four Years h 1829.

Articles.		1826.		1827.		1828.		1829.	
		Imp.	Out.	Imp.	Out.	Imp.	Out.	Imp.	Out.
- -	cwt.	7,275	4,141	8,050	7,885	6,677	6,372	4,085	5,235
- -	cwt.	69,935	88,265	161,920	136,720	129,035	130,535	128,650	148,500
a	cwt.	546	1,395	2,140	874	615	1,659	1,390	1,186
- -	serons	16	15	24	20	23	27	13	19
-	bales	33,256	28,130	29,972	37,136	40,090	34,880	40,439	42,782
-	cwt.	35,786	48,127	27,111	25,601	17,515	27,415	33,166	24,726
-	packages	692	415	392	403	766	646	449	401
-	pieces	20,000	32,000	- -	7,000	23,800	13,200	74,000	80,300
-	cwt.	23,325	14,539	9,770	12,410	12,218	13,018	11,847	11,540
-	cwt.	1,111	1,368	3,122	1,672	835	1,830	2,306	2,111
-	puncheons	294	489	663	573	1,554	1,044	1,086	1,076
-	boxes	498	217	143	143	236	316	467	237
and crus. -	hhds.	3,108	3,602	5,568	4,735	3,540	3,860	4,194	4,923
ıdia -	hhds.	2,371	1,511	1,411	1,641	4,335	4,172	4,504	3,235
-	chests	9,671	11,060	17,313	13,220	13,490	15,225	17,204	16,895
ah -	boxes	18,944	24,699	29,863	21,661	15,676	17,522	16,318	17,098
g all de-sions	cwt.	243,895	263,945	384,350	305,300	300,135	331,335	352,200	352,100

(From the *Price Current of P. and D. Terni and Co.*, Trieste, 7th of January, 1830.)

e Principal Articles imported into Trieste in 1830, specifying the Countries whence they came, and the Ships in which they were imported.

. — In 71 British vessels. Coffee, 535 tons Jamaica, 160 tons St. Domingo, 105 tons Rio, annah, 16 tons Demerara, 12 tons Porto Rico, 9 tons East India; sugar, 641 casks refined, rushed, 343 cases, 95 tierces white, 17 cases muscovado Brazil, 1,100 bags Santos, 121 boxes boxes yellow Havannah, 7,878 bags East India, 291 hhds. British plantation, 939 casks bas-a, 93 tons; cinnamon, 14 bales; cassia lignea, 94 tons; pepper, 7 tons; pimento, 81 tons; ons; indigo, 448 chests; rum, 372 puncheons; logwood, 466 tons; fustic, 60 tons; tin, 389 arrels bars, 4,954 boxes plates; iron, 1,143 tons; cotton, 95 bales American, 45 bales Brazil, t India, 453 bales Egyptian Mako; nankeens, 69,800 pieces; manufactures, 7,082 packages; l barrels; pilchards, 450 barrels.

— In 1 British and 15 American vessels. Coffee, 240 tons St. Domingo, 197 tons Porto Rico, uayra, 29 tons St. Jago, 19 tons Havannah; sugar, 3,865 bags Manilla, 283 hhds. West India; as; cassia lignea, 2 tons; pepper, 46 tons; indigo, 104 chests; rum, 266 puncheons; cotton, logwood, 626 tons; nankeens, 20,000 pieces.

56 British, 7 American, 6 Austrian, 5 Danish, 2 Portuguese, 1 Russian, 2 Sardinian, and ssels. Coffee, 3,243 tons Rio, 103 tons Bahia; sugar, 2,607 cases white, 942 cases muscovado, io, 6,760 cases white, 4,345 cases muscovado, 14 tierces and 60 bags Bahia, 3,897 cases white, iscovado, 115 hhds., 677 tierces, and 366 bags Pernambuco; cocoa, 108 tons Para; rum, s Bahia; hides, 1,283; cotton, 349 bales Rio, 1,875 bales Bahia, 2,255 bales Pernambuco, 194 fustic, 8 tons.

l other Ports of Cuba.—In 1 British, 18 American, and 2 Spanish vessels. Coffee, 1,067 tons tons Havannah, 11 tons Triage; sugar, 1,926 boxes white, 8,711 boxes yellow; logwood, ic, 18 tons.

In 8 British vessels. Coffee, 1,276 tons.

3 British vessels. Coffee, 137 tons; sugar, 250 hhds.; pimento, 37 tons; rum, 136 puncheons ons.

In 1 American vessel. Sugar, 455 casks, 54 tierces; fustic, 8 tons.

sels from Marseilles, 4 Bordeaux, and 1 Nantes). — In 1 British, 8 French, 11 Austrian, 1 Danish, 6 Neapolitan, 3 Roman, 3 Russian, 1 Spanish, 1 Swedish, and 2 Tuscan vessels. ns Porto Rico, 138 tons St. Jago, 25 tons Havannah, 11 tons St. Domingo, 4 tons Rio; sugar, fined, 3 casks crushed, 382 boxes yellow Havannah, 33 tierces, 110 bags Brazil, 7,386 bags cocoa, 38 tons; cloves, 457 packages; pimento, 92 bales; pepper, 242 tons; logwood, aragua wood, 3 tons; cotton, 100 bales; hides, 1,310; nankeens, 12,600 pieces; lead,

Spain. — In 2 British, 1 American, 1 Neapolitan, 1 Sardinian, and 7 Spanish vessels. Coffee, 1:
vannah, 3 tons Porto Rico; sugar, 413 boxes white, 348 boxes yellow Havannah; lead, 7,448
Portugal. — In 3 Austrian, 6 Danish, 5 Neapolitan, 1 Sardinian, and 6 Swedish vessels. Coffe
Rio; sugar, 2,639 cases white, 795 cases muscovado, 83 tierces Brazil; cocoa, 386 tons; co
bales Brazil; hides, 200; fustic, 4 tons.
Denmark, Norway, and Iceland. — In 2 British, 3 American, 4 Danish, 2 Dutch, 1 Russian, and I
vessels. Stockfish, 2,717 tons; herrings, 100 barrels.
Sweden. — In 2 Swedish vessels. Tar, 2,011 barrels; rosin, 10 barrels.
(From the *Circular of Lang, Freeland, c*

TRINITY-HOUSE. This Society was incorporated by Henry VIII.
for the promotion of commerce and navigation, by licensing and regulatin
and ordering and erecting beacons, light-houses, buoys, &c. A similar
for the like purposes, was afterwards established at Hull; and also an
Newcastle-upon-Tyne in 1537: which three establishments, says Haklu
in imitation of that founded by the Emperor Charles V. at Seville in Spai
observing the numerous shipwrecks in the voyages to and from the Wes
occasioned by the ignorance of seamen, established, at the *Casa de Cont*
lectures on navigation, and a pilot-major for the examination of other pi
mariners; having also directed books to be published on that subject foi
of navigators.

Henry VIII., by his charter, confirmed to the Deptford Trinity-house S
the ancient rights, privileges, &c. of the shipmen and mariners of Engl:
their several possessions at Deptford, from which it is plain that the Society h:
long previously. The Corporation was confirmed, in 1685, in the enjoyment :
vileges and possessions, by letters patent of the 1st of James II. by the name of th
Wardens, and Assistants of the Guild or Fraternity of the most glorious and v
Trinity, and of St. Clement's, in the Parish of Deptford Strond, in the County
At first the Corporation appears to have consisted of seamen only; but many g:
and some noblemen, are now amongst its members, or elder brethren. It is go
a master, 4 wardens, 8 assistants, and 31 elder brothers: but the inferior me
the fraternity, named younger brethren, are of an unlimited number; for every
mate, expert in navigation, may be admitted as such. Besides the power of
light-houses, and other seamarks, on the several coasts of the kingdom, for th
of navigation — (see LIGHT-HOUSES), — the master, wardens, assistants, and :
thren, are invested by charter with the following powers; viz. the examinati
mathematical scholars of Christ's Hospital, and of the masters of his Majest
the appointment of pilots to conduct ships into and out of the Thames; the an
of such unlicensed persons as presume to act as masters of ships of war, or pilot
cuniary fine; settling the several rates of pilotage; granting licences to poor s:
free of the city, or past going to sea, to row on the river Thames for their supp
venting aliens from serving on board English ships without licence; hearing and
ing the complaints of officers and seamen of British ships, subject to an appeal to
of the Admiralty, &c. To this company belongs the ballast office for cle:
deepening the Thames, by taking up a sufficient quantity of ballast for the
all ships that sail out of the river, for which they pay certain rates. — (See I
The Corporation is authorised to receive voluntary subscriptions, benefacti
and to purchase, in mortmain, lands, tenements, &c. to the amount of
annum. It is stated in Nightingale's "Account of London and Middlesex,"
in 1815, that about 3,000 poor seamen, their widows, and orphans, were an
lieved by this Society. The ancient Hall of the Trinity-house at Deptford,
meetings of the brethren were formerly held, was pulled down in 1787, and
building erected for the purpose in London, near the Tower.

Trinity-house Revenues, &c. — The revenues at the disposal of the Tri
are now very great, probably not less than from 150,000*l.* to 165,000*l.* a yea:
regulations of the Corporation as to fees on account of light-houses, pil:
exercise a very powerful influence over the commerce and navigation of th
and particularly over that of the metropolis. It seems highly expedient that
gation should be made into the affairs of this establishment. At present th
means of acquiring accurate information, either as to the amount of revenue de
light-houses, pilotage, &c., or as to the mode in which, and the purposes for v
expended. We have elsewhere—(see *antè*, p. 470. and p. 709.)—stated the :
which we are inclined to consider the charges on account of lights and :
quite exorbitant. Perhaps, however, were the accounts of the Corporation, :
tem of management, made public, it might be found that the charges refe:
really as reasonable as they can be made, consistently with the attainment of
of the institution, But at present, judging from the defective information
we come to a very different conclusion.

PANG, or SEA SLUG (*Biche de Mer*), a species of fish (of the genus
uria) found chiefly on coral reefs in the Eastern seas, and highly esteemed
a, into which it is imported in large quantities.

an unseemly looking substance, of a dirty brown colour, hard, rigid, scarcely
ng any power of locomotion, or appearance of animation. Sometimes the slug
ch as 2 feet in length, and from 7 to 8 inches in circumference. A span in
and 2 or 3 inches in girth, is, however, the ordinary size. The quality and
f the fish, however, does not by any means depend upon its size, but upon pro-
in it neither obvious to, nor discernible by, those who have not been long
ensively engaged in the trade. In shallow water the animal is taken out by
d, but in deeper water it is sometimes speared. When taken it is gutted, dried in
, and smoked over a wood fire; this being the only preparation it receives.
ery is carried on from the western shores of New Guinea, and the southern
f Australia, to Ceylon inclusive. Indeed, within the last few years it has been
ully prosecuted on the shores of the Mauritius. The whole produce goes to
In the market of Macassar, the great staple of this fishery, not less than *thirty*
are distinguished, varying in price from 5 Spanish dollars a *picul* (133⅓ lbs.) to
. that price, each variety being distinguished by well known names! The quan-
ipang sent annually to China from Macassar is about 7,000 piculs or 8,333 cwt.;
, usually varying from 8 dollars a picul to 110 and 115, according to quality.—
d's Indian Archipelago, vol. iii. p. 441.) In 1827, the export of tripang from
amounted to 2,480 piculs.
es tripang, *fish-maws* and *sharks' fins* are exported to China from every maritime
f India.

Y WEIGHT, one of the most ancient of the different kinds used in Britain.
und English Troy contains 12 ounces, or 5,760 grains. It is used in the
g of gold, silver, and jewels; the compounding of medicines; in experi-
a natural philosophy; in comparing different weights with each other;
w (by 5 Geo. 4. c. 74.) made the standard of weight.
WEIGHT, *Scotch*, was established by James VI. in the year 1618, who
that only one weight should be used in Scotland, viz. the French Troy
16 pounds, and 16 ounces to the pound. The pound contains 7,609 grains,
qual to 17 oz. 6 dr. avoirdupois. The cwt. or 112 lbs. avoirdupois, con-
y 103 lbs. 2½ oz. of this weight, though generally reckoned equal to 104 lbs.
ght is very nearly identical with that formerly used at Paris and Am-
 and is generally known by the name of Dutch weight. Though pro-
by the articles of Union, it has been used in most parts Scotland in
 iron, hemp, flax, and other Dutch and Baltic goods, meal, butchers' meat,
 —(See WEIGHTS and MEASURES.)

'FLES, a sort of vegetable production, like a mushroom, formed under
 A few have been found in England, in Northamptonshire; but they are
undant in Italy, the south of France, and several other countries. They
ned a great delicacy. — (*Rees's Cyclopædia*.)

ITH, or TURPETH, the cortical part of the root of a species of *con-*
brought from different parts of the East Indies. It is a longish root,
, thickness of the finger, resinous, heavy, and of a brownish hue without
ish within. It is imported cloven in the middle, lengthwise, and the
woody matter taken out. The best is ponderous, not wrinkled, easy to
d discovers to the eye a large quantity of resinous matter. At first it
 impression of sweetness on the taste; but, when chewed for some time,
 nauseous acrimony. It is used in medicine, but only to a small extent.
's Mat. Med.)

H (MINERAL), the name given by chemists to the subsulphate of

OT (*Pleuronectes maximus*), a well known and highly esteemed species
 Very considerable quantities of turbot are now taken on various parts
asts, from the Orkneys to the Land's End, yet a preference is given in
n markets to those caught by the Dutch. The latter are said to
times drawn as much as 80,000*l.* in a single year, for turbots sold in

urbots, however taken, or in whatever ship imported, may be imported
 ty. — (See FISH.)

TURKOISE, or TURQUOISE (Ger. *Türkiss;* Fr. *Turquoise;* It. *Turc* Sp. *Turquesa*), a precious stone in considerable estimation. Its colour, wh its principal recommendation, is a beautiful celestial blue, which migrates pale blue, and is sometimes tinged with green. Specific gravity, 3·127. destitute of lustre, opaque, and does not admit of a very high polish. It is cipally imported from Persia. It is much worn in necklaces, and in ever: of ornamental jewellery, from the size of a pin's head to that of an almo: contrasts beautifully with brilliants, or pearls, set in fine gold, and appears to advantage when cut spheroidal. — (*Mawe on Diamonds,* 2d ed. p. 129.)

TURMERIC, the root of the *Curcuma longa.* It is externally grayish, a: ternally of a deep lively yellow or saffron colour; very hard; and not unlike, in figure or size, to ginger. That should be preferred, which is large, new, res: difficult to break, and heavy. It is imported from Bengal, Java, China, &c some of a superior quality is said to have been brought from Tobago. quantities of it have also been grown in England. It has a slight aromatic not very agreeable smell; and a bitterish, slightly acrid, and somewhat taste. It used to be in considerable estimation as a medicine; but i: rope it is now used only as a dye. It yields a beautiful bright yellow c: which, however, is extremely fugitive, and no means have hitherto been disc: of fixing it. It is sometimes employed to heighten the yellows made with and to give an orange tint to scarlet; but the shade imparted by the tu: soon disappears. The Indians use it to colour and season their food.—(*I* *Mat. Med.; Bancroft on Colours,* vol. i. p. 276.)

The imports of turmeric from the East Indies, during the three years ending with 1828, amou an average, to 621,506 lbs. a year.

Its price in bond in the London market, January 1823, was — Bengal, per cwt. 10s. to 13s.; Jav: 18s.; China, 18s. to 1l. 4s.

The duty on turmeric is 2s. 4d. per cwt. on that brought from a British possession, and 10s. on that from a foreign country. The only effect of this distinction is to force the use of an article.

TURPENTINE (Ger. *Turpentin;* Fr. *Terebenthine;* It. *Trementina;* *Skipidar;* Pol. *Terpentyna*). There are several species of turpentine, bu: them possess the same general and chemical properties.

1. *Common Turpentine,* is a resinous juice which exudes from the Scotch Wild Pine (*Pinus Sylvestris*). The trees which are most exposed to the sun, an: the thickest barks, yield it in the greatest abundance. They begin to produce i: about 40 years old. The bark of the tree is wounded, and the turpentine flows drops which fall into a hole, or sort of cup, previously dug at the foot of the tre: ing about a pint and a half. It is purified by being exposed to liquefy in th: rays, in barrels perforated in the bottom, through which it filters. In the United the collection of turpentine is confided chiefly to negroes, each of whom l: charge of from 3,000 to 4,000 trees. The process lasts all year, although t: sions are not made in the trees till the middle of March, and the flow of t: pentine generally ceases about the end of October. The boxes are emptied fi: times during the year; and it is estimated that 250 boxes will produce a barrel ing 320 lbs. Turpentine has a strong, somewhat fragrant odour, and a bi: agreeable taste; its consistence is greater than that of honey; its colour dirty and it is more opaque than the other sorts. We import it almost entirely f: United States.

2. *Venice Turpentine,* is the produce of the Larch (*Pinus Larix*). It is obt: boring a hole into the heart of the tree about 2 feet from the ground, and fitting small tube through which the turpentine flows into vessels prepared for its recep: is purified by straining through cloths, or hair sieves. It is more fluid, having sistence of new honey, a yellowish colour, and is less unpleasant to the smell a: than the common turpentine. Genuine Venetian turpentine is principally obtai: the forests of Baye, in Provence; but much of that to be found in the shops con: America, and is, perhaps, obtained from a different species of fir.

3. *Canadian Balsam,* or *Turpentine,* is obtained from incisions in the bar: *Pinus Balsamea,* a native of the coldest regions of North America. It is i: in casks, each containing about 1 cwt. It has a strong, not disagreeable odou: bitterish taste; is transparent, whitish, and has the consistence of copaiva — (See BALSAM.)

4. *Chian,* or *Cyprus Turpentine,* is obtained from the *Pistacia Terebinthus,* of the north of Africa and the south of Europe, and cultivated in Chios and: It flows out of incisions made in the bark of the tree in the month of July subsequently strained and purified. It has a fragrant odour, a moderately wa:

acrimony or bitterness, and a white or very pale yellow colour; it has the
e of thick honey, is clear, transparent, and tenacious.　From its comparative
, Chian turpentine is seldom procured genuine, being for the most part adul-
th common turpentine.　The different species of turpentine may be dissolved
l spirit, or pure alcohol; and, by distillation, they all give similar oils, which,
being distilled (and not from any resemblance to alcohol, or spirits properly so
e vulgarly termed spirits of turpentine.　If the distillation be performed
, the produce is an essential oil, the common spirit of turpentine; and if
ation be carried on in a *retort*, without water, the product is more volatile
nt, — a concentrated oil, as it were, — and is called the ethereal spirit of
.　The residuum that is left, in both cases, is a brownish resinous mass,
able of being melted, highly inflammable, insoluble in water, but mixing freely
it is the common *rosin* of commerce. — (*Lib. of Entert. Knowledge, Vegetable
; Thomson's Dispensatory.*)

e imports of turpentine amounted to 304,792 cwt.; of which the United States furnished no
,174 cwt., and France the residue.　In 1829, the duty (4*s.* 4*d.* per cwt.) produced 59,110*l.*,
272,815 cwt. had been entered for home consumption.

ENTINE, OIL OF (Ger. *Terpentinöl;* Fr. *Eau de raze, Huile de tere-*
It. *Acqua di rasa;* Sp. *Aguarras*), the essential oil drawn from turpentine
ion.　There are two sorts of this oil: the best, red; and the second, white.
extensively used by house painters, and in the manufacture of varnish,
distillers have been charged with using it in the preparation of gin.　Oil
ine is very often adulterated.

NAGUE, the name given in commercial language to the zinc or spelter
—(See ZINC.)　This commodity used to be smuggled from China (the
n of unwrought metals from that empire being prohibited) to Hindos-
alay Archipelago, and neighbouring countries, to the amount, it is sup-
about 50,000 cwt. a year.　In 1820, the British free traders introduced
pelter for the first time into the Indian market.　In 1826, the import-
tenague from China into Calcutta ceased; and it has now been totally
l throughout India by spelter.　Of this latter commodity there were ex-
m British ports, at an average of the 3 years ending with 1828, 126,320
the declared value of 95,500*l.*, besides the quantities furnished by
, Rotterdam, Antwerp, and other continental ports.

U. V.

IA, a species of acorn, forming a very considerable article of export
Iorea and the Levant.　The more substance there is in the husk, or
acorn, the better.　It is of a bright drab colour, which it will always
hile it is kept dry: any dampness injures it; as it then turns black, and
its strength and value.　It is principally used by tanners, and is always
Though a very bulky article, it is uniformly bought and sold by weight.
only take a small proportion of her registered tonnage of valonia,
freight per ton is always high.　The price in the London market (May
d from 15*l.* to 17*l.* per ton.

wt. of valonia imported in 1828, 109,780 cwt. were brought from Turkey and Continental
ditto from Italy and the Italian islands (mostly at second hand), and 10,357 ditto from the
The duty on valonia (1*s.* 6*d.* per cwt.) produced, in 1829, 5,745*l.*, which shows that
been entered for home consumption.

RAISO, the principal sea-port of Chili, in lat. 33° 3′ S., lon. 72° 6′ W.
uncertain, perhaps 6,000 or 7,000.

in the bay is deep, and it affords a secure anchorage, except during northerly
violence of which it is exposed; but as the holding ground is good, and
he anchor is against a steep hill, accidents seldom occur to ships properly
hors and cables.　There is no mole or jetty; but the water close to the shore
at it is customary for the smaller class of vessels to carry out an anchor to
d, and to moor the ship with the stern ashore by another cable made fast to
Large ships lie a little further off, and load and unload by means of lighters.
lter is in that part called the fisherman's bay, lying between the castle and
onio, where, close to a clear shingle beach, there is 9 fathoms water.　In

the very worst weather a landing may be effected in this part of the bay.—(Se
Travels in Chili and La Plata, vol. i. p. 440., where there is a plan of Valparais
harbours of Valdivia and Concepcion are much superior to that of Valparaiso ; th
being, indeed, not only the best in Chili, but second to few in any part of th
But Valparaiso being near the capital, Santiago, and being the central *depôt* fo
sources of the province, is most frequented. The town is inconveniently sit
the extremity of a mountainous ridge ; most of the houses being built either
acclivity or in its breaches. Large quantities of corn and other articles of
are shipped here for Callao and Panama, but principally for the former. E
of wheat, the principal articles of export are tallow and hides, copper, the preciou
indigo, wool, sarsaparilla, &c. According to Mr. Jacob, the produce of the
silver mines of Chili may be estimated, at an average of the last twenty years, at I
a year.—(*Jacob on the Precious Metals*, vol. ii. p. 261.) There is a great want of c
the country ; and the anarchy and insecurity that have prevailed since the comme
of the revolutionary war have been very unfavourable to all sorts of industry.
can, however, be no doubt that Chili has already gained considerably, and
will every day gain more, by her emancipation from the yoke of Old Spain.
we carry on with this distant country already amounts to above 1,200,000*l.* a ye
there can be no doubt that it will become far more extensive. In 1829, the de
real value of the exports of British produce and manufactures from this country
amounted to 818,950*l.* ; of this sum the exports of cotton goods amounted
600,000*l.*, those of woollens to 126,000*l.*, linen to 28,000*l.* &c. Chili also
spices, tea, wine, sugar, coffee, tobacco, &c. A small part, however, of the
are re-exported for Peru.

A country with a scanty population, which imports so extensively, cannot
wretched condition that Mr. Miers and other disappointed travellers would ha
believe. The candour and good sense of M. de la Perouse are above all quest
every one who compares his remarks on the condition of Chili, with what has
stated, must see that its commerce, at least, has gained prodigiously by the revo

" The influence of the government is in constant opposition to that of the
The system of prohibition exists at Chili in its fullest extent. This kingdom,
the productions would, if increased to their maximum, supply all Europe; wh
would be sufficient for the manufactures of France and England ; and whose he
verted into salt provisions, would produce a vast revenue ; — this kingdom, ala
commerce. Four or five small vessels bring every year from Lima, tobacco, s
some articles of European manufacture, which the miserable inhabitants can ob
at second or third hand, after they have been charged with heavy customs dutie
at Lima, and, lastly, at their arrival in Chili ; in exchange they give their tall
some deals, and their wheat, which, however, is at so low a price, that the cult
no inducement to extend his tillage. Thus Chili, with all its gold, and artic
change, can scarcely procure sugars, tobacco, stuffs, linens, cambrics, and
necessary to the ordinary wants of life." — (*Perouse's Voyage*, vol. i. p. 50. F

Instead, however, of 4 or 5 small ships from Lima, in 1828, 69 British ships
12,746 tons, entered Valparaiso only, besides several at the other ports ! A
European goods are carried direct to Chili, and are admitted at reasonable du
advantages resulting from this extensive intercourse with foreigners, and from
ment of English adventurers in the country, have been already immense, and
day become more visible. It was impossible, considering the ignorance of th
the people, that the old system of tyranny and superstition could be pulled
without a good deal of violence and mischief; but the foundations of a bett
things have been laid ; nor can there be a doubt that Chili is destined to becor
lent and a flourishing country.

Monies, Weights, and *Measures* of Chili are the same as those of Spain ; for
CADIZ. The quintal of 4 arrobas, or 100 lbs. = 101·44 lbs. avoirdupois. T
or principal corn measure, contains 3,439 English cubic inches, and is th
1.599 Winch. bushels. Hence 5 fanegas = 1 Winch. quarter very nearly.
or measure of length = 33·384 Eng. inches.

VAN DIEMEN'S LAND, a large island belonging to Great Britai
part of Australia, lying between 41° 20′ and 43° 40′ S. lat., and 14
148° 20′ W. lon. It is supposed to contain about 15,000,000 acres.—
Mercator's Chart prefixed to this work.)

This land was discovered by the Dutch navigator Tasman, in 1642
named in honour of Anthony Van Diemen, at that time governor-gen
Dutch possessions in the East Indies. Previously to 1798, it was su
form part of New Holland, but it was then ascertained to be an islan

possession of by the British in 1803; and in 1804, Hobart Town, the
was founded.

surface is generally hilly and mountainous; but there are several fertile plains,
ood deal of the hilly ground is susceptible of being cultivated. On the whole,
·, it is not supposed that more than about a third part of the entire surface of the
an be considered arable; but about a third more may be advantageously used as
asture. It is well watered; the climate delightful, and suitable for European
tions. The wheat raised here is superior to that produced in New South Wales,
siderable quantities are exported to Sydney. Wool, however, is at present the
·oduce of the colony.

Diemen's Land, like New South Wales, was originally intended to serve as a
lony, and convicts are still sent to it; latterly, however, it has received a very
able number of free settlers. In 1830, the total population of the island, ex-
f aborigines, amounted to 21,125, of whom about 10,000 were convicts. The
· between the sexes is not quite so great here as in New South Wales.

rosperity of the colony was formerly a good deal retarded by the enormities
ed by a banditti of runaway convicts, known by the name of bush-rangers; and
ently by the hostilities of the natives. Vigorous measures have, however, been
for the suppression of such outrages, by confining the natives within a limited
and it is to be hoped that they may be effectual.

t Town is situated in the southern part of the island, on the west side of the
·went, near its junction with Storm Bay. The water is deep, and the anchorage
A jetty has been constructed, accessible to the largest ships. The situation
o have been very well chosen; and the town has been judiciously laid out. In
1831, it contained 6,000 inhabitants, distributed as follows: viz. 1,400 free
lts, 600 ditto under age; 1,100 free female adults, 400 ditto under age; 1,900
oners, and 600 female ditto. There were in all 785 houses, supposed to be
: an average, 50l. a year. There are 3 printing establishments in the town,
· 4 newspapers, some of them very well conducted. There is also a Book
a Mechanics' Institute, and several respectable schools and academies. The
·men's Land banking company has its office in Hobart Town.

eston, the second town in the island, is situated in the northern part, at the head
vigable river Tamar, which falls into Port Dalrymple. Its population may
o about 2,000. It has a considerable trade with Sydney and Hobart Town,
tly it has begun to trade direct to England.

of Van Diemen's Land. — Drunkenness is very prevalent among the convict
he population; and malt liquors, rum, brandy, and wine, form the principal
·e imports into the colony. Next to them are piece goods, hardware, tea, sugar,
total real value of the imports in 1830, was estimated at 300,000l.; and that of
ts at 170,000l. The latter consisted of

	£		£
- - - -	48,000	Hides - - - - - -	600
- - - -	40,000	Seal Skins - - - -	400
- - - -	17,000	Opossum and Kangaroo ditto -	400
- - - -	6,000	Mimosa Bark - - -	2,000
- - - -	3,000	Timber - - - -	1,000
- - - -	5,000	Unenumerated Goods - -	41,600
- - - -	4,500		
Oats - - - -	500	Total -	£170,000

antity of wool imported into the United Kingdom in 1830, from Van Diemen's
· 993,979 lbs., being about 20,000 lbs. more than the quantity imported from
h Wales,—an extraordinary importation from a country into which sheep were
l for the first time in 1804.

·eights, and Measures, same as in England. The Spanish dollar circulates at

·, &c. — In 1830, there belonged to the island 26 vessels, of the aggregate
2,151 tons. In the same year, 65 ships, of 22,587 tons and 1,633 men, cleared
Great Britain for New South Wales and Van Diemen's Land, in about equal
s for each.

, &c. — The customs duties collected in the colony amount to about 45,000l.
d the whole revenue is about 65,000l.

regulations as to the granting of land in Van Diemen's Land, &c., see

etails, and those on the following page, have been, for the most part, abstracted
Hobart Town Almanack for 1831.

Custom-house Regulations.

(Hours for public business from 10 to 3 daily, excepting on Saturday, from 10 to 12.)

	L.	s.	d.
Entry of a British vessel, not colonial, with merchandise	1	10	0
Entry of any foreign vessel	3	0	0
Permission to trade	1	1	0
Dues on each bond	0	10	0
Dues on port clearance and fee	0	7	6
Transports are free from port charges.			
Colonial Vessels. — Entry and clearance to the out ports	0	4	0
Fee on ditto	0	2	0
Entry and clearance to the fishery or the out settlement	0	10	0
Fee on ditto	0	2	0
Clearance of an open boat	0	1	0
Annual licence for a boat	0	2	6
Duties. — On brandy, per gallon	0	10	0
On Hollands or Geneva, per gallon	0	10	0
On rum, per gallon, the produce of the West Indian colonies	0	7	6
On British gin, per gallon	0	7	6
On tobacco, per lb.	0	1	6

The duty on all spirits, either British or foreign, is increased in proportion to strength, if over proof, according to Sykes's hydrometer.

On all merchandise of foreign produce or manufacture, an *ad valorem* duty of 5 per cent. on importation, agreeably to the act of 4 Geo. 4. c. 96. with the exception of wine, which is subjected to a duty of 15 per cent. Goods of British manufacture are not subjected to any duty.

	L.	s.	d.
Wharfage. — On landing each cask, bale, or package	0	0	9
On landing iron, per ton	0	9	0
On landing salt, per ton	0	3	0
On landing timber, per 1,000 feet	0	2	0
On shipping each cask, bale, or package	0	0	3
On shipping iron, per ton	0	3	0
On shipping salt, per ton	0	1	0

Colonial produce, when landed or shipped, is not subjected to any charge, except for a sufferance.

	L.	s.	d.
Fees. — A sufferance to land or ship goods	0	1	0
A warrant to remove goods from under bond	0	1	0
On landing each cask or package of spirits or wine	0	0	6
On the registry of vessels not exceeding 40 tons	2	0	0
On the registry of vessels above 40 tons, per ton	0	1	0
To the chief clerk on the registry of vessels	0	10	0
On endorsing change of master	0	10	0

Warehouse Rent and Charges. — A government order, published 7th February 1826, fixes the following rents on spirits and tobacco, in the king's bonded stores, viz.: —

1st. All spirituous liquors, 1*s.* 3*d.* per tun of 252 gallons, for every week, or any period less than a week, during which the same shall be deposited.

2dly. Tobacco, 6*d.* per ton for every week, or any period less than a week, during which the same shall be deposited.

3dly. The amount of all such warehouse rent, in respect of any cask or package required to be delivered, must be paid before the same can be so delivered.

4thly. No allowance whatsoever will at any time be made in respect of, nor will the government be answerable for, any loss by fire, leakage, robbery, or casualty of any kind.

Government Order, 28th February, 1829. — Representations having been made to the lieutenant-governor of the inconvenience and delay attending the stowing and unstowing of goods in the bonded warehouses, a gang of men has been appointed to be employed under the storekeeper for this purpose exclusively, and the following scale of charges will be required to be paid: —

For Spirits. — Per pipe, three quarter pipe, or puncheon, each, stowing 9*d.*, unstowing 1*s.* 6*d.*

Per half pipe, hogshead, or barrel, stowing 6*d.*, unstowing 2*s.*

Per case containing 3 or more dozen bottles, stowing 3*d.*, unstowing 4*d.*

Per case containing a less quantity than 3 dozen, st unstowing 3*d.*

For Tobacco. — In large seroons, each, stowing 6d ing 9*d.*

In cases, each, stowing 3*d.*, unstowing, 4*d.*

In kegs, each, stowing 2*d.*, unstowing, 3*d.*

In baskets, rolls, or small seroons, stowing 1d ing 1*d.*

In consequence of this arrangement it is to be u that no labourers are to be admitted into, or emplo bonded warehouse, except the storekeeper's gang.

Goods intended to be warehoused under bond landed before 12 o'clock.

Hours of attendance at the Custom-house qua o'clock till 4 from the 1st of September to the 30th and from 9 till 4 from 1st of May till 31st of August

The appointed days for opening the bonding war the delivery of goods, are, Mondays and Thursday week, at 1 o'clock, on which days the duties mus prior to 12 o'clock. Tobacco is issued on the same 10 to 12 o'clock.

Rates of Pilotage at the Derwent.

Draught of water.	Into. L.	s.	d.
10 Feet and under	3	0	$11\frac{1}{3}$
11 ditto	3	3	$4\frac{1}{2}$
12 ditto	3	8	3
13 ditto	3	15	$6\frac{3}{4}$
14 ditto	4	5	$3\frac{1}{4}$
15 ditto	4	19	$11\frac{1}{4}$
16 ditto	5	17	0
17 ditto	7	1	$4\frac{1}{2}$
18 ditto	8	13	$0\frac{3}{4}$
19 ditto	10	14	6
20 ditto	13	3	3

At Port Dalrymple.

Proceeding above Whirlpool Reach.	L.	s.	d.	F be po
7 Feet and under	2	5	6	
Above 7 feet, per foot	0	6	6	

If the pilot does not board the vessel outside ground at the Heads at George Town, or the weath mitting his going outside, if he be not ready to channel by keeping his boat in the fair way until t be boarded, he shall forfeit one half the pilotage in

For every number of inches below 6, no charg made; for half a foot and upwards, 1 foot is to be ch

Colonial vessels are exempted from the payment unless the master shall make the signal for a pilot his service.

Harbour Dues at the Derwent.

For mooring and unmooring a vessel within th harbour, per register ton

For each removal of the ship within the harbour per register ton

Colonial vessels under 80 tons, per register, to be from the payment of the foregoing dues, unless th the harbour master be specifically required.

At Port Dalrymple.

For each removal of a ship or vessel from anchorag or moorings, to other anchorage or moorings under 200 tons
200 tons and under 300
300 tons and under 400
400 tons and under 500
500 tons and upwards

Each vessel entering the harbour will be ch 2 removes.

Vessels belonging to the port are not to pay harb

No vessels to be deemed colonial that are not Van Diemen's Land.

VANILLA, the fruit of the *Epidendrum Vanilla*, a species of vine ext cultivated in Mexico.

It has a trailing stem, not unlike the common ivy, but not so woody, which itself to any tree that grows near it. The Indians propagate it by planting cu the foot of trees selected for that purpose. It rises to the height of 18 or 20 flowers are of a greenish yellow colour, mixed with white; the fruit is ab 10 inches long, of a yellow colour when gathered, but dark brown or black ported into Europe; it is wrinkled on the outside, and full of a vast number like grains of sand, having, when properly prepared, a peculiar and delicious fl It is principally used for mixing with and perfuming chocolate; and is, on that largely imported into Spain; but as chocolate, owing to oppressive duties, is li in England, vanilla is not much known in this country.

Vanilla is principally gathered in the intendancy of Vera Cruz, in Mexic santla, Colipa, Vacuatla, and other places. It is collected by the Indians, who the whites (*gente de razon*), who prepare it for market. They spread it to d sun for some hours, then wrap it in woollen cloths to sweat. Like pepper, i its colour in this operation — becoming almost black. It is finally dried by ex to the sun for a day. There are four varieties of vanilla, all differing in pric cellence; viz. the *vanilla fina*, the *zacate*, the *rezacate*, and the *vasura*. The b

orests surrounding the village of Zentila, in the intendancy of Oaxaca. Accord-
mboldt, the mean exportation of vanilla from Vera Cruz may amount to from
00 millares, worth at Vera Cruz from 30,000 to 40,000 dollars. Vanilla is also
from Brazil, but it is very inferior. The finest Mexican vanilla is extremely
d. All sorts are loaded in this country with the enormous prohibitory duty
, per lb! — (See *Humboldt, Nouvelle Espagne,* 2d edit. tome iii. pp. 37. 46.;
Notes on Mexico, p. 194., &c.)

UM, a species of fine parchment. — (See PARCHMENT.)

CE, a famous city of Austrian Italy, formerly the capital of the republic
me, situated on a cluster of small islands towards the northern extremity
ciatic, in lat. 45° 25¼' N., lon. 12° 21' E. Population about 100,000. The
of Venice, once the most extensive of any European city, is now com-
trifling; and the population is gradually diminishing both in numbers
h. Her imports are principally confined to hardware, linen, and other
res, from the north of Europe; East and West India goods direct, or
he medium of Malta; and salt fish, from Newfoundland or England, for
mption of the inhabitants during fast days and Lent. The exports
consist of raw and wrought silk, oil, fruits, cheese, &c., the products
oining provinces of Italy. Her manufactures, so famous in the middle
ow much decayed.

Formerly there were various methods of accounting here; but now accounts are kept, as at
e Italiane, divided into centesimi, or hundred parts. The lira is supposed to be of the same
ess, and, consequently, value as the franc. But the coins *actually in circulation,* denominated
ectively equal in sterling value to about 5d. and 4¼d. The latter are coined by the Austrian

d *Measures.* — The commercial weights are here, as at Genoa, of two sorts; the *peso sottile*
grosso. The French kilogramme, called the libbra Italiana, is also sometimes introduced.

grosso =	105·186 lbs. avoirdupois.	100 lbs. peso sottile =	66·428 lbs. avoirdupois.
—	127·830 lbs. Troy.	—	80·728 lbs. Troy.
—	47·398 kilogrammes.	—	30·123 kilogrammes.
—	98·485 lbs. of Hamburgh.	—	62·196 lbs. of Hamburgh.
—	96·569 lbs. of Amsterdam.	—	60·986 lbs. of Amsterdam.

o, or measure for corn, is divided into 4 staja, 16 quarte, or 64 quartaroli. The staja = 2·27
ls.
re for wine, anfora = 4 bigonzi, or 8 mastelli, or 48 sechii, or 192 bozze, or 768 quartuzzi. It
nglish wine gallons.
= 5 bigonzi. Oil is sold by weight or measure. The botta contains 2 migliaja, or 80 mire of
osso. The miro = 4·028 English wine gallons.
, or long measure for woollens = 26·6 English inches; the braccio for silks = 24·8 do. The
e = 13·68 English inches. (*Nelkenbrecher,* and *Dr. Kelly.*)

l *Notice.* — Venice was the earliest, and for a lengthened period the most
e, commercial city of modern Europe. Her origin dates from the invasion of
tila in 452. A number of the inhabitants of Aquileia, and the neighbouring
ying from the ravages of the barbarians, found a poor but secure asylum in
of small islands opposite to the mouth of the Brenta, near the head of the
ulf. In this situation they were forced to cultivate commerce and its sub-
as the only means by which they could maintain themselves. At a very
, they began to trade with Constantinople and the Levant; and notwith-
e competition of the Genoese and Pisans, they continued to engross the
de in Eastern products, till the discovery of a route to India by the Cape of
e turned this traffic into a totally new channel. The crusades contributed
the wealth, and to extend the commerce and the possessions of Venice.
e middle of the 15th century, when the Turkish sultan, Mahomet II.,
stantinople sword in hand, and placed himself on the throne of Constantine
ian, the power of the Venetians had attained its maximum. At that period,
ral extensive, populous, and well cultivated provinces in Lombardy, the
mistress of Crete and Cyprus, of the greater part of the Morea, and most
n the Egean Sea. She had secured a chain of forts and factories that ex-
; the coasts of Greece from the Morea to Dalmatia; while she monopolised
hole foreign trade of Egypt. The preservation of this monopoly, of the
inion she had early usurped over the Adriatic, and of the dependence of
and distant establishments, were amongst the principal objects of the Ve-
nment; and the measures they adopted in that view were at once skilfully
prosecuted with inflexible constancy. With the single exception of Rome,
e 15th century, was by far the richest and most magnificent of European
er singular situation in the midst of the sea, on which she seems to float,
o impress those who visited her with still higher notions of her wealth and
annazarius is not the only one who has preferred Venice to the ancient
world; but none have so beautifully expressed their preference.

Viderat Adriacis Venetam Neptunus in undis,
    Stare urbem, et toto ponere jura mari.
Nunc mihi Tarpeïas quantumvis, Jupiter, arces
    Objice, et illa tua mœnia martis, ait :
Si Tiberim pelago præfers, urbem aspice utramque,
    Illam homines dicas, hanc possuisse Deos.

Though justly regarded as one of the principal bulwarks of Christendom ag
Turks, Venice had to contend, in the early part of the 16th century, agains*
bination of the European powers. The famous League of Cambray, of whi
Julius II. was the real author, was formed for the avowed purpose of effecting *
subjugation of the Venetians, and the partition of their territories. The emp
the kings of France and Spain joined this powerful confederacy. But owir
the valour of the Venetians, than to dissensions amongst their enemies, the Le:
speedily dissolved without materially weakening the power of the republic. F
period the policy of Venice was comparatively pacific and cautious. But
standing her efforts to keep on good terms with the Turks, the latter invaded (
1570; and conquered it after a gallant resistance continued for 11 years.
netians had the principal share in the decisive victory gained over the Turks at
in 1571. But owing to the discordant views of the confederates, it was not
followed up, and could not prevent the fall of Cyprus.

The war with the Turks in Candia commenced in 1645, and continued t
The Venetians exerted all their energies in defence of this valuable island; a*
quisition cost the Turks above 200,000 men. The loss of Candia, and the
cline of the commerce of the republic, now almost wholly turned into other
reduced Venice, at the close of the 17th century, to a state of great exhaustion.
be said, indeed, to have owed the last 100 years of her existence more to the fo
and jealousies of others than to any strength of her own. Nothing, howev
avert that fate she had seen overwhelm so many once powerful states. In
" maiden city" submitted to the yoke of the conqueror: and the last surviving *
antiquity — the link that united the ancient to the modern world — stripped
pendence, of commerce, and of wealth, is now slowly sinking into the waves w'
arose.

The foundation of Venice is described by Gibbon, c. 35.; and in his 60th chapter he has elo
picted her prosperity in the year 1200. Mr. Hallam, in his work on the Middle Ages (vol. i. pp
has given a brief account of the changes of the Venetian government. Her history occupies a ·
space in the voluminous work of M. Sismondi on the Italian Republics; but his details as to h·
commercial policy are singularly meagre and uninteresting. All previous histories of Venice
ever, been thrown into the shade by the admirable work of M. Daru (Histoire de la Républiqu
2d ed. 8 vols. 8vo. Paris, 1821). Having had access to genuine sources of information, inaccessi!
predecessors, M. Daru's work is as superior to theirs in accuracy, as it is in most other quali*
in a history.

Trade, Navigation, and Manufactures of the Venetians in the 15th Century. —
netian ships of the largest class were denominated galeasses, and were fitted
double purpose of war and commerce. Some of them carried 50 pieces of ca
crews of 600 men. These vessels were sometimes, also, called argosers or argo*
had early an intercourse with England; and argosies used to be common in
In 1325, Edward II. entered into a commercial treaty with Venice, in ·
liberty is given to them, for 10 years, to sell their merchandise in England, an·
home in safety, without being made answerable, as was the practice in thos·
the crimes or debts of other strangers. — (*Anderson's Chron. Deduction, A*
Sir William Monson mentions, that the last argosie that sailed from Venic·
land was lost, with a rich cargo and many passengers, on the coast of the Isle
in 1587.

In the beginning of the 15th century, the annual value of the goods exp
Venice by sea, exclusive of those exported to the states adjoining her provinc·
bardy, was estimated, by contemporary writers, at 10,000,000 ducats; the pr·
out and home voyage, including freight, being estimated at 4,000,000 d
the period in question, the Venetian shipping consisted of 3,000 vessels o!
to 200 tons burthen, carrying 17,000 sailors; 300 ships with 8,000 sailor·
galleys of various size, kept afloat by the republic for the protection of her·
having 11,000 men on board. In the dock-yard, 16,000 labourers were *
ployed. The trade to Syria and Egypt seems to have been conducted pri·
ready money; for 500,000 ducats are said to have been annually export·
countries; 100,000 were sent to England. —(*Daru*, tome ii. p. 283., tome iii. p·
The vessels of Venice visited every port of the Mediterranean, and every coast ·
and her maritime commerce was, probably, not much inferior to that of all·
Christendom. So late as 1518, five Venetian galeasses arrived at Antwerp,·
spices, drugs, silks, &c. for the fair at that city.

Venetians did not, however, confine themselves to the supply of Europe with the ... ities of the East, and to the extension and improvement of navigation. They ... ed new arts, and prosecuted them with vigour and success, at a period when ... re entirely unknown in other European countries. The glass manufacture ... ce was the first, and for a long time the most celebrated, of any in Europe ; and ... ufactures of silk, cloth of gold, leather, refined sugar, &c. were deservedly ... d. The jealousy of the government, and their intolerance of any thing like ... cussion, was unfavourable to the production of great literary works. Every ... s, however, aware of the fame which Venice early acquired by the perfection ... h she carried the art of printing. The classics that issued from the Aldine ... are still universally and justly admired for their beauty and correctness. The ... Venice was established in the 12th century. It continued throughout a bank ... it merely, and was skilfully conducted.

... he policy of government, though favourable to the introduction and establish- ... manufactures, was fatal to their progressive advancement. The importation of ... manufactured commodities into the territories of the republic for domestic con- ... a was forbidden under the severest penalties. The processes to be followed ... anufacture of most articles were regulated by law. — " Dès l'année 1172, un ... avoit été créé pour la police des arts et métiers, la qualité et la quantité des matières ... igneusement déterminées." — (Daru, tome iii. p. 153.) Having, in this way, ... ear from foreign competition, and being tied down to a system of routine, there ... ing left to stimulate invention and discovery ; and during the last century the ... ures of Venice were chiefly remarkable as evincing the extraordinary perfection ... they had early arrived, and the absence of all recent improvements. An unex- ... le judge, M. Berthollet, employed by the French government to report on the ... he arts of Venice, observed, " Que l'industrie des Vénitiens, comme celle des ... avoit été précoce, mais était restée stationnaire." — (Daru, tome iii. p. 161.) ... aru has given the following extract from an article in the statutes of the State ... n, which strikingly displays the real character of the Venetian government, ... jealousy of foreigners : — " If any workman or artisan carry his art to a foreign ... to the prejudice of the republic, he shall be ordered to return ; if he do not ... nearest relations shall be imprisoned, that his regard for them may induce him ... ack. If he return, the past shall be forgiven, and employment shall be pro- ... him at Venice. If, in despite of the imprisonment of his relations, he perse- ... s absence, an *emissary shall be employed to despatch him ;* and after his death ... ns shall be set at liberty ! "—(Tom. iii. p. 150.)

book of M. Daru's history contains a comprehensive and well-digested account of the com-
ufactures, and navigation of Venice. But it was not possible, in a work on the general history
lic, to enter so fully into the details as to these subjects as their importance would have jus-
Storia Civile e Politica del Commercio de' Veneziani, di Carlo Antonio Marin, in 8 vols. 8vo.
t Venice at different periods, from 1798 to 1808, is unworthy of the title. It contains, indeed,
y curious statements ; but it is exceedingly prolix ; and while the most unimportant and
cts are frequently discussed at extreme length, many of great interest are either entirely omit-
treated in a very brief and unsatisfactory manner. The commercial history of Venice re-
o be written ; and were it executed by a person of competent attainments, it would be a
le acquisition.

A CRUZ, the principal sea-port on the western coast of Mexico ; lat. ... N., lon. 100° 49⅓' W. Population (supposed) 16,000. Opposite the ... the distance of about 400 fathoms, is a small island, on which is built ... g castle of St. Juan d'Ulloa, which commands the town. The harbour, ... between the town and the castle, is exceedingly insecure ; the anchorage ... ery bad, that no vessel is considered safe unless made fast to rings fixed for ... se in the castle wall ; and even this is not always a sufficient protection ... fury of the northerly winds (*los nortes*), which sometimes blow with tre- ... violence. Humboldt mentions, in proof of what is now stated, that a ... he line, moored by 9 cables to the castle, tore, during a tempest, the ... s from the wall, and was dashed to pieces on the opposite shore.— ... *Espagne*, ed. 2de, tome iv. p. 59.) Its extreme unhealthiness is, how- ... ore serious drawback upon Vera Cruz, than the badness of its port. ... to be the original seat of the yellow fever. The city is well built, and ... s clean ; but it is surrounded by sand hills and ponds of stagnant water, ... thin the tropics, are quite enough to generate disease. The inhabitants, ... accustomed to the climate, are not subject to this formidable disorder ; ... rangers, even those from Havannah and the West India islands, are ... he infection. No precautions can prevent its attack ; and many have ... alapa, on the road to Mexico, who merely passed through this pesti- ... t. During the period that the foreign trade of Mexico was carried on

exclusively by the *flota*, which sailed periodically from Cadiz, Vera Cru
celebrated for its fair, held at the arrival of the ships. It was then crowded
dealers from Mexico, and most parts of Spanish America; but the abolit
the system of regular fleets in 1778, proved fatal to this fair, as well as to th
more celebrated fair of Portobello.

The distance in a direct line from Mexico to Vera Cruz is 69 leagues; but
road it is considerably greater. Mexico being situated on a *plateau* elevated
8,000 feet above the level of the sea, and the country being in many places very r
the road originally was so bad as to be hardly practicable, even for mules. I
the last 30 years, immense sums have been laid out on its improvement; and
siderable part of it has been completed in the best, and, indeed, most splendid ma
but in many places it is still rough and unfinished, and does not admit of ca
being used. M. Humboldt seems to think, that were this road completed, whe
flour brought from the table land of Mexico might be shipped at Vera Cruz, an
in the West Indies cheaper than the wheat and flour of the United States.
agree with Mr. Poinsett in regarding any such expectation as quite chimerical. T
the advantage on the side of Mexico in respect of superior fertility of soil and
ness of labour were decidedly greater than it really is, it would not balance the enc
expense of 300 miles of land carriage upon such bulky and heavy articles, more esp
as the wagons would, in most cases, have to return empty. It is plain, howeve
the advantage of getting the produce of the mines, and the peculiar productions
country, as cochineal, indigo, sugar, vanilla, tobacco, &c., conveyed with comp
facility to market, and of getting back European goods at a proportionally less ex
will more than indemnify all the outlay that may be required to perfect the roa
will be of the very greatest importance to the republic; but it is quite out of the q
to imagine that Vera Cruz is ever destined to become a rival of New Orleans
exportation of corn and flour.

For a considerable period after the town of Vera Cruz had thrown off the S
yoke, the castle of St. Juan d'Ulloa continued in possession of the Spaniards.
this interval, the commerce of Vera Cruz was almost entirely transferred to the
Alvarado, 12 leagues to the south-east. Alvarado is built upon the left ban
river of the same name. The bar at the mouth of the river, about 1½ miles bel
town, renders it inaccessible for vessels drawing above 10 or 12 feet water. Larg
are obliged to anchor in the roads, where they are exposed to all the violence
north winds, loading and unloading by means of lighters. Alvarado is suppose
probably without much foundation, to be a little healthier than Vera Cruz. Th
has now mostly reverted to its old channel.

Exports and Imports. — The precious metals have always formed the principal
of export from Mexico. During the 10 years ending with 1801, the average
produce of the Mexican mines amounted, according to M. Humboldt, to 23,0
dollars — (*Nouvelle Espagne*, tome iv. p. 137.); and in 1805, the produ
27,165,888 dollars. — (*Id.* tome iv. p. 83.) But during the revolutionary w
old Spanish capitalists, to whom most of the mines belonged, being proscribe
grated with all the property they could scrape together: and this withdrawal of
from the mines, added to the injury several of them sustained by the destruction
works during the contest, the interruption of all regular pursuits which it occ
and the insecurity and anarchy that have since prevailed, have caused an extrac
falling off in the produce of the mines; so much so that it is not supposed to am
present to more than 12,000,000 dollars, being less than *half* the quantity it ar
to previously to the breaking out of the disturbances! — (*Jacob on the Precious*
vol. ii. p. 239.) The operations of the English mining companies have not
had any perceptible influence in increasing the produce of the mines. — (See
Companies.)

Besides the precious metals, cochineal, sugar, flour, indigo, provisions, lea
saparilla, vanilla, jalap, soap, logwood, and pimento, are the principal articles
from Vera Cruz.

The imports consist principally of linen, cotton, woollen, and silk goods
brandy, cacao, quicksilver, iron, steel, wine, wax, &c.

According to the statement published by the Mexican government, the value of the im
exports at Vera Cruz and Alvarado, in 1824, was as follows: —

	Doll
Imports from other Mexican ports	28
from American ports	4,36
from European and other foreign ports	7,43
Total	12,08

Dollars.

ts for other Mexican ports   -   -   -   -   202,042
for American ports   -   -   -   -   -   3,022,422
for European and other ports   -   -   -   -   1,468,093

Total   -   -   -   4,592,557

count is exclusive of the imports by government on account of the loan ne-
London.

ng to Humboldt, the imports at Vera Cruz, before the revolutionary struggles,
stimated, at an average, at about 15,000,000 dollars, and the exports at about
ditto.

however, be observed that this statement refers only to the *registered* articles,
that paid the duties on importation and exportation. But exclusive of these,
f the articles clandestinely imported by the ports on the gulf, previously to
ion, was estimated at 4,500,000 dollars a year; and 2,500,000 dollars were
o be annually smuggled out of the country in plate and bars, and ingots of
lver. A regular contraband trade used to be carried on between Vera Cruz
ca: and notwithstanding all the efforts of government for their exclusion, and
ve severity of its laws against smuggling, the shops of Mexico were always
supplied with the products of England and Germany. — (*Humboldt, Nou-
ne*, tome iv. p. 125.; *Poinsett's Notes on Mexico*, p. 133.)

nboldt states, that the total population of Mexico, exclusive of Guatemala, may
d at about 7,000,000. Of this number about a half are Indians, the rest being
, or descendants of Europeans, and mixed races. But notwithstanding this
nt of population, the trade we carry on with Mexico is but trifling compared
ch we carry on with Brazil; and does not amount even to half our trade with
n the Rio de la Plata, or with Chili. The following is an account of the
ared value of all sorts of British produce and manufactures exported to the
ntral and Southern America, in 1829: —

	£		£
- - -	303,562	States of the Rio de la Plata	758,540
- - -	nil.	Chili - - -	818,950
- - -	232,703	Peru - - -	300,171
- - -	2,516,040		

rts of British goods at second hand into Mexico and Colombia, from Ja-
the other West India islands, are no longer of any considerable importance.
eing, with the exception of the United States, the richest and most populous
merican countries, the smallness of its trade with England may justly excite
t originates principally, we believe, in the want of large cities on the coast,
tance and difficulty of the roads from Vera Cruz and other ports to the
elevated part of the country. These circumstances, coupled with the ob-
h the restrictive policy of the Spaniards threw in the way of the importation
roducts, led to the establishment of manufactures in the interior. Previously
encement of the revolutionary struggles, some of these manufactures were
vanced state; and were sufficient to supply the population with most of the
other articles required for their consumption. They have since declined
; but as it is pretty certain that the wealth of the inhabitants has declined
his circumstance has had little effect in increasing importation.

ghts, and *Measures*, same as in Spain; for which, see CADIZ.
t *Vera Cruz.* — The Mexican government issued, on the 16th of November, 1827, a new
the following regulations were prefixed: —

Regulations as to the Mexican Tariff.

nations in amity with the United States of Mexico will be admitted to entry at the privi-
he republic, upon payment of the duties, and subject to the regulations to be observed at
ustom-house, according to this tariff.
ge duty is abolished, and all vessels arriving from foreign ports are to pay 17 rials per ton

els will not be allowed to trade coastways with the ports of the republic.
utting into any of the ports of this republic, by stress of weather or for refitment, will be
uisite time to complete their repairs or provisions, and will only have to pay such charges
ry.
their arrival are to present their manifests by triplicate, specifying the marks and numbers
, with the particulars of their respective contents.
ill be levied on all goods according to their specification in the manifest, whether they are
and any article that shall be found not specified in the manifest, or any alteration in the
lity, will subject such goods to seizure.
and measures designated in the tariff are those used in Mexico; and any article exceeding
annexed to the same shall, for every eighth of such excess in measurement, pay an eighth
duty affixed to the said article.
ot specified or enumerated in the tariff shall pay a duty of 40 per cent. on the valuation
ed on the same at the port of entry; and for every such valuation three brokers shall be
of whom is to be chosen by the importer, and the other two on the part of the Custom-

The *averia*, and all other duties lately payable in this republic under various denominations (the state duty), are abolished.

The importer shall be liable for the whole amount of the duties, one half of which is to be p 90 days from the day the goods are landed, and the other half within 90 days after the expira latter period. No article will be allowed to be taken out of the Custom-house until the d have been paid, or security given for the due payment of the same, to the satisfaction of authorities.

All articles imported prior to this law taking effect are liable to the international duties as be

After the duties have been once paid, no deduction or allowance whatever can be made on excepting in cases where an error may have occurred.

No article will be allowed to be re-exported without previous payment of the import duties.

All goods that may arrive damaged shall be examined in presence of the proper authorit allowance made according to the damage such goods shall have sustained.

All goods arriving direct from the place of their growth or manufacture, in vessels under th flag, are to pay one sixth less duty than in foreign vessels.

The tariff may be altered at any time, whenever the Congress shall deem it expedient so to c alteration which may be prejudicial to commerce in general shall be put in force until 6 m such alteration shall have been decided upon.

The basis contained in the preceding articles are not intended to interfere with any separat commerce which has or may be entered into by this nation.

These regulations are to be put in force within 60 days from the date hereof.

Articles admitted into Mexico Duty free.

Quicksilver.	Philosophical, mathematical, and optical instruments.	Implements for agricultur artificers.
Carts upon foreign construction.	Slates of all sorts.	Carding wire.
Wooden frames for houses.		Plants and seeds.
Printed books, maps, and music.		

Articles prohibited to be imported into Mexico.

Aniseeds, cummins, and caraways.	Tallow.	Flour and wheat.
Rum and molasses.	Soap, hard or soft.	Vermicelli.
Sugar, raw or refined.	Epaulets, gold and silver lace, galloons, &c.	Cotton thread, under No. 2
Coffee and chocolate.		Stone ware.
Rice.	Tapes of cotton.	Trunks and portmanteaus
Leather.	Shawls of silk or cotton.	Woollen cloths, coarse and
Boots and shoes.	Beds, bedding, and bed linen, made up, of every kind and description.	Parchment.
Saddlery of every description.		Wearing apparel of every
Salted and dried meats of all kinds.	Copper, in sheets or pigs.	Common salt.
Lard.	Lead, in sheet, pigs, or shot.	Hats, common, stuff, and
Wax, wrought.	Biscuit.	Tobacco, in leaf or manuf

Export Duties. — All articles, the growth and produce of this republic, are free of duty on exportation, excepting gold in coin, or wrought, which pays 2 per cent. *ad valorem*; silver in coin, or wrought, which pays 3½ per cent. *ad valorem*.

N. B. — Gold and silver ore, or in ingots or du bited under penalty of seizure.

Notices to Masters of Vessels and Passengers proceeding to any Mexican Port.

Notice is hereby given to all masters of vessels proceeding from London to any port or United States of Mexico, that the passengers they take out should be provided with passport his Excellency the minister of the republic, otherwise the vessels will be liable to detenti arrival at those ports, and the passengers on board unprovided with such passports will not b to land in the ports of Mexico. No plea for the want of them will be admitted.

Masters of vessels proceeding to and from those states are required to have on board a papers and vouchers, which, according to the orders conveyed through his Excellency t minister plenipotentiary at the court of his Britannic Majesty, to this consulate, ought to co sides the regular ship's papers, all the invoices of shippers, with the corresponding bills of la chandise found on board, which should not appear inserted in the invoices certified by the co otherwise is falsely described, either in quality or quantity, shall be considered and dealt wi band.

A bill of health, certified by the consul, will also be required from vessels on arrival, by th at the Mexican ports.

The above regulations are to be in force from the date of this notice.

J. SCHEIDNAGEL, Vi

Consulate of the United States of Mexico in London, 20. Austin-friars, Nov. 28. 1830.

Notice is hereby given, that the Congrés of the United States of Mexico decreed, the 12th the last year, that the Mexican envoys and consular agents must henceforward charge for e to Mexico 2 dollars, and for each certification and signature 4 dollars.

20. Austin-friars, 9th Jan. 1831.　　　　　　　The Vice-Consul, J. SCHEI

VERDIGRIS (Ger. *Grünspan;* Fr. *Vert-de-gris, Verdet;* It. *Verder Cardenillo, Verdete, Verde-gris;* Rus. *Jar*), a kind of rust of copper, of a bluish green colour, formed from the corrosion of copper by fermented Its specific gravity is 1·78. Its taste is disagreeably metallic; and, l compounds into which copper enters, it is poisonous. It was kno ancients, and various ways of preparing it are described by Pliny. It i tensively used by painters, and in dyeing; it is also used to some medicine. The best verdigris is made at Montpellier; the wines of I being particularly well suited for corroding copper, and forming this It is generally exported in cakes of about 25 lbs. weight each. It is a factured in this country, by means of the refuse of cider, &c.; the hi 2s. per lb. on the foreign article giving the home producers a pretty monopoly of the market. The goodness of verdigris is judged of from ness and brightness of its colour, its dryness, and its forming, when rub hand with a little water or saliva, smooth paste, free from grittiness. — (Chemistry; Rees's Cyclopædia.)

VERJUICE (Ger. *Agrest;* Fr. *Verjus;* It. *Agresto;* Sp. *Agraz*), harsh, austere vinegar, made of the expressed juice of the wild appl

rench give this name to unripe grapes, and to the sour liquor obtained
em.

RMICELLI, (Ger. *Nudeln;* Du. *Meelneepen, Proppen;* Fr. *Vermicelli;* It.
lli, Tagliolini; Sp. *Aletrias*), an Italian mixture, prepared of flour, cheese,
f eggs, sugar, and saffron; and reduced into little long pieces, or threads
rms, by forcing it with a piston through a number of little holes in the end
e made for that purpose. It is much used in Italy, and other countries,
s, broths, &c.

RMILION. See Cinnabar.

EGAR (Ger. *Essig;* Du. *Azyn;* Fr. *Vinaigre;* It. *Aceto;* Sp. and Port.
; Rus. *Ukzus;* Lat. *Acetum*).—(See Acid (Acetic), for a description of
) A duty being imposed on vinegar of 2*d.* the gallon, its manufacture
under the control of the excise. A licence, costing 5*l.*, and renewable
, has to be taken out by every maker of vinegar, or acetous acid.

es for manufacturing or keeping vinegar must be entered, under a penalty of 50*l.* No vinegar
o receive any vinegar, or acetous acid, or sugar wash, or any preparation for vinegar, without
hours' notice to the excise, under penalty of 100*l.* Any person sending out or receiving vinegar
ss the duty on it be paid, and it be accompanied by a permit, forfeit 200*l.* All vinegar makers
e entries at the next Excise-office of the quantity made within each month, and are bound to
he duties within a month of such entry, on pain of double duties. — (See 58 Geo. 3. c. 65., and
tice of the Peace, Marriott's ed.) The nett produce of the duties on vinegar, in 1829, amounted
12*s.* 10*d.*

RIOL. See Copperas.

RIOL, OIL OF. See Acid (Sulphuric).

RAMARINE (Ger. *Ultramarin;* Fr. *Bleu d'outremer;* It. *Oltramarino;*
amar; Rus. *Ultramarin*), a very fine blue powder made from the blue
lapis lazuli. It has the valuable property of neither fading, nor be-
tarnished, on exposure to the air, or a moderate heat; and on this account
prized by painters. Owing to its great price, it is very apt to be adul-
It was introduced about the end of the fifteenth century.

NCE, a period of *one, two,* or *three* months, or of so many days, after
of a bill of exchange, according to the custom of different places,
e bill becomes due. Double or treble usance, is double or treble the
he; and half usance is half the time. When a month is divided, the
ce, notwithstanding the differences in the lengths of the months, is uni-
days. Usances are calculated exclusive of the date of the bill. Bills
nge drawn at usance are allowed the usual days of grace, and on the last
ree days the bill should be presented for payment. — (See Exchange.)

RY. See Interest and Annuities.

W.

GHEES, sometimes called Japan Canes, a species of cane imported
na. They should be chosen pliable, tough, round, and taper; the knots
distances from each other; and the heavier the better. Such as are dark
badly glazed, and light, should be rejected. — (*Milburn's Orient. Com.*)

EHOUSING SYSTEM. By this system is meant the provisions made
ng imported articles in public warehouses, at a reasonable rent, without
of the duties on importation till they be withdrawn for home consump-
re-exported, no duty is ever paid.

liency and Origin of the Warehousing System. — It is laid down by Dr. Smith,
his justly celebrated maxims on the subject of taxation, that " Every tax
e levied at the time and in the manner that is most likely to be convenient for
utor to pay it."— (*Wealth of Nations,* vol. iii. p. 368.) No one can doubt
ness of this maxim; and yet it was very strangely neglected, down to 1803, in
ement of the customs. Previously to this period, the duties on most goods
ad either to be paid at the moment of their importation, or a *bond,* with suffi-
rity for their future payment, had to be given to the revenue officers. The
d inconvenience of such a system is obvious. It was often very difficult to
es; and the merchant, in order to raise funds to pay the duties, was fre-
duced to the ruinous necessity of selling his goods immediately on their
en, perhaps, the market was already glutted. Neither was this the only incon-

venience that grew out of this system; for the duties having to be paid all a
and not by degrees as the goods were sold for consumption, their price was ra
the amount of the profit on the capital advanced in payment of the duties; comp
too, was diminished in consequence of the greater command of funds required t
on trade under such disadvantages; and a few rich individuals were enabled to
polise the importation of those commodities on which heavy duties were payable.
system had, besides, an obvious tendency to discourage the carrying trade. It pre
this country from becoming an *entrepôt* for foreign products, by hindering the i
ation of such as were not immediately wanted for home consumption ; and thus
to lessen the resort of foreigners to our markets, inasmuch as it rendered it diffic
rather impossible, for them to complete an assorted cargo.   And in addition to al
circumstances, the difficulty of granting a really equivalent drawback to the expo
such commodities as had paid duty, opened a door for the commission of every spe
fraud.

But these disadvantages and drawbacks, obvious as they may now appear,
attract the public attention till a comparatively late period. Sir Robert Walpole
to have been one of the first who had a clear perception of their injurious influenc
it was the principal object of the famous *Excise Scheme*, proposed by him in 1
oblige the importers of tobacco and wine to deposit them in public warehouses ;
ing them, however, from the necessity of paying the duties chargeable on them t
were withdrawn for home consumption.

No doubt can now remain in the mind of any one, that the adoption of this
would have been of the greatest advantage to the commerce and industry of the c
But so powerful was the delusion generated in the public mind with respect to
its proposal well nigh caused a rebellion. Most of the merchants of the d
availed themselves of the facilities which the existing system afforded of defraud
revenue ; and they dexterously endeavoured to thwart the success of a scheme
would have given a serious check to such practices, by making the public believe
would be fatal to the commercial prosperity of the country.   The efforts of th
chants were powerfully seconded by the spirit of party, which then ran very high
political opponents of the ministry, anxious for an opportunity to prejudice them
public estimation, contended that the scheme was only the first step towards the
duction of such a universal system of excise as would inevitably prove alike sub
of the comfort and liberty of the people.   In consequence of these artful misre
ations, the most violent clamours were every where excited against the schem
one occasion Sir Robert Walpole narrowly escaped falling a sacrifice to the ungov
fury of the mob, which beset all the avenues to the House of Commons; an
many violent and lengthened debates, the scheme was ultimately abandoned.

The disadvantages of the old plan, and the benefits to be derived from the establ
of a voluntary warehousing system, were most ably pointed out by Dean Tucke
" Essay on the Comparative Advantages and Disadvantages of Great Britain and
with respect to Trade," published in 1750.   But so powerful was the im
made by the violent opposition to Sir Robert Walpole's scheme, and such is
of prejudice, that it was not till 1803 that this obvious and signal improve
the greatest, perhaps, that has been made in our commercial and financial sy
could be safely adopted.

2. *Regulations as to Warehousing.* — The statute of 43 Geo. 3. c. 132. laid the
ations of this system ; but it was much improved and extended by subsequent
the regulations of which have been embodied in the act 6 Geo. 4. c. 112., wh
effect on the 6th of January, 1826.

This act empowers the commissioners of the customs, under the authority a
tion of the Lords of the Treasury, to nominate the ports at which goods may
housed without payment of duty, and the warehouses in which particular descri
goods may be deposited.   It also fixes the time during which goods are allow
main in the warehouse; and prescribes the regulations as to their removal fror
port, their sale and stowage in the warehouse, the remission of the duties i
loss by accident, the allowances for waste, &c.   But as this statute is of much
ance, we subjoin a full abstract of it.

ABSTRACT OF THE ACT 6 GEO. 4. c. 112. FOR THE WAREHOUSING OF GOODS.

Commencement of the act, 5th of January, 1826. — § 1.
Treasury to appoint Warehousing Ports. — It shall be lawful for the commissioners of the t
their warrant, to appoint the ports which shall be warehousing ports for the purposes of this
it shall be lawful for the commissioners of customs, subject to the directions of the commission
treasury, by their order from time to time to appoint in what warehouses of special security,
nary security, in such ports, and in what different parts of such warehouses, and in what m
goods, and what sorts of goods, may and may only be warehoused and secured upon the
thereof, or for exportation only, in cases wherein the same may be prohibited to be importe
use; and also in such order to direct in what cases (if any) security by bond, in manner herei
vided, shall be required in respect of any warehouse so appointed. — § 2.

e of special Security. — Whenever any warehouse shall have been approved of by the said
ers as being a warehouse of special security, it shall be stated, in their order of appointment,
arehouse is appointed as a warehouse of special security: Provided that all warehouses con-
wharfs for the landing of the goods, and enclosed together with such wharfs within walls,
or shall be required by any act for the constructing of such warehouses and wharfs, and being
be legal quays, shall without any order of the commissioners of customs be warehouses for
of this act, for all goods landed at such wharfs or quays, at any port appointed by the com-
of the treasury to be a warehousing port, and all such warehouses shall be warehouses for
ity. — § 3.

n in respect of Goods warehoused, to continue in Force. — All appointments of warehouses for
using of goods under the authority of an act in force at the time of the commencement of
ll continue in force as if the same had been made under this act, and all bonds given in
ay goods warehoused or entered to be warehoused under any act in force at the commence-
act, shall continue in force for the purposes of this act. — § 4.

ners to provide Warehouses for Tobacco. — The commissioners of customs shall, out of the
stoms, provide warehouses for the warehousing of tobacco at the ports into which tobacco
ly imported : Provided that for every hogshead, chest, or case of tobacco so warehoused, the
proprietor shall pay for warehouse rent such sum, not exceeding any sum payable under any
at the time of the commencement of this act, and at such periods and in such manner as the
rs of the treasury shall by their warrant direct, and all such sums shall be paid and appro-
ities of customs. — § 5.

evoke or alter Appointment. — It shall be lawful for the commissioners of the treasury by
for the commissioners of customs by order, to revoke any former warrant, or any former
make any alteration in or addition to any former warrant or order. — § 6.

n in Gazette. — Every order made by the commissioners of customs in respect of warehouses
curity, as well those of original appointment, as those of revocation, alteration, or addition,
lished in the London Gazette, for such as shall be appointed in Great Britain ; and in the
tte, for such as shall be appointed in Ireland. — § 7.

Keeper may give general Bond, if willing. — Before any goods shall be entered to be ware-
y warehouse, in respect of which security by bond shall be required, the proprietor or occu-
warehouse, if he be willing, shall give general security by bond, with two sureties, for the
he full duties of importation, or for the due exportation thereof ; and if such proprietor or
not willing, the different importers shall, upon each importation, give such security in
e particular goods imported by them, before such goods shall be entered to be warehoused. —

ods in Warehouse by Proprietor. — If any goods lodged in any warehouse shall be the pro-
occupier, and shall be *bonâ fide* sold by him, and upon such sale there shall have been a
ment signed by the parties, or a written contract of the sale made, executed, and delivered
or person authorised on behalf of the parties, and the amount of the price shall have been
or secured to be paid by the purchaser, every such sale shall be valid, although such goods
in such warehouse, provided that a transfer of such goods shall have been entered in a book,
the officer of the customs having charge of such warehouse, who is to enter such transfers,
s thereof, upon application of the owners, and produce such book upon demand. — § 9.

Warehouse to afford easy Access. — All goods warehoused shall be stowed in such manner
ccess may be had to every package or parcel, and if the occupier shall omit so to stow the
ll forfeit 5l. ; and if any goods shall be taken out of any warehouse without due entry with
icers of customs, the occupier shall be liable to the payment of the duties. — § 10.

dulently concealed or removed. — If any goods warehoused shall be fraudulently concealed
d from the warehouse, the same shall be forfeited ; and if any importer or proprietor of
used, or any person in his employ, shall, by any contrivance, fraudulently open the ware-
access to the goods except in the presence of the proper officer, such importer or proprietor
00l. — § 11.

n on Entry and Landing. — Marking Package. — Within one month after any tobacco
oused, and upon the entry and landing of any other goods to be warehoused, the officer may
take a particular account of the same, and shall mark the contents on each package, and
word " prohibited " on such as contain goods prohibited to be imported for home use ; and
be warehoused and kept in the packages in which imported, and no alteration shall be
ackages or the packing of any goods in the warehouse, except in cases herein-after provided.

carried to Warehouse under Authority of Officers of Customs. — All goods entered to be
or to be rewarehoused, shall be carried to the warehouse under the care or with the autho-
cer of the customs, and in such manner, and by such persons, and by such roads or ways,
ch time, as the officer shall authorise ; and all goods not so carried shall be forfeited. —

cleared in Three Years, and Ships' Stores in One Year. — All goods warehoused shall be
for exportation or for home use, within 3 years, and all surplus stores of ships within
e first entry (unless further time be given by the commissioners of the treasury), and if
not so cleared, it shall be lawful for the commissioners of customs to cause the same to be
roduce shall be applied to the payment of warehouse rent and other charges, and the over-
e proprietor ; and such goods, when sold, shall be held subject to all the conditions to which
ect previous to such sale, except that a further time of 3 months from the date of sale be
purchaser for clearing from the warehouse ; and if the goods so sold shall not be cleared
months, the same shall be forfeited : Provided that if the goods shall have been imported
dia Company, or shall be of the description called " piece goods," imported from places
ts of their charter into the port of London, the same shall, at the requisition of the com-
ustoms, be exposed to sale by the said Company at their next ensuing sale, and shall be
he highest price offered. — § 14.

landing or shipping Goods. — If any goods entered to be warehoused, or entered to be
the warehouse, shall be lost or destroyed by any unavoidable accident, either on shipboard or
or shipping, or in the receiving into or delivering from the warehouse, it shall be lawful
sioners of customs to remit or return the duties on the quantity so lost or destroyed. —

portation or Home Use. — No goods warehoused shall be taken from the warehouse, except
y. and under care of officers for exportation, or upon due entry and payment of the full
e use, if they be such goods as may be used in the United Kingdom. — § 16.

*res, and surplus Stores, may be shipped without Entry, if borne on Victualling Bill ; or
ate Use.* — Any rum of the British plantations may be delivered into the charge of the
shipped as stores for any ship without entry or payment of any duty, and any surplus stores
y be delivered into the charge of the searcher to be reshipped as stores for the same ship,
master in another ship, without entry or payment of any duty (being duly borne upon the
, and if the ship, for the future use of which any surplus stores have been warehoused,
broken up or sold, such stores may be delivered for the use of any other ship belonging

to the same owners, or may be entered for payment of duty, and delivered for the private u
owners, or of the master or purser. — § 17.

Duties to be paid on original Quantities. — Upon the entry of any such goods to be cleared
warehouse, if for home use, the person entering inwards shall deliver a bill of the entry and
thereof, in like manner as in the case of goods entered to be landed, as far as applicable, and a
shall pay down to the officer of customs the full duties, and not being less in amount than ac
the amount of the quantity first taken, at the time of the first entry and landing, without any
on account of deficiency, except as by this act provided; and if the entry be for exportation
moval to any other warehouse, and any of the packages be deficient of the quantities, accord
account first taken, a like entry inwards shall also be passed in respect of the quantities deficien
full duties shall be paid on the amount thereof, before such packages shall be delivered o
exportation or removal, except as by this act provided; and if any goods deficient in quanti
such as are charged to pay duty according to the value, such value shall be estimated at the
which the like sorts of goods of the best quality shall have been last or lately sold, either at
the East India Company, or in any other manner. — § 18.

Importer to enter Goods for Home Use or for Exportation, although not warehoused. — I
goods shall have been entered and landed to be warehoused, and before the same shall have bee
deposited, the importer shall further enter the same for home use or for exportation, the goods
shall be considered as virtually warehoused, although not actually deposited, and may be deli
taken for home use and for exportation, as the case may be. — § 19.

Goods may be removed to other Ports to be rewarehoused. — Any goods which have been war
some port may be removed by sea or inland carriage to any other port, in which the like goo
warehoused upon importation, to be rewarehoused at such other port, and again to any other
to be rewarehoused, subject to the regulations herein-after mentioned; (that is to say,) 12 hour
writing of the intention to remove such goods shall be given to the warehouse officer, specifyi
ticular goods, and the marks, numbers, and descriptions of the packages, in what ship impo
and by whom entered inwards to be warehoused; and if subsequently rewarehoused, when an
rewarehoused, and to what port the same are to be removed; and thereupon the warehouse c
take a particular account of such goods, and shall mark the contents on every package in prep
the delivering of the same for the purposes of such removal, and previous to the delivery th
cause the proper seals of office to be affixed thereto: Provided always, that tobacco, the proc
British possessions in America, or of the United States of America, and purchased for the
Majesty's navy, may be removed, by the purser of any ship of war in actual service, to t
Rochester, Portsmouth, or Plymouth, to be there rewarehoused, in name of such purser, in
house as shall be approved for that purpose by the commissioners of customs. — § 20.

Entry for Removal. — Before such goods shall be delivered to be removed, due entry of the
be made, and a proper bill of such entry, with duplicates thereof, be delivered to the collecte
troller, containing the before-mentioned particulars, and an exact account of the quantities of t
sorts of goods, and such bill of the entry, signed by the collector and comptroller, shall be t
for the removal; and an account of such goods, containing all such particulars, shall be tran
the officers of the port of removal to the officers of the port of destination; and upon the arri
goods at the port of destination, entry of the same to be rewarehoused shall in like manner be
the collector and comptroller at such port, containing all the particulars and accounts before
together with the name of the port from which such goods have been removed, and the desc
situation of the warehouse in which they are to be warehoused; and the bill of such entry
such collector and comptroller, shall be the warrant to the landing officer and the warehou
admit such goods to be there rewarehoused, under such examination as is made of the like
first warehoused upon importation; and the particulars to be contained in such notice and in s
shall be written and arranged in such form and manner as the collector and comptroller sh
and the officers at the port of arrival shall transmit to the officers at the port of removal an
the goods so arrived, according as they shall upon examination prove to be, and the warehous
the port of removal shall notify such arrival in their books. — § 21.

Bond to rewarehouse may be given at either Port. — The persons removing such goods s
time of entering the same, give bond, with one surety, for the due arrival and rewarehous
goods within a reasonable time (with reference to the distance, to be fixed by the comm
customs), which bond may be taken by the collector and comptroller either of the port of r
the port of destination, as shall best suit the residence or convenience of the persons intere
such bond shall have been given at the port of destination, a certificate thereof, under the h
collector and comptroller, shall, at the time of entering such goods, be produced to the collec
troller of the port of removal. — § 22.

Bond how to be discharged. — Such bond shall not be discharged unless such goods shall ha
rewarehoused at the port of destination within the time allowed, or shall have been otherwis
for to the satisfaction of the commissioners; nor until the full duties due upon any deficienc
been paid; nor until fresh security shall have been given, in manner herein-after provided,
goods shall have been lodged in some warehouse in respect of which general security sha
given by the proprietor or occupier, or in some warehouse in respect of which no security is
§ 23.

Goods rewarehoused held as first warehoused. — Such goods, when so rewarehoused, may
and shipped for exportation, or entered and delivered for home use, as the like goods n
first warehoused upon importation, and the time which such goods shall be allowed to ren
housed at such port shall be reckoned from the day when the same were first entered to be
— § 24.

*On Arrival, after Forms of rewarehousing, Parties may enter to export, or take for Hon
out first carrying to the Warehouse.* — If upon the arrival of such goods at the port of de
parties shall be desirous forthwith to export the same, or to pay duty thereon for home
actually lodging the same in warehouse, it shall be lawful for the officers of the customs
after all the formalities of entering and examining for rewarehousing have been performe
labour of carrying and of lodging the same in warehouse), to consider the same as virtually r
and to permit the same to be entered and shipped for exportation, or to be entered and delive
use, upon payment of the duties, in like manner as if such goods had been actually lodged i
and the account taken for the rewarehousing may serve as the account for delivering t
from the warehouse, either for shipment or for payment of duties; and all goods so ex
which the duties have been so paid, shall be deemed to have been duly cleared from the v
§ 25.

Removal in the same Port. — Any goods which have been warehoused in the port of Lond
the permission of the commissioners of customs, be removed to any other warehouse in th
which like goods may be warehoused on importation; and any goods which have been w
some warehouse in any other port may, with the permission of the collector or comptrolle
to any other warehouse in the same port in which like goods may be warehoused on impo
such general regulations as the commissioners of customs shall direct. — § 26.

Goods and Parties subject to original Conditions. — All goods removed from one wareho
another, whether in the same port or in a different port, and all proprietors of such goods
ject to all the conditions to which they would have been subject if such goods had remained
house where originally warehoused. — § 27.

old, new Owner may give Bond, and release the original Bonder. — If any goods warehoused in
" which general security by bond, as before provided, shall not have been given by the proprietor
er of such warehouse, and particular security, as in such case is required, shall have been given
porter, and such goods shall have been sold, so that the original bonder shall be no longer
, it shall be lawful for the officers to admit fresh security to be given by the bond of the new
, with his sufficient surety, and to cancel the bond given by the original bonder, or to exonerate
his surety to the extent of the fresh security. — § 28.

Remover to be in force in new Warehouse. — If the person removing any goods from one port to
nd who shall have given bond in respect of such removal and rewarehousing, shall be interested
ods, after the same shall have been rewarehoused, and such goods shall have been rewarehoused
'arehouse in respect of which security is required, and the proprietor or occupier shall not have
eral security, the bond in respect of such removal and rewarehousing shall be conditional and
in force for the rewarehousing, until fresh bond be given by some new proprietor or other person,
c before provided. — § 29.

ment of Goods while in Warehouse in which the same were imported. — It shall be lawful in the
e to sort, separate, pack, and repack any goods, and to make such alterations therein, or arrange-
reof, as may be necessary either for the preservation of such goods, or in order to the sale, ship-
egal disposal of the same; provided that such goods be repacked in the same packages, or in
of entire quantity equal thereto, or in such other packages as the commissioners of customs shall
ot being less in any case than may be required by law for the importation); and also in the
e to draw off any wine or any rum of the British plantations into reputed quart bottles or
int bottles, and to pack the same in cases containing not less than 3 dozen quart bottles or 6
t bottles each, for the purpose only of being exported from the warehouse; and also in such
e to draw off any such rum into casks containing not less than 20 gallons each, for the purpose
ing disposed of as stores for ships; and also in the warehouse to draw off and mix with any
once, but not oftener, any brandy secured in the same warehouse, not exceeding 10 gallons of
100 gallons of wine, for the purpose only of being exported from the warehouse; and also in
house to fill up any casks of wine or spirits from any other casks secured in the same ware-
e but not oftener, for the purpose either of home use or of exportation, and once again for the
ly of exportation; and also in the warehouse to take such moderate samples of goods as may
by the commissioners of customs, without entry and without payment of duty, except as may
become payable, as on a deficiency of the original quantity. — § 30.

ation to be made in Goods or Packages but according to such Regulations as the Commissioners
No alteration shall he made in any such goods or packages, nor shall any such wine, rum,
spirits be bottled, drawn off, mixed, or filled up, nor shall any such samples be taken except
notices given by the importers or proprietors, and at such times, and in such manner, and
a regulations as the commissioners of customs shall direct. — § 31.

ng in proper Packages. — After goods have been repacked in proper packages, it shall be lawful
mmissioners of customs, at the request of the importer or proprietor, to cause any of such
naged, or surplus goods, not contained in any of such packages, to be destroyed; and if the
ach as may be delivered for home use, the duties shall be immediately paid upon such surplus,
ne shall be delivered for home use; and if they be such as may not be so delivered, such sur-
y so remain shall be disposed of for the purpose of exportation in such manner as the com-
of the customs shall direct; and thereupon the quantity contained in each of such packages
ertained and marked upon the same, and the deficiency shall be ascertained by a comparison
a quantity in such proper packages with the total quantity first warehoused, and the proportion
a deficiency may bear to the quantity in each package shall also be marked on the same, and
ach quantity, and the total shall be deemed to be the imported contents of such package, and
ject to the full duties of importation, except as otherwise in any case provided by this act:
ways, that it shall be lawful for the commissioners of customs to accept the abandonment, for
of any quantity of tobacco or coffee, and also of any whole packages of other goods, and to
a quantity from the total quantity of the same importation, in computing the amount of the
of such total quantity. — § 32.

n Casks, &c. to be used for repacking, unless Duties have been paid, &c. — No foreign casks,
ks, packages, or materials whatever, except any in which some goods have been bonded
used, shall be used in the repacking of any goods in the warehouse, unless the full duties shall
irst paid thereon. — § 33.

g Goods to be cleaned. — If any stuffs or fabric of silk, linen, cotton, wool, or mixture of them
her material, which may not be taken out of the warehouse for home use, shall have been
for exportation, it shall be lawful for the commissioners of customs to permit such goods to
it to be cleaned, refreshed, dyed, stained, or calendered, under security by bond, to their
that such goods shall be returned within the time which they shall appoint. — § 34.

Bulk delivered. — No parcels of goods so warehoused which were imported in bulk shall be
xcept in the whole quantity of each parcel, or in a quantity not less than one ton weight,
ecial leave of the officers of the customs. — § 35.

to be marked before Delivery. — No goods so warehoused shall be delivered, unless the
packages containing the same shall have been marked in such distinguishing manner as the
ers of customs shall been deemed necessary and direct. — § 36.

and Increase may be ascertained and allowed. — It shall be lawful for the commissioners of
to make regulations for ascertaining the amount of decrease and increase of the quantity of
lar sorts of goods, and to direct in what proportion any abatement of duty for deficiencies
the exportation of such goods, be made on account of such decrease: Provided always, that
s be lodged in warehouses declared to be of special security, no
e be charged for any amount of deficiency on the exportation thereof, except in cases where
all arise that part of such goods has been clandestinely conveyed away, nor shall any such
s they be wine or spirits) be measured, counted, weighed, or gauged for exportation, except
s of suspicion. — § 37.

s for natural Waste of Wine, Spirits, &c. in Warehouses not of special Security. — For any
, coffee, cocoa nuts, or pepper, lodged in warehouses not being declared to be of special secu-
owing allowances for natural waste in proportion to the time during which any such goods
emained in the warehouse, shall be made upon the exportation thereof, according as such
re herein-after set forth. — § 38.

every cask; viz.		
ay time not exceeding 1 year	-	1 gallon.
y time exceeding 1 year, and not exceeding 2 years - -	-	2 —
y time exceeding 2 years - - - -	-	3 —
every 100 gallons hydrometer proof; viz.		
ay time not exceeding 6 months - - -	-	1 —
y time exceeding 6 months, and not exceeding 12 months	-	2 —
y time exceeding 12 months, and not exceeding 18 months	-	3 —
y time exceeding 18 months, and not exceeding 2 years -	-	4 —
ay time exceeding 2 years - - - - -	-	5 —
nuts, pepper, for every 100 lbs. and so in proportion for any less quantity	-	2 lbs.

In Cases of Embezzlement and Waste through Misconduct of Officers, Damages to be made goo Proprietor. — In case any embezzlement, waste, spoil, or destruction shall be made of or in an which shall be warehoused, through any wilful misconduct of any officer of customs or exci officer shall be guilty of a misdemeanor, and shall upon conviction suffer such punishment as inflicted in cases of misdemeanor; and if such officer shall be so prosecuted to conviction by porter, consignee, or proprietor, then no duty of customs or excise shall be payable, and no forfe seizure shall take place of any goods so warehoused in respect of any deficiency caused by such en ment, waste, spoil, or destruction, and the damage shall be repaid and made good to such import signee, or proprietor, by the commissioners of customs or excise, under such regulations as shall by the commissioners of the treasury. — § 39.

On Entry outwards Bond for due shipping and landing shall be given. — Upon the entry out any goods to be exported from the warehouse to parts beyond the seas, and before cocket be gran person in whose name the same be entered shall give security by bond in double the value, with c cient surety, that such goods shall be duly shipped and exported, and shall be landed at the which they shall be entered outwards, or otherwise accounted for to the satisfaction of the commi of customs. — § 40.

Restriction as to the Isle of Man. — No goods shall be exported from the warehouse to the Isle except such goods as may be imported into the said island with licence of the commissioners of c and in virtue of such licence first obtained. — § 41.

Limiting the Quantity of Tobacco to be exported to Guernsey, &c. — No tobacco shall be expor the warehouse to the islands of Guernsey, Jersey, Alderney, or Sark, without the licence of tl missioners of customs, nor in greater quantities in any one year to the said islands respectively quantities herein-after mentioned; (that is to say,)

To Jersey, 40,000 lbs. weight.	To Alderney, 5,000 lbs. weight.
Guernsey, 35,000 lbs. weight.	Sark, 1,000 lbs. weight.

And the said commissioners are, upon application in writing, to grant their licences under the (to be in force 30 days and no longer) to any subjects, to export any of such quantities. — § 42. — (N. clause is repealed by the act 7 Geo. 4. c. 48. § 88.)

Goods removed from Warehouse for Shipment under Care of Customs Officers. — All goods tak the warehouse for removal or for exportation, shall be removed to be shipped under the care or authority of the officer of the customs, and in such manner, and by such persons, and within suc of time, and by such roads or ways, as the officer of customs shall authorise or direct; and all su not so removed or carried shall be forfeited. — § 43.

Ships for exporting warehoused Goods. — It shall not be lawful for any person to export any warehoused, nor to enter for exportation to parts beyond the seas, any goods so warehoused, in which shall not be of the burthen of 70 tons or upwards. — § 44.

Goods landed in Docks liable to Claims for Freight as before landing. — All goods landed in de lodged in the custody of the proprietors of the docks, under this act, not being goods seized as shall, when so landed, continue liable to the same claim for freight in favour of the master and the ship, or of any other person interested in the freight, as such goods were subject to whilst were on board such ships and before the landing; and the directors and proprietors of such their servants or agents, shall, upon due notice in that behalf given to them by such master o or other person aforesaid, detain and keep such goods, not being seized as forfeited, in the wa belonging to the said docks, until the freights to which the same shall be liable shall be paid, with the charges to which the same shall have been subject, or until a deposit shall have been the owners, or consignees, equal in amount to the claim made by the master, or owners, or perso said, for freight; which deposit the said directors or proprietors of such docks, or their a directed to receive and hold in trust, until the claim for freight shall have been satisfied; upor which, and demand made by the persons by whom the deposit shall have been made, and the ch upon the said goods being first paid, the said deposit shall be returned by the said directors or p or their agents. — § 45.

DELIVERY OF SUGAR *from the Warehouses for refining.* — The two following to the delivery of sugar from the warehouses for refining have expired. Ther no doubt, however, that a new act will be again brought in, with such altera may be deemed necessary. But it is most probable that any future enactmen subject will very much resemble the following, which we therefore insert.

How Sugar may be delivered for refining. — Upon the application of any person actually carryi business of a sugar refiner in the ports of London, Liverpool, Bristol, or Glasgow, and having at least at work upon the same premises, it shall be lawful for the officers of the customs at t respectively, at any time before July 5. 1829, to deliver to such person any quantity of foreign of sugar the produce of the East Indies, not exceeding the quantity hereinafter expressed, to refined, under the regulations and upon the conditions herein-after mentioned. — (9 *Geo.* 4. c. s

Average Price. — The prices of brown or Muscovado sugar, the produce of the British poss America, shall from time to time be ascertained and taken in manner herein-after mentioned; importer of such sugar within the city of London or the bills of mortality, who shall, by hims sworn broker or other agent acting in his behalf, buy or sell any such brown or Muscovado su by himself, or his sworn broker or other agent acting in his behalf, deliver in, upon oath before Mayor or any of the aldermen of the city of London (which oath the said Lord Mayor or ald hereby respectively authorised to administer), to the clerk of the Grocers' Company, on or befo in every week, a true account of the quantities of such brown or Muscovado sugar bought him, or his sworn broker or other agent acting in his behalf, in the preceding week, specifying of the ship in which such sugar was imported, and the name of the master of such ship, a marks and packages, and the sum total of the nett landing weights of such sugar, as far as the be made out, and the price paid for each quantity respectively, exclusive of the duty of custom clerk of the Grocers' Company is hereby required to compute and make up in every week accounts so delivered to him of the quantities and prices of such sugar bought or sold by the i his sworn broker or agent, in the week immediately preceding, the average price of such suga cause such average price to be published every Friday in the London Gazette; and such av shall be deemed to be the price of brown or Muscovado sugar for the purposes of this act. — §

Register. — A register or book shall be kept by the clerk of the Grocers' Company, contain accounts so received by him from time to time from the importer, or sworn broker, or agent of the average prices by him computed and made up from the same; which register or book may at convenient times be inspected by any person whatever, upon paying the fee of 1s. a for the same. — § 3.

Negligence. — If the clerk of the Grocers' Company shall neglect to do what he is required to do, he shall forfeit for every such neglect 50l., to be recovered by action of debt, bill, plain mation, in any of his Majesty's courts of record at Westminster, wherein no essoign, protec of law, or any more than one imparlance shall be granted or allowed. — § 4.

Returns not made. — If any importer, or sworn broker, or agent acting in his behalf, sha neglect to deliver upon oath a true account of the quantities of brown or Muscovado sugar by

:ifying the name of the ship in which such sugar was imported, and the name of the master
), and also the marks and packages, and the sum total of the nett landing weights of such
` as the same can be made out, and the price paid for each quantity, as herein-before required,
e actual buyer or seller of such sugar, shall forfeit for every cask of sugar for which he shall
 neglect to deliver in an account 5*l.*, to any one who will prosecute and sue for the same,
red bfore the Lord Mayor or an alderman of the said city, on the oath of any one or more
nesses. — § 5.

r may be seized. — It shall be lawful for the officers of customs to detain any sugar entered for
t of such duties, and within five days from the time of such detention to take the same for
e crown ; and for every cwt. of sugar which shall be so taken there shall be paid to the pro-
:of, in full satisfaction for the same, a sum of money to be computed in manner following ;
sugar shall have been entered as not being of greater value than the average price of British
ugar, then the sum to be paid shall be 2s. the cwt. less than such average price ; and if
hall have been entered as not being of greater value than such average price, then there shall
such sum the number of shillings by which such sugar shall have been entered as being of
e than such average price ; and there shall also be returned to such proprietor the duty which
d upon the entry of such sugar. — § 6.

Bond. — Upon the entry of any sugar for duty under this act, the person entering the same
ond to the satisfaction of the officers of the customs, in the penalty of 20*s.* for every cwt.
r, that the whole of such sugar shall be actually subjected to the process of refinement ; and
four months from the time and date of such bond, for every cwt. of sugar so entered and
efined, there shall be by him exported, or delivered into warehouse to be exported, 107 lbs.
igar and treacle in the following relative proportions, viz. if such sugar shall be entered as
greater value than the average price of sugar as aforesaid, then there shall be so exported
61 lbs. of refined sugar in loaves or lumps, 18 lbs. of bastard sugar, and 28 lbs. of treacle ;
y shilling by which such sugar shall be entered as being of greater value than such average
hall be so exported or delivered 3 lbs. the more of refined sugar in loaves or lumps, and 1 lb.
stard sugar, and 2 lbs. the less of treacle : Provided always, that no entry for any such sugar
e except in the name of the refiner on whose premises the same is to be refined, nor unless
 of such premises be stated in such entry. — § 7.

f Packages, and undue Removal. — Before any package of sugar be delivered for the purposes
he officers of customs shall mark the same in some conspicuous manner, and shall also, upon
ver to the carrier of the same a cartage note, setting forth the particulars of every package
 the time of delivery, and the description or situation of the premises to which the same is
ed ; and if any sugar delivered for the purposes of this act be found without such mark on
or removing without a proper cartage note for the same, or unloading at any place other
e to which it ought to have been taken, or out of the line of road leading to such place,
all be forfeited, and the person to whom such sugar was delivered to be refined shall also
n respect of every package of sugar so forfeited or liable to forfeiture. — § 8.

Sugar. — No greater quantity of sugar shall be delivered, under the authority of this act,
, so as to be at any one time in his possession, than 1,000 cwt. for every pan actually at work
nises : Provided, that every quantity of refined sugar by him exported, or warehoused to be
ill be deemed to be sugar no longer in his possession, and shall be deducted from the quan-
ad been delivered to him as aforesaid. — § 9.

may be delivered to be refined. — Upon the application of any person actually carrying on
of a sugar refiner in the ports of London, Liverpool, Bristol, or Glasgow, and having two
t work upon the same premises, it shall be lawful for the officers of customs at those ports
t any time before 5th July, 1831, to deliver to such person any quantity of foreign sugar, or
roduce of the East Indies, not exceeding the quantity specified in the preceding act of
. to be by him refined, under the regulations, and upon the conditions, and in the manner
:t directed, upon payment of the following duties, in lieu of the duties specified in the said

Duties on Sugar delivered to be refined.	£	s.	d.
scovado or clayed sugar, not being of greater value than the average price of of the British plantations in America, the cwt. -		1 4	0
ther, in respect of every shilling by which such sugar shall be of greater value such average price, the cwt. - - - - -		0 0	6

auses, penalties, forfeitures, and things, contained in the former act, shall extend to this act,
nner as if the same had been repeated and re-enacted in the body of this act, and had
reof.

for Delivery of Sugar to be refined. — 1st. That on the approval of any premises by the
 purposes of the act above-mentioned, and the requisite security being entered into, due
 be given to the landing surveyor for the office, in order that he may open an account in
he refiner whose premises shall have been so approved.

:vious to the delivery of any sugar from the bonded warehouses for the purpose of being
rties requiring the same do give notice to the landing surveyor, specifying thereon the
narks and numbers of the packages, the name of the importing ship, master's name, and
mported.

 landing surveyor do certify upon such notice the quantity of sugar the party is entitled to
s premises for the purpose of being refined, and insert the same in his book, and after-
uch notice to the party for the information of the long-room officers in passing the entry
y certified thereon.

e warrant of entry be forwarded by the long-room officers, in the first instance, to the
or, to be recorded by him in his book, and then forwarded to the officers of the department
igar is warehoused, as their authority for the delivery thereof.

on refined sugar being brought to the warehouse or quays for exportation, a certificate of
d quality of such sugar delivered into the charge of the officers of the revenue, be for-
searchers to the landing surveyor, as his authority for discharging the same from the
refiner. — (1 *Will.* 4. c. 72.)

ng Ports, &c. — Certain ports only are warehousing ports; nor may all sorts
warehoused in every warehousing port. We subjoin a list of the ware-
s in Great Britain and Ireland, and a specification of the goods that may
ed in each, classed in tables.

ENGLAND.
Table C.
ods except tobacco, East India goods, and
, other than sugar.
Table A, wine and spirits in Table B, and
 spirits in Table B.

Bridgewater—Wine and spirits in Table B, and wood and tar
 in Table C, rum, and tallow.
Bristol—East India goods, and goods in Tables A, B, C, D,
 and E.
Chepstow—Timber, deals, hemp, linseed, staves, tallow, and
 tar.
Chester—Wine and spirits in Table B.

Chichester—Wood, pitch, tar, and iron in Table C, and wool in Table E.

Colchester—Rum in Table A, and wine and spirits in Table B.

Cowes—Goods in Tables A, B, and D; and timber and deals in Table C.

Dartmouth—Goods in Tables A, B, C, and D (except tobacco).

Dover—Goods in Table B (except tobacco), and timber and wood in Table C.

Exeter—Rum in Table A, goods in Table B (except tobacco), tallow and bristles in Table C, and oil of olives in Table E; bark, hair, hides, horns, skins, valonia, timber, deals, and clover seeds.

Falmouth—Goods in Tables A, B, C, and D.

Gloucester—Spirits in Table A, wine and spirits in Table B, tallow in Table C, and barilla in Table E; sugar not East India, and all other goods not East India produce, and not in Table A.

Goole, near Hull,—All articles, except tobacco and snuff.

Grimsby, ditto—Goods in Tables A, B, C, D, and E (except tobacco).

Hull—East India goods, and goods in Tables A, B, C, D, and E.

Ipswich—Wine and spirits in Tables A and B, and barilla.

Lancaster—Goods in Tables A, B, C, and D.

Liverpool—East India goods, and goods in Tables A, B, C, D, E, and F.

London—East India goods, and goods in Tables A, B, C, D, E, and F.

Lynn—Wine and spirits in Table B, and timber and wood in Table C.

Maldon—Wood goods.

Milford—Goods in Tables C and D.

Newcastle—Goods in Tables A, B, C, D, and E.

Newhaven—Rum in Table A, wine and spirits in Table B, and timber and wood in Table C.

Plymouth—Goods in Tables A, B, C, D, and E.

Pool—Goods in Tables A, B, C, D, and E (except tobacco).

Portsmouth—Goods in Tables A, B, C, and D, (except tobacco), and hides in Table D.

Rochester—Rum in Table A, wine and spirits in Table B, and timber and wood goods in Table C.

Rye—Wood in Table C, and clover seed in Table E.

Southampton—Spirits in Table A, wine and spirits in Table B, goods in Tables C, D, and E, and East India goods removed for exportation to Guernsey and Jersey.

Shoreham—Goods in Table C.

Stockton—Rum in Table A, wine and spirits in Table B, timber and goods in Table C, clover seed and green fruit in Table E.

Sunderland—Goods in Tables A, B, C, and D (except tobacco).

Swansea—Goods in Table C.

Weymouth—Rum in Table A, wine and spirits in Table B; almonds of all sorts, barilla, clover seed, currants, figs, oil of olives, salad oil, prunes, raisins of all sorts, and liquorice juice in Table E.

Whitby—Goods in Tables C and D.

Whitehaven—Goods in Tables A, B, C, and E.

Wisbech—Wood goods.

Yarmouth—Rum in Table A, wine and spirits in Table B, hemp and iron in Table C, and goods in Table E.

SCOTLAND.

Aberdeen—Goods in Tables A and B; brimstone, hemp undressed, iron in bars, timber and wood, in Table C; almonds, ashes, black or Dantzic beer, barilla, currants, cotton wool, figs, gum Arabic, gum Senegal, linen plain (except sail-cloth), oil of olives, and raisins of all sorts, in Table C.

Borrowstoness—Timber and wood in Table C.

Dumfries—Wine in Table B.

Dundee—Wine and spirits in Tables A and B; iron, pitch, tar, timber, and wood, in Table C.

Glasgow—East India goods, and goods in Tables A, B, C, D, and E.

Grangemouth—Fustic, hemp, iron, logwood, mahogany, pitch, rosin, staves, tar, tallow, tow, turpentine, timber, and wood, in Table C, and flax in Table E.

Greenock—East India goods, and goods in Tables A, B, C, D, and E.

Leith—East India goods, and goods in Tables A, B, C, D, and E.

Montrose—Wines, spirits, and sugar ; and goods in Tables C and D; ashes, butter, cheese, coffee, feathers, hams, hides, honey, spruce beer, seeds, vinegar, and yarn.

Port Glasgow—East India goods, and goods in Tables A, B, C, and E.

IRELAND.

Dublin }
Belfast } East India and all other goods, at Cork; also vinegar.
Cork. }

Coleraine—All goods, except East India goods and tobacco.

Drogheda }
Dundalk }
Galway }
Limerick } All goods (except East India goods, and the
Londonderry } articles enumerated in Table F, with the
Newry } exception of sugar).
Sligo }
Waterford }

Wexford—Wine, sugar, hemp, iron, tallow, foreign spirits, and vinegar.

TABLE A.

Annatto or rocou	Cocoa nuts	Sugar
Cassia fistula	Coffee	

Not being the produce of, nor imported from, any place within the limits of the East India Company's charter.

Angustura bark	Indigo	Pimento
Cotton wool	Mahogany	Rum
Ginger	Molasses	Wine

Imported from the West Indies.

Cocoa nuts	Indigo	Pimento
Coffee	Mahogany	Rum
Cotton wool	Molasses	Sugar
Ginger		

The growth and produce of, and imported direct from, any of the territories or dominions of the crown of Portugal.

TABLE B.

Brandy	Rice	T
Geneva, and other spirits	Shrub	W

Not being the produce of, nor imported from, any the limits of the East India Company's charter wine excepted), or not being imported from the

Cocoa nuts	Indigo	Pi
Coffee	Mahogany	R
Cotton wool	Molasses	Su
Ginger		

Being the growth or produce of, and imported any of the territories or dominions of the crown

Spirits and wine

Being the produce of any place within the limit India Company's charter, and imported otherwi said Company.

TABLE C.

Brimstone	Kelp	Stave
Cork	Linseed	Tallo
Hemp, undressed	Mahogany	Tar
Iron, in bars or slit, or hammered into rods, and iron drawn or hammered less than ¼ of an inch square	Marble blocks	Timb
	Oil of turpentine	Tow
	Pitch	Turpe
	Rapeseed	Wood
	Rosin	Zaffre

Not being the produce of, nor imported from wit of, the East India Company's charter, nor impo West Indies.

TABLE D.

Hides	Blubber of British fishing	sha
Oil of British fishing		and
Oil of spermaceti, or head matter	Whale fins of Bri- tish fishing	sort
Train oil, and all other fish oil	Indian deer skins, half dressed or	taw
		way

Not being the produce of, nor imported from wit of, the East India Company's charter, and ported from the West Indies.

TABLE E.

Alkermes	Hams	Oils,
Almonds	Harp-strings	per
Anchovies	Hones	othe
Angustura bark	Jalap	me
Aniseed	Jesuits' bark	Opiu
Annatto or rocou	Jet	Orang
Arrowroot	India rubber	o
Ashes	Indigo	Ottar
Balsam of all sorts	Isinglass	Pearl
Barilla	Juice of lemons	Pictu
Beads of amber and of coral	Limes and oranges	Pigs'
	Juniper berries	fac
Bees' wax	Lamp black	Pime
Black or Dantzic beer	Plain linen (except sail-cloth)	Pitch Plat
Bristles, undressed	Linseed cakes	ch
Buck wheat	Liquorice powder	Pots
Cantharides	Maccaroni	Prur
Carpets, Turkey	Madder, ground	Quic
Cassia fistula	Mahogany	Rad
Catlings or lute-strings	Manna	Rag
Cheese	Mercury	Rais
Chip hats	Mohair yarn	Rap
Citrate of lime	Molasses	Rhi
Citron in salt and water	Oil of almonds amber	Rhu Rur
Clover seed	aniseed	Sacc
Cochineal and co-chineal dust	bay	Saff
	cajeputa	Sal
Cocoa nuts	carraway	
Coffee	cassia	
Copal	castor	
Cotton wool and cotton yarn	cinnamon	
	cloves	
Currants	jessamine	Sap
Elephants' teeth	juniper	Sar
Essence of bergamot and of lemon	lavender	Sen
	linseed	Silk
Essence of British America spruce, imported from thence	mace	or
	marjoram	Sm
	nutmegs	Stra
	olives	Suc
Euphorbium	oranges	Sug
Feathers for beds	palm	Tap
Figs	pine	Tar
Flax	rock	Tor
German sausages	rosemary and rosewood	Toy
Ginger	salad	Ver
Ginseng	sassafras	Ver
Granilla	spike	Var
Gum arabic	thyme	oi
Guaiacum and Se-negal	turpentine and walnut	n

Not being the produce of, nor imported from India Company's charter, and not being in West Indies.

TABLE F.

Agates, rough and polished	Bugles of all kinds	Ca
Almond paste	Cambric	Ch
Aloes	Camphor	C
Ambra liquida	Cantharides	Cr
Ambergris	Cardamoms	Ci
Balsams of all sorts	Cards'	
Beads of all kinds	Carmine	C
Beer	Cassia buds	C
Benjamin	lignea	C
Bottles	fistula	

	Jet	Powder of bronze	Turbith	Vinegar	and strong, of all
dicus	Jewels, emeralds,	and of brass	Vanelloes	Watches of all sorts	sorts
a	rubies, and all	Powder, not other-	Vellum	Watch glasses	Wires
ot	other precious	wise enumerated,	Verdigris	Waters, mineral	Yarn, mohair
sorts	stones, except dia-	which will serve			
y made	monds	for the same use			
s	Inkle, wrought	as starch			

And also all goods and merchandise of every description, which, under the provisions of the warehousing act, may be imported for the purpose of exportation only; all which goods may be deposited only in warehouses inclosed by and surrounded with walls, or in other warehouses, or in places of special security, especially to be approved, by the commissioners of the treasury.

gne	Lace of all kinds	Quicksilver
	Mace, imported by	Radix ipecacuanhæ
all sorts	licence	and rhataniæ
all sorts	Manna	Resina jalapæ
ostrich	Mercury	Rhubarb
rs, not	Metheglin	Saffron
enu-	Morels	Sal limonum and
dressed	Musical boxes	succini
ed	Musk	Scammony
tificial	Nutmegs, imported	Silk, raw and or-
	by licence	ganzined
kinds	Nux vomica	Snuff
erved	Opium	Soap
kinds	Or molu	Spikenard
aradise	Ottar of roses	Starch
nea	Paper	Stones, bezoar
ax	Pearls	Storax of all kinds
n	Perry	Succades
	Pictures	Sugar
onnets	Plate	Threads of all kinds
	Platina	Tobacco
	Platting of all sorts	Tortoise shell
		Treacle of Venice
		Truffles

WAREHOUSE RENT.

Rates for warehouse rent on goods deposited in the king's warehouses at the several out-ports, viz.—

On large cases and vats containing toys or other merchandise, and packages of wine and other liquids, per week, 6d. each.

Packages of baggage, small packages of presents, viz. boxes, kegs, jars, &c., per week, 2d. each.

All other packages not before described (except tobacco), per week, 4d. each.

For every hogshead of tobacco deposited in the king's warehouse at London, 2s.; and for every hogshead taken out of the same, 2s.

For every hogshead of tobacco warehoused in the king's warehouse at the out-ports, 1½d. per week.— *Treasury Orders*, Nov. 27. 1824, and March 19. 1830.

CHES (Ger. *Uhren, Taschenuhren;* Fr. *Montres;* It. *Oriuoli da tasca, o occia;* Sp. *Relojes de faltriquera;* Rus. *Karmannüe tschasü*), portable s, generally of a small size and round shape, that measure and indicate essive portions of time, having, for the most part, their motions regulated al spring. When constructed on the most approved principles, and ex- the best manner, a watch is not only an exceedingly useful, but a most le piece of mechanism. It has exercised the skill and invention of the lful mechanics, as well as of some of the ablest mathematicians, for nearly nturies. And considering the smallness of its size, its capacity of being bout uninjured in every variety of position, the number and complexity vements, and the extraordinary accuracy with which it represents the suc- portions of time as determined by the rotation of the earth on its axis, not wonder at Dr. Paley having referred to it as a striking specimen of ngenuity.

watches are constructed nearly on the same principle as pendulum Instead of the pendulum in the latter, a spring is used in the former, the sm of the vibrations of which corrects the unequal motions of the

cal Notice. — The invention of spring watches dates from about the the sixteenth century, and has been warmly contested for Huygens and The English writers generally incline in favour of the latter. Dr. Hut- (*Mathematical Dictionary*, art. *Watch*), that the words " Rob. Hooke 658," were inscribed on the dial plate of a watch presented to Charles 75. But Montucla affirms (*Histoire des Mathématiques*, tome ii. p. 413. , that Huygens made this " *belle découverte* " in 1656, and presented a tch to the States of Holland in 1657. Comparing these statements, it appears that the claim of Huygens to the priority of the discovery is the ablished of the two. We do not, however, believe that either of those hed persons owed, in this respect, any thing to the other. The pro- eems to be that the happy idea of employing a spring to regulate the watches occurred to them both nearly at the same time.

ement of Watches. — Owing to the facility with which the longitude may ined by the aid of accurately going watches, it is of great importance em made as perfect as possible. In this view liberal premiums have to the makers of the best marine watches, or chronometers, by the nts of England, France, Spain, &c. And to such perfection has the art nat some of the chronometers employed by navigators, though carried nost opposite climates, have not varied to the extent of two seconds in n rate of going throughout the year.

meters are tried at the Royal Observatory at Greenwich; and a pre- 300*l.* is annually awarded to the best of those whose variations are ithin certain limits.

Manufacture. — The watch-making business is carried on to a great ex- ondon; the artists of which have attained to an unrivalled degree of in this department. There are about 14,000 gold and 85,000 silver

watches annually assayed at Goldsmith's Hall, London — (*Jacob on the P*[
Metals, vol. ii. p. 413.) ; the aggregate value of which is, probably, not much
1,000,000*l.* The manufacture is also carried on to a considerable ext
Liverpool, Coventry, Edinburgh, &c. Watch movements used to be exter
manufactured at Prescot in Lancashire ; but latterly, we believe, the ma
turers have been withdrawing to Liverpool.

On the Continent, watches are principally manufactured at Paris, Genev
in Neufchâtel. Some of the French and Swiss watches are excellent ; but,
rally speaking, they are slight, and inferior to those made in London. Pa
Geneva watches are largely exported to foreign countries ; and are every
in high estimation, particularly among the ladies.

Watches impressed with any mark or stamp, appearing to be or to represent any legal Briti
mark or stamp, or purporting by any mark or appearance to be of the manufacture of the Unit
dom, or not having the name and place of abode of some foreign maker abroad visible on the fr
also on the face, or not being in a complete state, with all the parts properly fixed in the case, ma
imported into the United Kingdom, even for the purpose of being warehoused. — (6 *Geo.* 4. c. 1
See *antè*, p. 609.)

WATER. It may be thought unnecessary, perhaps, to say any thin
work of this sort with respect to a fluid so well known and so abundant.
besides being an indispensable necessary of life, water is, in most large cit
important commercial article. It is in the latter point of view, principally, t
mean to consider it. Inasmuch, however, as the mode of supplying d
places with water, and its price, necessarily vary in every possible way, w
limit our remarks on these subjects to the metropolis only. The few r
we intend to offer of a general nature will apply indifferently to any po
place, the supply of which with water occasions a considerable expense.

1. *Quality of Water.* — Dr. Ure has made the following statements with res
he quality of water : — " Water," says he, " is a very transparent fluid, posse
moderate degree of activity with regard to organised substances, which renders it
to animal and vegetable life, for both which it is, indeed, indispensably necessary.
it acts but slightly on the organs of sense, and is therefore said to have neither ta
smell. It appears to possess considerable elasticity, and yields in a perceptible
to the pressure of air in the condensing machine.

" Native water is seldom, if ever, found perfectly pure. The waters that flow
or upon the surface of the earth contain various earthy, saline, metallic, veget
animal particles, according to the substances over or through which they pass.
and snow waters are much purer than these, although they also contain whateve
in the air, or has been exhaled along with the watery vapours.

" The purity of water may be known by the following marks or properties
water : —

" 1. Pure water is lighter than water that is not pure.

" 2. Pure water is more fluid than water that is not pure.

" 3. It has no colour, smell, or taste.

" 4. It wets more easily than the waters containing metallic and earthy salt
hard waters, and feels softer when touched.

" 5. Soap, or a solution of soap in alcohol, mixes easily and perfectly with

" 6. It is not rendered turbid by adding to it a solution of gold in aqua regia ;
lution of silver, or of lead, or of mercury, in nitric acid ; or a solution of acetate
in water.

" Water was, till modern times, considered as an elementary or simple substar
it is now ascertained to be a compound of oxygen and hydrogen."

2. *Supply of Water.* — London was very ill supplied with water previousl
early part of the seventeenth century, when the New River water was introdu
the city. This exceedingly useful work was planned and carried into effec
famous Sir Hugh Middleton, who expended his whole fortune on the project ;
like many other public benefactors, entailed poverty on himself and his pos
embarking in an undertaking productive of vast wealth to others, and of gre
utility. The New River has its principal source near Chadwell, between Her
Ware, about 20 miles from London ; but the artificial channel in which the
conveyed is about 40 miles in length. Sir Hugh Middleton encountered inn
difficulties during the progress of the undertaking, which it is probable would I
abandoned, at least for a time, but for the aid afforded by James I. The N
Company was incorporated in 1619, 6 years after the water had been brough
reservoir at Islington. The undertaking yielded very little profit for a cor
number of years ; but it has since become extremely profitable ; so much s
original 500*l.* share has been sold for 13,000*l.* !

elsea Water-Works Company was formed in 1723, and (with the aid of three
mpanies, none of which are now in existence) it, and the New River, supplied
rt of the metropolis north of the Thames with water, down to the year 1810.
ar, however, three new companies, the East London, West Middlesex, and
nction, were established, under the authority of different acts of parliament.
oment the metropolis is supplied with water by the following companies : —

New River,	Grand Junction,
Chelsea,	Lambeth,
East London,	Vauxhall, or South London, and
West Middlesex,	Southwark Water-Works.

owing statements with respect to these companies are taken from Mr. Wade's
reatise on the police of the metropolis. The Report of the commissioners
by government in 1827, to inquire into the state of the supply of water in
olis, is the principal authority on which they are founded.

New River Company get their supply from the spring at Chadwell, between
nd Ware. It comes in an open channel, of about 40 miles in length, to
t Clerkenwell. There are two reservoirs, having between them a surface of
es, and an average depth of 10 feet. These reservoirs are 84½ feet above
mark in the Thames; and, by means of steam engines and a stand-pipe, an
height of 60 feet can be given to the water, so that all the mains belonging
ipany are kept full by a considerable pressure of water. The highest service
ne New River is the cistern on the top of Covent Garden Theatre. The
y which the water is brought has only a fall of 2 inches per mile; thus it
evaporation, during the drought of summer, and is impeded by frost in the
t these times the Company pump an additional supply from the Thames,
Wharf, between Blackfriars and Southwark Bridges. To this, however,
n have recourse; and their engine, erected since the works at London
e broken down, has worked only 176 hours in the year. The New River
supply 66,600 houses with water, at an annual average of about 1,100
each, or, in all, about 75,000,000 hogsheads annually.

ast London Water-Works are situated at Old Ford, on the river Lea, about
n the Thames, and a little below the point to which the tide flows up the
he act of parliament, this Company must take its water when the tide runs
mills below have ceased working. The water is pumped into reservoirs and
settle; and a supply of 6,000,000 gallons is daily distributed to about
ses. This Company supply no water at a greater elevation than 30 feet, and
eight at which the delivery is made to the tenants is 6 feet above the pave-
have 200 miles of iron pipes, which, in some places, cost them 7
ard. This and the New River are the only companies which do not draw
of water entirely from the Thames.

st Middlesex derive their supply of water from the Thames, at the upper
mersmith, 9½ miles above London Bridge, and where the bed of the
ravel. The water is forced by engines to a reservoir at Kensington, 309
3 wide, and 20 deep, paved and lined with bricks, and elevated about 120
w water in the Thames. They have another reservoir on Little Primrose
70 feet higher, and containing 88,000 hogsheads of water, under the pres-
ch the drains are kept charged, in case of fires. They serve about 15,000
the average daily supply is about 2,250,000 gallons.

lsea Water-Works derive their supply from the Thames, about a quarter of
f Chelsea Hospital; and they have two reservoirs — one in the Green Park
in Hyde Park — the former having an elevation of 44 feet, and the latter
se reservoirs, till within these few months, had never been cleaned, nor had
my preparation made for that purpose in their construction. About one
vater served out by this Company is allowed to settle in these reservoirs, and
ng two thirds are sent directly from the Thames. Latterly, the Company
aking preparations for filtering the water; and also for allowing it to settle
, at Chelsea, before it is delivered in the mains. The Chelsea Company
2,400 houses, and the average daily supply is 1,760,000 gallons.

nd Junction Company derive the whole of their supply from the Thames,
adjoining Chelsea Hospital; thence it is pumped, without any filtration
into three reservoirs at Paddington. These reservoirs are about 71, 86,
t above high water mark in the Thames; their united contents are
gallons; and by means of a stand-pipe, the water is forced to the height of
about 61 feet above the average height in the reservoir. The number of
ied by the Grand Junction Company is 7,700, and the average daily
out 2,800,000 gallons.

" *The Lambeth Company* take their supply from the Thames, between Wes and Waterloo Bridges. It is drawn from the bed of the river by a suction-p delivered to the tenants without being allowed to subside; there being only a c 400 barrels at the works, as a temporary supply, until the engines can be starte greatest height to which the Company force water is about 40 feet; the nu houses that they supply is 16,000, and the average service is 1,244,000 gallons c

" *The South London*, or *Vauxhall Company*, take their supply from the river by a tunnel, which is laid 6 feet below low water mark, and as far into the riv third arch of Vauxhall Bridge. At that particular place, the bed of the Tham scribed as being always clean, and without any of those depositions of mud a offensive substances that are found in many other places. Besides the greater the bed of the Thames here than where any other Company on the south side t supply, the Company allow the water to settle in reservoirs. The Vauxhall C supply about 10,000 houses, with about 1,000,000 gallons of water daily.

" *The Southwark Water-Works* (the property of an individual) are supplied middle of the Thames, below Southwark and London Bridges; and the w taken is sent out to the tenants without standing to settle, or any filtration furr it receives from passing through wire grates and small holes in metallic plat number of houses supplied by these works is about 7,000, and the average dail about 720,000 gallons."

The results may be collected into a table, as follows : —

Companies.	Services.	Average per Day. Gallons.	Gallons Annually.	Av House
1. New River - -	67,000	13,000,000	4,056,000,000	
2. East London - -	42,000	6,000,000	1,872,000,000	
3. West Middlesex - -	15,000	2,250,000	702,000,000	
4. Chelsea - -	12,400	1,760,000	549,120,000	
5. Grand Junction - -	7,700	2,800,000	873,600,000	
6. Lambeth - -	16,000	1,244,000	388,128,000	
7. South London - -	10,000	1,000,000	312,000,000	
8. Southwark - -	7,000	720,000	224,540,000	
Total - -	183,100	28,774,000	8,977,388,000	

Average per house north of the river   -   196 gallons.
Average per house south of the river   -   93 ditto.

It would appear from this table, as if the supply of water were either excess Middlesex side of the river, or very deficient on the Surrey side. But this di is more apparent than real. The inhabitants in the northern districts are, generally, decidedly richer than those in the southern district; they have, parti the west end of the town, larger families, and a much greater number of horse is also a much larger expenditure of water upon the roads in Middlesex than i Still, however, we believe that there is a more liberal supply in the former t latter.

Monopoly of the Water Companies. — The sanction of parliament was giv three new companies formed in 1810, not so much in the view of increasing supply of water, as of checking monopoly, and reducing the rates by their co But these expectations have not been realised. For a while, indeed, the com the several companies was exceedingly injurious to their interests, and occa total destruction of some of the inferior ones; but no sooner had this happene others discovered that their interests were in reality the same, and that the t promote them was to concert measures together. In furtherance of this c five companies for the supply of that part of the metropolis north of the river to divide the town into as many districts, binding themselves, under heavy *not to encroach on each other's estates :* and having in this way gone far to se selves against any new competitors, their next measure was to add *five and* cent. to the rates established in 1810; and these have, in several instances further augmented ! The benefits that were expected to result from their mu have, therefore, proved quite imaginary; and though the supply of water increased, it is neither so cheap nor so good as it might have been under system.

The following statement of the rates and profits of the five principal Water in 1820 and 1827, is extracted from the Report of the select committee of of Commons on the supply of water in 1828.

Comparative Returns of 1820 with 1827.

Houses.	Average Rate per House.	Gross Annual Income.	Gross Expenditure.	Nett Profit.	Remarks.
	s.	£ *s. d.*	£ *s. d.*	£ *s. d.*	
		West Middlesex.			
10,350	47	24,252 6 10	9,000 0 0	15,252 6 10	
14,500	51	37,000 0 0	13,000 0 0	24,000 0 0	
		Grand Junction.			
7,180	57	20,153 11 7	8,916 6 5	11,237 5 7	
7,809	61	24,702 5 0	10,674 8 4	14,027 16 8	
		Chelsea.			
8,631	35	15,150 7 11	12,255 11 0	2,894 16 11	
12,409	30	18,589 16 1	12,532 2 9	6,057 13 4	
		East London.			There was also a non-permanent expenditure in 1827, amounting to 23,217*l.* 18*s.* 2*d.*
32,071	22	35,358 14 9	16,336 1 0	19,022 13 9	
42,000	21	45,442 19 5	14,050 6 3	31,392 13 2	
		New River.			
52,082	25	67,275 2 4	48,109 18 4	19,165 4 0	
66,600	28	95,657 15 10	59,204 13 3	36,453 2 7	
		South London.			
5,200	18	4,708 3 4	-	-	Incomplete.
10,000	16	8,293 2 7	7,991 13 7	301 9 0	
		Lambeth.			
11,487	16	9,335 0 0	8,552 0 0	783 0 0	
15,987	16	12,370 0 0	9,500 0 0	2,870 0 0	
		Southwark.			} Returns incomplete.
6,900	-	-	-	-	

Total North of the Thames.

Years.	Houses.	Gross Annual Income.	Gross Expenditure.	Nett Profit.
		£ *s. d.*	£ *s. d.*	£ *s. d.*
1820	110,314	162,190 3 5	94,617 16 4	67,572 7 1
1827	143,318	221,392 16 4	109,461 10 7	111,931 5 9

Total South of the Thames. — Returns not complete.

ıth is, as we endeavoured to show in the article COMPANIES, that certain restric-
ht, in almost all cases, to be imposed on companies for the supply of water to
ty. These are not undertakings that can be safely trusted to the free principles
generally be relied upon. If there be only one set of springs adjacent to a
if there be certain springs more conveniently situated for supplying it with
n any other, a company acquiring a right to such springs, and incorporated for
se of conveying the water to town, would thereby gain an *exclusive advantage ;*
limits were set to its dividends, its partners might make an enormous profit at
se of the public, and without its being possible materially to reduce them by
competition. What has happened in the case of the New River Company
y evinces the truth of what has now been stated. Had its dividends been
any thing like a reasonable profit, the water that is at present supplied by its
ght have been furnished for a small part of what it actually costs. But in
his sort, priority of occupation, even without any other peculiar advantage,
● exclude all regular and wholesome competition. A company that has got
down in the streets may, if threatened by the competition of another company,
ates so as to make the latter withdraw from the field ; and as soon as this is
ay revert to its old, or even to higher charges. It is not, in fact, possible, in
concerns of this sort, to have any thing like competition in the ordinary sense
ı ; and experience shows that whenever it is attempted, it only continues for
●eriod, and is sure to be in the end effectually suppressed. We are, therefore,
opinion, that no company ought ever to be formed for the conveyance of water
ge city, without a maximum being set both to the rates and the dividends ;
company an option, in the event of the maximum rate yielding more than the
dividend, either to reduce the rate, or to apply the surplus to the purchase of
ny's stock ; so that ultimately the charge on account of the dividends may be

glad to have to add, that we are supported in what is now stated by the
the select committee of the House of Commons on the supply of water for
olis, printed in 1821. It is there said — " The public is at present without
ion even against a further indefinite extension of demand. In cases of dispute,
● tribunal but the Boards of the companies themselves, to which individuals
; there are no regulations but such as the companies may have voluntarily
●on themselves, and may therefore at any time revoke, for the continuance of
in its present state, or for defining the cases in which it may be withdrawn
ouseholder. All these points, and some others of the same nature, indis-
quire legislative regulation, where the subject matter is an article of the first

necessity, and the supply has, from peculiar circumstances, got into such a cou
it is not under the operation of those principles which govern supply and dem
other cases.

" The principle of the acts under which these companies were instituted,
encourage competition; and certainly in this, as in other cases, it is only from cc
tion, or the expectation of competition, that a perfect security can be had for
supply. But your committee are satisfied, that, from the peculiar nature of these
takings, the principle of competition requires to be guarded by particular chec
limits in its application to them, in order to render it effectual, without the
destruction to the competing parties, and thereby, ultimately, of a serious injury
public." And the committee proceeds to remark — " The submission of their ac
annually to parliament, for a few years, would necessarily throw light on this par
question."

We think that it would be highly expedient to adopt the suggestion of the com
by calling upon the companies to lay annually detailed statements of their affairs
parliament. They should be obliged in these statements to give an account of th
charged by them, and to make a special report as to every case in which they hav
drawn water from a householder. It is to no purpose to repeat, in opposition
proposal, the commonplaces about competition securing for the citizens a su
supply of water at the lowest prices, in the same way that the competition of
and butchers secures them supplies of beef and bread! The statements alread
show that there is no analogy whatever in the circumstances under which these
are supplied. If a man be dissatisfied with any particular butcher or baker, he
to another; but *it is not possible for him to change his water merchant,* unless
change the place of his residence. No water company will encroach upon the
assigned to another; and supposing an individual unlucky enough to quarrel wit
who have the absolute *monopoly* of the supply of the district in which he resides,
either migrate to another, or be without water, unless he can get a supply upon
premises! Such being the actual state of things, it is quite ludicrous to tal
competition affording any real security against extortion and abuse. Even the pub
of the proceedings of the companies would be a very inadequate check on their cc
but such as it is, it is perhaps the only one that can now be resorted to; and as i
have considerable influence, it ought not, certainly, to be neglected.

3. *Quality of the London Water.* — All the companies, with the exception of t
River and East London Companies, derive their supplies of water from the T
and in consequence of their taking it up within the limits to which the tide flo
necessarily, in the first instance, loaded with many impurities. But the repo
were recently so very prevalent, with respect to the deleterious quality of the wat
from the river, have been shown to be very greatly exaggerated. The state
Dr. Bostock, given in the Report of the commissioners, shows that by far the
part of the impurities in the Thames water are mechanically suspended in,
chemically combined with, it; and that they may be separated from it by filtr
by merely allowing it to stand at rest. Most of the companies have recently ma
siderable efforts to improve their water; and though they have not done in this
as much as they might and ought to have done, a considerable improvement has
whole, been effected : and notwithstanding all that has been said to the cont:
have been assured, by those best qualified to form an opinion on such a subj
though not nearly so pure as a little pains would render it, there is not the
foundation for the notion that its impurities have been such as to affect, in any
the health of the inhabitants.

WAX (Ger. *Wachs;* Fr. *Cire;* It. and Sp. *Cera;* Rus. *Wosk*), a vegeta
duct. Several plants contains wax in such abundance, as to make it wor
to extract it from them. But bees' wax is by far the most generally know
honey is first pressed from the comb, and the wax is then melted into ca
has a slight odour of honey, is insipid, and of a bright yellow hue. It i
yet soft, and somewhat unctuous to the touch. It is often adulterated wit
pea-meal, resin, &c. The presence of the former may be suspected w
cake is very brittle, or when its colour inclines more to gray than to yell
the presence of resin may be suspected when the fracture appears sm
shining, instead of being granulated. Wax, when bleached or purified,
perfectly insipid, inodorous, and somewhat translucent; it is harder, less u
to the touch, heavier, and less fusible, than yellow wax. It is sometim
terated with the white oxide of lead to increase its weight, with white tal
with potato starch. The first is detected by melting the wax in water,
oxide falls to the bottom; the presence of tallow is indicated by the wax

ique white, and wanting the transparency which distinguishes pure wax; h may be detected by applying sulphuric acid to the suspected wax, as arbonises the starch, without acting on the wax.—(*Thomson's Chemistry,* *. T. Thomson's Dispensatory.*)

anding the large supply of wax produced at home, a considerable quantity is imported from i there can be no doubt that the import would be much greater, were it not for the f the duty, which, notwithstanding its late reduction, still amounts to 1*l.* 18*s.* per cwt. The y imported, in 1828, amounted to 9,209 cwt., of which 4,632 cwt. were retained at home. Of 1,247 cwt. came from Russia, 954 from the Netherlands, 1,018 from the northern coast of from the western coast of ditto, and 1,326 from Cuba and the United States. The nett ved from wax amounted, in 1830, to 5,893*l.* 2*s.* 6*d.* The price of wax varies from 5*l.* to :wt.

HTS AND MEASURES. Weights are used to ascertain the gravity ,—a quality depending partly on their magnitude, and partly on their Measures are used to determine the magnitude of bodies, or the space y occupy.

account of the weights and measures used in foreign countries, and their in English weights and measures, see the notices of the great sea-port ersed throughout this work. Thus, for the Russian weights and measures, sBURGH; for those of China, see CANTON, &c.)

the magnitude nor the weight of any one body can be determined, unless by it with some other body selected as a standard. It is impossible, indeed, to dea in respect of magnitude or weight, except in relation to some definite eight with which we are acquainted. We say that one article weighs one other two pounds, a third three, and so on; meaning not only that these to each other as 1, 2, 3, &c., but also that the weight or specific gravity of equal to the known and determinate weight denominated a pound, that the qual to two pounds, and so on.

s of Weight and Measure. — Standards of lineal measure must have been at the earliest period, and appear to have consisted principally of parts of the ly, — as the cubit, or length of the arm from the elbow to the tip of the er; the foot; the *ulna,* arm, or yard; the span; the digit, or finger; the space from the extremity of one hand to that of the other, when they are both opposite directions; the pace, &c. Large spaces were estimated by mea- ed out of multiples of the smaller ones; and sometimes in days' journeys, ace which it was supposed an ordinary man might travel in a day, using a degree of diligence.

al measures can only be used to determine the magnitude of solid bodies; de of bodies in a liquid or fluid state has to be determined by what are ures of capacity. It is probable that, in the infancy of society, shells, or w instruments afforded by nature, were used as standards. But the inac- he conclusions drawn from referring to them must soon have become ob- it early occurred, that to obtain an accurate measure of liquids nothing more ry than to constitute an artificial one, the dimensions, and consequently the which should be determined by the lineal measures previously adopted.

ermination of the gravity or weight of different bodies, supposes the the balance. Nothing is known of the steps which led to its introduc- was used in the remotest antiquity. It seems probable that, at first, me common lineal measure, as a foot, or the fraction of a foot, formed iron, or some other metal, were used as standards of weight. When the s selected, if it was desired to ascertain the specific gravity or weight of rticle, all that was necessary was to put it into one of the scales of the d as many cubes, or parts of cubes, on the other, as might be necessary to it.

have, however, been frequently derived from grains of corn. Hence, in ome other European countries, the lowest denomination of weight is a *grain;* ese grains are directed, by the ancient statute called *compositio mensurarum,* a pennyweight, whereof 20 make an ounce, 12 ounces a pound, and so

country in which commercial transactions are extensively carried on, the im- having weights and measures determined by some fixed standard becomes very one. But as the size of different parts of the human body differ in viduals, it is necessary to select some durable article, — a metallic rod, for of the length of an ordinary cubit, foot, &c., and to make it a standard with e other cubits, feet, &c. used in mensuration shall correspond. These ve always been preserved with the greatest care: at Rome, they were emple of Jupiter; and among the Jews, their custody was intrusted to Aaron. — (*Paucton, Métrologie,* p. 223.)

The principal standards used in the ancient world, were, the cubit of the Je which their other measures of length, capacity, and weight were derived; an the Greeks and Romans.

In England, our ancient historians tell us that a new, or rather a revived, sta lineal measure was introduced by Henry I., who ordered that the ulna, or ar which corresponds to the modern yard, should be made of the exact length o arm, and that the other measures of length should be raised upon it. This has been maintained without any sensible variation. In 1742, the Royal So a yard made, from a very careful comparison of the standard ells or yards of of Henry VII. and Elizabeth kept at the Exchequer. In 1758, an exact made of the Royal Society's yard; and this copy having been examined by a c of the House of Commons, and reported by them to be equal to the standard was marked as such; and this identical yard is declared, by the act 5 Geo. to be the standard of lineal measure in Great Britain. The clause in the follows: —

"From and after the 1st of May, 1825 (subsequently extended to the 1st of January, 1826), line or distance between the centres of the two points in the gold studs in the straight brass rod, custody of the clerk of the House of Commons, whereon the words and figures ' STANDARD Y are engraved, shall be the original and genuine standard of that measure of length or lines called a yard; and the same straight line or distance between the centres of the said two point gold studs in the said brass rod, the brass being at the temperature of 62° by Fahrenheit's th shall be and is hereby denominated the ' IMPERIAL STANDARD YARD', and shall be and is herel to be the unit or only standard measure of extension, wherefrom or whereby all other n extension whatsoever, whether the same be lineal, superficial, or solid, shall be derived, com ascertained; and that all measures of length shall be taken in parts or multiples or certain of the said standard yard; and that ⅓d part of the said standard yard shall be a foot, and th of such foot shall be an inch; and that the pole or perch in length shall contain 5½ such furlong 220 such yards, and the mile 1,760 such yards."— § I.

The superficial measures are formed on the basis of the square of this stan being enacted, that

"the rood of land shall contain 1,210 square yards, according to the said standard yard; a acre of land shall contain 4,840 such square yards, being 160 square perches, poles, or rods." –

Uniformity of Weights and Measures. — The confusion and inconvenience the use of weights and measures of the same denomination, but of different ma was early remarked; and there is hardly a country in which efforts have not b to reduce them to the same uniform system. Numerous acts of parliament l passed, having this object in view, and enjoining the use of the same we measures, under very severe penalties. But owing to the inveteracy of an toms, and the difficulty of enforcing new regulations, these statutes have a a very limited influence, and the greatest diversity has continued to preva in lineal measures. But the statute of 5 Geo. 4. c. 74. seems to have, at lengt what former statutes failed of accomplishing. It is, perhaps, indebted fo cess in this respect to the moderate nature of the changes which it introdu have already seen that it made no alteration in the lineal measures previou Neither did it affect the previously existing system of weights: both the Tr Avoirdupois weights having been preserved.

"The Troy weight," says Mr. Davies Gilbert, President of the Royal Society, " appeare Commissioners of Weights and Measures) to be the ancient weight of this kingdom, having reason to suppose, existed in the same state from the time of St. Edward the Confessor; a reasons, moreover, to believe, that the word Troy has no reference to any town in France, I the monkish name given to London, of Troy Novant, founded on the legend of Brute. therefore, according to this etymology, is, in fact, London weight. We were induced, more serve the Troy weight, because all the coinage has been uniformly regulated by it; and all scriptions or formulæ now are, and always have been, estimated by Troy weight, under a p division, which the College of Physicians have expressed themselves most anxious to preserv

It was resolved, therefore, to continue the use of Troy weight, and also, on account of the the Troy standard, to raise the Avoirdupois weight from this basis.

"We found," said Mr. Davies Gilbert, " the Avoirdupois weight, by which all heavy goo for a long time weighed (probably derived from Avoirs (Averia), the ancient name for goo and Poids, weight), to be universally used throughout the kingdom. This weight, however, have been preserved with such scrupulous accuracy as Troy weight, by which more precious been weighed; but we had reason to believe that the pound cannot differ by more than one, grains, from 7,000 grains Troy; some being in excess, and others, though in a less degree, in def case amounting to above one, two, or three grains. It therefore occurred to us, that we sh ing no violence to this system of weights, if we declared that 7,000 grains Troy should be h sidered as the pound Avoirdupois."

In accordance with these views, it was enacted, — "That from and after the 1st day the standard brass weight of one pound Troy weight, made in the year 1758, now in the c Clerk of the House of Commons, shall be, and the same is hereby declared to be, the original standard measure of weight, and that such brass weight shall be, and is hereby denomina perial Standard Troy pound, and shall be, and the same is hereby declared to be, the unit or measure of weight, from which all other weights shall be derived, computed, and ascertain one twelfth part of the said Troy pound shall be an ounce; and that one twentieth part o shall be a pennyweight; and that one twenty fourth part of such pennyweight shall be that 5,760 such grains shall be a Troy pound, and that 7,000 such grains shall be, and they a clared to be, a pound Avoirdupois, and that one sixteenth part of such ounce shall be a dra

The measures of capacity were found to be, at the period of passing the l in the greatest confusion; and a considerable change has consequently be

The wine gallon formerly amounted to 231 cubic inches, the corn gallon to
nd the ale gallon to 282. But these are superseded by the Imperial gallon,
ntains 277·274 cubic inches, or 277¼ very nearly. It is deduced as follows: —

tandard measure of capacity, as well for liquids as for dry goods not measured by heaped
shall be THE GALLON, containing 10 lbs. avoirdupois weight of distilled water weighed in air, at
rature of 62° of Fahrenheit's thermometer, the barometer being at 30 inches ; and a measure
rthwith made of brass, of such contents as aforesaid, under the directions of the Lord High
or the commissioners of his Majesty's treasury ; and such brass measure shall be and is
clared to be the Imperial standard gallon, and shall be and is hereby declared to be the unit
tandard measure of capacity, from which all other measures of capacity to be used, as well for
, ale, spirits, and all sorts of liquids, as for dry goods not measured by heap measure, shall be
omputed, and ascertained ; and that all measures shall be taken in parts or multiples or
oportions of the said imperial standard gallon, and the quart shall be ¼th part of such standard
d the pint shall be ⅛th of such standard gallon, and 2 such gallons shall be a peck, and 8 such
ll be a bushel, and 8 such bushels a quarter of corn or other dry goods, not measured by
easure." — § 6.

oin a table showing the contents of the different gallons, both in measure and weight.

	Cubic Inches.	Avoirdupois Weight.			Troy Weight.			
		Lbs.	oz.	dr.	Lbs.	oz.	dwt.	grs.
mperial gallon -	277·274	10	0	0	12	1	16	16
orn gallon - - -	268·8	9	10	1¾	11	9	7	12
Vine gallon - - -	231	8	5	6½	10	1	9	22
le gallon - - -	282	10	2	11½	12	4	6	8

l Measures. — The greatest blemish, by far, in the new act, is the continuance
mnation of the practice of selling by heaped measure. We are astonished at the
of such a barbarous custom. All articles that may be sold by heaped measure
be sold by weight. In Scotland, indeed, the use of heaped measure was legally
above 200 years since ; and the present ill-advised attempt to revive a practice
e of nothing but fraud has been universally rejected in that country. The
the act as to heaped measure are as follow : —

dard measure of capacity for *coals, culm, lime, fish, potatoes, or fruit, and all other goods
commonly sold by heaped measure,* shall be the aforesaid bushel, containing 80 lbs. avoirdupois
aforesaid, the same being made round, with a plain and even bottom, and being 19½ inches
e to outside of such standard measure as aforesaid. — § 7.
g use of such bushel, all coals and other goods and things commonly sold by heaped measure,
y heaped up in such bushel, in the form of a cone, such cone to be of the height of at least
ad the outside of the bushel to be the extremity of the base of such cone ; and that 3 bushels
ack, and 12 such sacks shall be a chaldron. — § 8. It was further enacted, by stat. 6 Geo. 4.
rom and after the 1st of January, 1826, all such heaped measures shall be made cylindrical,
ameter of such measures shall be at the least double the depth thereof, and the height of the
p shall be equal to ⅔ths of the depth of the said measure, the outside of the measure being
ty of or base of such cone. — § 2.
of Weight, or Heaped Measure, to be used for Wheat. — Provided always, that any contracts,
les, and dealings, made or had for or with respect to any coals, culm, lime, fish, potatoes, or
l other goods and things commonly sold by heaped measure, sold, delivered, done, or agreed
e sold, delivered ,done, or agreed for, by weight or measure, shall and may be either according
standard of weight, or the said standard for heaped measure ; but all contracts, bargains,
ealings, made or had for any other goods, wares, or merchandise, or other thing done or agreed
sold, delivered, done, or agreed for by weight or measure, shall be made and had according
tandard of weight, or to the said gallon, or the parts, multiples, or proportions thereof ; and
e same the measures shall not be heaped, but shall be stricken with a round stick or roller,
d of the same diameter from end to end. — (5 Geo. 4. c. 74. § 9.)
The 12th section of the act directs models of the standard weights and measures to be kept
ent counties, cities, burghs, &c. for the verification of the weights and measures in use in

for Sale, &c., by Weight or Measure.—All contracts, bargains, sales, and dealings, which shall
had within any part of the United Kingdom, for any work to be done, or for any goods,
handise, or other thing to be sold, delivered, done, or agreed for by weight or measure, where
greement shall be made to the contrary, shall be deemed to be made and had according to the
ghts and measures ascertained by this act ; and in all cases where any special agreement
e, with reference to any weight or measure established by local custom, the ratio or pro-
h every such local weight or measure shall bear to any of the said standard weights or
all be expressed, declared, and specified in such agreement, or otherwise such agreement
and void. — § 15.
Veights and Measures may be used, being marked. — And as it is expedient that persons
lowed to use the several weights and measures which they may have in their possession,
h weights and measures may not be in conformity with the standard weights and measures
y this act ; it is therefore enacted, that it shall be lawful for any person or persons to buy
s and merchandise by any weights or measures established either by local custom, or founded
greement : Provided that, in order that the ratio or proportion which all such measures and
bear to the standard weights and measures established by this act, shall be and become a
nmon notoriety, the ratio or proportion which all such customary measures and weights
the said standard weights and measures shall be painted or marked upon all such customary
measures respectively ; but nothing herein contained shall extend to permit any maker of
easures, or any person or persons whomsoever, to make any weight or measure, at any time
day of May, 1825, except in conformity with the standard weights and measures established
t. — § 16.
ficient Weights, &c. — The 21st section declares that all the powers, rules, and regulations
rmer acts for preventing the use of false and deficient measures are to be applied and put
except such as are expressly repealed or altered by this act.

le or Natural Standards. — As the standards adopted in most countries have
reat degree arbitrary, it has long been the opinion of scientific men, that, to
more perfect system of weights and measures, some natural and unchangeable

basis should be adopted. It has, indeed, been contended by Paucton and Bail the measures of the ancients were deduced from a basis of this sort: and t *stadium* always formed an aliquot part of the earth's circumference, that part di amongst different nations and authors. But no learning or ingenuity can any one to believe what is so obviously incredible. The ancients had no m determining the earth's circumference with any thing like the accuracy required der it the great unit of a system of measures; and, what is equally decisive, no author ever makes the slightest allusion to any such standard.

In more modern times, however, the idea of seeking for a unit of weight an sure in some unchanging natural object has been practically carried into effect. standards that have been usually proposed for this object, have been some aliqu of the quadrant of the meridian, or the length of a pendulum vibrating seconds i given latitude. The latter has been in so far adopted into the existing sy weights and measures established by the act of 1823, that the length of the st yard, as compared with that of a pendulum vibrating seconds in the latitude of L is specified in the act as follows: —

"Whereas it has been ascertained by the commissioners appointed by his Majesty to enquire subject of Weights and Measures, that the said yard hereby declared to be the Imperial stand when compared with a pendulum vibrating seconds of mean time in the latitude of London, in a at the level of the sea, is in the proportion of thirty-six inches to thirty-nine inches, and one three hundred and ninety-three ten thousandth parts of an inch: be it therefore enacted and That if at any time hereafter the said Imperial standard yard shall be lost, or shall be in any m stroyed, defaced, or otherwise injured, it shall and may be restored by making, under the directi Lord High Treasurer, or the Commissioners of his Majesty's Treasury of the United Kingdom Britain and Ireland, or any three of them for the time being, a new standard yard, bearing the portion to such pendulum as aforesaid, as the said Imperial standard yard bears to such pendulu

TABLES OF ENGLISH WEIGHTS AND MEASURES, ACCORDING TO THE NEW OR IMPERIAL STANDARD.

IMPERIAL TROY WEIGHT.

The standard pound containing 5,760 grs.

			French Grammes.
	1 Grain	- =	0·0648
24 Grains	- 1 Pennyweight	=	1·5552
20 Pennyweights	1 Ounce	- =	31·1027
12 Ounces	- 1 Pound	- =	373·2330

Troy weight is used in the weighing of gold, silver, jewels, &c. It is also used in ascertaining the strength of spirituous liquors; in philosophical experiments; and in comparing different weights with each other.

APOTHECARIES' WEIGHT.

				Fr. Gram.
		1 Grain	- - =	0·0648
20 Grains	=	1 Scruple	- - =	1·296
3 Scruples	=	1 Dram	- - =	3·888
8 Drams	=	1 Ounce	- - =	31·102
12 Ounces	=	1 Pound	- - =	373·233

This weight is essentially the same as Troy weight, but differently divided. It is chiefly used for medical prescriptions; but drugs are mostly bought and sold by avoirdupois weight.

DIAMOND WEIGHT. — Diamonds and other precious stones are weighed by carats, the carat being divided into 4 grains, and the grain into 16 parts The diamond carat weighs $3\frac{1}{5}$ grains Troy: thus,

Diamond Weight.		Troy Weight.	Decigrammes.
16 Parts	- 1 Grain	- $0\frac{8}{10}$ Grains	- = $51\frac{1}{3}$
4 Grains	- 1 Carat	- $3\frac{1}{5}$ Grains	- = $205\frac{1}{4}$

IMPERIAL AVOIRDUPOIS WEIGHT.

			Fr. Gram.
	1 Dram	- =	1·771
16 Drams	= 1 Ounce	- =	28·346
16 Ounces	= 1 Pound	- =	453·544
28 Pounds	= 1 Quarter	=	12·699 kilog.
4 Quarters	= 1 Hundred wt.	=	50·796
20 Hundred wt.	1 Ton	- =	1015·920

The dram is subdivided into 3 scruples, and each scruple into 10 grains; the pound, or 7,680 grains avoirdupois, equa grains Troy, and hence 1 grain Tro 1·097 grains avoirdupois.

Hence also 144 lbs. avoird. = 175 lb
and - 192 oz. ditto = 175 o

The stone is generally 14 lbs. avoirdupo but for butcher's meat or fish it is 8 lbs the hundred equals 8 stone of 14 lbs. or 1 8 lbs.

A stone of glass is 5 lbs. A seam o stone, or 120 lbs.

Hay and straw are sold by the load of
The truss of hay weighs 56 lbs. and o lbs. The truss of new hay is 60 lbs. un of September.

The custom of allowing more than 16 the pound of butter used to be very g several parts of the country.

WOOL WEIGHT.

Like all other bulky articles wool is by avoirdupois weight, but the divisio thus

7 Pounds -	=	1 Clove.	$6\frac{1}{2}$ Tods	=	
2 Cloves -	=	1 Stone.	2 Weys	=	
2 Stone -	=	1 Tod.	12 Sacks	=	

A pack of wool contains 240 lbs.

CHEESE AND BUTTER.

8 Pounds	- =	1 Clove.
32 Cloves	- =	1 Wey in Es
42 Do. -	- =	1 Do. in Suf
56 Pounds	=	1 Firkin of B

IMPERIAL LONG MEASURE.

12 Inches	= 1 Foot	- =
3 Feet	= 1 Yard	=
$5\frac{1}{2}$ Yards	= 1 Pole or Rod	=
40 Poles	= 1 Furlong	=
8 Furlongs	= 1 Mile	- = 1
3 Miles -	1 League	- = 4
60 Geographical, or $69\frac{1}{9}$ English Miles -	1 Degree	= 11

Besides the above, there are which equals 3 inches; the hand, the span, 9 inches; and the fatho

IAL SUPERFICIAL MEASURE.

		Fr. Sq. Metres.
s	=1 Sq. foot =	0·0929
e feet	=1 Sq. yard =	0·8361
e yards	=1 Sq. pole =	25·2916
e poles	=1 Rood =	1011·6662
	=1 Acre =	4046·6648

n is generally divided, on scales, , or decimal parts; but in squar- nensions of artificers' work, the l system is adopted; the inch led into 12 parts or lines, each 2 seconds, and each second into

usually measured by a chain of 22 yards, which is divided into 10 chains in length and 1 in ake an acre, which equals 160' hes, or 4,840 square yards.

BIC OR SOLID MEASURE.

		Fr. Cubic Metres.
nches	=1 Cubic foot - =	·0283
et	=1 Cubic yard - =	·7645
rough } , or } wn do. }	1 Load or ton =	{ 1·1326 / 1·4157
et	1 Ton of shipping =	1·1892

measure, marble, stone, timber, ma- artificers' works of length, breadth, , are measured, and also the contents es of capacity, both liquid and dry.

L LIQUID AND DRY MEASURE,

m the Standard Gallon, containing ght of distilled water, temperature ter 30 inches.

Cubic Inches.	Gills.	Pints.	Quarts.	Pottles.	Gallons.	Pecks.	Bushels.	Cooms.	Quarter.
8·665	1								
34·659	4	1							
69·318	8	2	1						
138·637	16	4	2	1					
277·274	32	8	4	2	1				
554·548	64	16	8	4	2	1			
2218·191	256	64	32	16	8	4	1		
8872·763	1,024	256	128	64	32	16	4	1	
17745·526	2,048	512	256	128	64	32	8	2	1

ons of the Imperial standard bushel —The outer diameter 19¼ inches, diameter 18¼. The depth is 8¼, and he cone, for heaped measure, is 6 ntents of the Imperial heaped bushel ubic inches. The subdivisions and n the same proportion.

URES SUPERSEDED BY THE MPERIAL SYSTEM.

D WINE MEASURE.

		Cub. In.		Fr. Litres.
Pint	- -	28·875	- =	0·4731
Quart	- -	57·75	— =	0·9463
Gallon	-	231·	— =	3·3785
Tierce	-	5·614 Feet	=	158·9673
Puncheon	-	11·228	— =	317·9345
Hogshead	-	8·421	— =	238·4509
Pipe or Butt		16·842	— =	476·9018
Tun	-	33·684	— =	953·8036

bdivided into halves and quarters; led a gill. A rundlet is 18 gallons,

Conversion of Old Wine Measure into Imperial Measure.—The old wine gallon contains 231 cubic inches, and the Imperial gallon 277·274 ditto. Hence, to convert wine gallons into Imperial gallons, multiply by $\frac{231}{277·274}$, or by ·83311; and to convert Imperial gallons into wine gallons, multiply by the reciprocal fraction $\frac{277·274}{231}$, or by 1·20032. But for most practical purposes, wine measure multiplied by 5 and divided by 6 will give Imperial measure with sufficient accuracy, and conversely.

N. B.—The multipliers and divisors employed to reduce old wine, ale, &c. measures to Imperial measure, serve also to reduce prices by the former to the latter.

We subjoin, from the very complete and valuable work of Mr. Buchanan of Edinburgh, on Weights and Measures, a

Table of English Wine Gallons, from 1 to 100, with their Equivalents in Imperial Gallons.

Wine Gallons.	Equivalents in Imperial Galls.	Wine Gallons.	Equivalents in Imperial Galls.	Wine Gallons.	Equivalents in Imperial Galls.	Wine Gallons.	Equivalents in Imperial Galls.
1	0·83311	26	21·66038	51	42·48866	76	63·31643
2	1·66622	27	22·49399	52	43·32177	77	64·14954
3	2·49933	28	23·32711	53	44·15488	78	64·98265
4	3·33244	29	24·16022	54	44·98799	79	65·81576
5	4·16555	30	24·99333	55	45·82110	80	66·64887
6	4·99867	31	25·82644	56	46·65421	81	67·48198
7	5·83178	32	26·65955	57	47·48732	82	68·31509
8	6·66489	33	27·49266	58	48·32043	83	69·14820
9	7·49800	34	28·32577	59	49·15354	84	69·98131
10	8·33111	35	29·15888	60	49·98665	85	70·81443
11	9·16422	36	29·99199	61	50·81976	86	71·64754
12	9·99733	37	30·82510	62	51·65288	87	72·48065
13	10·83044	38	31·65821	63	52·48599	88	73·31376
14	11·66355	39	32·49133	64	53·31910	89	74·14687
15	12·49666	40	33·32444	65	54·15221	90	74·97998
16	13·32977	41	34·15755	66	54·98532	91	75·81309
17	14·16289	42	34·99066	67	55·81843	92	76·64620
18	14·99600	43	35·82377	68	56·65154	93	77·47931
19	15·82910	44	36·65688	69	57·48465	94	78·31242
20	16·66222	45	37·48999	70	58·31776	95	79·14554
21	17·49533	46	38·32310	71	59·15087	96	79·97865
22	18·32844	47	39·15626	72	59·98398	97	80·81176
23	19·16155	48	39·98932	73	60·81710	98	81·64487
24	19·99466	49	40·82243	74	61·65021	99	82·47798
25	20·82777	50	41·65555	75	62·48332	100	83·31109

Hence, supposing the former denominations to be preserved, a tierce of wine = 35 imperial gallons very nearly; a puncheon = 70 ditto very nearly; a hogshead = 52½ ditto very nearly; a pipe or butt = 105 ditto very nearly; and a tun = 210 ditto very nearly.

OLD ALE AND BEER MEASURE.

			Cub. In.		Fr. Litres.
		1 Pint -	35·25	=	0·5776
2 Pints	-	1 Quart -	70·5	=	1·1552
4 Quarts	-	1 Gallon -	282·	=	4·6208
8 Gallons	-	1 Firkin ale	1·305 Feet	=	36·9669
9 Gallons	-	1 ditto beer	1·468 —	=	41·5872
2 Firkins	-	1 Kilderkin	2·937 —	=	83·1744
2 Kilderkins		1 Barrel -	5·875 —	=	166·3488
1½ Barrel	-	1 Hogshead	8·812 —	=	249·5232
2 Barrels	-	1 Puncheon	10·750 —	=	332·6876
2 Hogsheads		1 Butt -	17·624 —	=	499·0464
2 Butts	-	1 Tun -	35·248 —	=	998·0928

Conversion of Old Ale and Beer Measure into Imperial Measure.—The old ale gallon contains 282 cubic inches, and the Imperial standard gallon 277·274 ditto. Hence, to convert ale gallons into Imperial gallons, multiply by $\frac{282}{277·274}$, or by 1·0170445; and to convert Imperial gallons into ale gallons, multiply by the reciprocal fraction $\frac{277·274}{282}$, or by ·9832411. Unless extreme accuracy be required, the first three decimals need only be used. And for most practical purposes, ale measure multiplied by 59 and divided by 60 will give Imperial measure with sufficient accuracy, and conversely

Table of English Ale Gallons, from 1 to 100, with their Equivalents in Imperial Gallons.

Ale Gallons.	Equivalents in Imperial Galls.	Ale Gallons.	Equivalents in Imperial Galls.	Ale Gallons.	Equivalents in Imperial Galls.	Ale Gallons.	Equivalents in Imperial Galls.
1	1·01704	26	26·44316	51	51·86927	76	77·29538
2	2·03409	27	27·46020	52	52·88631	77	78·31243
3	3·05113	28	28·47725	53	53·90356	78	79·32947
4	4·06818	29	29·49429	54	54·92040	79	80·34652
5	5·08522	30	30·51134	55	55·93745	80	81·36356
6	6·10227	31	31·52838	56	56·95449	81	82·38060
7	7·11931	32	32·54542	57	57·97154	82	83·39765
8	8·13636	33	33·56247	58	58·98858	83	84·41469
9	9·15340	34	34·57951	59	60·00563	84	85·43174
10	10·17045	35	35·59656	60	61·02267	85	86·44878
11	11·18749	36	36·61360	61	62·03971	86	87·46583
12	12·20453	37	37·63065	62	63·05676	87	88·48287
13	13·22158	38	38·64769	63	64·07380	88	89·49992
14	14·23862	39	39·66474	64	65·09085	89	90·51696
15	15·25567	40	40·68178	65	66·10789	90	91·53401
16	16·27271	41	41·69882	66	67·12494	91	92·55105
17	17·28976	42	42·71587	67	68·14198	92	93·56809
18	18·30680	43	43·73291	68	69·15903	93	94·58514
19	19·32385	44	44·74996	69	70·17607	94	95·60218
20	20·34089	45	45·76700	70	71·19312	95	96·61923
21	21·35793	46	46·78404	71	72·21016	96	97·63627
22	22·37498	47	47·80109	72	73·22720	97	98·65332
23	23·39202	48	48·81814	73	74·24425	98	99·67036
24	24·40907	49	49·83518	74	75·26129	99	100·68741
25	25·42611	50	50·85223	75	76·27834	100	101·70145

OLD DRY OR WINCHESTER MEASURE.

			Cub. In.		Fr. Litres.
4 Gills	-	1 Pint	33·6	=	0·55053
2 Pints	-	1 Quart	67·2	=	1·10107
2 Quarts	-	1 Pottle	134·4	=	2·20214
2 Pottles	-	1 Gallon	268·8	=	4·40428
2 Gallons	-	1 Peck	537·6	=	8·80856
4 Pecks	-	1 Bushel	2150·42	=	35·23430
4 Bushels	-	1 Coom	4·977 Feet	=	140·93721
2 Cooms	-	1 Quarter	9·954	=	281·87443
5 Quarters	-	1 Wey or Load	49·770	—	1409·37216
2 Weys	-	1 Last	99·540	—	2818·74432

The Winchester bushel is 18½ inches wide, and 8 inches deep. Corn and seeds are measured by striking the bushel from the brim, with a round piece of light wood, about 2 inches in diameter, and of equal thickness from one end to the other. All other dry goods are heaped.

Table of Winchester Quarters, from 1 to 100, with their Equivalents in Imperial Quarters.

Winchester Quarters.	Equivalents in Imperial Qrs.	Winchester Quarters.	Equivalents in Imperial Qrs.	Winchester Quarters.	Equivalents in Imperial Qrs.	Winchester Quarters.	Equivalents in Imperial Qrs.
1	0·9615	26	25·20562	51	49·44180	76	73·67797
2	1·93889	27	26·17507	52	50·41124	77	74·64742
3	2·90831	28	27·14452	53	51·38069	78	75·61687
4	3·87779	29	28·11396	54	52·35014	79	76·58631
5	4·84724	30	29·08341	55	53·31959	80	77·55576
6	5·81668	31	30·05286	56	54·28903	81	78·52521
7	6·78613	32	31·02230	57	55·25848	82	79·49165
8	7·75558	33	31·99175	58	56·22793	83	80·46410
9	8·72502	34	32·96120	59	57·19737	84	81·43355
10	9·69447	35	33·93055	60	58·16682	85	82·40300
11	10·66392	36	34·90009	61	59·13627	86	83·37241
12	11·63336	37	35·86954	62	60·10571	87	84·34189
13	12·60281	38	36·83899	63	61·07516	88	85·31134
14	13·57226	39	37·80843	64	62·04461	89	86·28078
15	14·54171	40	38·77788	65	63·01406	90	87·25023
16	15·51115	41	39·74733	66	63·98350	91	88·21968
17	16·48060	42	40·71677	67	64·95295	92	89·18912
18	17·45005	43	41·68622	68	65·92240	93	90·15857
19	18·41949	44	42·65567	69	66·89184	94	91·12802
20	19·38894	45	43·62512	70	67·86129	95	92·09747
21	20·35839	46	44·59456	71	68·83074	96	93·06691
22	21·32783	47	45·56401	72	69·80018	97	94·03637
23	22·29728	48	46·53345	73	70·76963	98	95·00581
24	23·26673	49	47·50290	74	71·73908	99	95·97525
25	24·23618	50	48·47235	75	72·70853	100	96·94470

Conversion of Winchester Bushels into [Imperial] Bushels.— The Winchester bushel conta[ins] cubic inches, and the Imperial standa[rd] 2218·192 ditto. Hence, to convert W[inchester] bushels into Imperial bushels, multiply by [...] or by ·969447; and to convert Imperial b[ushels into] Winchester bushels, multiply by the fraction $\frac{2218\cdot192}{2150\cdot42}$, or 1·0315157. For prac[tical pur]poses, multiply Winchester measure by [...] vide by 32 for Imperial measure, and the [...]

In some markets corn is sold by weigh[t ...] the fairest mode of dealing, though not [...] convenient in practice. Even where me[asure is] used, it is customary to weigh certain qu[antities or] proportions, and to regulate the prices ac[cordingly.] The average bushel of wheat is generally [reckoned] at 60 lbs.— of barley 47 lbs.— of oats [...] peas 64, beans 63, clover 68, rye and [...] and rape 48 lbs. In some places a load [of ...] a man, is reckoned 5 bushels, and a c[...] bushels.

COAL MEASURE.

Coals were formerly sold by the chald[ron, which] bears a certain proportion to Winchester [measure.]

4 Pecks	-	=	1 Bus[hel]
3 Bushels	-	=	1 Sack
3 Sacks	-	=	1 Vat
4 Vats	-	=	1 Cha[ldron]
21 Chaldron	-	=	1 Sco[re]

The coal bushel holds 1 Winchester [...] than the Winchester bushel; its con[tents] 2217·62 cubic inches. It is 19½ inches [...] outside to outside, and 8 inches deep. I[n measuring] coals, it was heaped up in the form of a [cone to a] height of at least 6 inches above the brim [according] to a regulation passed at Guildhall, in 18[..] side of the bushel being the extremity [...] so that the bushel should contain an [...] cubic inches, nearly equal to the Imp[erial] bushel. Hence the chaldron does m[...] cubic feet.

But the sale of coals by measure ha[s, in conse]quence of the frauds to which it le[d (see] p. 277.), been abolished; and they are [...] weight.

Of Wood Fuel, English Measure.— [Wood is] assized into shids, billets, faggot, fa[ggot, and] cord wood. A shid is to be 4 feet long, [and, accord]ing as they are marked and notched, [a propor]tion must be in the girth; viz. if the [... one] notch, they must be 16 inches in th[e girth; if] of two; the first is 7 inches, the secon[d ...] notches, 23 inches; if three notches, [...] 4 notches, 33 inches; and if 5 notche[s, ...] about. Billets are to be 3 feet long, [and ...] should be three sorts; viz. a single cas[t ...] and the third 14 inches, about: they ar[e ...] 100 of 5 score. Faggots are to be 3 fee[t long,] the band 24 inches about; besides the [...] faggots, 50 go to the load. Bavins an[d ...] are sold by the 100, which are accou[nted ...] Cord wood is the bigger sort of fire w[ood,] measured by a cord, or line, whereof [...] measures; that of 14 feet in length, 3 fe[et ...] and 3 feet in height. The other is 8 f[eet ...] 4 feet in height, and 4 feet in breadth.

MEASURES OF WOOD.

1,000 Billets of wood	-	=	1 Cord
10 Cwt. of ditto	-	=	1 Cor[d]
1 Cord of wood	-	=	½ Cha[ldron]
100 Pounds of wood	-	=	1 Qui[ntal]

French System of Weights and Measures. — The new metrical system est[ablished in] France subsequently to the Revolution, is founded on the measurement of th[e length] of the meridian, or of the distance from the pole to the equator. This dista[nce having] been determined with the greatest care, the ten millionth part of it was assu[med the] *metre*, or unit of length, all the other lineal measures being multiples, or su[bmultiples] of it in decimal proportion. The metre corresponds pretty nearly to [the] French *aune*, or yard, being equal to 3·07844 French feet, or 3·281 Engl[ish feet, or] 39·3708 English inches.

it of weight is the *gramme*, which is a timetre, or the 100th part of a metre of vater of the temperature of melting ice; 15·434 English Troy grains.

to express the decimal proportion, the vocabulary of names has been adopted, the terms for multiplying are Greek, and lividing are Latin.

ltipliers, the word

a prefixed means	-	10 times.
to -	-	100 —
-	-	1,000 —
ia - -	-	10,000 —

ontrary, for divisors,

word *Deci* expresses the		10th part.
Centi	- -	100th —
Milli	- -	1,000th —

ecametre means 10 metres.
ecimetre — the 10th part of a metre.
ilogramme — 1,000 grammes, &c.

is the element of square measure, being ecametre, equal to 3·955 English perches.
is the element of cube measure, and 5·317 cubic feet English.
is the element of all measures of ca- is a cubic decimetre, and equals 2·1135 nts. 100 litres make the hectolitre, als 26·419 Wine gallons, or 2·838 Win- hels.

USUEL, OR BINARY SYSTEM.—This new the metrical standards for its basis, but ons are binary, that is, by 2, 4, 8, &c.; of the new vocabulary, the names of weights and measures are used, annex- m *usuel* to each. Thus the half kilo- called the livre usuelle, and the double toise usuelle.

wing Tables show the proportions be- ew or metrical French system and the tem:—

of FRENCH and ENGLISH WEIGHTS and s, containing the New or Metrical and Measures of France, with their n to those of England, both according cimal System and the Système Usuel.

DECIMAL SYSTEM.

Long Measures.

		English.
-	- =	0·03937 inches.
-	- =	0·39371 —
-	- =	3·93710 —
- -	- =	39·37100 —
-	- =	32·80916 feet.
-	- =	328·09167 —
-	- =	1093·63890 yards.
.	- =	10936·38900 — or 6 miles 1 furlong 28 poles.

Measures of Capacity.

-	- =	0·06103 cubic inches.
-	- =	0·61028 —
-	- =	6·10280 —
ic }	- =	{ 61·02803 — or 2·1135 wine pints.
.	- =	610·28028 cubic inches, or 2·642 wine gallons.
-	- =	3·5317 cubic feet, or ·419 wine gallons, 22 Imperial gallons, or 2·839 Winchester bushels.
-	- =	35·3171 cubic feet, or 1 tun and 12 wine gallons.
-	- =	353·17146 cubic feet.

Superficial Measures.

Centiare	- - =	1·1960 sq. yards.
Are (a square decametre)	=	119·6046 —
Decare	- - =	1196·0460 —
Hectare	- - =	11960·4604 — or 2 acres 1 rood 35 perches.

Solid Measures.

Decistere	- - =	3·5317 cubic feet.
Stere (a cubic metre)	- =	35·3174 —
Decastere	- - =	353·1714 —

Weights.

Milligramme	- - =	0·0154 grains.
Centigramme	- - =	0·1543 —
Decigramme	- - - =	1·5434 —
Gramme	- - - =	15·4340 —
Decagramme	- - - =	154·3402 — or 5·64 drams avoirdupois.
Hectogramme	- - =	3·2154 oz. Troy, or 3·527 oz. avoirdupois.
Kilogramme	- =	2 lbs. 8 oz. 3 dwt. 2 grs. Troy, or 2 lbs. 3 oz. 4·428 drams avoirdupois.
Myriagramme	- - =	26·795 lbs. troy, or 22·0485 lbs. avoirdupois.
Quintal	- - =	1 cwt. 3 qrs. 25 lbs. nearly.
Millier, or Bar	- =	9 tons 16 cwt. 3 qrs. 12 lbs.

SYSTEME USUEL.

Comparison of Weight.

	Grammes.		Troy Weight. Lbs.	oz.	dwt.	gr.	Avoirdupois. Lbs.	oz.	dr.
Kilogramme	1,000	=	2	8	3	2	2	3	4⅜
Livre usuelle	500	=	1	4	1	13	1	1	10¼
Half -	250	=		8	0	18·5		8	13⅛
Quarter -	125	=		4	0	9·25		4	6½
Eighth -	62·5	=		2	0	4·5		2	3¼
Once -	31·3	=		1	0	2·25		1	1⅝
Half -	15·6	=			10	1·125			8⅞
Quarter -	7·8	=			5	0·5			4½
Gros -	3·9	=			2	12·25			2¼

Comparison of Lineur Measures.

Mesures usuelles.	Metres.		English Measure. Feet.	Inch.	Parts.
Toise usuelle -	2	=	6	6	9
Pied, or Foot -	0⅙	=	1	1	1½
Inch - - -	$0\frac{1}{72}$	=	1	1	1⅛
Aune - -	1⅕	=	3	11	3
Half - -	0⅗	=	1	11	7½
Quarter - -	$0\frac{3}{10}$	=	0	11	9¾
Eighth - -	$0\frac{3}{20}$	=	0	5	10⅞
Sixteenth - -	$0\frac{3}{40}$	=	0	2	$11\frac{1}{16}$
One third of an aune	0⅖	=	1	3	9
Sixth - -	0⅕	=	0	7	10½
Twelfth - -	$0\frac{1}{10}$	=	0	3	11¼

Comparison of Measures of Capacity.

	Litres.		Eng. Winch. Bush.
Boisseau usuel -	12·5	=	0.35474

With halves and quarters in proportion.

	Paris Pinte.		English Pint.
Litron usuel -	1·074	-	$2\frac{1}{9}$

With halves and quarters in proportion.

eights and Measures.—This subject is involved in considerable difficulty; and to enter fully be quite inconsistent with our objects and limits. But the following details, abstracted from horities, may be useful to such of our readers as have occasion to look into any of the ors.

rious Ancient Weights according to different Authorities.

	English Troy grains.	
-	{ 8·2	Christiani.
	9·1	Arbuthnot.
a	{ 51·9	Chr.
	54·6	Arb.
	69·	Paucton.
-	- 3,892·	Chr.
-	{ 5,189·	Chr.
	5,464·	Arb.
	6,900·	Pauc.

Medical mina - -	6,994· gr.	Arb.
Talent = 60 minæ = ⅜ cwt. English.		
Old Greek drachm -	{ 146·5 Eng. Troy gr.	Arb.
	62·5 = Roman denarius,	Arb.
Old Greek mina - -	6,425·	Do.
Egyptian mina - -	8,326·	Do.
Ptolemaic mina of Cleopatra }	8,985·	Do.
Alexandrian mina of Dioscorides - }	9,992·	Do.
Roman denarius	{ 51·9 = ⅛ Rom. oz.	Chr.
	62·5 = ⅛ Rom. oz.	Arb.

English Troy grains.		
Denarius of Nero	54·	Pauc.
Papyrius	61·7	Do.
Ounce	415·1	Chr.
	437·2	Arb.
	431·2	Pauc.
Pound of 10 oz.	4,150·	Chr.
12 oz.	4,981·	Chr.
	5,246·	Arb.
	5,174·4	Pauc.

ROMAN MEASURES OF LENGTH. — (*Arbuthnot and Hutton.*)

	Eng. inches.
Digitus transversus	0·72525
Uncia, the ounce	0·967
Palmus minor	2·901
Pes, the foot	11·604
	Eng. feet.
Palmipes	1·20875
Cubitus	1·4505
Gradus	2·4175
	Paces.
Passus	0·967
Stadium	120·875
Milliare	967·0

SCRIPTURE MEASURES OF LENGTH. — (*Arbuthnot and Hutton.*)

	Inches.
Digit	0·7425
Palm	2·97
Span	8·91
	Eng. feet.
Lesser cubit	1·485
Sacred cubit	1·7325
	Yards.
Fathom	2·31
Ezekiel's reed	3·465
Arabian pole	4·62
Schœnus	46·2
Stadium	231·0
Sabbath day's journey	1155·0
	Miles.
Eastern mile	1·886
Parasang	4·158
Day's journey	33·264

GRECIAN MEASURES OF LENGTH. — (*Arbuthnot and Hutton.*)

	Inches.
Dactylos	0·75546
Doron, Dochme	3·02187
Dichas	7·55468
Orthodoron	8·31015
	Eng. inches.
Spithame	9·06562
Pous	12·0875
	Eng. feet.
Pous	1·00729
Pygme	1·13203
Pygon	1·25911
Pechys	1·51093

En...

Orgya	-	-	-
Stadios, Dulos	-	-	1
Milion	-	-	8

ROMAN DRY MEASURES. — (*Arbuthnot and ...*)
En

Hemina	-	-	-
Sextarius	-	-	-
			En
Modius	-	-	-

ATTIC DRY MEASURES.
Er

Xestes	-	-	-
Chenix	-	-	-
			Win...
Medimnus	-	-	-

JEWISH DRY MEASURES, ACCORDING TO JOS...
Er

Gachal	-	-	-
Cab	-	-	-
Gomer	-	-	-
			E
Seah	-	-	-
			Win
Ephah	-	-	-
Latech	-	-	-
Corom, Chomer	-	-	-

ROMAN MEASURES FOR LIQUIDS. — (*Arbut... Hutton.*)
E

Hemina	-	-	-
Sextarius	-	-	-
Congius	-	-	-
			Win
Urna	-	-	-
Amphora	-	-	-
Culeus	-	-	-

ATTIC MEASURES FOR LIQUIDS.
E

Cotylus	-	-
Xestes	-	-
Chous	-	-
Meteotes	-	-

JEWISH MEASURES FOR LIQUIDS.
E

Caph	-	-
Log	-	-
Cab	-	-
Hin	-	-
Seah	-	-
Bath	-	-
Coron	-	-

WELD, or **DYERS' WEED** (Ger. *Wau;* Du. *Wouw, Wouwe;* Fr. It. *Guadarella;* Lat. *Luteola*), is an imperfect biennial, with small fusiforn and a leafy stem from 1 to 3 feet in height. It is a native of Britain, It: various parts of Europe; and is cultivated for the sake of its stalk, flow leaves, which are employed in the dyeing of yellow, whence its botanic *Reséda Luteola*. Weld requires the growth of nearly two summers before to maturity; and the crop is liable to fail from so many causes, and is be exhausting, that its cultivation is by no means profitable, and is only carrie this country at least, to a small extent, principally in Essex. Weld is to all other substances in giving the lively green lemon yellow. It is, expensive; and it is found, when employed in topical dyeing, to degrade terfere with madder colours more than other yellows, and to stain the part to be kept white. Hence quercitron bark is now employed in calico pri the almost total exclusion of weld. It is still, however, employed in dy a golden yellow, and in paper staining. — (*Loudon's Ency. of Agriculture;* on Colours, vol. ii. pp. 95—100.; *Rees's Cyclopædia.*)

WHALEBONE, a substance of the nature of horn, adhering in thin laminæ to the upper jaw of the whale. These vary in size from 3 to

he breadth of the largest at the thick end, where they are attached to
is about a foot.   They are extremely elastic.   All above 6 feet in length
ize bone.

ebone bore anciently a very high price, when the rigid stays and the expanded
ur grandmothers produced an extensive demand for this commodity.   The
ve occasionally obtained 700l. per ton, and were accustomed to draw
annually from England for this one article.   Even in 1763, it still brought
t soon fell, and has never risen again to the same value.   During the present
e price has varied between 60l. and 300l. ;   seldom falling to the lowest rate,
exceeding 150l.   Mr. Scoresby reckons the price, in the five years ending
at 90l. ; while at present (July, 1830), it is stated from the different ports to
30l. to 180l.   This is for what is called the *size bone*, or such pieces as mea-
or upwards in length ; those below this standard are usually sold at half
may appear singular that whalebone should rise, while oil has been so de-
vered ; but the one change, it is obvious, causes the other.   Oil, being the
ct of the fishery, regulates its extent, which being diminished by the low
quantity of whalebone is lessened, while the demand for it continuing as great
the value consequently rises."—(*Polar Seas and Regions*, p. 321., *Edin.*

e worth while to remark, as evincing the ignorance that at one time prevailed
t to the whale, that, by an old feudal law, the *tail* of all whales belonged to
s a perquisite, to furnish her Majesty's wardrobe with whalebone !—(*Black-*
, p. 233.)
lebone was worth, in the London market, in January, 1832, 180l. a ton.

E (COMMON), the *Balæna Mysticetus* of Linnæus, a fish of the ce-
ecies, and the largest of all the animals with which men are acquainted.
has sometimes, it is affirmed, been found 160 feet in length ; but this
bably an exaggeration.   In the Northern seas, it is at present seldom
ve 60 feet long : being now, however, generally killed before it arrives
rowth, this is no proof that the animal may not formerly have attained
larger size.   The bodies of whales are covered, immediately under the
a layer of fat or *blubber*, which, in large fish, is from 12 to 18 inches thick.
hales this fatty matter resembles hog's lard, but in old ones it is of a
our.   This is the valuable part of the whale ; and the desire to possess
pted man to attempt the capture of this mighty animal.   The blubber
xpression, nearly its own weight of a thick viscid oil (train oil).   The
hale is now rarely found, except within the arctic circle ; but at a
od it was not unfrequently met with on our coasts.   There is a good
the common whale, and of the manner in which the fishery is carried
John Laing's " Voyage to Spitzbergen ;" one of the shortest, cheapest,
the innumerable books published on this hackneyed subject.
seter macrocephalus, or black-headed spermaceti whale, is chiefly found
thern Ocean.   It usually measures about 60 feet in length, and 30 in
ce at the thickest part.   The valuable part of the fish is the spongy,
ug from the cavity of the head ; this is crude spermaceti ; and of it an
ed whale will yield about 12 large barrels.
E FISHERY.   We do not propose entering, in this article, into any
o the mode in which the fishery is carried on ; but mean to confine
a brief sketch of its history and value in a commercial point of

bly true, as has been sometimes contended, that the Norwegians occasionally
whale before any other European nation engaged in so perilous an enter-
the early efforts of the Norwegians were not conducted on any systematic
ould be regarded only in the same point of view as the fishing expeditions
maux.   The Biscayans were certainly the first people who prosecuted the
y as a regular commercial pursuit.   They carried it on with great vigour
n the twelfth, thirteenth, and fourteenth centuries.   In 1261, a tithe was
ie tongues of whales imported into Bayonne — they being then a highly
cies of food.   In 1338, Edward III. relinquished to Peter de Puyanne a
erling a whale, laid on those brought into the port of Biarritz, to indem-
the extraordinary expenses he had incurred in fitting out a fleet for the ser-
Majesty.   This fact proves beyond dispute that the fishery carried on from
e period referred to must have been very considerable indeed ; and it was

also prosecuted to a great extent from Cibourre, Vieux Boucan, and subsequen
Rochelle and other places. *

The whales captured by the Biscayans were not so large as those that are take
Polar seas, and are supposed to have been attracted southward in pursuit of I
They were not very productive of oil, but their flesh was used as an article
and the whalebone was applied to a variety of useful purposes, and brough
high price.

This branch of industry ceased long since, and from the same cause that I
sioned the cessation of the whale fishery in many other places — the want
Whether it were that the whales, from a sense of the dangers to which they
themselves in coming southwards, no longer left the Icy Sea, or that the breed
nearly destroyed, certain it is that they gradually became less numerous in th
Biscay, and at length ceased almost entirely to frequent that sea ; and the fish
obliged to pursue their prey upon the banks of Newfoundland and the coasts of
the French fishery rapidly fell off.

The voyages of the Dutch and English to the Northern Ocean, in order, if
to discover a passage through it to India, though they failed of their main ob
open the haunts of the whale. The companions of Barentz, who discovere
bergen in 1596, and of Hudson, who soon after explored the same seas, repres
their countrymen the amazing number of whales with which they were crowde
sels were in consequence fitted out for the Northern Whale Fishery by the En
Dutch, the harpooners and a part of the crew being Biscayans. They did I
ever, confine their efforts to a fair competition with each other as fishers. The
Company obtained a royal charter, prohibiting the ships of all other nations fro
in the seas round Spitzbergen, on pretext of its having been first discovered by I
Willoughby. There can, however, be no doubt that Barentz, and not Sir Hug
original discoverer ; though, supposing that the fact had been otherwise, th
to exclude other nations from the surrounding seas, on such a ground, was no
could be tolerated. The Dutch, who were at the time prompt to embark
commercial pursuit that gave any hopes of success, eagerly entered on this ne
and sent out ships fitted equally for the purposes of fishing, and of defence ag
attacks of others. The Muscovy Company having attempted to vindicate it
sions by force, several encounters took place between their ships and those of th
The conviction at length became general, that there was room enough for all
the Northern seas ; and in order to avoid the chance of coming into collision
other, they parcelled Spitzbergen and the adjacent ocean into districts, wl
respectively assigned to the English, Dutch, Hamburghers, French, Danes, &

The Dutch being thus left to prosecute the fishery without having their
diverted by hostile attacks, speedily acquired a decided superiority over
competitors.

When the Europeans first began to prosecute the fishery on the coast of Sp
whales were every where found in vast numbers. Ignorant of the strength a
gems of the formidable foe by whom they were now assailed, instead of betr
symptoms of fear, they surrounded the ships and crowded all the bays. The
was in consequence a comparatively easy task, and many were killed which it
wards necessary to abandon, from the ships being already full.

While fish were thus easily obtained, it was the practice to boil the b
shore in the North, and to fetch home only the oil and whalebone. And
nothing can give a more vivid idea of the extent and importance of the Dut
in the middle of the seventeenth century, than the fact that they constructe
derable village, the houses of which were all previously prepared in Holla
Isle of Amsterdam, on the northern shore of Spitzbergen, to which they gave
priate name of *Smeerenberg* (from *smeeren*, to melt, and *berg*, a mountain).
the grand rendezvous of the Dutch whale ships, and was amply provided wi
tanks, and every sort of apparatus required for preparing the oil and the b
this was not all. The whale fleets were attended by a number of provision
cargoes of which were landed at Smeerenberg ; which abounded during the b
with well-furnished shops, good inns, &c. ; so that many of the conveni
enjoyments of Amsterdam were found within about 11 degrees of the Pole !
ticularly mentioned, that the sailors and others were every morning supplied
a Dutchman regards as a very great luxury — *hot rolls* for breakfast. B
Smeerenberg were founded nearly at the same period, and it was for a c
time doubted whether the latter was not the most important establishme
Reste, Histoire des Pêches, &c. tome i. p. 42.)

* See *Mémoire sur l'Antiquité de la Pêche de la Balcine, par Noel*, 12mo. Paris, 1

g the flourishing period of the Dutch fishery, the quantity of oil made in the
as so great that it could not be carried home by the whale ships; and every
sels were sent out in ballast to assist in importing the produce of the fishery.

he same cause that had destroyed the fishery of the Biscayans, ruined that which
ied on in the immediate neighbourhood of Spitzbergen. Whales became grass common, and more and more timid and difficult to catch. They retreated
e open seas, and then to the great banks of ice on the eastern coast of Green-
Vhen the site of the fishery had been thus removed to a very great distance
tzbergen, it was found most economical to send the blubber direct to Holland.
berg was in consequence totally deserted, and its position is now with difficulty
ble.

hough very extensive, the Dutch whale fishery was not, during the first 30
its existence, very profitable, This arose from the circumstance of the right
t on having been conceded, in 1614, to an exclusive company. The expense in-
from such great associations, the wastefulness and unfaithfulness of their ser-
to were much more intent upon advancing their own interests than those of
any, increased the outlays so much, that the returns, great as they were,
ttle more than adequate to defray them, and the fishery was confined within
ver limits than it would otherwise have reached. But after various prolong-
the charter of the first company, and the formation of some new ones, the
finally thrown open in 1642. The effects of this measure were most salu-
afford one of the most striking examples to be met with of the advantages of
etition. Within a few years the fishery was vastly extended; and though it
rogressively more and more difficult from the growing scarcity of fish, it
otwithstanding these disadvantages, more profitable to the private adventurers
d ever been to the company; and continued for above a century to be prose-
h equal energy and success. The famous John de Witt has alluded as follows
ange in the mode of conducting the trade : —

respect," says he, " it is worthy of observation, that the authorised Greenland Company
fore little profit by their fishery, because of the great charge of setting out their ships; and that
l, blubber, and whale fins were not well made, handled, or cured; and being brought hither
to warehouses, were not sold soon enough, nor to the Company's best advantage. Whereas
ery one equips their vessels at the cheapest rate, follow their fishing diligently, and manage
y, the blubber, train oil, and whale fins are employed for so many uses in several countries,
n sell them with that conveniency, that though *there are now fifteen ships for one that for-*
out of Holland on that account, and consequently each of them could not take so many
eretofore, and notwithstanding the new prohibition of France and other countries to import
odities, and though there is greater plenty of them imported by our fishers — yet those com-
e so much raised in the value above what they were whilst there was a company, that the
habitants do exercise that fishery with profit, to the much greater benefit of our country
it was (under the management of a company) carried on but by a few." — (*True Interest*
p. 63. 8vo ed. London, 1746.)

vate ships sent by the Dutch to the whale fishery were fitted out on a prin-
secured the utmost economy and vigilance on the part of every one con-
h them. The hull of the vessel was furnished by an individual who commonly
himself the office of captain, a sail-maker supplied the sails, a cooper the
The parties engaged as adventurers in the undertaking. The cargo being
Holland and disposed of, each person shared in the produce according to
tion of the outfit. The crew was hired on the same principle; so that every
motive to exert himself, to see that all unnecessary expenses were avoided,
hose that were necessary were confined within the narrowest limits. This
s been imitated to some extent in this and some other countries, but in none
n carried so far as in Holland. It appears to us that it might be advan-
introduced into other adventures.

i its most flourishing state, towards the year 1680, the Dutch whale fishery
about 260 ships and 14,000 sailors.

iglish whale fishery, like that of Holland, was originally carried on by an
association. The Muscovy Company was, indeed, speedily driven from the
it was immediately succeeded by others that did not prove more fortunate.
he South Sea Company embarked largely in the trade, and prosecuted it for
the end of which, having lost a large sum, they gave it up. But the legis-
ing resolved to support the trade, granted, in 1732, a bounty of 20s. a ton
ip of more than 200 tons burthen engaged in it; but this premium being in-
t was raised, in 1749, to 40s. a ton, when a number of ships were fitted out,
ertainly in the intention of catching the bounty as of catching fish. De-
he prosperous appearance of the fishery, parliament imagined that it was
blished, and in 1777 the bounty was reduced to 30s. The effects of this
showed the factitious nature of the trade, the vessels engaged in it having
n the course of the next 5 years from 105 to 39! To arrest this alarming
bounty was raised to its old level in 1781, and of course the trade was soon

restored to its previous state of apparent prosperity. The hostilities occasioned
American war reduced the Dutch fishery to less than half its previous amoun
gave a proportional extension to that of England. The bounty, which had in
quence become very heavy, was reduced, in 1787, to 30s. a ton; in 1792 it was
reduced to 25s.; and in 1795 it was reduced to 20s., at which sum it continu
1824, when it ceased.

It appears from accounts given in Macpherson's "Annals of Commerce," (v
p. 511., vol. iv. p. 130.), that the total bounties paid for the encouragement of the
fishery, in the interval between 1750 and 1788, amounted to no less than 1,57
It will be seen from the official account which follows, that there are no means of fu
ing any accurate account of the sums paid as bounties from the year 1789 to 1813 inc
but it is, notwithstanding, abundantly certain that the total bounties paid during the
from 1789 to 1824 considerably exceeded a million. Here, then, we have a sum
wards of TWO MILLIONS AND A HALF laid out since 1750 in promoting the whale f
Now we believe that if we estimate the entire average value of the *gross* produce
Northern whale fishery (and it is to it only that the preceding statements apply),
the last three or four years, at 375,000*l.* a year, we shall be about the mark. But
2,500,000*l.* expended in bolstering up this branch of industry been laid out as ca
any ordinary employment, it would have produced 125,000*l.* a year of *nett* profi
deducting this sum from the above, there remains only 250,000*l.* to replace the
wasted and ships lost in carrying on the fishery, and to afford *a clear national*
Whatever, therefore, may be the value of the whale fishery as a nursery for seame
absurd to regard it as contributing any thing to the public wealth. The rem
Dr. Franklin, that he that draws a fish out of the sea draws out a piece of si
ever in the mouths of those who are clamouring for bounties and protection
competition. But we apprehend that even Franklin himself, sagacious as h
would have found it rather difficult to show how the wealth of those is to be inc
who, in fishing up one piece of silver, are obliged to throw another of equa
into the sea. We subjoin

An Account of the Number of Ships annually fitted out in Great Britain for the Norther
Fishery, of the Tonnage and Crews of such Ships, and of the Bounties paid on their Accou
1789 to 1824.

Years.	Ships.	Tons.	Men.	Bounties paid.	Years.	Ships.	Tons.	Men.	Bounties p
1789	161	46,599	4,482		1807		There are no documents in this of			
1790	116	33,232	4,520		to		which the account for these years			
1791	116	33,906	4,520		1813		rendered.			
1792	93	26,983	4,667						£ s.
1793	82	23,487	3,210	The documents	1814	112	36,576	4,708	43,799 1
1794	60	16,386	2,250	from which the	1815	134	43,320	5,783	41,487 14
1795	44	11,748	1,601	amount of boun-	1816	130	41,767	5,542	42,746 13
1796	51	13,833	1,910	ties paid in these	1817	135	43,548	5,768	43,461 6
1797	60	16,371	2,265	years could be	1818		45,040	5,903	45,806 1
1798	66	18,754	2,633	shown, were de-	1819	140	45,093	6,291	43,051 8
1799	67	19,360	2,683	stroyed in the fire	1820	140	45,092	6,137	44,749 18
1800	61	17,729	2,459	at the late Cus-	1821	142	44,864	6,074	42,164 0
1801	64	18,568	2,544	tom-house.	1822	140	38,182	5,234	32,347 4
1802	79	23,539	3,129		1823	124	37,628	4,984	32,980 9
1803	95	28,608	3,806		1824	120	35,194	4,867	29,131 13
1804	92	28,054	3,597			112			
1805	91	27,570	3,636						
1806	91	27,697	3,715						

Office of Registrar General of Shipping,   JOHN COVE
    Custom-house, London, 16th Dec. 1830.   Reg. Gen. of Sh

It is not even certain whether the expenditure of 2,500,000*l.* upon bountie
really have had the effect of establishing the whale fishery upon a solid foundat
for the occupation of Holland by the French, and the consequent hostilities
she was involved with this country. These did more to promote and consoli
British fishery than any thing else. The war entirely annihilated that of the
And our government having wisely offered to the fishers of Holland all the im
enjoyed by the citizens of Great Britain in the event of their settling amongst u
availed themselves of the invitation, bringing with them their capital, indus
skill. In consequence of this signal encouragement, the whale fishery of Eng
prosecuted with greater success than at any previous period: and at the ter
of the late war, in 1815, there were 134 valuable ships and about 5,800
engaged in the Northern fishery, and about 30 ships and 800 men in that to th

After peace was restored, the English capitalists and others became apprehe
the Dutch should engage anew with their ancient vigour and success in t
fishery. But these apprehensions were without any real foundation. The H
during the 30 years they had been excluded from the sea, had lost all that

ce with the details of the fishery, for which they had long been so famous,
is so essential to its success. The government attempted to rouse their dor-
gies by the offer of considerable premiums and other advantages to those who
in the trade. Three companies were in consequence formed for carrying it
Rotterdam, one at Harlingen, and one in South Holland. But their efforts
very limited, and altogether unfortunate. In 1826, the company of South
was dissolved, while that of Harlingen despatched 4 ships, and that of
2. In 1827, Rotterdam sent only 1 ship, and Harlingen 2: and in
litary ship sailed from Holland — a feeble and last effort of the company
en !

been the fate of the Dutch whale fishery. The attempts to revive it failed,
e the ships sent out were ill calculated for the service, but because they were
unskilful seamen. In the early ages of the fishery, this difficulty would
got over, because, owing to the fewness of competitors, and the scanty supply
whalebone, even a small cargo brought a high price; but at present, when the
prosecuted on a very large scale and at a very low rate of profit by the
e Americans, the Hamburghers, &c., no new competitor coming into the
expect to maintain himself unless he had nearly equal advantages. The
e, therefore, done wisely in withdrawing from the trade. Any attempt to
by the aid of bounties and other artificial encouragements would be one of
ultimate success must be very doubtful, and which could lead to no really
lt. During the 20 years preceding the late French war, the fishery of Hol-
radually declining, and had, in a great measure, ceased to be profitable. It
lly to endeavour to raise anew, and at a great expense, a branch of industry
come unproductive at a former period, when there is no ground for supposing
ld be more productive at this moment.

already noticed several changes of the localities in which the whale fishery
rried on at different periods; within these few years another has taken place
mportant. The seas between Spitzbergen and Greenland are now nearly
by the whalers, who resort in preference to Davis's Straits and Baffin's Bay,
which washes the coast of West Greenland. The Dutch fishers first began
Davis's Straits in 1719; and as the whales had not hitherto been pursued
st recess, they were found in greater numbers than in the seas round Spitz-
rom about this period it was usually resorted to by about three tenths of the
.. It was not till a comparatively late period that Davis's Straits began to
ed by English whalers; and even so late as 1820, when Captain Scoresby
is elaborate and valuable work on the whale fishery, that carried on in the
seas was by far the most considerable. But within the last few years the
ishery has been almost entirely deserted. The various discoveries made by
ons recently fitted out by government for exploring the seas and inlets to the
f Davis's Straits and Baffin's Bay, have made the fishers acquainted with
and advantageous situations for the prosecution of their business. What
lutions the fishery may be destined to undergo, it is impossible to foresee;
n be little doubt that the same results that have happened elsewhere will
Davis's Straits, and that it will be necessary to pursue the whale to new and
more inaccessible haunts.

n Davis's Straits is less incommoded with field ice than the Greenland and
seas, but it abounds with icebergs; and the fishery, when carried on in
y and Lancaster Sound, is more dangerous, perhaps, than any that has
attempted.

ving table gives a view of the produce of the Northern whale fishery during
nding with 1827 : —

Years.	Number of Ships despatched.	Number of Whales captured.	Quantity of Oil.	Quantity of Whalebone.
			Tons.	Tons.
1825	110	501	6,597	360
1826	94	510	7,087	390
1827	88	1,155	13,179	732

s from this and the previous table, that the number of ships sent out has
rly a half since 1820. The bounty was repealed in 1824, and the ships
ve since fallen off in the ratio of 112 to 88 or 90. This is a sufficient proof
re foundation on which the trade had previously rested.
e fishery has for a lengthened period partaken more of the nature of a
venture than of a regular industrious pursuit. Sometimes the ships do not
rgo, and sometimes they come home *clean*. The risk of shipwreck is also
able. It appears from Mr. Scoresby's tables (vol. ii. p. 131.), that of 586

ships sent to the North during the 4 years ending with 1817, *eight* were los
period was, however, uncommonly free from disaster. It would seem, too,
risk of shipwreck is greater in Davis's Straits than in the seas to the east of Gr
In 1819, of 63 ships sent to Davis's Straits, no fewer than 10 were lost; in 1
of 79 ships, 11 were lost; and in 1822, out of 60 ships, 7 were lost. B
has in this respect been the most disastrous. — Of 87 ships that sailed fo
Straits, no less than 18, or 22 per cent. of the whole, have been totally lost; 24
clean, or without having caught a single fish; and of the remainder not 1 h
cargo, only 1 or 2 being *half fished!* If we estimate the value of the ships c
including the outfit, at 7,000*l.* each, the loss from shipwreck only will be 126,0
seems very doubtful whether, in the present critical state of the fishery, it w
recover from so dreadful a blow.

A little work on "Discovery and Adventures in the Polar Seas and I
forming part of the "Edinburgh Cabinet Library," and compiled with great
ability, was published in 1830. We borrow from it the following instructiv
with respect to the fishery of 1829, and the changes that have taken place d
last 20 years in the ports at which the fishery ships are fitted out: —

Result of the Fishery of 1829.

Ports.	No. of Ships.	Tonnage.	Fish.	Oil.	B
				Tons.	Tons.
Aberdeen - - - -	11	3,322	84	1,171	63
Berwick - - - -	1	309	11	147	8
Dundee - - - -	9	3,031	77	1,005	54
Hull - - - -	33	10,899	339	3,982	235
Kirkcaldy - - - -	4	1,261	51	649	37
Leith - - - -	7	2,393	71	862	48
London - - - -	2	714	2	32	2
Montrose - - - -	4	1,301	39	481	27
Newcastle - - - -	3	1,103	45	541	29
Peterhead - - - -	12	3,429	118	1,445	78
Whitby - - - -	3	1,050	34	357	21
Totals - - -	89	28,812	871	10,672	607

Estimated Value.

		£
10,672 Tons of oil, at 25*l.* - - -		266,800
607½ Tons of whalebone, at 180*l.* - - -		109,350
		£ 376,150

In the commercial tables printed by the House of Commons in 1830, the entire proce
are stated at 428,591*l.* 6*s.* 6*d.*; but this, of course, includes also the Southern fishery. Of th
there were exported to foreign countries, *oil* to the value of 73,749*l.* 10*s.* 6*d.*, and *whalebone*
to 40,666*l.* 15*s.* 6*d.*; making in all, 114,416*l.* 6*s.*

There has also been a somewhat singular change in the ports from which the fishery is ch
on. In London were undertaken all the discoveries which led to its establishment; and for s
complete monopoly was enjoyed by the great companies formed in that city. Even betwee
1780 and 1790, the metropolis sent out four times the number of vessels that sailed from any
It was observed, however, that her fishery was, on the whole, less fortunate than that of the
which had sprung up; and her merchants were so much discouraged, that in Mr. Scoresby
equipped only 17 or 18 vessels. They have since almost entirely abandoned the trade, emp
year and the present not more than 2 ships.

Hull early became a rival to London, having sent out vessels at the very commencement of
Although checked at first by the monopoly of the great companies, as soon as the trade beca
prosecuted it with distinguished success. In the end of the last century, that town attained, a
since preserved, the character of the first whale-fishing port in Britain.

Whitby engaged in this pursuit in 1753, and carried it on for some time with more than c
cess; but her operations have since been much limited. Liverpool, after embarking in the
with spirit, has now entirely relinquished it. Meantime the eastern ports of Scotland h
carried on, and even extended, their transactions, while those of the country at large were
The increase has been most remarkable at Peterhead; and indeed this town, as compare
with London, must derive a great advantage from avoiding, both in the outward and homew
600 miles of somewhat difficult navigation.

The following summary has been collected from Mr. Scoresby, as the average quantity
fitted out in the different ports for nine years, ending with 1818; and the comparison of
number sent out in 1830 will show the present state of the trade: —

	Average of 1810—18.	1830.		Average of 1810—18.
England — Berwick -	1⅞ -	- 1	Scotland — Burntisland	0 -
Grimsby -	1⅘ -	- 0	Dundee -	7⅝ -
Hull - -	53¼ -	- 33	Greenock -	⅝ -
Liverpool -	1⅝ -	- 0	Kirkcaldy -	7 -
London -	17⅞ -	- 2	Kirkwall -	⅝ -
Lynn - -	1⅘ -	- 0	Leith - -	8⅞ -
Newcastle -	4⅞ -	- 3	Montrose -	2⅞ -
Whitby -	8⅝ -	- 2	Peterhead -	6⅞ -
	— 91⅗	— 41		— 40
Scotland — Aberdeen -	10⅝ -	- 10		
Banff - -	⅝ -	- 0	Total - -	13

e 91 ships fitted out in 1830, 4 only were for Greenland.

ave already seen that, as a source of national wealth, the whale fishery is of gly little importance. Neither does it seem to be of so much consequence rsery for seamen as is commonly supposed. The number employed in the 1 fishery does not exceed 4,500; and it may be doubted whether the casualties they are exposed do not, in a public point of view, more than balance the l skill and hardihood they acquire in so perilous an occupation.

seems no reason to apprehend any deficiency in the supply of oil from a T in the fishery. We have seen, from the foregoing statements, that the fish rted in 1829, amounted to 10,672 tons. But at present about half this quan- live oil is annually imported; and as olive oil is loaded with a duty of 8*l.* 8*s.* a obvious that if this duty were reduced, as it ought to be, to 2*l.* or 3*l.* a ton, ased quantity imported would go far to balance any falling-off in the supply oil. When a coarser species is required, rape and linseed oil may be advan- substituted for that of the whale. Tallow may also be applied to several to the exclusion of train oil. Although, therefore, the whale fishery should we need not fear that any material injury will thence arise to the industry of ry. And it would be most impolitic to attempt to bolster it up, either by to the exploded system of bounties, or by laying heavy duties on oil or ported from other countries.

ɔuth Sea fishery was not prosecuted by the English till about the beginning of rican war. And as the Americans had already entered on it with vigour and 1 American harpooners were sent out in each vessel. In 1791, 75 whale e sent to the South Sea; but the number has not been so great since. In y 31 ships were sent out, of the burthen of 10,997 tons, and carrying 937 men. rocephalus, or spermaceti whale, is particularly abundant in the neighbourhood of Islands; and Mr. Crawford, in his valuable work on the Eastern Archipelago, ɔ. 447.), has entered into some details to show that the fishery carried on there ter importance than the spice trade. Unluckily, however, the statements on r. Crawfurd founded his comparisons were entirely erroneous, neither the the men employed amounting to more than a fifth or sixth part of what ɔresented.

rors of this sort abound in the works of those who had better means of the truth. Mr. Barrow, in an article on the Fisheries, in the *Supplement to* ɔpædia Britannica, states the number of ships fitted out for the Northern whale 1814 at 143, and their crews at 7,150; and he further states the number of d out for the Southern fishery in 1815 at 107, and their crews at 3,210. In ɔct, however, only 112 whale ships cleared out for the North in 1814, carrying 1; and in 1815, only 22 whale ships cleared out for the South, carrying 592 ɔw Mr. Barrow, who has access to official documents, should have given the ɔf his authority to so erroneous an estimate, we know not. In the same r. Barrow estimates the entire annual value of the British fisheries of all sorts ɔ0*l.* But it might be very easily shown that, in rating it at 3,500,000*l.*, we tainly be up to the mark, or rather, perhaps, beyond it.—(See Fɪsʜ.)

ɪex a detailed account of the progress of the southern whale fishery since

t of the Number of Ships annually fitted out in Great Britain, with their Tonnage and the Southern Whale Fishery, and of the Bounties on their Account from 1814 to 1824 ɔive.

.	Ships.	Tons.	Men.	Bounties paid.	Years.	Ships.	Tons.	Men.	Bounties paid.
				£					£
	30	8,999	794	5,600	1820	68	19,755	1,827	9,100
	22	6,985	592	8,000	1821	55	14,398	1,396	8,300
	34	10,332	852	4,500	1822	44	11,432	1,022	7,400
	42	14,785	1,201	10,000	1823	59	17,669	1,536	6,800
	58	18,214	1,643	6,600	1824	31	9,122	796	7,300
	47	14,668	1,345	9,100					

of the Number of Ships fitted out in the different Ports of Great Britain (specifying the the Southern Whale Fishery, their Tonnage, and the Number of Men on board, during the rs ending 5th January, 1830.

Ports.	Year ending 5th January, 1828.			Year ending 5th January, 1829.			Year ending 5th January, 1830.		
	Ships.	Tons.	Men.	Ships.	Tons.	Men.	Ships.	Tons.	Men.
- - - -	31	10,158	874	21	7,000	604	31	10,997	937
	2	216	28		nil.			nil.	

egistrar General of Shipping, ɔuse, London, Dec. 16. 1830.

JOHN COVEY, Reg. Gen. of Shipping.

For a lengthened period the Americans have prosecuted the whale fisher
greater vigour and success than, perhaps, any other people. They commence
1690, and for about 50 years found an ample supply of fish on their own shores.
the whale having abandoned them, the American navigators entered with extrao
ardour into the fisheries carried on in the Northern and Southern Oceans. From
to 1775, Massachusetts employed annually 183 vessels, carrying 13,820 tons,
former; and 121 vessels, carrying 14,026 tons, in the latter. Mr. Burke, in his
speech on American affairs in 1774, adverted to this wonderful display of
enterprise as follows: —

" As to the wealth," said he, " which the colonists have drawn from the sea by their fisher
had all that matter fully opened at your bar. You surely thought these acquisitions of value,
seemed to excite your envy; and yet the spirit by which that enterprising employment has been e
ought rather, in my opinion, to have raised esteem and admiration. And pray, Sir, what in the
equal to it? Pass by the other parts, and look at the manner in which the New England people
the whale fishery. While we follow them among the trembling mountains of ice, and behold the
trating into the deepest frozen recesses of Hudson's and Davis's Straits; while we are looking f
beneath the Arctic Circle, we hear that they have pierced into the opposite region of polar col
they are at the antipodes, and engaged under the frozen serpent of the South. Falkland Island
seemed too remote and too romantic an object for the grasp of national ambition, is but a st
resting-place for their victorious industry. Nor is the equinoctial heat more discouraging to the
the accumulated winter of both poles. We learn, that while some of them draw the line or st
harpoon on the coast of Africa, others run the longitude and pursue their gigantic game along t
of Brazil. No sea, but what is vexed with their fisheries. No climate, that is not witness of the
Neither the perseverance of Holland, nor the activity of France, nor the dexterous and firm sag
English enterprise, ever carried this most perilous mode of hardy industry to the extent to
has been pursued by this recent people; a people who are still in the gristle, and not harder
manhood."

The unfortunate war that broke out soon after this speech was delivered, chec
a while the progress of the fishery; but it was resumed with renewed vigour as
peace was restored. The American fishery has been principally carried on fron
tucket and New Bedford in Massachusetts; and for a considerable time past th
have mostly resorted to the southern seas. " Although," says Mr. Pitkin,
Britain has, at various times, given large bounties to her ships employed in this
yet the whalemen of Nantucket and New Bedford, unprotected and unsuppor
any thing but their own industry and enterprise, have generally been able t
their competitors in a foreign market." —(Commerce of the United States, 2d. ed.

France, which preceded the other nations of Europe in the whale fishe
hardly be said, for many years past, to have had any share in it. In 1784, Loui
endeavoured to revive it. With this view he fitted out 6 ships at Dunkirk on
account, which were furnished with harpooners and a number of experienced
brought at a great expense from Nantucket. The adventure was more successf
could have been reasonably expected, considering the auspices under which it v
ried on. Several private individuals followed the example of his Majesty, and
France had about 40 ships employed in the fishery. The revolutionary war de
every vestige of this rising trade. Since the peace, the government has mad
efforts for its renewal, but hitherto without success; and it is singular, that,
exception of an American house established at Dunkirk, hardly any one has the
sending out a ship.

(This article has been copied, with little variation, from the Foreign Quarte
view, No. 14., to which publication it was contributed by the author of this w

WHARF, a sort of quay constructed of wood or stone, on the mar
roadstead or harbour, alongside of which ships or lighters are brought
sake of being conveniently loaded or unloaded.

There are two denominations of wharfs, viz. *legal quays* and *sufferance wharfs*. The former
wharfs in all sea ports, at which all goods are required by the 1 Eliz. c. 11. to be landed and shi
they were set out for that purpose by commission out of the court of Exchequer, in the reign of
and subsequent sovereigns. Many others have been legalised by act of parliament. In som
Chepstow, Gloucester, &c., certain wharfs are deemed legal quays by immemorial practice, t
set out by commission, or legalised by act of parliament.
Sufferance wharfs are places where certain goods may be landed and shipped; such as hemp,
and other bulky goods; by special sufferance granted by the crown for that purpose.

WHARFAGE, the fee paid for landing goods on a wharf, or for shippi
off. The stat. 22 Chas. 2. c. 11., after providing for the establishment o
and quays, makes it lawful for any person to lade or unlade goods, or
wharfage and cranage at the rates appointed by the king in council.

WHEAT (Ger. *Weitzen*; Du. *Tarw*; Da. *Hvede*; Sw. *Hvete*; Fr.
Bled, Blé; It. *Grano, Formento*; Sp. and Port. *Trigo*; Rus. *Pschenis*
Pszenica), a species of bread corn (*Triticum*, Lin.), by far the most inp
any cultivated in Europe. We are totally ignorant of the country whe
valuable grain was first derived; but it was very early cultivated in Si

n almost every part of the temperate zones, and in some places as high
eet above the level of the sea.

ds of wheat sown are numerous, but they may be classed under four heads :
or bearded wheat, which, however, is now little cultivated ; white wheat, of
re are innumerable varieties, the *white Dantzic* being considered one of the
wheat, which is seldom sown where the climate is good and early, and the land
ondition ; and spring wheat. A greater number of people are nourished by
by wheat ; but owing to the greater quantity of gluten which the latter
t makes by far the best bread. Rye comes nearer to wheat in its bread-
ualities than any other sort of grain ; still, however, it is very inferior to it.
 samples of wheat are small in the berry, thin skinned, fresh, plump, and
ping readily through the fingers.

ery extensively cultivated on soils of very various qualities, and frequently with
fect preparation, the produce of wheat crops in Great Britain varies from about
t 56 bushels an acre.

nties most distinguished for the quantity and quality of their wheat are, Kent,
folk, Rutland, Hertfordshire, Berkshire, Hampshire, and Herefordshire, in
and Berwickshire, and the Lothians, in Scotland. In the northern counties it
g generally, of an inferior quality, being cold to the feel, dark coloured, thick
d yielding comparatively little flour. In the best wheat counties, and in good
veight of a Winchester bushel of wheat is from 60 to 62 lbs. In the isle of
Kent (where, perhaps, the best samples of wheat sent to the London mar-
oduced), this grain, in some favourable seasons, weighs 64 lbs. a bushel.
climate is colder, wetter, or more backward, or in bad seasons, the weight of
of wheat is not more than 56 or 57 lbs. It is calculated that the average
he bushel of good English wheat is 58½ lbs. ; and that the average yield of
bs. of flour to 14 lbs. of grain. — (See Mr. Stevenson's very valuable article
, in *Brewster's Encyclopædia*, vol. viii. p. 720 ; *Loudon's Ency. of Agricul-*

w of the regulations with respect to the importation and exportation of wheat,
rn Laws and Corn Trade.

oreign Wheat, and Wheat Flour, into Great Britain in 1829 and 1830, specifying the
Countries whence they came, and the Quantities imported from each.

ries.	1829. Wheat, and Wheat Flour.	1830. Wheat, and Wheat Flour.	Countries.	1829. Wheat, and Wheat Flour.	1830. Wheat, and Wheat Flour.
	Qrs. bush.	Qrs. bush.		Qrs. bush.	Qrs. bush.
	341,567 1	235,108 0	Cape of Good Hope	4,803 6	
	16,590 5	2,960 5	Mauritius -	668 2	3 0
	425 0		East Indies and China	70 0	672 0
	83,288 7	88,103 1	Van Diemen's Land -		4
	355,958 6	519,575 0	British North American		
	306,966 1	365,981 1	Colonies -	5,649 6	76,654 1
ls -	144,549 0	76,711 3	British West Indies -		1 0
	48,939 7¼	14,742 2	United States of America	113,818 5	184,100 0
ne Azores		5	Brazil -	1 5	1
	150,080 3¼	40,953 7	Isles of Guernsey,⎫ Foreign	13,500 5	17,349 0
		1,141 6	Jersey, Alder- ⎬	8,598 1	13,491 0
	75,604 0		ney, and Man ⎭ Native		
	65 4¼	28,612 5			
	6,931 0	7,268 6			
		1	Total -	1,676,077 1	1,675,430 0

s from all countries in 1831 - - - - 2,319,461 qrs. 2 bushels.
e of Wheat per Imperial quarter in 1831, 66s. 4d. For further details as to the imports
heat, see *ante*, pp. 398—402.

Y, a spirit obtained by distillation from corn, sugar, or molasses,
erally from the former. Whisky is the *national spirit*, if we may so
Scotland, and Ireland ; but that distilled in the former is generally
aperior to that of the latter. — (See Spirits.)

(Ger. *Wein;* Fr. *Vin;* It. and Sp. *Vino;* Port. *Vinho;* Rus. *Wino,*
e *winoe;* Lat. *Vinum;* Gr Οινος; Arab. *Khumr*), the fermented juice
, or berries of the vine (*Vitis vinifera*).

is indigenous to Persia and the Levant ; but it is now found in most
egions. The limits within which it is cultivated in the northern
of the Old World vary from about 15° to 48° and 52° ; but in North
s not cultivated farther north than 38° or 40°. It is rarely grown at
titude than 3,000 feet. From Asia the vine was introduced into
l thence into Italy. The Phoceans, who founded Marseilles, carried
the south of France ; but it is doubtful whether it was introduced

into Burgundy till the age of the Antonines.* The species of *vitis* indig⋯
North America are very different from the *vitis vinifera*. In favourable⋯
the vine ripens in the open air in England; and in the eleventh and twe⋯
turies, considerable quantities of inferior wine were made from native⋯
Vineyards are now, however, unknown in this country; but the grapes⋯
hot-houses, and used in desserts, are excellent.

The vine grows in every sort of soil; but that which is light and gravel⋯
best suited for the production of fine wines. It succeeds extremely⋯
volcanic countries. The best wines of Italy are produced in the neighb⋯
of Vesuvius: the famous Tokay wine is also made in a volcanic distric⋯
several of the best French wines; many parts of the south of France⋯
evident marks of extinct volcanoes. Hermitage is grown among the⋯
granite rocks. The most favourable situation for a vineyard is upon⋯
ground or hill facing the south-east, and the situation should not be too c⋯

——————— apertos
Bacchus amat colles.

The art of expressing and fermenting the juice of the grape appears⋯
been practised from the remotest antiquity. The sacred writings tell⋯
Noah planted a vineyard soon after the deluge — (*Gen.* ch. ix. v. 20.)⋯
modern Latin poet ingeniously represents the vine as a gift from Heaven⋯
sole mankind for the miseries entailed upon them by that grand catastro⋯

> Omnia vastatis ergo quum cerneret arvis
> Desolata Deus; nobis felicia vini
> Dona dedit; tristes hominum quo munere fovit
> Reliquias, mundi solatus vite ruinam!
>
> *Vanierii Præd. Rusticu*⋯

Species of Wine. — There are a great variety of vines; and this circu⋯
combined with differences of soil, climate, mode of preparation, &c., occ⋯
extreme variety in the different species of wine. But even between p⋯
mediately contiguous to each other, and where a cursory observer wou⋯
remark any difference, the qualities of the wines, though produced by⋯
species of grape, and treated in the same way, are often very different.⋯
deal evidently depends upon the aspect of the vineyard; and it is prob⋯
a good deal depends on peculiarities of soil. But whatever may be t⋯
it is certain that there are wines raised in a few limited districts, such⋯
Johannisberger, Constantia, the best Burgundy, Champagne, claret, &c., t⋯
or care has hitherto succeeded in producing of equal goodness in other⋯

ANCIENT WINES. — The wines of Lesbos and Chios among the Greek⋯
Falernian and Cecuban among the Romans, have acquired an immortality⋯
Great uncertainty, however, prevails as to the nature of these wines. Dr.⋯
thinks that the most celebrated of them all, the Falernian, approached, in⋯
essential characters, near to Madeira. In preparing their wines, the anci⋯
inspissated them till they became of the consistence of honey, or even thicke⋯
were diluted with water previously to their being drunk; and, indeed, t⋯
mixing wine with water seems to have prevailed much more in antiquity than⋯
times.

MODERN WINES. — The principal wines made use of in this country are p⋯
claret, champagne, madeira, hock, &c.

Port, the wine most commonly used in England, is produced in the provinc⋯
Douro, in Portugal; and is shipped at Oporto, whence its name. When it arr⋯
country, it is of a dark purple or inky colour, has a full, rough body, with an⋯
bitter sweet taste, and a strong flavour and odour of brandy. After it has rem⋯
years longer in the wood, the sweetness, roughness, and astringency of the flav⋯
but it is only after it has been kept 10 or 15 years in bottle, that the od⋯
brandy is completely subdued, and the genuine aroma of the wine developed.⋯
to too great an age, it becomes tawny, and loses its peculiar flavour. During th⋯
melioration, a considerable portion of the extractive and colouring matter is⋯
on the sides of the vessels in the form of crust. In some wines this cha⋯
much earlier than in others.

* The ancient writers give the most contradictory accounts with respect to the introducti⋯
into Gaul. — (See the learned and excellent work of Le Grand d'Aussy, *Vie Privée des Fra*⋯
pp. 329—333.) The statement given above seems the most probable.

ge quantity of brandy is always mixed with the wine shipped from Oporto for
. Genuine unmixed port wine is very rarely met with in this country. We
n so long accustomed to the compounded article, that, were it possible to pro-
nmixed, it is doubtful whether it would be at all suited to our taste. Accord-
Mr. Brande's analysis, on which, however, owing to the differences in the
f the wine, no great stress can be laid, port, as used in England, contains about
ent. of alcohol.

Wine Company. — The quality of the wine shipped from Oporto has been materially injured
onopoly so long enjoyed by the Oporto Wine Company. This company was founded in
ng the administration of the Marquis Pombal. A certain extent of territory is marked out
ter as the only district on the Douro in which wine is to be raised for exportation : the entire
te disposal of the wines raised in this district is placed in the hands of the Company ; who are
thorised to fix the prices to be paid for them to the cultivators, to prepare them for exportation,
the price at which they shall be sold to foreigners ! It is obvious that a company with such
not be any thing else than an intolerable nuisance. What could be more arbitrary and unjust
terdict the export of all wines raised out of the limits of the Company's territory ? But even
district, its proceedings have been most oppressive and injurious. The Company annually fix,
f their own, two rates of prices — one for the *vinho de feitoria*, or wine for exportation, and
or *vinho de ramo*, or wine for home consumption — at which the cultivators are to be paid,
may be the quality of their wines ! They have, therefore, no motive to exert superior skill
uity ; but content themselves with endeavouring to raise, at the least possible expense, the
pply of *vinho de feitoria*, for which the Company allow the highest price. All emulation is thus
extinguished, and the proprietors who possess vineyards of a superior quality invariably adul-
r wines with inferior growths, so as to reduce them to the average standard. " In this way,"
enderson, " the finer products of the Douro vintages have remained in a great measure unknown
port wine has come to be considered as a single liquor, if I may use the expression, of nearly
vour and strength ; varying, it is true, to a certain extent in quality, but still always approach-
efinite standard, and admitting of few degrees of excellence. The manipulations, the
— in one word, the *adulterations*—to which the best wines of the Cimo do Douro are subjected,
the same effect as if all the growths of Burgundy were to be mingled in one immense vat,
into the world as the only true Burgundian wine. The delicious produce of Romanée,
1, and the Clos-vougeot, would disappear, and in their places we should find nothing better than
te Beaune or Maçon wine." — (*History of Ancient and Modern Wines*, p. 210.)

however, have the Oporto Wine Company deteriorated the quality, but they have also raised
' their wines to an enormous height. Secured against the competition of their countrymen,
g down to the *present year* a monopoly of the British markets by means of the high duties on
nes, they have filled their pockets at our expense. At *the very moment when the company
hipping wine for England at* 40*l. a pipe, they have frequently shipped the same wine to other
: 20l. !* — (*Fleetwood Williams on the Wine Trade.*) And the authentic tables published by
that the price of wine has been trebled or quadrupled under the management of this corpo-
ssai Statistique sur le Royaume de Portugal, tome 1. p. 157.)

gh the abuses inherent in the constitution of the Company have been carried of late years to
s extent, it is long since its injurious effects on the commerce of this country were distinctly
nd pointed out. So far back as 1767, the Board of Trade laid a memorial before his Majesty in
which they state, " With respect to many particular regulations of the Oporto Company,
think justly objected to by the merchants as highly grievous and oppressive, we have not
necessary to enter into a minute description of them, being of opinion that one general and
on lies against them all ; viz. — that *they all contribute to establish in the Company a monopoly
r Majesty's subjects, from which by treaty they have a right to be exempted.*"
thstanding this authoritative exposition of the injury done to the English by this monopoly,
erience which every subsequent year afforded of its mischievous influence, such has been the
f ancient prejudice, that it was not till last session (1831) that we took the only step by which
ope to rid ourselves of its evils, as well as of a host of others, by equalising the duties on
Portuguese wines ; and putting an end to the absurd and injurious preference in favour of
stablished by the Methuen treaty.

nd Brazil are the only countries to which any considerable quantity of port wine is exported.
have recently varied from about 17,000 to 20,000 pipes — of which, however, a portion is sub-
ported ; while the exports from Portugal to all other countries exclusive of Brazil, do not
500 pipes. It may, however, be fairly anticipated, now that there is no discriminating duty
port, that its consumption in this country will gradually fall off, its place being filled by
other wines — a change that will not be in any point of view undesirable.

s of a deep amber colour ; when good, it has a fine aromatic odour ; its
rm, with some degree of the agreeable bitterness of the peach kernel. When
tes harsh and fiery ; it is mellowed by being allowed to remain 4 or 5 years
n the wood ; but it does not attain to its full flavour and perfection, until it
15 or 20 years. It is a very strong wine, containing about 19 per cent. of
It is principally produced in the vicinity of Xeres, not far from Cadiz, in
: is very extensively used in this country as a dinner wine. Dry sherry, or
, when genuine and old, fetches a very high price. Perhaps no wine is
adulterated as sherry. Its consumption is very large, amounting to above
Imperial gallons.

– the term generally used in England to designate the red wines, the pro-
e Bordelais. Of these, the Lafitte, Latour, Château-Margaux, and Haut-
so generally esteemed, that they always sell from 20 to 25 per cent. higher
thers of the province. The first mentioned is the most choice and delicate,
aracterised by its silky softness on the palate, and its charming perfume,
akes of the nature of the violet and the raspberry. The Latour has a fuller
at the same time a considerable aroma, but wants the softness of the Lafitte.
au-Margaux, on the other hand, is lighter, and possesses all the delicate qua-
e Lafitte, except that it has not quite so high a flavour. The Haut-Brion,
more spirit and body than any of the preceding, but is rough when new, and

requires to be kept 6 or 7 years in the wood; while the others become fit for b
in much less time.

Among the second-rate wines, that of Rozan, in the parish of St. Margau
proaches in some respects to the growth of the Château-Margaux; while that of
in the same territory, is little inferior to the Latour; and the vineyards of L
Larose, Bran-mouton, and Pichon-Longueville, in the canton of Pauillac,
light wines of good flavour, which, in favourable years, have much of the excell
the finer growths. In the Entre-deux-Mers, the wines of Canon and St. Emil
the vicinity of Libourne, are deemed the best, being of a full body and very d
When new, these wines are always harsh and astringent; but they acquire an ag
softness, and are characterised by a peculiar flavour, which has been not unaptl
pared to the smell of burning wax. The aroma of the first growths is seldom
developed till after they have been kept 8 or 9 years: but the secondary qualitie
to perfection a year or two sooner. The colour often grows darker as the wi
vances in age, in consequence of the deposition of a portion of its tartar; but, whe
made, and thoroughly fined, it seldom deposits any crust.

These particulars are borrowed from the excellent work of *Dr. Henderson, on*
and Modern Wines (p. 184). We have given, in a previous article — (see Borde
full and authentic details as to the trade in claret. We beg, also, to refer the re
that article for some observations on the wine trade of France, and on the inju
to it by the restrictive system of commerce.

There is generally a very good supply of claret in bond in the docks in London. It will be s
the statement of prices annexed to this article, that they at present, (January, 1832) vary, from
hogshead for the inferior, to 50*l.* and 55*l.* per hogshead for the superior growths. What are call
or shipping clarets may be bought at from 6*l.* to 10*l.* per hogshead. The finest case claret sells in
about 50*s.* per dozen; but parcels of very well flavoured wine may be bought at 25*s.*

Champagne, so called from the province of France of which it is the produce,
of the most deservedly esteemed of the French wines. The wines of Champa
divided into the two grand classes of white and red wines; and each of these ag
still and sparkling: but there is a great variety in the flavour of the produce o
ent vineyards. Sillery is universally allowed to be the best of the still wines
dry, of a light amber colour, has a considerable body, and a charming aroma.
corps," (says M. Jullien,) " le spiritueux, le charmant bouquet, et les vertus t
dont il est pourvu, lui assurent la priorité sur tous les autres."— (*Topographie de*
Vignobles, p. 30.) Dr Henderson agrees with M. Jullien, in considering it a
the wholesomest of the Champagne wines. The sparkling wines are, however, i
popular, at least in this country. Of these the wine of Ay, 5 leagues south from
is, perhaps, the best. It is lighter and sweeter than Sillery, and has an e
flavour and aroma. That which merely creams on the surface (*demi-mousseux*)
ferred to the full frothing wine (*grand-mousseux*). Being bright, clear, and spar
is as pleasing to the eye as it is grateful to the palate.

> " Cernis micanti concolor ut vitro
>   Latex in auras, gemmeus aspici,
>   Scintillet exultim; utque dulces
>   Naribus illecebras propinet
> " Succi latentis proditor halitus!
>   Ut spuma motu lactea turbido
>   Crystallinum lætis referre
>   Mox oculis properet nitorem."

Hautvilliers, about 4 leagues from Rheims and one from Epernay, used
to produce wine that equalled, and sometimes surpassed, the wine of Ay. Bu
longer cultivated with the same care; so that, though still very good, it now on
in the second class.

The best of the red wines of Champagne are those of Verzy, Verzenay, Maily
and St. Basle. " Ils ont une belle couleur, du corps, du spiritueux, et surto
coup de finesse, de sève, et de bouquet." — (*Jullien*, p. 27.) The Clos St. Th
the vicinity of Rheims, produces wine which, according to M. Jullien, unites t
and the aroma of Burgundy to the lightness of Champagne.

The province of Champagne produces altogether about 1,100,000 hectolitres
of which, however, the finest growths make but a small part. The principal
wine is carried on at Rheims, Avise, and Epernay. The vaults in which the
are stored are excavated in a rock of calcareous tufa to the depth of 30 or 40 fee
of M. Moet, at Epernay, are the most extensive, and few travellers pass thr
place without going to see them. The briskest wines (*grands-mousseux*) keep t
— (*Jullien*, p. 34.)

Burgundy. The best wines of this province, though not so popular in E
those of Champagne, enjoy the highest reputation. " In richness of flavour

all the more delicate qualities of the juice of the grape, they unquestionably first in the world; and it was not without reason that the dukes of Bur- former times, were designated as the *princes des bons vins.*" — (*Henderson,* M. Jullien is not less decided : — " Les vins des premiers crus, lorsqu'ils pro- 'une bonne année, réunissent, dans de justes proportions, *toutes les qualités qui les vins parfaits;* ils n'ont besoin d'aucun mélange, d'aucun préparation, pour ur plus haut degré de perfection. Ces opérations, que l'on qualifie dans s pays de soins *qui aident* à la qualité, sont toujours nuisibles aux vins de ?." — (p. 104.)

-Conti, Chambertin, the Clos Vougeôt, and Richebourg, are the most cele- he RED wines of Burgundy. Chambertin was the favourite wine of Louis XIV. oleon. It is the produce of a vineyard of that name situated 7 miles to the ijon, and furnishing each year from 130 to 150 puncheons, from an extent 5 acres. It has a fuller body and colour, and greater durability, than the vith an aroma nearly as fragrant.

te wines of Burgundy are less numerous, and, consequently, less generally n the others : but they maintain the highest rank among French white wines, t inferior to the red either in aroma or flavour.

ire annual produce of wine in Burgundy and Beaujolais may at present d, at an average, at nearly 3,000,000 hectolitres, of which about 750,000 he consumption of the inhabitants. Since the Revolution, the cultivation of s been greatly extended in the province. Many of the new vineyards having been planted in comparatively unfavourable situations, a notion has been ound that the wines of Burgundy were degenerating. This, however, is 2. On the contrary, the quantity of *bons crus,* instead of being diminished, 'd considerably ; though, as the supply of inferior wines has increased in a degree, the fine wines bear a less proportion to the whole than they did :o the Revolution. — (*Jullien,* p. 90.)

icipal trade in Burgundy is carried on at Dijon, Gevrey, Châlons-sur-

he above, France has a great variety of other excellent wines. Hermitage, t. Péry, &c. are well known in England; and deservedly enjoy, particu- st, a high degree of reputation.

the Comparative Merit of Champagne and Burgundy. —The question whether the wines of of Burgundy were entitled to the preference, was agitated during the reign of Louis XIV. with keenness. The celebrated Charles Coffin, rector of the University of Beauvais, published, dur- versy, the classical ode, partly quoted above, in which Champagne is eulogised, and its supe- ted, with a spirit, vivacity, and delicacy worthy of the theme. The citizens of Rheims ateful to the poet; but liberally rewarded him with an appropriate and munificent donation e had so happily panegyrised. Gréneau wrote an ode in praise of Burgundy ; but, unlike 'as flat and insipid, and failed to procure any recompence to its author. The different pieces g controversy were collected and published in octavo, at Paris, in 1712. — (See *Le Grand 'rivée des Français,* tom. iii. p. 39., and the *Biographie Universelle,* tom. ix. art. *Coffin*) asmus attributes the restoration of his health to his having drunk liberally of Burgundy ; ised it in the most extravagant terms. An epistle of his, quoted by Le Grand d'Aussy, staff and he might have spent an evening together less disagreeably than might have been e premier qui enseigna l'art de faire ce vin (Bourgogne), ou qui en fit present, ne doit-il point our nous avoir donné la vie que pour nous avoir gratifié d'une liqueur." — (*Vie Privée des* e iii. p. 9.)

of French Wine in England. Discriminating Duties. — Owing to the intimate connection veen England and France for several centuries after the Conquest, the wines of the latter lmost exclusive possession of the English market : but the extension of commerce gradu- introduction of other species ; and in the reigns of Elizabeth and James I., the dry white seem to have been held in the highest estimation. This, however, was only a temporary ubsequently to the Restoration, the wines of France regained their former ascendancy. mportations amounted to 15,518, in 1688 to 14,218, and in 1689 to 11,106 tuns. It is ex- tful whether so much as a single pipe of port had ever found its way to England previously -(*Henderson,* p. 313.) ; and it is most probable that the wines of France would have continued ir ascendancy in our markets, had not their importation been artificially checked.

th France had occasionally been prohibited previously to the accession of William III. ; until 1693 that any distinction was made between the duties payable on French and other ouis XIV. having espoused the cause of the exiled family of Stuart, the British govern- ritation of the moment, and without reflecting that the blow aimed at the French would upon themselves, imposed, at the period above-mentioned, a discriminating duty of 8l. h wines, and in 1697 increased it to 33l. ! In consequence of this enormous augmentation nch wines, the merchants began to import wine from Oporto as a substitute for the red eaux, excluded by the high duties. It is probable, however, that these discriminating ave been repealed as soon as the excitement which produced them had subsided, and that t have returned to its old channels, had not the stipulations in the famous commercial tugal, negotiated by Mr. Methuen in 1703, given them permanence. Such, however, was ase : for, according to this treaty, we bound ourselves to charge in future *one third* higher ines of France than on those of Portugal; the Portuguese, by way of compensation, bind- to admit our woollens into their markets in preference to those of other countries, at a lable rate of duty.

generally regarded at the time as the highest effort of diplomatic skill and address, the was certainly founded on the narrowest views of national interest, and has proved, in no e, injurious to both parties, but especially to England. By binding ourselves to receive

Portuguese wines for *two thirds* of the duty payable on those of France, we, in effect, gave
guese growers a monopoly of the British market, and thereby attracted too great a proportion
ficient capital of Portugal to the production of wine; while, on the other hand, we not only
one of the principal equivalents the French had to offer for our commodities, and proclaimed to
that we considered it better to deal with *two* millions of poor beggarly customers, than with *thir*
of rich ones, but we also provoked the retaliation of the French, who forthwith excluded m
articles from their markets!

The injurious effects of the regulations in the Methuen treaty were distinctly pointed of
Davenant and Mr. Hume. The latter, in his " Essay on the Balance of Trade," published in
" Our jealousy and hatred of France are without bounds. These passions have occasioned in
barriers and obstructions on commerce, where we are commonly accused of being the aggres
what have we gained by the bargain ? *We lost the French market for our woollen manufac*
transferred the commerce of wine to Spain and Portugal *where we buy much worse liquor*
higher price! There are few Englishmen who would not think their country absolutely ru
French wine sold in England so cheap, and in such abundance, as to supplant ale and other hor
liquors. But would we lay aside prejudice, it would not be difficult to prove that nothing cou
innocent, perhaps more advantageous. Each new acre of vineyard planted in France, in orde
England with wine, would make it requisite for the French to take an equivalent in English
the sale of which we should be equally benefited."

In consequence of the preference so unwisely given to the wines of Portugal over those of
—a preference continued in defiance of every principle of sound policy and common sense, de
year (1831), — the imports of French wine were for many years reduced to a mere trifle; an
standing their increased consumption, occasioned by the reduction of the duties in 1825, th
made use of has not recently exceeded 360,000 gallons, or 1,714 tuns; while the consumption of I
wines amounts to about 3,000,000 imperial gallons, or 14,300 tuns! This is the most strikin
perhaps, in the history of commerce, of the influence of custom duties in diverting trade into
nels, and altering the taste of a people. All but the most opulent classes having been compe
long series of years, either to renounce wine, or to use port, the taste for the latter has be
rooted; the beverage that was originally forced upon us by necessity having become cong
habit. We have little doubt, however, now that the discriminating duty in favour of port is
that the incontestable superiority of the French wines will ultimately regain for them some por
favour in the English market they formerly enjoyed.[*]

Madeira, so called from the island of that name, is a wine that has long bee
tensive use in this and other countries. Plants of the vine were conveyed from
Madeira in 1421, and have succeeded extremely well. There is a considerable of
in the flavour and other qualities of the wines of Madeira: the best are produce
south side of the island. Though naturally strong, they receive an addition of
when racked from the vessels in which they have been fermented, and anothe
is thrown in previously to their exportation. This is said to be required to su
wine in the high temperature to which it is subjected in its passage to and fre
and China, to which large quantities of it are sent; it being found that it is mell
its flavour materially improved by the voyage. It does not, however, necessari
that the wines which have made the longest voyages are always the best. M
obviously depend on the original quality of the wine; and many of the parce
to be sent to India are so inferior, that the wine, when brought to London,
rank so high as that which has been imported direct. But when the parce
has been well chosen, it is very much matured and improved by the voyage;
only fetches a higher price, but is in all respects superior to the direct imp
Most of the adventitious spirit is dissipated in the course of the Indian voyage

Madeira wines may be kept for a very long period. " Like the ancient vi
the Surrentine hills, they are truly *firmissima vina,* retaining their qualities u
in both extremes of climate, suffering no decay, and constantly improving as
vance in age. Indeed, they cannot be pronounced in condition until they I
kept for 10 years in the wood, and afterwards allowed to mellow nearly twice
in bottle: and even then they will hardly have reached the utmost perfection
they are susceptible. When of good quality, and matured as above described,
all their original harshness, and acquire that agreeable pungency, that bitter swe
which was so highly prized in the choicest wines of antiquity: uniting gree
and richness of flavour with an exceedingly fragrant and diffusible aroma.
taste, which is often very marked, is not communicated, as some have ima
means of bitter almonds, but is inherent in the wine." — (*Henderson,* p. 253.)

The wines of Madeira have latterly fallen into disrepute in England. T
of the island is very limited, not exceeding 20,000 pipes, of which a considera
tity goes to the West Indies and America. Hence, when Madeira was a f
wine in England, every sort of deception was practised with respect to it,
quantities of spurious trash were disposed of for the genuine vintage of t
This naturally brought the wine into discredit; so that sherry has been for se
the fashionable white wine. It is difficult, however, to imagine that adulte
ever practised to a greater extent upon Madeira than it is now practised up
It is, therefore probable, that a re-action will take place in favour of Made
quantity consumed amounts at present to about 230,000 gallons.

---

[*] The mischievous operation of the Methuen treaty, and of the discriminating duty on F
were very strikingly exhibited by Mr. Hyde Villiers, in his very able speech on the 15th of
It is highly deserving of the reader's attention.

sey, a very rich luscious species of the Madeira, is made from grapes grown on ounds exposed to the full influence of the sun's rays, and allowed to remain ne till they are over ripe.

rade in Madeira wine is carried on at Funchal, the capital of the island, in lat. N., lon. 17° 6′ W. Weights and measures same as at Lisbon.

iffe wine, so called from the island of that name, resembles Madeira, and is not ntly substituted in its place; but it wants the full body and rich flavour of the vths of Madeira.

n Wines. — The wines of Germany imported into England are principally t on the banks of the Rhine and the Moselle. The Rhine wines constitute a order by themselves. They are drier than the French white wines, and are ised by a delicate flavour and aroma, called in the country *gäre*, which is quite to them, and of which it would, therefore, be in vain to attempt the description. prevails that they are naturally acid; and the inferior kinds, no doubt, are so: s not the constant character of the Rhine wines, which in good years have no le acidity to the taste, at least not more than is common to them with the of warmer regions. Their chief distinction is their extreme durability. The de in warm dry years are always in great demand, and fetch very high prices. hannisberger stands at the head of the Rhine wines. It has a very choice d perfume, and is characterised by an almost total want of acidity. The vine- e property of Prince Metternich. The Steinberger ranks next to the Johan- It is the strongest of all the Rhenish wines, and in favourable years has our and delicacy.

oduce of certain vineyards on the banks of the Moselle is of superior quality. r sorts are clear and dry, with a light pleasant flavour and high aroma; but times contract a slaty taste from the strata on which they grow. They arrive ty in 5 or 6 years; though, when made in a favourable season, they will keep time, without experiencing any deterioration. —(*Henderson*, p. 226.)

so called from a town in Hungary near which it is produced, is but little England. It is luscious, possessing at the same time a high degree of flavour a. It is scarce and dear; and very apt to be counterfeited.

ines. — Of the remaining wines imported into England, those of the Cape of pe form the largest proportion; the quantity annually entered for home con- being about 540,000 imperial gallons. The famous Constantia wine is the f two contiguous farms of that name, at the base of Table Mountain, between niles from Cape Town. The wine is very rich and luscious; though, ac- Dr. Henderson, it yields, in point of flavour and aroma, to the muscadine Languedoc and Roussillon. But with this exception, most of the Cape wines o England have an earthy disagreeable taste, are often acid, want flavour and d are, in fact, altogether execrable. And yet this vile trash, being the produce h possession, enjoys peculiar advantages in our markets; for while the duty vine is only 2s. 9d. a gallon, that on all other wines is 5s. 6d. The conse- this unjust preference are doubly mischievous: in the first place, it forces tation of an article of which little is directly consumed, but which is exten- loyed as a convenient menstruum for adulterating and degrading sherry, and other good wines; and, in the second place, it prevents the improvement e; for, while the legislature thinks fit to give a bounty on the importation or an article, is it to be supposed that the colonists should exert themselves to y thing better? It is not easy to imagine a more preposterous and absurd . The act enforcing it ought to be entitled, an act for the adulteration of Great Britain, and for encouraging the growth of bad wine in the Cape

es of Italy and Greece are but little imported into England. They are, single exception, in all respects very inferior to those of France. The natives stow no care upon the culture of the vine; and their ignorance, obstinacy, and ill in the preparation of wine, are said to be almost incredible. In some he art is, no doubt, better understood than in others; but had the Falernian, and other famous ancient wines, not been incomparably better than the best of are now produced, they never would have elicited the glowing panegyrics of

on of Wine in Great Britain. — Duties. — We have repeatedly had occasion, in the course of call the reader's attention to the injurious operation of unequal and exorbitant duties. Per- er, the trade in wine has suffered more from this cause than any other department of industry. eady endeavoured to point out some of the effects resulting from the inequality of the duties, reference so long given to the inferior wines of Portugal and Spain over the superior wines But the exorbitance of the duties was, if possible, still more objectionable than the partial which they were imposed. It appears from the subjoined table, that during the 3 years 1792, when the duty on French wines was 3s. 9d., and on Portuguese 2s. 6d. per wine gallon, tion in Great Britain amounted, at an average, to 7,410,947 gallons a year, producing about

900,000l. of revenue. It is probable, had the increase taken place *gradually*, that these duties mig
been doubled without any material diminution of consumption. But in 1795 and 1796 they wer
to 8s. 6d. per gallon on French, and to 5s. 8½d. per gallon on Portuguese and Spanish wine; and
sequence of this sudden and inordinate increase, as exhibited in the table, was, that the consump
from nearly 7,000,000 gallons in 1795, to 5,732,383 gallons in 1796, and to 3,970,901 in 1797!
unanswerable demonstration of the ruinous effect of heavy and sudden additions to the duties did
vent them from being raised, in 1804, to 11s. 3½d. on French, and to 7s. 8d. on Portuguese and
wine. They continued at this rate till 1825; and such was their influence, that, notwithstanding
increase of wealth and population since 1790, and the general improvement in the style of li
total consumption of wine during the 3 years ending with 1824, amounted, at an average, to only
gallons a year; being no less than 2,162,180 gallons under the annual consumption of the 3 year
with 1792! It may, therefore, be truly said, making allowance for the increase of population,
consumption of wine in Great Britain fell off more than fifty per cent. between 1790 and 1824!

Had Mr. Vansittart continued in power, it is difficult to say when this system might have term
but no sooner had Mr. Robinson (now Lord Goderich) become Chancellor of the Exchequer,
resolved upon the effectual reduction of the wine duties. In pursuance of this wise determ
Mr. Robinson took, in 1825, nearly 50 per cent. from the previously existing duties; and notwith
the spirit duties were at the same time reduced in a still greater degree, the consumption of wine
Britain has been increased from little more than 5,000,000 to above 6,500,000 gallons, while th
revenue has been but inconsiderable. We are, therefore, justified in affirming that this measure
signally successful, and that it is a most valuable example of the superior productiveness of low

The duties, as reduced by Mr Robinson, were 7s. 3d. per imperial gallon on French wines, 4s.
do. on all other foreign wines, and 2s. 5d. on those of the Cape of Good Hope. They continued
footing till the late equalisation act (1 & 2 Will. 4. c. 30.) which imposes a duty of 5s. 6d. per
gallon on all foreign wines, and of 2s. 9d. on those of the Cape.

But though this act be an immense improvement upon the old system, the wine trade will not l
on a fair footing till the duty is imposed on an *ad valorem* principle. The imposition of the sa
on inferior and cheap wines worth 10l. a hogshead, as on the choicest Burgundy and Champagr
50l. or 60l. a hogshead, is so utterly subversive of all principle, that one is astonished it should
tained for an instant. Its absurdity would not be exceeded, were the same duty charged on s
that is charged on gin! The effect of this apparently equal, but really *most unequal* duty, is to
all low priced wines from the English markets; and to deprive the middle classes of the gra
derivable from their use. Commercially speaking, Bordeaux is much nearer to London than
and, but for this preposterous system, the cheap wines of the Gironde, Languedoc, and Provenc
be bought here at a less price than in most parts of France. Were it necessary for the sake of
to continue the present system, it might be reluctantly submitted to; but it is abundantly cert
a fairly assessed *ad valorem* duty would, by increasing the consumption of the middle classe
much larger amount of revenue than is produced by the constant duty: and it is not to be endu
the trade of the country should be deeply injured, and the enjoyments of the great bulk of
munity materially impaired, for no purpose of public utility, but merely that injustice and absur
be prolonged! It is said, indeed, that the imposition of an *ad valorem* duty would lead to the
sion of fraud; but we have been assured, by those familiar with the customs, that such precautio
easily be adopted as would prevent any danger on this head. And though it were otherwise
a few thousand gallons of wine were to be admitted for home consumption at a somewhat lo
than they ought to have paid — the injury would be of the most trivial kind, and would hardl
deserve a moment's attention. In the United States, most duties are imposed on an *ad valorem*
and it is not alleged that any real difficulty has to be encountered in their collection.

Consumption of Wine in Ireland. — Duties. — In 1790, the duties on wine consumed in Irel
considerably below the level of those imposed in Great Britain, and the average annual quan
sorts retained for home consumption in that country amounted to about 1,400,000 gallons, produc
135,000l. a year of revenue. Had those to whom the government of Ireland was intrusted pos
slightest knowledge of the merest elements of finance, or of the condition of the Irish pe
would not have attempted to add to the public revenue by augmenting the duties on wine. Ow
limited number of the middle classes in Ireland, an increase of duty could not be expected
ductive; and though it had yielded 50,000l., or even 100,000l. a year of additional revenue,
have been no compensation for the injury it was sure to do in checking the diffusion of that
luxuries and enjoyments so essential to the improvement of the people. But those who had to
the affairs of Ireland were insensible to such considerations; and never doubted that two and
four in the arithmetic of the customs as well as in Cocker! Such, indeed, was their almost
rapacity, that in the interval between 1791 and 1814, they raised the duty on French wine fro
tun to 144l. 7s. 6d.; and that on port from 22l. 4s. 8d. to 95l. 11s.! This was a much more rapi
than had taken place in England; and as the country was far less able to bear even the sam
the consequences have been proportionably mischievous. In 1815, the quantity of wine retaine
consumption in Ireland had declined, notwithstanding the population had been doubled,
gallons, or to about *half* the quantity consumed in 1790; and in 1824, the consumption ha
564,529l. gallons, while the revenue only amounted to 185,000l.!

It is unnecessary to make any commentary on such statements. But it is mortifying to refle
legislature of a civilised country like Great Britain should have obstinately persevered in suc
for about a quarter of a century. We venture to affirm, that those who ransack the financia
Turkey and Spain, will find nothing in them evincing in every part greater rapacity, ignoranc
tempt for the public interest, than is displayed in the history of Irish taxation from 1790 to 181

The reduction of the duties in 1825 has *more than doubled* the consumption of wine in Irelar
added considerably to the revenue! The Irish, however, are particularly attached to French
were the duty imposed on an *ad valorem* principle, we believe the consumption would be ve
quadrupled.

Adulteration of Wine. — We have already alluded to this practice. It was prosecuted to a
extent previously to the reduction of the duties in 1825, and is still very far from being suppre
believed that at this moment more than *a third* of all the sherry consumed in London is the
the *home presses!* Indeed, wines are every day offered for sale at prices at which every one
with the trade knows they could not be afforded were they genuine. Mr. Fleetwood Williams
in his valuable pamphlet on the Wine Trade (1824), some curious details on this subject.

The imposition of the duties on an *ad valorem* principle, by allowing genuine wine to be so
price, would put an effectual stop to the practices of the adulterators. The increase of the du
reigns of William and Anne first gave birth to this discreditable fraternity (see a curiou
Addison's, Tatler, No. 131.); and it will continue to flourish as long as the duties are maintaine
present footing.

---

* An article in the Edinburgh Review, No. 80., contributed to bring about this measure.
excellent tract on the wine trade, by Mr. Warre, published in 1824.

the Quantity of French and other Sorts of Wine retained for Home Consumption in Great
from 1789 to 1828, specifying the Produce of the Duty, and the Rates of Duty thereon.

es retained for Home Consumption.		Rates of Duty.						Nett Revenue.		
Other Sorts.	Total.	French.	Madeira.	Portuguese & Spanish.	Rhenish.	Cape.	Other Sorts.	French.	Other Sorts.	Total.
Wine Gallons.	*Wine Gallons.*	*Wine Gall.*	*Wine Gall.*	*Wine Gall.*	*Wine Gall.*	*Wine Gall.*	*Wine Gall.*	£	£	£
5,580,366	5,814,665	3 9	2 $5\frac{11}{12}$	2 $5\frac{11}{12}$	4 1	2 $11\frac{2}{3}$	3 9	36,549	684,969	721,518
6,245,983	6,492,313	- -	- -	- -	- -	- -	- -	41,352	779,209	820,562
7,407,437	7,658,276	- -	- -	- -	- -	- -	- -	43,417	873,351	916,769
7,778,522	8,082,249	- -	- -	- -	- -	- -	- -	59,693	959,951	1,019,645
6,634,750	6,890,910	- -	- -	- -	- -	- -	- -	30,308	660,377	690,686
6,700,102	6,799,220	- -	- -	- -	- -	- -	- -	14,487	780,536	795,023
6,808,534	6,927,121	6 $1\frac{1}{2}$	4 $1\frac{1}{8}$	4 $1\frac{1}{8}$	5 8	4 $6\frac{2}{3}$	5 4	55,579	1,375,143	1,430,722
5,681,502	5,732,383	8 6	5 $8\frac{1}{4}$	5 $8\frac{1}{4}$	7 3	6 $1\frac{3}{4}$	6 11	25,253	1,134,270	1,159,523
} 3,975,775	3,970,901	- -	- -	- -	- -	- -	- -	36,232	1,347,432	1,383,665
4,715,290	4,760,657	8 $9\frac{1}{8}$	5 11	5 $9\frac{1}{8}$	7 $6\frac{3}{4}$	6 3	7 $0\frac{1}{8}$	33,247	1,339,414	1,372,661
4,726,505	4,777,631	- -	- -	- -	- -	- -	- -	31,316	1,661,510	1,692,826
7,645,400	7,728,871	- -	- -	- -	- -	- -	- -	42,341	1,924,871	1,967,213
6,864,617	7,006,310	8 6	5 $8\frac{1}{2}$	5 $8\frac{1}{2}$	7 3	6 $1\frac{3}{4}$	6 11	84,686	1,908,310	1,992,097
6,226,469	6,355,749	8 10	5 $11\frac{1}{2}$	5 $10\frac{1}{2}$	7 $7\frac{1}{8}$	6 $3\frac{3}{4}$	7 1	61,514	1,870,358	1,931,872
7,989,330	8,181,466	10 4	6 $11\frac{1}{4}$	6 $10\frac{1}{4}$	8 $7\frac{1}{4}$	6 $10\frac{1}{4}$	6 $10\frac{1}{4}$	72,103	2,069,252	2,141,356
4,818,915	4,840,719	11 $3\frac{1}{8}$	7 7	7 6	9 3	7 6	7 6	34,423	1,779,899	1,814,323
4,501,565	4,565,551	11 5	7 8	7 7	9 $4\frac{1}{8}$	7 7	7 7	81,386	1,922,480	2,003,866
5,780,233	5,936,235	- -	- -	- -	- -	- -	- -	94,813	2,225,615	2,320,428
5,762,223	5,922,337	- -	- -	- -	- -	- -	- -	89,139	2,245,058	2,334,197
6,221,590	6,408,534	- -	- -	- -	- -	- -	- -	126,936	2,226,800	2,353,736
5,682,821	5,808,087	- -	- -	- -	- -	- -	- -	The nett receipt of duty on French and other descriptions of wine cannot be separately stated for these years, in consequence of the destruction of the customs records by fire.		2,361,113
6,614,359	6,805,276	- -	- -	- -	- -	- -	- -			2,313,615
5,797,653	5,860,874	- -	- -	- -	- -	- -	- -			2,169,871
5,059,178	5,136,490	- -	- -	- -	- -	- -	- -			1,911,352
4,531,821	4,718,568	16 5	7 8	7 7	9 $4\frac{1}{8}$	2 $6\frac{1}{3}$	7 7			Customs records destroyed.
4,904,783	4,941,663	11 5	7 8	7 7	9 $4\frac{1}{8}$	2 $6\frac{1}{3}$	7 7	73,185	1,959,655	2,032,840
5,667,411	5,968,435	- -	- -	- -	- -	- -	- -	122,662	1,972,637	2,095,299
4,294,182	4,420,807	- -	- -	- -	- -	- -	- -	76,046	1,534,252	1,610,299
5,466,951	5,614,622	- -	- -	- -	- -	- -	- -	87,475	1,936,244	2,023,720
5,873,066	6,139,490	- -	- -	- -	- -	- -	- -	155,370	2,086,010	2,241,380
4,762,754	4,978,600	11 $5\frac{1}{8}$	7 8	7 7	9 5	2 $6\frac{1}{3}$	7 7	126,667	1,675,429	1,802,097
4,837,785	5,019,960	- -	- -	- -	- -	- -	- -	106,892	1,711,503	1,818,396
4,850,778	5,016,569	- -	- -	- -	- -	- -	- -	97,486	1,700,004	1,797,491
4,797,401	4,975,159	- -	- -	- -	- -	- -	- -	104,425	1,689,588	1,794,013
5,108,114	5,291,410	- -	- -	- -	- -	- -	- -	106,982	1,800,484	1,907,466
5,274,831	5,479,732	- -	- -	- -	- -	- -	- -	117,202	1,850,751	1,967,953
8,121,978	8,655,993	6 0	4 0	4 0	4 0	2 0	4 0	166,184	1,648,869	1,815,053
								Allowances for stock in hand		1,021,044
										794,009
6,093,968	6,450,814	Per Imperial Gallon.						107,292	1,162,825	1,270,118
6,921,639	7,262,110	7 3	4 10	4 10	4 10	2 5	4 10	102,509	1,324,040	1,426,550
7,129,264	7,580,625	equal to the former duties per wine gallon						136,024	1,370,098	1,506,122

he Number of Gallons of Foreign Wine upon which Duty has been paid for Home
n in the United Kingdom, and the Rate of Duty per Gallon, stated in Imperial Measure,
r ending 5th January, 1831; distinguishing Cape, French, Madeira, Portugal, Spanish,
d other Sorts, and stating the Gross and Nett Produce of Duty for the Year. — (*Parl.*
345. Sess. 1831.)

e entered for Home Consumption in the United Kingdom, in the Year ending 5th January, 1831.

tions of Wine.	Quantity upon which Duty has been paid for Home Consumption.	Rates of Duty chargeable per Imperial Gallon.	Amount of Duty received. Gross Amount.	Nett Amount.
	Imperial Gallons.	£ s. d.	£ s. d.	£ s. d.
- - -	537,188	0 2 5	64,694 10 2	64,399 4 8
- - -	337,093	0 7 3	121,074 19 3	110,417 6 5
- - -	228,221	0 4 10	55,318 13 3	52,385 9 8
- - -	2,933,176	- -	708,468 1 8	692,905 11 11
- -	2,153,031	- -	519,492 10 6	502,011 9 10
- - -	71,423	- -	17,335 18 5	16,447 12 3
- - -	105,875	- -	25,615 8 5	24,606 19 1
- -	2,780	- -	666 16 9	666 16 9
&c. - -	259,709	- -	62,771 8 4	60,337 7 8
- - -	6,628,496	- -	1,575,438 6 9	1,524,177 18 3

Price of Wine in London. — The following account of the price of wine in bond in Lond 13th of January, 1832, is taken from the Circular of the eminent brokers, Matthew Keeling : —

	L.	s.	L.	s.	
Port, very superior old	45	0 to	50	0	per pipe.
good do.	30	0 —	38	0	—
other qualities do.	23	0 —	26	0	—
very superior young	40	0 —	42	0	—
good do.	26	0 —	30	0	—
other qualities do.	22	0 —	24	0	—
Hermitage, red and white (highest growth)	50	0 —	55	0	per hhd.
2d quality	38	0 —	40	0	—
3d do.	28	0 —	30	0	—
Clarets, 1st growths	50	0 —	52	0	—
2d quality	38	0 —	40	0	—
3d do.	26	0 —	30	0	—
4th do. and 5th do.	10	0 —	20	0	—
cargo	5	0 —	6	0	—
French white, Sauterne, Barsac, &c. 1st qual'ty	31	0 —	36	0	—
2d quality	26	0 —	30	0	—
3d do.	20	0 —	22	0	—
4th do. and 5th do.	10	0 —	16	0	—
cargo	5	0 —	6	0	—
Champagne, 1st quality	2	0 —	2	10	per doz.
good do. and other qualities	1	2 —	1	10	—
Burgundy, red	40	0 —	45	0	per hhd.
white	48	0 —	50	0	—
Hock, superior old	45	0 —	50	0	per aum.
2d quality	31	0 —	35	0	—
3d do. and 4th do.	18	0 —	28	0	—
Moselle, 1st quality	18	0 —	21	0	—
2d do.	14	0 —	16	0	—
Sherry, very superior	60	0 —	80	0	per butt.
1st class	50	0 —	55	0	—
2d do.	40	0 —	45	0	—
3d do.	25	0 —	35	0	—
4th do. and other qualities	17	0 —	24	0	—

	L.	s.	L.	
Madeira, East India, 1st quality, very superior		none		
do. good	50	0 —	60	
other qualities	30	0 —	40	
West India, 1st quality, very superior		none		
do. good	40	0 —	45	
other qualities	25	0 —	35	
direct London part. 1st quality, superior	50	0 —	55	
good	30	0 —	35	
other qualities	18	0 —	28	
Lisbon	23	0 —	26	
Bucellas	25	0 —	35	
Carcavellos	30	0 —	35	
Mountain, London particular	25	0 —	30	
cargo	17	0 —	19	
Teneriffe, London particular	20	0 —	22	
2d quality	14	0 —	16	
cargo	9	0 —	10	
Figuera, red	14	0 —	14	
Spanish, red	12	0 —	14	
Sicilian, red	10	0 —	14	
white		none		
Bronti or Marsala	14	0 —	15	
Cape white, superior	14	0 —	15	
good quality	10	0 —	12	
other qualities	8	0 —	9	
Cape red, superior	14	0 —	15	
good quality		none		
other do.		none		
Fayal, Madeira, good		none		
cargo		none		

Measures. — According to the system of wine measures that prevailed down to 1826, th tained 231 cubic inches; the tierce, 42 gallons ; the puncheon, 84 gallons; the hogshead, 63 g pipe or butt, 126 gallons; and the tun, 252 gallons. But in the new system of measures introd act 5 Geo. 4. c. 74., the Imperial standard gallon contains 277·274 cubic inches: so that the (very nearly) Imperial gallons; the puncheon = 70 (very nearly) do. ; the hogshead = 52½ (v do. ; the pipe or butt = 105 (very nearly) do.; and the tun = 210 (very nearly) do. — (See W. MEASURES.)

A very great quantity of wine is sold to the consumer in dozens; much more, indeed, thar any other way; and yet there is no regulation as to the size of bottles, — a defect which has c great deal of abuse. No one doubts the propriety of making all gallons, bushels, &c. of the sam and why should not similar regulations be enforced in the case of measures so universally used

Regulations as to Importation.—Wine is not to be imported, unless in a vessel of the burthe or upwards, under penalty of forfeiture. — (6 *Geo.* 4. c. 107.)

Wine the produce of Europe may not be imported for home consumption, except in British ships of the country of which the wine is the produce, or of the country from which it is i (6 *Geo.* 4. c. 109.)

Wines of the growth of France or Germany, Spain, the Canaries, Portugal, Madeira, and t islands, imported in foreign ships, shall be deemed *alien goods*, and shall pay town and port c ingly. — (6 *Geo.* 4. c. 111.)

No abatement of duties made on account of any damage received by wine. — (6 *Geo.* 4. c. 1(

Wine from the Cape must be accompanied by a certificate of its production. — (See *antè*, p.

Wine for Officers of Navy. — For the quantity of duty-free wine to be allowed to officers and the regulations under which it is to be allowed, see *antè*, p. 612.

Regulations as to mixing, bottling, &c. in Warehouses. — 1. Wines, when deposited in wa special security, or in warehouses situated near the places of landing and shipping, and dec order of approval to be substantially built, and capable of affording general accommodation t may be allowed to be fitted up, fined, and racked, as often as the owners may deem necessary be destroyed without payment of duty, the quantities destroyed being correctly ascertained pose of being eventually deducted from the official accounts.

2. Bonded brandy may be allowed to be added to wine in the bonded stores for its pre improvement, and the whole to pay duty as wine upon being taken out for home consumptio the whole quantity of brandy contained in the wine, at the time of entry for home consum exceed 20 per cent. ; and that a proper sample for the purpose of ascertaining the strength t be taken out by the proper officers.

3. Wines may be allowed to be mixed with wines of the same description as often as necessa preservation or improvement; provided that wine so mixed be kept separate from other wi the packages containing the same be branded as *mixed wine*, and the brand or other marks of shipper be effaced. — (*Treasury Order,* 20th May, 1830.)

Wine may be bottled for exportation in the vaults of the London, West India, and St. docks, upon giving 24 hours' notice; but no foreign bottles, corks, or packages may be used, in which the wine may have been imported and warehoused, unless the full duties shall ha on the same; and that not less than 3 dozen reputed quarts, or 6 dozen reputed pint bot exported in each package; and if any surplus or sediment remain, it is to be immediately des presence of the officer, or the full duties paid upon it. — (6 *Geo.* 4. c. 112., and *Customs M* 1828.)

The brands or marks on the casks into which wines or spirits may be racked at the bonde are to be effaced, and no other brand or mark to be retained thereon, than those which were when originally imported. — (*Treasury Order,* 29th June, 1830.)

WOAD (Ger. *Waid;* Du. *Weede;* Fr. *Pastel, Guéde, Vouéde;* It. *Guado, Glastro;* Sp. *Pastel, Glasto*), the *Isatis tinctoria* of botanists, plant, with a fusiform fibrous root, and smooth branchy stem, rising fr feet in height. Woad is indigenous to most parts of Europe; and was e used from a very remote period, down to the general introduction of the dyeing of blue. It is still cultivated to a considerable extent i but in this country its cultivation is chiefly restricted to a few c Lincolnshire. After being bruised by machinery, to express the watery

nto balls, which ferment and fall into a dry powder, which is sold to the
Woad is now seldom employed without a mixture of indigo. By itself, it
ble of giving a bright and deep blue colour; but the colour which it does
ery durable. The best methods of conducting the fermentation and pre-
of woad are still so very ill understood, that the goodness of any parcel
never be ascertained till it be actually used; so that it has the disadvan-
being purchased under the greatest uncertainty as to its true value. At
er age, indigo plants yield about thirty times as much colouring matter,
, far superior quality, as an equal weight of woad; so that there is no
that any improvement that may be made in its preparation will ever
, either in goodness or cheapness, a rival of the former. — (*Loudon's*
Agriculture; Bancroft on Colours, vol. i. p. 167.) We have previously—
ıGO) — given some account of the efforts made by the woad growers to
the use of indigo.

D. See TIMBER.

L (Ger. *Wolle;* Du. *Wol;* Da. *Uld;* Sw. *Ull;* Fr. *Laine;* It. and Sp.
'ort. *Lā, Lāa;* Rus. *Wolna, Scherst;* Pol. *Welna;* Lat. *Lana*), a kind of
or down. The term is not very well defined. It is applied both
ıe hair of animals, as sheep, rabbits, some species of goats, the vicuna,
d to fine vegetable fibres, as cotton. In this article, however, we
ly to the wool of sheep,—an article which has continued, from the
ıeriod down to the present day, to be of primary importance — having
ɔrmed the principal part of the clothing of mankind in most temperate

of Wool. — It has been customary in this country to divide wool into two
ses — long and short wools; and these again into subordinate classes, according
ness of the fibre.

vool is used in the cloth manufacture, and is, therefore, frequently called
vool. It may vary in length from 1 to 3 or 4 inches: if it be longer, it re-
ɛe cut or broken to prepare it for the manufacture.

'ting property of wool is known to every one. The process of hat making,
le, depends entirely upon it. The wool of which hats are made is neither
voven; but locks of it, being thoroughly intermixed and compressed in warm
ere and form a solid tenacious substance.

nd woollen goods are made from wool possessing this property; the wool is
ın, woven, and then being put into the fulling mill, the process of felting
ɛ. The strokes of the mill make the fibres cohere; the piece subjected to the
contracts in length and breadth, and its texture becomes more compact and
This process is essential to the beauty and strength of woollen cloth. But
'ool of which stuffs and worsted goods are made is deprived of its felting pro-
This is done by passing the wool through heated iron combs, which takes away
ɛ or feathery part of the wool, and approximates it to the nature of silk or

r combing wool may vary in length from 3 to 8 inches. The shorter comb-
are principally used for hose, and are spun softer than the long combing
ɛ former being made into what is called hard, and the latter into soft worsted

ness of the hair or fibre can rarely be estimated, at least for any useful pur-
ɔt by the wool sorter or dealer, accustomed by long habit to discern those
'erences that are quite inappreciable by common observers. In sorting wools,
'equently eight or ten different species in a single fleece; and if the best wool
ɛe be not equal to the finest sort, it is thrown to a second, third, or fourth, or
ɔwer sort, of an equal degree of fineness with it. The best English short
es, such as the fine Norfolk and South Down, are generally divided by the
r into the following sorts, all varying in fineness from each other: viz.
2. Choice; 3. Super; 4. Head; 5. Downrights; 6. Seconds; 7. Fine
Coarse Abb; 9. Livery; 10. Short coarse or breech wool. The relative
ch varies, according to the greater demand for coarse, fine, or middle cloths.
ness of the fibre is a quality of great importance. It is not dependent on the
the fibre; and consists of a peculiar feel, approaching to that of silk or down.
ınce in the value of two pieces of cloth made of two kinds of wool equally

ıres quadrupedes, ovilli pecoris secunda ratio est, quæ prima sit, si ad utilitatem magnitu-
ıs. Nam id præcipue nos contra frigoris violentiam protegit; corporibusque nostris
ɛbet velamina. — (*Columella,* lib. 7. cap. 2.)

fine, but one distinguished for its softness and the other for the opposite quality, i
that, with the same process and expense of manufacture, the one will be worth from
25 per cent. more than the other. Mr. Bakewell showed that the degree of softn
pends principally on the nature of the soil on which sheep are fed: that she
tured on chalk districts, or light calcareous soils, usually produce hard wool; wl
wool of those that are pastured on rich, loamy, argillaceous soils, is always disting
by its softness. Of the foreign wools, the Saxon is generally softer than the S
Hard wools are all defective in their *felting* properties.

In clothing wool, the colour of the fleece should always approach as much as
to the purest white; because such wool is not only necessary for cloths dressed
but for all cloths that are to be dyed bright colours, for which a clear white gr
required to give a due degree of richness and lustre. Some of the English fine
sheep, as the Norfolk and South Down, have black or gray faces and legs.
such sheep there is a tendency to grow gray wool on some part of the body, or
duce some gray fibres intermixed with the fleece, which renders the wool unfit fo
kinds of white goods; for though the black hairs may be too few and minute to
tected by the wool sorter, yet when the cloth is stoved they become visible, f
reddish spots, by which its colour is much injured. The Herefordshire sheep
have white faces, are entirely free from this defect, and yield a fleece without any
ture of gray hairs.

The cleanness of the wool is an important consideration. The Spanish wool,
ample, is always scoured after it is shorn; whereas the English wool is only imp
washed on the sheep previously to its being shorn. In consequence, it is said tha
a pack of English clothing wool of 240 lbs. weight will waste about 70 lbs. in the
facture, the same quantity of Spanish will not waste more than 48 lbs. Cle
therefore, is an object of much importance to the buyer.

Before the recent improvements in the spinning of wool by machinery, great
and strength of staple was considered indispensable in most combing wools. Th
of the long woolled sheep, fed in the rich marshes of Kent and Lincoln,
be reckoned peculiarly suitable for the purposes of the wool comber: but t
provements alluded to have effected a very great change in this respect; an
enabled the manufacturer to substitute short wool of 3 inches staple, in the place
combing wool, in the preparation of most worsted articles. A great alteration
consequence, taken place in the proportion of long to short wool since 1800
having been, in the interim, according to Mr. Hubbard's calculations — (see
an increase of 132,053 packs in the quantity of the former produced in Engla
a decrease of 72,820 in the quantity of the latter.

Whiteness of fleece is of less importance in the long combing than in clothin
provided it be free from gray hairs. Sometimes, however, the fleece has a ding
colour, called a *winter stain*, which is a sure indication that the wool is not in a tho
sound state. Such fleeces are carefully thrown out by the wool sorter; being
only for goods that are to be dyed black. The fineness of heavy combing wool
so much consequence as its other qualities.

The Merino or Spanish breed of sheep was introduced into this country ab
close of last century. George III. was a great patron of this breed, which
several years a very great favourite. But it has been ascertained that, though t
does not much degenerate here, the carcase, which is naturally ill formed, an
comparatively little weight of meat, does not improve; and as the farmer, in the
sheep which he keeps, must look not only to the produce of wool, but als
butcher market, he has found it his interest rather to return to the native bree
own country, and to give up the Spanish sheep. They have, however, been of c
able service to the flocks of England; having been judiciously crossed with t
Down, Ryeland, &c.

Deterioration of British Wool. — It appears to be sufficiently established, by
dence taken before the House of Lords in 1828, and other authorities, tha
siderable deterioration has taken place in the quality of British wool, particularl
the last 30 years. The great object of the agriculturist has been to increase th
of the carcase and the quantity of the wool; and it seems very difficult, if not
possible, to accomplish this without injuring the fineness of the fleece. M
says, that the Herefordshire sheep that produce the finest wool are kept lean,
1¼ lb. each; he adds, " if they be better kept, they grow large and produce m
but of an inferior quality." This would seem to be universally true. The
tension of the turnip husbandry, and the general introduction of a larger breed
appears, in every instance, to have lessened the value of the fleece. Speaki
Norfolk fleeces, Mr. Fison, a wool sorter, says, that 25 years ago the weight w
a fleece, and that now it is 3 lbs. or 3½ lbs.—(*Report*, p. 356.) But according

by the same gentleman, containing the results of his experience, it appears
tods, or 420 lbs. of clothing wool grown in Norfolk in 1790, 200 lbs. were
ile in 1828 the same quantity of Norfolk wool only yielded 14 lbs. prime !
p. 207.) The statements of other witnesses are to the same effect. — (*Report*,
0. and 644.) According to the estimate in Mr. Luccock's " Treatise on Eng-
' which has always enjoyed the highest reputation, the produce of all sorts of
gland, in 1800, was 384,000 packs, of 240 lbs. a pack. But Mr. Hubbard,
lligent and extensive wool-stapler at Leeds, has shown, that, supposing
ck's estimate of the number of sheep to be correct, the quantity of wool now
annot, owing to the greater weight of the fleece, be estimated at less than
cks ; being an increase of 20 per cent. ! It is, therefore, probable, notwith-
e decline in the price of wool, that, taking into account the greater weight of
, and the greater weight of the fleece, sheep produce more at present to the
at any former period.

of Sheep in Great Britain. — It is not possible to form any accurate estimate,
e number of sheep, or of the quantity of wool annually produced. With the
f Mr. Luccock's, most of the statements put forth with respect to both these
a much exaggerated. But Mr. L.'s estimate, which is considerably under
d previously appeared, was drawn up with great care ; and is supposed by
son, a high authority upon such matters, to approach very near to accuracy.
gland, *Edin. Ency.* vol. viii. p. 731.) According to Mr. Luccock, the

ber of long woolled sheep in England and } Wales in 1800, was	4,153,308	
hort-woolled ditto	14,854,299	
Total number shorn		19,007,607
hter of short woolled sheep per annum	4,221,748	
n of ditto	211,087	
hter of long woolled ditto	1,180,413	
n of ditto	59,020	
ter of lambs	1,400,560	
n of ditto	70,028	
		7,140,856
Total number of sheep and lambs		26,148,463

parts of England there has been an increase in the number of sheep since
n others they have decreased. But we have been assured by competent
on the whole, the number has not materially varied in the interim.
e last half century a very decided increase has taken place in the number of
tland, and a very great improvement in the breed, particularly in the High-
this district many of the proprietors have let their estates in large farms to
, who have introduced the Cheviot breed of sheep, in the place of the small
heath breed that was formerly the only one to be met with. We may re-
way, that a good deal of unmerited odium has attached to the patrons of this
though it be true that in a few instances the peasantry were rudely ejected
ttle possessions, there can be no doubt that it has, on the whole, been de-
ntageous. Besides rendering large tracts of country more valuable to the
nd the public generally, the condition and habits of the peasantry have been
proved. Instead of loitering away more than half their time, as was their
ice, they have now either become the servants of the large farmers, or have
owns and villages, and been metamorphosed into industrious tradesmen,
c. A very small proportion of the whole has emigrated ; and the country is
us at present than before the sheep farming system began.
neral Report of Scotland (vol. iii. Appen. p. 6.), the number of sheep is es-
650,000 ; and, allowing for the increase that has taken place since 1814,
haps, estimate the total number of sheep in that part of the empire at this
,500,000.
to Mr. Wakefield, there is not a single flock of breeding sheep in the
ce of Ulster. — (*Account of Ireland*, vol. i. p. 341.) And though there be
flocks, in Roscommon and other counties, we believe, that if we estimate the
r of sheep in Ireland at 2,000,000, we shall be a good deal beyond the mark.
ole, therefore, if we are right in these estimates, the total number of sheep
itain and Ireland may be taken at about 32,000,000. This estimate is
under that given by Dr. Colquhoun for 1812 ; but that learned person
ounds whatever for his estimate, which is utterly inconsistent with all the
tic information on the subject. It is curious enough to observe the Ger-

man statistical writers referring to Dr. Colquhoun's statements as if they were of authority. They would be about as near the mark, were they to quote the Nights in proof of any disputed historical fact.

British Trade in Wool. — From 1660 down to 1825 the export of wool w. prohibited. A notion grew up towards the end of the 17th, and continue ground during the first half of last century, that the wool of England was so that of every other country; that long wool could not be produced any where that, if we succeeded in keeping the raw material at home, we should infall: mand the market of the world for our woollen manufactures. In consequen merable statutes were passed, — the enactments in some of which were the n trary and severe that can be imagined,— to prevent the clandestine exportation Mr. John Smith was one of the first who, in his excellent work entitled " M Wool*," exposed the injustice and absurdity of this system, by proving that wh: vantages the manufacturers might gain by preventing the exportation of wool, v than lost by the agriculturists. But in despite of Mr. Smith's reasonings, w! enforced by many later writers, and which experience had proved to be in al accurate, the prohibition of the exportation of wool was continued till 18: Mr. Huskisson happily succeeded in procuring the abolition of this miserable of a barbarous policy. The improvement of machinery, by enabling short or wool to be applied to most of those purposes for which long or combing been exclusively appropriated, had annihilated the only apparently tenable : on which the prohibition of exportation had ever been vindicated; and it will be observed, applied only to a small proportion of the whole wool in England.

Down to 1802, the importation of foreign wool into Great Britain had b free; and, being the raw material of an important manufacture, the policy of al to be imported free of duty is obvious. In 1802, however, a duty of *5s.* 3 was laid on all foreign wool imported. In 1813, this duty was raised to 6s. in 1819, Mr. Vansittart raised it to the enormous amount of *56s.* a cwt., or to 6d Had English wool sufficed for all the purposes of the manufacture, such a du have been less objectionable; but the very reverse was the case. The use c wool had become, owing to the deterioration of British wool, and other circu quite indispensable to the prosecution of the manufacture : and as our superi the foreigner in several departments of the trade was by no means decided, that the imposition of a duty which amounted to about 50 per cent. upon the considerable quantity of the wool we were obliged to import, must, had it been p in, have ruined the manufacture. It occasioned, indeed, during the period c tinuance, a considerable decline of the exports of woollens, and was productiv mischievous effects, from which the manufacture is still suffering.

The evidence as to the absolute necessity of employing foreign wool, tak the Lords' committee, is as decisive as can well be imagined. Mr. Gott, of I of the most extensive and best informed manufacturers of the empire, informe mittee, that, in his own works, he used only foreign wool. On being a: ther he could carry on an export trade to the same extent as at present, if factured his cloth of British wool, Mr. G. replied, that, in certain description " *he could not make an article that would be merchantable at all for the foreign even for the home market, except of foreign wool.*" We subjoin a few addition from the evidence of this most competent witness.

" Can you give the committee any information with respect to the compe now exists between foreigners and this country in woollen cloths?" — " I thin! petition is very strong. In some instances the foreigner has, probably, the adva: in others, the superiority of the British manufacture, I think, has greatly the a that would apply, I should say, particularly to the fine cloths of Great B: pared with foreign cloths; in some descriptions of low cloths, the foreigners on a footing, and in some instances, perhaps, superior to us."

" Speaking of the finer cloths, is the competition such as to render an addi on the importation of foreign wool likely to injure the export trade." — " *I ha: speaking on my oath, that it would be fatal to the foreign cloth trade of the c* would say further, that it would be equally injurious to coarse manufactures made of English wool. The competition now with foreigners is as nearly possible; and the disturbing operation of attacks of that description would enable the foreigner to buy his wool cheaper than we should do it in this co result would be, that foreigners would, by such a premium, be enabled to e manufactures, to the exclusion of British manufactures of all descriptions."

---

* This learned and accurate work contains a great deal of information with respect to t! manufactures and commerce in England.

other part of his evidence, Mr. Gott says, " If two pieces of cloth, at 10s. a
re put before a customer — one made of British wool, the other of foreign
ne would be sold, and the other would remain on hand : I could not ex-
order with it. If any person sent to me for cloth of 7s. or 8s. a yard, and it
le of English wool, it would be sent back to me, and I should resort to foreign
foreign mixed with British, to execute that order."

r. Gott being asked whether, in his opinion, the price of British wool would
n greater or less than it actually is, had the duty of 6d. per lb. on foreign
n continued, he answered, — " My opinion is, that the price of British wool
ve been less at this time ; the demand for British wool would have been very
s. *British manufactures would have been shut out of every foreign market;*
tock of wool would have accumulated, as it will do if ever that duty be im-
in." — (*Mr. Gott's Evidence*, pp. 292. 293.)

ew taken by Mr. Gott of the effect of the importation of foreign wool on the
British wool is supported by the concurrent testimony of all the manufacturing
examined by the committee. Blankets, flannels of all sorts, baizes, carpets, bear-
are made principally of English wool; and the command of foreign wool enables
facturers to use a considerable quantity of English wool in the manufacture of
scriptions of cloth, which, if made entirely of it, would be quite unsaleable.
Goodman, a wool-stapler of Leeds, being asked whether, if a duty were laid on
ool, it would force the use of English wool in the manufacture of cloths, from
s now excluded, he answered, — " Certainly not : we could not get people to
a a cloth ; they want a better, finer cloth ; it is so much handsomer in its wear,
ch more durable." — (p. 241.) Mr. Francis, of Heytesbury, declared that there
mand for cloth made wholly of British wool ; that it was principally applicable
nufacture of blankets, baizes, &c.; and that the exclusion of foreign wool
y injure the manufacture, without raising the price of British wool. — (p. 268.)
s to the same effect were made by Mr. Webb (p. 270.), Mr. Sheppard
Mr. Ireland (p. 319.), and, in short, by every one of the witnesses conversant
manufacture.

Wool imported into England. — A very great change has taken place, within
of the present century, not only as respects the quantity of foreign wool im-
at as respects the countries whence it is derived. Previously to 1800, our
mports of wool did not much exceed 3,000,000 lbs., mostly brought from
e wool of which has long maintained a high character. In 1800, our imports
to near 9,000,000 lbs. ; and they have since gone on gradually increasing, till
amount to between 25,000,000 and 32,000,000 lbs. Instead, however, of
cipally derived from Spain, as was the case down to 1814, the greater part of
ase supply of foreign wool is now furnished by Germany. The late king of
hen elector, introduced the breed of Merino sheep into his dominions, and
mself to promote the growth of this valuable race of animals. His praise-
orts have been crowned with the most signal success. The Merino sheep
cceed better in Saxony and other German states than in Spain ; and have
so rapidly, that the Spanish wool trade has become insignificant com-
that of Germany ! The importations of German wool were quite trifling
war — amounting, in 1812, to only 28 lbs. ; but since the peace they have in-
yond all precedent. In 1814, they amounted to 3,432,456 lbs. ; in 1820, they
3,442 lbs. ; in 1825, they reached the enormous amount of 28,799,661 lbs. ; but
a year of overtrading, they declined, in 1826, to 10,545,232 lbs. They have
ever, recovered from this depression ; and, in 1830, amounted to 26,073,882 lbs.
is a very good account of the German wool trade in the " Foreign Quarterly
No. XI. art. 8.

ed of sheep that was carried out to New South Wales and Van Diemen's Land
ded remarkably well ; and Australia promises, at no distant day, to be one of
al wool growing countries of the world. The imports into Great Britain
rapidly increasing. In 1830, they amounted to 1,967,309 lbs., while the
m Spain only amounted to 1,643,515 lbs. The Spanish flocks suffered
ring the campaigns in Spain ; and the best Spanish wool does not now
than half the price of the best German wool.

Number of Sheep and Quantity of Sheep's Wool produced in England, according to Mr. I
Tables, revised by Mr. Hubbard, and made applicable to 1828.

	1800.					1828.		
County.	Number of Short Wool Sheep.	Weight of Fleece.	Number of Packs.	Number of Long Wool Sheep.	Number of Packs.	Weight of Fleece.	Number of Packs of Short Wool.	Nu P. Lon
Northumberland -	538,162	5½	12,333	- -	- -	5½	6,167	
Durham - -	159,385	5	3,320	- -	- -	5¾	- -	
Ditto - - -	- -	9	- -	67,200	2,520	8½	- -	
Cumberland - -	378,400	3¾	5,915	- -	- -	5	7,883	
Westmorland -	223,725	3½	3,262	-	- -	5	4,660	
York, West Riding -	383,122	var.	6,678	- -	- -	5½	4,390	
—— East Ditto -	306,240	5	6,380	- -	- -	6	- -	
—— North Ditto -	365,326	var.	5,939	- -	- -	5	5,708	
Holderness - -	- -	8	- -	84,000	2,800	8	- -	
Other Part of Yorkshire	- -	8	- -	14,310	477	8	- -	
Lancaster - -	310,000	3½	4,522	- -	- -	4½	5,812	
Chester - -	65,000	var.	926	- -	-	4½	1,218	
Derby - - -	362,400	3	4,530	- -	- -	6	- -	
Nottingham - -	255,147	var.	4,112	-	- -	6½	- -	
Lincoln - -	123,648	5½	2,833	- -	- -	6	-	
Ditto, Rich Land -	- -	9	- -	1,241,625	46,561	9	-	
Ditto, Marshes - -	- -	8	- -	87,500	2,916	9	- -	
Ditto, Miscellaneous Land - -	- -	8	- -	505,657	16,855	6	- -	
Rutland - - -	- -	5	-	114,000	2,370	6	-	
Northampton - -	- -	6	- -	640,000	16,000	6	- -	
Warwick - -	182,962	3	2,287	- -	- -	6 (Warwick and Ditto)	- -	
Ditto - - -	- -	5	-	160,000	3,333			
Leicester - -	20,000	3½	291	- -	- -	6 (Leicester and Ditto)	- -	
Ditto - - -	- -	7	- -	380,528	11,100			
Oxford - -	304,584	var.	5,303	-	-	5	- -	
Bucks - - -	222,968	3	2,787	- -	- -	5	- -	
Gloucester - -	355,000	var.	5,400	- -	- -	6	-	
Ditto - - -	- -	8	- -	200,000	6,666	8	- -	
Somerset - -	500,700	4½	9,388	- -	-	5	5,215	
Worcester - -	330,504	3½	4,820	- -	- -	4¾		
Monmouth - -	177,619	var.	1,431	- -	-	4	- -	
Hereford - - -	500,000	2	4,200	-	- -	4	2,778	
Shropshire - -	422,034	2½	4,397	- -	- -	4	2,344	
Stafford - - -	183,120	2	1,526	- -	- -	4½ (Stafford and Ditto)	- -	
Ditto - - -	- -	7	- -	3,720	113			
Bedford - - -	204,000	5	4,250	- -	- -	5	- -	
Berks - - -	306,600	3¼	4,151	-	- -	3½	4,471	
Huntingdon - -	108,000	4½	2,000	-	- -	5½ (Huntingdon and Ditto)	- -	
Ditto - -	- -	7	- -	87,500	2,552			
Cambridge - -	67,744	4	1,128	- -	- -	4½	1,270	
Ditto - - -	- -	8	- -	41,688	1,390	8	- -	
Suffolk - -	497,000	2½	5,176	- -		4¼	8,801	
Norfolk - - -	683,704	2	5,697	- -	- -	4½	4,273	
Ditto - - -	- -	7	-	38,500	1,123	7½	- -	
Essex - - -	519,000	3	6,486	- -	- -	4	8,650	
Hertford - - -	277,000	4½	5,297	-	- -	5	2,885	
Middlesex - -	45,000	4	750	- -	- -	5	937	
Kent - - -	524,475	3¼	7,000	- -	-	4¾	.	
Ditto, Romney Market	- -	7	- -	185,000	5,400	6½	- -	
Ditto, the Marsh - -	- -	7	- -	108,330	3,160	6½	- -	
Surrey - -	283,000	3	3,540	- -	- -	3½	4,127	
Sussex Downs - -	316,800	2	2,540	- -	-	3	3,960	
Ditto Lowlands -	547,000	3	6,837	-	- -	3	6,837	
Hampshire - -	516,600	3	6,457	-	- -	3	6,457	
Isle of Wight - -	61,000	3¼	800	-	- -	4	1,016	
Wilts, Downs - -	583,500	2¾	6,684	- -	- -	2¾	6,685	
Ditto, Pasture -	117,500	3	1,460	- -	- -	4	1,958	
Dorset - -	632,240	3¾	9,880	-	-	3¾	9,878	
Devon - - -	436,850	4	7,280	- -	- -	5	2,275	
Ditto - - -	- -	8	- -	193,750	6,458	8	- -	
Cornwall -	203,000	4	3,382	-	-	7	- -	
Total -	14,854,299		193,475	4,153,308	131,794		120,655	

1800—Short Fleeces - -	193,475	1828—Short Fleeces - - -	
Long Fleeces -	131,794	Long Fleeces - - -	
	325,269		
Short and Long, Skin and Lambs' Wool - -	58,705	Short and Long, Skin and Lambs' Wool - -	
	383,974		
Part of Wales not included in the above Tables -	9,262		
Increase from 1800 to 1828 -	69,933	Wales, taken as before -	
	463,169		

1800 — Packs of Short Wool -	193,475	1800 — Packs of Long Wool - -	
1828 — Ditto ditto -	120,655	1828 — Ditto ditto - - -	
Decrease -	72,820	Increase -	

1800 — Total Quantity of Short Wool	-	193,475	
Ditto ditto of Long Wool	-	131,794	
			325,269
1828 — Total Quantity of Short Wool	-	120,655	
Ditto ditto of Long Wool	-	263,847	
			384,502

Increase of Wool - - -	59,233	Fleeces.
Increase of Skin and Lambs' Wool -	10,700	
Total Increase - -	69,933	

wool from slaughtered sheep and carrion not mentioned in this table; but allowed for above.

Sheep and Lambs' Wool imported into Great Britain from Foreign Parts.

1810.	1815.	1820.	1825.	1827.	1830.
Lbs.	*Lbs.*	*Lbs.*	*Lbs.*	*Lbs.*	*Lbs.*
59,503	371,484	75,614	1,995,900	607,558	203,231
351,741	424,822	13,527	554,213	59,826	179,717
123,057	105,073	107,101	131,100	786,410	713,246
778,835	3,137,438	5,113,442	28,799,661	21,220,788	26,073,882
2,873	432,832	186,051	1,059,243	392,454	939,123
-	756,427	230,909	436,678	345,360	45,093
018,961	1,146,607	95,187	953,793	451,637	461,942
952,107	6,929,579	3,539,229	8,206,427	3,898,006	1,643,515
349,053	12,891	3,851	19,250	18,988	
21,554	97,679	2,815	227,453	177,269	9,461
40,040	55,804	5,050	72,131	5,565	
-	- -	-	25,983		
-	12,513	189,584	513,414	315,807	
41,407	6,264	19,015	22,266	26,949	7,745
701	- -	8,056	- -	5,219	
167	73,171	99,415	323,995	512,758	1,967,309
29,717	23,363	13,869	27,619	44,441	33,407
4,111	8,590	1,477	80,538	87,187	9,038
-	-	- -	14,313	165,955	5,741
-		14,792	2		
116,173	45,838	73,036	331,302	270	20,589
23,837					
914,137	13,640,375	9,789,020	43,795,281	29,122,447	32,313,059
.. *s. d.*	*L. s. d.*	*L. s. d.*	*L. s. d.*	*L. s. d.*	*L. s.d.*
580 4 3	48,238 4 8	181,860 19 6	163,799 16 7½	106,367 8 3	120,420 8 0

Rates of Duty chargeable.	
Until 5 July 1803	Free.
From 5 July 1803, to June 1804 -	5*s.* 3*d.* per cwt.
— 1 June 1804, to 5 April 1805 - -	5*s.* 10*d.* —
— 5 April 1805, to 10 May 1806 - -	5*s.* 11*d.* 8-20ths
— 10 May 1806, to 5 July 1809 -	6*s.* 4*d.* 2-30ths
— 5 July 1809, to 15 April 1813 - -	6*s.* 8*d.* per cwt.
— 15 April 1813, to 5 July 1819 - -	7*s.* 11*d.* —
— 5 July 1819, to 10 October 1819 -	1*d.* per lb.
Of British Possessions.	Of Foreign Countries.
Per lb.	
From 10 Oct. 1819, to 5 Jan. 1823 - 1*d.*	6*d.* per lb.
From 5 Jan. 1823, to 10 Sept. 1824 3*d.*	6*d.* —
From 10 Septem. 1825, to 10 Dec. 1824 - - 1*d.*	3*d.* —
From 10 Dec. 1824, to 5 July 1825 - 1*d.*	1*d.* —
From 5 July 1825, free	½*d.* per lb. on wool not of the value of 1*s.* per lb. 1*d.* per lb. on wool of the value of 1*s.* per lb, & upwards.

the Quantity of *British* Sheep and Lamb's Wool exported from Great Britain in 1830. mbs' wool 2,951,100 lbs.; woollen and worsted yarn, 1,108,023 lbs. By far the larger portion ts was destined for France and the Netherlands.

Price of South Down Wool per lb. from 1784 to 1827, both inclusive.

Year.	Price of Wool.	Year.	Price of Wool.	Year.	Price of Wool.	Year.	Price of Wool.
	s. d.		*s. d.*		*s. d.*		*s. d.*
1784	0 8½	1795	1 3	1806	1 10	1817	2 7
1785	0 9	1796	1 4	1807	2 0	1818	2 6
1786	0 9	1797	1 3	1808	1 9	1819	1 7
1787	0 11	1798	1 3	1809	3 0	1820	1 5
1788	1 0	1799	1 9	1810	2 4	1821	1 3
1789	1 0	1800	1 5	1811	1 5	1822	1 3
1790	1 0½	1801	1 7	1812	1 8	1823	1 3½
1791	0 11½	1802	1 7	1813	1 11	1824	1 2
1792	1 4	1803	1 8	1814	2 2	1825	1 4
1793	0 11½	1804	1 10	1815	1 11	1826	0 10
1794	1 1	1805	2 3	1816	1 6	1827	0 9

(See *Mr. Bischoff's* able pamphlet on the *Wool Question*, London, 1828, p. 73.)

Prices of Wool in the London Market, March, 1832.

		£ s. d.		£ s. d.
-	per lb.			
st and 2d				
Electoral	—	0 4 0	to	0 6 6
'rima -	—	0 2 6	—	0 3 6
ecunda -	—	0 1 9	—	0 2 3
'ertia -	—	0 1 6	—	0 1 9
Elector.	—	0 4 0	—	0 5 6
Prima	—	0 2 4	—	0 3 9
Secunda	—	0 1 9	—	0 2 3
Tertia	—	0 1 3	—	0 1 9
- -	—	0 1 6	—	0 3 9
- -	—	0 1 6	—	0 2 6
-	—	0 1 3	—	0 1 9
- -	—	0 1 6	—	0 2 6
a -	—	0 2 0	—	0 2 9
- -	—	0 2 0	—	0 2 4

		£ s. d.		£ s. d.
Soriana - -	per lb.	0 1 10	to	0 2 0
Caceres - -	—	0 2 0	—	0 2 3
Seville - -	—	0 1 8	—	0 1 10
Portugal - -	—	0 1 2	—	0 1 4
Lambs' - -	—	0 1 4	—	0 2 0
Australian, best -	—	0 2 0	—	0 5 0
2d and inferior	—	0 1 2	—	0 2 0
Lambs - -	—	0 1 2	—	0 2 1
Van Diemen's Land				
Greasy & inferior	—	0 0 9	—	0 1 0
Clean and better	—	0 1 3	—	0 1 9
Eng. Merino, washed	—	0 1 9	—	0 2 6
In the Grease -	—		none	
South Down -	—	0 1 0	—	0 1 4
Goats' Wool, Turkey	—	0 1 4	—	0 1 8

WOOLLEN MANUFACTURE, the art of forming wool into c
stuffs. This has always ranked as an important branch of national i
and, until it was recently surpassed by the cotton manufacture, was
the most important of all the manufactures carried on in England.

Rise and Progress of the British Woollen Manufacture. — Exports. — The
no doubt that the arts of spinning wool, and manufacturing the yarn into cl
introduced into England by the Romans, the inhabitants being previously clo
in skins. From the period of the Romans quitting England, down to the 10th
there are no notices of the manufacture; and those relating to the period from
to the 13th century are but few and imperfect. It is certain, however, that
facture of broad cloths was established soon after the year 1200, if not previ
(*Smith's Memoirs of Wool*, vol. i. p. 17.) But the woollen manufactures of
being at this period, and long afterwards, in a comparatively advanced state
wool was exported in large quantities to Bruges and other Flemish cities, wh
cloths and other products were brought back in exchange. Edward III. took
judicious measures for improving the English manufacture, by inviting ove
weavers, fullers, dyers, and others, and protecting them from the assaults of th
Shortly after the first emigration of Flemings, or in 1337, an act was pas
hibiting the wear of any cloths made beyond sea, and interdicting the export o
wool. — (*Smith*, vol. i. p. 25.) But in these turbulent times such restraining
little better than a dead letter; and this, indeed, was soon after repealed.— (*Sm*
pp. 32. 39.) From this remote period the manufacture has always been rega
primary importance, and has been the object of the especial solicitude of the le
It may be doubted, however, whether it has derived any real advantage from
berless statutes that have been passed in the view of contributing to its adva
With the exception, indeed, of the prohibition of the export of English wool, v
finally put a stop to in 1660, the other acts, being mostly intended for the reg
the manufacture, could not be otherwise than mischievous: and the benefit o
the manufacturers from the prohibition was more apparent than real; inasm
occasioned a diminished growth of wool, at the same time that it was impossib
vent its clandestine exportation. Mr. Smith has proved that the manufactu
far more rapid progress during the reign of Elizabeth, when wool might be f
ried out of the kingdom, than it ever did during any equal period subseque
restriction on exportation. Foreign wool began to be imported in small qu
the 13th century.

At first, the manufacture seems to have been pretty equally distributed
country. In an insurrection that took place in 1525, more than 4,000 we
other tradesmen are said to have assembled out of Laneham, Sudbury, and othe
Suffolk. The manufacture had been previously introduced into Yorkshire. I
act was passed (34 & 35 Hen. 8. c. 10.), reciting, "that the city of York afore
had been upholden principally by making and weaving of coverlets, and the po
daily set on work in spinning, carding, dyeing, weaving, &c.;" that the ma
having spread into other parts, was "thereby debased and discredited;" and ena
remedy for this evil, that henceforth "none shall make coverlets in Yorkshire,
bitants of the city of York!" This may be taken as a fair specimen of the c
legislation of the time. Indeed, it was enacted, nearly at the same period, tha
nufacture should be restricted, in Worcestershire, to Worcester and four ot
Worsted goods, so called from Worsted, now an inconsiderable town in Norf
the manufacture was first set on foot, were produced in the reign of Edwa
perhaps earlier; but Norwich soon after became, and has since continued to be
cipal seat of this branch of the manufacture. In an act of Henry VIII. (3
c. 16.), worsted yarn is described as "the private commodity of the city of
In 1614, a great improvement took place in the woollen manufacture of
England, by the invention of what is called medley or mixed cloth, for which
tershire is still famous. During the reign of Charles II. there were man
unfounded, complaints of the decay of the manufacture; and by way of en
it, an act was passed (30 Car. 2. st. i. c. 3.), ordering that all persons should
in woollen shrouds! This act, the provisions of which were subsequently
preserved its place on the statute book for more than 130 years!

Towards the end of the 17th century, Mr. Gregory King and Dr. D
(*Davenant's Works*, Whitworth's ed. vol. ii. p. 233.) —estimated the value c
shorn in England at 2,000,000*l.* a year; and they supposed that the value o
(including that imported from abroad) was quadrupled in the manufacture
the entire value of the woollen articles annually produced in England a
8,000,000*l.* of which about 2,000,000*l.* were exported. In 1700 and 1701,
value of the woollens exported amounted to about 3,000,000*l.* a year. Ow

ase in the wealth and population of the country, the manufacture must have been
tly extended during last century ; but the increase in the amount of the exports
comparatively inconsiderable. At an average of the 6 years ending with 1789,
ıl official value of the exports was 3,544,160*l.* a year, being an increase of only
0,000*l.* on the amount exported in 1700. The extraordinary increase of the
ınufacture soon after 1780, and the extent to which cotton articles then began
stituted for those of wool, though it did not occasion any absolute decline of the
ure, no doubt contributed powerfully to check its progress. In 1802, the
lue of the exports rose to 7,321,012*l.* being the largest amount they have ever
In 1812, they sunk to 4,376,479*l.* During the 3 years ending with 1830,
.l and the declared or real values of the woollen manufactures exported from
.d Kingdom have been as under : —

	1828.	1829.	1830.
ılue of woollen manufactures exported	£5,728,969	£5,372,490	£5,558,709
or real value of ditto - -	5,125,984	4,661,259	4,850,884

f the Manufacture. — Number of Persons employed. — The most discordant
have been given as to both these points. For the most part, however, they
grossly exaggerated. In a tract published in 1739, entitled *Considerations on
ng* (Smuggling) *of Wool,* the number of persons engaged in the manufacture is
1,500,000, and their wages at 11,737,500*l.* a year. Dr. Campbell, in his " Po-
vey of Great Britain," published in 1774,—observes," Many computations have
e upon this important subject, and, amongst others, one about 30 years since,
that time, was thought to be pretty near the truth. According to the best in-
that can be obtained, there may be from 10,000,000 to 12,000,000 of sheep in
some think more. The value of their wool may, one year with another,
₃ 3,000,000*l.* ; the expense of manufacturing this may probably be 9,000,000*l.*,
tal value 12,000,000*l.* We may export annually to the value of 3,000,000*l.*,
₁e year we exported more than 4,000,000*l.* In reference to the number of per-
are maintained by this manufacture, they are probably upwards of 1,000,000.
₁men will judge these computations too low, and few will believe them too
'Vol. ii. p. 158.) But the moderation displayed in this estimate was very soon
₃f. In 1800, the woollen manufacturers objected strenuously to some of the
in the treaty of Union between Great Britain and Ireland, and were allowed
₂ir objections at the bar of the House of Lords, and to produce evidence in
₁ort. Mr. Law, afterwards Lord Ellenborough, the counsel employed by the
₁rers on this occasion, stated in his address to their Lordships, on information
₁ated to him by his clients, that 600,000 packs of wool were annually produced
₁d and Wales, worth, at 11*l.* a pack, 6,600,000*l.* ; that the value of the manu-
₁ods was three times as great, or 19,800,000*l.* ; that not less then 1,500,000
₁ere immediately engaged in the operative branches of the manufacture ; and
₁de collaterally employed about the same number of hands. — (*Account of the
s of the Merchants, Manufacturers, &c.* p. 34.)
₁onishing that reasonable men, conversant with the manufacture, should have
uch ludicrously absurd statements. We have already seen that the quantity of
₁ced in England and Wales, in 1800, did not really amount to 400,000 packs ;
₁tion that *three* out of the *nine* millions of people then in the country were
₁d indirectly employed in the manufacture, is too ridiculous to deserve notice,
₁was generally acquiesced in at the time.—(See *Middleton's Survey of Middlesex,*
₁644.; *Adolphus's Political State of the British Empire,* vol. iii. p. 236.)
₁venson, who is one of the very few writers on British statistics to whose state-
₁h deference is due, after a careful examination into the subject, has given the
₁stimate of the value of the woollen manufactured goods annually produced in
₁nd Wales, and of the interest, &c. of the capital, and the number of persons
₁n the manufacture : —

₁tal value of manufactured articles - -		£18,000,000
lue of raw material - - -	£6,000,000	
₂erest on capital, sum to replace its wear and tear, and		
₁manufacturers' profits - - -	2,400,000	
₁ages of workmen - - -	9,600,000	
		18,000,000

₁Number of people employed, 480,000, or perhaps 500,000.

₁ve, however, taking Scotland into account, and looking at the probable an-
₁diture of each individual on woollens, that the total value of the manufactured
₁ually produced in Great Britain may, at present, be moderately calculated at
₁*l.* or 22,000,000*l.* But, on the other hand, Mr Stevenson has materially
₁the proportion of the entire value of the manufacture falling to the share of
₁sts, and required to indemnify them for their various outgoings, and to yield

them ordinary profits. We learn, too, from good authority, that in estimating the
of the persons employed at about 8s. a week, or 20l. a year, he is below the mar
that 10s. a week, or 26l. a year, would be a more correct average. On the wh
are pretty well satisfied that the number of persons *employed* in the manufactu
not much exceed, if it do not fall short of, 400,000.

Most of the innumerable statutes formerly passed for the regulation of the d
processes of the manufacture have been repealed within these few years ; and the
every vestige of the remainder disappears from the statute book, the better.

Account of the Quantity and Declared Value of the Woollen Manufactures exported from th
Kingdom in 1829; specifying the Countries to which they were exported, and the Quant
Values sent to each.

Countries to which Exported.	Entered by the Piece.		Entered by the Yard.		Hosiery and Small Wares.	Countries to which Exported.	Entered by the Piece.		Entered by
	Quantity.	Declared Value.	Quantity.	Declared Value.	Declared Value.		Quantity.	Declared Value.	Quantity.
	Pieces.	*L.*	*Yards*	*L.*	*L.*		*Pieces.*	*L.*	*Yards.*
Russia - -	39,729	93,985	90,348	7,071	5,655	Sumatra, Java, and			
Sweden - -	2,607	5,022	3,425	301	199	other Islands of			
Norway - -	3,440	11,584	13,286	931	802	the Indian Seas	13,898	117,992	200
Denmark - -	1,554	2,311	5,274	397	529	New South Wales,			
Prussia - -	147	444	1,726	141	102	Van Diemen's			
Germany - -	566,936	532,775	526,410	38,009	42,341	Land, and Swan			
The Netherlands	132,654	220,338	657,633	46,479	34,753	River - -	1,856	9,526	58,422
France - -	4,705	8,71	19,602	3,060	197	British Northern			
Portugal, Proper	67,695	228,340	68,592	5,835	3,454	Colonies - -	52,785	179,958	824,953
——, Azores	2,536	8,507	6,060	565	2	——— West Indies	32,364	96,598	260,410
——, Madeira	1,087	4,118	2,683	243	117	Hayti - -	1,620	3,800	4,331
Spain and the						Cuba and other			
Balearic Islands	59,488	127,495	98,172	11,038	4,222	Foreign West			
——— Canaries	2,488	7,618	25,987	2,199	78	Indies - -	9,547	28,362	141,004
Gibraltar - -	9,227	30,303	81,760	7,364	2,016	United States of			
Italy and the Ita-						America	307,786	815,642	1,601,519
lian Islands	91,210	192,192	84,804	8,671	3,233	States of Central			
Malta - -	2,051	9,297	5,828	544	478	and Southern			
Ionian Islands	162	1,290	760	78	313	America, viz.			
Turkey and Con-						Mexico - -	2,960	11,699	9,285
tinental Greece	2,999	4,618	11,529	840	7	Colombia - -	9,021	32,939	58,632
Egypt(Ports on the						Brazil	62,275	230,543	115,939
Mediterranean)	78	852				States of the Rio			
Western Coast of						de la Plata	21,052	93,640	98,315
Africa	467	1,528	1,530	98	1,757	Chili - -	26,026	115,878	33,078
Cape of Good Hope	8,314	26,517	47,446	3,140	1,495	Peru - -	13,961	80,475	36,714
St. Helena	116	623	800	63	25	Isles of Guernsey,			
Mauritius -	3,318	8,352	11,925	834	509	Jersey, Alder-			
East India Com-						ney, Man, &c. -	7,614	29,436	92,377
pany's Territo-									
ries,Ceylon, and									
China - -	208,381	685,123	197,336	17,153	3,585	Total exported -	1,773,060	4,056,266	5,298,495

WRECK, in navigation, is usually understood to mean any ship or
driven ashore, or found floating at sea in a deserted or unmanageable co
But in the legal sense of the word in England, *wreck* must have come t
when at sea, it is distinguished by the barbarous appellations of *flotsam*,
and *ligan.* — (See FLOTSAM.)

In nothing, perhaps, has the beneficial influence of the advance of society
isation been more apparent than in the regulations with respect to the per
property of shipwrecked individuals. In most rude and uncivilised countr
treatment has been cruel in the extreme. Amongst the early Greeks and
strangers and enemies were regarded in the same point of view. — (*Hostis apud
peregrinus dicebatur.* — *Pomp. Festus ;* see also *Cicero de Offic.* lib. i. c. 12.) Wh
inhospitable sentiments prevailed, the conduct observed towards those that w
wrecked could not be otherwise than barbarous ; and in fact they were, in most i
either put to death or sold as slaves. But as law and good order grew up, a
merce and navigation were extended, those who escaped from the perils of the
treated in a way less repugnant to the dictates of humanity : and at length the
law made it a capital offence to destroy persons shipwrecked, or to prev
saving the ship ; and the stealing even of a plank from a vessel shipwrecked or in
made the party liable to answer for the whole ship and cargo. — (*Pand.* 47. 9.

During the gloomy period which followed the subversion of the Roman em
the establishment of the northern nations in the southern parts of Europe, the
barbarous practices with respect to shipwreck were every where renewed. Th
survived were in most countries reduced to servitude ; and their goods were eve
confiscated for the use of the lord on whose manor they had been thrown. —
son's Charles V. vol. i. note 29.) But nothing, perhaps, can so strongly evince
valence and nature of these enormities, as the efforts that were made, as soon as
ments began to acquire authority, for their suppression. The regulations as
wreck in the laws of Oleron are, in this respect, most remarkable. The 35th
articles state, that " Pilots, in order to ingratiate themselves with their lords,

d treacherous villains, sometimes willingly run the ship upon the rocks, &c.;"
offence they are held to be accursed and excommunicated, and punished as
robbers.   The fate of the lord is still more severe.   " He is to be appre-
s goods confiscated and sold, and himself fastened to a post or stake in the
is own mansion house, which being fired at the four corners, all shall be
gether, the walls thereof be demolished; the stones pulled down; and the
ed into a market place, for the sale only of hogs and swine, to all posterity."
article recites, that when a vessel was lost by running on shore, and the
ad landed, they often, instead of meeting with help, " were attacked by
e barbarous, cruel, and inhuman, than mad dogs; who, to gain their monies,
d other goods, did sometimes murder and destroy these poor distressed sea-
this case, the lord of the country is to execute justice, by punishing them in
ns and their estates; and is commanded to plunge them in the sea till
lf dead, and then to have them drawn forth out of the sea, and stoned to

re the dreadful severities by which it was attempted to put a stop to the
inst which they were directed.   The violence of the remedy shows better
ing else how inveterate the disease had become.

England, like that of other modern countries, adjudged wrecks to belong to the king. But
injustice of this law was modified so early as the reign of Henry I., when it was ruled, that
escaped alive out of the ship, it should be no wreck. And after various modifications, it was
e reign of Henry III., that if goods were cast on shore, having any marks by which they
ified, they were to revert to the owners, if claimed any time within a year and a day. By
Edw. 3. c. 13., if a ship be lost and the goods come to land, they are to be delivered to the
ying only a reasonable reward or SALVAGE (which see) to those who saved or preserved them.
ent statutes, owing to the confusion and disorder of the times, were very ill enforced; and
practices previously alluded to, continued to the middle of last century. A statute of
. st. 2. c. 18.), confirmed by the 4 Geo. 1. c. 12., in order to put a stop to the atrocities in question,
officers and others of the towns near the sea, upon application made to them, to summon
s as are necessary, and send them to the relief of any ship in distress, on forfeiture of 100l. ;
assistance given, salvage is to be assessed by three justices, and paid by the owners. Persons
goods cast ashore are to forfeit treble their value; and if they wilfully do any act whereby
or destroyed, they are guilty of felony without benefit of clergy. But even this statute
ave been sufficient to accomplish the end in view; and in 1753, a new statute (26 Geo. 2.
cted, the preamble of which is as follows:—" Whereas, notwithstanding the good and salu-
y in being against plundering and destroying vessels in distress, and against taking away
lost, or stranded goods, many wicked enormities have been committed, to the disgrace of
the grievous damage of merchants and mariners of our own and other countries, be it,
then enacted, that the preventing of the escape of any person endeavouring to save his
ng him with intent to destroy him, or putting out false lights in order to bring any vessel
hall be capital felony. By the same statute, the pilfering of any goods cast ashore is
ceny.
& 2 Geo. 4. c. 75. it is enacted, that any person or persons wilfully cutting away, injuring, or
buoy or buoy rope attached to any anchor or cable belonging to any ship, whether in dis-
ise, shall be judged guilty of felony, and may upon conviction be transported for 7 years.
unt of the sums to be paid to those assisting in the saving of wreck, see art. SALVAGE in
, see also the chapter on Salvage in Mr. Abbott's (Lord Tenterden's) work on the Law

Y.

a long measure used in England, of 3 feet, or 36 inches. — (See
ND MEASURES.)
(Ger. Garn; Du. Garen; Fr. Fil; It. Filato; Sp. Hilo; Port. Fio;
), wool, cotton, flax, &c. spun into thread.

Z.

R, OR ZAFFRE. After the sulphur, arsenic, and other volatile
alt have been expelled by calcination, the residuum is sold, mixed or
th fine sand, under the above name.   When the residuum is melted
is earth and potash, it forms a kind of blue glass, known by the name
(see SMALTZ), — of great importance in the arts.   When smaltz is
fine, it receives in commerce the name of *powder blue*.   Zaffer, like
mployed in the manufacture of earthenware and China, for painting
of the pieces a blue colour.   It suffers no change from the most vio-
t is also employed to tinge the crystal glasses made in imitation of
transparent precious stones of a blue colour.

4 D

ZEA, INDIAN CORN, or MAIZE. See MAIZE.

ZEDOARY (Ger. *Zittwer;* Fr. *Zédoaire;* It. *Zedoaria;* Sp. *Cedoari Judwar;* Hind. *Nirbisi*), the root of a plant which grows in Malabar Cochin-China, &c., of which there are three distinct species. It is brou in pieces of various sizes, externally wrinkled, and of an ash colour, but i of a brownish red. Those roots which are heavy and free from worms chosen; rejecting those which are decayed and broken. The odour of z fragrant, and somewhat like that of camphor; the taste biting, aromatic terish, with some degree of acrimony. It was formerly employed in medi is scarcely ever used by modern practitioners. — (*Milburn's Orient. Com*

ZINC, or SPELTER (Ger. *Zink;* Fr. *Zinc;* It. *Zinco;* Sp. *Zinc* Rus. *Schpiauter;* Lat. *Zincum*), a metal of a brilliant white colour, wit of blue, composed of a number of thin plates adhering together. When i is rubbed for some time between the fingers, they acquire a peculiar t emit a very perceptible smell. It is rather soft; tinging the fingers, whe upon them, with a black colour. The specific gravity of melted zinc va 6·861 to 7·1, the lightest being esteemed the purest. When hammered, it as high as 7·1908. This metal forms, as it were, the limit between the b the malleable metals. Its malleability is by no means to be compared of copper, lead, or tin; yet it is not brittle, like antimony or arsenic struck with a hammer, it does not break, but yields, and becomes some ter; and by a cautious and equal pressure, it may be reduced to pretty th which are supple and elastic, but cannot be folded without breaking heated to about 400°, it becomes so brittle that it may be reduced to p a mortar. It possesses a certain degree of ductility, and may with care out into wire. Its tenacity is such, that a wire whose diameter is equal t an inch is capable of supporting a weight of about 26 lbs. Zinc has n found in a state of purity. There are three works in this country whe separated from its ore; two in the neighbourhood of Bristol, and one at The word zinc occurs for the first time in the writings of Paracelsus, in 1541; but the method of extracting it from its ores was not knov early part of last century. — (*Thomson's Chemistry.*) The compounds o copper are of great importance. — (See BRASS.)

APPENDIX.

)NIES. Since the articles COLONIES and QUEBEC were printed, the
oners for emigration have issued the following information for the use of
ntending to emigrate to the British Colonies in North America.

Colonial Office, 9th February, 1832.

t of the present notice is to afford such information as is likely to be useful to persons who
r to emigrate, or to assist others to emigrate, to the British possessions in North America.
st place, it seems desirable to define the nature of the assistance to be expected from govern-
rsons proceeding to these colonies. No pecuniary aid will be allowed by government to emi-
e North American colonies; nor after their arrival will they receive grants of land, or gifts of
upply of provisions. Hopes of all these things have been sometimes held out to emigrants by
in this country, desirous of making a profit by their conveyance to North America, and willing
pose to delude them with unfounded expectations, regardless of their subsequent disappoint-
the wish of government is to furnish those who emigrate, with a real knowledge of the cir-
they will find in the countries to which they are going.
nce of the extraordinary extent above described is allowed, because, in colonies, where those
o work cannot fail to do well for themselves, none such is needed. Land, indeed, used for-
granted gratuitously; but when it was taken by poor people, they found that they had not the
ing during the interval necessary to raise their crops; and further, that they knew not enough
er of farming in the colonies, to make any progress. After all, therefore, they were obliged
wages, until they could make a few savings, and could learn a little of the way of farming in
ut now, land is not disposed of except by sale. The produce of sales, although the price is
te, is likely to become a considerable fund, which can be turned to the benefit of the colonies,
re of the emigrants; while yet no hardship is inflicted on the poor emigrant, who will work
st as he did before, and may after a while acquire land, if land be his object, by the savings
gh wages in these colonies enable him speedily to make.
the reasons why government does not think it necessary to give away land in a country,
e lowness of its price, the plentifulness of work, and the high rates of wages, an industrious
n enough in a few seasons to become a freeholder by means of his own acquisitions.
which is for sale will be open to public competition, and of course, therefore, its price must
a the offers that may be made; but it will generally not be sold for less than from 4s. to 5s. per
s situations where roads have been made, or the ground has been partially cleared, the com-
lately have been 7s. 6d., 10s., and 15s. Further particulars will be best learned upon the
every endeavour will be made to meet the different circumstances and views of different

government will not make any gifts at the public expense to emigrants to North America,
be maintained at the principal colonial ports, whose duty it will be, without fee or reward
e individuals, to protect emigrants against imposition upon their first landing, to acquaint
he demand for labour in different districts, to point out the most advantageous routes, and to
n generally with all useful advice upon the objects which they have had in view in emigrating.
private engagement cannot be immediately obtained, employment will be afforded on some
works in progress in the colonies. Persons newly arrived should not omit to consult the
agent for emigrants, and as much as possible should avoid detention in the ports, where they
to all kinds of impositions, and of pretexts for keeping them at taverns till any money they
has been expended. — For the same purpose of guarding against the frauds practised on new
of preventing an improvident expenditure at the first moment of arrival, it seems very desir-
lividuals who may wish to furnish emigrants with money for their use in the colony should
ans of making the money payable there, instead of giving it into the hands of the emigrants
ry. The commissioners for emigration are engaged in effecting general arrangements for
, and due notice will be given to the public when they shall be completed. Agents for emi-
been appointed at St. John's, St. Andrew's, and Miramichi in New Brunswick, and at Quebec
Canada. On the whole subject of the manner of proceeding upon landing, it may be ob-
nclusion, that no effort will be spared to exempt emigrants from any necessity for delay
of disembarkation, and from uncertainty as to the opportunities of at once turning their labour

explanation of the extent of the aid to be expected from government, the following state-
bjoined of the ordinary charges for passage to the North American colonies, as well as of the
f wages and usual prices in them, in order that every individual may have the means of judging
f the inducements to emigrate to these parts of the British dominions.
- Passages to Quebec or New Brunswick may either be engaged *inclusive* of provisions, or *ex-*
ovisions, in which case the ship owner finds nothing but water, fuel, and bed places, without
uildren under 14 years of age are charged one half, and under 7 years of age one third, of the
nd for children under 12 months of age no charge is made. Upon these conditions the price
om London, or from places on the east coast of Great Britain, has generally been 6l. with pro-
without. From Liverpool, Greenock, and the principal ports of Ireland, as the chances of
er, the charge is somewhat lower; this year it will probably be from 2l. to 2l. 10s. without
from 4l. to 5l. including provisions. It is possible that in March and April passages may be
a Dublin for 35s. or even 30s.; but the prices always grow higher as the season advances. In
from Scotland or Ireland, it has mostly been the custom for passengers to find their own pro-
this practice has not been so general in London; and some ship owners, sensible of the
istakes which may be made in this matter through ignorance, are very averse to receive pas-
will not agree to be victualled by the ship. Those who do resolve to supply their own pro-
'd at least be careful not to lay in an insufficient stock; 50 days is the shortest period for
.fe to provide; and from London the passage is sometimes prolonged to 75 days.

The best months for leaving England are certainly March and April; the later emigrants find employment so abundant, and have less time in the colony before the commencement of wint
Various frauds are attempted upon emigrants, which can only be effectually defeated by the goo of the parties against whom they are contrived. Sometimes agents take payment from the emigr his passage, and then recommend him to some tavern, where he is detained from day to day und pretences for delay, until, before the departure of the ship, the whole of his money is extracted fro This of course cannot happen with agents connected with respectable houses; but the best securi name in the bargain for passage a particular day, after which, whether or not the ship sails, the pa is to be received on board and victualled by the owners. In this manner the emigrant cannot be tionally brought to the place of embarkation too soon, and be compelled to spend his money at public by false accounts of the time of sailing; for from the very day of his arrival at the port, being the d viously agreed upon, the ship becomes his home.

The conveyance of passengers to the British possessions in North America is regulated by an act liament (9 Geo. 4. c. 21.), of which the following are the principal provisions: — Ships are not allo carry passengers to these colonies unless they be of the height of 5½ feet between decks; and the not carry more than 3 passengers for every 4 tons of the registered burthen; there must be on b least 50 gallons of pure water, and 50 pounds of bread, biscuit, oatmeal, or bread stuff, for each pas When the ship carries the full number of passengers allowed by law, no part of the cargo, and no st provisions, may be carried between decks; but if there be less than the complete number of pass goods may be stowed between decks in a proportion not exceeding 3 cubical feet for each passenge ing of the highest number. Masters of vessels who land passengers, unless with their own conse place different from that originally agreed upon, are subject to a penalty of 20*l*., recoverable by su process before two justices of the peace in any of the North American colonies.

The enforcement of this law rests chiefly with the officers of his Majesty's customs; and persons complaints to make of its infraction, should address themselves to the nearest Custom-house.

Besides the sea voyage from England, persons proceeding to Canada should be provided with the of paying for the journey which they may have to make after their arrival at Quebec. The cost journey must, of course, depend upon the situation of the place where the individual may find e ment, or where he may have previously formed a wish to settle; but to all it will probably be us possess the following report of the prices of conveyance, during the last season, on the route from to York, the capital of Upper Canada. From Quebec to Montreal (180 miles), by steam-bo charge for an adult was 6*s*. 6*d*.; from Montreal to Prescot (120 miles), by boats or barges, 7*s*.; fro cot to York (250 miles), by steam-boat, 7*s*. The journey, performed in this manner, usually occupi 12 days; adding, therefore, 11*s*. for provisions, the total cost from Quebec to York (a distance miles) may be stated, according to the charges of last year, at 1*l*. 11*s*. 6*d*. Persons who are poss sufficient means prefer to travel by land that part of the route where the river St. Lawrence is n gable by steam-boats, and the journey is then usually performed in 6 days, at a cost of 6*l*. It mus served, that the prices of conveyance are necessarily fluctuating, and that the foregoing account presented as sufficiently accurate for purposes of information in this country, leaving it to the gove agent at Quebec to supply emigrants with more exact particulars, according to the circumstance time at which they may arrive.

Rates of Wages and Market Prices. — The colonies in North America, to which emigrants c advantage proceed, are Lower Canada, Upper Canada, and New Brunswick. From the reports from the other British colonies in North America, namely, Prince Edward's Island, Newfoundlan Scotia, and Cape Breton, it appears that they do not contain the means either of affording emp at wages to a considerable number of emigrants, or of settling them upon land.

Lower Canada. — From Lower Canada the commissioners for emigration have not received th reports which were required from the North American colonies, for the purpose of compiling the statement. They believe, however, that the following account of the prices of grain and of wa be relied upon for its general correctness: —

		s.	*d.*
Wheat	per bushel	4	6
Rye	—	3	0
Maize	—	2	6
Oats	—	1	3
Wages of labourers	per day	2	6
Ship-builders, carpenters, joiners, coopers, masons, and tailors		5	0

Upper Canada. — The following table exhibits the lowest and the highest price which the sev cles therein named bore, during the year 1831, in each of the principal districts of Upper Canada

	Eastern District.		Johnstown ditto.		Bathurst ditto.		Newcastle ditto.		Home ditto.		Gore ditto.		Ni
	Lowest Price in 1831.	Highest Ditto.	Lowest.	Highest	Lowest.	Highest	Lowest.	Highest	Lowest.	Highest	Lowest.	Highest	Lowe
	L. s. d.	*L. s. d.*	*L. s. d.*	*L. s. d.*	*L. s. d.*	*L. s. d.*	*L. s. d.*	*L. s. d.*	*L. s. d.*	*L. s. d.*	*L. s. d.*	*L. s. d.*	*L. s*
Wheat, per bu.	0 5 0	0 5 6	0 5 3	0 6 9	0 5 0	0 5 0	0 3 6	0 6 3	0 3 9	0 5 3	0 4 4½	0 6 3	0 3
Maize —	0 2 6	0 3 0	0 1 9	0 2 3	0 2 6	0 3 0	0 2 0	0 3 0	0 2 0	0 2 9	0 2 6	0 2 6	0 2
Oats —	0 1 3	0 1 8	0 1 3	0 1 6	0 1 6	0 2 0	0 1 3	0 2 0	0 0 10	0 1 10½	0 1 3	0 1 10½	0 1
Barley —	0 2 6	0 2 6	0 1 9	0 4 0	0 3 0	0 3 6	0 2 6	0 3 1	0 2 3	0 3 9	0 2 6	0 2 6	0 2
Potatoes cwt.	0 1 3 per bushel.	0 1 6 per bushel.	0 1 3	0 1 9	0 1 3	0 1 9	0 2 0	0 3 0	0 0 10	0 2 6	0 1 3	0 1 6	0 1
Butter (fr.) lb.	0 0 7½	0 0 9	0 0 6	0 0 9	0 0 6	0 0 8	0 0 7½	0 0 9	0 0 7½	0 1 0	0 0 7½	0 0 7½	0 0
Ditto (salt) —	0 0 7½	0 0 7½	0 0 7½	0 0 10	0 0 7½	0 0 7½	0 0 7½	0 0 9	0 0 9	0 0 10	0 0 6	0 0 7½	0 0
Cheese —	0 0 6	0 0 6	0 0 1	0 0 6	0 0 6	0 0 6	0 0 5	0 0 7½	0 0 6	0 0 6	0 0 5	0 0 7½	0 0
Eggs, per doz.	0 0 5	0 0 9	0 0 6	0 0 10	0 0 4	0 0 8	0 0 6	0 0 7½	0 0 7½	0 1 10½	0 0 6	0 0 7½	0 0
Ducks, per pair	0 1 8	0 1 8	0 1 6	0 2 0	0 2 6	0 3 0	0 2 0	0 2 6	0 1 3	0 1 10½	0 2 6	0 2 6	0 1
Fowls —	0 1 4	0 1 6	0 1 0	0 1 3	0 1 8	0 2 3	0 1 3	0 1 3	0 1 3	0 1 6	0 1 3	0 1 3	0 1
Geese —	0 4 0	0 5 0	0 2 4	0 2 6	0 4 0	0 4 0	0 2 6	0 3 9	0 3 3	0 5 0	0 3 9	0 3 9	0 3
Turkeys —	0 5 0	0 6 0	0 3 6	0 4 0	0 4 0	0 4 0	0 2 3	0 3 9	0 5 0	0 10 0	0 5 0	0 5 0	0 5
Hay - per ton	1 15 0	2 5 0	1 10 0	2 10 0	2 0 0	2 10 0	1 10 0	3 10 0	1 10 0	2 10 0	2 0 0	2 0 0	1 15
Straw, per load	0 16 8	0 16 8	0 5 0	0 10 0	0 7 6	0 7 6	0 5 0	0 5 0	0 15 0	0 15 0	0 7 6	0 7 6	0 5
Bread, 4lb. lf.	0 0 9	0 0 10	0 0 6	0 0 8	0 0 10	0 0 10	0 0 7½	0 0 7½	0 0 4½	0 0 7	0 0 7½	0 0 7½	0 0
Meat, per lb.													
Beef - -	0 0 2½	0 0 3½	0 0 2½	0 0 4	0 0 4	0 0 4	0 0 2½	0 0 3	0 0 3	0 0 5	0 0 3	0 0 3½	0 0
Mutton -	0 0 3	0 0 4	0 0 2½	0 0 4	0 0 4	0 0 4	0 0 2½	0 0 3	0 0 5	0 0 7½	0 0 3	0 0 3½	0 0
Pork - -	0 0 4	0 0 5	0 0 4	0 0 6	0 0 3	0 0 3	0 0 3	0 0 4	0 0 3	0 0 6	0 0 2	0 0 2½	0 0
Veal - -	0 0 3	0 0 3	0 0 2½	0 0 3	0 0 4	0 0 4	0 0 3	0 0 3½	0 0 3	0 0 5	0 0 3	0 0 3½	0 0
Flour, 100 lbs.													
Fine - -	0 15 0	0 17 6	0 15 0	0 17 6	0 12 6	0 16 0	0 12 6	0 17 6	0 12 6	0 15 0	0 14 6	0 15 0	0 12
Seconds -	0 12 6	0 12 6	0 12 6	0 15 0	0 10 6	0 12 6	0 10 0	0 15 0	0 11 3	0 12 6	0 12 0	0 12 6	0 12

mparison of all the documents before the commissioners for emigration, it appears that the
of labourers in Upper Canada, hired by the year, are from 27l. to 30l.; that their monthly
erent situations and at different seasons, range from 1l. 10s. to 3l. 10s. per month; and that
ange from 2s. to 3s. 9d.   In all these rates of wages, board and lodging are found by the em-
hout board, daily wages vary from 3s. 6d. out of harvest to 5s. during harvest; 6s. 3d., besides
sometimes given to harvest men.   The wages of mechanics may be stated universally at from
er day.

wick — The following is a list of prices compiled from documents sent in from various parts
swick :—

	L. s. d.	L. s. d.			L. s. d.	L. s. d.
per bushel	0 5 0 to	0 10 0	Bread	per 4 lb. loaf	0 0 10 to	0 1 0
—	0 4 6 —	0 5 0	Beef	per stone	0 3 3 —	0 4 0
—	0 1 6 —	0 2 6	Mutton	—	0 2 4 —	0 4 0
—	0 4 0 —	0 5 0	Pork	—	0 2 0½ —	0 4 0
per cwt.	0 1 3 —	0 3 6	Veal	—	0 2 4 —	0 4 8
per lb.	0 0 9 —	0 1 0	Flour	per 100 lbs.	0 16 0 —	0 17 6
—	0 0 8 —	0 0 10	Salt Pork	per barrel	4 15 0 —	5 5 0
—	0 0 4 —	0 0 7	Ditto Beef	—	3 0 0 —	3 10 0
per dozen	0 0 7½ —	0 1 0	Malt	per bushel	0 6 2 —	0 6 4
per pair	0 2 0 —	0 3 6	Rye Flour	per barrel	1 2 6	
—	0 1 6 —	0 2 6	Indian ditto	—	1 2 6	
—	0 3 0 —	0 5 0	Oatmeal	per cwt.	0 16 0 —	0 18 0
—	0 7 6 —	0 10 0	Salt Cod	per 112 lbs.	0 10 0 —	0 12 0
per ton	1 10 0 —	2 10 0	Ditto Mackarel	per barrel	0 17 0 —	1 0 0
—	1 0 0 —	1 5 0	Ditto Alewives	—	0 10 0 —	0 12 0

ld at 30s. per chaldron.   House rent is from 5l. to 6l. per annum for families occupying one
r families occupying two rooms, from 6l. to 10l.   Common labourers receive from 3s. to 4s. a
heir own subsistence; but when employed at the ports in loading vessels, their subsistence
em.   Mechanics receive from 5s. to 7s. 6d. per day, and superior workmen from 7s. 6d.

regoing statements, it must be observed that emigrants, especially such of them as are agri-
rers, should not expect the highest wages named until they have become accustomed to the
lony.   The mechanics most in demand are those connected with the business of house-
oemakers and tailors, and ship-builders, also find abundant employment.

By order of the Commissioners,
T. FREDERICK ELLIOT,
Secretary to the Commission.

Since the article LACE was printed, Mr. Heathcoat has been pointed
s the original inventor of the bobbin net machine; and it is affirmed,
o his patent being obtained, bobbin net made by machinery was un-
ough numerous attempts had been made for many years previously
it by its means.   Mr. Brunel, engineer, who was examined as a witness
on *Boville v. Moore,* tried before Sir Vicary Gibbs, in March, 1816,
eference to this machine, that when Mr. Heathcoat had separated one
threads, and placed them on a beam as warp threads, and made the
ich carried the other half of the threads, act between those warp
as to produce Buckinghamshire or pillow lace, *the lace machine was*
Relying upon the authenticity of this statement, we feel it due to Mr.
to give this explanation.

-HOUSES.   Since the article LIGHT-HOUSES was written, the dues on
the North and South Foreland lights have been abolished, at the sugges-
:. Poulett Thomson, Chairman of the Commissioners of Greenwich

ATION.   Having had frequent occasion, in the course of this work,
the population of Great Britain, we subjoin, for the convenience of
s, an account of the results of the enumerations taken in 1801, 1811,
1831.   Most part of our work having been printed previously to the
of last census, we estimated the population at 16,000,000; an estimate
een proved to be sufficiently accurate for all practical purposes.

Population of Great Britain.

	Population, 1801.	Increase per Cent.	Population, 1811.	Increase per Cent.	Population, 1821.	Increase per Cent.	Population, 1831.
- -	8,331,434	14½	9,551,888	17½	11,261,437	16	13,098,338
-	541,546	13	611,788	17	717,438	12	805,236
&c.	1,599,068	14	1,805,688	16	2,093,456	13	2,365,807
-	470,598	- -	640,500	- -	319,300	- -	277,017
	10,942,646	15½	12,609,864	14	14,391,631	15	16,537,398

the Parliamentary Paper (No. 60. Sess. 1832), the population of Ireland in 1831 was
as some of the returns were not complete, it may be taken at about 8,000,000.

'UE AND EXPENDITURE.   The following comprehensive state-
: revenue and expenditure during the three years ending with 1830,
ail of being acceptable to our readers.

PUBLIC INCOME AND EXPENDITURE

Heads of Income.	Income. 1828. L. s. d.	1828. L. s. d.	1829. L. s. d.	1829. L. s. d.	L. s.
Customs and Excise.					
Spirits — Foreign	1,558,406 10 11		1,519,572 8 7		1,480,507 3
Spirits — Rum	1,392,553 7 2		1,434,782 13 1		1,599,445 6
Spirits — British	4,969,685 7 0¼		4,783,951 2 1		5,185,574 4
Malt	4,623,113 19 3½		3,814,305 1 5¼		3,436,272 14
Beer	3,256,186 12 11½		3,055,453 15 11½		2,345,122 10
Hops	260,578 18 0		242,658 0 10½		118,912 5
Wine	1,500,051 6 1		1,473,607 11 4		1,524,177
Sugar and Molasses	5,193,148 14 5		5,089,315 0 3		4,927,025
Tea	3,448,814 2 9¼		3,321,722 2 6		3,387,097 18
Coffee	440,244 13 10		498,951 8 1		579,363
Tobacco and Snuff	2,793,874 11 8	29,436,658 4 1½	2,849,706 7 8	28,084,025 11 10¼	2,924,264
Butter	195,743 13 5		147,839 3 4		102,752
Cheese	112,049 0 11		87,122 14 4		54,870
Currants and Raisins	436,581 5 11		388,102 2 6		420,217
Corn	193,250 12 8		898,793 15 2		790,109
Cotton Wool and Sheep's Wool imported	395,773 5 3		317,074 10 5		482,274
Silks	345,278 1 2		205,615 9 0		209,047
Printed Goods	657,741 5 4½		552,270 12 4½		570,330
Hides and Skins	474,391 6 10¾		452,768 15 7		255,278
Paper	727,377 4 9¾		684,563 10 11¾		690,610
Soap	1,212,092 7 2½		1,152,245 11 1½		1,251,021
Candles and Tallow	665,758 6 5½		652,971 16 11½		662,944
Coals, Sea-borne	935,911 5 5		983,919 9 2¼		1,021,862
Glass	616,534 14 10		670,494 12 9¾		567,632 1
Bricks, Tiles, and Slates	392,365 10 9¾		398,145 14 8¼		383,985
Timber	1,488,498 0 1¼		1,394,407 19 11¼		1,319,233
Auctions	275,564 4 3¾		251,562 19 6¾		234,854
Excise Licences	845,160 2 7¾		845,390 18 3¼		848,469
Miscellaneous Duties, Customs and Excise	2,321,050 19 8½		1,892,668 2 4		1,971,223
		12,291,121 7 11		11,975,957 18 6¾	
Total of Customs and Excise		41,727,779 12 0½		40,059,983 10 5	
Stamps.					
Deeds and other Instruments	1,686,315 9 8¾		1,663,145 14 6½		1,621,427
Probates and Legacies	2,043,268 4 9½		2,035,719 0 4		2,084,432
Insurance — Marine	243,359 0 9		226,897 6 6½		219,565
Insurance — Fire	745,710 15 1¾		764,939 0 11¼		760,931
Bills of Exchange, Bankers' Notes, &c.	603,237 12 2		593,485 1 1½		568,546
Newspapers and Advertisements	581,526 18 5		433,385 5 10½		613,848
Stage Coaches	407,529 10 10¾		426,472 1 3		418,598
Post Horses	238,858 0 4		252,772 2 8		220,357
Receipts	236,531 6 6		225,996 2 6		223,660
Other Stamp Duties	531,272 9 2¾	7,317,609 7 11½	663,164 5 9½	7,285,976 1 7½	516,716
Assessed and Land Taxes.					
Land Taxes	1,210,227 17 10½		1,200,159 10 11¼		1,184,790
Houses	1,295,550 12 10		1,324,327 18 9¾		1,361,625
Windows	1,164,010 13 7½		1,163,760 17 8		1,185,283
Servants	277,759 5 4¾		286,552 7 0		295,087
Horses	400,676 9 3		405,678 1 9		425,125
Carriages	352,478 16 9		374,677 14 0		397,613
Dogs	182,944 17 11¾		183,060 8 4		186,102
Other Assessed Taxes	279,224 16 0	5,162,873 9 8½	268,175 2 9	5,206,392 1 8	259,242
Post Office		2,207,998 11 5		2,184,667 2 4	
Crown Lands		448,792 17 7		465,481 4 5½	
Other Ordinary Revenues and Resources		620,542 3 11		622,302 0 0¼	
Grand Total	L.	57,485,596 2 7½		55,824,802 0 1½	

KINGDOM, IN THE YEARS 1828, 1829, 1830.

ture.	Expenditure. 1828.		1829.		1830.	
	L. s. d.	L. s. d.	L. s. d.	L. s. d.	L. s. d.	L. s. d.
ollection. rtments	1,184,378 4 7½		1,100,050 8 10¾		1,027,870 17 1½	
Service	262,940 5 0¾		268,478 10 3½		260,940 1 4½	
	1,446,318 9 8½		1,368,528 19 2½		1,287,913 18 6	
	1,226,403 6 7¾		1,240,948 12 0		1,225,429 10 9½	
	225,515 1 3		193,279 13 9		190,159 7 1¾	
axes	280,812 6 1½		287,183 2 2		281,939 12 1	
nues (ex-	45,589 8 4½		28,162 10 6½		28,782 2 10	
e		3,225,638 12 0½		3,118,102 17 8		3,014,224 11 4½
t Debt	25,332,782 11 4¾		25,318,866 10 7½		24,091,750 7 10	
Termin-	1,981,034 17 0		1,854,695 8 4		1,843,106 11 7	
Life An- ities for	650,851 13 9		826,402 13 10		1,453,269 2 5	
	949,429 13 7		878,494 1 3¾		813,300 16 5	
r Bills	275,877 16 10		275,143 7 1¾		275,179 3 4	
ot		29,189,976 12 6¾		29,153,602 1 3		28,476,606 1 7
nt. s, Privy Trades- ass, Sala- lousehold	409,700 0 0		409,700 0 0		401,628 16 10¾	
Junior Royal Fa- Leopold Prince of	248,500 0 0		247,974 4 6¼		245,923 1 6¼	
Ireland's	67,935 1 8		67,935 1 8		32,749 9 3¾	
penses of ot(includ-	123,094 17 5		141,599 18 5		144,374 6 5	
in Great f those in and Ord-	345,320 15 6¾		328,706 0 1¼		320,045 1 8½	
solidated evenue	208,218 3 11½		204,870 7 9		264,247 3 2¼	
England, and	195,259 8 2		196,114 4 11		170,000 0 0	
rnment		1,598,028 6 9		1,596,899 17 4½		1,578,967 19 0½
England, and	446,683 19 10		496,828 16 2		407,801 9 9½	
Prosecu-	187,361 19 9		203,639 11 3		222,450 9 4	
ome and	135,783 12 9		145,925 18 3		140,305 16 1	
S. Wales	167,500 0 0		167,500 6 0		167,500 0 0	
s	63,263 6 1		60,704 12 8		55,620 6 11¾	
stice		1,000,592 18 6		1,004,598 18 4		993,678 2 2¼
d Allow- inisters	236,950 0 0		224,950 0 0		220,932 15 9¾	
uls	127,870 0 0		119,470 0 0		117,595 0 0	
No. 1, 2, 3.	63,191 13 7		59,118 5 2		37,097 7 1	
atic		428,011 13 7		403,538 5 2		375,625 2 10¾
er of Men	(89,047.)		(85,721.)		(84,172.)	
e	5,146,463 8 3½		4,829,282 12 4½		4,492,687 5 7½	
er of Men	(96,916.)		(96,595.)		(96,081.)	
e	2,903,476 0 0		2,939,896 0 0		2,939,606 9 6	
Army	8,049,939 8 3½		7,769,178 12 4½		7,432,294 15 1½	
er of Men	(8,906.)		(8,879.)		(8,878.)	
e	1,223,770 0 0		1,363,282 0 0		1,332,354 0 0	
er of Men	(12,439.)		(12,494.)		(12,364.)	
e	372,380 0 0		365,626 0 0		357,090 0 0	
dnance	1,596,150 0 0		1,728,908 0 0		1,689,444 0 0	
er of Men	(31,818.)		(32,458.)		(31,444.)	
e	4,400,135 7 7		4,299,645 11 11		4,067,308 7 8½	
er of Men	(31,136.)		(30,467.)		(29,922.)	
e	1,595,830 0 0		1,579,149 0 0		1,531,646 17 11¾	
	5,995,965 7 7		5,878,794 11 11		5,594,955 5 8	
s		15,642,054 15 10½		15,376,881 4 3½		14,716,694 0 9½
ng Fishe- ifactures, the Gross		276,226 8 6		236,898 3 0¾		207,966 10 1½
		727,615 0 10		606,396 8 4		474,242 0 1
Revenue for Im- iousPub-		421,838 17 6		427,015 2 5½		252,601 5 7½
of Collec- ments		681,368 7 2½		696,801 16 11¾		718,359 8 6½
rehousing		159,709 4 9½		191,852 18 2½		214,037 14 6¾
anted by				200,000 0 0		
ces, not foregoing of Grants nents out d Fund, Lists of , and Ire-		1,485,840 12 8¾		1,336,287 16 7		1,988,530 7 8½
otal	L.	54,836,901 10 9½		54,348,875 9 8½		53,011,533 3 5½
ife An- e		2,631,886 10 9		2,681,098 2 2		3,296,375 14 0
uities, as nlaison		1,798,617 10 9		1,811,529 15 9		2,143,685 13 6
	L.	833,269 0 0		869,568 6 5		1,152,689 0 6

THE END.

LONDON :
Printed by A. & R. Spottiswoode,
New-Street-Square.

For EU product safety concerns, contact us at Calle de José Abascal, 56–1°,
28003 Madrid, Spain or eugpsr@cambridge.org.

www.ingramcontent.com/pod-product-compliance
Ingram Content Group UK Ltd.
Pitfield, Milton Keynes, MK11 3LW, UK
UKHW012156180425
457623UK00018B/213